WITHDRAWAL

University Libraries, University of Memphis

FAMOUS FIRST FACTS

Other Titles from the H.W. Wilson Company

Other titles by Joseph Nathan Kane

Facts About the Presidents, Sixth Edition

Other titles by Joseph Nathan Kane, Steven Anzovin, & Janet Podell in the Wilson Facts Series

Facts About the States, Second Edition
Facts About the Presidents, Seventh Edition

Other H.W. Wilson titles by Steven Anzovin & Janet Podell

Old Worlds to New: The Age of Exploration and Discovery (authors)
Speeches of the American Presidents, Second Edition (editors)

Other titles in the Wilson Facts Series

Facts About American Immigration
Facts About the American Wars
Facts About the British Prime Ministers
Facts About Canada, Its Provinces and Territories
Facts About China
Facts About the Cities, Second Edition
Facts About the Congress
Facts About the Supreme Court of the United States
Facts About the Twentieth Century
Famous First Facts, International Edition

JOSEPH NATHAN KANE

STEVEN ANZOVIN & JANET PODELL

FAMOUS FIRST FACTS

Sixth Edition

A Record of First Happenings, Discoveries, and Inventions in American History

The H.W. Wilson Company
New York • Dublin
2006

Copyright © 1933, 1935, 1950, 1964, 1981 by Joseph Nathan Kane

Copyright © renewed 1961, 1963, 1978 by Joseph Nathan Kane

First Edition 1933
Second Edition 1950
Third Edition 1964
Fourth Edition 1981
Fifth Edition 1997
Sixth Edition 2006

Copyright © 2006 by The H.W. Wilson Company

All rights reserved. No part of this work may be reproduced or copied in any form or by any means, including but not restricted to graphic, electronic, and mechanical-for example, photocopying, recording, taping, or information and retrieval systems-without the express written permission of the publisher, except that a reviewer may quote and a magazine, newspaper, or electronic information service may print brief passages as part of a review written specifically for inclusion in that magazine, newspaper, or electronic service.

ISBN 13: 978-0-8242-10656
ISBN 10: 0-8242-1065-4

Library of Congress Cataloging-in-Publication Data

Kane, Joseph Nathan, 1899–
Famous first facts / Jospeh Nathan Kane, Steven Anzovin, Janet Podell.—6th ed.
p. cm.
Includes index.
ISBN 0-8242-1065-4
1. Encyclopedias and dictionaries. I. Anzovin, Steven. II. Podell, Janet. III. Title.
AG5.K315 2006
031.02—dc22

2006003096

Printed in the United States of America

The H.W. Wilson Company
950 University Avenue
Bronx, NY 10452
www.hwwilson.com

Ref.
AG
5
.K315
2006

Contents

4/30/2007 #63807624 LF

Preface

This edition of *Famous First Facts*, the sixth, takes the popular reference book into a new century, one in which scientific, technological, and medical advances are occurring with greater speed than ever before. It contains more than 7,500 entries, with five indexes to assist readers in locating information.

The present volume also includes several new features that distinguish it from previous editions. There are over 1,000 new entries describing "firsts" in science, technology, military history, politics, and more, that have occurred since the publication of the Fifth Edition, along with events from earlier years that had not been covered previously. Sidebars highlighting interesting details about selected events are also attached to many of the new firsts, while several existing entries have been updated. In addition, some 100 images illustrating the individuals, inventions, and moments covered in new and existing entries visually augment the text.

The book's overall structure has been revised as well—entries have also been reorganized into 16 chapters, with chapter headings appearing atop right-hand pages for easier browsing. A more detailed discussion of the book's arrangement is presented in the section entitled "How to Use This Book," which appears on page ix. Finally, the subject index has also been reorganized into a more conventional, topic-oriented index, so that a single entry can be listed in more than one place.

Since *Famous First Facts* is a book of firsts, it is appropriate to mention its first edition, which was published by the H.W. Wilson Company in 1933. It was the brainchild of Joseph Nathan Kane, then a freelance, self-syndicated journalist. In the course of a decade of research for a book on the history of American inventions, he accumulated 3,000 "firsts" which he organized into a manuscript. Eleven publishers rejected it; finally, Halsey W. Wilson accepted it after receiving multiple requests for the book from reference librarians.

That first edition of *Famous First Facts* was so successful that in 1938–39 it was turned into a radio program of the same name, hosted by Mr. Kane, who subsequently became a consultant to radio and television quiz shows. He also compiled additional books for the H.W. Wilson Company, including *Facts About the Presidents* and *Facts About the States,* both of which quickly became—and remain to this day—standard reference volumes in schools and libraries. The world changed so rapidly during the 20th century that it became necessary to issue a second, updated edition of *Famous First Facts* by 1950, followed by a third in 1964, a fourth in 1981, and a fifth in 1997.

Now, a personal note. The preparation of this edition was undertaken by an editorial team consisting of myself and my husband, Steve Anzovin. The two of us had collaborated for many years on book projects for the H.W. Wilson Company, including the fifth edition of *Famous First Facts.* We were in the early stages of the current revision when Steve was diagnosed with metastatic colon cancer, which took his life on December 25, 2005. I carried on the work with the help of a number of people to whom I would like to express my gratitude. At H.W. Wilson, I had the good fortune to work with General Reference Editor Lynn Messina, the most tactful of editors even under the most challenging circumstances, and her assistants Paul McCaffrey and Richard Stein. At the B. Davis Schwartz Memorial Library, C.W. Post Campus, Long Island University, I received assistance from Masako Yukawa, head of the Government Information Department, who answered many factual questions; Robert Delaney, Reference Associate, who furnished advice on photo research; and my mother, Diane Podell, who researched hundreds of possible new firsts. Computer programming for the indexes was started by Morgan Robinson and completed by Hypercard magician Brian Kendall.

In addition to my mother, the rest of the family pitched in. Roger and Sheri Podell, my brother and sister-in-law, looked up new state firsts. My son Rafael took over some of my tasks at Anzovin Studio, the computer animation company he founded with Steve. My daughter Miriam, a student at the University of Massachusetts, served as my picture researcher. My daughter Hannah proofread entries with me late into the night and supplied me with her nourishing homemade cookies. Both of them kept me going with their constant demonstrations of encouragement and love. So did my brother, David Podell; my cousin, Susanne Barkan; my friend Karen Anolik; and my father, Larry Podell, who died shortly before this book was finished.

Steve and I were married for 31 years. Steve, this book is dedicated to you.

JANET PODELL
Amherst, Massachusetts
November 2006

How to Use This Book

The entries in this edition of *Famous First Facts* are grouped into 16 chapters, each of which is divided into a number of sections. In response to requests from readers of the previous edition, we have kept the number of sections within the chapters to a minimum. These sections are arranged in alphabetical order; within each one, the entries are arranged in chronological order. Each entry begins with a four-digit indexing number, starting with 1001. (For a complete list of chapters and their sections, please refer to the Expanded Contents.)

History is a complicated subject, and classification is an inexact science. In the many cases in which an entry could potentially be placed in more than one chapter, priorities were established that will quickly become evident to the reader. Entries about military academies, for example, could have been placed either in "Military and War" or in "Education." They were assigned to the latter, in a subchapter entitled "Education—Military."

At the back of the book, the reader will find five indexes: Subject Index, Index by Years, Index by Days, Index to Personal Names, and Geographical Index. In all five, entries are identified by the four-digit indexing number, printed in italics.

The Subject Index has been reorganized for this edition, again in response to reader requests. Each entry is indexed under one or more keywords. Thus, the entry **Two-way telegraph** is indexed under *Telegraph.* The entry **Novel by an American to depict Native Americans in a realistic manner** is indexed under both *Novel* and *Native American.*

To prevent the Subject Index from becoming excessively large, the keywords have been chosen for the greatest possible precision. Thus, **African-American opera singer to sing a white role** is indexed under *African-American* and *Opera,* but not under *Music* (though many other nonoperatic entries will be found in the Index under *Music).* Ship voyages around the globe are listed under *Circumnavigation,* but other circuits of the globe that do not involve navigation will be found under *Round-the-world* (such as, for instance, **Round-the-world bicycle trip**).

Expanded Contents

Arts and Entertainment

Amusement Parks

1001. Carousel patent was granted on July 25, 1871, to Willhelm Schneider of Davenport, IA. It was a two-story carousel and not very successful or practical.

1002. Roller coaster was invented by Lemarcus Adna Thompson, a former Sunday school teacher, and put in operation in June 1884 by the L.A. Thompson Scenic Railway Company at Coney Island, NY (now part of New York City). It traveled along a wooden and steel track 450 feet long at a speed of six miles per hour. The cars started from a peak and ran downgrade, the momentum carrying the cars up an incline. The passengers got out, the attendants pushed the train over a switch to a higher point on a second track, and the passengers returned. The highest drop was only 30 feet. Thompson obtained a patent on January 20, 1885, on a roller-coasting structure and another patent on December 22, 1885 on a gravity switchback railway. The first high-speed roller coaster was The Cyclone, which opened at Coney Island on June 26, 1927. Its one-and-a-half minute ride hit speeds of up to 60 miles per hour.

1003. Mechanized shooting gallery that was fully automatic was invented in 1890 by Charles Wallace Parker of Abilene, KS, whose first sale was made to Leon Brownie of Houston, TX.

1004. Ferris wheel was invented in 1892 by George Washington Gale Ferris, a railroad and bridge engineer. It was erected on the Midway at the World's Columbian Exposition in Chicago, IL, in 1893. It consisted of 36 cars, each capable of holding 60 passengers. The highest point of the wheel was 264 feet. The total weight of the wheels and cars was 2,100 tons, of the levers and machinery 2,200 tons, and of the passengers per trip 150 tons.

1005. Shoot-the-chutes was built by Captain Paul Boyton and opened on July 6, 1895, at the amusement park at Coney Island, NY (now part of New York City). Each passenger toboggan held 16 persons. The inclined railway was 80 feet high with a 50 percent grade to the surface of a large body of water.

1006. Roller coaster with a loop-the-loop was a centrifugal railway invented by Edwin Prescott of Arlington, MA, who received a patent for it on August 16, 1898. It was known as Boyton's Centrifugal Railway and was installed at the amusement park on Coney Island, NY (now part of New York City), in 1900. It had a 75-foot incline and a 20-foot-wide loop.

1007. Skee-ball alley was built in 1914 by the National Skee-Ball Company of Coney Island, New York City, and the first battery was operated by William A. Norwood in April 1914 at the Coney Island amusement park.

1008. Theme park was Santa Claus Land, a Christmas-themed park in Santa Claus, IN, founded by retired businessman Louis J. Koch. The park, which opened on August 3, 1946, offered rides, food treats, an antique toy collection, and a wax museum, as well as a Santa Claus impersonator. The name was changed to Holiday World in 1984.

Art

1009. Cave paintings known to have been made in what is now the United States were painted in caves near the Pecos River in southwest Texas circa 1970 B.C.E. The caves had been inhabited for more than 3,000 years when the paintings were made, and continued to be inhabited until the arrival of the Spanish in the 16th century. The date of the paintings was established using a technique developed by Marvin Rowe, Marian Hyman, and Jon Russ of Texas A&M University that separates organic materials in the paint from inorganic substances in the rock.

1010. Artist to come to America was Jacques Le Moyne de Morgues, a cartographer attached to the French Huguenot expedition to Florida under René Goulaine de Laudonnière. They sailed from Havre de Grace, France, on April 20, 1564, and reached Florida (then called New France) on June 22, remaining until September 20, 1565, when the Spanish destroyed their settlement and killed its inhabitants. Le Moyne's work consisted principally of scenic and historical views.

1011. Painting of an American scene by a European painter was painted near what is now St. Augustine, FL, on June 27, 1564, by Jacques Le Moyne de Morgues, a cartographer who accompanied the French Huguenot expedition to Florida under René Goulaine de Laudonnière. The work, titled *Laudonnierus et Rex Athore ante Columnam a Praefecto Prima Navigatione Locatam Quamque Venerantur Floridenses*, was painted in gouache and metallic pigments on vellum. It shows Laudonnière being welcomed by a party of Native Americans led by Chief Athore.

1012. Artist in the English colonies was the English painter and cartographer John White, who came to North Carolina in 1585 as part of Sir Walter Raleigh's expedition. He recorded Native American life in his paintings and made maps of the coast as far south as Florida. He returned in 1587 as governor of Raleigh's Roanoke colony, which disappeared while White was back in England getting supplies. Among the vanished colonists was Virginia Dare, the first child of European descent known to have been born in America, who was White's grandchild.

1013. Woodcut was a likeness of the Reverend Richard Mather, the leader of Congregationalism in the Massachusetts Bay Colony, made just prior to his death in April 1669. The engraver, John Foster, cut away from the surface of a flat wooden block those parts which were to appear white in the print, leaving the actual design in raised outline on the block. The print was 5 by 6 inches.

1014. Self-portrait from the English colonies known to exist was painted circa 1670 by Captain Thomas Smith, a Puritan mariner of Boston, MA. The painting, in a style taken from Dutch portraiture, shows Smith resting his hand on a skull, which in turn rests on a poem that discusses Smith's own death.

1015. Engraving of any artistic merit was a line-engraving copperplate portrait of Increase Mather, made in 1701 by Thomas Emmes. It was used as a frontispiece to a sermon, "The Blessed Hope," published in Boston, MA, in 1701 by Timothy Green for Nicholas Boone.

1016. Pastelist was Henrietta Johnston of Charlestown, SC, who was active between 1707 and 1720. She worked with colored chalk. Her subjects were principally colonial women of South Carolina. Her most celebrated piece of work, done in 1718, was a portrait entitled *His Excellency Robert Johnson Captain General, Governor and Commander-in-Chief in and over His Majesty's Province of Carolina.*

1017. Painter to obtain a public commission was Gustavus Hesselius. His painting *The Last Supper*, an oil on canvas, 117.5 inches wide and 35 inches high, was commissioned on September 5, 1721, by the Vestry of St. Barnabas' Church, Queen Anne's Parish, Prince Georges County, MD. It was put in place as an altarpiece on November 26, 1722. Hesselius was paid "£17 currt. money" for the painting and installation. It was also the first important commission in America for a painting with more than one figure.

1018. Mezzotint engraving was a portrait of Cotton Mather about 13.5 by 10 inches, made by Peter Pelham in 1727.

1019. Artist of importance to be born in America was John Singleton Copley, the great portraitist, who was born in Boston, MA, in 1738, and emigrated to England in 1774. He painted many of the prominent people of his era, including Samuel Adams, John Adams, John Quincy Adams, John Hancock, and the King and Queen of England. He is credited with more than 269 oil paintings, 35 crayons, and 14 miniatures.

1020. Historical print engraved in America was *A Prospective Plan of the Battle Fought Near Lake George*, which presented a bird's-eye view showing the march of troops at the left, the camp and battle at the right, and Forts William Henry and Edward in the upper right-hand corner. It was a hand-colored line engraving by Thomas Johnston after a painting by Samuel Blodget, and was printed by Richard Draper in Boston, MA, in 1755.

1021. Caricature was Nathaniel Hurd's *The True Profile of the Notorious Doctor Seth Hudson*, published in 1762 in Boston, MA. It depicted Dr. Hudson in the pillory and Howe, his assistant, at the whipping post, in punishment for forging paper money.

1022. Commercial artist who was successful was Matthew Pratt, who painted signboards in Philadelphia, PA, in 1768. From 1764 to 1768 he had been an art student in London, where he studied under the American expatriate artist Benjamin West.

1023. Engraving to achieve popularity was *The Bloody Massacre Perpetrated in King Street, Boston, on March 5, 1770,* which was engraved, printed, and sold by Paul Revere. It depicted the shooting of five Americans in Boston, MA, by British troops—the famous Boston Massacre—and has appeared in countless children's textbooks and general works on American history.

1024. Artist of American birth to head the Royal Academy of London was Benjamin West, who became president of the Royal Academy on March 24, 1792, succeeding Sir Joshua Reynolds. Born on October 10, 1738, near Springfield, PA, he went to Italy in 1760 for three years of study and afterward settled in London, where he gained fame as a painter of historical subjects. In 1772 he became historical painter to King George III.

1025. Professional illustrator was Alexander Anderson of New York City. A trained physician, he was also a highly skilled wood engraver who illustrated hundreds of books, periodicals, and newspapers. The earliest engravings of Anderson's to be published appeared in 1794 in Arnaud Berquin's children's book *The Looking-Glass for the Mind.* Anderson's engraving of Father Time appeared on the cover of the *Farmer's Almanac* in various forms and re-engravings for 190 years.

1026. Professional portrait painter who was African-American was Joshua Johnson (or Johnston), a free man, possibly a former slave, who worked in Baltimore, MD, between 1795 and 1825. More than 80 of his portraits are known to exist, most of them depicting individuals or families from the city's mercantile elite.

1027. Landscape painter of renown was Thomas Cole, born in 1801 in England and recognized as the founder of American landscape painting. The leader of the Hudson Valley School of artists, Cole specialized in painting the scenery of New York State. His later works were often done in a grandiose neoclassical style.

1028. Lithograph was *A Water Mill,* by Bass Otis of Philadelphia, PA, published July 1819 in the *Analectic Magazine.*

1029. Painting movement was the Hudson River School, a group of American landscape painters who were active between 1825 and 1875. Their main subject was the Hudson River Valley and other grand vistas of the American landscape. Among the most important members of the school were Thomas Cole, Albert Bierstadt, Asher Brown Durand, Samuel Finley Breese Morse, and Frederic Edwin Church.

1030. National organization of artists was the National Academy of Design, whose first president was the inventor and artist Samuel Finley Breese Morse. It was organized on January 18, 1826, by 15 members of the New York Drawing Association, which had been formed on November 8, 1825, in New York City.

1031. Etcher of skill was William Dunlap of New York City, a painter who studied under Benjamin West in London and whose success in 1830 inspired others to practice the art of etching. He was also a prominent playwright and historian.

1032. Marble statuary group was *The Chanting Cherubs,* designed in 1830 by Horatio Greenough for James Fenimore Cooper. The subject was suggested by a portion of a Raphael painting but incurred hostility because of the nudity of the figures.

1033. Sculptor to obtain a federal commission was John Frazee. A federal appropriation of $400 was granted to him on March 2, 1831, for a bust of John Jay for the Supreme Court, Washington, DC.

1034. Sculptor of renown was Hiram Powers of Vermont, who got his start as a sculptor in a waxworks museum. His chief sculptures were produced from 1835 to 1873. In addition to neoclassical statues entitled *Eve Disconsolate, Greek Slave, Proserpine, Il Penseroso, A Californian,* and *An American,* he made busts of George Washington for Louisiana, of John Caldwell Calhoun for South Carolina, and of Daniel Webster for Boston. His busts of Benjamin Franklin and Thomas Jefferson were installed in the Capitol in Washington, D.C. He also made busts of John Quincy Adams, Andrew Jackson, Chief Justice John Marshall, Martin Van Buren, and other distinguished Americans.

1035. Art magazine of merit was *The Illustrated Magazine of Art*, which contained "selections from the various departments of painting, sculpture, architecture, history, biography, art-industry, manufactures, scientific inventions and discoveries, local and domestic scenes, ornamental works, etc." It was published by Alexander Montgomery in New York City from January 1853 to December 4, 1854. The first issue contained 60 pages.

1036. Chromolithograph was made in 1861 of John Banvard's painting *The Orison*, which depicted the interior of the St. Eustace convent in Italy. It was 16 by 24 inches and was chromolithographed by Sarony, Major and Knapp. Proofs were $10, prints $5.

1037. Halftone engraving was made by Stephen Henry Horgan and appeared in the *New York Daily Graphic* on March 4, 1880. It was entitled *Scene in Shantytown, NY*. The basis of the invention was a screen gradated from transparency to opacity.

1038. Abstract paintings by a modern artist were the work of Arthur Dove, born in Geneva, NY. In 1910, he created a series of six paintings on linen, such as *Nature Symbolized, No. 1*, that took their inspiration from landscape but showed no clearly recognizable representational forms.

1039. Modern art exhibition of importance opened at the 69th Regiment Armory in New York City on February 17, 1913. The controversial exhibition, organized chiefly by the American modernist painter Arthur Bowen Davies, scandalized the public with such avant-garde works as Marcel Duchamp's *Nude Descending a Spiral Staircase*. More than 250,000 visitors received their first look at paintings by Paul Cèzanne, Paul Gauguin, Vincent van Gogh, Edward Hopper, Henri Matisse, John Marin, Charles Sheeler, and others.

1040. Cover of the *Saturday Evening Post* by Norman Rockwell appeared on the issue dated May 20, 1916. It depicted a boy pushing a baby carriage past a group of jeering pals. Rockwell, a native New Yorker who became famous for his anecdotal scenes of small-town American life, painted 319 more covers for the magazine. The last appeared in 1963.

1041. Native American art exhibition of importance was the Exposition of Indian Tribal Arts, a traveling show assembled by artist John Sloan and writer Oliver La Farge in 1931. The highlight of the show was the collection of Navajo textiles of the Classic Period, worth up to $1,000 apiece at the time. The first major museum show of Native American art took place in 1940 at the Museum of Modern Art, New York City.

1042. Exhibition of the *Mona Lisa* in the United States took place on January 8, 1962, in the National Gallery of Art, Washington, DC. The painting, Leonardo da Vinci's masterpiece of 1506, was owned by the Louvre, in Paris. The loan of the painting was arranged by First Lady Jacqueline Kennedy and André Malraux, the French minister of culture. On the first day, 2,000 dignitaries were allowed to view the painting. The exhibition was opened to the public on January 9 and received 518,535 viewers during its three-week stay. The *Mona Lisa* was then moved to the Metropolitan Museum of Art in New York City, where it was seen by 1,077,051 visitors.

1043. Major solo show of work by an African-American artist was a 90-piece exibition of the paintings of Henry Ossawa Tanner, co-sponsored by the National Collection of Fine Arts and the Frederick Douglass Institute. It opened in Washington, D.C., in 1969 and traveled to seven other major American museums. Tanner painted genre scenes depicting African-American life and scenes from the Bible.

1044. Light sculpture created with a cityscape was *Night/Light*, created by artist James Pelletier to commemorate the centennial of the invention of the light bulb by Thomas Edison. The sculpture involved a dozen office buildings along the East River waterfront in lower Manhattan, each of which was provided with a pattern of windows to illuminate. The result, which lasted for three hours on the night of October 21, 1979, was a display of geometrical forms that were reflected in the river.

1045. Sale of an American painting at a price comparable to that of European paintings took place at an auction at Sotheby's, in New York City, on December 1, 1999. The painting was *Polo Crowd*, a 1910 work by George Bellows. The buyer was

Microsoft founder Bill Gates, who paid $27,502,400, a record price for a painting by an American artist.

Dance

1046. Ballet performed in the United States took place in Charleston, SC, in 1735. An English dance company led by Henry Holt performed The Adventures of Harlequin and Scaramouche and The Burgomaster Trick'd at the Exchange Building.

1047. Professional American dancer was John Durang of Lancaster, PA, a multi-talented entertainer renowned for his dancing, acting, directing, stage managing, clowning, puppeteering, and acrobatics. He began performing in 1784 in Philadelphia, PA, and traveled extensively with dance and theater companies and circuses. His star turn was "Durang's Hornpipe," a dance to music written by Franz Hoffmeister.

1048. Ballerina in the United States was Suzanne Vaillande, also known as Madame Placide. In 1792 she danced in a season of ballets and pantomimes staged by her lover, the impresario Alexandre Placide, at the John Street Theatre in New York City.

1049. Tap dancer of renown was William Henry Lane of Providence, RI, an African-American entertainer who went by the stage name Juba during the 1840s. Billed as "The Wonder of the World, Juba . . . the King of All Dancers," Lane derived his tapping style by combining fast steps from jigs and reels with West African *giouba*, a kind of step-dance. He was the first African-American to headline a troupe of white dancers. Bill "Bojangles" Robinson, born Luther Robinson in Richmond, VA, in 1878, was the first dancer to bring tap into modern stage and film entertainment.

1050. Modern dancer was Isadora Duncan, born Angela Duncan in 1878 in San Francisco, CA. She trained in classical ballet, but rejected it in favor of a personal, freely interpretive style, often based on Greek classical art, that attempted to synthesize music, poetry, and natural imagery into a symbolism of movement. She preferred to dance barefoot, wearing a loose, flowing tunic and scarves. In 1899 she left the United States and traveled to England, Germany, and, in 1905, Russia, where she met her greatest success. Her only important tour of the United States, in 1922, was a complete failure.

1051. Ballet choreographer of international renown to work in the United States was George Balanchine, born Georgi Meilitonovitch in 1904 in Russia. Balanchine defected from the Soviet Union in 1924 to join Sergei Pavlovich Diaghilev's Ballets Russes. He settled in 1933 in New York City, where he cofounded the School of American Ballet with Lincoln Kirstein. In 1948 he became artistic director and principal choreographer of the New York City Ballet. Balanchine's works, of which there were more than 100, were noted for their abstract themes and simplicity of movement.

1052. Modern dance troupe that was all-male was Ted Shawn and His Men Dancers, founded by dance pioneer Ted Shawn in Becket, MA. The lead dancer was Barton Mumaw. Shawn was the choreographer. Their first performance took place in Boston, MA, in March 1933. Until 1940, when the group disbanded, they toured extensively in the United States and overseas.

1053. Ballet on an American theme by an American choreographer that was set to American music and performed by an American ballet company was *Billy the Kid*, a work depicting the violent career of the Western folk hero. The choreographer was Eugene Loring of Milwaukee, WI. The music was composed by Aaron Copland. The ballet was first performed at the Chicago Civic Opera House on October 9, 1938, by Lincoln Kirstein's Ballet Caravan.

1054. Theater designed for dance performances was the Ted Shawn Theatre, designed by Joseph Franz and built at Jacob's Pillow, Shawn's dance retreat in Becket, MA. It was built of pine with a smooth maple floor. The first performance was given there on July 9, 1942.

1055. Copyright registered for a choreographic score was presented on microfilm by Hanya Holm, New York City, and registered on February 25, 1952, as an unpublished dramatic-musical composition. It was a complete score of her choreography for Cole Porter's musical comedy *Kiss Me, Kate*, which opened on December 30, 1948, at the Century Theater, New York City. The score was recorded in Labanotation, the notation system invented by Rudolf Laban.

1056. Ballet transmitted by satellite to be shown in the United States was the Royal Ballet's "The Royal Ballet Salutes the U.S.A.," hosted by Gene Kelly from Covent Garden, London, and broadcast over WNEW-TV, New York City, at 8 P.M. on July 22, 1978, and at 3 P.M. on July 23. The program was a Metromedia Television–British Broadcasting Company television coproduction and was sponsored by the Irving Trust Company.

1057. Powwow at the National Mall in Washington, DC, was held over the weekend of September 14–15, 2002, near the construction site of the National Museum of the American Indian. The event was a contest of traditional dance, with more than 400 participants of all ages competing in eight categories. Drumming accompaniment was provided by Black Lodge (Blackfeet) and Cozad (Kiowa) drummers. The event was organized by George Horse Capture, a curator at the museum.

Courtesy of the Indian Health Service, U.S. Department of Health and Human Services

An Indian powwow.

Literature

1058. Book written in America was *A True Relation of Such Occurrences and Accidents of Noate as Hath Happened in Virginia Since the First Planting of That Collony*, printed for I. Tappe in 1608 in London. The author was Captain John Smith, who used the pseudonym Th. Watson. A plain, unadorned account of hardships, it is generally regarded as more reliable than his later work *A Generall Historie of Virginia* (1624), which includes the romantic, and possibly fabricated, tale of his rescue by Pocahontas.

1059. Poetry translation prepared in America was made by George Sandys, treasurer of the Virginia Company, who made his translation while he was a member of the English colony at Jamestown, VA. His translation of Ovid's *Metamorphoses* was published in 1626 in London as *Ovid's Metamorphoses Englished, Mytholized and Represented in Figures*. A second edition was published in 1632, to which was added a translation of Virgil's *Aeneid*.

1060. Poetry collection by an American poet was Anne Dudley Bradstreet's volume *Several Poems compiled with great variety of Wit and Learning, full of delight; wherein especially is contained a compleat Discourse, and Description of the Four Elements, Constitutions, Ages of Man, Seasons of the Year, together with an exact Epitome of the Three first Monarchyes, Viz. The Assyrian, Persian, Grecian, and beginning of the Romane Common-wealth to the end of their last King: With diverse other pleasant & serious Poems. By a Gentlewoman in New-England*. The book was published in Massachusetts in 1640. Bradstreet was born in Northampton, England, circa 1612 and came in 1630 to Massachusetts, where her husband later served as governor.

1061. Book published in America was the *Bay Psalm Book*, printed by Stephen Day of Cambridge, MA, the first colonial printer. Its full title was *The Whole Booke of Psalmes, Faithfully Translated into English Metre whereunto is prefixed a Discourse declaring not only the lawfullness, but also the necessity of the heavenly ordinance of singing scripture psalmes in the Churches of God*. The book, 5.5 by 7 inches, contained 296 pages and was published in July 1640. It was a new metrical version of the psalms, a revision of those of Sternhold and Hopkins. Seventeen hundred copies were printed and sold for 20 pence each, netting a profit of almost £80. This was also the first hymn book published in America.

1062. Children's book was John Cotton's catechism *Milk for Babes, Drawn out of the Breasts of Both Testaments, Chiefly for the Spiritual Nourishment of Boston Babes in either England: But may be of like use for any children,* printed by Stephen Day in Cambridge, MA, 1641–45.

1063. Book intended for circulation in the English colonies was Martin Luther's *Little Catechism,* translated into the Algonkian Native American language in 1656 by Johannes Campanius, a clergyman, who dedicated it to King Karl X Gustav of Sweden. It contained 132 pages of text and 27 pages of dictionary. About 600 copies of the book were printed in 1696, 40 years later, in Stockholm, Sweden, by Thomas Campanius Holm, Campanius's grandson. The title was *Lutheri Cathechismus oswersatt pä American-Virginiste Sprätet.* It was intended for missionary work among the Native Americans in the colony of New Sweden, in what is now New Jersey and Delaware, and also contained a small vocabulary in the Algonkian language.

1064. Poetry collection by an American poet who was a man was *New Englands Crisis, or a Brief Narrative of New Englands Lamentable Estate at present, compar'd with the former (but few) years of Prosperity. Occasioned by many unheard of Crueltyes practised upon the Persons and Estates of its united Colonyes, without respect of Sex, Age or Quality of Persons, by the Barbarous Heathen thereof.* The author was Benjamin Tompson, who was graduated from Harvard College, Cambridge, MA, in 1662. This work, a 31-page book of poems about King Philip's War, was published in 1676 in Boston, MA. It was printed and sold by John Foster.

1065. Poem to be printed in a newspaper was "The Seminary at Quebeck," a Latin poem published on December 24, 1705, in the *Boston News Letter.* It was four lines long and described a fire whose flames engulfed a church: *Gallica crux aequam flammam sentive coacta est.*

1066. Story serialized in a newspaper appeared in Samuel Keimer's *Pennsylvania Gazette* in Philadelphia in 1729. It was entitled "Religious Courtship" and was written by Daniel Defoe, author of *Robinson Crusoe.* It was reprinted from his book of the same title, published in 1722 in London.

1067. Translation of a classic was Marcus Porcius Cato's *Moral Distichs Englished in Couplets,* which was translated by James Logan, president of the Council and chief justice of the province of Philadelphia. It was printed and sold in 1735 by Benjamin Franklin, Philadelphia, PA, for one shilling. It consisted of 24 pages of precepts of morality and moral apothegms. An announcement in the pages of the *Pennsylvania Gazette* of December 11 and December 18, 1735, stated that it was "very proper to be put into the Hands of Young Persons."

1068. Poetry collection by an African-American writer was *Poems on Various Subjects, Religious and Moral* by Phillis Wheatley, published in London in 1773 and dedicated to the Countess of Huntingdon. Wheatley was born in Africa, possibly in Senegal, about 1753. She was kidnapped by slavers as a child and taken to Boston, MA, where she became personal servant to the wife of tailor John Wheatley. She began to write in English at the age of 13. Her first poem, "An Elegiac Poem on the Death of George Whitefield," was published in 1770.

1069. Novel by a writer born in America was *The Life of Harriot Stuart,* by Charlotte Ramsay Lennox, published in two volumes in London in 1751. The author, whose father was a British army officer, was born in 1720 in New York State and moved to England at the age of 15. This novel, her first, was a semiautobiographical romance. Samuel Johnson, the eminent English writer and lexicographer, was a personal friend of hers, and celebrated the book's publication by throwing an all-night party.

1070. Philosophy book printed in America was *Elementa Philosophica: Containing Chiefly, Noetica, or Things Relating to the Mind or Understanding: and Ethica, or Things Relating to the Moral Behaviour,* by Samuel Johnson. It contained 103 pages and was printed in 1752 in Philadelphia, PA, by Benjamin Franklin and D. Hall.

1071. Published literary work by an African-American was "An Evening Thought. Salvation by Christ with Penitential Cries: Composed by Jupiter Hammon, a Negro belonging to Mr. Lloyd of Queen's Village, on Long Island, the 25th of December, 1760," published as a broadside in 1761. Hammon, though a slave, was educated by a minister, Nehemiah Bull, and himself served as preacher.

1072. Work of satirical fiction was a 16-page pamphlet by Francis Hopkinson entitled *A Pretty Story, Written in the Year of Our Lord 1774 by Peter Grievous, Esquire, ABCDE. Velunti in Speculo.* It was a political satire on the administration of the British colonies in North America and the causes of the American Revolution. It was printed in Williamsburg, VA, in 1774 by John Pinkney, for the benefit of Clementine Rind's children.

1073. Novel by an American writer to be translated into a foreign language was *Adventures of Alonso: Containing Some Striking Anecdotes of the Present Prime Minister of Portugal* (Sebastião José de Carvalho e Mello, Marquis de Pombal) by "A Native of Maryland, some years resident in Lisbon." The work is attributed to Thomas Atwood Digges of Warburton Manor, MD. The original edition consisted of two volumes, 148 pages and 129 pages, and was printed for John Bew in London in 1775. It was published in Leipzig, Germany, in 1787 by Schwickert as *Alonzo's Abenteur.*

1074. Travel writer was John Ledyard of Hartford, CT. After sailing through the Mediterranean and the Caribbean as a seaman with the British Navy, he circumnavigated the globe as a marine under Captain James Cook; then, with the encouragement of Thomas Jefferson, he made his way on foot from London to Yakutsk, Siberia, taking notes as he went. His last trip was an expedition to Egypt. His *Journal of Captain Cook's Last Voyage to the Pacific Ocean* was published in 1783.

1075. Professional writer who was a woman was Hannah Adams, born in Medfield, MA, in 1755. Her income from this source was very limited. Her first book, *Alphabetical Compendium of the Various Sects which Have Appeared from the Beginning of the Christian Era to the Present Day,* appeared in 1784.

1076. Bibliography of Americana in English was *Bibliotheca Americana; or a Chronological Catalogue of the most curious and interesting books, pamphlets, state papers, etc. upon the subject of North and South America, from the earliest period to the present in print,* published in 1789 in London for J. Debrett. It contained 271 pages and included an introductory study on the state of literature in North and South America.

1077. Novel by an American writer to be published in America was *The Power of Sympathy or the Triumph of Nature Founded in Truth,* dedicated "to the young ladies of America." It was printed in 1789 in Boston, MA, by Isaiah Thomas and Company and sold at the company's bookstore, 45 Newbury Street. Publication was announced in the *Independent Chronicle* of January 21, 1789. The novel appeared in two volumes of 138 and 158 pages. No author's name appeared on the first edition. Later editions bore the name of Mrs. Sarah Wentworth Apthorp Morton, but literary scholars attribute the novel to William Hill Brown. Brown, the son of a Boston clockmaker who had emigrated from England, was a friend of the Apthorp family and embarrassed them by including in his novel a thinly disguised version of a real event, the seduction and suicide of one of the daughters.

1078. Anthology of American literature was *American Poems, Selected and Original,* 304 pages, compiled by Elihu Hubbard Smith, published in 1793 in Litchfield, CT, by [Thomas] Collier and [David] Buel. An earlier anthology, *Select Poems on Various Occasions, Chiefly American,* printed by S. Hall, Boston, MA, in 1787, contained English as well as American poems.

1079. Fiction best-seller was *Charlotte, a Tale of Truth,* by Susanna Haswell Rowson, an actress at the New Theatre, Philadelphia, PA, and the author of several previous novels. *Charlotte* was printed by D. Humphreys for M. Carey, Philadelphia, PA, in two volumes in 1794. An English edition of *Charlotte* was printed in London in 1790. Later it was entitled *Charlotte Temple.* About 200 editions have been printed.

1080. Writer whose livelihood was obtained exclusively by writing was Charles Brockden Brown of New York and Philadelphia. His first book was *Alcuin, a Dialogue,* one of the earliest known works by an American to champion the rights of women. It was published anonymously and was first announced on April 28, 1798, by T. and J. Swords, New York City. His first novel was *Wieland, or the Transformation*, the first American example of the Gothic horror novel, which was published in New York City in 1798.

1081. True-crime bestseller was Narrative of Patrick Lyon Who Suffered Three Months Severe Imprisonment in Philadelphia Gaol on Merely a Vague Suspicion of Being Concerned in a Robbery of the Bank of Pennsylvania With his Remarks Thereon, printed by Francis and Robert Bailey in Philadelphia, PA, in 1799. This was Lyon's account of his wrongful imprisonment for the sensational robbery of the Bank of Pennsylvania on September 1, 1798. The book, written after he was cleared by a grand jury, recounted the story of the robbery as he had it from his own communications with the thieves. It was a popular success, portraying as it did the persecution of a common citizen by the wealthy and powerful.

1082. Book on Americanisms was John Pickering's *A Vocabulary, or Collection of Words and Phrases Which Have Been Supposed to Be Peculiar to the United States of America; to which is prefixed an essay on the present state of the English language in the United States*, a 206-page book published in 1816 by Cummings and Hilliard, Boston, MA.

1083. Historical novel was James Fenimore Cooper's *The Spy*, the story of an itinerant peddler who spies for George Washington during the Revolution. It was published in 1821. The New York–born author, then 32, wrote it after making a bet with his wife that he could pen a more exciting story than the English novel she was reading at the time.

1084. Rhyming dictionary was *A Rhyming Dictionary, containing all the perfect rhymes of a different orthography, and allowable rhymes of a different sound, throughout the language, with authorities for the usage of them from our best poets*, published in 1823 by F. and R. Lockwood, New York City. It was an American edition of John Walker's *A Dictionary of the English language answering at once the purposes of rhyming, spelling and pronouncing on a plan not hitherto attempted*, first published in London in 1775.

1085. Novel about whaling was *Miriam Coffin; or, The Whale-Fishermen*, by Massachusetts author Joseph C. Hart, written in 1834. The novel was set in Nantucket and New Bedford.

1086. Novel by an American to depict Native Americans in a realistic manner was *The Yemassee*, written in 1835 by South Carolina author William Gilmore Simms. Simms, a planter, politician, and leading secessionist, wrote more than 80 books, most of which concern some aspect of South Carolina history and manners. *The Yemassee* describes the Yemassee rebellion of 1715–18.

1087. Transcendentalist literary work was *Nature*, an essay by the philosopher Ralph Waldo Emerson of Concord, MA, published anonymously on September 9, 1836.

Library of Congress, Prints & Photographs Division LC-USZ61-225

Ralph Waldo Emerson

1088. Detective story to achieve popularity was Edgar Allan Poe's "The Murders in the Rue Morgue," published in April 1841 in *Graham's Magazine*, Philadelphia, PA.

1089. Humor writer who was a woman was Frances Miriam Berry Whitcher, who contributed humorous pieces to Joseph Clay Neal's *Saturday Gazette* in 1846 under the nom de plume "Frank." Her "Widow Bedott" papers, republished in book form in 1855, sold over 100,000 copies.

1090. Book to sell more than 1 million copies was *Uncle Tom's Cabin; or, Life Among the Lowly*, the antislavery novel by Harriet Beecher Stowe. It had already appeared as a weekly serial in the *National Era* newspaper when it was published in book form in March 1852 by John P. Jewett & Co., Boston, MA. It became an instant and sold almost 1.5 million copies worldwide, particularly in England, where there was a strong antislavery movement.

1091. Novel by an African-American writer was William Wells Brown's *Clotel, or the President's Daughter, a Narrative of Slave Life in the United States*, the story of a slave woman represented as the housekeeper of Thomas Jefferson. In the novel one of the woman's two daughters drowns herself in the Potomac River to elude pursuing slavers. The book was published in London in 1853, and reprinted with slight changes in 1864 in Boston, MA, under the title of *Clotelle, A Tale of the Southern States*. It was published by James Redpath, contained 104 pages, and sold for 10 cents.

1092. Novel by an African-American woman is thought to have been *The Bondwoman's Narrative, by Hannah Crafts, a Fugitive Slave, Recently Escaped from North Carolina*, apparently a work of fictionalized autobiography. The author used a pseudonym. Professor Henry Louis Gates, Jr., who located the manuscript in 2001, dated its composition to the period 1855–59. The book was published by Warner Books on April 2, 2002. If the dating of the manuscript proves to be incorrent, the first known novel would be *Our Nig; or, Sketches from the life of a Free Black, in a two-storey white house, North. Showing that Slavery's Shadows Fall Even There*. It was written by Harriet E. Wilson and published by Geo. C. Rand & Avery in Boston, MA, in 1859.

1093. Poem to win national acclaim was Henry Wadsworth Longfellow's *Song of Hiawatha*, which was published in book form on November 10, 1855, by Ticknor and Fields, Boston, MA. In four weeks 10,000 copies were sold, and in 18 months, 30,000.

1094. Book tour of the United States by an author was made by the English writer Charles Dickens. He first visited the United States in 1842. On November 19, 1867, he arrived in Boston, MA, to begin a book tour in which he stopped at major cities to perform readings from his works. He was paid $3,000 per reading, and his performances, which were wildly popular, stimulated sales of his books. He left in April 1868.

1095. American poet honored in Westminster Abbey in London, England, was Henry Wadsworth Longellow, a descendant of English immigrants. Longellow died in 1882 and was buried in Cambridge, MA. In 1884, a white marble bust sculpted by Sir Thomas Brock was placed in the abbey's Poets' Corner "by the English admirers of an American poet," as the inscription read.

1096. Novel by a woman of Native American descent was *Wynema: A Child of the Forest*, by S. Alice Callahan, an Oklahoma teacher who was the daughter of a Muscogee (Creek) mother and an Irish-American father. It was published in 1891.

1097. Nonfiction best-seller other than a textbook or purely theological work was *In His Steps, or What Would Jesus Do?* by the Reverend Charles Monroe Sheldon. It was written in the winter of 1896 and was a utopian fantasy of what the world might be like if people lived literally according to the teachings of Jesus. It was read by the author a chapter at a

Library of Congress, Prints & Photographs Division
LC-USZ61-225

Henry Wadsworth Longfellow

time to his Sunday evening congregation in the Central Congregational Church, Topeka, KS. He sold the story for $75 to the Chicago *Advance* and it was printed as a serial in 1897. As only parts of the serial were sent to the copyright office, the copyright was declared defective. Over 8 million copies in various editions were published by different publishers.

1098. Comic books were published in 1904 by Cupples and Leon, New York City. They were collections of cartoons that had previously been published in newspapers. The books were 10 inches high and 15 inches long, contained 40 pages, and retailed for 75 cents. The titles of some of the books were *Alphonse and Gaston and Their Friend Leon* and *Happy Hooligan* by Frederick Burr Opper, *The Naughty Adventures of Vicious Mr. Jack* by James Swinnerton, and *The Katzenjammer Kids* by Rudolph Dirks. The first comic book containing original material was *More Fun*, published in 1935 by National Periodical Publications, which later became Detective Comics (DC).

1099. Book-of-the-Month Club selection was *Lolly Willowes, or the Loving Huntsman*, by Sylvia Townsend Warner, published by Viking Press, which was distributed to 4,750 members of the club on April 16, 1926. The club was established in New York City in April 1926 by Harry Scherman, with Robert Haas as president. The original book judges were Dorothy Canfield, Heywood Broun, Henry Seidel Canby, William Allen White, and Christopher Morley.

1100. Comics studio for the mass production of comics was started in 1936 by Will Eisner and Jerry Iger in New York City. Eisner, the creator of "The Spirit," mentored other comic-book artists such as satirist Jules Feiffer, Bob Kane, the creator of "Batman," and Art Spiegelman, the author of *Maus*.

1101. Comic book hero with superpowers was Superman, created by writer Jerry Siegel and artist Joe Shuster, childhood friends from Cleveland, OH, who shared an interest in science fiction. Both were on the staff of D.C. Comics in New York City, working on other people's comic strips, when the company's publisher decided to take a chance on their unusual superhero character. Superman was featured in the first volume of Action Comics, which appeared in June 1938.

Jerry Siegel and Joe Shuster's original Superman was a superpowered villain. In 1933 they decided he would make a better hero, so they created a comic strip for him. It was rejected by all the newspaper comics syndicates.

1102. Batman comic book was *Detective Comics* issue #27 (May 1939), published by Manhattan-based National Publications (later DC Comics, acquired by Warner Communications in 1976). Originally billed as "The Bat-Man," the Caped Crusader was co-created by artist Bob Kane and writer Bill Finger, though only Kane received official credit. It was Finger, however, who conceived of the bat connection and who suggested the character's cowled headgear and black cape. Batman's sidekick, Robin (also the creation of Finger), did not appear until issue #38 (April 1940). By 2005, a mint copy of *Detective Comics* #27 was worth more than $300,000 to collectors.

1103. Comic book versions of literary works were created by Albert Kanter, founder of the Gilberton Company. In 1940, Kanter began publishing *Classic Comics*, a line of great books in comic-book format that proved popular with GIs. The name was changed to *Classics Illustrated* in 1947. Among the works adapted were *Moby-Dick*, *Frankenstein*, and *Romeo and Juliet*.

1104. Book censorship board established by a state was appointed by Georgia in March 1953 under authority of an act approved on February 19, 1953, with the power to make recommendations for prosecution. The first chairman of the three-member committee was James Wesberry. Newspapers were not subject to review or censorship.

1105. Beat Generation literary event of note was a poetry reading at the Six Gallery in San Francisco, CA, on October 7, 1955. Hosted by Kenneth Rexroth, it featured five readers, including Allen Ginsberg, who electrified the crowd of about 150 listeners with his recitation of "Howl."

1106. Spider-Man comic book was issue #15 (August 1962) of *Amazing Fantasy* (formerly *Amazing Adventures*, then *Amazing*

Adult Fantasy), published by Marvel Comics, New York, NY. Spider-Man, described in the Marvel copy as "America's most different new teen-age idol!," was created by writer-editor Stan Lee and designed by artist Steve Ditko. The *Amazing Fantasy* story introduced readers to troubled high school student Peter Parker and explained how he gained his superpowers from a radioactive spider. The value of a mint edition of *Amazing Fantasy* was more than $42,000 in 2005. Spider-Man proved to be so popular that he was given his own title, *The Amazing Spider-Man*, starting in March 1963.

1107. Underground comic book of note was the Apex Novelty Company's *Zap*, which appeared on newsstands in San Francisco, CA, beginning on October 3, 1967, and ran for several issues. It featured sexually frank, politically radical drawings and stories by Robert Crumb, Gilbert Shelton, S. Clay Wilson, Spain, and other artists. One issue was impounded for obscenity in Berkeley, CA, by the police.

1108. Graphic novel has a variety of claimants, but the honor is usually given to *A Contract with God, And Other Tenement Stories* by Will Eisner, published by Baronet Books, New York, NY, in October 1978. Eisner, a veteran comic-book artist and writer, intended his work to be viewed as a form of literature, "to call attention to things that human beings must deal with in the struggle for survival." The four stories that make up the book deal with Jewish life in the Bronx of the 1930s, where Eisner grew up.

1109. Poet laureate of the United States was Robert Penn Warren, who was named the country's first official poet laureate on February 26, 1986, in Washington, DC, by the Librarian of Congress, Daniel J. Boorstin. Warren was born in Guthrie, KY, in 1905 and won three Pulitzer Prizes, two for volumes of poetry and one for his 1946 novel *All the King's Men*. The first woman to hold the post was Mona Van Duyn, designated in 1992, the sixth person to receive that honor. The first African-American poet laureate, named in 1993, was Rita Dove, who in 1985 had become the second African-American woman to win a Pulitzer Prize for poetry.

1110. Language to have its entire literature digitized was Yiddish, the language of the Jews of eastern Europe. Beginning in January 1999, the National Yiddish Book Center in Amherst, MA, digitized 35,000 books in Yiddish by running the pages through an automatic scanning machine, making it possible to reproduce any of the books electronically in 30 seconds. Most of the world's Yiddish-speaking Jews were killed by the Nazis and their collaborators during the Holocaust (1938–45), so this project helped to ensure that their language did not die with them. The center was founded by Aaron Lansky in 1980.

1111. Book to sell 5 million copies in a single day was *Harry Potter and the Order of the Phoenix* by J. K. Rowling, published in the United States by Scholastic, New York, NY. The novel was published on June 21, 2003. Sales exceeded $5 million on that day in the U.S. alone.

Movies

1112. Movie made in the United States was *Monkeyshines, No. 1*, a brief test film made in November 1890 by William Kennedy Laurie Dickson and William Heise using Dickson's Kinetograph camera. The film, showing a lab worker clowning around, was made in West Orange, NJ, at the Edison Laboratory. It was never shown to the public.

1113. Movie studio was a frame cabin covered with black roofing paper, built on Thomas Alva Edison's property in West Orange, NJ, in 1892. The structure was built so that it could be pivoted to enable the stage to secure the maximum sunlight. It was called a "revolving photographic building" and was completed on February 1, 1893, at a cost of $638. It was nicknamed Black Maria.

1114. Movie exhibition was held on May 9, 1893, before 400 people at the Department of Physics, Brooklyn Institute, Brooklyn, NY (now part of New York City). Thomas Alva Edison's Kinetograph was used. An optical lantern projector showed moving images of a blacksmith and his two helpers passing a bottle and forging a piece of iron. Each filmstrip had 700 images, each of which appeared for about 0.01 seconds. The equipment that was to have provided sound accompaniment failed to operate at this showing.

1115. Movie to be copyrighted consisted of 47 successive frames showing Fred Ott sneezing. The images had been filmed on February 2, 1893, at the Edison studio, West Orange, NJ, by William Kennedy Laurie Dickson. The copyright was recorded as follows: "Edison Kinetoscopic Record of a Sneeze, January 7, 1894. Entered in the name of W. K. L. Dickson, under No. 2,887, January 9, 1894." This was also the first movie closeup. Earlier, on August 28, 1882, a series of photographs showing sequential motion had been copyrighted by Eadweard J. Muybridge. They could not be projected, but could be arranged to simulate movement when viewed in an electrical tachyscope.

1116. Actor to have an exclusive movie contract for a single appearance in a movie was the prizefighter James John Corbett, engaged by the Kinetoscope Exhibition Company to appear in a six-round fight, one minute each round, with Pete Courtney of Trenton, NJ, in August 1894.

1117. Movie recorded on film to be shown on a screen was exhibited by Woodville Latham, who demonstrated his Pantoptikon at 35 Frankfort Street, New York City, on April 21, 1895. A continuous roll of film, with hole perforations on the sides for spokes of the sprocket, was reeled in front of an electric light contained in a projector of the magic lantern type. On May 5, 1895, Latham filmed a staged bout of four minutes' duration between Young Griffo and Battling Charles Barnett on the roof of Madison Square Garden, New York City. The film was exhibited on May 20 at 153 Broadway, New York City, after which it was shown in a tent on Surf Avenue on Coney Island for the rest of the summer.

1118. Movies with color were exhibited in September 1895 by Thomas Alva Edison at the Cotton States Exposition, Atlanta, GA. One of them was *Annabelle, the Dancer*. The film was hand-colored at Edison's studios in West Orange, NJ, in 1894. The first movies to use a color-sensitive film process were exhibited on December 11, 1909, at the Madison Square Garden Concert Hall, New York City. They were run through red and green screens at about twice the present speed and were very hard on the eyes. The presentation was about 10 minutes long and was composed of short subjects and views. The pictures used the Kinemacolor film invented by Charles Urban and G. Albert Smith of England and licensed to Gilbert Henry Aymer and James Klein Bowen of Allentown, PA.

1119. Movie production company formed expressly to make and distribute movies was the American Mutoscope and Biograph Company, founded in New York City on December 27, 1895, by William Kennedy Laurie Dickson, formerly an associate of Thomas Edison, and three others. The company made twelve feature films and thousands of shorts. Its first release, in 1896, was *Empire State Express*.

1120. Movie kiss happened in *The Kiss*, a 20-second short made by Thomas Edison's Black Maria studio. It featured two famous actors of the time, May Irwin and John Rice, who were currently appearing on Broadway in J. J. McNally's musical comedy *The Widow Jones*. The kiss that their characters share at the end of the play was filmed by cameraman William Heise at the studio in West Orange, NJ, in April 1896.

1121. Movie exhibition in a theater to a paying audience was held on April 23, 1896, in Koster and Bial's Music Hall, 34th Street, New York City. Thomas Alva Edison's Vitascope depicted a series of short scenes, including a ballet scene, a burlesque boxing match, surf breaking on the shore, and a comic allegory entitled *The Monroe Doctrine*. The images were about half life-size and were shown in conjunction with other acts. The audience called for Edison, but he did not appear and refused to take a bow.

1122. Movie western was a 46-second short, *Cripple Creek Bar-Room Scene*, made at the Edison studio in West Orange, NJ, in March and April 1899. James White was the producer. The scene was set in a Colorado bar, where a barmaid (played by a man) subdues a drunken miner by spraying him with vichy water.

1123. Theater to show movies was the Electric Theater, 262 South Main Street, Los Angeles, CA, a circus front tent-show called a "black top," which was opened on April 2, 1902, by Thomas Lincoln Tally. Among the first pictures shown were *The Capture of the Biddle Brothers* and *New York in a Blizzard*. The show lasted about one hour; the admission was 10 cents.

1124. Movie star was Max Aronson, known as Bronco Billy, Max Anderson, and Gilbert M. Anderson. His first film appearance was in 1903 in *The Great Train Robbery*, in which he played the roles of the bandit, the brakeman, and the passenger who was shot. His first starring role was in *The Messenger Boy's Mistake*, for which he was paid 50 cents an hour.

1125. Movie with multiple plot lines was *The Great Train Robbery*, directed by Edwin Stanton Porter for the Edison Company and shot in New Jersey in the fall of 1903. The movie, about 10 minutes long, followed the violent exploits of a gang of bandits as they rob a passenger train and stage a climactic shootout with a sheriff's posse. Porter introduced the use of jump cuts between parallel lines of action and shocking images that later became movie clichés, including the tossing of a body from a moving train. The film starred "Broncho Billy" Anderson (Max H. Aronson).

1126. Movie theater was the Nickelodeon, which was opened on June 19, 1905, by Harry Davis in an empty store at 433–435 Smithfield Street, Pittsburgh, PA. It had 96 seats taken from Davis's other theaters. Among the first films shown were *Poor But Honest* and *The Baffled Burglar*. A profit of over $1,000 was netted the first week. John Paul Harris was general manager and Isaac Lisbon manager.

1127. Movie spoof was the Edison Company's 12-minute short *The Little Train Robbery*, filmed in Connellsville, PA, in August 1905 by Edwin Stanton Porter as a parody of his own 1903 film *The Great Train Robbery*. In this version, all the characters are children, including the robbers, the passengers, and the police.

1128. Movie star who was a woman was Florence Lawrence, whose first performance in films was in 1907 for the Edison company. She then worked for the Vitagraph Company. In 1909 she went to the Biograph Company and was featured as "The Biograph Girl." Later she became known as "The IMP Girl," working for the Independent Moving Picture Company.

1129. Movie censorship board at the national level was the National Board of Censorship of Motion Pictures, organized in March 1909 by the People's Institute of New York City, which had been founded on May 15, 1897. Producing companies agreed to prorate a review charge among their member companies based on a fee of $3.50 for each negative reel of 1,000 feet. The fund was applied to the office expenses of the board. In 1916 the name was changed to the National Board of Review of Motion Pictures.

1130. Movie director who was a woman was Alice Guy Blaché. A pioneer filmmaker for the Gaumont studio in Paris, France, she founded her own production company, the Solax Company, in 1910 in New York City, and built a state-of-the-art studio in Fort Lee, NJ. She directed some 35 films for Solax and served as producer for many more.

1131. Movie made in Hollywood was *In Old California*, a silent 17-minute melodrama by D. W. Griffith and shot by Billy Blitzer. It was released by Biograph in 1910.

1132. Movie star who was an inventor was Florence Lawrence (born Florence Annie Bridgwood), who became the leading actress of the IMP Company, an early movie studio, in 1910. She invented a set of mechanical turn signals for automobiles as well as a rear-end stop sign that was activated when the driver braked. These were the precursors of electric turn signals and brake lights.

1133. Movie censorship board established by a state was the State Board of Censors, created in Pennsylvania by act of June 19, 1911. No appropriation was made until April 4, 1913, when $7,500 was provided. Censors were appointed on February 1, 1914. Ohio approved an act on May 3, 1913, providing for a three-member censorship board. Kansas approved an act on March 13, 1913, but no provisions to enforce it were made until 1915. The Supreme Court in February 1915 held the Ohio and Kansas censorship laws unconstitutional.

1134. Movie version of a Shakespeare play to be made in the United States was *Richard III*, produced in 1912. The movie was the second feature-length American film. It starred English actor Frederick Warde and cost $30,000, a huge budget for the time. A print of the long-lost film was donated to the American Film Institute, Los Angeles, CA, on September 17, 1996, by William Buffum, a 77-year-old former projectionist living in Portland, OR.

1135. Movie photographed from an airplane was shot on February 16, 1912, by Frank Trenholm Coffin in a hydroplane flying over lower Manhattan and New York Harbor.

Still photographs from the movie were shown on a full page of the *New York Times* issue of February 18, 1912.

1136. Foreign feature film exhibited was *Queen Elizabeth*, shown to an invited audience on July 12, 1912, at the Lyceum Theatre, New York City, and commercially exhibited on August 12, 1912, at the Powers Theater, Chicago, IL. It was a four-reel feature made in France that starred Sarah Bernhardt as Queen Elizabeth and Lou Tellegen as Robert Devereux, Earl of Essex. It was released by Famous Players Film Company, of which Adolph Zukor was president and Daniel Frohman managing director.

1137. Movie censorship law enacted by Congress was the act of July 31, 1912, "to prohibit the importation and the interstate transportation of films or other pictorial representations of prize fights." The penalty for violation was not more than $1,000, or one year at hard labor, or both.

1138. Movie of feature length made in Hollywood was *The Squaw Man*, shot in 1913 in a rented stable when Hollywood was still a quiet village. Dustin Farnum played the lead, and Cecil B. DeMille directed. The movie was the first to be produced by Samuel Goldfish, later known as Samuel Goldwyn.

1139. Serial movie with installments longer than one reel was *The Adventures of Kathlyn*, issued by Selig's Polyscope Company, Chicago, IL, on December 29, 1913. The first installment was a two-part drama, "The Unwelcome Throne," in three reels, featuring Kathlyn Williams, Tom Santochi, Charles Clary, William Carpenter, and Goldie Caldwell. Twelve other installments of two reels each followed. F. J. Grandon was the director. The film was adapted by Gilson Willets from a story by Harold MacGrath that appeared in the Hearst newspapers in 1913 and that was published in book form by the Bobbs-Merrill Company, Indianapolis, IN, in 1914.

1140. Movie comedy of feature length was *Tillie's Punctured Romance*, released on December 21, 1914, by the Alco Film Corporation. It took four weeks to produce. The director was Mack Sennett and the stars were Marie Dressler, Mabel Normand, Charles Chaplin, and Mack Swain.

1141. Movie blockbuster was *The Birth of a Nation*, directed by D. W. Griffith and based on two novels by Thomas F. Dixon, Jr. The movie premiered in Los Angeles, CA, on February 8, 1915. It was a three-hour silent epic about the South in the aftermath of the Civil War and used innovative editing techniques to create an unprecedented level of visual and emotional excitement. Audiences came in droves to see it, while the NAACP protested its racial stereotyping and its glorification of the Ku Klux Klan. It remained the biggest money-earner in film history until 1937.

THE BIRTH OF A NATION provoked riots against African-Americans by skillfully playing on many white people's fears, and it was responsible for the resurgence of the Ku Klux Klan as a domestic terrorist organization.

1142. Movie featuring an African-American actor was *Natural Born Gambler*, produced by Biograph in 1916. It starred Bert Williams, leading comedian of the Ziegfeld Follies from 1909 to 1919. The first movie with sound to feature African-American entertainers was *Snappy Tunes*, featuring Noble Sissle and Eubie Blake, which was released in 1923. It used the Phonofilm system invented by Dr. Lee De Forest.

1143. Movie sex shocker was *A Daughter of the Gods*, directed by Herbert Brenon, with music by Robert Hood Bowers, which was shown at the Lyric Theatre, New York City, on October 17, 1916. It featured Annette Kellerman, about whom a reviewer wrote that she "wanders disconsolately . . . through the film, all undressed and nowhere to go."

1144. Movie director who was African-American was Oscar Micheaux, a South Dakota writer. In 1918 he started the Micheaux Book and Film Company to make a film version of his novel *The Homesteader*. His 1919 film *Within Our Gates* was his reply to D. W. Griffith's film *The Birth of a Nation*, depicting the same era—Reconstruction—but from another point of view. One scene of attempted rape from *The Birth of a Nation* was re-created by Micheaux, but with the races of the characters switched. In all, Micheaux directed 44 films, for which he also served as writer and producer.

WITHIN OUR GATES is the oldest extant film by an African-American director.

1145. Movie in Technicolor that was really successful was *The Toll of the Sea*, released on December 3, 1922, at the Rialto Theatre, New York City. The process was developed by Dr. Herbert Thomas Kalmus, president and general manager of Technicolor Motion Picture Corporation from its inception until 1959.

1146. Movie with sound recorded on the film was Dr. Lee De Forest's Phonofilm, demonstrated on March 12, 1923, for the press and on April 4, 1923, before the New York Electrical Society in New York City. Pictures were shown with music, but no voices were heard. The pictures were shown on April 15 to an invited audience at the Rivoli Theatre, New York City. Presented on the film were "The Gavotte" (a man and woman dancing to old-time music); "The Serenade" (four musicians playing on wind, percussion, and string instruments); and an Egyptian dancer. The sound occupied a narrow margin of the film on which the pictures appeared.

1147. Movie with sound to be released as a feature or "talking picture" was presented on August 5, 1926, at an invitation performance at the Warner Theatre, New York City. On August 6, a gala premiere was held at which seats sold for $10. The show used the Vitaphone system, meaning that the film did not carry a sound recording but was synchronized with disc phonograph records of the musical score. The main feature was *Don Juan*, directed by Alan Crosland, which starred John Barrymore, Mary Astor, Warner Oland, Estelle Taylor, and Myrna Loy. The musical score was played by the New York Philharmonic Orchestra. It was preceded by a number of short features showing performances by Mischa Elman, Efrem Zimbalist, a marimba band, and other musicians.

1148. Celebrities to leave handprints at Grauman's Chinese Theatre in Hollywood, CA, were Mary Pickford and Douglas Fairbanks, who pressed their palms into wet cement on April 20, 1927. Along with Sid Grauman, the two were part owners of the theater, which opened to the public on May 18, 1927.

1149. Feature film with recorded music and dialogue was *The Jazz Singer*, which premiered in New York City on October 6, 1927. Directed by Alan Crosland for Warner Bros., it starred Al Jolson as the musically talented cantor's son whose father can't forgive him for deserting the synagogue in search of applause on Broadway. The film, originally planned as a mainly silent movie with musical sequences, was altered to include scenes with dialogue after Jolson ad-libbed his signature line, "You ain't heard nothin' yet!"

Al Jolson's own life paralleled that of the character he played in THE JAZZ SINGER. Born Asa Yoelson in Lithuania, he was himself the son of a cantor and became an entertainer after the family moved to the United States.

1150. Movie of feature length made outdoors was *In Old Arizona*, a film version of O. Henry's "The Caballero's Way," a Fox Movietone with sound recorded on the film. It was released on January 20, 1929. Most of the production was shot on location in Zion National Park and Bryce Canyon, Utah; in California's Mojave desert; and at the old San Fernando mission in California. It was directed by Raoul Walsh and Irving Cummings and featured Edmund Lowe, Warner Baxter, and Dorothy Burgess.

1151. Movie by a major company for an African-American audience was the William Fox Movietone feature *Hearts In Dixie*, a musical comedy drama of the South featuring 200 entertainers, which was first shown on February 27, 1929, at the Gaiety Theatre, New York City. It was a Paul Sloane production, written and directed by Eugene Walter, with story and dialogue by Walter Weems. The featured actor was Stephen "Stepin'" Fetchit. The entire cast, with one exception, was African-American.

1152. Oscar for best picture was awarded to *Wings*, an aviation adventure released by Paramount Pictures in 1927. It was directed by William A. Wellman and starred Clara Bow, Charles "Buddy" Rogers, Richard Arlen, and Gary Cooper. The award was presented to Wellman by the Academy of Motion Picture Arts and Sciences in Hollywood, CA, on May 16, 1929.

1153. Oscars for best acting were presented to Emil Jannings (*The Last Command*, *The Way of All Flesh*) and Janet Gaynor (*Seventh Heaven*, *Street Angel*, *Sunrise*) by the Academy of Motion Picture Arts and Sciences in Hollywood, CA, on May 16, 1929, "for the best acting in pictures released in Los Angeles, CA, between August 1, 1927, and July 31, 1928." Ten similar awards and two special awards were presented to others for excellence in allied fields, such as cinematography, art direction, engineering effects, and direction.

1154. Oscars for best movie director were given to Frank Borzage for the drama *Seventh Heaven* and Lewis Milestone for the comedy *Two Arabian Knights*. The awards were presented by the Academy of Motion Picture Arts and Sciences in Hollywood, CA, on May 16, 1929.

1155. Movie with both sound and color was Warner Brothers' Vitaphone Technicolor film *On With the Show*, exhibited on May 28, 1929, at the Winter Garden, New York City. The cast included Betty Compson, Joe E. Brown, and Ethel Waters. It was directed by Alan Crosland and was based on a story by Humphrey Pearson.

1156. Movie entertainment shown on an airplane was a newsreel and two cartoon comedies. They were shown on October 8, 1929, by the Transcontinental Air Transport Company in a Ford transport plane 5,000 feet in the air. The projector was installed by J. Frankenberg, its originator. It weighed about eight pounds; the entire apparatus together with batteries weighed less than 34 pounds. It utilized a delicate filament lamp, specially designed to operate on low voltage, which was unaffected by the vibration of the engines. Regular in-flight movie service began on July 19, 1961, on a Trans World Airlines flight between New York City and Los Angeles. The movie was *By Love Possessed*.

1157. Newsreel theater was the Embassy, on Broadway and 46th Street, New York City, which opened on November 2, 1929.

1158. Theater designed and built for the rear projection of movies was the Trans-Lux Theatre at 58th Street and Madison Avenue, New York City, which was opened on March 14, 1931. The first rear-projection screen of theater size had been installed on March 11, 1927, for the opening night of the Roxy Theatre, New York City. It was a Trans-Lux screen 18 by 22 feet which at first was used only for silhouette work, because the lens of the projector was imperfect.

1159. Drive-in movie theater was opened on June 6, 1933, on a 10-acre plot on Admiral Wilson Boulevard, Camden, NJ, by Richard Milton Hollingshead, Jr., and Willis Warren Smith of Riverton, NJ. Two shows were presented nightly on a screen 40 by 50 feet. Nine rows of inclined planes with aisles 45 feet deep accommodated 500 cars. The sound equipment was supplied by the RCA-Victor Company, Camden, NJ.

1160. Movie associated with a merchandise marketing campaign was the Disney animated feature *Snow White and the Seven Dwarfs*, which premiered in Los Angeles on December 21, 1937. Figurines and toys inspired by the movie were sold at the premiere.

1161. Movie to earn $1 billion was Walt Disney's animated film *Snow White and the Seven Dwarfs*, first exhibited on December 21, 1937, in Los Angeles, CA. In its nine theatrical releases between 1937 and 1994, it earned approximately $1 billion. The home video version of *Snow White* was officially released on October 28, 1994, after receiving about 27 million retail orders, making it the top-selling video up to that time.

1162. Movie to be shown on a television screen was Alexander Korda's *The Return of the Scarlet Pimpernel*, a 1.5-hour film shown by NBC on May 31, 1938. The image was 7 by 10 inches. Preceding the film, five actors produced a 20-minute play for children entitled *Sauce for the Gander*.

1163. Movie premiere festivities to be shown on television were presented on December 19, 1939, on station W2XBS of the National Broadcasting Company on the occasion of the New York opening of *Gone With the Wind*. Two cameras, one on the sidewalk outside the Capitol Theatre, New York City, and the other in the lobby, recorded interviews with celebrities. Ben Grauer was the master of ceremonies. The film, based on Margaret Mitchell's novel, was produced by David Oliver Selznick and starred Clark Gable and Vivien Leigh.

1164. Oscar awarded to an African-American performer was won by Hattie McDaniel, who played Scarlett O'Hara's "mammy" in the movie version of Margaret Mitchell's *Gone With the Wind*. The award, for the best performance by a supporting actress, was presented by the Academy of Motion Picture Arts and Sciences on February 29, 1940, in Hollywood, CA.

1165. Noir film is widely considered to have been the 1941 version of *The Maltese Falcon*, directed by John Huston for Warner Bros., Hollywood, CA, and based on the novel by Dashiell Hammett, with Humphrey Bogart starring as private detective Sam Spade. Noir films featured a brooding visual esthetic derived from early German Expressionist films and a generally dark view of human nature.

1166. Movie star who was a weapons inventor was Hedy Lamarr, born Hedwig Eva Maria Kiesler in Vienna, Austria, about 1914. While under contract with the MGM studio in Hollywood, CA, she developed the concept of "frequency hopping" as a means of controlling torpedoes by radio. The method was highly resistant to jamming and eavesdropping because it utilized quick and unpredictable changes in the frequency of the controlling radio transmission. Co-inventor George Antheil, an avant-garde composer born in New Jersey, came up with the idea of using punched paper rolls like those in player pianos to synchronize the frequency changes between transmitter and receiver. They received a patent for the system on August 11, 1942. Although it was not used during World War II, the technique of frequency hopping later became a standard feature of military wireless remote-control systems.

1167. Movie to premiere on television was a two-reel short, *Patrolling the Ether*, that was televised on April 10, 1944, simultaneously by WNBT of New York City, WRGB of Schenectady, NY, and WPTZ of Philadelphia. The film depicted the wartime activities of the radio intelligence division of the Federal Communications Commission in tracing illegal and espionage radio transmitters. It was produced by Metro-Goldwyn-Mayer and released to theaters on April 22, 1944, 12 days after its premiere on television. The first full-length American film to receive its premiere on television was *The Constant Husband*, directed by Sir Alexander Korda and starring Rex Harrison and Margaret Leighton, which was shown coast-to-coast by the National Broadcasting Company from WNBT-TV, New York City, on November 6, 1955.

1168. Movie in Cinemascope was Henry Koster's *The Robe*, a biblical epic released in 1953 and starring Richard Burton, Jean Simmons, and Victor Mature. The Cinemascope screen was wider than conventional screens, providing viewers with a greater sense of immersion in the movie. However, production was more costly than for traditional films, and relatively few Cinemascope theaters were built. Cinemascope was eventually abandoned by Hollywood when it failed to lure viewers away from the newer medium of television.

1169. Three-dimensional feature movie was *Bwana Devil*, produced, directed, and written by Arch Oboler of Arch Oboler Productions and released by United Artists in 1953. It was a Natural Vision-Magnetic Sound Track picture requiring Polaroid viewers. It opened on February 18, 1953, at Loew's State Theatre, New York City. It was the story of a British engineer who tracked two man-eating lions that were disrupting the construction of the first railroad in East Africa at the turn of the century. The cast included Robert Stack, Barbara Britton, Nigel Bruce, and Ramsay Hill.

1170. Oscar awards ceremony to be telecast took place on March 19, 1953, when pick-ups of the 25th ceremony of the Academy of Motion Picture Arts and Sciences were made from New York City and Hollywood, CA, and broadcast over 174 stations. Oscar winners included *The Greatest Show on Earth* for best picture, Gary Cooper as best actor for his performance in *High Noon*, and Shirley Booth as best actress for her performance in *Come Back, Little Sheba*. The first color telecast of the Academy Awards took place in 1966.

1171. Three-dimensional feature movie in color produced by a major studio was *House of Wax*, starring Vincent Price, first exhibited on April 10, 1953, at the Paramount Theatre, New York City. It was a remake of the 1933 movie *Mystery of the Wax Museum*. *House of Wax* was in Warnercolor and was seen through Polaroid viewers.

1172. Movie to be shown simultaneously on pay television and in movie theaters was Paramount's *Forever Female*, directed by Pat Duggan and starring William Holden, Ginger Rogers, and Paul Douglas. It was transmitted on November 28, 1953, to 70 Telemeter receiving sets in Palm Springs, CA. At the same time, it was shown at the Plaza Theatre in Palm Springs. The telecast fee, $1.35, was placed in a coin box attached to each set.

1173. Oscar for best picture awarded to a movie that was independently produced was won by *Marty*, the 1955 film version of a television play by Paddy Chayefsky. The film was produced by an independent company founded by Burt Lancaster and Harold Hecht.

1174. Movie with scent was *Behind the Great Wall*, a travelog of modern China, presented on December 8, 1959, at the De Mille Theatre, New York City. The film depicted a tiger hunt, fishing with cormorants, a May Day parade in Beijing, and other scenes. The scent was forced through ceiling vents by the Aromarama process.

1175. Movie premiered simultaneously in major cities throughout the world was *On the Beach*, an adaptation of the novel by Nevil Shute, which had its premiere on December 17, 1959, at New York City's Astor Theatre and in 17 other cities. The 134-minute film was produced by Stanley Kramer and written by John Paxton. It starred Gregory Peck, Ava Gardner, Fred Astaire, and Anthony Perkins.

1176. Oscar for best actor awarded to an African-American performer was won by Sidney Poitier, who played an itinerant construction worker in *Lilies of the Field*. He received his Oscar on April 13, 1964. The first African-American to win the Oscar for best actress was Halle Berry, who won on March 24, 2002, for her performance in *Monster's Ball*.

MONSTER'S BALL was the first Oscar-winning film produced by a sole African-American producer, Lee Daniels.

1177. Hollywood movie directed by an African-American was *The Learning Tree*, released by Warner Brothers–Seven Arts, Hollywood, CA, in 1969. The director was Gordon Parks, who based it on his autobiographical novel of the same name. Parks was also the producer, the scriptwriter, and the composer.

1178. Oscar for best picture awarded to an X-rated movie was given to *Midnight Cowboy*, a 1969 film directed by John Schlesinger and starring Jon Voight and Dustin Hoffman.

1179. Movie to be digitally restored was the 1937 Disney animated feature *Snow White and the Seven Dwarfs*. Before its re-release by Disney in 1993, it was made into a digital version so that it could be restored using computer graphics tools.

1180. Movie broadcast on the Internet was *Wax: Or the Discovery of Television Among the Bees*, a cult science-fiction film by director David Blair. Blair uploaded the film in digital video format on May 22, 1993, for viewing worldwide.

1181. Movie that cost more than $100 million to make was *True Lies*, a 20th Century–Fox action-adventure film directed by James Cameron and starring Arnold Schwarzenegger. It opened nationwide on July 15, 1994. Though exact figures were not released by the studio, the film was estimated to have cost $115 million.

1182. Movie rated NC-17 was *Showgirls*, directed by Paul Verhoeven and released by MGM/UA on September 22, 1995. The NC-17 rating from the Motion Picture Association of America restricted films to viewers over 17 years old. Although many theaters shunned films rated NC-17 as having too limited an audience, *Showgirls*, a lurid drama about Las Vegas strippers, debuted in 1,000 theaters, far more than any previous NC-17 movie. Despite extensive pre-release publicity, *Showgirls* was a resounding flop at the box office.

1183. Movie to earn more than $400 million in the United States market was *Star Wars*, a 1977 science-fiction film directed by George Lucas for 20th Century–Fox. It reached the $400 million mark after it was re-released in February 1997 in a 20th-anniversary edition with enhanced special effects.

1184. Movie to earn $1 billion in its first worldwide theatrical release was *Titanic*, an epic romance about the doomed luxury liner. The 1997 film was written, produced, and directed by James Cameron and distributed by two Hollywood studios—Paramount Pictures and Twentieth Century Fox. By March 2, 1998, the film had earned $575.7 million in the international box office and $427 million in North American theaters, for a total of $1,002,706,625. It was the highest-grossing film of all time, as well as the highest-grossing film in more than 50 countries.

1185. Web site constructed to authenticate a film was *www.haxan.com*, launched in June 1998 before the release of the film it supported, *The Blair Witch Project*. The film, a low-budget work of fiction made by Daniel Myrick and Eduardo Sanchez, purported to be actual footage taken by a trio of young filmmakers who had disappeared while investigating a local witchcraft legend. The Web site covered the "legend" in detail, as if it were historical, and made no mention of the movie.

THE BLAIR WITCH PROJECT was the highest grossing film of 1999.

1186. Feature film to premiere simultaneously in a theater and on the Internet was *Dead Broke*, a low-budget drama written and directed by Edward Vilga and starring Paul Sorvino, Tony Roberts, and John Glover. On May 5, 1999, it was made available for viewing anywhere in the world via the Web site of iFilm Network, an online community of independent filmmakers and film fans. Simultaneously, the film was downloaded by satellite feed to a digital projection system at the Tribeca Film Center, a movie theater in New York City.

1187. Digital projection of a major motion picture took place on June 18, 1999, when four theaters—two in New Jersey and two in California—screened George Lucas's science fantasy film *Star Wars: Episode 1—The Phantom Menace* using experimental filmless digital projection systems from competing manufacturers CineComm and Texas Instruments. In both systems, a computerized projector delivered images to the screen directly from a motion graphics file stored on a high-capacity hard disk or downloaded from a satellite transmission.

1188. Major motion picture produced and exhibited entirely with digital technology was Walt Disney Pictures' animated feature *Tarzan*, based on the Edgar Rice Burroughs story. Produced and mastered entirely digitally using animation, composition, and editing software, it began a run using filmless digital projection systems at three theaters—one in Orlando, FL, one in Burbank, CA, and one in Irvine, CA—on July 23, 1999.

1189. Movie on videocassette to be released worldwide in one week was *Star Wars: Episode I: The Phantom Menace,* directed by George Lucas. The distributors, Twentieth Century Fox Home Entertainment, Century City, CA, and Lucasfilm Ltd., San Francisco, CA, made the videocassettes available for sale in most countries during the week of April 3 through April 8, 2000.

1190. Movie to gross $100 million in its opening weekend was *Spider-Man*, directed by Sam Raimi for Columbia Pictures, Culver City, CA. On the weekend beginning May 3, 2002, it appeared in 3,615 theaters in the United States and Canada, earning $114.8 million in gross box-office receipts.

1191. Movie sold simultaneously as a downloadable product and a DVD after its original theatrical release was *Brokeback Mountain*. On April 4, 2006, it became available in DVD format at retail stores and in downloadable format from Movielink.com, a Web site supported by six major Hollywood studios. Customers could download the movie to their computer hard drives and view it repeatedly on their monitors.

Animations

1192. Animated picture machine was the Zoetrope, the Wheel of Life, patented on April 23, 1867, by William E. Lincoln of Providence, RI, who assigned it to Milton Bradley and Company, Springfield, MA. It consisted of a horizontal wheel with a series of animated drawings showing successive steps at right angles to the circumference. The drawings were viewed through a slit and, when the wheel revolved, appeared to show animation.

1193. Animated photograph projection before a theater audience was shown on February 5, 1870, at the Academy of Music, Philadelphia, PA, at the Ninth Annual Entertainment of the Young Men's Society of St. Mark's Evangelical Lutheran Church of Philadelphia, by Henry Renno Heyl. Heyl used his Phasmatrope, a converted projecting lantern in front of which was a revolving disc containing 16 openings near the edge on which photographic plates were placed. The first plate showed dancers who appeared to move as the revolving wheel showed successive motions. The pictures were continuous and did not change.

1194. Flicker animation was patented by Henry Van Hoevenbergh of Elizabeth, NJ, who obtained a patent on May 16, 1882, on an "optical toy." The flicker was a series of successive drawings bound together in book form that, when riffled front-to-back, appeared to show animation. On June 20, 1882, Van Hoevenbergh obtained a patent on an improvement combining two or more series of superimposed leaves. Alternate leaves were indented and cut.

1195. Animated cartoon was James Stuart Blackton's *Humorous Phases of Funny Faces*, containing about 8,000 drawings showing a man rolling his eyes and blowing smoke at a girl, a dog jumping over a hoop, and similar scenes. The final scene was a chalk-type drawing that the artist started as a sketch of one object, but that ended as a sketch of another. The film was released by Vitagraph in 1906.

1196. Animated cartoon made with cel animation using clear sheets of celluloid or acetate was *The Artist's Dream*, also known as *The Dachshund*, released on June 12, 1913, by Pathé Frères. It was produced by John Randolph Bray of New York City, who received a patent for the technique on August 11, 1914. The cartoon showed Bray drawing a dachshund that ate sausages until he exploded.

1197. Animated cartoon in color was *The Debut of Thomas Kat*, the story of a kitten taught by his mother to catch mice who confidently and tragically tackled a rat. The cartoon was produced by the Bray Pictures Corporation, New York City, and was released in 1916 by Paramount. The drawings were made on transparent celluloid, with the colors painted on the reverse side, and were photographed with a regular color camera. The Brewster color process was used.

1198. Animation for technical purposes was produced in 1916 by the Bray Pictures Corporation of New York City. Animated sequences permitted the visualization of "unseeable" phenomena such as the flow of invisible gases and radio waves.

1199. Animated cartoon with sound was Walt Disney's *Steamboat Willie*, produced in Hollywood, CA, depicting the antics of Mickey Mouse. It was shown on September 19, 1928, at the Colony Theatre, New York City.

1200. Animated feature-length cartoon in Technicolor was Walt Disney's *Snow White and the Seven Dwarfs*, based on the fairy tale. It was first exhibited on December 21, 1937, at the Carthay Circle Theatre, Los Angeles, CA. The running time was 75 minutes.

1201. Animated three-dimensional cartoon in Technicolor was Walt Disney's *Melody*, distributed by RKO Radio Pictures. Its world premiere took place on May 28, 1953, at the Hollywood Theatre and the Downtown Paramount Theatre, Los Angeles, CA.

1202. Animated film inducted into the National Film Registry was "What's Opera, Doc?," an animated short directed by Chuck Jones in 1957 for the Warner Bros. animation studio. It featured a Siegfried-like Elmer Fudd invoking the elements against Bugs Bunny in a parody of Wagnerian opera. On December 4, 1992, the short was inducted into the National Film Registry in Washington, DC, for being "among the most culturally, historically or aesthetically significant films of our time," an honor bestowed on only 100 films up to that time.

1203. Movie that was entirely computer-animated was *Toy Story*, 81 minutes long, released on November 21, 1995, by Walt Disney Pictures, Burbank, CA. It was produced at Pixar Corporation and directed by former Disney animator John Lasseter. The plot involves the adventures of two dolls, a cowboy and a space hero, who are rivals for the attention of a young boy. *Toy Story* was one of the year's top-grossing films, earning close to $300 million worldwide in its first 12 months of release.

Technology

1204. Photographic attempt to show motion was made by Dr. Coleman Sellers of Philadelphia, PA, who obtained a patent on February 5, 1861, on the Kinematoscope, an "improvement in exhibiting stereoscopic pictures of moving objects." A series of still pictures with successive stages of action was mounted on blades of a paddle and viewed through slits passed under the lens of a stereoscope revolved at right angles. The pictures were not reflected on a screen, and were visible only in the cabinet. The whole of the picture was not seen at once, but only by degrees as the cylinder revolved.

1205. Movie projector patent was awarded to O. B. Brown of Malden, MA, on August 10, 1869, for an "optical instrument." It combined the principles of the phenakistoscope and the magic lantern.

1206. Movie film was manufactured beginning on March 26, 1885, by the Eastman Dry Plate and Film Company of Rochester, NY, which was also the first to produce, manufacture, and market films in continuous strips on reels.

1207. Klieg light unit for movie production was invented by John Hugh Kliegl and Anton Tiberius Kliegl and placed in use in 1911. The unit used two 35-ampere arcs operating in series and equipped with an automatic arc-feed arrangement, using white flame carbons. It gave four times as much light as other available sources. The lights were first used by the Carlton Motion Picture Laboratory, Coney Island, New York City; the Lubin Manufacturing Company, Philadelphia, PA; and Thomas Alva Edison's Decatur Avenue Studio, New York City. The name was not adopted until later.

1208. Portable movie projector was invented by Dr. Herman Adolf De Vry and produced in 1913 in Chicago, IL. It weighed approximately 26 pounds, cost $200, and was known as "the projector in a suitcase."

1209. Portable movie camera was the Victor Cine Camera, manufactured by the Victor Animatograph Company, Davenport, IA, in 1923. It was 3 by 6 by 8 inches, weighed 5 pounds, and cost $55. It was advertised on August 12, 1923.

Music

1210. Music book printed with bars was *The Grounds and Rules of Musick Explained; or, an Introduction to the art of singing by note. Fitted to the Meanest Capacities. Recommended by Several Ministers*, by the Reverend Thomas Walter of Roxbury, MA. It was an oblong book containing 19 pages of songs with the reverse pages blank, and was printed in 1721 by James Franklin, Boston, MA.

1211. Vocal instruction book was *A Very Plain and Easy Introduction to the Art of Singing Psalm-tunes; with the cantus or trebles of twenty-eight psalm-tunes, contrived in such a manner as that the learner may attain the skill of singing them, with the greatest ease and speed imaginable*, by John Tufts, pastor of Newburyport, MA. It was printed by James Franklin for Samuel Gerrish in Boston, MA, in 1721. Letters took the place of notes on the staff, with F, S, L, substituting for fa, sol, la, and so on.

1212. Concert was "a concert of music on sundry instruments" held at six o'clock at Peter Pelham's "great room" near the Sun Tavern in Boston, MA, on December 30, 1731. Tickets cost five shillings each.

1213. Music society of importance was the St. Cecilia Society of Charleston, SC, organized in 1737 as an amateur concert society and formally organized in 1762 to give annual concerts and balls.

1214. Orchestra was the Collegium Musicum of Bethlehem, PA, formed in 1744. There were 14 players, including two first violins, two second violins, two violas, two flutes, two trumpets, two French horns, one cello, and one double bass. The orchestra believed to have been the original Philharmonic Orchestra was founded about 1810–11 in Boston, MA, by Johann Christian Gottlieb Graupner. Its last concert was given at the Pantheon, Boylston Square, Boston, on November 24, 1824.

1215. Orchestra in a theater was employed in 1750 at the Nassau Street Theater, located between John Street and Maiden Lane, New York City. The instruments were German flutes, horns, and drums. The theater, a two-story gabled structure, was illuminated by a chandelier made of a barrel hoop through which a dozen nails were driven to serve as candle holders. It had 10 box seats at eight shillings each, 161 pit seats at five shillings each, and 121 gallery seats at three shillings each. The stage was set five feet above the floor level.

1216. Composer born in America was Francis Hopkinson, one of the signers of the Declaration of Independence, who was born in Philadelphia, PA, in 1737 and graduated in 1757 from the College of Philadelphia. He was also a lawyer, judge, and writer of political commentary and satire. His first important song was "My Days Have Been So Wondrous Free," composed in 1759, one of the earliest secular compositions extant. In 1763, his book *A Collection of Psalm Tunes, with a few anthems and hymns, some of them entirely new, for the use of the United Churches of Christ Church and St. Peter's Church in Philadelphia* was printed by W. Dunlop, Philadelphia, PA. He was the author of the first book of secular songs by an American-born composer, *Seven Songs for the Harpsichord or Forte Piano*, published in 1788.

1217. Musical instrument dealer was Michael Hillegas, who opened a shop in Philadelphia, PA, in 1759. On December 13, 1759, he advertised instruments, music, and musical supplies in the *Pennsylvania Gazette*. Musical instruments, however, had been sold previously and were advertised for sale at a dancing school in Boston, MA, in 1716.

1218. Music book by an author born in America was *Urania; or a Choice Collection of Psalm-Tunes, Anthems, and Hymns, in Two, Three and Four parts; the whole peculiarly adapted to the use of churches and private families—to which are prefix'd the plainest and most necessary rules of Psalmody*, by James Lyon, A.B. It was published in 1761 in Philadelphia and contained 198 songs in its 220 pages.

1219. Music book printed from type was *The Psalms of David, with the ten commandments, creed, Lord's prayer, etc. In Metre, also the catechism, confession of faith, liturgy etc.*, printed by James Parker, New York City, in 1767. It had 479 pages and contained all 150 psalms, translated from the Dutch for the use of the Reformed Protestant Dutch Church of the city of New York. It was edited by Francis Hopkinson and had a preface by Johannes Ritzema. The type for the music notes was obtained from Amsterdam, Holland.

1220. Book of music by a composer born in America was *The New England Psalm-Singer or American Chorister containing a number of psalm tunes, anthems, and canons in four and five parts*, composed by William Billings. It was printed by Edes and Gill, Boston, MA, in 1770, consisted of 112 pages, and sold for eight shillings.

1221. Music printed in a magazine was "The Hill Tops, a New Hunting Song," printed in the April 1774 issue of the *Royal American Magazine or Universal Repository of Instruction and Amusement*, published by Isaiah Thomas in Boston, MA.

1222. Music magazine was the *American Musical Magazine*, which was published in May 1786 in New Haven, CT. It was issued regularly and was a collection of tunes and hymns. It was published and sold by Amos Doolittle and Daniel Read. The first issue, six pages long, contained the selection "The Seasons Moralized."

1223. Songbook of secular songs was Alexander Reinagle's *A Selection of the Most Favorite Scots Tunes*, published in August 1787 by Thomas Dobson, Philadelphia, PA.

1224. Songbook of secular songs by an American-born composer was Francis Hopkinson's *Seven Songs for the Harpsichord or Forte Piano*, which was dedicated to George Washington and published in 1788 by Thomas Dobson, Philadelphia, PA. An advertisement in the *Federal Gazette* stated: "These songs are composed in an easy familiar style, intended for young practitioners on the harpsichord or forte piano, and is the first work of this kind attempted in the U.S."

1225. Music publishers to deal exclusively in music were John C. Moller and Henri Capron of Philadelphia, PA, whose publishing business was established in 1790. They also had a music store and offered musical instruction.

1226. Singing contest in America took place in 1790 in Dorchester, MA, between the singers of the First Parish of Dorchester and the singing society of Stoughton. The Stoughtonians began with Jacob French's "Heavenly Vision," the author of which was their fellow townsman. When they finally sang Handel's *Hallelujah Chorus* without books, the Dorchestrians gave up the contest and gracefully acknowledged defeat.

1227. College orchestra was founded at Harvard University, Cambridge, MA. The minutes record that "at a meeting held on March 6, 1808, by a number of students of Harvard University, they unanimously agreed to institute a society for their mutual improvement in instrumental music." It was known as the Pierian Sodality, as it was not the custom

Library of Congress, Prints & Photographs Division
LC-USZ62-5252

Harvard Hall, on the campus of Harvard University, in the 1820s.

then for any extracurricular activity to take the name of the college. The orchestra is now known as the Harvard University Orchestra.

1228. Music festival is claimed to have been given in Boston, MA, to celebrate the signing of the Treaty of Ghent, which ended the War of 1812 between the United States and Great Britain. The treaty was signed on December 25, 1814. The news reached Boston on February 13, 1815. A concert of sacred music was played on February 16 at the Reverend Dr. Baldwin's house in Boston. It included the first part of Haydn's *Creation*, Handel's *Hallelujah Chorus*, parts of Handel's *Judas Maccabeus*, and the Dettingen *Te Deum* and *Ode to St. Cecilia's Day*.

1229. Bandleader of renown in the United States was Francis B. Johnson, also known as Frank Johnson, a free African-American whose band was in constant demand in Philadelphia, PA, among both blacks and whites, beginning circa 1818. The group played at concerts, dances, church gatherings, and numerous public events, toured widely, and introduced promenade concerts, better known today as pops concerts. Johnson himself played a variety of instruments, including bugle and violin.

Bandleader Francis B. Johnson and some of his band members became the first professional musicians from the United States to play in Europe when they visited England in 1837 to perform for Queen Victoria at Buckingham Palace.

1230. Composer who was African-American was Francis B. Johnson, better known as Frank Johnson, a free African-American from Philadelphia, PA, who wrote more than 300 musical works, including dances, marches, overtures, band music (he led the nation's first concert band), and commemorative salutes. His first composition to be published was *A Collection of New Cotillions*, which appeared in 1818.

1231. Oratorio performance was a presentation of George Frideric Handel's *Messiah* on December 25, 1818, by the Handel and Haydn Society, Boylston Hall, Boston, MA, with a chorus of approximately 200 singers. The soloists were the Misses Sumner and Bennett, Mr. J. Sharp, and Master White. Benjamin Holt, the president of the society, conducted the concert.

1232. Music book for children was the *Juvenile Lyre: or Hymns and Songs, Religious, Moral and Cheerful, set to appropriate music, for the use of primary and common schools*, by Lowell Mason, published in 1831 by Richardson, Lord and Holbrook, Boston, MA. It contained 61 songs and was copyrighted February 1, 1831, in the District of Massachusetts.

1233. Performance of "America the Beautiful" in public took place on July 4, 1832, in the Park Street Church, Boston, MA, where it was sung by the schoolchildren of Boston. The song was written on a scrap of paper in half an hour by Dr. Samuel Francis Smith, a Baptist minister. The original manuscript is in the Harvard University Library.

1234. Orchestra of international stature was the Philharmonic Society of New York, later called the New York Philharmonic. On December 7, 1842, the 63-member orchestra gave its first public performance in New York City's Apollo Room, playing Beethoven's Fifth Symphony. Ureli Corelli Hill was the conductor.

1235. Minstrel show troupe was the Virginia Minstrels, organized by Daniel Decatur Emmett, composer of "Dixie." In 1843 they gave performances at the Chatham Theatre, New York City, which was located on Chatham Street between Roosevelt and James streets, and at the Bowery Amphitheatre. Frank Brower played the bones, Richard Pelham the tambourine, Daniel Emmett the violin, and William Whitlock the banjo. They wore white trousers, striped calico shirts, and long blue calico swallowtail coats, and they blackened their faces to give themselves the appearance of African-Americans. Their popular songs included "Old Dan Tucker," "Happy Uncle Tom," and "The Raccoon Hunt."

1236. Chamber music ensemble was the Mendelssohn Quintette Club of Boston, MA. Its first concert was given at Chickering Hall on December 14, 1849.

1237. Musician born in America to achieve fame in Europe was the pianist Louis Moreau Gottschalk, who in 1852 gave concerts in the leading music centers of the world. Born in New Orleans, LA, in 1829, he exhibited an interest in music at the age of four and played an organ in church when he was six. In April 1845 he appeared in Paris, in 1846–47 in Italy, and in 1850 in Switzerland. He was also a composer who wrote piano pieces, songs, symphonies, and other instrumental and orchestral works.

1238. School band was formed in 1857 by the Boston Asylum and Farm School for Indigent Boys, located on Thompson Island in Boston Bay, MA. Musical sounds were produced by singing through paper-covered combs. Later, three violins, a bass violin, saxhorn, cornopean, and drum were added. Beginning in 1859, the band participated in street parades in Boston and elsewhere. In 1860 they had 14 brass pieces and a bass drum. On June 10, 1907, the name of the school was changed to the Farm and Trades School and in 1956 to Thompson Academy.

1239. Collection of spirituals was *Slave Songs of the United States*, edited by William Francis Allen, Charles Pickard Ware, and Lucy McKim Garrison, and published in 1867 by A. Simpson & Co., New York. It was an anthology of 136 songs that had been collected from African-American singers during the Civil War.

1240. Choral concerts featuring spirituals were offered by the Jubilee Singers, a group of nine students from the recently founded Fisk University, Nashville, TN. In 1871, they toured the Northeast and Europe in a fundraising campaign. The proceeds of the concerts were used for the construction of academic buildings.

1241. Oratorio by an American was John Knowles Paine's *Oratorio of St. Peter*, performed on June 3, 1873, at the City Hall, Portland, ME, by the Haydn Society of Portland, assisted by eminent artists from abroad and the 41-member Harvard orchestra of Cambridge, MA.

1242. Symphonic work by an American composer was the *Symphony in C minor*, Opus 23, by John Knowles Paine, presented in January 1876 in Boston, MA, by Theodore Thomas and his orchestra.

1243. Telephone concert held long-distance was held on March 31, 1877, at Steinway Hall, New York City. Music played in Philadelphia, PA, was heard by means of Elisha Gray's so-called Transmission of Music by Telegraph. The audience heard "Home, Sweet Home," "The Last Rose of Summer," "Yankee Doodle," and other songs.

1244. Catalog of recordings on disk was offered by the United States Gramophone Company, Washington, DC, the successor to Emile Berliner's American Gramophone Company. Dated November 1, 1894, the single-sheet catalog listed selections of band, instrumental, vocal, and folk music. Each disk sold for 60 cents, about half the cost of a cylinder recording.

1245. Music by Native Americans to be recorded were two disk recordings of "Indian Songs," both titled "Three Melodies from the Ghost Dance." They were listed in the first catalog, dated November 1, 1894, of the United States Gramophone Company, Washington, DC. No examples of these recordings are known to have survived.

1246. Composer born in America to win an international reputation was Edward Alexander MacDowell, born in New York City in 1861. A protege of Franz Liszt, MacDowell wrote symphonic poems, concertos, orchestral suites, songs, and piano sonatas, including *Woodland Sketches*, composed in 1896, and *Sea Pieces*, composed in 1898. He taught at Columbia University, New York City, from 1896 to 1904.

1247. Symphonic work by an American woman was the Gaelic Symphony in E Minor, Op. 32, by Amy (Cheney) Beach. It was first performed on October 30, 1896, by the Boston Symphony Orchestra.

1248. Performance of "The Stars and Stripes Forever" by John Philip Sousa took place at the Academy of Music in Philadelphia, PA, on May 14, 1897. Sousa's greatest march was such a smashing success that the audience asked to hear it twice more. One newspaper account praised it as "stirring enough to rouse the American eagle from his crag and set him to shriek exultantly while he hurls his arrows at the aurora borealis." Some musicologists believe the march was first performed in public in Augusta, ME, on May 1, two weeks earlier.

Library of Congress, Prints & Photographs Division LC-USZ61-143

John Philip Sousa

1249. Sheet music to sell millions of copies was "Maple Leaf Rag," a ragtime composition for piano by composer Scott Joplin, who was then living in Sedalia, MO. It was published in 1899.

1250. Singer whose voice was broadcast over radio was Eugenia H. Farrar, whose voice was broadcast by Lee De Forest on December 16, 1907, from the Brooklyn Navy Yard, Brooklyn, New York City, on the occasion of the departure of Admiral Robley Dunglison Evans on a cruise with the fleet.

1251. Jazz composer was William Christopher "W.C." Handy, whose *Memphis Blues* was composed in 1911 and published on September 27, 1912. An African-American born in Florence, AL, he was known as the "father of the blues," having composed numerous other pieces in that idiom, among them *St. Louis Blues* and *Beale Street Blues.*

1252. Community chorus was established in 1912 in Rochester, NY, by Harry Barnhart, who appeared by permission of the mayor of Rochester at a band concert at the Convention Hall, where he introduced the idea of community singing.

1253. Orchestra conductor who was a woman in the United States, and possibly in the world, was Mary Davenport-Engberg, who founded the Bellingham Symphony Orchestra in Bellingham, WA, in 1914, and served as its conductor. The group had 85 musicians. In 1921 she became conductor of the Seattle Symphony Orchestra.

1254. Music society for the protection of composers and song writers was the American Society of Composers, Authors and Publishers, which was formed on February 13, 1914, in New York City. The object of the society was to protect the copyrighted musical compositions of its members against illegal public performance for profit and other forms of infringement, and to collect license fees for authorized performances in public amusement establishments for distribution among its members. The society was an unincorporated voluntary association and was affiliated with similar societies functioning in foreign countries. George Maxwell was the first president.

1255. City orchestra supported by taxes was the Baltimore Symphony Orchestra, Baltimore, MD, formed in 1915 with a Board of Estimate appropriation of $6,000. It was managed by Frederick R. Huber, who took office on July 13, 1915, as the municipal director of music. The first concert master was J. C. van Hulsteyn, the first soloist Mabel Garrison, and the first conductor Gustav Strube. The first concert was presented on February 11, 1916.

1256. Jazz record sold to the public was recorded by the Original Dixieland Jass Band, a group of five white musicians led by cornetist Nick La Rocca, the son of an Italian cobbler. The session was recorded on a Victor 78 disk by the Victor Company in New York City in February 1917. It featured two tunes, "Dixieland Jass Band One-Step" and "Livery Stable Blues," in which La Rocca made his horn sound like a horse whinnying.

1257. Orchestra from the United States to make a European tour was the Symphony Society of New York, which sailed for Europe on April 22, 1920. Under the leadership of Walter Johannes Damrosch, 34 concerts were given in 21 cities in France, Italy, Belgium, Holland, and England. The first concert was given on May 4, 1920, at the Paris Opera House. The last was given on June 20, 1920, at the Royal Albert Hall, London. The Symphony Society merged with the New York Philharmonic on March 30, 1928, to form the Philharmonic Society of New York, with Arturo Toscanini as conductor in chief.

1258. Radio orchestra was the Detroit News Orchestra of Detroit, MI, a 16-piece symphonic ensemble that began broadcasting on May 28, 1922. It was composed principally of members of the Detroit Symphony Orchestra. Otto Krueger, piccolo player, was the conductor. The broadcasts were sponsored by the Detroit Bank on station WWJ.

1259. Swing band to achieve wide popular success was the Fletcher Henderson Orchestra, the regular band at the Roseland Ballroom in New York City. The group developed a swing sound in 1924 when Louis Armstrong joined the group on trumpet. Their arranger, Don Redman, was a veteran of an earlier group with a swing sound, McKinney's Cotton Pickers.

1260. Gospel composer of importance was Thomas Andrew Dorsey, born in 1899 in Villa Rica, GA. Known as "the father of gospel music," Dorsey began his career as a blues pianist and songwriter with the stage name of Georgia Tom and was later a church choir director in Chicago, IL. In 1926, after the death of a close friend, he composed "If You See My Savior, Tell Him That You Saw Me," considered the first true gospel song. Dorsey's achievement was to bring a strong blues and ragtime sound to religious song. Among his best-known compositions are "Take My Hand, Precious Lord," "The Lord Will Make a Way Somehow," and "Peace in the Valley."

1261. Symphony on an African-American folk theme was the Symphony No. 1, known as the *Negro Folk Symphony*, composed by the African-American conductor William Levi Dawson. It was first presented on November 14, 1934, by the Philadelphia Orchestra under the direction of Leopold Stokowski at the Academy of Music, Philadelphia, PA.

1262. Original movie soundtrack recording was *Snow White and the Seven Dwarfs*, released by RCA in 1937 to accompany the premiere of the Walt Disney animated film. The soundtrack featured songs with lyrics by Larry Morey and music by Frank Churchill.

1263. Symphony orchestra devoted exclusively to radio broadcasting was the National Broadcasting Company (NBC) Symphony Orchestra, formed on November 13, 1937. The conductor was Arturo Toscanini. The orchestra made its debut at 10 P.M. on December 25, 1937, over the NBC stations WEAF and WJZ, New York City. The program consisted of the first symphony of Johannes Brahms, Wolfgang Amadeus Mozart's G minor symphony, and Antonio Vivaldi's *Concerto Grosso*.

1264. White band leader to hire an African-American woman vocalist was Artie Shaw, leader of the Artie Shaw Band, an ensemble of white musicians. In 1938, he hired Billie Holiday, a newcomer to the New York jazz scene.

1265. Jazz concert at Carnegie Hall in New York City took place on January 16, 1938, when Benny Goodman and His Orchestra played with guest performers Jess Stacy, Count Basie, and members of the Basie and Duke Ellington orchestras.

1266. Bluegrass musician of renown was William Smith "Bill" Monroe, the "father of bluegrass music," born 1911 in Rosine, KY. In 1939, Monroe formed a band called the Blue Grass Boys and developed the blend of Appalachian melodies, folk music, and jazz that came to be called bluegrass. He wrote more than 500 songs, including the classic bluegrass tune "Blue Moon of Kentucky." In 1983 he received the first Grammy Award in the category of Best Bluegrass Recording from the National Academy of Recording Arts and Sciences.

1267. American conductor of an American orchestra was Leonard Bernstein, a native New Yorker, who began a three-year stint as music director of the New York City Symphony Orchestra on October 8, 1945. Bernstein later spent 11 years as director of the New York Philharmonic.

1268. Gospel singer of importance was Mahalia Jackson, born in New Orleans, LA, in 1911. Jackson began singing in a church children's choir when she was four years old. Her first recording, "I Will Move On Up A Little Higher," issued in 1946, sold close to 2 million copies. Of her total of 31 recordings, 12 sold more than one million copies. Her rendition of "We Shall Overcome" became the unofficial anthem of the civil rights movement of the 1960s.

1269. Symphonic concert to be shown on television was transmitted on March 20, 1948, by the Columbia Broadcasting System. At 5 P.M., Eugene Ormandy conducted the Philadelphia Symphony Orchestra in a concert televised by WCAU-TV, Philadelphia, PA, on CBS. At 6:30 P.M. that same day, Arturo Toscanini conducted the NBC Symphony Orchestra in an all-Wagner concert televised by WNBT-TV, New York City, over the National Broadcasting Company system.

1270. Musical composition consisting entirely of silence was *4'33"*, a piece by avant-garde composer John Cage. The score, composed in 1952, was entirely blank. It was meant to be "performed" by a musician sitting silently for 4 minutes and 33 seconds in front of a piano or any other instrument. Cage's intent was to employ the ambient sounds in the concert hall as his "music."

1271. Televised performance by Elvis Presley took place on January 28, 1956, on "Stage Show," a weekly music program broadcast by CBS. Elvis sang three songs, including "Shake, Rattle & Roll." He received $1,250 for his performance. After five more appearances on the show, he was sufficiently popular to be booked on the Milton Berle and Steve Allen shows before making his famous appearance on the Ed Sullivan show on September 9.

1272. Grammy awards for musical recordings were awarded in 1958 by the National Academy of Recording Arts and Sciences, Burbank, CA. The winning single recording was *Nel Blu Dipinto Di Blu (Volare)* by Domenico Modugno. The winning album was *The Music From Peter Gunn* by Henry Mancini.

1273. Jazz composition to appear on the Top 40 charts was pianist Dave Brubeck's instrumental piece *Take Five*, which entered the Top 40 popular music chart published by the trade newspaper *Billboard* on October 23, 1961. It eventually reached No. 25.

1274. Psychedelic music album was "This Is IT" by Alan Watts, released in Sausalito, CA, in 1962 on the Musical Engineering Association (MEA) label. Watts, an English expatriate and Zen Buddhism proponent living in California, described "This Is IT" as a "spontaneous musical happening" that purportedly was recorded under the influence of the psychedelic drug LSD. Participants were Watts, supplying incantations; Roger Somers, drums and chanting; Leah Ananda, conga drum; Joel Andrews, falsetto and evocations; Henry Jacobs, piano and French horn; and William Loughborough, bass marimba and lujon.

1275. Performance by a British rock group was a televised set by the Beatles on the CBS variety series *The Ed Sullivan Show*, broadcast on February 7, 1964, from New York City. The Beatles performed their top single "I Want to Hold Your Hand" from their album *Meet the Beatles*, which, at the time, was the fastest-selling album in American history.

1276. Rock and roll broadcast on FM radio took place on April 7, 1967, in San Francisco, CA, on KMPX-FM, a foreign-language station. The disk jockey, Tom Donahue, played a program of San Francisco–area psychedelic rock and other underground music.

1277. Rock music festival was the Monterey International Pop Festival, held on June 15–18, 1967, at the Monterey, CA, fairgrounds. Promoter Alan Pariser and booking agent Ben Shapiro assembled the largest roster of rock and soul acts up to that time, including The Who, the Grateful Dead, Otis Redding, Jefferson Airplane, Big Brother and the Holding Company with Janis Joplin, and the Jimi Hendrix Experience. More than 50,000 fans attended the nonprofit event, which inaugurated a decade of ever-larger rock festivals.

1278. Disco dance suite was an 18-minute medley created by Tom Moulton for singer Gloria Gaynor that occupied one entire side of her 1974 MGM album *Never Can Say Goodbye.* It was constructed from three three-minute songs. Moulton, an innovative sound mixer, doubled the song times by rearranging their instrumental tracks and bridged the songs into an extended suite for the use of dancers in disco clubs.

1279. Music video on MTV was "Video Killed the Radio Star" by The Buggles, a duo consisting of Trevor Horn and Geoff Downes. The song was cowritten by them and Bruce

Woolley, and the video was directed by Russell Mulcahy. It was broadcast on August 1, 1981, the launch day for the MTV (Music Television) cable channel, which was based in New York City.

1280. Rap album to attract a mass audience was *Run-D.M.C.*, recorded by the rap group of the same name. Run-D.M.C.'s members were "Jam Master" Jason Mizell, Joseph "Run" Simmons, and "MC" Darryl "D" McDaniels, all of New York City. The album was released by Profile Records in June 1984 and went gold on December 17 of that year.

1281. MTV Video Music Awards were given out on September 14, 1984, at New York's Radio City Music Hall. The cohosts were actor Dan Aykroyd and singer Bette Midler. "You Might Think" by The Cars was named best video of the year. David Bowie won the best male video award for "China Girl," Cyndi Lauper the best female video award for "Girls Just Want to Have Fun," Herbie Hancock the best concept video award for "Rockit," and ZZ Top the best group video award for "Legs." ZZ Top's "Sharp Dressed Man" took top honors for best direction.

1282. Grammy Award to be retracted was revoked on November 20, 1990, when the National Academy of Recording Arts & Sciences stripped the 1989 Best New Artist Grammy from Rob Pilatus and Fabrice Morvan, the duo known as Milli Vanilli, because neither actually sang on their debut album, *Girl You Know It's True*. Pilatus and Morvan had been hired by producer Frank Fabian to impersonate the actual singers, who were talented but insufficiently attractive.

1283. Internet record label was J-Bird Records, launched at www.j-birdrecords.com by record executive Jay Barbieri on October 21, 1996. J-Bird, based in Wilton, CT, sought artists via the Internet and worked to develop methods of promoting and distributing their work online.

1284. American orchestra to play for a pope at the Vatican was the Pittsburgh Symphony Orchestra, which played a concert at the Vatican on January 17, 2004, to mark 25 years of the pontificate of Pope John Paul II. The concert, dedicated to the theme of interfaith dialogue among the three Abrahamic faiths (Judaism, Islam, and Christianity), included Symphony No. 2, "Resurrection," by Gustav Mahler. Financing for the orchestra's trip was provided by a Catholic group, the Knights of Columbus. The conductor was Gilbert Levine.

1285. American orchestra to make all its recordings downloadable from the Internet through digital music distributors was the Milwaukee Symphony Orchestra, Milwaukee, WI. On October 4, 2005, the orchestra introduced its own e-label, MSO Classics, a collection of recordings made between 1970 and 2005 during live performances that were broadcast on radio. They were sold through electronic services affiliated with the Independent Online Distribution Alliance.

1286. Live concert for astronauts took place on November 13, 2005, when two astronauts aboard the international space station, in orbit 220 miles above the Earth, heard a transmission of Paul McCartney singing "Good Day Sunshine" and "English Tea" to an audience in Anaheim, CA. The astronauts, Bill McArthur of the United States and Valery Tokarev of Russia, were on the 44th day of a six-month mission.

Musical Instruments

1287. Organs were brought to the United States in 1700 by the Episcopal Church of Port Royal, PA, and the Gloria Dei Church of Philadelphia, PA, a Swedish Lutheran church. Priority is claimed for each.

1288. Bell foundry in colonial America was probably the foundry opened in Boston, MA, in 1736 by William Coffin. He also manufactured the first tower clocks and the first self-winding clock, a "machine that winds itself up by help of the air and will continue to do so without any other aid or assistance."

1289. Organ built in the United States was constructed by Johann Gottlob Klemm, also known as John Clemm, of Philadelphia, PA, who proposed building an organ on June 1, 1739, for Trinity Church, New York City. His proposition was accepted, and in May 1740 the pipe organ was installed in the West Gallery. It had three manuals and 26 stops: 10 in the great organ, 10 in the choir, and six in the swell. It cost about £520.

1290. Carillon was installed in the belfry of the Old North Church (now Christ Church), Boston, MA, in 1745. Eight bells were ordered in 1744 from Abell Rudhall's foundry, Gloucester, England, by Thomas Gunther, who put up a bond to guarantee payment. They were shipped on the *Two Friends* on March 9, 1745, the total cost being £560, four shillings, 10 pence.

1291. Trombone was played at the funeral of a child on November 15, 1754, at Bethlehem, PA. Trombones were also used on March 30, 1755, in the church's Easter services.

1292. Church bells made in America on a regular basis were manufactured in Abington, MA, in 1769, at a foundry owned by Colonel Aaron Hobart. He employed Thomas Gillimore, a bell founder from England who had deserted from the British Army. One of Hobart's sons taught the technique to Paul Revere, who became the country's first bellmaker of importance.

1293. Harpsichord made in the United States was made by John Harris. It was called a spinet and was described in the *Boston Gazette* of September 18, 1769. It had only three or four octaves. Each jack was provided with a little spur of goose-quill that plucked the thin wire to cause vibration.

1294. Iron piano frame was made in 1837 in Boston, MA, by Jonas Chickering. It was designed to resist the tremendous tension of the modern piano without allowing the wires to deflect from pitch.

1295. Melodeon patent was granted to C. Austin of Concord, NH, on June 19, 1849. The melodeon was a small kind of reed organ and employed a suction bellows worked by treadles that drew the air through the reeds.

1296. Piano wire was produced at the factory of Ichabod Washburn, Grove Street, Worcester, MA, in 1850. This plant was later part of the Washburn and Moen Manufacturing Company, afterward absorbed by the American Steel and Wire Company.

1297. Calliope was invented by Joshua C. Stoddard of Worcester, MA, who on October 9, 1855, received a patent on a "new musical instrument to be played by the agency of steam or highly compressed air." He formed the American Steam Music Company in Worcester, MA, in 1855.

1298. Grand piano with a cast-metal plate designed to withstand the pull of high-tension strings was invented by the German-American piano maker Henry Engelhard Steinweg in 1859. The new grand piano, manufactured in Steinweg's New York City factory, yielded a fuller tone than earlier instruments. Steinweg began calling himself Steinway beginning in 1865, and his company became Steinway & Sons.

1299. Zither factory was established by Franz Schwartzer in Washington, MO, in 1866. In the first 20 years, he sold about 3,000 zithers, ranging in price from $50 to $500.

1300. Electric organ was built by Hilborne Lewis Roosevelt in 1876, and installed in Chickering Hall, Fifth Avenue and 18th Street, New York City. It was operated by storage batteries. It had 31 ranks: 10 in the great organ, eight in the swell organ, five in the solo organ, three in the echo organ, and five in the pedal organ.

1301. Organ with color display was invented by Bainbridge Bishop of New Russia, NY, who obtained a patent on January 16, 1877, on an "attachment for key-board musical instruments" for typifying musical sounds by the display of colors.

1302. Player piano was invented by John McTammany, Jr., of Cambridge, MA, who received a patent on June 14, 1881, on a "mechanical musical instrument." He constructed a mechanism for automatic playing of organs using narrow sheets of perforated flexible paper that governed the notes to be played.

1303. Player piano that was completely automatic was the Angelus, made by the Wilcox and White Company, Meriden, CT, in February 1897. It was invented by Edward H. Leveaux of Surrey, England. Leveaux obtained a British patent on February 27, 1879, and an American patent on October 4, 1881, on an "apparatus for storing and transmitting motive power."

1304. Saxophone production was undertaken in 1889 at Charles Gerard Conn's instrument factory in Elkhart, IN. The saxophone had been invented in 1846 by Adolphe Saxe of Belgium. Conn's first saxophone was made by Ferdinand Buescher, Conn's foreman, for E.A. Lefebre, a musician who was a friend of Saxe. The instruments were made of brass, had two octave keys, and descended to B-flat. Originally they were used only by military bands.

1305. Metal clarinet was manufactured by Charles Gerard Conn of Elkhart, IN, who obtained a patent on August 27, 1889, on a "clarionet." Previously, all clarinets had been made of wood. Conn's clarinet was made with double metal walls in the old Albert system.

1306. Pneumatic piano player that was practical was the Pianola, invented in 1896 by Edwin S. Votey of Detroit, MI, who received a patent on May 22, 1900. His original model was larger than the piano to which it was attached. The patent was for an attachment of practical and economical construction that could be applied to and removed from any piano. It was introduced by the Aeolian Company.

1307. Music synthesizer powered by electricity was the Telharmonium, also known as the Dynamophone, invented by Thaddeus Cahill and first demonstrated publicly in 1906 at Telharmonic Hall in New York City. The huge, 200-ton instrument, consisting of 140 dynamos and tone mixers powered by electrically driven gears, was controlled by an organ-style keyboard and foot pedals. When the player pressed the keys, current produced by the dynamos was converted into musical tones. The machinery itself was so noisy it had to be placed in the basement of the building. The sound was transmitted by telephone lines to subscribing restaurants, hotels, and homes, marking the first use of electronic equipment to distribute music.

1308. Sousaphone was manufactured by the C.G. Conn Company, Elkhart, IN, from designs suggested by John Philip Sousa. The first models had the bell pointing up. The first instrument with the bell in front was made in 1908.

1309. Modern carillon was installed in the Church of Our Lady of Good Voyage, Gloucester, MA, and blessed by Cardinal O'Connell on July 2, 1922. The bells and apparatus, weighing 28,000 pounds, were made and installed by John Taylor and Company, Loughborough, England, and consisted of 31 bells, the largest weighing 2,826 pounds. They were played for the first time by carillonneur George B. Stevens.

1310. Pipeless organ was invented by Laurens Hammond, who received a patent on April 24, 1934, covering 74 claims. The organ was manufactured by the Hammond Clock Company, Chicago, IL, and was first exhibited at the Industrial Arts Exposition, New York City, on April 15, 1935. The organ consisted of a two-manual console with pedal clavier and an electric power cabinet. It had neither reeds, pipes, nor vibrating parts. It weighed 275 pounds and cost less than one cent an hour to operate.

1311. Electric guitar to be widely marketed was the Rickenbacker Electro Spanish guitar of 1935, designed by Adolph Rickenbacker (also spelled Rickenbacher), George Beauchamp, and Doc Kauffman of the Electro Company, Los Angeles, CA. It was made of cast Bakelite, a synthetic resin, and featured a one-piece body, molded fittings, and a bolt-on neck. A patent was filed by Beauchamp in 1936 and granted in 1939. Credit for the first electric guitar of any kind is claimed by several inventors. Between 1920 and 1924, acoustical engineer Lloyd Loar experimented with microphone pickups for acoustic guitars, and in the early 1930s he designed for the Vivi-Tone company an acoustic-electric Spanish-neck guitar made out of solid wood. Les Paul electrified acoustic guitars in 1929 using a phonograph needle. George Beauchamp patented the electrified Fry Pan Hawaiian guitar, which was made of solid aluminum, in 1931, the same year that Dobro introduced its own electric solid-body Hawaiian guitar.

1312. Musical instrument capable of making any audible sound was the RCA Electronic Music Synthesizer, developed at the Columbia–Princeton Electronic Music Center in New York City in 1955. It could generate electronically all the physical characteristics of any sound and produce an infinite variety of sound combinations. The instrument was operated by a teleprinter-style alphanumeric keyboard.

Opera

1313. Opera performed in America was Colley Cibber's ballad opera *Flora, or Hob in the Well*, presented on February 18, 1735, at the Courtroom, Charleston, SC. It was advertised in the *South Carolina Gazette* and was shown with a pantomime entertainment billed as *The Adventure of Harlequin Scaramouche*.

1314. Opera performed by a professional visiting troupe was *The Beggar's Opera*, a three-act burlesque by John Gay, performed on December 3, 1750, by the Walter Murray and Thomas Kean Company at the Nassau Street Theatre, New York City. The principal songs were "Let Us Take to the Road," "Lillibullero," "Green Sleeves," "Hither Dear Husband," and "When a Wife's in a Pout." Entertainment was presented between the acts.

1315. Comic opera written for the American stage was Andrew Barton's *The Disappointment, or The Force of Credulity,* a satirical comedy in two acts with a prologue and epilogue, inspired by "the infrequency of dramatic compositions in America, the necessity of contributing to the entertainment of the city, and to put a stop (if possible) to the foolish and pernicious practice of searching after supposed hidden treasures." The satire was directed against seekers of the pirate Blackbeard's treasure. The opera contained 18 songs and was arranged with seven scenes in the first act and five in the second. A performance was scheduled to take place on April 20, 1767, in Philadelphia, PA, but at the last moment the work was withdrawn for fear of offending. The libretto, published later that year in New York City, was the first opera libretto published in America.

1316. Opera of a serious nature produced in America was James Hewitt's *Tammany, or The Indian Chief,* based on the book by Anne Julia Kemble Hatton. The opera was produced on March 3, 1794, by Charles Ciceri, under the auspices of the Tammany Society, by the Old American Company at the John Street Theatre, New York City.

1317. Opera by an American composer was *The Archers, or the Mountaineers of Switzerland,* about the exploits of William Tell, which was performed in New York City on April 18, 1796, with a libretto by William Dunlap and music by Benjamin Carr. The first one of importance was *Leonora,* a lyrical drama in three acts with a libretto by Joseph Reese Fry and music by William Henry Fry, which was performed on June 4, 1845, at the Chestnut Street Theatre, Philadelphia, PA. The plot was based on Bulwer-Lytton's *The Lady of Lyons.* It was sung in English and had a chorus of 75 and an orchestra of 50.

1318. Italian opera to be produced in the United States in Italian, with Italian singers, was Gioacchino Antonio Rossini's *Il Barbiere di Siviglia,* performed on November 29, 1825, at the Park Theatre, New York City. The libretto was by Cesare Sterbini. The singers were Manuel de Populo Vicente, De Rosich, Manuel Crivelli, Maria Felicita Garcia, and Manuel Garcia, Jr. The orchestra of 25 musicians was conducted by Nathaniel De Luce. Performances were given at 7:30 P.M. The prices were listed as follows: boxes, $2.00; orchestra, $1.00; gallery, 25 cents. Twenty-three performances were given. The largest receipts for a single performance were $1,962, and the smallest $250.

1319. Opera produced at the Metropolitan Opera House in New York City was Charles François Gounod's *Faust,* sung in Italian on October 22, 1883. Augusto Vianesi was the conductor. Faust was sung by Italo Campanini, Mephistopheles by Franco Novara, Valentin by Giuseppe Del Puente, Wagner by Ludovico Contini, Siebel by Sofia Scalchi, Marthe by Louise Lablache, and Marguerite by Christine Nilsson. Admission was priced at $6 for orchestra stalls, $3 for the balcony, and $2 for the family circle.

1320. Opera composed by a woman to be performed at the Metropolitan Opera House was the one-act opera *Der Wald,* by the English composer Dame Ethel Mary Smyth, performed on March 11, 1903, in New York City. Alfred Hertz was the conductor. Johanna Gadski sang Roschen, and Georg Anther sang Heinrich.

1321. Opera by an American composer to be performed at the Metropolitan Opera House in New York City was *The Pipe of Desire,* by Frederick Shepherd Converse, which was produced on March 18, 1910. The libretto was by George Edward Barton. The cast included Riccardo Martin, Louise Homer, Clarence Whitehill, Leonora Sparkes, Lillia Snelling, Glenn Hall, and Herbert Witherspoon. The opera had been produced previously in Boston in 1906.

1322. Opera broadcast over the radio in its entirety was presented on May 19, 1921, during Music Week, from the Auditorium, Denver, CO. A municipal chorus of 150 voices presented *Martha* over station 9ZAF. The first by a professional cast was *Samson et Dalila* by Camille Saint-Saëns, broadcast on November 14, 1921, over station KYW, Chicago, IL, from the Chicago Auditorium. Lucien Muratore and Marguerite D'Alvarez were the leads; Giorgio Polacco conducted. The Metropolitan Opera House's first full opera broadcast was Engelbert Humperdinck's *Hansel and Gretel,* presented on December 25, 1931, through the

National Broadcasting Company, New York City. Editha Fleischer was Hansel, Queena Mario was Gretel, and Karl Riedel conducted.

1323. City opera house was the War Memorial Opera House of San Francisco, CA, which opened on October 15, 1932, with a performance of *Tosca* by the San Francisco Opera Company.

1324. Opera prima donna who was African-American was Caterina Jarboro, who appeared on July 22, 1933, as Aida, the Ethiopian slave, in Giuseppe Verdi's opera *Aida*, presented by Alfredo Salmaggi's Chicago Opera Company at the New York Hippodrome, Sixth Avenue and 43rd Street, New York City.

1325. Opera to be televised in its entirety was Engelbert Humperdinck's *Hansel and Gretel*, presented on December 23, 1943, by WRGB of the General Electric Company, Schenectady, NY.

1326. African-American opera singer to sing a white role with a white cast was Robert Todd Duncan, a baritone of Washington, DC, who first appeared as Tonio in *I Pagliacci* on September 28, 1945, and as Escamillo in *Carmen* on September 30, 1945, in the New York City Opera Company's presentation at the City Center of Music and Drama, New York City. Both operas were included in the 1945 fall season. *I Pagliacci* was performed five times and *Carmen* seven.

1327. Opera to be televised from the Metropolitan Opera House was Giuseppe Verdi's *Otello*, a three-and-a-half-hour performance that was televised on November 29, 1948, over WJZ-TV, New York City. It was sponsored by the Texaco Company It starred Licia Albanese, Ramon Vinay, Leonard Warren, Martha Lipton, John Garris, and Nicola Moscona and was conducted by Fritz Busch. Milton Cross was the commentator. The telecast was also seen at network outlets in Philadelphia, Baltimore, Washington, and Boston. On March 10, 1940, station W2XBS, New York City, presented a condensed version of the first act of Ruggiero Leoncavallo's opera *I Pagliacci*, performed by members of the Metropolitan Opera Company and broadcast from a Radio City studio.

1328. Opera written for television was *Amahl and the Night Visitors*, by Gian-Carlo Menotti, first televised on December 24, 1951, by the National Broadcasting Company from WNBT-TV, New York City. The program was sponsored by Hallmark Greeting Cards. Thomas Schippers was the conductor and Chet Allen, a 12-year-old boy soprano, the featured singer. The opera tells the story of the Three Wise Men and the miraculous cure of a disabled boy.

1329. Metropolitan Opera singer who was African-American was Marian Anderson, contralto, who sang the role of the fortune teller Ulrica in Giuseppe Verdi's *Un Ballo in Maschera*, presented on January 7, 1955, at the Metropolitan Opera House, New York City.

1330. Metropolitan Opera orchestra conductor who was African-American was Henry Lewis, who conducted Giacomo Puccini's *La Bohème* on October 16, 1972, in New York City.

1331. Metropolitan Opera orchestra conductor who was a woman was Sarah Caldwell, who conducted *La Traviata* by Giuseppi Verdi on January 13, 1976. The cast included Beverly Sills as Violetta, Stuart Burrows as Alfredo, and William Walker as Germont.

Songs

1332. Patriotic song to achieve national popularity was "Yankee Doodle," written in 1755 by Dr. Richard Shuckburgh, regimental surgeon to General Edward Braddock, commander in chief of the British forces during the French and Indian War. The verses were written at Albany, NY, and set to an ancient English tune, "The World Turned Upside Down." Shuckburgh intended to ridicule the "homely clad colonials," but the song was taken up by the colonists themselves, and was played at the victory celebration in Yorktown in 1781 when Lord Cornwallis surrendered at the end of the Revolutionary War.

1333. Secular song by a composer born in America was "My Days Have Been So Wondrous Free," composed in 1759 by Francis Hopkinson of Philadelphia, PA. It was based on a poem by Thomas Parnell. Despite its popularity, it was not published until the 20th century.

1334. Patriotic song by an American was "The Liberty Song," also known as "In Freedom We're Born," published by John Mein and John Fleming in July 1768 in Boston, MA.

The lyrics were by John Dickinson, set to the tune of "Hearts of Oak" by William Boyce of London. The words were published in the *Boston Gazette* of July 18, 1768.

1335. War song was "Chester," composed in 1778 by William Billings of Boston, MA. The song was published in Billings's *The Singing Master's Assistant, or Key to Practical Music*, printed by Draper and Folsom, Boston, in 1778. "Chester" contains the following chorus: "Let tyrants shake their iron rod; / And Slav'ry clank her galling chains, / We fear them not; / We trust in God, / New England's God forever reigns."

1336. Orchestral song to be printed contained parts for a first viol, a second viol, a first clarinet, a second clarinet, E-flat horns, and other instruments, and was tipped in after page 186 of the *Massachusetts Magazine*, published in Boston, MA, in March 1791. The song was "The Death Song of an Indian Chief," by Hans Gram of Boston. It was based upon *Ouabi*, a tale of the Native Americans in four cantos by "Philenia, a lady of Boston" (Sarah Wentworth Apthorp Morton).

1337. Secular song hit with words and music by an American was "The Ministrel's Return from the War," by John Hill Hewitt, composed in Greenville, SC, in 1825. It was published in 1827 by James L. Hewitt and Company, Boston, MA, but was not copyrighted, as its importance was not anticipated.

1338. Song popular in the Confederate States was "I Wish I Was in Dixie's Land" (better known as "Dixie"), written and composed by Daniel Decatur Emmett, a Northerner, expressly for Bryant's Minstrels, who performed at 472 Broadway, New York City. It was announced as a plantation song and dance. According to some sources, it was based on a song of lament sung by the slaves of a Dutch planter named Dixye, who sold them away to a farmer in Piedmont County, South Carolina, after trying unsuccessfully to grow tobacco in Harlem, New Amsterdam (the future New York City). The song was introduced by Emmett on April 4, 1859, at Mechanics Hall, New York City, and was published by Firth Pond and Company, New York City. It was sung at the inauguration of Jefferson Davis as president of the Confederate States on February 18, 1861.

Library of Congress, Prints & Photographs Division LC-USZ62-2565

The Montgomery, AL, state house, site of the inauguration of Jefferson Davis in 1861.

1339. Taps played as a military signal, indicating "lights out" at night and "farewell" at military funerals, was originally played on a drum, whence its name. The musical form of "Taps," which is performed as a bugle call and also as a song, was written toward the beginning of July 1862 in a Union Army camp. General Daniel Butterfield wrote the music on the back of a torn envelope and whistled the tune to Oliver Willcox Norton, bugler and aide-de-camp of General Strong Vincent, commander of the 83rd Regiment Pennsylvania Volunteers of the Army of the Potomac. They were resting in camp at Harrison's Landing on the James River in Virginia, immediately after the seven days of fighting near Richmond.

1340. Song to hit No. 1 in the pop charts was Tommy Dorsey's "I'll Never Smile Again," sung by Frank Sinatra. Pop music record charts for single songs were published by the music trade newspaper *Billboard* beginning on July 20, 1940.

1341. Rock and roll song was probably "Rocket 88," recorded in 1951 by Jackie Brenston for Chess Records, Chicago, IL.

1342. Single by Elvis Presley was "That's All Right Mama," recorded at Sun Studios in Memphis, TN, and released on July 19, 1954, by Sun Records. The recording was produced by Sam Phillips. Presley was backed by guitarist Scotty Moore and bassist Bill Black. "That's All Right Mama" was written by bluesman Arthur "Big Boy" Crudup and was recorded by him in 1946. Presley's cover is considered by many to be the first widely influential rock-and-roll recording.

1343. Rock and roll song to hit No. 1 in the pop charts was "Rock Around the Clock," recorded by Bill Haley and the Comets, one of the first all-white acts to play rock and roll. It was recorded on April 12, 1954, and reached No. 1 on June 29, 1955.

1344. Civil rights anthem to achieve fame was "We Shall Overcome." It was originally published in Chicago, IL, in May 1945 as a gospel song, "I'll Overcome Someday," with music by Atrong Twigg and revised lyrics and music by Kenneth Morris. The tune was based on the melody of a hymn dating from the colonial era. The words were adapted from another hymn that included the line: "If in my heart, I do not yield, I'll overcome some day." African-American workers sang the song on a picket line in Charleston, SC, in 1945. The song became the anthem of the civil rights movement in the 1960s.

Spectacles

1345. Fireworks were used in 1608 by Captain John Smith, who fired a few rockets to entertain the Native Americans living near Jamestown, VA. In 1781, the city of Newport, RI, became the first city to celebrate the Fourth of July with fireworks.

1346. Lion exhibited to the public was exhibited on November 26, 1716, in Boston, MA, by Captain Arthur Savage. A notice in a Boston newspaper invited the public to Savage's house on Brattle Street, "where is to be shewn by William Nichols, a Lyon of Barbary, with many other rarities, the like never before in America."

1347. Camel exhibited to the public was an "African camel . . . 7 feet high and 12 feet long," exhibited in Boston, MA, and advertised in the *Boston Gazette* of October 2, 1721.

1348. Polar bear to be exhibited was Ursa Major, a nine-month-old cub caught in Davis Strait, on the western coast of Greenland, which was exhibited on January 18, 1733, at Clark's Wharf, North End of Boston, MA. It was brought by Captain Atkins from Greenland and kept in a large cage. It was shipped to London on February 27, 1734.

1349. Automaton to be shown in colonial America was advertised in the *New York Weekly Journal* on July 18, 1743. "To be Seen. At Mr. Pacheco's WareHouse, in Marketfield Street, commonly known by the Name of Petticoat Lane, opposite the Cross Guns, near the Fort. A Curious Musical machine, arriv'd from England, the third Day of May last, which performs several strange and diverting Motions to the Admiration of the Spectators, viz. The Doors fly open of their own accord, and there appear six Ringers in white Shirts all busy pulling the Bell-Ropes, and playing several Tunes, Chimes and Changes: They first appear with black Caps and black Beards, at one Corner there is a Barbers Shop and a Barbers Pole hung out, and at the Shop Door stands the Barber's Boy, who, at the Word of Command, gives three Knocks at his Master's Door, out comes the Barber with his Rasor and Baton to shave the Ringers, then the Doors shut themselves whilst the Barber is Shaving them, then the Doors open themselves." Exhibitions were held at 4 P.M. and 7 P.M., admission one shilling one pence.

1350. Waxworks was opened by James Wyatt in New York City in June 1749. The figures were imported from England and exhibited from June to December 1749 at "the Sign of the Dolphin, Privateer, near the Work-House." Effigies were shown of King George II and Frederick, Prince of Wales, "both dressed in Royal Robes . . . as when sitting in the Parliament House," the Duke of Cumberland "in his Regimentals," the "famous present actress" Miss Peggy Woffington, nuns, friars, British and Hungarian-Bohemian royal personages, and several others.

1351. Monkey trained to perform was "a creature called a Japanese, of about two feet high, his body resembling a human body in all parts except the feet and tail," exhibited on February 25, 1751, at the house of Edward Willet, New York City. Admission of a shilling was charged for the performance, in which the monkey walked a tightrope, exercised a gun, and danced.

1352. Saint Patrick's Day parade was held in New York City on March 17, 1762, by the city's Irish population.

1353. Horseriding exhibition was given by John Sharp in 1771. He rode two horses at a time at full speed, standing on the saddles. He also rode three horses, standing with one foot on each of the outside horses. He gave exhibitions in Boston and Salem, MA, and other cities.

1354. Dwarf exhibited as a theatrical attraction was a man, 53 years of age and 22 inches high, who was shown at the house of Widow Bignall, next door to King's Head Tavern, a little above Mr. Hancock's wharf in Boston, MA. Admission was one shilling. His appearance was advertised in the *Massachusetts Spy* on August 22, 1771.

1355. Panorama show was *Jerusalem*, exhibited in 1790 at Lawrence Hyer's Tavern, 62 Chatham Street, New York City, "between the Gaol and the Tea Water Pump." It was open from 10 in the morning until 10 at night. According to advertisements in the *Daily Advertiser*, the sight was "most brilliant by candlelight."

1356. Circus was owned by John Bill Ricketts and known as Ricketts' Circus. A building was erected especially for his use at 12th and Market streets, Philadelphia, PA, where he gave exhibitions as early as 1792. President George Washington attended Ricketts' Circus on April 22, 1793. Ricketts erected a larger building called the Art Pantheon and Amphitheatre, which was opened to the public October 19, 1795. In 1797 he built an Amphitheatre on Greenwich Street in New York City and exhibited in other towns as far north as Albany, NY.

1357. Elephant to be exhibited arrived in New York City on the *America* on April 13, 1796, from Bengal, India. She was two years old, 6.5 feet high, and was exhibited by Jacob Crowninshield at the corner of Beaver Street and Broadway. The elephant's habits were described as follows: "It eats thirty pounds of rice besides hay and straw—drinks all kinds of wine and spirituous liquors, and eats every sort of vegetable; it will also draw a cork from a bottle with its trunk."

1358. Gaslights for display were introduced in Philadelphia, PA, in August 1796. The inflammable gas was manufactured by Michael Ambroise and Company on Mulberry Street, Philadephia, between Eighth and Ninth streets. The light showed "a grand fire-work by means of light composed of inflammable air," arranged so as to form an Italian parterre and Masonic figures and emblems. The jets of light were made to issue from orifices in pipes bent into the requisite shapes. The gas was not used for illuminating purposes.

1359. Leopard to be exhibited was exhibited on February 2, 1802, by Othello Pollard, near the Columbian Museum, Boston, MA. An admission fee of 25 cents was charged to see the "import from Bengal."

1360. Magic lantern book was *The Expositor, or Many Mysteries Unravelled; delineated in a series of letters between a friend and his correspondent, comprising the learned pig, invisible lady and acoustic temple, philosophical swan penetrating spy glasses, optical and magnetic, and various other curiosities on similar principles; also a few of the most wonderful feats as performed by the art of legerdemain, with some reflections on ventriloquism*, by William Frederick Pinchbeck. It was 100 pages long and was printed in Boston, MA, in 1805.

1361. Magician of note was Richard Potter, who was said to have demonstrated "upward of one hundred curious but mysterious experiments with cards, eggs, money, etc." He was also a ventriloquist and performed at the Columbian Museum, Boston, MA, in November 1811.

1362. Sword swallower was Senaa Samma, "an Indian juggler from Madras and late from London," who performed at St. John's Hall, New York City, on November 11, 1817. Admission was $1, children half price. On November 25, 1817, Samma swallowed "a sword manufactured by Mr. William Pyle of New York as a substitute for the one lately stolen from him by some villain."

1363. Tightrope performer who was a woman was Madame Adolphe of Paris, who, accompanied by Monsieur Godau, appeared on June 1, 1819, at the Anthony Street Theatre, New York City.

1364. Giant exhibited as a theatrical attraction was Patrick Magee, "just arrived from Ireland," who went on exhibition on October 6, 1825, at 13 Park, Park Exchange, New York City, from 7 A.M. until 10 P.M. A charge of 25 cents was made to see the giant, "conspicuous for the masculine beauty of his form and his surprising strength."

1365. Rhinoceros to be exhibited was exhibited on September 13, 1826, at Peale's Museum and Gallery of the Fine Arts, New York City. Advertisements stated that "its body and limbs are covered with a skin so hard and impervious that he fears neither the claws of the tiger nor the proboscis of the elephant; it will turn the edge of a scimitar and even resist the force of a musket ball." The exhibit, scheduled to close on October 13, was extended to November 25.

1366. Daredevil jumper of note was Sam Patch, a former sailor and mill hand who joined the national jumping craze of the early 19th century. Patch began his public career with a dive from a 90-foot-high bridge spanning the Passaic River in Passaic, NJ, where he worked in the Hamilton Mills. He followed that up with a jump partway down Niagara Falls. A well-publicized jump off the 125-foot-high Genesee Falls in Genesee, NY, in November 1829 turned out to be his last. His body was recovered from Lake Ontario the following spring.

1367. Parade held by a mystic society was held by the Cowbellian de Rakian Society, organized on December 31, 1830, in Mobile, AL. It started as an impromptu raid on a hardware store staged by a score of young bloods, who were led, according to tradition, by Michael Krafft. The peculiar feature of this society and those which followed later was that absolute secrecy was maintained about their members, who never appeared in public except in costume and mask. Parades by the mystic societies were held annually in Mobile on New Year's Eve until 1867, when the city switched to daylight parades held on Mardi Gras (Shrove Tuesday), the day initiating the penitential Christian season of Lent.

1368. Flea circus was an "Extraordinary Exhibition of the Industrious Fleas" at 187 Broadway, New York City, which opened on January 1835. Admission was 50 cents and performances were given from 11 A.M. to 3 P.M. and from 5 P.M. to 9 P.M. A cold spell forced the exhibit to close to enable the exhibitor "to fill up the vacancies that grim death had made." It was reopened on January 20, 1835, for one week.

1369. Tattooed man exhibited as a theatrical attraction was James F. O'Connell, whose appearance at the Franklin Theatre, Chatham Square, New York City, on October 21, 1849, was advertised as follows in the *New York Herald*: "The manager has at an enormous expense engaged Mr. J. F. O'Connell, the wonderful 'Tattooed Man' who will go through a variety of performances peculiar to himself, and perfectly original."

1370. Horse show was the Upperville Colt and Horse Show, Upperville, VA, established in 1853 by Colonel Richard Hunter Dulany. Shows were held annually in June until the Civil War. The first show after the war was held on November 10, 1869.

1371. Daredevil to cross Niagara Falls on a tightrope was Jean François Gravelet, a Frenchman better known by his professional name, Émile Blondin, whose first exhibition took place on June 30, 1859, before a crowd of 5,000 people. Wearing pink tights and a spangled tunic of yellow silk, he crossed a cable about two inches in diameter and 1,100 feet long, strung below the suspension bridge with a series of parallel ropes alongside. In 1859 and 1860 Blondin gave a series of "ascensions." They included carrying a man on his back across the cable, trundling a loaded wheelbarrow across, walking across in a sack, and pushing a wheelbarrow while dressed as an ape. He usually carried a long pole that helped him to balance himself and that could also serve as a guard in case he fell, since it would be supported by the parallel ropes and thus prevent him from falling into the river.

1372. Peep show machine was patented by Samuel D. Goodale of Cincinnati, OH, who obtained a patent on February 5, 1861, on a hand-operated stereoscope device. Pictures were placed on leaves fastened by one edge to an axis in such a way that they stood out like spokes. As the shaft revolved, different images were seen in motion. The device was incorporated in the Mutoscope, a popular attraction that cost viewers a penny to use.

1373. Circus to feature a car as an attraction was Wheeler, Hatch and Hitchcock's Circus and Royal Hippodrome, which toured New York, Massachusetts, Connecticut, and Rhode Island in 1864. It advertised the car as a "tremendous novelty, never seen before, of an ordinary road carriage driven over the common high-ways without the aid of horses or other draught animals, being beyond doubt the most simple, useful and ingenious piece of mechanism ever put into practical use."

1374. Parade with float tableaux was held in Mobile, AL, on the evening of Mardi Gras day, February 24, 1868. The Order of Myths produced the first pageant, followed the next day by the Infant Mystics and the Knights of Revelry. These groups were among the original mystic societies of Mobile.

1375. Rodeo for roping and tying steers is a matter of considerable debate, since ranch hands working on cattle ranches often took part in impromptu tests of working skills. The first known organized competition was held on July 4, 1869, at Deer Trail, CO. The winner, who was crowned with the title Champion Bronc Buster of the Plains, was Emilnie Gardenshire.

1376. Prehistoric hoax was the Cardiff Giant, a sensational stunt perpetrated by George Hull (or Hall), a tobacco farmer from Binghamton, NY. In 1868, Hull arranged for a block of gypsum to be carved in the shape of a 10-foot-tall man. It was buried secretly near Cardiff, NY, on a farm that was owned by William C. Newell, who was in on the hoax. On October 16, 1869, the statue was "discovered" by unsuspecting workmen hired by Newell to dig a well. Hull and Newell spread the rumor that it was a petrified man from biblical times. The figure was exhibited at $1 per viewing to large crowds in Syracuse, Albany, New York City, and Boston before the hoax was exposed by Yale University paleontologist Othniel C. Marsh, who noted that the statue was "of very recent origin, and a decided humbug." In 1948, the Cardiff Giant was put on display in the Farmers' Museum in Cooperstown, NY.

1377. Human cannonball was an American named Eddie Rivers, who in 1871 was fired from a cannon at the Royal Cremorne Music Hall in London. Rivers used the stage name "Lulu."

1378. Dog show of importance was the New York Bench Show of Dogs, held at the Hippodrome (Gilmore's Garden), 26th Street and Madison Avenue, New York City, on May 8, 1877, under the auspices of the Westminster Kennel Club. Charles Lincoln was superintendent of this show, at which there were 1,201 entries.

Champion Warren Remedy, a female Smooth Fox Terrier, took the first Best In Show prize ever given at the Westminster Dog Show, in 1907.

1379. Labor Day parade was held in New York City on September 5, 1882, under the auspices of the Central Labor Union. It featured musical bands and 10,000 marchers who carried placards reading "Less Work and More Pay," "Less Hours More Pay," "Labor Pays All Taxes," "Labor Creates All Wealth," "To the Workers Should Belong the Wealth," and "Laborer Must Receive and Enjoy the Full Fruit of His Labor."

1380. Rodeo at which cash prizes were awarded was a contest among local cowboys that took place in Pecos, TX, on July 4, 1883. Forty dollars in prize money was handed out.

1381. Wild West Show was put together by William Frederick Cody, more familiarly known as "Buffalo Bill," and presented in North Platte, NE, as part of a Fourth of July celebration in 1883. The following year, Cody commercialized the show and took it on tour, starting in Omaha. Exhibitions and contests celebrating frontier life in the West were a frequent feature of local fairs and holidays before the Wild West Show was developed.

1382. Cowgirl was Lucille Mulhall, born October 21, 1885. She was the daughter of Zachary Mulhall, an Oklahoma cattleman and impresario who owned a ranch near the town of Alfred (later Mulhall) in the Oklahoma Territory. Lucille showed an early aptitude for bronco-busting, branding, steer-roping, and other rodeo skills, and in 1899, at the age of 13, began performing with her father's Wild West show, "The Congress of Rough Riders and Ropers." Unlike other female Western stars of the time, Mulhall performed alongside male cowboys in the roughest riding and roping events. Mulhall became the top female rodeo performer of her day, appearing in New York's Madison Square Garden in 1905 and eventually forming her own company, Lucille Mulhall's Round-up. Among her admirers were Theodore Roosevelt, Tom Mix, Geronimo, and Will Rogers, who may have coined the word "cowgirl" to describe her.

1383. Daredevil to jump off the Brooklyn Bridge and survive may have been Stephen Brodie, a 23-year-old unemployed Irish immigrant. On July 23, 1886, Brodie was pulled from the East River, claiming that he had just jumped from the bridge. Although Brodie was unable to produce any objective witnesses to say he had performed the feat—he was accused of having his friends drop a dummy from the bridge while he slipped unnoticed into the water from the riverbank—he became famous anyway. In 1894, he starred in a play called *On the Bowery*, during which he rescued the heroine by jumping off a bridge built on stage.

1384. Ticker-tape parade took place in lower Manhattan on October 28, 1886, the day that the Statue of Liberty was dedicated. The day had been declared a public holiday in the city, and a parade of 20,000 people headed for the Battery, viewed by a crowd of more than 1 million. The streets were draped with red, white, and blue bunting in the designs of the French and American flags. As the parade came down Wall Street, according to the *New York Times*, workers in the financial houses "from a hundred windows began to unreel the spools of tape that record the fateful messages of the 'ticker.' In a moment the air was white with curling streamers."

1385. Rodeo to charge admission was held on July 4, 1888, at the racetrack at Prescott, AZ. This was the first rodeo to be formally organized as a spectator sport. The winner was Juan Leivas, who took home a silver shield as the prize.

1386. Peep show using film in a vending machine or cabinet was exhibited by Andrew M. Holland of the Holland Brothers at 1155 Broadway, New York City, on April 14, 1894. The machine was invented by Thomas Alva Edison, who utilized film prepared by George Eastman. The films were made in the Edison laboratories. The pictures were viewed directly, rather than reflected, and were visible to only one person at a time. Annie Oakley, Sandow, Buffalo Bill, Ruth St. Denis, and other celebrities were shown.

1387. Magic lantern feature show was *Miss Jerry*, previewed October 9, 1894, at the Carbon Studio, New York City. Alexander Black was the author, scenario writer, director, camera man, and titler. The leads were taken by Blanche Bayliss, who played Jerry, William Courtenay as the hero, and Ernest Hastings as the villain. Slides were shown at the rate of five a second.

1388. Cat show was held at Madison Square Garden, New York City, on May 8–11, 1895. Over 200 cats were exhibited in cages. The owners could take their cats home overnight upon payment of a $5 bond guaranteeing they would be brought back the following day. Prizes and money were awarded for each class—for example, the best litter of kittens, the best homeless cat

1389. Parade of automobiles was held at Newport, RI, September 7, 1899. Society leaders of Boston, New York, and Philadelphia participated. Nineteen cars were in the line, profusely decorated with flowers and flags. A prize was awarded to Mrs. Hermann Oelrichs, whose automobile, hung with wisteria, appeared to be drawn by a flock of pure white doves perched on the radiator.

1390. Ticker-tape parade for a celebrity was held in New York City on September 30, 1899, to celebrate the return of Admiral George Dewey after his victory in the Spanish-American War. There were two previous ticker-tape parades, both in New York City: an impromptu one on October 28, 1886, during the dedication of the Statue of Liberty, and another on April 29, 1889, as part of the centennial observance of President George Washington's inauguration.

1391. Daredevil to go over Niagara Falls in a barrel was Anna Edson Taylor, who went over the Horseshoe Falls on the Canadian side on October 24, 1901, in a barrel 4.5 feet high and 3 feet in diameter. A leather harness and cushions were placed inside the barrel to protect her.

1392. Fashion show is thought to have been a special event held in 1903 by Ehrich Brothers, a clothing store in New York City. Another possibility is the Fashion Fete that was held on November 4, 1914, at New York's Ritz-Carlton Hotel to raise money for charity. The organizer was Edna Woodman Chase, editor of *Vogue* magazine.

1393. Stuntman was Frederick Rodman Law, a steeplejack, who staged a parachute jump from the Statue of Liberty on Bedloe's Island in New York Harbor on February 2, 1912, for Pathé News. On April 14, 1912, he jumped from the Brooklyn Bridge, and on November 12, 1912, from a dynamited balloon into the Hudson River.

1394. Beauty pageant to be held nationwide was the Inter-City Beauty Contest, sponsored by the Businessmen's League of Atlantic City, NJ, and, held on September 7–8, 1921, at a two-day carnival at Keith's Theatre on the Garden Pier. The award to the most beautiful contestant was made to Margaret Gorman of Washington, DC, 16 years old. The name "Miss America" was bestowed by a local journalist and was later applied to the contest, which became an annual event. The first Jewish winner was Bess Myerson, in 1945; the first African-American winner was Vanessa Williams in 1983; the first winner with a disability was Heather Whitestone in 1994; and the first winner of Asian descent was Angela Perez Baraquio in 2001.

1395. Platypus to be exhibited was shown on July 15, 1922, at the Bronx Zoo, New York City. It arrived at San Francisco, CA, from Australia.

1396. Radio broadcast from a circus was made from the menagerie of the Ringling Brothers Barnum and Bailey circus in the basement of Madison Square Garden, New York City, on April 10, 1924. Lew Graham was the circus announcer. The broadcast was transmitted from station WJZ, Aeolian Hall, New York City, to station WGY, Schenectady, NY. The roar of the animals at feeding time and the music of the calliope were broadcast.

1397. Macy's Thanksgiving Day Parade was held in New York City on November 27, 1924, along a two-mile stretch of Broadway from Central Park West to Herald Square. The event was intended to boost holiday sales and bring customers to R. H. Macy's recently expanded flagship store at Herald Square.

The first floating balloon character to participate in the parade was Felix the Cat, in 1927. The first African-American balloon character was Little Bill, introduced in 2002.

1398. City in miniature was Tiny Town, in Grant Beach Park, Springfield, MO. It was built on June 6, 1925, by 10,000 children under the direction of William H. Johnson, on a carefully prepared townsite of five acres, with avenues, electric lights, and water mains, all to a scale of one inch to one foot. The town had 1,200 miniature structures, covering every aspect of a modern city. Schoolchildren served as the officers of the town, which had the manager-commission form of government. Conceived and constructed as an incentive to building, Tiny Town boosted building permits in Springfield from a $280 daily average for the 90 days preceding its exhibition to $1,843 per day for the 90 days immediately following. Six years before the townsite was selected, a miniature village was exhibited by Johnson on the floor of the convention hall in Springfield.

1399. Frog-jumping jubilee was held at Angels Camp, Calaveras County, CA, on May 19–20, 1928, in commemoration of Mark Twain's famous story, "The Celebrated Jumping Frog of Calaveras County." Fifty-one frogs were entered in the contest. "The Pride of San Joaquin," a frog owned by Louis R. Fischer of Stockton, CA, was the winner with a jump of 3 feet 4 inches.

1400. Daredevil to go over Niagara Falls in a rubber ball was Jean Lussier, who made the descent on July 4, 1928, in a ball of his own construction weighing 750 pounds and costing $1,485. It was equipped with oxygen tanks and reinforced with cushions. It was set adrift from a launch and went over the Horseshoe Falls.

1401. Cow flown in an airplane was Elm Farm Ollie, a Guernsey, who went aloft on February 18, 1930, with a corps of reporters. She was milked during the flight and the milk was sealed in paper containers and parachuted over St. Louis, MO.

1402. Railroad mystery excursion was run by the Missouri Pacific Railroad on May 21, 1932. The trip was from St. Louis to Arcadia, MO, a distance of 92 miles, but the passengers were not told in advance where they were going. The round trip fare was $2.50, which included a barbecue at Arcadia.

1403. Fashion show to be shown on television took place on May 17, 1939, at the Ritz-Carlton Hotel, New York City. Renee Macready was the fashion coordinator. It was shown on WNBT-TV, New York City, in cooperation with the Swiss Fabric Group and the Ostrich Feather Group.

1404. Beauty pageant to be shown on television was the Fairest of the Fair contest, held at 7 P.M. on June 22, 1939, on the Wild West Show and Rodeo platform of the New York World's Fair, Flushing, Queens, New York City. The first national contest to be televised was the Miss America Pageant, telecast from Convention Hall, Atlantic City, NJ, on September 11, 1954, by ABC, using six cameras. Bess Myerson and John (Charles) Daly narrated and Bert Parks was master of ceremonies. The winner was Lee Ann Meriwether of San Francisco.

1405. Circus to be shown on television was the Ringling Brothers Barnum and Bailey circus, which gave a three-hour show on April 25, 1940, at Madison Square Garden, New York City. It was televised by station W2XBS, New York City, using two cameras.

1406. Be-In took place on January 17, 1967, in Golden Gate Park, San Francisco, CA, where as many as 20,000 hippies gathered to make music, dance, and use recreational drugs.

1407. Tightrope walker to span two skyscrapers was Philippe Petit of Nemours, France, who walked across a tightrope at a height of 1,350 feet between the two towers of the World Trade Center, New York City, on August 7, 1974, at 7:15 A.M. As he arrived at the second tower, he was taken into custody by the police. His sentence was suspended on condition that he give a public demonstration of his skill under controlled conditions in Central Park, New York City.

1408. Motorcycle jump across a river canyon was accomplished by stunt rider Robert Craig "Evel" Knievel, who successfully jumped the Snake River Canyon in Twin Falls, ID, on September 8, 1974.

1409. Parade in which the marching music was supplied by transistor radios was held from 11 A.M. to 12 noon on July 4, 1977, at Streamwood, IL. The marchers carried portable transistor radios that were all tuned to receive music broadcast by radio station WRMN, Elgin, IL. The parade was witnessed by thousands and telecast over channel 2 and channel 5.

1410. Human chain across the United States was attempted on May 21, 1986, when millions of Americans participated in Hands Across America, a fund-raising event sponsored by a consortium of charities and corporations. The chain of hand-holders, which had some gaps, stretched from Battery Park in New York City to Long Beach, CA, a distance of 4,150 miles.

Theater

1411. Theatrical performance by nonprofessional actors was *The Bare and The Cubb*, a satire by Philip Alexander Bruce, which was performed on August 27, 1665, at Accomack, VA. The actors, Cornelius Watkinson, Philip Howard, and William Darby, were accused of sedition and were summoned to appear in court on November 16, 1665, "in those habilements that they then acted in and give a draught of such verses or other speeches and passages which were then acted by them." They were found not guilty, and Edward Martin, who had informed on them, was ordered "to pay all the expenses of the presentment."

1412. Play of note written by an American and produced in America was *Gustavus Vasa*, a tragedy by Benjamin Colman. Harvard College students gave a performance of it in 1690 in Cambridge, MA.

1413. Play written in America that was printed was Governor Robert Hunter's *Androboros*, a biographical farce in three acts, printed in 1714 by William Bradford in New York City. The text contained 27 pages, quarto size. Androboros means "man-eater." New York City was disguised in the play as Monoropolis, meaning "Fool's town."

1414. Theater was built in 1718 by William Levingston at Williamsburg, VA. He acquired the lots from the Trustees of Williamsburg on November 5, 1716 and began making plans for the construction of a playhouse where comedies, drolls, and stage plays would be presented. He contracted with Charles Stagg, a dancing master, and Mary Stagg, his wife, to put on plays and teach acting. The finished theater was 86.5 feet long and 30 feet wide. Governor Alexander Spotswood entertained a number of guests at the theater in 1718.

1415. Play presented by professional players was given at the New Theatre, New York City, on December 6, 1732. It was *The Recruiting Officer*, by the Irish dramatist George Farquhar. The part of Worth was played by Thomas Heady, a barber.

1416. Puppet show to which admission was charged was held on February 12, 1738, in Henry Holt's room at Broad and Pearl streets, New York City. The show was entitled *The Adventures of Harlequin and Scaramouche, or The Spaniard Trick'd*. Admission was five shillings. The room was 39 feet long, 19 feet wide, and nine feet high.

1417. Play by William Shakespeare to be produced is supposed to have been *Richard III*, which was presented at the Nassau Street Theatre, New York City, on March 5, 1750, by Walter Murray and Thomas Kean. The play was "altered" by the poet Colley Cibber. The performance began at 6:30 P.M. Admission to the pit was five shillings and to the gallery three shillings.

1418. Publicist for a theater company was Robert Upton, who left London in October 1750 for New York City to publicize an upcoming tour by the Hallam Company. Instead, he joined the theater company of Walter Murray and Thomas Kean, which was performing in New York City.

1419. Benefit performance of a play was given on January 7, 1751, at the Nassau Street Theatre, New York City, for Walter Murray, one of the managers. It was advertised in the December 31, 1750, issue of the *Weekly Post-Boy*: "By his Excellency's Permission (for the benefit of Mr. Murray). On Monday, the seventh of January, will be performed, a comedy, called, 'A Bold Stroke For A Wife,' (being the last time of its being perform'd this season) to which will be added, an Entertainment called 'The Devil To Pay, Or, The Wives Metamorphos'd.'"

1420. Theater building of brick construction was the Southwark Theatre, on South Street above 4th, Philadelphia, PA, built by David Douglass. It opened on November 21, 1766, with Lewis Hallam of the American Company in *The Gamester*. The walls and the first story were built of brick. The building was used as a hospital in the Revolutionary War and was partly destroyed by fire on May 9, 1821.

1421. Playwright to write professionally was William Dunlap, who wrote or adapted 63 dramatic pieces, many of which appeared at the Park Theatre, New York City. His first comedy, *Modest Soldier, or Love in New York*, was written in a few weeks in 1787. He went bankrupt in 1805. He was also a painter and a historian. His books included *The History of the American Theatre*, published in 1832.

1422. Play by an American writer to be successfully presented by an established company on a regular stage was Royall Tyler's five-act play *The Contrast*. It was first produced on April 16, 1787, at the John Street Theatre, New York City, by the American Company under the management of Lewis Hallam and John Henry. It depicted the contrast between the meretricious standards of the fashionable world and the simple, straightforward ideals of the true American. The play was published in 1790 for Thomas Wignell in Philadelphia, PA, by Prichard and Hall.

1423. Actor of American birth was John Martin, who appeared at the Old Southwark Theatre, Philadelphia, PA, on March 13, 1790, in a play entitled *Douglas*.

1424. Play about a Native American written by an American was James Nelson Barker's *The Indian Princess, or La Belle Sauvage*, a three-act operatic melodrama on the life of Pocahontas, based on Captain John Smith's *General History of Virginia*. It was first produced on April 6, 1808, at the Chestnut Street Theatre, Philadelphia, PA.

1425. English actor of note to perform in America was George Frederick Cooke of Covent Garden, London, who made his debut on November 21, 1810, as Richard III in the play of the same name at the Park Theatre, New York City, before 2,000 people. His manager, Thomas Apthorpe Cooper, paid him $125 a week for 10 months, a traveling fee of 25 cents per mile, and expenses. Cooke died in New York City on September 26, 1812.

1426. Showboat theater was a keel boat converted by Noah Miller Ludlow in 1817 at a cost of $200. It left Nashville, TN, on October 20, 1817, to travel on the Cumberland, Ohio, and Mississippi rivers. The first plays presented were David Garrick's *The Honeymoon* and *The Lying Valet*, which were performed on November 15, 1817. The first showboat of importance was *The Floating Palace*, a flat scow with a superstructure, which plied the Mississippi River in 1852. It was operated by Spalding and Rogers. The dress circle had 1,100 cane-bottom chairs, the family circle 500 cushioned settees, and the gallery 900 seats. It was heated by steam.

1427. Actor to receive curtain applause was Edmund Kean, the famous English actor, who appeared in a group of special performances in Boston, MA, in 1821.

1428. Theater lighted by gas was the Chatham Garden and Theatre, New York City. Gas lighting had been used previously in theaters, but as a novelty rather than as illumination. The *New York Post and Mirror* on May 9, 1825, stated that the whole theater was lighted by gas, "which sheds a clear soft light over the audience and stage." The illumination "elicited the loudest plaudits from all present."

1429. Actor to appear abroad was James Henry Hackett, who made his English debut on April 5, 1827, at Covent Garden, London. He had made his professional debut the previous year in New York City.

1430. Play performed 1,000 times was *The Gladiator*, a five-act tragedy in blank verse, set in ancient Rome. It was written by Dr. Robert Montgomery Bird and was first performed on September 26, 1831, at the Park Theatre, New York City, with Edwin Forrest as Spartacus. By 1853 it had been performed 1,000 times.

1431. Theater history of importance was *A History of the American Theatre*, by William Dunlap, published in 1832 in New York City by J. and J. Harper. It contained 430 pages.

1432. Aquatic play was *The Pirate's Signal, or The Bridge of Death*, presented on July 4, 1840, at the Bowery Theatre, New York City. At the end of the fifth act, at the upper entrance of the stage, a full-rigged ship appeared, floated on water down to the footlights, turned, and went up the stage and off at the upper entrance.

1433. Theater ticket scalpers began plying their trade in New York City prior to the first appearance of the Swedish singer and celebrity Jenny Lind at Castle Garden on September 11, 1850. The seats were auctioned by Phineas Taylor Barnum, who charged 25 cents admission to the auction. The first ticket was sold to John Nicholas Genin for $225. One thousand tickets sold for a total of $10,141. Some ticket holders resold their tickets at high premiums. Gross receipts for the performance were $17,864. Jenny Lind donated her share of the gross to New York charities.

1434. Chinese theatrical performance was offered by the Tong Hook Tong Dramatic Company under the management of Mr. Tiksoon, Norman Assing, and Tong Chick at the American Theatre, Sansom Street, San Francisco, CA, on October 18, 1852. The company consisted of 123 performers and musicians who were shareholders in the theatrical enterprise. The performance contained four parts: *The Eight Genii Offering Their Congratulations to the High Ruler Yuk Hwang on His Birthday, Too Tsin Made High Minister by the Six States, Parting at the Bridge of Parkew of Kwan Wanchang and Tsow*, and *Defeated Revenge*.

1435. Chinese theater was the theater of "Celestial John," on Telegraph Hill, fronting Dupont Street, San Francisco, CA, which opened on December 23, 1852. It consisted of one vast pit or parquet and had a seating capacity of 1,400. There were no tiers of boxes. No scenery was used.

1436. Folding theater chair was invented by Aaron H. Allen of Boston, MA, who obtained a patent on December 5, 1854, on an "improvement in seats for public buildings."

1437. Play in which a horse race was run on stage was *Herne, the Hunter*, presented on February 18, 1856, in the Old Broadway Theatre, 326-328 Broadway, New York City. A chariot pulled by six horses was used. Many injuries occurred. One horse caused the collapse of a platform, another fell off the proscenium onto spikes, and there were many similar mishaps. The theater had 4,000 seats with no backs and room for 500 spectators to stand. Admission was 25 cents.

1438. Theater ticket agency was an office at Macoy and Herwig, Stationers, 112–114 Broadway, New York City, which was open from 8 A.M. to 4 P.M. The agency advertised in the *New York Times* on September 9, 1866, that patrons could obtain reserved seats for theaters in New York and Brooklyn, and choice seats and tickets at all times and in advance, when required.

1439. Broadway hit musical was *The Black Crook*, an original magical and spectacular drama in four acts by Charles M. Barras, with the scene laid in and around the Hartz Mountains about the year 1600. The musical show was produced by Barras and William Wheatley and featured 100 scantily clad young women playing a troupe of dancing fairies. It opened on September 12, 1866, at Niblo's Garden, New York City, and ran for an unprecedented 16 months, closing on January 4, 1868, after playing 475 performances and grossing $1.3 million.

1440. Musical with an American theme and original score was *Evangeline, the Belle of Acadia,* first performed at Niblo's Theatre, New York City, on July 27, 1874. It was based on Henry Wadsworth Longfellow's poem "Evangeline." The book and lyrics were by J. Cheever Goodwin. It ran for two weeks and featured bare-legged dancing. George K. Fortesque was the female impersonator playing the ponderous Catherine.

1441. Actors' home was the Forrest Home, Philadelphia, opened on October 2, 1876. The property consisted of 90 acres of farmland and 20 acres of lawn. The first superintendent was Joseph McArdle.

1442. Play presented by a Jewish professional acting troupe was *Die Hexe (The Sorceress),* by Arthur Firzer, which was staged by the Hebrew Opera and Dramatic Company at the Bowery Garten Theater, 113 Broadway, New York City, on September 25 and 27, 1880. It was directed by Leon Golubok, the 17-year-old comedian who played the part of the 80-year-old witch. An advertisement of August 12, 1882, stated that a performance would be given for the benefit of 10 poor Russian immigrant families.

1443. Greek drama produced in Greek was *Oedipus Tyrannus* by Sophocles. It was presented at Harvard University, Cambridge, MA, in May 1881. George Riddle played the part of Oedipus.

1444. Yiddish theater performance took place in New York City on August 18, 1882, when a Yiddish acting troupe from Russia staged a performance of *Koldunya (The Witch),* by Abraham Goldfaden, at Turner Hall on East Fourth Street. The cast included Boris Thomashefsky, who afterwards became one of the leaders of New York's thriving Yiddish theater scene.

1445. Theater lighted by electricity was the Bijou Theatre, 545 Washington Street, Boston, MA, which was lighted by an Edison isolated plant on December 11, 1882. Six hundred and fifty lamps were used. The proscenium was surrounded by 192 lights, and 140 were used in the borders. The first performance in the theater was Gilbert and Sullivan's *Iolanthe,* presented by Colliers' Standard Opera Company.

1446. Vaudeville show took place in 1883 in Boston, MA, where Benjamin Franklin Keith opened a small museum next to the old Adams House in Washington Street which he called the "Gaiety Museum." One of its principal attractions was "Baby Alice," a midget.

1447. Theater to employ women as ushers was the Third Avenue Theatre, New York City, which opened on August 30, 1884, with *49,* starring Mr. and Mrs. McKee Rankin. The young women wore white caps and aprons.

1448. Theater operated by a city was the Academy of Music of Northampton, MA, which was accepted by the City of Northampton as a gift from Edward Hutchinson Robbins Lyman on February 9, 1893. Visiting companies and traveling troupes performed there. The first stock company was that of Jessie Bonstelle and Bertram Harrison, who played from 1912 to 1917.

1449. Musical comedy written by African-Americans for African-American performers was *A Trip to Coontown,* a musical comedy in two acts by Bob Cole and Billy Johnson, produced at the Third Avenue Theatre at 31st Street in New York City on April 4, 1898. Cole played the part of the tramp Willie Wayside, and Johnson played Jim Flimflammer, the bunco steerer.

1450. Original cast recording of a stage performance was a 10-inch single-face disc record of "Old Folks at Home" ("Swanee River"), sung in Act I of the spectacular military operetta *When Johnny Comes Marching Home,* which was recorded in 1904 and released by the Victor Talking Machine Company, Camden, NJ. The libretto was by Stanislaus Stange, the music by Julian Edwards, and the production by the Whitney Opera Company.

1451. Drama broadcast on radio was *The Wolf,* by Eugene Walter, broadcast on August 3, 1922, by station WGY, Schenectady, NY. The two-and-a-half-hour performance was directed by Edward H. Smith.

1452. Full-length play by an African-American writer to be performed in New York City was *Appearances,* by Garland Anderson, a three-act protest against lynching, which was produced on October 13, 1925, at the Frolic Theatre atop the New Amsterdam Theatre, New York City. It was produced by Lester W. Sager and lasted 23 performances.

1453. Puppet show to be televised was a two-minute symbolic one-act play with puppet characters, produced on August 21, 1928, by WOR, Newark, NJ, a radio station owned by L. Bamberger and Company of Newark. In the play, a character symbolizing "Creative Genius" produced an apparatus that brought forth "The Spirit of Television," a winged sprite holding a globe. Sight and sound were synchronized. Viewers heard the narrator and musical accompaniment through earphones.

1454. Play to be shown on television was *The Queen's Messenger*, by J. Hartley Manners, presented on September 11, 1928, by radio station WGY of the General Electric Company, Schenectady, NY. The telecast was under the direction of Mortimer Stewart, with Izetta Jewell and Maurice Randall as the principal performers. The performance went out on three wavelengths, the picture on 379.5 meters and 21.4 meters and the voices on 31.96 meters. Several semicommercial 24-line receivers were set up in the WGY studios. Three cameras were used. The image was 3 by 3 inches.

1455. Theater built and named for a living actress was the Ethel Barrymore Theatre, New York City, which opened on December 20, 1928, with a performance of *The Kingdom of God*, a translation of a Spanish play by Gregorio Martinez Sierra entitled *Reino de Dios*. Barrymore played Sister Gracia, the lead.

1456. Drama broadcast on radio from a regular stage with full scenery and a cast in costume was *Roses and Drums*, a dramatic story of the unsuccessful Union attempt in 1864 to capture Jefferson Davis and free the Union prisoners from Libby Prison. It was presented by WABC, New York City, on September 24, 1933.

1457. Theatrical presentation sponsored by the federal government was *The Family Upstairs*, first produced on January 30, 1934, by a cast of players operating under the Civil Works Administration at the Central School of Business and Arts, New York City. An appropriation of $28,000 for wages was made on January 12, 1934. The project was under the direction of Margaret Smith. Other plays were presented later the same day. By March 25, 1934, 864,000 persons had witnessed 576 performances of 17 plays produced under this program in 107 schools, clubs, and museums.

1458. Musical comedy broadcast on radio with specially composed music was *The Gibson Family*, sponsored by the Procter and Gamble Company of Cincinnati, OH, and introduced over the National Broadcasting Company network on September 15, 1934. The comedy was composed by Arthur Schwartz and the lyrics were written by Howard Dietz. The musical comedy was booked for a 39-week period and was broadcast from station WEAF, New York City.

1459. Lighting designer for the stage was Jean Rosenthal of New York City, who devised a dramatic lighting plan in 1937 for a production of *Julius Caesar* at Orson Welles's Mercury Theatre. Until then, lighting in stage productions was arranged for the sole purpose of illuminating the action, rather than for dramatic effect. Rosenthal also invented a notation system for recording the placement and use of lights that allowed the original lighting plan for a play or dance performance to be duplicated in subsequent productions.

1460. Broadway play shown in a television version with its original cast was Rachel Crothers's comedy *Susan and God*, presented on June 7, 1938, over station W2XBS. The play was produced by the Radio Corporation of America in cooperation with John Golden, the Broadway producer. Featured in the cast were Gertrude Lawrence, Paul McGrath, and Nancy Coleman, then playing in *Susan and God* at the Plymouth Theater, New York City. Exact replicas of the stage settings were built for the telecast from the National Broadcasting Company's studio in the RCA building, New York City. The first to be televised in color was James Matthew Barrie's *Peter Pan*, starring Mary Martin as Peter Pan and Cyril Ritchard as Captain Hook, which was telecast on March 7, 1955, from 7:30 to 9:30 P.M. by WRCA, Channel 4, New York City, on *Producer's Showcase*. It could also be seen in black and white on the NBC network.

1461. Broadway play starring an African-American actress was *Mamba's Daughters*, a play by Dorothy and DuBose Heyward, in which the blues singer Ethel

Waters played the leading role. The play opened in New York City in January 1939. Waters took 17 curtain calls on opening night.

1462. Musical comedy to be shown on television was a performance of "Topsy and Eva—Television Edition," presented on July 25, 1939, by station W2XBS of the National Broadcasting Company, New York City. The entertainers who appeared on the program were the Duncan sisters, Billy Kent, Florence Auer, Winfield Hoeney, Edwin Vail, the Southernaires, and the Chansonettes.

1463. Musical comedy written for television was *The Boys from Boise*, produced by the Charles M. Storm Company for *Esquire* magazine on September 28, 1944, over WABD, New York City. The program was directed by Ray Nelson.

1464. Tony Awards ceremony honoring excellence in Broadway theater was held in the Grand Ballroom of the Waldorf-Astoria Hotel in New York City on April 6, 1947. The award was named for Antoinette Perry, the recently deceased head of the American Theater Wing. The program was broadcast on radio by WOR and the Mutual Network. The winners, who received a scroll and a small gift, included actors David Wayne, for *Finian's Rainbow*; Fredric March, for *Years Ago*; and Jose Ferrer, for *Cyrano de Bergerac*; actresses Patricia Neal, for *Another Part of the Forest*; Ingrid Bergman, for *Joan of Lorraine*; and Helen Hayes, for *Happy Birthday*; playwright Arthur Miller, for *All My Sons*; choreographers Agnes de Mille, for *Brigadoon*; and Michael Kidd, for *Finian's Rainbow*; composer Kurt Weill, for *Street Scene*; costume designer Lucinda Ballard, for five different plays; director Elia Kazan, for *All My Sons*; and scenic designer David Folks, for *Henry VIII*.

1465. Broadway play written by an African-American woman was *Raisin in the Sun*, by Lorraine Hansberry, which opened on March 11, 1959, at the Ethel Barrymore Theatre, New York City. It was a story about an African-American family living in the Southside area of Chicago and starred Sidney Poitier, Ruby Dee, and Claudia McNeil.

1466. Musical to run for more than 3,000 performances was *Fiddler on the Roof*, based on stories by the Yiddish writer Sholem Aleichem (pen name of Sholem Yakov Rabinowitz). It opened on September 22, 1964, at the Imperial Theatre, New York City, and ran for 3,242 performances. Zero Mostel took the part of Tevye. It was presented by Harold Prince, with choreography by Jerome Robbins, music by Jerry Bock, lyrics by Sheldon Harnick, and book by Joseph Stein.

1467. Rock musical was *Hair, An American Tribal Love–Rock Musical*, which opened at the Public Theater in New York City on October 29, 1967. The composer was Galt MacDermott. The book and lyrics were written by Jerome Ragni and James Rado. The musical, which appeared during the Vietnam War, carried an antiwar message and aroused some controversy for its glorification of "hippie" values, including a nude scene at the end of the first act. The production moved to Broadway's Biltmore Theatre in April 1968.

1468. American theater company to perform Shakespeare at Stratford was the Theatre for a New Audience, based in New York City. In November 2001, the group brought its production of Shakespeare's *Cymbeline* to a playhouse run by the Royal Shakespeare Company in Stratford-upon-Avon, Shakespeare's birthplace. The play was directed by Bartlett Sher.

BUSINESS AND INDUSTRY

1469. Trade monopoly was the fur trade established in Vermont by the explorer Samuel de Champlain, acting as the agent of fur dealers in France. In 1609, he set up trading operations in the Lake Champlain area with the local Hurons and Algonkians. The first trade monopoly among manufacturers was probably the United Company of Spermaceti Candlers, formed by nine New England spermaceti candle manufacturers in 1761. The group set a maximum price at which whale oil products could be sold.

1470. Commercial corporation was the New York Fishing Company, which was chartered on January 8, 1675, by the Governor and Council of New York, acting for the Duke of York "for settleing a fishery in these parts." Shares of the capital stock were £10 each.

1471. Price regulation agreement by colonists was signed by 21 coopers of New York City on December 17, 1679. The coopers agreed upon "the Rate and Prizes of Caske, this is to Say, for every Dry halfe Baril one shilling Six Pence." The agreement concluded: "And Wee, the Under Written, Doo Joyntly and Seavorally Bind ourselves, that for Every one that shall sell any cask Beefore mentioned under the Rate or Prizes above, Sd., that for every Such Default ffivety Shillinges he or they shall pay for use of the poore, as Wittnes our hands, this 17th Day of December, 1679." The coopers' action was condemned and they were brought to trial in the Council Chamber on January 8, 1680. The compact was annulled and the following verdict issued: "They are adjudged guilty, all that have signed the Contract, and are To pay each 50s, & either of them in publick employ to be dismist. The paym't to be to the Church or pious uses."

1472. Arbitration law was "an act for the more easy and effectually finishing of controversies by arbitration," passed at the legislative session held from October 11 to November 2, 1753, in New Haven, CT. Three arbitrators were appointed, one by each side and one by the court. The court was granted power to levy and collect the awards.

1473. Arbitration tribunal was established by the Chamber of Commerce, New York City, on May 3, 1768, and consisted of seven members. It was charged with adjusting "any differences between parties agreeing to leave such disputes to this Chamber." A different committee was appointed for each meeting.

1474. Chamber of Commerce was incorporated on March 13, 1770, under a royal charter from King George III. Its motto was *Non nobis nate solum* ("not born for ourselves alone"). The Chamber of Commerce of the United States was founded in 1912 by approximately 500 representatives of commercial organizations, trade associations, and individual establishments, who were invited to participate in a series of discussions by President William Howard Taft and Secretary of Commerce and Labor Charles Nagel. The headquarters of the Chamber of Commerce of the United States was dedicated on May 20, 1925.

1475. Trade directory was *Aitken's General American Register, and the Gentleman's and Tradesman's Complete Annual Account Book and Calendar for . . . 1773.* It was printed by J. Crukshank for Robert Aitken in Philadelphia, PA, in 1772–73, and contained 110 unnumbered pages. The contents included a calendar, an account book for the year, a list of public officers of the various colonies, and space for memoranda.

1476. Price regulation law enacted by a colony was enacted by Rhode Island at Providence on December 31, 1776. It was "an act to prevent monopolies and oppression by excessive and unreasonable prices for many of the necessaries and conveniencies of life, and for preventing engrossers, and for the better supply of our troops in the army with such necessaries as may be wanted." The law regulated prices on farm labor, beef, hides, shoes, cotton, sugar, salt, coffee, cheese, butter, beans, peas, potatoes, pork, wool, flannel, towcloths, flax, tallow, rum, molasses, oats, stockings, wheat, rye, maize, salted pork, and similar commodites. Lawbreakers were assessed fines equivalent to the value of the merchandise. The fines were distributed equally to the state and to informers.

1477. Arbitration law enacted by a state was passed on December 15, 1778, by the General Assembly of Maryland, in Annapolis, which ruled that "it shall be lawful to and for such court to give judgment upon the award of the person or persons to whom such submission and reference shall be made."

1478. Corporate body chartered by a special act of Congress was the President, Directors and Company of the Bank of the United States, chartered on February 25, 1791, by the First Congress, in session in New York City.

1479. Bankruptcy act was the act of Congress of April 4, 1800, "to establish a uniform system of bankruptcy in the United States." It contained 64 sections and applied to "any merchant or other person residing within the United States, actually using the trade of merchandise, by buying and selling in gross, or by retail, or dealing in exchange as a banker, broker, factor, underwriter or marine insurer." It was repealed in December 1803. It did not permit voluntary bankruptcy and applied to traders only.

1480. Capitalized corporation formed in the United States was the Boston Manufacturing Company, formed by Francis Cabot Lowell in 1813 to raise money for his project of building a cotton mill near the Charles River in Waltham, MA. He secured $400,000 in capital from the Boston Associates, a group of Boston aristocrats.

1481. Trust was the salt trust, organized on November 10, 1817, by the salt manufacturers of Kanawha, WV. It went into active operation on January 1, 1818, at the Kanawha Salt Company. It was formed for the purpose of controlling the quantity of salt manufactured, the method of manufacture, the packing, and the production. The company disbanded on January 1, 1822.

1482. Manufacturers' fair was held in the Masonic Hall, New York City, on October 24, 1828, under the auspices of the American Institute in the City of New York. The institute was incorporated on May 2, 1829, to encourage and promote domestic industry in the United States in agriculture, commerce, manufacturing, and the arts.

1483. Credit protection group was the Merchants' Vigilance Association, formed in 1842 by importers and commission houses in New York City. The association distributed reports prepared by Sheldon P. Church. William C. Dusenbury, who later formed the Mercantile Agency of Woodward and Dusenbury, was the secretary.

1484. Trade association of importance was the American Brass Association, which was organized in the Naugatuck Valley of Connecticut in February 1853. Headquarters were opened in Waterbury, CT. The original object of the association was to regulate prices, but in 1856 it also attempted to regulate production. The association ceased to function in 1869.

1485. World's fair was held in New York City in 1853, modeled after the 1851 World's Fair held in London. The exposition, sponsored by the Association for the Exhibition of the Industry of All Nations, was held at Reservoir Square, in a specially erected two-story building with an area of 249,691 square feet that occupied the space from 40th Street to 42nd Street and between Fifth and Sixth avenues. The exposition was opened by President Franklin Pierce on July 14, 1853. Admission was 50 cents for a single ticket, $2.50 monthly, $10 per person; children under 12 were admitted for 25 cents each. The building was destroyed by fire on October 5, 1858.

1486. Metric system usage to be approved by Congress was approved on July 28, 1866. The act provided that it "shall be lawful throughout the United States of America to employ the weights and measures of the metric system."

1487. State chamber of commerce was the New York Chamber of Commerce, formed on April 5, 1868, by 20 merchants at a meeting at Fraunces Tavern, New York City, for "promoting and encouraging commerce, supporting industry, adjusting disputes relative to trade and navigation, and procuring such laws and regulations as may be found necessary for the benefit of trade in general." John Cruger was the first president.

1488. Patent list was the *Official Gazette of the U.S. Patent Office*, issued weekly, which gave the numbers, titles, and claims of the patents issued during the week immediately preceding, together with the names and addresses of the patentees. The first issue was dated January 3, 1872.

1489. National measurement organization to improve systems of weights and measures was the American Metrological Society, formed on December 30, 1873, at Columbia University, New York City, by Wolcott Gibbs, Frederick Augustus Porter Barnard, and Hubert Anson Newton.

1490. Centennial exhibition was the International Exhibition, which occupied 236 acres in Fairmount Park, Philadelphia, PA. It opened on May 10, 1876, and was host to 76,172 cash customers and 110,500 free customers. It closed on November 10, 1876. It attracted 60,000 exhibitors and 9,010,916 visitors.

1491. Antitrust law enacted by a state was an act "to prevent monopolies in the transportation of freight, and to secure free and fair competition in the same," approved on February 23, 1883, by Alabama. The first general law was passed on March 9, 1889, by Kansas, "to declare unlawful trusts and combinations in restraint of trade and products, and to provide penalties therefor."

1492. Holding companies authorized by a state were authorized by New Jersey in a law passed on April 4, 1888. It provided that it was "lawful for any corporation of this state, or of any other state, doing business in this state and authorized by law to own and hold shares of stocks and bonds of corporations of other states, to own and hold and dispose thereof in the same manner and with all the rights, powers and privileges of individual owners of shares of the capital stock and bonds or other evidences of indebtedness of corporations of this state."

1493. Antitrust law enacted by Congress was an "act to protect trade and commerce against unlawful restraints and monopolies," passed by Congress on July 2, 1890. It provided that "every contract combination in the form of trust or otherwise, or conspiracy, in restraint of trade or commerce among the several states, or with foreign nations, is hereby declared to be illegal." The act is popularly known as the Sherman Act.

1494. National manufacturing association representing members of diversified industries was the National Association of Manufacturers of the United States, organized on January 22, 1895, at a convention held in Cincinnati, OH. The first president elected was Thomas P. Dolan.

1495. Industrial research laboratory was the General Electric Research Laboratory, Schenectady, NY, opened in September 1900. It was supervised by Dr. Willis Rodney Whitney, former instructor at the Massachusetts Institute of Technology.

1496. National business organization for African-Americans was the National Negro Business League, founded in Boston, MA, on August 23, 1900, by Booker T. Washington. Four hundred delegates from 34 states attended the founding conference, which promoted the growth of African-American–owned businesses. Washington was elected the first president of the organization.

1497. Corporation with a capitalization of $1 billion was the United States Steel Corporation. It was incorporated on February 25, 1901, and was ready for business on April 1, 1901, with an authorized capitalization of $1.4 billion. The original member companies were the Carnegie Company, Federal Steel Company, National Steel Company, National Tube Company, American Steel and Wire Company of New Jersey, American Tin Plate Company, American Steel Hoop Company, American Sheet Steel Company, Lake Superior Consolidated Iron Mines, and American Bridge Company. The first president was Charles M. Schwab.

1498. Boycott prevention law enacted by a state was passed on September 26, 1903, by Alabama, "to prohibit boycotting, unfair lists, picketting, or other interference with the lawful business or occupation of others, and to provide a penalty therefor." The law declared it a misdemeanor for two or more persons to conspire to prevent persons from carrying on a lawful business, to print or circulate stickers, cards, etc., and to use threats. The penalty was a fine of not less than $50 nor more than $500, or imprisonment of not more than 60 days at hard labor.

1499. Rotary Club meeting took place on February 23, 1905, in Chicago, IL. The group's founder was a lawyer, Paul Percy Harris, who invited three friends, a coal dealer, a tailor, and a mining engineer. Meetings were held in each member's place of business in rotation, so that each could obtain some knowledge of the others' businesses. A convention of 16 Rotary clubs met in Chicago in August 1910 to form a national association. An international association was formed in August 1912 in Duluth, MN, to provide charters for Winnipeg,

Canada, and London, England. The constitution was revised in June 1922, when Rotary International was adopted as the group's new name.

1500. Consumer protection law enacted by Congress was "an act forbidding the importation, exportation or carriage in interstate commerce of falsely or spuriously stamped articles of merchandise made of gold or silver or their alloys." It was enacted on June 13, 1906.

1501. Price regulation law enacted by a state was enacted by Louisiana and approved on July 2, 1908, by Governor Jared Young Sanders. It prohibited "unfair commercial discrimination between different sections, communities, cities, or localities in the State of Louisiana or unfair competition therein."

1502. Blue-sky laws enacted by a state were passed by Kansas on March 10, 1911, "for the regulation and supervision of investment companies and providing penalties for the violation thereof."

1503. Advertising association to combat business abuses by advancing truth and fair practice in business was the Vigilance Committee of the Advertising Club of New York, New York City, organized at a meeting called on December 1911 by Lewellyn E. Pratt, program committee chairman.

1504. Junior chamber of commerce was organized on October 13, 1915, as the Young Men's Progressive Civic Association, St. Louis, MO. In 1918, the name was changed to the Junior Chamber of Commerce. On January 21, 1921, delegates from 24 cities assembled in St. Louis to establish the United States Junior Chamber of Commerce. The first national convention was held in St. Louis on June 17–19, 1920. Henry Giessenbier, Jr., was elected president.

1505. Arbitration law enacted by Congress was "an act to make valid and enforceable written provisions or agreements for arbitration of disputes arising out of contracts, maritime transactions or commerce among the States or Territories or with foreign nations," approved on February 12, 1925.

1506. Woman's World Fair was held in Chicago, IL, April 18–25, 1925, to demonstrate women's progress in 70 industries. At the Chicago World's Fair of 1893, women's handicrafts had been featured only at the sewing exhibit. The Woman's World Fair was officially opened by Grace Coolidge, the wife of President Calvin Coolidge.

1507. Resale price maintenance law enacted by a state was California's Fair Trade Act, approved on May 8, 1931, which provided "that the buyer will not resell [a] commodity except at the price stipulated by the vendor." The title of the act is "an act to protect trade-mark owners, distributors and the public against injurious and uneconomic practices in the distribution of articles of standard quality under a distinguished trade-mark, brand or name."

1508. Director of a major corporation who was a woman was Lettie Pate Whitehead, named a director of the Coca-Cola Company in 1934. She was the widow of Joseph Brown Whitehead, who had made his fortune bottling and marketing Coca-Cola and whose business she operated following his death.

1509. Cartel of corporations listed by that name was the Pacific Coast Gasolene Cartel. The cartel was an association of the companies selling 95 percent of the gasoline in the states of California, Washington, Oregon, Arizona, and Nevada, and the territories of Hawaii and Alaska. The agreement, which regulated competition, was approved by the secretary of the interior on February 13, 1934. A committee of seven persons was chosen to manage the activities of the cartel. The first chairman was Ralph Kenneth Davies of San Francisco, director of the Standard Oil Company of California, who was elected on February 24, 1934. The government representative on the board was William Herbert Eaton. The cartel became effective on March 1, 1934, but was abandoned before the end of the month.

1510. Corporation with a net income of more than $1 billion in one year was the General Motors Corporation, Detroit, MI, whose net income in 1955 was $1,189,477,082 (9.6 percent of net sales amounting to $12,443,277,420). It exceeded $1.5 billion in 1963, with a net income of $1,591,823,085 (9.7 percent of net sales of $16,494,818,184). In 1965, net income exceeded $2 billion, with the corporation reporting a net income of $2,125,606,400 (10.3 percent of net sales of $20,733,982,295).

1511. Installment sales law enacted by a state to protect consumers in practically all types of time sales was signed by Governor William Averell Harriman of New York on April 17, 1957. It placed a limit on credit service charges, required all charges to be clearly itemized, and prohibited fine print in the contracts.

1512. World's Fair that was financially successful was the Century 21 Exposition, held from April 21 to October 21, 1962, in Seattle, WA. It was opened by remote control by President John Fitzgerald Kennedy in conjunction with a speech he transmitted by telephone from Palm Beach, FL. The fair paid for its entire operating expenses, had a surplus of about a million dollars, and left a number of very valuable buildings and improvements on the site of the present Seattle Center.

1513. Product liability lawsuit to result in a criminal trial was filed by the relatives of three women who were killed in 1978 in an auto accident involving a Ford Pinto. The Ford Motor Company was charged with reckless homicide for knowingly selling vehicles that were unsafe. On March 13, 1981, a jury in Winimac, ID, found the company not guilty.

1514. Fortune 1000 company to be owned and chaired by a woman was the Warnaco Group of New York City, a company specializing in women's apparel. Linda Wachner headed a $480 million leveraged buyout of Warnaco in 1986 and proceeded to turn it into one of the most profitable companies in the industry.

1515. Company to pay a fine of $100 million for a price-fixing scheme was the Archer Daniels Midland Company, Decatur, IL, a maker of agricultural commodities. The Justice Department imposed the fine on the company on October 14, 1996, as a penalty for conspiring with other companies to fix the prices of two food additives, lysine and citric acid. The company admitted the charges. It was by far the largest such fine up to that time.

Advertising

1516. Patent medicine advertisement appeared in the 1692 *Boston Almanack*, printed by Benjamin Harris and John Allen: "That Excellent Antidote against all manner of Gripings called Aqua anti torminales, which if timely taken, it not only cures the Griping of the Guts, and the Wind Cholick; but preventeth that woful Distemper of the Dry Belly Ach; With printed directions for the use of it. Sold by Benjamin Harris at the London-Coffee House in Boston. Price three shillings the half pint Bottle."

1517. Newspaper advertisement appeared from May 1 to May 8, 1704, in the *Boston News-Letter*, Boston, MA. Three ads occupied four inches in a single column. The only display was a two-line initial letter in the text and the word "Advertisement" above the ads. One offered "At Oysterbay on Long Island in the Province of New York . . . a very good Fulling Mill to be Let or Sold, as also a Plantation, having on it a large new Brick house, and other good house by it for a Kitchin and workhouse, etc." Another offered a reward for the capture of a thief and the return of certain wearing apparel, and the third was a notice of the loss of two anvils.

1518. Medicine advertisement in booklet form was *A Short Treatise of the Virtues of Dr. Bateman's Pectoral Drops: The Nature of the Distemper They Cure, and the Manner of Their Operation.* It contained 36 pages, including 15 pages of testimonials and a four-page abstract of the royal patent granted to the inventor, Benjamin Okell, and his associates. The catalog was originally printed by J. Cluer in Bow-Churchyard, London, and was reprinted by John Peter Zenger in New York in 1731. The medicine was sold wholesale and retail by James Wallace of New York City, for cases of "the rheumatism, stone and gravel pains, colds, agues, and fevers, gout, jaundice, ailments of the breast, and asthmas."

1519. Magician's advertisement appeared on March 18, 1734, in the *New York Weekly Journal.* It announced that on that day Joseph Broome would "perform Wonders of the World by Dexterity of Hand" at the home of Charles Sleigh, on Duke Street, New York City, and invited "all to be Spectators of his Ingenuity." The admission fees were one shilling, ninepence, and sixpence.

1520. Newspaper advertisement across two columns appeared in the *New York Weekly Journal*, New York City, on July 18, 1743, announcing the exhibition of a musical automaton imported from England—the first automaton seen in this country. It was also the first advertisement to occupy a half-page space in a periodical.

1521. Price sheet for commodities was the *South-Carolina Price-Current*, a broadside issued by Crouch and Gray, commission merchants, Charleston, SC, on a sheet 6 by 12 inches, two columns wide. The first known copy, that of July 30, 1774, listed 168 commodities with their prices.

1522. Advertising agency was opened in 1841 in Philadelphia, PA, by Volney B. Palmer, who thus became the first commercial advertising agent.

1523. Advertising magazine was the *Advertising Agency Circular*, a monthly founded by George Presbury Rowell and published by George P. Rowell and Company, New York City. It was issued from 1865 until December 1866, when the name was changed to the *Advertiser's Gazette*. It became a weekly on Thursday, April 1, 1875.

1524. Premiums given away with merchandise were successfully introduced by Benjamin Talbert Babbitt of New York City in 1865, to help him sell soap in wrappers. People felt that they were paying extra for the wrappers, so he printed the word "coupon" on them and offered to give away a "beautiful lithograph picture" for 10 coupons. Eventually his company ran a premium department, which carried as many as a thousand different items in stock.

1525. Trademark for food registered by the Patent Office was granted in 1867 to William Underwood and Company of Boston, MA. The mark depicted a red devil and was printed on the packaging for Underwood's canned "deviled entremets," or deviled meats, introduced the same year.

1526. Newspaper premiums were chromolithograph pictures, offered between 1870 and 1881 by the *Christian Union*, edited by Henry Ward Beecher. They were credited with raising the paper's circulation from 10,000 to 100,000. Premiums were also offered by the *New York Recorder*, New York City, whose issue of March 25, 1893, printed the first of a series of coupons offering 17-by-25-inch color reproductions of celebrated paintings. Ten different subjects were offered, any one of which could be had for 20 coupons. Coupons and bonus prizes were also offered for ad insertions; prizes included a $10 gold piece, five silver watches, and 10 plush ottomans.

1527. Bandwagon used for the distribution of samples and advertising matter was employed in 1871 by Benjamin Talbert Babbitt, who used eight imported white Arabian stallions to pull the wagon. The band was seated on top of the wagon. His slogan, "For All Nations," was prominently featured on advertising cards over the doors of Broadway streetcars in New York City. Babbitt had the distinction of being one of the first to advertise in streetcars and buses.

1528. Trading stamp was originated in 1891 by Thomas Alexander Sperry, who in 1896 organized the Sperry and Hutchinson Company of Bridgeport, CT. The company was incorporated in 1900. Trading stamps were issued by merchants as an incentive to customers. The more a customer spent, the greater the number of trading stamps earned. Books of collected stamps could be exchanged for free merchandise.

1529. Electric sign of large dimensions was designed and constructed by the Edison General Electric Company and installed in June 1892 on the wall of a nine-story building near Broadway and 23rd Street, New York City. The sign occupied a surface area 60 by 68 feet and was composed of 107 galvanized iron boxes varying in height from 3 to 6 feet. The front of each box was cut out to form the desired letter. Inside the boxes were 1,457 16-candlepower Edison bulbs in red, blue, green, and frosted white. The sign read: "BUY HOMES ON / LONG ISLAND / SWEPT BY OCEAN BREEZES / MANHATTAN BEACH / ORIENTAL HOTEL / MANHATTAN HOTEL/ GILMORE'S BAND / BROCK'S FIREWORKS." Current was supplied by the Edison Electric Illuminating Company. The sign was illuminated from dusk to 11 P.M. One line went on at a time until all the lights were on, then all the lights went out and the cycle began again.

1530. Trademark character impersonated by an actor as an advertising ploy was Aunt Jemima. The original Aunt Jemima was a character in a song. Chris Rutt, the inventor of the first ready-made pancake mix, borrowed the name to represent his product because he thought it suggested the image of an expert family cook. In 1893, when the Davis Milling Company, manufacturers of the mix, set up a promotional booth at the World's Columbian Exposition in Chicago, IL, it hired a local woman named Nancy Green to cook pancakes for visitors. Green continued to play the role for the rest of her life.

1531. Full-page magazine advertisement for a food product was printed in several national magazines in 1894. The product was Van Camp Pork and Beans, manufactured by the Van Camp Seafood Company of Indianapolis, IN. The ad offered a sample can for six cents.

1532. Truth-in-advertising law enacted by a state was "an act to regulate the sale of merchandise and to prevent misleading and dishonest representations in connection therewith," passed by New York on April 30, 1898. Those whose advertisements are "intended to have the appearance of an advantageous offer, which is untrue or calculated to mislead, shall be guilty of a misdemeanor."

1533. Car advertisement in a specialty magazine appeared in *Scientific American* on July 30, 1898. It was a one-column advertisement by the Winton Motor Car Company, Cleveland, OH, under the caption "Dispense with a Horse."

1534. Car advertisement in a national magazine of general circulation appeared in the *Saturday Evening Post* on March 31, 1900. The W.E. Roach Company of Philadelphia, PA, ran an ad featuring its slogan, "Automobiles That Give Satisfaction."

1535. Advertising show to be held annually took place May 3–9, 1906, in Madison Square Garden, New York City. Its slogan was "If your business isn't with advertising, advertise it for sale."

1536. Advertising campaign based on sex appeal was the "skin you love to touch" campaign, created by Helen Resor of the J. Walter Thompson Agency in New York for Woodbury Facial Soap. The first quarter-page ad appeared in the May 1911 *Ladies' Home Journal*. It showed a painting by Alonzo Kimball of a well-dressed man passionately embracing a woman who coyly looks away. The copy read in part, "A skin you love to touch . . . Your skin, like the rest of your body, is changing every day. As old skin dies, new forms. This is your opportunity. By the proper external treatment, you can make this new skin just what you would love to have it." A full-page color version first appeared in the September 1915 *Ladies' Home Journal*.

1537. Radio commercial was sponsored by the Queensboro Realty Corporation, Jackson Heights, NY, on August 28, 1922, over station WEAF, the experimental station of the American Telephone and Telegraph Company, New York City. The advertising rate was $100 for 10 minutes. Listeners heard H.M. Blackwell speak for 10 minutes about Hawthorne Court, a dwelling in Jackson Heights.

1538. Skywriting advertisement exhibition took place at noon over Times Square, New York City, on November 28, 1922. The skywriting was done by Captain Cyril Turner of the Royal Air Force, who spelled out the message "Hello, U.S.A. Call Vanderbilt 7200" in letters a half mile high at an altitude of 10,000 feet. The message resulted in 47,000 telephone calls in 2.5 hours. The letters were written upside down in white smoke released from the rear of the airplane. The vapors formed when oil hit a hot exhaust pipe. The release of the oil was controlled by levers.

1539. Neon advertising sign was installed on a marquee at the Cosmopolitan Theatre, 59th Street and Columbus Circle, New York City, in July 1923. This sign advertised the theatrical production *Little Old New York*, in which Marion Davies played the leading role. A patent on this tube was granted to George Claude of Paris, France, on January 19, 1915.

1540. Radio network program sponsored by commercial advertising was "The Eveready Hour," first broadcast on February 12, 1924, from station WEAF, New York City, to stations WCAP, Washington, DC, and WJAR, Providence, RI, under the sponsorship of the National Carbon Company.

1541. Radio jingle was a commercial for Pepsi-Cola that aired in 1940. It ran: "Pepsi-Cola hits the spot / Twelve full ounces, that's a lot / Twice as much for a nickle, too / Pepsi-Cola is the drink for you." The authors were Alan Bradley Kent and Austen Herbert Croom-Johnson. The jingle was eventually heard in 55 languages.

1542. Electric flashing sign installed was the Motograph News Bulletin, placed in service on the four sides of the *New York Times* building, New York City, on November 6, 1928, when election returns were flashed. The system was invented by Francis E. J. Wilde of Meadowmere Park, NY, who obtained a patent on May 3, 1927, on an "electric sign control" designed "to permit changing of sign without interruption." It was installed by the Motorgram Corporation, New York City, and was 360 feet long and 5 feet high. It had 14,800 lamps, 88,000 soldered connections, 1,386,000 feet of wire, and 39,000 contact brushes that created 21,925,664 lamp flashes an hour.

1543. Athlete depicted on a Wheaties box was Lou Gehrig, baseball player for the New York Yankees, whose picture appeared on the back of Wheaties cereal boxes in 1934. The first woman featured on a Wheaties box was aviator Elinor Smith, also in 1934. Wheaties, invented in Minneapolis, MN, and introduced to the market in 1924 as Washburn's Gold Medal Whole Wheat Flakes, found a lucrative market among sports fans after it was advertised in 1933 on a billboard at a local baseball stadium.

Wheaties boxes began featuring athletes on the front of the box in 1958, starting with decathlon champion Bob Richards.

1544. Newspaper advertisement scented with perfume was issued on March 25, 1937, by the *Daily News*, Washington, DC. It contained a one-page advertisement of the Peoples Drug Stores featuring flowers.

1545. Electric sign showing an animated cartoon was displayed April 28, 1937, by Douglas Leigh on the front of a building on Broadway, New York City. It contained 2,000 bulbs and presented a four-minute show depicting, among other things, a cavorting horse and ball-tossing cats.

1546. Radio jingle played nationwide on network radio for an on-the-air commercial most probably was "Have You Tried Wheaties?," sung by a quartet on December 25, 1926, over WCCO, Minneapolis, MN. Washburn Crosby Company (later called General Mills), the maker of Wheaties, also owned the radio station. The melody was based on that of a popular song, "Jazz Baby."

1547. Television commercial that was sanctioned by the Federal Communications Commission and legally broadcast on a commercial station was aired on July 1, 1941, by WNBT, the National Broadcasting Company affiliate in New York City. During a break in a game between the Dodgers and the Phillies at Ebbets Field in Brooklyn, New York City, the camera focused in on a ticking Bulova watch while an announcer read the time. The Bulova Watch Company was billed $9 for the airtime and station charges. Advertisements not sanctioned by the FCC had been appearing on noncommercial stations for at least a decade.

1548. Department store sales demonstrations using television on a large scale were staged at Gimbel Brothers, Philadelphia, PA, from October 24 to November 14, 1945, with RCA-Victor equipment. Approximately 25,000 people viewed the demonstrations at the auditorium and at 20 television sites placed at strategic locations on the seven floors of the department store. There were 11 daily demonstrations lasting about 10 minutes and showing millinery, home furnishings, shoes, scarves, furs, nursery furniture, toys, curtains, interior decorating, and hair styling.

1549. Movie trailer to be shown on television appeared on September 20, 1946, on WNBT-TV, New York City. It advertised a Columbia Pictures film, *The Jolson Story*.

1550. Television show to be sponsored by a commercial advertiser was "Geographically Speaking," sponsored by the Bristol-Myers Company and broadcast on October 27, 1946, on WNBT, New York, and WPTZ, Philadelphia. The first in color was Colgate Palmolive's *Colgate Comedy Hour*, telecast on November 22, 1953, from the Colonial Theater, New York City, by WNBT-TV, New York City, on the NBC network from 8 to 9 P.M. It starred Donald O'Connor, Corinne Calvet, Ralph Bellamy, Dorothy Dandridge, and Sidney Miller.

1551. Newspaper advertisement that looked three-dimensional was published on June 12, 1953, in the *Daily Freeman*, Waukesha, WI. A decorating company, Hale-Frame Associates, used a full page to advertise carpets. A cardboard cutout with red and blue lenses with which to view the three-dimensional effect was supplied with the newspaper.

1552. Television commercial in color to appear on a local show was commissioned on March 9, 1954, by Castro Decorators, New York City, in a contract with WNBT-TV, New York City, for spot announcements. The first telecast was on August 6, 1954.

1553. Newspaper advertisement printed on aluminum foil appeared in the *Milwaukee Sentinel*, Milwaukee, WI, on March 18, 1958. It was a lamination of Reynolds aluminum foil on one side and paper on the other. The foil side was printed in seven colors at the gravure plant of the Reynolds Metal Company in St. Louis, MO, while the paper side was printed by the *Sentinel* in one color and black.

Agriculture

1554. Tobacco cultivation was undertaken at Jamestown, VA, in 1612 by John Rolfe, the future husband of Pocahontas, who had arrived from England with 107 other settlers on May 13, 1607. Rolfe was the first settler to come up with a method of curing tobacco, which made it possible to grow tobacco crops for export to England.

1555. Maize to be produced in quantity by English colonists was grown on a 40-acre tract planted in Jamestown, VA, in 1609. It had been grown by Native American peoples for many thousands of years. Maize is indigenous to America, and records of its growth and use were made by the explorers Christopher Columbus and Giovanni da Verrazano in the late 15th and early 16th centuries.

1556. Sheep were imported into America in 1609, when the London Company brought over a shipment to Jamestown, VA. Merino sheep were imported from Portugal in 1802 by Colonel David Humphreys, U.S. minister to Spain (although three merino sheep are reported to have been smuggled into the United States in 1793 and eaten). Karakul sheep were imported in 1908 from Russia.

1557. Corn found by English settlers was discovered on November 16, 1620, on the future site of Provincetown, MA, by 16 Pilgrims led by Myles Standish, William Bradford, Stephen Hopkins, and Edward Tilley at a place they named Corn Hill.

1558. Potato is believed by some authorities to have been imported from Bermuda by Virginia colonists in December 1621 or January 1622. The first potatoes are said to have been used for food rather than for planting.

1559. Cattle to be imported were brought over from Dover, England, in March 1624 by Edward Winslow, governor of the Plymouth Colony in Massachusetts. Cows were raised principally for their hides; secondly, for meat; and only very incidentally for their milk. Guernsey cattle were first imported in 1831; purebred shorthorns in 1833; Aberdeen-Angus cattle in 1873; and Afrikaaner cattle in 1931.

1560. Pear and peach trees were brought to America by Walloon settlers from Belgium in the early 17th century. They were first cultivated in what is now New Jersey and New York.

1561. Apples were imported from England in 1629 by John Winthrop, colonial governor of Massachusetts. The first apples grown by colonists were probably obtained from trees planted in Boston, MA, from which "ten fair pippins" were plucked on October 10, 1639.

1562. Crop limitation law was passed on October 16, 1629, by the Virginia General Assembly. Act Five limited the planting of tobacco.

1563. Crop surplus destruction ordered by a government was ordered on January 6, 1639, by the Virginia General Assembly: "Tobacco by reason of excessive quantities made, being so low that the planters could not subsist by it or be enabled to raise more staple commodities or pay their debts, enacted that the tobacco of that year be viewed by sworn viewers and the rotten and unmerchantable, and half the good to be burned, so the whole quantity made would come to 1,500,000 pounds without stripping and smoothing."

1564. Agricultural fair held annually was authorized by the director and council of New Netherlands (now New York) on September 30, 1641. They "ordained that henceforth there shall be held annually at Fort Amsterdam a Cattle Fair on the 15th of October; and a fair for Hogs on the 1st of November. Whosoever hath any things to sell or to buy can regulate himself accordingly."

1565. Branding law was enacted on February 5, 1644, by Connecticut. It provided that all cattle and swine older than six months be earmarked or branded before May 1, 1644, and that the marks be registered. The penalty for violation was five shillings a head, two of which were paid to informers.

1566. Rice to be imported was brought to America by Sir William Berkeley, governor of Virginia, in 1647. He directed that a half bushel of seeds be planted. The yield was 16 bushels.

1567. Livestock pounds for stray animals were required by Connecticut on May 1650. It decreed "that there shall be one sufficient pound or more made and maintained in every town and village within this jurisdiction, for the impounding of all swine and cattle as shall be found in any cornfield or other inclosure."

1568. Indigo crop was planted and harvested in South Carolina prior to 1690, when a petition was presented by Governor Seth Sothell to the Lords Proprietors asking that the inhabitants of South Carolina might be allowed to "pay their rents in the most valuable and merchantable produce of their lands" and enumerating such products as silk, cotton, rice, and indigo. Indigo, from which blue dye is derived, was not a successful crop until Elizabeth Lucas Pinckney began cultivating it on her family's two South Carolina plantations in 1740.

1569. Book on agriculture was *The Husbandman's Guide: In Four Parts. Part First. Containing many Excellent Rules for Setting and Planting of Orchards, Gardens and Woods, the times to Sow Corn, and all sorts of Seeds. Part Second. Choice Physical Receipts for divers dangerous Distempers in Men, Women and Children. Part Third. The Experienc'd Farrier. . . . Part Fourth. Certain rare Receipts to make Cordial Waters, Conserves, Preserves.* It was a 107-page reprint of an English book and was published in 1710 for Eleazar Phillips by John Allen, Boston, MA.

1570. Potatoes to be cultivated were planted in 1719 at Londonderry Common Field (now Derry), NH, by Scotch-Irish immigrants.

1571. Hemp to be exported was shipped to England in 1730. It consisted of 50 hundredweight of hemp raised in New England and Carolina, and 3 hundredweight from Virginia.

1572. Agricultural experiment farm was established on 10 acres set aside by Savannah, GA, in 1735. A skillful botanist was appointed "to collect the seeds of drugs and dying-stuffs in other countries in the same climate, in order to cultivate such of them as shall be found to thrive well in Georgia."

1573. Tomatoes eaten in America were given public approval as an edible food by Dr. John Siccary, a Portuguese Jewish physician who came to Virginia in 1745. Until he recognized their nutritional value, tomatoes were thought by the American colonists to be poisonous. The leaves are indeed toxic, though not the fruit. Siccary's fellow Virginian, Thomas Jefferson, grew tomatoes on his estate and helped to publicize their safety.

1574. Sugar cane was brought to Louisiana by Jesuit priests in 1751 from the island of Hispaniola (present-day Santo Domingo). It was used for making taffia, a kind of rum. The sugar industry started with the work of Étienne de Bore, who planted sugar cane in 1794 and in 1795 harvested a crop of sugar that sold for $12,000. At his death, his wealth was estimated at $300,000, all from sugar.

1575. Cattle to be exported were 16 steers shipped from Savannah, GA, in 1755. It is possible that prior shipments were made, but there is no record of them.

1576. Agricultural book that was distinctly American was *Essays upon Field Husbandry in New England*, by Jared Eliot. It consisted of six essays, originally printed separately, which were printed and sold by Edes and Gill in Boston, MA, in 1760.

1577. Cotton crop exported to England consisted of eight bales from Charleston, SC, which were seized by the custom house in England in 1764 on the grounds that the American colony could not have produced so much.

1578. Greenhouse was erected by James Beekman in New York City in 1764. It is claimed that Andrew Faneuil erected a glass house at Boston, MA, prior to 1737.

1579. Rhubarb was shipped by Benjamin Franklin from London, England, to John Bartram in Philadelphia, PA, on January 11, 1770.

1580. Oyster propagation under state auspices began in Rhode Island, which in June 1779 set aside part of the public domain for the cultivation and propagation of oysters.

1581. Seed business regularly established was organized on January 7, 1784, by David Landreth in Philadelphia, PA. Previously, seeds had been imported from Europe or saved from each crop by individual farmers. The firm, incorporated in 1904 as the D. Landreth Seed Company, later became a subsidiary of the Robert Buist Company, founded in Philadelphia in 1828.

1582. Agriculture society was the Philadelphia Society for the Promotion of Agriculture, which was organized on March 1, 1785. Meetings were scheduled every two months. Earlier, in 1781, the New Jersey Society for Promoting Agriculture, Commerce and Arts had undertaken the promotion of agriculture as one of its functions.

1583. Mule born in the United States was bred from a jackass sent to President George Washington. The exportation of full-blooded jacks from Spain was prohibited, but King Charles III of Spain, learning of Washington's interest, sent him two jacks and two jennets, which arrived in Boston, MA, on October 26, 1785.

1584. Agricultural dictionary published in the United States was Samuel Deane's *The New England Farmer; or, georgical dictionary: containing a compendious account of the ways and methods in which the most important art of husbandry, in all its branches is, or may be practised to the greatest advantage in this country*, a 335-page double-column book, published in 1790 by Isaiah Thomas in Worcester, MA. It was copyrighted on September 13, 1790, in the 3rd Massachusetts District.

1585. Cotton gin to separate the seed from the cotton was invented in 1792 by Eli Whitney at Mulberry Grove, a plantation near Savannah, GA, possibly using ideas furnished by his financial patron, Catherine Littlefield Greene. He formed a partnership with Greene's second husband, Phineas Miller, to manufacture the gin, but his model was stolen by dishonest manufacturers who produced many units. Although Whitney received a patent on March 14, 1794, he was unable to stop the infringement of his rights because the gin was so successful, greatly increasing cotton production in the South. The patent was not renewed when it expired because of the power exerted by those who had been enriched by Whitney's invention.

1586. Alfalfa is supposed to have been introduced into California in 1854 from Chile, but John Spurrier described alfalfa (which he called "lucerne") in his book *The Practical Farmer*, which was dedicated to Thomas Jefferson and published at Wilmington, DE, in 1793.

1587. Plow patent was granted on June 26, 1797, to Charles Newbold, a farmer of Burlington County, NJ. The plow was of solid cast iron, excepting the handles and beam, and consisted of a bar, a sheath, and a moldplate. It was the first cast-iron plow made. The invention did not meet with great success, as many farmers believed that the iron poisoned the land.

1588. Vineyard that was successful was established on August 28, 1798, by John James Dufour on a tract of land consisting of about 630 acres situated 25 miles from Lexington, KY. He called it "The First Vineyard." Dufour was one of the pioneer viticulturists in America. Attempts to establish vineyards had been made as early as 1619 in Virginia.

1589. Fruit culture treatise was *A Treatise on the Culture and Management of Fruit Trees; in which a new method of pruning and training is fully described. Together with observations on the diseases, defects and injuries in all kind of fruit and forest trees*, by William Forsyth, published for J. Morgan in 1802 in Philadelphia, PA. The book also contained *An Introduction and Notes Adapting the Rules of the Treatise to the Climates and Seasons of the United States* by William Cobbett.

1590. Agricultural encyclopedia was Anthony Florian Madinger Willich's *The Domestic Encyclopedia, or A Dictionary of Facts, and useful knowledge, comprehending a concise view of the latest discoveries, inventions and improvements, chiefly applicable to rural and domestic economy*. The encyclopedia was a five-volume set, published in Philadelphia, PA, in 1804 by William Young Birch and Abraham Small. It had originally appeared in England.

1591. Bananas are recorded as having arrived in 1804, when the schooner *Reynard* brought 30 bundles of bananas from Cuba.

1592. Agricultural journal was the *Agricultural Museum*, a 16-page octavo first issued on July 4, 1810, under the sponsorship of the Columbia Agricultural Society. It was edited by the Reverend David Wiley and printed by W.A. Rind at Georgetown, DC (now part of Washington, DC). Beginning with Volume 2, it was issued monthly. Subscription was $2.50 for 24 numbers. Publication ceased in May 1812. The first agricultural journal to attain prominence was the *American Farmer*, an eight-page quarto-size weekly, which was founded in Baltimore, MD, on April 2, 1819, by John Stuart Skinner. It flourished under various names until 1897.

1593. Cattle fair was held on October 1, 1810, in Pittsfield, MA. It was promoted by Elkanah Watson and was known as the Berkshire Cattle Show. There were 383 sheep, 20 bulls, and 15 yoke of oxen entered for premiums amounting to $70. After the fair, there was a grand procession a half mile long of 60 yoke of prime oxen.

1594. Horticulture society was the New York Horticultural Society, founded in 1818. It existed about 15 years. The first permanent organization was the Pennsylvania Horticultural Society, organized on November 24, 1827, in Philadelphia, PA, with a membership of 53. Horace Binney was the first president. The first exhibition open to the public was held on June 6, 1829.

1595. Melons and cantaloupes were grown in Germantown, PA, at the residence of E. B. Gardette on Wissahickon Avenue. The seed was brought over from Tripoli by Commodore James Barron in 1818.

1596. Cranberry cultivation was attempted about 1820 by Captain Henry Hall of Dennis, Cape Cod, MA. Cranberries grow wild on Cape Cod and were probably eaten by the Pilgrims.

1597. Sugar beets were grown about 1830 at Ensfield, PA, by the Beet Sugar Society of Philadelphia, of which James Donaldson was president.

1598. Reaper machine that was practical was built by Cyrus Hall McCormick in 1831 and demonstrated at a public trial in a field near Walnut Grove, VA. The owner of the field feared that the machine would rattle the heads off his wheat and stopped the demonstration. Another neighbor whose ground was more level invited McCormick to his field, where the machine worked splendidly, cutting six acres of wheat in half a day—as much as six men would have done. The reaper was patented on June 21, 1834, but farmers remained suspicious of it, and McCormick did not make his first sale until 1841. He began manufacturing it on a large scale in Chicago, IL, in 1847. An earlier reaper machine had been invented by Henry Ogle in 1826, but it was not practical. It consisted of a straight scythe blade that moved against a series of triangular fingers. The cut grain fell on a collecting board.

1599. Guano for use as a soil fertilizer was imported from Peru in 1832. Guano is the deposits of droppings of sea birds and bats, found in caves or above ground in areas where there is little or no rain.

1600. Horticultural magazine was the *Floral Magazine and Botanical Repository*, published in May 1832 in Philadelphia, PA, by David and Cuthbert Landreth, nurserymen and seedsmen. Publication ceased after 80 pages and 31 colored lithograph prints had been issued.

1601. Avocado was imported by Henry Perrine in 1833 and planted at Santa Barbara, CA.

1602. Gardener's manual was the *Young Gardener's Assistant, containing a catalogue of garden and flower seeds, with practical directions under each head, for the cultivation of culinary vegetables and flowers, also directions for cultivating fruit trees, the grape vine, etc.*, by Thomas Bridgeman, published in 1835 in New York City.

1603. Agricultural seed distribution on a national scale was undertaken in 1836–37 by the Commissioner of Patents, Henry Leavitt Ellsworth, at his own expense and without congressional authorization. In 1838 the cost was $126.40. In 1839 about 30,000 packets were distributed, the expense being about $1,000. Yearly seed distribution continued until 1923.

1604. Steel plow with a steel moldboard was made in 1837 by John Deere, a blacksmith, who tested it on the farm of Lewis Crandall, near Grand Detour, IL. Deere used steel from a broken saw blade. In 1843, he imported rolled steel from England, which cost about $300 a ton. In 1847 he began manufacturing the plows in Moline, IL, using steel produced by the Jones and Quiggs Steel Works, Pittsburgh, PA. His company was incorporated in 1868 as Deere and Company.

1605. Threshing machine to employ steam was patented by John A. Pitts and Hiram Abial Pitts of Winthrop, ME, who received a patent on December 29, 1837, on a "machine for threshing or cleaning grain." The machine separated grain from the straw and chaff.

1606. Seeding machine that was practical was invented by Joseph Gibbons of Adrian, MI, who received a patent on August 25, 1840. His machine was a grain drill with cavities to deliver seed and a device for regulating the volume. An earlier gravity-fed device, patented by Eliakim Spooner of Vermont on January 25, 1799, was not practical.

1607. Egg incubator for hatching chickens by artificial heat was patented on March 30, 1843, by Napoleon E. Guerin of New York City, who invented a "mode of distributing steam heat, purifying air, etc."

1608. Grain elevator operated by steam to transfer and store grain for commercial purposes was designed by Robert Dunbar and made by Jewett and Root for Joseph Dart, Buffalo, NY, in 1842. The first cargo of corn was unloaded on June 22, 1843, from the *South America.*

1609. Herd book for livestock was the *American Herd Book, containing pedigrees of short horn cattle to which is prefixed a concise history, of English and American short horns,* 240 pages, edited by Lewis Falley Allen and published in 1846 in Buffalo, NY.

1610. Synthetic fertilizer was developed by Professor James Jay Mapes, who experimented with fertilizers in 1847 on his 20-acre farm at Newark, NJ. He applied for a patent in 1849 on a superphosphate of lime made from charred bone (the waste products of sugar refineries), to which were added sulfate of ammonia and Peruvian guano. The patent was granted on November 22, 1859.

1611. Poultry show was the Grand Show of Domestic Poultry and Convention of Fowl Breeders and Fanciers, held on November 15–16, 1849, at the Public Garden, Boston, MA, with 1,423 specimens in 219 cages. More than 10,000 persons attended.

1612. Beehive with removable frames was patented by Lorenzo Lorraine Langstroth, a former pastor in Oxford, OH, on October 5, 1852. Langstroth's hive design revolutionized beekeeping because it was the first that allowed bees to build combs on wooden frames that could be removed, stripped of honey and wax, and then replaced. His key discovery was the "bee space," the minimum air space that bees would not bridge with wax or bee glue. By setting up his frames at this distance, he prevented the bees from building connections between them. This allowed him to remove one frame at a time without damaging the adjacent frames, and enabled him to maximize the amount of honeycomb in the hive.

1613. Grape vines planted in California for wine-making were planted in Buena Vista, CA, in 1857 by Count Agoston Haraszthy de Moksa, who imported Tokay, Zinfandel, and Shiras grape varieties from his native Hungary. These were the first varietal grapevines in the United States. In 1861, at the request of the California State Legislature, de Moksa imported 100,000 cuttings of 300 varieties of European wine grapes.

1614. Scientific publication issued by an agriculture bureau was *A Report on the Chemical Analysis of Grapes,* a four-page leaflet by Charles Mayer Wetherill, Ph.D., M.D., dated October 15, 1862, printed by the Government Printing Office, Washington, DC.

1615. Farmers' institute sponsored by a state was held by the Massachusetts State Board of Agriculture in Springfield, MA. The institute opened on December 8, 1863, and continued for four days. Lectures and discussions pertaining to agriculture occupied the meetings.

1616. Fish hatchery to breed salmon was an experimental laboratory established in 1864 under the supervision of James B. Johnson. He imported from Europe salmon eggs, which were hatched in his New York City laboratory.

1617. Fur-bearing animals raised commercially were minks reared in Oneida County, NY, in 1866 by H. Ressegue. Prices of skins were high, and live animals for breeding stock brought $30 a pair.

1618. Irrigation law enacted by Congress was the act of July 26, 1866, which ruled that control of waterways was a matter of state control subject to "local customs, laws and decisions of the court."

1619. National organization of farmers was the National Grange of the Patrons of Husbandry, which was organized in Washington, DC, December 4, 1867, with William Saunders of the Department of Agriculture as master and Oliver Hudson Kelley, a native of Boston, MA, as secretary. This was the first important cooperation undertaken by farmers. The movements and meetings of the society were carried on in secret.

1620. Jute culture was introduced by the Department of Agriculture in 1869–70. A quantity of seed was imported from France and India and planted from the Carolinas to Texas.

1621. State dairy association was the Vermont Dairymen's Association, organized on October 27, 1869, at Montpelier, VT.

1622. Oranges of the seedless navel variety grown in the United States were grown from a dozen budded saplings brought from Bahia, Brazil, in 1871 by William Saunders, horticulturist of the Department of Agriculture. Two of the trees, which were obtained by Jonathan and Eliza C. Tibbets in 1873, started the industry in Riverside, CA. Other types of oranges, however, had been grown earlier in Florida.

1623. Fish hatchery run by the federal government was established in 1872 at Bucksport, ME, under the supervision of Charles Grandison Atkins, for the propagation of Atlantic salmon. It was a joint activity, with the cooperation of state agencies of Maine, Massachusetts, and Connecticut, and was a continuation of experiments initiated by these agencies in 1871. It was later moved to East Orland, ME.

1624. Silo on record was constructed by Fred L. Hatch in 1873 in McHenry County, IL.

1625. State agricultural experiment station was the Connecticut Agricultural Experiment Station, established in Connecticut by an act approved on July 20, 1875. Orange Judd, editor and proprietor of the *American Agriculturist*, offered $1,000 and the trustees of Wesleyan University at Middletown, CT, offered the free use of the chemical laboratory of the university's Orange Judd Hall on condition that the legislature appropriate $2,800 per year for two years. The appropriation was made on October 1, 1875, and work began on January 1, 1876. Professor Wilbur Olin Atwater was the first director.

1626. Fruit spraying was done in 1878 when an apple grower in Niagara County, NY, sprayed his apple trees with Paris green for the control of canker worms.

1627. Loganberry was introduced in 1881 by Judge James Harvey Logan in Santa Cruz, CA, and given to the public in 1893 by the University of California. The loganberry is a cross between a California wild blackberry and a red raspberry.

1628. Fence made of woven wire was constructed in 1883 by John Wallace Page on his farm in Lenawee County, MI. The fence was made of wires that were interlaced horizontally and vertically. There were so many calls for similar fences from Page's neighbors that he opened a factory in Adrian, MI.

1629. Ostrich farm was established at South Pasadena, CA, by Edwin Cawston in 1886. He imported 50 ostriches from Africa, 18 of which survived the trip and were landed at Galveston, TX, in 1886. In order to discourage the exportation of ostriches from Africa, an export tax of $500 was placed on each ostrich and $25 on each egg, but this shipment escaped the tax, as the boat sailed from Africa a few hours before it went into effect.

1630. Sweet potato was brought to California in 1888 by John B. Avila, a native of the Portuguese Azores. Avila planted a 20-acre plot of *Ipomoea batatas*, a species originally native to Central and South America that was probably introduced to Europe by Christopher Columbus.

1631. Steam tractor was made by Daniel Best of San Leandro, CA, in 1886. One of his Best tractors was loaded on a car at San Leandro on February 8, 1889.

1632. Alligator farm was established in 1892 at Anastasia Island, St. Johns County, FL, by George Reddington.

1633. Boll weevil was introduced into the United States from Central America about 1892, probably through Brownsville, TX. The weevil is a species of beetle that causes extensive damage to cotton plants but is immune to most insecticides.

1634. Gasoline tractor was manufactured in 1892 by John Froelich of Froelich, IA. On September 6, 1892, he shipped one of his tractors to Langford, SD, where it was employed from September 24 to November 16 in threshing. It had a Van Duzen vertical single-cylinder gasoline engine mounted on wooden beams to operate a J.I. Case threshing machine. In 1893, Froelich formed the Waterloo Gasoline Traction Engine Company, Waterloo, IA, which was later acquired by the John Deere Plow Company.

1635. Horse farm operated by the federal government was the United States Morgan Horse Farm, Middlebury, VT, established in 1907 on 400 acres donated by Colonel Joseph Battell of Middlebury. The first 270 acres of land were deeded to the United States by Battell on February 1, 1907. Horse breeding under the Bureau of Animal Industry began in December 1904 as a cooperative enterprise with the Colorado Experiment Station to develop an American utility horse.

1636. Japanese cherry trees were a gift to the United States from the people of Tokyo, Japan. The first shipment arrived in 1909 but had to be destroyed because of insect infestation. A second shipment was planted in 1912 in Potomac Park, Washington, DC.

1637. Farm bureau was the Broome County Farm Bureau, established on March 20, 1911, in Binghamton, NY. The bureau's first officer was John H. Barron, an agent of the Department of Agriculture, who worked in cooperation with the State College of Agriculture at Cornell University, the Binghamton Chamber of Commerce, and the Delaware, Lackawanna and Western Railway. On May 24, 1913, an act appropriating $25,000 for assisting the farm bureaus was passed by New York, the first state to pass an act of this kind.

1638. Japanese beetle appeared in Riverton, NJ, in 1916. Its grubs were believed to have arrived in the roots of imported nursery stock.

1639. Hybrid seed corn shipment was sold to Samuel Ramsay, Jacobsburg, OH, on April 13, 1916, by Funk Brothers Seed Company, Bloomington, IL. The price was $15 a bushel.

1640. Soybean processing plant that was commercially successful was built by Augustus Eugene Staley in Decatur, IL, in 1922. The beans were run through an expeller, which removed the oil to within 4 percent, and the residue was sold to the feed industry for use in commercial animal feeds or to farmers, who mixed the meal with other ingredients as a protein supplement for livestock.

1641. Chinchilla farm that was successful was established on February 22, 1923, at Los Angeles, CA, by Mathias Farrell Chapman with 11 chinchillas imported from Peru and Chile. The farm, which was later moved to Inglewood, CA, contained about 1,300 animals.

1642. Corn-husking championship was held on November 24, 1924, on a farm near Alleman, Polk County, IA. There were six contestants. The winner was Fred Stanek of Webster County, IA, who husked 1,891 pounds in 90 minutes.

1643. Radio broadcast of a livestock auction took place at the International Livestock Exposition, Chicago, IL, on December 18, 1924. The auction, which sold pigs, sheep, lamb, and cattle, was broadcast by WLS, Chicago, IL, on 345-meter wavelength.

1644. Citrons grown commercially in any large quantity were raised by Edwin Giles Hart, who planted 6,000 trees at La Habra, CA, in 1925.

1645. Mechanical cotton picker of importance was the Rust Cotton Picker, a horse-drawn picker built by John Daniel Rust in Weatherford, TX, in 1928. In 1929 it was rebuilt into a self-propelled model powered by a Model T motor. In 1935 a tractor model was built, and in 1937 an improved model picked 13 bales of cotton in one day.

1646. Rotating milking platform was the Rotolactor, invented by Henry W. Jeffers and installed on November 13, 1930, in the lactorium of the Walker Gordon Laboratory Company at Plainsboro, NJ. It permitted 1,680 cows to be milked in seven hours by means of a revolving platform that brought them into position with the milking machines.

1647. Private hydroponic garden where vegetables and flowers were grown in nutrient-enriched water was created in 1931 by William Frederick Gericke at his home in Berkeley, CA. Gericke's article "Aquaculture, A

Means of Crop Production," published in December 1929 in the *American Journal of Botany*, was the first description of hydroponic agriculture. The term "hydroponics" for soilless crop production was first used in Gericke's article "Hydroponics—Crop Production in Liquid Culture Media," published on February 12, 1937, in *Science*. Early attempts at hydroponic growing of crops had used sand beds, mounted over tanks containing nutrient solutions, to hold the plantings.

1648. Plant patent was awarded to Henry F. Bosenberg of New Brunswick, NJ, on August 18, 1931. It covered a climbing rose named New Dawn that blooms successively throughout the season instead of in June only, as does its parent, Dr. Van Fleet.

1649. Diesel-powered tractor offered on the market was the Caterpillar Diesel Tractor, manufactured by the Caterpillar Tractor Company, Peoria, IL. It was a track-type, weighed 24,390 pounds, and developed 68 maximum drawbar horsepower. It was powered with a four-cylinder, four-cycle diesel engine. The first one was delivered in October 1931.

1650. Fruit tree patent was issued on February 16, 1932, to James E. Markham and assigned to the Stark Brothers Nurseries and Orchards Company of Louisiana, MO. The patent was obtained on a peach tree, the fruit of which ripened later than ordinary peaches.

1651. Commercial production of hydroponic plants using water instead of soil was undertaken by the firm of Vetterle and Reinelt of Capitola, CA, in February 1934. The company constructed a greenhouse 100 by 33 feet, with 100 tanks. The first planting consisted of about 2,000 begonias, which, as a result of precise regulation of humidity and food supply, grew more rapidly than if soil-planted. On October 12, 1935, the growers set out tomato plantings that grew to 15 feet in height within six to eight months. A commercial hydroponicum on a large scale was established in Montebello, CA, on December 5, 1935, by Ernest Walfrid Brundin and Frank Farrington Lyon, who installed a water-circulating system. They obtained a patent on December 1, 1936, on a "system of water culture" and incorporated the company on October 19, 1937, as the Chemi-Culture Company.

1652. Farm cooperative for artificial insemination of livestock in the United States was a cow-breeding organization founded by Enos Perry, a professor at Rutgers University, New Brunswick, NJ. The cooperative began operations at Clinton, NJ, on May 17, 1938.

1653. Tetraploid (giant) flower produced by the use of chemicals was publicly exhibited by David Burpee of the W. Atlee Burpee Company, Philadelphia, PA, on January 29, 1940, at the New York City Flower Show. A marigold was treated with colchicine, a chemical extracted from the roots of the fall crocus, with the result that it was one and a half times as large in diameter as the Guinea Gold from which it started.

1654. Genetically altered plants were approved for outdoor testing by the Department of Agriculture in 1986. The cultivars were high-yield tobacco plants.

1655. Tomatoes from space were grown from 6,000 tomato seeds that orbited the earth for nearly six years aboard NASA's Long-Duration Exposure Facility, which was recovered by the space shuttle in January 1990. The space-exposed seeds were distributed to 64,000 teachers and 3.3 million students in the United States and abroad. Compared to Earth-bound control seeds, the space-exposed seeds germinated slightly faster. The resulting plants grew faster for the first few weeks, exhibited premature chlorophyll development, and had greater levels of chlorophyll.

Courtesy of NASA

LDEF at Kennedy Space Center.

1656. State law decriminalizing hemp cultivation was signed into law by Governor Ed Schafer of North Dakota on April 22, 1999. All states had previously banned the growing of hemp because, like marijuana, it is a variant of the plant genus *Cannabis*, though it does not contain a high level of psychoactive cannabinoids. The North Dakota law allowed farmers to grow industrial hemp as long as they had no prior criminal record and submitted to random inspections.

1657. Felony conviction for cruelty against farm animals occurred on January 13, 2003, when Alejo Pena pleaded guilty to three counts of animal cruelty. Pena was the former manager of Seaboard Farms, a pig farm in Guymon, OK. The charges were brought after an undercover investigation by People for the Ethical Treatment of Animals showed him beating animals with a hammer. Their videotape also showed workers skinning pigs alive and cutting off limbs while they were still conscious.

1658. County ban on genetically modified farming was passed by voter initiative in Mendocino County, CA, on March 2, 2004. The ordinance made it illegal "for any person, firm, or corporation to propagate, cultivate, raise, or grow genetically modified organisms in Mendocino County."

1659. State to require the labeling of genetically modified seeds was Vermont, on April 26, 2004. The law mandated that manufacturers of GMO seeds put descriptive labels on their products, adopt safe-handling techniques for transporting and storing them, and file an annual report of their sales with the state secretary of agriculture.

1660. County to require its public agencies to purchase locally grown organic food was Woodbury County in Iowa. On January 10, 2006, the county's Board of Supervisors voted to require county departments to meet their food needs by purchasing food grown by a cooperative of local farmers, with priority given to organic food. The term "local" referred to the region within 100 miles of Sioux City, IA.

1661. Permanent protective vault for crops and seeds was an artificial cave created in a mountainside in the Svalbard Archipelago in Norway, above the Arctic Circle. It was intended to preserve 3 million seeds from every region of the Earth, with the subzero climate protecting them against possible refrigeration failures. The plan was conceived by Cary Fowler of Memphis, TN, executive secretary of the Global Crop Diversity Trust. Construction began on June 19, 2006.

Business Equipment

1662. Typewriter was patented on July 23, 1829, by William Austin Burt of Mount Vernon, MI, who received a patent on his invention of a "typographer." The first letter written on the machine was sent by John P. Sheldon, editor of the *Michigan Gazette*, Detroit, MI, to Martin Van Buren, secretary of state, on May 25, 1829.

1663. Platform scale was built in St. Johnsbury, VT, in 1830 by Thaddeus Fairbanks. It was patented on June 30, 1831, by Erastus and Thaddeus Fairbanks. Previously, even-balance and steelyard types of scales had been used.

1664. Fireproof safe worthy of the name was the Salamander Safe, invented by Charles A. Gayler of New York City, who obtained a patent on April 12, 1833, on a "fire-proof iron chest." It consisted of two chests, one within the other, with a space between to "inclose air or any non-conductors of heat."

1665. Adding machine to employ depressible keys was made by Du Bois D. Parmelee of New Paltz, NY, who received a patent for it on February 5, 1850. He called his machine a "calculator." It was neither practical nor widely used.

1666. Safe deposit vault was opened on June 5, 1865, by the Safe Deposit Company of New York, 140–146 Broadway, New York City. Four vaults were located on the ground floor of the building and were constantly guarded. One of the vaults was devoted exclusively to the reception of deposits of valuable articles, for which the rates ranged from $1.50 to $2.50 per year for every $1,000 represented. The three other vaults contained individual safe deposit vaults, which cost from $30 to $40 annually. Each subscriber was provided with an individual key to open his vault box.

1667. Typewriter that was practical was invented in 1867 by Christopher Latham Sholes, who also coined the word "type-writer." The machine was patented on June 23, 1868, and was known commercially as The Type-Writer. This machine had a movable carriage, a lever for turning paper from line to line, and a converging type bar. The keyboard, similar to that of a piano, had two rows of black walnut keys with letters painted in white. The machine had all the letters in capitals, figures from 2 to 9, a comma, and a period. It was manufactured by E. Remington and Sons of Ilion, NY, under contract dated March 1, 1873. The first machine was completed on September 12, 1873. A few years later, the firm sold its typewriter business to Wyckoff, Seamans and Benedict, who afterward organized the Remington Typewriter Company.

1668. Adding machine to print totals and subtotals was made in 1872 by Edmund D. Barbour of Boston, MA. His machine, which was called a "calculating machine," was not practical.

1669. Cash carrier system was invented by David Brown of Lebanon, NJ, who obtained a patent on July 13, 1875, on "an apparatus for transmission of goods, packages, etc." It had a wire rail with endless rope pulleys. William Stickney Lamson installed it in his ladies' furnishing store in Lowell, MA, in February 1879. By means of two overhead wires, a small basket was conveyed from the salesman to the cashier. In the spring of 1881, he organized the Lamson Consolidated Store Service Company to manufacture these carriers for others, and in January 1882 he incorporated the Lamson Cash Railway Company.

1670. Stenotype device for printing a legible text in the English alphabet at a high reporting speed was invented by John Celinergos Zachos of New York City, who received a patent on April 11, 1876, on a "typewriter and phonotypic notation." The type was fixed on eighteen shuttle bars, several of which might be simultaneously placed in position. The impression was given by a plunger common to all the bars.

1671. Electric turnstile with a rachet was used at the Philadelphia Centennial, Philadelphia, PA, which opened on May 10, 1876. The attendant released the brake by foot pressure to allow visitors to enter. The number of turns was registered on a machine in the central office.

1672. Cash register was invented in 1879 by James J. Ritty, a businessman from Dayton, OH, who while on a trip to Europe observed the workings of a recording device on the steamship that marked the revolutions of the ship's propeller and gave the officers an accurate daily record of the speed of the boat. Back in the United States, he invented a machine for registering receipts of cash and totaling them. It was not accurate, but the following year, 1880, he produced a machine that gave some evidence of being practical. In 1884 the National Cash Register Company took over the business.

1673. Vending machine that dispensed liquid automatically was patented on December 16, 1884, by William Henry Fruen of Minneapolis, MN. When a coin was inserted in the slot, a uniform supply of liquid was released from a reservoir.

1674. Adding machine successfully marketed was invented by William Seward Burroughs of St. Louis, MO. In January 1886 he incorporated his business as the American Arithmometer Corporation of St. Louis, MO, with an authorized capitalization of $100,000. This company was acquired on January 16, 1905, by the Burroughs Adding Machine Company, organized under the laws of Michigan with a capital stock of $5 million.

1675. Typewriter ribbon was patented on September 14, 1886, by George K. Anderson of Memphis, TN.

1676. Key time recorder was invented by Willard L. Bundy of Auburn, NY, who obtained a patent on November 20, 1888. A key bearing the workman's number was inserted in the mechanism, which printed both the number and the time on a paper tape. Bundy formed the Bundy Manufacturing Company, which later became a division of IBM Corporation.

1677. Electric tabulating machine was invented by Dr. Herman Hollerith of New York City, who received a patent on January 8, 1889, on a system of recording separate statistical items by means of holes, or combinations of holes, punched in cards, and then counting or tallying such statistical items either separately or in combination by means of electrical counters operated by electromagnets, the circuits being controlled by the perforated cards. The first extensive use of the electric tabulating system was in the compilation of the statistics of population for the 11th federal census, in 1890.

1678. Dial time recorder was invented in 1888 by Dr. Alexander Dey of Glasgow, Scotland, who obtained a U.S. patent on September 24, 1889. Numbers assigned to the various employees appeared around the circumference of a large ring on the front of the machine. A pivoted pointer arm was pressed into a guide hole, which caused the machine to print the time opposite the number on a prepared sheet. In 1893, Alexander Dey formed the Dey Patents Company of Syracuse, NY, along with his two brothers, John and Robert, who operated a department store in Syracuse. The company later changed its name to the Dey Time Register Company.

1679. Vending machine to dispense postage stamps was manufactured in 1892 by the United States Postage Stamp Delivery Company, Boston, MA, of which Carroll Davidson Wright was president. It was a quartered-oak case 20 inches high, 9.75 inches wide, and 5.4 inches deep. Upon insertion of a nickel, it delivered a capsule containing four cents' worth of stamps and a coupon that could be redeemed for merchandise from advertisers.

1680. Portable typewriter was the Blickensderfer, which was patented on April 12, 1892, by George C. Blickensderfer of Stamford, CT.

1681. Typewriter to produce a line of writing visible as it was being typed was invented by Herman L. Wagner of Brooklyn, NY (now part of New York City), who obtained a patent on it on May 16, 1893. This machine went through an experimental period with the Wagner Typewriter Company and then was sold to John T. Underwood, who had been associated with Wagner's father in the ribbon and carbon business of John Underwood and Company. The Underwood Typewriter Company, incorporated in March 1895, undertook the manufacture of Wagner's machine in New York City.

1682. Card time recorder was invented by Daniel M. Cooper of Rochester, NY, who received a patent on October 30, 1894. The employee pressed a lever on the machine to record the time on specially printed cards divided by horizontal lines into seven equal spaces for the days of the week. The recorder, known as the Rochester, was manufactured by the Willard and Frick Manufacturing Company.

1683. Vending machine to sell food from bulk was the Automatic Clerk, a wooden cabinet six feet high, which dispensed hot peanuts in bags. The machine was equipped with a heater and a weighing device. It was invented in 1897 by T.S. Wheatcraft of Rush, PA.

1684. Vending machine law enacted by a city was approved by Omaha, NE, on May 10, 1898, by Mayor Frank Edward Moores. The law made all vending machines subject to a $5 permit fee.

1685. Automatic computing pendulum scale was invented by Allen De Vilbiss, Jr., of Toledo, OH, who received a patent on the fan-type automatic computing scale on May 22, 1900. In 1899 he organized the De Vilbiss Scale Company, which later developed into the Toledo Scale Company. This company was the first to produce an adjustable automatic indicator controller for bringing the hand to a quick stop.

1686. Public locker plant was established in 1903 by A. G. Eames of the Chico Ice and Cold Storage Company, Chico, CA. Individual lockers, each with a lock and key, were rented to the public. The company was purchased in 1913 by the Union Ice Company of San Francisco, CA.

1687. Multigraph was invented by Harry Christian Gammeter of Cleveland, OH, who obtained a patent on March 10, 1903, on a "duplicating machine." It was the first successful machine designed to simplify the printing processes, so that the ordinary layman could print from type, either with ribbon or with ink. Commercial manufacture was undertaken on December 12, 1902, by the American Multigraph Sales Company, Cleveland, OH.

1688. Photographic copying machine was known by the trade name Photostat and was commercially manufactured in 1910 by the Eastman Kodak Company, Rochester, NY, under the supervision of John S. Greene of the Photostat Corporation. It photographed the subject to be copied directly upon a roll of sensitized paper and eliminated the necessity for the use of any glass plate or film negative. It was capable of making a print 11.5 by 14 inches. The process was not new, but was simplified.

1689. Coin-operated locker was invented by Willis S. Farnsworth of Petaluma, CA, who received a patent on March 7, 1911, which he assigned to the Coin Controlled Lock Company. He also secured a patent jointly with William H. Reed on a coin receptacle "magazine-hinge and conveyor" on the same date. The insertion of a coin in a slot released a key to open and close the locker.

1690. Electric typewriter that was commercially successful was the Model 01, introduced by IBM, Armonk, NY, in 1935. It was a redesign of a machine made by Electromatic Typewriters, acquired by IBM in 1933.

1691. Shopping cart was the invention of Sylvan N. Goldman, the owner of the Standard Food Stores chain of Oklahoma City, OK. Seeking a way to make it easier for consumers to buy larger quantities of goods, Goldman got the idea for a folding basket on wheels after seeing a pair of folding chairs atop a wheeled dolly. After several months of tinkering, he introduced the finished design into his stores in June 1937.

1692. Bar code scanner was invented by Bernard Silver and N. J. Woodland, who in 1949 filed a patent application entitled "Classifying Apparatus and Method." It described techniques for creating machine-readable product identification codes. The first bar code scanner in commercial use was installed by Sylvania General Telephone on the Boston and Maine Railroad in 1961. The unit read red, white, blue, and black bars that identified gravel train cars and commuter cars. The first scanner used in a retail store was installed in a Kroger supermarket in Cincinnati, OH, in 1967.

1693. Copy machine that was commercially successfully was the Model 914, introduced in 1950 by the Haloid Company of Rochester, NY. An earlier Haloid copier, the Model A, was too slow and complicated to be successful. In 1961, Haloid changed its name to the Xerox Corporation.

1694. Correction fluid for typewriters was Liquid Paper, invented in 1951 by Bette Nesmith Graham, an executive secretary at the Texas Bank and Trust Company in Dallas, TX, who saved erasing time by applying a dab of white tempera water base paint over her typing mistakes. Her bottled version of the paint was originally called "Mistake Out." Changes to the formula made it quick-drying and virtually invisible.

1695. Valeteria for pressing and storing clothes was made by the United States Hoffman Machinery Corporation and displayed on September 19, 1951, in the lobby of the Bulkley Building, Cleveland, OH. The device had a control unit equipped with a telephone and a series of lockers in which garments could be hung. It was designed to open doors, accept payments, and give correct change without any manual aid. It was based on an invention of Ross L. Timms of Akron, OH.

1696. Newspaper vending machine to deliver a single copy with the insertion of the proper coins was the NewsVend, manufactured by the United Sound and Signal Company, Columbia, PA, and leased on March 20, 1954, to the *Chicago Tribune*, the *New York Journal American*, the *New York Mirror*, the *Philadelphia Bulletin*, and the *Washington Times-Herald*. It had 30 compartments, each capable of holding any size paper or magazine up to 300 pages, and was available in any coin combination, returning pennies or nickels in change when required. All newspaper vending machines prior to this time had a mechanism that unlocked a single compartment, allowing dishonest customers to remove more than one copy.

1697. Electric portable typewriter was manufactured by Smith-Corona, Syracuse, NY. It was announced on October 9, 1956, and placed on sale on February 4, 1957. It weighed about 19 pounds and retailed at $190.

1698. Typewriter without type arms was the Selectric typewriter, introduced in 1961 by International Business Machines, Armonk, NY. Designed by Eliot Fette Noyes, it utilized an interchangeable element about the same size and shape as a golf ball with an entire font of type embossed on its surface. The ball moved parallel to a stationary platen and oriented itself to hit the ribbon with each letter typed. The Selectric was faster and less likely to jam than conventional electric typewriters with type arms.

1699. Vending machine to dispense fresh flowers was placed in the Grand Central Terminal, New York City, on October 20, 1961, by the Automated Flowers Company, Greenwich, CT. It was six feet high, three feet wide, and two feet deep. The machine, which was manufactured by Wittenborg of Denmark, was a self-contained refrigerated unit that required no plumbing.

1700. Typewriter that could retype text automatically was an adaptation of the Selectric typewriter. In 1964, the IBM Corporation, Armonk, NY, began selling a magnetic tape recorder and controller device that attached to certain Selectric models. The device recorded each keystroke of the typist. When played back, the tape caused the Selectric to retype the text automatically. It was the first crude word processor. The combined unit cost $10,000.

1701. Vending machine for art was the Vend'art machine, invented by Ona Linquist. Linquist reconditioned ice cream vending machines from the 1950s and filled them with inexpensive original artworks commissioned from working artists. The first Vend'art machine was installed in a Greenwich Village movie theater in New York City in 1985.

Finance

1702. Financial "corner" took place in New Amsterdam (the future New York City) in 1666. Frederick Phillipse cornered the market in wampum by creating a shortage. He buried several hogsheads of it in order to force those who had to use this medium of exchange to purchase wampum from him at a higher price.

1703. Credit report book was prepared by Sheldon P. Church and published anonymously in 1844 in New York City. It was distributed to subscribers only and contained commercial information about merchants in southern and midwestern states.

1704. Millionaire with a fortune greater than $100 million was Cornelius Vanderbilt, who was born in Staten Island, NY (now part of New York City), in 1794. As a boy, Vanderbilt worked on a ferry in New York harbor, and later entered the steamboat and shipping business. His strategy of cutting rates below those of his competitors earned him $20 million by 1860. He followed the same practice after entering the railroad business in 1865 and within two years gained control of the New York Central Railroad. At his death in 1877, his estate was valued at more than $100 million.

1705. Accounting society was the Institute of Accountants and Bookkeepers, organized on July 28, 1882, in New York City.

1706. National accounting society was the American Association of Public Accountants, formed in New York City on December 22, 1886. The first president was James Yalden.

1707. Certified public accountant was Frank Broaker of New York City, who received certificate No. 1 on December 1, 1896, from the New York State Board of Certified Public Accountant Examiners.

1708. State accounting society was the New York State Society of Certified Public Accountants, which was organized in New York City on March 30, 1897, following the passage of the New York State Certified Public Account Law of April 17, 1896. Charles Waldo Haskins, president of the state's CPA board of examiners, was the first president.

1709. Certified public accountant who was a woman was Christine Ross of New York City, who received Certificate No. 143 on December 27, 1899, after passing the state accounting examination.

1710. Millionaire who was an African-American woman was Sarah Breedlove, who, under her married name, Madame C. J. Walker, founded the first successful cosmetics company that catered exclusively to African-American customers. She invented the first hair-straightening tonic and began selling it to African-American women in Denver, CO, in 1906. Within five years, she had opened two factories and expanded her business nationally, using uniformed saleswomen to sell her line of grooming products door-to-door. The company moved to Indianapolis, IN, in 1910.

1711. Billionaire was John Davison Rockefeller, born in 1839 in Richford, NY. In 1863 he established an oil refinery that became the Standard Oil Company of Ohio. Rockefeller bought out most of his competitors and came to dominate the U.S. oil-refining industry. In 1899 he consolidated his companies into the Standard Oil Company of New Jersey, which became the target of a celebrated antitrust lawsuit by the federal government in 1911. Rockefeller retired in 1911 with a fortune estimated at well over a billion dollars.

1712. Certified public accountant who was African-American was John W. Cromwell, Jr., of Washington, DC, a Phi Beta Kappa graduate of Dartmouth College and a teacher of mathematics. Both Maryland and Virginia, the states nearest to the District of Columbia, required their CPA applicants to have work experience, but none of the local accounting companies would hire him. He took his examination in New Hampshire in 1921 because that state had no work requirement.

1713. Certified public accountant who was an African-American woman was Mary T. Washington of Chicago, IL, who passed the state CPA exam in 1943. The firm she founded, Mary T. Washington and Company (later known as Washington, Pittman & McKeever), became the largest African-American–owned business in Chicago and for many years was virtually the only company in the nation that would hire young African-American accountants, enabling them to acquire the work experience needed to become CPAs themselves.

1714. Billionaires who were African-American were Robert L. Johnson and Sheila Crump Johnson, cofounders of the cable network Black Entertainment Television, Washington DC. Their company, BET Holdings, was sold to Viacom on November 3, 2000, for $2.3 billion in stock, and they split the proceeds.

Banking

1715. Bank chartered by Congress was the Bank of North America in Philadelphia, PA, which was organized on November 1, 1781. It began business on January 7, 1782, with a total capital of $400,000, of which the government subscribed $250,000. Thomas Willing was elected president, and Tench Francis cashier. Later the bank entered the National Banking System.

1716. Bank of the United States was sponsored by the Federalist Party and was chartered in Philadelphia, PA, on February 25, 1791, by "an act to incorporate the subscribers to the Bank of the United States." Although the charter made no specific provision for the deposit of government funds, the secretary of the treasury, Alexander Hamilton, used the bank as a fiscal agent. The charter expired in 1811 and was not renewed by Congress because of the opposition of the Democratic-Republicans. The closing of the bank was partly responsible for the panic of 1814. The second Bank of the United States was authorized on April 10, 1816, and was opened on January 7, 1817. It ceased functioning as a national institution in March 1836.

1717. Savings bank was the Bank for Savings in the City of New York, which was conceived on November 29, 1816, but for which the charter was not granted until March 26, 1819. The bank opened for business on July 3, 1819. The deposits on the first day, received from 80 depositors, amounted to $2,807. The statement for the first six months showed a loss of $27 suffered as a result of the bank's accepting counterfeit money and a short change loss of $23.92.

1718. Savings bank to receive money on deposit was the Philadelphia Saving Fund Society, Philadelphia, PA, which opened for business on December 2, 1816, in the office of George Billington, the secretary-treasurer, on the west side of Sixth Street. Billington received a salary of $250 a year. The affairs of the bank were conducted by 12 managers. Andrew Bayard was the first president. The bank was chartered February 25, 1819.

1719. Trust company permitted to do a trust business was the Farmer's Fire Insurance and Loan Company of New York City, which was incorporated on February 28, 1822. The first company to use "Trust Company" as part of its title was the New York Life Insurance and Trust Company of New York City, which was chartered on March 9, 1830, with an authorized capital of $1 million. The first company organized to do a trust business exclusively was the United States Trust Company of New York, which was incorporated on April 12, 1853.

1720. Bank deposit insurance law enacted by a state was the Safety Fund Banking Law of New York, "an act to create a fund for the benefit of the creditors of certain monied corporations," enacted on April 2, 1829. Banking organizations were assessed one-half of 1 percent of the capital stock, until 3 percent was set aside for a bank fund. Three commissioners, known as Bank Commissioners of the State of New York, were appointed for two-year terms at an annual salary of $1,500. Banks, their officers, and their servants were required to be examined under oath at least once every four months.

1721. Building and loan association was the Oxford Provident Building Association, which was organized on January 3, 1831, in Thomas Sidebotham's Tavern, 4219 Frankford Avenue, Frankford, PA. The organizers were Jesse Castor, secretary, Samuel Pilling, treasurer, and Jeremiah Horrocks. The company was succeeded by the Decatur Building Association. The first loan was $500, made on April 11, 1831, to Comly Rich, a lamplighter from Philadelphia, PA.

1722. Bank clearinghouse was the New York Clearing House, organized on August 23, 1853, by representatives of 38 banks, who met at the Merchants Bank, New York City. The exchange was opened on October 11 at 14 Wall Street. Total clearings the first day exceeded $22 million, and the balances exceeded $1.3 million. Clearings for the year ending September 30, 1854, were $5.7 billion; for the same period, ending in 1980, they were $38 trillion.

1723. National bank under the national banking law of February 25, 1863, an "act to provide a national currency," was the First National Bank of Davenport, IA, later called the Union Savings Bank and Trust Company. Subscription books were opened on May 25, and in three days the capital stock of $100,000 had been subscribed. The bank was opened on June 29. The first president was Austin Corbin. For two days the bank was the only national bank in operation under the new act.

1724. Bank for freed African-American slaves was the Freedman's Savings and Trust Company, for the Negro, chartered by Congress on March 3, 1865. A central bank was established in Washington, DC, with branches in 34 cities. The bank was in operation about eight years, during which time it received deposits amounting to $57 million. The depreciation in security values due to the panic of 1873 caused the trustees to vote to close the bank, the affairs of which were placed in the hands of three commissioners.

1725. National bank to fail was the First National Bank of Attica, NY, placed in receivership on April 14, 1865. The failure was due to injudicious banking and failure of large debtors. The receivership was terminated on January 2, 1867.

1726. Check protectors were manufactured in 1870 and consisted of punches that perforated figure holes in paper to help protect against forgeries. In June 1899 Libanus McLouth Todd completed the model of a different kind of check protector in a woodshed at 384 Gregory Street, Rochester, NY. The machine forced ink into the paper under pressure, making it part of the fiber of the document. The machine, called the Protectograph, went on the market in the fall of that year. Todd obtained a patent on August 9, 1904.

1727. National banking association was the American Bankers Association, which was organized on May 24, 1875. The first national convention was held at Saratoga, NY, on July 20–22, 1875, at which time Charles Bingley Hall was elected president. The objects of the association were self-protection against frauds, standardization of rules, and bettering of conditions between the banks and their clients.

1728. Savings group for children to teach them to save their money in a methodical manner was started on March 16, 1885, by Professor John Henry Thiry of Long Island City, NY (now part of Queens, New York City), who established a system of fund collections in schools and a school savings bank.

1729. State banking association was the Texas Bankers' Association, which was organized on July 23, 1885, at Lampasas, TX, with an initial membership of 31. The first president was James Francis Miller.

1730. Bank for African-Americans operated by African-Americans was the savings bank of the Grand Fountain of the United Order of True Reformers, a group founded by William W. Browne, which was incorporated in 1881 in Richmond, VA. The bank was chartered on March 2, 1888, and began operations on April 3, with a paid-up capital of $4,000. The first day's deposits were $1,268.69. The board of directors was elected by the society.

1731. Travelers checks were issued on August 5, 1891, by the American Express Company, making it possible for American travelers in Europe to obtain cash in places where a letter of credit from a banker was not accepted. The checks were available in $10, $20, $50, and $100 denominations.

1732. Bank president who was a woman was Maggie Lena Walker, the daughter of an African-American slave, who founded the Saint Luke Penny Savings Bank, Richmond, VA, incorporated on July 28, 1903. It had a paid-in capital of $25,000. The first day's deposits exceeded $8,000. The bank later became the Consolidated Bank and Trust Company.

1733. Bank open day and night was the Night and Day Bank, New York City, opened on May 1, 1906, with a capital of $200,000, a surplus of $200,000, and a reserve of $100,000. Oakleigh Thorne was the first president. The idea was originated by Thomas Benedict Clarke.

1734. Credit union was founded by Alphonse Desjardins in Manchester, NH, on December 16, 1908. It was known as "La Caisse Populaire Ste. Marie" and was chartered April 6, 1909. Ninety-nine percent of the depositors were French Canadians.

1735. Credit union law enacted by a state was sponsored by Pierre Jay, the first bank commissioner of Massachusetts, and was passed by the Massachusetts legislature. It was approved on May 21, 1909, by Governor Eben Sumner Draper.

1736. Christmas savings club at a bank was started by the Carlisle Trust Company, Carlisle, PA, in 1909. The idea originated with Merkel Landis, the bank's treasurer. The first payment was received December 1, 1909.

1737. Bank to establish a branch in a foreign country was the National City Bank of New York, which opened a branch in Buenos Aires, Argentina, on November 10, 1914. The Federal Reserve Act, approved December 23, 1913, permitted American banks to establish branches abroad.

1738. Federal reserve banks were formally opened on November 16, 1914, inaugurating the federal reserve system. The Federal Reserve Act, approved on December 23, 1913, was an "act to provide for the establishment of Federal Reserve Banks, to furnish an elastic currency . . . to establish a more effective supervision of banking in the United States." The 12 regional district banks were under the supervision of a seven-member Board of Governors.

1739. Joint stock land bank chartered was the Iowa Joint Stock Land Bank of Sioux City, IA. It was chartered on April 24, 1917, and authorized to do business in the states of Iowa and South Dakota. The charter was granted under the Federal Farm Loan Act of July 17, 1916.

1740. Bank wholly owned and operated by a state was the Bank of North Dakota, Bismarck, ND, established by special referendum election on June 26, 1919, under jurisdiction of the federal Industrial Commission, and opened on July 28. It was the only legal depository of all state funds and those of state institutions.

1741. Bank with resources exceeding 1 billion dollars was the National City Bank (later Citibank), New York City, whose assets on November 17, 1919, were $1,027,938,114.31.

1742. Check photographing device was the Checkograph, a microfilm device invented by George Lewis McCarthy, who received a patent for it on February 25, 1930. Commercial manufacture was undertaken on May 1, 1927, by the Eastman Kodak Company, Rochester, NY, which marketed the device as the Recordak and made the first installation on May 1, 1928, at the Empire Trust Company, New York City. The machine photographed checks on 16mm motion picture film. The first application of the machine other than by banking institutions was made in 1929 by the Treasury.

1743. Bank deposit insurance law enacted by Congress was the Glass-Steagall Act, known as the Banking Act of 1933, which was passed by Congress on June 16, 1933, "to provide for the safer and more effective use of the assets of banks, to regulate interbank control, and to prevent the undue diversion of funds into speculative operation." It insured deposits up to $2,500 each in all Federal Reserve banks. Deposits in approved banks were insured on a sliding scale: 100 percent up to $10,000; 75 percent from $10,000 to $50,000; and 50 percent over $50,000. A later law, entitled "an act to provide for the sound, effective and uninterrupted operation of the banking system, and for other purposes," approved on August 23, 1935, limited the insurance to $5,000 for any one depositor.

1744. Savings and loan association established by the federal government was the First Federal Savings and Loan Association of Miami, FL, which was chartered on August 8, 1933. The creation of savings and loan institutions had been authorized by the Home Owners Loan Act of June 13, 1933, to provide a convenient place for the investment of small and large sums and to lend money to local applicants for first mortgages.

1745. Payment by the Federal Deposit Insurance Corporation to depositors of a closed insured bank was a payment of $125,000 to 1,789 depositors of the Fond du Lac State Bank of East Peoria, IL, which suspended business on May 28, 1934, and went into receivership on June 25, 1935. The first depositor to receive her share of the payment was a widow, Lydia Lobsiger, whose check arrived on July 3, 1934. The corporation had been created by the Banking Act of 1933.

1746. Federal credit union chartered under the Federal Credit Union Act approved on June 26, 1934, was the Morris Shepard Federal Credit Union in Texarkana, TX, named in honor of the law's sponsor, which held its organizational meeting on October 1, 1934. The purpose of the law was "to establish a further market for securities of the United States and to make more available to people of small means credit for provident purposes through a national system of cooperative credit, thereby helping to stabilize the credit structure of the United States."

1747. Bank president of a national bank who was a woman was Frances Estelle Mason Moulton, who was elected on January 11, 1938, as president of the Limerick National Bank, Limerick, ME, to fill the vacancy caused by the death of her father, Jeremiah Miller Mason.

1748. Drive-in banking service was instituted on November 12, 1946, by the Exchange National Bank of Chicago, IL. Ten tellers' windows protected by heavy bulletproof glass and impregnable corrugated steel were equipped with automatic slide-out drawers to enable motorists to transact business without leaving their cars.

1749. Bank to operate a window in a subway station for the convenience of subway riders was the Bowery Savings Bank, New York City, which opened two tellers' windows in a glass-enclosed cubicle in the Grand Central station of the Interborough Rapid Transit subway on September 26, 1955. The windows had bullet-resistant glass. They were equipped with special receptacles for passing money and bankbooks that permitted only one side to be open at a time.

1750. Bank to open a branch in a trailer was the Meadow Brook National Bank, West Hempstead, NY, which opened a branch at Locust Grove, NY, on May 26, 1956, in a 46-foot air-conditioned trailer. It had four tellers' windows opening out on one side of the trailer. Over $100,000 was received in deposits on the first day. The trailer was used while a permanent structure was built.

1751. Bank of importance to lease personal property was the Bank of America, San Francisco, CA, which instituted the service on July 22, 1963, under the direction of Robert D'Oyly Syer. James Joseph Saxon, comptroller of the currency, advised national banks on March 18, 1963, that they were permitted to lease personal property, buying equipment and leasing it directly to customers.

1752. ATM machine was installed by the Chemical Bank, New York City, which placed its first machine in operation at Rockville Center, Long Island, NY, on January 1969. A coded card inserted in an opening dispensed a package envelope containing a set sum of cash.

1753. Bank to be automated was the Civic Center branch of the Surety National Bank, Los Angeles, CA, which opened April 27, 1970. It contained six telestations equipped with closed-circuit television and monitored by a teller. A "validator" provided instant validation of checks by code rather than by signature. A money machine dispensed cash in an envelope.

1754. Bank to provide movies for customers waiting in line was the Chemical Bank, New York City. On December 22, 1972, movies were projected on 4-by-5-foot screens at three different branches: 2681 Broadway, 86th Street and Lexington Avenue, and 67 Broad Street.

1755. Federally chartered bank owned and managed by women was the Women's National Bank of Washington, DC, founded in 1977. Barbara Davis Blum was the first chief executive officer. The bank's name was changed to the Abigail Adams National Bank in 1986, following the incorporation of its holding company, the Abigail Adams National Bancorp, in Delaware on July 22, 1981. The name change was a move to alter the public perception that the bank existed exclusively to serve the banking needs of women.

Loans and Credit

1756. Loan by a colony was authorized on December 10, 1690, by the Massachusetts Bay Colony, which issued tax anticipation certificates that did not have a maturity date or bear interest. They were not redeemable in metal and were not considered legal tender.

1757. Loan for war purposes by a central governmental agency was negotiated with France by the Continental Congress. A resolution of December 23, 1776, authorized the loan of $181,500 (1 million livres), which was used for the purchasing of supplies and construction of cruisers. The length of the loan was indefinite. Bonds were sold at par. The rate of interest was 5 percent, payable annually. The loan was received on June 4, 1777. The final redemption was made on December 31, 1793, when the balance due was merged into the general account of the French debt.

1758. Loan to the United States was negotiated by Alexander Hamilton. Between September 13, 1789, and February 17, 1790, he obtained from the Bank of New York and the Bank of North America a total of $191,609. It was known as the Temporary Loan of 1789 and was obtained without authority of law. The money was used to pay salaries of the president, senators, representatives, and officers of the first Congress during the first session under the Constitution. The interest rate was 6 percent. The final redemption of the loan was made on June 8, 1790.

1759. Installment finance company to purchase installment contracts from retail dealers was the Fidelity Contract Company, Rochester, NY, which held its first directors' meeting on April 7, 1904. The company, organized by Lee Richmond, Frederick Zoller, and George Gale Foster, became the Bankers Commercial Corporation of New York City.

1760. Car finance company was the Bankers Commercial Corporation, New York City, organized on February 1915, an affiliate of the Commercial Security Company of Chicago.

1761. Loan made by the federal Government to a war ally was a loan of $200 million at 3.5 percent made to Great Britain on April 25, 1917.

1762. Liberty loan subscriptions were taken on May 2, 1917. The first loan was authorized by act of April 24, 1917, "an act to authorize an issue of bonds to meet expenditure for the national security and defense, and for the purpose of assisting in the prosecution of the war, to extend credit to foreign governments and for other purposes." A subscription of $2 billion was required. The program continued through June 15, 1917, during which time approximately 4 million people subscribed for more than $3 billion in bonds to yield 3.5 percent.

1763. Credit card to be nationally accepted was the Diners Club card, originated in 1950 by Frank X. McNamara, a credit specialist for a credit company in New York City, and Ralph Scheider, an attorney. Previous credit cards had been limited in use to one retail establishment or chain, such as a gas station or department store. Owners of the Diners Club card could use the card at a variety of restaurants and retail outlets.

1764. Bank to issue a credit card was the Franklin National Bank, Franklin Square, NY, which did so on April 15, 1952. Purchases were charged to the bank, which made the payments and then billed the card holders. The service was extended to its branches. The first bank credit card to gain national acceptance was the BankAmericard (later called Visa), issued by the Bank of America, San Francisco, CA, in 1959. There was no membership fee or service charge. Full-scale services were offered to cardholders and merchants.

1765. Smart card in the United States was the "Blue" card, introduced in September 1999 by the American Express Company. Resembling a credit card, the "Blue" card contained a data-storing computer chip that gave it multiple electronic capabilities.

Stocks and Bonds

1766. Bonds issued by the federal government were interest-bearing obligations that were authorized by the congressional act of August 4, 1790, for the refunding of the domestic debt and for that part of the state debt which was assumed by the federal government. The total issue amounted to $64,456,963.90, of which $30,088,397.75 drew interest at 6 percent, $19,719,237.39 at 3 percent, and $14,649,328.76 at 6 percent after 1800. Practically the entire issue was retired by 1836.

1767. Stock exchange was the New York Stock Exchange, the outgrowth of an agreement signed on May 17, 1792, by 24 brokers to fix the rates of commission on stocks and bonds. The first meeting was held at the Merchants Coffee House, Second and Gold streets, New York City. The first president was Matthew McConnell. This protective league existed until March 8, 1817, when the New York Stock and Exchange Board adopted its constitution, organized on its present lines. On January 29, 1863, the name was changed to the New York Stock Exchange. A securities exchange was informally organized in Philadelphia in 1791.

1768. War bond issued by the federal government aside from the refunding of the Revolutionary War debts was authorized on March 14, 1812, for the purchase of weapons and equipment and the enlargement of the Army in preparation for the impending War of 1812 against Britain. The amount authorized was $11 million. Bonds were issued to the amount of $8,134,700 and sold exclusively in the United States.

1769. Treasury notes bearing interest were authorized by an act of Congress of June 30, 1812. The president was authorized to issue treasury notes to an amount not exceeding $5 million. The interest was fixed at "five and two-fifths per centum a year."

1770. Commercial rating agency was established in New York City on August 1, 1841, as the Mercantile Agency, by Lewis Tappan, who had founded the *Journal of Commerce* in 1828. The first place of business of the agency was at the corner of Hanover Street and Exchange Place. Branch houses were later opened, the first in Boston, MA, in February 1843. On May 1, 1859, the firm was taken over by R.G. Dun and Company.

1771. Stock price indicator used on Wall Street in New York City was the Gold Indicator, invented by Samuel Spahr Laws, president of the Gold Exchange, to announce changes in the price of gold. It was installed at the exchange in 1867.

1772. Stock brokerage concern to use a stock ticker was David Groesbeck and Company, a member of the New York Stock Exchange. The ticker was the invention of Edward A. Callahan of the American Telegraph Company and was the first device to use ticker tape. It was installed on December 29, 1867, by the Gold and Stock Telegraph Company, New York City. A rental of $6 a week was charged for the service, which was operated by Daniel Drew.

1773. Brokerage office owned by women was Woodhull, Claflin and Company, New York City, opened in 1869 by the sisters and social reformers Victoria Claflin Woodhull and Tennessee Celeste Claflin. The company showed a net profit of $750,000 for the first six weeks. A contemporary newspaper cartoon depicted them driving a chariot drawn by bulls and bears with human heads—the heads of the largest financiers of the time—while other financiers were crushed under the wheels.

1774. Clearinghouse for stocks and bonds was the Philadelphia Clearing House, which was organized in Philadelphia, PA, in August 1870 as an adjunct of the Board of Brokers of the Philadelphia stock exchange.

1775. Wall Street stock index was the Dow Jones Transportation Average, an index of 11 stocks that included railroad companies and Western Union. It was created by two New York financial reporters, Charles Dow and Edward Jones, to help their readers understand changes in the values of publicly traded stocks. Their publication, *The Customer's Afternoon Letter*, forerunner of *The Wall Street Journal*, first printed the index on July 3, 1884.

The most widely used of the Dow Jones indicators, the Dow Jones Industrial Average, first appeared on May 26, 1896.

1776. Stock exchange at which more than a million shares were traded in one day was the New York Stock Exchange, New York City, whose transactions on December 15, 1886, totaled 1,096,509 shares.

1777. Stock quotation boards were made of slate and were manufactured by Mount and Robertson of New York City in 1889.

1778. Investment trust is claimed to have been the New York Stock Trust, New York City, a general portfolio statutory trust, formed on April 1, 1889, with 50,000 shares at $10 a share.

1779. Bonds payable specifically in United States gold coins were issued under authority of a financial bill enacted on March 14, 1900, an "act to define and fix the standard of value, to maintain the parity of all forms of money issued or coined by the United States, to refund the public debt."

1780. Automatic electric stock quotation board was manufactured in 1929 by the Teleregister Corporation (later the Bunker-Ramo Corporation), Stamford, CT, and placed in operation on May 21, 1929, in the brokerage office of Sutro Brothers and Company, New York City. The board automatically shifted figures as changes were made. It showed open, high, low, and last prices of each stock listed.

1781. Commodity exchange member who was a woman was Gretchen B. Schoenleber of the Ambrosia Chocolate Company, Milwaukee, WI, who was admitted September 3, 1935, to membership in the New York Cocoa Exchange, New York City.

1782. Stock brokerage concern of importance whose president was a woman was A. M. Kidder and Company, New York City. Josephine Perfect Bay became chairman and president of the company on December 1, 1956.

1783. Stock exchange director who was a woman was Mary Gindhart Roebling of the Trenton Trust Company, Trenton, NJ. On October 28, 1958, she became one of the 32 governors of the American Stock Exchange, New York City, which entitled her to go on the floor of the exchange. She was one of the three so-called "public" members, not connected with the Wall Street community. The first women to become official members of the American Stock Exchange were Julia Montgomery Walsh, general partner of Ferris and Company, Washington, DC, and Phyllis Kathryn Smith Peterson, general partner of Sade and Company, Washington, DC, both of whom were elected on November 18, 1965.

1784. Stockholder meetings televised coast-to-coast simultaneously were meetings of General Mills stockholders that took place on October 29, 1959, in New York City, Minneapolis, Chicago, Los Angeles, San Francisco, Boston, and Buffalo, NY. By means of a closed-circuit television system, stockholders in each city were able to ask questions of Gerald S. Kennedy, chairman of the company, who presided at the New York meeting, and Charles Heffelfinger Bell, the company's president, who presided at the meeting in Minneapolis.

1785. New York Stock Exchange seat owner who was a woman was Muriel Siebert, who paid $445,000 plus a $7,515 initiation fee on November 18, 1967. She was admitted on December 28, 1967, as a full member with privilege to handle customers' orders on the floor. The first woman to serve as a director of the New York Stock Exchange was Dr. Juanita Morris Kreps, professor of economics and dean of the Women's College, Duke University, Durham, NC, who was nominated on June 6, 1972, and elected on July 5.

1786. New York Stock Exchange member who was African-American was Joseph Louis Searles III, a partner in the brokerage firm of Newburger, Loeb and Company, New York City, whose admission was approved by the board of governors on February 13, 1969. The first African-American director of the New York Stock Exchange was Dr. Jerome Heartwell Holland, retired U.S. ambassador to Sweden and one of the 10 public nominees on the 21-member board, who was nominated on June 6, 1972, and elected on July 5.

1787. Brokerage firm whose shares were traded by a major stock exchange was Merrill Lynch, Pierce, Fenner and Smith. The stock opened on the New York Stock Exchange on July 27, 1971, at 38.25, and closed at 37. There were 47,500 shares traded the first day. Previous transactions had been made over the counter.

1788. Dow Jones Industrial Average to exceed 1,000 points occurred on November 14, 1972, when the Dow closed at 1003.16. It first exceeded 2,000 points on January 8, 1987, when it finished at 2002.25 after climbing more than 100 points the previous week. This record was successively topped for the next 13 days in some of the most frenzied trading in New York Stock Exchange history. The Dow topped the 3,000 mark on July 16, 1990, during the course of the day's trading. The closing average was 2999.75.

1789. Dow Jones Industrial Average over 7,000 occurred on February 13, 1997. On that day, the Dow climbed 60.81 points to close at 7,022.44. It was the fastest

1,000-point rise ever to occur on Wall Street. The Dow had reached the 6,000-point level just 82 days earlier.

1790. Dow Jones Industrial Average to exceed 10,000 points took place on March 29, 1999, when the stock market index reached 10,006.78. A few weeks later, on May 3, 1999, the stock market index exceeded 11,000 points when it reached a high of 11,014.70.

Fishing and Whaling

1791. Commercial fishery is believed to have been established at Medford, MA. On April 17, 1629, the colonists were given instructions to let the fish "be well saved with the said salt, and packed up in hogsheads; and send it home by the 'Talbot' or 'Lion's Whelpe.'" The industry flourished and on May 28, 1639, received "salt, lines, hooks, knives, boots, etc., for the fishermen." Fishing had also been attempted elsewhere by the first colonists.

1792. Whaling industry established by a city was organized on March 7, 1644, by Southampton, NY, a town on the coast of Long Island where whales were often cast ashore. The town was divided into four wards of 11 persons each to attend to the whales. Two persons from each ward were employed to cut them up so that each inhabitant obtained an equal portion. A whaling franchise was granted to a Mr. Whiting in 1647 for the waters of Long Island Sound between Stonington, CT, and Montauk Point, NY.

1793. Sperm whale captured at sea was captured in 1711 by a whaling vessel out of Nantucket, MA. This was the beginning of an industry that numbered over 700 vessels by 1846.

1794. Whaling expedition on record set sail from Nantucket, MA, about 1715. Six sloops, of 30 to 40 tons burden each, returned with cargoes amounting to 600 barrels of oil and 11,000 pounds of bone, the total value of which was £1,100 sterling. There were whaling trips by single boats prior to this expedition.

1795. Ship sunk by a whale was the whaler *Essex*, which sailed from Nantucket, MA, on August 12, 1819, headed for the whaling grounds off the coast of Chile. According to the account of first mate Owen Chase, on November 20, 1820, the *Essex* was hunting sperm whales at latitude 0 degrees 40 minutes S, longitude 119 degrees W, when an enraged bull whale rammed the ship twice and capsized it. The crew escaped in open boats, but only five of them survived the 4,500-mile journey to Peru, which took 83 days. The story of the *Essex* was one of the inspirations for Herman Melville's novel *Moby-Dick.*

Gambling

1796. Lottery of importance was held on June 26, 1614, by the Virginia Company. The first Great Prize was 4,500 crowns.

1797. Gambling law for ministers enacted by a colony was passed in 1624 by the Virginia Assembly. It specified that "mynisters shall not give themselves to excesse in drinking or yette spend their tyme idelie by day or by night, playing at dice, cards or any unlawful game."

1798. Gambling law for residents enacted by a colony was passed on March 22, 1630, in Boston, MA: "It is . . . ordered that all persons whatsoever that have cards, dice or tables in their houses, shall make away with them before the next court under pain of punishment."

1799. Lottery held by the Continental Congress was held on April 10, 1777, in Philadelphia, PA, for the purpose of raising funds. The lottery was approved on November 1, 1776, and seven managers were appointed to conduct it. Treasury bank notes were awarded as prizes, payable at the end of five years. Funds were obtained by lottery by individual colonies at various times prior to this national lottery.

1800. Craps was introduced in New Orleans, LA, about 1813 by Bernard Xavier Philippe de Marigny de Mandeville, who had seen the game played in France as "hazards." As a common nickname for a Creole man was Johnny Crapaud, the game became known as Crapaud's game, which later was abbreviated to "craps." Mandeville lost a fortune at the game. He was obliged to cut a street through his property and to sell lots on both sides to obtain funds to pay his debts. Maps show this street as Craps Street, later changed to Burgundy Street.

1801. **Federal law hostile to lotteries** was the act of Congress of March 2, 1827, which provided "that no postmaster or assistant postmaster shall act as agent for lottery offices or under any color of purchase, or otherwise, send lottery tickets; nor shall any postmaster receive free of postage or frank lottery schemes, circulars or tickets."

1802. **Slot machine** operated by a pull handle and incorporating three spinning wheels was invented in 1895 by Charles Fey of San Francisco, CA. Early slot machines were installed in drugstores, gas stations, bars, and clubs. Lewis C. Thompson of Washington, DC, was the first person to win more than $1 million from a slot machine. In 1988, after playing just eight quarters, he hit the $1.1 million Quartermania jackpot at the Ramada Express Hotel Casino in Laughlin, NV.

1803. **Casino in Las Vegas** was the Flamingo Hotel, built in 1946 on a strip of Nevada desert (the future intersection of Las Vegas Boulevard and Flamingo Road) by mobster Benjamin "Bugsy" Siegel. Financing was provided by Murder Incorporated co-founder Meyer Lansky. The property was acquired by the Hilton Hotels Corporation on July 14, 1970. A $140 million expansion begun in 1993 demolished Siegel's former quarters and added such amenities as an outdoor habitat of live Chilean flamingos and African penguins.

1804. **State lottery** in the modern era was a horse-racing sweepstakes enacted in New Hampshire on April 30, 1963, to raise money for state schools. The law gave cities and towns the opportunity to decide, by referendum, whether or not to allow the sale of sweepstakes tickets in their jurisdictions. Most of them voted in favor. The first ticket was bought by Governor John W. King on March 12, 1964.

1805. **Lottery in which the top prize was $1 million** was conducted by New York State on October 8, 1970, and was won by George and Genevieve Ashton and their son Glenn, of West Hempstead, NY. The lottery was based on the results of a horse race at the Belmont Track on September 24, 1970. The sale of lottery tickets amounted to $16,724,931.

1806. **Off-track betting operation** that was legal was started by New York City on April 8, 1971. Betting parlors were set up in retail store locations throughout the city.

1807. **Casino outside the state of Nevada** was opened in Atlantic City, NJ, on May 28, 1978, after the state's voters approved legalized casino gambling in 1977. Resorts International opened the casino in a hotel on the Atlantic City boardwalk. The first week's take was $2.6 million.

1808. **Casino run by a Native American tribe** was Hollywood Seminole Bingo in Hollywood, FL, which opened on December 14, 1979. It was the idea of Howard Tommie, the tribal chairman, who realized that Native American tribes, as sovereign nations, were free to offer jackpots much higher than those allowed by state law.

Hospitality

1809. **Building built to serve as a hotel** was the City Hotel, with 70 rooms, opened in 1794 on Broadway, just below Wall Street, New York City.

1810. **Gourmet restaurant** was Delmonico's of New York City, founded by two Swiss-born brothers, Giovanni and Pietro Del-Monico, in 1827. At first the brothers ran a wine, coffee, and chocolate shop on Williams Street in the Battery section of Manhattan. In 1831 they opened a "Restaurant François." By the 1860s, under the direction of Lorenzo Delmonico and principal chef Charles Ranhofer, the restaurant had become a mecca for well-to-do Americans seeking the best food and wine. Unable to thrive under Prohibition, when alcoholic beverages were banned, Delmonico's closed its doors on May 21, 1923.

1811. **Hotel recognized as a modern first-class hotel** was the Tremont House in Boston, MA, which celebrated its opening with an elaborate dinner on October 16, 1829. It covered 12,839 square feet and contained 170 rooms. The rate was $2 a day, including four meals. Travelers were permitted to rent a single private room instead of having to double up with strangers. Other innovations at the Tremont House were a key for each room, a washbowl, a pitcher, a free cake of soap for every guest, and gaslights. In addition, the Tremont was the first hotel outfitted with plumbing, including indoor bathrooms and toilets. It had eight "privies" and eight bathing rooms in the basement, to which there was a separate entrance. The kitchen and laundry had cold running water. Each of the two cisterns in the attic contained three hogsheads of rainwater, one for the baths and the other for various outlets. The plumbers were Thomas Philpott and Thomas Pollard. The cornerstone of the hotel was laid July 4, 1828, by Samuel Turell Armstrong, president of the Massachusetts Charitable Mechanic Association.

1812. Tourist guide for train travelers was *The Traveller's Guide Through the State of New York, Canada, etc., embracing a general description of the city of New York; the Hudson River Guide, and the fashionable tour to the springs and Niagara Falls: with steam-boat, rail-road, and stage routes, accompanied by correct maps.* It was 72 pages long and was published in 1836 by J. Disturnell, New York City. It contained a folded map of New York State and another of the Hudson River vicinity, lists of canal routes, stage routes, and railroad routes, lists of railroads, cemeteries, monuments, colleges, museums, hotels, amusements, and other notable places, and a general description of New York City.

1813. Tourist guide with train schedules showing the arrival and departure times of trains was Doggett's *United States Railroad and Ocean Steam Navigation Guide, Illustrated with a map of the United States, showing the working lines of Railroad*, published in September 1847 by John Doggett, Jr., of New York City. It contained 132 pages and a folding map and sold for 12.5 cents.

1814. Chinese restaurant was the Macao and Woosung, opened in 1849 in San Francisco, CA, by Norman Asing, a Chinese-American businessman from Charleston, SC. Most Chinese restaurants of the period identified themselves by flying small yellow flags, as was traditional in China.

1815. Ornamented soda fountain for restaurants was made of white Italian marble and produced in 1858 by Gustavus D. Dows of Lowell, MA. It was adorned with spread eagles perched on the syrup cocks. In 1862, Dows invented the double-stream draft arm and cock, which allowed the choice of a large or small stream. In 1863, Dows embarked on the manufacture of these fountains, which he sold for $225 each. His first patent was obtained on January 25, 1870.

1816. Hotel with an elevator was installed in the six-story Fifth Avenue Hotel, New York City, which opened on August 23, 1859. The elevator operated on the principle of an Archimedean screw. It was viewed and inspected by Albert Edward, Prince of Wales, on October 11, 1860.

1817. Chinaware for restaurant use was made by the Greenwood Pottery Company of Trenton, NJ, in 1862. It combined the best qualities of both porcelain and stoneware.

1818. Hotel with safe deposit boxes was the New England Hotel, Boston, MA. In 1866, Lambert Maynard, the manager, purchased a Salamander safe in which he installed compartments with individual locks.

1819. Lunch wagon was introduced in Providence, RI, in 1872 by Walter Scott. He drove a wagon to a location on Westminster Street, where he sold coffee, sandwiches, pies, and cakes. In order to comply with Board of Health regulations and to secure running water, the operators of lunch wagons obtained desirable vacant sites where they hooked up to a water supply. Individual wagons were constructed until 1887, when they were commercially manufactured in Providence, RI, by Ruel B. Jones, who also operated a chain of lunch wagons.

1820. Hotel that was fireproof was the Palmer House, Chicago, IL, opened in November 1873 by Potter Palmer. The building cost approximately $2 million, the land $1 million, and the furnishings $500,000. It replaced the Palmer House that had been destroyed by fire on October 8, 1871, a year after it opened.

1821. Hotel for women was the Women's Hotel, New York City, founded by Alexander Turney Stewart and inspected by 20,000 visitors on its opening day, April 2, 1878. It was a nine-story building of brick, iron, and stone built around a courtyard, 197 feet by 205 feet in area and 155 feet high, with five steam elevators. Guests could choose from among 115 large rooms at $12 a week, 34 medium-sized rooms at $10, and 354 small rooms at $7 a week, board included. The main dining room accommodated 600 diners and also supplied meals to be taken out. Breakfast was 35 cents, lunch 25 cents, dinner 50 cents. There were 250 servants. The cost of the hotel was $3.7

million. Any profit was to be used to reduce the rates and any deficit was covered by a fund. On June 8, 1878, it became a commercial hotel accommodating both sexes.

1822. Hotel to install electric lights was the Prospect House, Blue Mountain Lake, NY. In 1881 the electricity was installed, but the lights were not entirely dependable. On October 12, 1882, the Duke of Veranga and his party arrived after dark to celebrate Columbus Day. As they were shown to their rooms the lights went out, but after a slight delay the lights went on again. The hotel was owned by Howard M. Durant and operated by George Tunnicliffe. The name was later changed to the Eutowana.

1823. Self-service restaurant was opened on September 4, 1885, at 7 New Street, New York City, opposite the New York Stock Exchange. It was called the Exchange Buffet.

1824. Hotel transported from one location to another was the Brighton Beach Hotel, Brooklyn, NY (now part of New York City), which was moved 600 feet inland, the operation taking place from April 3 to July 29, 1888. The hotel was jacked up on railroad cars on 24 parallel tracks and moved by six locomotives in two teams of three each. The building, which was 500 feet long and weighed 6,000 tons, was moved 124 feet the first day.

1825. Cafeteria was opened in 1895 in Chicago, IL, on Adams Street between Clark and La Salle streets, by Ernest Kimball. In 1899 he moved it to the basement of the New York Life Building, where it was located until 1925.

1826. Penny restaurant where most items were sold for one cent was opened by Bernarr Adolphus Macfadden at 487 Pearl Street, New York City, in the winter of 1900. In 1901 he opened a larger one. He continued opening branches and by 1906 he had 30 in operation. They were known as the Macfadden Physical Culture Restaurants.

1827. Restaurant with an automatic arrangement for vending food was the Automat Restaurant, which was opened by the Horn and Hardart Baking Company at 818 Chestnut Street, Philadelphia, PA, on June 9, 1902. The mechanism, which cost $30,000, was imported from Germany, where the patents were acquired from their Swedish originators. The company then opened a chain of Automat restaurants in cities across the nation, including New York City, where a branch opened in 1912 at 1515 Broadway. These Automats used a different mechanism that was patented and manufactured by Horn and Hardart. Customers were presented with an array of little compartments, each containing a dish of prepared food visible through a glass door. When the customer dropped a nickel in the proper slot, the door popped open, allowing the customer to remove the dish. The compartments were refilled from behind by restaurant workers.

1828. Hotel with individually controlled air conditioning and heating in every room was the St. Regis Hotel, New York City, opened on September 4, 1904. Six dynamos operated six metallic fans, each seven feet in diameter. The building cost approximately $4 million, $5.5 million when equipped.

1829. Pizzeria was G. Lombardi, which opened on Spring Street in New York City in 1905 (some give the date as 1895). The first deep-dish, Chicago-style pizza was created in 1943 by Ike Sewell and Ric Riccardo of Pizzeria Uno, Chicago, IL.

1830. Motel was the Motel Inn, built in 1924 on Neil Cook's property on the north side of San Luis Obispo, CA, and opened on December 12, 1925. Arthur S. Heineman was the architect. The building featured a sign with flashing lights that alternated the letters *H* and *M* preceding the letters *otel* to spell out "Hotel" and "Motel." It had accommodations for 160 guests in individual chalets with garage, bathroom, and telephone.

1831. Hotel at an airport was the Oakland Airport Inn, in Oakland, CA, built by the Board of Port Commissioners. It was opened on July 15, 1929, and operated by the Interstate Company.

1832. Franchise chain was Howard Johnson's. The chain got its start in 1925, when Howard Dearing Johnson, the proprietor of a drugstore in Quincy, MA, began making ice cream with a hand-held crank to sell at the soda fountain. Unable to finance additional restaurants on his own, he began franchising his name and the formulas for his ice cream and other specialties. The first restaurant to which he granted a franchise, in 1932, was on Cape Cod. Eventually, the chain had 600 restaurants across the country. Johnson's innovations included the use of a central commissary to supply all franchisees with food of consistent quality and the siting of diners along highways.

1833. Dunkin' Donuts was opened in 1950 in Quincy, MA, by entrepreneur William Rosenberg, who had previously run a luncheon service that brought meals to area factories. The shop was originally called the Open Kettle. Rosenberg's key insight was to franchise the donut-and-coffee breakfast concept. His first franchise agreement, for a shop in Worcester, MA, was signed in 1955. By 2005 there were more than 6,000 Dunkin' Donuts locations worldwide.

1834. Holiday Inn was opened in 1952 on U.S. Highway 70 in Memphis, TN. The owner was Kemmons Wilson. It was the first motel with all the major features of a modern motel chain: a swimming pool, air conditioning and television in every room, free ice, and no charge for children under 12.

1835. McDonald's restaurant was opened by Ray Kroc on April 15, 1955, in Des Plaines, IL. The idea for a fast-food restaurant originated with two brothers in the restaurant business, Richard and Maurice McDonald of San Bernardino, CA, who granted a franchise to Kroc, a milkshake-supplies salesman. In 1961, Kroc bought out the brothers for $14 million. By the 1980s, he had built McDonald's into a multi-billion-dollar, multinational burger empire that was widely considered America's most successful modern export. The original drive-up building in Des Plaines was replaced by a modern design that retained the building's golden arch, which became the symbol of the corporation.

1836. Revolving restaurant was The Top of the Needle, located at the 500-foot level of the 600-foot-high steel and glass tower dedicated on May 22, 1961, at the Century 21 Exposition, Seattle, WA. It contained 260 seats and revolved 360 degrees in an hour. Above the restaurant was an observation deck and above that a beacon. It was designed by John Graham and Company.

1837. Singles bar was T.G.I. Fridays, opened on First Avenue in New York City by Alan Stillman on March 15, 1965. It was the first bar specifically intended as a place for unmarried professionals to meet one another.

1838. Discothèque was the Whisky a Go Go, opened by club owner Elmer Valentine in Los Angeles, CA, on January 16, 1965. A discothèque is a dance club in which the music is provided by a disk jockey playing recordings, not by a live band. Valentine borrowed the discotheque concept from a club in Paris, which was also called the Whiskey a-Go-Go.

1839. Hotel built over a pier was the Flagship Hotel, Galveston, TX, opened on June 30, 1965. The hotel, containing 240 rooms, was built on a pier 1,500 feet long and 340 feet wide, extending into the Gulf of Mexico.

1840. Horse motel was opened on June 10, 1967, by Wayne Biggs at Marshfield, MO. It was 100 feet long and 89 feet wide, with an addition of 24 by 48 feet on the back side. The price was $7 a night with feed and care, or $5 for lodging. About 40 horses could be accommodated in one night.

1841. Dog hotel was the Kennelworth, opened on November 12, 1975, in New York City by Leo Wiener. The 116 air-conditioned rooms had different color schemes and were built around a circular court. They measured 28, 37, and 55 feet square and rented for $10, $12, and $14 a day, respectively. Proof of distemper and rabies shots was required.

1842. Undersea hotel was Jules' Undersea Lodge, located at the bottom of 30-foot-deep Bora Bora Lagoon off Key Largo, FL. The hotel was opened in 1987 by Gary Gerberg, who renovated a former marine research station into a luxury hotel for up to six people. For $195 to $295 a night, guests could stay in an 8- by-10-foot bedroom complete with a refrigerator, television, VCR, and compact-disc player. Each room also had a 42-inch porthole for viewing marine life. The hotel had its own air supply. Guests could use special air hoses to go diving without bulky tanks, but standard diving gear was required to get to the hotel from the surface.

1843. Cyber cafe was the Electronic Cafe International, founded by video artists Sherrie Rabinowitz and Kit Galloway. It opened in Santa Monica, CA, in 1988 and offered computers with modems and other telecommunications gear for the use of patrons, plus a coffeehouse menu and artistic events. The first kosher cyber cafe, the IDT Megabite Cafe in New York City's diamond district, opened in the spring of 1997.

1844. Fast-food corporation to require humane animal treatment from its suppliers was McDonald's, the international fast-food giant based in Oak Brook, IL. With the encouragement of animal welfare groups, McDonald's agreed in September 2000 to require its egg suppliers to adopt humane practices. These included giving hens more room, stopping the debeaking of chicks, and stopping forced molting through starvation.

1845. Ice hotel in the United States was built by entrepreneur and resort owner Bernie Karl at Chena Hot Springs, AK, about 60 miles northeast of Fairbanks. A 14,000-ton, 30-foot-high carved ice structure in the form of a Gothic palace, the Aurora Ice Hotel was designed by world champion ice carver Steve Brice of Fairbanks. After a battle with the state fire marshal over egress requirements and fire-code violations, it opened for guests on December 31, 2003. The hotel melted in the spring and was rebuilt in winter 2004–2005 as a museum, with a permanent coolant system.

Industrial Equipment

1846. Steam engine for industrial use was imported from England by the pioneer steam engineer Josiah Hornblower. Hornblower left London on the S.S. *Irene* on June 6, 1753, and arrived in New York City on September 9. The engine was delivered to the copper mine of Colonel John Schuyler in New Barbadoes Neck (now North Arlington), NJ, on September 25, 1753. It was assembled, installed, and placed in service on March 12, 1755, to pump water from the mine.

1847. Pile driver was patented on March 10, 1791, by John Stone of Concord, MA, who obtained his patent on "driving pile for bridges."

1848. Belt conveyor system was described by Oliver Evans in his book *The Young Millwright and Millers Guide*, published in Philadelphia, PA, in 1795. Evans illustrated a flat belt receiving material on its upper run and discharging it over the end, on a broad endless strap of thin pliant leather or canvas revolving over two pulleys in a case or trough.

1849. Steam engine for industrial use that was practical was manufactured by Oliver Evans of Philadelphia in 1795. In 1799, he introduced a high-pressure engine that was light and cheap, and thus was ideally suited to the needs of the simple colonial industries.

1850. Belting sold to manufacturers is recorded in the account books of Pliny Jewell, a leather dealer of Hartford, CT. There is an entry in 1826 recording the sale of a leather belt three inches wide. Manufacturers who required belting usually bought skins, cut them to the desired thickness, and stretched them taut by nailing the ends of the pieces to the floor when wet and driving wedges between the leather and floor halfway between the ends.

1851. Leather belts for transmitting power from shaft to shaft were devised by Paul Moody, who used them in the Appleton cotton mill in Lowell, MA, in 1828. Up to this time all transmissions had been by means of iron gears. Belting, however, had previously been used in some mills to carry power from shafts that in turn were driven by gears from a water wheel.

1852. Sandpaper patent was granted to Isaac Fischer, Jr., of Springfield, VT, on June 14, 1834. His invention was covered by four different patents, all issued on the same date.

1853. Bellows for smiths and furnace fires was invented by John R. Morrison of Springfield, OH, who was granted a patent on December 23, 1834.

1854. Safety fuse was manufactured in 1836 by the firm of Bacon, Bickford, Eales and Company, Simsbury, CT, on a spinning bench machine with traveling jennies that drew and twisted the yarn. Powder was fed to the center of the twisting strands and the resulting fuse lengths were afterwards "countered" and coated with waterproof compounds. The machine was imported from England.

1855. Steam shovel was invented in 1838 by William S. Otis of Philadelphia, PA, who obtained a patent on February 24, 1839, on a crane for excavating and removing earth. It was first used on the Western Railroad in Massachusetts.

1856. Wire rope factory was erected in Saxonburg, PA, in 1841 by John Augustus Roebling, who also created the machinery. The wire was spliced and wound onto reels.

Seven separate strands were then drawn together and twisted into one large rope. The twisting machine was out in the open and operated by hand power. The wire rope was used in the construction of suspension bridges, including several for which Roebling served as designer and engineer.

1857. Turbine successfully operated by waterpower was invented in 1844 by Uriah Atherton Boyden and was installed in the cotton mills of the Appleton Company at Lowell, MA. It was an improvement on the turbine waterwheel invented by the French engineer Benoit Fourneyron and utilized approximately 80 percent of the power expended.

1858. Spring manufacturer was Edward Lucian Dunbar, whose factory in Bristol, CT, opened in 1845. He specialized in coiled clock springs, which were tempered by a process invented by Silas Burnham Terry. At the time, weights were generally used in large clocks and imported springs in smaller clocks.

1859. Percussion rock drill was patented on March 27, 1849, by Joseph James Couch. The drill was driven by steam power and was independent of gravity. The machine was stationary and the drill was thrown against the rock, the tool being seized at the end of the blow by means of friction-grips.

1860. Gas mask resembling the modern type was patented by Lewis Phectic Haslett of Louisville, KY, who received a patent on June 12, 1849, on an "inhaler or lung protector." It had a filter of woolen fabric or other porous substance to purify the air and remove dust. A gas mask with a self-contained breathing apparatus was patented on July 2, 1850, by Benjamin J. Lane of Cambridge, MA.

1861. Dynamite was manufactured in 1866 in San Francisco, CA, on a site that is now in Golden Gate Park, by Julius Bandmann, using the patents granted to the inventor of dynamite, Alfred Nobel. The company, known as Bandmann Neilson and Company, became the Giant Powder Company in 1867.

1862. Machine for cutting and straightening wire was invented in 1866 by John Adt, who established a small plant in Wolcottville, CT. Before this invention, wire had been straightened by drawing it between two corrugated wooden blocks or through holes in several wooden blocks. The cutting was done by hand. Adt's machine did the work mechanically. His company was absorbed in 1895 by the F.B. Shuster Company of New Haven, CT.

1863. Sawmill to use a band saw was operated in 1867 by the Hoffman Brothers of Fort Wayne, IN. The band saw was 40 feet in length, and the ends were joined so that it revolved continuously. The saw blades, from four to five inches wide, were obtained from Sweden. The design was patented by Jacob Rosecrans Hoffman of Fort Wayne on July 6, 1869.

1864. Barbed wire commercial production was begun on November 1, 1873, in De Kalb, IL, by Joseph Farwell Glidden, who obtained a patent for his invention on November 24, 1874. The barbs were cut from sheet metal and were inserted between two twisted wires.

1865. Cold storage plant operated by mechanical refrigeration was opened in 1881 by the Mechanical Refrigerating Company at Boston, MA.

1866. Crane was manufactured in 1883 by the Yale and Towne Manufacturing Company, Stamford, CT, for the Pittsburgh Bessemer Steel Company. This two-ton machine was a full-revolving, self-propelling steam crane mounted on a four-wheel standard-gauge truck.

1867. Wrecking crane was built by the Industrial Brownhoist Corporation, Bay City, MI, in 1883. It had a capacity of 20 tons and was mounted on a nonpropelling car that operated on a standard-gauge track. In 1886 an adaptation of the revolving crane was developed. This was a 15-ton steam-railway-type crane in which the crane was mounted at one end of the car and the boiler at the other.

1868. Gasoline pump was the "Self-measuring Gasoline Storage Pump" made by Sylvanus F. Bowser of Fort Wayne, IN, in 1905. The design, which was based on Bowser's earlier design for a kerosene pump, consisted of a ventilated wooden box containing a 50-gallon metal tank. The gasoline was suction-pumped by hand through a hose.

1869. Spring winding machine in which the size of the spring helix was determined solely by the angle at which the wire was forced between guides was developed and built in 1892 by Clinton S. Marshall of the Washburn and Moen Manufacturing Company, Worcester, MA.

1870. **Sawmill driven by electricity** that operated successfully was designed and operated in 1896 by the Allis-Chalmers Manufacturing Company for the American River Land and Lumber Company, Folsom, CA.

1871. **Air conditioner patent** was obtained on January 2, 1906, by Willis Haviland Carrier, a mechanical engineer with the Buffalo Forge Company, Buffalo, NY. Carrier had done earlier research on the effect of humidity on heat absorption by air, and he developed the first machinery that was able to both cool the air and control humidity. Carrier designed the first climate-control systems beginning in 1908, and the first home air-conditioning units in 1927.

1872. **Steam-operated pressing machine** was invented by Adon J. Hoffman, who received a patent on July 13, 1909. The machine was equipped with a "buck," or lower pressing surface, and a "head," or upper pressing surface, which was heated by gas. It was necessary to lay a damp cloth over the goods, as when pressing with a hand iron. The machine was first marketed in 1907 by the United States Hoffman Company of Seattle, WA.

1873. **Ice-loading machinery** for icing refrigerator railway cars was operated in May 1917 by the William Metz Ice Company of Pittsburgh, PA. The machines were manufactured by the Thomas Wright Company of Jersey City, NJ. Wright obtained a patent on April 22, 1913, on a "body elevating mechanism." It consisted of a truck with an extension top adjustable to any position to enable ice to be placed in the uppermost section of the car, making it possible for one man to do all the loading without the help of assistants.

1874. **Wrecking crane operated from a car** was devised in 1917 by Robert E. Manley. The car had a tilting beam that permitted adjustment of height and overhang to suit various conditions and a swivel nose that permitted direct pull from any angle. The crane had six leverages and speeds and two sets of controls so that it could be operated from either side of the car. Manley later formed the Manley Manufacturing Company, York, PA, which in 1928 was absorbed by the American Chain and Cable Company.

1875. **Explosion of Thermit to break up ice jams** was effected on February 24, 1925, when a 250,000-ton ice jam in the St. Lawrence River at Waddington, NY, was moved in a few hours after the reaction of three Thermit charges of 90 pounds each. Thermit is a mixture of finely powdered aluminum metal and oxide of iron. When properly ignited, it reacts vigorously, generating very high temperatures and producing extremely hot liquid iron. This method of using Thermit in ice-breaking work was first applied by Howard Turner Barnes, professor of physics at McGill University, Montreal, Canada.

1876. **Self-computing gasoline pump** was marketed by the Wayne Oil Tank and Pump Company, Fort Wayne, IN, on November 1, 1932. The pump was invented by Robert Joseph Jauch, Ivan Richard Farnham, and Ross Harper Arnold, who received a patent on November 22, 1932, on a "liquid dispensing apparatus." Using a mechanical calculator, the pump accurately computed and indicated the exact quantity delivered in gallons and the price in dollars and cents as delivery was made. Total gallons dispensed and cash received were recorded by two totalizers.

1877. **Textile-wrapped detonating fuse** was manufactured in 1936 by the Ensign-Bickford Company, Simsbury, CT. It was known as Primacord and consisted of a core of pentaerythrite tetranitrate enclosed in textile wrappings suitably protected by waterproof coverings. It had a velocity of detonation of approximately 20,000 feet per second.

1878. **Belt conveyor more than four miles long** was manufactured by the Goodyear Tire and Rubber Company, Akron, OH, for the National Mines Corporation, to convey coal 10,900 feet from a West Virginia mine to the Monongahela River. The conveyor was installed in 1949. It was a single loop of belting more than four miles in total circumference. It traveled at a speed of 300 feet a minute to deliver 300 tons of coal an hour.

1879. **Welding machine for aluminum pipes** was a MIG (metal inert-gas) welder jointly developed by the Reynolds Metal Company and the Air Reduction Company. A finished model was tested in 1957 at Corpus Christi, TX. It welded 2,880 feet of four-inch pipe in a four-hour period with no supplemental hand-welding needed at any point. A unit mounted on a tractor rotated around the pipe carrying a shielded electric arc. Inert gas was released to blanket the area being welded.

1880. Computer-aided manufacturing system was developed in 1959 by researchers in the Servomechanics Laboratory at the Massachusetts Institute of Technology, Cambridge, MA. In the first public demonstration, a computer issued instructions in a custom programming language to an automated milling machine, which turned out a batch of aluminum ashtrays.

Industrial Processes

1881. Sulfuric acid was produced by John Harrison in 1793 in a little shop at Third and Green Streets, Philadelphia, PA. At first the acid was concentrated in fragile glass retorts. Later, platinum containers were used instead. The business founded by Harrison, known as Harrison Brothers and Company, was purchased in 1917 by the E.I. du Pont de Nemours and Company of Wilmington, DE.

1882. Glue factory to produce glue from animal parts was established in 1807 at Boston, MA, by Roger Upton. It was absorbed by the American Glue Company of Boston, MA, and later taken over by the Peter Cooper Corporation, Gowanda, NY.

1883. Varnish manufacturer to produce varnish exclusively was Christian Schrack, a carriage maker, who opened a shop in 1815 in Philadelphia, PA. Furniture had previously been finished with shellac or oil.

1884. Boiler plates were made between 1816 and 1825 by Dr. Charles Lukens's mill, the Brandywine Mill at Coatesville, PA. The mill was originally started at Rokeby, PA, by Isaac Pennock in 1790 as the Federal Slitting Mill. Iron slabs were heated in an open charcoal fire, rolled out into plates, and then slit up into rods for general use by blacksmiths. In 1810, Pennock purchased a sawmill at Brandywine, which he converted into the Brandywine Iron Mill. The organization remained in the hands of Lukens's descendants and became known as the Lukens Steel Company, one of the world's largest plate mills.

1885. Rubber company was the Roxbury India Rubber Company of Roxbury, MA, which began manufacturing various rubber products in 1832. It was incorporated on February 11, 1833, by Lemuel Blake, Luke Baldwin, Edwin M. Chaffee, and Charles Davis, Jr. The rubber was affected by heat and cold and had a disagreeable odor, and the company was unable to find a market for its products.

1886. Gutta-percha was imported from Calcutta in 1840 by William Bartlett, supercargo of the *Mary Parker*. Bartlett presented a whip made of gutta-percha to William Rider of New York City, who subsequently organized William Rider and Brothers to handle the new commodity. On June 1, 1852, John Rider obtained a patent on "vulcanized rubber," and in 1855 the North American Gutta Percha Company, New York City, was formed by the Rider brothers with a capitalization of $500,000.

1887. Vulcanized rubber was successfully produced by Charles Goodyear of New York City, who obtained a patent on June 15, 1844, on an "improvement in India-rubber fabrics." He had received a previous patent on June 17, 1837, for a method of destroying the adhesive properties of rubber by applying bismuth, nitric acid with copper, or other materials.

1888. Pressure-sensitive adhesive was a combination of ingredients that included India rubber, pine gum, and spirits of turpentine. It was patented by Dr. Henry Day in 1845.

1889. Coal oil factory to manufacture coal oil from coal tar was started in 1853 by the U.S. Chemical Manufacturing Company in Waltham, MA. The light fractions from this coal oil distillation were called coal oil, and used for illuminating purposes. The oil made in connection with picric acid, benzol, and other products from coal tar was named Coup Oil by Luther Atwood, the inventor. When Edwin Drake demonstrated, in 1859, that petroleum could be secured by drilling, the coal oil industry died a natural death.

1890. Artificial-ice manufacturing plant was the Louisiana Ice Manufacturing Company, built in 1868 on Delachaise Street and the Mississippi River, in New Orleans, LA. The process was kept secret and the factory was guarded.

1891. Dye plant was the Albany Aniline and Chemical Company, Albany, NY, which opened in 1868. It later moved to Rensselaer, NY, and was acquired by the General Aniline and Film Corporation.

1892. Celluloid was invented by John Wesley Hyatt of Albany, NY, and Isaiah Smith Hyatt of Rockford, IL, who obtained a patent for it on June 15, 1869. This invention won a $10,000 prize offered by Phelan and Collender of New York City for a substitute for ivory in billiard balls. The inventors dissolved pyroxyline and camphor in alcohol, then subjected the mixture to heat and pressure in molds. They began manufacturing it in 1872, organized the Newark Celluloid Manufacturing Company, and obtained a trademark registration on the word "celluloid," a word they coined to mean "cellulose-like."

1893. Sandblasting process for cleaning, engraving, cutting, and boring glass, stone, metal, and other hard substances was invented by Benjamin Chew Tilghman of Philadelphia, PA, who received a patent on October 18, 1870, for "cutting and engraving stone, metal, glass, etc." with "sand used as a projectile."

1894. Welding by the electric processwas invented by Professor Elihu Thomson of Lynn, MA, who obtained a patent on August 10, 1886, on "an apparatus for electric welding." His electric welder was widely used in the auto, shipbuilding, construction, and consumer appliance industries as a substitute for riveting.

1895. Centralized refrigeration service that was successful was put into operation in March 1889 by the Colorado Automatic Refrigerating Company of Denver, CO. A 30-ton ice machine and a 50,000-foot cold storage warehouse supplied refrigeration to local businesses via two miles of street mains. The refrigerant was liquid ammonia.

1896. Acetylene gas was made on May 4, 1892, by Thomas Leopold Wilson of the Wilson Aluminum Company in Spray, NC. He was trying to produce metallic calcium by fusing lime and coal tar in an electric furnace. The experiment was unsuccessful. When the molten slaglike mass was dumped into a nearby stream, a gas was liberated which was recognized as acetylene. The manufacturing of acetylene on a commercial scale was begun soon afterward.

1897. Carbide factory to manufacture commercial quantities of carbide was established in 1894 by Thomas Leopold Willson in Spray, NC. He obtained two patents on June 18, 1895, on calcium carbide, a compound of calcium and carbide. He produced it by fusing calcium or lime with coke at a very high temperature.

1898. Carbon tetrachloride was manufactured by Charles Ernest Acker, who introduced his process in 1908. He also invented the Acker process of manufacturing caustic soda by the electrolysis of molten salt in 1896, for which he received the Elliott Cresson Gold Medal of the Franklin Institute in 1902. He was also the first to produce carbon and tin tetrachloride on a commercial scale.

1899. Thermosetting resin was patented by the Belgian-American chemist Leo Hendrik Baekeland on December 7, 1909. Working in his private laboratory in Yonkers, NY, Baekeland invented a method of controlling the reaction of phenol and formaldehyde to produce a soft resin that hardened permanently with the application of heat. The commercial product, called Bakelite, found many industrial and consumer uses.

1900. Synthetic rubber was made by Lucas Petrou Kyrides and Dr. Richard Blair Earle in 1913 for the Hood Rubber Company, East Watertown, MA. They prepared a number of polymerized hydrocarbons having rubberlike qualities, of which dimethyl butadiene had the most promising commercial possibilities.

1901. Dry ice manufactured commercially was made by the Prest-Air Devices Company of Long Island City, NY (part of Queens, New York City), in 1925, through the efforts of Thomas Benton Slate. Dry ice is solid carbon dioxide. When compressed and cooled, gaseous carbon dioxide changes to a liquid, then to a solid. Its temperature is 109 degrees below zero. It does not melt but instead turns to gas. Dry ice was first used by Schrafft's, 181 Broadway, New York City, in July 1925 to keep ice cream from melting. The first large sale of dry ice was made later in the year to the Breyer Ice Cream Company of New York City.

1902. Synthetic rubber for manufacture was isolated on April 10, 1930, by Dr. Arnold M. Collins, who isolated a chemical called chloroprene and observed its polymerization. It was synthesized by E.I. du Pont de Nemours and Company, Wilmington, DE, after chemists working under Dr. Elmer K. Bolton discovered that chloroprene could be produced by treating vinylacetylene with other substances. Du Pont began manufacturing a synthetic rubber called Du Prene on November 2, 1931, at its plant in Deepwater, NJ. The first commercial production of various articles from Du Prene began in May 1932, when the Manhattan Rubber Manufacturing Division of Raybestos-Manhattan, of Passaic, NJ, made oil hose from Du Prene and offered it for sale to oil companies. Experimental tires were made of this material in February 1934 by the Dayton Rubber Manufacturing Company of Dayton, OH.

1903. Products made of vinyl were shock absorber seals that were first marketed in 1931. A synthetic substitute for rubber, vinyl was invented in 1926 by Waldo L. Semon, a chemical engineer with the BF Goodrich Company, Akron, OH. By dissolving polyvinyl chloride in a solvent, Semon produced a pliable, waterproof plastic gel that could be molded to make myriad household and industrial products.

1904. Abrasive for commercial use to perform work that previously was possible only with diamond dust was boron carbide. It is lighter than aluminum and its density is 2.52 grams per cubic centimeter. It was produced by the research laboratories of the Norton Company, Worcester, MA, and introduced to the world through a technical paper read before the Electrochemical Society in New York City on September 27, 1934.

1905. Casein fiber was produced in December 1935 by Earle Ovando Whittier and Stephen Philip Gould of Washington, DC, who obtained a patent on December 13, 1938, and dedicated it "to the free use of the people of the United States of America." Casein is a derivative of milk protein used to make plastics and adhesives.

1906. Lucite commercially manufactured was made by E.I. du Pont de Nemours and Company, Wilmington, DE, beginning on May 21, 1936. Lucite, or polymethyl methacrylate, is a plastic that is low in moisture absorption, highly nonconducting, and crystal clear, and that possesses the interesting property of bending light rays as they pass through it.

1907. Teflon created in a laboratory was discovered by chemical engineer Roy J. Plunkett in 1938 at E.I. du Pont de Nemours and Company, Wilmington, DE. Teflon's chemical name is polymer of tetralourethylene, or PTFE. It is a plastic with a nonstick surface that can be sprayed onto utensils or formed into machinery components. It was first used in commercial products in 1954.

1908. Coal hydrogenation plant designed specifically for converting coal into chemicals was opened on May 8, 1952, in Institute, WV, by the Carbide and Carbon Chemicals Company. Coal was pulverized and mixed with oil to form a paste, then converted under heat and pressure in combination with hydrogen gas into liquid chemical intermediate products. The $11 million plant had a production capacity of 300 tons of coal a day. Some of the principal products were cresols, higher phenols, naphthalene, and aromatic hydrocarbon.

1909. Plastic wrap was polyvinylidene chloride, a nonporous membrane that was discovered accidentally at the Dow Chemical Company, Midland, MI, in 1933. Under the brand name Saran, it was used as a protective coating on planes during World War II. A version designed for household kitchen use was marketed as Saran Wrap in 1953.

1910. Polystyrene was commercially produced by the Koppers Company, Kobuta, PA, in 1954. Polystyrene is produced in small beads. When placed in molds and heated, the beads expand and take the shape of the enclosure.

1911. Polycarbonate products were manufactured in 1958. The new material was discovered in 1953 by two scientists working independently, Hermann Schnell in Germany and Daniel Wayne Fox at General Electric, Pittsfield, MA. Polycarbonate is a transparent, hard, impact-resistant plastic.

Metals

1912. Ironworks was erected at Falling Creek, VA, near Richmond, in 1619 by the Virginia Company. It operated only a short time, however, because of the colony's troubles with the local Native American tribes, and its charter was revoked in 1624. John Berkeley was in charge of operations.

1913. Ironworks that was successful was constructed in 1643 by John Winthrop, Jr., and 10 others who were known as the Company of Undertakers for the Iron Works. The operation was established near the Saugus River, near Lynn, MA. It produced eight tons of iron per week from the neighboring bog ore. It was managed by Captain Robert Bridges and Thomas Dextor. A forge was later installed.

1914. Manufacturer of metal goods was Joseph Jencks, who made the first kitchen utensils, metal tools, and machines in the New World. He opened a brass and iron foundry, the Iron Works, in Lynn, MA, in 1645.

1915. Iron exportation was made in 1650, when Samuel Hutchinson, a Massachusetts merchant, shipped 172 bars of iron to London on the *Charles*. This iron was probably made in Lynn, MA.

1916. Steel was manufactured in May 1728 by Samuel Higley of Simsbury, CT, and Joseph Dewey of Hebron, CT. Higley employed three workmen in a "curious art, by which to convert, change and transmute common iron into good steel, sufficient for any use."

1917. Iron casting is credited to Joseph Mallinson of Dusboro, PA, who introduced it in 1739 and received a grant of 200 acres of unimproved land in recognition of his services.

1918. Iron rolling mill was the Sarum ironworks, established in 1746 by John Taylor in Chester, PA. Three stacks worked full blast.

1919. White lead manufacturer was Samuel Wetherill of Philadelphia, PA, who began production in 1789. White lead was used primarily in paint and to some extent for medicinal purposes.

1920. Copper rolling mill was built by the former silversmith Paul Revere on the Neponset River at Canton, MA, where he produced his first sheets of copper on October 24, 1801. Revere copper was used to sheath the hulls of the earliest ships built for the U.S. Navy, including the *Constitution*, and to roof the domes of important public buildings.

1921. Brass was rolled in 1802 by Abel Porter and Company of Waterbury, CT. The factory was owned by Abel and Levi Porter, who were also the first to make brass by the direct fusion of copper and zinc.

1922. Iron mill to puddle and roll iron was the Plumstock Rolling Mill on Redstone Creek between Connellsville and Brownsville, PA, in Fayette County, put into operation on September 15, 1817, by Isaac Meason. It was wrecked by floods in 1824 and was not rebuilt.

1923. Malleable iron castings were produced in Newark, NJ, on July 4, 1826, by Seth Boyden. At first the iron was melted in crucibles, with lime used as a flux and heated in charcoal or hard coal fires.

1924. Brass wire and tubing were manufactured in 1831 on machinery imported from England by Israel Holmes for his firm, Holmes and Hotchkiss, of Waterbury, CT. The first company to manufacture brass wire successfully was the Wolcottville Brass Company, founded in 1841 with a capital investment of $56,000.

1925. Iron blast furnace to use anthracite coal in smelting was a furnace operated by the Lehigh Coal and Navigation Company at Mauch Chunk, PA, in 1837. The anthracite coal used was approximately 80 percent of the fuel consumed. On August 27, 1838, another blast furnace was erected in which anthracite was used exclusively.

1926. Iron blast furnace to use anthracite coal successfully was the Pioneer furnace in Pottsville, PA, which was blown on October 19, 1839, by Benjamin Perry. About 28 tons of foundry iron were produced a week. The furnace was built by William Lyman of Boston, MA.

1927. Hammered iron was made in 1842 at the Weymouth Iron Works, founded in 1754 on New Jersey's Great Egg Harbor River. The iron was hammered at the forge by two great trip hammers operated by waterpower.

Stephen Colwell received a medal from the Academy of Natural Sciences for developing the machinery used in this plant.

1928. **Cast steel for plows** was made by William Woods at the steel works of Jones and Quigg, Pittsburgh, PA, in 1846. The plows were made by John Deere at Moline, IL.

1929. **Silver plating factory** to be successful was Rogers Brothers, Hartford, CT, established in 1847 by three brothers, William, Asa, and Simeon S. Rogers. In 1862, the factory was moved to Meriden, CT, and they associated themselves with the Meriden Britannia Company, which in 1898 was succeeded by the International Silver Company. Silver plate consists of a hard metal that is plated or coated with silver. The base metal is usually nickel-silver, a combination of copper, zinc, and nickel. Prior to the introduction of silver-plated ware, silverware was made from coin silver.

1930. **Brass and copper seamless tubes** were manufactured in 1851 by the American Tube Works at Somerville, MA. The process was introduced by Joseph Fox. Previously, strips of rounded metal with brazed edges had been used.

1931. **Brass spinning** was invented by Hiram Washington Hayden of Waterbury, CT, who obtained a patent on December 16, 1851, on machinery for making kettles and articles of like character from discs of metal. A disc was mounted in a chuck that was rotated at a uniform speed. A tool was then pressed against the metal, which was thus shaped to the die. The process was first attempted at Wolcottville (now Torrington), CT, and was later sold to the Waterbury Brass Company.

1932. **Silver mill** to treat silver ore successfully, as well as the first reducing mill to treat ore-bearing quartz, was established by the Washoe Gold and Silver Mining Company, No. 1, near Virginia City, NV. The mill, operated by waterpower, was built by Almarin B. Paul, who began the construction work on May 25, 1860, and completed it on August 9, 1860. It consisted of 24 stamps that began to crush ore on August 11, 1860.

1933. **Bessemer steel converter** used commercially was erected by the Eureka Iron and Steel Works in 1864 in Wyandotte, MI, on the future site of the public library. The steel was made in a 2.5-ton experimental converter by William Franklin Durfee by means of the Kelly pneumatic process.

1934. **Zinc sheet mill** was erected in Bethlehem, PA. Production began in March 1865.

1935. **Open-hearth furnace for the manufacture of steel** by the Siemens-Martin process was built in 1868 by Frederick J. Slade for Cooper Hewitt and Company, owners of the New Jersey Steel and Iron Company, Trenton, NJ. The furnace was ready for operation in December 1868.

1936. **Nickel plating** was invented by William H. Remington of Boston, MA, who obtained a patent on October 6, 1868, on a "process of electroplating with nickel." He used a solution prepared by dissolving refined nickel in nitric acid, then precipitating the nickel by the addition of carbonate of potash, washing the precipitate with water, dissolving it in a solution of salammoniac, and filtering it.

1937. **Brass rod** was drawn in 1873 by the Coe Brass Company of Torrington, CT.

1938. **Tin factory** for the manufacture of black plate, as well as tin and terne plate, was established in 1874 by Rogers and Burchheld in Leechburg, PA.

1939. **Copper refinery furnace** to operate by the use of gaseous fuel was constructed in 1878 by William Franklin Durfee for the Wheeler and Wilson Company in Ansonia, CT.

1940. **Steel mill to install an electrical machine** was the Edgar Thomson Works of the Carnegie Steel Company, Braddock, PA. A two-light arc machine, operated by belt drive from a line shaft, was installed in the blast furnace machine shop in 1882. (Other claims to primacy were made by the Carnegie Steel Company's Homestead Works and other plants in the East.) The first installation of rolls driven by electric motor was made in the No. 3 mill of the Edgar Thomson Works in October 1905.

1941. **Aluminum in metallic form** produced in commercial quantities was made in November 1888 by the Pittsburgh Reduction Company, Pittsburgh, PA, which later developed into the Aluminum Company of America. It was based upon Charles Martin Hall's invention, in February 1886, of a method of reducing aluminum by electrolysis. Hall produced aluminum electrically instead of chemically, greatly reducing its cost. He dissolved alumina in a bath of molten cryolite (the double fluoride of aluminum and sodium) and passed an electric current through the solution.

1942. Manganese steel was manufactured in 1892 by the Taylor Iron and Steel Company in High Bridge, NJ.

1943. Steel mill to produce continuous sheets was designed by John Butler Tytus and built by the American Rolling Mill Company, Ashland, KY, in 1922. The plant consisted of an arrangement of machines that passed sheet steel through a series of mills in a tandem train at a high speed. The process replaced much slower methods. Operations began in 1924.

1944. Chromium plating process for commercial use was invented in 1924 at Columbia University, New York City, by Dr. Colin Garfield Fink, who obtained a patent for it on April 20, 1926. He also received a patent on April 28, 1931, on a process of electro-depositing chromium, which he assigned to the Chemical Treatment Company.

1945. Titanium plant fully self-contained and fully integrated was opened on June 1, 1951, in Henderson, NV, by the Titanium Metals Corporation of America. Titanium ore was converted at the plant to titanium sponge, which was melted and cast into ingots of titanium metal.

1946. Vacuum-cast steel was poured on July 2, 1957, by the Bethlehem Steel Corporation, Bethlehem, PA, in the form of a 93,900-pound ingot 78 inches in diameter. Vacuum-cast steel was melted in either an electric or an open-hearth furnace and poured into ingots. The gases were entrapped by vacuum-stream degassing with equipment designed by the F.J. Stokes Corporation, Philadelphia, PA.

1947. Titanium mill for rolling and forging titanium was opened on November 2, 1957, in Toronto, OH, by the Titanium Metals Corporation of America, owned by the National Lead Company and the Allegheny Ludlum Steel Corporation.

1948. Molybdenum centrifugal casting was made on November 4, 1958, when a hollow molybdenum cylinder 4.5 inches wide and 8 inches long was cast at the Albany Metallurgy Research Center of the Bureau of Mines, Albany, OR. The cast metal weighed about 10 pounds. Although molybdenum had previously been arc-melted in water-cooled copper crucibles to form cylindrical ingots, this was the first reported production of a shaped casting obtained from poured metal.

Insurance

1949. Insurance book of importance was *Ways and Means for the Inhabitants of Delaware to Become Rich, wherein the several growths and products of these countries are demonstrated to be a sufficient fund for a flourishing trade*, 65 pages, printed in Philadelphia, PA, in 1725, by S. Keimer. The author was Francis Rawle, who advocated the establishment by the legislature of an insurance office in Philadelphia for the purpose of providing marine insurance for merchants.

1950. Insurance regulation enacted by a state was enacted by Massachusetts on February 13, 1799, pursuant to a law establishing the Massachusetts Fire Insurance Company." It required that the company "shall, when and as often required by the legislature of the Commonwealth, lay before them such a statement of their affairs as the said legislature may deem it expedient to require, and submit to an examination hereon under oath."

1951. Insurance agency was opened by Israel Whelan in New York City in 1804. He was a representative of the Phoenix Fire Office of London.

1952. Insurance company owned by African-Americans was the African Insurance Company of Philadelphia, PA, organized in 1810 with a capital stock of $5,000 in $50 shares. It specialized in insuring African-Americans. Joseph Randolph was the first president. The company was not incorporated but was a voluntary association.

1953. Marine insurance law enacted by a state was approved by Massachusetts on February 16, 1818. An act was passed defining the powers, duties, and restrictions of insurance companies. It applied only to companies writing marine insurance and provided for annual publication by the president and directors of the amount of their stock, the risks against which they meant to insure, and the amounts of the single risks. They were also required to report to the legislature whenever so directed and were forbidden to write in any risk a sum exceeding 10 percent of the capital stock of the company.

1954. Insurance board established by a state government was the New Hampshire Insurance Department, established on July 1, 1851, which authorized the governor to appoint three suitable residents of the state to examine personally each year the affairs of all insurance companies and report to the legislature. Each member was appointed to a one-year term. The first board consisted of Albert S. Scott, Jacob E. Ela, and Timo Hoskins.

1955. Insurance journal was *Tuckett's Monthly Insurance Journal*, published in 1852 in Philadelphia, PA.

1956. Accident insurance company was the Travelers Insurance Company of Hartford, CT, chartered June 17, 1863, through the efforts of James Goodwin Batterson. The charter provided for the issuance of accident insurance to cover travel accidents only. In 1864 this was amended to include accidents of every description. The first policy was issued to James Bolter of Hartford for $1,000 in 1864 and covered only the period he spent walking from the post office to his home on Buckingham Street. The premium was two cents. The agreement was oral.

1957. Boiler insurance company was the Hartford Steam Boiler Inspection and Insurance Company of Hartford, CT, chartered in June 1866. The first president of the company was Enoch Roberts. The first policy was issued on February 14, 1867.

1958. Insurance rate standardization was effected on July 18, 1866, in New York City by the National Board of Fire Underwriters, an organization of 75 fire insurance companies. The first annual meeting was held on February 20, 1867, in New York City, and the first president was James McLean.

1959. Plate-glass insurance was written by the United States Plate Glass Insurance Company of Philadelphia, PA, incorporated on April 12, 1867, with an original capital of $20,000. The first president was John Van Dusen.

1960. Fraternal group insurance of consequence was issued in 1869 by the Metropolitan Life Insurance Company, New York City, to the Hildise Bund, an organization of German-American wage earners, which collected weekly premiums from its members. The premiums are said to have amounted at one time to about $7,500 a week.

1961. Title guaranty insurance company was the Real Estate Title Insurance and Trust Company, organized in Philadelphia, PA, on March 31, 1876. It offered security against errors in titles. The original capital was $250,000, half of which was paid in. The first president was Joshua H. Morris.

1962. Bonding company was the American Surety Company, New York City, incorporated on December 7, 1881. It began business on April 15, 1884.

1963. Credit insurance was briefly attempted in New York State in 1887. The first company that operated for any length of time was the U.S. Credit System Company of New York, organized in 1889.

1964. Mutual liability insurance company was the American Mutual Liability Insurance Company, Boston, MA, incorporated on March 30, 1887, and opened for business on October 1, when 22 policies were written covering liability of employers to injured workers. The rate was 30 cents per $100 of payroll. The first president was William Croad Lovering.

1965. Car insurance policy was issued by the Travelers Insurance Company of Hartford, CT, on February 1, 1898, to Dr. Truman J. Martin of Buffalo, NY. The premium was $11.25, covering $5,000 to $10,000 liability.

1966. Numerical system of insurance rating was originated by the New York Life Insurance Company of New York City about 1903. Values were assigned to various factors affecting the insurability of an applicant, to aid a company in determining under its rules whether the applicant was insurable, and if so, at what rates of premium.

1967. Hail insurance law enacted by a state was enacted by the legislature of North Dakota and approved on March 18, 1911. The number of policies issued the first year was 1,011, representing risks of about $1 million. The losses during the first year exceeded the premiums by nearly 18 percent, and the losses, as adjusted, had to be prorated at 70 percent.

1968. Bonding law enacted by a state for the bonding of all officers, deputies, and state employees was enacted by North Dakota on March 1, 1913, but was declared unconstitutional in 1914. Another law was approved on March 5, 1919. The premiums were 25 cents a year for each $100 of the required bond. A state bonding fund was created which in the first year showed a net income of $63,172. The first claim was filed on August 4, 1919, by Riggin Township, Benson County, for $1,000 for misappropriations of funds. It was paid on February 4, 1920.

1969. Aircraft liability and property damage insurance was issued by the Travelers Insurance Company of Hartford, CT, to a New York manufacturer in 1919.

1970. Car insurance law enacted by a state was "an act requiring owners of certain motor vehicles and trailers to furnish security for their civil liability on account of personal injury caused by their motor vehicles and trailers," approved on May 1, 1925, by Massachusetts. Automobiles were required to carry $5,000 to $10,000 liability.

1971. Babysitters' insurance policy was issued on January 26, 1950, by the American Associated Insurance Companies, St. Louis, MO. It covered sitters available through the Missouri State Employment Service, who were bonded up to $2,500 each for fraud and dishonesty.

1972. Insurance company to insure the lives of animals exclusively was the Animal Insurance Company of America, New York City, founded on August 1, 1957, by Milton M. Weiss. Coverage was extended only to pedigreed dogs and cats until May 1958, at which time the company added insurance for livestock classes of horses and cattle. Policies on animals were previously written by general insurance companies.

1973. No-fault car insurance law enacted by a state was enacted by Massachusetts, "an act providing for compulsory personal injury protection for all registered motor vehicles, defining such protection, restricting the right to claim damages for pain and suffering in certain actions of tort, regulating further the premium charges for compulsory automobile insurance and amending certain laws relating thereto." The act was approved by Governor Francis Williams Sargent on August 13, 1970. It permitted policyholders to collect up to $2,000 for medical expenses and out-of-pocket costs including wages, to be paid directly by the insurance company, irrespective of fault. A similar law had been enacted previously by Puerto Rico.

Fire

1974. Fire insurance agent is said to have been John Copson of High Street, Philadelphia, PA, who inserted an advertisement on May 25, 1721, in the *American Weekly Mercury* announcing that he would open an office for insurance on "vessels, goods and merchandise."

1975. Fire insurance company was organized in 1735 in Charleston, SC, as the Friendly Society for the Mutual Insurance of Houses Against Fire, and received subscriptions beginning on January 1, 1735. This company issued policies and conducted business over a period of about six years, as evidenced by advertisements and notices in the *South Carolina Gazette* from November 15, 1735, to February 19, 1741. On November 18, 1740, there was a conflagration that consumed half the town and probably ruined the society, as the last advertisement stated that "the bonds given by the members will be put in suit unless paid."

1976. Fire insurance company to receive a charter was the Philadelphia Contributionship for the Insurance of Houses from Loss by Fire, Philadelphia, PA, which was organized on April 13, 1752, when 12 directors and a treasurer were elected. Its first fire insurance policy was issued on June 1 to John Smith of Philadelphia, the company's treasurer, who for £1 insured his house, valued at £1,000. A charter was granted by the lieutenant governor and proprietaries of the province of Pennsylvania on February 20, 1768, and was subsequently confirmed by King George III of Great Britain upon the advice of his privy council. The first name subscribed to the Articles of Association was that of Lieutenant Governor James Hamilton; the first private name was that of Benjamin Franklin. Each insured house displayed a wooden shield showing the company's seal, "four Hands united."

1977. Fire insurance joint-stock company was the American Fire Insurance Company, organized on February 28, 1810, in Philadelphia, PA. The first president was

Captain William Jones, who later became secretary of the navy under President James Madison.

1978. Mutual fire insurance company for insuring factories was the Manufacturers' Mutual Fire Insurance Company of Rhode Island, located in Providence, RI, and incorporated on October 31, 1835. The first policy was issued on December 3, 1835, to Zachariah Allen for $2,500 at a cash premium deposit rate of 60 cents per year. At the expiration of the policy, a 51 percent dividend was declared, resulting in an insurance cost of 29.4 cents per $100 for the year.

1979. Fire and tornado insurance fund enacted by a state was established by North Dakota and began to function on July 1, 1919. For the first five months, the gross income was $28,909 and the losses paid were $3,773. The net income, after expenses were paid, amounted to $24,144. The first loss was $1,500, paid on October 23, 1919, to Conway, SD, to compensate for damage caused by an overheated furnace. The law provided that no policy over $100,000 could be written. When necessary, additional insurance was obtained from private companies.

Health

1980. Health insurance company was the Massachusetts Health Insurance Company of Boston, MA, organized on April 21, 1847. The company existed for a very short period.

1981. Hospital insurance group plan was effected by Baylor University Hospital, Dallas, TX, on December 21, 1929. The plan was inaugurated by Dr. Justin Ford Kimball, executive vice president of Baylor University. The first group insured were the Dallas public school teachers, who paid 50 cents per month for 21 days of hospital treatment.

1982. Blue Cross and Blue Shield plans were distinguished from other group health insurance plans because they were nonprofit plans and their membership was not restricted to a particular organization or occupation. The Blue Cross symbol was first used by E. A. van Steenwyk, an executive of the Hospital Service Assocation of Minnesota, in 1934. The Blue Shield symbol was adopted by a health plan in Buffalo, NY, in 1939.

1983. Medical insurance group policy for college students covering medical, surgical, and hospital expenses was issued February 1, 1936, by the Ocean Accident and Guarantee Corporation to Vassar College, Poughkeepsie, NY. The plan was sponsored by the college for voluntary participation, and 565 students were included at a premium of $12 each for the year. Known as the Students' Reimbursement Plan, it was organized and managed by the A.W.G. Dewar Company of Boston, MA, whose Tuition Refund Plan in 1929 had first introduced the insurance of school fees in American private schools.

1984. Health insurance clause in a labor contract was put into effect on August 25, 1941, by the International Ladies Garment Workers Union in a contract with the Waist and Dress Manufacturers Association of Philadelphia, PA. The clause set aside 2.5 percent of the payroll to establish a system of weekly sick benefits and a medical clinic to supervise the health of the workers. About 10,000 cotton-dress and -blouse workers in Philadelphia were covered.

1985. Health maintenance organization in which members prepaid for comprehensive medical services was the Kaiser-Permanente Medical Care Program, begun in 1942 by Henry J. Kaiser and Dr. Sidney R. Garfield. The first two programs, in the Pacific Northwest and California, were administered by Kaiser's Permanente Foundations. They were originally intended for groups of employees. Enrollment was opened to the public in 1945.

1986. Health insurance law enacted by a state was the Rhode Island Cash Sickness Compensation act, approved on April 29, 1942. It required employers to collect 1 percent from employees after June 1, 1942, on salaries up to $3,000 paid in any calendar year, and granted benefits ranging from $6.75 to $18 a week.

1987. State to mandate universal health insurance for all its citizens was Massachusetts. On April 4, 2006, the state legislature enacted a law to establish coverage for the entire population by July 1, 2007. It required employers with more than 10 employees either to offer them health insurance coverage or to make contributions to a state fund that would subsidize low-cost policies from private insurers. Tax penalties would apply to any person who elected to remain without coverage.

Life

1988. Life insurance company was the Corporation for the Relief of Poor and Distressed Presbyterian Ministers and of the Poor and Distressed Widows and Children of Presbyterian Ministers, incorporated on January 11, 1759, in Philadelphia, PA. The Reverend Robert Cross was the first president. The first policy was issued on May 22, 1761, to Francis Alison. Survivor annuities were granted at the death of the policyholder, the beneficiary receiving £10 to £35 for the duration of his or her life. The annual premium required was one-fifth of the annuity. The first commercial company specializing in life insurance was the Pennsylvania Company for Insurance on Lives and Granting Annuities, incorporated in Philadelphia in 1812.

1989. Life insurance offered by a general insurance company was offered by the Insurance Company of North America, organized in Philadelphia, PA, on December 10, 1792, with a capital of $600,000, and chartered on April 14, 1794. The first policy was issued on December 15, 1792. Only six policies were written in five years, and in 1804 the life insurance feature was discontinued. The first president was John Maxwell Nesbitt.

1990. Mutual life insurance company was the Mutual Life Insurance Company of New York City, which was chartered on April 12, 1842. The first policy was issued on February 1, 1843, to Thomas N. Ayres. The first president was Morris Robinson. Policyholders were entitled to a share in the management through the election of directors. All profits belonged to the policyholders. The New England Mutual Life Insurance Company of Boston, MA, was chartered earlier, on April 1, 1835, but did not do business until December 1, 1843, and issued its first policy on February 1, 1844.

1991. Life insurance policy rated substandard was issued on July 1, 1896, by the New York Life Insurance Company of New York City. A substandard policy is one issued on a life that because of a medical impairment, hazardous occupation, or some other reason is "substandard" and therefore not insurable at "standard," or normal, rates of premium.

1992. Savings bank life insurance was launched by act of the Massachusetts legislature dated June 26, 1907. The plan was originated by Louis Dembitz Brandeis, then a Boston lawyer, and later associate justice of the Supreme Court. The first savings bank to establish an insurance department was the Whitman Savings Bank in Whitman, MA. The department was established on June 18, 1908, and the first policy written on June 22. Savings bank life insurance is legal reserve insurance that is sold "over the counter" by certain mutual savings banks. No solicitors are employed.

1993. Life insurance group policy was written by William J. Graham of the Equitable Life Assurance Society of the United States on June 1, 1911, under one blanket contract. Without medical examination, 121 employees of the Pantasote Leather Company of Passaic, NJ, were insured as a group for $87,030. Each employee was given insurance protection amounting to a year's salary and a funeral benefit of $100. The following year, the same insurance company underwrote the first large-scale group contract, whereby 3,000 employees of Montgomery Ward and Company, Chicago, IL, were insured as a group for approximately $6 million without medical examination.

Packaging

1994. Bottle blown in America was made in a factory set up in the woods one mile from Jamestown, VA, in 1608. The common glass bottle bears the distinction of being the first manufactured product exported from this country.

1995. Paper bag machine was invented by schoolteacher Francis Wolle of Bethlehem, PA, who spent $15.99 in the process. He received a patent for the device in 1852 and cofounded the Union Paper Bag Machine Company in 1869.

1996. Tin can with a key opener was invented by J. Osterhoudt of New York City, who obtained a patent on October 2, 1866, for an "improved method of opening tin cans." The can had a projecting lip and key.

1997. Paper bags with flat bottoms were made by a machine that was patented in 1870 by Margaret Knight of New Hampshire.

1998. Milk bottles were made by Louis Porter Whiteman, owner of the Warren Glass Works, Cumberland, MD, who manufactured a product he called Glass Air Tight Milk Jars in 1879. They were used by the Echo Farms Dairy Company, New York City. To commemorate the event, the Pennsylvania State Agricultural Society presented a plaque to Whiteman.

1999. Bottle cap with a cork crown was invented in 1892 by William Painter, founder of the Crown Cork and Seal Company, Baltimore, MD, who obtained a patent for the product on February 2, 1892. It was a simple bit of tin with a corrugated rim or skirt into which was inserted a disc of natural or composition cork.

2000. Practical paper beverage carton was invented by toy manufacturer John Van Wormer of Toledo, OH. On October 19, 1915, he received a patent for a coated, spoutless "paper bottle" that he called the Pure-Pak. However, a machine capable of making and filling the Pure-Pak was not perfected until 1929, and full production did not begin until 1937, when 42 million units were sold.

2001. Bottle with a screw cap and a pour lip was patented on May 5, 1936, by Edward A. Ravenscroft, Glencoe, IL. The bottles were manufactured by the Abbott Laboratories, North Chicago, IL.

2002. Spray can was invented by Julian Seth Kahn of New York City, who received a patent on August 22, 1939, for an "apparatus for mixing a liquid with gas." It was equipped with an inexpensive disposable valve mechanism. Under controlled pressure, it dispensed such items as whipped cream, paints, pharmaceuticals, and insecticides.

2003. Aluminum can with a pull-tab pop-top was introduced in 1962 by Iron City Beer, Pittsburgh, PA. The tab was the invention of Ermal Cleon Fraze, owner of Dayton Reliable Tool & Manufacturing Company, Dayton, OH, who received a patent for the pull tab on June 29, 1965, and for the pop-top can on December 13, 1966. The removable metal tabs, with their sharp edges, proved to be a safety hazard as well as a source of litter.

The pop-top's problems were solved in 1976 with the invention of the Sta-Tab, a pull tab that remained attached to the can after opening. The inventor was Daniel F. Cudzik of the Reynolds Metal Company, Richmond, VA.

2004. Aluminum soda can was manufactured in 1963 by the Reynolds Metals Company, Troutdale, OR. A "Vitamin C enriched" diet cola called Slenderella was the first to appear on the market in an 8-ounce Reynolds can. The first national brand to adopt the aluminum can was Royal Crown Cola. Aluminum cans had the advantage of being lighter than steel cans, easier to print on, and made from fewer pieces.

2005. Plastic soda bottle was patented in 1973 by Nathaniel Wyeth, an engineer for the E.I. du Pont de Nemours Company, Wilmington, DE. It was made of polyethylene terephthalate (PET), a highly elastic polymer that was strengthened to enable it to withstand the pressure of carbonated beverages.

Paper and Printing

2006. Paper mill was built in 1690 by William Rittenhouse, Samuel Carpenter, Robert Turner, Thomas Tresse, and William Bradford in Germantown, PA, on a rivulet called Paper Mill Run, about two miles above the junction of the Wissahickon River with the Schuylkill. The mill was built on 20 acres of land leased from Samuel Carpenter at an annual rental of five shillings. The paper was made by hand from linen rags that were pounded into pulp in stone mortars. Each sheet was made separately. The production rate was about 250 pounds a day.

2007. Watermark in paper was the single word "company," which was formed in the paper manufactured in 1690 by William Rittenhouse in his mill on Paper Mill Run, Germantown, PA. Afterwards he used several other watermarks to distinguish his paper.

2008. Printer who was a woman was Dinah Nuthead of Annapolis, MD, who successfully petitioned the Assembly on May 5, 1696, for license to print and carry on the printing trade of her late husband, William Nuthead.

2009. Printer's ink was successfully manufactured in America by Charles Eneu Johnson, who began manufacturing inks in Philadelphia, PA, in 1804. His concern later became part of the United Carbon Company.

2010. Paper made by machine in the United States was produced in Thomas Gilpen's paper mill at Brandywine, DE. Previously, paper had been made by hand in small sizes because of limited facilities and molds. Gilpin's cylinder machine, which he built in August 1817, permitted paper to be made in unlimited lengths and widths.

2011. Fourdrinier papermaking machine capable of making an endless roll of paper in any size was imported from England and set up in Joseph Pickering's shop in North Windham, CT, in January 1828. The first such machine to be manufactured in the United States was built in 1829 in South Windham, CT, by James Phelps and George Spafford, who formed the firm of Phelps and Spafford. Aided by Charles Smith, they produced a machine that was set up in May 1829 in the mill of Amos H. Hubbard of Norwich Falls, CT. The machine had no driers. The paper was run off wet and hung up to dry. The firm name was changed to Smith, Winchester and Company in 1837.

2012. Straw paper was made from straw and grass in 1829 by George Augustus Shryrock of Philadelphia, PA, in the Hollywell mill near Chambersburg, PA. He also invented a machine for producing it.

2013. Envelope manufacturer was a Mr. Pierson of New York City, who manufactured envelopes in a little store on Fulton Street in 1839. Prior to the manufacture of envelopes, letters were folded and sealed and the name and address written on the blank side.

2014. Manila paper was invented by John Mark and Lyman Hollingsworth of South Braintree, MA, partners under the firm name of J.M. and L. Hollingsworth, who received a patent on December 4, 1843. They manufactured it from hemp sails, canvas, and rope.

2015. Envelope folding machine that proved practical commercially was patented on January 21, 1853, by Dr. Russell L. Hawes of Worcester, MA. It was not self-gumming, but nevertheless it enabled three girls to produce the finished product at the rate of about 25,000 envelopes in 10 hours.

2016. Paper for printing made from rags and wood-pulp fiber was manufactured by William Orr at his paper mill in Troy, NY, in 1854. The composition of the paper was three-fourths rag and one-fourth wood fiber.

2017. Paper made from wood pulp was made of basswood by John Beardsley of Buffalo, NY. He exhibited three samples of it on December 26, 1854, to the editor of the *Buffalo Democrat*.

2018. Magazine for professional printers was the *Typographic Advertiser*, a quarterly published by L. Johnson and Company, Philadelphia, PA, which appeared in April 1855.

2019. Blotting paper was made in New Haven, CT, by Joseph Parker and Son in 1856 at the West Rock Paper Mill on a Fourdrinier machine. Until this time, only small quantities had been imported from England. Most people used sand to dry their ink.

2020. Paper folding machine to fold paper for books and newspapers was invented by Cyrus Chambers, Jr., of Kennet Square, PA, who obtained a patent on October 7, 1856. It was for plain three-fold right-angle work and delivered a 16-page folded signature to the packing box. It was installed in the Bible printing house of Jasper Harding and Son, Philadelphia, PA.

2021. Perforated wrapping paper was patented on July 25, 1871, by Seth Wheeler of Albany, NY. The paper was wound into rolls and could easily be torn off at the perforations.

2022. Corrugated paper was invented by Albert L. Jones of New York City, who received a patent on December 19, 1871, on an "improvement in paper for packing." His patent covered corrugated sheets only and made no mention of backing or facing sheets. Later a facing sheet was applied to one side, and then to both sides, making single-face and double-face corrugated cardboard. Jones assigned his patent to the Thompson and Norris Company of Brooklyn, NY (now part of New York City), which was the first manufacturer of corrugated paper in the United States. Corrugated paper boxes came into use about 1890.

2023. Crepe paper was manufactured in 1890 by Charles T. Bainbridge's Sons, Brooklyn, NY (now part of New York City). It was made of rag paper with only one ratio of stretch. It was made in a variety of colors and sold to the trade for 50 cents a roll. Each roll was 20 inches wide and 10 feet long.

2024. Envelope folding and gumming machine was patented on February 8, 1898, by John Ames Sherman of Worcester, MA. It reduced the cost of a completely gummed envelope ready for market from 60 cents to 8 cents per 1,000.

2025. Envelope with a window was patented by Americus F. Callahan of Chicago, IL, on June 10, 1902. It was first manufactured in July 1902 by the U.S. Envelope Company of Springfield, MA, which had leased the patent.

2026. Ink paste was invented by Frank Buckley Cooney of Minneapolis, MN, who obtained a patent on January 1, 1924. The paste, known as Cooney's Ink Paste, was manufactured on February 10, 1923, by the Standard Ink Manufacturing Company, Minneapolis, MN. The inventor sold rights to manufacture to the American Crayon Company.

2027. Copy made by xerography was made by Chester Floyd Carlson, a research physicist from New York City. Xerography is the process of making dry paper copies based on principles of photoconductivity and electrostatics. While doing some work in the patent office for P.R. Mallory and Company, an electronics firm, Carlson saw the need for a high-volume copying process that was more economical and easier to handle than photostats and carbon copies. On October 22, 1938, in Astoria, Queens, New York City, Carlson made the first electrophotographic image on wax paper pressed against an electrostatically charged, sulfur-coated zinc plate dusted with fine dark powder. The image consisted of the message "10-22-38 Astoria." Carlson patented the process, which he called xerography, on October 6, 1942.

2028. Sticky notes were Post-it Notes, introduced by 3M of St. Paul, MN. The adhesive was invented in 1968 at 3M's Corporate Research Labs by chemist Spencer Silver. It was composed of tiny acrylic spheres that formed a temporary bond with paper. No product application could be found for it until 1974, when another 3M employee, chemical engineer Arthur Fry, realized that he could mark book pages in his choir hymnal using slips of paper backed with Silver's weak adhesive. The company began marketing its new product by giving away samples and quickly built up a demand. Sales began nationwide in 1980.

Technology

2029. Printing press was imported from England in the summer of 1638 by the Reverend Jesse "Jose" Glover of Sutton, England. Glover hired Stephen Day, a printer skilled in the operation of the press, to sail to Massachusetts in the same ship, together with his wife and children. Glover died on board the ship. The press was set in operation in March 1639 at Cambridge, MA, and Day became the first printer in colonial America.

2030. Hebrew type was used in the *Bay Psalm Book*, the first book to be published in America, printed by Stephen Day and issued in 1640 by the Cambridge Press, Cambridge, MA.

2031. Stereotype printing was tried in 1745 in Philadelphia, PA, by Benjamin Mecom, a nephew of Benjamin Franklin. He commenced casting plates for the New Testament but never finished the task. The first successful stereotypers were David and George Bruce, who established the firm of D. and G. Bruce in New York City in 1813. They designed machinery and molds patterned after those in use in England and had them cast in New York City. The business remained in the family until 1895, when it was sold.

2032. Type foundry in America belonged to Abel Buell, who cast his first font on April 1, 1769, at Killingworth, CT. It is said that the statue of King George III that was torn down in New York City was brought to Buell's foundry to be cast into type.

2033. Dollar marks to be made in type were cast in 1797 by Archibald Binny and James Ronaldson, type-founders of Philadelphia, PA, who started in business on November 1, 1796.

2034. Printing press invented in the United States was the Columbian Press, an iron hand-printing press that was operated by a combination of compound levers instead of a screw to give the downward pressure. It was invented by George E. Clymer of Philadelphia, PA, in 1816. The first to be successful was the Washington Press, invented in 1827 by Samuel Rust of New York City, and valued for its usefulness in taking fine proofs. Rust obtained patents on May 13, 1821, March 2, 1826, and April 17, 1829. The machine was manufactured by R. Hoe and Company, New York City.

2035. Steam-powered printing press was made by Daniel Treadwell of Boston, MA, in 1822. Only three or four were manufactured.

2036. Printing press for printing wallpaper in color was invented by Peter Force of Washington, DC, who patented it on August 22, 1822.

2037. Cylinder printing press was made by R. Hoe and Company, New York City, in 1831 and was operated initially by hand power and later by steam. It was used to print the *Temperance Recorder*, a monthly that was first published on March 6, 1832, in Albany, NY.

2038. Embossing press was a standing hand-lever press built in New York City in 1838 by Bernard Sheridan. An object placed between the descending die and the bed was given a raised surface when pressure was applied. The press sold for $200.

2039. Electric printing press was invented by Thomas Davenport of Brandon, VT, and used in 1839 in New York City. It was a rotary press operated by an engine weighing less than 100 pounds. Beginning in January 1840, he used it to print the journal *Electro-Magnet and Mechanics Intelligencer*, of which he was the editor. He obtained a patent on February 25, 1837, on an "electrical motor."

2040. Cylinder and flatbed combination printing press was manufactured in 1844 by R. Hoe and Company, New York City. It was invented by Robert Hoe, who obtained a patent on April 17, 1844. The circumference of the cylinder was equivalent to the entire travel of the bed forward and backward. The cylinder made one revolution for each impression in printing without stopping.

2041. Printing press for polychromatic printing was invented by Thomas F. Adams of Philadelphia, PA, who obtained a patent for it on September 17, 1844. Different color rollers, operating in parallel, were used to produce linear work.

2042. Rotary printing press was the double-cylinder machine invented by Richard March Hoe of New York City. It was first used in the office of the *Philadelphia Ledger*, Philadelphia, PA, in 1846. The bed was of such length that the form of type passed backward and forward under both cylinders. The central cylinder was placed in a horizontal position. The output was 2,000 sheets per hour for each of four feeders. A patent was obtained on July 24, 1847.

2043. Curved stereotype plate was cast by Charles Craske in 1854 in New York City for a Hoe rotary press. It was used by the *New York Tribune*. On August 31, 1861, full pages of the *Tribune* were printed from curved plates.

2044. Typesetting machine that actually operated was invented by Timothy Alden of New York City, who obtained a patent on September 15, 1857. The type was arranged in cells around the circumference of a horizontal wheel. As the wheel revolved, several receivers also started to rotate. The desired type was picked up and dropped in proper order in a line.

2045. Printing press to use a continuous web or roll of paper was the Bullock Press, produced by William Bullock of Pittsburgh, PA, in 1865. It was the first machine built especially for curved stereotype plates. It printed both sides of the sheet, and cut it either before or after printing. A patent on the machine was granted on April 14, 1863. The press was first used by the *New York Sun*.

2046. Rotary printing press with a continuous-roll feed to be perfected was produced in 1871 by R. Hoe and Company, New York City, and utilized the first gathering and delivery cylinder patented by Stephen D. Tucker of New York City. The press was installed in the *New York Tribune* plant and produced as many as 18,000 newspapers an hour.

2047. High-speed newspaper printing and folding machine utilizing the gathering cylinder with a rotary folding cylinder was installed in 1876 on the presses of the *Philadelphia Times*, Philadelphia, PA. It printed and folded four-page sheets at the rate of 400 a minute. The press was shown in operation at the Philadelphia Centennial Exposition in 1876.

2048. Mimeograph was invented by Thomas Alva Edison of Menlo Park, NJ, who obtained a patent on August 8, 1876, on a "method of preparing autographic stencils for printing." On February 17, 1880, he obtained a second patent for an improved model.

2049. Halftone printing plate for reproducing photographs in books, magazines, and newspapers was the work of Frederic Eugene Ives, a photographer at Cornell University, Ithaca, NY, who received the first U.S. patent for the halftone printing screen and process on February 8, 1881. Earlier printers had conceived the idea of reproducing photographs by dividing them up into lines that could be transferred to a printer's plate. Ives was the first to devise a consistent method of producing halftones that could be applied to large printing operations. In 1878, he converted a photographic negative into a dot-screen gelatin relief from which he made a printing plate with good fidelity to the original image. The first halftone using the Ives process was printed in the June 1881 issue of the *Philadelphia Photographer.*

2050. Newspaper printing plant to install electricity was the *New York Times*, which turned on the current on September 4, 1882. Electricity was supplied by the Edison Electric Illuminating Company's central station at 257 Pearl Street, New York City. The editorial room had 27 electric lights, the counting room 25. The composing rooms and the press room were equipped later.

2051. Linotype machine was invented by Ottmar Mergenthaler of Baltimore, MD, who obtained a patent on August 26, 1884, on a "matrix making machine." The first Linotype machine to be used commercially was a blower machine installed on July 1, 1886, by the Mergenthaler Linotype Company in the printing plant of the *New York Tribune* and used to cast type for the July 3 issue. The machine had a keyboard assembling mechanism, a mechanism for casting a full line of type in a single bar, and a matrix lifting and distributing device. When the matrix was released from a vertical tube that resembled a pipe of an organ, it was carried by air blast along an inclined chute to its place in the assembling line of matrices.

2052. Newspaper page set by linotype was the *New York Daily Tribune*, whose editorial page was set by linotype on July 3, 1886.

2053. Monotype machine was invented by Tolbert Lanston of Washington, DC, who received five patents for it on June 7, 1887. The machine cast new type, letter by letter, from matrices that were used over and over.

2054. Web-fed four-color rotary printing press was made in 1890 by Walter Scott and Company, Plainfield, NJ, for the *Chicago Inter-Ocean* of Chicago, IL. It was placed in operation in 1892. Curved stereotype plates, cast to fit the cylinders, were used in printing a roll of paper two pages wide.

2055. Automatic plate-casting and finishing machine for stereotype printing was the Autoplate, invented by Henry Alexander Wise Wood, which greatly increased the speed at which newspapers could be printed. It was adopted by the *New York Herald* in 1900.

2056. Rotogravure press was imported in November 1904 by the American Photogravure Company of Philadelphia, PA. It had been built in Ramsbottom, England, by John Wood.

2057. Teletypesetter was manufactured by the Teletypesetter Corporation, Chicago, IL, and sold in October 1932 to a job printing plant in Detroit, MI. The teletypesetter consisted of two units: a perforator for preparing a paper tape and an operating unit for attachment to either a Linotype or an Intertype machine. As the tape was automatically fed into the operating unit, the keys of the line-casting machine were depressed and lines of type were steadily produced at a speed impossible to match by manual operation.

2058. Typesetting machine to dispense with metal type was the Intertype Fotosetter Photographic Line Composing Machine, manufactured by the Intertype Corporation, Brooklyn, New York City, and installed at the plant of Stecher-Traung Lithograph Corporation, Rochester, NY, in 1949. The machine was exhibited at the 6th Educational Graphic Arts Exposition, held at the International Amphitheater, Chicago, on September 11, 1950.

2059. Photographic type-composing machine was the Photon (Higonnet-Moyroud) machine, which was manufactured by Photon beginning in April 1953 under license from the Graphic Arts Research Foundation. The machine, operated from a standard typewriter keyboard at full electric-typewriter speed, delivered film negatives instead of type. The first book set by the Photon process was *The Wonderful World of Insects*, by Albro Tilton Gaul, offered for sale to the public on February 26, 1953, by Rinehart and Company, New York City. The first copy was presented to Dr. Karl Taylor Compton, chairman of the corporation of the Massachusetts Institute of Technology, on February 5, 1953, by Dr. Vannevar Bush, a director of the Graphic Arts Research Foundation, Boston, MA.

2060. Photoengraving high-speed process for making halftones, line plates, and combination plates was developed by the Dow Chemical Company of Freeport, TX, in cooperation with the American Newspaper Publishers Association Research Institute, Easton, PA. By means of this process, a machine could produce zinc or magnesium plates in about one-fifth the conventional time. The first commercial machine was placed in operation in February 1954 by the *Patriot-Ledger* of Quincy, MA.

Shipping

2061. Manufactured products to be exported from America were glass bottles exported to England. They were blown in 1608 at a small factory set up near the English settlement in Jamestown, VA. In addition to bottles, the eight German and Polish artisans who worked at the factory made glass beads that were traded to the Native Americans.

2062. Royal navigation act affecting the American colonies was passed by the English Parliament in 1651. The law allowed a three-year exemption from duty for all merchandise for the English-American plantations, on the condition that no colonial vessel could carry American produce to a foreign port. Except for intercolonial trade, all goods were to be carried in English ships.

2063. Customhouse in colonial America was established in Yorktown, VA. It was built about 1706 by Richard Ambler, who occupied it as "Collector of Ports for Yorktown" in 1720. At this period Yorktown was the port of entry for New York, Philadelphia, and other northern cities. A tombstone in Hampton, VA, badly obliterated but decipherable, reads "Peter Heyman, Collector of his Majesty's custom, died April 29, 1700." He is presumed to have been one of the early collectors of customs at Yorktown.

2064. Embargo act of the Continental Congress was the nonimportation act enacted on October 14, 1774. It stated: "After the first day of December next, there be no importation into British America, from Great Britain or Ireland, of any goods, wares or merchandize whatsoever, or from any other place of any such goods, wares or merchandize."

2065. Navigation act enacted by Congress was approved on July 20, 1789. It imposed a duty on the tonnage of vessels.

2066. Export report by the federal government covered the fiscal year ending September 30, 1791. The exports for the year amounted to $19 million, of which $18.5 million was for domestic merchandise and $512,041 for foreign goods. The imports for the same period amounted to $29.2 million, an excess of imports over exports of more than $10 million.

2067. Standardization of weights and measures for customs was established by Congress in an act dated March 2, 1799, which required the surveyor of customs of each port to standardize his measures to comply with the customs clause requiring "all duties, imposts, and excises [to] be uniform throughout the United States."

2068. Embargo act enacted by Congress was passed by Congress by a vote of 82–44 and approved by President Thomas Jefferson on December 22, 1807. The act required all American ships to refrain from international commerce. It was repealed on March 1, 1809. A later act substituted a requirement of nonintercourse with Great Britain and France.

2069. Year in which exports exceeded imports was the fiscal year ending September 30, 1811. The difference amounted to an excess of $7.9 million. Exports of domestic merchandise were worth $45.3 million and of foreign merchandise $16 million, making a grand total of exports of $61.3 million. The imports amounted to $53.4 million.

2070. Coastal shipping service was established in 1831 by Thomas Lowery Servoss. He outfitted five packet ships that ran regularly between New York City and New Orleans.

2071. Express delivery service was organized on February 23, 1839, by William Frederick Harnden of Boston, MA, who arranged for delivery service between Boston and New York City. The service was advertised to begin on March 4, 1839. The first shipment was a few suitcases. Shipments were made via the Boston and Providence Railway and Long Island Sound Steamboat.

2072. Express delivery service to the West was conducted from Buffalo, NY, by Wells & Co., formed in 1844 by Henry Wells. The first route went to Detroit, MI. William G. Fargo was the courier.

2073. Warehouse legislation enacted by Congress was passed by Congress on August 6, 1846. This act permitted duty-free storage of imported merchandise in warehouses owned or leased by the federal government, the duty to be paid upon withdrawal of the merchandise within a specified time of not more than one year. Another act, passed on March 28, 1854, extended bonded storage privileges to private warehouses approved by the secretary of the treasury. These warehouses were required to have proper customs officers in charge or to have joint custody with customs officers of all merchandise.

2074. Docks owned by a state were acquired by California by an act approved on April 24, 1863, "an act to provide for the improvement and protection of the wharves, docks and water front in the city and county of San Francisco." Three commissioners, one elected by the state, one elected by the city, and one appointed by the Senate and Assembly at a joint session, formed the Board of State Harbor Commissioners "to construct new wharves, to keep in good repair seawalls, embankments, wharves, piers, landings and thoroughfares for the advancement of commerce."

2075. Interstate commerce act enacted by Congress was approved on February 4, 1887, and was popularly known as the Cullom Act. Its principal objects were "to secure just and reasonable charges for [railroad] transportation; to prohibit unjust discrimination in the rendition of like services under similar circumstances and conditions; to prevent undue preferences to persons, corporations or localities; to inhibit greater compensation for shorter than for longer distances over the same lines; and to abolish combinations for the pooling of freights." The act established the Interstate Commerce Commission, which was organized on March 31, 1887.

2076. Express delivery service nationwide was Wells, Fargo & Co. Founded by Henry Wells and William G. Fargo in New York City in 1852, it employed agents who traveled to California by steamship, stagecoach, and eventually by rail. The company went nationwide in 1888.

2077. Intercity trucking service began on October 29, 1904, when William B. Chenoweth placed a six-cylinder motor truck in service between Colorado City, CO, and Snyder, TX.

2078. Shipment of merchandise by airplane was delivered to the Morehouse-Martens Company of Columbus, OH, by pilot Philip Parmelee. The shipment contained five bolts of Rajah silk manufactured by Rogers and Thompson of New York City and valued at $600. Parmelee took possession of the silk after it arrived in Dayton, OH, and brought it to Columbus in a Wright biplane, landing at the old Columbus Driving Park. The silk was cut up and the pieces were stamped with the legend, "This silk is a piece of the first merchandise ever carried in an airplane—Dayton to Columbus, November 7, 1910." The distance of 60 miles was made in 56 minutes. The delivery was a publicity stunt for which $5,000 was paid. The shipping rate was $71.42 a pound.

2079. Free port was opened on February 1, 1937, at Stapleton, Staten Island, New York City, under authority of a congressional act "to provide for the establishment, operation and maintenance of foreign-trade zones in ports of entry of the United States, to expedite and encourage foreign commerce, and for other purposes," approved on June 18, 1934. The port embraced an 18-acre tract around New York Municipal Piers Nos. 12, 13, 15, and 16, and was operated as a public utility by the Department of Docks, New York City, under the supervision of the Customs Service. Foreign merchandise was admitted in bond without payment of import duties. The first superintendent was John McKenzie.

2080. Containerized shipping was invented by Malcolm McLean of Maxton, NC, the owner of McLean Trucking, a large freight-trucking firm. He developed a large shipping container that could be packed with goods at the factory, hauled by truck to a port facility, carried on specially fitted ships to a port terminal, offloaded from the ship, and hitched directly to trucks or loaded on freight cars for cross-continental transport, all without unpacking the container's contents. McLean's first containership, the *Ideal X*, left the port of Newark, NJ, on April 25, 1956. The first containership facility was the Elizabeth–Port Authority Marine Terminal, operated by the Port of New York Authority. It opened for business on August 15, 1962, when Sea-Land Service's S.S. *Elizabethport* docked in Newark Bay, Elizabeth, NJ, on the south side of the Elizabeth Channel, south of Port Newark. During its first year, the facility handled 1.5 million tons of cargo on 242 vessels and employed 730 people, who earned a total of more than $4 million.

2081. Airborne express delivery service was Federal Express, founded in 1972 in Memphis, TN, by Frederick W. Smith. With $72 million in financing, Smith purchased eight aircraft and a fleet of trucks to deliver packages overnight to selected locations in the United States. Package deliveries began in April 1973. Federal Express delivered its first letters in 1981.

Stores

2082. Optical shop in the United States began doing business in 1799 in Philadelphia, PA. The proprietor was John McAllister, Sr., an immigrant from Scotland who was already established as a merchant of hickory canes and riding whips. He added spectacles to his inventory and by 1815 was making his own gold and silver frames. Eventually he became adept at measuring his customers' eyesight and began making lenses. His family continued the business for five generations.

> Both Thomas Jefferson and Andrew Jackson purchased their eyeglasses at John McAllister's optical shop.

2083. Cooperative store for consumers was organized in 1830 in New York City by William Bryan, treasurer of a cooperative in Brighton, England. He established a store in New York City that sold articles to members at prices generally below those prevailing at retail outlets.

2084. Department store was opened by Adam Gimbel, a German Jewish immigrant who began his career peddling household goods on foot in the Mississippi Valley. In 1842, he opened a store in Vincennes, IN, that offered a wide variety of goods under one roof, along with a money-back guarantee of satisfaction. Gimbel's seven sons imported the idea to cities across the country.

2085. Department store to occupy a city block was Alexander Turney Stewart's A.T. Stewart and Company department store, which opened in New York City in 1860. It occupied the block between 9th and 10th Streets and between Broadway and Fourth Avenue.

2086. Chain store organization with a long existence was the Great Atlantic and Pacific Tea Company, better known as A&P. George Huntington Hartford was in the hide and leather business in New York City in 1857, and in 1859 he added tea to his merchandise. In 1864 he originated the Great American Tea Company, which developed into the Great Atlantic and Pacific Tea Company in 1869. He remained president of the firm until his death on August 29, 1917. Despite the name, the first store on the Pacific coast was not opened until January 1930. The stores later became a chain of supermarkets.

2087. Mail-order business was established by Aaron Montgomery Ward in 1872 in a 12-by-14-foot room at 825 North Clark Street, Chicago, IL, with $2,400 capital, one-third of which was advanced by George R. Thorne. The first catalog consisted of a single-sheet price list, 8 by 12 inches, without illustrations. It was issued on August 18, 1872, and inaugurated a money-back guarantee policy. In 1873, the catalog was increased to four pages and listed 394 items. Afterward, catalogs with descriptive pictures were issued and a 15-cent charge made for them. The first free catalogs, more than 3 million weighing four pounds each, were mailed in 1904.

2088. Store with fixed prices was the Mechanic's Store, opened in Sacramento, CA, in 1874 by David Lubin, a Polish Jewish immigrant. Traders and storekeepers usually bargained with their customers. Lubin's innovation was to mark each item of merchandise with a fixed price based on its value plus a small profit. Lubin went on to found the International Institute for Agriculture, which promoted cooperation and information exchange among the farmers and growers of 45 member nations and was later absorbed into the United Nations Food and Agriculture Organization.

2089. Five-cent store was opened in Utica, NY, on February 22, 1879, by Frank Winfield Woolworth. The store was a great disappointment as its sales after a few weeks were as low as $2.50 a day. Woolworth moved his store in June 1879 to Lancaster, PA, where it proved a success. He came up with the idea for a five-cent store on September 24, 1878, in Watertown, NY, when he originated a "five-cent table" in the store of Moore and Smith during the week of the county fair. The first joint venture of the Woolworth brothers in Harrisburg, PA, was called the "Great 5 Cent Store."

2090. Cooperative store at a college was the Harvard Cooperative Society, Cambridge, MA. The store was managed by students and sold merchandise to members at prices below retail. The store's constitution was presented on February 28, 1882, and by March 15 it had 400 subscribers. The plan was proposed by Charles Hayden Kip. Frank Bolles was the first president.

2091. Price tags made by machine were the invention of Frederick Kohnle of Dayton, OH. On August 18, 1891, he received a patent for a device, called a pin-ticketing machine, that would both print the tag and affix it to the merchandise.

2092. Discount clothing store was Filene's Automatic Bargain Basement, which opened in Boston, MA, in 1909. It was owned by a Prussian-American merchant, William Filene, and his sons Edward P. Filene and Abraham Lincoln Filene. The store sold discount apparel and dry goods.

2093. Self-service grocery store was the Piggly Wiggly in Memphis, TN, founded by Clarence Saunders in 1916. The store had four aisles containing 605 items. Saunders patented the idea in 1917.

2094. Shopping mall was Country Club Plaza, built in 1922 by Jesse Clyde Nichols as part of a new residential development on the outskirts of Kansas City, MO. Customers had to drive to get there, as it was not accessible by public transportation. The first shopping plaza in which the stores faced in toward the promenade, rather than out toward the access road, was the Highland Park Shopping Village in Dallas, TX, built in 1931.

2095. Shopping center in a suburban business area planned to cater exclusively to customers with cars was the Country Club Plaza, Kansas City, MO, built by Jesse Clyde Nichols from the master plan drawn by Edward Buehler Delk on April 22, 1922. Construction began in November 1922, and the first tenant moved in in March 1923. The center occupied 40 acres and had 150 stores, a 2,000-seat auditorium, and a parking lot for 5,500 automobiles.

2096. Self-service supermarket was the Big Bear Super Market, Elizabeth, NJ, which was opened in 1932 in an empty car factory by Robert M. Otis and Roy O. Dawson. It was the first large discount self-service grocery store. Meats, produce, canned and packaged foods, radios, automobile accessories, and paints, all at cut prices, were displayed on long pine tables.

2097. Cooperative store operated by women was the Montgomery Farm Women's Cooperative Market, Bethesda, MD, incorporated in August 1932 by 29 women.

2098. Liquor stores run by a state government were established by Pennsylvania in 1933. An act was passed by a special session of the legislature and signed by Governor Gifford Pinchot on November 29, 1933. On January 2, 1934, 90 stores were opened in various parts of the state, stocked and ready to do business.

2099. Retail store whose sales in one day exceeded $1 million was the R.H. Macy Company, New York City, whose sales on December 7, 1944, exceeded $1 million. On December 14, 1957, they first exceeded $2 million; on December 18, 1965, $3 million; and on December 18, 1967, $4 million.

2100. Food-O-Mat was installed in the Grand Union Company store in Carlstadt, NJ, on May 24, 1945. It was invented by Lansing Peter Shield. The patented merchandise display fixture operated on a gravity-feed, rear-load principle. Stockmen working behind the unit placed cans, jars, and packages on inclined runways with the labels upright. The items reached the shopper with the brand name uppermost. As the customer picked out an item, another slid in place by gravity.

2101. Enclosed climate-controlled suburban shopping mall was Southdale, in the Minneapolis suburb of Edina, MN, opened in 1956. Designed by Victor Gruen, it had two levels and a central "garden court." The arrangement was copied by thousands of similar projects in suburbs across the country.

2102. Pedestrian shopping mall was constructed in 1959 along a section of Burdick Street in downtown Kalamazoo, MI, which thereafter called itself "Mall City, U.S.A." Based on a design by Victor Gruen of Victor Gruen Associates, the mall was intended to protect the town's commercial center from the threat posed by large suburban malls, but the attempt was a failure. The lack of parking drove customers away and led to the decline of the stores that lined the mall. Gruen had designed a pedestrian mall for Fort Worth, TX, seven years earlier, in 1952, but it was never built.

2103. Wal-Mart store was opened in 1962 by Samuel Moore Walton of Kingfisher, OK. Wal-Mart went public in 1970 and became the largest retailer in American history.

2104. Hydrogen refueling station in the United States was opened on November 11, 2004, at a Shell service station in Washington, DC, by Shell Hydrogen, a subsidiary of Royal/Dutch Shell Group, in partnership with General Motors Corporation. The station pumped liquid hydrogen mainly for use by experimental fuel-cell vehicles.

Textiles

2105. Leather tanning in America is credited to the Native Americans. The first of the known tanners of European ancestry was Experience Miller, who came to Plymouth, MA, on the *Ann* in 1623.

2106. Silk culture was started about 1623 in Virginia, where the Colonial Assembly directed the planting of mulberry trees. In 1656, an act was passed in which silk was described as the most profitable commodity for the country. It imposed "a penalty of ten pounds of tobacco . . . upon every planter who should fail to plant at least ten mulberry trees for every hundred acres of land in his possession."

2107. Cloth mill was built in 1638 by John Pearson in Rowley, MA. According to Captain Edward Johnson's book, *Wonder-Working Providences of Sion's Savior in New England*, published in London in 1654, "the Lord brought over the zealous affected and judicious servant of His, Master Ezekiel Rogers, who with an holy and humble people, made his progress to the northeastward and erected a town about six miles from Ipswich, called Rowley—they were the first people that set upon making cloth in this western world."

2108. Fulling mill for making wool cloth was established by John Pearson in Rowley, MA, in 1643. It cleaned, felted, and shrank the cloth until the desired consistency was obtained. The mill was operated by emigrants from Yorkshire, England.

2109. Worsted mill for making wool yarn was established in 1695 in Boston, MA, by John Cornish. The mill cleaned the wool and removed the noil, or short fibers. The spinning of the yarn was done by local farmers. An appraisal of Cornish's estate revealed "two pairs of combs, four looms and tackling, and two dye furnaces."

2110. Calico printery was established in Boston, MA, by George Leason and Thomas Webber, who advertised in the *Boston News Letter*, April 21–28, 1712, that they had "set up a Callender-Mill and Dye House in Cambridge Street, Boston, near the Bowling Green where all gentlemen, Merchants, and others may have all sorts of Linnens, callicoes, stuffs or Silks Callendered: Prints all sorts of Linnens."

2111. Silk export took place in 1735 when a shipment of raw silk weighing eight pounds was exported from Savannah, GA, to England. The Trustees of Georgia reported in 1736: "The raw silk from Georgia, organized by Sir Thomas Lombe, was made into a piece of silk and presented to the queen." This entry appears in the manuscript book of the trustees. It is possible that some silk may have been sent previously from Virginia, where silk cultivation was first introduced.

2112. Fustians, everlastings, and coating were made commercially by Samuel Wetherill, Jr., of Philadelphia, PA. Prior to April 3, 1782, his products were sold at his dwelling house and factory on what was then South Alley, between Market and Arch Streets.

2113. Spinning jenny for cotton was put into operation by Daniel Jackson, a coppersmith of Providence, RI, in 1786. At first it was set up in a private house, but it was afterward removed to the upper room in the Market House.

2114. Textile machine that could spin, card, and rope was manufactured in 1786 by Hugh Orr with the help of Robert and Alexander Barr in their workshop in Bridgewater, MA. On November 16, 1786, the Senate granted them £200 for their ingenuity, and afterward granted them a further compensation of six tickets in the land lottery of that period.

2115. Sailcloth factory was the Boston Sail Cloth Factory, Boston, MA, established in 1788. It was two stories high and 180 feet long. In 1789, 30 women and girls working 26 looms turned out 40 yards each a week.

2116. Worsted mill operated by waterpower and the first operated on a strictly commercial basis was the Hartford Woolen Manufactory, Hartford, CT, which was organized on April 15, 1788. A capital of 1,250 pounds was raised by subscription in nearby towns. The largest contributor was Jeremiah Wadsworth. A bounty of one penny per pound was given for all yarn spun in the factory before June 1, 1789, as a means of encouraging the new industry. Waterpower had previously been used to power fulling mills.

2117. Cotton mill was established in Beverly, MA, sometime in 1788 by a company of proprietors known as the Beverly Cotton Manufactory. The company was incorporated on February 3, 1789, and was visited on October 30, 1789, by President George Washington. The spinning jenny spun 60 threads at one time and the carding machine carded 40 pounds of cotton a day. The mill's products were the first cotton goods to be trademarked. On June 6, 1788, it was enacted "that all goods which may be manufactured by the said corporation, shall have a label of lead affixed to one end thereof, which shall have the same impression as the seal of the corporation, and that if any person shall knowingly use a like seal or label with that used by said corporation, by annexing same to any cotton or cotton and linen goods, not manufactured by said corporation with a view of vending or distributing thereof, as the proper manufacture of said corporation, every person so offending shall forfeit and pay treble the value of said goods to be sued for and recovered for the use of said corporation, by action of debt, in any court of record proper to try the same."

2118. Cotton mill to spin cotton yarn successfully was started on December 20, 1790, by Samuel Slater in Pawtucket, RI. It was 40 feet long, 26 feet wide, and two stories high, with an attic. Power was obtained from the old fulling mill water wheel in Ezekiel Carpenter's clothier's shop on the east bank of the Blackstone River. Secretary of the Treasury Alexander Hamilton, in his report of December 5, 1791, said, "The manufactory at Providence has the merit of being the first in introducing into the United States the celebrated cotton mill, which not only furnishes materials for the manufactory itself but for the supply of private families, for household manufacturing."

2119. Broadcloth was produced in Pittsfield, MA, in 1793, from fleeces of the merino sheep of Arthur and John Scholfield.

2120. Wool carding machine was built by John and Arthur Scholfield in Newburyport, MA, and installed in a mill in Byfield, MA, in 1793. It was 25 inches wide and had a single cylinder 33 inches in diameter. It carried two workers and strippers, a fancy, and a 14-inch doffer cover with card clothing sheets. A fluted cylinder of 13 inches was arranged behind the doffer.

2121. Textile machinery patent was a patent for a carding and spinning machine, granted on February 14, 1794, to James Davenport, who established the Globe Mills, Philadelphia, PA.

2122. Leather-splitting machine to split leather to any thickness was invented by Samuel Parker of Billerica, MA, who received patents on July 9, 1808, and April 26, 1809, on "currying and finishing leather." This invention doubled the use of leather.

2123. Leather tanning by the oil tan method of preparing buckskin and other leathers was originated by Talmadge Edwards in Johnstown, NY, in 1810.

2124. Silk mill was erected in 1810 for the Mansfield Silk Company by Rodney and Horatio Hanks in Mansfield, CT, in a building 12 by 12 feet.

2125. Cotton mill entirely powered by water was established in 1813 by the Boston Manufacturing Company in Waltham, MA. This was the first cotton mill in the world in which the entire process of cotton manufacturing, from spinning to weaving, was carried on by water power under a single management. The mill workers were organized into departments and paid a fixed wage. Nathan Appleton, Francis Cabot Lowell, and Patrick Tracy Jackson were the main sponsors of this organization. The machinery was constructed by Paul Moody.

The Waltham machines were copies of those already in use in the mills of Manchester, England. Francis Cabot Lowell visited Manchester in 1811, observed the machines, and reconstructed them entirely from memory.

2126. Patent leather was tanned in 1819 in Newark, NJ, by Seth Boyden at the tannery that he had established in 1813. At first the varnish was dried in the sun, but later it was dried in a warm room. In 1820, Boyden made an oven to hold 16 skins.

2127. Felt manufacturing mechanical process was invented by Thomas Robinson Williams of Newport, RI, in 1820. The wool was carded and placed in layers until the desired thickness was obtained, the outside rolls being the finest in texture. The mass was then placed between rollers and partly immersed in water while it was beaten, pressed, and oscillated. Dyeing and finishing completed the process.

2128. Silk power loom with the figure or pattern of the cloth made on a chain was invented by William Crompton of Taunton, MA, who obtained a patent on November 25, 1837, on a figure power loom.

2129. Bunting manufacture was undertaken in 1838 by Michael Hodge Simpson at the New England Worsted Company, Saxonville, MA.

2130. Silk dyers to achieve success were Edward Vallentine and Lewis Leigh, who emigrated from England in 1838. They began business at Gurleyville, CT, and achieved fame by producing silk dyed permanently black.

2131. Elastic webbing was produced by power machinery in the plant of the Russell Manufacturing Company of Middletown, CT, in 1841, through the efforts of Henry Griswold Hubbard. The concern was incorporated in 1834 with a capital stock of $40,000, nine-tenths of which was owned by Samuel Russell and Samuel D. Hubbard. Originally the company manufactured nonelastic webbing, a venture which was not profitable. The elastic webbing, however, proved very successful.

2132. Oilcloth factory that was successful was erected in 1845 in Winthrop, ME, by Ezekiel Bailey. It was known as C.M. Bailey Sons and Company. Within 10 years, it was doing an annual business of $200,000.

2133. Gingham factory was opened in Clinton, MA, by Erastus Brigham Bigelow in 1846. It was named Lancaster Mills and was capitalized at $500,000. On April 10, 1845, Bigelow received a patent for his invention of gingham manufacturing machinery. Previously, all gingham had been made by hand at home.

2134. Mohair from Angora goats was commercially manufactured by the Arlington Mills, Lawrence, MA, in 1872.

2135. Chrome tanning process for tanning hides and skins through the action of a metallic salt was invented by Augustus Schultz of New York City, who was granted two patents on January 8, 1884. His process enabled leather to be tanned thinner and stronger than was possible by vegetable tanning.

2136. Silk loom of importance was the Gem Silk Loom, built in 1887 by the Knowles Loom Works, Worcester, MA. On April 23, 1887, three 40-inch, four-by-four box loom machines were ordered by the Empire Silk Company, Paterson, NJ. Crepes, chiffons, and fancy pattern material requiring up to 20 harnesses could be woven on this loom.

2137. Chrome-tanned leather successfully marketed was produced in 1890 by Robert Herman Foerderer of Philadelphia, PA, who devised a method by which the fibrous and gelatinous matter in animal skin could be prepared to receive tanning agents and a second method to overcome the brittle effect.

2138. Kapok was commercially introduced by the Netherlands on May 1, 1893, at the formal opening of the World's Columbian Exposition, Chicago, IL.

2139. Rayon made from cellulose was commercially produced by the American Viscose Company in Marcus Hook, PA, on December 19, 1910. Production in 1911 amounted to 362,000 pounds. The patents were acquired from the General Artificial Silk Company, Lansdowne, PA, which started in 1901. The term "rayon" was adopted in 1924 to replace "artificial silk" and similar names.

2140. Crepe was produced in France in 1912 and was introduced into New York City in the same year by the firm of Haas Brothers, who registered the name "crepe georgette" at the patent office on December 30, 1913, and commenced production in the United States.

2141. Synthetic fiber produced entirely from chemicals was nylon, invented by Dr. Wallace Hume Carothers, a chemist at E.I. du Pont de Nemours and Company, Wilmington, DE, who obtained a patent for it on February 16, 1937. The patent covered synthetic linear condensation polymers capable of being drawn into strong, pliable fibers, as well as the process for making them.

2142. Nylon was introduced to the public by its manufacturer, the E.I. du Pont de Nemours Company, at the Golden Gate International Exposition held in San Francisco, CA, in 1939.

2143. Artificial leather was Corfam, a durable and permeable poromeric material that looked and felt like leather. It was introduced to the press by E.I. du Pont de Nemours and Company, Wilmington, DE, on October 2, 1963, and to stores in 20 cities on January 27, 1964. It was used mainly for shoe uppers.

2144. Synthetic fabric that was waterproof and breathable was Gore-Tex, a fabric developed by Wilbert L. Gore and his son Robert Gore in 1969. Derived from polymer of tetrafluorethylene (PTFE, also called Teflon), which Wilbert Gore had helped develop at E.I. du Pont de Nemours and Company, Wilmington, DE. Gore-Tex was a laminated fabric that allowed water vapor to pass through while completely blocking water droplets. Gore-Tex was used in sports clothing, shoes, electronics, and medical applications.

2145. Thread as strong as steel was Kevlar aramid fiber, invented in 1976 by Dr. Stephanie L. Kwolek, a chemist at E.I. Du Pont de Nemours and Company, Wilmington, DE. Kevlar was used in bulletproof vests, radial tires, structural composites for aircraft and space vehicles, and other products that required extremely high strength and low weight. For her work, Kwolek received the American Chemical Society Award for creative invention in 1980.

DAILY LIFE

Birth

2146. Midwife to practice professionally was Tryn Jonas, an immigrant from Norway. She was employed by the Dutch West India Company circa 1625 as a midwife for the colony of New Amsterdam (now New York City).

2147. Birth registration law enacted by a state was passed by Georgia on December 19, 1823. It required the "clerks of the court of ordinary, in each county respectively to enter and register in a book" the dates of births of all persons upon due proof made by affidavit or oath. The clerk was entitled to charge 25 cents for each registration.

2148. Conjoined twins to attain fame were Chang and Eng Bunker, brought to Boston, MA, by Robert Hunter on August 16, 1829. They were born on April 15, 1811, in Bangesau, Siam, joined at the waist by a cartilaginous band. They were exhibited throughout the United States and later in Europe. They settled in Mount Airy, NC, and were married in April 1843 to two sisters, Sarah and Adelaide Yates. Chang had 10 children and Eng nine children. The name "Siamese twins," meaning twins whose bodies are connected in any of a variety of ways, is derived from them.

2149. Sextuplets recorded were three boys and three girls born on September 8, 1866, in Chicago, IL, to James and Jennie A. Lewis Bushnell. The midwife was Priscilla Bancroft and the attending physician was Dr. James Edwards. One of the sextuplets, Lucy, died at the age of two months, and one, Laberto, died at eight months. Of the surviving four, Norberto died at 68, and three—Alberto, Alice Elizabeth, and Alincia—were over 70 when they died. There was a previous report, in the *Boston Medical and Surgical Journal* of 1847, of the birth of sextuplets on June 27, 1846, to Mrs. Marr of Phipsburg, ME, but the report may have been a hoax.

2150. Quintuplets recorded were five boys born on February 13, 1875, in Watertown, WI, to Mrs. Edna Beecham Kanouse, wife of Edward Cole Kanouse. All five died within two weeks. There are earlier, unverified claims for quintuplet births in Mars Bluff, SC, in 1776 and in Monticello, IL, in 1800.

2151. Maternity clinic in the United States was opened on East 79th Street in Manhattan by the Women's City Club, a group of affluent New Yorkers, in 1917. The staff included an obstetrician and three nurses. The center provided prenatal care, classes for expectant parents, five days of postpartum care, and housekeeping help.

2152. Nurse midwife to practice in the United States was Mary Breckinridge. In 1925 she founded the Frontier Nursing Service in a remote area of Kentucky that had neither doctors nor paved roads. The organization, privately funded and based in Wendover, KY, built a network of clinics and outposts staffed by nurse midwives who made home visits on horseback, delivering health care to entire families.

2153. City law requiring reporting of premature births was passed on March 5, 1935, by Chicago, IL. It required physicians to report the birth of all premature babies within an hour after the birth. A supplemental item was added to the official birth certificate to show whether or not a baby was born prematurely.

2154. Quadruplets delivered by cesarean operation were Maureen, Kathleen, Eileen, and Michael Cirminello, born to Mr. and Mrs. Joseph Cirminello on November 1, 1944, in Philadelphia, PA. The cesarean section was performed under spinal anesthesia. The obstetrician in charge was Dr. John Calvin Ullery of Upper Darby, PA.

2155. Method of natural childbirth to be taught in the United States originated with Dr. Grantly Dick-Read, a British obstetrician, whose book *Childbirth Without Fear* was published in 1933. In 1947 he visited the United States for a lecture tour. He attributed labor pain to unnecessary fear and tension and recommended that expectant mothers learn the physiology of childbirth.

2156. Birth to be shown on closed-circuit television was shown in color on June 14, 1951, as part of the American Medical Association meeting at Atlantic City, NJ. Two thousand physicians and their families watched the birth of Michael Gallagher, who weighed 9 pounds 12 ounces.

2157. Test for newborn health was the Newborn Scoring System, invented by Dr. Virginia Apgar, professor of anesthesiology at Columbia University, New York City, and introduced in 1952. Commonly known as the Apgar Score, the test allows attendants at a birth to identify problems with the baby's breathing, circulation, muscle tone, reflexes, and color.

2158. Birth to be televised for the public took place on December 2, 1952, and was televised by KOA, Denver, CO, over 49 stations of the National Broadcasting Company. The birth was that of Gordon Campbell Kerr, who weighed 5 pounds 7 ounces, and was delivered by cesarean section in the hospital delivery room of the Colorado General Hospital of the University of Colorado Medical School, Denver. The parents were Lillian Kerr and John R. Kerr of Denver. The telecast was part of the "March of Medicine" program presented in conjunction with the annual clinical meeting of the American Medical Association.

2159. Freestanding birth center was founded in Raymondville, TX, in 1972 by Sister Angela Murdaugh of the Franciscan Sisters of Mary. It was a program of Su Clínica Familiar, an outpatient clinic for migrant workers. The center was staffed by certified nurse-midwives.

2160. Major city with a freestanding birth center was New York City, where two centers opened in 1975: the Elizabeth Seton Childbearing Center, in lower Manhattan, and the Maternity Center Association's Childbearing Center, on the upper East Side. Both were staffed by certified nurse-midwives.

2161. Child born in the United States through in vitro fertilization was Elizabeth Jordan Carr, born on December 28, 1981, at Norfolk Hospital, Norfolk, VA. Assisting in the fertilization process were Howard and Georgeanna S. Jones of the In Vitro Fertilization Clinic, Eastern Virginia Medical School, Norfolk. In this procedure, an ovum extracted from a woman is placed in a glass dish and mixed with sperm. (The term *in vitro* means "in glass" in Latin.) The resulting embryo is implanted in the uterus of the mother, who then becomes pregnant. The world's first child produced by in vitro fertilization was Louise Brown, conceived in Bristol, England, on January 1, 1979.

2162. Septuplets were born on May 21, 1985, in Orange, CA, to Patti Frustaci, a 30-year-old schoolteacher. It was the largest multiple birth in the history of the United States. One child was stillborn and three more died within a month. Two boys and one girl survived. Frustaci and her husband later filed a malpractice suit against her doctors and the infertility clinic where she had been treated.

2163. Trial of a surrogate mother for refusing to give up her baby took place in New Jersey in 1987, when Mary Beth Whitehead of Brick Township was sued by William and Elizabeth Stern of Tenafly for breach of contract. Whitehead had signed a contract with the Sterns in which she agreed to accept $10,000 as compensation for undergoing artificial insemination, carrying the pregnancy to term, and giving up all parental rights. She changed her mind after giving birth to the baby, who was known in court records as "Baby M." On March 31, 1987, the trial judge upheld the legality of the contract, but his decision was overturned on February 3, 1988, by the state supreme court, which ruled unanimously that commercial contracts for surrogate motherhood were illegal. A lower court allowed the Sterns to retain custody of the baby, but gave visiting rights to the mother.

2164. Ban on surrogate motherhood enacted by a state was signed into law on June 27, 1988, by Governor James J. Blanchard of Michigan. The act made it illegal for women to enter into contracts that require them to bear other people's children in exchange for money.

2165. Grandmother to give birth to her own grandchild in the United States was 42-year-old librarian Arlette Schweitzer of Aberdeen, SD. Schweitzer's daughter, Christa Uchytil, age 22, had been born without a uterus. Ova taken from Christa were fertilized with sperm from her husband Kevin and implanted in Schweitzer's uterus at the University of Minnesota Hospital and Clinic in Minneapolis, MN. On October 12, 1991, she gave birth to twins named Chad and Chelsea.

2166. State to recognize midwifery as a separate profession was New York, which established a midwifery board in 1992 to regulate the licensing of midwives. It also planned the development of a four-year educational course for midwives, separate from nursing programs.

2167. Triplets born several weeks apart were delivered to Delvonda and Bernard Boldin of Florida. The first triplet, Kenard, was born on November 23, 1995. He weighed 1 pound 4 ounces and required emergency care. Doctors gave Delvonda drugs to stop her labor and stitched her cervix closed to allow the other babies more time to develop. Two daughters, each weighing less than two pounds, were born by cesarean section 23 days later.

2168. Live childbirth broadcast on the Internet occurred on June 16, 1998, at the Arnold Palmer Hospital for Women and Children in Orlando, FL. The mother, Elizabeth Oliver, gave birth to a boy named Sean at 10:40 A.M. Eastern Daylight Time after labor was induced at 6 A.M. The attending doctor was Dr. Steve Carlan. A live video feed of the birth was digitized and streamed to AHN.com, a World Wide Web site sponsored by America's Health Network, a healthcare information television cable network based in Orlando. Some 1.4 million people worldwide linked to the Web site. The camera was located behind the mother's head and the viewers saw the event from her point of view; they did not see the actual birth.

2169. Octuplets known to have survived birth were born at St. Luke's Episcopal Hospital in Houston, TX, to Nkem Chukwu, age 27, and her husband Iyke Louis Udobi, American citizens born in Nigeria. The children were conceived with the use of fertility drugs. One daughter, Chukwuebuka Nkemjika, was born twelve weeks prematurely on December 8, 1998. The others were born by cesarean section on December 20 and ranged in weight from 10.3 ounces to 1 pound 16 ounces. Five were girls and two were boys. The tiniest baby died of heart and lung failure a few days later.

2170. State whose businesses were required to offer paid family leave was California. According to a law passed in September 2002 and put into effect on January 1, 2004, employees with new babies or very sick relatives at home were entitled to take six weeks of short-term disability leave while receiving 55 percent of their salaries. The insurance fund set up to cover the costs of the program was funded by employee contributions.

2171. State law banning gifts of free formula to new mothers by the hospitals where they gave birth was enacted by Massachusetts on December 20, 2005. The law was passed after studies showed that the routine practice of giving new mothers free samples of formula provided by the product's manufacturers increased the likelihood that the mothers would stop breast-feeding their babies early or would not breast-feed at all.

Children

2172. Colonial provision for the care of orphans and widows was made in February 1653 in New Amsterdam, the present borough of Manhattan in New York City, where two deacons of the colony's Reformed Dutch Church were charged with guarding the welfare of fatherless families.

2173. Orphanage was established in New Amsterdam (now New York City) in June 1654. Fifty orphan children were sent from Holland in order to help populate Manhattan Island. They arrived on the *Pereboom* and the *Gelderse Blom*. A resolution was passed and signed by the colony's administrator, Peter Stuyvesant, on November 9, 1654, "to hire the house of Mr. [Isaac] Allerton and lodge there the children sent over by the Poor-masters." This orphanage also received the orphan children of the early colonists.

2174. Children's magazine was published in Hartford, CT, by Barzillai Hudson and George Goodwin. It was called the *Children's Magazine: Calculated for the Use of Families and Schools*. Four issues were printed from January to April 1789, each containing 48 pages, and presenting an "abridgement of geography, essays on morality, religion, manners, etc., familiar letters, dialogues and select pieces of poetry."

2175. Maternity book for women was *Letters to Married Women on Nursing and the Management of Children*, by Dr. Hugh Smith, published in 1792 in Philadelphia, PA, by Mathew Carey. It contained 167 pages on subjects such as birthmarks, miscarriages, mother's milk, nursing, and weaning. It was printed from the sixth London edition.

2176. Book on child-rearing was *The Maternal Physician; A Treatise on the Nurture and Management of Infants, from the Birth until Two Years Old, Being the Result of Sixteen Years' Experience in the Nursery*, published in Philadelphia, PA, in 1810 by "An American Matron."

2177. Children's magazine of literary merit was *The Juvenile Miscellany*, founded by Lydia Maria Frances Child in 1826. It was a bimonthly and appeared from September 1826 to January 1829. It was published by Putnam and Hunt in Boston, MA. The first issue contained 108 pages.

2178. Toy distribution center was opened on September 24, 1832, at the New York University community center, New York City. The organizers collected and repaired old toys for distribution to children. The first director was Mrs. Ida Cash.

2179. Baby bottle was patented in 1841 by Charles M. Windship, Roxbury, MA. It was made of glass and was designed to fit against the mother's breast. Rubber nipples did not appear until 1845, when a patent was issued to Elijah Pratt of New York City, but they had a strong odor and were unpleasant to use.

2180. Vacation fund to send poor children to the country was established in 1847 by the Reverend William Augustus Muhlenberg, rector of the Church of the Holy Communion, New York City.

2181. Baby carriage was made by Charles Burton in 1848 in New York City. Protests were heard because the people wheeling them showed a tendency to hit pedestrians. Burton moved to England, where he opened a factory and obtained orders for his "perambulator" from Queen Victoria, Queen Isabella II of Spain, and the pasha of Egypt. The first baby carriage factory to be successfully operated was started in 1858 in Leominster, MA, under the name of F.W. and F.A. Whitney. This later became the F.A. Whitney Carriage Company. The carriages had two wheels, with a long tongue and a supporting standard in front, and were made of wood. In the first year, 75 carriages were built.

2182. Orphan train to relocate homeless children from city slums to rural neighborhoods brought some 30 children from Boston to New Hampshire and Vermont in 1850. It was sponsored by the Children's Mission for the Children of the Destitute. New York's first orphan train, organized by Charles Loring Brace of the Children's Aid Society, brought 46 destitute children to Dowagiac, MI, in September 1854.

2183. State adoption law to consider the interests of the child was passed by Massachusetts and signed into law on May 24, 1851. The law stipulated that judges hearing adoption petitions should make inquiry into whether the adoptive parent or parents "are of sufficient ability to bring up the child, and furnish suitable nurture and education."

2184. Baby show was held at Springfield, OH, on October 5, 1854, more in a spirit of jest than with serious intent. It met with instant favor and 127 babies were entered. The prize baby was the 10-month-old daughter of William Ronemus of Vienna, OH, who was awarded a silver plate service including a large salver worth $300. Three other prizes were awarded.

2185. Camp for boys that stressed outdoor recreation was Camp Comfort, Welch's Point, Milford, CT, established in August 1861, when Frederick William Gunn, founder of the Gunnery School, took 50 boys on a two-week camping trip. The camp was organized again in August 1863 and in August 1865. In 1867 Gunn started another camp at Point Beautiful on Lake Waramaug, Washington, CT, which operated for a two-week period in August for 12 successive years.

2186. Playground was erected in Boston, MA, in 1886 in the yard of the Children's Mission. Three piles of yellow sand were brought there. The first Boston school appropriation for playgrounds was made in 1899.

2187. Pediatrics book written for parents of importance was Dr. Luther Emmett Holt's *The Care and Feeding of Children, a Catechism for the Use of Mothers and Children's Nurses*, 66 pages, published in 1894 by D. Appleton and Company, New York City. It was dedicated to Mrs. Chapin, "the founder of the first training school for nurses of infants in America."

2188. Teddy bear was created in 1902 by Morris Michtom, a Russian-born toy maker from Brooklyn, New York City. Michtom took a liking to a political cartoon that showed President Theodore Roosevelt refusing to shoot a bear cub, and he put the cartoon in the window of his store along with a stuffed toy bear with button eyes. He began manufacturing the "Teddy's Bear" in 1903. The same cartoon independently inspired a German toy maker, Margaret Stieff, to market a similar bear beginning in 1904.

2189. Child welfare congress was the International Congress in America for the Welfare of the Child, held on March 10–17, 1908, in Washington, DC, under the auspices of the National Congress of Mothers. President Theodore Roosevelt addressed the congress.

2190. Child delinquency law enacted by a state was passed on April 28, 1909, by Colorado. The law made it illegal to "encourage, cause or contribute to the dependency, neglect or delinquency of a child."

2191. Boy Scouts of America uniformed troop was organized at the Central YMCA, Troy, NY, in the fall of 1911. The uniform was designed by Charles M. Connally of Troy and has since become standard equipment. The Boy Scouts of America, an organization for boys from nine years upward, was founded by Daniel Carter Beard, the author of *Boy Pioneers and Sons of Daniel Boone*, who took his inspiration from the Boy Scouts movement that had recently begun in England. It was incorporated in Washington, DC, on February 8, 1910, and was granted a federal charter by an act of Congress of June 15, 1916. The first Eagle Scout was Arthur Rose Eldred of the Oceanside, NY, troop, who received this distinction on August 21, 1912. Others may have qualified at about the same time, but his name is the first recorded.

2192. State welfare program for single mothers was implemented by Illinois in 1911. Known as the mothers' pension program, it provided cash payments to families lacking a male breadwinner, with the intention of keeping the children in school and out of the poorhouse. The payments were originally considered compensation for the mother's work in taking care of her children, but the rules eventually required many mothers to work outside the home.

2193. Scouting organization for girls was the Girl Guides, founded on March 12, 1912, in Savannah, GA, by Juliette Gordon Low and adapted from the Girl Guides organization in England. The name was changed to Girl Scouts in 1913. The first Girl Guide was Mrs. Low's niece, Daisy Gordon. Another scouting organization, the Camp Fire Girls, was developed by Mrs. Luther Halsey Gulick at her camp at Lake Sebago, ME, and was made public on March 17, 1912. The group's watchword was "Wohelo," made from the first two letters of each of the words Work, Health, and Love.

2194. Home studies for foster and adoptive parents were required by Minnesota in 1917. The state board of control was given the responsibility for investigating the conditions in the home, as well as the adoptability of the child, and for submitting a written report giving its recommendations.

2195. Sale of Girl Scout cookies as a method of raising money for troop activities began in December 1917, when the Mistletoe Troop of Muskogee, OK, baked cookies and sold them in the high school cafeteria. Widespread door-to-door sales of Girl Scout cookies began after troop leader Florence E. Neil wrote an article in the July 1922 issue of *The American Girl* magazine, in which she suggested that batches of sugar cookies could be sold for 25 or 30 cents per dozen. In 1936 the national Girl Scout organization began licensing commercial bakers to produce Girl Scout–branded cookies for sale by local councils.

2196. Youth hostel was opened on December 27, 1934, in Northfield, MA, as the headquarters of the American Youth Hostels organization, incorporated on March 15, 1934, in Hartford, CT. The organization was the 18th member of the International Youth Hostels. Isabel and Monroe Smith were appointed directors of the American group.

2197. Federal directions for sealing birth records of adopted children and replacing them with amended records were made in 1949 by the U.S. Children's Bureau. The same report stated that the registrar in each state should maintain a record of the original birth certificate in case the adopted individual should require access to it.

2198. Disposable diapers were Boaters, invented in 1950 by a New York City mother, Marion Donovan. They consisted of an absorbent pad attached to a waterproof backing and were fastened on the baby with snaps. The first mass-market disposable diapers were Pampers, introduced in Peoria, IL, by Procter and Gamble of Cincinnati, OH, in 1961. They cost 10 cents each. After consumers complained about the price, the company withdrew them from the market and reintroduced them in Sacramento, CA, in 1966 for six cents each. The first disposable diapers with adhesive tabs to replace safety pins were Kimbies, made by Kimberly-Clark, Dallas, TX, in the early 1970s. Procter and Gamble's Luvs, introduced in 1976, were the first to come with an elastic fit.

2199. Barbie doll was invented in 1959 by Ruth and Eliot Handler, the founders of Mattel, a toy company in El Segundo, CA. The plastic doll, designed to appeal to fashion-conscious girls, was named after their daughter Barbara. They also introduced a male doll to serve as Barbie's boyfriend; he was named after their son Ken. The first human-sized Barbie was released by Mattel in 1992. It was three feet tall and sized to fit real girls' clothes.

2200. Toy action figure was G.I. Joe, introduced in February 1964 by Hasbro, Pawtucket, RI. It cost $2.49. It was the first mass-market doll intended exclusively for boys and, despite predictions to the contrary, was a great success, especially during the Vietnam War years.

2201. Organization for reuniting birthmothers and adopted children was the Adoptees' Liberty Movement Association, founded by Florence Ladden Fisher in New York City in 1971.

2202. Baby carrier to be mass-produced was the Snugli, a corduroy pouch that could be strapped on a parent's front or back. It was created by Ann Moore, a Peace Corps volunteer from Colorado who observed traditional African infant carriers when she was in Togo in the early 1960s. Moore patented the Snugli in 1977.

2203. State to decriminalize public breast-feeding was New York. In 1984 the legislature amended its laws against indecent exposure, affirming that they do not apply to mothers nursing their children.

2204. State to guarantee mothers the right to breast-feed in public was Florida. Its statute, which became law on March 9, 1993, encouraged breast-feeding as a natural act and protected breast-feeding mothers from being charged with obscenity or public nudity.

2205. State to mandate workplace accommodations for breast-feeding mothers was Minnesota. The 1998 law required employers of nursing mothers to give them a clean, private place in which to express milk and unpaid break time in which to do it.

2206. State law allowing sealed birth records of adopted children to be opened was passed on November 3, 1998, when Oregon voters passed Ballot Measure 58. It repealed a 1957 law that prevented adults who had been adopted from viewing and acquiring their original birth certificates.

2207. Sex discrimination case to establish the rights of fathers of newborn babies under the Federal Family and Medical Leave Act of 1993 was the result of a lawsuit brought by Kevin Knussman, a Maryland state trooper and helicopter paramedic, who was denied an extension of paid parental leave after the premature birth of his daughter and the hospitalization of his wife in December 1994. Although Maryland law allowed state employees with primary responsibility for newborns to take 30 days of sick leave, Knussman was not allowed to do so because he was the father, not the mother. On February 3, 1999, a jury ruled in his favor and awarded him $375,000.

Cleaning

2208. Soap manufacturer to render fats in his plant for soap stock was William Colgate, who opened a factory in 1806 at 6 Dutch Street, New York City. He had learned his trade at 50 Broadway, New York City, in the plant of John Slidell and Company.

2209. Brushes were manufactured at Medfield, MA, in 1808 by Artemas Woodward.

2210. Cakes of soap of uniform weight and individually wrapped were manufactured by Jessie Oakley of Newburgh, NY, about 1830. Cakes of soap were usually sold to grocers in large blocks from which pieces were cut as desired. Oakley prepared one-pound packages.

2211. Laundry was established in 1835 by Independence Starks, a manufacturer of Troy, NY, at 66 North Second Street, to wash and press the products of his own factory and of nearby collar makers.

2212. Soap powder in packages was introduced by Benjamin Talbert Babbitt about 1845. Rather than remelt the waste shavings of soap, he packaged the shavings in two-pound boxes. This innovation met with instant success at laundries and hotels.

2213. Chinese laundry opened in 1851 in San Francisco, CA. Most of its customers were gold miners. California miners had been sending their dirty clothes to Chinese laundries in Hawaii since the beginning of the Gold Rush in 1849.

2214. Washing machine with rotary motion was made by Hamilton Erastus Smith of Philadelphia, PA, who obtained a patent on October 26, 1858. It was equipped with a crank that was turned by hand, caused a perforated cylinder within a wooden shell to revolve. Smith continued to improve his machine and in 1863 secured patent protection on a self-reversing-motion attachment to the machine.

2215. Soap in liquid form was patented on August 22, 1865, by William Sheppard of New York City. It was made by mixing a pound of common soap with 100 pounds of ammonia solution or spirits of hartshorn. The soap was dissolved in water or by steam to the consistency of molasses.

2216. Vacuum cleaner that used suction was invented by Ives W. McGaffey of Chicago, IL, who obtained a patent on June 8, 1869, on a "sweeping machine," a light hand-powered suction device for surface cleaning.

2217. Carpet sweeper that was practical was invented in 1876 by Melville Reuben Bissell of Grand Rapids, MI, who obtained a patent for it on September 19, 1876. Although the idea had been introduced earlier, none of the early sweepers worked well. Bissell devised the "broom-action" principle, by which the application of variable pressure on the handle made the sweeper responsive to different grades of floor coverings. Bissell organized the Bissell Carpet Sweeper Company in Grand Rapids, MI.

2218. Dishwasher was invented by Josephine Cochrane of Shelbyville, IL, in 1886. Her initial design was a large copper tub outfitted with removable wire dish racks. Hot soapy water was pumped over the dishes by turning a crank. The Cochrane dishwasher was patented in December 1886 and won an award at the 1893 World's Columbian Exposition in Chicago.

2219. Vacuum cleaner driven by a motor was invented by John S. Thurman of the General Compressed Air and Vacuum Machinery Company, St. Louis, MO, who obtained a patent on October 3, 1899, on a "pneumatic carpet renovator."

2220. Laundry detergent packaged in a form that eliminated the need to slice up a bar of laundry soap was Lux Flakes, introduced by Lever Brothers in 1906. The first granulated detergent, Rinso, was introduced by Lever Brothers in 1918.

2221. Electric washing machine was a Thor machine, which was put on the market in 1907 by the Hurley Machine Company of Chicago, IL. A patent was granted on August 9, 1910, to Alva J. Fisher of Chicago, IL, for a "drive mechanism for washing machines."

2222. Vacuum cleaner with a disposable bag was made by the Air Way Sanitizer Company of Toledo, OH, in 1920. The bag, made of paper, was designed to fit inside a large cloth compartment that received the vacuumed dirt.

2223. Clothes dryer was an invention of J. Ross Moore of Devil's Lake, ND. To spare his mother from having to go outside to hang up the laundry in bone-chilling winter weather, he built an oil-heated drum that he set up in a shed next to the house. Beginning in 1930, he worked on a series of crude drying machines. He eventually sold the idea to the Hamilton Manufacturing Company, Two Rivers, WI, which began selling dryers in 1938.

2224. Synthetic laundry detergent whose formula included a surfactant to emulsify dirt was Dreft, first marketed on October 10, 1933, by the Procter and Gamble Company, Cincinnati, OH. It was a sodium alkyl sulfate made from chlorosulfonic acid and a fatty alcohol. The first effective powdered detergent made for use in washing machines, and the first to contain a phosphate compound as a water softener, was Tide, developed by Procter and Gamble in 1946.

2225. Laundromat was installed by J. F. Cantrell in a "washateria" in Fort Worth, TX, on April 18, 1934. Four electric washing machines were rented by the hour to those who wished to do their laundry. Hot water and electricity were supplied, but users were obliged to furnish their own soap.

2226. Cellulose sponge for household use was made in 1936 by Dr. William Orlin Kenyon of the Tennessee Eastman Company, Kingsport, TN, a division of the Eastman Kodak Company, Rochester, NY.

2227. Automatic washing machine was the Model S, introduced in 1937 at a county fair in Louisiana. The inventor was John Chamberlain, an engineer at Bendix Home Appliances, part of the Bendix Hydraulic Brake Company, South Bend, IN. The Model S required no more effort from the consumer than to load the soap and laundry and to set dials twice during the washing cycle. Bendix introduced a fully automatic model in 1947.

Clothing

2228. Shoes to be manufactured were made in 1628 by Thomas Beard, who came over on the *Mayflower*. Prior to that date, shoes were imported from England. The colonists also learned from the Native Americans how to make moccasins, which were so well liked that as early as 1650 they were exported to England.

2229. Shoe measuring stick was introduced as early as 1657. A dispute arose in court with regard to shoe sizes, and the court was informed that William Newman of Stamford, CT, "hath an instrument in his hand, which he brought out of England, which is thought to be right to determine the question between the buyer and the seller." The court "did ordain that the said instrument should be procured and sent to New Haven."

2230. Umbrella is believed to have been used in Windsor, CT, in 1740. It produced a riot of merriment and derision, with the neighbors parading after the user, carrying sieves balanced on broom handles. Umbrellas were invented by Jonas Hanway, a British merchant and philanthropist.

2231. Hat factory is believed to have been established in Danbury, CT, in 1780 by Zadoc Benedict. He employed one journeyman and two apprentices whose total output was about 18 hats a week. They were made from rabbit and beaver fur and sold for $6 to $10 apiece. They were described as being "without elegance, being heavy, rough and unwieldy."

2232. Buttons of pewter or block tin were manufactured in 1790 in Waterbury, CT, by Henry, Silas, and Samuel Grilley, three brothers who established a small factory on Waterbury's Bunker Hill. The buttons were cast in molds. The eyes were originally cast of the same material. Later, wire eyes were used.

2233. Straw hats were made in June 1798 by 12-year-old Betsey Metcalf of Providence, RI. She plaited seven strands of oat straws into braid and fashioned them into bonnets, which she trimmed with ribbons. The hats were lined with pink satin and sold for $1 to $1.25.

2234. Gilt buttons to be commercially manufactured were produced in 1802 by Abel Porter and Company of Waterbury, CT. This concern later developed into the Scovill Manufacturing Company of Waterbury, CT.

2235. Gloves manufactured in commercial quantities were made in 1809 by Talmadge Edwards of Johnstown, NY, whose small shop employed home-based stitchers.

2236. Shoe peg was invented by Joseph Walker of Hopkinton, MA, in 1818. Prior to his invention, all shoe soles were sewn.

2237. Detachable collar was made in 1825 in Troy, NY, by Hannah Lord Montague, who, tired of washing her husband's shirts merely because the collar was dirty, took scissors and performed the amputation that created a new style in men's apparel.

2238. Cloth-covered buttons were made by hand in Easthampton, MA, in 1826 by Mrs. Samuel Williston, who was the first to introduce their use commercially in the United States. Her husband formed a partnership with Joel Hayden, who invented the first machine for making covered buttons. The partnership lasted until 1848, when Williston bought out his partner and conducted the business alone.

2239. Circus tights are believed to have been introduced in 1828 by Nelson Hower, a bareback rider in the Buckley and Wicks Show, as the result of a mishap. The performers wore short jackets, knee breeches, and stockings, but Hower's costume failed to arrive and he appeared for the show in his long knit underwear.

2240. Collar manufacturer to make detachable collars was Ebenezer Brown, who started in Troy, NY, in 1829. He hired a number of women to make, wash, and iron the collars, giving in payment merchandise from his retail store, located at 285 River Street. These collars, which were known as string collars because they were tied about the neck with a string, were placed in paper boxes 16 or more inches in length, and were sold in his store.

2241. Hooks and eyes were successfully manufactured in 1836 in Waterbury, CT, by Holmes and Hotchkiss.

2242. Rubber shoe manufacturer was Leverett Candee, who established the L. Candee Shoe Factory in Hamden, CT, in 1842. He used the Goodyear vulcanizing patent. Prior attempts had been made in 1823 and 1831 to manufacture rubber footwear out of gum elastic, but the shoes were not serviceable. They melted and produced offensive odors.

2243. Shirt factory of importance was established in Boston, MA, in 1848 by Oliver Fisher Winchester.

2244. Bloomers were introduced at Lyceum Hall in Seneca Falls, NY, on July 19, 1848, during the First Woman's Rights Convention. They were long, full, ankle-length pants covered by a skirt that reached below the knees. The designer of the garment was Elizabeth Smith Miller, a well-to-do New York City housewife who wanted something practical to wear while she was gardening. The name was derived from the woman who first wore them in public, Amelia Jenks Bloomer, editor of the feminist magazine *Lily*, who was interested in reforming women's restrictive clothing customs.

2245. Derby hat was manufactured by James Henry Knapp of Knapp and Gilliam, South Norwalk, CT, in 1850. The first derbies were sold to New York jobbers Henderson and Bird, who sold 18 each of brown and black to a retail store on Broadway and Ninth Street, New York City. An English clerk suggested "Derby," after the famous English horse race, as the name of the hat. The word is pronounced "darby" in England and "derby" in the United States.

2246. Felt hats for women were introduced in New York City in 1851 by John Nicholas Genin, who took low-crowned soft black hats, fastened the left side of the brim of each to the crown, and ornamented it with a black feather. Prior to this time, women wore bonnets. Genin created the new style to celebrate the arrival of Lajos Kossuth, the Hungarian patriot, who arrived in New York City on December 5, 1851, on board the *Mississippi.*

2247. Paper collar was invented by Walter Hunt of New York City, who obtained a patent for it on July 25, 1854. He used a thin white cotton muslin and coated both sides with very thin white paper, with a layer of paste interposed between them. The collars were then varnished with a colorless bleached shellac that made them proof against perspiration; they could be wiped clean with a damp cloth.

2248. Shoe manufacturing machine was the McKay stitching machine, which revolutionized shoe manufacturing methods. It was invented by Lyman Reed Blake of Abington, MA, who obtained patents on July 6, 1858. The upper was lasted upon the insole by means of tacks driven through the insole and clinched against the steel bottom of the last. The outsole was then attached to the insole and upper by the McKay sewing machine, which made a chain stitch through and through to the inside of the shoe. The surface of the insole was then covered by a lining. The machine was introduced in the factory of William Porter and Sons, Lynn, MA, in 1861. It was probably operated by foot power.

2249. Cowboy hat was the invention of hatmaker John B. Stetson of Philadelphia, PA. In 1860, he designed the original wide-brimmed, high-crowned "10-gallon" hat to appeal to wealthy cattle ranchers who ordered their clothing back east. Before the Stetson, cowboys wore no special headgear.

2250. Snowshoe production for commercial purposes was undertaken in 1862 in Norway, ME, by Alanson Millen Dunham, Jr.

2251. Fashion magazine was *Harper's Bazaar*, "a Repository of Fashion, Pleasure and Instruction," whose first issue, 16 pages long, was published on November 2, 1867, by Harper and Brothers in New York City. It cost 10 cents a week or $4 a year. Potential readers were invited to write to the publishers to receive free copies of the first six issues. The magazine was edited by Mary Louise Booth and appeared as a weekly from November 1867 to April 1901, when it changed to a monthly. Within 10 years it had a circulation of 80,000.

2252. Earmuffs were invented in 1873 by Chester Greenwood of Farmington, ME, who commenced manufacturing them commercially the following year. He obtained a patent on March 13, 1877, on what he called "ear mufflers."

2253. Corset manufactured by a factory as a health item rather than a fashion article was made July 1874 by Warner Brothers, a partnership of Dr. Ira DeVer Warner and Dr. Lucien Calvin Warner, in McGraw, NY. The corset combined three garments in one—a corset, a skirt supporter, and self-adjusting pads—and had shoulder straps.

2254. Tuxedo coat was worn to the Autumn Ball at the Tuxedo Club in Tuxedo Park, NY, on October 10, 1886. Pierre Lorillard IV, heir to a tobacco fortune and the biggest landowner in town, asked his tailor to create four new formal black jackets modeled after the tailless red wool coats worn by English fox hunters. Lorillard declined to wear the result, but his son Griswold Lorillard and three of his friends did, along with waistcoats of scarlet satin, and the look caught on.

2255. Ready-made clothing for children was introduced in New York City by Louis Borgenicht, a Jewish immigrant from Poland who sold household goods out of a pushcart. He and his wife began sewing aprons and dresses for children in 1889.

2256. Slide fastener was invented by Whitcomb L. Judson of Chicago, IL, who obtained a patent on August 29, 1893, on a clasp locker for shoes. His design consisted of two metal chains made up of hook-and-eye locks that were fastened together by the movement of a slider. The patents were assigned to the Universal Fastener Company in Illinois. The fasteners were first manufactured in 1893 by the Automatic Hook and Eye Company of Meadville, PA, through the efforts of Colonel Lewis Walker. They jammed frequently and were not widely used.

2257. Uniforms for working women were made by Henry A. Dix, born Henry Dickstein in the Ukraine. Dix and his wife were shopkeepers in Millville, NJ, who went into business sewing ready-made dresses for women. In 1896 they switched their three factories to the production of uniforms for nurses, waitresses, maids, and saleswomen.

2258. Rubber shoe heel was made in Lowell, MA, by Humphrey O'Sullivan. He obtained a patent on January 24, 1899, on a "safety-heel."

2259. Maternity clothes to be manufactured were made by Lane Bryant (Lena Himmelstein), a New York City seamstress who had emigrated from Lithuania. Her first design for pregnant women, made circa 1904, was a dress with expandable accordion pleats, described as "A Self Adjustable Dress."

Since newspapers refused to run ads for maternity clothes, Lane Bryant and her husband, Albert Malsin, started the first mail-order catalog for maternity wear.

2260. Brassiere patent was granted in November 1914 to Mary Phelps Jacobs (later known as Caresse Crosby), a New York socialite, for the Backless Brassiere, which was designed to be worn under a sheer evening gown. Her original model was made of two white handkerchiefs, a length of satin ribbon, and some cord. In 1915 she sold her patent rights to the Warner Brothers Corset Company of Bridgeport, NY, for $1,500. Standardized sizes for bras were introduced in the 1920s by dressmaker Ida Kaganovich Rosenthal, a Russian-Jewish immigrant who founded the Maidenform company.

2261. Zipper was invented about 1906 by Gideon Sundback of Hoboken, NJ, an inventor of Swedish ancestry, who obtained a patent on April 29, 1913, on "separable fasteners." His design consisted of two flexible tapes, each of which carried a row of metal teeth with tiny hooks, and a slider that locked the two rows of hooks together. This fastener was improved upon by later patents obtained on March 20 and October 16, 1917, which were assigned to the Hookless Fastener Company of Meadville, PA, under the name "Talon." The first manufactured garments to incorporate zippers were rubber boots made by the B.F. Goodrich Company in 1923. The term "zipper" was coined by the English novelist Gilbert Frankau, who saw the device at a promotional luncheon and exclaimed: "Zip! It's open! Zip! It's closed!" The first fashion designer to use zippers was Elsa Schiaparelli, who added them to garments in her 1930 collection.

2262. Swimsuit of stretch fabric was made by the Portland Knitting Mills, Portland, OR, in 1915, using a lightweight woolen rib-knit cloth invented by Carl Jantzen, a Danish immigrant who was a partner in the company. He designed a body-hugging athletic costume for the Portland rowing team that was quickly adopted by swimmers. Bathing suits previously consisted of baggy clothes that covered the swimmer from neck to ankle.

2263. Sneakers with rubber soles and plain cloth uppers were sold from the early 1870s by Charles Goodyear of New York City, who developed the vulcanized rubber shoe sole, and by many other footwear companies. The first brand of sneakers was Keds, introduced in 1916 by the United States Rubber Company, the successor to Goodyear's shoe company. The first Keds had black soles and high-top brown canvas uppers, mimicking leather shoes. The name was a combination of "kids" and *ped*, the Latin word for "foot."

2264. Dictionary compiled by a woman was *The Language of Fashion*, edited by Mary Brooks Picken, published on February 2, 1940, in New York City. It contained 8,000 terms and 600 illustrations relating to clothing.

2265. Nylon stockings went on sale on May 15, 1940, "Nylon Day," at selected stores throughout the country. The merchandise was fought over by mobs of shoppers reacting to advertisements by the manufacturer of nylon, E.I. Du Pont de Nemours and Company of Wilmington, DE, which announced that nylon stockings, unlike silk, would be virtually indestructible. This was the first use of a synthetic fabric for an article of clothing. By the end of 1940, 36 million pairs of nylon stockings had been sold.

2266. Running shoes of the modern variety were introduced in 1962 by New Balance, Boston, MA, a company that specialized in orthopedic shoes. Known as Tracksters, they featured a one-piece rippled sole and a rubber shock-absorber in the heel.

2267. Clothing designer of international renown who was born in the United States was Roy Halston Frowick, born in Des Moines, IA, in 1932. He began his career as a milliner in Chicago, IL, and introduced his first complete line of women's apparel at Bergdorf Goodman in New York City in 1966, using the name Halston. In 1968 he became the first American designer to have his own freestanding couture establishment. He ceased to design professionally in 1984 and died of AIDS on March 26, 1990.

2268. Sports bra was invented in 1978 by Lisa Zobian-Lindahl, a runner, and Hinda Miller, a professional costume designer, both of Vermont. The product was called the Jogbra. The original consisted of two modified jock straps sewn together. Early commercial versions of the Jogbra were purchased for the permanent collections of the Smithsonian Institution, Washington, DC, and the Costume Collection of the Metropolitan Museum of Art, New York City.

Cooking

2269. Cooking pots made in America were cast-iron pots with three legs and a capacity of one quart. They were made in 1643 at the Saugus Iron Works, Lynn, MA.

2270. Tinware manufacturers are said to have been Edward and William Pattison, brothers who settled in Berlin, CT, about 1740 and manufactured kitchen vessels and household articles from sheet tin. They peddled their wares from house to house. The first successful tinware manufacturers were Lalance and Grosjean, who in 1860 established a factory at Woodhaven, NY, for the manufacture of deep tinware, such as milk pans, wash bowls, and dishpans.

2271. Refrigerator was invented in 1803 by Thomas Moore of Baltimore, MD. It consisted of two boxes, one inside the other, separated by insulating material. Ice and food were stored in the inner box. Moore granted manufacturing licenses for his invention, but gave poor people permission to copy it free of charge. The invention was described in a 28-page pamphlet, "An essay on the most eligible construction of ice houses, also, a description of the newly invented machine, called the Refrigerator."

2272. Apple parer was invented on February 14, 1803, by Moses Coats, a mechanic of Downington, PA.

2273. Brass kettles were made in 1834 in Wolcottville (now Torrington), CT, by Israel Coe, who organized the Coe Brass Company.

2274. Ice-making machine of the vapor compression type to be made in commercial quantities was invented in 1834 by Jacob Perkins, an American living in London. He obtained a British patent on August 14, 1834, for an "apparatus for producing ice and cooling liquids." Perkins showed that vapors or gases that do not ordinarily exist in liquid state may be liquefied upon being subjected to high pressure.

2275. Mechanical freezer patent was granted Dr. John Gorrie of Apalachicola, FL, on May 6, 1851, on an "improvement in the process for the artificial production of ice." At a dinner on July 14, 1850, at the Mansion House, Apalachicola, Gorrie produced blocks of ice the size of bricks. He installed his system in the U.S. Marine Hospital in Apalachicola.

2276. Can opener of practical value was invented by Ezra J. Warner of Waterbury, CT, in 1858. It was essentially a hook and a short blade attached to a handle. The user pierced the top of a sealed can with the hook and then ripped a hole with the blade, repeating the action all around the rim. Previously, people had used everything from knives to bayonets to a hammer and chisel to open cans. Warner's design was adopted by the army and used by soldiers in the Civil War. The first can opener of the modern type with a cutting wheel was patented by William W. Lyman in 1870. Electric can openers appeared in December 1931.

2277. Electric range was invented by George B. Simpson of Washington, DC, who received a patent on September 20, 1859, on an "electrical heating apparatus" that he called an electroheater. The machine generated heat by passing currents of electricity over coils of platina or other metallic wire.

2278. Coffee percolator was patented by James H. Nason of Franklin, MA, on December 26, 1865.

2279. Waffle iron patent was issued on August 24, 1869, to Cornelius Swarthout of Troy, NY.

2280. Doughnut cutter was invented by John F. Blondel of Thomaston, ME, who obtained a patent on July 9, 1872. A spring pushed the dough out of a center tube to make the hole.

2281. Slicing machine was patented on November 4, 1873, by Anthony Iske of Lancaster, PA, who obtained a patent on a "machine for slicing dried beef." It employed an oblique knife in a vertical sliding frame.

2282. Aluminum pots were made possible by Charles Martin Hall of Oberlin, OH, who on February 23, 1886, invented a simplified procedure for producing aluminum. His line of cast aluminum cookware, called Wear-Ever, met with indifference until 1903, when the Wanamaker's department store in Philadelphia, gave a demonstration in which a chef made apple butter in a a lightweight aluminum pan without needing to stir it. Aluminum pots quickly became standard kitchen equipment.

2283. Electric stove was a one-ring spiral-coiled conductor invented by William S. Hadaway, Jr., of New York City, who obtained a patent on June 30, 1896. It provided a uniform surface distribution of heat.

2284. Toaster with a pop-up action was developed by mechanic Charles Strite of Stillwater, MN. On May 29, 1919, he applied for a patent on a device that could toast and eject bread when positioned over a fire.

2285. Electric blender was invented by Stephen J. Paplawski of Racine, WI. In 1922 he patented an electric blender designed to make milkshakes for the burgeoning soda-fountain industry.

2286. Electric toaster of the household automatic pop-up type was marketed in June 1926 by the McGraw Electric Company, Minneapolis, MN, under the trademark Toastmaster. One lever lowered the bread into the toaster and another wound the timer. It received one slice of toast at a time. The retail price was $13.50.

2287. Gas refrigerator to be successfully introduced into the American market was the Electrolux, which was sponsored in 1926 by the Electrolux Refrigerator Sales Company of

Evansville, IN. A tiny gas flame and a tiny flow of water in the refrigerator took the place of all moving parts, circulating a liquid refrigerant that was hermetically sealed in rigid steel. The first patent issued to the Electrolux Servel Corporation on an absorption refrigerating apparatus was granted on December 7, 1926, to Baltzar Carl von Platen and Georg Munters of Stockholm, Sweden.

2288. Microwave oven for commercial food preparation was introduced by the Raytheon Company, Lexington, MA, in 1947. It was based on research into microwave-generating magnetron tubes by Raytheon scientist Percy Spencer. Spencer was standing near a magnetron when he noticed that a candy bar in his pants pocket had melted, although he had felt no heat. The first microwave oven for home use was the Tappan Oven, which was sold beginning in 1952 by the Tappan Corporation, Tappan, NY, for $1,295.

2289. Electronic range for domestic use was introduced at a press conference at the Hotel Pierre, New York City, on October 25, 1955, by the Tappan Stove Company, Mansfield, OH. A 220-volt electric current produced microwaves that cooked eggs in 22 seconds, bacon in 90 seconds, frozen broccoli in 4.5 minutes, and a five-pound roast in 30 minutes. The retail price of the range was $1,200.

2290. Food processor marketed in the United States was the Cuisinart, introduced in January 1973 at the Chicago Housewares Show, Chicago, IL. It was made by Carl Sontheimer, a Connecticut electronics engineer, who borrowed the basic idea from processing machines invented by the French chef Pierre Verdun. The Cuisinart had exchangeable blades that could divide and blend food in a multiplicity of ways, including grinding, chopping, slicing, mincing, mixing, and pureeing.

Death

2291. Autopsy was performed in what is now the state of Florida in 1536 on Philippe Rougement (Felipe de Rojamón), 22 years old, a victim of the plague or scurvy.

2292. Autopsy officially recorded took place at Salem, MA, in September 1639. In his *History of New England*, John Winthrop wrote: "This boy was ill-disposed, and his master gave him unreasonable correction and used him ill in his diet. After the boy gate a bruise on his head, so as there appeared a fracture in his skull, being dissected after his death." Marmaduke Perry of Salem was arraigned for the death of his apprentice.

2293. Lead coffins used in the New World were three caskets dating from the 17th century. Archeologists found them at St. Mary's City, MD, in the ruins of the first Catholic church built in England's North American colonies. They contained the remains of former Maryland governor Philip Calvert, his first wife, and his infant daughter by his second wife. Calvert died in 1661.

2294. Jewish cemetery was established in New York City by Congregation Shearith Israel, the first Jewish congregation in America, in 1656. The plot occupied a piece of ground in the section now known as Chatham Square. It was consecrated on February 22, 1656.

2295. Autopsy with verdict of a coroner's jury was recorded in Maryland on September 24, 1657. The surgeon received his fee of "one hogshead of tobacco" for "dissecting and viewing the corpse" of an African-American slave thought to have been murdered by his master.

2296. Identification of human remains using dental evidence was made in March 1776 by Paul Revere, the Boston silversmith and revolutionary. Revere supplemented his income by making false teeth out of ivory and other materials and wiring them in place using silver wire. One of his patients was Dr. Joseph Warren, a leader of the Boston rebels (in April 1775 he had sent Revere on his famous ride to Lexington to warn of the approach of the British army). Warren was shot in the face during the Battle of Bunker Hill at Charlestown, MA, on June 17, 1775, and was buried by the British in an unmarked grave. After the British ended their occupation of Boston and Charlestown the following March, Warren's two brothers and Revere located the grave and uncovered two decom-

Library of Congress, Prints & Photographs Division, LC-USZ62-4430

The Battle of Bunker Hill.

posing bodies. Revere recognized in one of them the two false teeth he had made for Dr. Warren, resulting in a positive identification.

2297. Cremation was that of Henry Laurens of Charleston, SC, an export merchant and delegate to the Continental Congress who served on diplomatic missions in France and England after the Revolutionary War. He died on December 8, 1792. His will read as follows: "I solemnly enjoin it upon my son as an indispensable duty that, as soon as he conveniently can after my decease, he cause my body to be wrapped in twelve yards of tow cloth, and burnt until it is entirely consumed, and then, collecting my ashes, deposit them wherever he may see proper."

2298. National cemetery was established in Washington, DC, in a section of Christ Church known as the Washington Parish Burial Ground. Records show that burials were made in 1804, but the date of the deed is recorded as March 31, 1812. In 1816, the federal government, seeking a burial place "for the interment of members of Congress, any heads of General Government and members of their familes," accepted the cemetery from the vestry of Christ Church. Located at 18th and E streets, SE, it is more familiarly known as the Congressional Cemetery and occupies 30 acres alongside the Anacostia River.

2299. Autopsy performed by a woman physician on a male corpse was performed by Dr. Bethenia Owens-Adair at Roseburg, OR, in 1870 and verified by six physicians. She was a graduate of two courses of medical lectures and had completed the course of study at the Eclectic School of Medicine, Philadelphia, PA.

2300. Crematory was erected by Francis Julius LeMoyne on his grounds in Washington, PA, in 1876. It was the only crematory in the United States until 1884. The first body incinerated was that of Baron Joseph Henry Louis de Palm, on December 6, 1876. LeMoyne died of diabetes on October 14, 1879, and two days later was cremated in his own crematory.

2301. State crematory was authorized by New York on May 21, 1888, when $20,000 was appropriated to build and equip a crematory on Swinburne Island in New York Harbor. It was built by Dr. Miles Lewis Davis of Lancaster, PA. In 1889, bodies buried at the Quarantine cemetery at Sequine's Point were disinterred and cremated.

2302. Federal cemetery to contain graves of both Union and Confederate soldiers was opened in Springfield, MO, by act of Congress dated March 3, 1911. Part of it was formerly a Confederate cemetery maintained by the state of Missouri, which deeded it to the federal government on June 21, 1911. A stone wall separates the graves of the Confederate troops from those of the Union soldiers. The cemetery contains over 3,100 graves.

2303. Burial at the Tomb of the Unknown Soldier in the National Cemetery at Arlington, VA, took place on November 11, 1921. President Warren Gamaliel Harding, accompanied by practically every prominent government officer, attended the services and the unveiling of the national shrine, which was built to honor the large number of American soldiers who lost their lives in World War I but whose bodies were never identified.

2304. Funeral home operated on the cooperative plan was the Collingwood Memorial, Toledo, OH, which opened on September 15, 1930. The expenses of operation were divided equally by the concerns using the building, thereby enabling funeral services to be provided more cheaply.

2305. Right-to-die society was the National Society for the Legalization of Euthanasia, formed on January 14, 1938, in New York City with the Reverend Charles

Francis Potter as president. The society was incorporated as the Euthanasia Society of America on November 30, 1938.

2306. Freezing of a corpse for future resuscitation took place in January 1967. Robert F. Nelson and others interested in cryonics used dry ice to freeze the body of James H. Bedford, a retired psychology professor.

2307. Right-to-die law enacted by a state was the Natural Death Act of California, enacted on September 30, 1976, which allowed physicians of terminally ill patients to withhold life-sustaining procedures under certain conditions.

2308. Death by suicide machine occurred in Detroit, MI, on June 4, 1990, when Janet Adkins of Portland, OR, took her own life using a device that administered a fatal dose of drugs when she pushed a button. The machine was invented by Dr. Jack Kevorkian, the crusader for doctor-assisted suicide. Kevorkian was on hand to assist Adkins, who suffered from Alzheimer's disease. Michigan was selected as the site because at that time the state had no law prohibiting doctor-assisted suicide.

2309. Judicial decision allowing physicians to end the lives of terminally ill patients at their request was issued on May 3, 1994, by federal judge Barbara Rothstein of Seattle, WA. In her decision, Rothstein held that the privacy of a terminally ill person is constitutionally protected, and that, as the law permits such people to refuse treatments aimed at prolonging life, it also permits them access to methods of hastening death.

2310. State to legalize physician-assisted suicide was Oregon, whose voters approved the Death with Dignity Act by a vote of 51 percent to 49 percent on November 8, 1994. The law specified that terminally ill, mentally competent adult patients with a life expectancy of less than six months could ask their physicians to prescribe them a lethal dose of medication. The request was required to be made in writing, to bear the signatures of two witnesses, and to be expressed orally twice. The law survived a series of legal challenges.

2311. Space burial took place on April 21, 1997, when small samples of the ashes of 24 people, including Timothy Leary and Gene Roddenberry, were carried into space along with Spain's first communications satellite. Leary, a psychologist famous for his espousal of psychedelic drugs, died on May 31, 1996. His final request was for "one last far-out trip." Roddenberry, who created the "Star Trek" television series, died on October 24, 1991. The remains were ejected in lipstick-sized capsules that were expected to orbit the earth for up to 10 years before burning up in the atmosphere.

2312. Moon burial took place on July 31, 1999, when a small container holding one ounce of the ashes of Eugene M. Shoemaker arrived on the moon aboard NASA's Lunar Prospector probe, launched on January 7, 1998. The burial was arranged by Space Services, Inc., Houston, TX. Shoemaker, an astrogeologist at the California Institute of Technology, Pasadena, CA, and the U.S. Geological Survey, Flagstaff, AZ, was the co-discoverer in 1993 of Comet Shoemaker-Levy 9. He died on July 18, 1997.

2313. Child removed from life support by court order despite a parent's wishes was Sun Hudson, who was born with thanatophoric dysplasia, an incurable skeletal disorder. He was born on September 25, 2004, at Texas Children's Hospital, Houston, TX, and was immediately placed on a ventilator. The hospital maintained that medical treatment was futile and that life support was prolonging the baby's suffering. His mother, Wanda Hudson, disagreed. After obtaining a judge's authorization under Texas law, the hospital removed the ventilator on March 15, 2005, and the baby died a few minutes later.

Food

2314. Beer was brewed at Sir Walter Raleigh's Roanoke colony in the future state of North Carolina in 1587. According to Thomas Hariot's account, "Wee made of the same [pagatowr, or maize] . . . some mault, whereof was brued as good ale as was to bee desired. So likewise by the help of hops thereof may bee made as good beere."

2315. Salt works was established in America in 1630 by Governor John Harvey of Virginia, who designed and established a factory for obtaining salt by evaporation of seawater. The factory was erected at Accomack, VA, on the eastern shore of Chesapeake Bay.

2316. Windmill for grinding grain was erected in 1632 in Cambridge, MA. As "it would not grind but with a westerly wind," it was moved in August 1632 to Copp's Hill (Boston Neck), Boston, MA.

2317. Meat packer was William Pynchon, who established a warehouse at Warehouse Point, Springfield, MA, in 1636. He dealt in mutton, tallow, and wool, but his chief business was pork packing. He also sold beaver skins. Competition was keen and "merchants encreased so many that it became little worth, by reason of their out-buying one another, which caused them to live on husbandry."

2318. Cornmeal machine for grinding maize was invented in 1712 by Sybilla Righton Masters, a Quaker woman from West New Jersey, and installed at Governor's Mill in Philadelphia, PA. Masters took out an English patent on it in 1715 in the name of her husband, Thomas. The machine, which could be run either by horsepower or waterpower, used a set of wooden cogwheels to stamp maize into powder, which Masters called "Tuscarora rice."

2319. Cookbook published in America was *The Compleat Housewife: or Accomplished Gentlewoman's Companion. Being a collection of upwards of Five Hundred of the most approved Receipts fit either for private Families, or such Publick-Spirited Gentlewomen as would be beneficent to their poor Neighbours*, published in 1742 in Williamsburg, VA, by William Parks. It was modeled after a cookbook printed by Mrs. E. Smith in England.

2320. Beef export was made from Savannah, GA, in 1755, when 40 barrels of beef were shipped out.

2321. Chocolate mill was erected beside the Neponset River at Dorchester, MA, in 1765 and was operated by John Hannan. In 1780 Dr. James Baker purchased the mill, originating the chocolate maker Walter Baker and Company.

2322. Cottonseed oil was produced in 1768 through the efforts of Dr. Otto, a Moravian, of Bethlehem, PA. He was able to get nine pints of oil from a bushel and a half of cotton seed. The first mill for producing cottonseed oil was established in Petersburg, VA, in 1829 by Francis Follet.

2323. Mustard was manufactured by Benjamin Jackson, who established the Globe Mills on Germantown Road, Philadelphia, PA, and sold his product in glass bottles with his label on them. He advertised in the *Pennsylvania Chronicle* of February 15, 1768, that he was "the original establisher of the mustard manufactory in America, and ... at present the only mustard manufacturer on the continent. I brought the art with me into the country."

2324. Cocktail is said to have been served in 1776 by Betsy Flanagan, a barmaid in Halls Corners, Elmsford, NY, who decorated the bar with tail feathers. An inebriate called for a glass of "those cocktails," so she prepared a mixed drink, and inserted one of the feathers.

2325. Ice cream to be made commercially was sold by Mr. Hall of 76 Chatham Street (now Park Row), New York City, who advertised it on June 8, 1786.

2326. Bourbon whiskey was distilled from corn in 1789 by a Baptist minister, Elijah Craig, in the bluegrass country of Kentucky. The area was later renamed Bourbon County.

2327. Flour mill equipped with elevators conveyors, drills, and a "hopper boy" was designed by Oliver Evans in 1789. With this equipment, the mill could be operated by one man instead of the four who were needed in the old-fashioned mills. The mill had an endless belt conveyor with buckets spaced a foot apart, each bucket holding a quart of grain.

2328. Sugar refinery that was practical was opened in New Orleans, LA, in 1791 by Antonio Méndez. Attempts had been made in 1759, 1764, 1765, and 1766, but because the exact crystallization point and the proper use of lime were not then known, the mills were unsuccessful and were abandoned. The first commercial mill began operation in New Orleans in 1795.

2329. Cracker bakery was that of Theodore Pearson of Newburyport, MA, which started in 1792. His products appealed chiefly because they kept better than bread.

2330. Cookbook by an American author was Amelia Simmons's *American Cookery, or the Art of Dressing Viands, Fish, Poultry and Vegetables, and the Best Modes of Making Puff-Pastes, Pies, Tarts, Puddings, Custards and Preserves, and All Kinds of Cakes, from the Imperial Plumb to Plain Cake—Adapted to This Country, and All Grades of Life.* It was printed for the author in 1796 by Hudson and Goodwin in Hartford, CT, and contained 46 pages.

2331. Ice shipped commercially was cut on Canal Street, New York City, in 1799, and shipped to Charleston, SC.

2332. Hard water crackers were made by hand in 1801 by Josiah Bent in his home in Milton, MA. They were made from winter wheat and cold water and were baked in ovens heated by bundles of hardwood sticks. Bent peddled them around the country and in 1827 sold his business, which became Bent and Company.

2333. Cheese factory cooperative was established by farmers of Cheshire, MA, in 1801. On July 20, 1801, a cheese was pressed at the farm of Elisha Brown, Jr., which on August 20 weighed 1,235 pounds. It was placed on a wagon drawn by six horses and on January 1, 1802, was presented to President Thomas Jefferson at the White House.

2334. Baked Alaska was served in the United States by President Thomas Jefferson. At a dinner he hosted at Monticello, his home near Charlottesville, VA, on February 6, 1802, he placed a confection of ice cream and baked crust before his guests. One of them, the scientist and clergyman Manasseh Cutler, described the dish as "ice cream very good, crust wholly dried, crumbled into thin flakes." In 1869 the chef at Delmonico's Restaurant in New York, Charles Ranhofer, created a baked ice cream dish to mark the purchase of Alaska by the United States. The term "baked Alaska" first appeared in print in 1905 in Fannie Farmer's cookbook.

2335. Macaroni and cheese casserole was served on February 6, 1802, to the scientist and clergyman Manasseh Cutler and the explorer Meriwether Lewis at a dinner given by President Thomas Jefferson at Monticello, his estate near Charlottesville, VA. "Dined at the President's," Cutler recorded, "a pie called macaroni, which appeared to be a rich crust filled with the strillions of onions, or shallots, which I took it to be, tasted very strong, and not agreeable . . . ; it was an Italian dish, and what appeared like onions was made of flour and butter, with a particularly strong liquor mixed with them." Cutler and Lewis probably mistook the Italian cheese included in the recipe for liquor.

2336. Distilling book was Michael August Krafft's *American Distiller, or The Theory and Practice of Distilling, according to the latest discoveries and improvements, including its most important methods of constructing stills and of rectification.* It contained 219 pages and six plates and was printed in 1804 by Thomas Dobson, Philadelphia, PA. The book was dedicated to Thomas Jefferson.

2337. Ice exported was shipped in August 1805 by Frederick Tudor, who sent 130 tons on the brig *Favorite* from Boston, MA, to the island of Martinique in the West Indies. His business increased, and in 1833 he commenced making shipments to the cities of Madras, Bombay, and Calcutta in India.

2338. Cider mill was patented by Isaac Quintard of Stanfield, CT, who obtained a patent on April 5, 1806, on a cider and bark mill.

2339. Soda water was prepared by Townsend Speakman of Philadelphia, PA, who was hired by the eminent surgeon Dr. Philip Syng Physick to make carbonated water as a medicinal treatment for his patients. In 1807, Speakman added fruit juices to make the drink more palatable. The soda water was dispensed regularly to patients from fountains. The cost was $1.50 a month for one glass a day.

Library of Congress, Prints & Photographs Division LC-USZ62-117117

Thomas Jefferson

2340. Canning book was a translation of Francois Appert's *L'Art de Conserver, pendant plusieurs années, toutes les substances animales et végétales*, published in 1812 by David Longworth, New York City.

2341. Canning of food was introduced in 1819 by Ezra Daggett and his nephew, Thomas Kensett, who canned salmon, oysters, and lobsters in New York City. On January 19, 1825, they obtained a patent to "preserve animal substances in tin." The vacuum canning process was invented in 1872 by writer and spiritualist Amanda Jones of Buffalo, NY, who received nine patents on it. Her company, the U.S. Women's Pure Food Vacuum Preserving Company, founded in 1890, produced canned pudding and lunch meat.

2342. Mineral water bottler was Elie Magloire Durand, who also invented a machine for bottling mineral water under pressure. Durand opened a drugstore in 1825 at the corner of Sixth and Chestnut streets, Philadelphia, PA.

2343. Coffee mill was patented on April 3, 1829, by James Carrington of Wallingford, CT.

2344. Glucose from potato starch was obtained in 1831 by Samuel Guthrie in a refinery at Sackets Harbor, NY.

2345. Soda water machine was manufactured by John Matthews, who opened a factory in New York City in 1834 exclusively for the manufacture of soda water apparatus. Various types of machines for making carbonated beverages had been made previously, however.

2346. Whole-wheat bread made at home from coarsely ground flour was the subject of a public campaign by the Reverend Sylvester Graham of Northampton, MA, whose book *Treatise on Bread and Bread-Making* was published in 1837. Graham accused the bakers of the era of adulterating the bread they sold and harming the public's health. At one of his lectures, delivered in Boston in 1847, the audience had to defend him from an assault by a mob of enraged bakers. He was also the inventor of Graham crackers.

2347. Sugar beet mill belonged to the Northampton Beet Sugar Company and was erected by David Lee Child in Northampton, MA, in 1838. In 1839, the mill produced 1,300 pounds of sugar from beets low in sucrose content. That year, the company received a $100 premium from the Massachusetts Agricultural Society and a silver medal at the exhibition of the Massachusetts Charitable Mechanics Association. The factory did not operate after 1840.

2348. Lager beer was manufactured in Philadelphia, PA, in 1840 by John Wagner, who had an eight-barrel kettle in his home. It was stored in a cellar under the brewhouse.

2349. Cornstarch made commercially from maize was made by Thomas Kingsford, who produced a small quantity in 1842 in Jersey City, NJ. He and his son, Thomas, Jr., erected a small cornstarch plant in Bergen, NJ, in 1846 and a larger one in Oswego, NY, in 1848.

2350. Ice cream freezer was invented by Nancy M. Johnson of New Jersey, who received a patent for it on September 9, 1843. It consisted of a container, equipped with a hand-cranked paddle, which was placed inside a larger container. The space between the two containers was filled with salt and ice. It was the model for all future hand-cranked ice cream makers.

A record of a purchase for "a cream machine for ice" is contained in George Washington's expense ledger under the date of May 17, 1784.

2351. Baking soda commercial production was undertaken in 1846 by John Dwight and Dr. Austin Church in New York City. In 1847 they organized John Dwight and Company.

2352. Chewing gum was the "State of Maine Pure Spruce Gum," manufactured in Bangor, ME, in 1848 by John Curtis and his brother on a Franklin stove. In 1850 they moved to Portland, ME, where they made paraffin gums under the brand names Licorice Lulu, Four-in-Hand, Sugar Cream, Biggest and Best, White Mountain, and spruce gums under the names Yankee Spruce, American Flag, Trunk Spruce, and 200 Lump Spruce.

2353. Macaroni factory was established by Antoine Zerega in Brooklyn, NY (now part of New York City), in 1848. It consisted of a small mill with crude mechanical equipment for grinding raw materials.

2354. Meat biscuit was invented by Gail Borden, Jr., of Elizabethport, NY, who baked flat, brittle cakes from concentrated meat extract combined with vegetable flour or meal. To make soup, the consumer added hot water and seasoning to the biscuit. Borden obtained a patent on July 30, 1850, on a "preparation of portable soup bread."

2355. Condensed milk was commercially produced in 1851 by Gail Borden of Brooklyn, NY (now part of New York City), who received a patent on August 19, 1856, on an "improvement in concentration of milk," although the patent office doubted the value of the invention. The first condensery was established at Wolcottville, CT, in 1856. It was not successful, and another attempt was made at Burrville, CT, in May 1857, but that was also a failure. A third attempt was made with an enlarged factory at Wassaic, NY, in June 1861. This venture was successful and later developed into the Borden Company, with factories throughout the country.

2356. Ice cream wholesale dealer was Jacob Fussel, a milk dealer in Baltimore, MD. In 1851, as a means of using up his surplus cream, he started manufacturing ice cream, which sold at 60 cents a quart.

2357. Cheese factory was established in Rome, NY, by Jesse Williams in 1851. It is referred to as the first permanent system of associated dairying in the United States. The first shipment of milk was received May 10, 1851.

2358. Matzoh made by machine for the Jewish holiday of Pesach (Passover) was introduced by Moses S. Cohen, a New York City baker, in 1852 or 1853, in his bakery on Front Street. Matzoh is traditionally made by hand. Rabbinical approval for machine-made matzoh was obtained from the Chief Rabbi of London. The first matzoh factory to package the product for widespread distribution was opened by Rabbi Dov Ber Manischewitz in Cincinnati, OH, in 1881.

2359. Potato chips are the subject of competing claims. According to some accounts, they were introduced in 1853 by George Crum, a Native American chef at Moon Lake Lodge, Saratoga Springs, NY, and were known as Saratoga Chips. According to others, they were first made by an African-American chef about 1865. The first plant constructed for the exclusive manufacture of potato chips was erected in Albany, NY, in 1925 by A. A. Walter and Company.

2360. Rolled oats were sold by the German Mills American Oatmeal Company, founded in Akron, OH, in 1856 by Ferdinand Schumacher, a German immigrant who ran a grocery store. To overcome the American perception of oats as horse food, Schumacher cooked the oat berries and flattened them between rollers.

2361. Creamery for commercial production was established by Alanson Slaughter at Wallkill, NY, in 1861.

2362. Pretzel bakery was founded by baker Julius Sturgis in Lititz, PA, in 1861.

2363. Salmon cannery was erected in 1864 at Washington, CA, on the banks of the Sacramento River, by Hapgood, Hume and Company. The firm consisted of Andrew S. Hapgood, George W. Hume, and William Hume. About 2,000 cases of salmon were canned the first year. Half of the first production spoiled because the cans were not hermetically sealed.

2364. Sugar and glucose from cornstarch were manufactured by the Union Sugar Company, New York City. The process was based on a patent, dated May 10, 1864, for a "sugar produced from corn and beets." The patent was granted to Frederick W. Gossling and assigned to Gossling, Henry F. Briggs, and Leman Bradley of Buffalo, NY. Gossling also received a patent on December 20, 1864, for a new and improved compound sugar made by a combination of cane sugar or cane syrup and corn syrup.

2365. Sweet crackers of American manufacture were introduced to the public in 1865 by Belcher and Larrabee of Albany, NY, in competition with English crackers, which were imported in increasing quantities. Soda crackers and salt crackers had been made previously.

2366. Root beer was manufactured in 1866 by Charles Elmer Hires, a student at the Jefferson Medical College, Philadelphia, PA, in cooperation with Dr. William Simpson and Dr. Henry Leffman. In 1869, Hires opened a drugstore in Philadelphia and placed a sign over his soda fountain offering a glass of root beer for five cents. In 1876, he started a national business selling root beer.

2367. Compressed fresh yeast was introduced in 1868 by Charles Fleischmann, whose firm, Gaff, Fleischmann and Company, manufactured it in Riverside, near Cincinnati, OH.

2368. Prepared-food producer to achieve great commercial success was Henry John Heinz, a chef of German descent, who in 1869 opened a factory at Sharpsburg, PA. His first product was grated horseradish, but his real breakthrough in the marketplace was bottled ketchup, which he introduced in 1876. The company, known since 1888 as the H.J. Heinz Company, eventually became a major firm that manufactured several hundred varieties of products.

2369. Baking powder manufacturer was Benjamin Talbert Babbitt, whose Star Yeast Powder was introduced to the public in 1870.

2370. Popcorn snack that was successful was Cracker Jack, invented by street vendor Frederick William Rueckheim in 1871. His confection of popcorn, peanuts, and molasses was marketed nationally after Rueckheim scored a success with it at the World's Columbian Exposition of 1893 in Chicago, IL. In 1912, Rueckheim started putting a prize—a miniature toy or book—into each box. The sailor boy on each Cracker Jack box was modeled after his grandson Robert, who died of pneumonia at the age of eight.

2371. Candy packaged in a factory was Smith Brothers Cough Drops, a medicinal candy made by William and Andrew Smith from a recipe handed down by their father James, a restaurant owner and candymaker in Poughkeepsie, NY. They began selling the cough drops locally in 1852. The product was so popular that in 1872 they began packaging it in small boxes for shipment. Until that time, storekeepers kept candies on their countertops in glass containers, from which customers made their selection.

2372. Dried milk patent was obtained by Samuel R. Percy of New York City, who obtained a patent on April 9, 1872, on a "process for the simultaneous atomizing and desiccating of fluids and solid substances," involving spray-drying of various liquid products. It was never used commercially in its original form.

2373. Margarine manufacturer who was successful was Alfred Paraf of New York City, who organized the Oleo-Margarin Manufacturing Company in 1871. On April 8, 1873, he obtained a patent on his process for purifying and separating fats. A previous patent had been granted on January 3, 1871, to Henry W. Bradley of Binghamton, NY, on a "compound for culinary use," composed of lard, vegetable butter, or shortening.

2374. Ice cream soda is supposed to have been introduced by Robert M. Green, the founder of Robert M. Green and Sons, manufacturers of soda fountains in Philadelphia, PA, who added ice cream to plain soda water. The first demonstration of the new beverage was made at the Semi-Centennial Celebration at Franklin Institute, Philadelphia, in the summer of 1874.

2375. Oat-crushing machine was patented on November 30, 1875, by Asmus J. Ehrrichson of Akron, OH, who obtained a patent on "an improvement in oatmeal machines." A hopper with a perforated bottom and a series of horizontal knives were the basis of his invention, which converted hulled kernels of oats into a cereal meal. The machine superseded the old method of crushing grain with burrs or millstones, which produced a product of inferior quality and reduced the grain to a fine flour of less value than the coarse meal.

2376. Animal crackers were an English confection originally called "zoologicals." They were first sold in the United States at the 1876 Centennial Exposition in Philadelphia, PA, by Philadelphia baker Walter G. Wilson. The earliest extant recipe for animal crackers appears in *Secrets of the Bakers and Confectioners' Trade* by J. D. Hounihan, published on April 1, 1883. The familiar animal cracker shapes and distinctive packaging, displaying P. T. Barnum's circus animals, were introduced in 1902 by the National Biscuit Company (now RJR Nabisco, East Hanover, NJ). Barnum himself was not involved in marketing the crackers and received nothing for the use of his name. The boxes were originally intended for use as Christmas ornaments, which is why each one has a string attached.

2377. Sardine cannery that was successful was established in 1876 in Eastport, ME, by Julius Wolff of Wolff and Reesing, New York City. The cans were made of three pieces, top, bottom, and side, which were soldered together.

2378. Margarine law was "an act for the protection of dairymen and to prevent deception in sales of butter," passed on June 5, 1877, by New York.

2379. Coffee in a can was a roasted blend packed in a sealed tin by the Chase and Sanborn Company of Boston, MA, in 1878.

2380. Milk delivery in glass bottles was made in 1878 in Brooklyn, NY (now part of New York City), by Alexander Campbell.

2381. Centrifugal cream separator was made in 1879 by David M. Weston and Edward Burnett of Boston, MA, and was used on the Deerfoot Farm, Southborough, MA. It made 1,600 revolutions a minute and had a 26-inch bowl. The machine had to be stopped to draw off the cream and skim milk after separation. Two years earlier, on September 25, 1877, an American patent was granted to Wilhelm C. L. Lefeldt and Carl G. O. Lentsch of Schoeningen, Germany, on an "improvement in centrifugal machines for creaming milk." It consisted of an electric rotator that forced the heavy milk to the base of the pan. A centrifugal cream separator with a continuous flow was invented by Carl Gustaf Patrik de Laval of Stockholm, Sweden, who received an American patent for it on October 4, 1881. The first machine of this type used in the United States was put in operation in 1881 by Theodore Augustus Havemeyer, sugar refiner and Jersey stock breeder, on his farm at Mahwah, NJ.

2382. Sugar substitute was saccharine, discovered by Constantine Fahlberg, who was working under the direction of Professor Ira Remsen at Johns Hopkins University, Baltimore, MD. Fahlberg described the discovery in an article entitled "On the Liquid Toluenesulphochloride," which he submitted to the *American Chemical Journal* on February 27, 1879. Saccharine is an edible substance 550 times sweeter than table sugar, but not absorbed by the body.

2383. Flour rolling mill was invented by John Stevens of Neenah, WI, who was granted a patent on a "grain crushing mill" on March 23, 1880. His method increased production 70 percent and produced a superior flour that sold for $2 more a barrel.

2384. Martini was mentioned in O. H. Byron's *The Modern Bartender's Guide*, published in New York in 1884. A martini is a cocktail made of gin or vodka and vermouth, with a dash of bitters. The origin of the name is in dispute. Byron called the drink a "Martinez" and described it as a Manhattan (a whiskey cocktail sweetened with vermouth) but made with gin rather than whiskey. It was first called a "Martini" in Henry Johnson's 1888 book *How to Mix Drinks in the Present Style*. The martini did not become "dry" until after World War I, when it became the fashion to use unsweetened French vermouth instead of the sweet Italian variety.

2385. Evaporated milk was produced by John B. Meyenberg of St. Louis, MO, who received a patent on November 25, 1884, for an "apparatus for preserving milk." On February 14, 1885, Meyenberg formed the Helvetia Milk Condensing Company of Highland, IL. Evaporated milk is milk from which approximately 60 percent of the water has been removed by evaporation.

2386. Cola drink was Coca-Cola, invented by pharmacist John Stith Pemberton in Atlanta, GA, as a patent medicine. It was a nonalcoholic version of a previous beverage he had popularized, Pemberton's French Coca Wine, and contained extracts of both kola nuts and cocaine. Jacobs' Pharmacy in Atlanta began selling it at the price of five cents a glass on May 8, 1886.

2387. Soup company to market canned, precooked liquid soups was the Franco-American Food Company of New York City, which was organized in November 1886 by Alphonse Biardot and his sons, Ernest and Octave.

2388. Malted milk was originally considered a health drink, as touted by its inventors, James and William Horlick of Racine, WI. In 1887 the Horlicks marketed a so-called "diastoid" tonic powder and tablet called "Horlick's Malted Milk," made from an extract of wheat and malted barley combined with milk. The Walgreens drugstore chain was the first to incorporate the powder in a chocolate malted.

2389. Ready-mix food to be sold commercially was Aunt Jemima Pancake Flour, invented at St. Joseph, MO, in 1889 by Chris L. Rutt and Charles G. Underwood. The original recipe consisted of hard wheat flour, corn flour, phosphate of lime, baking soda, and a pinch of salt. It was labeled "Self-Rising Pancake Flour" and sold in one-pound paper sacks. The name was changed to "Aunt Jemima" after Rutt saw a tune of the same name performed by two entertainers at a local minstrel show.

2390. Egg cream was the invention of Louis Auster, a Jewish immigrant who owned a candy store in Brooklyn, NY, on Avenue D. Family accounts claim that Auster invented the drink—a combination of seltzer, milk, and homemade chocolate syrup (no eggs or cream)—circa 1890; the exact recipe was kept secret despite efforts by soda-fountain chains to purchase it. The first printed reference to the egg cream dates from 1950. The egg cream made with Fox's U-Bet Chocolate Flavor Syrup, the classic commercial ingredient, dates from the 1920s.

2391. Hot dog was introduced to the United States by immigrants from Frankfurt, Germany, where local butchers had created the frankfurter, a thin variation of the traditional sausage, in 1852. One immigrant, Charles Feltman, settled in Coney Island, NY (now part of New York City), where he sold pies from a pushcart. In the 1890s he switched to selling boiled frankfurters on rolls topped with mustard and sauerkraut, which proved highly popular. The first entrepreneur to sell frankfurters at ball games was Harry Stevens, at New York City's Polo Grounds, where they were called dachshund sausages. A sketch by a newspaper cartoonist, Tad Dorgan, of a frankfurter in the shape of a dachshund gave rise to the term "hot dog."

2392. Milk butterfat tester of value for determining the percentage of butterfat in milk and cream was invented on May 15, 1890, by Stephen Moulton Babcock, professor of agricultural chemistry, University of Wisconsin, Madison, WI. He did not apply for a patent. Prior to this invention, the amount of butterfat in milk and cream was determined by a method that could be used only in a chemical laboratory and was entirely unsuitable for use in a creamery or milk plant.

2393. Fruit-filled cookies to be commercially manufactured were Fig Newtons, which began mass production circa April 10, 1892, at the Kennedy Biscuit Works in Cambridgeport, MA (now Cambridge, MA). The bakery used a funneling machine, invented in 1891 by Philadelphia baker James Henry Mitchell, that was capable of filling soft cookie dough with jam. The name "Fig Newton" was probably coined by bakery manager James Hazen in honor of the Boston suburb of Newton. The Kennedy Biscuit Works company was later purchased by the National Biscuit Company (now RJR Nabisco, East Hanover, NJ).

2394. Biscuits of shredded wheat were made by Henry D. Perky and William H. Ford of Watertown, NY, who obtained a patent on August 1, 1893, on a machine for making shreds or filaments of wheat. The Cereal Machine Company, Denver, CO, was formed in 1893 to manufacture them.

2395. Chocolate bars manufactured in the United States were produced in 1894 by candymaker Milton Snavely Hershey, using several German chocolate-making machines he purchased at the 1893 World's Columbian Exposition in Chicago. Hershey installed them in his caramel factory in Lancaster, PA. By 1900 he had given up on caramels to focus exclusively on chocolate bars, chocolate kisses, and chocolate cigars. Chocolate bars were originally manufactured on a large scale in Switzerland in 1819.

2396. Milk pasteurized commercially was processed in Bloomville, NY, in 1895 by the Sheffield Farms Company of New York City. The company used flash pasteurization, a very slow process and quite expensive due to the large quantity of ice used. Lewis Benjamin Halsey used two Champion coolers, one for the heating medium and the other for the cooling.

2397. Cereal sold as a breakfast food was Granose, introduced in February 1895 by John Harvey Kellogg and his brother Will Keith Kellogg of Battle Creek, MI. They boiled wheat, pressed it in a machine for rolling out dough, baked it into a thin film, cut it up, and sold the pieces as flakes in 10-ounce packages. John Harvey Kellogg, a champion of vegetarianism and a follower of Dr. Sylvester Graham, developed many other vegetarian foods, including the first granola, which he made in 1877 by grinding up cakes of wheat, oatmeal, and cornmeal, and the first cornflakes, introduced unsuccessfully in 1898. Kellogg's chief rival was Charles William Post, who produced Grape Nuts in 1897, Post Toasties in 1915, and Post's Bran in 1922.

2398. Recipes using standard measurements were invented in the 1880s by Fannie Merritt Farmer, a young woman who was working as a mother's helper in Boston, MA. The little girl in her care wanted to learn how to cook, but the process was slow, since most cooking directions referred only to such vague amounts as a pinch, a dash, a handful, or a spoonful. Farmer converted these measurements to standardized forms, so that all cooks could duplicate the ingredients of a dish in the right proportions. Her cookbook, *The Boston Cooking School Cook Book*, published in 1896, was the first to include standardized recipes.

2399. Chop suey was concocted in New York City on August 29, 1896, by the chef of Chinese Ambassador Li Hung-chang, who devised the dish to appeal to both American and Asian tastes. Chop suey was unknown in China at the time.

2400. Condensed soup for the consumer market was invented in 1897 by 24-year-old chemist John T. Dorrance of the Joseph Campbell Preserve Company, a cannery in Camden, NJ. His double-strength condensed soups had the advantage of being cheaper to distribute and sell because water, the weightiest part of the formula, was added by the consumer. The low-priced canned soups first appeared on the market in 1898, already sporting the company's characteristic red and white labels. In 1914, Dorrance became president of the company, which changed its name to the Campbell's Soup Company in 1924.

2401. Gelatin dessert packaged for commercial distribution was Jell-O, a powdered mixture of gelatin and fruit flavoring. It was created in 1897 by Pearle B. Wait, a carpenter in Le Roy, NY. The formula was purchased in 1899 by a marketing expert, Orator Frank Woodward, who turned Jell-O into a nationally distributed product.

2402. Ice cream sundae is said to have originated about 1897 in the Red Cross Pharmacy, State Street, Ithaca, NY, directly opposite the barroom of the Ithaca Hotel. As the barroom was closed on Sunday, thirsty patrons went to the drugstore, where a distinctive drink was sold as a sundae.

2403. Kosher wine made in the United States for sale to consumers was bottled on New York's Lower East Side beginning in 1899 by restaurateur Samuel Schapiro, an immigrant from Poland. His business, Schapiro's House of Kosher Wines, sold a famously sweet product known as "the kosher wine you can almost cut with a knife." Grapes were imported from upstate New York to ferment in huge cellars below Rivington Street, which produced up to 1,500 cases per day. The company is still run by members of the Schapiro family.

2404. Banana split is attributed variously to either David Strickler, who allegedly invented it in 1904 while he was a pharmacy apprentice in Latrobe, PA, or to Ernest Hazard, proprietor of Hazard's Restaurant in Wilmington, OH, who assembled a similar dessert in 1907. Both recipes have the essential banana split ingredients of bananas sliced longitudinally, three scoops of ice cream, chocolate syrup, and whipped cream.

2405. Hamburger evolved from the chopped-beef Hamburg steak of German invention, but the identity of the inventor of the American-style hamburger on a bun is uncertain. Hamburgers on buns, possibly with ketchup or mustard, may first have been served by German-born street vendors at the 1904 International Exposition in St. Louis, MO. Other claimants are Louis Lassen, the owner of the Louis Lunch diner in New Haven, CT, who began serving a broiled Hamburg steak sandwich on toasted bread in 1900, and Billy Ingram, who sold flattened meatballs for five cents each in Wichita, KS, in 1921, and eventually founded the White Castle chain of burger joints.

2406. Ice cream cone is said to have originated at the Louisiana Purchase Exposition in St. Louis, MO, in 1904. Charles E. Menches, a young ice cream salesman, gave an ice cream sandwich, as well as flowers, to the young lady he was escorting. Lacking a vase for the flowers, she took one of the layers of the sandwich and rolled it in the form of a cone to act as a vase. The remaining layer was similarly rolled to hold the ice cream, resulting in the invention of the ice cream cone. Similar claims have been made by other concessionaires.

2407. Bubble gum was invented by Frank Henry Fleer, founder of the Frank H. Fleer Corporation of Philadelphia, PA. In 1906 he developing a chewing gum called Blibber-Blubber. The recipe was perfected in 1928 by company employee Walter Diemer, who called his product Dubble Bubble for its ability to make large bubbles. Successful market testing began in Philadelphia on December 26, 1928.

2408. Canned tuna was packed in 1907 by a small cannery owned by A. P. Halfhill in San Pedro, CA, center of the American tuna industry. Canned tuna did not catch on as a staple of the American diet until 1926, when Van Camp Sea Food of San Pedro began packing yellow-fin tuna in cans and lowered the price.

Yellow-fin was a more economical and easier-to-catch fish than the white-fleshed albacore that canneries had packed until then.

2409. Confectionary machine for making candy "suckers," more familiarly known by the trade name "lollipops," was manufactured by the Racine Confectioners' Machinery Company, Racine, WI, in 1908. Its capacity at that time was 40 lollipops a minute, a rate that candy makers felt would produce more suckers in a week than they could sell in a year. The term "lollipops" was formerly an exclusive name used for candy produced by the Bradley-Smith Company of New Haven, CT, but it has since passed into the language as a generic term.

2410. Vichyssoise was served by Chef Louis Diat at the Ritz Carlton Hotel in New York City in 1910. Diat adapted his mother's recipe for a hot soup of leeks and potatoes, but offered it cold as a summer treat. The name is derived from Diat's birthplace in Vichy, France.

2411. Chocolate sandwich cookie with creme filling was the Hydrox "biscuit bonbon," introduced on January 1, 1910, by Jacob Leander Loose, cofounder of the Loose-Wiles Biscuit Company, Kansas City, KS. The company was later known as Sunshine Biscuits, which still produces the distinctive round sandwich cookie. Oreo cookies, designed by William Turner, were introduced as a response to the Hydrox product by the National Biscuit Company on March 6, 1912. Originally described as the "Oreo Biscuit—two beautifully embossed chocolate-flavored wafers with a rich cream filling," the Oreo's name was changed to "Oreo Creme Sandwich" in 1948.

2412. Bread factory that was completely automatic was opened on July 1, 1910, by the Ward Baking Company, Chicago, IL. The dough was not touched nor the bread handled except when it was placed on the wrapping machine.

2413. Hydrogenated vegetable shortening was introduced as Crisco by the Procter and Gamble Company, Cincinnati, OH, on August 15, 1911. It was a creamy-white all-vegetable shortening, odorless and tasteless, made from cottonseed oil.

2414. Puffed cereal commercially manufactured was Quaker Puffed Rice, introduced by the Quaker Oats Company, Akron, OH, in 1913. The puffing mechanism, which used pressure and heat, was invented by Ferdinand Schumacher. Popcorn, another puffed cereal, had been mixed with cream and eaten for breakfast in colonial times.

2415. Packaged popcorn sold commercially was Jolly Time Pop Corn, made by the American Pop Corn Company, Sioux City, IA, in 1914. The company started out as a home business run by the father-and-son team of Cloid and Howard Smith.

2416. Tomato juice was invented in 1917 by Louis Perrin, the chef at the French Lick Springs Resort and Spa in French Lick, IN, when his supply of oranges for orange juice ran out. The drink proved to be so popular with the resort's guests that a bottling plant was opened in French Lick the same year.

2417. White bread packaged for distribution to stores was Mary Maid, a one-pound loaf made by the Taggart Baking Company of Indianapolis, IN, in 1917.

2418. Acidophilus milk was devised early in 1920 by Dr. Leo Frederick Rettger and Harry Cheplin at Yale University, New Haven, CT. Commercial production was undertaken by the Fairlea Farms Company, Orange, CT, in February 1922 under the supervision of Dr. Rettger.

2419. Ice cream bar was invented by Christian K. Nelson of Onawa, IA, who obtained a patent on January 24, 1922. The pie was an ice cream confection containing a normally liquid material frozen to a substantially hard state and encased in a chocolate covering to maintain its original form during handling.

2420. Milky Way candy bar was introduced in 1923 by candymaker Frank C. Mars of Minneapolis, MN. The nougat bar was a mixture of milk chocolate, corn syrup, sugar, milk, hydrogenated vegetable oil, cocoa, butter, salt, malt, egg whites, and other ingredients, and was an immediate success. In 1930, Mars's company, Mars, Incorporated, began marketing the Snickers bar, which added peanuts to the Milky Way formula. In 1937, it introduced the five-cent Three Musketeers bar, which contained three bars in one wrapper, each with a different flavor of nougat.

2421. Frozen food for the mass market was developed by Clarence Birdseye, a biologist from Brooklyn, New York City. In 1916, Birdseye began to experiment with methods of retaining the flavor and nutrition of cabbage and fish over long periods by quick-freezing them in brine. In 1924, in Gloucester, MA, he perfected the belt-freezer, a device that subjected food to quick-freezing by pressing it between refrigerated plates. He received a patent for his invention on August 12, 1930. Frozen foods with the Birdseye trademark were first marketed in Springfield, MA, in 1930. Birdseye sold his trademark in 1929 to the Postum Company, later the General Foods Corporation, for $22 million.

2422. Popsicle was the descendant of frozen "hokey-pokey" treats sold by 19th-century Italian street vendors. In 1924, Frank Epperson of Oakland, CA, patented frozen fruit juice on a stick. Originally called the Epsicle and sold in six flavors, the name was later changed to Popsicle.

2423. Ice cream cone rolling machine was invented by Carl Rutherford Taylor of Cleveland, OH, who obtained a patent on January 29, 1924, on a "machine for spinning or turning a waffle."

2424. Caesar salad was the creation of Italian immigrant Caesar Cardini, a restaurateur living in San Diego, CA. To avoid Prohibition, as the story goes, Cardini operated an eatery in Tijuana, Mexico. There, on July 4, 1924, he concocted a salad of romaine, eggs, croutons, and Parmesan cheese, flavored with a dressing that included Worcestershire sauce (not anchovies, which were added by later chefs). The Cardini family later marketed a Caesar salad dressing to supermarkets. The recipe is also occasionally attributed to Giacomo Junia, an Italian-American chef in Chicago, IL, who allegedly invented it in 1903 and named it in honor of Julius Caesar.

2425. Reuben sandwich consisting of hot corned beef, swiss cheese, and sauerkraut on rye was likely assembled in 1925 by Reuben Kulakofsky, a grocer of Omaha, NE, for his poker pals. The sandwich was popularized by Charles Schimmel, owner of Omaha's Blackstone Hotel. Actual documentation for the Reuben exists on local Nebraskan menus from as early as 1937. A competing claim is made for New York deli owner Arnold Reuben, who may have come up with a sandwich called the Reuben Special (with cole slaw instead of sauerkraut) as early as 1914.

2426. Canned ham was marketed in 1926 under the name "Hormel Flavor-Sealed Ham" by George A. Hormel and Company of Austin, MN. In 1937, Hormel introduced Spam, the world's most popular canned meat. The name refers to the product's chief ingredients, pork shoulder and ham.

2427. Bagel bakery that was commercially successful was Lender's Bakery, which opened in 1927 in West Haven, CT. The owner was Harry Lender, who had just arrived from Lublin, Poland. Lender's introduced the first frozen bagels in 1963.

2428. Instant powdered soft drink was Kool-Aid (originally "Kool-Ade"), developed in 1927 by Edwin E. Perkins, a household products inventor living in Hastings, NE. Inspired by Jell-O, the instant gelatin dessert, Perkins mixed dextrose, citric acid, tartaric acid, flavoring, and food coloring into six original flavors: raspberry, cherry, grape, lemon, orange, and root beer. Perkins's key innovation was shelf-stable, lightweight packaging consisting of a soft waxed-paper inner liner and an outer envelope lithographed in bright colors. Retail sales began in June 1928. The name was changed to "Kool-Aid" in 1934. The Perkins Products Company was later sold to General Foods Corporation.

2429. Hydrogenated peanut butter was developed in 1928 by the E.K. Pond division of the Swift Packing Company under the brand name Peter Pan Peanut Butter. The hydrogenation process, invented in 1923 by J. L. Rosefield of Alameda, CA, and licensed exclusively to Swift, made the peanut butter smoother and prevented it from becoming rancid. The peanut butter was also homogenized, so that the peanut oil would not separate and rise to the top. In 1932, Rosefield canceled his agreement and began marketing his own brand of peanut butter, Skippy.

2430. Machine-sliced bread was introduced by the Chillecothe Baking Company of Chillicothe, MO, in July 1928. The slicing machine was the patented invention of Otto Frederick Rohwedder, with adjustments made by the bakery's owner, Frank Bench. It sliced fresh loaves without crushing them. The loaves were then secured at both ends with pins and wrapped.

2431. Yogurt dairy was the Colombo Dairy, Methuen, MA, established in 1929 by Sarkis Colombosian. The first year, about 4,000 quarts of yogurt were produced. At that time it was called *madzoon*, the Armenian name for yogurt.

2432. Rattlesnake meat in cans was packed in March 1931 by George Kenneth End of Arcadia, FL. Canned rattlesnake meat was served at an American Legionnaires dinner at the Hillsboro Hotel, Tampa, FL, on April 9. End founded the Floridian Products Corporation, which made its first sale of canned rattlesnake on May 22, 1931.

2433. Chocolate chip cookies were concocted by accident in 1933 by Ruth Graves Wakefield, the proprietor of an inn in Whitman, MA, who chopped chocolate squares into small pieces and mixed them into a batter for butter cookies, expecting them to melt. The finished cookies, with their unmelted chocolate chunks, proved popular with customers. Whitman named them Toll House cookies after her inn, which was originally a tollgate on the road to Boston. Packaged chocolate chips were introduced in 1939 by the Nestlé candy company.

2434. Monosodium glutamate commercial production began in 1934. Previously, American consumers used MSG from Japan, where the flavor-enhancing substance was first isolated from seaweed in 1908. MSG was first marketed commercially in 1947 under the Áccent brand name.

2435. Kosher soft drink was Coca-Cola, certified as kosher in 1935 by Rabbi Tobias Geffen, an Orthodox rabbi at Congregation Shearith Israel in Atlanta, GA. The Coca-Cola Company modified its secret recipe, eliminating an ingredient derived from beef tallow, in order to meet strict kosher standards.

2436. Beer in cans for retail sale was packed by the Krueger Brewing Company at Newark, NJ, and placed on sale in Richmond, VA, on January 24, 1935.

2437. Soda sold in cans was Cliquot Club Ginger Ale, introduced by Cliquot Club Beverages of Mills, MA, in 1938. The can was manufactured by the Continental Can Company in a cone-topped shape. Citric acid in the soda destroyed the can's lining and caused bad flavor, leaks, and occasional explosions. Pepsi-Cola was the first national soda brand to be introduced in a can, in 1948. Six-pack cartons of soda were first marketed in 1955 by the James Vernor Company of Detroit, MI.

2438. M&M candies were developed in 1940 for the armed forces by Forrest E. Mars and Bruce E. Murrie, whose initials supplied the candy with its name. M&M candies had a candy coating that kept the chocolate inside from melting in warm conditions.

2439. Frozen meals for air travelers were the invention of William L. Maxson of New York, NY, who introduced them to the Naval Air Transport Service in 1945. The meals were cooked, put into three-part trays made of plastic-coated cardboard, sealed with a cardboard lid, and frozen. They could be reheated in ovens on the plane. Each consisted of an entree, a side dish of potatoes, and a vegetable. Travelers had a choice of beef stew, hamburger, ham steak, roast lamb, Swiss steak, or veal cutlet.

2440. Food in an aerosol can that was nationally distributed was Reddi-wip, invented in 1948 by Aaron "Bunny" Lapin of St. Louis, MO. The product was a brand of sweetened whipped cream aerated and stored in pressurized cans. By pressing on a nozzle, the consumer could release the internal pressure and spray the cream.

2441. Popcorn was eaten by Native Americans. Small ears of popping corn, dated to about 3650 BCE, were discovered by Harvard graduate students Herbert Dick and Earle Smith at Bat Cave, NM, in 1948. The corn was popped by dropping the kernels in hot sand. Europeans were introduced to popcorn when Columbus returned from his journey of 1492.

> Popcorn was introduced to the English colonists at their first Thanksgiving dinner in 1621 by Quadequina, brother of Massasoit. His contribution to the dinner was a deerskin bag containing several bushels of popped corn.

2442. Frozen TV dinners (though not known by that name) were introduced to the retail market in 1949 by two brothers, Albert and Meyer Bernstein of Pittsburgh, PA. They marketed a line of frozen meals on three-part aluminum trays. Their original company, Frozen Dinners, Inc., was succeeded by Quaker

State Foods Corporation in 1952. The first company to bill its frozen meals specifically as TV dinners was C.A. Swanson & Sons of Omaha, NE, in 1954. Credit for the idea and its development is usually given to Gerry Thomas, a salesman for Swanson. It may also have been a company-wide effort initiated by the firm's owners, Gilbert and Clarke Swanson, to use up excess poultry inventory. Swanson's original TV Dinner, which cost 98 cents, consisted of turkey with cornbread dressing and gravy, a portion of sweet potatoes, and a portion of peas. Eventually, the entrees included fried chicken, meatloaf, and Salisbury steak. In the product's first year, the company sold 10 million units.

2443. Concentrated milk was Sealtest, which was first sold on November 30, 1950, by the Clover Dairy Company, Wilmington, DE, as a test. Two parts of water were added to one part fluid milk. The Clover Dairy Company was a division of the National Dairy Products Corporation.

2444. Sugar-free soft drinks were introduced in 1952. They were NoCal, introduced in 1952 by Hyman Kirsch of Kirsch Beverages, College Point, NY, and Diet-Rite Cola, introduced nationwide by Royal Crown Cola.

2445. Frozen bread was offered to stores on November 3, 1952, by Arnold Bakers, Port Chester, NY.

2446. Instant tea was White Rose Redi-Tea. The powdered beverage was marketed by Seeman Brothers of New York City beginning in 1953.

2447. Official use of the "Coke" trademark by the Coca-Cola Company, Atlanta, GA, was in 1955, 10 years after it registered the name "Coke" as a trademark.

2448. Powdered breakfast drink was Tang, patented in 1957 by General Foods Corporation, White Plains, NY. Tang was described in General Foods advertising as an "aromatic, orangy-tasting powder," comprised mainly of sugar, additives, and anticaking agents. Tang had its marketing breakthrough when it was supplied to astronauts on the Gemini IV and Gemini V space flights in the summer of 1965. Thereafter, General Foods promoted the powder as the first "space drink."

2449. Scooter Pies were trademarked by Burry's, a division of the Quaker Oats Company, on December 17, 1959. The chocolate-coated, marshmallow-filled pie was popular with schoolchildren in the 1960s; an important innovation by Burry's was to package each pie in its own cellophane bag, making it easy for mothers to pop one in the lunch box.

2450. Buffalo wings were most likely invented circa 1964 by Teressa Bellissimo at the Anchor Bar & Restaurant on the corner of East North and Main in Buffalo, NY. The savory appetizer of deep-fried chicken wings coated in spicy sauce, served with bleu cheese dressing and celery, was originally called "Buffalo chicken wings." No definite date of coinage has been determined for the simplified term "buffalo wings."

2451. Freeze-dried coffee was marketed in 1964 and made available nationally in 1968 by General Foods, White Plains, NY. This coffee was percolated and frozen at temperatures below zero. By sublimation, water passed under high vacuum directly from its solid icy state to vapor, bypassing entirely the liquid form.

2452. Microwave popcorn sold commercially was Act I, introduced by Golden Valley Microwave Foods, Edina, MN, in 1981. The popcorn was frozen and available only in vending machines. In October 1984 the same company introduced Act II. The kernels were mixed with soybean oil and packaged in bags that could be placed directly in a microwave oven for popping.

2453. Fat substitute in prepared foods was Simplesse, a low-calorie fat substitute developed by the Nutrasweet Company. Simplesse was made of proteins derived from egg whites and milk. It was approved by the Food and Drug Administration on February 22, 1990.

2454. Dolphin-free tuna became available in 1990, after environmentalists protested the mass drownings of dolphins caught in the long nets used by tuna fishermen. On April 12, representatives of three major canned tuna producers—Star-Kist Seafood, Bumble Bee Brands, and Van Camp Seafood (Chicken of the Sea)—announced that they would require their suppliers to switch to fishing methods that do not ensnare dolphins. Cans of tuna caught with these methods were marked with a "dolphin-free" logo.

2455. Genetically engineered product to appear in food that was widely consumed in the United States was bovine growth hormone (BGH), also called bovine somatotropin, produced from gene-altered bacteria by the Monsanto Company, St. Louis, MO, in the early 1990s. It was added to cattle feed to increase the milk production of cows by up to 25 percent. Milk from cows that had ingested BGH went on sale across the United States in February 1994 after approval by the Food and Drug Administration, but was shunned by many consumers.

2456. Genetically altered food was the Flavr Savr tomato, developed by Calgene, Davis, CA. The tomato contained a gene that caused it to ripen quickly on the vine. The company also claimed an improvement in the flavor. On May 18, 1994, the tomato was approved for sale by the Food and Drug Administration. It began appearing in stores about two weeks later.

Grooming and Hygiene

2457. Comb factory on a commercial scale was undertaken by Enoch Noyes of West Newbury, MA, in 1759. His combs were made from flattened animal horns, with their original color untouched.

2458. Comb made of ivory was made at Centerbrook, CT, by Andrew Lord in 1789. He cut the plates and teeth with a handsaw.

2459. Comb-cutting machine was invented by Phineas Pratt of Connecticut, who received a patent for it on April 12, 1799. Phineas Pratt and Abel Pratt cut the plates with handsaws and the teeth with circular saws operated by a water-powered windmill at Ivoryton, CT.

2460. Tattoo shop was opened in 1846 by Martin Hildebrandt on Oak Street between Oliver and James streets, New York City.

2461. Toilet paper was unbleached pearl-colored pure manila hemp paper made in 1857 by Joseph C. Gayetty of New York City, whose name was watermarked on each sheet. It sold at 500 sheets for 50 cents and was known as "Gayetty's Medicated Paper—a perfectly pure article for the toilet and for the prevention of piles." It did not catch on with the public. The first toilet paper to be marketed successfully was introduced by Edward and Clarence Scott of Philadelphia, PA, who sold it in small rolls.

2462. Toothpick manufacturing machine was developed by Charles Forster in Boston, MA. In 1869, while working for a shoe-peg manufacturer, he built a device to cut toothpicks from Maine white birch. A similar machine was patented on February 20, 1872, by Silas Noble and James P. Cooley of Granville, MA. The machine made it possible for "a block of wood, with little waste, at one operation, [to] be cut up into toothpicks ready for use."

2463. Dental floss dispenser was patented by Asahel M. Shurtleff in 1872. His company, Codman & Shurtleff of Randolph, MA, began selling dispensers of unwaxed silk floss in 1882.

2464. Electric tattoo machine was employed by Samuel F. O'Reilly in 1875 in his tattoo shop in Chatham Square on the Bowery, New York City. O'Reilly modified Thomas Edison's electric engraving pen to produce what he called "tattaugraphs."

2465. Hair clipper was manufactured by George Henry Coates of Worcester, MA, in 1876. His product was so superior to those imported from England and France that he received an initial manufacturing order for 5,000 clippers.

2466. Floating soap was made in 1878 by two cousins, Harley Procter and James Gamble, founders of the Procter and Gamble Company, Cincinnati, OH. It was invented by accident, when a factory worker forgot to turn off a mixing machine. The extra air that was whipped into the solution made the soap buoyant. It was known as White Soap until October 1879, when it was renamed Ivory Soap. A trademark was obtained for it on July 18, 1879. The advertising slogan "99 and 44-hundredths percent pure" was introduced on December 21, 1882.

2467. Antibacterial mouthwash to be widely used was Listerine, the invention of Dr. Joseph Lawrence of St. Louis, MO. Lawrence was inspired by the work of Sir Joseph Lister, the British pioneer in medical hygiene. He concocted an alcohol-based yellow mouth rinse and marketed it beginning in 1880 through the Lambert Pharmacal Company, St. Louis.

2468. Safety razor was the Star Safety Razor, made by Kampfe Brothers, New York City, in 1880, and consisted of a short portion of a hand-forged blade of a barber's straight razor inserted in a frame with full safety features. The first safety razor to be successfully marketed was invented by King Camp Gillette of Brookline, MA, in 1895 with the help of William Nickerson, a professor at the Massachusetts Institute of Technology, and manufactured by the Gillette Safety Razor Company. It was equipped with a flexible and movable blade that was punched out of thin steel and could be thrown away. The razors cost five dollars each when they went on sale in 1903. Consumers bought 300,000 of them in 1906.

2469. Avon Lady to sell cosmetics products door-to-door was Mrs. P. F. E. Albee of Winchester, NH. The founder of the company, David McConnell, was a door-to-door book salesman from Suffern, NY, who mixed his own perfume to give away as a premium to housewives. In 1886 he switched from selling books to selling the perfume and began hiring women to make sales in rural areas.

2470. Toothpaste tube was the invention of a dentist, Dr. Washington Wentworth Sheffield of New London, CT, who was seeking a method of packaging toothpaste that was more hygienic than the porcelain jars then in use. In 1892, he introduced a flexible, collapsible metal tube.

2471. Shampoo commercially produced was made by John Breck, a fire chief who had begun to lose his hair at the age of 25. In 1908 he opened a scalp-treatment center in Springfield, MA, where he began selling his own shampoos and massage oils. His products were receiving nationwide distribution by 1940.

2472. False eyelashes used in modern times were invented by the film director D. W. Griffith. In 1916, while filming *Intolerance*, Griffith wanted larger lashes for the actress Seena Owen, to make her eyes appear larger on film. The false eyelashes were constructed of human hair woven into fine gauze, which was then attached to the actress's eyelids with gum arabic.

2473. Blow dryer for hair was developed simultaneously by two Wisconsin companies, the Racine Universal Motor Company and Hamilton Beach, in 1920. Both companies were working on developing electric blenders, and both were aware that women were already using home vacuum cleaners to dry their hair. Combining these two technologies, plus a heating coil, yielded the earliest blow driers. The first widely successful model was introduced in the Sears-Roebuck Fall-Winter 1951 catalog. It featured a nozzle attached to a pink plastic bonnet that fit over the head.

2474. Sanitary napkin that was disposable was invented by army nurses during World War I. They adapted it from a crepe-cellulose surgical dressing made from wood pulp. The company that manufactured the dressing, the Kimberly and Clark Company (later called Kimberly-Clark, Dallas, TX), began marketing Kotex pads in 1920.

2475. Tampon to be mass-produced was the Tampax, patented in 1930 by Earl C. Haas, a gynecologist in Denver, CO. His design used a compressed cotton roll inside a cardboard applicator tube. Both the tube and the cotton were disposable. Tampons in various forms have been used since ancient times.

2476. Electric shaver was invented by Colonel Jacob Schick, who recognized that soldiers in the field needed a razor that did not require soap or hot water. He patented a tiny electric motor in 1923 and received patents on his "shaving implement" on November 6, 1928. The first razors manufactured by the Schick company of Stamford, CT, were delivered on March 18, 1931. The dual-headed electric shaver was introduced by Remington in 1940.

2477. Toothbrush with synthetic bristles was Dr. West's Miracle Tuft Toothbrush, made by the E.I. du Pont de Nemours and Company of Wilmington, DE, and first introduced to the retail trade in September 1938. The bristles were made from nylon, but were stiff enough to hurt the gums. Du Pont introduced a soft-bristle brush in the 1950s. Until the invention of nylon, people cleaned their teeth with hog-bristle brushes or with toothpicks.

2478. Commercial sunscreen product in the United States was Coppertone Suntan Cream, a mixture of cocoa butter and jasmine concocted in 1944 by Benjamin Green of

Miami Beach, FL. Green, a pharmacist, had had experience with sunburn while serving in the South Pacific during World War II.

2479. Deodorant soap was Dial Soap, produced by Armour and Company, Chicago, IL, in 1948. The white soap incorporated a bactericidal substance, hexachlorophene, that was developed during World War II for use in field hospitals.

2480. Toothpaste with fluoride was Crest, introduced by Procter and Gamble of Cincinnati, OH, in 1952. It contained stannous fluoride, a substance that research had shown to be effective in preventing tooth decay.

2481. Electric toothbrush was the Broxodent, made by the Squibb Company. It went on sale in 1961. A cordless electric toothbrush made by General Electric came on the market the following year.

2482. Anti-aging skin cream proven effective in a double-blind scientific trial was Retin-A, a retinoic acid derivative of vitamin A. It was first formulated by Albert Kligman, professor of dermatology at the University of Pennsylvania School of Medicine, Philadelphia, PA, and approved as a prescription acne medication in 1968. The first clear evidence of Retin-A's antiaging effects were reported in the January 22, 1988, issue of the *Journal of the American Medical Association* by John Voorhees and colleagues at the University of Michigan Medical Center. In the double-blind trial of 30 subjects, skin treated with Retin-A cream showed fewer wrinkles and sun spots than skin treated with a control cream.

2483. Horse grooming products sold for human use were marketed beginning in 1993 by Straight Arrow of Bethlehem, PA, owned by Roger Dunavant. Previously available only in feed and pet stores, the products, including Straight Arrow hoof strengthener and Mane 'n Tail shampoo, were made available in beauty salons, supermarkets, and drugstores. Dunavant thought of the idea when he learned that grooms were using the products on their own nails and hair.

Holidays

2484. Thanksgiving meal shared by European settlers and Native Americans was most likely a meal that took place in St. Augustine in what is now the state of Florida, on September 8, 1565, following a Catholic mass for 800 Spanish settlers led by Pedro Menendez de Aviles. The meal was shared by a group of Native Americans, the Seloy. Private celebrations of thanksgiving were made by the Spanish explorers who preceded Aviles, as well as by a French Huguenot colony that held its observance on June 30, 1564, near Jacksonville, FL, some months before they were decimated by the Spanish.

2485. Colonial law banning Christmas was instituted by the Puritan governing council of the Massachusetts Bay Colony in 1659. The law was repealed in 1681, but not because of popular demand. By then, Puritan leaders were confident that no one wanted to celebrate the holiday. The Puritans considered most Christmas celebrations to be of pagan origin, and thought the feasting and revelry associated with Christmas to be impious. Christmas was legalized in Massachusetts in 1856.

2486. Mardi Gras in the American colonies was celebrated by French soldiers at what is now Mobile, AL, in 1703, at which time it was known as *Boeuf Gras* (Fat Ox). The carnival traditions developed in Mobile were brought to New Orleans in 1857.

2487. National day of prayer was established on June 12, 1775, by the Continental Congress in Philadelphia, PA. The resolution recommended that all English colonists observe July 20 as a day of "public humiliation, fasting, and prayer" on which to "offer up our joint supplications to the all-wise, omnipotent, and merciful Disposer of all events," and to ask, among other things, for "a reconciliation with the parent state, on terms constitutional and honorable to both."

On July 20, 1775, all American troops under George Washington's command received orders to take part in services on the national day of prayer, bringing along "their arms, ammunition and accoutrements" in case of need.

2488. Christmas tree displayed in the United States is likely to have been the tree that was displayed in December 1777 on the Samuel Denslow farm in Windsor Locks, CT. It was set up by Hendrick Roddmore, a Hessian soldier in the British Army who was working as a laborer after having been taken prisoner by the Americans.

2489. National day of thanksgiving was authorized by the Continental Congress and held on December 18, 1777, to celebrate the surrender of Lieutenant General John Burgoyne on October 17 at Saratoga (now Schuylerville), NY. The first to be designated by presidential proclamation was November 26, 1789, which was appointed by President George Washington as a day of general thanksgiving for the adoption of the Constitution.

2490. Independence Day to be observed as a state holiday was celebrated by Massachusetts on July 4, 1781.

2491. Columbus Day was celebrated on October 12, 1792, to mark the tricentennial of Christopher Columbus's first landing in the New World. The second Columbus Day was celebrated a century later, in 1892. Annual celebrations began in 1893 during the World's Columbian Exposition in Chicago, IL.

2492. Valentines commercially produced in the United States were manufactured in 1834 by Robert H. Elton, an engraver, who opened Elton and Company in New York City, specializing in printing and publishing. Previously, valentines were handmade.

2493. Christmas cards made in the United States were designed and produced by Richard H. Pease, engraver and lithographer, at Albany, NY, in 1851. They were printed in black on white paper, 4.5 by 6 inches, with the message "A Merry Christmas and Happy New Year." The illustration showed a fanciful structure with a banner reading "Pease's Great Varety Store in the Temple of Fancy." (He misspelled "Variety." The cards were sent to his customers and friends.

2494. Presidential proclamation of a national day of prayer was made by Abraham Lincoln in Washington, DC, on March 30, 1863, in response to a request from the Senate. He asked citizens to observe April 30, 1863, as a day of national humiliation, fasting, and prayer, to be kept in their homes and places of worship, in the hope that "the united cry of the Nation will be heard on high, and answered with blessings, no less the pardon of our national sins, and restoration of our now divided and suffering country to its former happy condition of unity and peace."

2495. Thanksgiving Day was held in November 1863 to commemorate the feast of thanksgiving held by the Pilgrims at Plymouth, MA, in 1621. A proclamation by President Abraham Lincoln set aside the fourth Thursday in November for an annual nationwide observance. The establishment of Thanksgiving Day was the result of a long campaign by Sarah Josepha Hale, the editor of the popular magazine *Godey's Lady's Book*. The holiday was moved forward to the third Thursday in November in 1939 to accommodate merchants who wanted more time for the pre-Christmas shopping rush, but was returned to its traditional spot two years later.

2496. Commemoration of the birthday of Abraham Lincoln took place in Washington, DC, on February 12, 1866, ten months after President Lincoln's assassination. A joint session of Congress assembled at noon at the Capitol in the chamber of the House of Representatives, joined by President Andrew Johnson, most of his cabinet secretaries, the Justices of the Supreme Court, the governors of the various states, military officers, and other dignitaries. Following a brief performance by the Marine Band and a prayer by the House chaplain, the historian and diplomat George Bancroft delivered an address. Lincoln was born in Hardin County, KY, in 1809.

2497. Memorial Day as a national holiday was observed on May 30, 1868, by order of John A. Logan, commander in chief of the Grand Army of the Republic. The day, then called Decoration Day, was set aside to celebrate the lives of "comrades who died in defense of their country during the late rebellion." It was marked by a ceremony at Arlington National Cemetery. Tending the graves of the Civil War dead was a responsibility that had already been assumed in several states by local volunteer organizations, particularly women's memorial associations. The first state to adopt Memorial Day as a state holiday was New York, in 1873. Memorial Day was celebrated on May 30 until 1971, when Congress altered the date to the last Monday in May.

2498. Labor Day was inaugurated on December 28, 1869, by the Knights of Labor, a workers' organization formed in Philadelphia, PA. The first states to declare Labor Day a state holiday were Oregon, in February 1887; Colorado, in March 1887; and New York, in May 1887. The annual nationwide observance of Labor Day was sponsored by the American Federation of Labor, which resolved in convention at Chicago, IL, on October 7, 1884, "that the first Monday in September be set aside as a laborer's national holiday." On June 28, 1894, Congress designated the first Monday in September a legal holiday for federal employees and for the District of Columbia. The first Labor Day parade was held in New York City on September 5, 1882, under the auspices of the Central Labor Union. It featured musical bands and 10,000 marchers who carried placards reading "Less Work and More Pay," "Less Hours More Pay," "Labor Pays All Taxes," "Labor Creates All Wealth," "To the Workers Should Belong the Wealth," and "The Laborer Must Receive and Enjoy the Full Fruit of His Labor."

2499. Arbor Day was celebrated on April 10, 1872, in Nebraska. Governor Julius Sterling Morton suggested the holiday and helped celebrate it by having trees planted throughout the state. Arbor Day did not become a legal holiday in Nebraska until April 22, 1885, Morton's birthday.

2500. Christmas card to be printed in color in the United States were the work of Louis Prang, an emigrant from Prussia to Boston, MA. His printing shop, L. Prang and Company, specialized in chromolithography, using as many as 20 colors. He began selling expensive Christmas cards in 1875. They were designed by prominent painters and often contained verses by well-known poets.

2501. Centennial celebration of the Revolution was held at Lexington and Concord, MA, on April 19, 1875, to commemorate the 100th birthday of American liberty. The participants included President Ulysses Simpson Grant, three cabinet secretaries, and many state governors.

2502. Easter egg roll was held on April 2, 1877, at the Capitol grounds, Washington, DC, during President Rutherford Hayes's administration. The custom was carried on by later Presidents until it was discontinued by President Franklin Delano Roosevelt in 1942. It was reinstated on April 6, 1953, during the administration of President Dwight David Eisenhower.

2503. Flag Day remembrance took place on June 14, 1877. The Government requested that the flag be flown from all public buildings on that day in commemoration of the 100th anniversary of the adoption of the American flag. President Woodrow Wilson issued a proclamation in 1916 designating June 14 as Flag Day. The first state to make Flag Day a legal holiday was Pennsylvania, in 1937. A joint congressional resolution dated August 3, 1949, designated June 14 as an annual day of national observance.

Wilson's proclamation of Flag Day was the result of a popular movement begun by Bernard J. Cigrand, a teacher at Stony Hill School in Waubeka, WI.

2504. Christmas tree decorated with electric lights was installed in December 1882 in New York City in the house of Edward H. Johnson, an associate of Thomas Alva Edison.

2505. National holiday was April 30, 1889, authorized by act of Congress on March 21, 1889, in observance of the centennial of the inauguration of George Washington. The day was "hereby declared to be a national holiday throughout the United States." A committee of five senators and five representatives of the 51st Congress was appointed to arrange an appropriate celebration in Congress on December 11, 1889, at which Chief Justice Melville Weston Fuller was the guest speaker.

2506. Frontier Day celebration was the Cheyenne Frontier Day, held at the Fair Grounds in Cheyenne, WY, on September 23, 1897. From a one-day exhibition, the celebration grew to a six-day spectacle of ranch and range sports, Native American games and dances, military maneuvers, and races requiring the utmost skill in horsemanship. Other cities have similar celebrations under different names.

2507. Dropping of the ball in Times Square on New Year's Eve at one minute to midnight took place on December 31, 1907, when a 5-foot sphere weighing 700 pounds was lowered down a flagpole on the roof of

One Times Square in New York City. The sphere, a wood-and-iron contraption carrying 100 light bulbs, had been crafted by Jacob Starr, a Russian immigrant metalworker.

2508. Mother's Day celebration took place in Philadelphia, PA, on May 10, 1908. The idea was suggested by Anna Jarvis of Philadelphia at a public meeting in 1907. She proposed wearing a carnation in honor of mothers on the second Sunday of May. A joint resolution of Congress on May 8, 1914, established the second Sunday in May as Mother's Day. On May 9, President Woodrow Wilson proclaimed the date as a national holiday, which was held for the first time on May 10.

2509. Father's Day was celebrated on June 19, 1910. The idea originated with Mrs. John Bruce Dodd, and the holiday was launched by the Ministerial Association and the YMCA of Spokane, WA. It is now generally observed on the third Sunday in June.

2510. Indian Day celebration was held in New York State on May 13, 1916, sponsored by the Society of American Indians. The purpose was to recognize and honor the Native Americans and to improve their conditions.

2511. Veterans Day was observed nationally on November 11, 1919, on the anniversary of the day on which World War I was brought to an end. Public meetings, prayers, and parades were held, and two minutes of silence were observed at 11 A.M., the hour at which hostilities ceased. President Woodrow Wilson in 1920 declared the Sunday nearest to Armistice Day to be Armistice Sunday, an appropriate day for prayer for world peace. Until 1954, the annual commemoration was known as Armistice Day. It was made a legal holiday on May 13, 1938.

2512. Navy Day was celebrated on October 27, 1922, the anniversary of the birth of President Theodore Roosevelt. Celebrations were held in various parts of the United States. The idea was suggested by Mrs. William Hamilton to the Secretary of the Navy.

2513. National Christmas tree was the General Grant Tree, in General Grant National Park, CA, which was the site of a ceremony at noon on Christmas Day 1925. On May 1, 1926, Mayor Henry Leonard Suderman of Sanger, CA, officially dedicated it as "the Nation's Christmas Tree." The greatest horizontal diameter of the tree was 40.3 feet at the base. At 200 feet above the ground the diameter was about 12 feet. The tree was 267 feet high and 3,500-4,000 years old.

2514. Maritime Day took place on May 22, 1933. It was established by joint resolution of Congress on May 20, 1933. The resolution authorized and requested the President "annually to issue a proclamation calling upon the people of the United States to observe National Maritime Day by displaying the flag." The designated day was the anniversary of the sailing of the steamship *Savannah* from Savannah, GA, on May 22, 1819.

2515. Santa Claus school to train men to play the part of Santa Claus was a one-week program that opened on September 27, 1937, in Albion, NY, with an enrollment of six students. It was conducted by Charles Willis Howard.

2516. Halloween collection for UNICEF was called "Trick-or-Treat for UNICEF." It was made by a class of Sunday School children and their pastor in Philadelphia, PA, on October 31, 1950. As they went from door to door collecting candy treats, they also carried decorated milk cartons and asked for donations of coins for the United Nations International Children's Emergency Fund. They raised a total of $17.

2517. National Day of Prayer established by Congress was established by a unanimous joint resolution and was signed into law by President Harry S. Truman in Washington, DC, on April 17, 1952. The law was amended in 1988 to establish the first Thursday in May as the annual date of the event.

2518. Kwanzaa celebration was held on December 26, 1966, in California. It was the invention of black militant Ron Karenga, who drew upon African agricultural festivals to create a cultural festival for African-Americans. The name is a Swahili word meaning "first fruit of the harvest." Kwanzaa is held annually from December 26 to January 1. Each of the seven days celebrates a separate principle: unity, self-determination, collective work and responsibility, economic cooperation, purpose, creativity, and faith. A candle is lit on each night to represent the principle of the day.

2519. Earth Day was held nationwide on April 22, 1970, to increase public awareness of the world's environmental problems. Twenty million Americans participated in marches, educational programs, and rallies, including the students at some 2,000 colleges and 10,000 high schools.

2520. Martin Luther King Day was officially observed as a national holiday on January 20, 1986. It marked the birthday of the African-American minister and civil rights leader Martin Luther King, Jr., the champion of nonviolent social protest and winner of the 1964 Nobel Peace Prize, who was born on January 15, 1929, in Atlanta, GA. A bill to make his birthday a national holiday was submitted to Congress by Representative John Conyers of Michigan in April 1968, four days after Reverend King was assassinated. The observance was moved to the third Monday in January when the new holiday was created by Congress in November 1983.

> The first state to declare Martin Luther King's birthday a legal holiday was Illinois, which did so on September 17, 1973.

Library of Congress, Prints and Photographs Division
LC-DIG-ppmsc-01269

Martin Luther King , Jr.

2521. Native American Day was celebrated in South Dakota in place of Columbus Day on October 8, 1990.

2522. UNICEF Halloween collection that raised funds for American children took place on October 31, 2005, when trick-or-treaters in the United States raised $5.2 million. Half of that money was channeled to the U.S. Fund for UNICEF to help children in Gulf Coast states whose lives had been disrupted by Hurricane Katrina the previous August.

Houses

2523. Log cabins were constructed by the Swedish immigrants who built New Sweden, NJ (near the present site of Trenton), in 1638. Each cabin contained one room, about 12 feet by 14 feet, that housed a family and, in cold weather, its livestock.

2524. Summer home was the manor house erected in 1769 on the 4,000-acre tract of John Wentworth, last royal colonial governor of New Hampshire (1767–75). It was located on the shore of Lake Wentworth, Wolfeboro, NH.

2525. Tenement house was built in New York City in 1833 on Water Street, on a site later within the limits of Corlears Park. It was four stories high, with arrangements for one family on each floor. This was the beginning of the system of grouping many homes under one roof. A tenement is any house, or part of a house, occupied by three or more families living independently of each other and doing cooking on the premises. The term generally refers to buildings where the rents are low and the living conditions are substandard.

2526. Apartment house with a modern layout was erected in New York City in 1869. It was known as the Stuyvesant Apartments and was located at 142 East 18th Street. Every floor contained four apartment suites, each with a kitchen, dining room, parlor, and bedrooms, plus a servant's room and a dumbwaiter. The fifth and top floor was arranged for artists' studios. The annual rental for the apartments varied from $1,200 to $1,800 each; $200 was charged for the studios. The architect was Richard Morris Hunt; the owner, Rutherford Stuyvesant.

2527. Apartment house cooperative was the Gramercy, a 10-story apartment house at 34 Gramercy Park, New York City, constructed by James Campbell for the Gramercy Company. Each apartment was adjudged equal to a certain number of shares. Apartments sold for $4,500 to $8,000. The property, which became ready for occupancy in September 1883, was managed by seven trustees. The building had three hydraulic elevators and a restaurant on an upper floor that was leased in October 1883 to Louis Sherry.

2528. Apartment house to occupy a square city block was the Belnord Apartment House, a 12-story building in New York City, which became ready for occupancy on October 15, 1909. It was bounded by 86th Street on the south, 87th Street on the north, Broadway on the west, and Amsterdam Avenue on the east. At the time, it was the largest apartment house in the world. Its area was 64,614 square feet, with an interior court of 22,033 square feet. It contained six separate passenger elevators and 178 suites, each with 7 to 11 rooms and two to four baths. Every room was an outside room. Annual rentals ranged from $2,100 upwards. Philip Hiss and H. Hobart Weekes were the architects.

2529. House completely heated by solar energy was built in Dover, MA, and occupied on December 24, 1948. The house trapped the sun's energy through a unit consisting of a black sheet-metal collector behind two panes of glass. The solar heat was stored in a "heat bin" containing an inexpensive sodium compound. Electric fans blew the stored heat through vents as desired. The experiments were sponsored by Amelia Peabody. The house was designed by Eleanor Raymond and the heating system was developed by Dr. Maria Telkes.

2530. House with solar heating and radiation cooling was built by Raymond Whitcomb Bliss in Tucson, AZ. The system, built at a cost of nearly $4,000 for labor and materials, was placed in operation on January 15, 1955. A large slanting slab of steel and glass converted the sunlight into heat, which was brought into the house by ducts. The same fans, controls, and ducts were used for summer cooling.

2531. House with a built-in nuclear bomb shelter was exhibited on May 24, 1959, at Hi-Tor Woods, Pleasant Hills, PA. It was built by the Obie Construction Company, Pittsburgh, PA, and contained a fully equipped underground integral shelter, with bunks to sleep four persons, sanitary facilities, a food storage area and refrigerator, a transoceanic radio, a first-aid kit, a weather-warning device, a Geiger counter, a fire extinguisher, and other equipment. The main part of the shelter was 22 feet long and 8 feet wide. Another section contained an auxiliary power plant, heating equipment, an air filtering system, and an oxygen tank. The walls were made of concrete blocks 10 inches thick; lead was used for insulation against radiation. The shelter had a concrete escape tunnel.

2532. Year in which the average price of a new house topped $100,000 was 1984. In May of that year, the average price of a new single-family house was $101,000.

Housewares

2533. Fork brought to America was in a leather case with a bodkin and knife. Governor John Winthrop of Massachusetts introduced it into this country about 1630, following the style of eating which Queen Elizabeth of England had introduced despite the flaming denunciations of many eminent clergymen.

2534. Pottery made in America by settlers is believed to have been the work of John Pride of Salem, MA, who operated a pottery from 1641 to 1647. He made red earthenware from common brick clay. Another pottery was established by Dr. Daniel Coxe in Burlington, NJ, in 1680. It produced white and "chiney" ware for the local trade and also for export to Jamaica and Barbados. The factory was sold in 1691.

2535. Wallpaper was manufactured in 1739 by Plunket Fleeson of Philadelphia, PA. The design was stamped with wooden blocks on sheets of paper that were joined together. A paintbrush was used to apply the color. In August 1739, Fleeson advertised in the *Pennsylvania Gazette* the sale of "bedticks, choice live geese feathers, blankets, as well as paper-hangings."

2536. Heating stove was the Pennsylvania fireplace, invented by Benjamin Franklin in 1742 and now called the Franklin stove. It was a wood-burning open box of cast-iron that stood out from the chimney and caused heat from its back and sides to be thrown into the room. Smoke escaped over the top of a flat chamber behind the fire, and passed downward between it and the real back of the stove,

Library of Congress, Prints & Photographs Division LC-USZC4-623

Benjamin Franklin

then into the chimney. Franklin refused to patent his invention. The stoves were manufactured by Robert Grace, the master of the Warwick furnace in Chester County, PA.

2537. Candle factory for making spermaceti candles was established by Benjamin Crabb in Newport, RI, in 1748. It was destroyed by fire in 1750, after which the candles were manufactured in Newport by Jacob Rodriguez Rivera. Spermaceti candles, made from the oil obtained from the heads of sperm whales, burned better than the tallow candles then in general use. Rivera and other Sephardic Jewish immigrants made Newport the center of production of candles, soap, and other whale oil products.

2538. Rocking chair is believed to have been invented by Benjamin Franklin of Philadelphia, PA, about 1760. This date is not verified, but no authentic instance of a prior rocker has come to light.

2539. Venetian blinds are said to have been installed in 1761 in St. Peter's Church, Third and Pine streets, Philadelphia, PA. The first patent for them was granted to John Hampson of New Orleans, LA, on August 21, 1841, on a "manner of retaining in any desired position the slats of Venetian Blinds."

2540. Sieve was produced in 1768 in Philadelphia, PA, by John Sellers. His sieves were used principally by millers.

2541. Carpet mill was founded in 1791 by William Peter Sprague on North Second Street, Philadelphia, PA. He manufactured Axminster carpets on handlooms. One of his earliest designs represented the aims and achievements of the new republic of the United States.

2542. Glass crystal chandelier consisted of "six lights and shower upon shower of rainbow casting prisms." It was cut by William Peter Eichbaum at Bakewell's, Pittsburgh, PA, in 1810 and made in a 10-pot furnace. It sold for $300 to a Mr. Kerr, who hung it in his hostelry.

2543. Chair factory was established by Lambert Hitchcock in Hitchcockville (now Riverton), CT, in 1818. The chairs were generally hand-painted on the back. They were shipped disassembled. They sold extensively in the South.

2544. Cutlery shears were made in Elizabethport, NJ, in 1825 by Rochus Heinisch.

2545. Bedspring manufacturing patent was granted on August 25, 1831, to Josiah French of Ware, MA.

2546. Cutlery factory of importance was the Green River Works of John Russell and Company, Greenfield, MA, established about 1833 for the manufacture of chisels and table cutlery. It developed into the J. Russell Cutlery Company and had a branch office in New York City in 1840. A factory for making pocket cutlery was started at Lakeville, CT, by the Holley Manufacturing Company in 1845.

2547. Friction matches were made in Springfield, MA, in 1834 in a small establishment in the "L" of the Frederick Chapin house on Chicopee Street, Chicopee (then a part of Springfield), by Daniel M. Chapin and Alonzo Dwight Phillips. On October 24, 1836, Phillips received a patent for the product. The constituents of the match head were chalk, phosphorus, glue, and brimstone. The business was sold to Byam and Carlton of Boston, MA, and the product was thereafter known as the Boston Match. Before 1834, the only match in use had been a slender sulfur splint which was ignited by being drawn quickly through a double fold of sandpaper. Nontoxic friction matches, made with sesquisulfide of phosphorus rather than pure phosphorus, which is poisonous, were introduced by the Diamond Match Company in 1911.

2548. Wire sieves were manufactured commercially in 1834 by Edwin Gilbert of Gilbert, Bennett and Company at Georgetown, CT.

2549. Carpet power loom was invented by Erastus Brigham Bigelow of West Boylston, MA, who obtained a patent for it on April 20, 1837. It was used by the Lowell Manufacturing Company of Lowell, MA, in the weaving of carpets.

2550. Cotton twine factory was established in 1839 by Jacob Sloat of Sloatsburg, NY, at a mill where cotton cloth had been produced since 1815. During the factory's first year of operation it produced as much as 6,000 pounds of cotton twine each week.

2551. Reclining chair was patented on May 22, 1841, by Henry Peres Kennedy, a cabinet-maker and upholsterer of Philadelphia, PA. A spiral spring was placed horizontally between the back rail of the seat and the front rail of the chair.

2552. Safety pin was invented by Walter Hunt of New York City, who obtained a patent on April 10, 1849. Within the space of three hours, he conceived the idea, made a model, and sold his patent rights for $100. The pins were manufactured in New York City.

2553. Desk with a roll top was invented about 1850 by Abner Cutler, who formed the Cutler Desk Company of Buffalo, NY. The original patent showed the top very similar to the roll top of today. Flexible wooden curtains had been used previously. Cutler improved upon their manufacture by using a strong fabric held between an outer row of moldings and an inner row of soft wood slats, which made it possible to operate rolls six feet long and four feet wide.

2554. Blanket factory was the Burleigh Blanket Mills, established by Captain John H. Burleigh in 1854 on the Piscataqua River in Maine. The factory was located on the site originally used by the explorer Sir Ferdinando Gorges in 1620 for a grist mill, at what is now South Berwick, ME.

2555. Box spring was imported from France in 1857 by James Boyle, Chatham Square, New York City, a manufacturer of bedding. Made to be reversible, it was about 12 inches deep. The frame was made of boards joined together with strips of ticking.

2556. Oil lamp for burning kerosene was developed in 1857 by A.C. Ferris and Company, later the Tarentum Oil, Salt and Coal Company.

2557. Mason jar for canning was patented in 1858 by metalworker John Landis Mason of New York City. It was a reusable glass container with a wide, threaded mouth that could be tightly sealed with a flexible ring and a zinc lid. The first Mason jars were made by Whitney Glass Works of Glassboro, NJ.

2558. Corkscrew patent was granted on March 27, 1860, to M. L. Byrn of New York City. It covered a gimlet screw with a "T" handle.

2559. Decalcomania pictures that could be transferred from paper to other surfaces were imported in 1862 and used as playthings. The first commercial production of decalcomanias for decorating buggies, sleighs, bicycles, sewing machines, and other objects was undertaken in Philadelphia, PA, in 1890 by Thomas Burke, who established the National Decalcomania Company. The company was incorporated in 1922.

2560. Folding stepladder was patented by John H. Balsley, Dayton, OH, on January 7, 1862. Balsley replaced the typical ladder rungs with flat steps that were safer to use.

2561. Linoleum was manufactured in 1873 by the American Linoleum Manufacturing Company, Richmond, Staten Island, NY (now part of New York City). It was a British invention.

2562. Folding bed was successfully built in 1875–76 at Sixth and Filbert Streets, Philadelphia, PA, by the Hale and Kilburn Manufacturing Company. The folding bed was invented by a man in the company's employ named Everett and was improved upon by H. S. Hale. The bed was designed because apartment houses were becoming more popular and there was a need for economy in space. The beds were equipped with a flexible spring. They later used a "sectional spring bed," or the ordinary bedspring divided into three sections lengthwise, each of which was filled with springs and enclosed in a canvas covering. This spring developed into the box spring now in use.

2563. Electric fan was invented by Dr. Schuyler Skaats Wheeler, who in 1882 placed a fan or propeller on the shaft of an electric motor. In 1904, the Franklin Institute awarded him the John Scott medal for this invention.

2564. Dealer in Oriental rugs was Hagop Boghighian, an immigrant from Armenia, who began selling rugs in Boston, MA, in 1885.

2565. Drinking straws were made in 1886 by Marvin Chester Stone of Washington, DC, from paraffined manila paper rolled by hand. He obtained a patent on January 3, 1888. Rye straws had been used previously, but they proved unsatisfactory as they were generally unclean and cracked. Paper drinking straws were made by hand until 1905, when the first machine to manufacture them successfully was made by the Marvin C. Stone Estate.

2566. Pocket lighter was patented on October 29, 1889, by Elias Bernard Koopman. A similar model, patented by Koopman and William W. McKenney the following year, was identified as intended for "lighting cigars, lamps, gas-burners, and many other similar purposes." It was manufactured by the Magic Introduction Company, New York City.

2567. Deck chair for steamer passengers was introduced in 1891 by Heinrich Conried, impresario of the Metropolitan Opera House, New York City. He built 500 chairs and formed the Ocean Comfort Company to distribute and rent them. At one time 5,000 chairs were on rental to steamship companies. The first rental contract was signed with Albert Ballin, general director of the Hamburg-American lines.

2568. Matchbooks were made by the Diamond Match Company at its Barberton, OH, factory in 1896 under a patent granted on September 27, 1892, to Joshua Pusey, an attorney from Lima, PA. Although the patented design had the striking surface on the inside cover, the manufacturer moved it to the outside to prevent fires.

2569. Electric socket operated by a pull chain was patented on August 11, 1896, by Harvey Hubbell of Bridgeport, CT, who manufactured the sockets in Bridgeport.

2570. Thermos bottles made in the United States were manufactured in 1907 by the American Thermos Bottle Company, Brooklyn, New York, under license from a German firm. The company was founded by William B. Walker.

2571. Paper cup was developed in 1908 by Hugh Moore, who also invented an early type of water cooler and the Dixie Cup, a paper container for ice cream.

2572. Bed that could be hidden was manufactured by the Murphy Door Bed Company in San Francisco, CA, in 1909. The beds, known as In-a-Door Beds, operated on a pivot and could be swung out of sight behind doors or in closets.

2573. Linoleum manufacturing machine for manufacturing straight-line linoleum was installed in 1911 by Congoleum-Nairn at its Kearny, NJ, plant.

2574. Stainless steel flatware were knives manufactured by the Silver Company, Meriden, CT, in 1921. Most flatware up to that time was made of carbon steel or silver, which required frequent polishing.

2575. Cellophane was made in the early part of 1924 by the Du Pont Cellophane Company at its plant in Buffalo, NY, with machinery manufactured in its own shops. Cellophane originally sold for $2.65 a pound.

2576. Embossed inlaid linoleum was introduced in 1925 by the Armstrong Cork and Insulation Company of Lancaster, PA. The company manufactured the linoleum and then placed it under an embossing press in which parts of the design were compressed, so that the tile blocks or other portions of the pattern stood out in relief.

2577. Air conditioner for home use was designed in 1927 by Willis Haviland Carrier of Buffalo, NY. Carrier, an engineer, received a patent in 1906 for air-conditioning machinery.

2578. Cellophane transparent tape was invented by Richard Gurley Drew of St. Paul, MN, who obtained a patent on May 27, 1930, on "adhesive tape." The patent was assigned to the Minnesota Mining and Manufacturing Company of St. Paul, MN, better known as 3M. The tape was introduced to the market on September 8, 1930. The tape was developed from an earlier invention of Drew's, pressure-sensitive masking tape for use by car body shops.

2579. Mass-produced picture frames were made by the Metalcraft Corporation in Chicago, IL, in 1933. Composed of brass, the frames were sold at a reasonable price. The company, later known as Intercraft Industries, was founded by two brothers, Herman and Maurice Spertus.

2580. Lunch box featuring a licensed character was the Mickey Mouse box, an oval steel box with artwork done in four-color lithography. It was manufactured in 1935 by the Geuder, Paeschke & Frey Co. of Milwaukee, WI, under a contract with the Disney studio.

2581. Household product made entirely of plastic was a clear polyethylene water tumbler invented in 1945 by Massachusetts chemist Earl S. Tupper. In 1948 he began marketing Tupperware, a line of resealable, leak-proof polyethylene containers.

2582. Electric blanket was manufactured by the Simmons Company on October 9, 1946, in Petersburg, VA. Temperature was regulated by an "electronic" thermostatic control. It sold for $39.50.

2583. Aluminum foil was developed by R. S. Reynolds of Louisville, KY, the founder of Reynolds Metals. In 1947, Reynolds developed a thin foil of aluminum 12 inches wide and 0.0007 inches thick. He sold it on a roll for home use as a protective wrap for cooking and storage.

2584. Lunch box featuring a TV character was made by Aladdin Industries, Nashville, TN, in 1950. The character was Hopalong Cassidy, the cowboy played by William Boyd in the movies and on television and radio. The box, designed by Robert O. Burton, was made of enamel-covered steel and came in a choice of blue or red. Hopalong Cassidy appeared on a decal that was applied to the front of the box.

2585. Lunch box fully decorated with lithographed art was a steel box featuring Roy Rogers and Dale Evans, stars of television's "Roy Rogers Show." The scene on the front of the box showed Rogers riding Trigger in the foreground and Evans waving to them from the entrance to their ranch, all of it set in a Western landscape. It was introduced by the American Thermos Bottle Company, Brooklyn, NY, in 1953.

2586. Carpeting of tufted plastic was manufactured at La Fayette, GA, by the E.T. Barwick Mills and offered for sale on January 4, 1953. The carpeting, made of Saran fibers, was immune to moths, mildew, and fungi and was almost completely resistant to ink and other stains. It would soften, char, and decompose in flame, but would not support combustion.

Marriage

2587. Wedding of colonists in Virginia was that of Anne Burras, maid of Mistress Forrest, to John Laydon in 1609. The maid and her mistress had arrived in Jamestown, VA, in 1608 as the first female colonists in Virginia. No women came over with the original Jamestown settlers in 1607. The first wedding of African-Americans took place in Virginia in the early 1620s with the marriage of Antoney and Isabell, slaves (with the status of indentured servants) who had arrived in Jamestown in 1619.

2588. Wedding of colonists in New England was that of Edward Winslow and Susanna White, who were married on May 12, 1621 (new style May 22, 1621). Both were Pilgrims and members of the colony in Plymouth, MA, of which Winslow was the governor. His first wife, Elizabeth Barker, whom he had married in Holland in 1618, had died on March 24, 1621. Susanna White's first husband, William White, had died on February 21, 1621. Edward and Susanna Winslow had a son, Josiah Winslow, who became governor of New Plymouth Colony in 1673 and was thus the first American-born governor.

2589. Breach-of-promise suit was instituted on June 14, 1623, in the Virginia Council of State, Charles City County, VA. The Reverend Greville Pooley brought suit against Cicely Jordan, the widow of Captain Samuel Jordan, who had jilted him in favor of William Ferrar. The penalty for a third offense was either corporal punishment, a fine, or another punishment ordered by the court.

2590. Annulment of a marriage by court decree was passed on December 3, 1639, in Boston, MA, when "James Luxford, being presented for haveing two wifes, his last marriage was declared voyde, or a nullity thereof and to bee divorced, not to come to the sight of her whom hee last tooke, and hee to be sent away to England by the first opportunity; all that hee hath is appointed to her whom hee last married for here and her children; he is also fined 100 t. and to bee set in the stocks an houre upon a market day after the lecture, the next lecture day if the weather permit, or else the next lecture day after (3rd of the 10th month 1639)."

2591. Divorce was granted at a Quarter Court at Boston, MA, on the fifth day of the first month in the year 1643. "Anne Clarke, beeing deserted by Denis Clarke hir husband, and hee refusing to accompany with hir, she is graunted to bee divorced, his refusall was under his hand, and seale, which hee gave before Mr. John Winthrop, Junr. Mr. Emanuel Downing, Mr. Nehemiah Bo'ne [Bourne] and Richard Babington, alsoe hee confesseth hee liveth in adultery with one, by whom he hath had 2 and refuseth hir which hee had two children by."

2592. Married woman to keep her maiden name in the United States was probably Lucy Stone, a journalist and orator active in the movements for women's rights and abolition. Stone graduated from Oberlin College in 1850 and married abolitionist Henry Blackwell in Cincinnati, OH, on May 1, 1855.

2593. Wedding by telegraph took place at noon on April 12, 1900, in Kansas City, MO, when the Reverend Albert H. Linder performed a 25-minute long-distance ceremony for Andrew M. Candell of Washington, DC, who was in Kansas City with two friends, and Penelope Cundiff of Perkins, OK, who was in Mulhall, OK, with her mother and sister. A direct wire conveyed the ceremony a distance of about 200 miles.

2594. Wedding broadcast over the radio was performed on June 15, 1920, in the First Presbyterian Church, Detroit, MI, by the Reverend C. E. Mieras, who received $10 for his services. The bride was Mabelle E. Ebert. The groom, Seaman John R. Wichman, was aboard the U.S.S. *Birmingham* in the Pacific Ocean. A friend stood in as proxy for him at the wedding. The ceremony was telephoned to the telegraph office, wired to the Great Lakes Naval Training Station near Chicago, and sent by radio to the *Birmingham*.

2595. Wedding on television took place on October 14, 1928, in the radio studio at Des Plains, IL, where Cora Dennison and James Fowlkes of Kansas City, MO, were married by the Reverend Gustave A. Klenle of St. Luke's Evangelical Church. The ceremony was telecast.

2596. Wedding by transatlantic telephone took place on December 2, 1933, when Bertil Hjalmar Clason and Sigrid Sophis Margarete Carlson were married by Judge John Dennis Watts of the Wayne County Common Pleas Court in Detroit, MI. The groom was in Detroit and the bride was in Stockholm, Sweden. The ceremony was relayed from Detroit through New York to a Maine radio station, which sent it to Scotland to be relayed through London to Stockholm.

2597. No-fault divorce law enacted by a state was enacted by California on July 6, 1970. It allowed divorces in cases of incurable insanity and irreconcilable differences.

2598. Divorce rate of more than 1 million a year was reached in 1975, when 1,036,000 divorces were granted.

Library of Congress, Prints & Photographs Division
LC-USZ62-102264

Sending and receiving messages by telegraph.

2599. Marriage and divorce classes required by a state were mandated by Florida in May 1998. The law required high schools to include marriage skills education in the life management courses taken by the state's ninth- and tenth-graders. It also reduced the marriage license fee for couples who enroll in a marriage skills class and made divorce education mandatory for husbands and wives with minor children who are contemplating divorce.

Pets

2600. Cat domestically bred in America was probably the American shorthaired cat. It is believed to descend from cats brought to the New World by the early European explorers.

2601. Dog domestically bred was the American foxhound. All dogs of this breed descend from a pack of foxhounds imported from England by Robert Brooke, who settled in Maryland in 1650. The dogs were later crossed with other hound breeds from England, Ireland, and France.

2602. Commercial dog food was Spratt's Patent Meat Fibrine Dog Cakes, a biscuit made of wheat and vegetables mixed with beef blood. It was created by James Spratt of Cincinnati, OH, in 1860. Spratt, an electrician by trade, got the idea on a trip to London, England, where he observed dogs eating hardtack given to them by sailors on the docks. His product was made and sold in England for some 30 years before it was offered in the United States.

2603. Dog license law enacted by a state was "an act for the better protection of lost and strayed animals and for securing the rights of the owners thereof," passed on March 8, 1894, by New York. It authorized the American Society for the Prevention of Cruelty to Animals to carry out the provisions of the law and collect a $2 annual fee for dogs in cities with populations over 1.2 million. Unlicensed dogs were to be destroyed if not redeemed within 48 hours.

2604. Pet cemetery was the Pet Burial Grounds in Hartsdale, NY. The grounds were originally part of an orchard owned by veterinarian Samuel Johnson. In 1896 Johnson allowed a friend to bury her dog there. He was soon besieged by similar requests and established a cemetery at the location. As of 2005, some 70,000 pets had been buried there.

2605. Food for dogs on a special diet was formulated in 1943 by Mark Morris, a veterinarian in Edison, NJ, who used a low-protein, cereal-based mixture to treat dogs with kidney disease. It was packaged in cans by Louise Morris, his wife, for Morris Frank, the first blind person in the United States to have a seeing-eye dog. The formula, called Prescription Diet KD, was eventually produced commercially by the Hill Packing Company of Topeka, KS.

2606. Hospice for animals in the United States was Angel's Gate, established in Fort Salonga, NY, in 1992 by Susan Marino, a licensed veterinary technician. She provided care for terminally ill pets and wild animals.

2607. Cloned pet was CC, a kitten that was born by cesarean section on December 22, 2001, at Texas A&M University, College Station, TX. CC was a shorthaired calico cat cloned from the cells of Rainbow, an adult female. Gestation took place in the uterus of a second cat. The team that created CC was led by Mark Westhusin and funded by John Sperling, founder of a commercial animal-cloning company, Genetic Savings and Clone.

2608. Transgenic animal sold as a pet was the GloFish, a zebrafish whose genes had been altered to make it glow red when exposed to ultraviolet light. The added gene involved a fluorescent protein derived from sea anemones. The fish was patented in Singapore and was sold in the United States by Yorktown Technologies, Austin, TX. It reached the retail market in December 2003, except in California, where it was banned.

2609. Domestic violence protection law that included pets was signed into law in Portland, ME, by Governor James Baldacci on March 31, 2006. The law gave judges the power to issue protection orders against domestic abusers who threaten, injure, or kill animals belonging to their victims, a common occurrence in abusive relationships. Penalties included fines and imprisonment.

2610. State law requiring cats to be neutered was enacted by Rhode Island on June 9, 2006, to reduce the number of unwanted cats euthanized every year. Owners of cats six months old or older were required to have them spayed or neutered unless a veterinarian certified that it would harm the pet's health. The law also required breeders to obtain a permit from the town animal officer, at a cost of $100 per cat, and placed restrictions on the sale of cats. A surcharge of $1 was added to the fee for dog licenses in order to subsidize neutering programs for low-income pet owners. The penalty for violation of the law was $75 per month.

Sewing

2611. Cotton thread was made in Pawtucket, RI, in 1793 by Hannah Wilkinson Slater, who conceived the idea of twisting fine Surinam cotton yarn on spinning wheels. She manufactured No. 20 two-ply thread, which proved superior to the linen thread then in common use.

2612. Silk thread was manufactured in 1819 at Mansfield, CT, by Rodney Hanks and Horatio Hanks. It was sold in skeins. Silk thread on spools was first produced in 1849 by General Merritt Heminway at Bishop and Heminway, a factory in Watertown, CT, that had opened in 1822. The spools at first contained 12 yards of thread, and later 50 and 100 yards.

2613. Lock-stitch sewing machine was made in 1832–34 by Walter Hunt of New York, whose machine used two threads, one below the cloth and the other coming down through the cloth, thus interlocking with each other. He made no attempt to patent his machine until June 27, 1854, and his original application was refused on the ground of abandonment. Elias Howe obtained a patent on a lock-stitch machine on September 10, 1846.

2614. Machine for manufacturing pins that was practical was invented by John Ireland Howe of Derby, CT, who obtained a patent for it on June 22, 1832. The machine was exhibited at the American Institute Fair in New York City, and Howe received a silver medal for his contribution to manufacturing. In December 1835, he formed the Howe Manufacturing Company, New York City. He obtained a second patent on March 24, 1841, for an improved model.

2615. Pins manufactured with a solid head were made in 1838 by Samuel Slocum of Rhode Island, who invented the machine to manufacture them. He did not obtain a patent on it. One man tending two machines could produce 100,000 pins in 11 hours. He formed the firm of Slocum, Jilson and Company, Poughkeepsie, NY, in 1839. His products were known as "Poughkeepsie pins."

2616. Sewing machine manufacturer who was successful was Isaac Merritt Singer, who began business at 19 Harvard Place, Boston, MA, in 1851, with a capital of $40 supplied by George B. Zieber. His first machine was made in 11 days in the machine shop owned by Orson C. Phelps. He organized I.M. Singer and Company in 1851 and over the next 12 years patented a series of improvements that made his machine the most popular on the market.

2617. Sewing machine equipped with a rocking treadle or double treadle was invented by Isaac Merritt Singer of New York City, who obtained a patent on August 12, 1851. He used a treadle similar to that employed in old spinning wheels and attached it by means of a pitman to the handle on the driving gear of the machine.

2618. Sewing machine to stitch buttonholes was patented by Charles Miller of St. Louis, MO, on March 7, 1854.

2619. Paper sewing patterns using standardized sizes were invented by William and Ellen Curtis Demorest of New York City circa 1858. They cut apart stylish dresses and recreated them in tissue-paper versions packaged in large envelopes, which they sold mainly by mail order. A free pattern was included with each issue of their popular magazine, *Mme. Demorest's Mirror of Fashion.* Their company was notable in its time for being run jointly by a married couple and for employing African-Americans and whites equally. The business was eventually eclipsed by E. Butterick and Company, a New York City firm founded in 1867 by Ebenezer and Eleanor Butterick of Sterling, MA, who had received a patent for paper sewing patterns in 1863.

2620. Linen thread factory was established in Paterson, NJ, in 1865 by William Barbour and Sons of Lisburn, Ireland. The mill was driven by waterpower. The thread was used principally by shoe manufacturers and harness makers.

2621. Sewing needles made by machine were manufactured by the Excelsior Needle Company of Wolcottville, CT, which was organized on March 2, 1866, with $20,000 capital. By means of the cold swaging process, needles of a uniform size and shape were made at a cost very much lower than that of the crude needles previously made.

2622. Electric sewing machine was manufactured by the Singer Manufacturing Company in 1889 at its factory in Elizabethport, NJ.

2623. Nontwisted sewing thread was made commercially available in February 1946 by Belding Hemingway Corticelli, Putnam, CT. It was sold under the names Monocord and Nymo. It was the first nontwisted sewing thread made of nylon.

Time

2624. Clock to strike the hours was constructed in 1754 by Benjamin Banneker at Elkridge Landing, near Baltimore, MD. At the age of 23, without any tools except a jackknife, and without ever having seen anything similar but a sundial and a watch, Banneker constructed a wooden clock that kept time for more than 20 years. Banneker, an African-American, later became distinguished as a mathematician and astronomer.

2625. Clock that was self-winding was made by Benjamin Hanks at his farm at Litchfield, CT. On October 6, 1783, he petitioned the colonial assembly for the exclusive right to make and sell his clock, which "winds itself up by help of the air and will continue to do so without any other aid or assistance." He received a 14-year grant of rights. Hanks also made tower clocks.

2626. Alarm clock was made by Levi Hutchins of Concord, NH, in 1787. It was 29 inches high and 14 inches wide and had a pine case with a mirror in the door. The alarm rang at a specified time and could not be set or altered.

2627. Watchmaker was Luther Goddard, who in 1809 opened a shop in Shrewsbury, MA, his birthplace. He was aided by a law that forbade the importation of clocks and watches, and so was able to develop a small business. In reality, he assembled more watches from imported parts than he actually constructed. The real beginning of the watch industry came in 1849, when the American Horologe Company was formed in Roxbury, MA, by three men: Aaron L. Dennison of Boston, who was an experienced watchmaker; Edward Howard of Bingham, MA, who was skilled in making machinery for watches; and Samuel Curtis, who financed the enterprise, which later became the Waltham Watch Company.

2628. Brass clock works were invented in 1837 by Chauncey Jerome of the Jerome Clock Company, Bristol, CT, later known as the New Haven Clock Company. Jerome's production of standardized parts of pierced brass plates from steel dies enabled him to sell an eight-day metal clock for $4, cheaper than one-day wooden clocks that sold for $12.

2629. Watch made by machinery was placed on the market in 1838 by James and Henry Pitkin of Hartford, CT, the manufacturers. The factory was moved to New York, but in 1841 it was closed down, being unable to meet the competition of the imported Swiss watches.

2630. Standard time program went into effect in the United States at noon on November 18, 1883, when the Naval Observatory at Washington, DC, changed its daily telegraph signals to conform to the new system. The first standard time proposal, which was unsuccessful, was made by Charles Ferdinand Dowd of Saratoga Springs, NY, in 1870. It was raised again in 1879, and was finally adopted in 1883 on the initiative of the American Railway Association. The Uniform Time Act of 1966, enacted on April 13 and effective April 1, 1967, divided the United States into eight time zones: Eastern, Central, Mountain, Pacific, Yukon, Alaska, Hawaii, and Bering.

2631. Clock movement to be electrically wound and synchronized was made by H. Chester Pond in Chicago, IL, in the fall of 1885. In the summer of 1886, 50 of these movements were made and set up in New York City as a system. A high-grade master clock transmitted an hourly signal to the various self-winding or "subsidiary" clocks, correcting them hourly, and thereby maintaining in each clock location the same high degree of time accuracy that was inherent in the master clock.

2632. Daylight saving time program was put into operation in the United States on March 31, 1918, when clocks were set one hour ahead. The idea was sponsored by the National Daylight Saving Association. A bill to adjust the time in order to save daylight was introduced by Senator William Musgrave Calder of New York on April 17, 1917, but was defeated. It was passed without a roll call on June 27, 1917.

2633. Clock to operate by nuclear power was the Atomicron, made by the National Company, Malden, MA, and exhibited on October 2, 1956, at the Overseas Press Club, New York City. It was 84 inches high, 22 inches wide, and 18 inches deep, and was priced at $50,000. Its "pendulum" was the cesium atom, which oscillates at a never-changing frequency of 9,192,631,830 megacycles a second.

2634. Electric watch was made by the Hamilton Watch Company, Lancaster, PA, and introduced to the public on January 3, 1957. The movement was powered by a small energy cell guaranteed to operate the watch for a year. It had no mainspring and had 35 percent fewer parts than an automatic or self-winding watch.

2635. Electronic watch was produced by the Bulova Watch Company in its plant at Jackson Heights, NY, and placed on sale October 25, 1960. In place of mainspring, hairspring, and related gears, the watch had a precision tuning fork that vibrated exactly 360 times per second, transistorized electronic circuitry, and a miniature power cell to move the hands and maintain timekeeping accuracy (less than one minute per month was lost or gained). The watch was called the Accutron.

2636. Digital watch was the Pulsar, made by Hamilton Watch Company, Lancaster, PA, and Electro-Data Inc., Garland, TX, and offered for retail sale for $2,100 apiece in 1972. It was a quartz-controlled electronic watch that had no moving parts. Power came from a 4.5-volt rechargeable battery. The time was shown in the form of red digits in an LED display that appeared when the wearer pressed a button. The casing was sleekly metallic, giving the watch a futuristic look.

The Pulsar watch appeared in the 1973 film LIVE AND LET DIE as one of the space-age gadgets used by James Bond.

Tools and Hardware

2637. Steel shovel was manufactured in 1774 by Captain John Ames in West Bridgewater, MA.

2638. Nails were cold-cut in 1777 and were manufactured by Jeremiah Wilkinson of Cumberland, RI. The first nails were cut from an old chest lock with a pair of shears and were headed in a smith's vice. Later, Wilkinson began cutting small nails from sheet iron.

2639. Nail cutting and heading machine was patented on December 12, 1796, by George Chandler of Maryland.

2640. Ax factory was erected in 1800 at Johnstown, NY, by William Mann. The business was continued by his family at various locations and was sold in 1890 to the American Axe and Tool Company.

2641. Whips commercially manufactured were made in 1801 by Titus Pease and Thomas Rose in Westfield, MA. In 1808, Joseph Jokes of Westfield developed a new style of whip using hickory wood shafts, with a strip of horsehide fastened to the stock by a "keeper."

2642. Screw auger was manufactured in 1810 by Walter French in Seymour, CT. He was also the first to put a screw point on augers. Previously, only pod augers without screws had been used, and a gouge was required to start the hole before an auger could be made to work.

2643. Screw factory was established in 1810 by Aborn and Jackson at Bellefonte, RI. Screw manufacturing was a complicated matter. A blank was forged and the head of the screw was pinched between dies while hot, after which the threads were made by filing.

2644. Circular saw is supposed to have been produced by Benjamin Cummins in Bentonsville, NY, about 1814. His saws were originally used for cutting the teeth of clock wheels, and were later used for cutting wood.

2645. Lathe used for fashioning irregular forms was a profile lathe, patented by Thomas Blanchard of Middlebury, CT, on September 6, 1819, as a "machine for manufacturing gun stocks." The lathe did the work of 13 operators and made possible a great reduction in woodworking prices.

2646. File factory to manufacture files was started by Broadmeadow and Company in Pittsburgh, PA, in 1829. The files were made by hand. The first factory where files were successfully made by machine was the Nicholson File Company, organized in Providence, RI, in 1864. This company used a machine patented by William Nicholson of Providence on April 5, 1864. A file-making machine had been invented by Morris B. Belknap in 1812 in Greenfield, MA, but as far as is known, the machine was not a success.

2647. Wrench patent was obtained on August 17, 1835, by Solyman Merrick of Springfield, MA.

2648. Tool factory devoted exclusively to the manufacture of machinists' tools was established in 1838 by John H. Gage in the Water Street shop of the Nashua Manufacturing Company, Nashua, NH.

2649. Nuts and bolts factory was established by Micah Rugg and Martin Barnes in Marion, CT, in 1840, although they began making bolts and nuts for the market in 1838 in Rugg's blacksmith shop. Their factory was a one-story wooden building, 30 feet by 20 feet. They employed six operators, and the capacity production was 500 bolts a day. Prior to 1838, when they started making bolts commercially, these articles were hammered out and hand-finished by blacksmiths. Rugg invented a machine to trim the heads of nuts and bolts and obtained a patent for it on August 31, 1842. An earlier but impractical machine had been patented by David Wilkinson of Rhode Island.

2650. Collapsible tube was invented by John Rand, who received a patent on September 11, 1841, on a "mode of preserving paints, and other fluids, by confining them in close metallic vessels so constructed as to collapse with slight pressure, and thus force out the paint or fluid confined therein through proper openings for that purpose." The tubes, molded of lead and used to hold oil colors, were provided with caps to keep them airtight.

2651. Wire gauge for standardizing the sizes of drawn wire was a "V"-type gauge developed in 1849 by Ichabod Washburn of Worcester, MA. It was used by the Washburn and Moen Manufacturing Company (afterward part of the American Steel and Wire Company) and was the foundation for the steel wire gauge.

2652. Nail machine for making nails from wire was built under the supervision of Major Thomas Norton by Adolph and Felix Brown of New York City and was used in 1851 by William Hassall of New York City.

2653. Steel animal traps commercially manufactured were made in 1855 by Sewell Newhouse of the Oneida Community, Oneida, NY. He made them in eight different sizes, to trap animals ranging from the house rat to the grizzly bear, and sold them principally to Native Americans. Various types of traps had been made earlier by Newhouse and by others, but they had been devised for individual use and were not marketed. Newhouse was the author of *The Trapper's Guide: A Manual of Instructions for Capturing All Kinds of Fur-Bearing Animals and Curing Their Skins.*

2654. Screw machine to make pointed screws was devised by Cullen Whipple of Providence, RI, who obtained a patent on June 3, 1856. Prior to this invention, screws were blunt on their threaded ends, and it was necessary to bore a hole in order to insert them.

2655. Fishing line factory was established in 1859 in Harlem, New York City, by Henry Hall, who manufactured linen and silk lines. The company moved to Astoria, NY (now part of Queens, New York City), and later operated under the trade name Henry Hall and Sons.

2656. Paint ready-mixed was manufactured by the Averill Chemical Paint Company of New York City, using as a basis a patent granted on July 16, 1867, to D. R. Averill of Newburg, OH. The concern went out of business about 1900. It was unable to maintain a consistent standard of paint. The first manufacturer to do so was Henry Alden Sherwin, founder of the Sherwin-Williams Company, Cleveland, OH, which began producing paint in 1880.

2657. Tape measure was patented by Alvin J. Fellows of New Haven, CT, on July 14, 1868. The tape measure was enclosed in a circular case with a spring click lock to hold the tape at any desired point.

2658. Collapsible tube machine was built in 1873 at Philadelphia, PA, under the direction of August Herman Wirz. Wirz had seen tube-making machines in operation when he was U.S. Commissioner at the Industrial Exposition in Vienna, and had brought over the plans. The first machine-made tubes produced in the United States were used for cucumber jelly.

2659. Screw caliper was constructed by John Edson Sweet in 1874 in the shops of Sibley College, Cornell University, Ithaca, NY. The screw of the machine had 16 threads per inch and its divided circle had 625 readings, the calibration reading to 0.0001 inches. The machine stood on three legs.

2660. Pipe or screw wrench that was practical was the Stillson wrench, invented by Daniel C. Stillson of Somerville, MA, who obtained a patent on December 5, 1876. Stillson whittled the first model out of wood in 1869.

2661. Paint prepared from standard formulas for floors, woodwork, furniture, walls, and so on was manufactured by the Sherwin-Williams Company of Cleveland, OH, in 1880. Stains, enamels, varnishes, and varnish stains were later produced under uniform production methods.

2662. Steel-cut nails were manufactured in 1883 by the Riverside Iron Works of Wheeling, WV.

2663. Fishing rod of telescoping steel tubes was made by Everett Horton of Bristol, CT, who obtained a patent on March 8, 1887, on a fishing rod in "tubular metallic sections."

2664. Lawn mower that was practical was invented by Elwood McGuire of Richmond, IN, in the 1890s. He attached a set of sharp blades to a rotating reel with a cutting bed at the center. The grass was clipped off as it came between the bed and the blades. The first power mower was the Moto-Mower, a gasoline-powered machine invented by Edward George in 1919.

2665. Pneumatic hammer was invented by Charles Brady King of Detroit, MI, in 1890. Brady received a patent for it on January 30, 1894. The hammer was exhibited at the World's Columbian Exposition in Chicago, IL, in 1893.

2666. Flashlight was manufactured by the American Electric and Novelty Manufacturing Company of New York City, which started in business in 1896. The first flashlight was produced about 1898. The model consisted of a paper tube with metal fittings, a rough brass stamping used for a reflector, without any lens, and a spring contact switch. The lamp was handmade, as was the battery. The company later changed its name to the American Eveready Company and subsequently became a part of the National Carbon Company.

2667. Paint-spraying device commercially manufactured was made in 1909 by the De Vilbiss Company of Toledo, OH, using the same principle used in the De Vilbiss medical atomizer combined with compressed air.

2668. Electric hand drill. was invented in 1914 by S. Duncan Black and Alonzo G. Decker, founders of the Black and Decker Corporation of Towson, MD. The bulky but portable drill weighed 24 pounds and had a pistol grip and trigger switch. Black and Decker introduced the world's first portable half-inch electric drill in 1916 and the world's first cordless electric drill, powered by self-contained nickel-cadmium cells, in 1961.

In 1968 the Black and Decker Corporation developed the Apollo Lunar Surface Drill, the first cordless drill used on the moon. The power head for the drill was designed to remove core samples from the lunar surface.

2669. Fluorescent paint was invented in 1934 by two brothers, Robert and Joseph Switzer, who were students at the University of California, Berkeley, CA. They collected chemicals from their father's drugstore and checked them under ultraviolet light to identify naturally fluorescent organic compounds, which they mixed with shellac. During World War II the American military found many uses for their fluorescent paints and inks. Aircraft carrier runways were marked with fluorescent stripes, enabling American fighter planes to make night landings, and ground troops carried fluorescent signals that could be identified from the air by Allied dive bombers. Products made by the Day-Glo Color Corporation, which the Switzer brothers founded in Cleveland, OH, after the war, came to be used in hundreds of products, including toys, packaging, bathing suits, and traffic cones.

2670. Two-handed shovel was used on May 16, 1940, at the bridge dedication ceremonies at Niagara Falls. Mayor Ernst W. Mirrington, Jr., of Niagara Falls, NY, and Mayor George B. Ingles of Niagara Falls, Ontario, Canada, each held one of the handles.

2671. Soldering gun was invented by Carl E. Weller of Easton, PA, who received a patent on August 13, 1946, on an "electrical heating apparatus." The patent was assigned to the Weller Manufacturing Company, Easton, PA. Other electrically heated soldering irons were on the market at that time.

2672. Latex paint was Spred Satin, made by the Glidden Company in 1948. It was formulated with latex paint resin that had been developed by the Dow Chemical Company, Freeport, TX. The latex was a styrene-butadiene polymer suspended in a water-based solution. Latex paints were easier to apply than oil-based paints, dried faster, and did not emit strong solvent fumes. The first acrylic latex paint resin, which produced weather-resistant paints suitable for exterior walls, was made by the Rohm and Haas Company in 1953.

Writing Implements

2673. Invisible ink used in diplomatic correspondence was employed by Silas Deane in 1776. As a member of the Committee of Secret Correspondence, organized on November 29, 1775, "for the sole purpose of corresponding with our friends in Great Britain, Ireland, and other parts of the world," he left Philadelphia, PA, on March 5, 1776, and arrived in France on May 4 on a mission to purchase military supplies on credit. From France, he sent letters to John Jay, member of the Continental Congress, that were interlined with invisible ink, which was invented by Sir James Jay in 1776. Using this method, Deane sent the first authentic account that Congress received of the determination of the British to reduce the colonies to unconditional surrender. The writing was done with a solution of tannic acid. To make the ink visible, the paper was sponged with ferrous sulfate, which combined with the tannic acid to form a dark compound.

2674. Pencil factory was established by William Monroe of Concord, MA, in June 1812. He manufactured about 30 lead pencils of unfinished cedar, unpolished, very thin, with square leads, which he sold to Benjamin Adams, a hardware dealer of Union Street, Boston, MA. Adams then contracted to purchase all the pencils Monroe could produce.

2675. Ink was manufactured by the Thaddeus Davids Ink Company, established by Thaddeus Davids in New York City in 1825. The ink was bottled in various sizes and sold at retail. The first year, a few hundred bottles were manufactured.

2676. Steel pens commercially produced were manufactured by Richard Esterbrook, who founded the Esterbrook Steel Pen Manufacturing Company and established a factory in Camden, NJ, in 1858.

2677. Pencil with an attached eraser was patented by Hyman L. Lipman of Philadelphia, PA, who received a patent on March 30, 1858. The pencil had a groove into which was "secured a piece of prepared rubber, glued in at one end."

2678. Indelible pencil was invented by Edson P. Clark of Northampton, MA, who obtained a patent on July 10, 1866. It had a "filling composed of silver, black lead, calcined gypsum and lamp-black or asphaltum" that was shellacked to the groove in the wood.

2679. Fountain pen that was practical was invented by Lewis Edson Waterman and was manufactured in 1884 by the L.E. Waterman Company in New York City. The first year, about 200 fountain pens were manufactured. They were originally manufactured by hand. Waterman also invented the machinery to produce fountain pens in commercial quantities.

2680. Ball-point pen was patented on October 30, 1888, by John J. Loud of Weymouth, MA. The patent was on a pen having a spheroidal marking point capable of revolving in all directions.

2681. Pen with truly erasable ink was the Eraser Mate pen, which went on the market in April 1979. It was a refillable ball-point pen, a product of the Paper Mate Division of the Gillette Company, Boston, MA. The ink was 1 million times thicker than water. The pen was made under a patent issued on June 27, 1978, to Frank Andrew Miller of West Los Angeles and Henry Peper, Jr., of Pacific Palisades, CA, for "ball-point instruments writing with improved transitorially erasable trace and ink compositions therefor." The pen was produced in Santa Monica, CA.

EDUCATION

Colleges and Universities

2682. College founded in colonial America was established at Henrico (formerly Henricopolis), VA, part of the London Company's Virginia settlement. Ten thousand acres of land on the James River were set aside in 1618 for the campus, which was to include a college and university as well as a school for Native Americans. The Reverend Patrick Copland was appointed rector. In March 1622 the town was destroyed in an attack by Native Americans.

2683. College to open in America was Harvard College, established in 1636 by the General Court of Massachusetts Bay. On September 8, 1636, the Court appropriated £400 for the project, and in 1637 it appointed 12 of the principal men of the colony "to take orders for a college at New Towne." The institution was originally given the name Cambridge College. It was renamed in 1638 in honor of the Reverend John Harvard, who bequeathed the college about £800 and 300 books. The first building, erected in 1637, was known as "The Indian Collidge." It was made of brick and was 30 feet long and 200 feet wide.

2684. Hebrew instruction at a college was given to divinity students by the president and tutors of Harvard College, Cambridge, MA, in 1637. A chair of Hebrew and Oriental languages was endowed in 1655. The curriculum of 17th-century Harvard required students to study Hebrew and related languages one day each week for a total of three years. The Hebrew requirement was lifted in 1817.

2685. College library was created through a bequest from John Harvard of Charlestown, MA, who died on September 14, 1638, at the age of 31. He donated his private collection of 400 books, and a gift of money to maintain them, to the small college that had recently been founded in Newtowne (now Cambridge), MA. The college was afterwards named Harvard College in his honor.

2686. College president was Henry Dunster, who became the first president of Harvard College in 1640. His predecessor at Harvard, Nathaniel Eaton, was the first person to fulfill the job of a college president, though he was given the English title "master." Both Dunster and Eaton had been born and educated in England. Eaton was fired, allegedly for beating his assistant and serving the students tainted food, and Dunster was forced to resign after he refused to have his newborn son baptized, citing a change in his religious principles.

2687. Thesis directory was a broadside, "A List of Theses at the Commencement of Harvard College," published in 1642 by Stephen Day, Cambridge, MA. No copy is known to exist.

2688. Bachelor of Arts degree was conferred on September 23, 1642, by Harvard College, Cambridge, MA, on nine graduates: Tobias Barnard, Samuel Bellingham, Nathaniel Brewster, John Bulkley, George Downing, William Hubbard, Henry Saltonstall, John Wilson, and Benjamin Woodbridge.

2689. College student to work his way through college was Zechariah Brigden, 14 years old, who was graduated from Harvard College, Cambridge, MA, in 1657. He earned money by "ringing the bell and waytinge."

2690. College graduate who was Native American was Caleb Cheeshahteaumuck, the son of a Narragansett sachem of Holmes Hole in Martha's Vineyard, MA, who was graduated from Harvard College, Cambridge, MA, in 1665. He died of tuberculosis shortly after his graduation.

2691. College charter granted by the Crown under the Seal of the Privy Council was "their Majesties Royal College of William and Mary" in Williamsburg, VA, the charter for which was granted on February 8, 1693. The college was also the first to receive a coat of arms from the College of Heralds.

2692. Book catalog of a college was Harvard's *Catalogus Eorum Qui in Collegio Harvardino . . . Alicujus Gradus Laurea Donati Sunt*, printed in 1697 in Boston, MA, by Bartholomew Green and John Allen.

2693. Divinity professor at a college was Edward Wigglesworth, appointed on January 24, 1722, to the Thomas Hollis Professorship of Divinity at Harvard College, Cambridge, MA. He served until his death on January 16, 1765.

2694. College to have a full faculty was the College of William and Mary, Williamsburg, VA. On February 27, 1729, the college realty was transferred from the trustees to the faculty, which consisted of a president, six professors, an usher, and a writing master.

2695. French instruction at a college was offered in 1733 at Harvard College, Cambridge, MA. Louis Langloiserie was appointed instructor.

2696. College charter granted by a governor with only the assent of his council was issued on October 22, 1746, to 12 trustees of the College of New Jersey (now Princeton University), Princeton, NJ, by Governor John Hamilton, president of His Majesty's Council. The college opened the fourth week of May 1747. The first commencement was held on November 9, 1748. The Reverend Jonathan Dickinson was the first president.

2697. Academy to offer a broader curriculum than was taught in grammar schools was the Academy and College of Philadelphia, founded in 1749 in Philadelphia, PA, by Benjamin Franklin, who became its president. The academy opened on August 13, 1751, and offered English, mathematical, and classical courses of study. Seven men were graduated on May 17, 1757, at the first commencement, six as Bachelors of Arts and one as Master of Arts.

2698. German instruction at a college was given by William Creamer at the University of Pennsylvania, Philadelphia, PA, from 1754 to July 11, 1755.

2699. Law instruction at a college was offered by King's College (now Columbia University), New York City, in 1755. The fourth year of study was described as containing, among other things, "the Chief Principles of Law and Government together with History, Sacred and Profane."

2700. College literary society was the Cliosophic Society, founded at Princeton University, Princeton, NJ, in 1765. The first coeducational literary society at a college was the Alethezetean Society of Antioch College, Yellow Springs, OH, founded in December 1853. The society was disbanded in 1855 by vote of the faculty.

2701. Protest by college students of record was instigated in 1766 by Asa Dunbar, a student at Harvard College, Cambridge, MA. Dunbar complained about the food and raised the chant "Behold, our butter stinketh!" He was condemned for "the sin of insubordination" and responded by leading several followers off-campus to eat their breakfasts. Dunbar grew up to become the grandfather of the transcendentalist writer Henry David Thoreau.

2702. Botany professor at a college was Adam Kuhn, who was appointed in January 1768 by the Philadelphia College, Philadelphia, PA. He occupied his post for 21 years. His schooling was obtained in Sweden under Linnaeus.

2703. Chemistry professor at a college was Benjamin Rush, one of the signers of the Declaration of Independence. He gave lectures in chemistry at the Philadelphia Medical School, Philadelphia, PA, as early as 1769.

2704. College to confer medals as prizes was the College of William and Mary at Williamsburg, VA. In 1770 Lord Botetourt, governor of Virginia, presented two gold medals, one to be awarded to the best student in philosophy, the other to the best student in classics.

2705. College graduate who was Jewish was Isaac Abrahams, who was graduated from King's College (later called Columbia College), New York City, in 1774, receiving the A.B. degree. He delivered a Latin oration at the commencement exercises. Judah Monis, the Italian-born son of Portuguese Marranos (hidden Jews), was granted the degree of Master of Arts by Harvard College in 1720, probably on the strength of a manuscript that he had prepared on teaching Hebrew grammar. After his conversion to Christianity in 1722 he was appointed to the Harvard faculty as instructor in Hebrew.

2706. Scholastic fraternity at a college was Phi Beta Kappa, founded on December 5, 1776, at William and Mary College, Williamsburg, VA, with a nucleus of 50 members. In December 1779 it authorized the establishment of branches at Yale and Harvard. The first chapter to be established at an African-American university was formed on April 4, 1953, at Fisk University, Nashville, TN. Goodrich Cook White, president of the United Chapters of Phi Beta Kappa, presented the charter to eight charter members and two foundation members, both Fisk alumni. On April 8, 1953, a chapter was established at Howard University, Washington, DC.

2707. College to use the honor system during examinations was the College of William and Mary, Williamsburg, VA, in 1779.

2708. College with an elective system of study was the College of William and Mary, Williamsburg, VA. In 1779 students were permitted to choose the subjects they wanted to pursue.

2709. School of modern languages at a college was established by the College of William and Mary, Williamsburg, VA, in 1779.

2710. University legally designated as such was the University of the State of Pennsylvania, Philadelphia, PA. The original name of the institution was the College of Philadelphia. It was designated a university on November 27, 1779, by the Pennsylvania legislature. Since 1791, the name has been University of Pennsylvania. It is a privately endowed institution, not a state university. Whether it was in fact a university before it was designated as one, and whether it was the first institution to merit being called a university, are questions of definition.

2711. Law school at a college was established in 1779 at the College of William and Mary, Williamsburg, VA. Professors did not receive a stipulated amount from the college but were paid by the students attending the course. The first professor was George Wythe, who was appointed professor of law and police on December 4, 1779. The first college law school to be permanently organized was the Harvard College School of Law, Cambridge, MA, which was opened in 1817.

2712. College named after an American president was Washington College in Washington College, TN, founded in 1780 by the Reverend Dr. Samuel Doak, who became its first president. On April 24, 1783, it was chartered as Martin Academy by North Carolina, of which Tennessee was then a part. A second charter was received on March 31, 1785, from the state of Franklin, which was never officially recognized. A third charter, received on July 8, 1795, changed the name to Washington College. The name was proposed to the legislature of the "Territory of the United States South of the River Ohio" by General John Sevier.

2713. Political economy course at a college was given at the College of William and Mary of Williamsburg, VA, in 1784.

2714. Theology school was founded by the Dutch Reformed Church in 1784 with the appointment of Dr. John Henry Livingston of the Collegiate Church of New York City as professor of theology. In 1810, Livingston went to New Brunswick, NJ, under an agreement that allowed the school to share the campus of Queen's College (later Rutgers University). The theology school was named the New Brunswick Theological Seminary. The two institutions were not corporately connected and retained separate identities.

2715. State university to be chartered was the University of Georgia, Athens, GA. Although it was chartered on January 27, 1785, it was not opened to students until 1801. The first state university actually opened was the University of North Carolina, Chapel Hill, NC, which began operating on February 13, 1795.

2716. City college was the College of Charleston, Charleston, SC, which was founded in 1770, chartered on March 19, 1785, and opened in 1790 with the Reverend Robert Smith as the first principal. On December 20, 1837, it became a municipal university under municipal control. It opened on April 1, 1838, with 16 students. The first president was the Reverend Dr. William Theophilus Brantley, pastor of the Baptist Church.

2717. College founded as a Methodist institution was Cokesbury College, Abingdon, MD, named in honor of Bishops Thomas Coke and Francis Asbury. The building was 108 feet long, 40 feet wide, and three stories high. The first headmaster was the Reverend

Mr. Heath. The foundation sermon was delivered on June 5, 1785, and the building was opened on December 6, 1787.

2718. Mineralogy instruction at a college was given in 1786 by Dr. Benjamin Waterhouse at Rhode Island College, Providence, RI.

2719. College founded as a Catholic institution was Georgetown College, Washington, DC, established on January 23, 1789, and opened on November 15, 1791. The first student to register was William Gaston of Newberne, NC. Authority to grant degrees was authorized by act of Congress of March 1, 1815.

2720. Catholic seminary was St. Mary's Seminary and College, in Roland Park, Baltimore, MD. It was established on July 10, 1791, when Francis Charles Nagot, the first superintendent, arrived in Baltimore with three priests and five students. It became a pontifical university on May 1, 1822, when Pope Pius VII granted it the right and privilege of conferring degrees in divinity. The first degrees were granted on January 24, 1824.

2721. Agriculture professor at a college was Samuel Latham Mitchill, who was appointed by Columbia College, New York City, on July 9, 1792, as professor of natural history, chemistry, agriculture, and the other related sciences. Part of his course included the "theory of vegetation and application of its principles to practical agriculture, nutrition and food of plants, with the history of manures, multiplication, dissemination and habitations of plants. Chemical history of various vegetable products, Sap, Gum, Resin, Farina, etc., with their preparation and application to the uses of man. Vegetable colors, vegetable poisons, baking, brewing, tanning, etc."

2722. College that was nondenominational was Blount College, Knoxville, TN (now the University of Tennessee), chartered on September 10, 1794. The charter provided that the college "take effectual care that students of all denominations may and shall be admitted to the equal advantages of a liberal education and to the emoluments and honors of the college, so that they shall receive a like, fair, generous and equal treatment during their residence therein." The first president was Samuel Carrick. The second nondenominational college was Union College, Schenectady, NY, chartered on February 25, 1795, whose charter required that the majority of the 24 trustees "shall not at any time be composed of persons of the same religious sect or denomination." The Reverend John Blair Smith assumed office as the first president on December 8, 1795.

2723. English grammar instruction at a college was offered in 1795 at the University of North Carolina, Chapel Hill, NC.

2724. Italian instruction at a college was given at the College of William and Mary, Williamsburg, VA, in 1799 by Carlo Bellini, professor of modern languages.

2725. School of modern history at a college was established at the College of William and Mary, Williamsburg, VA, in 1803.

2726. Land grant university was Ohio University, Athens, OH, which was chartered on February 18, 1804, and opened on June 1, 1808, with three students. Governor Edward Tiffin presided at the first trustees' meeting. The first president was the Reverend Jacob Lindley. A contract dated October 27, 1787, between the Ohio Company of Associates and the federal government provided that the rental derived from land belonging to Ohio's townships should be set aside for the support of a university.

2727. College magazine was the *Literary Cabinet*, published on November 15, 1806, at Yale University in New Haven, CT. It was an eight-page biweekly and was edited by three college seniors. It sold for $1 a year. It folded after one year.

2728. College entrance requirement other than Greek, Latin, and arithmetic was geography, which was required in 1807 for admission to Harvard College, Cambridge, MA.

2729. Theology school that was nonsectarian was the Divinity School of Harvard College, Cambridge, MA, organized as a separate department of the college in 1816, although the faculty of the Divinity School was not appointed until 1819. Six students were graduated in 1817. Degrees were not conferred by the Divinity School until 1870. Theology had been taught since the opening of Harvard College.

2730. American to earn a Ph.D. was Edward Everett, a Harvard-educated Unitarian minister and future congressman, governor, ambassador, and secretary of state. After joining the faculty of Harvard as Eliot Professor of Greek Literature, he was sent by the college to do advanced studies at the University of Göttingen, Germany, which awarded him a doctorate in 1817.

2731. Theology school graduate who was African-American was Theodore Sedgwick Wright, born in Providence, RI, in 1797, who was graduated from the Princeton Theological Seminary, Princeton, NJ, in 1828. He was ordained in February 1829 and served for 18 years as pastor of the First Colored Presbyterian Church in New York City.

2732. Civil engineering course at a college was given in 1819 at Norwich University, Norwich, VT. The university was founded by Captain Alden Partridge on August 6, 1819, as the American Literary, Scientific and Military Academy. Courses in civil engineering included the construction of roads, canals, locks, and bridges, as well as architecture. The name was changed to Norwich University in 1834. In March 1866 the buildings were destroyed by fire and the college was moved to Northfield, VT.

2733. College alumni association established for any considerable period without suspending operations was the Society of Alumni of Williams College, Williamstown, MA, formed on September 1821. The first president was Dr. Asa Burbank of the class of 1797. The first full-time paid secretary of a college alumni association was Ralph C. McAllister, whose position was created on June 30, 1897, by the University of Michigan, Ann Arbor, MI, to foster service on the part of the alumni for the university.

2734. Ancient and modern history chair at a college was the McLean Professorship at Harvard College, Cambridge, MA, which was endowed in 1823 under the will of John McLean and established in 1838. The first incumbent was Professor Jared Sparks. The first integrated course in ancient and modern history at a women's college was given by Professor Woodrow Wilson at Bryn Mawr College, Bryn Mawr, PA, in 1885. The histories of Greece and Rome were taken as representative of ancient history, and of France and England as representative of medieval and modern history. The object was to "keep the student mindful of the broad views of history in which the events in the lives of individual nations stand related."

2735. College course without Greek or Latin was established in 1824 by Geneva College (now Hobart College), Geneva, NY. The course, known as the "English Course," was designed "for the practical business of life by which the Agriculturist, the Merchant and the Mechanic may receive a practical knowledge of what genius and experience have discovered, without passing through a tedious course of Classical studies." The first course diploma, in English, was awarded in 1827 to Henry Smith Attwater.

2736. Engineering college was the Rensselaer School, Troy, NY, founded on November 5, 1824, and opened on January 3, 1825. The first class of 10 students was graduated on April 26, 1826, with the degree of A.B. The first civil engineering degree was awarded in October 1835. Amos Eaton was senior professor and the first director. The name of the school was changed to Rensselaer Institute in 1832 and to Rensselaer Polytechnic Institute in 1861.

2737. Social fraternity at a college was Kappa Alpha, established on November 26, 1825, at Union College, Schenectady, NY. The first initiation was held on December 3, 1825. The first presiding officer was David White.

2738. College graduate who was African-American was Alexander Lucius Twilight, who was graduated from Middlebury College, Middlebury, VT, in 1823 with a B.A. degree.

2739. College founded as a Quaker institution was the Haverford School, Haverford, PA, which opened on October 28, 1833, under the sponsorship of members of the Society of Friends. The first superintendent was Samuel Hilles. The name was changed to Haverford College in 1856.

2740. College to enroll women and men on equal terms was Oberlin Collegiate Institute, Oberlin, OH, which opened on December 3, 1833, with 44 students, 29 men and 15 women. Equal status was granted to women on September 6, 1837, when 30 men matriculated along with four women: Elizabeth Smith Prall of New York City, Caroline Mary Rudd of Huntington, CT, Mary Hosford of Oberlin, OH, and Mary Fletcher Kellogg of Jamestown, NY. In 1841, the first three of these women graduated with the B.A. degree, having pursued a classical course equivalent to that at Yale. On March 21, 1850, the name of the school was changed to Oberlin College. It was the first school to advocate the abolition of slavery and to accept African-American men and women on equal terms with white students.

2741. College for women was Mount Holyoke College, South Hadley, MA, chartered on February 11, 1836, and opened on November 8, 1837, as the Mount Holyoke Female Seminary, with 80 students who paid $64 a year for tuition and board. They were required to do cooperative household tasks. The first principal was Mary Lyon, who served until 1849. The first commencement, at which four women were graduated, was held on August 23, 1838. Another women's college chartered in 1836 was Wesleyan College, Macon, GA, originally known as the Georgia Female College, which graduated its first class of 11 women on July 16, 1840. An earlier claim is made for the Elizabeth Female Academy, Washington, MS, which existed from 1818 to 1843.

2742. Model laboratory school at a college for student teaching was a three-story building opened on October 31, 1838, by Lafayette College, Easton, PA, and was known as West College. Its cost of $2,230 was paid by the college's president, George Junkin.

2743. Fraternity house at a college was occupied in 1839 by the Williams Chapter (Alpha Chapter of Massachusetts) of the Kappa Alpha Society at Williams College, Williamstown, MA. The chapter was founded on October 29, 1833, and used various quarters until 1839, when it hired a frame structure two stories high, an annex to the residence of Captain James Meachem. The first floor supplied space for social gatherings and a banquet room. A winding stair led to the second story, planned expressly for secret meetings.

2744. Library building at a university was the library of the University of South Carolina, Columbia, SC, completed on May 6, 1840. The university's first librarian was Elisha Hammond, who began to serve in 1805. The first librarian in the separate building was Dr. Thomas Park.

2745. Teaching methodology course at a college was offered beginning on December 1, 1841, when Alfred Saxe was appointed professor of normal instruction at Wesleyan University, Middletown, CT, for a term of two years "to prepare teachers more perfectly for the business of instruction." No tuition charge was made for the course, which was a one-year program of study.

2746. Applied chemistry professor at a college was Benjamin Silliman, Jr., who in 1846 was appointed to teach at the new Yale Analytical Laboratory, Yale University, New Haven, CT.

2747. Business economics course at a college was established by the University of Louisiana (now Tulane University), New Orleans, LA, in 1849. It was conducted by Professor James Dunwoody Brownson De Bow under the title "Commerce, Political Economy, and Statistics."

2748. American history chair at a college was established by the University of Pennsylvania, Philadelphia, PA, in 1850. The first incumbent was William Bradford Reed.

2749. College graduate who was an African-American woman was Lucy Ann Stanton of Cleveland, OH, who was graduated on December 8, 1850, from Oberlin College, Oberlin, OH, receiving the Bachelor of Literature degree.

2750. College to prohibit discrimination because of race, religion, or color was Cooper Union for the Advancement of Science and Art, New York City, whose deed of trust, dated April 29, 1851, prohibited discrimination in the acceptance of students for reasons of race, creed, or color. Peter Cooper was the first president.

2751. College secret society for women was the Adelphean Society, organized on May 15, 1851, at Wesleyan College, Macon, GA, with 16 charter members whose motto was "We live for one another." The founder was Eugenia Tucker Fitzgerald. The name was changed to Alpha Delta Phi Sorority in 1904, at which time the society had 60 active members and 3,000 alumnae. In 1913 it changed its name to the Alpha Delta Pi Sorority.

2752. College professor who was a woman and who was accorded the same privileges as male professors was Rebecca Mann Pennell, professor of physical geography, drawing, natural history, civil history, and didactics, who was appointed in September 1852 by Antioch College, Yellow Springs, OH. She conducted classes when the college opened on October 5, 1853. Other institutions employed women but did not allow them to attend faculty meetings.

2753. University on the Pacific coast was Willamette University, Salem, OR. It was organized on February 1, 1842, as the Oregon Institute, offering only elementary work, and opened on August 13, 1844, with five students. On January 12, 1853, it was chartered as a university by the Oregon Territorial Legislature. The Oregon Institute was continued as a preparatory school.

2754. College for African-American students was the Ashmun Institute, Chester County, PA, which was chartered by act of the legislature of Pennsylvania on April 29, 1854, to give theological, classical, and scientific training to African-Americans. It was named after Jehudi Ashmun, the reorganizer of the colony of Liberia. It opened on January 1, 1857. The first president was John Pym Carter. The charter was amended in 1866, changing the name to Lincoln University.

2755. College graduate of Asian ancestry was Yung Wing, who entered Yale University, New Haven, CT, in 1850 and was graduated on June 13, 1854, with a B.A. degree. He had been one of a group of three Chinese students who were brought to the United States in April 1847 by the Reverend Samuel Robbins Brown, head of the Morrison School, the first English-language school in China, to study at the Monson Academy, Monson, MA. They were the first Chinese students in the United States. Yung Wing later went on to serve as associate minister in the first Chinese embassy to the United States, which opened in Washington, DC, in October 1878.

2756. Comparative philology chair at a college was established by Lafayette College, Easton, PA, in 1856. The first professor was Francis Andrew March.

2757. College for deaf students was the National Deaf Mute College, Washington, DC, a department of the Columbia Institution for the Instruction of the Deaf, Dumb, and Blind, incorporated on February 16, 1857. On April 8, 1864, the parent school, now called the Columbia Institution for the Deaf, was authorized by a special act of Congress to confer degrees. The first graduate received his diploma in 1866. The name of the college was changed in 1894 to Gallaudet College in honor of Thomas Hopkins Gallaudet, who was the first principal of the first school for the deaf in America. His son, Dr. Edward Miner Gallaudet, served as president of the college from 1864 to 1910.

2758. Chemical laboratory at a college was opened at Boylston Hall, Harvard University, Cambridge, MA, in 1858. Josiah (Joseph) Parsons Cooke, author of numerous chemical books, was in charge of instruction.

2759. Agricultural college to be chartered by a state was the Farmers High School of Pennsylvania, incorporated on April 13, 1854. The school opened on February 16, 1859. In the first session, 119 students were admitted. The Bachelor of Scientific and Practical Agriculture degree was awarded to those who completed a four-year course and submitted a dissertation. The name was changed on May 6, 1862, to the Agricultural College of Pennsylvania. Another state agricultural school, the Agricultural College of Michigan in Lansing, MI, received its charter later, in 1855, but opened sooner, on May 13, 1857.

2760. Physical education and hygiene professorship at a college was established in 1860 by Amherst College, Amherst, MA.

2761. Doctoral degree awarded by an American university was awarded in 1861 by Yale University, New Haven, CT, to three graduates: Eugene Schuyler, James Morris Whiton, and Arthur Williams Wright. The degree had been authorized on July 24, 1860.

2762. Land grant for an agricultural college was proposed by Justin Smith Morrill, congressman from Vermont. He advocated giving each state an allotment of land, the income from which should be used to support at least one agricultural college in each state. The bill was vetoed by President James Buchanan in 1857, but was signed by President Abraham Lincoln on July 2, 1862, after certain modifications had been made. It was known as the Morrill Act.

2763. Fine arts department in a college was the School of Fine Arts, Yale University, New Haven, CT, which was established in 1864 and opened in 1869 with four students under John Ferguson Weir, appointed professor of painting and design. Until 1891, when the school's first Bachelor of Fine Arts degree was awarded to Josephine Miles Lewis, certificates were given to those who completed the three-year course. The College of Fine Arts at Syracuse University, Syracuse, NY, established June 24, 1873, was the first college fine arts department to grant degrees.

2764. Professional fraternity at a college was Theta Xi, founded on April 29, 1864, at the Rensselaer Polytechnic Institute, Troy, NY. Membership was confined to students of engineering and science. The fraternity was an offspring of Sigma Delta, a local society at Rensselaer Polytechnic Institute.

2765. Mines school at a college was opened on November 15, 1864, in the basement of the Columbia University building on East 49th Street, New York City. The first professor of mines and metallurgy was Thomas Egleston, who was appointed on February 1, 1864. It was through his efforts that the plan of the school was proposed and carried out.

2766. Architecture department at a college was established on February 20, 1865, by the Massachusetts Institute of Technology, Boston, MA. William Robert Ware was the first head of the department and received the title of professor.

2767. College to sponsor an endowed lecture series was the Union Theological Seminary, New York City, which on May 20, 1865, established the Morse Lectureship on the Relationship of the Bible to Any of the Sciences. The series was named in memory of the founder's father, Samuel Finley Breese Morse. The first lecture series was given in 1866 by Professor Arnold Guyot on "The First Chapter of Genesis." An endowed series known as the Elias P. Ely Lectureship on the Evidences of Christianity had previously been established by the same institution, but lectures were not given until 1867.

2768. African-American to earn a Ph.D. was Patrick Francis Healy, a Jesuit priest, who received his doctorate from Louvain University in Belgium on July 26, 1865. He later became president of Georgetown University, Washington, DC.

2769. Paleontology chair at a college was established by Yale University, New Haven, CT, in 1866, and was held by Professor Othniel Charles Marsh from that date to 1899. He was the first professor of vertebrate paleontology.

2770. University for African-American students with undergraduate, graduate, and professional schools was Howard University, Washington, DC, founded on November 20, 1866, as the Howard Theological Seminary. On January 8, 1867, the name was changed to Howard University. On May 1, 1867, the teacher-training department and the preparatory department opened in a leased frame structure with five students, all children of the trustees. It was incorporated on March 2, 1867, by act of Congress, which authorized the establishment of the teacher-training, preparatory, collegiate, theological, medical, law, and agricultural departments. The first president was the Reverend Charles Brandon Boynton. The first African-American president was Dr. Mordecai Wyatt Johnson of Charleston, WV, whose service began on September 1, 1926.

2771. State university supported by a direct property tax was the University of Michigan, Ann Arbor, MI. An act of the state legislature approved on March 15, 1867, assessed all taxable property one twentieth of a mill on each dollar of value, to be used for the use, aid, and maintenance of the university. The funds paid to the university in 1867 totaled $15,398.

2772. Theological school that was multisectarian and presented regular courses by scholars representing different denominations was the Boston Theological Seminary, Boston, MA, which opened in September 1867 with Catholic, Methodist, and Presbyterian professors, as well as faculty members of other faiths.

2773. Theological college for Jews was Maimonides College, Philadelphia, PA, which opened on October 27, 1867. It was sponsored by the Hebrew Education Society of Philadelphia and the Board of Delegates of American Israelites. The founder and first president was Rabbi Isaac Leeser, who also served as professor of homiletics, belles lettres, and comparative theology. It offered a five-year course leading to Bachelor's and Doctor of Divinity degrees. Tuition was $100, and board and lodging $200 per year. Dr. Marcus Jastrow was provost. The college closed in 1873.

2774. Journalism course at a college was given in 1869 by Professor Willard Fiske at Washington University (later Washington and Lee University), Lexington, VA. The idea was introduced by General Robert Edward Lee. A knowledge of shorthand and telegraphy was required, as well as practical experience in the university printing office.

2775. Law school at a university to admit women was the St. Louis Law School, now the School of Law, Washington University, St. Louis, MO. In 1869, two women students matriculated. One, Phoebe W. Couzins of St. Louis, was graduated from the school on June 15, 1871. Both eventually became members of the bar.

2776. State university to grant equal privileges to women was Indiana University, Bloomington, IN. Sarah Parke Morrison, who was graduated in 1869, was the first woman to enter the school and the first to receive a degree from it.

2777. Entomology professor at a college was Hermann August Hagen, who taught at Harvard University, Cambridge, MA, from 1870 to 1893.

2778. Sorority at a college was Kappa Alpha Theta, which was founded on January 27, 1870, at Indiana Asbury University, now DePauw University, in Greencastle, IN. The first sorority for African-American students was Alpha Kappa Alpha, founded on January 15, 1908, at Howard University, Washington, DC, by Ethel Hedgeman Lyle. The first president was Lucy Slowe.

2779. College summer school was established at Mount Union College, Alliance, OH. Lewis Miller of Akron, OH, presented the idea to the faculty in February 1870 and the summer school was started as a part of a four-term system in June 1870.

2780. Law school graduate who was a woman was Ada H. Kepley of Effingham, IL, who was graduated from the Union College of Law, Chicago, IL, on June 30, 1870.

2781. Land grant college for African-American students was the Alcorn Agricultural and Mechanical College in Rodney, MS, which was established by the state of Mississippi in 1871. The original name was Alcorn University. Under the Morrill Act of 1862, which gave each state an allotment of land on which to build an agricultural college, Mississippi received scrip for 210,000 acres, which it disposed of for $188,928. Three-fifths of the sum went to Alcorn University and the remaining two-fifths went to support the University of Mississippi.

2782. Political economy chair at a college was established at Harvard University, Cambridge, MA, in 1871. The first professor was Charles Franklin Dunbar. An earlier chair in moral philosophy and political economy was established in 1818 at Columbia College, New York City, with Professor John McVickar the first occupant.

2783. Theological school to admit women as students was the Boston University School of Theology, Boston, MA, founded on March 30, 1871, when the Boston Theological Seminary united with Boston University. The first female student matriculated on September 25, 1872. The first B.D. (Bachelor of Divinity) degree awarded to a woman was granted to Anna Oliver on June 7, 1876.

2784. College entrance plan using certified schools in which admission was based on the credentials of the applicant's preparatory school rather than the credentials of the applicant was the Michigan System, originated by Henry Simmons Frieze and introduced in September 1871 at the University of Michigan, Ann Arbor, MI. A student who graduated from an approved school was admitted without the necessity of taking individual examinations.

2785. Education department at a college was the Collegiate Department of Education, created by the University of Iowa, Iowa City, IA, in 1873, along with the first professorship of education. The department absorbed the university's former Normal Department, which had been in operation since 1855. A temporary department of education had been created by New York University in New York City in 1832.

2786. College president who was a woman was Frances Elizabeth Willard, professor of science at the Northwestern Female College, Evanston, IL. In February 1871, when the school was reorganized as the Evanston College for Ladies, she became president. All the members of the faculty and all the trustees were women. On June 25, 1873, the college was incorporated into Northwestern University as the Woman's College, with Miss Willard as the dean. The first woman to become president of a university was Hanna Holborn Gray, who became head of the University of Chicago on October 6, 1978.

2787. Mechanical engineering laboratory for research work was established at Stevens Institute of Technology at Hoboken, NJ, in 1874. It was proposed by Robert Henry Thurston, professor of mechanical engineering, who on January 30, 1874, outlined the usefulness of the laboratory to the community in a letter which he sent to the trustees of the school.

2788. College program of study abroad was introduced by Boston University, Boston, MA, which entered into reciprocal agreement on February 11, 1875, with the National University, Athens, Greece, and the Royal University, Rome, Italy. Students could attend these universities and have their credits applied towards degrees at their home institution. The first program offering a junior year abroad was instituted by the University of Delaware, Newark, DE, in 1923, when Professor Raymond Watson Kirkbride took a group of eight students to France for work at the University of Paris.

2789. Music professor at a college was John Knowles Paine, appointed to the chair in music established by Harvard University, Cambridge, MA, on August 30, 1875. On March 29, 1862, he had been appointed instructor in music, and on June 2, 1873, assistant professor. He served until his death, on April 25, 1906.

2790. Rabbinical college was Hebrew Union College, an institution of the Reform Jewish movement. It was established on October 3, 1875, in Cincinnati, OH, through the efforts of Dr. Isaac Mayer Wise, who served as president from 1875 to 1900. The first graduation was held on July 11, 1883.

2791. Doctoral degree awarded to an African-American by an American university was granted to Edward Alexander Bouchet by Yale University, New Haven, CT, in 1876, in physics. His thesis was entitled *Measuring Refractive Indices.* Bouchet was also the first African-American to be elected to Phi Beta Kappa, the national scholastic fraternity. He was graduated from Yale in 1874.

2792. Research university in the United States was Johns Hopkins University, which opened in Baltimore, MD, on February 22, 1876, with Daniel Coit Gilman as president. The school placed as much emphasis on faculty research and scholarship as on teaching.

2793. Chinese language and literature lectureship at a college was created by Yale University, New Haven, CT, in 1877. Samuel Wells Williams, Commodore Oliver Hazard Perry's secretary and interpreter in Japan, was the lecturer.

2794. Doctoral degree awarded to a woman by an American university was granted by Boston University, Boston, MA, on June 6, 1877, to Helen Magill. The title of her dissertation was *The Greek Drama.* She received her A.B. degree in 1875 from Swarthmore College.

2795. Business school at a college was the Wharton School of Commerce and Finance in Philadelphia, PA, established in 1881 by the University of Pennsylvania through a $100,000 gift of Joseph Wharton.

2796. Honors program offered by a university was held in September 1882 at the University of Michigan, Ann Arbor, MI. The program enabled students to take required work for two years and then, under faculty committee direction, to proceed within a limited range of subjects in a specialized course. Students who exhibited a thorough knowledge in their special fields were given bachelor's degrees or master's degrees upon passing a cumulative examination and completing a thesis.

2797. Electrical engineering school at a college was established on September 21, 1883, by the College of Engineering, Cornell University, Ithaca, NY. The college offered a four-year program leading to the degree of Bachelor of Science. Instruction was given in the theory of electricity; the construction and testing of telegraph lines, cables, and instruments; dynamo machines; and civil and mechanical engineering. Dr. Andrew White pledged his own resources for the school.

2798. Missionary training school was the Missionary Training College for Home and Foreign Missionaries and Evangelists, New York City, founded 1882 and formally opened on October 1, 1883, with an enrollment of four students. The course consisted of one year of study, including courses in English, Christian evidences, Bible study and interpretation, church history, and Christian life and work. The school was founded by Dr. Albert Benjamin Simpson, who was the first president. The name was changed to the Missionary Training Institute in April 1894.

2799. Dean of faculty at a college was Martha Carey Thomas, one of the four women in the world at that time to hold the Ph.D. degree, who was appointed at the January 1884 meeting of the trustees of Bryn Mawr College, Bryn Mawr, PA.

2800. State college for women was the Mississippi Industrial Institute and College, established in Columbus, MS, by act of the Mississippi legislature on March 12, 1884. The first graduation exercises took place in June 1889, at which time 10 A.B. degrees were conferred. The first president was Dr. Richard Watson Jones. In 1920 the name was changed to the Mississippi State College for Women.

2801. Graduate student who was a woman to receive a university fellowship was Harriet Elizabeth Grotecloss, who was awarded the Sage Fellowship in Entomology and Botany by Cornell University, Ithaca, NY, on June 19, 1884. The fellowship had a stipend of $400 per year, payable in six installments, and provided free tuition for graduate study.

2802. Biology course offered at a college was conducted by Edmund Beecher Wilson, professor of biology at Bryn Mawr College, Bryn Mawr, PA, beginning on September 23, 1885. Five lectures were given weekly, with eight hours of laboratory practice. The students examined the structure of typical animals and plants, first of familiar species, then of unicellular organisms, working thence progressively upward and taking the higher animals and plants, and ending with the embryological development of the chick. An advanced class was engaged in the study of animal morphology. Lectures on specific phases of biology had, however, been given earlier.

2803. Graduate school for women was Bryn Mawr College, Bryn Mawr, PA, which was organized in 1884 and formally opened on October 23, 1885. From its inception, Bryn Mawr offered graduate work leading to the M.A. and Ph.D. degrees, in addition to undergraduate programs.

2804. College for women to affiliate with a university was the H. Sophie Newcomb Memorial College, established on October 11, 1886, in New Orleans, LA. The college affiliated with Tulane University, also in New Orleans, in October 1887.

2805. Library school at a college was the School of Library Economy at Columbia University, New York City, which opened on January 5, 1887, through the efforts of Melvil Dewey. The school was transferred on April 1, 1889, to Albany, NY, where it was placed under the direction of the State University of New York as the New York State Library School. The first session was held on April 10, 1889, and the first public commencement and conferring of degrees took place on July 8, 1891. In 1926 the school was returned to Columbia University, where it was united with the Library School of the New York Public Library to form the School of Library Service, Columbia University.

2806. Catholic seminary under the supervision of the Pope was the Pontifical College Josephinum, Worthington, OH, a Roman Catholic institution immediately subject to the Holy See, established on September 1, 1888. Thirteen students enrolled in the courses in liberal arts and general professional theology.

2807. Animal husbandry professor at a college was John Alexander Craig of the Wisconsin Agricultural Experiment Station, University of Wisconsin, Madison, WI, who served from 1890 to 1897. His specialty was sheep husbandry.

2808. Dairy school at a college was opened on January 3, 1890, by the College of Agriculture, University of Wisconsin, Madison, WI, to supplement courses in testing milk and farm churning. The first instructor in charge of dairying was Professor John Wright Decker. The first year, the organized course was attended by only two students, but the following year 70 registered from nine states and Canada. Dairy certificates were awarded to those who passed the full course and had been in practical charge of a creamery or cheese factory for two seasons.

2809. Physical education department at a college on a par with other departments was established by the University of Chicago, Chicago, IL. Amos Alonzo Stagg was made assistant professor and director of the Department of Physical Culture and Athletics and a regular member of the faculty in 1892. In 1901 he was granted a full professorship. He and other members of the department coached the university athletic teams. Previously, in most colleges, athletics had been under the control of a student athletic association.

2810. Student government at a college was the Bryn Mawr Self-Government Association, chartered on February 23, 1892, by the trustees, subjecting student conduct outside the classrooms at Bryn Mawr, PA, to student rulings.

2811. Sociology professor at a college was Albion Woodbury Small, appointed professor and head of the Department of Sociology at the University of Chicago, Chicago, IL, effective October 1, 1892. Small held the position until his retirement on October 1, 1925. He was also dean of the Graduate School of Arts and Literature from 1905 to 1923. A course in sociology had been offered at Bryn Mawr College in 1892 by Franklin Henry Giddings, associate professor of political science.

2812. Public speaking department at a college was established in December 1892 at the University of Michigan, Ann Arbor, MI, with Thomas Clarkson Trueblood as professor of elocution and oratory. Similar courses had been given in 1887, but without departmental status.

2813. College extension courses granting college credits were offered on January 1, 1893, by the University Extension Division in the Class-Study Department of the University of Chicago, Chicago, IL, "with credit . . . given in the books of the University to properly qualified students who completed any course of instruction." Twenty-five academic or secondary school courses and 40 college courses were given. Admission requirements were the same as those of other parts of the university. The first director of the Extension Division was George Henderson.

2814. College course in the contemporary novel was given by Professor William Lyon Phelps at Yale University, New Haven, CT, in the academic year 1895–96. The course was called "Modern Novels" and was elected by 250 juniors and seniors.

2815. College for women founded as a Catholic institution was the College of Notre Dame of Maryland, Baltimore, MD, which opened on September 2, 1895. The first commencement was held on June 14, 1899, when four bachelor of arts degrees and two bachelor of literature degrees were awarded. Charles Joseph Bonaparte, a grandnephew of Napoleon, was the commencement speaker, his subject being "The Significance of the Bachelor's Degree."

2816. Forestry school at a college was established on September 19, 1898, at Cornell University, Ithaca, NY, as the New York State College of Forestry. Dr. Bernhard Eduard Fernow was director and dean. The law under which this school was established was signed by Governor Frank Swett Black on April 8, 1898, making New York the first state to establish a forestry course. The activities of the school were suspended in 1903. Lectures on forestry and tree culture were given at Yale University in 1873 and at Cornell in 1874.

2817. Foreign service school in a college was the School of Comparative Jurisprudence and Diplomacy of George Washington University, Washington, DC, which opened on November 15, 1898. It was discontinued as a separate school in 1913, though courses continued to be given by Columbian College. In September 1928, training in foreign service and governmental theory and administration was reestablished as a separate branch under the School of Government.

2818. University press was founded in 1899 by the Johns Hopkins University, Baltimore, MD. Its first publication was the *American Journal of Mathematics.*

2819. Rhodes Scholars took up residence at Oxford University, England, in 1904. The will of the British financier and industrialist Cecil Rhodes, dated July 1, 1899, established three-year scholarships to Oxford for outstanding students from the United States, Germany, and British colonies. The first year, 43 awards were made to students from 43 different states. The first African-American student to receive a Rhodes scholarship was Alain Le Roy Locke of Pennsylvania, who studied philosophy at Oxford's Hertford College from 1907 to 1910. He received his A.B. degree in 1908 from Harvard University. Women became eligible for Rhodes scholarships in 1977, after Rhodes's will was changed by an act of Parliament.

2820. Dean of students at a college was appointed at Whitman College, Walla Walla, WA, in 1901. Benjamin Harrison Brown, professor of physics and chemistry, was appointed dean of men, and Dr. Louis Francis Anderson, professor of Greek, was appointed dean of women.

2821. Technical college for women was Simmons College, Boston, MA, which was chartered in 1899 by the provisions of the will of John Simmons, a Boston merchant who died in 1870. The college opened in 1902 and the first class was graduated on June 13, 1906, when 32 B.S. degrees were conferred. The first president was Henry Lefavour.

2822. College varsity sports program in which letters were awarded was established on January 29, 1904, at the University of Chicago, Chicago, IL, by Amos Alonzo Stagg. It was known as the "order of the 'C.'" The practice of awarding blankets to lettermen who had completed their competition was initiated by Stagg at the University of Chicago following the football season of 1904.

2823. School of social work was the New York School of Philanthropy, which offered a one-year graduate course in association with Columbia University. It opened on October 3, 1904. The program originated in 1898 as the Charity Organization Society's Summer School in Philanthropic Work.

2824. National college fraternity for African-American men was Alpha Phi Alpha, formed on December 4, 1906, by members of a social study club formed in 1905. The first president was George B. Kelley. The first chapter was started at Cornell University, Ithaca, NY, and the second, in 1908, at Howard University, Washington, DC.

2825. Nonsectarian college under Jewish auspices was Dropsie College for Hebrew and Cognate Learning of Philadelphia, PA, chartered on June 6, 1907. The college was founded in accordance with the will of Moses Aaron Dropsie, who directed "that in the admission of students there shall be no distinction on account of creed, color or sex." The first president of the college was Dr. Cyrus Adler.

2826. Journalism school at a college offering a degree in journalism was opened on September 14, 1908, at the University of Missouri, Columbia, MO. Enrollment for the school year 1908–09 was 97, including 84 men and 13 women. The first degree, a Bachelor of Science in Journalism, was awarded in 1909 to Charles Arnold. The first dean was Walter Williams.

2827. Urban planning instruction at a college was offered in 1909 by Harvard University, Cambridge, MA, under James Sturgis Pray, professor of landscape architecture. In the fall of 1929, the Charles Dyer Norton Chair of Regional Planning was founded by a gift from James F. Curtis, and a separate School of City Planning was set up requiring a bachelor's degree for entrance and giving a Master of City Planning degree. The first degrees of Master in Landscape Architecture were conferred on June 18, 1925, and the first degrees of Master of City Planning on June 18, 1931.

2828. Climatology professor at a college was Robert De Courcy Ward, appointed in 1910 by Harvard University, Cambridge, MA.

2829. College foreign-language house was Deutsches Haus, a four-story brick building at Columbia University, New York City, opened in 1911. The first director was Rudolph Tombs, Jr. The house was suggested by Columbia's president, Nicholas Murray Butler.

2830. Oil and gas production course at a college was offered by the School of Engineering, University of Pittsburgh, Pittsburgh, PA, in 1912–13. The course was given by Professor Roswell Hill Johnson.

2831. Aeronautical engineering course at a college was given in 1913 by the Department of Naval Architecture and Marine Engineering, Massachusetts Institute of Technology, Cambridge, MA. Lectures in aeronautics were given in 1912 and 1913. The first regular instructor in aeronautical engineering was appointed in 1913. The aerodynamic laboratory was placed in operation and a graduate course was established leading to the degree of Master of Science in Aeronautical Engineering in 1914.

2832. College comprehensive senior examination program was adopted on May 26, 1913, by the faculty of Whitman College, Walla Walla, WA. Beginning with the class of 1914, every student graduated from Whitman College was required to pass an examination, either oral or oral and written, given by a committee of the faculty in the student's department and covering the entire field of study in student's major subject. The written examinations ran from 6 to 10 hours and the orals from 1 to 3.

2833. Civic design chair at a college was established by the University of Illinois, Urbana, IL, in 1912 as part of the landscape development program inaugurated in 1897 by Joseph Cullen Blair, in charge of the Department of Horticulture. The first incumbent of the chair was Professor Charles Mulford Robinson, who served as professor of civic design from September 1, 1913, until his death on December 30, 1917.

2834. Vocational guidance chair at a college was established in 1914 at Indiana University, Bloomington, IN. The first professor was Robert Josselyn Leonard, who served from June 1914 to April 1918.

2835. Fisheries school at a college was the College of Fisheries, University of Washington, Seattle, WA, established in March 1919. It offered practical training and a four-year program leading to a Bachelor of Fisheries degree. The first classes had an enrollment of 76 students. The first dean was John Nathan Cobb.

2836. Editor in chief of a law review who was a woman was Mary Honor Donlon, a student at the Cornell Law School, Ithaca, NY, who edited three issues of the *Cornell Law Quarterly* that were published in November 1919, January 1920, and March 1920.

2837. Geography school at a college was the Clark Graduate School of Geography, Clark University, Worcester, MA, which opened in the fall of 1921. Dr. Wallace Walter Atwood, president of the university, was appointed director of the school and professor of physical and regional geography.

2838. Civil rights chair at a college was established at Lafayette College, Easton, PA, through the gift of Fred Morgan Kirby. The first lectures were given in February 1921 by Professor Herbert Adams Gibbons.

2839. Hotel administration course at a college was offered by Cornell University, Ithaca, NY, in the fall of 1922, and included courses in accounting, administration, economics, engineering, food preparation, housekeeping, and languages. The course required four years and led to a B.S. degree. Professor Howard Bagnall Meek was the first professor of hotel administration.

2840. Business history chair at a college was the Isidor Straus Professorship of Business History, established in 1923 by the Graduate School of Business Administration, Harvard University, Cambridge, MA. The first incumbent was Norman Scott Brien Gras, appointed in 1927.

2841. Marriage course at a college was given by Professor Ernest Rutherford Groves in 1924 at the University of North Carolina, Chapel Hill, NC.

2842. Micropaleontology course at a college was given by Professor Jesse James Galloway at Columbia University, New York City, starting on September 25, 1924. It covered the principles of paleontology, classification and nomenclature, the use of paleontological literature, and the identification of small forms with the microscope.

2843. Citizenship and public affairs school at a college was opened on October 3, 1924, by Syracuse University, Syracuse, NY, through the generosity of George Holmes Maxwell. The first dean was William Eugene Mosher.

2844. Book course at a college was taught in the fall of 1926 at Rollins College, Winter Park, FL, by Dr. Edwin Osgood Grover, professor of books. The first instruction was given on September 22. The idea of a "professorship of books" was first suggested by Ralph Waldo Emerson in his essay "Books," which appeared in the *Atlantic Monthly* issue of January 1858.

2845. Dance major at a college was approved on November 11, 1926, by the Wisconsin Board of Regents and offered in the Department of Physical Education of Women, University of Wisconsin, Madison, WI. Margaret Newell H'Doubler was appointed chairman of the program.

2846. Propaganda course at a college was given by Professor Harold Dwight Lasswell of the Department of Political Science, University of Chicago, Chicago, IL, in 1927. It was entitled "Political Opinion and Propaganda."

2847. College founded as a Jewish institution was Yeshiva College, Amsterdam Avenue and 186th Street, New York City, chartered on March 29, 1928, by the board of Regents of the University of the State of New York. The first graduating class, consisting of 19 members, received bachelors' degrees on June 16, 1932. The first president was Rabbi Dr. Bernard Revel. On November 16, 1945, the college became Yeshiva University and was authorized to establish new graduate and undergraduate schools and to confer 15 kinds of degrees.

2848. Radio advertising course at a college was instituted by the School of Business and Civic Administration of the City College of New York on September 28, 1930, under the direction of Frank Atkinson Arnold, director of development of the National Broadcasting Company. The class consisted of 62 students.

2849. Greek Orthodox college and orphanage was the Monastery of St. Stephanos in Gastonia, NC, dedicated on September 18, 1932, by Archbishop Athenagaros of the Greek Orthodox Church in North and South America to the "oncoming generations of Greek youth."

2850. Game management chair at a college was established by the University of Wisconsin, Madison, WI, in August 1933, at which time Aldo Leopold was appointed to fill the post. The primary aim was to provide facilities for graduate research and a clearinghouse for the development of game production as a new use for Wisconsin land. The University of Michigan had established a school of conservation in 1927 and the University of Iowa had created the position of director of game research in 1932.

2851. Theater and dramatic criticism course at a college to award a Ph.D. degree was established by the Department of Drama, Yale University, New Haven, CT, on September 24, 1934. The first degrees were awarded to George Riley Kernodle, John Huber McDowell, and Virginia More Roediger on June 23, 1937. The normal minimum time required for the course was four full years of study and research. The first professor of the history of the drama was Allardyce Nicoll.

2852. College to dispense with credits, hours, points, and grades was Olivet College, Olivet, MI, which on October 1, 1934, substituted a system proposed by its president, Joseph Brewer. The system divided the college into junior and senior divisions and required candidates for the degree of Bachelor of Arts to have at least three years of instruction and to pass preliminary and final examinations. It also opened lectures to all members of the college without distinction and assigned tutors to guide each student's course while investing the responsibility for acquiring an education with the student.

2853. Drama school at a college that was operated in association with a professional theater was the Mohawk Drama Festival and Institute of the Theater, which offered its first courses on July 2, 1935, at Union College, Schenectady, NY. Seventy students enrolled in the intensive eight-week course, which covered history, theory, and practice. The director was Dr. Thomas Herbert Dickinson. Four plays were presented: *The Merry Wives of Windsor*, *Lysistrata*, *Rip Van Winkle*, and *Master of the Revels*. The course concluded on August 24, 1935, when 25 certificates of meritorious achievement were awarded. The school was chartered by the Regents of the University of the State of New York in 1938.

2854. Archival course at a college was "Archives and Historical Manuscripts," offered beginning on September 29, 1938, by Columbia University, New York City, under Dr. Solon Justus Buck, director of publications, National Archives, Washington, DC.

2855. Dean of a university graduate school who was a woman was Dr. Frieda Wunderlich, elected on January 4, 1939, as dean of the Graduate Faculty of Political and Social Science, part of the New School for Social Research, New York City.

2856. Radio production course at a college was part of a four-year combined program in liberal arts and radio leading to the degree of Bachelor of Arts, offered by New York University in September 1939 in the Washington Square College of Arts and Science. The course included instruction in writing, speaking, announcing, planning and production, news broadcasting, and broadcasting of special events.

2857. Television production course at a college was offered on September 26, 1940, in evening sessions at New York University, New York City. The instructor was Thomas H. Hutchinson of the National Broadcasting Company. The first day course was given by the School of Speech, Marquette University, Milwaukee, WI, in the fall of 1951. Fourteen students registered for instruction in programing, administrative duties, and coordination of writing, staging, directing, and acting. The course was conducted by Colby Lewis, assistant program manager of WTMJ-TV, Milwaukee.

2858. Film professorship at a college was established by the Washington Square College of Arts and Sciences of New York University, New York City, on May 26, 1941, when the appointment of Robert Gessner as assistant professor of motion pictures was approved for the term beginning on September 1, 1941. The title for the position was variously changed to professor of television, motion pictures and radio, and to professor of cinema.

2859. Industrial and labor relations school at a college was the New York State School of Industrial and Labor Relations, Cornell University, Ithaca, NY, opened for registration on November 2, 1945. Irving McNeil Ives was the first dean.

2860. College principally for war veterans was Champlain College, Plattsburgh, NY, opened on September 16, 1946. It was operated by the Associated Colleges of Upper New York, a corporation created by legislative act effective April 1, 1946, which also opened Mohawk College in Utica, NY, and Sampson College, in Sampson, NY, opened on October 23, 1946. The president was Asa Smallidge Knowles.

2861. Ballet technique course at a college was offered at Texas Christian University, Fort Worth, TX, in 1949, when instructor David Preston taught a class of 18 freshmen in the fall semester.

2862. Nuclear engineering course at a college was established by the North Carolina State College of Agriculture and Engineering of the University of North Carolina, Raleigh, NC, under the direction of Dr. Clifford Keith Beck, head of the physics department. The first students were accepted and enrolled on June 12, 1950.

2863. Yiddish professorship at a college was established on February 11, 1952, at Columbia University, New York City. The first incumbent was Uriel Weinreich, associate professor of Yiddish language, literature, and culture.

2864. Science fiction course at a college was offered at the City College of New York, New York City, in 1953. It was taught by Samuel Moskowitz.

2865. College Bowl competition on radio was "College Quiz Bowl," broadcast on October 10, 1953, on NBC. Two-four member teams participated, one from Columbia College, New York City, and the other from Northwestern University, Evanston, IL. The host was Allen Ludden. Northwestern beat Columbia by a score of 135 to 60.

2866. College student to receive federal aid as the child of a deceased veteran was George A. Turner, 19, of Brooklyn, New York City, who enrolled at the University of Oklahoma. He was the son of William G. Turner, who died in 1954 at the age of 43 from a disability incurred during the Normandy invasion in World War II. The law authorizing such grants was enacted by Congress on June 29, 1956, "to establish an educational assistance program for children of servicemen who died as a result of a disability or disease incurred in line of duty during World War One, World War Two, or the Korean conflict." It authorized the Veterans Administration to pay a subsistence grant of up to $110 a month not in excess of 36 months to a son or daughter between the ages of 18 and 23.

2867. State college for the performing artswas the North Carolina School of the Arts, Winston-Salem, NC, a conservatory established on June 21, 1963, by the North Carolina General Assembly. It began accepting students in 1965. The first president was composer Vittorio Giannini. The school was incorporated into the University of North Carolina system in 1972.

2868. Campus takeover by student protesters took place in September 1964 and was known as the Free Speech Movement. Students at the University of California, Berkeley, CA, occupied the administration building as a protest against the university's decision to ban various political activities on campus. More than 800 demonstrators were arrested by order of Governor Edmund G. Brown. Further building takeovers followed, as well as a general strike by faculty members and graduate students that shut down the university. The ban was rescinded.

2869. College on a Native American reservation was Navajo Community College, established in Tsaile, AZ, in 1969.

2870. College to offer a degree in human sexuality studies in the United States was San Francisco State University, San Francisco, CA. The program was started in 1970 by Bernard Goldstein, a professor of biology.

2871. President of a major university who was African-American was Clifton Reginald Wharton, Jr., who on January 2, 1970, became the 14th president of Michigan State University, East Lansing, MI, which had an enrollment of about 44,000.

2872. College whose tuition fees were based on family income was Beloit College, in Beloit, WI, which adopted the plan on October 11, 1971, for the term beginning in September 1972. Tuition in 1972–73 for families with no other children in college varied from $500 for those with an adjusted income of less than $7,000 to $1,650 for those with an adjusted income of $30,000 or more.

2873. College to offer courses to railroad commuters was Adelphi University, in Garden City, NY, which offered graduate courses in business statistics, microeconomic analysis, accounting, marketing, and the legal environment of business on trains of the Long Island Railroad between Huntington, NY, and New York City, beginning on October 18, 1971. The commuting classrooms contained swivel chairs, audiovisual systems, blackboards, and microphones. The fee was the same as on the campus, $246 for each three-point course, plus train fare. The Master of Business Administration degree was awarded on completion of the two-year program, which consisted of three classes a week for eight weeks, or two a week for 12 weeks. The 66-minute class began at 5:56 A.M. from Huntington; the 77-minute return-trip class from New York City began at 5:56 P.M. The courses, for which Adelphi received a $20,000 grant from the Long Island Trust Company, were under the direction of Dr. Peter Berman and Dean Julius Liff.

2874. College to offer athletic scholarships to women was the University of Miami, in Coral Gables, FL, which offered full-tuition scholarships, each worth $2,400 a year, to 15 athletes. The first recipient was Terry Williams of Homestead, FL, on May 5, 1973.

2875. College commencement exercises in a prison were held on January 20, 1975, in the Jackson State Prison, Jackson, MI. Twenty associate degrees were conferred by Jackson Community College.

2876. Year in which a higher percentage of female than male high school graduates enrolled in college was 1976, when 50.3 percent of the female graduates enrolled versus 47.2 percent of the male graduates. Since then, there have been different outcomes in different years: During the 1980s, in half the years the percentage of women was higher and in half the years the percentage of men was higher; during the 1990s, the percentage of women was higher in the majority of years.

2877. Year in which more women than men were enrolled in colleges and universities in the United States was 1979, when 5,683,000 men were enrolled and 5,887,000 women.

2878. Online college classes were offered by the New Jersey Institute of Technology (NJIT), Newark, NJ, in 1984, using the Electronic Information Exchange System developed by college personnel. The system included e-mail, instant messaging, and threaded discussion capabilities. NJIT trademarked the term "virtual classroom."

2879. Cyber university was Jones International University, headquartered in Englewood, CO, which offered courses on the Internet. On March 5, 1999, it received accreditation from the North Central Association of Colleges and Schools, an accreditation agency, as the first "cyber university," and was authorized to award the degree of Master of Business Administration. The courses were taught by professors at American colleges and were open to students anywhere in the world. The president of Jones International University was Pamela S. Pease.

2880. State to provide financial assistance to college students who are parents was Michigan, whose legislature created a fund for this purpose in a bill signed into law on December 29, 2004. The fund, a combination of state tax money and private donations, allowed colleges and universities to set up resource centers where pregnant students and those with children could access information about prenatal care, adoption services, and child-care options. The law took effect on March 30, 2005.

Elementary and

Secondary

2881. School run by missionaries in America was a classical school briefly operated by Spanish Franciscan priests in St. Augustine, FL, in 1606.

2882. School for colonial children in America is the subject of some dispute. A school is known to have been established by the Dutch West India Company on Manhattan Island in 1633, with Adam Roelantsen as its first master. Instruction was given in Dutch prior to 1775. In 1783 the school became known as the Collegiate School (formally the School of the Collegiate Reformed Dutch Church in the City of New York), the oldest school still in existence in the United States. Claims for earlier informal schools have been made on behalf of Jamestown, VA, where African-American and Native American children were taught in 1620, and the Pilgrim settlement at Plymouth, MA, where instruction was given to the children of colonists circa 1621.

2883. Free school funded by an endowment in the American colonies was the Syms-Eaton Academy, founded in Hampton, VA, in 1634 by Benjamin Syms (or Symmes). He donated "two hundred acres of land on Poquoson River with the milk and increase of eight cows for the maintenance of a learned and honest man to keep upon the said grounds a free school." In 1805 the name was changed to the Hampton Academy. Another early free school with an endowment was the Free Schoole in Roxburie, established in Roxbury, MA, in 1645. It was incorporated in 1789 as the "Grammar School in the Easterly Part of the Town of Roxbury."

2884. Public school with a continuous existence was the Boston Public Latin School for boys, established on February 13, 1635, and supported by voluntary contributions. The first schoolmaster was Philemon Pormort. Its original purpose was to prepare boys for the ministry by enabling them to "obtain a knowledge of the Scriptures and by acquaintance with the Ancient Tongues qualify them to discern the true sense and meaning of the original, however corrupted by false glosses."

2885. Property tax established by a colony to support public schools was established by vote of Dorchester, MA, on May 20, 1639: "It is ordered the 20th of May 1639, that there shall be a rent of twenty pounds a year for ever imposed upon Tomsons Island to be paid by every person that hath property in the said island according to the proportion that any such person shall from time to time enjoy and possess there."

2886. Catholic school was founded circa 1640 by the Jesuits at St. Mary's City, MD. The Catholic parochial school system is considered by some historians to have originated in a school started by St. Mary's Church, Philadelphia, PA, in 1782, while others date its beginnings from 1809, when Elizabeth Ann Seton, the first Catholic saint born in America, founded a school near Baltimore, MD.

2887. Compulsory education law in a colony was passed by Massachusetts on June 14, 1642. It stated: "This Court, taking into consideration the great neglect of many parents and masters in training up their children in learning and labor and other imployments which may be profittable to the common wealth, so hereupon order and decree, that in every towne the chosen men appointed for managing the prudentiall affayers of the same shall henceforth stand charged with the care of the redresse of this evil . . . and for this end . . . they shall have power to take account from time to time of all parents and masters, and of their children, concerning their calling and imployment of their children."

2888. Spelling book was printed by Stephen Day in 1643 in Cambridge, MA.

2889. School committee was elected in Dorchester, MA, in 1645. The members were elected for life, although the town reserved the right to remove any of them for "weighty reasons." They had charge of everything that pertained to the betterment of the school.

2890. Colonial law requiring towns to hire teachers and construct schools was passed on November 11, 1647, by Massachusetts. It "ordered that every township in this jurisdiction, after the Lord hath increased them to the number of fifty householders, shall then forthwith appoint one within their town to teach all such children as shall resort to him to write and read, whose wages shall be paid either by the parents or masters of such children, or by the inhabitants in general." Towns of 100 families were required to "set up a grammar school, the master thereof being able to instruct youths so far as they may be fitted for the university."

2891. Evening school for working children was established in New Amsterdam (now New York City) in 1661. Fees and regulations for instruction were contained in a report, *Instructions and Rules for Schoolmaster, Evert Pietersen*, which was drawn up by the burgomasters on November 4, 1661.

2892. Town trust fund for education was created by Burlington, NJ, in 1682. The assembly provided that a valuable island situated in the Delaware River above Burlington, and known as Matinicunk Island, "remain to and for the use of the town of Burlington . . . for the maintaining of a school for the education of youth."

2893. Schoolbook was the *New England Primer* of 1689–90. It was "printed by R. Pierce for, and sold by Benjamin Harris, at the London Coffee-House," Boston, MA.

2894. Blackboards for use in schools were introduced in 1714 by Christopher Dock of Skippack, PA. Dock, an immigrant from Germany, was the author of the first book on teaching methodology to be published in America.

2895. School for Native Americans to be permanently established was founded in 1720 in Williamsburg, VA, through the generosity of Robert Boyle, the eminent English scientist and formulator of Boyle's Law. To house the school, the Brafferton Building was erected at the College of William and Mary in 1723. The building was named after Boyle's estate in Yorkshire, England, which provided revenue from rents to support the school.

2896. School for girls in the future United States was the Ursuline Academy, New Orleans, LA. It was opened in the fall of 1727 by a group of Ursuline nuns who had emigrated from France a few months earlier. They offered instruction to Native Americans and to African-American slaves as well as to French colonists.

2897. School for Protestant girls was a boarding school established by Countess Benigna von Zinzendorf at Germantown, PA, in 1742, exclusively for girls of the Moravian Church. By 1800 this had become a noted seminary. It eventually became the Moravian College for Women.

2898. Textbook printed in America was Thomas Dilworth's *A New Guide to the English Tongue*, a combined reader, speller, and grammar, published in London in 1740 and reprinted by Benjamin Franklin's press in 1747 in Philadelphia, PA. It went through 26 editions before 1792. Dilworth was one of the first to provide word lists for spelling. Prior to this time, spelling had been taught incidentally with reading, using the Bible as an advanced reader.

2899. Book on teaching methodology was Christopher Dock's *Schul-ordnung; or A Simple and Thoroughly Prepared School-Management clearly setting forth not only in what manner children may best be taught in the branches usually given at school, but also how they may be well instructed in the knowledge of godliness.* The book was completed on August 3, 1750, but was not published until 20 years later. The preface was dated March 27, 1770. It was originally written in German and was printed by Christopher Saur in Germantown, PA.

2900. Manual training courses offered in a school were given at the Charity Workers' School, organized in Talbot County, MD, in 1750 by the Reverend Thomas Bacon. It opened on December 1, 1751, with an enrollment of six boys. It was financed through funds from a series of concerts given in Maryland and Virginia.

2901. Book advocating spelling reform was *A Scheme for a New Alphabet and Reformed Mode of Spelling; with Remarks and Examples*, written by Benjamin Franklin in 1768. He advocated dropping C, J, Q, W, X, and Y from the alphabet and substituting six other characters so "that there be no distinct sounds in the language without letters to express them."

2902. Land set aside for schools authorized by the Continental Congress was authorized by an ordinance of May 20, 1785: "There shall be reserved the lot No. 16 of every township for the maintenance of public schools within said township." This applied to the Western Reserve (now Ohio) and other unsurveyed lands to the west. A new system of surveying was established, with the land laid out in townships six miles square, subdivided into 36 numbered sections, each a mile square. Section No. 16 was popularly known as the "school section."

2903. Education association was the Middlesex County Association for the Improvement of Common Schools, organized on May

1799 in Middletown, CT, by the Reverend William Woodbridge, who served as its first president.

2904. Instruction for deaf students was given by the Reverend John Stanford in 1807 in the Almshouse, New York City. This instruction continued for about a year. Stanford's title was Chaplain to the Humane and Criminal Institutions. In 1817 a meeting was held at his home to organize the New York Institution for the Deaf, now the New York School for the Deaf, which opened in 1818.

2905. School for African-Americans in Washington, DC was the Bell School, founded in 1807 by three illiterate former slaves—George Bell, Nicholas Franklin, and Moses Liverpool—who built it themselves and solicited funds from private donors to hire a teacher. All three were caulkers at the Navy Yard.

2906. State superintendent of schools was Gideon Hawley, who was appointed state superintendent of common schools by New York in 1812. He began serving on January 14, 1813. An act was passed on April 15, 1814, making him secretary of the New York State Board of Regents at a salary of $400 a year. He was removed in 1821 because of political machinations, and the secretary of state was authorized to act as superintendent. In 1854 New York created the job of superintendent of public instruction.

2907. School for the higher education of women was the Middlebury Female Seminary, started by Emma Hart Willard in 1814 in her home in Middlebury, VT. The curriculum included academic subjects as well as household management. In 1819 she moved to Waterford, NY, and established the Waterford Academy. She had hoped for state aid, but no funds were appropriated. However, the citizens of Troy, NY, provided funds for a building, and in 1821 she opened the Troy Female Seminary, afterwards known as the Emma Willard School. Her book *Plan for Improving Female Education* was published in 1819.

2908. School for deaf students was started at Cobbs, Chesterfield County, VA, in 1815 by Colonel William Bolling with John Braidwood as instructor, but it lasted only two years.

2909. School for deaf students to be established on a permanent basis was the Connecticut Asylum in Hartford for the Education and Instruction of Deaf and Dumb Persons (now called the American School for the Deaf), which opened on April 15, 1817, in Hartford, CT, with seven pupils. The school was financed through the generosity of a few men, one of whom, Dr. Mason Fitch Cogswell, had a deaf daughter, Alice. Thomas Hopkins Gallaudet, the first principal, inaugurated the system of teaching with the collaboration of a Frenchman, Laurent Clerc. Sign language and finger spelling were the means of communication. The Clarke School for the Deaf, which was founded in 1867 in Northampton, MA, was the first permanent oral school for deaf students. It originated in 1865 in a small experimental school in Chelmsford, MA, founded by Harriet Rogers, who was its first principal.

2910. Education magazine that was successful was the *Education* magazine, a 16-page semimonthly, published from February 7, 1818, to January 29, 1820, in New York City. It was edited by Albert Picket and John W. Picket, president and corresponding secretary, respectively, of the Incorporated Society of Teachers, which published the magazine. It offered advice and comments on teaching, and cost $3 a year. The Pickets had previously published an unsuccessful magazine, the *Juvenile Mirror or Educational Magazine*, which made its first appearance in August 1811 but lasted less than a year.

2911. Industrial school on the Fellenberg plan was established in 1819 in Derby, CT, by Josiah Holbrook. The boys paid a portion of their tuition by laboring on the farm. In 1824, with the cooperation of the Reverend Truman Coe, Holbrook established the Agricultural Seminary. Neither of these enterprises was successful.

2912. State aid to special education was a grant provided by Connecticut to the American School for the Deaf, Hartford, CT, in 1819. The school had been founded on April 15, 1817, by Thomas Hopkins Gallaudet.

2913. Federal aid to special education took the form of a land grant for the benefit of the Ameircan School for the Deaf in Hartford, CT. Congress made the grant in 1820. The land was part of the Alabama Territory.

2914. High school was the English Classical School, opened in May 1820 in Boston, MA. The name was changed in 1824 to the English High School. Admittance was open to boys at least 12 years of age who were "well acquainted with reading, writing, English grammar in all its branches, and arithmetic, as far as simple proportions."

2915. Teacher training school was the Concord Academy, Concord, VT, opened on March 11, 1823, by the Reverend Samuel Read Hall, who conducted it as a teachers' seminary until 1830.

2916. Catholic school for Native Americans was the St. Regis Seminary, Florissant, MO, which opened on May 11, 1824, under the direction of Father Van Quickenborne. It was located in three buildings that cost about $2,000 to build. There were 40 to 60 students. It closed on June 30, 1831.

2917. Tax enacted by a state to support public schools was "an act providing for the establishment of free schools," enacted on January 15, 1825, by Illinois. It provided for a common school in each county, open to every class of white citizens between the ages of 5 and 21 years and supported by a tax of $2 of every $100 and five-sixths of the interest from the school fund.

2918. High school for girls was established in 1826 in Boston, MA, but was abolished in 1828. Instead, the course of study in the elementary schools was advanced.

2919. Nursery school was established in New York City in 1827 by the Infant School Society of the City of New York, founded on May 23, 1827, "to relieve parents of the laboring classes from the care of their children while engaged in the vocations by which they live, and provide for the children a protection from the weather, from idleness and the contamination of evil example besides affording them the means of early and efficient education." Children from 18 months to 5 years of age were accommodated, 448 receiving attention over the course of two years. Joanna Bethune was the first director.

2920. School for blind students was the New England Asylum for the Blind, Boston, MA, incorporated on March 2, 1829. The school was founded by Dr. John Dix Fisher and opened under Dr. Samuel Gridley Howe in August 1832 with six pupils. In 1839, the name was changed to the Perkins Institution and the Massachusetts Asylum for the Blind in honor of Thomas Handasyd Perkins, who in 1833 offered his Boston home for a school building, along with the open grounds around it. The school later moved to Watertown, MA, and was known as the New England Institution for the Education of the Blind.

2921. High school night classes were authorized in Ohio on March 16, 1829. Accordingly, three evening schools for boys opened in Cincinnati in November 1840. In 1855, schools for girls were also opened.

2922. National educational association was the American Institute of Instruction, formed at a preliminary meeting held March 15–19, 1830, and organized August 19–21, 1830, at a convention at Boston, MA, attended by delegates from 15 states. The first president was Francis Wayland, Jr., president of Brown University.

2923. City superintendent of schools was Roswell Willson Haskins, who was appointed "city superintendent of common schools" in 1836 by Buffalo, NY. He resigned before the end of the year, as the law was imperfect and restrictions hampered his work.

2924. State school for blind students was the Ohio Institution for the Blind, authorized on April 3, 1837, and opened on July 4, 1837, with five pupils, in the Presbyterian Church, Columbus, OH, in the presence of 900 people. Anson W. Penniman was the first teacher and William Chapin the first superintendent. In 1902, the name was changed to the Ohio State School for the Blind.

2925. State board of education was established by Massachusetts on April 30, 1837. The first secretary of the board, later designated as commissioner, was the educational reformer Horace Mann. He was appointed on June 29, 1837, and received $1,000 a year.

2926. Music instruction in a public school was conducted by Lowell Mason in November 1837 at the Hawes School, South Boston, MA. On August 28, 1838, the school board voted that a committee on music be instructed to contract with a teacher of vocal music for the several public schools of Boston. Mason was appointed and served from 1838 to 1841. He was in charge of four assistants.

2927. Teacher training school established by a state was the Normal School in Lexington, MA, which opened on July 3, 1839, with three pupils. Free tuition was offered to those who completed the one-year course and planned to teach in Massachusetts. Cyrus Pierce was the first principal. The school was started on the initiative of the educational reformer Horace Mann with the help of Edmund Dwight, who offered $10,000 on condition that the Commonwealth appropriate the same amount to be expended by the Board of Education in qualifying teachers for common schools. That amount was appropriated on April 19, 1838. On December 15, 1853, the school moved to Framingham, MA.

2928. Teachers' institute was held at Hartford, CT, in October 1839, when 26 male teachers attended a six-week course sponsored by Henry Barnard and received the "opportunity of critically reviewing the studies which they will be called upon to teach, with a full explanation of all the principles involved." Among the authorities who gave instruction were Charles Davies in higher mathematics and Thomas Hopkins Gallaudet in composition and school government.

2929. Handwriting teaching system widely used in schools was developed by Platt Rogers Spencer of East Fishkill, NY, between 1846 and 1850. Spencer based his ornate, rounded, strongly slanted letters on esthetic ideals he derived from Greek philosophy. He established "Spencerian" business colleges—the first schools to specialize in business communications—throughout the country. His handwriting copybooks and textbooks were used in the schools of 42 states.

2930. School to provide separate classrooms for each class was established in 1846 in Quincy, MA.

2931. School for children with mental disabilities was the Massachusetts School for the Idiotic and Feeble-Minded Youth, created through the efforts of Dr. Samuel Gridley Howe and established by a legislative resolution, approved on May 8, 1848, which appropriated $2,500 a year for three years. The first students were received on October 1, 1848. The name was later changed to the Massachusetts School for the Feeble-Minded and then to the Walter E. Fernald State School, named for Dr. Walter Elmore Fernald, the first resident superintendent.

2932. Compulsory education law enacted by a state was approved on May 18, 1852, by Governor George Sewall Boutwell of Massachusetts. It prescribed that children must attend school "between the ages of eight and fourteen years" for 12 weeks in the year, 6 of which must be consecutive.

2933. Physical education classes in elementary schools were required in 1853 in Boston, MA, where school officials ruled that "every scholar shall have daily in the forenoon and afternoon some kind of physical exercise."

2934. Truancy law enacted by a state was "an act to provide for the care and instruction of idle and truant children," enacted by New York on April 12, 1853. A $50 fine was levied against parents whose children between the ages of 5 and 15 were absent from school.

2935. Industrial school for girls was organized in Lancaster, MA, the funds being obtained by subscription undertaken in April 1854. The school was incorporated as a state institution on August 27, 1856, with Bradford K. Pierce as the first superintendent. This school was administered by the Department of Public Welfare.

2936. School for blind students to adopt the Braille system was the Missouri School for the Blind, St. Louis, MO. In 1859, Dr. Simon Pollak, a trustee of the school, introduced the system directly from Paris with a change in three letters. The system was adapted for use in music, spelling, etymology, and other subjects.

2937. Public school for Asian-American children was established in September 1859 in the basement of the Chinese Chapel, San Francisco, CA. James Denman was the superintendent of schools. The school had an enrollment of 67 boys and 8 girls, but the average daily attendance was only 12. The school was suspended in June 1860 and was reopened as an evening school.

2938. Boarding school on a Native American reservation was the Yakima Agency Boarding School, opened in November 1860 in the buildings of old Fort Simco on the Yakima Reservation, WA, under provision of the treaty with the Yakima Nation of June 8, 1855, proclaimed on April 18, 1859. James H. Wilbur was appointed superintendent of teaching. There were 25 pupils the first year.

2939. Teacher training school at which students conducted practice classes was the Oswego Training School for Primary Teachers, Oswego, NY, established on May 1, 1861, with an enrollment of nine students. Dr. Edward Austin Sheldon, who served from 1861 to 1897, was the first principal. On March 4, 1863, the New York legislature passed "an act for the support of a training school for primary teachers" that appropriated $3,000 for two years, calculated on an attendance of 50 pupils. On March 27, 1867, the state acquired the Oswego school as a state normal school and changed its name to the Oswego State Normal and Training School.

2940. School for freed slaves was established by the American Missionary Association at Fortress Monroe, VA, on September 17, 1861, with an African-American teacher, Mary S. Peake.

2941. Private school for children with disabilities was planned in 1861 by a Miss Cornelia and Dr. James Knight. It was opened on May 1, 1863, at the Hospital for the Ruptured and Crippled, New York City, under the auspices of the New York Society for the Relief of the Ruptured and Crippled.

2942. State ban on corporal punishment in schools was instituted by New Jersey in 1867.

2943. National organization of teachers was the National Teachers Association, which was organized on August 26, 1867, at a national convention attended by representatives of state teachers' associations, who met in the Hall of the Controllers of the Public Schools in Philadelphia, PA. The organization was intended "to elevate the character and advance the interest of the profession of teaching and to promote the cause of popular education in the United States." John L. Enos was chairman. At the convention held in Cleveland, OH, on August 15, 1870, the name was changed to the National Education Association.

2944. Kindergarten was established in Boston, MA, in 1868 by Elizabeth Palmer Peabody, who employed the Friedrich Froebel system of education used in Germany. An informal kindergarten group had been formed in December 1856 by Margarethe Meyer Schurz, wife of General Carl Schurz, in her home at Watertown, WI, for six children, two of whom were her own.

2945. Kindergarten manual was Edward Wiebe's *The Paradise of Childhood: A Manual for Self-Instruction in Friedrich Froebel's Educational Principles, and a Practical Guide to Kinder-Gartners*, printed in 1869 by Milton Bradley and Company, Springfield, MA. It was intended primarily for kindergarten teachers. Much of the material was translated from the German of Froebel, Marenholtz, Goldammer, and Morgenstern. The manual contained 86 pages and 74 full-page plates of illustrations.

2946. School for blind African-American students was the State School for the Blind and the Deaf, opened in Raleigh, NC, on January 4, 1869, with 26 pupils.

2947. School for African-American children established by a state was the Snowden School of Alexandria, VA. It was authorized by act of the legislature on July 11, 1870, and was under the guidance of William Frank Powell. It had only a short existence.

2948. Visible speech method of instruction for deaf students was used by the Horace Mann School in Boston, MA, in 1871. It was a form of phonetic writing invented by Alexander Melville Bell to show graphically any sound made by the human voice, and was used to facilitate pronunciation of foreign languages. The teachers at Horace Mann were instructed in the system by Bell's son, Alexander Graham Bell.

2949. Public school kindergarten that was successful was authorized on August 26, 1873, by the Board of Education of St. Louis, MO, and opened September 1873 in the Des Peres School, with an enrollment of 42. Susan Elizabeth Blow was the teacher. Dr. William Torrey Harris was the superintendent of schools.

2950. Free kindergarten was the Florence Kindergarten, which opened on January 3, 1876, in Florence, MA, in the home of its founder, Samuel Lapham Hill. The school was later known as the Hill Institute.

2951. School of prominence for Native American children was opened on November 1, 1879, at the old Army Barracks, Carlisle, PA, with 147 students. It was supported by private funds until March 3, 1881, when Congress appropriated $1,000 to pay Captain Richard Henry Pratt's salary as director. The school taught useful trades. The schoolwork did not go above the eighth grade, but students who were graduated were assisted in continuing their studies under the supervision of the school. At the end of the first year, 196 students were enrolled, 139 boys and 57 girls.

2952. Parent-teacher association was the Froebel Society of Brooklyn, NY (now part of New York City), founded in 1884 to further the "advancement of educational interests and the promotion of self-culture." It was named for the German educator Friedrich Wilhelm August Froebel.

2953. Yeshivah for Jewish religious study was Yeshivah Etz Chaim, founded in 1886 in New York City. It was not a congregational school, as previous Jewish schools had been, but an independent institution supported by an Orthodox Jewish community organization, the Hebra Machzikei Yeshivat Etz Chaim. It offered religious and secular studies at the elementary level. Graduates of the yeshivah formed the entering class of the first advanced-level yeshivah in America, the Rabbi Isaac Elchanan Theological Seminary (RIETS), incorporated in 1897. The schools merged in 1915 with Rabbi Dr. Bernard Revel as president. The following year, a secular high school program was added, the first to be sponsored by a yeshivah. RIETS became an affiliate of Yeshiva University in 1945.

2954. Kindergarten for blind children was established by the Perkins Institution and Massachusetts School for the Blind in Roxbury, MA, in 1887. The kindergarten was authorized on March 15, incorporated as a separate department of the school on March 30, and opened on May 2 with 10 children. The plan was proposed by Michael Anagnos, who became the first director.

2955. Business high school was the Washington Business High School, Washington, DC, authorized on June 11, 1889, by the Board of Education. It opened on September 22, 1890, in an unused grade school building of seven rooms. Allan Davis was the first principal.

2956. County high school was the Dickinson County Community High School, Chapman, KS, opened in September 1889. The first building was constructed entirely of limestone at a cost of $12,000. Enrollment the first year was 137. S.M. Cook, who taught mathematics, Latin, and Greek, was the first principal.

2957. National parent-teacher association was the National Congress of Mothers, organized on February 17, 1897, in Washington, DC, by Alice McLellan Birney and Phoebe Apperson Hearst at a meeting attended by 2,000 persons. At the annual meeting of March 9, 1908, the name was changed to the National Congress of Mothers and Parent-Teacher Associations. On May 9, 1924, the name was changed to the National Congress of Parents and Teachers.

2958. Country day school was the Country School for Boys of Baltimore, MD, a private school that opened in September 1897. The first headmaster was Frederick Winsor.

2959. Kindergarten for children with disabilities was opened at the Alta Settlement House, Cleveland, OH, in 1900.

2960. Public school for children with disabilities was the Tilden School, Chicago, IL, opened in 1900, with Emma Haskell as teacher. A horse-drawn wagon was used to transport the children.

2961. Trade school for girls was the Manhattan Trade School for Girls, New York City, opened in November 1902. The first director was Professor Mary Schenck Woolman, director of the domestic art department of Teachers College, Columbia University, New York City. Her staff consisted of an executive secretary, six supervisors, six instructors and foremen, six assistants, and four occasional workers. Twenty pupils enrolled the first day for courses in painting, hand sewing, and sewing machine operation. Night classes were begun in 1903.

2962. Vocational high school for girls was the Trade School for Girls, Boston, MA, opened in July 1904 as a summer experiment in training. Subjects taught were plain sewing, advanced sewing, dressmaking, millinery, machine operating, trade design, and domestic science. Florence M. Marshall was principal.

2963. Outdoor school for children with tuberculosis was the Meeting Street School, Providence, RI, which opened on January 27, 1908, as the Fresh Air School. Marie E. Powers was teacher and principal. Dr. Ellen R. Stone was the superintendent. Twenty children were in the first class, which comprised grades one through eight. Hot lunches furnished by the school supplemented lunches brought by the children.

2964. Junior high school was the Indianola Junior High School, Columbus, OH, opened on September 7, 1909. On July 6, 1909, the Columbus Board of Education directed Superintendent of Schools Jacob A. Shawan "to organize the new Indianola School primarily as a junior high school, with the 7th, 8th, and 9th grades as a unit, and only to admit such of the first six grades as might be necessary to relieve the neighboring districts." The ninth grade offered courses in English, German, algebra, elementary science, physical geography, manual training, domestic science, general history, and government of Ohio.

2965. School stadium was built in Tacoma, WA, and was dedicated on June 10, 1910. It was 250 feet wide at the narrowest point next to the curve and 400 feet wide at the open ends. It cost $150,000, of which $100,000 was paid by the school district and $50,000 was obtained through the sale of five-year passes at $10 each. Frederick Heath was the architect and L.A. Nicholson the engineer.

2966. Sex education program for high schools to be presented in a citywide system of public schools began in Chicago, IL, in 1913. It was devised by Ella Flagg Young, the superintendent of schools, who convinced the School Management Committee, a subcommittee of the Board of Education, to institute for all students in the city's secondary schools a series of lectures on "sex hygiene."

2967. International federation of students was the Pan American Student League, founded in New York City in 1920 to promote understanding among young people throughout the Americas. The first U.S. delegate to the group's International Council, and its first president, was Philip Leonard Green. The first secretary was J. Antonio Reyes of Peru.

2968. Correspondence school to offer instruction in Braille was the Hadley Correspondence School for the Blind, Winnetka, IL, founded by William Aaron Hadley. In August 1921 the school offered courses in English grammar, business correspondence, Bible study, and instruction in reading Braille printing.

2969. National Spelling Bee event was staged in Washington, DC, in 1925 by the *Courier-Journal* newspaper of Louisville, KY. There were nine young participants. The contest was won by Frank L. Neuhauser of Louisville, whose winning word was "gladiolus." He received a prize of $500.

2970. Trial of a teacher for violating a state ban on teaching the theory of evolution took place in July 1925. John Thomas Scopes, a high school science teacher in Dayton, TN, was convicted of breaking a law passed by the Tennessee legislature and signed on March 23, 1925, by Governor Austin Peay. It provided that "it shall be unlawful for any teacher in any of the universities, normal and all other public schools of the state which are supported in whole or in part by the public school funds of the state to teach any theory that denies the story of the Divine creation of man as taught in the Bible, and to teach instead that man has descended from a lower order of animals." Scopes was prosecuted by William Jennings Bryan and defended by Clarence Darrow. He was fined $100. The conviction was later overturned on technical grounds.

2971. Aviation course in a high school was instituted by Haaren High School, New York City, in September 1929, with 11 students under the direction of William Arnheim. In September 1931 an aviation annex was organized and the 833 boys enrolled in the aviation course were transferred to this building. In 1944, there were 3,500 students enrolled.

2972. Driving course in a high school was offered at State College High School, State College, PA, from February 17 to June 11, 1934. It included both classroom work and behind-the-wheel training. The first instructor was Amos Earl Neyhart. Students who completed the course received Pennsylvania automobile operators' licenses.

2973. Public school classes for children with epilepsy were organized in January 1935 in a small school building in Detroit, MI. In 1936 the courses were transferred to the White Special School, one of the divisions of Special Education of the Detroit Public Schools. The first teachers were Alice Mortimore and Edith Sargent.

2974. Public high school to specialize in the performing arts was the School of Performing Arts, a division of the Metropolitan Vocational High School, New York City, opened on September 13, 1948. Dr. Franklin J. Keller was the first principal. The school was conducted on the usual secondary school basis. However, half the time was given to practical work in the arts (music, dance, theater, and broadcasting) and the other half to college preparatory academic courses, with a diploma at the end of three years to those who had come from junior high schools and at the end of four years of study to those from eight-year elementary schools.

2975. Driver education in public schools was offered in Maryland in 1955. A state law enacted that year required all drivers younger than 18 to pass a driving course approved by the state department of education in order to obtain a license. The same law required all public high schools to offer the course.

2976. Air-conditioned public elementary school was the Belaire School, San Angelo, TX, which was opened in October 1955. The school, containing eight classrooms, was completely air-conditioned.

2977. Circular school building was St. Patrick Central High School, Kankakee, IL, opened on February 6, 1956. It was a two-story building, 200 feet in diameter, that housed classrooms and a gymnasium unit accommodating 2,000 spectators. It was connected to a small rectangular wing containing the administrative offices and library. The total cost of the school was $736,592. Belli and Belli of Chicago, IL, were the architects.

2978. Elementary schools to use closed-circuit televisions in teaching were eight public schools in Washington County, MD, which began using a closed-circuit system in September 1956. The schools served about 6,000 pupils. The system was expanded in September 1963, when all 45 public schools in the county were linked to the television circuit. The Fund for the Advancement of Education and the Ford Foundation contributed about $200,000 a year to the project over a five-year period. The equipment, worth $300,000, was provided by 75 manufacturers through the Electronics Industries Association.

2979. Federal aid program for primary and secondary schools was the Elementary and Secondary School Act, signed into law by President Lyndon Baines Johnson on April 11, 1965. The act allocated $1.3 billion for school districts according to the number of needy children they contained, and included funds for parochial and private schools.

2980. High school for pregnant teenage girls was the Educational Center of District 12, opened on June 23, 1967, in the Lincoln Hospital Neighborhood Maternity Center, New York City. The school opened with approximately 75 students and had a staff of one administrator, one guidance counselor, and five subject teachers. It was organized and started by project coordinator Martha Neilson for the Board of Education of the City of New York.

2981. Technical school for Native Americans was the Southwestern Indian Polytechnic Institute, Albuquerque, NM, a coeducational school that opened on September 16, 1971, with 700 Native American students from 64 tribes. It comprised 12 buildings on a 164-acre campus and cost $13 million. John L. Peterson was the first superintendent.

2982. Underground school was the Abo Elementary School, Artesia, NM, built underground in 1976 for safety from radiation and the effects of fallout. The roof was at ground level. The school was heated and air-conditioned during school hours. It had 16 teaching stations, a large library media center, and a multipurpose room with tables and seats that folded up into the wall. There were no distractions or outside noises, the lighting was near perfect, and the acoustics were excellent.

2983. Charter school was City Academy in St. Paul, MN, which opened in September 1992, following passage in 1991 of a state law permitting the establishment of charter schools. There were 17 students in the first graduating class. The academy, founded by English and Social Studies teacher Milo J. Cutter, was set up in a neighborhood recreation center and offered high school courses for youths who had already dropped out of the public school system. Each student signed a contract setting forth a scheduled plan of action. Initial funds for the school were provided by the Northern States Power Company.

2984. High school team to achieve a perfect score in the International Mathematical Olympiad were the six members of the 1994 U.S. team, drawn from the more than 350,000 high school students who took the American School Mathematics Examination that year. The 35th International Mathematical Olympiad was held in Hong Kong in July 1994. The U.S. team, all boys, scored a perfect 42 points in the two-day, nine-hour test of algebra, geometry, and number theory. Students from 68 other countries competed, including the favored Chinese and Russian teams, which took second and third place. The U.S. coach was Walter Mientka of the University of Nebraska, Lincoln, NE.

2985. School district put under state control by federal court order was the Cleveland Public School district in Cleveland, OH. In March 1995, supervision of the failing school system was removed from the city's elected school board and given to the Ohio State Superintendent of Schools to reform. It remained there until 1997, when it was transferred to a school board appointed by the mayor.

2986. Online high school was the Virtual High School, a cooperative venture of the Concord Consortium, a nonprofit organization in Concord, MA, and the public school system of Hudson, MA. The classes, taught by high school teachers with online experience, were available at any time of day. In its first year, 1996, the project provided elective courses to students already enrolled in high schools throughout the country.

2987. School voucher plan enacted by a state was Florida's Opportunity Scholarship Program, passed by the Florida legislature and signed into law by Governor Jeb Bush on June 21, 1999. The plan issued vouchers of up to $3,389 per year to students attending public schools if the schools failed to meet state criteria on standardized test scores two years in a row. The vouchers, funded by state tax revenue, could be used to pay tuition at private or parochial schools of the student's choice. On March 14, 2000, a state judge ruled that the program violated Florida's constitution. His ruling was upheld on November 16, 2004, by the 1st District Court of Appeals.

2988. School district to install surveillance cameras in all its classrooms was Biloxi, MS, which equipped each of its 500 classrooms with a dome-shaped ceiling camera that conveyed images to a website. Access to the website was limited to administrators and officials of the school board. The installation was completed in August 2003.

2989. School district to require mention of intelligent design in science classes was the Dover Area School District, Dover, PA. In October 2004 the board instituted a policy requiring ninth-grade students in evolution classes to hear a statement challenging the validity of the theory of evolution and suggesting intelligent design by a Creator as a reasonable alternative. On December 20, 2005, a federal judge ruled that the policy violated the concept of separation of church and state.

2990. State with an online learning requirement for high school students was Michigan. Under graduation standards set by the state legislature on April 20, 2006, all students had to have an "online learning experience" as defined by the state department of education.

2991. Online high school for gifted students to award a diploma was started by Stanford University, Stanford, CA. It offered courses for students in grades 10 through 12. The first group of students entered in September 2006. Annual tuition for the program was about $12,000.

Libraries

2992. Library founded with English donationswas the library of the planned college at Henrico, VA, founded in 1618 as part of the settlement at Jamestown. Gifts to this library included a copies of St. Augustine's *De Civitate Dei*, two Bibles, and *The Book of Common Prayer,* sent by an anonymous English donor in 1620 and 1621.

2993. Private libraries belonged to leaders of the Plymouth colony who arrived in Massachusetts in 1620. William Brewster, the group's preacher and the only member with a university education, owned a collection of books in Latin and English, as shown by an inventory of his possessions at the time of his death in 1644. Governor William Bradford, who died in 1657, left a collection of dozens of books, mostly on theological and historical subjects.

2994. Library bequeathed to the public by a philanthropist was donated by Robert Keayne to the town of Boston, MA, in 1653. Keayne was a successful merchant who had been punished by the Puritan authorities for using business practices they considered unethical. In his will, he left a third of his estate to the town for the construction of a building to be used as a city hall, an armory, and a church headquarters. One room was designated as a public library, to which Keayne left a selection of his own books. The building was erected in 1658 in Boston's Market Place.

2995. Library appropriation approved by a Town Meeting was voted by the citizens of Dorchester, MA, in 1665. They agreed to a proposal "whether the new impression of Mr. Mathers Catechismes should be payd for, out of a Towne Rate, and so the books to become the Towns."

2996. Lending library in colonial America was founded in Annapolis, MD, by Thomas Bray as part of his plan to establish a system of parochial (parish) libraries. Assisted by a financial donation from England's Queen Anne, Bray assembled a collection of 1,095 books and shipped them to Annapolis. They were placed in Maryland's State House by vote of the colonial Assembly on September 24, 1696. In all, Bray founded 80 parochial libraries in England and 39 in the English colonies.

2997. Library classification scheme for use in colonial America was proposed by the English minister Thomas Bray in his *Bibliothecæ Americanæ Quadripartitæ,* a manuscript from circa 1697. His "Compleat Scheme of the severall Sciences or Parts of necessary and Usefull Knowledge" divided all subjects into divine and humane, meaning those dealing with human life on Earth. The humane subjects were subdivided into those dealing with things (including ethics, economics, politics, law, history, physiology, medicine, chemistry, mathematics, and commerce) and those dealing with words (grammar, rhetoric, poetry, and logic).

2998. Publicly supported lending library was established in Charleston, SC, in 1698 through the efforts of Thomas Bray (later the representative in Maryland of the Bishop of London), who in 1696 forwarded religious books to the clergy. On November 16, 1700, Charleston passed an act "for securing the Provincial Library of Charlestown, by which commissioners and trustees were appointed for its preservation." The act authorized any inhabitants to "have liberty to borrow any book out of the said provincial library, giving a receipt."

2999. Library catalog in book form was compiled in Latin by Joshua Gee, librarian of Harvard College, Cambridge, MA, and published in 1723 at Boston by Bartholomew Green. It was entitled *Catalogus Librorum Bibliothecae Collegij Harvardini Quod Est Cantabrigiae in Nova Anglia.* Only 300 copies were printed. It contained 106 pages and listed books according to size (folio, quarto, octavo, duodecimo, and so on), then alphabetically through the first letter of the entry word.

3000. Social library was set up by the Library Company of Philadelphia, organized on July 1, 1731 by Benjamin Franklin through his society, the Junto. The first meeting was held November 8, 1731, at the house of Nicholas Scull. Fifty persons contributed 40 shillings each for purchasing the first parcel of books plus a fee of 10 shillings per year. The first books were ordered on March 31, 1732. An agreement to hire Lewis (Louis) Timothy as librarian was made on November 14, 1732. Timothy, a young French immigrant, worked every Wednesday from two to three o'clock and every Saturday from 10 to four. His salary was £3 sterling every trimester.

3001. Library building used exclusively as a library was a frame house erected by James Logan in 1725 on the west side of Sixth Street, between Chestnut and Walnut Streets, in Philadelphia, PA. Logan made this house available to the public as a reading room. On March 8, 1745, he turned over the property and 2,000 books to the city, but the library did not start to function as a public library until November 8, 1760. It was known as the Loganian Library, and William Logan, his son, was the first librarian. The library was closed after William Logan's death and on March 31, 1792, was incorporated into the Library Company of Philadelphia.

3002. Revolving library was a traveling collection that passed among three parishes in Maine. It was founded in 1751 as a joint stock company, with 26 participants. The prominent soldier and political leader Sir William Pepperell was among those who donated books.

3003. Library of Congress collection began with the appropriation on April 22, 1800, of $5,000 for the purchase of books and the furnishing of a reading room. An order for 152 books was shipped by the bookselling firm of Cadell and Davies from London in December 1800. The collection, expanded to 3,000 volumes by donations and purchases, was burned by the British during their invasion of

Washington, DC, in 1814, and was replaced by the personal library of Thomas Jefferson, who sold it to the government for $23,950.

Thomas Jefferson's book collection was transported to Washington for the Library of Congress in May 1815 in 10 wagons. It was stored for three years at a hotel while new government buildings were under construction.

3004. Catalog of the Library of Congress was *A Catalogue of Books, Maps, and Charts, Belonging to the Library of the Two Houses of Congress*, printed by William Duane, Washington, DC. It was dated April 1802 and listed 964 volumes and nine maps.

3005. Librarian of Congress was John James Beckley of Virginia, who was appointed on January 29, 1802, and served until his death on April 8, 1807. Until 1815, when George Watterston was appointed, the librarians were the clerks of the House of Representatives.

3006. Children's library was established in January 1803 in Salisbury, CT, through the generosity of Caleb Bingham of Boston, a native of Salisbury. He donated 150 volumes, the nucleus of the Bingham Library for Youth.

3007. Atheneum founded in the United States was the Boston Athenaeum, originally envisioned as a periodicals library for the city's Anthology Society. It was incorporated on February 13, 1807, and shortly thereafter was installed in Scollay's Buildings on Tremont Street, where it furnished its subscribers with a library, a reading room, and a museum. The first librarian was William Smith Shaw.

3008. Workers' library was opened in New York City in 1820 by the General Society of Mechanics and Tradesmen of the City of New York and was known as the Apprentice's Library. The name was changed in 1898 to the Free Library of the General Society of Mechanics and Tradesmen. Another library for apprentices was opened at Carpenters' Hall in Philadelphia, PA, by the Free Quakers on June 3, 1820. Horace Binney was the first president.

3009. Mercantile library was the Mercantile Library Association of the City of New York, organized at 49 Fulton Street, New York City, on November 9, 1820, with 150 sponsors in attendance. The library was founded to allow clerks and others engaged in mercantile business to enjoy the use of reading facilities. It opened on February 12, 1821. The first president was Lucius Bull.

3010. Library for seamen was inaugurated in March 1829 by the American Seamen's Friend Society of New York City, which was organized on May 5, 1828, to supply traveling libraries to ships. Smith Thomson was the first president. Loan libraries were placed on board American ships and on Coast Guard and naval vessels, as well as in Coast Guard lifesaving stations.

3011. Free public library established by a city was established in Peterborough, NH, on April 9, 1833. The funds for its creation came from state monies that had originally been appropriated for a state university and were then distributed to towns to use for educational purposes. The library was maintained by a public tax, controlled and managed by town vote, and open to all community members without restriction. An earlier but unsuccessful attempt to establish a free public library was made in New Orleans, LA, by the philanthropist Judah Touro, who founded the Touro Free Library Society in 1824.

3012. Periodical index was *An Alphabetical Index to Subjects Treated in the Reviews and Other Periodicals to Which No Indexes Have Been Published*, edited by William Frederick Poole and issued in 1848 by George Palmer Putnam in New York City. This was the forerunner of the famous *Poole's Index to Periodical Literature*, first shown in September 1853 at a library convention in New York City.

3013. Free public libraries authorized by a state were authorized by a New Hampshire bill approved on July 7, 1849. It provided that "the inhabitants of any school district in any city or town, and of any city or town not divided into school districts, in this Commonwealth, may, at any meeting called for that purpose, raise money for the purchase of libraries, in the same manner as school districts may raise money for erecting and repairing school houses in their respective districts . . . and that every public library established under provision of this act shall be open to the free use of every inhabitant of this town."

3014. Library newspaper room was opened on November 7, 1859, in the reading room in the great hall on the third floor of Cooper Union for the Advancement of Science and Art, Astor Place, New York City. It contained 12 New York dailies and 16 other dailies. The section was 125 feet long, 82 feet wide, and 32 feet high and was open from 8 A.M. to 10 P.M., free to all persons of good moral character for the use and instruction of the working classes. The attendance was about 3,000 people a week, a tenth of whom were women.

3015. Library journal was *Library Journal*, the monthly journal of the American Library Association, published by F. Leypoldt, New York City. The managing editor was Melvil Dewey and the general editor was Richard Rogers Bowker. The subscription price was 50 cents an issue, $5 a year. The first issue, dated September 30, 1876, contained 42 pages.

3016. National library association was the American Library Association, organized on October 6, 1876, at a meeting in Philadelphia, PA, attended by 103 librarians. The association was incorporated on December 10, 1879, under the laws of Massachusetts. The first president was Dr. Justin Winsor, and the first secretary was Melvil Dewey.

3017. Local library society was the New York Library Club, formed on June 18, 1885, at a meeting held at Columbia University, New York City, "to promote acquaintance and fraternal relations among librarians and those interested in library work and advance the interests of the libraries of New York and its vicinity." Richard Rogers Bowker was the first president.

3018. Children's department in a library is said to be that of the Minneapolis Public Library, which separated children's books from the rest of the collection in December 1889. A room was set aside for children in 1892, and in the fall of 1893 a whole corridor was equipped for their use.

3019. State library society was the New York Library Association, organized "to promote library interests of the state of New York" by 43 persons on July 11, 1890, at the New York State Library, Albany, NY. The first president was Melvil Dewey.

3020. County library successfully conducted was the Brumback Library of Van Wert County, Van Wert, OH, which was organized in 1898 and which opened a new building in 1901. Funds were secured from the County Commissioners through a tax levy.

3021. Librarian who was African-American who was professionally trained was Edward Christopher Williams, who attended New York State Library School in 1899–1900, before library schools were officially closed to African-American students. The first African-American woman to train as a librarian was Virginia Proctor Powell Florence, who attended Pittsburgh Carnegie Library School in 1922–23.

3022. Union catalog of books in American libraries was begun in 1901, when the Librarian of Congress authorized the exchange of printed catalog cards between the Library of Congress and other libraries holding books for which no Library of Congress cards were available. The catalog combined all holdings of the Library of Congress together with the holdings of over 600 other libraries in one author alphabet.

3023. Catalog cards from the Library of Congress were offered for sale on October 28, 1901. These were printed cards displaying cataloging information for books copyrighted after July 1, 1898. The first library to subscribe to the service was that of Amherst College, Amherst, MA, and the first card available described a 53-volume translation of the works of Balzac. The program was started by Herbert Putnam, eighth Librarian of Congress.

3024. National bibliography organization was the Bibliographical Society of America, organized on October 18, 1904, in St. Louis, MO, "to promote bibliographical research and to issue bibliographical publications." The first president was William Coolidge Lane.

3025. Bookwagon traveling library was started at the Washington County Free Library, Hagerstown, MD, in April 1905. A wagon that had previously been used for gathering eggs, butter, and produce was outfitted with shelves to carry books and was driven through the county three times a week by Mr. Thomas, the library's janitor.

3026. Union catalog of books in a state library was undertaken in 1909 by the California State Library, Sacramento, CA. The catalog covered periodicals available in California libraries and was later extended to books.

3027. Archivist of the United States was Robert Digges Wimberley Connor, appointed on October 10, 1934. The position was created by an act of Congress that established the Archives Bureau. Connor served until September 15, 1941. The archivist has an official seal and is chairman of a national publications committee.

3028. Federal aid to libraries was authorized by the Library Services Act of June 19, 1956, "to promote the further development of public library service in rural areas." It authorized the appropriation for the fiscal year ending June 30, 1957, and for each of the four succeeding fiscal years, of the sum of $7.5 million, to be used for making payments to states.

3029. Electronic book archive was Project Gutenberg (www.projectgutenberg.org), developed by Michael Hart, an undergraduate at the University of Illinois at Urbana-Champaign, with the purpose of making literary works, especially books, freely available on the Internet. Hart was provided with unlimited access to the Xerox Sigma V mainframe at the Materials Research Lab at the university. He keyed in Project Gutenberg's first entry, the full text of the Declaration of Independence, on July 4, 1971. As of September 2005, Project Gutenberg contained some 16,700 items in its collection, all keyed or scanned by volunteers. These items are either in the public domain or used with the permission of the copyright owner.

3030. State library to publish a master catalog of a major part of its holdings was the Oregon State Library, Salem, OR, which in 1974 published a 25-volume master catalog, with two-column pages measuring 8.5 by 11 inches. It contained the entries from over 3,500 catalog drawers of the Oregon State Library's adult nonfiction holdings, 190,000 separate titles in all, classified by author, title, and subject.

3031. Library to possess 100 million items was the Library of Congress, Washington, DC, which acquired its 100 millionth item in 1992. In 1996, its collections included 15 million books, 39 million manuscripts, 13 million photographs, 4 million maps, more than 3.5 million pieces of music, more than half a million motion pictures, and millions of other documents.

3032. Online library provided by a state was Delaware, whose Web site, DelAWARE: The Digital Library of the First State (www.state.lib.de.us), came online in 1996. The site offered links to numerous databases, reference texts, archives, and periodicals, as well as sources of information on history, literature, finances, health, and other subjects. It could be accessed at any time by residents possessing a barcoded library card.

Information Storage

3033. Microfilm reading device was invented by Bradley Allen Fiske of Washington, DC, who received a patent on March 28, 1922, on a "reading machine." It was known as a Fiskeoscope and could be carried in the pocket. A 2.5-inch newspaper column was reduced to 0.25 inches and 100,000 words were contained on a 40-inch tape.

3034. Book series microfilmed was *A Short Title Catalogue of Books Printed in England, Scotland and Ireland and of English Books Printed Abroad 1475–1640*, compiled by Alfred William Pollard and Gilbert Richard Redgrave, 609 pages, published in London in 1926. It was microfilmed by University Microfilms, Ann Arbor, MI, in 1935 from negatives made by the British Museum.

3035. Newspaper to store issues on microfilm was the *New York Times*, which in November 1935 microfilmed its issues from the years 1914 to 1927, in cooperation with the New York Public Library. The first newspaper to microfilm its current issues was the *New York Herald Tribune*, which began the service with the issue of January 1, 1936.

3036. Book issued on microcards was Fremont Rider's *The Scholar and the Future of the Research Library*, put on microcards by the Microcard Corporation, La Crosse, WI, in the fall of 1947. The 236-page book was reproduced on 3-by-5-inch cards containing about

80 pages to a card. These cards were not offered for sale but were given away to various individuals and institutions.

3037. Magazine on microfilm offered to subscribers was *Newsweek*, published in New York City, which offered a microfilm and microcard service to subscribers on June 1, 1949, for $15 a year. The microcard editions were printed on 3-by-5-inch cards. The microfilm editions were on 35mm reels in 100-foot lengths, 26 issues to a roll. Both editions were available in March and September of each year.

3038. Microfilm editions of federal publications and documents were offered as a regular service by University Microfilms, Ann Arbor, MI, in April 1952. The price was $900 for Hearings, Reports, Committee Prints for the 82nd Congress.

3039. Online library database was the Machine Readable Cataloging system, or MARC, developed by computer programmer Henriette Davidson Avram for the Library of Congress in 1968. The system, which made card catalogs obsolete, was adopted nationwide in 1971.

3040. Computerized library network in the world was OCLC, the Ohio College Library Center, established in 1971 at Ohio State University, Columbus, OH, by the Ohio College Association, a consortium of 54 academic libraries. Its first director was Frederick G. Kilgour, who created an electronic database that allowed all participating libraries to share cataloging and materials. After the network expanded nationwide and to more than 100 other countries, its name was changed to the Online College Library Center.

By 2006, the database had become a global network known as WorldCat, making millions of catalogued items available online.

Medicine

3041. Anatomy lectures to medical students were given by Dr. William Shippen at the College of Philadelphia, PA, from 1762 to 1765. Public lectures on anatomy were given in Boston, MA, in 1789 by John Jeffries, but public opinion was so much against his policy of dissecting bodies that at the second lecture a mob invaded the lecture room and carried off the body of a convict on which he was demonstrating. Further lectures were stopped as a result of public animosity.

3042. Medical college was the College of Philadelphia Department of Medicine, now the University of Pennsylvania School of Medicine, which was established in Philadelphia, PA, on May 3, 1765, principally through the efforts of Dr. William Shippen, Jr., and Dr. John Morgan, who became professor of the theory and practice of physic and professor of anatomy and surgery, respectively. The school was started in a wooden building known as Surgeons' Hall. At the first commencement, held on June 21, 1768, the first medical diplomas (Bachelor of Medicine) issued in America were presented to the 10 members of the graduating class.

3043. Midwifery professor at a college was Dr. John Van Brugh Tennent, appointed professor of midwifery at King's College (now Columbia University), New York City, in 1767.

3044. Physician to receive a Bachelor of Medicine degree was John Archer, who was the first of 10 students to be graduated on June 21, 1768, from the University of Pennsylvania, Philadelphia, PA. The university required a three-year waiting period before its medical graduates could return and receive the degree of Doctor of Medicine. Four of the 10 did so in 1771. The first M.D. degree was awarded in 1770 by King's College (now Columbia University), New York City, which required only one year to elapse before a student could return and for the M.D. degree. At both schools, the applicant for the higher degree was required to write a thesis in Latin or an inaugural dissertation and defend it satisfactorily before the faculty.

3045. Pharmacy professorship at a college was established in 1789 in Philadelphia, PA, at the Medical School of the College of Philadelphia (merged in 1791 with the University of Pennsylvania), when Dr. Samuel Powel Griffitts was appointed professor of materia medica and pharmacy. The first professorship devoted entirely to pharmacy was established in 1844 by the Maryland College of Pharmacy (now part of the University of

Maryland), Baltimore, MD. David Stewart was appointed to the chair of theory and practice of pharmacy.

3046. Nurses' training was given by Dr. Valentine Seaman of the New York Hospital, New York City, who gave lectures on anatomy, physiology, the care of children, and midwifery from 1798 to 1817. The first class consisted of 24 nurses.

3047. Medical jurisprudence course at a college was given by Dr. James Stringham, professor of medical jurisprudence at the College of Physicians and Surgeons, Columbia University, New York City, from 1813 to 1817. Prior to this appointment he served as professor of chemistry.

3048. Clinical instruction and bedside demonstration were introduced in 1818 by Alexander Hodgdon Stevens. It is said that in his operations as surgeon of the New York Hospital he often purposely avoided the neatness deemed so essential by other surgeons, in order to show his students that it was not essential to the recovery of the patient, provided the surgeon's skill and rapidity of manipulation were great enough.

3049. Hygiene lectures at a college were delivered in 1818 by Dr. James Jackson, Hersey professor of the theory and practice of physic, at Harvard College, Cambridge, MA. The committee decided on October 8, 1818, "that he be required to deliver a number of lectures on subjects relating to the care and preservation of health, and that they be this year delivered to the members of the two upper classes, at the hour appointed on Friday for a public lecture to those classes." The first professor of public hygiene was Dr. Thomas Bevan, appointed in 1868 by Northwestern University, Chicago, IL.

3050. Pharmacy college was the Philadelphia College of Apothecaries, established on February 23, 1821, at a meeting at Carpenters' Hall, Philadelphia, PA. Dr. Samuel Jackson was appointed professor of materia medica and pharmacy and Dr. Gerardt Troost professor of chemistry. Charles Marshall was elected president. The first class was held on November 9, 1821. The school was renamed the Philadelphia College of Pharmacy in 1822 and conferred the Ph.G. degree on its first three graduates on November 28, 1826. This was not the first time that degrees were granted to pharmacists: The University of Pennsylvania awarded honorary Master of Pharmacy degrees to 16 practicing apothecaries on April 5, 1821.

3051. Ophthalmology course at a college was established in 1823 at the Ophthalmic Clinic, Baltimore General Dispensary, University of Maryland, Baltimore, MD.

3052. Homeopathy school was the North American Academy of the Homeopathic Healing Art, founded on April 10, 1835, in Allentown, PA. The school was known as the Allentown Academy. The degree of Doctor of Homeopathia was conferred upon graduates. Instruction was in German. Constantine Hering, who came to Philadelphia in 1832 from Germany, was the first president and principal instructor.

3053. Clinic for teaching medical students was established in 1840 by Dr. Willard Parker, professor of surgery in the College of Physicians and Surgeons, New York City. He opened a dispensary where outpatients were brought to be examined and treated in the presence of the medical students.

3054. Dental college was the Baltimore College of Dental Surgery, organized in Baltimore, MD, in 1839 and formally opened on November 3, 1840, with five students. The faculty consisted of H. Willis Baxter, M.D., professor of anatomy and physiology; Thomas E. Bond, Jr., M.D., professor of special pathology and therapeutics; Chapin Aaron Harris, M.D., professor of practical dentistry; and Horace Henry Hayden, M.D., professor of dental physiology and pathology. This college is now the School of Dentistry, University of Maryland, Baltimore.

3055. Pathology chair at a college was established at Harvard University, Cambridge, MA, in 1847, when John Barnard Sweet Jackson was appointed professor of pathological anatomy and curator of the Warren Museum. The professorship was endowed by George Cheyne Shattuck in 1854. The first chair of modern pathology (after the field had been revolutionized by Louis Pasteur and his successors) was established in 1883 by Johns Hopkins University, Baltimore, MD. The first incumbent was Professor William Henry Welch.

3056. Medical school for women was the Boston Female Medical School, Boston, MA, which was organized through the initiative of Samuel Gregory. It opened on November 1,

1848, with 12 pupils and 2 teachers. On May 24, 1856, the school was incorporated as the New England Female Medical College, with power to confer degrees. In 1874 it was absorbed by the Boston University School of Medicine, founded the previous year as a school of homeopathy, which thus became the first coeducational medical school in the world.

3057. Physiology and hygiene courses at a liberal arts college were given in 1853 at Antioch College, Yellow Springs, OH. The college opened on October 5, 1853. Instruction was supervised by Professor Rebecca Mann Pennell and Acting Professor John Wesley Hoyt, M.D.

3058. Dissection of a living animal to demonstrate anatomy and physiology was performed about 1855 by Dr. John Call Dalton, who introduced the methods of vivisection in classroom demonstrations. In 1859 he published his *Treatise on Human Physiology*, and in 1860 he became professor of physiology and microscopic anatomy at the Long Island College Hospital, NY.

3059. Veterinary college was the Boston Veterinary Institute, Boston, MA, incorporated on April 28, 1855. The first president was Daniel Denison Slade, M.D. Courses were given in anatomy, physiology, chemistry, pharmacy, and the theory and practice of medicine and surgery.

3060. Pediatrics professor at a college was Dr. Abraham Jacobi, a Jewish immigrant from Germany, who lectured at the College of Physicians and Surgeons (now part of Columbia University), New York City, in 1857. He was appointed professor of infant pathology and therapeutics in 1860 and held the post of clinical professor of pediatrics from 1870 to 1899.

3061. Veterinary college of importance was the New York College of Veterinary Surgeons, New York City, incorporated on April 6, 1857. It did not go into active operation until 1865. The course of study, which embraced comparative anatomy, was given in two sections of five months each. The tuition fee was $135, of which $5 was for matriculation fees, $100 for lecture fees, $5 for the dissecting room fee, and $25 for the diploma. The president of the school was Eben Mason. The school had professors of histology, anatomy, physiology, theory and practice, surgical pathology, and operative surgery.

3062. Medical college on the Pacific Coast was the Medical Department of the University of the Pacific, opened at Santa Clara, CA, in 1858 by Dr. Elias Samuel Cooper.

3063. Laryngology instruction at a college was offered regularly by the Medical Department of the University of the City of New York in the autumn of 1861. Dr. Louis Elsberg lectured on the laryngoscope and diseases of the throat and larynx in 1863–64. From 1869 to 1873 he was clinical professor of diseases of the throat and from 1873 to 1881 professor of diseases of the throat and laryngology.

3064. Orthopedics chair at a college was established by Bellevue Hospital Medical College, New York City, in 1861. The first incumbent was Dr. Lewis Albert Sayre.

3065. Nursing school to award a diploma was the School of Nursing of the Woman's Hospital of Philadelphia, PA, chartered on March 22, 1861. The first diploma was awarded in 1865. The first nurse known to have received the diploma was Harriet N. Phillips.

3066. Professor of ophthalmology was Elkanah Williams, who was appointed by the Miami Medical College of Cincinnati, OH, in 1865.

3067. Dental school to be associated with a medical school and the first to be permanently established by a university was the Harvard School of Dental Medicine, Boston, MA, established on July 17, 1867. The first class began on November 4, 1868, with 16 students. Dr. Nathan Cooley Keep was the first dean, as well as the first professor of mechanical dentistry.

3068. Veterinary department at a college was the Department of Veterinary Science of Cornell University, Ithaca, NY, which offered courses by Professor James Law beginning on October 7, 1868.

3069. Dermatology chair at a college was established by Harvard University, Cambridge, MA, in 1871. The first incumbent was Dr. James Clarke White, instructor in medical chemistry, who later became the first president of the American Dermatological Association.

3070. Medical chemistry course at a college was offered in 1871 by Dr. Edward Stickney Wood, assistant professor of chemistry, at the Harvard Medical School, Cambridge, MA.

3071. Optometry school was the Illinois College of Optometry, Chicago, IL, founded in 1872 by George W. McFatrich, M.D., author of *Correction for Myopia*, who taught refraction. In 1907, Dr. William B. Needles founded the Needles Institute of Optometry, Kansas City, MO. These schools merged under the name of the Northern Illinois College of Optometry, chartered in 1927.

3072. Veterinary school established by a state was established on May 23, 1879, by the Board of Trustees of Iowa State College at Ames, IA. Lectures were given on veterinary anatomy, physiology, materia medica, pathology, disease and treatment, surgery, sanitary science, and practice. The first class of the veterinary school was graduated in 1880. The school was the first veterinary school in the United States to inaugurate a four-year program and the first to require as prerequisites for entrance diplomas from a high school and college.

3073. Pharmacist who was a woman to receive a degree from a pharmacy college was Susan Hayhurst of St. Michael's, MD, who graduated on March 16, 1883, from the Philadelphia College of Pharmacy with the Ph.G. degree. She went on to receive her M.D. degree in 1857 from the Female Medical College of Pennsylvania. She was the first female physician to graduate from a pharmacy college.

3074. Nursing school for African-American students was established at the Spelman Seminary, Atlanta, GA, founded in 1881 by Sophia Booker Packard and Harriet E. Giles of Boston, MA, as the Atlanta Baptist Female Seminary. A nurses' training department was established in 1886 in a two-room frame building set apart to serve as an infirmary and known as the Everts Ward. The first nurse received her certificate in 1888. The name of the school was changed in 1924 to Spelman College.

3075. Psychology professor at a college was James McKeen Cattell, who was appointed professor of psychology at the University of Pennsylvania, Philadelphia, PA, in 1888.

3076. Bacteriology courses at a college were given by the Hygienic Laboratory of the University of Michigan, Ann Arbor, MI. The laboratory was established in 1887, and the first class in bacteriology was instituted by Dr. Victor Clarence Vaughan and Dr. Frederick George Novy in January 1889. Classes were in session four hours daily for three months. In 1890–91 bacteriology became a required course for medical students. The first bacteriology lectures for medical school students were given in 1885 by Harold Clarence Ernst at the Harvard Medical School, Cambridge, MA.

3077. Osteopathy school was the American School of Osteopathy, chartered in Kirksville, MO, on May 10, 1892. The founders were Dr. Andrew Taylor Still and Dr. William Smith. It opened on October 3, 1892, in a little frame cottage with an enrollment of about 20 students. Its purpose, according to the articles of incorporation, was "to improve our system of surgery, midwifery, and treatment of general diseases—the adjustment of the bones is the leading feature of this school." Eighteen diplomas were granted to the first graduating class on March 2, 1894.

3078. Navy medical school was the Naval Laboratory and Department of Instruction, opened on August 1, 1893, at the U.S. Naval Hospital, Brooklyn, NY (now a borough of New York City). The first director was Henry M. Wells, appointed on August 21, 1893, with the relative rank of captain. An unofficial school had been authorized on May 19, 1823, and opened at the Navy Yard Hospital, Philadelphia, under the direction of Dr. Thomas Harris of Philadelphia's Pennsylvania Hospital, who taught naval hygiene, military surgery, customs and usage of the naval service, and so on. The secretary of the navy appropriated $400 for the support of the school, whose expenses were paid by Dr. Harris from his own income. The school was discontinued by order of January 31, 1843.

3079. Psychiatric institute organized for research and the training of physicians was the Pathological Institute, New York City, established by New York State on May 12, 1896. Dr. Ira Van Gieson was the first director. The name was changed in 1909 to the New York State Psychiatric Institute and Hospital. In 1927 it became the Psychiatric Department of the Columbia University–Presbyterian Hospital Medical Center and was housed in a new building dedicated December 3–4, 1929.

3080. **Chiropractic school** was the Palmer School of Chiropractic, Davenport, IA, which opened in 1900. It was established by Daniel David Palmer.

3081. **Professor at a first-class medical school who was a woman** was Dr. Florence Rena Sabin, who served on the faculty of the Johns Hopkins University School of Medicine, Baltimore, MD. She was appointed special fellow in anatomy in 1901 and became associate professor of anatomy in 1905 and professor of histology in 1917.

3082. **Nursing school at a college** was the School of Nursing, University of Minnesota, Minneapolis, MN, authorized by the Board of Regents on October 1, 1908, and established on March 1, 1909, through the efforts of Dr. Richard Olding Beard. The first director of the school was Bertha Erdmann.

3083. **Chiropody school of note** was the New York School of Chiropody, organized in 1910 by members of the Pedic Society of the State of New York. On January 1, 1913, it became the First Institute of Podiatry, with Dr. Maurice J. Lewi as president. Its first graduating class, in 1913, consisted of 13 men and 1 woman. On November 16, 1939, it became affiliated with Long Island University, awarding the degree of Pod.D. (Doctor of Podiatry).

3084. **Medical research chair at a college** was the John Herr Musser chair, established in 1910 by the School of Medicine, University of Pennsylvania, Philadelphia, PA. The first incumbent was Professor Richard Mills Pearce.

3085. **Optometry courses at a college** were given at Columbia University, New York City, which offered a two-year program beginning on September 28, 1910, following enactment of legislation by New York State on March 31, 1909, which required that optometrists be licensed. Instruction was given by Andrew Jay Cross, instructor in theoretic optometry, Frederick Albert Woll, and Charles F. Prentice, instructor in practical optics. Members of the university's departments of physics and mathematics gave instruction in those subjects to the optometry students.

3086. **Occupational therapy course at a college** was given in 1913 by the Milwaukee-Downer College of Milwaukee, WI. The subjects included psychology, physiology, sociology, design, metal work, leather work, and textile craft. Two students enrolled. The form of treatment called occupational therapy "includes any occupation, mental or physical, which is definitely prescribed and guided for the distinct purpose of contributing to, or hastening recovery from diseases or injury."

3087. **Chiropody school at a college** opened on September 20, 1915, at Temple University, Philadelphia, PA, where a chiropody clinic at the Garretson Hospital, an annex to Temple Hospital, had already been established. Four students completed the 34-week course in June 1916 and received the degree of M.Cp. The course was later changed to cover four years and lead to the degree of D.S.C. (Doctor of Surgical Chiropody). Dr. Frank Adoniram Thompson was the first dean of the school, and Dr. W. Ashton Kennedy and Dr. James Richardson Bennie were the first professors of chiropody.

3088. **Army nursing school** was the Army School of Nursing, authorized on May 25, 1918, by Secretary of War Newton Diehl Baker as a division of the surgeon general's office under the Medical Department of the Army. The first class of 402 graduates completed the course at Walter Reed Hospital, Washington, DC, on June 16, 1921. A three-year program of study was prescribed, with advanced credits offered to graduates of approved courses. The first dean of the school was Annie Warburton Goodrich. The school was discontinued on August 12, 1931.

3089. **Hygiene and public health school at a college** was established in 1916 at Johns Hopkins University, Baltimore, MD, under an endowment from the Rockefeller Foundation "for the advancement of knowledge and the training of investigators, teachers, officials and other workers" in the general field of hygiene and public health. This school was opened on October 1, 1918, with Dr. William Henry Welch as its first director.

3090. Plastic surgery professor at a college was Dr. Joseph Eastman Sheehan, who was appointed to that post in 1926 by the New York Postgraduate Medical School and Hospital, New York City.

3091. Medical center devoted to teaching, treatment, and research was the Columbia–Presbyterian Medical Center, on 168th Street west of Broadway, New York City, which opened on March 6, 1928. It had a library of 100,000 books and was designed to serve 600 students.

3092. History of medicine department at a college with a full salaried professor and staff was the Institute of the History of Medicine, inaugurated on October 18, 1929, by Johns Hopkins University, Baltimore, MD. Dr. William Henry Welch was the first professor of the history of medicine and Dr. Stephen d'Irsay was associate.

3093. School of nurse-midwifery in the United States was founded in 1931 in New York City by the Maternity Center Association.

3094. Medical college founded as a Jewish institution was the Albert Einstein College of Medicine of Yeshiva University, New York City, which offered instruction on September 12, 1935, to 56 men and women, although only one floor of the six-story building was completed. Dr. Marcus David Kogel was the first dean.

3095. Anesthesiology professor at a college was Dr. Virginia Apgar, who was appointed by Columbia University, New York City, in 1949. Apgar had previously spent 11 years as director of anesthesiology at an affiliated institution, Columbia–Presbyterian Medical Center.

Military

3096. Army academy was the United States Military Academy, established at West Point, NY, by act of Congress of March 16, 1802, for the purpose of educating and training young men in the theory and practice of military science. The first superintendent was Jonathan Williams.

3097. West Point graduate who was Jewish was Simon Magruder Levy of Maryland, who was appointed a cadet for his good conduct as orderly sergeant at the Battle of Maumee Rapids, August 20, 1794. He was one of the two cadets in the first graduating class on October 12, 1802, and was commissioned a second lieutenant in the Corps of Engineers. He resigned from the Army on September 30, 1805, because of ill health and died in 1807 in Georgia. The first Jewish woman to graduate from West Point was Cadet Donna Maller of Cockeysville, MD, one of 13 Jewish cadets who were graduated and commissioned on June 4, 1980, in a class of 831 men and 63 women.

3098. West Point graduates were Joseph Gardner Swift of Massachusetts and Simon Magruder Levy of Maryland. Both men were graduated from the U.S. Military Academy at West Point, NY, on October 12, 1802, and were appointed to the rank of second lieutenant. They were the only students to graduate of the original class of 10, which consisted of 5 men from Massachusetts and 1 each from Connecticut, Maryland, Missouri, New York, and Virginia. Levy resigned from the Army in 1805 because of ill health. Swift was brevetted a brigadier general on November 11, 1813, for his heroism in the battle at Chrystler's Field in upper Canada. On February 19, 1814, he was promoted to brigadier general for his meritorious service in the defense of New York in the War of 1812. He became head of the Military Academy in 1816 and retired from the Army on November 12, 1818. He died in 1865.

3099. West Point graduate killed in action was George Ronan, killed fighting against Native American allies of the British in the War of 1812. On August 15, 1812, he was mortally wounded during Captain Nathan Heald's desperate battle near Fort Chicago, IL, against a vastly superior force of Native Americans. Before he died, he killed two Native Americans in hand-to-hand fighting.

3100. Naval officers' training school was established on December 10, 1815, at the Navy Yard, Charlestown, MA. It was under the guidance of Commodore William Bainbridge, whose expertise as a naval leader had been demonstrated in the war with Tripoli.

3101. Military school was the American Literary, Scientific and Military Academy, founded by Captain Alden Partridge in Norwich, VT, on August 6, 1819. The cadets were required to wear uniforms, and received instruction in fencing, military drawing, topography, "the Laws of Nations, Military Law . . . the construction of Marine Batteries, Artillery duty, the Principles of Gunnery . . . etc." The first class entered on September 4, 1820. The first cadet enrolled was Cyril Pennock of Hartford, VT. No specific time for completing the course was required, but the enrollment period varied from one to six years according to the student's ability. The name was changed on November 6, 1834, to Norwich University. In March 1866, the buildings were destroyed by fire and the school was moved to Northfield, VT.

3102. West Point graduate who was Native American was David Moniac, a member of the Creek nation, who graduated and was commissioned a second lieutenant in 1822. He was killed in Florida in 1836 in the Battle of Wahoo Swamp, during the Army's campaign against the Seminoles. He had attained the rank of major.

3103. Military school established by a state was the Virginia Military Institute, Lexington, VA, established as an independent school at the Lexington Arsenal by act of March 29, 1839. It was governed by a board of visitors appointed by the governor, subject to approval by the state senate. The first corps of 28 cadets was mustered into service on November 11, 1839. The first superintendent was Professor (later Major General) Francis Henney Smith, who served until January 1, 1890.

3104. Military school operated by a church was the Catonsville Military Academy, founded in 1845 by Libertius Van Bokkelen in Catonsville, MD, and affiliated with St. Timothy's Protestant Episcopal Church.

3105. Naval academy was established at Windmill Point, Fort Severn, Annapolis, MD, on a nine-acre site that was transferred on August 15, 1845, from the War Department to the Navy Department. It was known as the Naval School and officially opened on October 10, 1845, with 56 students. The first superintendent was Commander Franklin Buchanan. As most of the midshipmen had already served some time at sea or otherwise in the Navy, the course of instruction varied in length, depending on the dates of their appointments. On July 1, 1850, the name was changed to the U.S. Naval Academy. The following year, the academy instituted a standard four-year program. The first official graduation was held on June 10, 1854. From May 9, 1861, to September 9, 1865, while Maryland was part of the Confederacy, the academy was transferred to Newport, RI.

3106. Coast Guard officers' training school was the Revenue Cutter Service School of Instruction, which was opened on July 31, 1876, in New Bedford, MA. The classes were held on board the revenue cutter *J.C. Dobbin*, which sailed on its first practice cruise on May 25, 1877, under Captain J. A. Henriques. In 1914 the name was changed to the Revenue Cutter Academy, and later, with the creation of the Coast Guard, to the Coast Guard Academy.

3107. West Point graduate who was African-American was Henry Ossian Flipper, born a slave on March 29, 1856, in Thomasville, GA. He was a cadet from May 20, 1873, to June 14, 1877. He was appointed a second lieutenant in the 10th Cavalry on June 15, 1877, and remained in service until June 30, 1882, when he was dismissed for conduct unbecoming an officer and a gentleman. In December 1976, the Army reviewed his court-martial charge and changed his discharge record from dishonorable to honorable. The first African-American admitted to West Point was James Webster Smith, who was appointed by Congressman Solomon Lafayette Hoge and who reported on May 31, 1870.

3108. Academy Academy graduate to attain the rank of rear admiral was Edward Simpson, who was graduated in 1846 in the first class. He became a lieutenant in 1855, a lieutenant commander in 1862, a commander in 1865, a commodore in 1878, and a rear admiral in 1884.

3109. Naval war college was established at Coaster's Harbor Island, Newport, RI, on October 6, 1884, by order of the Secretary of the Navy. Commander Stephen Bleecker Luce was the first superintendent. The college opened on September 3, 1885. It offered naval officers an 11-month course in military science, the art of naval warfare, and marine international law. On January 11, 1889, the college was consolidated with the Torpedo Station on Goat Island in Newport harbor.

3110. Army war college was authorized by the War Department on November 27, 1901, to furnish advanced military instruction to regularly commissioned army officers, using $20,000 that had been authorized by Congress on May 26, 1900. The first president was Major General Samuel Baldwin Marks Young. The first class of 16 officers was convened on November 1, 1904, and terminated on May 31, 1905. Classes were held in rented quarters until June 20, 1907, when a permanent building was opened in Washington, DC.

3111. Airplane flying school for military officers was opened by the Curtiss Exhibition Company at Lake Keuka, Hammondsport, NY, in September 1910. It gave military officers free instruction in flying. Glenn Hammond Curtiss was the instructor. The first army officer assigned to take the course was Captain Paul N. Beck, who became the first military aviator. The Navy Department also sent officers for instruction in flying.

3112. Naval air training school was the Navy Aeronautic Station, Pensacola, FL, opened on December 1, 1914, under the command of Captain Henry Croskey Mustin. The first staff consisted of three instructors and a dozen mechanics. The name was later changed to the Naval Air Station. From 1911 to 1914, flight training was given at a camp at Greensbury Point, near Annapolis, MD.

3113. ROTC unit was the Harvard Regiment, started at Harvard University, Cambridge, MA, in January 1916, with six French military instructors and more than 1,000 students. It became the first official ROTC unit when Congress formally established the Reserve Officers Training Corps in June 1916. Harvard's faculty voted to abolish the ROTC program in 1969. The oldest ROTC unit in continuous existence is the Paul Revere Battalion, founded at the Massachusetts Institute of Technology, Cambridge, MA, on December 10, 1917. MIT, like all land-grant institutions founded under the Morrill Act of 1862, already required its students to receive military training. ROTC became voluntary at MIT in 1958.

3114. Movie for training soldiers utilized by the Army was *School of the Soldier*, produced by the Bray Pictures Corporation of New York City at West Point, NY, in 1917.

3115. Army school for chaplains was the Army Chaplain School, Fort Monroe, VA, organized on February 9, 1918. Instruction was offered in military law, international law, and military science and tactics. The school was moved to Camp Taylor, KY, on April 9, 1918.

3116. Army language school began courses in Japanese on November 1, 1941, at Crissey Field, Presidio of San Francisco, CA. After moving to other locations, it was settled at the Presidio of Monterey, CA, in June 1946. In 1953 the school offered courses in 24 languages.

3117. Merchant marine academy was the Merchant Marine Academy at Kings Point, NY, dedicated on September 30, 1943. Previously, training had been held aboard ship and in temporary shore establishments. The cadet corps had been established on March 15, 1938, following the passage of the Merchant Marine Act of June 29, 1936. Upon completion of three years at the academy and one year at sea, the cadets received a Coast Guard license as Third Assistant Engineer or Third Mate, a B.S. degree, or a commission as ensign in the Naval Reserve, Merchant Marine Academy.

3118. Naval Academy graduate who was African-American was Wesley Anthony Brown of Washington, DC, who graduated on June 3, 1949, and received his commission as ensign. The first African-American midshipman at the Academy was James Henry Conyers of South Carolina, who attended from September 21, 1872, to November 11, 1873, but who did not graduate.

3119. Air Force academy was authorized on April 1, 1954. Temporary headquarters were established on July 11, 1955, at the Lowry Air Force Base, Denver, CO, where 306 candidates were sworn in. The first commandant was Lieutenant General Hubert Reilly Harmon. A $135 million academy was built at Colorado Springs, CO, and received its first cadets on August 29, 1958. The first graduating class of 207 cadets was commissioned on June 3, 1959. First in the graduating class was Bradley Clark Hosmer of Dunseith, ND. The four-year course consisted of 1,548 hours of the humanities, 1,629 hours of science, and 2,178 hours of airmanship.

3120. Air Force Academy graduate who was Native American was Leo Johnson of Fairfax, OK, who was one of the 297 graduates of the academy, Colorado Springs, CO, on June 6, 1962. He went on to earn the Air Force Commendation Medal as a pilot.

3121. Air Force Academy graduates who were African-American were Charles Vernon Bush, Isaac Sanders Payne IV, and Roger Bernard Sims, who were graduated from the academy in Colorado Springs, CO, on June 5, 1963, and received the Bachelor of Science degree.

3122. Naval War College students who were African-American were Commander Samuel Lee Gravely, Jr., of Richmond, VA, who attended the School of Naval Warfare for senior officers, and Lieutenant Commander George Irwin Thompson of Los Angeles, CA, who attended the School of Naval Command and Staff for mid-career officers. Both schools were given at the Naval War College, Newport, RI, from August 16, 1963, to June 17, 1964.

3123. Coast Guard Academy graduate who was African-American was Merle James Smith, Jr., of Baltimore, MD , part of the class of 113 cadets who were graduated on June 8, 1966. The ceremony was held at Jones Field, New London, CT. His commission was presented to him by his father, a colonel in the regular Army.

3124. West Point instructor who was a woman was Elizabeth Matthew Lewis, who taught a course entitled "Introduction to Fine Arts, including art history, appreciation and related activities," beginning on February 1, 1968. She had served since November 6, 1967, as fine arts librarian.

3125. Army War College graduates who were women were Lieutenant Colonel Frances V. Chaffin of Washington, DC, and Lieutenant Colonel Shirley Rowell Heinze of Houston, TX, of the Women's Army Corps, who were graduated on June 16, 1969, in a class of 224, at Carlisle, PA.

3126. Merchant Marine Academy cadets who were women were admitted on Acceptance Day, August 31, 1974, after having undergone two weeks of indoctrination and one month of general training at the academy in Kings Point, NY. The class of 1978 consisted of 15 women and 333 men.

3127. Air Force Academy cadets who were women were admitted to the academy at Colorado Springs, CO, on June 28, 1976, when 155 women were enrolled.

3128. Naval Academy students who were women were admitted on July 6, 1976, when 80 women were admitted. The first female midshipman at the Academy to graduate at the top of her class was Kristine Holderied, who graduated on May 23, 1984.

3129. West Point cadets who were women were accepted for admission on March 9, 1976, and enrolled on July 7, 1976. The graduating class on May 28, 1980, contained 62 women, who were commissioned second lieutenants.

3130. Naval War College president who was a former prisoner of war was Vice Admiral James Bond Stockdale, who served as president from October 13, 1977, to August 22, 1979. He was graduated from the U.S. Naval Academy, Annapolis, MD, on June 5, 1946. While serving during the Vietnam War, he parachuted from his stricken A-4 jet over North Vietnam and was captured. He endured 2,714 days of imprisonment, during which he was kept in solitary confinement for three years, suffering torture on numerous occasions. He was released on February 12, 1973, and on October 13, 1977, was promoted to the rank of vice admiral. In the presidential election of 1992, he was the running mate of the Texas businessman Ross Perot.

3131. Coast Guard Academy graduates who were women were 14 cadets who were graduated on May 21, 1980, in a class of 156. They were among a group of 38 women who had entered the Coast Guard Academy in New London, CT, on June 28, 1976, their admission having been authorized by a law enacted in October 1975. Completion of the four-year course entitled them to receive the bachelor of science degree in engineering and commissions as ensigns and second lieutenants at a salary of $660 a month. The first of the women to be graduated was Jean Marie Butler of Hershey, PA, since the graduates were called in alphabetical order.

3132. West Point cadet who was a woman to graduate at the top of her class was 21-year-old Rebecca Marier of New Orleans, LA, who was graduated from the United States Military Academy on June 3, 1995. She topped a class of 858 men and 130 women.

Museums

3133. Public museum in America was the Charleston Museum of Charleston, SC. It was organized on January 12, 1773, at the annual anniversary meeting of the Charleston Library Society. The first curators of the museum were the diplomat Charles Cotesworth Pinckney, the politician Thomas Heyward, and two physicians, Alexander Baron and Peter Fayssoux. Eventually the building was torn down, and the collection was moved to the College of Charleston. On August 29, 1850, the city council ratified an ordinance "to provide for the appointment of a Curator for the Museum of the College of Charleston." Francis Simmons Holmes was elected to the post on November 25, 1850, and was appointed professor of geology and paleontology at the college on December 28.

3134. Private museum in the United States was a museum of natural history featuring a collection of fossils, shells, minerals, and an assortment of live and preserved animal specimens, all of which had been put on display by the naturalist and painter Charles Willson Peale. The museum was opened to the public on July 18, 1786, at Peale's studio in Philadelphia, PA. Admission cost 25 cents. The collection contained many donations from President Thomas Jefferson and the Lewis and Clark expedition.

3135. Art museum of importance was the Pennsylvania Academy of Fine Arts, which was established in Philadelphia, PA, on December 26, 1805, "to promote the cultivation of the Fine Arts in the United States of America, by introducing correct and elegant copies from works of the first masters in sculpture and painting." The first president of the Academy was George Clymer.

3136. Museum especially constructed as a museum and art gallery was Peale's Baltimore Museum and Gallery of the Fine Arts, operated by Rembrandt Peale. It was a three-story building at 225 North Holliday Street, Baltimore, MD, and was designed by Robert Cary Long, Sr. The opening was advertised for August 15, 1814. The building was sold in 1830 to the City of Baltimore, which used it as its first City Hall.

3137. College art museum was the Yale University Art Gallery at 1111 Chapel Street, New Haven, CT, founded in 1832. It was known as the Trumbull Art Gallery of Yale University.

3138. Egyptian antiquities collection was imported in 1835 by Colonel Mendes I. Cohen of Baltimore, MD. It was not publicly displayed until 1884, when it was bequeathed to Johns Hopkins University, Baltimore.

3139. Free public art museum in continuous existence is the Wadsworth Atheneaum, located in Hartford, CT. It was founded by Daniel Wadsworth in 1842 to house his extensive collection of historical paintings, portraits, and American landscapes by John Trumbull, Frederic Edwin Church, Thomas Cole, and others. The Colt Memorial Wing, donated by Elizabeth Hart Jarvis Colt in 1907, was the first museum wing in the United States named for a woman.

3140. National hall of fame was National Statuary Hall, formerly the Hall of the United States House of Representatives in the Capitol at Washington, DC, which was established by act of Congress of July 2, 1864. Each state was invited to contribute marble or bronze statues of its most distinguished citizens.

3141. Art museum to sell reproductions of items in its collection was the Metropolitan Museum of Art in New York City. In 1871, the museum's trustees commissioned an engraver to make etchings of 10 recently acquired Old Master paintings. They were sold on consignment to raise money for the museum, which did not yet have a permanent home. Half a century later, in the 1920s, the museum, now well established in its Fifth Avenue location, began selling reproductions in its gift shop and through mail-order catalogs. During the 1980s and 1990s, it established retail stores in cities throughout the United States and other countries. In 1997, merchandising revenues for the Met reached $79 million.

3142. Zoo was the Philadelphia Zoological Garden, Philadelphia, PA, which was under the management of the Zoological Society of Philadelphia. The garden was opened to the public on July 1, 1874. Feature attractions were the bear pit and the lion house.

3143. Aquarium with an inland saltwater environment was installed by Marshall McDonald in Chicago, IL, for the 1893 World's Columbian Exposition. Medals were conferred upon him by Belgium, Britain, France, Germany, and Russia for his efforts to increase and better the hatching and propagation of fish.

3144. Commercial museum was the Philadelphia Commercial Museum, organized by city ordinance approved on June 15, 1894. It was developed by Dr. William Powell Wilson, who conceived the idea of the institution and who served as its director and executive head from 1894 to 1927. The Philadelphia Commercial Museum comprised the museum proper, the Department of Visual Education, the Foreign Trade Bureau, the Library, and the Exhibition Hall with its convention hall.

3145. Children's museum was the Brooklyn Children's Museum, Brooklyn Avenue and Park Place, New York City, in the Brower Park Building in the Crown Heights neighborhood. It opened on December 16, 1899.

3146. Academic hall of fame was the Hall of Fame, which was dedicated on May 30, 1901, on the University Heights campus of New York University, New York City. Twenty-nine tablets were unveiled. The oration was delivered by Senator Chauncey Mitchell Depew. The idea originated with Dr. Henry Mitchell MacCracken, chancellor of the university, who was aided in the project by a $250,000 endowment from Helen Miller Gould.

3147. Semitic museum was the Harvard University Semitic Museum, Cambridge, MA, which was formally opened on February 5, 1903, in the Peabody Museum of Archeology and Ethnology, though it had been opened to students and the public on May 13, 1891. It was founded by a donation from Jacob Henry Schiff. The collection included Syrian, Arabic, and Hebrew manuscripts.

3148. Museum of medieval art was The Cloisters, a building in upper Manhattan that was opened to the public in 1914 by sculptor George Grey Barnard to exhibit his private collection, which he had acquired during a sojourn in France. Oil magnate John D. Rockefeller, Jr., purchased the museum in 1925 on behalf of New York's Metropolitan Museum of Art and donated additional items from his own collection. To house it, he funded the construction of a museum complex, also called The Cloisters, which was designed by architect Charles Collens.

3149. Industrial museum was established by the Association for the Establishment and Maintenance for the People of the City of New York of a Museum of Peaceful Arts. It was incorporated on February 26, 1914. The name was changed in 1931 to the New York Museum of Science and Industry.

3150. Art museum for children was the Children's Art Center of Boston, MA, which was intended to serve poor children in the city's South End. It opened in 1918 under the auspices of the local settlement house, headed by Albert Kennedy. The artworks it exhibited were loaned by Boston galleries.

3151. Zoo habitat constructed of simulated rock formations without bars was started in 1915 at the City Park Zoo, Denver, CO, and was completed in 1918 at a cost of $60,000. Colored concrete and steel were used to simulate a mountain habitat. The floors of the enclosures were on ground level or above the outside walkway. The area was designed and supervised by Victor Borcherdt, the director of the zoo.

3152. Modern art museum was the Phillips Collection in Washington, DC. Duncan Phillips, whose collection of modern works formed the basis for the museum's permanent collection, directed the institution from its opening in 1921 until his death in 1966.

3153. Outdoor museum with nature trails was established in 1925 by Dr. Frank Eugene Lutz at the Station for the Study of Insects, located in the Ramapo Mountains in Tuxedo Park, NY. The nature trails were developed under the auspices of the American Museum of Natural History, New York City, with the cooperation of the Palisades Interstate Park Commission. There were two trails, the Training Trail and the Testing Trail, each half a mile long, which were posted with signs describing the trees, shrubs, flowering plants, and insects.

3154. Museum to feature a medieval building transported from Europe was the Worcester Art Museum, Worcester, MA. In 1927 the museum arranged to purchase the chapter house from the Benedictine Priory of Saint John in Le Bas-Nueil, France. The building, dating from the 12th century, was made of limestone with a six-part vaulted ceiling supported by two columns.

3155. Museum to install refrigerated vaults with automatic temperature control for the preservation of valuable specimens of furs and similar articles was the University of California Museum of Vertebrate Zoology, Berkeley, CA. The equipment was installed sometime before March 1930.

3156. Museum with interactive exhibits in the United States was the Museum of Science and Industry, Chicago, IL, which opened in 1933 with innovative hands-on science exhibits. The museum was founded by Julius Rosenwald, head of Sears Roebuck & Company, in the Palace of Fine Arts, a building that had originally been built for the 1893 Columbian Exposition.

3157. Costume museum was the Museum of Costume Arts, New York City, incorporated on April 28, 1937, to develop "cultural education in connection with those arts and industries which function in conjunction with design in form of apparel and accessories by applying to this field the ways and means now commonly used or applied by fine arts and industrial museum associations and foundations and musical societies of various kinds in their respective fields."

3158. Aquarium for large marine animals was Marineland, 18 miles south of St. Augustine, FL, built at an approximate cost of $500,000. Ground was broken on May 15, 1937, and the dedication and formal opening took place on June 23, 1938. The marine studios consisted of two adjacent open-air steel and concrete tanks (one rectangular, 100 feet by 40 feet, and 18 feet deep; the other circular, 75 feet in diameter and 11 feet deep) with 200 portholes.

3159. Museum devoted exclusively to nuclear energy was the American Museum of Atomic Energy, Oak Ridge, TN, opened to the public on March 19, 1949, the anniversary of the removal of the security fence from the city of Oak Ridge. During World War II, Oak Ridge was the site of a secret military installation where research into nuclear weapons was conducted. The museum was operated for the Atomic Energy Commission as a service to the public by the Oak Ridge Institute of Nuclear Studies, a nonprofit educational organization.

3160. Artmobile was conceived and designed by the Virginia Museum of Fine Arts, Richmond, VA, and began its tours on October 13, 1953, at Fredericksburg, VA, with an exhibition of art objects. It was an all-aluminum trailer weighing over five tons, measuring 34 feet in length and 7 feet 10 inches in height on the inside. When set up for exhibitions, it required a space 60 by 35 feet.

3161. Zoo with twilight conditions was dedicated on April 3, 1973, in Highland Park, Pittsburgh, PA, by the Pittsburgh Zoological Society. The zoo contained six ecological niches depicting nocturnal and diurnal scenes from various regions around the world. The same degree of lighting prevailed both day and night.

3162. Art museum devoted to work by women was the National Museum of Women in the Arts, Washington, DC, founded in December 1981, by Wilhelmina Cole Holladay, who became its first president. The museum was formally opened on April 7, 1987, with a collection of 500 works from the Renaissance to the modern era.

3163. Museum devoted solely to American political memorabilia was the Museum of American Political Life, which opened in 1989 at the University of Hartford campus in West Hartford, CT. The museum's mission was to collect, preserve, and exhibit artifacts and other materials relating to presidential campaigns, presidents, and the electoral process. The core of the museum's holdings were donated by collector J. Doyle Dewitt and included 60,000 artifacts, such as posters, buttons, banners, textiles, prints, medals, fine pottery, glassware, snuff-boxes, ribbons, torchlights, and a variety of other electoral paraphernalia.

3164. Museum commemorating the Holocaust was the U.S. Holocaust Memorial Museum, opened to the public on April 22, 1993, in Washington, DC. The museum combined innovative multimedia displays with one of the nation's largest repositories of documentary information about the Holocaust.

3165. Art museum of importance devoted to the work of an individual woman was the Georgia O'Keeffe Museum, which opened on July 17, 1997, in Santa Fe, NM. It housed major works by O'Keeffe, whose paintings of desert scenes and flowers made her the best-known 20th-century artist of the American Southwest. The museum, which contained 116 paintings and one sculpture, was housed in a sprawling adobe building renovated and expanded by architect Richard Gluckman. Peter H. Hassrick was the first director.

3166. Museum of espionage was the International Spy Museum in Washington, DC, which opened to the public in July 2002. It offered exhibits on eavesdropping devices, hidden cameras, escape techniques, cryptography machines, and other aspects of intelligence-gathering.

3167. Museum of children's book illustrations in the United States was the Eric Carle Museum of Picture Book Art, which opened in Amherst, MA, in November 2002.

Reference Works

3168. Almanac was *An Almanak for the Year of Our Lord,* 1639, Calculated for New England, by William Peirce, printed in 1638 at Cambridge, MA, by Stephen Day's Cambridge Press. The months began with March.

3169. Native American dictionary was *A Key into the Language of America, or an help to the language of the natives in that part of America called New England; together with briefe observations of the customes, manners and worships, etc., of the aforesaid natives,* by Roger Williams, the founder of Providence, RI. Williams prepared it on shipboard en route to Southampton, England, and it was published by Gregory Dexter, London, in 1643.

3170. Native American grammar was John Eliot's *The Indian Grammar Begun; or, An Essay to Bring the Indian Language into Rules, for the Help of Such as Desire to Learn the Same, for the Furtherance of Gospel Among Them,* published in Cambridge, MA, in 1666 by Marmaduke Johnson. It was written in the language of the Massachusetts peoples and consisted of 66 pages of text. About 500 copies were printed.

3171. Primer in a Native American dialect was *The Indian Primer; or, The Way of Training Up of Our Indian Youth in the Good Knowledge of God, in the Knowledge of the Scriptures and in an Ability to Read,* by John Eliot. It was printed in the Algonkian language spoken by the Native Americans of Massachusetts and was published in Cambridge, MA, in 1669 by Marmaduke Johnson. A similar edition by Eliot is believed to have been published in 1653–54 by Samuel Green, Cambridge, MA, but no known copies are in existence.

3172. Business manual was John Hill's *The Young Secretary's Guide; or a Speedy help to learning,* based on an English work and printed by Bartholomew Green and John Allen for S. Phillips in 1703 in Boston, MA. It contained 192 pages of instructions on writing business and social letters, punctuation rules, a dictionary of "hard words," and examples of bonds, bills, letters of attorney, deeds of sale, mortgage forms, warrants of attorney, deeds of gift, bills of sale, bills of exchange, assignments, and so on.

3173. Latin grammar was *A Short Introduction to the Latin Tongue.* For the use of the lower forms in the Latin School. Being the Accidence abbridg'd and compiled in that most easy and accurate method, wherein the famous Mr. Ezekiel Cheever taught and which he found the most advantageous by seventy years' experience. It was prepared by Ezekiel Cheever, master of the Boston Latin School, and published in 1709 in Boston, MA, by Bartholomew Green "for Benj. Eliot at his shop under the Town-house." It contained 64 pages and was 3 by 6 inches.

3174. English grammar by an American was *A Short English Grammar, an Accidence to the English Tongues,* by Hugh Jones, professor of mathematics at the College of William and Mary, Williamsburg, VA. It was published in London in 1724.

3175. Hebrew grammar was *Dickdook Leshon Gnebreet: A Grammar of the Hebrew Tongue, being an essay to bring the Hebrew Grammar into English, to facilitate the instruction of all those who are desirous of acquiring a clear idea of this primitive tongue by their own studies,* by Judah Monis, an instructor in Hebrew at Harvard College. It was 94 pages long, printed with type imported from England, and was published in 1735 in Boston, MA.

3176. Spanish grammar was *A Short Introduction to the Spanish Language; to which is added a vocabulary of familiar words for the more speedy improvement of the learner: with a preface shewing the usefulness of this language particularly in these parts,* by Garrat Noel, printed in New York City by James Parker in 1751.

3177. English grammar by an American published in America was Samuel Johnson's *The First Easy Rudiments of Grammar, Applied to the English Tongue.* By one who is extremely desirous to promote good literature in America, and especially a right English Education. For the Use of schools, 36 pages. It was published in 1765, in New York City by "J. Holt, near the Exchange in Broad Street." Dr. Johnson was the first president of King's College (now Columbia University).

3178. French grammar written and printed in America was *A New French and English Grammar, wherein the principles are methodically digested, with useful notes and observations, explaining the terms of grammar, and further improving its rules*, by John Mary, instructor at Harvard College. It was printed in 1784 by John Norman, Boston, MA, and sold by the author.

3179. Dictionary published in the United States was *The Royal Standard English Dictionary; the First American Dictionary, Carefully Revised and Corrected, from the Fourth British Edition*, by William Perry, lecturer in the Academy at Edinburgh, which was printed in 1788 in Worcester, MA, by and for Isaiah Thomas. It sold for seven shillings and contained 596 pages, including an appendix listing proper names in the Bible. There were 38 lines to a page, in double columns, and brief definitions, usually no longer than one line. The dictionary was dedicated to the American Academy of Arts and Sciences.

3180. Pocket dictionary was *William Perry's The Royal Standard English Dictionary, in which the words are . . . rationally divided into syllables, accurately accented, their parts of speech properly distinguished*, 596 pages, printed in 1788 by Isaiah Thomas, Worcester, MA. It was dedicated to the American Academy of Arts and Sciences and was based upon a British edition.

3181. Almanac with a continuous existence was *The Farmer's Almanack, Calculated on a New and Improved Plan, for the Year of Our Lord 1793; Being the First After Leap Year, and Seventeenth of the Independence of America*, founded by Robert Bailey Thomas of Sterling, MA, and printed at the Apollo Press in Boston, MA, by Belknap and Hall in 1792. The price was sixpence a copy, four shillings a dozen, 40 shillings a gross. Three thousand copies were printed. In 1832, the title was changed to *The Old Farmer's Almanac.*

3182. American gazetteer was compiled by Jedidiah Morse and was printed in 1795 in Boston, MA, by Isaiah Thomas and Ebenezer T. Andrews. It was titled *American Universal Geography, or a View of the Present State of All the Empires, Kingdoms, States and Republics in the Known World, and of the United States of America in Particular.* It contained 7,000 different subjects, "exhibiting in alphabetical order a much more full and accurate account than has been given of States, Provinces, Counties, Cities, Towns, etc."

3183. Encyclopedia printed in the United States was a reproduction of the third edition of the *Encyclopaedia Britannica*, originally published in Edinburgh between the years 1788 and 1797. The American reprint, however, was not called *Encyclopaedia Britannica*, but *Encyclopaedia; or a Dictionary of Arts, Sciences, and Miscellaneous Literature.* It consisted of 18 volumes and was completed in 1798 by Thomas Dobson in Philadelphia, PA. The first volume appeared in 1790 and contained 799 pages and 31 plates.

3184. Dictionary of the English language compiled by an American was Noah Webster's *A Compendious Dictionary of the English Language.* In which 5,000 words are added to the number found in the best English compends; the orthography is in some instances corrected: the pronunciations marked by an accent or other suitable direction; and the definitions of many words amended and improved. The dictionary was 408 pages long and was published in 1806 at New Haven, CT, by Sidney's Press for Hudson and Goodwin.

3185. Hebrew dictionary was Clement Clarke Moore's *A Compendious Lexicon of the Hebrew Language in Two Volumes; Volume 1, containing an explanation of every word which occurs in the Psalms with notes; Volume 2, being a lexicon and grammar of the whole language*, printed and sold in 1809 by Collins and Perkins, New York City.

3186. Encyclopedia compiled by American editors was the *Encyclopedia Americana*, edited by Francis Lieber. The set consisted of 13 volumes, of which the first was issued in 1829 and the last in 1833. It was published in Philadelphia, PA.

3187. Hebrew spelling book was *The Hebrew Reader: Hebrew and English Designed as an Easy Guide to the Hebrew*

Tongue for Jewish Children and Self-instruction, by Isaac Leeser, printed by Haswell, Barrington and Haswell at Philadelphia, PA, in 1838. It contained 48 pages.

3188. Gazetteer of the world was *Lippincott's Pronouncing Gazetteer of the World*, which was published in 1854 by Lippincott, Grambo and Company of Philadelphia, PA. It contained 1,364 pages.

3189. Phonetic dictionary was the *Phonetic Dictionary of the English Language adapted to the present state of literature and science, with pronouncing vocabularies of classical, scriptural and geographical names*, 776 pages, compiled by Daniel S. Smalley and published by Longley Brothers, phonetic publishers, Cincinnati, OH, in 1855.

3190. Braille encyclopedia was the *World Book Encyclopedia*, copyrighted in 1959 by the American Printing House for the Blind, Louisville, KY. The braille edition, comprising 30,467 pages, consisted of 145 volumes, which were issued between 1961 and 1972. Captions of illustrations were added to the text.

Schools

3191. Law school operated privately was opened in Litchfield, CT, in 1784 by Judge Tapping Reeve. He conducted it alone in a building near his home until 1789. The session was from 14 to 18 months, for which a tuition fee of $100 was charged for the first year and $60 for the balance of the course. About a dozen students were enrolled the first year.

3192. Technical institute was the Gardiner Lyceum, Gardiner, ME, founded by Robert Hallowell Gardiner in 1822 "for the purpose of giving to farmers and mechanics such a scientific education as would enable them to become skillful in their professions." Courses were offered in arithmetic, algebra, geometry, trigonometry, mensuration of surfaces and solids, bookkeeping, surveying, navigation, mechanics, hydrostatics, pneumatics, chemistry, natural philosophy, and "the higher branches of mathematics and natural history." The first lecturer was Benjamin Hale.

3193. Printing instruction at a school was given in the community school founded by Robert Owen in his utopian settlement at New Harmony, IN, in 1826. The subjects of study included printing, lithography, and engraving.

3194. Lyceum for adult education was founded by Josiah Holbrook in Millbury, MA, in October 1826. Its purpose was to afford adults an opportunity for mutual improvement through association and study, stimulate an interest in the schools, and contribute to the training of teachers and the dissemination of knowledge through libraries and museums. The Millbury Lyceum became part of the American Lyceum Association when it was organized on May 4, 1831, in New York City by delegates from Maine, Massachusetts, and New York.

3195. Nautical school was established on May 29, 1827, in Nantucket, MA, and was known as Admiral Sir Isaac Coffin's Lancasterian School. It was conducted by William Coffin, Jr., and Miss A. Meach and was located in a wooden schoolhouse. Courses on shipboard to train sailors had been offered previously.

3196. School for music teachers was the Boston Academy of Music, Boston, MA, founded on January 8, 1833. Samuel Atkins Eliot was the first president. The faculty consisted of Lowell Mason and George James Webb. The school used the teaching method that had been developed by the Swiss educator and reformer Johann Heinrich Pestalozzi.

3197. Business school was opened in Rochester, NY, in 1842 by George Washington Eastman, and was named the Eastman Commercial College.

3198. Nautical school established by a city was the Nautical School of the Port of New York, opened on January 11, 1875, in New York City on board the *St. Mary*, a 150-foot, three-masted, full-rigged vessel known as a sloop of war. It was built in 1844 to chase slavers. The main deck was less than 144 feet above the water line. The commanding officer was Commander Robert Lees Phythian. From July 22 to October 8, 1875, the school conducted a cruise of Long Island Sound. The school was authorized by New York State on April 24, 1873, and was supported by state funds.

3199. Cooking school was the New York Cooking School, which was opened in November 1876 by Juliet Corson at her residence on St. Mark's Place, New York City. In 1875 she gave cooking instruction in the Ladies' Cooking Class of the free Training School for Women, New York City.

3200. Typing school was opened by D. L. Scott-Browne at 737 Broadway, New York City, in 1878.

3201. Lipreading instruction for deaf people was given by Sarah Warren Keeler, a teacher at the Institution for the Improved Instruction of Deaf Mutes in New York City, who advertised lipreading lessons for adults in 1882. She lectured on the subject in 1884 and published her method in 1894. The first successful lipreading school for adults was established by Lillie Eginton Warren in 1890 in New York City. She obtained a patent in 1903 on a "means for teaching of the facial expressions which occur in speaking."

3202. Correspondence course of a serious nature was offered by the Literary and Scientific Circle of the Chautauqua Institution. The organization was founded by the first Sunday School Teachers Assembly on August 4, 1874, in Fair Point, NY, at the suggestion of John Heyl Vincent and Lewis Miller. A correspondence School of Theology was organized and in 1881 received its charter. On March 30, 1883, the Chautauqua College of Liberal Arts was given a charter by the legislature of the State of New York, conferring full authority to grant diplomas and to confer the usual college and university degrees.

3203. Manual training school entirely financed by public taxes was the Baltimore Manual Training School, established in Baltimore, MD, in 1884 under authority of municipal ordinance of October 20, 1883. Instruction and practice were given in carpentry, wood turning, pattern making, chipping and filing, forge work, molding, soldering and brazing, and other crafts.

3204. Drama school devoted exclusively to training performers for the professional stage was the Lyceum School of Acting in New York City, which was founded by Franklin Haven Sargent on October 1, 1884. It was renamed the American Academy of Dramatic Arts in 1890.

3205. Night school for immigrants was run by Henrietta Szold in Baltimore, MD, beginning in 1889. Szold, a teacher in a school for girls, taught English to Jewish refugees from czarist Russia. The first semester's enrollment was 50 students. The classes were taken over by the Baltimore board of education in 1898.

3206. Nautical school established by a state was the Massachusetts Nautical Training School, established by Massachusetts on June 11, 1891. On February 17, 1891, the governor was authorized to petition the secretary of the Navy for a suitable vessel, and on October 28, 1892, the steam sloop *Enterprise* was transferred to Massachusetts.

3207. Correspondence school for workers was started through the initiative of Thomas Jefferson Foster, proprietor and editor of the *Shenandoah Herald*, Shenandoah, PA, who issued a course in the fundamentals of coal mine development and operation as a way of educating workers. The first student was enrolled on October 16, 1891. The name was later changed to the International Correspondence Schools, with headquarters at Scranton, PA.

3208. Automobile school was established in 1903 by the education department of the Young Men's Christian Association, Boston, MA, to train chauffeurs, mechanics, and prospective car owners. The course consisted of lectures on the construction and operation of cars together with laboratory, machine shop, and repair work. Enrollment the first year was approximately 250 students.

3209. Apprentice continuation school funded by a public board of education was established in Cincinnati, OH, on August 30, 1909, to give tool apprentices the opportunity of a technical education along practical lines. Classes were conducted on the third story of a building at 12th and Jackson streets.

3210. State continuation school for adults was the Racine Continuation School, Racine, WI, which opened on November 3, 1911, to offer evening instruction to adults, as well as to children from 14 to 16 years of age who had permits to work.

3211. School of modern dance was the Denishawn Dance School, founded in 1915 in New York City by dancers Ruth St. Denis (born Ruth Dennis) and Ted Shawn. St. Denis's dances, based on Asian models, and

Shawn's works incorporating Native American themes strongly influenced the early course of modern dance in America. A second Denishawn School was founded in Los Angeles in 1920.

3212. Advertising school was established in 1920 by the members of the Poor Richard Club in their clubhouse in Philadelphia, PA. A diploma was awarded for the completion of the two-year course. In 1924, the name was changed to the Charles Morris Price School of Advertising and Journalism of the Poor Richard Club.

3213. Foreign language course broadcast on radio took place on March 21, 1924, when station WJZ, New York City, operating on a 455-meter wavelength, offered French lessons in cooperation with the Berlitz School of Languages.

3214. Modeling school to train young women to be models was officially opened in 1928 in Chicago, IL, and was known as *L'École de Mannequins*, the School of Modeling. Training was based upon the principles of mental control over body movements, a correct understanding of balance, poise, and gracefulness, and personality development.

3215. Cartooning school giving courses in the production of animated cartoons was the Hastings School of Animation, New York City, organized February 1938. Instruction began in April 1938.

3216. Truck driving school was opened in June 1954 by the Bedford Motor-Transport Drivers Training Program, Bedford, PA. The first class was graduated July 31, 1954.

3217. Circus clown training school was the "clown college" established on September 1, 1968, in Venice, FL, by Irvin Feld, president and producer of the Ringling Brothers and Barnum and Bailey Combined Shows. The eight-week tuition-free course was given during September, October, and November from 9 A.M. to 6 P.M. and included slaps and falls, juggling, stilt-walking, plate-spinning, makeup, mime and pantomime, acrobatics, equilibrium, and elephant riding.

ENGINEERING

3218. Architecture book printed in America was Abraham Swan's *British Architect; or the Builders Treasury of Staircases*, published in 1775 by Robert Bell in Philadelphia, PA, for J. Norman. It was a reprint of the edition published in London in 1745.

3219. Architect and engineer who worked professionally was Benjamin Henry Latrobe, born on May 1, 1764, near Leeds, England. After studying architecture in London, he left for America in 1795 and went into private practice in Virginia in 1796. Among his early projects was the design of Philadelphia's first water system. He is also credited with introducing to America the Gothic and Greek Revival styles of architecture. Latrobe is best known for his work on the Capitol Building in Washington, DC. His designs include the Hall of the House (now Statuary Hall), the Old Senate Chamber, and the Old Supreme Court Chamber.

3220. Architecture book distinctly American was *The Country Builders' Assistant; containing a collection of new designs of carpentry and architecture*, by Asher Benjamin. It contained 30 plates and was printed in 1797 by Thomas Dickman, Greenfield, MA.

3221. Transportation report was William Strickland's *Reports on Canals, Railways, Roads and Other Subjects made to the Pennsylvania Society for the Promotion of Internal Improvement*, a 51-page pamphlet containing 72 engraved plates, published in 1826 by H.C. Carey and I. Lea, Philadelphia, PA.

3222. Engineering society of importance was the Boston Society of Civil Engineers, organized at an informal meeting on April 26, 1848, at the United States Hotel, Boston, MA. The first regular meeting was held on July 3, 1848. The society was incorporated on April 24, 1851, for the purpose of "promoting science and instruction in the department of civil engineering." The first president was James Fowle Baldwin. Attempts had been made to form engineering societies in 1836 by engineers of the Cincinnati and Charleston Railroad, in 1839 by engineers in Baltimore, MD, and in 1841 in Albany, NY, but these sporadic attempts were not successful.

3223. National civil engineering society was the American Society of Civil Engineers, founded as the American Society of Civil Engineers and Architects on November 5, 1852, in New York City. Its purpose was "the advancement of the sciences of engineering and architecture in their several branches, the professional improvement of its members, the encouragement of intercourse between men of practical science, and the establishment of a central point of reference and union for its members." The first president was James Laurie.

3224. Engineer who was a woman in the United States was Emily Warren Roebling, whose husband, Washington Roebling, was chief engineer for the construction of the Brooklyn Bridge. In 1872, with her husband bedridden due to decompression sickness, she became the supervisor of the massive construction project. In 1882 she became the first woman to address the American Society of Civil Engineers. The first woman to earn a

Library of Congress, Prints & Photographs Division
LC-USZ62-4614

The Brooklyn Bridge

degree in engineering was Elizabeth Bragg, who graduated from the University of California in 1876.

3225. National mechanical engineering society was the American Society of Mechanical Engineers, founded February 16, 1880, by 40 men from eight states who met at the office of the *American Machinist* in New York City. An organizational meeting was held April 7, 1880, at the Assembly Hall of the Stevens Institute of Technology, Hoboken, NJ. The first president was Robert Henry Thurston.

3226. Architect who was a woman was Louise Blanchard Bethune, who opened an independent office in 1881 in Buffalo, NY. She was the first woman member of the American Institute of Architects, elected to full membership on September 15, 1890. The first woman to receive an architectural patent was Harriet Morrison Irwin, sister-in-law of General Stonewall Jackson, who in 1869 patented her design for a two-story hexagonal house, with all rooms connected by an airy central hallway. The house was built on West Fifth Street in Charlotte, NC.

Bridges

3227. Bridge was erected in 1634 over the Neponset River from Milton, MA, to Dorchester, MA, by Israel Stoughton. Authority to build a bridge and mill was extended April 1, 1634, by the Massachusetts General Court.

3228. Toll bridge was erected by Richard Thurlow (variously spelled Thorla, Thorlo, and Thurley) in 1654 over the Newbury River at Rowley, MA. He built the bridge with his own money. On May 3, 1654, the General Court of Massachusetts fixed a rate of toll for animals. Passengers were permitted free passage. The bridge remained a toll bridge until 1680.

3229. Stone arch bridge was the Frankford Avenue bridge over Pennypack Creek, built in 1697–98 at Pennepecka, near Germantown, Philadelphia, PA. William Penn wrote from Pennsburg on June 22, 1700, to "urge the justices about the bridge at Pennepecka and Poquessin forthwith for a carriage or I cannot come down" to attend a local meeting.

3230. Pile bridge was designed and constructed by Major Samuel Sewall and built across the York River at York, ME, in 1761. A 270-foot wooden bridge was erected atop 13 bands of piles, which were hammered upright, with the ends protruding above the water.

3231. Bridge on a large scale was the West Boston Bridge, connecting Boston, MA, and Cambridge, MA, begun on July 15, 1792, and opened for traffic on November 23, 1793. It rested on 180 piers. It was 3,483 feet long with a 3,344-foot causeway, and 40 feet wide with a railing on each side. The cost was $76,000. The toll right was granted to the proprietors for 70 years.

3232. Suspension bridge was erected in 1796 by James Finley across Jacob's Creek, Westmoreland County, PA. It had a 70-foot span and cost $6,000. Finley patented his design in 1801. The bridge was on the turnpike between Uniontown, PA, and Greensburg, PA.

3233. Pontoon bridge was floated into place at Collins' Pond, Lynn, MA, in 1804. The Board of Directors authorized Captain Moses Brown to bridge the pond, which was of great depth and which had a soft, peaty bottom that did not permit the use of supporting piers. The pontoon bridge built by Brown was 511 feet in length and 28 feet wide. It consisted of five layers of pine timber, each at right angles to the one below it. The whole mass was secured together by three-inch dowels. Including the top planking, it was about five feet thick.

3234. Suspension bridge of iron wire was the Schuylkill River bridge at Philadelphia, PA, designed and constructed by Erskine Hazard and Captain Josiah White. It was 408 feet long, with a board floor 18 inches wide. It had a 33-foot sag and could not support more than six or eight persons at a time. It weighed 4,702 pounds, cost $125, and was opened to traffic June 1816. A toll of one cent per person was charged until the tolls defrayed the cost.

3235. Stone arch railroad bridge in the world was the Carrollton Viaduct of the Baltimore and Ohio Railroad, spanning Gwynn's Falls at Baltimore, MD. It was named after Charles Carroll, who laid the last stone in the bridge several weeks prior to its official opening on December 21, 1829. It was 300 feet long and 70 feet high and had two arches: a large

80-foot span over the stream and a small arch through which, originally, a wagon road passed. The bridge was built by James Lloyd.

3236. Bridge of cast iron was built in 1835 over Dunlap's Creek at Brownsville, PA, by John Snowdon, from the design of and under the direction of his foreman, John Herbertson. It had five tubular arch ribs of 85-foot span and was 25 feet wide.

3237. Wooden railroad bridge of a purely truss type was built in 1838 by Benjamin Henry Latrobe for the Baltimore and Ohio Railroad Company across the Patapsco River at Elysville (now Alberton), MD. It consisted of two spans, each about 150 feet in length. The bridge was completed in 1839 and the wooden trusses were replaced in 1852 by iron Bollman trusses.

3238. Girder bridge of cast iron was built by Earl Trumbull over the Erie Canal at Frankfort, NY, in 1840. It had a span of 77 feet.

3239. Wire suspension bridge for general traffic was erected over the Schuylkill River at Fairmount, PA, by Charles Ellet. The bridge was opened on January 2, 1842. It had a 358-foot span, was supported by wire cables, five at each side, and had a width of 25 feet. It cost $35,000.

3240. Iron truss bridge with parallel chords and open web was designed by Richard Osborne, chief engineer of the Reading Company. Construction of trusses began in January 1845 at Pottstown, PA, and was completed in March. The bridge had a 34.2-foot foot span, with a four-foot space between tracks, and was erected a half mile east of Flat Rock Tunnel, north of the West Manayunk station. Erection was begun Saturday night, May 3, 1845, and the bridge was finished the next day. It remained on the main line of the Philadelphia and Reading Railroad Company until 1901.

3241. Twin covered bridges were built in 1849 by Peter Ent over Huntington Creek at Village Forks, PA, at a cost of $750. They were the 60-foot-long East Paden Bridge, which used a queen post form of truss, and the 92-foot-long West Paden Bridge, a Theodore Burr design. They were constructed of wood reinforced with iron.

3242. Railroad suspension bridge was the suspension bridge over the gorge at Niagara Falls, NY, which was completed in 1854. It had a span of 825 feet and two decks, the lower one carrying a highway 15 feet wide, partially enclosed at the side by timber stiffening trusses. The upper deck, 24 feet wide and 245 feet above high water, had a single railroad track in the center and was floored over to separate it from the highway below. The bridge was started in 1853 by Charles Ellet, who withdrew from the work. It was completed by John Augustus Roebling. The first train crossed the bridge on March 8, 1855.

3243. Railroad bridge across the Mississippi River was the Rock Island Railroad Bridge between Rock Island, IL, and Davenport, IA. It was built of wood resting on stone piers. The piers were completed June 1854. The bridge was fully completed on April 21, 1856. On April 22, a train consisting of three locomotives and eight passenger cars crossed as a test.

3244. Steel arch bridge was the Eads Bridge, built across the Mississippi River by James Buchanan Eads. It was built from St. Louis, MO, to East St. Louis, IL, at a cost of $6.5 million. Construction started in 1869. The center span was 520 feet, the two side spans 502 feet each. On May 24, 1874, more than 15,000 people paid a toll to walk across; on June 3, the upper roadway was ready for vehicles; and on July 4, President Ulysses Simpson Grant made the formal dedication speech. It was the first bridge construction project to use pneumatic caissons.

3245. Cantilever bridge was designed by Charles Shaler Smith for the Cincinnati Southern Railroad to cross the Kentucky River. It was built in 1876–77 near Harrodsburg in Mercer County, KY. A contract for an iron-truss bridge was let to the Baltimore Bridge Company on July 9, 1875, for $377,500. Construction started October 12, 1876, and was completed February 20, 1877. The bridge had three spans, each 375 feet long.

3246. Railroad bridge entirely of steel was the Glasgow Bridge, a 2,700-foot structure built by the Chicago and Alton Railroad Company over the Missouri River at Glasgow, MO. The contract for steel was dated October 12, 1878, and the bridge was placed in service about November 1, 1879.

3247. Highway bridge with concrete arches was designed by Carl A. Trik, superintendent of bridges for the Bureau of Highways, Philadelphia, PA, and erected in 1893 to carry Pine Road over Pennypack Creek, Philadelphia. It consisted of two arched spans, each 25 feet 4.75 inches wide, with a rise of 6 feet 6 inches, supported by concrete abutments and a concrete pier, built on a light skew. It was 34 feet wide and carried a 26-foot-wide macadam roadway with two granite-paved gutters on concrete foundations. The entire bridge, including the appurtenances and the thorough renovation of the retaining walls on both approaches, cost $9,288.

3248. Rolling lift bridge was the Van Buren Street bridge, located over the Chicago River, Chicago, IL, and was opened to traffic on February 4, 1895. It consisted of two arms meeting at the center of the river, which when open provided a clear channel 82 feet in width, measured along the line of the stream. Each arm consisted of three trusses that carried two roadways, each 18 feet wide, and two sidewalks, each eight feet wide. The bridge was operated by two 50-horsepower electric motors on each side of the river. The total construction cost was $169,700. The bridge's construction was patented by William Scherzer of Chicago.

3249. Suspension bridge with steel towers instead of masonry towers that was important was the Williamsburg Bridge, connecting the boroughs of Brooklyn and Manhattan in New York City. It was opened on December 19, 1903. The cost was $24 million for land and construction.

3250. Concrete cantilever bridge was erected over Indian Creek at Marion, IA, in 1905 for the Marion Street Railway Company. It had three 50-foot spans with two longitudinal ribs 12 inches wide supported on concrete columns and floor slabs on transverse beams.

3251. Aerial ferry was put in operation on April 9, 1905, over the ship canal from Lake Avenue, Duluth, MN, to Minnesota Point, MN. The car was suspended in the air from a superstructure which had a clear height over Lake Superior of 135 feet. The truss in the center was 51 feet, making a total height at the highest part of the superstructure of 186 feet above water level. The clear span was 393.75 feet in length. The car platform was 34 by 50 feet, with room enough to accommodate six automobiles and two glassed-in cabins for passengers, and with a carrying capacity of 125,000 pounds. The platform was 12 feet above the water line. The round trip could be made in 10 minutes.

3252. Double-deck bridge of importance was the Queensboro Bridge over the East River, New York City, which was opened to traffic on March 30, 1909. The Manhattan Suspension Bridge, also a double-deck bridge over the East River, was opened to traffic on December 31, 1909. The total cost of the land and construction of the Queensboro Bridge was approximately $17 million and of the Manhattan Suspension Bridge about $31 million.

3253. Bridge with piers sunk in the open sea was the Golden Gate suspension span, San Francisco, CA. Construction was officially started on January 5, 1933. Joseph Baermann Strauss was appointed chief engineer. The length of the main structure of the bridge was 8,940 feet, with towers 746 feet above water and a minimum clearance of 220 feet. The Golden Gate Bridge was the first built across the outer mouth of a major ocean harbor.

3254. Pontoon bridge of reinforced concrete was the Lake Washington Floating Bridge, Seattle, WA, begun on December 29, 1938, and dedicated on July 2, 1940. It was composed of 25 pontoons bolted together, each having two or more 65-ton anchors. Its total length was 34,021 feet. It was financed by a Public Works Administration grant of $3.8 million and a bond issue of $5.5 million to be repaid by toll charges.

3255. Bridge designed by computer was the Verrazano-Narrows Bridge, which spanned New York Harbor to connect Brooklyn and Staten Island, two boroughs of New York City. Construction began in 1959 under the supervision of Othmar H. Ammann. The main span, 4,260 feet long, was suspended from two towers 690 feet high. When it was completed in 1964, the bridge became the longest suspension bridge in the world.

3256. Bridge named for a woman was the Betsy Ross Bridge, which spanned three miles across the Delaware River, connecting Philadelphia and Pennsauken, NJ. It was officially opened on April 30, 1976. The construction cost about $105 million.

Buildings

3257. Brick building was erected in 1633 in the fort of New Amsterdam (the future New York City) as a residence for Wouter Van Twiller, the fifth Dutch governor. Several other brick structures were erected within the fort. The bricks were imported from Holland.

3258. Neoclassical building in the American colonies was the Redwood Library in Newport, RI, designed by Peter Harrison and dedicated in 1750. Harrison, an English seaman turned American merchant, owned a number of books on English architecture from which he derived his design.

3259. Industrial park was a planned industrial complex of 700 acres near the 70-foot waterfalls above and below the Great Falls of the Passaic River, Paterson, NJ. It opened in 1792. It was sponsored by Alexander Hamilton, who formed the Society for Establishing Useful Manufactures in 1791.

3260. Factory standardization to federal government specification was required on April 16, 1813, when a contract specifying interchangeable parts was drawn up between Callender Irvine, commissary general of the United States, and Colonel Simeon North of Berlin, CT, in Middletown, CT. The contract was for 20,000 pistols at $7 each to be produced within five years. It stipulated that "component parts of the pistols are to correspond so exactly that any limb or part of one pistol may be fitted to any other pistol of the 20,000." Colonel North established his pistol factory in 1810 in Staddle Hill, a suburb of Middletown. The factory produced about 10,000 pistols a year.

3261. Building in all-Gothic architecture was Trinity Episcopal Church, New Haven, CT, designed by Ithiel Town of New Haven in 1814. It had seamfaced traprock with brownstone trim.

3262. Building of fireproof construction was the Fireproof Building, which was designed and built by Robert Mills in 1822–23 on Meeting Street, between Queen and Broad streets, Charleston, SC. It was built for the preservation of the county records and was a stone and iron structure. Even the window sashes were made of iron.

3263. Arcade was the Philadelphia Arcade, which extended from Chestnut Street through to Carpenter Street between Sixth and Seventh Streets, Philadelphia, PA. It was erected by the Arcade Company, of which John Haviland was architect. The cornerstone was laid on May 3, 1826, and the building finished in September 1827. The cost of construction was $112,000; $42,500 was paid for the land.

3264. Split-level buildings were the Elfreth houses, three brownstone buildings on South Third Street, built in 1830 in Philadelphia, PA. The rooms in the rear were higher than those in the front.

3265. Mortised lock was introduced in 1835 by Philos Blake and Eli Whitney Blake of Blake Brothers, Westville, CT.

3266. Building with a high steeple was Trinity Church, New York City, which was begun on October 17, 1839, and dedicated on May 21, 1846, Ascension Day. The steeple was 284 feet above Broadway. The staircase to the top of the steeple had 308 steps, "with suitable resting places provided," and reached a point 34 feet below the peak. The Trinity spire was the highest point until 1894, when the Manhattan Life Insurance Company erected a 16-story building and tower that thrust its pinnacle 60 feet higher.

3267. Building heated by steam was the Eastern Hotel in Boston, MA, erected in 1845. Small wrought-iron pipes conveyed the steam and the heat was diffused by coils of pipe. The firm of Walworth and Nason (later known as the Walworth Company), founded by James Jones Walworth and Joseph Nason, established a plant in Boston in 1842 for the purpose of "warming and ventilating buildings by means of steam and hot water apparatus." At first they used hot water for the system, converting to steam in 1844.

3268. Monolithic concrete building was the Milton House, Milton, WI, a two-story hotel built in 1845 by Joseph Goodrich on the corduroy road between Chicago, IL, and Madison, WI. It replaced a log house built in 1837 and a frame building built in 1839. The walls were 18 inches thick. A hexagonal tower three stories high served as a lookout for the approach of Native Americans.

3269. Factory heated by steam was the Burlington Woolen Company at the Winooski River, Burlington, VT, built in 1846. The factory, sold at auction on October 20, 1852, was described in an advertisement in the *Burlington Free Press* as follows: "The factory building and dye houses were heated by steam conducted through iron pipes in the most modern and approved manner."

3270. Building constructed wholly of cast iron was a factory five stories high that was built by James Bogardus at the corner of Centre and Duane streets in New York City in May 1848.

3271. Elevator was a platform elevator made by Henry Waterman in 1850 in his shop on Duane Street, New York City. The elevator was installed in a building owned by Hecker and Brother, millers, at 203 Cherry Street, New York City, where it was used it to hoist barrels upstairs.

3272. Elevator with safety devices to prevent the car from falling in case the ropes should break was made by Elisha Graves Otis in 1853 and exhibited by him the same year at the Crystal Palace Exposition in New York City. The first such elevator was delivered on September 20, 1853, to Benjamin Newhouse, 275 Hudson Street, New York City.

3273. Building in which wrought-iron beams were used was erected for Harper and Brothers in New York City in 1854. Wrought-iron beams were rolled for the first time in the United States in 1854 at the Trenton Iron Works, Trenton, NJ, of which Peter Cooper was the principal owner. These beams were intended for the Cooper Union building in New York City, but they were not ready in time, as it took two years to prepare them. They were seven inches deep, weighed 81 pounds per yard, and were of the type known as deck beams. Previously, cast-iron beams had been used in construction work.

3274. Elevator with a completely enclosed car for conveying passengers to the upper floor of a building was installed in 1857 by Elisha Graves Otis in the store of E. V. Haughwout, at the corner of Broadway and Broome Streets, New York City.

3275. Building designed to be used by artists was the Tenth Street Studio Building in New York City, owned by businessman James Boorman Johnston. Johnston purchased a plot of land on 10th Street between Fifth and Sixth Avenues in Greenwich Village and hired architect Richard Morris Hunt to design a building to house artists' studios and galleries. Individual studios were arranged around a large central exhibition hall where new paintings could be shown to other tenants and collectors. The building opened in 1858. Among the artists who rented space there were Frederick Edwin Church, Sanford Gifford, Albert Bierstadt, Winslow Homer, and William Merritt Chase.

3276. Burglar alarm was installed by Edwin Thomas Holmes on February 21, 1858, in Boston, MA. The releasing of a spring by the opening of a door or window made a contact that caused a short circuit of the wires.

3277. Escalator patent was obtained by Nathan Ames of Saugus, MA, on August 9, 1859, on an improvement in revolving stairs. Steps or stairs were arranged upon an inclined endless belt or chain. Another escalator design was patented by Jesse W. Reno in March 1892. His Reno Inclined Elevator, an inclined conveyor belt with rubber cleats, was first installed at the Old Iron Pier on Coney Island, NY (now part of New York City), in 1896.

3278. Pin-tumbler cylinder lock was invented by Linus Yale, Jr., of Newport, NY, who obtained a patent on January 29, 1861, for his design. The pin-tumbler cylinder lock with a thin, flat key, still the basis for many combination locks today, was the most successful of Yale's many lock inventions, which included the first dial combination bank lock and a double bank lock that required two keys to open.

3279. Office building with an elevator was installed in 1868 in the original Equitable Life Assurance Society building, located on lower Broadway, New York City.

3280. Burglar alarm system in which the protected premises were connected by wire to a central office system that was immediately apprised of entry was installed by the Holmes Burglar Alarm Company, New York City, in 1872. The alarms served safe cabinets and bank vaults specifically, instead of providing general protection for stores and houses.

3281. Time lock was manufactured by Sargent and Greenleaf, Rochester, NY, and installed in May 1874 on the vault of the First National Bank of Morrison, IL. James Sargent of Rochester, NY, obtained a patent on July 20, 1875, on a "time-lock" and another on September 25, 1877, on "combined time-locks, and bolt-works for safes."

3282. Heating system to heat buildings from a central station was installed in Lockport, NY, in 1877 by Birdsall Holly. He ran a steam line through a trench for a distance of 100 feet from his house to an adjoining property and found that the heat was not lost by being carried through pipes. He subsequently formed the Holly Steam Combination Company, whose first plant was located at Elm and South streets, Lockport. The company was later operated by the New York State Electric and Gas Corporation, Lockport division.

3283. Building shaped like an elephant was James V. Lafferty's structure the Elephant, which was built in the form of an elephant with a covering of tin painted to resemble elephant hide. It was built in 1882 in Cedar Grove in Atlantic City, NJ, as an attraction to promote his real estate surrounding it. The hind legs contained a spiral staircase that led into a large room handsomely fitted with carved wood, where photographs and models of the property for sale were displayed. The front legs contained staircases leading to the eyes, through which the ocean was visible. The howdah, which was 65 feet above the sand, served as an observation tower. The structure cost $25,000 to build.

3284. Skyscraper was a 10-story steel-skeleton building erected by the Home Insurance Company of New York at La Salle and Adams streets, Chicago, IL. Designed by Major William Le Baron Jenney, it was started on May 1, 1884, and completed in the fall of 1885. It was constructed of marble and flanked by four columns of polished granite supporting a marble balcony. Two additional stories were added to it later. A steel frame supported the entire weight of the walls, instead of the walls themselves carrying the weight of the building.

3285. Steel-frame building was the Tacoma Building in Chicago, IL, completed in 1887. It was designed by Holabird and Roche and built by George Allon Fuller. This building embodied the principles upon which all modern skyscrapers are designed and erected.

3286. Revolving door was invented by Theophilus Van Kannel of Philadelphia, PA, who obtained a patent on August 7, 1888, on a "storm door structure." The first building to install a revolving door was an office building in Philadelphia.

3287. Electric elevator successfully operated was installed in 1889 by Otis Brothers and Company in the Demarest Building, Fifth Avenue and 33rd Street, New York City.

3288. Steel-frame residence was the Copper House, built in 1890 at Shore Road and 88th Street in the Bay Ridge section of Brooklyn, NY (now part of New York City). The house was constructed with copper sheets riveted to the exterior. It was built by Niels Poulson, who resided in it from 1890 until his death in 1911.

3289. Escalator of the modern type was manufactured by the Otis Elevator Company of New York City in 1900 and placed on exhibit at the Paris Exposition the same year. It was installed in 1901 in the Eighth Street store of Gimbel Brothers, Philadelphia, PA. The trade name Escalator was registered on May 29, 1900.

3290. Building with an all-marble dome was the Rhode Island State House in Providence, RI, occupied by the General Assembly and other state officers beginning on January 1, 1901. Ground was broken on September 16, 1895, and the cornerstone was laid on October 15, 1896. The architects were McKim, Mead and White, and the builders were Norcross Brothers, Worcester, MA. The dome was made of 327,000 cubic feet of white Georgia marble, and was 94 feet high. The diameter of the dome below the top of the gallery was 70 feet; the diameter above the top of the gallery, 56 feet; and the diameter of the dome proper, 50 feet.

3291. Factory with temperature and humidity control was the plant of the Sackett-Wilhelms Lithographing and Publishing Company, Brooklyn, New York City, which in 1902 installed a 30-ton fan-cooled dehumidifying unit designed by Willis Haviland Carrier. Its primary purpose was to stop the expansion and contraction of paper caused by varying weather conditions.

3292. Building with a large-scale clear-span dome was built in 1901 in West Baden (formerly Mile Lick), IN, by Colonel Lee Sinclair, a businessman and entrepreneur. Sinclair, who operated a resort near the town's sulfur springs, contracted with architect Harrison Albright and engineer Oliver J. Westcott to build the 708-room West Baden Springs Hotel complex, which featured a clear-span dome 130 feet high and 200 feet in diameter. The dome had no pillars, but was supported at the rim by 24 steel ribs weighing 8.5 tons each. The ribs were attached to the supporting walls by pivots that moved on tracks, thus allowing for thermal expansion and contraction of the dome. The hotel opened on September 1, 1902. It was the largest free-standing domed structure in the world until the opening of the Houston Astrodome in 1965.

3293. Factory cooled by air conditioning was the Gray Manufacturing Company's Gastonia, NC, plant, erected in 1905 with an air-conditioning system manufactured by Stuart W. Cramer of Charlotte, NC. This equipment drew in fresh air from outdoors, filtered and washed it, heated or cooled it, and corrected any variation in humidity. It completely changed the air in the factory about five times an hour.

3294. Stadium operated by a city was the Golden Gate Park Stadium, San Francisco, CA, completed in 1907. It was oval in shape and covered a 30-acre field. It had two entrances, one on the north and one on the south side, through tunnels 20 feet wide and 10 feet high. A three-quarter-mile trotting track 60 feet wide encircled the stadium. Bicycle races were held on November 29, 1906, before completion.

3295. Building of pressed structural steel was a two-story, 14-room building designed and built in June 1907 by the Taft-Howell Company of Cornwall Landing, NY, for the Tuxedo Park Association, Tuxedo Park, NY. The pressed steel, known by its trade name, Metal Lumber, was developed by Harry Merrill Naugle, chief engineer of the Berger Manufacturing Company, Canton, OH. The building had structural members substituting in every detail for what normally would be wood studs and joists in balloon frame construction for dwellings.

3296. Air rights lease was made by the New York Central Railroad Company in February 1910 to the Grand Central Palace, New York City, for $30,000 a year. The Palace was permitted to build its structure over the New York Central Railroad tracks. The idea of selling air rights over real estate was originated by Ira A. Place.

3297. Skyscraper higher than 750 feet was the Woolworth Building in New York City. It measured 791.5 feet high, 947 feet above sea level at high tide. At the time, it was the tallest structure in the world, with the exception of the Eiffel Tower in Paris. It was formally opened on April 24, 1913, at 7:30 P.M., when President Woodrow Wilson at the White House, Washington, DC, pressed a telegraph key that rang a bell in the engine room and dining hall and lit the electric lights on the 55 floors. The architect was Cass Gilbert.

3298. Air-conditioned office building was the Milam Building, San Antonio, TX, which opened on January 1, 1928. The building was 21 stories high, contained nearly 3 million cubic feet of space, and had 247,779 square feet of gross floor area. It was the first building in the world in which the air conditioning was a part of the original construction.

3299. Factory without windows was erected in Fitchburg, MA, in 1930. The plant, one story high and consisting of one room, was illuminated by hundreds of 1,000-watt electric lamps containing a small percentage of ultraviolet rays, which were considered healthful. The walls and ceilings were painted orange, blue, green, and white to increase visibility, and the floors were jet black. The building also lacked skylights. It was ventilated by a system that circulated 10 million cubic feet of washed, heated, and humidified air every 10 minutes. The walls were soundproofed by cork pads. The building was constructed by the Austin Company of Cleveland, OH, for the Simonds Saw and Steel Company at a cost of $1.5 million.

3300. Skyscraper higher than 1,250 feet was the Empire State Building, New York City, 102 stories high. It was dedicated on May 1, 1931, by President Herbert Clark Hoover, who pressed a button from the White House in Washington, DC, that switched on the lights. It was 1,250 feet high and cost about $52 million. The builder was Colonel William Aiken Starrett; the architect, William Frederick Lamb; the engineer, Homer Gage Balcom. In 1950, a 222-foot television sending-tower was constructed on the roof.

3301. Automatic swinging doors operated by a photoelectric cell were installed in Wilcox's Pier Restaurant, West Haven, CT. The Stanley Works of New Britain, CT, completed the installation on June 19, 1931. The "magic eye" provided fully automatic control and operation of swinging doors between the main dining room and kitchen.

3302. All-glass windowless structure was the Owens-Illinois Glass Company's packaging laboratory at Toledo, OH, completed on January 15, 1936. Eighty thousand translucent water-clear hollow glass blocks weighing about 150 tons were used in the two-story building, which had 39 rooms and an aggregate floor area of 20,000 square feet. The blocks were manufactured at the company's plant in Muncie, IN, and were a part of the structural strength of the building.

3303. Building built completely inside a factory and ready for occupancy, and the first building floated across a river, was a 41-ton five-room house and garage, 32 by 42 feet, fully equipped with furnace, cooling system, laundry, and plumbing, and partly furnished. It was built by the firm of R.G. Le Tourneau, Peoria, IL. It was towed across the Illinois River on its own bottom from Peoria to the Le Tourneau test farm in East Peoria, IL, on September 17, 1938.

3304. Quonset hut was built for the Navy in September 1941 at Quonset Point air station, Greenwich, RI, by the Great Lakes Steel Corporation, Stran-Steel Division, Detroit, MI. The structures were built around a framework of Stran-Steel members, a light steel building material distinguished by a patented groove into which nails could be driven. They were officially designated by the Navy as Navy Arch-Rib Huts.

3305. Building containing 6.5 million square feet of usable space was the Pentagon, Arlington, VA, built of reinforced concrete faced with Indiana limestone, and completed on January 15, 1943, at a cost of about $83 million. It is five stories high; each facade is 921 feet long; and each floor has a different color scheme. It has five rings of buildings intersected by 10 corridors. The length of the corridors is 17.5 miles. It covers 34 acres of land, with a five-acre pentagonal court in the center and 204 acres of lawns and terraces. It accommodates the headquarters of the Department of Defense. It was designed by George Edwin Bergstrom of Los Angeles, CA.

3306. Elevator with electronic signal controls was installed by the Otis Elevator Company in April 1948 at the Universal Pictures Building, New York City, after several years of experiment and development. Eight elevators, four local and four express, served the building's 22 stories. When a passenger touched a landing button, the call was registered by an electronic tube, which lit up to show that it had been activated. The stopping of the cars in response to these calls, the canceling of the calls as they were answered, and the operation of the cars were all controlled by means of electronic circuits.

3307. Burglar alarm operated by ultrasonic or radio waves using the Doppler effect was the Alertronic, invented by Samuel Bagno of New York City, who obtained a patent on October 13, 1953, on a movement detection system for intruders or fire. It was manufactured by the Alertronic Corporation of Long Island City, NY (part of Queens, New York City), and was first sold in June 1950. Reflected waves of 19,000 cycles a second, pitched too high for normal human ears, were recorded through a microphone into an alarm, generally stationed at a convenient location. The noise made by an intruder, having a slightly different frequency, would cause the alarm gong to sound.

3308. Building with its roof supported by cables was the J.S. Dorton Arena, in Raleigh, NC, which was completed and dedicated in 1953. The saddle-shaped roof was suspended on a network of cables that extended crosswise from the 90-foot parabolic arch. The 14-foot-wide arches reached a maximum height of 90 feet. They crossed each other at about 26 feet above ground, then extended into a tunnel below the surface at the east and west ends. The weight of the roof was equalized by tension cables, with 14-foot 2-inch strands connecting each end of the parabola through the stress tunnel. The roof was suspended in a way that eliminated any necessity for structural steel supports and presented no obstructions of view from any seat.

3309. Aluminum-faced building was the Alcoa Building, Pittsburgh, PA, a 30-story, 410-foot skyscraper, completed on August 1, 1953, for the Aluminum Company of America and dedicated on September 15, 1953. The exterior walls were thin stamped aluminum panels, 6 by 12 feet, bolted to angles on the spandrel beams and backed up with four inches of perlite-concrete sprayed on slotted aluminum lath and reinforcing bars. It had 183,000 square feet of exterior wall area. About 3 million pounds of aluminum were used. The elevators were of all-aluminum construction, the electrical wiring and conductors all-aluminum, and the plumbing 65 percent aluminum.

3310. Circular office building was the Capitol Tower, Hollywood and Vine streets, Los Angeles, CA, dedicated April 6, 1956. It was 150 feet high, with 13 stories, and had a diameter of 92 feet. Above the roof was a 90-foot spire from which a beacon light flashed the word *Hollywood* in Morse code. Welton Becket was the architect.

3311. Skyscraper of bronze and glass was the Seagram Building, a 519-foot structure, 38 stories high, at 375 Park Avenue, New York City. It contained 3,650,000 square feet of glass divided into 3,800 windows. The steel framework was put together with high-tensile steel bolts instead of steel rivets. Mies van der Rohe and Philip Johnson were the architects and Kahn and Jacobs the associated architects, with the George A. Fuller Company the general contractor. The highest point of steel construction was reached on December 17, 1956. The building was completed in November 1957.

3312. Civic center with an aluminum geodesic dome was the Virginia Beach Convention Center, Virginia Beach, VA, opened on May 15, 1957. It was renamed the Alan B. Shepard Convention Center on July 28, 1961.

3313. Commercial building with solar heating was the Solar Building, a single-story building in Albuquerque, NM. The heating system, designed by Frank Hillman Bridgers and Donald Paxton, was completed on August 1, 1957. One wall of the building, which was sheathed in glass tilted to face the sun, collected heat from the sun's rays. The heat warmed panels containing water, which flowed through a conventional heating system.

3314. Geodesic dome of substantial size was the Climatron, which opened in 1960 at the Missouri Botanical Garden in St. Louis, MO. The dome housed a tropical rainforest display, including streams, waterfalls, and some 1,200 species of plants in a natural setting. A geodesic dome is comprised of a complex network of triangles that form a roughly spherical surface. It is the structure with the highest ratio of enclosed area to external surface area. The geodesic dome was the invention of visionary architect and engineer Richard Buckminster Fuller, who received patents on it in 1947 and 1954. Fuller's original geodesic dome was constructed in Carbondale, IL, where he was a professor at Southern Illinois University.

3315. Building of large size with a retractable roof was the Civic Arena and Exhibit Hall, a stainless steel dome structure in Pittsburgh, PA, that was dedicated on September 17, 1961. The roof, which had no interior support, was divided radially into eight leaves, two of which were stationary and six of which rotated about a pin at the top as they rolled along curved rails laid on a reinforced concrete ring girder. There were approximately 2,950 tons of structural steel in the roof. The dome was constructed to open or close electrically in 2.5 minutes. It was nearly circular, 415 feet in diameter and 136 feet high at center. The arena could accommodate 13,000 spectators at a basketball game and 15,000 at a rally. It occupied a five-acre site and cost $22 million. The first event held there was the Ice Capades, September 18–30, 1961.

3316. Domed sports stadium that was fully enclosed was the Astrodome, Houston, TX, formally known as the Harris County Domed Stadium. Construction work started on March 18, 1963. The overall cost was $35.5 million. The building had a permanent translucent roof spanning 642 feet and covered with 4,596 plastic skylights. The distance to the top of the dome was 208 feet. The arena could accommodate 66,000 people at conventions and 48,000 at baseball games. The playing field was 466 feet by 288 feet, an area of 405,000 square feet. The first baseball game under the dome was played on April 9, 1965, between the Houston Astros and the New York Yankees, who lost 2–1. The first football game was played on September 11, 1965, when the University of Tulsa defeated the University of Houston 14–0.

3317. Elliptical office building was the $40 million Phoenix Mutual Building of the Phoenix Mutual Life Insurance Company, constructed as a part of the urban renewal project on Constitution Plaza, Hartford, CT. It contained 13 floors, each about 13,000 square feet. It measured 225 feet from end to end and 87 feet across at the widest point. It was designed by Wallace Kirkman Harrison and Max Abramovitz and was completed in November 1963. George A. Fuller was the contractor.

3318. Skyscraper higher than 1,400 feet was the 110-story Sears Building of Sears Roebuck and Company, measuring 1,454 feet high, located on Jackson Boulevard between Adams and Franklin streets in Chicago, IL, which was topped out on May 4, 1973, and completed in 1974.

3319. Adjustable stadium was the Aloha Stadium, Honolulu, HI, dedicated on September 12, 1975. It had seating accommodations for 50,000 people in six 147-foot-high grandstand sections, of which two were fixed (the north and the south) and four were removable (the east and west). Each section weighed 1,750 tons and was about 14 stories high. Three large compressors forced air into 416 discs, making it possible for hydraulic jacks to move any of the four sections a distance of 180 feet in 25 minutes. The stadium was designed by Charles Luckman Associates, Los Angeles, CA.

3320. Building with a combined heat and power energy system was the 200 Market Building, a 19-story office tower in Portland, OR. A CHP (combined heat and power) system was installed in it beginning in October 2001. The system used a microturbine to generate electricity. Heat produced by the microturbine was captured and used to power cooling and heating mechanisms.

Canals

3321. Canal for creating water power was dug by English settlers in 1639–40 at Dedham, MA, at Mill Creek, or Mother Brook as it is commonly called, and was used to run a mill. It conveyed water from the Charles River into the Neponset River. The order for the construction of the canal follows: "The 25th of the 1 month, Commonly Called March. 1639. . . . Ordered that a Ditch shalbe made at a Common Charge through purchased Medowe unto the East Brooke, that may both be a pticon fence in the same; as also may serve for a Course unto a water mill."

3322. Canal for boat transportation was built around the falls of the Connecticut River at South Hadley, MA, in 1793. It was chartered by "the Proprietors of the Upper Locks and Canals on the Connecticut River in the County of Hampshire." The canal was two miles long and was opened to traffic in 1794. Benjamin Prescott was the engineer. Boats were run into movable caissons filled with water and were hauled by cables operated by water power. The canal had two levels connected by an incline, along which boats were raised or lowered in a tank of water and propelled by cables operated by water wheels.

3323. Canal of importance was the Erie Canal, which connected the waters of Lake Erie at Buffalo with the waters of the Hudson River at Albany, NY. Lake Erie lies 550 feet above the level of tide water in the Hudson. The canal was 360 miles in length, 40 feet wide at the top and 28 feet wide at the bottom, and 4 feet deep. The canal was authorized on April 15, 1817, and construction started on July 4. The section between the towns of Rome and Utica carried its first boat on October 22, 1819. The canal, which cost about $9 million, was opened for traffic on October 26, 1825.

3324. Canal made of concrete were built by the federal government for the Illinois and Mississippi Canal (the Hennepin canal), which connected Lake Michigan at Chicago, IL, with the Mississippi River south of Rock Island, IL. Excavation work commenced July 1892 and the first section, the Milan section, was opened to traffic on April 17, 1895.

3325. Canal incorporated into a seaway was the 400-mile waterway between Montreal and Lake Erie, connecting the St. Lawrence River with the Great Lakes. It forms part of the St. Lawrence Seaway, 2,342 miles long, which allows oceangoing ships to travel from the Atlantic Ocean to Duluth, MN. It was opened on April 25, 1959.

Construction

3326. Brick kiln in America was established in Salem, MA, in 1629.

3327. Slate used for roofing material was obtained from Delta, PA, and Cardiff, MD, in 1734 by William and James Reese.

3328. Brick roofing tile was manufactured in 1735 by Hüster, a German tile maker in Montgomery County, PA.

3329. Rivet production on a commercial scale was attempted by Josiah Gilbert Pierson, who invented a "coldheader machine" on which he obtained a patent on March 23, 1794. His heading machine was a massive affair, with a heavy framework anchored to the floor and a large flywheel that operated on the toggle principle. His factory was located in New York City, on the later site of the New York Produce Exchange.

3330. Ball bearing commercial installation was made on October 30, 1794, on the weathervane topping the steeple of the Evangelical Lutheran Church of the Holy Trinity, Lancaster, PA. The bearings were of the antifriction roller type, with a pin through them.

3331. Natural cement rock was discovered in 1818 by Canvas White near Fayetteville, Onondaga County, NY. He obtained a patent on a cement manufacturing process, which he sold to New York State for $10,000.

3332. Angle iron was rolled in 1819 by Samuel Leonard at the Union Rolling Mill, on the Monongahela River at Pittsburgh, PA. The mill had four puddling furnaces.

3333. Concrete was patented as a building material by canal engineer Canvass White in 1820. His patent covered the use of cement made from "hydraulic lime" for underwater structures. Concrete mined in New York State's Madison, Cayuga, and Onondaga counties was first used in the construction of the Erie Canal that same year.

3334. Fire brick was made by the Salamander Works of Woodbridge, NJ, in 1825. Although definite records are not obtainable, it is believed an attempt was made to manufacture fire bricks in 1812.

3335. Fire brick to withstand high heat was manufactured in 1841 by the Mount Savage Fire Brick Works of Mount Savage, MD, later the Union Mining Company of Allegany County, MD.

3336. Wall and floor tiles were manufactured in 1845 by Abraham Miller, 7th and Zane streets, Philadelphia, PA. In 1810, he had succeeded Andrew Miller, who had conducted a pottery in Sugar Alley since 1791.

3337. Cork manufacturer is said to have been William King, whose factory in Brooklyn, NY (now part of New York City), produced cork products from 1850 to 1860.

3338. Terra cotta was manufactured by James Renwick in 1853 in New York City. He conceived the idea of introducing terra cotta as a building material and a substitute for cut stone work.

3339. Brick machine for the production of soft mud bricks was designed and built by Henry Martin in 1857 and installed in Hartford, CT. The clay was pushed from the press box through a die or jack mold into sanded wooden molds by a process similar to the method of pressing the clay by hand into wood or steel molds.

3340. Terra cotta factory to be successful was established by J. N. Glover in Louisville, KY, in 1867. After a series of successive changes of locale and management, it gradually developed into the Northwestern Terra Cotta Company, Chicago, IL.

3341. Cement was introduced into the United States from England about 1870. Because of its weight it was brought over as ballast. American portland cement was invented by David Oliver Saylor of Allentown, PA, who perfected a process for making hydraulic cement from argillo-magnesium and argillo calcareous limestone and received a patent on September 26, 1871. European cement was regarded as superior and it was not until 1897 that the use of American cement exceeded the use of cement imported from Europe.

3342. Corkboard patent to be issued on pure corkboard was granted to John T. Smith of Brooklyn, NY (now part of New York City), on July 14, 1891. Manufacture was begun in Brooklyn in 1894 by Stone and Duryea. Cork covering was produced first, followed by the manufacture of pure corkboard.

3343. Cork for covering steam pipes was manufactured in the United States in 1894 by Stone and Duryea of Brooklyn, NY (now part of New York City). The company moved to Bridgeport, CT, in 1896 and the following year produced cork covering for cold pipelines. It was succeeded by the Nonpareil Cork Manufacturing Company, which in turn was purchased by the Armstrong Cork Company in 1904.

3344. Rock wool insulation factory was the Crystal Chemical Works, Alexandria, IN, opened on June 1, 1897, by Charles Corydon Hall, who melted limestone rock in a specially designed water-jacketed cupola. The rock was blown by steam pressure into fine wool-like threads for use as insulating material. The Johns Manville Corporation acquired the works in 1929.

3345. Plywood commercially produced was marketed by the Portland Manufacturing Company in 1905 in St. Johns (now Portland), OR. They sold plywood panels of Oregon pine, and later of Columbian pine and Douglas fir. Plywood contains an odd number of veneer sheets bonded together, with the grain of each at right angles to the sheets above and below. Laminated sheets, all having the grain in the same direction, had been made earlier.

3346. Insulating brick was supplied to the trade by the Armstrong Cork Company of Lancaster, PA, in June 1913 under the trade name Nonpareil Insulating Brick. This brick was used in high-temperature equipment such as industrial furnaces, ovens, oil stills, blast furnaces, stoves, and similar apparatus. Diatomaceous earth was pulverized and mixed with finely ground cork, and a small quantity of clay was added for a binder. It was molded into brick form and then fired. The cork was consumed, leaving the finished brick terra-cotta in color and extremely cellular in structure. Because of the many small voids left when the particles of cork were burned out, and because of a large amount of noncirculating air, the ability of the brick to hold heat was exceptionally high.

3347. Sound-absorbing material made of rigid insulating board was invented by Carl Gebhard Muench of St. Paul, MN, who obtained a patent on September 14, 1915, on a "thermo non-conductor" known as Insulite. The invention consisted of a rigid thermal insulation with groundwood screenings as a fiber source. The first board machine built to make a fibrous board in one thick continuous layer was installed in International Falls, MN, where production was started on May 15, 1914. Sugar-cane bagasse was also found to be a satisfactory fiber for making insulation board. It was first used on August 10, 1921, in Marrero, LA, by the Celotex Corporation of Chicago, IL.

3348. Lightweight brick was developed in 1927 by Charles Frederick Burgess of the C.F. Burgess Laboratories, Madison, WI. It was porous, one-fifth the weight of ordinary brick, and yet resistant to the entrance of water. It floated in water and had adequate compressive strength for use in all types of buildings for load-bearing walls.

Dams

3349. Levees were built along the Mississippi River at New Orleans, LA, in 1724. They extended 18 miles above and 18 miles below New Orleans, but they were rudimentary dikes compared with the present mighty embankments. Sieur le Blond de la Tour, a knight of St. Louis and chief engineer of the colony, began construction of the levee in 1718. It was completed in 1727.

3350. Dam filled with rocks was built at Castlewood, CO, for the Denver Land and Water Company, and opened in November 1890. The upstream and downstream faces of the dam were built of dry or mortar rubble masonry. The core of the dam consisted of loosely dumped rock. The maximum height of the dam above the valley floor was about 70 feet, and the length about 600 feet. There was a spillway, located near the center of the dam, consisting of an opening four feet deep and 100 feet long. The outlets through the structure consisted of eight 12-inch cast-iron pipes, placed in pairs at four different elevations, with valves in a chamber built inside the dam. The reservoir capacity was about 3,400 acre-feet.

3351. Steel dam was the Ash Fork Dam in Johnson Canyon, four miles east of Ashfork, AZ, which was built in 1898 by the Atchison, Topeka and Santa Fe Railway Company. It was built of steel with masonry abutments. The west abutment was 84 feet long, and 16 feet high. The steel portion was 184 feet long. The height of the spillway crest was 30 feet above the reservoir bottom and 46 feet above the lowest bedrock. The width of the canyon at the stream bed was 40 feet. The top of the dam, aside from the spillway, was 300 feet. The capacity of this reservoir at spillway crest was 96.7 acre-feet. The canyon drained about 30 square miles.

Glass and Ceramics

3352. Glass factory was established in Jamestown, VA, in October 1608. Eight German and Polish mechanics were imported to start the new industry. Among the factory's products were glass beads for use in trade with the Native Americans. The factory remained in operation spasmodically for about seven years and was then disbanded, owing chiefly to the fact that the workers found it more profitable to grow tobacco for shipment to England. The London Company later sent Captain William Norton, accompanied by four Italians and two servants, to revive the Jamestown glass factory, which resumed operations on July 25, 1621. The massacre of the colonists by Native Americans in 1622 put an end to it.

3353. Window glass factory of importance was the Boston Crown Glass Company of Boston, MA, chartered in 1787. The manufacture of crown window glass began in 1792. The glass was blown through a pipe into a huge bulb, which was opened, flared out into a disc, and then cut into panes. The legislature gave this company the sole right to manufacture glass in Massachusetts for a 15-year period and exempted the company from taxes and the workers from military duty.

3354. Flint glass factory that was successful was founded in 1807 by George Robinson and Edward Ensel. It was located on the Monongahela River at the foot of Ross Street, Pittsburgh, PA. The first furnace held six 20-inch pots. The factory was sold to Bakewell and Page in 1808, and the name was later changed to Bakewell, Pears and Company.

3355. Porcelain to be manufactured successfully was made about 1825 by William Ellis Tucker at the American China Manufactory at the southwest corner of Sixth and Chestnut streets, Philadelphia, PA.

3356. Stained-glass window was made in 1844 by William Jay Bolton and John Bolton for Christ Church, Pelham Manor, NY. It depicted the Adoration of the Magi, over which was the legend "Behold the Lamb of God, which taketh away the sins of the world." It was placed in a window above the altar.

3357. Plate glass was manufactured about 1853 by James N. Richmond in the factory that he established in 1850 in Cheshire, MA, for the production of window glass. The plate glass was about half an inch thick and sold for 50 cents a square foot. To make 600 square feet of glass—one day's work—required 2,800 pounds of sand, 500 pounds of soda ash, and 800 pounds of lime. The factory operated about nine months a year until 1856, when it went out of business.

3358. Pottery to make sanitary ware was founded in Trenton, NJ, in 1853 by Milington and Astbury. On April 4, 1873, they consolidated with Thomas Maddock and Sons.

3359. Plate glass produced on a large scale was manufactured in 1883 by the New York City Plate Glass Company in Creighton, PA. The company was capitalized for $600,000 but was refinanced a few months later, when its name was changed to the Pittsburgh Plate Glass Company.

3360. Wire glass was invented by Frank Schuman of Philadelphia, PA, in 1892. He obtained a patent on September 20, 1892. While the glass was still malleable, he pressed a wire netting into it, smoothing the abrased surface. This glass was better able to withstand heat and shattering than was plain glass.

3361. Glass-blowing machine was patented on February 26, 1895, by Michael Joseph Owens of Toledo, OH. It operated five molds that circulated around the machine, each one surrounding the melted glass, which was placed in its proper position on the end of a pipe and simultaneously revolved so as to make a perfect article without seams or roughness.

3362. Cut glass made from pressed blanks was manufactured in 1902 by Henry Clay Fry, who organized the H.C. Fry Glass Company, Rochester, PA. The glass was pressed into a mold, the marks of the iron plunger remaining on the inside of the glass. Previously, cut glass had been blown.

3363. Heat-resistant glass was Pyrex, developed at the Corning Glass Works factory in Corning, NY, by researchers Eugene C. Sullivan and William C. Taylor. Boric acid added to the glass formula made it more resistant to thermal shock than ordinary glass. Pyrex was patented by Corning in 1915. It was used in laboratory glassware, cookware, and chemical manufacturing.

3364. Glass that was nonreflecting was developed by Katherine Burr Blodgett, a researcher at the General Electric laboratory in Schenectady, NY. Blodgett discovered that transparent glass coated with a gelatinous film one molecule thick would not reflect light and was therefore virtually invisible. She also invented a gauge that used gelatin-film technology to measure extremely thin substances with a precision of less than 0.000001 inches. Although Blodgett had developed the technology in 1933, the discovery was not announced by GE until December 1938, a few days before a similar discovery was announced by the Massachusetts Institute of Technology in Cambridge, MA.

3365. Invisible-glass installation was made in September 1935 at Marcus and Company, New York City. The glass window was bent at several different radius points. Mirrors flanked the window opening. The glass was covered by a patent granted on May 30, 1933, to Gerald Brown of London on a "means for nullifying or reducing window reflections," and another granted on June 4, 1935, to Gerald Brown and Edward Pollard of London on a "display window."

3366. Photosensitive glass was made in November 1937 by the Corning Glass Works, Corning, NY, and announced publicly 10 years later, on June 1, 1947. It was a crystal-clear glass in which submicroscopic metallic particles could be formed by exposure to ultraviolet light and subsequent heat treatment. Exposure through photographic negatives permitted development of positive images within the glass in a variety of colors, forming an image as permanent as the glass itself.

3367. Fiberglass and the machinery for its manufacture was invented by James Slayter and John H. Thomas of Newark, OH, who obtained four patents on October 11, 1938. On November 1, 1938, the Owens-Corning Fiberglas Corporation was founded by the Owens-Illinois Glass Company and the Corning Glass Works to market the product, used extensively for industrial equipment and building insulation. Fiberglass is also known as glass wool and spun glass.

Mining and Minerals

3368. Lead was mined and smelted in 1620 near Falling Creek, VA, to supply the local demand for bullets and shot at the Jamestown colony. Mining operations ceased after John Berkeley and 20 workmen were killed by Native Americans in May 1622.

3369. Lime was manufactured on January 27, 1662, in Providence, RI. Thomas Hackelton was granted liberty by the town to burn lime at a certain place on the commons. On October 27, 1665, the town ordered that the lime rocks about the limekiln should remain in common ownership.

3370. Copper mine known to have been worked was the Simsbury mine at Granby, CT, with a history dating back to 1705. A company to mine the ore was formed in 1709 by the younger John Winthrop and was the first mining company chartered in America. The mine was also known as the Granby mine and was worked for several years by convicts in the Newgate prison established there. In 1737 the copper obtained from this mine was used in the manufacture of the "Granby coppers," among the earliest colonial coins minted. The mine was worked at intervals until 1773.

3371. Gem-cutting machine was invented by Abel Buell of Killingworth, CT, in 1766. He claimed that his "method of grinding and polishing crystals and other stones of great value, all the growth of the Colony" would effect a great saving in money. The machine was called a lapidary.

3372. Marble quarry was operated in 1785 by Isaac Underhill on land owned by Reuben Bloomer in Dorset, VT. The quarry was first worked for stone for fire jambs, chimney backs, hearths, and lintels. A quarry was also opened in Rutland, VT, in 1785. Marble used before 1785 was obtained from exposed marble ledges.

3373. Jewelers' supply house of importance was established in 1794 by Nehemiah Dodge, silversmith, goldsmith, and watch repairer, in a shop on North Main Street, Providence, RI. In addition to his retail business, he sold gold plate made of a thin sheet of gold united with a thicker sheet of copper to manufacturing jewelers.

3374. Gold nugget was found in the Reed Mine, Cabarrus County, North Carolina, in 1799. For several years its nature was not known. The nugget was the size of a "small smoothing iron." Later another was found there that weighed 28 pounds. Gold in limited quantities had been discovered elsewhere, however. In 1782, Thomas Jefferson described a lump of ore of about four pounds, found four miles below the falls on the north side of the Rappahannock River in Virginia, that yielded 17 pennyweight of gold.

3375. Mica was obtained from the Ruggles mine, Isinglass Mountain, Grafton, NH, in 1803.

3376. Tungsten and tellurium were found in 1819 in a bismuth mine in Huntington, CT. The mine was owned by Ephraim Lane. Tungsten, a ferruginous metal known to mineralogists as wolfram, was found in the state of yellow oxide. Tellurium was found in the metallic state.

3377. Granite was quarried in Quincy, MA, in 1820 for the Bunker Hill Monument in Boston. About 9,000 tons in blocks 2.5 inches square and 12 feet long were transported by the Granite Railway Company from the Quincy quarry to the wharf at Charlestown, MA.

3378. Stone breaking machine was patented on April 13, 1831, by Benjamin F. Lodge and Ezekial T. Cox of Zanesville, OH.

3379. Zinc was produced in 1835–36 by John Hitz in the Arsenal at Washington, DC.

3380. Fluorspar commercial mining was attempted in 1837 at Trumbull, CT. It was used with magnetic iron pyrite in the smelting of copper ores and sold for $60 a ton.

3381. Silver mine was the Silver Hill Mine, discovered in 1838 about 10 miles from Lexington, NC. The company was incorporated on January 7, 1839, for $500,000.

3382. Graphite was produced commercially in 1840 at Ticonderoga, NY, which became the center of the graphite industry of the United States. Graphite occurs in association with igneous and metamorphic rocks.

3383. Gold discovered in California was found near the San Fernando Mission in 1842, but no importance was attached to it. On January 24, 1848, James Wilson Marshall found a nugget on property owned by John Augustus Sutter in a millrace on a branch of the Sacramento River near Coloma, CA. This was the discovery that started the gold rush of the Forty-Niners to California.

3384. Zinc commercial production was undertaken at the Pennsylvania and Lehigh Zinc Company Mill, which was opened in Bethlehem, PA, on October 13, 1853, by Samuel Wetherill. The zinc was obtained from calamine ores. Wetherill received patents on February 20, 1855, for an apparatus for separating zinc white; on November 13, 1855, for the process of making zinc white; on September 30, 1856, for a zinc white furnace; on January 6, 1857, for a process of reducing zinc ore; and on January 7, 1868, for the process of manufacturing white oxide of zinc.

3385. Borax was discovered by Dr. John A. Veatch, January 8, 1856, in mineral water from Tuscan Springs, Tehama County, CA. Commercial production began at Borax Lake, Lake County, CA, in 1864, when pure crystals were refined by immersion in solution and permitted to crystallize out again, thus disposing of an apparently very minute amount

A GOLD HUNTER ON HIS WAY TO CALIFORNIA, VIA, ST LOUIS.

Library of Congress, Prints & Photographs Division
LC-USZ62-760

A gold hunter on his way to California.

of impurities. This deposit supplied the United States until 1868, when larger deposits were found in Nevada.

3386. **Stone crusher** of value was built by Eli Whitney Blake of New Haven, CT, who obtained a patent on June 15, 1858, on an "improvement in machines for crushing stones." Blake's stone crusher had upright convergent jaws, one fixed and one movable. The stones descended by gravity into pits and were sorted by screens. The device was first used in 1859 in Hartford, CT, on a road construction job.

3387. **Sulfur deposit** was discovered in 1869 in a salt dome in Calcasieu Parish, LA. It was later developed as the Sulphur Dome of the Union Sulphur Company. Sulfur was first extracted from a well in the dome in October 1895 by Herman Frasch of Cleveland, OH. On October 20, 1891, he received two patents on "mining sulphur" and a third on "an apparatus for mining sulphur." Sulfur was melted in the ground and pumped to the surface in a liquid state to congeal in bins or blocks.

3388. **Fuller's earth** was imported in 1878 and used for refining edible oils and petroleum. A deposit of fuller's earth (also called bentonite) was discovered by John Olson in 1891 in Benton, AR. A claylike substance, it was used in cleansing (fulling) cloth, wool, and fur, and later in the bleaching, clarifying, and filtering of fats, greases, and oils.

3389. **Mineral segregation by oil flotation** was patented in 1886 by Carrie J. Everson, a Colorado schoolteacher. Her method, which was adopted by miners throughout the West, separated precious metals from rocky ore by running them through a bath of oily water. The particles of dross floated, but the particles of gold, silver, and copper sank.

3390. **Bauxite** was discovered in 1887 at a point a few miles northeast of Rome, Floyd County, GA. A few fragments of the unknown mineral were picked up on the Holland lot two miles north of the Ridge Valley Iron Company's furnace at Hermitage, GA. Bauxite mining began in April 1888, when the deposits on the Holland property were first opened and worked. The first shipments of the ore were made in May 1888 to the Pennsylvania Salt Company, Natrona, PA, and to Greenwich Point, PA. This ore is said to have been used for the manufacture of both alum and metallic aluminum.

3391. **Carborundum** was invented by Edward Goodrich Acheson in 1891 in Monongahela City, PA, as an abrasive to be used in place of emery, corundum, and other similar materials. By running a current of electricity through a mixture of silica and carbon, Acheson obtained a material hard enough for rough-polishing diamonds, rubies, sapphires, and other precious and semiprecious stones. He obtained a patent on February 28, 1893, on the production of artificial crystalline carbonaceous materials. The first sale of this material was 10 carats at the rate of 40 cents a carat or $880 a pound.

3392. **Diamonds in a meteorite** were found in June 1891 by Dr. George Augustus Koenig, professor of mineralogy and geology at the University of Pennsylvania, Philadelphia, PA, while cutting a meteorite found at Canon Diablo, AZ. In various cavities he found small black diamonds of little commercial value which cut through polished corundum.

3393. **Gold leaf** in roll form was patented on April 5, 1892, by Walter Hamilton Coe of Providence, RI. It was made by the W.H. Coe Manufacturing Company of Providence in rolls 67 feet in length and 0.00250 inches thick, varying in width from 0.06 inches to 3.75 inches.

3394. **Diamonds in actual rock** were found in peridotite on August 1, 1906, by John W. Huddleson at Murfreesboro, Pike County, AR. He found two diamonds, each weighing about three carats.

3395. **Ductile tungsten** was produced in 1908 by Dr. William David Coolidge of the General Electric Company, Schenectady, NY, who used high temperatures to draw the tungsten into fine filaments for incandescent lamps. Coolidge reported his findings in the issue of May 17, 1910, of the *Journal of the American Institute of Electrical Engineers* and obtained a patent on December 30, 1913, on "tungsten and method of making the same, for use as filaments of incandescent electric lamps."

3396. **Taconite production** was undertaken in November 1919 by the Mesabi Iron Company, Babbitt, MN. The first cargo, of 5,076 tons, was shipped on October 1 to the Ford Motor Company, River Rouge, MI. Taconite is a hard ferruginous rock containing 25 percent to 30 percent iron. The first large-scale commercial production was begun on September 13, 1956, by the E.W. Davis Works at Silver Bay, MN, built by the Reserve Mining Company, Duluth, MN, and owned jointly by the Armco Steel Corporation and the Republic Steel Corporation. Its capacity was rated at 3.75 million tons of iron ore pellets annually. The rock was crushed, ground, and processed by magnetic separation, producing small pellets containing 62.5 percent iron.

3397. Magnesium commercially produced from seawater was extracted on January 21, 1941, by the Dow Chemical Company, Freeport, TX. It sold for approximately 23 cents a pound.

3398. Synthetic mica was produced commercially by the Synthetic Mica Corporation, Caldwell Township, NJ, and offered for sale on May 17, 1956, under the trade name of Synthamica. It was a chemically pure synthetic fluorphlogopite mica capable of withstanding sustained temperatures as high as 2000 degrees F without physical or electrical failure. Research on synthetic mica was begun in 1947 by the Bureau of Mines in Norris, TN.

3399. Sulfur mine offshore was the Grand Isle offshore mine, 2,000 feet beneath the bottom of the Gulf of Mexico, about seven miles off the Louisiana coast. The mine was operated by means of a steel structure equipped with boilers, generators, and drilling rigs and situated in 50 feet of water. The deposit was discovered by the Humble Oil and Refining Company and the mine was built and operated by the Freeport Sulphur Company. The first sulfur was obtained on March 14, 1960.

3400. Mineral found on the moon before it was found on Earth was armalcolite, a member of the pseudobrookite group of minerals. It was discovered on July 20, 1969, by the astronauts of the *Apollo 11* mission and was named in the honor, using the first letters of their last names (Neil Armstrong, Buzz Aldrin, and Michael Collins). Subsequently, it was found in Montana, South Africa, Greenland, and Ukraine.

Roads and Highways

3401. Road pavement was laid at Pemaquid, in what is now the state of Maine, in 1625. It was 33 feet wide and consisted of stones, rocks, and cobblestones.

3402. Road construction law enacted by a colony was passed by the Virginia legislature on September 4, 1632, at James City. It provided that "highways shall be layd out in such convenient places as are requisite accordinge as the Governor and Counsell or the Commissioners for the monthlie corts shall appoynt, or accordinge as the parishoners of every parish shall agree."

3403. Stone pavement was laid in New York City in 1657 on Brouwere (Brewer Street), the location of many breweries. On January 24, 1658, Isaaq de Foreest and Jieronimus Ebbingh were authorized to contract for paving stones and to assess payment from each house in the street. Cobblestones were used and the street was consequently known as Stone Street.

3404. Hard-surfaced road extended about 100 miles from the Pahaquarry Mines, NJ, to Kingston, NY, through Warren and Sussex counties in New Jersey It was completed by the Dutch in 1663.

Courtesy of NASA

Launch of Apollo 11.

3405. Toll road was the Little River Turnpike in Virginia, which led from Alexandria to Snicker's Gap (or Snigger's Gap), a pass through the Blue Ridge Mountains leading into the Shenandoah Valley in the northwest part of the state. The General Assembly in October 1785 appointed nine commissioners to erect a chain of toll gates on the turnpike. The receipts were to be applied to clearing and repairing this road and the road between Alexandria and Georgetown. The road was not surfaced and by 1795 was completely worn out.

3406. One-way street appears to have been arranged temporarily in New York City on December 17, 1791, when the audience at a performance at the John Street Theatre received the following request: "Ladies and Gentlemen will order their Coachmen to take up and set down with their Horse Heads to the East River, to avoid Confusion."

3407. Road authorization by a state was made by Kentucky on December 14, 1793, when Daniel Weisiger, Bennett Pemberton, and Nathaniel Sanders were appointed "commissioners to receive subscriptions in money, labor or property, to raise a fund for clearing a wagon road from Frankfort, KY, to Cincinnati, OH."

3408. Macadam road was the Lancaster Turnpike, 62 miles long, connecting Philadelphia and Lancaster, PA. Work was begun in February 1793 by the Philadelphia and Lancaster Turnpike Railroad Company, of which William Bingham was the first president. The road was completed in December 1795 at an approximate cost of $7,500 a mile, a total of $465,000, which was provided by individual investors. The first two miles of the road were surfaced with coarse gravel. The remainder was surfaced with "pounded" or broken stone. It was 24 feet in width, 18 inches deep in the center, and 12 inches deep at the edge. Since the angular crushed stone was hard on the feet of horses, a dirt road 13 feet wide was built alongside the main road, to be used in good weather.

3409. Road appropriation of a specific sum by a state was made by Kentucky on December 19, 1795, when $2,000 was appropriated for the purpose of opening a wagon road from Crab Orchard to Cumberland Gap.

3410. Land subsidy by Congress for road improvements was authorized on April 30, 1802, by "an act to enable the people of the eastern division of the territory northwest of the river Ohio to form a constitution and state government, and for the admission of such state into the union on an equal footing with the original states." It authorized Ohio to appropriate a twentieth of the net proceeds of the funds received from the sale of public lands to the laying out and construction of public roads.

3411. Highway built by the federal government with funds from the national treasury was the Great National Pike, also known as the Cumberland Road, built in sections from 1806 to 1840 between Cumberland, MD, and Vandalia, IL. The first appropriation, of $30,000, was made by congressional act of March 29, 1806, and the last was made on May 25, 1838. The total appropriation was $6,821,246. In 1856 the road was turned over to the states through which it passed. Some of the money obtained from the sale of public lands was appropriated for state road work.

3412. Overland wagon road across the Rocky Mountains to the Pacific coast was the Oregon Trail. It followed Native American and buffalo trails and was blazed by many, but it may be considered to date from 1842, when John Charles Frémont made a survey of it for the government prior to the great covered-wagon expeditions. The Oregon Trail began in Independence, MO, on the Missouri River, followed the Sante Fe trail for a short distance, then extended for some 2,000 miles across Missouri, Kansas, Nebraska, Wyoming, Idaho, and Oregon to Vancouver on the north side of the Columbia River, in what is now the state of Washington.

3413. Plank road was completed on July 18, 1846, by the Salina and Central Square Plank Road Company between Syracuse and Central Square, NY. Trenches were dug slightly below the level of the road and a single track of hemlock planks about four inches thick and eight feet long was placed at right angles to the road. The track was covered with dirt as protection against horses' hoofs.

3414. Divided road was Savery's Avenue, a half-mile dirt road in Carver, MA, which was built in 1861–62 and presented to the public by William Savery. Trees were left standing between the roads "for shade and ornament for man and beast." Both roads were paved with macadam in 1907.

3415. Brick pavement on a city streetwas laid in Charleston, WV, in 1870 by a private citizen at his own expense. In 1873, the city extended the paving to include several streets.

3416. Boardwalk was dedicated on June 26, 1870, at Atlantic City, NJ. To finance it, $5,000 was obtained by the sale, at a 10 percent discount, of scrip which could be used to pay taxes. The boardwalk was eight feet wide and a mile long. It was built in eight-foot collapsible sections, which for 18 years were removed in September and stored for the winter. The idea for the boardwalk was conceived by a hotel man, Jacob Keim of the Chester County House, and Alexander Boardman, a railroad conductor on the Camden and Atlantic Railroad.

3417. Road pavement of sheet asphalt was laid on William Street, Newark, NJ, on July 29, 1870, by Professor Edward Joseph De Smedt of the American Asphalt Pavement Company, New York City. It was known as French asphalt pavement. On May 31, 1870, De Smedt obtained two patents, which he assigned to the New York Improved Anthracite Coal Company.

3418. Concrete road was built in Bellefontaine, OH, in 1892 on the west side of Main Street. A strip 10 feet wide and 220 feet long was put down. In 1893–94 the remainder of Main Street was paved, together with Columbus, Opera, and Court streets, which together formed the four sides of the public square.

3419. Moving sidewalk was installed at the World's Columbian Exposition in Chicago, IL, in 1893 to convey passengers from one part of the fairgrounds to the other. It traveled at two speeds, three and six miles per hour, and accommodated 5,610 persons.

3420. Coast-to-coast paved road was the Lincoln Highway, a 3,300-mile highway stretching from New York City to San Francisco, CA, opened on September 10, 1913. It was originally proposed by Carl Graham Fisher. The highway traversed 13 states—New York, New Jersey, Pennsylvania, Ohio, Indiana, Illinois, Iowa, Nebraska, Colorado, Wyoming, Utah, Nevada, and California—and cost about $10 million. The first complete coast-to-coast run over the official route was made by Neil Patterson.

3421. Grant-in-aid enacted by Congress to help the states build roads was the Federal Aid Road Act, "to provide that the United States shall aid the states in the construction of rural post roads, and for other purposes," passed on July 11, 1916. For the fiscal year ending June 30, 1917, $5 million was appropriated, an amount that was increased by $5 million every year until 1921, when the appropriation was $25 million. The first project was in Contra Costa County, CA, for 2.55 miles between the Alameda-Contra Costa boundary and the city limits of Richmond, CA. The contract was awarded on July 10, 1916. The work cost $53,938, of which $24,247 came from the federal appropriation.

3422. Nationwide highway numbering system was adopted on March 2, 1925, by Joint Board of State and Federal Highway officials appointed by the secretary of agriculture. To eliminate confusion caused by the motley array of signs in various localities, the board adopted the familiar shield-shaped numbered marker.

3423. Traffic rotary was built in Pennsauken, NJ, and opened to the public on July 1, 1927. It was known as Airport Circle.

3424. Traffic cloverleaf opened in 1929 in Woodbridge, NJ, at the intersection of State Highways 25 and 4 (presently U.S. 1/9 and NJ-35).

3425. Mosaic pavement similar to the mosaics of the ancient world was laid on Canal Street, New Orleans, LA. The mosaic effect was secured by mixing chipped metronite, crown point spar, and mica with the cement, then pouring the mixture into diamond-shaped brass-stripped forms, sanding it down, and polishing it. The work was completed on February 4, 1930, and was part of the project referred to as the "Beautification of Canal Street."

3426. Nationwide highway planning surveys authorized by Congress were included in the Hayden-Cartwright Act, approved on June 18, 1934. The surveys were designed to obtain traffic volume, load weight, and other information needed for the rational planning of a nationwide system of interstate highways. They were made by the Bureau of Public Roads of the Department of Agriculture, in cooperation with state highway departments.

3427. Concrete highway median barrier was a two-foot-tall parabolic divider introduced by the California Division of Highways in the mid-1940s on U.S. Highway 99, near Bakersfield, CA, a major truck route.

3428. Electronic road system to guide and control cars was conceived by Dr. Vladimir Kosma Zworykin at the RCA Laboratories, David Sarnoff Research Center, Princeton, NJ. Demonstrations were given in June 1953 with a controlled miniature car and on June 3, 1960, with a standard automobile. Wire cables buried under the pavement conveyed impulses to electronic circles in the automobiles in order to reduce speed automatically and thus prevent collisions.

3429. Highway interchange structure with four levels was built in Los Angeles, CA, and connected the Hollywood, Harbor, Santa Ana, and Arroyo Seco (now Pasadena) freeways. All sections were opened and in operation on September 22, 1953.

3430. Toll collection machine was placed in service on November 19, 1954, at the Union Toll Plaza on the Garden State Parkway of New Jersey, in the Newark-Irvington-Union area. Motorists paid the 25-cent toll by depositing coins in a wire mesh hopper. A green light flashed when the money was received, and an audible alarm sounded if the motorist failed to pay. A machine that could provide correct change went into operation at the extreme right lane of each direction of traffic.

3431. Two-way moving sidewalk was placed in service on January 30, 1958, at Love Field Air Terminal, Dallas, TX. It consisted of three loops totaling 1,435 feet of moving walkway. In each loop a continuous rubber carpet was attached to an endless train of wheeled pallets, flexibly interconnected so that they could follow vertical or horizontal curves as required. The walk was also known as a passenger conveyor.

3432. Metric distance markers on a state highway were put up by the Ohio Department of Transportation, which began the erection of four signs on February 12, 1973, on Interstate 71 between Cincinnati and Columbus and between Columbus and Cleveland. The signs showed the distance in both miles and kilometers.

3433. Border-to-border national highway was Interstate 75, which extended 1,564 miles from Canada to the Gulf of Mexico. The final section was dedicated on December 22, 1977.

3434. State with electronic toll collection on its highways was Oklahoma, which started its PIKEPASS system on January 1, 1991. Drivers using the system were eligible to use special lanes at toll plazas through which they could drive at highway speeds. Their toll charges were registered by means of a device mounted on their windshields. These charges were automatically debited from funds they kept on deposit with the state. The system was installed by TransCore of Harrisburg, PA.

Tunnels

3435. Tunnel was built as part of the Schuylkill Navigation Company's canal above Auburn, PA, at the Orwigsburg landing. Job Samson and Solomon Fudge were the contractors. Construction began in 1818 and the tunnel was opened to traffic in 1821. Cut through red shale, it was 20 feet wide, 18 feet high from the canal bottom, and 450 feet long. It was arched for about 75 feet inward from each portal. It was shortened to half its length in 1834 and was shortened once more in 1845. In 1856 it was again shortened "until nothing remained but air."

3436. Mining tunnel on a large scale was started as early as 1824 by the Lehigh Navigation Company. This was the Hacklebernie anthracite coal mine tunnel near Mauch Chunk, PA. It was driven by hand using black powder. Work stopped in 1827, when 790 feet had been penetrated. The opening was 16 feet wide and eight feet high. In 1846, work was resumed and the length was extended to 2,000 feet.

3437. Railroad tunnel was built in 1831 near Johnstown, PA, by the Allegheny Portage Railroad, the first railroad to go west of the Allegheny Mountains. The tunnel, driven through slate, was 901 feet long, 25 feet wide, and 21 feet high. It was lined throughout with masonry 18 inches thick. Construction began on April 12, 1831, and was completed on March 18, 1834. The segmented tunnel extended from Hollidaysburg to Johnstown, PA, a distance of 36.6 miles. The engineer was Solomon White Roberts.

3438. Underwater highway tunnel was the Washington Street Tunnel beneath the Chicago River, Chicago, IL, authorized on July 17, 1866, by the Board of Public Works. Construction began on November 30, 1866, and ended in 1869. The total length of the tunnel and its approaches was 1,520 feet. The contract price was $328,500, but the final cost was $512,709. The tunnel had two roadways, each 11 feet high and 13 feet wide, and a separate footway 10 feet high and 10 feet wide. It was lowered in 1907 to provide a clear draft of 27 feet in the Chicago River.

3439. Water supply tunnel for a city was the Chicago Lake Tunnel, which extended 10,587 feet under Lake Michigan to an inlet crib. It was five feet in diameter. Ellis Sylvester Chesbrough was the city engineer at the time of construction. The contract was given to Dull and Gowan of Philadelphia, PA, who started work on March 17, 1864. The tunnel was completed on December 6, 1866, at a cost of $380,785, and was put into operation on March 25, 1867. The pumping station at the intersection of Michigan Boulevard and Chicago Avenue escaped the fire of 1871.

3440. Tunnel construction using compressed air took place in 1879. This method was introduced by Dewitt Clinton Haskin and was used in the construction of the famous Hudson River tunnel between Hoboken, NJ, and Morton Street, New York City. The tunnel plans called for two tubes, each 16 feet wide and 18 feet high. During the construction, on July 21, 1880, the compressed air blew a hole through the soft silt of the roof about 360 feet from the Hoboken shaft, flooding the tubes and drowning 20 workmen. Work was discontinued. The tunnel was not opened until February 25, 1908.

3441. Underwater railroad tunnel to a foreign country was the St. Clair Railway tunnel between Port Huron, MI, and Sarnia, Ontario, Canada, which was opened for freight traffic on September 19, 1891, and for passenger traffic on December 7. The tunnel was designed and built under the supervision of Joseph Hobson, chief engineer of the Grand Trunk Railway (later the Canadian National Railways), at a cost of $2.7 million. Its length from portal to portal was 6,025 feet. The tunnel was equipped with electricity on May 17, 1908.

3442. Underwater highway tunnel with twin tubes was the Holland Tunnel between New York City and Jersey City, NJ, beneath the Hudson River. Construction began on October 12, 1920. The tunnel, which was named for the chief engineer, Clifford Milburn Holland, consisted of two tubes 9,250 feet long, of which 5,480 feet passed under the river, and was designed to accommodate 1,900 motor vehicles an hour. The ventilation system changed the air 42 times an hour, at the rate of 3,761,000 cubic feet per minute. The tunnel was opened on November 12, 1927, by President Calvin Coolidge, who gave the signal from the presidential yacht *Mayflower* anchored in the Potomac River off Washington, DC. In that first hour, 20,000 people walked through the tunnel from shore to shore. Vehicular traffic was allowed through on November 13, 1927. On April 21, 1930, all operation was turned over to the Port of New York Authority as agent for the states of New York and New Jersey.

3443. Vehicular tunnel to a foreign country was the Detroit-Windsor tunnel under the Detroit River between Detroit, MI, and Windsor, Ontario, Canada. It was 50 feet below the river and 5,135 feet from portal to portal, 2,200 feet of which were under water. The formal opening of the tunnel took place on November 1, 1930. It was opened to the public on November 2 and opened for traffic on November 3. The capacity was 1,000 motor cars per hour each way.

3444. Tunnel with television monitors was Memorial Tunnel, a section of the West Virginia Turnpike near Standard, WV. Opened on November 8, 1954, it also featured interior lights and an exhaust system. It was 2,800 feet long. In 2000, the obsolete tunnel was used as the site of the Center for National Response, a training center for first responders.

GOVERNMENT AND POLITICS

3445. Colonial council was held in Jamestown, VA, on May 13, 1607. Its members were Bartholomew Gosnold, Edward Maria Wingfield, Christopher Newport, John Smith, John Ratcliffe, John Martin, and George Kendall. They had been selected for the council by King James I, who had placed their names in a sealed box that was not to be opened until the colonists sponsored by the London Company arrived in America. The council elected Wingfield as the first president.

3446. Colonial government federation was the United Colonies of New England, organized on May 10, 1643, in Boston, MA, by the colonies of Connecticut, Massachusetts, New Haven, and Plymouth as "a firm and perpetual league of friendship and amity for offence and defence, mutual advice and succor, upon all occasions, both for preserving and propagating the truth and liberties of the gospel, and for their own mutual safety and welfare." A board of eight commissioners, two from each colony, formed the "consociation." Issues could be referred to the general courts for appeal if not approved by six votes. John Winthrop of Massachusetts was the first president. Massachusetts, the largest colony, gradually withdrew because it did not have proportional representation.

3447. Colonial act of defiance against the King of England was the decision of the legislature of the Massachusetts Bay Colony to authorize the minting of coins. British coins were in short supply and coins of other nations varied widely in value, yet the Crown showed no interest in alleviating the colonists' coin shortage and refused to allow them to mint coins of their own. The General Court of Massachusetts on May 27, 1652, authorized John Hull, an entrepreneurial silversmith, to establish a mint in Boston where he would coin twelvepence, sixpence, and threepence pieces.

3448. Statehouse was a building on Duke of Gloucester Street, Williamsburg, VA, in which the General Assembly met. The building was erected in 1698 by Governor Francis Nicholson, who was the first person to apply the term "capitol" to a government building.

3449. Independent civil government in America was the Watauga Commonwealth, an independent civil government. By the treaty of Fort Stanwix in 1768, the Six Nations confederacy of Native American tribes agreed to surrender all the lands between the Ohio and Tennessee rivers to the British. Inasmuch as there was some misunderstanding because the Iroquois had ceded land to which they had no legal right, the settlers organized a civil government of their own in May 1772 and drew up the "Articles of the Watauga Association," the first written constitution ever adopted by a community of American-born freemen. The settlers elected a representative assembly of 13 men, which in turn elected a committee of 5—John Sevier, James Robertson, Charles Robertson, Zachariah Isbell, and John Carter—who were vested with judicial and executive authority. This was the first free and independent community established on the American continent. The area was in North Carolina and the mountains of Tennessee.

3450. Independent government in an American colony was formed in March 1776 in Charleston, SC. John Rutledge was elected president, Henry Laurens vice president, and William Henry Drayton chief justice. An army and navy were created, a privy council and an assembly were elected, and the issue of $600,000 of paper money was authorized, as well as the issue of coin.

3451. Government on the Pacific Coast was authorized by the people of Willamette Valley at Champoeg, OR, on May 2, 1843, when American and Canadian residents met in a field to consider the report of an organizational committee that had been appointed the previous month. A committee of nine was chosen on July 5, 1843, to devise a plan of civil government. The first governor was George Abernethy, who served from June 12, 1845, to March 3, 1849, when the United States took over jurisdiction of the Oregon territory.

Americana

3452. Letter containing a description of America was probably written by the explorer Christopher Columbus, who sailed on August 3, 1492, from the harbor of Palos, Spain, with three small caravels and about 90 men, and returned 224 days later, on March 14, 1493, to Lisbon, Portugal. From Lisbon, he dispatched two letters of identical content, one to Raphael Sanchez and the other to Luis de Santangel.

Library of Congress, Prints & Photographs Division, LC-USZ62-1784

Christopher Columbus

3453. Use of "America" as a geographical designation was made by the German mapmaker Martin H. Waldseemüller, also called Ilacomilus or Hylacomylus, in his book *Cosmographiae Introductio*, published in April 1507 at St. Dié in the Vosges Mountains of Alsace. The book contained an account by the Italian explorer Amerigo Vespucci of his discoveries in South America. Waldseemüller coined the name in his honor.

3454. Letters written in English in America are claimed to be the four letters of Ralph Lane, the first commander of Raleigh's first colony at Roanoke Island, NC. The letters were written on August 12, 1585, from Porte Ferdynando. They were not published until 1860.

3455. Constitution to declare that "the foundation of authority is in the free consent of the people" was the first constitution of colonial Connecticut, known as the "fundamental orders," drawn up by Roger Ludlow and adopted on January 14, 1639, in Hartford, CT, by representatives of Wethersfield, Windsor, and Hartford. Ludlow was influenced by a sermon delivered May 31, 1638, by the Reverend Thomas Hooker at Hartford's Center Church.

3456. Document known to have been printed in America was the "Oath of a Free Man," printed in March 1639 by the Stephen Day Press, Cambridge, MA. It was a one-page sheet that read: "I doe solemnly bind myself in the sight of God, that when I shall be called to give my voice touching any subject of this State, in which Freemen are to deal, I will give my vote and suffrage as I shall judge in mine own conscience may best conduce and tend to the publick weal of the body, without respect of persons, or favour of any man."

3457. Written constitution adopted by a community of American-born freemen is known as the "Articles of the Watauga Association." It was written in May 1772 by colonists from North Carolina and Tennessee who formed an independent civil government called the Watauga Commonwealth.

3458. Declaration of independence by citizens of an American colony was formally made on July 12, 1774, in the First Presbyterian Church in Carlisle, PA, at a meeting of freeholders and freemen from the several townships. The Reverend John Montgomery presided. A similar statement was the Mecklenburg Declaration of Independence, adopted by local citizens on May 20, 1775, in Charlotte, Mecklenburg County, NC.

3459. Declaration of rights was passed by the First Continental Congress in Philadelphia, PA, on October 14, 1774, and was known as the "Declaration and Resolves of the First Continental Congress." It stated that the the colonists "are entitled to life, liberty and property; and they have never ceded to any foreign power whatsoever a right to dispose of either without their consent."

3460. State constitution was that of Massachusetts, adopted on May 16, 1775, by the Provincial Congress of Massachusetts. The motto of the state was *Ense petit placidam sub libertate quietem* ("with the sword she seeks peace under liberty"). The constitution was temporary. A new one was framed in Boston on September 1, 1779, and was completed on March 2, 1780, and ratified by a two-thirds vote.

3461. Declaration of independence by a colonial government was made on April 12, 1776, when the Provincial Congress in session at Halifax, NC, by unanimous action empowered the delegates to the Continental Congress to concur with delegates of other provinces in declaring independence from Great Britain.

3462. Congressional vote on a declaration of independence took place in Philadelphia, PA, on July 1, 1776, after the delegates, meeting as a committee, debated a resolution that had been introduced on June 7 by Richard Henry Lee of Virginia and seconded by John Adams of Massachusetts. The motion was carried, but not unanimously; negative votes were cast by Pennsylvania, South Carolina, and some of the delegates from Delaware. On the following day, Congress, meeting in formal session, took a second vote, with 12 states in favor, one abstaining, and none opposed. The delegates then debated the document written by Thomas Jefferson, which they adopted, with amendations, on July 4.

3463. Design for the Great Seal of the United States was entrusted by the Continental Congress on July 4, 1776, to a committee consisting of Benjamin Franklin, Thomas Jefferson, and John Adams. Franklin suggested an image from the Bible showing the triumph of Moses over Pharaoh at the Red Sea, with the motto "Rebellion to Tyrants is Obedience to God." Jefferson suggested an image of the Israelites following the Pillar of Cloud and the Pillar of Fire through the wil-

Library of Congress, Prints & Photographs Division, LC-USZ62-3736

The signing of the Declaration of Independence, July 4, 1776, as rendered by John Trumbull.

derness. Adams preferred an engraving of "The Judgment of Hercules," a story from Xenophon.

The design that was ultimately accepted for the federal seal was made by Charles Thomson and adopted on June 20, 1782. It shows a spread eagle, bearing on its breast a shield with 13 red and white stripes, with an olive branch in its right talon and 13 arrows in its left. In its beak is a ribbon bearing the legend E PLURIBUS UNUM ("from many, one"). Over its head, a golden light breaks through a cloud surrounding 13 stars that form a constellation on a blue field.

3464. Signer of the Declaration of Independence was John Hancock of Massachusetts, president of the Continental Congress, who signed it on July 4, 1776, in Philadelphia, PA. It was also signed by secretary Charles Thomson, who was not a delegate. The parchment copy was signed by the delegates on August 2, 1776.

3465. Printing of the Declaration of Independence was done on July 5, 1776, in Philadelphia, PA, by John Dunlop in a folio broadside and distributed the same day. On July 4, Congress, acting as a Committee of the Whole, approved the Declaration and ordered that it be printed and that copies be "sent to the several assemblies, conventions and committees or counsels of safety and to the several commanding officers of the Continental troops that it be proclaimed in each of the United States and at the head of the army."

3466. Newspaper to publish the Declaration of Independence was the *Pennsylvania Evening Post* of Philadelphia, PA, which printed the text in its edition of July 6, 1776.

3467. Public reading of the Declaration of Independence took place on July 8, 1776, when Colonel John Nixon, delegated by the high sheriff of Philadelphia, read it in the old State House yard (now Independence Square). The "Liberty Bell," which bore the biblical inscription "Proclaim liberty throughout all the land unto all the inhabitants thereof," was rung to call the citizens together to hear the reading.

3468. Publication of the Declaration of Independence in another language took place in Philadelphia, PA, on July 9, 1776, when a translation of the Declaration was published in the *Staatsbote*, a German-language newspaper.

3469. Use of the name United States instead of United Colonies was authorized on September 9, 1776, by the Second Continental Congress: "That in all continental commissions and other instruments where heretofore the words, 'United Colonies' have been used, the style be altered, for the future, to the 'United States.'" The colonies were first definitely proclaimed to be united in a resolution adopted by the Second Continental Congress on June 7, 1775: "On motion, resolved, that Thursday, the 20th of July next, be observed throughout the Twelve United Colonies as a day of humiliation, fasting and prayer." Only 12 of the 13 colonies were represented because Georgia did not send delegates to the First and Second Continental Congresses.

3470. American flag saluted by a foreigner was the Continental Union flag flown by the brig *Andrea Doria* at St. Eustatius, Dutch West Indies, on November 16, 1776. It was saluted by Johannes de Graeff, governor of the colony. The brig was captained by Nicholas Biddle, who had been sent to St. Eustatius to transport arms and ammunition for the American army.

3471. American flag to represent the United States was formally adopted as the National Standard by Congress on June 14, 1777. Except for the adding of a new star for each new state and changes in the arrangement of the stars, the flag displayed today is the same as the first flag. Claims have been made that the first flag was made by Betsy Ross (Elizabeth Griscom Ross) in her little shop at 239 Arch Street, Philadelphia, PA, at the request of George Washington, Robert Morris, and Colonel George Ross, for the Continental Congress.

3472. American flag displayed on a man-of-war was flown in Portsmouth Harbor, NH, when a group of young women presented to Captain John Paul Jones a flag they had made, using cloth taken from their own and their mothers' gowns. Captain Jones raised it to the mast of his ship, the *Ranger*, on July 4, 1777.

3473. American flag flown in battle was carried on September 3, 1777, by a detachment of light infantry and cavalry under General William Maxwell at Cooch's Bridge, DE, where they met an advance guard of British and Hessian troops under Generals Richard Howe, Charles Cornwallis, and Wilhelm von Knyphausen.

3474. American flag on the high seas was carried by Captain Thomas Thompson of the American sloop *Raleigh,* who, on September 4, 1777, engaged in an encounter with a British vessel.

3475. American flag saluted by a foreign nation was flown from the top mast of the *Ranger*, under the command of Captain John Paul Jones. The *Ranger* sailed for France on November 1, 1777, with dispatches announcing the surrender of British general John Burgoyne. On February 14, 1778, the *Ranger* saluted the French flag in the harbor of Quiberon, France, with 13 guns. The salute was returned by Admiral La Motte Piquet with nine guns, the same salute authorized by the French court to be given in honor of an admiral of Holland or of any other republic.

3476. Articles of Confederation were adopted on November 15, 1777, and were formally engrossed on July 9, 1778, in Philadelphia, PA. South Carolina was the first of the 13 states to ratify them, on February 5, 1778, and Maryland was the last, on January 30, 1781. The articles were formally announced to the public on March 1, 1781.

3477. Seal of a military department of the federal government was the seal of the Board of Admiralty, which was in charge of the Continental Navy. On May 4, 1780, the Continental Congress adopted a seal that showed a chevron of alternating red and white bars on a field of blue, with an anchor below it and a sailing ship atop it. At the bottom was the motto *Sustentans et Sustentatus* ("Sustaining and Sustained"). Around the circumference was the legend *U.S.A. Sigil. Naval,* "Seal of the Navy of the United States of America." The Navy Department, which was founded in 1798, 13 years after the Continental Navy was disbanded, used a different seal.

3478. Die for the Great Seal of the United States was cut from brass sometime between June and September 1782 and showed the obverse of the seal. The engraver may have been Robert Scot of Philadelphia. Though the designers intended the seal to show a bald eagle, the die portrayed a crested eagle. In 1841, this die was replaced with a steel die whose engraver mistakenly reduced the number of arrows from 13 to six and had five-pointed stars instead of the intended six-pointed stars. These irregularities were not fixed until 1885, when James Horton Whitehouse of Tiffany & Co. designed a new die, the one on which the current seal is based.

3479. Keeper of the Great Seal of the United States was Charles Thomson, secretary of the Continental Congress, who had helped design the seal. He was in charge of it from September 1782, when it was adopted by Congress, until 1789, when Thomas Jefferson, head of the newly formed Department of State, took possession of it.

3480. Impression made by the Great Seal of the United States was made on September 16, 1782, on the upper left corner of a document authorizing General George Washington to negotiate and sign an agreement with the British for the exchange, subsistence, and better treatment of prisoners of war. The document bore the signatures of John Hanson, president of the Continental Congress, and Charles Thomson, secretary.

3481. Illustrations of both sides of the Great Seal of the United States were engravings made by a Philadelphia artist, James Trenchard. His engraving of the obverse side of the seal (the eagle side) appeared in *The Columbian Magazine* in September 1786. His engraving of the reverse (the pyramid side) appeared in the same magazine in October. No actual die of the reverse side had ever been cut, so Trenchard's drawing was based on the written description approved by Congress. When the Great Seal Centennial Medal was struck in 1882, Trenchard's engraving of the reverse was used as the model.

The creation of the 1882 Great Seal Centennial Medal marked the first time that the federal government required both sides of the seal to be imprinted. When the seal is impressed on treaties and other documents, only the obverse is visible.

3482. Printed copies of the Constitution were printed from plates engraved by Jacob Shallus, assistant clerk of the Pennsylvania Assembly, who received $30 for the work. Sixty proof sheets were printed August 1–3, 1787, and laid before the Constitutional Convention on August 6.

3483. Constitution of the United States was signed at the conclusion of the Constitutional Convention, which met at Philadelphia, PA, from May 25, 1787, to September 17. Of the original 55 delegates, only 41 remained to the conclusion, and three of them refused to sign. It was agreed that the Constitution would become binding on the 13 former colonies when it was ratified by nine states. This took place on June 21, 1788, when the legislature of New Hampshire approved ratification by a 57–47 vote. The Constitution was declared to be in effect on March 4, 1789.

3484. Newspaper to publish the Constitution was the *Pennsylvania Packet and Daily Advertiser*, Philadelphia, PA, published by John Dunlap and David C. Claypoole. The text of the Constitution was published in the issue dated September 19, 1787.

3485. Ship to carry the American flag around the world was the *Columbia*, a 212-ton vessel under Captain Kendrick that sailed from Boston, MA, on September 30, 1787, on a fur-trading mission to Canada. It was accompanied by the sloop *Washington*, under Captain Robert Gray, who exchanged commands with Captain Kendrick and completed the trip, returning to Boston on August 9, 1790. The trip took nearly three years and covered a distance of 41,899 miles. The crew explored the Queen Charlotte Islands and discovered the straits of Juan de Fuca and the mouth of the Columbia River.

3486. Federalist Paper was printed in the *New York Independent Journal* on October 27, 1787. The author, writing under the pseudonym Publius, was Alexander Hamilton. Over the next 10 months, 85 essays were published under the name Publius in New York newspapers, most of them by Hamilton, others by James Madison and John Jay. Their aim was to persuade the public that ratification of the Constitution and the advent of a strong central government were essential to the success of the American political experiment.

3487. State to ratify the federal Constitution was Delaware, on December 6, 1787. The constitution was ratified on December 6 and signed on December 7 by all 30 members of the Constitutional Convention.

3488. Seal of a nonmilitary department of the federal government was the seal of the Treasury Department. It was adopted in 1789, when the future department was the Board of Treasury under the Articles of Confederation. The seal, probably designed by Francis Hopkinson, showed a golden shield bearing a pair of balanced scales, a chevron bearing 13 stars, and a key. Around the circumference was the Latin phrase *Thesauri Americae Septentrionalist Sigillum*, abbreviated as *Thesaur. Amer. Septent. Sigil.*, meaning "the seal of the treasury of North America." In 1968, when the design was modernized, the phrase "The Department of the Treasury, 1789," was substituted for the Latin legend.

3489. Constitutional amendments to fail the ratification process were the first two of 12 proposed articles of amendment that were adopted by Congress and submitted to the states on September 25, 1789. The remaining 10 articles were ratified by the states and enacted into law on December 15, 1791, as the Bill of Rights. Article I, if ratified, would have established a minimum of 200 congressional representatives and a maximum of one for every 50,000 persons. Article II, if ratified, would have prevented Congress from voting midterm pay raises for its own members. Article II was resubmitted to the states nearly two centuries later, was declared ratified on May 7, 1992, and was incorporated into the Constitution as the 27th Amendment. Its text reads: "No law varying the compensation for the services of the Senators and Representatives shall take effect until an election of Representatives shall have intervened.

3490. Constitutional amendments to be ratified were declared in force on December 15, 1791, having been passed by both houses of Congress and ratified by the required number of states. These 10 amendments, drawn up by James Madison, are collectively known as the Bill of Rights. The first of them established religious freedom, freedom of speech and press, the right to assemble, and the right to petition the government. The amendments were submitted to the states by the First Congress on September 25, 1789. The first state to ratify was New Jersey, which acted on November 20, 1789. Originally 12 amendments were passed by both houses, but two of them—on the proportionment of representatives and on compensation—failed to secure the requisite number of state ratifications.

3491. Changes in the American flag to be authorized by Congress were passed by Congress on January 13, 1794, an "act making an alteration in the flag of the United States" and providing "that from and after the first day of May 1795, the Flag of the United States be fifteen stripes, alternate red and white; and that the union be fifteen stars, white, in a blue field." The change was made so that Vermont and Kentucky would be represented on the flag. A law passed on April 4, 1818, reduced the number of stripes to 13 to represent the original 13 states, as in the first American flag, and provided one star for each state. A new star was to be added on the Fourth of July following the admission of each new state.

3492. American flag flown over conquered hostile territory was flown on April 27, 1805, when Lieutenant Presley Neville O'Bannon of the Marines raised the colors over the Tripolitan fortress at Derna, on the north coast of Africa (now in Libya). The American attack on the fortress was part of a successful plan to recue the crew of the USS *Philadelphia*, who had been imprisoned there by the Pasha of Tripoli.

3493. American flag flown over a schoolhouse was flown in May 1812 over the log schoolhouse at Catamount Hill, Colrain, MA. It was cut and made by Rhoda Shippee, Mrs. Lois Shippee, Mrs. Sophia Willis, and Mrs. Stephen Hale at the home of Captain Amasa Shippee, who instructed the women in the arrangement of the stars and stripes.

3494. Star-Spangled Banner was sewn in the first two weeks of September 1814, during the War of 1812, by Mary Young Pickersgill, a seamstress in Baltimore, MD, with the assistance of her daughter and two nieces. The commission came from Commodore Joshua Barney and Brigadier General John Strickland of nearby Fort McHenry, who ordered a giant flag that would be visible to the British in Chesapeake Bay. Mrs. Pickersgill's flag, made from more than 400 yards of wool bunting, measured 30 feet by 42 feet. It was flying above Fort McHenry on September 13, 1814, when 16 British warships began a bombardment that lasted until dawn the following

Library of Congress, Prints & Photographs Division, LC-USZC4-2705

Bombardment of Tripoli.

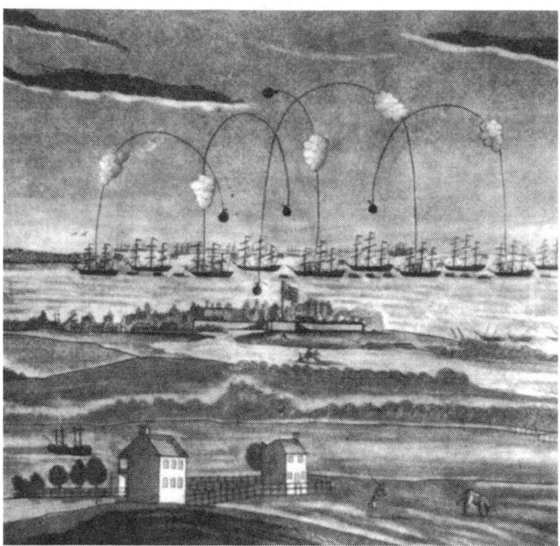

Library of Congress, Prints & Photographs Division
LC-USZ62-61

Fort McHenry

day but failed to dislodge the Americans. This episode, witnessed by a young American lawyer, Francis Scott Key, was the inspiration for his poem "The Defense of Fort McHenry," which was later set to music as "The Star-Spangled Banner" and adopted as the national anthem. Mrs. Pickersgill was paid $405.90 for her work on the flag, which is now on display at the National Museum of American History of the Smithsonian Institution in Washington, DC.

3495. Constitutional amendment proposal to bear the signature of a president was an amendment that would have prevented Congress from banning or regulating slavery in the states. It was signed by President Abraham Lincoln on March 2, 1861, in the hope of averting a civil war. It read: "No amendment shall be made to the Consitution which will authorize or give to Congress, the power to abolish or interfere, within any State, with the domestic institutions thereof, including that of persons held to labor or service by the laws of said State." The proposal was not ratified.

3496. Battle flag was that of the Confederate Army, adopted on March 4, 1861, by the Confederate Convention in Montgomery, AL. It set a blue St. Andrew's Cross and 13 stars against a red field. The battle flag was adopted after the Battle of Bull Run (July 16–21, 1861), in which soldiers were confused by the similarities between the Confederate flag, which consisted of seven stars and three stripes, and the stars and stripes of the Union flag.

3497. Construction of the Statue of Liberty on site at Bedloe's Island (now Liberty Island) in New York Harbor began in May 1886. The disassembled statue had arrived from France on June 19, 1885, packed in 214 wooden crates. It took six months to assemble the huge copper statue on its massive base. The Statue of Liberty was unveiled for public view on October 28, 1886. The bronze plaque with Emma Lazarus's poem "The New Colossus" was not added until 1903.

3498. Dedication ceremony for the Statue of Liberty took place on October 28, 1886, at Bedloe's Island (now Liberty Island) in New York Harbor. Twenty thousand people headed for the Battery in a ticker-tape parade, the first ever held. The harbor was crowded with ships of the United States and France. The festivities were attended by President Grover Cleveland, French prime minister Jules Ferry, and sculptor Frédéric-Auguste Bartholdi, who waited in

Library of Congress, Prints & Photographs Division
LC-DIG-ppmsca-02957

The colossal hand and torch of "Liberty."

the head of the statue. At a signal from a boy on the ground, Bartholdi was to pull a rope that would drop the huge French flag that veiled her face. The boy's cue was the completion of a speech by Senator William M. Evarts, known to be exceptionally long-winded. Evarts began, paused to take a breath, and the boy signaled Bartholdi, who dropped the flag, setting off a thunderous cacophony of cannon blasts, whistles, shouts, and applause.

3499. Salute to the flag by schoolchildren was the American Patriotic Salute, created by Civil War veteran Colonel George T. Balch and introduced on Flag Day, June 14, 1889, at the New York City free kindergarten of which he was the founder and director. It ran: "We give our heads and our hearts to God and our country. One country, one language, one flag." The ceremony, performed in unison with accompanying gestures, was intended to instill a sense of patriotism in immigrant children.

3500. Version of the Pledge of Allegiance was published anonymously on September 8, 1892, in a popular Boston magazine, *The Youth's Companion*, as part of a campaign to develop flag-raising ceremonies to be used in the upcoming National Public School Celebration of Columbus Day. Its author was Francis Bellamy, a Baptist minister with Christian Socialist views. The text read: "I pledge allegiance to my Flag and the Republic for which it stands, one nation, indivisible, with liberty and justice for all."

The text of the Pledge of Allegiance was altered to specify "the Flag of the United States" in 1923 and "the Flag of the United States of America" in 1924. The phrase "under God" was added by Congress in 1954.

3501. Recitation of the Pledge of Allegiance by schoolchildren took place on Columbus Day, October 12, 1892, as part of the nationwide celebration of the quadricentennial of the arrival of Christopher Columbus. The first public recitation by adults took place at the National Liberty Pole and Flag Raising Ceremony held at Navesink, NJ, on April 25, 1893, with the pledge's author, Francis Bellamy, in attendance.

The original flag salute during the Pledge of Allegiance required the right arm to be raised straight ahead, at an angle. The rise in Germany of the Nazi salute, a nearly identical gesture, prompted the American salute to be changed to hand-over-heart.

3502. State law requiring schoolchildren to salute the American flag in public schools was passed in April 1898 by the New York legislature during the furor over the start of the Spanish-American War.

3503. Use of "American" as an adjective instead of "United States" was officially recommended by John Hay, secretary of state, who instructed American diplomatic and consular officers under date of August 3, 1904, to adopt it. The adjective form of designation is not used in strictly formal documents and in notarial acts performed by consular officers; instead, the full name of the country is given, as, for example: Government of the United States of America, Embassy of the United States of America.

3504. American flag displayed from the right hand of the Statue of Liberty in honor of an individual was flown on June 13, 1927, designated as Lindbergh Day, in honor of Charles Augustus Lindbergh's transatlantic solo flight. The flag was hoisted to the peak of the right arm of the Statue of Liberty in unison with the raising of the Post Flag and the discharge of the Morning Gun at Governors Island, and was lowered in unison with Post Retreat ceremonies.

3505. Constitutional amendment to be repealed was the 18th Amendment, known as Prohibition, which instituted the ban on intoxicating liquors. It had been declared ratified on January 29, 1919, and became effective on January 16, 1920. A bill to repeal the amendment, and thereby end Prohibition, was passed in the Senate on February 16, 1933, and in the House on February 20. Congress then offered it as a proposal to the states. It was declared ratified on December 5, 1933.

3506. American flag to orbit the earth was carried in the capsule of the satellite *Discoverer 8*, which was launched on August 10, 1960, by the Air Force at Vandenberg Air Force Base, CA. A 300-pound reentry capsule was ejected on August 11, 1960, on the 17th orbit and was recovered the same day by the U.S.S. *Haiti Victory*, whose frogmen used a helicopter. The flag was presented to President Dwight David Eisenhower on August 15, 1960. The orbital time of the satellite was 94.1 minutes; its perigee was 161 miles, its apogee 436 miles.

3507. Popular vote on a national emblem to represent the United States was the National Tree Election, sponsored by the National Arbor Day Foundation. Twenty-one trees appeared on the ballot, which was available from the foundation or on its Web site. Nearly 445,000 ballots were received, and were tallied on April 27, 2001. The winner was the oak, which received 101,146 votes. The four runners-up were redwood, flowering dogwood, maple, and pine. The designation of the oak as the national tree became effective after Congress approved legislation in November 2004.

Cities

3508. City incorporated in the colonies was Georgeana (now York), ME. On December 2, 1631, Sir Ferdinando Gorges received a grant of 24,000 acres on both sides of the Agamenticus, or York, River and founded a town named after the river on April 10, 1641. The name was changed to Georgeana when the city was incorporated on March 1, 1642, and was later changed again to York. The charter embraced a territory of 21 square miles and the inhabitants were formed into a body politic. This was the first English charter for a city in America. Kittery, ME, was the first and oldest town in the state, but Georgeana was incorporated as a city rather than as a town.

3509. Mayor of New York City was Thomas Willett, who was appointed in 1665 by Richard Nicolls, the English colonial governor. New York's mayors continued to be appointed until 1820, when Stephen Allen was elected by the city's Common Council. The first mayor of metropolitan New York City, formed from the consolidation of the five boroughs of Manhattan, Queens, Brooklyn, the Bronx, and Staten Island on January 1, 1898, was Robert van Wyck, who had been handpicked by Richard Croker, the head of Tammany Hall, the city's powerful Democratic machine.

3510. Communistic settlement with a religious basis was a monastic commune established in the colony of Ephrata, eight miles from Lancaster, PA, in 1733 by Johann Conrad Beissel. A convent for women was similarly established. The group, known as the Ephrata Society, was an offshoot of the Dunkards (also known as Brethren or German Baptists).

3511. Town built by free African-Americans in an area now in the United States was Fort Mose, near St. Augustine, FL. In 1738, Spanish authorities established a free militia of 100 former slaves, including men, women, and children, who had escaped from British territory in what is now Georgia. They built Fort Mose, a 65-foot-square structure in the salt marshes north of St. Augustine. In 1740 they were driven away by a British attack, but rebuilt and enlarged the fort in 1752. In 1763, when Spanish Florida was ceded to England, the residents of Fort Mose moved to Cuba . The fort was declared a national historic landmark in 1994.

3512. Milestones between cities were set by the directors of an insurance company known as The Philadelphia Contributionship for the Insurance of Houses from Loss by Fire. On February 17, 1761, they agreed "to apply their fines (a forfeiture of one shilling for not meeting precisely at the hour appointed, and two shillings for total absence) in purchasing Stones to be erected on the Road leading from Philadelphia toward Trenton, the distance of a mile one from another with the Number of miles from Philadelphia, to be cut in each stone, and Tho. Wharton and Jacob Lewis are requested to Contract for the same." On May 15, 1764, at five o'clock in the morning, the two men started out from Front and Market streets, taking with them the Surveyor General of the Province, and planted a stone at the end of every mile. They planted the 29th milestone near the edge of the Delaware River, and gave their two remaining stones to be planted on the Jersey side of the road to New York.

3513. Local political machine was organized in Boston, MA, where caucus clubs held secret meetings as early as 1763 (the year when the activities of one such club were described by John Adams in his diary). The members—usually propertied men and merchants—gathered before elections to identify the candidates most likely to benefit their interests and encouraged the intended outcome by exerting influence over other voters and distributing ballots selectively. Similar groups were active in other New England and Middle Atlantic towns.

3514. Town named for George Washington was a North Carolina town originally known as Forks of Tar River, which had been founded on November 20, 1771, by James Bonner. It changed its name to Washington in 1775 and was incorporated in 1782. The first town to be incorporated under the name of Washington was a town in Wilkes County, GA, that was incorporated on January 23, 1780.

3515. Town named for Benjamin Franklin was the Town of Franklin, MA, now a suburban industrial community 22 miles southwest of Boston. Formerly part of the Town of Wrentham, it was incorporated as the Town of Franklin on February 16, 1778.

3516. City founded by an African-American pioneer was Chicago, which got its start in 1779 when a trading post was established on the shore of Lake Michigan. The trader was Jean Baptiste Point du Sable, a settler from Haiti whose mother was Haitian and father French. In 1800 he sold his lands to John Kinzie for $1,200 and moved to Missouri to farm. By 1834, prime waterfront property in Chicago sold for more than $20,000 an acre.

3517. City directory was *Macpherson's Directory for the City and Suburbs of Philadelphia Extending to Prime Street, Southward; and Maiden Street, Northward; and From the River Delaware to Tenth Street Westward,* published on October 1, 1785, by John Macpherson. It was printed by Francis Bailey at Loick's Head, 65 Market Street, Philadelphia, PA, and contained 6,250 names, of which 686 were subscribers. William Bradford of Philadelphia also published a directory of that city the same year. It contained 83 pages with 43 names to the page, making a total of 3,569 names.

3518. Government of Washington, DC was established by Congress in 1802. It consisted of a mayor appointed by the president of the United States and a city council whose members were elected by the voters. (The first president to appoint a mayor of Washington, DC, was thus Thomas Jefferson.) Between 1812 and 1820 the mayor was elected by the council. Ultimate authority for enacting legislation affecting Washington, DC, rested with Congress, and the local government had few real powers.

3519. Town founded by a woman was Tangipahoa, LA, settled in 1806 by Rhoda Holly Singleton Mixon, who came from South Carolina accompanied by her daughters and slaves. Her grandchildren sold their property in 1869.

3520. Communistic settlement that was not religious was established at New Harmony, IN, in 1825, by the utopian thinker Robert Owen and his associates, who purchased for approximately $150,000 the village that had been founded by the German pietist George Rapp in 1805. It had about 1,000 members and existed until May 1827.

3521. City mayor elected by popular vote was Cornelius Van Wyck Lawrence, a Democrat, who defeated Gulian Crommelin Verplanck, a Whig, in the three-day election held on April 8–10, 1834, in New York City. There were 34,988 votes cast, of which 17,573 were for Lawrence, 17,393 for Verplanck, and 22 for others. Seven other municipal officers were also elected. Previously, mayors had been chosen by a board of the Common Council.

3522. Cow town was Abilene, KS. In the late 1860s, Abilene was the terminus of the Kansas Pacific Railway. In 1867, Illinois cattleman Joseph Geating McCoy bought the entire town for $2,400 and turned it into a central shipping depot for cattle driven north from rural Texas along the Chisholm Trail. The first rail shipment took place on September 5, 1867, when 20 Kansas Pacific Railway cars full of Texas longhorns embarked for slaughterhouses in Kansas City and Chicago. The first year, 35,000 head of cattle were shipped through Abilene.

3523. African-American town in continuous existence is Nicodemus, KS, the oldest town entirely populated by African-American residents and the only such town west of the Mississippi. A tiny settlement with 50 permanent residents, it was founded in 1877 and was named after an African prince who was reputed to be the first slave to buy his freedom. The town was designated a national historic landmark in 1976.

3524. City with a population of more than 1 million was New York City, whose population according to the census of 1880 was 1,206,299. This number was for Manhattan alone. Brooklyn was then an independent city. Brooklyn and three other areas (the Bronx, Queens, and Staten Island) were combined with Manhattan in 1898 to form the five boroughs of New York City. The population of the city in 1920 was 5,620,048, making it the first city with a population exceeding 5 million.

3525. Settlement house in a poor city neighborhood was the University Settlement, established by Stanton Coit in 1886 in a Forsythe Street tenement, New York City. The idea was that intellectuals would settle in a slum area and by living and working with their tenement neighbors would be able to help them raise their standard of living. Playgrounds were provided for children, instruction in English was given to immigrants, and other educational programs were established.

3526. Mayor who was a woman was Susanna Medora Salter, elected mayor of Argonia, KS, on April 4, 1887. Her name was submitted without her knowledge by the Woman's Christian Temperance Union, and she did not know that she was a candidate until she went to the polls and found her name listed on the ballot. Although only 27 years of age, she received a two-thirds majority of the votes. She served one year for $1. The first woman to serve as a mayor with a town council consisting entirely of women was Mrs. Mary D. Lowman, elected in April 1888 in Oskaloosa, KS. Her council consisted of Sadie Balsley, Millie Golden, Emma Hamilton, Carrie Johnson, and Hannah Morse.

3527. Settlement house serving an Hispanic population was El Hogar Feliz, founded by Katherine and Adelaide Rowan in Los Angeles, CA, in 1897. The organization, which offered health and educational services, was part of the Los Angeles Catholic Center.

3528. City government using the commission plan originated in Galveston, TX, in 1901 as an emergency measure following a disastrous flood. The legislature granted Galveston a charter on April 19, 1901, and the system went into operation on September 18. Under this form, large powers both legislative and executive are vested in a single group of officers, elected by the whole body of voters within the city without regard to political party.

3529. City manager was Charles Edward Ashburner of Richmond, VA, who on April 2, 1908, was elected general manager by the city council of Staunton, VA. He opened his office on April 15, 1908. His first year's salary was $2,000; the second year's, $2,500. He served until July 1911.

3530. Mayor of a major city who was a Socialist was Emil Seidel, who served as mayor of Milwaukee, WI, from April 1910 to April 1912.

3531. City government using the manager plan was adopted by Sumter, SC, in June 1912, when the voters, in a regular election, adopted the manager-commission form of government. The commission was composed of a mayor and two councilmen, all elected at large. The commission employed a city manager to whom active administration of the affairs of the city was entrusted and who was accountable to the commission.

3532. Tract housing development was Concrest, a development of 100 identical six-room houses near East Rochester, NY. It was built by Kate Gleason, a local machine-shop saleswoman turned contractor, beginning in 1913. Gleason had seen car engines mass-produced on an assembly line and decided to apply the method to the construction of low-cost housing.

3533. Zoning ordinance was put into effect in New York City on July 25, 1916, in the wake of concern over the unprecedented size of the 39-story Equitable Building, erected in lower Manhattan in 1915. The ordinance restricted the height and mass of skyscrapers and required buildings to be set back from the street, with the amount of setback calculated from the height and area of the building site. The total floor area of skyscrapers was also limited to no more than 12 times the area of the building site.

3534. Mayor of a major city who was a woman was Bertha Knight Landes, a Republican, who was elected mayor of Seattle, WA, on March 9, 1926. She had previously served as president of the city council and as acting mayor. A strong anticorruption activist, she was defeated for reelection after one term in office.

3535. Sister city partnership was established in 1931 between Toledo, OH, and Toledo, Spain, through The Association of Two Toledos. It predated the founding of the sister-city movement in the United States, which began in 1956 with People-to-People, a project of the National League of Cities. In 1967 the organization became an independent nonprofit corporation, Sister Cities International.

3536. Federally funded low-income housing project was Techwood Homes, which provided 604 units on 25 acres of land in Atlanta, GA. It replaced about 13 city blocks of downtown slums. The project was designed by the architectural firm of Burge and Stevens and was built by the J. A. Jones Construction Company of Charlotte, NC. Total construction cost was $2,108,337, or about $3,500 for each of the 604 units. Occupants, who could not qualify if they earned more than five times the rent charged, moved in beginning August 15, 1936. The project was dedicated by President Franklin Delano Roosevelt on November 29, 1935, before a crowd of over 50,000.

3537. Retirement colony was dedicated on October 23, 1936, at Roosevelt Park, Millville, NJ. The project, which was completed on January 1, 1937, contained seven houses for couples, which rented for $7 a month; six houses for single people, which rented for $5; and a community house. The city of Millville supplied the land, which had been taken over for taxes; the federal government's Works Progress Administration supplied $34,571. The city collected rent and agreed to keep the houses in repair. Residents received $15 monthly from the state under the Old Age Assistance Act. The plan was originated by Effie Morrison, deputy director of the Cumberland County Welfare Board.

3538. Planned suburban development was Levittown, NY, a tract of 17,447 identical four-room houses constructed between 1947 and 1951 on former potato fields in Nassau County, Long Island, by builder William Jaird Levitt. Along with the houses, which sold initially for $7,990 each, Levittown contained seven village greens and shopping centers, 14 playgrounds, nine swimming pools, two bowling alleys, and a town hall. Levittown and other suburban developments were built to meet the need for housing by veterans of World War II who returned home to marry and start families. Levitt was a Navy Seabee during the war and adapted the Seabees' rapid construction techniques in his developments.

3539. Urban master plan in the United States was adopted by the city council of Berkeley, CA, in April 1955. The plan divided the city into 28 neighborhoods and required the development of a local plan for each one.

3540. Private housing development designed as a complete community was LeFrak City, in Queens, New York City, a 40-acre complex containing high-rise apartment buildings, an office park, schools, stores, and recreational facilities. It was built by Samuel Jayson LeFrak, a real estate developer, and was opened in 1961. The complex cost $150 million to build and contained 5,000 apartments housing 25,000 people.

3541. Mayor of a major city who was African-American was Carl Burton Stokes, a Democrat, elected on November 7, 1967, by the citizens of Cleveland, OH. He was sworn in on November 13, 1967, in the City Council Chamber. Also in 1967, Walter E. Washington was elected mayor of Washington, DC, and Richard G. Hatcher was elected mayor of Gary, IN. The first African-American mayor of a major city in the South was Maynard Jackson, who was elected mayor of Atlanta, GA, on October 16, 1973.

3542. Mayor of a major city with a population over 500,000 who was a woman was Patience Sewell Latting, sworn in on April 13, 1971, as mayor of Oklahoma City, OK. Her salary was $2,000 a year. The city's population exceeded 366,000. The first woman to be elected mayor of a city with a population over 500,000 was Janet Gray Hayes of San Jose, CA, elected on November 6, 1974, on the Democratic ticket.

3543. Mayor of a major city who was of Mexican descent was Henry Gabriel Cisneros, who was elected mayor of San Antonio, TX, on April 4, 1981.

3544. Mayor of New York City who was African-American was David N. Dinkins, 63, the Manhattan borough president, who was elected on November 7, 1989, as a Democrat. He served one term. He was defeated in his 1993 bid for reelection by Republican candidate Rudolph Giuliani, whom he had beaten in 1989.

3545. City with a fleet of personal mobility machines was Atlanta, GA. On April 23, 2002, the city began providing battery-powered Segway Human Transporters for the use of its police force and three other government agencies.

3546. Municipal downsizing plan was adopted by Youngstown, OH, a manufacturing city with a population that had been in steady decline since the 1980s. In December 2002 the Youngstown city council adopted an initiative prepared by the city planning department and Youngstown State University to reduce infrastructure in parts of the city.

Congress

3547. Colonial congress met at Albany, NY, from June 19 to July 11, 1754, to form a plan of union and to negotiate a treaty with the Six Nations of the Iroquois. Seven colonies attended. Massachusetts Bay sent four delegates, New Hampshire four, New York four, Pennsylvania four, Connecticut three, Maryland two, and Rhode Island two.

3548. Continental Congress session began on September 5, 1774, at Carpenters' Hall, Philadelphia, PA. The participants were 44 delegates from 11 colonies. Delegates from Georgia and North Carolina did not attend until later sessions. The Congress adjourned on October 26, 1774, recommending another session to begin on May 10, 1775, in Philadelphia, PA.

3549. President of the Continental Congress was Peyton Randolph, a delegate from Virginia, who was elected on September 5, 1774, the day the Congress assembled. He resigned on October 22, 1774, to attend the Virginia State Legislature, and his place was taken on the same day by Henry Middleton of South Carolina.

3550. Continental Congress assembly to be opened with prayer was held on September 7, 1774, at Carpenters' Hall, Philadelphia, PA. The Reverend Jacob Duche, an Episcopalian minister, rector of Christ Church, appeared in his canonicals, attended by his clerk. The morning service of the Episcopal Church was read, with the clerk making the responses. The Psalter for the seventh day of the month includes the 35th Psalm, wherein David prays for protection against his enemies: "Plead my cause, O Lord, with them that strive with me; fight against them that fight against me." The rector concluded with an appeal so heartfelt that Congress gave him a vote of thanks.

3551. Medal awarded by the Continental Congress was granted to General George Washington for his exploit of March 17, 1776, in compelling the British forces to evacuate Boston, MA. The date of the resolution authorizing the medal was March 25, 1776. It was struck in Paris. The obverse showed Washington in profile. The reverse showed Washington and his officers on horseback viewing the town of Boston in the distance with the British fleet in view under sail. The medal was not presented to Washington until 1786.

3552. Medal awarded by the Continental Congress to a foreigner was a silver medal presented to Lieutenant Colonel François Louis Teisseidre de Fleury, who commanded the first of the storming parties in the assault upon Stony Point, NY, on July 15, 1779. He was the first man to enter the main fort and strike the British flag with his own hands. Fleury, who had been in the French military service, joined the Continental Army in 1777. The date of the congressional resolution was July 26, 1779, and the presentation was made on October 1.

3553. Meeting place of Congress was Federal Hall in New York City, located at 26 Wall Street, at the intersection with Nassau Street. It had been built in 1699 as the city hall and had since been used as a courthouse, prison, and provincial capitol. In 1788, after New York City was chosen to be the temporary home of Congress, the building was renovated for its use, with $32,000 of financing donated by wealthy New Yorkers (another $33,000 was later raised from taxes and a lottery). The architect was Pierre Charles L'Enfant, soon to be famous as the architect of Washington, DC. The renovations included the addition of a second-story balcony, where George Washington took the oath of office as president on April 30, 1789. Congress assembled there for the first time on March 4, 1789. The building reverted to its use as City Hall when Congress left for Philadelphia in 1790 and was torn down in 1812.

3554. Session of Congress took place in New York City from March 4, 1789, to September 29, 1789. The 13 states were represented by 26 senators and 65 representatives.

The largest number of representatives from any state was 10, from Virginia. The first quorum of the House of Representatives met on April 1, when 30 members were present, and the first Senate quorum assembled on April 6. The final session in New York City was held on August 12, 1790. The capital was then moved to Philadelphia, PA. The first session to meet in Philadelphia was held on December 6, 1790, and the final session on May 14, 1800. The act of April 24, 1800, provided for the removal of the government to Washington, DC, and on November 17, 1800, the second session of the Sixth Congress convened there. On February 27, 1801, Congress assumed jurisdiction over the District of Columbia.

3555. Joint meeting of the Senate and the House of Representatives was held on April 6, 1789, in the Senate Chamber, New York City. The House of Representatives attended the opening of the Senate session and the counting by the Senate of the electoral votes for president and vice president in the country's first presidential election. The electoral votes were cast as follows: George Washington 69, John Adams 34, Samuel Huntingdon 2, John Jay 9, John Hancock 4, Robert H. Harrison 6, George Clinton 3, John Rutledge 6, John Milton 2, James Armstrong 1, Edward Telfair 1, and Benjamin Lincoln 1.

3556. Contact between the president and the Congress took place on April 23, 1789, a week before George Washington was inaugurated as president. As Washington embarked from Elizabeth Town, NJ, to cross New York Harbor on the way to his future home in New York City, he was escorted by an eight-member joint congressional committee, including three senators and five representatives. A similar committee, composed of two senators and three representatives, greeted John Adams, the vice president–elect.

3557. Congressional chaplain was the Reverend William Linn, a Presbyterian minister, who served in the First Congress from May 1, 1789, to December 10, 1790.

3558. Congressional act was "An Act to regulate the Time and Manner of administering certain Oaths," which was approved by President George Washington on June 1, 1789. The first Congress (March 4, 1789–March 3, 1791) enacted 118 acts, comprising 94 public acts, 14 public resolutions, 8 private acts, and 2 private resolutions.

3559. Congressional act declared unconstitutional by the Supreme Court was the act of September 24, 1789, which authorized the Supreme Court to issue writs of mandamus (written orders) to American courts and public officials. The Court's ruling held that this statute extended the Supreme Court's powers beyond what was specified in the Constitution.

3560. Meeting place of Congress that is still in existence was Congress Hall, a two-story brick building at the corner of Sixth and Chestnut streets in Philadelphia, PA, near Independence Hall. In July 1790 Congress voted to move the seat of federal government from New York City to Philadelphia for a 10-year period while a permanent federal city was constructed. Congress began meeting there on December 6, 1790, the Senate occupying a courtroom on the second floor and the House a larger courtroom, with a spectators' gallery, on the ground floor. When the House, reapportioned after the 1790 census, grew from 69 to 105 members in 1793, the building was enlarged to accomodate them. Congress continued to meet there until May 4, 1800, after which the hall became a courthouse again.

Library of Congress, Prints and Photographs Division
LC-USZC4-12011

George Washington arrives for his inauguration at Congress Hall in Philadelphia, 1793.

3561. Designs for the building of the Capitol were submitted in 1792 to the Commissioners of the District of Columbia, in response to a March 14 advertisement announcing a competition for the best design. The prize was $500 and a building lot in the city of Washington; second prize was $250. Sixteen entries are known to have been submitted, but none of them met with the approval of President George Washington and Secretary of State Thomas Jefferson. The winning entry was a low-domed Palladian design by a young physician and painter, William Thornton, who turned in his plan in 1793 and was named to the post of Architect of the Capitol.

Courtesy of Lynn Messina

The U.S. Capitol building, Washington, DC.

3562. Congressional investigation was authorized on March 27, 1792, after troops under the command of Major General Arthur St. Clair were defeated by Native American forces near the Ohio-Indiana border on November 4, 1791. The House of Representatives, by a vote of 44–10, resolved "that a committee be appointed to inquire into the causes of the failure of the late expedition under Major General St. Clair; and that the said committee be empowered to call for such persons, papers and records as may be necessary to assist their inquires." The seven-member committee, which was headed by Thomas Fitzsimons, a Federalist of Pennsylvania, absolved St. Clair and ruled that his defeat "can in no respect be imputed to his conduct either at any time before or during the action." St. Clair nonetheless resigned his army command, retaining his post as governor of the Northwest Territory.

3563. Special session of Congress was held on May 15, 1797, in Philadelphia, PA. President John Adams had issued a proclamation on March 25 for convening the Senate and the House of Representatives to consider the difficulty with France.

3564. Guide to parliamentary rules of order was Thomas Jefferson's *A Manual of Parliamentary Practice, for the Use of the Senate of the United States*, a 199-page book, printed in 1801 by Samuel Harrison Smith in Washington, DC.

3565. Congressional chaplain who was Catholic was Father Charles Constantine Pise, ordained in 1825, who served the 22nd Congress from March 4, 1831, to March 3, 1832.

3566. Congress in which 1,000 bills were introduced was the 22nd Congress, held from December 5, 1831, to July 16, 1832 (226 days) and December 3, 1832, to March 2, 1833 (91 days). Of the 976 bills and 24 joint resolutions introduced, 462 were passed, comprising 175 public acts, 16 public resolutions, 270 private acts, and 1 private resolution.

3567. Congressional lobbyist who was a woman was Dorothea Lynde Dix, who in the 1840s and 1850s championed the care of the indigent insane. On June 23, 1848, she presented a petition to Congress for a grant of 5 million acres for "the relief and support of the indigent insane in the United States." By courtesy of Congress, a special alcove in the Capitol Library was set apart for her use, where she could converse with members.

3568. Body to lie in state in the Capitol rotunda was that of Senator Henry Clay, who died in Washington, DC, at the age of 75 on June 29, 1852. His body was placed in the rotunda, where it was displayed July 1, 1852, prior to interment in Lexington Cemetery, Lexington, KY.

3569. Congressional medal awarded to a physician was presented to Frederick Henry Rose of the British Navy. In April 1858, in Jamaica, yellow fever broke out on the U.S.S. *Susquehanna*. Rose offered his services and sailed to New York with the stricken crew. On May 11, 1858, Congress authorized a gold medal to be presented to him for his kindness and humanity to the officers and crew.

3570. Officer to preside over both of the branches of Congress was Schuyler Colfax of Indiana, who served as speaker of the House of Representatives in the 38th, 39th, and 40th Congresses (March 4, 1863–March 3, 1869), and who presided over the Senate as President Ulysses Simpson Grant's vice president (March 4, 1869–March 3, 1873).

3571. Congressional directory published by the federal government was authorized by act of February 14, 1865, and published in 1865 for the first session of the 39th Congress. It was compiled by Benjamin Perley Poore. In addition to a roster of congressmen, the 57-page directory contained information about Washington banks, insurance companies, hotels, express offices, churches, railroads, steamboats, and mail service.

3572. Congress to appropriate $1 billion was the 52nd Congress, which lasted from March 4, 1891, to March 3, 1893. It appropriated $507,376,398 in the first session for the fiscal year 1893 and $519,535,293 in the second session for the fiscal year 1894. The appropriations included funds for the postal service, payable from postal revenues, and estimated permanent annual appropriations, including sinking-fund requirements.

3573. Naturalized citizen to lie in state in the Capitol rotunda was Pierre (Peter) Charles L'Enfant, the French-born architect, engineer, and soldier who came to colonial America in 1776 to join the Continental Army during the Revolutionary War, rising to the rank of major, and afterward was commissioned by President George Washington to design the new federal city of Washington, DC. He died in poverty and obscurity on June 4, 1825, and was buried on a friend's Maryland farm. In 1908 Congress unanimously authorized his reburial in Arlington National Cemetery, Arlington, VA. His body was exhumed on April 22, 1909, and lay in state in the Capitol on April 28 prior to reinterment.

3574. Radio broadcast of an open session of Congress took place on December 3, 1923, from noon to 12:45 P.M., during the first session of the 68th Congress. The swearing-in ceremony was broadcast by radio station WRC, Washington, DC, from the Senate. Three newly elected senators—Alva Blanchard Adams of Colorado, a Democrat; Magnus Johnson of Minnesota, a member of the Farmer-Labor Party; and Porter Hinman Dale of Vermont, a Republican—were sworn in alphabetically. The session adjourned in memory of the recently deceased senators whose seats they were taking—Samuel Danford Nicholson, Knute Nelson, and William Paul Dillingham, respectively.

3575. Congress to enact more than 1,000 laws was the 70th Congress, which met from March 4, 1927, to March 3, 1929. It enacted 1,722 acts, comprising 1,037 public acts, 108 public resolutions, 568 private acts, and 9 private resolutions.

3576. Physician to Congress was Dr. George Wehnes Calver, a retired rear admiral. He reported for duty at the Capitol in Washington, DC, on December 8, 1928, in response to a resolution of the 70th Congress, passed December 4, requesting the secretary of the Navy to detail a medical officer to be in attendance at the sessions of Congress. His title was "the attending physician."

3577. Congress in session a full year was the third session of the 76th congress, in session from January 3, 1940, to January 3, 1941, a total of 366 days. The first session of the 77th Congress lasted 365 days, from January 3, 1941, to January 2, 1942.

3578. Congressional opening session to be televised was the joint session of the 80th Congress that met on January 3, 1947. The proceedings were televised by the major networks.

3579. Terrorist shootings in the Capitol Building took place on March 1, 1954, when four Puerto Rican nationalists shouting "Freedom for Puerto Rico!" fired more than 30 rounds at the floor of the House of Representatives from a visitors' gallery. Alvin Bentley of Michigan, George Fallon of Maryland, Ben Jensen of Iowa, Clifford Davis of Tennessee, and Kenneth Roberts of Alabama were all wounded. The nationalists—Lolita Lebrón, Rafael Cancel Miranda, Andrés Figueroa Cordero, and Irving Flores—served 25 years of their 50-year sentences before they were pardoned on September 6, 1979, by President Jimmy Carter.

3580. Capitol Police Officers killed in the line of duty were Special Agent John Michael Gibson, 42, and Police Private First Class Jacob Joseph Chestnut, 58. Both were shot on July 24, 1998, by a deranged Montana man named Russell Weston, Jr. Weston entered the Capitol and shot Chestnut point blank, then exchanged fire with Gibson, killing him before collapsing of his own wounds. The bodies of the two officers were displayed in the Capitol Rotunda on July 27, and were then buried in Arlington National Cemetery.

House of Representatives

3581. Congressional representative appointed to a presidential cabinet was James Madison of Virginia, who served in Congress from March 4, 1789, to March 3, 1797, and as Thomas Jefferson's secretary of state from May 2, 1801, to March 3, 1809.

3582. Congressional representative who was Catholic was Thomas FitzSimons of Pennsylvania, who was elected as a Federalist to the first three Congresses. He served from March 4, 1789, to March 3, 1795. Another Catholic, Charles Carroll of Maryland, also served in the First Congress.

3583. Session of the House of Representatives met in New York City on March 4, 1789. It was attended by four delegates from Massachusetts, three from Connecticut, four from Pennsylvania, one from Virginia, and one from South Carolina. Meetings were constantly called and adjourned for lack of a quorum. The first quorum gathered on April 1, 1789, and the first business transacted was the balloting for the office of speaker of the House.

3584. Clerk of the House of Representatives was John James Beckley of Virginia, who served from April 1, 1789, to May 15, 1797, in the First through the Fifth Congresses, and from January 10, 1803, to October 26, 1807, in the Seventh through the 10th Congresses.

3585. Speaker of the House was Frederick Augustus Conrad Muhlenberg of Pennsylvania, who served as speaker in the First Congress from April 1, 1789, to October 23, 1791, and in the Third Congress from December 2, 1793, to December 6, 1795. He represented Pennsylvania in the House from March 4, 1789, to March 3, 1797.

3586. Congressional committee was the Committee on Elections, a standing committee, appointed on April 2, 1789, to determine the eligibility and rights of admission of those who had been elected. It was resolved "that a committee be appointed to prepare and report such standing rules and orders of proceedings as may be proper to be observed."

3587. House of Representatives election that was contested was the race between David Ramsay and William Loughton Smith of South Carolina. Smith took his seat on April 13, 1789. On April 15, 1789, Ramsay presented a petition that Smith be declared ineligible, on the ground that he had not been "seven years a citizen of the United States," as he had studied abroad during that period. The dispute was referred to April 18, 1789, to the Committee on Elections, which ruled that Smith was entitled to his seat.

3588. Filibuster in the House of Representatives for the purpose of delaying legislative action occurred on June 11, 1790, when Elbridge Gerry of Massachusetts and William Loughton Smith of South Carolina made long speeches during consideration of the resolution to change the seat of government.

3589. Congressional representative who was Jewish was Israel Jacobs, who was elected by Pennsylvania to sit in the Second Congress. He served from March 4, 1791, to March 3, 1793. (There were two men named Israel Jacobs from Pennsylvania, and confusion exists as to which one served.) The next was Lewis Charles Levin, representative from Pennsylvania, who was elected as a candidate of the American Party and served from March 4, 1845, to March 3, 1851.

3590. Congressional apportionment of representatives under the Constitution was authorized by act of April 14, 1792, an "act for apportioning representatives among the several states according to the first enumeration." The first apportionment was made in 1793. It was based on the results of the first decennial census, the census of 1790, and provided for 106 representatives, one for every 33,000 of population. The first Congress, which met before this apportionment was made, had consisted of 65 representatives, one for every 30,000.

3591. Congressional representative to serve before his 25th birthday in contravention of the constitutional requirement was William Charles Cole Claiborne of Tennessee, a Jeffersonian Democrat, who served from March 4, 1797, to March 3, 1801. He was born in Sussex County, VA, in 1775.

3592. Brawl in the House of Representatives took place in Philadelphia, PA, on January 30, 1798, when Matthew Lyon of Vermont had an argument with Roger Griswold of Connecticut and spat in Griswold's face. A resolution was introduced to expel Lyon. Lyon acted as his own attorney and defended himself in the proceedings, which lasted from January 30 to February 12, 1798, and occupied practically all the attention of the House. The resolution was carried by a vote of 52 to 44, but because expulsion requires a two-thirds vote, Lyon was not expelled.

3593. Congressional caucus was held secretly in 1800 by the Federalist party at the instigation of Alexander Hamilton for the purpose of reelecting President John Adams in the third presidential election. The Democratic-Republicans later held their own caucus and nominated Thomas Jefferson. Adams and Jefferson each received 73 electoral votes, whereupon the election was turned over to the House of Representatives. After 37 ballots taken between February 11 and 17, 1801, the House elected Thomas Jefferson of Virginia as president and Aaron Burr of New York as vice president. The first congressional caucus to meet openly, rather than in secret, was held on February 25, 1804, by the Democratic-Republicans, who nominated Thomas Jefferson. Jefferson received 162 of the 176 electoral votes.

3594. Duel between representatives in Congress was held on the famous Bladensburg, MD, dueling field in 1808, when George Washington Campbell of Tennessee shot Barent Gardenier of New York through the body. Gardenier had accused Congress of being under the influence of France, which Campbell denied, at the same time assailing Gardenier with a torrent of personal abuse. Gardenier challenged him to a duel, was wounded, and after his recovery returned to his attacks with more animosity than before. Campbell served in Congress from October 17, 1803, to March 3, 1809; Gardenier served from March 4, 1807, to March 3, 1811.

3595. Congressional representative who was Hispanic was Joseph Marion Hernández (born Joseph Mariano Hernández) of St. Augustine, FL, the son of immigrants from Minorca. The Spanish colony of Florida became a U.S. territory in 1821, and Hernández was elected the territory's congressional delegate in 1822.

3596. Congressional representative to be refused a seat was John Bailey of Canton, MA, an Independent, who was elected in 1823. He was excluded on the ground that he was not a resident of the district he purported to represent. An election was held to fill the resulting vacancy, and Bailey ran and won again. He was seated on December 13, 1824, was reelected three times, and served to March 3, 1831.

3597. Congressional representative to be censured was William Stanberry, a member of the Anti-Jacksonian Party from Ohio, who was censured on July 11, 1832, for having insulted Speaker of the House Andrew Stevenson on the previous day. In the course of a speech on the House floor, he had said that "the eyes of the Speaker were too frequently directed towards the White House," meaning that he courted favor with President Andrew Jackson. The vote in favor of censure was 92 to 44.

Representative John Quincy Adams of Massachusetts, the former President, refused to participate in the vote on William Stanberry's censure and was nearly censured himself as a result.

3598. Gag rule in the House of Representatives was adopted on May 26, 1836, when the House voted 117 to 68 to ban any consideration of the contentious subject of slavery. The resolution read: "Whereas it is extremely important and desirable that the agitation of this subject should be finally arrested, for the purpose of restoring tranquility to the public mind, your committee respectfully recommend the adoption of the following additional resolution: Resolved that all petitions, memorials, resolutions, propositions, or papers, relating in any way, or to any extent whatever, to the subject of slavery, or the abolition of slavery, shall without being either printed or referred, be laid upon the table, and that no further action whatever shall be had thereon."

3599. Killing of one congressional representative by another took place on the duelling ground at Bladensburg, MD, near Washington, DC, on February 12, 1838. Jonathan Cilley, a Democrat from Maine, was called out by William J. Graves, a Whig from Kentucky, for a supposed aspersion on the character of James Watson Webb, the editor of the *New York Courier and Enquirer*. Cilley was shot during the third round of rifle fire and bled to death. Resolutions in the House to expel Graves and censure his second, Virginia congressman Henry Wise, failed by a vote of 103 to 78.

3600. Brothers to serve as representatives in Congress simultaneously were the three Washburn brothers, each of whom represented a different state. Israel Washburn, Jr., of Maine, served two terms as a Whig and three terms as a Republican, from March 4, 1851, to January 1, 1861. Elihu Benjamin Washburne of Illinois, who spelled his name with a final *e*, served as a Whig from March 4, 1853, to March 6, 1869. Cadwallader Colden Washburn of Wisconsin served as a Republican from March 4, 1855, to March 3, 1861. The three brothers served simultaneously as congressmen from March 4, 1855, to January 1, 1861. Another brother, William Drew Washburn of Minnesota, served as a Republican from March 4, 1879, to March 3, 1885.

3601. Congressman censured for assaulting another was Laurence Massillon Keitt, Democrat from South Carolina, who assisted his colleague from South Carolina, Preston Brooks, in his attack on Massachusetts antislavery senator Charles Sumner on May 22, 1856. Brooks and Keitt approached Sumner in the Senate chamber after the Senate was adjourned, and Brooks beat Sumner into unconsciousness with a cane while Keitt protected him from interference. Keitt was censured on July 15, 1856, by a vote of 106-96. A vote to censure Brooks failed, 121 to 95.

3602. Rabbi to open the House of Representatives with prayer was Rabbi Morris Jacob Raphall, rabbi of Congregation B'nai Jeshurun, New York City, who delivered the invocation on February 1, 1860, at the first session of the 36th Congress.

3603. Congressional representative to be expelled was Benjamin Whittemore, Republican from South Carolina. Together with two other Republicans, John T. Deweese of North Carolina and Roderick R. Butler of Tennessee, Whittemore was accused of collecting money in exchange for appointing certain prospective cadets to the U.S. military and naval academies. He resigned on February 24, 1870, and was censured by the House the same day by a vote of 187 to 0. His district reelected him, but he was not permitted by the House to take his seat. Butler too was censured, and Deweese was censured after his resignation.

3604. African-American preacher to deliver a sermon in the House of Representatives was the Reverend Dr. Henry Highland Garnet, pastor of the 15th Street Presbyterian Church, Washington, DC. President Abraham Lincoln, with the unanimous consent of his Cabinet and the two congressional chaplains, arranged for the special Sunday morning service. The chaplain of the House, the Reverend William Henry Channing, extended an invitation to Dr. Garnet to preach a sermon commemorating the triumph of the Union Army and the deliverance of the country from chattel slavery. He delivered the sermon on Sunday, February 12, 1865, to a crowded chamber. He was also the first African-American allowed in the House, as previously African-Americans had been forbidden to enter the grounds.

3605. Congressional representative censured for corruption was Benjamin Whittemore, Republican from South Carolina. Together with two other Republicans, John T. Deweese of North Carolina and Roderick R. Butler of Tennessee, Whittemore was accused of collecting money in exchange for appointing certain prospective cadets to the U.S. military and naval academies. He resigned on February 24, 1870, and was censured by the House the same day by a vote of 187 to 0. His district reelected him, but he was not permitted by the House to take his seat. Butler too was censured, and Deweese was censured after his resignation.

3606. Congressional representative who was African-American was Joseph Hayne Rainey of Georgetown, SC, a Republican, who was sworn in on December 12, 1870, to fill the vacancy caused by the action of the House of Representatives in declaring the seat of Benjamin Franklin Whittemore vacant. Rainey served 10 years, until March 3, 1879. The first African-American representative from a northern state was Oscar Stanton De Priest of Chicago, IL, a Republican, who served from March 4, 1929, to January 3, 1935. The first from the Democratic Party was Arthur Wergs Mitchell of Illinois, who served from January 3, 1935, to January 3, 1943.

3607. Speech delivered before the House of Representatives by an African-American representative was made on February 1, 1871, by Jefferson Franklin Long, Republican, a former slave who had won a special election to fill Georgia's vacant seat in Congress, thus becoming the second African-American congressional representative. In his speech, he sought to persuade Congress to reject a bill intended to make it possible for former members of the Confederacy to hold public office, including those who were actively terrorizing African-Americans and federal Reconstruction agents. Congress approved the bill by a vote of 118 to 90.

3608. Congressional representative to serve a single day was George Augustus Sheridan of Lake Providence, LA, elected as a Liberal on November 5, 1872, to the 43rd Congress, which ran from March 4, 1873, through March 3, 1875. He finally took his seat on March 3, 1875, the last day of the session, after an unsuccessful challenge by Pinckney Benton Stewart Pinchback.

3609. House majority leader was Sereno Elisha Payne, Republican of Auburn, NY, who served in the House from March 4, 1883, through March 3, 1887, and again from December 2, 1889, until his death on December 10, 1914. He was majority leader from 1889 through 1911.

3610. Congressional representative elected by prohibitionists was Kittel Halvorson, born in Telemarken, Norway, who was elected as the candidate of the Farmers' Alliance and the prohibitionists. He served as a representative from Minnesota from March 4, 1891, to March 3, 1893.

3611. Voting machines in congressional elections were approved by Congress in a bill signed by President William McKinley on February 14, 1899. It provided that "all votes for representatives in Congress must be by written or printed ballot, or voting machines, the use of which has been duly authorized by the state."

3612. Congressional representative who was a Socialist was Victor Louis Berger of Wisconsin, who served from March 4, 1911, to March 3, 1913, in the 62nd Congress. He was elected to the 66th and 67th congresses, but was not permitted to take his seat. He was subsequently elected to the 68th, 69th, and 70th congresses and served from March 4, 1923, to March 3, 1929.

3613. Congressional representative who was a woman was Jeannette Rankin, who was elected as a Republican from Montana and served from March 4, 1917, to March 4, 1919, and from January 3, 1941, to January 3, 1943. She was the first representative to vote twice against entry into war, on April 6, 1917, and December 8, 1941.

Courtesy of Images of American Political History

Jeannette Rankin

3614. Congressional representative who was a mother was Winnifred Sprague Mason Huck, a Republican from Chicago, IL, who was elected on November 7, 1922, to fill the vacancy caused by the death of her father, William Ernest Mason, on June 16, 1921. She served from November 20, 1922, to March 3, 1923, in the 67th Congress.

3615. Congressional representative who was a Jewish woman was Florence Prag Kahn, the widow of Julius Kahn, who represented San Francisco, CA, in the House for 26 years. She won a special election to fill his seat and was reelected five times, serving from February 17, 1925, through January 3,

1937. Both were Republicans. Kahn was the first woman to serve on the Military Affairs Committee.

3616. Congressional page who was female was Gene Cox, 13 years old, the daughter of Representative Edward Eugene Cox of Georgia, who served on January 3, 1939, the first day of the 76th Congress, and received a check for $4 for her services.

3617. Congressional standing committee headed by an African-American was the Committee on Expenditures in the Executive Departments, to which William Levi Dawson of Chicago, IL, was appointed on January 18, 1949.

3618. Mother and son simultaneously elected to Congress were Ohio Republicans elected on November 4, 1952, to serve in the 83rd Congress. Frances Payne Bolton, 67, represented Ohio's 22nd District, and had served since February 27, 1940, when she was elected to fill the vacancy caused by the death of her husband, Chester Castle Bolton. Her son, Oliver Payne Bolton, 35, represented Ohio's 11th District.

3619. Congressional representative reelected after serving a prison term was Thomas Joseph Lane, a Democrat of Massachusetts, who was elected to the 77th Congress at a special election on December 30, 1941, and served eight terms before being convicted of income tax evasion and sentenced to four months in jail. He served his sentence in the Federal Correctional Institution, Danbury, CT, from May 7, 1956, to September 4, 1956. He was subsequently elected on November 6, 1956, to serve his ninth term.

3620. Congressional representative of Asian ancestry was Dalip Singh Saund, a Democrat representing the 29th district of California. A Sikh, he was born in Amritsar, India, and held a doctorate in mathematics from the University of California at Berkeley. He was elected on November 6, 1956, and reelected in 1958 and 1960.

3621. Congressional representative who was a woman of Asian descent was Patsy Takemoto Mink, the granddaughter of Japanese immigrants, who was elected to Congress as a Democrat from Hawaii in November 1964. She served from January 3, 1965, through January 3, 1977, then was returned to Congress in 1990 and served until her death in September 2002; in the November election, she was posthumously reelected.

3622. Congressional page who was African-American was Frank Mitchell, age 15, of Springfield, IL, who was appointed on August 14, 1965, by Representative Paul Findley, Republican of Illinois.

3623. Congressional representative who was an African-American woman was Shirley Anita St. Hill Chisholm, a Democrat, who was elected on November 5, 1968, from New York City's 12th District, in the Bedford-Stuyvesant section of Brooklyn. She was sworn in on January 3, 1969, and was reelected six times, leaving the House of Representatives in 1982. The first female African-American representative from a southern state was Barbara Charline Jordan, elected as a Democrat from the 18th District of Texas in 1972. Jordan, who held degrees in political science, history, and law, had served in the Texas state senate from 1966 to 1972. In 1976 she became the first African-American speaker to deliver the keynote speech at a Democratic National Convention.

3624. Congressional representative of Puerto Rican ancestry was Herman Badillo, a Democrat, who was born on August 21, 1929, in Caguas, Puerto Rico. He was elected on November 3, 1970, by the 21st district of New York. He served in the 92nd, 93rd, 94th, and 95th congresses and resigned on December 31, 1977.

3625. Vote in the House of Representatives to be tallied by machine took place on March 3, 1971, when 391 votes were cast on a motion to pass the Wright Patman amendment to delete an interest rate section in a proposed piece of debt-ceiling legislation. Representatives displayed a green card if they were in favor, a red card if they were against. The name of the voter appeared on each card. There were 180 green cards and 211 red.

3626. Congressional candidate elected while missing was Thomas Hale Boggs, Democrat of Louisiana and House majority leader, who was elected to his 15th term on November 7, 1972. He had been missing since October 16, when the small plane in which he was a passenger disappeared. He was declared dead, and his wife, Corinne Claiborne "Lindy" Boggs, was elected in his stead on March 20, 1973.

3627. Vote in the House of Representatives to be recorded electronically took place on January 23, 1973, when 331 members recorded their presence at a quorum call. Forty-four voting stations were located throughout the House Chamber. Each member placed a personalized plastic identification card in one of the vote stations to vote yea, nay, or present. A large panel on the south wall of the room, above the Speaker's podium, displayed the names of all the representatives and indicated their presence by means of light signals. The recorder, which cost $1.1 million, was designed by Dr. Frank B. Ryan, director of the House Information Systems.

3628. Congressional representative to give birth while holding office was Yvonne Braithwaite Burke, 41, Democrat of California, who gave birth to a daughter, Autumn Roxanne Burke, in Los Angeles, CA, on November 23, 1973. She had been elected to the 93rd Congress on November 7, 1972, and reelected to serve in the 94th and 95th congresses. Previously, she was the first African-American woman to be elected to the General Assembly of California.

3629. Congressional representative who was a grandmother was Millicent Hammond Fenwick, a Republican of New Jersey, who was elected to the 94th Congress on November 5, 1974, and was reelected to two subsequent terms. She was born on February 25, 1910. She had eight grandchildren.

3630. Congressional representatives to marry each other were Martha Elizabeth Keys, Democrat of Kansas, and Andrew Jacobs, Jr., Democrat of Indiana. Both were elected on November 5, 1974, to the 94th Congress. They were married on January 3, 1976, at Topeka, KS. He had first been elected on November 3, 1964, and had served in the 89th, 90th, 91st, and 92nd congresses; he was subsequently elected to the 95th and 96th Congresses. She was reelected to serve in the 95th Congress.

3631. Bilingual report of a congressional committee was the 215-page report of a hearing that took place on March 28, 1978, at Miami, FL. It was entitled *Needs of the Hispanic Elderly, hearing before the Select Committee on Aging, House of Representatives, Ninety-Fifth Congress, second session*, and was simultaneously printed in Spanish under the title *Las Necesidades de los Ancianos Hispanos*.

3632. Congressional representative expelled for corruption was Michael J. Myers, one of seven national politicians (six congressmen and one senator) who were convicted of accepting bribes during an FBI sting operation known as Abscam. Myers was convicted on August 30, 1980, and was expelled from the House by a vote of 376 to 30 on October 2, 1980.

3633. Congressional representatives censured for sexual misconduct were Gerry Studds, Democrat from Massachusetts, and Daniel Crane, Republican from Illinois. They were both censured by a vote of 421 to 3 on July 20, 1983, after an investigation by the House ethics committee uncovered evidence that they had both had sex with 17-year-old congressional pages, Studds with a male page in 1973 and Crane with a female page in 1980. Crane, a married man with six children, apologized to the House; he ran for reelection when his term expired but was defeated. Studds insisted that he had done no wrong and should not have been disciplined. He was reelected many times and retired in 1996.

3634. Congressional representative who was a Hispanic woman was Ileana Ros-Lehtinen, Republican of Florida. Born in Cuba, she came to the United States as a refugee when she was a child. She entered Congress on August 29, 1989, after winning a special election to fill a vacancy in the 18th District. In the 104th Congress, she became the first Hispanic woman appointed to chair a subcommittee, the Africa Subcommittee. Previously, she was the first Hispanic women elected to the Florida state legislature.

3635. Congresswoman who was a veteran of the armed forces and the first graduate of the Air Force Academy of either sex to serve in Congress was Representative Heather Wilson of Albuquerque, NM, who took her seat from New Mexico's 1st Congressional District on June 23, 1998 (she was reelected in 2000, becoming the first woman from New Mexico to serve more than one term in Congress). Wilson, the daughter and granddaughter of military airmen, enlisted in the USAF at age 17 and graduated from the Air Force Academy in 1982, then earned her doctorate at Oxford University on a Rhodes scholarship. From 1989 to 1991 she was director for European Defense Policy and Arms Control on the National Security Council staff at the White House.

3636. Midterm election since World War II in which the president's party gained seats in the House of Representatives was the election of November 3, 1998, during the presidency of Bill Clinton, in which Democrats picked up five House seats, maintained their seats in the Senate, and won the coveted governorship of California. The last time the president's party showed a net gain in a midterm election was in 1934, under Franklin Delano Roosevelt. Typically, the president's party loses seats in Congress in the midterms, especially if it is the president's final term in office.

3637. Former speaker of the House to become a television news commentator was Newt Gingrich, Republican of Georgia, who was hired in October 1999 by Fox News to provide political commentary for its news shows and to host programs on a variety of topics. Gingrich resigned as speaker of the House of Representatives in January 1999 after the Republican Party sustained losses in the 1998 congressional elections.

3638. Year in which the majority of states were represented by at least one congresswoman in the House of Representatives was 2001, when women participated in the congressional delegations of 27 of the 50 states.

3639. Political party leader in Congress who was a woman was Nancy Pelosi, elected in 1987 to the House of Representatives from California's 8th District. In November 2002, the House Democrats chose her as minority leader.

3640. Congressional representatives who were sisters were Loretta Sanchez and Linda T. Sánchez, both Democrats from California. Loretta Sanchez entered Congress on January 3, 1997, representing the state's 47th congressional district. She was subsequently reelected and was still in office when Linda T. Sánchez entered Congress on January 3, 2003, representing the 39th congressional district.

3641. FBI raid on the office of a congressional representative took place on May 23, 2006, when 15 FBI agents entered and searched the office of Louisiana's Democratic congressman, William J. Jefferson, in the Rayburn House Office Building in Washington, DC. Jefferson had been accused of accepting bribes from a company that wanted his help in making business connections in Africa and was said to have hidden $90,000 in the freezer in his apartment.

Senate

3642. Senate of the United States Congress were elected in 1788 by their state legislatures, in accordance with the Constitution. There were 26 senators, two from each of the 13 states. Their average age was 48, the oldest being 62, the youngest 34. Eleven of them had graduated from college and 12 others had had some higher education. The majority were veterans of state legislatures and constitutional conventions. Nineteen had served in the Continental Congress or the Congress of the Confederation, seven had been officers in the Continental Army, and four had signed the Declaration of Independence. The senators were aligned into two general groups, one designated as the Administration Party, the other as the Opposition Party, with 17 senators belonging to the former and nine to the latter.

3643. Senate journal was the *Journal of the First Session of the Senate of the United States. Begun and Held at the City of New York, March 4, 1789*, published in 1789 in New York City.

3644. Senator who was Catholic was Daniel Carroll, a Federalist of Maryland, who served from March 4, 1789, to March 3, 1791. His brother was John Carroll, the first Catholic bishop in the United States.

3645. Session of the Senate met in New York City on March 4, 1789. The only members present were Senators John Langdon and Paine Wingate of New Hampshire, William Samuel Johnson and Oliver Ellsworth of Connecticut, William Maclay and Robert Morris of Pennsylvania, Caleb Strong of Massachusetts, and William Few of Georgia. Various sessions were called but had to be adjourned because no quorum was present. The first session of the Senate at which there was a quorum was held on April 6, 1789, at which meeting John Langdon of New Hampshire was elected president pro tempore.

3646. Senate president pro tempore was John Langdon of New Hampshire, who held the office on April 6, 1789, during the counting of the votes for president and vice president in the first presidential election. April 6 was the first occasion on which a Senate quorum assembled. The counting resulted in the election of George Washington as president and the runner-up, John Adams, as vice president. Since the Constitution provides that the vice president shall act as president of the Senate, Adams took over the office on April 21, 1789.

3647. Secretary of the Senate was Samuel Allyne Otis of Massachusetts, who was elected on April 8, 1789, and continued in his post until April 22, 1814. All the administrative, financial, and record-keeping tasks associated with the Senate were under his supervision.

3648. Government accounting book was a notebook known as S-1, in which were marked down the salary and mileage payments made to the members of the Senate, beginning in 1790 and ending in 1881. It was originally kept by Samuel Alleyne Otis, the first secretary of the Senate.

3649. Senator appointed by a governor was John Walker of Virginia, who was appointed on March 31, 1790, by Governor Beverley Randolph. Walker was appointed to the Senate to fill the vacancy caused by the death of William Grayson. He produced his credentials, took his seat April 26, 1790, and served until November 9, 1790, when James Monroe was elected to fill the unexpired term ending March 3, 1791.

3650. Special session of the Senate was held on March 4, 1791, at the Senate Chamber, Philadelpia, PA. It was summoned by President George Washington to transact urgent business: the nomination of district supervisors, of military officers, and of the various officers necessary to put the federal government into operation in the newly admitted state of Vermont.

3651. Legislator to serve in both houses of Congress was Roger Sherman of New Haven, CT, the first congressman to become a senator. He represented Connecticut in the First Congress, from March 4, 1789, to March 3, 1791. On June 13, 1791, he entered the Senate to fill a vacancy caused by another senator's resignation. The first senator to become a congressman was Paine Wingate of Stratham, NH, who represented New Hampshire in the Senate from March 4, 1789, through March 3, 1793, when he was sworn in as the congressional representative from New Hampshire. Both men had been members of the Continental Congress during the Revolution.

Roger Sherman was the only delegate to the Continental Congress whose signature appears on the Declaration of 1774, the Declaration of Independence, the Articles of Confederation, and the Constitution.

3652. Senate election that was contested was that of Abraham Alfonse Albert Gallatin of Pennsylvania, who was born in Switzerland and emigrated to the United States in 1780. He was elected to the Senate from Pennsylvania and presented his credentials on February 28, 1793. No action was taken during the Second Congress, which adjourned March 2, but on December 2 a petition was presented alleging that he had not been a citizen of the United States for the nine years required by the Constitution. The trial began on February 20, 1794, and on February 28 the Senate declared his election void. Gallatin was later elected to the House of Representatives, where he served from March 4, 1795, to March 3, 1801. Gallatin's trial was the first occasion on which members of the public were admitted to the Senate. A motion passed on the first day of the trial required that the Senate chamber "be provided with galleries which shall be permitted to be open every morning so long as the Senate shall be engaged in their legislative capacity, unless in such cases as may in the opinion of the Senate require secrecy."

3653. Senators elected but not seated were William Blount and William Cocke of Tennessee, elected by the Tennessee legislature, who presented their credentials on May 9, 1796. They were refused seats because Tennessee was not admitted to the Union until June 1, 1796. They were elected again on August 2, 1796, and took their seats on December 6, 1796.

3654. Senator to be expelled was William Blount, the first senator from Tennessee, who was elected on August 2, 1796, and served from December 6, 1796, until July 8, 1797, when he was expelled. Blount was convicted of entering into a conspiracy with British officers to divert part of Louisiana from Spain to Great Britain, "a high misdemeanor, entirely inconsistent with his public trust and duty as a Senator." While Congress was considering impeachment charges against him, Blount was elected to serve in the Tennessee state senate, and at the opening session in 1798 was chosen to be its speaker.

3655. Senator to serve in contravention to the age limit was Henry Clay of Kentucky, who served from November 19, 1806, to March 3, 1807. He was born on April 12, 1777, in Hanover County, VA, and was 29 years 221 days old when he took office, although the Constitution states that "no person shall be a Senator who shall not have attained to the age of thirty years."

3656. Senator to be censured was Timothy Pickering, a Federalist of Massachusetts, and a former postmaster general, secretary of war, and secretary of state. On January 2, 1811, the Senate approved a motion to censure him, by a vote of 20 to 7. The motion stated that Pickering, who "read from his place certain documents confidentially communicated by the President of the United States to the Senate, the injunction of secrecy having been removed, has, in so doing, committed a violation of this body." He served in the Senate from March 4, 1803, to March 3, 1811, and in the House of Representatives from March 4, 1813, to March 3, 1817.

3657. Senate filibuster took place February 11–21, 1811, to disrupt the Senate's debate over the Bank of the United States. The filibuster was not continuous, as other business was transacted during the period. The bank's charter had been approved on February 25, 1791. The Senate's first continuous filibuster extended from February 18, 1841, to March 11, 1841. The topic was the dismissal of the printers of the Senate and the election of a public printer.

3658. Father and son who were senators at the same session were Henry Dodge of Wisconsin and his son Augustus Caesar Dodge of Iowa, who sat together from December 7, 1848, to February 22, 1855, in the 30th to 33rd Congresses. Previously they had served as delegates to the House of Representatives in the 27th and 28th Congresses, from March 4, 1841, to March 3, 1845, prior to the statehood of their territories. Henry Dodge continued to serve in the Senate until March 3, 1857.

3659. Senator to serve three states was James Shields of Illinois, Minnesota, and Missouri. He was elected as a Democrat to serve Illinois in the 33rd Congress for the term commencing March 4, 1849. His election was declared void because he had not been a citizen for the requisite number of years. He was then reelected for the same term and served from October 27, 1849, to March 3, 1855. In the 35th Congress, he represented Minnesota, serving from May 12, 1858, to March 3, 1859. He was elected by Missouri on January 22, 1879, to fill the vacancy caused by the death of Lewis Vital Bogy, and served in the 44th Congress from January 27, 1879, to March 3, 1879.

3660. Senator who was returned to the Senate after being defeated for the presidency was Henry Clay of Kentucky, who served in the Senate in 1806–07 and 1810–11, spent many years in the House of Representatives and as secretary of state, served again in the Senate from 1831 to 1842, ran unsuccessfully for president as the candidate of the Whig Party in the election of November 5, 1844, and was returned to the Senate on March 4, 1849, serving until 1852.

3661. Senator who was Jewish was Judah Philip Benjamin of New Orleans, LA, who was elected to the Senate in 1852 and reelected in 1856. He resigned his seat in 1861, after Louisiana seceded from the Union, and was appointed attorney general of the Confederacy and then its secretary of war. A previous senator of Jewish descent was David Levy Yulee, a Democrat from Florida who had converted to Christianity. He served from 1845 to 1851 and again from 1855 to 1861.

3662. Assault by a congressman on a senator took place on May 22, 1856, when Preston Brooks, a Democratic congressman from South Carolina, entered the Senate chamber and beat Massachusetts senator Charles Sumner into unconsciousness with a guttapercha cane. Brooks claimed that this was an act of revenge for Sumner's verbal attacks on Brooks's relative, South Carolina senator Albert Butler. The question of disciplinary action was taken up in the House, where an investigating committee recommended that

Brooks be expelled, but the resolution fell short of a majority vote. Brooks then resigned and was promptly reelected.

> Senator Charles Sumner was trapped at his desk when Congressman Preston Brooks attacked him. The first blow opened a four-inch gash in Sumner's head. In all, Brooks hit Sumner between 12 and 20 blows, breaking his cane into pieces as he did so.

3663. Mass expulsion from the Senate took place on July 11, 1861, when the Senate, by a vote of 32 to 10, voted to expel 10 senators who had not taken their seats because their states had withdrawn from the Union. They were James Mason Murray, the president pro tempore of the Senate, and Robert M. T. Hunter, both of Virginia; Thomas L. Clingman and Thomas Bragg of North Carolina; James Chesnut, Jr., of South Carolina; Alfred O. P. Nicholson of Tennessee; William K. Sebastian and Charles B. Mitchel of Arkansas; and John Hemphill and Louis T. Wigfall of Texas. All were Democrats. Sebastian's expulsion was later reversed.

3664. Senator to address the Senate in military uniform was Edward Dickinson Baker, Republican of Oregon. On August 11, 1861, he was drilling his regiment at Meridian Hill when he was summoned to refute Senator John Breckinridge, Democrat of Kentucky, who was speaking against a proposal to send troops against the South. Baker did not have time to change into civilian attire but removed his sword prior to delivering his speech. He was killed at the Battle of Balls Bluff, VA, on October 21, 1861.

3665. Senate hearing witness who was a woman was Elizabeth Cady Stanton, who addressed the Senate District Committee on January 20, 1869, in a plea to save the women of the District of Columbia from being debarred from voting.

3666. Senator who was African-American was Hiram Rhoades Revels, Republican of Natchez, MS, who was elected to the Senate on January 20, 1870, by the legislature of Mississippi for the unexpired term beginning March 4, 1865, and ending March 3, 1871. He was sworn in on February 25, 1870. After his Senate service he became president of Alcorn Agriculture and Mechanical College in Lorman, MS. The first African-American senator to serve a full term was Blanche Kelso Bruce, Republican of Mississippi, who served from March 4, 1875, to March 3, 1881. He had been born a slave in Virginia.

3667. Fistfight in the Senate took place on February 28, 1902, between two South Carolina senators, Benjamin Tillman and John McLaurin. Tillman accused McLaurin of changing his position on a treaty for political gain. McLaurin called Tillman a liar, and a brawl ensued. The Senate later adopted a rule prohibiting in its members any words or behavior deemed "unworthy or unbecoming a Senator."

3668. Senator convicted of a crime was Joseph Ralph Burton, Republican of Kansas. In 1904 he was convicted by a federal court in St. Louis, MO, of having accepted four checks of $500 each from the Rialto Grain & Securities Company in exchange for using his influence to persuade the U.S. Post Office not to punish the company for mail fraud. His conviction was overturned by the Supreme Court and the matter was sent back for retrial; he was convicted again in November 1905, and this time his conviction was upheld. He resigned from the Senate on June 4, 1906, and served a five-month prison term.

Library of Congress, Prints & Photographs Division LC-USZ62-48965

Elizabeth Cady Stanton and her daughter, Harriet, from a daguerreotype, 1856.

3669. Senator who was Native American was Charles Curtis of Kansas, who served from January 23, 1907, to March 3, 1913, and from March 4, 1915, to March 3, 1929, when he resigned to assume the vice presidency under President Herbert Clark Hoover. His mother was the great-granddaughter of the Kansas-Kaw chief White Plume and came from a family that had intermarried for several generations with French Canadians. Curtis spent part of his childhood living near the Kaw reservation in Council Grove, KS.

3670. Senator expelled for corrupt election practices was William Lorimer of Illinois, elected in 1909. Two lengthy investigations by the Committee on Privileges and Elections concluded that his election was valid and in accordance with "existing political conditions in the State of Illinois." However, a resolution declaring his election invalid was put to a vote on July 13, 1912, and passed by a vote of 55 to 28.

3671. Senate whip was Senator James Hamilton Lewis of Illinois, who was appointed on May 28, 1913, by the Democratic Party to see that Democrats were present or paired at every roll call. The first whip of the Republican Party was Senator James Wolcott Wadsworth of New York, who served one week in 1915 until Senator Charles Curtis of Kansas was named his successor.

3672. Senator elected by popular vote after the passage of the 17th Amendment to the Constitution was Augustus Octavius Bacon, Democrat of Georgia, who was elected on July 15, 1913, and sworn in on July 28. Section 3, Article 1 of the Constitution provided for the election of senators by the state legislatures. The 17th Amendment, which required senators to be elected by popular vote, was passed in the House of Representatives on April 13, 1912, and by the Senate on June 12, 1912. The 36th state to ratify the amendment was Wisconsin, on May 9, 1913, and the amendment was declared in force May 31, 1913. The first general election in which senators were elected by popular vote took place on November 4, 1913.

3673. Senator who was a woman was Rebecca Latimer Felton, a Democrat, who was appointed temporarily to the Senate by Governor Thomas William Hardwick of Georgia on October 3, 1922, to fill the vacancy caused by the death of Thomas Edward Watson; she served only two days. The first woman to win election to the Senate was Hattie Ophelia Wyatt Caraway, a Democrat from Jonesboro, AR. After having been appointed in November 1931 to fill the vacancy caused by the death of her husband, Senator Thaddeus Horatio Caraway, she was then elected in her own right on January 12, 1932, and reelected in 1938.

3674. Senate majority leader was Charles Curtis, Republican of Kansas, who served in the Senate from January 29, 1907, through March 3, 1913, and again from March 4, 1915, through March 3, 1929. He was elected majority leader on November 28, 1924, and served in that post until he left the Senate to become vice president under Herbert Hoover.

3675. Senator unseated after a recount was Smith Wildman Brookhart, Republican of Iowa, the presumed winner of the election of November 4, 1924. He presented his credentials as a senator-elect for the term commencing March 4, 1925, and served until April 12, 1926, when he was ousted by a Senate vote of 45–41. A recount had proved the winner to be Daniel Frederic Steck, the Democrat candidate, who served from April 12, 1926, to March 3, 1931.

3676. Senate election in which neither candidate was seated after a recount was the election of November 2, 1926, in Pennsylvania. William Bauchop Wilson, a Democrat, was narrowly defeated by William Scott Vare, a Republican, who presented his credentials as senator-elect for the term beginning March 4, 1927. The Senate, on December 6, 1929, decided by a vote of 58–22 that Vare was not entitled to the seat. Governor John Stuchell Fisher appointed Joseph Ridgway Grundy, a Republican, to the vacant seat. Grundy served from December 11, 1929, to December 1, 1930.

3677. Senator who was Hispanic was Octaviano Larrazolo, Republican of New Mexico, who served in the 70th Congress from December 7, 1928, to March 3, 1929. Larrazolo was born in 1859 in the Mexican state of Chihuahua and in 1875 emigrated to the United States, where he studied law and later served in a series of local and statewide elective posts. In 1918 he became governor of New Mexico, and in 1928 he was elected to fill the unexpired term of Democratic senator Andieus A. Jones, who had died in office.

3678. Radio broadcast from the Senate chamber in the Capitol building, Washington, DC, was made on March 4, 1929, in connection with the inauguration ceremonies of President Herbert Clark Hoover. The retiring vice president, Charles Gates Dawes, and the incoming vice president, Charles Curtis, were both heard.

3679. Senate parliamentarian was Charles Lee Watkins, who was formally appointed on July 1, 1937, although he had served as parliamentarian and journal clerk since July 1, 1935, and in other capacities in the Senate since July 16, 1914. He resigned on January 1, 1965, and was designated parliamentarian emeritus by Senate Resolution No. 4 on January 4, 1965.

3680. Legislator who was a woman to serve in both houses of Congress was Margaret Chase Smith, Republican of Skowhegan, ME. Her husband, Clyde H. Smith, was representing Maine in the House of Representatives when he died in 1940. On June 3, 1940, she won his seat in a special election. She was reelected to the House four times. In the primary election of 1948, she defeated three men to become the Republican candidate in the Maine senatorial race, and on November 2, 1948, she won election to the Senate. She was elected three more times before being unseated in 1972. The first woman from the Democratic Party to serve in both houses was Barbara Ann Mikulsi of Maryland, who took her seat in the House on January 3, 1977, and in the Senate on January 6, 1987.

3681. Senator to win a seat that had been occupied by his father and his mother was Russell Long of Louisiana, who was elected on November 2, 1948, and sworn in on December 31, 1948, for the term expiring January 2, 1951. His father, Huey Pierce Long, the boss of the Democratic party machine in Louisiana, was elected on November 4, 1930, and took the oath of office on January 25, 1932. He was assassinated in 1935. Rose McConnell Long, wife of Huey Long and mother of Russell Long, was appointed on January 31, 1936, to fill the seat left vacant by the assassination. She served until January 2, 1937.

3682. Three brothers from one family to serve in the Senate were the three sons of Joseph Patrick Kennedy and Rose Kennedy of Boston, MA: John Fitzgerald Kennedy, senator from Massachusetts, who was sworn in on January 3, 1953; Edward Moore Kennedy, also from Massachusetts, who was sworn in on January 9, 1963; and Robert Francis Kennedy, senator from New York, who was sworn in on January 3, 1965.

3683. Senator elected by a write-in vote was James Strom Thurmond, Democrat of South Carolina, who was elected on November 2, 1954, for the term ending January 3, 1961. Thurmond received 139,106 votes, defeating Edgar Brown, the official candidate of the Democratic Party, who received 80,956 votes.

3684. Senate filibuster to last for more than 24 hours was conducted by Senator James Strom Thurmond, Democrat of South Carolina, who spoke against civil rights legislation for 24 hours and 18 minutes on August 28–29, 1957.

3685. Senator of Asian ancestry was Hiram Leong Fong, a Republican of Chinese ancestry who was elected on July 29, 1959, by Hawaii, which joined the Union on August 21. He was sworn in on August 24. His parents, emigrants from China, were laborers on sugar plantations.

3686. Senate election race in which both candidates were women was held on November 8, 1960, in Maine. Incumbent Margaret Chase Smith, Republican, defeated Lucia Marie Cormier, Democrat, by a vote of 255,890 to 159,809.

3687. Senate page who was African-American was Lawrence Wallace Bradford, Jr., age 16, of New York City, who was appointed by Senator Jacob Javits of New York on April 13, 1965.

3688. Senator who was African-American to be elected by popular vote was Edward William Brooke, the attorney general of Massachusetts, who was elected on November 8, 1966, by a plurality of approximately 439,000 votes. He was seated on January 10, 1967.

3689. Senator to act in the movies was Everett McKinley Dirksen of Illinois, who appeared in *The Monitors*, a satire released on October 9, 1969. It was a 91-minute film produced by Bell and Howell Productions in association with Commonwealth United Entertainment. The film depicted a pacifistic nonviolent United States dominated from the White House down by a horde of robot-like young men in bowlers. It featured Ed Begley as the president, Keenan Wynn as the general, and Larry Storch as the colonel.

3690. Senator who had been an astronaut was John Herschel Glenn, Jr., of New Concord, OH, the first astronaut to orbit the earth, who was elected as a Democrat on November 5, 1974. He was the pilot of the Mercury spacecraft *Friendship*, launched on February 20, 1962, by an Atlas booster. He made three orbits in 4 hours 55 minutes and landed east of the Bahamas in the Atlantic Ocean.

3691. Senate proceeding to be shown on television was the installation ceremony for Nelson Aldrich Rockefeller of New York, who was sworn in as the 41st vice president of the United States on December 19, 1974, in the Senate chamber, Washington, DC, immediately after being confirmed. He was selected by President Gerald Rudolph Ford on August 20, 1974, 11 days after Ford took office following the resignation of President Richard Milhous Nixon.

3692. Senator who was an African-American woman was Carol Mosely Braun, a Democrat from Chicago, IL, who was elected on November 3, 1992.

3693. Senators who were Jewish women were Barbara Boxer and Dianne Feinstein, elected to the Senate as Democrats from California on November 3, 1992.

3694. Arms control treaty rejected by the Senate was the Comprehensive Test Ban Treaty, signed by President Bill Clinton in September 1996. On October 13, 1999, the Senate refused to ratify the treaty. The vote was 51 against, 48 in favor, and 1 vote of "present"; 67 votes were required for passage.

3695. First Lady elected to the Senate was Hillary Rodham Clinton, First Lady from 1993 to 2001. While still First Lady, she was nominated by the Democratic Party as a candidate for the Senate from New York State. She was elected on November 7, 2000, and took office on January 3, 2001.

3696. Senate candidate elected posthumously was Mel Carnahan, the governor of Missouri. Carnahan, a Democrat, challenged incumbent senator John Ashcroft in the 2000 election. On October 16, 2000, in the midst of the campaign, Carnahan, his son, and an aide were killed when their plane crashed near Goldman, MO. His wife Jean ran in his stead, but it was too late, according to Missouri law, to remove Carnahan's name from the ballot. He defeated Ashcroft in the election on November 7.

3697. Senator to change political control of the Senate by switching parties was Jim Jeffords of Vermont, originally elected as a Republican. On May 24, 2001, he announced that he was leaving the GOP to become an independent. Because the 2000 election left the Senate evenly divided between Republicans and Democrats, with 50 on each side, Jeffords's switch made the Democrats the majority party.

3698. Senate election in which both candidates were African-American was the election of November 2, 2004, for an open Senate seat from Illinois. The winner was Barack Obama, the Democratic candidate. His Republican opponent was political commentator Alan Keyes. Obama's father was born in Kenya; his mother was white. Keyes's parents were both from Jamaica.

Courts

3699. Grand jury convened on September 1, 1635, at New Towne (now Cambridge), MA, to investigate accusations against persons charged with crimes and indict them for trial before a petit jury if there was sufficient evidence.

3700. Jury composed of women was ordered by the General Provinciall Court at the session held on September 22, 1656, at Patuxent, MD. The jury was composed of seven married women and four single women who tried Judith Catchpole for the murder of her child. The order read: "Whereas Judith Catchpole being brought before the Court upon Suspicion of Murdering a Child which She is accused to have brought forth, and denying the fact or that She ever had Child, the Court hath ordered that a Jury of able women be Impannelled and to give in their Verdict to the best of their Judgment whether She the said Judith hath ever had a Child or not." The jury's verdict was "not guilty" and the court ordered that "the said Judith Catchpole be acquitted of that charge unless further evidence appear."

3701. Judge to be impeached was Nicolas More, chief justice of colonial Philadelphia. He fell under such displeasure that the assembly on May 15, 1685, presented 10 charges of impeachment against him to the council. Among other offenses he was charged with "assuming to himself an unlimited and arbitrary power in office." He was expelled on June 2, 1685, but the council refused to sanction the impeachment proceedings.

3702. Creation of federal courts was accomplished through the first Judiciary Act, drafted by William Paterson of New Jersey and Oliver Ellsworth of Connecticut, and enacted on September 24, 1789. It established a federal judicial system consisting of district courts (one for each state), circuit courts (one for each of three regions), a six-member Supreme Court, and the post of attorney general.

3703. Attorney of the United States was Samuel Sherburne, Jr., of New Hampshire, who was appointed United States attorney in and for the New Hampshire District on September 26, 1789. Twelve other attorneys, one for each state district, were appointed on the same date.

3704. Federal judge to be impeached was John Pickering, judge of the U.S. District Court for the district of New Hampshire, who was removed from office after his conviction by the Senate on March 12, 1804, on charges of drunkenness, profanity, and violence on the bench. The vote was 19–7.

3705. Civil trial featuring celebrity lawyers took place in Philadelphia, PA, in 1805, when Patrick Lyon sued the president of the Bank of Pennsylvania, its head cashier, a board member, and a constable for framing him for a 1798 bank robbery. The trial was an all-star showcase for the top legal talent of the day. Lyon was represented by two distinguished trial lawyers: Alexander J. Dallas, a future secretary of the Treasury, and Joseph Hopkinson, future congressman from Pennsylvania and son of Francis Hopkinson, a signer of the Declaration of Independence. The attorneys for the defense were Jared Ingersoll, former and future attorney general of Pennsylvania and a signer of the Constitution, and William Rawle, former U.S. district attorney for Pennsylvania.

The jury in the Lyon case returned a verdict of guilty and awarded him unprecedented damages of $12,000, later reduced to $9,000 on appeal. This was one of the largest trial awards of the age and enabled Lyon to set up as a successful manufacturer of fire engines.

3706. Claims court established by the federal government was established by an act "to establish a court for the investigation of claims against the United States," signed on February 24, 1855, by President Franklin Pierce. It required the appointment by the president, with the consent of the Senate, of three judges with life tenure. President Pierce appointed Isaac Blackford of Indiana and John James Gilchrist of New Hampshire on March 3, 1855, and George P. Scarborough of Virginia on May 8, 1855. The judges received $4,000 annually. The court was organized on May 11, 1855, with Judge Gilchrist as presiding judge. It was reorganized by act of March 3, 1863. Until March 3, 1887, it was the only court in which cases could be prosecuted against the government.

3707. Interracial jury composed of both white and African-American jurors was the grand jury that indicted Jefferson Davis, the president of the Confederacy, on a treason charge on May 8, 1866. The petit jury in this case was the second interracial jury. Davis, his wife, and their four children were captured at Irwinville, GA, on May 10, 1865, by Lieutenant Colonel Benjamin Dudley Pritchard, commanding the 4th Michigan Cavalry. Davis was imprisoned and indicted for treason. In 1867 he was released on bond. The case was finally brought to trial on December 3, 1868, in the Circuit Court of the United States at Richmond, VA, before Judges Salmon Portland Chase and John Curtiss Underwood, but was dismissed because of President Andrew Johnson's general amnesty proclamation, issued on December 25, 1868. The charge was dropped by the district attorney on February 15, 1869.

3708. State supreme court justice who was African-American was Jonathan Jasper Wright of Beaufort, SC, who served as one of the three members of the court from February 2, 1870, to December 1, 1877. The first African-American chief justice of a state supreme court was James Benton Parsons, who became chief justice of the Illinois Supreme Court on April 18, 1975.

3709. Justice of the peace who was a woman was Esther Hobart Morris of South Pass City, WY, who was appointed on February 17, 1870, by the county commissioners.

3710. Juvenile court was the Juvenile Court of Cook County, known as the Chicago Juvenile Court, authorized on April 21, 1899, and opened on July 1, 1899, with Richard Stanley Tuthill as judge. This was the first juvenile court in the world. During the first year, about 2,300 cases were heard. Cases involving girls were tried by a female judge, Mary Margaret Bartelme, beginning on March 3, 1913.

3711. Night court was opened in New York City on September 1, 1907. It was a magistrates' court, the Jefferson Market Court at Ninth Street and Sixth Avenue, presided over by Charles Nathan Harris. Sessions were held from 8 P.M. to 3 A.M. until September 1, 1910, when the closing hour was fixed at 1 A.M.

3712. Domestic relations court was established in Buffalo, NY, in 1909 by Simon Augustine Nash, judge of Police Court, who privately heard domestic relations cases in his chambers instead of in open court. A state law approved on May 29, 1909, formally established the City Court of Buffalo, and the domestic relations division was opened on January 1, 1910.

3713. Commerce court established by the federal government was established by act of Congress on June 18, 1910. A presiding judge and five associates were appointed by President William Howard Taft for terms that extended from one to five years. The court was organized on February 8, 1911, and opened on February 15 in Washington, DC. Appeal of its decisions could be made only to the Supreme Court. Because of various abuses, the court was abolished on December 31, 1913.

3714. Small claims court was a state court for small debtors, authorized on March 15, 1913, by Kansas, to deal with cases involving not more than $20. Plaintiffs and defendants appeared without legal representation. Judges served without fee, pay, or award and were not required to be lawyers. Appeals could be taken to the district court. The first court was at Topeka, KS, with W. H. Kemper as judge. The first city conciliation tribunal for small claims was the Conciliation Branch of the Municipal Court of Cleveland, OH, also established on March 15, 1913. The complainant could not be represented by counsel but had to present his own case. Strict rules of evidence and procedure were waived. The judgment rendered had the same force and effect, and was as binding, as a judgment rendered in any court of record.

3715. District attorney who was a woman was Annette Abbott Adams, who served as U.S. district attorney in the Northern California District from July 25, 1918, to June 26, 1920.

3716. Judge to impose the death penalty who was a woman was Florence Ellinwood Allen, a judge of the Court of Common Pleas of the County of Cuyahoga, Cleveland, OH. She gave a sentence of death by electrocution to Frank Motto, who had been convicted by a jury on a charge of first-degree murder on May 14, 1921. The sentence was carried out on August 20, 1921.

3717. State supreme court justice who was a woman was Florence Ellinwood Allen of Cleveland, OH, who was elected on December 16, 1922, to the Ohio Supreme Court.

3718. State supreme court in which all the judges were women was the Special Supreme Court of Texas, appointed by Governor Pat Morris Neff on January 8, 1925. When an application for writ of error in the case of *W. T. Johnson, et al. v. J. M. Darr, et al.*, from El Paso County (a Woodmen of the World case), reached the Supreme Court of Texas, all three judges found themselves disqualified to consider it and immediately certified their disqualifications to the governor as required by law. The governor appointed Hortense Ward of Houston as special chief justice and Hattie L. Henenberg of Dallas and Ruth Brazzil of Galveston as special associate justices. The case was decided on May 23, 1925, affirming the judgment of the Court of Civil Appeals.

3719. Federal judge who was a woman was Genevieve Rose Cline of the U.S. Customs Court, New York, who was appointed on May 4, 1928, by President Calvin Coolidge. The first justice of the Circuit Court of Appeals who was a woman was Florence Ellinwood Allen, nominated on March 6, 1934, by President Franklin Delano Roosevelt to fill the vacancy brought about by the death of Judge

Smith Hickenlooper. She was sworn in on April 9, 1934. She served in the sixth judicial court.

3720. Grand jury foreman who was a woman was Julia Isabelle Sims of Newark, NJ, who served on the federal grand jury in the U.S. District Court for the District of New Jersey in session at Newark from April 6, 1937, to October 19, 1937. Judge William Clark presided.

3721. Judge who was an African-American woman was Jane Matilda Bolin, who on July 22, 1939, was appointed judge of the Court of Domestic Relations by Mayor Fiorello La Guardia of New York City. She was also the first African-American woman to graduate from Yale Law School and the first to be admitted to the New York City bar. The first African-American woman to be elected to a judgeship, rather than appointed, was Edith Spurlock Sampson, elected associate judge of the Municipal Court of Chicago, IL, on November 8, 1962, and sworn in on December 3, 1962. She became an associate judge of the Circuit Court of Cook County, Chicago, IL, on January 1, 1964.

3722. Federal appellate judge who was African-American was William Henry Hastie, former governor of the U.S. Virgin Islands, who was unanimously confirmed by the Senate on July 19, 1950, for a recess appointment to the Courts of Appeals for the Third Judicial Circuit (Pennsylvania, New Jersey, Delaware, and the Virgin Islands). He was sworn in by Chief Judge John Biggs, Jr., in Philadelphia, PA.

3723. Television eyewitness allowed to testify in a federal court was Mrs. Sophie Eisenberg of Brooklyn, New York City, who testified in U.S. Federal Court, New York City, on January 29, 1951, before Judge Irving Robert Kaufman. The lawsuit before the court had been brought by Jonas Walvisch of New York City, who had been a spectator at a hockey game between the Montreal Canadiens and the New York Rangers at Madison Square Garden on March 16, 1947. Walvisch accused Emile "Butch" Bouchard, the captain of the Canadiens, of hitting him, and sued him for $75,000. Mrs. Eisenberg testified that she was watching the game on television when she saw Bouchard hit Walvisch. The spectator, however, lost his suit.

3724. Judge of Asian ancestry was Delbert E. Wong, appointed to the municipal bench of Los Angeles, CA, by Governor Edmund Brown in 1959.

3725. District attorney who was African-American was Cecil Francis Poole, who was sworn in July 6, 1961, at San Francisco, as attorney for the northern district of California. He retired February 3, 1970. Previously, four African-Americans had served as United States attorney in the U.S. Virgin Islands, which are territorial possessions of the United States.

3726. Federal district court judge who was African-American was Judge James Benton Parsons, who was sworn in on September 22, 1961, at Chicago, IL, as a U.S. district judge for the Northern District of Illinois. His appointment had been confirmed by the Senate on August 30, 1961. The first African-American woman to serve as judge of a federal district court was Constance Baker Motley, nominated by President Lyndon Baines Johnson on April 4, 1966, confirmed on August 30 by the Senate Judiciary Committee, and sworn in at the U.S. Court House, Foley Square, New York City on September 9, 1966. She served in the Southern District of New York. In 1982 she was appointed chief judge. Previously, she had been the first African-American woman elected to the New York State Senate.

3727. Courtroom verdict to be televised was delivered on March 14, 1964, at the 3rd Criminal District Court of Dallas County, Dallas, TX. The telecast took place from 12:37 to 2 P.M. Judge Joseph Brantley Brown sentenced Jack Ruby (Jacob L. Rubenstein) to die in the electric chair for the murder with malice of Lee Harvey Oswald, the alleged assassin of President John Fitzgerald Kennedy, on November 24, 1963. The broadcast was pooled by the Columbia Broadcasting System, sent to New York City, and shared with the NBC and ABC networks.

3728. State supreme court chief justice who was a woman was Lorna Elizabeth Lockwood of Douglas, AZ, who was elected as chief justice of the Arizona Supreme Court by unanimous vote of the other justices on January 8, 1965, as chief justice of the Arizona Supreme Court. She served as chief justice from 1965 to 1975. She had been elected an associate justice of the court in 1961.

3729. Judge who had served time in prison was Robert A. "Bob" Young, who was elected to serve the term from January 3, 1977, to December 31, 1983, as judge of the Justice Court, Loomis, CA. He had been convicted at the age of 19 of stealing a credit card out of the mail and had served 20 months in federal prison and four years on parole. He was graduated from law school in 1970 and after a two-year investigation was admitted to the bar.

3730. Civil lawsuit against American organizations brought by American victims of terrorism was filed in May 2000 by Stanley and Joyce Boim, whose 17-year-old son David was shot dead near Jerusalem, Israel, in May 1996 by a gunman from the Palestinian group Hamas. The suit accused four American organizations—the Holy Land Foundation for Relief and Development, the Islamic Association for Palestine, the American Muslim Society, and the Quranic Literacy Institute—of raising funds to help Hamas pay for its terror activities, including the murder of David Boim. All four were held liable by a federal judge and jury in Chicago, IL. On December 8, 2004, U.S. Magistrate Judge Arlander Keys tripled the jury's $52 million award for damages, resulting in a penalty of $156 million. Also held liable for raising and laundering money was an individual, Mohammad Salah of Bridgeview, IL.

Supreme Court

3731. Supreme Court chief justice was John Jay of New York, who was appointed by President George Washington on September 24, 1789. His appointment was confirmed on September 26, 1789, and he served until June 29, 1795.

3732. Supreme Court of the United States consisted of Chief Justice John Jay of New York (1789–95), and associate justices John Rutledge of South Carolina (1789–91), William Cushing of Massachusetts (1789–1810), James Wilson of Pennsylvania (1789–98), John Blair of Virginia (1789–96), and Robert Hanson Harrison of Maryland (1789–90). The appointments were made by President George Washington on September 24, and confirmed by the Senate on September 26. The Judiciary Act of 1789, which implemented the clause in the Constitution providing for the Supreme Court, was passed on September 24. It provided for six justices, four of whom constituted a quorum. The first session began on February 1, 1790, in the Royal Exchange Building on Broad Street, New York City, and lasted 10 days. Two sessions were held each year, beginning on the first Monday of February and of August.

3733. Supreme Court clerk was John Tucker of Boston, MA, appointed on February 3, 1790. It was required "that he reside and keep his office at the seat of the national government, and that he do not practice, either as an attorney or a counsellor in this court, while he shall continue to be clerk of the same."

3734. Supreme Court decision was *West v. Barnes*, tried in the August 1791 term. The motion was refused, as "writs of error made by clerk of the circuit court for Rhode Island district to remove causes to this court from inferior courts, can regularly issue only from the clerk's office of court." No cases were argued during the first four terms of the court (February 1790, August 1790, February 1791, August 1791).

3735. Supreme Court nominee who was rejected by the Senate was William Paterson of New Jersey, who was nominated on February 20, 1793, by President George Washington. His name was sent to the Senate for approval on February 27, but he was rejected on a technicality (he had been serving as senator from New Jersey when the office of associate justice was created). On March 4, 1793, Washington renominated Paterson under a recess appointment. He was confirmed, and served from March 14, 1793, to September 9, 1806.

3736. Supreme Court chief justice whose nomination was not confirmed was John Rutledge of South Carolina, a Federalist, who was appointed chief justice by President George Washington during the adjournment of Congress. He served at a salary of $4,000 a year beginning on July 1, 1795, and presided at the August 1795 term. On December 15, 1795, the Senate rejected the nomination. Rutledge had served as an associate justice from September 26, 1789, to March 5, 1791, at a salary of $3,500 a year, and had resigned to become chief justice of South Carolina.

3737. Supreme Court chief justice who had been a congressional representative was John Marshall of Virginia, who served in the House of Representatives from March 4, 1799, to June 7, 1800, and as chief justice from Febuary 4, 1801, to July 6, 1835, when he died.

3738. Supreme Court decision in a matter between states was the result of a bill in equity between New York and Connecticut in the term that began on August 5, 1799. Chief Justice Oliver Ellsworth presided. The decision read: "As the state of New York was not a party to the suit, nor interested in the decision of these suits, an injunction ought not to issue."

3739. Supreme Court chief justice to serve in a presidential cabinet was John Marshall of Virginia, who was chief justice from February 4, 1801, to July 6, 1835. For the first month, until March 4, 1801, he continued to serve as President John Adams's secretary of state, the job he had held since June 1800.

3740. Supreme Court decision voiding an act of Congress was *Marbury vs. Madison*, which was heard in the term beginning on February 3, 1803, and concerned the congressional act of September 24, 1789. President John Adams appointed William Marbury justice of the peace. President Thomas Jefferson instructed Secretary of State James Madison not to deliver the commission.

James Madison

3741. Supreme Court justice to be impeached was Samuel Chase, against whom charges were brought on March 12, 1804, by the House of Representatives. The accusation consisted of eight articles, of which the majority had to do with high-handed conduct displayed by Chase in two treason and sedition trials. There were also political reasons for the impeachment, which was encouraged by President Thomas Jefferson. The trial began on January 30, 1805. Chase was acquitted and served until his death on June 19, 1811, at the age of 70.

3742. Supreme Court decision establishing the power of the federal government as greater than that of the individual states was made on February 20, 1809, when Chief Justice John Marshall, in *United States v. Judge Peters*, rendered an opinion sustaining the federal power and ordered a writ of mandamus issued to carry a previous decree into effect. Judge Richard Peters of the U.S. District Court of Pennsylvania had decreed that a certain sum of prize money be paid to a Mr. Olmstead of Connecticut for his capture of a British sloop during the Revolutionary War. The state of Pennsylvania refused to recognize Olmstead's claim, and the state militia was called out to stop a federal marshal from serving the judge's order. The Supreme Court decided that a state legislature of a state cannot annul the judgment or determine the jurisdiction of a federal court.

3743. Supreme Court decision declaring a state law unconstitutional was made on March 16, 1810, in the case of Robert Fletcher of Amherst, NH, who bought 13,000 acres of land for $3,000 on May 14, 1803, from John Peck of Boston, MA. The court ruled that Georgia's rescinding act violated the contract clause of Article 1, Section 10, of the Constitution. Chief Justice John Marshall decided that "the Union has a constitution, the supremacy of which all acknowledge, and which imposes limits to the legislation of the several states, which none claim a right to pass."

3744. Supreme Court decision reversing the ruling of a state supreme court was rendered in 1813 in the case of *Fairfax's Devisee v. Hunter's Lessee*. The case concerned the Virginia estate of a wealthy loyalist, Lord Thomas Fairfax, which had been confiscated by Virginia during the Revolutionary War. The Virginia Court of Appeals held that the confiscation was illegal. A writ of error was obtained and the case was argued as *Martin v. Hunter's Lessee*. The Supreme Court in 1816 unanimously sustained the validity of the 25th section of Chapter 20 of the act of September 24, 1789, which established the judicial system and established for all time the right of the Supreme Court to review the determinations of the highest state courts in cases involving the Constitution and federal laws or treaties.

3745. Supreme Court decision in a commerce case was *Thomas Gibbons v. Aaron Ogden*, for which the opinion was written by Chief Justice John Marshall in February 1824. The decision determined that navigation from one state to another is a form of interstate commerce. It reversed a lower court ruling that prevented Gibbons from sailing his steamboats in New York State waters.

3746. Supreme Court justice who was Catholic was Roger Brooke Taney of Frederick, MD, who was appointed by President Andrew Jackson to succeed John Marshall as chief justice. He served from March 28, 1836, until his death on October 12, 1864.

3747. Supreme Court decision in a state boundary case was made in 1846, when Chief Justice Roger Brooke Taney ruled that a bill "should be dismissed upon the ground that this court under the Constitution of the United States have not the power to try such a question between states, or redress a wrong, even if the wrong is proved to have been done." On March 16, 1832, Rhode Island, the complainant, had petitioned the Supreme Court to settle a boundary controversy with Massachusetts.

3748. Supreme Court nominee to die before taking office was Edwin McMasters Stanton, appointed by President Ulysses Simpson Grant on December 20, 1869, and confirmed the same day by a vote of 46 to 11. Stanton died on December 24.

3749. Supreme Court justice to be appointed chief justice was Edward Douglass White, who was appointed associate justice on March 12, 1894, and chief justice on December 12, 1910. He took his seat on December 19 and served until May 2, 1921, a week before his death. In 1795, President George Washington had appointed former associate justice John Rutledge to be chief justice, but the appointment was rejected by the Senate after Rutledge had already served during one session.

3750. Supreme Court justice who was Jewish was Louis Dembitz Brandeis of Boston, MA, who was appointed on January 28, 1916, by President Woodrow Wilson. The nomination was confirmed by the Senate on June 1, 1916, and Brandeis was sworn in on June 3. He served until 1939. The first Jewish woman to serve on the Supreme Court was Ruth Bader Ginsburg of the U.S. Appeals Court for the District of Columbia, nominated by President William Jefferson Clinton on June 14, 1993. She filled the seat vacated by Justice Byron White. She was the second woman to serve on the Supreme Court and the first Jewish justice since the resignation of Abe Fortas in 1969.

3751. Supreme Court justice who was African-American was Thurgood Marshall of Maryland, appointed on June 13, 1967, by President Lyndon Baines Johnson. He was confirmed by the Senate by a vote of 69–11 on August 30, 1967, and sworn in on September 1 in a private ceremony. He was publicly sworn in at the opening ceremony of the new term on October 2, 1967. He was the 96th justice.

3752. Supreme Court justice who was a woman was Sandra Day O'Connor of Arizona, nominated as an associate justice by President Ronald Reagan on July 7, 1981. The Senate approved her appointment by a vote of 99–0 on September 21. O'Connor took her seat on September 25 after taking the oath of office administered by Chief Justice Warren E. Burger.

3753. Supreme Court decision on inclusion of candidates in televised political debates was *Arkansas Educational Television Commission v. Forbes*, decided on May 19, 1998. The case concerned a candidates' debate that was sponsored by a state-owned public television station during the congressional election campaign of 1992. The station did not permit an independent candidate, Ralph Forbes, to participate in the debate along with the candidates of the major parties, although he had qualified to appear on the ballot. The Rehnquist Court, by a vote of 6 to 3, agreed with a lower court that the First Amendment allowed the station to give selective access to candidates as long as it did not target specific political views for discrimination.

3754. Supreme Court with a majority of Catholic justices was the Roberts Court of 2006. When Samuel A. Alito was sworn in on January 31, 2006, he became the fifth Catholic jurist on the nine-member panel, together with Antonin Scalia, Anthony Kennedy, Clarence Thomas, and Chief Justice John G. Roberts.

Elections

3755. Election held in a colony took place on May 18, 1631, when John Winthrop was elected governor of Massachusetts. It is believed, however, that in 1619 the Virginia Assembly was selected by means of votes.

3756. Colonial election held in defiance of the Royal Courts was held on April 11, 1640, in Wethersfield, CT, when Matthew Mitchell was elected recorder. The King's Court at Hartford refused to recognize the election and penalized Wethersfield £5 and the recorder 40 nobles. The fines were not paid.

3757. Ban on convicts holding public office was passed on March 2, 1642, by Virginia. It stated: "Be it also enacted that no person or persons whatsoever for any offence already committed or to be committed shall be hereafter adjudged to serve the collony."

3758. Woman in America to appeal for the right to vote was Margaret Brent, a niece of Lord Baltimore, the founder of the colony of Maryland. She came to America from England in January 1638 and was the first woman in Maryland to own property in her own name. She became one of the colony's principal landowners and a person of influence, raising a troop of soldiers in 1644. On June 24, 1647, she appealed for the right to vote in the colonial assembly by virtue of her position as secretary to Governor Leonard Calvert, asking for a "place and voyce," but was ejected from the meetings. At the death of Calvert, she became his executor and acting governor, presiding over the General Assembly, but was refused a voice in the affairs of the government as "it would set a bad example to the wives of the colony." She moved to Virginia in 1650.

3759. Corrupt election practices law enacted by a colony was passed on May 22, 1649, by the General Court in Warwick, RI. It provided that "no one should bring in any votes that he did not receive from the voters' own hands, and that all votes should be field by the Recorder in the presence of the Assembly." A committee of four freemen was authorized to determine violations of the law and "to examine parties and present to this court what they find in the case."

3760. Woman whose vote was recorded was the widow of Josiah Taft of Uxbridge, MA, who participated in a town referendum in 1756. She was granted this privilege because her son, Bazaleel, was a minor. She voted in favor of levying a town tax.

3761. Election law enacted by a colony granting voting rights to women was passed by New Jersey. Its new constitution, adopted on July 2, 1776, provided "that all the inhabitants of this Colony of full age who are worth 50 Pounds Proclamation money, with clear estate in the same, and have resided within the county in which they claim a vote for twelve months immediately preceding the election" were entitled to vote at the general election. In 1790 this was interpreted to mean both men and women. It did not, however, apply to married women, but only to spinsters and widows. On November 16, 1807, the General Assembly passed laws providing that only free white male citizens could exercise the franchise.

3762. Election law enacted by a state to grant universal voting rights to freemen without restriction as to property or wealth was Vermont. The state constitution adopted at a general convention held on July 28, 1777, at Windsor, VT, permitted all freemen who were natural-born citizens over 21 years of age to elect officers and to be elected to office.

3763. Book advocating voting rights for women was a reprint of *A Vindication of the Rights of Women, with Strictures on Political and Moral Subjects*, by Mary Wollstonecraft Godwin, 276 pages, printed in 1792 in Philadelphia, PA, by William Gibbons. Another edition, of 340 pages, was published in Boston, MA, by Peter Edes with a slight subtitle variation. The book was originally published in England in 1790.

3764. Printed ballot was authorized by the "act to regulate the general elections within this commonwealth," enacted on February 15, 1799, by Pennsylvania. The law provided that "every elector may deliver written or printed tickets." The ballots were prepared by political parties and were known as "vest pocket tickets." They contained only the names of the issuing party's candidates.

3765. Voting registration law enacted by a state was enacted by Massachusetts and signed on March 7, 1801, by Governor Caleb Strong.

3766. State nominating convention assembled at Utica, NY, in 1824 for the purpose of nominating candidates for governor and lieutenant governor. The number of delegates corresponded to the number of representatives in the assembly. De Witt Clinton was nominated by the Democratic-Republican Party and was elected on November 3, 1824. He served as governor from January 1, 1825, to his death on February 11, 1828. He had previously served as governor from January 1, 1818, to December 31, 1822.

3767. African-American to hold elective office was John Mercer Langston, elected town clerk by the voters of Brownhelm, OH, in 1855. Langston, the son of a plantation owner and a freed slave, was an Oberlin-educated lawyer. He went on to serve as law professor and dean of Howard University, minister to Haiti and chargé d'affaires to Santo Domingo (1877–85), and president of the Virginia Normal and Collegiate Institute. He was the first African-American to represent Virginia in the House of Representatives, in 1890–91.

3768. Literacy qualification for voting was required by Massachusetts. An amendment was passed on May 1, 1857, by a vote of 23,833 for and 13,746 against, providing that "no person shall have the right to vote, or to be eligible to office under the constitution of this commonwealth, who shall not be able to read the constitution in the English language, and write his name," excepting those unable to qualify because of physical disability or those over 60 years of age.

3769. National voting rights organization to advocate universal voting rights was the American Equal Rights Association, organized in 1866 to advocate the extension of the voting rights to all citizens, regardless of race, color, or sex. Lucretia Mott was president and Susan Brownell Anthony secretary. In 1869 the association split over the question of whether to place priority on securing voting rights for women or for African-Americans. The result was the formation of two new organizations, the American Woman Suffrage Association, led by Lucy Stone and Julia Ward Howe, and the National Woman Suffrage Association, led by Elizabeth Cady Stanton and Susan B. Anthony. Some 20 years later, the two were reunited to form the National American Woman Suffrage Association.

Library of Congress, Prints & Photographs Division
LC-USZ62-83145

Susan B. Anthony

3770. Corrupt election practices law enacted by a state was passed by the legislature of California and signed by Governor Frederick Low on March 26, 1866. The first state law requiring candidates to file itemized accounts of campaign expenditures, under penalty of imprisonment and loss of office, was passed by New York State and signed by Governor Theodore Roosevelt on April 4, 1890.

3771. Election law granting African-American men the right to vote was the congressional act of January 8, 1867, amending voting practices in Washington, DC. Every male citizen of the city who was 21 years of age or over was given the right to vote, except paupers, those under guardianship, men convicted of infamous crimes, and men who gave voluntary comfort to the rebels during the Civil War. The bill was vetoed by

President Andrew Johnson on January 5, 1867. His veto was overridden in the Senate by a vote of 29 to 10 and in the House by a vote of 112 to 38.

3772. African-American to vote under authority of the 15th Amendment to the Constitution was Thomas Peterson-Mundy of Perth Amboy, NJ, who voted in Perth Amboy on March 31, 1870, in a special election for ratification or rejection of a city charter. The charter was adopted and he was appointed to the committee to revise the charter. The 15th Amendment to the Constitution, allowing African-American male citizens to vote, became law on March 30, 1870.

3773. Election law enacted by a state to grant voting rights to women after the adoption of the Constitution was Wyoming, which became a state on July 10, 1890. Women had voted in Wyoming from the beginning of its existence as a territory. The first territorial legislature extended the vote to women on December 10, 1869.

3774. Voting machines were authorized for use in New York State on March 15, 1892, by an act "to secure independence of voters at town meetings, secrecy of the ballot and provide for the use of Myers' automatic ballot cabinet." Later legislation extended the use of the machine to cities. The machines were first used on April 12, 1892, at Lockport, NY, where 3,271 votes were cast for the office of mayor and other town offices. The machine was invented by Jacob H. Myers and manufactured by the American Ballot Machine Company, which was later absorbed by the Automatic Voting Machine Corporation of Jamestown, NY.

3775. Absentee voting law enacted by a state was enacted by Vermont on November 24, 1896. According to its provisions, a voter could obtain a certificate declaring that he was qualified to vote in the state. He could then vote for state officers at any election booth in the state.

3776. Primary election law enacted by a state was passed by Minnesota on April 20, 1899. It applied to candidates for city and county offices, judges, and elective members of school, library, and park boards in counties having a population of 200,000 or more. Hennepin County was the only one that had the required population when the law went into effect. In 1903 Wisconsin became the first state to establish statewide primary elections.

3777. Corrupt election practices law enacted by Congress was passed on January 26, 1907. It prohibited corporations from contributing to candidates' campaign funds in presidential and congressional races. An act passed on March 4, 1909, further prohibited national banks and corporations from making financial contributions to campaign funds in connection with any election to any political office.

Library of Congress, Prints & Photographs Division
LC-USZ62-24065

A suffrage parade in Yonkers, NY, 1913.

3778. Election using the preferential ballot system took place in Grand Junction, CO. The charter that contained the preferential ballot provision was adopted on September 14, 1909, and the first election using the system took place on November 2. Opposite the name of each candidate were three columns headed "First Choice," "Second Choice," and "Third Choice." Any person receiving more than half of all the votes cast for first choice was elected; if no one received more than half the first choices, the lowest candidate was dropped and the first and second choices were added together. If any remaining candidate received a majority of the combined votes, he was elected, but if not, then the lowest candidate was again dropped, and all choices for each candidate then added together, and the person receiving the largest total vote was elected. In case of a tie, priority in choice determined election.

3779. Election using proportional representation was held on November 2, 1915, in Ashtabula, OH, to elect seven council members. The votes were counted so that each group consisting of one-seventh of all the voters secured a representative.

3780. Constitutional amendment proposal guaranteeing women the right to vote was submitted in 1868 and at intervals thereafter without success. The woman suffrage amendment that eventually became law was passed by the House of Representatives on May 21, 1919, and by the Senate on June 4. It was ratified by Illinois, Wisconsin, and Michigan on June 10. Tennessee was the 36th state to ratify, on August 18, 1920, completing the necessary three-quarters of the states to put the amendment into effect. On August 26, 1920, the 19th amendment to the Constitution was proclaimed to be in effect.

Sixty-sixth Congress of the United States of America;

At the First Session,

Begun and held at the City of Washington on Monday, the nineteenth day of May, one thousand nine hundred and nineteen.

JOINT RESOLUTION

Proposing an amendment to the Constitution extending the right of suffrage to women.

Resolved by the Senate and House of Representatives of the United States of America in Congress assembled (two-thirds of each House concurring therein), That the following article is proposed as an amendment to the Constitution, which shall be valid to all intents and purposes as part of the Constitution when ratified by the legislatures of three-fourths of the several States.

"ARTICLE ———.

"The right of citizens of the United States to vote shall not be denied or abridged by the United States or by any State on account of sex.

"Congress shall have power to enforce this article by appropriate legislation."

F. H. Gillett

Speaker of the House of Representatives.

Thos. R. Marshall

Vice President of the United States and President of the Senate.

Courtesy of Images of American Political History and the Library of Congress

The 19th Amendment.

3781. Election campaign using radio was undertaken by Senator Harry Stewart New, Republican of Indiana, who waged an unsuccessful campaign for reelection in 1922. He made a number of radio speeches during the campaign, and hired several halls in which the speeches could be heard over loudspeakers. He was defeated by Samuel Moffett Ralston, the Democratic candidate.

3782. Negative election campaign run by media specialists took place during the California governor's race of 1934. The Democratic candidate was the writer and social reformer Upton Beall Sinclair, a Socialist, whose platform was called EPIC ("End Poverty in California"). The Republican Party, for the first time in any major American election, hired outside political consultants and advertising specialists to conduct a wholly negative campaign. It included attack ads on radio and film, thousands of negative cartoons and leaflets comparing Sinclair to Hitler and Stalin, and a secret dirty tricks squad that tapped his phones. The Republican candidate, Frank Merriam, won by more than 250,000 votes.

3783. Election law lowering the voting age in a state to 18 was enacted on March 3, 1943, as an amendment to the Georgia state constitution. It was approved by popular vote on August 4, 1943, by a 3–1 majority. The first election held under this law took place on November 7, 1944. The national voting age was lowered to 18 in 1971, when the 26th Amendment to the Constitution was ratified by the required number of states. It became law on July 5, 1971.

3784. Governor of Puerto Rico to be elected was Luis Muñoz Marín, journalist and founder of Puerto Rico's Partido Popular Democratico (PPD), the island's ruling party from 1970 to 1977. Muñoz Marín was elected governor in San Juan, PR, in 1948, having previously served as president of the senate since 1942. He was instrumental in securing commonwealth status for Puerto Rico in 1952.

3785. Election in the District of Columbia was the primary election held on Wednesday, May 6, 1964, when the Reverend Edward Franklin Jackson, a Methodist minister who was African-American, defeated Frank Daniel Reeves for the office of Democratic committeeman.

3786. Year when citizens of the District of Columbia could vote in a presidential election was 1964. Residents of Washington, DC, went to the polls on November 3, 1964, to choose between Democrat Lyndon Baines Johnson and Republican Barry Goldwater. Johnson received 85.6 percent of their votes.

3787. Voting rights in space were authorized by the Texas legislature in July 1997. The law was enacted after astronaut John Blaha, a registered voter in Houston, TX, requested the opportunity to vote in the election of November 1996 while he was millions of miles from home aboard the Russian space station *Mir*. Absentee ballots were not available when his mission began, and existing communications technology did not permit him to cast a secret ballot, as required by law. On August 25, 1997, Texas secretary of state Tony Garza announced a new computer program that would allow NASA to collect coded votes from astronauts in space by email. Soviet cosmonauts had already participated in elections while in space, but their votes were not secret.

3788. Vote cast from space in an American election was cast by astronaut David Wolf, a resident of Houston, TX, who was aboard the Mir space station on Election Day, November 4, 1997. Using an email ballot that was authorized by Texas law, Wolf was able to vote in Houston's municipal elections. His ballot was forwarded in both directions through the Russian space agency.

Courtesy of NASA

Space Shuttle Atlantis *with the* Mir *space station.*

3789. State to eliminate polling places in statewide elections was Oregon, where voters approved a proposal to replace voting machines with universal mail-in ballots on November 3, 1998.

3790. Governor of Puerto Rico who was a woman was Sila M. Calderón of San Juan, PR, a member of Popular Democratic Party, who took the oath of office on January 2, 2001. She had previously served as the mayor of San Juan, Puerto Rico's capital city.

3791. State to require paper receipts for electronic voting machines was Nevada. The secretary of state, Dean Heller, announced on December 10, 2003, that the state had ordered touch-screen, direct-recording electronic voting machines to replace its punch-card voting machines, and that each new machine would be able to print paper receipts, allowing voters to compare the votes they made with the votes that were recorded. The machines were manufactured by Sequoia Voting Systems, Oakland, CA. They were first used statewide in the presidential elections on November 2, 2004.

3792. State to require proof of citizenship for voters was Arizona, on November 2, 2004, when Proposition 200 was approved in a referendum. Under the proposition, a person registering to vote for the first time, and anyone coming to vote at a polling place, had to furnish a document such as a birth certificate or passport to prove that he or she was an American citizen.

Presidential

3793. Presidential election was authorized on September 13, 1788, by the Constitutional Convention, which "resolved that the first Wednesday in January next be the day for appointing electors in the several states, which, before the said day, shall have ratified the said Constitution; that the first Wednesday in February next be the day for the electors to assemble in their respective states, and vote for a President; and that the first Wednesday in March next be the time, and the present seat of Congress the place for commencing the proceedings under the said Constitution." Congress was then located in New

York City. The presidential election authorized in this resolution took place on February 4, 1789.

3794. President to receive the unanimous vote of the presidential electors was George Washington of Mount Vernon, Virginia, who received all of the 69 votes cast by the electors from the 10 states that voted on February 4, 1789. A nearly unanimous vote took place in November 1816, when James Monroe of Virginia received 231 of the 232 votes cast by the electors from 24 states. The dissenting vote was cast by William Plumer of New Hampshire.

3795. Electoral vote cast contrary to instructions was cast by Samuel Miles, a Pennsylvania Federalist, in the presidential election of 1796. Instead of voting for John Adams, the Federalist candidate, Miles voted for Thomas Jefferson, a Democratic-Republican. The electors were pledged, but not legally bound, to support a candidate belonging to their party. On March 25, 1969, Maine became the first state to require presidential electors to cast their ballots for the presidential and vice presidential candidates of the political party for which they were chosen.

3796. Presidential election in which more than one candidate declared for the presidency was the election of 1797, in which John Adams received 71 electoral votes and was elected president, and Thomas Jefferson received 68 electoral votes and was elected vice president. In the elections of 1789 and 1793, George Washington was the only avowed presidential candidate.

3797. Presidential candidate nominated at a caucus was Thomas Jefferson of Virginia. The Democratic-Republican Party held a caucus on February 25, 1804, in Washington, DC, at which Jefferson was unanimously nominated for president and George Clinton of New York for vice president. This was the first nominating caucus attended by leaders of a political party. The Federalists did not hold a caucus, but supported Charles Cotesworth Pinckney of South Carolina for president and Rufus King of New York for vice president. At the election in November 1804, Jefferson received 162 electoral votes and Pinckney 14.

3798. Presidential election in which candidates were nominated for the vice presidency was held on November 6, 1804. Prior to the adoption of the 12th Amendment to the Constitution on September 25, 1804, the candidate for president receiving the highest number of votes became president, and the candidate receiving the second highest number became vice president. Thomas Jefferson and George Clinton were the candidates of the Democratic-Republican Party and Charles Cotesworth Pinckney and Rufus King the candidates of the Federalist Party.

3799. Vice presidential candidate to decline the nomination was John Langdon of New Hampshire, who was nominated in Washington, DC, on May 12, 1812, by the congressional caucus of the Republican Party, which gave him 64 votes to James Madison's 82. Langdon declined to run, and a second caucus was held at which Elbridge Gerry was nominated.

3800. Presidential election in which a loser won took place in November 1824, the first election in which popular votes were counted as well as electoral votes. Andrew Jackson received 153,544 popular and 99 electoral votes, John Quincy Adams received 108,740 popular and 84 electoral votes, and William Harris Crawford and Henry Clay received 42 and 37 electoral votes respectively. Since no candidate had a majority of the electoral votes, the House of Representatives was called on to exercise its constitutional responsibility to choose from the highest three. In the meantime, Crawford became ill and was practically eliminated, and Clay agreed to use his influence to have Adams elected, provided that Adams promised to appoint him secretary of state. The balloting in the House of Representatives was 13 states for Adams, seven for Jackson, and four for Crawford.

3801. Presidential candidate nominated at a national convention was Andrew Jackson of Tennessee, who was nominated by the Democrats at their national convention in Baltimore, MD, in 1832. Martin Van Buren of New York was nominated as the Democratic candidate for vice president.

3802. Presidential candidate to make a campaign speech was William Henry Harrison, the Whig candidate in the election of 1840, who spoke on June 6, 1840, from the steps of the National Hotel in Columbus, OH.

Library of Congress, Prints & Photographs Division LC-USZC2-3178

William Henry Harrison

Before that time, candidates gave no speeches themselves, but let others in the party speak on their behalf. Harrison gave 23 stump speeches in all, mostly at rallies held in his home state of Ohio.

3803. President who was a "dark horse" candidate was James Knox Polk. His name appeared for the first time on the eighth ballot at the Democratic convention on May 29, 1844, in Baltimore, MD. On the ninth ballot, amid great confusion, the convention stampeded for him.

3804. Presidential candidate to be assassinated was Joseph Smith of Nauvoo, IL, founder and leader of the Church of Jesus Christ of Latter-day Saints (Mormon Church), whose candidacy was advocated in January 1844 by the church's Council of Twelve. The National Reform Party confirmed the nomination in a state convention at Nauvoo on May 17, with Sidney Rigdon of Pennsylvania as his running mate. Smith was killed on June 27, when a mob shot him after breaking into the jail at Carthage, IL, where he was confined while awaiting trial on charges brought against him by his personal enemies and by seceders from the church.

3805. Election day for presidential voting held nationwide was authorized by act of January 23, 1845, "an act to establish a uniform time for holding elections for electors of President and Vice President in all the states of the Union." The day selected for voting was "the Tuesday next after the first Monday in the month of November of the year in which they are to be appointed." The first election under the act was held on November 7, 1848.

3806. Year in which two presidents were elected was 1861, after the formation of the Confederacy as a rival government. Both presidents were from Kentucky. Abraham Lincoln, born on February 12, 1809, in Hardin County, KY, became president of the United States on March 4, 1861. Jefferson Davis, born in Todd County, KY, on June 3, 1808, was chosen president of the Confederacy by the provisional congress on February 18, 1861. He was inaugurated at Richmond, VA, on February 22, 1862, after he was elected by popular vote.

3807. Presidential election in which soldiers in the field were allowed to vote was the election of 1864. Of a total of 150,635 votes cast by the soldiers on November 8, 116,887 were for Abraham Lincoln, Republican, and 33,748 for George Brinton McClellan, Democrat.

3808. Presidential candidate who was a woman was Victoria Claflin Woodhull, who was nominated by the Equal Rights Party at a convention held on May 10, 1872, at Apollo Hall, New York City. She was not, however, old enough to hold office, had she been elected. The first female presidential candidate eligible to hold office was Belva Ann Bennett Lockwood of the District of Columbia, nominated by the Equal Rights Party on September 20, 1884, in San Francisco, CA.

3809. Vice presidential candidate who was African-American was Frederick Douglass, who was nominated on May 10, 1872, by the Equal Rights Party, assembled at Apollo Hall, New York City. The presidential nominee was Victoria Claflin Woodhull.

3810. Presidential candidate who was Catholic was Charles O'Conor of New York, who was nominated at the Democratic convention at Louisville, KY, on September 3, 1872, by a wing of Democrats who refused to accept the nomination of Horace Greeley that had already been made at Baltimore, MD.

O'Conor declined the nomination, but his name nevertheless was listed and he received approximately 30,000 votes from 23 states.

3811. Presidential candidate to make campaign speeches in a foreign language was James Abram Garfield of Ohio, who made several political speeches in German. He was elected in November 1880.

3812. Vice presidential candidate who was a woman was Marietta Lizzie Bell Stow of California, nominated by the Equal Rights Party in San Francisco, CA, on September 20, 1884.

3813. Presidential nominee who was African-American was Frederick Douglass of Rochester, NY, who received one vote on June 23, 1888, on the fourth ballot of the Republican national convention. On June 25, on the eighth ballot, the convention nominated Benjamin Harrison, who was elected as the 23rd president. Douglass was later appointed U.S. minister to Haiti.

Courtesy of Images of American Political History and the National Archives and Records Administration

Frederick Douglass

3814. Presidential candidate to ride in a car was William Jennings Bryan, who was given a ride in 1896 at Decatur, IL, in an automobile made by the Mueller Manufacturing Company, accompanied by his wife. There were only 10 cars in the United States at that time.

3815. Presidential candidate to appear in movie footage was William Jennings Bryan, who was filmed receiving congratulations at his residence at Fairview, NE, after his nomination on July 10, 1908. The film was shown on July 12, 1908, at Hammerstein's Roof, 42nd Street and Broadway, New York City, having been developed on the train heading east.

3816. Election in which returns were broadcast on radio was the presidential election of November 7, 1916. An experimental station, the De Forest Radio Laboratory in the Highbridge section of the Bronx, New York City, broadcast bulletins from the *New York American* on the results of the presidential race for approximately six hours. The broadcasters signed off about 11 P.M. with the announcement that Charles Evans Hughes had been elected. In fact, Woodrow Wilson was the winner. The first widespread radio broadcast of election results took place on August 31, 1920, when station WWJ of Detroit, MI, broadcast the results of congressional and county primaries. On November 2, 1920, Leo H. Rosenberg of station KDKA of Pittsburgh, PA, broadcast the results of the Harding–Cox presidential election.

3817. Presidential nomination ceremony broadcast on radio was the ceremony held at Leland Stanford Junior University Stadium, Palo Alto, CA, on August 11, 1928, when Herbert Hoover was formally notified of his nomination for the presidency by the Republican Party and accepted. The broadcast was carried by more than 107 stations.

3818. Presidential candidate to give an acceptance speech at a national convention was Franklin Delano Roosevelt, who flew from Albany, NY, to Chicago, IL, on July 2, 1932, to address the Democratic National Convention. This was the first time a candidate accepted his party's nomination in person.

3819. Presidential campaign manager who was a woman was Ruth Hanna McCormick Simms, daughter of Republican senator Mark Hanna, who was named one of two managers of Thomas Edmund Dewey's campaign on December 2, 1939. The other manager was J. Russel Sprague, Republican leader of Nassau County, NY.

3820. Political action committee (PAC) was the Congress of Industrial Organizations Political Action Committee, organized by CIO leader Sidney Hillman in 1944 to assist the reelection campaign of President Franklin Delano Roosevelt. The committee effectively marshalled the support of organized labor on behalf of the Democrats, paid for advertisements and publications about the labor movement, conducted a door-to-door voter registration drive, had a hand in the drafting of the party platform, and was influential in the choice of Harry S. Truman as the vice presidential nominee at the Democratic National Convention, held in July 1944 in Chicago, IL.

3821. Presidential candidate who was renominated after a defeat was Thomas Edmund Dewey of New York, who was defeated in the election of November 7, 1944, by the incumbent president, Franklin Delano Roosevelt, and went on to be nominated by the Republican national convention at Philadelphia, PA, on June 24, 1948. He was defeated in the 1948 election by Harry S. Truman.

3822. Vice presidential candidate who was an African-American woman was Charlotta A. Bass, who was nominated on July 5, 1952, by the Progressive Party at its convention in the International Amphitheatre, Chicago, IL.

3823. Presidential election in which a computer was used to predict the outcome was the 1952 presidential race between Dwight David Eisenhower and Adlai Ewing Stevenson. The CBS television network employed the UNIVAC to choose the winner. Only an hour after the polls had closed, when less than 10 percent of the votes had been counted, the computer correctly projected Eisenhower's landslide victory, trumping human experts who had predicted a close race.

3824. Presidential election debates to be shown on television were the debates between Richard Milhous Nixon, the Republican candidate, and John Fitzgerald Kennedy, the Democratic candidate, that took place during the 1960 presidential campaign. The first of four debates was held on September 26 in a Chicago studio; the second on October 7 in a Washington, DC, studio; the third on October 13, with Kennedy in New York City and Nixon in Hollywood, CA; and the fourth on October 21 in a New York City studio.

3825. Presidential election in which votes were tallied electronically was the election of November 3, 1964, when Coleman Vote Tally Systems were used in Hamilton County (Cincinnati), OH; Orange County (Santa Ana-Anaheim), CA; and Contra Costa (Martinez), CA. They counted 600 ballots a minute. Data from each machine and counting center were automatically transmitted by wire to a central computer in the Registrar of Voters office, where countywide returns were made available as fast as the votes were counted.

3826. Presidential candidate who was an African-American woman was Charlene Mitchell of California, nominated by the Communist Party USA during its convention in New York City, July 3-7, 1968. She won 415 votes in Minnesota and 23 in Ohio.

3827. Presidential campaigner to be assassinated while campaigning for his party's nomination as candidate for president was Senator Robert Francis Kennedy of New York, who was assassinated by Sirhan Bishara Sirhan, a Palestinian-Jordanian terrorist, on June 6, 1968, at the Biltmore Hotel, Los Angeles, CA.

3828. Vice presidential candidate of a major political party to resign before the election was Senator Thomas Francis Eagleton of Missouri, who was nominated on July 13, 1972, at the Democratic National Convention at Miami Beach, FL. He submitted his resignation on August 1, 1972. The National Democratic Committee nominated Robert Sargent Shriver of Maryland in his stead.

3829. Electoral vote for a woman was cast by Roger L. McBride of Charlottesville, VA, whose vote for Theodora Nathan of Oregon, vice presidential candidate of the Libertarian Party, was counted on January 6, 1973.

3830. Presidential election debate between an incumbent president and a challenger to be televised was held on September 23, 1976, when three networks pooled their efforts to telecast a debate between President Gerald Rudolph Ford, a Republican, and Jimmy Carter, the Democratic candidate, at the Walnut Street Theatre, Philadelphia, PA. The debate, limited to domestic issues, was sponsored by the League of Women Voters. A second debate took place on October 6, 1976, from the Palace of Fine Arts Theatre, San Francisco, CA. A third debate took place on

October 22, 1976, from the stage of Phi Beta Kappa Hall on the campus of the College of William and Mary, Williamsburg, VA. Each confrontation was 90 minutes long.

3831. Debate among party hopefuls for the presidential nomination to be shown on television took place on January 5, 1980, in Des Moines, IA, where six Republican competitors faced each other in a two-hour debate. The six were John Anderson of Illinois, Howard Baker, Jr., of Tennessee, George Herbert Walker Bush of Texas, John Connally of Texas, Philip Crane of Illinois, and Robert Dole of Kansas. Ronald Wilson Reagan was absent. The confrontation was sponsored by the *Des Moines Register and Tribune*.

3832. Presidential candidate who had been an astronaut was Ohio senator John Herschel Glenn, Jr., the first American to orbit the earth, who sought the Democratic nomination in 1984. Glenn entered the race on April 21, 1983, with a speech in his hometown of New Concord, OH, but failed to generate widespread interest in his campaign, despite the release in 1984 of a Hollywood film, *The Right Stuff*, celebrating his status as an American hero. He tried again, also without success, in 1988.

3833. Vice presidential candidate from a major political party who was a woman was Geraldine Ferraro, congressional representative from New York State. She was chosen by Democratic presidential nominee Walter F. Mondale as his running mate on July 12, 1984, at the Democratic National Convention.

3834. Presidential election in which the winning candidate received a greater percentage of women's votes than men's took place on November 5, 1996, when incumbent president Bill Clinton defeated Senator Robert Dole and various third-party candidates. Male voters were fairly evenly split between Clinton (43 percent) and Dole (44 percent). Female voters were much more likely to vote for Clinton (54 percent) than for Dole (38 percent). Clinton was even more popular with unmarried women (62 percent).

3835. Presidential election in which all candidates operated sites on the Internet was the election of 2000. This was also the first presidential election in which major polling organizations took polls on the Internet and in which every candidate made significant efforts to solicit Web-based donations.

3836. Vote cast from space in a presidential election was cast by Dr. Leroy Chiao on October 31, 2004, when he was aboard the International Space Station as commander of Expedition 10. He used an electronic ballot that traveled to space and back through NASA's Houston, TX, headquarters by means of an encrypted email connection.

3837. Presidential election observed by international monitors was the election of November 2, 2004. A team of 92 monitors from the Organization for Security and Cooperation in Europe visited polling places at the invitation of the Bush administation. Their conclusions, published on the OSCE website, were that the elections "were conducted in an environment that reflects a longstanding democratic tradition, including institutions governed by rule of law, free and professional media and an active civil society involved in all aspects of the election process.

Federal Government

3838. Federal law enforcement agency was the Marshals Service, whose creation was authorized by Congress in the Judiciary Act of September 24, 1789. The act mandated the appointment of marshals and deputy marshals in regional districts, charged with making sure that laws and court orders were enforced. Their duties included making arrests, serving summonses and subpoenas, managing the courts, and carrying out the census (until 1870). In some frontier territories, where there was no organized police force, federal marshals were the only law enforcement agents.

3839. Building erected by the federal government was a structure for the United States Mint in Philadelphia, PA, authorized by act of Congress on April 2, 1792. This was a plain brick edifice on the east side of Seventh Street, near Arch, containing rolling and drawing machines and a smelting furnace. The cornerstone was laid by David Rittenhouse, director of the Mint, on July 31, 1792. Additional buildings, both brick and wood-frame, were constructed nearby to house the Mint's vaults, an assayer's furnace, deposit and weighing rooms, press rooms, milling machines, planchet cutters, a smithy, a coal house, machine shops, a horse mill, and stables. The property and its buildings were sold at auction in 1835 after the Mint was expanded at another location.

3840. Building erected in Washington, DC, by the federal government was the White House, originally known as the Executive Mansion. It was modeled after the palace of the Duke of Leinster in Ireland and was designed by James Hoban. The cornerstone was laid on October 13, 1792. The Executive Mansion was first occupied by President John Adams in 1800, and the first New Year's reception there was held on January 1, 1801. The mansion was burned by the British in 1814, during the War of 1812, and only the four walls were left standing. It was restored in 1818. In order to obliterate the marks of fire, the stones were painted white. Since that time, the Executive Mansion has been known as the White House. When Adams first took occupancy, there was only a path through an elder swamp leading from the President's house to the Capitol.

3841. Federal government employees who were women were Sarah Waldrake and Rachael Summers, who were employed in 1795 by the Mint in Philadelphia, PA, as adjusters to weigh gold coins. Their pay was 50 cents a day.

3842. Secret service established by the federal government was the Treasury Department's Secret Service Division, created on July 5, 1865, to combat the efforts of criminals to counterfeit United States money. Its first chief was William P. Wood. After the assassination of President William McKinley in 1901, the Secret Service was given the duty of guarding the president. It currently protects the president, his immediate family, the vice president, ex-presidents and their wives, widows, and minor children, winners of the presidential election before they are sworn in, major candidates, foreign diplomatic missions, visiting heads of state, and government envoys performing special missions abroad.

The Federal Bureau of Investigation was created in 1908 to supplement the anti-fraud work of the Secret Service.

Courtesy of Images of American Political History and the Library of Congress

The White House, Washington, DC.

On March 1, 2003, the Secret Service was transferred to the Department of Homeland Security.

3843. Indian Affairs Commissioner who was Native American was Brigadier General Ely Samuel Parker (Donehogawa), a prominent civil engineer and chief of the Tonawanda Seneca who had served as military secretary to General Ulysses S. Grant during the Civil War. As President, Grant appointed Parker to the post of commissioner of Indian affairs on April 21, 1869. He served until December 1871. The first Native American superintendent of an agency of the Bureau of Indian Affairs was Shirley Plume, an Oglala Sioux, who was designated as acting superintendent of the Standing Rock Agency at Fort Yates, ND, on August 20, 1973. She was appointed superintendent on January 24, 1974.

Library of Congress, Prints & Photographs Division
LC-DIG-cwpb-02956

Brig. Gen. Ely Samuel Parker

3844. Catalog of government publications was *A Descriptive Catalogue of the Government Publications of the U.S.—Sept. 5, 1774–March 4, 1881*, compiled by order of Congress. The work was given to printer Benjamin Perley Poore on March 1, 1883, and was finished in 1885. It was arranged chronologically with a general index and was published by the Government Printing Office, Washington, DC.

3845. Secret Service agent killed in the line of duty was Joseph A. Walker, head of the Secret Service branch headquartered at Denver, CO. He was shot in the back on November 3, 1906, during an investigation of a land fraud case. The first female agent to be killed in the line of duty was Julie Yvonne Cross, who was engaged in undercover surveillance of a counterfeiting operation when she was fatally wounded by gunfire on June 4, 1980, in Los Angeles, CA. The first Secret Service agent killed while protecting the President was Leslie William Coffelt, who stopped an assassination attempt on President Harry S. Truman at the cost of his own life. On November 1, 1950, while he was guarding Blair House (Truman's temporary residence), he was shot at close range by Griselio Torresola, but managed to shoot and kill Torresola before he lost consciousness.

3846. Federal agency director who was a woman was Julia Lathrop, who was appointed the first chief of the U.S. Children's Bureau, established by Congress on April 8, 1912. Lathrop was a veteran activist for children's welfare and had long been associated with Hull House, the pioneering settlement house in Chicago, IL.

3847. Factories operated by the federal government in peacetime were part of a relief effort during the Great Depression. The factories, both located in Millville, MA, were a jersey cloth mill formerly operated by the Famb Knitting Company and a large hall known as Forester's Hall, in which the Massachusetts branch of the Federal Emergency Relief Administration established sewing and stock rooms. The project was started on June 4, 1934, by authority of Joseph P. Carney, emergency relief administrator of Massachusetts, who detailed Thomas E. Wye as factory supervisor to organize and start the project. The products were not sold but were distributed to different welfare divisions of the cities and towns in Massachusetts.

3848. Federal family assistance program was Aid to Dependent Children (later known as Aid to Families with Dependent Children), established as part of the Social Security Act of August 14, 1935. The federal government issued grants to the states to be used for the support of poor families. In its first month of operation, February 1936, the program paid out $1.7 million to assist more than 140,000 children in 12 states and Washington, DC.

3849. National identification scheme for American citizens was the Social Security number, made possible under the Social Security Act approved by President Franklin Delano Roosevelt on August 14, 1935. The act authorized some form of record-keeping scheme for participants in the program. A number scheme was formalized under Treasury Decision 4704 of 1936, which required the issuance of an account number to each employee covered by Social Security. Approximately 30 million applications for SSNs were processed between November 1936 and June 30, 1937. Although the federal government has resisted calling the Social Security Number a "national identifier," the SSN has functioned unofficially in that capacity since 1943, when Executive Order 9397 required all federal agencies and organizations to use the SSN exclusively whenever it was advisable to set up a new identification system for individuals.

3850. Magazine of the federal government was the daily *Federal Register*, first issued on March 14, 1936. The masthead was decorated with the eagle shield and the Latin motto *Littera scripta manet* ("the written word endures"). It was published in Washington, DC, by the National Archives under the Federal Register Act approved on July 26, 1935, and contained 16 two-column pages containing federal laws, orders, and reports.

3851. Federal administrator who was an African-American woman was Mary Jane McLeod Bethune, born in Mayesville, SC, in 1875, the daughter of slaves. On June 24, 1936, she was named director of the Negro Division of the National Youth Administration by President Franklin Delano Roosevelt, thus becoming the first African-American woman to receive a major federal appointment. In 1904, Bethune founded the Daytona Normal and Industrial Institute for Negro Girls, later known as Bethune-Cookman College, located in Daytona Beach, FL. She was also the founder and first president of the National Council of Negro Women. In 1991, her home and offices in Washington, DC, were designated a national historic landmark.

3852. Food stamps were introduced in May 1939 by the Department of Agriculture as a pilot program for the hungry in Rochester, NY. The program continued until 1943. On May 29, 1961, as part of a national test program, food stamps were distributed in Welch, WV. The first recipients were Chloe and Alderson Muncy, who accepted $95 worth of food stamps from Secretary of Agriculture Orville Freeman. The Muncys immediately used their stamps at a local grocery store.

3853. Social security monthly payment was made to Ida May Fuller of Ludlow, VT, who received check No. 00-000-001 for $22.54, dated January 31, 1940. By 1975, when she died at the age of 100, Fuller had received more than $20,000 in benefits. The Social Security Act was approved by President Franklin Delano Roosevelt on August 14, 1935. It authorized the appointment of a three-member board to administer a federal system of old-age insurance benefits, to approve state unemployment compensation laws, and to administer grants-in-aid to the states to help the needy aged, the blind, and dependent children. These programs, and others added later, were funded by mandatory contributions by workers, employers, and the self-employed, and provided coverage to people with a documented history of employment. Several groups of unemployment insurance cards were issued simultaneously, so that the recipient of the first social security card is not known.

3854. Federal government building built to withstand a nuclear attack was the laboratory for the Armed Forces Institute of Pathology, Walter Reed Army Medical Center, Washington, DC, which was occupied on March 13, 1955, and dedicated by President Dwight David Eisenhower on May 23. The eight-story reinforced concrete bomb-resistant building contained eight floors, five above ground and three underground. It had a gross area of approximately 215,000 square feet and a net usable area of 130,000 square feet. It was constructed by the Cramer-Vollmerhousen Company of Washington, DC.

3855. Affirmative action order issued by the federal government was Executive Order 10925, signed by President John Fitzgerald Kennedy on March 6, 1961. The order required all federal contractors to "take affirmative action to ensure that applicants are treated equally without regard to race, color, religion, sex, or national origin." The order created the President's Committee on Equal Employment Opportunity with the mandate "to realize more fully the national policy of nondiscrimination within the executive branch of the Government." Affirmative action for businesses owned by women was mandated by Executive Order 12138, signed by President Jimmy Carter in 1979.

3856. Health insurance plan enacted by Congress was Medicare, enacted on July 30, 1965, as part of the federal Social Security system, to help pay the cost of medical care for people aged 65 and over. Payments are made from a fund made up of mandatory contributions from employers, employees, and the self-employed, as well as contributions from the general revenue of the federal government. The first payments were made on July 1, 1966. The first payments for skilled nursing facilities, made under the extended care benefit provision of the statute, were made on January 2, 1967. The first Medicare identification cards were presented to former President Harry S. Truman and his wife, Bess Wallace Truman, by President Lyndon Baines Johnson at the Truman Library, Independence, MO, on January 20, 1966.

3857. Presidential order enforcing affirmative action was Executive Order 11246, issued on September 24, 1965, by President Lyndon Baines Johnson. The order required federal government contractors to "take affirmative action" toward the hiring and promotion of minority employees.

3858. National Endowment for the Arts grant was delivered to the American Ballet Theatre, New York, NY, on December 20, 1965. The grant of $100,000 saved the organization from closing down for lack of funds. The NEA was founded by act of Congress on September 9, 1965, with Roger Stevens as its first chairman.

3859. National Endowment for the Humanities grants were issued in 1966 to the American Society of Papyrologists, Cincinnati, OH, an academic organization specializing in Greek and Latin papyri, and the American Council of Learned Societies, New York, NY. The NEH was founded by act of Congress on September 9, 1965, with Barnaby C. Keeney as its first chairman.

3860. Secret Service agents who were women were Laurie B. Anderson, Sue A. Baker, Kathryn I. Clark, Holly A. Hufschmidt, and Phyllis Frances Shantz, former agents of the Executive Protective Service, who were sworn in as special agents on December 15, 1971, in Washington, DC.

3861. Year in which the public debt of the United States exceeded $1 trillion was 1981, following the energy crisis of the 1970s, tax cuts, and the beginning of "Reaganomics." On December 31, 1981, the debt was $1,028,729,000,000, rounded to millions.

3862. Year in which the federal budget exceeded $1 trillion was fiscal year 1988. The budget submitted to Congress on January 5, 1987, by President Ronald Wilson Reagan totaled $1,024.3 billion, or $1.024 trillion, which included revenues of $916.6 billion and a projected deficit of $107.8 billion.

3863. Detailed financial statement for the federal government showing all aspects of the government's assets and liabilities was publicly released on March 31, 1998, by the Clinton administration. Previously, the federal government provided to the public a general summary of its financial condition but did not release full details.

3864. Ruling requiring retention of all electronic records of the federal governmentwas handed down on April 9, 1998, by Judge Paul L. Friedman of the U.S. District Court for the District of Columbia, who ordered the archivist of the United States, John W. Carlin, to instruct federal agencies not to destroy electronic records without special approval. The ruling reinforced an earlier decision by Friedman nullifying General Records Schedule 20, a federal regulation allowing the destruction of federal electronic records according to a set schedule as long as paper copies were available.

3865. Federal payment over the Internet was a $32,000 contract payment issued on June 30, 1998, by the U.S. Treasury's Financial Management Service to a unit of the GTE Corporation. The electronic checking system was developed by the nonprofit Financial Services Technology Consortium.

3866. Government report posted on the Internet before its publication on paper was "Referral to the United States House of Representatives Pursuant to United States Code, S 595(c) Submitted by The Office of the Independent Counsel, September 9, 1998," commonly known as the Starr Report. The 445-page report by independent prosecutor Kenneth Starr on the Clinton-Lewinsky affair claimed to contain "substantial and credible information that may constitute grounds for impeachment" of President Bill Clinton.

3867. Year in which Medicare spending declined was fiscal year 1999, which ended on September 30, 1999. The Treasury Department reported that spending for Medicare by the federal government declined by 1 percent during that period, decreasing from $213.6 billion in fiscal year 1998 to $212 billion, $19 billion less than was predicted by the Congressional Budget Office. The Medicare program, founded in 1965 to provide health-care benefits to elderly and disabled people, reached an annual increase rate of 10 percent during the 1990s.

3868. Internet march on Washington was the Billion Byte March, which took place on January 20, 1999. It was sponsored by Third Millennium and Economic Security 2000, two organizations concerned with rescuing the Social Security system. Participants sent the following e-mail message to the White House and Congress from the Web site of Economic Security 2000: "With 76 million Baby Boomers retiring, Social Security is in trouble. Save the safety net for all seniors, survivors and the disabled. Add individual accounts to open meaningful savings to all Americans. Fix Social Security this year." According to the organizers, tens of thousands of messages were sent.

3869. Customer satisfaction survey by the federal government was published in December 1999 as the *Federal Agencies Government-wide Customer Satisfaction Report for the General Services Administration.* One of its features was the American Customer Satisfaction Index. Of the various federal agencies examined, the IRS had the lowest score, with 51 percent, and the U.S. Mint had the highest, with 86 percent. The general aggregate score was 68.6 percent.

3870. Federal agency overseeing all border control was the U.S. Customs and Border Protection (CPB), established on March 1, 2003, as part of the Department of Homeland Security. The agency's mandate was to exercise unified oversight of all border questions, including immigration, food imports, and customs. It comprised the Office of Field Operations, the Office of Border Patrol, and the Office of CPB Air & Marine. W. Ralph Basham was the first commissioners.

3871. Comprehensive database of federal research projects was RaDiUS, developed by the RAND Corporation, a nonprofit institution, in the early 1990s. It allowed policy makers to identify current federal expenditures in science and technology research and development without waiting for the publication of after-the-fact reports. Access was provided to the public at no charge. The database was officially recognized by the federal Office of Management and Budget in March 2005.

Foreign Relations

3872. Government intelligence agency was formed on November 29, 1775, when the Continental Congress voted "that a committee of five be appointed for the sole purpose of corresponding with our friends in Great Britain, Ireland and other parts of the world." The members of this secret Committee of Correspondence were William Samuel Johnson of Connecticut, John Jay of New York, John Dickinson of Pennsylvania, Benjamin Harrison of Virginia, and Benjamin Franklin of Pennsylvania, who was the chairman. The committee established a network of agents in Europe who ran espionage missions, including covert operations and interception of communications. This group became the Committee for Foreign Affairs in 1777and the Department of Foreign Affairs in 1781.

3873. Foreign nation to recognize the independence of the United States was Morocco, whose leader, Sultan Sidi Muhammad Ben Abdullah, was interested in attracting foreign trade. On December 20, 1777, he ordered his country's ports to allow entry to all ships flying the American flag. When this did not result in a trade agreement, he applied pressure by taking hostage the crew of an American ship. A Treaty of Peace and Friendship was signed by Morocco and the United States in 1787. This treaty, revised in 1836, is the oldest continuing treaty in the history of the United States.

3874. Alliance between the United States and another country was formalized in the treaties of amity and alliance with France, drafted in Paris on February 6, 1778. The only alliance established by the United States until the 20th century, the relationship was negotiated mainly by the French foreign minister, Charles Gravier, Comte de Vergennes, and the U.S. minister to France, Benjamin Franklin. France supplied sorely needed funds and supplies to the Continental Army, as well as troops; Washington commanded an army almost evenly divided between American and French forces at the siege of Yorktown, the decisive battle of the Revolutionary War, where he defeated the British on October 19, 1781.

3875. Treaties entered into by the federal government were A Treaty of Amity and Commerce and a Treaty of Alliance, signed by the United States and France in Paris on February 6, 1778. Benjamin Franklin, Silas Deane, and Arthur Lee represented the United States, and Conrad Alexandre Gérard, first secretary to France's foreign minister, signed for France. These pacts were the first treaties made by the federal government with a foreign power. The treaty was ratified by the Second Continental Congress at York, PA, on May 4, 1778, and by France on July 16, 1778. Ratifications were exchanged in Paris on July 17, 1778, and the treaty was declared in force. The treaty was abrogated on July 7, 1798, when Congress passed an act "to declare the treaties heretofore concluded with France no longer obligatory on the United States."

Library of Congress, Prints & Photographs Division
LC-USZC4-623

Benjamin Franklin's reception at the court of France.

3876. Representative of a foreign country to the United States was Conrad Alexandre Gérard of France, who arrived in July 1778. He was styled minister plenipotentiary and also bore a commission as consul general.

3877. Minister plenipotentiary was Benjamin Franklin of Philadelphia, PA, who was elected by the Continental Congress on September 14, 1778, to represent the United States in the court of France. Thomas Jefferson was the first minister plenipotentiary after the Revolutionary War. He was appointed on March 10, 1785, and served in Paris until October 1789.

3878. Salute fired by Great Britain in honor of an officer of the United States was fired on May 8, 1783, when General George Washington and Governor George Clinton arrived at the British ship *Ceres*, commanded by Sir Guy Carleton, in New York Harbor to arrange for the British evacuation. When they departed, 17 guns were fired in honor of Washington's rank. New York was evacuated by the British on November 25, 1783.

3879. Treaty between the federal government and a nation with which it had been at war was the armistice with Great Britain that ended the Revolutionary War. Preliminary articles of peace were signed on November 30, 1782, in Paris. Hostilities ceased on January 20, 1783. The treaty was proclaimed by the Continental Congress on April 11, 1783. The definite treaty of peace was signed in Paris on September 3, 1783, by David Hartley, plenipotentiary of Great Britain, and Benjamin Franklin and John Adams of the United States. The treaty was ratified and proclaimed on January 14, 1784. It set the borders of the United States as Canada in the north, Spanish Florida in the south, and the Mississippi River in the west. It also granted the Americans fishing rights off the Newfoundland coast.

3880. Hostage crisis involving a foreign government began on October 11, 1784, when Morocco, by order of its sultan, Sidi Muhammad ben Abdullah, captured the American merchant ship *Betsey* and took its crew hostage. His intent was to pressure Congress into moving forward with negotiations on a long-delayed treaty. The ship and crew were released on July 9, 1785.

From 1785 through 1793, the Barbary state of Algiers captured 126 Americans, holding them until the United States agreed to a cash payment of nearly $650,000 plus annual contributions of money and naval supplies.

3881. **Minister to Great Britain** was John Adams of Quincy, MA, who on June 1, 1785, was introduced by the Marquis of Carmarthen to the King of Great Britain as ambassador extraordinary from the United States of America to the Court of London. The first minister plenipotentiary to Great Britain was Thomas Pinckney of South Carolina, who was appointed on January 12, 1792.

3882. **Treaty entered into by the federal government after independence** was concluded with Prussia and signed at the Hague on September 10, 1785, by Benjamin Franklin, John Adams, and Thomas Jefferson, representing the United States. The treaty was ratified by Congress on May 17, 1786, and the ratifications were exchanged in October 1786.

3883. **Consul** was Major Samuel Shaw of Massachusetts, who was appointed consul to Canton, China, on January 1, 1786, prior to the ratification of the Constitution, and confirmed on February 10, 1790.

3884. **Neutrality proclamation by the federal government** was made by President George Washington on April 22, 1793: "Whereas it appears that a state of war exists between Austria, Prussia, Sardinia, Great Britain and the United Netherlands on the one part and France on the other," citizens of the United States will be "liable to punishment or forfeiture under the law of nations by committing, aiding or abetting hostilities against any of the said powers."

3885. **Neutrality regulation enacted by Congress that governed the actions of citizens** was passed by act of Congress on June 5, 1794. The act provided that any citizen who "accepts and exercises a commission to serve a foreign prince, state, colony, district or people, with whom the United States are at peace shall be fined not more than $2,000 and imprisoned not more than three years." The first conviction was that of Isaac Williams of Norwich, CT, who accepted a commission in a French armed vessel and served against Great Britain. He was tried in September 1799 at Hartford, CT, in U.S. Circuit Court, found guilty under two counts, and sentenced on each count to a fine of $1,000 and imprisonment for four months.

3886. **Extradition treaty with a foreign country** was the Treaty of Amity, Commerce and Navigation, popularly known as the Jay Treaty, between the United States and Great Britain, which was signed in London on November 19, 1794. Article XXVII provided for the apprehension and delivery of persons charged with certain crimes. The signatory for the United States was John Jay, and for Great Britain, William Wyndham Grenville, Baron Grenville of Wotton, one of His Majesty's Privy Council and His Majesty's Principal Secretary of State for Foreign Affairs. The treaty was ratified by the Senate on June 24, 1795, and signed by President George Washington on October 28, 1795. The ratification was proclaimed on February 29, 1796.

3887. **Treaty between the federal government and a South American nation** was the General Convention of Peace, Amity, Navigation and Commerce between the United States and the Republic of Colombia, which was signed at Bogotá, Colombia, on October 3, 1824. The Republic of Colombia then included Venezuela and Ecuador. The treaty was submitted to the Senate on February 22, 1825, and ratified on March 7. It was ratified by Colombia on March 26, 1825. The treaty was proclaimed on May 31, 1825. The plenipotentiaries who signed the treaty were Richard Clough Anderson, minister plenipotentiary of the United States to the Republic of Colombia, and Pedro Gual, secretary of state and foreign relations of Colombia.

3888. **Treaty rejected by the Senate** was a pact with Colombia for suppressing the African slave trade, which was rejected on February 22, 1825, by a vote of 40–0.

3889. **Ambassador to Mexico** was Joel Roberts Poinsett, appointed to the post of minister to Mexico by President James Monroe. A native of Charleston, SC, he had been serving as a congressman from South Carolina and resigned his seat on March 7, 1825, in order to accept Monroe's appointment. He gave his name to the poinsettia plant, which he was the first to import from Mexico to the United States. Poinsett later served as secretary of war, from 1837 to 1841.

3890. Conference of American republics was the General Congress of South American States, assembled on March 14, 1826, at Panama. Convoked by Simon Bolivar, who sent invitations in December 1824, it was attended by delegates from Mexico, Colombia, Peru, and Central America. Richard Clough Anderson and John Sargeant were appointed delegates from the United States in July 1825, but their appointment was not confirmed until December 6, 1825, and the conference adjourned before they reached it. The first such conference initiated by the United States was the First International Conference of American States, which opened in Washington, DC on October 2, 1889, at the invitation of Secretary of State James Gillespie Blaine. Ten participating nations signed an arbitration treaty.

3891. Treaty between the federal government and an Asian nation was the Treaty of Amity and Commerce with Siam (now called Thailand), concluded on March 20, 1833, the last day of the fourth month of the Siamese year 1194, called Pi-Marông-chat-tava-sôk, or the year of the Dragon. One copy of the treaty was in Siamese and one in English, with a Portuguese and a Chinese translation annexed. Edmund Roberts was the envoy of the United States. Ratifications were exchanged on April 14, 1836, in the royal city of Bangkok, and the treaty was proclaimed on June 24, 1837, by President Martin Van Buren.

3892. Consul to California was Thomas Oliver Larkin, who was appointed consul to Monterey, CA, on May 1, 1843, and special agent on October 17, 1845.

3893. Diplomat who was African-American was Ebenezer Don Carlos Bassett, consul general to Haiti, where he served from April 16, 1869, to November 27, 1877.

3894. Ambassador who was Jewish was Oscar Solomon Straus of New York City, who was appointed envoy extraordinary and minister plenipotentiary to Turkey on March 24, 1887, and served again during crises in 1890, 1897, and 1909. The first Jew to represent the United States in a high diplomatic post was Mordecai Manuel Noah, who served from 1813 to 1816 as consul to Tunis, where he negotiated the release of American sailors held prisoner by Barbary pirates.

3895. Conference of great powers to be held on American soil and affecting American interests was the Conference on the Limitation of Armaments, which assembled in at Memorial Continental Hall in Washington, DC, from November 12, 1921, to February 6, 1922. Nine nations took part in the conference: the United States, Great Britain, France, Italy, Japan, China, Holland, Belgium, and Portugal. The American delegation was headed by Secretary of State Charles Evans Hughes.

3896. Diplomat who was a woman in the United States was Ruth Bryan Owen. From May 9, 1933, through June 27, 1936, she served as chief of mission, with the rank of minister, at the U.S. embassy in Copenhagen, Denmark. She had previously been the first woman to represent Florida in Congress.

3897. Ambassador to Canada was William Phillips, a career Foreign Service officer from Massachusetts who was appointed envoy extraordinary and minister plenipotentiary on February 17, 1927. The first person to hold the formal title of ambassador to Canada was Ray Atherton, named envoy extraordinary on July 7, 1943, and promoted to the rank of ambassador extraordinary and plenipotentiary on November 18, 1943. He held this office until his resignation and mandatory retirement on August 30, 1948.

3898. Treaty signed by a woman on behalf of the U.S. government was the Charter of the United Nations, signed on June 26, 1945, at San Francisco, CA, by Virginia Crocheron Gildersleeve, a delegate to the United Nations Conference on International Organization.

3899. Ambassador to the United States who was a woman was Her Excellency Shrimati Vijaya Lakshmi Pandit, ambassador of India, who presented her letter of credence to President Harry S. Truman on May 12, 1949.

3900. Ambassador from the United States who was a woman was Eugenie Moore Anderson of Red Wing, MN, who was sworn in on October 28, 1949, in Washington, DC, as ambassador to Denmark.

3901. United Nations delegate who was African-American was Edith Spurlock Sampson, who was appointed alternate delegate to the fifth General Assembly on August 24, 1950. Her first assignment, on September 28, 1950, was to the Social, Humanitarian and Cultural Committee.

3902. Nuclear arms-control treaty was the Nuclear Test Ban Treaty, formally the Treaty Banning Nuclear Weapons Tests in the Atmosphere, in Outer Space and Under Water. It was signed in Moscow on August 5, 1963, by the United States, the Soviet Union, and the United Kingdom. The treaty banned tests of nuclear weapons above ground, in the ocean, and in outer space but did allow testing underground. It made no allowance for verification of compliance. More than 100 nations ratified the treaty. Two nations that did not were France and the People's Republic of China, both of which continued to conduct above-ground tests.

3903. United Nations ambassador who was a woman was Marietta Peabody Tree, who was sworn in on October 28, 1964, to the Trusteeship Council of the United Nations. She had served since 1961 as a United Nations delegate.

3904. Ambassador who was an African-American woman was Patricia Roberts Harris, who was sworn in on July 9, 1965, in Washington, DC, as ambassador to Luxembourg.

3905. Space treaty signed by the United States was the Treaty on Principles Governing the Activities of States in the Exploration and Use of Outer Space, Including the Moon and Other Celestial Bodies, endorsed by the United Nations General Assembly on December 19, 1966. The treaty was signed by the United States, the Soviet Union, the United Kingdom, and other countries beginning on January 27, 1967. Signatories were prohibited from placing weapons of mass destruction into space and agreed not to claim sovereignty over other celestial bodies.

3906. Ambassador assassinated in office was John Gordon Mein, ambassador to Guatemala, who was attacked and killed in his automobile on August 27, 1968, about 10 blocks away from the American embassy in the downtown section of Guatemala City, Guatemala.

3907. United Nations Security Council resolution vetoed by the United States was a resolution to condemn Great Britain for not using force to overthrow the white minority government of Rhodesia. The veto was cast on March 17, 1970, by Ambassador Charles Woodruff Yost. Great Britain also rejected the resolution. The Security Council met at the United Nations headquarters in New York City.

3908. Radiation attacks against an American embassy were confirmed by American officials on February 10, 1976, when it was revealed that Soviet KGB agents had been bombarding the U.S. embassy in Moscow with nonionizing microwave radiation since the mid-1950s. The radiation was blamed for the deaths of at least two U.S. ambassadors and for an unusually high level of cancers among embassy personnel. The CIA learned of the attacks circa 1962, but for security reasons, American diplomatic staff were not informed of the danger. After the attacks, Soviet officials reluctantly admitted to the practice, claiming that the microwaves were only employed to damage American surveillance devices.

3909. Hostage crisis in the modern era in which a large number of American citizens were held prisoner by representatives of a foreign government in peacetime began on November 4, 1979, when the U.S. embassy in Teheran, Iran, was occupied by Islamic revolutionary troops. The occupiers, acting on behalf of Iran's dictator, Ayatollah Ruhollah Khomeini, demanded the forced return of the Shah of Iran, Mohammed Reza Pahlavi, whose regime had been overthrown in January. Pahlavi was in the United States undergoing treatment for cancer. President Jimmy Carter imposed economic sanctions on Iran and ordered a military rescue effort that failed. The 52 hostages were released on January 21, 1981.

3910. Permanent ambassador to the United Nations who was a woman was political scientist Jeanne Duane Jordan Kirkpatrick. In 1981, she was chosen by President Ronald Wilson Reagan to be the U.S. representative to the United Nations. She returned to her academic position at Georgetown University, Washington, DC, in 1985.

3911. Elimination of an entire class of nuclear weapons by treaty was carried out between August and September 1988 in accordance with the provisions of the Intermediate-Range Nuclear Forces (INF) Treaty, signed on December 8, 1987, at Washington, DC, by President Ronald Reagan and Soviet General Secretary Mikhail Gorbachev. In August 1988 the Soviet Union destroyed the first of its SS-12 missiles at Saryozek, in the presence of American inspectors. On September 8, 1988, in the presence of Soviet inspectors, the United States began eliminating its stockpile of Pershing missiles at Longhorn Army Ammunition Plant near Marshall, TX, starting with Pershing II and Pershing 1a first-stage rocket motors. The destruction of missiles by both sides was accomplished by May 1991.

3912. Chemical arms control treaty was signed on June 1, 1990, at a summit meeting in Washington, DC, by President George H. W. Bush and Soviet leader Mikhail Gorbachev. The treaty called for an 80-percent reduction of each country's chemical weapon arsenal and provided for on-site inspectors to observe the destruction of weapons stockpiles.

3913. Payment by the United States to a foreign nation for destroying nuclear weapons was arranged between the United States and Ukraine. The deal was made public on January 10, 1994, while President Bill Clinton was visiting Kiev. Clinton announced that Ukraine would receive cash from the United States in return for dismantling its nuclear arsenal, the third largest in the world.

3914. Ambassador to Vietnam after the end of the Vietnam War was Peter Peterson, who presented his portfolio in Hanoi on May 9, 1997. Peterson, a former Air Force captain, had been held as a prisoner of war in Vietnam for 6.5 years after his bomber was shot down near Hanoi in 1966. He was released in March 1973. The United States had not maintained formal diplomatic relations with Vietnam since its previous ambassador, Graham Martin, left Saigon by helicopter in 1975 as the city fell to North Vietnamese forces.

3915. Ambassador who was Muslim was M. Osman Siddique, nominated by President Bill Clinton to be U.S. ambassador to the Fiji Islands (the Republic of Fiji, the Republic of Nauru, the Kingdom of Tonga, and Tuvalu) and sworn in on August 17, 1999. He was the first American ambassador to take the oath of office with his hand on the Koran. He was born in Dhaka, Bangladesh.

3916. American civil administrator of a Middle Eastern country was retired U.S. Army general Jay Montgomery Garner, appointed director of reconstruction and humanitarian assistance for Iraq on April 21, 2003, following the occupation of Iraq by Coalition forces. Garner, a native of Arcadia, FL, was replaced by L. Paul Bremer on May 11, 2003.

3917. Foreign flag flown at the State Department was the British flag, raised by police officers at the State Department offices in Washington, DC, on July 7, 2005, in remembrance of those killed in the Islamist suicide bombings that had taken place on the London transportation system earlier that day.

Nobles and Heads of State

3918. Knighthood conferred on a person born in America was awarded at Windsor Castle, England, on June 28, 1687, by King James II to William Phips [Phipps] for his fair distribution of 34 tons of silver, gold, and jewels valued at $1,350,000 that he salvaged from a sunken Spanish ship that had lain in the sea near the Bahama Islands for 44 years. Phips's share amounted to $72,000. He was born on February 2, 1651, at Pemaquid (now Bristol), ME.

3919. Knighthood conferred on a soldier born in America was awarded on September 23, 1745, to General William Pepperell, who was born in Kittery, ME. He was made a baronet by Great Britain because of his military exploit on April 29, 1745, when he undertook the siege and reduction of Louisburg, a French fortress on the island of Cape Breton, Nova Scotia, built at a cost of $6 million. The siege, a joint American and British campaign, lasted 49 days. The fortress capitulated on June 16, 1745.

3920. Knighthood conferred on American soil was awarded to Major General Jeffery Amherst for his campaign against the French and for his capture of Montreal on September 8, 1760. He was awarded the thanks of Parliament, and on May 26, 1761, King George III made him a knight of the Bath, with Sir Charles Cotterel-Dormer serving as his proxy. Major Robert Monckton, governor of New York, conferred the award in a special ceremony on October 25, 1761, at Staten Island, NY (now part of New York City). Amherst served as commander in chief of the British army from 1772 to 1795.

3921. American woman to become a countess was Sarah Thompson, who became the Countess of Rumford when her father, Benjamin Thompson, an American physicist born in North Woburn, MA, was knighted as Count Rumford on February 23, 1784, by King George III of England. He was also created a count of the Holy Roman Empire in 1791 by Charles Philip Frederick, Duke of Bavaria. The Countess of Rumford had the privilege of residing in any country she chose and receiving half of her father's pension of 2,000 florins.

3922. President of the Republic of Texas was Sam Houston, who was elected on September 5, 1836, and who took the oath of office on October 22, 1836 in Columbia, TX. He served until December 10, 1838, and was succeeded by Mirabeau Buonaparte Lamar. Houston was reelected and served from December 14, 1841, to December 9, 1844. Upon the admission of Texas on December 29, 1845, as the 28th state of the United States, Houston was elected as a Democrat to the Senate, where he served from February 21, 1846, to March 3, 1859.

3923. Prince of Wales to visit the United States was Albert Edward, Prince of Wales (later King Edward VII), who left Plymouth, England, on July 10, 1860, and arrived in Detroit, MI, on September 20 from Hamilton, Ontario, Canada. He was received by Moses Wisner, governor of Michigan, and Mayor Christian Buhl of Detroit. After touring the United States, he sailed from Portland, ME, on October 20. He used the name Baron Renfrew during his travels.

3924. Queen to visit the United States was Queen Emma, widow of King Kamehameha IV of the Sandwich Islands (Hawaii), who arrived in New York City from England on August 8, 1866, on the Cunard liner *Java*. She was received on August 14, 1866, by President Andrew Johnson and introduced to his family.

3925. Reigning king to visit the United States was David Kalakaua, King of the Sandwich Islands (Hawaii), who was elected king on February 12, 1874, by a vote of 39–6. He embarked on the U.S.S. *Benicia* on November 17, 1874, and was received at the White House, Washington, DC, by President Ulysses Simpson Grant on December 15. Congress tendered him a reception on December 18. He arranged for a treaty of reciprocity, which was concluded on January 30, 1875. He returned to his country on February 15 on the U.S.S. *Pensacola*.

3926. Royal palace in the United States was Hale Alii (House of the Chief), built by King Kalakaua of Hawaii and completed in December 1882. An Italianate mansion, it featured a throne room, a state dining room, a music room, and private residential suites. Now known as Iolani Palace, it is located in downtown Honolulu.

3927. Coronation on territory that would later become part of the United States took place on February 12, 1883, when King Kalakaua and Queen Kapiolani were crowned king and queen of the Hawaiian Islands at Iolani Palace, Honolulu.

3928. American woman of European descent to be made a Native American chief was Harriet Maxwell Converse, who was made a chief of the Six Nations on September 18, 1891, at the Tonawanda Reservation, NY, in a ceremony known as the Condolence. In recognition of her services to the Native Americans, she was given the name Gaiswanoh, meaning "the watcher." In 1884, Mrs. Converse had been adopted as a member of the Seneca in appreciation of her efforts on their behalf.

3929. American woman to become a member of the British Parliament was Lady Astor, born Nancy Witcher Langhorne in Danville, VA. She succeeded her second husband, Waldorf Astor, in the House of Commons when he moved to the House of Lords in 1919 after becoming Viscount Astor of Hever on the death of his father. She was elected to represent the Plymouth constituency and took her oath of office on December 1, 1919. She was not only the first American-born woman to sit in Parliament, but the first woman of any nationality.

3930. Queen to visit the United States during her reign was Queen Marie of Rumania, who arrived in New York City on October 18, 1926, on the *Leviathan* and received a 21-gun salute from the fort at Governors Island. She was accompanied by Prince Nicholas and Princess Ileana. They returned on November 24 on the *Berengaria.*

3931. King born in the United States was Bhumibol Adulyadej (Phumiphon Aduldet), king of Thailand, who was born on December 5, 1927, at Mount Auburn Hospital, Cambridge, MA. He was crowned on May 5, 1950, as King Rama IX. He was the son of Prince Mahidol.

3932. Absolute monarch to visit the United States was King Prajadhipok of Siam, who crossed from Canada to Portal, ND, on April 29, 1931, accompanied by his wife, Queen Rambai Barni, and the royal entourage. President Herbert Clark Hoover received him on April 29, 1931. The king had visited the United States in 1924, when he was a prince.

3933. Pope to visit the United States before his election was Eugenio Pacelli, the future Pope Pius XII, who visited America from October 8 to November 7, 1936, while serving as papal secretary of state. His headquarters were at Inisfada, the Long Island mansion of the Papal Duchess Genevieve Garvan Brady.

3934. Woman of American ancestry to become a queen was Countess Geraldine Apponyi of Hungary, who married King Zog of Albania on April 27, 1938, at the Royal Palace, Tirana, Albania. The marriage was proclaimed by Heqmet Delvina, vice president of the Albanian Parliament. The countess was the daughter of Count Julius Apponyi, a Hungarian nobleman, and Virginia Gladys Stewart, his American-born wife.

3935. King of Great Britain to visit the United States were King George VI and his wife, Elizabeth, who crossed the international border from Canada at 10:39 P.M. on June 7, 1939, at the Suspension Bridge Station, Niagara Falls, NY. They visited New York City and Washington, DC, and recrossed the border at 5:22 A.M. on June 12. They sailed from Halifax, Nova Scotia, on June 15.

3936. King and queen to be shown on television were King George VI and Queen Elizabeth of Great Britain, who visited the New York World's Fair, New York City, on June 10, 1939, during "British Week." They were pictured visiting the exhibits.

3937. President of a Sub-Saharan African country to visit the United States was President Edwin James Barclay of the Republic of Liberia, who addressed the Senate on May 27, 1943, the day following his arrival. He was accompanied by the vice president, William Vacanarat Shadrach Tubman, who was also the president-elect. They were welcomed by President Franklin Delano Roosevelt.

3938. Pope to visit the United States was Pope Paul VI, who arrived at Kennedy International Airport, New York City, on October 4, 1965, at 9:27 A.M. He went to Saint Patrick's Cathedral and Cardinal Spellman's residence at 11:44 A.M., conferred with President Lyndon Baines Johnson at the Waldorf-Astoria Hotel at 1:40 P.M., addressed the General Assembly of the United Nations in French at 3:30 P.M., attended a public Mass at Yankee Stadium at 8:20 P.M., visited the Vatican Pavilion at the New York World's Fair at 10:25 P.M., and returned to Rome the same day at 11 P.M. on an Alitalia jet liner. He was seen by about 1 million persons and by 100 million on television.

3939. European king buried in the United States was King Peter II of Yugoslavia, who died on November 4, 1970, in the Colorado General Hospital, Denver, CO, and was buried at the Liberty Eastern Serbian Orthodox Monastery, Liberty, IL. His Serbian name was Petar Karadjordjevíc. He became king on October 11, 1934. He left Yugoslavia in 1941 after it was invaded by Germany, and headed the exiled Yugoslav government during World War II. After 1945, when Yugoslavia became a republic, he lived in New York City.

3940. Emperor of Japan to visit the United States was Emperor Hirohito of Japan, who landed at Patrick Henry Airport, Williamsburg, VA, on September 30, 1975, accompanied by his wife. In 1971, he had stopped briefly at Alaska on his way to Europe.

3941. Pope to visit the White House in Washington, DC, was Pope John Paul II, who flew across the Atlantic in the *Shepherd 1*, landing in Boston, MA, on October 1, 1979. In six days, he visited Boston, New York, Philadelphia, Urbandale, IA, Chicago, and Washington. He returned to Rome from Andrews Air Force Base, near Washington, on October 6.

3942. Principal chief of a major Native American tribe who was a woman was Wilma P. Mankiller, born in Tahlequah, OK. She was elected principal chief of the Cherokee Nation of Oklahoma, the second largest Native American tribe in the United States, in July 1987.

3943. American to hug the Queen of England was Alice Frazier, an African-American woman who affectionately wrapped her arms around Queen Elizabeth II of Great Britain when the queen visited Frazier's new government-subsidized home on Drake's Place in Washington, DC, in 1991. Under British protocol, people are restricted from touching the queen, though they may shake her hand if she extends it. The event attracted so much international media attention that neighborhood officials decided to rename the street "Queen's Stroll" to commemorate the event.

3944. Criminal conviction of a foreign head of state took place in Miami, FL, on April 9, 1992, when Panama's dictator, General Manuel Noriega, was convicted by a jury on charges of racketeering, drug trafficking, and money laundering. A former collaborator with the CIA, he had been indicted by a federal grand jury in Miami in 1988 and had been captured during the U.S. invasion of Panama in 1989. He was sentenced to 40 years in prison.

3945. American mayor to be knighted was Rudolph Giuliani, the former mayor of New York City. He was granted an honorary knighthood on February 13, 2002, by Queen Elizabeth II of Great Britain for the leadership he displayed in the aftermath of the attack on the World Trade Center by Islamic terrorists on September 11, 2001.

3946. President to attend the funeral of a pope during his term of office was George W. Bush. On April 8, 2005, he was one of about 80 heads of state to attend the funeral of Pope John Paul II. The service was held in St. Peter's Square, Vatican City. Two former presidents were also present—George Herbert Walker Bush and William Jefferson Clinton—as well as First Lady Laura Bush.

Law

3947. Lawyer disbarred was Thomas Lechford, who was engaged by William and Elizabeth Cole in the summer of 1639 for the prosecution of an action against Mrs. Cole's brother, Francis Doughty of Taunton, MA. In a Quarter Court held in Boston on September 3, 1639, Lechford was disbarred by the General Court of Massachusetts because he spoke privately with members of the jury. The records state that "M. Thomas Lechford, for going to the Jewry, pleading with them out of Court, is debarred from pleading any man's cause thereafter, unless his owne, and admonished not to presume to meddle beyond what hee shalbee called to by the Courts." Lechford was pardoned, but a year later was again disbarred for the same offense, and again pardoned.

3948. Law book of colonial laws was *The Book of the General Lawes and Libertyes concerning the inhabitants of the Massachusets, collected out of the records of the General Court for the several years wherein they were made and established and now revised by the same Court and disposed into an Alphabetical order and published by the same Authoritie in the General Court held at Boston the fourteenth of the first month Anno 1647.* The work was published in Cambridge, MA, in 1648 and sold by Hezekiah Usher in Boston, MA.

3949. Shorthand account of a trial was made in Maryland by John Llywellin, clerk of the Council, who was instructed by Lord Baltimore to record the proceedings held in the Provinciall Court, St. Johns, MD, on November 15, 1681. The Justices Tailoor, Stevens, and Diggens found Josias Fendall guilty of mutiny on March 26, 1681, and sentenced him to pay "40,000 pounds of Tobacco for a fine, Be kept in safe custody at your own proper costes and charges until you shall have paid the same and after the same is paid to be for ever banished out of this Province."

3950. Law history book published was William Penn's *The Excellent Priviledge of Liberty and Property being the birth-right of the free-born subjects of England. Containing 1. Magna Charta, with a learned comment upon it. 2. The confirmation of the charters of the Liberties of England and of the Forrest, made in the 35th year of Edward the first. 3. A statute made the 34 Edw. 1. commonly called De*

Tallageo non concedendo; wherein all fundamental laws, liberties and customs are confirmed. With a comment upon it. 4. An abstract of the pattent granted by the king to William Penn and his heirs and assigns for the province of Pennsylvania. 5. And lastly, the charter of liberties granted by the said William Penn to the freemen and inhabitants of the province of Pennsylvania and territories thereunto annexed, in America. A sextodecimo book containing 83 pages, it was printed by William Bradford in Philadelphia, PA, in 1687.

3951. State organization of lawyers was the New York Bar Association, New York City, which operated from 1747 to 1770. Its purpose was to develop collective opinion on the economic issues prior to the Revolutionary War and to control admission to practice.

3952. Laws of entail and primogeniture to be abolished by a state were abolished by Georgia, whose constitution of February 5, 1777, abrogated those two bulwarks of legal tradition. Entail is a means of willing property to a specified and unchangeable hierarchy of inheritors. Primogeniture is the right of the eldest child in a family, usually the eldest son, to inherit his parent's entire estate.

3953. Insurance law treatise was a reprint of an English book, *A System of the Law of Marine Insurances; with three chapters on bottomry, on insurance on lives and on insurances against fire*, by Sir James Alan Park, published in Philadelphia, PA, in 1789.

3954. Law report was Ephraim *Kirby's Reports of Cases Adjudged in the Superior Court of the State of Connecticut from the year 1785 to May 1788 with some determinations in the Supreme Court of Errors*, published in 1789 by Collier and Adam, Litchfield, CT. It consisted of 456 pages of text, 12 pages of index, and a five-page list of subscribers. Volume 1 of Harris and McHenry's *Maryland Reports*, published in 1809, reported cases from as far back as 1658.

3955. Lawyers admitted to practice before the Supreme Court were Elias Boudinot of New Jersey, Thomas Hartly of Pennsylvania, and Richard Harrison of New York, who were admitted on February 5, 1790. The requirements for admittance were "membership for three years past in the Supreme Court of the State in which they respectively belong, and that their private and professional character shall appear to be fair."

3956. Law book of federal laws was *Acts passed at a Congress of the United States of America, begun and held at the City of New York, on Wednesday the fourth of March 1789, being the acts passed at the first session ofthe First Congress of the United States, to wit, New Hampshire, Massachusetts, Connecticut, New York, New Jersey, Pennsylvania, Delaware, Maryland, Virginia, South Carolina and Georgia, which eleven states ratified the Constitution of Government for the United States.* The book contained 486 pages and was published in Hartford, CT, in 1791 by Barzillai Hudson and George Goodwin.

3957. Legal treatise published in the United States was *A System of the Laws of the State of Connecticut*, written by Zephaniah Smith, future judge of the Connecticut Superior Court. It was published by John Byrne at Windham, CT, in two volumes, in 1795 and 1796.

3958. Digest of American law was *An Abridgement of the Laws of the United States or a complete digest of all such acts of Congress as concern the United States at large, to which is added an appendix containing all existing treaties, the Declaration of Independence, the Articles of Confederation, the rules and articles for the government of the army and the ordinance for the government of the territory north-west of Ohio.* It was edited by William Graydon and published in Harrisburg, PA, in 1803. It contained 650 pages.

3959. Legal treatise analyzing the Constitution was St. George Tucker's *American Blackstone*, published in Philadelphia, PA, in 1803. The five-volume work included a lengthy appendix on the character and interpretation of the new federal Constitution. Much of Tucker's commentary was written as early as 1790, and therefore was nearly contemporaneous with the writing of the Constitution itself. His views are generally accepted as the definitive source for original intent by the Supreme Court, which has cited Tucker in more than 40 major cases.

3960. Law magazine was the *American Law Journal*, which was published in Baltimore, MD, from 1808 to 1817. It was edited by John Elihu Hall.

3961. Medical jurisprudence treatise accepted as authoritative was Theodoric Romeyn Beck's *Elements of Medical Jurisprudence,* a two-volume work published in 1823 in Albany, NY.

3962. Law code adopted by a state was the Louisiana Code of 1825, *A System of Penal Law, Divided into Code of Crimes and Punishments, Code of Procedure, Code of Evidence, Code of Reform and Prison Discipline, Beside a Book of Definitions.* On March 14, 1822, the legislature appointed L. Moreau Lislet, Edward Livingston, and Pierre Derbigny to remodel the colonial code of 1808. The code was approved on April 12, 1824 and promulgated on June 13, 1825.

3963. Dictionary of American law was John Bouvier's *A Law Dictionary Adapted to the Constitution and Laws of the United States of America and of the Several States of the American Union With References to the Civil and Other Systems of Foreign Law.* It was published in two volumes in Philadelphia, PA, in 1839.

3964. Law book of federal laws then in force was *The Public Statutes at Large of the United States of America, from the organization of the government in 1789 to March 3, 1845, arranged in chronological order with references to the matter of each act and to the subsequent acts on the same subject, and copious notes of the decisions of the Courts of the United States construing those acts and upon the subjects of the laws with an index to the contents of each volume.* The first volume, containing 777 pages, was published in 1845 in Boston, MA, by Charles C. Little and James Brown. It was edited by Richard Peters. Publication was authorized by act of March 3, 1845, "a resolution to authorize the Attorney General to contract for copies of a proposed edition of the laws and treaties of the United States."

3965. Lawyer formally admitted to the bar who was African-American was Macon B. Allen, who passed his legal examination in Worcester, MA, and was admitted on May 3, 1845. He had practiced for two years previously in Maine, where no license was required.

3966. Lawyer admitted to practice before the Supreme Court who was African-American was John S. Rock, who was admitted on February 1, 1865. His admittance was moved by Senator Charles Sumner of Massachusetts. Chief Justice Salmon Portland Chase presided. The first African-American female lawyer admitted was Violette Neatly Anderson of Chicago, IL, who was admitted on January 29, 1926.

3967. Lawyer who was a woman was Arabella A. Mansfield of Mount Pleasant, IA, who was admitted to practice law in June 1869. She had studied in a law office and at home. Previously, women were considered ineligible for admission to the bar because the Iowa Code of 1851 allowed admission to "any white male person." That clause was repealed by an act approved on January 5, 1853, which held that "the affirmative declaration that male persons may be admitted is not an implied denial to the right of females." Mrs. Mansfield was admitted to practice and on March 8, 1870, the words "white male" were omitted from the statute.

3968. Lawyer who was an African-American woman was Charlotte E. Ray, who received an LL.B. degree from the School of Law, Howard University, Washington, DC, on February 27, 1872. On April 23, 1872, she was admitted to the Supreme Court of the District of Columbia, the first African-American woman to be admitted to the Washington bar.

3969. National society of lawyers was the American Bar Association, organized on August 21, 1878, at an informal meeting in Saratoga, NY, at the suggestion of Judge Simeon Eben Baldwin. At the close of the meeting, the membership consisted of 291 lawyers from 29 states. The first president was James Overton Broadhead of St. Louis, MO.

3970. Lawyer who was a woman to be admitted to practice before the Supreme Court was Belva Ann Bennett Lockwood, who was admitted on March 3, 1879. The bill admitting women passed the House of Representatives on February 21, 1878, and the Senate on February 7, 1879. It was titled an "act to relieve certain legal disabilities of women" and was signed on February 15, 1879, by President Rutherford Birchard Hayes. It provided that any female member of the bar of good moral character who had practiced for three years before a state supreme court was eligible for admittance to practice before the Supreme Court of the United States.

3971. American Bar Association members who were women were Mary Belle Grossman of Cleveland, OH, and Mary Florence Lathrop of Denver, CO, who were admitted by unanimous vote at the ABA annual meeting in Cleveland on August 28, 1918. Three other women were admitted later that same year. Mary Belle Grossman had received the LL.B. degree from the Cleveland Law School of Baldwin-Wallace College in 1912; she later served for 36 years as a municipal court judge in Cleveland. Mary Florence Lathrop had received her LL.B. degree from the University of Denver in 1896; her law practice in Denver was the first in the state to be owned by a woman.

3972. National arbitration organization devoted exclusively to advancing principle and practice in this field was the Arbitration Society of America, formed in New York City on May 15, 1922. On January 29, 1926, this group merged with two others to form the American Arbitration Association, whose first president was Anson W. Burchard.

3973. Public defender hired by a state was Peter Murray, appointed director of the Office of State Public Defender by Governor Richard Joseph Hughes of New Jersey on June 20, 1967, for a five-year term. A deputy public defender was appointed for each of New Jersey's 21 counties.

Copyright

3974. Colonial copyright law securing benefit of copyright was passed on May 15, 1672, by the General Court of Massachusetts assembled in Boston, MA, which granted John Usher, a bookseller, the privilege of publishing on his own account a revised edition of *The General Laws and Liberties of the Massachusetts Colony*. It was ordered "that for at least seven years, unless he shall have sold them all before that time, there shall be no other or further impression made by any person thereof in this jurisdiction." The penalty for violation of the copyright was treble the whole charges of printing and paper.

3975. Book to be afforded copyright protection in the United States was *Journal of Captain Cook's last voyage to the Pacific Ocean, and in quest of a North-west passage between Asia & America, performed in the Years 1776, 1777, 1778, and 1779,* by John Ledyard of Hartford, CT. The book was printed by Nathaniel Patten in Hartford in 1783. It was protected by a Connecticut statute that was passed on January 29, 1783.

3976. Copyright law enacted by a state was "an act for the encouragement of literature and genius," passed on January 29, 1783, by the General Court of Assembly of the Governor and Company of the State of Connecticut, Hartford, CT. The law gave authors sole right of publication for 14 years with power of renewal. Massachusetts passed a copyright law on March 17, 1783, for a 21-year period. Both laws extended rights only to other states having reciprocal legislation.

3977. Copyright law enacted by Congress was an act "for the encouragement of learning by securing the copies of maps, charts and books to the authors and proprietors of such copies during the times therein mentioned." The bill was signed by the speaker and the president of the Senate on May 25, 1790, laid before President George Washington on May 27, and signed on May 31. Rights were granted only to citizens of the United States, a policy which continued until 1891. Protection was extended over a 14-year period, renewal rights being granted only if the author was still alive.

3978. Book entered for copyright with the federal government was *The Philadelphia Spelling Book arranged upon a plan entirely new, adapted to the capacities of children and designed as an immediate improvement in spelling and reading the English language*, which was registered in the clerk's office of the first district of Pennsylvania on June 9, 1790, by John Barry, the author. It was printed in Philadelphia, PA, in 1790 by Carey, Stewart and Company. It was also issued as *The American Spelling Book*.

3979. Copyright law on photographs enacted by Congress was enacted on March 2, 1861, and signed the next day by President James Buchanan.

3980. Trademark registered in the United States was registered with the federal government on July 8, 1870, by the Averill Chemical Paint Company, New York City. The logo depicted an eagle with a pot of paint.

3981. International copyright agreement was the Platt-Simonds Copyright Act, passed on March 4, 1891. The act enabled citizens of Switzerland, France, Belgium, and Great Britain to obtain copyright protection in the

United States. The United States had been represented by Boyd Winchester at the Bern International Copyright Convention in 1886, but had not become a signatory to the convention.

3982. Sound trademark registered with the federal government consisted of a sequence of three notes that were used by the National Broadcasting Company, New York City, to cue the announcers and technicians on its radio network. The registration took effect on April 4, 1950.

3983. Online filing system for registering trademarks in the world was the Trademark Electronic Application System, which became available at the U.S. Patent and Trademark Office, Alexandria, VA, on a limited basis on November 30, 1997, and full-time on October 1, 1998. The website was www.uspto.gov/teas/index.html.

3984. Trademark registered in the 21st century was registered at the U.S. Patent and Trademark Organization on January 4, 2000, by Origins Natural Resources Inc., New York City, a company that sells personal care products. The company's logo showed a pair of trees, the firm's name, and the trademarked slogan "The genius of nature."

Patents

3985. Patent granted by a colony was awarded to Samuel Winslow in 1641 by Massachusetts for a new method of extracting salt: "Whereas Samuel Winslow hath made a proposition to this Court to furnish the contrey with salt at more easy rates then otherwise can bee had, & to make it by a meanes & way which hitherto hath not bene discovered, it is therefore ordered, that if the said Samuel shall, within the space of one yeare, set upon the said worke, hee shall enjoy the same, to him & his associates, for the space of ten yeares, so as it shall not bee lawfull to any other pson to make salt after the same way during the said yeares; pvided, nevthelesse, that it shall bee lawfull for any pson to bring in any salt, or to make salt after any othrway, dureing the said tearme."

3986. English patent granted to a resident of America was issued on November 25, 1715, to "Thomas Masters, Planter of Pennsylvania, for an invention found out by Sibylla his wife for cleaning and curing the Indian Corn growing in several colonies in America."

3987. Patent granted by the federal government was issued to Samuel Hopkins of Vermont on July 31, 1790, for a process of making potash and pearl ashes. The document bore the signatures of George Washington, president; Thomas Jefferson, secretary of state; and Edmund Randolph, attorney general. Under an act approved on April 10, 1790, "to promote the progress of useful arts," the holders of these three offices constituted a patent commission empowered to issue patents. Only three patents were issued that first year. In May 1802 the Patent Office was organized with Dr. William Thornton as superintendent. In 1833, after 9,000 patents had been issued, the head of the Patent Office said that he wanted to resign because "everything seems to have been done."

3988. Patent recipient to obtain more than one patent was Samuel Mulliken of Philadelphia, PA, who was granted four patents on March 11, 1791. They were on a "machine for threshing grain and corn," a "machine for breaking and swingling hemp," a "machine for cutting and polishing marble," and a "machine for raising a nap on cloths."

3989. Patent granted jointly to a father and son was awarded on August 2, 1791, to Samuel Briggs, Sr. and Jr., of Philadelphia, PA, on a machine for making nails.

3990. Patent granted to an inventor who was a woman was granted in 1793 to Hannah Wilkinson Slater of Pawtucket, RI, on a method of spinning cotton thread on spinning wheels. Her husband, Samuel Slater, operated a cotton mill on the Blackstone River.

3991. Patent granted to an African-American inventor was Patent No. 3306X, issued to Thomas Jennings of New York City on March 3, 1821. Jennings was a free man who ran a dry-cleaning business. His patent was entitled "Dry Scouring of Clothes."

3992. Numbering system for patents was introduced on July 13, 1836. Prior to that time, 9,957 unnumbered patents had been issued. Patent No. 1 under the consecutive numbering system was issued on July 13, 1836, to John Ruggles of Thomaston, ME, for "traction wheels for locomotive steam-engine for rail and other roads." Ruggles was chairman of the Senate Committee on Patents.

3993. Design patent was issued on November 9, 1842, to George Bruce of New York City for a typeface.

3994. Patent issued by the Confederate States of America was issued on August 1, 1861, to James J. Van Houten of Savannah, GA, on a breech-loading gun.

3995. Patent issued to Thomas Alva Edison was issued on July 1, 1869, for an "Electrographic Vote-Recorder and Register," a switch-operated device intended for use by legislatures.

3996. Patent examiner who was a woman was Anna R. G. Nichols of Melrose, MA, a clerk in the Patent Office, who took office on July 1, 1873, as an assistant examiner. On August 24, 1971, Brereton Sturtevant, of Wilmington, DE, became the first woman to hold the position of examiner-in-chief of the Patent Office.

3997. Label patent was issued on August 1, 1874, to the Baltimore Pearl Hominy Company of Baltimore, MD, for a label to be attached to the sack, barrel, or box in which the firm's breakfast hominy was sold.

3998. Patent granted to an inventor who was an African-American woman was a patent for a fold-out cabinet bed, awarded on July 14, 1885, to Sarah E. Goode, who ran a furniture store in Chicago, IL. The cabinet functioned as a desk in the daytime and a bed at night.

3999. Print patent was issued on March 7, 1893, to the H.J. Heinz Company of Pittsburgh, PA, for the phrase "Heinz's Preserves, Celery Sauce, Ketchup" in the shape of a pickle with three designs in circles. A patented print can be used in advertisements but cannot be used as a trademark.

4000. Patent on a living organism was issued on March 31, 1981, to Ananda Mohan Chakrabarty, a biologist working for General Electric, Waukesha, WI. Chakrabarty's invention, created through genetic engineering, was *Burkholderia cepacia* (then known as *pseudomonas*), a bacterium with the ability to break down crude oil. The U.S. Patent and Trademark Office initially refused him a patent. On June 16, 1980, the U.S. Supreme Court ruled that artificially created microorganisms are indeed patentable.

4001. Patent registered in the 21st century was issued to Leonard Siprut, San Diego, CA, on January 4, 2000. His invention was a form of protective headgear for extreme sports that combined multiple adjustable elements, including a headband, visor, eye shield, hood, mask, and cord.

Money

4002. Coins made in colonial America were made in 1652 for the General Court of Massachusetts, which established a mint in Boston by act of May 27, 1652, to give the residents of Massachusetts Bay Colony relief from a drastic shortage of coins. John Hull was the mint master. The dies were produced by Joseph Jencks at the Iron Works of Lynn, MA, and were used to make silver coins worth three, six, and twelve pence, "forme flatt," with "N.E. Anno 1652" and a Roman numeral denoting the value on the obverse side. On the reverse was the word "Massachusetts" and the image of a tree (probably an oak tree originally, then a pine or a willow). The mint continued in operation for some 30 years, but the date of 1652 remained on its coins, since the British refused to allow colonial coining and the mint was expected to be shut down at any time.

4003. Paper money was issued in the colonies. On February 3, 1690, Massachusetts established a provincial bank and issued money in denominations from two shillings to £5 to pay the soldiers who served in the war with Quebec. Other colonies and states also issued paper money without any basis, so that in 1780 the ratio of paper to silver was 40 to 1.

4004. Copper coins were made from copper obtained from the Simsbury mine in Granby, CT, by John Higley in 1737. They were stamped upon planchets of the pure copper, and in consequence were in demand by goldsmiths for alloy. The obverse side showed a standing deer, facing left, occupying the whole field, with the legend, "Value me as you please." The reverse side showed three hammers, each bearing a crown upon the head with the legend "I am good copper—1737."

4005. Paper money issued by the Continental Congress was an issue of $3 million, of which $2 million was issued on June 22, 1775, and $1 million on July 25, 1775. Additional millions were issued at intervals until January 14, 1779. The largest share of the original issue, $434,244, was given to Massachusetts, and the next largest share was the $372,208 awarded to Pennsylvania. Only 12 states were granted money. Georgia was not included, as it was not represented in the Congress. The notes were issued in denominations of 1, 2, 3, 4, 5, 6, 7, and 8 dollars; 20 dollars; and from 30 to 35 dollars in five-dollar increments. There were also fractional notes of two-thirds, one-half, one-third, and one-sixth. Since these notes had little of value to back them, they were not widely accepted, and Congress had to pass a resolution in January 1776 making the refusal to accept them a treasonable act.

4006. Copper cents minted by a state were issued by Vermont. On June 15, 1785, the state granted authority to Reuben Harmon, Jr., to make these coins for two years, beginning on July 1, 1785. The copper coins were to be one-third of an ounce each, troy weight. Harmon established a mint at Rupert, VT, where he lived. In October 1785, Connecticut authorized the coinage of 10,000 pounds of copper cents at the mint at New Haven, which was operated by Samuel Bishop and John Goodrich of New Haven and Joseph Hopkins of Waterbury, CT.

4007. Decimal system of money with the dollar as a unit was adopted on July 6, 1785, by the Continental Congress, which established "that the money unit of the United States of America be one dollar; that the smallest coin be of copper, of which two hundred shall pass for one dollar; that the several pieces shall increase in a decimal ratio." On August 8, 1786, it was voted "that the standard of the United States of America for gold and silver, shall be eleven parts fine and one part alloy."

4008. Coin to use *E pluribus unum* as a motto was the cent issued by New Jersey in 1786, the obverse of which showed a horse's head above a plow with the date of coinage and the name of the state in Latin, *Nova Caesarea*. The reverse showed a heart-shaped shield of the United States and the national motto *E pluribus unum* ("from many, one"). The first United States coin bearing the motto was the half eagle, authorized by act of Congress of April 2, 1792, and coined in 1795. The obverse showed the draped bust of Liberty facing right, with long, loose hair, and a liberty cap; above, "Liberty" and 15 stars; below, "1795." The reverse displayed an eagle, bearing the shield of the United States on its breast, with arrows in right claw and olive branch in left; in its beak, a scroll inscribed *E pluribus unum*; above the head, 16 stars; beneath, an arch of clouds. The coin had a reeded edge and weighed 135 grains.

4009. Coins issued by the United States were copper cents authorized by Congress on April 21, 1787, when the Articles of Confederation were still in force. The design was accepted on July 6, 1787. One side showed a chain of 13 links surrounding a circle bearing the phrase "United States," with the words "We Are One" in the center. The other side showed a meridian sun shining over a sundial, with "1787" to the right, the Latin word *Fugio* on the left, and the words "Mind Your Business" below. *Fugio*, meaning "I Fly," refers to time, and the phrase "Mind Your Business" was a reminder to Americans to attend to their work, rather than an admonition to busybodies. Since the federal government had not yet established a mint, a contract for the production of 300 copper coins was awarded to James Jarvis, whose father-in-law ran a mint in New Haven, CT. His first delivery, consisting of 400,000 Fugio Cents, was turned over to the Treasurer of the United States on May 21, 1788. He was unable to obtain sufficient quantities of copper and eventually defaulted on his contract.

4010. Trade tokens were issued in 1789 by William and John Mott, manufacturers and dealers in watches and jewelry, Water Street, New York City. They were smaller in size than the ordinary copper cent and beautifully engraved. On the obverse was a regulator supported by two columns and surmounted by a small eagle. The inscription read "Motts, NY. Importers, Dealers, Manufacturers of Gold and Silver Ware." On the reverse was an eagle with expanded wings, facing to the left, holding an olive branch in one talon and three barbed arrows in the other, the shield of the United States upon its breast. The date "1789" was above the eagle, while below was the inscription "Watches, Jewelry, Silver Ware, Chronometers, Clocks."

4011. Coin bearing the likeness of a president were struck in December 1791 and included silver half-dollars and copper cents that displayed a portrait of the current president, George Washington. They were requested by Robert Morris, head of the Senate committee on coinage, who wanted to distribute them to his colleagues in Congress before a bill to establish a federal mint came up for a vote. They were designed by silversmith Peter Getz and were struck in the basement of a Philadelphia saw factory. The depiction of a country's leader on its coins was thought to be more appropriate for a monarchy than for a republic, and the coins did not enter circulation. Copper coins displaying Washington's portrait had already been struck by a company in Birmingham, England, in a bid to win a coining contract from the federal government.

Library of Congress, Prints & Photographs Division
LC-USZ62-11716

George Washington

4012. Gold price fixed by Congress was $19.39 an ounce, authorized on April 2, 1792. Except for the period between August 1814 and February 1817, this value remained firm until June 28, 1834, when the value of an ounce of gold was raised to $20.67. This price remained firm until May 29, 1933, except during the panics of 1837 and 1857 and from February 25, 1862, to January 1, 1879.

4013. Minting of coins by the federal government was proposed by Robert Morris, head of the Finance Department of the federal government, who laid a plan for American money coinage before Congress on January 15, 1782. Through his efforts and the cooperation of Thomas Jefferson and Alexander Hamilton, an act "establishing a mint and regulating the coins of the United States" was approved by both houses and signed by George Washington at Philadelphia, PA, on April 2, 1792. This act authorized the coinage of half-cents, cents, half-dismes, dismes, quarters, half-dollars, dollars, quarter eagles ($2.50), half eagles ($5), and eagles ($10). It also required all coins to display "an impression emblematic of Liberty, with an inscription of the word Liberty, and the year of coinage; and upon the reverse of each of the gold and silver coins shall be the representation of an eagle," with the words "United States of America.

4014. Mint of the United States was located at Philadelphia, PA. Robert Morris, as head of the Finance Department of the federal government, laid a plan for American money coinage before Congress on January 15, 1782. Through his efforts and the cooperation of Thomas Jefferson and Alexander Hamilton, an act "establishing a mint and regulating the coins of the United States" was approved by both houses and signed by George Washington on April 2, 1792. The cornerstone was laid on July 31, 1792, and construction was completed on September 7.

4015. Metal purchased for coinage was six pounds of old copper, purchased at the price of one shilling and three pence per pound, which was obtained on September 12, 1792, by Henry Voigt (or Voight), the first coiner of the United States Mint. It was coined and delivered to the Treasurer in 1793. Available quantities of local copper proved inadequate for the Mint's needs, and additional copper was bought from Sweden.

4016. Coins struck by the U.S. Mint in Philadelphia, PA, were struck in October 1792, but they did not enter circulation. A batch of silver dimes and half-dimes were struck, most probably from sterling silver tableware owned by George and Martha Washington. Also coined at the same time were a number of copper cents. All three coins bore a figure of Lady Liberty that was probably modeled on a portrait of Martha Washington.

4017. Director of the U.S. Mint was David Rittenhouse of Philadelphia, PA, who was appointed by President George Washington in 1793 and retired in 1795. Rittenhouse had had a long career as a scientist and surveyor. He was treasurer of Pennsylvania from 1777 to 1789 and president of the American Philosophical Society. The first woman to serve as director was Nellie Tayloe Ross, who assumed office on May 3, 1933.

4018. Coins struck by the United States Mint to enter circulation were 11,178 copper cents, each containing 11 pennyweights of copper. They were authorized by congressional act on April 2, 1792, and were delivered to the Treasury by the Mint in March 1793. One side showed a chain encircling the words "One Cent," with the legend "United States of America." The other side showed the profile of a woman, with the legends "Liberty" and "1793." Public opinion denounced these images as offensive—the chain because it was inappropriate for a free people, the head of Lady Liberty because it looked ghoulish—and other designs were quickly substituted.

4019. Silver deposit for coinage was made by the Bank of Maryland on July 18, 1794. It consisted of coins of France worth $80,716 as silver bullion. The first return of American silver coins to the Treasury was made on October 15, 1794.

4020. Gold bullion deposit for coinage was made by Moses Brown, a merchant of Boston, MA, on February 12, 1795. It was of gold ingots worth $2,276.72, which were paid for in silver coins.

4021. Peace medals struck by the U.S. Mint in Philadelphia, PA, were made at the request of President Thomas Jefferson for use by the Corps of Discovery, the transcontinental expedition led by Meriwether Lewis and William Clark. Made of silver, they were intended as tokens of good will to be delivered to leaders of the Native American tribes. The obverse showed the likeness of Jefferson in profile. The reverse showed a handshake and a peace pipe crossed over a tomahawk, with the legend "Peace and Friendship." The Corps took with them 32 of these medals in three sizes. The first gift of them was made on August 3, 1804, to leaders of the Oto and Missouri.

Some of the recipients of the peace medals believed them to be transmitters of bad luck and passed them along to their enemies.

4022. Paper money issued by the Native Americans is believed to have been issued about 1840 or 1850 by the Arapahos in Oregon. A later specimen bears the following inscription: "Office of Discount at Arrapahos Way in the Far West. The President and Directors of the Oregon State Bank promise to pay five dollars on demand." The Cherokee Nation in Oklahoma also issued paper money. The only known specimen is a one-dollar note, on which was inscribed, in ink, the date June 18, 1862, and the number 592. It bore the legend "Lewis Ross—Cherokee Nation" and was payable "in notes of the Confederated States at Tahlequah." It also bore numerous Cherokee symbols.

4023. Private mint authorized by the federal government was the Moffat Assay Office, Mount Ophir, Mariposa County, CA, built in 1850 by John L. Moffat. The mint manufactured $50 hexagonal gold ingots used as legal tender to replace gold dust and nuggets. Beginning on February 20, 1851, the ingots were made under the supervision of the United States Assayer, and on July 3, 1852, Congress passed an "act to establish a branch of the mint of the United States in California." Augustus Humbert of New York was appointed United States Assayer to place the government stamp upon the ingots produced by Moffat and Company. In 1852 the mint became the United States Assay Office.

4024. Fifty-dollar gold pieces were manufactured on February 20, 1851, by the Moffat Assay Office, Mount Ophir, Mariposa County, CA. They were octagonal. On the obverse was an eagle surrounded by the words "United States of America." Above it was the legend "887 thous," indicating the fineness of the gold, and at the bottom, "50 D C." On the reverse, a number of radii extended from a center in which was stamped in small figures "50." Around the edge was the phrase "The United States Assayer."

4025. Confederate coin was a silver half dollar produced at the mint in New Orleans, LA, in 1861. Only four pieces were minted. On the obverse was the Confederate shield with a liberty cap and a wreath of sugar cane and cotton branches. On the reverse side was the regular United States die.

4026. Confederate paper money was issued under the Confederate States Act of March 9, 1861, at Mobile, AL, authorizing $1 million in treasury notes in denominations of

$50, $100, $500, and $1,000. The $50 note featured three African-American slaves in a field, two of them hoeing; the $100 note, a train of cars at a depot, at the right, and Liberty standing, at the left; the $500 note, a rural scene with cattle wading in a brook; and the $1,000 note, busts of Andrew Jackson and John Caldwell Calhoun.

4027. Paper money issued by the federal government was authorized by acts of Congress of July 17, 1861, and August 5, 1861, in the amount of $50 million. The notes were first issued on March 10, 1862. The denominations were $5 (Hamilton), $10 (Lincoln), and $20 (Liberty). They were called "demand notes" because they were payable on demand at certain designated subtreasuries. They were not legal tender when first issued but were made so by act of March 17, 1862.

4028. Bill bearing the likeness of a president was the $10 bill issued on March 10, 1862, which bore a portrait of Abraham Lincoln.

4029. Paper money fractional currency was issued from August 21, 1862, to May 27, 1863, in denominations of 5 cents, 10 cents, 25 cents, and 50 cents. The bills were originally issued with perforated edges, but later were cut plain. They were also known as "postage currency," as they depicted postage stamps. They were receivable in payment for all dues to the United States less than $5 and were exchangeable for United States notes by any assistant treasurer or designated U.S. Depository in sums not less than $5.

4030. Gold certificates were authorized by act of Congress of March 3, 1863. Gold certificates of one- and two-year notes, and of compound interest notes, and certificates under the fifth section of the act were used for clearing-house purposes soon after the passage of the national bank act. They were issued on November 13, 1865, and were authorized to be received at par in payment of duties.

4031. Notes wholly engraved and printed at the Bureau of Engraving and Printing in Washington, DC, were those of the fractional currency authorized by act of Congress of March 3, 1863. Over 3 million sheets of this currency, with a monetary value of more than $13 million, had been printed by November 26, 1864.

4032. Coin to use the motto "In God We Trust" was the two-cent piece of 1864. Salmon Portland Chase, secretary of the treasury, addressed a letter to the director of the Mint at Philadelphia, PA, stating that American coinage should bear a motto expressing in the fewest words possible that no nation can be strong except in the strength of God. Congress established the motto by act of April 22, 1864, which authorized the director of the Mint to fix the shape, mottoes, and devices to be used. On July 11, 1955, Congress enacted a law to provide that "all United States currency (and coins) shall bear the inscription 'In God We Trust.'" The phrase was made the national motto of the United States on July 30, 1956, when President Dwight David Eisenhower signed a joint resolution of Congress.

4033. Nickel five-cent piece was authorized on May 16, 1866. It weighed 77.16 grains and was composed of 75 percent copper and 25 percent nickel. The obverse showed a United States shield surmounted by a cross, an olive branch pendant at each side; in back of the base of the shield were two arrows, only the heads and feathers visible; beneath, "1866"; above in the field, "In God We Trust." The reverse showed the figure "5" within a circle of 13 stars and rays, and the words "United States of America."

4034. Trade dollars were authorized by act of Congress of February 12, 1873, and were not intended for circulation in the United States, but for export to China. Each dollar weighed 420 grains, 900 fine. When its coinage was authorized it was inadvertently made legal tender in the amount of five dollars, but this was repealed on July 22, 1876. The trade dollar was discontinued on March 3, 1887.

4035. Coins manufactured for a foreign government were made for Venezuela in 1876 by the Mint in Philadelphia, PA. They comprised 10 million pieces of *un centavo* of the nominal value of $100,000 and 2 million pieces of *dos y medio centavos* of the nominal value of $50,000. The coins were composed of copper, nickel, and zinc and had a diameter of 23 millimeters and 19 millimeters respectively. The charge for the manufacture was equal to the expense, including labor and use of machinery. The production was authorized on January 29, 1874, by an act providing for coinage to be executed for foreign countries at the mints of the United States and stipulating that such production was not to interfere with the required coinage for the United States.

4036. Bill bearing the likeness of a woman was the one-dollar silver certificate, series of 1886, delivered by the Bureau of Engraving and Printing to the Department of the Treasury in September 1886. It had a portrait of Martha Washington. The reverse was in green, covered with ornamental lathe work.

4037. Commemorative coin was the Columbus silver half dollar authorized by the congressional act of August 5, 1892, for the World's Columbian Exposition, held in Chicago, IL. It was first issued in November 1892. The Isabella silver quarter, issued for the same exposition, was authorized by act of March 3, 1893. Charles E. Barber designed the obverse; George T. Morgan, the reverse.

4038. Coin bearing the likeness of a foreign monarch was the Isabella silver quarter issued for the World's Columbian Exposition in Chicago, IL. The coin was authorized on March 3, 1893, and issued in June 1893. It bore on its obverse a crowned bust of Queen Isabella, facing left, with "1893" to the right in the field. About the center design was the inscription "United States of America." On the reverse, a spinner was pictured kneeling to the left, holding a distaff in her left hand and a spindle in her right. Below was the inscription "Columbian Quar. Dol."

4039. Fifty-dollar gold pieces minted by the federal government were coined on June 15, 1915, at the mint at San Francisco, CA, for the Panama Pacific International Exposition. They were designed by Robert Aitken. About 3,000 were produced. Half were octagonal and half were round. The main design was a bust of Minerva with crested helmet.

4040. Coin bearing the likeness of a president to enter circulation was the 1909 Lincoln penny, a copper cent, designed by Victor David Brenner and based on a photograph of President Abraham Lincoln taken in 1864 by Mathew B. Brady. The design was adopted in April 1909 and in May 1909 coinage began at the Mint in Philadelphia, PA. The first delivery of the coins was made on June 30, 1909, to the Cashier of the Mint, and distribution began on August 2. The reverse was redesigned in 1959 to show the Lincoln Memorial. The first coin to bear the likeness of a living President was the 1926 Sesquicentennial half dollar, the obverse of which bore the heads of Presidents George Washington and Calvin Coolidge. The reverse depicted the original Liberty Bell. The net coinage was 141,120 pieces, struck at the Mint at Philadelphia, PA.

4041. Coin bearing the likeness of a living person to enter circulation was the 1921 Alabama Centennial commemorative half dollar, of which 70,000 were struck at the Mint at Philadelphia, PA. The obverse showed the heads of William Wyatt Bibb, the first governor of Alabama, and Thomas Erby Kilby, governor in office at the time of the centennial. The reverse depicted an American eagle.

4042. Wooden money was issued at Tenino, WA, in February 1932. When the Citizens Bank of Tenino closed its doors on December 5, 1931, during the Depression, the town was without ready cash to do business. The Tenino Chamber of Commerce, through three trustees and the State Supervisor of Banking, devised the assignment of scrip. By this plan a depositor could assign to the Chamber a certain amount of his own proven deposit in exchange for a similar amount of scrip, which the Chamber guaranteed to redeem when the liquidation of the bank paid them the necessary funds. The first scrip was printed on lithographed sheets by the *Thurston County Independent* in December 1931. In February 1932, wooden money in denominations of 25 cents, 50 cents, and $1 was printed on three-ply sitka spruce wood. Red cedar and Port Orford cedar were used afterward.

4043. Bill of $100,000 denomination was the gold certificate bearing the portrait of President Woodrow Wilson and delivered by the Bureau of Engraving and Printing in January 1935 to the Department of the Treasury. These bills were not issued for general circulation but were used within the Federal Reserve System.

4044. Bill to depict both sides of the Great Seal of the United States was the one-dollar silver certificate, series of 1935, issued on December 18, 1935. The steel plates from which the bills were printed did not carry the signature of the Secretary of the Treasury or the Treasurer. The signatures were printed in a blank space on the face of bills at the same time that the bills were numbered and sealed.

4045. Coin bearing the likeness of an African-American was the 50-cent silver commemorative honoring Booker Taliaferro Washington, the founder of Tuskegee Institute. It was authorized on August 7, 1946. The first coin was presented to President Harry S. Truman on December 17, 1946. The obverse showed the head of Washington and the reverse a stylized Hall of Fame, under which were the words "From Slave Cabin to Hall of Fame." Centered under this wording was a slave cabin, to the left of which was the inscription "In God We Trust," and to the right, "Franklin County, Va." Around the rim was the inscription "Booker T. Washington Birthplace Memorial—Liberty." The coin was designed by Isaac Scott Hathaway.

4046. Coins bearing dates other than the year of issue were authorized by Congress on July 23, 1965. The statute provided that "any coins minted after the enactment of the Coinage Act of 1965 from .900 fine coin silver shall be inscribed with the year 1964." The first of these coins were issued on November 1, 1965, at the Mint in Philadelphia, PA.

4047. Coin bearing the likeness of an American woman was a copper- and nickel-clad dollar coin depicting Susan Brownell Anthony, founder of the National Woman Suffrage Association. The coin was authorized by act of Congress of October 10, 1978, and was issued on December 13, 1978, at the Mint in Philadelphia, PA. The coin, which was round, featured an 11-sided frame on both sides. A profile of Anthony was depicted within the frame on the obverse. The reverse showed an eagle symbolizing the Apollo 11 spacecraft (dubbed *The Eagle*) landing on the moon. The weight was 0.3 ounce, the diameter 1.04 inches. The coin was also produced at the Denver and San Francisco mints. It was placed in circulation on July 1, 1979, but was withdrawn after some years because its small size made it easy to confuse with quarters.

4048. Electronic anticounterfeiting features in U.S. currency were security threads and microprinting, added in the series 1990 notes. The security thread contained electronic information that identified authentic currency, and microprinting was extremely difficult to reproduce with typical counterfeiting methods. Additional anticounterfeiting features were incorporated into a series of redesigned notes that first appeared in 1996 with the $100 note. The revamped $50 and $20 notes appeared in 1997 and 1998, respectively.

4049. Coins depicting state symbols were approved by Congress through the 50 States Quarters Program Act of 1997. The act provided for the redesign of the reverse side of quarters to depict emblems of each of the 50 states, with a separate design for each state. The 50 new designs were to be introduced into general circulation at the rate of five per year, starting in 1999 and ending in 2008. They were issued in the order in which the states signed the Constitution or joined the Union.

4050. Year in which two different coins showed portraits of the same president was 2003, and the president was Abraham Lincoln. The penny that was first issued in 1909, showing the head of President Lincoln facing right, was still in circulation. On January 6, 2003, the United States Mint unveiled the Illinois quarter, part of its 50 State Quarters Program. This coin showed Lincoln as a young man, standing in a border in the shape of Illinois. The likeness of Lincoln was adapted from a sculpture by Avard Fairbanks.

4051. Coin showing a president in frontal view was a nickel issued by the U.S. Mint in Washington, DC, on October 4, 2005. It showed a portrait of Thomas Jefferson facing nearly frontward, with the inscriptions "Liberty" and "In God We Trust." The reverse showed the image of Jefferson's home, Monticello. The portrait of Jefferson was drawn by Jamie Franki of Concord, NC.

4052. Year in which the value of a penny was less than its cost of manufacture was 2006. During the fiscal year ending September 30, 2006, it cost the United States Mint 1.23 cents to produce each penny it minted. Included in the cost of manufacture were expenditures for labor, processing, and transportation, as well as the price of the metal. Similarly, the Mint paid 5.73 cents for every five-cent nickel it produced.

Parties

4053. Quids political faction was organized during the administration of President Thomas Jefferson. Its members took an extreme position in favor of states' rights and were opposed to Jefferson's attempts to acquire West Florida. They were led from 1804 to 1808 by John Randolph of Roanoke, VA. In 1808 they ran James Monroe as a presidential candidate against James Madison. The name is derived from the Latin *tertium quid* ("a third thing"), indicating separation from both existing political parties, or from both administration and opposition forces.

4054. Political machine that was well organized was the Albany Regency, made up of a group of Democrats who, from 1820 to 1854, exercised a controlling influence over the politics of New York State. Their headquarters were in Albany, NY, but their power extended into national politics. Prominent among them were Martin Van Buren, William Learned Marcy, Silas Wright, and John Adams Dix.

4055. Anti-Masonic Party convention to nominate a presidential candidate took place at Baltimore, MD, on September 26, 1831. It was attended by 113 delegates from 13 states. William Wirt of Maryland was nominated for president and Amos Ellmaker of Pennsylvania for vice president. In the 1832 elections Wirt received 7 electoral votes as compared with 219 cast for the Democratic nominee, Andrew Jackson. The party had been formed in 1827 in western New York and held its first national convention in Philadelphia in 1830.

4056. National political platform was adopted on May 11, 1832, by a group of 295 Democratic-Republican delegates from 16 states and the District of Columbia, who assembled in Washington, DC, and drew up a list of resolutions for a platform. At the party's convention, held on December 12, 1831, in Baltimore, MD, Henry Clay was nominated for president and John Sergeant for vice president.

4057. Democratic Party national convention was held on May 21–23, 1832, in Baltimore, MD, under the name Republican Delegates from the Several States. Delegates from 21 states and the District of Columbia nominated Andrew Jackson for president and Martin Van Buren for vice president. The Democratic party received 687,502 votes in the election of November 6, 1832, and the National Republicans 530,189 votes. The use of the name "Republican" had come down from the time of Jefferson, and the party was popularly known as the Democratic-Republican party. In the party's early national conventions, the names "Democrat" and "Republican" were often used interchangeably. In 1840 the word "Republican" was dropped entirely and the official title of the convention became the Democratic National Convention, although even then speakers employed the name "Republican" when referring to what is now the Democratic party.

4058. National political convention to adopt the two-thirds rule was the Democratic-Republican convention, held May 21–22, 1832, at the Athenaeum, Baltimore, MD. The rule requires a candidate for nomination to receive two-thirds of the votes of the delegates. Robert Lucas of Ohio was chairman of the convention, which nominated Andrew Jackson for president and Martin Van Buren for vice president.

4059. Whig Party convention took place in Albany, NY, on February 3, 1836. William Henry Harrison of Ohio was unanimously nominated for president and Francis Granger of New York was nominated for vice president. This was a state convention attended by delegates from 32 of the 52 counties. The Whig Party of Ohio held a state convention in Columbus on February 22–23, 1836. In the election of November 8, Harrison received 73 electoral votes, compared with 170 cast for the winner, the Democratic candidate Martin Van Buren.

4060. Liberty Party convention to nominate presidential candidates took place in Warsaw, NY, on November 13, 1839. James Gillespie Birney of Kentucky was nominated for the presidency and Francis Julius LeMoyne for the vice presidency. The nominations were confirmed despite the unwillingness of the candidates to accept, and in the Harrison-Van Buren election of 1840 they polled 7,069 votes. The Liberty Party was the nation's first antislavery party.

4061. National political convention to adopt the unit rule was the Whig convention of 1840, held at Harrisburg, PA. The results of the balloting for the presidential nomination were 148 votes for William Henry Harrison of Ohio, 90 votes for Henry Clay, and 16 votes for Winfield Scott. John Tyler of Virginia was nominated for vice president. The unit rule had been adopted on December 4, 1839, when the party instructed each state to select a committee of three delegates who together formed a Committee of the Whole. The state delegates, meeting separately, gave instructions to the members of their committee, who later voted as a unit in the Committee of the Whole.

4062. Free Soil Party convention took place in Buffalo, NY, on August 9–10, 1848. In the election of 1848, the party's presidential candidate was Martin Van Buren of New York and the vice presidential candidate Charles Francis Adams of Massachusetts. Van Buren received 291,263 popular votes as compared with 1,360,099 cast for Zachary Taylor, the Whig candidate. The Free Soil Party was formed by the antislavery element of the Democratic Party and was supported by the Liberty Party. The party's slogan was "Free Soil, Free Speech, Free Labor, Free Men."

4063. Republican Party meeting took place on February 22, 1854, when the antislavery factions of the Whig and Free Democratic parties of Michigan held a preliminary organizational meeting. The new party was organized on February 28 in Ripon, WI, in protest against the Kansas-Nebraska bill, which permitted new territories to introduce slavery. The name Republican was suggested by Alvan Earle Bovay. The first convention formally organized under the name of Republican Party met in Strong, ME, on August 7, 1854. The first national meeting of the party was held in Pittsburgh, PA, on February 22, 1856, and the first national convention took place on June 17 at the Music Fund Hall in Philadelphia, where John Charles Fremont of California was nominated for the presidency, with William Lewis Dayton as his running mate.

4064. Know-Nothing (American) Party convention to nominate a presidential candidate was held on February 18, 1856, in Philadelphia, PA. The party had been founded in 1854 as a secret anti-immigrant organization. Members were required to be American-born and wholly unconnected with the Roman Catholic Church, and were obligated to vote as the society determined. The 1856 convention abolished the secret character of the organization and nominated former president Millard Fillmore of New York for president and Andrew Jackson Donelson of Tennessee for vice president. Fillmore received only eight electoral votes.

4065. Constitutional Union Party convention took place on May 9, 1860, in Baltimore, MD, the occasion on which the party may be said to have been definitely organized. This was the party's first and only convention. The platform declared for "the Constitution of the Country, the Union of the States and the Enforcement of the Laws." The delegates nominated John Bell of Tennessee for president and Edward Everett of Massachusetts for vice president. They received 12 electoral votes in the election of November 6, 1860. Abraham Lincoln, the Republican candidate, received 180.

4066. Delegate to a national political convention who was African-American was Frederick Douglass of Rochester, NY, who attended the National Loyalists' Loyal Union Convention at Philadelphia, PA, on September 6, 1866.

4067. Prohibition Party convention was the organizational meeting that took place on September 12, 1869, in Chicago, IL, attended by 194 delegates from nine states. The party was organized because neither of the major political parties had put a prohibition plank in its platform. The first national convention met in Columbus, OH, on February 22, 1872, and nominated James Black of Pennsylvania for president and John Russell of Michigan for vice president. The platform advocated prohibition, women's suffrage, a direct popular presidential vote, a sound currency, the encouragement of immigration, and a reduction of transportation rates. Black received 5,608 votes in the 1872 election, as compared with Grant, who received 3,597,132 votes. The organ of the party was *The Voice*, a magazine published in Chicago, the first issue of which appeared on September 25, 1884.

4068. Labor Reform Party national convention took place at Columbus, OH, on February 22, 1872. The presidential candidate was David Davis of Illinois, who received a single electoral vote in the 1872 election. Joel Parker of New Jersey was the vice presidential candidate. Both candidates declined to run, but received popular votes nevertheless. Labor Reform was the first national labor party. The first state labor party was the Workingmen's Party, which was organized in Philadelphia, PA, in July 1828, and held its first convention on August 25, 1828.

4069. Liberal Republican convention was held in Cincinnati, OH, on May 1, 1872, at which meeting the party was formed. Horace Greeley of New York was the presidential candidate and Benjamin Gratz Brown of Missouri the vice presidential candidate. In the election of November 5, 1872, Greeley (who was also the Democratic candidate) received 2,834,079 votes, as compared with 3,597,132 cast for Ulysses Simpson Grant, the Republican candidate.

4070. Greenback Party convention was held in Indianapolis, IN, on May 16–18, 1876. The first presidential candidate was Peter Cooper of New York, who received 81,737 votes in the 1876 election. Samuel Fenton Cary of Ohio was the vice presidential candidate. The party platform advocated the payment of the national debt of the government in greenbacks. The party, also known as the Independent Party, was organized on November 25, 1874, in Indianapolis.

4071. National political convention to be addressed by a woman was the Republican National Convention in Cincinnati, OH, in June 1876. On June 15, Sara Andrews Spencer made a speech against the disfranchisement of women and presented a memorial of the National Woman Suffrage Association stating "that the right to use the ballot inheres in the citizens of the United States."

4072. Socialist Labor Party of North America national convention was held in Newark, NJ, on December 26, 1877. The delegates nominated Simon Wing of Boston, MA, and Charles Horatio Matchett of New York City as the party's first presidential and vice presidential candidates. They received 21,512 votes in the election of November 8, 1892, compared to 5.55 million votes cast for Grover Cleveland, the Democratic candidate. The party was formed on July 4, 1874, as the Social Democratic Workmen's Party of North America, and changed its name in December 1877.

4073. Greenback Labor Party convention was held on June 9–11, 1880, in Chicago, IL. James Baird Weaver of Iowa was the nominee for president, Benjamin J. Chambers of Texas for vice president. The party was organized by members of the Labor Reform and Greenback parties on February 22, 1878, in Toledo, OH.

4074. Anti-Monopoly Party convention to nominate a presidential candidate was held in Chicago, IL, on May 14, 1884. The party was officially formed earlier that same day. General Benjamin Franklin Butler of Massachusetts was nominated for the presidency and General Absolom Madden West of Mississippi for the vice presidency; both were also the candidates of the Greenback Labor Party. In the 1884 election, Butler received 175,370 votes, as compared with 4,874,986 cast for Grover Cleveland of New York, the Democratic candidate. The existence of "The Anti-Monopoly Organization of the United States," as it was formally named, was of short duration, and its members joined the People's Party.

4075. Keynote speech by an African-American at a major party convention was delivered by John Roy Lynch of Natchez, MS, at the Republican National Convention that took place in Chicago, IL, on June 3–6, 1884. Lynch had served three terms in the U.S. House of Representatives and had been speaker of the house in the Mississippi state legislature. The first African-American woman to deliver the keynote speech before a major national convention was Barbara Charline Jordan of Texas, congresswoman from Texas and former member of the state senate, who spoke at the Democratic National Convention in 1976.

4076. National political convention of a major party presided over by an African-American met in the Exposition Building, Chicago, IL, on June 3, 1884. Mississippi congressman John Roy Lynch was nominated for temporary chairman of the Republican Party by Henry Cabot Lodge. The nomination was supported by Theodore Roosevelt and George William Curtis, and was carried by a vote of 424 for Lynch to 384 for Powell Clayton. John Brooks Henderson was the permanent chairman.

4077. Equal Rights Party convention took place on May 10, 1872, when 500 delegates from 26 states and four territories seceded from the National Woman Suffrage Association convention in New York City and nominated Victoria Claflin Woodhull of New York for president and Frederick Douglass for vice president.

4078. Union Labor Party convention took place on May 15–17, 1888, in Cincinnati, OH, when 274 delegates from 25 states nominated Alson Jenness Streeter of Illinois for president and Samuel Evans of Texas for vice president. Evans refused the nomination and Charles E. Cunningham of Arkansas was selected instead. They received 146,935 votes in the election of November 6, 1888, which was won by Benjamin Harrison of Indiana, the Republican candidate. The party was formed on February 22, 1887, when 300 delegates, including 10 women, attended the Industrial Labor Conference in Cincinnati. A platform was adopted the following day.

4079. **United Labor Party convention** took place on May 15–17, 1888, at the Grand Opera House, Cincinnati, OH. Robert Hall Cowdrey of Illinois was nominated for president and William H. T. Wakefield of Kansas for vice president. In the popular election of November 6, 1888, in which Benjamin Harrison, the Republican candidate, was elected president, Cowdrey received 2,818 votes. The party was formed at Clarendon Hall, New York City, on January 6, 1887, by secessionists from the Union Labor Party.

4080. **People's Party national convention** was held in Cincinnati, OH, on May 19, 1891, at which time the party was organized and the name adopted. At the second national convention, held on July 2–5, 1892, in Omaha, NE, James Baird Weaver of Iowa was nominated as the presidential candidate, with James Gaven Field of Virginia as his running mate. The People's Party was founded by members of the Farmers' Alliance and other industrial unions and later developed into the Populist Party.

4081. **Delegates to a national political convention who were women** were alternates Therese A. Jenkins of Cheyenne, WY, and Cora G. Carleton of Hilliard, WY, who attended the 10th Republican Party convention at Minneapolis, MN, on June 7–10, 1892.

4082. **Silverite national convention** was held in St. Louis, MO, on July 22, 1896. The delegates, who favored silver as a monetary standard, endorsed the Democratic candidates, William Jennings Bryan and Arthur Sewallt. The temporary chairman of the convention was Francis Griffith Newlands of Nevada, and the permanent chairman was William Pope St. John of New York.

4083. **Social Democracy of America Party national convention** was held on June 7, 1898, in Chicago, IL. The party was formed by the Brotherhood of the Cooperative Commonwealth, organized by Julius Augustus Wayland and members of the American Railway Union.

4084. **Social-Democratic Party of America national convention** was held in Rochester, NY, on January 27, 1900. The delegates nominated Eugene Victor Debs for president and Job Harriman for vice president. In the election of November 1900, the party received a popular vote of less than 100,000, compared with 7.2 million cast for the Republican candidate, William McKinley. The party was formed in 1898 by Debs, Victor Louis Berger, and Seymour Stedman, dissenters from the Social Democracy of America Party.

4085. **United Christian Party convention** took place on May 2, 1900, at which time Silas Comfort Swallow of Pennsylvania was nominated for president and John Granville Woolley of Illinois for vice president. The candidates withdrew, and were replaced by Jonah Fitz Randolph Leonard of Iowa for president and David H. Martin of Pennsylvania for vice president. The party's popular vote in the election of November 6, 1900, was 1,060, compared with 7.2 million cast for William McKinley, the Republican candidate. The party was organized in Rock Island, IL, and was devoted to the inculcation of religious and moral ideas as controlling forces in politics.

4086. **National political convention at which a woman made a seconding speech** was the Democratic National Convention, held at Kansas City, MO, in July 1900. On July 5, delegate Elizabeth Cohn of Utah seconded the nomination of William Jennings Bryan of Nebraska.

4087. **Union Reform Party convention** took place in Baltimore, MD, on September 3, 1900. Seth Hockett Ellis of Ohio was nominated for president and Samuel T. Nicholson of Pennsylvania for vice president. They received fewer than 6,000 votes, compared with 7.2 million cast for William McKinley of Ohio, the Republican candidate, in the election of November 6, 1900. The platform had been adopted on March 1, 1899, in Cincinnati, OH.

4088. **Socialist Party national convention** was held in Indianapolis, IN, on May 1, 1904. The party was formed on March 25, 1900, in Indianapolis, IN, by a group of Socialist Labor Party secessionists led by Morris Hillquit, who united his group with the Social-Democratic Party led by Eugene Victor Debs and Victor Louis Berger.

4089. **Progressive Party national convention** was held on August 6–7, 1912, at the Coliseum, Chicago, IL. It was attended by 1,800 delegates who nominated Theodore Roosevelt of New York for president and

Hiram Warren Johnson of California for vice president. Roosevelt received 4,126,000 popular and 88 electoral votes; William Howard Taft, the Republican candidate, 3,487,922 popular and 8 electoral votes; and Woodrow Wilson, the Democratic candidate, 6,297,099 popular and 435 electoral votes. The Progressive Party was organized on June 19, 1912, by seceding members of the Republican Party, and was nicknamed the Bull Moose Party. Its members reunited with the mainstream Republican Party in 1916.

4090. Communist Labor Party of America convention took place on September 1, 1919, in Chicago, IL. It was attended by 140 delegates representing 58,000 party members. The party had been formed the previous day to advance the principles laid down by the Third Internationale in Moscow. It adopted as its emblem a hammer and sickle surrounded by a wreath of wheat, and the motto "Workers of the world unite." Alfred Wagenknecht was made executive secretary.

4091. Communist Party of America convention took place on September 2, 1919, in Chicago, IL. Members of the party adopted as an emblem the figure of earth with a red flag across the face bearing the inscription "All power to the workers." Their program was the seizure of political power, the overthrow of capitalism, and the destruction of the bourgeois state.

4092. Red scare took place immediately after World War I, as the Bolshevik government tightened its grip on Russia. In the United States, a national hunt for alleged Communist radicals was led in 1919 and 1920 by Alexander Mitchell Palmer, U.S. attorney general in the last years of the Wilson administration. The so-called Palmer Raids culminated in an order on January 2, 1920, for the roundup of suspected subversives in 30 cities across the country. About 6,000 people were arrested, nearly half of whom were not formally charged with any crime. Nearly all were released by May 5, when the government ruled that membership in a communist or radical party was not in itself a crime.

4093. Farmer Labor Party convention took place on June 12, 1920, in Chicago, IL, when the organization was founded. The party was an outgrowth of the National Labor Party, which was formed in 1919. The first presidential candidate was Parley Parker Christensen of Utah and the vice presidential candidate was Maximilian Sebastian Hayes of Ohio. They received approximately 265,000 votes. The party merged with the Democratic Party in 1944.

4094. Political convention to be broadcast on radio took place on June 10, 1924, when the Republican Convention assembled at Cleveland, OH, to nominate Calvin Coolidge of Massachusetts and Charles Gates Dawes of Illinois for president and vice president. Graham McNamee was the announcer for the program, which was carried by 15 stations of the National Broadcasting Company from Boston, MA, to Kansas City, MO.

4095. National Union for Social Justice national convention was held on August 14, 1936, at the Public Auditorium, Cleveland, OH. The delegates voted 8,153–1 to support William Lemke and Thomas Charles O'Brien as candidates for president and vice president of the United States. The group was founded in November 1934 in Royal Oak, MI.

4096. Union Party convention took place on August 15, 1936, in Cleveland, OH. William Lemke was nominated for president and Thomas Charles O'Brien for vice president. The ticket was supported by liberals, the National Union of Social Justice, and Dr. Francis Everett Townsend, the social security insurance advocate, among others. The party was organized on June 18, 1936.

4097. Socialist Workers Party organizational meeting took place in Chicago, IL, on December 31, 1937. The organizers were former members of the Communist Party who had been expelled by order of the Soviet dictator Josef Stalin for adhering to the teachings of the Bolshevik leader Leon Trotsky. (Trotsky was murdered by an agent of Stalin three years later.) The party ran its first presidential campaign in 1948.

4098. Political convention to be televised was the 22nd Republican Convention, held on June 24–29, 1940, in Philadelphia, PA, at which Wendell Lewis Willkie of New York and Charles Linza McNary of Oregon were nominated for president and vice president. The telecast was made by station W2XBS of the National Broadcasting Company, New York City. The first to be telecast in color was the 29th Republican Convention, held on August 5–7, 1968, at Miami Beach,

FL. The proceedings were broadcast by both the National Broadcasting Company and the Columbia Broadcasting System.

4099. Neo-Nazi party in the United States was the American Nazi Party, founded in Arlington, VA, on March 8, 1959, by George Lincoln Rockwell, a naval officer and graphic artist who had been converted to Nazi beliefs after reading Adolf Hitler's *Mein Kampf* in 1951. He gave his first soapbox-style public address on the Mall in Washington, on April 3, 1960, and ran as the party's first presidential candidate in 1964. Rockwell was assassinated by a disgruntled former ANP member on August 25, 1967.

4100. Nominee who was a woman to receive votes at the national convention of a major party was Margaret Chase Smith, Republican senator from Maine. At the Republican National Convention, held in San Francisco, CA, on July 13–16, 1964, Maine's other senator, George Aiken, nominated her to be the party's presidential candidate. When the balloting was held, Smith received 27 votes, coming in second to Barry Goldwater of Arizona.

4101. Black Panther Party organizational meeting took place in Oakland, CA, on October 15, 1966. The founders were Robert "Bobby" Seale, Huey P. Newton, and David Hilliard, and the full name of the group was the Black Panther Party for Self-Defense. It was a Marxist revolutionary organization with a violent racialist agenda whose members took part in several bloody shootouts with police in the late 1960s. By the 1980s, many of its original members were dead or in prison for murder and other crimes.

4102. American Independent Party convention took place at Bakersfield, CA, on July 8, 1967, at the group's organizational meeting. George Corley Wallace, the former (and future) governor of Alabama, ran as AIP's presidential candidate in 1968. His third-party campaign appealed to conservative blue-collar whites who had been antagonized by inner-city riots and by the antiwar movement. Wallace returned to the Democratic Party after the election, in which he won 46 electoral votes. [but the party continued to exist, eventually splitting into two parties, one still called the American Independent Party, the other called the Independent American Party.

4103. National political convention to propose African-Americans for the offices of president and vice president was the 35th Democratic convention, held on August 26–29, 1968, at Chicago, IL. On August 28, 1968, the Reverend Channing Emery Phillips of Washington, DC, received 67.5 of the 2,622 votes cast for the presidential nomination. On August 29, Julian Bond of Atlanta, GA, was nominated but declined, as he did not fulfill the necessary age requirement.

4104. Right to Life Party organizational meeting took place in 1970 in Merrick, NY. The founders were a group of women who took up political activism after the legalization of abortion by the state legislature. They entered New York State politics in November 1970, when they ran Vincent Carey in the race for the fifth congressional district and won 5,000 votes. In 1978 RTLP candidate Mary Jane Tobin received 130,193 votes in New York's gubernatorial election. The party's first presidential campaign took place in 1980.

4105. People's Party convention was the organizational meeting that took place in Dallas, TX, in November 1971, with pediatrician and peace activist Dr. Benjamin Spock and author and gay activist Gore Vidal as co-chairmen. The delegates nominated Spock as their presidential candidate and African-American educator Julius Hobson as his running mate in the 1972 election. The platform called for an end to the Vietnam War and for "democratic and decentralized socialism." (This party is not to be confused with the original People's Party, later known as the Populist Party, that was organized in 1891.)

4106. Libertarian Party national convention took place in Denver, CO, in June 1972. The delegates chose John Hospers as their presidential candidate and Theodora Nathan as his running mate. They received one electoral vote in the election. The party was founded by David F. Nolan to promote a laissez-faire political philosophy that insisted on minimal government interference in the lives of individuals and the activities of corporations. It thus opposed a wide range of domestic government programs and called for disengagement of the United States from International affairs.

4107. Chairman of a major political party who was a woman was Frances Jean Miles Westwood of West Jordan, UT, elected chairman on July 14, 1972, at the Democratic National Committee meeting, Miami Beach, FL, which was attended by 303 members from 50 states. The first woman to serve as chairman of the Republican Party's national committee was Mary Louise Smith of Iowa, elected on September 16, 1974, at Washington, DC.

4108. Democratic Party convention between presidential elections was held in Kansas City, MO, on December 6–8, 1974. The party gathered to ratify its first major charter, which required affirmative action in all party affairs, with representation for women and minorities according to their proportion in the American electorate.

4109. Green Party organizational meeting took place at a conference of environmental activists in St. Paul, MN, in 1984. Originally known as the U.S. Green Party, it was a loosely organized affiliate of the left-wing environmentalist European Green movement. The name was later changed to the Green Party USA. The party achieved ballot status in Alaska in 1990 and California in 1992. At its first national convention, held in August 1996 in Los Angeles, delegates nominated a presidential ticket consisting of consumer advocate Ralph Nader and Native American activist Winona LaDuke. Nader refused to campaign and spent no more than $5,000 during the race, but he qualified for the ballot in 22 states and as a write-in candidate in 23 more. The Green ticket won more than 700,000 votes to take fourth place after Ross Perot in the November election.

4110. Chairman of a major political party who was African-American was Ronald H. Brown, who was elected chairman of the Democratic Party National Committee on February 10, 1989. Brown later served as secretary of commerce in the cabinet of President William Jefferson Clinton.

4111. Labor Party organizational meeting took place in June 1996. The party held its first national convention in Pittsburgh, PA, beginning on November 13, 1998. Attending were delegates from six international unions and 233 local unions. The Labor Party, not to be confused with various labor-oriented parties formed in the 19th and early 20th centuries, is a liberal political group created by unions, including the United Mine Workers, the Longshoremen, the American Federation of Government Employees, and the California Nurses Association. It endorsed its first state and federal candidates in 1998 in Wyoming under the "Green/Labor Alliance" banner.

4112. Year in which the heads of both major political parties were graduates of the same college was 2003. Terry McAuliffe, chair of the Democratic National Committee from February 2001 to February 2005, graduated from The Catholic University of America in Washington, DC, in 1979. Edward Gillespie, chair of the Republican National Committee from July 2003 to January 2005, graduated from the same institution in 1983. Both received their degrees in politics.

Presidents

4113. President elected under the Constitution was George Washington, who was inaugurated in the Federal Building on Wall Street in New York City and served from April 30, 1789, to March 4, 1797. He was not, however, the first person to be known as the president of the United States. After the adoption of the Articles of Confederation in 1781, the presidents of the sessions of the Continental Congress signed themselves "President of the United States in Congress Assembled." The first to do so was Thomas McKean of Delaware.

4114. Presidential inauguration took place on Thursday, April 30, 1789, in New York City, on the balcony of the Senate Chamber at Federal Hall, at the corner of Wall and Nassau streets. Robert R. Livingston, Chancellor of New York State, administered the oath of office to George Washington, whose right hand rested on a Bible borrowed from St. John's Lodge, Free and Accepted Masons. The Bible was opened to the first verse of Psalm 127. Washington, who wore a suit of homespun cloth, then delivered his inaugural address in the Senate Chamber. He had traveled to his inauguration from Elizabeth Town, NJ, on a barge rowed by 13 sailors.

4115. Inaugural ball was held on May 7, 1789, at the Assembly Rooms, on the east side of Broadway, a little way north of Wall Street,

New York City. A medallion portrait of President George Washington in profile on a fan was presented as a souvenir to the ladies.

4116. Presidential appointment was made by George Washington in June 1789, when he nominated William Short for the diplomatic post of *chargé d'affaires* for France. The first presidential appointment to be rejected was that of Benjamin Fishbourn, nominated to be naval officer of the port of Savannah, GA. On August 5, 1789, Congress refused to approve the nomination because Washington had failed to consult with Georgia's senators on the matter.

4117. President who had been a senator was James Monroe, who served as senator from Virginia from November 9, 1790, to May 27, 1794, filling the vacancy caused by the death of William Grayson on March 12, 1790.

4118. Presidential proclamation concerned the surveying of future site of the nation's capital, and was made in New York City on January 24, 1791, by George Washington. The proclamation directed surveyors "to survey and limit a part of the territory of ten miles square on both sides of the river Potomac, so as to comprehend Georgetown, in Maryland, and extend to the Eastern Branch."

4119. Presidential veto of a congressional bill was exercised by President George Washington on April 5, 1792, when he vetoed a bill for the apportionment of representation. The House of Representatives sustained the veto on April 6, 1792, by a vote of 33 to 22. A two-thirds vote of both houses is necessary to override a veto.

4120. Presidential commission was appointed by President George Washington to deal with the Whiskey Rebellion of 1794, in which the farmers of Washington and Allegheny counties, PA, attacked federal officers who were trying to collect an excise tax on whiskey. In sixth annual address, on November 19, 1794, he declared: "The report of the commissioners marks their firmness and abilities, and must unite all virtuous men, by shewing that the means of conciliation have been exhausted." The rebellion was then put down by an army of 13,000 militiamen.

4121. Presidential amnesty issued to rebellious citizens was issued by President George Washington on July 10, 1795, when he extended a full pardon to participants in the Whiskey Rebellion who were willing to sign an oath of allegiance to the United States. The first amnesty granted during the Civil War was issued by President Abraham Lincoln on December 8, 1863. He issued another on March 26, 1864. President Andrew Johnson issued supplementary proclamations on May 29, 1865; September 7, 1867; July 4, 1868; and December 25, 1868.

4122. President to reside in Washington was John Adams. On June 3, 1800, he took up residence at the Union Tavern, Georgetown, DC (now part of Washington, DC). In November 1800, he moved into the President's House, the Executive Mansion. George Washington was the only President who did not live in Washington, DC, as the Executive Mansion was not completed during his administration. In 1798 he did purchase two lots near the Capitol for $963, on the condition than he build two brick houses there. The houses were never built.

4123. President elected by the House of Representatives was Thomas Jefferson. After the election of 1800, the electoral vote stood as follows: Thomas Jefferson 73, Aaron Burr 73, John Adams 65, Charles Cotesworth Pinckney 64, and John Jay 1. The House of Representatives assembled on February 11, 1801, and on the 36th ballot elected Jefferson. Delaware and South Carolina cast blank ballots, with the result that the vote was 10 states for Jefferson and 4 for Burr.

4124. President inaugurated in the city of Washington was Thomas Jefferson, who was inaugurated on March 4, 1801. Jefferson walked from his boarding house to the unfinished Capitol building, where he was greeted with an artillery salute. He took the oath of office in the Senate chamber with the help of Chief Justice John Marshall. He then delivered his first inaugural address, in a voice so quiet that few in the audience could hear him.

4125. President to review the military forces at his residence was Thomas Jefferson. On July 4, 1801, he reviewed the Marines, led by the Marine Band, on the White House grounds.

4126. President to face enemy gunfire while in office and the first president actively to use his authority as commander-in-chief was James Madison. On August 25, 1814, he assumed command of Commodore Joshua Barney's battery, stationed a half mile north of Bladensburg, MD.

4127. Former president who was elected to the House of Representatives was John Quincy Adams, who served as president from March 4, 1825, to March 3, 1829. He represented the Plymouth, MA, district in Congress as a Whig for 17 years, from March 4, 1831, to February 23, 1848, when he died.

4128. Spoils system of presidential patronage was introduced by President Andrew Jackson as a reward to Simon Cameron of Pennsylvania and other supporters for their political assistance. The system allowed the president to appoint his supporters to public offices. Jackson served as president from March 4, 1829, to March 3, 1837.

4129. President to be censured by Congress was Andrew Jackson, who had incurred displeasure by his handling of the Bank of the United States matter. On March 28, 1834, by a vote of 26–20, the Senate passed a resolution declaring that President Jackson "in the last executive proceedings in relation to the public revenue, has assumed upon himself authority and power not conferred by the constitution and laws, but in derogation of both."

4130. Presidential protest was signed on April 15, 1834, by Andrew Jackson. He protested against the Senate resolution censuring him for his course in the bank controversy.

4131. Photograph of a former president was taken by the Southworth and Hawes Studio, Tremont Street, Boston, MA. It was a photograph of John Quincy Adams taken in 1843 at his home in the town of Braintree (now Quincy), MA. In 1845, Mathew B. Brady photographed Andrew Jackson at the Hermitage, Nashville, TN.

4132. Presidential veto to be overridden by Congress concerned "an act relating to revenue cutters and steamers," which provided that no revenue cutter could be built without prior appropriation. President John Tyler vetoed the bill on February 20, 1845, arguing that contracts for two revenue cutters had already been arranged, one with a firm in Richmond, VA, and another with a contractor in Pittsburgh, PA. The bill was reconsidered by the Senate and House on March 3, 1845. The Senate overrode the veto without debate by a vote of 41–1, and the House by a vote of 127–30.

4133. Photograph of a president in office was a picture of President James Knox Polk, made on February 14, 1849, in New York City by Mathew B. Brady.

4134. President who had received a patent was Abraham Lincoln. On March 10, 1849, in Springfield, IL, he applied for a patent on a device for "buoying vessels over shoals" by means of inflated cylinders. His application was granted on May 22, 1849.

4135. Former president to serve as an official of an enemy government was John Tyler of Virginia, president of the United States from 1841 to 1845. On August 1, 1861, he became a delegate to the Provisional Congress of the Confederate States. He was elected a member of the House of Representatives of the permanent Confederate Congress on November 7, 1861, but died on January 18, 1862, before taking his seat.

4136. President to be impeached was Andrew Johnson, the 17th President. The House of Representatives on February 24, 1868, voted to impeach him because he had dismissed Edwin McMasters Stanton, the secretary of war, and had declared several laws unconstitutional. The charges were usurpation of the law, corrupt use of the veto power, interference at elections, and misdemeanors. The trial was held in the Senate from March 13 to May 16, 1868, with Chief Justice Salmon Portland Chase presiding. Fifty-four senators took oaths as jurors. The vote was 35–19 against Johnson, but since this was one vote short of the two-thirds necessary for a conviction, he was acquitted. An earlier but unsuccessful attempt to bring impeachment proceedings against a president had been made on January 10, 1843, in the House of Representatives by John Minor Botts of Virginia, who introduced a resolution charging "John Tyler, Vice President acting as President" of corruption, misconduct in office, high crimes and misdemeanors. The nine charges were rejected and the resolution was not accepted by a vote of 83 ayes, 127 nays.

4137. Former president to become a senator was Andrew Johnson of Tennessee. Johnson was an unsuccessful candidate for election to the Senate in 1869 and to the House of Representatives in 1872. He was elected to the Senate from Tennessee in 1875 and served from March 4, 1875, until his death on July 31, 1875.

4138. President to use a telephone was James Abram Garfield, who first used a telephone while he was a member of Congress in 1878.

4139. Presidential seal was designed in 1880 for Rutherford B. Hayes and was intended to embellish official invitations from the White House. It was based on the obverse of the Great Seal of the United States and showed the American eagle holding the olive branch of peace in its right talon and the arrows of war in its left. Although the Great Seal shows the eagle's head facing right, the original Seal of the President of the United States showed the head facing left. It was changed to face right when the seal was redesigned in 1945.

4140. President elected for two nonconsecutive terms was Grover Cleveland, who served as the 22nd president (1885–89) and the 24th president (1893–97).

4141. President to pitch a ball to open the baseball season was William Howard Taft. On April 14, 1910, he threw the baseball that opened the American League's Washington–Philadelphia game, which Washington won 3–0. The crowd, which included 12,226 paying spectators, broke all previous baseball attendance records.

4142. Presidential flag was adopted on May 29, 1916, by Executive Order No. 2390 of President Woodrow Wilson. It showed the presidential seal in bronze on a field of blue, with a large white star in each corner.

4143. Former president to become chief justice of the Supreme Court was William Howard Taft, who was appointed chief justice on June 30, 1921. He resigned on February 3, 1930, a few weeks before his death.

4144. President to invite the president-elect to discuss government problems was Herbert Clark Hoover. On November 12, 1932, Hoover invited president-elect Franklin Delano Roosevelt to confer with him regarding the request made by Great Britain for suspension of payments of its war debt. An installment of $95 million was due on December 15, 1932. Roosevelt, then governor of New York, called on President Hoover on November 22, 1932.

4145. President to conduct religious services as commander-in-chief of the Navy was Franklin Delano Roosevelt, who read from the *Book of Common Prayer* of the Episcopal Church on Easter Sunday, April 1, 1934, while on the quarterdeck of Vincent Astor's yacht *Nourmahal* east of Key West, FL. The services were attended by the crew of the *Nourmahal* and the U.S.S. *Ellis*, a destroyer.

4146. President to go through the Panama Canal while in office was Franklin Delano Roosevelt. He passed through the canal on July 11, 1934, on the U.S.S. *Houston* on his way to Hawaii. He was greeted at Balboa, Panama, by President Harmodio Arias of Panama.

4147. President to read a veto message to Congress was Franklin Delano Roosevelt, who appeared before a joint session of Congress at Washington, DC, on May 22, 1935, to read his veto of the Patman Bonus Bill. The bill, introduced by Representative Wright Patman of Texas, provided for the immediate payment to veterans of the 1945 face value of their adjusted service certificates. Within an hour after the veto, the House voted to override it by a vote of 322–98 (the original vote on the measure had been 318–90). The following day, the Senate voted 54–40 to override the veto (the original vote had been 55–33).

4148. President inaugurated on January 20 in accordance with the 20th Amendment to the Constitution was Franklin Delano Roosevelt. The amendment was ratified on February 6, 1933, and President Roosevelt was inaugurated for his second term on January 20, 1937, in Washington, DC. Previously, presidents had been inaugurated in March.

4149. President elected for third and fourth terms was Franklin Delano Roosevelt. In the election of November 1940, when he was running for a third term, he received 27,241,939 popular votes, against Wendell Lewis Willkie's 22,304,755. In November 1944 he received 25,603,152 votes against Thomas Edmund Dewey's 22,006,616. He served only a few months of his fourth term, from January 20, 1945, until his death on April 12, 1945, when he was succeeded by his vice president, Harry S. Truman.

4150. Presidential library was the Franklin Delano Roosevelt Presidential Library, which opened in June 1941 at the Roosevelt family estate in Hyde Park, NY. Roosevelt had announced on December 10, 1938, that he would donate his papers to a library that would be open to the public. Previously, presidential papers had remained the private property of each chief executive's estate.

4151. Legal definition of the presidential seal was contained in Executive Order No. 9646, signed by President Harry S. Truman on October 25, 1945. The definition incorporated a number of design changes, including the addition of color and the reversal of the eagle's head to face toward the left. At the same time, the presidential flag was changed to include 48 stars, symbolizing the states.

4152. Pension for presidents and their widows was enacted by Congress on August 25, 1958. The act provided a pension of $25,000 for former presidents and $10,000 to their widows.

4153. Presidential hot line was installed on August 30, 1962, between the White House, Washington, DC, and the Kremlin, Moscow, during the administration of President John Fitzgerald Kennedy.

4154. President to witness the firing of a Polaris missile was John Fitzgerald Kennedy. On November 16, 1963, while aboard the U.S.S. *Observation Island* 32 miles off Cape Canaveral, FL, Kennedy watched the submerged nuclear submarine U.S.S. *Andrew Jackson* fire a Polaris A-2 missile, which broke through the surface of the water and headed on a 1,500-mile flight into the Caribbean.

4155. Former president to address the Senate was Harry S. Truman, who had served as a senator from Missouri (1935–45) and as the 33rd president (1945–53). On May 8, 1964, his 80th birthday, he was present in the Senate chamber in Washington, DC. His presence was formally acknowledged, and he responded with a 68-word speech.

4156. President to attend the launching of a manned space flight was Richard Milhous Nixon, who viewed the launching of *Apollo 12* at 11:22 A.M. on November 14, 1969, from Pad A at Cape Canaveral, FL.

4157. President to resign was Richard Milhous Nixon, who submitted his resignation to Secretary of State Henry Alfred Kissinger on August 8, 1974, and announced at 9:04 P.M., via radio and television, his intention to resign at noon on August 9, an intention that he carried out. He had been named an unindicted co-conspirator in the Watergate corruption case and was at risk of being impeached.

4158. President who came to the office through appointment rather than election was Gerald Rudolph Ford. Ford had been a longtime member of the House of Representatives when he was appointed by President Richard Milhous Nixon on October 12, 1973, to succeed Spiro T. Agnew, the vice president, who had resigned after he was charged with taking bribes. The president himself resigned on August 8, 1974, after he was named as an unindicted co-conspirator in the Watergate political burglary case. He was succeeded by Ford, who took the oath of office at noon on August 9 in the Oval Office of the White House, Washington, DC, as the 38th president.

4159. President to receive a presidential pardon was Richard Milhous Nixon, who accepted a pardon from his successor, Gerald Rudolph Ford, on September 8, 1974, exactly a month after Nixon resigned from the presidency in the wake of the Watergate scandal. Ford unconditionally pardoned Nixon for all federal offenses that the former president "committed or may have committed or taken part in" while in office.

4160. Presidential pardon for a person convicted of treason was granted by President Gerald R. Ford. On January 19, 1977, he issued an unconditional pardon to Iva Toguri. During World War II, Toguri, an American citizen living in Japan, had been pressed into making radio propaganda broadcasts alongside Allied prisoners of war. In 1949 she was convicted of treason for speaking "into a microphone concerning the loss of ships" and was imprisoned for six years. The witnesses against her, who had identified her as the mythical "Tokyo Rose," later confessed to perjury.

4161. President to take the oath of office using a nickname was Jimmy Carter, who was sworn into office in Washington, DC, on January 20, 1977, by Chief Justice Warren E. Burger. Instead of his formal name, James Earl Carter, Jr., he used his nickname, Jimmy.

4162. Pre-inaugural service at an African-American church took place on the morning of January 20, 1993, in Washington, DC. Traditionally, the president-elect attends a religious service before the inauguration. William Jefferson Clinton and his family attended an interfaith service held at the city's Metropolitan African Methodist Episcopal Church.

4163. President to use the line-item veto was William Jefferson Clinton, who used it on August 11, 1997, to eliminate three provisions from legislation that had been passed by Congress. One provision, deleted from a bipartisan bill to balance the federal budget, would have allowed the state of New York to tax Medicaid funding received by health-care providers. Two other provisions, deleted from a tax-cutting measure, would have allowed special tax deferrals for food-processing plants and financial service companies. The line-item veto, a power sought by presidents since Ulysses S. Grant, enables presidents to strike particular items from newly enacted federal laws without having to veto the entire bill. Congress passed the line-item veto in 1996.

4164. President to give testimony before a grand jury during his term in office was Bill Clinton, who on August 17, 1998, submitted to four and a half hours of questioning before a grand jury convened in Washington, DC, by special prosecutor Kenneth Starr. Starr was investigating whether Clinton lied under oath in earlier testimony given in connection with a sexual harassment lawsuit brought against the president by Paula Corbin Jones. In the grand jury session, Clinton admitted that he had had "inappropriate intimate physical contact" with White House intern Monica Lewinsky, a fact he had denied both in the Jones testimony and in public. However, Clinton maintained that he had not committed perjury because the "contact" did not fit the definition of sex used by the Jones lawyers.

Library of Congress, Prints & Photographs Division
LC-USZ62-107700

Bill Clinton

4165. Elected president to be impeached was Bill Clinton. At 1:22 P.M. on December 19, 1998, the House of Representatives approved by a vote of 228 to 206 the first of four articles of impeachment brought against him by the House Judiciary Committee, chaired by Henry J. Hyde of Illinois, on recommendation of independent prosecutor Kenneth Starr. The article accused Clinton of committing perjury while testifying before a Federal grand jury on August 17, 1998, about his relationship with White House intern Monica S. Lewinsky. In the Republican-dominated House, five Republicans voted against impeachment and five Democrats voted for it. A second article of impeachment charging Clinton with obstruction of justice was approved by 221 to 212, with 12 Republicans voting against impeachment. Two other articles were defeated.

4166. President to receive a bill from Congress by e-mail was Bill Clinton, who received a Y2K legal reform measure at his whitehouse.gov address on July 16, 1999. The bill was electronically signed by several members of Congress. At the time, there were no provisions in law for the president to officially receive an electronic version of a bill, so a paper version was also delivered.

4167. Chief White House counsel who was a woman was Beth Nolan, a native of Irvington, NY. She was named chief counsel of the White House on August 19, 1999, succeeding Charles F. C. Ruff. Nolan had been deputy attorney general of the United States since 1996 and was a former White House associate counsel.

Cabinet

4168. Cabinet was appointed by President George Washington during his first term, April 30, 1789, to March 3, 1793. Members of the Cabinet were Thomas Jefferson of Virginia, secretary of state; Alexander Hamilton of New York, secretary of the treasury; Henry Knox of Massachusetts, secretary of war; Samuel Osgood of Massachusetts, postmaster general; and Edmund Jennings Randolph of Virginia, attorney general. The seat of the federal government at that time was New York City.

4169. Secretary of the treasury was Alexander Hamilton of New York City, who was appointed by President George Washington on September 11, 1789, and who served until February 1, 1795. The Treasury Department was established by act of Congress on September 2, 1789.

4170. Attorney general of the United States was Edmund Jennings Randolph, who was appointed by President George Washington on September 26, 1789, entered on his duties on February 2, 1790, and served until January 1, 1794. The office was created by act of Congress of September 24, 1789, an "act to establish the Judicial Courts of the United States." His salary was $1,500 a year. He was required to provide his own quarters, law books, fuel, furniture, and stationery, and to pay a law clerk. The federal Department of Justice, on the cabinet level, was not established until July 1, 1870.

4171. Secretary of state was Thomas Jefferson, who was appointed by President George Washington. The State Department was created on July 27, 1789. John Jay, who served as secretary for foreign affairs for the Continental Congress from December 21, 1784, was held over without appointment or commission and continued, though not officially, to superintend the department under the Constitution until Jefferson took office as secretary of state on March 22, 1790.

4172. Secretary of War was Henry Knox of Massachusetts, who took office on September 12, 1790. The Department of War, established by Congress in New York City on August 7, 1789, was the second executive department to be created. The secretary's salary was $3,000 a year.

4173. Cabinet member to serve in two or more cabinet posts was Timothy Pickering of Pennsylvania, who served in the two cabinets of President George Washington. Pickering became postmaster general on August 12, 1791, and was recommissioned on June 1, 1794. On January 2, 1795, he was sworn in as secretary of war. From December 10, 1795, to February 5, 1796, he served as secretary of war ad interim (temporarily). Meanwhile, on August 20, 1795, he also took office as secretary of state ad interim, and on December 10, 1795, he became the secretary of state.

4174. Secretary of the Navy was Benjamin Stoddert of Maryland, who was appointed to the post by President John Adams. He took office on June 18, 1798, and received an annual salary of $3,000. The Department of the Navy was established by Congress on April 30, 1798. Since 1789 the Navy had been the responsibility of the Department of War.

4175. Cabinet secretaries to be fired were Thomas Pickering of Pennsylvania, the secretary of state, and James McHenry of Maryland, the secretary of war. Both, on several occasions, opposed decisions that had been made by President John Adams and actively sought to have them reversed. On May 10, 1800, the president asked for their resignations. McHenry complied but Pickering refused and was dismissed by the president on May 12.

4176. Cabinet member who was Catholic was Roger Brooke Taney of Maryland, attorney general in President Andrew Jackson's cabinet from July 20, 1831, until September 23, 1833, and secretary of the treasury from September 23, 1833, until June 25, 1834.

4177. Cabinet appointee rejected by the Senate was Roger Brooke Taney of Maryland, appointed secretary of the treasury by President Andrew Jackson on September 23, 1833. This was a recess appointment, since Congress was not in session. Jackson submitted Taney's name on June 23, 1834, and it was rejected by a vote of 28 to 18 on September 24.

4178. Secretary of the interior was Thomas Ewing of Ohio, who was appointed by President Zachary Taylor on March 8, 1849, and who served until July 23, 1850. The department was then known as the Home Department. It was established by Congress on March 3, 1849.

4179. Cabinet member who had served as a Confederate officer was David McKendree Key, a senator from Tennessee, who served from March 12, 1877, to August 24, 1880, as postmaster general in the cabinet of President Rutherford Birchard Hayes. He had been a lieutenant colonel in the 43rd Regiment of Tennessee and had been wounded and captured at Vicksburg.

4180. Secretary of Agriculture was Norman Jay Colman of Missouri, the former commissioner of agriculture, who was appointed on February 13, 1889, by President Grover Cleveland, who had only three weeks left in his term. Colman served until March 5, 1889.

4181. Secretary of commerce and labor was George Bruce Cortelyou of New York, who was appointed by President Theodore Roosevelt to head the Department of Commerce and Labor, established by Congress on February 14, 1903. Cortelyou took office on February 16. In 1913, commerce and labor were given separate executive departments.

4182. Cabinet member who was Jewish was Oscar Solomon Straus of New York, who was secretary of commerce and labor during President Theodore Roosevelt's second administration. He was appointed on December 12, 1906, and served from December 17, 1906, to March 3, 1909.

4183. Secretary of commerce was William Cox Redfield of New York, formerly the secretary of commerce and labor. Appointed by President Woodrow Wilson, he became secretary of commerce on March 5, 1913, the day after Congress authorized the division of the Department of Commerce and Labor into two departments. He served until March 5, 1921.

4184. Secretary of labor was William Bauchop Wilson of Pennsylvania, who served from March 5, 1913, until November 1, 1919. He was appointed by President Woodrow Wilson. Congress created the Department of Labor on March 4, 1913, when it abolished the old Department of Commerce and Labor.

4185. Father and son to occupy the same Cabinet post were Henry Cantwell Wallace, secretary of agriculture under Presidents Warren Gamaliel Harding and Calvin Coolidge from March 5, 1921, to October 25, 1924, and Henry Agard Wallace, secretary of agriculture under President Franklin Delano Roosevelt from March 4, 1933, to August 26, 1940.

4186. Cabinet member convicted of a crime committed during his tenure was Albert Bacon Fall, secretary of the interior in President Warren G. Harding's cabinet, who was tried in the District of Columbia Supreme Court in 1929. He was charged with accepting a bribe of $100,000 from Edward Laurence Doheny of the Pan-American Petroleum and Transport Company, who wanted Fall to grant his firm valuable oil leases in the Elk Hills Naval Oil Reserve in California. Fall was found guilty by Justice William Hitz on October 25, 1929. On November 1, he was sentenced to one year in prison and was fined $100,000.

4187. Cabinet in which all members were sworn in at the same time and place by the same official took office on March 4, 1933, when Justice Benjamin Nathan Cardozo of the Supreme Court swore in nine men and one woman as President Franklin Delano Roosevelt's cabinet in the library on the second floor of the White House.

4188. Cabinet member who was a woman was Frances Perkins, appointed secretary of labor by President Franklin Delano Roosevelt. She served from March 4, 1933, to June 30, 1945, the only cabinet member who served throughout all four terms of Roosevelt's administration. She had been state industrial commissioner for New York prior to this appointment.

4189. Cabinet member to address a joint session of Congress was Secretary of State Cordell Hull, who reported on November 18, 1943, that the tripartite conference at Moscow pointed toward the maintenance of peace and security in the postwar world. The two houses, being in recess, assembled to hear him, but technically it was not a "joint session."

4190. Secretary of defense was James Vincent Forrestal of New York. He was sworn in on September 17, 1947. The following day, John Laurence Sullivan was sworn in as Secretary of the Navy and William Stuart Symington as Secretary for Air. Kenneth Claiborne Royall had been sworn in nine weeks previously as Secretary of the Army. The Department of Defense, which replaced the War Department and the Navy Department, was authorized by Congress under the National Security Act of July 26, 1947.

4191. Secretary of health, education, and welfare was Oveta Culp Hobby of Houston, TX, who was sworn in on April 11, 1953, as the 10th officer in President Dwight D. Eisenhower's cabinet. Previously, she had been administrator of the Federal Security Agency. The Department of Health, Education, and Welfare was split into the Department of Health and Human Services and the Department of Education on May 4, 1980, by the Department of Education Organization Act.

4192. Cabinet conference to be telecast was presented on June 3, 1953, from the White House, Washington, DC. President Dwight David Eisenhower conferred for half an hour with Oveta Culp Hobby, secretary of health, education, and welfare; George Magoffin Humphrey, secretary of the treasury; Ezra Taft Benson, secretary of agriculture; and Herbert Brownell, attorney general. The telecast was carried by four networks.

4193. Cabinet session to be telecast and broadcast was recorded at the White House, Washington, DC, on October 25, 1954. The telecast showed a special meeting to hear the report of Secretary of State John Foster Dulles on agreements in regard to West Germany signed in Paris on October 23, 1954. All the members of President Dwight David Eisenhower's Cabinet were present, with the exception of Vice President Richard Milhous Nixon. The report was broadcast and telecast over the ABC, NBC, and CBS radio and television networks.

4194. Cabinet session held at a place other than the seat of the federal government was held on November 22, 1955, at President Dwight David Eisenhower's farm at Gettysburg, PA. It was attended by the President, the vice president, the 10 cabinet officers, and 4 other government officials.

4195. Cabinet member who was related to the president was Robert Francis Kennedy, who took office as attorney general in the cabinet of President John Fitzgerald Kennedy on January 21, 1961, in Washington, DC.

4196. Cabinet meeting attended by a foreign national was held on April 20, 1965, at Washington, DC. At the invitation of President Lyndon Baines Johnson, the meeting was attended by Aldo Moro, the visiting Italian premier; Amintore Fanfani, the Italian foreign minister; and Dr. Sergio Fenoaltea, the Italian ambassador to the United States.

4197. Cabinet member who was African-American was Robert Clifton Weaver of Washington, DC, sworn in on January 18, 1966, as secretary of housing and urban development.

4198. Secretary of housing and urban development was Robert Clifton Weaver of Washington, DC, who was nominated by President Lyndon Baines Johnson on January 13, 1966, and was sworn in on January 18, 1966. The Department of Housing and Urban Development had been authorized by Congress on September 9, 1965. Weaver was the first Cabinet member who was African-American.

4199. Secretary of Transportation was Alan Stephenson Boyd of Florida, who took office on January 16, 1967. He had been nominated by President Lyndon Baines Johnson. Congress authorized the creation of the Department of Transportation on October 15, 1966.

4200. Attorney general whose father also served as attorney general was William Ramsey Clark of Texas, sworn in on March 10, 1967, at Washington, DC. His father, Thomas Campbell Clark of Texas, who had served from June 30, 1945, to August 22, 1949, administered the oath to his son.

4201. Cabinet member to serve in four different capacities was Elliott Lee Richardson of Massachusetts, who was sworn in on June 24, 1970, as secretary of health, education and welfare; February 2, 1973, as secretary of defense; May 25, 1973, as attorney general; and February 2, 1976, as secretary of commerce. The first three posts were in the cabinet of President Richard Milhous Nixon, the fourth in the cabinet of President Gerald Rudolph Ford.

4202. Attorney general to plead guilty to a criminal offense was Richard Gordon Kleindienst of Arizona, who served in the administration of President Richard Milhous Nixon from June 12, 1972, to April 30, 1973, when he resigned, along with two other close associates of the president, as a result of the Watergate scandal. On May 18, 1974, in Federal District Court, Washington, DC, he pleaded guilty to charges that he had given inaccurate testimony before the Senate Judiciary Committee in March–April 1972, during its investigation into an antitrust settlement involving the International Telephone and Telegraph Corporation. He was convicted of a criminal misdemeanor.

4203. Secretary of state to serve simultaneously as national security advisor was Henry Alfred Kissinger, who was appointed President Richard M. Nixon's national security advisor in 1969 and who continued to hold that office after taking office as secretary of state on September 22, 1973. After President Nixon's resignation and replacement by Gerald R. Ford, Kissinger remained as national security advisor until 1975 and as secretary of state until 1977.

Kissinger emigrated to the United States from Germany in 1938 and became a citizen in 1943. He was the first secretary of state who was a naturalized citizen.

4204. Cabinet member who was an African-American woman was Patricia Roberts Harris of Washington, DC, appointed secretary of housing and urban development by President Jimmy Carter. She was sworn in on January 23, 1977.

4205. Attorney general to be incarcerated was John Newton Mitchell, attorney general during President Richard Milhous Nixon's first term in office, who was convicted of perjury, conspiracy, and obstruction of justice in connection with the Watergate burglary and cover-up. He entered the federal minimum security prison at Maxwell Air Force Base, near Montgomery, AL, on June 21, 1977. He was the 25th person convicted of crimes in connection with the Watergate scandal, which had forced the resignation of President Nixon in 1974.

4206. Secretary of energy was James Rodney Schlesinger of Virginia, who was appointed by President Jimmy Carter and sworn in on October 1, 1977. The Department of Energy had been authorized by Congress on August 4, 1977. Schlesinger had previously served as secretary of defense under Presidents Richard Nixon and Gerald Ford.

4207. Secretary of health and human services was Patricia Roberts Harris of Washington, DC. She had been appointed secretary of the Department of Health, Education, and Welfare by President Jimmy Carter in August 1979. On October 17, the department was split into the Department of Health and Human Services, with Harris in charge, and the Department of Education. Harris first entered President Carter's cabinet in 1977, when she was appointed secretary of housing and urban development.

4208. Secretary of education was Shirley Mount Hufstedler of California, formerly a circuit court judge. She took office on December 6, 1979, joining the cabinet of President Jimmy Carter. The department was created by Congress on October 17. A federal agency known as the Department of Education had existed from 1867 to 1869, but it did not have cabinet status.

4209. Cabinet member indicted while in office was Raymond L. Donovan, secretary of labor under President Ronald Wilson Reagan from 1981 to 1985. Facing a trial for larceny and fraud in New York, Donovan resigned on March 15, 1985. He was acquitted of all charges on May 25, 1987, after an eight-month trial in New York City.

4210. Secretary of veterans affairs was Edward Joseph Derwinski of Illinois, who took office on March 15, 1989, on the same day that Congress elevated the Veterans Administration to cabinet status as the Department of Veterans Affairs. He served through October 26, 1992.

4211. Attorney general who was a woman was Janet Reno of Miami, FL. She took the oath of office on March 12, 1993, after quick confirmation by the Senate on March 11. Reno had earned a law degree from Harvard University in 1963 and had been elected state attorney for Dade County, FL, in 1979.

4212. Secretary of state who was a woman was Madeleine Korbel Albright, born in Prague, Czechoslovakia, in 1937. Albright served as ambassador to the United Nations during the first administration of President William Jefferson Clinton. After a 99–0 vote of confirmation by the Senate, she was sworn into office by Vice President Albert Gore on January 23, 1997, at the White House, Washington, DC.

4213. Secretary of state who was African-American was Colin Powell, who served during the first term of President George W. Bush. Powell was sworn in on January 20, 2001, after being unanimously confirmed by the Senate. A career soldier and four-star general, he had previously served as National Security Advisor and as chairman of the Joint Chiefs of Staff. The first African-American woman to serve as secretary of state was Powell's successor, Condoleezza Rice, who was sworn in on January 26, 2005. A former professor of political science and university provost and an expert in international relations, she had served as President Bush's national securityadvisorsince2001.

Courtesy of Images of American Politial History, and the Library of Congress

Condoleezza Rice

4214. Secretary of homeland security was Tom Ridge, the former governor of Pennsylvania, who was chosen to head the newly formed United States Department of Homeland Security by President George W. Bush. The department, established on November 25, 2002, by the Homeland Security Act and in operation from January 24, 2003, consolidated various federal security organizations into a single cabinet agency. It superseded the Office of Homeland Security, which had been headed by Ridge since October 8, 2001.

First Ladies

4215. First Lady was Martha Dandridge Custis Washington, who was often known as Lady Washington. Her marriage to George Washington took place on January 6, 1759. She was 27 years old, the widow of a Virginia planter, and the mother of four children, two of whom had died in infancy. Washington was then 26 years old, a plantation owner in Mount Vernon, VA, and the former commander-in-chief of Virginia's army. They were both in their mid-fifties when Washington took the oath of office as president on April 30, 1789.

4216. First Lady to receive free mail franking privileges was Martha Washington of Mount Vernon, VA. On April 3, 1800, an "act to extend the privilege of franking letters and packages to Martha Washington" was passed. This privilege was granted her "for and during her life."

4217. First Lady to attend her husband's inauguration was Dolley Madison, wife of James Madison, the fourth president. Madison was inaugurated on March 4, 1809, in Washington, DC; Dolley Madison hosted the inaugural ball held that evening at Long's Hotel, on Capitol Hill, at 7 P.M.

4218. First Lady to write her autobiography was Louisa Catherine Adams, the wife of John Quincy Adams, who was president from 1825 to 1829. She wrote three unpublished autobiographical works: *Narrative of a Journey from Russia to France, 1815, Record of My Life* (1825), and *Adventures of a Nobody* (1840).

Library of Congress, Prints & Photographs Division
LC-USZ62-14438

Louisa Catherine Adams

4219. First Lady who was not born in the United States was Louisa Catherine Johnson, who married John Quincy Adams. She was born on February 12, 1775, in London. Her father was Joshua Johnson of Maryland, the first American consul in London. The wedding took place on July 26, 1797, at the Church of the Parish of All Hallows, Barking, England. At the time, Adams was serving as U.S. minister to Holland. Adams became president on March 4, 1825.

4220. First Lady who was the mother of a president was Abigail Adams, wife of John Adams, the second president, and the mother of John Quincy Adams, the sixth president. She gave birth to John Quincy Adams on July 11, 1767, in Braintree (now Quincy), MA. He took office on March 4, 1825.

4221. First Lady to have an occupation was Abigail Fillmore, who was a schoolteacher. She grew up in Sempronius, NY, where she was educated by her mother, and began teaching at the age of 16. Her future husband, Millard Fillmore, two years younger than she, was one of her students at New Hope Academy. She continued to teach during their long engagement and for two years after their marriage on February 5, 1826. Fillmore became a lawyer and politician and succeeded to the presidency on July 10, 1850.

Library of Congress, Prints & Photographs Division
LC-USZ62-1776

Abigail Powers Fillmore

4222. First Lady who was the grandmother of a president was Anna Tuthill Symmes Harrison. She was the wife of William Henry Harrison, whose presidency lasted a single month, March–April 1841. The Harrisons were the parents of 10 children. The fifth child, John Scott Harrison, born in 1804 in Vincennes, IN, had three children by his first wife, Lucretia Knapp Johnson Harrison, and 10 by his second, Elizabeth Ramsey Irwin Harrison. The second child of the second marriage was Benjamin Harrison, born on August 20, 1833, who became the 23rd president on March 4, 1889. Anna Harrison was alive when Benjamin Harrison was born. She died on February 25, 1864, at the age of 88.

4223. First Lady who was born an American citizen was Hannah Hoes Van Buren, childhood sweetheart of Martin Van Buren, who was his wife from February 21, 1807, to her death on February 5, 1819. She was born on March 8, 1783, in Kinderhook, NY. All first ladies before her were British subjects. She died before her husband took office, in 1837, and her place as White House hostess was filled by Van Buren's daughter-in-law Angelica, a relative of Dolley Madison.

4224. First Lady who attended school was Anna Tuthill Symmes Harrison, the wife of William Henry Harrison, president for 32 days in 1841. Born in 1775, she was educated at the Clinton Academy in Easthampton, Long Island, NY, and at Mrs. Isabella Graham's Boarding School for Young Ladies, located at 1 Broadway, New York City.

4225. First Lady to die during her husband's term in office was Letitia Christian Tyler, the wife of John Tyler. She died at Washington, DC, on September 10, 1842, at the age of 51, during Tyler's single term.

4226. First Lady to graduate from college was Lucy Ware Webb Hayes, the wife of Rutherford B. Hayes, president from 1877 to 1881. After taking classes at Ohio Wesleyan University in Delaware, OH, she matriculated at Wesleyan Female College in Cincinnati, from which she graduated with honors in

1850. As First Lady, she was active in the temperance movement and paid official visits to prisons and asylums.

Library of Congress, Prints & Photographs Division
LC-USZ62-1776

Lucy Ware Webb Hayes

4227. Pension granted to the widow of a president was authorized by an "act granting a pension to Mary Lincoln," approved on July 14, 1870. She received $3,000 a year. A congressional act of February 2, 1882, increased the annual pensions to $5,000 for the three widows then living and made a special grant of $15,000 to Mary Lincoln.

4228. Use of the term "First Lady" to refer to the president's wife was applied to Lucy Ware Webb Hayes, wife of President Rutherford B. Hayes, by journalist Mary Clemmer Ames in her newspaper account of the president's inauguration on March 5, 1877. The term was popularized by Charles Nirdlinger's musical comedy about Dolley Madison, *The First Lady in the Land*, which premiered at the Gaiety Theatre in New York, NY, on December 4, 1911.

4229. First Lady to give birth during her husband's term in office was Frances Folsom Cleveland, the wife of Grover Cleveland. They were married on June 2, 1886, during Cleveland's first term in office, which ended in 1889 after Cleveland lost his bid for reelection. Their first child, Ruth, was born on October 3, 1891, in New York City. She was known as "Baby Ruth," and her nickname was applied to a popular candy bar.

Library of Congress, Prints & Photographs Division
LC-USZ62-25797

Frances Folson Cleveland

4230. First lady to earn a college degree in a scientific field was Lou Henry Hoover, who received her degree in geology from Stanford University, Palo Alto, CA, in 1898. She translated Agricola's classical mining work *De Re Metallica* with her husband, Herbert Hoover, the future president, who had received his bachelor's degree in geology from Stanford three years earlier.

4231. First Lady to attend all her husband's cabinet meetings was Helen Herron Taft, the wife of William Howard Taft, the 27th president, who was inaugurated on March 4, 1909. A suffragist who claimed, with reference to her husband, that she "always had the satisfaction of knowing almost as much as he about the politics and intricacies of any situation," Helen Taft also attended many other political and official conferences.

Library of Congress, Prints & Photographs Division LC-USZ62-25804

Helen Taft

4232. First Lady whose autobiography was commercially published was Helen Herron Taft, the wife of William Howard Taft. Her book *Recollections of Full Years* appeared in 1914, soon after her husband left office. The publisher was the New York firm of Dodd, Mead & Company.

4233. First Lady to undertake a career of public service was Eleanor Roosevelt of New York, the wife of President Franklin Delano Roosevelt. She was already an experienced social-welfare and Democratic Party activist by the time her husband entered the White House in March 1933. During his long stay in office, as a speechmaker, columnist, and private lobbyist, she shaped public opinion and public policy on a wide range of issues, including civil rights, economic reform, the labor movement, and veterans' aid. She served as assistant director of the Office of Civilian Defense during World War II.

4234. First Lady to travel in an airplane to a foreign country was Eleanor Roosevelt, who left Miami, FL, in a commercial airplane on March 6, 1934, and visited Puerto Rico, the Virgin Islands, Port au Prince in Haiti, and Nuevitas in Cuba in the course of a trip of 2,836 air miles. She returned to the United States on March 16.

4235. First Lady appointed to a federal post after the death of her husband was Eleanor Roosevelt, whose husband, Franklin Delano Roosevelt, died in April 1945. On December 19, 1945, President Harry S. Truman named her to serve in the United States delegation to the United Nations General Assembly. She was elected chief of the United Nations Human Rights Commission on January 27, 1947.

4236. First Lady to earn a professional degree was Hillary Rodham Clinton, the wife of Bill Clinton, who was elected president in 1992 and again in 1996. She received a law degree from Yale Law School, New Haven, CT, in 1973. Bill Clinton, whom she married in 1975, was her classmate.

4237. First Lady who was also a federal official was Hillary Rodham Clinton, wife of President William Jefferson Clinton. On June 22, 1993, the U.S. Appeals Court in Washington, DC, ruled that Mrs. Clinton was a "de facto" federal official. The issue arose in the wake of controversy surrounding her chairmanship of a closed-door task force to revise the national health care system.

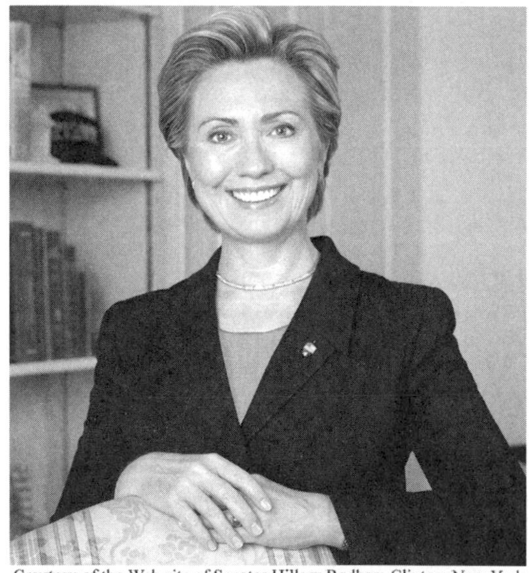

Courtesy of the Web site of Senator Hillary Rodham Clinton, New York

Hillary Rodham Clinton

4238. First Lady to be depicted on a monument to a president was Eleanor Roosevelt, the wife of Franklin Delano Roosevelt. The Franklin Delano Roosevelt Monument in Washington, DC, was dedicated on May 2, 1997. Eleanor Roosevelt was depicted in a sculpture in the fourth room of the monument, with the symbol of the United Nations in the background. The statue was sculpted by Neil Estern. The memorial was designed by Lawrence Halprin and occupied 7.5 acres between the Tidal Basin and the Potomac River.

4239. First lady to run for public office was Hillary Rodham Clinton, the wife of Bill Clinton. On February 6, 2000, she declared herself in the race for the seat being vacated by the retiring U.S. senator from New York, Daniel Patrick Moynihan, and on May 16, 2000, she received the Democratic state convention's unanimous nomination. The Clintons purchased a home in Chappaqua, NY, to enable Hillary Clinton to qualify as a resident of the state. She grew up in Illinois and lived most of her life in Arkansas or Washington, DC.

Lives and Deaths

4240. President born after the death of his father was Andrew Jackson. He was born on March 15, 1767, in Union County, NC, a few days after the death of his father.

4241. President born an American citizen was Martin Van Buren. He was born on December 5, 1782, in Kinderhook, NY.

4242. President whose son became president was John Adams, the second president, who was inaugurated on March 4, 1797. He was the father of John Quincy Adams, the sixth president, inauguarated on March 4, 1825.

4243. Congressional eulogy for a president was delivered by Representative Henry Lee of Virginia on December 26, 1799, before both houses of Congress, in honor of George Washington. This was the speech in which Washington was called "first in war, first in peace and first in the hearts of his countrymen."

4244. Biography of a president was *A History of the Life and Death, Virtues and Exploits, of General George Washington* by Mason Locke Weems, a Maryland-born Anglican pastor who earned his living as a publisher's agent and a hack writer of popular biographies. The first edition was published in 1800 to remarkable success, and the book has been through more than 80 editions altogether, despite the fact that it was recognized early on to be mainly a fabrication rather than a work of scholarship. To Weems we owe some of the best-known fictions about Washington, such as the story of the hatchet and the cherry tree, which was added to the fifth (1806) edition.

4245. President who had participated in a duel was Andrew Jackson. On May 30, 1806, at Harrison's Mills on the Red River, Logan County, KY, Jackson shot and killed Charles Dickinson. The combatants stood 24 feet apart. Dickinson fired first. The shot broke a couple of Jackson's ribs and grazed his breastbone. Despite the injury, Jackson fired and killed Dickinson. It was one of a hundred duels and brawls in which Jackson is said to have participated. Jackson served as president of the United States from March 4, 1829, to March 3, 1837.

4246. President born beyond the boundaries of the original 13 states was Abraham Lincoln. He was born near Hodgenville, KY, on February 12, 1809.

Library of Congress, Prints & Photographs Division
LC-USZ62-58516

Martin Van Buren

4247. President to be buried in a grave rather than in an above-ground crypt was Thomas Jefferson. George Washington was interred in 1799 in the family vault at Mount Vernon, VA, and was later reinterred in a new vault on the same property. John Adams was interred in the crypt of the United First Parish Church, Quincy, MA. Jefferson was buried in the family cemetery at Monticello, outside Charlottesville, VA. Adams and Jefferson both died on July 4, 1826, on the 50th anniversary of the signing of the Declaration of Independence.

4248. President whose assassination was attempted was Andrew Jackson. On January 30, 1835, Richard Lawrence fired two pistols at President Jackson as he attended the funeral of Representative Warren Ransom Davis of South Carolina at the Capitol in Washington, DC. Both weapons misfired.

4249. President whose grandson became president was William Henry Harrison, the ninth president (1841). His grandson, Benjamin Harrison, was the 23rd president (1888–93).

4250. President to die in Washington was William Henry Harrison, who died in the White House on April 4, 1841. He had caught pneumonia a month earlier at his inauguration on March 4, 1841.

4251. President married while in office was John Tyler. He married Julia Gardiner, daughter of a New York State senator, on June 25, 1844, at the Church of the Ascension, New York City. His first wife, Letitia Christian Polk, whom he had married on March 29, 1813, had died on September 10, 1842, in the White House.

4252. President to celebrate his silver wedding anniversary at the White House was Rutherford Birchard Hayes. The Reverend Dr. Lorenzo Dow McCabe of Ohio Wesleyan University, who had united him in marriage with Lucy Webb on December 30, 1852, performed the ceremony on December 31, 1877. Mrs. Hayes wore her wedding gown of white flowered satin.

4253. President who was a bachelor was James Buchanan, the 15th president. Buchanan was elected in 1856 and served as president until 1861.

4254. President to be assassinated was Abraham Lincoln. On April 14, 1865, a few days after the Civil War came to an end with the surrender of Confederate General Robert E. Lee, Lincoln attended a performance of *Our American Cousin* at Ford's Theatre, Washington, DC, where he was shot by the actor and Confederate sympathizer John Wilkes Booth. He died the following day, April 15, 1865.

4255. Body of a president to lie in state in the Capitol rotunda was that of Abraham Lincoln, who died from an assassin's bullet on April 15, 1865. His body was removed to the White House, where it remained until April 18, after which it was removed to the Capitol rotunda, where it lay in state on a catafalque on April 19 and 20. On April 21 it was taken to the railroad station and put aboard a train that conveyed it to Springfield, IL. Lincoln was buried on May 4, 1865, in Oak Ridge Cemetery, near Springfield.

4256. President whose mother lived at the White House was James Abram Garfield, who was elected in November 1880. His mother, Eliza Ballou Garfield, lived in the Executive Mansion with her son. Garfield died from an assassin's bullet in September 1881.

4257. Wedding of a president in the White House was Grover Cleveland's marriage to his ward, Frances Folsom, on June 2, 1886, during his first administration. Cleveland served as president from March 4, 1885, to March 4, 1889, and again from March 4, 1893, to March 4, 1897.

4258. President and First Lady to die during the term for which he had been elected were Warren Gamaliel Harding, who died on August 2, 1923, in San Francisco, CA, and Florence Kling De Wolfe Harding, who died on November 21, 1924, in Marion, OH. The term for which Harding had been elected was March 4, 1921–March 3, 1925.

4259. President buried in Washington was Woodrow Wilson. He was buried on February 5, 1924, in the National Cathedral, the Protestant Episcopal Cathedral of Sts. Peter and Paul, in Washington, DC.

Library of Congress, Prints & Photographs Division LC-USZ62-13028

Woodrow Wilson

4260. President to be born in a hospital was Jimmy Carter, the 39th President. The son of Lilian Gordy Carter and James Earl Carter, Sr., he was born on October 1, 1924, in Wise Sanitarium in the town of Plains, GA.

4261. President buried in the National Cemetery at Arlington, VA, was William Howard Taft. He was buried on March 11, 1930.

4262. President to become a godfather to a member of the British royal family was Franklin Delano Roosevelt. On August 4, 1942, the Duke of Kent, youngest brother of King George VI, served as proxy for President Roosevelt at the christening of his son, Michael George Charles Franklin, Prince George of Kent, who was born on July 4, 1942.

4263. Presidential pet to star in a movie was Fala, the black Scottie owned by President Franklin Delano Roosevelt. In 1943, the Metro-Goldwyn-Mayer movie studio made a short film about Fala's typical day at the White House, starting with the dog's morning biscuit, delivered to him on the presidential breakfast tray.

4264. President who had been divorced was Ronald Wilson Reagan, who was elected in November 1980. He had married his first wife, actress Jane Wyman, on January 24, 1940, when Reagan was a successful movie actor. They were divorced on July 19, 1949. They had two children, Michael and Maureen. Reagan married his second wife, Nancy Davis, on March 4, 1952.

4265. President who was Catholic was John Fitzgerald Kennedy, who was inaugurated on January 20, 1961, in Washington, DC, as the 35th president.

4266. Presidential physician who was a woman was Dr. Janet Graeme Travell of New York City, whose appointment was announced on January 25, 1961, by President John Fitzgerald Kennedy. She was the first woman to serve as a president's personal physician, but earlier presidents had received treatment from female medical practitioners. One of these was Dr. Susan Ann Edson, who was graduated from the Cleveland Homeopathic Medical College, Cleveland, OH, in 1854, treated President James Abram Garfield from July 2, 1881, the day he was shot by an assassin, to September 19, 1881, when he died.

4267. President with a brother in the Senate was John Fitzgerald Kennedy, whose brother Edward Moore Kennedy was elected on November 6, 1962, to fill his unexpired term as senator from Massachusetts after he was elected president.

4268. Assassination of a president captured on film was the murder of President John F. Kennedy in Dallas, TX, on November 22, 1963. Among the people in the crowd watching the presidential motorcade pass by was Abraham Zapruder, a dress manufacturer, who was taking pictures with an 8-millimeter home movie camera. His 26-second footage showed a clear view of President Kennedy at the moment he was shot by sniper Lee Harvey Oswald. The film was purchased by the U.S. government for safekeeping in the National Archives. An arbitration panel agreed on August 3, 1999, to pay Zapruder's heirs $16 million for it, the highest price ever paid for a historical American artifact.

4269. President who was a Rhodes Scholar was William Jefferson Clinton, a graduate of Georgetown University, Washington, DC, who attended University College, Oxford University, in Oxford, England, from 1968 to 1970 on a Rhodes Scholarship. He studied politics. The scholarship program, founded by bequest of the British colonial administrator and financier Cecil Rhodes, allows outstanding students from the British colonies, the United States, and Germany to study at Oxford. Oxford awarded Clinton an honorary doctorate in civil law in 1994.

4270. President who was a jet pilot was George W. Bush. He graduated from flight school at Moody Air Force Base, GA, on November 28, 1969, then trained to be an F-102 fighter pilot with the 147th Fighter Wing of the Texas Air National Guard at Ellington Air Force Base, Houston, TX, from December 1969 to June 27, 1970. From July 1970 to April 16, 1972, Bush took part in various drills and alerts at Ellington as a certified fighter pilot.

4271. President who had been a professional actor was Ronald Reagan. Reagan began his performing career as a radio sportscaster in Iowa and played a crusading radio announcer in his first Hollywood picture, *Love Is on the Air* (1937). His best-known movie roles were George Gipp, the doomed Notre Dame University football player in *Knute Rockne—All American* (1940), and Drake McHugh, whose legs are amputated in *Kings Row* (1941). In the latter picture, Reagan uttered the famous line, "Where's the rest of me?" which he later used as the title of his 1965 autobiography. Reagan was president of the Screen Actors' Guild (SAG) from 1947 to 1952 and again in 1959 and 1960.

4272. President to be wounded in an unsuccessful assassination attempt while in office was Ronald Wilson Reagan. On March 30, 1981, President Reagan was shot in the chest by a lone gunman, John Warnock Hinckley, Jr., as he was walking to his limousine from the Washington Hilton Hotel in Washington, DC. The president was rushed to nearby George Washington University Hospital, where a bullet was removed from his left lung. Three other people were wounded in the attack, including President Reagan's press secretary, James Brady, who was left paralyzed from the waist down.

4273. President whose body was exhumed was Zachary Taylor, the 12th president. Taylor died suddenly of acute gastrointestinal illness on July 9, 1850. Some historians suggested that he might have been poisoned. To test this theory, his remains were exhumed from a cemetery in Louisville, KY, on June 17, 1991. A coroner's report dated June 26 found no evidence of foul play.

4274. Internet camera showing the site of a presidential assassination went live on June 24, 1999, with a 24-hour-a-day webcast of the view from the window perch occupied by Lee Harvey Oswald when he shot President John F. Kennedy on November 22, 1963. The webcast was a joint project of Internet company Earthcam.com and the Sixth Floor Museum in the former Texas Book Depository on Dealey Plaza in Dallas, TX.

Mass Media

4275. President to appear on film was William McKinley. His inauguration on March 4, 1897, and his funeral in September 1901 were the first events of their kind to be filmed. Even before his election, during the 1896 campaign, he appeared in staged newsreel footage shot at his home in Canton, OH, re-creating the moment (a few weeks earlier) when he received the news that he had been nominated. The movie was made by Biograph, the New York City production company in which McKinley's brother had a financial interest.

4276. President to use a radio was Warren Gamaliel Harding, who had a vacuum-tube detector and two-stage amplifier receiving set installed in a bookcase in his study on the second floor of the White House, Washington, DC, on February 8, 1922.

4277. President to make a radio broadcast was Warren Gamaliel Harding. His speech at the dedication of the Francis Scott Key Memorial at Fort McHenry, Baltimore, MD, on June 14, 1922, was broadcast by WEAR, Baltimore, MD. His voice was carried over telephone lines to the studio and broadcast from there. On November 5, 1921, a message from President Harding had been broadcast from Washington, DC, to 28 countries. It was sent in code over the 25,000-volt RCA station at Rocky Point (near Port Jefferson), NY.

4278. Presidential message to Congress that was broadcast on radio was heard on December 6, 1923, when President Calvin Coolidge delivered his message to a joint session of Congress held in the House of Representatives, Washington, DC. It was broadcast by KSD, St. Louis, MO; WCAP, Washington, DC; WDAF, Kansas City, MO; WEAF, New York City; WFAA, Dallas, TX; and WJAR, Providence, RI. His voice was transmitted over telephone wires.

4279. President to make a radio broadcast from the White House was Calvin Coolidge, who delivered a speech from his study in the White House, Washington, DC, on February 22, 1924, on the occasion of George Washington's birthday. The speech was heard on 42 stations from coast to coast.

Library of Congress, Prints & Photographs Division LC-USZ62-5627

William McKinley

4280. Presidential inauguration to be broadcast on radio took place on March 4, 1925, when 24 stations broadcast the ceremony in which Calvin Coolidge and his vice president, Charles Gates Dawes, took the oath of office in Washington, DC. In the previous inauguration, on March 4, 1921, radio listeners heard Harold W. Arlin of station KDKA, Pittsburgh, PA, read a copy of President Warren Gamaliel Harding's 41-minute inaugural address at the same time that Harding was reading it. Arlin's reading was carried by 24 stations and heard by an audience estimated at 22.8 million.

4281. President to appear on television was Franklin Delano Roosevelt, who spoke at the Federal Building on the exposition grounds overlooking the Court of Peace at the opening session of the New York World's Fair, Flushing, Queens, New York City, on April 30, 1939, over WNBT-TV of the National Broadcasting Company, New York City. Two NBC mobile vans were used, one containing a transmitter and the other handling the pickup. Burke Crotty was the producer of the show, which lasted 3.5 hours. It began with a view of the World's Fair Trylon and the Perisphere. The first president to appear on color television was Dwight David Eisenhower, who addressed the 40th reunion of the U.S. Military Academy class of 1915 at West Point, NY, on June 6, 1955. The telecast was aired on June 7, 1955, from 11 A.M. to noon on the *Home Show* on NBC-TV.

4282. President to make a radio broadcast in a foreign language was Franklin Delano Roosevelt. He addressed the French people on November 7, 1942, from Washington, DC, at the same time that the American army was taking part in the invasion of French territorial possessions in Africa.

4283. Presidential address televised from the White House was a speech by President Harry S. Truman about food conservation and the world food crisis, delivered on October 5, 1947. The telecast was relayed from Washington, DC, to New York City, Philadelphia, and Schenectady. The president proposed meatless Tuesdays and eggless and poultryless Thursdays.

4284. Presidential press conference recorded on tape was held on January 25, 1951, at the White House, Washington, DC. Portions were released by consent of President Harry S. Truman. It was recorded for the White House archives by the Army Signal Corps unit that handled White House communications.

4285. Presidential news conference filmed for television and newsreels was held on January 19, 1955, in the treaty room of the State Department building, Washington, DC, where President Dwight David Eisenhower held a 33-minute conference. The film was cut to 28 minutes 25 seconds, plus introductory and closing remarks. The television film was recorded by the National Broadcasting Company on a pooled basis with the Columbia Broadcasting System, the American Broadcasting System, and the DuMont Network. The cost was prorated.

4286. Presidential news conference to be televised live was held on January 25, 1961, in the auditorium of the State Department building, Washington, DC. President John Fitzgerald Kennedy answered 31 questions in 38 minutes. The conference was also broadcast on radio.

Library of Congress, Prints & Photographs Division LC-USZ62-117124

John F. Kennedy

4287. Large-scale presidential media event was the trip by Richard M. Nixon to the People's Republic of China in February–March 1972. The White House carefully orchestrated the visit, the first by any president to the world's most populous nation. Nixon was accompanied by some 70 tons of transmitting equipment and an army of journalists who generated round-the-clock television, radio, and print coverage. Events were scheduled to begin and end within U.S. network prime-time hours for maximum domestic political impact.

4288. Radio broadcast in which citizens telephoned the president was the "Ask President Carter" show, in which President Jimmy Carter, sitting in the Oval Office in the White House, Washington, DC, replied to 42 listeners from 26 states who phoned in questions on the nationwide radio broadcast. The program was presented on March 5, 1977, on the CBS network. Walter Cronkite served as the moderator.

4289. Presidential inauguration broadcast live over the Internet was the second inauguration of William Jefferson Clinton, on January 20, 1997. Sun Microsystems, Inc,., of Santa Clara, CA, set up a website at www.inaugural97.org that allowed an international audience to see and hear the ceremony through live real-time streaming from Washington, DC.

4290. President to participate in a live chat over the Internet was President Bill Clinton. On November 8, 1999, he appeared on what was billed as a "virtual town meeting" on the Web site Excite@Home, answering questions that were sent to him by e-mail. While he sat on a stage at George Washington University in Washington, DC, a laptop computer streamed his image to the computer screens of the 50,000 participants, who also received a scrolling text of his remarks, transmitted by means of voice-recognition software. The moderator was Al From, president of the Democratic Leadership Council, which sponsored the event.

4291. Presidential inauguration broadcast on live high-definition TV was the first inauguration of George W. Bush on January 20, 2001, in Washington, DC. HDTV was offered by 26 stations affiliated with the Public Broadcasting Service, Alexandria, VA.

Transportation

4292. President to ride on a railroad train while in office was Andrew Jackson, who on June 6, 1833, took the stagecoach to Ellicott's Mills, where he boarded the Baltimore and Ohio train for Baltimore, MD, on a pleasure trip. John Quincy Adams had made a trip on the same line a few months earlier, after he had left the presidency.

4293. President to ride in a car was Theodore Roosevelt, who rode in a purple-lined Columbia Electric Victoria on August 22, 1902, at Hartford, CT. He was accompanied by Colonel Jacob Lyman Greene. Twenty carriages followed the presidential car during the tour of the city.

4294. President to hold an airplane pilot's license was Dwight David Eisenhower. He was issued pilot's license No. 93,258 on November 30, 1939, by the Civil Aeronautics Administration. He learned to fly in 1939 when he was a lieutenant colonel on General Douglas MacArthur's staff in the Philippines.

Courtesy of the U.S. Department of State

George W. Bush

4295. Presidential railroad car was U.S. Car No. 1, formerly known as the *Ferdinand Magellan*, built in 1942 by the Association of American Railroads. It was purchased for a nominal fee by the government and assigned to the White House. It weighed 285,000 pounds, was built on extra heavy trucks, and was sheathed throughout with armor plate 0.625 inches thick. It had bulletproof glass three inches thick in all of the windows and doors. The car had a lounge-observation compartment, a dining room seating 12 persons, a kitchen, and four bedrooms. It carried no identification marks other than the presidential seal on the brass-railed rear platform. A private railroad car had been built for Abraham Lincoln, but it was never accepted by him or assigned to the White House. It was used to bear his remains from Washington, DC, to Springfield, IL.

4296. President to fly in an airplane while in office was Franklin Delano Roosevelt, who in January 1943 flew 5,000 miles in a four-engine Boeing Flying Boat from Miami, FL, to the west coast of French Morocco to participate in the Casablanca Conference with British Prime Minister Winston Churchill. The first president, in or out of office, to fly in any kind of aircraft was Theodore Roosevelt. He was a passenger in a Wright biplane piloted by Archibald Hoxsey at the St. Louis Aviation Field, St. Louis, MO, on October 11, 1910, more than a year after he had left office. The flight lasted four minutes.

4297. Presidential airplane was the *Sacred Cow*, a four-engine Skymaster C-54 built at the Douglas Aircraft Company's plant in Santa Monica, CA, and delivered on June 1944 to the Air Transport Command. Its first mission outside the United States was to fly Henry Lewis Stimson, the secretary of war, from Washington, DC, to Naples, Italy, a distance of 4,200 miles, in 24 hours.

4298. President to travel underwater in a captured enemy submarine was Harry S. Truman. On November 21, 1946, he embarked at Key West, FL, in the *U-2513*, a captured German submarine. At sea off Key West, the vessel engaged in exercises during which it submerged.

4299. President to fly in a helicopter was Dwight David Eisenhower. On July 12, 1957, he flew in a three-seat Bell Ranger H-47J piloted by Major Joseph E. Barrett from the White House to an undisclosed site chosen for relocation of the White House during an atomic attack drill. He had previously flown in a helicopter while he was supreme Allied commander of the North Atlantic Treaty Organization.

Vice Presidents

4300. Vice president who was nominated specifically for that office was George Clinton, Governor of New York, who ran with Thomas Jefferson in the 1804 election. He served under Jefferson from 1805 to 1809, and again under James Madison from 1809 to 1812. Prior to the ratification of the 12th Amendment to the Constitution on September 24, 1804, the presidential candidate receiving the second highest number of votes became vice president. Clinton was also the first vice president to serve under two presidents.

4301. Former vice president to be arrested was Aaron Burr, who served under Thomas Jefferson from 1801 to 1805. In 1807, he was accused of organizing an expedition to invade Mexico and set up a separate republic in the Southwest. He was arrested on February 19, 1807, in Wakefield, AL, by Captain Edmund P. Gaines and taken to Richmond, VA, where he was brought before Chief Justice John Marshall of the U.S. Circuit Court on March 30. On June 24, he was indicted for treason. The trial began on August 3 and ended in an acquittal on September 1.

4302. Vice president to die in office was George Clinton, who served under President Thomas Jefferson from March 4, 1805, to March 4, 1809, and under President James Madison from March 4, 1809, to April 20, 1812, when he died in Washington, DC. William Harris Crawford acted as president pro tempore of the Senate for the unexpired portion of Clinton's term.

4303. Vice president who had served in the House of Representatives was Elbridge Gerry of Massachusetts, who served as a representative from March 4, 1789, to March 3, 1793, and as vice president from March 4, 1813, to November 23, 1814, when he died.

4304. Vice president to resign before the expiration of his term of office was John Caldwell Calhoun, who served as vice president under President John Quincy Adams from March 4, 1825, to March 4, 1829, and under President Andrew Jackson from March 4, 1829 to December 28, 1832. He resigned to fill the vacancy in the Senate caused by the resignation of Robert Young Hayne, senator from South Carolina. Calhoun was elected to fill the vacancy on December 12, 1832.

4305. Vice president elected by the Senate was Richard Mentor Johnson, who was chosen by the Senate on February 8, 1837, because no candidate had received a majority of the electoral votes. He served from March 4, 1837, to March 4, 1841, under President Martin Van Buren.

4306. Vice president to succeed to the presidency after the death of a president was John Tyler, the 10th president. Tyler succeeded William Henry Harrison, who died on April 4, 1841, a few weeks after his inauguration. Harrison served from March 4, 1841, to April 4, 1841, and Tyler from April 4, 1841, to March 4, 1845.

4307. Vice president sworn in on foreign soil was William Rufus de Vane King, a Democrat, the running mate of Franklin Pierce in the 1852 election. King took the oath of office on March 4, 1853, in Havana, Cuba, where he had gone for his health. The oath was administered by William L. Sharkey, the American consul in Havana. The privilege was extended to King by a special act of Congress. King's term of office was of short duration. He died on April 17, 1853, in Cahawba, AL.

4308. Vice president's widow to receive a pension was Lois I. Kimsey Marshall, widow of Thomas Riley Marshall, who died on June 1, 1925. A congressional act of January 25, 1929, awarded her an annual allowance of $3,000 and instructed the secretary of the interior to place her name on the pension roll.

4309. Vice president who was Native American was Charles Curtis of Kansas, a descendant on his mother's side from the Kansa-Kaw chief White Plume. He served under President Herbert Clark Hoover from March 4, 1929, to March 4, 1933.

4310. Vice president chosen under the 25th Amendment to the Constitution was Gerald Rudolph Ford, sworn into office as President Richard Milhous Nixon's vice president on December 6, 1973. The 25th Amendment, ratified on February 10, 1967, enables the president to appoint a vice president in the event that the office becomes vacant. On October 10, 1973, Vice President Spiro T.

Agnew resigned to face charges of income tax evasion, leaving the vice presidency open for the first time since the passage of the amendment.

Visits

4311. President to tour the country was George Washington, who traveled through the New England states from October 15 to November 13, 1789. He traveled in a hired coach accompanied by Major William Jackson, his aide-de-camp, and Tobias Lear, his private secretary, along with six servants, nine horses, and a luggage wagon. He went as far north as Kittery, ME (then part of Massachusetts). As Rhode Island and Vermont had not yet joined the new government, he did not visit those states. Washington's first tour of the southern states was made from April 7 to June 12, 1791, during which time he made a 1,887-mile trip from his estate in Mount Vernon, VA, through Philadelphia, south through Virginia and the Carolinas into Georgia, and back to Mount Vernon.

4312. President to visit a foreign country while in office was Theodore Roosevelt, who sailed to Panama on the U.S.S. *Louisiana* in 1906. He remained in Panama from November 14 to 17, after which he went to Puerto Rico.

4313. President to receive a passport while in office was Woodrow Wilson, whose passport was made out on November 27, 1918. He left the United States on December 5, 1918, on the transport *George Washington* and arrived at Brest, France, on December 13.

4314. President to visit Europe was Woodrow Wilson. He left Washington, DC, on December 4, 1918, on the S.S. *George Washington* and arrived at Brest, France, on December 13, returning to Boston, MA, on February 24, 1919. A few months later, Wilson made a second trip, leaving Hoboken, NJ, on March 5 and arriving at Brest on March 13, 1919. He returned to Hoboken on July 8.

4315. President to visit Alaska and Canada while in office was Warren Gamaliel Harding, who visited Metlakahtla, AK, on July 8, 1923, and Vancouver, British Columbia, Canada, on July 26, 1923. He sailed on the U.S. naval transport *Henderson*. Alaska was then a territory of the United States.

4316. President to visit South America while in office was Franklin Delano Roosevelt. He stopped off at Cartagena, Colombia, on July 10, 1934, to return the visit of President Enrique Olaya Herrera of Colombia, who had paid a formal visit to Roosevelt on board the cruiser U.S.S. *Houston*.

4317. President to visit Hawaii while in office was Franklin Delano Roosevelt, who landed on July 25, 1934, at Hilo, HI. He was officially welcomed by Governor Joseph Poindexter on board the cruiser U.S.S. *Houston*. Hawaii was then a territory of the United States.

4318. President to visit a foreign country in wartime was Franklin Delano Roosevelt, who flew from Miami, FL, to Trinidad, British West Indies, on January 10, 1943. From Trinidad, he continued on to Belém, Brazil; Bathurst, Gambia; and Casablanca, Morocco, where he arrived on January 14. He returned to Miami by plane via South Africa and Trinidad, and arrived in Washington, DC, by train on January 31.

4319. President to visit all 50 states was Richard M. Nixon, who did so in fulfillment of a campaign promise. The last state he visited was West Virginia, where he delivered an address on October 8, 1971, at the town of Elkins.

4320. President to visit a nation not recognized by the federal government was Richard Milhous Nixon, who visited the People's Republic of China in 1972. This was also the first trip to China, the world's most populous nation, by any American president. Accompanied by a small army of journalists, Nixon left the United States on February 17, 1972. He arrived in Beijing on February 21 for talks with Chairman Mao Zedong and Premier Zhou Enlai. Later that year, Nixon became the first president to visit the Soviet Union when he arrived in Moscow on May 22 for a summit with Soviet leaders. Among the agreements that were reached during the visit was the Strategic Arms Limitation Treaty, signed by President Nixon and the Soviet leader Leonid I. Brezhnev on May 26, which limited both nations to 200 antiballistic missiles each, divided between two defensive systems.

Library of Congress, Prints & Photographs Division LC-USZ62-13037

Richard M. Nixon

4321. Visit by an American president to a country on the U.S. list of terrorist states took place on October 27, 1994, when President Bill Clinton visited Damascus, Syria, to meet with that country's president, Hafez al-Assad. Clinton made the visit to urge Assad, a longtime foe of Israel, to take part in the peace process between the Jewish state and neighboring Arab states.

4322. President to visit Cuba after the Communist revolution in 1959 was former President Jimmy Carter, who arrived in Cuba on May 12, 2002, for a five-day visit with dictator Fidel Castro.

White House

4323. Presidential mansion was No. 1 Cherry Street, the Franklin House, at the corner of Franklin and Cherry streets (now Franklin Square), New York City. It was occupied by President and Mrs. George Washington from April 23, 1789, to February 23, 1790. It was originally the home of Samuel Osgood, the first commissioner of the treasury and later the first postmaster general.

4324. Child born in the White House was James Madison Randolph, born on January 17, 1806 in Washington, DC. He was the son of Thomas Mann Randolph and Martha (Jefferson) Randolph, the daughter of President Thomas Jefferson.

4325. Wedding in the White House took place on March 29, 1812, when Lucy Payne Washington was married to Thomas Todd, associate justice of the Supreme Court. Mrs. Washington was the widow of George Steptoe Washington, a nephew of George Washington. Her sister was Dolly Madison, the wife of James Madison, who was president at the time of the wedding.

4326. Gaslight in the White House in Washington, DC, was illuminated on December 29, 1848, during the administration of President James Knox Polk.

4327. Memoir of life in the White House was written by Paul Jennings, who had been born a slave on the estate of President James Madison and served as his valet. Entitled *A Colored Man's Reminiscences of James Madison*, it was published in 1865 by George Beadle in Brooklyn, NY.

4328. Child born in the White House who was the offspring of a president was Esther Cleveland, born on September 9, 1893 in Washington, DC. She was the second child of President Grover Cleveland and Frances Folsom Cleveland.

4329. Airplane to land on the White House lawn was the *Moth*, piloted by Harry Nelson Atwood, who landed on July 14, 1911, about 3 P.M., and was presented by President William Howard Taft with the gold medal of the Aero Club of Washington. Atwood circled the Capitol and the Library of Congress and flew down Pennsylvania Avenue and over the Washington Monument and the Executive Mansion.

4330. Movie shown in the White House was *The Birth of a Nation*, D. W. Griffith's fictionalized history of the South during and after the Civil War, which was screened for President Woodrow Wilson on March 21, 1915. The film was notorious for its biased presentation of the Ku Klux Klan as heroes saving the South from the menace of northern reformers and African-American former slaves. Wilson liked it enough to arrange for additional screenings for his cabinet secretaries and members of Congress.

Some of the screen titles in THE BIRTH OF A NATION were taken from President Woodrow Wilson's own book A HISTORY OF THE AMERICAN PEOPLE, published in 1902, in which he displayed much the same bias as D. W. Griffith.

4331. Dish set made in America for the White House was ordered by President Woodrow Wilson and delivered on July 31, 1918. The set, consisting of 1,700 pieces bearing the seal of the President of the United States, was manufactured by Walter Scott Lenox of Lenox Incorporated, Trenton, NJ.

4332. Swimming pool in the White House was built by popular subscription. It was located in the west terrace of the mansion and was 50 feet long and 15 feet wide, with a depth ranging from 4 to 8 feet. The pool was lined with aquamarine terra-cotta and a six-foot wainscot of pale green terra-cotta. The water was both filtered and sterilized. The pool was built under the direction of Lieutenant Colonel Ulysses Simpson Grant III, Director of Public Buildings, and was formally accepted by President Franklin Delano Roosevelt on June 2, 1933.

4333. State dinner televised from the White House took place at the Rose Garden of the White House, Washington, DC, on July 7, 1976. The dinner was held in honor of Queen Elizabeth II of England and Prince Philip, and was attended by 224 guests.

4334. Painting by an African-American artist to hang in the White House was *Dunes at Sunset, Atlantic City*, an 1885 landscape painting by Henry Ossawa Tanner. The painting was purchased for $100,000 by the White House Historical Association in 1996 and was put on display in the Green Room.

4335. Chef at the White House who was a woman was Cristeta Comerford, who was named Executive Chef of the White House by First Lady Laura Bush on August 14, 2005. Ms. Comerford, an immigrant from the Philippines, was promoted from the position of assistant chef, in which she had served for 10 years. She specialized in American, ethnic, and traditional French cuisine.

States

4336. Treaty between states after the Declaration of Independence was concluded between Georgia and South Carolina on May 20, 1777, at Dewitt's Corner, SC. Under its provisions, the Cherokees were forced to retire behind a line running southwest through Georgia from the straight part of Pickens County on the North to a point just below the mouth of the Tallulah at the western tip the state.

4337. State seal was the seal of Massachusetts, commissioned in 1780 and engraved by Paul Revere. It showed a Native American man holding a longbow and an arrow, with a star over his right shoulder symbolizing Massachusetts, and the state motto *Ense petit placidam sub libertate quietem* ("By the sword we seek peace under liberty").

4338. State denied admission into the Union was Franklin, formed on August 23, 1784, when it seceded from North Carolina. It was formed by three counties between the Bald Mountains and the Holston River, an area that is now in eastern Tennessee. Its citizens established a senate and a house of commons at Jonesboro and elected John Sevier as governor for a four-year term with an annual salary of £200 or 1,000 deerskins. Sevier was arrested in 1788 on charges of high treason. After his release, he was elected to the House of Representatives. He served as the first governor of Tennessee after it was admitted to the Union as the 16th state in 1796.

4339. State admitted to the Union after the ratification of the Constitution by the original 13 colonies was Vermont, which was authorized to join the Union by Congress on February 18, 1791, and which formally joined on March 4. Vermont was formed from the New Hampshire Grants, a region that was claimed by Massachusetts, New York, and New Hampshire. In 1777 it declared itself an independent commonwealth, the Republic of Vermont, and elected Thomas Chittenden as the first governor. All claims by other states were withdrawn by 1790. Chittenden went on to become the first state governor, serving to 1797.

4340. State nullification proceedings to obstruct federal legislation were the Kentucky Resolutions introduced by John Breckinridge. They were adopted by the Lower House of Kentucky on November 10, 1798, and by the Upper House on November 13, and approved by Governor James Garrard on November 16. Objection was taken to the congressional "act concerning aliens" of June 25, 1798, and the "act for the punishment of certain crimes against the United States" of July 14, 1798.

4341. Proposal in Congress that states should secede from the Union took place in the House of Representatives on June 4, 1811, during a debate on the proposal to create a state from the Orleans Territory, which entered the Union as Louisiana on April 30, 1812. The debate concerned the extension of slavery to the proposed state. Representative Josiah Quincy of Massachusetts declared: "It will be the right of all and the duty of some [of the states] definitely to prepare for a separation; amicably, if they can; violently, if they must." Representative Poindexter of Mississippi called Quincy to order, as did the speaker of the House. On appeal, the speaker's decision was reversed, and Quincy was sustained by a vote of 53 ayes to 56 nays on the point of order.

4342. Secession convention during the War of 1812 was held on December 15, 1814, at Hartford, CT, by delegates from Connecticut, Massachusetts, New Hampshire, Rhode Island, and Vermont who opposed the War of 1812 and planned secession from the United States.

4343. States with populations of more than 1 million were New York, with 1,372,812; Virginia, with 1,065,366; and Pennsylvania, with 1,049,456, according to the census of 1820. The first state to exceed 5 million in population was New York, which reached 5,082,871 in the census of 1880. It was also the first state to exceed the 10 million mark, which it reached in the 1920 census, when it had a population of 10,385,227.

4344. State west of the Mississippi River to be admitted to the Union was Missouri, which joined on August 10, 1821. The first governor of the new state was Alexander McNair, a Democrat, who served from 1820 to 1824. (Louisiana, the 18th state, admitted on April 30, 1812, is both east and west of the Mississippi.)

4345. Federal treasury surplus to be returned to the states was authorized by congressional act of June 23, 1836. Twenty-six states received a total of $28,101,645, which was distributed in proportion to their respective representation in the Senate and House and delivered in three installments. This money was supposed to remain on deposit until Congress directed otherwise, but no request for its return was ever made.

4346. State fair was the New York State Fair, held in Syracuse, NY, on September 29–30, 1841. The fair was organized by the New York State Agricultural Society and funded by the state legislature, which offered $8,000. The demonstrations and exhibits drew as many as 15,000 visitors. The fair has taken place annually ever since. Originally held in different cities, it was given a permanent home in Geddes in 1890 and has been under the control of a state commission since 1900.

4347. State to repudiate a debt was Mississippi, in 1842. The sovereign state of Mississippi sold $5 million worth of bonds in June 1838 to pay for 50,000 shares in the Union Bank of Mississippi. The bank became hopelessly insolvent in 1840, and in 1842 the legislature denied that the state was under legal or moral obligation to pay the bonds in question.

4348. State on the Pacific coast to be admitted to the Union was California, which joined on September 9, 1850. The first state governor was Peter Hardeman Burnett, a Democrat, who served from 1849 to 1851.

4349. Secession act at the start of the Civil War was the Ordinance of Secession, passed by the legislature of South Carolina on December 20, 1860.

4350. State to secede from the Union was South Carolina. On December 20, 1860, the state legislature passed the Ordinance of Secession, declaring: "We, the people of the State of South Carolina, in convention assembled, do declare and ordain, that the ordinance adopted by us in convention on the 23d day of May, in the year of our Lord 1788, whereby the Constitution of the United States was ratified, and also all acts and parts of the General Assembly of this State ratifying amendments of the said Constitution, are hereby repealed; and that the Union now subsisting between South Carolina and other States, under the name of the United States of America, is hereby dissolved." On December 24, the South Carolina delegation in Congress offered its resignation, but it was not accepted by the speaker of the House. A new state constitution was ratified on April 3, 1861, by a vote of 114–6.

4351. State readmitted to the Union after the Civil War was Tennessee, on July 24, 1866. A new constitution was adopted on January 9, 1865, and ratified on February 22.

4352. States admitted to the Union simultaneously were North and South Dakota, which were formed from the Dakota Territory. The act of admission was signed on February 22, 1889, by President Grover Cleveland. Each state held a constitutional convention beginning on July 4, 1889, and both held the ratifying election on October 1, 1889. President Benjamin Harrison signed the proclamations of admission on November 3, 1889, without knowing which was which. The first governors of both states were Republicans: John Miller, in North Dakota; Arthur Calvin Mellette, in South Dakota. Washington and Montana were admitted by the same enabling act, but the proclamations were not signed until a few days later.

4353. State named for a person born in America was Washington, the 42nd state, admitted into the Union on November 11, 1889.

4354. State seal designed by a woman was the Seal of Idaho, designed by Emma Sarah Edwards. The seal was officially adopted on March 14, 1891.

4355. Woman elected to statewide office was Laura J. Eisenhuth, a school superintendent in Carrington, ND. In 1892, running as a Democrat, she was elected North Dakota's superintendent of public instruction. Women in North Dakota had received the right to vote in school-related elections, but no others, in 1889.

4356. State-sponsored council for the arts was the Utah Arts Institute, established by Utah on March 9, 1899, at the instigation of state representative Alice Merrill Horne.

4357. State archival agency was the Alabama Department of Archives and History, established on March 2, 1901. The first director was Thomas Owen.

4358. Public archive building built for that purpose in the United States was the Kainina Building, constructed on the grounds of Iolani Palace in Honolulu, HI, in 1906.

4359. Treaty among more than two states was the Colorado River Compact, signed on November 24, 1922, at the Palace of the Governors, Santa FE, NM. The agreement, which set water allotments from the river, was negotiated by representatives from seven states--Arizona, California, Colorado, Nevada, New Mexico, Utah, and Wyoming—with the assistance of Commerce Secretary Herbert Hoover.

4360. State admitted to the Union that had no border with another state was Alaska, which was admitted as the 49th state on January 3, 1959, by proclamation of President Dwight David Eisenhower. Alaska had become a territory on August 24, 1912. A constitution was approved by popular vote on April 24, 1956, and was ratified by Congress on July 7, 1958. Voters approved statehood on August 26, 1958, and the first state election was held on November 25.

4361. State admitted to the Union that was separated by a substantial body of water from the contiguous United States was Hawaii, 2,090 miles across the Pacific from San Francisco, CA. It was voted into the Union by Congress on March 12, 1959, by a vote of 323–89. Hawaii was admitted as the 50th state by proclamation of President Dwight David Eisenhower on August 21, 1959.

4362. State to have a state sport was Maryland, which established jousting as the official state sport in 1962.

4363. State department of Indian affairs was established by the legislature of Maine to address the needs of the state's two main tribal groups, the Passamaquoddy and the Penobscot, neither of which fell under the jurisdiction of the established federal agencies for Native American affairs. The first commissioner took office on November 1, 1965.

4364. State to experience a natural decrease in population was West Virginia, which recorded 137 more deaths than births in 1977.

4365. State to have an official hero or heroine was Massachusetts, which named Deborah Bradford Sampson its official heroine on May 23, 1983, in a proclamation signed by Governor Michael J. Dukakis. Sampson (properly, but less commonly, spelled Samson) was a schoolteacher in Middleborough, MA, during the Revolutionary War. On May 20, 1782, the 21-year-old Sampson disguised herself as a man and enlisted in the Fourth Massachusetts Regiment, giving her name as Robert Shurtliff (also spelled Shurtleff). In a postwar skirmish with British forces near Tarrytown, NY, she received a bullet wound in the leg.

4366. State economic development agency that was partly privatized was that of Florida, which closed down its department of commerce in July 1996 in favor of a public-private partnership called Enterprise Florida, Inc., the main goal of which was to attract and retain high-growth businesses.

4367. State with a gross state product of $1 trillion was California, whose gross state product exceeded $1 trillion dollars in 1997.

4368. State government to completely privatize its computer services was Connecticut. In January 1999 the state awarded a $1 billion contract to Electronic Data Systems Corporation of Plano, TX, to handle all of its information technology services. The seven-year contract was expected to save some $400 million on computer systems and related services.

4369. State in which all of the top elected offices were held by women was Arizona. On January 4, 1999, at a ceremony at the state capitol in Phoenix, Republican Jane Dee Hull was sworn in as governor. Also taking office that day were Betsey Bayless, secretary of state; Carol Springer, treasurer; Lisa Graham Keegan, superintendent of public instruction; and Janet Napolitano, attorney general. (Arizona has no lieutenant governor.) All but Napolitano were Republicans. Administering the oath was Supreme Court Justice Sandra Day O'Connor, a resident of Arizona.

4370. State with $1 trillion in personal income was California, where personal income reached the $1 trillion mark in 2000.

4371. Comprehensive digital archive of state documents was opened by the state of Washington in October 2004 to salvage electronic records from extinction. Located on the campus of Eastern Washington University in Cheney, WA, the facility preserved the original electronic and digitized paper records of state birth, marriage, death, census, naturalization, military, institutional, legal, political, and historic data.

Governors

4372. Colonial governor who was born in America was Josiah Winslow of Plymouth, MA. He was elected governor of New Plymouth Colony in 1673 and served until his death in 1680. In 1675–76 he led the United Colonies forces against the Wampanoags and their allies in the conflict known as King Philip's War. His parents, Edward and Susanna Winslow, were the first English colonists to be married in New England.

4373. Brothers to serve simultaneously as governors of their respective states were Governor Levi Lincoln, Jr., who served as governor of the Commonwealth of Massachusetts from May 27, 1825, until January 21, 1834, and Governor Enoch Lincoln, who served as governor of Maine from January 4, 1827, until his death on October 8, 1829. Both were Whigs.

4374. State governor who was Catholic was Edward Douglass White, who served as governor of Louisiana from 1835 to 1839. Before and after his term, he served in the U.S. House of Representatives.

4375. State governor to be removed from office by a state supreme court was William Augustus Barstow, Democrat of Wisconsin, who served a full term from January 2, 1854, to January 7, 1856. He was installed for a second term on January 7, 1856. On March 20, 1856, the supreme court held that Coles Bashford, a Republican, was entitled to the office because of irregularities in the election. On March 21, Barstow resigned, and the lieutenant governor, Arthur MacArthur, was sworn in. The state assembly recognized Bashford on March 27, 1856.

4376. State governor to be impeached and acquitted was Charles Robinson, the first governor of Kansas (1861–63) and a leader of the Free State antislavery party. He was indicted for treason and conspiracy on a charge brought by the proslavery party. He was acquitted in 1862 by a federal grand jury and completed his term as governor.

4377. State governor who had also been governor of a territory was John White Geary, who served as governor of the Kansas territory from September 9, 1856, to March 4, 1857, and as governor of Pennsylvania from January 15, 1867, to January 21, 1873.

4378. State governor to be impeached and convicted was William Woods Holden, the 39th governor of North Carolina. On December 20, 1870, impeachment proceedings were brought against him in which he was charged with "high crimes and misdemeanors." The trial was conducted by Chief Justice Richmond Mumford Pearson. On March 22, 1871, he was ordered to be removed from office, two-thirds of the state Senate having found him guilty of six of the eight charges brought against him.

4379. Gubernatorial election in which two brothers were the opposing candidates was held on November 2, 1886, in Tennessee. Robert Love Taylor, the Democratic candidate, received 125,151 votes, defeating his brother, Alfred Alexander Taylor, the Republican candidate, who obtained 109,837 votes. Robert Love Taylor served as governor from January 17, 1887, to January 19, 1891, and from January 21, 1897, to January 16, 1899. Alfred Alexander Taylor defeated Albert Houston Roberts on November 2, 1920, and served as governor of Tennessee from January 15, 1921, to January 16, 1923.

4380. State governor who was Jewish was Moses Alexander of Idaho, a Democrat, who served from January 4, 1915, to January 6, 1919. A previous governor of Jewish descent was David Emanuel of Georgia, a convert to Christianity, who served from March 3, 1801, to November 7, 1801, after the resignation of Governor James Jackson. It is not clear whether he became governor by virtue of the fact that he was president of the senate when Governor Jackson resigned, or whether he was regularly elected.

4381. State governor who was a woman was Nellie Tayloe Ross, who was elected governor of Wyoming on November 4, 1924, to fill the unexpired term of her late husband, William Bradford Ross. The first woman to be elected state governor in her own right was Ella Grasso, a Democrat, elected on November 5, 1974, as the 83rd governor of Connecticut. She was reelected in November 1978 for a second term, which, because of illness, she did not complete. She resigned on December 31, 1980, and died on February 5, 1981.

4382. State governor to be granted almost dictatorial power was Paul Vories McNutt of Indiana. The Democrat-controlled legislature empowered him in February 1933 to organize the state government, which at that time was spread among 168 boards and commissions, into nine departments: Executive, State, Audit, Treasury, Law, Education, Public Works, Commerce, and Industry. He was authorized to hire and fire all state employees and to raise or lower salaries as he saw fit. His power was limited by legislative appropriations and by the authority of the courts to review and void his decisions.

4383. State governor who was African-American was L. Douglas Wilder, who was elected governor of Virginia on November 7, 1989. More than a century earlier, another African-American, Pinckney Benton Stewart Pinchback, the lieutenant governor of Louisiana, served as the state's governor from December 11, 1872, to January 14, 1873, during the impeachment of Governor Henry Clay Warmoth.

4384. State to elect two female governors in a row was Arizona, where Janet Napolitano, a Democrat, took office on January 3, 2003. She succeeded Jane Dee Hull, a Republican, who had served since September 5, 1997.

Legislatures

4385. Colonial legislative assembly was the House of Burgesses, which met in Jamestown, VA, on July 30, 1619. The location was the Old Church, a wooden structure 50 by 20 feet. The men sat with their hats on. It was decided that the new governor, Sir George Yeardley, was to summon a "General Assembly" elected by the inhabitants, with every free man voting. The assembly was to consist of 22 members, 2 from each borough. The speaker was Master John Pory. The session was opened with prayer by a Mr. Bucke. The first laws enacted were prohibitions against idleness, drunkenness, and gambling.

4386. Colonial legislature to establish two chambers convened in Massachusetts in 1644. "An Act of the Generall Court at Boston, March 7/17, 1644," established one house for magistrates and another for deputies.

4387. State legislator who was African-American was Alexander Lucius Twilight, a minister and schoolteacher in Vergennes and Brownington, VT. He was elected to the state General Assembly in 1836 from Orleans County.

4388. State legislator who was African-American to represent a constituency with a white majority was Bishop Benjamin William Arnett of the African Methodist Episcopal Church, Greene County, OH, who served in the lower house of the Ohio State Legislature from 1885 to 1887. He served in the 66th session, which convened on January 6, 1885, and adjourned on May 4, 1885, and the 67th, which convened on January 4, 1886, and adjourned on May 19, 1886.

4389. State legislators who were women were three Republicans elected to the Colorado General Assembly on November 6, 1894. This was the first election in Colorado in which women could vote. The three were Clara Cressingham, Carrie C. Holly, and Frances S. Klock.

4390. State senator who was a woman was Martha Hughes Cannon, elected to the second session of the Utah senate on November 3, 1896, and reelected to the third. She was a Democrat and represented the 6th Senatorial District, comprising Salt Lake County.

4391. State legislature to use an electric vote recorder was that of Wisconsin. The machine was installed on January 11, 1917, in the Wisconsin Assembly Chamber in Madison. It displayed green and white signal lights opposite the name of each legislator to show how he or she voted. A roll call could be recorded in 11 seconds, at a savings of more than 99 percent of the time previously consumed in roll calls. The acquisition of the vote recorder was approved on July 29, 1915.

4392. State speaker of the House who was a woman was Minnie Davenport Craig of Esmond, ND, a Republican, who was elected speaker on January 3, 1933. She served for one session, until March 31, 1933.

4393. State legislature with a single chamber in the post-Revolutionary era was that of Nebraska, which adopted a unicameral system by constitutional amendment on November 6, 1934. A single body of 43 members replaced a House of 100 members and a Senate of 33. The first bill, passed on January 21, 1937, appropriated $10,000 for mileage, postage, and incidental expenses for the members. All of the original states adopted bicameral systems at the formation of the United States, except Pennsylvania, Georgia, and Vermont, which changed to a bicameral system after 4, 12, and 58 years, respectively.

4394. State legislator who was an African-American woman was Crystal Bird Fauset of Philadelphia, PA, elected on November 8, 1938, to the Pennsylvania House of Representatives. Her term of office began on December 1, 1938, and she was sworn in and assumed her seat on January 3, 1939.

4395. Husband and wife to be elected simultaneously to both chambers of a state legislature were Richard Lewis Neuberger, state senator, and Maurine Brown Neuberger, state representative, both Democrats, elected to the Oregon legislature on November 7, 1950. Richard Neuberger had served previously as state senator, having been elected on November 2, 1948, to represent the 13th district.

4396. State legislative hearing to be shown on television was a hearing by the New Jersey senate's Committee on Federal and Interstate Relations that took place on April 11, 1954, and was aired from 7:30 to 8 P.M. on WATV, Newark, NJ. The subject was a proposal by Senator Malcolm Forbes to stop all new projects by the Port of New York Authority (later known as the Port Authority of New York and New Jersey). The proposal was defeated.

4397. State legislator expelled for campaign finance violations was David Burnell Smith, Republican of Scottsdale, AZ. Smith spent almost $32,000 on his 2004 primary campaign, $6,000 more than he was entitled to under Arizona's Clean Elections Act. The Citizens Clean Elections Commission voted to force him out of office on March 24, 2005. Their decision was upheld by the state's Superior Court on December 7, 2005.

Taxation

4398. Property tax levied by a colony was passed on May 14, 1634, and signed by Governor William Bradford of the Plymouth colony in Massachusetts: "It is further ordered that in all rates and public charges, the towns shall have respect to levy each man according to his estate, and with consideration of all other his abilities, whatsoever, and not according to the number of persons."

4399. Income tax levied by a colony was levied on the colonists of New Plymouth, MA, in 1643, giving the town the distinction of being the first place in America to impose an income tax.

4400. Tax on Britain's American colonists without their consent was levied in 1672, when the British Parliament passed a law imposing a duty on sugar, tobacco, ginger, coconuts, indigo, logwood fustic, wool, and cotton.

4401. Inheritance tax levied by a colony was levied by Virginia in 1687, when the Colony of Virginia provided that the governor of the colony should collect a fee of a cask and 200 pounds of tobacco for impressing documents with the public seal, without which they were invalid. These documents included probates, letters testamentary, and letters of administration.

4402. Direct tax on Britain's American colonists without their consent was the Stamp Act, enacted on March 22, 1765, by Parliament. It required colonists to buy revenue stamps for every pair of dice, every pack of playing cards, and every newspaper, document, and pamphlet. The purpose of the tax was to raise funds to pay for the upkeep of the British army in America. The first American locality to repudiate the act was Frederick County, MD. On November 23, 1765, 12 judges of the Court of Frederick County declared that "all proceedings shall be valid and effectual without the use of stamps." The act was repealed in March 1766 after the colonists mounted a sustained boycott of British goods.

4403. Free trade policy by the federal government was in effect from 1775 to 1780, but imports were taxed by the various states. Trade was free in Massachusetts from 1774 to 1781, in South Carolina from 1776 to 1783, in Maryland and Connecticut from 1776 to 1780. Although there were no federal restrictions, the situation was extremely complicated, and taxes were different in practically every state.

4404. Tariff legislation enacted by Congress after the adoption of the Constitution was the Tariff Act of July 4, 1789, an "act for laying a duty on goods, wares and merchandises imported into the United States." The main purpose was the collection of revenue, but protection was also extended to certain industries that the government wished to encourage, such as glass and earthenware. The act was signed by President George Washington and was to continue in force until July 1796. It laid specific duties on some articles and ad valorem duties on others, equivalent to an 8.5 percent ad valorem rate, with drawback, up to 1 percent of the duties on all articles exported within 12 months, except distilled spirits other than brandy and geneva.

4405. Internal revenue tax levied by Congress was imposed on March 3, 1791, as part of an act that established 14 revenue districts, one for each state. The law levied a tax on distilled spirits, both domestic and imported, of 11 to 30 cents a gallon, depending on alcoholic content prior to removal from the distillery. Carriages were also taxed. Subsequent early modifications of the act of 1791 imposed taxes on retail dealers in distilled spirits, as well as on refined sugar, snuff, property sold at auction, legal instruments, and bonds. On July 9, 1798, a direct tax was placed on real estate. The receipts for the fiscal year 1792 from internal revenue netted the government $208,943.

4406. Tax levied by Congress directly on the states was a direct pro rata tax upon the 16 states, authorized by act of July 14, 1798. It was levied on dwellings, land, and slaves. The amount to be collected was $2 million, which was apportioned to the states in direct ratio to the population.

4407. Tax rebellion occurred in February 1799, when John Fries raised an armed force in Northampton, Bucks, and Montgomery counties, PA, to protest a direct federal property tax that had been passed by Congress in July 1798 to raise funds for an expected war with France. Federal troops were called out by President John Adams to suppress the uprising. Fries was arrested in Bethlehem, PA, after resisting a federal marshal. He was convicted of treason and sentenced to death by Supreme Court Justice Samuel Chase. Adams pardoned Fries in 1800.

4408. Tariff passed by Congress for protection rather than primarily for revenue was the "act to regulate the duties on imports and tonnage," passed on April 27, 1816.

4409. Bachelor tax enacted by a state was levied by Missouri, which on December 20, 1820, placed a $1 tax "on every unmarried free white male, above the age of 21 years and under 50 years."

4410. Inheritance tax enacted by a state was passed by Pennsylvania on April 7, 1826, and signed by Governor John Andrew Shulze. It established a 2.5 percent collateral inheritance tax. The surviving spouse, the parents, and the descendants of the decedent were exempted.

4411. Tariff enacted by Congress to prevent the importation of obscene literature and pictures was the Tariff Act of August 30, 1842, an "act to provide revenue from imports." Section 28 stated: "The importation of all indecent and obscene prints, paintings, lithographs, engravings and transparencies is hereby prohibited . . . and all invoices and packages whereof any such article shall compose a part are . . . liable . . . to be seized and forfeited . . . and the said articles shall be forthwith destroyed."

4412. War tax resister of note was the writer Henry David Thoreau of Concord, MA. He was arrested and imprisoned in Concord, MA, on July 23, 1846, because he refused to pay the state poll tax, citing his opposition to the Mexican War. A relative paid the tax on his behalf.

4413. Income tax levied by Congress was imposed during the Civil War by act of August 5, 1861, effective January 1, 1862, which imposed a 3 percent tax on incomes exceeding $800 and a 1.5 percent tax on income derived from government securities. The income tax lists were open to public inspection by "all persons who may apply to inspect the same." This was interpreted in such a way as to eliminate idle curiosity seekers. The law was not enforced and was replaced the following year by another. It was rescinded in 1872 along with other Civil War taxes. An income tax law was passed by Congress on August 27, 1894, as part of the tariff act, but it was declared unconstitutional. The 16th Amendment to the Constitution, which was declared ratified on February 25, 1913, gave Congress the power to lay and collect income taxes.

4414. Inheritance tax levied by Congress was a part of the Internal Revenue Law of July 1, 1862, which assessed a tax on legacies and distributive shares of personal property.

4415. Revenue stamps issued by the federal government were issued in 1862 under authority of an act of Congress of July 1, 1862, "to provide Internal Revenue to support the government and to pay interest on the public debt." At first, specific taxes were identified on the stamps, such as bill of lading, foreign exchange, probate of will, warehouse receipt, and so on, but after December 25, 1862, they were used indiscriminately. Revenue stamps were issued in various sizes, in valuations from one cent to $200.

4416. Tariff commission established by Congress was authorized on June 7, 1882. Nine tariff commissioners at $10 a day and expenses were appointed from civil life to investigate tariff questions relating to agriculture, commerce, manufacturing, mining, and mercantile and industrial interests. The first chairman was John Lord.

4417. Single tax adopted by a city for local revenue purposes was adopted by Hyattsville, MD, which operated under this system from July 1892 to March 1893, under laws that were declared unconstitutional. The single tax system eliminates all government taxes except the tax on land.

4418. Corporation tax levied by Congress was passed on August 5, 1909. The act taxed all corporations with an income over $5,000. The law was passed prior to the adoption of the U.S. income tax amendment.

4419. Deadline for filing individual income tax returns after ratification of the 16th Amendment to the Constitution in 1913 was March 1, 1914. The Bureau of Internal Revenue, part of the Treasury Department, announced the previous January that individuals would be required to fill out a four-page form, then as now known as Form 1040. There were six income brackets, with people in the highest bracket (those who had a taxable income above $500,000) paying 6 percent. Each individual was allowed to take a $3,000 deducation, but married couples could deduct only $4,000. Most of the approximately 350,000 filers paid no tax.

4420. Tax levied by Congress on excess profits of corporations was passed on March 3, 1917, an "act to provide increased revenue to defray the expenses of the increased appropriation for the army and navy and the extension of fortifications." The act provided for taxation of the profits of all corporations in excess of 7 to 9 percent of the capital. The rates were progressive: 20 percent on excess profits up to 15 percent; 35 percent on the excess from 15 to 25 percent; 35 percent on the excess from 25 percent to 33 percent; and 60 percent on the excess above 33 percent. The act was repealed by the Revenue Act of 1917, approved on October 3, 1917.

4421. Gasoline tax levied by a state was enacted on February 25, 1919, when Oregon placed a tax of one cent per gallon on all motor fuel. The funds collected were used for road construction and maintenance.

4422. Sales tax enacted by a state was approved on May 3, 1921, by West Virginia, and became effective on July 1. The funds collected were used largely in place of funds from a tax on corporate net income. The rate was one-fifth of 1 percent on the gross income of banks, street railroads, telephones, telegraph, express, and electric light and power retailers, and two-fifths of 1 percent on timber, oil, coal, natural gas, and other minerals. Payments could be made to the state quarterly or annually.

4423. Tax on chain stores enacted by a state was levied by Indiana. This statute, commonly referred to as the Indiana Chain Store Tax Law, was signed on March 16, 1929, by Governor Harry Leslie. Under the statute, owners were required to pay an annual license fee of $3 to operate a store in Indiana. For two to five stores under the same management, supervision, or ownership, the tax was $10 for each additional store; for stores in excess of 5 but not in excess of 10, $15 for each additional store; for stores in excess of 10 but not in excess of 20, $20 for each additional store; for all stores in excess of 20, $25 plus a 50-cent filing fee for each additional store. An amendment to this act was signed on March 11, 1933, by Governor Paul Vories McNutt, requiring owners of stores in excess of 20 to pay $150 for each additional store.

4424. Gasoline tax levied by Congress was the Revenue Act of 1932, enacted on June 6, 1932, which placed a tax of one cent per gallon on gasoline and other motor fuel.

4425. Revenue stamp printed by the Post Office Department was the "Federal duck stamp," a $1 stamp required of all waterfowl hunters over 16 years of age, to be attached to game licenses as required by the Migratory Bird Conservation Act of March 16, 1934. The stamp went on sale on August 14, 1934. It depicted a male and female mallard coming to rest on a marshland and was drawn by Jay Norwood "Ding" Darling, chief of the Bureau of Biological Survey of the Department of Agriculture. Stamps of this class, as well as all other revenue stamps, had previously been issued by the Treasury Department. Although sold through the Post Office Department, the proceeds went to the Department of Agriculture, where 10 percent was used for the expense of printing and selling the stamps and the balance to lease or purchase marsh areas for waterfowl sanctuaries.

4426. Gambling permit stamp issued by the federal government was authorized on October 20, 1951, by the Revenue Act of 1951. The ungummed stamps measured 6.5 by 4 inches and cost $50 per year. In the first six months of issue, 22,401 stamps were purchased, mostly in Nevada.

MEDIA AND COMMUNICATIONS

Books

4427. Bookseller of importance was Hezekiah Usher, who started in business in Cambridge, MA, in 1639. He later obtained a monopoly on printing the laws of the General Court of Massachusetts and superintended the publications of the London Society for the Propagation of the Gospel Among the Indians.

4428. Book auction was authorized on April 18, 1662, by the Court of Burgomasters and Schepens of New Amsterdam, which declared that "Anna Claas Croezens, widow of Daniel Litschoe, deceased, requests by petition to be allowed to sell by the Baliff some books which she has belonging to Sir Henry Moedy, as according to obligation she has a claim on him for a considerable sum."

4429. Bookbinder was John Ratliffe of Massachusetts, who in 1663 was commissioned to bind missionary John Eliot's Algonkian translation of the Bible. His job was to "take care of the binding of 200 of them strongly and as speedily as may bee with leather, or as may bee most serviceable for the Indians." On August 30, 1664, he sent a letter to the Commissioners of New England stating that he was not well satisfied with the fees paid him for binding, and that three shillings four pence was the lowest price at which he could bind books.

4430. Book privately printed was John Eliot's *Communion of Churches; or, The Divine Management of Gospel-Churches by the Ordinance of Councils, Constituted in Order According to the Scriptures*, printed in 1665 by Marmaduke Johnson, Cambridge, MA. It contained 40 pages. It was not for general sale.

4431. Miniature book was William Secker's *A Wedding Ring, fit for the Finger, or the Salve of Divinity on the Sore of Humanity. With directions to those men that want wives, how to choose them; and to those women that have husbands, how to use them.* The book contained 92 pages and was published in 1705 in Boston, MA, by T. Green for Nicholas Butolph. The size was approximately 2 by 3.5 inches. It was a reprint of a work published in 1658 in London.

4432. Book auction catalog was mentioned in the *Boston News Letter*, Boston, MA, on May 18, 1713: "On Thursday next, the 28th current being the day after the election, there will be exposed to sale by public vendue or outcry at the house of Mr. Ambrose Vincent, silk dyer in Wings Lane, Boston, a good collection of books, to be seen at the said house two days before the sale, etc. Catalogues will be posted at public places."

4433. Printed book auction catalog was *A Catalog of Curious and Valuable Books Belonging to the Late Reverend and Learned Mr. Ebenezer Pemberton, Consisting of Divinity, Philosophy, History, Poetry and Generally Well Bound*, which described the books "to be sold by auction at the Brown Coffee House in Boston, Mass." on July 2, 1717, at 3 P.M. The catalog was printed by B. Green in 1717 and was obtainable free at the shop of Samuel Gerrish, bookseller.

4434. Book of folio size other than lawbooks was Samuel Willard's *A Compleat Body of Divinity in Two Hundred and Fifty Expository Lectures on the Assembly's Shorter Catechism wherein the doctrines of the Christian religion are unfolded, their truth confirm'd . . . etc.*, published posthumously in 1726 in Boston, MA, by Bartholomew Green and Samuel Kneeland. It contained 1,000 pages printed in two columns. There is an error in pagination, as the work was printed by two presses.

4435. German book printed in America was Johann Conrad Beissel's *Das Buchlein vom Sabbath*, printed in Philadelphia, PA, in 1728 by Andrew Bradford.

4436. Book plate by an American engraver of which there is any record was made by Nathaniel Hurd of Boston, MA, in 1740 for Thomas Dering.

4437. Book made with American paper, ink, and type was *The Impenetrable Secret*, printed and sold by Story and Humphreys in 1775 in Philadelphia. It was advertised on

June 23, 1775, in the *Pennsylvania Mercury* as "just published and printed with types, paper and ink manufactured in this Province."

4438. Book with color plates was *The City of Philadelphia in the State of Pennsylvania North America as it appeared in the year 1800, consisting of twenty-eight plates drawn and engraved by W. Birch and Son*, published on December 31, 1800, in Philadelphia, PA. It was a large oblong folio containing 26 separate views drawn and engraved and two preliminaries. It was originally issued in 14 numbers (two parts) in wrappers. It sold for $28 uncolored, $41.50 hand-tinted in unbound boards, and $44.50 bound.

4439. Organization of booksellers was the American Company of Booksellers, organized on June 7, 1801, in New York City "to improve quality, to avoid interference, to discontinue importations, to favor a literary fair, to recommend correspondence and to promote the general interest." The first president was Mathew Carey of Philadelphia, PA.

4440. Book fair was held in the Coffee House on Beaver Street, New York City, on June 1, 1802, to display offerings of publishers and booksellers. Hugh Gaines was chairman. This literary fair was attended by 46 booksellers and proved so successful that the following year a similar one was held in Philadelphia, PA, after which the fairs alternated between those cities.

4441. Book publishers' catalog was *The Catalogue of All the Books Printed in the United States, with the prices and places where published.* It was printed in January 1804 for the booksellers of Boston, MA, and contained 80 pages. It sold for 10 cents. The books were classified according to subjects: law, physic, divinity, Bibles, miscellanies, schoolbooks, and singing books. The first book catalog to contain the combined trade lists of American publishers in uniform size was *The American Bookseller's Complete Reference Trade List and Alphabetical Catalogue of Books Published in This Country with the Publishers' and Authors' Names and Prices Arranged in Classes for Quick and Convenient Reference*, 232 pages, compiled by Alexander Vietts Blake and published in 1847 by Simeon Ide, Claremont, NH.

4442. Cryptography book was A Dictionary to enable any two persons to maintain a correspondence with a secrecy, which is impossible for any other person to discover, a 4-page book published anonymously in 1805 in Hartford, CT.

4443. Type specimen book from an American type foundry is said to be that of Archibald Binny and James Ronaldson in Philadelphia, PA. It was printed in 1809 by Fry and Kammerer and titled *A Specimen of Metal Ornaments cast at the Letter Foundry of Binny and Ronaldson, Philadelphia.* Type faces were not shown, but about 100 ornaments were illustrated. In 1812, Binny and Ronaldson published *A Specimen of Printing Types*, in which type faces were shown.

4444. History of printing was Isaiah Thomas's *History of Printing in America, with a Biography of Printers, and an Account of Newspapers*, published in two volumes in 1810 in Worcester, MA.

4445. Stereotyped book was *The Larger Catechism*, which bore on the title page "The first book ever stereotyped in America. Stereotyped and printed by J. Watts and Company, New York, June 1813." The process was introduced by John Watts and was a combination of the systems of Firmin Didot and Charles Mahon, Earl of Stanhope.

4446. Pamphlet produced from a steel plate engraving was Jacob Perkins and Gideon Fairman's *Running Hand Stereographic Copies*, published in 1815 by Charles Whipple, Newburyport, MA. It contains a title page and seven pages of text that contain samples of handwriting.

4447. Book commercially bound in cloth was the fourth edition of Charlotte Anne Waldie Eaton's *Rome in the Nineteenth Century; containing a complete account of the ruins of the ancient city, the remains of the middle ages, and the monuments of modern times*, republished in 1827 by J. and J. Harper, New York City. It was first published in 1820 in Edinburgh and reprinted in 1822, 1823, and 1826.

4448. Antiquarian book business was established on July 10, 1830, in Boston, MA, by Samuel Gardner Drake, who specialized in writing about Native Americans.

4449. Book jacket was designed by John Keep for *The Keepsake; a Gift for the Holidays*, published in 1833 in New York City. It was variously called a book cover jacket, a book jacket, a dust cover, a dust jacket, and a wrapper.

4450. Book trade magazine was the *Bookseller's Advertiser & Monthly Chronicle of Literary Enterprises*, also known as the *Bookseller's Advertiser & Monthly Register of New Publications*, which appeared on January 1, 1834. It was published by West and Trow, New York City, and contained eight printed quarto pages. Subscription was $1 yearly. It listed 275 original American works published in 1833 and American reprints of foreign works.

4451. Index to books was the *American Book Circular*, published in 1843 by Wiley and Putnam, New York City. It contained 64 pages, of which 55 were devoted to a list of 1,172 original works in 2,474 volumes. It classified "some of the most important and recent American publications."

4452. Publishing society was the Seventy-Six Society, organized on September 5, 1854, in Philadelphia, PA. Its *Collections* dealt solely with subjects pertaining to the American Revolution. Henry J. Williams was president.

4453. Book trade magazine that was successful was the *American Publishers' Circular and Literary Gazette*, a weekly for booksellers and libraries, first issued on September 1, 1855, by the New York Book Publishers' Association, of which William Henry Appleton was president. It was later absorbed by *Publishers Weekly*.

4454. Mass-market paperback book was a work of fiction entitled *Malaeska: Indian Wife of the White Hunter*, by Mrs. Ann S. Stephens. It was published by Irwin P. Beadle and Company, New York City, and first advertised on June 7, 1860, in the *New York Tribune* as "Beadle's Dime Novels No. 1."

4455. Bibliophile magazine was *The Philobiblion, a Monthly Biographical and Literary Journal Containing Critical Notices of and Extracts from Rare, Curious and Valuable Old Books*, published on India paper by J.W. Bouton, New York City. The first issue was dated December 1861. George Philip Philes was the editor.

4456. Bookseller's guide was *The American Bookseller's Guide*, published monthly by the American News Company, New York City. The first issue was dated January 7, 1869. It was issued free to every publisher, bookseller, news dealer, music dealer, and stationer in the United States and Canada. The price to librarians and others not engaged in the trade was $1 a year.

4457. Book manuscript that was typewritten was the manuscript of *The Adventures of Tom Sawyer*, by Mark Twain (Samuel Langhorne Clemens). It was typed on a Remington typewriter in Hartford, CT, in 1875. *Life on The Mississippi* was also typewritten the same year. Twain did not publicize his use of the typewriter, as he did not want to write testimonials or explain the operation of the machine to the curious.

4458. Catalog of first American editions of American authors was the *Catalogue of First Editions of American Authors, Poets, Philosophers, Historians, Statesmen, Essayists, Dramatists, Novelists, Travellers, Humorists, etc.*, published in 1885 by Leon and Brother, booksellers, of New York City. It consisted of 58 pages and listed the various American authors in alphabetical order and the current prices for first editions of their works. In addition to the regularly issued catalog, there were also interleaved copies on handmade paper.

4459. Social register published was the *Society List and Club Register for the Season of 1886–7*, compiled by the Society List Publishing Company, New York City. It cost $3 and contained 381 pages, of which 276 pages contained lists of marriages, deaths, and subscription balls, and a directory of clubs and names, while 105 pages were devoted to advertisements.

4460. Book set by linotype was *The Tribune Book of Open Air Sports*, edited by Henry Hall and published in 1887 by the Tribune Association, New York City. The foreword states, "This book is printed without type—being the first product in book form of the Mergenthaler machine which wholly supersedes the use of movable type."

4461. Monthly cumulative index of books was the *Cumulative Book Index*, published in February 1898 by Morris and Wilson, Minneapolis, MN. It listed nine pages of books published during January 1898. The cumulative feature was begun a few months later, when all the books listed in previous issues were cumulated in one alphabet.

4462. Book series of small-size paperbacks was the Little Blue Books, 3.5 by 5 inches, published in 1919 by Haldeman-Julius Publications, Girard, KS. The books, priced at five cents each, contained from 32 to 128 pages; most were 64 pages. The first two booklets were *The Rubaiyat of Omar Khayyam* and *The Ballad of Reading Gaol* by Oscar Wilde. By 1931, 1,666 titles had been printed. By 1874, more than 300 million books had been sold.

4463. Book completed entirely by one man was *Old Papermaking,* by Dr. Dard Hunter, published in 1923 by the author at Chillicothe, OH. It consisted of 140 pages 9 by 11.5 inches in size and was printed on handmade paper from linen and cotton cloth. Not only was Dr. Hunter the author, but he manufactured the paper, designed the book, cut and cast the type, and printed and bound the sheets.

4464. Paperback publisher in the United States whose entire line was bound in paper was Pocket Books, launched by Robert de Graff in New York City in 1935. The first books issued by the company included reprints of *Wuthering Heights*, by Emily Bronte, *Five Great Tragedies*, by William Shakespeare, *The Murder of Roger Ackroyd,* by Agatha Christie, and *Bambi*, by Felix Salten. They were sold for a quarter each on newsstands and drugstore racks.

4465. Instant book compiled in haste and rushed to the bookstores after an event of major importance was *FDR: A Memorial*, published by Pocket Books, New York City, in April 1945, a few days after the death of President Franklin Delano Roosevelt. It was also the first book written for publication as a paperback. Previously, paperbound editions were reprints of books that had already been published in hardcover.

4466. Book set into type completely by electronic composition was *The Long Short Cut*, a 192-page suspense novel by Andrew Garve, which was published by Harper and Row, New York City, in April 1968. The type was composed and pages were produced by means of an electronic beam projected on the face of a high-resolution cathode ray tube at speeds of up to 600 characters per second. The book was produced by Haddon Craftsmen of Scranton, PA, who used an RCA Videocomp and computer system installed at Video Graphic Systems, Hauppauge, NY.

Faxes

4467. Radio fax patents were awarded on March 28, 1905, to Cornelius D. Ehret of Rosemont, PA, for "the art of transmitting intelligence" and "a system of transmitting intelligence."

4468. Transatlantic radio fax transmission of a photograph took place on June 11, 1922, when a photograph of Pope Pius XI was transmitted from Rome by Dr. Arthur Korn, a German physicist. It was published in the *New York World* the same day. The picture, a halftone 7 by 9.5 inches, was received 40 minutes after transmission at Bar Harbor, ME, by Chief Radioman Edmund H. Hansen of the Navy. Light falling on a selenium cell produced a group of shaded dots that formed a halftone.

4469. Transcontinental radio fax transmission of a photograph took place on March 4, 1925, when nine photographs taken in Washington, DC, of the inauguration of President Calvin Coolidge were sent to New York City, Chicago, and San Francisco by the American Telegraph and Telephone Company. One picture was sent every 12 minutes, and each photograph took 7 minutes to travel the distance.

4470. Transpacific radio fax transmission was made on May 6, 1925. It was also the first transcontinental radio fax transmission. Photographs of war games and of a general, an admiral, and a governor were transmitted by Alfred J. Koenig from Honolulu, HI, using a transmitter designed by Captain Richard Howland Ranger. The photographs went to Kahuku, HI, by wire; to Marshall, CA, by radio; to Bolinas, CA, by radio; to Riverhead, NY, by radio; and to New York City by wire. The total distance was 5,136 miles.

4471. Long-distance radio fax transmission of medical information was made on May 28, 1925, when the American Telegraph and Telephone Company transmitted stethogram and electrocardiogram pictures from its New York City office to a physician in Chicago.

4472. Fax transmission of movie film was a two-hour transmission of 10 feet of film showing the actress Vilma Banky, which was sent over telephone wires from Chicago, IL, on

April 4, 1928, to the American Telephone and Telegraph Company's New York City studio. The negatives were placed between glass plates, rephotographed, and reassembled. There were only eight telephone fax stations in the United States at the time. The feat had been attempted two years earlier, but the images received were blurred.

4473. High-speed radio fax transmission was demonstrated on October 21, 1948, by the Radio Corporation of America at the Library of Congress, Washington, DC, using Ultrafax, a system capable of transmitting a million words per minute. The first message was handwritten by David Sarnoff, president and chairman of the board of RCA. Margaret Mitchell's *Gone With the Wind*, a novel of 457,000 words and 1,047 pages, was transmitted from station WNBW, Washington, DC, to the Library of Congress, a distance of three miles, in 2 minutes 21 seconds.

Maps and Charts

4474. Map of a city within the present limits of the United States known to historians appeared in *Expeditis Francisco Draki Eqvitis Angli in Indias Occidentalis—1588*, an account of Sir Francis Drake's explorations. It was a line engraving depicting St. Augustine, FL.

4475. Native American map of record was a pen-and-ink drawing showing the location of rivers, roads, and pueblos in New Mexico. It was made in Mexico City in 1602 by a Native American man known to the Spanish as Miguel. He drew it during an inquiry by the Viceroy of New Spain into the results of Don Juan de Onate's expedition into territories north of New Mexico. Miguel had been captured at a Wichita Indian village on the Arkansas River, in present-day Kansas, after it was sacked by Escanxaque Indians who were serving as the expedition's guides. The place names on the map were written in by a notary. A copy of the map was forwarded to Spain, where it was preserved.

4476. Map made in America to be published in a book appeared in the Reverend William Hubbard's *The Present State of New England, being a narrative of the troubles with the Indians in New England, from the first planting thereof in the year 1607 to 1677*, published by John Foster, Boston, MA, in 1677. It was a topographical woodcut folding map and was known as the Wine Hills Map, since the English edition had "Wine Hills" instead of the "White Hills" of New Hampshire. It bore the inscription "Being the first that ever was here cut, and done by the best Pattern that could be had, which being in some places defective, it made the other less exact, yet doth it sufficiently shew the Scituation of the Countrey and conveniently well the distance of places." The name of the cartographer is unknown.

4477. Road map for public use was printed in *Tulley's Almanac* of 1698, published in Boston, MA, by John Tulley. The almanac showed a list of towns, roads, and distances from Boston. Later editions gave the names of the tavern keepers.

4478. War map was published in the December 24, 1733, issue of John Peter Zenger's *New York Weekly Journal*. It was a map of the harbor and fortifications of Louisburg, Nova Scotia.

4479. Map of the United States engraved in America was a wall map, 41 by 46.5 inches, made by Abel Buell in New Haven, CT, in 1783, after the Treaty of Paris. It was a line engraving, and was advertised for sale in the *Connecticut Journal* of March 31, 1784: "As this Map is the effect of the compiler's long and unwearied application, diligence and industry, and as perfection has been the great object of his labors, and it being the first ever compiled, engraved, and finished by any one man, and an American, he flatters himself, that every patriotic gentleman, and lover of geographical knowledge, will not hesitate to encourage the improvement of his country. Every favour will be most gratefully acknowledged, by the public's most obedient and very humble servant."

4480. Book of road maps was *A Survey of the Roads of the United States of America*, published in 1789 in New York City by Christopher Colles. It contained 86 plates and detailed the routes near the city.

4481. Cryptography chart was P. R. Wouves's *A Syllabical and Steganographical Table*, a chart 27 by 19.25 inches, with a list of syllables and words in English and French intended for secret correspondence. It contained 62 alphabetical columns of 6,138 two-letter combinations, numbered from 1 to

99 so that words could be converted into numerical figures. It had two title pages, one in English and one in French, and was published in 1797 by Benjamin Franklin Bache in Philadelphia, PA.

4482. Globe factory to produce terrestrial and celestial globes was started in 1813 by James Wilson in Bradford, VT. A large globe had been made in 1811 by Ira H. Hill of St. Albans, VT, for the Fairfield Academy of St. Albans.

4483. Atlas issued by a state was *The Atlas of the State of South Carolina, made under the authority of the Legislature; prefaced with a geographical statistical and historical map of the state*. It was prepared under the direction of Robert Mills and printed for the state in 1825 by John D. Toy, Baltimore, MD. It contained a map of the state of South Carolina and 28 district maps scaled 21 miles to the inch, which were engraved by H.S. Tanner and assistants. The atlas was 18 inches by 24 inches and included the location of the roads, rivers, bridges, ferries, factories, taverns, and many of the plantations.

4484. Relief map was made in 1871 by Edwin Eugene Howell and showed the island of San Domingo. In 1876, he made a relief map of the Grand Canyon of the Colorado as part of the Government Exhibit at the Philadelphia Centennial Exposition, Philadelphia, PA.

4485. Road map for motorists was produced by George Walker of Boston, MA, in 1900. His well-designed pocket maps for motorists were printed in color and were easy to fold. The first widely distributed road maps were published and distributed in 1914 by the Gulf Oil Company, Pittsburgh, PA. William B. Akin conceived the idea. The company distributed 10,000 maps showing roads and routes in Allegheny County, PA.

4486. Satellite composite map of the United States was the Earth Resources Technology photomosaic of the contiguous 48 states, constructed from 595 photographs taken from a 560-mile altitude by the *Landsat* satellite launched on July 23, 1972. It measured 10 feet by 16 feet and was assembled in November 1974 by the Department of Agriculture's Soil Cartographic Unit, Hyattsville, MD.

4487. High-resolution maps of the ocean floor were released in July 1995, when the Navy declassified satellite data from *Geosat*, an American satellite launched in 1985, and from the European Space Agency's *ERS-1* satellite. The data provided the first consistent and highly detailed view of the world's ocean basins, with information on many previously unknown submarine features.

News

4488. Broadsides were single sheets printed on one side with announcements of news. One of the earliest broadsides, and in some ways the most important, was *The Present State of the New English Affairs*. It was published by Samuel Green in Cambridge, MA, in 1689 "to prevent false reports." It consisted of a sheet of folio size, 8 by 14.5 inches, printed in two columns.

4489. Newspaper published in the British colonies was *Publick Occurrences, Both Foreign and Domestic*, which was printed by Richard Pierce in Boston, MA, for publisher Benjamin Harris. The first and only issue was distributed from Boston's London Coffee House on September 25, 1690. Although Harris had planned to publish the newspaper once a month, he was prevented from doing so by Governor Simon Bradstreet and other government officials, who objected to some of the first issue's contents. The paper had included a comment critical of the colony's employment of Mohawk Indians in a military raid against Quebec and a scurrilous reference to the king of France.

4490. Newspaper that was successful was the *Boston News-Letter*, the first issue of which was dated April 17–24, 1704. The editor was John Campbell, a New England postmaster, who earned the distinction of being America's first vendor of news. It was printed by Bartholomew Green in a back room of his home in Boston, MA. The page size was 7.5 by 12.5 inches. The text was set in small pica type. The paper was without competition for 15 years and reached a circulation of 300 copies.

4491. Editorial apology for false news to appear in a newspaper appeared in the Philadelphia, PA, *American Weekly Mercury* of April 20, 1721. It stated: "N.B. In our last week's *Mercury* No. 70, there is an account inserted from a private Letter sent to Boston, dated the 20th of September last, That the Government of Pennsilvania is Surrendered to the Crown, etc. These are to give Notice that we have now Letters from London, of a later Date, by which we find that the said Report concerning the Province of Pennsilvania is false and groundless and therefore was both by them and us too rashly inserted."

4492. Political newspaper was the *New York Weekly Journal*, established on November 5, 1733, by John Peter Zenger as a political organ to expose Governor William Cosby's corruption. Zenger was arrested on November 17, 1734, and charged with seditious libel. His acquittal was seen as a vindication of the right of free speech. The first political newspaper of national importance was the *Gazette of the United States*, the political organ of Alexander Hamilton, edited by John Fenno. The first issue appeared in New York City on April 15, 1789. The newspaper moved to Philadelphia when the government moved its headquarters there in 1790.

4493. Trial in which freedom of the press was upheld took place in New York City in 1735. John Peter Zenger, the German-born editor of the *New York Weekly Journal*, had reported that Governor William Cosby of New York had attempted to rig an election in Eastchester, PA, in 1733. Cosby brought suit against Zenger, charging him with seditious libel. Zenger was defended by lawyer Andrew Hamilton of Philadelphia, who convinced the jury that printing the truth does not constitute libel. Zenger's acquittal establishing a legal precedent for freedom of the press.

4494. Daily newspaper is claimed to have been the *Pennsylvania Evening Post and Daily Advertiser* of Philadelphia, PA, originally known as the *Pennsylvania Evening Post and Public Advertiser*, which started out as a triweekly in June 1775, became a semiweekly in January 1779, and switched to a daily in 1783. Benjamin Towne was editor and publisher. The claim of being the first daily newspaper is also made for the *Pennsylvania Packet and Daily Advertiser*, published by David C. Claypoole and John Dunlap in Philadelphia, PA, which appeared on September 21, 1784, and sold for fourpence a copy. It was founded in 1771 as a weekly, the *Pennsylvania Packet and General Advertiser*.

4495. Political newspaper to carry partisanship to extremes was the *Aurora* (originally called the *General Advertiser and Political, Commercial, Agricultural and Literary Journal*), founded in Philadelphia, PA, on October 1, 1790. The editor was Benjamin Franklin Bache, the grandson of Benjamin Franklin, who had himself been a printer and newspaper publisher. Bache, nicknamed "Lightning Rod Junior," was a rabid opponent of President George Washington and lampooned him mercilessly in comments and cartoons, for which he was assaulted by supporters of Washington on several occasions.

4496. Sunday newspaper was the *Sunday Monitor* of Baltimore, MD, published by Philip Edwards, which appeared on December 18, 1796. It consisted of four pages, 10.25 by 17 inches.

4497. Federal law intended to intimidate the press was the Sedition Act, enacted on July 14, 1798, during the escalating conflict with France. The Sedition Act threatened those opposing the war—the editors of the influential Democratic-Republican newspapers, many of whom were immigrants (or refugees) from France, England, and Ireland—with a fine of up to $2,000 and imprisonment up to two years if found guilty of publishing "any false, scandalous and malicious writing" against the government. Of the 25 people arrested under the act, 10 were convicted. They were pardoned by Thomas Jefferson when he became president in 1801, after the law had expired.

4498. Prosecution under the Sedition Act took place in October 1798. The defendant was Congressman Matthew Lyon of Vermont, a fervent opponent of the Federalist position in favor of war with France. Because his local newspaper refused to publish his opinions, Lyons founded his own outlet, *The Scourge of Aristocracy and Repository of Important Political Truths*. He was indicted four days later and charged with sedition for ridiculing President John Adams. Lyon was convicted and sentenced to a four-month jail term and a $1,000 fine. While he was in prison, he was overwhelmingly reelected to his seat in Congress, and as soon as he was released he went directly from the jail to Congress Hall, Philadelphia, with crowds of supporters cheering him along the way.

4499. Religious weekly newspaper was *The Religious Remembrancer*, first issued in Philadelphia, PA, on September 4, 1813, by John Welwood Scott. In 1840 the name was changed to *The Christian Observer*. In 1869 the offices were moved to Louisville, KY.

4500. News agency for gathering news was established in Boston, MA, in 1814, when Samuel Topliff became the owner of the Merchant's Reading Room (formerly Gilbert's Coffee House and Marine Diary), one of several Boston coffeehouses where customers read local weekly newspapers and discussed current news. Topliff maintained a correspondence with associates in foreign countries who supplied him with news. He kept a record of their reports for his own patrons and also distributed their reports to the newspapers for publication.

4501. Abolition newspaper was the *Philanthropist*, published and edited by Charles Osborn, which appeared in Mount Pleasant, OH, on August 29, 1817. It published "An Appeal to Philanthropists" by Benjamin Lundy, which is said by some to be the most powerful abolition appeal ever made.

4502. Opinion poll was published in the *Harrisburg Pennsylvanian* on July 24, 1824. Local voters were asked their preference in the presidential contest between Andrew Jackson and John Quincy Adams. Jackson was preferred by a wide majority. Adams won the election.

4503. Penny daily newspaper was *The Cent*, which was published in Philadelphia, PA, in 1830 by Dr. Christopher Columbus Conwell. The first successful penny paper was the *New York Sun*, published by Benjamin Henry Day, which appeared on September 3, 1833.

4504. Labor newspaper was *The Working Man's Advocate*, first published in New York City on February 18, 1834, by George Henry Evans. He advocated free homesteads, equal rights for women, and abolition of all laws governing collection of debts and imprisonment for debt. An earlier newspaper, the *Daily Sentinel*, first published on February 15, 1830, in New York City, was sympathetic to labor.

4505. News dispatch by telegraph was sent from Washington, DC, to the offices of the *Baltimore Patriot* on May 25, 1844. The message read: "One o'clock. There has just been made a motion in the House to go into committee of the whole on the Oregon question. Rejected. Ayes 79—Nays 86."

4506. Newspaper published on the Pacific Coast was the *Oregon Spectator*, a semimonthly issued in Oregon City, OR, beginning on February 5, 1846. Its slogan was "Westward the star of empire takes its way." The newspaper was published by the Oregon Printing Association and was nonpolitical. The first editor was Colonel William G. T'Vault. The first California newspaper was the *Californian*, published on August 15, 1846, in Monterey, CA, by Robert Semple and the Reverend Walter Colton.

4507. Social and political newspaper for women was *The Lily*. Founded by Amelia Jenks Bloomer, *The Lily* featured the writings of such women as Elizabeth Cady Stanton and Susan B. Anthony as well as Bloomer herself. Among the topics covered were temperance, suffrage, and marriage and motherhood . The first issue was published in Seneca Falls, NY, on January 1, 1849. The newspaper's circulation peaked at 6,000.

Amelia Bloomer

4508. Newspaper published by soldiers in the field was the *United States American Volunteer*, which first appeared on May 21, 1861, at De Soto, MO. It was published by members of Company A, 5th Regiment, Missouri Volunteers, commanded by Captain Nelson Cole. The issue consisted of a single page. It was printed on the back of a sheet of the *Jefferson County Herald*.

4509. Press censorship by military authorities occurred shortly after the beginning of the Civil War. Worried that press accounts of activities in Washington, DC, might prove helpful to the enemy, Winfield Scott, general in chief of the Union army, announced on July 8, 1861, that the Washington telegraph office would no longer carry "dispatches concerning the operations of the Army not permitted by the commanding general."

4510. Newspaper printed on a train was the *Weekly Herald*, a single sheet of approximately seven by eight inches, printed on both sides. It was issued by Thomas Alva Edison and distributed on the train between Port Huron and Detroit, MI. The first known issue was dated Port Huron, MI, February 3, 1862.

4511. Newspaper printed on wood-pulp paper was the *Boston Morning Journal* of Boston, MA, first published on January 15, 1863. It was a four-page, eight-column newspaper and sold for three cents a copy.

4512. Newspaper published at sea was the illustrated *Atlantic Telegraph*, printed on board the cablelaying *Great Eastern*, captained by James Anderson. It sold for five shillings for the series. Issues were published on July 29, August 5, and August 12, 1865. The first to use a radio news service was the *Transatlantic Times*, a four-page paper issued on November 15, 1899, on board the American ocean liner *St. Paul* by Guglielmo Marconi and two engineers. It sold for $1 a copy, with proceeds donated to the Seaman's Fund. The news was obtained by wireless from the Needles Station, Isle of Wight. The first daily paper published at sea to carry world news was the *Cunard Daily Bulletin*, inaugurated by Marconi in October 1902 on the liners S.S. *Campania* and the S.S. *Lucania*. The news was obtained from the wireless stations at Poldhu, Cornwall, England, and Glace Bay, Canada.

4513. Newspaper index separately published was *The Index to the New York Times for 1865*, published in 1866 by Henry J. Raymond and Company, New York City. It contained 182 pages. Earlier indexes had been printed primarily for staff use.

4514. Financial news agency was the Kiernan Financial News Agency, established in 1869 by John James Kiernan at 21 Wall Street, New York City. In 1882, the service was extended to include results of athletic contests, arrivals of steamships, commodity quotations abroad, and similar items.

4515. Illustrated daily newspaper was the *New York Daily Graphic*, an illustrated evening newspaper that sold for five cents a copy. It was issued on March 4, 1873, from 41 Park Place, New York City, and consisted of eight pages printed by chromolithography using zinc plates.

4516. News dispatch by telephone was sent from Salem, MA, on February 12, 1877, to the *Boston Globe*, Boston, MA, using equipment provided by Alexander Graham Bell. The *Globe* reported: "This special dispatch to the *Globe* has been transmitted by telephone in the presence of twenty people who have

Library of Congress, Prints & Photographs Divsion
LC-USZ62-3205

Alexander Graham Bell

thus been witnesses to a feat never before attempted—the sending of news over the space of 16 miles by the human voice."

4517. College daily newspaper was the *Yale News*, which was first published in New Haven, CT, on January 28, 1878.

4518. Newspaper delivery train was operated by the International Great Northern Railroad over the Galveston, Houston and Henderson Railroad, in 1883 to deliver the *Galveston News* to subscribers located between Galveston and Houston, TX. The *News* paid $500 a month for the exclusive lease of the train.

4519. Newsboy was Barney Flaherty, a 10-year-old who answered the advertisement, "To the Unemployed—A number of steady men can find employment by vending this paper. A liberal discount is allowed to those who buy to sell again," inserted in the *New York Sun*, New York City, on September 4, 1883, by Benjamin Day, the publisher.

4520. Newspaper clipping bureau was opened at 60 Ann Street, New York City, on April 15, 1884, by Samuel Leavitt. The business was absorbed by Henry Romeike, who had established a similar service in June 1881 in London. It was known as Henry Romeike's Press Cuttings.

4521. Newspaper syndicate to supply articles and stories was started on November 8, 1884, by Samuel Sidney McClure of New York City, who organized the McClure Syndicate. The syndicate paid writers directly and distributed their articles to its membership of daily newspapers throughout the country. The first attempt at syndication took place in 1841, when Moses Yale Beach of New York City printed up President John Tyler's December 7 message to the second session of the 27th Congress. He sold the sheets to the *Advertiser* of Albany, NY, the *Whig* of Troy, NY, the *Gazette* of Salem, MA, the *Times* of Boston, MA, and other papers. Each newspaper printed its own name in the blank space provided for that purpose.

4522. European edition of an American newspaper was the Paris edition of the *New York Herald*, first published on October 4, 1887. It consisted of four six-column pages, of which the last page was devoted to advertisements.

4523. Book review newspaper supplement was the Book Review Supplement of the *New York Times*, first issued on Saturday, October 10, 1896. It contained eight pages of four columns each. The first editor was Francis Whiting Halsey. On January 29, 1911, it began appearing on Sunday as a 16-page supplement.

4524. Newsreel was the Pathé Weekly, later known as Pathé News, which was first shown in November 1910. Herbert Case Hoagland was the editor. Moving pictures of historic events had, however, been taken earlier, including films of the McKinley inaugural parade of 1896, the funeral procession in Colón, Cuba, of the *Maine* victims in 1898, and the embarkation of Theodore Roosevelt's Rough Riders.

4525. Newspaper circulation audit was made by a group of advertisers who organized the Association of American Advertisers to verify circulation figures. On August 21, 1914, the Audit Bureau of Circulations was formed in Chicago, IL, as a cooperative nonprofit organization. Membership was composed of advertisers, advertising agencies, and publishers. Of the 25 directors, four were from daily newspapers, two from magazines, two from business papers, two from farm papers, two from advertising agencies, and 13 from various advertisers.

4526. Illustrated tabloid was the *Illustrated Daily News* of New York City, which appeared on June 26, 1919. It was published by Robert Rutherford McCormick and Joseph Medill Patterson.

4527. News program on radio was an announcement of local election returns, broadcast on August 31, 1920, by station 8MK (later WWJ), Detroit, MI.

4528. Airplane used for newspaper reporting was a Canadian Curtiss biplane, piloted by Lieutenant William D. Tipton, which was placed in service by the *Evening Sun* of Baltimore, MD, on September 1, 1920, when it reported a railroad wreck at Back River. Two days later it flew out to sea and located the submarine *S-5*, in trouble off the Delaware Capes.

4529. Daily news program on radio began broadcasting on September 1, 1922, by station WBAY, American Telegraph and Telephone Company, New York City, between 4:30 P.M. and 5:30 P.M. It was known as "The Radio

Digest" and was edited by George F. Thompson. Questions and answers concerning radio were also broadcast.

4530. Mimeographed daily newspaper was the *Kellogg Daily Reminder*, published on July 25, 1923, by Eaton's Letter Shop, Kellogg, ID. The founder and first editor was Marson M. Eaton, Jr. The first issue consisted of one sheet printed on both sides.

4531. Combined newspaper was issued in September 1923 during a citywide newspaper strike and bore on its masthead the names *New York American, New York Herald, The Journal of Commerce, The Daily News, The Morning Telegraph, The New York Times, The New York Tribune, The World, The New York Staats-Zeitung, Il Progresso Italo-Americano,* and *Americand.*

4532. Newsreels showing presidential candidates were filmed on August 11, 1924, by Theodore W. Case and Lee De Forest. They showed the Republican incumbent, President Calvin Coolidge, on the grounds of the White House in Washington, DC, and his Progressive opponent, Senator Robert Marion La Follette, on the steps of the Capitol. The Democratic candidate, John William Davis, was photographed at Locust Valley, NY. The newsreel was shown in various theaters in September 1924.

4533. Fax transmission by a press syndicate direct to newspaper offices was an 8-by-10-inch aerial view of an American Airlines Curtiss Condor transport plane that had crashed in the Adirondack mountains 10 miles from Newhouseville, NY, on a flight from Cleveland, OH, to Boston, MA. The facsimile was transmitted simultaneously to eight newspapers in 24 cities by the Wirephoto service of the Associated Press on January 1, 1935.

4534. Unscheduled event to be televised as it occurred was an outdoor scene of firemen answering an alarm on April 24, 1936, in Camden, NJ. It was shown in green tint, 5 by 7 inches, 24 pictures per second, on a 343-line screen. The pictures were taken by engineers from the RCA-Victor Company, Camden.

4535. News magazine featuring photographs was *Life*, the weekly magazine founded by Henry Luce and published by Time, Incorporated, in New York City. Luce had conceived of a new kind of magazine in which "the cream of the world's pictures" would be edited into a coherent story. The first issue went on sale on November 19, 1936, with a cover by photojournalist Margaret Bourke-White depicting Montana's Fort Peck Dam. The first printing of 200,000 copies sold out by the end of the day. This magazine had no connection to an earlier publication called *Life*, a magazine of satire and humor published in 1883 in New York City by John Mitchell.

4536. Newspaper printed on pine-pulp paper in color was the *Dallas News* of Dallas, TX, a daily, which printed a pine-paper edition on March 31, 1937.

4537. Coast-to-coast radio news broadcast to be recorded was made on May 6, 1937, by Herbert Morrison, who described the explosion of the dirigible *Hindenburg* at Lakehurst, NJ. The recording was flown to New York City and was broadcast over both networks, the Red and the Blue, of the National Broadcasting Company.

4538. Radio facsimile newspaper was transmitted by KSTP, St. Paul, MN, on December 17, 1937. It consisted of a roll of sensitized paper nearly five inches wide, with perforations at the sides, that issued from a receiving set.

4539. Transoceanic newspaper was the *Daily Mail*, a weekly digest of the *Daily Mail* of London, which first appeared on January 5, 1944. It was made up and edited in London, microfilmed, and flown to New York City, where it was enlarged and printed. It contained 12 pages, 9 by 12 inches, four columns wide.

4540. Newsreel in color was a Warner Brothers-Pathé newsreel taken on January 1, 1948, of the Tournament of Roses and the Rose Bowl Game, Pasadena, CA. It was made by Cinecolor process and released on January 5, 1948.

4541. Newsreel telecast presented daily was the 20th Century–Fox Movietone News telecast, first presented on February 16, 1948, over the National Broadcasting Company's East Coast network. The program was sponsored by the R.J. Reynolds Tobacco Company.

4542. Editorial to be broadcast over radio and television was made from 8 P.M. to 8:15 P.M. on August 26, 1954, over the Columbia Broadcasting System network. Dr. Frank Stanton, the network's president, protested the Senate's decision to bar radio and television coverage of its hearings into the conduct of Senator Joseph Raymond McCarthy, Republican of Wisconsin.

4543. Newspaper reproduced commercially and regularly by radio facsimile was the San Francisco edition of *The Wall Street Journal*, which was prepared by conventional methods until the spring of 1962. Experimental editions, not distributed to the public, first appeared on April 10, and regular daily fax operations began on May 28. Page proofs were telecast by coaxial cable through microwave circuits to Riverside, CA, where they were reproduced by photoetching, using zinc plates.

4544. Large-type weekly newspaper for persons with impaired vision was the *New York Times Large Type Weekly*, 28 pages long, first published on March 6, 1967. It was printed in New York City in 18-point type and was priced at $29 a year.

4545. Television newsmagazine was *60 Minutes*, produced for the CBS television network by Don Hewitt. The biweekly program premiered on September 24, 1968, with hosts Mike Wallace and Harry Reasoner. The first interview was with Attorney General Ramsey Clark.

4546. Space-to-ground news conference telecast took place at 7:30 P.M. on November 23, 1969, when *Apollo 12* was 108,000 miles from earth, traveling earthward at 3,670 miles per hour. Commanders Charles Conrad, Jr., Alan La Vern Bean, and Richard Francis Gordon, Jr., answered questions submitted in writing by reporters at the Manned Spacecraft Center, Houston, TX, to Lieutenant Colonel Gerald P. Carr, who read them to the astronauts. *Apollo 12* took off on November 14, 1969, and splashed down on November 24.

4547. Newspaper whose contents were transmitted by a communications satellite was the *Wall Street Journal*, set in type at Chicopee, MA, and sent to Orlando, FL, via the *Westar* communications satellite at 3.5 minutes per page. Dedication ceremonies for the new system were held on November 20, 1978.

4548. All-news television network in the world was Cable News Network (CNN), headquartered in Atlanta, GA. It was founded in June 1980 by Robert Edward Turner III, better known as Ted Turner, head of the Turner Broadcasting System. CNN used satellite feeds to provide live coverage of global events, supplied by a network of news bureaus in cities worldwide. The network broadcast 24 hours a day.

4549. Newspaper to publish an Internet edition was the *Columbus Dispatch*, based in Columbus, OH. In July 1980 the newspaper became the first of eleven Associated Press members to upload an experimental electronic edition to the consumer online service CompuServe, also based in Columbus. A maximum of 10,000 dial-up subscribers took part, each of whom paid up to $5 per hour after 5 P.M. to read the text-only edition. The experiment was ended in 1982.

4550. Major network news program broadcast in high-definition television was "Good Morning America," ABC's morning news show. It was produced in HDTV beginning with the edition of November 3, 2005.

Ethnic Newspapers

4551. German newspaper was published on May 6, 1732, by Benjamin Franklin in Germantown, PA, and was entitled *Philadelphische Zeitung*. It was a small four-page sheet, with the text set in double columns and in Roman type. The editor was Lewis (Louis) Timothy. Christopher Saur's newspaper *Der Hoch-Deutsch Pennsylvanische Geschichts-Schreiber, oder Sammlung wichtiger Nachrichten aus dem Natur-und-Kirchen-Reich* ("The High German Pennsylvania Recorder of Events or Collection of Important News from the Kingdom of Nature and of the Church"), first published on August 20, 1739, in Germantown, PA, is usually considered the first German newspaper. The first daily was the *New Yorker Staats-Zeitung*, introduced in New York City on January 26, 1850. It had begun publication on December 24, 1834, as a weekly. The first editor was Gustav Adolf Neumann.

4552. French newspaper was the *Courier de l'Amérique* of Philadelphia, PA, published from July 27, 1784, to October 26, 1784. The first French newspaper to be published daily was the *Courrier Français* of Philadelphia, PA, established on April 15, 1794, which was published triweekly between August 24 and October 26, 1795, and was discontinued on July 3, 1798. The first successful French daily was the *Courrier des États Unis*, which appeared on June 10, 1851, in New York City, with Paul Arpin as editor. It was started as a weekly on March 1, 1828, by E. William Hoskin, the founder and first editor.

4553. Newspaper for Jewish readers was *The Jew*, published monthly in New York City from March 1823 to March 1825. Solomon Henry Jackson, the first Jewish printer in New York, was the editor. Subscriptions cost $1.50 per year. Editorials in the paper were intended to counteract the activities of the American Society for Meliorating the Condition of the Jews, a missionary group. The first Jewish weekly in English was *The Asmonean*, which called itself "a family journal of commerce, politics, religion, and literature." It was first issued on October 26, 1849, in New York City. It was published by Robert Lyon and sold for $3 a year. It was eight pages long, with three columns on a page.

4554. Newspaper for African-American readers edited by African-Americans was *Freedom's Journal*, a four-page weekly published in New York City from March 16, 1827, to March 28, 1829, and edited by John Brown Russwurm and Samuel E. Cornish. The first African-American daily newspaper was the *New Orleans Tribune*, founded by Louis C. Roudanez, which appeared on October 14, 1864, in New Orleans, LA. It was printed in both French and English.

4555. Spanish newspaper was *El Redactor*, first published on July 1, 1827, in New York City. The first editor was Juan José de Lerena.

4556. Native American newspaper was the *Cherokee Phoenix*, a weekly newspaper in English and Cherokee, published from February 21, 1828, to October 1835 in New Echota, GA, the capital of the Cherokee nation. The paper was edited by Elias Boudinot, a Cherokee who had been educated at the foreign mission school in Cornwall, CT, with the help of a philanthropist whose name he adopted. It was printed in the Cherokee writing symbols invented by Sikwayi (Sequoyah), a silversmith, painter, and soldier.

4557. Norwegian newspaper was *Nordlyset* ("The Northern Light"), first published on July 29, 1847, in Muskego, WI. James De Noon Reymert was the first editor.

4558. Chinese newspaper was *Kim Shan Jit San Luk* ("San Francisco Golden Hills News"), published in San Francisco, CA, beginning in 1854. The bilingual *China World*, in Chinese and English, appeared in San Francisco in 1891. The first daily Chinese newspaper was San Francisco's *Chung Sai Yat Po* ("The Chinese Western Daily Paper"), whose first issue appeared on February 16, 1900. It was 15 by 22 inches and consisted of four pages. The founder of the paper was Ng Poon Chew, who served as the president and managing editor until his death in 1931.

4559. Czech newspaper was *Slovan Amerikansky*, a small folio weekly sheet edited by Frank Korizek. It was first issued on January 1, 1860, in Racine, WI.

4560. Yiddish newspaper was the weekly *Yiddisher Zeitung* "Jewish Times"), founded in New York City in 1870 by J.K. Buchner. The first daily newspaper in Yiddish was the *Yiddishes Tageblatt* ("Jewish Daily News"), published in New York City beginning in 1885 by Kasriel Hersch Sarasohn. It merged with the *Yiddishe Morgen Zhurnal* ("Jewish Morning Journal") in 1928 and continued publication until 1952.

4561. Hebrew newspaper was *Ha-Tzofeh be-Eretz ha-Chadash* ("The New World Scout"), edited by Hirsch Bernstein and published in New York City from 1871 to 1876. It was eight pages long and cost 10 cents.

4562. Danish newspaper was *Den Danske Pioneer*, first published in 1872.

4563. Lithuanian newspaper was *Lietuwiszka Gazieta*, published in 1874 in Shamokin, PA.

4564. Italian newspaper was *Il Progresso Italo-Americano*, first issued in New York City in September 1880. The first owner and editor was Charles Barsotti.

4565. Armenian newspaper was *Arekag* ("The Sun"), published in Jersey City, NJ. The first issue appeared in May 1888.

4566. Greek newspaper was the *Atlantis*, first issued on March 3, 1894, from 2 Stone Street, New York City, as a four-page weekly of tabloid size. On January 3, 1905, it became a full-sized four-page daily. It

THE ATLANTIS was the first publication in the world to use typesetting machinery for the Greek alphabet.

was the first Greek publication in America. Its founder and first editor was Solon John Vlasto.

4567. Latvian newspaper was *Amerikas Vestnesis*, published in Boston, MA, in 1896.

4568. Arabic daily newspaper was *Al-Hoda*, founded as a weekly on February 22, 1898, in Philadelphia, PA, by Naoum Anthony Mokarzel. On August 25, 1902, it started publication as a daily in New York City. Mokarzel was the owner and editor-in-chief until his death in 1932.

4569. Hungarian daily newspaper was the *Amerikai Magyar Népszava*, first published on October 18, 1904, in New York City. Its founder and editor in chief was Geza David Berko. It was originally established in March 1899 as a weekly.

4570. Flemish newspaper was *De Gazette van Moline*, which appeared in 1907 in Moline, IL. Flemish is one of the languages spoken in Belgium.

4571. Russian newspaper was *Novoye Russkoye Slovo*, which began publication in New York City in 1910. A biweekly newspaper in Russian and English was circulated in San Francisco in 1868.

4572. Japanese newspaper in continuous publication was the *Utah Nippo*, founded in Salt Lake City, UT, in 1914 by Kuniko Terasawa, who served as its publisher, editor, reporter, typesetter, and proofreader. By the 1990s, it was the only remaining Japanese-language newspaper in the United States that had once been read by the early immigrants from Japan. It continued to be published in old-style, pre-World War II characters no longer used by most Japanese.

4573. Ukrainian daily newspaper was the *Ukrainian Daily News*, established on January 31, 1920, in New York City. The first editor was M. Tkach.

Illustrations

4574. Newspaper cartoon was "Join or Die," designed by Benjamin Franklin and published in Philadelphia, PA, in his newspaper, the *Pennsylvania Gazette*, on May 9, 1754. It was printed in the first column of the second page. It depicted a snake cut up into segments representing South Carolina, North Carolina, Virginia, Maryland, Pennsylvania, New Jersey, New York, and New England.

4575. Political cartoon featuring Uncle Sam appeared in 1834 and was entitled "Uncle Sam in Danger." It showed President Andrew Jackson, Vice President Martin Van Buren, Senator Thomas Hart Benton, and Amos Kendall, a Jackson aide soon to be named postmaster general, in the guise of ignorant doctors bleeding a sick man sitting in a chair. The patient is Uncle Sam, who appears as a cleanshaven man with dark hair, wearing a cap and surrounded by a striped robe that looks something like the American flag. In other early cartoons he was often dressed like Benjamin Franklin. By the 1840s he was portrayed with striped trousers, a top hat, and a long coat, but he was still cleanshaven. It was many decades before he took on his current image as an elderly but vigorous man with a long white beard.

Library of Congress, Prints & Photographs Division
LC-USZ62-117120

Andrew Jackson

4576. Political cartoon showing the Democratic Party as a donkey was "The Modern Balaam and His Ass," published in 1837. It shows Andrew Jackson as the biblical Balaam, riding a donkey and beating it with his hickory stick because it refuses to go forward. In the donkey's path is an angel labeled "Bankruptcy of 1837," "The Regency," "Deposit Banks," and other references to contentious issues of the day. Some four decades later, the great cartoonist Thomas Nast used the donkey to represent northern Democrats who sympathized with the South. His first cartoon to do so was "A Live Jackass Kicking a Dead Lion," a wood engraving that appeared in *Harper's Weekly* on January 15, 1870. The jackass was tagged "Copperhead papers" and the dead lion represented Edwin McMasters Stanton, the former secretary of war, who had clashed with President Andrew Johnson over his refusal to enforce tougher measures in the South.

4577. Line drawing to illustrate a newspaper article appeared on January 15, 1840, in the *New York Sun* of New York City. A four-page supplement showed a drawing under the five-column headline "Steamboat Lexington Burnt!! One Hundred and Fifty Lives Lost."

4578. Newspaper with a full page of woodcut engravings was the *Weekly Herald* of New York City, whose edition of June 28, 1845, printed six woodcuts depicting the grand funeral procession of Andrew Jackson.

4579. Political cartoon showing the Republican Party as an elephant was drawn by Thomas Nast and appeared in *Harper's Weekly*, New York City, on November 7, 1874. It was entitled "The Third-Term Panic" and referred to the possibility that President Ulysses S. Grant might seek a third term. It depicted an ass labeled "N.Y. Herald" in a lion's skin labeled "Caesarism," frightening numerous timid animals labeled "N.Y. Times," "N.Y. Trib.," etc., while a berserk elephant, labeled "Republican vote," about to fall into "Chaos," tossed platform planks to right and left. The quotation accompanying the title read: "An Ass having put on the Lion's skin, roamed about the Forest, and amused himself by frightening all the foolish Animals he met with in his wanderings."

4580. Comic strip in a newspaper was published on September 11, 1875, in the *New York Daily Graphic*, New York City, and showed 17 successive pictures on one full page. It was entitled "Professor Tigwissel's Burglar Alarm."

4581. Sunday comics section in a newspaper was published in 1893 by the *New York World*, New York City. The drawings were made by Richard Felton Outcault and depicted a humorous set of characters under the title of "Hogan's Alley." On November 18, 1894, the newspaper published the first of his six-box cartoon series "The Origin of a New Species." This was the first successful colored newspaper section.

4582. Newspaper with a color page was in the *New York Recorder*, whose issue of Sunday, April 2, 1893, carried on page 13 a full-page advertisement for R.H. Macy, 14th Street and 6th Avenue, New York City, showing a large star printed in red. The first illustrated color page in a newspaper appeared in the *New York World* of Sunday, May 21, 1893. One large sheet, printed in color and folded once, made up four pages. Page 29 showed a Walt McDougall cartoon in color, "Broadway Cable Car Possibilities." Page 32 was a full-page color reproduction of a painting of the Spanish ship *The Santa Maria*.

4583. Newspaper colored supplement was issued by the *New York World* on Sunday, November 19, 1893, and consisted of a four-page section, the outside pages of which were printed in five colors. Two half-page drawings in color featured "A Scene in Atlantic Gardens, Saturday Night," and "The Cathedral at Eleven O'Clock Mass." The inside pages were printed in black.

4584. Comic strip in continuous newspaper publication was "The Katzenjammer Kids," created by Rudolph Dirks. The strip first appeared in the *New York Journal* on December 12, 1897, and was still in syndication in 1996.

4585. Newspaper rotogravure sections were simultaneously instituted by seven newspapers on March 29, 1914, when an eight-page supplement showing 13 masterpieces of the Altman Collection in the Metropolitan Museum of Art, New York City, was included with the *New York Times*, the *Boston Sun-Herald*, the *Philadelphia Public Ledger*, the *Chicago Tribune*, the *Cleveland Plain Dealer*, the *St. Louis Post-Dispatch*, and the *Kansas City Star*.

4586. Transatlantic radio fax of a drawing was a sketch of Ambassador Alanson Bigelow Houghton, drawn on April 30, 1926, by Augustus John, which was transmitted in 58 minutes from London to the offices of the *New York Times* in New York City on May 2, 1926.

4587. Color news photograph transmitted by radio fax for publication was a photograph of President Harry S. Truman, Soviet leader Josef Stalin, and British Prime Minister Clement Richard Attlee, taken at the Potsdam Conference in Germany and transmitted on August 3, 1945, to Washington, DC. A one-shot camera exposed three negatives simultaneously. From the negatives, three black and white prints were made, and each was placed on a cylinder representing one of the three primary colors, red, blue, and yellow.

Journalists

4588. Newspaper publisher was Benjamin Harris, "the father of American newspapers." His paper, *Publick Occurrances, Both Foreign and Domestic*, issued from the London Coffee House, Boston, MA, was printed by R. Pierce on September 25, 1690. It was promptly suppressed because of certain "reflexions" distasteful to Governor Simon Bradstreet of Massachusetts. Harris had intended to issue it monthly "or if any Glut of Occurrances happen, oftener," but only the one issue appeared. It was a one-sheet paper folded to present four pages, containing news in double columns. The last page was blank. There were no advertisements.

4589. Newspaper editor who was a woman was Elizabeth Timothy of Charleston, SC. Her husband, Lewis (or Louis) Timothy, was a protege of Benjamin Franklin, who arranged for him to become the editor, publisher, and printer of the *South Carolina Gazette* in 1734. After her husband's death in 1738, Elizabeth Timothy, the mother of seven children, continued to run both his newspaper and his printing business for the next seven years, until her eldest son was able to take over. The first issue she published was dated January 4, 1739.

4590. Washington news correspondent of importance was James Gordon Bennett (the elder), whose articles first appeared on January 2, 1828, in the *New York Enquirer*, later known as the *Courier and Enquirer*.

4591. Sportswriter was Henry William Herbert, who used the *nom de plume* Frank Forester, and who acquired fame in 1834 as an authority on outdoor sports.

4592. Book review editor was the author and literary critic Margaret Fuller, formerly the editor of the Transcendentalist magazine *Dial*, who was hired in December 1844 by Horace Greeley for his *New York Tribune*. Fuller served until 1846. She was killed in 1850 in the wreck of a ship off Fire Island, NY, together with her husband and child.

4593. War correspondent was George Wilkins Kendall, founder and coeditor of the *Picayune* of New Orleans, LA. During the Mexican War of 1846-50, Kendall joined the American army as a participant, not an observer, and was wounded in battle. He wrote daily stories about his experiences and sent them back to New Orleans by messenger.

4594. News reporter at a political convention who was a woman was Mary Ashton Rice Livermore, one of the editors of the *New Covenant*, who covered the Republican National Convention, May 12–18, 1860, at the Chicago Wigwam, Chicago, IL, which nominated Abraham Lincoln.

4595. News reporter tried as a spy was Thomas Wallace Knox, staff war correspondent of the *New York Herald*, who was tried on February 5, 1863, at Young's Point, LA, before a military court composed of a brigadier general, four colonels, and a major. He was charged with giving information to the enemy, being a spy, and disobeying orders. The trial lasted 14 days. Knox was found guilty on the first two charges and not guilty on the third, and was banished from General Grant's and General Sherman's theater of war. The sentence was revoked by President Abraham Lincoln.

4596. News correspondent accredited to the White House was Emily Edson Briggs, correspondent for the *Philadelphia Press* of Philadelphia, PA, who wrote a series of letters that were published between January 1866 and January 1882, during the administrations of Presidents Johnson, Grant, Hayes, and Garfield. She wrote under the pseudonym "Olivia."

4597. Organization of newspaper publishers was the American Newspaper Publishers Association, organized on November 17, 1886, in Detroit, MI. The call was made by William Henry Brearley of the *Detroit News*. The first convention was held on February 16–17, 1887, in Rochester, NY, and was attended by 51 delegates.

4598. Photojournalist was Jacob Riis, a Danish-born reporter for the *New York Tribune* and *New York Evening Sun*, who wrote articles about the living conditions in New York City's slum neighborhoods and documented his observations with photographs. His 1890 book *How the Other Half Lives* helped persuade reformers and legislators to aid the city's poor.

4599. News correspondent who was African-American was Joel Augustus Rogers, who was sent to Addis Ababa, Ethiopia, by the *Pittsburgh Courier* of Pittsburgh, PA, in October 1935. He returned on April 21, 1936. The first African-American correspondent accredited to the White House was Harry McAlpin, representing the *Daily World* of Atlanta, GA, and the press service of the Negro Newspaper Publishers Association, who attended his first White House press conference on February 8, 1944. The first to be admitted to the congressional press gallery was Percival L. Prattis, representative of *Our World*, New York City, who was accredited on February 3, 1947.

4600. News anchor on radio was Robert Trout of the CBS Radio Network, based in New York City. On the evening of March 13, 1938, Trout emceed a special show in which he introduced a series of live shortwave reports from journalists in London, Vienna, and other European cities. The subject was Nazi Germany's annexation of Austria two days before. This became the first edition of *CBS World News Roundup*, a twice-daily broadcast with Trout as host.

The first newscaster to be known by the term "anchor" was Walter Cronkite. The title was applied when he headed the CBS reporting teams at the Republican and Democratic National Conventions in July 1952.

4601. News anchor on television was Douglas Edwards, a CBS radio newscaster who made the switch to television in 1946 as host of a new weekly show, *The CBS Television News*. On August 15, 1948, the show became a nightly program under the title *Douglas Edwards and the News*. The program was seen nationwide starting in September 1951. Edwards also anchored CBS's coverage of the national party nominating conventions in the summer of 1948.

4602. Television news commentator who was African-American was Malvin Russell "Mel" Goode of Pittsburgh, PA, who was assigned on August 29, 1962, by WABC-TV to the United Nations staff, New York City.

4603. Television newswoman to report from Capitol Hill was Nancy Dickerson, a correspondent for the CBS and NBC networks. In 1960, working for CBS, she became the first woman television reporter to cover a national political convention. In 1963 she joined the Washington bureau of NBC; her first major story was the 1963 March on Washington. She was active as a reporter and commentator until 1996.

4604. Television network evening news program anchor who was a woman was Barbara Walters, who co-hosted the *ABC Evening News* with Harry Reasoner beginning in 1976. Her $1 million salary was at that time the largest ever paid to any broadcast journalist.

4605. Editor of a major daily newspaper who was a woman was Mary Anne Dolan, who edited the *Los Angeles Herald Examiner*, Los Angeles, CA, from 1981 to 1989, when the paper ceased publication.

Periodicals

4606. Magazine published in America was *The American Magazine, or a Monthly View of the Political State of the British Colonies*, edited by John Webbe and published by Andrew Bradford in Philadelphia, PA. It was published monthly for three months in the spring of 1741. On the title page was an illustration of the Philadelphia waterfront. The first issue appeared in the middle of February, about three days prior to Benjamin Franklin's *General Magazine and Historical Chronicle for All the British Plantations in America*, which was also published in Philadelphia.

4607. Comic magazine was *The Wasp*, edited by Robert Rusticoat, Esq. (also known as "Rusty-Turncoat"), and printed by Harry Crosswell, Hudson, NY. The first issue, dated July 7, 1802, consisted of four pages and lampooned politics and politicians.

4608. Magazine containing a fashion plate was *The Port Folio*, published by Bradford and Inskeep, Philadelphia, PA, and Inskeep and Bradford, New York City. The June 1809 issue contained two engravings, one page showing a full dress and one showing the front and back views of "Fontarabian robes of Saragossa brown net."

4609. Quarterly magazine was *The American Review of History and Politics and General Repository of Literature and State Papers*, edited by Robert Walsh and published in Philadelphia, PA. The first issue, dated January 1811, contained 200 pages and a 60-page appendix. Subscription was $6 a year. The last issue was published in October 1812.

4610. Magazine for women to continue publication for more than five years was the *Ladies' Magazine*, which was founded in Boston, MA, in 1828 by Sarah Josepha Hale, who became its editor. In 1837, the magazine merged with *Godey's Lady's Book*, which Mrs. Hale continued to edit in Philadelphia until 1877.

Library of Congress, Prints & Photographs Division LC-USZ62-69592

A page from Godey's Lady's Book.

4611. Trade journal was the *Rail-road Advocate*, published biweekly from July 4, 1831, to June 14, 1832, in Rogersville, TN, by "an association of gentlemen." The first issue contained eight pages measuring 12.5 by 9.75 inches. Its main objects were "to advocate railroads and other internal improvements that would connect East Tennessee with markets for its surplus produce" and "end its isolation from the rest of the country," and to collect and publish "all the information that can be collected on this interesting subject."

4612. Illustrated weekly magazine was *Brother Jonathan, a Weekly Compend of Belles Lettres and the Fine Arts, Standard Literature and General Intelligence*, first issued on January 1, 1842. It consisted of 28 pages plus a 32-page supplement containing the first installment of "Adventures of Tom Stapleton," by John M. Moore. It was founded by Benjamin Henry Day and Nathaniel Parker Willis and was published by Wilson and Company, New York City. It was not the first magazine to contain illustrations, but the first to make them a fundamental part of the presentation.

4613. Comic weekly was *The John Donkey*, 16 pages, published by G.B. Zieber and Company of Philadelphia,st six cents a copy or $3 a year. It was edited by Thomas Dunn English and George G. Foster and was illustrated by Felix Octavius Carr Darley and Henry Louis Stephens.

4614. All-fiction pulp magazine was the October 1896 issue of *Argosy*, 192 pages, 7 by 10 inches. It was an outgrowth of an eight-page illustrated weekly for boys and girls edited by Frank Andrew Munsey entitled *The Golden Argosy*, which first appeared on December 9, 1882. It was published in New York City.

4615. Science fiction magazine was *Amazing Stories*, published by radio and television pioneer and science proselytizer Hugo Gernsback, who is credited with coining the term "science fiction." The first issue was dated April 1926 and was published from the New York City offices of Gernsback's Experimenter Publishing Company. It billed itself as the first "Magazine of Scientifiction," a blend of "charming romance intermingled with scientific fact and prophetic vision." Early issues of *Amazing Stories* depended heavily on reprints. Later issues contained original tales by Gernsback and others that were noted for their technological prescience, if not for their sophisticated prose. *Amazing Stories* continued publication under various names until 1994.

4616. Magazine to contain a phonograph record was the November 1955 issue of *Pageant*, published in New York City, which went on sale on October 10, 1955. It contained a 78-r.p.m. acetate recording of "If You Don't Want My Love," sung by Jaye P. Morgan to the accompaniment of Hugo Winterhalter's orchestra. Approximately 1.1 million copies were issued.

4617. Photograph taken in the United States was a daguerreotype, a form of image recording invented by Louis Jacques Mandé Daguerre of France in 1839. The first published description of the method appeared in the *London Globe*, which arrived in the United States on September 20, 1839, on the *British Queen*. Among those who are credited with taking the first daguerreotype are the inventor and artist Samuel Finley Breese Morse, Amasa Holcomb, a Philadelphia lamp maker named Robert Cornelius, and Joseph Saxton, a balance maker at the Philadelphia mint. A picture taken by Dr. John William Draper of his sister Dorothy Catherine Draper in the summer of 1840, using a six-minute sunlight exposure, is believed to be the first daguerreotype portrait.

4618. Commercial photography studio was opened on March 4, 1840, in New York City by Alexander S. Wolcott and John Johnson. On May 8, 1840, Wolcott received the first photography patent, for "a method of taking likenesses by means of a concave reflector and plates so prepared that luminous or other rays will act thereon." The photographs, 1.75 by 2.5 inches, were not reversed, as were daguerreotypes with refracting lenses.

4619. Class photograph was taken by Professor Samuel Finley Breese Morse on August 18, 1840. It showed the Yale College class of 1810 at their 30th reunion in New Haven, CT. He made 35 daguerreotypes, each a half-inch square.

4620. Photograph to gain world fame was a daguerreotype panorama of Niagara Falls, NY, taken in July 1845 by William and Frederick Langenheim of the Philadelphia Daguerrotype Establishment, Philadelphia, PA, from a site near the Clifton House on the Canadian side of the falls. Sets were made and presented to Louis Jacques Mandé Daguerre, President James Knox Polk, Queen Victoria, the kings of Prussia, Saxony, and Wurtemberg, and the Duke of Brunswick.

4621. Photography book was *The History and Practice of the Art of Photography: or, the Production of Pictures Through the Agency of Light, Containing All the Instructions Necessary for the Complete Practice of the Daguerrean and Photogenic Art, Both on Metallic Plates and on Paper*, by Henry Hunt Snelling, published by G.P. Putnam, New York City, in 1849. It contained 139 pages of text.

4622. Photography magazine was the *Daguerreian Journal; devoted to the Daguerreian and Photogenic Arts, also embracing the Sciences, Arts and Literature*, a 32-page octavo fortnightly that was first published on November 1, 1850, in New York City. It sold for 25 cents a copy or $3 a year. S. D. Humphrey was the editor and publisher and William S. Dorr the printer.

4623. Aerial photograph was "Boston as the Eagle and the Wild Goose See It," taken on October 13, 1860, by James Wallace Black of Boston, MA, from a balloon navigated by Samuel Archer King of Providence, RI. The balloon, *The Queen of the Air*, was held by a cable 1,200 feet above the city. Eight pictures were taken, only one of which was good. It showed an area bounded by Brattle Street on the north, the harbor on the east, Sumner Street on the south, and Park Street on the west. Wet plates were used, which were prepared in the balloon before each exposure.

4624. Photographs of combat were two pictures taken during the siege of Charleston, SC, in the summer of 1863 by Southern photographer G. S. Cook. One photograph, taken from the parapet of Fort Moultrie, shows Union gunboats in the act of shelling the fort. The other depicts a shell bursting inside Fort Sumter. No known Civil War photograph shows men in combat.

4625. News photographs of distinction were made during the Civil War by Mathew B. Brady of New York City who, with the permission of President Abraham Lincoln and the Secret Service, followed the Union Army and photographed it in action. He took more than 7,000 pictures, 2,000 of which were purchased by the Government for $25,000. Many of these photographs appeared in a book, *Brady's National Photographic Collection*, in 1870. Brady studied photography with Samuel Finley Breese Morse and had a studio,

Brady's Daguerrian Miniature Gallery, at Broadway and Fulton Street in New York City.

4626. Book showing photographs of movements in sequence was *An Electro-Photographic Investigation of Consecutive Phases of Animal Movements*, by Eadweard Muybridge, begun in 1872, completed in 1885 and published in 11 volumes under the auspices of the University of Pennsylvania in 1887. The 781 plates, comprising 20,000 figures of men, women, children, animals, and birds, were printed by the Photo-Gravure Company of New York.

4627. Photographs showing action were taken by Eadweard Muybridge in 1872 on a stock farm owned by Leland Stanford at Palo Alto, CA. He used a series of 12 clocks for breaking electric circuits connected with camera shutters. This enabled him to take a series of photographs at regular intervals, in rapid succession, of a racehorse in action.

4628. Photograph taken from an airplane was taken by Major H.A. "Jimmie" Erickson on January 10, 1911, in a Curtiss biplane piloted by Charles Hamilton over San Diego, CA.

4629. Photographs taken under the sea that were successful were obtained by John Ernest Williamson at Chesapeake Bay, VA, in 1913 with the use of the Williamson Submarine Tube and Photosphere.

4630. Photograph taken from an airplane at night was taken on November 20, 1925, over Rochester, NY, by Lieutenant George Goddard in cooperation with the Eastman Kodak Company, which supplied a photometer by which the intensity of light was measured. The photographs were taken from a 3,000-foot altitude and showed about three square miles of the city's area. A light bomb was dropped that made a flash lasting 0.05 seconds.

4631. Photographs taken under the sea in natural colors were made for the magazine *National Geographic* off the Tortugas of the Florida Keys on July 16, 1926, and were published in the January 1927 issue. The work was carried out by Dr. William Harding Longley of Goucher College and Charles Martin, chief of the National Geographic Society's photographic laboratory. The camera used in making these autochromes was enclosed in a brass case with a plate-glass window in front of the lens. A supplementary hood was fitted above the regulation reflector. The photographer was able to focus his instrument by means of an acute-angle mirror.

4632. Aerial photograph in natural colors was made in July 1930 by Melville Bell Grosvenor, assistant chief of illustrations of *National Geographic* magazine, and published in the September 1930 issue.

4633. Infrared photograph taken in the dark with a short exposure was made in the Eastman Kodak Research Laboratories in Rochester, NY, on October 7, 1931. A photograph was taken with a one-second exposure, in apparently total darkness, of a group of 50 visitors to the laboratories. The room was flooded with invisible infrared rays, and a new photographic emulsion sensitive to infrared was used.

4634. Aerial photograph showing the lateral curvature of the horizon and the beginning of the stratosphere was taken by Captain Albert William Stevens from the gondola of the stratosphere balloon *Explorer 11*, which was sent up on November 11, 1935, by the National Geographic Society and the Army Air Corps. The photograph was made from an altitude of 72,395 feet, or 13.71 miles, above sea level. It was the first photograph of the horizon taken from such a great altitude; the first photograph for which the line of sight was entirely in the stratosphere; and the first photograph showing the extreme top of the "dust sphere" that marks the dividing line between the lower atmosphere with its clouds and dust and the stratosphere, which is clear. The balloon took off from Rapid City, SD, and landed 8 hours 13 minutes later at White Lake, SD.

4635. Photographer to receive the John Simon Guggenheim Memorial Foundation award was Edward Weston of Los Angeles, CA, who received a $2,500 grant for his series of photographic documents of the West. Announcement of the award was made on March 28, 1937. The photographs, taken with an 8-by-10-inch camera using panchromatic film, were used as illustrations for *California and the West*, by Charis Wilson Weston and Edward Weston, published by Duell, Sloan and Pearce, New York City, in 1940.

4636. Photograph bounced off the moon was transmitted by the Navy from Hawaii and received on January 28, 1960, at Washington, DC.

4637. Photograph bounced off a satellite was a photograph of President Dwight David Eisenhower. On August 18, 1960, it was beamed 1,000 miles up to the satellite *Echo 1* from a dish antenna by the Collins Radio Company, Cedar Rapids, IA. It was received on standard Associated Press Wirephoto equipment by the Alpha Corporation near Dallas, TX.

Technology

4638. Camera exposure scale was prepared by D. W. Seager and published in the March 1840 issue of the *American Repertory of Arts, Sciences, and Manufactures.* The shortest tabulated exposure was five minutes at noon on a very brilliant and clear day; the longest was 50–70 minutes at 3 P.M. on a cloudy day.

4639. Achromatic lenses were made in 1844 in Cambridgeport, MA, by Alvan Clark.

4640. Tintype camera was patented by Professor Hamilton Lamphere Smith, professor of natural sciences, Kenyon College, Gambier, OH, who obtained a patent on February 19, 1856, on "photographic pictures on japanned surfaces." The photographs were collodion positives on black or chocolate-colored iron plates.

4641. Photograph taken by incandescent electric light was a portrait of Charles Batchelor made in December 1879 in Menlo Park, NJ.

4642. Film rolls for cameras were patented by David Henderson Houston of Cambria, WI, who obtained a patent on October 11, 1881, for a "photographic apparatus." He had a camera with a receptacle or box at its inner end containing a "roll of sensitized paper or any other suitable tissue, such as gelatine or any more durable material that may be discovered, and an empty reel, upon which the sensitized band is wound as rapidly as it has been acted upon by the light." The purpose of the camera was "to facilitate taking a number of photographic views successively in a short time."

4643. Camera to use film rolls was Kodak No. 1, a fixed-focus box camera, announced in June 1888 by George Eastman of Rochester, NY. It weighed 22 ounces and had a lens fast enough to make instantaneous exposures. It used a roll of film of 100 exposures and took a round picture 2.5 inches in diameter. It did not require a table or tripod for support. The camera was covered by a patent dated September 4, 1888, and the name Kodak was registered on the same date.

4644. Celluloid photographic film and the process for producing it were invented by the Reverend Hannibal Williston Goodwin of Newark, NJ, who received a patent on September 13, 1898, on "nitro cellulose transparent flexible photographic film pellicles." He received an order from Thomas Alva Edison for one roll at $2.50 on September 2, 1889.

4645. Filmpack camera was the Premo Film Camera, a box camera introduced in 1903 by the Rochester Optical and Camera Company, Rochester, NY. It cost $4. In 1905 the Premo Folding Film bellows camera was offered at $10.

4646. Film-developing machine that was fully automatic was the Photomaton, invented by Anatol M. Josepho, who constructed the first model in a loft building on 125th Street, New York City. He received a patent on January 17, 1928, on an apparatus for developing photographic film strips. The first Photomaton studio was opened to the public at 1659 Broadway, New York City, in September 1926.

4647. Stroboscopic lamp for high-speed photography was invented in 1927 by Harold Eugene "Doc" Edgerton, a graduate student at the Massachusetts Institute of Technology in Cambridge, MA. Edgerton's stroboscope, or strobe, emitted a bright light for a tiny fraction of a second. Previous researchers had conceived of a fast-flashing light, but Edgerton was the first to synchronize a strobe light to the shutter of a camera and develop the techniques of high-speed photography. His stop-action photographs of the splash of a single milk droplet, a bullet in mid-flight, and other previously invisible events revealed a world of unknown natural phenomena. The holder of 47 patents, Edgerton also invented specialized sonar, underwater cameras, and high-intensity lamps.

4648. Photographic flashbulbs that were fireless, smokeless, odorless, and noiseless, similar to incandescent lamp bulbs, were made by the General Electric Company of Schenectady, NY, on August 1, 1930, under a patent awarded on September 23, 1930, to Johannes Ostermeier of Althegnenberg, Germany. A small filament in the bulb, when connected to a source of electricity, became heated and ignited the foil and oxygen, causing a flash of light of high intensity and short duration. The bulb was the size of a 150-watt incandescent bulb.

4649. Camera exposure meter was invented in 1931 by William Nelson Goodwin, Jr., of the Weston Electrical Instrument Corporation, Newark, NJ, who obtained a patent on February 21, 1932, on a thermal ammeter. The first one, manufactured in February 1932, was called the photronic photoelectric cell, popularly known as a camera exposure meter. It contained a dial calculating device for translating brightness values into camera aperture settings. It required no battery for its operation, as it changed light energy directly into electrical energy.

4650. Color film that was commercially successful was Kodachrome, developed by Leopold Godowsky, Jr., and Leopold Damrosch Mannes at the Kodak Research Laboratories in Rochester, NY. Godowsky and Mannes improved on earlier color film products by developing a reversal-process color film with three emulsion layers that was simpler and less expensive to process while yielding good color fidelity. Kodak released Kodachrome 16mm movie film in April 1935 and 35mm still film in August 1936.

4651. Instant camera was the Polaroid camera, invented by Edwin Herbert Land and demonstrated on February 21, 1947, at a meeting of the Optical Society of America at the Hotel Pennsylvania, New York City. The camera contained a specially prepared photographic paper with "pods" of developer and hypo sandwiched with the film. The turning of a knob squeezed open one of the pods, which developed the negative and made the print. The picture was produced in about one minute.

4652. Flashbulb device with multiple flashbulbs was made by the Sylvania Electric Company, Montoursville, PA, and introduced on July 8, 1965, at a press conference at the Waldorf-Astoria Hotel, New York City. It was known as the Flashcube and contained four flash bulbs set in a single socket. A sleeve of three cubes retailed for $1.95. The cubes were presented jointly by Sylvania Electric Products and the Eastman Kodak Company.

Postal Service

4653. Post office in a colony for the collection of mail was established by order of the General Court of Massachusetts on November 5, 1639, in Boston, MA, at the house of Richard Fairbanks for "all letters which are brought from beyond the seas, or are to be sent thither." He was allowed a penny for the transmission of each letter and was accountable to the authorities in charge of the colony.

4654. Postal route between cities was the route between New York City and Boston, MA. On December 10, 1672, Governor Francis Lovelace of New York announced that monthly service would be inaugurated on January 1, 1673. The first post rider left New York City on January 22, 1673, and arrived in Boston three weeks later.

4655. Parliamentary act to establish a colonial post office in the American colonies was passed in April 1692. A royal patent had been granted to Thomas Neale on February 17, 1691, by the English sovereigns William and Mary, with "full power and authority to erect, settle and establish within the chief parts of their Majesties' colonies and plantations in America, an office or offices for the receiving and dispatching of letters and pacquets, and to receive, send and deliver the same under such rates and sums of money as the planters shall agree to give, and to hold and enjoy the same for the term of 21 years." Neale did not come to America but named Andrew Hamilton as postmaster general, an appointment that was confirmed on April 4, 1692, by the English postmaster general.

4656. Postmaster who was a woman was Mary Katherine Goddard, appointed postmaster at Baltimore, MD, in 1775. She served until November 14, 1789. The first woman to be appointed postmaster after the adoption of the Constitution was Sarah De Crow, who was made postmaster at Hertford, NC, on September 27, 1792. She was the only woman among 195 postmasters.

4657. Postmaster general under the Continental Congress was Benjamin Franklin, who was appointed on July 26, 1775, by the Second Continental Congress at a salary of $1,000 a year and who served until November 7, 1776. He had served the crown as deputy postmaster at Philadelphia, PA, from 1737 to 1753, and as deputy postmaster general for the colonies from 1753 to 1774.

4658. Mail franking privilege allowing free use of the mail was granted to members of Congress and private soldiers in service on November 8, 1775. Regulations of January 9, 1776, provided that soldiers' mail was to be franked by the officer in charge. On April 3, 1800, free franking of mail during her natural life was granted to Martha Washington.

4659. Postmaster general of the United States was Samuel Osgood, who was appointed by President George Washington and who served from September 26, 1789, to August 19, 1791. His office was authorized by act of Congress of September 22, 1789, which gave the general supervision of the post office to a postmaster general under the direction of the President. Other postmasters under Washington's administration were Timothy Pickering, appointed in 1791, and Joseph Habersham, in 1797.

4660. Postal service law enacted by Congress was signed by President George Washington on February 20, 1792. This act set the rates at 6 cents for letters to be carried not more than 30 miles, 8 cents between 30 and 60 miles, 10 cents between 60 and 100 miles, and 12.5 cents between 100 and 150 miles.

4661. Mailbox see-through locker was invented in 1810 by Thomas Brown, who was governor of Florida from 1849 to 1853. His mailboxes consisted of a series of numbered pigeonholes with glass fronts. People who owned or rented boxes were thus able to see whether there was any mail waiting for them without having to open the box.

4662. Mail delivery by steamboat was authorized by act of Congress of February 27, 1813. The postmaster general was granted the power to transport mail in steamboats as long as the expense was not more, "taking into consideration distance, expedition and frequency, than is paid for carrying the mail by stages on the post road, or roads, adjacent to the course of such steamboats."

4663. Dead letter office of the Post Office Department was organized in 1825 in Washington, DC. A dead letter is a letter that is unclaimed and undeliverable.

4664. Post office building built for that purpose was the Custom House and Post Office in Newport, RI, built in 1829 and occupied in 1830. An act of Congress approved on May 24, 1828, authorized the erection of the building. The title to the site was vested in the government on November 12, 1828.

4665. Ocean mail contracts were authorized by act of Congress of March 3, 1845, "to provide for the transportation of the mail between the United States and foreign countries." The first contract was made in 1847 with the Ocean Navigation Company, which agreed to transport United States mail once a month between the ports of New York City; Southampton, England; and Bremen, Germany. Compensation was $16,666 for each round trip. The *Washington*, pioneer of American ocean steamers, started this service on June 1, 1847. The contract expired on June 1, 1857.

4666. Postal directory was *A List of Post Offices in the United States with the Names of the Postmasters on the first of July 1855, also the Principal Regulations of the Post Office Department*, compiled by Daniel Tompkins Leech of the Post Office Department and printed by George S. Gideon, Washington, DC, in 1855. It contained 146 pages of directory, 48 pages of regulations, and six pages of miscellaneous material.

4667. Registered mail was authorized by act of Congress of March 3, 1855. The system was placed in operation on July 1, 1855. The fee was five cents.

4668. Street letter box was invented by Albert Potts of Philadelphia, PA, who obtained a patent on March 9, 1858, on "a mode of attaching metallic letter-boxes." The box had a center hole through which the shaft of an ordinary cast-iron lamppost was placed. Boxes were erected on August 2, 1858, in Boston and New York City.

4669. Overland mail service to the Pacific Coast was begun on September 15, 1858, by the Overland Mail coaches, the old John Butterfield stage line. Stages left Tipton, MO, and San Francisco, CA, simultaneously every Monday and Thursday. The route was operated under government contract, authorized by act of Congress of March 3, 1857. The contract was signed on September 16, 1857, and specified payment of $600,000 a year for six years, for semiweekly trips in both directions, in "good fourhorse post coaches or spring wagons suitable for the convenience of passengers as well as safety and security of the mails." The specified running time for the 2,800 miles was a maximum of 25 days. The first trips were made in a little less than 24 days.

4670. Airmail dispatched from a post office in a balloon and bearing postage stamps was sent in the *Jupiter*, piloted by John Wise. On July 1, 1859, Wise endeavored to fly mail from St. Louis, MO, to New York City, but he jettisoned it in a storm over Lake Ontario. On August 17, he left Lafayette, IN, carrying 123 letters and 23 circulars in a pouch. His destination was New York City, but instead he landed at Crawfordsville, IN, about 27 miles south of the takeoff point.

4671. Pony Express mail left St. Joseph, MO, and Sacramento, CA, simultaneously on April 3, 1860, carried by Henry Wallace riding west and John Roff riding east. The westbound packet was delivered in 10 days, the eastbound in 12. (According to some accounts, the first rider westward was William Richardson or John Frey, and the first rider eastward was Samuel Hamilton, who rode 20 miles in 59 minutes.) The route went through Fort Kearney, Fort Laramie, Fort Bridger, Salt Lake City, Camp Floyd, Carson City, Washoe Silver Mines, and Placerville. Until the service was discontinued on October 24, 1861, riders left St. Joseph every day at noon and Sacramento every day at 8 A.M. except on Sundays. It was a private enterprise under a charter granted by the state of Kansas to the Central Overland and Pike's Peak Express Company. The charge was $5 a half ounce.

Library of Congress, Prints & Photographs Division LC-USZ62-5398

The overland Pony Express.

4672. Newspaper wrappers for mailing newspapers were issued in October 1861 under act of Congress of February 27, 1861. They were manila and buff, and bore a one-cent blue stamp with the head of Benjamin Franklin. In 1863, a two-cent wrapper was added, bearing a black stamp with the head of Andrew Jackson.

4673. Postage stamp catalog was compiled by A. C. Kline, 824 Walnut Street, Philadelphia, PA, in 1862. It listed 1,500 varieties of stamps. Its title was *The Stamp Collector's Manual, Being a complete guide to the collectors of American and Foreign postage and despatch stamps.*

4674. Railroad post office was placed in operation on July 28, 1862, on Missouri's Hannibal and St. Joseph Railroad during the administration of Postmaster General Montgomery Blair. The idea was originated by William Augustine Davis and the mail was car built at Hannibal, MO.

4675. Free mail delivery in cities was authorized by congressional act of March 3, 1863. City delivery service was placed in operation on July 1, 1863, in 49 major cities, using 440 carriers at an annual cost of $300,000. On January 3, 1887, free delivery service was extended to cities with populations of 50,000 or more and was permitted in places having a population of at least 10,000 and postal receipts of $10,000.

4676. Money order system was established on November 1, 1864, in order to promote public convenience and ensure safety in the transfer by mail of small sums of money. Foreign service was authorized on July 27, 1868. The first agreement was made with Switzerland, effective September 1, 1869. Service was extended to Great Britain in October 1871 and to Germany in October 1872.

4677. Stamp collection magazine was the *Stamp Collector's Record*, which consisted of four pages, 5.5 by 8.25 inches, two columns to a page, first published on December 15, 1864, at Albany, NY, by Samuel Allan Taylor. It was issued on the 15th of every month and sold for 50 cents a year. The rate for advertising was 15 cents a line.

4678. Uniforms for mail carriers were authorized by Congress on July 27, 1868, by an act that authorized the postmaster general "to prescribe a uniform dress to be worn by the letter-carriers." A standard uniform was approved on October 31, 1868.

4679. Mail fraud law enacted by Congress was enacted on June 8, 1872. It outlawed any "fraudulent lottery, gift enterprise, or scheme for the distribution of money, or of any real or personal property, by lot, chance, or drawing of any kind, or in conducting any other scheme or device for obtaining money through the mails by means of false or fraudulent pretenses, representations, or promises." The postmaster general was authorized to stamp mail, registered mail, and money orders "fraudulent" and return them to the sender instead of making the delivery to the addressee.

4680. Postal card was issued on May 1, 1873, under act of Congress of June 8, 1872. A one-cent stamp printed on the upper right-hand corner showed a profile of the Goddess of Liberty looking to the left and surrounded by a lathework border with the words "U.S. Postage" inserted above, and the words "One Cent" below. The body of the card was light buff, the printing velvet brown. The size of the card was 3 by 5.125 inches. The cards were made by the Morgan Envelope Company, Springfield, MA. The first known cancellation was May 12, 1873.

4681. Mail chute for dropping mail from the upper stories of office buildings, hotels, apartment houses, and other tall structures was installed in 1883 in the Elwood Building, Rochester, NY, following plans prepared by James Goold Cutler, the architect of the building, who received a patent for a mail chute on September 11, 1883. The device was later developed and suited to the requirements of the Post Office and public use by Joseph Warren Cutler under a series of about 30 patents issued to him.

4682. Special delivery mail service was authorized by congressional act of March 3, 1885. The service was established on October 1, 1885, and at first was restricted to free delivery offices in towns of 4,000 or more inhabitants. An additional charge of 10 cents a letter was made for this service, and a blue special delivery stamp was required. On August 4, 1886, the service was extended to all free delivery offices.

4683. Reply-paid card was the one-cent black on buff reply card attached to a one-cent black on buff message card issued on October 25, 1892, as a souvenir of the World's Columbian Exposition held in Chicago, IL. It showed a likeness of President Ulysses Simpson Grant. It was sold as two unsevered cards, one for the message and one for the reply. The message card had originally been issued as a single card on December 16, 1891.

4684. Rural free mail delivery was established on October 1, 1896, when three routes were designated in West Virginia: one from Charles Town, one from Uvilla, and one from Halltown.

4685. Postcard privately printed and mailed was authorized on May 19, 1898. The regulation allowed the use of private mailing cards of the same form, quality, and weight as postal cards printed by the government. Postcards, unlike postal cards, required a one-cent stamp.

4686. Mail truck built especially for mail collection was constructed by the Winton Motor Vehicle Company of Cleveland, OH, in 1899. A test was made in Cleveland over a 22-mile route, when mail was collected from 120 boxes. Although the test was made in a severe snowstorm under adverse conditions, the trip took only 2 hours 27 minutes. A horse and wagon took six hours to make the same trip.

4687. Bulk mail was authorized by Congress on April 28, 1904, and went into use on October 1, 1904. It permitted 2,000 or more identical pieces of third-class or fourth-class mail to be mailed without stamps affixed, in exchange for a fee. The denomination of the postage, the place of mailing, and the permit issued by the post office for the mailing was printed in place of the stamp.

4688. Navy mail service was established on May 27, 1908, when an appropriation was made for the year ending June 30, 1909, to designate enlisted men of the Navy as naval mail clerks for an extra $500 in pay and assistant naval mail clerks for an extra $300. The U.S.S. *Illinois, Prairie*, and *Rhode Island* were the first vessels equipped with postal facilities, beginning on August 15, 1908.

4689. Post office aboard a naval vessel was established on August 20, 1908, on the U.S.S. *Nebraska.*

4690. Airmail pilot was Earl Lewis Ovington, who was sworn in on September 23, 1911, at Garden City, Long Island, NY, as "air mail pilot number one." In his Blériot monoplane, *Dragonfly*, he delivered airmail from Postmaster General Frank Harris Hitchcock in Garden City to postmaster William McCarthy in Mineola, NY, a distance of six miles, inaugurating the first official airmail service authorized by the Post Office Department. The first mail consisted of 640 letters and 1,280 postcards that bore the cancellation "Aeroplane No. 1, Garden City Estates, NY."

4691. Parcel post service was authorized on August 24, 1912, when appropriations were made for the service that started on January 1, 1913. Previously the weight limit of mail had been four pounds. The rates of the parcel post service depended upon the weight of the package and the distance carried.

4692. Airmail regular service was established on August 12, 1918, by the Post Office Department between New York City and Washington, DC. Ben B. Lipsner was the first superintendent of airmail. The pilots were Edward V. Gardner, Maurice Newton, Max Miller, and Robert F. Shank.

4693. International airmail was inaugurated on March 3, 1919, between Seattle, WA, and Victoria, British Columbia, Canada, a distance of 74 miles, by Edward Hubbard of the Hubbard Air Service, who piloted a Boeing Type C open cockpit biplane with pontoons. William Edward Boeing was a passenger on the flight. Regular service under contract began on October 14, 1920, and continued under successive contracts until June 30, 1937.

4694. Postage meter was officially set at Stamford, CT, by the Pitney-Bowes Postage Meter Company on November 16, 1920. Although the idea of metered mail originated in 1900, when the American Postage Meter Company was organized in Chicago, it was not until September 1, 1920, that the Post Office Department approved it. About $2 million was spent on research and development of the machine.

4695. Transcontinental airmail flight was from San Francisco, CA, to New York City. The plane left San Francisco at 4:30 A.M. on February 22, 1921, and arrived at Hazelhurst Field, Long Island, NY, at 4:50 P.M. on February 23, 33 hours 20 minutes later. The actual flying time was 25 hours 16 minutes; the average speed for the 2,629 miles was 104 miles per hour.

4696. Transcontinental regular airmail service was established between New York City and San Francisco, CA on July 1, 1924, when the airmail-railroad service was discontinued. The first westward flight of this service was made by Wesley Leland Smith, who flew from New York City to Cleveland, OH, and the first eastward flight by Claire K. Vance, who flew from San Francisco, CA, to Reno, NV. The service was daily including Sunday, with 14 stops en route.

4697. Drive-up mailbox enabling motorists to mail letters without moving from the seats of their cars was installed in July 1927 at Houston, TX. The box had metal handles 8 to 10 inches long and was tilted 4 inches. The boxes were known as "courtesy collection boxes."

4698. Airmail service from ship to shore was inaugurated on August 13, 1928, by the Trans-Atlantic Aerial Company when an amphibian was launched from the *Ile de France*, 400 miles at sea. Three sacks of mail, including two packages of films, were delivered to New York City 15 hours before the ship docked. Service was discontinued on September 28, 1928.

4699. International dogsled mail left Lewiston, ME, on December 20, 1928, with Alden William Pulsifer, postmaster of Minot, ME, in charge, and arrived on January 14, 1929, at Montreal, Canada. The mail traveled in a regular eight-foot mushing sled weighing 200 pounds, pulled by six blackhead Eskimo dogs. They averaged nine miles an hour (seven to eight on bare ground) and covered from 40 to 60 miles a day. The mail pouch contained 385 letters in government-stamped canceled envelopes. The trip was not an official one. The sled returned to Lewiston on February 2, 1929, having passed through 118 cities and covered 600 miles, of which 90 percent was bare of snow.

4700. Airmail letter sheet depicted an airplane in blue on white stock and was placed on sale on January 12, 1929. The stamped sheet, issued by the Post Office Department, was designed to be folded and serve as an envelope. It cost five cents.

4701. Transpacific airmail flight and the first air crossing from California to the Philippines was made by the *China Clipper* of Pan American Airways, commanded by Edwin Charles Musick. The plane left San Francisco, CA, on November 22, 1935, at 3:46 A.M. and made stops at Honolulu, Midway, Wake, and Guam, landing at Manila, Philippine Islands, on November 28 at 11:31 P.M., having covered 8,210 miles in 59 hours 48 minutes. It carried 58 sacks of mail containing 110,865 letters. The return trip started on December 1, 1935, from Manila and was completed on December 6 at 10:37 A.M. at San Francisco, CA. The eastbound flight was made in 63 hours 24 minutes. The total flying time was 123 hours 12 minutes.

4702. Letter to circumnavigate the world by commercial airmail was dispatched from New York City on April 19, 1937. It was routed via San Francisco, Hong Kong, Penang, Amsterdam, and Brazil and was returned to New York on May 25, 1937.

4703. Coin-operated mailbox was the Mailomat, combining a postage meter with a U.S. letter box. Manufactured by the Pitney-Bowes Postage Meter Company, Stamford, CT, the first machine was installed at the General Post Office, New York City, on May 17, 1939. It was covered by a patent granted on July 28, 1942, to Linden A. Thatcher of Stamford, CT. Coins were dropped in slots, the desired stamp denomination was dialed, and the letter was inserted in a letter slot. The machine did the rest automatically, printing a meter stamp with postmark and date of mailing and holding the letter for scheduled collection. It provided postage from 1 cent to 33 cents, including airmail, special delivery, and other services. It obviated the need for ordinary adhesive stamps, operated day or night, and speeded mail delivery because metered mail needs no post office "facing," canceling, or postmarking.

4704. Transatlantic airmail service was inaugurated by Pan American Airways on May 20, 1939, when the *Yankee Clipper*, a four-engine, 41.5-ton flying boat, took off from Manhasset Bay, Port Washington, NY, at 9:07 P.M. It made one stop at Horta, in the Azores, and arrived at Lisbon, Portugal, on May 21 at 8:42 P.M. The elapsed time was 26.5 hours, the flying time 20 hours 16 minutes. It was commanded by Captain Arthur Earl La Porte and carried a crew of 14, 3 airline employees, and 1,680 pounds of mail.

4705. Jet airplane to transport mail was a P-80 Shooting Star that on June 22, 1946, carried a letter addressed to President Harry S. Truman. It was piloted by Captain Robert Atkinson Baird III of Clarksdale, MS, who left the Schenectady County Airport, Schenectady, NY, and arrived at the National Airport, Washington, DC, a distance of 370 miles, in 49 minutes. Another jet-propelled P-80, piloted by Major Kenneth Oscar Chilstrom of Elmhurst, IL, left for Dayton, OH, with a letter for Orville Wright and, after a stopover at Wright Field, arrived at Chicago, IL, in 2 hours 2 minutes.

4706. Parcel post international air service was inaugurated on March 15, 1948, between the United States and 21 countries in Europe and Africa. Service to South America was instituted on September 4, 1948, and to the Pacific area on September 11.

4707. Parcel post domestic air service was authorized on June 29, 1948, and began on September 1, 1948. Overnight delivery of packages was planned. The country was divided into eight postal zones, with a maximum rate of 80 cents for the first pound and 65 cents for each additional pound or fraction thereof.

4708. Airmail postal card was the four-cent card issued on January 10, 1949. It depicted an eagle in flight, printed in orange-red on buff stock.

4709. Commemorative postal card depicted the uplifted arm of the Statue of Liberty holding a flaming torch. It was issued on May 4, 1956, at New York City to commemorate the Fifth International Philatelic Exhibit, held at the Coliseum, New York City, from April 28 to May 6, 1956. It was a two-cent deep carmine and dark blue triangular design on buff stock.

4710. Airmail by missile to be officially dispatched was sent from the submarine U.S.S. *Barbero*, about 100 miles at sea off the Atlantic coast, to the Mayport Naval Auxiliary Station near Jacksonville, FL, on June 8, 1959. Bearing four-cent postage rather than seven-cent airmail stamps, 3,000 letters were shot in a 36-foot Regulus 1 winged missile at about 600 miles per hour. The missile landed 22 minutes after being launched. The letters, signed by Postmaster General Arthur Ellsworth Summerfield, were addressed to President Dwight David Eisenhower and to other government officials and important personages. The project was under the supervision of Captain Arnold Schade.

4711. Post office fully mechanized was opened on October 20, 1960, in Providence, RI. A $20 million experimental installation designated Project Turnkey and built by Intelex Systems, a subsidiary of the International Telephone and Telegraph Corporation, was leased to the Post Office Department for 20 years. Letters were electronically faced and canceled and automatically transported to 300 destination bins at the rate of 18,000 per hour.

4712. Zip codes to speed mail delivery were inaugurated in July 1963. The system assigned five-digit codes to each location in the United States, with the first digit indicating the region. The word "zip" stands for "Zone Improvement Plan." It was preceded by a two-digit system that was put into use by the Post Office Department on May 1, 1943, at Pittsburgh, PA, and later in 125 of its large-volume offices.

4713. International postal card was the 7-cent single and identical 14-cent reply-paid postal card designed by Suren H. Ermoyan and placed on sale at New York City on August 30, 1963. It depicted a map of North America, highlighting Alaska and the continental United States, and was printed on white stock by offset. It bore the slogan "World vacationland, USA" against a bright blue background to publicize the Visit USA program.

4714. Self-service post office was an unattended unit installed in the Wheaton Plaza Regional Shopping Center at Wheaton, MD, on October 17, 1964. Located on a concrete island in the parking area, it dispensed stamps, envelopes, and postal cards at the same price as at stamp windows. It had a machine to make change for coins and bills, a scale for weighing letters and parcels up to 50 pounds, and a zone map for calculating parcel postage.

4715. Pictorial postal cards printed by the Government Printing Office, Washington, DC, were issued on June 29, 1972, at Boston, MA, in observance of Tourism Year of the Americas. There were five pictorial cards, each 6 by 4.25 inches, printed in black and dull orange on beige stock: three 6-cent cards for regular domestic surface mail; a 9-cent airpost card for domestic airmail, including Canada and Mexico; and a 15-cent card for international airmail beyond Canada and Mexico. Each featured four outstanding tourist attractions on the reverse side.

Stamps

4716. Adhesive postage stamps were used by the City Despatch Post, established on February 15, 1842, by Alexander M. Greig, with its principal office at 46 William Street, New York City. They were engraved by Rawdon, Wright and Hatch, New York City, and printed in sheets of 42. They were a three-cent denomination and sold for $2.50 for a hundred stamps.

4717. Postage stamps issued by the Post Office Department were authorized by act of Congress of March 3, 1847, and were placed on sale in New York City on July 1, 1847. The issue consisted of two stamps, a 5-cent red-brown stamp depicting Benjamin Franklin and a 10-cent black stamp bearing the likeness of George Washington. These were the first stamps that bore the likeness of a president. They were printed by Rawdon, Wright, Hatch and Edson of New York City. They were withdrawn from use on June 30, 1851. The issue consisted of 3,712,200 of the 5-cent denomination and 891,000 of the 10-cent denomination. The first stamps printed by the Bureau of Engraving and Printing were the 1894 issue of the "triangle" design stamps.

4718. Postage stamps depicting the American eagle were the one-cent carrier's stamps in blue, issued on November 17, 1851.

4719. Stamped envelopes were issued in June 1853 under congressional act of August 31, 1852, and were manufactured by George F. Nesbitt and Company of New York City under a contract dated October 25, 1852. They showed the profile of George Washington in an oval, the value above, and "cents" below.

They were printed on white and buff paper. The first series included a 3-cent red, a 6-cent red and green, and a 10-cent green.

4720. Postage stamp issued with perforations was the one-cent blue Benjamin Franklin, issued on February 24, 1857. Originally issued in sheets on July 1, 1851, the stamp bore the inscriptions "U.S. Postage" and "One Cent." The picture on the stamp was modeled after the bust of Franklin by Jean Jacques Caffieri. All U.S. postage stamps issued previously were imperforate, as were many after 1857.

4721. Mourning postage stamp was the 15-cent black postage stamp depicting the assassinated President Abraham Lincoln, issued on June 17, 1866. A 10-cent and a 12-cent black stamp showing portraits of George Washington had been issued on July 1, 1847, and July 1, 1851, but these were not mourning stamps.

4722. Stamp collection society was the New York Philatelic Society, organized on March 21, 1867, in New York City, by eight collectors of postage stamps. The first president was the Reverend J. A. Morley, D.D., LL.D.

4723. Postage stamps depicting scenes were the series of 1869, issued from March 1, 1869, to April 9, 1870. The designs were furnished by the National Bank Note Company of New York City, which received a contract on December 12, 1868, for furnishing the stamps. There were 10 denominations. The 2-cent stamp depicted a post horse and rider, the 3-cent brown a locomotive, the 12-cent ultramarine blue and green a steamboat, the 15-cent Prussian blue the landing of Columbus, and the 24-cent light green the signing of the Declaration of Independence. The 1-cent ocher, 6-cent ultramarine blue, and 90-cent black and carmine stamps carried portraits of Franklin, Washington, and Lincoln, respectively. The 10-cent orange and 30-cent carmine and blue stamps pictured an eagle resting on a shield.

4724. Postage stamp depicting the American flag was the 30-cent blue and carmine stamp issued on May 15, 1869. It depicted an eagle with outstretched wings, facing to the left, resting on a shield with flags grouped on either side.

4725. Stamp auction was held on the evening of May 28, 1870, at the Clinton Hall Book Sales Rooms and Art Galleries, New York City, by Leavitt, Streibeigh and Company, auctioneers. About 14,000 stamps in 269 lots were offered for sale. The highest price for a single lot was $38 for 1,800 stamps. The highest price for a single stamp was $11, the lowest 35 cents. The bid for the first lot, 100 foreign stamps, started at 25 cents and closed at 60 cents. The total receipts for the day were approximately $500.

4726. Public exhibition of postage stamps was held from May 10 to November 10, 1876, in the United States Building at the Centennial Exhibition at Fairmount Park, Philadelphia, PA. It was arranged by John Walter Scott. The first important exhibit by collectors opened on March 11, 1889, at the Eden Musée, New York City, where 31 exhibitors showed 272 sheets of stamps from 161 countries, valued in excess of $200,000.

4727. Commemorative postage stamps issued by the Post Office Department were the Columbian series of 1893, which depicted incidents in the discovery of America by Christopher Columbus. The stamps were of 16 denominations and ranged in value from one cent to $5. They were issued on January 2, 1893, with the exception of the eight-cent stamp, which was issued on March 3. The World's Columbian Exposition at Chicago, IL, was held from May 1 to October 30, 1893, to celebrate the 400th anniversary of Columbus's voyage of discovery.

4728. Postage stamps depicting a woman were the Columbus commemorative stamps of 1893. Queen Isabella was depicted on three varieties that were placed on sale on January 2, 1893. The 5-cent stamp (35,248,250 issued) was in chocolate brown and depicted "Columbus Soliciting the Aid of Isabella"; the $1 stamp (55,050 issued) was in rose salmon and showed "Isabella Pledging Her Jewels"; and the $4 stamp (26,350 issued) was in carmine, with portraits of Columbus and Isabella. Women were also shown as characters in group scenes in this set, but their identity was not given.

4729. Books of postage stamps were issued on April 16, 1900. They contained two-cent stamps. Books containing 12 stamps cost 25 cents each; books containing 24 stamps cost 49 cents; and books containing 48 stamps cost 97 cents.

4730. Postage stamp depicting an American woman was a violet-black eight-cent stamp, issued on December 6, 1902, that showed the likeness of Martha Washington. The portrait was based on a painting by Gilbert Stuart.

4731. Postage stamp depicting a Native American was the five-cent Jamestown Commemorative issued on May 7, 1907, to honor the first permanent English settlement in America, at Jamestown, VA, in 1607. It showed a likeness of Pocahontas, who is said to have saved the life of Captain John Smith when he was captured by warriors of the Powhatan Confederacy, ruled by her father, Chief Powhatan. She later married the colonist John Rolfe and visited England, where she was received with royal honors and where she died in 1617 at the age of about 22.

Library of Congress, Prints & Photographs Division
LC-USZ62-5258

The wedding of Pocahontas and John Rolfe.

4732. Postage stamps in coils were issued on February 18, 1908. They were coarsely perforated, 8.5 holes to two centimeters, and were printed by the Bureau of Engraving and Printing, Washington, DC, for the Post Office Department. The first coils prepared from sheets had appeared in 1902. They were made from sheets of 400 stamps cut into strips of 20 and spliced together into rolls to be used in vending and affixing machines by commercial organizations.

4733. Memorial postage stamp was the Lincoln two-cent memorial issue, commemorating the 100th anniversary of the birth of Abraham Lincoln, that was placed on sale on February 12, 1909. This stamp was red, the size and shape of the regular issue of postage stamps. It depicted a profile of the head of Lincoln from Saint-Gaudens's statue in an oval with the words "1809 Feb. 12 1909" on a ribbon below.

4734. Airmail stamps were issued on May 13, 1918, and consisted of three denominations: 6-cent orange, 16-cent green, and 24-cent carmine, rose, and blue, all with airplanes depicted on them. The 24-cent stamp was placed on sale on May 13, the 16-cent on July 11, and the 6-cent on December 6.

4735. Precanceled stamps printed on rotary presses at the Bureau of Engraving and Printing, Washington, DC, were issued on April 21, 1923. This initial order embraced one-cent stamps of the 1923 series. One-cent precanceled stamps in coils were first issued on January 7, 1924. Prior to the addition of precanceling devices to rotary presses, the Bureau of Engraving and Printing precanceled one-cent stamps in sheets for a limited number of post offices with electrotype plates containing 400 stamps each. The records indicate that Bureau-precanceled stamps of this style were first issued to the post offices in New Orleans, LA, Augusta, ME, and Springfield, MA, in January 1917.

4736. Sheet of souvenir postage stamps was the White Plains Commemorative, issued to commemorate the 150th anniversary of the Battle of White Plains. The sheet consisted of 25 two-cent horizontal rectangle stamps printed in red ink. The margins of each sheet bore the inscription "International Philatelic Exhibition, October 16 to 23, 1926, New York, NY, U.S.A." The sheets were placed on sale on October 18, 1926, and were not issued to postmasters for sale to the general public. They were printed in sheets of 100 subjects in four panes of 25 two-cent stamps, each separated by one-inch gutters with central guidelines. The regular sheets containing 100 stamps were also placed on sale on the same date.

4737. First-day special cancellation of a postage stamp was prepared for the Virginia Dare commemorative stamp, released on August 18, 1937, at Manteo, NC. The one-inch-square blue five-cent stamp commemorated the 350th anniversary of her birth. Virginia Dare, the child of English settlers in Sir Walter Raleigh's Roanoke colony, was the first English child born in America.

4738. Postage stamp depicting an African-American showed the educator Booker Taliaferro Washington, whose likeness was on the 10-cent brown stamp first placed on sale on April 7, 1940, at Tuskegee Institute, AL. The stamp was one of the Famous American Commemorative series issue of 1940. A three-cent deep blue stamp depicting the log cabin in which Washington lived had been issued on April 5, 1936.

Courtesy of Images of American Political History

Booker T. Washington

4739. Postage stamp depicting a Jew commemorated the labor leader Samuel Gompers, one of the founders of the American Federation of Labor. The three-cent, bright red-violet postage stamp was issued on January 27, 1950, at Washington, DC, to commemorate the centenary of Gompers' birth. The stamps were printed by rotary press, 70 stamps to the pane.

4740. United Nations postage stamps in U.S. denominations were placed on sale on October 24, 1951, on United Nations Day in New York City. Six stamps were issued on that date: 1-cent magenta, 1.5-cent blue green, 3-cent magenta and blue, 5-cent blue, 25-cent olive gray and blue, and $1 red. Five stamps were issued on November 16, 1951: 2-cent purple, 10-cent chocolate, 15-cent violet and blue, 20-cent dark brown, and 50-cent indigo. The stamps were only valid for use from United Nations headquarters.

4741. Postage stamp issued jointly by two countries was the four-cent green and rose Mexican Independence stamp commemorating the 150th anniversary of Mexican independence, issued by the United States and Mexico on September 16, 1960, in Los Angeles, CA. It was designed by Leon Helguera and Charles Chickering. The first holiday stamp jointly issued by the United States and another country was the USPS/Israeli Holiday Celebration Series Chanukah stamp, simultaneously issued in Washington, DC, and Jerusalem on October 23, 1996. The stamp art, identical in its American and Israeli versions, portrayed a Chanukah menorah.

4742. Postage stamp featuring a work of art in true color was the four-cent stamp placed on sale on October 4, 1961, at Washington, DC, to commemorate the 100th anniversary of the birth of Frederic Remington, artist of the West. Shown on the stamp is

Courtesy of Images of American Political History and the Library of Congress

Samuel Gompers

a portion of Remington's oil painting *The Smoke Signal*, from the Amon Carter Museum of Western Art, Fort Worth, TX. The stamp was printed on Giori presses in gradations of red, blue, and yellow on white paper.

4743. Postage stamp issued on the date of the event it commemorated was the Project Mercury commemorative of 1962, placed on sale throughout the nation on February 20, 1962. This four-cent dark blue and yellow stamp showed the spaceship in which Colonel John Glenn orbited the earth. Three million covers were canceled the first day at Cape Canaveral, FL.

4744. Christmas postage stamp regular issue was placed on sale on November 1, 1962, at Pittsburgh, PA. It was a four-cent red and green stamp, showing burning candles and an evergreen wreath with a red bow and the inscription "Christmas 1962." It was designed by Jim Crawford and printed by the Giori press, 400 subjects to a sheet, in four panes of 100 each. The first Christmas stamp series to depict both a religious and a nonreligious subject was the eight-cent series issued on November 10, 1971, at Washington, DC. The religious stamp, multicolored with gold, was an adaptation of Giorgione's *Adoration of the Shepherds*, designed by Bradbury Thompson. The nonreligious stamp was dark green, red, and multicolored, designed by Jamie Wyeth and printed by rotogravure on the Andreotti rotary press. It was entitled *A Partridge in a Pear Tree*.

4745. Postage stamp with fluorescent tagging was the eight-cent fire-red stamp issued on August 1, 1963, at Dayton, OH. It depicted a jet airplane soaring past the dome of the Capitol. Under fluorescent light, the stamp glowed an orange red. The stamp was the regular airmail stamp issued on December 5, 1962, at Washington, DC, to meet new postal rates that would take effect on January 7, 1963.

4746. Commemorative postage stamp depicting a president's wife was the five-cent light purple stamp issued on October 11, 1963, at Washington, DC, on the anniversary of the birthday of Eleanor Roosevelt, the wife of Franklin Delano Roosevelt.

4747. Postage stamps of four different designs sold as a single sheet of regular size was the 1964 Christmas issue of five-cent green and carmine postage stamps, depicting holly, mistletoe, poinsettia, and a sprig of conifer. Each pane of 100 contained 25 blocks of four different stamps. They were placed on sale at Bethlehem, PA, on November 9, 1964.

4748. Postage stamp issued in the United States and canceled by a foreign country was the five-cent multicolored postage stamp commemorating the 100th anniversary of Canada's achievement of federation, issued on May 25, 1967, at the United States Pavillion at Expo 67, Montreal, Canada. The date of issue and cancelation coincided with President Lyndon Baines Johnson's visit to Ottawa and Montreal. The stamp was designed by Ivan Chermayeff of New York City and showed a symbolic depiction of the scenic grandeur of Canada.

4749. Twin postage stamps were issued on September 29, 1967, and were first placed on sale at the Kennedy Space Center, at a branch of the Orlando, FL, post office. A single horizontal design picture was perforated through the center. Each half was of the five-cent denomination and could be used separately. The pair could also be used as a 10-cent stamp. The stamp on the left depicted an astronaut in space and the stamp on the right showed the Gemini spaceship with the earth in the background. It was designed by Paul Calle of Stamford, CT. Each sheet contained 200 subjects in four panes of 50 each.

4750. Gravure-printed postage stamp was a horizontal five-cent stamp printed by the Bureau of Engraving and Printing, Washington, DC, and issued on November 2, 1967,

Library of Congress, Prints & Photographs Division
LC-USZ62-25812

Eleanor Roosevelt

at Washington, DC. It was printed with red, yellow, blue, and black inks and featured a photographic reproduction of Thomas Eakins's oil painting *The Biglin Brothers Racing* surrounded by a gold frame. The original picture, which depicts a sculling scene on the Schuylkill River near Philadelphia, PA, hangs in the National Gallery of Art, Washington, DC.

4751. Postage stamp depicting a living American was the multicolored 10-cent airmail stamp, 1.05 by 1.8 inches, issued on September 9, 1969, to commemorate the moon landing of *Apollo 11* on July 20, 1969. It showed astronaut Neil Alden Armstrong stepping onto the moon from the *Eagle*. The stamp was printed in sheets of 128 and panes of 32 stamps, instead of the usual sheets of 200 and panes of 50, and was a horizontal stamp. The plates used for printing the stamp were made from a master steel die that had been on board the *Apollo 11* landing module and had made the round-trip journey to the moon.

4752. Books of postage stamps with humidity-resistant adhesive that eliminated the need for tissue paper between the leaves were booklets of one-cent and six-cent stamps issued on March 1, 1971, at Washington, DC. The adhesive gum had a dull finish instead of the conventional glossy finish. The booklet cost $2 each and contained four panes of eight 6-cent stamps and one pane of eight 1-cent stamps. The first production order was for 2 million booklets.

4753. Self-adhesive postage stamp was the 10-cent Dove of Peace precanceled Christmas stamp issued on November 15, 1974, at New York City. It depicted a dove weather vane.

4754. Postage stamps without a denomination were the Christmas stamps printed in plates of 200 subjects in four panes of 50 each and issued on October 14, 1975, in Washington, DC. The stamps sold for 10 cents each and were printed before the postage rate was increased to 13 cents. One was based on a painting by Domenico Ghirlandaio in the National Gallery of Art, Washington, DC, the other on a Christmas greeting card produced by Louis Prang in Boston in 1878.

4755. Postage stamps of 50 different designs sold as a single sheet were part of the American Bicentennial Issue, displaying 50 state flags in varied colors, issued on February 23, 1976. They were sold in plates of 200 in four panes of 50 each. The designer was Walt Reed.

4756. Postage stamp depicting an African-American woman was issued on February 1, 1978, at Washington, DC. It showed the likeness of Harriet Tubman, the escaped slave and abolitionist who led more than 300 slaves to freedom along the Underground Railroad.

Library of Congress, Prints & Photographs Division
LC-USZ62-7816

Harriet Tubman

4757. Postage stamp whose design was decided by popular vote was the Elvis Presley stamp, issued in 1992. The Postal Service solicited votes on which of two portraits of the singer would be used: one of Presley as a young man, or one of him as a mature entertainer. On June 4, 1992, the results were announced: 1.1 million voters picked the younger Presley by a margin of three to one.

4758. Fundraising (semipostal) stamp issued by the U.S. Postal Service went on sale on July 29, 1998, to raise funds for breast cancer research. The stamp was intended for use as a regular 32-cent first-class stamp. The price was 40 cents, with the additional eight cents donated to the National Institutes of Health and the Department of Defense Medical Research Program. The stamp, a line drawing of a woman on a multicolored background bearing the legend "Fund the fight. Find a cure," was designed by Ethel Kessler and illustrated by Whitney Sherman. A total of $7.8 million was raised in the stamp's first year of use.

4759. Stamp honoring a Muslim holiday was the 34-cent Eid Stamp, part of the Holiday Celebrations series routinely released by the U.S. Postal Service in the fall. It went on sale on September 1, 2001, in Des Plaines, IL. The stamp, intended to honor the two Muslim Eid holidays, Eid al-Fitr (Festival of Fast-Breaking, which closes Ramadan) and Eid al-Adha (Festival of Sacrifice), was designed by calligrapher Mohamed Zakariya of Arlington, VA. The Arabic calligraphy on the stamp read *Eid mubarak* ("May your religious holiday be blessed").

Pulitzer Prizes

4760. Pulitzer Prize awarded to a newspaper reporter was won by Herbert Bayard Swope of the *New York World* for his stories on the internal situation in the German empire. The $500 award was announced by Columbia University, New York City, on June 4, 1917.

4761. Pulitzer Prize for a newspaper editorial was won by an editorial by Frank Herbert Simonds that was published in the *New York Tribune* on May 7, 1916, the first anniversary of the sinking of the *Lusitania*. The $500 award was announced by Columbia University, New York City, on June 4, 1917.

4762. Pulitzer Prize for fiction was won by *His Family*, by Ernest Poole, published in 1917 by the Macmillan Company, New York City. It was about a New York man and his three daughters. The $500 award was announced by Columbia University, New York City, on June 4, 1917.

4763. Fiction writer to win the Pulitzer Prize twice was Booth Tarkington, who won the 1919 award for his novel *The Magnificent Ambersons* and the 1921 award for *Alice Adams*. Both prizes were awarded in New York City.

4764. Pulitzer Prize awarded to a newspaper was given to the *New York Times*. The award was presented on June 5, 1918, at the graduation ceremony at Columbia University, New York City.

4765. Pulitzer Prize for drama was awarded to *Why Marry?*, a three-act comedy by Jesse Lynch Williams and produced by Selwyn and Company. It opened on December 25, 1917, at the Astor Theatre, New York City. It starred Nat C. Goodwin as Uncle Everett, Lotus Robb as Jean, Edmund Breese as John, and Harold West as Rex. It was adapted for the stage from a 1914 novel entitled *And So They Were Married*. The award was announced on June 3, 1918, and awarded on June 5.

4766. Pulitzer Prize for a novel written by a woman was presented in 1921 to Edith Newbold Jones Wharton for her novel *The Age of Innocence*, published in 1920 by D. Appleton and Company.

4767. Pulitzer Prize for an editorial cartoon was awarded to "On the Road to Moscow" by Rollin Kirby, which appeared on August 5, 1921, in the *New York World*. The award of the $500 prize was announced on May 21, 1922.

4768. Pulitzer Prize awarded to a musical was given to the two-act comedy *Of Thee I Sing* by George Simon Kaufman, Morrie Ryskind, George Gershwin, and Ira Gershwin, on May 2, 1932. It was produced by Sam H. Harris at the Music Box Theatre, New York City, on December 26, 1931, and starred Victor Moore as Alexander Throttlebottom and William Gaxton as John P. Wintergreen. It played for 441 performances.

4769. Poet to win a Pulitzer Prize four times was Robert Frost, who was awarded the prize in New York City on May 3, 1943, for *A Witness Tree*. His other awards were in 1924 for *New Hampshire: A Poem With Notes and Grace Notes*, in 1931 for *Collected Poems*, and in 1937 for *A Further Range*.

4770. Writer to win the Pulitzer Prize in both fiction and poetry was Robert Penn Warren, who won the fiction award for *All the King's Men* in 1947 and the poetry award for *Promises: Poems 1954*–1956 in New York City in 1958.

4771. Poet who was an African-American woman to win the Pulitzer Prize was Gwendolyn Brooks of Chicago, IL, who received the award on May 1, 1950, for *Annie Allen*, a collection of poems about a woman as daughter, wife, and mother.

4772. Writer to win a Pulitzer Prize four times for drama was Eugene Gladstone O'Neill, who was awarded the prize for the fourth time on May 6, 1957, for his play *Long Day's Journey Into Night*. His other awards were in 1920 for *Beyond The Horizon*, in 1922 for *Anna Christie*, and in 1928 for *Strange Interlude*. Robert Emmet Sherwood won three Pulitzer Prizes for drama—for *Idiot's Delight* in 1936, *Abe Lincoln in Illinois* in 1939, and *There Shall Be No Night* in 1941—and the Pulitzer Prize for biography in 1949, for *Roosevelt and Hopkins: An Intimate History*.

4773. Pulitzer Prize awarded to a comic book was a special prize in journalism that was awarded in 1990 to *Maus*, by Art Spiegelman. *Maus* used the comic-book format to recount the experiences and suffering of Spiegelman's father and mother during the Holocaust, with Jews depicted as mice and Nazis as cats.

4774. Pulitzer Prize awarded to a science book was awarded in 1991 to *The Ants*, a comprehensive guide to myrmecology by biologists Edward O. Wilson and Bert Holldobler, both of Harvard University, Cambridge, MA. Wilson was the first scientist to win two Pulitzer prizes. His first was for *On Human Nature* (1979).

Radio

4775. Radio broadcast demonstration was made by Nathan B. Stubblefield of Murray, KY, in 1892. He was the first person to transmit a voice by air without the aid of wires. He gave a public exhibition of his invention on January 1, 1902. At another exhibition on May 30, 1902, in Fairmont Park, Philadelphia, PA, his voice was heard a mile away from the transmitter. He obtained a patent on May 12, 1908, but he was something of an eccentric and did not permit knowledge of his invention to be spread abroad.

4776. Message sent by wireless transmission in the United States was the Morse code for the letter "S." It was sent in April 1899 from a transmitter at Notre Dame University, South Bend, IN, to a receiver at St. Mary's College, a distance of one mile. The wiring was done by Jerome S. Green, an electrical engineer at Notre Dame.

4777. Transatlantic radio broadcast was sent in code on January 19, 1903, between Cape Cod, MA, and Cornwall, England. Greetings were exchanged between King Edward VII and President Theodore Roosevelt. Experimental broadcasts had been made earlier. The first transatlantic broadcast in which a voice was transmitted took place on December 31, 1923, when station KDKA of Pittsburgh, PA, broadcast the voice of Dr. Harry Phillips Davis, vice president of the Westinghouse Electric and Manufacturing Company, via short wave. It was received by 2AZ, a station operated by the Metropolitan Vickers Company, Manchester, England, and rebroadcast to London.

4778. Radio program broadcast was sent by Professor Reginald Aubrey Fessenden on December 24, 1906, from Brant Rock, MA. The general call "CQ" was heard, followed by a song, a poetry reading, a violin solo, a speech, and an invitation to listeners to report on the reception. Fessenden used a 40-horsepower steam engine driving a 35-kilowatt, 125-cycle alternator, with rotary spark at a frequency of 250 per second. The antenna consisted of a single straight tube, 36 inches in outside diameter and 429 feet high, in eight-foot sections bolted together.

4779. Transatlantic radio message of the regular westward service was sent in code by Privy Councillor Lord Avebury, formerly Sir John Lubbock, to the *New York Times* from Clifden, Ireland, via Glace Bay, Nova Scotia, on October 17, 1907, on regular Marconi transatlantic service. The message included the statement: "Trust introduction wireless more closely unite people States Great Britain who seem form one Nation though under two Governments and whose interests are really identical." This occurred six years after the first transatlantic radio signal, consisting of the letter *S* in Morse code, was sent by Guglielmo Marconi from Poldhu, Cornwall, to St. Johns, Newfoundland, in December 1901.

4780. Radio society was the Wireless Association of America, formed in New York City in November 1908, with Dr. Lee De Forest as president and Hugo Gernsback as chairman and business manager. There were no dues and no obligations. Within a few months, more than 3,000 members were enrolled.

4781. Radio contest was held by the United Wireless Telegraph Company in Philadelphia, PA, on February 23, 1910. Contestants demonstrated their speed and accuracy in receiving and transmitting signals in Morse telegraphic code. The winner was Robert F.

Miller of the United Wireless Company. Harvey Williams of Western Union was the runner-up.

4782. Radio broadcast sent from an airplane was dispatched on August 27, 1910, by James A. Macready from an airplane above the racetrack in Sheepshead Bay, NY. The message was "Another chapter in aerial achievement is hereby written in the receiving of this first message ever recorded from an airplane in flight."

4783. Transpacific radio conversation was transmitted on October 6, 1911, from the steamer *Chive Maru* to the wireless station on Hokkaido Island in the northern part of Japan and thence to the Hillcrest station, San Francisco, CA, approximately 6,000 miles away. The operators exchanged messages.

4784. Radio broadcast from a submerged submarine was made on October 5, 1919, from the U.S.S. *Nautilus* while it was submerged in the Hudson River. The demonstration was conducted by Lieutenant C. Clark Withers. Communication could be received within 50 miles.

4785. Radio program theme song was sung on October 21, 1921, by Billy Jones and Ernie Hare to introduce their program "The Happiness Boys," sponsored by Happiness Candy. The first line was: "How do you do, everybody, how do you do?"

4786. Radio broadcast of a debate was made on May 23, 1922, over station WJH of the White and Boyer Company, Washington, DC. Both sides were argued by students of the National University Law School, Washington, DC. The affirmative, "Resolved, That daylight saving is an advantage," was taken by Calvin Ira Kephart, representing the Miller Debating Society, and the negative by Thomas E. Rhodes, representing the Alvey Debating Society. The audience was requested to act as judge.

4787. Chain radio broadcast was accomplished on October 7, 1922, when station WJZ and station WGY transmitted a World Series baseball game from the Polo Grounds, New York City, where the New York Giants were playing the New York Yankees. Ordinary telegraph lines from Newark, NJ, and Schenectady, NY, were connected with the field, where they picked up sounds through a microphone. It was not possible to transmit the highest and lowest frequencies. Graham McNamee was the announcer.

4788. Transatlantic radio program received from Great Britain was transmitted from eight stations in Bournemouth, Cardiff, Glasgow, Birmingham, Newcastle, Manchester, Aberdeen, and Liverpool, and rebroadcast from London. It consisted of the words "Hello America" and piano selections. The program was received from 10 to 10:30 P.M. on November 25, 1923, at Garden City, NY, Chatham, MA, Quincy, MA, and Tarrytown, NY. All radio stations in the United States went off the air during this period to enable the broadcast to be heard.

4789. Coast-to-coast radio hookup took place on February 8, 1924, when General John Joseph Carty, vice president and chief of research of the Bell Telephone system, spoke from the meeting of the Bond Men's Club at the Congress Hotel, Chicago, IL. The speech was broadcast by WJAR, Providence, RI; WEAF, New York City; WCAP, Washington, DC; WMAQ, Chicago, IL; KLX, Oakland, CA; and KTO, San Francisco, CA. It was heard by some 50 million people.

4790. Radio two-way broadcast from an airplane was accomplished on August 14, 1924, in New York City by station WJZ. A conversation was broadcast between Major William Nicholas Hensley, commandant of Mitchel Field, who was aloft in a plane, and Major Lester Durand Gardner, who was on the ground in Central Park, New York City.

4791. Radio network broadcast received on the Pacific Coast was the speech of President Calvin Coolidge on October 23, 1924, at the dedication of the Chamber of Commerce of the United States building, Washington, DC. The 45-minute speech was broadcast by 23 stations, including stations in Los Angeles, CA; Portland, OR; and Seattle, WA.

4792. Radio show with a plot and with repeating characters who had different adventures each week was *Amos 'n' Andy*, a comedy show in which two white actors, Freeman Gosden and Charles Correll, played the parts of two African-American taxi drivers. The show originated in 1926 on WMAQ, Chicago, IL, as *Sam 'n' Henry*. It moved to WGN in March 1928 in search of a wider audience and premiered on the NBC Blue network in August 1929 after the manufacturers of Pepsodent toothpaste agreed to sponsor it. Previously, all radio programs were either variety shows or broadcasts of events like ball games and church services.

4793. Grand Ole Opry broadcast took place live on December 10, 1927, over radio station WSM, Nashville, TN. The show had already been on the air as "WSM Barn Dance" since November 28, 1925. Radio announcer George Dewey Hay suggested the name change to point up the difference between his own country-music show and the classical music program that had just preceded it on the air ("The Music Appreciation Hour," with Walter Damrosch conducting the NBC Symphony Orchestra). The first musician to perform on the renamed show was harmonica master DeFord Bailey, who played his composition "Pan American Blues."

> On that December night in 1927, Nashville radio personality George Dewey Hay told his audience, "For the past hour, we have been listening to music taken largely from Grand Opera, but from now on we will present 'The Grand Ole Opry.'"

4794. Round-the-world radio broadcast was accomplished in 0.125 seconds on June 30, 1930, by a series of radio relays. Clyde Decker Wagoner spoke into a short-wave microphone from station W2XAD, Schenectady, NY. His voice was relayed to Holland, to Java, to Australia, across the Pacific Ocean to North America, and back to Schenectady.

4795. Radio variety show with a live studio audience who interacted with the host and laughed audibly at his jokes was *The Chase and Sanborn Hour*, which aired on the NBC network starting in 1931 with the vaudeville comedian Eddie Cantor as the host. Cantor also introduced scripted jokes in place of off-the-cuff banter.

4796. Radio broadcast from a moving train of a regular program on a national network was made by station WABC at 9 P.M., March 27, 1932, from a train on the Baltimore and Ohio Railroad. Pickup points were at Beltsville, MD, and Laurel, MD. The transmitter was operated on a frequency of 1542 kilocycles, employing high-percentage modulation and running on 50 watts of power. Belle Baker and Jack Denny's orchestra were featured on the program.

4797. Soap opera on radio was "Ma Perkins," a weekly show that ran from 1933 to 1956. It featured melodramatic stories interspersed with commercials for Oxydol laundry detergent. For years, soap operas were aired on Monday, the traditional laundry day of a homemaker's week.

4798. Radio broadcast heard in both the Arctic and the Antarctic regions was made on September 23, 1934, by W2XAF, the short-wave station of the General Electric Company, Schenectady, NY. The program, broadcast by the New York Coffee House, was sent to the American artist Rockwell Kent, who was near Labrador. It was also heard by Admiral Richard Evelyn Byrd, who was with his second Antarctic expedition at Little America.

4799. Radio broadcast from a tape recording was made by WQXR, the station of the Interstate Broadcasting Company, New York City, on August 26, 1938, from 6:30 P.M. to 7 P.M. A sapphire stylus engraved a 15-minute program on 1,000 feet of tape. The recording used Millertape, the invention of James Arthur Miller of the Miller Broadcasting System, New York City, which allowed editing and cutting.

4800. Radio program simultaneously transmitted over 24 AM and FM stations, and telecast over five, was presented on March 20, 1948, when a sustaining feature, the NBC Symphony, was broadcast. The first commercial program similarly aired was *The Voice of Firestone* on March 22, 1948. The New York City outlet was WNBC.

4801. Radio broadcast using an orbiting satellite was made on December 19, 1958, when a tape recording of the voice of President Dwight David Eisenhower delivering Christmas greetings was broadcast on frequencies of 107.97 and 107.94 megacycles from a rocket revolving around the earth.

4802. Coast-to-coast solar-powered two-way radio conversation was accomplished on June 23, 1960, by the Army Signal Corps, when Colonel Leon J.D. Rouge at Fort Monmouth, NJ, conversed with Sheldon Stern, who was manning the transmitter on the roof of the Hoffman Electronics plant at El

Monte, CA. Each terminal station had a 20-foot square panel with 7,800 individual solar cells.

4803. Transatlantic undersea radio conversation took place on October 2, 1965, between aquanauts in *Sealab 2*, at a depth of 205 feet in the Pacific Ocean off La Jolla, CA, and French divers in *Conshelf 3*, at a depth of 330 feet in the Mediterranean Sea off Cape Ferrat, France.

4804. Packet radio network was ALOHAnet, developed by computer scientist Norman Abramson of the University of Hawaii, Honolulu, HI. ALOHAnet became operational in July 1970 at 9,600 bits per second throughout the state of Hawaii. Other network innovations developed by Abramson's team included the first packet radio sensors, the first satellite packet network, the first packet radio repeaters, and the first radio access to the Internet.

4805. Auction of radio spectrum for satellite services took place on January 24, 1996. The Federal Communications Commission solicited bids for rights to two of the eight orbital slots given to the United States by international agreement for direct broadcast satellite services in the 12.2–12.7 GHz range. One of the slots sold was the last unused slot that could provide satellites with a view of the whole continental United States.

Stations

4806. Radio license granted to an individual was given to George Hill Lewis of Cincinnati, OH, in 1911.

4807. City radio station was WRR, Dallas, TX (50 watts), established in 1920 to broadcast fire alarms. The station played phonograph records so that owners of radio receivers could check to determine whether they were tuned in. In 1925 the station began selling time to sponsors.

4808. Commercial radio station licensed was station 8MK, which instituted daily service in Detroit, MI, on August 20, 1920, with the program "Tonight's Dinner." The station was owned by the *Detroit News*, the first newspaper to operate a radio station. The call letters were changed later to WWJ. Station KDKA, Pittsburgh, PA, was licensed on October 27, 1920, and began offering a semiweekly broadcast on November 2, 1920.

4809. College radio station was WRUC, Union College, Schenectady, NY, which went on the air on October 14, 1920, playing weekly music programs from phonograph records. The programs were broadcast from 8 P.M. to 8:30 P.M. with a three-minute interval. They were initially heard within a 50-mile radius, which increased under favorable weather conditions. The station used a U-tube transmitter with five 50-watt tubes. Frederic L. Ganter was president of the Radio Club of Union College, Wendell W. King the chief engineer, and Francis J. Campbell the chief operator. The station was owned by the trustees of the college.

4810. International radio broadcasting license issued by the Federal Communications Commission was granted on October 15, 1927, to the Experimenter Publishing Company, New York City. The frequency was 9,700 kilocycles and the power 500 watts. The station was taken over in 1929 and subsequently moved to Boston, MA, where it was operated as W1XAL by the World Wide Broadcasting Corporation.

4811. FM radio transmitter to receive a commercial license was station W47NV, Nashville, TN, which operated on a frequency of 44,700 kilocycles with a power of 20,000 watts. It was licensed to cover a 16,000-square-mile radius. It began operations on March 1, 1941, when it presented a commercial for the Standard Candy Company, Nashville.

4812. Radio station owned and operated by African-Americans was WERD, Atlanta, GA (1,000 watts), which opened on October 3, 1949. It was owned by Radio Atlanta, of which Jesse Bee Blayton was president. It became WXAT in 1972.

4813. Local radio network was formed on May 15, 1950, by five local stations: WARL, Arlington, VA, 1,000 watts; WGAY, Silver Spring, MD, 1,000 watts; WPIK, Alexandria, VA, 1,000 watts; WBCC, Bethesda, MD, 250 watts; and WFAX, Falls Church, VA, 250 watts. Time on all five stations was offered at $300 an hour.

4814. Radio network for African-Americans was the National Negro Network, formed on January 20, 1954. The first program was "The Story of Ruby Valentine," starring Juanita Hall, which was broadcast on January 25 on 40 stations. It was sponsored five days a week alternately by Philip Morris and Company and the Pet Milk Company. The New York outlet was WOV.

4815. All-news radio station was WINS in New York City, which began broadcasting news 24 hours a day at the 1010 AM frequency on April 19, 1965. Previously, it had broadcast rock and roll. The news-only format was quickly copied by WCBS, another New York station, and then by AM stations throughout the country.

4816. Radio station with all-podcast programming was KYOU 1550, an AM station run by Infinity Broadcasting in San Francisco, CA. The podcasts, which included music, monologues, and other audio programs, were uploaded over the Internet by the station's listeners. The format was launched in May 2005.

Technology

4817. Radio impulse transmission was accomplished by Joseph Henry in Princeton, NJ, in December 1840. Current obtained from a group of Leyden jars was passed through a wire which, by means of a magnetized needle, produced a vibration on another line about 100 feet away. The lines were not connected with each other; the transmission was the result of induction.

4818. Radio patent of importance was granted on December 29, 1891, to Thomas Alva Edison of Menlo Park, NJ, for a "means for transmitting signals electrically." In the patent, he stated that "signalling between distant points can be carried on by induction without the use of wires connecting such distant points."

4819. Radio receiver advertised was the Telimco, a $7.50 outfit announced in a one-inch advertisement in the January 13, 1906, issue of the *Scientific American.* The receiver was made by Hugo Gernsback's Electro Importing Company of New York. The advertisement offered a "complete outfit comprising one inch spark coil, balls, key, coherer with auto decoherer and sounder, 50 ohm relay, 4 cell dry battery, send and catch wires and connections with instructions and diagrams. Will work up to one mile. Unprecedented introduction prices. Agents wanted. Illustrated pamphlet."

4820. Carbon microphone used in radio broadcasting was employed by Dr. Lee De Forest in 1907 in his laboratory at the Parker Building, 19th Street and Fourth Avenue, New York City. It was of the ordinary telephone variety.

4821. Portable radio to be commercially successful was produced in 1924 by the Zenith Electronics Corporation, Chicago, IL.

4822. Car radio was invented in 1929 by Paul Vincent Galvin, 34, an engineer, in a garage in Chicago, IL. The radio was roughly the size of a large toolbox and had a speaker that was installed under the car's floorboards. It had poor sound but was a commercial success. Galvin went on to found the Motorola Company.

4823. FM radio was the invention of Edwin Howard Armstrong, an electrical engineer and researcher at Columbia University in New York City. In 1933, he devised a method of transmitting static-free radio signals using frequency modulation (FM), a system superior to the older amplitude modulation (AM) method. He received patents for this technology on December 26, 1933. Armstrong had previously received important patents for other radio devices, including the feedback receiver and the superheterodyne receiver.

4824. Transistor radio receiver to be mass-produced was the Regency Radio, manufactured by the Regency Division of Industrial Development Engineering Associates, Indianapolis, IN. The first shipments to dealers were made in October 1954. The receiver was 3 by 5 by 1.25 inches and weighed 12 ounces. It had no tubes but instead contained four transistors. It was powered entirely by a 22.5-volt B battery.

4825. Radio receiver with an auxiliary solar-cell power unit to convert solar rays into electrical power was the Sun Power Pak, made by the Admiral Corporation, Chicago, IL, which was first developed in October 1955 and offered for sale on April 16, 1956. The radio weighed 5.25 pounds and contained six transistors in place of vacuum tubes. It was 2.875 inches thick, 8.75 inches high, and 10.375 inches long and cost $59.95. It was operated by six ordinary flashlight batteries lasting from 700 to 1,000 hours. The auxiliary Sun Power Pak, which converted solar energy into power, cost $185. It had a silicon "solar cell element" to pick up rays from the sun or from an incandescent bulb.

4826. Master skyscraper antenna was erected in 1965 on the 102nd floor of the Empire State Building in New York City, at the 1,250-foot level. The antenna was built at an estimated cost of $30,000 by the Alfred Manufacturing Company of Boston. It enabled 17 frequency modulation stations to broadcast simultaneously. The first were WQXR-FM, WHOM-FM, WLIB-FM, and WNCM-FM. Transmissions were made beginning in mid-October 1965. The transmitters were located on the 81st floor.

Sound Recording

4827. Phonograph was invented by Thomas Alva Edison of Menlo Park, NJ, who secured a patent on February 19, 1878, on a "phonograph or speaking machine." His original idea had been to invent a telegraph repeater, and he had given construction directions to one of his mechanics, John Kreusi, on August 12, 1877. The first cylinder, operated by a hand crank, was wrapped in tin foil, with which two needles fastened to diaphragms made contact. The first verse recorded on the new instrument was "Mary Had a Little Lamb." A clock spring motor and waxlike record were invented some 10 years later.

Library of Congress, Prints & Photographs Division
The Brady-Handy Collection, LC-DIG-cwpbh-04043

Thomas Edison with his phonograph.

4828. Phonograph that was practical was the Graphophone, manufactured by the firm of Bell and Tainter, Washington, DC. On May 4, 1886, Chichester Bell and Charles Sumner Tainter received a patent "for recording and reproducing speech and other sounds." Patents on "reproducing sounds from phonograph records" and on "transmitting and recording sounds by radiant energy" were also received on May 4, 1886, jointly with Alexander Graham Bell.

4829. Phonograph record of the modern disk type was invented by Emile Berliner of Washington, DC, and first publicly demonstrated before the Franklin Institute in Philadelphia, PA, on May 16, 1888. Berliner's "Gramophone" record was a flat disk in which the grooves were cut in a lateral spiral, making it much easier to duplicate for the mass market than Edison's recording cylinder.

4830. Jukebox was a coin-operated phonograph player installed in the Palais Royale, San Francisco, CA, on November 23, 1889, by Louis Glas. The first widely successful jukebox manufacturer was the Rudolph Wurlitzer Company of North Tonawanda, NY. The company's most popular model was the Wurlitzer Model 1015, designed in 1946 by Paul Fuller. Among its novel features were curved plastic tubes containing a fluid with a low boiling point. Small heaters kept the fluid bubbling. Wurlitzer sold 56,246 of the Model 1015 at $750 each.

4831. Phonograph trade magazine was *The Phonogram*, "official organ of the phonograph companies of the United States," edited by V. H. McRae. It was published monthly in New York City from January 1891 to January 1893. The first issue contained an article by Thomas Alva Edison entitled "How Sound Is Reproduced."

4832. Phonograph with an automatic record changer was introduced by the Victor Talking Machine Company, Camden, NJ, in March 1927. It played twelve 10-inch or 12-inch records and stopped automatically after the last record had been played.

4833. Tape recorders imported into the United States were two Magnetophon recorders that were transported from Occupied Germany in 1945 and rebuilt by an American engineer, John Mullin. They arrived with 50 reels of BASF Luvitherm tape (plastic tape coated with magnetite). Although wire recording was well known in the United States, audio tape-recording technology had not yet been used in any commercial sound-recording equipment. The Magnetophon ran at 30 inches per second and had a frequency response of up to 15 KHz.

4834. Tape recorder built in the United States for commercial use was the Model 200, developed by the Ampex Corporation, Redwood City, CA, in 1948. The Model 200 was invented to make pre-recordings of Bing Crosby's national radio series of 1947–48. The first American-made audio tape was Scotch 111, developed by the 3M Corporation, St. Paul, MN, for use with the Ampex recorder.

4835. Long-playing microgroove phonograph records that were successfully manufactured were made by Columbia Records, Bridgeport, CT, a division of the Columbia Broadcasting System, and introduced to the public on June 21, 1948, at the Waldorf-Astoria Hotel, New York City. CBS engineer Peter Goldmark was the inventor of the nonbreakable Vinylite plastic disks, which played at a speed of 33.3 revolutions per minute. One side of a 12-inch "LP" played for 23 minutes, compared to 4 minutes for one side of a standard 78-r.p.m. record; 78s were quickly supplanted by the new technology.

4836. Tape-recording machine for mass production of tapes was announced on January 26, 1949, by the Minnesota Mining and Manufacturing Company (3M), St. Paul, MN. The machine taped 48 hours of recorded music in one hour.

4837. Cassette audio tape recorder was the CarryCorder 150, sold in the United States beginning in 1965 by Norelco, the North American division of the Philips Company, a Dutch consumer-products manufacturer. It was battery-powered and was the first machine to use the quarter-inch tape cassette format that later became standard in the consumer audio industry.

4838. Compact disc players were introduced in the United States in 1983. They were manufactured by the Japanese firm Sony using technology pioneered in 1979 by the Dutch firm Philips. To make CD recordings, sounds were digitally rendered on magnetic tape as electronic signals in binary form. These signals were encoded as microscopic pits in the reflective surface of a five-inch disc made from plastic and aluminum. The sound was played back by focusing a laser beam on the spinning disc. When the beam encountered the pits, it was reflected back at an angle to a detector that converted it into an analog signal for output to a hi-fi stereo system.

4839. MP3 player available in the United States was the Eiger Labs MPMan F10/F20 (there were two versions of the same device). It was manufactured by the Korean electronic firm Saehan Information Systems and released in the U.S. in July 1998. The MPMan models contained up to 32 megabytes of flash memory storage, enough to hold about three hours of MP3-compressed audio at low quality or about one compact disk's worth of songs at high quality.

Telegraph

4840. Semaphore telegraph system was invented in 1799 by Jonathan Grout of Belchertown, MA, who installed a series of towers, each within sight of the next, between Boston and Martha's Vineyard, 90 miles distant. By means of a combination of the semaphore and flag systems, he was able to ask a question and receive an answer within 10 minutes. This system did not involve the use of an electric telegraph line.

4841. Telegraph system was constructed in 1827 by Harrison Gray Dyar, who operated a two-mile telegraph system at the racecourse at Long Island City, NY (now part of Queens, New York City). Iron wire attached to glass insulators on wooden posts enabled the current to produce a red mark on litmus paper at the receiving station. The lapse of time between the sparks indicated the different letters.

4842. Electromagnetic telegraph was invented by Joseph Henry, who exhibited it in 1831 at the Albany Academy, Albany, NY. The device was 14 inches long. At each excitation of the electric magnet, one end of a compass rod or needle remained in contact with a limb of the soft iron core. Near the opposite end of the compass rod was a small stationary office bell. When the current was reversed, the compass rod moved back to the opposite limb of the electromagnet. Signals were transmitted by means of the electromagnet through more than a mile of wire. The invention was not put to practical use; it merely demonstrated the possibility of transmitting signals.

4843. Telegraphic system in which dots and dashes represented letters was invented by Alfred Vail of Morristown, NJ, in September 1837. On January 8, 1838, the message "A patient waiter is no loser" was transmitted. On January 24, in a public demonstration given at New York University, New York City, the message "Attention the Universe. By Kingdom's Right Wheel" was transmitted through a circuit of 10 miles. Previously, words had been assigned numbers, with the marks appearing as acutely angulated lines like the letter V or V in reverse, which appeared on cylinders at the receiving station.

4844. Telegraph cable was an insulated copper wire laid on October 18, 1842, by Samuel Finley Breese Morse in New York Harbor between the Battery and Governors Island. On the following day, while transmitting signals, the cable stopped working because a vessel, in raising its anchor, had caught and wrecked 200 feet of it. Another cable was laid in New York Harbor for commercial use in 1843 by Samuel Colt. It was insulated with cotton yarn, beeswax, and asphaltum encased in a lead pipe, and connected New York City with both Fire Island and Coney Island.

4845. Telegraph appropriation by Congress was made on March 3, 1843. A sum of $30,000 was appropriated "to test the practicability of establishing a system of electromagnetic telegraphs by the United States."

4846. Telegraph station was opened in Washington, DC, in 1844 under the direction of Samuel Finley Breese Morse. The station was located between Seventh and Eighth Streets and E and F Streets.

4847. Commercial telegraph service was inaugurated on May 24, 1844, by Professor Samuel Finley Breese Morse, who sent a message from the Supreme Court room in the Capitol, Washington, DC, to Alfred Vail at the Mount Clare station of the Baltimore and Ohio Railroad Company, Baltimore, MD. Vail retransmitted it to Morse. The message, "What hath God wrought," was selected from the 23rd verse of the 23rd chapter of the biblical Book of Numbers by Annie Ellsworth, daughter of the commissioner of patents.

4848. Underwater telegraph cable that was practical was laid by Ezra Cornell, an associate of Samuel Finley Breese Morse. In 1845 he laid 12 miles of cable enclosed in lead pipes across the Hudson River, connecting Fort Lee, NJ, with New York City. This cable was carried away by ice in 1846. Before the cable was installed, messages for Philadelphia, PA, and Washington, DC, were carried across the Hudson by messengers in boats.

4849. Telegrapher who was a woman was Sarah G. Bagley, who was in charge of the Lowell, MA, office of the New York and Boston Magnetic Telegraph Association when the line opened on February 21, 1846, between Boston and Lowell.

4850. Telegraph company was the Magnetic Telegraph Company, incorporated on February 4, 1847, under the laws of Maryland. The first president was Amos Kendall. Offices were rented in New York City at a cost of $250 a year, in Philadelphia for $150, in Baltimore for $150, and in Washington, DC, for $50. At first, messages were sent by pigeons across the Hudson River from Jersey City, NJ, to New York City. Later, a lead pipe enclosing a covered wire saturated with pitch was laid under the river. The rates from Baltimore to Washington were 10 cents for the first 10 words and 1 cent for each additional word. The rates from New York to Washington were 50 cents for the first 10 words and 5 cents for each additional word.

4851. Telegraph used by a railroad was used on September 22, 1851, when Charles Minot, superintendent of the Erie Railroad, telegraphed 14 miles to Goshen, NY, to delay a train so that his own train would not have to wait. Trains were run on the interval system.

4852. Telegraph ticker to print type successfully was invented by David Edward Hughes of Louisville, KY, who received a patent on May 20, 1856. He had sold his rights to the Commercial Company for $100,000 on November 1, 1855.

4853. Transatlantic telegraph cable was completed on August 5, 1858, through the efforts of Cyrus West Field, after two unsuccessful attempts. On July 28, 1858, a splice was made in midocean, and on the following day four ships belonging to Britain and the United States paid out the cable as they sailed for home—the *Agamemnon* and *Valorous*, bound for Valentia, Ireland, and the *Niagara* and *Gorgon*, bound for Trinity Bay, Newfoundland. These destinations were to be the terminals of the cable. The cable was 1,950 statute miles long and more than two-thirds of it was laid more than 2 miles deep. Introductory and complimentary messages were exchanged by President James Buchanan and Queen Victoria on August 16, 1858. The cable was weak and the current insufficient, and service was suspended on September 1, 1858.

4854. Telegram dispatched from an aerial station was sent from the balloon *Enterprise* on June 18, 1861, to President Abraham Lincoln by Professor Thaddeus Sobieski Coulincourt Lowe, who acknowledged his indebtedness "for the opportunity of demonstrating the availability of the science of aeronautics in the military service of the country."

4855. Transcontinental telegraph line was placed in operation by the Western Union Telegraph Company on October 24, 1861, when Stephen Johnson Field, chief justice of California, sent a message to President Abraham Lincoln. On October 25, 1861, telegrams were exchanged between Mayor Fernando Wood of New York City and Mayor H. F. Teschemacher of San Francisco, CA. Rates during the first week were $1 a word between San Francisco and the Missouri River. Later the rates were reduced: 10 words from San Francisco to New York City cost $6, and each additional word cost 75 cents.

4856. Two-way telegraph that was practical was invented by Thomas Alva Edison of Newark, NJ, who obtained a patent on August 9, 1892, in the United States, after receiving patents in Britain, France, Italy, Austria-Hungary, and Russia. The telegraph enabled "two operators to simultaneously send over one wire in one direction, by reversal of a battery current in one instance and increasing and decreasing the strength of the current in the other instance, and the connections are so arranged that the party at the receiving station can signal to the sender to repeat in case of inaccuracy."

4857. Transpacific telegraph cable was paid out beginning on December 14, 1902, between San Francisco, CA, and Honolulu, HI, a distance of 2,277 nautical miles (2,620 miles), by the cableship *Silverton*. It was landed on the beach near Honolulu on January 1, 1903. The first message was sent at 11:03 P.M. San Francisco time on that day. On January 5, the cable was opened for public use.

4858. Telegraph message sent around the world by commercial telegraph was "This message sent around the world," sent at 7 P.M. on August 20, 1911, from the 17th floor of the New York Times building, New York City, by the *New York Times* and received by the *Times* at 7:16:30 P.M. The message traveled over 28,613 miles and 16 relays by way of the Azores, Gibraltar, Bombay, Philippine Islands, Midway, Guam, Honolulu, and San Francisco.

4859. Coaxial cable was invented by Lloyd Espenschied of Kew Gardens, NY, and Herman A. Affel of Ridgewood, NJ. On May 23, 1929, they applied for a patent on a "concentric conducting system." The patent was granted on December 8, 1931, and was assigned to the American Telegraph and Telephone Company, New York City.

4860. Teletype commercial service was inaugurated on November 20, 1931, by the American Telegraph and Telephone Company. Messages typed on tape were transmitted automatically to a central office and retransmitted to their destinations. The charges were based on the time required to transmit each message, not on the number of words. On December 1, 1931, the teletype systems of the Postal Telegraph Company and the Western Union Telegraph Company cooperated in "Timed Wire Service" so that a patron of one service could transmit to a patron of the other service.

4861. Singing telegram was introduced by the Western Union Telegraph Company, New York City, on July 28, 1933. The innovation, opposed by a company executive, proved popular with customers. Many telegrams were sung by messengers in person, but after 1950 all singing was done by telephone.

4862. Submarine cable plow was patented on January 12, 1937, by Chester S. Lawton of Ridgewood, NJ, and Captain Melville H. Bloomer of Halifax, Nova Scotia, Canada, who assigned it to the Western Union Telegraph Company. The plow dug a trench in the bed of the ocean and simultaneously fed the cable into the furrow. The plow could be used in depths as great as half a mile. The first transatlantic cable of a high-speed permalloy was buried on June 14, 1938.

Telephones

4863. Voice synthesizer was demonstrated to the public on December 22, 1845, at the Musical Fund Hall in Philadelphia, PA, by Joseph Faber, an inventor recently arrived from Germany. His device took 17 years to develop. It consisted of a keyboard that by mechanical means operated a series of reeds, bellows, and chambers, designed to work like the human mouth, tongue, teeth, glottis, larynx, and lungs. Passing air through the device produced sixteen basic phonemes, enough to pronounce accurately any word in any European language. The machine's slow, sepulchral voice seemed to emerge from a mechanical head that was fixed to the frame. In 1846, Phineas T. Barnum exhibited Faber's invention, dubbed the Euphonium, in London, where it was viewed by Melville Bell, the father of Alexander Graham Bell, inventor of the telephone.

4864. Telephone message that was distinguishable was "Mr. Watson, come here, I want you," spoken into the telephone on March 10, 1876, by Alexander Graham Bell and received by his associate Thomas Augustus Watson on another floor in Bell's home at 5 Exeter Place, Boston, MA. This was the world's first telephone conversation. Three days earlier, on March 7, Bell had received the first telephone patent, for an "improvement in telegraphy."

4865. Telephone conversation over outdoor wires took place on October 9, 1876, between Alexander Graham Bell in Boston, MA, and Thomas Augustus Watson in Cambridge. The sound traveled over the private telegraph wire of the Walworth Manufacturing Company from Boston to Cambridgeport, a distance of two miles. Parallel accounts of the conversation, as recorded separately by both Bell and Watson, were published in the *Boston Advertiser* on October 19, 1876, in answer to the skeptics who did not believe that the telephone was as reliable as the telegraph.

4866. Telephone for domestic use was installed in April 1877 at the home of Charles Williams, Jr., of Somerville, MA, at the corner of Arlington and Lincoln streets. Williams also had a telephone installed at the same time in his office at 109 Court Street, Boston, MA.

4867. Interstate telephone call took place on May 17, 1877, when a call was made from New Brunswick, NJ, to Dr. Alexander Graham Bell at Chickering Hall, New York City.

4868. Telephone switchboard or exchange was put in operation on May 17, 1877. It was located at 342 Washington Street, Boston, MA, where Edwin Thomas Holmes was operating an electrical burglar alarm business. Holmes's office was connected by wire to a number of banks and similar institutions, and the telephones were placed in the offices of six of his subscribers and connected to these wires. The system served as a telephone system by day and as a burglar alarm system at night. The telephones were connected only in the daytime.

4869. Telephone directory was issued on February 21, 1878, by the New Haven District Telephone Company, New Haven, CT. It listed about 50 names.

4870. Telephone operator who was a woman was Emma M. Nutt, who went to work for the Telephone Despatch Company, Boston, MA, on September 1, 1878. Previously, all operators had been men.

4871. Automatic telephone system was patented on December 5, 1879, by Daniel Connolly of Philadelphia, PA, Thomas A. Connolly of Washington, DC, and Thomas J. McTighe of Pittsburgh, PA. The system employed a single-line wire, a battery of cells located at each telephone, and a dial-switching mechanism for each line. The system could accommodate only a few lines and was not commercially applied. The first successful system was invented by Almon B. Strowger. It was installed at La Porte, IN, where it was formally opened to the public on November 3, 1892. The first exchange equipped with a rotating dial was an interior system in the City Hall of Milwaukee, WI, which was installed in 1896.

4872. Pay station telephone service began on June 1, 1880, in the office of the Connecticut Telephone Company, Yale Bank Building, State and Chapel streets, New Haven, CT. The toll was given to an attendant.

4873. International commercial telephone service was begun on July 1, 1881, when service was inaugurated by the National Bell Telephone Company of the State of Maine between Calais, ME, and St. Stephen, New Brunswick, Canada, two points separated by the St. Croix River, the international boundary line between the United States and Canada.

4874. Yellow pages telephone directory was published in Cheyenne, WY, in 1883. The directory contained listings for businesses. It was printed on yellow paper and bound into a residential telephone directory,

4875. Long-distance telephone call was made on March 27, 1884, by branch managers of the American Bell Telephone Company in Boston, MA, and New York City. Said a contemporary account: "The words were heard as perfectly as though the speakers were standing close by, while no extra effort was needed at the other end of the line to accomplish the result."

4876. Pay telephone was invented by William Gray of Hartford, CT, who received a patent on August 13, 1889, on a "coin-controlled apparatus for telephones." The first machine in commercial use was installed in the lobby of the Hartford Bank in 1889 under the supervision of Ellis Benjamin Baker, superintendent of the Southern New England Telephone Company. In 1891, Gray, with Amos Whitney and Francis Pratt, incorporated the Gray Telephone Pay Station Company (later the Gray Manufacturing Company) and installed the telephones in stores on a rental basis. The company rented out pay phones for 25 percent of the take. Ten percent of the take went to the place of business in which the telephones were installed and 65 percent went to the telephone company.

4877. Long-distance telephone call over underground cables took place on February 26, 1914, between Boston, MA, and Washington, DC.

4878. Transcontinental telephone demonstration took place on January 25, 1915, when Alexander Graham Bell, calling from the offices of the American Telephone and Telegraph Company in New York City and using a model of the first telephone, spoke with his associate, Thomas Augustus Watson, in San Francisco, about 3,000 miles away. Bell repeated the words "Mr. Watson, come here, I want you," the phrase he had spoken 40 years earlier, in March 1876, during the world's first telephone conversation. Later, Mayor John Purroy Mitchel of New York City talked with Mayor James Rolph, Jr., of San Francisco.

4879. Mobile telephone one-way communication was established by Bell System engineers on April 4, 1915, from Montauk Point, NY, to Wilmington, DE, a distance of 250 miles.

4880. Transcontinental commercial telephone service from New York to California was inaugurated on April 7, 1915, at a cost of $20.70 for the first three minutes and $6.75 for each minute thereafter.

4881. Transcontinental demonstration of radio telephone operation was given on September 29, 1915, when speech was transmitted from New York City to Arlington, VA, thence to Mare Island, San Francisco, 2,500 miles away, and on to Honolulu that night.

4882. Transatlantic message over radio telephone was transmitted on October 21, 1915, from Arlington, VA, to Paris, France. The voice of B. B. Webb was heard by Herbert E. Shreeve and Austen M. Custis of the American Telephone and Telegraph Company and by Lieutenant Colonel Ferrie of the French government at the receiving station installed in the Eiffel Tower by Bell System engineers.

4883. Ship-to-shore conversation over radio telephone took place on May 6, 1916, over the regular telephone network to demonstrate a way of mobilizing the telephone and telegraph in case of war. Captain Lloyd Horwitz Chandler of the battleship *New Hampshire*, while at sea off Hampton Roads, VA, reported to, and received orders from, Secretary of the Navy Josephus Daniels and Admiral William Shepherd Benson, who were in Washington, DC.

4884. Radio telephone communication from an airplane took place on July 2, 1917, at Langley Field, VA, where speech of good volume and quality was received from a transmitting plane two miles away. On July 4, speech from the ground was received by L. M. Clement of the Western Electric Company in a plane several miles away. On August 18, the first two-way communication was established between a plane and the ground, and on August 20, 1917, between two planes. Both events took place at Langley Field.

4885. Two-way radio conversation between a submerged submarine and another vessel took place on October 5, 1919, between the U.S. submarine *H-2*, commanded by Lieutenant Commander Clark Withers, and the destroyer *Blakey*. The submarine was submerged in the Hudson River off 96th Street, New York City.

4886. Radio telephone commercial service was inaugurated on July 16, 1920, between Los Angeles and Santa Catalina Island, CA. A radio link connected the town of Avalon on the island to telephone lines in Long Beach, CA. The service was maintained by the Bell Telephone System for three years. It was replaced by cable because "speech-scrambling" devices had not yet been developed and messages sent over the radio could be picked up by anyone capable of tuning a receiving set.

4887. Telephone cable deep-sea service was established on April 11, 1921, between Key West, FL, and Havana, Cuba. It was officially opened by President Warren Gamaliel Harding, who placed the first call from the Pan American Building, Washington, DC, to Cuba's President Mario García Menocal at Havana.

4888. Transatlantic commercial telephone service was established between New York City and London, England. It was inaugurated on January 7, 1927, when Walter Sherman Gifford, president of the American Telephone and Telegraph Company, who was in New York, talked to Sir George Evelyn Pemberton Murray, secretary of the British Post Office, who was in London. Thirty-one commercial calls were made the first day. The charge was $75 for a three-minute conversation. The first private conversation was made by Adolph Simon Ochs, publisher of the *New York Times*, to Geoffrey Dawson, editor of the *Times* of London. The messages were transmitted from Rocky Point, NY.

4889. Telephone switchboard with Braille markings and devices to enable a blind person to operate it by touch and sound was designed by the Western Electric Company and installed by the New York Telephone Company on April 1, 1928, in the New York Institute for the Education of the Blind, the Bronx, New York City. The first operator was Frances Sievert, who held the position for more than 25 years.

4890. Ship-to-shore mobile telephone commercial service was inaugurated on December 8, 1929, when Walter Sherman Gifford, president of the American Telephone and Telegraph Company, lifted a receiver in New York City and spoke to Commodore Harold A. Cunningham of the S.S. *Leviathan*. The first personal call was made by William Hector Rankin, a New York advertising man, to Sir Thomas Lipton, who was a passenger aboard the liner. The rate varied from $7 to $11 a minute, depending upon the zone.

4891. Walkie-Talkie two-way radio device was built in 1933 at the Signal Corps Engineering Laboratories, Fort Monmouth, NJ. Its official name was the portable superregenerative receiver and transmitter. The personnel principally concerned with this project were John Hessel, radio mechanic; C. W. Hayhurst, mechanical design engineer; and John Reid, shop mechanic. Commercial production was undertaken in 1934 by the Allen D. Cardwell Company, Brooklyn, New York City.

4892. Round-the-world telephone conversation was held on April 25, 1935, between Walter Sherman Gifford, president of the American Telephone Company, in his office in New York City, and T. G. Miller, a company vice president, who was in an office about 50 feet away. The call was routed over 23,000 miles of telephone wire as well as by radio through San Francisco, Java, Amsterdam, and London and back to New York.

4893. Electronic voice mechanism capable of creating complex sounds of speech in an intelligible manner was Pedro, the Voder, designed by Homer Walter Dudley, Robert Richard Riesz, and Stanley Sylvester Alexander Watkins of the Bell Telephone Laboratories, New York City, and publicly exhibited on June 5, 1938, at the Franklin Institute, Philadelphia, PA.

4894. Mobile telephone commercial service was inaugurated on June 17, 1946, by the Southwestern Bell Telephone Company, St. Louis, MO. Installations were completed in the automobiles of two subscribers, the Monsanto Chemical Company and Henry L. Perkinson, a contractor. Conversation was possible with any Bell Telephone System or connecting company telephone.

4895. Mobile overseas telephone call from a moving vehicle was made on July 16, 1946, by Roger Pierce from St. Louis, MO, to Honolulu, HI.

4896. Long-distance car-to-car telephone conversation was made on September 11, 1946, when a reporter with the *Houston Post* of Houston, TX, telephoned a reporter with the *St. Louis Globe Democrat* of St. Louis, MO.

4897. Area code was 201, the number assigned to the state of New Jersey. Area codes were developed in 1947 by an engineering team at American Telephone & Telegraph (AT&T), which devised the North American Numbering Plan to facilitate direct-dialed long-distance calling by customers, using automated switching systems instead of operators. Each area was assigned a three-digit code, of which the first digit was a number between 2 and 9 and the second digit was either 0 or 1. In 1951, when the area codes were put into use, there were 90 of them.

4898. Transatlantic mobile telephone call between two cars was made on June 26, 1947, by U.S. Ambassador James Clement Dunn from Milan, Italy, to Vincent R. Impellitteri, president of the New York City Council, on the occasion of Marconi Day at the Milan Fair.

4899. Commercial telephone service on railroad trains for passengers was placed in operation on August 15, 1947, on the Baltimore and Ohio Railroad Company's *Royal Blue* and the Pennsylvania Railroad Company's *Congressional Limited* between New York City and Washington, DC. Two-way radio telephone conversations could be carried on in the same way as ordinary telephone calls.

4900. Mobile telephone call between an airplane in flight and a moving car made with commercial equipment over commercial communication lines was accomplished on October 9, 1947, by executives of the Hercules Power Company, Wilmington, DE, from an airplane 2,000 feet in the air to an automobile about 5 miles west of Wilmington, on the Lancaster Pike (Route 41).

4901. Telephone recording devices were authorized by the Federal Communications Commission on June 30, 1948. They were required to have a tone-warning device that produced a distinctive "beep" signal at regular intervals, to let those taking part in the conversation know that their voices were being recorded. Recording devices had been used previously by government and business.

4902. Long-distance dial telephone service began on October 17, 1949, when Mark Sullivan, president of the Pacific Telephone and Telegraph Company, dialed Oakland, CA, from New York City. He spoke to Dr. Oliver E. Buckley, president of the Bell Telephone Laboratories, and Keith S. McHugh, president of the New York Telephone Company. It took less than one minute to complete the call.

4903. Radio paging service was instituted on October 15, 1950, in the New York City area by Aircall. The first call was for a doctor who was on a golf course 25 miles away. Subscribers equipped with six-ounce Aircall pocket radio receivers could hear their call numbers repeated in numerical sequence on the air at least once per minute within a 30-mile area.

4904. Telephone company answering service was provided by the Ohio Bell Telephone Company, which marketed a recording machine and offered service at $12.50 a month, plus a $15 installment fee. As many as twenty 30-second messages could be recorded on a cylinder, which could then be cleaned and used again. The service was offered to the public in March 1951.

4905. Transcontinental direct-dialed phone call was placed by M. Leslie Denning, the mayor of Englewood, NJ, to Frank P. Osborn, the mayor of Alameda, CA, on November 10, 1951. After an 18-second delay, the connection was made and the conversation began. Raymond J. Neiligan was the manager of the Englewood exchange.

This phone call marked the first time a customer dialed a phone number using an area code.

4906. Transatlantic telephone service using the transoceanic cable began with a conversation between Samuel H. Berlin of New York City and John Blackburn Batley of England. The rate was $12 for a three-minute call. The transatlantic cable, which ran for a distance of about 2,250 miles between Clarenville, Newfoundland, Canada, and Oban, Scotland, was laid by the *Monarch* from June 22 to September 26, 1955.

4907. Transatlantic telephone call carried by the transoceanic telephone cable took place on September 25, 1956, when Cleo Frank Craig, chairman of the board of the American Telegraph and Telephone Company, who was in New York City, spoke to Dr. Charles Hill, the British postmaster general, who was at Lancaster House, London. The cable, designed to carry 36 conversations at the same time, was the joint undertaking of the Bell System, the British Post Office (operator of the telephone service in Great Britain), and the Canadian Overseas Telecommunications Corporation.

4908. Air-to-ground public telephone service began on September 15, 1957, in the Chicago–Detroit area, when about 20 airplanes were equipped for the two-way service. The rates varied from $1.50 to $4.25 for a three-minute call, depending on the location of the airplane and of the telephone on the ground.

4909. Telephone call conveyed by a privately owned satellite was made on July 10, 1962, at 7:28 P.M. by Frederick Russell Kappel, board chairman of the American Telephone and Telegraph Company, to Vice President Lyndon Baines Johnson in Washington, DC, on the sixth orbit of the satellite *Telstar 1*. Kappel's voice went from Andover, ME, to the satellite, bounced back to Andover, and then was carried by land line to Washington, DC. Johnson's voice was carried by land line to Andover.

4910. Trimline telephone was placed in service by the Michigan Bell Telephone Company, Detroit, MI, at Jackson, MI, on October 21, 1963. The phone became commercially available on an optional basis throughout the company's territory on August 2, 1965, at a monthly charge of $1. The dial was mounted in the receiver midway between the mouth and the ear pieces, eliminating the need to reach for the base when dialing.

4911. Telephone with push buttons instead of a rotary dial was the Touch-Tone Telephone with 10 push buttons, manufactured by the Western Electric Manufacturing and Supply Unit of the Bell System and placed in commercial service in Carnegie and Greensburg, PA, on November 18, 1963, following marketing trials in Ohio and Pennsylvania. Touch-Tone service was offered at an extra charge on an optional basis.

4912. Transcontinental Picturephone call was made on April 20, 1964, when William Leonard Laurence, science consultant to the New York World's Fair, New York City, spoke to Donald Shaffer, managing editor of the *Anaheim Bulletin*, at Disneyland, Anaheim, CA. The set was about 12 inches across, 7 inches high, and 13 inches deep.

4913. Transpacific telephone service using the transoceanic cable began on June 18, 1964, when President Lyndon Baines Johnson in Washington, DC, spoke to Premier Hayato Ikeda in Tokyo, Japan. The cable, with a capacity of 138 voice channels, stretched 5,300 nautical miles from Oahu, Hawaii, to Japan via Midway, Wake, and Guam, and joined existing cables to the United States mainland, Canada, and Australia. Partners in the $80-million cable project were the American Telephone and Telegraph Company, Kokusai Denshin Denwa Company of Japan, the Hawaiian Telephone Company, and RCA Communications.

4914. Picturephone commercial service was inaugurated on June 24, 1964, in New York City, Chicago, and Washington, DC, when Lady Bird Johnson, wife of President Lyndon Baines Johnson, spoke in Washington, DC, to Dr. Elizabeth A. Wood of the Bell Laboratories in New York City. The picturephone had three parts: a chassis containing the camera, loudspeaker, and screen, which was 4.375 inches wide and 5.75 inches high; a control unit; and the power supply. It was possible to both hear and see the person talking. Service for the general public opened on June 25, 1964. Rates for calls were $16 for the initial three-minute period between New York and Washington, $21 between Washington and Chicago, and $27 between Chicago and New York.

4915. Mobile telephone call to the moon was made by President Richard Milhous Nixon on July 20, 1969, to astronauts Neil Alden Armstrong and Edwin Eugene Aldrin, Jr., aboard *Apollo 11* during the first moon-landing mission.

4916. Phone call made on a cell phone was placed by Martin Cooper on April 3, 1973, to Joel Engel, head of research at Bell Labs. Cooper, a project manager at Motorola, Chicago, IL, had come to New York City to demonstrate his new invention, a handheld cell phone. He connected to the phone system through a base station he had installed in a Manhattan skyscraper. This first model weighed 2.5 pounds and took 10 hours to recharge. Cooper received a patent for the phone on September 16, 1975.

4917. Cell phone marketed commercially was the DynaTAC 8000X, made by Motorola, Schaumburg, IL, to be used with Motorola's cellular system. It was approved by the Federal Communications Commission in 1983 and went on the market the following year. The handset weighed 28 ounces. The price for the phone was $3,500.

4918. Cellular telephone system began operation in Chicago, IL, in 1983. It was a microwave-based radiotelephone system in which the service area was divided into geographic "cells," each of which was assigned a transmission frequency. The first such system in the world was put into service in Tokyo in 1979.

4919. Transoceanic fiber-optic telecommunications cable was the TAT-8, brought online on December 8, 1988, by the telecom companies American Telephone & Telegraph (AT&T), Standard Communications Laboratories, and Submarcom, a French firm. TAT-8, so called because it was the eighth transatlantic cable laid by AT&T, was capable of carrying 40,000 simultaneous telephone calls between the United States and France.

4920. Prepaid phone card to require a PIN was introduced in 1990 by NYNEX, the Bell regional phone company that served New York and New England. The user accessed the phone lines through an 800 number.

4921. Telephone directory with internet addresses was issued for Westchester County, NY, in February 1997 by Nynex, a New York regional telephone utility company serving New York and New England. The directory included names, addresses, phone numbers, fax numbers, email addresses, and World Wide Web addresses. Similar information had been provided by on-line computerized directories beginning in 1995.

4922. Prepaid disposable cell phone was sold by Hop-On.com Inc., Garden Grove, CA, and New Horizons Technologies International Inc., Orlando, FL, in 2002. The phones, which cost about $40, were preprogrammed with a set number of minutes and could be reused if additional minutes were purchased.

Television

4923. Telecast of an object in motion was sent on June 13, 1925, from radio station NOF, Bellevue, DC (now part of Washington, DC), and was received at the laboratory of Charles Francis Jenkins, 1519 Connecticut Avenue, Washington. The apparatus used was Vision-by-Radio, invented by Jenkins. The image showed a small model windmill with its blades in motion.

4924. Weather map to be telecast from a land sending station to a land receiving station was sent on August 18, 1926, from radio station NAA, Arlington, VA, and received at the Weather Bureau Office, Washington, DC. The demonstration was arranged by the Jenkins Laboratory, Washington, DC. The first weather map to be telecast to a transatlantic steamer was sent by the Radiomarine Corporation station, New York City, on June 20, 1930, to the S.S. *America*, nearly 3,000 miles distant.

4925. Telecast of image and sound transmitted over any considerable distance was demonstrated on April 7, 1927, when Secretary of Commerce Herbert Clark Hoover, at 1208 H Street, Washington, DC, read a speech into a telephone and was both seen and heard by a large group gathered in the auditorium of the Bell Telephone Laboratories, New York City. The picture was 2 by 3 inches and was transmitted at the rate of 18 images per second.

4926. Woman to appear on television was Edna Mae Horner, a telephone operator for the Chesapeake and Potomac Telephone Company. On April 27, 1927, during Bell Telephone's first long-distance telecast, she appeared on camera working a telephone switchboard. The event transmitted images and sound from Washington, DC, to New York City.

4927. Image transmitted by television was a straight line that was telecast on September 7, 1927, by Philo T. Farnsworth using his camera tube, the Image Dissector. This was the first use of an all-electronic television transmitter and receiver. The parts were in separate rooms of Farnsworth's lab in San Francisco, CA.

In 1929 Philo T. Farnsworth telecast the first human images ever seen on television, including an image of his wife, Elma Gardner Farnsworth, that was transmitted on October 19, 1929.

4928. Television sets to be installed in homes on an experimental basis were installed in Schenectady, NY, on January 13, 1928, by the Radio Corporation of America and the General Electric Company. Three sets were installed. The images were transmitted over a wavelength of 37.8 meters and the sound sent simultaneously over a wavelength of 379.5 meters. The picture was 1.5 inches square. The television receiver's elements were a light source, a scanning device, and a synchronizing system.

4929. Television station was run by the Charles Francis Jenkins Laboratories. A license was issued to the laboratories on February 25, 1928, by the Federal Radio Commission for the operation of a television broadcast station at 1519 Connecticut Avenue, NW, Washington, DC, using the call letters W3XK. In 1929, the station was authorized to move its transmitter to a location between Silver Spring and Wheaton, MD. The station ceased to operate on October 31, 1932.

4930. Television programs to be shown regularly began appearing on May 11, 1928, from the General Electric Station, WGY, at Schenectady, NY. The programs were shown three times a week. The image consisted of 24 scanning lines repeated 20 times a second.

4931. Outdoor scenes to be televised were viewed in the offices of the Bell Telephone Laboratories, New York City, on July 12, 1928. Scenes enacted in the open air were almost as clear as those taken in specially designed studios.

4932. Standard broadcast station to transmit a television image was Hugo Gernsback's station WRNY, Coytesville, NJ, which transmitted a 1.5-inch square image of the face of Mrs. John Geloso on August 13, 1928. The image was viewed at Philosophy Hall, New York University, New York City, by 500 persons. It was magnified by a lens to twice the size.

4933. Remote television pickup took place on August 22, 1928, from the New York State Assembly chamber at Albany, NY, where the presidential candidate of the Democratic Party, Alfred Emanuel Smith, was notified of his nomination. Television images of his acceptance were transmitted from Schenectady, NY, and relayed by short wave over 2XAF and 2XAD by the General Electric Company. It was the first televised news broadcast.

4934. Speaker to address an organization by television was Dr. Peter Irving Wold, president of the Fortnightly Club, Schenectady, NY, who conducted a meeting of the club from the television station at the General Electric Laboratory on April 1, 1930. The members were assembled at the home of Dr. Ernst Fredrik Werner Alexanderson in Schenectady.

4935. Television theater to be licensed was the Massachusetts Television Institute, Boston, MA. It opened on July 13, 1938, with a 45-minute show witnessed by 200 people who had paid a 25-cent admission fee. The show consisted of vocal, instrumental, and dance numbers. They were performed in a room above the auditorium and transmitted by a wire to a 9-by-12-inch screen on which black and white images appeared, accompanied by sound.

4936. Cathode ray tubes were invented by the Russian-American electrical engineer Vladimir Kosma Zworykin, who received the two essential television patents on December 20, 1938. One patent was for the iconoscope, a cathode-ray transmitting tube that was the heart of all television cameras until the late 1980s. The second patent was for the kinescope, or cathode-ray receiving tube, the device that displays the image on all televisions and most computer monitors.

4937. Sports event to be televised live was a Columbia–Princeton baseball game that was played on May 17, 1939, at Columbia's Baker Field in New York City. An Iconoscope camera mounted near third base fed signals to station W2XBS in the Empire State Building. Commentary was provided by a radio announcer, Bill Stern. The camera was unable to follow the ball with sufficient speed, and the audience—mostly visitors to the New York World's Fair in Flushing, Queens, New York City—saw little more than white dots and streaks on a gray background.

4938. Commercial television licenses were granted to 10 stations on May 2, 1941, by the Federal Communications Commission, with permission to begin operations on July 1, 1941. The first license, No. 1, was issued to W2XBS, NBC, which telecast from the Empire State Building using Channel 1. The station had four sponsors: Lever Brothers, for Spry; Proctor and Gamble, for Ivory Soap; the Sun Oil Company; and the Bulova Watch Company.

4939. Television variety talent show series was telecast by WNBT-TV, New York City, for Standard Brands on Thursday nights from May 9, 1946, until March 6, 1947. The first episode, "The Hour Glass," starred Edgar Bergen, Paul Douglas, Joe Besser, and Evelyn Knight. The first variety talent show series with an African-American cast was "Happy Pappy," which was first televised on April 1, 1949, over WENR-TV, Chicago, IL. The program featured Ray Grant as master of ceremonies, the Four Vagabonds, and the Modern Modes.

4940. Commercial program telecast on a network was "Geographically Speaking," sponsored by the Bristol-Myers Company and first broadcast on October 27, 1946, on WNBT, New York, and WPTZ, Philadelphia, PA.

4941. Commercial television station west of the Mississippi River was KTLA-TV, Hollywood, Los Angeles, CA, which began operations on January 22, 1947, at 8:30 P.M., from a converted garage. Dick Lane was the announcer.

4942. Television drama program regularly scheduled was *Kraft Television Theater*, telecast on the National Broadcasting Company's network from May 7, 1947, to October 1, 1958, from 7:30 to 8:30 P.M. The program ran for 11 years, during which time it presented 650 plays that required 5,236 sets and the participation of 3,955 actors. The first drama was *Double Door*, starring John Baragrey.

4943. Western series on television was *Hopalong Cassidy*, which first aired on November 28, 1948, on NBC-TV. Actor Bill Boyd, 53, starred in the title role.

4944. Animated cartoon made for television was *Crusader Rabbit*, which premiered in 1949. It was the creation of animator Jay Ward, who with writer Bill Scott also produced *Rocky and His Friends* for the ABC network in 1959.

4945. Sitcom television show was *The Goldbergs*, which debuted on January 17, 1949, and aired weekly until June 1951. It was derived from the radio show of the same name. The star was Molly Berg. The term "sitcom" is short for "situation comedy."

4946. Emmy awards for excellence in television were presented by the National Academy of Television Arts and Sciences on January 25, 1949, at the Hollywood Athletic Club, Los Angeles, CA. Walter O'Keefe was the host. Most of the awards were won by programs originating at station KTLA, Los Angeles, CA, including the award for the most popular television program, *Pantomine Quiz Time*; the award for the most outstanding television personality, Shirley Dinsdale and her puppet Judy Splinters; and the award for the best film made for television, *The Necklace*, which appeared on the KTLA series *Your Show Time*. KTLA won an additional award for outstanding overall achievements in 1948.

4947. Soap opera on daytime television was *These Are My Children*, by Irna Phillips, which was aired between 5 and 5:15 P.M. every weekday from January 31 to February 25, 1949, by NBC from Chicago, IL.

4948. Television series in which an African-American performer had a starring role was the 1950 sitcom *Beulah*, which starred Ethel Waters.

4949. Illegal television station closed by the Federal Communications Commission was operated by the Tube Division of Sylvania Electric Products at Emporium, PA. It was shut down on October 19, 1950. The station, which used a 90-foot transmission tower on top of Whittemore Mountain, had televised programs from WJAC-TV, Johnstown, PA, without authorization.

4950. Pay television system was Phonovision, first demonstrated on January 1, 1951, by station KS2KSBS of the Zenith Radio Corporation, Chicago, IL, under authority of the Federal Communications Commission. The station transmitted a scrambled radio signal that could be received only by customers whose home television sets were activated by a "key signal" sent by a telephone circuit. The demonstration consisted of three movies: *April Showers*, with Jack Carson, shown at 4 P.M.; *Welcome Stranger*, with Bing Crosby, at 7 P.M.; and *Homecoming*, with Clark Gable and Lana Turner, at 9 P.M. A charge of $1 was made for each full-length feature program. During the first four weeks, 2,561 sales were made. The test was limited to 300 families chosen from 51,000 applicants by the National Opinion Research Council of the University of Chicago.

4951. Television program in color to be presented daily was Ivan T. Sanderson's *The World Is Yours*, first seen on the CBS network over Channel 2 (W2CBS) on June 26, 1951, from 4:30 to 5 P.M. It depicted the earth's natural treasures. The first regular prime-time series broadcast in color was *Bonanza*, which aired on NBC from 1959 to 1973.

4952. Transcontinental telecast received on the East Coast was transmitted from the War Memorial Opera House, San Francisco, CA, on September 4, 1951, at 10:30 P.M. by a pool of the four networks to 94 of the 107 television stations then in operation. The telecast was transmitted by microwave relays to Omaha, NE, and then by coaxial cables to stations in the east, north, and south. Secretary of State Dean Acheson introduced President Harry S. Truman, who made an address from the Opera House in conjunction with the signing of the Japanese peace treaty.

4953. Transcontinental telecast received on the West Coast was the Columbia Broadcasting System program *Crusade for Freedom*, transmitted from WCBS-TV, New York City, on September 23, 1951. General Lucius DuBignon Clay was chairman of the program.

4954. Telecast from a foreign country took place on October 15, 1951, from 10:45 to 11:15 A.M., when WWJ-TV, Detroit, MI, had its mobile unit cover the informal reception given to Princess Elizabeth of Great Britain and Philip, Duke of Edinburgh, on Government Dock, Windsor, Canada. Budd Lynch was the announcer. The program was carried by the National Broadcasting Company and the American Broadcasting Company on Channel 4 and Channel 7. The first live telecast from a noncontiguous foreign country was transmitted on November 13, 1955, by CMQ, Havana, Cuba. A five-minute aerial view of Havana was televised from an airplane to CMQ and relayed by airplanes to WIOD, Miami, FL, for telecasting on Dave Garroway's show *Wide Wide World* on the National Broadcasting System network.

4955. Pay television presentation of a sports event was the closed-circuit coast-to-coast telecast of the Jersey Joe Walcott–Rocky Marciano fight at the Municipal Stadium, Philadelphia, PA, on September 23, 1952. Marciano won the heavyweight title by a knockout 43 seconds into the 13th round. The telecast was viewed by 40,379 persons in 49 theaters located in 31 cities. Ticket sales totaled $504,645.

4956. Year in which television industry profits exceeded those of radio was 1953. According to the Federal Communications Commission, profits for that year were $68 million for television and $55 million for radio.

4957. Three-dimensional telecast was presented on April 29, 1953, from KECA-TV, Los Angeles, CA, by American Broadcasting–Paramount Theatres. The audience was 70 newspaper and trade publishers attending the 31st annual convention of the National Association of Radio and Television Broadcasters at the Biltmore Hotel, Los Angeles, where special receivers had been installed. The one-hour telecast included a live performance of *Space Patrol* and Lloyd Nolan's prologue to the motion picture *Bwana Devil*. The three-dimension effect was achieved by showing two offscreen images simultaneously. The images appeared blurred unless viewed through polaroid lenses.

4958. Educational television station was KUHT, University of Houston, Houston, TX, which broadcast test patterns on May 12, 1953. Programming began on May 25, 1953, from 5 to 9 P.M. five days a week over Channel 8, on the very-high-frequency band. The station was licensed jointly by the University of

Houston and the Houston public school system on April 14, 1952. John Schwarzwalder was director.

4959. Coast-to-coast live telecast in color was transmitted on November 3, 1953, from the Colonial Theatre, New York City, by WNBT-TV, New York City. The program, which starred Nanette Fabray, was sent in compatible color over the radio relay circuit system of the Bell Telephone Company and was received by 14-inch receivers at Burbank, CA.

4960. Educational television station sponsored by a city was WQED, Channel 13, Pittsburgh, PA, which received its license on May 13, 1953, and went on the air on April 1, 1954. A second education channel, WQEX, Channel 16, was granted a license on July 16, 1958, making Pittsburgh the first city with two educational television stations.

4961. Microwave television station was KTRE-TV, Lufkin, TX, owned by the Forest Capital Broadcasting Company, which began operations on August 31, 1955, on Channel 9, on the very-high-frequency band. Signals from KPRC-TV, Houston, TX, on Channel 2, were deflected to booster equipment at the bottom of a tower at Coldspring, 60 miles away. There the signals were amplified and sent to the next relay tower, at Carmona, 30 miles away, where they were again amplified and sent to Lufkin, another 30 miles away. Richman Lewin was general manager of KTRE-TV.

4962. All-color television station to televise live local programs was WNBQ-TV, Channel 5, Chicago, IL, which began operations in color on April 15, 1956. Three color studios were equipped with five color cameras and two color-film projector chains for 16mm and 35mm films. The station had started showing black and white telecasts on January 7, 1949, and had begun the conversion to color on November 3, 1955.

4963. Video recording on magnetic tape televised coast-to-coast was *The Jonathan Winters Show*, televised from 7:30 to 7:45 P.M. on October 23, 1956, by WRCA-TV, New York City. The process was developed by RCA for NBC. Instead of film, the system utilized instantaneous tape with pictures that could be played back immediately after recording. The telecast was shown in full compatible color and also in black-and-white.

4964. Network variety show hosted by an African-American was the *Nat King Cole Show*, starring the singer and jazz pianist Nat King Cole (the stage name of Nathaniel Adams Coles). It was a weekly showcase for musical talent, broadcast on NBC starting on November 5, 1956. No national sponsors bought commercial time for fear of offending white viewers, and the show went off the air after 13 months.

4965. Telecast received from England was transmitted via cable on June 18, 1959, from London to Montreal, Canada, and relayed by the Canadian Broadcasting Company to the National Broadcasting Company in New York City, which sent it out over the entire NBC network. The film showed the departure from London of Queen Elizabeth and Prince Philip, who were on their way to attend the opening ceremonies for the St. Lawrence Seaway. The Motion Picture Facsimile process used in the telecast was developed by the BBC. Each frame required eight seconds for transmission. The film was seen 2 hours and 21 minutes after the recording was made.

4966. Animated cartoon series on prime-time television was *The Flintstones*, which debuted on September 30, 1960, on the ABC television network. The half-hour show, produced by William Hanna and Joseph Barbera, featured the antics of two prehistoric families.

4967. Pay television dramatic program was shown on June 29, 1962, by WHCT-TV, Channel 18, Hartford, CT, on ultrahigh frequency. The program consisted of a play, *Sunrise at Campobello*, starring Ralph Bellamy as President Franklin Delano Roosevelt, plus a Czechoslovakian presentation of William Shakespeare's *Midsummer Night's Dream*. No commercials were shown. Subscribers, who had decoders installed on their sets, paid a $1 fee. The station operated under a test license granted on February 24, 1961, for three years by the Federal Communications Commission, effective when 2,000 paying customers signed up.

4968. Live telecast to Europe by satellite was transmitted by the American Broadcasting System, the National Broadcasting System, and the Columbia Broadcasting System by *Telstar 1* on July 23, 1962, to the Eurovision network of 18 nations. The program was narrated in seven languages and showed sequences picturing the Statue of Liberty, buffalo on the western plains, the Phillies–Cubs baseball game at Chicago, President John Fitzgerald Kennedy's news conference, the Abraham Lincoln carving at Mount Rushmore, the Mormon Tabernacle Choir, astronaut Lieutenant Commander Walter Marty Schirra, a small boy admiring a Native American chief, and similar scenes. Three hours later, a 20-minute telecast was received from Europe, showing Big Ben and the House of Commons, reindeer in the Arctic Circle, Swiss guards at the Sistine Chapel, the entrance to the Louvre, the Colosseum in Rome, a painting in the National Museum of Belgrade, and fishermen in Sicily.

4969. Telecast transmitted by satellite to Japan was a 15-minute news program beamed at 7 P.M. on November 22, 1963, from the U.S. ground station in the Mojave Desert. It was relayed by the communications satellite *Relay 1* and received by the Space Communications Laboratory north of Tokyo, Japan, from 5:16 to 5:46 A.M. on November 23. ABC and NBC shared in producing the program. Japanese viewers saw scenic and cultural sequences and heard taped messages from Ryuji Takeuchi, the Japanese ambassador, and James Edwin Webb, director of the National Aeronautics and Space Administration. The first telecast transmitted by satellite from Japan to the United States was beamed over the satellite *Relay 2* and viewed simultaneously on three national networks. It was rebroadcast on the *Today Show* on March 25, 1964, from 7:32 to 7:40 A.M. The telecast showed Prime Minister Hayato Ikeda.

4970. Soap opera on prime-time television was *Peyton Place*, which first aired on the CBS network on September 15, 1964, and continued to run for five years. The series was based on the 1956 novel by Grace Metalious, which also spawned a popular 1957 Hollywood film. It detailed the steamy doings in a small New England town.

4971. Made-for-TV movie was *See How They Run*, which starred John Forsythe and Jane Wyman. It aired on the NBC network on October 7, 1964. The joint NBC–Universal Studios production was not a ratings success.

4972. Television dramatic series starring an African-American performer was *I Spy*, which starred Bill Cosby as secret agent Alexander Scott. The show premiered on the NBC network on September 15, 1965, and ran until September 2, 1968.

4973. British-made television series to be shown coast-to-coast on an American network in prime time as part of the regular weekly schedule, rather than as a replacement for a canceled series, was *The Avengers*, starring Patrick Macnee and Diana Rigg. It was aired by ABC beginning in 1967. The show, which had been on the air in Britain since 1961, already had an audience of more than 30 million viewers in 40 countries. The first 13 episodes shown in the United States were filmed in black and white, the remaining episodes in color.

4974. Educational television network operated as a nonprofit corporation was National Educational Television (NET), New York City, which started in 1952 as a nonprofit Illinois corporation, the Educational Television and Radio Center. On January 10, 1967, NET interconnected 70 of its 100 independent affiliated educational stations for a live broadcast and analysis of President Lyndon Baines Johnson's State of the Union message. Regularly scheduled noncommercial network broadcasting began on November 5, 1967, with the premiere of the Public Broadcast Laboratory over the NET network.

4975. Worldwide live television program was *Our World*, shown in 26 countries on June 25, 1967, via four satellites. The two-hour production involved 10,000 technicians and 300 cameras in 14 countries on five continents. It opened with glimpses of births in Mexico, Canada, Denmark, and Japan. The rest of the program featured clips of Leonard Bernstein and Van Cliburn rehearsing a Rachmaninoff concerto at New York City's Lincoln Center, the Beatles recording a song in London, a rehearsal of *Lohengrin* in Bayreuth, Germany, the making of a movie in Italy, and other presentations. The American outlet was the National Educational Television network. The program cost about $5 million.

4976. Year in which color television sets outsold black and white sets was 1968, when 11.4 million sets were sold, 5.8 color and 5.5 million black and white.

4977. Episode of *Sesame Street* to be shown on television aired on November 10, 1969, on the Public Television System. The show was produced by the Children's Television Workshop. It used techniques borrowed from commercial television to teach letters and numbers to preschoolers.

4978. Stereo telecast was a double-channel telecast made on December 28, 1972, from 11:30 P.M. to midnight over WNEW-TV (Channel 5) and WNET (Channel 13), New York City. The program was entitled *Two's Better Than One* and featured four playlets: *Boxes, Are You There?*, *What a Life*, and *The Yin and Yang of It*. The hosts were Bob Elliott on Channel 5, where half the action took place, and Ray Goulding on Channel 13, for the other half.

4979. All-politics television network was C-SPAN, the Cable-Satellite Public Affairs Network, founded by Brian P. Lamb. It began broadcasting live coverage of proceedings in the House of Representatives on March 19, 1979, and in the Senate on June 2, 1986. Its coverage also included congressional hearings, major party conventions, important speeches and briefings, and some political activities in other countries.

4980. TV program broadcast on the Internet was the 85th episode of a public-access television series called "ROX," which debuted in cyberspace on April 15, 1995, at a Web site called The Rox Quarry (www.rox.com/quarry/) in the digital QuickTime format. "ROX," a home-grown program of social and political satire, was produced by Joe Nickell and Bart Everson of Bloomington, IN. The first professionally produced television show to appear on the Internet was Computer Chronicles, a program about personal computing hosted by Stewart Cheifet. Its first cyberspace episode was also broadcast in 1995.

4981. High-definition television broadcasting license was granted to WRAL-TV, Raleigh, NC, by the Federal Communications Commission on June 19, 1996. The experimental HDTV station, with the call sign "WRAL-HD," operated on channel 32 and could be viewed with proper equipment in the Raleigh, Durham, Fayetteville, and Chapel Hill areas. James F. Goodmon was president and CEO of WRAL's parent company, Capitol Broadcasting Co., Inc.; Capitol's HDTV Project Manager was John L. Greene. On Jan. 28, 2001, WRAL became the world's first high-definition TV newsgathering operation with the debut of the station's all-digital HD newsroom.

4982. Television station to regularly broadcast high-definition television was WRAL, a CBS affiliate in Raleigh, NC. On July 23, 1996, WRAL-HD, an experimental station, began broadcasting high-definition digital television data from a spectrum analyzer. WHD-TV, an experimental station at NBC affiliate WRC-TV in Washington, DC, broadcast the first full high-definition television pictures a week later. A high-definition version of the long-running news show *Meet the Press* was broadcast by WHD-TV beginning in February 1997.

4983. Movie shown on a television network without interruption by commercials was *Schindler's List*, a 1993 film about the Holocaust directed by Steven Spielberg. It was broadcast by the NBC network on Sunday, February 23, 1997. The sponsor, Ford Motor Company, presented one commercial before the film and one afterward, but none during the telecast. This was also the first broadcast rated TV-M (for "mature" audiences) under the television ratings system implemented by broadcasters in late 1996.

4984. Major network program broadcast in high-definition television was "The Wonderful World of Disney: 101 Dalmations," which aired on ABC on November 1, 1998.

4985. TV drama about an actual war in progress was *Over There*, a series about an infantry squad of American soldiers fighting in Iraq. It was conceived and produced by Stephen Bochco and was shown on the FX cable network. The first episode appeared on July 27, 2005. After a three-month season, the show was canceled by FX because of a steep decline in viewers.

Technology

4986. Miniature television tube was the "peanut tube," an N-type tube, 2 inches high and 0.625 inches in diameter, operated on a single dry cell. The tube was created by Howard W. Weinhart of Elizabeth, NJ, who obtained a patent on August 25, 1925, on an "electric discharge device." The patent was assigned to the Western Electric Company, New York City.

4987. Public demonstration of color television was given on June 27, 1929, in the Bell Telephone Laboratories, New York City. Some of the objects shown in color were an American flag, a watermelon, and a bunch of roses. The images were of low definition and were mechanically scanned. The equipment demonstrated utilized three complete systems of photoelectric cells, amplifiers, and glow tubes. Each system had a red, blue, or green screen. A system of mirrors superposed the three monochromatic images to make one combined picture in color.

4988. Demonstration of home reception of television was given in New York City on August 20, 1930, when a half-hour program broadcast from two stations was received on screens placed in a store in the Hotel Ansonia at Broadway and 73d Street, in the Hearst Building at Eighth Avenue and 57th Street, and in a residence at 98 Riverside Drive. On these screens appeared the images of performers talking and singing in the studios of the Jenkins W2XCR television station at Jersey City, NJ, and the De Forest W2XCD station at Passaic, NJ. The distance, approximately six miles, was the greatest over which pictures had yet been transmitted by television. The cartoonist Harry Hirschfeld was master of ceremonies.

4989. Telecast using coaxial cable was sent on June 10, 1936, from the Radio City complex, New York City, to the transmitter atop the Empire State Building, a distance of approximately 1.5 miles.

4990. High-definition telecast was made on June 29, 1936, by station W2XBS from the Empire State Building, New York City, at the rate of 30 pictures per second with a 343-line screen. On July 7, 1936, David Sarnoff, president of the Radio Corporation of America, and Major General James Guthrie Harbord, chairman of the board of RCA, opened for invited guests a program in which Henry Hull, Graham McNamee, Ed Wynn, and members of the Water Lily Ensemble appeared as performers. A fashion show and a film were also presented.

4991. Mobile television unit for outdoor events consisted of two large motor vans containing television control apparatus and a microwave transmitter. The unit was completed by the RCA Manufacturing Company, Camden, NJ, and turned over to station W2XBT of the National Broadcasting Company, New York City, on December 12, 1937. The telecasts were relayed by microwave to a tower transmitter in the Empire State Building, New York City, and rebroadcast from there. The first mobile color units were placed in operation on January 1, 1954, by the National Broadcasting Company's station WNBT, New York City, and consisted of two three-color mobile units with complete audio-video control, housed in a van 35 feet long, 8 feet wide, and 10 feet 7 inches high.

4992. Public telecast made over telephone wires took place on May 20, 1939, when the National Broadcasting Company televised bicycle races at Madison Square Garden, New York City. The images were transmitted from Madison Square Garden to the NBC studio at the Radio City complex in New York City via the Circle telephone exchange at Ninth Avenue and 50th Street. When the images were received at the studio over telephone wire, they were conveyed over a coaxial cable to the transmitter in the tower of the Empire State Building, from which they were telecast.

4993. Coin-operated television receiver was the Tradio-Vision, manufactured by Tradio, Asbury Park, NJ, and publicly exhibited on November 7, 1946, in New York City. The receiver, housed in a metal cabinet 16 inches high, 8 inches deep, and 9 inches wide, contained 20 tubes and a 5-inch cathode tube that reflected a 500-line image on a mirror on the lid. The apparatus was designed to operate after a 25-cent coin was inserted.

4994. Television image using a split screen was exhibited on December 8, 1948, by the NBC at the Television Broadcasters Association Clinic held at the Waldorf-Astoria Hotel, New York City. The technique presented two pictures from different points of origin side by side on the same kinescope picture tube. The telecast showed John Cameron Swayze, in New York City, interviewing Representative Karl Earl Mundt of South Dakota, who was in Washington, DC.

4995. Rectangular television tube that was practical was announced to the trade on July 10, 1949, by the Kimble Glass Company, a subsidiary of Owens-Illinois in Toledo, OH. The bulb faces of the tube were approximately 12 by 16 inches. The tube sold for approximately $12. The first deliveries were made on October 1, 1949.

4996. Television remote control was the Lazy Bones, which was introduced by the Zenith Radio Corporation, Chicago, IL, in 1950. The idea came from Zenith's president, Eugene F. McDonald, Jr., who wanted to give customers a convenient way to change channels in order to avoid commercials. The handset was connected to the television set by a cable. The device cost $50.

4997. Video recording on high-definition magnetic tape was made on October 3, 1952, when the electronics division of Bing Crosby Enterprises, Los Angeles, CA, recorded images on magnetic tape, rewound the tape, and immediately reproduced the picture through a standard television monitor tube. A one-inch tape with 12 tracks, 1 for sound and 11 for pictures, was used. The cost was one-third that of photographic processes.

4998. Television receiver that showed two programs simultaneously was the Duoscopic, publicly demonstrated on January 7, 1954, in New York City and Chicago, IL, by the Allen B. Du Mont Laboratories. Two superimposed images were projected onto the screen by two cathode ray tubes set at right angles. The images were viewed through polaroid glasses. Contrast controls were separate, and two separate systems were used to carry sounds through personalized earpieces. Each speaker could be turned off independently. The viewer could choose to watch only one image, as in standard sets, or to watch one picture on the screen and listen to the other through the earpiece. The system was announced for sale in a full-page advertisement that ran on January 21, 1954, in the *New York Times*.

4999. Wireless television remote control was the Flashmatic, which was invented by Eugene Polley, an engineer at the Zenith Radio Corporation, Chicago, IL, and went on sale in 1955. The handset was a flashlight in the shape of a gun that could be used to activate photo cells hidden in the corners of the screen. The Flashmatic was superceded the following year by Space Command, the first ultrasonic remote control device, invented by another Zenith engineer, Robert Adler.

5000. Television receivers to project large images up to 9 by 12 feet were installed in April 1955 in seven Sheraton Hotels. The receivers, built by the Fleetwood Corporation, Toledo, OH, were 4 feet high, 2 feet wide, and 3 feet deep and weighed 400 pounds. They were mounted on rubber-tired casters so that they could be moved easily. They were designed to show closed-circuit programs in ballrooms, conference rooms, and places of assembly.

5001. Video tape recorder for sounds and pictures was manufactured by the Ampex Corporation, Redwood City, CA, and demonstrated simultaneously in Redwood City and Chicago, IL, on April 14, 1956. The tape, 2 inches wide, moved at a speed of 15 inches per second. A single 14-inch reel accommodated a 65-minute recording. The developers were Charles P. Ginsberg, Charles E. Anderson, and Ray Dolby. The Columbia Broadcasting System purchased three of the video tape recorders at $75,000 each in 1956.

5002. Telecast from the stratosphere was made on July 26, 1958, from the 17-story Navy plastic balloon *Strato-Lab High III* at an altitude of 60,000 feet over Minnesota. The images were transmitted by Commander Malcolm Ross and Commander Morton Lee Lewis and received by KSTP-TV, St. Paul, MN. The balloon took off from an open-pit mine at Crosby, MN, soared to 82,000 feet, and remained aloft for 34 hours 29 minutes, establishing an endurance record, before landing at Jamestown, ND.

5003. Coast-to-coast telecast by satellite was accomplished on April 24, 1962, when the Massachusetts Institute of Technology's Lincoln Laboratory field station at Camp Parks, CA, transmitted airwaves to the two-year-old orbiting balloon *Echo I*, which bounced them back to earth. They were received at Millstone Hill, Westford, MA. The pictures were of poor quality but were recognizable.

5004. Transoceanic telecast by satellite was transmitted on July 10, 1962, from Andover, ME. It was bounced off the 170-pound orbiting relay communications satellite *Telstar 1* and was received at various stations in Europe and the United States. The following day, a telecast from Pleumeur-Bodou, France, was received at Andover received by means of the 380-ton horn-shaped antenna. The satellite was launched on July 10 from Cape Canaveral, FL.

5005. Television receiver and transmitter operated by laser beam was demonstrated on February 20, 1963, by the General Telephone and Electronics Corporation, Bayside, NY, where it was developed by Samuel M. Stone and Louis Richard Bloom. A laser device produces a narrow highly-intense beam of light that can be focused and directed over long distances. The first network television show to be transmitted by laser was the Columbia Broadcasting System show *I've Got a Secret*, telecast on May 14, 1963, from New York City. An electronic signal from a studio television camera was fed into a laser transmitter, carried across a two-foot space on a light beam, picked up by a laser receiver, and transmitted via the studio control room over the national television network.

5006. Video cassette recorder for home use was the Betamax, which was sold in the United States by the Sony Corporation of Japan beginning in November 1975. It was built into a console that also contained a Sony color television set. The tape was contained in a plastic cassette to make it easy to handle. Sony had marketed the first open-reel video tape recorder for home use, the TCV-2010, beginning in 1966. The device required a separate camera set up on a tripod, as well as a separate microphone to record sound.

5007. Satellite dish for personal use was designed by electronics engineer Taylor Howard in 1976. The dish enabled the user to receive broadcast signals directly from communications satellites.

MEDICINE AND HEALTH

5008. Physician in the colony of Virginia was Lawrence Bohune, who arrived in the first half of 1610. He was the first physician of the London Company. He was killed on March 19, 1622, on board the *Margaret and John* when the vessel was attacked by Spanish ships.

5009. Physician in the New England colonies was Dr. Samuel Fuller, who arrived on board the *Mayflower* on December 21, 1620, and was one of the signers of the Mayflower Compact. For some time he was the sole physician in Massachusetts. In a letter dated June 28, 1630, written at Salem, MA, to Governor William Bradford of Plymouth, he described one of the customary treatments, in which he "let some twenty of these people blood."

5010. Medical regulations enacted by a colony were passed by Virginia on October 21, 1639, in an "act to compel physicians and surgeons to declare on oath the value of their medicines." Another law, enacted May 3, 1649, in Massachusetts, was directed to "physicians, chirurgians, midwives or others" and forbade them "to exercise or put forth any act contrary to the known rules of art, nor exercise any force, violence, or cruelty upon or towards the bodies of any, whether young or old." The act was "not intended to discourage the lawful use of their skill but to encourage and direct them in the right use thereof and to inhibit and restrain the presumptious arrogance of such as . . . exercise violence upon . . . bodies."

5011. Physician who was Jewish was Jacob Lumbrozo, who settled in Maryland on January 24, 1656. He was a native of Lisbon, Portugal. He died in May 1666. The first Jewish physician to head an asylum for the mentally ill was Dr. John de Sequeyra, a Portugese physician educated in Holland, who was appointed in 1770 at Williamsburg, VA.

5012. Pharmacist who was a woman was Elizabeth Marshall, daughter of Charles Marshall, the president of the Philadelphia College of Pharmacy. She became manager of the apothecary originally established by her grandfather, Christopher Marshall, in 1729 in Philadelphia, PA. She served from 1804 until 1825, when the store was sold.

5013. Physician born in America who was graduated from a foreign medical school was Dr. William Bull of Charleston, SC. He received his degree from Leyden University, Leyden, the Netherlands, on August 18, 1734. The title of his thesis was "Colica pictonum."

5014. Pharmacist to fill prescriptions other than his own was Jonathan Roberts, who served from May 1754 to May 1755 as apothecary in the Pennsylvania Hospital, Philadelphia, PA. Previously, each apothecary had prepared remedies to use in his own practice.

5015. Medical licensing law enacted by a city that was actually enforced was an "act to regulate the practice of Physick and Surgery in the City of New York," passed on June 10, 1760. It provided that "no person whatsoever shall practice as a physician or surgeon . . . before he shall first have been examined in physick or surgery and approved of and admitted by one of His Majesty's Council, the Judges of the Supreme Court, the King's Attorney General and the Mayor of the City of New York for the time being or by any three or more of them." Violators were subject to a penalty of £5, half of which went to the informer and the remainder to the funds for the poor.

5016. Medical licensing law enacted by a colony was New Jersey's law of September 26, 1772. The act was effective for a five-year period. It authorized a licensing board consisting of two judges of the Supreme Court of New Jersey and a third individual appointed by them, and forbade the practice of medicine without a license. Very severe fines were imposed upon violators, but the law did not apply to those who drew teeth, bled patients, or gave medical assistance for which they received no fee or compensation.

5017. Physician who was African-American was James Derham, a slave who was trained by his owner, a doctor, and who practiced circa 1783 in New Orleans, LA, and later in Philadelphia, PA. The first African-American with formal medical training was James McCune Smith, who received his medical degree in 1837 from the University of Glasgow, Scotland, with financial aid from the Glasgow Emancipation Society. He became a physician and pharmacist in New York City, as well as a prominent abolitionist. The first to receive a medical degree from an American school was David Jones Peck, who graduated in 1847 from Rush Medical College, Chicago, IL.

5018. Quack doctor of note was Dr. Elisha Perkins, born in 1740, who invented Perkins' Patented Metallic Tractor, a contraption of metallic rods intended to "pull" diseases from the body. Among his better-known patients were President George Washington and Supreme Court Chief Justice Oliver Ellsworth. Perkins died in 1799 from yellow fever, four weeks after bringing his Tractor to New York City to cure an epidemic of that disease.

5019. Physiologist of note was Dr. William Beaumont, a surgeon in the Army, whose book *Experiments and Observations on the Gastric Juice and the Physiology of Digestion* was published in 1833 in Plattsburgh, NY. He achieved fame by his treatment of Alexis St. Martin (also called Samata or San Maten), who was shot in the stomach on June 6, 1822, at the Fort Mackinac trading post. Dr. Beaumont was able to watch the digestive process through the opening in the patient's stomach wall and to find by experiment the effect of different foods and medicines. He found that gastric juices were secreted only when there was food in the stomach and that simple irritation of the mucous membrane would not initiate a flow of gastric juices.

5020. Homeopathy practitioner was Dr. Hans Burch Gram, a Dutch homeopathy doctor who emigrated to New York City in 1825. In 1828, Gram was elected a member of the New York Medical and Philosophical Society, and in 1829 he became its president.

5021. Phrenologist of importance to visit the United States was Johann Gaspar Spurzheim, an associate of Dr. Franz Joseph Gall, the German physician who originated the now-discredited theory of phrenology, which posited that an individual's character and personality could be determined from the shape of the skull. Spurzheim arrived in New York City on August 6, 1832, and gave a series of lectures in Boston and Cambridge, MA. He died on November 10. His funeral was attended by the Boston Medical Association as a group.

5022. Chiropodist was Nehemiah Kenison, who, together with his brother and a cousin, opened an office in 1840 directly opposite the Old South Church on Washington Street, Boston, MA. They developed instruments and protective dressings to aid in the relief of the pain caused by corns and other foot conditions.

5023. Dental surgeons to be licensed by a state were those of Alabama, under a law passed on December 31, 1841. It provided for the establishment of "medical boards of the state to examine and to issue a license to applicants to practice dental surgery under the same rules and regulations, and subject to the same restrictions as those who apply for license to practice medicine."

5024. Physician who was a woman was Dr. Elizabeth Blackwell, a native of Bristol, England, who came to the United States in her youth and received her M.D. degree from the Geneva Medical College (later known as Hobart College), Geneva, NY, on January 23, 1849, receiving the highest grades in her class. She opened a private dispensary in New York City in 1853 and afterwards became professor of gynecology at the London School of Medicine for Women.

5025. Ophthalmologist of note was Dr. Edward Delafield. In 1818 he formulated a plan to establish the New York Eye Infirmary, which opened in 1820 in two rooms at 45 Chatham Street, treating 436 patients in the first seven months. In 1864, he became the first president of the American Ophthalmological Society.

5026. Physician who was an African-American woman was Rebecca Lee Crumpler, who received an M.D. degree on March 1, 1864, from the New England Female Medical College, Boston, MA.

5027. Surgeon who was a woman was Dr. Mary Harris Thompson, who received her M.D. degree in 1863 from the New England Medical College, Boston, MA. In May 1865 she founded the Mary Thompson Hospital in Chicago, IL, to care for widows and children of the poor, to sustain a free dispensary, and to train competent nurses. The hospital had 14 beds. It was destroyed by fire on October 9, 1871, but the patients were removed to another location and operation resumed the same day. The hospital is now the Women's and Children's Hospital, Chicago, IL.

5028. Nurse to receiving formal training was Linda Ann Judson Richards, first in a class of five to register as a student nurse at the Training School of the New England Hospital for Women and Children, Roxbury, MA, on September 1, 1872. The school offered a one-year program in medical, surgical, and obstetric nursing. After graduation, Richards served as night superintendent at Bellevue Hospital, New York City, and as superintendent of the Training School of the Massachusetts General Hospital, Boston, MA. The first trained nurse who was African-American was Mary Eliza Mahoney, who graduated in 1879 from the same program.

5029. Osteopathic physician was Dr. Andrew Taylor Still of Macon, MO, who cured a case of "flux" on June 22, 1874. He was instrumental in founding both a college and a magazine devoted to osteopathy.

5030. District nurse was employed by the Woman's Branch of the New York City Mission Society, New York City, in 1877.

5031. Visiting nurses were organized by Lillian Wald in 1892 to help the poor in New York City's Lower East Side tenement district. The service, later known as the Visiting Nurses' Service, eventually operated out of Wald's Henry Street Settlement.

5032. Osteopathic physicians who were women were Jenette Hubbard Bolles, Mamie B. Carter and Lou J. Kern, who were graduated on March 1, 1894, from the American School of Osteopathy, Kirksville, MO.

5033. Chiropractor was Daniel David Palmer, who gave the first adjustment treatment of vertebrae to Harvey Lillard in Davenport, IA, on September 18, 1895.

5034. Company nurse hired by a firm to attend to the health of its employees was Ada Stewart, who was employed by the Vermont Marble Company of Proctor, VT, in 1896.

5035. Physician who was a Chinese woman was Dr. Mary Stone (Shih Mai-yu), who was graduated from the Medical School of the University of Michigan, Ann Arbor, MI, on June 22, 1896. She founded the Women's Hospital at Kiukiang, China, under the auspices of the Methodist Foreign Mission and served as its head for 25 years.

5036. School nurses in public schools were employed in November 1902 by the New York City Department of Health.

5037. Nurses to be registered by a state were those of North Carolina, under a law ratified on March 3, 1903. It provided for voluntary registration with the county clerk of the Superior Court of any licensed trained nurse and for an examining and licensing board composed of two physicians and three registered nurses.

5038. Pharmacists to be regulated by a state were those of New York. A law enacted on May 3, 1904, required pharmacists to have two years of training and four years of practical experience.

5039. Nurse appointed to a college professorship was Mary Adelaide Nutting, who was appointed professor of household administration at Teachers College, Columbia University, New York City, in 1906. From 1910 to 1923 she served as professor of nursing education, and from 1923 to 1925 as professor of nursing education at the Helen Hartley Foundation.

5040. Chiropractic regulation law enacted by a state was passed on March 18, 1913, by Kansas. It regulated the practice of chiropractic, provided for licensing and examination of chiropractors, and created a three-member board for examination and regulation. Applicants were required to be graduates of a chartered chiropractic school or college having a course of three years, with actual attendance of more than six months each year.

5041. Dental hygienists to be licensed by a state were those of Connecticut, which passed a licensing law during the January 1915 session. It was approved on May 19, 1915. The first examination for dental hygienists was given by the State Board in June 1918, since no hygienists applied for a license prior to that date.

5042. Consumer protection medical alert listing medical quacks, manufacturers of spurious "cure-alls," peddlers of nostrums, "inventors" of worthless diets and exercises, and others who prey on the ill and the gullible was started in January 1930 by the New York

City Department of Health and is said to be the first of its kind in the world. The "rogue's gallery" was compiled by the National Better Business Bureau, at the suggestion of Special Deputy Health Commissioner Edward Fisher Brown.

5043. Physician with a mobile medical office for his private patients was Dr. Huerta Cortez Neals, cardiovascular specialist of the Jersey City Medical Center, who placed a motor home in service on June 23, 1970, in Jersey City, NJ, equipped with a bathroom, refrigerator, heating unit, air conditioner, 30-gallon water tank, electrocardiograph, blood-pressure apparatus, scale, blood Auto-Analyzer, and other instruments.

Ambulances

5044. Ambulance service for hospitals was introduced by the Commercial Hospital (now the General Hospital), Cincinnati, OH, prior to 1865. The list of employees for the year ending February 28, 1866, names James A. Jackson, employee No. 27, as "driver of ambulance" at an annual salary of $360. A similar service was started in June 1869 by Bellevue Hospital, New York City.

5045. Ambulance air service to transport sick people by airplane to hospitals was organized on October 21, 1929, by the Colonial Flying Service and the Scully Walton Ambulance Company of New York City.

5046. Ambulance service with an incubator for the transportation of premature infants was instituted by the city of Chicago, IL. The ambulance was ordered on February 26, 1935, and made its first run on March 21, 1935.

5047. Ambulance equipped for mobile coronary care was ordered by St. Vincent's Hospital and Medical Center of New York City and went into operation in October 1968. It brought doctors, nurses, and paramedics along with defibrillator, respirator, and electrocardiograph equipment to the patient's side within moments after a heart attack. The concept of on-site treatment of cardiac cases was created by Dr. William Joseph Grace.

5048. Ambulance ship for first aid to boaters and pleasure craft was the *Star of Life No. 1*, a 31-foot Uniflite cruiser owned by Fairfield Medical Products Corporation of Stamford, CT, and launched on April 2, 1976. Its equipment consisted of a Fairfield Heart Defibrillator, a coronary surveillance unit, and resuscitator (oxygen and aspirator) vacuum systems. The onboard equipment was equal to that of a typical hospital emergency room. The boat was made of fire-retardant fiberglass and was capable of a top speed exceeding 35 miles per hour. It was used in patrol and rescue duty on Long Island Sound between Greenwich and Norwalk, CT, and Glen Cove and Port Jefferson, NY, covering more than 150 square miles.

Anesthesia

5049. General anesthetic was sulfuric ether, used by Dr. Crawford Williamson Long of Jefferson, GA, in December 1841. On March 30, 1842, he removed a cystic tumor about half an inch in diameter from the back of the neck of James M. Venable, applying ether under a towel. His bill for the operation amounted to $2.25: for sulfuric ether 25 cents and for excising the tumor $2. The discovery was not reported, however, until 1852, when the Georgia State Medical Society was notified.

5050. Anesthetic in dentistry was used by Dr. Horace Wells, a dentist of Hartford, CT, who discovered the anesthetic property of nitrous oxide (laughing) gas. On December 11, 1844, while under the influence of gas, he had one of his teeth extracted by Dr. John M. Riggs. The use of the gas was not successful, as he did not know that it had to be combined with oxygen, a discovery that was not made until 24 years later.

5051. Anesthetic administered in childbirth was ether, employed on December 27, 1845, by Dr. Crawford Williamson Long during the delivery of his second child, Fanny, at Jefferson, GA.

5052. Demonstration of surgery under anesthesia was given on October 16, 1846, at the Massachusetts General Hospital, Boston, MA. Dr. John Collins Warren operated on Gilbert Abbott, who had a swelling on the right side of his jaw, and removed a tumor, using a drug supplied by William Thomas Green Morton, a dentist of Charleston, MA. Morton was refused admission to hospitals until he divulged the name of the secret drug, which was sulfuric ether. Although he is credited with the discovery of anesthetics, 8 or 10 others have also claimed the honor.

5053. Local anesthetic was pioneered in 1885 by Dr. William Stewart Halsted of Baltimore, MD. Experimenting with the technique of conduction, or block, anesthesia (the production of insensibility in a part of the body by interrupting the conduction of a sensory nerve leading to it), he injected a preparation made from the leaves of the coca plant into a nerve trunk in his own arm. As a result of his experiments, Halsted became addicted to cocaine and morphine.

Blood and Tissue

5054. Blood serum made of dried human blood was prepared by Dr. Earl William Flosdorf and Dr. Stuart Mudd of the School of Medicine, University of Pennsylvania, Philadelphia, PA, on December 21, 1933, with glass apparatus made by them. The powdered dried blood serum was used successfully in transfusions for the prevention and treatment of children's diseases at a hospital at Philadelphia, PA. The method was first described at a meeting of the American Chemical Society at St. Petersburg, FL, in April 1934.

5055. Blood bank to preserve blood by refrigeration for future use in transfusions was established on March 15, 1937, by the Cook County Hospital, Chicago, IL. The use of dehydrated plasma in blood banking was originated by Dr. Charles Richard Drew at Columbia Medical Center in New York City.

> As head of the Blood for Britain campaign during World War II, Dr. Charles Richard Drew came up with the idea for refrigerated Bloodmobiles.

5056. Rh factor discovery was made in 1940 by Karl Landsteiner and Alexander S. Wiener at the Rockefeller Institute for Medical Research in New York City. Rh factor is a protein substance found on red blood cells that can produce a severe antibody reaction in babies during gestation. It was named after the rhesus monkeys used in the research. Landsteiner, while still working in his native Austria, had established the existence of different blood types in 1909.

5057. Eye bank was opened on May 9, 1944, at New York Hospital, New York City, through the efforts of Dr. Richard Townley Paton of Manhattan Eye, Ear and Throat Hospital and Dr. John McLean of New York Hospital. Twenty-one hospitals in the metropolitan area offered cooperation in obtaining eyes and sending them to the bank.

5058. Bone bank was established in April 1946 by Dr. Leonard Franklin Bush and Dr. Clarence Zent Garber at the New York Orthopaedic Hospital and Dispensary, New York City, and by Dr. Philip Duncan Wilson at the Hospital for Special Surgery, New York City.

5059. Tissue bank to apply the freeze-drying principle to the storage of human tissue grafts was undertaken in 1954 at the Naval Medical School, National Naval Center, Bethesda, MD. Tissues were procured for storage in a centralized unit. The bank was under the supervision of Lieutenant Commander George William Hyatt.

5060. Transfusion of artificial blood took place at the University of Minnesota Hospital, Minneapolis, MN, on November 20, 1979. The patient was a Jehovah's Witness who on religious grounds refused a transfusion of real blood. Dr. Robert Anderson injected the patient with Fluosol, an artificial blood substitute developed in Japan.

5061. Functioning human organ grown in a laboratory was a urinary bladder that was implanted in 1999 in a young patient suffering from myelomeningocele, a congenital birth defect. Researchers at the Institute for Regenerative Medicine at the Wake Forest University School of Medicine created the bladder by culturing the patient's own cells and shaping the resulting tissue over a biodegradable structure. In 2006 the director of the Institute, Anthony Atala, M.D., announced that seven children and teenagers had received lab-grown bladders, all of which were functioning properly.

5062. Heart attack treatment using the patient's own stem cells occurred at William Beaumont Hospital in Royal Oak, MI, beginning on February 17, 2003. The patient, Dmitri Bonnville, 16, had been shot in the heart with a 3-inch nail fired from a nail gun. He suffered a heart attack after the nail was surgically removed. To repair the damaged tissue, doctors injected him with stem cells that had been harvested from his own blood.

5063. Public blood bank for collecting umbilical cord and placental blood for stem cell research was founded on October 18, 2005, by executive order of Governor Richard J. Codey of New Jersey. The order directed the state Department of Health and Social Services to create two collection depots, one in Paramus and one in Camden, where hospitals could send umbilical cord blood and placental blood donated by birthing mothers. Stem cells extracted from the blood were given to biomedical researchers.

Clinics

5064. Pediatric clinic was established in 1862 at the College of Physicians and Surgeons (now part of Columbia University), New York City, by Dr. Abraham Jacobi, a member of the faculty.

5065. Laryngology clinic was established in March 1863 by the Medical Faculty of the University of the City of New York under the supervision of Dr. Louis Elsberg.

5066. General medical clinic of importance was opened by the Johns Hopkins Medical School, Baltimore, MD, in October 1889, five months after the opening of the Johns Hopkins Hospital. The first director was Sir William Osler, Regius Professor of Medicine at Oxford University, who also served as physician in chief of the hospital and professor of medicine at the medical school.

5067. Birth control clinic was opened on October 16, 1916, at 46 Amboy Street, in the Brownsville section of Brooklyn, New York City, by Fania Mindell, Ethel Byrne, and Margaret Sanger. The handbill announcing its opening was printed in English, Yiddish, and Italian. Sanger was jailed for operating the clinic. The first birth-control clinic staffed entirely by doctors opened in 1923.

5068. Flying medical clinic left the United States in January 1930 to attend the Pan American Medical Association convention in Panama City, Panama. It was composed of physicians who demonstrated the latest methods in surgery and medicine in local hospitals in Guatemala, Nicaragua, Panama, Colombia, Venezuela, and other Latin American countries. The first demonstration of an operation was made on January 25, 1930, by Dr. Fred Houdlett Albee.

5069. Ophthalmology clinic was opened by the Fifth Avenue Hospital, New York City, in September 1932. The clinic was devoted to the treatment of ocular muscle imbalances, including some types of strabismus (cross-eye). The clinic was under the direction of Le Grand Haven Hardy, M.D., director of the Eye Service.

5070. Birth control clinic run by a state government was opened on March 15, 1937, in Raleigh, NC, when the North Carolina State Board of Health officially introduced a program setting up contraceptive clinics for poor married women in local maternity and child health services. The first director was Dr. George Marion Cooper of the Division of Preventive Medicine. Roberta Pratt, a Raleigh nurse, was hired to work with the health officers.

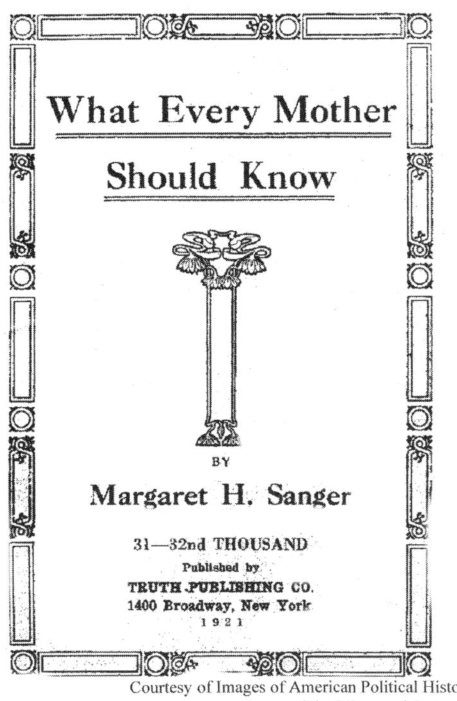

What Every Mother
Should Know
BY
Margaret H. Sanger
31—32nd THOUSAND
Published by
TRUTH PUBLISHING CO.
1400 Broadway, New York
1921

Courtesy of Images of American Political History and the Library of Congress

5071. Genetics clinic was opened on November 12, 1941, by the Department of Human Heredity, a research unit of the Laboratory of Vertebrate Genetics, University of Michigan, Ann Arbor, MI, under the direction of Dr. Lee Raymond Dice. It secured data on the role that heredity plays and furnished advice to families about matters in which heredity is a factor.

5072. Traveling cancer clinic was established on February 14, 1946, by the Oklahoma Division of the American Cancer Society, Oklahoma City, OK. A school bus was remodeled to convey equipment and instruments for four examination rooms, which were presided over by an internist, a dermatologist, a gynecologist, and a surgeon. All services were rendered free of charge, and the physicians and nurses serving on the staff donated their time and expenses. Clinics were usually set up in church classrooms. The first clinic was set up in Tonkawa, Kay County, OK.

5073. Cancer prevention clinic for children was the Kate Depew Strang Foundation Prevention Clinic, opened on January 3, 1947, in the Prevention Clinic of Memorial Hospital, New York City.

5074. Vasectomy outpatient service was opened on October 3, 1969, by the Margaret Sanger Research Bureau, New York City, under the direction of the bureau's director, Dr. Aquiles Jose Sobrero. The clinical director was Dr. Joseph Edward Davis.

5075. Acupuncture treatment center was the Acupuncture Center of New York, which opened on July 12, 1972, and was quickly closed as a result of legal complications. It reopened on December 27, 1972, as the Acupuncture Center of Washington, Washington, DC.

5076. Natural medicine clinic subsidized by a government was established in Seattle, WA, by the Kings County Council in 1995. Patients at the clinic were treated according to the principles of naturopathy, which seeks to strengthen the body's own immune system rather than eradicate symptoms. Treatments included diet, exercise, and acupuncture.

Dentistry

5077. Dentist who was born in the United States was Josiah Flagg, who started practicing dentistry in Boston, MA, in 1782, at the age of 18. In 1785 he advertised as follows: "Dr. Flagg transplants teeth, cures ulcers and eases them from pain without drawing; fastens those that are loose; mends teeth with foil or gold to be as lasting and useful as the sound teeth . . . sells, by wholesale and retail, dentifrices, tinctures, chew-sticks, mastics, teeth and gum brushes, suitable for every age, complaint and climate, with directions for their use."

5078. Porcelain teeth were introduced about 1785, owing principally to the efforts of Dr. John Greenwood of New York City. He advertised "artificial teeth set in so firm (without drawing stumps or causing the least pain) as to eat with them, and so exact as not to be distinguished from natural." Greenwood also invented the foot-powered drill. One of his patients was George Washington.

5079. Dental drill was invented in 1790 by John Greenwood of New York City. It was adapted from the spinning wheel. Power was obtained by means of a foot treadle.

5080. Dental dispensary was the City Dispensary for the Medical Relief of the Poor, New York City, which opened on February 1, 1791. Isaac Roosevelt was the first president. From February 1 to November 23, 1791, 310 patients were admitted. The fee for extracting teeth and for filling cavities with silver or lead foil was 50 cents; the fee for filling cavities with gold or for a good set of front teeth was $1.

5081. Dental amalgam for filling teeth was introduced by Messrs. Crawcour and Sons, who advertised it in the *New York Commercial Advertiser* of August 12, 1834, as "Royal Mineral Succedaneum for filling decayed teeth without the slightest pain, heat or pressure." They paid little attention to caries and filled all cavities without first removing decay. Their work was unsatisfactory and they were obliged to flee the country.

5082. Dental chair that provided such necessary conveniences as a headrest and adjustments in height and position was designed by M. Waldo Hanchett of Syracuse, NY, who received a patent on it on August 15, 1848.

5083. **Dental filling made of gold** was advocated by Dr. Robert Arthur. In 1855 he discovered the cohesive property of annealed gold foil, a discovery that revolutionized the dental profession. He described it in an 86-page book, *A Treatise on the Use of Adhesive Gold Foil,* published in 1857 in Philadelphia, PA.

5084. **Dentist who was a woman** to maintain a dental office independently was Dr. Emeline Roberts Jones, who began practice in Danielsonville (now Danielson), CT, in May 1855 as an assistant to her husband, Dr. Daniel Albion Jones. In 1859 she became his partner and after he died in 1864 she carried on the practice alone.

5085. **Dentist who was a woman to obtain a D.D.S. degree** from a dental college was Lucy B. Hobbs, who was graduated on February 21, 1866, from the Ohio College of Dental Surgery, Cincinnati, OH. She became the first female member of a dental society when she was elected a member of the Iowa State Dental Society in July 1865.

5086. **Dental crown made of gold** was made by Dr. William Newton Morrison, corresponding secretary of the Missouri State Dental Association, who described his process in the May 1869 issue of the *Missouri Dental Journal.* The first patent for such a crown was granted on November 4, 1873, to Dr. John B. Beers of San Francisco, CA.

5087. **Dental drill powered by electricity** was invented by George F. Green of Kalamazoo, MI, who obtained a patent on January 26, 1875, on "electro-magnetic dental tools" used for sawing, filing, dressing, and polishing teeth. The patent was assigned to Samuel S. White of Philadelphia, PA. The engines were too heavy and the batteries too expensive for general use.

5088. **Dental inlay made of gold** was described by William H. Taggart, a Chicago dentist, before the New York Odontological Society on January 15, 1907. He invented the method of casting gold inlays by the inverted pattern procedure, using the ancient principle of the "disappearing core."

5089. **Tooth-wear gauge** was invented in 1990 by Mark F. Teaford of Johns Hopkins University, Baltimore, MD. The gauge directly measured daily or weekly rates of tooth wear by using a scanning electron microscope to examine casts of teeth. The examination detected minute scratches and pits in the tooth enamel caused by chewing.

Epidemics

5090. **Smallpox epidemic** of importance occurred in 1616–17 and swept away the Native Americans of New England from the Penobscot River to Narragansett Bay, reducing the fighting force from 3,000 to some 50 men. About a century later, in May 1721, an outbreak of smallpox killed up to a quarter of the population of Boston, MA, and nearby cities.

5091. **Influenza epidemic** occurred in 1733 and was most serious in Philadelphia, PA, and New York City. About three-fourths of the entire population was affected.

5092. **Medical record of an epidemic** was Benjamin Rush's *An Account of the Bilious Remitting Yellow Fever, as It Appeared in the city of Philadelphia, in the year 1793.* The book, which had 363 pages, was printed in 1794 by Thomas Dobson in Philadelphia, PA. About 4,000 people died between August and November 1793.

5093. **Cholera epidemic** occurred in 1832. Individual cases are said to have developed in several cities, but the real force of the epidemic was manifested in the larger cities such as New York City, Boston, MA, and Philadelphia, PA. The first case in New York City appeared on June 28, 1832. From July 5 to August 29, 5,835 cases developed, of which 2,251 resulted in death. On July 21, New York City reported 311 cases and 100 deaths.

5094. **Polio epidemic** occurred in Vermont in 1894. Between June 17 and September 1, 123 cases appeared in Rutland and Wallingford. The first major urban polio epidemic took place in the summer of 1916 in New York City, where 9,000 children were stricken and 2,400 died.

5095. **AIDS epidemic** began in the spring of 1981, when the first cases were reported to the Centers for Disease Control in Atlanta,

GA, by doctors in San Francisco and New York City. The initial patients were all young, previously healthy gay men who died from rare opportunistic illnesses because their immune systems had been suppressed. AIDS stands for "acquired immunodeficiency syndrome."

5096. AIDS antidiscrimination law was enacted on August 15, 1985, by the city council of Los Angeles. The statute levied civil damages on anyone who denied AIDS patients their right to medical care, employment, education, housing, or service in public accommodations such as restaurants. To enforce the law, the city attorney's officer set up a special unit, the first of its kind in the United States, in 1986.

Hospitals

5097. Hospital was the Pennsylvania Hospital, opened in Philadelphia, PA, through the efforts of Benjamin Franklin and Dr. Thomas Bond. A temporary hospital was erected in 1751 in a private house on High (now Market) Street before the permanent building opened on February 11, 1752. This was the first hospital to give free treatment to the poor. The care of the sick, however, had been undertaken earlier by both secular and religious agencies. In 1565, the Spanish settlement at St. Augustine, FL, set aside six beds in a home for the poor; on December 20, 1656, the Dutch West India Company appointed Master Jacob Hendrickszen Varrevanger surgeon in New Amsterdam to look after the sick; and on July 17, 1734, the Ursulines of New Orleans, LA, opened an infirmary without restrictions, under the supervision of Sister Xavier Herbert.

5098. Hospital for insane patients established by a colony was the Publick Hospital for Persons of Insane and Disordered Minds, incorporated in Williamsburg, VA, in 1768. It was opened on October 12, 1773, and received as its first patient Zachariah Mallory of Hanover County, VA. The hospital was maintained by the colony from the beginning and later became known as the Eastern State Hospital.

5099. Independent dispensary to furnish free medicine to the needy was the Philadelphia Dispensary, established in Philadelphia, PA, on April 12, 1786, by Bishop William White. The Philadelphia Dispensary affiliated with the Pennsylvania Hospital in 1922.

5100. Hospital for insane patients operated privately was founded by the Religious Society of Friends (Quakers) in Philadelphia, PA, on April 14, 1813, as The Asylum for the Relief of Persons Deprived of the Use of Their Reason. The grounds were located 5 miles from Philadelphia and 1 mile west of Frankford and covered 52 acres, 30 of which were cultivated, the balance in woodland. No manacles, handcuffs, iron grates, or bars were used. The name was changed in 1888 to the Friends Asylum for the Insane, and in 1914 to Friends Hospital. A home for insane patients had been established by the Quakers in Philadelphia as early as 1709.

5101. Eye infirmary was established in New London, CT, in 1817 by Elisha North, a medical student.

5102. Eye hospital was the New York Eye Infirmary, a two-room hospital on the second floor at 45 Chatham Street, New York City, which was opened on August 14, 1820. The chief surgeons were Dr. Edward Delafield and Dr. John Kearney Rodgers. William Few was the first president. By January 1, 1822, the infirmary had treated 1,120 cases and cured 801. On April 30, 1864, the name was changed to the New York Eye and Ear Infirmary.

5103. Hospital for treatment of the mentally ill established by a state was the Worcester Hospital, Worcester, MA, authorized by the Massachusetts legislature on March 10, 1830. The act appropriated $30,000 and approved the appointment of three commissioners to build and supervise an asylum for "one hundred and twenty lunatics or persons furiously mad." The chief advocate of the project was Horace Mann of Boston, who sought to ensure humane treatment for people who were incapacitated by mental illness. The hospital was declared open on January 10, 1833, when it began receiving patients who had previously been confined in prisons.

5104. Hospital and asylum for African-Americans founded by whites was chartered on December 24, 1832, in Savannah, GA, as the Georgia Infirmary for the Relief and Protection of Aged and Afflicted Negroes. The organizational meeting was held at the Exchange on January 15, 1833, and the first president was Richard F. Williams.

5105. Homeopathic hospital was the Homeopathic Hospital of Pennsylvania, Philadelphia, PA, incorporated on September 20, 1850. It was opened for service in 1852 with 30 beds. Vincent L. Bradford was the first president.

5106. Hospital under Jewish auspices was Mount Sinai Hospital in New York, organized and incorporated on January 15, 1852, as the Jews' Hospital in New York City for "benevolent, charitable and scientific purposes." The founder and first president was Sampson Simson, a lawyer, who held the distinction of being the first Jew to be graduated from Columbia College and the first to pass the New York bar examination. The first patients were received on June 8, 1855, in the hospital's first building, a four-story brownstone on West 28th Street, New York City. Julius Raymond was the superintendent. Dr. Mark Blumenthal was the attending and resident physician. Operating expenses during the first year totalled $5,494, and 225 patients were treated. The hospital moved uptown in 1872 and became nonsectarian in 1886.

5107. Infirmary for women staffed by physicians who were women was the New York Infirmary for Women and Children, New York City, incorporated on December 13, 1853, "to provide for poor women the medical advice of competent physicians of their own sex." A one-room infirmary was opened in Tompkins Square. On May 12, 1857, a hospital was opened. The physicians were the sisters Dr. Elizabeth Blackwell and Dr. Emily Blackwell, and Dr. Marie Elizabeth Zakrzewska.

5108. Children's hospital was established in 1854 in New York City and was known as the Nursery and Child's Hospital. It originated from a society founded by Sarah Platt Doremus and Mrs. Cornelius Du Bois "for the maintenance and care of the children of wet-nurses, and the daily charge of infants whose parents labor away from home."

5109. Asylum for alcoholics was the United States Inebriate Asylum "for the reformation of the poor and destitute inebriates," incorporated on April 15, 1854, and organized on May 15, 1854, in Binghamton, NY, by Dr. James Edward Turner. In 1857 the name was changed to the New York State Inebriate Asylum. John D. Wright was the first president of the corporation.

5110. Hospital for women in the world, founded by women for the exclusive use of women, was the Woman's Hospital of New York City. On February 10, 1855, a constitution was adopted by 30 women who formed the Woman's Hospital Association. The Woman's Hospital was opened with 40 beds on May 4, 1855, in a hired building at Madison Avenue and 29th Street, with Dr. James Marion Sims as resident surgeon. A permanent building on West 110th Street was opened on December 5, 1906.

5111. Hospital record system was introduced at the Bellevue Training School for Nurses, New York City, in 1874 by the head nurse, Linda Ann Judson Richards. Record was made of symptoms, diagnosis, medication, temperature, and pulse rate for all patients in the hospital.

5112. Floating hospital was the *Emma Abbott*, which made her trial trip on July 19, 1875. The ship cost $20,000, was 215 feet long with a 40-foot breadth of beam, and had three decks, one of which served as a dining room. It was known as the "poor children's yacht" and was operated by St. John's Guild, New York City. The ship served until 1902, when it was replaced with a more modern ship. The idea for the hospital originated in the summer of 1873, when the guild hired a barge and gave two excursions for sick children. The following summer it gave 18 excursions to 15,202 sick children and their mothers. The health benefits were so obvious that the guild decided to operate its own floating hospitals.

5113. Hospital designed exclusively for infants was the Babies Hospital of the City of New York, which was chartered on June 23, 1887. The hospital opened in a house at 161 East 36th Street, New York City, with eight beds.

5114. Cancer hospital was the New York Cancer Hospital, 106th Street and Central Park West, New York City. The hospital had its beginning at a meeting held on February 7, 1884, at the residence of Mrs. Elizabeth Hamilton Cullum. It was opened for patients on December 7, 1887. In 1916 its name was changed to the Memorial Hospital for the Treatment of Cancer and Allied Diseases. The first attending surgeons were Dr. James Bradbridge Hunter, Dr. Clement Cleveland, and Dr. William Tillinghast Bull. The first president was John E. Parsons. The hospital later affiliated with Memorial Sloan-Kettering Cancer Center.

5115. Hospital open to all races as a matter of policy was the Provident Hospital, Chicago, IL, opened on May 4, 1891. Although primarily for African-Americans, there was no racial barrier to the admission of patients or staff appointments of physicians. Dr. Frank Billings was chief consulting physician; Dr. Christian Fenger, chief consulting surgeon; and Drs. Ralph N. Isham and Daniel Hale Williams, attending surgeons. A nursing school, the Provident Hospital Training School Association, was connected with the hospital.

5116. Leprosy hospital was the Louisiana Leper Home, Carville, LA, founded in 1894 by an act of the Louisiana legislature. It consisted of a plantation of about 200 acres on which were seven cottages, an elevated pavilion, dining hall, kitchen, and quarters for the Sisters of Charity of the order of St. Vincent de Paul, four of whom took care of the patients. The home accommodated 25 patients and was controlled by a Board of Officers. The first president was M. D. Lagan and the first resident physician was Dr. Elihu Morgan Hooper. The home was purchased by the federal government from the state of Louisiana on January 3, 1921, to be operated as a 300-bed hospital by the Public Health Service, with nursing care supplied by the Sisters of Charity.

5117. Hospital for disabled children established by a state was the Gillette State Hospital for Crippled Children, St. Paul, MN, authorized on April 23, 1897, with an appropriation of $5,000. The hospital was named in honor of Dr. Arthur Jay Gillette.

5118. Cancer research fund was the Collis P. Huntington Fund for cancer research, established in 1902 by Mrs. Collis Potter Huntington. The fund, amounting to $100,000, was used by the New York Cancer Hospital, New York City. It enabled the hospital to administer X-ray treatments and install new equipment.

5119. Centralized system of medical records for hospitals was developed by Dr. Henry Plummer and Mabel Root at the Mayo Clinic, Rochester, MN, and went into operation on July 1, 1907. The system gave each patient a unified file that contained all records of hospital treatment, including lab test results, enabling medical staff to review the patient's entire history. Previously, each department maintained its own files on patients.

5120. Neurological disease research institute was the Neurological Institute of New York, incorporated on April 5, 1909, which opened its hospital on October 1, 1909, in New York City. The first superintendent was Alexander H. Candlish.

5121. Intensive care unit in the United States for critically ill patients is a matter of definition. The Johns Hopkins University, Baltimore, MD, had a separate unit for postoperative neurosurgery patients in 1928. At the Mary Hitchcock Memorial Hospital, Lebanon, NH, Dr. William Mosenthal set up an 18-bed Special Care Unit in 1955 with round-the-clock care provided by nurses with advanced training.

5122. Hospital with circular wards was Rochester Methodist Hospital in Rochester, MN. An experimental ward, known as the Special Observation Unit, was built in 1957. It featured a central nursing station surrounded by 12 patient rooms, all easily visible. Additional circular wards were incorporated into the hospital's new wing in 1966.

5123. Children's hospital for research and treatment of catastrophic childhood diseases was St. Jude Children's Research Hospital, Memphis, TN, which opened on February 4, 1962. It was founded by actor Danny Thomas, its first president. There were no charges to patients for treatment, hospitalization, or consultation.

Tuberculosis

5124. Tuberculosis patients' home was the Channing Home, Boston, MA, opened on May 1857 through the benevolence of Harriet Ryan. The home accommodated 12 patients and was not a sanatorium. It also accommodated patients with other chronic diseases.

5125. Tuberculosis sanatorium privately operated was the Mountain Sanatorium for Pulmonary Diseases, opened in 1875 in Asheville, NC, by Dr. William Gleitsmann.

5126. Tuberculosis sanatorium using modern treatment methods was the Trudeau Sanatorium, sometimes called the Adirondack Cottage Sanatorium, a one-room cottage 14 by 18 feet with two cot beds and heated by a wood stove, built at Saranac Lake, NY, for Dr. Edward Livingston Trudeau at a cost of $400. It was opened on February 1, 1885.

5127. Tuberculosis hospital for the poor established by a city was the Branch Hospital of the Cincinnati Hospital (later Cincinnati General Hospital), which opened on July 8, 1897, in Cincinnati, OH, with a capacity of 20 beds. John Fehrenbach was the superintendent and Dr. Benjamin Lyle the chief physician. The name was later changed to the Hamilton County Tuberculosis Hospital.

5128. Tuberculosis sanatorium established by a state was the Massachusetts Hospital for Consumptives and Tuberculosis Patients, Rutland, MA, completed on September 23, 1898. It received its first patient on October 3, 1898. Dr. Walter John Marcley was the first medical director.

5129. Tuberculosis hospital established by Congress was opened at Fort Stanton, NM, on April 27, 1899. The first patient was received on November 18. The hospital was suggested and founded by Walter Wyman. It was not exclusively for men in military service but afforded care and treatment to all beneficiaries of the Public Health Service, most of whom at that time were seamen.

5130. Tuberculosis hospital for needy patients to provide medical and surgical care on a free, nationwide, nonsectarian basis was the National Jewish Hospital, Denver, CO, which opened on December 10, 1899, with 58 beds, under the auspices of the B'nai B'rith organization. An earlier attempt, in 1892, by the Jewish Hospital Association of Colorado to establish such a hospital had failed for lack of funds.

Imaging

5131. X-ray photograph was made on January 12, 1896, by Dr. Henry Louis Smith, professor of physics and astronomy, Davidson College, Davidson, NC. Smith obtained the hand of a corpse, fired a bullet into it, and then took a 15-minute exposure which, when developed, revealed the exact location of the bullet.

5132. X-ray of the entire body of a living person made in a single exposure was taken by Dr. William James Morton of New York City in April 1897. The film was a coated single sheet three feet by six feet, made by the Eastman Kodak Company of Rochester, NY. The apparatus employed was a 12-inch induction coil that used the 117-volt Edison current. At each revolution of the break wheel, which made 5,000 revolutions per minute, the coil afforded a free discharge of sparks across a five-inch air gap. The distance of the tube from the film was 4 feet 6 inches. The tube was run steadily for the first 10 minutes; then the current was turned off several times a minute to allow it to cool. The total time consumed, including stoppages, was 30 minutes. The heavier regions of the body, such as the pelvis, spine, and thighs, were underexposed, while the thinner portions, such as the hands, were overexposed.

5133. Diagnostic procedure using radioactive tracers was performed in 1925 by Hermann Blumgart at Harvard University, Cambridge, MA. After first testing the procedure on himself, he injected a radium preparation into the veins of 15 patients and observed the rate of blood circulation with an electroscope. From this he was able to identify those who suffered from cardiac disease.

5134. X-ray photograph of the entire body of a living person taken in a one-second exposure under ordinary clinical conditions available to the average hospital or average radiographer, and the first in which a selective filter was used, was a full-length, full-size, one-piece radiograph taken on July 1, 1934, by Arthur Wolfram Fuchs of the Eastman Kodak Company, Rochester, NY. The size of the film was 32 by 72 inches. The radiograph was exhibited by the Chicago Roentgen Society at the Century of Progress Exposition, Chicago, IL.

5135. X-ray photograph showing the complete arterial circulation in an adult human was completed on July 16, 1936, in Rochester, NY, by Dr. Edmond John Faris of the Wistar Institute of Anatomy and Biology, Philadelphia, PA, and Arthur Wolfram Fuchs of the Medical Division, Eastman Kodak Company, Rochester, NY. A radio-opaque medium was injected into the arteries of a cadaver by Faris. Fuchs made several full-body radiographs on film 32 by 72 inches, employing 30 seconds of exposure at a distance of 12 feet. Ultra-high-speed X-ray intensifying screens were also used in a large cassette made to accommodate the film and screen.

5136. X-ray movies of human organs in action were made by Drs. William Holmes Stewart, William Joseph Hoffman, and Francis Henshall Ghiselin, all of New York City, who set a movie camera in front of a fluoroscopic screen. The pictures showed the motion of the heart, stomach, diaphragm, lungs, and other organs and structures. They were exhibited on October 2, 1937, in New York City, at a convention of the American Roentgen Ray Society.

5137. Photograph of genes was taken by Dr. Daniel Chapin Pease and Dr. Richard Freligh Baker at the University of Southern California, Los Angeles, CA, and announced on January 7, 1949. The tissue sections in the photograph were magnified 120,000 times. Genes are the particles that carry DNA, transmitting physical characteristics from one generation to another.

5138. Nuclear medicine imaging device was the rectilinear scanner, invented in 1950 by Benedict Cassen at the University of California at Los Angeles. A motorized scanner, the device recorded the levels of radioisotopes in an organ as a series of lines and printed them out as a complete image. It was originally used at the Veterans Administration Medical Center in West Los Angeles to examine patients' thyroid glands.

5139. Movie showing the inside of a living heart was made at Montefiore Hospital, New York City, by Dr. Elliott Samuel Hurwitt, Dr. Adrian Kantrowitz, and Anatol Herskovitz, the photographer. The movie showed the opening and closing of the mitral valve of a dog. The official title of the 9.5-minute color film was *A Cinematographic Study of the Function of the Mitral Valve in Situ*. It was first shown on October 16, 1951, at the clinical session of the New York Academy of Medicine Post Graduate Fortnightly held at Montefiore Hospital.

5140. Gamma camera for imaging the body was invented by Hal Oscar Anger at the University of California at Berkeley. It was first demonstrated in 1958. Its use requires the patient to be injected with a radioactive isotope that emits gamma rays, which are then collected by the camera and converted into a computerized image in which metabolic activity appears as a bright area. The gamma camera was the basis for many subsequent imaging techniques.

5141. X-ray three-dimensional stereo fluoroscopic system was installed at the University of Oregon Medical Center, Portland, OR, by Richard J. Kuhn on April 15, 1966. The development engineer was Joseph Quinn. The $30,000 device was primarily intended to be used in heart catherization. It was exhibited on September 27, 1966, at the American Roentgen Ray Society at San Francisco, CA, by the X-ray Department of the General Electric Company, Milwaukee, WI. The "stereo fluoricon" consisted of a single anode dual cathode X-ray tube, an image intensifier with polarizers, and a synchronized analyzer. The 3D image was observed through a viewing mirror without the use of special glasses.

5142. CT scanner in a U.S. medical facility was installed in 1973 at the Mayo Clinic, Rochester, MN. The CT scanner (an abbreviation for "computerized axial tomography") builds a three-dimensional image of the patient's body using stacks of cross-sectional x-rays. It was independently developed by Allen MacLeod Cormack, a South African–born professor of physics at Tufts University, Medford, MA, and British researcher Godfrey Newbold Hounsfield, who shared the Nobel Prize for Physiology or Medicine in 1979.

5143. PET scanner was installed at the University of California at Los Angeles in December 1976. PET is an abbreviation for "positron emission tomography," an imaging technique that identifies areas of metabolic activity by tracking positrons emitted by radioactive isotopes injected into the patient. The scanner, widely used for brain imaging and cancer detection, was invented by Michael Phelps and Edward Hoffman at Washington University, St. Louis, MO, in 1974.

5144. Radioimmunoassay test was developed by Solomon Aaron Berson and Rosalyn Sussman Yalow at the Bronx Veterans Administration Hospital in New York City. Their method involved taking a blood sample from the patient and using radioactive tagging to measure the presence of a particular hormone, drug, or biological substance. Originally developed as a way of measuring the rate at which the thyroid gland removes iodine from the bloodstream, it proved applicable to many other diagnostic questions, of which the first was the level of insulin in the blood of diabetics. Yalow won the Nobel Prize in Medicine in 1977 for her contribution.

5145. Magnetic resonance image of a human body was made on July 3, 1977, by Dr. Raymond Damadian, founder of the FONAR Corporation in Melville, NY. Working independently, Damadian and Paul C. Lauterbur of the University of Illinois at Urbana-Champaign, IL, developed the application of magnetic resonance imaging (MRI) technology to noninvasive medical diagnosis. MRI scanners produce detailed images of soft tissues, including blood vessels, blood flow, cartilage, bone marrow, muscles, ligaments, the spinal cord, and fluids in the brain and spine, that do not show up well on X-rays.

5146. Laboratory test to identify patients with Alzheimer's disease or those at high risk for developing the disease was the work of a team headed by Katherine K. Sanford (Katherine Sanford Mifflin) at the Laboratory of Cellular and Molecular Biology at the National Cancer Institute, Bethesda, MD. The team's study, published in May 1996, showed that the skin fibroblasts of patients with Alzheimer's were less capable of repairing DNA damage, which was induced by exposure to fluorescent light.

5147. Comprehensive digital atlas of the human body was the Visible Human Project, led by Victor Spitzer and David Whitlock of the University of Colorado Health Sciences Center in Denver, CO. The body of an executed murderer, 39-year-old Joseph Paul Jernigan, was sliced into ultrathin cross-sections. Detailed views of these cross-sections were made by photography, magnetic resonance imaging, and computer tomography. These views were made available to medical schools, hospitals, and researchers on CD-ROMs and specialized computer networks. (A woman's body was incorporated into the atlas at a later date.) A CD-ROM entitled *Body Voyage* was released to the public in 1997. The program was financed by the National Library of Medicine, a unit of the National Institutes of Health.

Immunizations

5148. Inoculation against smallpox using material from human smallpox pustules was introduced into America by Dr. Zabdiel Boylston of Boston, MA. On June 26, 1721, Boylston inoculated his six-year-old son, Thomas, and two African-American servants. In 1721 and 1722, Boylston inoculated 247 individuals. The public acceptance of inoculation was due in large measure to the efforts of Cotton Mather, the Boston minister and scientist, who persistently advocated it.

5149. Vaccination against smallpox using cowpox as originated in England by Dr. Edward Jenner was introduced by Dr. Benjamin Waterhouse of Cambridge, MA, professor of the theory and practice of medicine at Harvard, who inoculated his son, Daniel Oliver Waterhouse, and three children and three servants on July 8, 1800.

5150. Smallpox vaccine clinic for research into the smallpox virus and free distribution of the vaccine to the poor was opened by Dr. James Smith in Baltimore, MD, on March 25, 1802.

5151. Vaccination program offered by a city was conducted by the Massachusetts towns of Milton and Bedford, which offered free inoculations against smallpox. A committee chosen on July 8, 1809, authorized Dr. Amos Holbrook to charge a 25-cent fee for his services. He inoculated the entire population of Milton, 337 individuals, and pledged that the people "are for ever secure against Small Pox."

5152. Vaccination law enacted by a state was "an act to diffuse the benefits of inoculation for the Cow-Pox," enacted on March 6, 1810, by Massachusetts, which required every town, district, and plantation to guard against smallpox by choosing "three or more suitable persons, whose duty it shall be to superintend the inoculation of the inhabitants . . . with the cowpox."

5153. Vaccination law enacted by Congress was the act of February 27, 1813, to encourage vaccination against smallpox. It authorized the president to appoint a vaccine agent to furnish vaccine through the Post Office to any citizen of the United States who might apply for it. The act was repealed on May 4, 1822.

5154. Vaccination program by the federal government to protect Native Americans against smallpox was authorized by congressional act of May 5, 1832, "an act to provide the means of extending the benefits of vaccination, as a preventive of the smallpox, to the Native American tribes, and thereby, as far as possible, to save them from the destructive ravages of that disease." An appropriation of $12,000 was made. Physicians were paid $6 a day for their services.

5155. Tuberculosis vaccine produced in the United States that was effective was developed in 1928 by Dr. William Hallock Park, director of the research laboratory of the New York City Health Department and professor of preventive medicine at New York University. The vaccine was manufactured at the research laboratories of the Department of Health and was first used in January 1928.

5156. Yellow fever vaccine for human immunization was developed by Drs. Wilbur Augustus Sawyer, Wray Devere Marr Lloyd, and Stuart Fordyce Kitchen and publicly announced on April 28, 1932, at a meeting of the American Societies for Experimental Biology, Philadelphia, PA. The work was sponsored by the Rockefeller Foundation. The first test vaccinations were made in May 1931.

5157. Polio vaccine was produced by Dr. Maurice Brodie of New York City in February 1933. It was obtained from the spinal cords of rare Indian monkeys that had been infected with poliomyelitis. The spinal cords were excised and made into an emulsion that was treated with formalin to kill the virus.

5158. Anthrax vaccine for human immunization was developed in 1948 by Dr. George Green Wright of the Biological Laboratory of the Army Chemical Laboratory. Anthrax is a rare bacterial disease that infects both humans and animals.

5159. Mass immunizations for polio began on February 23, 1954, with the vaccination of schoolchildren in Pittsburgh, PA. The vaccine had been developed in 1952 by Jonas Edward Salk, director of the Virus Research Laboratory at the University of Pittsburgh's School of Medicine, who employed a method of virus culture developed by bacteriologists John Franklin Enders, Frederick Chapman Robbins, and Thomas Huckle Weller. For their work, the four shared the 1954 Nobel Prize in physiology or medicine. The vaccine was licensed for public use on April 12, 1955.

5160. Vaccine against a form of cancer was the hepatitis B vaccine, developed in 1968 by Baruch S. Blumberg and Irving Millman at the Fox Chase Cancer Center in Philadelphia, PA. They had identified the hepatitis B virus the previous year. The vaccine, which went into clinical use in 1981, helped prevent the onset of hepatocellular carcinoma, a form of liver cancer.

5161. Chicken pox vaccine was approved for public use by the Food and Drug Administration on March 17, 1995. Marketed by Merck and Company, Whitehouse Station, NJ, under the trade name Varivax, the vaccine was believed to be 70 to 90 percent effective.

5162. State ban on mercury in children's vaccines was enacted by Iowa on April 14, 2004, and took effect on January 1, 2006. The bill required all vaccines regularly administered to children, with the exception of flu vaccine, to be free from thimerosal, a mercury compound used in pharmaceuticals as a preservative. Mercury is toxic to the neurological system.

Laboratories

5163. Physiology laboratory was established in the Sheffield Scientific School at Yale University, New Haven, CT, in 1874 under the direction of Russell Henry Chittenden.

5164. Psychology laboratory was established at Johns Hopkins University, Baltimore, MD, in 1881 by Granville Stanley Hall. It was discontinued in 1888 when Dr. Hall was appointed president of Clark University. A larger laboratory was established at Johns Hopkins in 1904 by Professor George Malcolm Stratton.

5165. Bacteriology laboratory was the Hoagland Laboratory, 335 Henry Street, Brooklyn, NY (now part of New York City), incorporated on February 21, 1887, and opened for experimentation in February 1889. The first director was Dr. George Miller Sternberg, who demonstrated the microbe of pneumonia in saliva. A privately endowed institution, the laboratory later became affiliated with the Long Island College of Medicine in Brooklyn. This was the first bacteriology laboratory run by an institution; private laboratories had been established earlier by individual physicians.

5166. Tuberculosis research laboratory was the Saranac Laboratory, established in 1894 by Dr. Edward Livingston Trudeau in a room in his home at Saranac Lake, NY.

5167. Cancer laboratory exclusively for the study of cancer was the New York State Pathological Laboratory for the Study of Cancer, established in May 1898 at the University of Buffalo under a $10,000 appropriation made by the New York State legislature on April 29. Dr. Roswell Park was the first director.

5168. Laboratory for the study of human parasites was the Hygienic Laboratory, Washington, DC (later incorporated into the National Institutes of Health). It was established on August 16, 1902, by the Public Health Service. Dr. Charles Wardell Stiles was chief of the division of zoology.

5169. Sleep laboratory was founded at the University of Chicago, IL, in 1925 by Nathaniel Kleitman.

5170. Microbiology laboratory was the Institute of Microbiology, Rutgers University, New Brunswick, NJ, dedicated on June 7, 1954. The cost of the building was approximately $3,050,000 and that of the equipment $450,000. Classroom and seminar instruction was offered to graduate students. The first director was Dr. Selman Abraham Waksman.

Medical Equipment

5171. Adhesive and medicated plaster used in the treatment of fractures was reported in *Anatomy, Physiology and Diseases of the Bones and Joints* by Samuel David Gross, published in 1830 in Philadelphia, PA. The first patent for such a plaster was issued on March 26, 1845, to Dr. Horace Harrel Day of Jersey City, NJ, and Dr. William H. Shecut. They dissolved rubber in a solvent, such as benzine, turpentine, and bisulphide of carbon, which they spread with a brush on fabric. They sold the process to Dr. Thomas Allcock, who introduced Allcock's Porous Plaster.

5172. Silver wire suture in place of silk thread was used by Dr. James Marion Sims of Montgomery, AL, who reported his experiments in an article, "On the Treatment of Vesico-vaginal Fistula," in the *American Journal of the Medical Sciences* of January 1852. Sims had begun his experiments on December 9, 1845. He performed a vesico-vaginal fistula operation on June 21, 1849. The suture was removed on the eighth day after the operation.

5173. Silk sutures and ligatures used instead of catgut in operations were used in 1882 by Dr. William Stewart Halsted of Baltimore, MD. He advocated black silk, which he introduced in 1889 at the Johns Hopkins Hospital, Baltimore.

5174. Antiseptic surgical dressings commercially manufactured were adhesive plasters made by Johnson & Johnson in New Brunswick, NJ, in 1887.

5175. Incubator for premature babies was constructed by Dr. William Champion Deming, in charge of the maternity ward of the State Emigrant Hospital, Ward's Island, New York City, in 1888, by order of Dr. Allan M. Thomas. It was called a "hatching cradle" and was 3 feet square and 4 feet high and built in two sections, one of which contained 15 gallons of water. The first child placed in it was Edith Eleanor McLean, who weighed 2 pounds 7 ounces when she was born on September 7, 1888.

5176. Sterile hospital product commercially manufactured was a cotton-and-gauze dressing produced in 1891 by Johnson & Johnson in New Brunswick, NJ.

5177. Electric heating pad was patented by S. I. Russell in 1912. It was intended for use in tuberculosis sanitariums, to keep the patients' chests warm.

5178. Bandage with built-in adhesive was the Band-Aid, the invention of Earle Dickson, of the Johnson & Johnson Company, New Brunswick, NJ. In 1921, while preparing a dressing for his accident-prone wife, Dickson came up with the idea of a small, ready-to-apply bandage made of a wad of sterile gauze backed by a strip of surgical adhesive. Dickson's key innovation was the use of a removable nonstick material to protect the sticky side of the adhesive tape. Another Johnson & Johnson employee, W. Johnson Kenyon, suggested the name "Band-Aid."

5179. Portable electric stethoscope to amplify the sounds of the human body was demonstrated to 500 doctors by the Western Electric Company of New York City on June 10, 1924, at the Municipal Pier, Chicago, IL. It was developed by Western Electric in cooperation with Bell System engineers and Dr. Horatio Burt Williams, professor of physiology, Columbia University, New York City. The stethoscope was first marketed in October 1925.

5180. Iron lung respirator was invented by Professor Philip Drinker and Louis Agassiz Shaw, who made the original model in April 1927. It consisted of a cheap galvanized iron box with a bed made from "garage creepers" and two household vacuum cleaners with hand-operated valves as the source of alternate positive and negative pressure. The Consolidated Gas Company of New York donated $7,000 to Harvard University, Cambridge, MA, to produce a second model, which was first used on October 12, 1928, at the Children's Hospital, Boston, MA, to help a little girl suffering from respiratory failure caused by poliomyelitis. The machine was manufactured by Warren E. Collins, Boston, MA.

5181. Electric sterilamp was introduced in March 1938 by the Lamp Division of the Westinghouse Electric and Manufacturing Company, Bloomfield, NJ. It was designed to reduce the germ population of the air by bactericidal ultraviolet radiation.

5182. Fiberglass sutures were used by Dr. Roy Philip Scholz of St. Louis, MO, on July 19, 1939, in a mastoid operation. The caliber of the suture was that of #00 silk. It had a carrying strength of 7.4 pounds.

5183. Home health testing kit was Clinitest, which allowed diabetics to measure the level of sugar in their urine using a reagent tablet. Copper sulfate in the tablet reacted with glucose in the urine, causing it to change color. The kit was made by Ames, a division of Miles Laboratories, Elkhart, IN, and was sold to consumers beginning in 1941.

5184. Cellulose sponge for medical and surgical use was marketed by Parke Davis and Company, Detroit, MI, under the trademark Oxycel, on June 5, 1946. It was a hemostatic material used as a surgical dressing, which converted to an absorbable form when left in contact with incised body tissues.

5185. Nuclear reactor used in medical therapy was the Atomic Energy Commission's Brookhaven National Laboratory unit in Upton, near Brookhaven, NY, placed in operation on February 15, 1951.

5186. Catgut substitute for medical use was Dexon, a polyglycolic acid suture, a virtually nonirritating synthetic absorbable, produced in April 1966 by the Davis and Geck department of Lederle Laboratories, Pearl River, NY, a division of the American Cyanamid Company. Work began in January 1962 at Cyanamid's Central Research Laboratory in Stamford, CT.

5187. Wearable infusion pump was invented in 1972 for the purpose of delivering chemotherapy to cancer patients. The inventor was Dean Kamen, an undergraduate at Worcester Polytechnic Institute, Worcester, MA. The pump, a lightweight, portable device carried by the patient in a pouch, could be programmed to deliver doses of medication into a vein at specified intervals.

5188. Home pregnancy test sold in the United States was e.p.t, or "early pregancy test." Made by Warner Chilcott, a UK-based company, the product was approved by the Food and Drug Administration (FDA) in 1976 and appeared in drugstores late the following year.

5189. Home screening kit for HIV infection was approved on May 14, 1996, by the Food and Drug Administration. The kit, sold under the name Confide, was developed by Direct Access Diagnostics, a subsidiary of Johnson & Johnson, New Brunswick, NJ. Users pricked their fingers to get a drop of blood and sent the sample to a laboratory, then called a week later for the results and counseling. HIV (Human Immunodeficiency Virus) is the retrovirus that causes AIDS.

5190. Powder capable of stopping a lethal hemorrhage was QuikClot, developed by Z-Medica Corporation, Wallingford, CT, in cooperation with branches of the U.S. armed forces and approved by the FDA in March 2002. Granulated minerals in the powder absorbed water from blood, allowing clotting agents to work faster.

5191. Bandage capable of stopping a lethal hemorrhage was the chitosan hemostatic dressing, developed by the Oregon Medical Caser Center and manufactured by HemCon Inc., Portland, OR. It was approved by the FDA for use by the U.S. armed forces in the fall of 2003. The bandage was a 4-by-4 inch square made from chitosan, a polymer component of shrimp shells. The combination of positively charged chitosan molecules and negatively charged red blood cells produced a clot powerful enough to seal blood vessels.

Military

5192. Navy doctor was Dr. Joseph Harrison, appointed in 1775 in Philadelphia, PA, to serve on the *Alfred*.

5193. Naval surgeon was Dr. George Balfour, who was ordered to Norfolk, VA, in 1801 to take charge of the first marine hospital. He had entered the Army on April 11, 1792, and was transferred to the Navy on March 9, 1798. He resigned on April 12, 1804, to enter private practice.

5194. Naval hospital established by Congress was authorized on February 26, 1811, with an appropriation of $50,000. On April 2, 1827, the cornerstone was laid at Portsmouth, VA. One wing was ready for occupancy in July 1830, and the building was completed and dedicated in 1833.

5195. Army medical corps is generally claimed to have been established by the Reorganization Act of April 14, 1818. From 1789 to 1798, individual medical officers were appointed for regiments as they were authorized by Congress, beginning with Richard Allison of Pennsylvania, who was appointed surgeon of a corps of 700 rank and file which the first Congress authorized in September 1789.

5196. Navy bureau of medicine and surgery was authorized by act of Congress on August 31, 1842. It was organized in 1842 by Dr. William Paul Crillon Barton, who served as its first chief.

5197. Army field hospital was a tent hospital established by Brigadier General Bernard John Dowling Irwin of the Army Medical Corps at Shiloh, TN, prior to the Civil War battle of April 6–7, 1862, when the Union army suffered more than 13,000 casualties.

5198. Army ambulance corps was established on August 2, 1862, by Major General George Brinton McClellan, who issued General Order No. 147 authorizing one captain to each army corps as the commandant of the Ambulance Corps, a first lieutenant for a division, a second lieutenant for a brigade, and a sergeant for each regiment. The members of the corps wore a green band on the cap and a green half chevron two inches broad on each arm above the elbow. On March 11, 1864, Congress approved a law providing each army corps with two-horse ambulances in accordance with its strength. Infantry regiments of 200 to 500 men were entitled to two ambulances, those of more than 500 men to three; cavalry regiments with fewer than 500 men were entitled to one ambulance, those of more than 500 to two.

5199. Hospital ship operated by the Navy was the U.S.S. *Red Rover*, which was captured from the Confederate forces on September 20, 1862. On December 26, 1862, it was converted into a hospital ship. It remained in service until August 12, 1865.

5200. Military hospital was the Army and Navy Hospital, Hot Springs, AR, which opened for the reception of patients on January 17, 1887. The appropriation was authorized by act of Congress of June 30, 1882. The hospital had five separate buildings, which were connected by verandas.

5201. Dentist officially employed in the Army was Dr. W. H. Ware, an enlisted man in the Medical Department, who served as a dental surgeon in the army in the Philippine Islands in 1898.

5202. Ambulance ship operated by the Navy was the U.S.S. *Solace*, of 5,700 tons, placed in service on April 14, 1898, and used in naval warfare in the Spanish-American War. Formerly the S.S. *Creole*, it was purchased on April 7, 1898. The *Solace* was the creation of Admiral William Knickerbocker Van Reypen. It was fitted out under the terms of the Geneva Convention and was the first designated ambulance ship, used for transporting as well as caring for the sick and wounded, and the first to carry the Geneva Cross flag at the fore. It was removed from the Navy list on August 6, 1930, and sold on November 6, 1930.

5203. Army dental corps was authorized by the Army Reorganization Act of February 2, 1901, "an act to increase the efficiency of the permanent military establishments of the United States." It authorized the employment of contract dental surgeons "not to exceed one to every 30,000 of said army, and not to exceed 30 in all." The first three contract dental surgeons were Drs. John Sayre Marshall, Robert T. Oliver, and Robert W. Morgan. Commissions in the Army Dental Corps were authorized by act of Congress on March 3, 1911.

5204. Army nurse corps for women was established as a permanent organization of the Army on February 2, 1901. Two years earlier, Anita Newcomb McGee, acting assistant surgeon of the Army, had organized the nurses who remained with the Army after the Spanish-American War into a corps under the surgeon general. The 1901 law provided for one superintendent who would receive annual compensation of $1,800 and nurses and reserve nurses who would receive $40 a month within the continental limits of the United States and $50 a month when on foreign service. Quarters, subsistence, and medical attendance were also provided. The first superintendent was Mrs. Dita H. Kinney.

5205. Navy nurses' corps was established on May 13, 1908, in the Navy Medical Department. Navy nurses received the same pay allowances, emoluments, and privileges as the nurse corps of the Army. The first superintendent was Esther Voorhees Hasson. Women had been serving as contract nurses aboard American naval vessels as early as the War of 1812.

5206. Navy dental corps was authorized by act of Congress of August 22, 1912, which provided for not more than 30 dental surgeons to be part of the medical department of the Navy and to provide professional services for navy personnel. They received the rank of lieutenant, junior grade.

5207. Dentist in the Navy to serve aboard a naval ship was Dr. Harry Edward Harvey, who was assigned to the hospital ship U.S.S. *Solace* on March 5, 1913. He served until October 1915.

5208. Army veterinary corps was established as part of the Medical Department of the Army by the National Defense Act of 1916, enacted on June 3, 1916. The legislation authorized two officers for each regiment of cavalry, one for every three batteries of field artillery, and one for each mounted battalion of engineers.

5209. Ambulance ship designed and built by the Navy as a hospital for the transportation of sick and wounded naval men was the U.S.S. *Relief*. Congress authorized the construction of the *Relief* on August 29, 1916. The keel was laid on July 4, 1917. The vessel was launched on December 23, 1919, and delivered to the Navy on December 28, 1920. The overall length of the *Relief* was 484 feet and it had a displacement of 9,750 tons and a speed of 16 knots. The hospital capacity was 515 beds in 14 wards and 15 officers' rooms.

5210. Doctor in the regular Navy who was a woman was Dr. Frances Lois Willoughby of Pitman, NJ, appointed a lieutenant commander on October 15, 1948. During World War II, women were accepted in the Medical Corps of the Naval Reserve on a temporary basis.

Organizations

5211. Medical society was founded in Boston, MA, prior to 1735, and functioned until 1741. It was not very effective and was only local in character.

5212. State medical society of consequence was the Massachusetts Medical Society, which was incorporated in Boston, MA, on

November 1, 1781. Membership was limited to 70 fellows. The first president was Dr. Edward Augustus Holyoke. The charter was signed by Samuel Adams as president of the Senate, and by John Hancock as governor of the Commonwealth. The first African-American member was Dr. John Van Surlay DeGrasse, who was admitted in 1854.

5213. Homeopathic medical society was the Hahnemann Society, organized on April 10, 1833, in Philadelphia, PA, by Drs. Carl Ihm, George H. Bute, Charles F. Matlack, Constantine Hering, and William Wesselhoeft.

5214. Dental society of a city was the Society of Surgeon-Dentists of the City and State of New York, which was formed on December 3, 1834, with Dr. Eleazar Parmly as the first president and Dr. Solyman Brown as the first corresponding secretary. Both men were also on the publishing committee of the first dental journal, the *American Journal of Dental Science.*

5215. Physiology society was the American Physiological Society, organized on February 11, 1837, in Boston, MA, by 124 men and 39 women who signed the constitution. The object was to acquire and diffuse a knowledge of the laws of life and of the means of promoting human health and longevity. Dues were $1 per year. The first monthly meeting was held on March 7, 1837. The first president was William Andrus Alcott.

5216. National dental society was the American Society of Dental Surgeons, organized on August 18, 1840, at a meeting held at the American Hotel, New York City. Dr. Horace Henry Hayden of Baltimore, MD, was the first president. The society disbanded in 1856.

5217. National psychiatry association was the Association of Medical Superintendents of American Institutions for the Insane, formed on October 16, 1844, in Philadelphia, PA, by 13 members. The first president was Samuel B. Woodward. The name of the association was changed in 1892 to the American Medico-Psychological Association and in 1921 to the American Psychiatric Association.

5218. National medical society was the National Medical Association, which was organized on May 5, 1846, with Dr. Jonathan Knight as the first president. Two hundred and fifty delegates attended, representing 22 states, 28 medical schools, and 40 medical societies. The American Medical Association was founded the following year, on May 5, 1847, in Philadelphia, PA, as an outgrowth of the National Medical Association. The first female member of the AMA was Dr. Sarah Hackett Stevenson, who was graduated from the Woman's Medical College of Chicago in 1874 and was elected to membership in the AMA in 1876 as a delegate from the Illinois State Medical Society.

5219. Medical society for women was the American Medical Educational Society of Boston, MA, organized by Samuel Gregory on November 23, 1848, with six members "to provide and promote the education of midwives, nurses and woman physicians, and to diffuse among women generally a knowledge of physiology and the principles and means of preserving and restoring health." Timothy Gilbert was president. Membership was not confined to the professions.

5220. National pharmacy society was the American Pharmaceutical Association, organized on October 6, 1852, in Philadelphia, PA, with Daniel B. Smith as the first president. The first annual meeting was held in Boston, MA, on August 24, 1853.

5221. Medical society for African-Americans was the Medico-Chirurgical Society of the District of Columbia, organized on April 24, 1884, at the office of Dr. Robert Reyburn, Washington, DC. Reyburn was the first president. The society was revived and incorporated on January 15, 1895. Three of the eight incorporators were white.

5222. Nursing society was the Philomena Society, organized on November 24, 1885, in New York City. It disbanded in 1887.

5223. National physiology society was the American Physiological Society, organized in New York City on December 30, 1887, with Silas Weir Mitchell of Philadelphia as president and Henry Newell Martin, professor of biology at Johns Hopkins University, as secretary. Their proceedings, the *American Journal of Physiology*, were first published on January 3, 1898. This society was unrelated to the local society of the same name that was founded in Boston in 1837.

5224. Tuberculosis research and prevention society was the Pennsylvania Society for the Prevention of Tuberculosis, founded on April 10, 1892, in Philadelphia, PA, by Lawrence Francis Flick.

5225. National psychology society was the American Psychological Association, organized on July 8, 1892, at Clark University, Worcester, MA, to advance psychology as a science. Professor Granville Stanley Hall was the first president. The first scientific meeting was held on December 27, 1892, at the University of Pennsylvania, Philadelphia, PA.

5226. National optometry society was the American Association of Opticians, organized on October 10, 1898, by 183 charter members from 31 states and Canada in the Broadway Central Hotel, New York City. Charles Lembke of New York City was the first president. The name was changed in 1910 to the American Optical Association and in 1919 to the American Optometric Association.

5227. Orthodontists' society was the American Society of Orthodontists, founded in June 1900 in St. Louis, MO. The first president was Dr. Edward Hartley Angle of St. Louis. The society was incorporated on February 23, 1917, in Pennsylvania, and the name changed on April 21, 1937, to the American Association of Orthodontists.

5228. Disease research and treatment organization composed of physicians and laymen was the National Tuberculosis Association, organized on June 6, 1904, in Atlantic City, NJ. It had about 400 members. The first annual meeting was held on May 18–19, 1905, in Washington, DC. The first president was Dr. Edward Livingston Trudeau.

5229. National surgery society was the American College of Surgeons, incorporated on November 25, 1912, in Springfield, IL, and organized in Washington, DC, on May 5, 1913, "to elevate the standard of surgery, to establish a standard of competency and of character for practitioners of surgery, and to educate the public and the profession to understand that the practice of surgery calls for special training." Dr. John Miller Turpin Finney of Baltimore, MD, was the first president. The first annual convocation for the admission of fellows took place in Chicago, IL, on November 13, 1913. An African-American surgeon, Dr. Daniel Hale Williams, was in the first group of fellows admitted. The first female surgeons to become fellows were Dr. Alice Gertrude Bryant and Dr. Florence West Duckering, both of Boston, MA, who were admitted along with 1,093 other candidates on June 22, 1914.

5230. Immunology society was the American Association of Immunologists, organized in Minneapolis, MN, on June 19, 1913, with Dr. Gerald Bertram Webb as temporary chairman. The first annual meeting was held on June 22, 1914, in Atlantic City, NJ. The original goal of the society was to bring together vaccine therapists, but in 1915 it developed into a scientific organization covering the whole field of immunology. Its purpose was to study problems of immunology and its application to clinical medicine.

5231. President of a major medical society who was a woman was Dr. Emma Sadler Moss of the Charity Hospital, New Orleans, LA, who was installed as president of the American Society of Clinical Pathologists on October 13, 1955, at the 34th annual meeting.

Pharmaceuticals

5232. Cod-liver oil was described in Thomas Morton's *New English Canaan*, published in 1637, an account of the author's adventures in what is now Quincy, MA. A "great store of traine oyle is mayd of the livers of the Codd, and is a commodity that without question will enrich the inhabitants of New England quicly and is therefore a principall commodity."

5233. Patented pills were introduced in 1796 by Samuel Lee, Jr., of Connecticut, and were known as Lee's Windham Pills and Lee's New London Bilious Pills. On April 30, 1796, he obtained a patent on a "composition of bilious pills."

5234. Drug mill was established in 1812 in Philadelphia, PA, by Charles V. Hagner, who used waterpower for grinding. He was able to perform in one day work that previously would have required months of hand powdering in mortars. His first task of importance was the grinding of several tons of cream of tartar, for which Dr. Haral, a druggist, paid him three cents a pound.

5235. Quinine was manufactured in 1822 by John Farr and Abraham Kunzi in Philadelphia, PA.

5236. Chloroform was distilled in 1831 by Dr. Samuel Guthrie in Sackets Harbor, NY. He called it "chloric ether," and obtained it by distilling chloride of lime with alcohol in a copper still. He described it in "A New Mode of Preparing a Spirituous Solution of Chloric Ether." It is a colorless liquid known chemically as trichloromethane.

5237. Homeopathic pharmacy was established by J. G. Wesselhoeft at 9 Broad Street, Philadelphia, PA, in 1834. In 1835 he opened a branch at 498 Greenwich Street, New York City, which was purchased by William Radde, his clerk. Dr. Francis E. Boericke acquired the business and in 1869 formed a partnership with Adolph J. Tafel as Boericke and Tafel.

5238. Compressed pills or tablets to be commercially manufactured were made in 1863–64 by Jacob Dunton, a wholesale druggist of Philadelphia, PA, who employed a machine in their manufacture. The formulas that were sold in tablet form consisted principally of simple chemicals such as potassium chlorate and ammonium chloride. Dunton sold his products to dispensing druggists and did not attempt to market them under his own name until 1869. His entire production from 1869 to 1876 was less than that now made daily in the laboratories of this country.

5239. Petroleum jelly or petrolatum, a semisolid gel derived from petroleum and used as a lubricant and skin emollient, was developed in 1870 by Robert Augustus Chesebrough, a chemist from Brooklyn, NY (now part of New York City), after a trip to the Pennsylvania oil fields, where he was shown a gummy waste product that was thought to heal wounds. He coined the word Vaseline for his gel and registered it on May 14, 1878, as a trademark. On May 10, 1880, he organized the Chesebrough Manufacturing Company, New York City, which he headed until 1909.

5240. Patent medicine to achieve nationwide popularity was Lydia E. Pinkham's Vegetable Compound, a bottled elixir of herbal extracts, preserved in 19 percent alcohol, that attracted thousands of customers. The ingredients included black cohosh, fenugreek, and unicorn root. The formula, which, despite its name, was never patented, was a household remedy used by a Massachusetts mother, Lydia Estes Pinkham, to cure the ailments of her own four children. Pinkham began selling the compound by mail order in 1876, when she placed her first advertisement in the *Boston Herald*.

5241. Eye wash commercially manufactured was Murine, a solution of muriate of berberine. It was packaged in 1891 by Drs. James and George McFatrich, two brothers who were both ophthalmologists, and Otis Hall, a banker from Spokane, WA. Hall had used the solution at the suggestion of the doctors to heal an eye wound caused by a blow from a horse's tail.

5242. Laxative in candy form was Ex-Lax, invented in 1905 in New York City by Max Kiss, a Hungarian-born pharmacist. He combined chocolate with phenolphthalein, a chemical with a relaxing effect on the intestines. The name is a contraction of"Excellent Laxative."

5243. Vitamin to be commercially synthesized and manufactured was vitamin D, which was manufactured by Mead, Johnson and Company, Evansville, IN, beginning in 1927 and was marketed in the spring of 1928. It was made by exposing a solution of ergosterol to ultraviolet light.

5244. Sulfanilamide production took place in December 1930 at the Jackson Laboratory of E.I. du Pont de Nemours and Company, Wilmington, DE, for use in dyeing cellulose acetate fibers. Sulfanilamide was not used in medicine until 1935, when Dr. Ashley Weech of Babies Hospital, New York City, used it as a treatment for streptococcic infections, but without formally reporting it. Dr. Perrin Hamilton Long of Johns Hopkins Hospital, Baltimore, MD, obtained a one-pound vial from the Du Pont company on November 9, 1936, and together with Eleanor Bliss used it to treat a seven-year-old child with erysipelas. They reported their use of the drug to the Southern Medical Association, Baltimore, MD, on November 17, 1936.

5245. Fizzing cold remedy was Alka-Seltzer. In 1931, Hubert Beardsley, president of Dr. Miles Laboratories, Elkhart, IN, was told about a local cold remedy combining aspirin and baking soda. He asked Miles's chief chemist, Maurice Treneer, to develop an analgesic tablet that would fizz when dropped in water. It went on sale that year as Alka-Seltzer. The original formula contained baking soda, monocalcium phosphate (an antacid), aspirin, and citric acid. Alka-Seltzer achieved nationwide popularity at the end of Prohibition as a cure for hangovers.

5246. Pituitary hormone isolated in chemically pure crystalline form was announced on July 23, 1937, in *Science* by Drs. Abraham White, Hubert Ralph Catchpole, and Cyril Norman Hugh Long of the Laboratories of Physiological Chemistry and Physiology, Yale University School of Medicine, New Haven, CT.

5247. Antibiotic discovered in America was streptomycin, isolated from a culture of a soil microbe known as *Streptomyces griseus* by Dr. Selman Abraham Waksman and four students—Albert Schatz, Elizabeth Bugie, Doris Jones, and H. Christine Reilly—at the New Jersey Agricultural Experiment Station, Rutgers University, New Brunswick, NJ, in January 1944. It was first manufactured commercially by Merck and Company, Rahway, NJ, in September 1944. This antibiotic is active against both gram-positive and gram-negative bacteria as well as upon acid-fast bacteria, of which the most important is the organism that causes tuberculosis. Waksman, a Jewish immigrant from the Ukraine, won the Nobel Prize in physiology and medicine in 1952.

5248. Synthetic quinine was produced on April 10, 1944, by Dr. Robert Burns Woodward and Dr. William von Eggers Doering at the Converse Memorial Laboratory, Harvard University, Cambridge, MA. It consists of 20 atoms of carbon, 24 atoms of hydrogen, 2 atoms of oxygen, and 2 atoms of nitrogen.

5249. Antihistamine drug for allergy symptoms was diphenhydramine hydrochloride, invented by chemical engineer George Rieveschl of the University of Cincinnati in Ohio. The compound blocks the body's production of histamine, an immune-response chemical that is triggered by the presence of an allergen such as pollen. The drug, under the name Benadryl, was marketed as a prescription medication by Parke, Davis and Company in 1946.

5250. Fungicide used medicinally was nystatin, discovered in 1948 by microbiologists Elizabeth Hazen and Rachel Brown in soil from a Virginia farm. Nystatin proved to have applications in medicine, agriculture, and even art restoration (it was used in 1966 to protect artworks damaged by flooding in Florence, Italy).

5251. Broad-spectrum antibiotic was aureomycin chlortetracycline, released to American physicians in November 1948. It was developed and produced by Lederle Laboratories, a division of the American Cyanamid Company, Pearl River, NY. Discovered by Dr. Benjamin Minge Duggar, the antibiotic is a yellow crystalline substance obtained from a mold named *Streptomyces aureofaciens*.

5252. Cortisone synthesis was achieved by chemist Percy Lavon Julian at the Glidden Company, Chicago, IL, in October 1949. The previous year, Edward Kendall at the Mayo Clinic had succeeded in isolating cortisone, a steroid that relieves symptoms of rheumatoid arthritis and other immune-system disorders. It was difficult to obtain and hence expensive. Julian's discovery made possible its widespread use in medicine.

5253. Antibiotic synthetically manufactured for commercial production was chloromycetin. A laboratory to produce chloromycetin by chemical means was opened on March 13, 1952, by Parke Davis and Company, Holland, MI. The main processing building was longer than a football field and had a 40-foot ceiling.

5254. Polypeptide hormone synthesized was oxytocin, a protein-like compound made up of eight amino acids that stimulates uterine contractions in a mother giving birth and starts the flow of her milk. Dr. Vincent du Vigneaud, biochemist of Cornell University Medical College, New York City, and his co-workers isolated oxytocin and synthetically reproduced the hormone. The announcement of the synthesis was made in the fall of 1953. On November 2, 1955, Dr. du Vigneaud was awarded the Nobel Prize in chemistry for this and other work on the chemistry and metabolism of sulfur compounds.

5255. Antidepressant was iproniazid phosphate, a monoamine oxidase inhibitor originally developed to treat tuberculosis. Its effect on depression was revealed when the tuberculosis patients who took it experienced an improvement in their moods. It was approved for prescription as an antidepressant in 1958.

5256. Blockbuster prescription drug was the tranquilizer Valium, invented in 1959 and approved by the FDA in 1963. Valium belongs to a class of chemical compounds, the benzodiazepines, that reduce feelings of anxiety by influencing the activity of the neurotransmitter GABA. They were developed beginning in 1954 by Leo Henryk Sternbach, a chemist employed by Hoffman-LaRoche, Nutley, NJ. The first of the benzodiazepines to be approved for prescription use, in 1960, was Librium. Valium, the second to be approved, was the most popular prescription drug in the United States for more than a decade and earned billions of dollars annually.

5257. Medicine produced using recombinant DNA was human insulin, produced in 1978 by the City of Hope Medical Center, Duarte, CA, in a joint venture with the biotechnology firm Genentech. The insulin was created using bacteria that had been implanted with human DNA. The Food and Drug Administration did not approve use of the bioengineered insulin until 1982.

5258. Human antibodies produced artificially were announced by Dr. Henry Kaplan and Dr. Lennart Olson on July 29, 1980, at the Stanford University Medical School, Stanford, CA. Kaplan and Olson, seeking a method of manufacturing pure human antibodies to help diagnose and treat disease, created a line of antibody-producing hybrid cells by fusing bone-marrow cancer cells with human spleen cells.

5259. Transdermal patch was Transderm-Scop, a motion-sickness remedy marketed by CibaGeigy, Ardsley, NY. It was developed by ALZA Corporation, Mountain View, CA, and received FDA approval in 1981. The patch delivered a continuous dose of scopolamine, a drug that suppresses nausea and vomiting, through the patient's skin.

5260. Drug for treating AIDS to win the approval of the Food and Drug Administration was AZT (azidothymidine). Approval was given on March 20, 1987. The drug was made by Burroughs Wellcome and initially cost more than $10,000 a year for each patient.

5261. SSRI antidepressant was fluoxetine hydrochloride, better known by its brand name, Prozac. Drugs in the SSRI family, the selective serotonin reuptake inhibitors, reduce feelings of anxiety and depression by adjusting the levels in the body of the neurotransmitter serotonin. Fluoxetine was invented by organic chemists Klaus K. Schmiegel and Bryan B. Molloy at Eli Lilly and Company, Indianapolis, IN. It entered the United States market in January 1988 as a prescription drug.

5262. Oral medicine for erectile dysfunction that was effective was Viagra, approved for use by the Food and Drug Administration on March 27, 1998. Viagra was the trade name for sildenafil citrate, developed by Pfizer, Inc., New York, NY. It quickly became the world's most popular prescription drug.

5263. Cancer-preventing drug was tamoxifen citrate, a selective estrogen receptor modulator, developed by Zeneca Pharmaceutical of Wilmington, DE, under the trade name Nolvadex. In April 1998 the National Cancer Institute released findings from the National Adjuvant Breast and Bowel Project's Breast Cancer Prevention Trial that showed tamoxifen cut the risk of breast cancer nearly in half among more than 13,000 women at high risk for the disease. The U.S. Food and Drug Administration approved tamoxifen on October 29, 1998, for the reduction of breast cancer risk in healthy women.

Prosthetics

5264. Bifocal eyeglasses were invented by Benjamin Franklin of Philadelphia, PA, who was annoyed at having to carry two pairs of glasses. He took a frame and equipped it with lenses that consisted of two parts with different focusing powers. On May 23, 1785, from Passy, France, he wrote to George Whatley, "I have only to move my eyes up and down as I want to see distinctly far or near." Inasmuch as ordinary spectacles in the colonies cost as much as $100 each, his invention did not receive a ready popular response. Eyeglass frames were invented by a London optician in 1727.

5265. Artificial leg patent was granted to Benjamin F. Palmer of Meredith, NH, on November 4, 1846. The leg had a pliable joint that worked noiselessly and preserved its contour in all positions. Artificial legs had been made previously. Howland and Company, of Brookfield, MA, exhibited one in 1837 at the Massachusetts Charitable Mechanics Association.

5266. Artificial eyes were manufactured by Pierre Gougelman in 1851 at Van Dam Street, New York City, from glass imported from France. The business was later known as Mager and Gougelman.

5267. Hearing aid other than ear trumpets was the Audiphone, a fanlike device held against the teeth, patented on September 23, 1879, by Richard S. Rhodes of River Park, IL.

5268. Electrical hearing aid produced commercially was the Acousticon, invented by Miller Reese Hutchinson of New York City in 1901. On April 27, 1880, Francis D. Clarke and M. G. Foster had secured a patent on a "device for aiding the deaf to hear" that made its own electricity and operated by bone conduction.

5269. Contact lenses were imported for commercial purposes in New York City in 1924 from Jena, Germany, where they were manufactured by Carl Zeiss. The lenses were ground rather than blown. They were thin saucer-shaped shells of optical glass that were worn under the eyelid in direct contact with the eye itself.

5270. Artificial lens for cataract patients was fitted on March 18, 1952, at Wills Eye Hospital, Philadelphia, PA, by Dr. Warren Snyder Reese. He performed the Ridley operation, developed by Frederick Thomas Ridley, which involved the insertion of a plastic lens approximately eight millimeters in diameter into the eye of a patient whose diseased lens had been removed.

5271. Hearing aid using transistors was manufactured by the Sonotone Corporation, Elmsford, NY, and offered for sale on December 29, 1952. It weighted 3.5 ounces and was three inches long.

5272. Bifocal contact lenses was developed by Newton K. Wesley, O.D., of the Eye Research Foundation and the Plastic Contact Lens Company, Chicago, IL. They were officially introduced in May 1958. Prescriptions for distant vision were ground in the center of the lens, and reading prescriptions were ground on the outer circle. The cost of a pair ranged from $200 to $400.

5273. Soft contact lens available in the United States was the Soflens, introduced by Bausch & Lomb, Rochester, NY, in 1971. The soft lens had been invented in 1961 by chemist Otto Wichterle in Czechoslovakia. A political dissident in a Communist nation, Wichterle had been fired from his laboratory and had to create his prototypes on his kitchen table with homemade equipment.

5274. Eyeglasses with polycarbonate lenses were made by Gentex Corporation, Simpson, PA, in 1983. They were thin, light, and resistant to breaking, but not as optically clear as glass lenses.

5275. Thought control of a computer was achieved in October 1998, when John Ray, a construction worker paralyzed by a stroke, employed a small electronic brain implant to move the cursor on a computer screen. The implant was developed by Dr. Phillip Kennedy of Emory University in Atlanta, GA. It consisted of two tiny glass cones containing electrodes. When the patient thought about moving the cursor, the electrodes read the electrical activity in his brain and, via a transmitter in his scalp, sent a command to the computer. Ray had received the implant in an operation performed by Dr. Roy Bakay in March 1998. He died four years later of a brain aneurysm.

5276. Bionic artificial arm operated by thought control was developed by Dr. Todd Kuiken of the Rehabilitation Institute of Chicago, IL, and fitted in January 2003 to Jesse Sullivan of Dayton, TN. Sullivan had lost both his arms in a work accident. While his right arm was replaced by a conventional prosthetic limb, his left arm was replaced by Kuiken's myoelectric device, which responded to his thoughts much as a normal arm would do. The device used muscle to receive and transmit brain-generated impulses.

5277. Thought control of mechanical devices was accomplished by quadriplegic Matthew Nagle of Weymouth, MA. In June 2004, in a test of the BrainGate Neural Interface System, a sensor 4 millimeters square and containing 100 electrodes was implanted in the motor cortex of his brain, together with a connection device that protruded from his skull. The device had a port for a fiberoptic computer cable. The interface enabled Nagle to operate a robotic arm, control a television set, and play video games using thought alone. BrainGate was developed by Cyberkinetics Neurotechnology Systems Inc., Foxborough, MA, a firm founded by John Donoghue and other neuroscientists from Brown University.

Publications

5278. Medical pamphlet written by an American was *On Baths and Mineral Waters* by Dr. John Bell, printed in two volumes in 1831 in Philadelphia, PA. Volume 1 (374 pages) was "a full account of the hygienic and curative powers of cold, tepid, warm, hot and vapour baths and of sea bathing." Volume 2 (158 pages) was "a history of the chemical composition and medicinal properties of the chief mineral springs of the United States and Europe."

5279. Hydrotherapy book was On Baths and Mineral Waters by Dr. John Bell, printed in two volumes in 1831 in Philadelphia, PA. Volume 1 (374 pages) was "a full account of the hygienic and curative powers of cold, tepid, warm, hot and vapour baths and of sea bathing." Volume 2 (158 pages) was "a history of the chemical composition and medicinal properties of the chief mineral springs of the United States and Europe."

5280. Epidemiology report was *The Practical History of a New Epidemical Eruptive Military Fever, with an Angina Ulcusulosa which prevailed in Boston, New-England in the years 1735 and 1736*, a 24-page thesis by William Douglass, M.D., printed and sold by Thomas Fleet at the Sign of the Heart and Crown in Cornhill, Boston, MA, in 1736. "This distemper did emerge 20th May 1735 in Kingston Township, fifty miles eastward from Boston, and affected one-fourth of the inhabitants."

5281. Dissection report appeared in 1750. It was a report by Dr. John Bard and Dr. Peter Middleton, who dissected the body of Hermanus Carroll, a criminal executed for murder, in New York City.

5282. Medical education book was printed by William Bradford, Philadelphia, PA, in 1765. It contained 63 pages of text and was entitled *A Discourse Upon the Institution of Medical Schools in America*, by John Morgan, M.D., professor of the theory and practice of medicine in the College of Philadelphia. The discourse was delivered at a public anniversary commencement held in the College of Philadelphia in May 1765, and was prefaced by "The Author's Apology for attempting to introduce the regular mode of practicing Physic in Philadelphia."

5283. History of medicine was printed in New York City in 1769 by Hugh Gaine. It was entitled *A Medical Discourse, or An Historical Inquiry into the ancient and present State of Medicine: The Substance of which Was delivered at opening the Medical School in the City of New York*, by Peter Middleton, M.D., professor of the theory of physic in King's College (now Columbia University). It contained a two-page dedication and 72 pages of text.

5284. Medical ethics book was *A Discourse Upon the Duties of a Physician, with Some Sentiments on the Usefulness and Necessity of a Public Hospital, delivered before the President and Governors of King's College* [now Columbia University] *at the commencement held on the 16th of May, 1769. As advice to those gentlemen who then received the first medical degrees conferred by that university*, by Samuel Bard, M.D., and printed by A. and J. Robertson, New York City, in 1769. It consisted of 18 printed pages.

5285. Surgery manual was *Plain, Concise Practical Remarks on the Treatment of Wounds and Fractures; to which is added a short appendix on camp and military hospitals; principally designed for the use of young military surgeons in North America*, 92 pages, printed in 1775 by John Holt, New York City. The author was Dr. John Jones, professor of surgery in King's College (now Columbia University), New York City.

5286. Pharmacopoeia was the work of Dr. William Brown, physician-general to the hospitals of the United States, who wrote it for the use of the Military Hospital of the Army at Lititz, PA. It was entitled *Pharmacopoeia simpliciorum et efficaciorum, in usum nosocomii militaris*. It was entirely in Latin and was published in Philadelphia, PA, in 1778. There were 32 pages. The page size was 4.25 by 2.5 inches.

5287. Army medical book was *A Journal of the Practice of Medicine, Surgery and Pharmacy in the Military Hospitals of France, published by order of the King. Reviewed and digested by M. De Horne, under the inspection of the Royal Society*. The 120-page octavo book, printed in 1790 by J. M. McLean and Company, New York City, was translated from the French by Joseph Browne and consisted of one volume. The French edition, consisting of seven volumes, was published from 1782 to 1788.

5288. Anatomy book was *A Compendious System of Anatomy*, published in 1792 by Thomas Dobson in Philadelphia, PA. It contained 438 pages and 12 anatomical plates and was divided into six parts covering osteology, the muscles, the abdomen, the thorax, the brain and nerves, and the senses. The text was an extract from the American edition of the *Encyclopaedia Britannica.* The first anatomy book written as such, also published in Philadelphia by Dobson, was *A System of Anatomy for the Use of Students of Medicine*, by Dr. Caspar Wistar, professor of anatomy at the medical school of the University of Pennsylvania from 1808 to 1818. The book contained 422 pages.

Courtesy of the United States National Library of Medicine, B026493

Dr. Caspar Wistar

5289. Dentistry book written by an American was Richard Cort Skinner's *A Treatise on the Human Teeth, Concisely Explaining Their Structure and Cause of Disease and Decay*, copyrighted in 1801 by Johnson and Stryker, New York City. It contained 26 pages and sold for 30 cents. Originally published in 1794, it claimed to obviate every disease of the teeth and gums. The first dentistry book to become popular was Josiah Foster Flagg's *The Family Dentist: Containing a Brief Description of the Structure, Formation, Diseases and Treatment of the Human Teeth*, 82 pages, printed and published in 1822 in Boston, MA, by Joseph W. Ingraham.

5290. Pediatrics monograph was Charles Caldwell's *An Attempt to Establish the Original Sameness of Those Phenomena of Fever, (Principally confined to Infants and Children) Described by Medical Writers Under the Several Names of Hydrocephalus Internus, Cynanche Trachealis and Diarrhoea Infantum*, a thesis presented on May 17, 1796, for a degree at the University of Pennsylvania Medical School, Philadelphia, PA. It was published in Philadelphia by Thomas Dobson.

5291. Medical journal was published in New York City on August 8, 1797, and was called *The Medical Repository*, a "depository of facts and reasonings relative to Natural History, Agriculture and Medicine." Printed by T. and J. Swords, printers to The Faculty of Physicians of Columbia College, it was published quarterly and appeared until 1824. It was also the first scientific periodical published in the United States. The first editor was Dr. Samuel Latham Mitchill, who continued in this capacity for 16 years. Drs. Edward Miller and Elihu Hubbard Smith were also active in the founding of this journal.

5292. Herbal book was Samuel Stearns's *The American Herbal or Materia Medica wherein the virtues of the mineral, vegetable and animal productions of North and South America are laid open*, printed in 1801 in Walpole, NH, by David Carlisle for Thomas and Thomas and the author. It contained 360 pages.

5293. Gastroenterology treatise was *An Experimental Inquiry into the Principles of Nutrition and the Digestive Processes*, a 48-page graduation thesis submitted by John Richardson Young at the University of Pennsylvania, Philadelphia, PA. It was published by Eaken and Mecum, Philadelphia, PA, in 1803.

5294. Hemophilia treatise was prepared by Dr. John Conrad Otto of Philadelphia, PA, who stated that the hemorrhagic tendency was transmitted through the females to the males but that the females were not susceptible themselves. His report appeared in 1803 in the *Medical Repository & Review of American Publications on Medicine and Surgery*, and was entitled "An Account of an Haemorrhagic Disposition Existing in Certain Families." The magazine was published in New York City.

5295. Pharmacopoeia prepared by a medical association for the use of its members was authorized October 3, 1805, by the Massachusetts Medical Society, Boston, MA. It contained 286 pages and was edited by Dr. James Jackson and Dr. John Collins Warren. It was published in 1808 in Boston, MA, as *The Pharmacopoeia of the Massachusetts Medical Society.*

5296. Pharmaceuticals book was the *American Dispensatory, Containing the Operations of Pharmacy, Together With the Natural, Chemical, Pharmaceutical and Medical History of the Different Substances Employed in Medicine*, by John Redman Coxe. It was printed in 1806 in Philadelphia, PA, by A. Bartram for Thomas Dobson. It was a simplified arrangement of Dr. Duncan's *Edinburgh New Dispensatory*, and contained 787 pages and six plates. The first entirely American pharmaceuticals book was *Dispensatory of the United States of America*, 1092 pages, published in 1833 in Philadelphia, PA, by Grigg and Elliot. It was prepared by Dr. George Bacon Wood, professor of materia medica and pharmacy, and Dr. Franklin Bache, professor of chemistry, both of the Philadelphia College of Pharmacy.

5297. Obstetrics book was Samuel Bard's *A Compendium of the Theory and Practice of Midwifery*, a 239-page book published in 1807 by Collins and Perkins, New York City. It contained "practical instructions for the management of women during pregnancy, in labor, and in child-bed, calculated to correct the errors, and to improve the practice of midwives as well as to serve as an introduction to the study of this art for students and young practitioners."

5298. Medical book by a Navy medical officer was *Observations on the Means of Preserving the Health of Soldiers and Sailors; and on the Duties of the Medical Department of the Army and Navy; with remarks on hospitals and their internal arrangement*, by Edward Cutbush. It was printed by Thomas Dobson in Philadelphia, PA, in 1808. It contained 336 pages and a 14-page supplement by Dr. Benjamin Rush.

5299. Psychiatry book was *Medical Inquiries and Observations Upon the Diseases of the Mind*, by Benjamin Rush, M.D., which was published by Kimber and Richardson, Philadelphia, PA, in 1812. This comprehensive book on mental illness contained 367 pages plus four pages listing books issued by the publishers. Dr. Rush was professor of the institutes and practice of medicine and of clinical practice at the University of Pennsylvania.

5300. Therapeutics book was *Discourses on the Elements of Therapeutics and Materia Medica*, published in 1817 in Philadelphia, PA, by Nathaniel Chapman.

5301. General pharmacopoeia was *The Pharmacopoeia of the United States of America.* It was published on December 15, 1820, in both English and Latin by Wells and Lilly of Boston, MA, and copyrighted by Ewer and Bedlington of Boston. It listed 217 drugs. It consisted of 274 pages printed on rather porous paper, 6 by 10 inches. The chairman in charge of the work was Dr. Lyman Spalding, who had proposed the work on January 8, 1817, to the New York County Medical Society.

5302. Ophthalmology book was *A Treatise on the Diseases of the Eye; Including the Doctrines and Practice of the Most Eminent Modern Surgeons, and Particularly those of Professor [George Joseph] Beer*, by Dr. George Frick, ophthalmic surgeon to the Baltimore General Dispensary, Baltimore, MD. It was published by Fielding Lucas, Jr., and printed by John D. Toy in Baltimore in 1823. It consisted of 320 pages.

5303. Homeopathic treatise was Christian Friedrich Samuel Hahnemann's *Geist der Homöopathischen Heil-Lehre*, translated by

Courtesy of the United States National Library of Medicine. B022630

Dr. Benjamin Rush

Dr. Hans Birch Gram and published as a 24-page pamphlet entitled *The Characteristic of Homöopathia.* The book was issued in December 1825 by J. and J. Harper, New York City.

5304. Pharmacy journal was *The Journal of the Philadelphia College of Pharmacy,* which appeared in December 1825. Its first editor was Daniel B. Smith. The magazine contained 32 pages of "original and selected papers on subjects connected with pharmacy and chemistry," and sold for 25 cents.

5305. Dental surgery textbook was *A System of Dental Surgery in three parts: 1. Dental surgery as a science; 2. Operative dental surgery; 3. Pharmacy connected with dental surgery,* by Samuel Sheldon Fitch, a surgeon dentist of Philadelphia, PA. The work, which contained 568 pages, was published in 1829 in New York City by G. and C.H. Carvill.

5306. Pathology textbook was *A Treatise on Pathological Anatomy,* published in Philadelphia, PA, in 1829. It contained 460 pages. The author was William Edmonds Horner, who in 1831 was appointed professor of anatomy in the medical school of the University of Pennsylvania, Philadelphia.

5307. Phrenology book was *Outlines of Phrenology* by Johann Gaspar Spurzheim, M.D., of the universities of Vienna and Paris, licentiate of the Royal College of Physicians of London. It was published in 1832 by Marsh, Capen and Lyon, Boston, MA. It was divided into three sections covering general principles of phrenology, special facilities of the mind, and practical applications of phrenology.

5308. Medical dictionary was *A Dictionary of Medical Science* by Robley Dunglison, published in 1833 in Philadelphia, PA.

5309. Homeopathy journal was the *American Journal of Homeopathia,* 48 pages, issued in February 1835. It was edited by Drs. John F. Gray and Amos Gerald Hull and published by Moore and Payne, New York City. Subscription was $4 a year. Only four issues were printed: February, April, June, and August, 1835.

5310. Medical encyclopedia was the *American Cyclopedia of Practical Medicine and Surgery; A Digest of Medical Literature,* edited by Isaac Hays, surgeon to Wills' Hospital and physician to the Philadelphia Orphan Asylum, published by Carey, Lea and Blanchard, Philadelphia, PA. Only two volumes of the work were published, covering "A to Azygores": Volume 1, 1834, 560 pages, and Volume 2, 1836, 589 pages.

5311. Phrenology journal was published by Nathan Allen in October 1838 in Philadelphia, PA. It was entitled the *American Phrenological Journal and Miscellany* and enjoyed a good circulation until its discontinuance in January 1911.

5312. Cranioscopy book was Dr. Samuel George Morton's *Crania Americana; or A Comparative View of the Skulls of Various Aboriginal Nations of North and South America to Which Is Prefixed an Essay on the Varieties of the Human Species,* published in 1839 by J. Dobson, Philadelphia, PA. It was a tall folio containing a five-page preface, 297 pages of text, and four blank sheets. It had 71 full pages of lithograph plates.

5313. Dental journal was *The American Journal of Dental Science,* 24 pages long, which made its appearance in July 1839. Dr. Chapin Aaron Harris was the first editor. It was published in New York City.

5314. Embalming book was *History of Embalming, and of Preparations in Anatomy, Pathology and Natural History; including an account of a new process for embalming,* 264 pages, published in 1840 in Philadelphia, PA, by Judah Dobson. It was a translation by Richard Harlan, M.D., of a book by Jean Nicolas Gannal that had been published in 1838 in Paris.

5315. Orthodontia treatise to be printed was *An Essay on the Importance of Regulating the Teeth of Children Before the Fourteenth Year; or the Period of Life when the Second Set of Teeth Become Perfectly Developed,* by Solyman Brown, M.D., which was printed in 1841 in New York City.

5316. Health journal to advocate water cures was the *Water Cure Journal,* devoted to the "proper explanation of hydropathy, or water cure, including bathing in its various forms, attention to diet, drink, air, exercise, cleanliness, and clothing, as affecting bodily and mental health." Edited by Joel Shew, M.D., and T. D. Pierson, M.D., this 16-page semimonthly was first published in New York City on December 1, 1845, at $1 a copy.

5317. Bronchitis treatise was published in 1846 by Horace Green, professor of theory and practice of medicine at the New York Medical College. It was entitled *Treatise on the Diseases of the Air Passages comprising an Inquiry into the History, Pathology, Causes and Treatment of those affections of the Throat called Bronchitis, Chronic Laryngitis, Clergyman's Sore Throat.*

5318. Psychiatry textbook was *A Manual of Psychological Medicine*, by John Charles Bucknill and Daniel Hack Tuke, published in Philadelphia, PA, in 1858. It contained 536 pages. The chapters on history, nosology, description, and statistics were written by Tuke; the chapters in the last half of the book on diagnosis, pathology, and treatment of insanity, as well as the appendix of cases, by Bucknill.

5319. Chiropody book was *Surgical and Practical observations on the Diseases of the Human Foot*, by Issachar Zacharie, published in 1860 in New York City.

5320. Electrotherapy book was Dr. Alfred Charles Garratt's *Electro-Physiology and Electro-Therapeutics, showing the best methods for the medical uses of electricity*, 712 pages, published in 1860 by Ticknor and Fields, Boston, MA.

5321. Pediatrics journal was the *American Journal of Obstetrics and Diseases of Women and Children*, a quarterly, started in May 1868 in New York City. It was edited by Dr. Emil Jacob Noeggerath and Dr. Benjamin Frederick Dawson. The first issue contained 96 pages, including an article by Dr. Abraham Jacobi on "The Pathology and Treatment of the Different Forms of Croup."

5322. Neurology textbook was Dr. William Alexander Hammond's *The Diseases of the Nervous System*, edited by Dr. Thaddeus M. B. Cross and published in 1871 in New York City. It was divided into five sections covering diseases of the brain, spinal cord, cerebrospinal system, nerve cells, and peripheral nerves. The book consisted of Hammond's lectures delivered at the New York State Hospital for Diseases of the Nervous System and Bellevue Hospital Medical College, New York City.

5323. Allergy book was Morrill Wyman's *Autumnal Catarrh—Hay Fever*, published in 1872 by Hurd and Houghton, New York City. It was dedicated to Jeffries Wyman, professor of anatomy at the Harvard University School of Medicine, and contained 173 pages and three maps.

5324. Dermatology treatise was *The Atlas of Skin Diseases* by Dr. Louis Adolphus Duhring, professor of skin diseases at the medical school of the University of Pennsylvania. The first section was published in 1876 in Philadelphia, PA.

5325. Bacteriology textbook was *Bacteria*, by Dr. Antoine Magnin, translated from the French by George Miller Sternberg, M.D., surgeon of the Army. The 227-page book was published in 1880 by Little, Brown and Company, Boston, MA.

5326. Laryngology journal was the *Archives of Laryngology*, a 108-page quarterly, published in New York City in March 1880. It was edited by Dr. Louis Elsberg of New York City, Dr. George Morewood Lefferts of New York City, Dr. Jacob Solis-Cohen of Philadelphia, PA, and Dr. Frederick Irving Knight of Boston, MA.

5327. Neurasthenia book was George Miller Beard's *A Practical Treatise on Nervous Exhaustion (Neurasthenia); Its symptoms, nature, sequences and treatment*. It contained 198 pages and was published in 1880 by M.

Courtesy of the United States National Library of Medicine
B026393

Dr. William Alexander Hammond

Wood and Company, New York City. Beard's first article on this subject appeared on April 29, 1869, in the *Boston Medical and Surgical Journal*.

5328. Nursing magazine was *The Nightingale*, "a paper in the interests of the methodical nursing of the sick," which appeared on March 6, 1886, in New York City. The first issue consisted of four pages. It was a monthly, edited by Sarah E. Post of the Graduate Training School for Nurses, Bellevue Hospital, New York City. The subscription price was $2 a year.

5329. Psychology journal was the *American Journal of Psychology*, a quarterly first published in Baltimore, MD, in November 1887 under the editorship of Granville Stanley Hall. The subscription price was $3 a year.

5330. Opticians' journal was *The Optician*, a 16-page monthly, edited and published by Frederick Boger, New York City, beginning in January 1891. The subscription price was 50 cents a year. In May 1892 the name was changed to *The Optician and Allied Interests* and in October 1892 to *The Optician and Jeweler*.

5331. Medical journal published by an African-American was the *Medical and Surgical Observer*, 32 pages, published in Jackson, TN, in December 1892. It appeared regularly for 18 months. The first editor was Vandahurst Lynk, M.D.

5332. Osteopathy journal was the *Journal of Osteopathy*, which was started in May 1894 by the American School of Osteopathy in Kirksville, MO. The first editor was Dr. Jenette Hubbard Bolles.

5333. Physiology journal was *The American Journal of Physiology*, 144 pages, the first issue of which was dated February 1898. It was published by Ginn and Company, Boston, MA.

5334. Orthodontia journal was the *International Journal of Orthodontia*, edited by Dr. Martin Dewey. The first issue was published in January 1915 in St. Louis, MO, and contained 44 pages. The title was changed to the *American Journal of Orthodontics and Oral Surgery* in January 1938.

5335. Dental hygiene book was *Mouth Hygiene*, compiled and edited by Dr. Alfred Civilion Fones and associate editors Robert Hallock Wright Strang and Edward Cameron Kirk. It was a course of instruction for dental hygienists and consisted of 530 pages with 278 illustrations and seven plates. It was published by Lea and Febiger, Philadelphia and New York, in 1916.

5336. Allergy journal was the *Journal of Allergy*, published in November 1929 in St. Louis, MO. It was edited by Dr. Harry Louis Alexander. The first issue contained 112 pages.

5337. Medical slang dictionary was the *Dictionary of Medical Slang and Related Esoteric Expressions*, 207 pages long, by Jacob Edward Schmidt, published in 1959 in Springfield, IL.

Surgery

5338. Cesarean operation that was successful was performed by Dr. Jessee Bennett on his wife, Elizabeth Hog Bennett, on January 14, 1794, in Edom, VA. Bennett had asked Dr. Alexander Humphreys of Staunton, VA, to assist in performing the operation, but because of the low chance of success, Humphreys had declined. Dr. Bennett performed the operation with the assistance of two slaves, who held the patient. She was placed on a table made of two planks laid on a couple of barrels and was given laudanum in lieu of an anesthetic.

5339. Abdominal operation other than a cesarean section was an ovariotomy, the surgical removal of an ovarian tumor. It was performed by Dr. Ephraim McDowell on December 13, 1809, at Danville, KY. The operation was performed without anesthetic. The patient, Jane Todd Crawford, sang hymns to distract her mind. She was 45 years of age at the time of the operation, and lived to be 78.

5340. Plastic and reconstructive surgeon in the United States was Dr. John Peter Mettauer of Prince Edward Courthouse, VA, who made his own surgical instruments. He mended a cleft palate in 1827 and was a pioneer in the repair of gynecological fistulas as well as the founder of a medical school.

5341. Skin grafting was suggested in 1847 by Dr. Frank Hastings Hamilton of Buffalo, NY. In 1854 he reported a case in which he had succesfully grafted skin on a large raw surface of a man's leg that had been injured by a heavy stone.

5342. Mastoid operation to relieve infected ears was performed on June 15, 1859, at the Brooklyn City Hospital, Brooklyn, NY (now part of New York City), by Dr. Joseph Chrisman Hutchison, and was described by him at the April 1865 meeting of the Medical Society of Kings County, Brooklyn. His report, entitled "Otitis; Perforating of Mastoid Process with a Trephine," appeared in the *Transactions of the Medical Society of Kings County* in April 1865 and in the *Buffalo Medical and Surgical Journal* in October 1865.

5343. Gallstone operation was performed on June 15, 1867, by Dr. John Stough Bobbs, known as "the father of cholecystotomy," in Indianapolis, IN, and was reported to the Indiana Medical Society on May 19–20, 1868. The patient was Mary E. Wiggins of McCordsville, IN,

5344. Appendectomy to remove a perforated appendix was performed in Davenport, IA, on January 4, 1885, by Dr. William West Grant. The patient was Mary Gartside, age 22. The patient lived until 1919, when she died of a quite different illness.

5345. Surgical repair of a stab wound to the heart that was successful was accomplished on July 9, 1893, at the Provident Hospital, Chicago, IL. The patient was James Cornish, whose internal mammary artery had been damaged by a knife wound. Dr. Daniel Hale Williams sutured the pericardium. The operation, which was witnessed by six doctors, was described in March 27, 1897, in the *Medical Record*.

5346. Suturing of a heart wound in the United States was accomplished by Dr. Luther Leonidas Hill of Montgomery, AL, on September 15, 1902. The patient was Henry Myrick, a 13-year-old who had been stabbed in the heart. A team of seven doctors headed by Hill placed two sutures in his torn left ventricle. The operation was performed on a rickety kitchen table by the light of kerosene lamps.

5347. Peritonitis preventive that was successful was amniotic fluid, first used to prevent postoperative peritonitis and adhesions in 1922 by Dr. Herbert Lester Johnson of Boston, MA. The first fluid was of human origin, from cesarean operations, but the widespread use of this new principle of preventive medicine resulted in the development of a commercial preparation known as Amniotic Fluid Concentrate, made from bovine amniotic fluid.

5348. Lung removal was performed on April 5, 1933, at the Barnes Hospital, St. Louis, MO, by Dr. Evarts Ambrose Graham of St. Louis, who removed the left lung of Dr. Robert Gilmore, a Pittsburgh obstetrician. Seven ribs were also removed for the purpose of allowing the soft tissues of the chest wall to collapse against the bronchial stump and therefore to obliterate as much as possible of the pleural cavity.

5349. Surgical elevation of the skull to treat epilepsy was demonstrated on November 2, 1933, at the Flower Hospital, New York City, by Dr. Karl Winfield Ney, professor of neurosurgery at the New York Medical College and Flower Hospital in New York City, before the members of the Eastern Homeopathic Medical Association and Clinical Congress. The top of the patient's skull was cut through almost all the way around, lifted slightly, and then replaced.

5350. Heart pump was a spirally coiled glass tube and pump invented in 1935 by Dr. Alexis Carrel, assisted by Colonel Charles Augustus Lindbergh. The apparatus consisted of a culture chamber and the electrically operated glass pump. A surgically removed heart was suspended in the culture chamber and the main artery and vein were connected with the glass tubes of the pump, which circulated a nutritive fluid through the organ and kept it alive. The experiments were carried on in the Rockefeller Institute in New York City.

5351. Heart operation for the relief of angina pectoris was performed on February 13, 1935, by Dr. Claude Schaeffer Beck, associate professor of surgery at Western Reserve University, on a patient at the Lakeside Hospital, Cleveland, OH. Dr. Beck resected one of the pectoral muscles in the chest and fastened the cut end to the heart wall, to provide an additional source of blood for the heart.

5352. Surgical operation televised on a closed circuit was a half-hour hernia operation that took place on March 21, 1939, at the Israel Zion Hospital, Brooklyn, New York City. It was filmed by the American Television Corporation using a television camera and a microphone suspended above the operating table and was transmitted to medical students 500 feet away in another building of the hospital. The first closed-circuit telecast of surgery that was viewed by physicians, rather than by students, was shown on February 27, 1947, at a meeting of the Johns Hopkins Medical and Surgical Association held at the Johns Hopkins Hospital, Baltimore, MD. There were four heart operations and one on the spinal vertebra. The images were transmitted to 10 receivers in four classrooms.

5353. Pacemaker was invented in 1952 by Paul M. Zoll, a cardiologist at Beth Israel Hospital in Boston, MA. He was seeking a way to aid cardiac patients suffering from Stokes-Adams attacks, also called complete heart block, a breakdown of the heart's ability to beat regularly. Zoll inserted a bare wire into the recipient's heart to convey electrical pulses provided by an external pulse generator. Since the generator had to be plugged into an electrical outlet, the patient's mobility was severely limited. The first battery-powered external pulse generator was developed in 1958 by electrical engineer Earl Bakken at the request of C. Walton Lillehei, an open-heart surgeon at the University of Minnesota medical school. It was the size of a transistor radio and ran on flashlight batteries.

5354. Surgical operation shown on a local television program for the general public was performed by Dr. Isador Schwaner Ravdin at the University of Pennsylvania Hospital, Philadelphia, PA, on March 16, 1952. It was a peptic ulcer operation that lasted 2.5 hours. Ten minutes of the operation were shown by WPTZ, Philadelphia.

5355. Surgical operation televised coast-to-coast was transmitted on June 10, 1952, from the Wesley Memorial Hospital, Chicago, IL, in connection with the 101st annual meeting of the American Medical Association at the Palmer House, Chicago, IL. The program showed an eight-minute portion of a 3.5-hour duodenal ulcer operation performed on a 60-year-old man by Dr. Samuel Julian Fogelson. The program was sponsored by Smith, Kline and French Laboratories, and presented by the National Broadcasting Company.

5356. Mitral valve corrective surgery was carried out on July 3, 1952, by Dr. Forest Dewey Dodrill at the Harper Hospital, Detroit, MI. The patient was a 41-year-old man. The Michigan Heart was used as a substitute for the lower left ventricle during the operation, which was the first to involve prolonged exposure of the mitral valve.

5357. Heart operation in which the deep-freezing technique was employed was a 58-minute operation performed on September 2, 1952, by Dr. Floyd John Lewis, associate professor of surgery at the Medical School of the University of Minnesota, Minneapolis, MN. The patient was a five-year-old girl. During the operation, her body temperature was reduced to 79 degrees F, except in her head. She recovered and left the hospital 11 days after the operation.

5358. Artificial aortic valve was made by Dr. Charles Anthony Hufnagel of the Georgetown University Medical Center, Washington, DC, and successfully fitted on a 30-year-old patient on September 11, 1952. It was made of Flexiglas and contained a float 0.75 inches in diameter. When blood was forced into the aorta during the upbeat of the heart's pumping cycle, the float rose and slipped into one of three sockets in the side of the valve sleeve.

5359. Conjoined twins separated successfully by surgery were Carolyn Anne and Catherine Anne Mouton, daughters of Ashton and Rosa Mouton. The girls were born in Lafayette, LA, on July 22, 1953. Their lower intestines were connected and their lower spinal bone structure and dural membrane were joined. On September 17, 1953, a team of 15 doctors worked for more than two hours at the Ochsner Foundation Hospital, New Orleans, LA, to separate them. The operation was successful, and on October 14 they were discharged from the hospital.

5360. Kidney transplant and the first organ transplant that was successful was performed at the Peter Brent Brigham Hospital, Boston, MA, on December 23, 1954. The surgery was conducted by Joseph E. Murray of Harvard University, who transplanted a kidney from one identical twin to another. The recipient lived for seven years. For his work in transplantation, Murray was awarded the Nobel Prize in physiology or medicine on December 10, 1990. He was the first graduate of a Jesuit college to receive the prize.

5361. Heart operation in which the elective cardiac arrest technique was employed was performed in May 1956 on a 17-month-old boy at the Cleveland Clinic, Cleveland, OH, by Dr. Donald Brian Effler and a task force of 15 doctors and nurses. The boy's heartbeat was temporarily stopped by an application of potassium citrate.

5362. Prefrontal lobotomy was performed by Dr. James Winston Watts and Dr. Walter Freeman on September 14, 1956, at George Washington University Hospital, Washington, DC. The patient was a 63-year-old woman. The operation involved the cutting of nerve pathways in the frontal lobe of the brain to relieve symptoms of mental illness.

5363. Pacemaker to be implanted in a patient's body was invented by Dr. William M. Chardack and engineer Wilson Greatbatch, both of Buffalo, NY. On April 18, 1960, Chardack inserted a wire implant into the heart of Frank Henefelt, a cardiac patient, to test the pacemaker's reliability. The battery-powered pulse generator unit tested successfully and was implanted into Henefelt's abdomen on June 6. He lived for 2.5 years with the device. Swedish doctors first implanted a similar device in 1958.

5364. Limb reattachment that was successful was performed on May 23, 1962, by surgeons Donald A. Malt and J. McKhann of Massachusetts General Hospital, Boston, MA. They reattached the severed right arm of a 12-year-old boy.

5365. Liver transplant was performed as an experimental procedure on March 1, 1963, by a team led by surgeon Thomas Earl Starzl at the University of Colorado Health Sciences Center, Denver, CO. Starzl went on to perform scores of hepatic transplants, including the first baboon-to-human liver transplant. He was the author of *Experience in Hepatic Transplantation* (1969), the first full published account of liver grafting.

5366. Lung transplant in the United States was performed on June 11, 1963, at the University of Mississippi Medical Center in Jackson, MS. In a three-hour operation, a team of doctors headed by Dr. James D. Hardy replaced the left lung of John Richard Russell. He survived for 18 days.

5367. Transplant of an animal organ into a human being took place at the University of Mississippi Medical Center in Jackson, MS, on January 23, 1964, when a team of 12 doctors headed by Dr. James D. Hardy transplanted the heart of a chimpanzee into the body of a 64-year-old patient. The patient, whose name was not made public, died 90 minutes later.

5368. Heart transplant in the United States was performed at Maimonides Hospital in Brooklyn, New York City, on December 6, 1967. The surgeon was Dr. Adrian Kantrowitz, and the patient was a two-week-old baby boy, who lived for 6.5 hours after the operation. The transplant took place three days after Dr. Christiaan Barnard performed the first heart transplant in history in Cape Town, South Africa. The first heart transplant performed on an adult in the United States took place on January 6, 1968, at the Stanford Medical Center, Palo Alto, CA. The patient was Mike Kasperak and the surgeon was Dr. Norman Shumway.

5369. Bone marrow transplant in the world was performed in 1968 by Dr. Robert A. Good at the University of Minnesota, Minneapolis. The patient was a four-month-old baby suffering from an inherited immune deficiency. The baby's sister donated the bone marrow. The operation was successful.

5370. Hip-replacement operation in the United States that was authorized by the federal Food and Drug Administration was performed by Dr. Mark Coventry on March 10, 1969, at Rochester Methodist Hospital, Rochester, MN.

5371. Heart transplant using an artificial heart took place at St. Luke's Episcopal Hospital in Houston, TX , on April 4, 1969. Dr. Denton A. Cooley implanted the world's first entirely artificial heart into Haskell Karp, age 47, from Skokie, IL. The prosthetic heart was made of Dacron and plastic. Karp lived with the heart for three days, when it was replaced by a transplanted human heart. He died on April 8.

5372. Transplant of artificial skin took place at Massachusetts General Hospital, Boston, MA, on April 23, 1981. Doctors reported that an artificial skin composed of cowhide, shark cartilage, and plastic was applied with successful results to 10 burn patients, 3 of whom would have died without the treatment. The artificial skin was developed by Ioannis V. Yannas and a team of researchers at the Massachusetts Institute of Technology, Cambridge, MA.

5373. Baby whose life was saved by surgery while still in the womb was Michael Skinner, born on May 10, 1981, to Rosa Skinner of San Francisco, CA. Two weeks before his birth, at seven months' gestation, he was operated on by Dr. Michael Harrison at the University of California at San Francisco Medical Center to relieve a blockage in his urinary tract. The surgeon placed a tiny catheter in his bladder, saving his kidneys from hydronephrosis. The operation was complicated by the fact that Michael shared the womb with a twin sister, Mary.

5374. Heart transplant using an artificial heart that was intended to be permanent was performed on December 2, 1982, when a team of doctors at the University of Utah Medical Center, Salt Lake City, UT, headed by Dr. William C. DeVries, implanted a mechanical heart into Barney B. Clark, 61, a retired dentist from Des Moines, IA. The device, called the Jarvik-7, was designed by Dr. Robert K. Jarvik. Clark survived for nearly four months before dying of vascular collapse on March 23, 1983.

5375. Heart transplant using a baboon heart was performed by Dr. Leonard L. Bailey at the Loma Linda University Medical Center, Loma Linda, CA, on October 16, 1984. The patient was a 15-day-old baby girl known to the public as "Baby Fae." Her body rejected the transplant and she died on November 15.

5376. Liver transplant from a live donor was performed at the University of Chicago Medical Center, Chicago, IL, on November 27, 1989. The patient was Alyssa Leanne Smith, 21 months old, who had been diagnosed as having biliary atresia, a fatal liver disease. In a 14-hour transplant, Alyssa's diseased liver was removed by Dr. Christoph Erich Broelsch and replaced with a section of liver donated by her mother, Teri Smith of Schertz, TX. This was the first mother-to-daughter liver transplant in the United States.

5377. Liver transplant using a baboon liver took place at the University of Pittsburgh Medical Center, Pittsburgh, PA, in July 1992. A team of surgeons led by Thomas Earl Starzl transplanted the liver of a baboon into a 35-year-old patient infected with human immune deficiency virus (HIV) whose liver had been destroyed by hepatitis B. A human liver could not be used because it too would have been destroyed by the hepatitis. The patient died two months later, apparently of unrelated causes.

5378. Transplant of human embryo tissue to be done in the United States took place at the University of Florida's Brain Institute at Shands Hospital in Gainesville, FL, on July 11, 1997. Neurosurgeon Richard Fessler injected spinal cord cells from a human embryo into a patient suffering from syringomyelia, a paralytic spinal disease.

5379. Live surgery broadcast on the Internet was a coronary bypass operation performed on August 19, 1998, at a hospital in Houston, TX. The patient's first name was given as Rena. The surgeon was Dr. Denton A. Cooley. The operation took 3 hours 40 minutes. It was viewed by more than 150,000 people on AHN.com, a Web site operated by a cable TV channel, America's Health Network, based in Orlando, FL. Other live transmissions pioneered on the same Web site include the birth of a child, on June 16, 1998; a hair transplant, on September 30, 1998; a knee operation, on November 11, 1998; surgery on a herniated disk, on December 3, 1998; brain surgery, on January 7, 1999; repair of an aneurysm, on February 18, 1999; and a knee replacement operation, on February 23, 1999. Footage of heart surgery was uploaded to the Internet on August 18, 1998, from the Providence Seattle Medical Center, Seattle, WA, but the operation was not shown live.

5380. Magnetic surgery was a biopsy performed on December 17, 1998, at the Barnes-Jewish Hospital in St. Louis, MO. The patient was a 31-year-old man with a tumor of the frontal lobe, in a part of the brain that is difficult to reach directly. Using superconducting magnets, neurosurgeon Ralph Dacey guided a magnet-tipped catheter along a complex path, avoiding areas of the brain that surgeons wanted to leave untouched. Magnetic-resonance images were used as a map to the tumor. The procedure, called the Magnetic Surgery System, was developed by Matthew A. Howard III and a team of researchers at Stereotaxis, Inc., St. Louis, MO.

5381. Hand transplant that was successful was completed on January 25, 1999, at Jewish Hospital, Louisville, KY. Recipient Matthew Scott, a 37-year-old paramedic from New Jersey, received a new left hand in a 15-hour operation performed by a team of surgeons from the University of Louisville and Kleinert, Kutz and Associates Hand Care Center. The chief surgeon was Dr. Warren Breidenbach. A year later, Scott was able to use the hand to tie his shoe, deal cards, and sign his name with a pen. The world's first hand transplant operation was carried out on a New Zealand man, Clint Hallam, in France in 1998, but in 2001 surgeons removed the transplanted hand at his request.

5382. Bloodless liver transplant from a living donor was made on June 15, 1999, at the University of Southern California, Los Angeles, CA, by surgeons Rick Selby, Nicolas Jabbour, and Yuri Genyk. The patient, Bill Jennings of Parker, AZ, received a lobe from the liver of his brother Scott. According to the tenets of his religious group, Jehovah's Witnesses, Jennings could not receive blood transfusions during the operation. To minimize bleeding, he was given supplements and medications to increase his red blood cell count and a shunt was implanted in his liver to decrease his blood pressure. The transplant was successful and both healthy lobes, the one in the donor and the one in the recipient, regenerated into complete functioning livers.

5383. Dual kidney and liver transplants from children to a parent were made by Dr. Rick Selby in October 2000 at the University of Southern California, Los Angeles, CA. The recipient was Maria Alvarez. She received a kidney from her adult daughter, Rosario Proscia, and a liver lobe from her adult son, Jose Alvarez.

5384. Self-contained artificial heart that was entirely enclosed within the body was the AbioCor Implantable Replacement Heart, developed by ABIOMED Inc. of Danvers, MA. The AbioCor consisted of an internal thoracic unit, an internal rechargeable battery, an internal miniaturized electronics package, and an external battery pack. It could operate for up to 30 minutes on internal batteries only, and could draw power from the external power pack via induction coils without needing to be wired into the patient's body. On July 2, 2001, during a seven-hour operation at Jewish Hospital and the University of Louisville, Louisville, KY, the device was implanted in patient Robert Tools by research team leaders Laman A. Gray, Jr., and Robert D. Dowling. Tools died on November 30, 2001.

5385. Transatlantic telesurgery took place on September 7, 2001, and involved the successful removal of a diseased gallbladder from a 68-year-old woman. The patient was anesthetized in a hospital operating room in Strasbourg, France. The two surgeons, Jacques Marescaux and Michel Gagner, conducted the 45-minute laparoscopic operation from Mount Sinai Medical Center in New York City using the Zeus Robotic Surgical System, made by Computer Motion Inc., Santa Barbara, CA. Viewing the patient on computer screens, they manipulated joysticks whose micromovements were instantaneously transmitted to the Zeus robot by satellite.

Therapies

5386. Spa at a mineral spring opened to the public was deeded to the colony of Virginia in 1756 by Thomas Fairfax, sixth Baron Fairfax, "to be forever free to the publick for the welfare of suffering humanity." The spa was located in Bath, Berkeley County, VA (now Berkeley Springs, Morgan County, WV), and was chartered in October 1776. George Washington had visited the mineral springs on March 18, 1748.

5387. Steam baths for curing disease were advocated by Samuel Thomson, who in 1796 experimented with steam in the treatment of his daughter, whom physicians were unable to cure. He traveled on horseback through New Hampshire, Maine, Vermont, and Massachusetts, advocating treatment by steam as well as by the use of herbs.

5388. Stomach washing with a tube or syringe was accomplished by Dr. Philip Syng Physick in 1800 in Philadelphia, PA. His procedure is described in his article "Account of a New Mode of Extracting Poisonous Substances from the Stomach," which appeared in the *Eclectic Report and Analytic Review* in 1813.

5389. Water cures were advocated by David Campbell, originator of the *Water Cure Journal*, who opened a water-cure resort in 1843 at 63 Barclay Street, New York City. Joel Shew, M.D., was the physician. The therapeutic use of baths was popular at the time.

5390. Artificial insemination of a woman resulting in conception was made in 1866 by Dr. James Marion Sims, gynecologist and chief of the Woman's Hospital, New York City. Sims gave 54 other injections in 1866 and 1867.

5391. Occupational therapy treatment was given by Susan Edith Tracy, author of *Studies in Invalid Occupation*, at the Training School for Nurses of the Adams Nervine Asylum, Jamaica Plain, Boston, MA. The school had been established under the will of Seth Adams, who died on December 7, 1873, and was incorporated on March 16, 1877. The first patients were admitted in April 1880.

5392. Hospice for incurable cancer patients operated free of charge was established in a room in an apartment on Scammel Street, New York City, on September 15, 1896, by Rose Hawthorne Lathrop (later Sister Mary Alphonsa, O.D.), who was afterward assisted by Alice Huber (later Sister Mary Rose, O.D.). They organized the Servants of Relief for Incurable Cancer. On May 1, 1899, they opened St. Rose's Free Home for Incurable Cancer in New York City, with accommodations for 15 patients. On June 1, 1901, a building in the country was acquired to carry on the work under the name of Rosary Hill Home at Sherman Park (now Hawthorne), NY.

5393. Radium treatment for cancer instead of surgery was advocated by Dr. Robert Abbe, who published his conclusions in the June 1904 *Yale Medical Journal*. He held professorships of surgery in the Women's Medical College and the New York Post Graduate School of New York City.

5394. Radioactive isotope medicine was phosphorus 32, artificially produced in a 37-inch cyclotron. It was administered on December 24, 1936, to a 28-year-old woman with chronic leukemia by Dr. John Hunsdale Lawrence, director of the Donner Laboratory at the University of California at Berkeley.

5395. Psychodrama treatment for psychiatric patients was instituted by Dr. Jacob L. Moreno in Beacon, NY, in 1937. The treatment was designed to enable the psychiatric worker to achieve a clearer understanding of the patient's mental processes. None but interested participants and doctors were privileged to see the reenactment of cases.

5396. Chemotherapy to successfully achieve remission of cancer was given in November 1947 by Dr. Sidney Farber to a group of 16 children with acute leukemia at the Children's Medical Center, Boston, MA. The children received doses of aminopterin, a drug that blocks folic acid, in an attempt to stop the production in their bones of abnormal bone marrow, the source of malignant white blood cells. Ten of the children went into temporary remission.

5397. Artificial insemination for women to be permitted by a state was allowed under legislation enacted by Oklahoma and signed on May 18, 1967, by Governor Dewey Follett Bartlett.

5398. Hospice home-care program in the United States was the Connecticut Hospice in New Haven, CT, which opened in March 1974. Founded by Florence Wald, the former dean of the Yale University School of Nursing, and her husband, Henry Wald, it was modeled on St. Christopher's Hospice in London.

5399. Gene therapy was conducted on September 14, 1990, by W. French Anderson, chief of the Molecular Hematology Branch of the National Heart, Lung, and Blood Institute in Bethesda, MD, and Drs. Kenneth Culver and Michael Blaese. The gene procedure was intended to correct a genetic immunodeficiency disease, adenosine deaminase deficiency, inherited by a four-year-old girl. Samples of her white blood cells were cultured and exposed to an engineered retrovirus that carried a healthy version of the gene that produces adenosine deaminase. The virus transferred the gene to her cells, which were then reinjected into her.

5400. Alternative medicine department in a federal research institution was the Office of Alternative Medicine, established in 1992 by the National Institutes of Health, Bethesda, MD. Joe Jacobs, a pediatrician, was the first director. Among the healing therapies studied by the department were acupuncture, acupressure, herbal medicine, chiropractic, massage, aromatherapy, Tai Chi, meditation, and prayer.

5401. Biotechnology treatment for cancer was rituximab, a monoclonal antibody that was approved by the FDA on November 26, 1997, to treat a particular form of non-Hodgkin's lymphoma. A chimeric antibody containing mouse genes, it attacked a cancer-causing antigen in the patients' white blood cells. It was developed by IDEC Pharmaceuticals Corporation, San Diego, CA, and Genentech, Inc, San Francisco, CA, and was marketed as Rituxan.

5402. State to offer free cancer treatment for uninsured residents was Delaware, whose Delaware Cancer Treatment Program was announced by Gov. Ruth Ann Minner on September 14, 2004. The program paid the costs of cancer treatment during the first year of illness for eligible residents who lacked health insurance and who could not afford medical care. It was run by the state Division of Public Health.

Veterinary

5403. Veterinary hospital was opened by Charles C. Grice in 1830 on Pearl Street, New York City. In later years, he moved it to White Street and then to Macdougal Street. Grice was graduated from the Royal Veterinary College of England in 1826 and came to America in 1830. He was the first veterinary graduate to practice his profession in the United States.

5404. Laboratory for the study of parasites in livestock was opened on August 1, 1886, in Washington, DC, in the Bureau of Animal Industry of the Department of Agriculture, with Dr. Cooper Curtice in charge. Dr. Charles Wardell Stiles took over the supervision in 1891, when the laboratory was designated a "zoological laboratory."

5405. Cattle tuberculosis test was made on March 3, 1892, on a herd of cattle belonging to Dr. J. E. Gillingham, Claremont Farms, Villanova, PA. The herd was tested with tuberculin brought from Europe by Dr. Leonard Pearson, dean of the Veterinary Department of the University of Pennsylvania, Philadelphia.

5406. Animal disease of American origin was tularemia, an epizootic of wild rabbits and other animals, which was recognized in 1910 in ground squirrels of Tulare County, CA, by Dr. George Walter McCoy. He and Dr. Charles Willard Chapin named the organism *Bacterium tularense*. The disease was named by Dr. Edward Francis of the Public Health Service, who was awarded a gold medal by the American Medical Association for his research into it.

5407. Surgical operation on a bull to correct a sperm block was performed on July 25, 1965, by Dr. James Hicks and Dr. Donald F. Walker at the Auburn University School of Veterinary Medicine, Auburn, AL, on Linderis Evulse, a $176,000 Aberdeen-Angus bull. The bull, owned by the Black Watch Farms, Wappinger Falls, NY, was strapped on a hydraulic operating table for the operation.

5408. Veterinary hospital established by a city was the Spay and Neuter Clinic of the Los Angeles City Department of Animal Regulation, Los Angeles, CA, which opened on February 17, 1971. The cost for spaying was $17.50 and for neutering $11.50. The first head of the hospital was Walter E. Ziegler, D.V.M., chief of veterinary services. The general manager was Robert I. Rush.

5409. Zoo hospital with a CT scanner was the Steffee Center for Zoological Medicine at the Cleveland Metroparks Zoo, Cleveland, OH. The scanner was donated by Philips Medical Systems of Highland Heights, OH.

Military and War

Army

5410. Military field strategy manual was Roger Stevenson's *Military Instructions for Officers detached in the field, containing a scheme for forming a corps of a partisan, illustrated with plans of the manoeuvres necessary in carrying on the Petite Guerre*. The 232-page book was printed in 1775 by Robert Aitken, Philadelphia, PA.

5411. Army engineering department was authorized by the Continental Congress on June 16, 1775. It established a separate engineering department in the Continental Army, composed of a chief engineer, who received $60 a month, and two assistant engineers at $20 a month. The first chief engineer was Colonel Richard Gridley. A formal Corps of Engineers was established on March 11, 1779, but was disbanded on November 3, 1783, upon the dissolution of the Revolutionary Army.

5412. Military drill manual was Baron von Steuben's *Regulations for the Order and Discipline of the Troops of the United States*, 154 pages, printed in 1779 in Philadelphia, PA, by Melchior Styner and Charles Cist.

5413. Army uniform was standardized by order of the Continental Army in October 1779, when George Washington, as the commander in chief, prescribed a uniform through a general order. The coat was blue. The facings for the infantry were varied—white, buff, red, and blue; the artillery and artificers' coats were faced with scarlet and had scarlet linings; and the light dragoons' coats were faced with white and had white buttons and linings.

5414. Army organization under the Constitution was enacted on April 30, 1789. It provided for one regiment of infantry to consist of three battalions of four companies each, one battalion of artillery with four companies, and a total strength not to exceed 1,216 noncommissioned officers, privates, and musicians. The monthly authorized pay was $60 for the lieutenant colonel commandant, majors $40, captains $30, lieutenants $22, corporals $4, privates $3, and musicians $3.

5415. Army engineer corps was established by Act of March 16, 1802, "fixing the military peace establishments of the United States." The corps consisted of one engineer (major), two assistant engineers (captains), two other assistants (second lieutenants), and 10 cadets. The first engineer in charge was Major Jonathan Williams, appointed on April 13, 1802.

5416. Military dictionary was *A Military Dictionary, or explanation of the several systems of Discipline of different kinds of troops, infantry, artillery and cavalry, the principles of fortification and all the modern improvements in the science of tactics*, by William Duane, a retired lieutenant colonel, published in 1810 in Philadelphia, PA. It contained 748 pages.

5417. Army cavalry unit to be formally established was the Regiment of Dragoons, later known as the 1st Regiment of Dragoons, organized at Jefferson Barracks, MO, in August 1833, with Colonel Henry Dodge in command. The designation of this organization was changed to the 1st Cavalry by act of Congress of August 3, 1861. Earlier, in March 1792, Congress had given the president power to raise a squadron of cavalry at his direction to serve for three years.

5418. Camels imported for military purposes were landed on May 14, 1856, at Indianola, TX. Lieutenant David Dixon Porter of Chester, PA, brought them from Izmir, Turkey, on the *Supply*, a Navy storeship. The shipment consisted of 34 camels—one more than left Smyrna. On March 3, 1855, Congress had appropriated $30,000 to the War Department for the purchase and importation of camels and dromedaries to be employed for military purposes.

5419. Army signal corps was established under act of June 1, 1860, which appropriated $2,000 "for the manufacture or purchase of apparatus and equipment for field signals" and the appointment of one signal officer. On June 27, 1860, Assistant Surgeon Albert James Myer was appointed signal officer, with the rank of major. The corps became a separate branch of the Army by act of Congress of March 3, 1863.

5420. Army secret service bureau was inaugurated in 1861 by President Abraham Lincoln, who appointed the prominent detective Allan Pinkerton to be in charge. The identity of Pinkerton was not revealed, and he served as "Major Allan." He was attached to the staff of General George Brinton McClellan.

5421. Military service by African-Americans to be authorized by Congress was authorized by an act introduced on July 16, 1862, by Senator Henry Wilson of Massachusetts and signed on July 17, 1862, by President Abraham Lincoln. It empowered the president to accept "persons of African descent, for the purpose of constructing intrenchments or performing camp competent."

5422. State law prohibiting discrimination against soldiers was passed on May 5, 1908, by Rhode Island. The bill, sponsored by Theodore Francis Green, imposed a penalty for excluding soldiers in uniform from public places.

5423. Radio car for military use was designed in 1911 by Colonel Royal Page Davidson at Lake Geneva, WI, and was equipped with telescopic masts for radio broadcasting. Current for the operation of the radio was generated by the automobile motor. The car was also equipped with rapid-fire machine guns and two powerful electric searchlights with helix shutters for flashlight signaling.

5424. Army training camp for African-American officers was established on June 15, 1917, at Fort Des Moines, Des Moines, IA, and was known as the 17th Provisional Training Regiment. On October 15, 1917, the first commissions were granted, with 106 African-Americans commissioned as second lieutenants.

5425. Army gas regiment was authorized on August 15, 1917, by General Order No. 108, and was organized by Colonel Earl James Atkisson. The first year it was known as the 30th Engineers; afterwards, as the 1st Gas Regiment. The first battalion was organized on October 16, 1917. Its first independent action took place on June 18, 1918, against Germans in the Toul sector, France, during World War I.

5426. Army armored car unit was Troop A, 1st Armored Car Squadron, which was organized at Fort Meade, MD, in 1928. It was commanded by Captain Harold G. Holt.

5427. Army corps for women was the Women's Army Auxiliary Corps, authorized on May 14, 1942, to allow women to serve in the Army. The first director was Oveta Culp Hobby. The first training course took place at Fort Des Moines, Des Moines, IA, from July 20 to August 29, 1942, when 346 women were commissioned third officers. The corps was renamed the Women's Army Corps on September 30, 1943.

5428. Military band leader who was a woman was Sergeant MaryBelle Johns Nissly, inducted into the Women's Army Auxiliary Corps in the summer of 1942 at Fort Des Moines, IA. In early 1943, five all-female bands were formed, and Nissly was appointed band director. When the WAAC was absorbed into the Women's Army Corps in January 1944, Congress had to give Nissly the rank of warrant officer, a prerequisite for anyone holding the job of Army bandleader. The Women's Army Bands played for servicemen returning from overseas, usually performing a musical salute from a ship that met the troop transport vessels in New York Harbor. Nissly later went on to found the USAF WAF Band.

5429. Army specialist corps for women was the Women's Army Medical Specialist Corps, authorized under the Army–Navy Nurses Act of 1947, dated April 16, 1947, which established a dietitians' section, a physical therapists' section, and an occupational therapists' section to consist of 24 majors and 385 captains and first and second lieutenants.

5430. Army ballistic missile operational unit was the 259th Field Artillery Missile Battalion, which completed training in November 1954 at Fort Bliss, TX. The unit was deployed to Europe in February 1955 to provide guided missile support for units in the Seventh Army.

5431. Armored division transported by airplanes to a foreign country was the 2nd Armored Division, commanded by Major General Edwin Hess Hurba, who took off with 62 men of his staff on October 22, 1963, in a C-135 Stratolifter from the Bergstrom Air

Force Base, near Austin, TX, for the Rhein-Main Air Base in West Germany as part of Operation Big Lift. In 63 hours and 20 minutes, 196 airplanes, including 23 jets, transported 15,268 combat-ready troops in 235 missions. The division returned to Texas from November 12 to 21, 1963. Major General Archie J. Old, Jr., of the 15th Air Force was the overall commander of the flight.

5432. Military police officer who was a woman was Adrienne Lee Goodmanson, who joined the U.S. Army as a WAC in 1973. Goodmanson attended military police school in Fort Gordon, GA, and in 1974 served as the first female military police officer at Redstone Arsenal, AL. In 1976, at Ft. Leonard Wood, MO, she was promoted to become the first woman MP Investigator.

Officers

5433. General of the Continental Army was George Washington, who was appointed commander of all continental armies on June 15, 1775, by the Second Continental Congress assembled at the State House, Philadelphia, PA. Congress resolved "that five hundred dollars per month be allowed for the pay and expenses of the general." Washington took command the following month at Cambridge, MA, and led the American forces for six years during the Revolutionary War. After forcing Britain's Lord Cornwallis to surrender in October 1781, he served until December 23, 1783, when he resigned his commission.

5434. Army chief engineer of the Continental Army was Colonel Richard Gridley, who served from June 17, 1775, to August 5, 1776. On June 16, 1775, the Continental Congress authorized one chief engineer at $60 a month, and two assistants at $20.

5435. Paymaster general of the Continental Army was James Warren of Massachusetts, appointed on June 27, 1775. On June 16, 1775, the Continental Congress established a separate department in the Army to take care of payments to troops. The department consisted of the paymaster general, who received $100 a month, and a deputy at $50 a month. Warren resigned on April 19, 1776.

5436. Surgeon general of the Continental Army was Benjamin Church, who served from July 27 to October 16, 1775. He held the position of director general and chief physician and received compensation of four dollars a day. On November 1, 1775, he was jailed for treason. The first surgeon general of the Army to whom the title was officially applied was James Tilton of Delaware, the author of *Economical Observations on Military Hospitals*, who served from June 11, 1813, until June 15, 1815.

5437. Quartermaster of the Continental Army was Major Thomas Mifflin, who served from August 14, 1775, to November 7, 1777.

5438. Brevet commission in the Army was authorized by the Continental Congress on July 20, 1776, for Jacques Antoine de Franchessin, a Knight of the Order of St. Louis, an experienced officer in the service of France, who received a brevet commission of lieutenant colonel.

5439. Army lieutenant general was George Washington of Mount Vernon, VA, appointed on July 11, 1798, by President John Adams, under authorization of the act of May 28, 1798, as lieutenant-general and commander in chief of all the armies raised for the service of the United States. He was authorized to receive a salary of $250 monthly, $50 monthly allowance for forage, and 40 rations per day, or money in lieu thereof at the current price. He served from July 3, 1798, to December 14, 1799, when he died.

5440. Army general to become an admiral in the Navy was Samuel Powhatan Carter, who served in the Navy from 1840 to 1862. In 1861, during the Civil War, he organized the Tennessee Brigade militia. He became Army brigadier general of volunteers on May 1, 1862, and was breveted major general in March 1865 for gallantry and meritorious service as a cavalry commander. He returned to the Navy and was appointed lieutenant commander in charge of the gunboat *Monocacy* on the Asiatic station. He was appointed rear admiral on May 16, 1882, and retired on August 6, 1882.

5441. Army major who was African-American was Martin Robinson Delany, who received his commission on February 8, 1865. On April 5, 1865, he was ordered to report to Charleston, SC.

5442. General of the U.S. Army was Ulysses Simpson Grant, commander of the Union forces during the Civil War, who was appointed on July 25, 1866. He served until March 4, 1869, when he was inaugurated as President of the United States.

Library of Congress, Prints and Photographs Division
LC-USZ62-13018 DLC

Ulysses S. Grant

5443. General of the Armies of the United States was General John Joseph Pershing, commander in chief of the American expeditionary forces during World War I, whose appointment was unanimously confirmed by the Senate on September 4, 1919.

5444. Army officer to occupy both the nation's highest military post and the highest nonelective civilian post was General George Catlett Marshall of Pennsylvania. He was the Army's chief of staff with rank of major general from September 1, 1939, to November 20, 1945; secretary of state from January 21, 1947, to January 20, 1949; and secretary of defense from September 21, 1950, to September 12, 1951.

5445. Army general who was African-American was Benjamin Oliver Davis, commanding officer of Harlem's 369th Coast Artillery (National Guard), who was appointed on October 25, 1940, to command a brigade in the 2nd Cavalry Division at Fort Riley, KS, with the rank of brigadier general.

5446. Army general who rose from draftee was Keith L. Ware, who was drafted on November 23, 1940. He attended Officer's Candidate School, Fort Benning, GA, and rose to commander of the 1st Infantry Division in Vietnam, becoming brigadier general on November 28, 1967. He, his staff of three, and four helicopter crewmen were killed on September 13, 1968, when his helicopter was shot down about 60 miles north of Saigon during the battle of Locninh. He was the fourth general killed in the Vietnam War.

5447. Army general appointed from civilian rank was William Signius Knudsen, director general of Office of Priority Management, appointed a lieutenant general on January 16, 1942, by President Franklin Delano Roosevelt.

5448. Army generals to wear the five-star insignia were Henry Harley Arnold, Dwight David Eisenhower, Douglas MacArthur, and George Catlett Marshall, whose appointments were ratified on December 15, 1944, by the Senate. The grade of General of the Army was established by act of Congress on December 14, 1944.

5449. Army officer who was a woman was Florence Aby Blanchfield, who on July 9, 1947, was appointed lieutenant colonel in the Army with permanent rank under authority of the Army Nurses Law of April 16, 1947. The ceremony was held at the Pentagon, Washington, DC. General Dwight David Eisenhower, Chief of Staff, presented her with her commission. On June 1, 1943, she had been appointed superintendent of army nurses. The first nonmedical female army officer to be sworn into the regular Army was Colonel Mary Agnes Hallaren, who took the oath of office on December 3, 1948. She became director of the Women's Army Corps, Regular Army.

5450. Doctor commissioned in the regular Army who was a woman was First Lieutenant Fae Margaret Adams of San Jose, CA, sworn in on March 11, 1953, in Washington, DC. Previously, she had been a WAC reserve medical officer. She obtained her degree under the GI Bill of Rights.

5451. Sergeant major of the Army was William O. Wooldridge, a native of Shawnee, OK, who served in the Army starting in 1940, fought in World War II, in Korea, and in Vietnam, and was sworn in on July 11, 1966, to present the enlisted man's point of view to the army chief of staff, General Harold Keith Johnson.

5452. Army general who was African-American to lead an infantry brigade in combat was Major General Frederic Ellis Davison, who led the 199th Light Infantry brigade in the Tet offensive at Long Binh, Vietnam, in February 1968. Fourteen Americans and about 900 attacking troops were killed.

5453. Army general who was a woman was Anna Mae Hays, chief of the Army Nurse Corps, who was promoted to brigadier general on June 11, 1970. On the same day, Elizabeth P. Hoisington, director of the Women's Army Corps, was elevated to the same rank.

5454. General of the Armies of the United States with the rank of six stars was George Washington, whose posthumous promotion to General of the Armies was signed by President Gerald Rudolph Ford on October 19, 1976. The appointment was authorized by a joint congressional resolution enacted on October 11, 1976, to take effect on July 4, 1976.

5455. Army general who was an African-American woman was Hazel Winifred Johnson, who was promoted to the rank of brigadier general in 1979. Johnson was also the first African-American to head the Army Nurse Corps. The first African-American woman to become a brigadier general by rising through the ranks of the regular Army was Sherian Grace Cadoria, who received her promotion in 1985.

5456. Chairman of the Joint Chiefs of Staff who was African-American was Army General Colin Powell, appointed by President George Herbert Walker Bush on August 9, 1989. Powell, born in New York City in 1937, served from 1987 to 1989 as national security advisor to President Ronald Wilson Reagan. In 1989, he was promoted to four-star general, thus becoming the highest-ranking African-American officer up to that time. During his service as chairman he oversaw the 1991 Gulf War military campaign. He resigned in 1993.

Courtesy of the U.S. Department of State

Colin Powell

Aviation

5457. Airship bombing plan was a scheme to capture the Mexican port of Veracruz that was thought up by balloonist John Wise of Lancaster, PA. He proposed to send out a ship that would serve as the launch site for a tethered balloon from which bombs could be dropped on the city. Wise petitioned Congress in 1851 for funds with which to carry out the plan, but was turned down.

5458. Army balloon corps was the Balloon (Aeronautic) Corps of five balloons and 50 men under the command of Thaddeus Sobieski Coulincourt Lowe, chief aeronaut of the Army of the Potomac, formed on October 1, 1861, during the Civil War. Four balloons were ready for service on November 10, 1861, and were used for reconnaissance and for directing artillery fire via telegraph in Virginia.

5459. Artillery fire to be directed from the air was directed by Professor Thaddeus Sobieski Coulincourt Lowe, who communicated with Union artillery units by telegraph on May 24, 1862, during the Civil War. Lowe made his first official ascent on July 24, 1861, and saw the movements of the Confederate troops after the battle of Manassas, VA. He also detected a Confederate maneuver to attack the troops of General Heintzelman, who was separated from the main force at Fair Oaks.

5460. Balloon destroyed by enemy gunfire was shot down by the Spanish on July 1, 1898, at Santiago, Cuba. It was piloted by Colonel George Derby of the Army Engineer Department, who reported on the enemy's movements as he floated above the American troops. The soldiers were glad that it was brought down, as it had been drawing fire in their direction.

5461. Airplane unit in the Army was the Aeronautical Division, founded on August 1, 1907, as part of the U.S. Army Signal Corps. Its aviation equipment consisted of 10 balloons and an airship until August 2, 1909, when it acquired a single airplane from Wilbur and Orville Wright. The entire division initially consisted of two men-Lieutenant Benjamin D. Foulois, a pilot, and Corporal Edward Ward, the first enlisted airman. In 1914 it was replaced by the newly founded Aviation Section of the Signal Corps.

5462. Army pilot to fly solo in an airplane was Second Lieutenant Frederic Erastus Humphreys, who on October 26, 1909, at College Park, MD, made two circuits of the field in three minutes. He was followed by Lieutenant Frank Purdy Lahm, who went six times around and made some small circles as well, remaining aloft 13 minutes. Lieutenant Humphreys then resumed his solo flying for eight minutes.

5463. Airplane bombing experiment was made over Lake Keuka, Hammondsport, NY, on June 30, 1910, by Glenn Hammond Curtiss under the auspices of the *New York World*. Curtiss released lead missiles attached to colored streamers from a height of 50 feet toward a target 500 feet by 90 feet. He scored 10 hits and 4 misses. The tests were witnessed by Admiral William Wirt Kimball.

5464. Pilot to fire a gun from an airplane was Lieutenant Jacob Earl Fickel of the 29th Infantry, who fired rifle shots at a target on August 20, 1910, at the Sheepshead Bay Race Track, New York City, from a single-seater Curtiss plane piloted by Glenn Hammond Curtiss.

5465. Navy pilot was Lieutenant Theodore Gordon Ellyson, a submarine officer, who volunteered to attend the flight school run by aviation pioneer Glenn Hammond Curtiss in San Diego, CA. He reported for training in January 1911. Curtiss had offered to train an officer without charge.

5466. Fatal airplane accident in a solo military airplane took the life of Second Lieutenant George E. Maurice Kelly of the Signal Corps, who crashed to the ground in a Curtiss airplane about 7:30 A.M. on May 10, 1911, in San Antonio, TX. He suffered a fractured skull and was rushed to Fort Sam Houston Hospital, where he died one hour later.

5467. Naval airplane was the Curtiss Amphibian Triad with dual controls, delivered July 1911. It was purchased with funds from a $25,000 congressional appropriation passed on March 4, 1911, "for experimental work in the development of aviation for naval purposes." The plane was tested at Lake Keuka, Hammondsport, NY.

5468. Airplane outfitted with a machine gun was a Wright biplane, flown at College Park, MD, on May 7, 1912, by pilot Lieutenant Thomas de Witt Milling. It was equipped with a Lewis machine gun manned by Charles de Forest Chandler of the Army Signal Corps.

5469. Air combat unit of the Army was the 1st Aero Squadron, established in Galveston, TX, on March 3, 1913. In 1916 it was ordered to proceed to Casa Grandes, Mexico, for active duty with the punitive expedition against Pancho Villa commanded by General John Joseph Pershing. The pilots served mainly as couriers. The squadron flew to Europe on August 5, 1917, to serve with the U.S. Expeditionary Force in World War I. It is still in existence, renamed the 1st Reconnaissance Squadron.

5470. Coast Guard aviation unit was formed under an act of Congress of August 29, 1916, which authorized the secretary of the treasury "to establish, equip, and maintain aviation stations, not exceeding ten in number, for the purpose of saving life and property along the coasts of the United States and at sea contiguous thereto."

5471. Air combat unit of the Navy was the 1st Aeronautic Detachment, a group of seven officers and 122 enlisted men. It left the naval air station at Pensacola, FL, in May

1917 and arrived in June 1917 in France, where it was commanded by Rear Admiral H. B. Wilson. The unit began making patrol flights along the French coast on November 23, 1917, from the air station at Le Croisic, and was also engaged in escorting troop convoys.

5472. Pilot who was African-American was Eugene Bullard, born in Columbus, GA, on October 9, 1894. After emigrating to France, he joined the French Army and received his flying certification on May 5, 1917. His first flight, a reconnaissance mission over the city of Metz, took place on September 8. Bullard was credited with one confirmed "kill," a German Pfalz he shot down over Verdun in November 1917.

5473. Air combat unit of the Marine Corps was the Marine Aeronautic Company, comprising 12 officers and 133 enlisted men, which landed on January 21, 1918, at Punta Delgada, San Miguel, Azores. The commanding officer was Captain Francis T. Evans. The unit carried out antisubmarine patrols. The first Marine aviation unit to see combat was the 1st Marine Aviation Force under Major Alfred A. Cunningham, which arrived in France on July 30, 1918, with 107 officers and 654 enlisted men. Until their own planes arrived, they flew bombing missions over Germany with British squadrons. They began flying independently on October 14, 1918.

5474. Army pilot to win a victory over an enemy airplane was First Lieutenant Stephen W. Thompson of the 1st Aero Squadron, who downed an Albatross pursuit plane on February 5, 1918, at Saarbrucken, Germany.

5475. Air combat arm of the Army was the Air Service of the U.S. Army. It was created on May 24, 1918, when aviation responsibilities were transferred from the Signal Corps to the War Department. It became a combatant arm under the Army Reorganization Act of 1920. By congressional act dated July 2, 1926, it was renamed the Army Air Corps, and on June 20, 1941, it came under the command of the Army Air Forces.

5476. Fighter plane was the Kirkham Fighter, designed by Charles Kirkham, manufactured by the Curtiss Aeroplane and Motor Company, Garden City, NY, and tested at Garden City on August 19, 1918, when it attained a speed of 162 miles per hour. It established a world's record on October 11, 1918, when it made a ceiling climb of 26,300 feet.

5477. Radio compass on a naval airplane was used on July 7, 1920, when a Curtiss F-5-L naval seaplane flew from Norfolk, VA, to the battleship *Ohio*, 95 miles at sea, and returned, guided entirely by radio signals.

5478. Air defense military organization was the Air Defense Command, created on February 26, 1940, with headquarters at Mitchel Field, Long Island, NY, pursuant to War Department Orders dated February 26, 1940, for defense against air attack through the practical application of the coordinated effort of aviation, antiaircraft artillery, and aircraft warning agencies, including fixed military and civilian installations. It was charged with the development of a system for unified air defense of an area and the determination of tasks within the capabilities of the various combinations of tactical units that might be assembled for the air defense of cities, continental bases, manufacturing and industrial areas, or of armies in the field. The first commander was Brigadier General James Eugene Chaney.

5479. Army parachute battalion was the 501st, organized on October 1, 1940, at Fort Benning, GA, under the command of Major William Maynadier Miley.

5480. Parachute fatality in the Army occurred on March 6, 1941, at Fort Benning, Columbus, GA, when Sergeant Floyd S. Beard, age 28, of Coleman, GA, a parachutist of Company C of the 501st Parachute Battalion, participated in a mass jump with 35 others. His parachute failed to function and he fell 750 feet to his death.

5481. African-American air unit was the Army Air Corps' 99th Pursuit Squadron, first unit of the Tuskegee Airmen. The formation of the 99th was announced on January 16, 1941, by Undersecretary Robert P. Patterson of the War Department, and the unit was officially activated on March 19, 1941. Pilots were trained at Tuskegee Army Air Field, Tuskegee, AL. The first class of aviation cadets graduated on March 7, 1942. Colonel (later General) Benjamin O. Davis, Jr., one of the graduates, was made the 99th's commanding officer. The 99th flew its first combat mission in North Africa on June 2, 1943, against the island of Pantelleria. The Tuskegee Airmen also included the 332nd Fighter Group as well as various support units and staff, including navigators, gunners, bombardiers, and mechanics.

5482. Pilots of military aircraft who were women were the 28 members of the Women's Auxiliary Flying Squadron, formed in September 1942 under the leadership of Nancy Harkness Love. In August 1943, this group was merged with the much larger Women's Flying Training Detachment under Jacqueline Cochran to form the Women Airforce Service Pilots (WASP), based in Sweetwater, TX. Though the pilots were officially civilians, they handled a wide variety of aviation duties for the Army Air Corps, including ferrying aircraft, performing searchlight missions, and serving as flight instructors. Thirty-eight were killed in the course of World War II.

5483. African-American paratroop unit was the 555th Parachute Infantry Battalion of the Army Air Corps. Known as the Triple Nickles, the 555th was constituted on February 25, 1943, and activated on December 30, 1943, at Fort Benning, GA. Trained for overseas combat, the Triple Nickles were deployed in 1944 as smoke-jumping firefighters on the West Coast, fighting forest fires started by Japanese balloon-borne incendiary bombs. The unit was integrated into the 82nd Airborne Division after World War II.

5484. Jet-propelled fighter plane to be accepted by the Army Air Force for combat purposes was the P-80 Shooting Star, designed by Clarence L. Johnson and constructed in 143 days by the Lockheed Aircraft Corporation, Burbank, CA. It had a wingspan of 38 feet 10.5 inches, an overall length of 34 feet 6 inches, and a height of 11 feet 4 inches. The first flight was made on January 1944. In February 1945, the Army declared that it had been perfected for actual combat.

5485. Rocket airplane for military use was the MX-324, built by the Northrop Aircraft, Hawthorne, CA, and flown July 5, 1944, by Harry Crosby, pilot. It had a prone cockpit in which the pilot lay flat to withstand the pull. An Aerojet XCAL-200 rocket motor was used with monoethylaniline as fuel. The craft was known as the Rocket Ram. It was originally tested as a glider on October 2, 1943, by John Myers.

5486. Rocket plane for manned supersonic flight built in the United States was the Army XS-1, manufactured by the Bell Aircraft Corporation, Buffalo, NY. The craft was an orange-colored needle-nose plane 31 feet long, with a 28-foot wingspan and a 210-pound engine. It carried both fuel and oxygen. After a series of glide tests, the XS-1 made its first powered flight on December 9, 1946, when it was released from a B-29 bomber at 25,000 feet. It remained aloft 19 minutes, seven of which were under power. The test pilot, Chalmers Goodlin of New Alexandria, PA, landed the plane at the army air field in Muroc, CA.

5487. Navy jet airplane squadron was Fighter Squadron 17-A, which received its first jet airplane, a McDonnell FH-1 Phantom, at the Naval Air Station, Quonset Point, RI, on July 23, 1947. On May 5, 1948, at the close of three days of operations aboard the USS *Saipan*, the squadron became the first Navy jet squadron to qualify aboard a carrier.

5488. Independent aviation branch of the U.S. armed forces was the United States Air Force, established on September 18, 1947, under the National Security Act of 1947, which made the Air Force part of the newly created Defense Department along with the Army and the Navy. Its first chief of staff, appointed on September 26, 1947, was General Carl A. Spaatz.

5489. Army helicopter battalion to be activated was the 8th Transportation Battalion, consisting of three helicopter companies and one maintenance company, formed on April 1, 1954, at Fort Bragg, NC, under command of Major Robert Kolb.

5490. Military heliport was the Fort Eustis Heliport, Felker Field, Fort Eustis, VA, dedicated December 7, 1954. The field was named for Warrant Officer Alfred Charles Felker, a graduate of the first army helicopter pilot course, who was killed in an airplane flight in February 1953. The heliport was built in the shape of a huge wheel, with 600-foot runways forming the spokes and a circular taxiway composing the rim. The first commanding officer was Lieutenant Colonel Robert C. Spiedel, Jr.

5491. Human to fly above 100,000 feet was Captain Iven Carl Kincheloe, Jr., a USAF test pilot based at Edwards Air Force Base, Muroc, CA. On Sept. 7, 1956, Kincheloe flew a

Bell X-2 experimental rocket plane to a record altitude of 23.9 miles (126,200 feet). At that time, Kincheloe was hailed as having reached "the edge of space", although space is now considered to begin at 50 miles (264,000 feet) above the surface of the earth. On July 26, 1958, Kincheloe was killed in the crash of an F-104 jet.

5492. Stealth aircraft used in combat were deployed in the early hours of December 20, 1989, during the U.S. invasion of Panama. On December 23, 1989, the Department of Defense, Washington, DC, said that two F-117A Stealth bombers, aircraft equipped with advanced sensor-evasion technology, had bombed a barracks in the Panama City area.

5493. Pilot of a B-52 bomber who was a woman was Air Force Second Lieutenant Kelly Jean Flinn. In 1996, she flew Secretary of the Air Force Dr. Sheila Widnall in a Boeing B-52 strategic bomber stationed at Minot Air Force Base in Minot, ND.

Officers

5494. Air Force general who was African-American was Benjamin Oliver Davis, Jr., of Washington, DC, director of operations and training of the Far East Air Force, who was named brigadier general on October 27, 1954. He was the son of Brigadier General Benjamin Oliver Davis of the Army.

5495. Air Force chairman of the Joint Chiefs of Staff was General Nathan Farragut Twining, who was sworn in on August 15, 1957, in Washington, DC, by President Dwight David Eisenhower. On September 29, 1960, the day before Twining retired as chief of staff, President Eisenhower decorated him with the Distinguished Service Medal.

5496. Air Force Reserve officer who was a nun was Sister Nancy Ann Eagan, a nurse, who became a lieutenant on May 5, 1970. She was assigned to the 932d Aeromedical Airlift Group, Scott Air Force Base, IL.

5497. Air Force general who was a woman was Brigadier General Jeanne Marjorie Holm of Portland, OR, nominated on December 12, 1970, by President John Fitzgerald Kennedy. She received her silver stars at the Pentagon, Washington, DC, on July 16, 1971. Holm had served since 1965 as Director of Women in the Air Force.

5498. Air Force general who was an African-American woman was Marcelite Jordan Harris, who attained the rank of general in 1991. In 1995 she was promoted to major general, with overall responsibility for maintenance on every USAF base. She thus became the first African-American woman to attain the rank of major general in any of the nation's armed forces. In 1969, Harris had served with the 36th Tactical Wing at Bitburg Air Base, West Germany, where she became the first female aircraft maintenance officer in the air force.

5499. Head of one of the armed services who was a woman was Sheila E. Widnall, who was sworn in on August 6, 1993, as secretary of the Air Force. She oversaw an annual budget of $62 billion, a force of 380,000 men and women on active duty, the 251,000 members of the Air National Guard and the Air Reserve, and 184,000 civilian employees. Previously, Widnall spent nearly three decades as a professor of aeronautics and astronautics at the Massachusetts Institute of Technology, Cambridge, MA.

Awards

5500. Purple Heart was awarded to Sergeants Daniel Bissell, William Brown, and Elijah Churchill of Connecticut regiments, decorated on May 9, 1783, for singularly meritorious action in the Revolutionary War. They were entitled "to wear on facings over the left breast, the figure of a heart in purple cloth or silk, with narrow lace or binding." The Order of the Purple Heart, a decoration for "military merit," was established by George Washington on August 7, 1782, at Newburgh, NY, and was the first honor badge for enlisted men and noncommissioned officers.

5501. Combat action that earned the Medal of Honor took place February 13–14, 1861, at Apache Pass, AZ, when Colonel Bernard John Dowling Irwin, assistant surgeon, "voluntarily took command of troops and attacked and defeated the hostile Indians (Chiricahua) he met on the way." This action occurred before the medal was authorized on July 12, 1862. The award was made on January 21, 1894.

5502. Civil War combat action that earned the Medal of Honor was awarded on May 24, 1861, to Francis E. Brownell of Troy, NY, a private in the 11th New York Infantry Regiment, better known as the New York Fire Zouaves. The group was commanded by Col. Ephraim Elmer Ellsworth. On May 24, 1861, one day after Virginia's secession, the Zouaves entered Alexandria, VA. Ellsworth, accompanied by Brownell and three others, entered a hotel and tore down a Confederate flag. The hotel's proprietor, James W. Jackson, retaliated by shooting Ellsworth in the chest with a shotgun, killing him. Brownell immediately shot Jackson and bayoneted his body."

5503. Proposal for a Medal of Honor to pay national tribute to gallantry, courage, and self-sacrifice in battle was made on December 9, 1861, when Sen. James W. Grimes of Iowa introduced a bill to authorize the awarding of such medals to Navy and Marine Corps personnel who distinguished themselves in action during the Civil War. The bill passed and was signed into law on December 21, 1861. A similar bill for Army privates, introduced on February 17, 1862, by Sen. Henry Wilson of Massachusetts, became law the following July 12; its provisions were extended to officers on March 3, 1863. Before the Medal of Honor was authorized, the only recognition available to private soldiers was a certificate of merit, introduced in 1847."

5504. Medal of Honor awarded to an Army soldier was awarded to Pvt. Jacob Parrott of Company K, 33rd Ohio Infantry, on March 25, 1863, by Secretary of War Edwin Stanton in Washington, DC. Parrott and five other Union soldiers, who also received the Medal of Honor, had just been released from Confederate prisons. They were the surviving participants of the Andrews Raid, a famous exploit that had taken place the previous April. James J. Andrews, a civilian spy for the Union, had led 20 soldiers on a raid into eastern Tennessee prior to the Union invasion of Chattanooga. Stealing a locomotive while the conductor and engineer were at breakfast, they steamed through enemy territory, cutting rail lines and telegraph wires, but before they could succeed in burning two important bridges, they were overtaken by Confederates who chased them in a second locomotive that was running in reverse. All were either hanged or imprisoned.

5505. Medal of Honor awarded to a member of the Naval Service was given on April 3, 1863 to John Williams, captain of the maintop of the USS *Pawnee* during an attack on Matthias Point, VA, on June 26, 1861.

5506. Medal of Honor awarded to a Marine was presented to Sergeant John Freeman Mackie by Commander Henry Rolando July 10, 1861. During the attack on Fort Darling at Drewrys Bluff, James River, VA, on May 15, 1862, Mackie rallied the Marine Guard on the USS *Galena* after the entire 3rd Division was killed or wounded. He cleared the deck and resumed the action without awaiting orders.

5507. Medal of Honor winner to receive two awards was Thomas W. Custer, Second Lieutenant, Company B, 6th Michigan Cavalry, who was awarded the medal on May 3, 1865, for the capture of a flag at Namozine Church, VA, on May 10, 1863, and a second medal on May 26, 1865, for his heroism at Sailors Creek, VA, on April 6, 1865, when he jumped his horse over the enemy's works and captured two stands of colors despite the fact that his horse was shot under him and he received a severe wound.

5508. Medal of Honor awarded to a woman was awarded to Mary Edwards Walker, a physician from Rome, NY, who volunteered to serve with the Union Army during the Civil War and worked as a surgeon in field hospitals. For four months she was a Confederate prisoner of war. She received the Medal of Honor on November 11, 1865. It was revoked in 1917 because she had not participated in combat, but was restored posthumously on June 10, 1977.

5509. Medal of Honor awarded to a Jewish soldier was conferred upon Sergeant Leopold Karpeles of Springfield, MA, of Company E, 57th Massachusetts Infantry, who, while serving as flag bearer, rallied the retreating troops at the Battle of the Wilderness, near Fredericksburg, VA, on May 6, 1864, and persuaded them to check the enemy's advance. The award was authorized July 12, 1864, and the date of issue was April 30, 1870.

5510. Military campaign medal was the Dewey Medal, authorized by act of Congress of June 3, 1898, to be presented to all officers and men under the command of Commodore George Dewey who participated in the Battle

Library of Congress, Prints & Photographs Division
LC-USZ62-5534

Commodore George Dewey

of Manila Bay on May 1, 1898. Unlike medals suspended from ribbons, this bronze medal was suspended from a bar that bore the design of an American eagle with its wings spread over the sea.

5511. Medal of Honor awarded to an African-American soldier was issued on June 23, 1899, to Private George Henry Wanton, Troop M, 10th U.S. Cavalry. During the Spanish-American War, he voluntarily went ashore at Tayabacoa, Cuba, on June 30, 1898, "in the face of the enemy and aided in the rescue of his wounded comrades, this after several previous attempts at rescue had been frustrated."

5512. Medal of Honor awarded to an African-American soldier for an action in the Civil War was issued on May 23, 1900, to Sergeant William Harvey Carney for his bravery on July 18, 1863, while a member of Company C, 54th Massachusetts Colored Infantry, at Fort Wagner, SC. He was wounded twice while planting the flag on a parapet and removing it when the troops fell back under a fierce fire in which he was severely wounded. He was discharged on June 30, 1864, with disability. Although he was the first African-American soldier to earn the Medal of Honor, he was the second to receive it, since he had to wait 36 years before his medal was granted.

5513. Croix de Guerre awarded to an American was given on May 24, 1918, to two African-American soldiers who fought with the American Expeditionary Force in France during World War I. They were members of Company C, 369th Infantry, 93rd Division. Henry Johnson of Albany, NY, and Needham Roberts of Trenton, NJ, were on sentry duty on the front lines when they were attacked by a group of Germans. Despite being wounded, they drove off the enemy with hand grenades and a bolo, and Johnson saved Roberts from capture.

5514. Croix de Guerre awarded to an American woman was awarded in 1919 to Natalie Vivian Scott of New Orleans, LA, who served as a Red Cross volunteer in France during World War I. The battlefield hospital where she worked as a nurse was bombed nightly by the Germans. Scott saved the lives of numreous wounded soldiers whom she brought out of the debris.

5515. Medal of Honor awarded to a pilot was given to Second Lieutenant Frank Luke, for extraordinary heroism in action at Murvaux, France, September 12–15, 1918, when he destroyed eight enemy balloons in four days. The award was made on April 14, 1919, and was posthumously presented at Phoenix, AZ, on May 29, 1919, to his father, Frank

Library of Congress, Prints & Photographs Division
LC-USZC4-507

Storming Fort Wagner.

Luke, Sr. Luke was a member of the 27th Aero Squadron when he was killed in action. He is officially credited with 18 victories, a record that was surpassed in World War I only by Captain Edward Vernon Rickenbacker.

5516. Medal of Honor awarded in World War I was presented in Washington, DC, on May 21, 1919, to Ernest August Janson, gunnery sergeant, who served under the name of Charles F. Hoffman, of Brooklyn, New York City, in the 49th Company, 5th Regiment, 2nd Division, Marine Corps. On June 6, 1918, near Chateau-Thierry, France, he saw 12 enemy soldiers with light machine guns and bayoneted two of them, forcing the others to flee and abandon their guns.

5517. Purple Heart awarded to a woman was awarded to First Lieutenant Annie G. Fox of the Army Nurse Corps, head nurse of Hickam Hospital at Pearl Harbor, HI, who supervised the treatment and evacuation of the wounded during the Japanese attack on December 7, 1941.

5518. Medal of Honor awarded in World War II was posthumously awarded to Second Lieutenant Alexander Ramsey "Sandy" Nininger, Jr., for heroism in action in the vicinity of Abucay, Bataan, Philippine Islands, on January 12, 1942. It was presented on February 10, 1942, at Tampa, FL, to his father, Alexander Ramsey Nininger. The first Medal of Honor awarded to a Marine in World War II was presented posthumously to First Lieutenant George "Ham" Hammon Cannon of Ann Arbor, MI, battery commander of Battery H, 6th Defense Battalion Fleet Marine Force, Marine Corps, on March 14, 1942. He was mortally wounded by shell fire on December 7, 1941, at the bombardment of Sand Island, Midway Islands, by Japanese forces, and refused to be evacuated from his post until his own men who had been wounded by the same shell were evacuated. He continued to direct the reorganization of his command post until he was forcibly removed. He died from loss of blood.

5519. Navy Cross awarded to a Coast Guard officer in World War II was presented on June 4, 1942, to Lieutenant Maurice D. Jester, who, while in command of the 165-foot Coast Guard *Icarus* off the Carolina coast, sank an enemy submarine, captured the commanding officer, his first mate, and 31 members of the crew, and brought them as prisoners to Charleston, SC.

5520. Distinguished Service Cross awarded in enemy-occupied territory was presented on July 11, 1942, to Captain Charles C. Kegelman of El Reno, OK, for "his heroism, his flying skill, his intimate knowledge of his equipment and his great coolness and judgment in action" against the enemy on July 4, 1941. Although one motor in his aircraft was shot to pieces, the tail riddled with bullets, and a hole made in the cabin, he saved his aircraft and his crew. His rank was raised to that of major on July 9, 1942.

5521. Navy–Marine Corps Medals for Heroism awarded to Marines were awarded to Sergeant Norman C. S. Pearson of Minneapolis, MN, and Corporal Gordon Miller of Cincinnati, OH, who risked their lives to save a gunner sergeant imprisoned in a fallen and burning airplane. They were specially commended on September 21, 1942, by Lieutenant General Thomas Holcomb, commandant of the Marine Corps, and promoted a grade.

5522. Silver Star awarded to a civilian was presented by General Douglas MacArthur to Vern Haugland, Associated Press correspondent, on October 3, 1942. He was a passenger on an army airplane forced to descend in New Guinea during World War II. After 43 days in the jungle, he reached civilization.

5523. Soldier's Medal awarded to a woman was conferred on nurse Edith Greenwood on June 21, 1943, for heroism in saving the lives of her patients in a fire in a station hospital near Yuma, AZ, on April 17, 1943. A Soldier's Medal was presented on November 17, 1943, at Allied Headquarters, Algiers, to Private Margaret Helen Maloney of Rochester, NY, a member of the Women's Army Corps, for rescuing Private Kenneth J. Jacobs from a pool of burning gasoline.

5524. Distinguished Service Cross awarded to an animal was authorized under General Order No. 79 of the 3rd Infantry Division dated October 24, 1943, and conferred by Major General Lucian Truscott on Chips, a half-shepherd and half-husky dog owned by Mr. and Mrs. Edward Wren of Pleasantville, NY, for "courageous action in singlehandedly eliminating a dangerous machine-gun nest and causing surrender of the crew." The award was rescinded on February 3, 1944, after a War Department circular dated January 19, 1944, prohibited the awarding of decorations to animals.

5525. Silver Star awarded to a woman was awarded in February 1944 to 1st Lieut. Mary Roberts (later Mary Roberts Wilson), a nurse from Dallas, TX, who volunteered for military duty after Pearl Harbor and was assigned to the Army's 56th Evacuation Unit as the operating room supervisor. On February 10, 1944, her field hospital on the beach at Anzio, Italy, came under heavy German artillery fire. Roberts and her staff kept the hospital functioning and led 42 patients to safety. Three other nurses—2nd Lieuts. Elaine Roe, Virginia Rourke, and, posthumously, Ellen Ainsworth—also received Silver Stars for their actions on that day. Ainsworth was killed in the attack."

5526. Army officer to receive the three highest decorations was Captain Maurice L. Britt of Lonoke, AR, infantry, the recipient of the Medal of Honor, the Silver Star, the Purple Heart with three Oak Leaf clusters, and the Military Cross of the British Empire, who was presented with the Distinguished Service Cross on December 7, 1944, by Major General Frank L. Walker for gallantry in action.

5527. Presidential citation to an entire armed forces division was made on March 15, 1945, to the 101st Airborne Division, the heroes of Bastogne, by General Dwight David Eisenhower, somewhere on the western front. From December 18 to December 27, 1944, the division withstood tremendous odds during the Battle of the Bulge.

5528. Medal of Honor awarded to a conscientious objector was presented on October 12, 1945, to Private First Class Desmond T. Doss of Lynchburg, VA, for outstanding bravery as a medical corpsman on Okinawa in specific acts between April 29 and May 21, 1945.

5529. Medal of Honor awarded to a chaplain was presented to Reverend Timothy O'Callahan, of Cambridge, MA, on January 23, 1946, at Washington, DC. He gave the last rites, organized rescue parties, and carried ammunition when the USS *Franklin* was set afire by an aerial bombing by kamikaze pilots on March 19, 1945, off the Japanese coast.

5530. Medal of Honor awarded to a soldier of Japanese ancestry was conferred upon Private First Class Sadao S. Munemori of Company A, 100th Infantry Battalion, 442nd Combat Team, for action near Seravezza, Italy, on April 5, 1945, when he knocked out two machine guns with grenades and saved the lives of two of his companions by diving on an exploding grenade. The medal was presented posthumously on March 13, 1946, to his mother, Mrs. Nawa Munemori.

5531. Medal of Honor awarded in the Korean War was presented on September 30, 1950, to Major General William Frische Dean of Berkeley, CA, commanding general of the 24th Infantry Division, who at the battle for Taejon on July 20–21, 1950, personally and alone attacked an enemy tank while armed with only a hand grenade. Other recipients at the ceremony were Private First Class Melvin L. Brown of Mahaffey, PA, and First Lieutenant Frederick F. Henry of Clinton, OK. Posthumous awards were also made to Sergeant Charles W. Turner of Boston, MA, and Master Sergeant Travis E. Watkins of Gladewater, TX.

5532. Medal of Honor given to a Marine in the Korean War was presented to Lieutenant Henry Alfred Commiskey of Hattiesburg, MS, who killed seven enemy soldiers in hand-to-hand combat, armed only with a pistol, on September 20, 1950, near Yongdungpo, outside Seoul, Korea. The medal, the 30th medal award of the Korean War, was presented on August 1, 1951, by President Harry S. Truman at the White House, Washington, DC.

5533. Air Force Medal of Honor for action in the Korean War was awarded posthumously to Major Louis J. Sebille of Chicago, IL, who was killed on August 5, 1951, in an F-51 Mustang which he crashed into the ground amid a group of enemy armored vehicles near Hamchang, Korea. The award was presented to his widow, Mrs. Elizabeth J. Sebille, on August 24, 1951, at March Air Force Base, Riverside, CA.

5534. Navy–Marine Corps Medal for Heroism awarded to a woman was presented on August 7, 1953, to Staff Sergeant Barbara Olive Barnwell, of Pittsburgh, PA, Marine Corps Reserve, in Washington, DC. She saved Private First Class Frederick G. Romann from drowning on June 7, 1952, at Onslow Beach, Camp Lejeune, NC.

5535. Medal of Honor awarded in the Vietnam war was presented on December 5, 1964, to Army Captain Roger Hugh Donlon of Saugerties, NY. He was wounded four times (in the stomach, leg, shoulder, and face) at Nam Dong, about 20 miles from the Laotian frontier. The award was the first since the Korean War, the first in a counterinsurgency effort, and the first to a soldier with a friendly foreign force engaged in an armed conflict in which the United States was not a belligerent.

5536. Medal of Honor awarded to a Seabee was presented posthumously on September 13, 1966, in Washington, DC, to Marvin Glen Shields of Port Townsend, WA, for heroism in the 14-hour battle at Dongzoal, Vietnam, on June 10, 1965, during which he saved the lives of many of his companions. The medal was accepted by his widow, Joan Elaine Shields.

5537. Silver Star awarded to a Navy chaplain for gallantry was presented on April 18, 1968, to Lieutenant Richard M. Lyons, a Roman Catholic priest, who braved enemy fire to administer last rites to wounded marines during the battle for Hue, South Vietnam.

5538. Medals of Honor awarded to African-American servicemen for service in World War II were awarded on January 13, 1996, by President William Jefferson Clinton at a ceremony in the White House, Washington, DC. None of the 1.7 million African-Americans who served in World War II had received a Medal of Honor despite the many documented cases of bravery that were presented to officials of the armed forces. Of the seven servicemen who received the medal at the ceremony, the only one still alive was Vernon Baker, a 77-year-old retired career Army officer. Medals were awarded posthumously to Staff Sergeant Edward A. Carter, Jr., of Los Angeles, First Lieutenant Charles L. Thomas of Detroit, Private George Watson of Birmingham, AL, First Lieutenant John R. Fox of Boston, Private First Class Willy F. James, Jr., of Kansas City, KS, and Staff Sergeant Ruben Rivers of Tecumseh, OK.

5539. Medal of Honor awarded to a soldier in the Iraq war was awarded posthumously to U.S. Army Sergeant First Class Paul Ray Smith of Holiday, FL, squad leader of Bravo Company, 11th Engineer Battalion, First Brigade, Third Infantry Division. On April 4, 2003, as his unit was working near the Baghdad airport, it was attacked by Iraqi Republican Guards. Smith held them off with machine-gun fire for 90 minutes while his wounded men were evacuated. He killed between 30 and 50 enemy soldiers before he was himself killed, and was credited with saving the lives of 100 of his men. His family received the Medal of Honor from President George W. Bush at a White House ceremony on April 4, 2005.

5540. Silver Star awarded to a woman for actions in combat was awarded to Sgt. Leigh Ann Hester of Nashville, TN, on June 16, 2005. Hester, a member of the Kentucky National Guard's 617th Military Policy Company, was the commander of one of three armored Humvees that were shadowing a convoy of supply trucks south of Baghdad, Iraq, on March 20, 2005. A group of insurgents ambushed the convoy, firing rifles, machine guns, and rocket-propelled grenades. Hester and others in her unit attacked the group. In a 45-minute firefight, they killed 27 of the enemy, wounded six, captured one, and took control of a large arms cache. Two other soldiers in the unit, Staff Sgt. Timothy Nein and Spc. Jason Mike, also received Silver Stars, and other soldiers received medals."

5541. Medals of Honor issued by a state to honor service members killed in Iraq and Afghanistan were awarded by Hawaii on April 28, 2006, at a joint session of the state legislature in Honolulu. Relatives and friends of 49 service members killed between March 2003 and March 2006 received a framed medal of silver and gold. Seventy-one additional medals were delivered to families who could not attend.

Coast Guard

5542. Coast guard service was the Revenue Cutter Service, organized by an act of Congress of August 4, 1790, "an act to provide more effectually for the collection of the duties imposed by law on goods, wares and merchandise imported into the United States and on the tonnage of ships and vessels." The Life Saving Service was authorized by an act of June 18, 1878. The two services were combined on January 28, 1915, into the Coast Guard. The motto of the Coast Guard is *Semper paratus (Always Ready)*. The first commandant was Alexander V. Fraser.

5543. Coast Guard serviceman who was African-American was Michael A. Healy of Georgia, who was appointed on March 7, 1865, to the Revenue Cutter Service, the predecessor of the Coast Guard. He was appointed second lieutenant on June 6, 1866, first lieutenant on July 20, 1870, and captain on March 3, 1883. He was commanding officer of the *Bear* from 1886 to 1895. He retired on September 22, 1903.

5544. Coast Guard inland station was opened on November 3, 1881, when four surfmen were employed on Station No. 10 of the 9th Life Saving District, embracing Lake Erie and Lake Ontario, at Louisville, KY, near the falls of the Ohio River. The station was commanded by Captain William M. Devan. The first rescue was made on November 7, four days after the station opened, when the 1,603-ton steamer *City of Baton Rouge* of St. Louis, MO, valued at $125,000, with 26 persons on board, was stranded on the left-hand reef of the falls. The vessel was finally floated off the rocks on November 24.

5545. Coast Guard unit for women was the Coast Guard Women's Reserve, called SPARS, from the initials of the Coast Guard motto *Semper Paratus (Always Ready).* It was authorized on November 23, 1942, and placed under the command of Lieutenant Commander Dorothy Constance Stratton. The first recruit was Dorothy Edith Lorne Tuttle, who enlisted on December 7, 1942, as a yeoman third class.

5546. Coast Guard officers who were women who served aboard ships other than hospital ships were Ensign Beverly Gwin Kelley of Bonita Springs, FL, assigned to the seagoing cutter *Morgenthau*, and Petty Officer Third Class Debra Lee Wilson of San Jose, CA, assigned to the seagoing cutter *Gallatin*, on June 22, 1977.

5547. Coast Guard ship commander who was a woman was Lieutenant (j.g.) Beverly Kelley, who was appointed on April 16, 1979, to command the 95-foot cutter *Cape Newagen*, with a crew of 14, based in Maalaea, Maui, HI. Her assignment included search missions, boating safety, antipollution patrols, and law enforcement. The first woman to command a Coast Guard ship on regular patrol was Lieutenant (j.g.) Susan Ingalls Moritz, who assumed command of the USS *Cape Current* on June 8, 1979. The ship operated in the Straits of Florida, where smuggling of drugs and immigrants was a constant problem.

Courts

5548. Court-martial in a colony was held on August 24, 1676, in Newport, RI, by Governor Walter Clarke, Deputy Governor John Crayton, and their assistants. Edmund Calverly was the attorney general. Quanpen, a Native American sachem also known as Sowagonish, was found guilty of participation in King Philip's War against the colonists and ordered shot on August 26. Others who had participated in the war were sentenced to various penalties.

5549. Execution by the Army occurred on June 27, 1776. A guard, Thomas Hickey, plotted with others to capture George Washington and deliver him to Sir William Howe. Hickey was tried, convicted, and hanged in New York City. The execution took place at a field near Bowery Lane in the presence of 20,000 persons, including an armed assembly of all the off-duty officers and men of four brigades.

5550. Court-martial by the Army was held on January 20, 1778, in Cambridge, MA. Colonel David Henley, commanding officer of the American troops in Cambridge, was accused "of a general tenor of language and conduct heinously criminal as an officer, and unbecoming a man, of the most indecent, violent, vindictive severity against unarmed men, and of intentional murder." The trial was concluded on February 25, when Henley was found not guilty. Brigadier General John Glover was the presiding officer at the trial.

5551. Court-martial at which the judges included enlisted men was convened at 8:30 A.M. on February 1, 1949, in Heidelberg, Germany, to try Private First Class Andrew D. Byrd of Orlando, FL, and Private First Class Oscar B. Gannon of Hanging Rock, OH, on the charge of premeditated murder of a German civilian and assault on another in a brawl. The military court consisted of four sergeants and six officers. The defendants were convicted on February 3 of manslaughter and sentenced to serve seven years at hard labor and to receive dishonorable discharges.

5552. Court-martial of an officer for collaborating with his captors was held on September 23, 1954, at Fort Sheridan, IL. A court of eight colonels and three lieutenant colonels sentenced Lieutenant Colonel Harry Fleming, reserve officer, of Racine, WI, to "involuntary discharge" for collaborating with Communists during the Korean War. On February 8, 1957, the Court of Military Appeals upheld the conviction and agreed with the court-martial and military board of review.

Draft

5553. Draft law enacted by a colony was enacted on April 18, 1637, in Boston, MA, by the Massachusetts Bay Colony legislature, which provided "there shalbee 160 men pvided to be chosen out of the severall townes according to the portion underwritten," to serve in the conflict known as the Pequot War. The conscription call was as follows: Boston 26, Salem 18, Ipswich 17, Saugus 16, Watertown 14, Dorchester 13, Charlestown 12, Roxbury 10, Cambridge 9, Newbury 8, Hingham 6, Weymouth 5, Medford 3, and Marblehead 3.

5554. Conscientious objectors who refused for religious reasons to participate in war were the Shakers, members of a pacifist Christian sect that had originated in England. The group's formal title was "The United Society of Believers in Christ's Second Appearing." A group of Shakers, led by their founder, Ann Lee, had emigrated from England in 1774 and settled in Watervliet, NY. They refused to aid the colonies in the Revolutionary War, with the result that they were accused of treason and imprisoned without trial in the old fort in Albany, NY. On December 20, 1780, they were all released from prison with the exception of Ann Lee, who was transferred to the jail at Poughkeepsie, NY. She was released soon thereafter.

5555. Draft of civilians by Congress was authorized by the act of May 8, 1792, "effectually to provide for the National Defense by establishing a uniform militia throughout the United States." Every free able-bodied white male citizen between the ages of 18 and 45 was required to be enrolled in the militia of the United States and to supply himself with a gun and no fewer than 24 cartridges suited to the bore of his musket. There was no penalty for noncompliance. This law left the militia under the command of the states.

5556. Draft law enacted by Congress during wartime was passed on March 3, 1863, "an act for enrolling and calling out the national forces, and for other purposes." It required men 20 to 45 years of age to be enrolled on April 1, 1863, by provost marshals. Exemptions could be bought for $300. The first draft call was made on July 7, 1863. Earlier draft bills had been passed by the House and Senate during the War of 1812, but the need to produce a compromise bill ended with the signing of a peace treaty on December 24, 1814.

5557. Draft law enacted by Congress in preparation for war was passed on September 14, 1940, by a vote of 47–35 in the Senate and 232–124 in the House. It called for a total of 900,000 men to be trained in any given year. Registration was required of all men who had attained the age of 21 and who had not reached the age of 36 on October 16, 1940. Each registrant was assigned a number, so that quotas of soldiers could be filled by lottery. The first drawing of numbers was made on October 29, 1940, in Washington, DC. The first number to come up, No. 158, was drawn by Secretary of War Henry Lewis Stimson. On November 15, the government issued a call for 75,000 men. The director of the draft was Dr. Clarence Addison Dykstra.

5558. Camp for conscientious objectors was the Patapsco Civilian Public Service Camp, Relay Post Office, MD, opened on May 15, 1941, to house 26 men of various faiths and beliefs who chose to do public service rather than participate in war. The director was Dr. Ernest Atkins Wildman, professor of chemistry, Earlham College, Richmond, IN. Inmates worked in the neighboring Patapsco State Park and in the State Forestry Nursery. Similar camps were later opened by the National Service Board for Religious Objectors.

Marine Corps

5559. British marine corps of American colonists was organized in 1740 when three regiments of American colonists were recruited in New York to serve under the British flag. They wore green swallowtail coats faced with red, white waistcoats, buff trousers, crossed white belts, and three-cornered hats.

5560. Marines were organized in two battalions on November 10, 1775, under authority of the Continental Congress. They were called the 1st and 2nd Battalions of American Marines, and were commanded by a colonel, two lieutenant colonels, and two majors. The first marine officer was Samuel Nicholas, a Philadelphia Quaker, commissioned captain on November 28, 1775, at $32 a month. The Marines were under the jurisdiction of the War Department until April 30, 1798, when Congress created the Navy Department. The present Marine Corps was created by act of July 11, 1798, which authorized a major, 4 captains, 16 first lieutenants, 12 second lieutenants, 48 sergeants, 48 corporals, 32 drums and fifes, and 720 privates, including enlisted men. The first major was William Ward Burrows of South Carolina, who was appointed July 12, 1798, and served nearly 6 years.

5561. Marine officer killed in service was John Fitzpatrick, a second lieutenant in the Continental Marines, who was killed on April 6, 1777, when the *Alfred*, a 24-gun frigate under command of Captain Samuel Nicholas, was attacked off Block Island, RI, by the 20-gun H.M.S. *Glasgow*.

5562. Marine band was authorized by act of Congress of July 11, 1798, which allowed the appointment of a drum major, a fife major, and 32 drummers and fifers. William Farr was leader of the Marine band from January 21, 1799, to November 22, 1804. The first president to review the band from his residence was John Adams on January 1, 1801.

5563. Marine Corps commando raid was made on February 16, 1804, in North Africa by Lieutenent Stephen Decatur, who led 74 volunteers, including 8 Marines under Sergeant Solomon Wren, in a 20-minute raid to burn the USS *Philadelphia*, which had been captured by the Tripolitans and was lying under the protection of their shore guns. The raiders killed or captured all the enemy but two and set the *Philadelphia* afire.

5564. Marine who was a woman was Lucy Brewer, alias George Baker and Louisa Baker, who concealed her sex and served on board the *Constitution* in its battle with the *Guerrière* on August 19, 1812.

5565. Marine pilot was Lieutenant Alfred Austell Cunningham, assigned for training and instruction to the Navy Aviation Camp, Annapolis, MD, on July 9, 1912. He made his first solo flight on August 1, 1912, received seaplane license certificate No. 2, and became naval aviator No. 5. From November 17, 1919, to December 12, 1920, he served as director of Marine Corps Aviation.

5566. Marine reserve member who was a woman was Mrs. Opha May Johnson, who enrolled on August 13, 1918, as a private and was assigned to duty as a clerk at the headquarters of the Marine Corps Quartermaster Corps, Washington, DC, following an order from the secretary of the navy allowing women to enroll in the Marine Corps Reserve for clerical duty. She was appointed sergeant on September 11, 1918, and was honorably discharged on February 28, 1919.

5567. Marine general to wear four stars was Major General Thomas Holcomb, commandant of the Marine Corps, who was advanced to lieutenant general on January 20, 1942. On January 1, 1944, he was placed on the retired list and his rank was raised to that of full general. The first four-star general in active service was Lieutenant General Alexander Archer Vandegrift, appointed on April 4, 1945, with date of rank from March 21, 1945.

5568. Commissioned officer in the Marine Corps who was African-American was John Earl Rudder, a midshipman in the regular Naval Reserve Officers' Training Corps at Purdue University, Lafayette, IN, who was commissioned on June 8, 1948, as a second lieutenant. He had served as an enlisted man in the Marine Corps Reserve from July 24, 1943, to June 26, 1946.

5569. Marine who was an African-American woman was Annie Neal Graham (nee Gilliard), who enlisted on September 8, 1949, and trained at Paris Island, SC. At the time of her discharge in 1952 she had attained the rank of sergeant.

5570. Marine general who was a woman was Brigadier General Margaret Ann Brewer, nominated on April 6, 1978, by President Jimmy Carter and sworn in on May 11, 1978, as director of the division of information.

5571. Marine general who was African-American was Colonel Frank E. Petersen, Jr., of Topeka, KS, nominated on February 23, 1979, for brigadier general by President Jimmy Carter. He was the thirtieth African-American to achieve the rank of general or admiral.

Navy

5572. Navy fleet was authorized on October 13, 1775, when the Continental Congress appointed a marine committee consisting of John Adams, John Langdon, and Silas Deane to be in complete control of naval affairs. Although open hostilities against the British began on April 19, 1775, little consideration was given to protection by sea until October 5, when the Congress received news that a British naval fleet was on its way. The Continental Navy was organized on December 22, 1775, and consisted of two 24-gun frigates, the *Alfred* and the *Columbus*, as well as two 14-gun brigs, the *Andrea Doria* and the *Cabot*, and the schooners *Hornet*, *Wasp*, and *Fly*. Esek Hopkins was commissioned commander of the fleet and his pay was set at $125 a month. Sailors received $8 a month.

5573. American warship named after a foreigner was the Alfred, the first ship acquired by the Continental Navy. Originally a merchant vessel called Black Prince, it was purchased by the Naval Committee on November 4, 1775, renamed and refitted, and commissioned on December 3. The name was chosen in honor of Alfred the Great, ninth-century king of the English realm of West Sussex, who became known as the Father of the Royal Navy because of his prescience in building ships to defend his coast.

5574. Navy uniforms to be standardized were adopted by the Marine Committee on September 5, 1776. The uniform of captains in the Navy consisted of a coat of blue with red lapels, slashed cuffs, a stand-up collar, flat yellow buttons, blue breeches, and a red waistcoat with yellow lace. The sailors or mariners were to have green coats faced with white, round cuffs, slashed sleeves and pockets, with buttons around the cuff, a silver epaulet on the right shoulder, shirt collars turned back, buttons to match the facings, white waistcoats and breeches edged with green, black gaiters, and garters. The men were also to have green shirts, "if they can be procured."

5575. Navy recruiting campaign began at Portsmouth, NH, where John Paul Jones was looking for sailors to man a new ship, the 20-gun Ranger. On July 26, 1777, an advertisement written by Jones appeared in the town's newspaper, the *Freeman's Journal*. He also distributed recruitment handbills in Providence, RI, and Boston, MA.

Library of Congress, Prints & Photographs Division LC-USZ61-288

John Paul Jones

5576. Naval protection was afforded by the Revenue Cutter Service, which was organized on August 4, 1790, under an act of Congress approved by President George Washington. It operated under the general direction of the secretary of the treasury. Commissions were granted on March 21, 1791, to captains to command "a cutter in the Service of the United States of America." For nearly seven years, the revenue cutters formed the only armed force of the United States afloat. The service was later merged with the Coast Guard.

5577. Warship builder was Joshua Humphreys, "father of the American Navy," who was appointed master builder on June 28, 1794, at an annual salary of $2,000. On March

27, 1794, Congress passed an "act to provide a naval armament," which authorized four ships of 44 guns and two of 36 guns. Humphreys constructed *Constitution*, *Constellation*, *Chesapeake*, *President*, *United States*, and numerous other ships. He served until October 26, 1801.

5578. Navy yard acquired after the establishment of the Navy Department on April 30, 1798, was the Portsmouth Navy Yard, Portsmouth, NH, which was purchased on June 12, 1800, from William Dennet and his wife for $5,500. It embraced 58.18 acres and had previously been used for building man-of-war ships.

5579. Prize money awarded by the Navy was granted to the USS *Delaware*, commanded by Captain Stephen Decatur, Sr., which captured the French schooner *Croyable* in June 1798 off the Delaware Capes during the undeclared naval war with France (1798–1801). By act of Congress on June 28, 1798, cases involving captured ships were tried in federal district courts. The act provided that after the condemnation of a captured ship, the part accruing to the United States was to be paid into the public treasury, and the amount due the officers and crews was to be distributed among them in the proportions which the president should direct. Prize money had been awarded as early as the Revolution to men on the vessels of the Continental and state navies and privateers.

5580. Shipbuilding law enacted by Congress was the shipbuilding act of February 25, 1799, which authorized the president to direct a sum "not exceeding $200,000 to be laid out in the purchase of growing or other timber, or of lands on which timber was growing, suitable for the navy." On December 19, 1799, a tract of 350 acres on Grover's Island, GA, was purchased for $7,500.

5581. Standardization of nomenclature for naval vessels was mandated by a congressional resolution passed on March 3, 1819, which provided that "the Secretary of the Navy shall name ships of the first class for states, of the second class for rivers, and of the third class for cities and towns."

5582. Navy contract for armor plate was awarded to the Bethlehem Iron Company, South Bethlehem, PA, on June 1, 1887. A total of 6,700 tons was ordered at $536 a ton for the battleships *Maine* and *Texas* and the monitors *Puritan*, *Amphitrite*, *Monadnock*, and *Terror*.

5583. Naval militia established by a state was the Massachusetts Naval Battalion, organized under executive order of March 18, 1890, authorizing the formation of four companies. The companies were formed on March 25, 1890, with Thomas A. DeBlois, William M. Paul, William M. Wood, and John W. Weeks, all of Boston, commanding companies A, B, C, and D, respectively. On May 7, 1890, John Codman Soley, a graduate of the U.S. Naval Academy, was commissioned lieutenant commander of the naval battalion.

5584. Naval radio station was established in 1903 at the Highlands, Navesink, NJ. Chief Radioman Jack Scanlin was in charge.

5585. Navy task force assembled for foreign service was Task Force 19, consisting of 25 ships commanded by Rear Admiral David McDougal Le Breton. Formed at Argentina, it sailed on July 1, 1941. It included the battleships *Arkansas* and *New York*, the light cruisers *Brooklyn* and *Nashville*, and destroyers.

5586. Naval patrol bomber launched like a ship was the *Mars*, a 140,000-pound XPB2M-1 made by the Glenn L. Martin Company and launched on November 8, 1941, at Baltimore, MD. The keel was laid August 22, 1940. The bomber had a 200-foot wingspan and four engines of 2,000 horsepower each. It was the first flying boat accorded Navy keel-laying and launching ceremonies.

5587. Navy personnel in the regular Navy who were women took their oaths of office on July 7, 1948, in Washington, DC. They were Frances Teresa Devaney, Ruth Flora, Kay Louise Langdon, Wilma Juanita Marchal, Doris Roberta Robertson, and Edna Earle Young, all of whom were transferred from the Naval Reserve.

5588. Navy task force to fight undersea craft was Task Force Alfa, which consisted of an aircraft carrier with a group of antisubmarine aircraft, a helicopter squadron, destroyers, shore-based patrol planes, and submarines. The task force was created on March 24, 1958, under the command of Rear Admiral John Smith Thach and placed in operation in April 1958.

5589. Navy nuclear submarine division was Atomic Submarine Division 102, formed on March 31, 1958, at New London, CT, under command of Commander Robert Glennwood Black. The division consisted of the atomic submarines *Nautilus*, *Sea Wolf*, and *Skate*, and the conventional submarines *Hardhead*, *Bang*, and *Half-break*.

5590. Navy SEAL units were formed on January 1, 1962, to conduct commando operations in Vietnam. Personnel for the two teams were recruited from the Navy's Underwater Demolition Teams, which had been operating since World War II. SEAL is an acronym for "sea, air, and land."

5591. Navy divers to submerge for 10 days were Lieutenant Commander Robert E. Thompson of the Medical Corps, Gunners Mate First Class Lester E. Anderson, Chief Quartermaster Robert A. Barth, and Chief Hospital Corpsman Sanders W. Manning, who descended in *Sealab 1* to a depth of 192 feet, 30 miles off Hamilton, Bermuda, on July 22, 1964. *Sealab 1* was a 40-foot compartment nine feet in diameter. The divers breathed air that was a mixture of 80 percent helium, 4 percent oxygen, and 16 percent nitrogen at 86 pounds of pressure. They surfaced on July 31, 1964.

5592. Navy nuclear task force to circumnavigate the globe without refueling or other logistic support was Task Force One, consisting of the attack carrier USS *Enterprise*, the guided missile cruiser USS *Long Beach*, and the guided missile frigate USS *Bainbridge*. The task force left Norfolk, VA, on July 31, 1964, and returned on October 3, completing Operation Sea Orbit, a 30,000-knot trip that included 18 cities in 10 countries by way of the Cape of Good Hope and Cape Horn. The crew of 6,000 men was under the command of Rear Admiral Bernard Max Strean.

5593. Sailors assigned to regular Navy shipboard duty who were women were Ensign Rosemary Elaine Nelson, assistant supply officer, and Lieutenant (j.g.) Ann Kerr, personnel officer, who were respectively assigned on August 11 and October 25, 1972, to the hospital ship USS *Sanctuary*.

Officers

5594. Commander-in-chief of the Continental Navy was Esek Hopkins of Rhode Island, who served from December 22, 1775, to January 2, 1778.

5595. Navy officer commissioned was Captain Hopley Yeaton of New Hampshire, appointed on March 21, 1791, by George Washington to command "a cutter in the service of the United States of America." He was assigned to the *Scammel*, built at Portsmouth, NH.

5596. Commodore in the Navy was John Barry, senior officer in the Navy, who was appointed in 1794 after the Navy was reorganized.

5597. Navy officer to abolish corporal punishment on his ship was Uriah Phillips Levy, the son of a prominent Sephardic Jewish family of Philadelphia, PA. He joined the service as a sailing master on October 21, 1812, during the War of 1812. As captain of the USS *Vandalia*, he proved that it was possible to maintain discipline on a ship without flogging. He captured 21 British merchant ships before being taken prisoner and continued his naval career when the war ended. In 1860, after becoming the nation's first Jewish commodore, he persuaded the Navy to abolish corporal punishment throughout the service.

5598. Navy officer to become an engineer was Charles Haynes Haswell. He was commissioned on February 19, 1836, by Secretary of the Navy Mahlon Dickerson, and was appointed to design steam-power equipment. He was made chief engineer on July 12, 1836, and engineer-in-chief on October 3, 1844.

5599. Navy officer condemned for mutiny was Midshipman Philip Spencer, son of the Secretary of War, who was hanged on December 1, 1842, from the yardarm of the USS *Somers*, a brig of war, while at sea in West Indian waters. Boatswain Samuel Cromwell and Seaman Elisha Small were hanged at the same time. They were convicted, at a court-martial held on shipboard, of conspiring to organize a mutiny, murder the officers, and turn the ship into a pirate cruiser. The commander of the *Somers* was Alexander Slidell Mackenzie, who was exonerated by a court of inquiry.

5600. Judge advocate of the Navy was William Eaton Chandler of New Hampshire, who on March 6, 1865, was appointed by President Abraham Lincoln to be solicitor and naval judge advocate general under act of March 2, 1865. His salary was $3,500 a year.

5601. Navy officer to become an admiral was David Glasgow Farragut, who received his appointment on July 25, 1866. On July 16, 1862, Farragut had been given the rank of rear admiral, with rank comparable to that of major general in the Army, at a compensation of $5,000 a year at sea, $4,000 on shore duty and leave of absence, or $3,000 awaiting orders. On December 13, 1864, he had received the title of vice admiral, for which the pay was $7,000 at sea, $6,000 on shore duty, and $5,000 when awaiting orders. On July 25, 1866, the Navy was authorized by Congress to have 10 rear admirals, a vice admiral, and an admiral.

5602. Naval attaché was Lieutenant Commander French Ensor Chadwick. He was sent to London on November 15, 1882, and remained there until April 3, 1889.

5603. Admiral of the Navy was Admiral George Dewey, who served from March 3, 1899, until his death on January 16, 1917. The rank was conferred by act of Congress, passed on March 2, 1899.

5604. Navy admiral who was Jewish was Rear Admiral Adolph Marix, who was advanced to the rank of rear admiral on July 4, 1908. He had entered the service as a midshipman on September 26, 1864.

5605. Navy petty officer who was a woman was Loretta Walsh, age 18, of Philadelphia, PA, who was sworn in as chief yeoman on March 21, 1917. She assumed office on March 22, 1917, and was in charge of recruiting for the Naval Coast Defense Reserve.

5606. Navy officer commissioned in the U.S. Naval Reserve who was a woman was Mildred Helen McAfee, who was appointed lieutenant commander on August 3, 1942, to serve as director of the Women's Reserve, U.S. Naval Reserve. Members of this unit were nicknamed WAVES (Women Accepted for Volunteer Emergency Service). On November 13, 1943, McAfee became the first woman in the Navy to hold the rank of captain as a line officer.

5607. Navy admirals to wear the five-star insignia as Admirals of the Fleet were Ernest Joseph King, William Daniel Leahy, and Chester William Nimitz, whose appointments were ratified on December 15, 1944, by the Senate. The grade of fleet admiral of the Navy was established by act of Congress on December 14, 1944.

5608. Navy commissioned officer who was African-American was Ensign John W. Lee of Indianapolis, IN, who was commissioned on March 15, 1947, and assigned to the USS *Kearsarge*. The first African-American commissioned officer in the Naval Reserve was Bernard Whitfield Robinson, a medical student at Harvard University, Cambridge, MA, who was commissioned ensign on June 18, 1942.

5609. Medical officer assigned to a naval vessel who was a woman was Lieutenant Commander Bernice Rosenthal Walters of New York, an officer in the Medical Corps, Naval Reserve, who was assigned on March 8, 1950, to the Hospital Ship USS *Consolation* and reported for duty on July 13, 1950. She had served during World War II at the Naval Shipyards in Boston, MA; the Naval Air Station in Weymouth, MA; and the Naval Hospital in Bainbridge, MD.

5610. Navy chairman of the Joint Chiefs of Staff was Admiral Arthur William Radford, who served from August 15, 1953, to August 15, 1957.

5611. Commander of a combat ship who was African-American was Lieutenant Commander Samuel Lee Gravely, Jr., of Richmond, VA, who on January 31, 1961, assumed command of the destroyer escort USS *Falgout*, one of the vessels of Escort Squadron 5 on duty with the barrier Pacific force. The ship had a crew of 150 and 13 officers.

5612. Navy captain who was African-American was Thomas David Parham, Jr., of Newport News, VA, a Presbyterian chaplain, whose rank was raised from commander to captain on February 1, 1966.

5613. Navy admiral who was African-American was Samuel Lee Gravely, Jr., of Richmond, VA, whose date of rank was July 1, 1972.

5614. Navy officer who was a woman to hold a major command was Captain Robin Lindsay Quigley, who assumed command on May 17, 1973, of the Navy Service School, San Diego, CA, supervising 30,000 students.

5615. Navy officer who was a woman to command a ship at sea was Lieutenant Commander Darlene Iskra, who took command of the USS *Opportune* in 1991.

5616. Sailor to become a four-star admiral was Jeremy M. "Mike" Boorda, the only man in the Navy's history to rise from the lowest rank of sailor to the highest rank of admiral. Boorda, who enlisted in the Navy in 1956, became chief of naval operations in April 1994.

5617. Executive officer of a man-of-war who was a woman was Lieutenant Commander Claire V. Bloom, who served as the executive officer of the frigate USS *Constitution*, the flagship of the Navy, during its 200th-anniversary voyage that began on July 21, 1997, in Marblehead, MA.

Veterans

5618. Military pension awarded to a disabled soldier who was a woman was awarded to Margaret Cochran Corbin of Pennsylvania. During the Revolutionary War, she volunteered to serve as a nurse in the First Company of Pennsylvania Artillery, the regiment of her husband, John Corbin. The Corbins manned a cannon together on November 16, 1776, during the regiment's doomed defense of Fort Washington. Margaret continued to fire after John was killed, and received grapeshot wounds to her jaw, chest, and shoulder that cost her the use of her left arm. The Supreme Council of Pennsylvania awarded her a military pension of $30 in July 1779, and the Continental Congress approved a lifetime pension amounting to half the disability pay of a regular soldier. Corbin died in 1800 and was buried at the U.S. Military Academy Cemetery at West Point.

5619. Revolutionary War national veterans' organization was the Society of the Cincinnati, founded on May 13, 1783, at the Verplanck house, near Fishkill, NY. The first general meeting was held on May 7, 1784, in Philadelphia. Membership was limited to officers who had served three years in the Continental army or who had been honorably discharged for disability. George Washington was elected the first president general in 1783; he remained in office until his death and was succeeded by Major General Alexander Hamilton. The first state branches were established in New York and Massachusetts on June 9, 1783. The French branch was organized on January 7, 1784, in Paris. The name was derived from Lucius Quinctius Cincinnatus, the distinguished Roman who, called from the plow, "left all to save the republic."

5620. Widower of a veteran of the armed services to receive a pension was Benjamin Gannett of Sharon, MA, the widower of Deborah Bradford Sampson (or Samson) Gannett, who had served in the Revolutionary War under the name Robert Shurtliff (or Shurtleff). She died on April 29, 1827. On March 4, 1831, he received the first installment of a lifetime government pension of $80 a year. He died in January 1837. Her son and two daughters received a final payment of $466.66 following a special act of Congress dated July 7, 1838.

5621. Soldiers' homes established by Congress for disabled veterans were authorized by act of Congress of March 21, 1866, an "act to incorporate a national military and naval asylum for the relief of the totally disabled officers and men of the volunteer forces of the United States." The first homes, which began operating in 1867, were the Eastern Home, Togus, ME; the Central Home, Dayton, OH; and the Northwestern Home, Milwaukee, WI. The first female resident of such a home was Private First Class Regina C. Jones of the Women's Army Corps, who was admitted to the Soldiers' and Airmen's Home, Washington, DC, on September 2, 1955.

5622. Grand Army of the Republic post for veterans of the Civil War was established in Decatur, IL, on April 6, 1866. The organization was founded principally through the efforts of Dr. Benjamin Franklin Stephenson, surgeon, and the Reverend William J. Rutledge, chaplain, both of the 14th Illinois Infantry. The first state convention was held on July 12, 1866, in Springfield, IL. Stephen Augustus Hurlbut was elected the first national commander in chief.

5623. Veterans of Foreign Wars of the United States meeting took place on August 18–20, 1913, in Denver, CO, where the organization was founded. It was composed of Army,

Navy, and Marine Corps veterans who served in time of war in theaters of operation. Rice W. Means was the first commander in chief. The VFW was an amalgamation of three separate groups: the American Veterans of Foreign Service, organized in September 1899; the Army of the Philippines, organized in December 1899; and the American Veterans of Foreign Service, organized on September 10–12, 1903, which was itself a combination of the Philippine War Veterans, organized in October 1901, and the American Veterans of the Philippines and China Wars, organized in July 1902.

5624. American Legion convention of veterans of World War I was held in Minneapolis, MN, on November 10–12, 1919. The group had been organized in Paris on February 15–16, 1919. It was incorporated by act of Congress of September 16, 1919, "to uphold and defend the Constitution of the United States; to maintain law and order; to foster and perpetuate one hundred per cent Americanism; to preserve our memories of incidents in the Great War; to inculcate a sense of individual obligation to the community, state and nation; to safeguard and transmit to posterity the principles of justice, freedom and democracy; to consecrate and sanctify our comradeship by our devotion to mutual helpfulness."

5625. World War II veterans' society officially recognized by Congress was the American Veterans of World War II, which was founded on December 12, 1944, in Kansas City, MO, as an amalgamation of 11 groups with a membership of about 1,700. The first national commander was Elmo Woodrow Keel. The organization was chartered by Congress on July 23, 1947.

Wars: 16th Century

5626. Battle between Native Americans and European soldiers occurred in May 1539 in Clarke County, AL, when Hernando de Soto's Spanish forces killed several thousand Native Americans, members of a war party under Chief Tuscaloosa, in nine hours of fighting at the Battle of Mauvilla. The Spanish loss was 70 killed and 900 wounded, including de Soto.

Library of Congress, Prints & Photographs Division, LC-USZ62-5312

The burial of de Soto.

5627. Colonial warfare between European powers in America took place in 1565 between Spain and France. Pedro Menéndez de Avilés and 400 Spaniards arrived on the northeastern coast of Florida from Cadiz, Spain, on August 28, 1565, and proceeded overland to the St. Johns River, where they surprised and captured the French Huguenot settlement at Fort Caroline (near the present site of Jacksonville) on September 20. The French, commanded by René Goulaine de Laudonnière, lost 140 men in the attack. The Spanish lost none.

5628. Truce violation occurred on September 20, 1565, when Pedro Menéndez de Avilés, the Spanish navigator, captured the French Huguenot colony at Fort Caroline, near present-day Jacksonville, FL. The French surrendered under the terms of a truce that guaranteed them amnesty, but Menéndez hanged them, putting a sign over the bodies that read: "I do this not to Frenchmen but to Lutherans." In 1568, the fort was recaptured by a Huguenot corsair, Dominique de Gourges, who took his revenge by killing all his prisoners. His sign read: "I do this not to Spaniards . . . but as to traitors, robbers, and murderers."

Wars: 17th Century

5629. Rebellion in the English colonies was attempted in 1607 at the colony in Jamestown, VA. George Kendall, one of the original first councilors appointed in England, "was put off from being of the Council, and committed to prison; for that it did manyfestly appear he did practize to sew discord between the President and Council." He was shot to death for mutiny.

5630. Battle between English colonists and Native Americans took place on May 27, 1607, when the English settlers of Jamestown, VA, repulsed an attack by 200 Native American warriors. It is recorded that the English leader, Captain Edward Maria Wingfield, "was shot clean through his beard."

5631. Naval expedition mounted by an English colony was undertaken in 1613 against a French settlement in Nova Scotia. It consisted of 11 vessels carrying a total of 14 light guns, and was commanded by Samuel Argall of Virginia. The expedition captured Mount Desert, St. Croix, and Port Royal, Nova Scotia.

5632. Colonial warfare between England and France in America occurred in 1613 at Mount Desert, ME, where Father Pierre Biard, superior of Saint Sauveur, had established a settlement of French Jesuits. The settlement was attacked by an English expedition under the command of Captain Samuel Argall. His aim was to suppress piracy and to defend England's claim to the country, which was based on explorations made by John and Sebastian Cabot in the 15th and 16th centuries. A brief description of the conflict records that an English "vessel and forty soldiers landed at a place called Mount Desert in Nova Scotia, near St. John's River, or Tweed, possessed by the French; they killed some French, took away their guns and dismantled the Fort."

5633. Military leader of the English settlers was Miles Standish, one of the Mayflower Pilgrims, who in 1621 was unanimously chosen military captain of the colony.

5634. Massacre of settlers by Native Americans took place at Jamestown, VA, on March 22, 1622, when 347 colonists out of a population of 1,240 were slain.

5635. Militia was established by the Court of Assistants of the Massachusetts Bay Colony, Boston, MA, which ordered on April 12, 1631, "that there shall be a watch of 4 kept [every] night att Dorchester and another of 4 att Waterton, the watches to begin att sunset."

5636. Naval battle between colonists took place on April 23, 1635, when *The Cockatrice*, a pinnace commanded by Lieutenant Ratcliff Warren, attacked two pinnaces commanded by Captain Thomas Cornwallis, the *St. Helen* and the *St. Margaret*, in the Little Pocomoke or Wicomoco River at St. Mary's, on the eastern shore of Maryland.

5637. Military organization established by a colony was the Ancient and Honorable Artillery Company, chartered in Boston, MA, on March 13, 1638. At the first elections, in June 1638, Captain Robert Keayne was elected commander; Daniel Haugh (Howe), lieutenant; and Joseph Weld, ensign.

5638. Rebellion by colonists against an English governor took place in Delaware against Governor Francis Lovelace and was led by Marcus Jacobson, "The Long Finne," who claimed to be the son of the Swedish general Hans Christoph Konigsmark. He was trapped and turned over to the English commandant. On December 20, 1669, he was condemned for insurrection in the first trial by jury in Delaware. He was lashed in public, branded with the letter *R*, and sold in chains as a slave in Barbados.

Wars: 18th Century

5639. Mass scalping of Native Americans by colonists took place on February 20, 1725. A posse of New Hampshire volunteers ran across a band of 10 sleeping Native Americans and scalped them all. The posse entered Dover in triumph with the 10 scalps stretched on hoops and elevated on poles. A bounty of £100 for each scalp was paid in Boston out of the public treasury. Individual scalps had been brought in earlier.

5640. Bloodshed in the French and Indian War occurred on May 28, 1754, on an isolated mountainside a few miles east of Uniontown, PA. Lieutenant Colonel George Washington, at the head of several companies of Virginia militia, reached the Monongahela River and overtook a French reconnoitering party from Fort Duquesne (the future site of Pittsburgh). Jumonville, the French commander, was slain and his force captured.

5641. Battle in the French and Indian War took place on the Great Meadows in southwestern Pennsylvania, near the present site of Uniontown, where Lieutenant Colonel George Washington, commanding 400 Virginia and South Carolina provincial troops, had built a small entrenchment known as Fort Necessity. On July 3, 1754, the fort was attacked by the French commander Coulon de Villiers and his army of 1,600 French regulars, French Canadian militia, and Native Americans. Washington surrendered on July 4.

5642. Attack on British soldiers by civilians in the Revolution was made in New York City on January 18, 1770, by the Sons of Liberty, a crowd of Americans who attacked a group of 40 to 50 soldiers because they had cut down the liberty poles that the Americans had erected. The soldiers used their bayonets and dispersed them. No one was killed, but several persons on both sides were seriously injured. The mob fight has been termed the Battle of Golden Hill.

5643. Child to be killed in the Revolution was Christopher Snider, an 11-year-old boy who was killed on February 22, 1770, in Boston, MA. A man named Theophilus Lille had violated the merchants' agreement against importing and his house had been marked as a punishment. These marks were removed by another man, Ebenezer Richardson. A mob gathered to attack Richardson's house and Richardson fired into it, killing the boy and wounding another person. Shops and schools were closed on the day of the funeral. Richardson was convicted of murder and sentenced to two years in prison.

5644. Americans killed by British soldiers in the Revolution were shot on March 5, 1770, at Boston, MA, when British soldiers of the 29th Regiment of Foot fired at a taunting crowd, killing Crispus Attucks, James Caldwell, Patrick Carr, Samuel Gray, and Samuel Maverick. The incident became known as the Boston Massacre. The soldiers were tried for murder and were defended by John Adams and Josiah Quincy, Jr. Two soldiers were found guilty, branded on the hand, and discharged. Six other soldiers and an officer were acquitted.

5645. Naval attack in the Revolutionary War was made on June 9, 1772, against the British revenue cutter *Gaspee*, commanded by Lieutenant William Duddingston, which ran aground while chasing the packet *Hanna* off Namquit Point, Providence, RI, in Narragansett Bay. During the night, merchant John Brown and a number of others rowed out in eight longboats captained by Abraham Whipple, boarded the *Gaspee*, and set it on fire.

5646. Shot fired by an American combatant to wound a British combatant in the conflict over independence was the musket shot fired on June 9, 1772, by Joseph Bucklin V, which wounded Lieutenant William Dudingston of the British Navy. Dudingston was commander of the cutter Gaspee, which ran aground off Namquit Point near Providence, RI, in Narragansett Bay, while chasing the packet Hannah. During the night, merchant John Brown and a number of others rowed out to the Gaspee in eight longboats captained by Abraham Whipple. As Dudingston stood on deck, refusing Whipple's order to surrender, Bucklin shot him. The Americans then boarded the ship and set it on fire.

5647. Military organization formed to oppose the British was the Light Horse of the City of Philadelphia, PA, organized on November 17, 1774, by 28 gentlemen, three of whom were members of the Committee of Correspondence of the first Congress of America, to resist the aggressions of the British crown.

5648. Ground attack in the Revolutionary War occurred on December 13, 1774, when Major John Sullivan of the Granite State Volunteers, later a major general in the Continental Army, and 400 patriots attacked Fort William and Mary at New Castle, NH, in Portsmouth harbor. They bound the commander of the fort and frightened the soldiers away, capturing 100 casks of powder and small arms. This attack took place some four months before the battle of Lexington.

5649. Battle in the Revolutionary War was the Battle of Lexington, a skirmish at Lexington, MA, on April 19, 1775, between 70 Minutemen volunteers under Captain John Parker and about 700 British Regulars under Major John Pitcairn, who were on their way to destroy illegal military stores at nearby Concord. The Americans were ordered to disperse.

As they were doing so, one of them fired a shot. The British returned fire, killing 8 Minutemen and wounding 10.

5650. American capture of a British fort in the Revolutionary War occurred on May 10, 1775, when Ethan Allen and 83 men who called themselves the Green Mountain Boys crossed Lake Champlain from Vermont in scows, entered Fort Ticonderoga, NY, through the south gate, and swarmed into the barracks while the soldiers were asleep. Allen demanded the surrender of the fort "in the name of the Great Jehovah and the Continental Congress." The fort, commanded by Captain William Delaplace and Lieutenant Jocelyn Feltham, was captured with 78 guns, 6 mortars, 3 howitzers, thousands of cannon balls, 30,000 flints, and other supplies.

5651. Naval battle in the Revolutionary War took place on June 12, 1775, when Captain James Moore of the British schooner *Margaretta* arrived in the harbor of Machias, ME, and ordered the inhabitants to take down a liberty pole they had erected. The townspeople, led by Jeremiah and John O'Brien, set out in a confiscated sloop, the *Unity*, and in a hand-to-hand encounter captured the *Margaretta* and confiscated her cannons. The captured crew was marched overland to Cambridge, MA, where they were turned over to General George Washington. The American loss was four killed and eight wounded.

5652. Volunteer detachment in the Revolutionary War to arrive in Cambridge, MA, to fight the British was the Reading Riflemen of Reading, PA, which arrived on July 18, 1775. The Riflemen of York, PA, arrived on July 25.

5653. Warship to receive definite orders to attack the enemy was the 78-ton schooner *Hannah*, commanded by Captain Nicholson Broughton of Marblehead, MA. His order was dated September 2, 1775. The crew consisted of a detachment of soldiers from the Essex County Regiment of Marblehead. They sailed on September 5, 1775, from Beverly, MA, and on September 6 they captured the 260-ton British ship *Unity* en route from Portsmouth to Boston.

5654. American woman to be killed in action on the battlefield was Jemima Warner, whose husband was a member of a rifle battalion from Cumberland, PA, during the Revolutionary War. In 1775, she accompanied her husband as he marched with his unit as part of Benedict Arnold's invasion of Canada. He died on the way, but she remained with the battalion, and delivered the army's surrender demand to the British inside the fortress of Quebec. She was killed by British fire on December 11, 1775.

5655. American prisoners of war were thousands of seamen and other Americans, including women and children, who were captured by the British during the Revolution and incarcerated in prison ships at Wallabout Bay, near the future site of the Brooklyn Navy Yard, beginning in late 1776. There were hundreds of these floating prisons, each holding more than 1,000 inmates in airless holds under terrible conditions. Some 11,500 people are estimated to have died aboard them. They were buried in mass graves on the Brooklyn shore. A monument to their memory was raised in Brooklyn by the Tammany Society of New York after the war. The current monument, the Prison Ship Martyrs Memorial, in nearby Fort Greene Park, was dedicated in 1908.

5656. Marine engagement in battle took place on March 4, 1776, during the Revolutionary War, when Captain Samuel Nicholas and approximately 200 marines captured Fort Nassau in the Bahamas. Nicholas was assisted by 50 sailors under Lieutenant Thomas Weaver of the *Cabot*. The assault was a surprise attack and the fort surrendered without conflict. The Americans captured large military stores, including about 100 cannon, 15 mortars, 5,400 shells, and 11,000 rounds of ammunition, and brought them back to New London, CT, on April 8. This naval expedition, which left the Delaware Capes on February 17, 1776, was under the command of Esek Hopkins of the *Alfred*.

5657. Capture of an enemy warship by a commissioned American naval officer took place on April 17, 1776, when the brig *Lexington* under Captain John Barry met the British warship *Edward* off the Virginia coast, captured it, and conveyed it to Philadelphia, PA. The *Lexington* had been purchased by the federal government in February 1776.

5658. Jewish soldier killed in the Revolutionary War was Francis Salvador, known as the Southern Paul Revere for having warned of the approach of the British fleet at Charleston, SC. On August 1, 1776, while he was leading the militia under the command of

Major Andrew Wilkinson, his group was ambushed by Native Americans and loyalists near Esseneka (Seneca). Salvador was shot through the body and the left leg and was scalped by a group of Cherokees who sided with the British.

5659. Military intelligence unit and special forces unit was called Knowlton's Rangers, after its first leader, Lieutenant Colonel Thomas Knowlton of Ashford, CT. Knowlton, a veteran of the Battle of Bunker Hill, was asked on August 12, 1776, to form a reconnaissance squad that would report to General George Washington. The group had 130 picked members. Knowlton was killed in combat a month later, just a few days before the execution of Nathan Hale, a Ranger who was caught spying.

5660. Land grant to deserters from the British Army during the Revolutionary War was authorized by the act of the Continental Congress of August 14, 1776. The act offered American citizenship to British and Hessian deserters from the British Army and gave each deserter or his heirs 50 acres of unappropriated land in certain states. On August 27, 1776, a similar act was passed to encourage officers in the British forces to desert.

5661. Major battle lost by American forces was the Battle of Long Island, fought on August 27, 1776, between soldiers under British general Lord William Howe, commander in chief of the British Army in North America, and the Continental Army under George Washington. The American forces, outnumbered two to one, were outflanked by Howe, who took 1,200 American prisoners and inflicted about 400 casualties. However, rather than pursue a complete victory, Howe elected to lay siege, allowing Washington and his remaining men to escape to Manhattan under cover of fog.

5662. American executed as a spy was Nathan Hale, a young schoolteacher from Connecticut. Hale joined the Connecticut militia in July 1775 and was promoted to captain under Thomas Knowlton's Rangers. Volunteering in August 1776 to observe British troop movements on Long Island, he crossed the British lines posing as a Dutch schoolteacher. On September 21, as he made his way back to the American position at Harlem Heights, he was betrayed and captured. Hale was hanged the next morning without a trial

Library of Congress, Prints & Photographs Division
LC-USZ62-3754

The execution of Nathan Hale.

by order of General William Howe, the British commander. His famous last words—"I only regret that I have but one life to lose for my country"—were adapted from "Cato, a play by Joseph Addison."

5663. American soldier to commit treason was William Demont (or Dement), a member of the 5th Pennsylvania Battalion, who was appointed adjutant in Colonel Robert Magraw's battalion on February 29, 1776. He deserted on November 2, 1776, and notified the British of the position of Fort Washington (now a neighborhood in New York City). Demont's act enabled the British general Sir William Howe to conquer the fort with a force of 8,900 men on November 16, 1776. They captured 2,818 American officers and men, 43 guns, and 2,800 muskets.

5664. Capture of an enemy ship in enemy waters was accomplished by the 16-gun brig *Reprisal*, which sailed for France on December 4, 1776, under the command of Captain Lambert Wickes. One of the passengers was Benjamin Franklin, who was traveling incognito to Auray, France, to obtain French assistance. On the way over, the *Reprisal* captured two British vessels. It captured two others in the Bay of Biscay, one of which was the King's packet plying between Falmouth and Lisbon. This was the first time an American warship entered enemy waters and the first attempt to block and destroy British commerce at the source.

5665. Army chaplain killed in action was John Rosbrugh of Allen Township, PA, who served as chaplain of Northampton County. He was commissioned on December 26, 1776, and was killed at the battle of Assunpink, or the Second Battle of Trenton, on January 2, 1777. He was bayoneted by Hessian troops.

5666. Government expert on codes and ciphers was James Lovell of Boston, MA, who was appointed to the Committee for Foreign Affairs by the Continental Congress in May 1777. The committee was in charge of gathering intelligence. Lovell created elaborate ciphers to be used by the Americans who were running the Continental government and armed forces, some so complicated that even Benjamin Franklin found them annoying. Lovell was also an expert cryptanalyst who broke the ciphers used by the British.

5667. Warship captured overseas was the *Lexington*, which had made the first American capture of an enemy warship in April 1776. The ship was 86 feet long and 24 feet 6 inches wide, and carried a 16 guns and a complement of 110. On September 20, 1777, the ship was becalmed in the English Channel. Captain Henry Johnson, who was out of ammunition, surrendered the ship to the British cutter H.M.S. *Alert*, commanded by Lieutenant John Bazely.

5668. Major American victory in the Revolutionary War occurred at the Battle of Saratoga, actually a series of battles fought in 1777 in upstate New York. The British general John Burgoyne was pushing down from Canada along the Hudson River with an army of 6,000 regulars and auxiliaries with the plan of cutting off New England from the rest of the colonies. Ranged against him was a smaller American force commanded by General Gates. After several failed British assaults, Burgoyne made a last attempt at a breakthrough at the Battle of Bemis Heights, also called the Second Battle of Freeman's Farm, fought on October 7, 1777. Gates's forces threw back the British, killing some 700 men, about four times the American losses. On October 17, 1777, Burgoyne and his remaining army surrendered to Gates at Saratoga. The victory, a turning point in the war, prevented the British from pursuing a divide-and-conquer strategy and encouraged the French to offer aid to the new nation."

5669. American naval victory in British waters during the Revolutionary War took place on April 24, 1778. John Paul Jones, in command of the Continental Navy's 18-gun sloop Ranger out of Portsmouth, NH, defeated a 20-gun British sloop, HMS Drake, in the Irish Sea off Carrickfergus, Ireland. There were 40 British dead, including the captain of the Drake, George Burdon, and two Americans. Jones took the Drake to France as a prize of war.

5670. Blockade of enemy ships that was effective was completed on April 30, 1778, stretching from West Point, NY, to Constitution Island, NY. A huge chain was forged at the Sterling Iron Works in Orange County, NY, from ore mined in the same county and was carried in sections to West Point, where it was joined and stretched across the Hudson River to prevent British ships from passing. The chain weighed 180 tons and was 1,700 feet long; each link was 2.5 inches wide and 30 inches long. It was placed in position on April 16 and on April 30 was secured at both ends. Earlier in the war, in the summer of 1776, a chain of chevaux-de-frise and sunken ships had been extended between Fort Washington,

Library of Congress, Prints & Photographs Division
LC-USZ62-3615

Horatio Gates, a general of the American forces.

NY, and Fort Lee, NJ, to serve as a blockade, but the British passed it on October 9, 1776, without firing a gun.

5671. Revolutionary War conflict in which American and British troops met on equal terms was the Battle of Monmouth Courthouse, Freehold, NJ, on June 28, 1778. The Americans under General George Washington lost 69 killed and 160 wounded; the British under Sir Henry Clinton lost 300 killed and 100 wounded or captured.

5672. Revolutionary War bayonet charge occurred on July 16, 1779, when General Anthony Wayne, known as "Mad Anthony," charged the British garrison at Stony Point, NY, with 1,200 men and forced it to surrender. He was slightly wounded. The British loss was 63 killed and 553 wounded; the American loss, 15 killed and 83 wounded.

5673. Naval hero was John Paul Jones, the Scottish-born captain who led a series of spectacular actions against the British during the Revolutionary War. The most famous took place on September 23, 1779, when Jones, commanding the "Bonhomme Richard" at the head of a four-ship squadron, captured the warship "Serapis" and its convoy of merchant vessels in a three-hour battle off the coast of Britain. He won the victory despite long odds, and his retort to the enemy's call for his surrender—"I have not yet begun to fight"—was made part of American folklore. He was decorated by the United States and the king of France, became a rear admiral in the Russian Navy after political infighting put an end to his American career, and died in obscurity in Paris.

5674. American imprisoned in the Tower of London as an enemy agent was Henry Laurens of Charlestown, SC, president of the Continental Congress from 1777 to 1778. On August 13, 1780, Laurens sailed from Philadelphia, PA, on the brigantine *Mercury* en route to Holland, where he was to negotiate a loan and treaty. Three weeks later, he was captured by the British off Newfoundland. He threw his papers overboard, but they were recovered and led to the British declaration of war against Holland. From October 6, 1780, to December 31, 1781, he was imprisoned in the Tower on suspicion of high treason, and was forced to pay for his room, board, and guard. He was released in exchange for the British army leader Lord Cornwallis, who had surrendered to General George Washington at Yorktown, VA. Laurens, with Benjamin Franklin and John Jay, drew up the preliminary treaty of peace with Great Britain on November 30, 1782, to terminate the Revolutionary War.

5675. Rebellion against the federal government took place in Massachusetts in 1786, when Daniel Shays of Pelham, MA, organized a group of malcontents into an armed force that overthrew courts and committed other acts of violence. They were protesting the depreciation of paper money, the insistence of creditors on being paid in silver money, and the imprisonment of debtors. On December 5, 1786, the rebels seized Worcester. By February 1787, however, they were completely routed.

5676. Battle fought by federal troops after the formation of the Union was the Miami Expedition. On October 19, 1790, Colonel John Hardin, under Brigadier General Josiah Harmar, led 400 troops against 150 Native Americans in the Great Lakes region northwest of Ohio, but because of poor leadership, insufficient training, and unworkable guns, the attack ended in a retreat.

5677. Arsenal of the federal government was the Springfield Armory, Springfield, MA, founded in April 1778 as a laboratory for the preparation of all kinds of ammunition and established on April 2, 1794, as a national armory for the manufacture of small arms. The first superintendent was David Ames and the master armorer was Robert Orr. It took a month to complete the first 20 muskets. Two hundred and forty-five muskets were made the first year.

Wars: 19th Century

5678. War fought by the United States against a foreign power was the Tripolitan War, also called the Barbary War. The Pasha of Tripoli (the future Libya), one of four Islamic states on the North African coast of the Mediterranean, declared war on the United States on May 14, 1801, after President Thomas Jefferson refused to continue paying him extortionate sums to protect American shipping from his own pirate fleets. Following an American military campaign that included a naval blockade, artillery bombardment, and a land attack, the Pasha signed a treaty on June 4, 1805.

5679. Members of the U.S. armed forces to die in combat on an overseas mission were naval officer Richard Somers and his crew, who had been sent to Tripoli (modern Libya) as part of the U.S. campaign to free itself from state-sponsored terrorism against shipping in the Mediterranean. On September 4, 1804, Somers and 12 crew members sailed a "floating bomb" into the harbor of Tripoli in order to blow up the enemy fleet. All died when the ship exploded before reaching its destination.

5680. Naval ship to surrender in peacetime was the USS Chesapeake, on June 22, 1807. Sailing from Norfolk, VA, en route to the Mediterranean, the Chesapeake was stopped by a British ship, HMS Leopard, and ordered to give up four crew members who had deserted from the Royal Navy. Three of the four were American sailors who had been impressed, against their will, out of American ships. James Barron, captain of the Chesapeake, refused the order, but surrendered after his ship received seven broadsides from the Leopard's guns.

5681. Naval battle in the War of 1812 took place before war was declared, on May 16, 1811, in the Atlantic Ocean about 40 miles off Cape Cod, MA. The 18-gun British sloop *Little Belt* under Captain A.B. Bingham attacked the 44-gun American frigate *President* under Commodore John Rodgers, striking the mainmast and the foremast and wounding one man. The *President* returned fire, killing or wounding 20 of the crew of the *Little Belt.* The first naval battle after the United States declaration of war of June 18, 1812, took place in the Atlantic on June 23 between the *President* and the *Belvidera* under Captain Richard Byron. The *President* closed in for the telling shot, but one of its guns exploded, killing or wounding 22 men. The *Belvidera* escaped in the confusion.

5682. Naval action of importance in the War of 1812 took place in the Atlantic Ocean about 750 miles east of Boston, MA, on August 19, 1812, when the *Constitution*, commanded by Captain Isaac Hull, met the British 38-gun frigate *Guerrière*, commanded by Captain James Richard Dacres. The *Constitution*, built in Boston in 1797, was rated as a frigate of 1,576 tons, with an armament of 44 guns. Within a quarter of an hour the mizzenmast of the *Guerrière* had been shot away, and its spars, sails, and rigging torn to shreds. The American loss was 14 killed or wounded; the British, 79 killed or wounded. On March 3, 1813, Congress awarded $50,000 to Hull and the crew for the victory over the *Guerrière.*

5683. Prisoners captured in the War of 1812 were taken by Lieutenant William Learned Marcy, who captured a corps of Canadian militia at St. Regis, NY, on October 22–23, 1812.

5684. Capture of a British frigate in the War of 1812 was accomplished by the frigate *United States*, 44 guns, under Captain Stephen Decatur, which captured the *Macedonian*, 38 guns, under Captain John Surnam Garden, near the Madeira Islands, off the Moroccan coast, on October 25, 1812. The *Macedonian* sustained a loss of 36 killed and 68 wounded, of whom 53 later died of wounds. The *United States* suffered six killed and seven wounded. The captured *Macedonian* was taken into the harbor of New London, CT, on December 4, 1812, and was later brought to the East River, New York City.

5685. Defeat of a British naval squadron in the War of 1812 and in all of British history was the Battle of Lake Erie, which took place on September 10, 1813. The American naval officer Oliver Hazard Perry left Erie, PA, with a fleet of nine ships and encountered a squadron of six British warships off Put-in-Bay, OH. Perry's attack was hampered by his short-range guns, and his ship was battered to a hulk with only a handful of capable men left. He renewed the fight from a sister ship, the *Niagara*, and had the satisfaction of seeing the British strike their colors. His message of victory contained the famous phrase, "We have met the enemy and they are ours."

5686. War to receive daily newspaper coverage was the Mexican War of 1846-50. An express system of couriers traveling by horse, rail, and steam carried articles written by correspondents in the war zone to newspaper editors in distant cities. The system proved to be more effective than the army's own messenger service.

5687. War that began before a declaration of war was made by Congress started when American soldiers led by Zachary Taylor, acting under orders from President James K. Polk, entered a disputed area along the Rio

Grande River to construct a fort. On April 25, 1846, they were attacked by Mexican cavalrymen. Polk then appealed to Congress, which declared war on May 13.

5688. Unit of American deserters to join an enemy army was Los San Patricios, a group of Catholic immigrants, mostly from Ireland, who switched sides during the Mexican War. They fought as an artillery unit under John Riley at the Battle of Monterrey, September 21, 1846, and later as an infantry unit. Most died in battle or were captured and executed.

5689. War fought mostly on foreign soil was the Mexican War, which was fought almost entirely on Mexican territory. Some of that territory, including California, was ceded to the United States by the terms of the peace treaty that concluded the war on February 2, 1848.

5690. Act inaugurating the Civil War took place on January 9, 1861, when a detachment of Confederate forces at Morris Island, in Charleston Harbor, Charleston, SC, fired upon the *Star of the West*, a merchant steam vessel. The vessel had been chartered by the federal government to convey supplies and men to reinforce Major Robert Anderson at Fort Sumter, Charleston Harbor, although the announced destinations were Savannah, GA, and New Orleans, LA. It left New York harbor January 5, 1861, and was fired on within two miles of Forts Sumter and Moultrie. Its captain, John McGowan, retired from the scene after 17 shots had been fired at his ship. The first shot was fired by Cadet George E. Haynesworth of Sumter, SC, who was ordered to fire by Major P. F. Stevens.

5691. Confederate congressional session took place in Montgomery, AL, from February 4, 1861, to March 16, 1861. Its official title was Congress of the Confederate States. The president of the Senate was Alexander Hamilton Stephens of Georgia, the president pro tempore was Robert Mercer Taliaferro Hunter of Virginia, and the secretary of the Senate was James H. Nash of South Carolina. The House of Representatives under the permanent constitution met in Richmond, VA, on February 18, 1861. Emmet Dixon of Georgia was elected clerk and Thomas Salem Bocock of Virginia was elected speaker. The session adjourned on April 21, 1862.

5692. Confederate government bond was authorized by act of February 28, 1861, "to raise money for the support of the government and to provide for the defense of the Confederate States of America." The bond issue limit was $15 million.

5693. Civil War attack was made on Fort Sumter, SC. The first gun was fired on the morning of April 12, 1861, by Edmund Ruffin, a 67-year-old Virginian. There were no casualties.

5694. Naval skirmish in the Civil War took place on April 12, 1861, off Charleston, SC, when the Union side-wheeler *Harriet Lane* fired a shot across the bow of the merchantman steamer *Nashville* to force it to show its colors. The *Nashville* hoisted a U.S. ensign and was allowed to proceed, even though it was a Confederate ship. The *Harriet Lane*, 270 feet long with a 22-foot beam, had been built by William Henry Webb in 1857 as a Treasury Department revenue cutter and was transferred to the Navy in 1858. It was named after a niece of President James Buchanan and was the first federal steamer named for a woman. On January 1, 1863, the *Harriet Lane* was captured by Confederate forces in Galveston Bay after desperately resisting boarding parties from four rebel ships.

5695. Civil War call for volunteers was made by President Abraham Lincoln on April 15, 1861, the day after the surrender of Fort Sumter, SC. His call was for 75,000 volunteers. The first regiment to respond to the call was the Ringgold Light Artillery of Reading, PA, known as the First Defenders, commanded by Dr. John Keys. They reported to Governor Eli Slifer at Harrisburg, PA, on April 16. Their first engagement took place on September 24, 1861, at Hanging Rocks, WV. They and the other Pennsylvania regiments were the first state militias to arrive at Washington, DC.

5696. Civil War bloodshed occurred on April 19, 1861, near Baltimore, MD. When President Abraham Lincoln issued his proclamation on April 15, 1861, declaring a state of insurrection and calling for volunteers, Governor John Albion Andrew of Massachusetts sent five regiments of infantry, a battalion of riflemen, and a battery of artillery to Washington, DC. While they were passing through

Baltimore, a mob attacked them, killing 4 soldiers and injuring 20. Nine casualties were reported among the mob.

5697. Union soldier killed by enemy action in the Civil War was Bailey Thornsberry Brown, Company B, 2nd West Virginia Volunteer Infantry. On May 22, 1861, while engaged in obtaining recruits, he was shot by Confederate pickets at Fetterman, near Grafton, WV. He was given a military funeral and buried in a temporary cemetery on upper Maple Avenue in Fetterman. In 1900, Reno Post No. 7 of the Grand Army of the Republic, a veterans' organization, erected a shaft to Brown's memory on Pearl Street in Grafton, and in 1928 the Betsy Ross Tent Daughters of the Union Veterans erected a monument in Fetterman on the spot where Brown fell.

5698. Union officer killed in the Civil War was Ephraim Elmer Ellsworth of Chicago, IL. Ellsworth had studied law in the office of Abraham Lincoln and became his personal friend. He was also a military enthusiast who led the U.S. Zouave Cadets, an acclaimed drill performance team. In 1861, at the outbreak of the Civil War, he organized a regiment of New York City firefighters known as the New York Fire Zouaves. The group was ordered to secure Alexandria, VA, on May 24, 1861, following Virginia's secession from the Union. Ellsworth had just torn down a Confederate flag that was flying over a hotel building when he was shot in the chest by the hotel's owner, James W. Jackson. Jackson, in turn, was killed by Francis E. Brownell, one of the Zouaves. Ellsworth's body was given the honor of lying in state at the White House and at New York's City Hall, and his death prompted the formation of another regiment, the Ellsworth Avengers.

5699. Confederate cruiser to raid Union commerce was the *Sumter*, commanded by Captain Raphael Semmes. The *Sumter* was a merchantman that had been fitted out in 1861 at New Orleans, LA, with five small guns. Beginning in June 1861, the *Sumter* captured 18 vessels, of which 8 were burned.

5700. Confederate officer killed in the Civil War was Captain John Quincy Marr of Warrenton, VA, commander of the Warrenton Rifle Guards (designated Company K of the 17th Virginia Infantry Regiment), who was killed on June 1, 1861, in a skirmish at Fairfax Court House, VA. Marr was actually a lieutenant colonel, having been commissioned on May 2, 1861, but his letter of commission from Governor John Letcher had not been delivered to him.

5701. Land battle in the Civil War fought by organized troops took place at Philippi, VA (now West Virginia), on the night of June 3, 1861. Two groups of Union soldiers under Colonels Benjamin F. Kelley and Ebenezer Dumont converged on Philippi and forced out a Confederate occupation force under Colonel George A. Porterfield. Battlefield surgeons afterwards performed two amputations, the first of the Civil War.

5702. Civilian welfare effort for soldiers organized on a large scale was undertaken during the Civil War by the U.S. Sanitary Commission, a volunteer group begun by New York City women in April 1861 and accepted as a federal agency on June 18, 1861. The group had two main branches: a 21-member board of physicians who inspected military camps for proper drainage, ventilation, nutrition, and cleanliness, and a relief effort run by women that provided regiments and individual soldiers with equipment, extra food and clothing, medical supplies, blankets, and similar items.

5703. Union naval officer killed in the Civil War was Captain James Harmon Ward of the *Thomas Freeborn*, who landed at Mathias Point, VA, on the Potomac River about 50 miles south of Washington, DC, on June 27, 1861, with about 35 men and 250 sandbags to erect breastworks to unload a cannon. They were surprised by 1,500 infantrymen who attacked them and drove them off. Ward was hit in the breast by a Minié ball and died from an internal hemorrhage. He had been appointed on May 16, 1861, to command the Potomac flotilla.

5704. Confederate general killed in the Civil War was Robert Selden Garnett, a graduate of the United States Military Academy at West Point, who resigned from the Army on April 30, 1861, and was appointed a brigadier general of the Confederate States on June 6, 1861. He was killed July 13, 1861, at the battle of Carrick's Ford, VA (now near Parsons, WV).

5705. Major battle of the Civil War was the First Battle of Bull Run, fought on July 21, 1861, along a stream named Bull Run outside Manassas, VA, an important rail junction. About 37,000 Union soldiers led by General Irvin McDowell attempted to break through the 35,000-man Confederate line under the leadship of General P. G. T. Beauregard. Arrival of Confederate reinforcements forced the retirement of McDowell's troops, resulting in the first important Confederate victory of the war.

5706. African-American to enlist in the United States armed forces during the Civil War was probably James Stone, who enlisted on August 23, 1861, in the 1st Fight Artillery of Ohio. He had escaped from slavery in Kentucky. African-Americans were not allowed to enlist in the Army until the following year, but Stone, who had fair skin, was accepted as white. He died in 1862.

5707. Confederate forts to surrender in the Civil War were Fort Clark and Fort Hatteras on Hatteras Island, NC, guarding Pamlico Sound. They surrendered on August 29, 1861, to Flag Officer Silas H. Stringham and General Benjamin Franklin Butler, who had captured the garrison with 715 men, 31 heavy guns, and 1,000 stands of arms.

5708. Naval battle in the Civil War took place on September 14, 1861, at Pensacola, FL. Lieutenant John Henry Russell, leading a detachment of the crew of the USS *Colorado*, descended upon the Confederate navy yard at Pensacola at 2 A.M. They burned the five-gun steamer *Judah*, lying at anchor, and spiked the only gun in the yard. There were no Confederate casualties. Three of the Union troops were killed and four wounded.

5709. Union ship captured in the Civil War was the USS *Fanny*, an Army steam tug that grounded on a shoal on October 1, 1861, in Pamlico Sound, NC, while it was en route to Chicomacomica, the encampment of the 20th Indiana Regiment. The pilot and deckhand escaped by swimming ashore, but the ship was captured by Confederate naval forces. Also captured were the *Raleigh*, a small

Library of Congress, Prints & Photographs Division, LC-USZ62-8376

The first Battle of Bull Run, VA, Sunday afternoon, July 21, 1861.

iron-hull propeller-driven towing steamer; the *Junaluska*, a vessel of 79 tons; and the *Culew*, 260 tons.

5710. Regiment of free African-Americans organized during the Civil War was the Louisiana Native Guards, also known as the Corps d'Afrique, a group of men from New Orleans, LA, who fought for the Confederacy. The unit, consisting of 33 officers and 731 enlisted men, joined the Louisiana militia on November 23, 1861. The Confederate Army did not officially accept them, and they saw little action other than the defense of the city's French Quarter during the Union attack in April 1862. They subsequently decided to fight for the Union.

When the 1st Regiment of the Louisiana Native Guards was mustered into the Union Army on September 27, 1862, its members became the first African-American soldiers to be sworn into federal service during the Civil War.

5711. Navy chaplain killed in action was Chaplain John L. Lenhart, who was commissioned chaplain on February 27, 1847. At that time chaplains did not hold naval rank and were known simply as chaplains. On March 8, 1862, the Confederate ironclad *Merrimac* encountered the Union frigate *Cumberland* off Hampton Roads, VA. The *Merrimac* crushed the *Cumberland* by driving her iron prow through the side of the *Cumberland*, at the same time pouring in a fire of shells. Chaplain Lenhart died with his sinking ship.

5712. Naval battle between ironclad vessels in the Civil War was fought between the *Monitor* and the *Merrimac* at Hampton Roads, VA, on March 9, 1862. The *Monitor* was a 172-foot Union ship with a crew of 58 under the command of Lieutenant John Lorimer Worden, who was partially blinded by a shot while observing action and was superseded by Lieutenant S. Dana Greene. It had been designed by John Ericsson and had a revolving gun turret. The *Merrimac* was a 275-foot Confederate ship with a crew of 300 under the command of Captain Franklin Buchanan, who was wounded and superseded by Lieutenant Catesby ap Roger Jones. It was a scuttled Union steam frigate that had been

Library of Congress, Prints & Photographs Division
LC-USZ62-294

Battle between the Monitor *and* Merrimac *at Hampton Roads, near Norfolk, VA.*

salvaged and armored by the Confederates and renamed the *Virginia*. The battle ended with the sinking of the *Merrimac*.

5713. Confederate ship surrendered to the Union was the *Planter*, a 313-ton side-wheel steamer serving as an armed dispatch boat. It was surrendered on May 12, 1862, off the harbor in Charleston, SC, by Robert Smalls, an African-American slave who was its pilot. He and the African-American crew took charge of the ship while the captain was ashore. Flying the Confederate flag, they saluted the forts on their voyage northward. When out of reach of ammunition, Smalls hoisted a white flag of truce and turned over the ship to the USS *Onward*. In appreciation, a special act of Congress was passed on May 30, 1862, awarding Smalls and his partners one-half the value of the *Planter* and its cargo.

5714. Army field telegraph used in warfare was employed on May 24, 1862, in the Peninsula campaign during the Civil War. A wire several miles long extended from the headquarters of General George Brinton McClellan near Williamsport, VA, to an advance guard at Mechanicsville, VA, commanded by General George Stoneman, chief of cavalry in the Army of the Potomac.

5715. Photographs of an American battlefield showing the bodies of the dead were taken by Alexander Gardner, a photographer working for Civil War chronicler Mathew Brady. His subject was the battlefield at Antietam, MD, where Union troops had turned back an attempted invasion of the North by Confederate troops led by Robert E. Lee. The battle, fought on September 17, 1862, left 3,650 men dead and 17,300 wounded. The dead were still unburied two days later when Gardner arrived with his camera. He made 70 photographs.

Library of Congress, Prints & Photographs Division, LC-USZ62-5331

The Battle of Antietam.

5716. African-American unit in the Union Army to see combat was the 1st Kansas Colored Volunteer Infantry, a regiment of escaped slaves. They were recruited beginning in 1862 by Kansas senator James H. Lane, and first went into combat at the Battle of Island Mound in Missouri on October 27, 1862. They were formally mustered into service on January 13, 1863. Later that year, the 1st Kansas, led by a white officer, James M. Williams, fought alongside white Union troops at Cabin Creek in Indian Territory. The regiment was renamed the 79th U.S. Colored Infantry in December 1864.

African-American soldiers were actively recruited by the United States beginning in May 1863, when the Bureau of Colored Troops was established.

5717. Warship sunk by an underwater torpedo mine was sunk during the Civil War. The target was the ironclad Union gunboat *Cairo*, built by James Eads and Company, Mound City, IL, and commissioned on January 25, 1862. It was 175 feet long with a beam of 51 feet 2 inches, had a 512-ton displacement, and carried a crew of 251 officers and men. While clearing mines from the Yazoo River, near Vicksburg, MS, on December 12, 1862, the ship struck a bottle containing cannon powder that was floating beneath the surface. It sank in 30 feet of water within 12 minutes. The crew was rescued by the gunboat *Queen of the West*. An earlier but unsuccessful attack had been made on July 7, 1861, at Acquia Creek on the Potomac River, when Confederate forces attempted to destroy the Union ship *Pawnee* by floating a torpedo mine down the river on pieces of cork. The first Confederate vessel lost to a torpedo mine was a torpedo boat that was destroyed on February 17, 1864, off Charleston, SC.

5718. Civil War bloodshed north of the Mason-Dixon Line was a battle that took place on June 30, 1863, between Brigadier General Judson Kilpatrick's 3rd Cavalry Division, Army of the Potomac, and Major General James Ewell Brown Stuart's Cavalry Division, Army of Northern Virginia, at Hanover, PA. About 11,000 troops were in this cavalry and artillery engagement, which resulted in more than 300 casualties. This battle was one of the determining factors that enabled the North to win the battle at Gettysburg, PA, in July 1863.

5719. Submarine to sink a warship was CSS *H. L. Hunley*, named after its inventor, Horace Lawson Hunley. The company of Parks & Lyons, Mobile, AL, manufactured it in 1863 for the Confederacy. On February 17, 1864, the *Hunley* attacked a Union ship, the USS *Housatonic*, a steam sloop-of-war that was blockading the harbor of Charleston, SC. Using a pole some 20 feet long, the *Hunley* rammed the *Housatonic* and drove an explosive device into its hull. The detonation sank the Union ship with the loss of five lives; most of the crew survived. The *Hunley*, for reasons unknown, sank soon after, taking all nine crew members with it.

On August 8, 2000, the HUNLEY was raised by marine archeologists. The remains of the crew were buried at Magnolia Cemetery in Charleston on April 17, 2004. The event was called the last Confederate funeral.

5720. War in which more than 500,000 American combatants died was the Civil War, which ended on April 9, 1865. The number of combatant deaths in the Revolutionary War is estimated at 4,435; the War of 1812, 2,260; and the Mexican War, 13,283, of whom 1,733 died in combat and the remainder of disease and other causes. The number of combatant deaths in the Civil War, according to the Civil War Center, is estimated at 558,052, of whom 184,594 died in combat and 373,458 died of other causes.

5721. Trial of a war criminal by the federal government was held in Washington, DC, from August 23 to November 4, 1865. The defendant was Captain Henry Wirz, superintendent of the Confederate prison at Andersonville, GA, who was accused of conspiring to torture, injure, and murder Union prisoners. He was tried under 13 separate specifications by a military commission presided over by General Lewis Wallace, U.S. Volunteers. Wirz was convicted and sentenced to death by hanging. He was executed on November 10, 1865, and buried in Mount Olivet Cemetery, Washington, DC.

5722. National cemetery for Civil War dead was the Grafton National Cemetery in Grafton, WV. The idea originated in 1865 with Iowa congressman Swinton Burdett, commander-in-chief of the Grand Army of the Republic. The cemetery, a little more than three acres in area, was established by act of Congress. A total of 1,251 bodies, both Union and Confederate, were removed from their graves and reburied at Grafton. Memorial services were held on June 14, 1868. The cemetery continued to receive the remains of war dead until 1961, when it reached capacity.

5723. Documentary movies of an American war were made by the American Mutoscope & Biograph Company of New York City and the Edison Manufacturing Company of Menlo Park, NJ. Cameramen from both companies began filming soon after the USS *Maine* was sunk in the harbor of Havana, Cuba, on February 15, 1898. Their movie footage, showing war preparations, troops

Library of Congress, Prints & Photographs Division, LC-USZ62-783

Destruction of the USS Housatonic *by the CSS* H. L. Hunley.

Library of Congress, Prints & Photographs Division
LC-USZC4-1572

Explosion of the Maine.

landing, wounded soldiers, and other aspects of the Spanish-American War, were taken in Cuba, Washington, DC, and Tampa, FL.

5724. Capture of a ship in the Spanish-American War was made by the American gunboat *Nashville*, which took the Spanish ship *Buena Ventura* on April 22, 1898. On April 24, Spain declared that a state of war existed with the United States. The following day, Congress declared that a state of war had existed since April 21.

5725. Navy officer killed in action in the Spanish-American War was Ensign Worth Bagley, executive officer of the torpedo boat USS *Winslow*, who was killed on May 11, 1898. The *Winslow* had been sent to the wharves at Cardenas, Cuba, for a closer inspection of the docks, and was fired upon simultaneously by a shore battery and a Spanish gunboat. Also killed was a sailor, George Burton Meek, to whose memory a monument was erected in the McPherson Cemetery, Clyde, OH.

5726. Military expeditionary force to be sent beyond the Western Hemisphere sailed on May 25, 1898, from San Francisco, CA, on the *Australia*, *City of Pekin*, and *City of Sydney*, bound for Manila, Philippines, a distance of 6,220 miles. The expeditionary force consisted of 115 officers and 2,386 enlisted men commanded by General Wesley Merritt. They arrived off Manila on June 30 and landed on July 1. Admiral George Dewey and General Merritt demanded the surrender of Manila on August 7. The city complied on August 13.

5727. Army officer killed in battle in the Spanish-American War was Captain Allen Kissam Capron, who was killed in action on June 24, 1898, at Las Guásimas, Cuba.

5728. Land battle in the Spanish-American War took place on June 24, 1898, at Las Guásimas, Cuba. The 1st Cavalry, the 10th Cavalry, and the Rough Riders, all unmounted, took part. Juragua was captured and 11 Spanish dead were left on the field. Sixteen Americans were killed and 52 wounded.

Library of Congress, Prints & Photographs Division
LC-USZC4-1316

The Rough Riders.

Wars: 20th Century

5729. American to sail to Europe to fight in World War I was Denis Patrick Dowd, Jr., of Sea Cliff, NY, who enlisted on August 6, 1914. He fought with the French Foreign Legion, was transferred to a line regiment when the battered legion was withdrawn, was wounded, and upon recovery was transferred to the Lafayette Escadrille, the squadron of American volunteer airmen attached to the French air force. He died on August 11, 1916, when his plane crashed in a nosedive at Buc, near Paris, the day before he was to fly to the front. He was buried in the Memorial Cemetery of the Lafayette Escadrille in the Parc du Villeneuve l'Étang near St. Cloud, France.

5730. Ship from the United States lost in World War I was the *William P. Frye*, a steel sailing vessel of 3,374 gross tons, built in 1901 and owned by Arthur Sewall and Company of Maine. The ship left Seattle, WA, on November 4, 1914, bound for England, with a cargo of 186,950 bushels of wheat. It was sunk on January 28, 1915, by the German cruiser *Prinz Eitel Friedrich*.

5731. American combatant to die in World War I was Edward Mandell Stone of Chicago, IL, an expatriate living in Paris who enlisted in the French Foreign Legion and was assigned to the second regiment. He served at Champagne and in the Aisne, where he was mortally wounded on February 17, 1915. He died on February 27. He was posthumously awarded the Croix de Guerre and the Military Medal.

5732. Cargo ship from the United States attacked by a German submarine in World War I was the *Nantucket Chief* from Port Arthur, TX, a 5,189-ton tanker 360 feet long with a net tonnage of 3,262 tons. It was carrying a cargo of oil bound for Rouen, France, when it was torpedoed by the German submarine *U-30* off the Scilly Isles, England, on May 1, 1915. The first to be sunk by a submerged German submarine was the SS *Frederick R. Kellogg*, 7,127 tons, owned by the Pan-American Petroleum and Transportation Company, which was sunk 12 miles north of Barnegat Light, NJ, on August 13, 1918, when a torpedo struck the engine room. The ship sank in 15 seconds.

5733. Pilot from the United States shot down in World War I was H. Clyde Balsley of the Lafayette Escadrille volunteer air unit, who was attacked by a German squadron at a height of 10,000 feet above Verdun, France, on June 18, 1916. Although wounded, he managed to land his airplane within the Allied lines. He received the Military Medal and the War Cross for his bravery.

5734. Pilot from the United States killed in World War I while serving in the Lafayette Escadrille was Victor Emmanuel Chapman, who was shot down on June 23, 1916, northeast of Douamont, France, in the Verdun sector. He had served for a year in the Foreign Legion before joining the Lafayette Escadrille.

5735. War in which the armed services of the United States were deployed in defense of another nation was World War I, which began as a conflict among European nations. The United States entered the war on April 6, 1917, to assist Britain, France, Belgium, and the Netherlands in repelling Germany's invasion. In the course of the war, nearly 5 million Americans served in the armed forces, of whom 126,000 were killed in action.

5736. Shot fired by the Navy in World War I was fired on April 7, 1917, at Guam Island. Commander William Alden Hall, in command of a prize crew, left the USS *Supply* and proceeded to the port town of Piti with orders to follow the governor's aide, who had boarded the interned German cruiser *Cormorant* in Apra harbor under a flag of truce to demand its surrender. The Americans sighted a German launch with a cutter in tow and fired two warning shots across her bow, both of which were disregarded. After several shots, the launch hove to and was ordered to Piti to surrender to the authorities there. The Germans refused and blew up their ship. Seven crew members were killed and the rest were captured and sent as prisoners to an army camp in Utah.

5737. Army general to fly over enemy lines was Brigadier General William Lendrum Mitchell, who took off at 5:30 P.M. from La Cheppe, France, on April 24, 1917, in an airplane piloted by Lieutenant François Lafont and flew over the German lines at an altitude of 6,000 feet, returning at 7 P.M.

5738. Troops from the United States to sail to Europe in World War I were members of the American Expeditionary Force under General John Joseph Pershing. The group included 40 regular army officers, 17 reserve officers, 2 Marine Corps officers, 67 enlisted men, 36 field clerks, 20 civilians, 3 interpreters, and 3 news correspondents. They left New York City on May 28, 1917, on the *Baltic*, docked at Liverpool, England, on June 8, and reached Paris on June 13. The United States had been in a state of war with Germany since April 6, 1917, when it became the 13th nation to declare war against the Central Powers.

5739. Marine regiment to land in Europe in World War I was the 5th Regiment of Marines, commanded by Colonel Charles A. Doyen, which sailed from New York City on board the *Henderson*, *De Kalb*, and *Hancock* on June 14, 1917. By July 2, 1917, the entire regiment had arrived at St. Nazaire, France. The regiment was detached for service in France by executive order of May 25, 1917.

5740. Organization of parents of servicemen and servicewomen was the American War Mothers, founded in Indiana on September 27, 1917, during World War I. Mothers who joined the organization put in their front windows a white flag showing a blue star. Members undertook a variety of support activities, including visiting hospitalized soldiers and sending care packages to soldiers overseas. The group was chartered by Congress on February 24, 1925, with Alice French as the first national president.

5741. Navy enlisted man killed in World War I action was Gunners Mate First Class Osmond Kelly Ingram of Pratt City, AL, a member of the crew of the destroyer USS *Cassin*, which was on patrol duty. On October 16, 1917, Ingram was blown overboard by a torpedo fired by a German submarine from a distance of five miles, which hit the stern of the *Cassin*, knocked out the engine, and wounded five other sailors. A destroyer, the *Osmond Ingram*, was named in his honor. It was laid down on October 15, 1918, by the Bethlehem Shipbuilding Company, Quincy, MA, launched on February 23, 1919, and commissioned on June 28, 1919, at Boston. It was the first naval ship to be named for an enlisted man.

5742. Army division to go into battle in World War I was the 1st Division, which entered the trenches on October 21, 1917, in the Lunéville sector, near Nancy, France. Each unit was attached to a corresponding French unit.

5743. Shot fired by American infantry in World War I was fired at 6:05 A.M. on October 23, 1917, by Battery C of the 6th Field Artillery under the command of Sergeant Alexander L. Arch of South Bend, IN. Corporal Robert E. Bralet is credited with having jerked the lanyard on a French 75mm gun to send the first shot into a German trench half a mile away.

5744. Soldiers in the American army killed in combat in World War I were Corporal James B. Gresham of Evansville, IN, and Privates Thomas F. Enright of Pittsburgh, PA, and Merle D. Hay of Glidden, IA, members of Company F, 16th Infantry, 1st Division. They met death when the Germans raided the 16th Infantry's trenches near Bathelémont, France, on the night of November 2–3, 1917. On November 3, General Bordeaux of the French Army commended their heroism and sacrifice. Earlier, on September 4, 1917, a group of American soldiers assigned to a field hospital operated by the British Expeditionary Force at Dannes-Camiers, France, had been killed when the hospital was bombed by a German airplane. They were First Lieutenant William Thomas Fitzsimons of Kansas City, MO, and enlisted men Rudolph Rubino, Jr., of the Bronx, New York City, Oscar Le Tugo of Boston, MA, and Leslie G. Woods of Streator, IL.

5745. Naval vessels to sink an enemy submarine in the Atlantic were the USS *Fanning* and the USS *Nicholson*. On November 17, 1917, at 4:10 P.M., in latitude 57 degrees 37 minutes N, longitude 8 degrees 12 minutes W, the *Fanning*, while in convoy, sighted the periscope of a submarine. The *Fanning* headed for the spot and dropped depth charges. The *Nicholson*, one of the vessels of the convoy, speeded to the spot and also dropped depth charges. The German submarine *U-58* came to the surface. The *Nicholson* fired three shots from her stern while the *Fanning* headed for the submarine and fired its bow gun. After three shots, the crew of the submarine came on deck and surrendered. The submarine sank shortly afterward. The commanding officer of the *Fanning* was Lieutenant Commander Arthur Schuyler Carpenter, and the commanding officer of the *Nicholson* was Lieutenant Commander Frank Dunn Berrien.

5746. Troop ship from the United States torpedoed by a German submarine in World War I was the SS *Tuscania*, carrying 119 officers and 2,037 men. It was torpedoed and sunk by the submarine *U-77* on February 15, 1918, off the north coast of Ireland, with a loss of 183 men.

5747. Air squadron of the Army in World War I was Squadron No. 1, also known as the 1st Aero Squadron, assigned to the front on April 8, 1918, for observation duty. The first combat action took place on April 12, 1918, when the squadron was attacked while on a reconnaissance mission.

5748. Combat mission of American pilots ordered to battle in World War I by an American squadron commander was the 94th Aero Pursuit Squadron, the "Hat-in-the-Ring Squadron." On April 13, 1918, Major John Huffer ordered Captain David Peterson, Lieutenant Reed Chambers, and Lieutenant Edward Vernon Rickenbacker to make a two-hour patrol from Pont-à-Mousson to St. Mihiel, France, at 6 A.M. the following day.

5749. Pilots in American units to participate in air combat in World War I were Alan Francis Winslow and Douglas Campbell, who shot down two German single-seaters almost directly over the Squadron Aerodrome at Toul, France, on April 14, 1918.

5750. Gold Star mothers were mothers of soldiers serving in World War I. The term was first used by President Woodrow Wilson on May 28, 1918. It originated in a proposal by the Women's Committee of the Council of National Defenses that bereaved mothers should wear an armband with a gold star, and in the efforts of the American War Mothers organization to designate the homes of soldiers on active duty by blue stars and the homes of fallen soldiers by gold stars. A national organization, the American Gold Star Mothers, was founded in 1928 by a group of 25 women headed by Grace Darling Siebold of Washington, DC, whose son George was killed in France in 1918.

5751. American air ace was Lieutenant Douglas Campbell of San Jose, CA, who shot down a German pilot on April 14, 1918. His fifth victory, which qualified him as an ace, occurred on May 31, 1918. He was a member of the 94th Pursuit Squadron, known as the "Hat-in-the-Ring."

5752. Airplane bombing raid by an American air unit was made by six airplanes of the Army's 96th Aero Squadron. The unit left the airdrome at Amanty, France, in Breguet airplanes on June 12, 1918. Five airplanes dropped 80 bombs on a railroad junction at Dommary-Baroncourt, about 40 miles inside enemy territory. Lieutenant Howard Grant Rath was the lead observer.

5753. Shots fired by German forces to land on American soil in World War I were fired on July 21, 1918, by the German submarine *U-156*. The target was the tugboat *Perth Amboy* and four barges loaded with stone off Nauset Bluffs, Orleans, MA. About 70 or 80 shots were fired three miles offshore. A few shots landed on shore at Meeting House Pond.

5754. Ace of Aces from the United States was Captain Edward Vernon Rickenbacker of Columbus, OH, a former professional race car driver, who was credited with 26 victories, including 22 airplanes and four balloons. He was member and later commander of the 94th Pursuit Squadron. His first victory took place in the Baussant region, in the Toul sector, France, on April 29, 1918, and his last in the St. Juvin region, on October 30, 1918.

5755. American division to cross the Rhine River in World War I was the 1st Division, which passed over the pontoon bridge at Coblentz on the morning of December 13, 1918, led by Company M, 18th Infantry, commanded by Lieutenant Donald McClure.

5756. Submarine from the United States destroyed in World War II was the *Sealion*, launched on May 25, 1939, at the Electric Boat Division of General Dynamics at Groton, CT, and commissioned on November 27, 1939. The ship, 311 feet long with a 2,350-ton displacement, was docked at Machina Wharf at the Navy Yard at Cavite, Philippine Islands, on December 10, 1941, when a group of 54 Japanese airplanes dropped bombs on it. Four men were lost and the ship was badly damaged. Since the closest repair facilities were at Pearl Harbor, Honolulu, HI, the *Sealion* was towed out to sea, where it was exploded on December 25 by three depth charges placed inside. Lieutenant Commander Richard G. Voge was the commanding officer.

5757. Ship from the United States sunk by a German submarine in World War II was the *Robin Moor*, 4,985 tons, operated by the Robin Line of New York, which sailed on May 6, 1941, from New York City for Cape Town, South Africa, with 8 passengers and a crew of 38 under Captain Edward Myers. It was sunk on May 21 in the South Atlantic, 400 miles south of the Cape Verde Islands and 900 miles due west of Monrovia, Liberia.

5758. Capture of a German ship by an American ship in World War II was accomplished by the Coast Guard cutter *Northland*, captained by Commander Carl Christian von Paulsen, which captured the 60-ton trawler *Busko* at Mackenzie Bay, Greenland, on September 12, 1941. The *Busko* had entered U.S. waters without proper documentation and had radioed weather reports and other information to Germany. The captured ship was sent under the escort of the Navy-manned USS *Bear* under Lieutenant Commander Joseph Gainard to Commonwealth Pier, Boston, MA, where its crew of 20 men and 1 woman was held without bail.

5759. Warship convoy across the Atlantic Ocean in World War II was convoy HX-150, consisting of the destroyers *Dallas*, *Eberle*, *Ellis*, *Ericsson*, and *Upshur*, commanded by Captain Morton L. Deyo. On September 17, 1941, the warships assumed charge of 50 merchant ships that had left Nova Scotia, Canada, the previous day.

5760. Destroyer from the United States torpedoed in World War II was the *Kearny*, commanded by Lieutenant Commander Anthony Leo Danis, which was attacked on October 17, 1941, 350 miles southwest of Iceland. Eleven of the crew were killed, two were seriously wounded, and eight sustained minor wounds, but the *Kearny* remained afloat and arrived at Iceland on October 19. The first American destroyer torpedoed and sunk while on convoy duty was the *Reuben James*, commanded by Lieutenant Commander Heywood Lane Edwards, which was attacked on October 30, 1941, off the western coast of Ireland by the German submarine *U-562*. The torpedo hit a magazine on the port side and exploded, sinking the destroyer with the loss of 115 of the crew of 160.

5761. American losses in the Pacific in World War II took place on December 7, 1941, when Japan carried out a surprise attack against the American fleet at Pearl Harbor, HI. The United States lost five battleships, three destroyers, a minelayer, and a target vessel. Many other ships were damaged and about 400 airplanes were destroyed. American casualties totaled 2,117 killed, 1,272 wounded, and 960 missing.

5762. Navy admiral killed in action in World War II was Rear Admiral Isaac Campbell Kidd, staff aide to Admiral Husband Edward Kimmel, commander in chief of the United States Fleet. Kidd was killed on December 7, 1941, when the USS *Arizona* blew up during the Japanese attack on Pearl Harbor, HI.

5763. Radar used to detect enemy airplanes was employed at Pearl Harbor, HI, on December 7, 1941. At 7:20 A.M., Private Joseph L. Lockard of Williamsport, PA, reported to his superiors that he heard the approach of planes. The planes were assumed to be friendly and proper precautions were not taken, with the result that the Japanese succeeded in making a devastating surprise attack on the United States fleet. On February 8, 1942, Lockard received the Distinguished Service Medal and was sent to Officer Training School, Fort Monmouth, NJ.

5764. Ship from the United States to sink a Japanese submarine in World War II was the USS *Ward*, which hit the Japanese submarine *I-170* with fire from a four-inch gun on December 7, 1941, during the Japanese attack on Pearl Harbor, HI.

5765. World War II air hero was Second Lieutenant George S. Welch of Wilmington, DE, who shot down four Japanese airplanes at Oahu, HI, during the surprise attack on Pearl Harbor on December 7, 1941. He was awarded the Distinguished Service Cross on December 16, and received the congratulations of President Franklin Delano Roosevelt at the White House on May 25, 1942. In 33 months, he shot down 18 enemy aircraft.

5766. Ship from the United States to surrender to the Japanese in World War II was the 370-ton shallow-draft river gunboat *Wake*, which carried two three-inch pieces. The ship was the target of a surprise assault on December 8, 1941, at Shanghai. The crew attempted in vain to scuttle the ship before surrendering. The captured ship, renamed *Tataru* by the Japanese, was turned over in 1945 to the United States, which gave it to the navy of the Republic of China, which in turn renamed it *Tai Yuan*. During the civil war in China it fell into the hands of the Chinese Communists and was added to their navy.

5767. Bombing mission by American forces in Asia in World War II took place on December 9, 1941, two days after the Japanese attack on Pearl Harbor, when B-17 airplanes of the 19th Bombardment Group attacked Japanese ships off the east coast of Vigan, Luzon, Philippine Islands.

5768. Fighter plane from the United States to destroy a Japanese airplane in World War II was a Grumman F4F Wildcat fighter of the Marines, which downed a twin-engine bomber on December 9, 1941, off Wake Island.

5769. General of the American armed forces killed in World War II was Major General Herbert Arthur Dargue, who was killed on December 12, 1941, in an airplane that crashed en route to the Pacific area.

5770. World War II ace was First Lieutenant Boyd David Wagner of Johnstown, PA. While serving in the Army Air Corps in the Philippines, Wagner was attacked on December 13, 1941, by five Japanese pursuit planes. He shot two planes out of the air and machine-gunned 12 on the ground, leaving five burning. He was awarded the Distinguished Service Cross.

5771. Submarine from the United States to sink a Japanese ship in World War II was the USS *Swordfish*, commanded by Lieutenant Chester Carl Smith, which torpedoed the 8,662-ton Japanese freighter *Atsutusan Maru* on December 16, 1941, off the coast of Indochina. The *Swordfish* was 311 feet long and displaced 2,350 tons. It was launched on April 1, 1939, and commissioned on July 22. The ship was destroyed by a mine on its 13th patrol in January 1945, near Okinawa, with the loss of all aboard.

5772. Coded military radio transmissions using a Native American language began in 1942, when the Allied and Axis powers were competing to devise communications codes that could not be deciphered by the enemy. Philip Johnston, a missionary's son who had grown up on the Navajo reservation, proposed the idea of using the Navajo language, a complicated system in which the meaning of a word is often determined by expression and pronunciation. Marine Major General Clayton B. Vogel approved the plan and recruited 420 Navajo "code talkers" to handle coded radio communications in the Pacific theater. The codes combined everyday Navajo words with about 400 special terms made up by the code talkers. Members of other tribes were employed as well. The Japanese were aware of the Navajo codes, but never broke them. They were kept top secret until 1968. The first National Navajo Code Talkers Day was held on August 14, 1982.

5773. American expeditionary force to land in Europe in World War II arrived in Ireland on January 26, 1942, and was greeted by Sir Archibald Sinclair, the British air minister. The first officer to land was Major General Russell Peter Hartle. The first enlisted man to land was Private Milburn Henke of Hutchinson, MN.

5774. Bombing raid on the continental United States in World War II was made on February 23, 1942, at about 7 P.M. P.S.T., while President Franklin Delano Roosevelt was delivering his weekly "fireside chat" by radio to the American public. The Japanese submarine *I-17*, captained by Captain Kozo Nishino, fired 12 to 15 shots during the space of 20 minutes at the Barnsdall Oil Refinery in Ellwood, CA, about 12 miles west of Santa Barbara. The submarine was about half a mile offshore. One shell made a direct hit on the rigging and pumping equipment of an oil well, causing damage of about $500. Other shells made crater holes, one of which was about five feet deep. No one was injured.

5775. Naval counterattack by American forces against the Japanese in World War II was a surface engagement known as the Battle of Balikpapan, or the Battle of the Makassar Strait, which took place on February 23–24, 1942, in the harbor of Balikpapan, East Borneo. The U.S. destroyers *John D. Ford*, *Parrott*, *Pope*, and *Paul Jones*, under the command of Lieutenant Commander Paul H. Talbot, came in at night at high speed and sank a patrol craft and the transports *Tatsukami Maru* (7,064 tons), *Tsuruga Maru* (6,988 tons), *Kuretake Maru* (5,175 tons), and *Somanouri Maru* (3,519 tons).

5776. Pilot from the United States to sink a German submarine was Ensign William Tepuni, Naval Reserve, who was flying a Lockhead-Hudson airplane of Squadron VP-82 when he attacked and sank the German submarine *U-656* off Cape Race, Newfoundland, Canada, on March 1, 1942.

5777. Naval vessel from the United States to sink a German submarine in World War II was the destroyer *Roper*, captained by Lieutenant Commander Hamilton Wilcox Howe, which sank the German submarine *U-85* on April 13–14, 1942, off Wimble Shoal, near Hatteras, NC.

5778. Air attack against the Japanese homeland in World War II was made on April 18, 1942, by 16 B-25 airplanes of the 17th Bombardment Group, 8th Air Force. The bombers, led by Colonel James Harold Doolittle, took off from the U.S. *Hornet*. Traveling low over the water, they dropped bombs on the cities of Tokyo, Kobe, and Nagoya, then continued straight on until they ran out of fuel and crash-landed in the Chinese countryside. The raid took the Japanese military establishment by surprise and demonstrated for the first time the vulnerability of the Japanese home islands.

5779. Sea battle in World War II fought solely by air power was the Battle of the Coral Sea, which took place on May 4–8, 1942, between Navy Task Force 17 and Vice Admiral Takeo Takagi's Japanese Carrier Striking Force. American planes took off from carriers 180 miles away from each other. The Japanese lost 39 ships. The United States lost the aircraft carrier *Lexington*. The attack was planned by Admiral Chester W. Nimitz.

5780. Aircraft carrier from the United States sunk in World War II was the 33,000-ton *Lexington*, commanded by Rear Admiral Frederick Carl Sherman, which was hit on May 8, 1942, in the Coral Sea by two bombs and two aircraft torpedoes launched from Japanese aircraft. Some 150 men were killed.

5781. American territory occupied by the Japanese in World War II was the undefended island of Attu and the island of Kiska in the Western Aleutians, which were captured on June 7, 1942. The capture was announced by the Navy on June 13. The islands were retaken by American forces in May 1943 in the only battle fought on U.S. soil during World War II.

5782. American expeditionary force to land in Africa in World War II was the 41st Engineers General Service Regiment, which landed on June 17, 1942, at Port Takoradi, Gold Coast, Africa. The first man to land was Private Napoleon Edward Taylor of Baltimore, MD, orderly of Major Charles S. Ward.

5783. Bombing mission by American forces over enemy-occupied territory in Europe in World War II took place on July 4, 1942, when a Royal Air Force group of twelve A-20 Boston bombers, six manned by British crews and six by American crews, made a daylight attack against three German airfields in the Netherlands.

5784. Capture of an American ship captain by a German submarine in World War II took place on July 9, 1942, when the Grace Line's *Santa Rita* was sunk by a U-boat torpedo about 500 miles south of Bermuda. The captain, Henry Stephenson of Larchmont, NY, was removed from a lifeboat as it pulled away from the sinking ship. He was taken prisoner and interned until February 1945, when he was repatriated. He was then 69 years old.

5785. American offensive in the Pacific in World War II was undertaken on August 7, 1942, at Guadalcanal, Solomon Islands, by the Marines under Lieutenant General Alexander Archer Vandergrift. The Marines landed at Floria, Gavutu, Guadalcanal, Tanambogo, and Tulagi. The overall commander was Vice Admiral Robert Lee Ghormley, South Pacific commander.

5786. Enemy saboteurs executed in the United States were six Germans who were electrocuted on August 8, 1942, in a jail in Washington, DC. They were part of a group of eight who were tried by a military commission of seven generals. One saboteur, George John Dasch, was sentenced to 30 years in prison, and another, Ernest Peter Burger, received a life sentence. All eight were found guilty of landing in rubber boats from enemy submarines, carrying explosives, incendiaries, fuses, detonators, timing devices, acids, and similar materials. Four of them landed on June 13, 1942, at Amagansett, NY, on Long Island, and were discovered by Seaman Second Class John C. Cullen of the Amagansett Coast Guard Station. Four others landed on June 17, 1942, at Ponte Vedra Beach near Jacksonville, FL.

5787. Pilot from the United States to shoot down a German fighter plane in World War II was Second Lieutenant Sam F. Junkin of Natchez, MS, who shot down a Focke-Wulf-190 plane over Dieppe, France, in a Commando-Ranger raid on August 19, 1942. Junkin was wounded and jumped from his disabled plane. He was picked up by a returning Commando barge. On the same date, a similar plane was shot down by Frank A. Hill of the 31st Fighter Group, but it was listed as "probably destroyed," since observers did not see the plane hit the ground or explode in the air, or see the pilot bail out.

5788. Soldier from the United States to land on French soil in World War II was Corporal Franklin M. Koons of Iowa, one of the Rangers who accompanied Lieutenant Colonel Lord Lovat's Commandos in a raid on Dieppe on August 19, 1942. Koons destroyed a German 155mm gun and was awarded the British Military Medal for "conspicuous gallantry and admirable leadership" on October 2, 1942.

5789. Air attack on Germany by the Army Air Force in World War II was made on January 27, 1943, by the 8th Air Force led by Brigadier General Haywood Shepherd Hansell III from bases in England. The targets were naval bases and docks at Wilhelmshaven and factories in Emden in northwest Germany. The Americans lost three planes on the mission, two Liberators and one Flying Fortress. The German loss was 22 fighter airplanes and 3 bombers.

5790. American land victory without infantry in World War II was won on June 11, 1943, when the Italian fortress on the island of Pantelleria in the Mediterranean Sea, about 70 miles southwest of Sicily, surrendered to the Northwest African Air Forces of the Anglo-American Air Command, which had dropped 6,200 tons of bombs in more than 5,000 sorties. The island was occupied 22 minutes after landing. Lieutenant General Carl Andrew Spaatz commanded the operation.

5791. Army pilot who was African-American to shoot down an Axis airplane in World War II was First Lieutenant Charles Hall of Brazil, IN, who shot down a German Focke-Wulf 190 over Sicily on July 2, 1943. He was flying a Warhawk as part of a fighter squadron escorting bombers. The squadron commander was Lieutenant Colonel Benjamin Oliver Davis, Jr., who later became the first African-American general of the Air Force.

5792. Airship from the United States lost to enemy action in World War II was the K-74, a nonrigid blimp on patrol over the East Coast that attacked a German submarine submerged in the Caribbean on July 18, 1943. The airship was destroyed by gunfire and was forced to alight on the water. All of the 11-man crew was saved with the exception of Isadore Stessel of Brooklyn, New York City, Aviation Machinist First Class.

5793. Submarine from the United States sunk by an enemy submarine was the *Corvina*, of Task Force 72. Its length was 311 feet 9 inches, its breadth 27 feet 3 inches, its draft 15 feet 3 inches, and its displacement 2,424 tons. It was launched on May 9, 1943, at the Electric Boat Company, Groton, CT, and commissioned on August 6. It left Pearl Harbor, HI, on its first war patrol on November 4, 1943, and was torpedoed south of the Truk Islands on November 16 by Japanese submarine *I-176*, which fired three torpedoes, two of which hit. The ship, with a crew of 82, was officially presumed lost as of December 23, 1943, and the loss was announced on March 14, 1944. Commander Roderick Shanahan Rooney was in command.

5794. Capture and boarding of an enemy submarine on the high seas by American forces took place on June 4, 1944, when the 740-ton German submarine *U-505* was attacked and captured by airplanes and ships under the command of Captain Daniel Vincent Gallery of the aircraft carrier USS *Guadalcanal* off Cape Blanco on the west coast of Africa, between Cape Verde and the Canary Islands. The submarine was boarded by Lieutenant (j.g.) Albert Leroy David and eight crewmen from the destroyer USS *Pillsbury*, commanded by George W. Cassleman. The *Guadalcanal* towed the *U-505* more than 1,700 miles across the Atlantic Ocean to Port Royal Bay, Bermuda, where it arrived on June 19, 1944.

5795. American civilians killed in the continental United States in World War II were Elsie Mitchell and five neighborhood children of Lakeview, OR, who tried to drag a Japanese balloon out of the woods on May 5, 1945. The balloon was armed and it exploded, killing all six. On June 7, 1949, Congress awarded $5,000 to Elsie Mitchell's husband as compensation for his loss, and $3,000 to the parents of each of the children: Edward Milian Engen, Jay Gifford, Ethel Jean Patzke, Richard Joe Patzke, and Sherman Shoemaker.

5796. Naval bombardment of the Japanese homeland in World War II was made on July 14, 1945, by the U.S. Pacific Fleet under the immediate tactical command of Rear Admiral John Franklin Shafroth. The battleships *Massachusetts*, *Indiana*, and

South Dakota, the heavy cruisers *Chicago* and *Quincy*, and nine destroyers bombed the iron works in the coastal city of Kamaishi, Honshu, 275 miles northeast of Tokyo. Damage was inflicted on 342 airplanes, 4 ships, and 15 airfields.

5797. Atomic bomb explosion over enemy territory took place on August 6, 1945, over Hiroshima, Japan, from the *Enola Gay*, a B-29 airplane. The pilot was Colonel Paul Warfield Tibbets, Jr., of Miami, FL, and the bombardier was Major Thomas W. Ferebee of Mocksville, NC.

5798. CARE packages were cartons of surplus U.S. military meals that were collected and delivered by the Cooperative for American Remittances to Europe, a consortium of 22 humanitarian groups. The first 20,000 boxes arrived at Le Havre, France, on May 11, 1946. They contained food that had been prepared in anticipation of the American invasion of Japan.

5799. Military think tank was the RAND Corporation, founded on October 1, 1946, at Hamilton Field, San Francisco, CA, by a group of scientists and researchers associated with the Army Air Force under the direction of General Henry Harley "Hap" Arnold. Arnold appropriated $10 million from leftover wartime research funds to establish a semi-independent organization devoted to the scientific study of national security issues. The acronym RAND stood for "research and development." Frank Collbohm was RAND's first president. In May 1948, RAND became an independent nonprofit enterprise.

5800. United Nations peacekeeping mission in which the United States participated was the first such mission ever undertaken by the United Nations. Called UNTSO, the United Nations Truce Supervision Organization, it was formed on May 29, 1948, by resolution of the United Nations Security Council to maintain the armistice agreements that brought a halt to the invasion of the newly created state of Israel by Arab armies. The first Americans to lose their lives in a U. N. peacekeeping mission were Army Sergeant Lester Welling of Hampton, VA, and Air Force Corporal Charles F. Smith, Wilmette, IL, who died near Jerusalem in a car accident on December 7, 1948.

5801. Pilot to destroy an enemy airplane in the Korean War was First Lieutenant William G. Hudson of the 68th Fighter Squadron, who shot down a YAK-9 on June 26, 1950, while flying an F-82 airplane over Kimpo to provide cover for its evacuation. The war began on June 25, when South Korea was invaded by Communist forces from North Korea. The defense of South Korea was assisted by the United States as part of a United Nations effort.

5802. Combat mission in the Korean War involving an exchange of fire occurred on June 27, 1950, between Communist forces and an F-80C airplane from the 8th Fighter-Bomber Group, 5th Air Force, which was based at Itazuke Air Base in southern Japan.

5803. Soldier killed in action in the Korean War was Private Kenneth Shadrick, 19, of Skin Fork, WV, a member of a bazooka squad, who was killed on July 5, 1950, near Sojong, Korea, by a bullet fired from an enemy tank.

5804. Officer killed in action in the Korean War was Colonel Robert R. Martin of Toledo, OH, who was killed on July 8, 1950, while leading a rocket and grenade attack against an enemy tank. He was awarded the first Distinguished Service Cross of the Korean War, posthumously presented to his son, Robert, a cadet at the U.S. Military Academy.

5805. Helicopter rescue of an American pilot behind enemy lines was effected in Korea on September 4, 1950, by First Lieutenant Paul Van Boven of San Mateo, CA, and hospital corpsman Corporal John Fuentz of Kansas City, MO, who rescued Captain Robert Earl Wayne of Garden City, NY, shot down on his 95th mission.

5806. Tank crew to cross the 38th parallel in the Korean War was a patrol of the 1st Cavalry Division that crossed into the Kaesong Area, about 85 miles south of the Communist capital of Pyongsang, at 3:14 P.M. on October 7, 1950. The crew members were Sergeant Homer Lee of Evansville, IN, Private First Class James Emerich of Sutton, WV, Sergeant Walter Hill of Fairmont, ND, Sergeant Charles Gissendanner of Autaughville, AL, and Corporal Clarence Johnson of Taylorsville, NC. The 38th parallel was the line of latitude that had divided North Korea from South Korea since the end of World War II.

5807. Pilot of a jet fighter to win a dogfight in the Korean War was First Lieutenant Russell John Brown of Pasadena, CA, the pilot of an Air Force F-80, who destroyed a MiG-15 over North Korea in jet-versus-jet combat on November 8, 1950.

5808. Ace to fly a jet was Captain James Jabara of Wichita, KS, a member of the Fourth Fighter Interceptor Wing, who shot down his fifth and sixth enemy MiG jet airplanes on May 20, 1951, in battle over Sinuiju, northwest Korea. He was flying an F-86 Sabre Jet airplane. He eventually defeated 15 MiGs over Korea and became the second triple jet ace.

5809. Triple jet ace was Captain Joseph Christopher McConnell, Jr., who shot down 16 MiG-15s in his F-86 Sabre Jet. On May 18, 1953, he downed three in one day. He completed 106 missions in Korea. On August 10, 1953, a residence known as Appreciation House was presented to him by his neighbors in Apple Valley, CA, who built it in 45 hours. He was killed on August 25, 1954, at Edwards Air Force Base, Muroc, CA, while testing a new plane, an F-86 H.

5810. Navy ace in Korea was Lieutenant Guy Bordelon, who achieved his fifth victory on July 17, 1953, in a World-War-II-vintage propeller-driven F-4U Corsair. He was awarded the Navy Cross.

5811. Civilian pilot wounded in Vietnam was Paul Robert Holden of Greenleaf, KS, who was wounded in the right thigh and arm by 37mm antiaircraft shells over Dien Bien Phu on April 24, 1954. Holden was flying a C-119 Flying Boxcar for the Civil Air Transport, delivering supplies to the French. His copilot, Wallace Abbott Buford, of Kansas City, KS, managed to land the plane safely in French territory. Buford was killed on May 7, 1954, near Dien Bien Phu.

5812. Troops sent to Vietnam, were 425 helicopter crewmen sent by President John Fitzgerald Kennedy on December 11, 1961, to provide support and training for South Vietnamese forces.

5813. Navy pilot shot down and captured in North Vietnam was Lieutenant (j.g.) Everett Alvarez, Jr., 26, of San Jose, CA, aviator on the USS *Constellation*, who was shot down on August 5, 1964, and parachuted into the ocean. He was rescued by the crew of a small Vietnamese boat, to whom he surrendered. He was confined in the Hon Gay naval base and later in the Hoa Lo prison. He was returned to the United States on February 13, 1973.

5814. Ground troops sent to Vietnam were 3,500 Marines who landed at the port of Da Nang in South Vietnam on March 8, 1965. The Marines' mission was to guard the air base there. They raised the total U.S. troop strength in Vietnam to 27,000.

5815. Demonstration in Washington against the Vietnam War took place in April 1965, when 20,000 protesters organized by the radical group Students for a Democratic Society picketed the White House and marched from the Washington Monument to the steps of the Capitol building. The first campus teach-in was also held that month, at the University of Michigan at Ann Arbor.

5816. General killed in Vietnam by enemy fire was Major General Bruno Arthur Hochmuth, commander of the 3rd Marine Division, killed on November 14, 1967, at Hué, Vietnam, when ground fire downed the helicopter in which he was a passenger. Two American pilots, an American crew chief, and a Vietnamese interpreter were also killed in the crash.

5817. Hijacking of an American airliner by terrorists took place on August 29, 1969. The airliner was a Boeing 707 traveling from Rome, Italy, to Athens, Greece, as TWA Flight 840. Two members of the Marxist-Leninist group Popular Front for the Liberation of Palestine forced the pilot to land the plane in Damascus, Syria. Once the passengers and crew had been taken off, the plane was wrecked by a bomb planted by the hijackers. One hundred and five passengers and crew left Damascus on a chartered plane the following day. Four Israeli passengers were held until September 1. Two others were held by Syria until December 5, when they were released as part of a prisoner exchange.

5818. Vietnam War Moratorium Day demonstration took place on October 15, 1969. Millions of antiwar protesters wearing black armbands marched in major cities across the country. The largest protest was in Washington, DC, where 250,000 demonstrators gathered and were led in a candlelight march past the White House by Coretta Scott King, the widow of Martin Luther King, Jr.

5819. Air Force ace in Vietnam was Captain Richard Stephen Ritchie of Reidsville, NC, who downed his fifth MIG-21 aircraft in North Vietnam on August 28, 1972, in an air-to-air missile battle southwest of Hanoi. He flew an F-4 Phantom with the 555th Tactical Fighter Squadron of the 432d Tactical Reconnaissance Wing based in Thailand. His other "kills" occurred May 10th, May 31st, and two on July 8, 1972.

5820. Compensation of Japanese-Americans interned during World War II was enacted by Congress and signed into law on August 10, 1988. The bill provided for a payment of $20,000 to each surviving internee and a formal apology from the federal government. More than 110,000 men, women, and children of Japanese descent, including both American citizens and aliens, were rounded up from their homes in California, Arizona, Oregon, and Washington in the spring of 1942 and confined in rural internment camps until the end of the war, on suspicion that they might collaborate with Japan. The evacuation was carried out by executive order of President Franklin D. Roosevelt.

5821. War that was predicted by pizza orders was Operation Desert Storm, which was launched on Wednesday, January 16, 1991, by a United Nations coalition led by the United States. At 5 A.M. that morning, the Domino's Pizza fast-food chain put out a warning to its franchisees that war was likely later that day, based on record orders of pizza the previous night from the Pentagon. The Pentagon is the headquarters of the Department of Defense in Washington, DC.

5822. Pilot to destroy an enemy airplane in the Gulf War was F-15C pilot Jon Kelk, who shot down an Iraqi Soviet-built MIG fighter over southern Iraq on January 16, 1991. Flying combat air patrol with three other F-15Cs, Kelk spotted an unidentified aircraft on radar and fired a radar-guided missile that brought the craft down before it could return fire.

5823. Serviceman killed in the Gulf War was Navy pilot Scott Speicher. His F-18 Hornet fighter was shot down over Iraq by antiaircraft fire on January 17, 1991.

5824. Pilot who was a woman to die in a combat zone was Army Major Marie T. Rossi-Cayton, whose supply helicopter crashed on March 1, 1991, over Iraq during the Gulf War. In 1992, Rossi-Cayton was inducted into the Army Aviation Hall of Fame, becoming the first woman so honored.

5825. Serviceman killed in the peacekeeping mission in Somalia was Private First Class Domingo Arroyo, a 21-year-old Marine from Elizabeth, NJ. He was shot by an unknown gunman while on night patrol at the airport near the Somali capital of Mogadishu in January 1993.

5826. Bombing of a skyscraper by foreign terrorists occurred at 12:18 P.M. on February 26, 1993, when a truck bomb exploded in the parking garage of the World Trade Center in New York City. The bomb left a crater 200 feet wide and and caused interior walls and floors of the twin towers to collapse, but the main structures were not seriously damaged. Six people were killed and several hundred were injured. Some 50,000 people were evacuated from the buildings in a rescue effort that disrupted the city's economy and transportation. An FBI manhunt led to the arrest and eventual conviction of several suspects from the Middle East, including the radical Islamic cleric Sheik Omar Abdel Rahman and the plan's mastermind, Ramzi Yousef.

5827. Members of a foreign terrorist organization indicted for planning attacks within the United States were Zein Isa, Tawfiz Musa, Saij Nijmeh, and Luie Nijmeh, indicted on April 1, 1993, on charges of conspiring to blow up the Israeli embassy in Washington, DC. The four were members of the Palestinian terrorist group known as the Abu Nidal Organization and ran a secret ANO cell in St. Louis, MO. Three of the four defendants accepted a plea bargain that allowed them to avoid jail terms. The fourth, Isa, had all charges against him dropped because he had already been convicted of the murder of his 16-year-old daughter Palestina, whom he had stabbed to death because she applied for a part-time job without his permission. The sounds of the murder were captured on tape during the electronic surveillance.

5828. Emergency activation of a Russian nuclear response to a presumed American attack took place on January 25, 1995, when Russian radar screens showed what appeared to be a missile headed for Moscow. The rocket was actually Black Brant XII, a research probe launched by Norway and NASA to investigate the aurora borealis. Norway's foreign ministry had sent out a routine international alert before the launch, but it had been missed by the Russian authorities. President Boris Yeltsin activated the "nuclear briefcase," enabling the firing of retaliatory missiles, before the situation was clarified.

5829. Serviceman killed in the peacekeeping mission in Bosnia was Sergeant First Class Donald Allen Dugan of Ridgeway, OH, a member of the peacekeeping force organized by the North Atlantic Treaty Organization that entered Bosnia-Herzegovina in December 1995. Dugan was killed in an explosion in Sarajevo, Bosnia, on February 3, 1996. The cause of the explosion was not determined.

5830. Bounty of $5 million for an enemy of the United States was posted on November 5, 1998, for information leading to the arrest and conviction of the Saudi Arabian national Osama bin Laden. Bin Laden was charged in a Manhattan court with a 238-count indictment for masterminding the bombings on August 7 of American embassies in Nairobi, Kenya, and Dar es Salaam, Tanzania. The $5 million reward was the largest ever offered by the State Department.

5831. Fighter pilot who was a woman to fire a missile in combat was Lieutenant Kendra Williams of the U.S. Navy air wing based on the USS *Enterprise* aircraft carrier. On the night of December 16–17, 1998, she launched a laser-guided missile from her FA/18 Hornet jet fighter at an anti-aircraft emplacement in Iraq.

5832. Terrorist attack on the U.S. Navy took place on October 12, 2000, when agents of the Islamic terror organization Al Qaeda attacked the USS *Cole*, a Navy destroyer moored at the fuel station in the port of Aden, Yemen. Two Arab suicide bombers, Ibrahim al-Thawr and Abdullah al-Misawa, detonated a small craft packed with explosives next to the *Cole*, blowing a large hole in its side. The blast killed 17 crew members and wounded 39. The masterminds of the attack were Abu Ali al-Harithi and Abd al-Rahim al-Nashiri. Al-Harithi was killed in 2002 in the Yemeni desert by a CIA Predator drone missile, and al-Nashiri was captured and sentenced to death by a Yemeni court.

5833. Bioterror attacks by mail were the anthrax letter attacks of September–October 2001. On September 18, 2001—a week after Al Qaeda's attack on the World Trade Center and the Pentagon—mail containing a granular weapons-grade preparation of anthrax, a deadly bacterial agent, was sent from a post office in Trenton, NJ, to the New York offices of ABC News, CBS News, NBC News, the *New York Post*, and the *National Enquirer*. The first case of anthrax infection was reported publicly on October 4, although it was not realized until October 10 that mail might be the vector for infection. On October 9, additional anthrax letters were received in the Washington, DC, offices of Senators Tom Daschle of South Dakota and Patrick Leahy of Vermont. In all, five people died from inhalation of the anthrax grains, and several people, including an infant, were made ill by cutaneous anthrax infection. It was never discovered who sent the letters.

5834. Color-coded federal warning system was the Homeland Security Advisory System, a terrorism risk advisory instituted on March 12, 2002, and administered by the Department of Homeland Security beginning January 24, 2003. Intended as a "comprehensive and effective means to disseminate information regarding the risk of terrorist acts to Federal, State, and local authorities and to the American people," the Homeland Security Advisory System issued terrorist threat warnings keyed to five colors: red (severe), orange (high), yellow (elevated), blue (guarded), and green (low).

5835. Islamic terrorist who was born in America was the so-called "American Taliban," John Phillip Walker Lindh. Raised in suburban Maryland and San Anselmo, CA, by Roman Catholic parents, Lindh converted to Islam at the age of 16, studied at religious schools in Yemen and Pakistan, and trained with Osama bin Laden's Al Qaeda terrorist organization. In late 2001, when the United States invaded Afghanistan in reprisal for Al Qaeda's September 11 attack on the World Trade Center and the Pentagon, Lindh served as a soldier for the Taliban, Afghanistan's radical Islamic rulers. He was captured and returned to the United States for trial. On

July 15, 2002, he pleaded guilty to supplying aid to the enemy and possessing explosives during the commission of a felony. He received a 10-year sentence for each count.

5836. Ground battle in the Iraq War began on March 19, 2003, after Iraqi dictator Saddam Hussein and his sons refused to leave the country as demanded by the opposing Coalition forces. The U.S. land assault was led by Marine forces in southern Iraq along the Shatt el Arb River towards the Iraqi naval base and town of Umm Qasr. The first clash of the war occurred at the mouth of the Khawr al-Zubayr river, just south of Umm Qasr.

Weapons and Equipment

5837. Gunpowder mill was operated by Edward Rawson, to whom the General Court of Massachusetts granted 500 acres of land at Pecoit, MA, on June 6, 1639, on which to erect it.

5838. Germ warfare was suggested in July 1763 by Major General Jeffery Amherst, commander of the British army in North America, after a series of Native American uprisings in the Great Lakes area. Amherst suggested to Colonel Henry Bouquet that he distribute to the tribes blankets that had been used by smallpox victims. "Could it not be contrived to send the Small Pox among these disaffected tribes of Indians?" he wrote to Bouquet, who responded on July 13, 1763, "I will try to inoculate [them] with Some Blankets that may fall into their Hands." It is not known whether this strategem was carried out. Another British officer, Captain Ecuyer, the commander of Fort Pitt (now Pittsburgh, PA), claimed to have given two infected blankets to hostile chiefs during the summer of 1763.

5839. Mine barrage was the invention of David Bushnell, who conceived the idea of floating kegs containing explosives and equipped with a gunlock and hammer that would ignite upon contact with ships. In August 1777 he attached a series of mines together in Black Point Bay, near New London, CT. Members of the crew of the British frigate *Cerberus*, commanded by Captain J. Symons, noticed a rope alongside their ship. They hauled it in, not realizing that a mine was attached to the other end. They hoisted the mine on board and it exploded, killing three of the crew and blowing a fourth into the water.

5840. Muskets produced at a government arsenal were made in 1795 at the Springfield Armory, Springfield, MA, under the direction of David Ames, the first superintendent, and Robert Orr, a master armorer. The first gunlock was filed by Alexander Crawford after a struggle of three days and was hand-stocked by Richard Beebe. In the first year, the armory produced 245 muskets.

5841. Government contract authorized by Congress for pistols was authorized on May 4, 1798, when Congress appropriated $800,000 for guns, pistols, and other weapons. The first contract was made on March 9, 1799, with Simeon North of Berlin, CT, for 500 horse pistols at $6.50 each. A second contract for 1,500 additional pistols of the same type was signed on February 6, 1880.

5842. Revolving gun was made by John Gill of Newberne, NC, in 1829. It had 14 chambers and was a percussion gun. It was never patented. The first patent for this type of gun was granted to David G. Colburn of Canton Canal, NY, on June 29, 1833.

5843. Rifled gun was made in 1834 by Cyrus Alger, who had made the first perfect bronze cannon for the Ordnance Department in 1827 at the foundry of the South Boston Iron Company.

5844. Bowie knife was invented by Colonel James Bowie in Texas about 1835. It is variously claimed that he made a weapon out of a file; that the knife was originally used by the Mexicans; and that in an encounter with Mexicans his original sword broke to within 20 inches of the hilt, leaving a shortened blade that was easier to handle. The knife had one edge and a curved point, which necessitated its being carried in a sheath.

5845. Revolver pistol with a revolving cylinder was invented in 1830 by Samuel Colt while he was traveling on the S. S. *Corlo*. With a pocket knife he whittled a wood model. He obtained a patent from England in 1835 and another from the United States on February 25, 1836, on "an improvement in revolving fire-arms." He formed the Patent Arms Manufacturing Company of Paterson, NJ, capitalized at $230,000, to manufacture them. The first revolvers produced by the factory were .34-caliber models.

5846. Land mines were invented by Captain Gabriel Jones Rains and were used against the Seminole peoples in Florida in 1840. They were later employed in the retreat from Yorktown, VA, on May 3, 1862, by Rains's Brigade under Major General John Bankhead "Jeb" Magruder during the Civil War. They were also known as booby traps and land torpedoes. They were not considered a proper or effective method of war and were outlawed, except at river defenses.

5847. Underwater torpedo operated by electric current was invented by Samuel Colt of Hartford, CT, who informed President John Tyler in a letter dated June 19, 1841, that he could sink ships by mines. He sank the gunboat *Boxer* in New York Harbor on July 4, 1842, and the 300-ton brig *Volta* on October 18, 1842. On April 13, 1843, in the presence of President Tyler, his Cabinet, General Winfield Scott, and other officials, Colt blew up a schooner on the Potomac River by an electric mine from a distance of five miles. His invention was a combination of Robert Fulton's stationary torpedo and Professor Robert Hare's galvanic current.

5848. Breech-loading cannon was invented by Benjamin Chambers, Sr., who obtained a patent on July 31, 1849, on "an improvement in movable breeches for fire-arms and the locks and appurtenances of the same." His wooden model was discovered in an old smithy and became part of the collection of the Virginia Historical Society.

5849. Signal flares for communication between ships over long distances were developed in the late 1850s by Martha Hunt Coston of Washington, DC, widow of inventor Benjamin Coston, who came up with the original idea. Her Coston Telegraphic Signals, in white, red, and green, were used by the Union navy during the Civil War.

5850. Rifled breech-loading steel cannon was made in 1854 by James Richards Haskell. He sold 25 to the Mexican government.

5851. Revolver that was self-cocking was the Rider model, invented by John Rider and manufactured in 1856 by E. Remington and Sons of Ilion, NY.

5852. Machine gun was invented by Charles E. Barnes of Lowell, MA, who obtained a patent on July 8, 1856, on an "improved automatic cannon." It was operated by a crank, the speed of firing depending upon the speed with which the crank was turned.

5853. Metal gun cartridge successfully produced was made by Daniel Baird Wesson of the Smith and Wesson Company, Springfield, MA, in 1857, based upon a patent granted to him on August 8, 1854. In 1860, additional patents were granted on a cartridge in which the fulminate was enclosed in the hollow annular projecting case. Metal cartridges revolutionized the firearms industry and made the breech-loading rifle possible.

5854. Revolving gun turret for ships was invented by Theodore Ruggles Timby of Brooklyn, NY (now part of New York City), who was also the first to advocate the use of iron in the construction of ships. He showed the War Department an ivory model of a revolving battery in April 1841 and filed a caveat in 1843 for "a revolving tower for offensive and defensive warfare to be used on land and water." The design was adapted from the shape of Castle Williams in New York. Twenty years elapsed before the War Department adopted the idea for use during the Civil War. Timby's revolving gun turret was installed on the Union ship *Monitor*, which defeated the Confederate ship *Merrimac* on March 9, 1862, at Hampton Roads, VA, in the first Civil War battle between ironclad ships.

5855. Rapid-fire machine gun was the Gatling gun, invented by Richard Jordan Gatling of Indianapolis, IN, who obtained a patent on November 4, 1862, on "an improvement in revolving battery guns." The first gun, which fired 250 shots a minute, was made in Indianapolis.

5856. Periscope was invented by Thomas Doughty, acting chief engineer of the Navy, in 1864. During Nathaniel Prentiss Banks's Red River expedition, Doughty was on the turreted monitor *Osage*. Annoyed by bushwhackers and snipers who could not be seen yet did deadly work, Doughty rigged up a sheet-iron tube extending from a few feet above the deck to the engine room below, with an internal arrangement of mirrors that allowed him to see the shore. When attacked, he would signal the gunners to fire. Admiral David Dixon Porter officially thanked him for his invention.

5857. Cartridge belt patent was granted on August 20, 1867, to Anson Mills, brevet lieutenant colonel in the Army, Fort Bridger,

UT. Moisture had previously affected cartridge belts. Mills invented a woven cartridge belt, and the machinery for making it, which was adopted by both the Army and Navy.

5858. Air gun was the "Chicago," a wooden gun marketed in March 1886 by the Markham Manufacturing Company, Plymouth, MI. It fired a size "BB" shot. In 1888 a metal gun was manufactured and on January 16, 1889, sales rights were granted to the Plymouth Iron Windmill Company.

5859. Shot tower used by an American manufacturer of ammunition was erected in 1895 by the Peters Cartridge Company at Kings Mills, OH. The factory was organized by G. Moore Peters and was incorporated on January 24, 1887.

5860. Army field range drawn by horses, known as a "moving kitchen," was introduced by Captain Daniel Frank Craig of the Army's 4th Field Artillery on a 21-day march in May 1908, while he was serving on the staff of Colonel Alexander Brydie Dyer at Vancouver, WA. It was mounted on a two-wheeled truck or trailer and was drawn behind a rations wagon. Though extensively used, it was never officially adopted by the War Department.

5861. Airplane torpedo was invented by Bradley Allen Fiske of the Navy, who obtained a patent on July 16, 1912, on a "method of and apparatus for delivering submarine torpedoes from airships." The torpedo, held rigidly in place with its bow pointing in the same direction as the airplane, was dropped under its own power.

5862. Submachine gun was the .45-caliber Thompson submachine gun, known as the "Tommy gun." It was invented by Brigadier General John Taliaferro Thompson, who organized the Auto-Ordnance Company in 1915 to build lightweight semiautomatic infantry shoulder rifles. The first model was proof-fired at the Warner and Swasey Company, Cleveland, OH, where the first gun was built. The gun weighed approximately 10 pounds and had a cyclic rate of fire of between 600 and 800 shots a minute.

5863. Tank operated by Army troops was the French-built Renault tank used in the Battle of St. Mihiel on September 12, 1918. The first chief of the Tank Corps was Brigadier General Samuel Dickerson Rockenbach, appointed in June 1919. No American-built tanks were used in World War I.

5864. Airplane bombing experiment to sink a battleship took place on July 21, 1921, near Hampton Roads, VA, in an Army bombing demonstration conducted by General William Mitchell. The target was the *Ostfriesland*, a former German battleship. Martin bombers dropped seven 2,000-pound bombs on the battleship and nearby, causing it to turn on its port side and sink stern first within 21 minutes. This was the first of several demonstrations by Mitchell with the goal of persuading military leaders to strengthen the air power of the armed forces.

5865. Smokescreen for concealing the movement of troops and ships was invented in 1923 by Thomas Buck Hine. It was first demonstrated publicly on September 5, 1923, during naval bombing tests off Cape Hatteras, NC.

5866. Semiautomatic rifle adopted as standard by the Army was the U.S. Rifle Caliber .30, M1, known as the Garand Semi-Automatic Shoulder Rifle. It was invented by John C. Garand of Somerset, MD, who obtained a patent on October 19, 1926, on an "automatic gun." It was adopted by the Army on January 9, 1936.

5867. General purpose military vehicle was the jeep, designed in 1940 by Karl K. Pabst, consulting engineer to the American Bantam Company, Butler, PA. That summer, the army had asked for prototypes of a "low-silhouette scout car" that was powerful, light, rugged, and easy to service. The Bantam prototype featured a four-cylinder Continental engine, four-wheel drive, and a fold-down windshield. Similar models were manufactured by Willys-Overland and the Ford Motor Company. Almost 650,000 jeeps were manufactured by the end of World War II. The basic jeep design was abandoned by the military in the 1970s but persisted in consumer vehicles. The name jeep derived from the initials of "General Purpose."

5868. Automatic aircraft cannon of 20 millimeters was manufactured by the Eclipse Machine Division of the Bendix Aviation Corporation, Elmira, NY, and was delivered to the Army on May 16, 1941.

5869. Heavy tank built in the United States for the Army was constructed by the Baldwin Locomotive Works, Eddystone, PA, and presented by William Henry Harman, vice president of the company, to Brigadier General Gladeon Marcus Barnes of the Army Ordnance Department on December 8, 1941. It weighed 60 tons and had a 75-millimeter (three-inch) cannon in the turret.

5870. Handheld rocket launcher was developed by Capt. L. A. Skinner and C. N. Hickman and produced on June 14, 1942, by the General Electric Company, Bridgeport, CT. Dubbed the "bazooka," after a crude wind instrument made of pipes invented by American comedian Bob Burns, it weighed 12 pounds and was operated by a two-man team. It consisted of a smoothbore steel tube about 50 inches long and 2.5 inches in diameter, open at both ends. Attached to the tube were a shoulder stock and front and rear grips for the gunner, together with sights and an electric battery that set off the rocket-propelled charge when the launcher trigger was squeezed. The rocket was nearly two feet long. It fired about 300 yards. The first 5,000 bazookas were completed within 30 days and were used in the field mainly against tanks and armored vehicles.

5871. Atomic bomb explosion occurred on July 16, 1945, in a desert area at Alamogordo Air Base, 120 miles southeast of Albuquerque, NM. The shot, designated "Trinity," was part of Operation Trinity. It was a tower shot with a 100-foot height of burst.

5872. Atomic bomb dropped from an airplane over water was released from *Dave's Dream*, an Air Force B-29 Superfortress, on June 30, 1946 (21:01 Greenwich Civil Time), over the Bikini Lagoon in the Pacific Ocean. The shot, designated "Able," was part of Operation Crossroads. It had a 520-foot height of burst and caused the sinking of two transports (the *Gilliam* and the *Carlisle*) and damage to 18 other ships that were among a group of 73 vessels used as a target.

5873. Atomic bomb underwater explosion took place on July 24, 1946, in the Pacific Ocean, three miles off Bikini. The bomb was dropped from an airplane at a height of 7,000 feet and exploded 90 feet underwater. The shot, designated "Baker," was part of Operation Crossroads. It resulted in the sinking of 10 vessels (including the battleship *Arkansas*) that were set up as a target.

5874. Ballistic missile was a Corporal, fired on May 22, 1947, at the White Sands Proving Ground, NM. It responded accurately to guidance commands and reached a range of 63 miles.

5875. Atomic bomb explosion to be shown on television took place on February 1, 1951, at Frenchman Flat, NV. It was the third blast set off by the Atomic Energy Commission. A camera on Mount Wilson, 300 miles away, telecast the explosion for station KTLA, Los Angeles, CA. It was shown on Channel 4 of the NBC network.

5876. Air-to-air rocket was the Mighty Mouse, created by the Navy's Bureau of Ordnance for use by interceptor planes to destroy bombers. The rocket, which was placed in production in October 1951, was 4 feet long, weighed 18 pounds, and had a diameter of 2.75 inches. The rockets could be fired one at a time or in salvos of 6, 12, 18, or 24.

5877. Rocket to intercept an airplane was a Nike, fired on November 27, 1951, at the White Sands Proving Ground, NM, at an aerial target. The missile detonated about 25 feet from the target, which was flying at a range of about 15 miles at an altitude of 33,000 feet and a speed of 300 miles per hour.

5878. Atomic bomb underground explosion was detonated on November 29, 1951, at Frenchman Flat, NV, and witnessed by a group consisting of some members of Congress and some military officers headed by Chief of Staff General Joseph Lawton Collins. The explosion, which produced a hole about 800 feet in diameter and 100 feet deep, was designated as "Uncle," a part of Operation Buster-Jangle.

5879. Hydrogen bomb was detonated on October 31, 1952, and designated as "Mike," part of Operation Ivy. It was a tower shot with a burst of 20 feet at the Elugelab Atoll at the Eniwetok Proving Ground, Marshall Islands.

5880. Nuclear cannon was a 40-foot, 85-ton cannon known as Atomic Annie or Amazon Annie, which was electronically fired at 8:30 A.M. on May 25, 1953, at Frenchman Flat, NV. A 280-millimeter projectile, 11 inches by 3 feet, was loaded by a crew of nine from the 52nd Field Artillery Group, Fort Sill, OK, and aimed at a target seven miles away. The shot produced an eight-second fireball visible for a distance of 65 miles despite the bright sunshine. The charge was touched off by scientists of the Atomic Energy Commission from a site 10 miles away. The explosion was witnessed from points three to seven miles from the target area by the secretary of defense and other executives and by 100 members of Congress.

5881. **Hydrogen bomb dropped from an airplane** exploded on May 20, 1956, over Namu Atoll at the northwest edge of the Bikini Atoll. It was designated as "Cherokee," a part of Operation Redwing. It created a fireball four miles in diameter.

5882. **Intermediate-range ballistic missile** was a Jupiter, fired on May 31, 1957, from the Atlantic Missile Range, Cape Canaveral, FL. The firing was conducted by the Jet Propulsion Laboratories and the Army Ballistic Missile Agency.

5883. **Nuclear warhead mounted on a rocket** was installed on an MB-I, known as the Genie, that was fired on July 19, 1957, at Yucca Flat, NV. It was an air-to-air rocket and contained a built-in guidance mechanism. It was made by the Douglas Aircraft Company, Santa Monica, CA, and was fired from an F89 Scorpion jet.

5884. **Rocket to intercept a supersonic target missile** was a Nike Hercules missile, fired in November 1958, that destroyed a supersonic target missile traveling faster than 1,500 miles per hour at an altitude greater than 60,000 feet.

5885. **Ship to fire a Polaris missile** was the *Observation Island*, commissioned on December 5, 1958. It was 563 feet long overall and had a beam of 76 feet, a full load displacement of 16,100 tons, a draft of 24 feet, and a speed of 20 knots. It was commanded by Captain Leslie Slack. Formerly, it had been the SS *Empire State Mariner*, a merchant cargo ship that had been launched on August 15, 1953, by the New York Shipbuilding Corporation, Camden, NJ, and transferred to the Navy on September 10, 1956. On August 27, 1959, a Polaris missile was launched from the *Observation Island* seven miles off Cape Canaveral, FL. The missile, fired by compressed air, ignited successfully at 70 feet and sped 700 miles to the target area. It was a solid-propellant two-stage missile, 28 feet long and 4 feet 6 inches in diameter.

5886. **Guided missile launched from a nuclear submarine** was a Regulus I, launched on March 25, 1960, from the *Halibut* off Oahu, HI. The missile was guided over its simulated target on Lehua Island, 120 miles away, before landing, about 15 minutes after launching, at Bonham Air Force Base, Kauai, HI, 20 miles beyond the target.

5887. **Submerged submarine to fire a Polaris missile** was the USS *George Washington*, commanded by Commander James Butler Osborn, which submerged to a depth of 90 feet about 30 miles off Cape Canaveral, FL, on July 20, 1960, and fired a 28,500-pound Polaris missile at 1:39 P.M. The 28-foot two-stage rocket traveled 1,150 statute miles eastward in less than 14 minutes. A second missile was fired at 4:32 P.M. News of the firing was sent to President Dwight David Eisenhower: "Polaris . . . from out of the deep to target. Perfect."

5888. **Nuclear warhead fired from a Polaris submarine** was fired on May 6, 1962, from the USS *Ethan Allen*, submerged off Christmas Island in the Pacific test area. The missile sped skyward in a parabolic trajectory and then exploded. It carried a force estimated at 500,000 tons of TNT.

5889. **Launching silos for Atlas F missiles** were built by General Dynamics–Astronautics and turned over to the Strategic Air Command on September 13, 1962. Twelve underground silos, 175 feet deep, were built around Salina, KS. The complex cost about $150 million. The missiles had a range of 6,000 miles.

5890. **Tank with a turbine engine** was the XM-1, known as the Abrams tank. It was powered by an AVCO Lycoming rotary diesel-fuel turbine engine that was rolled out on February 29, 1980, at the Chrysler Corporation's factory in Lima, OH. The tank had Chobham-type armor and a laser range-finder on its main gun, could attain 20 miles per hour in six seconds, and could cruise at 45 miles per hour. It cost $1.5 million. The first unit recipient was H Company, 2nd Squadron, 6th Armored Cavalry Lightning Brigade.

5891. **MX intercontinental ballistic missile base** was built in 1986 at Warren Air Force Base, WY. The MX were multiple-warhead nuclear missiles capable of being transported underground by rail to any of thousands of secret launch sites. The MX system was designed to survive an enemy's nuclear first strike and to give the United States a first-strike capability of its own. The $30 billion system, approved on June 7, 1979, by President Jimmy Carter, was only partially completed.

5892. **Cruise missiles used in war** were launched on January 16, 1991, the first day of the Gulf War, when approximately 100 Tomahawk cruise missiles were fired from American ships in the Persian Gulf. They struck targets in Baghdad, Iraq.

5893. **Destruction of an attacking missile by a defensive missile in combat** occurred on January 18, 1991, when a SCUD missile launched from Iraq during the Gulf War was blown out of the sky over northern Saudi Arabia by an American-made Patriot antimissile missile.

5894. **Ray gun to shoot down an armed missile** was the U.S. Army's Tactical High Energy Laser/Advanced Concept Technology Demonstrator (THEL/ACTD) weapon, a high-energy chemical laser projector co-developed with the U.S. defense contractor TRW Space & Electronics Group and the Israel Ministry of Defense. On June 6, 2000, at the Army's High Energy Laser Systems Test Facility in White Sands, NM, the laser successfully intercepted and destroyed a Russian-made Katyusha short-range rocket armed with a live warhead.

5895. **Lightweight bulletproof body armor** was Interceptor Body Armor, developed for the U.S. Army and the U.S. Marine Corps in 2003. The vest, made of Kevlar, weighed 8.4 pounds and came in various sizes. It could be enhanced by the addition of 4-pound boron carbide ceramic plates at the chest and back.

NATURE AND ENVIRONMENT

5896. Flood of record was the flooding of the Mississippi River in 1543, which was observed by the Spanish explorer Hernando de Soto. He noted that the river began overflowing its banks on March 18 and continued until it crested on April 20. By the end of May, the flood had receded.

5897. Hurricane of record occurred on August 15, 1635, when a fierce storm ravaged New England. It was described by both William Bradford, governor of Plymouth Colony, and John Winthrop, governor of Massachusetts Bay Colony, who wrote that it "blew with such violence, with such abundance of rain, that it blew down many hundred of trees, overthrew some houses, and drave ships from their anchors."

5898. Earthquake of record is described in *History of the Plymouth Plantation* by William Bradford, the colony's first governor. The earthquake occurred on Friday, June 1, 1638, at 2 p.m. at Plymouth, MA, and is described in part as follows: "However, it was very terrible for the time; and as the men were set talking in the house, some women and others were without the doors, and the earth shooke with the violence as they could not stand without catching hold of the posts and pails that stood next them, but the violence lasted not long. And about halfe an hower, or less, came an other noyse & shaking, but neither so loud nor strong as the former, but quickly passed over, and so it ceased." In 1638 several Native Americans described to Roger Williams, founder of Providence, RI, an earthquake that had occurred there in 1558. No accurate record exists prior to this date.

5899. Cyclone of record occurred on August 27, 1667, at Jamestown, VA. According to one observer, it produced "such violence that it overturned many houses burying in the ruins much goods and many people, beating to the grounds such as were any ways employed in the fields, blowing many cattle that were near the sea or rivers, into them, whereby unknown numbers have perished, to the great affliction of all people . . . . the sea swelled twelve foot above the normal eight, drowning the whole country before it, with many of the inhabitants, their cattle and feed."

5900. Tornado of record occurred at New Haven, CT, on June 10, 1682, about 2:30 P.M. Sir Walter Raleigh's Virginia colonists are believed to have seen a tornado off the coast of North Carolina on June 23, 1586.

5901. Landscape architect was John Reid, gardener to Sir George Mackenzie of Rosebaugh, lord advocate under Charles II. Reid left Aberdeen, Scotland, on August 28, 1683, on the *Exchange*, accompanied by his wife and three daughters, and landed at Staten Island, NY (now part of New York City), on December 19, 1683.

5902. Volcanic eruption for which a date can be estimated occurred at Cinder Cone, in the Lassen Peak district of California, about 1694.

5903. Drought of record occurred in New England in 1727, when there was hardly any rainfall from the second week of April through the middle of July.

5904. Hailstone shower of record that was fatal took place on May 8, 1784, at Winnsborough, SC, when "an extraordinary shower of hail, attended with thunder and lightning," killed several people, as well as sheep and fowl.

5905. Coast survey book was Captain Lawrence Furlong's *The American Coast Pilot, containing the courses and distance from Boston to all the principal harbours, capes and headlands included between Passamaquady and the Capes of Virginia with directions for sailing into, and out of, all the principal ports and harbours, with the sounding on the coast,* 121 pages, printed in March 1796 in Newburyport, MA, by Edward March Blunt and Angier March.

5906. Environmental protection law enacted by a state in connection with advertising was passed by New York on March 28, 1865, amending an 1853 law entitled "an act for the more effectual prevention of wanton and malicious mischief and to prevent the defacement of natural scenery." The amendment declared that painting and printing upon stones, rocks, or trees and the defacement of natural scenery in certain localities constituted a misdemeanor punishable by a fine not exceeding $250, or six months' imprisonment, or both.

5907. Photograph of a tornado that is known was taken on August 28, 1884, 22 miles west of Howard, SD (which, at that time, was still part of the Dakota Territory). The photographer was F. N. Robinson. The picture is a sepia-toned image of a cloud with two partial funnels and a third one making contact with the ground.

5908. Earthquake of consequence to be recorded was felt on August 31, 1886, throughout the eastern part of the United States. The epicenter was 15 miles northwest of Charleston, SC, where 41 people died, 90 percent of the city's 6,956 brick buildings were damaged, and nearly all of its 14,000 chimneys were broken off at the roof. Altogether, the earthquake claimed some 100 lives. A series of earthquakes beginning on December 16, 1811, were the most severe in U.S. history—they changed the course of the Mississippi River and created many new lakes—but the epicenter was in a sparsely populated region and caused no known casualties.

5909. Dam disaster of great consequence occurred on May 31, 1889, at Johnstown, PA, when the South Fork Dam burst and flooded the city with a wall of water reaching 75 feet high and half a mile wide. The flood caused 2,205 deaths and property damage of about $10 million. The dam had held back the waters of Conemaugh Lake, which was about 2.5 miles long and 1.5 miles wide, with an average depth of 50 feet.

5910. Conservationist of note was the naturalist John Muir, born in 1838 in Scotland. Muir came to the United States in 1849 and spent many years traveling through the interior as a botanist. He founded the Sierra Club and campaigned successfully for the establishment of protected national parks and forests, including Yosemite National Park in California, which was formed by act of Congress in 1890. Muir Woods National Monument in California and Alaska's Muir Glacier were named for him.

5911. Nonprofit land conservation trust was the Trustees of Public Reservations, established on May 21, 1891, for the purpose of acquiring and preserving places of historic interest and places of great natural beauty. It was the brainchild of Charles Eliot, a Boston landscape architect. The group was created by a vote of the state legislature, but because it was a private organization, the word "Public" was eventually deleted from its name. The Boston Metropolitan Parks System was a direct result of its work.

5912. Audubon society for the protection of birds and, more generally, of the natural environment, was the Massachusetts Audubon Society, founded in Boston, MA, in 1896 by Harriet Lawrence Hemenway and others. This was the start of the national Audubon movement, which spread to most states by the end of the century. The National Association of Audubon Societies for the Protection of Wild Birds and Animals was organized in New York in 1905. In 1940 the organization's name was changed to the National Audubon Society.

5913. Garbage incinerator that was successful was established in 1897 in St. Louis, MO, by a private contractor who had a contract with the city for the collection and disposal of garbage. The Merz process was used. The water was drained off, cans, bottles, and rags were taken out, and grease was extracted by means of naphtha.

5914. Hurricane to cause extensive destruction since records have been kept was the Galveston Hurricane, which had gathered enough strength in the Gulf of Mexico to form a Category 4 hurricane by the time it smashed into the coast of Texas on September 8, 1900. Galveston was flooded by storm tides that reached up to 15 feet. The storm caused an estimed 8,000 to 12,000 deaths and $30 million of property damage.

5915. Tornado disaster on a large scale occurred on March 18, 1925, when tornados struck Indiana, Illinois, Kentucky, and Tennessee. Over the course of three hours, 689 people died, 13,000 were injured, and $16–18 million worth of damage occurred.

5916. Volcanic eruption to be broadcast on radio was the eruption of the Mount Kilauea volcano in Hawaii. The sound was transmitted via short wave by station KGU, Honolulu, HI, whose wires extended 3.5 miles from the mouth of the volcano to the transmitter. The broadcast was picked up in San Francisco and relayed to WJZ, New York City, where it was heard at 4:15 P.M. on December 28, 1931. Thomas A. Jaggar, a volcanologist, likened the sound of the erupting volcano to the roar of Niagara Falls and reported that in six days about 260,000 cubic feet of lava had been disgorged.

5917. Deposits on bottles were instituted in 1934 by the National Recovery Administration, a federal agency. The deposits were two cents or five cents, depending on the size of the bottle.

5918. Category 5 hurricane to make landfall in United States territory since record-keeping began was the hurricane that hit the upper Florida Keys, centering on the town of Islamorada, on September 2, 1935. (As the naming of hurricanes did not begin until 1950, this storm is known as the Labor Day Hurricane.) Among the 423 dead were 259 veterans of World War I who were working on a bridge-construction projects for the federal government and who were living in rickety barracks that were demolished by the 160-mph winds. The train that had been sent to evacuate them was washed away by floodwaters.

5919. Public service symbol of the federal government was Smokey Bear. During World War II, the Forest Service sought advertising help to educate the public about the danger of forest fires. On August 9, 1944, Albert Staehle, an illustrator of animals, came up with the image of a fire-fighting bear. The slogan "Only you can prevent forest fires" was coined by a Los Angeles ad agency in 1947. Smokey Bear appeared on posters and comic books distributed to schoolchildren and on television commercials. In 1950, a bear cub rescued from a forest fire in New Mexico was dubbed "Smokey Bear." He was exhibited in the National Zoo in Washington, DC, and died in 1976.

5920. Deaths from smog occurred in October 1947 in Donora, PA. A thermal inversion trapped pollutants over the heavily industrialized town, which is set in a natural basin. The inversion ended four days later, leaving 20 people dead and 6,000 in need of medical treatment.

5921. Water pollution law enacted by Congress was the Water Pollution Control Act, which took effect on June 30, 1948. It provided funds for sewage treatment systems and pollution research and empowered the Justice Department to file suit against polluters.

5922. State law regulating beverage containers was Vermont's ban on disposable beer bottles, passed in 1953 and repealed in 1957. Its purpose was, in part, to prevent dairy cattle from ingesting broken glass.

5923. Ecology book of wide influence was *Silent Spring* by biologist Rachel Louise Carson. The book, published in 1962 by the Houghton Mifflin Company, Boston, MA, detailed the harm to wildlife caused by the widespread use of the persistent pesticide DDT. It is credited with launching the environmental movement in the United States.

5924. Smog chamber for air pollution research built by an industrial organization was placed in operation in July 1962 by General Motors Research Laboratories, Warren, MI. The cylindrical chamber contained 300 cubic feet of space irradiated by 247 fluorescent lamps that simulated noonday sunlight.

5925. Air pollution law of importance enacted by Congress was the Clean Air Act of 1963, signed into law on December 17, 1963. It authorized $93 million in matching grants for state-funded air pollution prevention and control programs. The Clean Air Act of 1970, signed into law on December 31, 1970, was the first to set national standards for air polluting emissions from motor vehicles.

5926. Comprehensive wilderness law was the Wilderness Act of 1964, which led to the creation of a system of wilderness preserves. The act was the culmination of the work of several government conservationists, including Arthur Carhart, Aldo Leopold, and Robert Marshall of the Forest Service, and Howard Zahniser of the Bureau of Biological Survey.

5927. Endangered species list issued by the federal government was issued by the Department of the Interior in 1966. It listed 78 species of rare and endangered plants, reptiles, birds, and mammals.

5928. State bottle deposit law aimed at reducing litter was enacted by Oregon on July 2, 1971. The law required a five-cent deposit on containers for carbonated and malt beverages. The bill outlawed pull-tab cans and non-returnable bottles.

5929. Noise-control law enacted by a state was New Jersey's Noise Control Act of 1971, signed on January 24, 1972, by Governor William Thomas Cahill. The act empowered the state Department of Environmental Protection to promulgate codes, rules, and regulations to lessen noise pollution, created a Noise Control Council, and made a $100,000 appropriation.

5930. Volcano known to claim human life in the contiguous 48 states was Mount St. Helens, located in the Cascade Range of Washington state. During the massive eruption of May 18, 1980, 61 people were asphyxiated by the rain of hot ash, buried by pyroclastic flows of superheated gas and mud, or drowned in flash floods.

5931. Year when half of the nation's agricultural counties were designated disaster areas was 1988. By the end of June, much of the United States was suffering through the worst drought in five decades.

5932. Billion-dollar settlement in an environmental lawsuit was reached on October 22, 1998, by the Environmental Protection Agency and the Justice Department with seven diesel truck engine manufacturers—Caterpillar Inc., Cummins Engine Co. Inc., Navistar International Corp., the Detroit Diesel Corp., Mack Trucks, Renault SA, and Volvo—charged with violating clean air laws. The manufacturers were alleged to have sold as many as 1.3 million engines designed to evade motor vehicle pollution standards.

5933. Ban on the sale of mercury thermometers to reduce mercury toxicity in the waste stream was enacted on March 6, 2000, by Duluth, MN. The ordinance also banned the sale of other medical and scientific devices that use mercury, including sphygmomanometers (blood-pressure cuffs), and prohibited the city's schools from buying mercury in bulk.

5934. Municipal recycling of diapers and incontinence products in the United States was undertaken in Santa Clarita, CA, in November 2002. A Canadian company, Knowaste, collected diapers and similar products and removed the recyclable components, such as wood pulp and plastic.

5935. City to require "green" construction for low-income housing was San Francisco, CA, whose mayor, Gavin Newsom, announced the policy on August 2, 2005. Assisted by a grant from the Enterprise Foundation, the city offered financing to nonprofit developers to create 600 new low-income housing units using recycled materials, solar heating panels, and energy-efficient appliances.

5936. Natural disaster to cause the evacuation of an entire city was Hurricane Katrina, a Category 3 hurricane that hit New Orleans, LA, in 2005. On August 27, as the storm approached, Mayor Ray Nagin asked residents to leave the city voluntarily. The following day, he ordered the mandatory evacuation of every resident. Those without private transportation were unable to comply. Katrina arrived on August 29, wrecking the city's system of levees and sinking New Orleans under floodwaters up to 20 feet high.

Animals

5937. Furs exported were shipped to England on the S.S. *Fortune* on December 13, 1621, under the charge of Robert Cushman, one of the Plymouth colonists. The cargo, valued at $2,450, consisted of furs, sassafras, clapboards, and wainscot. The boat was captured by the French and the cargo seized.

5938. Hunting law enacted by a colony was passed on March 24, 1629, by Virginia and provided that "no . . . hides or skins whatever be sent or carried out of this colony upon forfeiture of thrice the value, whereof the half to the informer and the other half to public use."

5939. Wolf bounty was granted under authority of the General Assembly held at James City, VA, on October 5, 1646. It was signed by Sir William Berkeley, Knight Governor, and provided that "what person soever shall after publication hereof kill a wolfe and bring in the head to any commissioner, upon certificate of said communication to the county court, he or they shall receive one hundred pounds of tobacco for so doing to be raised out of the County where the wolfe is killed."

5940. Fish protection law enacted by a city was an act for "preserving fish in fresh water ponds," enacted on May 28, 1734, by New York City. Fishing by hoop-net, draw-net, purse-net, catching-net, cod-net, bley-net or with any other engine, machine, arts, or ways and means whatsoever, other than by angling with angle-rod, hook, and line, was subject to a fine of 20 shillings.

5941. Bird banding was done in 1803 at Mill Grove Farm, Montgomery County, 24 miles northwest of Philadelphia, PA, by John James Audubon, who used silver wire to band a brood of phoebes and was fortunate in obtaining two returns.

5942. Sparrows were imported in 1850 under the auspices of Nicholas Pike and other directors of the Brooklyn Institute, Brooklyn, NY (now part of New York City), for the purpose of protecting shade trees from foliage-eating caterpillars. Eight pairs of English, or house, sparrows (*Passer domesticus*) were imported. The birds were kept in cages until liberated in the spring of 1851. They did not thrive, and in 1852 a larger number were imported.

5943. Bird refuge established by a state was established at Lake Merritt, Oakland, CA, by authority of a law enacted on February 14, 1872.

5944. Game warden to be paid a salary was William Alden Smith of Grand Rapids, MI, appointed for a four-year term at $1,200 annually plus expenses under a state law approved March 15, 1887, "an act to provide for the appointment of a game and fish warden and to prescribe his powers and duties to enforce the statutes of this state for the preservation of moose, wapiti, deer, birds and fish." Wisconsin approved a similar law on April 12, 1887, authorizing appointment of four game wardens for two-year terms at an annual salary of $600 with a maximum of $250 for expenses.

5945. Pronghorn antelope bred and reared in captivity was born in the City Park Zoo, Denver, CO, in 1903. The event was noted by Theodore Roosevelt, who congratulated the zoo director, Alfred Hill.

5946. Bird reservation established by the federal government was established by executive order of President Theodore Roosevelt on March 14, 1903, at Pelican Island, situated in the Indian River near Sebastian, FL. Its goal was to protect a nesting colony of pelicans and herons. This wildlife refuge was enlarged in 1909 to include adjacent mangrove islands and swamps.

5947. Bird for which a definite crossing of the Atlantic was recorded was a common tern (*Sterna hirundo*) that was banded at Eastern Egg Rock, ME, on July 3, 1913, and found dead in August 1917 at the mouth of the Niger River, West Africa.

5948. Bird banding by federal authorities was done by the United States Biological Survey. Bands were attached to different species of ducks and other water birds during the summer of 1914 by Dr. Alexander Wetmore, who was making investigations of the duck sickness at the Bear River marshes in Utah.

5949. Extinction by humans of a native American animal in modern times was that of the the American passenger pigeon (*Ectopistes migratorius*). Until the mid-1800s the most numerous bird on earth, the passenger pigeon was hunted extensively for meat and vanished from the wild by 1890. The last known specimen, named Martha, died on September 1, 1914, in the Cincinnati Zoo, Cincinnati, OH.

5950. Bird protection international treaty was the Migratory Bird Treaty for the protection of migratory birds in the United States and Canada, signed on August 16, 1916, by the United States and Great Britain at Washington, DC. It was signed by President Woodrow Wilson on September 1, 1916, ratified by Great Britain on October 20, and proclaimed on December 8.

5951. Musk ox born in captivity was a calf born on September 5, 1925, at the Bronx Zoo, New York City.

5952. Reindeer born in the United States was a jet-black calf born on May 31, 1929, at Lodgepole Ranch, the estate of Otis Emerson Dunham at North Beverly, MA.

5953. Raptor sanctuary was Hawk Mountain Sanctuary, founded in 1934 on the Kittatinny Ridge near Harrisburg, PA. It was the first bird sanctuary in the world to protect migrating hawks and eagles.

5954. Snow goose bred in captivity was hatched in 1934 in the City Park Zoo, Denver, CO.

5955. Ptarmigan hatched and reared in captivity was hatched on July 24, 1934, at Ithaca, NY, from one of 10 eggs obtained from Churchill, Manitoba, Canada, by Arthur Augustus Allen, professor of ornithology, Cornell University, Ithaca, NY. The ptarmigan was 110 days old when it died of enterohepatitis.

5956. Giant panda was Su-Lin, imported from China by Mrs. William H. Harkness, Jr., on the *President McKinley*. It weighed about five pounds when it arrived at San Francisco, CA, December 18, 1936. Su-Lin died on April 1, 1938, in the Brookfield Zoo, Chicago, IL, which had purchased it for $8,750.44. Giant pandas, though bearlike in appearance, are related to raccoons. They were first discovered in China in November 1936.

5957. Okapi was imported on August 4, 1937, when it arrived at New York City. It was 21 months old, weighed 235 pounds, and was 49 inches tall at the shoulder. It resembled a cross between a zebra and a giraffe, and had a mahogany-red body with white stripes on its buttocks and upper legs. It consumed eight bananas, four heads of cabbage, three bunches of carrots, and six liters of condensed milk and water daily. It was captured in the Belgian Congo and shipped on July 22, 1937, on the Red Star liner *Pennland*, under the personal care of Dr. William Reid Blair, director of the Bronx Zoo, New York City, to which it was delivered.

5958. Game preserve appropriation by the federal government to assist state wildlife restoration projects was passed on September 2, 1937. A million dollars was appropriated on June 16, 1938. The federal government paid 75 percent of the costs of such projects and the state 25 percent. The first project was the Utah Fish and Game Commission's plan to stabilize the water levels on some 2,000 acres of land bordering Great Salt Lake, approved on July 23, 1938, by the Fish and Wildlife Service.

5959. Quetzal bird (*Pharomacrus costaricensis*) was imported on October 4, 1940, by Dr. Victor Wolfgang Von Hagen, New York City, who had captured it. It was exhibited at the Bronx Zoo, New York City, for three days before being acquired by the St. Louis Zoo, St. Louis, MO. It was a male, three years old, pigeon-sized, with a crimson breast, emerald back and head, jet black wings, a black-and-white tail, and a green train about a yard long. On October 29, 1937, Von Hagen had brought back nine young quetzals, which were shown at the Bronx Zoo until April 1939, when the last one died.

5960. King cobra snakes born in captivity in the United States were hatched on July 4, 1955, at the Bronx Zoo, New York City. The parent snakes were mated on March 10, 1955, and on April 25, the female snake laid 41 eggs. Nine eggs hatched, the first on July 4 and the last on July 12. The infant cobras were mottled white and brown and felt leathery to the touch.

5961. Dugong arrived at the Steinhart Aquarium, San Francisco, CA, on November 16, 1955, and was on display until December 27, 1955, when it died. The dugong is a sea mammal similar to a manatee.

5962. Forest horse born in the United States was Pepin, sired by Charlemagne and foaled by Siegling on May 18, 1956, at the Chicago Zoological Park, Brookfield, IL. This extinct forest breed had been re-created by a program of crossbreeding that involved more than 300 Iceland ponies, Shetland ponies, Dartmoor ponies, Norwegian duns, Hanover coach horses, feral horses from Patagonia, and Koniks of Poland. Forest horses were first imported into the United States in 1955.

5963. Gorilla born in captivity in the United States was Colo, born on December 22, 1956, at the zoo in Columbus, OH. She weighed 3.25 pounds and was the offspring of Baron (11 years old, 380 pounds) and Christiana (9 years old, 260 pounds).

5964. Whooping crane born in captivity was Dawn, a six-inch-tall crane born on May 28, 1975, at the Rare and Endangered Bird Research Center, Laurel, MD.

5965. Orca born in captivity was a six-foot, 125-pound calf born on February 28, 1977, at Marineland, Los Angeles, CA. She was the offspring of Cork, a 16-year-old, 11-ton orca. Orcas are also known as killer whales.

5966. Wolf to be reintroduced into the wild was the red wolf (*Canis rufus*), believed to be the only species of wolf that evolved completely in North America. Once common in the southwestern United States, the red wolf had been extinct in the wild since the 1970s. The only surviving individuals were maintained in captive breeding programs. In 1987, four breeding pairs and their pups were released in the Alligator River National Wildlife Refuge, NC, by the Fish and Wildlife Service.

5967. Zebra mussels were accidentally introduced from Europe in the mid-1980s. The first specimen of the prolific shellfish (*Dreissena polymorpha*) was identified in 1988 in Lake St. Clair, near Detroit, MI. The mussels quickly spread through Lake Erie into Lake Ontario and connected bodies of water, replacing native species and causing damage to underwater structures and marine equipment.

5968. Killer bees entered the United States from Mexico in October 1990. More properly called Africanized honeybees, the aggressive species, a hybrid of European honeybees and African honeybees, had been migrating north since their origin in Brazil in 1956. By the 1990s, they had caused more than 1,000 human deaths.

5969. Sea otter conceived and born in captivity to survive was Oz, born to sea otters Thelma and Eddie at the Oregon Zoo in Portland, OR, on January 3, 2001.

5970. Endangered species to be cloned was the gaur, a wild ox from Asia. On January 8, 2001, a male baby gaur was born to a cow that had served as his surrogate mother. He had been cloned by scientists led by Philip Damiani at Advanced Cell Technologies, Worcester, MA. The calf died of a bacterial infection two days after birth.

5971. Rediscovery of a bird thought to be extinct in the United States occurred on February 11, 2004, when Gene Sparling, an outdoorsman from Hot Springs, AK, saw an ivory-billed woodpecker in Big Woods, an Arkansas nature reserve. Once found throughout swamps and forests in the southeastern states, the ivory-billed woodpecker had been considered extinct since 1944, though sightings were occasionally reported. The discovery was authenticated by a team of Cornell University ornithologists, who began a campaign to save what remained of the woodpecker's habitat.

Forests

5972. Forestry law enacted by a colony was the act of March 29, 1626, passed by the Plymouth Colony, which required the approval of the governor and the council to sell or transport lumber out of the colony.

5973. Community forest was established in 1710 in Newington, NH. An area of 110 acres of pine trees was set aside as a "town forest."

5974. Forest fire of consequence that was recorded occurred on October 8, 1871, at Peshtigo, WI, north of Green Bay. The fire, which was eight to 10 miles wide, destroyed 1.28 acres of timberland. The forests were dry, since there had been no rain for three months.

5975. National forestry association was the American Forestry Association, organized on September 10, 1875, in Chicago, IL. The American Forestry Congress merged with the association in 1882.

5976. State forestry association was the Minnesota Forestry Association, organized on January 12, 1876, in St. Paul, MN, to promote the planting of forest trees. E. R. Drake was the first president. On March 2, 1876, the state appropriated $2,500 to carry on the work.

5977. Forestry book was Franklin Benjamin Hough's *Elements of Forestry; designed to afford information concerning the planting and care of forest trees for ornament or profit and giving suggestions upon the creation and care of woodlands with the view of securing the greatest benefit for the longest time, particularly adapted to the wants and conditions of the United States*. It contained 381 pages and was published in 1882 by R. Clarke and Company, Cincinnati, OH.

5978. Forest reserve established by a state was the New York State Forest Preserve, designated on May 15, 1885. Legislation prohibiting the sale of state lands in certain counties in the Adirondack Mountains area was passed on February 6, 1883. This forest reserve functioned as a state park, where logging and other commercial forms of exploitation were prohibited.

5979. Forest management on a professional scale was begun in 1891 in Asheville, NC, on the Biltmore estate of George Washington Vanderbilt.

5980. Forest planting by the federal government was begun in 1891 in the sand hills of Nebraska in cooperation with private individuals. A small plantation of jack and Norway pines was established four miles west of Swan, NE, for the purpose of forming shelter belts to hold the sand in place. The land was acquired under authority of the act of March 3, 1891, "an act to repeal timber culture laws, and for other purposes."

5981. National forest was the Shoshone National Forest in Wyoming, established by President Benjamin Harrison on March 30, 1891, by presidential proclamation.

5982. National forest reserve was the Yellowstone Park Timberland Reserve, which was so designated by an act of Congress passed on March 30, 1891, and signed by President Benjamin Harrison. It was placed under the administration of the Land Office of the Department of the Interior.

5983. Forest fire lookout tower was a log cabin with a flat roof erected by the M.G. Shaw Lumber Company, Greenville, ME, on Squaw Mountain, southwest of Moosehead Lake. The first watchman was William Hilton of Bangor, ME, whose service started on June 10, 1905.

5984. Forest Service aerial patrol was established by the Department of Agriculture on June 1, 1919. Two patrols a day were operated out of March Field, Riverside, CA. Five routes were covered, for each of which there was one airplane. The expense was borne mainly by the Army. From June 1 to October 30, the airplanes flew 2,457 hours and covered 202,009 miles. The patrol was discontinued on October 31, 1919.

5985. Dutch elm disease breakout was observed in 1930 in Cleveland and Cincinnati, OH, where it began killing American elm trees, *Ulmus americanus*. The blight, caused by the Asiatic fungus *Ceratocystis ulmi*, was imported to the United States in elm logs shipped from Europe. It spread rapidly, decimating the North American elm population and changing the appearance of many American cities.

5986. Forest fire drenched by artificial rain produced by seeding cumulus clouds with dry ice was attacked on October 29, 1947, at Concord, NH. Seeders from the General Electric Company, Schenectady, NY, flew over the burning area in "rain-making" planes and caused rain to fall. The experiment was Project Cirrus, a joint weather research program of the Army Signal Corps and the Office of Naval Research. General rain caused by natural conditions followed, so it was impossible to determine the extent of artificial rainfall.

5987. Forest canopy crane to be used in North America was erected in the Wind River Experimental Forest, part of the Gifford Pinchot National Forest in Washington State's southern Cascade Range, in 1995. The 285-foot-tall crane, the largest of the world's three canopy cranes, raised researchers to the canopy of an old-growth conifer forest that was impossible to reach by climbing. It was the first time such a crane was used to study a temperate forest canopy.

Parks

5988. Parkland purchased by a city was Elm Park, containing 27 acres, which was sold to Worcester, MA, on March 17 and March 20, 1854, by Levi Lincoln and John Hammond.

5989. State park was the Yosemite Valley park in California, an area embracing the valley itself and the Mariposa Grove of Big Trees some miles south of it. It was granted to the state of California by act of Congress of June 30, 1864, but actual control of the area and its development were delayed some 10 years by the adverse claims of settlers in the area. The Yosemite National Park was created in 1890, and in 1905 the California State Legislature passed an act of retrocession by which the valley and grove were returned to the federal government to be included in the national park.

Courtesy of PDPhoto.org

Half Dome, at Yosemite National Park in California.

5990. National park was the Yellowstone National Park in Wyoming, authorized on March 1, 1872, by "an act to set aside a certain tract of land (2,142,720 acres) lying near the headwaters of the Yellowstone River as a public park." The first superintendent was Nathaniel Pitt Langford. The first ranger, hired in 1880, was Harry Yount, a Civil War veteran. Additional grants of land to Yellowstone Park were later made in Wyoming, Montana, and Idaho. Hot Springs National Park in Arkansas, consisting of 911 acres with 46 hot springs, was established as a reservation by an act of Congress on April 20, 1832, but was not designated as a national park until March 4, 1921.

5991. National park east of the Mississippi River and the first located on an ocean is the Acadia National Park, on the island of Mount Desert about a mile south of Bar Harbor, ME. It was established by President Woodrow Wilson on July 8, 1916, as the Sieur de Monts National Monument and became the Lafayette National Park on February 26, 1919. The name was changed on January 19, 1929, to Acadia National Park. It contains 27,871 acres.

5992. National park to contain an active volcano was the Lassen Volcanic National Park in the Sierra Nevada in California, a tract of 104,526 acres. It was established by an act of Congress approved August 9, 1916. Lassen Peak, 10,457 feet high, at the southern end of the Cascade mountain range, erupted in 1914–16 and is the only active volcano in the 48 contiguous states.

5993. International peace park was Waterton-Glacier International Peace Park, created in 1932 by the governments of the United States and Canada as a gesture of friendship. It was formed by the combination of Glacier National Park in Montana, established in 1910, and Waterton Lakes National Park in Alberta, established in 1895. The area was designated a World Heritage Site in 1995.

5994. National seashore was Cape Hatteras National Seashore, an area of 30,319 acres along the coast of North Carolina. Set aside by Congress in 1937, it was one of the longest stretches of undeveloped shoreline on the Atlantic seaboard.

5995. Undersea park established by the federal government was the Key Largo Coral Reef Preserve, an area 21 miles long and 3.5 miles wide in the Atlantic Ocean off Key Largo, FL, which was established on March 15, 1960, by presidential proclamation of President Dwight David Eisenhower. This wildlife refuge contains 40 of the 52 known coral species. Previously, it had been the John Pennekamp Coral Reef State Park, the title to which had been obtained on December 3, 1959, by the Florida Board of Parks and Historic Monuments.

5996. National park in the Southern Hemisphere was the National Park of American Samoa, established in 1993, when the National Park Service leased land from a number of villages. Of the park's 9,000 acres, 2,500 were under water. Most of the remainder were covered by tropical rainforest.

5997. American Heritage Rivers were 14 rivers and watersheds designated in 1998 by the federal government for protection. They included the New River in North Carolina, the oldest extant river in the United States; the Willamette River in Oregon; the Blackstone and Woonasquatucket Rivers in Massachusetts and Rhode Island; the Cuyahoga River in Ohio; the Detroit River in Michigan; the Hanalei River in Hawaii; the Hudson River in New York; the Rio Grande in Texas; the Potomac River in the District of Columbia, Maryland, Pennsylvania, Virginia, and West Virginia; the St. Johns River in Florida; the Upper Mississippi River in Iowa, Illinois, Minnesota, Missouri, and Wisconsin; the Lower Mississippi River in Louisiana and Tennessee; and the Upper Susquehanna and Lackawanna Rivers in Pennsylvania.

POPULATION AND SETTLEMENT

5998. Human construction in North America known to archeologists was built more than nine millennia ago, beginning approximately in the year 7000 B.C.E., at Watson Brake, LA, on the flood plain of the Ouachita River. The structure, which covered an area about 900 feet in diameter, consisted of 11 mounds of earth connected by low earthen ridges. A team of scientists led by Dr. Joe W. Saunders, professor of geosciences at Northeast Louisiana University, Monroe, LA, opened the site and found plant seeds, fish bones, and animal bones. Their findings were announced on September 20, 1997. The mounds were not used for habitation and their purpose could not be identified. They were some 1,500 years older than other early Native American sites.

5999. European to sight America was probably Bjarni Herjolffson, a trader from Iceland who was on his way to Greenland about the year 986 when his ship was blown off course by a storm. He and his men found themselves near an unknown tree-covered land, which they did not stop to investigate. His account of this adventure inspired Leif Eriksson to undertake a voyage of exploration some years later.

Library of Congress, Prints & Photographs Division LC-USZ62-3032

The discovery of Greenland.

6000. European settlement in America was Vinland, founded by the Icelandic Viking explorer Leif Eriksson circa 1000 somewhere on the northeastern coast of North America, with guesses ranging from as far south as Virginia and as far north as Newfoundland. It was, according to the account given in an Icelandic saga, a land with hardwood forests, ample pastureland, and wild grapes. Leif and his crew wintered there and returned to Greenland in the spring with a cargo of timber. A group of colonists led by Leif's sister Freydis Erikssdottir returned to the area in 1004 and again circa 1007. The settlement was abandoned by 1015.

6001. Child born of European parents on American soil was Snorri, the son of Thorfinn Karlsefni and Gudrid, widow of Leif Eriksson's brother Thorstein Eriksson. They were among 160 volunteers from Iceland who arrived in America circa 1007 to colonize a region they called Vinland, which had been explored by Leif Eriksson some years before. Historians have placed Vinland in various parts of the Atlantic coast, including Nova Scotia, Maine, and Massachusetts.

6002. Settlement in America in continuous habitation is the mountain village of Acoma, NM. First settled in the 11th century by Indians from nearby Enchanted Mesa, Acoma still has a few dozen permanent residents.

6003. European to set foot on the North American continent after the Vikings was John Cabot (also spelled Caboto, Cabotto, Caboote, Gabote, Calbot, or Talbot), a mariner who was probably born in Genoa, Italy. In 1496, King Henry VII of England granted Cabot a charter to sail west to Asia and set up a spice-trade monopoly. Cabot's ship, a 70-foot caravel called the *Mathew*, embarked from Bristol, England, on May 20, 1497, and arrived on the coast of Newfoundland—or possibly Maine—on June 24. After planting the

English and Venetian flags, Cabot and his men spent a few hours exploring the landing site, then returned to their ship.

6004. Exploration of the Mississippi River by a European was made by Hernando de Soto, the Spanish explorer. On May 21, 1541, he and his crew arrived at a village called Chisca, where they erected a huge cross. Shortly afterward de Soto died near what is now Ferriday, LA, and was buried in the "Father of Waters," the first European to be buried in the Mississippi. In 1519 Alonso Alvarez de Piñeda, who was sent out by Francisco de Garay, governor of Jamaica, entered the mouth of the river, which he called the Rio de Espiritu Santo.

Library of Congress, Prints & Photographs Division LC-USZ62-3013

De Soto arrives at the settlements along the Mississippi.

6005. Exploration of land on the Pacific coast by a European who made actual contact with it was made by Juan Rodríguez Cabrillo, who left Navidad, Mexico, on June 27, 1542, and landed on September 28 at what is now known as Ballast Point, San Diego, CA. Other Europeans had encountered the Pacific Ocean previously, including Vasco Nuñez de Balboa, who had laid eyes on the Pacific in 1513, and Ferdinand Magellan, who had sailed across the Pacific in 1520–21 during the first circumnavigation of the world.

6006. League of Native American nations was the Iroquois Confederacy, located in what is now New York State and the surrounding area. According to tradition, the Confederacy was formed in about the year 1550 by Hiawatha (Haio-hwat'ha), a Mohawk Indian, and his mentor, Dekanawida, a Huron. It included the Cayuga, Mohawk, and Oneida tribes, which were later joined by the Seneca and the Onondaga. The Tuscarora joined the Confederacy in 1715. The league was formed on cooperative principles, with each tribe represented at a policy-making council.

6007. French to arrive in America were explorers and traders who came in the 16th century. The first French settlement, located on Parris Island, SC, was established in 1562 by Huguenots (Protestants) seeking refuge from France's religious wars. It lasted two years. Another Huguenot settlement, at Fort Caroline, FL, founded in 1564, was attacked and destroyed by the Spanish the following year and its inhabitants massacred.

6008. Permanent European settlement in America was St. Augustine, FL, founded on September 8, 1565, by the sea captain Pedro Menéndez de Avilés. He left Cadiz, Spain, on July 28, 1565, on a mission to stop the settlement activities of the French Huguenots. He sighted land off the Florida coast on August 28, the feast day of St. Augustine of Hippo, for whom he named the garrison that he built nearby. The city of St. Augustine is the oldest colonial site to be continuously inhabited and the first permanent site of Catholic settlement.

6009. Surveyor in America was the English mathematician Thomas Harriot (or Hariot), surveyor and historian of Sir Walter Raleigh's first colony at Roanoke, who arrived in 1585. He remained a year and returned to England in July 1586 with the fleet commanded by Sir Richard Grenville. He published his observations in London in 1588 as *A Briefe and True Report of the New Found Land of Virginia, of the Commodities There Found and to be Raysed, As Well Merchantable, As Others for Victuall, Building and Other Necessarie Uses For Those That Are and Shalbe the Planters There . . . .*

6010. Child born of English parents in America was Virginia Dare. She was born at Roanoke Island, in the future state of North Carolina, on August 18, 1587, and was the daughter of Ananias Dare and Eleanor (White) Dare. Her maternal grandfather was John White, governor of the colony. Only the first nine days of her life are known to history. Her parents were part of a group of 150 settlers, including 25 women and children, who left England on May 8, 1587, in three vessels. They landed at Cape Hatteras on July 22 and cruised up what is now Pamlico Sound to the "iland called Roanoac." Two vessels returned to England immediately. The third, with John White aboard, sailed for England on August 27, nine days after Virginia Dare's birth, to acquire more supplies. When White returned in 1590, the colonists had vanished and their fort was in ruins.

6011. Exploration of the New England region by an Englishman was made by Captain Bartholomew Gosnold, who left Falmouth, England, on March 26, 1602, in the *Concord* with a crew of 31. On May 15, 1602, he landed on the southern Maine coast near what is now Cape Porpoise.

6012. European settlement in the northeast after the Vikings was on Neutral Island at Calais, ME, on the St. Croix River at the head of Passamaquoddy Bay. It was founded in 1604 by Pierre du Guast, Sieur de Monts, the French explorer.

6013. Permanent English settlement in America was established at Jamestown, VA, on May 13, 1607, with the arrival of the colonists who had been sent out by the London Company from Blackwell, England, on December 19, 1606. A total of 105 colonists arrived on the *Susan Constant*, 100 tons, under Captain Christopher Newport; the *Godspeed,* 40 tons, under Captain Bartholomew Gosnold; and the *Discovery*, 20 tons, under Captain John Ratcliffe.

6014. Colonists who were women in Jamestown were Mistress Forrest, the wife of Thomas Forrest, and Anne Burras, her maid. They arrived in Jamestown, VA, in October 1608, with the "Second Supply" of reinforcements, since so many of the original settlers had died. Anne Burras married and bore at least one child; records show she was still alive in 1625. Mistress Forrest, on the other hand, did not survive more than a few months. Her remains were found by archeologists in 1998.

6015. Polish settlers in America were artisans recruited by the sponsors of the English colony in Jamestown, VA, to produce items for export. Their number included glassblowers, soap makers, and pitch makers. They arrived on the *Mary and Margaret* in 1609.

6016. Dutch settlement in America was a trading post set up in 1614 at what is now Albany, NY, following the explorations of the Dutch explorer Henry Hudson in 1609. The Dutch West India Company established Fort Orange at Albany in 1624. The entire colony, stretching along the Hudson River, was called New Netherland and had its capital at New Amsterdam, on Manhattan Island. Lack of interest by Dutch people in emigrating to New Netherland forced the company to recruit volunteers from France, Belgium, Sweden, and other Western European countries. The first director general of the colony was Peter Minuit.

Library of Congress, Pritns & Photographs Division
LC-USZ62-3024

Henry Hudson encounters the native peoples.

6017. Child born of English parents in New England was Peregrine White, born on board the *Mayflower* off Cape Cod harbor on November 20, 1620. He was the son of Susanna and William White.

6018. Greeting addressed to the Pilgrims by a Native American was a phrase in the English language: "Welcome, Englishmen." It was spoken by Samoset, an Abenaki Indian, on March 16, 1621, when he entered the Pilgrim settlement at what is now Plymouth, MA. Samoset was a sagamore of the Pemaquid tribe who had learned some English from the fishermen who harvested cod off the coast of Maine. He was in Massachusetts as a guest of the Wampanoag chief Massasoit, whose territories included Plymouth. Samoset introduced the Pilgrims to

Massasoit and to Tisquantum (also known as Squanto), the English-speaking Patuxet Indian who instructed the settlers in agriculture.

6019. Colonial treaty with the Native Americans was a defensive alliance made on April 1, 1621, on Strawberry Hill, Plymouth, MA, between Massasoit, chief of the Wampanoags, and the Plymouth colonists, acting in behalf of King James I. They promised not to "doe hurt" to one another. If a Wampanoag broke the law, he was sent to Plymouth for punishment; if a colonist was the offender, he was sent to the Wampanoags. The agreement in all its parts was kept by both parties for more than half a century.

6020. Belgian immigrants were Walloons, led by Jesse de Forest, who came to New Amsterdam (later New York City) in 1624 aboard the ship *New Netherland*. They settled in New Amsterdam, Brooklyn, Albany, and in Gloucester, NJ, becoming the first European residents in what is now the Middle Atlantic region.

6021. Child born of African-American parents in America was William Tucker, born in Elizabeth City, VA, to Antoney and Isabell, two of the first 20 Africans to arrive in Jamestown in 1619 and the first Africans to marry. William was baptized in Jamestown in 1624.

6022. Land sale by Native Americans to Europeans known to have taken place occurred in July 1625, when John Brown of New Harbor, ME, purchased 12,000 acres of Pemaquid land in Maine. The deed was signed by two leaders of the Pemaquid, Samoset and Unungoit.

6023. Land sale swindle was the sale of Manhattan Island to Dutch colonists under Peter Minuit in 1626. The Canarsie chiefs who accepted 60 guilders' worth of trinkets for the island (a sum worth several thousand dollars, not $24 as is often reported) had no claim to it. They hailed from the area that is now called Brooklyn. The future site of New York City belonged to the Manhattans (also called the Manados), and Minuit had to pay them separately.

6024. Fur trading post was established by the Pilgrims of Plymouth Colony in Augusta, ME, in 1628. Trade was carried on with the Norridgewock tribe of Native Americans. Most of the pelts were exported to England.

6025. Deportation took place in 1628, when Thomas Morton was sent back to England by the Plymouth Colony for being a troublemaker. Morton, an Englishman who had emigrated in 1624, had built a house at Merry Mount, in what is now Quincy, MA, where he hosted wild parties, earned a reputation as "the lord of misrule," and taunted the Pilgrims, calling Miles Standish "Captain Shrimp." In 1627, the Pilgrims cut down a Maypole he erected "upon the festival day of Philip and Jacob" when he regaled some Native Americans with a "barrel of excellent beer." He was also accused of supplying them with guns. He was deported to England on June 9, 1628, came back and was again deported, came back a third time and was jailed in Boston. His book *New English Canaan*, containing satirical remarks about the colonies, was published in England in 1637.

6026. Czech settler in America may have been Augustine Herrmann, who disembarked in New Amsterdam (the future New York City) in 1633 and eventually made his home in Maryland.

6027. Swedes to arrive in America landed in 1638. The Dutch colonial administrator Peter Minuit led an expedition that sailed from Gothenburg, Sweden, on November 20, 1637, in two Dutch vessels, *Kalmar Nyckel* and *Vogel Grip*, with Jan Hendricksen van de Waeter as skipper. The expedition landed in March 1638 at "The Rocks" on the Christina River (the future site of Wilmington, DE). Fort Christina, built nearby, was named in honor of the Swedish queen. Another settlement, New Sweden, was built on the Delaware River, near the present site of Trenton, NJ.

6028. Danish settlers in America arrived early in the 17th century. One of the first was Jonas Bronck, who settled in 1641 in the area north of Manhattan Island. It is now known as the Bronx and is one of New York City's five boroughs.

6029. Expedition of Englishmen to cross the Allegheny Mountains began on August 27, 1650, at Fort Henry, at the falls of the Appomattox River, VA, and returned on September 4. The party consisted of Captain Abraham Wood and his servant Henry Newcombe; Edward Bland, merchant, and his servant Robert Farmer; Elias Pennant and

Sackford Brewster; and two guides, Oyeocker, a Nottaway chief, and Pyancha, an Appamattuck war captain.

6030. Jews to arrive in America were Marranos, Spanish Jews who had converted to Christianity in order to escape torture and death under the Inquisition. Marranos were part of Columbus's voyage of discovery in 1492 and of Spanish explorations and settlements in the 16th century. A handful of Jews came to the English colonies in Virginia and Massachusetts in the first half of the 17th century, but most historians consider the first permanent Jewish settler in America to have been Jacob Barsimson of Holland, who landed at the Dutch colony of New Amsterdam (the future New York City) on August 22, 1654. A month later, a group of 23 Jews from Recife, Brazil, arrived in New Amsterdam seeking refuge from Portuguese persecution. Against the wishes of the colony's governor, Peter Stuyvesant, the Dutch West India Company allowed them to stay, provided "the poor among them should not become a burden to the Company or the community, but be supported by their own nation."

6031. Jew to win full citizenship was Asser Levy of New Amsterdam (later New York City). After the first Jews arrived in the city in 1654, the Council of New Amsterdam passed a law denying them the privilege of standing guard and keeping watch, compulsory for all other citizens, and taxed them for the exemption. Asser Levy and Jacob Barsimson objected to the discrimination and a decision was rendered against them. Levy appealed the decision after doing guard duty voluntarily and on April 20, 1657, was admitted to the status of a burgher, or town citizen. He became a prosperous trader, the first Jew to own land in America and the first to serve on a jury (in 1671, after the colony had been taken over by the English).

6032. Colonial badges issued to friendly Native Americans were authorized in Virginia by the Act of 1661, which authorized "silver and plated placques to be worn by the Indians when visiting the settlements." One of these has a crude representation of a tobacco plant and scrolls, above which is "The King Of" on the obverse, while on the reverse is a similarly engraved plant and the word "Patomeck" with the *e* overlined. The surface edges were engraved to represent scrolls and foldings, while the medal was holed for suspension. On December 2, 1662, an act "prohibiting the entertainment of Indians without badges" was passed by the Assembly at James City, VA.

6033. Naturalization act in the American colonies was provided for on March 12, 1664, in the letters patent of King Charles II of England to James, the Duke of York, who was permitted to bring in subjects of the realm as well as "any other subjects who would become subjects."

6034. Swiss settlement in America was established in 1670 near Charleston, SC. A Swiss mercenary, Diebold von Erlach, who was employed by Spain, had arrived in Florida more than a century earlier, in 1562.

6035. Irish to arrive in America were explorers and settlers: William Ayers, from Galway, who was a sailor in Columbus's crew in 1492; Francis Maguire, who was a member of the colony in Jamestown, VA, in 1607; and John Coleman, who sailed with Henry Hudson in 1609. The first community of Irish settlers to arrive, in 1678, were a group of 100 families who had been working as laborers in Barbados after the English government forced them off their land. They became indentured servants in Virginia and the Carolinas.

6036. Settler heroine publicly rewarded was Hannah Duston, who was captured in a Native American attack on Haverhill, MA, on March 16, 1697, in which 40 settlers were murdered or taken prisoner. The attackers killed Duston's week-old baby by dashing it against a tree. On April 29, she escaped from a guarded campsite after killing 10 Native Americans with a tomahawk, scalping them as proof of her deed. The Great and General Court of Massachusetts on June 8, 1697, voted to pay her a reward of £25. Smaller rewards were given to two people who helped her: Mary Neff, the baby's nurse, who had been captured at the same time, and Samuel Leonardson, a young boy from Worcester, MA, who had been held prisoner for two years.

6037. Slovak settler in America to take up permanent residence was Anton Schmidt, a member of the Moravian brotherhood. He emigrated to Bethlehem, PA, in 1746 and served as a missionary to the Native Americans.

6038. Colonial settlement west of the Allegheny Mountains other than military forts and outposts was established by the Loyal Land Company of Virginia in 1750. On

March 6, a group of six men in the employ of the company, led by Dr. Thomas Walker, a physician, started out from Charlottesville, VA. They reached the future site of Barbourville, KY, on April 23, and built a house that was completed on April 30.

6039. Reservation for Native Americans established by a state was set aside on August 29, 1758, when the New Jersey Legislature appropriated 1,600 acres of a tract of 3,044 acres in the township of Evesham, Burlington County, NJ, to be used as a reservation for the Native Americans of New Jersey. Governor Francis Bernard named the tract Brotherton. About 200 Native Americans, probably Lenapes and Unamis, were settled on it. In 1801, the land was sold and the Native Americans moved to the Lake Oneida Reservation.

6040. Greek settlement was New Smyrna, FL, founded in 1767 by some 1,400 Greek and Italian farmers led by Andrew Turnbull. The colony was named for Smyrna, Greece, the birthplace of Turnbull's wife.

6041. Treaty entered into by the federal government with Native American tribes was a treaty with the Delaware Nation, signed on September 17, 1778. The signers were Andrew and Thomas Lewis, commissioners for the United States, and Captain White Eyes, Captain Pipe, and Captain John Kill Buck on behalf of the Delawares. This treaty, agreed upon at Fort Pitt, PA (now Pittsburgh), contained the following provisions: all offenses were to be mutually forgiven; peace and friendship were to be perpetual; in case of war, each party was to assist the other; the United States was to have free passage to forts and towns of former enemies, and such warriors as could be spared were to join the troops of the United States; neither party was to inflict punishment without an impartial trial; an agent was to be appointed by the United States to trade with the Delaware Nation; the United States was to guarantee all territorial rights granted by former treaties and to allow a Delaware representative in Congress under certain conditions.

6042. Territory owned by the federal government was the Northwest Territory, also known as the Old Northwest, an area of land about 248,000 square miles around the Great Lakes and the Mississippi River, which was acquired by the United States in the Treaty of Paris of 1783 that ended the Revolutionary War. Between 1781 and 1802, pieces of the territory claimed by New York, Virginia, Massachusetts, Connecticut, and other states were ceded to the federal government. Arthur St. Clair was appointed the first governor of the Northwest Territory in October 1787. The first territorial legislature assembled on September 24, 1799. A separate entity, the Indiana Territory, was formed from part of it in 1800. The area was divided into states beginning with Ohio in 1803, followed by Indiana, Illinois, Michigan, Wisconsin, and Minnesota.

6043. Russian settlement was Three Saints Bay on Kodiak Island, AK, founded by Grigori Shelikhov, a fur trader, in 1784, before Alaska was claimed by Russia. Shelikhov lived there with his wife, Natalia, and 190 men. The first Russian settlement in what would be the continental United States was established on March 15, 1812, at Cazadero, 18 miles north of Bodega Bay on the Russian River in California. The party consisted of 95 Russians and 80 Aleut hunters from Sitka, AK, under the command of Ivan Alexandrovich Kuskof. They built Fort Rumiantzof, a compound of nine buildings surrounded by a 12-foot spiked stockade, as well as 50 buildings outside the stockade. The fort was dedicated on September 11, 1812. On April 15, 1839, the Russians decided to abandon it, and it was sold to the German-American pioneer John Augustus Sutter for $30,000. The Russians evacuated the fort in December and sailed from San Francisco on January 1, 1842. The Spaniards called the settlement Fuerto de los Rusos, the Americans, Fort Ross. Sutter built a trading post there called Sutter's Mill, the site of the 1849 Gold Rush.

6044. Citizenship conferred by special grant was awarded to the Marquis de Lafayette, Washington's French ally in the Revolutionary War, by the General Assembly of Maryland at the session held on November 1, 1784, to January 22, 1785, at Annapolis, MD. It provided that "the Marquis de Lafayette and his heirs male for ever, shall be, and they and each of them are hereby deemed, adjudged, and taken to be, natural born citizens of this state, and shall henceforth be entitled to all the immunities, rights and privileges, of natural born citizens thereof."

6045. Sale of federal land authorized by Congress was authorized by a law enacted on May 20, 1785. It provided for the sale of land in the Northwest Territory.

6046. Survey of public lands was authorized by the Ordinance of 1785, which was passed by the Continental Congress on May 20, 1785. The first surveys were made in the Seven Ranges in the Western Reserve. The Ordinance of 1785 provided for the division of all public lands into townships six miles square, numbered east and west from primary meridians and north and south from base lines. This rectangular system of surveying prevails throughout the United States except in the original 13 states and in Maine, Vermont, Kentucky, Tennessee, and West Virginia.

6047. Reservation for Native Americans established by the federal government was set aside in 1786. The first official notice of the removal of Native Americans residing east of the Mississippi River to reservations west of the river was contained in the act of March 26, 1804. Reservations established by executive order without an act of Congress were not held to be permanent before the general allotment act of February 8, 1887, an "act to provide for the allotment of lands . . . severally to Indians on the various reservations, and to extend the protection of the laws of the United States and the territories over the Indians."

6048. Land office was established in 1789 by Oliver Phelps and Nathaniel Gorham, who purchased 2,600,000 acres in the "Great American Wilderness" at Canandaigua, NY, for resale to settlers. William Walker was the agent.

6049. Naturalization act enacted by Congress was passed on March 26, 1790. It authorized courts of record to "entertain the applications" of alien free white persons who had resided in the United States for two years or more, one year of which should be in a particular state, on proof of good character and on their taking an oath or affirmation to support the Constitution.

6050. Exploration by ship of the mouth of the Columbia River in Oregon took place on May 11, 1792, when Robert Gray, a fur trader on his second commercial voyage to the northwest coast of America, rounded Cape Disappointment and sailed the *Columbia Rediviva* 22 miles up the river. Earlier explorers had passed the Columbia's mouth but had not recognized it as such.

6051. Sale of federal land to an individual was authorized by act of Congress of May 17, 1796, "an act providing for the sale of the lands of the United States in the territory northwest of the River Ohio, and above the mouth of the Kentucky River." Congress granted Ebenezer Zane three tracts of land in Ohio, each one mile square, for the purpose of operating ferries: one on the Muskingum River, one on the Sciota, and one on the Hockhocking. These grants were confirmed and patented to Zane on February 14, 1800, in return for his activities in opening Zane's "trail" or "trace" in 1797. The trail, about 200 miles long, led from Wheeling, WV, through Ohio to Limestone (now Maysville), KY.

6052. Protection of Native American hunting grounds authorized by Congress was included in an act approved on May 19, 1796, "to regulate the trade and intercourse with the Native American tribes and to preserve peace on the frontiers." The penalty for crossing the line to hunt or destroy game within Native American territory was a fine of $100 and six months in jail. A later treaty with the Native Americans signed in 1832 is generally regarded as the first national hunting law.

6053. Passport recorded in the Passport Division of the State Department is dated July 8, 1796. The passport was issued to Francis Maria Barrere, "a citizen of the United States having occasion to pass into foreign countries about his lawful affairs," and was signed by Thomas Pickering, secretary of state.

6054. Immigration law enacted by Congress requiring the recording of data pertaining to the arrival of aliens in the United States was the act of June 25, 1798, which required the master or commander of a vessel to make a written report to the customs officer in charge of the port of entry, giving the names of all arriving aliens and other prescribed data pertaining to them.

6055. Deportation of aliens authorized by Congress was authorized by the act passed on July 6, 1798, which required that aliens above the age of 14 who were "not actually naturalized shall be liable to be apprehended, restrained, rescued and removed as alien enemies."

6056. District land office opened on July 2, 1800, in Steubenville, OH, with David Hoge as the first registrar. It was established under the act of May 10, 1800, which also authorized district land offices in Ohio in Cincinnati, Chillicothe, and Marietta.

6057. Grant of federal land to a foreigner was enacted by Congress on March 3, 1803. The act authorized the secretary of war to issue land warrants to the Marquis de Lafayette (Major General Marie Joseph Paul Yves Roch Gilbert du Motier) for 11,520 acres, which at his option were to be located, surveyed, and patented in conformity with the provisions of the act regulating the grants of land appropriated for military services.

6058. Territory annexed by the federal government was the Louisiana Purchase, a tract of land bought from France on April 30, 1803, for $15 million. It covered 1,171,931 square miles and included the entire Mississippi Valley from the Mississippi River to the Rocky Mountains and from the Gulf of Mexico to Canada. This territory included the present states of Louisiana, Arkansas, Missouri, Iowa, North and South Dakota, Nebraska, Kansas, and Oklahoma, part of Colorado and Wyoming, and most of Montana and Minnesota. The treaty was arranged by Robert R. Livingston, minister at Paris, and James Monroe, who had been sent by President Thomas Jefferson as a special envoy to assist Livingston. The tract was also claimed by Spain, which ceded it to France on November 30, 1803. On December 20, France formally delivered the colony to the American representatives.

6059. Coast survey was authorized by act of Congress of February 10, 1807, "an act to provide for surveying the coasts of the United States," which appropriated a sum not exceeding $50,000. The first superintendent of the survey was Ferdinand Rudolph Hassler, who was appointed on August 3, 1816. Hassler received $3,000 a year and $2,000 for personal expenses in the field.

6060. Settlers to reach the Pacific coast left New York City on September 6, 1810, on the S.S. *Tonquin*, a 290-ton vessel captained by Jonathan Thorn. They rounded Cape Horn on December 25, 1810, landing on April 12, 1811, at Cape Disappointment, WA, a promontory at the mouth of the Columbia River. The enterprise was sponsored by John Jacob Astor.

6061. Land office established by Congress was established in the Department of the Treasury by act of April 25, 1812. The salary of the commissioner was $2,250 a year.

6062. Native American language to be given a written form was the Cherokee language. The inventor of its written form was Sikwayi (also called Sequoyah), a Cherokee silversmith born circa 1776 in the East Tennessee settlement of Tuskegee. His father was Nathaniel Gist, a French trader. Sikwayi, though illiterate, was fascinated by books, and understood the immense advantage that a system of writing gave to European settlers. Over many years, he developed a syllabary in which 85 characters derived from English, Hebrew, and Greek were assigned to serve as symbols for Cherokee sounds, allowing the Cherokee to write in their own language for the first time. Although his writing was at first considered witchcraft, the syllabary was adopted by the Tribal Council in 1821 and was used to produce the first Native American newspaper in 1828. Specimens of Sikwayi's writings are preserved in the Sequoyah Birthplace Museum near Vonore, TN.

6063. Overland trip to California (other than by Native Americans) was made in 1826, when Jebediah S. Smith led a group of trappers out from Utah, much to the displeasure of the Mexican governor of the territory. Smith and two others became the first non-Native Americans to cross the Sierra Nevada the following year.

6064. Settlers to cross the continent who were women were Narcissa Prentiss Whitman and Eliza Hart Spalding, who crossed the Continental Divide at South Pass, WY, on July 4, 1836. They reached Fort Walla Walla, WA, on September 1, 1836. They were accompanied by their husbands, Marcus Whitman, M.D., and the Reverend Henry Harmon Spalding, Presbyterian missionaries sent by the American Board of Commissioners for Foreign Missions. The Whitmans and 12 others were murdered by the Cayuse in 1847.

6065. Japanese to enter the United States was Manjiro Nakahama, a 15-year-old boy who was one of five Japanese shipwrecked in 1841 and rescued by American sailors. After the other four were landed at Honolulu,

HI, Nakaham was brought to Fairhaven, MA, where he attended school for six years. He returned to Japan and was beaten for having left his country. When Commodore Matthew Calbraith Perry went to Japan on a diplomatic mission in 1853, Nakahama acted as interpreter. The first naturalized citizen of Japanese birth was another castaway, Hikozo Hamada, who became an American citizen in 1850.

6066. Wagon train to California left Sapling Grove in what is now Kansas in the spring of 1841 and arrived at Mount Diablo, 50 miles from San Francisco, on November 4, 1841. The party of settlers was led by John Batleson and Paul Geddes and traveled part of the way with Father Pierre-Jean De Smet, the Jesuit missionary, and the mountain man Thomas Fitzpatrick.

6067. Chinese immigrants to America were two men and a woman who arrived in San Francisco, CA, in 1848, on the brig *Eagle*. According to some historians, there were Chinese shipbuilders on the West Coast as early as 1571, and Chinese laborers there toward the end of the 18th century.

6068. Community leader to exercise the authority of king and high priest was James J. Strang, an expelled Mormon elder who organized a dissident sect of 5,000 Mormons. In 1847 the group settled on Big Beaver Island, MI, where Strang crowned himself King James I in 1850. He was elected to the Michigan legislature in 1852. Strang was assassinated by two of his followers on June 16, 1856.

6069. Traveler's aid program was instituted in 1851, when Bryan Mullanphy of St. Louis, MO, willed approximately one-third of his fortune of more than $1 million to a trust fund to be administered by the City Council for the purpose of assisting those who were "traveling to the west." St. Louis was the usual starting point for westward-bound settlers. In 1885, William Collins and Edward Prior, of the Society of Friends (the Quakers), paid the salary of the first employed worker among travelers.

6070. Chinese labor immigration was arranged through the efforts of William Kelly of Pittsburgh, PA, who in 1854 induced 12 Chinese laborers to work in his foundries. They were willing to work for extremely low wages.

6071. Homestead law enacted by Congress was the Homestead Act, "an act to secure homesteads to actual settlers on the public domain," passed by both houses of Congress on May 19, 1862, and approved on May 20, 1862, by President Abraham Lincoln. Under this law, any man or woman of 21 years or older could secure title to 160 acres of public land by living on it for five years, making certain improvements, and paying fees of approximately $18. The first homestead granted under the act was taken by Daniel Freeman, a Union soldier, on January 1, 1863, near Beatrice, NE.

6072. Passport fee was levied under the Internal Revenue Act of July 1, 1862, "to provide internal revenue to support the government and to pay interest on the public debt." It fixed a fee of $3 for "every passport issued in the office of the Secretary of State." Prior to this time, consuls in foreign countries charged a fee not exceeding $1 for passports they issued, but passports issued in the United States were free.

6073. Territory annexed by the federal government that was noncontiguous was Alaska, which was purchased from Russia on June 20, 1867, for $7.2 million. General Lovell Harrison Rousseau, the first military governor of the territory, took formal possession of Alaska in October 1867.

6074. Territory annexed by the federal government beyond the nation's continental limits was Midway Island in the North Pacific Ocean, claimed on August 28, 1867, by Captain William Reynolds of the Navy for the United States.

6075. Native American to win territorial concessions from the federal government was Red Cloud, a chief of the Oglala Sioux. After years of leading successful assaults against U.S. forts in the Powder River area of Montana, Red Cloud signed a treaty at Fort

Library of Congress, Prints & Photographs Division
LC-USZ62-1134

Fort Laramie in Montana.

Laramie on November 6, 1868. The treaty provided for the abandonment of Forts Reno, Kearney, and C. F. Smith.

6076. Lithuanian settlement was founded by four Lithuanian immigrants in Danville, PA, in 1869.

6077. Federal law restricting immigration was the Page Law, passed by Congress on March 3, 1875. This law barred prostitutes and convicted felons from entry into the United States. The law required American officials to ascertain whether "the immigration of any subject of China, Japan, or any Oriental country, to the United States, is free and voluntary." Chinese women applying to emigrate had to obtain certification that they were not traveling for purposes of prostitution or polygamy.

6078. Court case to establish the personhood of Native Americans was Standing Bear v. Crook, decided by Judge Elmer Scipio Dundy in Lincoln, NE, on May 12, 1879. Standing Bear, a chief of the Ponca tribe, had been arrested in Oklahoma for attempting to return to his ancestral lands in Nebraska. The judge ruled that Native Americans qualified as persons under federal law and were protected from detention by the 14th Amendment.

6079. Restrictions by Congress on immigration of Chinese laborers were passed on May 6, 1882, suspending Chinese immigration for a 10-year period and forbidding naturalization. According to the provisions of a treaty between China and the United States, signed on May 9, 1881, by President Chester Alan Arthur and proclaimed on October 5, it was agreed that the United States could "regulate, limit or suspend" the immigration of Chinese labor, but not prohibit it altogether. The Chinese exclusion acts were repealed on December 17, 1943.

6080. Immigration ban enacted by Congress was passed on August 3, 1882. The law denied entry to convicts, paupers, and people with physical or mental defects, and required each immigrant to pay a tax of 50 cents. In 1903 the fee was $2; in 1907, $4; and in 1918, $8.

Library of Congress, Prints & Photographs Division
LC-USZ62-37784

The immigrant landing station at Ellis Island, NY.

6081. County created by federal law was Latah County in Idaho, authorized by Congress in a bill enacted on May 14, 1888. The bill set aside a portion of Nez Perce County in Idaho to become Latah County, with the county seat at Moscow.

6082. Formal declaration of the closing of the American frontier was made by the superintendent of the census, Robert Porter, in his report on the findings of the 1890 census: "Up to and including 1880 the country had a frontier of settlement, but at present the unsettled area has been so broken into by isolated bodies of settlement that there can hardly be said to be a frontier line. In the discussion of its extent, its westward movement, etc., it can not, therefore, any longer have a place in the census reports."

6083. Island territory annexed by the federal government was the Hawaiian Islands, which were formally annexed on August 12, 1898. The treaty was signed on June 16, 1897, by John Sherman, secretary of state. A joint congressional resolution to provide for the annexation was passed on July 7, 1898.

6084. Border patrol officer was Jefferson Davis Milton of the Immigration and Naturalization Service, who served from April 13, 1904, to June 30, 1932. He was appointed under authority of annual appropriation acts before the border patrol was formally established by act of Congress on May 28, 1924. His job was to prevent the smuggling of illegal Asian immigrants across the Mexican border.

6085. Old age home for pioneers was the Home for Aged and Infirm Arizona Pioneers, Prescott, AZ, authorized by the legislative assembly of the Territory of Arizona on March 10, 1909. Applicants for admission were required to be residents of Arizona not less than 35 years or over 60 years of age who were citizens of the United States for at least 5 years prior to the date of application, who were active in the development in Arizona, and who were unable to provide themselves with the necessities and comforts of life because of adverse circumstances or failing health. The home was opened for guests on February 6, 1911. The first superintendent was Major A. J. Doran.

6086. Alien land law was enacted by the state legislature of California in 1913. It barred any alien who was ineligible for citizenship from owning or leasing land. In practice the statute targeted Asian immigrants. The law was repealed in 1956.

6087. Passport photographs were required by a regulation effective on November 20, 1914.

6088. Immigration quota enacted by Congress was the act of May 19, 1921, which limited immigration to 3 percent of the number of foreign-born persons of any given nationality in the United States as shown in the 1910 census. Not more than 20 percent of any country's quota was permitted to arrive in one month.

6089. State law to establish English as an official language was the Illinois law enacted on June 19, 1923, which stated that "the official language of the State of Illinois shall be known hereafter as the 'American' language."

6090. Citizenship statute for Native Americans was enacted by Congress on June 2, 1924. It provided that "all non-citizen Indians born within the territorial limits of the United States be, and they are hereby declared to be, citizens of the United States."

6091. Registration of aliens by the federal government was authorized by Congress under the Alien Registration Act of 1940, approved on June 28, 1940, "to amend certain provisions of law with respect to the admission and deportation of aliens; to require the fingerprinting and registration of aliens." The registration was conducted by the Alien Registration Division of the Immigration and Naturalization Service. Earl Grant Harrison was the director in charge of registration. During the period from August 27, 1940, to December 26, 1940, the number of noncitizens who registered was 4,741,971.

6092. Citizenship granted on foreign soil was conferred on December 4, 1942, in the Panama Canal Zone by Thomas Buckman Shoemaker, assistant commissioner of the Immigration and Naturalization Service, on Private James Alexander Finnell Hoey, who had been born in Ireland. The Second War Powers Act of March 27, 1942, authorized the commissioner of Immigration and Naturalization to designate a representative who shall have power to naturalize "any person entitled to naturalization, who while serving honorably in the military or naval forces of the United States is not within the jurisdiction of any court authorized to naturalize aliens."

6093. Chinese person granted citizenship after the repeal of the Chinese exclusion act was Edward Bing Kan of Chicago, IL, an interpreter for the Immigration and Naturalization Service, who filed his application on December 18, 1943, and was naturalized on January 18, 1944, in Chicago. On December 17, 1943, President Franklin Delano Roosevelt signed the Chinese Act, which made Chinese residents eligible for naturalization and permitted the annual immigration of a quota of 105 Chinese nationals.

6094. Nazi collaborator to be deported by the Immigration and Naturalization Service was Ferenc Vajta, a Hungarian newspaper editor who had helped to plan the arrangements by which more than half a million Hungarian Jews were sent to Nazi death camps and forced labor camps during the Holocaust. After World War II he did espionage work for the United States and was allowed to enter the country. He was arrested in 1948 and was deported to Colombia in February 1950.

6095. Commonwealth of the United States was Puerto Rico, which ratified its status as a commonwealth in a constitution adopted on July 25, 1952. Residents of Puerto Rico possess all the rights of U.S. citizens except that of voting in federal elections.

6096. Japanese person to receive an immigration visa after World War II was Sozaburo Kujiraoka of Tokyo, Japan, who was given a visa on February 22, 1953. The McCarran-Walter Immigration and Nationality Act of June 27, 1952, allowed an annual quota of 100 immigrants from Japan.

6097. Refugee to arrive under the Refugee Relief Act of 1953 was Stamatoula Roumanis, a 12-year-old Greek girl, who arrived at Idlewild International Airport, New York City, on January 1, 1954. The law had been enacted by Congress on August 7, 1953, "for the relief of certain refugees and orphans, and for other purposes."

6098. Honorary citizenship authorized by Congress was conferred on Sir Winston Churchill, the former prime minister of Great Britain, by proclamation of April 9, 1963, by President John Fitzgerald Kennedy.

6099. Occupation of federal territory by Native American protesters in the modern era lasted for four hours on March 9, 1964, when five Sioux led by Richard McKenzie took over Alcatraz Island in San Francisco Bay, off San Francisco, CA, demanding the establishment of a cultural center and university on the island. On November 20, 1969, these demands were raised again by Richard Oakes and a group of about 100 Native Americans, mostly college students, who began an organized occupation of Alcatraz that lasted 19 months.

6100. Naturalization ceremony in the White House was held on November 23, 1968, when 54 immigrants from 26 nations became citizens. The youngest was an 8-year-old Filipino girl and the oldest was a 72-year-old Chinese laundry worker.

6101. Birth rate resulting in negative population growth occurred in the first quarter of 1972, when for the first time in American history the birth rate declined below the rate necessary to maintain the population. Among the causes cited by demographers were easy access to contraception and abortion and the entry of more women into the workforce.

6102. Armed occupation by Native American protesters in the modern era began on February 27, 1973, when 200 members of the American Indian Movement, led by Russell Means and Dennis Banks, occupied Wounded Knee, SD, a town on the Pine Ridge Indian Reservation. Their demands included a review of treaties between the federal government and indigenous peoples, a Senate investigation into the treatment of Native Americans, and free elections of tribal leaders. The occupation ended on May 8 when the group surrendered to federal marshals. Gunfights during the siege killed one marshal and two protesters. Wounded Knee was the site of a massacre in December 1890 when Army troops machine-gunned 200 Sioux men, women, and children.

6103. Nazi death camp guard to be deported by the Immigration and Naturalization Service was Hermine Braunsteiner Ryan of New York City. During the Holocaust, she worked as a guard at Nazi concentration camps in Poland, where she tortured and murdered prisoners with extreme cruelty. She became a naturalized American citizen in 1963. After her crimes were made public by the Nazi-hunter Simon Wiesenthal, she became the subject of an INS investigation and gave up her citizenship. She was deported in August 1973 to Germany, where she stood trial along with 14 other defendants. She was convicted of murder in 1981 and received a life prison term.

6104. State services to refugees were offered by Wisconsin, whose Office of Refugee Services opened in 1975, when the state began taking in Hmong people who had fled Laos in the wake of the Vietnam War.

6105. Cuban boatlift began on April 21, 1980, when the Carter Administration agreed to accept into the United States a large number of refugees seeking political asylum from Cuba's communist regime. Most of the 125,262 immigrants traveled in small boats to Key West, FL, from the Cuban port of Mariel. The boatlift lasted until September 26, when Mariel was closed by Cuban authorities to further emigration.

6106. Political asylum granted on grounds of sexual orientation was given to Jose Garcia (a pseudonym), a Mexican citizen, who was granted asylum by the Immigration and Naturalization Service on March 25, 1994. Garcia was a homosexual who said that he had been harassed and raped by Mexican police.

6107. Political asylum granted to avoid genital mutilation was given on June 13, 1996, to Fauziya Kasinga, 19, a citizen of the West African country of Togo. Kasinga was kept in immigration detention centers for more than a year before the Immigration Service's Board of Immigration Appeals decided that fear of genital mutilation represented a legitimate ground for asylum. Mutilation of the genitals of girls and young women for religious and cultural reasons is a common practice in many parts of Africa.

6108. Honorary citizen who was a woman was Agnes Gonxha Bojaxhiu, better known as Mother Teresa, the Albanian nun and human rights advocate. Congress voted her the honor on September 17, 1996; she received it in November of that year from the U.S. ambassador to India, Frank G. Wisner, at the Missionaries of Charity in Calcutta, the congregation Mother Teresa formed in 1949. A person of exceptional merit who is not a citizen of the United States may be declared an honorary citizen by the president, pursuant to an act of Congress.

6109. Year in which people of Hispanic descent became the largest minority group in the United States was 2000. The census taken that year showed that there were 35.3 million people claiming Hispanic or Latino ancestry, representing 12.5 percent of the total population. Historically, the largest minority group was African-Americans, who numbered 34.7 million in 2000, or 12.3 percent of the total population. However, the statistics are complicated by the fact that Hispanic people may be of any race.

African-Americans

6110. Escape of slaves from a colony in what is now U.S. territory took place at San Miguel de Guadalupe, the first Spanish (and first European) settlement in the continental United States, probably located at Winyah Bay in South Carolina, at the mouth of the Pee Dee River. Among the 500 settlers who arrived in July 1526 from Hispaniola with the founder, Lucas Vazquez de Ayllón, were a number of African slaves. In November, after the death of Ayllón, some of them escaped from the settlement, presumably to live with local Native Americans. The remaining Spanish colonists returned to Hispaniola.

6111. African slaves in the English colonies in America were introduced in Jamestown, VA, in August 1619 by a Dutch man-of-war that sold 20 kidnapped Africans to the planter colonists. They were treated as indentured servants, since slavery was not legalized in Virginia for several decades. Forms of slavery were also practiced among Native American peoples from ancient times.

6112. African-American who was free was Anthony Johnson, one of the first 20 Africans to arrive in Jamestown, VA, in 1619. In accordance with common practice of the time, he was released after a fixed term of indentured labor. In 1622 he was recorded as a free citizen of Old Accomack, VA. He married a white Englishwoman, Mary Johnson, and on July 24, 1651, was granted 250 acres of farmland in Virginia's Northampton County, making him the first African-American to become a landowner of substance. An individual named Anthony Johnson—probably the same man—began importing European and African indentured servants to Virginia in 1651.

6113. Colony to legalize slavery was Massachusetts, whose law code of 1641, the *Body of Liberties*, recognized as lawful the enslavement of Native Americans and Africans as long as "unjust violence" was not employed.

6114. Slavery emancipation law enacted by a colony was enacted by Rhode Island. It was one of several "Acts and Orders made at the General Court of Election held at Warwick, RI, this 18th day of May, anno 1652." It contained the following provision: "No blacke mankind or white . . . [may be] forced by covenant bond or otherwise to serve any man or his assignes longer than ten years, or until they come to be 24 years of age, if they be taken in under 14, from the time of their coming within the Liberties of the Collonie, and at the end or terme of ten years . . . [are to be set] free, as is the manner with the English servants. And that man that will not let them goe free, or shall sell them away elsewhere, to that end that they may be enslaved to others for a long time, he or they shall forfeit to the Collonie forty pounds."

6115. Colonial laws making slavery lifelong and hereditary were enacted in Virginia. A 1661 law prescribed lifelong servitude for slaves of African descent and their children. The following year, Virginia passed a law that made the status of a child dependent on the status of his or her mother, making a slave of any child whose mother was an African slave but whose father was an English colonist. This was a reversal of English law, which determined that one's freedom or servitude should pass through the father.

6116. Protest against slavery of importance was made on February 18, 1688, by the German Friends, or Quakers, at a meeting in Germantown, PA. They protested against the "traffic in the bodies of men" and considered the question of the "lawfulness and unlawfulness of buying and keeping Negroes." Some of the protesters were Francis Daniel Pastorius, Dirck op den Graeff, Abraham op den Graeff, and Gerhard Hendricks.

6117. Rebellion of African-American slaves in a major city occurred on April 6, 1712, in New York City. Six whites were killed. The militia was called out to suppress the revolt. Twenty-one African-American slaves (some accounts say 12) were executed by hanging, and 6 committed suicide.

6118. Slave importation ban enacted by a colony was passed on June 13, 1774, by the Rhode Island General Assembly in Newport, RI. It provided that "no Negro or mulatto slave shall be brought in to this colony, and in case any slave shall be brought in, he or she shall be, and are hereby, rendered immediately free, so far as respects personal freedom, and the enjoyment of private property, in the same manner as the native Indians."

6119. Abolition organization was the Society for the Relief of Free Negroes Unlawfully Held in Bondage, formed on April 14, 1775, in Philadelphia, PA. The first president was John Baldwin. The society was incorporated in 1789 as the Pennsylvania Society for Promoting the Abolition of Slavery and for the Relief of Free Negroes Unlawfully Held in Bondage and for Improving the Condition of the African Race.

6120. Slavery emancipation law enacted by a state was enacted by Vermont, whose constitution of July 2, 1777, provided that "no male person born in this country or brought from over sea, ought to be holden by law, to serve any person as a servant, slave or apprentice, after he arrives to the age of twenty-one years, nor female, in like manner, after she arrives to the age of eighteen years, unless they are bound by their own consent, after they arrive to such age, or bound by law, for the payment of debts, damages, fines, costs or the like."

6121. Slave to be emancipated by a court was Elizabeth Freeman, known as Mum (or Marm) Bett, who was owned by Hannah Hogeboom Ashley, the wife of Colonel John Ashley of Sheffield, MA. In 1780, Hannah Ashley endeavored to strike Lizzie, Elizabeth's sister, with a red-hot kitchen shovel. Elizabeth interfered and received the blow on her arm, where she was scarred for life. She ran away to the home of lawyer Theodore Sedgwick, whom she had seen at the Ashley house discussing the rights of man with a group of Sheffield notables, and obtained his help in suing for her freedom. The case was tried in Great Barrington, MA, on August 21, 1781. The jury granted her freedom. She died on December 28, 1829, and was buried in the Sedgwick family plot.

6122. Slavery ban enacted for a territory of the United States was prepared by Nathan Dane of Massachusetts and enacted on July 13, 1787, by the Continental Congress. The law prohibited slavery forever within the borders of the Northwest Territory, a region east of the Mississippi River, north of the Ohio River, south and west of the Great Lakes, and west of Pennsylvania.

6123. Fugitive slave law enacted by Congress was passed on February 12, 1793. It required the forcible return of slaves who had escaped. The law stated: "No person held to service or labor in one state, under the laws thereof, escaping into another, shall, in consequence of any law or regulation therein, be discharged from such service or labor, but shall be delivered up on claim of the party to whom such service or labor may be due."

6124. State in which slavery was illegal from the time it was admitted to the Union was Ohio, which was admitted on March 1, 1803. The following year, however, it became the first of the northern states to pass statutes impairing the civil rights of African-Americans, including restricting their freedom of movement and banning them from testifying in court.

6125. Federal ban on the importation of African slaves was enacted by Congress on March 2, 1807, effective January 1, 1808. The bill made it unlawful to import African slaves and to fit out vessels for transporting them, though it did not outlaw the owning of slaves. Congress had been prevented by the Constitution (Article I, Section 9) from legislating an end to the African slave trade before the year 1808.

6126. Antislavery magazine was *The Emancipator*, issued monthly from April 30 to October 31, 1820. It was edited and published by Elihu Embree and cost $1 a year.

6127. National convention of African-Americans assembled at Bethel African Methodist Episcopal Church, Philadelphia, PA, on September 15, 1830. It was attended by delegates from seven states. Bishop Richard Allen presided. The convention was organized to protest the work of the American Colonization Society, which was calling for the return to Africa of free African-Americans.

6128. Slave rebellion after the Revolution on a large scale took place beginning August 21, 1831, in Southampton County, VA. It was led by Nat Turner, an African-American slave and religious visionary who believed that he was divinely chosen to lead his fellow slaves to freedom. With seven accomplices, Turner killed his owner, Joseph Travis, and the Travis family in their sleep, then led more than 70 followers in a two-day revolt in which 55 to 60 whites were killed. State militiamen and armed whites confronted the rebels near Jerusalem, VA, and killed as many as 100 slaves, a number of whom had not taken part

Library of Congress, Prints & Photographs Division
LC-USZ62-2582

A slave auction in the South.

in the rebellion. Turner escaped, but was caught six weeks later and hanged on November 11.

6129. Antislavery book was published in Boston, MA, in 1833 by Allen and Ticknor. It was written by Lydia Maria Francis Child and entitled *An Appeal in Favor of That Class of Americans Called Africans.*

6130. African-American magazine was *The Mirror of Liberty*, a quarterly of 16 pages, edited and published in New York City by David Ruggles. The first issue was dated July 1838.

6131. Senator elected on an antislavery ticket was John Parker Hale of New Hampshire, who was elected on June 9, 1846, for the six-year term that began on March 4, 1847. Previously, he had served as a Democrat in the House of Representatives from March 4, 1843, to March 3, 1845.

6132. Escaped slave legally recaptured in New England under the Fugitive Slave Law of 1850 was Shadrach Minkins, who had escaped from John DeBree of Norfolk, VA, and was living in Boston, MA. On February 15, 1851, as he was leaving the coffeehouse where he worked, he was seized by federal marshals and hustled into the courthouse. Rescued by a crowd of African-American men, he was turned over to the Underground Railroad, which brought him to Canada. A number of his rescuers were caught, tried, and acquitted.

6133. Federal law to emancipate slaves during the Civil War was the confiscation act passed on August 6, 1861, which gave immediate freedom to slaves whose owners had assigned them to work for the Confederate war effort. Further congressional action taken in 1862 abolished slavery in the District of Columbia (April 16) and in U.S. territories (June 19) and liberated the slaves of rebellious citizens (July 17).

6134. Emancipation proclamation made by President Abraham Lincoln was the Preliminary Emancipation Proclamation, issued on September 22, 1862, to take effect on January 1, 1863. It declared that "all Persons held as Slaves" in all the Confederate states, excepting a number of counties under federal control, were to be considered "forever Free." It also enjoined members of the federal armed forces from returning fugitive slaves to their owners. The Emancipation Proclamation in its final form was signed on January 1, 1863.

Library of Congress, Prints & Photographs Division
LC-USZ6-2356

The Emancipation Proclamation, signed on January 1, 1863.

6135. Ku Klux Klan meeting took place in 1865 in Pulaski, TN. It was originally founded as a social organization, but quickly became a terrorist group that tried to enforce white supremacy by means of intimidation and violence. The first Grand Wizard was the Confederate general Nathan Bedford Forrest.

6136. Civil rights law enacted by Congress was an "Act to Protect all Persons in the United States in their Civil Rights and Furnish the Means of Their Vindication," enacted on April 9, 1866, during the first session of the 39th Congress. The act conferred citizenship upon African-Americans, allowing them to hold property, engage in lawsuits, make contracts, and serve as witnesses in court. The law was widely ignored for the next hundred years.

6137. Jim Crow law intended specifically to discriminate against African-Americans was enacted by the Tennessee legislature in 1875 and was struck down as unconstitutional in 1880 by a federal circuit court. In 1881, Tennessee passed another law that segregated African-American passengers on railroads, establishing a precedent that was quickly imitated by other Southern states. The constitutionality of Jim Crow laws was upheld on May 18, 1896, by the Supreme Court in the case of *Plessy v. Ferguson*. The result was a flurry of state laws that segregated everything from restaurants to drinking fountains. The term "Jim Crow" was borrowed from a character in a minstrel show.

6138. Lynching ban enacted by a state was a statute approved on December 20, 1893, by Georgia, "an act to prevent mob violence in this state, to prescribe a punishment for the same, to provide a means for carrying this act into effect, to punish a failure to comply with its requirements, and for other purposes." Violators were guilty of a felony punishable by imprisonment of up to 20 years. If death resulted, a murder charge could be instituted.

6139. Freedom ride by civil rights activists was the Journey of Reconciliation, organized by Bayard Rustin and George Houser. From April 7 to April 23, 1947, a team of 16 riders, eight black and eight white, traveled through Virginia, North Carolina, Tennessee, and Kentucky, relying on a recent

Supreme Court decision that disallowed segregation on interstate buses. Confrontations with the police resulted in multiple arrests, with some riders serving time on chain gangs.

6140. Year in which there were no reported lynchings of African-Americans was 1952. Record-keeping began in 1881.

6141. Mass boycott by civil rights protesters took place in Montgomery, AL, over a period of 381 days in 1955–56, when the African-American residents of the city refused to ride the municipal buses. The boycott was organized to protest the arrest on December 1, 1955, of an African-American seamstress, Rosa Parks, for refusing to give up her seat to a white passenger, as required by law. The protest was led by a young minister, the Reverend Dr. Martin Luther King, Jr. Eventually the city agreed to treat all riders equally and to hire African-Americans as bus drivers.

6142. Civil rights sit-in occurred on February 1, 1960, when four African-American freshmen from the Agricultural and Technical College in Greensboro, NC--Joseph McNeil, Izell Blair, Franklin McCain, and David Richmond--sat down at the lunch counter of the Woolworth's in Charlotte, NC. They were protesting the store's policy of refusing to allow African-American customers to sit down. The students were denied service but sat at the counter until closing time. Within weeks, similar "sit-in" protests were held in other Southern cities.

6143. Freedom ride in the 1960s was organized by the Congress of Racial Equality and the Student Nonviolent Coordinating Committee as a challenge to segregation. A group of 13 activists, seven black and six white, left Washington, DC, on May 4, 1961, intending to ride through the South on commercial buses to New Orleans, LA. On May 14 one of their buses was firebombed and the other was assaulted by a mob. The ride was continued by a second group as far as Montgomery, AL, where they, too, were attacked.

6144. Town to voluntarily desegregate its schools was Teaneck, NJ, a predominantly white suburb with one predominantly African-American neighborhood. To stop the resulting racial segregation of the local elementary schools, the head of Teaneck's school board, Bernard Confer, proposed a plan that would combine all sixth-graders in one school and mix the populations of the lower grades through a busing program. At a public meeting held on May 13, 1964, before a largely hostile audience, the board voted 7–2 in favor of the plan.

6145. Comprehensive civil rights law enacted by Congress was the Civil Rights Act of 1964, introduced in Congress after the March on Washington of August 28, 1963, at which the Reverend Dr. Martin Luther King, Jr., gave his "I Have a Dream" speech before a crowd of 200,000. The act was signed by President Lyndon B. Johnson on July 2, 1964. It barred racial discrimination in public accommodations, public schools and facilities, and employment, and extended some federal protection to African-American voting rights.

6146. State law to end de facto segregation in schools was "an act providing for the elimination of racial imbalance in the public schools," enacted in Massachusetts on August 18, 1965.

6147. Black Power advocate was Stokely Carmichael, chairman of the Student Nonviolent Coordinating Committee, based in Atlanta, GA. In June 1966 he issued a call urging African-Americans to reject integration as a goal of the civil rights movement and to adopt militant action instead of the pacifist methods of Martin Luther King, Jr.

6148. School district to implement court-ordered busing to achieve racial integration was Charlotte, NC, which began busing its students on September 9, 1970. The program was the result of a lawsuit brought against the school board by Vera and Darius Swann, whose six-year-old son James had been denied a place in the school closest to his home because he was African-American and the school was designated for white students. In 1969 a federal district court judge ordered the school board to comply with federal law by desegregating its schools. The school board refused and was then ordered to implement a plan that involved busing students to different schools so that each building would accommodate a set percentage of black and white students. The case was appealed to the Supreme Court, which unanimously upheld the lower court's ruling on April 20, 1971.

6149. African-American history trail was the Black History Trail, dedicated in Washington, DC, in 1988. The seven-and-a-half-mile trail visited important sites in African-American history. It was the brainchild of Willard Andre Hutt, who came up with the idea in 1978, when he was a 17-year-old Boy Scout.

Census

6150. Census of the United States was authorized by act of Congress of March 1, 1790, "providing for the enumeration of the inhabitants of the United States." The census compilation cost $44,377 and utilized the services of 17 marshals and 650 assistants. Marshals received from $100 to $500 and assistants received $1 for every 150 persons in county districts and $3 for every 300 in cities and towns. The enumeration, as of August 1, 1790, showed a population of 3,939,326 located in 16 states and the Ohio territory. Virginia, with 747,610, was the most populous state; Rhode Island, with 68,825, the least. New York City had a population of 33,131, Philadelphia had a population of 28,522, and Boston had a population of 18,320.

6151. Census to use racial categories was the original census of 1790, authorized by Congress on March 1, 1790. Respondents were identified as free whites, as slaves, or as all other free persons.

6152. Census in which the national population exceeded 10 million was the fifth census, the census of 1830, which showed a population of 12,866,620. The first census to show a population of more than 50 million was the 10th census, the census of 1880, which listed the population as 50,155,783. The first census over 100 million was the census of 1920, which showed a population of 105,710,620. The first census over 150 million was that of 1950, which showed a population of 150,697,361. The first census over 200 million was that of 1970, which showed a population of 203,184,772, later revised to 203,211,926. A public ceremony was held on November 20, 1967, at the Department of Commerce, Washington, DC, when the nation's population reached 200 million persons.

6153. Census that included deaf, mute, and blind people was taken in 1830. Previously, people with these disabilities were not enumerated at all.

6154. Census compiled by machines was the 1890 census, which recorded a population of 62,979,766 on June 1, 1890.

6155. Census to show more people living in cities than in rural areas was the census of 1920. Of a total population of 106,021,537, the census showed that 54,253,282, or 51.2 percent, lived in urban areas and 51,768,255, or 48.8 percent, lived in the country.

6156. Census proven to have been inaccurate was the census of 1940. When federal officials compared the number of men eligible for the military draft, as counted in the census, with the number of men who had actually registered for the draft, they discovered that the latter group was larger than the former. The population of young men was thus shown to have been undercounted in the census, with African-American men undercounted at a higher rate than white men.

> The results of all censuses after 1940 have been checked for accuracy by comparing them against other sources of demographic information, including birth and death certificates.

6157. Census compiled in part from statistics obtained by mail was the 19th decennial census, mailed on April 1, 1970.

6158. Census to collect information over the phone was the census of 2000, which allowed respondents to deliver the answers to their questionnaires using a toll-free number.

6159. Multiracial census category was included in the 2000 census, according to rules issued by the Office of Management and Budget for listing racial and ethnic makeup on federal forms. Respondents were allowed to identify themselves as members of more than one race. Previously, respondents had to choose a single racial category or select "other."

6160. Person to be counted in the 2000 census was Stanton Katchatag, an 82-year-old resident of Unalakleet, AK. He was interviewed on January 20, 2000, by Kenneth Prewitt, director of the Census Bureau, who arrived in the village by dogsled. Unalakleet lies 450 miles northwest of Anchorage and has 800 residents, most of them Inuit Native Americans.

6161. Census to be replicated was the census of 1890, whose results were lost in 1921 in a fire at the Commerce Building in Washington, DC. On March 14, 2000, the organization Ancestry.com launched a cooperative project, the 1890 Census Substitute, that was intended to provide genealogical researchers with a database of comparable information culled from a variety of historical sources, including city directories and tax lists. The project was proposed by Curt B. Witcher and overseen by Andre Brummer.

RELIGION

6162. Christian in America was Leif Eriksson, who founded the Icelandic settlement of Vinland on the North American coast about the year 1000. Leif was born into a Viking family that adhered to the pagan Norse religion and was converted to Christianity on a visit to Norway shortly before his journey.

6163. Muslim traveler in America was the slave Estevanico al-Zemmouri. A Morrocan Berber, he came to Florida with his Spanish master, Andrés Dorantes de Carranza, in 1528, as part of the doomed expedition of Panfilo de Narváez. After crossing Texas with a small group of shipwreck survivors, he accompanied the Franciscan friar Marcos de Niza through Arizona in 1539 and was killed there by the Zuni.

6164. Baptism in America was performed in March 1540 by Spanish priests who were part of the expedition of Hernando de Soto. Two Native American guides were baptized in the Ocmulgee River near Macon, GA, and given the names Peter and Mark.

6165. Christian martyr on American soil was Fray Juan de Padilla, a Spanish Franciscan missionary accompanying the expedition of Francis Vasquez Coronado. He was murdered by the Kansas tribe of Native Americans in 1542 near what is now Lyon, KS.

6166. Catholic mass to take place in what is now the continental United States was celebrated on August 28, 1565, the feast day of St. Augustine of Hippo, by priests who accompanied the expedition of Pedro Menéndez de Avilés to Florida. The garrison built by Menéndez de Avilés was given the name St. Augustine.

6167. Catholic parish in the future United States was the parish of St. Augustine, FL, founded on September 8, 1565, on the day of the Feast of the Nativity of the Blessed Virgin, by Pedro Menéndez de Avilés. The first parish register is also owned by this church and consists of 15 volumes beginning January 1, 1594, and continuing down to the time of the British occupation of Florida in 1763. The first parish priest was Martin Francisco López de Mendozo Grajales.

6168. Christian religious service in English on the Pacific Coast was the Holy Communion service conducted on June 24, 1579, at San Francisco Bay, CA, by the Reverend Francis Fletcher, who read from the *Book of Common Prayer* of the Church of England. Fletcher was chaplain on Sir Francis Drake's ship, the *Golden Hind*, during its voyage of circumnavigation from 1577 to 1580. Drake named the place Nova Albion, Latin for New England. A 57-foot marble cross commemorates the event in Golden Gate Park, San Francisco, CA.

6169. Native American to become a Protestant was Manteo, chief of the Hatteras, who was baptized into the Christian faith as a member of the Church of England on August 13, 1587. He was invested by Sir Walter Raleigh with the power of Lord of Roanoke and of Dasamonguepeuk. There were earlier baptisms of Native Americans by Roman Catholic priests in Florida.

6170. Catholic bishop to exercise episcopal functions in the future United States was Fray Juan Cabezas de Altamirano, son of Juan Cabezas and Doña Ana Calzado, appointed Bishop of Santiago de Cuba in 1603. He visited the Provinces of Florida in 1607 and at St. Augustine administered the sacrament of confirmation to many Spaniards and converted Native Americans.

6171. Episcopal church service in an English colony took place at Cape Henry, near Jamestown, VA, on May 9, 1607, when the Reverend Robert Hunt celebrated the Eucharist. The event was reported as follows: "We did hang an awning (which is an old saile) to three or four trees, to shadow us from the sunne, our walles were railes of wood, our seats unhewed trees till we cut plankes; our Pulpit a bar of wood nailed to two neighboring trees." The founding of the Episcopal Church in America dates from April 29, 1607, when Captain Gabriel Archer, Christopher Newport, George Percy, Bartholomew Gosnold, Edward Maria Wingfield, and 25 other

English colonists set up a cross at Cape Henry. The first parish was started at Jamestown on June 21. The Episcopal Church originated in the Church of England, also known as the Anglican Church.

6172. Thanksgiving worship service was held on August 9, 1607, at Phippsburg, ME, by colonists on *The Gift of God* and the *Mary and John*, who landed at "St. Georges Illand" under the leadership of George Popham. Services were held by the Reverend Richard Seymour, "gyvinge God thanks for our happy metinge & saffe aryval into the country."

6173. Presbyterian church was established in 1611 in Virginia. The Reverend Alexander Whitaker was installed as pastor of the church, which was governed by him and a few of the most religious men of the colony.

6174. Sabbath law enacted by a colony was enacted by the first legislative body assembled in America, the Virginia House of Burgesses, at its first session in 1619. The law provided that "all persons whatsoever upon the Sabbath days shall frequent divine service and sermons, both forenoon and afternoon." The Anglican Church was made the sole legal religion, and the creed of the church was the rule of the colony.

6175. Congregational church was founded at Plymouth Colony (the future Plymouth, MA) in 1620 by 102 English Separatists under the leadership of William Brewster, William Bradford, and Edward Winslow, upon their arrival at Plymouth. Ralph Smith was the first pastor. The Separatists, who had withdrawn from the established Church of England for theological reasons, made up the greater part of the group of settlers known as the Pilgrims.

6176. Dutch Reformed church was established by Jonas Michaëlius in 1628 in New Amsterdam (now New York City). It was a Calvinist Presbyterian group under the authority of the Church of Holland.

6177. Catholics to settle in the English colonies in America arrived in Maryland in March 1634 on the ships *Ark* and *Dove*. They established St. Mary's Village, the first colonial settlement in Maryland. Their leader was Leonard Calvert. His brother, Cecil Calvert, Lord Baltimore, had founded Maryland in 1632 as a haven for Roman Catholics, who were unwelcome in England. The colony allowed freedom of religion for Christians of any denomination that accepted the doctrine of the Trinity.

6178. Religious leader in the American colonies who was a white woman was Anne Hutchinson, born Anne Marbury in England. She and her family arrived in the Massachusetts Bay Colony on September 18, 1634. She organized groups of women who met at her house and led them in the discussion of secular and theological questions. She taught that each person could attain understanding in matters of faith and therefore owed no obedience to church law. Her influence became so great that in November 1637 she was brought to trial in Cambridge for undermining the authority of the colony's Puritan ministers. Banished from the colony, she was given a safe haven in Roger Williams's settlement (the future Providence, RI) along with 70 followers. In 1642 she moved to the wilderness near what is now Pelham Bay, NY, where she and her family were killed by Native Americans.

6179. Religious refuge for people of all faiths to be founded anywhere in the world was Providence, RI, established in 1636 by Roger Williams. Williams, an English-born minister, emigrated to Massachusetts Bay Colony in 1630 and served briefly as pastor of Plymouth and then of Salem. He was banished from Massachusetts in 1635 for holding dissident religious and political opinions. With the help of the Narragansett tribe of Native Americans, he founded the town of Providence and the colony of Rhode Island as a refuge "for such as were destitute for conscience' sake." Among those who found a haven there were Anne Hutchinson, who was exiled from Massachusetts for theological reasons; some of the first families of Jews to settle in North America; and the Quakers, who were a persecuted sect in Massachusetts.

6180. Synod held in America met at Mr. Shepard's church, Cambridge (then Newtowne), MA, on August 30, 1637, to condemn the preaching of Anne Hutchinson, the first female religious leader in the American colonies. Eighty-two errors in her teachings were enumerated and condemned. The synod adjourned on September 22, 1637. Hutchinson was brought to trial on the strength of this condemnation and was exiled from the Massachusetts Bay Colony.

6181. Baptist church was the Baptist Church of Newport, RI, founded in 1638 by Dr. John Clarke, an emigrant from Bedfordshire, England. The principles of the Baptist faith had already been introduced in Providence, RI, by its founder, Roger Williams, "the Apostle of Religious Liberty," who had been banned from the Massachusetts Bay Colony for his dissident religious and political views.

6182. Blue laws prohibiting activities on Sunday were enacted in New Haven, CT, in 1638. They established Sunday as the day of rest and restricted various activities on that day in accordance with biblical teachings. The term "blue laws" derives from the blue paper with which the printed laws were bound.

6183. Lutheran pastor was Reorus Torkillus from Mölndal, Sweden, who came over on the *Kalmar Nyckel* with Governor Peter Hollander Ridder, landing on April 17, 1640, at Fort Christina, DE. He died of the plague in 1643. The first Lutheran pastor ordained in America was Justus Falckner, ordained in Gloria Dei Church at Wicaco, Philadelphia, PA, on November 24, 1703, with Andrew Rudman, Erick Biörck, and Andrew Sandel as officiating clergymen.

6184. Catholic priest born in America was Father Francisco de Florencia, who joined the Jesuit order in 1643. He was born in St. Augustine, FL, in 1620.

6185. Lutheran church was dedicated by the Reverend Johannes Campanius at Christina (Tinicum Island), near the present site of Essington, PA, on September 4, 1645. Before the church was built, Campanius had conducted services in a small blockhouse at Fort Göteborg.

6186. Ecumenical synod was held at Cambridge, MA, in 1646, and protracted its sessions by adjournments until 1648, when the Cambridge Platform was adopted. It was a platform of church discipline recommended to the General Court and to the churches. The synod was attended by 25 churchmen who discussed 80 subjects in an effort to reconcile Presbyterianism and Congregationalism.

6187. Ban on Jesuits to be enacted by a colony was passed in Puritan Massachusetts on May 26, 1647. It provided that "no Jesuit or eclesiasticl person ordayned by the authoritie of the pope shall henceforth come within our jurisdiction" excepting survivors of shipwrecks and traders who "behave themselves inoffencively during their abode here." A second offense was punishable by death.

6188. Religious "toleration" law enacted by a colony was the Tolerance Act, enacted by Maryland in April 1649. It ordered toleration for all who professed faith in Jesus Christ and subscribed to the orthodox interpretation of the Trinity, but prescribed the death penalty for Arian heretics, atheists, and Jews. It stated that "whatsoever person or persons within this province and the islands thereunto belonging shall from henceforth blaspheme God or deny our Saviour Jesus Christ to be the Son of God, or shall deny the Holy Trinity, the Father, Son and Holy Ghost, or the Godhead of any of these said persons of the Trinity, or the unity of the Godhead, shall be punished with death and forfeiture of all his or her lands and goods to the Lord Proprietary." The Arians were Christians who did not believe that Jesus was of the same substance as God.

6189. Missionary society established for the English colonies was the New England Protestant Missionary Society, chartered in July 1649 by Parliament to propagate the gospel. Missionary work among the Native Americans had been carried on earlier by John Eliot, John Cotton, Henry Dunster, and others.

6190. Jewish congregation was Congregation Shearith Israel ("Remnant of Israel"), established in 1655 in New Amsterdam (later New York City) by Sephardic Jews seeking refuge from persecution in Portuguese Brazil. It was formed despite a law prohibiting all religious assemblies except those of the Dutch Reformed Church. Sephardic Jews, whose name derives from *Sfard*, the Hebrew word for Spain, are those whose families originated in Spain and Portugal.

6191. Quakers to arrive in America were two Englishwomen, Ann Austin and Mary Fisher, who landed at Boston, MA, on July 11, 1656. They had come from Barbados, where the Quakers had established a center for missionary work. After five weeks' imprisonment, they were deported to Barbados. The Quakers were followers of George Fox, who preached reliance on the "inner light" over the authority of the church.

6192. Ban on Quakers enacted by a colony was passed by the General Court of the Massachusetts Bay Colony on October 14, 1656, at the urging of Governor John Endecott. The law provided for a fine of £100 for any ship captain who delivered Quakers "or any other blasphemous heretics" to the colony. Possessing Quaker books and coming to the defense of Quakers was also outlawed and punished with fines, whipping, and jailing. Subsequent anti-Quaker laws included the penalties of having the ears cut off and the tongue bored through with a hot iron.

6193. Quakers executed for their religious beliefs were William Robinson and Marmaduke Stevenson, English Quakers who had come to America in 1656. They were hanged from an elm tree on Boston Common, Boston, MA, on October 27, 1659. They were condemned by the Massachusetts General Court under a law passed on October 19, 1658, that banished Quakers from the colony under pain of death. Also condemned, but reprieved at the last moment, was Mary Dyer, who returned to Boston the following year and was hanged on June 1, 1660.

A

DECLARATION

Of the SAD and GREAT

Perſecution and Martyrdom

Of the People of God, called

QUAKERS, in *NEW-ENGLAND*,

for the Worſhipping of God.

Whereof
22 have been Baniſhed upon pain of Death.
03 have been MARTYRED.
03 have had their Right-Ears cut.
01 hath been burned in the Hand with the letter H.
31 Perſons have received 650 Stripes.
01 was beat while his Body was like a jelly.
Several were beat with Pitched Ropes.
Five Appeals made to *England*, were denied by the Rulers of *Boſton*.
One thouſand forty four pounds worth of Goods hath been taken from them (being poor men) for meeting together in the fear of the Lord, and for keeping the Commands of Chriſt.
One now lyeth in Iron-fetters, condemned to dye.

ALSO

Some CONSIDERATIONS, preſented to the KING, which is in *Anſwer* to a Petition and Addreſs, which was preſented unto Him by the General Court at *Boſton*: Subſcribed by *J. Endicot*, the chief Perſecutor there; thinking thereby to cover themſelves from the Blood of the Innocent.

Gal. 4. 29. *But as then, he that was born after the fleſh, perſecuted him that was born after the Spirit, even ſo it is now.*

God hath no reſpect to *Cains Sacrifice*, that killed his Brother about Religion

London, Printed for *Robert Wilſon*, in *Martins Le Grand*.

Courtesy of Images of American Political History

Title page from a work on the persecution of Quakers in New England.

6194. Church for Native Americans in New England was established in Natick, MA, by John Eliot in 1660. Six other "praying towns" were established before 1674.

6195. Quaker annual meeting was held in Scituate, MA, in 1660. The first monthly meeting is believed to have been held in Sandwich, MA, on June 25, 1672. It is possible that earlier meetings were held, but no records of them have been preserved.

6196. Colonial charter of religious freedom for all faiths was the royal charter issued by King Charles II in 1663 to Roger Williams's colony of Rhode Island. The charter guaranteed that "no person within the said colony, at any time hereafter shall be any wise molested, punished, disquieted, or called in question, for any differences in opinion in matters of religion," and that each persom may "freely and fully have and enjoy his and their own judgments and consciences, in matters of religious concernments." The charter was in effect from July 8, 1663, until the state constitution, adopted in November 1842, became operative on the first Tuesday of May 1843.

6197. Native American preacher of Christianity was Hiacoomes, who was taught to read and write by Thomas Mayhew. He was ordained on August 22, 1670, by John Eliot and John Cotton, and preached to his countrymen in a small church in Martha's Vineyard, MA.

6198. Seventh Day Baptist Church was organized at Newport, RI, in 1671 by Stephen Mumford, an English Sabbatarian Baptist. The first deacon was William Weeden.

6199. Catholic holy orders were conferred by Gabriel Diaz Vara Calderón, Bishop of Santiago de Cuba, on a visit to St. Augustine, FL, on August 24, 1675. Minor orders were conferred on seven candidates.

6200. Quaker meeting house was most likely the house of Nicholas Easton in Newport, RI, which he willed to the local members of the Society of Friends in 1676. The first building designed to serve as a meeting house was the Great Friends Meeting House, constructed nearby in 1699 and still extant.

6201. Labadist community was established at Bohemia Manor, MD, in 1683, by followers of the French religious reformer Jean de Labadie, a former Jesuit priest who called for a return to the original forms of Christianity. The first Labadists were P. Vorstman and J. Shilders, who arrived on September 23, 1679, in New Netherlands on the *Charles.*

6202. Jewish synagogue was a one-room house in New York City, on Beaver Street, that was rented by Congregation Shearith Israel in 1682 after the repeal of a law forbidding public worship by anyone except members of the Dutch Reformed Church. The first permanent Jewish house of worship in America was a small stone building built by the congregation on Mill Street (now South William Street) and completed on April 8, 1730. Saul Pardo, the first prayer leader, received a salary of £50, six cords of wood, and a supply of unleavened bread for Passover. The congregation's present synagogue is located at Central Park West and 70th Street.

6203. Mennonites to arrive in America were 13 German and Dutch families from Krefeld, Germany, led by Francis Daniel Pastorius, who disembarked on October 6, 1683, from the *Concord.* They were induced to come to America through the generosity of William Penn, who offered them 5,000 acres of land in Pennsylvania and freedom from religious persecution. Their settlement, called Germantown, is now a neighborhood in Philadelphia.

6204. Episcopal church organized in New England was King's Chapel, at the corner of Tremont and School Streets, Boston, MA, built in 1686.

6205. Christian worship services organized by African-American slaves took place in Massachusetts in 1693, when the Puritan minister Cotton Mather wrote his "Rules for the Society of Negroes" at the request of a group of slaves who wanted to adopt Christian practices and hold their own prayer meetings. The rules stipulated that religious meetings would be held on Sabbath evenings between the hours of seven and nine, at a convenient time for the slaves' masters. Mather wrote a treatise on the subject, *The Negro Christianized,* that was published in 1701. Many slaveowners opposed missionary efforts to the slaves for fear that baptized slaves would someday be freed by law.

6206. Lutheran services in English were held in 1694 in Germantown and Philadelphia, PA, by Heinrich Bernhard Koester.

6207. Rosicrucian Order lodge as well as temple and laboratories were erected in 1694 in what is now Fairmount Park, Philadelphia, PA, by Magister Kelpius. The order, also known as the Ancient Mystical Order of the Rosy Cross, originated in Europe and promotes esoteric teachings which it claims to have derived from ancient sources. The national headquarters of the Grand Lodge of the Rosicrucian Order of the North and South Jurisdiction is located at Rosicrucian Park, San Jose, CA. Each jurisdiction is under the direction of an imperator who has a Supreme Council as an advisory board that charters lodges and chapters.

6208. Presbyterian presbytery met in Philadelphia, PA, in 1705 and was composed of 7 ministers—Francis Makemie, John Hampton, George McNish, Samuel Davis, Nathaniel Taylor, John Wilson, and Jedidiah Andrews—and 34 others. The first known ordination, which took place in 1706, was that of John Boyd, who settled in Freehold, NJ.

6209. Mennonite meetinghouse was built in 1708 on the east side of Germantown Avenue, above Herman Street, Germantown, PA. It was succeeded in 1770 by a stone building. The first minister was William Rittenhouse (Rittinghuysen), who served for two years.

6210. Brethren (also known as Dunkards, Dunkers, Tunkers, and German Baptists) arrived in America in 1719 and settled in the area of Germantown, PA. They held their first immersion on December 25, 1723, at Wissahickon Creek in Germantown. The first chosen elder was Peter Becker. The first congregation was the Coventry Congregation, which met on September 7, 1724. The group originated in Schwarzenau, Germany, in 1708. The official name Church of the Brethren was adopted in 1908.

6211. Reformed Church meeting took place in Falkner Swamp, Montgomery County, PA, on October 15, 1725, when the new denomination was organized by John Philip Boehm.

6212. Catholic nuns to arrive in the future United States were 12 members of the Ursuline order who emigrated from Rouen, France. They arrived in New Orleans, LA, in July 1727. The group founded a girls' school, an orphanage, and an infirmary.

6213. Catholic convent permanently established was in New Orleans, LA, in a two-story frame building with six apartments on each floor. It was occupied on August 6, 1727, by the Ursulines. On August 9, Mass was offered there for the first time. The superioress was Mother Marie (Tranchepain) of St. Augustine, FL.

6214. Jewish religious school for children was Yeshivat Minhat Areb, founded in 1728 by New York City's Congregation Shearith Israel, the first Jewish congregation in North America. Its successor, the Shearith Israel Congregation School, opened in 1755 with a curriculum combining religious and secular studies (arithmetic, Spanish, and English). The first Jewish Sunday school, held for 50 pupils, was the Hebrew Sunday School of Philadelphia, PA, organized on March 4, 1838, by Rebecca Gratz for "the religious instruction and general improvement of children of the Jewish faith." Philadelphia's Gratz College was the first to offer training for teachers in Jewish schools, beginning in 1897.

The much-admired and famously beautiful Rebecca Gratz was the model for the character Rebecca in Sir Walter Scott's novel IVANHOE.

6215. Catholic nun who professed her vows in the United States was Sister St. Stanislas Hachard of the Ursuline Convent, New Orleans, LA, who took her vows on March 15, 1729. The first nun born in the United States was Mary Turpin of Illinois, born in 1731, who entered the Ursuline Convent in 1748. She began her novitiate on July 2, 1749, and made her profession of faith on January 31, 1752. She died on November 20, 1761, at the age of 30.

6216. Schwenkfelder to arrive in America was George Schultz, who arrived at Philadelphia, PA, in 1731. He was followed three years later by 180 Schwenkfelders who had been exiled from Silesia. They formally organized a church in 1782. The Schwenkfelders were followers of Kaspar Schwenkfeld von Ossig, a 16th-century nobleman and mystic.

6217. Catholic church in the English colonies to be used for public worship was St. Joseph's Church, founded in Philadelphia, PA, in 1733.

6218. Great Awakening of religious revival began in Northampton, MA, in 1734, when pastor Jonathan Edwards began preaching sermons on the transforming action of divine grace on the human spirit. It was brought to a fever pitch by the preaching tour of English minister George Whitefield, who arrived in Georgia in 1739. His oratory, as he traveled throughout Britain's American colonies, produced thousands of conversions and helped create an atmosphere of ferment that gave rise to several new religions and denominations.

6219. Moravian settlement in America began with the arrival of George Boehnischt in Pennsylvania on September 22, 1734. The following year, a group of Moravians led by Augustus Gottlieb Spangenberg came to Georgia for the purpose of converting Native Americans. Their first church was built in 1735 in Savannah, GA, where General James Edward Oglethorpe had given 600 acres of land for a colony. Bishop David Nitschmann arrived from Germany in 1736 and ordained Anton Sieffert as pastor, the first ordination by a Protestant bishop in America. The group soon relocated to Pennsylvania and built a settlement in Bethlehem, PA, in 1741. Spangenberg became the Moravians' first American bishop in 1744. Moravians are followers of Jan Hus, the 15th-century Bohemian religious reformer, and call themselves the Church of the Brethren, or Unitas Fratrum.

6220. Protestant Sunday school was opened in Christ Church, Savannah, GA, in 1736 by John Wesley and was under the leadership of Charles Delamotte. Before the Sunday evening services, Wesley instructed between 30 and 40 children and heard them recite their catechism. Prior to this, religious instruction had been given to children individually and in small unorganized groups.

6221. Methodist preacher was John Wesley, the founder of Methodism, who arrived in the English colony of Georgia on February 6, 1736. At Savannah, GA, he established the first Methodist parish and parsonage, preaching his first service on March 7, 1736. He returned to England in 1738.

6222. Missionary society organized in the English colonies was the Society for the Propagation of Christian Knowledge Among the Indians of North America, which was founded in 1762 in the Massachusetts Bay Colony. The Archbishop of Canterbury persuaded King George III to cancel the charter, fearing it might become a channel of influence for churches that did not adhere to Church of England teachings.

6223. Methodist meetinghouse was the log cabin of Robert Strawbridge in New Windsor, MD, built in 1764. (When John Wesley, the founder of Methodism, sojourned in Georgia in 1736–38, he preached in Savannah's Town Hall.) The oldest meetinghouse in continuous use is Wesley Chapel in New York City, also known as the John Street Church, built by a group of Irish Methodists and dedicated by Philip Embury, the first minister, on October 30, 1768. It was a small frame house, 42 by 60 feet and one and a half stories high, built in antique Dutch style. It accommodated 700 people.

6224. Methodist Society in America was founded by Irish immigrant and itinerant preacher Robert Strawbridge in New Windsor, MD, circa 1764. The oldest one in continuous existence in the United States was founded in 1766 in New York City by two cousins, also emigrants from Ireland, Philip Embury and Barbara Ruckle Heck.

6225. United Brethren in Christ meeting took place on May 18, 1766, in Isaac Long's barn in Lancaster, PA. The church was founded by the Reverend Martin Boehm and the Reverend Philip William Otterbein, who were elected bishops in September 1800.

6226. Catholic mission in California was dedicated and blessed by Father Junipero Serra on July 16, 1769. After high mass, the royal standard of Spain was unfurled over the mission, which was named in honor of San Diego de Alcala. The mission, located in what is now San Diego, CA, was the first of a chain of 21 that were erected.

6227. Protestant church west of the Alleghenies was built in 1772 at Schoenbrunn, OH, by Moravian missionaries. The first communion service was held on June 9, 1772, although the church was not finished until September 19. A larger church was dedicated on October 24, 1773. The same missionaries built the first schoolhouse west of the Alleghenies, completing it on July 29, 1773. The Reverend David Zeisberger was the church's first preacher and the school's first teacher.

6228. Baptist churches for African-Americans were part of the Separatist (or New Light) Baptist movement, which emphasized independent congregations. The earliest congregation for African-Americans in the South was established in 1756 on a plantation at Lunenburg, VA. The first to have a major influence was the plantation congregation founded in 1773 at Silver Bluff, SC, from which came a number of "exhorters," or African-American preachers, who went on to found Baptist churches in other locations, including Jamaica and the African nation of Sierre Leone.

6229. Universalist church services were held in 1774. The church was formally organized on January 1, 1779, when the articles of association were signed by 31 men and 30 women led by the Reverend John Murray, who was made the first minister. A church built in Winthrop Sargent's garden, Water Street, Gloucester, MA, was dedicated on December 25, 1780. It contained 30 box pews.

6230. Shaker religious community was founded in Watervliet, NY, in 1776 by Ann Lee of Manchester, England, and eight others who left Liverpool on the *Mariah* and arrived in New York City on August 6, 1774. The group's full name was "The United Society of Believers in Christ's Second Appearing." Its followers believed in pacifist principles and a celibate communal life. The rules of the Society stated that "the head of the Shaker Order is Christ, Represented in a Dual Order of Leaders, Ministry, Elders and Trustees." Women and men had different responsibilities but were treated as equals. Shaker communities were founded in New Hampshire, Ohio, and in other locations in New York. They began to decline after the Civil War.

6231. Catholic funeral attended by the Continental Congress was that of Philippe Charles Jean Baptiste Tronson du Coudray, a French officer who was serving as inspector general of the American army. On September 15, 1777, while crossing the Schuykill River in Pennsylvania on a ferry to join Washington's army, his horse became frightened and plunged overboard, and Tronson du Coudray was drowned. Congress resolved that he should be buried with military honors and that the members of Congress should attend his funeral, which was held in Philadelphia, PA, on September 17.

6232. Methodist minister who was African-American was Richard Allen, who was accepted as a minister by Bishop Francis Asbury in 1784 at the first general conference of American Methodists, held in Baltimore, MD. He was ordained a deacon in 1799 and eventually became an elder. In 1816 he became the founder and first bishop of the African Methodist Episcopal Church. An earlier African-American preacher, Harry Hosier, traveled with Francis Asbury, the bishop who carried Methodism throughout the English colonies in the late 18th century. The first African-American minister of an all-white Methodist congregation was the Reverend Simon Peter Montgomery of Pineville, SC, who assumed the pulpit of the Old Mystic Methodist Church, Old Mystic, CT, on October 2, 1955.

6233. Episcopal bishop was Samuel Seabury, consecrated on November 14, 1784, at Aberdeen, Scotland, by the Scottish bishops Robert Kilgour, Arthur Petrie, and John Skinner. He was rector of St. James Church, New London, CT, and bishop of Rhode Island and Connecticut from that date until his death on February 25, 1796. The first to be consecrated in the United States was the Reverend Thomas John Claggett, founder of the Trinity Episcopal Church, Upper Marlboro, MD. He was consecrated on September 17, 1792, at Trinity Church, New York City, by Bishops Seabury, White, Provoost, and Madison.

6234. Methodist bishop was Francis Asbury, who was appointed in 1784 by Thomas Coke, to whom the title really belonged. They were known as the joint bishops of the Church in North America. Bishop Asbury was elected by the first General Conference, called the Christmas Conference, which met on December 24, 1784, in the Light Street Church, Baltimore, MD.

6235. Congregational Church minister who was African-American was the Reverend Lemuel Haynes, who was ordained in 1785. Until 1833, he served as pastor to several congregations in New York, Connecticut, and Vermont. Most of the members of these congregations were white.

6236. Unitarian church was King's Chapel, Boston, MA, originally founded in 1686 as the first Church of England (Episcopalian) church organized in Puritan New England. In 1785 the congregation abandoned the Anglican ritual in favor of Unitarian principles and reordained its minister, James Freeman. The first Unitarian church to be identified as such in its name was the Society of Unitarian Christians, organized in Philadelphia on June 12, 1796, under the leadership of Joseph Priestley. An organized movement of Unitarians was founded by William Ellery Channing in 1819. The first woman ordained as a Unitarian minister was Celia C. Burleigh, who was given a parish in Brooklyn, CT, on October 5, 1871.

6237. Missionary to the Native Americans who was African-American was John Marrant of New York, ordained on May 15, 1785, as a Methodist minister in London. Among his converts were the chief of the Cherokees and his daughter.

6238. Methodist churches for African-Americans were founded in Baltimore, MD, after the formation of the Colored Methodist Society in 1787. The congregants were former members of the city's Methodist meeting houses who objected to segregated seating and insulting treatment. The first Methodist church in the North to be organized by African-Americans, and for the same reasons, was the Mother Bethel Church, founded in August 1794 by Richard Allen, a former slave, at Sixth and Lombard streets, Philadelphia, PA.

6239. Catholic diocese and archdiocese was the diocese of Baltimore, MD, established on April 6, 1789, and raised to the dignity of the first archdiocese in the United States on April 8, 1808. By a decree of the Sacred Congregation of the Propaganda, approved by Pope Pius IX on July 5, 1858, prerogative of place was conferred on the archdiocese of Baltimore, so that it is known as the Premier See of the country.

6240. Catholic bishop appointed to serve in the United States was the Right Reverend John Carroll of Maryland. A petition for appointment of an American bishop was sent to Pope Pius VI on March 12, 1788, and was voted upon favorably. The result was confirmed by the Pope on November 6, 1789. The Right Reverend Charles Walmesley consecrated Carroll bishop of Baltimore, MD, on

August 15, 1790, in the chapel of Lulworth Castle, Dorset, England. On April 8, 1808, he became an archbishop.

6241. Presidential tribute to freedom of religion was a letter written by George Washington on August 17, 1790. It was a reply to a letter he had received from Moses Seixas on behalf of the congregation of Touro Synagogue in Newport, RI, thanking the United States for being a haven against persecution and asking for divine blessing on its leader. Washington emphasized that the government "gives to bigotry no sanction, to persecution no assistance," and, quoting the Hebrew Bible, referred to the United States as a country where "every one shall sit in safety under his own vine and figtree, and there shall be none to make him afraid."

6242. Eastern Orthodox church was founded in 1792 at Kodiak Island in southeastern Alaska, the capital of Russian America. In 1808 the capital was moved to Novoarkhangelsk (Sitka), where the Cathedral of St. Michael was built in 1848. Novoarkhangelsk was the seat of the Bishop of Kamchatka, Alaska, and the Kurile and Aleutian Islands, an expanse of more than 1 million square miles.

6243. Catholic African-Americans were French-speaking Catholics from Haiti, who came to Baltimore, MD, in 1793 as refugees from Haiti's revolution.

6244. Catholic priest ordained in the United States was Father Stephen Theodore Badin, ordained on May 25, 1793, by Bishop John Carroll in Baltimore, MD. He was appointed to the mission of Kentucky and held his first mass there on the first Sunday of Advent, 1793, in the house of Dennis McCarthy in Lexington, KY. The first priest to receive his full theological training in the United States was Demetrius Augustine Gallitzin (Dimitri Augustin Golitzyn), who was ordained a bishop by Bishop Carroll on March 18, 1795, in Baltimore.

6245. Swedenborgian or New Church temple was erected at the southwest corner of Exeter and Baltimore Streets, Baltimore, MD, in 1799. The brick structure was built with funds supplied by citizens of the community. The first church service was held on Sunday, January 5, 1800. The New Church group in Baltimore was led by Robert Carter, a member of the Virginia Colonial Council, which began meeting in 1792. The first New Church ministers ordained in America were the Reverend Ralph Mather, formerly of England, and the Reverend John Hargrove, a former preacher of the Methodist Episcopal Church who was also the Baltimore City registrar. Hargrove became the first pastor. The first General Convention met in 1817 in Philadelphia, PA, where Hargrove was chosen as the first president.

6246. Catholic bishop consecrated in the United States was Leonard Neale, who was consecrated bishop of Gortyna, Crete, in the procathedral of St. Peter's in Baltimore, MD, on December 7, 1800.

6247. Ashkenazic Jewish congregation was Congregation Rodeph Shalom ("Seeker of Peace") of Philadelphia, PA, founded on October 10, 1802. Ashkenazic Jews, whose name derives from *Ashkenaz*, the Hebrew word for Germany, are those whose families originated in central and eastern Europe.

6248. Camp meeting was held in 1803 by James M'Geary, William McGee (a Presbyterian), and John McGee (a Methodist) in a little log church on the Gaspar River in Logan County, KY.

6249. Religious tract society was the Massachusetts Society for Promoting Christian Knowledge, instituted in Boston, MA, on September 1, 1803, at the suggestion of Samuel Phillips and Professor D. Tappan.

6250. Evangelical Church conference took place on November 15, 1807, at the house of Samuel Becker in Muhlbach, PA (now Kleinfeltersville). It was attended by church officials, five itinerant ministers, three local preachers, and 20 class leaders and exhorters. Jacob Albright, who had founded the group in 1800, was elected bishop. The first church building was the Evangelical Church, a structure 34 by 38 feet, erected in 1816 in New Berlin, PA. The Reverend John Dreisbach preached the sermon at the dedication on March 2, 1817. The denomination changed its name to the Evangelical Association at its general conference in October 1816, in Buffalo Valley, PA.

6251. Bible society was the Bible Society of Philadelphia, organized on December 12, 1808, at Philadelphia, PA. The name was changed to the Pennsylvania Bible Society in 1840. The Reverend William White was the first president and B.B. Hopkins the first secretary. The initiation fee was $5 and the dues $2 a year. Life membership was $50.

6252. Disciples of Christ meeting was held on August 17, 1809, in Washington, PA, when a group of Presbyterians headed by Thomas Campbell formed themselves into the Christian Association of Washington. On May 4, 1811, a church was established in Brush Run, PA, with Thomas Campbell as elder and Alexander Campbell, his son, as preacher. No attempt at forming a separate and distinct denomination was made until 1823, when Alexander Campbell and several members of the Brush Run Church founded a church in Wellsburg, WV.

6253. Foreign missionary society was the American Board of Commissioners for Foreign Missions, organized on June 29, 1810, by the General Association of Massachusetts at its annual meeting in Bradford, MA. The board received its charter in 1812 from Massachusetts.

6254. African Methodist church was the African Union Methodist Church, was founded in 1813 by the Reverend Peter Spencer in Wilmington, DE.

6255. African Methodist Episcopal bishop was Richard Allen, who was elected on April 11, 1816, at the church's founding convention in Philadelphia, PA, when 16 delegates from five independent churches met to form an African-American denomination based on the principles of Methodism. Allen had been born into slavery in 1760, when his family was owned by the chief justice of Pennsylvania, and had purchased his freedom in 1786 after converting his current owner to Methodism. He became a licensed exhorter, or traveling preacher, and was accepted as a minister in 1784. Ten years later, he established an independent congregation of African-Americans, which led to the founding in 1816 of the African Methodist Episcopal denomination.

6256. National bible society was the American Bible Society, formed by delegates from 35 Bible societies for the purpose of increasing the circulation of the Holy Scriptures. The delegates met on May 8, 1816, in New York City, and organized the society on May 11, 1816. The first president was Elias Boudinot, who served from 1816 to 1821. In the first year, 6,140 Bibles were distributed.

6257. African Methodist Episcopal preacher who was a woman was Jarena Lee of Bethel Church, Philadelphia, PA. In 1809, having felt a call to preach, she asked permission from Bishop Richard Allen, who responded that he had no authority to allow it. Eight years later, in 1817, she was moved to stand up in church and speak. Allen then gave her an informal license to travel as a missionary, preaching to camp meetings and churches.

6258. Prayers in sign language were offered by the Reverend Thomas Hopkins Gallaudet, a Congregational minister and teacher of the deaf, in 1817 at the American Institution for the Deaf, Hartford, CT. His son, the Reverend Thomas Gallaudet, an Episcopal priest, held the first church service for deaf worshippers on October 3, 1852, in the small chapel of New York University, New York City. He held spoken worship services in the morning, services using American Sign Language in the afternoon. The first church whose purpose was to serve deaf people was St. Ann's Church for Deaf-Mutes, which held its first services on August 7, 1859. The first ordained clergyman who was deaf was the Reverend Henry Winter Syle, who became a deacon in 1876 and a priest in 1883. He founded All Souls' Church for the Deaf, Philadelphia, PA, in 1885.

6259. Methodist missionary was Ebenezer Brown, sent out by the Methodist Missionary Society. In 1819 he was assigned a residence in New Orleans, LA, to preach to the French people of Louisiana.

6260. Mariners' church was built on June 4, 1820, by the New York Port Society, as a nonsectarian, interdenominational church. The society was organized in May 1818 and was chartered on April 13, 1819, as the Society for Promoting the Gospel Among Seamen in the Port of New York. The first pastor was the Reverend Ward Stafford, who preached from 1818 to 1821.

6261. Cathedral was the Cathedral of the Assumption of the Blessed Virgin Mary, in Baltimore, MD, a primatial see of the Catholic Church. The cornerstone was laid July 7, 1806, and the building was dedicated on May 31, 1821, by Archbishop Ambrose Marechal. It was completed in 1851. In 1936, the Baltimore Cathedral was raised to the rank of a minor basilica by Pope Pius XI.

6262. Reform Jewish congregation was the Reform Society of Israelites, organized on November 21, 1824, by dissident members of Congregation Beth Elohim of Charleston, SC, an Orthodox synagogue that had been founded by Sephardic Jews in 1750. The group was formed after the trustees of the synagogue refused a request to modernize the prayer service. Its leader was Isaac Harby, a teacher and journalist. The society disbanded in 1833, but many of its members rejoined the synagogue after the arrival of Rabbi Gustav Poznanski, who approved radical alterations in the service.

6263. National religious tract society was the American Tract Society, organized on May 11, 1825, in New York City. It was formed from a combination of about 50 large and small tract societies. The society was organized to minister to all classes and conditions of people, in many languages, through the medium of the printed page. The first president was Sampson Vryling Stoddard and the first secretary the Reverend William Allen Hallock.

6264. Catholic community of African-American nuns was the Oblate Sisters of Providence, founded by Jacques Hector Nicholas Joubert de la Muraille on July 2, 1829, in Baltimore, MD. Pope Gregory XVI approved the order on October 2, 1831. The nuns were members of Baltimore's Haitian community. The first convent to admit African-American women as sisters was the Sisters of Loretto, Loretto, KY. The Reverend Charles Nerinck in May 1824 admitted to the novitiate five African-American women who followed the same community exercises as the other sisters but lived apart from them.

6265. Mormon Church meeting took place on April 6, 1830, in Fayette, NY, in the home of Peter Whitmer. Joseph Smith, the founder of the church, declared that an angel of God had shown him gold plates on which was engraved a divine scripture, *The Book of Mormon*, which he had translated. The official title of the Mormon Church is the Church of Jesus Christ of Latter-day Saints.

6266. Mormon temple was built in Kirtland, OH, by Joseph Smith, the founder of the Church of Jesus Christ of Latter-Day Saints (or Mormon Church), who had moved to Ohio from New York with about 50 families. The temple's cornerstone was laid on July 23, 1833, and it was dedicated on March 27, 1836. It measured 59 by 79 feet and was 50 feet high. It had a tower 110 feet high.

6267. Floating church was the Floating Church of Our Saviour, constructed in 1843 and moored in the East River at the foot of Pike Street, New York City. The church was organized by the Young Men's Church Missionary Society, an auxiliary of the City Mission Society. The society dissolved in 1844 and deeded the church to the Protestant Episcopal Church Missionary Society for Seamen in the City and Port of New York, an organization that emanated from the original group.

6268. Adventist church to accept Saturday as the Sabbath was the Adventist church in Washington Center, NH, which began to keep the seventh day as the Sabbath in the spring of 1844 under the influence of its minister, Frederick Wheeler. The first general conference of Seventh-Day Adventists was organized on May 21, 1863.

6269. Spiritualist was John D. Fox of Hydeville, Wayne County, NY. In 1848, his house attracted hordes of the curious who wanted to hear spirit knockings and rappings. Fox's daughters, Margaret and Catherine, continued his work and acted as mediums.

6270. Scandinavian Methodist Episcopal church was organized in Cambridge, WI, in April 1851 by the Reverend Christian B. Willerup with an initial membership of 52. The denomination was incorporated on May 3, 1851, and a stone building costing $4,000 was dedicated in the summer of 1852. This church is the oldest Methodist Episcopal church built by Scandinavians in this or any other country.

6271. Minister who was a woman was the Reverend Antoinette Brown Blackwell, who was ordained on September 15, 1853, at the Congregational Church, South Butler, NY.

6272. Buddhist temple in the United States was the Kong Chow Temple in San Francisco, CA, which was built by the Sze Yap Company, a group of Chinese immigrants.

6273. Foreign missionary society organized by women to send unmarried missionaries to Asia was the Woman's Union Missionary Society of America for Heathen Lands, organized in November 1860 in Boston, MA, by Mrs. Ellen H. B. Mason and nine other women. In May 1861, a similar society was formed in Philadelphia, PA, which united with the Boston group to form the Woman's Union Missionary Society for Heathen Lands. The first president was Mrs. Sarah B. Doremus. The first missionary was Sarah H. Marston, who sailed in November 1861 for Tounghoo, Burma.

6274. Episcopal cathedral was the Cathedral of Our Merciful Saviour, Faribault, MN, built by the Right Reverend Henry Benjamin Whipple, First Bishop of Minnesota, as his own church. The cathedral was begun in 1862 and completed in 1869 at a cost of $100,000. A tower was added in 1902.

6275. Catholic parish church for African-Americans was St. Francis Xavier's Church, Baltimore, MD, purchased on October 10, 1863, and dedicated on February 21, 1864.

6276. Greek Orthodox church was the Holy Trinity Church, 1222 North Dorgenois Street, New Orleans, LA, founded in 1867. The first pastor was Paisios Ferentinos.

6277. Hutterites arrived in New York City from Europe in 1874 and went on to found the Bonhomme community in Yankton, SD. They went on to found some 200 additional communities in North and South Dakota, Minnesota, Montana, Washington, and Canada. The Hutterites are a separatist Anabaptist sect who live in farming communes, where they hold all property in common. They follow the teachings of Jakob Hutter, who was martyred in 1536.

6278. Catholic priest from the United States to be made a cardinal was John McCloskey, born in Brooklyn to Irish immigrant parents, and ordained a priest in 1834. In May 1864 he was appoined archbishop of the archdiocese of New York. On March 15, 1875, Pope Pius IX elevated him to the rank of cardinal, the first from the Western Hemisphere.

6279. Catholic bishop who was African-American was James Augustine Healy, born in Georgia, who was consecrated on June 21, 1875, as bishop of Portland, ME. The first African-American archbishop was Eugene Antonio Marino, appointed archbishop of Atlanta, GA, on March 15, 1988, by Pope John Paul II.

> Healy's father was an Irish immigrant, his mother a slave; legally, they could not marry. Six of their children became priests or nuns, and another son became a Coast Guard captain.

6280. Christian Science church was founded by Mary Baker Eddy in Boston, MA, in 1879, following her founding of Christian Science as a religion and her publication of its textbook, *Science and Health*, with Key to the Scriptures, in 1875.

6281. Salvation Army services took place at Castle Garden, New York City, on March 10, 1880, after Commissioner George Scott Railton and seven women arrived on the *Australia* at the Battery in lower Manhattan. Early services were held at street meetings and between performances of *Uncle Tom's Cabin* at Harry Hill's Gentleman's Sporting Theatre. The Salvation Army is a missionary group founded by William Booth in London in 1865 under the name of the East London Mission.

6282. Catholic hillside shrine similar to those in European Catholic countries was "The Way of the Cross," built in New Ulm, MN, in 1884. Connected with the shrine were the Loretto Hospital and the St. Alexander Home for the Aged.

6283. Episcopal bishop who was African-American was the Reverend Samuel David Ferguson, who was elected to the House of Bishops of the Protestant Episcopal Church in 1884. He was consecrated on June 24, 1885, at Grace Church, New York City, as the successor of the Missionary Bishop of Liberia.

6284. Catholic priest who was African-American and assigned to work in the United States was the Reverend Augustus Tolton. He was ordained at the College of Propaganda, Rome, Italy, on April 24, 1886, and opened a mission in Quincy, IL, in the diocese of Springfield, IL. The first African-American priest to be ordained in the United States was Charles Randolph Uncles, who was ordained in the Baltimore Cathedral, Baltimore, MD, on December 19, 1891, by Cardinal Gibbons.

6285. Vedanta Center for spreading the teachings of the Vedanta movement, a form of the Hindu religion, was founded in 1894 in New York City by Swami Vivekananda. He became the first Hindu spiritual leader to visit America when he came to Chicago in 1893 to attend the World's Parliament of Religions at the Columbian Exposition.

6286. National Zionist organization was the United American Zionists, formed on October 22, 1897, in New York City by 10 local societies. The first convention was held on July 4, 1898, in New York City. Local Zionist societies, known as Chovevei Tzion or Chibat Tzion ("Lovers of Zion"), had been formed as early as 1882 to advocate the return of the Jewish people to their homeland.

6287. Portable church was the Chapel of the Transfiguration, which was consecrated on June 3, 1899, at Conanicut Island, RI. An Episcopal church, it was 27 feet long and 18 feet wide and contained 14 benches, 20 chairs, a platform, and an altar. The interior, including the pews, prayer desk, and altar, was made of oak. The church was built on a wooden chassis with four wheels and was drawn from place to place by horses. The first preacher was the Reverend Charles E. Preston of St. Matthew's Church. The first service was held on April 23, 1899.

6288. Catholic mass for night workers was held on May 5, 1901, at the Church of St. Andrew, New York City. Father Luke J. Evers obtained special permission from the Pope to institute this service, as church law did not permit mass before sunrise.

6289. Hindu temple in the United States was built on Webster Street in San Francisco, CA, by Swami Trigunatita and the Vedanta Society of Northern California. It was opened on January 7, 1906.

6290. Bibles in hotel rooms were placed in the Superior Hotel, Iron Mountain (now Superior), MT, in October 1908, by the Gideons, the Christian Commercial Traveling Men's Association. The organization was founded in 1899 at Boscobel, WI. The first president was Samuel Eugene Hill. The work was extended to include distribution to hotels, hospitals, penal institutions, and public schools.

6291. Church without theology, creed, or dogma was organized by Richard Wolfe of Denver, CO, in 1912. The First Liberal Church of Denver, the first of the new sect, was organized in 1922. Wolfe became the first bishop of the Liberal Church of America.

6292. Sikh gurdwara in the United States was the Stockton Gurdwara, in Stockton, CA. Religious services began in 1912 in a private house. On November 21, 1915, a two-story building was dedicated as the permanent gurdwara, or temple. The Granthi was Bhola Singh. The building, constructed through the efforts of the Pacific Coast Khalsa Diwan Society, included a kitchen that offered free meals to the needy.

6293. Church organized by Native Americans was the First American Church, incorporated on October 10, 1918, with its principal seat of government and place of business at El Reno, Canadian County, OK. The organizers, all residents of the state of Oklahoma, were Mack Haag and Sidney White Crane of the Cheyenne; Charles W. Dailey, George Pipestem and Charles N. Moore of the Oto; Frank Eagle of the Ponca; William Peawa and Manwat of the Comanche; Kiowa Charlie of the Kiowa; and Apache Ben of the Apache.

6294. Orthodox rabbi born in America was Sol B. Friedman, who received rabbinical ordination in New York City on March 23, 1919, along with four other graduates of the Rabbi Isaac Elchanan Theological Seminary.

6295. Religious service broadcast on radio took place on January 2, 1921, when the Calvary Episcopal Church of Pittsburgh, PA, broadcast its services through station KDKA. The preacher was the Reverend Edwin Jan Van Etten.

6296. Radio church was established on November 27, 1921, when services of the Radio Church of America were broadcast by Walter J. Garvey from his home at 2000 University Avenue, the Bronx, New York City. Hospitals, military installations, and radio operators were alerted to the program. The sermon was preached by Richard Jay Ward, assisted by Dr. M. H. Leventhal. Solos were sung by Clara Brookhurst and Adele Lauriat Barrow.

6297. Catholic nuns in a cloistered community were the Magdalen Sisters at the Convent of the Good Shepherd, Baltimore, MD, founded on April 24, 1922.

6298. Episcopal bishop deposed for heresy in the United States was William Montgomery Brown, Protestant Episcopal Bishop of Arkansas and the author of *Communism and Christianity*, who was deposed for heresy at New Orleans, LA, on October 12, 1925. The deposition was imposed by the Right Reverend Ethelbert Talbot, presiding officer of the House of Bishops of the Protestant Episcopal Church. The Secretary of the House, Dr. Charles Laban Pardee, drew a line through Brown's name on the record. He was not excommunicated.

6299. Catholic church to become a basilica was the Sanctuary of Our Lady of Victory, Lackawanna, in the diocese of Buffalo, NY. It was dedicated and consecrated on May 25, 1926, as Our Lady of Victory Shrine, and on July 28, by apostolic decree of Pope Pius XI, it was dignified with the title of "Basilica of Our Blessed Lady of Victory."

6300. Presbyterian elder who was a woman was Sarah E. Dickson of the Wauwatosa Presbyterian Church of Milwaukee, WI, who was elected on June 2, 1930, and served until January 1, 1934. Her election was permitted by the church's General Assembly in its meeting at Cincinnati, OH, on May 31, 1930.

6301. Catholic saints who were active in North America were canonized in a three-day celebration commencing on June 30, 1930. Each of those canonized was credited with having performed two miracles and having met a heroic death. Among them were two laymen, René Goupil and John Lalande, and six Jesuit priests: Isaac Jogues, John De Brébeuf, Noel Chabanel, Anthony Daniel, Gabriel Lalemant, and Charles Garnier. The Pontifical Mass was celebrated at the Vatican by Archbishop Forbes of Ottawa, Canada.

6302. Baha'i house of worship was opened at Wilmette, IL, for public lectures and guided tours on May 1, 1931. The site had been blessed on May 1, 1912, by Abdu'l-Baha, the son of Baha'u'llah, founder of the Baha'i religion.

6303. Mosque of importance was the Islamic Center, Washington, DC, whose cornerstone was laid on January 11, 1949. It had a minaret 160 feet above street level from which calls to prayer were announced through a loudspeaker. A colonnade cloister joined the mosque to two wings that housed an institute containing a library, a museum, classrooms, and administrative offices. An auditorium in the basement of the mosque was designed to accommodate 300 people. The first director was Dr. Mahmoud Hoballah.

6304. Children's church that was built to scale and intended to be operated by children was the Children's Church, Milton, MA, dedicated on November 14, 1937, by the Reverend Vivian Towse Pomeroy, pastor of the First Parish Unitarian Church, Milton, MA. The miniature church was 18 feet by 32 feet, complete with steeple, belfry, organ, spire, and pews 2 feet 8 inches in height. It cost in excess of $5,000. The first pastor was the Reverend Mrs. Dorothy Pomeroy.

6305. Catholic beatification of a Native American took place on May 9, 1939, when the Cardinals of the Congregation of Rites in Rome, Italy, recommended the beatification of Kateri Tekakwitha, the "lily of the Mohawks." Their decision was sanctioned by Pope Pius XII on May 19, 1939. Kateri Tekakwitha was born in 1656 at Ossernenon, near the future Auriesville, NY.

6306. Religious services to be shown on television were produced on March 24, 1940, by station W2XBS of the National Broadcasting Company, New York City. At 11:30 A.M., the station aired a Protestant Easter service led by the Reverend Dr. Samuel McCrea Cavert of the Federal Council of the Churches of Christ in America, with music provided by the Westminster Choir, directed by Dr. John Finley Williamson. At 12:30, the station aired a Roman Catholic Easter service led by the Right Reverend Monsignor Fulton John Sheen of the Catholic University of America, Washington, DC, with music provided by the Paulist Choristers under the direction of Father William Joseph Finn, C.S.P., in cooperation with the National Council of Catholic Men. Other Easter services were televised from the Hollywood Bowl, Hollywood, CA, and from Central Park, New York City.

6307. Passover seder to be shown on television took place on April 25, 1940, in New York City, in the studio of the National Broadcasting Company, which had been set up as a dining room. Rabbi Saul Bezalel Applebaum of Central Synagogue, New York City, led seven participants in the seder; Lazar Weiner directed the music and the Central Synagogue choir. The program was produced with the cooperation of the United Jewish Layman's Committee.

6308. Serbian Orthodox cathedral was the Cathedral of St. Sava, New York City, which was elevated on June 11, 1944, from a pro-cathedral. On the same day, Bishop Dionisije Milivojevich conferred the Gold Cross and the title Stravrophor on Rector Doushan Jefta Shoukletovich and elevated him to dean. The cathedral was the diocesan headquarters of the Serbian Orthodox Church in Canada and the United States.

6309. Catholic saint who was an American citizen was Frances Xavier Cabrini, known as Mother Cabrini, founder of the Institute of the Missionary Sisters of the Sacred Heart. Born Maria Francesca Cabrini on July 15, 1850, in Italy, she came to the United States in 1889 and became a citizen in 1909. She was responsible for establishing hospitals, schools, and orphanages throughout the United States and South America. She died on December 22, 1917. She was declared venerable in November 1937, was beatified on November 13, 1938 (the first beatification of an American citizen), and was canonized a saint on July 7, 1946, by Pope Pius XII in Rome.

6310. Religious service to be televised from a church was the candlelight service on December 24, 1946, at Grace Episcopal Church, Broadway at 10th Street, New York City, which was telecast at 8:30 P.M. by WABD on the New York–Philadelphia–Washington network. The service was led by the Reverend Louis W. Pitt. The choir of 50 men and boys was led by the organist, Ernest Mitchell.

6311. Muslim cemetery in the United States was the Muslim National Cemetery, established in Cedar Rapids, IA, in 1948.

6312. Catholic midnight mass to be televised was transmitted on December 24, 1948, from St. Patrick's Cathedral, New York City, by stations WNBT-TV, WJZ-TV, and WCBS-TV.

6313. Mosque of importance in the United States was the Moslem Temple in Cedar Rapids, IA. Dedicated on February 15, 1934, the Moslem Temple was built by Sunni Muslims whose families had emigrated from Lebanon beginning in the 1870s. The building is now known as the Mother Mosque of America and contains a museum.

6314. Reform rabbi who was a woman was Paula Ackerman of Meridian, MS, who was appointed on January 26, 1951, to serve in the place of her late husband as rabbi of Temple Beth Israel. The first woman to receive ordination as a Reform rabbi was Sally Jane Priesand, who was ordained on June 3, 1972, in the Isaac M. Wise Temple, Cincinnati, OH. The Conservative movement ordained its first female rabbi, Amy Eilberg, on May 12, 1985, at the Jewish Theological Seminary in New York City. The first woman to serve as a cantor in a Reform temple was Betty Robbins of Massapequa, NY, whose sang on September 15, 1955, the eve of Rosh Hashanah, the Jewish New Year, at Temple Avodah, Oceanside, NY.

6315. Jewish prayer services to be televised in their entirety were shown on November 4, 1951, by WPIX-TV, New York City. The services were held at Temple Israel in New York City, a Reform synagogue. Rabbi William Franklin Rosenblum preached the sermon. Cantor Harold Orbach of Temple Israel, New Rochelle, NY, conducted the musical portions. This service, as well as three others on successive Saturdays, was arranged by the Radio and Television Division of the American Jewish Committee.

6316. Religious radio program broadcast by a husband and wife was conducted by Dr. Norman Vincent Peale, minister of the Marble Collegiate Church, New York City, and Mrs. Ruth Peale. On October 1, 1952, they began a television series entitled "What's Your Trouble?" The program was produced by the Broadcasting and Film Commission of the National Council of the Churches of Christ in the United States and presented on the Columbia Broadcasting System.

6317. Catholic cardinal whose see was west of the Rockies was James Francis Cardinal McIntyre, Archbishop of Los Angeles, CA, who was elevated to the Sacred College of Cardinals on January 12, 1953, by Pope Pius XII.

6318. Jewish mobile synagogue was the Circuit Riding Rabbi Bus, dedicated on March 27, 1955, at the Amity Country Club, Charlotte, NC. It was the project of the North Carolina Association of Jewish Men. The first rabbi was Harold A. Friedman. The bus was equipped with desks, blackboards, maps, a projection machine, a record player, and a library.

6319. Catholic prelate named to the Roman Curia who was American-born was Samuel Alphonsus Cardinal Stritch, archbishop of Chicago, IL, nominated on March 1, 1958, by Pope Pius XII to head one of the 12 departments of the Church's central administration, the Sacred Congregation for the Propagation of the Faith. He arrived in Rome on April 25, 1958, and on April 26 was admitted to the Sanatrix Clinic, where he died on May 27 before he could take up his post.

6320. Television station owned by a religious organization was WYAR-TV, Channel 27, Portsmouth, VA, a nonprofit station that began operating on October 1, 1961. It was founded by M. G. Robertson as the Christian Broadcasting Network. The station was on the air on Sundays from 1 to 6 P.M. and on weekdays, except Mondays, from 7 to 10 P.M.

6321. Catholic mass in English was celebrated on August 24, 1964, in Kiel Auditorium, St. Louis, MO, by the Reverend Frederick Richard McManus of the Catholic University of America. The Gloria, most of the responses, the Creed, and the Agnus Dei (Lamb of God) prayer were in English. Joseph Elmer Cardinal Ritter, the archbishop of St. Louis, authorized the celebration to mark the 25th annual Liturgical Week, attended by about 11,000 bishops, priests, nuns, and laymen.

6322. Russian Orthodox saint canonized in the United States was the Reverend John Sergiev, known as Father John of Cronstadt, who was canonized on November 1, 1964, in a ceremony in the Cathedral of Our Lady of the Sign, New York City. The canonization ceremony was presided over by Metropolitan Philaret, primate of the Russian Orthodox Church Outside of Russia. Father John died in 1909 at the age of 80.

6323. Zen Buddhist monastery was Tassajara, also called Zenshinji or Zen Mountain Center, officially opened in July 1967 at Tassajara Springs, CA. The first abbot was Shunryu Suzuki and the first director was Richard Baker.

6324. Armenian Orthodox cathedral was the Armenian Cathedral of St. Vartan, New York City, consecrated on April 28, 1968, by His Holiness Vasken I, Supreme Patriarch and Catholicos of All Armenians. The Most Reverend Torkom Manoogian was the first upon whom the Catholicos personally bestowed the rank of archbishop in the United States.

6325. Religious ritual on the moon was conducted by Buzz Aldrin, after he and Neil Armstrong landed on the lunar surface on July 20, 1969, during the Apollo 11 mission. Aldrin, a Presbyterian, had carried with him a home Communion kit, consisting of a tiny portion of wine and a miniature Host wafer. After asking on the radio for a moment of silence, he silently offered a prayer and consumed the wafer and the wine.

6326. Catholic saint who was born in America was Elizabeth Ann Bayley Seton, who was born into an Episcopalian family in New York City on August 28, 1774. The mother of five children, she founded the Society for the Relief of Poor Widows with Small Children in 1797. She converted to Roman Catholicism in New York City in 1805 and founded an order of nuns, the Sisters of Charity of St. Joseph. She died on January 4, 1821, in Emmitsburg, MD, was beatified on March 17, 1963, at the Vatican, Rome, by Pope John XXIII, and was canonized on September 14, 1975.

6327. Episcopal priest who was a woman was Jacqueline Means, who received her ordination on January 1, 1977, three years after an irregular ordination of 11 women in Philadelphia, PA, that was not recognized by the church's House of Bishops. The first female Episcopal bishop was Barbara C. Harris, who was elected suffragan bishop of the Diocese of Massachusetts on September 24, 1988.

6328. Catholic saint who was a male American citizen was John Nepomucene Neumann, born in Bohemia on March 28, 1811, who arrived in New York City in January 1836 and was ordained in St. Patrick's Cathedral, Mott Street, New York City. In 1848 he became an American citizen. From 1852 until his death in 1860 he served as the fourth bishop of Philadelphia. He was responsible for organizing the first diocesan school system in America and for building schools, churches, and asylums. He was declared venerable in 1896. In 1963 he became the first male American citizen to be beatified, and on June 19, 1977, he was canonized in Rome by Pope Paul VI.

6329. Mormon man ordained to the priesthood who was African-American was Joseph Freeman, Jr., who was ordained on June 11, 1978, in Salt Lake City, UT. He was a lay minister, a regular member of his congregation, not a pastor. The Mormon Church had observed a long-standing tradition of barring African-Americans from entering the priesthood, although ordinations of African-Americans had taken place in the Church's earliest years. On June 9, 1978, the Church's First Presidency announced that, through prayer and revelation, the priesthood had been opened to men of all races.

6330. Methodist bishop who was a woman was the Reverend Marjorie Swank Matthews of Traverse City, MI, elected bishop of the United Methodist Church on July 17, 1980, at Dayton, OH. She was consecrated on July 18, 1980, at Selinsgrove, PA. The first Methodist bishop who was an African-American woman was Leontine T. C. Kelly, elected by the United Methodist Church in 1984. She served a San Francisco–area diocese of nearly 400 churches and 100,000 members.

6331. American to be recognized by Tibetan Buddhists as a reincarnated lama was Catharine Burroughs of Poolesville, MD, who was formally recognized in September 1988 as the reincarnation of Ahkon Lhamo, a Tibetan Buddhist saint of the 17th century. Her divinity was announced in 1987 by His Holiness the Third Drubwang Padma Norbu Rinpoche, the supreme head of the Palyul lineage of Nyingmapa Tibetan Buddhism. She was the first Western woman to be so honored in the religion's 1,200-year history.

6332. Coptic Orthodox Church bishop was Bishop Serapion, appointed by the Patriarch of the Coptic Orthodox Church in Egypt to become the first Coptic Orthodox bishop in North America. On December 30, 1995, he was welcomed by the congregation of the Coptic Orthodox Church in Los Angeles, CA.

6333. Summit conference of world religions was the Millennium World Peace Summit of Religious and Spiritual Leaders, which took place from August 28 to 31, 2000, at the General Assembly Hall of the United Nations complex in New York, NY. There were some 2,000 delegates from more than 100 countries in attendance. The participants issued a Declaration of World Peace that called on religious leaders to take active measures to bring about reconciliation and cooperation in troubled areas and to preserve human rights. The Secretary-General of the summit was Bawa Jain of India.

6334. Church with a weekly attendance exceeding 30,000 in the United States was Lakewood Church in Houston, TX. The congregation was originally housed in a neighborhood feed store. Its membership exceeded 25,000 in 2004 and 32,000 in 2005. Joel Osteen was the pastor.

6335. Year in which Protestants were no longer a majority of the United States population was 2005, according to expert estimates. Studies by the National Opinion Research Center at the University of Chicago showed that the percentage of Americans identifying themselves as members of Protestant churches decreased over the period between 1993 and 2002 from 63 percent to 52 percent and would probably fall below 50 percent by mid-decade.

6336. Muslim prayer service led by a woman acting as Imam with a congregation of both sexes took place in New York, NY, on March 18, 2005. Jumah, the obligatory Friday public prayer service, was led by an African-American woman, Dr. Amina Wadud, a professor of Islamic studies. The service was organized by the Progressive Muslim Union.

Publications

6337. Sermon to be printed was "The Sin and Danger of Self-Love, a Discourse," based on the text from I Cor.10:24, "Let no man seek his own; But every man another's wealth." It was delivered on December 9, 1621, by Robert Cushman in Plymouth, MA, in "an assembly of His Majesty's faithful subjects, there inhabiting," and was printed in London in 1622. It was reprinted by S. Kneeland, Boston, MA, in 1724.

6338. Hymnbook published in America was Stephen Day's *The Whole Booke of Psalmes, Faithfully Translated into English Metre whereunto is prefixed a Discourse declaring not only the lawfullness, but also the necessity of the heavenly ordinances of singing scripture psalmes in the Churches of God*, better known as the *Bay Psalm Book*. It was published in July 1640 in Cambridge, MA, and was the first book of any kind published in America.

6339. Bible printed in America was a translation into Algonkian, a Native American language, made by John Eliot, the "Apostle to the North American Indians." Finished in 1661, it was entitled *The New Testament of Our Lord and Saviour Jesus Christ* and bore a dedication in English to England's King Charles II. It contained 130 printed leaves without pagination and two title pages, one in English and the other in the Algonkian language. The text was in double columns with marginal references. In 1663 *The Holy Bible, Containing the Old Testament and the New, Translated into the Indian Language* was printed in quarto size and contained 540 leaves. Both Bibles were "ordered to be printed by the Commissioners of the United Colonies in New England, at the charge and with the consent of the corporation in England for the propagation of the gospel amongst the Native Americans in New England," and were printed in Cambridge, MA, by Samuel Green and Marmaduke Johnson.

6340. Bible concordance was a reprint of an edition published in London in 1643. It was published in Cambridge, MA, in 1683. In 1720 it was published as the *Cambridge Concordance* by Samuel Newman of Cambridge, MA.

6341. Theological treatise of importance was *Vier kleine doch ungemeine und sehr nützliche Tractätlein*, by Francis Daniel Pastorius, published in 1690 in Germantown, PA. It contained an outline of the saints, an account of the bishops and saints, and a review of the church councils and the bishops and patriarchs of Constantinople.

6342. ***Book of Common Prayer*** **in the Mohawk language** was *The morning and evening prayer, the litany, church catechism, family prayers, and several chapters of the Old and New Testament, translated into the Mahaque Indian language by Lawrence Claesse, interpreter to William Andrews, Missionary to the Indians from the Honourable and Reverend the Society for the Propagation of the Gospel in Foreign Parts*. The book contained 115 pages and was published in 1715 by William Bradford in New York City.

6343. Catalog of theological and biblical literature appeared in Cotton Mather's *Manuductio Ad Ministerium; directions for a candidate of the ministry, wherein first, a right foundation is laid for his future improvement, and, then, rules are offered for such a management of his academical and preparatory studies, and thereupon, for such a conduct after his appearance in the world, as may render him a skilful and useful minister of the gospel*. The work was printed in 1726 for Thomas Hancock and sold at his shop in Ann Street, Boston, MA. It contained 151 pages and a catalog for a young student's library.

6344. Bible printed in German was printed by Christoph Sower in Germantown, PA, in 1743, from the text of the 32nd Halle edition, with type obtained from Frankfurt, Germany. Its abbreviated title was *Biblia Das ist; Die Heilige Schrift altes und Neues Testaments, Nach der Deutschen Uebersetzung D. Martin Luthers*.

6345. Religious magazine was *The Christian History*, published weekly in Boston, MA, from March 5, 1743, to February 23, 1745, "containing accounts of the revival and propagation of religion in Great Britain and America." The editor was Thomas Prince, Jr. It was eight pages long and was printed by Samuel Kneeland and Bartholomew Green.

6346. Jewish prayer book published in America was *Prayers for Shabbath, Rosh-Hashanah and Yom Kippur, or the Sabbath, the beginning of the year and the Day of Atonements; with the Amidah and Musaph of the Moadim, or Solemn Seasons according to the order of the Spanish and Portuguese Jews*, translated by Isaac Pinto and printed for him in 1766 (the year 5526 according to the Hebrew calendar) by John Holt, New York City. The book contained 196 pages.

6347. Bible printed in English was printed by Robert Aitken of Philadelphia, PA, in 1782. It was entitled *The Holy Bible, containing the Old and New Testaments—newly translated out of the original tongues; and with the former translations diligently compared and revised*. The frontispiece noted that it was "printed and sold by R. Aitken, at Pope's Head, Three doors above the Coffee House, in Market Street, Philadelphia, PA, 1782." It was a duodecimo of 353 pages without pagination. The venture, though authorized by Congress on September 21, 1782, was financially unsuccessful. The New Testament alone was printed in 1781 by Aitken.

6348. Episcopal catechism published after the separation of the American synod from the British church was *The ABC with the Church* *of England Catechism. To which are annexed, prayers used in the academy of the Protestant Episcopal Church in Philadelphia. Also a Hymn on the Nativity of our Saviour; and another for Easterday.* It was 12 pages long and was printed in 1785 by Young, Stewart and M'Cullough in Philadelphia, PA. On page six, instead of the words "king" and "him," dotted lines were printed so that the title of the head of government could be written in.

6349. Unitarian prayer book was *A Liturgy, Collected Principally From the Book of Common Prayer, for the use of the first Episcopal Church in Boston; together with the Psalter or Psalms of David*, compiled by the Reverend James Freeman and printed in 1785 by Peter Edes of Boston, MA, for King's Chapel, Boston.

6350. Catholic magazine was the weekly journal *Courier de Boston*, which appeared on April 23, 1789, and continued publication weekly for six months. It was published in French in Boston, MA, and was edited by Paul Joseph Guérard de Nancrède, instructor in French at Harvard University.

6351. Publisher of denominational religious books was the Methodist Book Concern, organized at a conference in the John Street Methodist Episcopal Church, New York City, in May 1789. The Reverend John Dickins advanced the capital, $600, from his private savings and started publishing in Philadelphia, PA. The first book issued was *The Christian's Pattern*, John Wesley's version of Thomas à Kempis's *Imitation of Christ*.

6352. Catholic Bible in English was a 990-page quarto printed by Carey, Stewart and Company, Philadelphia, PA, in 1790. It was printed from new type cast in the foundry of John Baine, Philadelphia, and was intended to be issued in 48-page sections every Saturday. The first section was issued on December 12, 1789. The title was *The Holy Bible, translated from the Latin Vulgate: diligently compared with the Hebrew, Greek and other editions, in divers languages; and first published by the English College at Douai, anno 1609. Newly revised and corrected, according to the Clementine edition of the Scriptures, with annotations for elucidating the principal difficulties of Holy Writ.* It was based on the New Testament published in 1582 in Reims, France, and the Old Testament published in Douai, Flanders, in 1609.

6353. Lutheran hymnbook in English was Johann Christoff Kunze's *A Hymn and Prayer Book for the Use of Such Lutheran Churches as Use the English Language*, printed and sold by Hurlin and Commardinger, 450 Pearl Street, New York City, in 1795. Its 300 pages contained 240 hymns, 70 of which were of English origin. Kunze was the senior of the Lutheran clergy in New York State. A Lutheran hymnbook in German, *Erbauliche Lieder-Sammlung zum Gottesdienstlichten Gebrauch in den Vereinigten Evangelisch-Lutherischen Gemeinken in Nord-America*, was published in 1786 in Germantown, PA. It contained 707 hymns compiled by the Reverend Henry Melchior Muhlenberg. It was copyrighted on October 2, 1786, by Peter Leibert and Michael Billmeyer.

6354. Hymnbook with music was the ninth edition of *The Psalms, Hymns & Spiritual Songs of the Old and New Testament; Faithfully Translated into English Meetre. For the Use, Edification and Comfort of the Saints in publick and private especially in New England*, 420 pages, printed in 1798 by Bartholomew Green and J. Allen, Boston, MA, for Michael Perry. The book contained 13 tunes.

6355. Greek Testament was *The New Testament in Greek*, 478 pages, printed in 1800 by Isaiah Thomas, Worcester, MA.

6356. Hymnbook compiled by an African-American editor was *A Collection of Spiritual Songs and Hymns, Selected from Various Authors*, published in Philadelphia, PA, in 1801. The compiler was Richard Allen, the first African-American minister in the Methodist Church and the founder of the African Methodist Episcopal Church.

6357. Bible translated into English in America was *The Holy Bible, containing the old and new covenant, commonly called the Old and New Testament; translated from the Greek*, issued in four volumes with unnumbered pages. It was printed in Philadelphia, PA, by Jane Aitken in 1808. It was copyrighted on September 12, 1808, in the District of Pennsylvania by the translator, Charles Thomson, who had been secretary to the Continental Congress.

6358. Catholic magazine in English was the *Michigan Essay or Impartial Observer*, a weekly, which was issued on August 31, 1809. It was printed and published in Detroit, MI, by James M. Miller and was only semi-Catholic in scope. The idea was advocated by the Reverend Gabriel Richard of Detroit. The weekly consisted of four pages, of which a small part was printed in French. The rates were $5 a year for subscribers living in the city, $4.50 in upper Canada, and $4 elsewhere.

6359. Bible in Hebrew published in America was *Biblia Hebraica*, printed in 1814 by Thomas Dobson, Philadelphia, PA, from type imported from Amsterdam, Holland.

6360. Bible for the blind in embossed form using the old line letter system was issued in 1835 by the American Bible Society, New York City. This society was also the first to supply the blind with the Bible in New York Point, and in the more recent Braille.

6361. Hebrew book other than the Bible published in America was *Abne Yehoshua* ("Stones of Joshua"), by Joshua Ben Mordecai ha-Cohen Falk, published in 1860 in New York City. It contained 108 pages.

6362. Bible translation by a woman was made by Julia Evelina Smith of Glastonbury, CT, and published in Hartford, CT, in 1876 by the American Publishing Company. The full title was *The Holy Bible, containing the Old and New Testaments: translated literally from the original tongues*. The book contained 1,168 pages.

SCIENCE AND TECHNOLOGY

Astronomy

6363. Planetarium to show mechanically the movement of celestial bodies within the solar system was imported from England in 1732 and was presented by Thomas Hollis to Harvard College, Cambridge, MA. It was built by Joseph Page and was "a very costly orrery, an instrument that this, or any other part of America, as far as we can learn, has never before been favored with."

6364. Astronomer of note was John Winthrop, Jr., of Cambridge, MA, a professor at Harvard College, who made sunspot observations on April 19, 20, and 22, 1739. No observations were made on April 21, as it was cloudy. The observations consist of one-page reports in the University Archives, Harvard University Library, and have never been published. Winthrop observed the transits of Mercury in 1740, 1743, and 1769 and of Venus in 1761 and 1769. In 1746 he established the first laboratory of experimental physics in America.

6365. Planetarium built in America was constructed in 1743 by Thomas Clap, president of Yale College, New Haven, CT. In the center was a globe three inches in diameter, from which extended 12 wooden arms about seven feet long. The sun, planets, satellites, and other celestial bodies were represented. The orrery had no gear work and was operated by hand.

6366. Scientific expedition sponsored by a colony was outfitted by the Commonwealth of Massachusetts in 1761. John Winthrop, Jr., the Harvard College astronomer and physicist, went to Newfoundland in a vessel in the Provincial Service to make astronomical observations. His expenses were defrayed by the colonial government.

6367. Astronomer to acquire international fame was David Rittenhouse, born near Philadelphia, PA, in 1732. Trained as a clockmaker, Rittenhouse crafted precise scientific instruments, including compass verniers, surveying devices, and orreries. He observed the transit of Venus in 1769, charted the position of Uranus after its discovery in 1781, and invented the first light diffraction grating. Rittenhouse also served as a member of Pennsylvania's constitutional convention, the treasurer of Pennsylvania, the first director of the United States Mint, and the president of the American Philosophical Society.

6368. Observatory was built by self-taught astronomer and mathematician David Rittenhouse at his family farm in Norriton, PA, in order to observe the transit of Venus across the sun on June 3, 1769. His measurements were taken with quadrants and telescopes of his own invention. He was professor of astronomy at the University of Pennsylvania from 1777 to 1789, and in 1793 he discovered a comet.

6369. Astronomical expedition to record an eclipse of the sun consisted of Professors Samuel Williams, Stephen Sewall, James Winthrop, Fortesque Vernon, and six students, who were sent on October 9, 1780, from Harvard College, Cambridge, MA, to Penobscot Bay (then in Massachusetts, now in Maine). The Commonwealth of Massachusetts supplied a boat. Although the country was at war with Britain, the British officer in command at Penobscot Bay permitted the expedition to land and observe the eclipse of October 27, 1780, which lasted from 11:11 A.M. to 1:50 P.M.

6370. Reflecting telescope was manufactured by Amasa Holcomb of Southwick, MA, about 1826. The first one, made to order for John A. Fulton of Chillicothe, OH, was 14 feet long, with a 10-inch aperture and six eyepieces that magnified from 90 to 960 times. Telescopes were later made in four standard sizes. The reflecting telescope was invented by Isaac Newton.

6371. Observatory operated by a college was built in 1830 by Joseph Caldwell, president of the University of North Carolina, Chapel Hill, NC. It contained a meridian transit telescope, a zenith telescope, a refracting telescope, an astronomical clock, a sextant, a reflecting circle, and a Hadley's quadrant. The observatory was completed in 1831, having been built with Caldwell's own funds at a cost of $430. Caldwell was eventually reimbursed by the trustees of the college.

6372. Observatory established by the federal government was established by the Navy on December 6, 1830, in Washington, DC. The first instrument installed was a 30-inch portable transit telescope, which was made by Richard Patten of New York. Lieutenant Louis Malesherbes Goldsborough was appointed the first officer in charge of the observatory and served until 1833.

6373. Observatory on a mountaintop was the Lick Observatory on Mount Hamilton in California. Founded by wealthy financier and philanthropist James Lick in 1876 and completed in 1888, it was the world's first mountaintop modern astronomical observatory and housed what was then the world's largest telescope, a 36-inch refractor. Lick, who died in 1876, was buried in a tomb directly under the telescope.

6374. Astronomer to measure the size of a fixed star was Dr. Francis Gladheim Pease, who on December 13, 1920, at Mount Wilson Observatory, Mount Wilson, CA, measured Betelgeuse, the bright red star in the right shoulder of Orion, by means of an inferometer designed by Professor Albert Abraham Michelson. He found the star to be 260 million miles in diameter.

6375. Planetarium open to the publicwas the Adler Planetarium and Astronomical Museum, presented to the city of Chicago, IL, by Max Adler, a local businessman. The dome was 68 feet in diameter and seated 450 people. It was under the direction of Professor Philip Fox and was opened to the public on May 10, 1930. The projector was manufactured by Carl Zeiss of Jena, Germany. It was the first modern planetarium in the western hemisphere.

6376. Radio astronomer was radio engineer Grote Reber, born in 1911, who in 1937 built the world's first radio telescope in his backyard in Wheaton, IL. With the scope, a bowl-shaped antenna 31 feet in diameter, he discovered the first point radio sources in the sky. He worked virtually alone in the field until after World War II, when radiotelescopy became a valuable and widespread tool for astronomers.

6377. Telescope lens 200 inches in diameter was installed in a telescope at the Mount Palomar Observatory on Palomar Mountain, San Diego County, CA, in 1947. The lens was molded by the Corning Glass Works, Corning, NY. On December 2, 1934, molten glass at 2,700 degrees F was poured into a ceramic mold that had taken several months to construct. The temperature of 20-ton disc was lowered gradually over a period of 11 months. It was ground and polished at the California Institute of Technology over a period of 11 years and was completed on October 3, 1947. The telescope and observatory were dedicated on June 3, 1948, at which time the instrument was named the Hale telescope in memory of Dr. George Ellery Hale, who had conceived and promoted it. The telescope was first used on February 1, 1949, to observe the constellation of Coma Berenices, near the north pole of the Milky Way, and objects 6 sextillion (6 billion trillion) miles away.

6378. Scientific program to search for extraterrestrial life was SETI (Search for Extraterrestrial Intelligence), conducted over a three-month period in 1960 at the National Radio Astronomy Observatory in Green Bank, WV. Astronomer Frank Drake was the lead researcher. Two nearby stars, Tau Ceti and Epsilon Eridani, were scanned on radio bands for signals indicating intelligent life, but none were discovered.

6379. Archeoastronomer was Gerald Stanley Hopkins, a professor of physics and astronomy at Boston University, Boston, MA. In 1961 Hopkins compared the placement of the megaliths at Stonehenge to a computerized chart of the sky over England in 1500 BCE and concluded that Stonehenge was built as an observatory. He later applied similar techniques to analyze sites in Peru and Egypt.

6380. Vacuum telescope was the Vacuum Tower Telescope, designed by astronomer Richard B. Dunn and installed at the Sacramento Peak Observatory in Sunspot, NM, in October 1969. The evacuation of air from the telescope tube eliminated a longstanding problem in astronomy—the distortion of celestial images by atmospheric turbulence and by heat-induced turbulence within the telescope itself.

6381. Orbiting observatory of importance was the Hubble Space Telescope, named after American astronomer Edwin Powell Hubble. The $1.5 billion orbiting optical observatory was launched from Space Shuttle *Discovery* on April 25, 1990, in an orbit 381 miles above the earth. Fourteen feet wide and 43 feet long, the Hubble contained a 94.5-inch primary mirror and five main instrument packages, plus additional cameras sensitive to various parts of the electromagnetic spectrum. Early technical problems, including a flaw in the primary mirror, were repaired in December 1993 by a team of astronauts on Space Shuttle *Endeavour*.

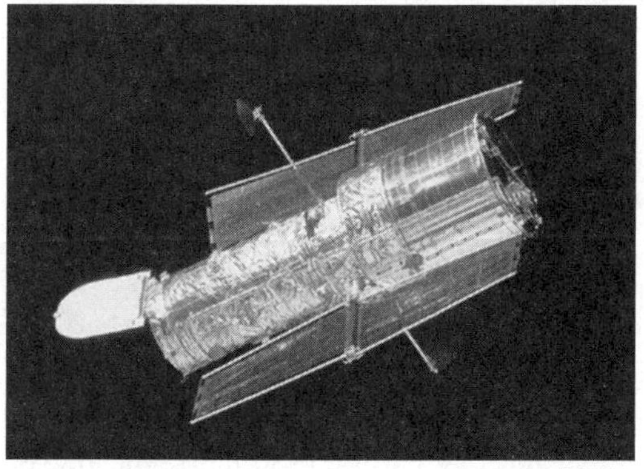

Courtesy of NASA

The Hubble Space Telescope.

6382. Telescope of importance with a compound objective mirror was the William M. Keck I telescope on Mauna Kea, HI. It had a 394-inch main objective mirror of 36 hexagonal segments that could be precisely positioned by computer. An interferometer combined the light from the 36 segments into a single focused image. The first astronomical image from the Keck was produced on November 24, 1990, when nine of the segments were in place.

Discoveries

6383. Comet recorded was seen in November 1618. Edward Johnson, in his *Johnson's Wonder-working Providence*, described it as "that perspicuous bright blazing comet; anon after Sun set it appeared as they say in the South-west, about three houres, continuing in her horizon for the space of thirty sleepes."

6384. Meteor shower on record was observed by Andrew Ellicott on November 12, 1799, off the Florida Keys. In his journal, Ellicott wrote that the "whole heaven appeared as if illuminated with sky rockets, flying in an infinity of directions, and I was in constant expectation of some of them falling on the vessel. They continued until put out by the light of the sun after day break."

6385. Meteorite whose landing was recorded fell at 6:30 A.M. on December 14, 1807, at Weston (now Easton), CT, making a hole 5 feet long and 4.5 feet wide.

6386. Asteroid named for an American president was Hooveria. It was discovered in March 1920 by Professor Johann Palisan of the University of Vienna, Austria, and named for Herbert Hoover, who at that time was engaged in feeding the distressed European peoples.

6387. Cosmic ray to be discovered was detected in 1925 by Robert Andrews Millikan at the California Institute of Technology, Pasadena, CA. The formal announcement of the discovery was made on November 11, 1925, before the National Academy of Sciences assembled in convention at Madison, WI.

6388. Planet found beyond Neptune was Pluto, discovered at the Lowell Observatory, Flagstaff, AZ, on February 18, 1930, by Clyde William Tombaugh, on photographic plates made as part of a long-term systematic search begun under the direction of the late Dr. Percival Lowell. Lowell had mathematically predicted the location of the planet many years before, almost exactly in the position where it was ultimately found. Even after the planet had been observed many times, the announcement of its discovery was withheld until March 13, 1930, the anniversary of Lowell's birth (and of William Herschel's discovery of Uranus).

> On August 24, 2006, the International Astronomical Union decided to rescind Pluto's status as a planet and reclassify it as another entity called a "dwarf planet."

6389. Radio waves from space to be observed were discovered in 1931 by Karl Guthe Jansky, a physicist at the Bell Telephone Laboratories in Holmdel, NJ. Asked to identify and classify sources of radio interference, Jansky found one source of static that moved across the sky each day. He eventually found that this source emanated from the center of the galaxy in the constellation of Sagittarius. Jansky moved on to other work when Bell Telephone rejected his proposal for a 100-foot-wide dish-shaped radiotelescope.

6390. Meteorite known to have struck a person crashed through the roof of a house at Sylacauga, AL, on November 30, 1954, bounced off a radio, and struck Mrs. Elizabeth Hodges on the hip. She was not permanently injured. The space rock was a sulfide meteorite weighing 8.5 pounds and measuring seven inches long. It was put on display in the University of Alabama Museum of Natural History, Moundville, AL.

6391. Calculation of the surface temperature of Venus that proved to be accurate was made in 1958 by Cornell H. Mayer at the Naval Research Laboratory in Washington, DC, using a 50-foot radio telescope. His measurements of the thermal radiation on the surface of Venus showed that the temperature was more than 600 degrees Fahrenheit, too hot for habitation. Space probes later confirmed his findings.

6392. Quasar to be observed was discovered by Allan Rex Sandage, an astronomer with the Mount Wilson and Palomar Observatories, Palomar, CA. In 1961, Sandage and radio astronomer Thomas A. Matthews recorded signals from an extremely distant starlike object that was a strong emitter of radio waves, and located it with a large optical telescope. To describe the new object, Sandage coined the term "quasar," short for "quasi-stellar radio source."

6393. Brown dwarf star to be discovered was detected in the constellation of the Pleiades by Gibor Basri and James R. Graham of the University of California, Berkeley, CA, and Geoffrey W. Marcy of San Francisco State University. At a meeting of the American Astronomical Society held in Pittsburgh, PA, on June 13, 1995, the team presented evidence for the existence of a brown dwarf, a substellar object midway between a large planet and a small star. The object was the first major discovery by the Keck Observatory on Mauna Kea in Hawaii.

6394. Solar system with multiple planets to be discovered (other than our own) was a system of three planets in orbit around the star Upsilon Andromedae, about 44 light-years distant in the constellation Andromeda. Its discovery was announced in April 1999. The innermost planet, discovered in 1996, has about three-quarters of the mass of Jupiter and is so close to the star that it completes an orbit in the equivalent of 4.6 earth days. The middle planet has at least twice the mass of Jupiter and completes an orbit every 242 earth days. The outermost planet has at least four times the mass of Jupiter and completes an orbit about once every four earth years. The planets, too small to be seen with any telescope of the time, were detected by studying the effects of their gravitational pulls on Upsilon Andromedae. The planets' existence was discovered independently by two teams of astronomers, one at San Francisco State University, San Francisco, CA, and the other at Harvard-Smithsonian Center for Astrophysics, Cambridge, MA, and at the National Center for Atmospheric Research, Boulder, CO.

6395. Discovery of a meteorite on another planet was announced on January 19, 2005, by the Jet Propulsion Laboratory, Pasadena, CA. It was found by *Opportunity*, one of NASA's two Mars Exploration Rovers. A rock about the size of a basketball, located in the area of Mars called Meridiani Planum, it was made chiefly of iron and nickel. The identification was made by spectrometers aboard the rover. The principal science investigator for the rover was Steve Squyres, Cornell University, Ithaca, NY.

6396. Capture of comet particles was made by *Stardust*, a NASA spacecraft, during its third orbit around the sun. Passing close to a comet known as Wild 2, it collected more than a million microscopic particles in an absorbent substance called aerogel, which was then sent back to Earth in a robotic capsule. The capsule made a parachute landing in Utah on January 15, 2006, and the first images of the particles were released by NASA on January 20.

6397. Detection of water ice on the surface of a comet was announced on February 2, 2006, by Scientists for *Deep Impact* at the University of Maryland. *Deep Impact*, a NASA spacecraft, was deliberately crashed into the side of the comet Tempel 1 in July 2005. Analysis of data collected during the crash provided evidence that water ice was present in small quantities in three places on the comet's surface. The team's principal investigator was Michael A'Hearn.

Imaging

6398. Astronomy photograph was a daguerreotype of the moon taken on December 18, 1839, by John William Draper, professor of chemistry at New York University, New York City. He exposed the plate for 20 minutes. The image was one inch in diameter. He presented the photographs on March 23, 1840, to the Lyceum of Natural History of New York City.

6399. Photograph of a star other than the sun was a picture of Vega, Alpha Lyrae, made at the Harvard College Observatory, Cambridge, MA, on July 17, 1850, by Whipple, a professional photographer, under the direction of William Cranch Bond, the first director of the observatory. A 15-inch telescope was used as a camera lens and the daguerreotype plate was set up at the eye end.

6400. Photograph of a solar eclipse was made on March 25, 1857, by Frederick Langenheim of Philadelphia, PA, who took eight pictures in sequence. The first photograph of a total solar eclipse was taken on August 7, 1869, by Professor Edward Charles Pickering at Mount Pleasant, IA. Using a portrait lens, he made the first successful photographs of the corona. The eclipse crossed America diagonally from Alaska to North Carolina.

6401. Photograph of a lightning flash was taken by W. C. Gurley of the Marietta observatory in Marietta, OH, on the evening of May 4, 1884. The lightning was about three miles away.

6402. Photograph of a meteor taken in the United States was made on August 10, 1889, by the Harvard College Observatory, Harvard University, Cambridge, MA. The meteor appeared as a straight dense line. The exposure, 13 hours 50 minutes long, was taken by a Gundlach camera strapped to an 11-inch telescope.

6403. Movie of a solar eclipse taken from an airship was photographed from the Navy dirigible *Los Angeles* on January 24, 1925, when it was about 4,500 feet in the air about 18.75 miles east of Montauk Point, NY. The total eclipse of the sun, which lasted 2 minutes 4.6 seconds, was recorded by four astronomical cameras, two moving picture cameras, and one spectrograph.

6404. Movie showing another planet was made in October 1926 by William Hammond Wright at the Lick Observatory, Mount Hamilton, CA, with the aid of the Crossley telescope, and showed the planet Mars. Another was made in September 1927 of Jupiter. Exposures were made every three minutes, so that at the rate of 32 frames a minute, the movement of the planet took as many seconds on the screen as it did hours in the sky. The photographs were taken in several colors, ranging from ultraviolet to infrared, and illustrated alterations in the appearance of the planets.

6405. Movie of a solar eclipse taken from an airplane was made on April 28, 1930, by Lieutenant Leslie Edward Gehres and Chief Photographer J. M. F. Haase of the Navy, flying approximately 18,000 feet over Honey Lake, CA. The flight was sponsored by the U.S. Naval Observatory. The totality of the eclipse was 1.5 seconds. An attempt to take similar pictures had been made on September 10, 1923, at Santa Catalina, CA, by Captain Albert Ware Marshall, Lieutenant Ben Harrison Wyatt, and Chief Photographer Haase, but the weather was cloudy and the pictures were of little value.

6406. Movie of the sun when not in eclipse was taken by Robert Raynolds McMath at the McMath-Hulbert Observatory of the University of Michigan at Lake Angelus, Pontiac, MI, on June 19, 1934, with the Spectroheliokinematograph. The pictures, which showed solar prominences or sunspots in motion as well as activity in connection with sunspot groups, were first shown publicly before the American Astronomical Society on September 10, 1934, at Connecticut College, New London, CT.

6407. Ultraviolet pictures of the sun were taken on March 13, 1959, from an Aerobee-Hi research rocket at an altitude of 123 miles over the White Sands Proving Ground, NM, under the direction of the Naval Research Laboratory. A camera with spectroscopic mirrors reflected out the visible light of the sun, leaving only the Lyman-Alpha radiation to fall on the special film.

6408. Astronomy photographs in color to be published in a magazine appeared in the May 1959 issue of *National Geographic*, Washington, DC, and showed the Great Nebula in Orion, the Crab Nebula, and the Veil Nebula in Cygnus. They were taken by William C. Miller, research photographer of the

Mount Wilson and Palomar Observatories in California, using Super Anscochrome film and the 200-inch Hale telescope on Palomar Mountain.

6409. Photograph from space showing the earth was transmitted on August 14, 1959, when the cameras in the paddlewheel satellite *Explorer 6* sent back pictures showing a 20,000-square-mile area of the earth. The satellite was launched on August 7 and had a total weight of 142 pounds.

6410. Color photograph of the earth taken from space was taken on December 1, 1959, from the nose cone of a Thor missile launched from Cape Canaveral, FL. The camera was found on February 16, 1960, in the data capsule on the beach of Mayaguana Island, Bahama Islands, approximately 1,700 miles from the takeoff point.

6411. Photographs of the moon in close-up were taken on July 31, 1964, by six RCA-TV cameras aboard the Ranger 7 rocket, which was launched on July 28, 1964, from Cape Canaveral, FL. The pictures were received by the National Aeronautics and Space Administration's receiving station in the Mojave Desert, CA. The cameras took 4,316 close-up still pictures over the course of 17 minutes before Ranger 7 crashed in the area northwest of the Sea of Clouds.

6412. Photograph of the earth taken from the moon was made by a camera aboard the space probe *Lunar Orbiter 1*, which was launched from Cape Canaveral, FL, on August 10, 1966. Between August 18 and August 29, the probe generated 207 photographs. The first image of Earth, showing the home planet from a distance of 380,000 km, was returned on August 23.

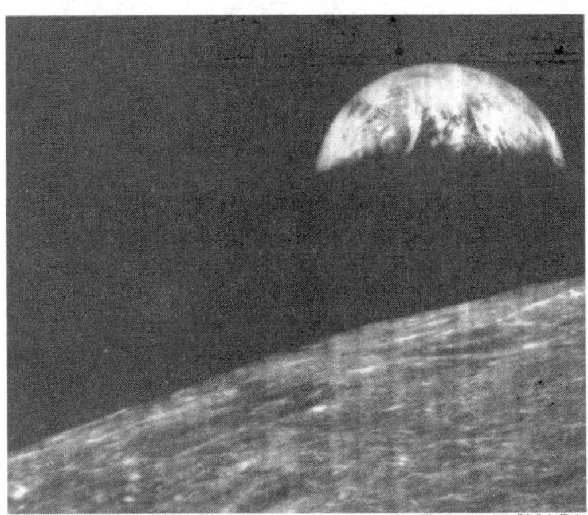

Courtesy of NASA

Earth-rise, as seen from the Moon.

6413. Live telecast from space was made on October 14, 1968, during the flight of *Apollo 7*, which had been launched on October 11 from the Kennedy Space Center at Cape Canaveral, FL. The astronauts, Captain Walter Marty Schirra, Jr., Major Donn Fulton Eisele, and Major Ronnie Walter Cunningham, showed views of the inside of the capsule and views through the windows.

6414. Photograph of a comet taken from space was made of the comet Kohoutek on December 29, 1973, by Dr. Edward George Gibson and Lieutenant Colonel Gerald Paul Carr from the space station *Skylab 3*.

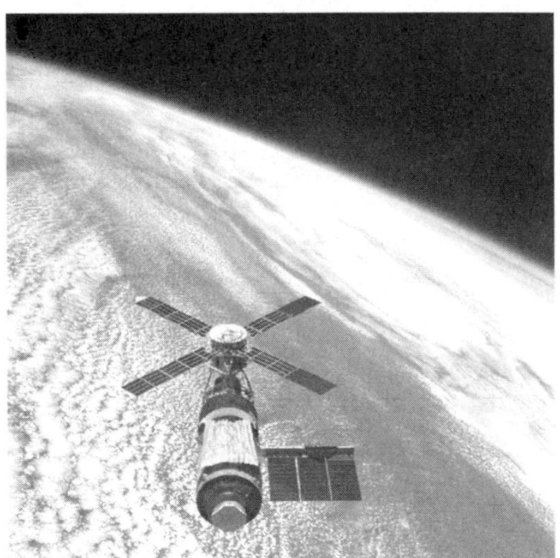

Courtesy of NASA

Skylab *and Earth.*

6415. Photograph taken on Mars was a 340-degree panorama taken by the two cameras aboard the 1,300-pound, 10-foot *Viking 1* lander, which was launched on August 20, 1975, and landed on Chryse Planitia (the Plain of Gold) on Mars on July 20, 1976. The pictures, taken on July 20, were transmitted to the *Viking* mother ship in orbit around Mars, which sent them to the Jet Propulsion Laboratory in Pasadena, CA, via a radio telescope in Spain.

6416. Photograph taken close up of an asteroid in space was taken on October 29, 1991, by the American space probe *Galileo*, and showed the asteroid Gaspara. The *Galileo* was launched from Space Shuttle *Atlantis* on October 18, 1989, on a multi-year mission to Jupiter.

6417. Images of the surface of Mars to be televised live were transmitted by the *Pathfinder* spacecraft on July 4, 1997. The craft landed in the flood plain known as Ares Vallis and immediately began transmitting photographs back to NASA over a distance of 119 million miles. NASA then broadcast them over the Cable News Network (CNN), based in Pasadena, CA.

Courtesy of NASA

A 360-degree panorama of the Mars Pathfinder *landing site.*

6418. Image of a planet outside Earth's solar system was released on May 28, 1998, by a team under Susan Terebey of the Extrasolar Research Corporation in Pasadena, CA, using the Hubble Space Telescope's Near Infrared Camera and Multi-Object Spectrometer. Dubbed TMR-1C, the planet is located about 450 light-years distant in the constellation Taurus, near an evolving pair of binary stars. It is estimated to be a young gas-giant planet up to three times the mass of Jupiter.

6419. Image of Mars at night was made by the Thermal Emission Imaging System aboard the NASA spacecraft *Odyssey*. The camera used infrared light, allowing scientists to see below the dusty top layer of the planet. The image was released on March 1, 2002. Odyssey, launched on April 7, 2001, was on a three-year mapping exploration of Mars.

6420. Image of Earth as seen from Mars was photographed by a camera on the Mars Global Surveyor spacecraft on May 8, 2003. The photograph showed Earth from a distance of 86 million miles, with North, Central, and South America visible under cloud cover. A half moon and the planet Jupiter were also captured on the same image. The spacecraft was launched by NASA and the camera was run by Malin Space Science Systems, San Diego, CA.

6421. Photograph of a planet in another solar system was taken late in 2004 at the European Southern Observatory in Chile by a combined European and American team. The planet orbits 2N1207, a brown dwarf star 200 light years from Earth near the constellation Hydra. It is estimated to be five times the size of Jupiter and to be sufficiently distant from its star to make life impossible. Confirmation of the finding was announced on April 30, 2005.

Computers

6422. Computing device with electronic components was constructed in 1930 by Vannevar Bush, a professor at the Massachusetts Institute of Technology, Cambridge, MA. His "differential analyzer" used vacuum tubes in which numerical values could be stored as voltages. Bush, who later served as science advisor to President Franklin Delano Roosevelt, also designed the "memex device," an electromechanical information appliance. The memex, which was never built, presaged many of the features of the personal computer and the Internet.

6423. Computer bug was an actual bug, a moth that got into the circuits of a Mark II computer at Harvard University, Cambridge, MA. On September 9, 1945, the moth was located by Grace Murray Hopper and her assistants and was removed with tweezers. The moth is preserved in the Naval Museum at Dahlgren, VA. The computer terms "bug" and "debug" do not derive from this incident, however. The use of "bug" to refer to a defect in an apparatus or its operation dates from the early 1800s.

6424. Electronic computer was the Electronic Numerical Integrator and Computer (ENIAC), designed and built under the direction of J. Presper Eckert, Jr., and John W. Mauchly of the Moore School of Electrical Engineering at the University of Pennsylvania, Philadelphia, PA. It was given its first public demonstration on February 14, 1946. The ENIAC was subsequently used by the Army Ordinance Department at Aberdeen,

MD. It was housed in a room 30 by 50 feet, contained approximately 18,000 vacuum tubes, and required 130 kilowatts per hour to operate.

6425. Electronic computer for commercial use was the UNIVAC I (Universal Automatic Computer), introduced by J. Presper Eckert, Jr., and John W. Mauchly in 1951, and manufactured by the Remington Rand Corporation, Philadelphia, PA. It was demonstrated and dedicated at the Bureau of the Census in Philadelphia on June 14, 1951. The key to its success was the use of inexpensive magnetic tape for data input and output. It could retain a maximum of 1,000 separate numbers, accept information contained on magnetic tape at the rate of more than 10,000 characters per second, add, subtract, multiply, divide, sort, collate, and take square and cube roots as needed. More than 50 units were sold in all.

6426. Electronic computer with solid-state components was developed in 1958 by Remington Rand Univac, a division of the Sperry Rand Corporation, at the company's laboratories in Philadelphia, PA, and was built at Ilion, NY. Because solid-state elements such as transistors, Ferractor amplifiers, and magnetic cores were used in its construction, the computer occupied about one-sixth the space of its predecessor, the UNIVAC, though it had 100 times the capacity and 10 times the speed.

6427. Military computer network was SAGE (Semi-Automatic Ground Environment), a network for U.S. air defense. Developed in 1958 by researchers at the Massachusetts Institute of Technology, Cambridge, MA, SAGE provided computer communications over telephone lines for 27 regional command centers controlling more than 100 radar and surface-to-air missile sites.

6428. Interactive computer sold commercially was the PDP-1 (for Program, Data, Processor) minicomputer, introduced by the Digital Equipment Corporation (DEC) of Maynard, MA, in 1960. The price was $120,000. It was designed by electronics engineer Ben Gurley. The PDP-1 was described as "a compact, solid state general purpose computer with an internal instruction execution rate of 100,000 to 200,000 operations per second. PDP-1 is a single address, single construction, stored program machine with a word length of 18-bits operating in parallel on 1's complement binary numbers." As the first commercial computer to incorporate a keyboard and a cathode ray tube monitor, it allowed users to enter code quickly and see the results instantly. The first unit was delivered to Bolt, Beranek and Newman (BBN), a computer consulting firm in Cambridge, MA.

6429. Mobile computer center was established by Remington Rand Univac, a division of the Sperry Rand Corporation, New York City, which equipped a motor van with a UNIVAC Solid-State 90 computer. The first assignment was undertaken on March 27, 1961, for the Douglas Aircraft Corporation, Charlotte, NC.

6430. Computer graphics software was Sketchpad, invented by Ivan Sutherland for his doctoral thesis at the Massachusetts Institute of Technology, Cambridge, MA, in 1963. An artist using Sketchpad could draw geometric shapes directly on a computer screen with a lightpen and then interactively modify them to create a finished design.

6431. Supercomputer was the Control Data 6600, designed by a team under Seymour R. Cray at a division of the Control Data Corporation located in Chippewa Falls, MN. The CDC 6600, introduced in August 1963, was far faster than competing mainframe computers of the time. It was purchased by the military to simulate nuclear explosions and break Soviet codes. Scientists also used the 6600 and later Cray-designed supercomputers to model complex phenomena such as hurricanes and the formation of galaxies.

6432. Computer-aided design (CAD) software was DAC (Design Augmented by Computer), a system developed jointly in 1964 by the General Motors Corporation of Detroit, MI, and the International Business Machines Corporation of Armonk, NY. The DAC system was geared to automobile prototyping. It was first used to design the trunk lids for GM's 1965 line of Cadillacs.

6433. Large commercial computer network was the SABRE airline reservation system, developed in 1964 by the International Business Machines Corporation, Armonk, NY, for American Airlines. SABRE allowed airlines and travel agents to check schedules and book reservations for passengers on any participating airline.

6434. Educational computer programming language was BASIC (Beginner's All-purpose Symbolic Instruction Code), invented by John Kemeny and Thomas Kurtz of Dartmouth College, Dartmouth, NH, as a simple programming language for student instruction. It was introduced in 1965 and soon gained wide popularity with hobbyists.

6435. Minicomputer that was commercially successful was the PDP-8, introduced by the Digital Equipment Corporation of Maynard, MA, in 1965. The $18,000 minicomputer was smaller and less expensive than competing mainframe computers, but was almost as powerful. It was purchased primarily by institutions, smaller businesses, and researchers.

6436. Computer modem that was practical was demonstrated by John van Geen at the Stanford Research Institute, Stanford, CA, in 1966. A modem, short for "modulator/demodulator," is a device that converts digital computer information to a signal that can be transmitted to another computer over a telephone line. Van Geen's acoustical coupler modem design was able to receive data signals accurately over telephone lines despite random noise and static, a problem that earlier modem researchers had been unable to solve.

6437. Computer programming language for children was Logo, invented by Seymour Papert at the Massachusetts Institute of Technology, Cambridge, MA, in 1967. With Logo, children could write simple programs to make a mechanical turtle move around on the floor.

6438. Computer mouse was invented by Douglas Engelbart of the Palo Alto Research Center, Palo Alto, CA. A mouse is a hand-operated pointing device that enables the computer user to manipulate text or images on a computer screen. Prior to the mouse, the user interacted with the computer screen by typing commands on a keyboard. Engelbart first publicly demonstrated a three-button mouse in San Francisco in 1968.

6439. Use of the term "personal computer" appeared in *Science* magazine in the issue dated October 4, 1968. An advertisement for Hewlett-Packard's first programmable scientific desktop calculator, the $4,900 Model 911A, used the phrase "the new Hewlett-Packard 911A personal computer."

6440. Home computer commercially available was the H316 "Kitchen Computer," a minicomputer made by Honeywell in Minneapolis, MN, and released in 1969. Priced at $10,600, it was available through the Neiman Marcus catalog, which featured it on the cover. The "Kitchen Computer" was essentially a recipe-filing device that could plan meals for the cook to prepare. Ad copy for the device read, "If she can only cook as well as Honeywell can compute." Using the device required owners to pass a two-week programming course.

6441. Computer operating system for multiple users that was practical was Unix, developed by Ken Thompson, Dennis Ritchie, and Rudd Canaday of Bell Telephone Labs, Holmdel, NJ, between April and June of 1969. A full working implementation of Unix was demonstrated in the summer of 1970 on a Digital Equipment PDP-11/20. The first written documentation for Unix was the *Unix Programmer's Manual*, dated November 3, 1971. Because it allowed any number of users to access a computer at one time, and because it was relatively easy to program, Unix became the preferred operating system for large academic and engineering computer installations.

6442. General-purpose computer network was ARPANET, a data communications network developed by J. C. R. Licklider, Robert Taylor, and other researchers for the Department of Defense's Advanced Research Projects Agency. The first ARPANET link was put into service on November 21, 1969. It connected a computer in the computer science department at the University of California at Los Angeles with a laboratory computer at the Stanford Research Institute, Stanford, CA. Over the next decade, ARPANET grew to include many government and university computers. In 1973, Dr. Vinton Cerf and Robert E. Kahn were commissioned by the federal government to create a national computer network for military, governmental, and institutional use. The network was based on ARPANET sites and employed packet-switching, flow-control, and fault-tolerance techniques developed by ARPANET. This was the origin of the Internet.

6443. E-mail was sent in 1971 by computer engineer Ray Tomlinson, an engineer at the technology firm of Bolt Beranek and Newman, Cambridge, MA, across the ARPANET, the

U.S. Army-built precursor to the Internet. The message was sent by Tomlinson to himself as a test of the ARPANET's messaging capabilities and contained no memorable content.

6444. Floppy disk was developed in 1971 by researcher Alan Shugart for the International Business Machines Corporation of Armonk, NY. The eight-inch disk was made of polyester sheet coated with fine magnetic particles and encased in a cardboard sleeve. It was the first form of digital information storage that was cheap, portable, and high-density.

6445. Use of @ in an e-mail address occurred in 1971, when Ray Tomlinson, a computer engineer at Bolt Beranek and Newman, Cambridge, MA, succeeded in sending a message from one computer to another over a network. He needed a marker to designate the name of the network host and chose the @ sign, largely because it is a keyboard sign that is not used in people's names.

6446. Laser printer was the so-called EARS printer designed by Gary K. Starkweather, a researcher at the Xerox Corporation's Palo Alto Research Center in Palo Alto, CA. Starkweather built on the xerographic plain-paper copier technology first developed by Xerox founder Chester Carlson. Starkweather's team produced a working version in November 1971. However, the first laser printer brought to market was the IBM model 3800, a room-sized unit introduced in 1975. Xerox's own commercial laser printer, the 9700 Electronic Printing System, was released in 1977; it was the first laser printer intended for use with a single computer.

6447. Conversation between two computers in which two software programs appeared to chat with each other over a network took place on September 18, 1972, as monitored at the University of California at Los Angeles. A program called PARRY, written in 1972 by Stanford University psychiatrist Kenneth Colby to emulate the responses of a paranoid schizophrenic, was "interviewed" by a program called ELIZA (or "the Doctor"), a parody of a Rogerian psychiatrist written in 1966 by Joseph Weizenbaum. The programs communicated by teletype.

6448. Personal computer operating system was CP/M (Control Program for Microcomputers), developed by Gary Kildall in 1974. The first version was the CP/M-80 operating system, which simplified the tasks of writing and debugging software for Intel 8080-compatible microprocessors. It was the first operating system suited to computer hobbyists. A version of CP/M was available for the Altair 8800, the first personal computer.

6449. Magazine for home computer users was *Creative Computing*, founded by David Hollerith Ahl, a marketing manager for American Telephone and Telegraph (AT&T), based in Morristown, NJ. Ahl was an early advocate of personal computing. The first issue began shipping on November 1, 1974, to 600 subscribers, about two months before Altair began marketing the first personal computer kit.

6450. Personal computer was the Altair 8800, sold in kit form beginning on December 19, 1974, when it was featured on the cover of the January 1975 issue of *Popular Electronics* magazine. It was developed by Edward Roberts at Micro Instrumentation and Telemetry Systems (MITS) of Albuquerque, NM. The kit cost $397. The first personal computer that was commercially successful was the Commodore PET, developed by Commodore Business Machines of Westchester, PA, and marketed to consumers beginning in early 1977. It sold for $595. The Apple II, developed by Steven Jobs and Steven Wozniak of Apple Computer, Cupertino, CA, is often considered the first successful PC, but it was not released until later in 1977.

6451. Commercial software for personal computers was a program that enabled the Altair 8800 personal computer to understand software written in the BASIC computer language. It was developed in 1975 by William Henry Gates III, age 19, and Paul Gardner Allen, age 22, in Seattle, WA. Microsoft, the company they founded to market the software, was the world's first personal computer software company.

6452. Computer virus is generally considered to have been Pervade, which was created by UNIVAC programmer John Walker in January 1975. Walker developed Pervade as a means of distributing *Animal*, a popular mainframe computer game. Pervade copied *Animal* to any UNIVAC computer that ran the game. However, a virus named Creeper is rumored to have infected the Defense Department's ARPANET system some years before.

6453. Personal computer users group was the Homebrew Computer Club (also called the Amateur Computer User's Group), founded by Fred Moore and Gordon French. The first meeting, attended by 32 computer enthusiasts including Apple Computer co-founder Steven Wozniak, was held on March 5, 1975, in Menlo Park, CA, in French's garage. An Altair desktop computer was demonstrated by Robert Albrecht.

6454. Computer store was the Arrow Head Computer Company, also known as The Computer Store, founded by Richard Heiser in Los Angeles, CA. It opened for business in July 1975 and sold preassembled Altair computers, as well as other computer items.

6455. Word processor for computers was the Electric Pencil, written in 1976 by Michael Shrayer, inventor of the Altair microcomputer. The first word processor that was widely popular was WordStar, introduced in April 1979 by MicroPro International Inc., San Rafael, CA. The program was written by MicroPro founder Seymour Rubenstein together with Rob Barnaby and Jim Fox.

6456. Voice reader for reading printed matter aloud was invented by Raymond Kurzweil. It was first demonstrated publicly on January 13, 1976, and was tested by the National Federation for the Blind. The machine, manufactured by Kurzweil Computer Products, Cambridge, MA, converted ordinary printed materials, including books, magazines, and typewritten correspondence, directly into spoken English at 150 words per minute. It used a camera to scan the pages into a computer that analyzed the letters and pronounced them.

6457. Computer camp was Camp Retupmoc ("computer" spelled backwards), a week-long camp for high school students. It was organized by mathematics teacher Jack Kinney of the Rose-Hulman Institute of Technology and held in June 1977 in Terre Haute, IN.

6458. Computer bulletin board was inaugurated in February 1978 by Ward Christianson and Randy Suess of Chicago, IL. Called the Computerized Bulletin Board System, it allowed computer users equipped with a modem to log on to the site and exchange information.

6459. Spreadsheet program for computers was VisiCalc Spreadsheet Software, invented by Dan Bricklin and Bob Frankston. Bricklin was attending the MBA program at Harvard Business School, Cambridge, MA, when he realized the need for an electronic spreadsheet that would perform all necessary recalculations when any single figure was changed. He and Frankston founded Software Arts Inc. in Arlington, MA, to develop the program, which was published by a Cambridge company, Personal Software. VisiCalc for Apple II computers went on sale in October 1979.

VisiCalc was the basis for the popular Lotus 1-2-3 spreadsheet, published by the Lotus Development Corporation.

6460. Graphical user interface for a commercial computer was used in the Star, developed by the Xerox Corporation at its Palo Alto Research Center, Palo Alto, CA, and put on the market in 1981. The Star had many of the interface features later incorporated into nearly all personal computers, including a mouse input device and a screen with icons, windows, and menus.

6461. Computer software patent in the United States was issued to Satya Pal Asija of St. Paul, MN, on May 26, 1981, for a data storage and retrieval system, which he dubbed SWIFT-ANSWER, an acronym for Special Word Indexed Full Text Alpha Numeric Storage With Easy Retrieval. The program provided answers in ordinary language to questions posed by users.

6462. IBM personal computer was the Model 5150, announced by International Business Machines Corporation, Armonk, NY, on August 12, 1981. It was the first microcomputer that was widely accepted in the business world and was the basis for imitations, called PC "clones," made by other electronics companies. Its operating system was provided by Microsoft. The first of the PC clones was the MPC 1600-1, marketed by Columbia Data Products in 1982. IBM sold its computer division in 2005.

6463. Computer virus in personal computers was Elk Cloner, which traveled between Apple II computers on floppy disks. It was created by Richard Skrenta, a ninth-grader from Pittsburgh, PA, in 1982 in order to annoy his friends. An infected disk would crash the computer and cause a mischievous poem to pop up on the screen. The virus also infected other disks used in the same machine.

6464. Emoticon comment sign for computer users was the smiley face, made up of a colon, a dash, and an end parenthesis, which was intended to be read sideways so that it formed an expressive face. It was suggested by Scott E. Fahlman in a post to an online bulletin board at Carnegie Mellon University, Pittsburgh, PA, on September 19, 1982. In the same post, Fahlman also proposed a frowny face, made up a colon, a dash, and an open parenthesis.

6465. Thermal inkjet printer was the HP ThinkJet, developed by Hewlett-Packard Company, Palo Alto, CA. It reached the market in 1984.

6466. Internet domain was symbolics.com, registered on March 15, 1985, by Symbolics, Inc., a computer hardware and software developer located in Cambridge, MA, and Chatsworth, CA.

6467. Desktop publishing software that was commercially successful was Aldus PageMaker, introduced by Aldus Corporation, Seattle, WA, on July 15, 1985. The software was written by Paul Brainerd for use on Macintosh computers coupled with Apple LaserWriter printers. The application allowed any person trained in its use to create publishing layouts, including graphic design tasks, on computer.

6468. Interactive multimedia authoring program was HyperCard, written by William Atkinson for Apple Computer of Cupertino, CA, and introduced for the Macintosh computer in September 1987. HyperCard enabled computer users who were unfamiliar with programming to create their own information databases with hypertextual links, audio-visual effects, and true interactivity.

6469. E-mail program with a graphic interface was Eudora, written in 1988 by Steve Dorner, a computer programmer at the University of Illinois at Urbana-Champaign. The program, a year in development, was originally called UIUCMail. It was available at no charge until the rights to it were purchased by the communications firm QUALCOMM, which marketed it as a consumer product.

6470. Major worm attack on the Internet took place on November 2, 1988, when a worm (a form of self-propagating computer virus) was released into the Internet as an experiment by Robert Tappan Morris, Jr., a graduate student at Cornell University, Ithaca, NY. The worm replicated much more quickly than expected and within a few hours had shut down some 6,000 of the 60,000 hosts then on the Internet. The cost to repair the damage caused by the worm ranged from $200 to more than $53,000 per host site. Morris was later convicted of violating the United States Computer Fraud and Abuse Act.

6471. Commercial provider of dial-up Internet services was The World (world.std.com), a public dial-up Internet Service Provider (ISP) operated by Software Tool and Die and based in Brookline, MA. The World began offering Internet access to customers with telephones and modems in 1989.

6472. Internet search engine was Archie, invented in 1989 by Alan Emtage, a student at McGill University in Canada who later became the chief technical officer at New York's Mediapolis, Inc. Archie was programmed to visit public FTP (file transfer protocol) sites and compile an online index of them for the convenience of the computer user.

6473. Machine controlled via the Internetwas the Internet Toaster, devised by computer scientist John Romkey. Responding to a 1989 challenge by Dan Lynch, president of the INTEROP Internet networking convention, Romkey and co-researcher Simon Hackett modified a Sunbeam Deluxe Automatic Radiant Control toaster so its power supply could be controlled via a Simple Networking Management Protocol Management Information Base (SNMP MIB), an early Internet protocol. Typing the appropriate command on a networked computer allowed Romkey to turn the toaster on or off; the longer the power was on, the darker the toast became. This system still required a human being to manually drop in and pop out the bread. The Internet Toaster was first shown publicly at the INTEROP convention held in San Jose, CA, in October 1990. At the 1991 INTEROP, an Internet-controlled robotic arm built of LEGO blocks was added that would pick up and drop a piece of bread into the toaster without human assistance.

6474. Educational multimedia CD-ROM was *Mixed-Up Mother Goose*, published by Sierra Online of Bellevue, WA, in the spring of 1991. The disc featured animated Mother Goose characters with digitized voices. It sold for $59.95.

6475. Optical computer that stored its programs and processed information entirely by means of light rather than electricity was demonstrated by electrical engineers Harry F. Jordan and Vincent P. Heuring of the University of Colorado, Boulder, CO, in January 1993. The complex array of lasers, switches, and optical fibers was the size of a small car and had the computing ability of a 1960s-era minicomputer. Its limited memory rendered it unable to perform complex calculations.

6476. Holographic data storage system was demonstrated by Lambertus Hesselink, John Heanue, and Matthew Bashaw of Stanford University, Stanford, CA, in the summer of 1994. It was a crystal the size of a large lump of sugar in which was stored a digitized image of the "Mona Lisa." Hesselink founded a company named Optitek to commercialize the invention, which had the potential to store information more compactly than any current data storage system.

6477. Banner ads on the Internet appeared on the site hotwired.com beginning October 25, 1994, in a rectangular 468 by 60 pixel format that fit conveniently within the layout of the hotwired Web page. This size subsequently became the most common for all Web banners. The first banner to appear was for the telecommunications company American Telephone and Telegraph (AT&T); the message, meant to forecast the future of Internet advertising, was: "Have you ever clicked your mouse right here? You will." Clicking on the ad did not actually lead to a hyperlink. The ad was created for Modem Media/AT&T by TANGENT Design/Communications of Westport, CT, by a team under creative director Joe McCambley.

6478. Wiki Web site was the Portland Pattern Repository, a site on the World Wide Web dedicated to "the theory and practice of developing urban, architectural and other design patterns." It was launched on March 25, 1995, by Howard G. (Ward) Cunningham, a software programmer from Portland, OR, using the Internet domain c2.com owned by his company Cunningham & Cunningham, Inc. Wiki Web sites are open to public contribution and modification and are particularly appropriate for repositories of free information. *Wiki-wiki* is a Hawaiian word meaning "quick."

6479. American banned from the Internet was 24-year-old Chris Lamprecht (aka "Minor Threat"), who on May 5, 1995, was sentenced by U.S. District Court judge Sam Sparks to 70 months in the Federal Correctional Institution in Bastrop, TX, for money laundering and computer hacking. Lamprecht was forbidden any access to the Internet for a period of eight years.

6480. Computer software application on Digital Video Disc was the PhoneDisc PowerFinder USA ONE, an electronic phone directory for the entire United States, announced by Digital Directory Assistance, Bethesda, MD, on January 18, 1996. It contained on a single digital video disc, or DVD, information that previously required the storage capacity of six CD-ROM discs.

6481. Censorship of the Internet was attempted under the Communications Decency Act, signed into law by President Bill Clinton on February 8, 1996.

6482. Webmail service was Hotmail, launched on July 4, 1996, by company founders Sanbeer Bhatia and Jack Smith. The Hotmail service allowed members to check their e-mail via the World Wide Web anywhere in the world without the need for a personal e-mail client. Hotmail was sold to the Microsoft Corporation of Redmond, WA, in January 1998 for $400 million.

6483. Teraflop computer capable of performing a trillion mathematical operations per second was the Janus, built by the Intel Corporation, Santa Clara, CA. The computer, housed in 84 cabinets, contained 9,072 Pentium Pro processors and had hundreds of billions of bytes of memory, enough to generate simulations of complex and massive events in four dimensions with extreme detail. It was installed in July 1997 at Sandia National Laboratories in Albuquerque, NM. The cost was $55 million.

6484. Computer virus spread by e-mail was Melissa, developed by David L. Smith of Aberdeen Township, NJ. Members of an Internet newsgroup called Alt.Sex received an anonymous post in March 1999 inviting them to download a pornography-related document. The virus was transmitted with the document and, once downloaded, e-mailed itself to addresses in the computer's mail program.

By clogging the e-mail facilities of several large corporations, the Melissa virus caused $80 million in damages. Smith was caught, pleaded guilty, and reduced his jail sentence from 40 years to 20 months by becoming an undercover virus specialist for the FBI.

Earth Sciences

6485. Aurora borealis display recorded in America took place in New England on December 11, 1719. A contemporary account in the collection of the Massachusetts Historical Society contained this description: "This evening, about eight o'clock, there arose a bright and red light in the E. N. E. like the light which arises from an house when on fire (as I am told by several credible persons who saw it, when it first arose) which soon spread itself through the heavens from east to west, reaching about 43 or 44 degrees in height, and was equally broad."

6486. Weather observations to be systematically recorded were made by Dr. John Lining, a physician of Charleston, SC, who took daily observations at 6:30 A.M., 3 P.M., and 10 P.M. in January 1738. He recorded temperature, rainfall, atmospheric pressure, humidity, wind direction and force, and the state of the weather, as well as the effect of the weather on the human body, communicating his reports to the Royal Society of London.

6487. Lightning demonstration showing the relationship between lightning and electricity was made on June 15, 1752, in Philadelphia, PA, by Benjamin Franklin. His letter to Peter Collison, dated October 19, 1752, describing his experiments was read before the Royal Society of London in December 1752.

6488. Geographer of the United States was Thomas Hutchins, appointed under an ordinance of May 20, 1785. He was the first and only incumbent of this office. He was in charge of surveys of land in the public domain.

6489. Geological survey for a state government was undertaken by Edward Hitchcock for Massachusetts from 1830 to 1833.

6490. Diving suit that was practical was invented by Leonard Norcross of Dixfield, ME, who obtained a patent on June 14, 1834, on a "water-dress." It consisted of an airtight rubber garment to which was attached a brass cap or helmet that rested on the shoulders. The cap was connected to an air pump on the boat by means of a rubber hose. The feet were weighted with heavy lead shot.

6491. Geological survey authorized by Congress was authorized on June 28, 1834, when Congress appropriated $5,000 to be applied to geological and mineralogical survey and research. The funds were used in making a geological survey of the country between the Missouri and the Red rivers. George William Featherstonhaugh was in charge of the survey.

6492. Geodetic survey was undertaken by Simeon Borden and completed by him in 1841. In 1830 he made an apparatus for measuring the base line for the trigonometrical survey required by Massachusetts. The apparatus was 50 feet long and was enclosed in a tube. It was also fitted with four compound microscopes, everything being adjustable to permit movement in any direction.

6493. Seismograph was installed at the Lick Observatory, University of California, Mount Hamilton, CA, and exhibited at the formal opening of the building on June 1, 1888. The equipment consisted of a three-component Ewing seismograph, a Gray seismograph, and a Duplex seismograph.

6494. Geologist who was a woman was Florence Bascom. After receiving her Ph.D. in geology (the first doctorate awarded by Johns Hopkins University to any woman), she started the geology department of Bryn Mawr College. In 1896 she became the first woman to join the staff of the U.S. Geological Survey, where she specialized in mapping and petrographic analysis of the Appalachian Mountain area in the mid-Atlantic states.

6495. Oceanography institution was the Scripps Institution of Oceanography of the University of California, located at La Jolla, CA. It developed from the Scripps Institution for Biological Research of the University of California, which was established in 1912. Its investigations covered the circulation of the waters in the ocean, the interrelation of the sea and the atmosphere, the chemistry of ocean water, the sediments on the sea floor, and the life of marine organisms.

6496. Weather forecast broadcast on radio was made on January 3, 1921, by station 9XM of the University of Wisconsin, Madison, WI. The first radio weather forecasts made for the federal government were broadcast on April 26, 1921, by station WEW, St. Louis, MO.

6497. Fathometer to measure the depth of water was invented by Herbert Grove Dorsey of the U.S. Coast and Geodetic Survey, who received a patent on April 24, 1928. The device measured depth by means of a series of electrical sounds and light signals.

6498. Fluorescent mineral exhibit was opened on April 26, 1929, at the Academy of Natural Sciences of Philadelphia, PA. Carbon arc lamps with Corning filters were used by Samuel George Gordon, associate professor of minerals, to activate a display of minerals.

6499. Deep-sea exploration vessel was the bathysphere, developed by William Beebe, director of tropical research at the New York Zoological Society, and inventor Otis Barton in the early 1930s. A reinforced steel sphere with windows, an air supply, and a telephone, it was suspended by cable from a ship. The first descent by Beebe and Barton was made off the coast of Bermuda on June 11, 1930, when the bathysphere reached a depth of 1,300 feet (400 meters). A few days later, one of their team members, ichthyologist Gloria Hollister, became the first woman to dive in the bathysphere, making observations from 410 feet below the surface with colleague John Tee-Van.

6500. Artificial lightning demonstration was conducted on June 10, 1932, in Pittsfield, MA, by the General Electric Company, using 10 million volts of artificial lightning. Five million volts had been the previous maximum voltage attained in the laboratory.

6501. Lightning observatory was erected during the summer of 1935 on top of the Pittsfield Works, the General Electric Company's building in Pittsfield, MA. It was built almost entirely of metal and enclosed a circular area 14 feet in diameter. Within was a lightproof room seven feet square that contained a periscope with a brilliantly silvered area reflecting lightning flashes from any direction and sending their images to a mirror set at an angle of 45 degrees. A 12-lens motor-operated high-speed camera recorded on a moving strip of film any flash of lightning within range.

6502. Weather forecasting service by telephone was inaugurated on April 8, 1939, at New York City. A steel tape recorder, developed by the Bell Telephone Laboratories, was equipped to answer 30,000 inquiries a day. The forecasts were based on reports obtained from the New York City Weather Bureau.

6503. Lightning bolt to be scientifically measured was trapped by engineers of the Westinghouse Company in Pittsburgh, PA, during an electrical storm on September 15, 1939. The bolt contained enough electrical energy to power 40,000 light bulbs of 100 watts.

6504. Artificial snow from a natural cloud was produced on November 13, 1946, by Vincent Joseph Schaefer of the General Electric Company, who flew in an airplane over Mount Greylock, MA. He dispensed small dry-ice pellets over a tract of cloud about three miles long from a height of about 14,000 feet. The cloud produced snow, which fell for an estimated distance of 3,000 feet, but the dryness of the atmosphere beneath the cloud caused the snow to evaporate before it reached the ground. Schaefer had already succeeded in producing snow in a cold chamber, on July 12, 1946.

6505. Hurricanes to receive names in alphabetical order were those of 1950, when they were given names from the World War II phonetic alphabet, beginning Able, Baker, Charlie, Dog. In 1953 forecasters began using lists of female names (Alice, Barbara, Carol, Dolly, Edna, Florence, Gilda, Hazel, Irene, Jill, Katherine, Lucy, Mabel, Norma, Orpha, Patsy, Queen, Rachel, Susie, Tina, Una, Vicky, Wallis). The rules were changed in 1979 to allow for alternating female and male names, as well as names from French and

Spanish. The agency charged with nomenclature for tropical storms and hurricanes is the World Meteorological Organization.

6506. Hurricane name to be retired was Carol. The names of the most lethal storms are taken off the name lists issued by the World Meteorological Organization. Hurricane Carol pulverized the coasts of New York, New England, and Quebec in late August 1954, causing damages of $4.1 billion. Another name, Hazel, was also retired that year.

6507. Ship outfitted for hurricane research was the *Crawford*, a 125-foot converted cutter, which was placed in service on July 3, 1956, by the Oceanographic Institution, Woods Hole, MA, to study how hurricanes originate. It carried a crew of 14 and 8 scientists. The first captain was David Casiles.

6508. Ship with a floating scientific instrument platform was developed by the Navy and the Marine Physical Laboratory of the Scripps Institution of Oceanography, University of California, San Diego, CA, with financial support from the Office of Naval Research, and was built at the Gunderson Brothers Engineering Corporation yard in Portland, OR. It was called a FLIP ship, for "floating instrument platform." It was launched on June 22, 1962. The ship towed like a log and could turn on end with only 55 of its 355-foot length above water. It weighed about 750 tons and cost less than $600,000. It was placed in service in September 1962. Commander Earl D. Bronson supervised the construction and developed operating techniques.

6509. Geologist to reach the moon was Dr. Harrison Hagan Schmitt, who accompanied Captain Eugene A. Cernan and Commander Ronald E. Evans, both of the Navy, in *Apollo 17*, which was launched on December 7, 1972, at 12:33 A.M. at Cape Canaveral, FL. Schmitt stepped out onto the surface of the moon from the lunar landing module Challenger on December 11. He and Cernan spent three days on the surface of the moon gathering scientific data.

6510. Oceanographer of distinction who was a woman was marine biologist and environmentalist Sylvia A. Earle. In 1991 and 1992, she served as the first female chief scientist of the National Oceanographic and Atmospheric Administration (NOAA), Washington, DC. In 1979, Earle made the world's deepest untethered dive when she walked along the ocean floor off Oahu, HI, for 2.5 hours at a depth of 1,250 feet.

6511. Three-dimensional maps of the ocean floor were created in 1981 by William F. Haxby at Columbia University's Lamont-Doherty Earth Observatory in New York City. The maps were based on data supplied by *SEASAT*, a NASA satellite.

6512. Municipal Heat-Health Warning forecasting system was established in Philadelphia, PA, in July 1995, to prevent summer heatwave deaths. The system, developed by the Center for Climatic Research at the University of Delaware, evaluates a broad set of meteorological data with sufficient speed to warn residents of the approach of lethal heat conditions.

6513. Interactive topographical maps of the United States were offered in 1999 on *www.topozone.com* by Maps a la Carte, Inc. Information used in the creation of the maps was provided by the United States Geological Survey.

6514. Year in which hurricane forecasters ran out of names on the annual alphabetical list was 2005, when 26 tropical storms and hurricanes occurred. Hurricane Wilma, the 21st storm of the year, was followed by Tropical Storms Alpha, Beta, Gamma, Delta, and Epsilon, as meteorologists switched to using the names of the letters of the Greek alphabet. (The letters Q, U, X, Y, and Z are usually not used in the annual list of names.)

Electronics

6515. Electron tube to enable humans to see in the dark was invented by Dr. Vladimir Kosma Zworykin and Dr. George Arthur Morton and described on January 2, 1936, at a meeting of the American Association for the Advancement of Science in St. Louis, MO. The device was sensitive to ultraviolet and infrared rays, and converted light rays from motion pictures into electrons.

6516. Electronic digital calculator was invented by John Vincent Atanasoff, a professor at Iowa State University, Ames, IA. The device was a digital calculator designed to solve linear equations using vacuum tubes for arithmetic units, condensers for memory, and a punch-card input/output system. Atanasoff began working on the calculator in September 1939 and performed the first calculations with it in October of that year.

6517. Transistor was invented at the Bell Telephone Laboratories, Murray Hill, NJ, by John Bardeen, Walter Houser Brattain, and William Shockley. The first demonstration took place on June 30, 1948. The essential element of the device was a tiny wafer of germanium, a semiconductor. Transistors perform the same functions as vacuum tubes, but occupy a fraction of the space and operate on greatly reduced amounts of power. The three inventors shared the Nobel Prize in physics in 1956

6518. Phototransistor operated by light rather than electric current was invented by Dr. John Northrup Shive of the Bell Telephone Laboratories, Murray Hill, NJ, and announced on March 30, 1950. It was composed of a midget disk of germanium with only a single collector wire. Light focused on one side of the disk controlled the flow of current to the opposite side, the side to which the wire was attached.

6519. Transistors produced commercially for a specific product were made in October 1951 by the Western Electric Company, Allentown, PA, for long-distance dialing equipment of the Bell Telephone System. Experimental transistors had been manufactured and distributed to military and civilian engineering organizations in 1948 for early circuit development work.

6520. Automaton to operate by long-distance control was a machine nicknamed Yes Man. It was made by the General Electric Company's General Engineering Laboratory, Schenectady, NY, for the Aircraft Nuclear Propulsion Department under contract with the Air Force, and its manufacture was announced on May 23, 1956. It was electronically geared to duplicate simultaneously the exact motions of a master machine at long distances. The machine was designed to perform mechanical jobs in dangerously radioactive areas from any required distance by remote control.

6521. Laser was the invention of Charles Hard Townes of New York City and Arthur Leonard Schawlow of Madison, NJ. In 1951, Townes, a physicist with Columbia University, New York City, first conceived of the maser, a practical device for amplifying the stimulated emission of microwaves, basing his idea on the earlier work of English physicist Paul Dirac and others. Townes and his brother-in-law Schawlow developed the first "optical maser," or laser, in September 1957. They filed for a patent on July 30, 1958, which was granted on March 22, 1960. Gordon Gould, a graduate student at Columbia, independently conceived of the laser in October 1957, but did not apply for a patent until April 1959. The first working laser was demonstrated in public on July 7, 1960, by Theodore Harold Maiman, a researcher at the Hughes Aircraft Company in Malibu, CA. Maiman designed a ruby cylinder with polished ends. It was partially silvered on the outside with a small hole at one end for the beam to exit. When illuminated by a powerful xenon lamp, the ruby emitted a coherent beam of red light. The word "maser" is an acronym for "microwave amplification by stimulated emission of radiation." The word "laser" is an acronym for "light amplification by stimulated emission of radiation."

6522. Integrated circuit was invented independently by Jack Kilby of Texas Instruments, Dallas, TX, and Robert Noyce of Fairchild Semiconductor, Mountain View, CA. On September 12, 1958, Kilby tested a working integrated circuit. Between March and June of 1959, Noyce improved on Kilby's cruder device by designing the first reliable, mass-produceable integrated circuit. Noyce was awarded the patent after a 10-year lawsuit between the two men.

6523. Industrial robot that was practical was the Unimate, developed by physicist Joseph F. Engelberger and engineer George C. Devol. The first unit to be produced was installed in 1961 at a General Motors plant to work with heated die-casting machines. That year, Engelberger and Devol founded Unimation, the first commercial company to make robots, and Devol filed the first American robot patent.

6524. Microprocessor was built in late 1970 by the Intel Corporation, Santa Clara, CA, for the Busicom Corporation of Japan. Designed by a team of Intel engineers including Ted Hoff, Stan Mazor, Masatoshi Shima, and Federico Faggin, the Intel 4004 crammed 2300 transistors onto one silicon chip smaller than a thumbtack and ran at a clock speed of 750 kilohertz. It was the first general-purpose computing device that was small enough, cheap enough, and powerful enough to be used as the brain of a wide variety of devices, including computers, calculators, cars, and appliances. Intel announced the 4004 to the public on November 15, 1971.

6525. Electronic pocket calculator was a battery-powered model introduced on August 20, 1971, by Texas Instruments, Dallas, TX. It weighed about 2.5 pounds and cost $149. It could add, subtract, multiply, and divide, displaying the results in an LED (light-emitting diode) window.

6526. Robot to make pizza was developed in 1990 by K. G. Engelhardt and a team of researchers at Carnegie-Mellon University, Pittsburgh, PA. Dubbed PizzaBot, it was intended to help people with disabilities manage fast-food restaurants. The robot used a simple voice-recognition system to interpret orders called out by the manager.

6527. Haptic computer interface to give a sense of virtual tangibility was the PHANTOM, invented by Thomas Massie as an undergraduate at the Massachusetts Institute of Technology, Cambridge, MA, and his professor, Kenneth Salisbury. A device approximately the size and shape of a desk lamp, the PHANTOM gave users the physical sensation of touching 3D objects displayed on a computer screen. Later improvements allowed users to "sense" textures and temperatures and to alter the object's characteristics. Massie's development and marketing company, SensAble Technologies, was incorporated in 1993.

6528. Robot to perform surgery was Robodoc, the world's first robotic device that actively performed surgical procedures. It was developed by Howard "Hap" Paul, a veterinarian-surgeon at the Sacramento Animal Medical Group in Carmichael, CA, and William Bargar, an orthopedic surgeon at Sutter General Hospital, Sacramento, CA, and was manufactured by Integrated Surgical Systems. Robodoc was capable of cutting bone 40 times more precisely than human doctors. In 1995, the $500,000 robot was authorized by the Food and Drug Administration to perform 300 hip replacement procedures on humans.

6529. Robot to grade essays on a standardized test was the E-rater, invented in 1996 by Jill Burstein and other scientists at the Educational Testing Service, Princeton, NJ. It was used for the first time on February 10, 1999, to help score handwritten responses to the Graduate Management Admission Test (GMAT), given to American business-school applicants. The robot was programmed to look for such things as errors in spelling and grammar, inaccurate sentence structure, and illogical or disorganized arguments. Each test was graded by a human reader as well as the robot. If their results differed by more than one point on a grading scale of 0 to 6, a second human reader was asked to arbitrate. The introduction of electronic scoring was intended to save labor costs and time and to reduce the subjectivity of human grading.

6530. Transmission of touch signals over a long distance took place on May 23, 2002, between researchers at the Massachusetts Institute of Technology, Cambridge, MA, and their counterparts at University College London across the Atlantic. They employed a virtual reality haptic device, the PHANTOM, which provides a realistic sense of force and touch. The researchers, each using a robotic arm, picked up a computerized box visible on their screens, each feeling the other one's actions so that they could lift the box together.

6531. Robot Olympics was the ROBOlympics (later renamed RoboGames), held on March 21 and 22, 2004, in San Francisco, CA, under the sponsorship of the Robotics Society of America. Participants from 11 countries entered their robots in 31 events, including sumo, soccer, combat, and wrestling.

6532. Winner of the Grand Challenge robotic vehicle race was a modified Volkswagen Touareg nicknamed "Stanley," customized by researchers from Stanford University under team leader Sebastian Thrun. The competition was held on October 8, 2005, along a rugged 131.6-mile desert course north of Primm, CA. It was sponsored by the federal Defense Advanced Research Projects Agency, which offered a $2 million purse, and was meant to spur development of unmanned robot transports for military use. The robots had to navigate the course unaided, without human intervention or remote control, in less than 10 hours. Of the 23 vehicles that qualified for the race, only five reached the finish line. This was the second Grand Challenge held; no vehicle was able to complete the course in the first competition.

6533. Wireless microchip receiver-transmitter for making digital information part of a nondigital object was the Memory Spot, made by Hewlett Packard, Palo Alto, CA. Two prototype models, one with 256 kilobits of storage and the other with 4 megabits, were demonstrated on July 17, 2006. The minuscule silicon chips were intended to be embedded in paper and plastic items, such as pill bottles and business cards, or in office equipment, such as printers, where the digital audio and video files stored in them could be accessed by readers in people's cell phones and PDAs.

Energy

Electricity

6534. Electric cooking experiment was performed by Benjamin Franklin on the banks of the Schuylkill River, Philadelphia, PA, in 1749. In a letter dated April 29, 1749, Franklin wrote: "A turkey is to be killed for our dinner by the electrical shock and roasted by the electrical jack, before a fire kindled by the electrified bottle; when the healths of all the famous electricians in England, Holland, France and Germany are to be drank in electrified bumpers, under the discharge of guns from the electrical battery."

6535. Electromagnet was invented by Joseph Henry, who exhibited one before the Albany Institute, Albany, NY, in June 1828. It was closely wound with silk-covered wire about 0.026 inches in diameter.

6536. Electric motor using direct current was invented by Thomas Davenport of Brandon, VT, in July 1834. Davenport, a prosperous blacksmith, had traveled to the Penfield Iron Works in Crown Point, NY, to purchase some iron. He saw one of the first electromagnets there, and was so fascinated that he bought it on the spot. After several months of experiments, he built the first practical electric motor. It consisted of a rotating disk with two electromagnets as the spokes, supported by a spindle rising from a base on which were fixed two other electromagnets. When Davenport rapidly switched the direction of the current back and forth, the disk spun at speeds up to 30 revolutions per second. Davenport obtained a patent on the device in 1835.

6537. Electric light for household illumination was probably used by Professor Moses Gerrish Farmer at 11 Pearl Street, Salem, MA. In July 1859 he arranged a series of lamps in his parlor, the current for which was generated by a galvanic battery of some three dozen six-gallon jars in his cellar. The lamps could be turned on individually. He also invented an incandescent lamp that consisted of a strip of sheet platinum operating in air.

6538. Dynamo for a direct-current outdoor lighting system was built in 1875 at Cornell University, Ithaca, NY, by Professor William Arnold Anthony and a graduate student, George Sylvanus Moler. It was exhibited at the Philadelphia Centennial in 1876 and was made from designs of the original Gramme machine. It was used to supply the current to light the Cornell campus in 1875.

6539. Electric company was the Edison Electric Light Company, 65 Fifth Avenue, New York City, incorporated on October 15, 1878. Three thousand shares with a par value of $100 each were issued for the express purpose of financing Thomas Alva Edison's work on the incandescent lamp. The Edison Electric Illuminating Company was incorporated on December 17, 1880, with a capitalization of $1 million for the purpose of furnishing electric light in New York City. The first president of the company was Dr. Norvin Green.

6540. Electric light in a store was installed in the Philadelphia, PA, establishment of John Wanamaker on December 26, 1878, in the Grand Depot. Twenty-eight arc lamps were used, with eight dynamos supplying the current.

6541. Electricity generated by Niagara Falls waterpower was made in 1879, when 16 arc lights in Prospect Park, Niagara Falls, NY, were lit by a small dynamo powered by the falls. The first large-scale use was made by the Niagara River Hydraulic Tunnel Power and Sewer Company (later the Niagara Falls Power Company), which broke ground on October 4, 1890, for a power plant. On October 24, 1893, a contract was executed with the Westinghouse Electric and Manufacturing Company of Pittsburgh, PA, for three 5,000-horsepower generators delivering two-phase currents at 2,200 volts, 25 cycles. On August 26, 1895, power was first transmitted commercially, the current being employed by the Pittsburgh Reduction Company in the reduction of aluminum ore. The city of Buffalo, NY, received its first power for commercial purposes on November 15, 1896.

6542. Electric company organized to produce and sell electricity was the California Electric Light Company, San Francisco, CA, organized on June 30, 1879. In September 1879, it furnished current from a central generating station for lighting Brush arc light lamps.

6543. Incandescent lamp of practical value was invented on October 21, 1879, by Thomas Alva Edison of Menlo Park, NJ. After 13 months of experimenting, he utilized carbonized cotton filaments and produced a light bulb that would burn 40 hours in a vacuum inside a glass bulb. The Pennsylvania Railroad Company ran special trains to Menlo Park on December 31, 1879, to enable the public to view a public demonstration of the lamp. Patent papers on this invention were granted on January 27, 1880.

6544. Hydroelectric power plant to furnish arc lighting service was the Grand Rapids Electric Light and Power Company, Grand Rapids, MI, organized on March 22, 1880, and placed in operation on July 23, 1880. The first president and organizer was William T. Powers. The first generating equipment was a 16-arc-light Brush generator, driven by a water wheel, which supplied power to the factory of the Wolverine Chair Company. On August 1, 1881, a new building was occupied from which current was generated to supply street lighting. This plant furnished arc lighting service for the first four years of its operations.

6545. Incandescent lamp factory was the Edison Lamp Works, Menlo Park, NJ, opened on October 1, 1880. More than 130,000 bulbs had been manufactured by April 1, 1882, when the factory moved to Harrison, NJ.

6546. Incandescent light bulbs in widespread use were developed by Lewis Howard Latimer of the U.S. Electric Lighting Company, Bridgeport, CT, as an improvement on the bulbs invented by Thomas Edison. By placing the carbon filament inside a protective jacket made of cardboard, Latimer extended the useful life of the bulbs and brought down their price, making possible the installation of electric lighting systems in cities. A patent for his improvement was issued on September 13, 1881. Latimer was the son of former slaves.

6547. Electric light from a power plant in a residence was generated by an independent plant installed in the home of James Hood Wright in the Fort Washington section of New York City sometime before December 1881. Other New York residences that were equipped with power generators were those of William Henry Vanderbilt and John Pierpont Morgan.

6548. Electric power plant operated by a city was purchased in 1882 by Fairfield, IA. It supplied power to 13 streetlights and six Brush arc lamps of 2,000 candlepower that were situated on a 185-foot tower. City operation was supervised by Al Robb and James McQuiston. The illumination cost $70 annually per arc. A windstorm blew the tower down on May 9, 1883.

6549. Dynamo that was successful was Jumbo No. 1, a direct-current steam dynamo, which was built in 1881 at the Edison Machine Works, Goerck Street, New York City. It weighed 27 tons, 6 tons of which was the armature. When the armature was air-cooled, the dynamo's capacity was 700 lamps of 16-candlepower each. The dynamo was put in operation September 4, 1882.

6550. Electric power station with a central source was the Edison Electric Illuminating Company of 257 Pearl Street, New York City, which opened on Saturday evening, September 4, 1882. It had one engine, which generated power for 800 electric light bulbs. Within 14 months, the service had 508 subscribers and 12,732 bulbs.

6551. Power plant using alternating current was placed in operation in Great Barrington, MA, on March 6, 1886. The transformers were built by William Stanley in his Great Barrington laboratory and were successfully operated for a considerable time, but an accident disabled the generators and the plant was discontinued. The first such plant to be commercially successful was built in Buffalo, NY, in November 1886 by the Westinghouse Electric and Manufacturing Company, Pittsburgh, PA. The station, located on Wilkerson Street, Buffalo, was placed in operation on November 30, 1886, by the Brush Electric Light Company.

6552. Electric meter indicating the amount of electrical energy dispensed or applied was invented by Oliver B. Shallenberger of Rochester, PA, who obtained a patent on August 14, 1888. Commercial production of the meters was started in August 1888 by the Westinghouse Electric and Manufacturing Company, Pittsburgh, PA.

6553. Hydroelectric power plant generating alternating current to operate over a long distance was built by the Willamette Falls Electric Company at Willamette Falls, Oregon City, OR. It operated two 300-horsepower Stilwell and Bierce water wheels belted to a single-phase generator rated at 720 kilowatts. On June 2, 1889, it supplied current to Portland, OR, a distance of 13 miles from the plant.

6554. Power transmission installation using alternating current was made in 1890 at Telluride, CO, by the Westinghouse Electric and Manufacturing Company. The generator was a 100-horsepower, 88.33-cycle, single-phase, 3,000-volt unit driven by water power. A three-mile transmission line was erected and a single-phase synchronous motor was installed at the end of the line. The motor lacked a starting torque, and a necessary adjunct was a starting motor to bring the unloaded synchronized motor to its normal speed.

6555. Electric alternator in parallel successfully operated was installed in 1896 by the Hartford Electric Light Company in its station at Hartford, CT. It was used in connection with a waterpower unit.

6556. Hydroelectric power plant to use a storage battery was installed by the Hartford Electric Light Company, Hartford, CT, in 1896. The storage battery made it possible to supply the company's peak load requirements from water power that would otherwise have gone to waste during the periods of relatively small demand.

6557. Steam turbine operated by a public utility to produce electricity was a 1,500-kilowatt steam turbine installed in April 1901 by the Hartford Electric Light Company, Hartford, CT, at its Pearl Street station. The turbine, manufactured by the Westinghouse Electric and Manufacturing Company, East Pittsburgh, PA, began to generate electricity in October 1901.

6558. Mercury vapor lamp was invented by Peter Cooper Hewitt of New York City, who received eight patents on September 17, 1901. It consisted of an elongated vacuum glass tube with a mercury electrode at one end and an iron electrode at the other end. The light was obtained from the gas or vapor of the mercury, through which an electric current passed. The lamps lacked red rays. They were manufactured by the Cooper Hewitt Electric Company in New York City beginning in December 1902.

6559. Hydroelectric power plant built by the federal government was the Minidoka Dam on the Snake River in Idaho, constructed by the Bureau of Reclamation, Department of the Interior. The first unit of the power plant was started on May 1, 1909, and had a capacity of 1,400 kilovolt amperes.

6560. Alkaline dry cell battery was developed by Thomas Alva Edison in 1914 at his laboratory in West Orange, NJ. It used an alkaline electrolyte of basic nickel-iron and nickel-cadmium, not an acid electrolyte, as in lead storage-cell batteries. Edison did not commercialize the alkaline cell, and it did not become widely used until the 1970s.

6561. Electric power line commercial carrier was placed in operation on December 6, 1922, by the Utica Gas and Electric Company, Utica, NY. The plant was built by the General Electric Company, Schenectady, NY, and consisted of the transmitters, the power lines, and the associated receivers. The transmission lines carried both voices and power. A single power line could carry several different carrier frequencies simultaneously, making possible distant supervisory control of various types of electric equipment.

6562. Machine to make glass light bulbs was invented by Benjamin D. Chamberlin of Washington, DC, who received a patent on September 1, 1925, on an "apparatus for gathering glass and the treatment thereof on blowpipes," which was assigned to the Hartford-Empire Company, Hartford, CT. The first commercial machine was the result of several individuals' work and went into regular use about 1914 at the main plant of the Corning Glass Works, Corning, NY.

6563. Photoelectric cell or tube was publicly demonstrated on October 21, 1925, by the Westinghouse Electric and Manufacturing Company at the Electrical Show at Grand

Central Palace in New York City. The photoelectric cell, which is sensitive to light, was used to count objects as they interrupted a light beam in passing, to open doors as a person or car approached, and to perform similar functions.

6564. Electric light bulb frosted on the inside with sufficient strength for commercial handling was invented by Marvin Pipkin of the Incandescent Lamp Department of the General Electric Company at Nela Park, OH. He received a patent for it on October 16, 1928. Inside-frosted bulbs have a number of distinct advantages over outside-frosted bulbs, among which are less absorption of light and less collection of dust. Pipkin found that bulbs frosted by previous methods were weak because the etched surface was made up of minute, sharp-angled pits or depressions, and that he could strengthen the bulb by changing these into rounded pits, either by treating the bulb with a weaker etching solution or by using the strong solution for a shorter period of time.

6565. Hydroelectric power plant operated by a county was placed in operation by the people of Crisp County, GA, on August 1, 1930. The plant was 14 miles southwest of Cordele on the Flint River and was built under government license. Emmet Stephen Killebrew was the chief engineer. It had a capacity of 14,000 horsepower and produced 47 million kilowatt-hours per year.

6566. Floating electric power plant was the *Jacona*, a 7,000-ton steam-driven cargo vessel, 396 feet long and 53 feet wide, built in 1919 by the Todd Dry Dock and Shipbuilding Company, Tacoma, WA, for the United States Shipping Board and rebuilt in 1930 at the Newport News Shipbuilding and Dry Dock Company, Newport News, VA, which installed two 10,000-kilowatt turbines. The *Jacona* was towed by tug to Bucksport, ME, where it supplied a paper mill with 24,121,000-kilowatt hours of power from November 1930 to March 1931, at which time power was obtained from the Central Maine Power Company's Wyman Dam. The idea for the floating power plant was conceived by Walter Scott Wyman and the design engineering done by Nepsco Services.

6567. Sodium vapor lamps were installed on June 13, 1933, on the Balltown Road, near Schenectady, NY, by the General Electric Company and the New York Power and Light Corporation. The lamps were monochromatic and glowed in one color, giving 2.5 times the light output of incandescent lamps of the same wattage. The lamp wattage was about 80 to 90 watts and the light output about 4,000 lumens.

6568. Electric power contract between a city and the federal government was signed by J.P. Nanney, mayor of Tupelo, MS, and Arthur Ernest Morgan, chairman of the Tennessee Valley Authority, on November 11, 1933. It went into effect on February 7, 1934. The 20-year contract required the city to purchase electricity from TVA and sell it to its customers at rates agreed upon with the Authority. The electricity cost the city of Tupelo about 5.5 mills per kilowatt hour.

6569. Fluorescent lamp successfully developed was made by Arthur Compton at the General Electric Company, Schenectady, NY, in 1934. His fluorescent bulb sent electric current through an argon-filled glass tube that was coated on the inside with phosphor. Mercury vapor inside the tube emitted ultraviolet waves that were changed by the phosphor into visible light. General Electric displayed the lamps at the 1939 New York World's Fair.

6570. Hydroelectric power plant to produce a million kilowatts was the Boulder Dam, Boulder City, NV, which reached this production peak in June 1943. The Bureau of Reclamation of the Department of the Interior awarded a contract on March 11, 1931, for a concrete arch-gravity dam. The first of its four generators was placed in operation on October 26, 1936, to serve the Los Angeles area. In 1947 its name was changed to the Hoover Dam.

6571. Gas turbine used by an electrical utility company was a General Electric turbine that was placed in service on July 29, 1949, in the Belle Isle station of the Oklahoma Gas and Electric Company, Oklahoma City, OK. The unit attained full capacity in 17 minutes.

6572. Battery to convert radioactive energy into electrical energy was a radioelectric cell invented by Philip Edwin Ohmart of Cincinnati, OH, and announced on December 31, 1951. It consisted of two electrochemically dissimilar electrodes separated by a filling gas that was ionized by exposure to nuclear energy to produce an electrical current.

6573. Electric power using municipal garbage as a boiler fuel was obtained by the Union Electric Company's Meramec Plant, St. Louis, MO, on April 4, 1972. Refuse was shredded and burned with coal to generate electricity. In the first month, 200,000 kilowatt hours of electricity were generated.

Fossil Fuels

6574. Oil spring of record in America was marked on a map of territory near Cuba, NY, in 1627 by Fran|Accois Dollier de Casson and René de Brehant de Galinée, Catholic missionaries of the Order of St. Sulpice. The map was sent by them to Jean Talon, intendant of Canada. A description of the oil spring is contained in a letter written by the Franciscan missionary Joseph de la Roche d'Allion dated July 18, 1627, reproduced in Gabriel Sagard-Théodat's *Histoire du Canada et Voyages que les Frères Mineurs Recollects y ont Faicts pour la Conversion des Infidelles*, published in 1636.

6575. Coal is said to have been discovered by Father Louis Hennepin during a journey of exploration from 1673 to 1680. It is asserted that he noticed coal on the bluffs of the Illinois River not far from the future towns of Ottawa and La Salle, IL.

6576. Fire in a mine was chronicled by the Reverend Charles Beatty in 1765. He reported that a fire had been burning for at least a year in a coal mine known as Spot Hill, the opening of which was somewhere between the Point Bridge and the Smithfield Street Bridge, on the south side of the Monongahela River in that part of Pittsburgh now known as Mount Washington.

6577. Anthracite coal was discovered accidentally in 1791 by Philip Ginter, a hunter, near Sharp Mountain, Carbon County, PA. It was regarded as a species of black stone. Its value was not appreciated fully, as the coal was difficult to kindle and produced such a high heat that it endangered the old-time boilers, which were designed principally for burning wood.

6578. Anthracite coal used commercially was successfully burned in 1812 in a heating furnace at White and Hazard's Fairmount Nail and Wire Works near Philadelphia, PA. The coal was supplied by Colonel George Shoemaker of Pottsville, PA, who loaded nine wagons from his mine at Centreville. A second wagonload was sold to Mellon and Bishop of the Delaware County Rolling Mill. The remaining seven loads were given away because no one would buy hard coal.

6579. Oil well was drilled unintentionally in 1818 at the mouth of Troublesome Creek, on the Big South Fork of the Cumberland River 28 miles southeast of Monticello, KY, by Martin Beatty, who was seeking brine. The drillers, Marcus Huling and Andrew Zimmerman, searching for salt, drilled a five-inch hole with pole and auger to a depth of 536 feet. The oil had no known value and sand was thrown down the well to plug it up. The "devil's tar," as Beatty called the oil, was allowed to flow into the Cumberland River and covered its surface for a distance of 35 miles. The oil became ignited and an enormous fire ensued that destroyed trees along the banks of the river, as well as the salt works.

6580. Natural gas used as an illuminant was tried in Fredonia, NY, on June 4, 1825, at the Taylor House, which was lit up in honor of the arrival of General Lafayette. The general arrived at 2 A.M. and found the house brilliantly illuminated, using about 30 burners of 60 candlepower. This was regarded as a great curiosity. The gas was fed through a pipeline from a 27-foot well that had been dug near a gas spring in 1821. It was later walled up because its odor was offensive.

6581. Gas meter to record the amount of gas used was a "gasometer" patented on October 17, 1834, by James Bogardus of New York City. It operated on the principle of a bellows, alternately being filled with gas and emptied, while the pulsations were counted on a register.

6582. Coke used successfully as a blast furnace fuel was tested in 1835 by William Firmstone at the Mary Ann Furnace in Huntingdon County, PA.

6583. Oil company was the Pennsylvania Rock Oil Company, incorporated on December 30, 1854, in New York City by George Henry Bissell of New Haven, CT, with a capital stock of $250,000.

6584. Oil refinery was started by Dr. Samuel M. Kier, a druggist of Pittsburgh, PA, to refine petroleum. He built a small refinery in 1855, using the oil, which he called Kier's Rock Oil, for medicinal purposes. Eventually he distilled the oil in his drugstore using laboratory equipment, bottled the product, and sold it for 50 cents a half pint. He also discovered that the light fractions from the crude oil would burn, and that the heavy fractions or bottoms were good for cleaning wool.

6585. Kerosene distilled from bituminous shale and cannel coal for illuminating purposes was obtained by Dr. Abraham Gesner, who secured a patent on March 27, 1855, covering his process. The product was manufactured by the North American Kerosene Gaslight Company at Newton Creek, NY. Gesner received patents on June 27, 1854, on a process for obtaining kerosene by heat distillation. The name "kerosene" is derived from *keros*, the Greek word for wax, referring to the use of paraffin in the distillation process.

6586. Oil well that was commercially productive was discovered on August 27, 1859, at Titusville, PA, when E. B. Bowditch and Edwin Laurentine Drake of the Seneca Oil Company bored through rock in a section known as Oil Creek. The well produced about 400 gallons a day from a depth of 69.5 feet. Drake was the first to tap petroleum at its source and to offer proof of the occurrence of oil in reservoirs beneath the earth's surface.

6587. Commercial oil refinery was erected by William Barnsdall and William Hawkins Abbott in Oil Creek Valley, PA, in June 1860. The only product saved was the kerosene. The small amount of gasoline manufactured was run into Oil Creek. The kerosene was sold in competition with whale oil and rock oil for use in lamps. In 1864 the refinery and some property were sold for $50,000 to six men who organized an oil company.

6588. Fire in an oil well occurred on April 17, 1861, when the Little and Merrick well on the Buchanan farm near Rouseville, PA, at Oil Creek, caught fire shortly after it gushed. It burned for three days and 19 persons lost their lives. The well produced about 3,000 barrels a day.

6589. Petroleum exported to Europe was shipped in barrels on the *Elizabeth Watts*, a 224-ton brig captained by Charles Bryant. On November 12, 1861, Messrs. Peter Wright and Sons of Philadelphia, PA, chartered this brig from Messrs. Edmund A. Sander and Company. The shipment was made from Philadelphia, PA, on November 19, 1861, and arrived at the Victoria Docks, London, on January 9, 1862, with 1,329 barrels of oil. It was not easy to recruit a crew, since men would not work above a cargo of oil, so a crew was kidnapped.

6590. Oil pipeline was laid in 1862 by Barrows and Company under the direction of J.L. Hutchins. It ran from the James Tarr farm at Oil Creek, PA, a distance of 2.5 miles to the Humboldt refinery at Plumer, PA, on Cherry Run. The pipeline had lead sockets and a two-inch diameter. It was completed on February 19, 1863, but was abandoned because of leakage.

6591. Natural gas corporation was the Fredonia Gas Light and Water Works Company, organized in Fredonia, NY, in 1865.

6592. Oil pipeline of importance to transport crude petroleum successfully was completed on October 9, 1865, by Samuel Van Syckel of Titusville, PA. It was about five miles long and extended from Miller's Farm on Oil Creek to Pithole, PA. Wrought iron pipes two inches in diameter were laid underground in 15-foot sections. Two pumping stations supplied the power.

6593. Oil drill offshore rig was patented by Thomas F. Rowland of Greenpoint, NY, who obtained a patent on May 4, 1869, on a "submarine drilling apparatus."

6594. Coal mine disaster with large loss of life occurred in Avondale, PA, early in the morning of September 6, 1869. A fire broke out in the mineshaft, cutting off the miners' escape route and their only source of air. The trapped miners tried to keep toxic fumes out of the tunnel by building a wall of boxes, barrels, and their own clothing, but the effort was hopeless. The death toll was 110 men and boys.

6595. Natural gas for manufacturing was used in Olean, NY, in 1870. The first use of natural gas in ironworking occurred at the Leechburg, PA, works of the Rogers and Burchfield Iron Mill, where it was extensively used in 1873 in both iron and puddle mill furnaces.

6596. Natural gas plant operated by a city was acquired by Wheeling, WV, which appointed a board of trustees on June 23, 1871, to operate the gasworks. It had been incorporated on March 18, 1850, as the Wheeling Gas Company, and had received a city franchise on April 13. The company was organized with a capital stock of $50,000, the city subscribing $15,000. After considerable litigation, the city acquired the gas plant in 1871.

6597. Natural gas pipeline constructed over a long distance was a two-inch pipe five miles in length, extending from Newton Wells to Titusville, PA. It was completed on August 1, 1872.

6598. Steam distribution plant of importance was the New York Steam Corporation, 16 Cortlandt Street, New York City, formed on July 26, 1880. The first boiler plant was erected in the New York City block bounded by Cortlandt, Dey, Greenwich, and Washington streets. It contained 48 coal-burning boilers of 250 horsepower each and a chimney 225 feet high. On September 19, 1881, the company was consolidated with the Steam Heating and Power Company of New York, a smaller organization. The first distribution of steam from a central plant in New York City was made on March 3, 1882, to the United Bank Building, 88–92 Broadway. Within nine months, the service had been extended to 62 customers.

6599. State gas commission was established by Massachusetts by a law approved on June 11, 1885. The Department of Public Utilities, later called the Department of Public Works, was established to regulate the industry, to supervise the issue of capital stock, to hear consumer complaints, to reduce the price of gas and electricity to consumers, and to require gas companies to file annual returns with the commission. The department of Public Utilities was quasi-judicial in character.

6600. Gas conservation law enacted by a state was enacted on March 2, 1891, by Indiana, "making it unlawful to burn natural gas in what are known as flambeau lights." Violation was considered a misdemeanor subject to a fine not exceeding $25; a second offense was subject to a fine not exceeding $200.

6601. Oil wells successfully drilled in the ocean were drilled off Summerland, Santa Barbara County, CA, in 1896.

6602. Gasoline obtained from crude petroleum by the cracking process was obtained by William M. Burton of Chicago, IL, the inventor of the process, who received a patent on January 7, 1913, on the "manufacture of gasoline." His method of treating the residue of the paraffin group of petroleum by distillation and condensation of the vapors was used by the Standard Oil Company of Indiana, to whom the patent was assigned.

6603. Oil and gas conservation law enacted by a state was enacted by Oklahoma on May 17, 1913. It provided for a chief deputy inspector of oil and gas wells and pipelines to supervise their use and operation.

6604. Ethyl gasoline to be marketed was sold in Dayton, OH, on February 2, 1923. Tetraethyl lead, made from alcohol and lead, was found to influence the combustion rate of gasoline by Thomas Midgley, Jr., of the General Motors Research Laboratories, Dayton. During seven years of experimenting in the development of ethyl gasoline, at least 33,000 compounds were tested to determine their antiknock effect.

6605. Coal mine to be automated was the Butler Consolidated Coal Company's Wildwood mine, Wildwood, PA, which opened in October 1930. The drilling, crushing, loading, screening of sizes, mechanical cleaning, dumping, and transportation operations were accomplished mechanically. Rubber conveyor belts carried the coal.

6606. Fuel alcohol plant was established by the Bailor Manufacturing Company, Atchison, KS, which began selling fuel alcohol on October 2, 1936. Five percent of the total output was butyl alcohol and acetone, which were blended with ethyl alcohol, which in turn was blended with gasoline. Raw materials used were rye, oats, sweet potatoes, barley, milo, kafir corn, molasses, and rice.

6607. Gas turbine to pump natural gas was installed by the Mississippi River Fuel Corporation of St. Louis, MO, at Wilmar, AR, on May 13, 1949. The unit was later moved to Bonne Terre, MO, and placed in operation on January 19, 1951.

6608. Plastic oil pipeline was placed in service on October 19, 1953, by the C.C. Thomas Company to carry oil from Williston Basin, near Poplar, MT, to a railroad car siding of the Great Northern Railway, a distance of nine miles. Its capacity was 2,500 barrels a day. It was a smooth, flexible three-inch pipe of Tenite butyrate plastic produced by the extrusion process. A 20-foot section of the pipe weighed 13 pounds, compared to 153 pounds of steel pipe. It withstood a pressure of 90 pounds per square inch.

6609. Oil refinery with a carbon monoxide boiler to achieve complete conversion of waste gases into useful power was the Sinclair Oil Corporation's refinery in Houston, TX. The boiler, which was designed and developed by the company, was placed in operation in November 1953. Carbon monoxide was converted into carbon dioxide by injecting a stream of air into the waste gases from the generator. The catalyst was regenerated in the catalytic oil cracking process.

6610. Oil drill seagoing rig for drilling in more than 100 feet of water was built in the Beaumont Yard of the Bethlehem Steel Company, Bethlehem, PA, for the C.G. Glasscock Drilling Company. The rig could drive piles with a force of 827 tons and could pull with the force of 942 tons. It was placed in service March 24, 1955.

6611. Coal pipeline was completed on September 12, 1956, and placed in commercial operation on June 4, 1957. It extended 108 miles from the Georgetown Preparation Plant of the Hanna Coal Company, a division of the Pittsburgh Consolidation Coal Company, near Cadiz, OH, to the Eastlake Power Station of the Cleveland Illuminating Company, Eastlake, OH. The pipeline, 10.75 inches in diameter, was originally designed to move an equal mixture of coal and water at the rate of 150 tons of coal per hour.

6612. Oil spill with disastrous consequences occurred on January 28, 1969, when Offshore Well A-21, owned by the Union Oil Company, burst and began leaking crude oil along a 200-mile stretch of coast centered on Santa Barbara, CA. The leak, which took 11 days to plug, fouled beaches and caused widespread loss of animal life.

6613. Coal miner who was a woman to be killed in a mining accident was Marilyn J. McCusker, killed by falling rocks while working as a roof-bolter on October 2, 1979, in the Rushton Mining Company mine, Coalport, PA.

6614. Synthetic fuels plant on a commercial scale was constructed beginning in 1980 at Beulah, ND. It was designed to convert lignite into natural gas. In 1985, with the default of $1.5 billion in federally guaranteed loans, the plant passed into the hands of the Department of Energy, which was unable to find a buyer.

6615. Offshore port for oil supertankers was the Louisiana Offshore Oil Port, which opened in 1981. It was the first facility in the United States capable of servicing very large crude carriers (VLCCs), the largest type of supertanker. Financed and built by a consortium of corporations, LOOP is located in the Gulf of Mexico about 16 miles southeast of Port Fourchon, LA. Oil offloaded from tankers is pumped via pipeline to the mainland.

6616. Shipment of oil directly from Russia to the United States arrived on March 7, 2002, at the Port of Houston, TX, via the supertanker *Astro Lupus*. The shipment signaled the two countries' desire to establish a petroleum trading relationship that bypassed the Middle East.

Nuclear

6617. Civilian to die in a nuclear accident was 24-year-old Harry K. Daghlian, Jr., a researcher at the Omega Site laboratory in Los Alamos, NM, who was fatally irradiated while performing a plutonium experiment on August 21, 1945. Daghlian was testing the critical masses of a 6.2-kilogram sphere of plutonium surrounded by a structure of tungsten carbide bricks. He accidentally dropped one of the bricks onto the sphere, triggering a dangerous supercritical state, and instinctively reached in with his bare hand to remove the brick. Daghlian's total-body radiation exposure was about 480 roentgens of soft x-rays and 110 roentgens of gamma rays, a fatal dose; the hand he used to push the brick away was exposed to an extremely high dose of 20,000 to 40,000 rem. He died on September 15, 1945, less than four weeks later. The official announcement of his death attributed it to chemical burns rather than acute radiation sickness.

6618. Nuclear product for peacetime use was developed by Clinton Laboratories, Chicago, IL, which delivered one millicurie of carbon-14 to Barnard Free Skin and Cancer Hospital, St. Louis, MO, on August 2, 1946, for use in medical treatment. The radioactive carbon has a half-life of 10,000 to 25,000 years and gives off millions of beta particles. It was a white powder, in a quantity too small to be seen by the naked eye, and was placed in aluminum and steel containers.

6619. Electric power from nuclear energy was obtained through the use of Experimental Breeder Reactor I, placed in operation during the summer of 1951 at the National Reactor Testing Station operated by the Atomic Energy Commission near Idaho Falls, ID. EBR-I was a fast breeder reactor—the first practical breeder reactor in the nation—designed and operated by the Argonne National Laboratory, Argonne, IL. The core in use at the time of the first production of electricity enabled the reactor to produce 1,400 thermal kilowatts and 150 electrical kilowatts. On December 20, 1951, the reactor supplied steam to a turbogenerator that produced more than 100,000 watts of electricity. This operated the pumps and other reactor equipment and provided light and electrical facilities for the building in which the reactor was housed.

6620. Electric power generated from nuclear energy to illuminate a town was obtained from the Utah Power and Light Company's station at Arco, ID, on July 17, 1955. At 11:28 P.M., the station released steam from a borax reactor into a turbine that drove a 3,500 kilowatt-capacity generator to supply current for the 1,200 inhabitants of Arco. The power, which lasted only one hour, was the sole source of the town's light. The news was withheld until August 11, 1955, when it was announced at the Atoms for Peace Conference at Geneva, Switzerland.

6621. Electric power generated from nuclear energy to be sold commercially was delivered by the Atomic Energy Commission at West Milton, NY, to the Niagara Mohawk Power Corporation, which supplied power on July 18, 1955, to homes and industry at three mills per kilowatt hour. The power was obtained from a nuclear reactor, the prototype of the reactor used in the submarine *Seawolf*. A capacity of about 10,000 kilowatts was integrated with the regular current.

6622. Nuclear reactor built for private industrial research was a 50,000-watt research reactor designed and built by Atomics International, a division of North American Aviation, which began operating on June 28, 1956. The reactor was located on the campus of the Illinois Institute of Technology, Chicago, IL, and operated by the Armour Research Foundation. It was of the "solution" type, fueled by enriched uranium, with a reactor core surrounded by graphite bars arranged in a stack (8 feet by 5 feet by 5 feet) that acts as a reflector. The rate of fission in the reactor was controlled by four boron bars. The reactor produced neutrons and gamma rays and was not used to generate electrical power. Twenty-four industrial companies contributed about $20,000 each toward the total cost of $700,000. The first director of the project was Dr. Richard Franklin Humphreys.

6623. Sodium reactor was built on an experimental basis by Atomics International, a division of North American Aviation, for the Atomic Energy Commission in the Santa Susana Mountains, about 30 miles northwest of Los Angeles, CA. The atomic power reactor reached criticality on April 25, 1957. It generated about 6,000 kilowatts of electricity.

6624. Nuclear power plant devoted exclusively to peaceful uses was the Shippingport Atomic Power Station, Shippingport, PA, whose reactor attained criticality on December 2, 1957. The plant produced its full rated capacity of 60,000 net kilowatts on December 23. It consisted of a single pressurized water-type reactor and its associated systems, four steam generators heated by the reactor, a single turbine-generator and associated systems, a radioactive waste disposal system, laboratory, shops, and administrative facilities. The station was designed to supply an initial electrical output of 60,000 kilowatts net, enough to provide for the residential needs of a city of 250,000 people. To allow for increased output from future nuclear fuel loadings, the turbine generator was designed with a capacity of 1 million kilowatts. President Dwight David Eisenhower broke ground for the station by remote control from Denver, CO, on September 6, 1954, and formally dedicated the plant by remote control from Washington, DC, on May 26, 1958.

6625. Nuclear reactor operated commercially was the $57 million Yankee Atomic Electric Company's plant at Rowe, MA, on the Deerfield River, which began producing power for distribution on November 10, 1960. A pressurized light water reactor, it produced 135,000 kilowatts of atomic-fueled electricity. The company was formed by 12 New England utility companies, which signed a contract on June 4, 1956, with the Westinghouse Electric Corporation, principal contractor. The reactor became critical on August 19, 1960. It was permanently shut down for safety reasons in 1995.

6626. Deaths in an American nuclear reactor occurred on January 3, 1961, when three workers were killed by high levels of radiation from an experimental reactor at a federal installation near Idaho Falls, ID.

6627. Nuclear reactor fueled by plutonium that produced useful amounts of electricity was installed in the experimental reactor of the Argonne National Laboratory's Idaho division, near Idaho Falls, ID. It was announced on June 30, 1963.

6628. Nuclear commercial power plant licensed operator who was a woman was Roberta A. Kankus, a graduate of Rensselaer Polytechnic Institute, Troy, NY, who was licensed on February 12, 1976, by the Nuclear Regulatory Commission, Washington, DC, after 14 months of on-the-job training at the Philadelphia Electric Company's Peach Bottom atomic power plant, 60 miles southwest of Philadelphia, PA. Her title was engineer in the Generating Division.

6629. Nuclear power plant to sustain a major accident was the Three Mile Island nuclear reactor complex near Middletown, PA. On March 28, 1979, homes in nearby neighborhoods were evacuated after the reactor suffered a loss of coolant and a partial core meltdown caused by a series of equipment failures and human errors.

6630. Nuclear waste storage site deep underground was the Waste Isolation Pilot Plant, located in salt beds 2,150 feet (655 meters) under the desert near Carlsbad, NM. The site, created to store hundreds of thousands of barrels of radioactive waste materials generated by the production of nuclear weapons, was licensed for plutonium storage by the U.S. government on May 13, 1998.

Renewable

6631. Waterpower development grant to a colonist was part of a charter obtained from the English crown in 1620 by the English mariner Sir Ferdinando Gorges, who planned to start new fiefdoms and noble estates in New England. The charter gave him the right to develop the territory lying between the 40th and 48th parallels, north latitude, from sea to sea, and required him to develop waterpower. Gorges constructed a log dam at the future site of South Berwick, ME, on that part of the Piscataqua River known as the Newwichawanick River. He erected a grist mill and sent some of the meal to England as proof that he was conforming to the agreement. The establishment of the colonies of Plymouth and Massachusetts ruined his plans, though he retained his claim to Maine.

6632. Utilization of Niagara Falls waterpower for industrial purposes was made in 1757 by Chabert Joncaire, who dug a ditch so that the water would operate an overshot waterwheel to drive a crude sawmill.

6633. Wind turbine to generate energy for a central power system producing alternating current was placed in service at Grandpa's Knob, VT, on October 19, 1941, when it was phased into the Central Vermont Public Service Corporation's system. Synchronized operation continued for two hours, during which a maximum output of 800 kilowatts was delivered. The wind velocity indicated by the anemometers at this load was 26 miles per hour. Palmer Cosslet Putnam was the inventor.

6634. Solar energy battery to convert the sun's energy into useful amounts of electricity was invented by Gerald Leondus Pearson, Calvin Souther Fuller, and Daryl M. Chapin at the Bell Telephone Laboratories, New York City, and announced on April 25, 1954. Made of specially treated strips of silicon, the battery needed no fuel other than the light of the sun. It had no moving parts, nothing in it was consumed or destroyed, and theoretically it was possible for it to last indefinitely.

6635. Solar energy battery to be manufactured commercially was made by National Fabricated Products, Chicago, IL, in 1955. It consisted of a disc, the size of a half dollar, which was hermetically sealed. It generated a half volt from its two terminals. The battery was first advertised on May 20, 1955, in *Electronic Design*, and the first shipment was made June 1, 1955.

6636. Power plant using solar cells was dedicated on June 7, 1980, by Governor Scott Matheson at Natural Bridges National Monument, UT. The $3 million photovoltaic system had 266,029 solar cells mounted in 12 long rows. They produced a 100-kilowatt output that supplied current for six staff residences, maintenance facilities, a water sanitation system, and a visitors' center. The plant was a joint venture of the National Park System, the Department of Energy, and the Massachusetts Institute of Technology's Lincoln Laboratory. It was 38 miles from the nearest power line.

6637. Power plant generating electricity from peat began operation in Deblois, ME, in 1989. Run by Worcester Power/Worcester Peat (formerly Down East Peat, L.P.), the 28-megawatt Worcester Power Plant drew fuel from the on-site 1,000-acre Denbo Heath sphagnum peat bog.

6638. City to derive all its energy needs from renewable sources was Santa Monica, CA, where the city council initiated the policy in February 1999. Power for municipal buildings and traffic lights came from geothermal, solar, wind, photovoltaic, and biomass installations. The city's gasoline-powered vehicles were likewise replaced with solar-powered electric SUVs.

Exploration

6639. Arctic expedition to seek the Northwest Passage for the £20,000 reward offered by Parliament for proof of its existence sailed in March 1753 from Philadelphia, PA. Captain Charles Swaine made the voyage in the *Argo*, a 60-ton schooner. Swaine encountered ice off Cape Farewell and entered Hudson Strait in the latter part of June 1753. He returned to Philadelphia in November 1753, and made a second voyage the following year.

6640. Transcontinental expedition to the Pacific coast was undertaken by Captains Meriwether Lewis and William Clark, who left St. Louis, MO, on May 14, 1804, reached the mouth of the Columbia River on November 8, 1805, and returned to St. Louis on September 23, 1806. The expedition consisted of 9 Kentucky men, 14 army men, 2 French voyageurs, an African-American servant, and a Shoshone guide, Sacagawea, who was married to one of the voyageurs.

6641. Discovery of Antarctica by an American was made on November 18, 1820, by Captain Nathaniel Brown Palmer in the *Hero*, a sloop of 44 tons, with a crew of six men including the captain and the mate. He sailed from Stonington, CT, on July 25, 1820, and returned on May 8, 1821. His discovery of the Antarctic peninsula now called Palmer's Peninsula was made at a point near latitude 64 degrees S and longitude 60 degrees W. Palmer did not realize he had seen a continent. The first American to set foot on Antarctica was probably John Davis, a seal hunter, who went ashore at Hughes Bay on February 7, 1821. Antarctica had already been seen from a distance by the English explorer James Cook and the crew of his ship, the *Endeavour*, which circumnavigated the continent between 1773 and 1775.

6642. Scientific expedition fitted out by the federal government was authorized by Congress on May 14, 1836. An appropriation of $150,000 was made for a surveying and exploring expedition to the Pacific Ocean and the South Seas. Instructions were received on August 11, 1838. The expedition left Hampton Roads, VA, on August 18, with Lieutenant Charles Wilkes in command, explored the South Seas, and returned to New York City on June 10, 1842. The explorers saw the Antarctic continent on January 16, 1840.

6643. Arctic expedition by an American explorer was made by Elisha Kent Kane and his crew, who left New York City on May 31, 1853, in the *Advance*. They arrived at Cape Constitution, where they remained for 21 months while their ship remained frozen in the ice pack. After disease broke out on board, the crew made a 1,000-mile trek to the nearest Eskimo village.

6644. Exploration of the Grand Canyon of the Colorado by a man other than a Native American was made by Major John Wesley Powell, who left Green River City, above the head of the Colorado River, on May 24, 1869, and emerged from the lower end of the Grand Canyon on August 29, 1869, with five of the nine men who had started with him. The following year he was appointed chief of the Topographical and Geological Survey of the Colorado River of the West. The Grand Canyon had been observed by Spanish explorers in 1540 and described by the Sitgreaves expedition in 1851. A War Department team had explored navigable waters from the south in 1858, but had stopped at the foot of the canyon.

6645. Polar expedition of which a woman was a member was the Peary Expedition, led by Robert Edwin Peary, who sailed in the *Kite* on June 6, 1891, from New York City, with his wife, Josephine Peary, among the crew. This expedition did not reach the Pole.

6646. Discovery of the North Pole was long thought to have been made on April 6, 1909, by a dogsled expedition led by Robert Edwin Peary, who was accompanied by his African-American assistant, Matthew Alexander Henson, and four Eskimos. This claim was disputed by Frederick A. Cook, who maintained that he had reached the Pole by dogsled on April 21, 1908. Both claims were ruled incorrect in 1997 by historian Robert M. Bryce, who said that neither explorer succeeded in reaching 90 latitude N. The first person known to have set foot on the Pole was Lieutenant Colonel Joseph Otis Fletcher of Shawnee, OK, who arrived by plane on May 3, 1952.

6647. Airplane flight over the North Pole was claimed to have been made by Navy Lieutenant Commander Richard Evelyn Byrd and his pilot, aviator Floyd Bennett, on May 9, 1926. In the *Josephine Ford*, a triple-engine Fokker monoplane, they flew from King's Bay, Spitzbergen, to the Pole and back, without stopping, covering 1,545 miles in 15 hours 30 minutes. Both received the Medal of Honor. However, Byrd's diary, analyzed in 1996, indicated that he turned back 150 miles short of the Pole. If so, Italy's Umberto Nobile and his co-adventurers, Norwegian explorer Roald Amundsen and U.S. coal-mining heir Lincoln Ellsworth, would receive the credit for their flight over the North Pole on May 12, 1926.

6648. Airplane flight over the South Pole was made in a Ford tri-motor airplane on November 28, 1929, by Navy Lieutenant Commander Richard Evelyn Byrd, who took off from Little America, his base in the Antarctic, at 10:29 P.M. E.S.T. The crew consisted of Bernt Balchen, pilot, Harold I. June, radio operator, and Captain Ashley C. McKinley, photographer. They reported that they reached the Pole about 8:55 A.M. on November 29 and dropped an American flag there, returning at 5:10 P.M.

6649. American base in Antarctica that was permanent was East Base, built in 1940 on Stonington Island, Antarctica, and used for exploration, mapping, and scientific research. The two expeditions that used the camp were led by Richard Black and Finn Ronne. By the time of the explorers' final departure in 1948, they had carried out epic dogsled journeys as well as dangerous airplane expeditions to map some of the last unknown areas of the continent. The first women in Antarctica were Edith "Jackie" Ronne, Finn Ronne's wife, and Jennie Darlington, the wife of pilot Harry Darlington, who were part of a private 23-person expedition assembled in 1947 that spent a year on East Base.

6650. Airplane flight to land at the North Pole was made by a ski-wheeled Air Force C-47, which landed on May 3, 1952. It took off from Fletcher's Ice Island, about 115 miles from the Pole, carrying 10 air force officials and scientists. It was piloted by Lieutenant Colonel William Pershing Benedict of San Rafael, CA, and copilot Lieutenant Colonel Joseph Otis Fletcher of Shawnee, OK. In 1997, historian Robert M. Bryce published the results of research indicating that no previous explorer succeeded in reaching the Pole, despite two longstanding claims, and that Fletcher was the first human known to set foot on it.

6651. Explorer to set foot on both the North and South Poles was Dr. Albert Paddock Crary. On May 3, 1952, he visited the North Pole by aircraft. On Febrary 12, 1961, he reached the South Pole by tracked vehicle as part of a scientific expedition.

6652. Airplane flight to land at the South Pole landed on October 31, 1956, at 8:30 A.M. Greenwich time. Rear Admiral George John Dufek and six officers landed in the *Que Sera Sera*, a twin-engine Douglas R4D Skytrain transport plane. The flight was part of Operation Deepfreeze, commanded by Admiral Richard Evelyn Byrd and undertaken in connection with the International Geophysical Year 1957–58. Dufek, commander of the Naval Support Force, was in charge of logistic support for the scientific body of the expedition. He became the first American to set foot on the South Pole.

6653. Charting of the Northwest Passage between the Atlantic and the Pacific oceans was accomplished in the period from June to September 1957 by three Coast Guard cutters, the *Bramble*, the *Spar*, and the *Storis*, which were led by the *Labrador*, a Canadian ice patrol ship, through Beloit Strait between Boothia Peninsula and Somerset Island. The commanding officer was Commander Harold L. Wood.

Life Sciences

6654. Botanical garden was planned and made by John Bartram, who laid out five or six acres with his own hands in 1728. The garden was located at 43rd and Eastwick streets, Philadelphia, PA, on the banks of the Schuylkill River. Bartram at one time acted as botanist to King George III of England.

6655. Botanist of note who was a woman was Jane Colden, daughter of Cadwallader Colden, the lieutenant governor of New York and an accomplished botanist. She manifested her interest in botany in 1728, at the age of four. By the time she was 34, in 1758, she had described 400 plants according to the Linnaean method, using English terms (since her father had prevented her from learning Latin). She was the first to identify and name the gardenia.

6656. Botanic expedition to study and classify botanical species was made in the New England area by Manasseh Cutler, who set out from Ipswich, MA, on July 19, 1784. At Mount Washington, NH, he examined 350 species and classified them according to the Linnaean method.

6657. Prehistoric animal skeleton to be displayed in the United States was that of a mastodon, whose bones were excavated from a farm near Newburgh, NY, in the summer of 1801. The organizer of the excavation was the painter and naturalist Charles Willson Peale, who reconstructed the skeleton at his natural history museum in Philadelphia, PA. The skeleton was 11 feet tall and more than 17 feet long. Peale called it a mammoth and began displaying it on December 24, 1801.

6658. Dinosaur fossils found in the United States were three-toed footprints discovered in 1802 in sandstone near the town of South Hadley, MA, in the Connecticut River valley. A boy named Pliny Moody found the tracks, which were so much like those of birds that local people believed them to be the footprints of Noah's raven. Edward Hitchcock, a professor at Amherst College, Amherst, MA, believed the tracks were left by large, flightless birds. His analysis, *Ichnology of New England: A Report on the Sandstone of the Connecticut Valley, Especially its Fossil Footprints*, published in 1858, was the first scholarly work on fossil footprints.

6659. Entomologist hired by a state was Asa Fitch. The New York State Legislature on April 15, 1854, made an appropriation of $1,000 to pay for an examination and description of the insects of New York State, particularly those harmful to plants. The executive committee of the New York State Agricultural Society, meeting at the Astor House, New York City, on May 4, 1854, appointed Asa Fitch to do this work. His report appeared in the Agricultural Society's report for 1855.

6660. Entomologist hired by the federal government was Townend Glover, who was commissioned on June 14, 1854. He was the "expert for collecting statistics and other information on seeds, fruits and insects of the United States." His first report, which appeared under the imprint of the Patent Office, was *Insects Injurious and Beneficial to Vegetation*, printed in 1854.

6661. Dinosaur skeleton found in the United States was that of a hadrosaur, a duck-billed dinosaur of the Cretaceous period. The skeleton consisted of most of the animal's left side plus 28 vertebrae and nine teeth. The bones were unearthed in 1858 by William Parker Foulke, a member of the Academy of Natural Sciences in Philadelphia, PA, on the farm of John Hopkins in Haddonfield, NJ. They were first described by Joseph Leidy, professor of anatomy at the University of Pennsylvania, who gave the animal the name *Hadrosaurus foulkii* in honor of Foulke, and who connected this discovery with the dinosaur skeleton that had been found earlier in Britain. The hadrosaur skeleton was assembled for display at the academy by Benjamin Waterhouse Hawkins. The missing bones were sculpted in plaster.

6662. Anatomy research institute was the Wistar Institute of Anatomy and Biology, which was established in Philadelphia, PA, on July 20, 1891, with a $20,000 gift from General Isaac Jones Wistar. The first building was dedicated on May 21, 1894.

6663. Taxidermy method of stuffing animals was devised by Carl Ethan Akeley in 1902. He mounted skins on specially constructed forms, lifelike and true in all details to the living animals. His first important work, "The Four Seasons," representing four groups of Virginia deer and their appropriate surroundings in spring, summer, autumn, and winter, was prepared for the Field Museum of Natural History, Chicago, IL.

6664. Formation of a new animal by transplantation was accomplished by Ethel Browne (later Ethel Browne Harvey) in 1909, when she was a graduate student at Columbia University in New York City. Working with freshwater polyps called hydra, she found that transplanting a tentacle into the midsection of a hydranth, or grafting mouth tissue of one hydranth into the midsection of another, could stimulate production of a new organism from parts of the host.

6665. Anthropology laboratory was the Laboratory of Anthropology, formally opened to the public on September 1, 1931, at Santa Fe, NM. Jesse Logan Nusbaum was in charge.

6666. Virus obtained in crystalline form was a plant virus, the tobacco mosaic virus, which was crystallized by Dr. Wendell Meredith Stanley at the Rockefeller Institute for Medical Research, Princeton, NJ. The research was reported in *Science* magazine on June 28, 1935. The first human virus to be crystallized was the poliomyelitis virus, which was crystallized by Dr. Carlton Everett Schwerdt of the Virus Laboratory, University of California, Berkeley. The achievement was announced on November 3, 1955, at the meeting of the National Academy of Sciences held at the California Institute of Technology, Pasadena, CA.

6667. Flea laboratory was opened on January 1, 1939, at the University of California's Hooper Foundation for Medical Research, San Francisco, CA. It was a flea-tight, rodent-tight, two-story concrete building, air-conditioned at a constant temperature. The first director was Dr. Karl Friedrich Meyer.

6668. Surrogate birth experiment with an animal resulted from experiments by Dr. Gregory Pincus of Clark University, Worcester, MA, conducted at Harvard University, Cambridge, MA, in November 1939 under the auspices of the Dazian and Josiah Macy, Jr., Foundation. Pincus removed an egg from the ovary of a female rabbit, fertilized it with a salt solution, and transferred it to the uterus of a second rabbit that acted as an "incubator." The second rabbit gave birth in October 1939. Pincus exhibited the baby rabbit on November 1, 1939, at the 12th annual Graduate Fortnight at the New York Academy of Medicine.

6669. Cloning of a mammalian cell was accomplished by Katherine K. Sanford (Katherine Sanford Mifflin) at the National Cancer Institute, Bethesda, MD, in March 1948. Using Strain L, a strain of cells derived from the connective tissue of a male mouse, she isolated and cultured in vitro a single cell, producing cloned fibroblasts after 929 attempts.

Dr. Katherine K. Sanford's L929 was the first pure cell line developed through cloning, paving the way for subsequent advances in biomedical research.

6670. Cloning experiment was conducted at the Institute for Cancer Research, Philadelphia, PA, by Robert Briggs and Thomas J. King. The researchers removed the nuclei from eggs of the frog species *Rana pipiens* and replaced them with nuclei from various parts of embryonic frogs. The majority of these altered eggs produced normal tadpoles.

6671. Discovery of different sleep states was announced on September 4, 1953, when the magazine *Science* published a report by physiologists Nathaniel Kleitman and Eugene Aserinsky of the University of Chicago, IL. Their study, for which they measured the eye movements of sleeping subjects, established the existence of rapid-eye-movement (REM) sleep, its occurrence in 90-minute cycles, and its connection to dreaming.

6672. Use of tobacco to produce cancer in laboratory animals took place at Memorial Sloan-Kettering Institute, New York, NY, where a team of researchers headed by Dr. Ernst Wynder applied components of cigarette smoke to the skin on a group of mice. Cancerous tumors developed in 44 percent of the mice. The results were published in December 1953 in *Cancer Research.*

6673. Virus separated into component parts which on reconstruction yielded a material as effective as it was in its original form was the tobacco virus, which causes a disease in tobacco and many other plants. The research was performed by Drs. Heinz Ludwig Fraenkel-Conrat and Robley Cook Williams of the Virus Laboratory of the University of California at Berkeley early in 1955. It was reported on June 10, 1955.

6674. Chromosomal abnormality linked to cancer was discovered in 1960 in Philadelphia, PA, by Dr. Peter Nowell of the University of Pennsylvania and Dr. David Hungerford of the Fox Chase Cancer Center. While analyzing the cells of patients with chronic myelogenous leukemia, a blood cancer, they observed that chromosome 22 lacked a segment of DNA.

6675. Isolation of a single gene from an organism is often credited to molecular biologist Jonathan Beckwith at Harvard Medical School, Cambridge, MA. He and his team announced in 1969 that they had isolated a lactose-controlling gene, called lacZ, from the bacterium *Escherichia coli*. Other colleagues give credit for the isolation of this gene to another Harvard researcher, Garret Ihler.

After announcing their achievement, Jonathan Beckwith and his colleagues held a press conference to express their concern with the potentially horrific consequences of genetic engineering.

6676. Recombinant DNA molecule was created in 1972 at Stanford University, Palo Alto, CA, by Janet Mertz, a graduate student working under biochemist Paul Berg. Using a restriction enzyme, EcoRI, as a chemical knife, she removed sections of DNA from two different species (a bacterial virus and a mammalian virus), then joined their ends together with another enzyme, ligase, to create an entirely new molecule of DNA.

6677. Artificial gene was produced in 1973 by Har Gobind Khorana at the Massachusetts Institute of Technology, Cambridge, MA. The gene, created in a series of replications using transfer-ribonucleic acid, was a 207-base-pair chain identical to a virus gene.

6678. Gene splicing (also known as recombinant DNA cloning) took place in March 1973. Herbert Boyer at the University of California, San Francisco, and Stanley Cohen and Annie Chang at Stanford University, Stanford, CA, created an entirely new organism by inserting a DNA molecule called a plasmid into a host bacterium, *Escherichia coli*. The plasmid contained viral and bacterial genes that cause resistance to antibiotics. The host bacterium acquired the same characteristic and passed it to all its descendants.

6679. Transgenic animal was a mouse that was born in 1980 in the laboratory of Frank Ruddle at Yale University, New Haven, CT. The mouse had originated as a fertilized egg that was removed from its mother, injected with a transfer gene derived from the herpes virus, and reimplanted in the mother's uterus to gestate. When born, all its cells contained the foreign gene. The term "transgenic" was coined by Ruddle.

6680. Isolation of embryonic stem cells in a mammal was achieved in 1981 by Gail Martin at the University of California at San Francisco, and independently by Martin Evans at the University of Cambridge in England, both of whom isolated stem cells from the embryos of mice. The term "stem cell" was coined by Martin.

6681. DNA chain polymerization was invented in 1983 by Kary B. Mullis, a staff chemist for the Cetus Corporation in Emeryville, CA. The DNA polymerase chain reaction enabled Mullis to replicate an entire chain of deoxyribonucleic acid (DNA) as many times as needed from a single original DNA strand. The technique had many practical applications in genetic engineering, human genome mapping, DNA fingerprinting, evolutionary science, and genetic diagnosis. Mullis won the 1993 Nobel Prize in chemistry for his work.

6682. Identification of the AIDS virus was announced by two scientific teams in March 1983. The human immune deficiency virus (HIV), the retrovirus that causes AIDS, was isolated and reported by Dr. Robert Gallo of the National Cancer Institute in Bethesda, MD, and by Dr. Luc Montagnier at the Institute Pasteur in Paris. AIDS is an abbreviation for acquired immunodeficiency syndrome.

6683. Genetically altered virus approved for use in a vaccine was approved by the Department of Agriculture on April 22, 1986. The virus was used in veterinary medicine to fight a form of swine herpes.

6684. Patent on an animal was awarded to Harvard University, Cambridge, MA, in April 1988. Developed by geneticists Philip Leder and Timothy A. Stewart, the animal was a genetically engineered "oncomouse" that was highly susceptible to breast cancer. The use of oncomice in testing anticancer therapies was intended to reduce the number of animals used in medical experimentation and to improve the accuracy of experimental results. E.I. du Pont de Nemours and Company, Wilmington, DE, had commercial rights to the animals and initially sold them for $50 each. Patents on nonhuman animals created by reproductive technologies were authorized by the federal government on April 16, 1987, making the United States the first nation in the world to allow applications for such patents.

6685. Bacterium to be discovered that was visible to the naked eye was found by scientists at the University of Indiana, Bloomington, IN. The organism, *Epulopiscium fishelsoni*, which lives in the gut of surgeonfish, was first identified in 1985 as a protozoan. Some of these organisms can grow to visible size. In a paper published in the March 18, 1993, issue of the journal *Nature*, Norman R. Pace and Esther R. Angert analyzed the creature's genetic material and proved it to be a bacterium of unprecented size—.015 inches across, or about the size of a period in a small-print book.

6686. Isolation of embryonic stem cells in a primate was announced in November 1995 by the University of Wisconsin, Madison, where molecular biologist James A. Thomson isolated and cultivated the stem cells of rhesus monkeys.

6687. Commercial DNA bank was founded in 1996 by GeneLink, Margate, NJ, a company owned by John R. DePhillipo and Dr. Richard Ricciardi, a microbiologist. GeneLink maintained a long-term repository at the University of North Texas Health Science Center in Fort Worth, TX, where DNA samples swabbed from the cheeks of recently deceased people were kept on ice at a cost of $175 to $295.

6688. Cloning of a primate from an embryo was announced on March 2, 1997, by M. Susan Smith and Donald Wolf of the Oregon Regional Primate Research Center, Beaverton, OR. Two rhesus monkeys were cloned by the process known as nuclear transfer, which produced two genetically identical monkeys from chromosomes extracted from a single monkey embryo.

6689. Ban on federal funding for human cloning research was imposed on March 4, 1997, by President William Jefferson Clinton. The ban followed the successful cloning of a sheep in Scotland and two rhesus monkeys in Oregon.

6690. Complete DNA sequencing of a free-living organism was achieved by a team led by J. Craig Venter of the Institute for Genomic Research in Gaithersburg, MD, and Hamilton O. Smith of the Johns Hopkins University School of Medicine, Baltimore, MD. In May 1997, the researchers announced that they had determined the complete genetic blueprint of *Hemophilus influenzae*, a bacterium that can cause human infections, including a form of meningitis. The organism's DNA was comprised of 1,830,137 base pairs, containing the coded instructions for 1,743 genes.

6691. Human embryonic stem cell lines were developed by Dr. John D. Gearhart and a team of researchers at the Johns Hopkins University, Baltimore, MD, using tissue taken from aborted human embryos. Stem cells are the basic, unspecialized cells from which all other cells in the body develop during the growth of a baby in the womb. The announcement of the discovery was made on July 25, 1997.

6692. Cultivation of human stem cells in a laboratory was achieved in 1998 by two separate teams of researchers, the first led by James A. Thomson at the University of Wisconsin, Madison, and the second by John D. Gearhart at the Johns Hopkins University, Baltimore, MD. Both teams were funded by Geron Corporation of Menlo Park, CA. The Wisconsin group succeeded in growing stem cells taken from blastocysts—fertilized eggs in the process of cell division—donated by couples undergoing fertility treatments. The Baltimore group used germ cells, the cells that become the individual's future eggs or sperm, taken from aborted fetuses.

6693. Genome sequencing of a multicellular organism was made by an international consortium of scientists from the federal government's National Human Genome Research Institute, Bethesda, MD, and other institutions. The organism, which was found to contain 19,000 genes in some 100 million DNA base pairs, was the nematode *Caenorhabditis elegans*, also known as the roundworm. The findings were announced on December 11, 1998.

6694. Plant DNA bank was the Tropical Plant DNA Bank, opened in 1999 at the Center for Tropical Plant Conservation at Fairchild Tropical Botanical Gardens, Coral Gables, FL, as a joint project with Florida International University. The bank collects, stores, analyzes, and shares DNA samples from tropical plants worldwide, including more than 1,000 species of palms.

6695. Complete sequencing of a human chromosome was announced on December 1, 1999, by researchers in the Human Genome Project, who had determined the complete sequence of 679 genes in chromosome 22, the second smallest of the human autosomes. Research was led by Dr. Francis Collins, director of the National Genome Research Institute at the National Institutes of Health, Bethesda, MD. The project involved an international consortium of research institutions, including the Sanger Centre near Cambridge, England; Keio University in Tokyo; the department of chemistry and biochemistry at the University of Oklahoma, OK; and the Genome Sequencing Center at Washington University School of Medicine, St. Louis, MO.

6696. Genome sequencing of a plant was published on December 14, 2000. The plant was *Arabidopsis thaliana,* a member of the mustard family. The project was made by the Arabidopsis Genome Initiative, an international team of researchers.

6697. State to approve funding for biomedical research using stem cells derived from human embryos was California, whose voters approved Proposition 71 on November 2, 2004. The plan authorized the state to sell bonds in order to raise $3 billion for stem cell research, including funds to establish the California Institute for Regenerative Medicine. The sale of bonds was deferred until the courts could hear lawsuits brought by people who opposed the use of human embryos for research purposes.

6698. Genome sequencing and analysis of a bird was published on December 9, 2004, by the International Chicken Genome Sequencing Consortium and the National Human Genome Research Institute in Bethesda, MD. The bird was *Gallus gallus*, also known as the red jungle fowl, to which chickens are related. According to the research, G. gallus has 1 billion DNA base pairs containing between 20,000 and 23,000 genes.

6699. Experiment that showed separate brain sites involved in processing nouns and verbs was conducted at Harvard Medical School by psychology professor Alfonso Caramazza. He used an MRI scanner to examine the brain functions of ten volunteers while they recited phrases containing either nouns or verbs. The results, published in January 2005, identified specific brain sites that are responsible for handling these different parts of speech.

6700. Neanderthal skeleton reconstructed from actual bones and with articulated joints was put together by anthropologists G. J. Sawyer of the American Museum of Natural History, New York City, and Blaine Maley of Washington University, St. Louis, MO. They made casts of a Neanderthal skeleton found in 1909 in France, with missing parts supplemented by casts from other individuals. A report on the skeleton was published on March 11, 2005.

6701. Comprehensive comparison of the human and chimpanzee genomes was announced on August 31, 2005 by the Chimpanzee Sequencing and Analysis Consortium, an international research team. Their results showed that 96 percent of human DNA is also present in chimps. The lead author was Tarjei S. Mikkelsen of the Massachusetts Institute of Technology.

6702. Chimpanzee fossils to be discovered were three teeth estimated at half a million years old. They were found in Kenya by two American scientists, Nina G. Jablonski and Sally McBrearty. The discovery was announced on September 1, 2005.

6703. State to disburse funding for biomedical research using stem cells derived from human embryos was New Jersey. On December 16, 2005, the state's Commission on Science and Technology made grants totalling $5 million to 17 stem cell research projects, including three that derived stem cells from human embryos. The grantees included universities and private companies.

6704. Proof that a human brain can restore impaired functions by growing new networks of nerve fibers was collected by a team of researchers headed by Henning Voss and Nicholas Schiff at Cornell University's Weill Medical College in New York City and was published on July 3, 2006, in the *Journal of Clinical Investigation*. The evidence was furnished by Terry Wallis of Mountain View, AR, who spent 19 years in a minimally conscious state after suffering a traumatic brain injury in a car wreck. Nerve cells in his brain slowly developed new connections that eventually formed a network of fibers, enabling him to regain some of his powers of speech and motion.

6705. Regeneration of spinal cord connections in animals was achieved by John D. Houle of Drexel University, Philadelphia, PA, and Jerry Silver of Case Western Reserve University, Cleveland, OH. They severed the spinal cords of rats who consequently lost the use of their forelimbs. Nerves from the animals' legs were then partially transplanted across the severed spinal nerve endings. In rats who received an enzyme that destroys scar tissue, the transplanted nerves grew neural connections, enabling the forelimbs to regain some function. The results of the experiment were published on July 12, 2006.

Mathematics

6706. Mathematical theory of economic decision-making was the theory of games, described in 1944 by the Hungarian-American mathematician John von Neumann (born Janos von Neumann) of the Institute for Advance Study, Princeton, NJ, and the German-American economist Oskar Morgenstern in their book *Theory of Games and Economic Behavior*. Games theory provided a theoretical framework for applying statistical logic to the choice of strategies in any competitive situation, including the marketplace.

6707. Quantum theory of electromagnetic radiation that was successful was quantum electrodynamics, developed in 1948 by two American physicists, Richard Phillips Feynman of Cornell University, Ithaca, NY, and Julian Seymour Schwinger of Harvard University, Cambridge, MA, together with a Japanese physicist, Tomonaga Shinichiro. They shared the 1965 Nobel Prize in physics for their work. Quantum electrodynamics describes the quantum properties of electromagnetic radiation, especially light, and its interaction with electrically charged particles.

6708. Factoring of a 100-digit number was accomplished on October 11, 1988, when Mark Manasse of the Systems Research Center of the Digital Equipment Corporation in Palo Alto, CA, and Arjen Lenstra of the University of Chicago announced that they had succeeded in fully factoring a huge number, 11 to the 104th power plus 1. They used the "quadratic sieve" factoring method invented by Carl Pomerance of the University of Georgia at Athens. The work was calculated by a network of hundreds of computers in the United States, Europe, and Australia.

6709. Mathematical proof of Fermat's last theorem was announced in June 1993 by mathematician Andrew Wiles of Princeton University, Princeton, NJ, at the Isaac Newton Institute in Cambridge, England. Fermat's last theorem, proposed in 1637 by Pierre Fermat, is an extension of the Pythagorean theorem. It states that no number raised to any power higher than two can be the sum of two other numbers raised to like powers. Mathematicians seeking to prove the deceptively simple theorem, the most famous unsolved problem in mathematics, had been frustrated for centuries. Wiles's 200-page proof was so specialized that only a few dozen mathematicians in the world could understand it. It was published in the May 1994 issue of *Annals of Mathematics*.

6710. Encyclopedia of integer sequences was published in 1995 by Neil J. A. Sloane of AT&T Bell Laboratories in Murray Hill, NJ, and Simon Plouffe of the University of Quebec in Montreal. Each entry in the encyclopedia gave the first dozen or more numbers from a particular sequence, the sequence's name, a mathematical formula showing how to obtain successive terms, and citations indicating where the sequence had appeared in the mathematical or scientific literature.

6711. Patent on a number was granted by the Patent Office to mathematician Roger Schlafly of Real Software, Soquel, CA, in 1995. The number was nearly 150 digits long. It was useful in speeding up mathematical calculations performed within the Diffie-Hellman public-key data encryption system.

6712. Theory of fair division was published by political scientist Steven Brams of New York University, New York City, and mathematician Alan Taylor of Union College, Schenectady, NY, in the January 1995 issue of *American Mathematical Monthly*. Their technique made it possible to fairly divide anything—from cakes to war reparations—even among parties that strongly disagree.

Organizations

6713. Science society was the Boston Philosophical Society, which was founded by Increase Mather in 1683 in Boston, MA. He wrote that it was "a philosophical society of agreeable gentlemen who met once a fortnight for a conference upon improvements in philosophy and additions to the stores of natural history." The first one of importance was the American Philosophical Society, organized in 1743 in Philadelphia, PA, by Benjamin Franklin. On May 14, 1743, he issued a broadside, "A Proposal for Promoting Useful Knowledge Among the British Plantations in America," as a prospectus. The organization was an outgrowth of the Junto, a Philadelphia society that he had organized in 1727.

6714. Chemistry society in the world was the Chemical Society of Philadelphia, founded in Philadelphia, PA, in 1792 by James Woodhouse.

6715. National geology society was the American Geological Society, founded in 1819 at Yale College, New Haven, CT. The society functioned until 1828. The first president was William Maclure.

6716. Statistical society of importance was the American Statistical Association, organized on November 27, 1839, in Boston, MA, "to collect, preserve and diffuse statistical information in the different departments of human knowledge." The first president was Richard Fletcher.

6717. National science society was the American Association for the Advancement of Science, organized on September 20, 1848, in Philadelphia, PA, for the purpose of advancing science in every way. The first president was William Charles Redfield.

6718. National science institute was the National Academy of Sciences, incorporated by act of Congress and approved by President Abraham Lincoln on March 3, 1863, with the stipulation that "the Academy shall, whenever called upon by any department of the Government, investigate, examine, experiment, and report upon any subject of science or art, the actual expense of such investigations, examinations, experiments, and reports to be paid from appropriations which may be made for the purpose, but the Academy shall receive no compensation whatever for any services to the Government of the United States." The Academy's first president was Alexander Dallas Bache. The first woman elected to the Academy was Dr. Florence Rena Sabin, elected on April 29, 1925. At the time she was professor of histology at Johns Hopkins University, Baltimore, MD.

6719. National social science society was the American Social Science Association, founded in 1865 and incorporated by act of Congress on January 28, 1899. One of its departments, organized in 1912, was the National Institute of Social Sciences, whose first president was Hamilton Wright Mabie. Since 1926, when the federal charter was amended, the National Institute of Social Sciences has operated as the main organization.

6720. National philology society was the American Philological Association, organized in New York City on November 13, 1868, to promote the advancement and diffusion of philological knowledge. The first convention was held on July 27, 1869, in Poughkeepsie, NY, and the first president was William Dwight Whitney.

6721. National chemistry organization was the American Chemical Society, organized in New York City on April 20, 1876. The first president was John William Draper.

6722. National archeology organization was the Archaeological Institute of America, which was founded on May 10, 1879, at Boston, MA, to promote and direct archeological research. The first president was Charles Eliot Norton.

6723. Economics association was the American Economic Association, founded on September 9, 1885, in Saratoga, NY. The purpose of the association was to encourage "economic research and freedom of economic discussion." The first president was Francis Amasa Walker.

6724. National physics association was the American Physical Society for the advancement and diffusion of the knowledge of physics, formed on May 20, 1899, at Columbia University, New York City, by physicists from 17 institutions. The first president was Henry Augustus Rowland. The society admitted 59 fellows the first year.

6725. National political science association was the American Political Science Association, founded in New Orleans, LA, on December 30, 1903, for the encouragement of the scientific study of politics, public law, administration, and diplomacy. The first president was Professor Frank Johnson Goodnow.

6726. National sociology society was the American Sociological Society, organized in Baltimore, MD, in December 1905, for the "encouragement of sociological research and discussion, and the promotion of intercourse between persons engaged in the scientific study of society." The first president was Lester Frank Ward. The first annual meeting was held in Providence, RI, on December 27–29, 1906.

6727. National research society was the National Research Council, established in 1916 by the National Academy of Sciences at the request of President Woodrow Wilson "to bring into co-operation existing governmental, educational, industrial and other research organizations, with the object of encouraging the investigation of natural phenomena, the increased use of scientific research in the development of American industries, the employment of scientific methods in strengthening the national defense, and such other applications of science as will promote the national security and welfare." The original membership numbered 44, including 10 officers of the federal government assigned by President Wilson. The council held its first meeting on September 20, 1916, in New York City.

Physical Sciences

6728. Blowpipe was invented in 1801 by Professor Robert Hare of Philadelphia, PA, who called it a "hydrostatic blowpipe." He reported his discovery to the Chemical Society of Philadelphia in *A Memoir of the Supply and Application of the Blow-Pipe, Containing an Account of the new method of supplying the Blow-Pipe either with common air or oxygen gas; and also of the effects of the intense heat produced by the combustion of the hydrogen and oxygen gases.*

6729. Helium plant was the United States Production Plant, Fort Worth, TX, completed in April 1921 under the cognizance of the Navy Department. It was operated by the Linde Air Products Company using its own process. The Bureau of Mines assumed the supervision of this plant on July 1, 1925, and operated it until 1929, when it was closed on account of insufficient gas supply.

6730. Cyclotron spiral atom smasher was developed by Professor Ernest Orlando Lawrence at the University of California, Berkeley, CA, in 1934 to study the nuclear structure of the atom. A magnetic whirling machine using an 80-ton magnet produced 10-million- to 15-million-volt rays and sent a stream of high-energy bullets from the nuclei of helium gas atoms or alpha particles in the form of a beam of light a foot from the machine.

6731. Spectrophotometer was invented by Professor Arthur Cobb Hardy of Wellesley, MA, who received a patent on January 8, 1935, on a "photometric apparatus." This electronic device detected 2 million different shades of color and produced for permanent records a chart of each color. The patent was assigned to the General Electric Company, Schenectady, NY, which sold the first machine on May 24, 1935.

6732. Electron microscope was invented by Dr. Vladimir Kosma Zworykin of the RCA Laboratory, Camden, NJ, and was first publicly demonstrated by Dr. Ladislaus Morton on April 20, 1940, at the American Philosophical Society convention in Philadelphia, PA. The instrument was 10 feet high, weighed about 1,000 pounds, and magnified up to 100,000 diameters.

6733. Betatron was built at the University of Illinois, Urbana, IL, by Professor Donald William Kerst and placed in operation on July 15, 1940. It had an output energy of 2.3 million electron volts. The betatron is a machine to accelerate electrons by the use of a magnetic field and can produce either a sharp beam of high-energy X rays or a free beam of high-energy electrons.

6734. Synchrotron was constructed by the General Electric Research Laboratory, Schenectady, NY, by Dr. Herbert Chermside Pollock and Willem Fredrik Westendorp, and installed at the Radiation Laboratory, University of California, Berkeley, CA, where it released its full energy on January 17, 1949. It was invented by Edwin Mattison McMillan of the university. It weighed about eight tons and had a betatron-type magnet and accelerated electrons that had negative charges.

6735. Nuclear reactor privately operated was the Raleigh Research Reactor, Raleigh, NC, placed in operation on September 5, 1953, by the North Carolina State College of Agriculture and Engineering and the University of North Carolina. Completely independent of the Atomic Energy Commission and other federal government financial support, the reactor was free of secret or classified data and was available without restriction to the general public for observation and to students and staff for study and research.

6736. Nuclear reactor patent was granted on May 17, 1955, to Enrico Fermi of Santa Fe, NM, and Leo Szilard of Chicago, IL, assigned to the United States of America as represented by the Atomic Energy Commission.

6737. Instrument for observing radiation in total darkness that was nonelectronic was the Evaporograph, built by Baird Associates, Cambridge, MA, an affiliate of the American Research and Development Corporation, and announced to the public on February 15, 1956. It cost $9,500 and was housed in a cabinet 18 by 14 by 11 inches. It was designed to observe radiation differences corresponding to temperature variations of one to several thousand degrees Fahrenheit.

6738. Nuclear reactor for research and development was part of the Plutonium Recycle Program conducted by the General Electric Company for the Atomic Energy Commission at the Hanford Atomic Products Operation, Richland, WA. It reached criticality on November 25, 1960. It was designed to determine the feasibility of plutonium-containing fuels for power reactors. The use of plutonium-239 as an enrichment material instead of uranium-235 was intended to permit the operation of enriched-fuel reactors without dependence on expensive uranium isotope separation facilities, to increase the amount of energy recovered from a given amount of raw uranium, and to provide a way of utilizing for peaceful purposes plutonium not needed for weapons use.

6739. Superconducting motor using high-temperature superconductors was developed by Reliance Electric of Cleveland, OH, and American Superconductor of Watertown, MA, and was first demonstrated in 1991. Reliance built the motor with coils of flexible wire that American Superconductor fashioned from a superconducting bismuth compound. The prototype produced 25 watts of power.

6740. Molecular measuring machine was announced in 1995 by physicist Clayton Teague of the National Institute of Standards and Technology in Gaithersburg, MD. The machine could measure distances as large as a millimeter or as small as the width of a few atoms. It combined a scanning tunneling microscope with a laser interferometer that allowed researchers to track the position of the microscope tip with extreme accuracy to within 20 to 40 nanometers (billionths of a meter).

Discoveries

6741. Universal constant in physics to be measured by American scientists was *C*, the speed of light, 186,282 miles per second, which was calculated with high precision in 1881 by physicists Albert A. Michelson and Edward W. Morley of the Case Institute of Technology in Cleveland, OH. The "Michelson-Morley experiment," one of the most famous in the history of physics, used an optical interferometer invented by Michelson to detect the existence of the "luminiferous ether," a hypothetical universal medium that was thought to be necessary for the transmission of light waves. No ether was detected, but the experiment did determine the speed of light with unprecedented accuracy. It was Albert Einstein's determination in 1905 that the speed of light is a universal constant.

6742. Helium in natural gas was discovered in 1905 by Professor Hamilton Perkins Cady and Dr. David Ford McFarland of the University of Kansas. They tested the residuum from a gas well at Dexter, KS, and found that it had a 1.84 percent helium content.

6743. Heavy water to be identified was discovered by Harold Clayton Urey in the autumn of 1931 and subsequently named deuterium. The first public scientific announcement of the discovery was made at a meeting of the American Association for the Advancement of Science in New Orleans, LA, on December 29, 1931. Heavy water is a water molecule that contains a hydrogen atom with an extra neutron in its nucleus.

6744. Antimatter to be observed was discovered in 1932 by Dr. Carl David Anderson at the California Institute of Technology, Pasadena, CA. While working with cosmic rays, he noticed a line that curved in the wrong direction, a trailing vapor in a "cloud expansion chamber." He identified it as a positively charged particle with the same mass and energy as the electron, which has a negative charge, and gave it the name "positron." Anderson, who received a Nobel Prize in physics in 1936, was also the co-discoverer in 1936 of the meson, a particle intermediate in mass between the proton and electron.

6745. Radioactive substance produced synthetically was radium E, made by Dr. John Jacob Livingood of the University of California, Berkeley, CA, on February 4, 1936. Radium E is one of the intermediary products in the slow deterioration of radium. Synthetic radium E was obtained through the bombardment of common inert bismuth with deuterons at an energy of approximately 5.5 million volts. Radiobismuth made synthetically is theoretically identical with natural radium E.

6746. Element created artificially was technetium, created in 1937 by Ernest O. Lawrence at the University of California at Berkeley. The element had not yet been found in nature. It was created by bombarding molybdenum with nuclei of deuterium in a cyclotron. The resulting sample was sent for analysis to Italy, where it was identified by mineralogist Carlo Perrier and physicist Emilio Segrè as an element with the atomic weight of 43. The name technetium was derived from the Greek word for "artificial."

6747. Plutonium (Element 94, symbol Pu, atomic weight 242) was discovered in 1940 at the University of California at Berkeley, CA, by Dr. Glenn Theodore Seaborg and Dr. Edwin Mattison McMillan. They received the 1951 Nobel Prize in chemistry for their discovery.

6748. Self-sustaining nuclear chain reaction demonstration was made on December 2, 1942, by Enrico Fermi and his staff at the Metallurgical Laboratory of the University of Chicago, Chicago, IL, before approximately 40 persons. Atomic particles known as neutrons, spontaneously released by atoms of metallic uranium or uranium oxide, embedded in a suitable pattern throughout a block of graphite, were permitted to collide with neighboring atoms of uranium or uranium oxide, causing these neighboring atoms to split. The split atoms released additional neutrons, which caused further reactions with still other uranium atoms, and so on at a rapidly increasing rate.

6749. Quark to be observed was discovered by Jerome Friedman and Henry Kendall of the Massachusetts Institute of Technology, Cambridge, MA, and Richard Taylor of the Stanford Linear Accelerator Center (SLAC), Stanford, CA, during experiments performed at the SLAC between 1967 and 1973. They found unexpectedly large numbers of electrons being scattered at large angles--clear evidence for hard subparticles, called quarks, within protons. The existence of quarks, the building blocks of subatomic particles, was first proposed in the early 1960s by Murray Gell-Mann of the California Institute of Technology, Pasadena, CA, who took the name from James Joyce's linguistically playful novel *Finnegans Wake*. Friedman, Kendall, and Taylor received the 1990 Nobel Prize in physics for their work.

6750. Fullerenes to be observed were identified by the American chemists Richard E. Smalley and Robert F. Curl, Jr., of Rice University, Houston, TX, in 1985. They are carbon molecules in the shape of closed spheres or cylinders. The first to be discovered was a large molecule of 60 carbon atoms in the shape of a truncated icosahedron, the basic shape of a geodesic sphere. It was produced as a byproduct of experiments in which graphite was vaporized using a laser. Smalley and Curl gave the molecule the name "buckminsterfullerene" (usually shortened to "fullerene") in honor of Buckminster Fuller, the inventor of the geodesic dome. Fullerenes are produced in nature as a result of lightning strikes. Scientists refer to the spherical type as "buckyballs" and to the cylindrical type as "buckytubes."

6751. Superconducting material that operated at relatively high temperatures was developed in February 1987 by research teams under Paul Chu of the University of Houston, Houston, TX, and Maw-Kuen Wu at the University of Alabama, Huntsville, AL. Previously, the operation of superconductors required frigid temperatures near absolute zero that were hard to reach and maintain. Searching for superconductors that could perform at higher temperatures, the researchers mixed yttrium, barium, copper, and oxygen to form a compound that lost its electrical resistance at 90 degrees K (-297 degrees F), an unprecedentedly high temperature. The discovery was officially reported in the March 2, 1988, issue of *Physical Review Letters*.

6752. Physical manipulation of individual atoms was achieved by Donald M. Eigler and Erhard K. Schweizer of the IBM Almaden Research Center, San Jose, CA. In January 1990, it was announced that the two had used a scanning tunneling microscope to position 35 individual atoms of xenon on a nickel surface to spell the initials "IBM." A photograph of the initials clearly showed "bumps" indicating the presence of individual atoms.

6753. Teleportation experiment in which a range of physical properties was instantaneously transferred from one physical entity to another without apparently crossing the intervening space was demonstrated successfully by researchers on October 23, 1998, at the California Institute of Technology in Pasadena, CA. A team led by physics professor Jeff Kimble replicated the quantum properties of a beam of light in another light beam across a laboratory bench, taking advantage of the quantum property known as entanglement, in which photons or other particles somehow share characteristics and fates even though they may exist at opposite ends of the universe.

Publications

6754. Paleontology report was prepared by the Reverend Cotton Mather in 1713. The subject was three teeth and a 17-foot thigh bone that had been unearthed in Albany, NY, in 1705, and which Mather thought to be the remains of a race of giants. The report was read before the Royal Society of London in 1714. On the basis of his scientific work *Curiosa Americana*, Mather was elected a member of the Royal Society, the first American to receive this distinction.

6755. Botanical report on plant hybridization was authored by the minister and scientist Cotton Mather of Boston, MA, and published on September 24, 1716. He described the hybridization of Indian corn and squash.

6756. Arithmetic book printed in America was James Hodder's *Arithmetick; or that necessary art made most easy. Being explained in a way familiar to the capacity of any that desire to learn it in a little time*, printed by James Franklin, Boston, MA, in 1719 for S. Phillips. It had originally been published in London in 1661.

6757. Arithmetic book by an American-born author was Isaac Greenwood's *Arithmetick—Vulgar and Decimal with the Application Thereof to a Variety of Cases in Trade and Commerce*, which was published in 1729 in Boston, MA, by S. Kneeland and T. Green for T. Hancock at the Sign of the Bible and Three Crowns in Ann Street. It contained 158 pages, four pages of index, and four pages of advertisements.

6758. Algebra book was *Arithmetic, or the art of ciphering, according to the coins, measures and weights of New York, together with a short treatise on algebra*, a Dutch textbook by Pieter Venema, printed by John Peter Zenger in 1730 in New York City. The Dutch title was *Arithmetica of Cyffer-Konst, Volgens de Munten Maten en Gewigten, te Nieu York, gebruykelyk als mede een kort ontwerp van de Algebra*.

6759. Logic book was William Brattle's *Compendium Logicae Secundum Principia, D. Renati Cartesii Plerumque Efformatum, et Catechistice Propositum*, published in Boston, MA, in 1735. The text was in Latin and contained 64 pages.

6760. Slide rule book was Thomas Abel's *Subtensial Plain Trigonometry, Wrought with a Sliding-Rule, with Gunter's Lines: and also arithmetically in a very concise manner. And this method apply'd to Navigation and Surveying, to which is added, 1. Mensuration of masons work, 2. A solution of rota, or Aristotle's wheel. 3. A brief discourse upon gravity*, printed in 1761 by Andrew Stuart, Philadelphia, PA. It contained 86 pages and seven folding plates.

6761. Chemistry textbook was Benjamin Rush's *Syllabus of a Course of Lectures on Chemistry*, published in 1770 in Philadelphia, PA.

6762. Engineering book was a translation of Louis André de la Mamie de Clairac's *L'Ingénieur de Compagne; or Field Engineer*. It contained 256 pages and a variety of copperplates. It was translated by Major Lewis Nicola and was published in 1776 by Robert Aitken, Philadelphia, Pa.

6763. Geography book was Jedidiah Morse's *Geography Made Easy, being a short but comprehensive system of that useful and agreeable science*, a 214-page duodecimo published in 1784 in New Haven, CT, by Meigs, Bowen and Dana.

6764. Botany book by an American-born author and printed in this country was *Arbustrum Americanum; the American Grove, or an alphabetical catalogue of forest trees and shrubs, natives of the American United States . . . also some hints of their uses in medicines, dyes and domestic economy*, 174 pages, by Humphry Marshall of Chester County, PA, published in 1785 by Joseph Crukshank, Philadelphia, PA.

6765. Algebra book by an American-born author was Nicholas Pike's *A New and Complete System of Arithmetic, composed for the use of the citizens of the United States*, published in 1788 by John Mycall, Newburyport, MA. It contained 512 pages, of which 39 were devoted to algebra.

6766. Chemistry laboratory manual was James Woodhouse's *Young Chemist's Pocket Companion*, a 56-page book that contained about 100 experiments. It was published in 1797 in Philadelphia, PA.

6767. Geology book of importance was *Observations on the Geology of the United States*, which was read by William Maclure on January 20, 1809 before the American Philosophical Society. It was published in revised form in 1817 in Philadelphia, PA, and contained the first chart of United States territory that divided the land into rock types. It was the first true geological map of any part of North America and one of the world's earliest geological maps. Maclure was a wealthy businessman and amateur geologist who emigrated from Scotland and became a citizen in 1796. He is considered the first American geologist of note.

6768. Mineralogy journal was the *American Mineralogical Journal*, founded by Archibald Bruce. The first number was printed in New York City in January 1810. This was followed by three other issues, the last of which appeared in 1814. These four numbers, comprising 270 pages, constitute the first and only volume that was published.

6769. Chemistry magazine was the *Memories of the Columbian Chemical Society of Philadelphia*, which was printed by Isaac Peirce, 3 South Fourth Street, Philadelphia, PA, in 1813–14. The first volume consisted of 221 pages. The society was founded in 1811.

6770. Mineralogy textbook was *An Elementary Treatise on Mineralogy, being an introduction to the study of these sciences, and designed for the use of pupils,—for persons attending lectures on these subjects,--and as a companion for travellers in the United States of America*, by Parker Cleaveland, professor of mathematics and natural philosophy at Bowdoin College. It was published in 1816 by Cummings and Hilliard, Boston, MA, and printed by Hilliard and Metcalf at the University Press, Cambridge, MA. The book contained 668 pages and six illustrated plates.

6771. Geology textbook was *The Index to the Geology of the Northern States*, by Amos Eaton, which was published in 1818 in Leicester, MA.

6772. Science journal was the *American Journal of Science and Art*, printed in New York City and first issued in July 1818. It was edited by Benjamin Silliman. The first volume of four numbers contained 448 pages.

6773. Entomology book was Thomas Say's *American Entomology, or Descriptions of the Insects of North America*, three volumes, published in Philadelphia, PA, by Samuel Augustus Mitchell. The first volume was published in 1824, the second in 1825, and the third in 1828. Each contained 18 plates.

6774. Fireworks book was *A System of Pyrotechny, comprehending the theory and practice with the application of chemistry, designed for exhibition and for war, adapted to the military and naval officer, the man of science and the artificer*. The book contained 612 pages, including a 44-page introduction. It was written by James Cutbush, acting professor of chemistry and mineralogy at the U.S. Military Academy, and was published by Clara F. Cutbush in Philadelphia, PA, in 1825.

6775. Magazine for mechanics was *The American Mechanics' Magazine*, "containing useful original matter, on subjects connected with manufactures, the arts, and sciences; as well as selections from the most approved domestic and foreign journals," first published in New York City by J. V. Seaman on February 5, 1825. From 1826 to 1828 its title was

The Franklin Journal and American Mechanics' Magazine, and afterwards *The Journal of the Franklin Institute*.

6776. Astronomical observations book was James Melville Gillis's *Astronomical Observations made at the Naval Observatory, Washington, under Orders of the Honorable Secretary of the Navy, Dated August 13, 1838*. It contained 671 pages and was a catalog of 1,248 stars. It was printed in Washington, DC.

6777. Electricity journal was *The Electro-Magnetic and Mechanics Intelligencer*, which appeared on January 18, 1840. It was printed in New York City on a press "propelled by electro-magnetism." The editor of the magazine and the inventor of the electrical printing press was Thomas Davenport.

6778. Astronomy magazine presenting a popular exposition of astronomy was *The Sidereal Messenger*, published by Ormsby MacKnight Mitchel, editor and director of the Cincinnati Observatory. It cost $3 a year. The first issue was published in July 1846 by Derby Bradley and Company, Cincinnati, OH, and consisted of eight pages. Publication ceased in October 1848.

6779. Mechanics textbook was *The Elements of Analytical Mechanics*, 445 pages, by William Holmes Chambers Bartlett, professor of natural and experimental philosophy at the U.S. Military Academy, West Point, NY, published by A.S. Barnes and Company, New York City, in 1853.

6780. Gas journal was the *American Gas-Light Journal*, a monthly devoted to light, water supply, and sewerage, published by John B. Murray and Company, New York City, at $3 a year. The first issue, dated July 1, 1859, contained 16 pages. It listed 183 gaslight companies in the United States and 5 in Canada. The second issue, dated August 1, 1859, was larger in size and was described as the "Representative of Light, Water, and the Public Health." In 1917 the name was changed to *American Gas Engineering Journal* and in 1921 to *American Gas Journal*.

6781. Entomology journal devoted to applied entomology was the *Practical Entomologist*, the first issue of which was published in Philadelphia, PA, in October 1865 by the Entomological Society of Philadelphia (later known as the American Entomological Society). The original editors were Ezra Townsend Cresson, Augustus Radcliffe Grote, and James W. McAllister. The journal ceased publication after two years.

6782. Popular science magazine to report news of laboratory and workshop developments in popular terms was *Popular Science Monthly*, published by D. Appleton and Company, New York City, and first issued in May 1872. The first editor was Edward Livingston Youmans. The monthly contained 128 pages and sold for 50 cents. Some of the articles in the first issue were "Early Superstitions of Medicine," "The Study of Sociology," "The Causes of Dyspepsia," "Disinfection and Disinfectants," and "Science and Immortality."

6783. Economics journal was the *Quarterly Journal of Economics*, published in Boston, MA, for Harvard University. The first number appeared in October 1886.

6784. Geography magazine was *National Geographic*, founded in October 1888 by the National Geographic Society, Washington, DC. Alexander Graham Bell, an early editor of the magazine, originated the idea of paying famous explorers to write personal accounts of their exploits.

6785. Oil journal was the *Oil Investors' Journal*, a semimonthly whose first issue was published on May 24, 1902, at Beaumont, TX. Holland S. Reavis was the founder and editor. The first issue contained 16 pages. The subscription price was $1 a year. In 1910, it became the *Oil and Gas Journal*.

6786. Radio magazine was *Modern Electrics*, first published in April 1908 by Hugo Gernsback in New York City. The first issue contained 36 pages. The subscription price was $1 a year.

6787. Television magazine was *Television, America's First Television Journal*, first published in June 1928 by the Television Publishing Company, New York City. It contained 32 pages plus cover and sold for 35 cents a copy.

Space

6788. Rocket flight using liquid fuel was made on March 16, 1926, at Auburn, MA, under the direction of Professor Robert Hutchins Goddard. Pressure was produced internally by an outside pressure tank, and after launching by an alcohol heater on the rocket.

The rocket traversed 184 feet in 2.5 seconds, moving along the trajectory at about 60 miles an hour. The flight was reported to the Smithsonian Institution on May 5, 1926. As early as 1920, Goddard, working under a grant from Clark University, Worcester, MA, had demonstrated the lifting force of rockets using liquid oxygen and ether.

6789. Rocket to break the sound barrier was Rocket No. 4, flown on September 9, 1934, at Marine Park, Staten Island, New York City, by the American Rocket Society. It climbed 400 feet and traveled 1,600 feet horizontally, reaching a speed of 700 miles per hour.

6790. Radar signal to the moon was beamed by the Army Signal Corps on January 10, 1946, from the Evans Signal Laboratories, Belmar, NJ. The experiment was supervised by Lieutenant Colonel John H. De Witt. An echo was received 2.4 seconds later that consisted of a 180-cycle note of a quarter-second duration.

6791. Rocket to attain a 100-mile altitude was a captured German V-2 rocket, fired on July 30, 1946, from the White Sands Proving Ground, NM. It descended 69 miles north of the launching platform, having attained an altitude of 104 miles.

6792. Rocket to reach outer space was a two-stage rocket consisting of a WAC Corporal set in the nose of a captured German V-2. It was fired on February 24, 1949, from the White Sands Proving Ground, NM, by a team of scientists under Dr. Wernher von Braun. It reached an altitude of 250 miles.

6793. Rocket launched from Cape Canaveral in Florida was launched on July 24, 1950, by the U.S. armed forces and the General Electric Company. The rocket, called the Bumper 2, was a two-stage vehicle. The base, a V-2 missile, fired a WAC Corporal upper-stage rocket to an altitude of 400 kilometers.

6794. Rocket-driven sled on rails was tested on March 19, 1954, by Air Force Lieutenant Colonel John Paul Stapp, chief of the Aero Medical Field Laboratory of the Holloman Air Development Center at the Holloman Air Force Base, Alamogordo, NM. It was known as the "abrupt deceleration vehicle." It was designed by Northrop Aircraft to determine the effect upon fliers of bailing out at very high altitudes at supersonic speeds. The sled was propelled by six rockets at 421 miles per hour, which was eventually increased to over 3,000 miles per hour. It moved along heavy rails mounted in concrete and was halted by water scooped in vents in the bottom of the sled. The water trough was 5 feet wide and 18 inches deep.

6795. Space cabin simulator was a hermetically sealed cabin with equipment that supplied oxygen, removed waste products by chemical means, and recirculated body moisture to cool the cabin's temperature. It was used at the Air Force School of Aviation Medicine at Randolph Air Force Base, TX. The cabin simulated the conditions that an astronaut would meet in the sealed cabin of a rocket ship in space. The first person to spend 24 hours in the cabin, living in outer-space conditions, was Dalton F. Smith of New Orleans, LA, an aeromedical technician, who was observed through glass ports from 3 P.M. on March 31, 1956, to 3 P.M. on April 1.

6796. Radar signal bounced off the sun was transmitted on April 7, 1959, at Stanford University, Stanford, CA, by Professor Von Russel Eshleman, Lieutenant Colonel Robert Charles Barthle, and Dr. Philip Benjamin Gallagher, who used a 40,000-watt transmitter. The signals reached the sun's corona about a half million miles above the visible part of the sun. They required 1,000 seconds for transmission in both directions. The signals consisted of a series of dots and dashes that were detected by an electronic computer even though they were much weaker than the radio noise from the sun.

6797. Animals to survive a space flight were Able and Baker, two one-pound female monkeys, one a rhesus, the other a spider monkey, who survived a 15-minute flight in separate containers in the nose cone of a Jupiter rocket launched on May 28, 1959, from Cape Canaveral, FL. The cone was shot 300 miles into space and was recovered about 90 minutes later off the island of Antigua, about 1,500 miles away, by Navy frogmen from the tug *Kiowa*. A previous attempt made on December 13, 1958, had been unsuccessful.

6798. Animal fired into space to orbit the earth was Enos, a 37.5-pound five-year-old male chimpanzee, sent aloft at 1:28 P.M. on November 29, 1961, from Cape Canaveral, FL, in a capsule atop a Mercury–Atlas 5 rocket. The satellite orbited the earth twice at a speed of 17,500 miles per hour in a flight lasting 3 hours 21 minutes. It landed in the ocean near Puerto Rico and was recovered by the U.S.S. *Stormes.*

6799. Rocket with an electrostatic (ion) engine to produce thrust in space was SERT 1 (Space Electric Rocket Test), 375 pounds, launched on July 20, 1964, from Wallops Island, VA. The rocket climbed 2,500 miles, had a 48-minute suborbital flight, and fell to earth 2,000 miles away from the launch site. The mercury-propelled engine performed in space for 16 minutes, generating 0.0055 pounds of thrust.

6800. Scientific evidence for life on Mars was announced by Daniel Goldin, administrator of the National Aeronautics and Space Administration, on August 6, 1996. The discovery was made by Dr. Roberta Score and a team of American scientists. Using electron microscopes, they examined a 4.5-billion-year-old Martian meteorite that struck Antarctica 13,000 years ago and found fossils of what appeared to be "a primitive form of microscopic life."

6801. Rocket built by college students to be launched from Cape Canaveral in Florida was a Pathfinder rocket designed and constructed by a team of students from Florida Institute of Technology, Melbourne, FL. It was launched on June 28, 2006, and landed in the Atlantic Ocean. The team was preparing to compete for the Space Pioneer Cup, an award sponsored by the Florida Space Authority and the U.S. Air Force 45th Space Wing.

Astronauts

6802. Astronauts trained by the United States were chosen by the National Aeronautics and Space Administration for the first manned space program, Project Mercury. They were Air Force Captains Leroy Gordon Cooper, Jr., of Carbondale, CO, Virgil Ivan Grissom of Mitchell, IN, and Donald Kent Slayton of Sparta, WI; Navy Lieutenants Malcolm Scott Carpenter of Boulder, CO, and Walter Marty Schirra, Jr., of Hackensack, NJ; Navy Lieutenant Commander Alan Bartlett Shepard, Jr., of East Derry, NH; and Lieutenant Colonel of Marines John Herschel Glenn, Jr., of New Concord, OH. The selection of the seven men was announced on April 7, 1959. The group trained at the Langley Research Center, Hampton, VA.

6803. Astronaut to be launched into space was Commander Alan Bartlett Shepard, Jr. His capsule, *Freedom 7,* launched on May 5, 1961, by a Mercury–Redstone 3 rocket from Cape Canaveral, FL, reached a height of 1,165 miles. The capsule, weighing slightly more than 2,000 pounds, made a 302-mile trip at a ground speed of 4,500 miles per hour; it reached an altitude of 115 miles before reentering the earth's atmosphere. Shepard experienced a five-minute period of weightlessness. The first human to fly in space was the Russian cosmonaut Yury Gagarin, who was launched into orbit on April 12, 1961.

6804. Astronaut to orbit the earth was Lieutenant Colonel John Herschel Glenn, Jr., of New Concord, OH, who was blasted off at 9:48 A.M. on February 20, 1962, from Cape Canaveral, FL, in an Atlas D rocket 93 feet high. The bell-shaped capsule traveled around the earth three times, covering 83,450 miles at an average speed of 17,400 miles per hour. The capsule came down at 2:43 P.M. in the Atlantic Ocean. Two Soviet cosmonauts had orbited the earth previously.

6805. Astronaut to walk in space was Major Edward Higgins White II, who opened the hatch of *Gemini 4* at 3:42 P.M. on June 3, 1965, stepped out into space at a 120-mile altitude at 3:45 P.M., and remained outside for 20 minutes, until 4:05 P.M., attached to the craft by a 25-foot tether. A hand-held 7.5-pound oxygen jet propulsion gun operated by pressure on a trigger gave him control over his movements. Command pilot Major James Alton McDivitt remained inside *Gemini 4.* The spacecraft was launched on June 3, 1965, at 11:16 A.M. from Cape Canaveral, FL, made 62 revolutions in a flight lasting 97 hours and 56 minutes, and touched down on June 7 at 1:14 P.M. in the Atlantic Ocean. The first human to walk in space was cosmonaut Aleksei A. Leonov, who stepped out of his *Voshkod 2* spacecraft on March 18, 1965.

6806. Astronaut to orbit the earth on two trips was Lieutenant Colonel Leroy Gordon Cooper, whose first trip was made from Cape Canaveral, FL, on May 15–16, 1963, in *Faith 7,* when he made 22 orbits in 34 hours 19 minutes 45 seconds. His second flight was made on August 21–29, 1965, when he and Lieutenant Commander Charles Conrad, Jr., made a two-man spaceflight of 120 orbits in 190 hours 55 minutes 14 seconds in *Gemini 5.*

6807. Astronaut to converse with an aquanaut while each performed in his respective field was Lieutenant Colonel Leroy Gordon Cooper, who spoke from spacecraft *Gemini 5* 100 miles above the earth on August 29, 1965, on its 117th orbit. He spoke by radio to Commander Malcolm Scott Carpenter, who was in *Sealab 2*, a 12-by-58-foot steel capsule resting 205 feet beneath the surface of the Pacific Ocean, about 1,000 yards off La Jolla, CA.

Courtesy of NASA

Launch of Gemini 5 *on August 21, 1965.*

6808. Astronauts to rendezvous in space with another spacecraft were Captain Walter Marty Schirra, Jr., and Major Thomas Patten Stafford, who took off on December 15, 1965, at 8:43 A.M. from Cape Canaveral, FL, in *Gemini 6* to meet *Gemini 7*, which was orbiting the earth with Major Frank Borman and Lieutenant Commander James Arthur Lovell, Jr., aboard. The two *Gemini* spacecraft flew in formation within 20 to 100 feet of each other for 5 hours 16 minutes, during which the astronauts photographed each others' crafts, sighted a fire in Madagascar, and conversed. *Gemini 6* reentered the atmosphere and landed in the Atlantic Ocean on December 16 after 25 hours 52 minutes and 16 revolutions.

6809. Astronaut who was a civilian to orbit the earth was Neil Alden Armstrong, who orbited for 10 hours 42 minutes in *Gemini 8*, accompanied by Major David Randolph Scott. The spacecraft was launched at 9 A.M. on March 16, 1966, from Cape Canaveral, FL, achieved the world's first docking in space, and splashed down on March 17.

6810. Astronauts to die in a spacecraft were Lieutenant Colonel Virgil Ivan Grissom, Lieutenant Colonel Edward Higgins White II, and Lieutenant Commander Roger Bruce Chaffee, who died on January 27, 1967, when a flash fire caused by electrical arcing erupted inside the *Apollo 1* spacecraft command module on the ground at the Kennedy Space Center, Cape Canaveral, FL. The astronauts had been participating in a simulation of the *Apollo 1* flight scheduled for February 21.

6811. Astronaut international rescue agreement was the Agreement on the Rescue of Astronauts, the Return of Astronauts and the Return of Objects Launched into Outer Space, signed by Dean Rusk, secretary of state, at a ceremony held on April 22, 1968, and ratified by the Senate on October 8 by a vote of 66 to 0. President Lyndon Baines Johnson announced on December 3, 1968, that it was in force. The signatories were the United States, the United Kingdom, and the Union of Soviet Socialist Republics.

6812. Astronauts to orbit the moon were Colonel Frank Borman, Captain James Arthur Lovell, Jr., and Major William Alison Anders, who made 10 lunar orbits in *Apollo 7*, launched by a three-stage Saturn 5 rocket from Cape Canaveral, FL, at 7:51 A.M. on December 21, 1968. The spacecraft reentered the atmosphere and splashed down in the Pacific Ocean 147 hours 11 seconds later.

6813. Astronauts to transfer from one spacecraft to another while in orbit were Russell Louis Schweickart and Colonel James Alton McDivitt, who made an intravehicular transfer from *Gumdrop*, the *Apollo 9* command ship, to *Spider*, the lunar module, on March 6, 1969, leaving the pilot, Colonel David Randolph Scott, in the command ship. A Saturn 5 rocket launched the satellite at 11 A.M. on March 3, 1969, from Cape Canaveral, FL. It redocked at 2 P.M. It made a 10-day orbit (241 hours 40 minutes 53 seconds) and landed on March 13 in the Atlantic Ocean, 250 miles east southeast of Bermuda.

6814. Astronauts to land on the moon were Neil Alden Armstrong and Lieutenant Colonel Edwin Eugene Aldrin, Jr., the first human beings to set foot on land beyond the earth. Together with Lieutenant Colonel Michael Collins, they were lifted off in *Apollo 11* at 9:32 A.M. by a Saturn 5 rocket on July 16, 1969, from Kennedy Space Center, Cape Canaveral, FL, with Armstrong as flight commander. The flight reached the moon on Sunday, July 20. Collins remained in orbit as pilot of the command module *Columbia* while the other two, with Aldrin as pilot, descended to the surface of the moon in the lunar module *Eagle*. At 4:17:42 P.M. E.D.T. the *Eagle* touched down on the moon's Sea of Tranquility. At 10:56 P.M. Armstrong came down the ladder, placed his foot on the moon, and said: "That's one small step for a man, one giant leap for mankind." He was joined on the lunar surface by Aldrin at 11:14 P.M. They placed a plaque on the moon and erected an 8-foot aluminum staff with a 3-by-5-foot nylon United States flag. They also set up scientific instruments, collected rocks, and took photographs. At 1:34 P.M. on July 21 the *Eagle* lifted off the lunar surface to rejoin the mother ship. The *Columbia* splashed down at 12:50 P.M. E.D.T. on July 24 in the Pacific Ocean, about 920 miles southwest of Hawaii. The astronauts were taken on board the U.S.S. *Hornet* at 2:12 P.M. and entered a mobile quarantine facility, where they remained until August 11.

6815. Human beings to see the sun eclipsed by the Earth were Charles Conrad, Jr., Richard F. Gordon, Jr., and Alan L. Bean, the astronauts aboard the *Apollo 12* moon flight, November 14–24, 1969. As they were returning home, they passed into the shadow of the Earth and photographed a solar eclipse made by their own planet.

6816. Astronauts to retrieve a manmade object from the moon were Commanders Charles Conrad, Jr., mission leader, and Alan La Vern Bean, lunar landing module pilot, who on November 19, 1969, recovered a piece of the unmanned spacecraft *Surveyor 3*, which had landed on the Ocean of Storms of the Moon on April 19, 1967. They were two of the three astronauts on *Apollo 12*, which was launched by a Saturn 5 rocket from Cape Canaveral, FL, at 11:22 A.M. on November 14, 1969. While Commander Richard Francis Gordon, Jr., remained in orbit to pilot the command module, Conrad and Bean descended to the moon's surface in the lunar module *Intrepid* and remained there for one day, the second time that human beings landed on the moon. Splashdown took place on November 24, 1969, 400 miles from Samoa, after a flight of 244 hours 36 minutes 25 seconds.

The boots with which Neil Armstrong took his "small step for man" were left on the moon when the Eagle departed. In all, there are 10 pairs of astronaut boots on the lunar surface.

6817. Astronauts to ride a vehicle on the moon were Colonel David Randolph Scott and Lieutenant Colonel James Benson Irwin, who on July 31, 1971, rode the four-wheeled electric cart Rover, an LRV (Lunar Roving Vehicle), alongside the 1,200-foot-deep canyon Hadley Hills on the moon. With Major Alfred Merrill Worden, they were launched on July 26, 1971, at 9:34 A.M. from Cape Canaveral, FL, in *Apollo 15* and landed on August 7, 1971.

6818. Physician to practice as an astronaut in space was Navy Commander Dr. Joseph Peter Kerwin, who flew aboard *Skylab 2*, which took off from Cape Canaveral, FL, on May 25, 1973, and splashed down on June 22 in the Pacific Ocean. The duration of the flight was 28 days 49 minutes 49 seconds. Kerwin made daily routine medical tests on his fellow astronauts, Charles Conrad, Jr., and Paul Weitz.

6819. Haircut in space took place aboard the Skylab 2 space station during a 28-day mission by astronauts Charles Conrad, Jr., Joseph P. Kerwin, and Paul J. Weitz in May and June of 1973. Conrad trimmed the hair of Weitz, who held a vacuum device to collect the clippings.

6820. Astronauts to participate in an international spaceflight were Thomas Patten Stafford, mission commander, Donald Kent Slayton, pilot of the docking module, and Vance Devoe Brand, pilot of the command module, who participated in the joint Soviet-American Apollo-Soyuz Test Project. They took off from Cape Canaveral, FL on July 15, 1975, and returned on July 24, traveling 217 hours 28 minutes 24 seconds. Their craft, *Apollo 18*, docked with the Soviet spacecraft *Soyuz 19*, manned by Aleksei Arkhipovich Leonov and Valery Nikolayevich Kubasov, on July 17.

6821. Astronauts who were women were selected by the National Aeronautics and Space Administration in 1977 and announced on January 16, 1978. They were Anna L. Fisher of Rancho Palos Verdes, CA; Shannon W. Lucid of Oklahoma City, OK; Judith A. Resnik of Akron, OH; Sally K. Ride of Stanford, CA; Margaret R. Seddon of Memphis, TN; and Kathryn D. Sullivan of Paterson, NJ. They were chosen from 3,000 applicants.

6822. Astronaut who was Jewish was biomedical and electrical engineer Judith A. Resnik, who joined the NASA astronaut corps in August 1979. Her first Space Shuttle flight, on which she served as a mission specialist, was launched on August 30, 1984, when she became the second woman to fly in space. She was a member of the crew of the Space Shuttle *Challenger*, which exploded after liftoff on January 28, 1986.

6823. Astronaut who was of Asian descent was Ellison Shoji Onizuka, a lieutenant colonel in the U.S. Air Force, who joined the NASA astronaut corps in August 1979. He was of Japanese ancestry. His first Space Shuttle flight was launched on January 24, 1985. He was one of the six crew members who died on January 28, 1986, in the explosion of the Space Shuttle *Challenger*.

6824. Astronaut who was Hispanic was Franklin R. Chang-Dìaz, who grew up in Venezuela and Costa Rica (his paternal grandfather was Chinese). After receiving his doctorate in applied plasma physics, he entered the astronaut corps in August 1981. He participated in seven Space Shuttle flights between 1986 and 2002, including three space walks.

Franklin R. Chang-Dìaz was the first American astronaut who was a naturalized citizen. He emigrated from Costa Rica as a teenager in the hope of becoming an astronaut.

6825. Astronaut who was a woman to fly in space was Dr. Sally K. Ride of Stanford, CA, who served as a crew member aboard Space Shuttle *Challenger* when it was launched on June 18, 1983. Ride trained as an astrophysicist and in 1978 joined NASA, where she helped design the robot arm for the space shuttle. She retired from the astronaut corps in 1987. Valentina V. Tereshkova of the Soviet Union, who crewed *Vostok 6* on June 16, 1963, was the first woman from any country to fly in space.

6826. Astronaut to fly in space who was African-American was Air Force Lieutenant Colonel Guion Bluford, a mission specialist on the third flight of Space Shuttle *Challenger*, launched on August 30, 1983, from Cape Canaveral, FL. The main activity of the mission was to deploy a communications satellite built for India. The first African-American woman to fly in space was Dr. Mae Carol Jemison, a physician who also held degrees in chemical engineering and African-American studies. Jemison, who left private practice to join NASA in 1987, made her first space flight on September 12, 1992, as a payload mission specialist on Space Shuttle *Endeavour*. She performed experiments on space motion sickness and bone cell loss in the space environment.

6827. Astronauts to fly free in space were Navy Captain Bruce McCandless and Army Lieutenant Colonel Robert Stewart. On February 7, 1984, while in orbit over the earth, McCandless exited Space Shuttle *Challenger* and maneuvered freely, without a tether, using a rocket pack of his own design. Stewart also used the rocket pack to fly untethered later that day.

6828. Astronaut who was a woman to walk in space was Kathryn D. Sullivan, who exited Space Shuttle *Challenger* on a tether and flew in space for 3.5 hours on October 11, 1984. A female cosmonaut had walked in spae in July 1984.

6829. Astronaut who was a mother was Dr. Anna L. Fisher, a member of the crew of Space Shuttle *Discovery* mission that lifted off on November 16, 1984, from Cape Canaveral, FL. She participated in the world's first satellite retrieval and repair operation.

6830. Senator to fly in space was Jake Garn, Republican senator from Utah, who joined the crew of Space Shuttle *Discovery* as a "congressional observer" when the shuttle lifted off from Cape Canaveral, FL, on April 12, 1985. A former Navy pilot, Garn had taken several months of astronaut training. Another senator, John Herschel Glenn, Jr., of Ohio, was an astronaut in the 1960s, before he entered politics.

6831. Astronaut who was a Hispanic woman was Ellen Ochoa of La Mesa, CA, whose paternal grandparents were Mexican. She joined the astronaut corps in July 1991 after earning her doctorate in electrical engineering and flew on her first Space Shuttle flight in April 1993. She also earned a number of patents for optical inventions.

6832. Husband and wife to fly in space together were Mission Specialist N. Jan Davis, an engineer, and Air Force Lieutenant Colonel Mark C. Lee, who served as crew members aboard the mission of Space Shuttle *Endeavour* that began on September 12, 1992. Although NASA has a rule forbidding married couples to take part in the same mission, the rule was waived for Davis and Lee because they had no children and both had trained as astronauts for several years before they were married.

6833. Cosmonaut on an American space mission was Sergei K. Krikalev, a veteran of several Russian space missions. Krikalev flew as a specialist aboard Space Shuttle *Discovery* on Flight STS-60, the first joint U.S./Russian Space Shuttle mission, which was launched on February 11, 1994, from Cape Canaveral, FL. Krikalev operated the Remote Manipulator System during the flight. He also was a crewmember on board STS-88 (launched December 4, 1998), the first International Space Station assembly mission.

6834. Astronaut who was a woman to pilot the space shuttle was Lieutenant Colonel Eileen Marie Collins, a 1990 graduate of the Air Force Test Pilot School, who joined NASA in July 1991. On her initial mission, on February 3, 1995, she served as pilot of the Space Shuttle *Discovery*, which docked with the Russian space station *Mir* in the first flight of the joint Russian-American space program. She became the first woman to serve as commander of a space flight on July 23, 1999, when the Space Shuttle *Columbia* lifted off from Cape Canaveral, FL, to loft the Chandra X-Ray Observatory into a high elliptical earth orbit.

6835. Astronaut to receive training in Russia's space program was Dr. Norman Earl Thagard of Jacksonville, FL. After training with cosmonauts in Star City, Russia, Thagard and the Russian members of the *Mir 18* mission left the launch pad in Baikonaur, Kazakhstan, on March 14, 1995, to rendezvous with the *Mir* space station.

6836. Astronaut from the United States to live in a space stationwas Dr. Norman Earl Thagard of Jacksonville, FL, who reached the *Mir* space station on March 16, 1995, and remained there for 115 days to conduct 28 experiments. He left on June 29, 1995, aboard the Space Shuttle *Orbiter*.

6837. Astronaut from the United States who was a woman to live in a space station was biochemist Dr. Shannon W. Lucid, 53, of Bethany, OK. On March 24, 1996, Lucid transferred from Space Shuttle *Atlantis* to the Russian space station *Mir* for a planned five-month stay. It was the first time the shuttle returned to earth with one less person aboard than had been present at the launch. Lucid remained on the station for 188 days, the longest space sojourn by any American and any woman until that time. Her return was delayed more than six weeks by emergency repairs to the booster rockets of the *Atlantis* and by a hurricane. She came home in the *Atlantis*, which touched down at Edwards Air Force Base, Muroc, CA, on September 26, 1996.

6838. Joint space walk by American and Russian astronauts took place in earth orbit on April 29, 1997, when Dr. Jerry L. Linenger and Vasily Tsibliyev collected cosmic dust samples and installed a radiation meter outside the Russian space station *Mir*.

6839. Space tourist was millionaire businessman Dennis A. Tito, a former aeronautics engineer and founder of Wilshire Associates Incorporated, an investment analysis firm in Santa Monica, CA. Tito paid $20 million to the Russian space program to fly aboard a Soyuz spacecraft to the International Space Station. The eight-day trip took place from April 29 to May 7, 2001.

6840. Astronaut to fly in space who was Native American was John Bennett Herrington, a member of the Chickasaw Nation. He flew aboard Space Shuttle *Endeavour* on November 23, 2002, to the International Space Station, where he made three space walks in the course of the mission.

6841. Astronaut lost in a U.S. space mission who was not an American was Colonel Ilan Ramon, the first Israeli astronaut, who died in the breakup of the Space Shuttle *Columbia* on February 1, 2003, as it was descending toward a landing at the Kennedy Space Center, Cape Canaveral, FL, after a 16-day mission. Ramon, the son of a Holocaust survivor, was a fighter pilot in the Israeli Air Force. He began astronaut training at the Johnson Space Center in Houston, TX, in 1998.

6842. Astronauts to make a ground landing in a capsule were NASA astronauts Kenneth Bowersox and Donald Pettit. The two had arrived at the International Space Station in November 2002 aboard Space Shuttle *Endeavour* and were stranded there when shuttle flights were cancelled after the explosion of the shuttle *Columbia*. Together with cosmonaut Nikolai Budarin, they came home in the space station's lifeboat, the Russian spacecraft *Soyuz TMA-1*. The capsule containing all three men came down in a remote part of Kazakhstan on May 4, 2003. All previous U.S. capsule landings had taken place at sea.

6843. Podcast from space was transmitted on August 7, 2005, by Mission Specialist Stephen Kern Robinson aboard the Space Shuttle *Discovery* during Mission STS-114. Robinson made the podcast on the shuttle's last day of orbit around Earth. He ended his message by sending "a greeting to all Earthlings."

Satellites

6844. Satellite placed in orbit by the United States was *Explorer 1*, launched on January 31, 1958, from Cape Canaveral, FL, by a Jupiter C Army missile. It was a bullet-shaped tubular rocket 80 inches long that weighed 30.8 pounds. The weight of the satellite proper was 18.13 pounds; the weight of the final stage of rocket after burnout, 12.67 pounds. The satellite was airborne at 10:48:16 A.M. and went into orbit around the earth at 10:55 A.M., traveling at a speed ranging from 18,000 to 19,000 miles per hour.

6845. Satellite to transmit photographs of the earth was *Explorer 6*, launched on August 7, 1959, from the Atlantic Missile Range, Cape Canaveral, FL. The pictures, received in Hawaii, took 40 minutes to transmit. They were released on September 28, 1959, by the National Aeronautics and Space Administration, and depicted a crescent shape of part of the earth in sunlight. They were taken about 19,500 miles over Mexico from a position facing the Pacific Ocean. The velocity of the satellite at perigee was 23,031 miles per hour. The perigee was 156 miles and the apogee 26,357 miles.

6846. Weather satellite to provide cloud-cover photographs was *Tiros 1* (Television and Infra Red Observatory Satellite), launched by a Thor-Able rocket on April 1, 1960, from Cape Canaveral, FL. It took photographs of the earth's cloud cover from an altitude of 450 miles. The last transmission took place on June 17, 1960.

6847. Navigational satellite was *Transit 1*-B, launched on April 13, 1960, by a Thor-Able-Star rocket from Cape Canaveral, FL. The payload, weighing 265 pounds, included two ultrastable oscillators, two telemetry transmitters and receivers, batteries, and solar cells.

6848. Spy satellite that was successful was *Midas 2*, launched on May 24, 1960, at 12:37 P.M. from Cape Canaveral, FL, by a two-stage Atlas-Agena rocket. *Midas 2* was 122 feet long and 5 feet in diameter and weighed 5,000 pounds. It circled the earth every 94.34 minutes. Its apogee was 292 miles, its perigee 322 miles. It was intended to replace the U-2 reconnaissance aircraft in gathering intelligence on the Soviet Union.

6849. Multisatellite launching of several satellites in one shot was made at 1:54 A.M. on June 22, 1960, from Cape Canaveral, FL, by a Navy Thor-Able-Star rocket. The main satellite, designated *Transit 2-A*, carried two instrumented payload satellites: *Eta 1*, a 36-inch sphere that weighed 223 pounds, and *Eta 2*, a 20-inch sphere that weighed 42 pounds.

6850. Space capsule recovered from an orbiting satellite was located on August 11, 1960, in the Pacific Ocean. It was recovered from *Discoverer 8*, a satellite that had been launched by a Thor-Agena rocket from Vandenberg Air Force Base, CA, on August 10, 1960. The capsule, which measured 27 by 33 inches and weighed 350 pounds, was ejected from the satellite during its 17th polar orbit at a height of 200 miles over latitude 70 degrees N. The descent of the capsule was slowed down by a parachute, which opened at about

50,000 feet. The capsule was recovered by a Navy frogman, Boatswain's Mate Third Class Robert W. Carroll of Keene, NH, who dived from a helicopter that took off from the naval vessel *Haiti Victory*.

6851. Communications satellite was *Echo 1*, a 26.5-inch magnesium sphere launched by a Thor-Delta rocket at 5:39 A.M. on August 12, 1960, from Cape Canaveral, FL. The satellite went into orbit at 7:45 A.M. after the three stages of the rocket had been fired successfully. A taped message was transmitted from Goldstone, CA, bounced off the satellite, and received by the Bell Telephone laboratory at Holmdel, NJ.

6852. Space capsule recovered in midair from an orbiting satellite was a 300-pound capsule ejected from the satellite *Discoverer 14* and retrieved on August 19, 1960. The capsule dropped back to earth by parachute and was snatched at 8,000 feet by an Air Force C-119 airplane piloted by Captain Harold E. Mitchell about 360 miles southwest of Honolulu, HI. *Discoverer 14* was launched by a Thor-Agena rocket on August 18, 1960, from Vandenberg Air Force Base, CA.

6853. Communications satellite with signal reception and transmission equipment was *Courier 1B*, a delayed repeater satellite weighing 500 pounds that was launched at 1:50 P.M. on October 4, 1960, from Cape Canaveral, FL, by a two-stage Thor-Able-Star launch vehicle. On its second orbit, it received and recorded from Fort Monmouth, NJ, a transcribed message by President Dwight David Eisenhower to Secretary of State Christian Archibald Herter at the United Nations in New York City, who delivered it to Frederick Henry Boland, president of the General Assembly. The first attempt to launch such a satellite had ended in an explosion on August 18, 1960. Early communications satellites were for testing purposes only.

6854. Orbiting solar observatory was *OSO 1*, launched by a Thor-Delta booster on March 7, 1962, at 11:06 A.M. from Cape Canaveral, FL. It was 37 inches tall and weighed 458 pounds. It transmitted data on solar flares and was stabilized and sun-oriented, so that the instruments always pointed toward the sun. Its apogee was 370 miles, its perigee 340 miles.

6855. International satellite was the United States–United Kingdom satellite *Ariel 1*, launched at 1 P.M. on April 26, 1962, from the Atlantic Missile Range, Cape Canaveral, FL, by a Thor-Delta booster. The 132-pound cylinder payload was 23 inches in diameter and less than 11 inches long. It carried six British experiments: three to measure electron density, temperatures, and the composition of positive ions in the ionshere; two to monitor intensity of radiation from the sun; and one to measure cosmic rays. Its apogee was 754.2 miles and its perigee 242.1 miles.

6856. Satellite from the United States to impact the moon was the *Ranger IV*, launched on April 23, 1962, at 3:50 P.M. from the Atlantic Missile Range, Cape Canaveral, FL. It was launched by an Atlas-Agena B, 102 feet high, with a 16-foot base diameter and a liftoff weight of 275,000 pounds. It traveled an estimated 229,541 miles and impacted the moon at 7:49:53 A.M. E.S.T. on April 26, 1962. The velocity at lunar impact was 5,963 miles per hour.

6857. Commercial satellite was *Telstar 1*, an active relay-communications satellite that was designed and built by the Bell Telephone Laboratories for the American Telephone and Telegraph Company. An application permit was filed on October 21, 1960, and an experimental license was granted on January 19, 1961. The satellite was launched on July 10, 1962, at 4:35 A.M. from Cape Canaveral, FL, by the National Aeronautics and Space Administration (NASA), using a three-stage Thor-Delta rocket. The satellite payload was a sphere 34.5 inches in diameter that weighed 170 pounds. The perigee was 593 miles and the apogee 3,503 miles. Orbit time was 157.8 minutes.

6858. Geodetic satellite was *Anna 1B*, 350 pounds, launched by a Thor-Able-Star rocket at 3:08 A.M. on October 31, 1962, from Cape Canaveral, FL. It had four flashing lights that gave off five flashes spaced 5.6 seconds apart. It had an apogee of 727 miles and a perigee of 670 miles. Distances on the earth were computed by triangulation. The name Anna is an acronym for Army, Navy, NASA, and Air Force.

6859. Geosynchronous satellite was *Syncom 2*, launched at 10:33 A.M. on July 26, 1963, from the Atlantic Missile Range, Cape Canaveral, FL, by NASA. It was conceived and designed by the Hughes Aircraft Company. The cylinder was 28 inches in diameter and 15.5 inches high and weighed 147 pounds. Its orbital period was 23.9 hours. Its apogee was 22,239 miles and its perigee 22,230 miles, almost equal to the time required for the earth to rotate once on its axis so that it seems to stand still in space.

6860. Orbiting geophysical observatory was *OGO 1*, launched on September 4, 1964, at 9:23 P.M. from Cape Canaveral, FL, by an Atlas-Agena B rocket. The payload weighed 1,073 pounds and was 6 feet long and 3 feet wide. The satellite carried 13 protruding appendages and had 32,250 solar cells and two 28-volt nickel cadmium batteries. Its velocity varied from 1,124 miles per hour at the apogee of 92,827 miles to 23,180 miles per hour at the perigee of 175 miles.

6861. Satellite with a nuclear reactor to orbit the earth was *Snapshot I*, a 970-pound satellite, 12 feet long with a base 5 feet in diameter, that was launched by an Atlas-Agena booster from Vandenberg Air Force Base, CA, on April 3, 1965. It contained a System for Nuclear Auxiliary Power reactor (SNAP 10A), 15.5 inches high and 9 inches in diameter, that weighed 250 pounds and generated 500 watts of power after it was in stable orbit. The reactor operated for 43 days, until May 16, 1965, and produced 500,000 watt-hours of electricity. It orbited the earth every 112 minutes at an apogee of 820 miles and a perigee of 788 miles. SNAP 10A was developed by the Atomics International division of North American Aviation at Canoga Park, CA.

6862. Satellite launched from the earth to orbit another planet was *Mariner 9*, an unmanned American spacecraft that was sent to Mars to photograph the surface and to study the planet's thin atmosphere, clouds, and hazes, surface chemistry, and seasonable changes. The satellite entered Martian orbit at 7:33 P.M. E.S.T. on November 13, 1971. It mapped 70 percent of the planet's surface.

6863. Satellite repair in orbit was performed by the crew of the fifth mission of Space Shuttle *Challenger*. On April 10, 1984, using the shuttle's robot arm, the crew hooked an ailing science satellite, the *Solar Max*, and brought it into the cargo bay. Mission specialists George Nelson and James Van Hoften replaced the satellite's attitude control module, then returned the *Solar Max* to orbit on April 12. The shuttle landed on April 13.

6864. Astronomical phenomenon caused by space debris was identified by Paul D. Maley, an astronomer at the NASA Johnson Space Center Astronomical Society, Houston, TX. In a paper published in 1987, he demonstrated that flashes of light observed by astronomers in 1985 in the neighborhood of the constellations Aries and Perseus were caused by the passage of obsolete manmade satellites.

6865. Global Positioning System (GPS) satellite that could be used for civilian purposes was placed in orbit on February 14, 1989. Launched from Cape Canaveral, FL, atop a Delta II booster, it was the first of 24 so-called Block II satellites (all manufactured by Rockwell International) that were intended to provide precise, three-dimensional location and navigation information for any GPS-compatible transceiver on the surface of the earth or in near-earth space. The GPS system was originally developed by the federal Department of Defense to meet military requirements.

Spacecraft

6866. Spacecraft placed in solar orbit to investigate interplanetary space between the orbits of Earth and Venus was *Pioneer 5*, launched on March 11, 1960, from Cape Canaveral, FL, by a three-stage Thor-Able IV rocket. The payload was a 26-inch sphere plus four vanes covered by 4,800 solar cells with a total weight of 94.8 pounds, including approximately 40 pounds of instruments. The spacecraft orbited the sun in 311.6 days. Its velocity at the third-stage burnout was 24,689 miles per hour. It was 74.9 million miles from the sun in perigee and 92.3 million miles in apogee. Its last message was received on June 26, 1960, when it was 22.5 million miles from earth and had transmitted data for 138.9 hours.

6867. Spacecraft to transmit data from Venus was *Mariner 2*, a 447-pound spacecraft that was launched on August 27, 1962, at 2:53 A.M. from Cape Canaveral, FL, by an Atlas-Agena B rocket. On December 14, 1962, it passed within approximately 21,600 miles of the planet Venus and measured temperatures and other characteristics of the Venusian surface and its atmosphere.

6868. Spacecraft to transmit close-up photographs of the lunar surface was *Ranger 7,* launched on July 28, 1964, from Cape Canaveral, FL. The payload weighed 806 pounds, measured 8.25 feet high with a 5-foot diameter, and included six RCA-TV cameras. It impacted the moon's surface in the area northwest of the Sea of Clouds at 9:25 A.M. E.D.T. on July 31, after taking 4,316 pictures of the moon's surface. The total elapsed flight time to the moon, 240,000 miles away, was 68 hours 36 minutes.

6869. Spacecraft to transmit close-up photographs of Mars was *Mariner 4,* a 574-pound spacecraft that was launched at 9:22 A.M. on November 28, 1964, from Cape Canaveral, FL, by a two-stage Atlas-Agena D rocket. On July 14, 1965, when the satellite was 134 million miles away from earth and 10,500 miles from Mars, it sent a transmission of photographs consisting of 8.3 dots per second of varying degrees of darkness. The transmission lasted for 8.5 hours and depicted the regions on Mars known as Cebrenia, Arcadia, and Amazonis.

6870. Manned docking of two spacecraft was effected on March 16, 1966, by *Gemini 8,* which made a rendezvous and docking on its fourth orbit, 6.5 hours after launching, with a 26-foot Agena target vehicle launched at 9 A.M. the same day. *Gemini 8* was launched from Cape Canaveral, FL, at 10:41 A.M. by a two-stage Titan II. It made seven orbits in 10 hours 42 minutes, landing in the Pacific Ocean at 10:23 P.M. E.S.T. near Okinawa, where it was picked up 3.5 hours after splashdown and hauled on to the deck of U.S.S. *Leonard F. Mason* at 1:38 A.M. on March 17. Its apogee was 164 miles, its perigee 99 miles. Neil Alden Armstrong was the command pilot and Major David Randolph Scott the pilot.

6871. Space probe to achieve lunar orbit launched by the United States was *Lunar Orbiter 1,* which entered moon orbit on August 14, 1966, and moved to a closer orbit on August 21. It had been launched from Cape Canaveral, FL, on August 10, the first of five probes that were intended to map the surface of the moon in preparation for a manned lunar mission. It returned 207 photographs. *Lunar Orbiter 1* was crashed into the moon's far side on October 29 to make way for the next launch.

6872. Spacecraft to carry an extraterrestrial message intended to be read by living beings elsewhere in the universe was *Pioneer 10,* the planetary probe that was launched from Cape Canaveral, FL, on March 2, 1972, by NASA. Bolted to the probe's exterior wall was a gold-anodized plaque, six by nine inches in area, that carried a number of illustrations: drawings of a human man and woman, a star map marked with the location of the sun, and a second map showing the flight path of *Pioneer 10.* The message was designed by astronomer Carl Sagan.

6873. Space station launched by the United States was *Skylab 2,* which lifted off on May 25, 1973, from Cape Canaveral, FL. Three astronauts, Charles Conrad, Jr., Joseph P. Kerwin, and Paul J. Weitz, spent nearly a month in the station conducting long-duration flight tests and other scientific experiments. The mission ended successfully on June 22 when the astronauts returned to earth, leaving *Skylab* in orbit. It later disintegrated in the earth's upper atmosphere. The first manned space stations were launched by the Soviet Union beginning in 1971.

6874. Spacecraft to land on Mars was the American planetary probe *Viking 1,* launched on August 20, 1975, from Cape Canaveral, FL. Its sister craft *Viking 2* was launched on September 9, 1975. *Viking 1* touched down on Mars on July 20, 1976, and began sending photographs back to Earth. The probe operated for 6.5 years. *Viking 2* landed on September 3, 1976, and functioned for 3.5 years.

6875. Reusable manned spacecraft was Space Shuttle *Columbia,* piloted by astronauts Robert L. Crippen and John W. Young, which was launched at 7 A.M. on April 12, 1981, from Cape Canaveral, FL. After a 54-hour, 22-minute flight of 36 orbits, the 80-ton shuttle touched down on the dry lake bed at Edwards Air Force Base, Muroc, CA, on April 14, 1981, at 10:21 A.M. Development of the hybrid spacecraft-airplane cost almost $10 billion and took nine years. The first free atmospheric flight by a space shuttle took place on August 12, 1977, when Space Shuttle *Enterprise* was lifted to a height of 25,000 feet by a Boeing 747 airplane and glided back to Edwards Air Force Base, Muroc, CA, piloted by astronauts C. Gordon Fullerton and Fred W. Haise, Jr.

6876. Private space launch took place on September 9, 1982, when Space Services, Inc., Houston, TX, launched the *Conestoga* I from Matagorda Island in the Gulf of Mexico. *Conestoga*, a 37-foot rocket with a 1,097-pound payload, climbed to a height of 196 miles and came down in the sea 10 minutes after launching. The cost of the flight, borne by private investors, was $2.5 million.

6877. Spacecraft to leave the solar system was the planetary probe *Pioneer 10*, launched on March 2, 1972, from Cape Canaveral, FL. *Pioneer 10* passed Jupiter on December 3, 1973, taking the first close-up pictures of the giant planet. It left the solar system on June 14, 1983, and sent back the first data from interstellar space. The 25th anniversary of the launch took place on March 3, 1997, when *Pioneer 10* became the world's oldest functioning spacecraft. It was also the farthest man-made object from Earth, having traveled a distance of 6 billion miles. NASA officially ended the mission on March 31, 1997, but *Pioneer 10* continued to travel. In the year 34600, the probe will pass within three light years of the star Ross 246.

6878. Salvage operation in space was performed by astronauts Joseph Allen and Dale Gardner. On November 12, 1984, during the second flight of Space Shuttle *Discovery*, they used the shuttle's robot arm to snare an orbiting satellite and bring it into the cargo bay for repair.

6879. Space shuttle disaster occurred on January 28, 1986, when Space Shuttle *Challenger* exploded off the coast of Florida 74 seconds after liftoff. It was the largest single space disaster in history. All six astronauts on board—Francis R. Scobee, Michael J. Smith, Ronald E. McNair, Ellison S. Onizuka, Judith A. Resnik, and Gregory B. Jarvis—were killed. Also killed was Christa McAuliffe, a New Hampshire elementary school teacher who had won a competition to become the first ordinary civilian to fly in space, and who thus became the first civilian to die in a spacecraft accident. The cause of the explosion was cold weather on the morning of the launch. The icy temperatures had reduced the elasticity of o-ring seals on the shuttle's solid fuel boosters and the seals had cracked, allowing exploding gases to escape. An inquiry revealed that NASA had relaxed its own safety regulations to advance the launch date.

6880. Spacecraft launched by the United States to dock with a Russian space station was Space Shuttle *Atlantis*, commanded by Navy Captain Robert L. Gibson. At 8 A.M. on June 29, 1995, the 122-foot-long shuttle docked with the 112-foot-long Russian space station *Mir* 245 miles above the earth, forming the largest structure ever assembled in space up to that time. The station's two Russian cosmonauts and one American astronaut, combined with the shuttle's five Americans and two Russians, also constituted the largest human population that had ever been in orbit.

6881. Planetary probe to enter the atmosphere of Jupiter was a 746-pound probe carried on the *Galileo* spacecraft, launched in October 1989 from Cape Canaveral, FL. The probe, outfitted with instruments to measure the temperature, pressure, and composition of Jupiter's atmosphere, detached from *Galileo* in July 1995 and entered Jupiter's upper cloud layer on December 5, 1995. It descended by parachute several hundred miles before being crushed and vaporized under intense atmospheric pressure. Analysis of the probe data revealed that Jupiter's composition was closer to the sun's than had been supposed, and that its atmosphere lacked water and complex organic molecules. *Galileo* itself was the first spacecraft to orbit one of the giant outer planets for a long-term survey.

6882. Robot to conduct a roving exploration of the surface of another planet was Sojourner, a 25-pound, six-wheeled robot designed to explore and analyze the surface of Mars. The *Pathfinder* mission, which carried Sojourner into space, was launched from Cape Canaveral, FL, on December 4, 1996. On July 4, 1997, *Pathfinder* landed on the Ares Vallis, an ancient Martian floodplain. Upon landing, the craft was renamed the Sagan Memorial Station, in honor of the late American astronomer Carl Sagan. On July 6, Sojourner rolled away from *Pathfinder* and began conducting an analysis of soil and rocks in the immediate area. The $23 million robot was named for Sojourner Truth, the African-American abolitionist.

6883. Spacecraft with ion propulsion system was *Deep Space 1*, launched from Cape Canaveral, FL, on October 24, 1998, as a test of 12 advanced technologies. These included the innovative NSTAR electrostatic ion drive, which used high voltage electrodes to accelerate ions, achieving low-powered but efficient thrust. Under project manager Marc Rayman, the probe went on to encounter Comet Borrelly, returning high-quality images and other science data. The spacecraft was retired on December 18, 2001.

6884. International space station was *Freedom*, a joint project of the U.S. space agency, NASA, and its partners, including the European Space Agency (a consortium of 13 countries), Canada, and Japan. The station was originally proposed in a 1984 speech by President Ronald Reagan. An agreement of cooperation with the international partners was signed in 1985. Russia joined the project in 1993 when it agreed to merge its *Mir* space station program with the Western effort. Construction began in space on November 20, 1998, and was expected to continue until circa 2012.

Library of Congress, Prints & Photographs Division LC-USZ62-13040

Ronald Reagan

6885. Space probe mission headed entirely by women was a planetary exploration project, the Deep Space–2 mission, sponsored by the U.S. National Aeronautics and Space Administration (NASA) in the late 1990s. The team, working at the Jet Propulsion Laboratory in Pasadena, CA, built two electronic microprobes that were launched in December 1999 from the Mars Polar Lander. The microprobes, each surrounded by an aeroshell, were designed to crash into Mars at a speed of 400 miles per hour, burrow into the surface, and relay information about the planet's soil composition. The mission was run by project manager Sarah A. Gavit, chief mission engineer Kari A. Lewis, and lead scientist Suzanne E. Smrekar.

6886. Spacecraft to land on an asteroid was NASA's Near Earth Asteroid Rendezvous–Shoemaker spacecraft, launched on February 17, 1996, from Cape Canaveral, FL. Named for planetary scientist Eugene M. Shoemaker, NEAR-Shoemaker touched down on the asteroid 433 EROS in its "saddle" region on February 12, 2001. A gamma-ray spectrometer was used to collect data about the asteroid's surface. Previously, NEAR-Shoemaker had been the first space probe to orbit an asteroid.

6887. Manned spacecraft to explode over the U.S. mainland was the Space Shuttle *Columbia*, which had been launched from the Kennedy Space Center in Cape Canaveral, FL, on January 16, 2003. The crew conducted some 80 experiments during 16 days in space. On February 1, 2003, during her landing descent over east Texas en route to the Kennedy Space Center, the shuttle broke apart. The spacecraft was destroyed and her entire crew of seven were lost: Rick D. Husband, commander; William C. McCool, pilot; Michael P. Anderson, payload commander; David M. Brown, Kalpana Chawla, and Laurel Blair Salton Clark, mission specialists; and Ilan Ramon, payload specialist. An investigation revealed that the *Columbia* had been damaged by heat-shielding tiles dislodged during liftoff. Some 83,800 pieces of debris from the craft were recovered, analyzed, and stored at the Kennedy Space Center.

6888. Privately funded spacecraft to fly in space was *SpaceShipOne*, a suborbital spaceplane entirely funded by private investors, with no government support. Designed by Burt Rutan's Scaled Composites aerospace firm, *SpaceShipOne* (Scaled Composites Model 316) was a three-seat, stub-winged craft constructed of composite materials and powered by a single N2O/HTPB SpaceDev Hybrid Solid rocket engine. The craft was lifted to the stratosphere by a jetliner, then continued under its own rocket propulsion system to higher altitudes before gliding back to earth. On April 1, 2004, Scaled Composites received the first license for suborbital piloted rocket flights ever issued by the federal Department of Transportation. On June 21, 2004, flying from the Mojave Airport Civilian

Flight Test Center in Mojave, CA, pilot Mike Melville flew *SpaceShipOne* to an altitude of 62 miles (100 kilometers), the altitude at which space is considered to begin. Melville thereby became the first civilian pilot to fly a craft into space. On October 4, 2004, *SpaceShipOne* won the $10 million manned spaceflight Ansari X Prize by reaching 100 kilometers in altitude twice in a two-week period.

6889. Spacecraft to land on the moon of another planet was the Huygens probe, which landed on Titan, the largest moon of Saturn, on January 14, 2005. The probe was part of the Cassini Orbiter mission to Saturn, a joint venture by NASA, the European Space Agency, and the Italian Space Agency. Cassini was launched by rocket on October 15, 1997, from Cape Canaveral, FL. It reached the Saturnian system after a seven-year trip and began orbiting Saturn on July 1, 2004. The Huygens probe was detached on December 25 and began transmitting images as it parachuted through Titan's atmosphere. The mission manager for the Huygens probe was Jean-Pierre Lebreton.

Courtesy of NASA

Saturn and its moon Titan.

6890. Solar sail aircraft was *Cosmos 1*, a project of the Planetary Society, Pasadena, CA, a private nonprofit group founded by Carl Sagan and Ann Druyan to develop a method of fuelless space travel. The craft, shaped like a pinwheel with eight remote-controlled Mylar wings, was designed to be propelled by the pressure of photon particles in sunlight. It was launched on June 21, 2005, on a Russian-made booster rocket from a submarine submerged in the Barents Sea, but the rocket malfunctioned shortly after takeoff and the craft never reached orbit.

6891. In-flight repair of a space shuttle exterior took place on August 3, 2005, during Mission STS-114, when Mission Specialist Stephen Kern Robinson was lifted out of the Space Shuttle *Discovery* on a 55-foot crane operated by fellow astronaut James Kelly. Spacewalking underneath the vehicle, which was docked to the orbiting International Space Station, he pulled off two loose pieces of filler from between the tiles of the shuttle's heat shield.

6892. Private space station prototype was *Genesis 1*, made by Bigelow Aerospace, Las Vegas, NV. It was a prefabricated inflatable module that was launched on July 14, 2006, at Yasny, Russia, using a recycled Soviet ICBM rocket. Once in orbit, the craft was expanded to its full length of 14 feet by compressed air carried in onboard tanks. *Genesis 1* was the prototype for a future inflatable space station to be run as a commercial venture. The project was financed largely by the company's president, Robert Bigelow.

SOCIETY

Awards

6893. Copley Medal awarded to an American was presented to Benjamin Franklin of Philadelphia, PA, in 1753 for his "curious experiments and observations on electricity." The medal, the highest distinction given by England for scientific research, was awarded by the Royal Society of London.

6894. American to be named a Chevalier of the Legion d'Honneur by the government of France was Thomas Wiltberger Evans of Philadelphia, PA. An expert dentist, he spent his career in Paris, where he counted among his clients the Emperor Napoleon III and many other members of Europe's royalty and nobility. He also served as the emperor's personal envoy on a variety of missions and was his confidant in political matters. He was named to the Legion d'Honneur in 1854.

6895. Albert Medal presented to a person born in America was awarded on June 10, 1884, to James Buchanan Eads for his plan for deepening the Mississippi River as far as the mouth of the Ohio River by jetties. The Albert Medal was established in 1862 in memory of Prince Albert, consort of Queen Victoria, and was awarded by the (British) Society for the Encouragement of Arts, Manufactures and Commerce.

6896. Carnegie Hero Fund Commission awards were given in 1904 to E. Ralph Adams, 15, and Ernestine F. Atwood, 17. Adams died trying to save two younger boys from drowning in a freezing lake in Decatur, MI, on December 7, 1904. Atwood was boating in Boston Harbor on August 22, 1904, when she dived off her rowboat and saved Harry M. Smith, a coachman, who was trapped under a float 200 feet from shore. The fund was founded in 1904 by Andrew Carnegie, the Pittsburgh steelmaker and philanthropist. Moved by the self-sacrifice of two rescuers in a coal-mine disaster, he gave $5 million to provide recognition and financial assistance to civilian heroes.

6897. Interstate Commerce Commission Medal of Honor was a bronze medal awarded on December 5, 1905, to George H. Poell of Grand Island, NE. On June 26, 1905, while a fireman on the St. Joseph and Grand Island Railway, he climbed out on the pilot of his engine and rescued a child on the tracks. Poell was seriously injured and one foot had to be amputated. The medal was authorized by act of Congress of February 23, 1905, for presentation to those "who shall hereafter, by extreme daring, endanger their own lives in saving, or endeavoring to save lives from any wreck, disaster or grave accident, or in preventing or endeavoring to prevent" accidents. Four degrees were established: chief commander, commander, officer, and legionnaire.

6898. Nobel Prize awarded to an American was the Nobel Peace Prize, granted in 1906 to President Theodore Roosevelt for his service in the cause of peace in concluding the treaty between Russia and Japan at the end of the Russo-Japanese War. The Nobel Prizes, established by the Swedish inventor Alfred Nobel, are awarded annually in six fields to individuals or institutions whose accomplishments have been of great benefit to humanity.

6899. National Geographic Society gold medal was the Hubbard medal, presented on December 15, 1906, in Washington, DC, by President Theodore Roosevelt to Commander Robert Edwin Peary for his Arctic explorations. On December 15, 1909, Peary received a second medal for his discovery of the North Pole the previous April 6. The first woman to receive the Hubbard medal was Anne Morrow Lindbergh, copilot and radio operator of the Charles A. Lindbergh Aerial Survey, on March 31, 1934. The National Geographic Society awarded a special gold medal on June 21, 1932, to Amelia Earhart for her achievement in becoming the first woman to make a solo transatlantic flight.

6900. Nobel Prize in physics awarded to an American was granted in 1907 to Albert Abraham Michelson of the University of Chicago, Chicago, IL, "for his optical instruments of precision, and the spectroscopic and metrologic investigations which he carried out by means of them."

6901. Nobel Prize in medicine and physiology awarded to an American was granted in 1912 to Dr. Alexis Carrel of the Rockefeller Institute for Medical Research, New York City, "for his work on vascular ligature and on the grafting of blood vessels and organs."

6902. Nobel Prize in chemistry awarded to an American was granted in 1914 to Theodore William Richards of Harvard University, Cambridge, MA, "in recognition of his accurate determination of the atomic weight of a large number of chemical elements." The prize of 146,900 Swedish kroner was presented on November 12, 1915, in Stockholm.

6903. Distinguished Flying Cross was presented to Charles Lindbergh by President Calvin Coolidge in Washington, DC, on June 11, 1927, in recognition of his pioneering solo flight from New York to Paris that had taken place the previous month. The first woman aviator to receive the award was Amelia Earhart, in recognition of her own solo flight across the Atlantic; she received it on July 29, 1932, in Los Angeles, CA.

6904. Nobel Prize in literature awarded to an American was granted in 1930 to Sinclair Lewis "for his great and living art in painting life, with a talent for creating types with wit and humor." The first American woman to win the prize was Pearl Sydenstricker Buck, author of *The Good Earth* and other novels about China. She received it on December 10, 1938, at the Concert House, Stockholm, Sweden.

6905. Nobel Peace Prize awarded to an American woman was granted to Jane Addams, the pioneering social worker who founded Hull House in Chicago, IL, to serve the city's poor residents. She received the award jointly with Dr. Nicholas Murray Butler, president of Columbia University, for founding the American Civil Liberties Union in 1920. It was accepted for them at Oslo, Norway, on December 10, 1931, by Hoffman Philips, U.S. minister to Norway. The first woman to receive the peace prize was Bertha von Suttner of Austria in 1905.

6906. Nobel Prize shared by an American husband and wife was the Nobel Prize in medicine, awarded to Dr. Carl Ferdinand Cori and Dr. Gerty Theresa Cori of the Washington University School of Medicine, St. Louis, MO, who discovered how sugar in the human system is coverted into glycogen through an enzyme or biological catalyst called phosphorylase. The award was announced on October 23, 1947. The Coris shared the prize with Dr. Bernardo Alberto Houssay of the Buenos Aires Institute of Biology and Experimental Medicine, who was recognized for his work on the relation between the pancreas and the pituitary gland.

Courtesy of the United States National Library of Medicine, B05351

Dr. Ferdinand Cori

6907. Nobel Peace Prize awarded to an African-American was awarded to Dr. Ralph Johnson Bunche, whose mediations in 1949 between Israel and the Arab nations that attacked it resulted in an armistice settlement. On December 10, 1950, at Oslo, Norway, he received the Nobel Medal and diploma and a cash award equivalent to $31,674.

6908. Nobel Peace Prize awarded to a professional soldier was awarded to General George Catlett Marshall on December 10, 1953, at Oslo University, Oslo, Norway. Marshall was the chief of staff of the Army during World War II and the sponsor of the postwar European Recovery Program.

6909. Nobel Prize winner to receive awards in two different categories was Dr. Linus Carl Pauling of the California Institute of Technology, Pasadena, CA, who was presented with the award for chemistry on December 10, 1954, at Stockholm, Sweden, and the Peace Prize on December 10, 1963, at Oslo, Norway. The awards were worth $35,000 and $50,000 respectively.

6910. Presidential Unit Citation award in peacetime was made by President Dwight David Eisenhower on August 8, 1958, to the crew of the submarine *Nautilus* for its voyage from June 8 to August 5, 1958, across the top of the world from the Bering Sea to the Greenland Sea, passing submerged beneath the geographic North Pole. Her crew was entitled to wear a citation ribbon and a special clasp in the form of a golden *N*.

6911. Federal employee to win a Nobel Prize was Marshall Warren Nirenberg, who joined the staff of the National Institutes of Health in Bethesda, MD, in 1960. On October 16, 1968, he received the year's Nobel Prize in Physiology or Medicine for his work in understanding the relationship between messenger RNA and protein synthesis, a discovery crucial to the deciphering of the genetic code. The prize was shared with two others.

6912. Nobel Prize in Economics awarded to an American was awarded on December 10, 1970, to Paul Anthony Samuelson of the Massachusetts Institute of Technology, Cambridge, MA, for his work in applying scientific and mathematic analyses to the study of economics.

6913. Nobel Prize winner to win twice in the same field was physicist John Bardeen of Champaign, IL. He and two co-winners, Dr. William Shockley and Dr. William Houser Bralton, received the Nobel Prize in physics at Stockholm, Sweden, on December 10, 1956, for their work on semiconductors and the discrepancy of the transistor effect. Bardeen also shared the 1972 prize with Leon N. Cooper and John Robert Schrieffer for their explanation of superconductivity leading to more efficient transmission of electrical power.

6914. Presidential Citizen Medal was presented on May 14, 1973, to the widow of Roberto Walker Clemente, star outfielder of the Pittsburgh Pirates, who was killed December 31, 1972, in the crash of a DC-7 four-engined cargo plane off San Juan International Airport, San Juan, PR, while delivering aid to victims of the earthquake in Managua, Nicaragua. The medal was established by executive order on November 13, 1969, by President Richard Milhous Nixon for "citizens of the United States of America who have performed exemplary deeds of service for their country or their fellow citizens."

6915. Year in which Nobel Prizes were won by Americans in five of six categories was 1976. On December 10, 1976, in Stockholm, Sweden, King Carl XVI Gustaf presented medals to William Nunn Lipscomb, Jr., in chemistry; Saul Bellow, literature; Milton Friedman, economics; Baruch Samuel Blumberg and Daniel Carleton Gajdusek, medicine; Burton Richter and Samuel Chao Chung Ting, physics. The Nobel Peace Prize went to Mairead Corrigan and Betty Williams of Northern Ireland.

6916. Charles Stark Draper Prize for engineering and technology was awarded in February 1990 to Robert N. Noyce and Jack S. Kilby, who, working independently, invented the integrated circuit and developed its commercial potential. The $350,000 prize, which included a gold medal, was established by the National Academy of Engineering in 1989 to honor engineers who contribute "to the advancement of human welfare and freedom."

6917. Medal of Technology awarded to a woman was won by Rear Admiral Grace Murray Hopper in 1991, when she was 85. During World War II, Hopper was assigned by the Navy to the Bureau of Ordnance Computation Project at Harvard University, Cambridge, MA. Later she became a senior mathematician for the Eckert-Mauchly Corporation in Philadelphia, PA, working on UNIVAC, the world's first fully electronic commercial computer. In 1955, she developed a prototype compiler, a computer language for automatically generating programs in the low-level machine code understood by a computer's central processing unit. This was the basis for COBOL (Common Business Oriented Language), the first widely used programming language for business. The medal is the highest award for technological achievement awarded by the federal government.

6918. Nobel Prize in literature awarded to an African-American writer was awarded in 1993 to the novelist Toni Morrison. Morrison, born in 1931, won the Pulitzer Prize in 1988 for her novel *Beloved*.

6919. American honored by Yad Vashem in Jerusalem, Israel's Holocaust memorial, was Varian Fry, a New York City editor who had witnessed the persecution of Jews in Germany. In 1940-41, he ran a clandestine rescue network in Marseilles, France, that used forged documents and underground routes to bring some 2,000 people out of Nazi-occupied Europe. He was posthumously named one of the Righteous Among the Nations by Yad Vashem in February 1996.

6920. American woman honored by Yad Vashem in Jerusalem, Israel, was Martha Sharp of Wellesley, MA. On June 13, 2006, she and her husband, Unitarian minister Waitstill Sharp, were posthumously honored as two of the Righteous Among the Nations for their work in helping refugees escape Europe and for risking their lives to smuggle the German writer Lion Feuchtwanger to freedom.

Crime

6921. Kidnapping is recorded in a letter dated July 8, 1524, from Giovanni da Verrazano, the Florentine explorer, to Francis I, king of France. The letter, which was sent from Dieppe, France, chronicled Verrazano's discoveries in America. Verrazano relates that in 1524 his crew "tooke a [Native American] childe from . . . [an] olde woman to bring into France, and going about to take . . . [a] young woman which was very beautiful and of tall stature, they could not possibly, for the great outcries that she made, bring her to the sea; and especially having great woods to pass through and being farre from the ship, we purposed to leave her behinde, beareing away the childe only."

6922. Slander proceedings were instituted on September 17, 1607, by John Robinson, who accused Edward Maria Wingfield, the first governor of the colony at Jamestown, VA, "of having said he, with others, consented to run awaye with the shallop to Newfoundland." A verdict was rendered in favor of Robinson.

6923. Duel of which there is any record took place on June 18, 1621, between two servants of Stephen Hopkins, one of the leaders of the Plymouth Colony. Governor William Bradford's decision was rendered as follows: "The Second Offense is the first Duel fought in New England, upon a Challenge at Single Combat with Sword and Dagger between Edward Dotey and Edward Leister, Servants of Mr. Hopkins; Both being wounded, the one in the Hand, the other in the Thigh; they are adjudg'd by the whole Company to have their Head and Feet tied together, and so to lie for 24 hours, without Meat or Drink; which is begun to be inflicted, but within an Hour, because of their great Pains, at their own and their Master's humble request, upon Promise of better Carriage, they are Released by the Governor."

6924. Pirate on the Atlantic seaboard was Dixie Bull, an English colonist who had received a grant of land at York, ME. In June 1632, while he was away in Penobscot Bay, a French pinnace arrived and seized his shallop and stock of "coats, ruggs, blanketts, bisketts, etc." Bull avenged himself by becoming a pirate and looting Bristol, ME.

6925. Treason trial by a colony was held on May 7, 1634, when the Virginia Assembly heard complaints against Sir John Harvey, governor of Virginia. On April 28, 1635, he was removed from the governorship as a traitor and replaced by Captain John West. Harvey was returned to England, where his case was considered. On April 2, 1636, he returned to assume his post, which he held until November 1639.

6926. American "Robin Hood" was a thief named Tom Cook, born in 1741 in Westborough, MA. For years, Cook stole from the rich and gave to the poor in scores of New England towns. He called himself "the Leveller." He was finally caught roasting a stolen goose in an abandoned schoolhouse in Brookline, MA. As punishment, Cook was offered the choice of staying in jail or running the gauntlet between two rows of his former victims, all of whom were armed with whips. He chose the gauntlet, which he survived.

6927. Street gangs were formed in the New York City slums beginning about 1785. The members were young tradesmen who claimed various streets as their territory and fought one another over these claims. The first organized gang of street criminals was the Forty Thieves, formed by Edward Coleman in 1826 in Five Points, an Irish slum neighborhood in lower Manhattan. The gangs of Five Points began the custom of having identifiable clothing, hand signals, and rituals.

6928. Bank robbery took place in Philadelphia on the night of August 31–September 1, 1798, when $162,821 was stolen from vaults of the Bank of Pennsylvania at Carpenters' Hall. The largest theft of money to take place in North America in the 18th century, it was an inside job, involving Isaac Davis, who had assisted in the bank's move to Carpenters' Hall, and bank porter Thomas Cunningham, who was on duty the night of the robbery. Davis was confronted by police when he deposited some of the stolen cash into an account at the bank he had just robbed. He made a full confession and returned all but $5,000 of the money; in exchange, he was pardoned and never served a day in prison. Patrick Lyon, a locksmith who was wrongly accused of being an accomplice, spent three months in jail and later wrote a book about his ordeal that became the first true-crime bestseller.

6929. Dueling law enacted by a state was an "act to prevent the evil practice of duelling," passed by the Fourth General Assembly held at Knoxville, TN, and signed on November 10, 1801, by Governor Archibald Roane.

6930. Conscience fund for people with nagging consciences was started in 1811 during President James Madison's administration by an unknown person who claimed to have defrauded the government and the Treasury of $5 and who wanted to pay it. Other deposits in that year increased the total to $250. No further deposits were received until 1827, when $6 was forwarded. The largest amount collected in one year was received in 1950, when $370,285 was sent in. For statistical and accounting purposes, funds are listed as "Miscellaneous Receipts."

6931. Piracy law enacted by Congress was "an act to protect the commerce of the United States and punish the crime of piracy," enacted on March 3, 1819. Offenders convicted by a circuit court could be punished by death.

6932. Gun control law enacted by a state was a ban on the ownership of pistols small enough to be concealed, enacted by Georgia in 1837. It was struck down by the state Supreme Court as unconstitutional. The law also outlawed Bowie knives.

6933. Temporary insanity defense in a criminal case was used by Daniel Sickles, a congressman from New York. On February 25, 1859, Sickles shot and killed Philip Barton Key, the son of Francis Scott Key, author of "The Star-Spangled Banner," after he learned that the younger Key was having an affair with his wife. His lawyer, James T. Brady, offered the defense of "temporary insanity." Sickles was acquitted. He eventually became a general in the Civil War, in which he lost a leg, and served as minister to Spain.

6934. Robbery of a disabled train took place on May 5, 1865, when an Ohio and Mississippi Railroad train en route from St. Louis, MO, to Cincinnati, OH, overturned at North Bend, OH, 14 miles from Cincinnati, and was robbed by looters.

6935. Bank and train robbery gang that was well organized was the James Gang, which operated in Missouri after the Civil War. The gang included the James brothers, Frank and Jesse, and the Younger brothers, Cole, James, and Robert. Their first bank holdup took place on February 13, 1866, at the Clay County Savings and Loan Association in Liberty, MO. The cashiers, brothers Greenup and William Bird, were locked in the bank's vault, while the robbers joked that "all birds should be caged." They made off with $60,000 in currency and securities. It was the first of more than 26 raids by the James Gang that yielded more than $500,000 in loot.

6936. Robbery of a train in motion took place on October 6, 1866, when Frank Sparks, John Reno, and Simeon Reno boarded an Ohio and Mississippi Railroad baggage and express car while it was getting into motion and threw off two safes, one containing $15,000 and the other $30,000. The second safe was recovered. The bandits were arrested, freed on bail, and never tried, although they were later convicted of other crimes.

6937. Tong organized crime gang was the Kwong Dock Tong of San Francisco, CA, organized about 1870. Tongs were secret societies formed by Chinese immigrants. The first tong war broke out in 1873 as a result of an attack made on Ming Long, a member of the Kwong Dock Tong, by Low Sing, a member of the Suey Sing Tong. The dispute arose in connection with the gangs' traffic in forced prostitution. At Ross Valley and Waverly Place, San Francisco, the two factions met by appointment and began shooting. Six members of the Kwong Dock Tong were wounded, three of them fatally, and one of the Suey Sing Tong men was killed.

6938. Fingerprint conviction in a crime was recorded on February 1, 1911, in the Criminal Court of Cook County, IL, when Thomas Jennings was found guilty and sentenced to death for the murder of Clarence B. Hiller on September 19, 1910. The conviction was upheld by the Illinois Supreme Court on December 21, 1911, when the court ruled that fingerprint evidence was admissible. Jennings was hanged in the Cook County jail on February 16, 1912.

6939. Airplane bombing raid by criminals occurred on November 12, 1926, during a Prohibition feud between rival illicit beer and rum factions, the Sheltons and the Birgers, in Williamson County, IL. A plane swooped low and dropped three crude bombs on the farmhouse of Charles Birger. They failed to explode, which probably saved the lives of Birger and his companions, for the marksmanship of the flyer was unusually good.

6940. Armored truck holdup was staged on March 11, 1927, by the Flatheads gang, about seven miles from Pittsburgh, PA, on the Bethel Road on the way to Coverdale. An armored truck carrying a $104,250 payroll of the Pittsburgh Terminal Coal Company blew up when it drove over a mine planted under the roadbed by the bandits. Five guards were badly injured.

6941. Airplane bombing raid by a mercenary soldier took place in 1929, when Patrick Murphy, an American pilot in the pay of Mexican rebels, dropped bombs on Naco, AZ. Murphy apologized to the United States, claiming that he had meant to bomb the town of Naco in Sonora, Mexico, just across the border, but he bombed the American town several more times anyway. When the 1929 Mexican revolution collapsed, Murphy disappeared.

6942. Organized crime massacre of national notoriety was the St. Valentine's Day Massacre, which took place in Chicago, IL, on February 14, 1929. In a gangland struggle for control of the Chicago trade in bootleg liquor, gunmen in the employ of mobster Al Capone machine-gunned seven members of the George "Bugs" Moran gang in a garage on North Clark Street.

6943. Mobster convicted for tax evasion was Alphonse Capone, better known as Al Capone, who ruled Chicago's illicit beer and liquor trade during Prohibition. Capone's crime organization netted him more than $100 million a year in the late 1920s, little of which he declared to the government. On October 24, 1931, he was sentenced in a federal court in Chicago to 11 years' imprisonment and a $50,000 fine for failing to pay $231,000 in federal income taxes.

6944. Federal gun control regulation was enacted by Congress on June 26, 1934, as part of a revision of the Internal Revenue Code. Known as the National Firearms Act, it required owners of certain classes of weapons, including fully automatic firearms, silencers, and short-barrelled rifles and shotguns, to register them with the federal Bureau of Alcohol, Tobacco, Firearms, and Explosives in Washington, DC. It also imposed taxes on the manufacture and transfer of these weapons, and required purchasers to be fingerprinted and to receive clearance from the bureau and from local law enforcement.

6945. Public Enemy Number 1 so labeled by the Federal Bureau of Investigation was Indiana-born bank robber John Dillinger, the most notorious criminal of the 1930s. In 1933–34, the charismatic, nattily dressed Dillinger held up banks throughout the Midwest and made spectacular escapes from prisons in Indiana and Ohio. He was finally shot and killed by federal agents on July 22, 1934, as he emerged from the Biograph Movie Theater in Chicago, IL.

6946. Lie detector used as evidence in a court of law for consideration by a jury was the Keeler Polygraph, invented by Leonarde Keeler of the Scientific Crime Detection Laboratory, Northwestern University School of Law, Chicago, IL. Keeler conducted a test on February 2, 1935, in Portage, WI, and produced graphs of the test in the case of *Wisconsin State v. Cecil Loniello and Tony Grignano* that was being heard in the Circuit Court of Columbia County, WI. Both defendants were found guilty of assault. Tests of a similar nature had been used in minor civil and criminal cases as early as 1924, when blood pressure readings were made with a Tycos sphygmomanometer.

6947. Ten Most Wanted list was issued by the Federal Bureau of Investigation in March 1950 at the urging of the International News

Service, which asked the FBI for information on most-wanted fugitives for a series of articles. It was largely a publicity stunt, but one that paid off: Two of the men were caught within the month, based on tips from the public.

6948. Criminal on the FBI's Ten Most Wanted list was Thomas James Holden, who headed the first list, issued on March 14, 1950. Holden had been accused of committing a triple murder in Chicago, IL, and had fled the state to avoid arrest. He was caught in 1951 after the FBI received a tip from a citizen who had seen his photograph in a newspaper. The first woman to be placed on the Ten Most Wanted list was Ruth Eisemann-Schier, accused in the kidnapping for ransom of Barbara Jane Mackle from a motel in Decatur, GA, on December 17, 1968. Mackle was found alive about 80 hours after the abduction, buried in a box underground. Eisemann-Schier was arrested in Norman, OK, on March 5, 1969, convicted, and sentenced to a seven-year prison term.

6949. Destruction of an American airliner by a criminal took place on November 1, 1955, when United Airlines Flight 629, en route from Denver, CO, to Portland, OR, exploded 11 minutes after takeoff. All 44 people aboard were killed. Their murderer was identified as Jack Gilbert Graham, whose mother was one of the passengers. In her suitcase he had hidden a dynamite bomb operated by a timer. His intention had been to collect her life insurance money. He was executed on January 11, 1957.

6950. Murder trial to be televised was the trial of Harry Washburn, held on December 5–9, 1955, in the District Court, Waco, TX, with Judge Drummond William Bartlett presiding. The defendant was accused of killing his former mother-in-law, Helen Harris Weaver, with a car bomb at San Angelo, TX. The defense and prosecution agreed to allow one camera to be placed on a balcony. The entire 25-hour proceedings were televised by KWTX-TV, Waco, TX, as a public service to the community. Washburn was convicted on December 10 and sentenced to life imprisonment.

6951. Skyjacking of a commercial American airplane took place on May 1, 1961, during the flight of a National Airlines twin-engine Convair CV 440 from Miami, FL, to Key West, FL. The plane left Marathon, FL, at 3:23 P.M. with eight passengers. The crew consisted of pilot Francis X. Riley, copilot J. T. Richardson, and flight attendant Inez Barlow. A passenger named Antulio Ramirez Ortiz threatened the crew and passengers with a pistol and a knife. The plane landed in Havana and returned to Key West at 8:35 P.M., 4.5 hours late. The string of airplane highjackings that followed were dubbed "skyjackings" by the press and led to the U.S.'s first air piracy law, passed in September 1961.

6952. Murder to be captured live on television took place at 12:20 P.M. on November 24, 1963, in the police headquarters at Dallas, TX. While television news cameras were rolling, a Dallas police officer brought in Lee Harvey Oswald, the alleged assassin of President John Fitzgerald Kennedy. Oswald was in the process of being transferred to the county jail. A man in the crowd stepped forward and fired a concealed pistol at Oswald, killing him. The crime was witnessed by millions of people. The murderer was Jack Ruby (Jacob L. Rubenstein), a Dallas nightclub owner.

6953. Shelter for abused women was Haven House Inc., a privately funded project of Alcoholics Anonymous in Pasadena, CA, where it opened in 1964. The shelter contracted with the state of California in 1974 to provide services, including counseling, for at-risk families.

6954. State payments to crime victims were made by the California Victim Compensation Program, established in 1965. The program used fines levied on criminals as part of their sentences to help victims with medical care, mental health counseling, funeral expenses, lost worktime, and other needs.

6955. Rape crisis center was Bay Area Women Against Rape, a nonprofit organization founded in 1971 in Berkeley, CA, by Oleta Kirk Abrams after her foster daughter was sexually assaulted.

6956. Skyjacking in which the skyjacker disappeared took place on November 24, 1971, when D. B. Cooper commandeered a Northwest Airlines plane at 11 P.M. He parachuted near Woodland, WA, into a raging thunderstorm with winds up to 200 miles per hour and the temperature at seven degrees below zero, wearing only a light business suit. He escaped with 10,000 $20 bills. He was never found, and it is believed that he was killed.

6957. Trial in which lawyers appeared on a Picturephone took place in the Federal Court of Claims, Washington, DC. On October 16, 1975, a three-judge court, composed of Byron Skelton, Robert Kuntzig, and Philip Nichols, Jr., heard a claim for damages that had been in litigation for 15 years, involving $270,000. The lawyers, Rex E. Lee, assistant attorney general, and Bruce Mayor, counsel for the Merritt-Chapmann and Scott Company, presented their arguments before a picturephone located in the Bell Telephone Picturephone Service, 393 Seventh Avenue, New York City.

6958. State to make marital rape a crime was Nebraska, which did so in 1976. The traditional assumption held that marriage implies consent to sex and that a husband cannot be charged with rape for having sexual intercourse with his wife against her will. Nebraska's law abolished that defense.

> The first U.S. court to declare marriage a valid defense against a rape charge was the Supreme Judicial Court of Massachusetts in its 1857 decision in COMMONWEALTH V. FOGERTY.

6959. State to require arrests in cases of domestic violence was Oregon, in its Abuse Prevention Act of 1977. The law required a police officer responding to a domestic violence complaint to arrest anyone who had assaulted another person, threatened to commit assault, or violated a restraining order.

6960. FBI sting operation against corrupt politicians was Abscam. It began in 1978 when the FBI created a fake business, Abdul Enterprises, Ltd., and hired an experienced con man to run it. Undercover FBI operatives offered money to a number of politicians in exchange for their influence in shady business deals. The sting resulted in the convictions of one senator, six congressmen, and a number of lesser politicians

6961. Poisoning of store merchandise known to have resulted in numerous deaths took place in and around Chicago, IL. In a three-day period from September 29 to October 1, 1982, seven people died after taking Tylenol, a brand of acetaminophen, which they had bought at local drugstores and supermarkets. A murderer who was never apprehended had removed the bottles from store shelves, opened them, added cyanide to the capsules of Tylenol, and replaced them in the stores. The poisonings led to the introduction of wraps and seals on all pharmaceutical products and many other products as well.

6962. Bioterror attack on American soil in modern times was carried out by an armed isolationist cult, the Rajneeshee, in a bid to take political control of Wasco County, OR. Beginning on August 29, 1984, cultists infected two county commissioners with a toxic strain of bacteria, then contaminated the nearby town of The Dalles, using spray bottles to squirt salmonella on drinking glasses, doorknobs, urinal handles, supermarket produce, and salad bars. No one died, but 751 people fell ill of apparent food poisoning and 45 were hospitalized.

> The Rajneeshee bioterror plot was only discovered when cult members informed the FBI. Eight Rajneeshee were convicted, and the group's leader, Bhagwan Shri Rajneesh, was deported to India.

6963. National hotline for victims of domestic violence was a toll-free service that was started in 1987 by the National Coalition Against Domestic Violence in Washington, DC.

6964. Ban on cheap handguns enacted by a state was enacted in Maryland on May 23, 1988, effective January 1, 1990. The law banned the manufacture and sale of pistols that were unsafe or easy to conceal.

6965. Computer hacker to be convicted was Donald Burleson, the former director of computer security at a Texas insurance firm, USPA and IRA of Fort Worth, TX. Three days after Burleson was fired in 1985, the company discovered that 168,000 sales records had been erased from its computer system. Burleson used a type of computer virus called a "logic bomb" or "worm" to destroy the computer data. In September 1988, a Fort Worth jury convicted him on third-degree felony charges and sentenced him to seven years' probation and an $11,800 fine.

6966. American mercenaries convicted of planning a terrorist attack within the

United States on behalf of a foreign government were Jeff Fort, leader of the El Rukn gang in Chicago, IL, and his senior lieutenants in the gang hierarchy, who conspired with agents of Colonal Muammar Qaddafy, the dictator of Libya, to destroy police stations, government offices, and similar targets. Their payment was to have been $2.5 million and asylum in Libya. They were arrested after they attempted to purchase a shoulder-fired missile from an undercover FBI agent on July 31, 1986. Fort was found guilty in 1987 and sentenced to 80 years without parole. More than 50 El Rukn members were also prosecuted. The man who made the purchase, Melvin Edward Mays, eluded authorities and was placed on the FBI's Top Ten Most Wanted List in February 1989. He was apprehended by the FBI on March 9, 1995.

6967. International cyberespionage case involved the infiltration of government, corporate, and institutional computer systems in the United States, France, Switzerland, and West Germany by a group of West German hackers for the benefit of the KGB, the Soviet Union's spy agency. The first arrests in the case were made on March 2, 1989.

6968. Antistalking law enacted by a state was passed by California in 1990, to become effective on January 1, 1991. It criminalized the acts of following or harassing another person with the intent to inspire fear and allowed police officers to intervene before an act of violence was committed. The law was passed after actress Rebecca Schaeffer was killed in Los Angeles by a fan who had stalked her.

6969. Statewide registration of assault weapons was mandated under the Assault Weapons Control Act passed by California in 1989. Drafted by California Democratic state senator David A. Roberti, the law required all assault weapons to be registered with the state by January 1, 1991. By the deadline, only about 6 percent of the state's estimated 300,000 assault weapons had been registered, mainly because of resistance by individual owners but also because the state made little effort to enforce the law.

6970. Criminal convicted on the evidence of DNA matching was Timothy W. Spencer, who died in the electric chair in the Greensville Correctional Center, Greensville, VA, on April 27, 1994. Spencer was convicted of murdering four women in Richmond, VA, in 1987. DNA from his cells was matched with DNA found in evidence at the scene of the crime, a process also known as genetic fingerprinting.

6971. Reparations awarded to victims of a racially motivated massacre in the United States were authorized by the state of Florida on May 23, 1994, to compensate the survivors of an attack perpetrated against the African-American residents of Rosewood, FL, over the course of eight days in January 1923 when the town was destroyed by a white mob. A total of $2 million was appropriated.

6972. Bombing by domestic terrorists resulting in large loss of life occurred at 9:02 A.M. on April 19, 1995, when a massive truck bomb destroyed the Alfred R. Murrah Federal Building in Oklahoma City, OK. One hundred sixty-eight people were killed, including 19 children, and an estimated 850 were injured. The rescue effort lasted two weeks and involved more than 12,000 volunteers, one of whom was killed by falling debris. A nationwide manhunt resulted in the arrest of Timothy McVeigh and Terry Nichols, both of whom had connections to the far-right militia movement.

6973. Juvenile hacker charged under federal law was an unnamed Massachusetts teenager who used his PC to disrupt a communications computer at the Federal Aviation Administration control tower at Worcester Airport in Worcester, MA, on March 10, 1997. The airport's fire and security departments were also affected. The teenager received probation and was barred from using a computer modem for two years.

6974. Federal prosecution of a hate crime on the Internet was the case of Richard Machado of Los Angeles, CA, accused of violating the civil rights of 59 Asian students at the University of California at Irvine by sending them threatening, racist electronic mail. The case was tried in the federal district court at Santa Ana, CA. On November 25, 1997, the jury returned deadlocked and Judge Alicemarie H. Stotler declared a mistrial. Machado was tried a second time, convicted, and sentenced on May 4, 1998, to a year of probation and a $1,000 fine. Machado had already served a year in Federal custody for fleeing to Mexico after his indictment in November 1996.

6975. Law making identity theft a federal crime was the Identity Theft and Assumption Deterrence Act of 1998, which made transferring or using another person's means of identification a crime subject to federal penalties. Means of identification was defined as including name, social security number, date of birth, official state or federal driver's license or identification number, alien registration number, government passport number, and employer or taxpayer identification number.

6976. Murderer convicted on the basis of nationally televised evidence was retired pathologist Dr. Jack Kevorkian, the advocate for assisted suicide. On September 17, 1998, Kevorkian videotaped himself administering a lethal injection to Thomas Youk of Waterford Township, MI, who was terminally ill with amyotrophic lateral sclerosis, a paralyzing disease. The Michigan legislature had recently made assisted suicide a felony punishable by up to five years in prison. On November 22, the CBS newsmagazine *60 Minutes* televised Kevorkian's videotape, and on December 9, he was charged with murder, based mainly on the *60 Minutes* telecast. The defense argued that the patient's intense suffering prompted him to ask the doctor to assist in his death. Kevorkian was found guilty of second-degree murder on March 26, 1999, and was sentenced to 10 to 25 years.

6977. State criminal prosecution for the sale of confidential personal information took place on June 25, 1999, when private detective James J. Rapp and his wife, Regana L. Rapp, both of Aurora, CO, were indicted by a grand jury on two counts each of racketeering. They were believed to have sold personal information, including credit card records, confidential phone numbers, and bank account registers, to anyone willing to pay the price, including criminals. While it is not a federal crime to impersonate anyone except a law officer or government official, it is against the law in the state of Colorado to impersonate someone else for gain.

6978. Trial broadcast by the court over the Internet was the murder trial of Shirley Egan, age 68, a wheelchair-bound invalid, for the shooting death of her daughter, Georgette Smith, 42. The daughter had survived the shooting with paralysis from the neck down and had received court permission to have her life-support system turned off. After Smith died, Egan went on trial on August 16, 1999, in Orlando, FL, at the Orange County Courthouse. The courtroom was equipped with fiber-optics, audio and video output, and an Internet server, and the daily proceedings were available on a special Web site. Previous trials had been broadcast over the Internet by private companies; this was the first broadcast by the judicial system.

6979. Federal conviction for Internet piracy under federal law was Jeffrey Gerard Levy, 22, a senior at the University of Oregon in Eugene, OR. On August 20, 1999, Levy was found in violation of the No Electronic Theft Act of 1997 for illegally posting computer software programs, musical recordings, entertainment software programs, and digitally recorded movies on his Internet Web site, and allowing the general public to download and copy the copyrighted material.

6980. Antiglobalization protest of significance took place in Seattle, WA, in 1999 during a meeting of members of the World Trade Organization. From November 30, 1999, to December 3, 1999, masses of rioting protesters from the United States and around the world took Seattle police by surprise, committing widespread acts of vandalism and forcing the cancellation of the WTO's opening ceremonies.

6981. Criminal conviction in an airliner crash was handed down in federal court in December 1999 against SabreTech, St. Louis, MO, an aviation maintenance contractor. Employees of the company were responsible for mistakes that resulted in the illegal placement of 144 oxygen canisters in the cargo hold of ValuJet Flight 592, a passenger flight from Miami to Atlanta, in May 1996. The canisters exploded, causing a crash that killed 110 people. An appeals court threw out the guilty verdicts on eight of the nine charges, but upheld the firm's conviction on the charge of improperly training its workers in handling hazardous materials.

6982. Physician convicted of manslaughter for prescribing pain medication was James Graves of Pace, FL. He was convicted by a state jury on February 19, 2002, and sentenced to 63 years in prison for the deaths of four patients who had overdosed on the opioid painkiller OxyContin after filling prescriptions he had written. Two had injected it, contrary to instructions, and two had combined it with other drugs.

6983. Conviction by an American jury for crimes against humanity was handed down on October 15, 2003, in Miami, FL. The defendant was Armando Fernandez Larios, a former member of a military death squad in Chile. He was found liable for civil damages in the torture and murder of economist Winston Cabello, one of the 75 political prisoners killed in the aftermath of Augusto Pinochet's coup against Salvador Allende in September 1973. The jury awarded $4 million to Cabello's family. The plaintiffs and the defendant were all current residents of Florida. The decision was upheld by an appeals court in 2006.

6984. Law against human smuggling enacted by a state was passed by a bipartisan majority of the Arizona legislature and went into effect on August 12, 2005. The law, which was intended to stem the flow of illegal immigrants from Mexico, changed the crime of transporting people unlawfully across the border from a misdemeanor to a felony. In June 2006 a state court ruled that the law could be used to prosecute undocumented workers who pay smugglers to help them enter Arizona.

6985. Animal rights group convicted of terrorism was Stop Huntingdon Animal Cruelty, an organization formed to protest activities at animal testing facilities, including one in New Jersey that was operated by Huntingdon Life Sciences, a British company. On March 2, 2006, the group's director, Lauren Gazzola; its president, Kevin Kjonaas; and four other defendants were convicted by a federal jury in Trenton, NJ, of violating the 1992 Animal Enterprise Terror Act because their Web site encouraged violence against employees and clients of Huntingdon.

Punishment

6986. Execution in America was that of John Billington, one of the signers of the Pilgrims' compact, who was hanged in Plymouth, MA, on September 30, 1630. He was "arraigned, and both by grand and petie jurie found guilty of willful murder, by plaine and notorious evidence, and was for the same accordingly executed. This, as it was the first execution amongst them, so was it a matter of great sadness unto them. He way-laid a young man, one John Newcomin (about a former quarele), and shote him with a gune, whereof he dyed."

6987. Execution for witchcraft on record was that of Achsah Young of Massachusetts, who was hanged as a witch on May 27, 1647, although some histories of New England state that the first accused witch to be executed was Margaret Jones of Charlestown, MA, hanged in 1648.

6988. Prison was constructed in 1676 in Nantucket, MA. The court hired William Bunker on November 16, 1676, to keep the prison for one year and agreed to pay him "foeur pounds, halfe in wheat, the other in other graine."

6989. Colonist hanged for treason was Jacob Leisler, who led an insurrection against Governor Francis Nicholson of New York in 1689 "for the preservation of the Protestant religion" and in behalf of the sovereigns William and Mary. Through trickery, the aristocratic party regained power and in a manifestly unfair trial convicted Leisler of treason. He was hanged on May 16, 1691, from a scaffold erected in City Hall Park.

6990. Prison reform society to bring about changes in prison administration was the Philadelphia Society for Alleviating the Miseries of Public Prisons, formed on May 8, 1787, in the German School House on Cherry Street, Philadelphia, PA, by Philadelphia Quakers. The first president was William White. A similar organization for war prisoners was the Philadelphia Society for Relieving Distressed Prisoners Owing to the War of Independence, organized on February 7, 1776, which ceased operations in September 1777.

6991. Prison to have individual cells for prisoners was the Walnut Street prison in Philadelphia, PA, built in 1773, which was remodeled in 1790 in accordance with the act of April 5, 1790, of the Pennsylvania General Assembly. The remodeled prison contained 24 cells, each six feet wide, eight feet long, and seven feet high. The prisoners were kept in solitary confinement and were not allowed to leave their cells. The prison held about 110 prisoners.

6992. Death penalty ban by a state was enacted by Pennsylvania on April 22, 1794. The law abolished all executions except in cases of murder in the first degree. Michigan enacted a general ban on the death penalty on May 4, 1846, except in cases of treason against the state.

6993. Federal law exempting debtors from prison on processes issuing from a United States court amounting to less than $30 was "an act for the relief of persons imprisoned for debt," passed on May 28, 1796. On February 28, 1839, an act of Congress prohibited imprisonment for debt by a United States court in states where such imprisonment had been abolished.

6994. State law abolishing imprisonment for debt was passed by Kentucky on December 17, 1821.

6995. Prison treadmill was completed on September 7, 1822, for the New York City Prison. The treadmill was designed to be operated by eight to 16 persons and to grind 40 to 50 bushels of maize daily. The wheel was 5 feet 2 inches in diameter. The treadmill was placed in operation on September 23, 1822, in a two-story building 60 feet in length and 30 feet wide, with a garret that served as a granary. The idea for the treadmill was suggested to Stephen Allen, the mayor of New York, by Isaac Collins, one of the managers of the Society for the Prevention of Pauperism, and Stephen Greelet.

6996. Reformatory for juvenile delinquents was the New York House of Refuge, New York City, which officially opened on January 1, 1825, with three boys and six girls. It was under the supervision of the Society for the Reformation of Juvenile Offenders in the City of New York. The first president was Cadwallader David Colden. On April 9, 1825, the state authorized a grant of $2,000 annually for the next five years.

6997. Execution of a white criminal for the murder of a Native American on record took place on January 12, 1825, when James Hudson was hanged in Madison County, IN, for the murder of Logan, a Seneca chief. Logan and nine other Native Americans, incuding three women and four children, were killed on March 22, 1824, in what as known as the Fall Creek Massacre. Three other white men who participated were hanged and a fourth was pardoned.

6998. Branding punishment by a federal court was imposed at Pensacola, FL, in 1844. Jonathan Walker, a ship captain, was convicted of stealing seven slaves, whom he carried into his 30-foot schooner. He set sail on June 23, 1844, intending to go to Nassau, but was captured by the U.S. steamer *General Taylor* and taken to Pensacola on July 20. He was imprisoned, tried in the District Court, and placed in the pillory on the public highway to be pelted with rotten eggs. He was sentenced to one year in jail for each of the seven slaves and was fined $600 for each slave plus all the costs of the trial. The initials SS, for "slave stealer," were branded on the palm of his right hand.

6999. Prison matrons for guarding women prisoners were appointed in 1845 through the efforts of the American Female Guardian Society. Four were assigned to Blackwell's Island, NY, and two the City Prison, New York City.

7000. Reformatory for boys established by a state was the reformatory school at Westborough, MA, later known as the Lyman School for Boys. It was authorized on April 9, 1847.

7001. Military prison on an island was Fort Jefferson, Monroe County, FL. Construction was begun in 1846 on an island in the Gulf of Mexico, 60 miles from Key West. It was a six-sided masonry structure with a huge courtyard in the center. The sides were 1,000 feet long, 80 feet high, and 60 feet thick. On January 19, 1861, it was garrisoned for the first time by Brevet Major Lewis Golding Arnold, 2nd U.S. Artillery, with four officers and 62 men. The fort had not been completed and was barely defensible. A prison for the confinement of U.S. military prisoners was established at Fort Jefferson in 1863. The prison, often called Dry Tortugas, was maintained during the Civil War.

7002. Execution for slave trading carried out by the federal government was the hanging of Nathaniel Gordon at the Tombs prison, New York City, on February 21, 1862. He had been tried and convicted of piracy under the law of May 15, 1820, which defined slave trading as piracy. Gordon, a native of Portland, ME, was the captain of the *Erie*. His ship was stopped by the U.S. *Mohican* about 50 miles off the African coast and was found to be carrying 890 Africans, including 600 children, to a slave market. The captives were released in Liberia and Gordon's ship was brought to New York City, where his trial was held.

7003. Citizen of the United States to be hanged for treason was William Bruce Mumford, a retired gambler. During the Civil War, Captain Theodorus Bailey was sent by Admiral David Glasgow Farragut to New Orleans, LA, where he hoisted the American flag over the mint on April 28, 1862. After the troops left, Mumford tore down the flag. On May 1, General Benjamin Franklin Butler arrived in New Orleans with 2,000 troops and took possession of the St. Charles Hotel. A crowd gathered in front of it, among them Mumford, who boasted of his exploit in humbling the "old rag of the United States." Mumford was arrested, tried under the direction of the provost marshal of the district of New Orleans, convicted, and hanged on June 7, 1862.

7004. Execution of a woman by hanging by the federal government took place on July 7, 1865. The condemned woman was Mary Eugenia Surratt, the proprietor of a boardinghouse in Washington, DC. Her son was a friend of the actor John Wilkes Booth and met with him and other plotters in the boardinghouse to plan the assassination of President Abraham Lincoln. The assassination was carried out on April 14, 1865. Mrs. Surratt was arrested and tried for conspiracy by a military commission of nine army officers headed by Major General David Hunter. The trial began on May 9 and ended on June 30 with a conviction and the death sentence. Four conspirators, including Mrs. Surratt, were hanged on July 7. Her guilt is still a subject of controversy. Her son was brought to trial, but the government failed to obtain an indictment, and he was released.

7005. State probation officer for juvenile delinquents was hired under a Massachusetts law enacted on June 23, 1869. The law required the governor to appoint a visiting agent at $2,500 a year to work for the welfare and redemption of delinquents, rather than for their punishment. The visiting agent or his deputies were directed to visit all children maintained wholly or in part by the Commonwealth of Massachusetts once every three months.

7006. Prison built for women and managed by women was the Indiana Reformatory Institution for Women and Girls, Indianapolis, IN, which received its first 17 prisoners on October 8, 1873. The first superintendent was Sarah J. Smith. In 1907 the name was changed to the Indiana Women's Prison. Beginning in January 1877, all members of the Board of Trustees were women.

7007. Probation system for criminals of all ages was legally established as a judicial policy by Boston, MA, in 1878 and by Massachusetts in 1880. This was the first such system in the world.

7008. Rotary jail was the Montgomery County Jail, built in 1882 in Crawfordsville, IN. The two-level cell block was constructed as a rotating cylinder divided into 16 cells (eight on each level), all radiating from the center. To access a cell, the jailer would rotate the block until the cell door lined up with the central opening. The turntable mechanism was responsible for numerous injuries and was stopped in 1939, but the jail continued to serve as the county lockup until it was converted to a museum in 1975. It is now on the National Register of Historic Places. The idea for the rotary jail was patented on July 12, 1881, by its inventors, Indianapolis businessmen William H. Brown and Benjamin F. Haugh, whose company built the Crawfordsville jail and several others.

7009. Execution by electrocution was that of William Kemmler, alias John Hart, who died on August 6, 1890, at Auburn Prison, Auburn, NY. He had been convicted of the first-degree murder of Matilda Ziegler. The electric chair used at the prison was invented by Dr. Alphonse David Rockwell. An autopsy was performed three hours after the execution under the direction of Dr. Carlos Frederick MacDonald. The first woman to be executed by electrocution was Martha M. Place of Brooklyn, New York City, who was electrocuted at Sing Sing Prison, Ossining, NY, on March 20, 1899, for the murder of her stepdaughter Ida.

7010. Federal penitentiary was the Federal Penitentiary at Atlanta, GA, which was authorized in 1899 and completed in January 1902. The Federal Penitentiary at Leavenworth, KS, was authorized earlier, on March 3, 1891, but was not completed until February 1, 1906.

7011. Prison organized into community groups was Auburn Prison, Auburn, NY. In 1914, a Mutual Welfare League of prisoners was created on an experimental basis to assume the responsibility of discipline in the prison.

7012. Prisoners in a federal penitentiary to be employed in industry produced cotton duck for mail bags and other purposes at the Cotton Duck Mill operated by the Federal Penitentiary in Atlanta, GA, whose first loom started on July 11, 1919. The building covered an area of almost three acres. In the first year, 386,414 yards of duck were produced. The mill was authorized by act of Congress on July 10, 1918, which appropriated $650,000 for equipment and $150,000 as working capital. A wage system for inmates, established on April 29, 1921, set up a wage fund of two cents per yard that was divided among the inmates in proportion to their number of hours of service.

7013. Execution by lethal gas took place on February 8, 1924, in Carson City, NV. The executed man was a Chinese gang member, Gee Jon, who had been convicted of killing a rival tong man. Lethal gas as a means of execution had been adopted by Nevada on March 28, 1921.

7014. Federal prison for women was the Federal Industrial Institution for Women, Alderson, WV, established by act of Congress in 1926 and opened the same year. The first superintendent was Dr. Mary Belle Harris, sworn in on March 12, 1925. The compound contained 17 two-story brick dormitories, each designed to accommodate 30 persons, and built on the college plan. They cost over $2 million and occupied 500 acres of land. There were no prison walls or guards.

7015. Execution for kidnapping was imposed by the Circuit Court of Kansas City, MO, on July 27, 1933. Walter H. McGee was found guilty by a jury of having kidnapped Mary McElroy, daughter of the city manager of Kansas City. The prosecutor was Assistant County Prosecutor Michael W. O'Hern. The court applied a congressional act of May 18, 1934, regarding interstate kidnapping.

7016. Death penalty authorized by federal law made the killing of a federal officer a mandatory capital offense. The law was enacted on May 18, 1934. The first man executed under the law was George W. Barrett, for the murder of federal agent Nelson Bernard Klein in College Corner, IN, on August 16, 1935. He was tried before U.S. District Judge Robert C. Baltzell, convicted on December 14, 1935, and hanged on March 24, 1936, at the Marion County Jail, Indianapolis, IN.

7017. Execution of an organized crime leader in the electric chair was that of Louis Buchalter, better known as Louis Lepke, the head of Murder Incorporated, a gang of mob assassins based in New York City. Lepke surrendered to FBI chief J. Edgar Hoover on August 24, 1939, to face a charge of union racketeering. Under a secret agreement, he pleaded guilty to a lesser charge and was sentenced to a 14-year term in the federal penitentiary at Fort Leavenworth, KS. After New York State authorities found out from a mob informer about Lepke's career of murder, he was tried again and sentenced to death. On March 4, 1944, Lepke went to the electric chair at Sing Sing Prison in Ossining, NY.

7018. Peacetime death sentence for espionage was imposed on April 5, 1951, by Judge Irving Robert Kaufman of the U.S. District Court, Southern District, who sentenced Ethel and Julius Rosenberg to death for passing secret information about nuclear weapons to the Soviet Union. The trial began on March 6, 1951, and the jury rendered its verdict of guilty on March 29. The chief witness was Ethel Rosenberg's brother David Greenglass, an army sergeant who admitted that he had given them the information. The Rosenbergs were electrocuted on June 19, 1953, at Sing Sing Prison, Ossining, NY. They were the first native-born Americans executed for espionage by order of a civilian court.

7019. Prison commissioner who was a woman was Anna Moscowitz Kross, who was sworn in on January 1, 1954, as commissioner of correction, New York City. The first woman to direct a state prison system was Ward E. Murphy, who became director of the Maine Bureau of Corrections at Augusta, ME, in July 1970.

7020. Prison guard who was a woman to serve in a maximum security prison for men was Joan Wyatt Stewart of Burlington, IA, who was appointed correction officer on February 1, 1973, in the Iowa State Penitentiary, Fort Madison, IA.

7021. Execution by lethal injection took place on December 7, 1983, in the state penitentiary at Huntsville, TX. Charles Brooks, Jr., who had been convicted of murdering an auto mechanic, received an intravenous injection of sodium pentathol, the barbiturate also known as truth serum.

7022. Year in which the prison population exceeded 1 million was 1994, according to an announcement made by the Justice Department on October 27 of that year. The increase in prisoners made the United States second in the world to Russia with regard to incarceration rates.

7023. Prison to offer training in Vipassana meditation was the King County North Rehabilitation Facility in Shoreline, WA, where S. N. Goenka began teaching meditation to prisoners in November 1997. Eleven inmates completed the course.

7024. Federal judge to reduce a sentence as a protest against racial profiling by police departments was Nancy Gertner, judge of the Federal District Court in Boston, MA, who presided over the trial of Alexander Leviner. The defendant, an African-American man with a long record of minor drug offenses and traffic violations, was convicted of gun possession. The judge set aside the Federal sentencing guidelines, which calculate sentencing based on previous jail terms, because, she said, the defendant's arrests were the result of discriminatory racial profiling by the police and because the calculations did not take into account the severity of the offenses. Instead of the four- to six-year prison term he would have received under the guidelines, she sentenced him on December 3, 1998, to a term of two and a half years.

7025. State to enact a moratorium on executions was Illinois. On January 31, 2000, Governor George Ryan, a Republican, announced that the state would stop executing criminals on Death Row while a special panel conducted an investigation into the death penalty system.

7026. Execution to be televised in the United States was that of Timothy McVeigh, who died on June 11, 2001. He had been convicted of planting the bomb that destroyed the Alfred P. Murrah Federal Building in Oklahoma City, OK, on April 19, 1995, killing 168 people and wounding many others. A closed-circuit television feed was set up in Oklahoma City to allow nearly 300 survivors and family members of the victims to view the execution.

7027. Federal execution by lethal injection took place on June 11, 2001, when Timothy McVeigh was put to death at the federal penitentiary in Terre Haute, IN, for the bombing of the Alfred P. Murrah Federal Building in Oklahoma City, OK, in 1995, in which 168 people died. He was given a sedative, sodium pentothal, followed by injections of two drugs that stopped his breathing and heartbeat.

7028. Death penalty moratorium imposed by a state legislature was approved by the New Jersey state assembly in Trenton, NJ, on January 12, 2006, by a vote of 55 to 21. It had already been approved by the state senate the previous December by a vote of 30 to 6. The bill, signed into law by Gov. Richard J. Codey, stopped all executions for a period of at least nine months while a 13-member government commission conducted a study of the issue.

Disabilities

7029. Federal law providing services for people with disabilities was an act dated July 16, 1798, which established the Marine Hospital Service and empowered the President to appoint medical officers at ports and elsewhere to give medical treatment to disabled seamen. Funds were obtained by a tax of 20 cents a month deducted from the pay of those employed on American vessels. On April 20, 1801, Governor James Monroe of Virginia deeded the Norfolk Naval Hospital, Norfolk, VA, to the United States for this purpose.

7030. Book for the blind was the *Gospel of St. Mark*, published in 1833 in Philadelphia, PA, by the Pennsylvania Institution for the Instruction of the Blind. It was printed in embossed roman letters, upper and lower case. Jacob Snider, Jr., recording secretary of the Pennsylvania Institute, proposed the publication and the funds were donated by Nathan Dunn and Edward Coleman.

7031. Magazine for blind readers was the *Student's Magazine, a Periodical for the Blind*, published in January 1837 by the Pennsylvania Institution for the Instruction of the Blind, Philadelphia, PA. Embossed raised capital letters were used. It was a monthly and cost $3 a year.

7032. Magazine for and by patients with mental illness was the *Illuminator*, written and published in 1843 by patients in Pennsylvania Hospital, Philadelphia, PA. The first issue appeared on April 1, 1843, and contained 24 three-column pages, each in Spencerian handwriting.

7033. Magazine for and by deaf students was the *Deaf Mute Casket*, a four-page monthly edited by William D. Cooke. It was published in 1851 by the State School for the Blind and the Deaf in Raleigh, NC.

7034. Assistance to blind readers by the Library of Congress was initiated on November 8, 1897, when the library established a collection of 500 books in raised type and a program of reading aloud to people with impaired vision. The program evolved into the National Library Service for the Blind and Physically Handicapped.

> The "talking-book machines" distributed by the Library of Congress were maintained by the Telephone Pioneers of America, an all-volunteer group, beginning in 1960.

7035. National organization for the hard of hearing was the American Association for the Hard of Hearing, formed on February 27, 1919, in New York City. The first annual meeting was held in New York City on March 12, 1920. The name was changed to the American Society for the Hard of Hearing on June 5, 1935, at a meeting held in Cincinnati, OH.

7036. Electric motorized wheelchair was the Custer Invalid Chair, invented by Levitt Luzern Custer of Dayton, OH, for veterans of World War I. The chair, patented on October 7, 1919, had three wheels and was powered by a battery.

7037. Guide dog in the United States was Buddy, a German Shepherd. She was teamed with Morris Frank of Nashville, TN, a blind student at Vanderbilt University who traveled to Switzerland to obtain her. The pair arrived in New York City on June 11, 1928. They toured the country together for years, demonstrating how such dogs could assist the visually impaired and raising money for the establishment of a training school.

7038. School for guide dogs in the United States was The Seeing Eye, incorporated on January 29, 1929, in Nashville, TN. The school was founded by dog breeder Dorothy Harrison Eustis of Philadelphia, PA, and Morris Frank, the first American to own a guide dog, and was modeled on a German program that provided trained dogs for blinded veterans. Since 1931 the school has been located in Morristown, NJ.

7039. Music magazine published in Braillewas *The Musical Review for the Blind*, the first issue of which appeared in January 1930. It was published by the American Braille Press for War and Civilian Blind.

7040. Talking book for blind listeners was a collection of eight phonograph records of patriotic documents. It was issued in July 1934 by the American Foundation for the Blind, New York City, and was intended to be played on a specially designed phonograph. The Declaration of Independence and the Constitution of the United States were recorded on four double-faced records. The other four contained George Washington's Farewell Address to the Continental Army and his letter to the Congress of the United States.

7041. Organized civil rights protest by people with disabilities took place in New York City in 1935, when a group called the League for the Physically Handicapped, made up of 300 persons with polio, cerebral palsy, and other disabilities, occupied the offices of the Home Relief Bureau of New York City for nine days. LPH members had discovered that the Home Relief Bureau was stamping all their job requests with a special code that signalled the Works Progress Administration to deny them federal jobs.

7042. Telecommunication by deaf people that was both visual and oral was accomplished on October 13, 1940, when Bertha O'Donnell and Adele Costa conversed in sign language through two-way television sets at W2USA, the amateur television booth at the New York World's Fair, and W2HID, 220 East 42nd Street, New York City, eight miles away.

7043. Adaptive technologies for people with disabilities were developed at the Institute of Rehabilitation Medicine at New York University Medical Center in New York City, founded by Dr. Howard Rusk in 1951.

7044. State law prohibiting discrimination against the disabled in employment was passed by Wisconsin in 1965 as an amendment to the state's Fair Employment Law of 1945.

7045. Television show with open captions for hearing-impaired viewers was *The French Chef*, a cooking show starring Julia Child that aired on the Public Broadcasting System. Subtitles, called open captions, were added to the show in 1972.

7046. Television shows with closed captions for hearing-impaired viewers were aired on March 16, 1980, on three different networks: PBS, which showed *Masterpiece Theatre* and *Once Upon a Classic*; NBC, which showed *The Wonderful World of Disney*; and ABC, which showed *The ABC Sunday Night Movie*. Closed captioning is a process developed by the National Captioning Institute, Falls Church, VA, that places electronic messages in a blank area of the show's video signal. A device in the viewer's TV set decodes the messages and displays them as text.

7047. Comprehensive civil rights legislation for people with disabilities was the Americans with Disabilities Act, signed into law by President George H. W. Bush on July 26, 1990, at a White House ceremony. The wide-ranging legislation was intended to make American society more accessible to people with disabilities. The ADA is divided into five titles covering employment, public services, public accommodations, telecommunications, and miscellaneous issues. Its protection applies primarily, but not exclusively, to individuals with a physical or mental impairment or a history of disability that substantially limits their major life activities.

7048. Cablecasts of city meetings with realtime captioning for the hearing-impaired were initiated by Fremont, CA, on November 17, 1992. Realtime captioning was offered for all meetings of the city council and the board of education as they were broadcast on the community cable station. Funding was provided by a surcharge of seven cents a month on all cable TV bills.

7049. Robotic chair with balancing capability was the self-propelled iBOT Mobility System, invented by Dean Kamen in 1999 for people in wheelchairs. Using a system of gyroscopes and wheels connected to microprocessors, the chair could swivel its way up stairs and curbs, tilt safely in any direction, and raise the traveler to a standing position. It was marketed by Independence Technology of Endicott, NY.

7050. State to allow electric mobility devices on sidewalks was New Hampshire, which made sidewalk use of Electric Personal Assistive Mobility Devices legal on February 15, 2002.

7051. Court ruling requiring emergency evacuation plans for people with disabilities in all places of public accommodation was issued by Circuit Court judge John W. Debelius III on December 28, 2004. Katie Savage of Washington, DC, a wheelchair user, filed suit against a store and shopping mall in Silver Spring, MD, because they left her with no way to exit the mall during an emergency evacuation. The court ruled that retail businesses and other public accommodations are required by the Americans with Disabilities Act to take possible disabilities into account when preparing evacuation plans.

Drugs and Alcohol

7052. Alcohol prohibition enforcement officers were authorized by proclamation of Sir Francis Wyatt, governor of Virginia, on June 21, 1622: "We do ordaine an officer for that purpose to be sworne in every plantacion, to give information of all such, as shalbe so disordered: the moiety of the forfeitures to be given the sd officer so informing, or for default in him to any other that shall informe, and the other to the publique Threasury."

7053. Liquor reform movement was undertaken by the Dutch Reformed Church on Manhattan Island in 1623. It maintained a strong position against liquor, particularly with regard to excessive use.

7054. Alcohol temperance law enacted by a colony was signed on March 5, 1623, by Governor Sir Francis Wyatt of Virginia and 32 others. It provided that "the proclamations for swearing and drunkenness set out by the Governor and Counsell are confirmed by this assembly, and it is further ordered that the churchwardens shall be sworne to present them to the commanders of every plantation and that the forfeitures shall be collected by them to be for publique uses."

7055. Tobacco penalty enacted by a colony was authorized on October 3, 1632, by the Massachusetts Court of Assistants and General Court, which ruled in Boston "that no person shall take any tobacco publicly, under pain of punishment; also that everyone shall pay 1d. for every time he is convicted of taking tobacco in any place, and that any Assistant shall have power to receive evidence and give order for the levying of it, as also to give order for the levying of the officer's charge. This order to begin the tenth of November next."

7056. Antismoking ban enacted by a colony was the work of Willem Kieft, the third governor of New Netherlands (later New York City). In 1637, he introduced an ordinance to outlaw tobacco use and trade everywhere in the colony. On May 25, 1647, the colonial legislature of Connecticut passed a law forbidding smoking on the streets or in nearby fields, but permitted citizens to indulge freely at home, as long as no more than one other person "who useth and drinketh the same weed" was present.

7057. Temperance organization was formed in 1789 by the farmers of Litchfield County, CT. Their pledge read in part: "We do hereby associate and mutually agree that hereafter we will carry on our business without the use of distilled spirits as an article of refreshment, either for ourselves or for those whom we employ; and that, instead thereof, we will serve our workmen with wholesome food and the common simple drinks of our production."

7058. Tobacco tax enacted by Congress was levied in 1794, but after two years it was abandoned. A similar attempt was made in 1812 and repealed in 1816. The first federal tobacco tax for internal revenue purposes was levied by an act of Congress of July 1, 1862.

7059. Cigar factory of importance was established by Simeon Viets in 1810 in West Suffield, CT. He employed 15 women and a foreman. His popular brands were Windsors and Long Nines.

7060. Alcohol prohibition law enacted by a state was passed by Tennessee on January 26, 1838. The bill, an "act to repeal all laws licensing tippling houses," provided that "all persons convicted of the offense of retailing spirituous liquors shall be fined at the discretion of the court" and that the fines and forfeitures be used for the support of common schools.

7061. Narcotics tariff enacted by Congress was enacted by the Tariff Act of August 30, 1842, which placed a levy of 75 cents a pound on opium. Prior to this act, opium was exempted from duty by the act of July 14, 1832, and the act of March 2, 1833. The McKinley Tariff Act of October 1, 1890, provided for an internal revenue tax of $10 a pound upon all opium manufactured in the United States for smoking purposes, and limited the manufacture to United States citizens.

7062. State temperance society for women was the New York Women's State Temperance Society, founded on April 20, 1852, at a convention held in Rochester, NY, principally through the efforts of Susan Brownell Anthony. Approximately 500 women attended.

7063. Cigarette tax was levied by the United States under an act of Congress of June 30, 1864. The system of placing stamps on each package to indicate payment of tax was inaugurated in 1868.

7064. Corncob pipe commercial manufacture was undertaken in 1869 by Henry Tibbe of Washington, MO, who used plaster of paris to fill uneven surfaces in the pipe. He obtained a patent on July 9, 1878, on a "smoking pipe made of corncob, in which the interstices are filled with a plastic self-hardening cement." In 1872 he was joined by his son, Anton A. Tibbe, and they later incorporated as the Missouri Meerschaum Company.

7065. Cigarette-manufacturing machine was the Hook machine, which was invented by Albert H. Hook of New York City in 1872, but which did not come into practical commercial use until 1882. In 1875, 50 million cigarettes were made, according to revenue collection figures. The Hook machine was granted a patent on November 7, 1876. It unspooled a continuous ribbon of paper into which tobacco was fed before the edges were passed over a gummed wheel. The result was a very long cigarette that was afterwards cut into separate cigarettes.

7066. National temperance society for women was the National Woman's Christian Temperance Union, organized in the Second Presbyterian Church, Cleveland, OH, on November 18–20, 1874. The first president was Mrs. Annie T. Wittenmyer of Philadelphia, PA. The World Woman's Christian Temperance Union, an outgrowth of the national group, was organized at a convention held from October 31 to November 3, 1883, in Detroit, MI.

7067. Alcohol abuse programs required in schools by the federal government was put into place under a law enacted in 1882. The law, the first in the world, required "temperance education" to be included in the standard course of studies in public schools. Temperance education became mandatory in Washington, DC, in 1886. By 1900, similiar laws had been enacted by all the states.

7068. Cigar-rolling machine that was practical was invented by Oscar Hammerstein of New York City, who obtained a patent for it on February 27, 1883.

7069. Anti-saloon organization was the Anti-Saloon League, established on May 24, 1893, in the Oberlin College library building, Oberlin, OH. The group was founded by Howard Hyde Russell and 15 members of the Oberlin Temperance Alliance. The purpose of the society was to force the Ohio saloons out of business and to preach the benefits of temperance. On June 23, 1893, the Anti-Saloon League of the District of Columbia was formed in Washington, DC, with Major Samuel Hamilton Walker as the first president.

7070. National anti-saloon league was the Anti-Saloon League of America, formed December 17–18, 1895, at the Calvary Baptist Sunday School, Washington, DC, by a coalition of the Anti-Saloon League of the District of Columbia, the Anti-Saloon League of Ohio, and 45 other local temperance organizations. The first president was Hiram Price.

Library of Congress, Prints & Photographs Division
LC-USZ62-683

The temperance movement was considered "woman's holy war."

7071. Narcotics ban enacted by Congress was enacted on February 9, 1909. The act made it illegal to import opium and opium derivatives into the United States, except for medicinal purposes.

7072. Drug control law enacted by Congress was the Harrison Narcotics Act of 1914, sponsored by Representative Francis Burton Harrison of New York. It required sellers of narcotic drugs to register with the Internal Revenue Service.

7073. Alcohol prohibition vote taken in Congress that showed the House of Representatives with a dry majority was taken on December 22, 1914. The representatives voted 197–189 in favor of a resolution to provide a constitutional amendment banning the manufacture and sale of intoxicating beverages. The resolution, offered by Representative Richmond Pearson Hobson of Alabama, failed to win the necessary two-thirds majority.

7074. State to ratify the Prohibition Amendment to the Constitution was Mississippi, which ratified it on January 8, 1918. The amendment had been submitted by Congress to the legislatures of the states on December 18, 1917. Ratification by three-fourths of the states is required for any amendment to the Constitution. Nebraska became the 36th state to ratify the amendment on January 16, 1919. On January 29, the secretary of state proclaimed the amendment effective as of January 16, 1920. In 1933 it became the first constitutional amendment to be repealed.

7075. Alcohol prohibition law enacted by Congress forbidding the sale of intoxicating liquors except for export was the Wartime Prohibition Act, passed on November 21, 1918.

7076. Cigarette tax enacted by a state was established on April 11, 1921, when Iowa enacted a tax applicable to cigarettes, cigarette papers, and cigarette tubes. The tax on cigarettes was one mill on each cigarette ($1 per 1,000). This act repealed an existing law prohibiting the sale of cigarettes in Iowa.

7077. Drug treatment center for addicts established by Congress was the U.S. Narcotics Farm at Lexington, KY, which covered 11 acres of a 1,050-acre plot. The cornerstone was laid on July 29, 1933, and the building was dedicated on May 25, 1935, by the Public

Health Service. The first occupants were received on May 29, 1935. Dr. Lawrence Kolb was the first director.

7078. Twelve-step rehabilitation program was Alcoholics Anonymous, founded in New York City on June 10, 1935, by recovering alcoholics William "Bill W." Wilson and Dr. Robert H. Smith. They devised a plan to help alcoholics control their addiction through guided group discussion and confession, reliance on a "higher power," and a gradual return to sobriety. The first high school chapter of Alcoholics Anonymous was started in 1988 in Pacific Palisades, CA, by Palisades High School psychologist Linda Levine.

7079. Marijuana ban enacted by Congress was the Marijuana Traffic Act of 1937, which banned the possession, cultivation, and sale of the marijuana plant and its products. It was signed into law by President Franklin Delano Roosevelt on August 2, 1937.

7080. Major studies to show a link between smoking and lung cancer were published in the *Journal of the American Medical Association* on May 27, 1950. One was an epidemiological survey conducted in Buffalo, NY, by Morton Levin, who demonstrated that the risk of developing lung cancer was twice as high for smokers as for nonsmokers. The other, by Ernst L. Wynder and Evarts A Graham, showed that the vast majority in a group of 684 lung cancer patients had a history of smoking.

7081. Drug treatment center for minors offering full-scale long-term treatment was the Riverside Hospital, North Brother Island, New York City, which was converted for the purpose in November 1951. The first patients were received on July 1, 1952. The first superintendent was Dr. Jerome Louis Leon.

7082. Filter cigarette was Tareyton, made by the R.J. Reynolds Company of Winston-Salem, NC, and introduced in 1954. The filter contained charcoal. Another Reynolds filter cigarette, Winston, was introduced in the same year and eclipsed Tareyton in popularity.

7083. Methadone program for the rehabilitation of heroin addicts was established in New York City in 1964 by Vincent P. Dole and Marie Nyswander of Rockefeller University. Dole was awarded the Albert Lasker Medical Research award in 1988 for his work. Methadone, a synthetic opiate that blocks the euphoria of heroin and causes less severe withdrawal, was developed by German chemists during World War II.

7084. Major government report on tobacco smoking was "Smoking and Health: Report of the Advisory Committee to the Surgeon General," released on January 11, 1964. The report, commissioned by Surgeon General Luther Leonidas Terry, produced persuasive evidence that smoking has a causative effect on lung diseases such as cancer, emphysema, and bronchitis, as well as on cardiovascular diseases.

7085. Narcotics ban enacted by a state was enacted by Nevada on March 19, 1965. It stated that "the possession of dangerous drugs without a prescription is punishable as a gross misdemeanor upon first and second conviction and is punishable as a felony upon third conviction, and exempting physicians, dentists, chiropodists, veterinarians, pharmacists, manufacturers, wholesalers, jobbers and laboratories, and exempting ranchers under certain conditions."

7086. Magazine about recreational drugs was *High Times*, published and edited by Thomas Forcade of New York City in August 1974. Its stories described the risks and rewards of using marijuana, hashish, and psychedelic drugs.

7087. Nicotine replacement product approved by the FDA to help tobacco users break their nicotine addiction was nicotine polacrilex, marketed as Nicorette gum by the British company SmithKline Beecham. On January 13, 1984, the FDA authorized its sale by prescription. It was approved for over-the-counter sale on February 9, 1996. The gum released small doses of nicotine into the user's bloodstream through the mucous membranes of the mouth.

7088. Smoking ban on airplane flights went into effect on April 23, 1988. In compliance with rules issued by the Federal Aviation Administration, airlines banned smoking on domestic passenger flights lasting less than two hours, with the exception of chartered flights and travel club flights. Northwest Airlines voluntarily banned smoking on domestic passenger flights of all durations. The first commercial domestic air service that was entirely smoke-free, including the cockpit, was inaugurated by Delta Air Lines of Atlanta, GA, which banned smoking on all flights beginning January 1, 1995.

7089. Drug control chief appointed by the federal government was William J. Bennett, the former secretary of education, who was named to the newly created post of director of national drug control policy by President George Bush in 1989. The press quickly gave Bennett the informal title of "drug czar." At the time, an estimated 14.5 million Americans were using illegal drugs at least once a month. Bennett's plan, announced on September 5, 1989, included new policing efforts funded by the federal government.

7090. Tobacco sales to minors to be restricted by federal regulations were restricted as of February 28, 1997. The Food and Drug Administration implemented restrictions on retailers that required them to check the ages of all customers younger than 27 to prevent persons under 18 years of age from buying tobacco. Store owners caught selling cigarettes and other tobacco products to minors faced federal fines of $250 per violation. All states already had laws banning the sale of tobacco to persons under 18.

7091. Cigarette maker to agree to a lawsuit settlement was Liggett Group (formerly Liggett & Myers) of Durham, NC. On March 20, 1997, the company accepted terms that would allow it to settle lawsuits brought against it in 22 states. These terms included an admission that smoking tobacco is addictive and carcenogenic, a promise to stop marketing cigarettes to children, and a compensatory arrangement by which the 22 states would receive 25 percent of its gross profit annually for 25 years.

7092. Cigarette manufacturer to list ingredients on the label was Liggett Group Inc., Durham, NC. On December 16, 1997, the company placed detailed lists of ingredients on cartons of its L&M brand of cigarettes, in compliance with a recent Massachusetts law. In addition to tobacco, the list included flavorings such as licorice, chocolate, vanilla, menthol, and cedarwood, and chemicals such as propylene glycol and hexanoic acid. The law was declared unconstitutional by a federal judge in 2000.

7093. Major city to legalize possession of marijuana was Denver, CO. On November 1, 2005, Denver's voters approved a measure permitting adults over the age of 20 to possess a small amount of marijuana (up to an ounce). The ordinance could not take effect because possession of marijuana was still prohibited by the laws of the state of Colorado, which could not be superseded. The penalty in Colorado for possessing an ounce or less of marijuana was a fine of $100.

Labor Movement

7094. Pension law enacted by a colony was enacted by the Plymouth Colony in 1636. The legislation provided that "if any [man] shalbee sent forth as a souldier and shall returne maimed, hee shalbee maintained competently by the Collonie of New Plymouth during his life." The act applied particularly to the soldiers engaged in the Pequot Indian War, which concluded on November 20, 1637.

7095. Craft union was authorized on October 18, 1648, when the "shoomakers of Boston" were permitted "to assemble and meete together in Boston, at such time and times as they shall appoynt, who being so assembled, they, or the greatest number of them, shall have powre to chuse a master and two wardens, with fowre or six associats, a clarke, a sealer, a searcher, and a beadle. . . ." Similar permission was also extended to coopers.

7096. Labor protest in a colony took place in Gloucester County, VA, where a group of African-American slaves and English bond laborers decided to march to the governor to appeal for their freedom. The Englishmen were veterans of Oliver Cromwell's army who had been transported to the Virginia colony as punishment. The plan was betrayed on September 13, 1663, by one of the bondmen, and four of the participants were executed.

7097. Workers' compensation agreement was made on January 26, 1695, by Captain William Kidd of New York City, commander of the *Adventure Galley* of 787 tons burden. He promised to distribute to the crew one-fourth of all booty captured on privateering expeditions. According to the agreement, "If any man should Loose a Leg or Arm in the said service, he should have six hundred pieces of

Eight, or six able slaves; if any man should loose a joynt on the said service, he should have a hundred pieces of eight."

7098. Strike by workers took place in New York City in 1741, when the master bakers protested against municipal regulation of the price of bread. They were tried and convicted of unlawfully combining, but no sentence was passed.

7099. Pension law enacted by Congress was passed by the Continental Congress on August 26, 1776. It provided "that every commissioned officer, non-commissioned officer, and private soldier who shall have lost a limb in any engagement, or be so disabled in the service of the United States of America as to render him incapable afterwards of getting a livelihood, shall receive, during his life or the continuance of such disability, one half of his monthly pay from and after the time that his pay as an officer or soldier ceases." As the resources of the Continental Congress were meager, the states were asked to furnish the payments.

7100. Labor union to nominate its own political candidates was the Mechanics Union, which nominated candidates for the New York State Assembly in 1784. The first labor union whose candidates won an election was the New York Working Men's Party, whose candidate, Ebenezer Ford, president of the Carpenter's Union, was elected to the New York State Assembly on the Mechanic and Working Men's Ticket on November 7, 1829. Ford polled 6,166 votes.

7101. Strike benefit by a union was authorized on May 31, 1786, at the home of Henry Myers, Philadelphia, PA, when 26 members of the Typographical Society met to plan a protest against a reduction in wages. They agreed "that we will support such of our brethren as shall be thrown out of employment on account of their refusing to work for less than $6 per week." They won their demands.

7102. Pensions paid by the federal government were those paid under the act of September 29, 1789, which took up the obligation of paying the pensions granted by the Continental Congress and appropriated money for payments to invalids who were wounded and disabled in the Revolutionary War for one year from March 4, 1789. The act of July 16, 1790, continued the payment of pensions for another year. The act of April 30, 1790, provided for pensions to those wounded or disabled in the line of duty, and the act of March 23, 1792, provided for pensions of those suffering wounds or disabilities known to be of service origin.

7103. Child labor in a factory on record took place at the cotton mill of Almy, Brown, and Slater in Pawtucket, RI, in 1793. Samuel Slater, the mill's founder, hired children because their small hands could do finer work.

7104. Craft union contract between employers and organized labor was effected in 1799 by the Federal Society of Journeymen Cordwainers (shoemakers) of Philadelphia, PA, after a strike of 10 weeks. The union was formed in 1794 after an unsuccessful attempt in 1792. In 1806 the members were put on trial for conspiracy.

7105. Strike in which women participated took place in the textile mills in Pawtucket, RI, in 1824, when female weavers went on strike along with the male workers.

7106. Labor union for women was the United Tailoresses Society of New York, a protective association formed by tailors in 1825 in New York City. In June 1831 they went on strike for an increase in wages. About 600 women remained on strike for four or five weeks.

7107. Trade union organization established in a city was the Mechanics Union of Trade Associations, which was organized in Philadelphia, PA, in 1827. Invitations to join were sent to "those trades who are as yet destitute of trade societies." They were also urged to "organize and send delegates as soon as possible."

7108. Anarchist was Josiah Warren, who was known as the "father of anarchy." He was of the intellectual type and was not an advocate of violence. He was a veteran of the short-lived utopian colony in New Harmony, IN, whose failure convinced him that communistic social arrangements suppress individual initiative and responsibility. In May 1827 he opened his Equity Store in Cincinnati, OH, to vindicate his theory of "labor for labor," in which all labor is held to be equally valuable. The store sold merchandise at cost, plus seven percent for handling and the clerk's hire. Instead of money, the store also accepted "labor notes," in which the customer agreed to provide a specified amount of time and labor (for example, washing or carpentry) in exchange for merchandise. Warren also advocated the transference of government activities to private persons.

7109. Strike in which a militia was called out occurred in Paterson, NJ, on July 21, 1828, when the Godwin Guards of the national militia were ordered to keep peace during a strike brought about by the changing of the factory lunch hour from noon to one o'clock. The strikers were defeated, but the noon lunch hour was afterwards restored.

7110. Strike by women occurred at the Dover Manufacturing Company, Dover, NH, in 1828, when about 400 women went on strike against a wage cut and a 10-hour day in the needlework trades.

7111. Child labor law enacted by a state that included an education requirement was passed by Massachusetts on April 16, 1836. It required all children to attend school at least three months of the year until they reached the age of 15. Manufacturers were not allowed to hire children to work in their mills for more than nine months a year, but the children were conveniently transferred from mill to mill so that this legislation was not effective.

7112. Workers' compensation lawsuit involving the rights of an injured servant against his master was the case of *James Murray v. South Carolina Railroad Company*, which was tried before Judge Belton O'Neall at the July Extra Term, 1838, of Barnwell County, SC. The trial resulted in a verdict of $1,500 in favor of the plaintiff. The defendant appealed. The case was heard in February 1841 by the Court of Errors of South Carolina in Charleston, which reversed the decision and granted a new trial. The decision was written by Judge Josiah James Evans.

7113. Factory workers' magazine was *The Lowell Offering*, "a repository of original articles on various subjects, wholly written, edited and published by female operatives employed in the mills." It was published bimonthly and cost six and a quarter cents a copy. The first issue was published in October 1840 by Powers and Bagley.

7114. Child labor law enacted by a state that regulated hours of employment was approved by Massachusetts Governor John Davis on March 3, 1842. Massachusetts prohibited children under 12 years of age from working more than 10 hours a day. Connecticut enacted a similar law, which prohibited children under 14 years of age from working more than 10 hours a day.

7115. National labor congress was the First Industrial Congress of the United States, which convened in New York City on October 12, 1845. William E. Wait of Illinois was elected president. Annual meetings were held regularly until 1856.

7116. Workday of 10 hours to be mandated by a state was required by New Hampshire in a law dated July 9, 1847. It stated that "in all contracts relating to labor, ten hours actual labor shall be taken to be a day's work unless otherwise agreed by the parties." As a result of the bargaining provision, the law was ineffective.

7117. Child labor law enacted by a state that restricted the age of the worker was approved on March 28, 1848, by Governor Francis Rawn Shunk of Pennsylvania. The law prohibited children under 12 years of age from engaging in commercial labor. In 1849 the age limit was raised to 13 years. Similar legislation was enacted in 1853 by Rhode Island, in 1855 by Connecticut, and in 1866 by Massachusetts, with age limits of 12, 9, and 10 years, respectively.

7118. Working hours of women to be regulated by a state were set forth in a law enacted by Ohio on March 29, 1852. This law fixed 10 hours per day as the maximum number of working hours for manual labor by children under 18 and women. It was repealed in 1887, when a new code was adopted.

7119. Railroad union was formed in 1855 when 68 engineers from 45 different railroads in 13 states met in Baltimore, MD, from November 6 to 10 and organized the National Protective Association of the Brotherhood of Locomotive Engineers of the United States "to protect ourselves, the traveling public and our employers from the injurious effects resulting from persons of inferior qualifications being employed as locomotive engineers."

7120. Workday of eight hours to be authorized by Congress was authorized for government laborers in a law dated June 25, 1868, and signed by President Andrew Johnson. It provided, among other things, that "eight hours shall constitute a day's work for all laborers, workmen, and mechanics who may be employed by or on behalf of the Government of the United States." The eight-hour workday had been advocated by a variety of local unions since 1860, and the first unified proposal was made on August 20, 1866, in Baltimore, MD, by the National Labor Union at its first congress, which was attended by 77 delegates from 13 states.

7121. Labor bureau established by a state was the Massachusetts Bureau of Statistics of Labor, established by legislation approved on June 23, 1869, by Governor William Claflin. The duties of the bureau, under a chief and deputy, were "to collect, assort, systematize and present in annual reports to the legislature . . . statistical details relating to all departments of labor in the Commonwealth." Henry Kemble Oliver was appointed chief on July 31, 1869, at a salary of $2,500 a year.

7122. National union for women was the Daughters of St. Crispin, an organization of shoe operators. Their first convention was held at Lynn, MA, on July 28, 1869. The first president was Carrie Wilson of Lynn. Lynn had been the scene of a strike in March 1860, when 5,000 male shoe operators went on strike and were joined by 1,000 women.

7123. Labor union to admit workers other than craft workers was the Noble Order of the Knights of Labor, a secret society founded in Philadelphia, PA, on December 9, 1869, by six men. One of the founders, Uriah Smith Stevens, a tailor, became its first Master Workman. Membership was originally restricted to garment cutters. "Sojourners" were admitted for the first time on October 20, 1870. By January 5, 1871, there were 69 members.

7124. Half holiday on Saturday for factory workers was inaugurated by George Westinghouse, the inventor and manufacturer of the air brake, who established the custom in his factory in Pittsburgh, PA, in June 1871.

7125. Labor union label was adopted by the Cigar Makers' International Union and first came into use in San Francisco, CA, in 1874. The label was adopted to protect organized workers from employers who were importing Chinese laborers to do the same work at lower wages. The blue label of the Cigar Makers' International Union was adopted in 1880 at the 13th convention of the organization held in Chicago, IL, and was issued free of charge to all manufacturers who operated strictly union factories. In 1869 the Carpenters' Eight Hour League of San Francisco stamped the lumber produced by planing mills with an eight-hour workday to differentiate it from lumber produced by 10-hour mills.

7126. Pension plan was offered to employees of the American Express Company, New York, NY, in 1875. The plan included coverage of employees 60 years of age or older and with more than 20 years of employment. If approved for benefits, employees received 50 percent of the average salary they had earned over the preceding 10 years, with a cap of $500.

7127. Strike suppressed by federal troops in peacetime was an action by railroad employees that began on July 16, 1877. In response to requests for aid from the governors of West Virginia, Maryland, Pennsylvania, and other states, President Rutherford Birchard Hayes called out federal troops. Earlier, on January 29, 1834, President Andrew Jackson ordered federal troops to put down a "riotous assembly" among laborers on the Chesapeake and Ohio Canal.

7128. Factory inspection law enacted by a state was passed on April 30, 1879, by Massachusetts. It provided that the governor appoint two or more of the district police to act as inspectors of factories and public buildings.

7129. State ban on the employment of women in a dangerous occupation was "an act providing for the health and safety of persons employed in coal mines," passed and approved by Illinois on May 28, 1879. It prohibited the employment of women in mines in Illinois.

7130. National labor organization of importance was the American Federation of Labor, which was organized in Pittsburgh, PA, in 1881 as the Federation of Organized Trades and Labor Unions. It adopted the new title on December 8, 1886, in Columbus, OH, at a meeting attended by 25 officers of national craft unions representing over 300,000 members. The first woman to serve as a labor delegate to a national convention of the American Federation of Labor was Mary Burke, who represented the Retail Clerks' Union of Findlay, OH, at the convention held in Detroit, MI, December 8–13, 1890.

7131. Labor unions to be legalized by a state were legalized in New Jersey in "an act relative to persons combining and encouraging other persons to combine," approved on February 14, 1883. It provided that combinations organized to persuade workers to enter or leave employment were not unlawful.

7132. Labor mediation and arbitration board established by a state was the New York Board of Mediation and Arbitration, organized on June 1, 1886, under authority of an act of May 18, 1886. On June 2, 1886, Massachusetts authorized a state arbitration board "for the settlement of differences between employers and their employees."

7133. Sick-leave benefit funds for teachers were established in 1887 in both New York City and Brooklyn, which was then a separate city. The two organizations were the New York City Teachers Mutual Benefit Association and the Brooklyn Aid Association. The funds were built up from dues imposed on teachers' salaries.

7134. Accident reports by employers concerning personal injuries suffered by employees in their service were required by Massachusetts under the Employers' Liability Act, passed on May 14, 1887.

7135. Labor activists to be executed were four men accused of participating in the Haymarket Riot that occurred on May 4, 1886, in Chicago, IL. A labor rally had been called in Haymarket Square to protest the shooting of several strikers by Chicago police the previous day. Anarchist and communist speakers were addressing a crowd of several hundred mostly German-born workers when a squad of 180 police officers arrived to break up the rally. A bomb, thrown by a person who was never positively identified, fatally injured 7 officers and wounded 70. Police fired into the crowd, killing one worker and injuring more than a dozen. A grand jury indicted 31 suspected labor radicals in connection with the bombing. Eight men were tried for murder; seven were convicted. On November 11, 1887, four men—August Spies, Samuel Fielden, Adolph Fischer, and Albert Parsons—were executed by hanging. The other three were pardoned in 1893 by Illinois governor John Peter Altgeld.

7136. Employment service established by a state was created on April 28, 1890, by Ohio. Authorization was given to establish public employment offices in cities of the first and second class, including Cincinnati, Cleveland, Columbus, Dayton, and Toledo. The first office was opened June 4, 1890, in Toledo, with Charles W. Murphy as superintendent. The Commissioner of Labor Statistics, under whom the system of five offices was set up during the year 1890, was John McBride.

7137. Employment office established by a city was authorized by Seattle, WA, on March 5, 1894, by a vote of 2,058–523. John Lamb, the city's first labor commissioner, opened an office on April 1, 1894, in a rough board shanty containing one small room. The following year, the office moved to larger quarters in City Hall.

7138. Labor union discrimination law enacted by a state prohibiting employers from discriminating in matters of employment against members of trade unions was "an act in relation to the employment of labor by corporations," approved on May 15, 1894, by New Jersey. Violation was subject to a fine not to exceed $500 or three months' imprisonment.

7139. Actors' union was the Actors' National Protective Union, New York City, chartered by the American Federation of Labor on January 4, 1896. In August 1919 it combined with two other unions, the White Rats and the Actors' Equity Association, to form the Associated Actors and Artists of America. A strike was called on August 7, 1919, in 13 theaters in New York City and spread to other cities. The dispute was settled in the union's favor on September 6, 1919.

7140. Laborsaving machine approved by a labor union was the Autoplate stereotype platemaking machine, invented by Henry Alexander Wise Wood, which was approved in 1900 by the Stereotypers' Union. The machine enabled workers to avoid handling large quantities of molten metal type containing poisonous antimony and lead.

7141. Workers' compensation insurance law enacted by a state was enacted by Maryland in 1902, followed by Montana in 1909 and New York in 1910, but all three were declared unconstitutional. The first law to remain on the books was approved by Washington on March 14, 1911, but it did not go into effect until October 1. Meantime, Wisconsin passed a law on May 3, 1911, that went into effect on September 11. New Jersey's law was approved on April 4, 1911, and went into effect on July 4.

7142. Labor dispute resolved through presidential intervention was a strike by anthracite coal miners that began in May 1902. To avert a coal shortage, President Theodore Roosevelt held a meeting in Washington, DC, on October 3, 1902, between leaders of the United Mine Workers and mine owners. The impasse was broken by Roosevelt's threat to send Army troops to operate the mines. A commission appointed by Roosevelt worked out a compromise that ended the strike.

7143. Interracial labor union was the Japanese-Mexican Labor Association (or Japanese-Mexican Protective Association) of Oxnard, CA, composed of laborers in the sugar beet industry who were dependent on a job broker, the Western Agricultural Contracting Company. They called a strike on March 18, 1903, to force improvements in the subcontracting system. Their action was successful, but because the union included Japanese members, it was denied a charter from the American Federation of Labor.

7144. Workers' compensation insurance law enacted by Congress was approved on May 30, 1908. It was applicable to the following classes of federal employees: artisans or laborers in any manufacturing establishment, arsenal, or navy yard; employees in the construction of river and harbor fortifications; employees in hazardous employment on construction work in the reclamation of arid lands; and employees in hazardous employment under the Isthmian Canal Commission in Panama.

7145. Minimum wage law enacted by a state was enacted by Massachusetts on June 4, 1912. It established a three-member Minimum Wage Commission to be appointed by the governor with the advice of the Council. The act did not go into effect until July 1, 1913. Oregon, in advance of all other states, set up an administrative body to carry out the provisions of an act of February 17, 1913, which provided for the appointment, within 30 days, of a Welfare Commission to consist of three members, one representing the employer, one the employee, and one the public.

7146. Strike settlement mediated by the federal Department of Labor was a dispute by the railway clerks of the New York, New Haven and Hartford Railroad. Commissioners of conciliation had not yet been appointed by the board, but the secretary of labor assigned the dispute to Glossbrenner Wallace William Hanger, chief statistician of the Bureau of Labor Statistics, who entered the case on May 24, 1913, and effected a settlement on June 2.

7147. Child labor law enacted by Congress was passed on September 1, 1916, "an act to prevent interstate commerce in the products of child labor," the provisions of which were to be administered by the Children's Bureau. The government did not have the constitutional power to regulate labor directly, so the attempt was made to deal with the problem of child labor through the government's constitutional power to regulate interstate commerce. The act became effective on September 1, 1917, but on June 3, 1918, it was declared unconstitutional by the Supreme Court as an invasion of states' rights.

Courtesy of Images of American Political History and the National Archives and Records Administration

Child laborers, c. 1908.

7148. Massacre of strikebreakers by union members began on June 21, 1922, at the Southern Illinois Coal Company's strip mine near Herrin, IL. During a nationwide strike by the United Mine Workers (UMW), a group of recruited strikebreakers arrived at the mine. Fighting broke out, and one striker and two strikebreakers were killed. The mine was quickly surrounded by armed UMW members. On June 22, approximately 60 strikebreakers inside the mine surrendered to union members, who marched them to a barbed wire fence and gunned them down. A few who managed to escape were hunted down and slain in a nearby cemetery. Twenty-one strikebreakers and one mine official were killed, and most of the rest were severely wounded.

7149. Pension laws enacted by a state were enacted on March 5, 1923, by Montana and Nevada, whose respective governors signed their pension measures at the same hour on the same day. Montana instituted the first statewide mandatory system. It granted pensions of $25 a month to people who were over 70 years of age and who had been citizens and residents of the state for the previous 15 years. The funds were derived from the counties.

7150. Labor union of African-American workers to be recognized by a major corporation was the Brotherhood of Sleeping Car Porters and Maids, founded by A. Philip Randolph in New York City on August 25, 1925. The members were employees of the Pullman Company, Chicago, IL, which furnished sleeping and club cars for passenger trains throughout the United States and staffed them with underpaid African-Americans. The union received a charter from the American Federation of Labor in 1934 and was recognized by Pullman as its employees' bargaining agent on August 25, 1937.

7151. Housing cooperative sponsored by a labor union was the Amalgamated Houses, originally called the Amalgamated Cooperative Apartments, built by the Amalgamated Housing Corporation, which opened two buildings on November 1, 1927, in the Bronx, New York City. After additional buildings were erected, the project accommodated 1,495 families. The housing project was organized by Abraham Eli Kazan for the Amalgamated Clothing Workers of America.

7152. Unemployment insurance act passed by a state was enacted by Wisconsin on January 28, 1932, and signed by Governor Philip La Follette. Every employer of 10 or more was required to put 2 percent of the payroll aside until a fund accrued equaling $75 per eligible worker. An employee who lost his or her job could draw on the fund at the rate of $10 a week for a maximum of 10 weeks. The first payment was made on August 17, 1936. The chairman of the Industrial Commission, which regulated the department, was Voyta Wrabetz.

7153. Sit-down strike occurred in the packing plant of George A. Hormel and Company, Austin, MN, on November 13, 1933, when striking employees seized control of the plant. The Industrial Commission of Minnesota, of which Niels Henriksen Debel was chairman, held mediation hearings on November 16–18, 1933, and rendered a decision on December 8 affecting the specific issues involved. Various forms of stay-in strikes, slowdown strikes, and refusal-to-work strikes had been attempted previously in a variety of industries.

7154. Work week of 40 hours to be required by Congress was required by the Public Contract Act of 1936 "to provide conditions for the purchase of supplies and the making of contracts by the United States," approved on June 30, 1936. Workers on government contracts over $10,000 were required to receive overtime compensation at the rate of not less than time and a half for hours worked in excess of 40 a week or eight hours in any one day (if such compensation yielded a greater amount than on the weekly 40-hour basis). Workers were not to be paid less than the prevailing minimum wage of industry and locality. The act was known as the Walsh-Healy Act.

7155. Pensions paid by the federal government to workers in private industry were inaugurated on July 13, 1936, when checks totaling $901.56 were mailed to 18 retired railroad employees. This was done in accordance with the Railroad Retirement Act of August 29, 1935, which appropriated $46.7 million "to establish a retirement system for employees of carriers subject to the Interstate Commerce Act, and for other purposes."

7156. Federal law regulating ages and workload for child labor was the Fair Labor Standards Act of 1938. This act prevented employers in mining and other dangerous industries from hiring children under the age of 16. It also set 40 cents as the minimum wage paid to a child laborer and mandated a maximum work week of 40 hours.

7157. Minimum wage law enacted by Congress was one of the provisions of the Fair Labor Standards Act of 1938, "an act to provide for the establishment of fair labor standards in employment in and affecting interstate commerce," enacted on June 25, 1938.

7158. Labor antidiscrimination commission established by a state government was the New York State Commission Against Discrimination, appointed on July 1, 1945, "to formulate policies to eliminate and prevent discrimination in employment because of race, creed, color or national origin, either by employers, labor organizations, employment agencies or other persons." It consisted of five commissioners at $10,000 a year whose terms ranged from one to five years. The first chairman was Henry C. Turner.

7159. Strike to last longer than a year started on December 26, 1945, when Local 180 of the United Automobile Workers of America struck the J.I. Case Manufacturing Company, Racine, WI, a manufacturer of farm implements. On March 9, 1947, the workers voted 927–448 in favor of accepting the company offer of an increase in wages from 25 cents to 26 cents an hour.

7160. Labor dispute in which the Taft-Hartley Act was invoked took place in 1948 between the American Federation of Labor Atomic Trades and Labor Council and the Oak Ridge National Laboratory, Oak Ridge, TN. The Taft-Hartley Act, also known as the Labor-Management Relations Act of 1947, gave the president power to seek an 80-day injunction against strikes in cases of national emergency. On March 19, 1948, at Knoxville, TN, Federal Judge George Caldwell Taylor, responding to a request from President Harry S. Truman, issued an injunction to the Justice Department that restrained 900 members of the union from leaving their jobs on a walkout for an 80-day period, thus averting a strike by seven hours.

7161. Minimum hourly wage of one dollar was set by the federal government on August 12, 1955.

7162. Guaranteed 52-week wage in a major industry was signed into a contract between the American Can and Continental Can companies and the United Steel Workers union on August 13, 1955.

7163. Minimum wage law established by a city for public contract work was the City Contracts Minimum Wage law, approved by Mayor Robert Ferdinand Wagner of New York City on December 29, 1961. It applied to "every contract for or on behalf of the city for the manufacture, furnishing or purchase of supplies, material or equipment, or for the furnishing of work, labor or services, and entered into by public letting founded in sealed bids."

7164. Strike of postal employees was a wildcat strike of locals of the National Association of Letter Carriers that began in New York City on March 18, 1970, and spread to parts of New York, New Jersey, and Connecticut. On March 23, President Richard Milhous Nixon declared a state of national emergency and called out 30,000 troops to move the mail. The troops included 15,000 army, navy, and marine reservists from the New York City area; 12,000 members of the Army and Air National Guard in New York; and 2,500 men on active duty in New York. The strike ended on March 24.

7165. Strike by physicians against long working hours in hospitals began at 7 A.M. on March 17, 1975, when 21 of New York City's 91 voluntary and municipal hospitals were struck by interns and resident physicians demanding a reduction in work hours, not to exceed 40 hours.

7166. State to recognize unions for farmworkers was California. The Agricultural Labor Relations Act, signed into law by Governor Jerry Brown on June 5, 1975, allowed farmworkers to form unions and to engage in collective bargaining with growers.

7167. State welfare reform program was Wisconsin Works, started in 1997 with the aim of moving poor people into the workforce. Under the program, adults on welfare, except for mothers of newborns, were required either to find a job or to engage in activities that would prepare them to hold a job. Training and support services were offered.

Monuments

7168. Monument to Christopher Columbus was the Columbus Monument, dedicated on October 12, 1792, in Baltimore, MD, 300 years after his first journey to this continent.

7169. Monument to George Washington was the Washington monument of Baltimore, MD, the cornerstone of which was laid on July 4, 1815, with Masonic ceremony. The monument was not completed until October 19, 1829. Like the famous obelisk in Washington, DC, it was designed by Robert Mills. The Baltimore monument has a shaft 180 feet high and is surmounted by a 16-foot statue of George Washington. The site was donated by General John Eager Howard and the funds were raised by lottery. Another monument, begun later but completed earlier, was finished by Isaac C. Lutz in Boonsboro, MD, on July 4, 1827. It was a cairnlike structure, 54 feet in circumference at its base and 15 feet high. The wall of the monument was composed of huge stones, many weighing upward of a ton. A flight of steps ran to the top, which was also used as an observation tower.

7170. Bronze statue of full length was executed by Ball Hughes in 1847 and placed in the cemetery at Mount Auburn, Cambridge, MA. It represented the astronomer Nathaniel Bowditch, seated and holding a copy of his translated work, La Place's *Mécanique Céleste*, with a globe and a quadrant beside him. The statue was imperfect and was recast by Gruet Jne. Fondeur of Paris in 1886.

7171. Bronze equestrian statue was Clark Mills's statue of General Andrew Jackson, unveiled on January 8, 1853, in Lafayette Park, Washington, DC. It was cast from cannons captured by Jackson in the War of 1812.

7172. Monument to commemorate the Civil War was a plain brownstone shaft designed by Nelson Augustus Moore and dedicated in Kensington, CT, on July 25, 1863, two years before the end of the war, at a cost of $350. It was "erected to commemorate the death of those who perished in suppressing the Southern Rebellion," and eventually carried the names of 16 men.

7173. Monument ordered by the federal government from a sculptor who was a woman was a life-size model of Abraham Lincoln. An act of Congress of July 28, 1866, authorized the secretary of the interior to enter into contract with the sculptor Vinnie Ream. A contract was signed on August 30, 1866, to pay her $10,000, half upon presentation of the model in plaster and the balance upon completion of the marble statue. The statue was unveiled on January 25, 1871, in the Rotunda of the Capitol.

7174. Monument to an American poet was a full-length bronze statue of Fitz-Greene Halleck. It was the work of Wilson MacDonald and was presented to New York City by a committee of private citizens. It was unveiled in Central Park on May 15, 1877, 10 years after the death of Halleck, by President Rutherford Birchard Hayes.

7175. Obelisk to be brought to the United States was loaded in Alexandria, Egypt, on June 12, 1880, and arrived in New York City on July 20 on the U.S.S. *Dessoug* under Commander Henry Honeychurch Gorringe. A hole was cut in the starboard bow of the ship to accommodate the massive object. William Henry Vanderbilt paid the expenses of its removal. The obelisk was 90 feet high and weighed 443,000 pounds. It was built in Heliopolis, Egypt, between 1591 and 1565 B.C.E. and was removed about 22 B.C.E. to Alexandria, where it stood until it was brought to the United States as a present from the Khedive of Egypt. The cornerstone was laid with Masonic services on October 9, 1880, and the obelisk was erected on its pedes-

Courtesy of Richard J. Stein

Cleopatra's Needle, in New York's Central Park.

tal in Central Park, New York City, on January 22, 1881. It is popularly known as "Cleopatra's Needle."

7176. Statue cast by the federal government was a bronze statue of Admiral David Glasgow Farragut. On January 28, 1875, George Maxwell Robeson, secretary of the Navy, awarded a $20,000 contract to the sculptor Vinnie Ream. It was cast at the Washington Navy Yard, Washington, DC, and the mechanical work was performed by artisans employed by the government. It was accepted on April 25, 1881, by President James Abram Garfield. The base of the monument is formed of three tiers of uncut granite, the lower tier measuring 20 feet. The figure is of heroic size, standing in an easy position with one foot resting upon a pulley block around which a cable is coiled. In the hands is a telescope. The statue is located at Farragut Square, Washington, DC.

7177. Statue presented to the United States by a foreign country was Liberty Enlightening the World, popularly called the Statue of Liberty, which stands on Liberty Island (formerly Bedloe's Island) in New York Harbor, New York City. The statue, designed by the French sculptor Frédéric Auguste Bartholdi, was a gift of the people of France in commemoration of the hundredth anniversary of American independence. The right hand and torch of the statue were exhibited at the Centennial Exhibition in Philadelphia in 1876. The statue was put in place in 1885 and unveiled on October 28, 1886. It is 151 feet high and stands on a granite pedestal 155 feet high that was provided by popular subscription in the United States.

7178. Monument to a woman financed by women was dedicated on May 10, 1894, to "Mary, the Mother of Washington," over the grave of Mary Ball Washington, mother of President George Washington, in Fredericksburg, VA. The original monument had been raised in 1833 but had been neglected and had fallen into disrepair. The National Mary Washington Memorial Association, chartered on February 22, 1890, raised a fund of $11,500 to replace it. The new monument, a 40-foot monolith on bases and plinth 10 feet high, was designed and built by a Mr. Crawford. The cornerstone was laid on October 21, 1893.

7179. Statue officially sanctioned by the Pope was the figure of Our Lady of Prompt Succor, the Patroness of Louisiana, which was blessed by Archbishop Janssens in the name of Pope Leo XIII on November 10, 1895, at the Ursulines Convent, New Orleans, LA.

7180. Monument to commemorate the Spanish-American War was unveiled in Monroeville, OH, on Thursday, September 29, 1904.

7181. Statue of a woman installed in the Capitol's National Statuary Hall in Washington, DC, was the figure of Frances Elizabeth Willard, educator, editor, and temperance reformer, erected by Illinois and dedicated on February 17, 1905.

7182. National monument designated by the federal government was the Devils Tower, a massive fluted column of volcanic rock 865 feet tall in the Black Hills at Belle Fourche River, WY. The base of this gray igneous rock is 1,700 feet in diameter. President Theodore Roosevelt signed a bill on September 24, 1906, establishing 1,153 acres as a national monument.

7183. Monument to a bird was unveiled on October 1, 1913, at Salt Lake City, UT. It was designed by Mahonri Young, a grandson of Brigham Young, to commemorate the sea gulls from the Great Salt Lake that attacked a devouring horde of black crickets, or grasshoppers, that were destroying the wheat fields of the Mormon settlers in May 1848.

7184. Monument to an insect was dedicated on December 11, 1919, at Enterprise, AL. It was erected by the citizens of Enterprise, Coffee County, AL, "in profound appreciation of the Boll Weevil and what it has done as the herald of prosperity." The deadly destruction of cotton crops by the weevil had caused the farmers to diversify their crops, with the result that their income shortly jumped to triple the amount received in the best cotton years.

7185. National monument to Abraham Lincoln was the Lincoln Memorial in Potomac Park, Washington, DC, dedicated on Memorial Day, May 30, 1922. The idea originated in the celebrations that were held in February 1909 to mark the centenary of his birth. A bill to create a national memorial, introduced by Senator Shelby M. Cullom of Illinois, was passed in 1911. The building's architect, Henry Bacon, designed it to resemble the Parthenon in Athens, Greece; its 36 marble columns symbolize the states of the Union during Lincoln's presidency. The marble statue of Lincoln within is by the sculptor Daniel Chester French. Lincoln's Gettysburg Address is inscribed on the south wall, and the Second Inaugural Address on the north wall.

7186. Statue to commemorate literary characters was the Tom Sawyer and Huck Finn statue, a bronze group by Frederick Cleveland Hibbard, donated by Mr. and Mrs. George Addison Mahan and their son, Daniel Dulany Mahan. It was erected on a base of red granite on May 27, 1926, at Hannibal, MO.

7187. Monument to the American flag was dedicated at Schenley Park, Pittsburgh, PA, on June 14, 1927, on the 150th anniversary of the adoption of the Stars and Stripes as the national banner. It was designed by Harvey A. Schwab, dedicated by William T. Kerr, founder of the American Flag Day Association, and unveiled by Florence Bent of Pittsburgh's Bellefield High School.

7188. Monument to a comic-strip character was the Popeye statue in Popeye Park, Crystal City, TX, unveiled on March 26, 1937, during the Second Annual Spinach Festival. It was six feet tall, made of concrete, and colored to represent Elzie Crisler Segar's cartoon character "Popeye."

7189. National monument to Thomas Jefferson was the Thomas Jefferson Memorial in East Potomac Park in Washington, DC. Designed by John R. Pope, Otto R. Eggers, and Daniel P. Higgins, it was modeled after the Pantheon in Rome, in the domed classical style favored by Jefferson in his own architectural works. The monument was dedicated on April 13, 1943, for the 200th anniversary of Jefferson's birth. Under the central dome is a 19-foot bronze statue of Jefferson by sculptor Rudulph Evans, and inscribed on the interior walls are quotations taken from Jefferson's writings.

7190. National monument dedicated to an African-American was the George Washington Carver National Monument, authorized on July 14, 1943, officially established on June 14, 1951, and dedicated on July 14, 1953. It consists of 210 acres about 2.5 miles southwest of Diamond in Newton County, MO. It is administered by the National Park Service.

7191. Monument to a Native American was carved out of a granite mountain north of Custer, SD. The world's largest sculpture, it was a 563-foot-high, 600-foot-long monument to Crazy Horse, the Lakota chief who led the victory over Custer's forces at the Little Big Horn in 1876. In 1939, sculptor Korczak Ziolkowski, an assistant on the construction of the Mount Rushmore presidential monument, was asked by Lakota chief Henry Standing Bear to "caress a mountain so that the white man will know that the red man had heroes, too." Ziolkowski started work in 1948 and removed some 7 million tons of granite. He died in 1982, leaving the monument unfinished.

Library of Congress, Prints & Photographs Division, LC-USZC4-511

The Battle of the Big Horn.

7192. Monument to mothers of fallen soldiers was started on June 4, 2005, when the footing was poured for the granite pedestal of a statue in Putnam County Veterans Memorial Park, in Kent, NY. The lifesize bronze statue, sculpted by Andrew L. Chernak, a Vietnam veteran, depicts a mother of the World War II era crying in anguish as she receives the telegram informing her that her child has been killed in action.

Organizations

7193. Mason known to arrive in America was John Skene (or Skeen), member of a lodge in Aberdeen, Scotland. He came to New Jersey in 1682, settling in Burlington, and later became deputy governor of West Jersey. The first Mason born in America was Jonathan Belcher, a citizen of Boston, MA, who was made a Mason in England in 1704. Belcher served as royal governor of the Colony of Massachusetts Bay from 1730 to 1741 and royal governor of New Jersey from 1746 to 1757.

7194. Masonic lodge was St. John's Lodge, Philadelphia, PA, for which there are records dating back to 1730. The first lodge to receive a regular charter was St. John's Lodge of Boston, MA, organized by Henry Price and established on July 30, 1733. The first military lodge was formed at Crown Point, NY, under authority granted on April 13, 1759, by Provincial Grand Master Jeremy Gridley of Massachusetts. The first grand lodge was organized at Williamsburg, VA, on October 13, 1778, when the Grand Lodge of Virginia was established with Right Worshipful John Blair, past-master of Williamsburg Lodge No. 6, as the first grand master.

7195. Masonic book was printed and published by Benjamin Franklin in Philadelphia in 1734. It was advertised from May 9 to May 30, 1734, in the *Pennsylvania Gazette.* It was an American edition of Anderson's *Constitutions of the Freemasons; containing the History, Charges, Regulations, etc., of that most Ancient and Right Worshipful Fraternity.*

7196. Mason who was African-American was Prince Hall, initiated on March 6, 1775, in an army lodge that was stationed at Castle William under General Thomas Gage in or near Boston, MA. It operated under Irish constitutions. When the British evacuated Boston, Hall and his fellow members were given a permit to form African Lodge No. 1, which they did on July 3, 1776. On June 30, 1784, after the Revolution, Hall and others applied to the Grand Lodge of England for a warrant, which was issued on September 29, 1784, to African Lodge No. 459, with Prince Hall as Master. The first meeting under the charter was held on May 6, 1787, in Boston, MA. The lodge was not recognized by American masonry. The first African-American lodge to be recognized was the Alpha Lodge of New Jersey, No. 116 Free and Accepted Masons, the warrant for which was granted at the Annual Communication of the Grand Lodge in Trenton, NJ, on January 19, 1871.

7197. Interfaith charity organization was the Union Society, a cooperative effort of Protestants, Catholics, and Jews, formed in Savannah, GA, in 1776. Its purpose was to assist needy widows and orphans. The founder was Mordecai Sheftall, a Jewish businessman. Sheftall, who served as commissary general of the Georgia state militia during the Revolutionary War, was captured by the British during their attack on Savannah, but continued to hold meetings of the society as a prisoner of war.

7198. National arts and sciences organization was the American Academy of Arts and Sciences, founded in Boston, MA, and chartered on May 4, 1780, "to cultivate every art and science which may tend to advance the interest, dignity, honor and happiness of a free, independent and virtuous people." The first president was James Bowdoin, who served from 1780 to 1790. The first female member was Maria Mitchell, elected unanimously on May 30, 1848. On October 1, 1847, at Nantucket, MA, she had discovered a telescopic comet, for which King Frederick VI of Denmark presented her with a gold medal.

7199. Endowment for social service purposes was the White-Williams Foundation, established in February 1800 as the Magdalen Society, a Home for Girls, for the purpose of "providing more normal opportunities of development and inculcating good habits and to ameliorate the distressed condition of those unhappy females who have been seduced from the paths of virtue, and are desirous of returning to a life of rectitude."

7200. Women's club was the Female Charitable Society of Wiscasset, ME, which held its first meeting on November 18, 1805, at the home of Tempe Lee, wife of Judge Silas Lee, a member of Congress. Thirty women were present. A total of $78 was subscribed. The first president was Sally Sayward Wood, Maine's first female novelist.

7201. Masonic magazine was *Free-Masons Magazine and General Miscellany*, a monthly, published in April 1811 by Levis and Weaver, Philadelphia, PA. It was edited by George Richards.

7202. Peace society was the New York Peace Society, which was organized on August 16, 1815. David Low Dodge was its first president. Similar societies were formed elsewhere. On May 8, 1828, the New York Peace Society became a member of a national organization called the American Peace Society, which held its first annual meeting on May 13, 1829, in New York City.

7203. Odd Fellows lodge was Washington Lodge No. 1, established on April 26, 1819, in Baltimore, MD. It was organized by Thomas Wildey and acted under a charter obtained from the Duke of York Lodge of England. In 1821, Wildey organized the Grand Lodge of Maryland, of which he became grand master, and the Grand Lodge of the United States, of which he became grand sire.

7204. Fraternal society for Jews was B'nai B'rith (Sons of the Covenant), founded on October 13, 1843, in New York City by Henry Jones and 11 others. The first lodge was formed on November 12, 1843, at which time Isaac Dittenhoefer was elected president. The first national organization of Jewish women was the National Council of Jewish Women, founded in Chicago, IL, in January 1894, with Hannah Greenebaum Solomon as president.

7205. Young Men's Christian Association in the United States was organized on December 29, 1851, in Boston, MA. It was patterned after a similar organization started in London on June 6, 1844. The first gymnasium was opened in New York City in 1869, and in the same year the first separate boys' department was opened in Salem, MA. The first YMCA branch for African-American members was organized in Washington, DC, in 1853 by Anthony Bowen and Jerome Johnson, who served respectively as president and secretary.

7206. Village improvement society with a long-term existence was the Laurel Hill Association of Stockbridge, MA, founded by Mary Gross Hopkins. The society was organized on August 24, 1853, "to improve and ornament the streets and public parts of Stockbridge, by planting and cultivating trees and doing such other acts as shall tend to improve and beautify the village."

7207. Fund-raising organization to sell stamps was a group of women in Cleveland, OH, who came up with the idea of holding fairs where they would sell stamps as a way of raising money to aid soldiers wounded in the Civil War. They first met on April 20, 1861, eight days after the first gun was fired on Fort Sumter. Five days later, another group formed in New York City. Fairs were also held in Chicago, Albany, Boston, Stamford, and other cities, and special offices were established to sell the stamps, which were known as Sanitary Fair Stamps.

7208. Knights of Pythias meeting took place on February 19, 1864, in Washington, DC, when the organization was formed as a fraternal assocation by Justus Henry Rathbone and 12 associates. It was based on the Greek myth of Damon and Pythias and advocated toleration in religion, obedience to law, and loyalty to government. Washington Lodge No. 1 was the first lodge organized. The Supreme Lodge of the Knights of Pythias of the World was convened on August 11, 1868, in Washington, DC.

7209. Young Women's Christian Association was a local organization founded in Boston, MA, in 1866. In 1858 an organization called the Ladies Christian Association was formed in New York City, and a branch of this group later took the name of Young Women's Christian Association. In 1871 the local eastern associations met in national convention in Hartford, CT, and in 1886 a central group met in Lake Geneva, WI. These two national organizations came together as the YWCA of the United States of America. The first president of the national organization was Grace Hoadley Dodge of New York City.

7210. Animal humane society was the American Society for the Prevention of Cruelty to Animals, founded in New York City by Henry Bergh, formerly of the American Legation at St. Petersburg, Russia, who was appalled by the beatings which droshky drivers in Russia administered to their horses. When he returned to the United States he organized the A.S.P.C.A., incorporated April 10, 1866, and patterned after the Royal S.P.C.A. of London.

7211. Elks meeting that organized the Benevolent and Protective Order of Elks took place on February 16, 1868, in New York City. It derived from an older social and benevolent organization, the Jolly Corks. The first Exalted Ruler was George W. Thompson. The Grand Lodge was incorporated on March 10, 1871, in New York and the first Grand Exalted Ruler was George J. Green.

7212. Women's professional club was Sorosis, founded in New York City on March 21, 1868, by Jane Cunningham Croly and Ellen Demorest. The first president was Alice Carey.

7213. Organization to offer free lunches for the poor and sick was the New York Diet Kitchen Association. On April 24, 1873, the association opened a kitchen at 410 East 23rd Street, New York City, for the relief of the destitute sick. Beef tea, soup, milk-cooked rice, eggs, and oatmeal were served. The first president was Mrs. A.H. Gibbons.

7214. Young Men's Hebrew Association originated in the 1840s as the Young Men's Hebrew Literary Association. The first YMHA opened in Baltimore, MD, in 1854, but was unsuccessful. The first permanent YMHA was founded on March 22, 1874, by a group of German-Jewish businessmen and professionals headed by Dr. Simeon Newton Leo. The first president was Lewis May. A second club was started in Philadelphia in 1875.

7215. Child abuse prevention organization was the New York Society for the Prevention of Cruelty to Children, founded in New York City on December 15, 1874, by Henry Bergh, Elbridge Gerry, and James Wright. In its charter, the society's founding members pledged to shield "the unprotected children of this city and state from the cruelty and demoralization which neglect and abandonment engender." Initial funding was provided by Cornelius Vanderbilt. Bergh founded the American Society for the Prevention of Cruelty to Animals in 1866.

7216. Theosophical society was the American Theosophical Society, founded on November 17, 1875, by Helena Petrovna Blavatsky and Colonel Henry Steele Olcott in New York City. The society later was incorporated in Adyar, Madras, India, the city that became the international headquarters of the society. The American section of the organization had its headquarters in Wheaton, IL. Theosophy is a "synthesis of the principles underlying all religions and science." Its object is to form a nucleus of the "universal brotherhood of humanity," without distinctions of race, creed, sex, caste, or color; to encourage the study of comparative religion, philosophy, and science; and to investigate the unexplained laws of nature and the powers latent in humans.

7217. Ethical culture society was the New York Society for Ethical Culture, founded in New York City in May 1876 by Dr. Felix Adler. Additional groups were formed and in 1886 the American Ethical Union was organized.

7218. National animal humane society was the American Humane Association, which was organized on October 9, 1877, in Cleveland, OH, and was incorporated under the laws of the District of Columbia on November 12, 1903, as a federation of societies for the prevention of cruelty to animals, with the primary purpose of preventing cruelty in the transportation of livestock. The first president was Edwin Lee Brown of Chicago, IL.

7219. Red Cross meeting took place on May 21, 1881, at the home of Adolphus Simeon Solomons in Washington, D.C., where he and Clara Barton founded the American Association of the Red Cross as part of an international humanitarian movement to provide help to victims of war and natural disasters. The organization was made a part of the International Red Cross on March 16, 1882.

7220. Knights of Columbus meeting took place at St. Mary's Roman Catholic Church in New Haven, CT, on January 16, 1882, when the organization was founded as a fraternal benefit association for Catholic men by the Reverend Michael Joseph McGivney and nine parishioners.

7221. National animal rights organization was the American Anti-Vivisection Society, organized on February 23, 1883, at Philadelphia, PA. Its object, according to its charter, was "the restriction of the practice of vivisection within proper limits, and the prevention of the injudicious and needless infliction of suffering upon animals under the pretense of medical and scientific research." Vivisection is the practice of cutting open living, and often unanesthetized, animals. The founder of the society was Caroline Earle White. The first president was Dr. Thomas George Morton. The first annual meeting was held on January 30, 1884, in Philadelphia.

7222. Young Women's Hebrew Association was organized on February 6, 1902, in New York City. Mrs. Bella Unterberg was the founder and the first president. The first building used by the organization was at 1584 Lexington Avenue, New York City.

7223. National arts and letters organization was the National Institute of Arts and Letters, founded in September 1898. The first female member was Julia Ward Howe, author of "The Battle Hymn of the Republic," who was elected in January 1907. The first African-American member, elected in December 1943, was William Edward Burghardt Du Bois, head of the Department of Sociology of Atlanta University, and one of the founders of the National Association for the Advancement of Colored People. An important subsidiary organization, the American Academy of Arts and Letters, was founded in New York City on April 23, 1904, and counted among its original members William Dean Howells, Augustus Saint-Gaudens, Edmund Clarence Stedman, John La Farge, Mark Twain, John Hay, and Edward MacDowell.

7224. Fund-raising organization to sell Christmas seals was the Delaware chapter of the American National Red Cross, which sold them to raise funds to fight tuberculosis. The idea for the seals was proposed in 1907 by Emily Perkins Bissell of Wilmington, DE, who drew the designs and had them lithographed by Theo. Leonhardt and Son, Philadelphia, PA. They were first placed on sale on December 9, 1907, in the Wilmington post office. They were issued in perforated sheets, 228 seals to a sheet, in two types: "Merry Christmas" and "Merry Christmas and a Happy New Year." About $3,000 was realized from the project.

7225. Community trust charity was the Cleveland Foundation, Cleveland, OH, which was established on January 2, 1914, by the board of directors of the Cleveland Trust Company. The idea for a community fund-raising campaign was thought up by Frederick Harris Goff, the company's president. After various surveys of the community were conducted, the first distribution committee was appointed in May 1917, with Dr. James De Long Williamson as chairman. The first director of the Cleveland Foundation was Dr. Raymond Moley.

7226. Think tank in the United States was the Institute for Government Research, founded in 1916 in Washington, DC, by businessman Robert Somers Brookings for the purpose of conducting research in the social sciences and applying this research to public policy. In 1927 the organization merged with the Institute of Economics and the Robert Brookings Graduate School to become the Brookings Institution.

7227. Atheist organization of importance was the American Association for the Advancement of Atheism, the first society in the United States to use the word "atheism" or any of its forms as a title. The society was organized in New York City in October 1925, and was incorporated on November 16, 1925, in New York State. The charter was at first denied by the Supreme Court. The first president of the association was Charles Smith.

7228. Humanist association was the Humanist Society, established on January 13, 1929, in Hollywood, CA, "to humanize religion, disseminate science, stimulate thought and promote good will." The first director was the Reverend Theodore Curtis Abell. The first Humanist National Assembly was held in New York City, on October 10–11, 1934.

7229. Think tank for research and development was the RAND Corporation of Santa Monica, CA. Originally founded on October 1, 1945, as a collaborative project of the U.S. Army Air Forces and the Douglas Aircraft Company, RAND was reestablished as a nonprofit organization on May 14, 1948, with the aim of finding solutions to military, technological, and social problems through scientific analysis. Its first report, published in May 1946, was entitled "Preliminary Design of an Experimental World-Circling Spaceship."

7230. Poster child for a fundraising campaign was Donald Anderson, a toddler with poliomyelitis. In 1946 the March of Dimes, a campaign to help polio patients, issued a poster showing two photographs of Donald. In the first he is shown as a helpless invalid wearing a neck brace; in the second, as a confident walker. The legend read, "Your dimes did this for me!" Anderson grew up to become a postal worker in Seattle, WA.

7231. Daughters of the American Revolution member who was African-American was Karen Batchelor Farmer of Detroit, MI, who became the 623,128th member of the Daughters of the American Revolution in October 1977. She traced her ancestry to William Hood, who served in the militia of Lancaster, PA, during the Revolutionary War.

Public Health

7232. Quarantine law enacted by a colony was passed by the General Court of Massachusetts in March 1647 to protect against an epidemic that was raging in Barbados and the other islands of the West Indies and that took more than 6,000 lives. The court published an order that all ships coming from the West Indies should stay at the Castle at the entrance to the harbor and not land any passengers or goods without a license from three of the council, under a severe penalty. A like penalty was imposed upon any person visiting such quarantined vessel without permission. The act was repealed on May 2, 1649.

7233. Colonial law for the maintenance of an insane patient is found in the records of the Upland Court, Delaware County, PA, dated 1676. The act reads: "Jan Cornelissen of Amesland, Complayning to the Court that his son Erick is bereft of his naturall Senses and is turned quyt madd and that; he being a poore man is not able to maintaine him; Ordered: that three or four persons bee hired to build a little blockhouse at Amesland for to put in the said madman, and at the next Court, order will be taken that; a small Levy be Laid for to pay for the building of the house and the maintaining of the said madman according to the laws of the Government."

7234. Health board established by a city was appointed by Governor Thomas Sim Lee in 1792 for Baltimore, MD. Dr. John Ross was appointed quarantine physician for land and Dr. John Worthington for sea. On September 12 and 17, 1793, a quarantine was proclaimed against Philadelphia, PA, which had a yellow fever epidemic, and Governor Lee forbade all direct commerce. Beginning on April 24, 1795, the Board of Health was elected instead of appointed.

7235. Epidemiologist was Noah Webster, who is better known as the compiler of a famous dictionary. His *A Collection of Papers on the Subject of Bilious Fevers, Prevalent in the United States for a Few Years Past*, was printed in New York City by Hopkins, Webb and Company in 1797. A two-volume work, *A Brief History of Epidemics and Pestilential Diseases; with the Principal Phenomena of the Physical World, which Precede and Accompany Them, and Observations Deduced from the Facts Stated*, was published by Hudson and Goodwin, Hartford, CT, in 1799.

7236. Health service established by the federal government was the Marine Hospital Service, established by congressional act of July 16, 1798. The law provided that the master of every American merchant ship arriving from a foreign port should pay to the collector of customs the sum of 20 cents a month for each seaman, which he was authorized to deduct from the seamen's wages. The money was spent for health services in the district in which it was collected. The service was reorganized as a national hospital system, the Public Health Service, on June 29, 1870.

7237. Quarantine law enacted by Congress was passed on February 25, 1799. It required federal officers to aid and assist the enforcement of state and municipal regulations.

7238. Pure food and drug law established by Congress to prevent the importation of adulterated drugs was passed on June 26, 1848. It was enforced by the Treasury Department through the Customs Service.

7239. Public health report commissioned by a state was *The Report of the Sanitary Conditions of Massachusetts*, submitted to the state legislature in 1850 by statistical analyst Lemuel Shattuck. The report recommended the establishment of a network of local agencies to monitor public health issues and the installation in every city of clean water supplies and sewage removal systems.

7240. Public bathhouse and washhouse was opened on January 1, 1852, by the New York Association for Improving the Condition of the Poor in Mott Street, New York City, later known as the Community Service Society. The first year, 80,375 bathers and 10,038 washers availed themselves of the facilities. On August 17, 1891, the association opened the People's Bath, the first bathhouse to offer showers. The building cost $25,922. There was a charge of five cents for the use of a shower, including soap and towel. During the first 13 months there were 69,944 bathers.

7241. Quarantine board established by a state was a joint city and state board of health authorized by Louisiana and approved on March 15, 1855, by Governor Paul Octave Hebert. The board consisted of nine "competent citizens," six appointed by the governor with the consent of the senate and three elected by the council of New Orleans. The first president of the health board was Dr. A. Forster Axson.

7242. Milk purity law enacted by a state was "an act to punish fraud by the sale of adulterated milk," enacted by Massachusetts and signed on May 30, 1856, by Governor Henry Joseph Gardner.

7243. Milk inspection law enacted by a state was enacted by Massachusetts on April 6, 1859. An Inspector of Milk was appointed on August 10, 1859, by Boston, MA, "to prosecute before the proper tribunal all such violations as shall come to his knowledge."

7244. Turkish bath was opened on October 6, 1863, by Dr. Charles H. Shepard at 81 Columbia Heights, Brooklyn, NY (now part of New York City). It was known as "The Hammam," the name used in Turkey. Admission was a dollar. Only one bather came the first day. Fifty came the first month.

7245. Bathhouses owned and operated by a city were the L Street baths of Boston, MA, built in 1865. They were first opened to the general public in 1866 and were under the supervision of the Board of Bath Commissioners, which had charge of all baths and gymnasiums up to 1913.

7246. Ban by Congress on importation of diseased cattle from foreign countries was enacted on December 18, 1865. The first application of the law took place on July 31, 1875, when meat, cattle, and hides from Spain were excluded on account of the presence of foot-and-mouth disease in that country.

7247. Health board with emergency powers established by a city was the Metropolitan Board of Health, established in New York City by act of New York State Legislature passed on February 26, 1866, "an act to create a Metropolitan Sanitary District and Board of Health for the preservation of life and health therein, and to prevent the spread of disease therefrom." The first meeting of the board was held on March 5, 1866, and was presided over by Jackson Smith Schultz.

7248. Health board established by a state government was the Massachusetts State Board of Health and Vital Statistics, established on June 21, 1869. The first chairman was Henry Ingersoll Bowditch.

7249. Surgeon general was John Maynard Woodworth, appointed Supervising Surgeon of the Marine Hospital Service in April 1871. In 1870, Congress reorganized the MHS, previously a loose network of local hospitals, into a centrally controlled national health agency based in Washington, DC, under the administration of the Treasury Department. Woodworth, formerly the sanitary inspector for the Chicago Board of Health, had distinguished himself during the Civil War as army physician in charge of the ambulance train during General William Tecumseh Sherman's march through Georgia. Woodworth served in the new post until his death in March 1879. The title was changed to Supervising Surgeon General in 1875 and to Surgeon General in 1902.

7250. Quarantine law for plants enacted by a state was passed by California on March 4, 1881. Quarantine rules for the protection of fruit and fruit trees, covering both intrastate and interstate shipments, were issued on November 12, 1881. The quarantine was particularly designed against an insect known as *Phylloxera vastatrix*, which in 1873 had attacked the cultivated grapevines in the Sonoma Valley, and against the San Jose scale and codling moth, which in 1875 had caused serious damage to tree fruits.

7251. Pure food and drug law enacted by a state was "an act to prevent the adulteration of food or drugs," passed on May 28, 1881, by New York. Violators were guilty of a misdemeanor, subject to a fine up to $50 for the first offense and not exceeding $100 for each subsequent offense. Laws prohibiting the adulteration of specific products had been passed earlier.

7252. Home economist was Ellen Swallow Richards of Jamaica Plain, MA, also known as the founder of ecology as a field of study. Richards, a chemist trained at the Massachusetts Institute of Technology, pioneered the scientific study of conditions of domestic life. Her book *The Chemistry of Cooking and Cleaning: A Manual for House-keepers* was published by Estes & Lauriat, Boston, in 1882. In 1909 she cofounded the American Home Economics Association.

7253. Ecologist was Ellen Swallow Richards, who introduced the term "ecology" into the English language. Richards taught for decades at the Massachusetts Institute of Technology, Cambridge, MA, where she worked in the nation's first sanitary chemistry laboratory. From 1887 to 1897 she conducted water analyses for the state health board and was responsible for the establishment of the nation's first water-quality standards. She wrote a number of books explaining the effects of living and working conditions on human health.

Ellen Swallow Richards was the first woman admitted to a college of science, graduating from MIT. She also earned a doctorate there, which MIT withheld because she was female.

7254. Health laboratory established by a city was established on January 1, 1888, in Providence, RI. Dr. Charles Value Chapin was in charge. Dr. Gardner Taber Swarts was the medical inspector.

7255. Meat inspection law enacted by Congress was approved on August 30, 1890. It provided for the inspection of salted pork and bacon intended for export, as well as the inspection of export swine, cattle, sheep, and other ruminants.

7256. Milk pasteurizing stations were private laboratories set up in New York City in 1892 by the merchant and philanthropist Nathan Straus to kill bacteria in raw milk. He also started the Straus Milk Fund to distribute pasteurized milk to poor families. Some 34,000 bottles were distributed in the first year. The laboratories remained open until pasteurization and inspection of milk became required by law two decades later.

7257. Bacteriology diagnostic laboratory in a city health department was the Division of Pathology, Bacteriology and Disinfection, established by the Department of Health of New York City in 1892. The first director of the laboratory was Dr. Hermann Michael Biggs, who served from September 14, 1892, to February 3, 1902.

7258. Tuberculosis laboratory established by a city was authorized on December 13, 1893, and opened by the New York City Department of Health under the direction of Dr. Hermann Michael Biggs. The laboratory conducted diagnostic sputum examinations. It also administered reporting and registration procedures (compulsory for institutions, voluntary for physicians), official supervision of isolation, terminal disinfection, provision of hospital facilities, and public education.

7259. Dietary standards issued by the U.S. Department of Agriculture were published in 1894. The author was Wilbur O. Atwater, director of the USDA Office of Experiment Stations. The publication listed the nutrients in different foods and gave recommended dietary standards for adult males.

7260. Medical inspection of schoolchildren was established by the Board of Health, Boston, MA, in 1894. Eighty inspectors examined pupils sent to them by teachers and advised with regard to medical and surgical treatment. They also provided for exclusion and isolation in cases of contagious disease and imposed the conditions of readmission to school. This work was transferred to the School Committee in June 1915.

7261. Antitoxin laboratory established by a public health department was established in September 1894 by the New York City Department of Health. Dr. William Hallock Park was in charge. This was the first antitoxin laboratory in the world to be run by a public health organization and the first to provide for the free distribution of antitoxin to the poor.

7262. Bathhouses mandated by a state were required by New York in a law passed on April 18, 1895. The law provided for the establishment of free public baths in cities, villages, and towns of 50,000 or over, in such number as determined necessary by local health boards. It required the baths to be kept open not less than 14 hours a day and to be provided with hot and cold water. An earlier law, passed in 1892, had permitted cities to erect free public baths if they desired to do so.

7263. Milk sale regulations enacted by a city were passed by the New York City Department of Health in 1896. The sale of milk without a permit was prohibited. The department of health was also the first to organize a group of milk inspectors to undertake the inspection of dairies located beyond the political boundaries of the city that offered milk for sale in the city, beginning in June 1906.

7264. Health ordinance prohibiting spitting on the sidewalks or in other public places was passed on May 12, 1896, by the New York City Department of Health, as a way of preventing the spread of tuberculosis and other contagious diseases.

7265. Milk station operated by a city government to ensure clean, raw, tuberculin-tested milk for children during July and August and to raise the standard of the milk supply was established in 1897 in Rochester, NY, through the efforts of Dr. George Washington Goler.

7266. Water-quality standards enacted by a state were established in 1900 by the Massachusetts Board of Health, based on data collected by the Lawrence Experiment Station in Lawrence, MA, on the Merrimack River. Techniques for measuring microorganisms in water and sewage were developed there by William Thompson Sedgwick and Ellen Swallow Richards of the Massachusetts Institute of Technology.

7267. Hygiene department in a public school district to aid in instructing children in the fundamental laws of health and generally to improve health conditions was established in Boston, MA, in 1907. The department was in charge of physical training and athletics, as well as the newly organized nursing program.

7268. Rat extermination throughout an entire city was accomplished in San Francisco, CA, in 1907–08 by the Public Health Service, which saved the city and perhaps the nation by destroying the rats and ground squirrels that carried plague-bearing fleas.

7269. Safety congress was held on January 28, 1907, under the auspices of the American Institute of Social Science at the American Museum of Natural History, New York City. It included a public exhibition of safety appliances.

7270. Sterilization of humans by a state government as a matter of public policy was approved by Indiana on March 9, 1907. The law, which allowed sterilization for eugenic, punitive, and therapeutic reasons, was entitled "an act to prevent the procreation of criminals, idiots, imbeciles and rapists." One hundred and twenty operations were performed under the law. The constitutionality of the law was challenged, and on May 11, 1921, the Supreme Court of Indiana, in the case of *Williams v. Smith*, held it unconstitutional because it denied the appellee due process of law. A sterilization bill had been passed by the Pennsylvania legislature on March 21, 1905, but was vetoed by Governor Samuel Whitaker Pennypacker.

7271. Industrial toxicologist was Dr. Alice Hamilton of Chicago, IL, a physician who investigated toxic conditions in workplaces, first for the state of Illinois (from 1908 to 1911) and then for the federal Bureau of Labor (1911 to 1920). Her studies were the first to identify the dangers of lead, mercury, carbon monoxide, radium, and other poisonous substances to which workers were exposed in factories.

In 1911 Dr. Alice Hamilton joined the faculty of Harvard University. She was the first woman ever to teach there.

7272. Health department of a county organized on a full-time basis was established January 7, 1908, in Jefferson County, KY. The first full-time county health officer was Dr. Benjamin Wilson J. Smock, who received $150 a month.

7273. Child hygiene bureau was established in August 1908 in New York City with Dr. Sara Josephine Baker as director. It was the first time a municipal health department undertook to deal with the health of children from birth to legal working age. Dr. Baker's programs included nutrition and health education for residents of slum neighborhoods, health checks for schoolchildren, and licensing of midwives. The result was a drop in the infant mortality rate in poor neighborhoods from 1500 deaths a week to 300.

7274. Milk pasteurization law enacted by a city was passed in 1908 in Chicago, IL, through the efforts of Health Commissioner William A. Evans. The bill required that all milk sold in Chicago after January 1, 1909, be pasteurized, unless the cows producing the milk were tuberculin-tested. Many of the dairies serving Chicago refused to abide by the law.

7275. Quarantine law for plants enacted by Congress was the act of August 20, 1912, directed against dangerous plant diseases and injurious insect pests "new to or not theretofore widely prevalent or distributed within and throughout the United States." Plants that could transmit white-pine blister rust or potato wart, and plants that might harbor the Mediterranean fruit fly, were immediately affected. The first quarantine under the authority of this act was issued on September 16, 1912.

7276. National safety association grew out of the Cooperative Safety Congress, which was held from September 30 to October 5, 1912, in Milwaukee, WI. At the second congress, held on September 23–25, 1913, in New York City, the name was changed to the National Council for Industrial Safety, and the following year to the National Safety Council.

7277. Concept of food groups was introduced in "Food for Young Children" by Caroline Hunt, a 1916 publication by the U.S. Department of Agriculture. She identified five food groups, consisting of milk and meat, cereals, vegetables and fruits, fatty foods, and sugary foods.

7278. Blood testing laws enacted by a state were passed by New York in 1935. Three bills to empower courts to order blood tests were introduced by Assemblyman Charles H. Breitbart on January 9, 1935. They were amendments to the civil practice act, the inferior criminal courts act, and the domestic relations law. They were signed by Governor Herbert Henry Lehman on March 22, 1935.

7279. Blood tests for pregnant women to be required by a state were mandated by the Twomey-Newell bill, signed by Governor Herbert Henry Lehman on March 18, 1938.

7280. Blood tests for marriage license applicants to be required by a state were mandated by New York's Demond-Breitbart Law, signed on April 12, 1938, by Governor Herbert Henry Lehman. The blood tests, along with other medical tests, were intended to prevent the spread of syphilis.

7281. School completely irradiated with germicidal lamps was the Cato-Meridian Central School, Cato, NY. The lamps, made of special glass to permit ultraviolet bactericidal wavelengths to pass through, were made by the General Electric Company, Schenectady, NY, and were installed on January 3, 1945.

7282. Food bank was St. Mary's Food Bank, started by John van Hengel in Phoenix, AZ, in 1967. Van Hengel was working for a charity soup kitchen when he discovered that local grocery stores were routinely throwing out food that was slightly damaged but still edible. He turned a small warehouse into a collection and distribution site that gave away 250,000 pounds of donated food in its first year. Its success gave rise in 1976 to Second Harvest, a nationwide network of food banks, shelters, and other antihunger agencies.

7283. Surgeon general who was a woman was Dr. Antonia C. Novello, appointed by President George Herbert Walker Bush in October 1989. A native of Fajardo, Puerto Rico, she was also the first Latina to hold the post of surgeon general. Novello was previously a professor of pediatrics at Georgetown University Medical Center in Washington, DC, and deputy director of the National Institute of Child Health and Human Development.

7284. Food guide pyramid was published in August 1992 by the U.S. Department of Agriculture as a method of education the public about healthy eating. The broadest area was occupied by complex carbohydrates (bread, cereals, pasta, and rice). The next level consisted of vegetables and fruits. The third section up was divided between dairy products and other protein sources (meat, fish, eggs, beans, and nuts). At the top was a small area for fats, oils, and sweets.

7285. Nationwide nutritional labeling standards were detailed in the Nutrition Labeling and Education Act of 1990. The regulations were made public on December 28, 1992, and published in the *Federal Register* on January 6, 1993. The act required all packaged foods to bear nutrition labeling and all health claims for foods to be consistent with terms defined by the secretary of health and human services. The law preempted state requirements about food standards, nutrition labeling, and health claims and, for the first time, authorized some health claims for foods. The food ingredient panel, serving sizes, and terms such as "low fat" and "light" were standardized.

7286. AIDS policy coordinator for the federal government was Dr. Kristine Gebbie, appointed by President William Jefferson Clinton on June 25, 1993, in Washington, DC.

Gebbie had previously chaired the committee on HIV infection of the Centers for Disease Control and Prevention.

7287. Surgeon general who was African-American was Dr. Joycelyn Elders, born in 1933 in Schaal, AR. Elders, the former health director of the state of Arkansas, was confirmed by a Senate vote of 65 to 34 on September 7, 1993.

7288. Manufactured food product to carry a health claim on its label approved by the Food and Drug Administration (FDA) was oatmeal made by the Quaker Oats Company of Akron, OH. On January 4, 1996, the FDA granted permission to manufacturers of foods containing soluble fiber from whole oats to claim that such products "may reduce the risk of heart disease." The FDA's evaluation of the scientific data was prompted by a petition from the company.

7289. Mandatory AIDS testing for newborns enacted by a state was instituted by New York in 1996 and took effect on February 1, 1997. The law made it obligatory for all newborns to undergo a heel prick in order to draw blood for testing. If the blood proved to contain antibodies to human immunodeficiency virus, the organism that causes AIDS and that can be transmitted from mother to baby, the newborn was started on prophylactic medication to prevent *Pneumocystis carinii* pneumonia, a common illness in HIV-positive patients.

7290. Businessman convicted for importing unsafe toys was Steve Thai of Los Angeles, CA, who was convicted on April 9, 2002, in U.S. District Court. His company, Super Rambo Inc., imported toy vehicles and wind-up robots that had detachable small parts capable of choking a young child, in violation of the rules of the U.S. Consumer Product Safety Commission. He was fined $20,000 and given three years' probation.

7291. Company penalized for failing to report a hazardous product was Mirama Enterprises Inc., also known as Aroma Housewares Co., San Diego, CA. Judge Judith N. Keep of the U.S. District Court of Southern California ruled on July 2, 2002, that Mirama would be fined $300,000 as a civil penalty for its lateness in contacting the U.S. Consumer Product Safety Commission to report that its juicers had injured a number of people.

7292. City to import prescription drugs for its employees and retirees was Springfield, MA, whose mayor, Michael Albano, instituted the policy in July 2003. The city imported lower-cost drugs from Canada in defiance of federal law, saving $2.5 million in the program's first year.

7293. Outbreak of mad cow disease in the United States was announced by the U.S. Department of Agriculture on December 23, 2003. A single dairy cow from a farm in Mabton, WA, was found to have the disease, also called bovine spongiform encephalopathy. BSE is an incurable and fatal brain-wasting disorder that can be transmitted to humans who eat contaminated meat. Several countries, including Japan, Brazil, Australia, and Taiwan, immediately banned the import of U.S. beef.

7294. Dietary supplement to be banned by the Food and Drug Administration was ephedra (*Ephedra sinica*), an energy-boosting herb popular among athletes and dieters. Its active ingredient, ephedrine, was shown to promote strokes, heart attacks, and cardiac arrhythmias. Announced on February 11, 2004, the ban took effect on April 12. Ephedra had already been outlawed by various sports organizations, including the International Olympic Committee, as well as three states.

7295. State public health program to provide prescription drugs from Canada and Europe was I-Save Rx, established by Governor Rod Blagojevich of Illinois on October 4, 2004. Citizens enrolled in the program were able to buy more than 120 prescription drugs at discounted prices from certified pharmacies in Canada, England, and Ireland. Other states were also allowed to join the program.

7296. Campaign to promote citywide testing for the AIDS virus was launched in Washington, DC, on June 27, 2006, by the Mayor's Task Force on HIV and AIDS, established by Mayor Anthony A. Williams. Its goal was to encourage every resident between the ages of 14 and 84—about 400,000 people—to be screened for human immunodeficiency virus, the organism that causes AIDS, during routine medical examinations, using a quick-response oral swab. Washington's rate of HIV infection was higher than that of any other U.S. city. The campaign was expected to cost $8 million.

Public Safety

7297. Independent laboratory for evaluating consumer products was the Good Housekeeping Institute in Holyoke, MA, established in 1905 in association with *Good Housekeeping* magazine. The institute's original focus was on packaged foods. Products that were judged inferior could not run advertisements in the magazine.

7298. Air raid shelter was built by Howard Moyer Gounder at Fleetwood, PA, and completed on November 1, 1940. Stone walls 18 inches thick and set in concrete, with 18-inch retaining walls built alongside a mountain boulder, supported an eight-inch reinforced concrete roof, weather-conditioned with asphalt tar. Movable bunks on one wall accommodated six people. The floors were made of cement. Heavy double doors, one opening inward, the other outward, contained small windows. Electric wiring encased in iron pipes supplied illumination. A stove provided heating and cooking facilities, while ventilation was afforded by a protected chimney in the rear.

7299. State registry of convicted sex offenders was established by California in 1947. It was solely for the use of law enforcement officials, and the information it contained was not made public.

7300. Civil defense test held nationwide was held on June 14, 1954, in the continental United States, 10 provinces of Canada, Alaska, Hawaii, Puerto Rico, and the Virgin Islands from 10 to 10:10 A.M., when the all-clear signal was given.

7301. Air raid shelter for a community was the Highlands Community Shelter, Boise, ID, which was completed on July 1, 1961. It was designed to accommodate 1,000 people. Family membership cost $100. The shelter cost $142,000, of which $122,000 was government research funds obtained from the Office of Civil Defense.

7302. Emergency 911 phone system was installed in Haleyville, AL. A demonstration call, the first on a 911 system, was placed on February 16, 1968. The caller was Rankin Fite, Speaker of the House in the Alabama legislature, who called from the city hall in Haleyville, AL. The recipient was Tom Bevill, an Alabama congressman, who took the call at the police station. The demonstration was arranged by Robert Gallagher, president of the Alabama Telephone Company. The United Kingdom had had an emergency phone system since 1937.

7303. State to authorize incarceration of convicted sex offenders beyond their prison terms was Washington State, under the Community Protection Act, which took effect on February 28, 1990. The act allowed prosecutors to present evidence at a civil trial as to the likelihood that a convicted rapist would repeat the crime after his release from prison. A rapist who was declared a sexually violent predator could be confined indefinitely at the Special Commitment Center on McNeil Island. The U.S. Supreme Court upheld the constitutionality of the law in 2001.

7304. State to inform the public about the residences of released sex offenders was Washington State, which did so under the Community Protection Act, beginning on February 28, 1990. The law required police departments to keep track of the whereabouts of sex offenders who had been released from prison and to notify the public about the residences of the most dangerous of these offenders.

7305. Federal online privacy law was the Children's Online Privacy Protection Act, or COPPA, signed into law on October 21, 1998, and due to take effect on April 21, 2000. COPPA barred commercial Web sites from collecting personal information from customers younger than 13 without parental permission and gave parents various controls over that information. Violations were punishable with a $10,000 fine.

7306. State office of homeland security was established on September 26, 2001, in Missouri, by order of Governor Bob Holden. The first state with a homeland security department created by the state legislature was Alabama, on June 18, 2003.

7307. State consumer protection agency to combat identity theft was California's Office of Privacy Protection, which opened in Sacramento on November 21, 2001. Its mandate included providing education about identity theft, offering assistance to victims, and facilitating cooperation among law enforcement agencies. The director was Joanne

McNabb. Some 70,000 Californians were victims of identity theft in 2000, the year in which the legislature established the agency.

7308. State ban on the sale of violent video games to children was signed into law in Washington State on May 19, 2003, by Governor Gary Locke. The law set fines of $500 for retailers who sell or rent video and computer games depicting violence against police officers and/or firefighters to minors under the age of 17. A federal court struck down the law as unconstitutional the following year.

7309. Demonstration of wireless remote vehicle control as an antiterrorism tactic took place on November 4, 2003, at the California State Highway Patrol Academy in Sacramento, CA. A tanker truck fully loaded with petrochemicals and moving at high speed was instantly stopped by a remote-controlled signal delivered via satellite using Global Positioning System technology. The signal was sent from Satellite Security Systems, a tracking and monitoring firm, in San Diego, CA, 530 miles away.

7310. Antiterrorism security standards enacted by a state to protect its chemical plants were put in place by New Jersey on November 29, 2005. Managers at 140 chemical plants, with the participation of employees, were required to review their vulnerability to terrorist attacks, including physical access, access to information, storage of hazardous materials, and personnel issues, and to institute routine and emergency security practices.

Firefighting

7311. Fire prevention law enacted by a colony was enacted on March 17, 1631, by Cambridge (then called Newtowne), MA, as the result of a fire the previous day in Boston that had spread to an adjoining house. The legislation provided that "no man there shall build his chimney with wood, nor cover his house with thatch."

7312. Fire engine made in America was built in 1654 by Joseph Jencks, an iron maker of Lynn, MA. He made a contract with the selectmen of Boston for an "Ingine" to carry water in case of fire. It was a clumsy pump worked by relays of men at the handles. Its cistern was supplied with water by lines of bucket passers.

7313. Fire department established by a city was organized in 1659 by Peter Stuyvesant, governor of New Amsterdam (later New York City). He distributed 250 leather buckets and a supply of ladders and hooks that he had imported from Holland. A tax of one guilder for every chimney was imposed for the maintenance of this equipment. The fire alarm was given by the twirling of a rattle, with the result that the firemen became known as the Rattle Watch.

7314. Fire chief was the "brent-master," appointed in 1669 to lead the firemen of New Amsterdam (later New York City).

7315. Fire of serious consequence that was recorded occurred on November 27, 1676, when there "burned down to the ground 46 dwelling houses, besides other buildings, meeting house, etc.," in Boston, MA. Three years later, on August 8, 1679, another Boston fire destroyed 80 dwellings and 70 commercial buildings, the damage amounting to almost $1 million.

7316. Fire department to be paid was authorized in 1697 by New York City. Two fire wardens were authorized for every ward. A penalty of three shillings was imposed upon owners for neglecting to remedy defective flues and hearths. If a fire resulted after warning, the fine was 40 shillings, half of which went to the wardens and half to the city.

7317. Lightning rod was invented in 1749 by Benjamin Franklin, who installed it on his house at 141 Market Street, Philadelphia, PA. He described his experiments in his *Opinions and Conjectures concerning the Properties and Effects of the Electrical Matter, and the means of preserving Buildings, Ships, etc., from Lightning, arising from Experiments and Observations made at Philadelphia, 1749.*

7318. Fireboats were put in service in New York City in 1800. They were flat-bottom boats shaped like a scow, with sharp bows and square sterns. Each boat was powered by 12 rowers and was equipped with a hand-operated pump. Two of these boats were stationed at the foot of Roosevelt Street on the East River and patrolled the docks and waterfront of New York City. They were imported from England at a cost of $4,000 each and arrived in New York City on September 28, 1800.

7319. Fire patrol to protect property during fires was the Philadelphia Society for the Protection of Movable Property in Time of Fire, organized in Philadelphia, PA, in 1819 to prevent theft during fires and to salvage articles. The company had large baskets in which to place the articles saved and had vehicles for carrying the baskets away. The first fire patrol to be paid a salary was organized in New York City in 1835 and consisted of four men, each of whom received $250 a year.

7320. Fire hose of rubber-lined cotton web to replace old-fashioned hoses of riveted leather was invented by James Boyd of Boston, MA, who obtained a patent for it on May 30, 1821. In 1819 he established James Boyd and Sons in Boston, MA, to manufacture Boyd's Patent Double Fire Engine Hose.

7321. Fire engine with a steam boiler was designed and built by Paul Rapsey Hodge and publicly tested on March 27, 1841, at the City Hall, New York City. It was 14 feet long and weighed about 8 tons. It had two small wheels under the boiler in front and two huge wheels at the rear. Two horses were required to draw it on level ground. It was placed in service by the fire company known as Pearl Hose No. 28, but was abandoned because it was too heavy and because sparks poured from its stacks.

7322. Sprinkler system put into use was a perforated pipe system invented by the hydraulic engineer James Bicheno Francis. The first installation was made in 1852 at the plant of the Proprietors of the Locks and Canals on the Merrimack River at Lowell, MA.

7323. Fire engine that was practical was the Uncle Joe Ross, invented by Alexander Bonner Latta and manufactured by Latta, Shawk and Company in 1852 in Cincinnati, OH, in the shops of John H. McGowan. It took nine months to build, cost $10,000, and was tested on January 1, 1853, the date it went into service. It weighed 5 tons, was drawn by four horses and its own power, and had a square firebox, like that of a locomotive boiler, with a furnace open at the top, upon which the chimney was placed. It ran on three wheels, the front one revolving in the center of the car. It threw from one to six streams of water. In a single stream 1.75 inches in diameter, it threw water a distance of 240 feet.

7324. Fire department to be paid a salary was established by Cincinnati, OH, on April 1, 1853, through the efforts of Miles Greenwood. Members of the company received $60 a year, lieutenants $100, captains $150, pipemen and drivers $365. The chief engineer received $1,000 a year and assistant engineers $300.

7325. Fire alarm system operated by electricity was invented by William Francis Channing of Boston, MA, and Moses Gerrish Farmer of Salem, MA, who on May 19, 1857, received a patent for "a magnetic electric fire-alarm." The first city to adopt this system was Boston, which in June 1851 voted $10,000 to test the device.

7326. Fire escapes for tenements were required by New York State on April 17, 1860. The law was passed in the aftermath of a serious fire in Elm Street, New York City, on February 2, 1860, in which 20 persons were suffocated or burned to death.

7327. Boiler inspection law enacted by a state was approved on July 9, 1864, by Connecticut. It authorized the governor to appoint an Inspector of Boilers to check every steam boiler used for manufacturing or mechanical purposes.

7328. Sprinkler system patent was granted to Philip W. Pratt of Abington, MA, on September 17, 1872. The system operated by means of a valve to which cords and fuses were attached. When the cords and fuses melted, the valve opened, releasing a stream of water.

7329. Sprinkler head was invented by Henry S. Parmelee of New Haven, CT, who obtained a patent on August 11, 1874. It consisted of a perforated head containing a valve that was held closed against water pressure by a heavy spring made of low fusing material.

7330. Firehouse pole was installed on April 21, 1878, by Captain David B. Kenyon of Engine Company No. 21, New York City. A hole was cut in an upper floor to accommodate a greased pole three inches wide that extended between the two storeys, to enable the firemen slide down the pole instead of using the stairs.

7331. Fire extinguisher using vaporized chemicals was manufactured by the Pyrene Manufacturing Company, Newark, NJ, and introduced in 1905. The first model had a single-action pump, which had to be tilted down after each stroke in order to suck up liquid for the next discharge stroke.

7332. Fireworks law enacted by a city was passed by Cleveland, OH, on July 18, 1908. It provided that "no person, firm or corporation shall within the city, sell, offer for sale or have in his or its possession or custody any toy pistol, squib, rocket, cracker, Roman candle or fire balloon or other combustibles, or fireworks," under penalty of a $100 fine or 30 days' imprisonment or both. The Board of Public Service was permitted to give pyrotechnic displays when directed by the Council.

7333. Fireworks law enacted by a state was passed on March 29, 1929, by Michigan. It prohibited the use of fireworks by the general public but allowed displays by approved or licensed operators. Other states had partially restrictive laws.

7334. Fire department composed entirely of women was the Ashville Fire Department, Ashville, NY. In February 1943, 13 women replaced the department's male firefighters, who were serving in the armed forces or were working elsewhere. They served without pay. They operated a 500-gallon-per-minute pumper and were proficient in rescue work and other fire department procedures.

7335. Smoke alarm for residential use was the BRK SS68H, a battery-operated model that went on the market in 1968. It contained a photoelectric cell that set off an alarm if its voltage was raised by the presence of smoke particles. Heat detectors made by the Electric Heat Alarm Company were manufactured as far back as the 1890s.

Lifesaving

7336. Lighthouse was a conical masonry tower erected by the Province of Massachusetts in 1716 on Little Brewster Island at the entrance to Boston Harbor, at a cost of £2,285, 17shillings, and 8.5 pence. The lighthouse was authorized by act of July 23, 1715, and the light was first kindled by keeper George Worthylake on September 14, 1716. It had 16 spermaceti oil lamps in groups of four. To support its upkeep, a levy of a penny per ton was placed on all incoming and outgoing vessels except those engaged in coastal service. The lighthouse was rebuilt in 1783.

7337. Lifesaving service for distressed mariners was established in 1787 by the Humane Society of the Commonwealth of Massachusetts. Huts were erected at a cost of $40 each at Scituate Beach, Nantucket, MA, and at the west end of Lovell's Island, MA.

7338. Lighthouse built after American independence was located at Cape Henry, VA, at the entrance of Chesapeake Bay. On August 7, 1789, an act was passed "for the establishment and support of lighthouses, beacons, buoys and public piers." On March 31, 1791, a contract for the erection of the Cape Henry Lighthouse was made with John McComb, Jr. It was finished in 1792. The first lighthouse keeper was Laban Goffigan. The original fuel for illumination was fish oil, followed later by whale oil, colza oil, lard oil, kerosene, gas, and finally, electricity.

7339. Emergency first aid organization was the Humane Society of Philadelphia, PA, which was organized in 1780. The society was incorporated on January 23, 1793. Its object, according to the charter, was the "recovery of drowned persons, and of those whose animation may be suspended from other causes, as breathing air contaminated by burning charcoal, hanging, exposure to the choke-damp of wells, drinking cold water while warm in summer, strokes of the sun, lightning, swallowing laudanum, etc."

7340. Lifeboat was built in Nantucket, MA, by William Raymond under the supervision of Captain Gideon Gardner and was completed in 1807. It was built for the Humane Society of the Commonwealth of Massachusetts and cost $1,433. An additional $160 was used for a shed in Cohasset, MA, where the lifeboat remained until 1813.

7341. Lightship was placed in the Elizabeth River off Craney Island, VA, on July 14, 1820. The displacement was 70 tons. The ship was built at a cost of $6,000.

7342. Life preserver of cork was invented by Napoleon E. Guerin of New York City, who obtained a patent on November 16, 1841, on "an improvement in buoyant dresses or life-preservers." It was a jacket or waistcoat containing 18 to 20 quarts of rasped or grated cork.

The Neversink Cork Jacket, formed of granulated cork compressed under pressure, was invented by David Kahnweiler of New York City, tested in 1872 in the Potomac River, and patented on July 10, 1877. Life preservers of this type saved the lives of 287 persons when the S.S. *San Francisco* of the Pacific Mail Steamship Company was wrecked in the Pacific Ocean in 1877.

7343. Lighthouse on the Pacific coastwas the Spanish lighthouse erected in 1855 at Ballast Point on Point Loma, San Diego, CA.

7344. Lifesaving service established by the federal government was introduced in 1871 by Sumner Increase Kimball. An act of Congress of June 18, 1878, formally authorized the Life Saving Service as a separate and distinct service in the Treasury Department. This service and the Revenue Cutter Service were merged on January 28, 1915, to form the Coast Guard.

7345. Lifesaving medal awarded by the Treasury Department as authorized by act of June 20, 1874, was given on June 19, 1876, to Lucian M. Clemons, keeper of the United States Lifesaving Service Station at Marblehead, OH, for saving men from the schooner *Consuelo* on May 1, 1875. The award was established for "persons who should thereafter endanger their own lives in saving or endeavoring to save the lives of others from the perils of the sea within the United States or upon any American vessel."

7346. First aid instruction was given at the annual encampment of the New York State militia at Peekskill, NY, in 1885. The idea was proposed by George Ryerson Fowler.

7347. Electric lighthouse in the United States was the Statue of Liberty on Bedloe's Island in New York Harbor. During the statue's assembly, the Army Corps of Engineers equipped the torch with a set of lamps that were powered by an electric generator. They were lit on November 1, 1886, but did not provide much light.

7348. Radio distress signal from an American ship was sent on December 7, 1903, by Ludwig Arnson from the *Kroonland* of the Red Star line, bound from Antwerp, Belgium, to New York City. Heavy seas struck the rudder and broke the tiller on which the steering engine was mounted, leaving the ship out of control. The call, sent out 130 miles west of Fastnet on the Irish coast, was received by the British H.M.S. *Kent*, which arrived about two hours later and towed the disabled ship to Queenstown, Ireland.

7349. Radio distress signal officially established was the CQD signal, established on January 7, 1904, by the Marconi Company, effective February 1. "CQ" was the general signal for "Stop sending and listen." The popular interpretation of the call was "Come quick—danger." The SOS distress signal was adopted on November 22, 1906, at the International Radio Telegraphic Convention in Berlin, Germany, and superseded the CQD call in July 1908.

7350. Radio SOS call from an American ship was transmitted by Theodore D. Haubner, operator of the Clyde liner *Arapahoe*, a single-screw freight and passenger steamer of some 3,000 tons, bound for Charleston, SC, and Jacksonville, FL, from New York City. Its engines were disabled 21 miles southeast of Diamond Shoals, off Cape Hatteras, at 3:45 P.M. on August 11, 1909. Both the SOS and the CQD signals were sent. The SOS was first heard and acknowledged by R. J. Vosburg, wireless operator at station HA in Cape Hatteras, NC. Foreign registry ships had used SOS signals earlier.

7351. Atomic-powered lighthouse was the Baltimore Light in Chesapeake Bay, Baltimore Harbor, MD, which went into operation on May 20, 1964. A 60-watt radioisotope nuclear generator, 34.5 inches high and 22 inches in diameter, weighing 4,600 pounds (including shielding), was developed and produced by the Martin Company's Nuclear Division, Baltimore, MD, a division of the Martin Marietta Corporation, to supply a continuous flow of electricity for 10 years without refueling. It used 120 pairs of lead telluride thermo couples to convert heat from radioactive strontium titanate, a form of strontium-90, into electricity.

Police

7352. Extradition of criminals among colonies was established by the New England Confederation of 1643, which provided for extradition among the provinces of Massachusetts, Connecticut, Plymouth, and New Haven.

7353. Police force consisted of eight men employed by New Amsterdam (now New York City) in 1658.

7354. Police uniforms were authorized on July 8, 1693, by the Common Council of New York, which ordered that the mayor should provide the police "with a coat of the citty livery, with a badge of the city arms, shoes and stockings, and charge it to the account of the city."

7355. Secret service established in a colony was the Headquarters Secret Service, organized by Aaron Burr and Major Benjamin Tallmadge in June 1778. On July 4, 1778, General George Washington issued a special order making Burr head of the Department for Detecting and Defeating Conspiracies and ordered him "to proceed to Elizabeth Town to procure information of movements of the enemy's shipping about New York." This was the first official intelligence-gathering government service in the united colonies. Previously, information about the activities of the British had been gathered secretly by individuals and informal groups.

7356. Federal marshals were appointed by President George Washington, who signed their commissions in New York City on September 26, 1789. One marshal was appointed for each of the 13 regional judicial districts. The original marshals were Allan McLane, DE; Clement Biddle, PA; Thomas Lowry, NJ; Robert Forsyth, GA; Phillip Bradley, CT; Jonathan Jackson, MA; Nathaniel Ramsay, MD; Isaac Huger, SC; John Parker, NH; Edward Carrington, VA; William Smith, NY; Samuel McDowell, KY; and Henry Dearborn, ME. Two other marshals who were appointed in 1790 (Samuel Skinner, NC, and William Peck, RI), and one who was appointed in 1791 (Lewis R. Morris, VT), are also considered to belong to the first generation of U.S. marshals.

7357. Federal law officer killed in the line of duty was Robert Forsyth, the first U.S. marshal for Georgia, appointed in September 1789. On January 11, 1794, he and two deputies went to a house in Augusta, GA, to serve court papers on brothers William and Beverly Allen. Forsyth asked them to step outside; instead, they barricaded themselves in an upstairs bedroom. Beverly Allen put a pistol shot through the door and hit Forsyth in the head, killing him instantly. The Allen brothers were arrested but succeeded in escaping.

7358. Interstate anticrime pact was effected between New York and New Jersey and signed on September 16, 1833, in New York City by Benjamin Franklin Butler, Peter Augustus Jay, Henry Seymour, Theodore Frelinghuysen, James Parker, and Lucius Quintius Cincinnatus Elmer. The pact was ratified by act of Congress of June 28, 1834.

7359. State police were the Texas Rangers, who were authorized by the General Council of the Provisional Government of Texas to organize three Ranger companies in 1835. On November 9, 1835, G. W. Davis was commissioned to raise 20 more men for this new service. Texas was a province of Mexico at the time. It was admitted to the Union in 1845. The first African-American officer to serve as a Texas Ranger was Lee Roy Young, who joined the force in 1988.

7360. Traffic police squad was the old "Broadway Squad" of New York City, organized in 1860. This was the first unit of the Police Department to have special functions in the field of traffic regulation. The members of the squad were stationed on the sidewalks along Broadway from Bowling Green to 59th Street, at the intersections of the cross streets. It was their job to stop traffic and escort pedestrians across the street. The pavement of Broadway was made of cobblestones and most of the traffic consisted of horse-drawn vehicles.

7361. Federal marshal who was African-American was Frederick Douglass, who was appointed marshal for the District of Columbia on March 18, 1877, by President Rutherford B. Hayes. Douglass, who had been born into slavery in Maryland, had been an influential abolitionist before the Civil War.

7362. Police bureau of identification was established by Captain Michael Patrick Evans on January 1, 1884, for the Chicago Police Department, Chicago, IL. At its inception, only photographs were used. On June 1, 1887, the Alphonse Bertillon system of anthropometric identification was adopted, and on November 1, 1904, the Sir E. R. Henry system of fingerprinting was added. Evans was in charge of the Bureau of Identification from the time of its organization until the time of his death, October 6, 1931.

7363. Police officer who was a woman was Marie Owen, a patrolman's widow. In 1893 she was appointed to the Detroit Bureau of Police, Detroit, MI, by Morgan A. Collins, superintendent of police. The first policewoman under civil service was Alice Stebbins Wells, who was appointed by the Department of Police, Los Angeles, CA, on September 2, 1910.

7364. Police patrol wagon was designed by Frank Fowler Loomis of Akron, OH, and was placed in service by the Akron Police Department in June 1899. It had three speeds and could go 16 miles per hour. It was operated by electric power and weighed 5,500 pounds, including the batteries.

7365. State prison to take fingerprints of its prisoners was Sing Sing Prison, Ossining, NY, which commenced taking impressions on March 3, 1903.

7366. Police department to adopt the fingerprinting system was the St. Louis Metropolitan Police Department, St. Louis, MO, which on October 28, 1904, adopted the Sir E. R. Henry method to fingerprint persons arrested on serious charges. John M. Shea of the department was the first to qualify as a fingerprint expert connected with any police service.

7367. Fingerprinting in federal penitentiaries was undertaken on November 2, 1904, by the Bureau of Criminal Identification at the United States Penitentiary at Leavenworth, KS. This work was carried on until October 1, 1924, when it was taken over by the Federal Bureau of Investigation.

7368. Motorcycle police were Anthony L. Howe and Eugene Case of the New York Police Department, New York City, who were assigned to the police headquarters in the Bronx and Manhattan, respectively. They received official status on December 10, 1904.

7369. International exchange of fingerprints between the United States and Europe was made on July 6, 1905, when the St. Louis Metropolitan Police Department, St. Louis, MO, obtained the fingerprints of John Walker, alias Captain John Pearson, a frequent offender, from New Scotland Yard, London. The prints were later forwarded to New Orleans, LA, and introduced as part of his criminal record.

7370. Director of the Federal Bureau of Investigation was Alexander Bruce Bialaski, a Polish immigrant of Lithuanian extraction. He served from 1912 to 1919. The FBI was founded in 1908 as the Bureau of Investigation, a division of the Department of Justice, and was renamed the Federal Bureau of Investigation in 1935.

7371. Detective who was a woman was Isabella Goodwin, who was appointed as acting detective sergeant, first grade, on March 1, 1912, by the Police Department of New York City. She had served as a police matron since May 15, 1896.

7372. Police chief who was a woman was Dolly Spencer, who was appointed in 1914 by the mayor of Milford, OH.

7373. National file on suspected political radicals was assembled by J. Edgar Hoover, a former librarian, who between 1919 and 1921, as special assistant to Attorney General Alexander Mitchell Palmer, amassed a card file with some 450,000 entries on every known political radical, group, and publication. This card file made possible the mass "Red Scare" arrests carried out under Palmer's authority in 1920 and formed the basis of an expanded national database developed by the Justice Department's Bureau of Investigation (the Federal Bureau of Investigation from 1935) after Hoover became its director on May 10, 1924.

7374. Sheriff who was a woman was Mabel Chase of Haviland, KS. In 1926 she was elected sheriff of Kiowa County. Her husband had been elected sheriff in 1922 and 1924.

7375. State police radio system was established for the Michigan state police under the Radio Broadcasting Stations Act, which went into effect on August 28, 1929. It was the first such system in the world. The act, introduced by H. Earl McNitt, authorized appropriations for state-operated broadcasting and receiving equipment and allowed city governments to connect to the system.

7376. Teletypewriter system employed by a police department was opened by Governor John Stuchell Fisher of Pennsylvania and placed in service on December 23, 1929, at central headquarters, Harrisburgh, PA. It was connected to 95 cities and boroughs by 3,400 miles of telephone wires.

7377. State police officers who were women were appointed by the Division of State Police, Department of Public Safety, MA, on April 18, 1930. They were Lotta Caldwell, who served until April 13, 1940, and Mary Ramsdell, who served until April 18, 1950.

7378. Police bureau of criminal alien investigation was started by the New York Police Department, New York City, on December 23, 1930. The purpose was to bring to the attention of federal immigration authorities undesirable aliens who were subject to deportation under the Immigration Law, because of either their criminal records or their illegal entry into the United States.

7379. Police radio system connecting headquarters to patrol cars, patrol cars to headquarters, and the patrol cars to one another, was installed in Eastchester Township, NY, by Radio Engineering Laboratories, Long Island City, NY (part of Queens, New York City), in 1933. The company contracted with the township on May 8, 1933, to install one transmitter and receiver for police headquarters (20 watts, W2XCT) and two for police cars (4.5 volts, W2XCS and W2XEL). The cars were placed in operation on July 10 and were under the direction of Sergeant William E. Robinson.

7380. Community to fingerprint its citizens was Oskaloosa, IA, which acted upon the suggestion made by Police Chief Howard Ray Allgood on May 21, 1934. Although registration was not compulsory, a Personal Identification Bureau was established through which most of the town's residents had their fingerprints recorded.

7381. Identification of human beings from the pattern formed by the blood vessels of the retina was devised by Dr. Isidore Goldstein, ophthalmic surgeon of Mount Sinai Hospital, New York City, in collaboration with Dr. Carleton Simon, former deputy police commissioner of New York. The system was presented before the annual convention of the International Association of Chiefs of Police on July 7, 1935, in Atlantic City, NJ.

7382. National conference on crime was held on October 11–12, 1935, in Trenton, NJ, with a roster of delegates from 41 states and from the federal government. Its purpose was to curb crime throughout the country by developing reciprocal legislation and interstate cooperation agreements.

7383. High school to fingerprint its students was the Watertown Senior High School, Watertown, SD. The fingerprinting was started on October 19, 1936, as an outgrowth of a talk by a member of the Federal Bureau of Investigation.

7384. Police appeal for missing persons to be shown on television was made on October 3, 1943, by the Missing Persons Bureau of the Police Department of the City of New York on W2XWV, the DuMont station in New York City.

7385. Federal marshal who was a woman was Katherine Battle (later Katherine Battle Gordy), appointed a temporary marshal for the Southern District of Alabama on January 24, 1949. Women had served as deputy marshals in the 19th century in various locations. The first to be hired on a permanent basis were Jacqueline P. Balley, of Washington, DC, and Joanne Neely, of Oxon Hill, MD, sworn in on November 21, 1973, at Washington, DC.

7386. Parking meter enforcement division of a police department was appointed on June 1, 1960, by Mayor Robert Ferdinand Wagner of New York City. The "meter maids" underwent about two weeks of training and received salaries ranging from $3,150 to $4,830 a year. The first summons was issued on June 6, 1960.

7387. Sky marshals were appointed in accordance with President Richard Milhous Nixon's presidential directive of October 28, 1970, to deal with the proliferation of hijackings of commercial airplanes. The Treasury Law Enforcement Officers Training School graduated 46 marshals on December 23, 1970, and 81 marshals, including four women, on April 9, 1971.

7388. Police officer who was a woman to be killed in the line of duty was Gail A. Cobb of the Metropolitan Police Force, Washington, DC, murdered on September 20, 1974, in an underground garage at 20th and L Streets in Washington by a robbery suspect.

7389. Body farm for forensic research was the Anthropology Research Facility, founded in 1981 by William M. Bass at the University of Tennessee, Knoxville, TN. Now known as the Forensic Anthropology Center, the facility includes a wooded area in which donated bodies are allowed to decompose in a variety of conditions. Researchers collect information about the bodies' rates and forms of decay. The facility maintains a database for use by police scientists in solving murder cases.

7390. Federal lawsuit against a city for failure to protect a battered woman was brought by Tracey Thurman of Torrington, CT, who was stabbed and kicked by her husband in 1983 and left partially paralyzed from a broken neck. She had repeatedly asked the city's police department for protection against him, without success. The jury awarded her $2.3 million in 1985. The case resulted in the passage of the state's Family Violence Prevention and Response Act in 1986.

7391. Sheriff who was an African-American woman was Michelle B. Mitchell, elected sheriff in Richmond, VA, in November 1993. Mitchell ran unopposed for the post following a primary election in which she received 59 percent of the vote.

7392. Police 311 hotline was set up by the Baltimore, MD, police department on October 2, 1996, to handle routine calls. The 911 number was retained for emergency calls only. In 2001 the 311 number was expanded to include all municipal services.

7393. AMBER Alert System was started in Dallas–Fort Worth, TX, in July 1997, in response to the unsolved kidnapping and murder of nine-year-old Amber Hagerman. The system allowed police to communicate descriptions of abducted children to the public as soon as possible, using news bulletins on radio and television programs. In addition to honoring the murdered child, the word AMBER is an acronym for America's Missing: Broadcast Emergency Response. The plan was exported to all 50 states. In 2003 a national system was established under a federal coordinator. AMBER Alerts also appear on highway signs, lottery tickets, and other venues.

7394. National DNA database was brought online on October 13, 1998, by the Federal Bureau of Investigation. The database, a network of 50 state databases coordinated by FBI software, was maintained at computers in a secret location. The system made it possible for the first time to compare an identifying DNA sample from a crime in one state with all other DNA samples in the United States.

7395. State police department to be monitored for racial profiling was the New Jersey State Police, an organization with 2,700 officers. Following complaints made by the Black Ministers' Conference of New Jersey and other groups, the federal Justice Department charged the state police with violating the civil rights laws by targeting African-American and Hispanic drivers for traffic stops. To avoid a lawsuit, the state attorney general, Peter G. Verniero, negotiated a settlement in April 1999 committing the police to following a set of protocols intended to prevent discrimination.

7396. Urban business district with complete video surveillance was the downtown area of Wilmington, DE. The installation of a network of 25 cameras throughout the 60-square-block downtown district was completed on November 8, 2002, at a cost of $800,000. The cameras were monitored by the city's police department and led to a reduction in the rates of shoplifting, burglary, and car theft.

7397. City law restricting police inquiries into immigrant activities protected by the First Amendment was passed by the city council of Seattle, WA, on January 27, 2003. The ordinance instructed city employees, including the police, to refrain from collecting information about the opinions, associations, and legal status of immigrants as long as they were not suspected of criminal activity.

Public Services

7398. Curfew bell was introduced by Wilhelm Kieft, the third governor of New Netherlands (later New York City). In 1638 he instituted the custom of ringing the church bell nightly at nine o'clock to announce the hour of resting; every morning and evening to call persons to and from labor; and on Thursdays to summon prisoners to court.

7399. Water supply system built for a city was built in Boston, MA, by the Water Works Company in 1652. A series of wooden pipes was used to convey the water from nearby springs to a central reservoir, which was only 12 feet square.

7400. Water pumping plant was installed in Bethlehem, PA, on May 27, 1755. Water from a spring was pumped through wooden pipes into a 70-foot-high water tower. The plant was constructed by Hans Christopher Christiansen.

7401. Street-sweeping service was instituted in 1757 in Philadelphia, PA, by Benjamin Franklin, who reported: "After some inquiry, I found a poor industrious man who was willing to undertake keeping the pavement clean by sweeping it twice a week, carrying off the dirt from before the neighbors' doors, for the sum of six pence per month, to be paid by each house."

7402. Gas streetlights were installed in 1806 in Newport, RI, on Pelham Street, in front of the residence of David Melville. He patented his apparatus for making coal gas on March 18, 1813, about which time several important installations were made.

7403. Gas streetlights throughout a city were installed in Baltimore, MD, by the Gas Light Company in 1817. On June 19, 1816, the mayor and council authorized the company, whose officers included the artist Rembrandt Peale, to lay pipes for the manufacture and distribution of gas "to provide for more effectually lighting the streets, squares, lanes and alleys of the city of Baltimore." Coal gas was used. The first street was lighted on February 17, 1817. The first engineer of the company was David Pugh.

7404. Drinking water conduit to be built underwater was built in 1848 by the Water Department of Boston, MA. It was constructed on the shore, floated into place, and sunk into a prepared trench below the surface of the channel under the Dover Street Bridge, the Warren Avenue Bridge, the Chelsea Street South Bridge, and the Chelsea Street North Bridge. The wooden tunnels were approximately 4 feet 8.5 inches in diameter and some 50 feet or more in length. They contained cast-iron pipes 20 inches in diameter that carried drinking water from central Boston to the South Boston, Charlestown, and Chelsea sections of the city. All these pipes were in use before 1852.

7405. Street-cleaning machine of importance was employed by Philadelphia, PA, on December 15, 1854. According to a contemporary account, it consisted of "a series of brooms on a cylinder about two feet six inches wide, attached to two endless chains, running over an upper and lower set of pulleys, which are suspended on a light frame of wrought iron behind a cart, the body of which is near the ground. As the cart wheels revolve, a rotary motion is given to the pulleys conveying the endless chains, and series of brooms attached to them; which being made to bear on the ground successively sweep the surface and carry the soil up an incline or carrier plate, over the top of which it is dropped into the cart."

7406. Underground city sewer system was begun in Chicago, IL, in 1856 on the grid pattern. The sewers were of circular cross sections ranging from 3 to 6 feet in diameter and had brick walls 8.5 inches thick. Branch sewers were two feet in diameter, and the hose drains were four-inch and six-inch pipes or boxes made of wood planks. Manholes were provided every 100 feet, and in general the slope or gradient was 1 foot in 500. By June 30, 1860, about 46 miles had been completed. Single uncoordinated sewers had been used earlier.

7407. Dual sewer system for sewage and storm water was built in Brooklyn, NY (now a borough of New York City), in 1857 by Colonel Julius Adams. The size and capacity were scientifically calculated to care for a rainfall intensity of one inch per hour.

7408. Electric arc streetlights were made by Charles Francis Brush and were used in the Public Square, Cleveland, OH, on April 29, 1879. Twelve lamps of the carbon variety—two carbon points slightly separated—were used. The current jumped from carbon to carbon, giving off a dazzling white light.

7409. Sewage-disposal system separate from the city water system was built in Memphis, TN, under the direction of George Edwin Waring, beginning on January 21, 1880. Within four months, he had installed a system comprising 18 miles of pipe, with 152 flush tanks and four-inch connecting drains. The pipes were for sewage only and were kept constantly cleansed with water and well ventilated. Six-inch vitrified pipes emptied into larger pipes, which in turn emptied into increasingly larger ones until 20-inch pipes were used. An independent and separate set of pipes was provided for disposing of storm water. The total cost of 20 miles for the two main sewers, including labor, materials, engineering, superintending, and incidentals, was about $137,000. A similar system was adopted at about the same time by Pullman, IL (now a part of Chicago).

7410. Electric streetlight installed in a city was installed in Wabash, IN. On February 2, 1880, the city appropriated $100 to the Brush Electric Light Company of Cleveland, OH, to install a light on the dome of the courthouse. On March 31, four lights, each over 4,000 candlepower, were placed on a staff above the courthouse, and on April 8 a further payment of $1,800 was authorized.

7411. Plumbing law enacted by a state was enacted on May 30, 1881, by Illinois. It was "an act for the regulation and inspection of tenement and lodging houses or other places of habitation." In cities with a population of 50,000 or more, plumbers were required to receive a written certificate of instruction from the commissioner before commencing work on buildings. They were also required to work according to a prepared plan. Violations were punishable by a fine of not less than $100 for the first offense and $10 a day for noncompliance.

7412. Underground burial of electric wires to be required by a state was mandated under a law enacted on June 14, 1884, by New York. It required that "all telegraph, telephonic and electric light wires and cables in any incorporated city having a population of 500,000 or over . . . be placed under the surface of the streets, lanes and avenues." It also specified that telegraph poles be removed by November 1, 1885. Overhead wires had killed hundreds of people in New York City alone.

7413. Sewer district established by a city was the Sanitary District of Chicago, IL, authorized on November 5, 1889, by referendum vote to construct and operate the sewage system for the protection of the public water supply. Murray Nelson was the first president.

7414. Sewage disposal by chemical precipitation was undertaken in Worcester, MA, which installed the system in 1890. It used six chemical precipitation settling basins, each 66.67 by 100 by 7 feet. The raw sewage was screened and then treated with milk of lime. It was passed through a mixing channel into the six settling basins in series. The detention period was approximately six hours. After being quiescent for a few hours, the top water was drawn off, and the sludge was run to a six-inch centrifugal pump and discharged into lagoons.

7415. Water filtration system for bacterial purification of a city water supply was the Lawrence Filter, Lawrence, MA, designed by Hiram Francis Mills and completed in September 1893. It was an open filter of 2.75 acres that purified water from the Merrimack River by slow sand filtration. The idea dates from 1873, when an English-type slow sand filter was built at Poughkeepsie, NY, from plans prepared by James Pugh Kirkwood.

7416. Drinking water supply to be chemically treated with chlorine compounds on a practical scale was the water supply of Jersey City, NJ, which was chlorinated in 1908 under the supervision of George Arthur Johnson.

7417. Water supply to be fluoridated in order to reduce tooth decay was the water system of Grand Rapids, MI. Fluoridation started on January 25, 1945, with the addition of one part of fluoride ion to each million parts of water passing through the water treatment plant.

7418. Automatic streetlight system in which the lights individually turn themselves on and off was installed in New Milford, CT, on March 2, 1949, by the Connecticut Light and Power Company, New Milford, CT. Each streetlight was equipped with an electronic device that used a photoelectric cell. A total of 190 photoelectric-controlled streetlights were installed on approximately seven miles of streets by November 1949.

7419. Seawater conversion plant that was practical was opened on May 8, 1961, by the Office of Saline Water, Department of the Interior, at Freeport, TX. It was dedicated on June 21 by President John Fitzgerald Kennedy, who pressed a switch installed in his office at Washington, DC. The plant was set up to produce about a million gallons of water a day at a cost of $1 to $1.25 per 1,000 gallons.

7420. Statewide 211 help line was Infoline, a project of United Way of Connecticut. It went into effect in Connecticut in March 1999. Residents could call 24 hours a day to obtain information on community services, government agencies, and emergency assistance. The calls were fielded by caseworkers trained in crisis intervention. The service was started in 1976 using a toll-free 800 number but switched to 211 because it was simpler to use.

7421. City to use desalinated seawater as a source of drinking water was Tampa, FL, where a desalination plant, built by Tampa Bay Water at a cost of $110 million, began operating in 2003. It was designed to pass 44 million gallons of seawater per day through a reverse osmosis filtration system, converting it into 25 million gallons of potable water and 19 million gallons of supersalty brine. When operating at full capacity, the plant was expected to provide about 10 percent of the area's drinking water.

7422. City with complete WiFi coverage in the United States was Grand Haven, MI, a tourist destination on the Lake Michigan shore. The service, provided by Ottawa Wireless, Inc., became operative throughout the city on July 31, 2004. It made the Internet accessible everywhere in the city limits (six square miles) and 20 miles into the lake, replacing all previous Internet connections. Customers could purchase different levels of access, including residential, business, and roaming.

7423. City with a complete smart-card system in the United States was New Haven, CT, which voted in April 2005 to install it in the downtown area. The system was developed by Parcxmart Technologies, Inc., of Hampton Falls, NH, to replace cash and coins. It allowed residents and visitors to purchase a reloadable card, equipped with an electronic chip, that could be used for quick payment in parking meters, municipal parking garages, and retail locations.

7424. State to offer simultaneous access to multiple government databases was Virginia, whose Human Services Interface became operative on April 12, 2005. The software, designed by MITEM of Menlo Park, CA, helped government employees increase their efficiency by giving them a simple way to check and compare records from a variety of state agencies.

7425. City with a mobile mesh WiFi network for both public and municipal use was Granbury, TX. On October 27, 2005, the city council agreed to pay Frontier Broadband, a wireless Internet service provider, $305,000 for the right to use its network. Residents of Granbury received low-cost Internet access, and the city gained automated meter reading and other services.

7426. City with a free public WiFi system in the United States was New Orleans, LA, which deployed a wireless Internet system to boost recovery efforts in the aftermath of Hurricane Katrina. The French Quarter and the business district became the first parts of the city to receive the service on November 29, 2005. Internet connections were made at a speed of 512 kilobits per second by means of devices attached to streetlights. The equipment was provided by Tropos Networks Inc. of Sunnyvale, CA.

7427. Municipal wireless network paid for by advertisements was installed in Sunnyvale, CA, by MetroFi, a private company based in Mountain View, CA. Any computer with wireless capability could log on to the Internet at no charge. Operating expenses were paid for by revenues generated from ads that appeared in an onscreen window. Service began in some areas of Sunnyvale in December 2005.

7428. City to provide free citywide WiFi was St. Cloud, FL, a city of 15 square miles. The municipal service, called Cyber Spot, was developed by MRI and run by Hewlett Packard under contract with the city. Its installation and operation were funded by tax revenues.

Sex and Gender

7429. Prostitute is recorded as "this goodly creature of incontinency" in Thomas Morton's *New English Canaan*, published in England in 1637. Morton had been a colonist in Plymouth, MA, until the leaders of the colony deported him for leading a licentious life.

7430. Cross-dresser of note was Edward Hyde, Viscount Cornbury, the royal governor of the colonies of New York and New Jersey from 1702 to 1708. Cornbury was often seen parading about town in elegant women's dresses, gifts of his patron, Queen Anne of England.

7431. State law allowing married women to make wills was passed by Connecticut in 1809.

7432. Political activist who was an African-American woman was Maria W. Stewart of Boston, MA, the widow of an African-American businessman. In 1831, the abolitionist periodical *The Liberator* published her essay "Religion and the Pure Principles of Morality, the Sure Foundation on Which We Must Build." She began her speaking career on April 28, 1832, with an address to Boston's African-American Female Intelligence Society of America. Her abolitionist and feminist views were grounded in sources in the Christian Bible.

> On September 21, 1832, Maria W. Stewart delivered a speech before the New England Anti-Slavery Society. This was the first time that an American woman addressed an audience composed of both genders and both races.

7433. State law allowing married women to own property enacted in a state that had formerly been under English law was the Married Women's Property Act, passed in Mississippi in February 1839. It was chiefly concerned with slave ownership, and was the outgrowth of an 1837 court case (*Fisher v. Allen*) in which the state court ruled that a slave belonging to a Chickasaw woman, Elizabeth Love, could not be seized and sold at auction in order to satisfy a debt incurred by her white husband. The ruling was based on Chickasaw custom, which allowed spouses to maintain autonomy in ownership, contracts, and debts. Louisiana, a former French colony, followed French law in giving married women property rights under its constitution.

7434. Women's rights convention was held in the Wesleyan Chapel, Seneca Falls, NY, on July 19–20, 1848. The convention was assembled through the initiative of the reformers Lucretia Mott and Elizabeth Cady Stanton. A Declaration of Sentiments was read and a series of resolutions adopted, one of which called for woman suffrage. The first national convention of this kind was the National Woman's Rights Convention held at Brinley Hall in Worcester, MA, on October 23–24, 1850, "to consider the question of woman's rights, duties and relations."

7435. State law of significance to secure property rights for married women was the Married Women's Property Law of 1860, passed by New York State as an amendment to its 1848 law of the same name. The 1848 law allowed married women to keep property they had owned before marriage and to inherit property. The 1860 law went much farther, giving married women joint guardianship of their children. It also recognized their rights to own and control their own property and labor, including money earned through employment; to make contracts; and to engage in lawsuits. The law was the result of advocacy work by Elizabeth Cady Stanton and Susan B. Anthony.

7436. Polygamy ban enacted by Congress was enacted on July 1, 1862, "an act to punish and prevent the practice of polygamy in the territories of the United States and other places, and disapproving and annulling certain acts of the legislative assembly of the territory of Utah." Most of the settlers in Utah belonged to the Mormon Church (Church of Jesus Christ of Latter-day Saints), which encouraged men to marry multiple wives. Little effort was made to enforce this law. The first anti-polygamy law with teeth was the act of March 22, 1882, known as the Edmunds law, which defined simultaneous marriages as bigamy and prescribed loss of citizenship as a penalty. It legitimized children born in polygamy before January 1, 1883.

7437. Ban on sex discrimination in employment enacted by a state was passed by Illinois and approved by Governor John McAuley Palmer on March 22, 1872. The act provided that "no person shall be precluded or debarred from any occupation or employment (except military) on account of sex; Provided that this act shall not be construed to affect the eligibility of any person to an elective office. Nothing in this act shall be construed as requiring any female to work on streets or roads, or serve on juries. All laws inconsistent with this act are hereby repealed."

7438. Constitutional amendment proposal mandating equal legal rights for women and men was submitted to Congress in 1923. The author was Alice Paul. The amendment was reintroduced at every subsequent session of Congress without success until March 22, 1972, when the Senate passed the Equal Rights Amendment by a vote of 84–8. The first state to ratify the amendment was Hawaii, which did so later the same day. Ratification by three-fourths of the 50 states, or 38 states, was required for adoption. Although the deadline for ratification of the ERA was extended in 1978 to June 30, 1982, it fell short by three states.

7439. Gay rights organization in the United States was the Society for Human Rights, founded by Henry Gerber in Chicago, IL. It received a state charter on December 10, 1924.

7440. Scientific survey of sexual behavior among Americans was conducted by Alfred Charles Kinsey, a biologist at the University of Indiana. He described his results in *Sexual Behavior in the Human Male*, published in 1948, and *Sexual Behavior in the Human Female*, published in 1953. The reports presented data on human sexual behavior gathered nationwide through interviews with 18,500 men and women. Funding was provided by the National Research Council and the Rockefeller Foundation. The studies were considered highly flawed by many observers, in part because the respondents were mainly students and convicts. In 1942 Kinsey founded the University of Indiana's Institute for Sex Research, the first of its kind.

7441. National gay rights organization was the Mattachine Society, founded on November 11, 1950, in Los Angeles, CA, with chapters subsequently established in other cities. The co-founders were social activist Harry Hay and fashion designer Rudi Gernreich.

7442. Sex-change operation performed on an American was conducted by Dr. Christian Hamburger at Gentofte Hospital, Copenhagen, Denmark, on September 24, 1951, after a course of hormone treatments. The patient was George Jorgensen of New York City, 25 years old, who later adopted the name Christine Jorgensen. Two additional operations were needed to complete the change. The first hospital in the U.S. to offer sex-change surgery was the Johns Hopkins University, Baltimore, MD, which began performing operations in September 1966. The cost was about $1,500.

7443. Birth-control pill was developed by over a five-year period by Gregory Pincus, a biochemist at the Worcester Foundation for Experimental Biology, Shrewsbury, MA, and John Rock, a gynecologist at Harvard Medical School, Cambridge, MA. It used synthetic progesterone and estrogen to repress ovulation in women. Clinical tests were performed in 1954. The project was initially commissioned and funded by birth-control pioneer Margaret Sanger and heiress Katherine Dexter McCormick. The contraceptive was intended to be "without danger, sure, simple, practical, suitable for all women, and ethically acceptable for the couple." The first brand to be authorized for sale by prescription was Enovid-10, made by the G. D. Searle Company, Chicago, IL, which received approval by the Food and Drug Administration on May 9, 1960.

7444. National lesbian organization was the Daughters of Bilitis, founded in 1955 in San Francisco, CA, by Phyllis Lyon and Del Martin, the latter of whom served as the group's first president. Local chapters were started in other cities, and a national convention was held in San Francisco in 1960. Lyon was the first editor of the group's newsletter, *The Ladder*.

7445. State to repeal its ban on acts of sodomy was Illinois, which enacted the repeal on July 28, 1961, as part of a general revision of its criminal code. The law took effect on January 1, 1962. Although it decriminalized acts between consenting adults in private, it specifically did not allow sexual touching between persons of the same sex in public. Two years later, the law was changed to disallow public sexual touching by anyone.

7446. Ban on sex discrimination in wages enacted by Congress was the Equal Pay Act of 1963, enacted on June 10, 1963, "to prohibit discrimination on account of sex in the payment of wages by employers engaged in commerce or in the production of goods for commerce."

7447. Abortion legalized by a state as a medical procedure was legalized in an act signed on April 25, 1967, by Governor John Arthur Love of Colorado. It permitted therapeutic abortions in cases in which a three-doctor board of an accredited hospital licensed by the Colorado State Department of Health agreed unanimously.

7448. Gay rights protest took place on June 27, 1969, outside the Stonewall Inn in New York City's Greenwich Village neighborhood. Gay patrons and local residents rioted after a raid on the bar by Manhattan police. The first large-scale gay and lesbian protest took place in Washington, DC, on April 25, 1993. The march and rally drew an estimated 300,000 to 1 million demonstrators demanding a federal gay rights bill and more federal money to fight AIDS.

7449. Gay pride march took place on June 28, 1970, in New York City, in commemoration of the anniversary of the Stonewall Rebellion (the riot in lower Manhattan that marked the beginning of the gay rights movement in the United States). The march started in Greenwich Village and ended in Central Park. About 2,000 people participated. Gay pride marches were also held in three other cities, including Los Angeles, CA, where 1,200 took part.

7450. Minister who was openly gay was the Reverend William Johnson of the United Church of Christ, San Francisco, CA, a graduate of the Pacific School of Religion, Berkeley, CA, who announced his homosexuality in 1972. His ordination was sanctioned on April 30, 1972, by the Golden Gate Association by 62 of 96 votes.

7451. Openly gay politician elected to public office was Kathy Kozachenko, who was elected to a seat on the city council of Ann Arbor, MI, in January 1974 as a member of the Human Rights Party. She replaced Nancy Wechsler, a fellow HRP member who had been elected in 1972 and who publicly announced during her term in office that she was a lesbian.

7452. State legislator who was openly gay was Elaine Noble, a Democrat, who was elected on November 5, 1974, to the Massachusetts State Legislature from the 6th Suffolk district, the Fenway–Back Bay district of Boston, MA. She received 1,730 of the 2,931 votes cast. The first openly gay person to be elected to an important local office was Harvey Milk, who was elected to the board of supervisors of San Francisco in 1977. Milk was assassinated by former city supervisor Dan White in 1978.

7453. Sex discrimination law enacted by a state that affected high school athletic competitions was passed by Pennsylvania. On March 19, 1975, the Pennsylvania Commonwealth Court, by a five-to-three decision, upheld a law opening "interscholastic practice and competition to girls in all high school sports, including football and wrestling," and declaring "unconstitutional the ban against girls competing with boys in the bylaws of the Pennsylvania Interscholastic Athletic Association."

7454. Involuntary sterilization regulation enacted by a state was enacted on April 10, 1976, by the state of Virginia. It barred physicians from performing a vasectomy, salpingectomy, or other surgical sterilization procedure upon any person under the age of 21, or over 21 and legally incompetent.

7455. Gay rights march took place on October 14, 1979, in Washington, DC. More than 100,000 marchers participated.

7456. Openly gay member of Congress was Gerry Studds, Democratic representative from Massachusetts. He was elected in November 1972, at which time his sexual orientation was not public knowledge. An investigation by the House Ethics Committee revealed on July 14, 1983, that two representatives had had sexual relationships with congressional pages—Studds with a male, and Daniel Crane of Illinois with a female. Studds continued to serve in Congress until 1996.

7457. Parental leave law enacted by a state that applied to both mothers and fathers was passed by the Minnesota legislature in 1987. It allowed parents up to six weeks of unpaid leave from work.

7458. Condom commercials on television to be aired in a large urban market were broadcast on January 16, 1987, by KRON in San Francisco, CA. Stations in Detroit and Indianapolis showed the ads soon after. On February 16, 1987, the commercials were endorsed by Surgeon General C. Everett Koop. They were intended to encourage the use of condoms in preventing AIDS rather than in preventing conception.

7459. Transgendered person elected to public office in the United States is considered to have been Althea Garrison of Dorchester, MA, a Republican, who was elected to the Massachusetts House of Representatives on November 5, 1992, and served a single term. She did not identify herself as transgendered. Shortly after the election, a newspaper article reported that she had been born a male.

7460. Minister who was a transsexual in a mainstream Christian church was Erin Swenson, a Presbyterian minister who had received ordination as Eric Swenson before undergoing a sex-change procedure. On October 22, 1996, the Presbytery of Greater Atlanta, a Georgia branch of the Presbyterian Church (USA), decided by a vote of 186–161 to continue to recognize the ordination.

7461. Television network sitcom to feature a lead character who was gay was *Ellen*, an ABC network comedy starring Ellen DeGeneres. The series had been on the air for several seasons before the producers decided to air a show in which the character, Ellen Morgan, concluded that she was a lesbian. The show was aired on April 30, 1997. DeGeneres had recently announced that she was a lesbian in real life. The first regularly appearing gay character in a television situation comedy was Jodie Dallas, played by comedian Billy Crystal beginning in 1977 on the series *Soap*.

7462. State appeals court decision ordering the extension of insurance benefits to gay partners of government employees was made on December 9, 1998, when a three-judge panel of Oregon's State Court of Appeals upheld the 1996 ruling of a trial judge. The case involved three lesbian nurses who were employed by Oregon Health Sciences University, a public corporation that was formerly a state institution. Their 1991 applications for medical and dental insurance for their domestic partners were turned down because the university provided benefits to married spouses only. The court ruled that this denial violated the equal protection clause of the state constitution.

7463. State to establish civil unions for homosexual couples was Vermont. In December 1999 the state supreme court ruled that the state legislature must adopt some form of legal domestic partnership for same-sex couples that would afford them the rights, benefits, and obligations of marriage. The resulting bill was signed into law by Governor Howard Dean on April 26, 2000, to become effective on July 1. It provided for a statutory definition of marriage as a union between a man and a woman and at the same time set up a parallel legal institution for gay and lesbian couples, giving them the right to receive a license from a town clerk and to have that license certified by a justice of the peace or a member of the clergy. The union could be dissolved through Family Court in the same manner as marriages are dissolved. The new arrangement affected Vermont's adoption and inheritance laws.

7464. State to legalize gay marriage was Massachusetts. On November 18, 2003, by a vote of 4–3, the Supreme Judicial Court ruled in favor of seven gay couples who had sued for the right to marry. The first such marriage took place on May 17, 2004, in Cambridge, MA, between Marcia Kadish and Tanya McCloskey of Malden, MA.

Social Sciences

7465. History book of the colonial era was *A True Relation of such occurrences and accidents of noate as hath hapned in Virginia since the first planting of that Collony, which is now resident in the south part thereof, tille the last return from thence*, by Th. Watson for J. Tappe, published in London in 1608. Watson was a pseudonym for Captain John Smith.

7466. History of New England was Edward Johnson's *A History of New-England From the English Planting in the yeere 1628 untill, the yeere 1652, Declaring the Form of Their Government, Civil, Military and Ecclesiastique*, a 236-page book also known as *The Wonder-Working Providence of Sions Saviour in New England*, was published in London in 1654. The first history of New England to be published in New England was *New England's Memoriall, or a Brief Relation of the Most Memorable and Remarkable Passages of the Providence of God, Manifested to the Planters of New England in America: With Special Reference to the First Colony Therefore, Called New Plimouth*, published by Nathaniel Morton, secretary to the court for the Jurisdiction of New Plymouth. It was printed in 1669 in Cambridge, MA, by S. Green and M. Johnson, for John Usher of Boston, MA.

7467. Genealogy of an American family to be published separately was a 24-page pamphlet published in Hartford, CT, in 1771 by Ebenezer Watson. It was Luke Stebbins's *The Genealogy of the Family of Mr. Samuel Stebbins and Mrs. Hannah Stebbins, His Wife from the Year 1707 to 1771 with their names, time of their births, marriages, and deaths of those that are deceased.* In *The Memoirs of Captain Roger Clap*, 38 pages, published by Bartholomew Green in Boston, MA, in 1731, there was a 10-page supplement by James Blake, Jr., containing "a short account of the author and his family. Written by one that was acquainted therewith." Clap's family consisted of his wife and their six children.

7468. Historical hoaxes were perpetrated by the Reverend Sam Peters, Episcopalian rector of Hebron, CT, in the late 1700s. His best-known book, *General history of Connecticut, from its first settlement under George Fenwick to its latest period of amity with Great Britain prior to the Revolution . . . by a gentleman of the province*, published in 1781, was filled with deliberate falsehoods that represented the Puritan restrictions on Sabbath activities as even more stringent than they really were. He also described fanciful invasions of giant caterpillars and frogs. Peters's books were widely believed, and became such bestsellers that he was able to live off their royalties for the last two decades of his life.

7469. State historical society was the Massachusetts Historical Society, organized on August 26, 1790, in Boston, MA, by five persons under the leadership of the Reverend Jeremy Belknap. The main purpose of the society was to gather manuscript material to be preserved and published for general use and to establish a library that would carry on the founders' plan.

7470. American history book of importance whose author was a woman was a three-volume narrative history of the Revolutionary War entitled *History of the Rise, Progress, and Termination of the American Revolution, Interspersed with Biographical, Political and Moral Observation*, by Mercy Otis Warren. It was published in Boston, MA, in 1805.

7471. Comic history of the United States was *A Diverting History of John Bull and Brother Jonathan*, a 135-page book by Hector Bull-Us (pseudonym of James Kirke Paulding), published in 1812 in New York City by Inskeep and Bradford.

7472. National historical society was the American Antiquarian Society, founded in Worcester, MA, by Isaiah Thomas, the first printer of Worcester. Incorporated on October 24, 1812, it had the first great American historical collection. The first meeting was held on November 19, 1812, at the Exchange Coffee House, Boston, MA.

7473. Political history book was *A Political and Civil History of the U.S.A. from the year 1763 to the close of the administration of President Washington in March, 1797 including a summary view of the political and civil state of the North American colonies, prior to that period*, by Timothy Pitkin. It was published in two volumes by Hezekiah Howe and Durrie and Peck in 1828 at New Haven, CT.

7474. Genealogical collective work was Farmer's *Genealogical Register of the First Settlers of New England*, published in 1829 by John Farmer in Lancaster, MA.

7475. Sociology treatise was *A Treatise on Sociology; Theoretical and Practical*, by Henry Hughes of Mississippi. It was 292 pages long and was published in Philadelphia, PA, in 1854.

7476. History of African-Americans of a scholarly nature was *A History of the Negro Race in America from 1619 to 1880*, by George Washington Williams. The two-volume work was published in 1883. Williams, a pastor, journalist, and lawyer, was also the first African-American representative to serve in the Ohio legislature.

7477. Supreme Court case in which social-science research was accepted as evidence was *Brown v. Board of Education*, decided on May 17, 1954. The Court accepted testimony given before a lower court by the psychologists Kenneth Bancroft Clark and Mamie Phipps Clark of New York City. Their research involved African-American children who preferred white dolls to black dolls.

SPORTS AND RECREATION

Amateur

7478. Athlete to win the James E. Sullivan Memorial Trophy for outstanding amateur athlete of the year was golfer Robert Tyre "Bobby" Jones of Atlanta, GA. The award was made by the Amateur Athlete Union of the United States on December 16, 1930. The selecting committee of 600 considered 150 nominations. Jones received 1,625 votes, more than twice that of the runner-up. The award was presented on February 26, 1931, at the Medinah Athletic Club in Chicago, IL.

7479. African-American athlete to win the James E. Sullivan Memorial Trophy was Malvin Greston "Mal" Whitfield of the Los Angeles Athletic Club, a half-miler, who was the first choice on 252 of 657 ballots cast by a nationwide tribunal of sports authorities and tabulated on December 30, 1954. Whitfield set the Olympic record for 800 meters in London in 1948 and held the world 880-yard record and the 600-yard indoor record. The trophy, presented annually since 1930 by the Amateur Athletic Union, is the top award for amateur athletes in the United States.

7480. African-American athlete who was a woman to win the James E. Sullivan Memorial Trophy was Wilma Rudolph of Clarksville, TN. The presentation was made on February 23, 1962, at the New York Athletic Club, New York City. Rudolph won three gold medals in track at the 1960 Olympic Games in Rome.

Baseball

7481. Baseball book was Robin Carver's *The Book of Sports*, published in 1834 in Boston, MA, by Lilly, Wait, Colman, and Holden. It was based on an English edition of the *Boy's Own Book*.

7482. Baseball team was the Knickerbocker Club of New York, organized on September 23, 1845, by Alexander Joy Cartwright, the man who laid out the diamond-shaped baseball field and gave the game its modern form. Duncan F. Curry was the club's first president. The club played its first game in June 1846, losing 23–1. A previous team that played an earlier form of baseball was the Olympic Club of Philadelphia, PA, which played "cat ball," also known as town ball, from July 4, 1833, to the year 1860, when they changed to standard baseball. Town ball, a game similar to the British game of rounders, was the immediate forerunner of regular baseball in the United States.

7483. Baseball game to be played as part of an organized sport took place on June 19, 1846, at Elysian Fields, Hoboken, NJ, when the Knickerbocker Baseball Club of New York, the first organized baseball team, was defeated by an informal team called the New York Nine. The score was 23–1 in four innings. The umpire was Alexander Jay Cartwright, a member of the Knickerbocker team. Cartwright was the author of the first set of formal rules for baseball. He also laid out the sport's diamond-shaped field and established its nine playing positions. Early versions of baseball, based on the English games of rounders and cricket, were played in the English colonies of America as far back as the early 1700s.

> The widespread legend that attributes the founding of baseball to Abner Doubleday, a West Point cadet (later a general), at Cooperstown, NY, is false.

7484. Baseball uniforms were worn by the members of the Knickerbocker Club of New York, which adopted a blue and white uniform in 1848.

7485. Baseball rules standardizing the game were adopted in May 1858 in New York City by the National Baseball Association. The rules provided that the bat was not to exceed 2.5 inches in diameter and the ball 10.5 inches in circumference, the latter to weigh 6.5 ounces. The game was to last nine innings or until one team won 21 runs. Previously each team had played under its own set of rules. Three delegates from each of the following clubs attended the meeting: Atlantic, Baltic, Bedford, Continental, Eagle, Empire, Excelsior, Eckford, Gotham, Harmony, Knickerbocker, Nassau, Olympic, Putnam, and Union.

7486. Baseball game in which spectators were charged admission was the game of July 20, 1858, between two amateur teams at the Fashion Race Course in what is now the borough of Queens, in New York City, the opening game of the first series ever played. A 50-cent admission fee was charged each of the 1,500 people who attended to cover the cost of renting the racetrack.

7487. Baseball series was played July 20, August 17, and September 10, 1858, at the Fashion Race Course in what is now the borough of Queens, in New York City, between two amateur teams, the Brooklyn Brooklynites and the New York All Stars. New York won the first game 22–18 and took the series with two out of three games.

7488. Intercollegiate baseball game was played on July 1, 1859, between Amherst College and Williams College, in Pittsfield, MA. Amherst won by a score of 73–32. The game, played on a 60-foot square with the pitcher 35 feet from the batter, began at 11 A.M. and continued for four hours without interruption. Each team had 13 players and the game lasted 26 innings. The captain of Amherst was James Fitzgerald Claffin, the Williams captain Humphrey Stevenson Anderson.

7489. Baseball team to tour was the Brooklyn Excelsiors, under the management of Captain Joseph B. Leggett, who left on June 30, 1860, for Albany, NY. They played at Troy, Buffalo, and cities in the west and south.

7490. Baseball game of record in which a team scored no runs in nine innings was played on November 8, 1860, between the Brooklyn Excelsiors and the St. George Cricket Club. The score was 25–0 in favor of Brooklyn.

7491. Enclosed baseball park was the Union Grounds, Brooklyn, NY (now part of New York City), which opened on May 15, 1862, on a site at Lee Avenue and Rutledge Street that had been formerly used as a skating rink.

7492. Baseball game in which one team scored more than 100 runs was played on Sunday, October 1, 1865. In a nine-inning game in Philadelphia, PA, the Philadelphia Athletics defeated the Jersey City Nationals 114–2. About 500 women were among the 5,000 spectators.

7493. Baseball pitcher to throw a curve ball is reported to have been William Arthur Cummings, who introduced this innovation in 1866. He played with the Excelsior Junior Nine and the Stars of Brooklyn. Others for whom the claim is made are Fred Goldsmith of the Chicago White Stockings and George McConnell.

7494. Baseball teams for women were organized in the 1860s. In 1866, college women formed two baseball clubs, the Laurel Base Ball Club and the Abenakis, at Vassar Female College, Poughkeepsie, NY. A non-collegiate team was organized in Peterborough, NH, in 1868. The squad of 50 women wore short blue and white tunics reaching to the knees, white stockings, and straw hats. The captain of the senior team was Nannie Miller, who was also the catcher. Clara Mills was the pitcher; Mary Manning first base; Fran Richardson, second base; Bertha Powell, third base; Jennie Hand, shortstop; Hattie Ferris, left field; Maggie Marshall, right field; and Mary Frothingham, center field.

7495. Baseball team whose players received a regular salary was the Cincinnati Red Stockings, led by Harry and George Wright, who traveled in 1869 to various cities, engaging local teams. Through 1869 and up to June 1870, they played without losing a game. A salary of $1,400 was paid to the shortstop, $1,200 to the center fielder, $1,100 to the pitcher, $1,000 to the third baseman, and $800 each to the first and second basemen, the catcher, the left and right fielders, and the substitute.

7496. Baseball player to play as a professional was Alfred James Reach, outfielder of the Philadelphia Athletics of the National Association from 1871 to 1875. He played in 82 games. In 1874 he received $1,000 for playing 14 games.

7497. Baseball league of importance was the National Association of Professional Base-Ball Players, organized on March 17, 1871, at Collier's Cafe, New York City. James N. Kerns of Troy, NY, was elected president.

The member clubs were the Athletics of Philadelphia, the Mutuals of New York, the Kekiongas of Fort Wayne, the Olympics of Washington, the Haymakers of Troy, the Bostons of Boston, the White Stockings of Chicago, and teams from Cleveland and Rockford. Each club paid an entry fee of $10. The first game was played on May 4, 1871, at Fort Wayne, IN, and the score was Fort Wayne 2, Cleveland 0. The series consisted of three out of five games with the other teams. The champion team was the Athletics, under manager Elias Hicks Hayhurst, who won 22 games and lost seven (.759). Chicago was second, winning 20 games and losing nine (.690). Boston was third, winning 22 games and losing 10 (.688). The National League was started in 1876 and the American League in 1900.

7498. Baseball game between an all-white team and an all-African-American team was played in Chicago, IL, on July 6, 1871. The African-American Uniques beat the Alerts by a score of 17–16.

7499. Baseball player on a white team who was African-American was John Jackson, who played in 1872 on a white baseball team in New Castle, PA, under the name of John W. "Bud" Fowler. From 1872 to 1899 he usually played second base.

7500. Baseball teams to travel abroad were the Boston Red Stockings and the Philadelphia Athletic Blue Stockings, National Association teams that played a series of 15 exhibition games from July 30 to August 27, 1874, in England and Ireland.

7501. Baseball glove was worn by Charles Waite, first baseman of Boston, MA, in 1875. It was flesh-color so as not to be conspicuous and had a large round opening at the back for ventilation.

7502. Baseball game in which a team made no hits in nine innings was pitched by Joseph Emley Borden of the National Association's Philadelphia team on July 28, 1875, in Philadelphia, PA, against Chicago. The score was Philadelphia 4, Chicago 0.

7503. First baseball league game that was a shutout was the National League's Chicago vs. Louisville game, played on April 25, 1876, at Louisville, KY, before 2,000 spectators. Albert Goodwill Spalding, the Chicago White Stockings pitcher, pitched a seven-hitter and also made three of Chicago's eight hits off James Alexander Devlin. The score was Chicago 4, Louisville 0.

7504. Baseball players to hit home runs were Ross Barnes of the Chicago White Stockings and Charles Wesley "Baby" Jones of the Cincinnati Reds, on May 2, 1876, at Cincinnati, OH. Chicago won 15–9.

7505. Baseball catchers' chest protector was invented by William Gray of Hartford, CT, and used in 1878. He sold his rights in the 1880s to Albert Goodwill Spalding for $5,000.

7506. Baseball catcher's mask was invented by Frederick Winthrop Thayer of Waverly, MA, captain of the Harvard University Baseball Club, who obtained a patent on February 12, 1878, on a "face guard or safety mask." It was made by a tinsmith in Cambridge, MA, tried out in the gymnasium in the winter of 1876–77, and used by James Alexander Tyng in a game with the Live Oaks at Lynn, MA, April 12, 1877. Louis Trauschke, catcher of the Foster Baseball Club, Lawrence, MA, who had been hurt by a pitched ball, adopted the mask. Eventually it was manufactured by Peck and Snyder, New York City.

7507. Unassisted triple play in organized baseball took place on May 8, 1878, at Providence, RI, in a game between Providence and Boston. The play was made by Paul Hines, center fielder for the Providence team. Providence won 3–1.

7508. Major league baseball player who was African-American was Moses Fleetwood "Fleet" Walker, catcher on the Northwestern League Toledo team, who played with that team from 1883 to 1889. He played in 41 games in 1884 and hit .251. The team entered the American Association in 1884. He was also the first African-American college baseball player, playing for Oberlin College in 1881 and later for the University of Michigan, where he was a law student.

7509. Baseball game at night was played on June 2, 1883, at League Park, Fort Wayne, IN, between a club of boys known as the M. E. College and the Quincy professional team from Adams County, IL. The score was Quincy 19, College 11. The field was illuminated by 17 lights of 4,000 candlepower each. Seven innings were played. The game was witnessed by 2,000 people.

7510. Baseball championship was played at the Polo Grounds, New York City, in October 1884. The Providence Grays defeated the New York Metropolitans three games to none. Providence won the first game 6–0 in two hours on October 23, the second game 3–1 in 1 hour 35 minutes on October 24, the third game 11–2 in 1 hour 20 minutes on October 25.

7511. Baseball batting and fielding cage was built at Yale University, New Haven, CT, in the fall of 1885 by Captain Philip Battell Stewart. The building was about 70 feet long and 20 feet wide and had skylights protected by wire. It was the forerunner of the expensive cages and field houses now common in American colleges and universities.

7512. Baseball team of African-American players to play professionally was the Cuban Giants, organized in New York City by Frank P. Thompson in 1885. S. K. Govern was manager. The players received expenses and weekly salaries according to positions: pitchers and catchers, $18; infielders, $15; and outfielders, $12. The players also served as waiters during the summer season at the Argyle Hotel, Babylon, NY.

7513. Baseball player who was Native American was Jim Toy of the American Association, who played first base for the Cleveland team in 1887 and catcher for the Brooklyn and Baltimore teams in 1890.

Library of Congress, Prints & Photographs Division
LC-USZC4-2776

"A Base Ball Match," c. 1887.

7514. Baseball teams to go on a world tour were the Chicago and All America teams. They started their world tour on October 20, 1888, and returned on April 20, 1889. They played 53 games of four innings and over in Australia, Ceylon, Egypt, Italy, France, England, and the United States. Twenty-eight games were won by the All America team, 22 by the Chicago team, and three were tied. Their first game abroad was played on December 10, 1888, in Auckland, New Zealand.

7515. Baseball pinch hitter was John Joseph Doyle, a substitute catcher, ordered to bat in the ninth inning by Oliver Wendell Tebeau of the Cleveland Spiders in a game played on June 7, 1892, in Brooklyn, NY (now part of New York City), against the Brooklyn Ward's Wonders. Doyle made a single, advancing John Joseph O'Connor from first to third base. The 1891 rules allowed substitutions anywhere at any time during a game.

7516. Baseball player to catch a ball dropped from the Washington Monument in Washington, DC, from the 500-foot level, was William F. Schriver of the Chicago National League club, who accomplished this feat on August 29, 1892, and again on August 25, 1895. Charles Evard Street, catcher of the Washington club of the American League, caught a baseball dropped from the top of the monument on August 21, 1908.

7517. Baseball "Home Run King" to hit 25 home runs in one season was Bucky Freeman, outfielder of the Washington Club of the National League, who hit 25 home runs and 27 triples in 1899.

7518. World Series baseball game was played on October 1, 1903, at Boston, MA, when the Pittsburgh Pirates defeated the Boston Red Sox 7–3 before a crowd of 16,200 people. James Dennison Sebring of the Pirates hit a home run, the first in the World Series. The Pirates defeated the Boston Red Sox 7–3. Boston came back from a three-game loss and won the series on October 13 with five victories in seven games.

7519. World Series baseball game that was a shutout was played on October 13, 1905, at New York City between the New York Nationals and the Philadelphia Athletics of the American League. It was the fourth game in the 1905 series. Joseph Jerome McGinnity of New York shut out the Philadelphia team 1–0. New York won the series 4–1.

A shutout game had been played at an earlier World Series, on October 2, 1903, at Boston, when Samuel W. Leever of the Pittsburgh Nationals shut out the Boston Americans 3–0. This series, however, was not sanctioned by the leagues.

7520. Baseball league for children was the Waynesburg, PA, Juvenile Baseball League, formed in 1908 by three teams—the Colts, the North Side Cubs, and the Times Pirates (the last composed of carrier boys for the *Waynesburg Times*). An admission fee of 10 cents was charged for each game, the seasonal proceeds of $60 being donated to a library fund.

7521. Baseball with a cork center was invented by Benjamin F. Shibe of Bala, PA, who obtained a patent for it on June 15, 1909. It was manufactured by A.G. Spalding and Brothers, Chicago, IL, and was used in occasional league games in 1909 and in regular play in 1910. The ball was first used in a World Series game on October 20, 1910, in Chicago, IL.

7522. Fireproof baseball stadium built of concrete and steel was Forbes Field, Pittsburgh, PA. The stadium was named after Brigadier General John Forbes, the British officer who commanded the expeditionary force that captured Fort Duquesne, at what is now Pittsburgh. The first game to be played in the stadium took place on June 30, 1909, when the Pittsburgh Pirates defeated the Chicago Cubs 3–2 before a paying crowd of 30,338 spectators.

7523. Unassisted triple play in a major league baseball game was made by Cornelius Ball, shortstop of the American League's Cleveland team, on July 19, 1909, at Cleveland, OH, in the second inning of the first game of a doubleheader against the American League's Boston team. Ball caught Ambrose Moses McConnell's liner; touched second, retiring Charles F. Wagner, who was on his way to third; and tagged Garland Stahl as he came up to second. When Ball came to bat in the same inning, he hit a home run. Cleveland defeated Boston 6–1 in the first game. Boston defeated Cleveland 8–2 in the second game.

7524. Baseball players to win the Most Valuable Player award in the major leagues were Frank "Wildfire" Schulte of the Chicago Cubs and Ty Cobb of the Detroit Tigers, who won in 1911.

7525. Baseball strike took place on May 18, 1912, at Shibe Park, Philadelphia, PA, when 19 players of the Detroit Tigers refused to play the Athletics in sympathy for Ty Cobb, their outfielder, who had been suspended by Ban Johnson, president of the American League, because he mauled a spectator who had cursed him. The strikers were fined $50 a day, $100 for 48 hours. Hugh A. Jennings, the Detroit manager, recruited a scrub team that was defeated 24–2. There was not a regular Detroit player on the team.

7526. Major league baseball player killed in a game was Raymond Johnson Chapman, shortstop of the Cleveland Indians, who was accidentally hit on the left side of his head by a pitch thrown by Carl Mays of the New York Yankees in a game at the Polo Grounds, New York City, on August 16, 1920.

7527. Unassisted triple play in a World Series baseball game was made on October 10, 1920, at Cleveland, OH, in the fifth inning of the fifth game between the Cleveland Indians and the Brooklyn Dodgers. The Indians' second baseman, William Adolph Wambsganss, caught a line drive from Otto Miller's bat, tagged Peter John Kilduff at second base, then ran to first and tagged Clarence Elmer Mitchell. Cleveland defeated Brooklyn 8–1.

7528. Baseball commissioner was Judge Kenesaw Mountain Landis, elected on November 12, 1920, for a seven-year term from 1921 to 1928. He received a salary of $42,500 a year plus $10,000 for expenses to rule the 16 American and National League baseball clubs. He was re-elected three times and died in office on November 24, 1944.

7529. Radio broadcast of a baseball game with a play-by-play description took place at Pittsburgh, PA, on August 5, 1921, when the Pittsburgh Corsairs defeated Philadelphia by a score of 8–5 for their third straight victory. The baseball field was connected by wire to the broadcasting station of KDKA, Pittsburgh.

7530. Baseball manager to win pennants in both leagues was Joseph Vincent McCarthy, nonplaying manager of the Chicago National League team, which earned the pennant on October 6, 1929, by winning 98 games and losing 54. As manager of the New York American League team he won the pennant on September 23, 1932, winning 106 games and losing 46 games. New York went on to win the world championship on October 2, defeating Chicago in four straight games.

7531. Baseball pitcher who was a woman was Virne Beatrice "Jackie" Mitchell, who pitched a single game for the Chattanooga Baseball Club of the minor-league Southern Association. In an April 1, 1931, exhibition game against the New York Yankees, the 19-year-old Mitchell struck out Babe Ruth, Lou Gehrig, and Tony Lazzeri. After Mitchell was taken out of the game, Chattanooga lost 14 to 4.

7532. All-star major league baseball game was played on July 6, 1933, at Comiskey Park, Chicago, IL. The American League defeated the National League 4–2. The American runs were batted in by Earl Douglas Averill, Vernon Louis Gomez, and George Herman "Babe" Ruth, who hit two runs, one of which was a homer in the third inning. The National runs were made by Johnny Leonard, Roosevelt Martin, and Francis Frisch. The attendance was 49,200; receipts were $56,379.

7533. Baseball game at night by major league teams was played at Crosley Field, Cincinnati, OH, on May 24, 1935, when the Cincinnati Reds defeated the Philadelphia Phillies 2 to 1 before a paid attendance of 20,422. President Franklin Delano Roosevelt, in Washington, DC, pressed a button that turned on 363 lights of 1,000 kilowatts each on eight giant towers for this National League game.

7534. Major league baseball game to be shown on television was a double-header played at Ebbets Field, Brooklyn, New York City, on August 26, 1939, between the Cincinnati Reds and the Brooklyn Dodgers. Both games were televised by station W2XBS, New York City, using two cameras that alternated according to the play. During the intermission, there were appearances by Leo Durocher, manager of the Dodgers, William McKechnie, manager of the Reds, and several players. Walter L. "Red" Barber was the announcer. The first major-league baseball game to be shown in color was also a double-header played at Ebbets Field, where the Brooklyn Dodgers played the Boston Braves on August 11, 1951. The games were televised by WCBS-TV of the Columbia Broadcasting System, with Red Barber and Connie Desmond as the announcers.

7535. Major league no-hitter baseball game on opening day was played on April 16, 1940, in Chicago. Robert William Andrew Feller of the American League Cleveland Indians retired 15 men in a row from the fourth inning to the eighth inning against the Chicago White Sox.

7536. Baseball play-off series took place the first week of October 1946 in St. Louis, MO, and Brooklyn, New York City, after the Brooklyn Dodgers and the St. Louis Cardinals had tied on September 29, both teams having won 96 and lost 58 games for a .623 average in the National League. The Cardinals won the first two of the two-out-of-three series by the scores of 4–2 and 8–4, thus earning the National League pennant and the right to play the Boston Red Sox of the American League in the World Series. They beat the Red Sox in four out of seven games.

7537. Major league baseball player in the postwar era who was African-American was Jackie Robinson of the Brooklyn Dodgers, who played first base in an exhibition game on April 11, 1947, against the New York Yankees. In the course of the season he hit 12 home runs, stole 29 bases, and was voted Rookie of the Year. He won the Most Valuable Player award in 1949. His success opened the way for the racial integration of other baseball teams.

7538. World Series baseball game to be shown on television was the opening game of the 1947 series, played on September 30, 1947, between the New York Yankees and the Brooklyn Dodgers at Yankee Stadium, New York City. The game was transmitted to three stations (WABD, WCBS, and WNBT) in New York City and to all the television outlets along the Eastern seaboard. The entire series was telecast under the joint sponsorship of the Ford Motor Company and the Gillette Safety Razor Company at a cost of $65,000. The Yankees won the first game 5–3 and the series four games to three. The play-by-play descriptions were given by Bob Edge, Bob Stanton, and Bill Slater.

7539. Baseball player who was African-American to win the Most Valuable Player award in the major leagues was Jackie Robinson, second baseman of the National League's Brooklyn Dodgers, New York City, who won the Kenesaw Mountain Landis Memorial plaque on November 18, 1949, from the Baseball Writers Assocation.

The first African-American player in the American League to win the award was Elston Howard, catcher for the New York Yankees, on November 7, 1963.

7540. Umpire in organized baseball who was African-American was Emmett Littleton Ashford of the Class C Southwestern International League, who was authorized as a substitute umpire on February 20, 1952, by league president Les Powers. Ashford went on to become the first African-American umpire in the major leagues. He was purchased on September 15, 1965, from the Pacific Coast League by the American League. His salary was $7,500 a year plus $27 daily for expenses. He umpired at third base at the opening game of the season at Washington, DC, on April 12, 1966, between the Cleveland Indians and the Washington Senators.

7541. Major league baseball game in which the majority of the players on one team were African-American was played on July 17, 1954, between the Brooklyn Dodgers and the Milwaukee Braves at Milwaukee, WI. The Braves won 6 to 1. The black players on the Brooklyn team were Donald N. Newcombe, pitcher; Roy Campanella, catcher; James William Gilliam, second base; Jackie Robinson, third base; and Edmundo Isasi Amoros, left field.

7542. Baseball pitcher to pitch a perfect no-hit, no-run, no-walk World Series game was Donald James Larsen of the New York Yankees, who pitched a perfect game on October 8, 1956, at Yankee Stadium, New York City, in the fifth game of the World Series against the Brooklyn Dodgers. The score was New York 2, Brooklyn 0.

7543. Baseball player to win Most Valuable Player award in both major leagues was Frank Robinson. He was elected on November 22, 1961, by the Baseball Writers Association for his efforts as an outfielder with the National League's Cincinnati Reds. and again on November 8, 1966, unanimously, for services with the American League's Baltimore Orioles.

7544. Baseball player to steal more than 100 bases in a season was Maury Wills, shortstop for the Los Angeles Dodgers, who set the record during the 1962 season. He stole his first base on April 13 in Game 4 against Milwaukee and his 100th on September 26 in the third inning against the Houston Colts at Los Angeles, when he and left-fielder Tommy Davis pulled a double steal.

7545. Baseball coach in the major leagues who was African-American was John O'Neil, hired on May 29, 1962, by the Chicago Cubs as one of the team's six coaches. Previously he had served the team in various other capacities. The first African-American manager of a major league team was Frank Robinson, who was hired by the Cleveland Indians as both player and manager on October 3, 1974.

7546. Baseball player to play all nine positions in one game was Bert Campaneris of the Kansas City Athletics, who played all nine positions in a 13-inning night game at Kansas City, MO, on September 8, 1965. The Athletics were defeated by the California Angels 5–3.

7547. Designated hitter in a major league baseball game to bat for the pitcher was first baseman Ron Blomberg of the New York Yankees. On April 6, 1973, at Fenway Park, Boston, MA, he came to bat in the first inning and was walked by Luis Tiant of the Boston Red Sox. The first designated hitter to come to bat in a World Series game was Dan Driessen of the Cincinnati Reds. He stepped up to the plate in the opening game of the 1976 World Series between the Reds and the New York Yankees, but the runner at first base was picked off before a pitch was thrown, ending the inning for the Reds. The first player to serve as designated hitter for all games of a season was Rusty Staub of the Detroit Tigers, who played in all of the Tigers' 162 season games in 1978. The designated hitter rule was adopted on January 11, 1973, by American League club owners, whose teams at that time lagged behind those of the National League in batting prowess. The Triple-A International League had experimented successfully with the concept in 1969.

7548. Free agents in major league baseball were Andy Messersmith of the Los Angeles Dodgers and Dave McNally of the Montreal Expos. On December 23, 1974, a federal arbitrator ruled that the two players, and by extension other major league baseball players not bound to a current contract, were free to sell their services to the team that offered them the most money.

7549. World Series disrupted by an earthquake was the third game of the World Series between the San Francisco Giants and the Oakland Athletics on October 17, 1989, at Candlestick Park in San Francisco, CA. Minutes before the start of the game, a massive earthquake hit the San Francisco Bay area, causing scores of deaths and widespread damage. After a 10-day postponement, play resumed. The Athletics won games three and four for the first Series sweep in 13 years.

7550. Major league baseball player to hit grand slams from both sides of the plate in one game was Bill Mueller of the Boston Red Sox. In a game played at Arlington, TX, against the Texas Rangers on July 29, 2003, he hit three home runs. In the third inning, he hit a left-handed solo homer. He then hit a right-handed grand slam in the seventh inning and a left-handed grand slam in the eighth. The Red Sox won the game by a score of 14 to 7.

Basketball

7551. Basketball game was invented in 1892 by Dr. James Naismith, an instructor at the International Young Men's Christian Association Training School in Springfield, MA. The game was originally played with peach baskets mounted on poles. It was necessary for the players to use a ladder to remove the ball from the basket. The first game was played at the YMCA gymnasium on January 20, 1892. The first public game was played on March 11. The rules were standardized in 1894.

7552. Basketball played at a college was introduced in 1892 by Senda Berenson, director of physical education at Smith College, Northampton, MA. Several intercollegiate games were played against other colleges. The first college to have an official team was Mount Union College, Alliance, OH, in December 1892.

7553. Basketball rules were published in the *Triangle Magazine*, Springfield, MA, on January 15, 1892. The rules were later compiled in more complete form in a book, *Rules for Basketball*, by James Naismith, basketball's inventor. The book was published in 1892 by the Springfield Printing and Binding Company, Springfield, MA.

7554. Intercollegiate basketball game was played in Minnesota on February 9, 1895, when the Minnesota State School of Agriculture defeated Hamline College 9–3. The first intercollegiate basketball game with five-man teams was played on January 16, 1896, in Iowa City, IA. The University of Chicago team defeated the University of Iowa team 15–12. There were no substitutions.

7555. Basketball game at a large commercial sports arena was a benefit performance for the New York Relief Fund, played on January 19, 1931, at Madison Square Garden, New York City. Six college teams played. Columbia University defeated Fordham University 26–18, Manhattan College defeated New York University 16–14, and St. John's University defeated City College 17–8. About 15,000 persons attended, and $22,854 was raised.

7556. Basketball game to be shown on television was played on February 28, 1940, at Madison Square Garden and televised by station W2XBS, New York City. Fordham University played the University of Pittsburgh, which won the game by a score of 50–37. That game was followed by another in which New York University beat Georgetown University by a score of 50–27. Both games were televised.

7557. Basketball professional player who was African-American was Charles Henry Cooper, all-star player, who was drafted on April 24, 1950, by the Boston Celtics and who played his first game for that team on November 1, 1950, in Fort Wayne, IN.

7558. All-Star Game of the National Basketball Association was played on March 2, 1951, at the Boston Garden, Boston, MA, before a crowd of 10,094 patrons. The East team, coached by Joe Lapchick, defeated the West team, coached by John Kundla, by the score of 111–94.

7559. Basketball team to score more than 10,000 points in one season was the Philadelphia Warriors of the eastern division of the National Basketball Association, who scored 10,035 points in the 1961–62 season. In the 1966–67 season the team scored 10,143 points.

7560. Coach of a professional basketball team who was African-American was Bill Russell, who became coach of the Boston Celtics, Boston, MA, in 1966 and led the team to the National Basketball Association championship the following year.

7561. Basketball leagues for women to attract significant attendance at games were the American Basketball League (ABL), Palo Alto, CA, which originated in 1993, and the Women's National Basketball Association (WNBA), New York, NY, established on April 24, 1996.

7562. Player in the Women's National Basketball League was Sheryl Swoopes of Brownfield, TX, who was signed by the WNBA on October 23, 1996. The six-foot-tall Swoopes was assigned to the Houston Comets in the first player allocations on January 22, 1997. She won gold medals in women's basketball in the Olympic Games of 1996, 2000, and 2004.

7563. Women's National Basketball League game was played on June 21, 1997, at the Great Western Forum in Los Angeles, CA, between the New York Liberty and the Los Angeles Sparks. New York won 67–65.

7564. Women's National Basketball League champions were the Houston Comets. On August 30, 1997, they defeated the New York Liberty 65–51 at The Summit in Houston, TX.

Boating and Sailing

7565. Ice yacht was built by Oliver Booth at Poughkeepsie, NY, in 1790 and consisted of a square box mounted on three runners covered with iron, a sail, a rudder post, and a wooden tiller.

7566. Boat club was the Knickerbocker Boat Club of New York, organized in 1811. The club had a white boat with green gunwales and gilt stripes, named the *Knickerbocker*, built by John Baptist. John Palmerton was coxswain. The *Knickerbocker* raced the *Invincible*, built by John and William Chambers, from Harsimus, NJ, to the Battery, New York City. The club disbanded in 1812.

7567. Yacht club was the New York Yacht Club, organized on July 30, 1844, by four yachting enthusiasts in the cabin of John Cox Stevens's schooner *Gimcrack*. Stevens was elected commodore on March 17, 1845, and a clubhouse was opened at Elysian Fields, Hoboken, NJ, in 1846 (it was towed to Glen Cove, NY, in 1904). On August 7, 1848, the secretary of the Navy authorized the club's sloops and schooners to proceed from port to port in the United States without entering or clearing at the Custom House, provided that they did not transport merchandise for pay. An earlier yacht club, the Boston Yacht Club, founded in 1835 with Captain R. B. Forbes as commodore, was chiefly a fishing organization, and went out of existence in 1837.

7568. Regatta of importance was held by the New York Yacht Club, New York City, on July 16, 1845. The following contestants entered the competition: *Cygnet*, 45 tons; *Sybil*, 42 tons; *Spray*, 37 tons; *Newburg*, 33 tons; *Minra*, 30 tons; *Coquille*, 27 tons; *Gimcrack*, 25 tons; *Lancet*, 20 tons; and *Ada*, 17 tons. The yachts raced in the waters of New York from Robbin's Reef to Bay Ridge, thence to Stapleton, thence to the Southwest Spit buoy, and then back to the starting point.

7569. Yacht from the United States to win an international yacht race was *America*, owned by a syndicate headed by Commodore John Cox Stevens of the New York Yacht Club. It was designed by George Steers and built by William Henry Brown of New York. It was 101 feet 9 inches overall and 90 feet 3 inches at the waterline, with a beam of 23 feet 11 inches. The foremast measured 79 feet 6 inches and the mainmast 81 feet. The race, the first international yacht race ever held, took place in England on August 22, 1851, under the auspices of the Royal Yacht Squadron. The course circled the Isle of Wight, a distance of 53 miles. *America* covered the course in 10 hours 37 minutes, defeating 14 other contestants. It received a trophy valued at £100 sterling and known as the Queen's Cup, in honor of Queen Victoria.

7570. Ice yacht club was the Poughkeepsie Ice Yacht Club of Poughkeepsie, NY, which was organized in 1861. Regattas and races were held on the Hudson River.

7571. Transatlantic yacht race started on December 11, 1866. According to an agreement made on October 27, 1866, each of the three contestants put up $30,000, winner-take-all. The competing yachts were the *Henrietta*, 205 tons, owned by James Gordon Bennett; the *Vesta*, 201 tons, owned by Pierre Lorillard; and the *Fleetwing*, 212 tons, owned by George Osgood. The winner was the *Henrietta,* which made the trip from Sandy Hook, NJ, to Cowes, England, in 13 days 22 hours.

7572. Canoe club was the New York Canoe Club, founded in New York City in 1870. A clubhouse was built in 1879, during which year a regatta was held. The club was dissolved on August 3, 1880.

7573. Catamaran was patented by Nathanael Greene Herreshoff of Providence, RI, who received a patent on April 10, 1877, on two parallel hulls. A catamaran is a jointed boat, used principally by lifeguards at public beaches.

7574. Boat race for fishermen was held on May 1, 1886, over a triangular course. The start was off the Boston Light, Little Brewster Island, Boston, MA, to and around the Davis Ledge buoy off Minot's Ledge, thence to and around Half Way Rock off the Marblehead shore, and back to Boston Light. The *John H. McManus* won the first prize of $1,500, finishing two miles ahead of the *Sarah H. Prior,* which was a few minutes ahead of the *Gertie S. Windsor.* The pilot schooner *Hesper* won the race and the cup, but not the prize money, as it was not truly a fisherman's boat.

7575. Motorboat race under organized rules was held on June 23–24, 1904, under the jurisdiction of the Columbia Yacht Club, 86th Street and Hudson River, New York City. A 32-mile race was held for the Gold Cup of the Challenge Cup Series, from the clubhouse to a point 16 miles north and back. The trophy was won by C.C. Riotte in the *Standard,* a 100-horsepower motorboat 59 feet long, with an average speed of 22.57 statute miles (19.67 nautical miles) per hour. The contest was decided by a point system. The rules were formulated on April 22, 1903, by the American Power Boat Association, which was organized by seven yacht clubs on January 20, 1903.

7576. International lifeboat race was held on September 7, 1927, from the Statue of Liberty to Pier A, New York City, under the auspices of the Neptune Association. Eleven boats of different sizes, shapes, and weights from seven different nations competed. A prize cup was presented to Captain John F. Milliken of the M. S. *Segundo* of Norway, whose team of eight men covered the course in 15 minutes 27 seconds. Second honors went to the crew of the M. S. *Titania* of Norway and third place to the crew of the *De Grasse* of France. Later races developed uniform conditions.

7577. Motorboat ocean race under the rules of the Union of International Motorboating was the Sam Griffith Memorial Race, 172 miles, from Miami, FL, to Bimini, Bahamas, and back, on February 22, 1966. Although 31 boats started from Biscayne Bay, a 20-knot crosswind prevented 27 of them from reaching Bimini, and only two attempted the return trip. The *Thunderbird,* a 32-foot aluminum boat powered by two 500-horsepower United Aircraft gas turbine engines, with Jim Wynne and Walt Walters as codrivers, made the trip in 4 hours 45 minutes 23 seconds, at an average speed of 37 miles per hour. The *Thunderbird* was declared experimental and thus ineligible for the $3,000 prize. The award was made to Jerry Langer of the *No. 10,* which returned 2.5 hours after the *Thunderbird.*

7578. Human-powered submarine race was the International Submarine Race, which was organized by Henry Perry and took place in West Palm Beach, FL, on June 23–25, 1989. The race was run over a 5,396-foot underwater course and was intended to promote innovative design in submarine technology.

Bowling

7579. Bowling match recorded is that of January 1, 1840, played at the Knickerbocker Alleys, New York City.

7580. Bowling rule standardization was undertaken on November 13, 1875, when 27 delegates met at Germania Hall, New York City, and organized the National Bowling Association. The association soon went out of existence, however, as did the American Amateur Bowling Union, which was organized in 1890. The first important bowling convention to standardize rules was held by the American Bowling Congress, when it organized on September 9, 1895, in New York City.

7581. Bowling magazine was *Gut Holz,* first issued on August 9, 1893, in New York City. It was originally printed in German. On May 19, 1894, it became the *Bowlers' Journal.*

7582. Bowling with duckpins was introduced in the spring of 1900 at the Diamond Bowling Alleys, Howard Street, Baltimore,

MD, owned by Wilbert Robinson and John Joseph McGraw. A duckpins match at Schuetzen Park, Union Hill, NJ, on July 18, 1900, was won by Baltimore with 412 pins; the Stuyvesants of Brooklyn were second with 373 pins.

7583. Bowling tournament sponsored by the American Bowling Congress convened in Chicago, IL, on January 8–11, 1901. The participants were 41 five-man teams, 79 two-man teams, and 115 individuals. The prize money was $2,500. The individual winner was Frank "Pop" Breill (or Brill) of Chicago, with a score of 648. A two-man team, J. Voorhies and C. K. Starr of the Metropolitan Bowling Club of New York, rolled 1,203 points and won $80. The Standard Bowling Club of Chicago rolled 2,720 points, defeating the Crescents of Chicago, who had 2,692 points, and winning $200.

7584. Bowler to make a perfect score of 300 in an American Bowling Congress tournament was William Knox of Philadelphia, PA, who rolled a perfect game on March 10, 1913, in Toledo, OH, in the 13th international bowling tournament. It was the 14th perfect game recognized with a gold medal.

7585. Bowling tournament for women held under the auspices of the Women's International Bowling Congress was held on March 17, 1917, in St. Louis, MO. Eight five-woman teams, 16 two-woman teams, and 24 individuals participated. The individual high score was won by Mrs. M. Koester, with an average of 162. The Women's International Bowling Congress had been organized on November 29, 1916.

7586. Bowler to roll two perfect games in a sanctioned league competition was Frank Caruana of Buffalo, NY, who rolled two perfect games in succession on March 5, 1924, in Buffalo. He had five strikes on a third game, rolling 29 strikes in succession. His score for four games was 1,115 (300, 300, 268, 247).

7587. Bowler who was a woman to obtain a perfect score was Emma Fahning of the Germain Cleaning team, who bowled a perfect game on March 4, 1930, in Buffalo, NY. This was the first perfect score in a sanctioned competition under conditions of the Woman's International Bowling Congress. Rose Jacobs, who rolled a 300 in Schenectady, NY, in 1929, was the first woman of record to achieve that feat in unsanctioned competition.

7588. Bowling automatic scoring machine was the Brunswick Automatic Scorer, installed in September 1967 at Village Lanes, a 16-lane bowling center in Chicago, IL. It could automatically record pinfall, ball by ball, frame by frame; compute and total individual and team scores; and, in a fraction of a second, print scores on a permanent scorecard and project them onto an overhead screen. One console served four lanes. The machine was first used in sanctioned league games on October 10, 1967.

7589. Bowling Triple Crown winner was Billy Hardwick, who won the United States National Championship in 1963, the Firestone Tournament of Champions in 1965, and the United States Open in 1969.

Boxing

7590. Boxer to win distinction in the ring was Bill Richmond, born in Richmond, Staten Island, NY (now part of New York City), on August 5, 1763, the son of a slave owned by the Reverend Charlton. On July 8, 1805, Richmond knocked out Jack Holmes, alias Tom Tough, in the 26th round at Cricklewood Green, a short distance from Kilburn Wells, England. On October 8, 1805, he was defeated by Tom Cribb at Hailsham, Sussex. He never fought in the United States.

7591. Boxer of fame who was African-American was Tom Molineux, who grew up in slavery, probably on a plantation in Virginia, and who is said to have won his freedom by winning boxing bouts arranged by slaveholders. He had a wide following by the time he left for England in 1810 to fight the English champion Tom Cribb on December 10. Although he knocked Cribb out in the 23rd round, he was falsely accused of using lead weights in his gloves and the fight continued, ending in a victory for Cribb in the 40th round.

7592. Boxing arena was built near Worcester, MA, for the fight between Tom Springs and Jack Langan, the Irish champion, on January 7, 1824. It had about 4,000 seats and room for 22,000 people to stand. Admission was 10 shillings ($2.50), half of which went to the fighters.

7593. Boxer to die from blows inflicted in a fight was Andy Marsden, a British heavyweight, who fought a French heavyweight in New Orleans, LA, in 1834, and died the next morning of a fractured skull. The first known boxing death to take place in the ring occurred in a bare-knuckle fight on September 13, 1842, at Hastings, NY. Christopher Lilly, an Englishman, age 23, weighing 140 pounds, fought Thomas McCoy, an Irish-American, age 21, weighing 137, for a purse of $200. The fight lasted 2 hours 41 minutes (120 rounds). McCoy suffered internal wounds and suffocated in his own blood.

7594. Heavyweight boxing match to last longer than 100 rounds took place on September 9, 1841, at Caldwell's Landing, NY. Tom Hyer, son of fighter Jacob Hyer, defeated George "Country" McChester in a two-hour 55-minute match that lasted 101 rounds.

7595. Bare-knuckle world heavyweight boxing champion from the United States was Paddy Ryan, who won an undisputed title by knocking out Joe Goss of England in the 85th round on June 1, 1880, near Colliers, WV, about 300 yards from the Pennsylvania border. The fight, which lasted 1 hour 27 minutes, was witnessed by 300 spectators. The prize was $2,000.

7596. Prizefighting ban enacted by a state was passed by Louisiana on May 12, 1890. Although the act defined prizefighting as a crime, it did not "apply to exhibitions and glove contests between human beings, which may take place within the rooms of regularly chartered athletic clubs."

7597. Boxing match timed by automatic timer took place on May 21, 1891, at the California Athletic Club, San Francisco, CA, when Peter Jackson, an Australian, and James John Corbett met in a 61-round fight that ended in a draw. The timer sounded a gong at the expiration of each three-minute round.

7598. Boxing match under the Marquis of Queensberry rules requiring the use of gloves was the heavyweight championship fight between John Lawrence Sullivan and James John Corbett on September 7, 1892, at the New Orleans Olympic Club, New Orleans, LA, for a winner-take-all purse of $25,000 and an outside bet of $10,000. Five-ounce gloves were used. Corbett won in the 21st round. An unofficial match under the rules took place on August 29, 1885, at Chester Park, Cincinnati, OH, between Sullivan and Dominick F. McCaffery. It was billed as "six rounds to decide the Marquis of Queensberry glove contest for the championship of the world." Sullivan was the winner but "ascribed his failure to knock the youngster out to the latter's get-away tactics and to the restrictions of the Marquis of Queensberry Rules."

7599. Championship heavyweight boxing title won in the first round was won by Jim Jefferies, 250 pounds, who knocked out Jack Finnegan, 180 pounds, in 55 seconds of the first round at Detroit, MI, on April 6, 1900.

7600. Heavyweight boxing champion of the world who was African-American was Jack Johnson, who defeated Tommy Burns at Sydney, Australia, on December 26, 1908, in 14 rounds, technically winning the championship. The actual title was earned on July 4, 1910, when he defeated Jim Jefferies in 15 rounds at Reno, NV. Johnson lost his title on April 5, 1915, at Havana, Cuba, to Jess Willard in 26 rounds.

7601. Boxing match broadcast on radio was presented on September 6, 1920, by station WWJ, Detroit, MI. The fight took place in Benton Harbor, MI. Jack Dempsey knocked out Billy Miske in the third round of a scheduled 10-round fight.

7602. Boxing match broadcast on radio from ringside was presented on December 22, 1920, from Madison Square Garden, New York City, where Joe Lynch of New York City defended his bantamweight title against Peter Herman of New Orleans in a 15-round fight.

7603. Boxing match to gross $1 million was held on July 2, 1921, at Jersey City, NJ. Approximately 75,000 persons paid $1,626,580 in gate receipts to see Jack Dempsey fight Georges Carpentier in a match that was billed as "the battle of the century." Dempsey won by a knockout in the 57th second of the fourth round. He received $300,000 and Carpentier $200,000 as purses.

7604. Boxing match to attract 100,000 spectators was the Jack Dempsey–Gene Tunney fight, held on September 23, 1926, at the Sesquicentennial Stadium, Philadelphia, PA. The attendance was 120,757 and the gate receipts were $1,895,733. Tunney defeated Dempsey in a 10-round fight under the point system.

7605. Boxing match to be shown on television was the fight between Lou Nova and Max Baer at Yankee Stadium, New York City, on June 1, 1939, which was televised by WNBT-TV, New York City. Sam Taub was the announcer. Referee Frank Fullam halted the bout in the 11th round and awarded the decision to Nova. About 300 persons saw the telecast in the smoking room of the New Amsterdam Theatre, and about 20,000 saw it in stores and dealer display rooms.

7606. Boxing referee who was a woman was Belle Martell of Van Nuys, CA, who was granted a license on April 30, 1940, by the California State Athletic Commission. She also held an announcer's license and a timekeeper's license. Her first assignment was a complete show of eight bouts in San Bernardino, CA, on May 2, 1940. She retired the following month, on June 24, 1940. The first female referee to judge a heavyweight championship match was Eva Shain, who refereed the 15-round Muhammad Ali–Earnie Shavers prizefight on September 29, 1977, at Madison Square Garden, New York City. She voted nine rounds for Ali, six for Shavers. She had been licensed by the New York State Athletic Commission on January 6, 1975.

7607. Boxing referee in a heavyweight championship match who was African-American was Zack Clayton of Philadelphia, PA, who refereed the Jersey Joe Walcott–Ezzard Charles fight at Municipal Stadium, Philadelphia, PA, on June 5, 1952. Walcott outpointed Charles in the 15th round and retained his title.

7608. World heavyweight boxing champion to retire undefeated was Rocky Marciano, who won all his 49 professional bouts, notably the heavyweight championship in Philadelphia, PA, on September 23, 1952. Marciano retired following the sixth defense of his heavyweight title, in which he knocked out Archie Moore at Yankee Stadium on September 21, 1955.

7609. World heavyweight boxing champion to regain his crown was Floyd Patterson. The title had been relinquished by the undefeated Rocky Marciano at his retirement. Patterson won it on November 30, 1956, in the Chicago Stadium, Chicago, IL, when he knocked down Archie Moore twice in the fifth round before the referee stopped the fight. He lost the title on June 26, 1959, in Yankee Stadium, New York City, to Ingemar Johansson of Goteborg, Sweden, who won with a technical knockout in the third round after knocking Patterson down seven times. He regained it in a 15-round rematch held on June 20, 1960, at the Polo Grounds, New York City, by knocking out Johansson in 1 minute 51 seconds of the fifth round.

7610. Boxer to win five world titles in five weight divisions was Sugar Ray Leonard. He captured his first title, the World Boxing Council's welterweight championship, after knocking out Wilfredo Benitez of Puerto Rico in 1979. The next year he won the junior middleweight division in a victory over Ayub Kalule in Houston, TX. In 1987, he outpointed Marvin Hagler to win the middleweight title. In November 1988, he defeated Donny Lalonde of Canada to take the WBC light heavyweight and super middleweight titles. Leonard also won the gold medal in the light welterweight boxing event in the 1976 Summer Olympic Games in Montreal.

7611. Amateur boxing match for women officially sanctioned by the United States Amateur Boxing Association took place on October 30, 1993, at Edmonds Community College, Lynnwood, WA. Sixteen-year-old Dallas Molloy defeated Heather Poyner, a 20-year-old kick boxer. Each weighed 144 pounds.

7612. Boxer who was a woman to earn international recognition was Christy Martin, who fought Sue Chase in February 1996 in the first women's boxing match to be broadcast live on national television (by the Showtime cable network). In the following month she bested Deirdre Gogarty in front of a pay-per-view cable television audience of 1.1 million people, winning the World Boxing Council's women's championship belt.

Bullfighting

7613. Bullfight was held on July 4, 1884, in Dodge City, KS. The first bull put up a good fight but was not killed. The next four bulls showed little inclination to fight and likewise were spared. To appease the crowd, the first bull was returned to the ring and was killed by Captain Gregorio Gallardo. Among the bulls were Ringtailed Snorter, Iron Gall, Sheriff, Rustler, Loco Jim, Ku Klux, and Eat-em-up Richard. Another bullfight was held the following day. Earlier, on July 31, 1880, a steer-baiting contest had been held in New York City before 4,000 spectators, but rubber caps had been placed on the bulls' horns and the matadors were not permitted to kill the bulls. The rosettes were not stuck into the bulls, but glued on.

7614. Matador of American birth was Harper Baylor Lee, born James Harper Gillett in Ysleta, TX. He attended high school in Guadalajara, Mexico, where he learned bullfighting techniques, making his debut at the city bullring in 1908. He received the rank of matador at Monterrey, Mexico, on February 20, 1910.

7615. Bullfighter who was a woman to fight professionally was Patricia McCormick of Big Spring, TX, whose professional debut was made January 20, 1952, in Ciudad Juarez, Mexico. On that occasion she killed two bulls. In her first two years, she killed 80 bulls.

Car Racing

7616. Car race was held on Thanksgiving Day, November 28, 1895, over snowy roads from Chicago to Waukegan, IL, a distance of approximately 52 miles. The prize was $2,000, offered by the Chicago *Times-Herald*. Of the 80-odd entries, only 6 were able to start. The winner was James Franklin Duryea, who drove a gasoline-fueled automobile invented by his brother, Charles Edgar Duryea. It had a water-cooled engine with a water pump, a bevel-gear transmission with three speeds forward and reverse, and electric ignition. It was equipped with a rigid front axle with steering knuckles at the ends and was steered by a tiller handle, the up-and-down motion of which changed the speed. Only one other entry finished, an American-rebuilt Benz electric car, which had to be pushed many miles. The average speed in the race was 7.5 miles per hour.

7617. Car race on a racetrack was held on September 7, 1896, at Narragansett Park, Cranston, RI, as a feature of the Rhode Island State Fair, and was witnessed by 40,000 spectators. Six gasoline and two electric automobiles raced. There were five heats of five miles each on a one-mile dirt track, one heat to be raced each afternoon of the fair week for a prize of $1,000 each day. The winner was a Riker Electric Stanhope made by the Riker Electric Motor Car Company, Brooklyn, NY (now part of New York City), which won in 15 minutes 1.75 seconds with a speed of approximately 24 miles per hour. The driver was A. H. Whiting and the passenger was A. L. Riker, the owner.

7618. Car hill-climbing contest was sponsored by the Automobile Club of America and held on September 9, 1901, at Nelson Hill, just outside Peekskill, NY, as one of the feature events in the 500-mile test run from New York City to Buffalo, NY. The Class A race was won by the Grout brothers, automobile manufacturers of Orange, MA, who entered a steam-propelled open Stanhope automobile of their own manufacture. The car weighed 920 pounds and seated two people, including the driver. The climb took 2 minutes 45 seconds. The hill was 226 feet high and 2,372 feet long, with a slant varying from 12 to 17 degrees.

7619. Long-distance car race was held on September 9–14, 1901, under the auspices of the Automobile Club of America, which sponsored a 500-mile race from its clubhouse at Fifth Avenue and 58th Street, New York City, to Buffalo, NY. The exact mileage was 464.2 miles, divided into day trips, with stops at Poughkeepsie, Albany, Herkimer, Syracuse, Rochester, and Buffalo. There were 87 entries in the race, with 80 starters. The race was not a speed or endurance test but a reliability test. It was won by David Wolfe Bishop, who drove a Panhard automobile manufactured by Panhard-Levassor of Paris. The car carried one passenger and driver and was powered by gasoline. The average speed was 15 miles per hour.

7620. Car race from New York to Paris via Seattle and Yokohama started on February 12, 1908, from Times Square, New York City. Six automobiles were entered: three French, one Italian, one German, and one American. The race was won by George Schuster, driver, George J. Miller, mechanic, and Montague Roberts, assistant mechanic, in a car made by the E.R. Thomas Motor Company, Buffalo, NY. The elapsed time was 170 days, of which 88 were spent in actual driving. The average daily run was 152 miles, the longest daily run 420 miles. The Thomas car arrived in Paris on August 1 and returned to New York City on the SS *Lorraine*, arriving on

August 15. The race was sponsored by the *New York Times* and the Paris newspaper *Le Matin*.

7621. Transcontinental car race started on June 1, 1909, from New York City and ended on June 22 at Seattle, WA, scene of the Alaska-Yukon Pacific Exposition. Mayor George Brinton McClellan fired the starting gun. There were six entrants: an Acme, an Itala, a Shawmut, two Model T Fords, and a Stearns that failed to start. The race was won by Bert W. Scott and C. James Smith, who drove one of the Ford cars. They received a silver prize and a $2,000 award from H. Robert Guggenheim.

7622. Speedway with a board track was the Los Angeles Motordrome, near Playa del Rey, CA, opened on April 7, 1910. It was made of wood, with a circumference of 5,281 feet, and was under the direction of Fred Evans Moskovics.

7623. Indianapolis 500 race was the brainchild of Carl Graham Fisher, a car dealer in Indianapolis, IN, who built the Indianapolis Speedway in 1909 to promote his city as a center for automotive innovation. The speedway featured a 2.5-mile oval course. The first 500-mile race was run on May 30, 1911, when 40 cars competed for a prize of $25,000. There were multiple breakdowns in the scoring arrangements, making the actual winner a matter of controversy. Although the victory officially belongs to Ray Harroun, who drove a Marmon Wasp in six hours 42 minutes (an average of 74.7 miles per hour), the race may actually have been won by Ralph Mulford. One contestant was killed in an accident. The race was witnessed by 85,000 spectators.

7624. Asphalt-covered racetrack was opened on September 18, 1915, at the Narragansett Speedway, Cranston, RI, where two world records were broken.

7625. Soapbox derby was officially held in 1934 in Dayton, OH. It was the first racing event for children. The winner of the $500 prize was 11-year-old Bob Turner from Muncie, IN. The race was moved to Akron, OH, in 1935, after the *Akron Beacon-Journal* offered to build a permanent track. The first girl to win the derby was Karren Stead, in 1975. The first contestant to win two years in a row was Danielle Del Ferraro, who won the Kit Car division in 1993, the Masters division in 1994, and her division's award for best in construction both years.

The idea for the soapbox derby originated in 1933, when Dayton, OH, photojournalist Myron Scott snapped pictures of boys racing wooden crates with baby buggy wheels.

7626. Driver who was a woman to compete in the Indianapolis 500 was Janet Guthrie of Iowa City, IA, who qualified on May 22, 1977, at the Indianapolis Speedway with an average speed of 188.403 miles per hour for four consecutive laps. She drove a Lightning-Offenhauser. In the race, which was held on May 29, she reached a speed of 151.207 miles per hour, but was forced out by mechanical trouble after 27 laps, finishing 29th out of 33 entries. The following year, she qualified again and finished ninth. Guthrie was an aerospace engineer before she started competitive driving in the 1960s.

7627. Solar-powered car race held in the United States was the GM Sunrayce USA, which took place in July 1990 along an 1,800-mile route from Florida to Michigan. The competitors were college engineering students who constructed their own vehicles. There were 32 entrants. The winning team was fielded by the University of Michigan. The race, which has since become a biennial event known as the American Solar Challenge, was sponsored in part by the U.S. Department of Energy.

Cricket

7628. Cricket match was held in New York City, on the future site of Fulton Market, on May 1, 1751, between the Londoners and the New Yorkers. The New Yorkers made 80 and 86 and the Londoners 43 and 47. Cricket had been played by local teams on the same site about five years earlier.

7629. Cricket club was the Boston Cricket Club, founded in 1809 in Boston, MA. The first president was Andrew Allen.

7630. Cricket game played by a college team is said to have been played at Haverford College, Haverford, PA. The game was introduced in 1836 by William Carvill, the college gardener. The bats and balls were of home manufacture.

7631. International cricket tournament was held on October 3–5, 1859, at St. George's ground, Hoboken, NJ, between the All-England team, captained by George Parr, and the St. George's Cricket Club of New York, captained by J. Wisden. The American team was weak at bat and the English team won in one inning with a score of England 156, United States 92. A second game was played on October 10, 1859, at Philadelphia, PA, the English winning by seven wickets. The English team played two games in the United States and two in Canada.

7632. Cricket magazine was *The American Cricketer, a Journal Devoted to the Noble Game of Cricket*, four pages long, which was first published on June 28, 1877, at Philadelphia, PA. It was published weekly from May to November and monthly from November to May. The subscription price was $3 a year for 33 issues.

7633. College cricket club team to tour England was the Haverford College team, Haverford, PA, captained by John Lester, which competed from July 17 to July 31, 1896, against Harrow School, Eton College, Cambridge University, and others. They won four games, lost four games, and drew seven games. They returned to the United States on the *Belgenland* on August 5, 1896.

Curling

7634. Curling club was the Orchard Lake Curling Club, organized in the winter of 1831–32 near the present site of Pontiac, MI. Lacking genuine curling stones, the club improvised wooden blocks sawed from hickory and shaped with ax and chisel.

7635. Indoor curling rink devoted exclusively to curling was opened on December 19, 1920, by the Country Club, Brookline, MA.

7636. National curling championship competition was held on March 28–30, 1957, at the Stadium, Chicago, IL, with 10 teams competing. The winner was the Hibbing Curling Club from Hibbing, MN, which won eight games and lost one.

Cycling

7637. Bicycles were imported in 1819. The first one in New York City made its appearance on May 21, 1819. The Common Council met on August 19 and passed a law "to prevent the use of velocipedes in the public places and on the sidewalks of the city of New York." In their early years, bicycles were called velocipedes, curricles, or swift walkers.

7638. Bicycle patent was granted to William K. Clarkson, Jr., of New York City on June 26, 1819, for an "improved curricle."

7639. Bicycle with a rotary crank was patented on November 20, 1866, by Pierre Lallemont of Paris. It was known as a "bone shaker." He rode on it from Ansonia, CT, to New Haven, CT. The fore wheel was axled to the jaws of a depending bar, which was pivoted in the frame, and turned by a horizontal lever bar, which was revolved by a treadle crank.

7640. Bicycle school was opened in New York City on December 5, 1868, at 932 Broadway, by Pearsall Brothers.

7641. Bicycle factory was established by Colonel Albert Augustus Pope of Hartford, CT, who saw a bicycle at the 1876 Centennial Exposition in Philadelphia, PA, and commissioned W. S. Atwell of Boston, MA, to build a 70-pound model for him at a cost of $313. In 1878, he arranged with the Weed Sewing Machine Company of Hartford to produce 50 Standard Columbus bicycles, which he sold promptly.

7642. Bicycle magazine was *The American Bicycling Journal*, published December 22, 1877, in Boston, MA. It contained 16 pages and cost 10 cents a copy. It appeared every other Saturday. Frank William Weston was the editor and proprietor. It was eventually absorbed by *Bicycling World and Motor Cycle Review*.

7643. Bicycle club was the Boston Bicycle Club, formed on February 11, 1878, in Boston, MA, by 14 members. George B. Woodward was president and Thatcher Goddard captain. The uniform was a gray jacket, shirt, breeches, and stockings and a blue Glengarry Scotch cap with a small visor in front. The first meet was held on March 9, 1878.

7644. National bicycle organization was the League of American Wheelmen, formed on May 31, 1880, at Newport, RI, by 128 members representing 28 cycling clubs. The first president was Charles Ed Pratt of Boston, MA.

7645. Bicycle trip of 100 miles sponsored by a club took place on September 6, 1882, when the Boston Bicycle Club, Boston, MA, sponsored a trip from Worcester, MA, to Boston. The trip started at 4:38 A.M. and ended at 9:30 P.M., with frequent stop-offs for food, refreshments, and repairs. The elapsed time was 16 hours 52 minutes, of which 12 hours 6 minutes was the actual riding time. Seven men covered the complete 102.5 miles, but many others rode along for varying distances. The route was via South Framingham, Natick, Wellesley, Dedham, Stoughton, Brockton, Randolph, Braintree, Quincy, Mattapan, Waltham, and Newton.

7646. Round-the-world bicycle trip was made by Thomas Stevens, who started from San Francisco, CA, on April 22, 1884, on a 50-inch bicycle (the diameter of the large front wheel was 50 inches). He pedaled across the United States, arriving at Boston, MA, on August 24. He left for Europe by ship and visited England, France, Germany, Austria-Hungary, Serbia, Bulgaria, Turkey, Persia, India, China, and Japan. On December 17, 1886, he landed at Yokohama, Japan, having actually wheeled about 13,500 miles. He left Yokohama on the *City of Peking* and arrived at San Francisco on January 7, 1887.

7647. Six-day bicycle race held in the United States took place on February 11–16, 1889, at Madison Square Garden, New York City, under the management of William O'Brien. The week's proceeds amounted to $10,212, of which $1,635 went to the winner, Lottie Stanley, who rode for 624 miles. Riders from England and Ireland were among the contestants.

7648. Bicycle with a back-pedal brake was patented on December 24, 1889, by Daniel C. Stover and William A. Hance of Freeport, IL.

7649. Pneumatic bicycle tire was made in the tire factory of the George R. Bidwell Cycle Company of New York City in April 1891 for use on its bicycles.

7650. Six-day bicycle race for men held in the United States took place at Madison Square Garden, New York City, from midnight on Sunday, October 18, 1891, to midnight on Saturday, October 24, and was won by William "Plugger Bill" Martin of Detroit, MI, who rode a "high wheeler" bicycle. There were 40 contestants, but only 6 finished, all of whom won prizes. Martin covered 1,466 miles and won a $2,100 prize. The gate receipts were $26,000. The first two-man team event was held from February 12 to February 17, 1899, and was won by Charles Miller and Frank Waller, who rode a combined total of 2,733.4 miles.

7651. Bicycle tire made of cord was invented by John F. Palmer of Chicago, IL. On June 7, 1892, he obtained a patent on a self-healing tire in which the tread portion of the rubber was placed under compression, so that a puncture would tend to close rather than gape open. The tire was manufactured in 1892 by the B.F. Goodrich Company of Akron, OH, and was first exhibited at the Philadelphia Cycle Show in February 1893.

7652. Round-the-world bicycle trip by a woman was made by Annie Londonberry, who left on June 26, 1894, from the State House, Boston, MA, and ended her trip on September 12, 1895, at Chicago. She returned to Boston on September 24, 1895, to collect a $10,000 bet for completing the trip within 15 months, as well as $5,000 in lecture fees.

7653. Intercollegiate bicycle race was held on May 27, 1896, at the Manhattan Beach Track, New York City, under the auspices of the Intercollegiate Association of Amateur Athletes of America. Five races were held—a quarter mile, a half mile, one mile, one mile tandem, and five miles. Contestants scored five points for each first place, two points for each second place, and one point for each third place. The score was Columbia 20, Yale 8, Pennsylvania 5, Columbian University of Washington 5, and Harvard 2.

7654. Bicycle racer to attain the speed of a mile a minute was Charles Minthorn Murphy, known as Mile-A-Minute-Murphy, who on June 30, 1899, rode a mile in 57.8 seconds, riding behind a Long Island Railroad train from Farmingdale, NY, to Maywood, NY, on a three-mile measured track. The train was equipped with an extension top and sides so that Murphy raced in a comparative vacuum.

7655. Bicycle traffic court was held at Racine, WI, on June 18, 1936, under authority of Grover Cleveland Lutter, chief of police. The judges of the court were Sergeant Wilbur Hansen and Officer Alphonse Costabile of the Racine Police Department. Sessions were held Saturday mornings. A city law passed on May 4, 1937, required all bicycles to be registered with the police department.

7656. Bicycle champion who was a woman to win an event sponsored by the National Amateur Bicycle Association was Doris Kopsky of Belleville, NJ, who covered a mile in 4 minutes 22.4 seconds on September 4, 1937, in Buffalo, NY.

7657. Bicycle race to be shown on television was the six-day bicycle race at Madison Square Garden, New York City, which lasted from May 15 to May 21, 1939. The telecast was shown by W2XBS, National Broadcasting Company, on May 20 from 8:30 P.M. to 9 P.M. and showed 10 teams in action. Only 8 of the 12 teams of riders completed the race. The starting gun was fired by Joe DiMaggio, center fielder for the New York Yankees. Bill Stern was the announcer. The race, 2,388 miles long, was won by William and Doug Peden, who scored 1,498 points in sprints.

7658. Transcontinental bicycle trip made in less than three weeks was made in 1949 by Eugene McPherson, 22 years old, of Ohio State University, who left Santa Monica, CA, on September 1 and arrived at New York City on September 21, covering 3,054 miles in 20 days 4 hours 29 minutes.

7659. Mountain bike intended specifically for off-road use was constructed in 1953 by John Finley Scott, a sociology professor at the University of California–Davis, who later ran a bike shop in Cupertino, CA. His modified Schwinn Varsity bicycle, which he called the "Woodsie Bike," featured a diamond frame with cantilever brakes, flat handlebars, balloon tires, and nine-speed derailleur gears. Mountain biking did not catch on as a sport for another 25 years.

7660. Bicyclist from the United States to win the Tour de France was Gregory James LeMond of Los Angeles, CA. LeMond first won the Tour de France, world bicycling's premiere racing event, in 1986. He was seriously wounded in a hunting accident in 1987 but returned to win the tour again in 1989 and 1990. LeMond retired from professional cycling in 1994, suffering from a muscular disorder believed caused by lead pellets in his body.

Dog Racing

7661. Dog racetrack to use an imitation rabbit was opened on February 22, 1920, at Emeryville, CA. It was designed by R. S. Hawley and built by Owen Patrick Smith. The track was about 300 yards around. A car was run through a housing that covered the trolley and track. The arm carrying the rabbit extended from the car through a slot on the track side.

7662. Greyhound racing association was the International Greyhound Racing Association, formed on March 3, 1926, in Miami, FL, to systematize efforts and to conduct the races on the highest possible standard. The first high commissioner was Owen P. Smith.

7663. Dogsled race on an Olympic demonstration program was held on February 6–7, 1932, when the United States and Canada entered 13 teams. Contestants were required to cover a course of 25.1 miles on two consecutive days. First place was won by Emile St. Goddard of Canada, but the United States teams won 7 of the 12 points. The race was held at Lake Placid, NY.

7664. Iditarod sled dog race was held beginning March 3, 1973, along the Iditarod Trail, a 1,200-mile route through central Alaska from Anchorage to Nome. Thirty-four sled teams participated, following a long-abandoned trail that was only partially cleared. The winner was miner Dick Wilmarth of Red Devil, AK, who completed the course in 20 days, 49 minutes, 41 seconds. He earned a $12,000 purse.

During Alaska's frontier days, the Iditarod Trail was used by mushers and their sled-dog teams to transport mail and supplies, most famously in 1925 when a relay of dog teams delivered antitoxin serum to Nome during a diphtheria epidemic.

Fencing

7665. Fencing book was Edward Blackwell's *A Compleat System of Fencing; or the art of defence, in the use of the small sword; wherein the most necessary parts thereof are plainly laid down; chiefly for gentlemen, promoters and lovers of that science in North America*, printed in 1734 by William Parks, Williamsburg, VA. It was based on Henry Blackwell's *The English Fencing Master*, published in London in 1705.

7666. National fencing league was the Amateur Fencers League of America, organized on May 6, 1891 with Dr. Graeme M. Hammond of New York City as the first president. The first competition was held in 1892. The winners were W. Scott O'Connor of the Fencers Club, men's foils; Dr. B. F. O'Connor of the New York Athletic Club, dueling swords; and R. O. Haubold of the New York Athletic Club, sabers.

7667. Intercollegiate fencing championship competition was held by the International Fencing Association on May 5, 1894, at the Racquet and Tennis Club, New York City. Harvard defeated Columbia five matches to four and won the silver challenge cup. Yale, the only other entry in the competition, withdrew after an accident to one of the team. Fitzhugh Townsend of Columbia had the highest individual score.

7668. International fencing championship competition was held at the Racquet Club, Washington, DC, on November 18–19, 1921. The United States team defeated Great Britain 13–3 the first day. The U.S. team lost 10–4 on the second day. The finals were held on November 21 at the Hotel Astor, New York City, where the final score was 8–8. The United States won 25 of the 46 matches to win the Colonel Robert M. Thompson International Trophy.

Fishing

7669. Fishing club of more than temporary existence was the Schuylkill Fishing Company, founded in 1732 in Philadelphia, PA, with a limited membership of 25.

7670. Fishing treatise was a 22-page pamphlet, *A Discourse Utter'd In Part at Ammauskeeg Falls in the Fishing Season 1739*, by Joseph Seccombe ("Fluviatulis Piscator"), parish minister in Kingston, NH, published in 1743 in Boston, MA, by Samuel Kneeland and Timothy Green. It was dedicated "to the honourable Theodore Atkinson, Esq., and others, the worthy patrons of the fishing at Ammauskeeg."

7671. Fly casting tournament was held on June 18, 1861, in Utica, NY, by the New York State Sportsmen's Association. The "throwing the fly" competition was won by George Lenebacker of Utica, NY.

7672. Fishing magazine was the *American Angler*, a monthly magazine published in Philadelphia, PA, and edited by William Charles Harris. The first issue was published on October 15, 1881. On January 28, 1882, it became a weekly.

7673. Indoor fly casting tournament was held March 15–20, 1897, under the auspices of the Sportsmen's Association at Madison Square Garden, New York City. Competitions were held in casting for distance, casting for accuracy and distance, bass fly casting, and so on. A record for the first cast to exceed 100 feet was made by R. C. Leonard, who cast a distance of 101 feet 6 inches on March 17.

Flying

7674. Balloon cup race held in the United States for the James Gordon Bennett Aeronautic Cup took place on October 21, 1907, at St. Louis, MO, with a field of nine entrants. It was won by the German balloon *Pommern*, which flew 880 miles to Asbury Park, NJ, in 39 hours 59 minutes 25 seconds, with Oscar

Erbsl"oh and Henry Holm Clayton as pilots. The previous year's race, which was held in Europe, was the first to be won by an American. It took place on September 30, 1906, with a field of 16 balloons from seven countries. The route was from Paris, France, to Whitby, England, a distance of 410 miles. The winner was Lieutenant Frank Purdy Lahm, pilot of the balloon *United States*, who arrived in 22 hours 17 minutes.

7675. Airplane race won by an American in Europe was the First International Air Race held at Reims, France, during the week of August 22, 1909. The fastest time on the 20-kilometer course was 15 minutes 50.6 seconds. The race was won by Glenn Hammond Curtiss of Hammondsport, NY, in the *Golden Flyer* (length 31 feet 1 inch, wingspan 30 feet, height 11 feet).

7676. Airship race was held at St. Louis, MO, on October 4–9, 1909, when four dirigibles—all the existing dirigibles in the United States—flew from Forest Park and Clayton Road to Kingshighway and Lindell avenues and back. The first prize of $1,000 was won by Lincoln Beachey. Roy Knabenshue and Captain Thomas Baldwin were close runners-up. Cornwall Dixon, using foot power, was carried over the city and landed in East St. Louis. The four dirigibles were housed in improvised tents and were filled with hydrogen produced by a slow process with sulfuric acid and iron filings.

7677. Aviation meet was held on January 10–20, 1910, under the auspices of the Aero Club of California, at Dominguez Field in Los Angeles, where American planes were given an opportunity to prove their power in competition with foreign planes. The foreign exhibits included two Farman biplanes and two Blériot monoplanes. The American exhibits included three Curtiss biplanes, which were piloted by Glenn Hammond Curtiss, Charles Keeney Hamilton, and Charles Foster Willard. Louis Paulhan broke the world altitude record at the meet with a flight to 4,165 feet.

7678. Airplane race between cities was held on August 5, 1911, between New York City and Philadelphia, PA. Three Curtiss machines with Curtiss engines left Governors Island, NY. The race was won by Lincoln Beachey, who covered the 83 miles in 1 hour 50 minutes. Hugh Robinson completed the trip in 2 hours 8 minutes 47 seconds, while Eugene Burton Ely was forced to land at Princeton, NJ.

7679. Transcontinental air race was an aerial derby sponsored by the American Flying Club of New York. It began on October 8, 1919. Fifteen planes left the Presidio, San Francisco, CA, and 48 left Roosevelt Field, Mineola, NY, in a 5,400-mile race across the continent and back. The winner was Lieutenant Belvin W. Maynard, in a de Havilland-4 with a Liberty motor. He left Mineola at 9:24 A.M. on October 8 and reached the Presidio on October 11 with an elapsed time of 3 days 6 hours 4 minutes. On his return trip, he left the Presidio on October 14 at 1:19 P.M. and landed at Roosevelt Field on October 17 with elapsed time of 3 days 21 hours 31 minutes. His actual flying time for the round trip was 24 hours 59 minutes 48.5 seconds. Maynard won by elapsed time, but in his actual flying time he was eclipsed by three others.

7680. Parachute-jumping contest was held on October 12, 1923, at Mitchel Field, NY. Two men on a Martin bomber and two men on a de Havilland jumped from a 4,500-foot height and landed 400 feet from each other, 1.5 minutes apart. The first to land was Staff Sergeant Theodore Schieuming of Brooklyn, New York City. One thousand spectators witnessed the jump.

7681. Transcontinental air derby for women was the Powder Puff Air Derby, which began on August 18, 1929, when 19 pilots took off from Santa Monica, CA, in 10-minute intervals. Overnight stops were made at San Bernardino, CA; Phoenix and Douglas, AZ; Midland and Abilene, TX; Wichita, KS; East St. Louis, IL; and Columbus, OH. On August 26, 1929, 15 women completed the trip at Cleveland, a distance of 2,350 miles from the starting point. The winner was Louise McPhetridge Thaden of Pittsburgh, PA, whose time was 20 hours 19 minutes 10 seconds.

7682. Airplane race of importance in which both men and women were contestants was the National Air Race, held on August 30–31, 1931, from Los Angeles, CA, to Cleveland, OH, in which 36 men and 16 women competed. It was a handicap derby scored on the basis of comparative power of motor and speed of plane. It was won by

Phoebe Fairgrave Omlie of Memphis, TN. She also won the grand prize and the prize for the women's division.

7683. Round-the-world airplane passenger race started on September 30, 1936, from Lakehurst, NJ. Three reporters, Dorothy Kilgallen, Herbert Roslyn Ekins, and Leo Kiernan, made the trip by three different commercial flying routes as a test. The race was won by Ekins of the *New York World-Telegram*, who returned to Lakehurst on October 19, having covered 25,654 miles in 18 days 11 hours 14 minutes 33 seconds. The average speed was 127 miles per hour. The total flying time was 8 days 10 hours 6 minutes.

7684. Hang-gliding national championships were held on October 25, 1973, at the Angeles National Forest in Sylmar, CA. The distance winner was Chris Wills, a student from Santa Ana, CA.

Football

7685. Football club was the Oneida Football Club, which was organized in 1862 by Gerrit Smith Miller at Epes Sargent Dixwell's School in Boston, MA. The members played all comers from 1862 to 1865. They were never defeated, nor was their goal line crossed.

7686. Intercollegiate football contest in the world was played at Rutgers Field, New Brunswick, NJ, on November 6, 1869. Captain William Stryker Gummere '70 of Princeton University (later chief justice of New Jersey) challenged Captain William James Leggett of Rutgers to a friendly game. Each team consisted of 25 men. The rules were that each goal constituted a game and that six games would decide the match, which lasted one hour. The first team to score six goals was Rutgers, while Princeton scored four.

7687. Football rules were formulated at a meeting held on October 18, 1873, in New York City and attended by delegates from Columbia, Princeton, Rutgers, and Yale universities.

7688. International football game was played on December 6, 1873, at New Haven, CT. The Yale team defeated a team from Eton College, England, with a score of two goals to one.

7689. Football goalpost was used in the contest between McGill University and Harvard University that was played at Jarvis Field, Cambridge, MA, on May 14, 1874. The teams played rugby football under Harvard's rules, which stated that every goal constituted a game. McGill arrived with 11 men and Harvard with 15, four of whom were dropped to equalize the teams. Harvard won three games, the first two lasting about five minutes and the third about 12 minutes. As McGill is located in Montreal, Canada, this was the first international rugby football contest to be played, as well as the first instance in which an admission fee was charged at a collegiate sporting event. The proceeds were used for lavishly entertaining the McGill team. A second match was played the following day, and a third match was played in the fall in Montreal.

7690. Football uniforms worn in a game were worn on November 13, 1875, at New Haven, CT, by teams from Yale and Harvard colleges. The Yale team wore dark trousers, blue shirts, and yellow caps, while the Harvard team wore crimson shirts and stockings and knee breeches. Harvard won the game 4–0. The game at that time was closer to rugby than to present-day football. Each team had 15 players.

7691. Intercollegiate football championship was won in the fall of 1876 by Yale University, New Haven, CT, under Captain Eugene Voy Baker '77. Although it was not a member of the Intercollegiate Football Association, Yale played and defeated Columbia, Harvard, and Princeton. The standing of the teams was Yale 2, Princeton 2, Harvard 1, Columbia 0.

7692. Intercollegiate football association was the Intercollegiate Football Association, organized at the Massasoit House, Springfield, MA, on November 23, 1876, with Columbia, Harvard, and Princeton as its three charter members (Rutgers and Yale joined later). The association standardized the number of men on each team at 15 and set the area of the field at 140 by 70 yards.

7693. Penalty rule in football was passed in 1885. It required five points to be deducted from a team's score if one of its players crossed the scrimmage line before the ball was snapped. The rule was the invention of Walter Camp, the head of football at Yale University, New Haven, CT, who was hoping to discourage the kind of violent play that resulted in numerous deaths among student football players each year.

7694. Football dummy for tackling purposes was improvised by Amos Alonzo Stagg at Yale University, New Haven, CT, in the fall of 1889. He used an old gymnasium mat for the purpose.

7695. Tournament of Roses was held on January 1, 1890, at Pasadena, CA, under the auspices of the Valley Hunt Club. It was originally called the Battle of the Flowers and consisted of amateur sports contests held in the afternoon. The first college football contest at the Tournament, held on January 1, 1902, was a game between the University of Michigan and Stanford University, which was won by Michigan 49–0. Football games have been a regular annual event since January 1, 1916, when Washington State College defeated Brown University 14–0.

7696. Intercollegiate Army–Navy football game was played on November 29, 1890, at West Point, NY. The Army (U.S. Military Academy) captain was Dennis Michie '92, and the Navy (U.S. Naval Academy) captain was Charles Rulf Emerich '91. The score was Navy 24, Army 0.

7697. Football book was *American Football*, by Walter Chauncey Camp, published in 1891 by Harper and Brothers, New York City. It contained 175 pages with 31 portraits.

7698. Football game played indoors was played by the Young Men's Christian Association of Springfield, MA, against the Yale Consolidated Team of New Haven, CT, a team that had five of the Yale varsity players on it. The game was played as part of a three-day winter carnival at Madison Square Garden, New York City, after the close of the 1891 season. The score was 16–10 in Yale's favor.

7699. Football game at night was played on September 29, 1892, at the Mansfield Fair, Mansfield, PA, between the Mansfield Teachers College and the Wyoming Seminary of Kingston, PA. Twenty electric lights of 2,000 candlepower were used with a Thompson and Huston Dynamo Machine. The game lasted 70 minutes, but only one half was played, neither team scoring.

7700. Professional football game was played on September 3, 1895, at Latrobe, PA, between the Latrobe Young Men's Christian Association and the Jeannette Athletic Club, Jeannette, PA, which Latrobe won 12–0. Latrobe's captain was Harry Ryan and Jeannette's was "Posie" Flowers. Since the regular quarterback was unable to play, John K. Brallier of Indiana, PA, was paid $10 and expenses to fill in. The following year four men were paid, and in 1897 the entire team was paid.

7701. Intercollegiate football game between African-American colleges was played on January 1, 1897, at Brisbine Park, Atlanta, GA, between Atlanta University and Tuskegee Normal and Industrial Institute. Atlanta won 10–0. Atlanta's captain was George F. Porter, and Tuskegee's captain was Clarence Matthews.

7702. Football stadium was the Harvard Stadium, Cambridge, MA, constructed by the Aberthaw Construction Company, Boston, MA, under the direction of Professor Lewis Jerome Johnson and Joseph Ruggles, from a general architectural design worked out by George Bruns de Gersdorff. It was completed in the spring of 1904. The first stadium built specifically for football, it was also the first stadium built primarily of concrete and the largest steel-reinforced concrete structure in the world at the time of construction. The outer walls measured 527 by 420 feet and were divided into 37 reinforced concrete sections. A colonnade was added in 1910 and steel stands in 1929. The first football game played there was the Harvard–Dartmouth game of November 14, 1903, won by Dartmouth 11–0. The stadium had a seating capacity of 40,000.

7703. Football uniform numerals sewn on the players' uniforms to enable the spectators easily to distinguish the players were used by the University of Pittsburgh, Pittsburgh, PA, on December 5, 1908, for the game against Washington and Jefferson College. The score was 14–0 in favor of Washington and Jefferson.

7704. Professional football association was the American Professional Football Association, formed in Canton, OH, on September 17, 1920, by 11 clubs representing the following cities: Chicago, Decatur, and Rock Island, IL; Hammond and Muncie, IN; Rochester, NY; and Akron, Canton, Cleveland, Dayton, and Masillon, OH.

7705. Football game to be broadcast on radio with a play-by-play description was presented on November 25, 1920, by station WTAW of College Station, TX. The game was played at College Station on Thanksgiving Day between Texas University and the Agricultural and Mechanical College of Texas. At that time the station was operating under an experimental license and had the call letters 5XB. A spark transmitter was used and the transmission was in code.

7706. College football player to score 50 points in one game was Clark Hinkle of Bucknell University, Lewisburg, PA, who scored 50 points on November 28, 1929 at Lewisburg against Dickinson College, Carlisle, PA. He made eight touchdowns and two extra points. Bucknell won 78–0.

7707. World championship professional football game was played on December 17, 1933, at Wrigley Field, Chicago, IL, when the Chicago Bears of the Western Division defeated the New York Giants of the Eastern Division of the National Football League 23–21. The purse was divided, with 60 percent going to the players, 15 percent to each club, and 10 percent to the league. Shares for individual players were $210 for the Bears and $140 for the Giants.

7708. All-star football game was sponsored by Chicago Tribune Charities, a nonprofit organization, and was played on August 31, 1934, at Soldier Field, Chicago, IL. The Chicago Bears, coached by George Halas, played the College All-Stars, coached by Noble Kizer of Purdue, to a 0–0 tie. The players each received $150 and expenses. Attendance was 79,432.

7709. Football player to win the Heisman Trophy for excellence in college football was University of Chicago halfback John J. "Jay" Berwanger, who received the award from former University of Pennsylvania coach and football innovator John Heisman at the Downtown Athletic Club in New York City in 1935. The winner was chosen by sportswriters and sportscasters. The trophy, designed by Frank Eliscu of Brooklyn, New York City, was a bronze casting 21 inches high on a black onyx base and weighed approximately 70 pounds. It depicted a ball carrier with right hand extended to stiff-arm an opponent. Warren Mulrey of Fordham University was the model. The first casting cost $250. After Heisman's death in 1936, the name of the trophy was changed to the Heisman Memorial Trophy.

7710. Intercollegiate football game to be shown on television was played at Randall's Island, New York City, on September 30, 1939, between Fordham University and Waynesburg College. It was televised by station W2XBS, New York City. Fordham won 34–7.

7711. Professional football game to be shown on television took place on October 22, 1939, from Ebbets Field, Brooklyn, New York City, where the Brooklyn Dodgers defeated the Philadelphia Eagles by a score of 23–14. The game was transmitted by station W2XBS of the National Broadcasting Company, New York City. The first telecast of a pro football championship game was the Super Bowl game that took place on January 15, 1967, at Los Angeles, CA, where the Green Bay Packers defeated the Kansas City Chiefs by a score of 35–10. The telecast was pooled and shown by NBC-TV and CBS-TV.

7712. Professional football championship game broadcast on radio took place on December 8, 1940, at Griffith Stadium, Washington, DC. The Mutual Broadcasting System paid $25,000 for the rights to the game, which was broadcast by Walter Lanier "Red" Barber. The Chicago Bears defeated the Washington Redskins 73–0 and won the Ed Thorp Memorial Trophy.

7713. Championship game of the American Football League was played on January 1, 1961, at Houston, TX. The Houston Oilers of the Eastern Division defeated the Los Angeles Chargers of the Western Division 24–16. The Oilers received $1,025 per man and the Chargers $718. The attendance was approximately 32,200.

7714. Football player who was African-American to win the Heisman Memorial Trophy was Ernie Davis, halfback of Syracuse University, named on November 28, 1961, and presented with the award on December 6, 1961, at the Downtown Athletic Club, New York City. The Heisman trophy is awarded annually to the outstanding college player in the United States.

7715. Super Bowl football game between the National Football League and the American Football League for the world championship was played on January 15, 1967, at the

Memorial Coliseum, Los Angeles, CA, before 63,036 spectators. The Green Bay Packers (NFL) defeated the Kansas City Chiefs (AFL) 35–10. The winning Packers received $15,000 each, the Chiefs $7,500 each.

7716. Professional football game in which a woman participated took place on August 15, 1970, at Orlando, FL, when the Orlando Panthers of the Atlantic Coast League played the Bridgeport Jets. Patricia Palinkas, 27 years old, the wife of a player on the Panthers team, held the ball as her husband attempted to kick for the extra point. The 122-pound woman was forced to run with the ball and was brought down within seconds by a 235-pound tackle. The Panthers won 26–7.

7717. Football game to last longer than 80 minutes was the American Football League divisional playoff game on December 25, 1971, at Arrowhead Stadium, Kansas City, MO. The game had three halves (six quarters) and lasted 1 hour 22 minutes 40 seconds. The Miami Dolphins defeated the Kansas City Chiefs 27–24.

7718. Football game in which referees were allowed to check television instant replays was the Hall of Fame game played on July 29, 1978, at Canton, OH, when the Philadelphia Eagles defeated the Miami Dolphins 17–3. The game was telecast on Channel 7.

7719. Ball game to be declared a national special security event was Superbowl XXXVI, played in the Superdome, New Orleans, LA, on February 3, 2002, between the St. Louis Rams and the New England Patriots. The game took place five months after the terror attacks of September 11, 2001. The entire city was patrolled by security forces under the supervision of the Secret Service, with combat aircraft watching the sky, Coast Guard ships watching the waterways, concrete barriers protecting the Superdome, and police checkpoints where spectators were searched.

7720. Sportscaster who was a woman to be inducted into the Pro Football Hall of Fame was Lesley Visser, who received the organization's Pete Rozelle Radio-Television Award on August 5, 2006, in Canton, OH. Visser specialized in football reporting, starting out as a writer for the Boston Globe and continuing as a radio and TV commentator, including a longtime stint with Monday Night Football.

On June 26, 2004, Visser became the first female sportscaster to carry the Olympic torch on its way to the opening of the Olympic Games, taking it along Manhattan's Sixth Avenue.

Games

7721. Billiards were brought to America by the Spaniards who settled in St. Augustine, FL, in 1565.

7722. Game played in the English colonies in America that was recorded was "bowles," an early form of bowling, which was played by the settlers of Jamestown, VA, in May 1611, and observed by Sir Thomas Dale.

7723. Chess book was *Chess Made Easy—New Comprehensive Rules For Playing the Game of Chess with Examples from Philidor, Cunningham, etc. to which is prefixed a pleasing account of its origin; some interesting anecdotes of several exalted personages who have been admirers of it; and the Morals of Chess written by the ingenious Dr. Franklin.* It contained 106 pages, including eight pages of advertisements, and was printed and sold in 1802 by James Humphreys of Philadelphia, PA. Evidently it was a reprint of an English edition.

7724. Game manufacturing company to make games and children's books was the McLoughlin Company, organized in New York City in 1828 by John McLoughlin. In 1850 his sons, John and Edmund, were taken into partnership and the firm name became McLoughlin Brothers. In 1920 the company confined its activities to manufacturing books and moved to Springfield, MA.

7725. Whist rule book was *The Whist Player's Hand Book, containing most of the maxims of the old school and several new ones exemplified by opposite cases; with a method of acquiring a knowledge of the principles on which they are grounded to which are added observations on short whist, also the games of Boston and euchre.* The book was written by

Thomas Matthews and published in 1844 in Philadelphia, PA, by Isaac M. Moss. It contained 96 pages, 75 of which were devoted to whist.

7726. Billiards book was *Billiards Without a Master: a full and complete set of rules for the government of the game of billiards and the various games of pool, etc; hints to players, advice to amateurs, keepers of saloons, etc.*, by Michael Phelan, containing 127 pages and 50 copperplate diagrams. It was published in 1850 in New York City by D.D. Winant.

7727. Billiard match of importance was played on May 13, 1854, for a $200 stake at Malcolm Hall, Syracuse, NY, by Joseph N. White of New York City and George Smith of Watertown, NY. It was a four-ball carom game, 500 points up, on a 6-by-12-foot, four-pocket table. White won by a score of 500–484. The score of runs and averages was not kept.

7728. Chess tournament of importance was held from October 6 to November 10, 1857, by the American Chess Congress in New York City under the sponsorship of the New York Chess Club. The victor of the Grand Tournament was Paul Charles Morphy, who received the first prize, a silver service consisting of a pitcher, four goblets, and a salver.

7729. International chess champion from the United States was Paul Charles Morphy, 20 years old, of New Orleans, LA, who won first place at the chess tournament organized by the American Chess Congress, held in New York City from October 6 to November 10, 1857. In the years 1857–59, he played 95 games, including 68 victories, 14 draws, and 13 losses. He won the Grand Tournament of the First National Chess Association in England and France, held from July 19 to August 22, 1858. Technically, however, the world chess championship did not formally exist at that time. The first player to hold that title was Wilhelm Steinitz, in 1866.

7730. Real estate board game was The Landlord's Game, invented by Quaker activist Lizzie J. Magie (later known as Elizabeth Magie Phillips) to teach the principles advanced by the Single Tax advocate Henry George. All the properties on the board were available for rent, and as the game progressed, the landlords were enriched at the expense of the tenants. Magie received a patent for the game on January 5, 1904. It was afterwards adapted by Charles B. Darrow of Germantown, PA, and sold to the game company Parker Brothers, which began marketing it under the name Monopoly on November 5, 1935.

7731. Crossword puzzle was prepared by Arthur Wynne and was published in the Sunday supplement of the *New York World* of December 21, 1913.

7732. Auction duplicate bridge championship was held on July 9, 1914, at the Lake Placid Club, Lake Placid, NY. The four-man team of the New York Bridge Whist Club defeated the team of the Knickerbocker Whist Club of New York City by seven tricks on 48 boards to win the American Whist League's Hamilton Trophy, symbolic of the whist championship of the United States and Canada.

7733. Chess champion to play more than 100 games simultaneously was Frank James Marshall of New York City, who met 105 local players at the National Press Club, Washington, DC, on March 21, 1916. He won a total of 82 games, lost 8, and drew 15.

7734. Crossword puzzle book was the *Crossword Puzzle Book*, published by Simon and Schuster, New York City, on April 18, 1924. It was edited by Prosper Buranelli, F. Gregory Hatswick, and Margaret Petherbridge. It was an anthology of 50 puzzles from the *New York World*.

7735. Book on the game of bridge was *Laws of Contract Bridge 1927*, which was adopted and issued by the Whist Club, New York City. It was published by John C. Winston Company, New York City, and contained 57 pages. The rules became effective on September 15, 1927. The game was invented in 1925 by Harold Stirling Vanderbilt.

7736. Crossword game was Lexiko, developed beginning in 1931 by Alfred Mosher Butts after he was laid off from his New York job as an architect during the Depression. Lexiko consisted of a set of 100 wooden tiles, each displaying a letter of the alphabet, which players would arrange to make nine-letter words. The quantities of each letter were intended to reflect the frequency of their appearance in English words. Unable to find a company willing to manufacture his game, Butts spent years improving it. The result was called Criss-Cross Words. In 1947 he sold the rights to an entrepreneur, James Brunot, in exchange for a royalty. Brunot renamed the game Scrabble and licensed it to the game manufacturer Selchow & Righter. The popularity of the game took off in 1953 and has not abated since.

7737. Bridge table to shuffle and deal cards by electricity was patented on November 29, 1932, by Laurens Hammond of Chicago, IL, who obtained a patent for a "card table with an automatic dealing device." The unshuffled cards were placed in a sliding drawer that started the mechanism and delivered 13 cards to each player. The entire mechanism was concealed in the table. The table was manufactured by the Hammond Clock Company Chicago, IL, which marketed it in 1932.

7738. Bridge hand in which each player was dealt a perfect hand of 13 cards of the same suit occurred on March 12, 1954, at Cranston, RI. Irene Motta bid seven hearts and won the bid.

7739. Checkers champion of renown was Marion Tinsley of Tallahassee, FL, widely regarded as the best checkers player in history. A mathematics professor at Florida State University, Tinsley lost only nine games after winning his first world championship in 1955. In the final years of his career, there was no human opponent in his class. His last titles were won against checkers-playing computers.

7740. Billiard player to win a match in the first inning was Willie Mosconi of Philadelphia, PA, who ran 150 balls on April 17, 1956, at Kinston, NC, following the break by Jimmy Moore of Albuquerque, NM, who played a safety shot. Mosconi won each of his 14 matches and scored a 150–0 victory in the final match of the world pocket billiards tournament.

7741. Computer game was SPACEWAR, invented by Steve Russell, a graduate student at the Masschusetts Institute of Technology, Cambridge, MA, and first demonstrated publicly in 1962 at the university's Spring Open House. The game was based on the science-fiction stories of E. E. "Doc" Smith. Players used joysticks to control a computer graphics display showing two spaceships shooting at each other. The processing was done by a Digital Equipment Corporation PDP-1 minicomputer.

7742. Video game that was commercially successful was the arcade game Pong, an electronic version of ping-pong created by 29-year-old computer engineer Nolan K. Bushnell. Pong was introduced in 1972 by Bushnell's company, Atari Corporation. Bushnell placed the first unit in Andy Capp's Tavern in Sunnyvale, CA, where it was an instant hit. Pong became a national craze, making Bushnell a multimillionaire and inaugurating the video game industry. An early, noncommercial version of Pong was invented in 1958 by William Higinbotham, head of instrumentation design at the Brookhaven National Laboratory, Upton, NY. It was not patented.

7743. World chess champion from the United States was Robert James "Bobby" Fischer, born in Chicago, IL, in 1943. In 1972, Fischer captured the world championship title from Soviet grandmaster Boris Spassky at Reykjavik, Iceland. The score was 12.5 games to 8.5. Fischer won a record purse of $250,000. In 1992, Fischer defeated Spassky for a second time in an exhibition match held in Yugoslavia.

7744. Role-playing game was Dungeons and Dragons, invented by traveling salesman Gary Gygax and his friend Dave Arneson in 1973. To play the game, which required only a pair of dice and a rule book, players took on the roles of characters in a sword-and-sorcery fantasy and kept score according to elaborate rules of interaction. Many of the ideas in Dungeons and Dragons were based on *The Lord of the Rings* and other books by the English writer J. R. R. Tolkien. Gygax and Lorraine Williams formed a company, Tactical Studies Rules Hobbies, better known as TSR, to market the game.

7745. Chess computer to beat the world chess champion was Deep Blue, developed by a team of International Business Machines researchers based in Yorktown Heights, NY. Deep Blue was capable of evaluating 200 million chess moves per second, and could project every possible move within 10 to 15 moves. On February 10, 1996, in Philadelphia, PA, Deep Blue won the first game of a six-game match against Garry Kasparov, the world's ranking grandmaster. It was the first time a machine defeated the top human player under championship conditions. In that match, the computer won one game, lost three, and tied two. On May 11, 1997, Deep Blue won a rematch held at the Equitable Center in New York City. Kasparov, one of the strongest chess players in history, resigned the sixth and final game after just 19 moves. It was the first time that he was defeated in a multi-game match by any opponent, human or machine. The final score was 3.5 to 2.5 games. The match was officiated by the Association for Computing Machinery's chess committee.

7746. Chess grandmaster who was African-American was Maurice Ashley of Brooklyn, NY, a Jamaican-born immigrant who had been playing and studying chess since his teens. He earned the rank of grandmaster on March 15, 1999, in a tournament sponsored by the Manhattan Chess Club. The title of grandmaster is awarded by the International Chess Federation.

Golf

7747. Golf clubs for hitting balls are mentioned in an account of the estate of William Burnet, governor of New York and Massachusetts, who died in 1729. Among his possessions were "Nine Golf clubs, one iron ditto and seven dozen balls."

7748. Golf players' club was formed in Charleston, SC, in 1786.

7749. Golf mixed foursome was played on March 30, 1889, at the Grey Oaks course of the St. Andrews Golf Club, Yonkers, NY. John B. Upham and Carrie Low played John Reid and Mrs. John G. Reid.

7750. Golf course with nine holes was completed at Brenton's Point, near Newport, RI, in 1890.

7751. Golf course with 18 holes was designed and constructed by Charles Blair Macdonald for the Chicago Golf Club at Wheaton, IL. It was opened for play in 1893.

7752. Golf magazine was *Golfing*, a weekly that was introduced in 1894 in New York City by William L. Dudley, editor and publisher. It contained 32 pages and sold for 10 cents a copy or $4 a year.

7753. National championship stroke-play golf match was held on September 3–4, 1894, at the Newport Country Club, Newport, RI. The championship was won by W. G. Lawrence with a score of 188. The runner-up was Charles Blair Macdonald, whose score was 189.

7754. Amateur golf tournament was played on the Grey Oaks course of the St. Andrews Golf Club, Yonkers, NY, on October 13, 1894. Thirty-two contestants played an 18-hole match. The winner was Lawrence B. Stoddard of St. Andrews Golf Club, one up, and the runner-up was Charles Blair Macdonald of Chicago, IL. The first amateur tournament officially held under the rules of the United States Golf Association was played on October 12, 1895, at the Newport Country Club, Newport, RI. There were 32 entries. The winner was Charles Blair Macdonald and the runner-up Charles E. Sands.

7755. National golf association of importance was the United States Golf Association, formed in New York City on December 22, 1894, by the following charter members: Newport Golf Club, Newport, RI; Shinnecock Hills Golf Club, Southampton, NY; the Country Club, Brookline, MA; St. Andrews Golf Club, Mount Hope, NY; and the Chicago Golf Club, Wheaton, IL. The first president was Theodore A. Havemeyer of the Newport Golf Club.

7756. Golf book was *Golf in America*, a practical manual by James Parrish Lee, published on May 25, 1895, by Dodd, Mead and Company, New York City. It consisted of 194 pages and a frontispiece.

7757. Open golf championship tournament sponsored by the United States Golf Association was held on October 4, 1895, at the New Newport Country Club, Newport, RI. It was won by Horace Rawlins, age 19, of the club. His score was 173 for 36 holes (45–46–41–41). Rawlins defeated 10 professionals and 1 amateur. He won $150 and a gold medal.

7758. Amateur golf championship tournament for women was won by Mrs. Charles R. Brown in November 1895 at the Meadow Brook Golf Club, Westbury, NY. There were 13 entries in the unofficial match. Mrs. Brown scored 132 for 18 holes.

7759. Golf player in an official amateur tournament who was African-American was John M. Shippen, 16 years old, who played in a tournament held on July 18, 1896, at the Shinnecock Hills Golf Club, a 4,423-yard course in Southampton, NY, where he worked as a caddie. His score was 159 (78 and 81). The first prize of $200 was won by James Foulis of Chicago, IL, whose score was 152 (78 and 74).

7760. Golfer to win the United States Women's Amateur Championship was Beatrice Hoyt, who won by seven strokes at the Morris Country Club, Morristown, NJ, on October 7–9, 1896; by six strokes at the Essex Golf Club, Manchester, MA, on August 24–26, 1897; and by eight strokes at the Ardsley Golf Club, Ardsley, NY, on October 11–16, 1898.

7761. Intercollegiate golf association was formed in January 1897 by representatives from Columbia, Harvard, Princeton, and Yale. The first tournament was held on May 13–14, 1897, at the Ardsley Casino Golf Club, Ardsley-on-Hudson, NY. The team championship was won by Yale; the individual championship was won by Louis Pintard Bayard, Jr., of Princeton's class of 1898.

7762. Golf champion born in America to win the United States Amateur Golf Championship was Herbert M. Harriman of the Meadow Brook Golf Club, Hempstead, NY, who on July 8, 1899, defeated Findlay S. Douglas, the defending champion, by a score of 3–2. Ninety-eight entrants participated in the tournament, the fifth United States Championship, which was played at the Onwentsia Club, Lake Forest, IL. Harriman's scores were 81 and 82.

7763. Golf tee was invented by George F. Grant of Boston, MA, who obtained a patent on December 12, 1899, on a wooden tee with a tapering base portion and a flexible tubular concave shoulder to hold the golf ball.

7764. Professional open golf championship match under the rules of the United States Golf Association was held June 14, 15, and 17, 1901, at the Myopia Hunt Club, Hamilton, MA. Willie Anderson and Alex Smith tied for first place with 331 for 72 holes. An 18-hole playoff was won by Anderson 85–86.

7765. Golf club with a steel shaft was invented by Arthur F. Knight of Schenectady, NY, who obtained a patent on November 22, 1910, on a golf club with tapered and tempered steel tubing.

7766. Golfer to win both the U.S. Open and the U.S. Amateur in the same year was Charles "Chick" Evans, Jr., who won the national open championship at the Minikahda Country Club, Minneapolis, MN, on June 27th, 29th, and 30th, 1916, with a score of 286 (70, 69, 74, and 73), and the amateur championship at the Merion links, Philadelphia, PA, on September 9, 1916, defeating Bob Gardner 4 up 3 to play in the final round.

7767. Professional Golfers Association tournament was held from October 10 to October 14, 1916, at the Siwanoy Golf Club, Mount Vernon, NY, by James "Long Jim" Barnes of the Whitemarsh Country Club, Philadelphia, PA, who defeated runner-up Jock Hutchinson at medal play, one up. Barnes won the Rodman Wanamaker trophy, $500, a diamond-studded gold medal, and custody of a huge silver cup. There were 31 players in the 36-hole tournament.

7768. Golfer to play 180 holes in one day was Edward Styles, who started the marathon contest at 5:53 A.M. on July 11, 1919, at the Old York Road Country Club, Philadelphia, PA, played 180 holes, 10 rounds of golf, in 796 strokes, and finished playing at 8:32 P.M. The average time per round was 1 hour 19 minutes, the total playing time 13 hours 10 minutes. He walked nearly 40 miles and took time out three times for a change of shoes and for refreshments. His average score was 79.6 strokes per round.

7769. Golf champion to win both the U.S. Open and the Professional tournaments was Gene Sarazen, who won the United States Open Golf Championship on July 15, 1922, at the Skokie Country Club, Glencoe, IL, with a score of 288 for 72 holes, defeating 320 starters. He won the Professional Golfers' Tournament at the Oakmont Country Club, Oakmont, PA, on August 18, 1922, winning a diamond medal and a purse of $500.

7770. International golf match for the Walker Cup was held at the National Golf Links of America, Southampton, NY, on August 28–29, 1922. The course was 6,650 yards and 18 holes. The U.S. team, captained by William Clark Fownes, Jr., obtained eight points, five points in the singles and three points in the foursomes, while the team from Great Britain and Ireland, captained by R. Harris, obtained four points, three points in the singles and one point in the foursomes. The cup was presented by George Herbert Walker, president of the United States Golf Association. An informal competition had been held the preceding year.

7771. Miniature golf course is said to have been built in 1929 by John Garnet Carter near Chattanooga, TN. The greens were made of a compound of cottonseed hulls dyed green. Carter patented the name "Tom Thumb," which was the trade name of a midget golf course system that was leased and sold as an amusement game device. Small golf courses with fewer than nine holes and courses with short holes, however, had been established previously. The Tom Thumb system presented hazards, obstacles, and so on. The game was played exclusively with a putter.

7772. Golf champion to hold the four highest golf titles at one time was Bobby Jones of Atlanta, GA, who won the British Open Championship at Hoylake, England, on June 20, 1930; the British Amateur at St. Andrews, Scotland, on May 31, 1930; the United States Open at Minneapolis, MN, on July 12, 1930; and the United States Amateur at Philadelphia, PA, on September 27, 1930.

7773. Golfer born in America to win the British Women's Amateur Golf Tournament was Babe Didrikson Zaharias, who defeated Jacqueline Gordon on June 12, 1947, at Kullane, Scotland, to win the championship.

7774. Golfer to break 60 for 18 holes in a major tournament was Sam Snead, who shot a 59 (31 out, 28 coming home), 11 strokes under par, in the third round of the Sam Snead Festival golf tournament at White Sulphur Springs, WV, on May 16, 1959. He had a score of 196 for 54 holes and won $4,500. The tournament was originally named the Greenbrier Open.

7775. Golfer to play 24 hours continuously on a regulation course was James J. Johnson of Fort Worth, TX, who played 363 holes at the 6,101-yard course of the Abilene Country Club, Abilene, TX, on October 14–15, 1959. The rules enabled him to walk or run.

7776. Golfer to earn over $100,000 in one year in regular tournaments was Arnold Palmer, whose winnings in 1963 were $130,835, of which $128,230 was won in 20 official events and $2,605 in nine unofficial events.

7777. Illuminated nine-hole regulation golf course was the 3,230-yard course of the Tall Pines Golf Club, Sewell, NJ, illuminated on August 23, 1963, by 121 mercury flood lights of 1,000 watts each. It was a private course by day and open to the public at night.

7778. Sport played on the moon was golf. On January 31, 1971, astronaut Alan B. Shepard, Jr., commander of Apollo 14, used a six-iron to hit a golf ball on the moon. In the low lunar gravity, the ball kept going until it was far out of sight.

7779. Golfer to earn $100,000 in a contest was Miller Barber of Texas, who won the first prize of $100,000 in 144 strokes in the World Open at Pinehurst, NC, on November 8–17, 1973.

7780. Golfer to break 60 in a Professional Golfers Association tour was Allen L. Geiberger of California, who shot a 59 on June 10, 1977, in the second round of the Danny Thomas Memphis Open at the Colonial Country Club course, Memphis, TN (7,249 feet; par 72). His score was 273 and he won $40,000.

7781. Golfer to shoot below his age on a Professional Golfers Association Tour was Sam Snead, age 67, who shot a 66 on the fourth day of the Quad Cities Open tournament at Coal City, IL, on July 22, 1979. His score was 277 (70, 67, 74, and 66).

7782. Golf champion of African-American and Asian ancestry was Tiger Woods, 18, who won the U.S. Amateur Golf Championship, held at the Tournament Players Club–Sawgrass Stadium course in Ponte Vedra, FL, on August 28, 1994. He defeated 22-year-old Trip Kuehne to become the youngest winner in the 99-year history of the event. Woods went on to win two more amateur championships before turning professional in 1996. On April 13, 1997, Woods won the Masters Tournament at the Augusta National Golf Club, Augusta, GA, becoming at age 21 the youngest person ever to do so. His final round of 69 gave him a total score of 270, or 18 under par, the lowest in the history of the event. Woods's grandparents were African-American, Chinese, and Thai.

Gymnastics

7783. Gymnastics book was *Gymnastics for Youth; or a practical guide to healthful and amusing exercises for the use of schools*, by Johann Christoph Friedrich Guts Muths, translated from the original work in German, but erroneously credited to Christian Gotthelf Salzmann. It was published in 1802 by William Duane, Philadelphia, PA. It was illustrated with copper plates and contained 432 pages.

7784. Gymnasium to offer systematic instruction was started by the Round Hill School, Northampton, MA, which was opened on October 1, 1823, by John Green Cogswell and George Bancroft. Charles Beck was the instructor in Latin and gymnastics. Gymnastics was scheduled from 5 P.M. to 7 P.M.

7785. Gymnastics instruction at a college was offered in 1826 at Harvard University, Cambridge, MA. Charles Theodore Christian Follen, professor of German, was appointed superintendent of the gymnasium. He introduced Friedrich Ludwig Jahn's system of gymnastics.

7786. Gymnastics instruction at a college for women was offered in 1862 by Mount Holyoke College, South Hadley, MA. The first teacher of gymnastics was a Miss Evans. During the first year, the course was optional, and the instruction was given "in the long storeroom over the wood and coal shed at the northwest corner of the court." A gymnasium was erected in 1865. Courses in calisthenics had been introduced in 1835, but were replaced by the Dio Lewis system of gymnastics.

7787. Trampoline commercially manufactured was produced in 1937 by the Nissen Trampoline Company, Cedar Rapids, IA, a company founded by George P. and Paul F. Nissen. They were known as bouncing nets, bouncing tables, and rebound tumblers. The name was derived from the Spanish word for diving board.

Horse Racing

7788. Horse race run on a regular basis was held on the Newmarket Course, Hempstead Plains, NY, in 1665, when Governor Richard Nicolls, the first English governor of New York, established the course. He issued the order to measure off a mile course on the level prairie near the village and gave a cup to reward the owner of the swiftest-running horse, "not so much for the divertisement of youth as for encouraging the bettering of the breed of horses, which through neglect has been impaired."

7789. Horse racing ban by a colony was enacted on June 4, 1674, by Massachusetts. It provided "that whatsoever p'son shall run a race with any horse in any street or Comon road shall forfeite five shillings in Mony forthwith to be levied by the Constable or set in the stockes one houre if it be not payed."

7790. Horse breeders' society was the Massachusetts Society for Encouraging the Breed of Fine Horses, formed in Boston, MA, in 1810. Annual trials and competitions were held on October 23–25 at Boston's Washington course. The rules provided that "every driver shall be dressed at starting neatly with a jockey cap, silk jacket with sleeves."

7791. Horse race trotting course was established at Jamaica, NY (now part of the borough of Queens, New York City), in 1825 by the New York Trotting Club. On May 16, 1825, the main race was won by Screwdriver.

7792. Horse racing magazine was the *American Turf Register and Sporting Magazine*, published in Baltimore, MD, by John Stuart Skinner. The first issue appeared in September 1829 and contained 56 pages. Its purpose was "to serve as an authentic record of the performances and pedigrees of the bred horse."

7793. Race between a locomotive and a horse-drawn vehicle took place on August 25, 1830, between Relay and Baltimore, MD, a distance of nine miles. The locomotive was the *Tom Thumb*, an engine of the Baltimore and Ohio Railroad, driven by Peter Cooper. The *Tom Thumb* was involved in an accident, and the horse won.

7794. Harness horse race at night was held at the Beacon Track, Hoboken, NJ, on October 5, 1843. The winner of the two-mile race for the $300 purse was Dutchman, who won in 5:19. Hiram Woodruff was the driver. Americus (George Spicer, driver) was second and Lady Suffolk (Dave Bryan, driver) was third, having previously run a dead heat.

7795. Horse bred in the United States to win a major race abroad was Prioress, a four-year-old bay mare, winner of the Cesarewitch Handicap at Newmarket, England, on October 13, 1857. There were 37 starters, of which 3 tied. In the runoff after the regular daily program, Prioress won by a length and a half (4 minutes 15 seconds for the 2-mile 468-yard course). The odds were 100–1. Her owner was Richard Ten Broeck.

7796. Steeplechase was held on October 26, 1869, at Jerome Park, Westchester County, NY, by the American Jockey Club. Seven horses participated. The race was won by Oysterman, Jr., a five-year-old owned by Colonel D. McDaniel. Between 15,000 and 20,000 spectators witnessed the inaugural race.

7797. Kentucky Derby horse race was run on May 17, 1875, at the Churchill Downs Course at Louisville, KY. There were 15 starters. Aristides won a $2,850 purse covering the mile-and-a-half course in 2 minutes 37.75 seconds. Oliver Lewis was the jockey. Volcano was second, Verdigris third.

7798. Horse whose total purses exceeded $100,000 was Miss Woodford, foaled in 1880. She won 37 of 48 races between 1882 and 1886 for a purse of $118,270.00. The mare was the entry of the brothers Michael and Philip Dwyer.

7799. Horse bred in the United States to win the English Derby was Iroquois, a three-year-old, winner of the Epsom Derby at Epsom Downs, England, on June 1, 1881. There were 14 competitors. Fred Archer was the jockey. The horse was owned by Pierre Lorillard IV, inventor of the tuxedo.

7800. American Derby horse race was held at Washington Park Club, Chicago, IL, on June 28, 1884. The race for three-year-olds was won by Modesty, whose time for the 1.5-mile course was 2 minutes 42.75 seconds. He won $10,700 in a field of 12. Isaac Murphy was the jockey.

7801. Coursing club was the American Coursing Club, which was organized at Topeka, KS, on July 9, 1886, with Colonel Taylor of Emporia, KS, as president. There were 38 entries at the first inaugural meeting, which took place from October 10 to October 23, 1886, at Great Bend. The first all-age stake winner was Midnight, owned by Colonel Taylor.

7802. Race between a horse and a bicycle was the Great Velocipede Race of 1888, run over a gravel road between Silver City and Deming, NM, a distance of almost 60 miles. H. J. Kennedy of Denver, CO, rode the bicycle. His competitors were Billy King, a cowboy, who rode a horse named Rattler, and a rider on a pinto horse. The pinto won. King came in second but was so exhausted he collapsed and had to be put to bed. The bicyclist was last.

7803. Horse race of 1,000 miles started at 5:30 P.M. on June 13, 1893, at Chadron, NE. The destination was Chicago, IL, via Long Pine, Oneill, and Wausa, NE; Sioux City, Galva, Fort Dodge, Iowa Falls, Waterloo, Manchester, and Dubuque, IA; and Freeport and De Kalb, IL. Each contestant was allowed two race horses, one to ride and one to follow. The winner, John Berry, riding Poison, arrived on June 27 at 9:30 P.M., followed on June 28 by Emmet Albright at 11:15 A.M. and Joe Gillespie at 1:31 P.M.

7804. Horse race mutuel ticket to pay more than $1,000 was made on June 17, 1912, at the Latonia track, Covington, KY, when Wishing Ring, a four-year-old colt, paid $1,885.50 to win, $744.40 to place, and $172.40 to show. Only four $2 tickets were sold. The colt was owned by J. S. Respess and won the sixth race; the odds were 900–1.

7805. Filly to win the Kentucky Derby horse race at Churchill Downs, Louisville, KY, was Regret, Harry Payne Whitney's chestnut filly. She ran the mile and a quarter in 2 minutes 5.4 seconds on May 8, 1915, to win the 41st Kentucky Derby. There were 16 starters.

7806. Horse to win the Triple Crown for three-year-olds was Sir Barton. In 1919 he won a total of $57,275. He won $20,825 in the Kentucky Derby, Churchill Downs, KY, on May 1; $24,500 in the Preakness, Pimlico, MD, on May 14; and $11,950 in the Belmont Stakes, Elmont Park, NY, on June 11. At Belmont a new track record was set for the mile and three-furlong course. The rider in all three races was J. Loftus, making him the first jockey to win the Triple Crown.

7807. Hambletonian harness horse race for three-year-olds was won by Guy McKinney, a four-year old, winner of $45,868.42 of the $73,451.32 purse in 2 minutes 5.14 seconds at the initial stake on August 30, 1926, at the New York State Fair, Syracuse, NY. The horse was owned by Henry B. Rea of Pittsburgh, PA, and driven by Nat Ray.

7808. Horse to win a $100,000 purse in one race was Whichone, a two-year-old, son of Chicle and Flying Witch, who won the 40th Belmont Futurity at Belmont Park Race Track, Elmont Park, NY, on September 14, 1929. The time was 1 minute 19.6 seconds for 6.75 furlongs (approximately 0.88 mile). The purse was $105,730. Harry Payne Whitney was the owner and Sonny Workman the jockey. There were 17 starters in the race.

7809. Electric-eye camera installed at a racetrack to measure photo finishes was placed in operation on January 16, 1936, at the Hialeah Race Course, Hialeah, FL. Called the Futurity Foto-Finish Camera, it was invented by G. Harry Adalian, a rug dealer from Boston.

7810. Electric starting gate for horse races was invented by Clay Puett, who installed a two-stall working model on May 8, 1939, at Hollywood Park, Inglewood, CA. The first full-size gate was used at Bay Meadows Race Track, San Francisco, CA, on October 7, 1939. The gates were equipped with a bomb-release type of lock operated by solenoids. The front doors when closed formed a V and opened outward by means of springs.

7811. Horse stakes race ending in a triple dead heat was the 46th running of the Carter Handicap, the sixth race at Belmont Park, NY, on June 10, 1944. It was seven-furlong race (about 0.875 miles) for horses three years old or older. The winning time was 1 minute 23.4 seconds. The $11.700 purse was split equally between Eric Guerin on Joe W. Brown's Brownie, Jimmy Stout on Belair Stud's Bossuet, and G. L. Smith on William Ziegler, Jr.'s Wait-A-Bit.

7812. Horse to win $1 million in races was Citation, a six-year-old bay colt born and owned by Calumet Farms, which won the $100,000 Hollywood Gold Cup Handicap at Hollywood Park, Inglewood, CA, on July 14, 1951. His total earnings in 1947–48 and 1950–51 in 45 starts, resulting in 32 firsts, 10 seconds, 2 thirds, and 1 unplaced finish, amounted to $1,085,760.

7813. Jockey to win the Triple Crown twice was Eddie Arcaro, who rode Whirlaway in 1941 and Citation in 1948 to win the "Big Three": the Kentucky Derby at Churchill Downs, Louisville, KY, the Preakness at Pimlico, MD, and the Belmont Stakes at Belmont Park, Elmont, NY. The combined purses amounted to $150,410 in 1941 and $324,090 in 1948.

7814. Jockey to win the Kentucky Derby five times at Churchill Downs, Louisville, KY, was Eddie Arcaro. He rode Lawrin on May 7, 1938, to win $47,500; Whirlaway on May 3,1941, to win $61,275; Hoop Jr. on June 9, 1945, to win $64,850; Citation on May 1, 1948, to win $83,400; and Hill Gail on May 3, 1952, to win $96,300.

7815. Perfecta or Exacta horse race in which bettors select the first two horses in the same race paid $30.40 for a $2 winning ticket on Wednesday, June 30, 1965, at Monticello Raceway, Monticello, NY. Bayard was first and Sonny Ardin second. There were 481 winning tickets; $17,242 was bet.

7816. Jockey who was a woman to win on a regular parimutuel flat track was Barbara Jo Rubin of Miami Beach, FL, who rode Cohesian in the ninth race (6.5 furlongs) on February 22, 1969, at the Charles Town Race Track, Charles Town, WV, in 1 minute 20.2 seconds. Rubin was also the first woman to ride two winners in one day. On March 8, 1969, at Waterford Park, Chester, WV, she won the 5.5-furlong race on Co Zipper in the second race and the 5-furlong race on Cohesian in the 11th race. Both horses were owned by D. Forrest Lawson.

7817. Horse race parimutuel in which all the jockeys were women was the six-furlong Lady Godiva $10,000 handicap at Suffolk Downs, Boston, MA, on April 19, 1969. The third race, in which $115.044 was wagered, was won by Penny Ann Early on Royal Fillet, which paid $5.40. Second place was won by Diane Crump on Destiny's Twist, third place by Tuesee Testa on Critical.

7818. Jockey who was a woman to ride in the Kentucky Derby was Diane Crump of Oldsman, FL, who rode Fathom on May 2, 1970, in the 1.25-mile 96th Kentucky Derby, Churchill Downs, KY. In the 17-horse race, she finished 15th.

7819. Horse race for a purse of more than $1 million was the All American Futurity for quarter horses held on September 4, 1972, at Ruidoso Downs, Ruidoso, NM. It was won by Possumjet, a chestnut filly two-year-old quarter horse owned by Jack Byers of Blanchard, OK. Pete Herrera was the jockey. Possumjet won $336,629.70 of the $1,035,900 purse and returned $44.60, $16, and $7.20 across the boards. The time for the 400 yards was 20:04 seconds. Attendance was 14,338.

7820. Jockey who was a woman to win a major stakes race was Robyn Smith, who won the six-furlong Paumanauk Handicap ($27,450) on March 1, 1973. She rode North

Sea, a four-year-old colt, winning by four lengths at the Aqueduct Race Track, Aqueduct, NY. The horse, owned by Alfred Gwynn Vanderbilt, paid $26.20 on a $2 ticket.

7821. Jockey who was a woman to win a Triple Crown race was Julie Krone, who won the 1993 Belmont Stakes in Elmont, NY, riding Colonial Affair.

Hunting

7822. Fox hunting club was the Gloucester Fox Hunting Club, composed of residents of Philadelphia, PA, and Gloucester County, NJ. A group of 27 dog owners met on October 29, 1766, in Philadelphia and decided to formulate rules for a club, which began its activities on January 1, 1767. John Massey, huntsman, was appointed to keep the dogs. The club dissolved in 1818.

7823. Sports book of importance was *The Sportsman's Companion, or, an essay on shooting; illustratiously shewing in what manner to fire at birds of game, in various directions and situations—and, directions to gentlemen for the treatment and breaking their own pointers and spaniels.* The book was published in 1783 in New York City.

7824. Game protection society was the New York Sportsmen's Club, founded on May 20, 1844, in New York City. B.J. Meserole was president. On March 10, 1873, it became the New York Association for the Protection of Game.

7825. Game preserve was established by Judge John Dean Caton of Ottawa, IL, about 1860, on his own estate. The preserve was well stocked with all kinds and species of American native game.

7826. Hunting license required by a state was mandated by New York in a law passed on April 30, 1864. Deer hunters in Suffolk County were obliged to pay $10 for a license, the money to be "paid over to the overseers of the poor of such town for the benefit of the poor thereof."

7827. Bird hunting regulation law enacted by Congress was passed by Congress on March 4, 1909. It amplified state protections by prohibiting the interstate transportation of birds, parts, feathers, and so on. The first federal law regulating the shooting of migratory birds, known as the McLean Law, was passed by Congress on March 4, 1913.

Ice Hockey

7828. Professional hockey team was the Portage Lake Hockey Club of Houghton, MI, formed in 1896. It became a professional team in 1903 under the leadership of Dr. J. L. Gibson, a dentist. In 1903, the team won 24 of the 26 games it played.

7829. Hockey team from the United States to win the Stanley Cup was the Seattle Metropolitans, Seattle, WA, of the Pacific Coast League of Canada, which defeated the Montreal Canadiens of the National Hockey League on March 21, 24, and 27, 1917, winning three of the four games played to decide the series.

7830. National Hockey League team from the United States was the Boston Bruins, admitted to the NHL in 1924. Previously, only Canadian teams had qualified for the organization.

7831. Hockey game to be shown on television was played on February 25, 1940, at Madison Square Garden, New York City, between the New York Rangers and the Montreal Canadiens. It was televised by station W2XBS, New York City. The Rangers won, 6–2.

7832. Professional hockey player to score 50 goals in one season was Joseph Henri Maurice "Rocket" Richard of the National Hockey League's Montreal Canadiens, who scored his 50th goal on March 18, 1945, in the 17th minute 45th second of the third and last period against the Boston Bruins at the Boston Garden, Boston, MA. He retired in 1960 with 544 goals in 16 regular seasons.

7833. Professional hockey player who was African-American was forward Willie O'Ree of the National Hockey League's Boston Bruins, whose first game was played on January 18, 1958, against the Montreal Canadiens at the Forum, Montreal, Canada. Boston won 3–0. O'Ree participated in two games in 1957–58 and 43 games in 1960–61, when he scored 14 points (4 goals, 10 assists). The first African-American player on an amateur team was

Arthur Dorrington, who signed with the Atlantic City Seagulls of the Eastern Amateur League on November 15, 1950, in Atlantic City, NJ, and played for them in 1950 and 1951.

7834. Professional hockey player to reach a score of more than 1,000 points was Gordie Howe of the National Hockey League's Detroit Red Wings, who made two goals on November 27, 1960, at Detroit, MI, in a game against the Toronto Maple Leafs, bringing his score to 1,001 points. He became the first player to score more than 100 points in one season in 1968, when he scored 103 points (44 goals, 59 assists). In his NHL career, Howe scored 786 goals and made 1,023 assists, for a total of 1,809 points.

7835. Goalie in a National Hockey League team to score a goal was Bill Smith of the New York Islanders. On November 28, 1979, in a game against the Colorado Rockies at the Nassau Coliseum in Uniondale, NY, Smith stopped a shot that rebounded and slid all the way down the ice into the opposing team's goal.

7836. Professional hockey player who was a woman was Manon Rheaume, a 20-year-old goalie from Quebec. In September 1992, she became the first woman to play in a National Hockey League game when she minded the net for an American team, the Tampa Bay Lightning, in the first period of an exhibition contest. She gave up two goals and made seven saves.

7837. Sports league to cancel a season over a labor dispute was the National Hockey League. On February 16, 2005, hockey commissioner Gary Bettman announced at a news conference in New York, NY, that the league would cancel the entire 2004–2005 regular season and playoffs, owing to an insoluble salary-cap disagreement with the players' union.

Ice Skating

7838. Ice skating champion was Charles June of Newburgh, NY, who defeated recognized English contestants in 1849.

7839. Ice skating club was the Skaters' Club of the City and County of Philadelphia, formed on December 21, 1849, at Stigman's Hotel, Philadelphia, PA. The first president was James Page.

7840. Figure skater of note was former ballet master Jackson Haines, known as the "American Ice Master." He was born in New York City and moved to Europe in 1865 after winning the men's ice skating championship. Haines revolutionized the sport of ice skating with balletic turns, glides, and spirals that were unknown to skating at that time. The "Haines Method" is the basis for modern figure skating.

7841. Indoor ice skating rink was built by Thomas L. Rankin at Madison Square Garden, New York City, in 1879. It had 6,000 square feet of surface. On February 12, 1879, a gala carnival was presented.

7842. International championship figure skating tournament was held on March 20, 1914, at the Arena Ice Rink, New Haven, CT, under the rules of the Skating Union of America. The ladies' championship was won by Theresa Weld of the Skating Club of Boston, MA, the men's by Norman Scott of the Winter Club of Montreal, Canada. Other events were pair skating to music and waltzing.

7843. Figure skating champion from the United States to compete in the Olympic Games was Richard Button of Englewood, NJ, who earned the title on February 5, 1948, at the Fifth Winter Olympic Games, St. Moritz, Switzerland.

7844. World figure skating champion from the United States was Tenley Albright of Newton Center, MA, who won the title on February 15, 1953, at Davos, Switzerland. She was 17 years old.

7845. Artificial ice skating rink of Olympic size was formally opened by Vice President Richard Milhous Nixon on February 18, 1960, at Squaw Valley, CA, for the Eighth Olympic Winter Games. Freezing brine was piped into the rink through 70 miles of steel tubing. It had 300 feet of roof floating on cables suspended from 80-foot steel and concrete pillars.

Motorcycling

7846. Motorcycle endurance run was held July 4–5, 1902, covering a distance of 254 miles from Boston, MA, to New York City, through South Framingham, Worcester, Warren, and Springfield in Massachusetts, and Hartford (where there was an overnight stop), Meriden, New Haven, Bridgeport, and Greenwich in Connecticut. Of the 32 entries, 31 started, 13 finished, and 7 made a perfect score of 1,000 points. The winner was George N. Holly of Bradford, PA, who arrived at 5:18 P.M. on July 5, followed half a minute later by N. P. Bernard of Hartford, CT. The race was sponsored by the Metropole Cycling Club of New York.

7847. Motorcycle hill-climbing contest was staged in Riverdale, NY, on May 30, 1903, and was won by Glenn Hammond Curtiss, who received a gold medal from the New York Motorcycle Club. The race created quite a sensation because it was not believed that a motorcycle had much power.

7848. Motorcycle association was the Federation of American Motorcyclists, organized on September 7, 1903, at Manhattan Beach, NY. The first president was R. G. Betts of the New York Motor Cycle Club. About 200 delegates attended the first meeting.

7849. Motorcycle racer who was a woman and who was licensed by the American Motorcycle Association was Kerry Kleid, 21 years old, of Rye, NY, who received license No. 143B on August 22, 1971. Her debut was made on October 17, 1971, in the Mt. Peter motocross, six miles north of Greenwood Lake, NY.

Olympic Games

7850. Olympic athlete from the United States to win a gold medal was James Brendan Connolly of the Suffolk Athletic Club of South Boston, MA, who represented the United States in the hop, skip, and jump (triple jump) contest on April 6, 1896, at the Olympiad in Athens, Greece, the first Olympic Games held in the modern era. His jump of 45 feet exceeded that of his nearest competitor by 3 feet 3 inches. The American team of 10 men won 9 of the 12 events.

7851. Olympic athlete from the United States to win 10 medals was Ray Ewry of Lafayette, IN, who won the standing high jump and the standing broad jump at the games held in Paris in 1900, in St. Louis in 1904, in Athens in 1906, and in London in 1908. At the Paris and St. Louis Games, he also won the hop, step, and jump (now called the triple jump).

7852. Olympic Games held in the United States was the Third Olympiad, held in St. Louis, MO, from May 14 to August 1, 1904. The games were first awarded to Chicago, IL, but were later given to St. Louis to be staged in connection with the World's Fair. There were few entrants other than Americans in the 14 events. In the field competitions, the American athletes made a clean sweep of all the events with the exception of lifting the bar and throwing the 56-pound weight.

Library of Congress

A flyer advertizing the 1908 Olympic Games.

7853. Olympic medalist who was African-American was George C. Poage of the Milwaukee Athletic Club, Milwaukee, WI, who participated in the Third Olympiad at St. Louis, MO, in 1904. He placed third in the 400-meter hurdles on August 31 and third in the 200-meter hurdles on September 1. The first African-American athlete to win an individual event in the Olympic Games was William DeHart Hubbard of the University of Michigan, who won first place in the running long jump competition on July 8, 1924, in the Colombes stadium in Paris.

7854. Olympic athlete from the United States to win the marathon race was John J. Hayes, who won the marathon of the London Olympics on July 26, 1908, with a time of 2 hours 55 minutes 18.4 seconds.

7855. Olympic athlete from the United States to win the pentathlon and decathlon was Jim Thorpe of Prague, OK. Thorpe, of Irish, French, and Native American descent (his mother was the granddaughter of the Sauk chieftain Black Hawk), achieved this feat at the Olympic Games in Stockholm, Sweden, in 1912. His medals were revoked in 1913 on a technicality concerning his amateur status. His winning status was restored in 1982.

7856. Olympic gold medalist from the United States who was a woman was Ethelda Bleibtrey, who competed in the Seventh Olympiad, held in Antwerp, Belgium, in 1920. She won the 100-meter free-style swim on August 25 and the 300-meter free-style swim on August 26.

7857. Olympic gold medalist in both the Summer and Winter Olympics was Edward Eagan. He captured the gold medal in the light-heavyweight boxing competition at the 1920 summer games in Antwerp, Belgium, and was also a member of the winning four-man bobsled team in the 1932 winter games, held in Lake Placid, NY.

7858. Olympic Games competition to be held in the winter was held at Lake Placid, NY. Governor Franklin Delano Roosevelt of New York opened the games on February 4, 1932. The participants included 307 athletes from 17 nations.

7859. Olympic athlete from the United States to win four gold medals in one year was Jesse Owens. In the Olympic Games held in Berlin, Germany in 1936, he won the 100-meter run on August 3, the broad jump on August 4, the 200-meter run on August 5, and the 400-meter relay on August 9. The relay team consisted of Owens, Ralph Metcalfe, Foy Draper, and Frank Wykoff. Owens was African-American, and his success was considered a rebuke to the Nazi ideology of the Germans who hosted the games.

7860. Olympic gold medalist who was an African-American woman was Alice Coachman, who set a record in the women's high-jump competition with a jump of 5 feet 6.125 inches at the 1948 Summer Olympic Games in London. She was one of 100 American athletes to be honored at the 1996 Centennial Olympic Games in Atlanta, GA.

7861. State to refuse to host the Olympic Games was Colorado. On November 7, 1972, 62 percent of state voters rejected a $5 million bond issue that would have allowed Denver to play host to the 1976 Winter Olympics. Concerns over cost and pollution appeared to be the chief reasons. The games were held in Innsbruck, Austria, instead.

7862. American boycott of the Olympic Games took place in 1980, when the United States refused to send its athletes to the Summer Olympic Games in Moscow to protest the Soviet Union's invasion of Afghanistan. On April 22, 1980, at the urging of President Jimmy Carter, the U.S. Olympic Committee voted 1,604 to 797 to boycott the games. The following day, a number of athletes and coaches filed a class-action suit in U.S. District Court in Washington, DC, to block the boycott, but the suit was dismissed on May 16. The Soviet Union retaliated by boycotting the 1984 Summer Olympics in Los Angeles, CA.

7863. Olympic athlete to win two consecutive heptathlon events was Jackie Joyner-Kersee, widely regarded as America's greatest female track-and-field athlete. She won her first gold medal in the heptathlon event in the 1988 Summer Olympic Games in Seoul, South Korea, and won the gold again in 1992 at the summer games in Barcelona, Spain.

Pinball

7864. Toy pinball game machine was the Caille Log Tavern, built in 1910 by Adolph Caille of the Caille Brothers Company, Detroit, MI. The machine, which was placed flat on a table, had a slightly inclined board with pins on it. Marbles were shot up the board through an alley to top position, and would then roll down into scoring positions.

7865. Pinball game machine was the Whoopee Game, manufactured in 1930 by the In and Outdoor Games Company, Chicago, IL. It was 24 inches wide and 48 inches long and had adjustable legs. It sold for $175. The fee for playing was five cents for 10 balls. The game was modeled after the children's game known as Bagatelle.

7866. Pinball ban enacted by a city was approved on June 19, 1939, by Atlanta, GA, and was signed by Mayor William Berry Hartsfield. The act provided that any person convicted of a violation of this ordinance be subject to a fine not to exceed $20 and a sentence to the public works of the city for a period of 30 days, at the discretion of the recorder.

Polo

7867. Polo club was the Westchester Polo Club, organized in New York City in 1876. Matches were played at the Jerome Park racetrack in Westchester County, New York.

7868. Polo mallets and balls were imported from England in 1876 by the newspaper publisher James Gordon Bennett, who introduced polo to the United States. The first games were played in Dickel's Riding Academy, at the northeast corner of Fifth Avenue and 39th Street, New York City. The horses were brought up from Texas by Harry Blassan, a New York riding master.

7869. International polo series was played at Newport, RI, on August 25, 1886, between teams representing England and the United States. England won the series of two games with scores of 10–4 and 14–2. The American team consisted of Captain Thomas Hitchcock, Raymond Belmont, Foxhall P. Keene, and W. K. Thorne.

7870. National polo association was the United States Polo Association, formed on June 6, 1890, in New York City, by the Meadow Brook Club, Westbury, NY; the Philadelphia Country Club, Bala, PA; the Rockaway Hunting Club, Cedarhurst, NY; and the Westchester Polo Club, Newport, RI. The first chairman was H.L. Herbert and the first secretary-treasurer was Douglas Robinson.

7871. Intercollegiate indoor polo championship was won by Princeton University, which defeated Yale University on March 18, 1922, at the Squadron A Armory, New York City. Each team consisted of three players.

Roller Skating

7872. Roller skates were invented by Dr. James L. Plimpton of Medfield, MA, in 1863. Plimpton's patented wooden skates had with four wheels each and were strapped onto ordinary shoes. They earned him more than $2 million in royalties and license fees.

7873. Roller skating rink open to the public was opened at Newport, RI, in 1866 under the auspices of James Leonard Plimpton of Boston, MA, the inventor of the Plimpton skate. The skating rink was located in the Atlantic House, at the corner of Bellevue Avenue and Pelham Street, on the site later occupied by the Elks' Home.

7874. All-metal roller skate was marketed by Everett Hosmer Barney. In 1864 he started a business in Springfield, MA, as Barney and Berry. In 1919 the capital stock was purchased by the Winchester Repeating Arms Company, which in 1922 moved the manufacturing business to its plant in New Haven, CT. Barney was the first to conceive and develop the idea of fastening shoes to skates by means of metal clamps. He obtained a patent covering his invention of a screw-clamp skate on January 16, 1866.

7875. Roller derby was the Transcontinental Roller Derby, which opened on August 13, 1935, at the Coliseum, Chicago, IL, under the direction of Leo A. Seltzer. Fifty contestants, paired two to a team, endeavored to skate a distance equal to the distance from New York to California.

7876. In-line roller skate that was commercially successful was invented by Minnesota students Scott and Brennan Olson in 1980. Rummaging through a sporting goods store, they discovered an old in-line skate and decided that it would make a good off-season hockey training tool. Their design, an ice-hockey boot with three in-line wheels instead of a blade, was called the Rollerblade.

Rowing

7877. College to feature rowing as a sport was Yale, New Haven, CT, which in 1844 held races between various classes and students.

7878. Intercollegiate rowing race in eight-oared boats took place on August 3, 1852, between Yale and Harvard on a two-mile course on Lake Winnepesaukee, Centre Harbor, NH. Harvard's lone entry, the *Oneida*, a 38-foot boat captained by Joseph Mansfield Brown, won by two lengths over Yale's *Shawmut*, followed by Yale's *Undine* and *Atlanta*.

7879. Racing shell was the *Harvard*, a six-oared 40-foot rudderless round-bottom boat of white pine. It was built in 1857 by James Mackay of Brooklyn, NY (now part of New York City), for the Harvard Boat Club of Harvard College, Cambridge, MA. It was 26 inches wide and weighed 50 pounds.

7880. Intercollegiate regatta was held on July 26, 1859, at Lake Quinsigamond, Worcester, MA. Harvard defeated Yale and Brown over a three-mile course. A regatta had been scheduled for July 23 of the previous year at Springfield, MA, but was postponed because a member of the Yale crew had drowned the day before.

7881. Coxswain of a men's college varsity rowing team who was a woman was Sally Stearns of Rollins College, Winter Park, FL. She led the shell on May 27, 1936, against Marietta College and on June 1, 1936, against Manhattan College. The crew lost to Marietta by four lengths and beat Manhattan by a half length.

Shooting

7882. National rifle society was the National Rifle Association, organized and chartered on November 24, 1871, in New York City with 35 members. Its first shooting meet was held on April 25, 1873, at Creedmoor, NY. The contestants included nine regiments of the New York National Guard, one regiment of the New Jersey National Guard, the U.S. Engineers, and a squad of regular servicemen from Governors Island. The first president of the association was General Ambrose Everett Burnside, who had commanded the Army of the Potomac during the Civil War.

7883. International rifle tournament of consequence was held on September 26, 1874, at Creedmoor, NY, between an American team commanded by Colonel George Wood Wingate and an Irish team commanded by Captain Arthur Blennerhassett Leech. Each team was composed of six men who fired 15 shots each at targets set at distances of 800, 900, and 1,000 yards. The targets had square bull's-eyes and scores were rated at 4, 3, and 2 according to position. The maximum score possible was 1,080 points. The Americans, represented by the Amateur Rifle Club of New York, used American breechloaders and won the contest by a score of 934–931 points. Captain Leech of the Irish team presented a cup to the National Rifle Association. In 1875 Princess Louise, on behalf of Queen Victoria, presented the association with the Wimbledon Cup, which has been the trophy since that date.

7884. Clay pigeon target for trapshooting was invented by George Ligowsky of Cincinnati, OH, who obtained a patent on September 7, 1880, on a concave slotted "flying target."

7885. Grand American Trapshoot tournament using live birds was held in March 1893 at Dexter Park, Jamaica, Queens, NY (now part of New York City), with 21 entries. The winner was R. A. Welch, who killed 23 out of 25 birds from a distance of 23 yards.

7886. Grand American Trapshoot tournament with clay targets was held at Interstate Park, Queens, New York City, on June 12, 1900, and was won by Rolla O. "Pop" Heikes of Dayton, OH, who scored 91 targets out of a possible 100 from a distance of 22 yards. There were 74 entries. Walter S. Beaver of Berwyn, PA, was the first shooter to win the Grand American from the extreme distance of 25 yards. On August 25, 1933, he broke 99 out of 100 targets.

7887. Revolver shooting tournament was held on June 16, 1900, between teams representing the United States and France. Each contestant had 30 shots at targets placed at

150 feet and 52.5 feet. The American team won by 61 points. Out of a possible score of 6,000 points, the Americans received 4,889 and the Frenchmen 4,828. The contest was held at the shooting range in Armbruster Park, Greenville, NJ, and Gastinne-Renett's pistol range, Paris. The scores were cabled to the opposing teams.

7888. National skeet tournament sponsored by the National Skeet Association was won by Lovell S. Pratt of Indianapolis, IN, who led a field of 114 in Solon, OH, on August 31, 1935, to win the national all-bore with a score of 244 out of a possible 250. Second place was won by Phip Conway of Green Village, NJ, with 242 points. The women's title was won by Esther Abbie Ingalls of Hot Springs, VA, with a score of 95 out of 100.

Skiing

7889. Ski club association was the Central Organization, formed by 10 clubs in 1891. The first meeting and tournament were held at Ishpeming, MI, on January 16, 1891. The National Ski Association of America was formed at Ishpeming on February 21, 1904, with Carl Tellefsen of Ishpeming as president.

7890. Steel ski jump was built in November 1908 at Chippewa Falls, WI. It was 98 feet high, with a concrete foundation above the ground that raised it to 100 feet. In 1910, the national ski tournament was held on this jump.

7891. International ski meet of importance was held on February 10–13, 1932, at Lake Placid, NY, during the Olympic Games. Finland and Sweden each won an event and Norway won two events.

7892. Ski tow made of rope was built by Robert Royce and placed in operation on January 28, 1934, at Woodstock, VT. About 900 yards of manila rope 0.875 inches thick was spliced together, passed over pulleys and around a wheel attached to a tractor, and extended up the hill 300 yards.

7893. Ski lift was the Cannon Mountain Tramway at Franconia, NH, a 5,410-foot suspension ride that opened on June 17, 1938. It was suspended by giant cables 40 feet above the trees and ran from the base of Cannon Mountain to one of its peaks. It had two cars, each accommodating 27 persons, which made the trip up or down in eight minutes at the speed of a thousand feet a minute.

7894. Skimobile ski lift was invented in 1937 by George Morton of Goodrich Falls, NH. A 3,000-foot section was placed in operation on December 27, 1938, by Cranmore Skimobiles at North Conway, NH. One hundred and fifty toy cars, each seating one or two persons, were conveyed up a wide wood and steel trestle by a 6,000-foot endless steel cable 0.875 inches in diameter, which was propelled by electric motors. On August 1, 1939, another 2,000-foot unit was added to propel 60 cars from the halfway station to the summit of Cranmore Mountain. The system had a capacity of 1,000 passengers per hour. The vertical lift from bottom to top was 1,367 feet.

7895. Indoor ski school was the Bob Johnson Ski Center, opened on October 16, 1939, in the Wells Memorial Building, Boston, MA. About 300 square feet were covered with a special form of crystal plastic invented by Robert H. Johnson of Boston, MA, who received a patent for it on July 3, 1951. Johnson subsequently opened a larger school of 7,000 square feet at Framingham, MA.

7896. Ski lifts to be regulated by the state were those of New Hampshire, which approved a regulation law on September 17, 1959. It mandated the registration, inspection, and approval of all ski-lift devices and established a tramway safety board consisting of four appointed members and the commissioner of public works and highways.

7897. Indoor ski slope was the Ski-Dek Center, Buffalo, NY, which opened on January 17, 1962, in a former movie theater. It consisted of a huge bank of endlessly moving slopes that were treated to simulate two inches of powdered snow on a firm base. It had nine slopes and could accommodate 144 skiers.

Soccer

7898. Soccer team entirely made up of Americans is believed to have been the St. Louis Kensingtons, of St. Louis, MO, formed in 1890. Soccer had been played for at least two centuries in the Americas, and an American team from New Jersey was fielded for an international soccer match in 1886, but until 1890 all American teams included foreign players.

7899. Professional soccer organization recognized internationally was the United States Football Association (now known as the United States Soccer Federation), formed on April 5, 1913, in New York City. The first president was G. Randolph Manning, elected in June 1913. Later that year, the association was recognized by the Federation Internationale de Football Associations, the international governing body of soccer.

7900. Soccer player to score 12 points in one game was Giorgio Chinaglia of the New York Cosmos, who scored five goals for two points each and two assists for one point each in a game played on August 10, 1976, at Yankee Stadium, New York City, against the Miami Toros. The final score was Cosmos 8, Toros 2.

7901. Soccer world champion who was a woman was Michelle Akers, who led the U.S. national women's soccer team to its first World Cup title in 1991, the first year the competition was held. It was America's first world championship in soccer since 1862. From the beginning of her career through 1995, she scored 82 goals in 87 international games, a feat unmatched in women's or men's competition.

7902. World Cup soccer tournament held in the United States began on June 17, 1994, with a game at Soldier Field, Chicago, IL. Fourteen nations competed in the marathon tournament, with games held in nine American cities. Brazil won the cup after defeating Italy at the Rose Bowl in Pasadena, CA.

Squash

7903. Squash rackets champion to win the U. S. A. Squash Racquets Singles championship was John A. Miskey of the Overbrook Golf Club, Philadelphia, PA, who won the championship in 1907.

7904. National squash tennis organization was the National Squash Tennis Association, formed by 14 charter members on March 20, 1911, at the Harvard Club of New York City. The first president was John W. Prentiss.

7905. Squash tennis tournament sponsored by the National Squash Tennis Association was held at the Harvard Club, New York City, on April 8–10, 1911. Forty entries from 13 clubs played. The champion was Dr. Alfred Stillman II, who defeated John W. Prentiss on April 10 by scores of 15–5 and 17–15.

7906. Squash rackets champion who was a woman was Eleanora R. Sears of the Harvard Club, Boston, MA, who won the U. S. A. Women's Squash Racquets Singles Championship at the Round Hill Club, Greenwich, CT, on January 16–19, 1928, beating her opponent in three of four matches. Forty players entered.

Swimming

7907. Swimmer of note was Benjamin Franklin. In 1724, Franklin, then 18 years old, went to London to buy equipment for the printing business he was starting in Philadelphia, PA. His swimming feats on the Thames River astonished Londoners, one of whom offered to open a swimming school with Franklin as teacher. Franklin, who was known in England as "the watery American," was the first American to skin dive, invented a wet suit and webbed sandals made of reeds, and experimented with water skis. He also wrote a book on how to swim.

7908. Swimming school was opened on July 23, 1827, in Boston, MA. A boat beyond the Toll House on the Charles River conveyed the students to the Mill Dam, where the school was located. It was open from 5:30 A.M. to 7 A.M., from 9 A.M. to 1 P.M., and from 4 P.M. to 8 P.M. The method of instruction was described as follows: "A belt is placed about the bodies, under the arms, attached to a rope and pole, by which the head and body are kept in the proper position in the water, while the pupil is learning the use of his limbs."

7909. Amateur open swimming championship meet was held on September 30, 1877, on the Harlem River by the New York Athletic Club, New York City.

7910. Swimmer to cover 100 meters freestyle in less than one minute was Johnny Weissmuller of the Illinois Athletic Club, who swam the course in 58.3 seconds on July 9, 1922, at the Neptune Beach Tank, Alameda, CA. In the 1924 Olympics, he won a gold medal with a time of 59 seconds, and repeated the performance in 1928 for another gold medal with a time of 58.6 seconds.

7911. Swimmer from the United States to swim the English Channel was Henry F. Sullivan of Lowell, MA, who swam from Dover, England, to Cape Gris-Nez, France, a distance of 56 miles, in 27 hours 23 minutes on August 5–6, 1923. Sullivan was the fourth man to swim the Channel.

7912. Swimmer who was an American woman to swim the English Channel from France to England was Gertrude Caroline Ederle, born October 23, 1906, in New York City, who accomplished the feat on August 6, 1926. She swam from Gris-Nez, France, to Kingsdown, Dover, England, in 14 hours 34 minutes, beating the world record by nearly two hours. She suffered permanent hearing loss during the swim.

7913. Swimmer who was a woman to swim the English Channel in both directions was Florence Chadwick of San Diego, CA, who swam from Cape Gris-Nez, France, to Dover, England, in 13 hours 28 minutes on August 8, 1950, and from St. Margaret's Bay near Dover to Sangatte, France, in 16 hours 22 minutes on September 10, 1951.

7914. Swimmer to swim the English Channel underwater was Fred Baldasare of Cocoa Beach, FL, who left Cape Gris-Nez, France, at 1 P.M. on July 10, 1962, and arrived at Pegwell Bay, southwest of Ramsgate, England, about 8:15 A.M. on July 11, a little over 18 hours later. He used aqualung equipment and received tanks of air from his helpers, and was guided by a frame towed beneath the surface. Baldasare, a specialist in underwater long-distance swimming, was also the first to swim underwater across the Messina Strait, the Oresund Strait, the Bosphorus Strait round-trip, the Hellespont, Algeciras Bay, and the Strait of Gibraltar (all from June to December 1962), and the Laguna del Sol (in June 1964).

7915. Swimmer from the United States to make a round-trip crossing of the English Channel was Ted Erikson of Chicago, IL, 37 years old, who swam from St. Margaret's Bay, England, to the beach near Calais, France, in 14 hours 15 minutes on September 21, 1965. He stopped for three minutes to receive a fresh coating of grease and returned in 15 hours 48 minutes, taking a total of 30 hours 3 minutes for the round-trip swim.

7916. Swimmer to cross the Bering Strait was 30-year-old Lynne Cox. In August 1987 she swam 2.7 miles across the Bering Strait from Little Diomede Island off the coast of Alaska to Big Diomede Island off the coast of Soviet Siberia. The water temperature was 34 degrees to 39 degrees F, cold enough to send most unprotected swimmers into hypothermia. Cox's thick layer of subcutaneous fat, rapid freestyle crawl rhythm, and outstanding cardiovascular fitness kept her alive. She wore neither wetsuit nor grease. Her swim was the longest intentional cold-water ocean swim on record, and the only one to cross the International Date Line, which runs between the two islands. It was also the first time an American had set foot on the Soviet island of Big Diomede since 1948.

Tennis

7917. Lawn tennis was introduced in March 1874 by Mary Ewing Outerbridge, who imported rackets and other equipment from Bermuda. It is said that customs officials were unable to determine under what section of the Tariff Act the equipment belonged, and after a week's indecision permitted it to enter duty-free. A court was laid out in 1874 at the Staten Island Cricket and Baseball Club, New Brighton, NY (now part of New York City), to which Miss Outerbridge's family belonged. The first players were members of the family. Within seven years, tennis had become popular, and on May 21, 1881, Eugenius H. Outerbridge, Mary Outerbridge's brother, organized the United States Lawn Tennis Association, to which 33 tennis clubs sent delegates. General Robert Shaw Oliver of the Albany Tennis Club was elected the first president.

7918. Court tennis was introduced in Boston, MA, in 1876 by Hollis Hunnewell and Nathaniel Thayer, who built a court on Buckingham Street. Ted Hunt, an English professional, was in charge. The game is played with a racket on a court 110 feet long and 38 feet wide, usually enclosed, with an elaborate layout.

7919. Tennis tournament of national scope was held on September 1–4, 1880, at Camp Washington of the Staten Island Cricket and Baseball Club, New Brighton, NY (now part of New York City). Twenty-three entrants competed for the first prize, a silver cup valued at about $100, inscribed "The Champion Lawn Tennis Player of America." It was won by O. E. Woodhouse of England.

7920. National tennis society was the United States Lawn Tennis Association, formed on May 21, 1881, at the Fifth Avenue Hotel, New York City, by 34 clubs. It formulated the rules of play, standardized the height of the net and the size of the ball, and ruled on such matters as the service line and the size of the court. The first president was Robert Shaw Oliver of the Albany Tennis Club. In 1975 the name was changed to United States Tennis Association.

7921. National tennis championship matches were held at the Newport Casino, Newport, RI, on August 31, 1881, by the United States Lawn Tennis Association, which introduced the first national uniform conditions. The singles match was won by Richard Dudley Sears, who defeated W. E. Glyn 6–0, 6–3, and 6–2. The doubles were won by Clarence Monroe Clark and Frederick W. Taylor.

7922. Intercollegiate lawn tennis match was held on June 7–8, 1883, at Hartford, CT, on the grounds of Trinity College. Joseph Sill Clark of Philadelphia, PA, won the singles. The doubles were won by Clark and Howard Augustus Taylor of New York City. The winners represented Harvard. At a second series, played on September 2, 1883, Howard Augustus Taylor won the singles and teamed with R. E. Presbrey to win the doubles.

7923. National tennis championship match for women run by the United States Lawn Tennis Association was an outdoor singles match held at the Philadelphia Cricket Club, Philadelphia, PA, in 1887. It was won by Ellen F. Hansell, who defeated Laura Knight 6–1 and 6–0. The first women's doubles championship was played in 1890 and won by Ellen C. and Grace W. Roosevelt.

7924. International professional tennis contest was begun at the Newport Casino, Newport, RI, on August 29, 1889. George Kerr, an Irish professional, defeated Thomas Pettit 6–3, 6–1, 6–1. Pettit won 6–4, 2–6, 6–3, 6–4 on September 21, 1889, at Springfield, MA. The third match was held at the Longwood Cricket Club, Brookline, MA, on September 25, 1889, where Kerr won 6–3, 3–6, 6–4.

7925. Tennis champions who were brothers were Carr Baker Neel and Samuel R. Neel of Chicago, IL. On August 18, 1896, they won the United States Lawn Tennis Association outdoor men's doubles championship at Newport Casino, Newport, RI, defeating Robert D. Wrenn and M. G. Chace 6–3, 1–6, 6–1, 3–6, 6–1.

7926. International tennis matches for the Davis Cup challenge trophy were held at the Longwood Cricket Club, Brookline, MA, on August 8–10, 1900, under the auspices of the United States Lawn Tennis Association. The Davis Cup was first won by an American team consisting of Malcolm Douglass Whitman, Dwight Filley Davis, and Holcombe Ward, all of Harvard, who won three matches to none, 10 sets to one, and 76 games to 50 against England. The tournament called for one doubles match and four singles matches. The United States won the first three matches (rain spoiled the other two) and was declared victorious.

7927. Tennis match broadcast on radio was the Davis Cup match between Australia and Great Britain, broadcast on August 4, 1921, from the Allegheny Country Club, Sewickley, PA, by station KDKA, Pittsburgh, PA.

7928. Tennis champion to win the Grand Slam of four major titles in one year was John Donald Budge of Oakland, CA, who achieved this feat in 1938. He won the Australian title in Adelaide on January 29, the French title in Auteuil on June 11, the British title at Wimbledon, England, on July 1, and the American title at Forest Hills, Queens, New York City, on September 24.

7929. Tennis tournament to be shown on television was the Eastern Grass Court championship tournament that opened on August 9, 1939, at the Westchester Country Club, Rye, NY. Station W2XBS, New York City, used a telescopic lens in addition to the iconoscope to obtain closeups of important points. The first one to be televised in color was the Davis Cup match between Australia and the United States that was held at the West Side Tennis Club, Forest Hills, Queens, New York City, on August 26, 1955, which was televised by station WNBT-TV of the National Broadcasting Company.

7930. Tennis champion who was a woman to win the Grand Slam of four major titles in one year was Maureen "Little Mo" Connolly of San Diego, CA, who achieved this feat in 1953. She won the Australian title at Melbourne on January 17, the French title in Paris on May 30, the British title at Wimbledon, England, on July 4, and the American title at Forest Hills, Queens, New York City, on September 7.

7931. Intercollegiate court tennis match was played on May 4, 1954, at the Racquet and Tennis Club, New York City, between Yale University and Princeton University. James Laughlin of Yale defeated Kenley Webster of Princeton, Charles Watson of Yale defeated Gary Nash of Princeton, and Dozier Gardner of Princeton defeated Robert Easton of Yale. On May 23, at Manhasset, NY, Yale defeated Harvard 4–3 for the challenge bowl donated by James H. Van Alen.

7932. Tennis champion who was African-American was Althea Gibson, a sharecropper's daughter who grew up in New York City. In 1950, she became the first African-American tennis player to enter the U.S. Open tennis tournament at Forest Hills, Queens, New York City, and a year later, she became the first to play in the Wimbledon tournament in England. She won the women's singles championships at Wimbledon and Forest Hills in 1957 and again in 1958.

7933. Athlete who was a woman to earn more than $100,000 in one season was tennis player Billie Jean King, who earned $117,400 in 1971. That year, she won the U.S. Open women's singles and mixed doubles and the Wimbledon women's doubles and mixed doubles, as well as a number of other tournaments.

7934. Athlete who was a woman to earn more than $1 million in a year was Czech-born tennis star Martina Navratilova, who passed that landmark in 1982. In 1984 she earned $2,173,556 in prize money, the fourth highest gross for any athlete in any sport that year, and the highest for a woman in any sport up to that time. Her total prize earnings at the time of her retirement from singles tennis in 1994 were more than $20 million.

7935. Major sports facility named for a woman was the U.S. Tennis Association National Tennis Center in Flushing Meadows Corona Park, New York City. On August 28, 2006, the center was officially renamed the USTA Billie Jean King National Tennis Center. King, the winner of 39 Grand Slam titles and many other championships, was instrumental in popularizing women's tennis.

Track and Field

7936. Athletic club was the New York Athletic Club, which was organized on September 8, 1868, at the Knickerbocker Cottage, Sixth Avenue and 28th Street.

7937. Amateur athletic games held indoors took place on November 11, 1868, at the Empire City Skating Rink at 63rd Street and Third Avenue, New York City, sponsored by the New York Athletic Club. The events included the 75-yard race, the 220-yard race, the 440-yard race, the half-mile race, the one-mile walk, the standing broad jump, the standing high jump, the running broad jump, the running high jump, the shot put, and standing three-jumps. During the intermissions, Dodsworth's Band played. The rink was 350 feet long, 170 feet wide, 70 feet high, and had accommodations for 10,000 spectators.

7938. Amateur athletic games held outdoors were held on October 21, 1871, by the New York Athletic Club on its grounds at 130th Street and the Harlem River. This site was used afterward for the foundations of the Harlem Bridge.

7939. Intercollegiate athletic association of importance was the Intercollegiate Association of Amateur Athletes of America, organized in Saratoga, NY, in June 1876, when a track meet was held. The charter members were Amherst, Bowdoin, Brown, City College of New York, Columbia, Cornell, Dartmouth, Harvard, Pennsylvania, Princeton, Trinity, Union, Wesleyan, Williams, and Yale. The association originated in 1873, when the newspaper publisher James Gordon Bennett offered a cup to the best track athlete among various college rowing crews.

7940. Intercollegiate track meet was held in Saratoga, NY, on July 20–21, 1876, under the auspices of the Intercollegiate Association of Amateur Athletes of America. The participating teams represented Bowdoin, the City College of New York, Columbia, Dartmouth, Pennsylvania, Princeton, Wesleyan, Williams, and Yale. A silver cup was awarded annually to the winning team. The first meet was won by Princeton with four firsts and four seconds. The cup was given permanently to Harvard, which won 8 of the first 14 meets.

7941. Amateur athletic competition was held on September 27, 1879, by the National Association of Amateur Athletes of America at the New York Athletic Club's grounds in Mott Haven, the Bronx, NY (now part of New York City). Twenty games were on the program.

7942. Sports trainer to work professionally was Bob Rogers, who was engaged by the New York Athletic Club on May 1, 1883. He had previously been a trainer with the London Athletic Club.

7943. Cross-country championships were run on November 6, 1883, under the auspices of the New York Athletic Club.

7944. Relay race in a college track meet was held by the New Jersey Athletic Club at Bayonne, NJ, on May 30, 1893, before 5,000 spectators. The one-mile team race was won by Harvard in 3 minutes 25.4 seconds, three seconds faster than the record. Princeton was second, Yale third. Four men constituted a team, and each team member ran 440 yards.

7945. Discus-throwing competition in modern times took place in 1896 at the Olympic Games in Athens, Greece. Robert Garrett of Princeton University, representing the United States, won with a record throw of 95 feet 7.5 inches.

7946. Marathon race held annually was the American Marathon Race, now called the Boston Marathon. It was first run on April 19, 1897. The course began in Hopkinton, MA, and continued through Ashland, Framingham, Natick, Wellesley, and Newton to Exeter Street, Boston, a distance of 26 miles 385 feet. The winner was John J. McDermott of the Pastime Athletic Club of New York City, whose time was 2 hours 55 minutes 10 seconds.

7947. Broad jump to reach more than 25 feet was made on July 23, 1921, by Edward O. Gourdin of Harvard College, who jumped 25 feet 3 inches during the International Meet at Harvard Stadium, Cambridge, MA. The participants at the meet represented Harvard, Yale, Oxford, and Cambridge.

7948. Transcontinental foot race was the brainchild of promoter C. C. "Cash and Carry" Pyle, who conceived of the ultimate marathon race, a coast-to-coast run that he dubbed the Bunion Derby. The first Bunion Derby started from Ascot Park, Los Angeles, CA, on March 4, 1928, and ended on May 26, on its 84th day, inside Madison Square Garden, New York City, where a final 20-mile contest was held. A field of 275 runners started the race, and 55 runners completed it. The first prize of $25,000 was won by Andrew Payne, a Cherokee of Claremore, OK, whose time for the 3,422.3 miles was 573 hours 4 minutes 34 seconds. The runner-up and winner of the $10,000 prize was Long John Salo of Passaic, NJ, whose time was 588 hours 40 minutes 13 seconds. Philip Granville was third and won $5,000; Mike Joyce, fourth, won $2,500. Six additional prizes of $1,000 each were awarded.

Courtesy of Zserghei

Sculpture of a discus thrower, based on the original by Myron.

7949. Electrical timing device for foot races was tested on May 14, 1932, at Baker Field, New York City, in three events, when Columbia University defeated Syracuse University in a track meet. The results, however, were not accepted as final.

7950. Intercollegiate track meet to be shown on television was the 19th annual Intercollegiate Association of Amateur Athletes of America track and field championship meet at Madison Square Garden, New York City, televised on March 2, 1940, by station W2XBS. Twenty-three colleges participated in the various events, which included dashes, runs, relays, high hurdles, shot put, pole vault, weight throwing, broad jumps, and high jumps. New York University won, with 27 points.

7951. Pole vaulter to clear the bar at 15 feet was Cornelius Warmerdam of the San Francisco Olympic Club, who established this record on April 13, 1940, at Berkeley, CA, at the triangular meet of Washington State College, the Olympic Club of San Francisco, and the University of California. In 33 meets, 8 indoors and 25 outdoors, he duplicated or bettered this mark 43 times from 1940 through 1944.

7952. High-jump standards using electric eye detectors were constructed by a team headed by Lyle Hudson Bennett Peer of the General Electric Research Laboratory. They were used on May 31, 1941, at the Schenectady Patrolmen's Association interscholastic track meet, Schenectady, NY. A series of four parallel beams of light, one inch apart, recorded the height of each jump.

7953. Shot-put toss over 60 feet was made at Los Angeles on May 8, 1954, when Parry O'Brien, formerly of the University of Southern California, tossed the 16-pound shot 60 feet 5.25 inches at the University of California at Los Angeles—Southern California Pacific Coast Conference dual meet.

7954. High jump over seven feet was made on June 29, 1956, at the Coliseum, Los Angeles, CA, by Charles Dumas, a 19-year-old Compton College freshman, who jumped an official height of 7 feet .5 inch.

7955. Runner from the United States to run a mile in less than four minutes was Don Bowden of the University of California, who ran the mile in 3 minutes 58.7 seconds at the Pacific Amateur Athletic Union Meet at Stockton, CA, on June 1, 1957. He was the 11th man in the world to better the four-minute mile. The first runner to accomplish this feat indoors was James Tully "Jim" Beatty of the Los Angeles Track Club, who ran the mile in 3 minutes 58.9 seconds in the *Los Angeles Times* indoor track and field meet at the Los Angeles Memorial Sports Arena, Los Angeles, CA, on February 10, 1962.

7956. Marathon runner from the United States who was a woman was Roberta "Bobbi" Gibb, the first woman to run in the Boston Marathon. Gibb applied to enter the 1966 race but was turned down by the Boston Athletic Association, which cited its rule banning women from competition. Race officials claimed that women were physically unable to run a marathon. On the day of the race, Gibb slipped into the pack at the start and finished in 3 hours 21 minutes 40 seconds. In 1967, she again ran without registering. Another woman, Katherine Switzer, officially entered the marathon that year by inaccurately completing the registration form. She became widely known as the first woman to run the race, although Gibb beat Switzer's time by 59 minutes. Gibb's achievement was acknowledged in 1984, when she was invited to start at the first Women's Olympic Marathon Trials.

7957. New York City Marathon was held on September 23, 1970, in New York City. Queens fireman Gary Muhrcke won the race, which consisted of four laps around Central Park. The course was later changed to run from Staten Island to Central Park.

Various

7958. Surfing took place in Hawaii, where it was a traditional pastime. The first written description of surfing, made in 1779 by 1st Lieutenant James King, a member of Captain James Cook's third expedition, recounted his observations of Hawaiians surfing in Kealakehua Bay off Hawaii's Big Island. The first surfers in Southern California were three Hawaiian princes who tried the surf at Santa Cruz, CA, in 1885.

7959. Archery club was the United Bowmen of Philadelphia, founded in 1825 by Franklin Peale, Titian Ramsey Peale, Robert E. Griffith, M.D., Samuel P. Griffith, Jr., Jacob

M. Morris, and Thomas Sully. The club was not formally organized until 1828, when membership was limited to 25. Members dressed in frock coats of Lincoln green ornamented with gold braid and wore broad straw hats with three black ostrich plumes. The first national organization was the National Archery Association, formed on January 23, 1879, in Crawfordsville, IN, by representatives of eight archery clubs. The first president was Maurice Thompson. The first grand annual meeting and the first tournament were held on August 12–14 in Chicago, IL, at which 20 women and 69 men competed. High score was made by Will H. Thompson, who won with 172 hits and a score of 624.

7960. Team sport played in America was lacrosse, a favorite game among Native American tribes. The racquet was a wooden stick with a curve or loop that held a net made of animal skin. The ball was made of animal hide stuffed with hair. Team sizes and rules of play differed from tribe to tribe, with some groups providing extensive training and coaching for their athletes. In 1830, after observing the Seneca of New York State play the game, a white writer, Robert Bently Howe, noted in his description: "The players handled their racquets with great dexterity and out-maneuvered their opponents with such art and adroitness that frequently several minutes passed before the ball flew clear."

7961. Coaching club to encourage four-in-hand driving was the Coaching Club, formed by nine men on December 3, 1875, at the Knickerbocker Club, New York City. William Jay was the first president. The first meet, in which six coaches participated, was held April 22, 1876.

7962. Coach riding as a pastime was brought to the United States in 1875 by Colonel Delancey Astor Kane. A coach called the *Tallyho* was built by Holland and Holland of London and imported to New York City. Its first trip, on May 1, 1876, started from the Hotel Brunswick, Fifth Avenue and 26th Street, New York City, and ended at the Arcubarius Hotel, Pelham, NY. The fare was $1.50 each way. Some coaches had been imported earlier.

7963. Croquet league was the National Croquet League, organized on February 12, 1880, in Philadelphia, PA. The first president was George Washington Johnson of the Lemon Hill Croquet Club. Representatives from 18 clubs attended to standardize the game. Wickets were reduced in size and the balls reduced in diameter.

7964. Intercollegiate lacrosse association was the Intercollegiate Lacrosse Association, organized on March 11, 1882, in Princeton, NJ, with Columbia, Harvard, New York University, and Princeton as charter members. Each college team was scheduled to play one game with every other member. George William Gilmore of Princeton was president.

7965. Softball game was played on November 30, 1887, at the Farragut Boat Club, Chicago, IL. The game was invented by George W. Hancock, who devised a set of rules that gradually developed as the game progressed. A broomstick was used for the bat and a boxing glove for the ball. The game was known variously as Diamond Ball, Fast Ball, Kitten Ball, Playground Ball, and Recreation Ball. It was named softball by Walter C. Hakanson.

7966. Medicine ball was invented by Robert Jeffries Roberts, physical education director of the Boston Young Men's Christian Association, in 1895, and first used in Boston, MA.

7967. Volleyball was developed in 1895 as a game by Physical Director William George Morgan of the Young Men's Christian Association, Holyoke, MA. The game, at first called mintonette, was played with a basketball bladder over a rope. Later, a lightweight leather-covered ball was adopted, and an eight-foot net was substituted for the rope. Rules were adopted locally until 1900, when the Young Men's Christian Association Physical Directors' Association Volley Ball Committee developed standard rules. The first rules were published in the *Physical Education Magazine* in July 1896.

7968. Log-rolling national championship tournament was held on September 9, 1898, on the lagoon at the Trans-Mississippi Exposition, Omaha, NE, on Lumbermen's Day, by the Lumbermen's Association of America. There were six entries. The winner was Tommy Fleming of Eau Claire, WI. Log rolling is also known as birling.

7969. Intercollegiate wrestling association was formed on April 7, 1905, at the University of Pennsylvania, Philadelphia, PA, through the efforts of Leonard Mason, an instructor in gymnastics, who visited other eastern universities in search of members.

The first tournament, held on April 7, 1905, in the gymnasium of the University of Pennsylvania, was witnessed by over 1,000 spectators. Yale won, Columbia came in second, Princeton was third, and Pennsylvania was fourth.

7970. International horseshoe pitching contest open to all was held in Bronson, KS, in the summer of 1909. The contest was held on dirt courts. Pegs were 2 inches high and were spaced 38.5 feet apart. Frank Jackson of Blue Mound, KS, was awarded the World's Championship belt with miniature horseshoes attached to it. The first association of horseshoe pitchers was the Grand League of the American Horseshoe Pitchers Association, organized on May 16, 1914, in Kansas City, KS, to standardize the rules. Pegs were raised to 8 inches and spaced 38.5 feet apart. Ringers counted five points and leaners three points. The association's first championship tournament was held on October 23, 1915, in Kellerton, IA, and was won by Frank Jackson with 24 out of 25 games.

7971. Transcontinental journey on foot made entirely in one trip was accomplished by Edward Payson Weston, a professional walker. Payson began his trek in New York City on March 15, 1909. He reached San Francisco, CA, after a 3,795-mile journey that took 104 days 7 hours. The feat was all the more remarkable because Weston was 70 years old at the time. The next year, he walked the return route from Los Angeles, CA, to New York City, completing the trip in 76 days 23 hours.

7972. Dance marathon began on March 31, 1923, at 6:57 P.M., at the Audubon Ballroom, New York City, and continued until April 1 at 9:57 P.M., when the winner, Alma Cummings, concluded 27 hours of continuous dancing to a live band and phonograph music. She danced the fox-trot, one-step, and waltz, and tired out six partners. The first dance marathon to exceed 200 hours took place in St. Louis, MO, later that year. The winner was Bernie Brand of Dallas, TX, who danced continuously for 217 hours, beginning on June 1 and ending on June 10. He outlasted 21 other entrants.

7973. Snowmobile patent was obtained by Carl J. E. Eliason of Sayner, WI, who received a patent on November 22, 1927, on a "vehicle for snow travel."

7974. Nudist organization was the American League for Physical Culture, organized by three men on December 5, 1929, in New York City. The first nudist summer camp was opened by the American League in Central Valley, NY, in June 1930. There were approximately 30 participants.

7975. Bobsled run of international specifications was the Mountain Van Hoevenberg run at North Elba, NY, on the highway between Lake Placid and Elizabethtown, NY, designed by Stanislaus Zentzytzki. It was built for the New York State Olympic Winter Games Commission at a cost of more than $200,000. Work was begun on August 4, 1930, and the run was opened to the public on December 25 . It contained 26 curves and was 1.5 miles long. About 29,000 gallons of water were needed every 24 hours to spray the run. The first two-man competition was held on February 9–10, 1932, at the Olympic Winter Games, with 15 teams from eight nations. First place was won by the United States team of J. Hubert Stevens, driver, and Curtis Stevens, brakeman, in 8 minutes 14.74 seconds for the four heats. The first four-man competition took place at the Games on February 14–15, with 13 teams from six nations competing. First place was won by the United States team of William L. Fiske, driver, and Edward F. Eagan, Clifford B. Gray, and Jay O'Brien, brakemen, in a contest which covered the four heats in a total time of 7 minutes 53.68 seconds.

7976. Shuffleboard championship tournament was won by Carroll L. Bailey of Richmond, VA, who defeated 25 state champions at St. Petersburg, FL, on March 27, 1931, to win the U.S. shuffleboard title.

7977. Badminton championship tournament was sponsored by the United States Badminton Association and played in April 1937 at the Naval Pier in Chicago, IL. A field of 150 entrants competed in singles and doubles matches. Walter R. Kramer won the men's singles title and Del Barkhuff won the women's singles.

7978. Instructor of Japanese karate was Tsutomu Ohshima of Japan, a student of Gichin Funakoshi, the founder of the Shotokan style of karate. In 1956, as an economics student at the University of Southern California in Los Angeles, Ohshima taught informal classes. The following year, he was awarded the highest rank in Shotokan, fifth-degree black belt, and started the first karate club at an American college, at the California Institute of Technology. In 1959 he founded the Southern California Karate Association, which became Shotokan Karate of American, a national organization.

7979. Flying disk for use in throwing games was the Frisbee Flying Saucer, invented by Walter Frederick Morrison and sold by the Wham-O Company of San Gabriel, CA, starting on January 13, 1957. Inspired by the UFO craze then sweeping the nation, Morrison devised a lightweight metal throwing disk that looked like a flying saucer. Later versions were made of plastic. The name Frisbee was given to the disks by Wham-O president Richard Knerr. While traveling in New England, he saw college students tossing pie plates with the name "Frisbie" embossed on them. These were manufactured for the Frisbie Pie Company of Bridgeport, CT, founded in the 1870s. Knerr copyrighted an alternative spelling, "Frisbee," and had it embossed on each Wham-O disk.

7980. National wheelchair games were held on June 1, 1957, at Adelphi College, Garden City, NY. The athletes were paraplegics (people paralyzed from the chest down) from Ohio, Pennsylvania, and nearby states, as well as Canada, who competed in team and individual events. Some of the winners were Tony Mucci, Pan American Jets, 60-yard dash; Al Slootsky, Jersey Wheelers, javelin throwing; Sol Welger, Pan American Jets, table tennis (singles); and Pierre Brousseau, Montreal Wheel Chair Wonders, archery. Other events, including shot put, bowling, weight lifting, discus throwing, and adapted swimming, were added in subsequent years.

7981. Weight lifter to lift more than 6,000 pounds was Paul Anderson, age 22. On June 17, 1957, in Toccoa, GA, Anderson backlifted off the ground a table holding heavy automobile parts and a safe full of lead. The total weight was 6,270 pounds.

7982. Tae Kwon Do instructor in the United States was Jhoon Rhee, a native of Asan in South Chungchoeong Province, Korea (now in South Korea). Rhee was a captain in the Korean Army when he came to the United States for his undergraduate education. He was an engineering student at the University of Austin, TX, in 1959 when he began teaching tae kwon do to 184 students. Allen R. Steen was the first American to achieve a tae kwon do black belt under Rhee, who himself attained tenth-degree Grand Master rank. On June 28, 1962, Rhee opened the first professional Tae Kwon Do school, in Washington, DC. Among his students were Bruce Lee and Muhammad Ali.

7983. Ascent of Mount Everest by an American that was successful was made by James W. Whittaker of Redmond, WA. He was a leading member of the first American Mount Everest Expedition, which attempted the summit in the spring of 1963, 10 years after Sir Edmund Hillary and Tenzing Norgay made the first ascent of the 29,028-foot peak. Whittaker and his Sherpa climbing partner Nawang Gombu reached the top of Mount Everest at 1 P.M. on May 1, 1963. The first successful ascent by an American woman was made by Stacy Allison of the Northwest American Everest Expedition, who reached the summit on September 29, 1988. Peggy Luce, who was part of the same expedition, completed her ascent two days later.

7984. Snowmobile to exceed a speed of 125 miles per hour was a 1972 Ski-Doo Blizzard X2R driven by Yvon Duhamel of Valcourt, Quebec, Canada. On February 11, 1972, he reached a speed of 127.3 miles per hour at the Boonville Airport, Boonville, NY.

7985. Round-the-world journey on foot was made by David Kunst, who walked 14,450 miles across four continents between June 20, 1970, and October 5, 1974. Another American, George Matthew Schilling, claimed to have made a round-the-world walk beginning on August 3, 1897, but his achievement has not been verified. A Christian preacher, Arthur Blessitt of North Fort Myers, FL, walked to all seven continents over a period of 25 years beginning on December 25, 1969.

7986. Softball game of 365 innings was played at Summerville Field, Monticello, NY, on August 14–15, 1976, between teams representing Gager's Diner and the Bend n' Elbow Tavern. The game began at 10 A.M. on Friday and continued until 4 P.M. Saturday, when it was called because of rain and fog. About 70 players, including 20 women, participated. Some $4,000 was raised for the construction of a new softball field and for the Community General Hospital. The Gagers made 832 hits and scored 491 runs; the Elbows made 738 hits, scoring 467 runs. There were 31 home runs.

7987. Iron Man triathlon took place on February 18, 1978, at Kona, HI. The 15 contestants were required to swim for 2.4 miles, bike for 112 miles, and run for 26.2 miles. The winner was Gordon Haller, who reached the finish line after 11 hours 46 minutes. No prize money was offered.

7988. Walk from Canada to Mexico along the West Coast was completed in 2004 by Sarah Janes and Nate Olive, ecologists from the University of Georgia. Their 1,800-mile, three-month journey along the West Coast Trail began on June 8, 2004, at Cape Flattery, in northwestern Washington state, and ended on September 29, 2004, at the U.S.–Mexico border fence at Border Field State Park, San Diego County, CA.

7989. American to climb all 14 mountains higher than 8,000 meters (the equivalent of 26,240 feet) was Ed Viesturs of Seattle, WA, a high-altitude specialist who, unlike many mountaineers, did not rely on bottled oxygen. On May 12, 2005, he completed his campaign to climb all 14 when he reached the summit of Annapurna in Nepal. In all, the effort took 16 years, beginning with his climb of Kanchenjunga in May 1989. All 14 highest mountains are in the Himalayas.

Water Skiing

7990. Water skis that were practical were invented in 1922 by Ralph W. Samuelson, who steam-bent two eight-foot-long pine boards into skis. He took his first ride behind a motorboat on a lake in Lake City, MN.

Benjamin Franklin theorized that a person wearing barrel staves on his feet could be towed along the surface of the water by a large kite. He never put the idea into practice.

7991. National water skiing tournament was held at Jones Beach State Park, Long Island, NY, on June 22, 1939. Bruce Parker of Garden City, NY, won the men's championship and Esther Yates of Amityville, NY, the women's championship. The events included the slalom, jumping, and trick riding.

7992. Water skier to jump 100 feet was Warren Witherell of The Weirs, a northern suburb of Laconia, NH, who jumped 106 feet at Laconia on August 15, 1954.

TRANSPORTATION

Aviation

7993. Tethered balloon flight made in the United States was made by Edward Warren, 13 years old, on June 24, 1784, at Baltimore, MD. Warren went up in Peter Carnes's balloon, 35 feet in diameter and 30 feet high, made of silk of various colors. The air was rarefied by a cylindrical stove of iron suspended under the balloon. Carnes attempted a flight on July 17, 1784, at Philadelphia, but the balloon burst into flames.

7994. Untethered balloon flight made in the United States was a 40-minute flight made by Jean-Pierre Blanchard of France. He left Philadelphia, PA, at 10:16 A.M. on January 9, 1793, in the presence of President George Washington and other officials. He was permitted the use of the Walnut Street Prison courtyard at Germantown, Philadelphia, PA. The roar of artillery announced the moment of his departure. President Washington presented him with an order "To all to whom these presents shall come" directing that he be allowed "to pass in such direction and to descend in such places as circumstances may render most convenient." The balloon reached about one mile in altitude. He landed in Deptford Township, Gloucester County, NJ, about 15 miles away. It was his 45th ascension.

7995. Parachute jump from a balloon in the United States was made by Charles Guille, who ascended on August 2, 1819, from Vauxhall Gardens, New York City, in a wicker basket decorated with flowers and suspended from a 25,000-cubic-foot prepared-silk balloon that cost $3,000. Avoiding a squall, he jumped from a height of two miles with an umbrella-shaped parachute and fell 300 feet before it expanded. He drifted across the East River and in 15 minutes was out of sight, landing at New Bushwick, NY, on Long Island, four miles from the city. He carried two phials of hartshorn and cologne water to counteract dizziness.

7996. Professional American aeronaut was the balloonist Charles Ferson Durant. On September 9, 1830, he gave an exhibition in a balloon that he had constructed at his own home, flying from Castle Garden, New York City, to Perth Amboy, NJ. Durant was the first person to land on board a ship, a feat that he performed in Chesapeake Bay on the *Independence*. For his accomplishment he was awarded a gold medal in 1836 by the American Institute. The first leaflets to be dropped from the sky were poems written by Durant and tossed overboard from his balloon.

7997. Aviation book was John Wise's *A System of Aeronautics, Comprehending Its Earliest Investigations, and Modern Practice and Art; Designed as a History for the Common Reader, and Guide to the Student of the Art*, 310 pages, published in three parts in 1850 at Philadelphia by Joseph A. Speel.

7998. Transatlantic crossing attempted by a balloon took place on October 6, 1873, when the 300,000-cubic foot *Daily Graphic*, built by John Wise and funded by the *New York Daily Illustrated Graphic* newspaper, was launched in Capitoline Gardens, Brooklyn, NY (now part of New York City). Instead of a basket, the balloon carried a lifeboat supported by two slings. The crew consisted of Captain Washington Harrison Donaldson, George Ashton Lunt, and a newspaperman, Alfred Ford. The balloon left the earth at 9:19 A.M. A few hours later it ran into a storm. The crew jumped off at 1:15 P.M. near New Canaan, CT.

7999. Airship was designed and built by Caesar Spiegler. The flight was scheduled for July 3, 1878, with John Wise of Lancaster, PA, as the pilot. The dirigible was of the cigar shape and supported a wicker-cage partition with a door and window.

8000. Balloon pilot who was a woman was Mary H. Myers, who flew a balloon in 1880 at Little Falls, NY. Myers performed at fairs as Carlotta, the Lady Aeronaut. In 1886 she rose to a height of four miles—a world altitude record—in a balloon filled with natural gas.

8001. Glider flight ever made—and the first ever pilot-controlled flight of an aircraft heavier than air—was accomplished by John Joseph Montgomery on August 28, 1883, at Otay Mesa, near San Diego, CA. The weight of the glider was only 38 pounds and that of its rider 130 pounds. It traveled about 600 feet. A lever allowed Montgomery to change the position of the tail. The shape of the wings was modeled on that of the gulls he observed near his home, and he later received a patent for this "parabolic wing." Although Montgomery did not receive full recognition for his work at the time, probably because of lack of publicity, he nevertheless gained the title "Father of Gliding." He was also the first to the use the term "aeroplane" for a flying machine.

8002. Aviation magazine was *Aeronautics*, published from October 1893 to September 1894 by the *American Engineer and Railroad Journal*, New York City. It was edited by Matthias Nace Forney, and featured reports and articles about airplanes, gliders, and balloons. It contained 16 pages and sold for 10 cents a copy or $1 a year.

8003. Glider with cambered wings was invented in 1895 by Octave Chanute, who made about 2,000 glider flights without accident in 1896 and 1897 from his base at Miller's Station, IL, near Chicago.

8004. Airplane model to make a sustained flight under its own power was Samuel Pierpont Langley's model No. 5, which was tested on May 6, 1896, on the shores of the Potomac River. This unmanned model "aerodrome" weighed 26 pounds, was 16 feet in length, and had four cambered single-tier wings, each about 14 feet from tip to tip. It was driven by a one-horsepower steam engine. It was catapulted from a platform 20 feet above the water and flew a distance of about 0.75 miles, remaining aloft 1.5 minutes during one of its flights. As the fuel was exhausted, the plane descended gently to the water. It was picked up, dried off, refueled, and relaunched the same afternoon. This was the first flight anywhere in the world of a mechanically propelled machine that was heavier than air. Langley predicted that airplanes would eventually be used to carry humans, but his friends and the press scoffed.

8005. Airplane flight took place on December 17, 1903, at Kill Devil Hills, near Kitty Hawk, NC, with Orville Wright at the controls of a motor-powered airplane he had built with his brother Wilbur. The plane, which weighed 745 pounds and had a four-cylinder, 12-horsepower engine, was launched from a monorail after a 35- to 40-foot run. It remained aloft for 12 seconds and covered 120 feet. Three subsequent flights took place that day, of which the longest covered 852 feet in 59 seconds. The average speed was 31 miles per hour. Some historians respect the claim of Gustave Whitehead, who is said to have made four flights, one of which covered a distance of 1.5 miles, in his airplane *No. 21* on August 14, 1901, near Bridgeport, CT.

Library of Congress, Prints & Photographs Division
LC-DIG-ppprs-00626

Orville Wright takes off as brother Wilbur looks on at Kitty Hawk, NC.

8006. Airship disaster occurred on May 23, 1908, at Berkeley, CA, when the cigar-shaped balloon invented by John A. Morrell collapsed and exploded, injuring the inventor and 15 passengers. The airship was 450 feet long and 46 feet in diameter at the center and was powered by six gasoline engines that generated 200 horsepower each.

8007. Aviation trophy was awarded by the magazine *Scientific American* in New York City in 1908. It was valued at $2,500. It was to become the property of the flyer taking it three years in succession, the conditions for winning to be changed each year according to the progress of aviation. Flights were to be made before official witnesses at a preannounced time and place. Glenn Hammond Curtiss was the first trophy winner. His first flight for the trophy was made at 7:30 P.M. on July 4, 1908, at Hammondsport, NY, in his *June Bug* at a speed of 40 miles per hour. The

June Bug was equipped with an eight-cylinder air-cooled Curtiss engine with a six-foot propeller on the rear of its crankshaft.

8008. Airship ordered by the federal government was designed by Glenn Hammond Curtiss and built by Captain Thomas Scott Baldwin. It was 96 feet long, 19.5 feet in diameter, carried 19,500 cubic feet of hydrogen, and had a 10-foot wooden propeller and a 20-horsepower Curtiss engine. The body was covered by two layers of Japanese silk with vulcanized rubber. It was demonstrated to government representatives at Fort Myer, VA, on August 18, 1908, with Baldwin acting as pilot and Curtiss as engineer. It was subsequently purchased from Captain Baldwin and used by the Signal Corps at Omaha, NE. Its engine, the first water-cooled engine that Curtiss made, is now in the National Museum. It averaged 19.61 miles per hour and stayed aloft two hours. It was sold for $5,737.50.

8009. Airplane endurance flight exceeding one hour was made on September 9, 1908, by Orville Wright, who flew a Wright airplane with a Wright motor at Fort Myer, VA, for 1 hour 2 minutes 15 seconds.

8010. Fatal airplane accident occurred on September 17, 1908, at Fort Myer, Arlington Heights, VA, when a propeller blade struck an overhead wire because a fitting to which the guy wire was attached had worn through. Thomas Etholen Selfridge of the Army died from a skull fracture and Orville Wright received multiple hip and leg fractures.

8011. Aviation magazine devoted primarily to airplanes was *Fly*, first published in November 1908 in Philadelphia, PA, by Lawson and Kelley. It contained 20 pages and sold for 10 cents a copy or $1 a year. The magazine's first cover showed a girl seated on the back of an American eagle beckoning to two pilots.

8012. Airplane sold commercially was the *Gold Bug*, delivered by Glenn Hammond Curtiss to the New York Aeronautical Society at Hammondsport, NY, for $5,000 on June 16, 1909. Flying instructions were given to two members.

8013. Airplane purchased by the federal government was a Wright biplane that was given its first official flight on July 30, 1909, and accepted from Orville and Wilbur Wright of Dayton, OH, on August 2. The purchase price was $25,000, but a bonus of $5,000 was given because the specified speed, 40 miles per hour in still air, was exceeded. The plane, built at Dayton, was powered by a 25-horsepower motor. It was 28 feet long, with a wingspan of 36 feet 4 inches, and weighed 740 pounds (gross weight, 1,200 pounds). Its top speed was 44 miles per hour. It was known as *Miss Columbia.* Lieutenant Frank Purdy Lahm and Wilbur Wright made the first flight under government ownership at College Park, MD, on October 8, 1909.

8014. Monoplane was the Walden III, invented by Dr. Henry W. Walden and test-flown at Mineola, NY, on December 9, 1909. It was equipped with a 1909 Anzani three-cylinder motor that developed 22 horsepower and flew at a speed of 52 miles per hour.

8015. Pilot from the United States to establish an airplane altitude record was Louis Paulhan, who flew a Farman biplane on January 12, 1910, to a height of 3,967 feet at an aviation meet at Los Angeles, CA. About 50,000 spectators witnessed his flight, which lasted 50 minutes 46.2 seconds. His descent was made in 7 minutes 30 seconds.

8016. Night flight in an airplane was made by Walter Richard Brookins on April 18, 1910, at Montgomery, AL.

8017. Airplane round trip made in one day between two large cities took place on June 13, 1910, when Charles Keeney Hamilton, flying in a Curtiss biplane equipped with a Curtiss motor, made the round trip between Governors Island, New York City, and Philadelphia, PA. He left Governors Island at 7:36 A.M. and arrived at Front Street and Erie Avenue, Philadelphia, at 9:26 A.M. The average speed for his flight of 1 hour 50 minutes was 46.92 miles per hour. He left Philadelphia at 11:33 A.M. and, after a detour, landed at South Amboy, NJ, at 12:54 P.M., in a swamp instead of on a green. He repaired a broken spark plug, reascended at 6:17 P.M., and landed at Governors Island at 6:40 P.M. The flying time for the round trip was 3 hours 34 minutes. For this accomplishment he won a $10,000 prize offered by the *New York Times* and the *Philadelphia Ledger*.

8018. Airplane to fly higher than a mile in altitude was a Wright biplane flown by Walter Richard Brookins to an altitude of 6,234 feet on July 9, 1910, over Atlantic City, NJ. The gasoline gave out when he descended to 5,800 feet and the engine stopped, but Brookins glided the airplane to safety. He was in the air 1 hour 2 minutes 35 seconds. For his feat he won a $5,000 prize offered by the Atlantic City Aero Club.

8019. Airplane flight over water was made by Glenn Hammond Curtiss, who on August 31, 1910, flew in his biplane over Lake Erie from Euclid Beach Park, Cleveland, OH, to Cedar Point, Sandusky, OH. He flew at an altitude between 400 and 500 feet. The trip took 78 minutes nonstop over a distance of 70 miles.

8020. Transatlantic airship flight was attempted by Walter Wellman on October 15, 1910, when he and his companions left Atlantic City, NJ, in a nonrigid dirigible, *The America*, en route to Ireland. The dirigible was 228 feet long, with a 52-foot diameter. They were forced down by storms and fogs after flying 1,008 miles in 71.5 hours. The crew was rescued about 375 miles east of Cape Hatteras, NC.

8021. Airplane flight from a ship was made on November 14, 1910, when Eugene Burton Ely, a civilian pilot of the Curtiss Company, took off from the bow of the scout cruiser *Birmingham*, anchored at the Hampton Roads Yacht Clubhouse at Willoughby spit, and flew through fog and rain to Hampton Roads, VA. The runway was 83 feet long with a 5-degree slope, allowing only a 26-foot takeoff, as the length of the plane was 57 feet. Ely won a $5,000 prize.

8022. Airplane flight to the deck of a carrier was made on January 18, 1911, by Eugene Burton Ely of San Francisco, CA, who took off at 10:45 A.M. from Selfridge Field, Camp Selfridge, CA, flew 13 miles, and landed on a sloped wooden platform 130 feet long and 50 feet wide above the deck of the cruiser *Pennsylvania* in San Francisco Harbor. Ropes and sandbags were used to stop the airplane. Its speed was 35 miles per hour.

8023. Hydroplane that was successful was the *Flying Fish*, which was flown by its inventor, Glenn Hammond Curtiss, at San Diego, CA, on January 26, 1911.

8024. Airplane rescue at sea took place on January 30, 1911, 10 miles from Havana, Cuba. John Alexander Douglas McCurdy had been flying from Key West, FL, to Camp Columbia, Havana, making the first sea flight out of sight of land, when his biplane developed engine trouble as a result of a faulty oil connection. He landed the plane on the sea, where its pontoons kept it afloat, and within four minutes was picked up by the destroyer *Terry*.

8025. Pilot licensed by the Aero Club of America was Glenn Hammond Curtiss of Hammondsport, NY, who received License No. 1 on June 8, 1911.

8026. State aviation law was passed by Connecticut on June 8, 1911. It required all airships to be registered, for a $5 fee, and all applicants for a pilot's license to be tested, for a fee not more than $25. A license to operate and direct airships was required by each pilot, for a $2 fee. The law also established a penalty for noncompliance of a $100 fine and six months' imprisonment. An earlier law, passed by Tennessee in 1905, authorized a tax on aircraft, but did not attempt to regulate or control aircraft.

8027. Airplane flight under a bridge was made on June 27, 1911, by Lincoln Beachey, who flew in the rain in a 60-horsepower Curtiss biplane at Niagara Falls, NY, as a stunt for the international carnival. He took off from a baseball field on the American side of the Niagara River, crossed over the American Falls and the Horseshoe Falls at an altitude of 2,000 feet, and flew under the steel arch bridge, 168 feet high and 100 feet wide, at a height of some 15 feet above the water. He then flew down the gorge almost to the Whirlpool Rapids at a speed of 60 miles per hour and landed on the Canadian side. About 150,000 spectators witnessed the flight, which Beachey repeated two days later.

8028. Pilot licensed by the Aero Club of America who was a woman was Harriet Quimby, a New York City journalist, who passed the test on August 1, 1911, and received License No. 37. She was followed two weeks later by Matilde Moisant. Both joined the exhibition team founded by Moisant's brother, John Moisant. Quimby was the first woman to cross the English Channel in a plane, on April 16, 1912. She was killed three months later when she was thrown out of her plane during an air meet in Boston. The first American woman to make a solo flight was Blanche Scott, whose training airplane left the ground on September 2, 1910, despite the throttle block applied to it by Glenn Hammond Curtiss, Scott's instructor.

8029. Airplane rescue at sea by another airplane was made by Hugh Robinson on August 14, 1911. Pilot Rene Simon had been flying over Lake Michigan in a monoplane and dived down to wave to some motorboats. Unable to rise, he crashed into the lake. Robinson, in a Curtiss hydroplane, flew over to Simon and found him in his floating plane smoking a cigar. Robinson hailed several people in motorboats, and they towed Simon and his monoplane to the shore.

8030. Transcontinental airplane flight made in stages was made by Calbraith Perry Rodgers, who left Sheepshead Bay, NY, on September 17, 1911, in his Burgess-Wright biplane and spent 49 days en route to California, arriving in Pasadena on November 5. He was followed by a special train carrying spare parts. The distance was 3,417 miles, which he covered in 70 hops. His actual flying time was 3 days 10 hours 14 minutes. His best day's coverage was 231 miles and his best single flight was 133 miles, from Stovall, CA, to Imperial Junction, CA. Weather was responsible for the loss of 11 days, and 13.5 days were consumed in making repairs. On November 12, at Compton, CA, he crashed and was badly injured, but on December 10 he continued the journey.

8031. Parachute jump from an airplane was made on March 1, 1912, by Captain Albert Berry from a Benoist Pusher plane piloted by Antony Jannus, at Jefferson Barracks, St. Louis, MO. Berry jumped from an altitude of 1,500 feet while the plane was traveling at 50 miles per hour.

8032. Airplane round-trip flight over water was made by Glenn Luther Martin in a biplane on May 10, 1912. The trip was made in 37 minutes at an altitude in excess of 2,000 feet for an approximate distance of 31 miles over the Pacific Ocean from Newport Bay, CA, to Avalon, Santa Catalina Island, CA. The return flight was from Santa Catalina Island via San Pedro and down the coast to Newport Bay, covering 45 miles in 51 minutes. An inflated tire tube on the fuselage served as a life preserver.

8033. Fatal airplane accident involving a woman took the life of Julia Clark of Denver, CO, who was killed on June 17, 1912, at the Illinois State Fair Grounds, Springfield, IL, when her Curtiss biplane struck the limb of a tree and turned over while she was circling the field at 40 miles per hour on her first flight. Her death was the 151st in heavier-than-air aircraft.

8034. Parachute jump from an airplane by a woman was made by Georgia Broadwick, 18 years old, on June 21, 1913, over Griffith Field, Los Angeles, CA, from an airplane piloted by Glenn Martin and flying at a 1,000-foot altitude and a speed of 30 miles per hour. After a 100-foot drop, her 11-pound silken parachute opened and she landed in a barley field.

8035. Gyroscope that was successful in automatically stabilizing aircraft was demonstrated by Lawrence B. Sperry and Lieutenant Patrick Nelson Lynch Bellinger in August 1913 at Lake Keuka, Hammondsport, NY, in a Curtiss-F boat. Stabilization was longitudinal and lateral.

8036. Airplane loop-the-loop was made by Lincoln Beachey at North Island, San Diego, CA, on November 18, 1913. When he reached an altitude of 1,000 feet, he brought his machine up with a swoop and a moment later was flying head downward. The loop was completed at the 300-foot level. On November 28 he made a triple loop.

8037. Airplane flying school operated by a woman was the Stinson School of Flying, Stinson Field, San Antonio, TX, opened in 1914 by Emma Beaver Stinson. In 1916 the school moved to a field of about 200 acres that was leased from the city of San Antonio for $5 a year. The school trained Canadian pilots during World War I. The chief instructors were Mrs. Stinson's daughters, Marjorie and Katherine. Katherine was a famed stunt flyer who, in 1917, became the first female stunt pilot to tour China and Japan. Their brothers, Jack and Eddie, were also pilots and opened an aircraft manufacturing company in 1920.

8038. Hydroplane service started on January 1, 1914, between St. Petersburg, FL, and Tampa, FL. The planes were built by the Benoist Aircraft Company and were operated by the St. Petersburg–Tampa Airboat Line. Two round-trip flights were made daily. The regular round-trip fare was $10. Mayor Abram Cump Phiel of St. Petersburg paid $400 for the first round trip. The planes flew 80 feet above the water across Tampa Bay, an air distance of 18 miles, in 23 minutes.

8039. Airplane flight longer than 500 miles was made by Ruth Law, who flew a two-year-old obsolete Curtiss biplane 590 miles from Chicago, IL, to Hornell, NY, on November 19, 1916. She left at 8:25 A.M. and arrived at 2:10 P.M. in 5 hours 45 minutes' flying time. She landed and refueled and continued on to Binghamton, NY. Law, an accomplished stunt flyer, was the first American woman to fly at night. She and her husband later ran a three-plane flying troupe, Ruth Law's Flying Circus.

8040. Navy airship was the DNI, a twin-engine nonrigid 115,000-cubic-foot dirigible. The envelope was built at New Haven, CT, and the car at Boston, MA. It was acquired under contract of June 1, 1915, at a cost of $45,636. It was too overweight to leave the ground and the twin engine was replaced with a single engine. The first flight was made at Pensacola, FL, in April 1917. Only three flights were made, as the airship was damaged in handling and was not worth repairing.

8041. Municipal airport was Bader Field, in Atlantic City, NJ. It opened in 1918, serving seaplanes and regular planes. The town of Modesto, CA, had proposed building a municipal airport in 1910, but lack of funds delayed its construction until after the opening of Bader Field.

8042. Parachute known as the "free parachute" was developed by the Army Air Corps under the direction of Major Edward L. Hoffman. With this type of parachute, the operator jumps before pulling the rip cord. The first person to jump with the manually operated chute was Leslie Le Roy Irvin, who jumped on April 28, 1919, from a de Havilland DH-9 biplane at an altitude of 1,500 feet, flying at a speed of 100 miles per hour over McCook Field, Dayton, OH. He broke his ankle when he struck the ground. Floyd Smith was at the controls. Later Irvin founded the Irving Air Chute Company. His name was spelled incorrectly on the incorporation papers.

8043. Stowaway on an aircraft was William Ballantyne, a rigger, a member of the original crew of the British dirigible R-34. Ballantyne and two other men had been laid off in order to lighten the load for a transatlantic crossing to America, but Ballantyne stowed away on the flight. The R-34 left East Fortune, Scotland, at 2 A.M. on July 2, 1919, and arrived at 9:45 A.M. at Roosevelt Field, Long Island, NY, on July 6.

8044. Caterpillar Club member was John Boettner, pilot of the *Wing Foot* balloon of the Goodyear Tire and Rubber Company, Akron, OH, who parachuted 1,200 feet to safety on July 21, 1919, while his balloon crashed into a building at La Salle Street and Jackson Boulevard, Chicago, IL. The crash resulted in the death of three persons and injuries to 28. "Caterpillar Club" is a name used to designate those persons whose lives have been saved by parachute jumps from aircraft in distress.

8045. Airplane flight between New York and Alaska was made by four United States planes of the Alaskan Flying Expedition that left Mitchel Field, NY, on July 15, 1920, and arrived at Nome, AK, on August 25. The return trip began in Nome on August 29 and ended at Mitchel Field on October 20, with 16 stops en route. The distance was 4,345 miles each way. The average flying speed of the trip was 80 miles per hour. The expedition commander was Captain St. Clair Streett.

8046. Hydroplane international service was established by Aeromarine Airways on November 1, 1920, on a route from Key West, FL, to Havana, Cuba. The service employed two hydroplanes, each with the capacity to carry three people. The fare was $50. Mail was also carried.

8047. Transcontinental airplane flight made within 24 hours was made by Lieutenant William Devoe Coney of the 91st Aero Squadron, who took off from Rockwell Field, San Diego, CA, at 7 P.M., February 21, 1921. He was forced down at Bronte, TX, by a snowstorm. He completed his flight at Pablo Beach, Jacksonville, FL, on February 24 at 7:27 A.M. He covered 2,079 miles in an elapsed time of 36 hours 27 minutes and a flying time of 22 hours 27 minutes.

8048. Pilot who was an African-American woman was Bessie Coleman of Chicago, IL, the daughter of an African-American mother and a Native American father. Refused permission to enroll in aviation courses in the United States, she received her training in France and Germany and qualified for an international pilot's license on June 15, 1921. From 1922 until her death in a plane crash in 1926, she did exhibition stunt flying in air shows across the United States.

8049. Airship filled with helium gas was the semirigid cigar-shaped Navy dirigible C-7. It contained 181,000 cubic feet of gas and was powered by two motors. It was tested on December 1, 1921, at Hampton Roads Base, Hampton Roads, VA, and on December 4 made a round trip from Hampton Roads to Washington, DC. Lieutenant Commander R. F. Wood was the pilot.

8050. Helicopter flight of importance was made on June 16, 1922, by Henry Adler Berliner at College Park, MD, before representatives of the U.S. Bureau of Aeronautics. The machine raised itself three times to the height of seven feet. It had two lifting propellers in the front, the forward motion being obtained by tilting a propeller in the rear of the fuselage.

8051. Transcontinental airship flight was made by the C2, which left Langley Field, Newport News, VA, on September 14, 1922, and arrived at Ross Field, Arcadia, CA, on September 23. The dirigible was 192 feet long, 64 feet wide, and 67 feet high, and contained 172,000 cubic feet of hydrogen gas. It was powered by two 150-horsepower Wright motors and commanded by Major Harold A. Strauss and Captain George W. McEntire. On October 17, during the return trip, the bag ripped while the airship was being towed out of the hangar at San Antonio, TX, causing an explosion which injured seven of the eight-man crew.

8052. Pilot to bail out of a disabled airplane was Lieutenant Harold R. Harris, chief of the flying section of McCook Field, Dayton, OH, who jumped from a Loening monoplane on October 20, 1922, 2,000 feet over North Dayton, before his plane crashed.

8053. Transcontinental nonstop airplane flight was made by Lieutenants Oakley G. Kelly and John A. Macready of the Navy Air Service. On May 2, 1923, the pilots, flying a Fokker T2 monoplane equipped with a Liberty engine, took off from Roosevelt Field, NY, at 11:36 P.M. They arrived at Rockwell Field, Coronado Beach, CA, at 12:26 P.M. the next day, covering a distance of 2,700 miles in 26 hours 50 minutes.

8054. Airplane refueling attempt in midair was made at Rockwell Field, Coronado, CA, on June 27, 1923, at 4:43 A.M., from a De Havilland plane piloted by Air Corps Captain Lowell Herbert Smith, with Air Corps Lieutenant John Paul Richter as receiver of fuel. A 40-foot hose encased in steel wire was lowered to the fuel-receiving plane. After refueling in flight, the planes remained aloft 37 hours 15 minutes 14.8 seconds.

8055. Airport runway illumination was attempted on August 21, 1923, when 42 landing fields on the Chicago–Iowa City–Omaha–North Platte–Cheyenne route were lit by 30 six-inch electric arc beacons which made complete revolutions three times a minute. The lights were of 5.3 million candlepower and were visible for 50 miles.

8056. Rigid airship and the first of the Zeppelin type to use helium gas was *Shenandoah*—"daughter of the stars"—which was launched on August 20, 1923, and tested in flight on September 4, 1923, at Lakehurst, NJ. In 1924 it made the first transcontinental flight by a dirigible, leaving Lakehurst on October 7 under the command of Lieutenant Commander Zachary Lansdowne, arriving at San Diego, CA, on October 11, and finishing the return trip at Lakehurst on October 25. On September 3, 1925, it was destroyed in a storm over Caldwell, OH. Lansdowne and 14 members of the crew were killed.

8057. County airport was the Kern County Airport, Bakersfield, CA, developed in 1925 under the auspices of the Kern County Chamber of Commerce near Highway 99, about a mile west of the present site of Meadows Field.

8058. Airship with an enclosed cabin was the nonrigid dirigible *Pilgrim*, a 51,000-cubic-foot airship built by the Goodyear Tire and Rubber Company, Akron, OH. The car was fitted close to the envelope. The first flight was made on June 3, 1925, with John Maloney Yolton as pilot.

8059. Caterpillar Club member who was a woman was Irene McFarland, who jumped from her plane on June 28, 1925, over Grissard Field, Cincinnati, OH. She was testing a parachute that was packed in a container fastened to the plane, so that when she jumped her weight would cause the container to break and permit the parachute to slip and blow out. Officials also required her to use an army parachute. She jumped and her parachute jammed, suspending her under the fuselage, from which she swung like a pendulum. She could not release herself and Lieutenant Watson, her pilot, could not land. He motioned to her to release the army parachute, which she did, the force breaking the cords that held her tied to the airplane.

8060. Wind tunnel for testing airplane parts was completed in the summer of 1927 at the Langley Field Laboratory of the National Advisory Committee for Aeronautics, Langley Field, VA. The tunnel permitted the full-scale testing of engines and propellers, engine nacelles, wing combinations, and fuselages. It had an airstream 20 feet in diameter that traveled at speeds up to 110 miles per hour. A high-speed jet wind tunnel that allowed the testing of airfoils at a wind speed of about 600 miles per hour was completed on June 29, 1929.

8061. Scheduled passenger night flight by airplane was made on April 1, 1927, when a three-engine Fokker of the Colonial Air Transport Company took off for Boston, MA, from Hadley Field, NJ, then the only lighted airport with a lighted runway.

8062. State aviation department was established on May 10, 1927, when the Connecticut legislature authorized the organization of the Connecticut Department of Aviation, the first independent state department for the control and regulation of aeronautics in the United States. Offices were opened on July 1, 1927, at Brainard Field, Hartford, CT.

8063. Transatlantic solo airplane flight was made by Charles Augustus Lindbergh on May 20, 1927, from New York to Paris. He flew about 3,610 miles in 33 hours 32 minutes in the *Spirit of St. Louis*, a Ryan monoplane equipped with a single 225-horsepower Wright Whirlwind motor. He left Roosevelt Field, NY, at 7:52 A.M. on May 20 and arrived at 5:24 P.M. New York time the following day at Le Bourget field, Paris.

8064. Corporation to own its own airplane for transportation of its executives was the Standard Oil Company of Indiana, which paid $47,709 to the Stout Metal Aircraft Division of the Ford Motor Company, Detroit, MI, for a *Stanolind*, a 600-horsepower trimotor monoplane. The first flight was made on May 21, 1927, from Detroit to Chicago. The plane had a complete set of double controls, could carry 4,000 pounds, and could accommodate two pilots, one mechanic, and eight passengers.

8065. International airplane passenger station was established at Meacham Field, Key West, FL, in 1927. The airport consisted of a small frame building that served as the station and an even smaller frame building that served as a radio shack. Maintenance facilities were housed in an old fort nearby. Federal health, customs, and immigration officials came to the station when notified of the arrival or departure of a plane. The first flight to use the station was a Pan American World Airways flight on October 28, 1927.

8066. Pilot to die because of a lack of oxygen was Captain Hawthorne C. Gray of the Army Air Corps, who took off from Scott Field, Belleville, IL, on November 4, 1927, in a balloon that rose to 40,000 feet. Despite his oxygen mask, he died because he was unable to open a reserve oxygen cylinder. He was found near Sparta, TN, about 310 miles from Belleville, in the basket of his balloon.

8067. Airplane diesel engine was manufactured by the Packard Motor Car Company of Detroit, MI, in 1928. It was an air-cooled nine-cylinder 225-horsepower radial engine that weighed 510 pounds. It was used in a Stinson Detroiter airplane and made its first flight on September 19, 1928.

8068. Flight trainer for airplane pilots was the Link Trainer, a mechanical-electrical device complete with hooded cockpit, controls, and a full complement of flight instruments. The trainer simulated conditions in an aircraft without leaving the ground. It was invented by Edwin Albert Link. The first sale was made in 1929 to the Link Flying School, Binghamton, NY. It was adopted by the Navy in 1931 and by the Army Air Corps in 1934.

8069. Airship made completely of metal was the ZMC-2, which was constructed by the Detroit Aircraft Corporation, Detroit, MI, and delivered to the Navy. It was tested at Grosse Ile Airport, Grosse Ile, MI, on August 19, 1929, and was manned by Captain William E. Kepner and a crew of four who stayed aloft 49 minutes 55 seconds. The ship was 149 feet 5 inches long and 52 feet 8 inches in diameter and had a displacement of 202,200 cubic feet of helium gas. Its weight, empty, was 9,115 pounds. It carried a total load of 12,242 pounds. A congressional resolution signed by President Calvin Coolidge on June 24, 1926, had appropriated $300,000 toward its construction.

8070. Passenger transfer from an airship to an airplane was effected on August 29, 1929, at the Cleveland, OH, Air Show, when Lieutenant Calvin Bolster descended a ladder of metal girders lowered from the keel of the dirigible *Los Angeles* and boarded a plane flown by Navy Lieutenant Adolphus W. Gorton. The ladder ended in a hook which was attached to a hawser stretched between two uprights on the top wing of the plane.

8071. Automatic pilot on an airplane was installed on a Gates-Day Standard J5 airplane operated by the Pennsylvania-Central Airlines. It was first used on October 8, 1929, on a flight from Cleveland, OH, to Pittsburgh, PA, under the command of Captain Trow Sebree. Automatic pilot, an instrument which can be set to take over and relieve the pilot, was developed by William Green.

8072. Glider released from an airship was piloted by Lieutenant Ralph Stanton Barnaby of the Navy. The glider was cast loose on January 31, 1930, at Lakehurst, NJ, from the *Los Angeles*, commanded by Lieutenant Commander Herbert Victor Wiley, at an altitude of 3,000 feet. A perfect landing was made in 12 minutes.

8073. Glider flight indoors in "dead air" was made on March 2, 1930, when Harry Kuchins, a member of the St. Louis, MO, Glider Club, flew a glider inside the St. Louis Terminal building at a Boy Scout circus. The glider had been used by Colonel Charles Augustus Lindbergh in June 1929.

8074. Seaplane glider to be piloted in the air was loosed from a seaplane on March 15, 1930, at Port Washington, NY. It was built at Roosevelt Field, NY, and was fashioned after a flying boat. The first seaplane glider pilot was Frank Monroe Hawks, whose achievement was duplicated later the same day by Robert Atwater, flying a German-built converted glider.

8075. Transcontinental glider tow began on March 30, 1930, when Captain Frank Monroe Hawks took off from Lindbergh Field, San Diego, CA, in the *Eagle*, also known as the *Cloud-Hopping Choo Choo*, a glider designed for the Texas Company by Professor Roswell Earl Franklin of the University of Michigan. The glider was attached by a towline to a single-motor biplane piloted by J. D. "Duke" Jernigin, Jr. Stops were made at Tucson, AZ, Sweetwater, TX, Tulsa, OK, East St. Louis, IL, Columbus, OH, and Buffalo, NY. The glider landed in the rain before 15,000 people on April 6, 1930, at Van Cortlandt Park, New York City. Flying time was 36 hours 47 minutes.

8076. Airline flight attendant who was a woman was Ellen Church, a nurse from Cressbill, IA. In May 1930, she made her first flight between San Francisco, CA, and Cheyenne, WY, on Boeing Air Transport, a forerunner of United Air Lines. Requirements for the job were that she be not older than 25, not taller than 5 feet 4 inches, and that her weight be 115 pounds or less. The salary was $125 a month for 100 hours of flying. The first African-American woman hired as a flight attendant was Ruth Carol Taylor, a graduate nurse from Ithaca, NY, who made her first flight on February 11, 1958, from Ithaca to New York City on Mohawk Airlines.

8077. Airship for private commercial operation was delivered on May 22, 1930, by the Goodyear Zeppelin Corporation of Akron, OH, to the New England Airship Company of Bedford, MA. It was chartered by Bird and Son of East Walpole, MA, and as a goodwill messenger made 1,380 flights, carrying more than 6,000 passengers in less than five months.

8078. Radar detection of airplanes was accomplished on June 24, 1930, by Dr. Albert Hoyt Taylor and Leo C. Young of the Naval Aircraft Radio Laboratory, Anacostia, DC (now part of Washington, DC), who noted that airplanes reflect radio waves even though they fly above the transmitter and receiver, rather than between them.

8079. Airship to land and take off from an oceangoing steamship was the nonrigid dirigible *Mayflower*, a blimp of the Goodyear Fleet. On July 31, 1930, as the S.S. *Bremen* reached New York City, the *Mayflower* lowered itself to the deck and picked up a passenger, Paul Weeks Litchfield, president of the Goodyear Tire and Rubber Company. The railings of the ship were covered with mattresses to prevent the dirigible's sides from being punctured. The *Mayflower* was 128 feet long and 37 feet wide and contained 86,000 cubic feet of gas. The deck of the *Bremen* was 85 feet long and 36 feet wide.

8080. Transcontinental solo airplane flight by a woman was made by Laura Ingalls, who left Roosevelt Field, NY, on October 5, 1930, in a Moth biplane. She made nine stops before reaching Glendale, CA, on October 9. The flight took 30 hours 27 minutes. The return flight, which began on October 18, lasted 25 hours 35 minutes. Ingalls was also the first female pilot to make a nonstop transcontinental flight westbound. Her Wasp-powered Lockheed Orion monoplane, the *Auto da Fé*, left Floyd Bennett Field, Brooklyn, New York City, on July 10, 1935, and arrived at Burbank, CA, 18 hours 19.5 minutes later.

8081. Glider pilot's license issued by the National Aeronautic Association was awarded to Leonard A. Wiggins, Akron, OH, on October 7, 1930. He was the first to receive both the "A" license (for a flight of one-minute duration with two S curves and normal landing) and the "B" license (for a starting, 360-degree turn both to the left and the right).

8082. Glider license awarded to a woman by the National Aeronautic Association was No. 10 Class "A," issued to Maxine Dunlap on February 5, 1931. Requirements were a flight of one-minute duration with two S curves and a normal landing.

8083. Rocket glider flight that was successful was made at Atlantic City, NJ, on June 4, 1931, by William G. Swan. The 200-pound glider was equipped with pontoons. When it was up in the air, the pilot turned on a switch to ignite the rockets. He made a 1,000-foot hop at a 100-foot altitude. The next day he made an eight-minute flight at an altitude of 200 feet, using the full power of 12 rockets.

8084. Transpacific nonstop airplane flight was made by Clyde Pangborn and Hugh Herndon, Jr., who landed at Wenatchee, WA, on October 5, 1931, having flown from Sabishiro, Japan, a distance of 4,458 statute miles, in 41 hours 13 minutes. They flew in a single-motored 425-horsepower Bellanca monoplane. This was the last lap of their round-the-world trip.

8085. Parachute jump from an autogiro was made on November 15, 1931, by Frankie Hammond, a parachute jumper from West Paterson, NJ, who jumped from a Pitcairn Autogiro at an air circus at Curtiss Essex Airport, Caldwell, NJ. The air show was for the benefit of the family of Keyport pilot Victor Brooks, who was killed on November 1, 1931, when his plane crashed during a race at Stanhope, NJ.

8086. Transatlantic solo airplane flight by a woman was made by Amelia Earhart, a native of Atchison, KS, who left Harbor Grace, Newfoundland, Canada, at 5:50 P.M. on May 20, 1932, and arrived at Londonderry, Ireland, at 8:46 A.M. on May 21. She flew 2,026 miles in 14 hours 56 minutes. Her flight took place exactly five years after that of Charles Augustus Lindbergh, the first pilot to make a solo transatlantic crossing.

8087. Airport manager who was a woman was Laurette Schimmoler, appointed on May 28, 1932, at Port Bucyrus, OH, at a salary of $510 a year.

8088. Transcontinental nonstop airplane flight by a woman was accomplished by Amelia Earhart. She took off from Los Angeles, CA, on August 24, 1932, at 1:26 P.M., in her red Wasp-powered Lockheed airplane, and arrived at the Newark, NJ, Metropolitan Airport, at 11:32 A.M. She flew approximately 2,600 miles in 19 hours 5 minutes.

8089. Airplane sleeping berths were introduced by American Airways of Chicago, IL, in March 1933. Each berth was made by folding two of the plane's chairs to form a cot. The first airplane with nonconvertible sleeping berths was placed in service on October 5, 1933, by Eastern Air Transport on the route between Atlanta, GA, and New York City. The plane was a Curtiss-Wright Condor and was designed to contain eight berths and five seats, but on the initial trip only two berths were installed, an upper and a lower. The berths were 6 feet 5 inches long and 2 feet 4 inches wide. The first passengers to occupy the berths were the air ace Captain Edward Vernon Rickenbacker and Alexander Strong. The plane was equipped in the company's shops at the Atlanta Municipal Airport, where the first trip started.

8090. Round-the-world solo airplane flight was made by Wiley Hardeman Post in a Lockheed Vega monoplane, the *Winnie Mae*. He took off from Floyd Bennett Field, New York City, on Saturday, July 15, 1933, at 5:10 A.M. and landed in Berlin, Germany, at 6:55 A.M. the following day, after a flight of 25 hours 45 minutes. Other stops were at Konigsberg, Moscow, Novosibirsk, Irkutsk, Rukhlovo, Khabarovsk, Flat, Fairbanks, and

Edmonton. Post returned to Floyd Bennett Field on July 22 at 11:59:30 P.M., making the round-the-world circuit of 15,596 miles in 7 days 18 hours 49 minutes, of which 115 hours 36 minutes 30 seconds was flying time. His airplane was equipped with a Sperry automatic pilot and a directional radio. Post had previously made a round-the-world flight in the *Winnie Mae*, accompanied by Harold Gatty. Starting from Roosevelt Field, NY, on June 23, 1931, they covered a total of 15,474 miles before returning on July 1 after an elapsed time of 8 days 15 hours 51 minutes. Post was thus the first man to fly around the world twice.

8091. Transcontinental flight made by African-Americans in their own airplane was made by Charles Alfred Anderson of Bryn Mawr, PA, holder of a transport license, and Dr. Albert Ernest Forsythe of Atlantic City, NJ, a privately licensed pilot. They took off from Bader Airport, Atlantic City, on July 17, 1933, at 2:49 A.M. and arrived at Los Angeles, CA, on July 19 at 5:30 P.M.

8092. Pressure suit was flight-tested by aviator Wiley Hardeman Post in his plane, the *Willie Mae*, at Wright Field, Dayton, OH, in August 1934. Post was preparing for an air race from London, England, to Melbourne, Australia, in October and planned to fly most of the trip in the stratosphere. At that altitude, he needed to breathe pressurized oxygen to stay alive. After two tries, a workable suit was designed and sewn by engineer Russell Colley of the B.F. Goodrich Company. It was constructed of two layers of fabric, a balloon-like rubber layer containing the pressurized oxygen and an outer layer that protected the balloon and controlled its shape. Post wore a modified diver's helmet over his head.

8093. Pilot who was a woman to fly for a commericial airline was Helen Richey, who flew from Washington, DC, to Detroit, MI, via Pittsburgh and Cleveland on December 31, 1934. She was appointed a copilot by Central Airlines, Greensburg, PA, and flew a Tri-Motored Ford 12-passenger transport. She was ousted the following October after the company's male pilots prevented her from joining their union.

8094. Transpacific solo airplane flight by a woman was made by Amelia Earhart. She left Wheeler Field, Honolulu, HI, at 10:15 P.M. on January 11, 1935, and arrived at the Oakland Airport, Oakland, CA, at 4:31 P.M. the next day, covering 2,408 miles in 18 hours 16 minutes at an average speed of 133 miles per hour.

8095. Parachute tower for training jumpers was a free-drop tower built April 1935 in Hightstown, NJ, by the Safe Parachute Jump Company. The tower was 125 feet high, with a horizontal arm at the top capable of being rotated 360 degrees.

8096. Transport airplane designed for transoceanic service was the *Pan American Clipper*, a 19-ton flying boat powered by four Hornet air-cooled, geared, and supercharged engines, each developing 750 horsepower. It was an all-metal monoplane, 68 feet long, with a wingspread of 118 feet 2 inches. It carried within its hull and in the wings and pontoons a fuel load of more than 8.5 tons, adequate for a flight range of 3,500 miles. Under the command of Captain Edwin Charles Musick, the first Clipper took off April 16, 1935, at 6:50 P.M. from San Francisco, CA, and arrived 12:59 P.M. on April 17 at Pearl Harbor, Honolulu, HI, covering 2,301 air miles in 18 hours 39 minutes. The return trip was begun on April 22, 1935, at 8:59 P.M. from Pearl Harbor, and the transport landed at Alameda, CA, on April 23, at 5:59 P.M.

8097. Airplane instructor's license issued under the Civil Aeronautics Authority, created by the Civil Aeronautics Act of June 23, 1938, was a rerated license issued to Arthur J. Banks, Atlanta, GA, on September 27, 1939. The first woman licensed was Evelyn Pinckert Kilgore, San Bernardino, CA, who received her license on October 13, 1939. In the early days, "instructor" could be written on a private pilot's license after 200 hours of flight.

8098. Transatlantic commercial airplane service over the "southern route" was initiated by the 41.5-ton *Dixie Clipper* of Pan American Airways, commanded by Captain Robert Oliver Daniel Sullivan. It left Port Washington, NY, on June 28, 1939, at 1:59 P.M., with 12 crew members and 22 passengers. It was powered by four 1,550-horsepower Wright Cyclone engines. Stops were made at Horta, in the Azores, and at Lisbon, Portugal. The plane landed at Marseilles, France, on June 30, 1939, at 8:21 A.M. The fare was $375.

8099. Helicopter that was successful was the VS-300, constructed in October and November 1939 by Vought-Sikorsky Aircraft, Stratford, CT. A flight of 15 minutes and 3 seconds was made on July 18, 1940, by Igor Ivan Sikorsky at Stratford, CT, with a single main rotor powered by a 70-horsepower Franklin engine. The helicopter had three auxiliary tail rotors for control, one turning in a vertical plane for rudder control and the other two turning in a horizontal plane on outriggers on either side of the tail.

8100. Plastic bonded airplane to be awarded a Type certificate by the Civil Aeronautics Administration was an open two-place tandem low-wing full-cantilever type monoplane built by the Timm Aircraft Corporation, Van Nuys, CA, in July 1940. It was approved on April 5, 1941. It was a training plane, the fuselage, wings, and all control surfaces of which were fabricated from a special material formed by binding several laminations of plywood with liquid plastic and pressing in a precision mold to the exact contour and size desired. The entire airplane structure contained less than 7 percent aluminum.

8101. Helicopter flight of one-hour duration was made on April 15, 1941, by Igor Ivan Sikorsky, who hovered aloft in a Vought-Sikorsky VS-300 for 1 hour 5 minutes 14.5 seconds over Sniffen's Point, Stratford, CT. The main lift was supplied by a three-bladed propeller 28 feet in diameter. On May 6, 1941, the helicopter hovered over a tennis court for 1 hour 32 minutes 26.1 seconds.

8102. Helicopter flight from water was made on April 17, 1941, by Igor Ivan Sikorsky at Stratford, CT, in a Vought-Sikorsky VS-300 helicopter mounted on rubber bags so that it could land and take off on either land or water.

8103. Civilian airport owned and operated by the federal government was the Washington National Airport, Washington, DC, opened for regular traffic on June 16, 1941. The cornerstone of the Terminal Building was laid by President Franklin Delano Roosevelt on September 28, 1940. The Civil Aeronautics Administration was in charge, and John Groves was the manager.

8104. Test pilot who was a woman was Alma Heflin, who made her first production test flight November 12, 1941, for the Piper Aircraft Corporation, Lock Haven, PA.

8105. Round-the-world flight by a commercial airplane was made by the *Pacific Clipper*, of Pan American Airways, which left San Francisco, CA, on December 2, 1941, under Captain Robert Ford, with a 10-man crew, and returned to New York City on January 6, 1942. The plane covered 31,500 miles in a flying time of 209.5 hours. Because of war conditions, the return trip from New Zealand was over the Coral Sea, Netherlands East Indies, Indian Ocean, Java Sea, Bay of Bengal, Arabian Sea, Persian Gulf, Red Sea, the Nile and Congo rivers, overland to West Africa, thence to Brazil, and finally to New York.

8106. Long-distance helicopter flight was made in a two-place XR-4 Air Force helicopter designed by Igor Ivan Sikorsky, which took off on May 13, 1942, from Stratford, CT. It flew at low altitudes a distance of 761 miles and landed at Wright Field, Dayton, OH, on May 17, making 16 stops en route. Actual flying time was 16 hours 10 minutes. Charles Lester Morris, test pilot of Sikorsky Aircraft Division of the United Aircraft Corporation, was the pilot.

8107. Parachute jump using a nylon parachute was made on June 6, 1942, from an airplane at Brainard Field, Hartford, CT, by Adeline Gray, parachute rigger of the Pioneer Parachute Company, Manchester, CT.

8108. Jet airplane designed and built in the United States was the XP-59, an Airacomet, built by the Bell Aircraft Corporation, Buffalo, NY, and flown for the first time on October 1, 1942, at a secret testing base in Muroc, CA, by Robert Morris Stanley. It was rated over 400 miles per hour and in excess of 40,000 feet. The higher the altitude (up to a certain maximum), the faster it flew. It employed two turbojet engines built by the General Electric Company from designs made by Group Captain Frank Whittle, the British inventor. The fuel was generally kerosene, although anything that burned could be used as a substitute. There was no propeller.

8109. Amphibious seaplane glider was the XL-Q-1, manufactured by the Bristol Aeronautical Corporation, New Haven, CT, and flown on January 16, 1943, at the Navy Yard, Philadelphia, PA. It was designed as a troop transport and cargo carrier by the National Aircraft factory under Commander Ralph Stanton Barnaby at the Navy Yard. The glider was taken aloft behind a Catalina seaplane and released. It had an all-wood body, was 40 feet long with a 72-foot wingspan, and carried 12 men and their equipment.

8110. Airplane human pickup was accomplished on September 5, 1943, at the Clinton County Army Air Base at Wilmington, OH. Captain Norman Rintoul was the pilot. His plane was equipped with an electric reeling motor and a hook from which was suspended a 185-foot nylon rope half an inch thick. With this equipment, he succeeded in hoisting up paratrooper First Lieutenant Alexis Doster of Washington, DC.

8111. Gas-turbine propeller-driven airplane was the XP-81, a fighter, designed and produced by Consolidated Vultee Aircraft Corporation at Vultee Field, Downey, CA, and first flight-tested on February 11, 1945, at the Army Air Force base in Muroc, CA. Its wingspan was 50 feet 6 inches and its fuselage 44 feet 8 inches long. It weighed 19,500 pounds and traveled at a speed greater than 500 miles per hour. In the nose was a propeller-driven gas turbine built by the General Electric Company. Between the cockpit and the tail was a jet engine, also built by General Electric.

8112. Jet-propelled landing on an aircraft carrier was made on November 6, 1945, by Ensign Jake C. West in an FR-1 Fireball on the escort aircraft carrier *Wake Island* off San Diego, CA. The Fireball, a Ryan-built navy fighter plane, was powered by both a turbojet and a conventional reciprocating engine, and normally used its reciprocating power plant for takeoff and landing, switching over to the jet as either an exclusive or a supplementary propulsive force once it was in the air. As West was landing, the reciprocating engine power failed, and he landed using jet power.

8113. Helicopter hoist rescue took place off the coast of Fairfield, CT, in 1946. A Sikorsky R-5 helicopter equipped with an experimental hydraulic hoist was used to rescue two oil workers who were stranded on a barge that was being pounded against a reef by hurricane-force winds. Jimmy Viner, a nephew of helicopter pioneer Igor Sikorsky, piloted the helicopter, assisted by Jackson Beighle.

8114. Commercially designed helicopter was the S-51, a four-passenger helicopter designed and built by the Sikorsky Aircraft Division of the United Aircraft Corporation, Bridgeport, CT, which made its initial flight on February 16, 1946. It received its Approved Type Certificate from the Civil Aeronautics Authority on March 26, 1946. It cruised at 80 miles per hour and had a range of 150 miles with pilot, three passengers, and 70 pounds of baggage.

8115. Helicopter licensed for commercial use by the Civil Aeronautics Administration was a Bell 47B able to cruise at speeds of 1 to 100 miles per hour, fly forward, backward, or sideways, ascend or descend vertically, and hover. License No. 1 was granted on March 8, 1946, to the *New York Journal-American*, New York City, which used the helicopter for news coverage and photo delivery.

8116. Glider commercial freight service was inaugurated on April 24, 1946, by Winged Cargo of Philadelphia, PA. Colonel Fred Paul Dollenberg took off from Northeast Airport, Philadelphia, in a DC-3 Air Liner that towed a Waco glider at the end of a nylon towrope. The plane carried 5,000 pounds of freight and the glider 3,500 pounds. The average speed of the flight was 150 miles per hour. The first stop was at Miami, FL, with other stops at Havana, Cuba, and San Juan, Puerto Rico. Paul Myers Aubin piloted the glider.

8117. Transcontinental round-trip airplane flight made within 24 hours was made on June 12, 1946, by a jet-propelled P-80 Shooting Star fighter plane. The pilots were Colonel Leon Gray of Casa Grande, AZ, Major Robin Olds of Beverly Hills, CA, and Lieutenant Jack Richardson of Oklahoma City, OK. They flew from March Field, CA, to Andrews Field, MD, in 5 hours 31 minutes, with a 34-minute stop at Oklahoma City to refuel, and returned in 6 hours 45 minutes, with stops to refuel at Scott Field, IL, and Midland, TX. The trip of approximately 4,540 miles was made in 12 hours 15 minutes. Total elapsed time, including a drive to Washington, DC, for lunch, was 14 hours 51 minutes.

8118. Radar for commercial and private planes was developed by Howard Robard Hughes and the electronic engineers of the Hughes Aircraft Corporation, Culver City, CA, and was demonstrated on May 1, 1947, at Culver City on a TWA (Transcontinental and Western Air) plane. A brilliant red light on the instrument panel and a horn in the cockpit warned the pilot whenever he came too close to an obstacle.

8119. Round-the-world commercial airplane service began on June 17, 1947, when a Pan American airplane commanded by Hugh Gordon left La Guardia Field, New York City, with 21 passengers and a crew of 10. The route, 22,297 miles, was via Newfoundland, London, Istanbul, Karachi, Manila, Bangkok, Calcutta, Shanghai, Tokyo, Guam, Wake, Honolulu, and San Francisco. The first trip took 309 hours 21 minutes, with 101 hours 32 minutes of actual flying time. Round-trip fare for the world flight was $1,700.

8120. Transatlantic flight by a robot airplane was done by the Skymaster, an Army C-54 four-engine military transport that took off from Stephensville, Newfoundland, Canada, on September 22, 1947, and arrived 10 hours and 15 minutes later at Brise Norton, England, near London, a distance of 2,400 miles. The robot piloting device was not touched after the throttles were opened to start the airplane. The plane carried 14 persons, including Colonel James Milligan Gillespie, the pilot and commander.

8121. Pilot to break the sound barrier was Major Charles Elwood "Chuck" Yeager, who flew a Bell X-1, an army rocket airplane, at Edwards Air Force Base, Muroc, CA, on October 14, 1947. The rocket engine was built by Reaction Motors, Rockaway, NJ. The plane attained the speed of 750 miles per hour (Mach 1.06) and an altitude of 70,140 feet. Alcohol and liquid oxygen were used as fuel, forced into the burners by gaseous nitrogen. The plane was equipped with rockets that could keep it in the air only 10 minutes. It had to be dropped from a bomber while at a high altitude. Official announcement of the achievement was withheld until June 10, 1948. The first woman to break the sound barrier was Jacqueline Cochran, who flew a North American F-86 Saber over Edwards Air Force Base on May 18, 1953, at the speed of 760 miles per hour.

8122. Airplane with a delta wing was the Convair Model 7002, built by the Consolidated Vultee Aircraft Corporation in Downey, CA, and San Diego, CA. It was 42 feet 5 inches long, 17 feet 8 inches high, and had a 31 foot 3 inch wingspan. The wing had a 60-degree sweepback on its leading edge and had elevons on its straight trailing edge. The plane was powered by a single-jet Allison J33-A 29 engine. It made its first flight on September 18, 1948, at Muroc, CA (later Edwards Air Force Base). It was delivered to the Air Force on May 14, 1949, and designated XF 92A.

8123. Round-the-world nonstop flight by an airplane was made in 94 hours 1 minute by a B-50 Superfortress, *Lucky Lady II*, under the command of Captain James Gallagher. The plane left Carswell Air Force base, Fort Worth, TX, on February 26, 1949, at 11:21 A.M. It carried a crew of 14 and averaged 249 miles per hour on its 23,452-mile trip. It was refueled four times in the air by B-29 tanker planes and landed on March 2, 1949, at 9:22 A.M.

8124. Airport fog disposal unit was accepted by test on March 29, 1949, by the Los Angeles Airport, Los Angeles, CA. It consisted of 392 oil burners installed alongside runways. During World War II, the system was used in England and known as FIDO, Fog Investigation and Disposal Operation.

8125. Cargo airlines licensed by the Civil Aeronautics Board were the Flying Tiger Line, Slick Airways, United States Airlines, and Airnews, which were issued licenses on April 29, 1949, effective June 24, 1949.

8126. Heliport commercial base in a major city was Heliport No. 1 at Pier 41, New York City, leased from the Department of Marine Aviation by the Metropolitan Aviation Corporation. The seadrome was 161 by 60 feet. The first flight was May 18, 1949, the official opening of service, when pilot George Callahan and passenger Deputy Mayor John James Bennett flew in a Bell 47-B with a 605-pound payload capacity.

8127. Year in which air traffic volume exceeded first-class rail traffic volume was 1951, when scheduled United States domestic, territorial, and local-service (feeder) carriers flew 10,556,139,000 revenue passenger-miles, compared with parlor and sleeping car traffic of 10,225,525,000 miles on Class One railroads.

8128. Jet airplane passenger trip was made on January 10, 1951. An Avro Jetliner four-engine turbojet piloted by Donald Howard Rogers took off from Chicago, IL, at 11:07 A.M. and arrived at New York City in 1 hour 42 minutes, setting a new speed record of 442 miles per hour.

8129. Transatlantic helicopter flight was made by the Air Force Air Rescue Service in two H-19 (S-55) helicopters that left Westover Air Force Base, Chicopee, MA, on July 15, 1952, and arrived at the Air Force base at Wiesbaden, Germany, on August 4, after 51 hours 55 minutes of elapsed flight time. Leader of the flight was Captain Vincent Howard McGovern of Springfield, NJ, who with copilot Harry Celestine Jeffers of Newark, OH, piloted the project ship, *Hop-A-Long.* The accompanying aircraft, *Whirl-O-Way,* was piloted by First Lieutenant Harold W. Moore of Cincinnati, OH, and copiloted by Major George Okie Hambrick of Carter, OK. The 3,410-mile Atlantic crossing was made in 42 hours 25 minutes.

8130. Passenger to circle the world on commercial airlines in less than 100 hours was Major Horace C. Boren of Dallas, TX, who arrived at Idlewild International Airport, New York City, on June 25, 1953, having completed a round-the-world flight in 99 hours 16 minutes. Boren stopped at 19 airports on his 21,000-mile flight.

8131. Helicopter fully operated by remote control was the HTK-1, built by the Kaman Aircraft Corporation, Bloomfield, CT. In July 1953, at Windsor Locks, CT, it took off and landed, flew backward, sideways, and forward, and hovered at varying altitudes, speeds, and distances in compliance with commands from a remote-control station. The signals were sent by radio from a ground station to controls in the drone.

8132. Helicopter passenger service was instituted by New York Airways on July 9, 1953, at 9:15 A.M., when two passengers were transported between La Guardia Airport and Idlewild Airport, both in New York City. Twelve passengers were carried the first day. The captain was Jack S. Gallagher and the flight attendant was Neils Johnson. Freight service had been inaugurated on October 1, 1947, by Los Angeles Airways, which carried mail in the San Fernando Valley, CA.

8133. Transcontinental round-trip solo flight between sunrise and sunset was made on July 23, 1953, by Lieutenant Commander George H. Whisler, Jr. Whisler took off from the Naval Air Station, Norfolk, VA, in a Grumman F9F-6 Cougar jet fighter at 5:18 A.M., 17 minutes after sunrise. After stops at the Naval Air Station in Memphis, TN, and Webb Air Force Base, Big Spring, TX, he arrived at the Naval Air Station at North Island, San Diego, CA, at 9:05 A.M. On the return trip, he flew a Douglas F3D-2 Skyknight all-weather jet fighter, departing from San Diego at 9:55 A.M., refueling at the Naval Air Station in Dallas, TX, and arriving at the Norfolk, VA, airfield at 7:15 P.M., just before sunset. His elapsed flight time was 13 hours 57 minutes, with a flying time of 11.2 hours. The total distance covered was 4,930 statute miles. The flights in both directions were delivery trips for new planes.

8134. Transcontinental nonstop two-way airplane service was instituted on November 29, 1953, by American Airlines, using Douglas DC-7s, between International Airport, Los Angeles, CA, and Idlewild International Airport, New York City, a distance of 2,540 miles. The eastbound flight was scheduled for 7 hours 15 minutes and the westbound flight for 7 hours 55 minutes.

8135. Jet airplane used for commercial transport that was built in the United States was the Boeing Stratoliner Model 707, first tested July 15, 1954, by Alvin M. Johnston at Renton, WA, where it was built by the Boeing Airplane Company. It had four Pratt and Whitney J-57 engines with more than 10,000 pounds of thrust. It weighed 190,000 pounds and cost about $20 million. It was designed to carry about 150 passengers across the Atlantic Ocean at a speed of 550 miles per hour. The first transport was delivered on August 16, 1958, to Pan American Airways.

8136. Round-the-world flight over the North Pole on a regularly scheduled air route began on November 15, 1954, when the Scandinavian Airlines System, using DC-6B planes, inaugurated simultaneous service in both directions between Copenhagen, Denmark, and Los Angeles, CA. The eastbound flight, with 40 passengers, left International Airport, Los Angeles, CA, at 8:23 P.M. Greenwich Mean Time and arrived at Copenhagen on November 16 at 8:18 P.M. G.M.T., an elapsed time of 23 hours 55 minutes (20 hours 38 minutes' flying time) for the 5,800 miles. The westbound flight was made in 24 hours 11 minutes' flying time (27 hours' elapsed time).

8137. Pilot to bail out of an airplane flying at supersonic speed was George Franklin Smith of Manhattan Beach, CA, who was propelled into the air when his seat automatically detached itself from an F-100A Super Sabre Jet fighter on February 26, 1955, above the Los Angeles International Airport, Los Angeles, CA. He was flying at an altitude of 6,500 feet at the supersonic speed of 777 miles per hour. His clothes were cut to ribbons, and his socks, helmet, and oxygen mask were stripped off. He felt deceleration of 40 Gs, so that his organs weighed 40 times their normal weight. He landed in the ocean and was rescued by a passing boat off Laguna Beach, CA. He was hospitalized for about six months.

8138. Reconstruction of an airliner during a crash investigation was undertaken by the Civil Aeronautics Board, the Federal Bureau of Investigation, and the Douglas Aircraft Corporation after the explosion of United Airlines Flight 629 on November 1, 1955, near Longmont, CO. After retrieving the pieces of the airplane from the crash site, the investigators connected them together in a warehouse at Stapleton Airport, Denver, CO, using a wooden and wire framework. The reconstruction showed that the crash had been caused by a bomb hidden in a passenger's luggage by her son in an insurance-collection scheme.

8139. Aerocycle was built by De Lackner Helicopters, Mount Vernon, NY, and tested at Camp Kilmer, NJ, by the Army, which bought 12 on December 29, 1955. The aerocycle weighed about 200 pounds, carried a load of about 300 pounds, and had a top speed of 65 miles per hour and a range of about 150 miles. Handlebars controlled the ascent and descent, the pilot steering by leaning in the direction he wanted to go. The machine had helicopter blades, rose vertically, and was powered by a 41-horsepower outboard motor mounted above pontoons.

8140. Airplane disaster involving more than 100 persons occurred on June 30, 1956, when a Trans World Airlines Super Constellation en route from Los Angeles to Kansas City collided with a United Air Lines DC-7 traveling from Los Angeles to Chicago and Newark. The accident took place over the Grand Canyon in Arizona. There were 128 deaths.

8141. Transcontinental nonstop helicopter flight was made from Miramar Naval Air Station, San Diego, CA, on August 23, 1956, to Washington, DC, a distance of 2,610 miles, in 31 hours 40 minutes, by a twin-rotored H21. The helicopter was refueled four times in flight and twice while hovering. The crew was headed by Major Hugh Gaddis of Tulsa, OK. The helicopter, produced by the Vertol Aircraft Corporation of Morton, PA, weighed 3,300 pounds.

8142. Pilot on a scheduled passenger line who was African-American was Perry H. Young of Orangeburg, SC, who was hired as a flight crewman on December 17, 1956, by New York Airways, New York City. He started regular passenger flights on February 1, 1957, as a copilot in a 12-passenger S-58 helicopter between New York International, La Guardia, and Newark, NJ, airports.

8143. Round-the-world nonstop flight by a jet airplane was made by three B-52 Air Force Stratofortress bombers, which flew 24,325 miles in 45 hours 19 minutes at an average speed of 525 miles per hour under the command of Major General Archie J. Old, Jr., of the 15th Air Force. The takeoff was from Castle Air Force Base, Merced, CA, on January 16, 1957, and the landing was made at March Air Base, Riverside, CA, on January 18. The planes were refueled in flight by KC aerial tankers. Each eight-engine jet carried a crew of nine. The route was via Newfoundland, French Morocco, Saudi Arabia, the coasts of India and Ceylon, the Philippines, and Guam.

8144. Balloon flight to rise higher than 100,000 feet was made by the Winzen Research Balloon as part of Project Manhigh. It rose from Crosby, MN, on August 19, 1957, and descended at Elm Lake, SD, the following day, having reached an altitude of 101,516 feet during its 32 hours in the stratosphere. For approximately 26 hours its altitude was over 90,000 feet. Major David Goodman Simons, medical officer of the Air Force, was awarded the Distinguished Flying Cross for this flight on August 24, 1957.

8145. Transcontinental jet airplane passenger service began on January 25, 1959, when a four-engine American Airlines Boeing 707 made the trip between Los Angeles, CA, and New York City with 112 passengers and eight-member crew in 4 hours 3 minutes 3 seconds. The plane was piloted by Captain Charles Macatee of Huntington, NY. The fare was $158.85 one way plus tax and $301.90 round-trip plus tax.

8146. Jetway was installed on July 29, 1959 at International Airport, San Francisco, CA. It was a self-powered telescopic corridor that extended from 44 to 107 feet and swung into place to connect the terminal with aircraft, to protect passengers from wind and weather as they boarded or disembarked. The jetway could be extended from the terminal building to the aircraft door in less than 60 seconds.

8147. **Planned nationwide shutdown of air traffic** took place on September 10, 1960, while the North American Aerospace Defense Command conducted a military exercise called Sky Shield. No civil aircraft were allowed in the air for six hours, starting at 2:00 A.M., while fighter planes repelled a simulated attack by Soviet bombers.

8148. **Airline to carry 100 million passengers** was American Airlines, New York City, which selected pioneering aviator Lieutenant General James Harold Doolittle, chairman of the board of Space Technology Laboratories, Los Angeles, as the national symbol of the 100,000,000th passenger and presented him with a crystal bowl on December 28, 1961.

8149. **Pilot of an airplane to qualify as an astronaut by attaining a 50-mile altitude** was Major Robert Michael White of the Air Force, who piloted his X-15 rocket airplane to an altitude of 314,750 feet on July 17, 1962. He was launched from a B-52 at Edwards Air Force Base, Muroc, CA, and landed on Rogers Dry Lake after a flight lasting about 11 minutes. He was awarded astronaut wings on July 18, 1962. White was the fifth to qualify as an astronaut, having been preceded by Alan B. Shepard, Jr., Virgil Grissom, John H. Glenn, and Scott Carpenter.

8150. **Round-the-world solo airplane flight by a woman** was accomplished by Geraldine Mock of Columbus, OH, who flew a Cessna 180 monoplane, the *Spirit of Columbus*. She left Columbus on March 19, 1964, and returned on April 17, after a flight lasting 29 days 12 hours. She had a rival in Joan Merriam Smith, who was following the equatorial route that Amelia Earhart had attempted in 1937. Smith left Oakland, CA, on March 17, two days before Mock, and returned on May 12.

8151. **Parachute jumper snagged by airplane in midair** was Charles M. Alexander, a test parachutist for the Pioneer Parachute Company, Manchester, CT, who jumped from a single-engine Cessna 180 airplane at 10,000 feet on August 29, 1966, above the Sussex County Airport, Georgetown, DE. When he reached 9,000 feet, his parachute was snagged by a C-122 transport plane, piloted by Captain Arnold Olsen, that was traveling at 120 miles per hour. Alexander was taken aboard safely. The snag was done on purpose, to demonstrate a method of rescuing airmen who bail out over enemy territory.

8152. **Airplane made primarily of composite materials** was the Windecker Eagle 1, model A7-C, a four-seater civilian monoplane certified by the Federal Aviation Administration in December 1969. It was designed by Dr. Leo Windecker and his wife Dr. Fairfax Windecker, both dentists and aviation enthusiasts, who contracted with Dow Chemical Company in Freeport, TX, to develop a lightweight, foam-core, fiberglass-reinforced plastic airframe. The Windeckers founded Windecker Research Inc. in Midland, TX, to manufacture the Eagle from a composite called Fibaloy, producing a plane lighter and faster than competing all-metal models. Nine Eagle airplanes were produced in all, including two prototypes, six civilian versions, and one purchased by the U.S. Air Force. Military research on the Windecker (which the Air Force dubbed the YE-5) confirmed that the plastic craft had a very low radar profile. This formed the basis for stealth technology later incorporated into the B-2 Stealth Bomber. Windecker Eagle serial number 6 is preserved by the National Air and Space Museum at the Garber Facility in Suitland, MD.

8153. **Jumbo jet** was the Boeing 747, introduced for flight service by the Boeing Company of Seattle, WA, in 1970. The wide-bodied, two-decked aircraft was taller than a six-story building and could carry up to 490 passengers, more than could easily be handled by the terminal facilities of the time. The first 747s went into transatlantic service for Pan American Airlines beginning on January 21, 1970.

8154. **Airport baggage scanning system** that converted electronic data to a visible X-ray format was the Pep-720 baggage X-ray system manufactured by Princeton Electronic Products, New Brunswick, NJ. The first system to be installed was ordered by the Army's Picatinny Arsenal on August 9, 1971.

8155. **Fly-by-wire aircraft** in which all functions and flight surfaces were controlled by computer electronics rather than mechanical or hydraulic linkages was a modified Vought F-8C Crusader, first flight-tested by NASA research pilot Gary E. Krier on May 25,

1972. Systems developed for NASA's F-8 Digital Fly-By-Wire (DFBW) program, a joint effort between the NASA Flight Research Center, Edwards, CA (now the Dryden Flight Research Center), and the NASA Langley Research Center, Hampton, VA, were later incorporated into many military and civilian aircraft, including the Space Shuttle.

8156. Pilot on a regularly scheduled major airline who was a woman was Emily Howell Warner. She was hired by Frontier Airlines, Denver, CO, on January 29, 1973, as the second officer (co-pilot) on a Boeing 737. In 1976 she became the first woman pilot to earn the rank of captain.

8157. Balloon flight powered by solar energy was made at 8:30 A.M. on May 16, 1973, by Tracy Barnes, president of the Balloon Works, Statesville, NC. Barnes flew in the *Solar FireFly*, a 203,129-cubic-foot tetrahedron, or inverted pyramid. It used only solar energy to fly and did not employ a lifting gas or heat-producing device. The heat of the sun's rays was absorbed by the dark skin, and the solar energy dilated the air within the balloon, creating its buoyancy. The flight began at the soccer field of the University of North Carolina, Charlotte, NC, and lasted about 10 minutes.

8158. Transatlantic supersonic jet service to serve civilian passengers in the United States began operations on May 24, 1976, with the arrival of two Concorde jet airplanes at Dulles International Airport, Washington, DC. One plane had departed from Paris, the other from London. Passengers on the Concorde were able to cross the Atlantic in a mere three hours. Supersonic flights between France and New York City began on October 19, 1977.

8159. Human-powered aircraft that was successful was the *Gossamer Condor*, designed and built by a team under the direction of Paul MacCready, an aeronautical engineer living in Pasadena, CA. The ultra-lightweight craft was constructed primarily of cardboard, piano wire, aluminum tubing, and Mylar plastic sheeting. The power was supplied by the pilot, who continuously pushed a set of bicycle pedals. On August 23, 1977, bicyclist Bryan Allen pedaled over a three-mile course to win the $50,000 Kremer Prize, awarded for milestones in human-powered flight. On June 12, 1979, another MacCready design, the *Gossamer Albatross*, became the first human-powered aircraft to cross the English Channel. Allen piloted the plane from Folkestone, England, to Cap Gris-Nez, France, in 2 hours 55 minutes.

8160. Transatlantic balloon flight began on August 11, 1978, when Ben Abruzzo, Larry Newman, and Maxie Leroy Anderson, all of Albuquerque, NM, left Presque Isle, ME, in a helium-filled balloon, the *Double Eagle II*. They reached Paris on August 17 after a journey lasting 137 hours 18 minutes.

8161. Solar-powered long-distance airplane flight took place on December 3, 1979, when the *Solar Challenger* flew for 22 minutes over six miles of desert near Marana, AZ. The pilot was Janice Brown. The 210-pound aluminum and plastic aircraft drew power from 16,000 lightweight solar cells on its wings. On July 7, 1980, the *Solar Challenger*, with Stephen R. Ptacek at the controls, became the first solar-powered plane to cross the English Channel.

8162. Transcontinental nonstop balloon flight was made by Maxie Leroy Anderson and his son, Kris Anderson, of Albuquerque, NM, who took off from San Francisco at 12:30 A.M. on May 8, 1980, in the *Kitty Hawk*, a 75-foot-tall helium-filled plastic balloon, bound for Kitty Hawk, NC. They flew 3,100 miles—a straight distance of 2,817 miles—and landed on May 11 outside Matane, Quebec, on the Gaspé peninsula, more than 1,000 miles north of their original destination.

8163. Round-the-world helicopter flight was made by two Americans, Ross Perot, Jr., and Jay Coburn, in a helicopter called *The Spirit of Texas*. The flight began on September 1, 1982, and ended on September 30. It lasted 29 days 3 hours 8 minutes 13 seconds.

8164. Transatlantic solo balloon flight was completed on September 18, 1984, by Air Force Colonel Joe Kittinger. Flying the *Rosie O'Grady*, a 101,000-cubic-foot helium balloon, Kittinger navigated from Caribou, ME, to Montenotte, Italy, a flight of 3,543 miles, in 86 hours.

8165. Round-the-world nonstop airplane flight without refueling took place from December 15 to December 23, 1986, when Richard Rutan and Jeana Yeager circled the globe in *Voyager*, a front-and-rear-propeller plane constructed mainly of plastic. The 216-hour, 24,986-mile circumnavigation began and ended at Edwards Air Force Base,

Muroc, CA. Most of the fuel supply was stored in the plane's wings. The plane decreased in weight from 9,750 to 1,858 pounds as the fuel was consumed.

8166. Airship that was certified by the Federal Aviation Administration was *Skyship 600*, built by Airship Industries, which received certification on May 9, 1989. The $6 million airship first flew in 1984. Prior to 1987, the FAA set no criteria for lighter-than-air craft.

8167. Human-powered helicopter was developed by students at the California Polytechnic State University in San Luis Obispo, CA. The pedal-powered aircraft, which was constructed of graphite-epoxy, wood, and mylar, featured a 140-foot-long rotor driven by props at each end. It was named the Da Vinci 3, after Leonardo da Vinci, who first conceived of a rotary-wing flying vehicle. On December 10, 1989, in the school's gymnasium, the Da Vinci 3 made its first flight, which lasted 6.8 seconds and reached a height of seven inches.

8168. Ornithopter that succeeded in flying was designed by Jeremy Harris of the Battelle Memorial Institute, Columbus, OH, and James DeLaurier, a professor of aerospace engineering at the University of Toronto. In late 1991, after 20 years of work, they designed and flew the world's first true ornithopter, an 8.6-pound aircraft that flapped its wings and flew like a bird. The model ornithopter was made of wood, Kevlar, and carbon composites, and was radio-controlled. Its one-horsepower piston engine powered 10-foot wings made of three hinged panels. The first flight lasted 11.5 minutes.

8169. Commercial aircraft designed by computer was the Boeing 777-200 passenger jet, first flown on June 12, 1994. The Model 777, of which several versions were produced, was the first jetliner entirely designed, modeled, and "pre-assembled" with three-dimensional computer-aided design software, a process that saved the cost of constructing a full-scale mockup as well as thousands of hours of manual preassembly and testing. The twin-engine Model 777-200 held 305 passengers and had a range, fully loaded, of 5,210 miles. The Boeing Company's commercial aircraft division is located in Seattle, WA.

8170. Use of radar to investigate a plane crash took place on May 19, 1996, during the investigation into the crash of ValuJet Flight 592 in Everglades Holiday Park, FL, which had happened eight days earlier. The ground-penetrating radar system, made by Geophysical Survey Systems, North Salem, NH, and first used during the Vietnam War to locate underground tunnels, was used to search for the plane's voice cockpit recorder.

8171. Unplanned nationwide shutdown of air traffic was ordered by Jane Garvey, administrator of the Federal Aviation Administration in Washington, DC, on the morning of September 11, 2001, after the FAA received reports that two hijacked planes had been flown into the towers of the World Trade Center in New York City. All planes in the air were ordered to land, all takeoffs were cancelled, and all inbound international flights were diverted to airports in Canada.

8172. Solo balloon flight around the world was accomplished in his sixth attempt by American millionaire Steve Fossett, a native of Jackson, TN, in the hot-air balloon Bud Light Spirit of Freedom. Fossett, riding in a capsule measuring 7 feet long, 5.5 feet wide, and 5.5 feet high, departed from Northam, Western Australia, on June 19, 2002, and followed a route over southern waters for nearly the entire circumnavigation. He crossed 117 degrees east longitude, the same line where he began his trip, on July 2, 2002, at 9:40 EDT. Fossett touched down at Lake Yamma Yamma, a dry lake bed in Queensland. The total distance flown was 20,602 miles (32,963 kilometers), and the trip duration was 14 days 9 hours 51 minutes.

8173. Solo nonstop nonrefueled powered flight around the world took place from February 28, 2005, to March 3, 2005, when millionaire flight enthusiast Steve Fossett of Jackson, TN, flew the Virgin Atlantic GlobalFlyer from and to Salina Municipal Airport, Salina, KS, in 67 hours 2 minutes 38 seconds, [The GlobalFlyer, constructed from lightweight graphite epoxy and Aramid honeycomb materials, was designed by a team at Scaled Composites under Burt Rutan. Fossett took advantage of high-altitude jet stream tail winds to push the craft across the Atlantic to Britain before turning south and east over Egypt, Pakistan, India, China, and Japan.] for a total distance of 19,880 nautical miles (36,818 kilometers) at an average speed of 300 mph. The GlobalFlyer carried 13 fuel tanks, which accounted for 83 percent of its total weight at takeoff.

Horses

8174. Horses arrived with the Spanish conquerors in the 16th century. The first horses in the English colonies were imported in April 1629 by the Massachusetts Bay Colony. The agreement made by Matthewe Cradock, first governor of the company, required that "such cattle, both horses, mares, cowes, bulls, and goates, as are shipped by Mr. Cradock, are to bee devyded in equall halfes twixt him & the Companie."

8175. Traffic law enacted by a colony was passed on June 27, 1652, by New Amsterdam (the future New York City): "The Director General and Council of New Netherland in order to prevent accidents do hereby ordain that no Wagons, Carts or Sleighs shall be run, rode or driven at a gallop within this city of New Amsterdam, that the drivers and conductors of all Wagons, Carts and Sleighs within this city (the Broad Highway alone excepted) shall walk by the Wagons, Carts or Sleighs and so take and lead the horses, on the penalty of two pounds Flemish for the first time, and for the second time double, and for the third time to be arbitrarily corrected therefor and in addition to be responsible for all damages which may arise therefrom."

8176. Horse that was a thoroughbred is claimed to have been Bulle Rock, who was imported into Virginia in 1730. He was foaled in 1717 and was a son of Darley Arabian and the mare Byerly Turk. Another horse for which the same claim has been made was Spark, who was presented to Lord Baltimore by the Prince of Wales, the father of George III. Lord Baltimore gave Spark to Governor Samuel Ogle of Maryland about 1750.

8177. Conestoga wagon was manufactured in 1753 by German immigrants in Lancaster, PA, near Conestoga Creek. A century later, the canvas-roofed wagons became popular with settlers of the American West.

8178. Intercity stagecoach service was inaugurated on November 9, 1756, between Philadelphia, PA, and New York City by John Butler, Francis Holman, John Thompson, and William Waller.

8179. Morgan horse was named after its owner, Justin Morgan. It was foaled in 1789 in Randolph, VT, and got by True Briton, also known as Beautiful Bay. It died in 1821.

8180. Trotting horse was Messenger, a gray horse 15 hands 3 inches high, foaled in 1780. He was imported from England and arrived in Philadelphia, PA, in May 1788. He was buried with military honors on January 28, 1808.

8181. City carriage service ran along Broadway in New York City from Wall Street to Bleecker Street in what is now Greenwich Village. The proprietor was A. Brower. The first vehicle to run along the route was an open carriage, which was replaced in 1829 by the Sociable, a closed carriage pulled by two horses. It sat on double-deck springs and was so high off the ground that passengers had to climb six steps to get inside. Ten passengers could be accommodated on its long sideways seats. The fare was one shilling.

8182. Transcontinental solo trip on horseback by a woman was made by Nan Jane Aspinwall, who left San Francisco, CA, on September 1, 1910, carrying a letter from Mayor Patrick Henry McCarthy to Mayor William Jay Gaynor of New York City. She covered 4,500 miles in 301 days, 108 of which were spent traveling. She arrived in New York City on July 8, 1911.

Motor Vehicles

8183. Internal-combustion engine was invented by Captain Samuel Morey of Orford, NH, who received a patent on April 1, 1826, "on a gas or vapor engine." His engine had two cylinders, 180-degree cranks, poppet valves, a carburetor, an electric spark, and a water cooling device. He employed the vapor of spirits of turpentine and common air. A small tin dish contained the spirits, and the only heat he used was from a common table lamp. A rotary movement was obtained by means of a crank and flywheel, as in a steam engine.

8184. Gas engine was invented by Stuart Perry of New York City, who received a patent for it on May 25, 1844. He invented both air- and water-cooled types and used turpentine gases as fuel.

8185. Pneumatic tires were made in 1895 by the Hartford Rubber Works, Hartford, CT, owned by the Pope Manufacturing Company. They were used in March 1895 on the Duryea automobile that later won the first car race in the United States, the *Times-Herald* race in Chicago on Thanksgiving Day, 1895.

8186. Diesel engine built for commercial service was a two-cylinder 60-horsepower unit built in September 1898 in the plant of the St. Louis Iron and Marine Works, St. Louis, MO. The engine, which drove a direct-current generator, was erected and operated in the Second Street plant of the Anheuser Busch brewery and was the first diesel engine in the world to be placed in commercial service. Adolphus Busch bought Dr. Rudolf Diesel's American patent rights in 1897 for a sum of approximately $250,000. The next engines were built for the Diesel Motor Company of America, which was formed by Busch. These engines were built in the plant of the Hewes and Philips Iron Works, Newark, NJ, circa 1900, and were of one size. They had 11-by-20-inch cylinders that were designed to develop 20 horsepower when running at 200 revolutions per minute.

8187. Clincher tire was manufactured in 1899 by the B.F. Goodrich Company of Akron, OH, in sizes ranging from 28 by 2.5 inches to 36 by 3 inches. The tire was of 19-ply construction.

8188. Driver license board was the Board of Examiners of Operators of Automobiles, authorized on July 6, 1899, by the city of Chicago, IL, to ascertain the qualifications of persons seeking licenses. It included the city electrician, the city engineer, and the commissioner of health.

8189. License plates for vehicles were required by New York State under a law that took effect on April 25, 1901. Owners of automobiles were obliged to register their names and addresses and a description of their machines with the office of the secretary of state. The license plate had to be furnished by hte owner and had to display the owner's initials in letters at least three inches high. The registration fee was one dollar. In 1901 fees totaling $954 were received, and in 1902, $1,082.

8190. Speed limit for motor vehicles was passed by the General Assembly of Connecticut on May 21, 1901. The bill, which was introduced by State Representative Robert Woodruff of Orange, CT, provided that the speed of all motor vehicles should not exceed 12 miles per hour on country highways and eight miles per hour on highways within city limits.

8191. State to require driver licenses for motorists was Massachusetts, starting in June 1903. Missouri instituted similar measures later that year. Neither state required applicants to take a driving test.

8192. License plate issued by a state was issued to Frederick Tudor in September 1903 by Massachusetts. It was a dark blue plate showing the numeral one in white and the legend "Mass. Automobile Register."

8193. Printed traffic regulations were *Rules For Driving*, a four-page pamphlet about 3 by 6 inches in size. The regulations described in it were put into effect on October 30, 1903, by the New York City Police Department.

8194. Windshield wiper was the invention of Mary Anderson of Birmingham, AL, who received a patent on November 10, 1903. Her device consisted of a rubber blade attached to a down-swinging arm that was manually operated from inside the vehicle.

8195. Tire chains were invented by Harry D. Weed of Canastota, NY, who obtained a patent on August 23, 1904, on a "griptread for pneumatic tires." Weed licensed manufacture to the Weed Chain Tire Grip Company, which later was acquired by the American Chain and Cable Company.

8196. Gas station was opened in St. Louis, MO, in 1905 by Harry Grenner and Clem H. Laessig, founders of the Automobile Gasoline Company. The gasoline was stored in an elevated tank and was transferred into the vehicles through a garden hose.

8197. State competency test for drivers was introduced by Rhode Island in 1908, the same year that the state began requiring motorists to have a license.

8198. License plates with a graphic design were issued by Michigan in 1910. They were composed of porcelain and showed the state seal.

8199. State law prohibiting drunk driving was enacted by New York in 1910.

8200. Traffic lanes designated by painted lines were the invention of Edward Norris Hines, road commissioner for Wayne County, MI, who called his idea a "center line safety stripe." The lines were painted in white on River Road, near Trenton, MI, in the fall of 1911. A machine was later developed that painted the stripes at a reduced cost.

8201. Electric traffic light in the United States was invented by police detective Lester Farnsworth Wire of Salt Lake City, UT, in 1912 and installed there in 1914. It had two electric lights, one red and one green, fixed inside a wooden box and operated manually by a policeman. The device was automated in 1926.

8202. Demountable tire-carrying rim was invented by Louis Henry Perlman of New York City, who applied for a patent on May 21, 1906, and received it on February 4, 1913.

8203. Nonskid tires of the modern type were patented by Stacy G. Carkhuff of the Firestone Tire and Rubber Company, Akron, OH. The patent was applied for on September 4, 1908, and granted on April 14, 1914. The angle formation of the edges of the raised portions molded on the tire provided against skidding in all directions.

8204. Electric traffic lights equipped with noise signals were invented by James Hoge. They were installed on August 5, 1914, at Euclid Avenue and East 105th Street, Cleveland, OH, by the American Traffic Signal Company under the direction of Safety Director Alfred A. Benesch. Cross arms were installed 15 feet above the ground and equipped with red and green lights and buzzers. Two buzzes signalled Euclid Avenue traffic to proceed, and one buzz signalled the traffic on 105th Street.

8205. Automatic windshield wiper was the Storm Windshield Cleaner, a system of rubber rollers patented in 1917 by Charlotte Bridgwood of New York City.

8206. Three-colored traffic signal incorporating a yellow warning light in addition to a red "stop" light and a green "go" light was installed on Woodward Avenue in Detroit, MI, in 1920. The inventor was a Detroit police officer, William L. Potts.

8207. Balloon tire production on a regular basis was introduced on April 5, 1923, by the Firestone Tire and Rubber Company of Akron, OH. On several previous occasions, large-section, thin-walled tires with small bead diameters were used experimentally or for special purposes, but no commercial use was made of them.

8208. Diesel engine speed record that was official was made on March 20, 1930, by Clessie Lyle Cummins of the Cummins Engine Company, Columbus, IN, in a Packard roadster chassis equipped with a four-cylinder marine-type diesel engine with a bore and stroke of 4.5 by 6 inches and piston displacement of 381.5 cubic inches. The car was stripped of fenders, windshield, and spare tires and fitted with a fabric cover over the driver's compartment. Cummins averaged 80.398 miles per hour in the test at Daytona Beach, FL.

8209. Vanity license plates originated in 1937 in Connecticut. A motorist with a five-year history of safe driving was allowed to pick three letters—most often, the driver's initials—to be displayed on the plate.

8210. Synthetic rubber tires were commercially marketed by the B.F. Goodrich Company, Akron, OH. On June 5, 1940, the company exhibited passenger car tires made of butadiene, synthesized from soap, gas, petroleum, and air. These tires were trademarked Ameripol.

8211. Tubeless car tires were manufactured by the B.F. Goodrich Company, Akron, OH, which announced the manufacture on May 11, 1947. The tires automatically sealed themselves when punctured. They were marketed in Indiana, Kentucky, Ohio, and West Virginia before being offered for national distribution.

8212. Automatic headlight control was the "Autronic-Eye," developed by the Guide Lamp Division of General Motors Corporation, Anderson, IN, and offered to the public on January 25, 1952. Headlights automatically dimmed at the approach of an oncoming car and then flashed back to bright.

8213. Speed limit for highway traffic established by Congress was enacted in 1974 in an effort to conserve fuel during the energy crisis of the 1970s. The speed limit was set at 55 miles per hour. The law was repealed on November 28, 1995, after which most states proceeded to raise their speed limits to

65 miles per hour or higher, despite ample evidence that the lower speed limit resulted in fewer deaths in traffic accidents.

8214. License plate slogan to be challenged in the U.S. Supreme Court was "Live Free or Die," the motto of New Hampshire, which was added to the state's license plates in 1965. On April 20, 1977, the Court ruled in *Wooley v. Maynard* that the state had a right to place the motto on the plates and that a member of the Jehovah's Witness religious group who objected to the statement had the right to cover it up.

8215. State ban on the use of cell phones by drivers was enacted by the New York State legislature on June 25, 2001, and took effect on November 1, 2001. The law banned motorists from using handheld phones, but not speaker phones or headsets.

8216. Self-balancing personal vehicle was the Segway Human Transporter, invented by Dean Kamen. Introduced on December 3, 2001, by Segway LLC of Manchester, NH, it was equipped with an electric battery, a computer, and five gyroscopes, but no brakes. The machine, which functioned by sensing changes in the rider's center of gravity, had a top speed of 12 mph and could travel over various terrains.

8217. Digital-photography highway patrol was initiated on January 22, 2006, by Scottsdale, AZ, on a freeway known as Loop 101. Using digital equipment, the city photographed any vehicle traveling at 11 mph or more over the 65 mph speed limit. In February the city started sending traffic tickets to the photographed motorists.

Buses

8218. Sightseeing bus was the Motor Tally-Ho, built by the Mack Motor Truck Corporation, Brooklyn, New York City, in 1900 and sold for approximately $3,000 to Isaac Harris, who used it to take visitors on tours of Brooklyn's Prospect Park. It carried 19 passengers and the driver. It ran on gasoline and had a 60-horsepower engine.

8219. Double-deck bus was imported from France and introduced on Fifth Avenue, New York City, by the Fifth Avenue Coach Company in 1906. The company began manufacturing its own double-deck buses in 1915.

8220. Transcontinental bus service was offered by the Yelloway Bus Line, which began service on September 11, 1928, from Los Angeles, CA, to New York City. Three 26-passenger buses departed daily from each terminal, covering 3,433 miles in 5 days and 14 hours.

8221. Night coach was built by the Pickwick Corporation in Los Angeles, CA, and placed in service in July 1929 between Los Angeles and San Francisco, CA. The car was of metal construction, chiefly of Duralumin, and provided sleeping and seating accommodation for 26 people. The bus had two lavatories, a kitchen, and a pantry, and carried a crew of three: pilot, steward, and porter.

8222. Transcontinental express bus service was instituted on September 8, 1953, by Continental Trailways, which started its through service at 9 P.M. from the Port Authority Bus Terminal, New York City, to San Francisco, CA. The fare for the 3,154-mile trip was $56.70. The trip took 88 hours 50 minutes, of which 77 hours 19 minutes was actual riding time.

8223. Gas-turbine bus was the GM Turbocruiser, a modified coach built by the research staff of the General Motors Corporation, Detroit, MI, and publicly announced on June 10, 1954, after it had already logged more than 2,000 miles. The engine used a single burner and two turbine wheels, one to drive the centrifugal compressor, the other to drive a transmission that was connected to the rear wheels of the bus.

Cars

8224. Steam car was invented in 1866 by Henry Alonzo House. It was driven through the streets of Bridgeport, CT, and surrounding towns for several months. On October 6, 1866, House and his brother and co-inventor, James A. House, drove the car to Stratford, CT, taking a party of men to a vessel launching.

8225. Car with an electric storage battery was designed by William Morrison and built by Morrison and Schmidt, Des Moines, IA, in the summer of 1891. It was powered by 24 storage battery cells placed under the seats and could run continuously for 13 hours. The battery cells took 10 hours to charge. The car carried 12 people, had a four-horsepower motor, and was capable of a speed of 14 miles per hour. It was sold to J.B. McDonald, president of the American Battery Company of Chicago, in 1892.

8226. Car magazine was *The Horseless Age*, first published in November 1895 in New York City by Edward P. Ingersoll.

8227. Automobile club was the American Motor League, which held its preliminary meeting on November 1, 1895, in Chicago, IL, with 60 members. The first slate of officers included Charles Edgar Duryea, the car manufacturer, and Hiram Percy Maxim, car designer and inventor, as two of the four vice presidents, and the inventor Charles Brady King as treasurer.

8228. Car patent was filed on May 8, 1879, by George Baldwin Selden, an attorney of Rochester, NY. It was granted to him on November 5, 1895, and embodied his claims to the original application of the internal-combustion hydrocarbon motor to a road vehicle. His design resembled a horse-drawn carriage, with high wheels and a buckboard.

8229. Car produced for commercial sale was manufactured by Charles Edgar Duryea, America's pioneer automobile manufacturer. Duryea began building his first automobile in August 1891. It was completed at his shop in Springfield, MA, and was successfully operated on April 19, 1892. In 1895 he organized the Duryea Motor Wagon Company in Springfield to produce cars for sale. The first was sold in 1896.

Library of Congress, Prints & Photographs Division, LC-USZ62-3055

A car and horse-drawn carriage.

8230. Car accident occurred in New York City on May 30, 1896, when Henry Wells of Springfield, MA, driving a Duryea Motor Wagon, collided with Evylyn Thomas, a bicycle rider, who was taken to the Manhattan Hospital with a fractured leg. Wells spent the night in jail.

8231. Electric taxicabs were introduced in New York City in the spring of 1897 by the Electric Vehicle Company, whose office and garage were located at 1684 Broadway, New York City.

8232. Car driver who was a woman was Genevra Delphine Mudge, who drove a Waverly Electric in 1898 in New York City.

8233. Car exported from the United States was a steam-powered tricycle built in 1886 in Lansing, MI, by Ransom E. Olds, the founder of Oldsmobile. After adding a fourth wheel to it, he sold it in 1898 to a buyer in Bombay, India.

8234. Armored car was designed by Colonel Royal Page Davidson in May 1898. A Colt automatic machine gun was mounted on the car, which was intended for military use. The automobile was manufactured by the Duryea Automobile Company of Peoria, IL, and was used by the Northwestern Military and Naval Academy of Lake Geneva, WI.

8235. Car factory was an Oldsmobile factory, built in 1899 by Ransom Eli Olds in Detroit, MI. It manufactured 433 vehicles in 1901, 2,500 cars in 1902, and 5,508 cars in 1904.

8236. Driver arrested for speeding was Jacob German, operator of a taxicab for the Electric Vehicle Company, who was arrested on May 20, 1899, by Bicycle Roundsman Schuessler for driving at a "breakneck speed" of 12 miles per hour on Lexington Avenue, New York City. German was booked and jailed in the East 22nd Street station house.

8237. Public garage was established in Boston, MA, on May 24, 1899, by W. T. McCullough as the Back Bay Cycle and Motor Company. He advertised its opening as a "stable for renting, sale, storage and repair of motor vehicles."

8238. Car accident fatality was Henry H. Bliss, a real estate broker, 68 years old, who was knocked down and run over as he was alighting from a southbound streetcar at Central Park West and 74th Street, New York City, on September 13, 1899. He was taken to Roosevelt Hospital, where he died. Arthur Smith, the driver, was arrested and held on $1,000 bail.

8239. Car show was held at Madison Square Garden, New York City, on November 3–10, 1900, under the auspices of the Automobile Club of America. There were 51 exhibitors, of whom 31 showed cars, and the others showed accessories. A ramp was built to demonstrate the hill-climbing ability of the cars, and barrels were placed on the floor to demonstrate their steering. Braking contests and starting contests were held. Admission to the "horseless horse show" was 50 cents.

8240. Shaft-driven car was constructed in 1901 by the Autocar Company of Ardmore, PA. It was driven in 6 hours 15 minutes from Ardmore to Madison Square Garden, New York City, where it was exhibited in the New York Automobile Show of December 1901. The first 800 cars were equipped with steering levers, but the later ones were equipped with steering wheels.

8241. Car to exceed the speed of a mile a minute was driven on November 16, 1901, by A. C. Bostwick on a straightaway course at Ocean Parkway, Brooklyn, New York City, in a race sponsored by the Long Island Automobile Club. He covered the distance in 56.4 seconds. This record was held for only a few minutes, as Henry Fournier lowered it to 51.8 seconds in a 40-horsepower gasoline automobile. Foxhall Keene then lowered it to 54.6 seconds. Both Fournier and Keene raced in French automobiles. Bostwick used a 40-horsepower Winton.

8242. Transcontinental car trip by a nonprofessional driver in his own car was made by Dr. Horatio Nelson Jackson of Burlington, VT, a physician, with Sewell K. Crocker of Seattle, WA, as his mechanic. The car was a 20-horsepower $2,500 Winton, manufactured by the Winton Motor Carriage Company of Cleveland, OH. Jackson and Crocker left San Francisco, CA, on May 23, 1903, and arrived in New York City on July 26. The average daily run was 125 miles. The trip lasted 63 days, of which 44 were spent traveling and 19 awaiting supplies.

8243. Car with the steering wheel on the left side was the Northern four-cylinder car of 1907, manufactured by the Northern Motor Car Company of Detroit, MI. The automobile was also equipped with air brakes. The designer of these improvements was Charles Brady King, one of America's pioneer automobile inventors.

8244. Brake for four-wheeled cars was invented by Otto Zachow and William Besserdich of Clintonville, WI, who obtained a patent on December 29, 1908, on a "power applying mechanism."

8245. Year in which more than 100,000 passenger cars were produced was 1909, when 123,990 cars were manufactured. More than 1 million cars (1,525,578) were manufactured in 1916; more than 5 million cars (5,119,466) in 1949; more than 7 million cars (7,920,186) in 1955.

8246. Transcontinental car trip by women was made by Alice Huyler Ramsey of Hackensack, NJ, and Nettie R. Powell, Margaret Atwood, and Hermine Jahns, who left New York City on June 9, 1909, in a 30-horsepower Maxwell-Briscoe open car and arrived at San Francisco, CA, on August 6. Mrs. Ramsey was president of the Women's Motoring Club of New York.

8247. Electric-gasoline combination car was placed in service about 1910. It was equipped with the Owen magnetic drive and a generator in a combined unit.

8248. Electric self-starter used in cars was offered to the public in May 1911 by the Cadillac Motor Car Company of Detroit, MI. It was patented by Charles Franklin Kettering. The electric self-starter had been invented by Clyde Jay Coleman of New York City in 1899, but his invention was impractical.

8249. Transcontinental group tour by car was begun on June 26, 1911, when 10 Premier automobiles with 40 occupants, accompanied by a pilot car and a truck, left Atlantic City, NJ, on an "ocean to ocean" tour. They arrived at Los Angeles, CA, on August 10 and concluded the trip on August 13 at Venice, CA, having covered 4,617.6 miles.

8250. Sedan car was the 1913 Hudson Sedan, manufactured by the Hudson Motor Car Company, Detroit, MI. It was officially shown on January 11, 1913, at the 13th National Automobile Show, New York City. It carried all accessories as standard equipment.

8251. Armored car in commercial use was employed by Brink's Incorporated, Chicago, IL, in 1918. It had one thickness of armor-plate steel, but was not of all-steel construction throughout. The first armored car that was completely protected was put in service on February 1, 1920, by Michael Francis Sweeney of the Sweeney Detective Bureau, St. Paul, MN. Construction was started in March 1919 by the Boyd Auto Shops, Minneapolis, MN. The side walls and roof were steel, with welded-steel construction; no wooden walls or roof supports were used. The glass was "polished plate wired glass." The windshield and windows could be covered by hinged steel plates that fell into place when a catch was tripped.

8252. Car to exceed the speed of 200 miles per hour was a 1,000-horsepower *Mystery Sunbeam* driven by Major Henry O'Neil de Hane Segrave on March 29, 1927, at Daytona Beach, FL, at an average speed of 203.79 miles per hour both ways.

8253. Transcontinental car trip driven entirely in reverse was achieved by Charles Creighton and James Hargis, both of Maplewood, NJ. Between July 23 and August 13, 1930, t hey backed up a 1929 Ford Model A roadster from New York City to Los Angeles, CA, a distance of 3,340 miles, without once stopping the engine.

8254. Automatic parking meter was the Park-O-Meter, devised by Carlton Cole Magee, which was installed in Oklahoma City, OK, on July 16, 1935, by the Dual Parking Meter Company of Oklahoma City. Twenty-foot spaces were painted on the pavement and a parking meter that accepted nickels was installed at the head of each space. The city paid for the meters with funds collected from them.

8255. Car-airplane combination was the Arrowbile, built by the Waterman Arrowplane Corporation, Santa Monica, CA, and completed for testing on February 20, 1937. Delivery of five Arrowbiles was made on August 15, 1937, to the Studebaker Corporation, South Bend, IN. In the air, the Arrowbile's top speed was 120 miles per hour and its cruising speed was 105 miles per hour. It had a 6-cylinder, 100-horsepower Studebaker engine.

8256. Miniature car was offered for sale on April 28, 1939, by the Crosley Corporation of Cincinnati, OH. It had an 80-inch wheelbase and was 10 feet long from bumper to bumper. It had two cylinders, three forward speeds and a reverse, four-wheel mechanical brakes, a four-gallon capacity tank, and safety glass. The two-passenger convertible coupe and the four-passenger convertible sedan sold for $325 and $350. On June 19, 1939, the Crosley cars were put on sale in R.H. Macy's basement in New York City.

8257. Air-conditioned car was manufactured by the Packard Motor Car Company, Detroit, MI, and publicly exhibited on November 4–12, 1939, at the 40th Automobile Show, Chicago, IL. Air in the car was cooled to the temperature desired, dehumidified, filtered, and circulated. The refrigerating coils were located behind the rear seat in an air duct, with heating coils in another compartment of the same duct. The capacity of the unit was equivalent to 1.5 tons of ice in 24 hours when the car was driven at 60 miles per hour, or 2 tons at 80 miles per hour.

8258. Car with an automatic transmission was the Oldsmobile model of 1940, for which the Hydramatic automatic transmission, made by General Motors of Detroit, MI, was available as an option. An infinitely variable transmission, an earlier version of automatic transmission, had been offered on a few Austin cars between 1934 and 1936.

8259. Plastic car was manufactured by the Ford Motor Company, Dearborn, MI, in August 1941. Fourteen plastic panels were mounted on a tubular welded frame. Windows and windshield were of acrylic sheets, which resulted in an approximately 30 percent decrease in weight. On January 13, 1942, a patent was obtained by Henry Ford on the automobile body construction, an auto body chassis frame made from steel tubes or pipes designed for use with automobiles made from plastics.

8260. City parking garage was designed by Hassel T. Hicks and opened on September 1, 1941, in Welch, WV. It accommodated 232 cars and showed a profit the first year.

8261. Seat belts in cars were installed by Nash Motors in its 1949 models after their value was demonstrated by Cornell University's Crash Injury Research Program, but they were discontinued after customers complained about them. The first cars to have seat belts installed as standard equipment were the 1964 models manufactured by Studebaker-Packard, South Bend, IN. Three-point lap-and-shoulder belts were introduced by the Ford Motor Company in 1970 and were required by federal law in all American-made cars beginning with the 1974 models.

8262. Year in which more than 1 million passenger cars of one make were produced was 1949, when 1,109,958 Chevrolets were manufactured by the General Motors Corporation, Detroit, MI.

8263. Parking garage that was completely automated was the Park-O-Mat Garage, opened on December 5, 1951, in Washington, DC, by the Parking Services company. A car could be parked or returned in 50 seconds. The garage was an open building with 16 floors and 2 basement levels. Two elevators parked 72 cars on a lot 25 by 40 feet. There were no ramps, no aisles, no lanes, and only one attendant, who used push-button controls and did not enter the cars. The "vehicle parking apparatus" was patented on October 14, 1947, by Richard L. Sinclair of Los Angeles, CA.

8264. Mail delivery car with the steering wheel on the right was a Crosley, placed in service in Cincinnati, OH, on December 27, 1951. It is possible that prior to this date some mail delivery had been made using old automobiles manufactured with right-side drives.

8265. Sports car with a plastic laminated fiberglass body was the Chevrolet Corvette, produced on June 30, 1953, at Flint, MI, by the Chevrolet Motor Division of the General Motors Corporation. The list price was $3,250, including a 1953 powerglide automatic transmission as standard equipment. The car was only 33 inches at the door (body height), 70 inches wide, and 167 inches long on a 102-inch wheelbase. Its curb weight was approximately 2,900 pounds.

8266. Hydraulic-lift parking garage device was the Sky-Park, manufactured by Simmons Industries, Albany, NY. The first unit was installed in October 1954 in Washington, DC. A rigid central column with two hydraulically powered platforms operated by push-button controls raised automobiles, singly or doubly, thus providing double the parking space.

8267. Gas-turbine car was the XP-21 Firebird, built by the General Motors Corporation and tested by Mauri Rose in October 1953 at the GM Proving Ground, near Milford, MI. Its first public appearance took place on January 21–26, 1954, at the GM Motorama, Waldorf-Astoria Hotel, New York City. A 370-horsepower Whirlfire turbojet was installed in the rear of the car. The total weight of the engine unit, including the gasifier and the power sections, was 775 pounds, the overall weight of the entire car being 2,500 pounds. It had a plastic body and accommodated only the driver. Its speed was 150 miles per hour, but it was believed capable of 235 miles per hour. Since it consumed fuel faster than conventional cars, it was not commercially produced.

8268. Seat belt law enacted by a state requiring automobiles to be equipped with frame holes to which seat belts could be fastened was enacted by Illinois on June 27, 1955, and signed by Governor William Grant Stratton on July 6, 1955. The law provided that on or after July 1, 1956, no new motor vehicle could be registered unless equipped with seat belt attachments conforming to the specifications of the Society of Automotive Engineers.

8269. Solar-powered car was a 15-inch sunmobile built by William G. Cobb of the General Motors Corporation and publicly demonstrated on August 31, 1955, at the General Motors Powerama, Chicago, IL. It had 12 photoelectric cells made of selenium which converted light into electric current. The current powered a tiny electric motor with a driveshaft connected to the rear axle by a pulley.

8270. Car with front-wheel drive to be mass-produced as a full-size vehicle by a domestic manufacturer was the 1966 Oldsmobile Toronado, built by General Motors, Detroit, MI. The enormous front end, including V-8 engine, power train, drive train, and automatic transmission, weighed about 2,750 pounds. The two-door Toronado was also the first car with a single large window pane on each side, instead of a split window with a quarter vent in the front.

8271. Car equipped with an air bag marketed to the public was the 1973 Toronado, made by Oldsmobile in Lansing, MI. The air bag protected the passenger in the front seat.

8272. Diesel cars to be mass-produced were the Oldsmobile 88 and 98 diesel-engine models introduced by General Motors, Detroit, MI, on September 13, 1977.

8273. Child safety seat law enacted by a state was enacted by Tennessee in 1978. The law required parents to secure young children in safety restraints during car rides to prevent accidental deaths and injuries. The law's passage was the result of advocacy by Robert Sanders, M.D., a pediatrician and county health officer.

8274. Graduated driver licenses for teenagers were instituted in 1979 by Maryland, which adapted a plan designed by the National Highway Traffic Safety Administration. The law required teenage drivers under the age of 18 to earn a provisional license before they could receive a regular driver license. The provisional period, which mandated restrictions on nighttime driving, lasted six months.

8275. Rocket-powered car to break the sound barrier on land was the *Budweiser Rocket*, a three-wheeled, rocket-powered vehicle driven by stunt rider Stan Barrett. On December 16, 1979, Barrett clocked an unofficial speed of 739.666 mph, or Mach 1.01, on the dry lake bed at Edwards Air Force Base, Muroc, CA. The car, which cost about $800,000, was powered by a 48,000-horsepower rocket engine boosted by a 12,000-horsepower Sidewinder missile. It was brought to a stop by drag parachutes.

8276. Subcompact car with front wheel drive was the World Car, built by the Ford Motor Company's plant in Fort Wayne, MI. The first car off the assembly line was driven on August 11, 1980, by John Barson, president of the United Auto Workers Local 900.

8277. Air bag requirement by the federal government took effect on September 1, 1989, when all newly manufactured cars were required to have air bags installed on the driver's side.

8278. Car fueled by methanol was the Chevrolet Lumina Variable Fuel Vehicle, introduced by General Motors, Detroit, MI, in June 1992. The car could be powered by unleaded gas, by methanol (a fuel derived from plant fermentation that is similar to alcohol), or by any combination of the two. The first production model was delivered to Governor Tommy G. Thompson of Wisconsin.

8279. Electric car to be mass-produced using modern technology was the Electric Vehicle One, or EV1, marketed by General Motors, Detroit, MI, beginning on December 4, 1996. The first models were leased to customers in Los Angeles, CA, at a price tag of $34,000. The two-seater coupe was powered by a 137-horsepower, three-phase induction motor that ran on stored energy in a lead-acid battery pack. The EV1 could travel 70 to 90 miles between chargings, which took 3 to 12 hours.

8280. Family car with its own video entertainment systemavailable as a factory-installed option was the 1999 Oldsmobile Silhouette minivan, offered by General Motors, headquartered in Detroit, MI. The van could be equipped with a 5-inch (13-centimeter) LCD screen and a video cassette player.

8281. Fuel cell car that was practical was developed by automobile manufacturer DaimlerChrysler and publicly introduced on March 17, 1999, in Washington, DC. Called the NECAR 4, it used fuel cells built by Ballard Power Systems of Vancouver, Canada, to turn liquid hydrogen into electricity and water. Methanol or suitable reformulated gasoline could also be used in the fuel cell. The five-seater design, based on the Mercedes A-Class car, had a range of 280 miles between refuelings.

8282. Hybrid car for sale to the public in the United States was the Honda Insight, which debuted on December 15, 1999, at a price of $18,880. Powered by a 1.0-liter, 3-cylinder gasoline engine and an electric motor with an automatically recharged battery pack, the car got more than 70 miles per gallon in highway driving.

8283. State to require child booster seats for children who had outgrown infant seats was Washington. The legislature passed a law on March 28, 2000, effective on July 1, 2002, that required all children between four and six years old, or between 40 and 60 pounds, to be secured in a booster seat when they are passengers in a motor vehicle. The law was named for Anton Skeen, a four-year-old who was buckled into a regular seat belt when he died in a car crash.

8284. Hybrid sport utility vehicle was the Ford Escape, introduced in mid-2004. With a 2.3-liter, 4-cylinder engine and a 65-kilowatt electric motor, the Escape was the first American-made hybrid vehicle of any kind and could travel up to 500 miles on one tank of gas while producing less than one-sixtieth the emissions of a regular passenger car.

Motorcycles

8285. Steam-driven motorcycle was a two-wheeled vehicle invented by William A. Austin of Winthrop, MA, in 1868. The steam boiler was suspended amidships. The vehicle had a very limited traveling radius because of the small amount of steam generated.

8286. Motorcycle that was practical was manufactured by the E.R. Thomas Motor Company of Buffalo, NY, in 1900. A single-cylinder gasoline engine was attached to the transverse bar of an ordinary bicycle and a flat belt ran to a concentric pulley on the rear wheel.

8287. Motorcycle with a built-in gasoline engine was manufactured in Springfield, MA, by George M. Hendee, who formed the Hendee Manufacturing Company, which began to market the Indian motorcycle in 1901. Previously, motorcycles had been ordinary bicycles to which motors were attached. Three motorcycles were built in 1901. The following year, production was increased to 143. The motors were made by the Aurora Machine Company, Aurora, IL, and were mounted to the motorcycle frames in Springfield. The machines were first publicly demonstrated on June 1, 1901, in a hill-climbing exhibition.

8288. Transcontinental motorcycle trip was made by George A. Wyman of San Francisco, CA, on a Yale-California motorcycle built by L. W. Leavitt and Company, San Francisco. Wyman left San Francisco on May 16, 1903, and arrived in New York City on July 6. The motorcycle was a 3.5-horsepower single-cylinder machine with a belt drive.

8289. Twin-cycle motorcycle was an Indian, made in 1905 in Springfield, MA, by the Hendee Manufacturing Company. It had a spring-front fork, battery ignition, and a gravity-feed oiling system. The machine was started by pedaling. The gas tank was mounted on the rear fender.

8290. Transcontinental motorcycle trip by women was made by Adelina and Augusta Van Buren, who left New York City on July 5, 1916, and arrived in San Diego, CA, on September 12, traveling through Buffalo, Chicago, Omaha, Denver, and Salt Lake City.

8291. Motorcycle to exceed 200 miles per hour was ridden by Wilhelm Herz, who rode a measured mile over the salt flats at Wendover, UT, on August 4, 1956, at a speed of 210 miles per hour.

Trucks

8292. Truck was designed and built in Pittsburgh, PA, in 1898–99 by Louis Semple Clarke and his associates. They were organized as the Pittsburgh Motor Vehicle Company and later incorporated as the Autocar Company. The first truck was pictured and described in Autocar's 1899 catalog as "a delivery wagon which can be made of any size or design, that will be fitted with five to eight horsepower motors. Complete with motors it will weigh from 900 to 1400 pounds—so simple in construction that any driver of ordinary intelligence can operate it with more safety than he could drive a horse."

8293. Mobile home was designed in 1929 by aviation pioneer Glenn Hammond Curtiss. The streamlined, wheeled trailer was built by the Hudson Motor Car Company, Detroit, MI, and was put on display in dealer showrooms in New York City.

8294. Truck completely streamlined from the ground up was introduced by the White Motor Company, Cleveland, OH, on September 4, 1935.

8295. Refrigeration system for trucks was patented in 1949 by Fred Jones, an African-American inventor. His roof-mounted cooling device enabled trucks to carry perishable goods over long distances.

8296. Motor vehicles powered by natural gas were light utility trucks purchased by the Southern California Gas Company beginning on September 2, 1992. Fifty of the trucks, which were powered by liquid natural gas, were put into service by the company under a California law promoting the commercialization of vehicles using alternative fuels.

8297. Fuel cell truck was developed by General Motors at its research center in Honeoye Falls, NY, and delivered to the U.S. Army on April 1, 2005. The modified Chevrolet Silverado crew-cab pickup truck, powered by two hydrogen fuel cell stacks, required only hydrogen for fuel, had a top speed of 93 miles per hour, and had a range of 125 miles. It was deployed for noncombat testing at Fort Belvoir, VA, and Camp Pendleton, CA.

Railroads

8298. Inclined railroad was erected in 1764 at Lewiston, NY, by British soldiers under the command of Captain John Montresor, for transporting supplies between the Niagara portage and the lower Niagara River 300 feet below. The road consisted of two sets of parallel logs laid up the banks on stone piers from the ship wharf below to the portage above. The logs were deeply grooved to receive the wheels of two cradle cars. The cars were joined by heavy ropes passed around a revolving drum to provide balance when one car was at the bottom and the other at the top. Originally, the road was used solely for military purposes by the troops, but later it was used for transporting merchandise.

8299. Railroad for freight transportation was a tramroad built in 1809 by John Thompson for Thomas Leiper so that he could carry stone from his quarries on Crum Creek to Ridley Creek, PA, a distance of about 0.75 miles. It had wooden rails that rested on sleepers eight feet apart. The cars had grooved wheels and were pulled by horses. The service was in operation for 19 years.

8300. Railroad charter granted by a state was granted on February 6, 1815, by New Jersey, which passed "an act to incorporate a company to erect a rail-road from the river Delaware, near Trenton, to the river Raritan, at or near New Brunswick." The railroad, advocated by John Stevens of Hoboken, NJ, was not completed.

8301. Railroad owned by a state was the Philadelphia and Columbia Railway, constructed under a Pennsylvania act dated March 24, 1828, which required the state's canal commissioners to build a railroad from Philadelphia to Columbia by way of Lancaster and extending to the west end of York. The first locomotive trip was made on April 2, 1834, from Lancaster to Columbia. This line was completed in 1834 from Philadelphia to Pittsburgh, in four divisions, the first of which was the Columbia Railroad. The construction and regulation of this road was the responsibility of the Pennsylvania Board of Canal Commissioners until August 1, 1857, when the Pennsylvania Railroad purchased it from the state and the road came under private management and control.

8302. Railroad for commercial transportation of passengers and freight was the Baltimore and Ohio Railroad Company, incorporated in Maryland and Virginia in 1827. Construction began at Baltimore, MD, on July 4, 1828, and the first passenger revenue was obtained on January 7, 1830. Tickets were 9 cents each, or three for 25 cents, for a ride from Pratt Street in Baltimore to the Carrollton Viaduct. At first, passengers rode primarily for the novel experience.

8303. Interstate railroad was the Petersburg Railroad, chartered by special act of the General Assembly of Virginia on February 10, 1830, and by special act of the North Carolina Legislature on January 1, 1831. It was opened in 1833 on a route along the north bank of the Roanoke River from Petersburg, VA, to Blakely, NC, a distance of 59 miles. On November 21, 1898, it became part of the Atlantic Coast Line Railroad Company system.

8304. Railroad timetable advertised in a newspaper appeared in the *Baltimore American* of Baltimore, MD, on May 20, 1830, by the Baltimore and Ohio Railroad Company. The advertisement announced that on May 24, 1830, passenger transportation would be effected between Baltimore and Ellicott's Mills, MD, and that a brigade of train coaches would leave the company's depot on Pratt Street, Baltimore, at 7 A.M., 11 A.M., and 4 P.M. and would return from Ellicott's Mills at 9 A.M., 1 P.M., and 6 P.M. The price for the 26-mile trip was 75 cents. Because of a shortage of cars, passengers were obliged to return in the same coach and had to book passage for the whole trip. When additional cars were available, passengers could use any car and could engage passage for a shorter distance, if desired.

8305. Passenger train to run on a regular schedule was operated by the South Carolina Canal and Railroad Company in Charleston, SC, beginning on December 25, 1830. Passengers could catch a train at 8 a.m., 10 a.m., 1 p.m. and 3:30 p.m.

8306. Railroad to carry troops was the Baltimore and Ohio Railroad Company. On June 30, 1831, the railroad transported Brigadier General George H. Steuart, 1st Division Maryland Guards, and about 100 volunteer troops to Sykes Mills (now Sykesville), MD, where they quelled a riot of railroad workers who were striking for back pay due them. The troops arrested about 50 workers.

8307. Railroad accident occurred on July 25, 1832, on the Granite Railway, Quincy, MA. Four visitors, after seeing the process of transporting large and weighty loads of stone, were invited to ascend the inclined plane in one of the vacant returning cars. The cable chain snapped and they were precipitated over a cliff, a distance of 30 to 40 feet. One man was killed and the others seriously injured.

8308. State aid to railroads was granted by Illinois, which was empowered by Congress on March 2, 1833, to sell land it had acquired from the federal government and to use the proceeds to aid in the construction of railroads. This grant did not become effective and was not used by the state.

8309. Railroad to run west out of Chicago was the Galena and Chicago Union Railroad, a constituent company of the Chicago and North Western Railway. Its first train was hauled by *The Pioneer*, a 10-ton wood-burning locomotive, which left Chicago, IL, on October 25, 1848, for Oak Park, five miles away. The North Western rails reached the Missouri River at Council Bluffs, IA, in 1867. The first railroad to run west of the Mississippi River was the Pacific Railway of Missouri (later known as the Missouri Pacific), which began passenger service from St. Louis on December 23, 1852.

8310. Railroad excursion rates originated in 1849, during an exhibition in Boston, MA, of a panorama of the Saguenay, St. Lawrence, and Niagara Falls. Josiah Perham of Boston persuaded railroads to grant a one-day low excursion rate to visitors from outside the city who wanted to see the panorama.

8311. Railroad land grant of importance was authorized by act of September 20, 1850, "an act granting the right of way and making a grant of land to the states of Illinois, Mississippi and Alabama in aid of the construction of a railroad from Chicago to Mobile." Illinois received 2,595,133 acres of land and transferred them to the Illinois Central Railroad Company, which broke ground on December 23, 1851. The first 60-mile section of the railroad, from La Salle to Bloomington, IL, was completed on May 16, 1853.

8312. Railroad merger of importance was the agreement of May 17, 1853, in which 10 companies consolidated under the title of New York Central Railroad Company with an aggregate capital of $23.1 million. On April 2, 1853, an act was passed by the New York legislature "to authorize the consolidation of certain railroad companies." The equipment consisted of 187 first-class passenger coaches, 55 second-class coaches, 65 baggage, mail, and express cars, and 1,702 freight cars. There were 298 miles of main line, 236 miles of branch line, and 29 miles of leased road.

8313. Union passenger station used by several railroad companies was the Union Station in Indianapolis, IN, opened on September 20, 1853, for the trains of five railroad companies. The depot was 100 feet wide and 420 feet long, and contained five tracks inside and through the depot, and two tracks outside and north of the depot. The constructing engineer was Colonel T. A. Morris. Edwards and Copeland were the general contractors. The depot was owned and operated by the Indianapolis Union Railway Company, which ran the station, the tracks, and the Indianapolis Belt Railroad.

8314. Railroad safety law enacted by a state was passed by Georgia on March 5, 1856. The law, which made railroad companies liable for injuries to employees and passengers caused by negligence, was "an act to define the liability of the several railroad companies of this state for injuries to persons or property, to prescribe in what counties they may be sued, and how served with process."

8315. Cog railroad in the world was the Mount Washington Cog Railway, which ran to the summit of Mount Washington, NH. The railway was invented by Sylvester Marsh of Littleton, NH. Work was begun in May 1866. The first public demonstration was made at the base of the mountain on August 29, 1866, on a half-mile section of track. The railway was completed in July 1869 at a cost of $139,500.

8316. Elevated railroad was opened for traffic on July 2, 1867, in New York City. Charles T. Harvey built the first half-mile test section on single columns along the curb line of Greenwich Street, between Battery Place and Dey Street. The speed of the cars was from 12 to 15 miles per hour. The line was unsuccessful and was sold at a sheriff's sale. It was reorganized February 14, 1870, and placed in operation with steam power. Service was extended as far north as the New York Central Railroad Passenger station at 29th Street and Ninth Avenue.

8317. Railroad owned by a city was authorized by the Ohio legislature on May 4, 1869, with an "act to authorize cities of the first class to build railroads and to lease or operate the same." The first city to construct a railroad was Cincinnati. The Cincinnati Southern Railway started regular passenger service to Ludlow and Somerset, KY, on July 23, 1877. Freight service started on August 13. Freight service to Chattanooga, TN, was inaugurated on February 21, 1880, and through passenger trains on March 5. The railroad was leased on October 12, 1881, to the Cincinnati, New Orleans and Texas Pacific Railway Company for five five-year periods.

8318. Transcontinental railroad service became possible on May 10, 1869, when Senator Leland Stanford drove the last spike into the Union Pacific's rails at Promontory, UT, completing a rail network that stretched across the country and that was made up of numerous railroad companies.

8319. Electric elevated railroad was operated at the Chicago Railway Exposition in June 1883 by the Electric Railway Company of the United States. The *Judge*, a 15-horsepower electric locomotive, hauled the trains on a three-foot-gauge track around the outer edge of a gallery of the main exhibition building, curving sharply at either end on a radius of 56 feet. The total length of the track was 1,553 feet. The trial trip was made on June 2, 1883, but the line was not permitted to operate until June 9. It ceased operating on June 23, having run 118.75 hours. It made 1,588 trips, carried 26,805 passengers, and ran 446.24 miles. It was the first commercial electric line to operate. The first permanent electric elevated railroad was the Metropolitan West Side Elevated Railway in Chicago, which opened on May 17, 1895. It ran from Franklin Street to Logan Square, a distance of five miles.

8320. Piggyback railroad operation began on January 5, 1885, on the Long Island Rail Road in New York State. A produce train, consisting of eight flatcars for carrying farmers' wagons, eight cars to carry their horses, and a coach for teamsters, left Albertson's Station, a railroad station on Long Island. It arrived at 6:30 A.M. at Long Island City, where a ferry carried the wagons across the East River to New York City.

8321. Transcontinental daily railroad service was established in 1887. Passengers changed trains at Omaha, NE. On November 17, 1889, direct service was inaugurated between Chicago, IL, and Portland, OR, and between Chicago and San Francisco, CA, by the Union Pacific Railroad Company. This train was the *Overland Limited.*

8322. Railroad safety law enacted by Congress was the Safety Appliance Act, passed on March 2, 1893, "an act to promote the safety of employees and travelers upon railroads by compelling common carriers engaged in interstate commerce to equip their cars with automatic couplers and continuous brakes and their locomotives with driving wheel brakes, and for other purposes."

8323. Railroad to use an electric engine for a short distance in place of a steam engine was the Baltimore and Ohio, Baltimore, MD, which ran its first train with an electric engine through the Baltimore tunnel for a distance of 3.6 miles. The regular use of electric engines for freight trains for this distance was begun on August 4, 1894, and for passenger trains on May 1, 1895.

8324. Railroad operated by an electric third-rail system was the Lackawanna and Wyoming Valley Railroad Company (Laurel Company), which commenced operations in Scranton, PA, on May 25, 1903. After the system had been tried out successfully in Scranton, the elevated railway in New York City was electrified with a third rail.

8325. All-electric railroad was the Long Island Rail Road, which in 1905 installed a low-voltage third rail system on all its lines, eliminating the need for steam locomotion.

8326. Railroad operated by the federal government was the Alaska Railroad, acquired under the Alaska Railroad Enabling Act of March 12, 1914, from various private railroad companies. The golden spike marking the completion of the rail network was driven by President Warren Gamaliel Harding at Nenana, AK, on July 15, 1923. The railroad, which operated 478 miles of track, was under the control of the Federal Railroad Administration within the Department of Transportation.

8327. Railroad to be completely equipped with diesel-electric engines was the New York, Susquehanna and Western Railroad. The first diesel unit was placed in service on December 27, 1941. By May 25, 1945, all 16 engines in the fleet were diesel-electrics. They were built by the American Locomotive Company, New York City, and the General Electric Company, Schenectady, NY.

8328. Transcontinental Pullman sleeping car daily service requiring no change of cars was inaugurated on March 30, 1946, between New York City and Los Angeles, CA. The "Imperial Forest," a sleeping car of the *Twentieth Century Limited*, left New York City at 5:30 P.M. and arrived at Los Angeles on April 3, 1946, at 11:50 A.M., attached to the *Santa Fe Chief*. The hookup and transfer were made at Chicago. Eastward service ran from Los Angeles to New York. This service was discontinued in April 1958.

8329. Railroad freight yard that was fully automatic was the Elgin, Joliet and Eastern Railway Company's Kirk Yard at Gary, IN, which began operating under manual control on January 25, 1952, and changed to fully automatic operation on December 17, 1954. Radar and electronic brain circuits were used to sort out and assemble freight cars by destination, weigh them automatically, and couple them into trains. The equipment was installed by the General Railway Signal Company, Rochester, NY.

Locomotives

8330. Locomotive to pull a train on a track was a steam locomotive that was designed and built by John Stevens in 1824, when he was 76 years old. The locomotive could pull a 1,000-pound load at 12 miles per hour. It was operated on a circular track 220 feet in circumference on Stevens's estate at Hoboken, NJ. It moved by means of a large gear wheel engaging a toothed rack placed on the ties between the rails. The wheels had no flanges, so to keep the train from running off the track, Stevens affixed little horizontal friction rollers on the underside chassis that pressed and rolled along the inner vertical face of the wooden beams used for rails. The locomotive was completed on October 23, 1824.

8331. Locomotive for railroad use was the *Stourbridge Lion*, built by Foster, Rastrick and Company of Stourbridge, England. The diameter of the driving wheel was 48 inches. The gauge was 4 feet 3 inches. Horatio Allen was sent to England by the Delaware and Hudson Railroad Company to purchase it. The engine weighed seven tons and traveled at the speed of 10 miles per hour. Its first run in the United States took place on August 9, 1829, on the tracks of the Delaware and Hudson in Pennsylvania between Carbondale, a coal mining center, and Honesdale, the canal terminus. The locomotive was too heavy for the track.

8332. Passenger locomotive built in the United States was the *Tom Thumb*, designed and built by Peter Cooper in Baltimore, MD. It weighed six tons and had a 30-inch driving wheel. Its gauge was 4 feet 8.5 inches. On August 28, 1830, it carried 26 passengers a distance of 13 miles over the tracks of the Baltimore and Ohio Railroad in 1 hour 15 minutes. It returned with 30 passengers in 61 minutes, including a four-minute stop to take on water. Another American locomotive, the *Best Friend*, built at the West Point Foundry for use on the Charleston and Hamburg Railroad, made its initial trip on November 2, 1830, but it was derailed.

8333. Locomotive to burn coal was the *York*, invented by Phineas Davis, a watchmaker, and built at York, PA. Its first trial took place on February 19, 1831. It was the first locomotive that had coupled wheels and a double instead of a single pair of drivers. It weighed 3.5 tons and attained velocity by gearing, using a spur wheel and pinion on one of the axles of the wheels. The only accident in which it was involved occurred on September 27, 1835, as the result of a defective track. The accident killed Phineas Davis, who was riding on the locomotive.

8334. Locomotive with six or eight driving wheels attached to parallel axles was patented by Ross Winans on October 1, 1834. Winans was also the first to introduce eight-wheel cars in railroading. The first car was the *Columbus*, which was put into use by the Baltimore and Ohio Railroad Company, Baltimore, MD, on July 4, 1831.

8335. Locomotive with a cab for the engineer and crew was the *Samuel D. Ingham*, built in 1835–36 in Philadelphia, PA, for the Beaver Meadow Railroad (later the Lehigh Valley Railroad). It was of the eight-wheel type and had a peculiar valve motion, the reversing being done by a block sliding on the valve seats. It was designed by Andrew Eastwick. Abner Houston was the engineer, and Stephen Maxwell and "Squire Longshore" were the spragmen who pressed the brake blocks against the wheels to lessen the speed.

8336. Locomotive steam whistle was made by the Rogers Locomotive and Machine Works, Paterson, NJ, and used on October 6, 1837, by the Paterson and Hudson River Railroad on *The Sandusky*, a locomotive with a four-wheeled truck under the forward part of the engine. The whistle was so overworked on the locomotive's run from Paterson to New Brunswick, NJ, that the supply of steam was affected. The locomotive was sold to the Mad River and Lake Erie Railroad Company for $6,750 and on October 14, 1837, was packed in boxes and shipped by schooner.

8337. Electric locomotive made a trial round trip on April 29, 1851, on the Washington branch of the Baltimore and Ohio Railroad from Washington, DC, to Bladensburg, MD, five miles each way. It was designed by Charles Grafton Page of Salem, MA. It was 15 feet long and 6 feet wide, and had a platform truck of four wheels under the forward end and two 5-foot driving wheels under the rear end. It attained a speed of 19 miles per hour. It was operated by galvanized storage batteries, but was not practical, as it did not run any appreciable distance. The first electric freight locomotive was built by the Pullman Car Company at Pullman, IL, in 1888 for the Ansonia, Derby and Birmingham Electric Line, which later became part of the Connecticut Company and thus a part of Conrail (New Haven Division). It weighed 17.5 tons and was capable of hauling a train weighing about 35 tons at less than 10 miles per hour. The first trial took place on May 1, 1888.

8338. Narrow-gauge locomotive was constructed in Philadelphia, PA, by the Baldwin Locomotive Works. It was known as Engine No. 1, the *Montezuma*, and was first used by the Denver and Rio Grande Western Railroad Company on July 3, 1871. It had a 3-foot gauge, a length of 30 feet, and a total weight of 25,000 pounds.

8339. Locomotive to use oil for fuel was the *Young America*, an eight-wheeled wood-burning locomotive that was equipped with an oil burner from a San Francisco steamboat in 1879 by the Central Pacific Railroad. The fuel supply consisted of one barrel of crude oil mounted on a tender and connected to the burner with five hose lines.

8340. Locomotive to attain a speed of one mile in less than a minute was a No. 10 locomotive, built at Altoona, PA. During a 34-mile run from Huntingdon to Harrisburg, PA, on March 17, 1881, it covered one mile in 58 seconds and another mile in 59 seconds.

8341. Locomotive owned by an industrial company was ordered in June 1890 by the Whitin Machine Works, Whitinsville, MA, from the Thomson-Houston Electric Company, Lynn, MA, and placed in service on May 11, 1892, hauling freight cars to the plant. It could haul 60 tons at a speed of seven miles per hour.

8342. Diesel-electric locomotive was No. 1000, a 300-horsepower locomotive placed in service on December 17, 1924, by the Central Railroad of New Jersey at the Bronx terminal, New York City. The diesel engine was built by the Ingersoll-Rand Company, Phillipsburg, NJ, the electrical components by the General Electric Company, Elmira, NY, and the locomotive structure by the American Locomotive Company, Schenectady, NY. The locomotive remained in service until June 13, 1957. The first diesel-electric freight locomotive was constructed by the New York Central Lines in January 1928 and placed in operation in June 1928.

8343. Streamlined steam locomotive was introduced by the New York Central Lines on December 14, 1934, between Albany and Karner, NY. Built in West Albany, NY, it was named the *Commodore Vanderbilt* after the founder of the New York Central Lines. It was 96 feet long, weighed 228 tons, and developed 4,075 horsepower.

8344. Streamlined electric locomotive was No. 4800, type GG1, placed in service by the Pennsylvania Railroad Company on January 28, 1935, in a test run between Washington, DC, and Philadelphia, PA. The engine was 79.5 feet long, of all-steel construction, and weighed 230 tons. It operated on an 11,000-volt, 25-cycle, single-phase system, the current fed by overhead wires through a pantograph. The electric engine was placed in passenger service on February 10, 1935.

8345. Super-giant locomotive to carry the weight of 1 million pounds on drivers was the Class EL-2B No. 125, a 6,800-horsepower electric locomotive built by the General Electric Company, Erie, PA, and placed in operation on January 27, 1948, by the Virginia Railway Company, Norfolk, VA, between Roanoke, VA, and Mullens, WV. It had 16 driving axles and an overall length of 150 feet 8 inches.

8346. Gas-turbine-electric locomotive was track-tested on November 15, 1948, at Erie, PA. It was built by the American Locomotive Company for the Union Pacific Railroad Company and publicly demonstrated on June 16, 1949. The locomotive was 83 feet 7.5 inches long, weighed 500,000 pounds, and had a continuous tractive effort of 68,500 pounds at 20.4 miles per hour. Power from the generator was supplied to eight traction motors, each of which drove an axle. It was geared for 79 miles per hour, the locomotive carrying enough fuel for 12 hours of operation at 4,500 horsepower. The gas turbine power was rated at 4,800 horsepower.

Railroad Cars

8347. Double-deck railroad coaches were built by Richard Imlay in August 1830 and used on the Baltimore and Ohio Railroad between Baltimore, MD, and Ellicott's Mill, MD. They were called "Improved Passenger Cars." Each coach accommodated 12 passengers on the lower deck. An additional six people, including the driver, occupied outside seats at the end of the deck. The upper deck of each carriages was furnished with a double sofa that accommodated 12 more passengers, who were shaded by an awning stretched over an iron frame.

8348. Railroad car with a center aisle was the *Columbus*, introduced on July 4, 1831, by the Baltimore and Ohio Railroad Company, despite fears that the aisle would become one long spittoon. The car was designed by Ross Winans and built at Baltimore, MD.

8349. Railroad sleeping car was *The Chambersburg*, used in 1836 by the Cumberland Valley Railroad between Harrisburg and Chambersburg, PA. It included four sleeping sections, each of which had three bunks. No bedding was provided. It was common for persons traveling to sleep fully clothed and to cover themselves with shawls, which they carried with them for the purpose.

8350. Private railroad car was outfitted for the singer Jenny Lind, the "Swedish Nightingale," who made her first American appearance on September 11, 1850, at Castle Garden, New York City. The car was used on her tour of the country.

8351. Pullman sleeping car was "Old No. 9," built by Ben Field and George Mortimer Pullman in 1859 in Chicago, IL, and placed in service on September 1, 1859, on the Chicago and Alton Railroad between Bloomington and Chicago. It was a reconstructed day coach, little more than half the length of present coaches. Except for the wheels and axles, it was constructed almost entirely of wood. The roof was flat and low. The seats were adamantine. Two small wood-burning stoves furnished heat. The illumination was furnished by candles. There was a small lavatory at each end. The drinking faucet supplied water to a nonenclosed washbasin. There were 10 upper and 10 lower berths with mattresses and blankets but no sheets. The upper berth was suspended about halfway between the floor and ceiling at night, and by day was drawn up to the ceiling by pulleys.

8352. Oil tank railroad cars were introduced by Charles P. Hatch of the Empire Transportation Company, Philadelphia, PA, in 1864–65 and used on the Oil Creek Railroad, the Warren and Franklin Railroad, and other lines. Cars with three wooden tanks containing 3,500 gallons were used, but rain dissolved the glue coating and caused leakage. Later, riveted iron tanks mounted horizontally were used. On September 1, 1865, Amos Densmore mounted two wooden tanks over the trucks of a flatcar and used them to ship oil from Miller's Farm to New York City over the Atlantic and Great Western Railroad. The shipment consisted of two cars, each with two tanks, and each tank containing about 40 barrels.

8353. Pullman sleeping car that was comfortable was *The Pioneer*, built by George Mortimer Pullman in 1865 in Chicago, IL, at a cost of $18,000. It rested on 16 wheels (a later version of the car had 12 wheels). The car was longer, higher, and wider than its predecessors and had the first raised upper deck and folding upper berth. It was heated by hot air furnaces under the floor, lighted with candles, and ventilated through deck windows. It was fully carpeted, and the seats were covered with French plush upholstery.

8354. Refrigerated railroad car was patented by J. B. Sutherland of Detroit, MI, on November 26, 1867. He received a patent on an insulated car constructed with ice bunkers in each end. Air came in at the top, was passed through the ice chambers, and circulated through the car by means of gravity, controlled by the use of hanging flaps that created differences in air temperature. The first refrigerated railroad car to carry a load of fresh fruit was constructed in 1866 by Parker Earle of Cobden, IL, who built and shipped chests of strawberries on the Illinois Central Railroad. The chests had three layers of board and were airtight and watertight. They held 100 pounds of ice and 200 quarts of strawberries, which brought $2 a quart. In 1872, Earle shipped a full carload from Anna, IL, to Chicago.

8355. Railroad dining car ever operated in the world was the *Delmonico*, built in 1868 by the Pullman Palace Car Company, Pullman, IL, and placed in service between Chicago, IL, and St. Louis, MO, by the Chicago and Alton Railroad Company. It had tables and chairs and was serviced by a kitchen. Passengers on the Philadelphia–Baltimore run of the Philadelphia, Wilmington and Baltimore Railroad in 1863 were able to buy food at a 50-foot-long refreshment car fitted with an eating bar and steam box, where food prepared at the terminals was heated and sold.

8356. Railroad parlor car was the *Maritana*, built by George Mortimer Pullman and placed in operation in 1875. The chairs in the car were richly upholstered, with adjustable backs, and revolved on swivels.

8357. Railroad chapel car was the *Evangel*, dedicated on May 23, 1891, in Cincinnati, OH. The dedication address was delivered by Dr. Wayland Hoyt. The car was fitted out for religious services and was used on the Northern Pacific Railroad's tracks. Experimental services were held in St. Paul and Minneapolis, MN. The car was committed for the winter to the Reverend and Mrs. E. G. Wheeler, who conducted services in it on the Pacific Coast.

8358. Railroad tank car lined with glass for transporting milk was built in 1910 by the Pfaudler Company, Rochester, NY, for the Whiting Milk Company, Boston, MA. It was used on the Boston and Maine Railroad to collect milk from the country for city consumption.

8359. Air-conditioned railroad cars were installed by the Atchison, Topeka and Santa Fe Railway Company in 1914, when 15 new dining cars were put in service on the *California Limited* between Chicago, IL, and Los Angeles, CA. The system was known as the Duntley Air Washer and consisted of a motor-driven spray wheel partially submerged in ice water. Fresh air was drawn through the spray and delivered into the car by means of a fan and air ducts. This system lowered the temperature a few degrees, but the capacity was inadequate. An air-conditioning experiment was tried in 1854 by the New York and Erie Railroad, using a device that caught air through a funnel and passed it through a water tank underneath the car on its way to the car's interior. In winter, the air was heated by a stove. An opening in the rear of the car enabled the air to escape.

8360. Railroad car with an observation dome was placed in service on July 23, 1945, by the Chicago, Burlington and Quincy Railroad. It was a standard Budd stainless-steel coach equipped with three decks. A section of the top deck had a curved double glass roof called a VistaDome. The section was 19.5 feet long, extended the full width of the car, and seated 24 passengers. The first superdome observation cars were built by the Pullman-Standard Car Manufacturing Company and placed in service on January 1, 1953, by the Chicago, Milwaukee, St. Paul and Pacific Railroad. They were 85 feet long, 10 feet wide, and 15 feet 6 inches from top to rail. The dome section contained 625 square feet of curved safety glass in sections 3 feet wide and 5 feet high. The laminated glass consisted of polished plate glass and layers of plastic.

8361. Railroad dining car powered by electricity was the *Cafe St. Louis*, built in Chicago, IL, and placed in service on March 9, 1949, between Chicago and St. Louis, MO, by the Illinois Central Railroad. It had a self-contained electric power unit that developed approximately 50,000 watts, supplying the power for two broilers, two ranges, a hot food table, a coffee urn, plate and cup warmers, a deep-fry kettle, a dishwasher, a glass washer, mixers and fruit juice extractors, refrigerators, and a garbage disposal system.

8362. Railroad freight cars with compartments were developed jointly by the Western Pacific Railroad Company and the Pullman Standard Car Company and placed in service on September 12, 1952, between Chicago, IL, and San Francisco, CA. Four gates were installed in each car to separate the contents into sections and to prevent shifting and crushing.

8363. Adaptable railroad freight car was built by the American Car and Foundry Division of ACF Industries at Berwick, PA, and was placed in service on July 24, 1956, by the Chicago, Rock Island and Pacific Railroad Company between St. Louis, MO, and Wichita, KS. It was called an Adapto Car. Sections of various shapes and sizes were made to fit above the chassis of a flatcar. The sections could be removed along with their contents to allow reuse of the car without unloading.

Streetcars

8364. Streetcar company was the New York and Harlem Railway, New York City, incorporated on April 25, 1831, "to construct a single or double railroad." It was capitalized for $350,000 and received a 30-year franchise on December 22, 1831, from the Common Council. The first secretary was John Mason, who later became president.

8365. Streetcar was the *John Mason*, a horse-drawn conveyance designed and constructed by John Stephenson in Philadelphia, PA, and placed in service in New York City by the New York and Harlem Railway on November 26, 1832. Named for the prominent New York banker who organized the railway company, the *John Mason* was equipped with iron wheels and was drawn over iron rails laid in the center of the pavement. Lank O'Dell was the first driver. The car was divided into three nonconnecting compartments with 10 seats in each. The first of the three doors bore on its panel the name *New York*, the second *Yorkville*, and the third *Harlaem*. The fare was 12.5 cents. Tracks for the streetcar were laid along Fourth Avenue from Prince Street to 14th Street. In November 1835, a double track running north to Yorkville was completed.

8366. Cable car was invented by Eleazer A. Gardner of Philadelphia, PA, who obtained a patent on March 23, 1858, on an "improvement in tracks for city railways." The cable was housed in an underground tunnel with a series of pulleys inside.

8367. Coin box for streetcars was invented about 1870 in Louisville, KY, by Thomas Loftin Johnson, who rose from clerk to owner of a street railway in Indianapolis and became a large stockholder in railroad companies in New York City, Cleveland, and Detroit.

8368. Gas-powered streetcar was operated in 1873 in Providence, RI, from the car barns to Olneyville Square. Henry Thompson was the conductor. It had a gas and air engine, compressed by separate pumps. The engine was patented on April 2, 1872, by its designer, George B. Brayton of Boston, MA.

8369. Cable car put into service began operation on August 1, 1873, on Clay Street Hill, San Francisco, CA. The ride cost five cents. This was the first cable car put into service anywhere in the world. It was invented by Andrew Smith Hallidie, who obtained a patent on January 17, 1871, on an "endless-wire rope way."

8370. Electric streetcars commercially operated were those of the Baltimore and Hampden Line, a third-rail system that began operation on one line only on August 10, 1885, in Baltimore, MD. The line continued in service for more than a year. The first cars traveled on the Hampden Branch of the Baltimore Union Passenger Railway Company, which later became a part of the United Railways and Electric Company of Baltimore, MD.

8371. Double-deck streetcar was operated on July 4, 1892, on a trial trip in San Diego, CA. The upper deck was on the roof, with longitudinal seats facing outward that accommodated 12 people on each side. It was reached by a winding stairway at each end of the car, and shaded by a canopy. There were no sides or enclosures on the upper deck other than a railing.

8372. Printed streetcar transfers were invented by John Harry Stedman of Rochester, NY, who patented them on August 23, 1892. They were 1.875 by 2.5 inches and were first used on October 31, 1892, in Rochester.

8373. Interurban streetcar line was the Union Traction Company, established by Charles Lewis Henry. The company ran its first car on June 1, 1898, between Anderson and Alexandria, IN. The first conductor was Hadley Clifford.

8374. Trackless trolley system was built by Charles Mann and placed in operation on September 11, 1910, between "Bungalow Land" in Laurel Canyon, CA, and the terminal point of the Los Angeles Pacific Electric Railway Company in Los Angeles, a distance of 1.5 miles. Two automobile buses were used. On top of the buses were trolley poles making contact with overhead wires.

8375. Municipal streetcars were put into service on December 28, 1912, in San Francisco, CA. The Municipal Railway, an overhead trolley system, began operation with 10 cars on Geary Street, from Kearney Street to 33rd Avenue and Park. Thomas A. Cashin was superintendent. Mayor James Rolph, Jr., acted as motorman on the first car.

Subways

8376. Subway was the pneumatic subway invented by Alfred Ely Beach and was known as the Beach Pneumatic Underground Railway of New York City. The company was incorporated for freight traffic on June 1, 1868, and for passenger traffic on May 3, 1869, with a capital stock of $5 million. The system was opened to the public on February 26, 1870. The tunnel was 312 feet long and ran from the west curb line of Broadway at Warren Street down the middle of Broadway to a point south of Murray Street. It consisted of a circular tube nine feet in diameter. The straightaways were built of brick masonry, and the curves were built of iron plate. The cars, which were well upholstered, carried 22 persons each. They were propelled by a rotary blower that drove a blast of air through the tunnel against the rear of the car, carrying it along "like a sailboat before the wind."

8377. Municipal subway was the Tremont Street Subway, Boston, MA, construction of which was begun on March 28, 1895. The section between the Public Garden and Park Street was opened for traffic on September 1, 1897, and the section to North Station on September 3, 1898. The subway was built by the City of Boston at a cost of $4,369,000 and leased to the Boston Elevated Railway at an annual rental of 4.5 percent of construction cost.

8378. Rapid-transit subway was the Interborough Rapid Transit subway in New York City. The route ran north from City Hall (Brooklyn Bridge) under Lafayette Street and Park Avenue to Grand Central Station, west along 42nd Street to Times Square, then north on Broadway to 145th Street. The line was opened on October 27, 1904. At 7 P.M., 111,881 passengers paid a nickel each to ride for 26 minutes on the express train or 46 minutes on the local. The IRT's 300 subway motor cars and trailers were the first to have finish work, moldings, window panels, and other parts made of aluminum.

8379. Subway car with side doors was placed in service on February 16, 1909, when eight cars of the Interborough Rapid Transit of New York City left Lenox Avenue and 148th Street going south. The side doors, four feet from each end of the car, were opened and closed by a pneumatic-lever system. The cars cost $12,000 each. The doors were the invention of James McElroy of the Consolidated Car Heating Company.

8380. Subway train to run automatically without conductors or motormen was placed in operation in New York City on January 4, 1962, between Grand Central Station and Times Square. The train carried a motorman who stood by without performing any duties. This was a safety measure demanded by the transport workers' union, which was involved in a labor dispute with the New York City Transit Authority.

Tracks and Equipment

8381. Railroad track that was practical was laid in Philadelphia, PA, in 1809. It was made of wood laid on a steep grade of 1.5 inches to the yard and was 180 feet in length. On July 31, a carriage weighing 10,696 pounds with four grooved wheels was placed on the track at the lower end and a single horse walking on the loose dirt between the tracks pulled it up the slope.

8382. Railroad rails of T shape were invented in 1830 by Robert Livingston Stevens, president and engineer of the Camden and Amboy Railroad. They were made of malleable iron and weighed 36 pounds a yard. Their adoption was very slow, as the type of rail then preferred was the flat rail that was nailed to the ties.

8383. Locomotive cowcatcher was invented by Isaac Dripps and used in 1833 on the Camden and Amboy Railroad between Bordentown and Hightstown, NJ. It consisted originally of a small attachment on two wheels with projecting points, but since the prongs impaled animals, it was replaced by a heavy bar set at right angles to the rails.

Library of Congress, Prints & Photographs Division LC-USZC4-2365

A steam locomotive, with cowcatcher in front.

8384. Railroad rails of iron were rolled in 1844 at the Mount Savage Rolling Mill, Mount Savage, MD, and weighed 42 pounds a yard. Five hundred tons of the inverted U-type rails were rolled in 1845. They were laid between Mount Savage and Cumberland, MD, a distance of approximately nine miles. This rolling mill also produced T rails, which weighed 50 pounds a yard.

8385. Railroad rails of steel were used by the Pennsylvania Railroad. They weighed 56 pounds a yard and were placed in service in 1864 between Altoona and Pittsburgh, PA. The first rails of Bessemer steel were rolled at the North Chicago rolling mill, Chicago, IL, on May 24, 1865, from ingots made at the experimental steel works at Wyandotte, MI. Their manufacture was witnessed by members of the American Iron and Steel Association, who were assembled in conference at Chicago.

8386. Air brake was invented by George Westinghouse, Jr., of Schenectady, NY, who received a patent on April 13, 1869, on a "steam power brake." It was used on an experimental train carrying officials of the Panhandle Railroad. It immediately demonstrated its value. But inasmuch as it took longer for the air to reach the last cars of a train, each car stopped at a different time. A "triple air brake" that corrected this fault was patented by Westinghouse on March 5, 1872. He invented an automatic brake 15 years later.

8387. Railroad to install track water tanks to allow trains to take water on the run was the Pennsylvania Railroad, which placed a track tank in the northbound track at Sang Hollow on the Pittsburgh division during the early months of 1870, followed by a 1,200-foot tank in the southbound track at the same location. In the same year, the New York Central installed track tanks between Montrose and Albany.

8388. Railroad signal system with automatic electric block was invented by Thomas S. Hall of Stamford, CT, in 1867 and was installed on the New York and Harlem Railroad. Hall obtained a patent on June 7, 1870, for his electromagnetic railway signal apparatus. The wheels of the locomotive struck a lever fastened to the rail and this in turn set the signal at danger until the train was out of the block. The first signal system with a manual block had been installed in 1863 between Philadelphia, PA, and Trenton, NJ, on the Philadelphia and Trenton Railroad.

8389. Railroad coupler with which every railroad car in the United States, Canada, and Mexico was equipped was invented by Eli Hamilton Janney of Alexandria, VA, who obtained a patent on an "improvement in car-couplings" on April 29, 1873.

8390. Railroad interlocking signal machine was placed in service at Spuyten Duyvil, the Bronx, NY (now part of New York City), in 1874 by the New York Central and Hudson River Railroad. Levers operated from a central location controlled an arrangement of switch and signal appliances, providing a safe path for the movement of trains through switches, junctions, grade crossings, and terminal stations, and over drawbridges.

8391. Electric locomotive headlight was patented by Leonidas G. Woolley of Mendon, MI, on May 3, 1881. It was a polygonal lamp frame suspended in position by a series of opposing springs that neutralized the engine's jarring.

8392. Locomotive communications headlight was installed on November 6, 1934, on a Union Pacific six-car streamlined train, and was demonstrated the following day at the railway station in Schenectady, NY. The operator on the train aimed the beacon of his projector at a concave mirror mounted on the platform. Persons aboard the train were able to speak over the beam of light to others on the platform. The installation was made by the General Electric Company of Schenectady.

Trains

8393. Streamlined railroad train was invented by the Reverend Samuel R. Calthorp of Roxbury, MA, who obtained a patent on August 8, 1865, on an "air resister train." He gave "to the exterior surface of a railway train a form tapering from the center of the train toward either end, for the purpose of diminishing the atmosphere resistance." The front and rear ends of the train were pointed, and the wheels were enclosed in casing. The only projection was the smokestack. The tender was attached to the locomotive by an accordion hood.

8394. Train with electric lighting was the *Pennsylvania Limited* of the Pennsylvania Railroad Company, placed in service in June 1887 between Chicago, IL, and New York City. Steam from the engine was carried to a turbine in the forward compartment of the baggage car, where it drove an electric generator supplying current to the entire train.

8395. Air-conditioned train was installed by the Baltimore and Ohio Railroad Company. Air-conditioned service began on May 24, 1931, on the Washington–New York route, in both directions. The westbound train left New York City at 3:57 P.M. and the eastbound train left Washington, DC, at 4 P.M. Each train was made up of the following cars, all of which were air-conditioned and air-cooled: smoking car, coach, lounge car, colonial dining car, Pullman parlor car, and observation sunroom parlor car. The train was drawn by one of the President series of locomotives.

8396. Train to run 1,000 miles nonstop was the Chicago, Burlington and Quincy's streamlined train *Zephyr*, powered by a 660-horsepower diesel engine. The *Zephyr* left Union Station, Denver, CO, at 6:04 A.M. on May 26, 1934, and arrived at the Halsted Street station, Chicago, IL, in 13 hours 5 minutes 44 seconds. The trip covered a distance of 1,015 miles. The average speed was 77.6 miles per hour and the top speed 112 miles per hour. There were 65 persons aboard.

8397. Streamlined all-steel diesel-motor train was the *Zephyr*, 196 feet long and 208,061 pounds in weight, built by the Edward G. Budd Manufacturing Company of Philadelphia, PA, for the Chicago, Burlington and Quincy Railroad for service between Kansas City, MO, and Lincoln, NE. It was driven by a Winton 660-horsepower high-compression two-cycle eight-in-line diesel-electric motor. The first trip, on November 11, 1934, was a run from Lincoln to Kansas City via Omaha and back the same day.

8398. Train to transport passengers and their cars was the Auto-Train, which began daily service on December 6, 1971, between Lorton, VA, outside Washington, DC, and Sanford, FL, a town north of Orlando. At full complement, it consisted of 13 vehicle carriers, 2 buffet-movie cars, 5 coaches, 4 bedroom cars, 2 locomotives, a steam-generator car, and a kitchen car. Automobiles were loaded on two-level enclosed piggyback cars. Passengers rode in bi-level domed coaches and could have bedroom accommodations at an extra charge. One-way fare was $190 for an automobile and up to four people, with a charge of $15 for each additional passenger up to the legal maximum of the shipped auto's capacity. A buffet dinner, late-evening snacks, a continental breakfast, and movies were included in the charge. The train could transport 100 cars and 400 people.

8399. Train operated exclusively by women was placed in service on June 6, 1979, by the Long Island Rail Road. It started from Port Washington, NY, at 4:35 P.M. and arrived at Pennsylvania Station, New York City, at 5:07 P.M. The train's conductor was Deirdre Hickey, the first woman to qualify in yard, freight, and passenger service. Doreen Boyle was the fare collector; Beverly Terrillion and Eileen Denn, the brakemen.

Ships and Boats

8400. Ships built by Europeans in America were crude flatboats constructed by the Spanish expedition led by Pánfilo de Narváez between April 14, 1528, and the following September, near what is now the town of St. Marks, FL. The men reached the western shore of Florida on April 14 and traveled inland, but were unable to return to their supply ship. They spent six weeks building five boats, each 33 feet long. About 250 men embarked on these boats in the hope of finding their way to the Spanish settlement on the Panuco River in Mexico. Only four of them reached civilization.

8401. Ship built by English colonists in America was the *Virginia of Sagadahock*, launched in Maine from the banks of the Sagadahoc River (now the Kennebec) in Maine by the colonists of the short-lived Popham settlement in 1607. A ship of 30 tons, it was 30 feet long, had a beam of 13 feet, and drew 8 feet. Moss was used for caulking and shirts were used for its sails.

8402. Prefabricated ship built in America was an open shallop that was assembled by the London Company's Virginia colonists at the entrance to Chesapeake Bay. It was begun on April 17, 1607, and completed and launched on May 18. Captain John Smith, in his account of the colony, wrote that the shallop "had been shipped in portions easy to be fitted together."

8403. Decked ship built in America was built at the southern tip of what is now Manhattan Island, New York City, by the Dutch explorer Adriaen Block in the summer of 1614. He named it the *Onrust* ("Restless"). It was a 16-ton ship, 38 feet on the keel, 44.5 feet overall, and 11 feet in the beam, and was launched in the Hudson River.

8404. Great Lakes vessel was *Le Griffon*, a two-masted armored square-rigger built in 1679 by the explorer Robert Cavelier, Sieur de La Salle, at Cayuga Creek, near the Niagara River in New York. The keel was laid on January 26, 1679, and its first voyage was made on August 7. It was of 60 tons burden and sailed Lake Erie and Lake Michigan. It sank on September 18, 1679, in a gale in Mackinaw Strait and is believed to be resting in Mississagi Strait, Manitoulin Island, Canada.

8405. Schooner built in America was launched at Gloucester, Cape Ann, MA, in 1714. It was built by Henry Robinson.

8406. Steamboat was built by William Henry in 1763. He built an engine and a model stern-wheel boat that was tested unsuccessfully on the Conestoga Creek at Lancaster, PA.

8407. Nautical almanac was Samuel Stearns's *The Universal Kalendar, Comprehending the Landsman's and Seaman's Almanack for the Year 1783*, published on December 29, 1782, in Boston, MA, by Benjamin Edes and Son.

8408. Motorboat was invented by James Rumsey and exhibited by him in September 1784 on the Potomac River, in the presence of George Washington. It worked against the stream by mechanical means. He subsequently gave his attention to steam as a motive power and in March 1786 propelled a boat on the Potomac by a steam engine that produced motion by a pump at the stern. In December 1787 the experiment was successfully repeated on a larger scale.

8409. Steamboat to carry a man was built by John Fitch. On August 27, 1787, his boat plied up and down the Delaware River at the speed of three miles per hour. The boat was propelled by 12 large wooden paddles, 6 arranged in tandem along each side of the boat, alternately dipping into and drawing out of the water. The action of the paddles was the same as that used by the Native Americans in paddling a canoe.

8410. Steamboat patent was issued by the state of Georgia to Isaac Briggs and William Longstreet on February 1, 1788, through the General Assembly at Augusta, GA. This was the first and only patent issued by Georgia, authority having been vested by the Articles of Confederation, which were then in effect. The steamboat worked but was not practical. It was equipped with a boiler, two cylinders, and a condenser.

8411. Ship built on the Pacific coast was the *Northwest America*, a schooner of 40 tons, which was begun on June 11, 1788. It was built, launched, and equipped at Friendly Cove in King George's Sound (now Nootka Sound) abreast of the village of Nootka, British Columbia, Canada. Robert Funter was master. The ship was captured on June 9, 1789, by Spain.

8412. Federal revenue cutter was the *Massachusetts*, the keel of which was laid in 1791 in the yard of William Searle and Joseph Tyler at Newburyport, MA. It had one deck and two masts and cost $1,440. It was one of 10 revenue cutters authorized on August 4, 1790, at a cost of $10,000, to be paid out of the duties on goods imported. The master was John Foster Williams and the first mate Hezekiah Welch, both of whom were appointed on March 21, 1791.

8413. Yacht was the *Jefferson*, a 22-ton sloop that was constructed in Salem, MA, in 1801 by Christopher Turner for Captain George Crowninshield. It was 35 feet 10 inches long and 12 feet 4 inches wide, and had a 6-foot depth. It was rigged first as a schooner, afterward as a sloop.

8414. Steamboat with a twin-screw propeller was built by John Stevens at Hoboken, NJ, in 1803. He patented the engine on April 11, 1803, and successfully navigated in New York Harbor in 1804. The boat was 25 feet long and 4 feet wide and had two 5-foot screw propellers with four blades set at an angle of 35 degrees. It was operated by a double direct-acting noncondensing engine with a 4.5-inch cylinder and a 9-inch stroke.

8415. Dry dock for the repair of ships was constructed by Robert Fulton in 1805 in front of his foundry on the corner of Green and Morgan streets, in Jersey City, NJ. A block of ground was sold to him by the Associates of the Jersey Company for $1,000, allowing him five years on the purchase money without interest. The deed was dated November 3, 1804. An earlier dry dock had been authorized by Charlestown, MA, on October 30, 1677, to be constructed by James Russell, John Heyman, Samuel Ballard, and John Phillips, but it was never built.

8416. Steamboat to make regular trips was the *Clermont*, designed by Robert Fulton. The hull of the *Clermont* was built under his supervision by Charles Brown, a shipbuilder of New York. A Boulton and Watt engine was installed, and the boat began its trial trip to Albany, NY, on August 7, 1807. It made the 150-mile journey in 32 hours and returned in 30 hours.

8417. Steamboat to make an ocean voyage was the *Phoenix*, 100 feet long, built at Hoboken, NJ, by Robert Livingston Stevens with his father, John Stevens. On June 10, 1809, it went from New York City to Philadelphia, PA, by sea, navigating the Atlantic from Sandy Hook to Cape May, NJ, under the command of Moses Rogers.

8418. Steamboat to sail down the Mississippi was the *New Orleans*, which left Pittsburgh, PA, in September 1811 under the ownership and guidance of Nicholas J. Roosevelt. It arrived at New Orleans, LA, on October 1. The crew consisted of the captain, an engineer, a pilot, six sailors, two servants, a waiter, and a cook. Mr. and Mrs. Roosevelt were the only passengers. The *New Orleans* cost $38,000.

8419. Steam-propelled ferryboat was the *Juliana*, operated on October 11, 1811, by the engineers John Stevens and Robert Livingston Stevens, father and son, between Hoboken, NJ, and New York City.

8420. Transatlantic passenger line was the Black Ball Line, which ran regularly scheduled runs from New York City to Liverpool beginning on January 5, 1818, when the 400-ton *James Monroe* left New York Harbor. The line's other original ships were the *Amity*, the *Courier*, and the *Pacific*. The company was founded by New York merchant Isaac Wright and four partners, each of whom put up $25,000 in capital. They promised monthly crossings "on a certain day in every month throughout the year." Before that time, passengers had to book passage on a cargo ship and wait until the hold was full and the ship was ready to sail. During the first nine years, the Black Ball Line averaged 23 days for the transatlantic crossing.

8421. Double-deck steamboat was the stern-wheel Mississippi River flatboat *Washington*, built by Captain Henry Miller Shreve at the mouth of Wheeling Creek, Wheeling, VA (now in West Virginia). Its keel was laid on September 10, 1815, and it was launched on June 4, 1816. It arrived at its first destination, New Orleans, LA, on October 7, 1816. Each of the two side wheels was operated by a high-pressure engine with 24-inch cylinders and 6-foot strokes. They were unconnected, so that the pilot could go forward on one wheel and reverse on the other, thus turning the boat around in its own length of 148 feet. Instead of putting the engines in the hull in an upright position, Shreve placed them on the deck in a horizontal position and added another deck to carry the passengers and the horizontal boilers, thus creating the first double-deck steamboat.

8422. Steamboat on the Great Lakes was the *Frontenac*, built by Teabout and Chapman and launched on September 7, 1816. It plied Lake Ontario. The first steamboat to sail on all the Great Lakes was the *Walk-in-the-Walter*, 135 feet long with 388 tons of gross tonnage, built at Black Rock, Buffalo, NY, for McIntyre and Stewart and launched on April 4, 1818. Its first trip took place on October 10, 1818, when it left Buffalo with 100 passengers, bound for Detroit, MI.

8423. Tugboat powered by steam was the *Rufus King*, built in 1825 by Smith and Dimon for the New York Dry Dock Company to tow vessels to and from the railway at the foot of East 10th Street, New York City. It was 102 feet long and 19 feet wide and had a square engine with a 34-inch cylinder and a 4-inch stroke.

8424. Federal dry docks were constructed at Boston, MA, and Norfolk, VA, under authority of act of Congress of March 28, 1827. They were designed by Colonel Loammi Baldwin of Boston, MA, who was hired by Secretary of the Navy Samuel Southard. The dry docks were founded upon piles and were built entirely of stone faced with cut granite. Construction of the Boston dry dock was started on June 1827, the cornerstone laid on May 21, 1829, and the dry dock turned over to the commandant on September 9, 1833. It cost $677,090. The Norfolk dry dock was begun on November 1827 and completed on March 15, 1834. It cost $943,677. Earlier, in February 1799, Congress had approved the construction of federal dry docks, but failed to appropriate sufficient funds.

8425. Clipper ship was probably the *Ann McKim*, launched on June 3, 1833, for Isaac McKim by Kennard and Williamson of Fells Point, Baltimore, MD. It was 143 feet long and 31 feet wide and weighed 493 tons. The first master was Joseph Martin. Since definitions vary as to what constitutes a clipper ship, there are many other claims for primacy.

8426. Iron sailing vessel was the *John Randolph*, 122 tons, which was built in 1834 at Savannah, GA, by John Caut for Gazaway Bugg Lamar. The plates were made by John Laird of Birkenhead, England, and shipped in sections to Savannah, where they were riveted together. Two other iron vessels were also built in Savannah of iron manufactured in England: the *Chatham*, 198 tons, built by John Caut in 1836, and the *Lamar*, 196 tons, built by John Wade in 1838.

8427. Steamboat on the Pacific coast was the *Beaver*, tested on May 16, 1836, at Vancouver, WA. On May 31, during its maiden voyage, it entered the Willamette River in Oregon, ran down the river under steam, and entered the lower reaches of the Columbia River near Vancouver. It was 101.4 feet long and 20 feet in the beam, with a depth of 11 feet and a tonnage of 109. The engines were built by Boulton and Watt of England.

8428. Transatlantic steamboat service was started by the *Great Western* and the *Sirius*, both of which arrived in New York City on April 23, 1838. The *Sirius* made the trip from London in 19 days and the *Great Western* from Bristol in 15 days. They were built by Isambard Kingdom Brunel, the celebrated English engineer.

8429. Steamboat inspection service established by Congress was authorized on July 7, 1838, for the "better security of the lives of passengers on board of vessels propelled in whole or in part by steam." Inspectors were appointed by federal district judges and received $5 for each inspection. They gave the owners a certificate stating the age of the boat and the soundness of the vessel. An annual inspection was required.

8430. Iron steamship built for transatlantic service was the *Bangor*, constructed by Betts, Harlan and Hollingsworth at Wilmington, DE, for the Bangor Steam Navigation Company and launched in May 1844. It was 120 feet long with a burden of 231 tons. It was schooner-rigged, had three wooden masts, and carried eight sails.

8431. Steamship passenger line between American and European ports to fly the American flag was the Ocean Steam and Navigation Company. Service began on June 1, 1847, when the *Washington* sailed from New York City for Bremen, Germany, with 120 passengers. The 1,700-ton *Washington* had four decks, three masts, and a full-length effigy of George Washington as a figurehead. It was 260 feet long and had a 39-foot beam and a hold 31 feet deep. It was launched in 1847 from the East River yard of Wesstervelt and Mackary in New York City. The cost of the ship was $390,000. The *Hermann* was later added to the service.

8432. Steamboat service to California around Cape Horn was established by the Pacific Mail Steamship Company in 1849. The S.S. *California*, 1,050 tons, left New York City on October 6, 1848. It stopped at Rio de Janeiro, Brazil; Valparaiso, Chile; and Callao and Paita, Peru. On February 1, 1849, it arrived at Panama, where it took on 350 passengers. Further stops were made at Acapulco, San Blas, and Mazatlán, Mexico, and at San Diego and Monterey, CA. On February 28, 1849, the ship reached San Francisco, where most of the crew deserted to work in the gold fields. Captain Cleveland Forbes was in command. This trip started a semimonthly mail service between New York and Panama and a monthly service between Panama and Oregon.

8433. Steam whaler was the *Pioneer*, whose first trip was made from April 28 to November 14, 1866, under Captain Ebenezer Morgan. It had been converted in 1865 by Thomas W. Williams of New London, CT, from a government transport. It was crushed in the ice while on a whaling expedition in 1867.

8434. Transpacific side-wheeler steamer was the *Celestial Empire*, built by William Henry Webb for the Pacific Mail Steamship Company. The steamer's keel was laid on January 13, 1866, and the ship was launched on December 8. It made its trial trip on June 4, 1867, and sailed for Panama and San Francisco, CA, on July 1, 1867. The *Celestial Empire* was 360 feet long with a 47.4-foot beam, a depth of 23.3 feet, and a weight of 3,386 tons. It burned 45 tons of coal daily. The name was later changed to the *China*. The ship accommodated 1,200 passengers.

8435. Steamboat to employ electric lights successfully was the *Columbia*, built at Chester, PA, for the Oregon Railway and Navigation Company. Its length was 309 feet, its beam 38 feet 5 inches, its hold 23 feet 3 inches, and its net tonnage 1,746 tons. The *Columbia* plied between San Francisco, CA, and Portland, OR. An "A" type dynamo, placed in operation on May 2, 1880, illuminated the passenger rooms and main salons. It operated successfully for 15 years, until a larger dynamo was installed. An earlier attempt to employ electric lights had been made by the newspaper publisher James Gordon Bennett in his steamboat *Jeannette*, which he donated to the government for use in an expedition to the Bering Straits. The expedition left San Francisco, CA, on July 8, 1879. The electric system failed to work. On January 19, 1880, the ship sprang a leak from ice pressure. It sank on June 13, 1881.

8436. Steel-hulled ferryboat was the *Lackawanna*, built in 1881 at Newburgh, NY, by Ward Stanton at a cost of $76,000. It weighed 822 gross tons, 645 net tons, and was 200 feet long and 35 feet wide, with a 13-foot draft. The boat plied between Hoboken, NJ, and New York City.

8437. Motorboat pleasure craft was produced in 1885 by F. W. Ofeldt and manufactured by the Gas Engine and Power Company, New York City. The boat contained a two-horsepower engine, propelled by naphtha, which developed a speed of five to seven knots. It was 21 feet long and had a 64-inch beam and a draft of 22 inches.

8438. Motorboat with a storage battery was the *Magnet*, which was operated by one motor revolving a two-blade screw 18 inches in diameter. The battery consisted of 56 storage cells. A 10-hour charge ran the boat for 60 to 70 miles at a speed of 10 miles per hour. The *Magnet* was built in Newark, NJ, in 1888 and was owned by Anthony and Frederick Reckenzaun. It was 28 feet long, with a 6-foot beam, and was 3 feet deep amidships.

8439. Double-deck ferryboat was the *Bergen*, launched on October 25, 1888, at the Delmater Iron Works, Newburgh, NY. Its route went across the Hudson River from New York City to Hoboken, NJ. It was 203 feet in length and 62 feet wide, with a 10-foot draft, and was first piloted by Captain G. Beckwith.

8440. Steel sailing vessel was the *Dirigo*, built by Arthur Sewall and Company, Bath, ME, and launched on February 3, 1894. George W. Goodwin was the first captain. The *Dirigo* had a gross tonnage of 3,004 tons and a net tonnage of 2,855 tons. Its length was 310 feet, its width 45.15 feet, and its depth 25.6 feet. It had two full decks and carried 13,000 square yards of canvas.

8441. Steel seven-masted schooner was the *Thomas W. Lawson*, built at Quincy, MA, by the Fore River Ship and Engine Company for the Coastwise Transportation Company of Boston, MA. The keel was laid on November 1, 1901, and the ship was launched on July 10,

1902. Its overall length was 403 feet 4 inches, its beam 50 feet, and its depth 35 feet 3 inches. Its sail area was 40,617 square feet. The masts weighed about 17 tons apiece, and the rigging of each weighed three tons. The ship's tonnage was 4,914 net and 5,218 gross, and its carrying capacity was 8,100 tons.

8442. **Motorboat magazine** was *Motor Boat*, published by The Motor Boat Publishing Company, New York City. It covered all types of power craft. The first issue was dated April 10, 1904. It contained 40 pages and sold for 10 cents a copy.

8443. **Municipal ferryboats** were placed in operation in New York City on October 25, 1905, between Whitehall Street, Manhattan, and St. George, Staten Island.

8444. **Outboard motor** that was commercially successful was developed in Milwaukee, WI, in 1909 by Ole Evinrude. It was a single-cylinder, two-port, two-cycle, battery-ignited engine, developing 1.5 horsepower at about 1,000 revolutions per minute. It weighed 46 pounds.

8445. **Federal law requiring radios on ships** was the Wireless Ship Act of June 24, 1910, which required wireless equipment on all passenger vessels carrying 50 or more persons as passengers or crew.

8446. **Concrete seagoing ship** was the *Faith*, built by the San Francisco Shipbuilding Company at Redwood City, CA, and launched on March 14, 1918, six weeks after the pouring of the concrete had started. It cost $750,000 and was the first concrete ship to cross the Atlantic Ocean. The ship was 8,000 tons burden, 320 feet long, 44.6 feet wide, and 30 feet deep. The builder and owner was W. Leslie Comyn, president of the San Francisco Shipbuilding Company. The engineers were Allan MacDonald and Victor Poss.

8447. **Concrete barge** was the *Socony 200*, which was also the first reinforced-steel concrete barge for carrying oil in bulk. It was built to specifications for the Standard Oil Company of New York and was 98 feet long, 31 feet wide, and 9 feet 6 inches deep. The vessel was launched on July 27, 1918, and placed in service on August 12, 1918. It was built by the Fougner Shipbuilding Company, Flushing Bay, New York City.

8448. **Round-the-world steamboat passenger service** was inaugurated by the S.S. *President Harrison* of the Dollar Steamship Line, which sailed from San Francisco, CA, in February 1924. Previous trips were made irregularly by cruise steamers.

8449. **Ferryboat built exclusively to transport cars** was the *Governor Moore*, a diesel-electric ferry placed in service on November 8, 1926. It was built by the New York Shipbuilding Company of Camden, NJ, from plans conceived by Eads Johnson. Five other boats were built in 1926, each with capacity for 46 automobiles. They were operated by the Electric Ferries company on routes from 23rd Street in New York City to Edgewater, NJ, and Weehawken, NJ.

8450. **Tugboat with a diesel-electric engine** was placed in service in 1929 on the Warrior River, AL, by the Tennessee Coal, Iron and Railroad Company. The power plant included two 550-horsepower diesel engines. Each propeller was driven by a double motor rated at 400 horsepower. The length of the tow was limited to seven barges.

8451. **Seatrain** was built in 1928 by the Sun Shipbuilding Company of Chester, PA, for the Seatrain Lines, which inaugurated a service on January 12, 1929, between New Orleans, LA, and Havana, Cuba. Loaded freight cars were hoisted from the railroad rails and placed aboard the seatrain, which accommodated 95 railroad cars.

8452. **Passenger ship with a diesel engine** was *The City of New York*, built by the Sun Shipbuilding Company, Chester, PA, under the Merchant Marine Act of May 22, 1928, and tested on January 11, 1930, on the Delaware River. The ship was 470.8 feet long and 61.6 feet in the beam, with a 26-foot draft. It carried 61 first-class passengers and had a 10,000-ton deadweight tonnage. The ship was propelled by Sun-Doxford diesel engines that made 13 knots. The first direct voyage left Brooklyn, New York City, on February 1, 1930, for Capetown, South Africa, for the American South African Line.

8453. **Streamlined ferryboat** was the *Kalakala*, first placed in commercial operation on July 4, 1935, by the Puget Sound Navigation Company, Seattle, WA, between Seattle and Bremerton, WA, on Puget Sound, under the command of Captain Wallace H. Mangan. It was 276 feet long, had a beam of 55 feet 8 inches and a draft of 13 feet, and was designed to carry 2,000 passengers and 110 automobiles. The boat was built at the Lake Washington Shipyards at Houghton, WA, and was 97.75 percent steel in construction. The name Kalakala is a Chinook word meaning "flying bird." The accent is on the second syllable.

8454. Liberty ship built to carry cargo during World War II was the *Patrick Henry*, launched on September 27, 1941. It was built by the Bethlehem-Fairfield Shipbuilding Company, Baltimore, MD, in 244 days and delivered on December 30, 1941, to the U.S. Maritime Commission, which transferred it to the Lykes Brothers Steamship Company of New Orleans, LA. It had an overall length of 441 feet 6 inches, a beam of 57 feet, a depth of 37 feet 4 inches, a total displacement of 14,100 tons, and a general cargo capacity of 9,146 tons. It had single-screw steam reciprocating propulsion and on its first voyage, to Alexandria, Egypt, its average speed was 11.19 knots. The first captain was Richard Gailard Ellis.

8455. Ship completed in less than two weeks was the *Joseph N. Teal*, built by Henry John Kaiser's Oregon Shipbuilding Corporation at Portland, OR. It made a trial run on September 27, 1942, and was turned over to the Maritime Commission 13 days 23.5 hours after the laying of the keel. The previous record had been 29 days. Speedy construction of ships was essential to American efforts in World War II.

8456. Merchant ship commanded by an African-American captain was the *Booker T. Washington*, a Liberty ship launched by the California Shipbuilding Corporation at Wilmington, DE, on September 29, 1942. It was commanded by Captain Hugh Mulzac, the first African-American to hold an unlimited mariner's license. It arrived at its first port, London, on February 12, 1843.

8457. Victory ship launched was the *United Victory*, launched on January 12, 1944, at the yard of Henry J. Kaiser's Oregon Shipbuilding Corporation at Portland, OR. The Victory ships made 15 knots, which was faster than Liberty ships, and had three times as much power.

8458. Carrier for liquid bulk chemicals was the *Marine-Dow Chem*, a 16,500-ton oil tanker, 351 feet long, built by the Bethlehem Steel Company's shipbuilding division for the Marine Transport Lines, New York City, and under charter to the Dow Chemical Company. The ship arrived at New York City on its first run, on April 13, 1954, from Freeport, TX.

8459. Roll-on-roll-off carrier was the *Searoad*, placed in service on September 1, 1955, between Hyannis and Nantucket Island, MA, by the Searoad Transport Company, Hyannis, MA. It was 64 feet long, had a superstructure 14 feet high, and drew only 6.5 feet of water. Its 220-horsepower General Motors diesel engine attained a speed of nine knots. It was built by the Blount Marine Corporation of Warren, RI, and cost $65,000 to build and $25,000 to equip. The first skipper was Morris Johnson.

8460. Speedboat to exceed 200 miles per hour was the jet-powered *Bluebird*, piloted by Donald Malcolm Campbell, which averaged 216.2 miles per hour on November 16, 1955, on a measured kilometer course on Lake Mead, NV. The speed for one leg of the course was 239.5 miles per hour.

8461. Nuclear-powered merchant ship was the N.S. *Savannah*, 595 feet and 21,000 tons. It was built by the New York Shipbuilding Corporation, Camden, NJ, for the U.S. Maritime Commission. The pressurized waterpower reactor was built by the Babcock and Wilcox Company, New York City. The keel was laid on May 22, 1958, and the ship was launched on July 21, 1959.

8462. Cargo ship fully automated and flying the American flag was the 12,000-ton S.S. *Mormacargo*, whose keel was laid on April 22, 1963, at the Ingalls Shipbuilding Corporation, Pascagoula, MS. The ship, which cost in excess of $10 million, was launched on January 25, 1964. Its first run, from Pascagoula to Boston, started on August 28, 1964, and its first transatlantic trip started on September 11, 1964, from New York City. It was 550 feet 9 inches long overall, with a beam of 75 feet and a displacement of 19,800 tons. It had a bridge console with electronic control of speed, boiler temperatures, and reefer temperatures, and other automatic devices. Instead of the usual crew of 49, the crew numbered 32, each with a private room. Kenneth L. Chambers was the first captain.

8463. Automated tanker under the American flag was the *Texaco Rhode Island*, a 25,413-ton tanker built by the Bethlehem Steel Company at Sparrows Point, Baltimore, MD, for Texaco, Wilmington, DE, and launched on July 2, 1964. It was 575 feet long, 68 feet wide, 78 feet deep, and 33 feet 10 inches in draft. It had a centralized engine-room control system. An oil burner fueled the two-cylinder steam turbine.

8464. Commercial crude-oil carrier was the *Brooklyn*, built at the Brooklyn Navy Yard, New York City, by the Seatrain Shipbuilding Corporation and launched on June 30, 1973. The first test trip was made on October 22, 1973, in the East River. The ship was 1,094 feet long with a 226,200-ton displacement and cost $80 million. It could carry 1.5 million barrels of crude oil and could unload in 14 hours.

Military

8465. Naval ship of the line was the *America*, authorized by the Continental Congress on November 20, 1776. It was designed by Joshua Humphreys and laid down on May 1777 in John Langdon's shipyard in Portsmouth, NH. John Paul Jones was elected commander. On September 3, 1782, the *America* was presented to King Louis XVI of France in appreciation of his country's assistance during the Revolutionary War. It sailed for France on June 24, 1783.

8466. Frigate was the *United States*, which was built by Joshua Humphreys at what was formerly the Association Battery, Philadelphia, PA, and launched on May 10, 1797. President John Adams attended the launching. The vessel weighed 1,576 tons and was first captained by Commodore John Barry. It was scuttled on April 20, 1861, by federal forces abandoning the Norfolk Navy Yard in Norfolk, VA.

8467. Ship constructed by the federal government was the *Chesapeake*, built at the Navy Yard, Gosport, VA, under an act of Congress of March 27, 1794, "to provide a naval armament." The president was authorized to obtain six ships by purchase or otherwise and to equip and employ four ships of 44 guns each and two ships of 36 guns each to protect commerce. The marine yard was lent to the government by Virginia, and Captain Richard Dale was appointed its superintendent. Construction started in 1794, but as peace was concluded in 1796, the work was discontinued. Work was again undertaken in 1797, after materials on hand had been sold, with Commodore Samuel Barron as superintendent of the yard. The *Chesapeake* was launched on December 2, 1799.

8468. Steam-propelled frigate was the *Demologos*, or *Fulton, the First*, 2,475 tons, built by Robert Fulton for the Navy. Its keel was laid on June 20, 1814, and it was launched on October 29, 1814, without engines, at Brown's Ship Yard, New York City. It was propelled by its own steam and machinery for the first time on June 1, 1815. The vessel cost $320,000. It was made of wood five feet thick and had a center-wheel propulsion. Its length was 156 feet on deck, its breadth of beam was 56 feet, and its depth was 20 feet. It drew eight feet of water. It carried thirty 32-pound carronades and two columbiads, each of which fired a 100-pound red-hot ball. The guns were mounted in a battery protected by massive wooden sides.

8469. Iron vessel built for the Navy was an iron side-wheel steamer, the *Michigan*, built in Erie, PA, under authority of act of Congress of September 9, 1841. Construction began in 1842 with the building of sections in Pittsburgh, PA. These sections were transported to Erie, where the ship was completed. It was launched on December 5, 1843. The cost of the ship was $165,000. Its hull was designed and built by Stockhouse and Tomlinson, Pittsburgh. Its displacement was 685 tons; length, 163 feet 3 inches; breadth, 27 feet 1.5 inches; depth of hold, 13 feet 9 inches. It was renamed the *Wolverine* on June 17, 1905, and loaned to the city of Erie on July 19, 1927, by act of Congress of December 21, 1926. The vessel was stricken from the navy list on March 12, 1927.

8470. Warship with propelling machinery below the waterline and out of reach of hostile shot was the screw-warship *Princeton*, which was designed by John Ericsson in 1841. Its length on deck was 164 feet, its beam 30.5 feet, and its displacement 954 tons. Its wooden hull was built at the Navy Yard in Philadelphia, PA, under the supervision of Captain Robert Field Stockton. The propelling machinery was built by Merrick and Towne, Philadelphia. The *Princeton* cost $212,615 to construct and was launched on December 10, 1843. It carried two long 225-pound wrought-iron guns and twelve 42-pound carronades. On February 28, 1844, while the ship was on a demonstration run, one of its guns exploded, killing several of the distinguished visitors.

8471. Balloon carrier was the U.S.S. *Fanny*, an armed transport ship which John La Mountain used on August 3, 1861, to transport a balloon that was attached to a windlass at the stern. The balloon floated at a height of 2,000 feet and was used to observe military positions at Fortress Monroe, VA.

8472. Turreted frigate in the Navy was the U.S.S. *Roanoke*, originally a wooden screw steam frigate built at the Norfolk Navy Yard, Norfolk, VA, under authorization of Congress dated April 6, 1854. It was launched on December 13, 1855, and made its trial trip in 1857. It was altered to an ironclad in 1862–63 by the Novelty Iron Works, New York City, and was transferred to the New York Navy Yard on April 16, 1863. The alteration gave the *Roanoke* three revolving turrets of the design pioneered by John Ericsson, two pilothouses, and a battery of two 15-inch, two 11-inch, and two 150-pounder rifle guns. The hull proved to be too weak sustain the weight, and the ship was sold in 1883.

8473. Ironclad naval vessels were the *Benton* and the *Essex*, 1,000 tons each, and seven others of 512 tons each, delivered at St. Louis, MO, where they were accepted for the government by Captain Andrew Hull Foote on January 15, 1862. They were constructed under contract with James Buchanan Eads at Mound City and Cairo, IL, and added to the Western Flotilla, also known as the Gunboat Flotilla on Western Waters, or the Mississippi Squadron, which was organized on October 1, 1862.

8474. Ironclad seagoing naval warship was the *Galena*, built by Cornelius Scranton Bushnell and H. L. Bushnell of New Haven, CT, and launched on February 14, 1862, at the Maxson and Fish Yard, Mystic, CT. The ironclad vessel *Monitor* had been launched earlier, on January 30, 1862, but it was not a seagoing ironclad, merely a floating battery for harbor defense.

8475. Ironclad turreted vessel in the Navy was the U.S.S. *Monitor*, designed and built by John Ericsson, with a gun turret designed by Theodore Ruggles Timby. The terms of the contract, signed on October 4, 1861, provided that the ship was to be completed within 100 days. The keel was laid on October 22, 1861, and the ship was launched at Greenpoint, Brooklyn, NY (now part of New York City), on January 30, 1862. It was completed on February 19, 1862, and delivered to the Navy on February 20. It was 172 feet long and had two 11-inch guns in the turret that fired a solid shot weighing 180 pounds. It left New York City on March 6, 1862, with Lieutenant John Lorimer Worden in command and arrived at Hampton Roads, VA, on March 8. The next day it went into action against the Confederate ironclad ship *Merrimac*, the first battle between ironclad vessels in the Civil War, in which it was the victor.

8476. Torpedo boat worthy of the name was the *Lightning*, built in 1876 at Bristol, RI, by John Brown Herreshoff and Nathanael Greene Herreshoff. It was 58 feet long and had a speed of about 20 knots.

8477. Steel vessels of the Navy were the cruisers *Atlanta*, *Boston*, and *Chicago* and the dispatch boat *Dolphin*, authorized by Congress on March 3, 1883. The hulls were built by John Roach and Sons, Chester, PA, and the machinery was manufactured at the New York Navy Yard. The *Atlanta* and the *Boston* were 270 feet 3 inches long and 42 feet wide, and had horizontal back-acting engines and cylindrical tubular boilers. The *Chicago* was 325 feet long and 48 feet 2 inches wide. The *Atlanta* was launched on October 9, 1884, and commissioned on July 19, 1886; the *Boston* was launched on December 4, 1884, and commissioned on May 2, 1887.

8478. Battleship of importance was the U.S.S. *Maine*, authorized by act of Congress on August 3, 1886. It was built at the Brooklyn Navy Yard, Brooklyn, NY (now part of New York City). Its keel was laid on October 17, 1888, and it was launched on November 18, 1890, and commissioned on September 17, 1895. Its length was 319 feet, beam 57 feet, mean draft 21 feet 6 inches, displacement 6,682 tons. On the night of February 15, 1898, the *Maine* was mysteriously destroyed by an explosion in the harbor of Havana, Cuba, that killed 260 men of the 354-man crew.

8479. Turbine-propelled naval ship was the *Chester*, a scout cruiser, launched on July 26, 1907, and commissioned on April 25, 1908. It was built at the Bath Iron Works Company, Bath, ME. The contract price for the hull and machinery was $1,688,000. The *Chester* was equipped with four Parsons turbines. It had an overall length of 423 feet 1 inch and a displacement of 3,750 tons. Its trial speed was 26.52 knots.

8480. Electrically propelled naval ship was the U.S.S. *Jupiter*, built as a collier at the Navy Yard, Mare Island, CA. Its keel was laid on October 16, 1911, and it was launched on August 24, 1912, and commissioned on April 7, 1913. Its conversion to an aircraft carrier was authorized on July 11, 1919, when $2.5 million was appropriated. Its name was changed from *Jupiter* to *Langley* on April 21, 1920.

8481. Naval vessel equipped to lay mines was the cruiser *Baltimore*, which was commissioned on January 7, 1890. It was built by William Cramp and Sons, Philadelphia, PA, and its keel was laid on May 5, 1887. It was 252 feet 4 inches long. The captain was Winfield Scott Schley. The *Baltimore* served during the Spanish-American War as a cruiser. It was converted into a minelayer and recommissioned on March 8, 1915. During World War I, it saw considerable service in this assignment. The first naval vessel constructed as a minelayer was the U.S.S. *Terror*, launched on June 6, 1941, at the Philadelphia Navy Yard and commissioned on July 15, 1942. The ship, which had an overall length of 454 feet 10 inches, cruised at 20 knots and mounted four 5-inch .38-caliber dual-purpose guns and two twin 40mm antiaircraft guns. Howard W. Fitch was the commander.

8482. Warship propelled by electricity was the U.S.S. *New Mexico*, which was built at the Brooklyn Navy Yard, New York City. The keel was laid on October 14, 1915. The ship was launched on April 23, 1917, and commissioned on May 20, 1918. The *New Mexico* was 624 feet in length, displaced 30,000 tons, and carried twelve 14-inch guns and twelve 5-inch guns.

8483. Navy destroyer named for a Confederate officer was the *Buchanan*, named for Admiral Franklin Buchanan, ranking officer in the Confederate Navy. The ship was 314 feet 5 inches long, 31 feet 8 inches in breadth. It was launched at the Bath Iron Works, Bath, ME, on January 2, 1919, and commissioned on January 20. Lieutenant Howard Hartwell James Benson was the first in command.

8484. Aircraft carrier wholly designed and built as such was the *Ranger*, constructed by the Newport News Shipbuilding and Drydock Company, Newport News, VA. Its keel was laid on September 26, 1931, and it was launched on February 25, 1933. It was placed in service at Norfolk, VA, on June 4, 1934. The first captain was Arthur Leroy Bristol.

8485. Battleship equipped with radar was the U.S.S. New York, which was tested during battle maneuvers at sea in the months of January, February, and March of 1939. This radar set operated on a wavelength of 1.5 meters, detecting destroyers at a distance of approximately 8 miles. The first set to be installed on the New York was constructed at the Naval Research Laboratory at Washington, DC. The first contract was awarded in October 1939 to the Radio Corporation of America for the manufacture of six sets of aircraft detection equipment.

8486. Ship transported overland across the Rocky Mountains was the destroyer escort *Brennan*, which was prefabricated in Denver, CO, and shipped in sections by rail to the Mare Island Naval Shipyard, CA, where it was assembled and launched on August 22, 1942. On January 20, 1943, Lieutenant Commander H. A. Adams, Jr., was placed in temporary command. The *Brennan* was 289 feet 5 inches long with a breadth of 35 feet 1 inch and a displacement of 1,146 tons. The ship's complement was 156.

8487. Naval ship with a mixed company of male and female personnel was the U.S.S. *Sanctuary*, a 520-foot hospital ship with a hospital staff and ship's company of 70 officers and 460 enlisted personnel, including 2 female naval officers and 60 enlisted women. The ship was laid down as the U.S.S. *Marine Owl* by the Sun Shipbuilding and Dry Dock Company, Chester, PA, on August 15, 1944. It was converted and commissioned on June 20, 1945. On November 18, 1972, the ship was recommissioned at Hunter's Point Naval Shipyard, San Francisco, CA.

8488. Ship from which a long-range rocket was launched was the airplane carrier *Midway*. On September 6, 1947, a captured German V-2 rocket was fired from the flight deck while the ship was several hundred miles off the east coast of the United States. The rocket traveled about six miles. Rear Admiral John Jennings Ballentine commanded the task group of which the U.S.S. *Midway*, commanded by Captain Albert Kellogg Morehouse, was the flagship.

8489. Offshore radar warning station was built by the Bethlehem Steel Company's shipbuilding division at Fore River, Quincy, MA, for the Continental Air Defense Command. The keel was laid on January 10, 1955, and the station was launched on May 20. Known as a Texas Tower, it was a triangular 6,000-ton platform resting on three legs 87 feet above the water level, and served as a weather collecting and reporting station. It was turned over to the First Naval District of the Navy on December 2, 1955.

8490. Aircraft carrier with an angle deck was the supercarrier U.S.S. *Forrestal*, authorized in March 1951 and laid down on July 14, 1952. It was launched on December 11, 1954, by the Newport News Shipbuilding and Drydock Company at Newport News, VA, and was placed in service on October 1, 1955. The first captain was Captain Roy Lee Johnson. The carrier cost $198 million, was 1,046 feet long and 252 feet wide, and carried a crew of 3,500, including its own air group. Its height from keel to top of mast was equal to that of a 25-story building, and its flight deck had an area of nearly four acres. The carrier's displacement was 65,000 tons.

8491. Guided missile cruiser was the cruiser *Boston*, 13,600 tons standard, 17,200 tons full load, which was laid down on June 30, 1941, launched on August 26, 1942 at the Bethlehem Steel Company, Quincy, MA, and commissioned on June 30, 1943. It was converted to guided-missile use beginning on November 1, 1955. Its superstructure was entirely remodeled, including the removal of one of its two stacks to accommodate twin launchers capable of firing Terrier missiles. The ship was 673.5 feet long and had a 71-foot beam and a draft of 26 feet. Captain Charles Bowling Martell was the first commanding officer of the converted cruiser.

8492. Nuclear-powered cruiser was the Coast Guard cruiser *Long Beach*, 9,721 feet long, with a beam of 73 feet, a draft of 26 feet, a 14,000-ton standard displacement, and an 18,000-ton full-load displacement. The cost of construction was about $320 million. The keel was laid on December 2, 1957, and the ship launched on July 14, 1959, at the Fore River Shipyard of the Bethlehem Steel Company's shipyard at Quincy, MA. The ship, which had two nuclear reactors, attained a speed of 30 knots.

8493. Nuclear-powered aircraft carrier was the Enterprise, ordered on August 16, 1957, laid down on February 4, 1958, launched on September 24, 1960, and completed on December 20, 1961. It was 1,101 feet long and 252 feet wide, with a 133-foot beam, a 75,700-ton standard displacement, an 85,350-ton full-load displacement, and a draft of 37 feet. The carrier, built by the Newport News Shipbuilding and Dry Dock Company, Newport News, VA, had a complement of 440 officers and 4,160 enlisted men. It was equipped with eight pressurized water-cooled nuclear reactors and was capable of steaming for five years without refueling. Its flight deck was large enough to accommodate four football fields, and each of its four propellers was the height of a two-story building.

8494. Amphibious vehicle was the Marsh Screw Amphibian, designed and developed by the Chrysler Corporation's Defense Operations Division for the Navy Bureau of Ships under sponsorship of the Defense Department's Advanced Research Projects Agency. Two rotary aluminum pontoons fitted with spiral blades propel the amphibious craft forward, backward, and even sideways. It weighed 2,330 pounds without cargo or crew and was 13 feet 8 inches long and 8 feet 4 inches wide, with an overall height of 57 inches. It had an operational range of 10 continuous hours at full power and could carry six passengers plus the driver, or a cargo of approximately 1,050 pounds. It was first tested in March 1963 in Louisiana.

8495. Naval ship with a crew of mixed nationalities was the *Claude V. Ricketts*, a 3,370-ton guided-missile armed destroyer, which was named for Admiral Claude Vernon Ricketts. The ship sailed on January 4, 1965, from Norfolk, VA, on a three-week cruise to the Caribbean Sea for the North Atlantic Treaty Organization. The destroyer had a seven-nation crew comprising 336 officers and men, half of them American and half foreign. The ship was laid down by the New York Shipbuilding Corporation on May 18, 1959, launched on June 4, 1960, and completed on August 18, 1962. It was originally named the *William P. Biddle* and was renamed on July 28, 1964.

8496. Rocket-tracking ship was the *Vanguard*, a World War II tanker cut apart and fitted with a new mid-body at the Electric Boat Division of General Dynamics Corporation at the shipyard in Quincy, MA. It was 595 feet long and was used as an Apollo instrumentation ship by the Navy's Military Sea Transportation Service for the National Aeronautics and Space Administration. The ship completed initial trials in the Atlantic Ocean off Boston, MA, on January 31, 1966, and was then placed in service.

8497. Ship with a combined diesel and gas-turbine engine was the Coast Guard's twin-screw 2,800-ton cutter *Alexander Hamilton*, launched on December 18, 1965, at the Avondale Shipyards, New Orleans, LA. The ship's length was 378 feet 3 inches overall, the beam 42 feet, and the draft 20 feet. It had two 35,000-horsepower Fairbanks Morse diesel engines and two 18,000-horsepower Pratt and Whitney gas turbines. The ship cost $14.5 million. It was commissioned on March 18, 1967. The crew consisted of 15 officers and 137 men. The commanding officer was Captain William Francis Adams.

8498. Naval ship to be captured intact was the U.S.S. *Pueblo*, an electronic intelligence ship. The *Pueblo* had been launched on April 16, 1944, at Kewaunee, WI, by the Kewaunee Shipbuilding and Engineering Corporation. On January 23, 1968, while in North Korean waters, it was surrounded by three 50-knot torpedo boats and two subchasers and was brought into Wonsan, North Korea. Commander Lloyd Mark Bucher and several of the crew were wounded and fireman Duane D. Hodges of Creswell, OR, was killed when one of the subchasers fired 57mm cannons. Commander Bucher and 82 surviving crew members were released on December 22, 1968, but the ship was held.

Navigation

8499. Quadrant that was practical was invented in 1730 by Thomas Godfrey, who called it a "reflecting quadrant." It was used on vessels plying between the West Indies and the colonies in 1731–32. The invention was credited to John Hadley of England, but the Royal Society sent FL200 to Godfrey to make amends. A quadrant is an instrument that measures the altitude of the sun and the stars.

8500. Gyrocompass installed on an American naval vessel was placed on the U.S.S. *Delaware* and tested at sea on August 28, 1911. The installation consisted of a master gyrocompass, employing the meridian-seeking properties of a pendulous gyro. The master compass was designed to be installed in a protected station, with repeaters that followed the movements of the master located suitably for steering and taking bearings.

8501. Gyroscopic stabilizer was patented by Elmer Ambrose Sperry and Harry Laurence Tanner of Brooklyn, New York City, who obtained a patent on August 14, 1917. The patent was assigned to the Sperry Gyroscope Company of Brooklyn.

8502. Radio navigation beacons were originally known as radio fog signals. The first successful radio beacons, which sent out signals by radio in all directions around the horizon, were established by the U.S. Lighthouse Service at three stations in the approaches to New York Harbor: the Ambrose Channel Lightship, the Fire Island Lightship, and the Sea Girt Lighthouse at Sea Girt, NJ. They were placed in regular operation on May 1, 1921. Tests of radio fog signal transmitting sets leading to the installation of these stations were begun in 1916–17 at Navesink Light Station, Atlantic Highlands, NJ, by the Lighthouse Service and the Bureau of Standards. The tests were interrupted when the United States entered World War I but were resumed in the fall of 1919 and lasted until September 1920.

8503. Automatic steering gear for ships was installed on the *John D. Archibold* of the Standard Oil Company of New Jersey and tested on April 7, 1922. The device was called Gyro-Pilot, or Metalmike.

8504. Radar observations were made on September 27, 1922, by Dr. Albert Hoyt Taylor and Leo C. Young of the Naval Aircraft Radio Laboratory, Anacostia, DC (now part of Washington, DC). They reported to the Navy that radio detection equipment placed on any two ships could detect the passage of any vessel between them despite fog, darkness, or smoke screen, and that tall buildings reflect radio signals.

8505. Passenger ship equipped with radar was the flagship *New York* of the Hamburg-American Line. Two circular appendages three feet in diameter were installed atop the pilothouse of the ship. The equipment was placed in service on February 26, 1938.

8506. Radar installation aboard a commercial carrier operated by an American company was installed on April 27, 1946, on the S.S. *African Star* of the American South African Line, and placed in operation on May 1, 1946, at which time the ship made its maiden voyage from New York City. The equipment, supplied by the General Electric Company, Schenectady, NY, was known as the Mariner.

8507. Radio sextant was made by the Collins Radio Company, Cedar Rapids, IA, and announced on July 14, 1954, although it had already been used for two years as a secret device on naval ships. It determined the sun's position automatically and continuously through reception of microwave energy emitted from the sun.

Submarines

8508. Submarine built for use in war was the *American Turtle*, built in 1776 by David Bushnell of Saybrook, CT. The vessel, which was large enough to accommodate one operator, had a 24-inch two-bladed wooden screw propeller, operated by hand, that enabled it to travel forward or in reverse at three knots. A crank operated the rudder aft. Water was admitted for descent and forced out with a hand pump for surfacing. Another screw, on the bottom, moved the submarine vertically. On September 7, 1776, Ezra Lee used the craft to attach a torpedo time bomb to the hull of the British flagship, the 64-gun *Eagle*, in New York Harbor. An explosion resulted, but no serious damage occurred, as the bomb had drifted away from the ship.

8509. Submarine in the U.S. Navy was the U.S.S. *Alligator*, a 47-foot-long tube of green metal propelled by oars operated by a 20-man crew. It was designed by a French engineer, Brutus de Villeroi, completed at the Philadelphia Navy Yard, and launched on May 1, 1862. On the night of April 2, 1863, it disappeared in a storm off Cape Hatteras, in North Carolina, as it was being towed toward Charleston, SC.

The submarine U.S.S. ALLIGATOR was built to sink Confederate ironclads. It was equipped with an airtight passageway that allowed divers to exit on their way to attach an explosive mine to an enemy ship.

8510. Navy submarine contract was awarded to the John P. Holland Torpedo Boat Company of New York City by Navy Secretary Hilary Abner Herbert on March 13, 1895. The contractual amount was $150,000. Construction was started at the Columbian Iron Works, Baltimore, MD. The keel was laid on June 20, 1896, and the submarine was launched on August 7, 1897. It was 85 feet 3 inches in length and 11 feet 6 inches in extreme breadth, with a displacement of 168 tons, and was known as the *Plunger*. The project was abandoned and all expenses and advances returned to the government when the contract was canceled in April 1900. A new contract for another submarine was signed on November 7, 1900.

8511. Submarine fitted with an internal combustion engine was the *Argonaut*, invented by Simon Lake and built by the Columbian Iron Works and Dry Dock Company of Baltimore, MD, in 1897. A working model had been built by Lake in 1894. He patented the engine on April 7, 1896, and the submarine vessel on April 20, 1897. The *Argonaut* was also the first submarine to salvage sunken objects of value. On December 16, 1897, a demonstration was given on the Patapsco River during which 22 newspaper reporters made short descents ranging from 1.5 to 4 hours.

8512. Submarine that was practical and submersible was the *Holland No. 9*, built by the John P. Holland Torpedo Boat Company of New York City. Launched on March 17, 1898, it submerged off Staten Island, remaining under water for 1 hour 40 minutes. Its overall length was 53 feet 11 inches and its diameter 10 feet 3 inches. Its equipment included a dynamite gun and one torpedo tube. The vessel was purchased by the Navy on April 11,

1900, for $150,000 (though the actual cost of construction was greater) and was placed in commission on October 12.

8513. Diesel engine in a submarine was the Vickers air-injection type, a four-cycle, four-cylinder, non-airstarting and nonreversing unit. Two of these engines were placed in Submarines E-1 and E-2, built by the New London Ship and Engine Company of Groton, CT, in 1911.

8514. Submarine disaster occurred on March 25, 1915, when the *F-4*, commanded by Lieutenant Alfred L. Ede, sank with a loss of 21 men while approximately 1.5 miles out of Honolulu Harbor, HI.

8515. Submarine emergency air supply container was an oxygen bag with a canister of soda lime and tubes similar to those of an army gas mask. The invention, known as the submarine escape lung, was the result of the combined efforts of two naval officers, Lieutenant Charles Bowers Momsen and Chief Gunner Clarence Louis Tibbals, and a civilian, Frank M. Hobson, a civil engineer of the Naval Bureau of Construction and Repairs. Momsen and Tibbals tested the device on May 10, 1929, by using it to escape from depths of water as great as 206 feet. They were rewarded with the Distinguished Service Cross. Hobson received a year's pay for his part in the invention. The Navy tested the device under actual conditions in the Thames River at New London, CT, on August 30, 1929, when 26 officers and men successfully escaped from the after hatch of the submerged submarine *S-4*.

8516. Streamlined submarine was the U.S.S. *Nautilus*, built at the Navy Yard, Mare Island, Vallejo, CA. The keel was laid on May 10, 1927. The ship was launched on March 15, 1930, and commissioned on July 1. Its length was 371 feet, extreme beam 33 feet 3 inches, mean draft 15 feet 9 inches, and displacement 2,730 tons. It carried two six-inch .53-caliber guns and a complement of 88. (A nuclear submarine with the same name was constructed later.)

8517. Submarine escape training tank was placed in operation on August 15, 1930, at the U.S. Submarine Base, New London, CT. It was a cylindrical "water tower" column 100 feet deep, with a spiral stairway winding around it and an abutting elevator shaft. Candidates entered the tank through locks at various depths, wearing the submarine-escape lung, and climbed up a rope, hand over hand, in order to slow down their ascent sufficiently to let their bodies become gradually adjusted to the decrease in pressure.

8518. Submarine to be refloated was the U.S.S. *Squalus*, launched at Portsmouth, NH, on September 14, 1938. It foundered in 240 feet of water off Portsmouth on May 23, 1939, with a loss of 26 men. The ship was completely raised after a 113-day job and was towed back to Portsmouth on September 13, 1939. On May 5, 1940, its name was changed to the U.S.S. *Sailfish*.

8519. Submarine with a pressure hull of high-tensile steel was the U.S.S. *Balao*, authorized on December 23, 1941, laid down on June 26, 1942, launched on October 27, 1942, at the Portsmouth Naval Shipyard, Portsmouth, NH, and commissioned on Feburary 4, 1943. The ship was 311 feet 8 inches long, 273 feet 3 inches wide, and had a 2,424-ton displacement. The first commanding officer was Lieutenant Commander Richard H. Crane.

8520. Leaping submarine was the U.S.S. *Pickerel*, laid down on February 8, 1944, at the Boston Naval Shipyard, Boston, MA, and launched on December 15, 1944. The submarine was commissioned at the Portsmouth Shipyard, Portsmouth, NH, on April 4, 1949. It was 311 feet 8 inches long and 27 feet 3 inches wide, with a 2,015-ton displacement. The submarine's first sea trials took place between April 4 and July 25, 1949. The first commanding officer was Commander Paul Richard Schratz. The *Pickerel* surfaced from a depth of 150 feet with a 48-degree up-angle during a routine training exercise off Oahu, HI. Its bow seemed to leap up out of the water. It set a record for underwater travel in 1950 by snorkeling from Hong Kong to Pearl Harbor, Honolulu, HI, a distance of 5,200 miles, in 21 days, from March 16 to April 5.

8521. Nuclear-powered submarine was the *Nautilus*, built by the Electric Boat Company, a division of the General Dynamics Corporation, Groton, CT, under the supervision of Captain Hyman George Rickover. President Harry S. Truman participated in the keel-laying ceremony on June 14, 1952. The submarine, launched on January 21, 1954, on the Thames River at Groton, was commissioned on September 21, 1954, tested under nuclear power on January 17, 1955, and completed on

April 22, 1955. Its crew consisted of 11 officers and 85 enlisted men. The first commander was Eugene Parks Wilkinson. The steam turbines were powered by a liquid-cooled atomic reactor. The *Nautilus* was 323.25 feet overall. Its displacement was 2,975 tons light, 3,200 tons standard, and 3,747 tons submerged. It is now a national landmark, permanently berthed at Groton.

8522. Submarine expressly designed and built to fire guided missiles was the U.S.S. *Grayback*, ordered on June 19, 1952, laid down on July 1, 1954, launched on July 2, 1957, and commissioned on March 7, 1958, at Mare Island, CA. The *Grayback*, designed to fire Regulus I and Regulus II missiles, carried a crew of 85 officers and men. It was 322.5 feet long and had a displacement of 1,740 tons light, 2,287 tons surface, and 3,638 tons submerged.

8523. Submarine equipped with ballistic missiles was the nuclear-powered *George Washington*, laid down on November 7, 1957, launched on June 9, 1959, and commissioned on December 30, 1959, at Groton, CT, on the Thames River. The cost of construction was approximately $110 million. The first commander was James Butler Osborn. The submarine was 380 feet long and had a displacement of 5,400 tons light, 5,600 tons standard, and 6,700 tons submerged. It went on patrol duty on November 15, 1960, from Charleston, SC, and returned on January 21, 1961, having traveled 67 days underwater. It was equipped with 16 vertical Polaris missile tubes that were fired below the surface.

Voyages

8524. Ship built in America to cross the Atlantic Ocean was a pinnace, a light sailing ship, built by the Huguenots (French Protestants) of Jean Ribaut's colony at Port Royal, SC, in 1562. In the winter of 1562–63, about 30 of them endeavored to return to France in the pinnace. They ran out of food and water and killed La Chere, one of their crew, who was eaten by the rest. They reached the coast of France, which was hostile to Protestants, but were rescued by an English ship that took them to Queen Elizabeth.

8525. Trading ship sent to China was the *Empress of China*, a 360-ton privateer commanded by Captain John Green. It left New York City on February 22, 1784, arrived in Canton, China, on August 28, left China on the return voyage on December 28, and returned to New York on May 11, 1785. Its owners made a profit of $30,727 on a $120,000 investment, which was financed by Robert Morris, Peter Whiteside, and William Whiteside.

8526. Ship from the Atlantic coast to anchor in a California port was the *Otter* of Boston, MA, commanded by Captain Ebenezer Dorr. It carried six guns and 26 men and arrived on October 29, 1796, at Monterey, CA, where it remained until November 6, 1796.

8527. Transatlantic crossing by an American steamboat was made by the *Savannah*, a 350-ton full-rigged wooden boat designed by Daniel Dod of Elizabeth, NJ. It was built at Corlear's Hook, NY, at the shipyards of Crocker and Fickett, and was launched on August 22, 1818. It had one inclined direct-acting low-pressure engine of 90 horsepower. The trial trip from New York City to Savannah, GA, was made on March 28, 1819. The *Savannah* sailed on May 22, 1819, from Savannah, GA, and arrived at Liverpool, England, on June 20. Steam power was used for only 80 hours during the trip. Moses Rogers was the captain and Steven Rogers the first officer. The ship had 32 staterooms, but no passengers dared to make the trip.

8528. Circumnavigation of the globe by a warship was done by the three-masted U.S.S. *Vincennes*, a 16-gun sloop of war of 700 tons burden, which left New York City on August 31, 1826, under the command of Commander William Bolton Finch (afterward known as William Compton Bolton). It sailed to the Pacific by way of Cape Horn and returned in 1829 by way of the Cape of Good Hope, arriving at New York on June 8, 1830. The ship was 127 feet long and had a beam of 34 feet.

8529. Naval vessel to sail around the Cape of Good Hope to the west coast of the United States was the *Constellation*, which left Boston, MA, in December 1840. Stopping first at Rio de Janeiro, it proceeded to the Cape of Good Hope and thence to China. On the return voyage, it anchored in Monterey Bay, CA, on September 15, 1843.

8530. Circumnavigation of the world by a yacht was accomplished by the *North Star*, about 2,000 tons, owned by Cornelius Vanderbilt, which started its first voyage on May 21, 1853, from New York City. It went on the rocks at Corlears Hook and returned to dry dock for minor repairs, after which the trip was resumed. The ship made stops at Southampton, Copenhagen, Le Havre, Malaga, Leghorn, and Rome. It was not allowed to moor at Naples because the authorities did not believe it possible for a single individual to own the ship and feared a sinister design. Further stops were made at Malta, Constantinople, Gibraltar, Tangier, and Madeira. The *North Star* returned to New York City on September 23, 1853, after a trip of more than 15,000 miles. Asa Eldridge was the captain. The only untoward incident on the voyage was the death of the quartermaster, who was accidently knocked overboard and drowned.

8531. World tour by a woman traveling alone was made by the reporter Elizabeth Cochrane, better known as Nellie Bly, who made the tour in 1889–90 as a stunt for the *New York World*, trying to beat the record set by the hero of Jules Verne's novel *Around the World in Eighty Days*. She left New York City on November 14, 1889, sailing from Hoboken, NJ, on the *Augusta Victoria* for Southampton, England, and continued traveling eastward on a variety of conveyances, including boats, rickshaws, and mules. The *World* published daily reports on her progress. Bly returned to New York with much fanfare on January 25, 1890, on a chartered express train. The tour took 72 days 6 hours 11 minutes 14 seconds, of which 56 days 12 hours 41 minutes were spent in actual travel.

8532. Round-the-world solo sailing journey was accomplished by Captain Joshua Slocum, who sailed from Boston, MA, on April 24, 1895, in a little sloop called *The Spray*. It was 36 feet 9 inches long, 14 feet 2 inches wide, and 4 feet 2 inches deep. Its tonnage was nine tons net and its cost was $554. The round trip of 46,000 miles was completed on July 3, 1898, when Captain Slocum sailed into the harbor at Fairhaven, MA, where the ship had been built.

8533. Transatlantic trip by rowboat was accomplished by George Harbo and Frank Samuelson, who left Battery Park, New York City, on June 6, 1896, in a cedar boat 5 feet wide and 18 feet 4 inches long, with air tanks at both ends. It had oak timbers but no masts or sails. Provisions consisted of 60 gallons of water, 100 pounds of bread and canned meat, 6 gallons of oil, 2 gallons of signal oil, and one dozen night signals. Harbo and Samuelson arrived at St. Mary's, the Scilly Isles, off southwest England, on August 1, where they made a two-day stopover. They reached Le Havre, France, on August 7, ending a 3,250-mile voyage.

8534. Circumnavigation of the globe by a fleet of warships began on December 16, 1907, at Hampton Roads, VA, under the command of Rear Admiral Robley Dunglison Evans, who relinquished his command on May 9, 1908, to Rear Admiral Charles Stillman Sperry. The fleet left San Francisco, CA, on July 7, 1908, and returned to Hampton Roads on February 22, 1909, stopping at Honolulu, Auckland, Sydney, Melbourne, Manila, Yokohama, Amoy, Colombo, Suez, and Gibraltar en route. The fleet was made up of the *Connecticut*, *Vermont*, *Kansas*, *Minnesota*, *Georgia*, *Nebraska*, *New Jersey*, *Rhode Island*, *Louisiana*, *Virginia*, *Missouri*, *Ohio*, *Wisconsin*, *Illinois*, *Kentucky*, *Kearsarge*, and several auxiliary vessels.

8535. Transatlantic crossing by a submarine under its own power was made by the *E-1*, which was laid down on December 22, 1909 and launched on May 27, 1911, at the Fore River Shipbuilding Company, Quincy, MA. It was commissioned on February 14, 1912, and its first commander was Lieutenant Chester William Nimitz. The ship left Newport, RI, on December 4, 1917, for Ponta Delgada, the Azores, where it was ordered to protect the islands from German attack by submarines. It returned to New London, CT, on September 17, 1918. It was 135 feet 3 inches long and displaced 342 tons.

8536. Circumnavigation of the world by a cruise ship was accomplished by the Cunard liner *Laconia*, which left New York City on November 21, 1922, with 440 passengers and returned on March 30, 1923, after a 130-day cruise.

8537. Transatlantic solo boat journey by a woman was made by Ann Davidson in a 23-foot sailboat, the *Felicity Ann*, which left Plymouth, England, on May 18, 1952, and arrived at Miami, FL, on August 12, 1953. Davidson made stops en route at Douarnenez,

France; Vigo, Spain; Gilbraltar; and Dominica, Antigua, Nevis, St. Thomas, and Nassau, British West Indies.

8538. Circumnavigation of the world by a submarine was made by the *Gudgeon*, which sailed from Pearl Harbor, HI, on July 8, 1957, visited Asian, African, and European ports, and returned to Hawaii on February 21, 1958. It traveled approximately 25,000 miles in 228 days. The *Gudgeon* was 269 feet 2 inches long, had a complement of 83 and a 2,050-ton displacement, and was launched on June 11, 1952, at the Portsmouth Naval Shipyard, Portsmouth, NH. It was commissioned on November 21, 1952.

8539. Circumnavigation of the North American continent by a ship was achieved by the Coast Guard cutter *Spar*, of the Military Sea Transport Service task unit, based at Bristol, RI. In 1957 the cutter sailed to Seattle, WA, where it was joined by the *Bramble* and the *Storis*, all of which completed the Northwest Passage on September 7, 1957. They followed the *Labrador*, a Canadian ice-patrol ship that cleared Bellot Strait, the keystone of the Northwest Passage.

8540. Crossing of the North Pole underwater by a submerged submarine was accomplished on August 3, 1958, by the nuclear-powered submarine *Nautilus* under the command of Commander William Robert Anderson. The submarine carried 116 persons, including 14 officers, 98 crewmen, and 4 civilian scientists. It left Pearl Harbor, HI, on July 23, 1958, crossed the Pacific Ocean through the Bering Strait, surfaced, and went under the ice cap at Point Barrow, Alaska, on August 1, 1958, at 11:15 P.M. E.D.T. Traveling 1,830 miles under the ice in 96 hours, it arrived under the North Pole on August 3. The *Nautilus* then continued its voyage, reaching Iceland on August 7. The expedition was designated "Northwest Passage."

8541. Submarine to surface at the North Pole was the U.S.S. *Skate*, which left New London, CT, on March 4, 1959, traveled under the Arctic ice, and surfaced at the Pole on March 17.

8542. Circumnavigation of the earth by a submerged submarine was accomplished by the U.S.S. *Triton*, which left New London, CT, on February 16, 1960, crossed the equator on February 24, and completed the submerged circumnavigation on April 25, having traveled 41,500 miles in 84 days. It returned to New London on May 11. The hull of the submarine was submerged during the entire trip, but the upper portion broached the surface twice. The nuclear-powered *Triton* was 447 feet long and had a 37-foot beam. Its displacement was 5,650 tons light, 5,900 tons standard, and 7,750 tons submerged. It carried a crew of 13 officers and 135 men and was commanded by Captain Edward Latimer Beach. The *Triton* was laid down on May 21, 1956, launched on August 19, 1958, and commissioned on November 10, 1959.

8543. Submarine to make a submerged passage through the Northwest Passage from the Atlantic to the Pacific by way of the North Pole was the *Seadragon*, commanded by George P. Steele II which sailed from Portsmouth, NH, on August 1, 1960, cleared the ice pack on September 3, and docked at Pearl Harbor, HI, on September 14.

8544. Ship to pass both ways through the Northwest Passage was the Coast Guard icebreaker *Northwind*, an escort icebreaker that accompanied the oil tanker *Manhattan* in 1969. Built by the Western Pipe and Steel Company, San Pedro, CA, the icebreaker had been launched on February 25, 1945. It was 250 feet long, with a full load displacement of 6,515 tons.

8545. Transatlantic solo trip by rowboat was made by John Fairfax, who left Las Palmas in the Canary Islands, off the coast of Morocco, in the *Britannia*, a 22-foot rowboat, on January 20, 1969. He was swept down to the Cape Verde Islands, crossed the Atlantic, and landed in the surf at Hollywood, FL, at 1:48 P.M. on July 19, after a 180-day voyage.

8546. Transpacific solo sailboat crossing by a woman was made by Sharon Sites Adams, who sailed from Yokohama, Japan, on May 12, 1969, in a 31-foot fiberglass ketch, the *Sea Sharp*. She arrived at San Diego, CA, on July 25, having covered a distance of approximately 5,620 miles in 74 days 17 hours 15 minutes.

8547. Round-the-world solo sailing trip by an African-American was achieved by marketing executive and Coast Guard captain William Pinkney in the cutter *Commitment*. The 22-month voyage, across a distance of 32,000 nautical miles, began in Boston, MA, on August 5, 1990. Pinkney sailed south past the coast of South America, across the Atlantic Ocean to Capetown, South Africa, and on to the Australian island of Tasmania. After a nine-month break, he sailed around Cape Horn and back up the coast of South America. The *Commitment* was equipped with a satellite computer system and a shortwave radio that allowed 20,000 schoolchildren in Boston and Chicago to followed Pinkney's progress.

8548. Solo crossing of the Gulf of Mexico in a paddled boat was made by Arthur Hebert, Jr., of Gretna, LA, in a 17-foot (5-meter) kayak made of Kevlar and fiberglass. He left Mexico's Yucatán Peninsula on May 16, 1998, and reached Louisiana on June 4. The kayak drifted into the Mississippi River, where Hebert was picked up by a Coast Guard cutter. Hebert made the crossing to raise public awareness about juvenile rheumatoid arthritis.

8549. Solo row across an ocean by a woman and the first solo row across the Atlantic Ocean by an American was accomplished by Tori Murden (Victoria Murden McClure) of Louisville, KY, on December 3, 1999. In an unescorted voyage lasting 81 days 7 hours 46 minutes, she rowed a 23-foot boat from the Canary Islands near Africa to the Caribbean island of Guadeloupe.

SUBJECT INDEX

The Subject Index is a listing of the book's entries arranged by topic. To find an entry in the text, please go to the italicized number.

A

Abdominal operation, *5338*
- appendectomy, *5344*
- other than a cesarean section, *5339*
- peritonitis preventive, *5347*

Abolition
- abolitionist who was an African-American woman, *7432*
- antislavery book, *6129*
- antislavery magazine, *6126*
- newspaper, *4501*
- organization, *6119*
- *See also* Antislavery *and* Slavery

Abortion: legalization by a state for therapeutic reasons, *7447*
Abrasive for commercial use, *1904*
Absolute monarch to visit the United States, *3932*
Abstract paintings, *1038*
Academic hall of fame, *3146*
Academy, *2697*
- air force, *3119*
- army, *3096*
- coast guard, *3106*
- merchant marine, *3117*
- naval, *3105*

Accident insurance company, *1956*
Accounting
- national society, *1706*
- society, *1705*
- state society, *1708*

Acetylene gas, *1896*
Achromatic lenses, *4639*
Acidophilus milk, *2418*
Action figure, *2200*
Actor
- actors union, *7139*
- African-American movie actor, *1142*
- Broadway play starring an African-American actress, *1461*
- English, to perform in America, *1425*
- home for retired actors, *1441*
- movie star, *1124*
- of American birth, *1423*
- Oscar for best actor awarded to an African-American, *1176*
- Oscar for best actress awarded to an African-American, *1176*
- Oscars for best acting, *1153*
- tried for sedition, *1411*
- to appear abroad, *1429*
- to have an exclusive movie contract, *1116*
- to receive curtain applause, *1427*

Acupuncture treatment center, *5075*
Adding machine
- successfully marketed, *1674*
- to employ depressible keys, *1665*
- to print totals and subtotals, *1668*

Adhesive
- and medicated plaster, *5171*
- plaster, *5178*
- postage stamp that was self-adhesive, *4753*
- postage stamps, *4716*
- postage stamps with humidity-resistant, *4752*
- pressure-sensitive, *1888*

Admiral
- Jewish, *5604*
- who was a graduate of the Naval Academy, *3108*

Adoption
- federal directions for sealing birth records of adopted children, *2197*
- home studies for foster and adoptive parents, *2194*
- organization for reuniting birthmothers and adopted children, *2201*
- state law allowing sealed birth records of adopted children to be opened, *2206*
- state law to consider the interests of the child, *2183*

Adventist church to accept Saturday as the Sabbath, *6268*
Advertisement
- for a car in a national magazine, *1534*
- for a car in a specialty magazine, *1533*
- for a magician, *1519*
- for a medical product in booklet form, *1518*
- for a patent medicine, *1516*
- for a radio receiver, *4819*
- in a newspaper, *1517*
- for a railroad trip, *8304*

member of the NYSE, *1786*
Methodist church in the North, *6238*
Methodist churches, *6238*
Methodist minister, *6232*
Metropolitan Opera orchestra conductor, *1330*
Metropolitan Opera singer, *1329*
missionary to the Native Americans, *6237*
movie actor, *1142*
movie director, *1144*
movie for an African-American audience by a major company, *1151*
musical comedy by and for, *1449*
national business organization, *1496*
national college fraternity, *2824*
national convention, *6127*
national monument to an African-American, *7190*
Naval Academy graduate, *3118*
Naval Academy midshipman, *3118*
Naval War College students, *3122*
Navy admiral, *5613*
Navy captain, *5612*
news correspondent, *4599*
news correspondent accredited to the White House, *4599*
news correspondent admitted to the congressional press gallery, *4599*
newspaper, *4554*
nurse to receive formal training, *5028*
nursing school, *3074*
Olympic medalist, *7853*
Olympic medalist to win an individual event, *7853*
opera singer to sing a white role, *1326*
ordained to the Mormon priesthood, *6329*
Oscar for best actor, *1176*
Oscar for best actress, *1176*
painter whose work was hung in the White House, *4334*
paratroop unit, *5483*
pilot on a scheduled passenger line, *8142*
pilot, *5472*
poetry collection, *1068*
preacher to deliver a sermon in the House of Representatives, *3604*
president of a major university, *2871*
presidential nominee, *3813*
presidential order enforcing affirmative action, *3857*
presidential pre-inauguration church service, *4162*
pro hockey player, *7833*
professional basketball player, *7557*
professional portrait painter, *1026*
published literary work, *1071*
publisher of medical journal, *5331*
radio network, *4814*
radio station, *4812*
reparations awarded to victims of a racially motivated massacre, *6971*
Rhodes Scholar, *2819*
round-the-world solo sailing trip, *8547*
school for African-Americans in Washington, DC, *2905*
school for blind students, *2946*
secretary of state, *4213*
Senate election between two African-American candidates, *3698*
Senate page, *3687*
senator, *3666*
senator to be elected by popular vote, *3688*
senator to serve a full term, *3666*
sisters in a Catholic convent, *6264*
slave rebellion in a major city, *6117*
slaves to hold Christian worship services, *6205*
star of a dramatic series on television, *4972*
state ban on lynching, *6138*
state in the North to restrict civil rights, *6124*
state labor antidiscrimination commission, *7158*
state legislator to represent a constituency with a white majority, *4388*
state legislator, *4387*
state police department to be monitored for racial profiling, *7395*
state school for children, *2947*
state segregation law, *6137*
state supreme court chief justice, *3708*
state supreme court justice, *3708*
Supreme Court justice, *3751*
surgeon general, *7287*
tap dancer of renown, *1049*
television news commentator, *4602*
temporary governor, *4383*
tennis champion, *7932*
Texas Ranger, *7359*
theology school graduate, *2731*
to be nominated for the offices of president and vice president by a major party convention, *4103*
to become a landowner of substance, *6112*
to chair a major political party, *4110*
to direct a Hollywood movie, *1177*
to earn a doctoral degree at an American university, *2791*
to earn a doctoral degree, *2768*
to enlist in the Union armed forces during the Civil War, *5706*
to graduate from medical school, *5017*

AIDS
antidiscrimination law, *5096*
campaign to promote citywide testing, *7296*
drug treatment, *5260*
epidemic, *5095*
home screening kit, *5189*
identification of the AIDS virus, *6682*
mandatory testing for newborns enacted by a state, *7289*
policy coordinator for the federal government, *7286*
Air bag
federal requirement, *8277*
in a car, *8271*
Air combat
African-American unit, *5481*
arm of the Army, *5475*
Army unit, *5469*
Marine Corps unit, *5473*
Navy unit, *5471*
Air conditioner
for home use, *2577*
patent, *1871*
Air defense military organization, *5478*
Air Force, *5488*
African-American general, *5494*
African-American woman, *5498*
airplane with a delta wing, *8122*
chairman of the Joint Chiefs of Staff, *5495*
independent aviation branch of the U.S. armed forces, *5488*
Reserve officer who was a nun, *5496*
secretary who was woman, *5499*
woman general, *5497*
Air Force academy, *3119*
African-American graduates, *3121*
Native American graduate, *3120*
women cadets, *3127*
Air pollution
billion-dollar settlement in an environmental lawsuit, *5932*
deaths from smog, *5920*
federal law of importance, *5925*
smog chamber for research, *5924*
Air raid shelter, *7298*
for a community, *7301*
Air rights lease, *3296*
Air traffic
planned nationwide shutdown, *8147*
unplanned nationwide shutdown, *8171*
year in which air traffic volume exceeded first-class rail traffic volume, *8127*
Air-conditioned
car, *8257*
factory, *3293*
office building, *3298*
public elementary school, *2976*
railroad cars, *8359*
train, *8395*
Aircraft
human-powered, *8159*
in commercial use designed by computer, *8169*
liability and property damage insurance, *1969*
round-the-world solo nonstop nonrefueled powered flight, *8173*
Aircraft carrier, *8484*
nuclear-powered, *8493*
with an angle deck, *8490*
Airliner
bomb explosion set off by a murderer, *6949*
reconstructed during a crash investigation, *8138*
skyjacking, *6951*
skyjacking by terrorists, *5817*
smoking ban, *7088*
Airmail
by missile, *4710*
dispatched from a post office in a balloon, *4670*
international service, *4693*
letter sheet, *4700*
parcel post, *4707*
pilot, *4690*
postal card, *4708*
regular service, *4692*
service, *4690*
service from ship to shore, *4698*
stamps, *4734*
transatlantic service, *4704*
transcontinental flight, *4695*
transcontinental regular service, *4696*
transpacific flight, *4701*
transported by jet, *4705*
Airplane
ambulance service, *5045*
Army unit, *5461*
African-American woman flight attendant, *8076*
bombing experiment, *5463*
car-airplane combination, *8255*
commercial round-the-world service, *8119*
communications by radio phone, *4884*
crash investigated with radar, *8170*
disaster involving more than 100 persons, *8140*
fatal accident, *8010*
fatal accident in which a woman was killed, *8033*
fighter plane, *5476*

transcontinental flight made in stages, *8030*
transcontinental flight made within 24 hours, *8047*
transcontinental nonstop, *8053*
transcontinental nonstop flight by a woman, *8088*
transcontinental round-trip flight made within 24 hours, *8117*
transcontinental solo flight by a woman, *8080*
transpacific nonstop, *8084*
transpacific solo flight by a woman, *8094*
under a bridge, *8027*

Airplane race
between cities, *7678*
in Europe won by an American, *7675*
of importance in which both men and women were contestants, *7682*
transcontinental, *7679*

Airport
baggage scanning system, *8154*
city, *8041*
county, *8057*
fog disposal unit, *8124*
for civilians owned and operated by the federal government, *8103*
hotel, *1831*
international passenger station, *8065*
runway illumination, *8055*
woman manager, *8087*

Airship, *7999*
all-metal, *8069*
bombing plan, *5457*
certified by the FAA, *8166*
disaster, *8006*
filled with helium gas, *8049*
for private commercial operation, *8077*
Navy, *8040*
ordered by the federal government, *8008*
passenger to transfer to an airplne, *8070*
race, *7676*
rigid, *8056*
stowaway, *8043*
to land and take off from an oceangoing steamship, *8079*
transatlantic flight, *8020*
transcontinental flight, *8051*
transcontinental flight, *8056*
with an enclosed cabin, *8058*

Alarm clock, *2626*

Albert Medal, *6895*

Alcohol
abuse programs required in schools by the federal government, *7067*
Alcoholics Anonymous, *7078*
anti-saloon organization, *7069*
asylum for alcoholics, *5109*
congressional prohibition vote showing a dry majority, *7073*
federal prohibition law, *7075*
liquor reform movement, *7053*
national anti-saloon league, *7070*
national temperance society, *7066*
prohibition enforcement officers, *7052*
state law prohibiting drunk driving, *8199*
state prohibition law, *7060*
state temperance society for women, *7062*
state to ratify the Prohibition Amendment to the Constitution, *7074*
state-run liquor stores, *2098*
temperance law enacted by a colony, *7054*
temperance organization, *7057*
twelve-step rehabilitation program, *7078*

Alfalfa, *1586*

Algebra book, *6758*
by an American-born author, *6765*

All-glass windowless structure, *3302*

Allergy
book, *5323*
journal, *5336*

Alliance between the United States and another country, *3874*

Alligator farm, *1632*

Almanac, *3168*
nautical, *8407*
with a continuous existence, *3181*

Alternative medicine department in a federal research institution, *5400*

Aluminum
foil, *2583*
in metallic form, *1941*
pots, *2282*
soda can, *2004*
soda can with a pull-tab pop-top, *2003*

Amateur athlete
African-American to win the James E. Sullivan Memorial Trophy, *7479*
African-American woman to win the James E. Sullivan, *7480*
to win the James E. Sullivan Memorial Trophy, *7478*

Ambassador
African-American woman, *3904*
assassinated in office, *3906*
from the United States who was a woman, *3900*
Jewish, *3894*
Muslim, *3915*
to Canada, *3897*
to Mexico, *3889*
to the UN who was an American woman, *3903*

to the United States who was a woman, *3899*
to Vietnam, *3914*
woman permanent representative to the UN, *3910*
AMBER Alert System, *7393*
Ambulance
air service, *5045*
Army corps, *5198*
equipped for mobile coronary care, *5047*
Navy ship, *5202*
service for hospitals, *5044*
service with an incubator, *5046*
ship designed and built by the Navy as a hospital, *5209*
ship for first aid to boaters and pleasure craft, *5048*
America: use of the name as a geographical designation, *3453*
American: use of the word as an adjective, *3503*
American Bar Association, women members, *3971*
American College of Surgeons
African-American fellow, *5229*
woman fellow, *5229*
American flag
changes authorized by Congress, *3491*
depicted on a postage stamp, *4724*
displayed from the right hand of the Statue of Liberty, *3504*
displayed on a man-of-war, *3472*
flown by a cargo ship, *8462*
flown by an automated tanker, *8463*
flown in battle, *3473*
flown on the high seas, *3474*
flown over a schoolhouse, *3493*
flown over conquered hostile territory, *3492*
monument, *7187*
pledge of allegiance, *3500, 3501*
salute by a foreign nation, *3475*
salute by a foreigner, *3470*
salute by schoolchildren, *3499*
Star-Spangled Banner, *3494*
state law requiring salute by schoolchildren, *3502*
to circumnavigate the globe, *3485*
to orbit the earth, *3506*
to represent the United States, *3471*
American Heritage Rivers, *5997*
American history chair at a college, *2748*
American Revolution centennial celebration, *2501*
Americana: bibliography in English, *1076*
Amphibious vehicle, *8494*
Anarchist, *7108*
Anatomy
book, *5288*
dissection of a living animal, *3058*
lectures for medical students, *3041*
lectures for the public, *3041*
research institute, *6662*
Anesthesiology professor, *3095*
Anesthetic
administered in childbirth, *5051*
demonstration for surgical use, *5052*
general anesthetica, *5049*
in dentistry, *5050*
local, *5053*
Angle iron, *3332*
Anglican
Book of Common Prayer in the Mohawk language, *6342*
Christian religious service in English on the Pacific Coast, *6168*
church for deaf people, *6258*
ordained clergyman who was deaf, *6258*
Animal
disease of American origin, *5406*
fast-food corporation to require humane animal treatment from its suppliers, *1844*
fired into space to orbit the earth, *6798*
formation of a new animal by transplantation, *6664*
hospice, *2605*
life insurance, *1972*
prehistoric skeleton, *6657*
steel traps commercially manufactured, *2653*
surrogate birth experiment, *6668*
to be patented, *6684*
to survive a space flight, *6797*
transgenic, *6679*
Animal activism
felony conviction for cruelty against farm animals, *1657*
humane society, *7210*
national humane society, *7218*
rights organization, *7221*
Animal crackers, *2376*
in a circus box, *2376*
recipe, *2376*
Animal husbandry professor, *2807*
Animated
photograph projection before a theater audience, *1193*
picture machine, *1192*
Animated cartoon, *1195*
in an electric sign, *1545*
in color, *1197*
made with cel animation, *1196*
of feature-length in Technicolor, *1200*

joint space walk by an American astronaut and a Russian cosmonaut, *6838*
lost in a U.S. space mission who was not an American, *6841*
physician to practice in space, *6818*
Russian cosmonaut on an American space mission, *6833*
to be launched into space, American, *6803*
to become a senator, *3690*
to cast a vote from space, *3788*
to converse with an aquanaut, *6807*
to die in a spacecraft, *6810*
to fly free in space, *6827*
to fly in space who was Native American, *6840*
to get a haircut in space, *6819*
to hear a live concert, *1286*
to land on the moon, *6814*
to make a ground landing in a capsule, *6842*
to orbit the earth on two trips, *6806*
to orbit the earth, American, *6804*
to orbit the moon, *6812*
to participate in an international spaceflight, *6820*
to receiving training in Russia's space program, *6835*
to rendezvous in space with another spacecraft, *6808*
to retrieve a manmade object from the moon, *6816*
to ride a vehicle on the moon, *6817*
to see the sun eclipsed by the Earth, *6815*
to transfer from one spacecraft to another while in orbit, *6813*
to walk in space, American, *6805*
trained by the United States, *6802*
who was Hispanic, *6824*
who was of Asian descent, *6823*
woman from the United States to live in a space station, *6837*
woman to fly in space (American), *6825*
woman to pilot the space shuttle, *6834*
woman to serve as commander of a space flight, *6834*
woman to walk in space, *6825*

Astronomer
archeoastronomer, *6379*
of note, *6364*
radio, *6376*
to acquire international fame, *6367*
to calculate the surface temperature of Venus, *6391*
to measure the size of a fixed star, *6374*

Astronomical
observations book, *6776*
phenomenon caused by space debris, *6864*

Astronomy
color photograph of the earth taken from space, *6410*
color photographs published in a magazine, *6408*
expedition to record an eclipse of the sun, *6369*
image of a planet outside Earth's solar system, *6418*
image of Earth as seen from Mars, *6420*
image of Mars at night, *6419*
images of the surface of Mars to be televised live, *6417*
live telecast from space, *6413*
magazine, *6778*
movie of a solar eclipse taken from an airplane, *6405*
movie of a solar eclipse taken from an airship, *6403*
movie of the sun, *6406*
movie showing another planet, *6404*
photograph, *6398*
photograph from space showing the earth, *6409*
photograph of a comet taken from space, *6414*
photograph of a planet in another solar system, *6421*
photograph of the earth taken from the moon, *6412*
photograph taken close up of an asteroid in space, *6416*
photograph taken on Mars, *6415*
photographs of Jupiter, *6877*
photographs of the moon in close-up, *6411*
scientific program to search for extraterrestrial life, *6378*
ultraviolet pictures of the sun, *6407*

Asylum for alcoholics, *5109*

Atheneum, *3007*

Athlete
depicted on a Wheaties box, *1543*
woman to earn more than $1 million in a year, *7934*
woman to earn more than $100,000 in one season, *7933*

Atlas
issued by a state, *4483*
of the human body, *5147*

ATM machine, *1752*

Atomic bomb
dropped from an airplane over water, *5872*
explosion, *5871*
explosion over enemy territory, *5797*
explosion to be shown on television, *5875*
hydrogen, *5879*

B

Blood
bloodless liver transplant from a living donor, *5382*
powdered serum made of dried human blood, *5054*
transfusion of artificial blood, *5060*
Blood bank, *5055*
public, for collecting umbilical cord and placental blood for stem cell research, *5063*
Blood tests
for marriage license applicants to be required by a state, *7280*
for pregnant women to be required by a state, *7279*
required by a state, *7278*
Bloomers, *2244*
Blotting paper, *2019*
Blow dryer for hair, *2473*
Blue Cross and Blue Shield, *1982*
Blue-sky laws enacted by a state, *1502*
Bluegrass musician, *1266*
Boarding school on a Native American reservation, *2938*
Boardwalk, *3416*
Boat
club, *7566*
race for fishermen, *7574*
solo crossing of the Gulf of Mexico, *8548*
transatlantic solo boat journey by a woman, *8537*
Bobsled
American Olympic champions in four-man competition, *7975*
American Olympic champions in two-man competition, *7975*
four-man competition, *7975*
run, *7975*
two-man competition, *7975*
Boiler
state inspection law, *7327*
insurance company, *1957*
plates, *1884*
Boll weevil, *1633*
Bonding
company, *1962*
law enacted by a state, *1968*
Bonds
clearinghouse, *1774*
federal, *1766*
payable specifically in United States gold coins, *1779*
Bone
bank, *5058*
marrow transplant, *5369*
Book subjects
advocating spelling reform, *2901*
advocating voting rights for women, *3763*
almanac, *3168*
almanac with a continuous existence, *3181*
American history book of importance by a woman, *7470*
anthology of American literature, *1078*
catalog of theological and biblical literature, *6343*
children's, *1062*
coastal survey, *5905*
collective work of genealogy, *7474*
comic history of the United States, *7471*
containing a map made in America, *4476*
containing credit reports, *1703*
dental hygiene, *5335*
giving advice to mothers, *2175*
guide to parliamentary rules of order, *3564*
in German printed in America, *4435*
in Hebrew other than the Bible, *6361*
Masonic, *7195*
memoir of life in the White House, *4327*
music book printed with bars, *1210*
music, printed from type, *1219*
nautical almanac, *8407*
novel by a writer born in America, *1069*
of colonial laws, *3948*
of crossword puzzles, *7734*
of federal laws, *3956*
of music by a composer born in America, *1220*
of road maps, *4480*
of secular songs by an American-born composer, *1216*
on African-American history, *7476*
on agriculture that was distinctly American, *1576*
on agriculture, *1569*
on algebra, *6758*
on algebra by an American-born author, *6765*
on allergies, *5323*
on Americanisms, *1082*
on anatomy, *5288*
on architecture printed in America, *3218*
on arithmetic by an American-born author, *6757*
on arithmetic, printed in America, *6756*
on astronomical observations, *6776*
on aviation, *7997*
on baseball, *7481*
on billiards, *7726*
on botany by an American-born author, *6764*
on bridge, *7735*
on canning, *2340*

television version of a play with its original cast, *1460*
theater ticket agency, *1438*
Bronchitis treatise, *5317*
Brothers
opponents in a gubernatorial election, *4379*
tennis champions, *7925*
three from one family to serve in the Senate, *3682*
to serve as representatives in Congress simultaneously, *3600*
to serve simultaneously as state governors, *4373*
Brushes, *2209*
Bubble gum, *2407*
Buddhist
American to be recognized by Tibetan Buddhists as a reincarnated lama, *6331*
temple, *6272*
Zen monastery, *6323*
Buffalo wings, *2450*
Building
brick, *3257*
built completely inside a factory, *3303*
built to serve as a hotel, *1809*
commercial, with solar heating, *3313*
concrete monolithic, *3268*
constructed wholly of cast iron, *3270*
containing 6.5 million square feet of usable space, *3305*
designed as a post office, *4664*
designed to be used by artists, *3275*
elliptical office building, *3317*
erected by the federal government, *3839*
erected in Washington, DC, by the federal government, *3840*
faced with aluminum, *3309*
federal government, built to withstand a nuclear attack, *3854*
heated by steam, *3267*
in all-Gothic architecture, *3261*
in which wrought-iron beams were used, *3273*
library, *3001*
neoclassical, *3258*
of fireproof construction, *3262*
of large size with a retractable roof, *3315*
of pressed structural steel, *3295*
shaped like an elephant, *3283*
split-level, *3264*
steel-frame, *3285*
with a combined heat and power energy system, *3320*
with a high steeple, *3266*
with a large-scale clear-span dome, *3292*
with an all-marble dome, *3290*
with its roof supported by cables, *3308*
Building and loan association, *1721*
Bullfighter
bullfight, *7613*
matador of American birth, *7614*
woman to fight professionally, *7615*
Burglar alarm, *3276*
operated by ultrasonic or radio waves, *3307*
system, *3280*
Burial
at the Tomb of the Unknown Soldier, *2303*
in space, *2311*
on the moon, *2312*
Bus
double-deck, *8219*
night coach, *8221*
sightseeing, *8218*
transcontinental express service, *8222*
transcontinental service, *8220*
with a gas-turbine engine, *8223*
Business
business economics course at a college, *2747*
business history chair at a college, *2840*
high school, *2955*
manual, *3172*
national organization for African-Americans, *1496*
school, *3197*
school at a college, *2795*
Buttons
cloth-covered, *2238*
gilt, *2234*
of pewter or block tin, *2232*

C

Cabinet, *4168*
appointee rejected by the Senate, *4177*
conference to be telecast, *4192*
in which all members were sworn in at the same time and place, *4187*
meeting attended by a foreign national, *4196*
session held at a place other than the seat of the federal government, *4194*
session to be telecast and broadcast, *4193*
Cabinet member
African-American, *4197*
African-American woman, *4204*
Catholic, *4176*
convicted of a crime, *4186*

collar manufacturer, *2240*
collar, detachable, *2237*
collar, paper, *2247*
corset, *2253*
designer with a couture establishment, *2267*
discount store, *2092*
earmuffs, *2252*
gloves, *2235*
made of a synthetic fabric, *2265*
maternity clothes, *2259*
nylon stockings, *2265*
ready-made, for children, *2255*
shirt factory, *2243*
sports bra, *2268*
swimsuit, *2262*
Tuxedo jacket, *2254*
uniforms for working women, *2257*
valeteria, *1695*
Coach of a professional basketball team who was African-American, *7560*
Coach riding, *7962*
Coaching club, *7961*
Coal, *6575*
anthracite, *6577*
anthracite used commercially, *6578*
coal oil factory, *1889*
hydrogenation plant, *1908*
locomotive to burn, *8333*
mine disaster, *6594*
mine to be automated, *6605*
pipeline, *6611*
woman miner killed in a mining accident, *6613*
Coast
coast guard service, *5542*
federal survey, *6059*
survey book, *5905*
Coast Guard
African-American serviceman, *5543*
aviation unit, *5470*
inland station, *5544*
unit for women, *5545*
woman ship commander, *5547*
women officers, *5546*
Coast Guard Academy, *3106*
African-American graduate, *3123*
women graduates, *3131*
Coast-to-coast
British-made television series in prime time, *4973*
live telecast in color, *4959*
paved road, *3420*
radio hookup, *4789*
radio news broadcast to be recorded, *4537*
satellite telecast, *5003*
solar-powered two-way radio conversation, *4802*
video recording on magnetic tape, *4963*
Coaxial cable, *4859*
Coca-Cola, official use of trademark, *2447*
Cocktail, *2324*
Cod-liver oil, *5232*
Coffee
freeze-dried, *2451*
in a can, *2379*
mill, *2343*
percolator, *2278*
Coffins, lead, *2293*
Cog railroad, *8315*
Coke used successfully as a blast furnace fuel, *6582*
Cola drink, *2386*
Cold storage plant, *1865*
Cold War
presidential hot line to the Kremlin, *4153*
radiation attacks against an American embassy, *3908*
Collapsible tubes, *2650*
machine-made, *2658*
Collar
detachable, *2237*
manufacturer, *2240*
paper, *2247*
College
alumni association, *2733*
Army war, *3110*
art museum, *3137*
book catalog, *2692*
Catholic, for women, *2815*
chartered by a governor, *2696*
chartered by the Crown, *2691*
chemistry laboratory at a college, *2758*
city, *2716*
class photograph, *4619*
coat of arms, *2691*
coeducational literary society, *2700*
commencement exercises in a prison, *2875*
comprehensive senior examination program, *2832*
daily newspaper, *4517*
dean of students, *2820*
debate broadcast on radio, *4786*
dental, *3054*
entrance plan using certified schools, *2784*
entrance requirement other than Greek, Latin, and arithmetic, *2728*
extension courses, *2813*
for African-American students, *2754*
for deaf students, *2757*
for the performing arts, state, *2867*

Customs: standardization of weights and measures, *2067*
Cut glass, *3363*
Cutlery
  factory, *2546*
  pocket, *2546*
  shears, *2544*
Cyber cafe, *1843*
  kosher, *1843*
Cyber university, *2879*
Cyclone of record, *5899*
Czech
  newspaper, *4559*
  settler in America, *6026*

D

Dairy
  rotating milking platform, *1646*
  state association, *1621*
  school at a college, *2808*
Dam
  disaster of great consequence, *5909*
  filled with rocks, *3350*
  steel, *3351*
Dance
  ballet choreographer of international renown, *1051*
  ballet on an American theme by an American choreographer, *1053*
  ballet performed in the United States, *1046*
  ballet transmitted by satellite, *1056*
  copyright registered for a choreographic score, *1055*
  major at a college, *2845*
  modern, school, *3211*
  modern, troupe that was all-male, *1052*
  powwow at the National Mall, *1057*
  theater designed for dance performances, *1054*
Dance club/discotheque, *1838*
Dance marathon, *7972*
  to exceed 200 hours, *7972*
Dancer
  ballerina, *1048*
  modern, *1050*
  professional, *1047*
  tap, *1049*
Danish
  newspaper, *4562*
  settlers in America, *6028*
Daredevil
  jumper, *1366*
  to cross Niagara Falls on a tightrope, *1371*
  to go over Niagara Falls in a barrel, *1391*
  to go over Niagara Falls in a rubber ball, *1400*
  to jump off the Brooklyn Bridge and survive, *1383*
Database
  comprehensive database of federal research projects, *3871*
  computerized library network, *3040*
  national DNA, *7394*
  online library, *3039*
  ruling requiring retention of all electronic records of the federal government, *3864*
  state to offer simultaneous access to multiple government databases, *7424*
Daylight saving time, *2632*
Deadline for filing individual income tax returns, *4419*
Deaf
  cablecasts of city meetings with realtime captioning, *7048*
  church for deaf people, *6258*
  college for deaf students, *2757*
  instruction for deaf students, *2904*
  lipreading instruction, *3201*
  lipreading instruction for adults, *3201*
  magazine for and by deaf students, *7033*
  national organization for the hard of hearing, *7035*
  ordained clergyman, *6258*
  prayer service in sign language, *6258*
  school for deaf students, *2908*
  school to teach lip-reading, *2909*
  school using sign language, *2909*
  sign language conversation using TV, *7042*
  television show with open captions, *7045*
  television shows with closed captions, *7046*
  visible speech method of instruction, *2948*
Dean
  of students at a college, *2820*
  of a university graduate school who was a woman, *2855*
  of faculty at a college, *2799*
Death
  by suicide machine, *2308*
  hospice for incurable cancer patients, *5392*
  hospice home-care program, *5398*
Death penalty
  authorized by federal law, *7016*
  peacetime, for espionage, *7018*
  state ban, *6992*
  state legislature to impose a moratorium on executions, *7028*

Double-deck
bridge, *3252*
bus, *8219*
ferryboat, *8439*
railroad coaches, *8347*
steamboat, *8421*
streetcar, *8371*
Doughnut cutter, *2280*
Dow Jones Industrial Average
over 7,000, *1789*
to exceed 1,000 points, *1788*
to exceed 10,000 points, *1790*
Drama
broadcast on radio, *1451*
broadcast on radio from a regular stage, *1456*
school, *3204*
school at a college, *2853*
Draper Prize for engineering and technology, *6916*
Drill
cordless electric, *2668*
electric, *2668*
Drinking straws, *2565*
Drive-in
banking service, *1748*
movie theater, *1159*
Driver
arrested for speeding, *8236*
education in public schools, *2975*
Driver license
board, *8188*
graduated, for teenagers, *8274*
required by a state, *8191*
Driving
course in a high school, *2972*
state ban on driving while intoxicated, *8199*
state ban on driving while using a cell phone, *8215*
state competency test, *8197*
Drought of record, *5903*
Drug control
federal director, *7089*
federal law, *7072*
Drug treatment center
federal, *7077*
for minors, *7081*
Drugs, prescription
antibiotic manufactured commercially, *5247*
antidepressant, *5255*
antihistamine, *5249*
benzodiazepine tranquilizer, *5256*
broad-spectrum antibiotic, *5251*
cancer-prevention drug, *5263*
for treating AIDS, *5260*
federal purity law, *7238*
fungicide, *5250*
imported by a city for its employees, *7292*
mill, *5234*
oral medicine for erectile dysfunction, *5262*
SSRI antidepressant, *5261*
state public health program to provide drugs from Canada and Europe, *7295*
state purity law, *7251*
sulfanilamide, *5244*
synthetic antibiotic, *5253*
to achieve mass popularity, *5256*
transdermal patch, *5259*
Drugs, recreational
city to legalize possession of marijuana, *7093*
federal ban on marijuana, *7079*
methadone program for heroin addicts, *7083*
recreational, magazine, *7086*
state ban on narcotics, *7085*
state law decriminalizing hemp cultivation, *1656*
twelve-step rehabilitation program, *7078*
Drunk driving, state ban, *8199*
Dry dock, *8415*
federal, *8424*
Dry ice
manufactured commercially, *1901*
used in a restaurant, *1901*
Duel, *6923*
between congressional representatives that resulted in death, *3599*
between representatives in Congress, *3594*
president who had participated in, *4245*
state ban on duelling, *6929*
Dugong, *5961*
Dunkards: religious commune, *3510*
Dunkin' Donuts, *1833*
Dutch elm disease breakout, *5985*
Dutch
Reformed church, *6176*
settlement in America, *6016*
DVD: movie sold simultaneously as a downloadable product and a DVD, *1191*
Dwarf exhibited as a theatrical attraction, *1354*
Dye plant, *1891*
Dynamite, *1861*

E

E pluribus unum: use on coins, *4008*

car to be mass-produced, *8279*
Christmas tree lights, *2504*
clock movement, *2631*
cooking experiment, *6534*
cordless drill, *2668*
dental drill, *5087*
dynamo for a direct-current outdoor lighting system, *6538*
dynamo that was successful, *6549*
elevated railroad, *8319*
elevator, *3287*
eye detectors for high jump competitions, *7952*
fan, *2563*
fire alarm system, *7325*
flashing sign, *1542*
freight locomotive, *8337*
guitar, *1311*
hand drill, *2668*
hearing aid, *5268*
heating pad, *5177*
locomotive, *8337*
locomotive headlight, *8391*
locomotive with a gas-turbine-electric engine, *8346*
meter, *6552*
mobility devices allowed on sidewalks by a state, *7050*
mobility machines owned by a city, *3545*
motor using direct current, *6536*
motorized wheelchair, *7036*
music synthesizer, *1307*
naval ship, *8480*
newspaper printing plant, *2050*
organ, *1300*
portable typewriter, *1697*
power transmission installation using alternating current, *6554*
printing press, *2039*
railroad dining car, *8361*
railroad engine, *8323*
railroad that was all-electric, *8325*
range, *2277*
sawmill, *1870*
self-starter used in cars, *8248*
sewing machine, *2622*
shaver, *2476*
sign of large dimensions, *1529*
sign showing an animated cartoon, *1545*
socket operated by a pull chain, *2569*
starting gate for horse races, *7810*
stethoscope, *5179*
stove, *2283*
streamlined locomotive, *8344*
streetcars commercially operated, *8370*
table for shuffling and dealing cards, *7737*
tabulating machine, *1677*
taxicabs, *8231*
timing device for foot races, *7949*
toaster, *2286*
toothbrush, *2481*
traffic light, *8201*
traffic lights equipped with noise signals, *8204*
trains with a third rail, *8324*
turnstile with a rachet, *1671*
typewriter, *1690*
underwater torpedo, *5847*
warship, *8482*
washing machine, *2221*
watch, *2634*

Electric chair
execution of an organized crime leader, *7017*
used in an execution, *7009*
used in the execution of a woman, *7009*

Electric light
for household illumination, *6537*
from a power plant in a residence, *6547*
in a hotel, *1822*
in a lighthouse, *7347*
in a store, *6540*
in a theater, *1445*
in city streetlights, *7410*
on a steamboat, *8435*
on a train, *8394*

Electric power
commercial carrier, *6561*
company, *6539*
company organized to produce and sell electricity, *6542*
contract between a city and the federal government, *6568*
from nuclear energy, *6619*
generated by Niagara Falls waterpower, *6541*
generated from nuclear energy to be sold commercially, *6621*
generated from nuclear energy to illuminate a town, *6620*
state law requiring underground burial of wires, *7412*
using municipal garbage as a boiler fuel, *6573*

Electric power plant
floating, *6566*
generating electricity from peat, *6637*
operated by a city, *6548*
to use a gas turbine, *6571*
to use alternating current, *6551*
to use solar cells, *6636*
with a central source, *6550*

Electrical engineering school
at a college, *2797*

by lethal gas, *7013*
by lethal injection, *7021*
by the Army, *5549*
by the federal government using lethal injection, *7027*
colonist hanged for treason, *6989*
enemy saboteurs executed in the United States, *5786*
for kidnapping, *7015*
for slave trading carried out by the federal government, *7002*
for the murder of a federal officer, *7016*
for witchcraft, *6987*
in America, *6986*
of a white criminal for the murder of a Native American, *6997*
of a woman, *7009*
of a woman by hanging by the federal government, *7004*
of an organized crime leader in the electric chair, *7017*
of labor activists, *7135*
ordered by a woman judge, *3716*
to be televised, *7026*

Exhibition
major museum show of Native American art, *1041*
modern art, *1039*
Native American art, *1041*
of the *Mona Lisa, 1042*

Expedition
botanic, *6656*
of Englishmen to cross the Allegheny Mountains, *6029*
scientific, sponsored by a colony, *6366*
to record an eclipse of the sun, *6369*

Exploration
airplane flight over the North Pole, *6647*
airplane flight over the South Pole, *6648*
airplane flight to land at the North Pole, *6650*
airplane flight to land at the South Pole, *6652*
Arctic expedition by an American explorer, *6643*
Arctic expedition to seek the Northwest Passage, *6639*
by ship of the mouth of the Columbia River, *6050*
charting of the Northwest Passage, *6653*
deep-sea exploration vessel, *6499*
explorer to set foot on both the North and South Poles, *6651*
of land on the Pacific coast by a European, *6005*
of the Grand Canyon of the Colorado, *6644*
of the Mississippi River by a European, *6004*
of the New England region by an Englishman, *6011*
permanent American base in Antarctica, *6649*
polar expedition to include a woman, *6645*
scientific expedition fitted out by the federal government, *6642*
transcontinental expedition to the Pacific coast, *6640*
voyage to Antarctica by an American, *6641*
voyage to the North Pole, *6646*
women to participate in an Antarctic expedition, *6649*

Exports
beef, *2320*
car, *8233*
cattle, *1575*
cotton crop, *1577*
federal report, *2066*
furs, *5937*
glass bottles, *2061*
hemp, *1571*
ice, *2337*
manufactured products, *2061*
petroleum, *6589*
silk, *2111*
year in which exports exceeded imports, *2069*

Express delivery service, *2071*
airborne, *2081*
nationwide, *2076*
to the West, *2072*

Expulsion
from the Senate, mass, *3663*
of a congressional representative, *3603*
of a congressional representative for corruption, *3632*
of a senator, *3654*
of a senator for corrupt election practices, *3670*
of a state legislator for campaign financing violations, *4397*

Extinction by humans of a native American animal, *5949*

Extradition
of criminals among colonies, *7352*
treaty with a foreign country, *3886*

Eye
bank, *5057*
hospital, *5102*
infirmary, *5101*
wash, *5241*

Eyeglasses
bifocal, *5264*

with polycarbonate lenses, *5274*

F

Factory
bicycle, *7641*
child labor, *7103*
cooled by air conditioning, *3293*
federal standardization, *3260*
heated by steam, *3269*
operated by the federal government in peacetime, *3847*
state inspection law enacted, *7128*
to give workers a half holiday on Saturday, *7124*
with temperature and humidity control, *3291*
without windows, *3299*
False eyelashes, *2472*
Family assistance program, *3848*
Family leave, paid, required by a state, *2170*
Fan, *2563*
Farm
alligator, *1632*
bureau, *1637*
chinchilla, *1641*
cooperative for artificial insemination, *1652*
cruelty conviction of farmworkers
experimental, *1572*
federal horse farm, *1635*
ostrich, *1629*
Farmers
institute sponsored by a state, *1615*
national organization, *1619*
Fashion
designer to use zippers, *2261*
dictionary, *2264*
magazine, *2251*
plate in a magazine, *4608*
Fashion show, *1392*
for charity, *1392*
to be televised, *1403*
Fast-food corporation
Dunkin' Donuts, *1833*
franchise chain, *1832*
to require humane animal treatment from its suppliers, *1844*
Fat substitute in prepared foods, *2453*
Fatal
airplane accident, *8010*
airplane accident involving a woman, *8033*
airplane accident in a solo military airplane, *5466*
hailstone shower, *5904*
Father and son
to be awarded a joint patent, *3989*
to occupy the same Cabinet post, *4185*
who were senators at the same session of Congress, *3659*
Father's Day, *2509*
established by presidential proclamation, *2509*
Fax
high-speed radio fax transmission, *4473*
long-distance radio fax transmission of medical information, *4471*
patents, *4467*
transatlantic radio fax of a drawing, *4586*
transatlantic radio fax transmission of a photograph, *4468*
transcontinental radio fax transmission, *4470*
transcontinental radio fax transmission of a photograph, *4469*
transmission by a press syndicate direct to newspaper offices, *4533*
transmission of movie film, *4472*
transpacific radio fax transmission, *4470*
FBI
criminal on the Ten Most Wanted list, *6948*
director, *7370*
file on suspected political radicals, *7373*
Public Enemy Number 1, *6945*
raid on the office of a congressional representative, *3641*
sting operation against corrupt politicians, *6960*
Ten Most Wanted list, *6947*
woman on the Ten Most Wanted list, *6948*
Federal courts, *3702*
African-American appellate judge, *3722*
African-American district court judge, *3726*
African-American woman district court judge, *3726*
judge to be impeached, *3704*
judge to reduce a sentence to protest racial profiling, *7024*
to impose the punishment of branding, *6998*
woman judge, *3719*
woman judge on the Circuit Court of Appeals, *3719*
Federal government
affirmative action order issued, *3855*
African-American woman administrator, *3851*
agency director who was a woman, *3846*
agency overseeing all border control, *3870*

nationwide highway planning surveys, *3426*
naval hospital, *5194*
Native American commissioner of Indian Affairs, *3843*
Native American superintendent of a Bureau of Indian Affairs agency, *3843*
neutrality mandate to apply to American citizens, *3885*
nutrition standards, *7259*
observatory, *6372*
patent granted, *3987*
payment over the Internet, *3865*
penitentiary, *7010*
penitentiary whose prisoners were employed in industry, *7012*
pensions, *7102*
pensions paid to workers in private industry, *7155*
proclamation of neutrality, *3884*
public service symbol, *5919*
publications and documents on microfilm, *3038*
public railroad, *8326*
purchase of an airplane, *8013*
purchase of an airship, *8008*
quota on immigration, *6088*
rebellion by citizens, *5675*
records, court ruling requiring retention of electronic, *3684*
report posted on the Internet before its publication on paper, *3866*
report on exports, *2066*
report on health consequences of smoking, *7084*
research institution with a department of alternative medicine, *5400*
research projects, comprehensive database, *3871*
reservation for Native Americans, *6047*
restrictions on tobacco sale to minors, *7090*
revenue cutter, *8412*
savings and loan association, *1744*
secret service, *3842*
ship construction, *8467*
smallpox vaccination program to protect Native Americans, *5154*
Social Security monthly payment, *3853*
soldiers' homes, *5621*
speed limit for highways, *8213*
statue cast for a federal monument, *7176*
steamboat inspection service, *8429*
strike settlement mediated by the Department of Labor, *7146*
support for a scientific expedition, *6642*
support for a theatrical presentation, *1457*
suppression of a strike in peacetime, *7127*
Supreme Court decision establishing federal power, *3742*
tariff legislation, *4404*
telegraph appropriation, *4845*
territorial concessions to a Native American, *6075*
territory, *6042*
territory occupied by armed Native American protesters in the modern era, *6102*
territory occupied by Native American protesters in the modern era, *6099*
terrorism warning system using color codes, *5834*
treasury surplus to be returned to the states, *4345*
treaty with Native American tribes, *6041*
trial of a war criminal, *5721*
tuberculosis hospital, *5129*
war bond issue, *1768*
women employees, *3841*
year in which Medicare spending declined, *3867*
year in which the federal budget exceeded $1 trillion, *3862*
year in which the public debt exceeded $1 trillion, *3861*

Federal law
allowing duty-free storage of imported merchandise, *2073*
authorizing conveyance of vaccine through the mail, *5153*
authorizing deportation of aliens, *6055*
authorizing military service by African-Americans, *5421*
authorizing naturalization of citizens, *6049*
authorizing shipbuilding, *5580*
authorizing the death penalty, *7016*
banning immigration of particular people, *6080*
banning importation of adulterated drugs, *7238*
banning importation of diseased cattle, *7246*
banning mail fraud, *4679*
banning marijuana, *7079*
banning narcotics, *7071*
banning piracy, *6931*
banning polygamy, *7436*
banning polygamy that was enforced, *7436*
banning sex discrimination in wages, *7446*

to earn a college degree in a scientific field, *4230*
to earn a professional degree, *4236*
to give birth during her husband's term in office, *4229*
to graduate from college, *4226*
to have an occupation, *4221*
to receive free mail franking privileges, *4216*
to run for public office, *4239*
to travel in an airplane to a foreign country, *4234*
to undertake a career of public service, *4233*
to write her autobiography, *4218*
use of the term to refer to the president's wife, *4228*
who attended school, *4224*
who was also a federal official, *4237*
who was born an American citizen, *4223*
who was not born in the United States, *4219*
who was the grandmother of a president, *4222*
who was the mother of a president, *4220*
whose autobiography was commercially published, *4232*
Fish: city protection law, *5940*
Fish hatchery, *1616*
run by the federal government, *1623*
Fishery
commercial, *1791*
school at a college, *2835*
Fishing
club, *7669*
line factory, *2655*
magazine, *7672*
rod of telescoping steel tubes, *2663*
treatise, *7670*
Fizzing cold remedy, *5245*
Flag
battle, *3496*
of a foreign nation flown at the State Department, *3917*
presidential, *4142*
salute for schoolchildren, *3499*
state law requiring children to salute the flag, *3502*
See also American flag
Flag Day, *2503*
Flashbulb device with multiple flashbulbs, *4652*
Flashlight, *2666*
Flea
circus, *1368*
laboratory, *6667*
Flemish newspaper, *4570*
Flicker animation, *1194*
Flight trainer for airplane pilots, *8068*
Flint glass factory, *3354*
Floating
church, *6267*
electric power plant, *6566*
hospital, *5112*
soap, *2466*
Flood of record, *5896*
Flour
mill, *2327*
rolling mill, *2383*
Flowers
sold by vending machine, *1699*
tetraploid (giant), *1653*
Fluorescent
lamp, *6569*
mineral exhibit, *6498*
paint, *2669*
tagging for postage stamps, *4745*
Fluorspar, *3380*
Fly casting
indoor tournament, *7673*
tournament, *7671*
Flying
disk for use in throwing games, *7979*
medical clinic, *5068*
FM radio, *4823*
Folding
stepladder, *2560*
theater chair, *1436*
Food
advertised in a full-page magazine ad, *1531*
bank, *7282*
in an aerosol can, *2440*
prepared, *2368*
processor, *2290*
sold ready-mixed, *2389*
stamps, *3852*
state purity law, *7251*
to carry a trademark, *1525*
Food-O-Mat, *2100*
Foot journey
from Canada to Mexico, *7988*
round-the-world, *7985*
to all seven continents, *7985*
transcontinental journey in one trip, *7971*
Foot race
electric timing device, *7949*
transcontinental, *7948*
Football
AFL championship game, *7713*
all-star game, *7708*
Army-Navy game, *7696*
ball game to be declared a national special security event, *7719*

daily newspaper that was successful, *4552*
grammar, *3178*
instruction at a college, *2695*
newspaper, *4552*
to arrive in America, *6007*
French and Indian War
battle, *5641*
bloodshed, *5640*
Frigate, *8466*
steam-propelled, *8468*
with a turret, *8472*
Frog-jumping jubilee, *1399*
Front-wheel drive
in a car, *8270*
in a subcompact car, *8276*
Frontier Day, *2506*
Frozen
bread, *2445*
food for the mass market, *2421*
meals for air travelers, *2439*
TV dinners, *2442*
TV dinners known by that name, *2442*
Fruit
culture treatise, *1589*
spraying, *1626*
tree patent, *1650*
Fruit-filled cookies, *2393*
Fuel alcohol plant, *6606*
Fuel cell
truck, *8297*
car, *8281*
Fuller's earth, *3388*
Fulling mill, *2108*
Funeral home operated on the cooperative plan, *2304*
Fungicide used medicinally, *5250*
Fur
exported, *5937*
fur-bearing animals raised commercially, *1617*
trading post, *6024*
Fustians, everlastings, and coating, *2112*

G

Gallstone operation, *5343*
Gambling
law for ministers enacted by a colony, *1797*
law for residents enacted by a colony, *1798*
permit stamp issued by the federal government, *4426*
Game
federal appropriation, *5958*
management chair at a college, *2850*
preserve, *7825*
protection society, *7824*
warden, *5944*
Games
computer, *7741*
crossword, *7736*
manufacturing company, *7724*
played in the English colonies in America, *7722*
real estate board, *7730*
role-playing, *7744*
video, *7742*
Gamma camera for imaging the body, *5140*
Gang, *6927*
of organized street criminals, *6927*
specializing in bank and train robbery, *6935*
tong secret society, *6937*
Gangster
convicted for tax evasion, *6943*
executed in the electric chair, *7017*
massacre, *6942*
Garage, commercial, for motor vehicles, *8237*
Garbage
incinerator, *5913*
used as boiler fuel to generate electricity, *6573*
Garden, private hydroponic, *1647*
Gardening manual, *1602*
Gas
engine, *8184*
journal, *6780*
mask, *1860*
meter, *6581*
refrigerator, *2287*
station, *8196*
streetlights, *7402*
streetlights installed throughout a city, *7403*
Gas turbine
bus engine, *8223*
engine in a car, *8267*
locomotive with a gas-turbine-electric engine, *8346*
to pump natural gas, *6607*
used by an electrical utility company, *6571*
Gaslight
for display, *1358*
in a theater, *1428*
in the White House, *4326*
Gasoline
ethyl, *6604*
obtained from crude petroleum by the cracking process, *6602*
pump, *1868*

self-computing pump, *1876*
Gasoline tax
federal, *4424*
state, *4421*
Gastroenterology treatise, *5293*
Gay
marriage, *7464*
marriage legalized in a state, *7464*
member of Congress, *7456*
minister, *7450*
national gay rights organization, *7441*
national lesbian organization, *7444*
network sitcom to feature a gay lead character, *7461*
political asylum granted on grounds of sexual orientation, *6106*
politician elected to an important local office, *7452*
politician elected to public office, *7451*
politician to win an election, *7452*
pride march, *7449*
protest on a large scale, *7448*
regularly appearing character on a television show, *7461*
rights march, *7455*
rights organization, *7439*
rights protest, *7448*
state appeals court decision ordering the extension of insurance benefits to gay partners of government employees, *7462*
state to establish civil unions, *7463*
state to repeal its ban on acts of sodomy, *7445*
Gazetteer, *3182*
of the world, *3188*
Gelatin dessert, *2401*
Gem-cutting machine, *3371*
Gene
artificial, *6677*
isolation of a single gene from an organism, *6675*
splicing, *6678*
therapy, *5399*
to be photograhed, *5137*
Genealogy
collective work, *7474*
of an American family, *7467*
of an American family published as a pamphlet, *7467*
Genetic engineering
county ban on genetically modified farming, *1658*
food, *2456*
genetically altered plants, *1654*
genetically altered virus approved for use in a vaccine, *6683*
product to appear in food, *2455*
state to require labeling of genetically modified seeds, *1659*
Genetics clinic, *5071*
Genome sequencing
and analysis of a bird, *6698*
comprehensive comparison of the human and chimpanzee genomes, *6701*
of a human chromosome, *6695*
of a multicellular organism, *6693*
of a plant, *6696*
Geodesic dome of substantial size, *3314*
Geodetic survey, *6492*
Geographer of the United States, *6488*
Geography
book, *6763*
gazetteer, *3182*
gazetteer of the world, *3188*
magazine, *6784*
school at a college, *2837*
Geological
map of part of North America, *6767*
survey authorized by Congress, *6491*
survey for a state government, *6489*
Geologist
to reach the moon, *6509*
woman, *6494*
Geology
book, *6767*
national society, *6715*
textbook, *6771*
Germ warfare, *5838*
German
book printed in America, *4435*
daily newspaper, *4551*
instruction at a college, *2698*
newspaper, *4551*
Giant
exhibited as a theatrical attraction, *1364*
panda, *5956*
Gingham factory, *2133*
Girder bridge of cast iron, *3238*
Girl Scouts, *2193*
cookie sale, *2195*
Girls
congressional page, *3616*
high school, *2918*
high school for pregnant teenagers, *2980*
industrial school, *2935*
school, *2896*
school for Protestants, *2897*
trade school, *2961*
vocational high school, *2962*
Glass
cut glass, *3363*
factory, *3352*
flint glass factory, *3354*

of Puerto Rico who was a woman, *3790*
state to elect two female governors in a row, *4384*
temporary, who was African-American, *4383*
to be granted almost dictatorial power, *4382*
to be impeached and acquitted, *4376*
to be impeached and convicted, *4378*
to be removed from office by a state supreme court, *4375*
who was a woman, *4381*
who was African-American, *4383*
woman elected governor in her own right, *4381*
Grain elevator operated by steam, *1608*
Grammar
of a Native American language, *3170*
of English by an American, *3174*
of English by an American published in America, *3177*
of French, *3178*
of Hebrew, *3175*
of Latin, *3173*
of Spanish, *3176*
Grammy Award
for musical recordings, *1272*
to be retracted, *1282*
Grand jury, *3699*
foreman who was a woman, *3720*
Grandmother
to give birth to her own grandchild, *2165*
who was a congressional representative, *3629*
Granite, *3377*
Granola, *2397*
Grape vines planted in California for wine-making, *1613*
Graphic novel, *1108*
Graphite, *3382*
Gravure: printing of a postage stamp, *4750*
Great Awakening of religious revival, *6218*
Great Lakes
sailing ship, *8404*
steamboat, *8422*
Great Seal of the United States
design, *3463*
die to be cut, *3478*
illustrations of both sides, *3481*
impression, *3480*
keeper, *3479*
paper money to depict both sides, *4044*
Greek
daily newspaper, *4566*
drama produced in Greek, *1443*
newspaper, *4566*
settlement, *6040*
Testament, *6355*
Greek Orthodox
church, *6276*
college, *2849*
Greenhouse, *1578*
Greeting addressed to the Pilgrims by a Native American, *6018*
Greyhound racing association, *7662*
Grocery store, self-service, *2093*
Guided missile cruiser, *8491*
Guitar, electric, *1311*
Gulf War
cruise missiles used in war, *5892*
destruction of an attacking missile by a defensive missile in combat, *5893*
pilot to destroy an enemy airplane, *5822*
serviceman killed, *5823*
war that was predicted by pizza orders, *5821*
woman fighter pilot to fire a missile in combat, *5831*
woman pilot to die in a combat zone, *5824*
Gun control
federal regulations, *6944*
state law, *6932*
state law banning cheap handguns, *6964*
statewide registration of assault weapons, *6969*
Gunpowder mill, *5837*
Guns
air gun, *5858*
cartridge belt patent, *5857*
federal contract for pistols, *5841*
machine gun, *5852*
machine gun on an airplane, *5468*
metal gun cartridge, *5853*
muskets, *5840*
national rifle society, *7882*
rapid-fire machine gun, *5855*
revolver pistol, *5845*
revolving gun, *5842*
revolving turret for ships, *5854*
rifled, *5843*
self-cocking revolver, *5851*
semiautomatic rifle, *5866*
submachine gun, *5862*
Gutta-percha, *1886*
Gymnasium
at a YMCA, *7205*
to offer systematic instruction, *7784*
Gymnastics
book, *7783*
instruction at a college, *7785*
instruction at a college for women, *7786*
Gyrocompass, *8500*
Gyroscope, *8035*
Gyroscopic stabilizer, *8501*

H

flight, *8050*
freight service, *8132*
fully operated by remote control, *8131*
heliport commercial base, *8126*
hoist rescue, *8113*
human-powered, *8167*
licensed for commercial use, *8115*
military heliport, *5490*
passenger service, *8132*
president to fly in, *4299*
round-the-world flight, *8163*
transatlantic flight, *8129*
transcontinental nonstop flight, *8141*
Helicopter flight
from water, *8102*
long-distance, *8106*
of one-hour duration, *8101*
Hemophilia treatise, *5294*
Hemp
state law decriminalizing cultivation, *1656*
to be exported, *1571*
Heptathlon: Olympic athlete, *7863*
Herbal book, *5292*
Herd book, *1609*
High school, *2914*
aviation course, *2971*
business, *2955*
chapter of Alcoholics Anonymous, *7078*
county, *2956*
driving course, *2972*
for girls, *2918*
for pregnant teenage girls, *2980*
night classes, *2921*
online, *2986*
online, for gifted students, *2991*
public, to specialize in the performing arts, *2974*
sex discrimination ban enacted by a state that affected high school athletic competitions, *7453*
sex education program, *2966*
state law requiring online learning for students, *2990*
team to achieve a perfect score in the International Mathematical Olympiad, *2984*
to fingerprint its students, *7383*
vocational, for girls, *2962*
Highway
bridge with concrete arches, *3247*
built by the federal government, *3411*
coast-to-coast paved road, *3420*
concrete median barrier, *3427*
federal nationwide planning surveys, *3426*
interchange structure with four levels, *3429*
national border-to-border, *3433*
nationwide numbering system, *3422*
patrolled by digital photography, *8217*
state electronic toll collection, *3434*
with metric distance markers, state, *3432*
Highway tunnel
to a foreign country, *3443*
underwater, *3438*
underwater, with twin tubes, *3442*
with television monitors, *3444*
Hindu
spiritual leader to visit America, *6285*
temple, *6289*
Vedanta Center, *6285*
Hip-replacement operation, *5370*
Hispanic
astronaut, *6824*
congressional representative, *3595*
congressional representative who was a woman, *3634*
interracial labor union, *7143*
mayor of a major city who was of Mexican descent, *3543*
senator, *3677*
settlement house, *3527*
state police department to be monitored for racial profiling, *7395*
woman astronaut, *6831*
year in which people of Hispanic descent became the nation's largest minority group, *6109*
Historical
hoax, *7468*
novel, *1083*
print engraved in America, *1020*
Historical society
national, *7472*
state, *7469*
History
American history book of importance by a woman, *7470*
ancient and modern history chair at a college, *2734*
book of the colonial era, *7465*
modern history school at a college, *2725*
modern languages school at a college, *2709*
of African-Americans, *7476*
of medicine, *5283*
of medicine, department at a college, *3092*
of New England, *7466*
of New England published in New England, *7466*
of printing, *4444*

I

Irish people to arrive in America, *6035*
Iron
  blast furnace to use anthracite coal in smelting, *1925*
  blast furnace to use anthracite coal successfully, *1926*
  casting, *1917*
  exportation, *1915*
  hammered, *1927*
  malleable castings, *1923*
  mill to puddle and roll iron, *1922*
  piano frame, *1294*
  rolling mill, *1918*
  sailing vessel, *8426*
  truss bridge, *3240*
Iron lung respirator, *5180*
Iron Man triathlon, *7987*
Iron vessel built for the Navy, *8469*
Ironclad
  naval vessels, *8473*
  seagoing naval warship, *8474*
  turreted vessel, *8475*
Ironworks, *1912*
  that was successful, *1913*
  to use natural gas, *6595*
Irrigation: federal law, *1618*
Italian
  instruction at a college, *2724*
  newspaper, *4564*

J

Japanese
  beetle, *1638*
  cherry trees, *1636*
  citizen, *6065*
  Medal of Honor awarded to a soldier of Japanese ancestry, *5530*
  newspaper in continuous publication, *4572*
  person to receive an immigration visa after World War II, *6096*
  to enter the United States, *6065*
Jar, Mason, *2557*
Jazz
  composer, *1251*
  composition to appear on the Top 40 charts, *1273*
  concert at Carnegie Hall, *1265*
  record, *1256*
Jetway, *8146*
Jewelers' supply house, *3373*
Jewish
  admiral, *5604*
  ambassador, *3894*
  Ashkenazic congregation, *6247*
  astronaut, *6822*
  book in Hebrew, *6361*
  cabinet member, *4182*
  cemetery, *2294*
  cantor who was a Reform Jewish woman, 6314
  college, *2847*
  college graduate, *2705*
  commodore, *5597*
  congressional representative, *3589*
  congressional representative who was a woman, *3615*
  Conservative movement rabbi who was a woman, *6314*
  diplomat, *3894*
  fraternal society, *7204*
  governor, *4380*
  governor of Jewish descent, *4380*
  graduate of West Point, *3097*
  graduate of West Point who was a woman, *3097*
  Holocaust, museum to commemorate, *3164*
  hospital, *5106*
  hospital to provide free care for tuberculosis patients, *5130*
  master's degree earned by a Jew, *2705*
  matzah factory, *2358*
  matzah made by machine, *2358*
  medical college, *3094*
  mobile synagogue, *6318*
  national Zionist organization, *6286*
  newspaper published monthly, *4553*
  newspaper published weekly, *4553*
  nonsectarian college under Jewish auspices, *2825*
  organization for women, *7204*
  Orthodox rabbi born in America, *6294*
  Passover seder to be televised, *6307*
  person depicted on a postage stamp, *4739*
  person to arrive in America, *6030*
  person to win full citizenship, *6031*
  physician, *5011*
  physician to head an asylum for the mentally ill, *5011*
  play by a professional Yiddish theater troupe, *1444*
  play presented by a Jewish acting troupe, *1442*
  prayer book, *6346*
  prayer services to be televised in their entirety, *6315*
  rabbinical college, *2790*
  Reform cantor who was a woman, *6314*
  Reform congregation, *6262*
  Reform rabbi who was a woman, *6314*
  religious school for children, *6214*

senator, *3661*
senator of Jewish descent, *3661*
senators who were women, *3693*
Sephardic congregation, *6190*
soldier awarded the Medal of Honor, *5509*
soldier killed in the Revolutionary War, *5658*
Sunday school, *6214*
Supreme Court justice, *3750*
Supreme Court justice who was a woman, *3750*
synagogue, *6202*
synagogue that was permanent, *6202*
teacher training, *6214*
Yeshivah, *2953*
Yeshivah at an advanced level, *2953*
Yeshivah with a secular high school, *2953*
Jim Crow law, *6137*
Jockey
to win the Kentucky Derby five times, *7814*
to win the Triple Crown twice, *7813*
woman to ride in the Kentucky Derby, *7818*
woman to ride two winners in a day, *7816*
woman to win a major stakes race, *7820*
woman to win a Triple Crown race, *7821*
woman to win on a regular parimutuel flat track, *7816*
Journal
agricultural, *1592*
allergy, *5336*
dental, *5313*
economics, *6783*
electricity, *6777*
entomology, *6781*
gas, *6780*
health, to advocate water cures, *5316*
homeopathy, *5309*
insurance, *1955*
laryngology, *5326*
library, *3015*
medical, *5291*
medical, published by an African-American, *5331*
mineralogy, *6768*
oil, *6785*
opticians, *5330*
orthodontia, *5334*
osteopathy, *5332*
pediatrics, *5321*
pharmacy, *5304*
phrenology, *5311*
physiology, *5333*
psychology, *5329*
science, *6772*
Senate, *3643*
trade, *4611*
Journalism
course at a college, *2774*
school at a college, *2826*
Journalist
accredited to the White House, *4596*
admitted to the congressional press gallery, *4599*
African-American news correspondent, *4500*
African-American accredited to the White House, *4599*
African-American admitted to the congressional press gallery, *4599*
newspaper editor who was a woman, *4589*
newspaper publisher, *4588*
photojournalist, *2598*
radio news anchor, *4600*
reporter to receive a Pulitzer Prize, *4760*
sportswriter, *2591*
television news anchor, *4601*
television news anchor who was a woman, *4604*
television news commentator who had been Speaker of the House, *3637*
television news commentator who was African-American, *4602*
tried as a spy, *4595*
war correspondent, *4593*
Washington news correspondent, *4590*
woman sportscaster inducted into the Pro Football Hall of Fame, *7720*
woman to cover a political convention, *4594*
woman to edit a major daily newspaper, *4605*
woman to report from Capitol Hill, *4603*
Judge
African-American woman, *3721*
African-American woman to be elected, *3721*
of Asian ancestry, *3724*
to be impeached, *3701*
who had served time in prison, *3729*
woman to impose the death penalty, *3716*
Jukebox, *4830*
successful manufacturer, *4830*
Junior high school, *2964*
Jury
composed of women, *3700*
interracial, *3707*
Justice of the peace who was a woman, *3709*
Jute culture, *1620*
Juvenile court, *3710*

K

L

state workers' compensation insurance law that was not declared unconstitutional, *7141*
woman delegate to a national AFL convention, *7130*
work week of 40 hours to be required by Congress, *7154*
workday of eight hours authorized by Congress, *7120*
workers' compensation agreement, *7097*
workers' compensation lawsuit involving the rights of an injured servant against his master, *7112*
Labor Day, *2498*
federal holiday, *2498*
parade, *1379*
state holiday, *2498*
Labor union
craft union, *7095*
craft union contract, *7104*
for actors, *7139*
for women, *7106*
interracial union, *7143*
label, *7125*
legalized by a state, *7131*
massacre of strikebreakers by union members, *7148*
national union for women, *7122*
of African-American workers, *7150*
state law banning discrimination against union members, *7138*
state to recognize unions for farmworkers, *7166*
to admit workers other than craft workers, *7123*
to approve a laborsaving device, *7140*
to nominate its own political candidates, *7100*
to pay a strike benefit, *7101*
to sponsor a housing cooperative, *7151*
trade union organization established in a city, *7107*
Laboratory
anthropology, *6665*
antitoxin, *7261*
bacteriology, *5165*
cancer, *5167*
city tuberculosis lab, *7258*
flea, *6667*
for the study of human parasites, *5168*
for the study of parasites in livestock, *5404*
for tuberculosis research, *5166*
health, established by a city, *7254*
industrial research, *1495*
mechanical engineering, *2787*
microbiology, *5170*
physiology, *5163*
psychology, *5164*
sleep, *5169*
Lacrosse
intercollegiate association, *7964*
team sport played in America, *7960*
Ladder: folding stepladder, *2560*
Lager beer, *2348*
Lamp
fluorescent, *6569*
for sterilizing the air, *5181*
incandescent, *6543*
kerosene, *2556*
mercury vapor, *6558*
sodium vapor, *6567*
Land
alien land law, *6086*
nonprofit conservation trust, *5911*
sale of federal land authorized by Congress, *6045*
sale of federal land to an individual, *6051*
sale by Native Americans to Europeans, *6022*
set aside for schools authorized by the Continental Congress, *2902*
survey of public lands, *6046*
swindle, *6023*
Land grant
college for African-Americans, *2781*
federal aid to special education, *2913*
for an agricultural college, *2762*
to a foreigner of federal land, *6057*
to a railroad, *8311*
to British deserters during the Revolutionary War, *5660*
university, *2726*
Land mines, *5846*
Land office, *6048*
district, *6056*
federal, *6061*
Landscape
architect, *5901*
painter, *1027*
Language to have its entire literature digitized, *1110*
Laryngology
clinic, *5065*
instruction at a college, *3063*
journal, *5326*
Laser, *6521*
public demonstration, *6521*
television receiver and transmitter, *5005*
transmission of a television show, *5005*
Laser printer, *6446*
for use with a single computer, *6446*
marketed, *6446*
Latex paint, *2672*

Lathe, *2645*
Latin grammar, *3173*
Latvian newspaper, *4567*
Laundromat, *2225*
Laundry, *2211*
 Chinese, *2213*
Laundry detergent, *2220*
 granulated, *2220*
 synthetic, *2224*
Law
 code adopted by a state, *3962*
 dictionary of American, *3963*
 instruction at a college, *2699*
 magazine, *3960*
Law books
 collection of colonial laws, *3948*
 collection of federal laws, *3956*
 collection of federal laws currently in force, *3964*
 digest of American law, *3958*
 history of law, *3950*
 legal treatise, *3957*
 legal treatise analyzing the Constitution, *3959*
 report of cases, *3954*
 treatise on insurance law, *3953*
 treatise on medical jurisprudence, *3961*
Law school
 at a college, *2711*
 at a university to admit women, *2775*
 operated privately, *3191*
 permanently organized at a college, *2711*
 woman graduate, *2780*
 woman editor in chief of a law review, *2836*
Lawn mower, *2664*
 power, *2664*
Lawsuit
 against American organizations brought by American victims of terrorism, *3730*
 billion-dollar settlement in an environmental lawsuit, *5932*
 for slander, *6922*
 in a product safety case to result in a criminal trial, *1513*
Lawyer
 admitted to practice before the Supreme Court, *3955*
 African-American admitted to practice before the Supreme Court, *3966*
 African-American who was formally admitted to the bar, *3965*
 African-American woman, *3968*
 African-American woman admitted to practice before the Supreme Court, *3966*
 chief White House counsel who was a woman, *4167*
 disbarred, *3947*
 public defender hired by a state, *3973*
 woman, *3967*
 woman admitted to practice before the Supreme Court, *3970*
Lawyers
 national society, *3969*
 state organization, *3951*
 trial featuring celebrity lawyers, *3705*
Laxative in candy form, *5242*
Lead, *3368*
 coffins, *2293*
League of Native American nations, *6006*
Leather
 artificial, *2143*
 chrome tanning process, *2135*
 chrome-tanned, *2137*
 power belts, *1851*
 splitting machine, *2122*
 tanning, *2105*
 tanning by the oil tan method, *2123*
Legal treatise
 published in the United States, *3957*
 analyzing the Constitution, *3959*
Lending library, *2996*
Leopard to be exhibited, *1359*
Leprosy hospital, *5116*
Lesbian
 national organization, *7444*
 network sitcom to feature a lesbian lead character, *7461*
 politician elected to public office, *7451*
 politician to win an election, *7452*
 See also Gay
Letter
 containing a description of America, *3452*
 dead letter office, *4663*
 to circumnavigate the world by commercial airmail, *4702*
 typed on a typewriter, *1662*
 written in English in America, *3454*
Levees, *3349*
Liberty loan subscriptions, *1762*
Liberty ship, *8454*
Librarian
 of Congress, *3005*
 who was African-American, *3021*
 who was an African-American woman, *3021*
Library
 appropriation approved by a Town Meeting, *2995*
 atheneum, *3007*
 bequeathed to the public, *2994*
 bookwagon, *3025*

Lithuanian
newspaper, *4563*
settlement, *6076*
Liver
bloodless transplant from a living donor, *5382*
dual kidney and liver transplants from children to a parent, *5383*
transplant, *5365*
transplant from a live donor, *5376*
transplant of a baboon liver into a human, *5377*
Livestock
auction broadcast on radio, *1643*
farm cooperative for artificial insemination, *1652*
felony conviction for cruelty against farm animals, *1657*
pounds for stray animals, *1567*
Loan
by a colony, *1756*
for war purposes, *1757*
liberty, *1762*
made by the federal Government to a war ally, *1761*
to the United States, *1758*
Lobbyist, woman, in Congress, *3567*
Lobotomy, prefrontal, *5362*
Local political machine, *3513*
Locker
coin-operated, *1689*
rental, *1686*
Locomotive
communications headlight, *8392*
cowcatcher, *8383*
diesel-electric, *8342*
electric, *8337*
electric freight, *8337*
electric headlight, *8391*
for railroad use, *8331*
gas-turbine-electric, *8346*
narrow-gauge, *8338*
owned by an industrial company, *8341*
race with a horse-drawn vehicle, *7793*
steam whistle, *8336*
streamlined electric, *8344*
streamlined steam, *8343*
super-giant, *8345*
to attain a speed of one mile in less than a minute, *8340*
to burn coal, *8333*
to carry passengers, *8332*
to pull a train on a track, *8330*
to use oil for fuel, *8339*
with a cab, *8335*
with six or eight driving wheels, *8334*
Log cabins, *2523*
Log-rolling, national championship tournament, *7968*
Loganberry, *1627*
Logic book, *6759*
Lollipops, *2409*
Lookout tower for forest fires, *5983*
Lottery, *1796*
held by the Continental Congress, *1799*
in which the top prize was $1 million, *1805*
state, *1804*
Lucite commercially manufactured, *1906*
Lunch box
featuring a licensed character, *2580*
featuring a TV character, *2584*
fully decorated with lithographed art, *2585*
Lunch wagon, *1819*
Lung
removal, *5348*
transplant, *5366*
Lutheran
church, *6185*
hymnbook, *6353*
hymnbook in German, *6353*
pastor, *6183*
pastor ordained in American, *6183*
services in English, *6206*
Lyceum for adult education, *3194*
Lynching
state ban, *6138*
year in which there were no reported lynchings of African-Americans, *6140*

M

Macadam road, *3408*
Macaroni
and cheese casserole, *2335*
factory, *2353*
Macy's Thanksgiving Day Parade, *1397*
Magazine
about recreational drugs, *7086*
advertising, *1523*
African-American, *6130*
airplane, *8011*
antislavery, *6126*
art, *1035*
astronomy, *6778*
aviation, *8002*
bibliophile, *4455*
bicycle, *7642*
book trade, *4450*
book trade, *4453*
bowling, *7581*
by factory workers, *7113*

made in America to be published in a book, *4476*
Native American, *4475*
of a city within the present limits of the United States, *4474*
of the ocean floor, *4487*
of the ocean floor, three-dimensional, *6511*
of the United States, *4479*
relief, *4484*
war map, *4478*
Marathon
annual race, *7946*
New York City, *7957*
Olympic champion from the United States, *7854*
woman to run in the Boston Marathon, *7956*
Marble
quarry, *3372*
statuary group, *1032*
Mardi Gras, *2486*
in New Orleans, *2486*
Margarine
deception law, *2378*
manufacturer, *2373*
Marine Corps, *5560*
African-American commissioned officer, *5568*
African-American general, *5571*
African-American woman, *5569*
air combat unit, *5473*
band, *5562*
commando raid, *5563*
general in active service to wear four stars, *5567*
general to wear four stars, *5567*
major, *5560*
officer killed in service, *5561*
pilot, *5565*
woman, *5564*
woman general, *5570*
woman in the Reserve, *5566*
Marine insurance: state law, *1953*
Mariners' church, *6260*
Marines, *5560*
British marine corps of American colonists, *5559*
officer, *5560*
to participate in a Revolutionary War battle, *5656*
Maritime Day, *2514*
Marriage
annulment by court decree, *2590*
between two people of the same sex, *7464*
blood tests for marriage license applicants to be required by a state, *7280*
breach-of-promise suit, *2589*
by gay couples legalized by a state, *7464*
course at a college, *2841*
married woman to keep her maiden name, *2592*
president to marry while in office, *4251*
skills classes required by a state, *2599*
state law allowing married women to make wills, *7431*
state law allowing married women to own property, *7433*
state law to secure significant property rights for married women, *7435*
state to establish civil unions for gay couples, *7463*
state to outlaw marital rape, *6958*
Martial arts
karate instructor, *7978*
Tae Kwon Do instructor, *7982*
Martin Luther King Day, *2520*
Martini, *2384*
Mason
African-American, *7196*
born in America, *7193*
to arrive in America, *7193*
Mason jar, *2557*
Masonic
book, *7195*
lodge, *7194*
lodge of African-Americans, *7196*
lodge of African-Americans to be recognized, *7196*
magazine, *7201*
Mass-market paperback book, *4454*
Mastodon, *6657*
Mastoid operation, *5342*
Matador of American birth, *7614*
Matches
friction, *2547*
matchbooks, *2568*
nontoxic friction, *2547*
Maternity
book for women, *2175*
clinic, *2151*
clothes to be manufactured, *2259*
Mathematics
encyclopedia of integer sequences, *6710*
factoring of a 100-digit number, *6708*
high school team to achieve a perfect score in the International Mathematical Olympiad, *2984*
patent on a number, *6711*
proof of Fermat's last theorem, *6709*
quantum theory of electromagnetic radiation, *6707*
theory of economic decisionmaking, *6706*
theory of fair division, *6712*

Mexican War
unit of American deserters to join an enemy army, 5688
war fought mostly on foreign soil, 5689
war that began before a declaration of war was made by Congress, 5687
war to receive daily newspaper coverage, 5686
Mexico
ambassador to, 3889
mayor of a major city who was of Mexican descent, 3543
Mezzotint engraving, 1018
Mica, 3375
synthetic, 3398
Microbiology laboratory, 5170
Microcard
book issued on, 3036
version of magazine for subscribers, 3037
Microfilm
book series on, 3034
check photographing device, 1742
editions of federal publications and documents, 3038
reading device, 3033
used for current newspaper issues, 3035
used for newspaper archives, 3035
version of magazine for subscribers, 3037
Microwave
mobile TV transmitter unit, 4991
oven, 2288
oven for home use, 2288
popcorn, 2452
television station, 4961
Midwife
nurse-midwife, 2152
to practice professionally, 2146
Midwifery
professor, 3043
school of nurse-midwifery, 3093
state to recognize, as a separate profession, 2166
Milestones between cities, 3512
Military
African-American chairman of the Joint Chiefs of Staff, 5456
Air Force chairman of the Joint Chiefs of Staff, 5495
American servicemen to die in combat on an overseas mission, 5679
camels, 5418
campaign medal, 5510
computer network, 6427
dictionary, 5416
drill manual, 5412
field strategy manual, 5410
hospital, 5200
intelligence unit, 5659
leader of the English settlers, 5633
monument to mothers of fallen soldiers, 7192
Navy chairman of the Joint Chiefs of Staff, 5610
organization established by a colony, 5637
prison on an island, 7001
school, 3101
school established by a state, 3103
school operated by a church, 3104
service by African-Americans authorized by Congress, 5421
state law prohibiting discrimination against soldiers, 5422
think tank, 5799
woman band leader, 5428
Military decorations
Army officer to receive the three highest decorations, 5526
Distinguished Service Cross awarded in enemy-occupied territory, 5520
Distinguished Service Cross awarded to an animal, 5524
Navy Cross awarded to a Coast Guard officer in World War II, 5519
Navy-Marine Corps Medal for Heroism awarded to a woman, 5534
Navy-Marine Corps Medals for Heroism awarded to Marines, 5521
presidential citation to an entire armed forces division, 5527
Silver Star awarded to a woman, 5525
Silver Star awarded to a civilian, 5522
Silver Star awarded to a Navy chaplain, 5537
Silver Star awarded to a woman for actions in combat, 5540
Soldier's Medal awarded to a woman, 5523
Military draft
camp for conscientious objectors, 5558
conscientious objectors, 5554
enacted by Congress during wartime, 5556
enacted by Congress in preparation for war, 5557
instituted by a colony, 5553
into state militias, 5555
Militia, 5635
strike in which a militia was called out, 7109
Milk
acidophilus, 2418
bottles, 1998
butterfat tester, 2392

centrifugal cream separator, *2381*
centrifugal cream separator with continuous flow, *2381*
city pasteurization law, *7274*
city sale regulations, *7263*
concentrated, *2443*
condensed, *2355*
delivery in glass bottles, *2380*
dried milk paent, *2372*
evaporated, *2385*
genetically engineered product to appear in food, *2455*
malted, *2388*
pasteurized commercially, *2396*
pasteurizing stations, *7256*
state inspection law, *7243*
state purity law, *7242*
station operated by a city, *7265*
Milky Way candy bar, *2420*
Millionaire
African-American woman, *1710*
with a fortune greater than $100 million, *1704*
Mimeograph, *2048*
Mine
barrage, *5839*
land mines, 5846
Mineral
exhibit of fluorescent minerals, *6498*
found on the moon before it was found on Earth, *3400*
segregation by oil flotation, *3389*
Mineral water bottler, *2342*
Mineralogy
instruction at a college, *2718*
journal, *6768*
textbook, *6770*
Mines school at a college, *2765*
Miniature
book, *4431*
car, *8256*
church, *6304*
city, *1398*
golf course, *7771*
television tube, *4986*
Mining tunnel, *3436*
Minister
transgendered, *7460*
who was openly gay, *7450*
woman to be ordained, *6271*
Minister plenipotentiary, *3877*
after the Revolution, *3877*
to Great Britain, *3881*
Minister to Great Britain, *3881*
Minstrel show troupe, *1235*
Mint
director, *4017*
illegal colonial, *3447*
of the United States, *4014*
woman director, *4017*
Miss America, *1394*
contest to be televised, *1404*
Missile
armed, shot down by a ray gun, *5894*
ballistic, *5874*
cruise missiles used in war, *5892*
destruction of an attacking missile by a defensive missile in combat, *5893*
guided, launched from a nuclear submarine, *5886*
intermediate-range ballistic, *5882*
launching silos for the Atlas F, *5889*
MX intercontinental ballistic missile base, *5891*
Polaris, fired from a submerged submarine, *5887*
ship to fire a Polaris, *5885*
submarine designed and built to fire guided missiles, *8522*
submarine equipped with ballistic missiles, *8523*
to intercept a supersonic target missile, *5884*
Missionary
to cross the continent, *6064*
to the Native Americans who was African-American, *6237*
training school, *2798*
Missionary society
established for the English colonies, *6189*
foreign, *6253*
organized by women for foreign nations, *6273*
organized in the English colonies, *6222*
Mitral valve corrective surgery, *5356*
M&M candies, *2438*
Mobile
home, *8293*
medical office, *5043*
Mobile phone
commercial service, *4886*
commercial service, *4894*
one-way communication, *4879*
Model laboratory school at a college, *2742*
Modeling school, *3214*
Modern art
exhibition, *1039*
museum, *3152*
Modern dance
dancer, *1050*
school, *3211*
troupe that was all-male, *1052*
Mohair, *2134*
Molybdenum centrifugal casting, *1948*

to George Washington, *7169*
to George Washington to be completed, *7169*
to mothers of fallen soldiers, *7192*
to the American flag, *7187*
to Thomas Jefferson, national, *7189*

Moon
astronauts to retrieve a manmade object from the lunar surface, *6816*
astronauts to ride a vehicle on the lunar surface, *6817*
burial, *2312*
landing by astronauts, *6814*
mineral found on the moon before it was found on Earth, *3400*
orbited by astronauts, *6812*
photograph bounced off the mon, *4636*
photograph of, *6398*
radar signal to, *6790*
religious ritual on the moon, *6325*
satellite from the United States to impact the moon, *6856*
space probe to achieve lunar orbit, *6871*
spacecraft to transmit close-up photographs of the lunar surface, *6868*
sport played on the lunar surface, *7778*
telephone call, *4915*

Moravian
bishop, *6219*
church, *6219*
settlement in America, *6219*

Mormon
church meeting, *6265*
man ordained to the priesthood who was African-American, *6329*
temple, *6266*

Mortised lock, *3265*

Mosaic pavement, *3425*

Mosque
built for the purpose, *6303*
of importance, *6313*

Motel, *1830*
Holiday Inn, *1834*
horse, *1840*

Mother
and son simultaneously elected to Congress, *3618*
congressional representative to give birth while holding office, *3628*
trial of a surrogate mother for refusing to give up her baby, *2163*
who was a congressional representative, *3614*
who was an American astronaut, *6829*

Mother's Day, *2508*
established by presidential proclamation, *2508*

Mothers
Gold Star, *5750*
monument to mothers of fallen soldiers, *7192*
organization for reuniting birthmothers and adopted children, *2201*
organization of soldiers' mothers, *5740*
state welfare program for single mothers, *2192*

Motorboat, *8408*
magazine, *8442*
ocean race, *7577*
pleasure craft, *8437*
race under organized rules, *7575*
with a storage battery, *8438*

Motorcycle
association, *7848*
endurance run, *7846*
hill-climbing contest, *7847*
jump across a river canyon, *1408*
police, *7368*
steam-driven, *8285*
that was practical, *8286*
to exceed 200 miles per hour, *8291*
transcontinental trip, *8288*
transcontinental trip by women, *8290*
twin-cycle, *8289*
with a built-in gasoline engine, *8287*
woman racer, *7849*

Mountain bike, *7659*

Mountaineering
American ascent of Mount Everest, *7983*
American to climb all 14 mountains higher than 8,000 meters, *7989*
American woman to climb Mount Everest, *7983*

Mouthwash, *2467*

Movie
actor to have an exclusive contract, *1116*
American version of a Shakespeare play, *1134*
animated film inducted into the National Film Registry, *1202*
associated with a merchandise marketing campaign, *1160*
authenticated by a fraudulent Web site, *1185*
blockbuster, *1141*
broadcast on the Internet, *1180*
comedy of feature length, *1140*
digital projection of a major motion picture, *1187*
documentary of an American war, *5723*
drive-in theater, *1159*
exhibition, *1114*
exhibition in a theater to a paying audience, *1121*

N

Indian Affairs Commissioner who was Native American, *3843*
Indian Day, *2510*
issue of paper money, *4022*
land sale to Europeans, *6022*
language to be given a written form, *6062*
language used for coded military radio transmissions, *5772*
league, *6006*
major museum art show, *1041*
map of record, *4475*
mass scalping of Native Americans by colonists, *5639*
massacre of colonists, *5634*
monument to a Native American, *7191*
music to be recorded, *1245*
National Navajo Code Talkers Day, *5772*
Native American Day, *2521*
newspaper, *4556, 6062*
occupation of federal territory by protesters in the modern era, *6099*
personhood established by court ruling, *6078*
powwow at the National Mall, *1057*
preacher of Christianity, *6197*
principal chief of a major tribe who was a woman, *3942*
reservation established by a state, *6039*
school of prominence, *2951*
school to be permanently established, *2895*
senator, *3669*
settlement in America in continuous habitation, *6002*
state department of Indian affairs, *4363*
superintendent of a Bureau of Indian Affairs agency, *3843*
team sport adopted by European colonists, *7960*
technical school, *2981*
Thanksgiving meal shared with European settlers, *2484*
to address the Pilgrims, *6018*
to be beatified, *6305*
to become a Protestant, *6169*
to organize a church, *6293*
to receive colonial badges, *6032*
to win territorial concessions from the federal government, *6075*
treaty with the federal government, *6041*
West Point graduate, *3102*
woman author of a novel, *1096*
woman whose likeness appears on a coin, *4047*

Natural gas
corporation, *6591*
for use in ironworking, *6595*
for use in manufacturing, *6595*
motor vehicles powered by, *8296*
pipeline constructed over a long distance, *6597*
plant operated by a city, *6596*
pumped by a gas turbine, *6607*
state commission, *6599*
state conservation law, *6600*
used as an illuminant, *6580*

Natural history museum, *3134*

Naturalized citizen to lie in state in the Capitol rotunda, *3573*

Nature: museum with outdoor trails, *3153*

Nautical
almanac, *8407*
school, *3195*
school established by a state, *3206*
school run by a city, *3198*

Naval academy, *3105*
African-American graduate, *3118*
African-American midshipman, *3118*
graduate to attain the rank of rear admiral, *3108*
woman midshipman to graduate first in her class, *3128*
women students, *3128*

Naval aviation
air combat unit, *5471*
air training school, *3112*
airplane, *5467*
airship, *8040*
fleet, *5572*
jet airplane squadron, *5487*
pilot, *5465*

Naval war college, *3109*
African-American students, *3122*
president who was a former prisoner of war, *3130*

Navigation act, *2065*
royal act affecting the American colonies, *2062*

Navy
attack by terrorists, *5832*
award of prize money, *5579*
bureau of medicine and surgery, *5196*
contract for armor plate, *5582*
dental corps, *5206*
dentist to serve aboard ship, *5207*
divers to submerge for 10 days, *5591*
doctor, *5192*
federal hospital, *5194*
fleet, *5572*
mail service, *4688*
medical school, *3078*
nuclear submarine division, *5589*
nuclear task force to circumnavigate the globe without refueling, *5592*

transported overland across the Rocky Mountains, *8486*
turreted frigate, *8472*
warship named after a foreigner, *5573*
warship propelled by electricity, *8482*
warship that was a seagoing ironclad, *8474*
warship to circumnavigate the globe, *8528*
warship with propelling machinery below the waterline, *8470*
with a combined diesel and gas-turbine engine, *8497*
with a crew of mixed nationalities, *8495*
with a post office, *4689*
with a mixed company of male and female personnel, *8487*
Nazi
collaborator to be deported, *6094*
death camp guard to be deported, *6103*
Neanderthal skeleton reconstructed from actual bones, *6700*
Neon sign, *1539*
Neurasthenia book, *5327*
Neurological disease research institute, *5120*
Neurology
regeneration of spinal cord connections in animals, *6705*
textbook, *5322*
Neutrality
proclamation by the federal government, *3884*
regulation enacted by Congress that governed the actions of citizens, *3885*
New Year's Eve: dropping of the ball in Times Square, *2507*
New York City
mayor, *3509*
mayor elected by the council, *3509*
mayor of metropolitan New York City, *3509*
News
agency, *4500*
all-news radio station, *4815*
all-news television station, *4548*
anchor on radio, *4600*
anchor on television, *4601*
broadcast on radio, *4527*
broadcast on television, *4933*
daily radio program, *4529*
dispatch by telegraph, *4505*
dispatch by telephone, *4516*
financial news agency, *4514*
HDTV all-digital newsroom, *4981*
major network program broadcast in high-definition television, *4550*
news photograph transmitted in color by radio fax for publication, *4587*
space-to-ground news conference, *4546*
unscheduled event to be televised as it occurred, *4534*
News correspondent
accredited to the White House, *4596*
admitted to the congressional press gallery, *4599*
African-American accredited to the White House, *4599*
African-American admitted to the congressional press gallery, *4599*
to cover a war, *4593*
to report from Washington, *4590*
tried as a spy, *4595*
woman, at a political convention, *4594*
See also Journalist
News magazine
featuring photographs, *4535*
on television, *4545*
Newspaper, *4488*
book review supplement, *4523*
cartoon, *4574*
circulation audit, *4525*
clipping bureau, *4520*
colored supplement, *4583*
comic strip, *4580*
daily illustrated, *4515*
delivery train, *4518*
editor who was a woman, *4589*
editorial to win the Pulitzer Prize, *4761*
European edition of an American paper, *4522*
for African-American readers, *4554*
for Jewish readers published monthly, *4553*
for Jewish readers published weekly, *4553*
for Native American readers, *4556*
high-speed printing and folding machine, *2047*
illustrated tabloid, *4526*
in Arabic, *4568*
in Armenian, *4565*
in Chinese, *4558*
in Czech, *4559*
in Danish, *4562*
in Flemish, *4570*
in French, *4552*
in German, *4551*
in Greek, *4566*
in Hebrew, *4561*
in Hungarian, *4569*
in Italian, *4564*
in Japanese, *4572*
in Latvian, *4567*

Nurse-midwifery
school, *3093*
Nursery school, *2919*
Nursing
magazine, *5328*
society, *5222*
Nursing school, *5036*
Army, *3088*
at a college, *3082*
for African-American students, *3074*
to award a diploma, *3065*
Nutrition
concept of food groups, *7277*
dietary standards issued by the U.S. Department of Agriculture, *7259*
food guide pyramid, *7284*
food product to carry a health claim on its label, *7288*
nationwide labeling standards, *7285*
Nuts and bolts factory, *2649*
Nylon, *2142*
stockings, *2265*

O

Oats
crushing machine, *2375*
rolled, *2360*
Observatory, *6368*
established by the federal government, *6372*
in orbit above the Earth, *6381*
on a mountaintop, *6373*
operated by a college, *6371*
orbiting geophysical, *6860*
solar orbiting, *6854*
Obstetrics book, *5297*
Occupational
therapy course at a college, *3086*
therapy treatment, *5391*
Oceanographer, woman, *6510*
Oceanography
high-resolution maps of the ocean floor, *4487*
institution, *6495*
ship with a floating scientific instrument platform, *6508*
three-dimensional maps of the ocean floor, *6511*
Octuplets, *2169*
Off-track betting operation, *1806*
Office building with an elevator, *3279*
Oil
and gas production course at a college, *2830*
and gas state conservation law, *6603*
company, *6583*
journal, *6785*
lamp, *2556*
offshore port for supertankers, *6615*
offshore rig, *6593*
seagoing rig, *6610*
shipped directly from Russia to the United States, *6616*
spill with disastrous consequences, *6612*
spring, *6574*
tanker railroad freight cars, *8352*
Oil pipeline, *6590*
of importance, *6592*
plastic, *6608*
Oil refinery, *6584*
commercial, *6587*
with a carbon monoxide boiler, *6609*
Oil well, *6579*
fire, *6588*
successfully drilled in the ocean, *6601*
that was commercially productive, *6586*
Oilcloth factory, *2132*
Okapi, *5957*
Olympic athlete from the United States
to win a gold medal, *7850*
to win four gold medals in one year, *7859*
to win gold in both the Summer and Winter Olympics, *7857*
to win in bobsled, *7975*
to win in figure skating, *7843*
to win ten medals, *7851*
to win the discus competition, *7945*
to win the marathon race, *7854*
to win the pentathlon and decathlon, *7855*
to win two consecutive heptathlon events, *7863*
who was a woman gold medalist, *7856*
who was African-American to win a medal, *7853*
who was African-American to win an individual event, *7853*
who was an African-American woman gold medalist, *7860*
Olympic Games
American boycott, *7862*
competition to be held in the winter, *7858*
held in the United States, *7852*
state to refuse to act as host, *7861*
One-way street, *3406*
Online
college classes, *2878*
filing system for registering trademarks, *3983*
high school, *2986*
high school for gifted students, *2991*

P

mill, *2006*
perforated wrapping, *2021*
sewing patterns, *2619*
toilet, *2461*
with a watermark, *2007*
Paper bags
made by machine, *1995*
with flat bottoms, *1997*
Paperback
mass-market book, *4454*
publisher, *4464*
series, *4462*
Parachute
African-American paratroopers, *5483*
Army battalion, *5479*
Caterpillar Club member, *8044*
Caterpillar Club woman member, *8059*
fatality in the Army, *5480*
jump from a balloon, *7995*
jump from an airplane, *8031*
jump from an airplane by a woman, *8034*
jump from an autogiro, *8085*
jump using a nylon parachute, *8107*
jumper snagged by airplane in midair, *8151*
jumping contest, *7680*
known as the "free parachute," *8042*
tower for training jumpers, *8095*
Parade
held by a mystic society, *1367*
in which the marching music was supplied by transistor radios, *1409*
Labor Day, *1379*
Macy's Thanksgiving Day, *1397*
of automobiles, *1389*
Saint Patrick's Day, *1352*
ticker-tape, *1384*
ticker-tape, for a celebrity, *1390*
with float tableaux, *1374*
Parcel post
domestic air service, *4707*
international air service, *4706*
service, *4691*
Parent-teacher
association, *2952*
national association, *2957*
Parents
pediatrics book for, *2187*
state parental leave law that applied to both mothers and fathers, *7457*
state to provide financial assistance to parenting college students, *2880*
that was completely automated, *8263*
Parer, *2272*
Park
federal undersea, *5995*
international peace, *5993*
national monument designated by the federal government, *7182*
national, *5990*
national, east of the Mississippi River, *5991*
national, in the Southern Hemisphere, *5996*
national, to contain an active volcano, *5992*
parkland purchased by a city, *5988*
state, *5989*
Parking garage
city, *8260*
with a hydraulic lift, *8266*
Parking meter, automatic, *8254*
Parliament
act to establish a colonial post office, *4655*
woman elected to Britain's Parliament, *3929*
Parliamentary rules, *3564*
Parochial school, *2886*
Passenger
air travelers to receive frozen meals, *2439*
ship equipped with radar, *8505*
ship with a diesel engine, *8452*
to transfer from an airship to an airplane, *8070*
transcontinental daily train service, *8321*
transcontinental Pullman sleeping car daily service, *8328*
trains with commercial telephone service, *4899*
trip on a jet, *8128*
Passport, *6053*
fee, *6072*
photographs, *6087*
Pastelist, *1016*
Patent
artificial leg, *5265*
awarded to a future president, *4134*
granted by a colony, *3985*
granted by the federal government, *3987*
granted jointly to a father and son, *3989*
granted to a resident of America by England, *3986*
granted to a woman, *3990*
granted to an African-American, *3991*
issued by the Confederate States of America, *3994*
issued to an African-American woman, *3998*
issued to Thomas Alva Edison, *3995*
list, *1488*
numbering system, *3992*
on a car, *8228*
on a design, *3993*
on a fruit tree, *1650*

national society, *5220*
professor, *3045*
Phi Beta Kappa
African-American member, *2791*
chapter at an African-American university, *2706*
Philology national society, *6720*
Philosophy book printed in America, *1070*
Phone card, prepaid, for use with a PIN, *4920*
Phonetic dictionary, *3189*
Phonograph, *4827*
that was practical, *4828*
trade magazine, *4831*
with an automatic record changer, *4832*
Phonograph record, *4829*
in a magazine, *4616*
jazz, *1256*
long-playing microgroove, *4835*
original cast recording of a stage performance, *1450*
original movie soundtrack recording, *1262*
psychedelic music, *1274*
rap album, *1280*
single by Elvis Presley, *1342*
Photocopy, *2027*
Photoelectric cell, *6563*
Photoengraving: high-speed process, *2060*
Photograph
aerial, *4623*
astronomical, *6398*
bounced off a satellite, *4637*
bounced off the moon, *4636*
class, 4619
in a news magazine, *4535*
infrared, *4633*
news, *4625*
of a former president, *4131*
of a lightning flash, *6401*
of a meteor, *6402*
of a president in office, *4133*
of a solar eclipse, *6400*
of a star other than the sun, *6399*
of a tornado, *5907*
of an American battlefield showing bodies of the dead, *5715*
of cloud cover, *6846*
of combat, *4624*
of genes, *5137*
of the sun's corona made during a total solar eclipse, *6400*
series showing movement in sequence, *4626*
showing action, *4627*
taken by incandescent electric light, *4641*
taken from an airplane, *4628*
taken from an airplane at night, *4630*
taken in the United States, *4617*
taken under the sea, *4629*
taken under the sea in natural colors, *4631*
to gain world fame, *4620*
transatlantic radio fax transmission, *4468*
transcontinental radio fax transmission, *4469*
transmitted by satellite, *6845*
Photographer to receive the John Simon Guggenheim Memorial Foundation award, *4635*
Photographic
flashbulbs, *4648*
type-composing machine, *2059*
Photography
achromatic lenses, *4639*
attempt to show motion, *1204*
book, *4621*
commercial studio, *4618*
federal copyright law, *3979*
magazine, *4622*
Photojournalist, *4598*
Phrenologist, *5021*
Phrenology
book, *5307*
journal, *5311*
Physical education
and hygiene professorship at a college, *2760*
classes in elementary schools, *2933*
department at a college, *2809*
Physician
African-American, *5017*
African-American woman, *5026*
assisted suicide, *2308*
assisted suicide, state to legalize, *2310*
born in America to graduate from a foreign medical school, *5013*
Chinese woman, *5035*
convicted of manslaughter for prescribing pain medication, *6982*
in the colony of Virginia, *5008*
in the New England colonies, *5009*
Jewish, *5011*
Jewish, to head an asylum for the mentally ill, *5011*
osteopathic, *5029*
to Congress, *3576*
to practice as an astronaut in space, *6818*
to receive a Bachelor of Medicine degree, *3044*
to receive a congressional medal, *3569*
to receive an M.D. degree, *3044*
with a mobile medical office, *5043*
woman, *5024*

woman to be a personal presidential physician, *4266*
woman, to give medical treatment to a president, *4266*
Physics
betatron, *6733*
blowpipe, *6728*
cyclotron, *6730*
electron microscope, *6732*
element created artificially, *6746*
helium plant, *6729*
instrument for observing radiation in total darkness, *6737*
molecular measuring machine, *6740*
national association, *6724*
physical manipulation of individual atoms, *6752*
self-sustaining nuclear chain reaction demonstration, *6748*
spectrophotometer, *6731*
superconducting material that operated at high temperatures, *6751*
superconducting motor, *6739*
synchrotron, *6734*
teleportation experiment, *6753*
universal constant in physics to be measured by American scientists, *6741*
Physiologist, *5019*
Physiology
and hygiene courses at a liberal arts college, *3057*
dissection of a living animal, *3058*
journal, *5333*
laboratory, *5163*
national society, *5223*
society, *5215*
Piano
automatic player, *1303*
grand piano with a cast-metal plate, *1298*
iron frame, *1294*
player, *1302*
pneumatic piano player, *1306*
wire, *1296*
Picture frames, *2579*
Piggyback railroad operation, *8320*
Pile bridge, *3230*
Pile driver, *1847*
Pills
compressed, *5238*
to be patented, *5233*
Pilots
ace to fly a jet, *5808*
African-American, *5472*
African-American army pilot to shoot down an Axis airplane in World War II, *5791*
African-American woman, *8048*
African-American, on a scheduled passenger line, *8142*
Air Force ace in the Vietnam War, *5819*
American ace of aces, *5754*
American air ace, *5751*
American to establish an airplane altitude record, *8015*
awarded the Medal of Honor, *5515*
civilian to fly a craft into space, *6888*
civilian, wounded in Vietnam, *5811*
from the United States killed in World War I, *5734*
from the United States shot down in World War I, *5733*
from the United States to sink a German submarine in World War II, *5776*
in American units to participate in air combat in World War I, *5749*
in the Army to fly solo in an airplane, *5462*
in the Army to win a victory over an enemy airplane, *5474*
in the Navy, *5465*
killed in an airplane accident, *8010*
licensed by the Aero Club of America, *8025*
navy ace in the Korean War, *5810*
Navy pilot shot down and captured in North Vietnam, *5813*
of a B-52 bomber who was a woman, *5493*
of a jet fighter to win a dogfight in the Korean War, *5807*
of an airplane to qualify as an astronaut by attaining a 50-mile altitude, *8149*
of military aircraft who were women, *5482*
on regular airmail service, *4692*
to bail out of a disabled airplane, *8052*
to bail out of an airplane flying at supersonic speed, *8137*
to break the sound barrier, *8121*
to destroy an enemy airplane in the Gulf War, *5822*
to destroy an enemy airplane in the Korean War, *5801*
to die because of a lack of oxygen, *8066*
to fire a gun from an airplane, *5464*
to fly a seaplane glider, *8074*
to fly above 100,000 feet, *5491*
to fly airmail, *4690*
to receive a glider license, *8081*
to shoot down a German fighter plane in World War II, *5787*
triple jet ace, *5809*
woman fighter pilot to fire a missile in combat, *5831*

Poem
to be printed in a newspaper, *1065*
to win national acclaim, *1093*
Poet
from America honored in Westminster Abbey, *1095*
monument to an American poet, *7174*
to win a Pulitzer Prize four times, *4769*
who was an African-American woman to win the Pulitzer Prize, *4771*
Poet laureate, *1109*
African-American woman, *1109*
woman, *1109*
Poetry
Beat Generation literary event, *1105*
collection by an African-American writer, *1068*
collection by an American poet, *1060*
collection by an American poet who was a man, *1064*
published literary work by an African-American, *1071*
translation prepared in America, *1059*
Polar bear to be exhibited, *1348*
Police
311 hotline, *7392*
appeal for missing persons to be televised, *7384*
Capitol officers killed in the line of duty, *3580*
force, *7353*
patrol wagon, *7364*
printed traffic regulations, *8193*
radio system, *7379*
uniforms, *7354*
urban business district with complete video surveillance, *7396*
woman hired under civil service rules, *7363*
woman to be killed in the line of duty, *7388*
Police department
bureau of criminal alien investigation, *7378*
highway patrol using digital-photography, *8217*
identification bureau, *7362*
state unit, *7359*
to use a teletypewriter system, *7376*
with a parking meter enforcement division, *7386*
with a traffic police squad, *7360*
woman police chief, *7372*
Polio
epidemic, *5094*
mass immunizations, *5159*
vaccine, *5157*
Political
action committee (PAC), *3820*
cartoon featuring Uncle Sam, *4575*
cartoon showing the Democratic Party as a donkey, *4576*
cartoon showing the Republican Party as an elephant, *4579*
history book, *7473*
newspaper of national importance, *4492*
newspaper to carry partisanship to extremes, *4495*
platform adopted by a party, *4056*
Political economy
chair at a college, *2782*
course at a college, *2713*
Political machine, *4054*
local, *3513*
Political parties
African-American delegate to a national convention, *4066*
African-American to chair a major party, *4110*
African-American to preside over national convention of a major party, *4076*
American Independent, *4102*
American Nazi, *4099*
Anti-Masonic, *4055*
antislavery, *4060*
Black Panther, *4101*
Bull Moose, *4089*
Communist Labor Party of America, *4090*
Communist Party of America, *4091*
Constitutional Union, *4065*
Democratic, *4057*
Free Soil, *4062*
Green, *4109*
keynote speech by an African-American at a major party convention, *4075*
keynote speech by an African-American woman at a major party convention, *4075*
Know-Nothing (American), *4064*
Labor (modern), *4111*
Labor Reform, *4068*
Libertarian, *4106*
Liberty, *4060*
national convention broadcast on radio, *4094*
national convention to be televised, *4098*
national convention to adopt the two-thirds rule, *4058*
national convention to adopt the unit rule, *4061*
national convention to be addressed by a woman, *4071*
national platform, *4056*
National Union for Social Justice, *4095*

combination cylinder and flatbed, *2040*
cylinder, *2037*
electric, *2039*
for polychromatic printing, *2041*
for printing wallpaper in color, *2036*
invented in the United States, *2034*
invented in the United States that was successful, *2034*
powered by steam, *2035*
rotary, *2042*
rotary with a continuous-roll feed, *2046*
to use a continuous web or roll of paper, *2045*
web-fed four-color rotary, *2054*

Prison, *6988*
built for and managed by women, *7006*
college commencement exercises, *2875*
congressional representative reelected after serving a prison term, *3619*
federal abolition of imprisonment for debt, *6993*
federal penitentiary, *7010*
federal, for women, *7014*
matrons for guarding women prisoners, *6999*
military, on an island, *7001*
organized into community groups, *7011*
reform society, *6990*
reformatory for juvenile deliquents, *6996*
rotary jail, *7008*
state reformatory for boys, *7000*
to have individual cells for prisoners, *6991*
to offer training in Vipassana meditation, *7023*
treadmill, *6995*
woman commissioner of a city, *7019*
woman commissioner of a state, *7019*
woman guard to serve in a maximum security prison for men, *7020*
year in which the prison population exceeded 1 million, *7022*

Prisoners
American prisoners of war, *5655*
captured in the War of 1812 by the Americans, *5683*
in a federal penitentiary to be employed in industry, *7012*
Naval War College president who had been a POW, *3130*

Prizefighting: state ban, *7596*

Probation
officer for juvenile delinquents, *7005*
system, *7007*

Product safety
businessman convicted for importing unsafe toys, *7290*
cigarette maker to settle a lawsuit, *7091*
company penalized for failing to report a hazardous product, *7291*
dietary supplement to be banned by the FDA, *7294*
independent laboratory for evaluating consumer products, *7297*
liability lawsuit to result in a criminal trial, *1513*

Prohibition
congressional representative elected by prohibition advocates, *3610*
state to ratify the Prohibition Amendment to the Constitution, *7074*
See also Alcohol

Pronghorn antelope, *5945*

Propaganda course at a college, *2846*

Property tax
established by a colony to support public schools, *2885*
levied by a colony, *4398*

Prosecution under the Sedition Act, *4498*

Prostitute, *7429*

Protest
against forced labor in a colony, *7096*
against globalization, *6980*
against slavery, *6116*
armed occupation of federal territory by Native American protesters in the modern era, *6102*
by a president, *4130*
by college students, *2701*
by gay people against violations of their civil rights, *7448*
by gay people on a large scale, *7448*
by people with disabilities against violations of their civil rights, *7041*
campus takeover by students, *2868*
demonstration in Washington against the Vietnam War, *5815*
federal judge to reduce a sentence to protest racial profiling, *7024*
mass boycott by African-Americans over violations of civil rights, *6141*
Moratorium Day demonstration against the Vietnam War, *5818*
occupation of federal territory by Native American protesters in the modern era, *6099*
war tax resister, *4412*

Protestant
church west of of the Alleghenies, *6227*
missionary society established for the English colonies, *6189*
Native American to convert, *6169*
religious service to be televised, *6306*
Sunday school, *6220*

year in which Protestants were no longer a majority of the United States population, *6335*
Protestant Episcopal: military school operated by a church, *3104*
Psychedelic music album, *1274*
Psychiatric institute, *3079*
Psychiatry
book, *5299*
national association, *5217*
psychodrama treatment, *5395*
textbook, *5318*
Psychology
journal, *5329*
laboratory, *5164*
national society, *5225*
professor, *3075*
Ptarmigan, *5955*
Public
defender hired by a state, *3973*
health report commissioned by a state, *7239*
hygiene professor, *3049*
reading of the Declaration of Independence, *3467*
speaking department at a college, *2812*
Public school
classes for children with epilepsy, *2973*
for Asian-American children, *2937*
for children with disabilities, *2960*
with a continuous existence, *2884*
support by a property tax, *2885*
Publicist for a theater company, *1418*
Published literary work by an African-American, *1071*
Publisher
music, *1225*
of denominational religious books, *6351*
Publishing
house run by a university, *2818*
society, *4452*
Puerto Rico
congressional representative of Puerto Rican ancestry, *3624*
governor to be elected, *3784*
woman governor, *3790*
Puffed cereal commercially manufactured, *2414*
Pulitzer Prize
awarded four times to a poet, *4769*
awarded to a comic book, *4773*
awarded to a musical, *4768*
awarded to a newspaper, *4764*
awarded to a newspaper reporter, *4760*
awarded to a science book, *4774*
awarded to an African-American woman poet, *4771*
awarded twice to a scientist, *4774*
dramatist to win the Pulitzer Prize four times, *4772*
fiction writer to win twice, *4763*
for a newspaper editorial, *4761*
for a novel written by a woman, *4766*
for an editorial cartoon, *4767*
for drama, *4765*
for fiction, *4762*
won by a writer in both fiction and poetry, *4770*
Pullman sleeping car, *8351*
that was comfortable, *8353*
Pulp fiction magazine, *4614*
Pump
gasoline, *1868*
heart, *5350*
self-computing gasoline, *1876*
wearable infusion, for chemotherapy, *5187*
Puppet show, *1416*
to be televised, *1453*
Purple Heart, *5500*
awarded to a woman, *5517*

Q

Quack doctor, *5018*
Quadrant, *8499*
Quadruplets
delivered by cesarean operation, *2154*
Quaker
annual meeting, *6195*
ban enacted by a colony, *6192*
college, *2739*
executed for religious beliefs, *6193*
hospital for mentally ill patients, *5100*
library for workers, *3008*
meeting house, *6200*
prison reform society, *6990*
to arrive in America, *6191*
Quantum theory of electromagnetic radiation, *6707*
Quarantine
of plants by a state, *7250*
of plants enacted by Congress, *7275*
state board, *7241*
Quarantine law
enacted by a colony, *7232*
federal, *7237*
Queen
of England to receive a hug from an American, *3943*
to visit the United States, *3924*
to visit the United States during her reign, *3930*

who was a woman of American ancestry, *3934*
Quetzal bird, *5959*
Quinine, *5235*
synthetic, *5248*
Quintuplets, *2150*
Quonset hut, *3304*

R

Rabbi
to deliver the invocation in the House of Representatives, *3602*
Conservative woman, *6314*
Orthodox, born in America, *6294*
Reform woman, *6314*
Rabbinical college, *2790*
Radar
aboard a commercial carrier, *8506*
detection of airplanes, *8078*
for commercial and private planes, *8118*
in a battleship, *8485*
observations, *8504*
offshore warning station, *8489*
on a passenger ship, *8505*
signal bounced off the sun, *6796*
signal to the moon, *6790*
used to detect enemy airplanes, *5763*
used to investigate a plane crash, *8170*
Radio
advertising course at a college, *2848*
astronomer, *6376*
auction of radio spectrum for satellite services, *4805*
church, *6296*
compass on a naval airplane, *5477*
coast-to-coast hookup, *4789*
commercial, *1537*
contest, *4781*
distress signal from an American ship, *7348*
distress signal officially established, *7349*
fax of a newspaper, *4538*
federal law requiring radios on ships, *8445*
impulse transmission, *4817*
magazine, *6786*
master antenna on a skyscraper, *4826*
message sent by wireless transmission, *4776*
navigation beacons, *8502*
network program sponsored by commercial advertising, *1540*
orchestra, *1258*
packet network, *4804*
parade in which the marching music was supplied by transistor radios, *1409*
patent, *4818*
portable, *4821*
president to use a radio, *4276*
production course at a college, *2856*
receiver to be advertised, *4819*
receiver with an auxiliary solar-cell power unit, *4825*
sextant, *8507*
society, *4780*
SOS call from an American ship, *7350*
symphony orchestra, *1263*
system for state police, *7375*
theme song, *4785*
transatlantic message of the regular westward service, *4779*
transatlantic undersea conversation, *4803*
transpacific conversation, *4783*
year in which TV industry profits exceeded those of radio, *4956*
Radio broadcast
chain, *4787*
College Bowl, *2865*
demonstration, *4775*
foreign language course, *3213*
from a circus, *1396*
from a moving train, *4796*
from a submerged submarine, *4784*
from a tape recording, *4799*
from the Senate chamber, *3678*
heard in both the Arctic and the Antarctic regions, *4798*
in which citizens telephoned the president, *4288*
made by a president, *4277*
made by a president in a foreign language, *4282*
made by a presidentfrom the White House, *4279*
of a baseball game with a play-by-play description, *7529*
of a boxing match, *7601*
of a boxing match from ringside, *7602*
of a cabinet session that was simultaneously telecast, *4193*
of a championship football game, *7712*
of a debate, *4786*
of a drama, *1451*
of a football game with a play-by-play description, *7705*
of a livestock auction, *1643*
of a musical comedy, *1458*
of a national party convention, *4094*
of a play from a regular stage, *1456*
of a presidential inauguration, *4280*

operated by an electric third-rail system, *8324*
operated by the federal government, *8326*
owned by a city, *8317*
owned by a state, *8301*
piggyback operation, *8320*
post office, *4674*
rails of T shape, *8382*
safety law enacted by a state, *8314*
signal system with automatic electric block, *8388*
state aid, *8308*
steel rails, *8385*
timetable advertised in a newspaper, *8304*
to carry troops, *8306*
to delay a train by telegraph, *4851*
to install track water tanks, *8387*
to run west of the Mississippi River, *8309*
to run west out of Chicago, *8309*
to use an electric engine, *8323*
track that was practical, *8381*
transcontinental daily passenger train service, *8321*
transcontinental Pullman sleeping car daily service, *8328*
transcontinental service, *8318*
union passenger station used by several companies, *8313*
year in which air traffic volume exceeded first-class rail traffic volume, *8127*
Railroad bridge
across the Mississippi River, *3243*
steel, *3246*
stone arch, *3235*
suspension, *3242*
wooden truss, *3237*
Railroad car
adaptable freight car, *8363*
carrying oil tanks, *8352*
freight cars with compartments, *8362*
glass-lined tank car, *8358*
post office, *4674*
refrigerated, *8354*
refrigerated, to carry fresh fruit, *8354*
Railroad tunnel, *3437*
to a foreign country, *3441*
Rap album to attract a mass audience, *1280*
Rape
crisis center, *6955*
marital, state to outlaw, *6958*
state registry of sex offenders, *7299*
state to authorize incarceration of convicted sex offenders beyond their prison terms, *7303*
state to notify the public about the residences of released sex offenders, *7304*
Raptor sanctuary, *5953*
Rat extermination throughout an entire city, *7268*
Rattlesnake meat in cans, *2432*
Ray gun to shoot down an armed missile, *5894*
Rayon, *2139*
Ready-mix food, *2389*
Real estate board game, *7730*
Reaper machine, *1598*
Rebellion
against the federal government, *5675*
by colonists against an English governor, *5638*
in the English colonies, *5629*
Recipes using standard measurements, *2398*
Reclining chair, *2551*
Red scare, *4092*
Reformed Church meeting, *6211*
Refrigerated museum vaults, *3155*
Refrigeration
centralized service, *1895*
system for trucks, *8295*
Refrigerator, *2271*
gas, *2287*
Refugee
political asylum granted on grounds of sexual orientation, *6106*
political asylum granted to avoid genital mutilation of women, *6107*
state to offer services, *6104*
to arrive under the Refugee Relief Act of 1953, *6097*
Regatta, *7568*
Regiment
of free African-Americans during the Civil War, *5710*
to answer Lincoln's call for volunteers in the Civil War, *5695*
Reindeer, *5952*
Relief map, *4484*
Religion
interfaith charity organization, *7197*
national tract society, *6263*
publisher of denominational religious books, *6351*
summit conference of world religions, *6333*
year in which Protestants were no longer a majority of the United States population, *6335*
Religious
commune, *3510*
leader in the American colonies who was a white woman, *6178*
leader who exercised the authority of king and high priest, *6068*
magazine, *6345*

S

transpacific solo crossing by a woman, *8546*
Sailors, women, *5593*
Saint Patrick's Day parade, *1352*
Sale of an American painting at a price comparable to that of European paintings, *1045*
Salmon cannery, *2363*
Salt works, *2315*
Salute fired by Great Britain in honor of an officer of the United States, *3878*
Salvation Army services, *6281*
Sanatorium
for tuberculosis patients, *5125*
for tuberculosis patients established by a state, *5128*
for tuberculosis patients using modern treatment methods, *5126*
Sandblasting process, *1893*
Sandpaper patent, *1852*
Sanitary napkin, *2474*
Santa Claus school, *2515*
Sardine cannery, *2377*
Satellite
auction of radio spectrum for satellite services, *4805*
ballet transmission, *1056*
coast-to-coast transmission of airwaves, *5003*
commercial, *6857*
communications, *6851*
composite map of the United States, *4486*
dish for personal use, *5007*
for communication, with signal reception and transmission equipment, *6853*
for the Global Positioning System (GPS), *6865*
from the United States to impact the moon, *6856*
geodetic, *6858*
geosynchronous, *6859*
international, *6855*
launched from the earth to orbit another planet, *6862*
live telecast to Europe, *4968*
multisatellite launching, *6849*
navigational, *6847*
photograph bounced off a satellite, *4637*
placed in orbit by the United States, *6844*
private owned to convey a phone call, *4909*
repair in orbit, *6863*
spy, *6848*
telecast from Japan, *4969*
telecast to Japan, *4969*
to transmit a radio broadcast, *4801*
to transmit photographs of the earth, *6845*
transoceanic telecast, *5004*
weather satellite to provide cloud-cover photographs, *6846*
with a nuclear reactor to orbit the earth, *6861*
Saturday Evening Post cover by Norman Rockwell, *1040*
Savings group for children, *1728*
Savings and loan association, federal, *1744*
Savings bank, *1717*
life insurance, *1992*
to offer life insurance, *1992*
to receive money on deposit, *1718*
Sawmill
driven by electricity, *1870*
to use a band saw, *1863*
Saws, circular, *2644*
Saxophone production, *1304*
Scale
automatic computing pendulum, *1685*
camera exposure, *4638*
platform, *1663*
Scandinavian Methodist Episcopal church, *6270*
School
advertising, *3212*
Army chaplains, *3115*
Army language, *3116*
automobile, *3208*
band, *1238*
business, *3197*
cartooning, *3215*
Catholic, *2886*
Catholic, for Native Americans, *2916*
charter, *2983*
chiropody, *3083*
chiropractic, *3080*
circus clowns, *3217*
completely irradiated with germicidal lamps, *7281*
compulsory education law, *2887*
continuation for apprentices, *3209*
continuation for apprentices, *3210*
cooking, *3199*
drama, *3204*
elementary school with air conditioning, *2976*
elementary school to use closed-circuit TV, *2978*
for African-American children, state, *2947*
for African-Americans in Washington, DC, *2905*
for bicyclists, *7640*
for colonial children in America, *2882*

by German forces to land on American soil in World War I, *5753*
by the Navy in World War I, *5736*
in the Civil War, *5690*
Shot tower, *5859*
Shovel
steel, *2637*
two-handed, *2670*
Showboat, *1426*
of importance, *1426*
Shuffleboard championship tournament, *7976*
Siamese twins, *2148*
Sieve, *2540*
wire, *2548*
Sightseeing bus, *8218*
Sign
emoticon for computer users, *6464*
flashing electric, *1542*
neon, *1539*
use of @ in an e-mail address, *6445*
Sign language
prayers signed for deaf worshippers, *6258*
taught in a school for deaf students, *2909*
Signal flares, *5849*
Signer of the Declaration of Independence, *3464*
Sikh gurdwara, *6292*
Silk
culture, *2106*
dyers, *2130*
exported, *2111*
loom, *2136*
mill, *2124*
power loom, *2128*
sutures and ligatures, *5173*
thread, *2612*
Silo, *1624*
Silver
mill, *1932*
mine, *3381*
plating factory, *1929*
wire suture, *5172*
Singer whose voice was broadcast over radio, *1250*
Singing
contest, *1226*
vocal instruction book, *1211*
Single tax adopted by a city for local revenue purposes, *4417*
Singles bar, *1837*
Sister city partnership, *3535*
Sisters who were congressional representatives, *3640*
Sitcom television show, *4945*
Skee-ball alley, *1007*
Skeet: national tournament, *7888*
Ski
club association, *7889*
tow made of rope, *7892*
Ski lift, *7893*
for skimobiles, *7894*
state regulations, *7896*
Skiing
indoor school, *7895*
indoor slope, *7897*
international meet, *7891*
steel jump, *7890*
Skin
anti-aging cream, *2482*
artificial skin transplant, *5372*
grafting, *5341*
Sky marshals, *7387*
Skyjacking
in which the skyjacker disappeared, *6956*
of a commercial American airplane, *6951*
of an American airliner by terrorists, *5817*
Skyscraper, *3284*
antenna, *4826*
bombed by foreign terrorists, *5826*
higher than 1,250 feet, *3300*
higher than 1,400 feet, *3318*
higher than 750 feet, *3297*
of bronze and glass, *3311*
Skywriting, *1538*
Slavery
adoption of the gag rule by the House of Representatives, *3598*
African slaves in America, *6111*
African slaves in the English colonies, *6111*
antislavery party, *4060*
ban enacted for a federal territory, *6122*
colonial ban on slave importation, *6118*
colonial law making slavery lifelong and hereditary, *6115*
colony to legalize, *6113*
emancipation law enacted by a colony, *6114*
emancipation proclamation, *6134*
escape of slaves from a colony, *6110*
escaped slave legally recaptured in New England, *6132*
federal execution of a slave trader, *7002*
federal fugitive slave law, *6123*
federal law banning importation of African slaves, *6125*
federal law emancipating slaves, *6133*
protest, *6116*
school for freed slaves, *2940*
senator elected on an antislavery ticket, *6131*
slave rebellion after the Revolution, *6128*

radar signal bounced off, *6796*
Sunday
blue laws, *6182*
newspaper, *4496*
newspaper comics section, *4481*
school, Jewish, *6214*
school, Protestant, *6220*
Sunscreen product, *2478*
Superman comic book, *1101*
Supermarket, self-service, *2096*
Supersonic
airplane flight, *8121*
airplane flight by a woman, *8121*
manned rocket plane, *5486*
pilot to bail out of a plane flying at supersonic speed, *8137*
rocket, *6789*
rocket-powered car, *8275*
transatlantic jet passenger service, *8158*
Supreme Court of the United States, *3732*
African-American lawyer admitted to practice, *3966*
African-American woman lawyer admitted to practice, *3966*
case in which social-science research was accepted as evidence, *7477*
clerk, *3733*
lawyers admitted to practice, *3955*
nominee who was rejected by the Senate, *3735*
with a majority of Catholic justices, *3754*
woman lawyer admitted to practice, *3970*
Supreme Court chief justice, *3731*
to serve in a presidential cabinet, *3739*
who had been a congressional representative, *3737*
who had been a president, *4143*
whose nomination was not confirmed, *3736*
Supreme Court decision, *3734*
declaring a congressional act unconstitutional, *3559*
declaring a state law unconstitutional, *3743*
establishing the power of the federal government, *3742*
in a commerce case, *3745*
in a matter between states, *3738*
in a state boundary case, *3747*
on inclusion of candidates in televised political debates, *3753*
reversing the ruling of a state supreme court, *3744*
voiding an act of Congress, *3740*
Supreme Court justice
African-American, *3751*
Catholic, *3746*
Jewish, *3750*
Jewish woman, *3750*
nominee to die before taking office, *3748*
to be appointed chief justice, *3749*
to be impeached, *3741*
woman, *3752*
Supreme court, state
African-American chief justice, *3708*
African-American justice, *3708*
in which all the judges were women, *3718*
woman chief justice, *3728*
woman justice, *3717*
Surfing, *7958*
Surgeon
African-American fellow of the American College of Surgeons, *5229*
appointed by a colony, *5097*
plastic and reconstructive surgeon, *5340*
woman, *5027*
woman fellow of the American College of Surgeons, *5229*
Surgeon general, *7249*
African-American, *7287*
of the Army, *5436*
of the Continental Army, *5436*
woman, *7283*
Surgery
abdominal operation other than a cesarean section, *5339*
antiseptic dressings, *5174*
appendectomy, *5344*
artificial aortic valve, *5358*
artificial heart transplant, *5371*
artificial skin transplant, *5372*
baby whose life was saved by surgery while still in the womb, *5373*
battery-powered pacemaker, *5353*
bloodless liver transplant from a living donor, *5382*
bone marrow transplant, *5369*
cesarean operation, *5338*
conjoined twins separated successfully, *5359*
demonstration of anesthesia, *5052*
dual kidney and liver transplants from children to a parent, *5383*
elevation of the skull to treat epilepsy, *5349*
gallstone operation, *5343*
hand transplant, *5381*
heart operation for the relief of angina pectoris, *5351*
heart operation in which the deep-freezing technique was employed, *5357*
heart operation using the elective cardiac arrest technique, *5361*
heart pump, *5350*

Synod
ecumenical, *6186*
held in America, *6180*
Synthetic
fabric that was waterproof and breathable, *2144*
fabric used for clothing, *2265*
fertilizer, *1610*
fiber, *2141*
fuels plant, *6614*
laundry detergent, *2224*
mica, *3398*
radioactive substance, *6745*
rubber, *1900*
rubber for manufacture, *1902*
rubber tires, *8210*

T

Tabulating machine, *1677*
Taconite production, *3396*
Tampon to be mass-produced, *2475*
Tank
heavy tank, *5869*
operated by Army troops, *5863*
with a turbine engine, *5890*
Tanker, automated, under the American flag, *8463*
Tap dancer of renown, *1049*
Tape
cellophane, *2578*
measure, *2657*
Tape recorder, *4833*
built in the United States for commercial use, *4834*
machine for mass production of tapes, *4836*
open-reel video recorder for home use, *5006*
to use cassettes, *4837*
Tape recording used in a radio broadcast, *4799*
Taps bugle call, *1339*
Tariff
enacted by Congress to prevent the importation of obscene literature and pictures, *4411*
federal commission, *4416*
federal legislation, *4404*
passed by Congress for protection, *4408*
Tattoo
electric machine, *2464*
shop, *2460*
Tattooed man exhibited as a theatrical attraction, *1369*
Tax
British tax levied directly on American colonists without their consent, *4402*
British tax levied on American colonists without their consent, *4400*
colonial income tax, *4399*
colonial inheritance tax, *4401*
colonial property tax, *4398*
colonial property tax to support public schools, *2885*
deadline for filing individual income tax returns, *4419*
federal income tax, *4413*
federal inheritance tax, *4414*
federal internal revenue tax, *4405*
federal tax levied directly on the states, *4406*
federal tax on cigarettes, *7063*
federal tax on corporations, *4418*
federal tax on excess profits of corporations, *4420*
federal tax on gasoline, *4424*
federal tax on tobacco, *7058*
rebellion, *4407*
single tax dopted by a city, *4417*
state bachelor tax, *4409*
state inheritance tax, *4410*
state sales tax, *4422*
state tax on chain stores, *4423*
state tax on cigarettes, *7076*
state tax on gasoline, *4421*
state tax to support public schools, *2917*
war tax resister, *4412*
Taxicabs, electric, *8231*
Taxidermy: method of stuffing animals, *6663*
Tea, instant, *2446*
Teacher
national association, *2943*
national parent-teacher association, *2957*
parent-teacher association, *2952*
sick-leave benefit funds, *7133*
tried for violating a state ban on teaching the theory of evolution, *2970*
Teacher training
institute, *2928*
school, *2915*
school at which students conducted practice classes, *2939*
state school, *2927*
Teaching methodology
book, *2899*
course at a college, *2745*
Team sport played in America, *7960*
Technical
college for women, *2821*
institute, *3192*
school for Native Americans, *2981*

Truss bridge
iron, *3240*
wooden railroad, *3237*
Trust, *1481*
company, *1719*
Tuberculosis
cattle test, *5405*
city laboratory, *7258*
city rule prohibiting spitting, *7264*
home for patients, *5124*
hospital established by Congress, *5129*
hospital for the poor established by a city, *5127*
hospital to provide free care, *5130*
outdoor school for children, *2963*
research and prevention society, *5224*
research laboratory, *5166*
sanatorium, *5125*
sanatorium established by a state, *5128*
sanatorium using modern treatment methods, *5126*
vaccine, *5155*
Tubes
collapsible, *2650*
collapsible machine-made, *2658*
Tubing
brass, *1924*
brass and copper seamless tubes, *1930*
Tugboat
powered by steam, *8423*
with a diesel-electric engine, *8450*
Tuna
dolphin-free, *2454*
in cans, *2408*
Tungsten
and tellurium, *3376*
ductile, *3395*
Tunnel, *3435*
construction using compressed air, *3440*
for a city water supply, *3439*
highway tunnel with television monitors, 3444
mining tunnel on a large scale, 3436
railroad tunnel, 3437
underwater highway tunnel, 3438
underwater highway tunnel with twin tubes, 3442
underwater railroad tunnel to a foreign country, 3441
vehicular tunnel to a foreign country, 3443
wind tunnel for testing airplane parts, 8060
Turbine
successfully operated by waterpower, *1857*
tank engine, *5890*
Turbine-propelled naval ship, *8479*
Turnstile, electric, *1671*
Tuxedo jacket, *2254*
TV dinners, *2442*
Twelve-step rehabilitation program, *7078*
Twine, cotton, *2550*
Twins
conjoined, *2148*
conjoined twins separated successfully by surgery, *5359*
Type
foundry, *2032*
Hebrew, *2030*
specimen book from an American type foundry, *4443*
used in a music book, *1219*
Typesetting machine, *2044*
to dispense with metal type, *2058*
Typewriter
correction fluid, *1694*
electric, *1690*
portable, *1680*
portable electric, *1697*
ribbon, *1675*
that could retype text automatically, *1700*
that was practical, *1667*
to be patented, *1662*
to produce a line of writing visible as it was being typed, *1681*
used to write a book, *4457*
without type arms, *1698*
Typing school, *3200*

U

Ukrainian daily newspaper, *4573*
Ultrasonic television remote control, *4999*
Umbrella, *2230*
Umpire
African-American, in organized baseball, *7540*
baseball, *7483*
Underground
burial of electric wires, *7412*
cables to carry a long-distance telephone call, *4877*
city sewer system, *7406*
comic book, *1107*
deep nuclear waste storage site, *6630*
explosion of an atomic bomb, *5878*
school, *2982*
Undersea
hotel, *1842*
park established by the federal government, *5995*

Underwater
explosion of an atomic bomb, *5873*
highway tunnel, *3438*
highway tunnel with twin tubes, *3442*
railroad tunnel to a foreign country, *3441*
telegraph cable that was practical, *4848*
UNICEF
Halloween collection, *2516*
Halloween collection that raised funds for American children, *2522*
Uniform
Army, *5413*
baseball, *7484*
football, *7690*
for mail carriers, *4678*
for working women, *2257*
Navy, *5574*
police, *7354*
Union. *See* Labor union
Union
catalog of books in a state library, *3026*
catalog of books in American libraries, *3022*
station used by several railroad companies, *8313*
Unitarian
church, *6236*
church identified by that name, *6236*
prayer book, *6349*
woman minister, *6236*
United Brethren in Christ meeting, *6225*
United Nations
African-American delegate, *3901*
Americans to die in a UN peacekeeping mission, *5800*
peacekeeping mission in which the United States participated, *5800*
permanent American ambassador who was a woman, *3903*
Security Council resolution vetoed by the United States, *3907*
woman permanent representative from the United States, *3910*
United States: replacement of the name United Colonies, *3469*
United States Secret Service
agent killed in the line of duty, *3845*
agent killed while protecting the president, *3845*
ball game to be declared a national special security event, *7719*
established by the federal government, *3842*
woman agent killed in the line of duty, *3845*
women agents, *3860*
Universalist church services, *6229*
University
African-American president of a major university, *2871*
devoted to research, *2792*
doctorate awarded to an African-American, *2768*
doctorate awarded to an American, *2730*
doctorate awarded by an American university, *2761*
doctorate awarded to a woman, *2794*
doctorate awarded to an African-American by an American university, *2791*
doctorate in medicine, *3044*
for African-American students, *2770*
graduate school for women, *2803*
honors program, *2796*
land grant, *2726*
legally designated as such, *2710*
master's degree earned by a Jew, *2705*
on the Pacific Coast, *2753*
press, *2818*
state, supported by a direct property tax, *2771*
state, to be chartered, *2715*
state, to grant equal privileges to women, *2776*
state, to open, *2715*
woman graduate student to receive a university fellowship, *2801*
woman president, *2786*
Urban
master plan, *3539*
planning instruction at a college, *2827*

V

Vaccination
federal vaccination law, *5153*
federal vaccination program to protect Native Americans from smallpox, *5154*
mass immunizations for polio, *5159*
program offered by a city, *5151*
state ban on mercury in vaccine, *5162*
state vaccination law, *5152*
Vaccine
against a form of cancer, *5160*
anthrax, *5158*
chicken pox, *5161*
polio, *5157*
to use a genetically altered virus, *6683*
tuberculosis, *5155*
yellow fever, *5156*
Vacuum
canning process, *2341*
telescope, *6380*

W

celebration of a president's silver wedding anniversary, *4252*
chief counsel who was a woman, *4167*
child born in, *4324*
dish set made in America, *4331*
dwelling of president's mother, *4256*
Easter egg roll, *2502*
gaslight, *4326*
memoir of life in the White House, *4327*
movie shown, *4330*
naturalization ceremony, *6100*
painting by an African-American artist, *4334*
president to make a radio broadcast from, *4279*
president's child born, *4328*
state dinner televised from the White House, *4333*
swimming pool, *4332*
televised presidential address, *4283*
visit by a pope, *3941*
wedding, *4325*
wedding ceremony of a president, *4257*
woman chef, *4335*

White lead, *1919*

Whole-wheat bread, *2346*

Whooping crane, *5964*

Wild West Show, *1381*

Wilderness protection law, federal comprehensive, *5926*

Wind
tunnel for testing airplane parts, *8060*
turbine, *6633*

Windmill for grinding grain, *2316*

Window glass factory, *3353*

Windshield wiper, *8194*
automatic, *8205*

Wine, kosher, *2403*

Wire
brass, *1924*
gauge, *2651*
glass, *3361*
machine for cutting and straightening, *1862*
piano, *1296*
rope factory, *1856*
sieves, *2548*
suspension bridge, *3239*
woven wire fence, *1628*

Wireless
city to provide free citywide WiFi, *7428*
city with a free public WiFi system, *7426*
city with a mobile mesh WiFi network for both public and municipal use, *7425*
city with complete WiFi coverage, *7422*
demonstration of wireless remote vehicle control as an antiterrorism tactic, *7309*
message sent by wireless transmission, *4776*
municipal wireless network paid for by advertisements, *7427*
television remote control, *4999*
wireless microchip receiver-transmitter for making digital information part of a nondigital object, *6533*

Witchcraft: execution on record, *6987*

Wolf
bounty, *5939*
reintroduced into the wild, *5966*

Woman's World Fair, *1506*

Women
affirmative action order issued by the federal government, *3855*
African Methodist Episcopal preacher, *6257*
African-American, abolitionist, *7432*
African-American, Air Force general, *5498*
African-American, airline flight attendant, *8076*
African-American, amateur athlete to win the James E. Sullivan, *7480*
African-American, ambassador, *3904*
African-American, Army general, *5455*
African-American, astronaut to fly in space, *6826*
African-American, author of a novel, *1092*
African-American, billionaire, *1714*
African-American, cabinet member, *4204*
African-American, certified public accountant, *1713*
African-American, college graduate, *2749*
African-American, congressional representative from a Southern state, *3623*
African-American, congressional representative, *3623*
African-American, depicted on a postage stamp, *4756*
African-American, elected judge, *3721*
African-American, federal administrator, *3851*
African-American, federal district court judge, *3726*
African-American, general to rise through the ranks, *5455*
African-American, judge, *3721*
African-American, keynote speaker at a major party convention, *4075*
African-American, lawyer admitted to practice before the Supreme Court, *3966*
African-American, lawyer, *3968*
African-American, librarian, *3021*
African-American, Marine, *5569*

Coast Guard Academy graduates, *3131*
Coast Guard officers, *5546*
Coast Guard ship commander, *5547*
Coast Guard unit, *5545*
coeducational college literary society, *2700*
coeducational medical school, *3056*
college athletic scholarships for women, *2874*
college baseball team for women, *7494*
college for women, *2741*
college gymnastics instruction for women, *7786*
college president, *2786*
college professor, *2752*
college secret society for women, *2751*
colonial election law giving women voting rights, *3761*
colonist, *6014*
commissioned in the U.S. Naval Reserve, *5606*
composer whose opera was performed at the Metropolitan Opera House, *1320*
congressional lobbyist, *3567*
congressional representative of Asian descent, *3621*
congressional representative who was a veteran, *3635*
congressional representative who was Jewish, *3615*
congressional representative, *3613*
coxswain of a men's college varsity rowing team, *7881*
dean of a university graduate school, *2855*
delegate to a national political convention, *4081*
dentist, *5084*
depicted on a postage stamp, *4728*
detective, *7371*
diplomat, *3896*
director of a major corporation, *1508*
director of the U.S. Mint, *4017*
disabled soldier awarded a military pension, *5618*
district attorney, *3715*
editor in chief of a law review, *2836*
editor of a major daily newspaper, *4605*
elected to statewide office, *4355*
elected to the American Medical Association, *5218*
elected to the British Parliament, *3929*
elected to the National Academy of Sciences, *6718*
eligible presidential candidate, *3808*
engineer, *3224*
English colonists in America, *2587*
Episcopal priest, *6327*
executed in the electric chair, *7009*
executive naval officer of a man-of-war, *5617*
federal agency director, *3846*
federal appeals court judge, *3719*
federal government employee, *3841*
federal judge, *3719*
federal marshal, *7385*
federal prison for women, *7014*
fellow of the American College of Surgeons, *5229*
fire department that was all-women, *7334*
for whom a bridge is named, *3256*
foreman on a grand jury, *3720*
from the Democratic Party to serve in both houses of Congress, *3680*
geologist, *6494*
golfer to win the U.S. Women's Amateur Championship, *7760*
governor elected in her own right, *4381*
governor of Puerto Rico, *3790*
governor, *4381*
graduate school for women, *2803*
graduate student to receive a university fellowship, *2801*
hanged by the federal government, *7004*
Hispanic astronaut, *6831*
Hispanic congressional representative, *3634*
hospital for women, *5110*
hotel for women, *1821*
humor writer, *1089*
in America to appeal for the right to vote, *3758*
in the Marine Corps Reserve, *5566*
infirmary for women staffed by women physicians, *5107*
Jewish Conservative rabbi, *6314*
Jewish graduate of West Point, *3097*
Jewish Reform cantor, *6314*
Jewish Reform rabbi, *6314*
jockey to ride in the Kentucky Derby, *7818*
jockey to ride two winners in a day, *7816*
jockey to win a major stakes race, *7820*
jockey to win a Triple Crown race, *7821*
jockey to win on a regular parimutuel flat track, *7816*
judge to impose the death penalty, *3716*
jury panel in which all members were women, *3700*
justice of the peace, *3709*
labor delegate to a national AFL convention, *7130*
labor union for women, *7106*
law school graduate, *2780*

presidential nominee to receive votes at a major party convention, *4100*
presidential physician, *4266*
principal chief of a major Native American tribe, *3942*
printer, *2008*
prison built for and managed by women, *7006*
prison guard to serve in a maximum security prison for men, *7020*
professional bullfighter, *7615*
professional hockey player, *7836*
professional women's club, *7212*
professional writer, *1075*
professor at a first-class medical school, *3081*
proposal for a women's suffrage amendment to the Constitution, *3780*
religious leader in the American colonies who was a white woman, *6178*
sailor assigned to shipboard duty, *5593*
school of higher education for women, *2907*
sculptor to create a federal monument, *7173*
Secret Service agent, *3860*
Secret Service agent killed in the line of duty, *3845*
secretary of state, *4212*
senator, *3673*
senator elected, *3673*
senator who was Jewish, *3693*
settlers to cross the continent, *6064*
shelter for women abuse victims, *6953*
sheriff, *7374*
speaker of the house in a state legislature, *4392*
sportscaster inducted into the Pro Football Hall of Fame, *7720*
squash rackets champion, *7906*
state ban on women's employment in a dangerous occupation, *7129*
state college for women, *2800*
state in which women held all the top offices, *4369*
state law allowing married women to make wills, *7431*
state law allowing married women to own property, *7433*
state law granting women voting rights, *3773*
state law regulating women's working hours, *7118*
state law to secure significant property rights for married women, *7435*
state legislators, *4389*
state police officers, *7377*
state prison commissioner, *7019*
state senator, *4390*
state supreme court chief justice, *3728*
state supreme court in which all the judges were women, *3718*
state supreme court justice, *3717*
state temperance society of women, *7062*
state to elect two women governors in a row, *4384*
state university to grant equal privileges to women, *2776*
stock brokerage president, *1782*
stock exchange director, *1783*
strike by women, *7110*
strike in which women participated, *7105*
subject of a monument financed by women, *7178*
Supreme Court justice, *3752*
Supreme Court justice who was Jewish, *3750*
surgeon, *5027*
surgeon general, *7283*
team of women to head a space probe mission, *6885*
technical college for women, *2821*
telegrapher, *4849*
telephone operator, *4870*
television news anchor on a network evening news program, *4604*
television news correspondent to cover a national political convention, *4603*
television news correspondent to report from Capitol Hill, *4603*
test pilot, *8104*
theater ushers, *1447*
tightrope performer, *1363*
to address a national politican convention, *4071*
to appear on television, *4926*
to chair a major political party, *4107*
to compete in the Indianapolis 500, *7626*
to compile a dictionary, *2264*
to compose a symphony, *1247*
to drive a car, *8232*
to earn a D.D.S. degree, *5085*
to earn a doctoral degree, *2794*
to earn an airplane instructor's license, *8097*
to earn an engineering degree, *3224*
to found a town, *3519*
to give medical treatment to a president, *4266*
to head a branch of the armed forces, *5499*
to lead a Muslim prayer service, *6336*
to lead a political party in Congress, *3639*

naval counterattack by American forces against the Japanese, *5775*
Navy admiral killed in action, *5762*
Navy task force assembled for foreign service, *5585*
radar used to detect enemy airplanes, *5763*
sea battle fought solely by air power, *5779*
soldier from the United States to land on French soil, *5788*
warship convoy across the Atlantic Ocean, *5759*
World's fair, *1485*
for women, *1506*
that was financially successful, *1512*
Worsted mill, *2109*
operated by waterpower, *2116*
Wrecking crane, *1867*
operated from a car, *1874*
Wrench
patent, *2647*
pipe or screw, *2660*
Wrestling, intercollegiate association, *7969*
Writer
of fiction to win the Pulitzer Prize twice, *4763*
professional, who was a woman, *1075*
to win a Pulitzer Prize four times for drama, *4772*
to win the Pulitzer Prize in both fiction and poetry, *4770*
travel writer, *1074*
whose livelihood was obtained exclusively by writing, *1080*

X

X-ray
movies of human organs in action, *5136*
photograph, *5131*
photograph of the entire body of a living person made in a single exposure, *5132*
photograph of the entire body of a living person taken in a one-second exposure, *5134*
photograph showing the complete arterial circulation in an adult human, *5135*
three-dimensional stereo fluoroscopic system, *5141*

Y

Yacht, *8413*
circumnavigation of the globe, *8530*
club, *7567*
from the United States to win an international race, *7569*
transatlantic race, *7571*
Year
in which a higher percentage of female than male high school graduates enrolled in college, *2876*
in which air traffic volume exceeded first-class rail traffic volume, *8127*
in which citizens of the District of Columbia could vote in a presidential election, *3786*
in which color television sets outsold black and white sets, *4976*
in which Congress appropriated $1 billion, *3572*
in which exports exceeded imports, *2069*
in which half of the nation's agricultural counties were designated disaster areas, *5931*
in which hurricane forecasters ran out of names, *6514*
in which Medicare spending declined, *3867*
in which more than 1 million passenger cars of one make were produced, *8262*
in which more than 100,000 passenger cars were produced, *8245*
in which more women than men were enrolled in colleges and universities, *2877*
in which Nobel Prizes were won by Americans in five of six categories, *6915*
in which people of Hispanic descent became the largest minority group, *6109*
in which Protestants were no longer a majority of the United States population, *6335*
in which television industry profits exceeded those of radio, *4956*
in which the average price of a new house topped $100,000, *2532*
in which the federal budget exceeded $1 trillion, *3862*
in which the heads of both major political parties were graduates of the same college, *4112*
in which the majority of states were represented by at least one congresswoman, *3638*
in which the prison population exceeded 1 million, *7022*
in which the public debt of the United States exceeded $1 trillion, *3861*
in which the value of a penny was less than its cost of manufacture, *4052*

in which there were no reported lynchings of African-Americans, *6140*
in which two different coins showed portraits of the same president, *4050*
in which two presidents were elected, *3806*
Yeast for baking, *2367*
Yellow fever vaccine for human immunization, *5156*
Yellow pages telephone directory, *4874*
Yeshivah
advanced-level, *2953*
for Jewish religious study, *2953*
with a secular high school, *2953*
Yiddish
daily newspaper, *4560*
language to have its entire literature digitized, *1110*
newspaper, *4560*
play by a professional troupe, *1444*
play presented by a Jewish acting troupe, *1442*
professorship at a college, *2863*
Yogurt dairy, *2431*
Youth hostel, *2196*

Z

Zebra mussels, *5967*
Zen Buddhist monastery, *6323*
Zinc, *3379*
commercial production, *3384*
sheet mill, *1934*
Zip codes, *4712*
Zipper, *2261*
in designer clothes, *2261*
Zippered garments, *2261*
Zither factory, *1299*
Zoning ordinance, *3533*
Zoo, *3142*
habitat constructed of simulated rock formations without bars, *3151*
hospital to own a CT scanner, *5409*
with twilight conditions, *3161*

INDEX BY YEARS

The following is a chronological listing of entries, arranged by year. To find an entry in the main body of the text, please go to the italicized number.

College founded in colonial America, *2682*
Comet recorded, *6383*
Library founded with English donations, *2992*

1619

African slaves in the English colonies, *6111*
Colonial legislative assembly, *4385*
Ironworks, *1912*
Sabbath law enacted by a colony, *6174*

1620

Child born of English parents in New England, *6017*
Congregational church, *6175*
Corn found by English settlers, *1557*
Lead, *3368*
Physician in the New England colonies, *5009*
Private libraries, *2993*
Waterpower development grant to a colonist, *6631*
Wedding of African-Americans, *2587*

1621

Colonial treaty with the Native Americans, *6019*
Duel, *6923*
Furs exported, *5937*
Greeting addressed to the Pilgrims by a Native American, *6018*
Military leader of the English settlers, *5633*
Potato, *1558*
Sermon to be printed, *6337*
Wedding of colonists in New England, *2588*

1622

African-American who was free, *6112*
Alcohol prohibition enforcement officers, *7052*
Massacre of settlers by Native Americans, *5634*

1623

Alcohol temperance law enacted by a colony, *7054*
Breach-of-promise suit, *2589*
Leather tanning, *2105*
Liquor reform movement, *7053*
Silk culture, *2106*

1624

Belgian immigrants, *6020*
Cattle to be imported, *1559*
Child born of African-American parents in America, *6021*
Gambling law for ministers enacted by a colony, *1797*

1625

Land sale by Native Americans to Europeans, *6022*
Midwife to practice professionally, *2146*
Pear and peach trees, *1560*
Road pavement, *3401*

1626

Forestry law enacted by a colony, *5972*
Land sale swindle, *6023*
Poetry translation prepared in America, *1059*

1627

Oil spring, *6574*

1628

Deportation, *6025*
Dutch Reformed church, *6176*
Fur trading post, *6024*
Shoes to be manufactured, *2228*

1629

Apples, *1561*
Brick kiln, *3326*
Commercial fishery, *1791*
Crop limitation law, *1562*
Horses, *8174*
Hunting law enacted by a colony, *5938*

1630

Execution in America, *6986*
Fork, *2533*
Gambling law for residents enacted by a colony, *1798*
Salt works, *2315*

1631

Election held in a colony, *3755*
Fire prevention law enacted by a colony, *7311*
Militia, *5635*

1632

Pirate on the Atlantic seaboard, *6924*
Road construction law enacted by a colony, *3402*
Tobacco penalty enacted by a colony, *7055*
Windmill for grinding grain, *2316*

1633

Brick building, *3257*
Czech settler in America, *6026*
School for colonial children in America, *2882*

1634

Bridge, *3227*
Catholics to settle in the English colonies in America, *6177*
Free school funded by an endowment, *2883*
Property tax levied by a colony, *4398*
Religious leader in the American colonies who was a white woman, *6178*
Treason trial by a colony, *6925*

1635

Cod-liver oil, *5232*
Grand jury, *3699*
Hurricane of record, *5897*
Naval battle between colonists, *5636*
Public school with a continuous existence, *2884*

1636

College to open in America, *2683*
Meat packer, *2317*
Pension law enacted by a colony, *7094*
Religious refuge for people of all faiths, *6179*

1637

Antismoking ban enacted by a colony, *7056*
Draft law enacted by a colony, *5553*
Hebrew instruction at a college, *2684*
Prostitute, *7429*
Synod held in America, *6180*

1638

Almanac, *3168*
Baptist church, *6181*
Blue laws prohibiting activities on Sunday, *6182*
Cloth mill, *2107*
College library, *2685*
Curfew bell, *7398*
Earthquake of record, *5898*
Log cabins, *2523*
Military organization established by a colony, *5637*
Swedes to arrive in America, *6027*

1639

Annulment of a marriage by court decree, *2590*
Autopsy officially recorded, *2292*
Bookseller, *4427*
Canal for creating water power, *3321*
Constitution to declare that "the foundation of authority is in the free consent of the people," *3455*
Crop surplus destruction ordered by a government, *1563*
Document known to have been printed in America, *3456*
Gunpowder mill, *5837*
Lawyer disbarred, *3947*
Medical regulations enacted by a colony, *5010*
Post office in a colony, *4653*
Printing press, *2029*
Property tax established by a colony to support public schools, *2885*

1640

Book published in America, *1061*
Catholic school, *2886*
College president, *2686*
Colonial election held in defiance of the Royal Courts, *3756*
Hebrew type, *2030*
Hymnbook published in America, *6338*
Lutheran pastor, *6183*
Poetry collection by an American poet, *1060*

1641

Agricultural fair held annually, *1564*
Colony to legalize slavery, *6113*
Danish settlers in America, *6028*
Patent granted by a colony, *3985*
Pottery, *2534*

1642

Bachelor of Arts degree, *2688*
Ban on convicts holding public office, *3757*
City incorporated in the colonies, *3508*
Compulsory education law in a colony, *2887*
Thesis directory, *2687*

1643

Catholic priest born in America, *6184*
Colonial government federation, *3446*
Cooking pots made in America, *2269*
Divorce, *2591*
Extradition of criminals among colonies, *7352*
Fulling mill for making wool cloth, *2108*
Income tax levied by a colony, *4399*
Ironworks that was successful, *1913*
Native American dictionary, *3169*
Spelling book, *2888*

1644

Branding law, *1565*
Colonial legislature to establish two chambers, *4386*
Whaling industry established by a city, *1792*

1645

Lutheran church, *6185*
Manufacturer of metal goods, *1914*
School committee, *2889*

1646

Children's book, *1062*
Ecumenical synod, *6186*
Wolf bounty, *5939*

1647

Ban on Jesuits to be enacted by a colony, *6187*
Colonial law requiring towns to hire teachers and construct schools, *2890*
Execution for witchcraft, *6987*
Quarantine law enacted by a colony, *7232*
Rice to be imported, *1566*
Woman in America to appeal for the right to vote, *3758*

1648

Craft union, *7095*
Law book of colonial laws, *3948*

1649

Corrupt election practices law enacted by a colony, *3759*
Missionary society established for the English colonies, *6189*
Religious "toleration" law enacted by a colony, *6188*

1650

Dog domestically bred, *2601*
Expedition of Englishmen to cross the Allegheny Mountains, *6029*
Iron exportation, *1915*
Lead coffins, *2293*
Livestock pounds for stray animals, *1567*

1651

Royal navigation act affecting the American colonies, *2062*

1652

Coins made in colonial America, *4002*
Colonial act of defiance against the King of England, *3447*
Slavery emancipation law enacted by a colony, *6114*
Traffic law enacted by a colony, *8175*
Water supply system built for a city, *7399*

1653

Colonial provision for the care of orphans and widows, *2172*
Library bequeathed to the public, *2994*

1654

Fire engine, *7312*
History of New England, *7466*
Jews to arrive in America, *6030*
Orphanage, *2173*
Toll bridge, *3228*

1655

Jewish congregation, *6190*

1656

Ban on Quakers enacted by a colony, *6192*
Book intended for circulation in the English colonies, *1063*
Jewish cemetery, *2294*
Jury composed of women, *3700*
Physician who was Jewish, *5011*
Quakers to arrive in America, *6191*
Surgeon appointed by a colony, *5097*

1657

Autopsy with verdict of a coroner's jury, *2295*
College student to work his way through college, *2689*
Jew to win full citizenship, *6031*
Shoe measuring stick, *2229*
Stone pavement, *3403*

1658

Police force, *7353*

1659

Colonial law banning Christmas, *2485*
Fire department established by a city, *7313*
Quakers executed for their religious beliefs, *6193*

1660

Church for Native Americans in New England, *6194*
Quaker annual meeting, *6195*

1661

Bible printed in America, *6339*
Colonial laws making slavery lifelong and hereditary, *6115*
Evening school for working children, *2891*

1662

Book auction, *4428*
Colonial badges issued to friendly Native Americans, *6032*
Lime, *3369*

1663

Colonial charter of religious freedom for all faiths, *6196*
Hard-surfaced road, *3404*
Labor protest in a colony, *7096*

1664

Bookbinder, *4429*
Naturalization act in the American colonies, *6033*

1665

Book privately printed, *4430*
College graduate who was Native American, *2690*
Horse race run on a regular basis, *7788*
Library appropriation approved by a Town Meeting, *2995*
Mayor of New York City, *3509*
Theatrical performance, *1411*

1666

Financial "corner," *1702*
Native American grammar, *3170*

1667

Cyclone of record, *5899*

1669

Fire chief, *7314*
History of New England published in New England, *7466*
Primer in a Native American dialect, *3171*
Rebellion by colonists against an English governor, *5638*
Woodcut, *1013*

1670

Native American preacher of Christianity, *6197*
Self-portrait, *1014*
Swiss settlement in America, *6034*

1671

Seventh Day Baptist Church, *6198*

1672

Colonial copyright law, *3974*
Postal route between cities, *4654*
Tax on Britain's American colonists without their consent, *4400*

1673

Coal, *6575*
Colonial governor who was born in America, *4372*

1674

Horse racing ban by a colony, *7789*

1675

Catholic holy orders, *6199*
Commercial corporation, *1470*

1676

Colonial law for the maintenance of an insane patient, *7233*
Court-martial in a colony, *5548*
Fire of serious consequence, *7315*
Poetry collection by an American poet who was a man, *1064*
Prison, *6988*
Quaker meeting house, *6200*

1677

Map made in America to be published in a book, *4476*
Medical pamphlet, *5278*

1678

Irish to arrive in America, *6035*

1679

Great Lakes vessel, *8404*
Labadist community, *6201*
Price regulation agreement by colonists, *1471*

1681

Shorthand account of a trial, *3949*

1682

Jewish synagogue, *6202*
Mason, *7193*
Tornado of record, *5900*
Town trust fund for education, *2892*

1683

Bible concordance, *6340*
Landscape architect, *5901*

Mennonites to arrive in America, *6203*
Science society, *6713*

1685

Judge to be impeached, *3701*

1686

Episcopal church organized in New England, *6204*

1687

Inheritance tax levied by a colony, *4401*
Knighthood conferred on a person born in America, *3918*
Law history book, *3950*

1688

Protest against slavery, *6116*

1689

Broadsides, *4488*
Schoolbook, *2893*

1690

Indigo crop, *1568*
Loan by a colony, *1756*
Newspaper published in the British colonies, *4489*
Newspaper publisher, *4588*
Paper mill, *2006*
Paper money, *4003*
Play of note written by an American, *1412*
Theological treatise, *6341*
Watermark in paper, *2007*

1691

Colonist hanged for treason, *6989*

1692

Parliamentary act to establish a colonial post office, *4655*
Patent medicine advertisement, *1516*

1693

Christian worship services organized by African-American slaves, *6205*
College charter granted by the Crown, *2691*
Police uniforms, *7354*

1694

Lutheran services in English, *6206*
Rosicrucian Order lodge, *6207*
Volcanic eruption for which a date can be estimated, *5902*

1695

Workers' compensation agreement, *7097*
Worsted mill for making wool yarn, *2109*

1696

Lending library, *2996*
Printer who was a woman, *2008*

1697

Book catalog of a college, *2692*
Fire department to be paid, *7316*
Library classification scheme, *2997*
Settler heroine publicly rewarded, *6036*
Stone arch bridge, *3229*

1698

Publicly supported lending library, *2998*
Road map for public use, *4477*
Statehouse, *3448*

1700

Organs, *1287*

1701

Engraving of any artistic merit, *1015*

1702

Cross-dresser of note, *7430*

1703

Business manual, *3172*
Lutheran pastor ordained in American, *6183*
Mardi Gras, *2486*

1704

Mason born in America, *7193*
Newspaper advertisement, *1517*
Newspaper that was successful, *4490*

1705

Copper mine, *3370*
Miniature book, *4431*
Poem to be printed in a newspaper, *1065*
Presbyterian presbytery, *6208*

1706

Customhouse, *2063*

1707

Pastelist, *1016*

1708

Mennonite meetinghouse, *6209*

1709

Home for mentally ill patients, *5100*
Latin grammar, *3173*

1710

Book on agriculture, *1569*
Community forest, *5973*

1711

Sperm whale captured at sea, *1793*

1712

Calico printery, *2110*
Cornmeal machine for grinding maize, *2318*
Rebellion of African-American slaves in a major city, *6117*

1713

Book auction catalog, *4432*
Paleontology report, *6754*

1714

Blackboards for use in schools, *2894*
Play written in America that was printed, *1413*
Schooner built in America, *8405*
Scientist from America elected to the Royal Society of London, *6754*

1715

Book of Common Prayer in the Mohawk language, *6342*
English patent granted to a resident of America, *3986*
Whaling expedition, *1794*

1716

Botanical report on plant hybridization, *6755*
Lighthouse, *7336*
Lion exhibited to the public, *1346*

1717

Printed book auction catalog, *4433*

1718

Theater, *1414*

1719

Arithmetic book printed in America, *6756*
Aurora borealis display, *6485*
Brethren, *6210*
Potatoes to be cultivated, *1570*

1720

Master's degree recipient who was Jewish, *2705*
School for Native Americans to be permanently established, *2895*

1721

Camel exhibited to the public, *1347*
Editorial apology for false news to appear in a newspaper, *4491*
Fire insurance agent, *1974*
Inoculation against smallpox using material from human smallpox pustules, *5148*
Music book printed with bars, *1210*
Painter to obtain a public commission, *1017*
Vocal instruction book, *1211*

1722

Divinity professor at a college, *2693*

1723

Hydrotherapy book, *5279*
Library catalog in book form, *2999*

1724

Congregation of Brethren, *6210*
English grammar by an American, *3174*
Levees, *3349*
Swimmer of note, *7907*

1725

Insurance book, *1949*
Mass scalping of Native Americans by colonists, *5639*
Reformed Church meeting, *6211*

1726

Book of folio size, *4434*
Catalog of theological and biblical literature, *6343*

1727

Catholic convent, *6213*
Catholic nuns, *6212*
Drought of record, *5903*
Mezzotint engraving, *1018*
School for girls, *2896*

1741

American "Robin Hood," *6926*
Magazine published in America, *4606*
Moravian bishop, *6219*
Strike by workers, *7098*

1742

Cookbook published in America, *2319*
Heating stove, *2536*
School for Protestant girls, *2897*

1743

Automaton, *1349*
Bible printed in German, *6344*
Newspaper advertisement across two columns, *1520*
Planetarium built in America, *6365*
Religious magazine, *6345*
Science society of importance, *6713*

1744

Orchestra, *1214*

1745

Carillon, *1290*
Knighthood conferred on a soldier born in America, *3919*
Library building, *3001*
Stereotype printing, *2031*
Tomatoes eaten in America, *1573*

1746

College charter granted by a governor, *2696*
Iron rolling mill, *1918*
Poetry collection by an African-American writer, *1068*
Slovak settler in America, *6037*

1747

State organization of lawyers, *3951*
Textbook printed in America, *2898*

1748

Candle factory for making spermaceti candles, *2537*
Spa at a mineral spring, *5386*

1749

Electric cooking experiment, *6534*
Lightning rod, *7317*
Waxworks, *1350*

1750

Book on teaching methodology, *2899*
Colonial settlement west of the Allegheny Mountains, *6038*
Dissection report, *5281*
Neoclassical building, *3258*
Opera performed by a professional visiting troupe, *1314*
Orchestra in a theater, *1215*
Play by William Shakespeare, *1417*
Publicist for a theater company, *1418*

1751

Academy, *2697*
Benefit performance of a play, *1419*
Cricket match, *7628*
Manual training courses offered in a school, *2900*
Monkey trained to perform, *1351*
Novel by a writer born in America, *1069*
Revolving library, *3002*
Spanish grammar, *3176*
Sugar cane, *1574*

1752

Catholic nun born in the United States, *6215*
Hospital, *5097*
Lightning demonstration, *6487*
Philosophy book printed in America, *1070*

1753

Arbitration law, *1472*
Arctic expedition to seek the Northwest Passage, *6639*
Conestoga wagon, *8177*
Copley Medal awarded to an American, *6893*

1754

Battle in the French and Indian War, *5641*
Bloodshed in the French and Indian War, *5640*
Clock to strike the hours, *2624*
Colonial congress, *3547*
German instruction at a college, *2698*
Newspaper cartoon, *4574*
Pharmacist to fill prescriptions other than his own, *5014*
Trombone, *1291*

1755

Beef export, *2320*
Cattle to be exported, *1575*
Historical print engraved in America, *1020*
Law instruction at a college, *2699*

Patriotic song to achieve national popularity, *1332*
Steam engine for industrial use, *1846*
Water pumping plant, *7400*

1756

Intercity stagecoach service, *8178*
Woman whose vote was recorded, *3760*

1757

Street-sweeping service, *7401*
Utilization of Niagara Falls waterpower for industrial purposes, *6632*

1758

Botanist of note who was a woman, *6655*
Reservation for Native Americans established by a state, *6039*

1759

Comb factory, *2457*
Composer born in America, *1216*
Life insurance company, *1988*
Musical instrument dealer, *1217*
Secular song by a composer born in America, *1333*

1760

Agricultural book that was distinctly American, *1576*
Knighthood conferred on American soil, *3920*
Medical licensing law enacted by a city, *5015*
Rocking chair, *2538*

1761

Life insurance policy, *1988*
Milestones between cities, *3512*
Music book by an author born in America, *1218*
Pile bridge, *3230*
Published literary work by an African-American, *1071*
Scientific expedition sponsored by a colony, *6366*
Slide rule book, *6760*
Trade monopoly among manufacturers, *1469*
Venetian blinds, *2539*

1762

Anatomy lectures for medical students, *3041*
Caricature, *1021*
Missionary society organized in the English colonies, *6222*
Saint Patrick's Day parade, *1352*

1763

Germ warfare, *5838*
Local political machine, *3513*
Steamboat, *8406*

1764

Cotton crop exported, *1577*
Greenhouse, *1578*
Inclined railroad, *8298*
Methodist meetinghouse, *6223*
Methodist Society in America, *6224*

1765

Chocolate mill, *2321*
College literary society, *2700*
Direct tax on Britain's American colonists without their consent, *4402*
English grammar by an American published in America, *3177*
Fire in a mine, *6576*
Medical college, *3042*
Medical education book, *5282*

1766

Fox hunting club, *7822*
Gem-cutting machine, *3371*
Jewish prayer book, *6346*
Methodist Society in continuous existence in America, *6224*
Protest by college students, *2701*
Theater building of brick construction, *1420*
United Brethren in Christ meeting, *6225*

1767

Comic opera written for the American stage, *1315*
Greek settlement, *6040*
Midwifery professor at a college, *3043*
Music book printed from type, *1219*
Opera libretto published in America, *1315*
President born after the death of his father, *4240*

1768

Arbitration tribunal, *1473*
Book advocating spelling reform, *2901*
Botany professor at a college, *2702*
Commercial artist, *1022*
Cottonseed oil, *2322*
Fire insurance company to receive a charter, *1976*
Independent civil government in America, *3449*
Methodist meetinghouse in continuous use, *6223*

1768—*continued*

Mustard, *2323*
Patriotic song by an American, *1334*
Physician to receive a Bachelor of Medicine degree, *3044*
Sieve, *2540*

1769

Astronomer to acquire international fame, *6367*
Catholic mission in California, *6226*
Chemistry professor at a college, *2703*
Church bells, *1292*
Harpsichord, *1293*
History of medicine, *5283*
Medical ethics book, *5284*
Observatory, *6368*
Summer home, *2524*
Type foundry, *2032*

1770

Americans killed by British soldiers in the Revolution, *5644*
Attack on British soldiers by civilians in the Revolution, *5642*
Book of music by a composer born in America, *1220*
Chamber of Commerce, *1474*
Chemistry textbook, *6761*
Child to be killed in the Revolution, *5643*
College to confer medals as prizes, *2704*
Engraving to achieve popularity, *1023*
Jewish physician to head an asylum for the mentally ill, *5011*
Physician to receive an M.D. degree, *3044*
Rhubarb, *1579*

1771

Dwarf exhibited as a theatrical attraction, *1354*
Genealogy of an American family, *7467*
Horseriding exhibition, *1353*
Town named for George Washington, *3514*

1772

Medical licensing law enacted by a colony, *5016*
Naval attack in the Revolutionary War, *5645*
Protestant church west of of the Alleghenies, *6227*
Shot fired by an American combatant to wound a British combatant in the conflict over independence, *5646*
Trade directory, *1475*
Written constitution adopted by a community of American-born freemen, *3457*

1773

Baptist churches for African-Americans, *6228*
Hospital for insane patients established by a colony, *5098*
Public museum, *3133*
Schoolhouse west of the Alleghenies, *6227*

1774

College graduate who was Jewish, *2705*
Continental Congress assembly to be opened with prayer, *3550*
Continental Congress session, *3548*
Declaration of independence by citizens of an American colony, *3458*
Declaration of rights, *3459*
Embargo act of the Continental Congress, *2064*
Ground attack in the Revolutionary War, *5648*
Military organization formed to oppose the British, *5647*
Music printed in a magazine, *1221*
President of the Continental Congress, *3549*
Price sheet for commodities, *1521*
Slave importation ban enacted by a colony, *6118*
Steel shovel, *2637*
Universalist church services, *6229*
Work of satirical fiction, *1072*

1775

Abolition organization, *6119*
American capture of a British fort in the Revolutionary War, *5650*
American warship named after a foreigner, *5573*
American woman to be killed in action, *5654*
Architecture book printed in America, *3218*
Army chief engineer, *5434*
Army engineering department, *5411*
Battle in the Revolutionary War, *5649*
Book made with American paper, ink, and type, *4437*
Commander-in-chief of the Continental Navy, *5594*
Free trade policy by the federal government, *4403*
General of the Continental Army, *5433*
Government intelligence agency, *3872*
Mail franking privilege, *4658*
Marines, *5560*
Mason who was African-American, *7196*
Military field strategy manual, *5410*

National day of prayer, *2487*
Naval battle in the Revolutionary War, *5651*
Navy doctor, *5192*
Navy fleet, *5572*
Novel by an American writer to be translated into a foreign language, *1073*
Officer of marines, *5560*
Paper money issued by the Continental Congress, *4005*
Paymaster general of the Continental Army, *5435*
Postmaster general under the Continental Congress, *4657*
Postmaster who was a woman, *4656*
Quartermaster of the Continental Army, *5437*
State constitution, *3460*
Surgeon general of the Continental Army, *5436*
Surgery manual, *5285*
Volunteer detachment in the Revolutionary War, *5652*
Warship to receive definite orders to attack the enemy, *5653*

1776

American executed as a spy, *5662*
American flag saluted by a foreigner, *3470*
American prisoners of war, *5655*
American soldier to commit treason, *5663*
Blockade of enemy ships in the Revolutionary War, *5670*
Brevet commission in the Army, *5438*
Capture of an enemy ship in enemy waters, *5664*
Capture of an enemy warship by a commissioned American naval officer, *5657*
Cocktail, *2324*
Congressional vote on a declaration of independence, *3462*
Declaration of independence by a colonial government, *3461*
Design for the Great Seal of the United States, *3463*
Election law enacted by a colony granting voting rights to women, *3761*
Engineering book, *6762*
Execution by the Army, *5549*
Identification of human remains using dental evidence, *2296*
Independent government in an American colony, *3450*
Interfaith charity organization, *7197*
Invisible ink, *2673*
Jewish soldier killed in the Revolutionary War, *5658*
Land grant to deserters from the British Army during the Revolutionary War, *5660*
Loan for war purposes, *1757*
Major battle lost by American forces, *5661*
Marine engagement in battle, *5656*
Medal awarded by the Continental Congress, *3551*
Military intelligence unit, *5659*
Naval ship of the line, *8465*
Navy uniforms, *5574*
Newspaper to publish the Declaration of Independence, *3466*
Pension law enacted by Congress, *7099*
Price regulation law enacted by a colony, *1476*
Printing of the Declaration of Independence, *3465*
Public reading of the Declaration of Independence, *3467*
Publication of the Declaration of Independence in another language, *3468*
Scholastic fraternity at a college, *2706*
Shaker religious community, *6230*
Signer of the Declaration of Independence, *3464*
Submarine built for use in war, *8508*
Use of the name United States instead of United Colonies, *3469*

1777

American flag displayed on a man-of-war, *3472*
American flag flown in battle, *3473*
American flag on the high seas, *3474*
American flag saluted by a foreign nation, *3475*
American flag to represent the United States, *3471*
Army chaplain killed in action, *5665*
Articles of Confederation, *3476*
Catholic funeral attended by the Continental Congress, *6231*
Christmas tree displayed in the United States, *2488*
Election law enacted by a state to grant universal voting rights to freemen, *3762*
Foreign nation to recognize the independence of the United States, *3873*
Government expert on codes and ciphers, *5666*
Laws of entail and primogeniture to be abolished by a state, *3952*
Lottery held by the Continental Congress, *1799*
Major American victory in the Revolutionary War, *5668*
Marine officer killed in service, *5561*
Mine barrage, *5839*
Nails, *2638*
National day of thanksgiving, *2489*

1777—*continued*

Navy recruiting campaign, *5575*
Slavery emancipation law enacted by a state, *6120*
Treaty between states after the Declaration of Independence, *4336*
Warship captured overseas, *5667*

1778

Alliance between the United States and another country, *3874*
American naval victory in British waters during the Revolutionary War, *5669*
Arbitration law enacted by a state, *1477*
Blockade of enemy ships in the Revolutionary War that was effective, *5670*
Court-martial by the Army, *5550*
Minister plenipotentiary, *3877*
Pharmacopoeia, *5286*
Representative of a foreign country to the United States, *3876*
Revolutionary War conflict in which American and British troops met on equal terms, *5671*
Secret service established in a colony, *7355*
State to ratify the Articles of Confederation, *3476*
Town named for Benjamin Franklin, *3515*
Treaties entered into by the federal government, *3875*
Treaty entered into by the federal government with Native American tribes, *6041*
War song, *1335*

1779

Army uniform, *5413*
City founded by an African-American pioneer, *3516*
College to use the honor system during examinations, *2707*
College with an elective system of study, *2708*
Law school at a college, *2711*
Medal awarded by the Continental Congress to a foreigner, *3552*
Military drill manual, *5412*
Military pension awarded to a disabled soldier who was a woman, *5618*
Naval hero, *5673*
Oyster propagation, *1580*
Revolutionary War bayonet charge, *5672*
School of modern languages at a college, *2709*
Surfing in Hawaii, *7958*
University legally designated as such, *2710*

1780

American imprisoned in the Tower of London as an enemy agent, *5674*
Astronomical expedition to record an eclipse of the sun, *6369*
Conscientious objectors, *5554*
Hat factory, *2231*
National arts and sciences organization, *7198*
Seal of a military department of the federal government, *3477*
State seal, *4337*
Town named for George Washington to be incorporated, *3514*

1781

Bank chartered by Congress, *1715*
Fireworks display by a city on the Fourth of July, *1345*
Historical hoaxes, *7468*
Independence Day, *2490*
Slave to be emancipated by a court, *6121*
State medical society, *5212*

1782

Bible printed in English, *6347*
Dentist, *5077*
Die for the Great Seal of the United States, *3478*
Fustians, everlastings, and coating, *2112*
Impression made by the Great Seal of the United States, *3480*
Keeper of the Great Seal of the United States, *3479*
Nautical almanac, *8407*
Parochial school for Catholic children, *2886*
President born an American citizen, *4241*

1783

Book to be afforded copyright protection, *3975*
Clock that was self-winding, *2625*
College named after an American president, *2712*
Copyright law enacted by a state, *3976*
Daily newspaper, *4494*
Map of the United States, *4479*
Physician who was African-American, *5017*
Purple Heart, *5500*
Revolutionary War national veterans' organization, *5619*
Salute fired by Great Britain in honor of an officer of the United States, *3878*
Sports book, *7823*
Territory owned by the federal government, *6042*
Travel writer, *1074*

Treaty between the federal government and a nation with which it had been at war, *3879*

1784

American woman to become a countess, *3921*
Botanic expedition, *6656*
Citizenship conferred by special grant, *6044*
Episcopal bishop, *6233*
French grammar, *3178*
French newspaper, *4552*
Geography book, *6763*
Hailstone shower of record that was fatal, *5904*
Hostage crisis involving a foreign government, *3880*
Labor union to nominate its own political candidates, *7100*
Law school operated privately, *3191*
Masonic lodge of African-Americans, *7196*
Methodist bishop, *6234*
Methodist minister who was African-American, *6232*
Motorboat, *8408*
Political economy course at a college, *2713*
Professional American dancer, *1047*
Professional writer who was a woman, *1075*
Russian settlement, *6043*
Seed business, *1581*
State denied admission into the Union, *4338*
Tethered balloon flight, *7993*
Theology school, *2714*
Trading ship sent to China, *8525*

1785

Agriculture society, *1582*
Bifocal eyeglasses, *5264*
Botany book by an American-born author, *6764*
City college, *2716*
City directory, *3517*
College founded as a Methodist institution, *2717*
Congregational Church minister who was African-American, *6235*
Copper cents minted by a state, *4006*
Decimal system of money, *4007*
Episcopal catechism, *6348*
Geographer of the United States, *6488*
Land set-aside for schools authorized by the Continental Congress, *2902*
Marble quarry, *3372*
Minister plenipotentiary appointed after independence, *3877*
Minister to Great Britain, *3881*
Missionary to the Native Americans who was African-American, *6237*
Mule born in the United States, *1583*
Porcelain teeth, *5078*
Sale of federal land authorized by Congress, *6045*
State university to be chartered, *2715*
Street gangs, *6927*
Survey of public lands, *6046*
Toll road, *3405*
Treaty entered into by the federal government after independence, *3882*
Unitarian church, *6236*
Unitarian prayer book, *6349*

1786

Coin to use E pluribus unum as a motto, *4008*
Consul, *3883*
Golf players' club, *7748*
Ice cream to be made commercially, *2325*
Illustrations of both sides of the Great Seal of the United States, *3481*
Independent dispensary to furnish free medicine to the needy, *5099*
Lutheran hymnbook in German, *6353*
Mineralogy instruction at a college, *2718*
Music magazine, *1222*
Private museum, *3134*
Rebellion against the federal government, *5675*
Reservation for Native Americans established by the federal government, *6047*
Spinning jenny for cotton, *2113*
Strike benefit by a union, *7101*
Textile machine, *2114*

1787

Alarm clock, *2626*
Constitution of the United States, *3483*
Federalist Paper, *3486*
Lifesaving service for distressed mariners, *7337*
Methodist churches for African-Americans, *6238*
Newspaper to publish the Constitution, *3484*
Play by an American writer to be successfully presented by an established company, *1422*
Playwright to write professionally, *1421*
Printed copies of the Constitution, *3482*
Prison reform society, *6990*
Ship to carry the American flag around the world, *3485*
Slavery ban enacted for a territory of the United States, *6122*
Songbook of secular songs, *1223*
State to ratify the federal Constitution, *3487*
Steamboat to carry a man, *8409*
Territorial governor, *6042*

1787—*continued*

Window glass factory, *3353*

1788

Algebra book by an American-born author, *6765*
Book of secular songs by an American-born composer, *1216*
Coins issued by the United States, *4009*
Cotton mill, *2117*
Dictionary published in the United States, *3179*
Pocket dictionary, *3180*
Presidential election, *3793*
Sailcloth factory, *2115*
Senate of the United States Congress, *3642*
Ship built on the Pacific coast, *8411*
Songbook of secular songs by an American-born composer, *1224*
Steamboat patent, *8410*
Worsted mill operated by waterpower, *2116*

1789

Anatomy lectures for the public, *3041*
Army organization under the Constitution, *5414*
Attorney general of the United States, *4170*
Attorney of the United States, *3703*
Bibliography of Americana in English, *1076*
Book of road maps, *4480*
Bourbon whiskey, *2326*
Cabinet, *4168*
Catholic Bible in English, *6352*
Catholic diocese, *6239*
Catholic magazine, *6350*
Children's magazine, *2174*
Clerk of the House of Representatives, *3584*
College founded as a Catholic institution, *2719*
Comb made of ivory, *2458*
Congressional act, *3558*
Congressional act declared unconstitutional by the Supreme Court, *3559*
Congressional chaplain, *3557*
Congressional committee, *3586*
Congressional representative appointed to a presidential cabinet, *3581*
Congressional representative who was Catholic, *3582*
Constitutional amendments to fail the ratification process, *3489*
Contact between the president and the Congress, *3556*
Creation of federal courts, *3702*
Department of State, *4171*
Department of the Treasury, *4169*
Department of War, *4172*
Federal law enforcement agency, *3838*
Federal marshals, *7356*
First Lady, *4215*
Flour mill, *2327*
House of Representatives election that was contested, *3587*
Inaugural ball, *4115*
Insurance law treatise, *3953*
Joint meeting of the Senate and the House of Representatives, *3555*
Land office, *6048*
Law report, *3954*
Lighthouse built after American independence, *7338*
Loan to the United States, *1758*
Meeting place of Congress, *3553*
Morgan horse, *8179*
Navigation act enacted by Congress, *2065*
Novel by an American writer to be published in America, *1077*
Pensions paid by the federal government, *7102*
Pharmacy professorship at a college, *3045*
Political newspaper of national importance, *4492*
Postmaster general of the United States, *4659*
President elected under the Constitution, *4113*
President to receive the unanimous vote of the presidential electors, *3794*
President to tour the country, *4311*
Presidential appointment, *4116*
Presidential inauguration, *4114*
Presidential mansion, *4323*
Presidential proclamation of a national day of thanksgiving, *2489*
Publisher of denominational religious books, *6351*
Seal of a nonmilitary department of the federal government, *3488*
Secretary of the Senate, *3647*
Secretary of the treasury, *4169*
Senate journal, *3643*
Senate president pro tempore, *3646*
Senate session at which there was a quorum, *3645*
Senator who was Catholic, *3644*
Session of Congress, *3554*
Session of the House of Representatives, *3583*
Session of the House of Representatives at which there was a quorum, *3583*
Session of the Senate, *3645*
Speaker of the House, *3585*
Supreme Court chief justice, *3731*
Tariff legislation enacted by Congress, *4404*

1792—*continued*

Cremation, *2297*
Designs for the building of the Capitol, *3561*
Draft of civilians by Congress, *5555*
Eastern Orthodox church, *6242*
Episcopal bishop consecrated in America, *6233*
Exploration by ship of the mouth of the Columbia River, *6050*
Gold price fixed by Congress, *4012*
Industrial park, *3259*
Life insurance offered by a general insurance company, *1989*
Maternity book for women, *2175*
Metal purchased for coinage, *4015*
Minister plenipotentiary to Great Britain, *3881*
Mint of the United States, *4014*
Minting of coins by the federal government, *4013*
Monument to Christopher Columbus, *7168*
Postal service law enacted by Congress, *4660*
Presidential veto of a congressional bill, *4119*
Stock exchange, *1767*
Woman appointed postmaster after independence, *4656*

1793

Alfalfa, *1586*
Anthology of American literature, *1078*
Broadcloth, *2119*
Canal for boat transportation, *3322*
Catholic African-Americans, *6243*
Catholic priest, *6244*
Child labor in a factory, *7103*
Coins struck by the United States Mint to enter circulation, *4018*
Cotton thread, *2611*
Director of the U.S. Mint, *4017*
Emergency first aid organization, *7339*
Fugitive slave law enacted by Congress, *6123*
Neutrality proclamation by the federal government, *3884*
Patent granted to an inventor who was a woman, *3990*
Road authorization by a state, *3407*
Senate election that was contested, *3652*
Senator to become a congressional representative, *3651*
Sulfuric acid, *1881*
Supreme Court nominee who was rejected by the Senate, *3735*
Untethered balloon flight, *7994*
Wool carding machine, *2120*

1794

Arsenal of the federal government, *5677*
Ball bearing commercial installation, *3330*
Building built to serve as a hotel, *1809*
Cesarean operation, *5338*
Changes in the American flag to be authorized by Congress, *3491*
College that was nondenominational, *2722*
Commodore in the Navy, *5596*
Death penalty ban by a state, *6992*
Dentistry book, *5289*
Extradition treaty with a foreign country, *3886*
Federal law officer killed in the line of duty, *7357*
Fiction best-seller, *1079*
French daily newspaper, *4552*
Jewelers' supply house, *3373*
Medical record of an epidemic, *5092*
Methodist church for African-Americans in the North, *6238*
Neutrality regulation enacted by Congress that governed the actions of citizens, *3885*
Opera of a serious nature, *1316*
Presidential commission, *4120*
Professional illustrator, *1025*
Rivet production, *3329*
Silver deposit for coinage, *4019*
Textile machinery patent, *2121*
Tobacco tax enacted by Congress, *7058*
Warship builder, *5577*

1795

American gazetteer, *3182*
Belt conveyor system, *1848*
Cabinet member to serve in two or more cabinet posts, *4173*
Catholic priest trained in the United States, *6244*
English grammar instruction at a college, *2723*
Federal government employees who were women, *3841*
Gold bullion deposit for coinage, *4020*
Health board established by a city, *7234*
Legal treatise published in the United States, *3957*
Lutheran hymnbook, *6353*
Macadam road, *3408*
Muskets, *5840*
Presidential amnesty issued to rebellious citizens, *4121*
Professional portrait painter who was African-American, *1026*
Road appropriation of a specific sum by a state, *3409*

State university to open, *2715*
Steam engine for industrial use that was practical, *1849*
Supreme Court chief justice whose nomination was not confirmed, *3736*

1796

Architect and engineer who worked professionally, *3219*
Coast survey book, *5905*
Cookbook by an American author, *2330*
Dollar marks, *2033*
Electoral vote cast contrary to instructions, *3795*
Elephant to be exhibited, *1357*
Federal law exempting debtors from prison, *6993*
Gaslights for display, *1358*
Nail cutting and heading machine, *2639*
Opera by an American composer, *1317*
Passport, *6053*
Patented pills, *5233*
Pediatrics monograph, *5290*
Protection of Native American hunting grounds authorized by Congress, *6052*
Sale of federal land to an individual, *6051*
Senators elected but not seated, *3653*
Ship from the Atlantic coast to anchor in a California port, *8526*
Steam baths for curing disease, *5387*
Sunday newspaper, *4496*
Suspension bridge, *3232*
Unitarian church identified as such in its name, *6236*

1797

Architecture book distinctly American, *3220*
Chemistry laboratory manual, *6766*
Congressional representative to serve before his 25th birthday, *3591*
Cryptography chart, *4481*
Epidemiologist, *7235*
Frigate, *8466*
Medical journal, *5291*
Plow patent, *1587*
President whose son became president, *4242*
Presidential election in which more than one candidate declared for the presidency, *3796*
Special session of Congress, *3563*

1798

Army lieutenant general, *5439*
Bank robbery, *6928*
Brawl in the House of Representatives, *3592*
Department of the Navy, *4174*
Deportation of aliens authorized by Congress, *6055*
Encyclopedia printed in the United States, *3183*
Federal law intended to intimidate the press, *4497*
Health service established by the federal government, *7236*
Hymnbook with music, *6354*
Immigration law enacted by Congress, *6054*
Marine band, *5562*
Marine Corps major, *5560*
Naval surgeon, *5193*
Navy yard, *5578*
Nurses' training, *3046*
Prize money awarded by the Navy, *5579*
Prosecution under the Sedition Act, *4498*
Secretary of the Navy, *4174*
State nullification proceedings to obstruct federal legislation, *4340*
Straw hats, *2233*
Tax levied by Congress directly on the states, *4406*
Vineyard, *1588*
Writer whose livelihood was obtained exclusively by writing, *1080*

1799

Comb-cutting machine, *2459*
Congressional eulogy for a president, *4243*
Craft union contract, *7104*
Education association, *2903*
Gold nugget, *3374*
Government contract authorized by Congress for pistols, *5841*
Ice shipped commercially, *2331*
Insurance regulation enacted by a state, *1950*
Italian instruction at a college, *2724*
Meteor shower on record, *6384*
Optical shop, *2082*
Printed ballot, *3764*
Quack doctor of note, *5018*
Quarantine law enacted by Congress, *7237*
Semaphore telegraph system, *4840*
Senator to be expelled, *3654*
Ship constructed by the federal government, *8467*
Shipbuilding law enacted by Congress, *5580*
Standardization of weights and measures for customs, *2067*
Supreme Court chief justice who had been a congressional representative, *3737*
Supreme Court decision in a matter between states, *3738*
Swedenborgian or New Church temple, *6245*
Tax rebellion, *4407*
Territorial legislature, *6042*

Land grant university, *2726*
Marine Corps commando raid, *5563*
Members of the U.S. armed forces to die in combat on an overseas mission, *5679*
Peace medals struck by the United States Mint, *4021*
Pontoon bridge, *3233*
Presidential candidate nominated at a caucus, *3797*
Presidential election in which candidates were nominated for the vice presidency, *3798*
Printer's ink, *2009*
Quids political faction, *4053*
State in the North to restrict the civil rights of African-Americans, *6124*
Steamboat with a twin-screw propeller, *8414*
Supreme Court justice to be impeached, *3741*
Transcontinental expedition to the Pacific coast, *6640*
Vice president who was nominated specifically for that office, *4300*

1805

American flag flown over conquered hostile territory, *3492*
American history book of importance whose author was a woman, *7470*
Art museum, *3135*
Boxer to win distinction in the ring, *7590*
Civil trial featuring celebrity lawyers, *3705*
Cryptography book, *4442*
Dry dock, *8415*
Ice exported, *2337*
Magic lantern book, *1360*
Pharmacopoeia prepared by a medical association, *5295*
Women's club, *7200*

1806

Child born in the White House, *4324*
Cider mill, *2338*
College magazine, *2727*
Dictionary of the English language compiled by an American, *3184*
Highway built by the federal government, *3411*
Pharmaceuticals book, *5296*
President who had participated in a duel, *4245*
Senator to serve in contravention to the age limit, *3655*
Soap manufacturer to render fats in his plant, *2208*
Town founded by a woman, *3519*

1807

Atheneum, *3007*
Coast survey, *6059*
College entrance requirement other than Greek, Latin, and arithmetic, *2728*
Embargo act enacted by Congress, *2068*
Evangelical Church conference, *6250*
Federal ban on the importation of African slaves, *6125*
Flint glass factory, *3354*
Former vice president to be arrested, *4301*
Glue factory, *1882*
Instruction for deaf students, *2904*
Lifeboat, *7340*
Meteorite whose landing was recorded, *6385*
Naval ship to surrender in peacetime, *5680*
Obstetrics book, *5297*
School for African-Americans in Washington, DC, *2905*
Soda water, *2339*
Steamboat to make regular trips, *8416*

1808

Bible society, *6251*
Bible translated into English in America, *6357*
Brushes, *2209*
Catholic archdiocese, *6239*
College orchestra, *1227*
Duel between representatives in Congress, *3594*
Law magazine, *3960*
Leather-splitting machine, *2122*
Medical book by a Navy medical officer, *5298*
Play about a Native American, *1424*
Trotting horse, *8180*

1809

Abdominal operation other than a cesarean section, *5339*
Catholic magazine in English, *6358*
Cricket club, *7629*
Disciples of Christ meeting, *6252*
First Lady to attend her husband's inauguration, *4217*
Geology book, *6767*
Gloves, *2235*
Hebrew dictionary, *3185*
Magazine containing a fashion plate, *4608*
Parochial school for Catholic children, *2886*
President born beyond the boundaries of the original 13 states, *4246*
Railroad for freight transportation, *8299*
Railroad track that was practical, *8381*
State law allowing married women to make wills, *7431*

1809—*continued*

Steamboat to make an ocean voyage, *8417*
Supreme Court decision establishing the power of the federal government, *3742*
Type specimen book from an American type foundry, *4443*
Vaccination program offered by a city, *5151*
Vice president to serve under two presidents, *4300*
Watchmaker, *2627*

1810

Agricultural journal, *1592*
Book on child-rearing, *2176*
Boxer of fame who was African-American, *7591*
Cattle fair, *1593*
Cigar factory, *7059*
English actor of note to perform in America, *1425*
Fire insurance joint-stock company, *1977*
Foreign missionary society, *6253*
Glass crystal chandelier, *2542*
History of printing, *4444*
Horse breeders' society, *7790*
Insurance company owned by African-Americans, *1952*
Leather tanning by the oil tan method, *2123*
Mailbox see-through locker, *4661*
Military dictionary, *5416*
Mineralogy journal, *6768*
Screw auger, *2642*
Screw factory, *2643*
Silk mill, *2124*
Supreme Court decision declaring a state law unconstitutional, *3743*
Vaccination law enacted by a state, *5152*

1811

Boat club, *7566*
Conscience fund, *6930*
Disciples of Christ church, *6252*
Magician of note, *1361*
Masonic magazine, *7201*
Naval battle in the War of 1812, *5681*
Naval hospital established by Congress, *5194*
Proposal in Congress that states should secede from the Union, *4341*
Quarterly magazine, *4609*
Senate filibuster, *3657*
Senator to be censured, *3656*
Settlers to reach the Pacific coast, *6060*
Steam-propelled ferryboat, *8419*
Steamboat to sail down the Mississippi, *8418*
Year in which exports exceeded imports, *2069*

1812

American flag flown over a schoolhouse, *3493*
Anthracite coal used commercially, *6578*
Canning book, *2340*
Capture of a British frigate in the War of 1812, *5684*
Comic history of the United States, *7471*
Drug mill, *5234*
Land office established by Congress, *6061*
Life insurance commercial company, *1988*
Marine who was a woman, *5564*
National historical society, *7472*
Naval action of importance in the War of 1812, *5682*
Naval battle in the War of 1812 that took place after war was declared, *5681*
Navy officer to abolish corporal punishment on his ship, *5597*
Pencil factory, *2674*
Prisoners captured in the War of 1812, *5683*
Psychiatry book, *5299*
Russian settlement in the continental United States, *6043*
Treasury notes bearing interest, *1769*
Vice president to die in office, *4302*
Vice presidential candidate to decline the nomination, *3799*
War bond issued by the federal government, *1768*
Wedding in the White House, *4325*
West Point graduate killed in action, *3099*

1813

African Methodist church, *6254*
Capitalized corporation formed in the United States, *1480*
Chemistry magazine, *6769*
Cotton mill entirely powered by water, *2125*
Craps, *1800*
Defeat of a British naval squadron in the War of 1812, *5685*
Factory standardization to federal government specification, *3260*
Gas streetlights, *7402*
Globe factory, *4482*
Hospital for insane patients operated privately, *5100*
Jewish diplomat, *3894*
Mail delivery by steamboat, *4662*
Medical jurisprudence course at a college, *3047*
Religious weekly newspaper, *4499*
State superintendent of schools, *2906*
Stereotype printing that was successful, *2031*
Stereotyped book, *4445*

Supreme Court decision reversing the ruling of a state supreme court, *3744*
Surgeon general of the Army, *5436*
Vaccination law enacted by Congress, *5153*
Vice president who had served in the House of Representatives, *4303*

1814

Bible in Hebrew, *6359*
Building in all-Gothic architecture, *3261*
Circular saw, *2644*
Museum especially constructed as a museum and art gallery, *3136*
News agency, *4500*
President to face enemy gunfire while in office, *4126*
School for the higher education of women, *2907*
Secession convention during the War of 1812, *4342*
Star-Spangled Banner, *3494*

1815

First Lady to write her autobiography, *4218*
Monument to George Washington, *7169*
Music festival, *1228*
Naval officers' training school, *3100*
Pamphlet produced from a steel plate engraving, *4446*
Peace society, *7202*
Railroad charter granted by a state, *8300*
School for deaf students, *2908*
Steam-propelled frigate, *8468*
Varnish manufacturer, *1883*

1816

African Methodist Episcopal bishop, *6255*
Boiler plates, *1884*
Book on Americanisms, *1082*
Double-deck steamboat, *8421*
Mineralogy textbook, *6770*
National bible society, *6256*
National cemetery, *2298*
Printing press invented in the United States, *2034*
Savings bank, *1717*
Savings bank to receive money on deposit, *1718*
Steamboat on the Great Lakes, *8422*
Suspension bridge of iron wire, *3234*
Tariff passed by Congress for protection, *4408*
Theology school that was nonsectarian, *2729*
Transatlantic passenger line, *8420*

1817

Abolition newspaper, *4501*
African Methodist Episcopal preacher who was a woman, *6257*
American to earn a Ph.D., *2730*
Canal of importance, *3323*
Church built by the Evangelical Church, *6250*
Eye infirmary, *5101*
Gas streetlights throughout a city, *7403*
Iron mill to puddle and roll iron, *1922*
Law school at a college to be permanently organized, *2711*
Paper made by machine, *2010*
Prayers in sign language, *6258*
School for deaf students to be established on a permanent basis, *2909*
Showboat theater, *1426*
Sword swallower, *1362*
Therapeutics book, *5300*
Trust, *1481*

1818

Army medical corps, *5195*
Band leader of renown, *1229*
Chair factory, *2543*
Clinical instruction and bedside demonstration, *3048*
Composer who was African-American, *1230*
Education magazine, *2910*
Geology textbook, *6771*
Horticulture society, *1594*
Hygiene lectures at a college, *3049*
Marine insurance law enacted by a state, *1953*
Melons and cantaloupes, *1595*
Natural cement rock, *3331*
Oil well, *6579*
Oratorio performance, *1231*
Science journal, *6772*
Shoe peg, *2236*
Theology school graduate who was African-American, *2731*

1819

Agricultural journal to attain prominence, *1592*
Angle iron, *3332*
Bicycle patent, *7638*
Bicycles, *7637*
Canning of food, *2341*
Civil engineering course at a college, *2732*
Fire patrol to protect property during fires, *7319*
Industrial school, *2911*
Lathe, *2645*
Lithograph, *1028*
Methodist missionary, *6259*
Military school, *3101*
National geology society, *6715*

1819—*continued*

Odd Fellows lodge, *7203*
Parachute jump from a balloon, *7995*
Patent leather, *2126*
Piracy law enacted by Congress, *6931*
Silk thread, *2612*
Standardization of nomenclature for naval vessels, *5581*
State aid to special education, *2912*
Tightrope performer who was a woman, *1363*
Transatlantic crossing by an American steamboat, *8527*
Tungsten and tellurium, *3376*

1820

Antislavery magazine, *6126*
Bachelor tax enacted by a state, *4409*
Concrete, *3333*
Cranberry cultivation, *1596*
Discovery of Antarctica by an American, *6641*
Eye hospital, *5102*
Federal aid to special education, *2913*
Felt manufacturing mechanical process, *2127*
General pharmacopoeia, *5301*
Granite, *3377*
High school, *2914*
Lightship, *7341*
Mariners' church, *6260*
Mayor of New York City elected by the Common Council, *3509*
Mercantile library, *3009*
Political machine, *4054*
Ship sunk by a whale, *1795*
States with populations of more than 1 million, *4343*
Workers' library, *3008*

1821

Actor to receive curtain applause, *1427*
American to set foot on Antarctica, *6641*
Cathedral, *6261*
College alumni association, *2733*
Fire hose of rubber-lined cotton web, *7320*
Historical novel, *1083*
Native American language to be given a written form, *6062*
Patent granted to an African-American inventor, *3991*
Pharmacy college, *3050*
State law abolishing imprisonment for debt, *6994*
State west of the Mississippi River to be admitted to the Union, *4344*
Tunnel, *3435*

1822

Building of fireproof construction, *3262*
Congressional representative who was Hispanic, *3595*
Dentistry book to become popular, *5289*
Physiologist of note, *5019*
Printing press for printing wallpaper in color, *2036*
Prison treadmill, *6995*
Quinine, *5235*
Steam-powered printing press, *2035*
Technical institute, *3192*
Trust company, *1719*
West Point graduate who was Native American, *3102*

1823

Ancient and modern history chair at a college, *2734*
Birth registration law enacted by a state, *2147*
Congressional representative to be refused a seat, *3596*
Gymnasium to offer systematic instruction, *7784*
Medical jurisprudence treatise, *3961*
Newspaper for Jewish readers, *4553*
Ophthalmology book, *5302*
Ophthalmology course at a college, *3051*
Rhyming dictionary, *1084*
Teacher training school, *2915*

1824

Attempt to establish a free public library, *3011*
Boxing arena, *7592*
Catholic convent to admit African-American nuns, *6264*
Catholic school for Native Americans, *2916*
College course without Greek or Latin, *2735*
Engineering college, *2736*
Entomology book, *6773*
Locomotive to pull a train on a track, *8330*
Mining tunnel on a large scale, *3436*
Opinion poll, *4502*
Presidential election in which a loser won, *3800*
Reform Jewish congregation, *6262*
State nominating convention, *3766*
Strike in which women participated, *7105*
Supreme Court decision in a commerce case, *3745*
Treaty between the federal government and a South American nation, *3887*

1825

Ambassador to Mexico, *3889*
Archery club, *7959*
Atlas issued by a state, *4483*
Brothers to serve simultaneously as governors of their respective states, *4373*
Communistic settlement that was not religious, *3520*
Cutlery shears, *2544*
Dead letter office, *4663*
Detachable collar, *2237*
Execution of a white criminal for the murder of a Native American, *6997*
Fire brick, *3334*
Fireworks book, *6774*
First Lady who was not born in the United States, *4219*
First Lady who was the mother of a president, *4220*
Former president who was elected to the House of Representatives, *4127*
Giant exhibited as a theatrical attraction, *1364*
Homeopathic treatise, *5303*
Homeopathy practitioner, *5020*
Horse race trotting course, *7791*
Ink, *2675*
Italian opera, *1318*
Labor union for women, *7106*
Law code adopted by a state, *3962*
Magazine for mechanics, *6775*
Mineral water bottler, *2342*
National organization of artists, *1030*
National religious tract society, *6263*
Natural gas used as an illuminant, *6580*
Painting movement, *1029*
Pharmacy journal, *5304*
Porcelain, *3355*
Reformatory for juvenile deliquents, *6996*
Secular song hit, *1337*
Social fraternity at a college, *2737*
Tax enacted by a state to support public schools, *2917*
Theater lighted by gas, *1428*
Treaty rejected by the Senate, *3888*
Tugboat powered by steam, *8423*

1826

Arcade, *3263*
Belting, *1850*
Children's magazine of literary merit, *2177*
Circumnavigation of the globe by a warship, *8528*
Cloth-covered buttons, *2238*
College graduate who was African-American, *2738*
Conference of American republics, *3890*
First Lady to have an occupation, *4221*
Gymnastics instruction at a college, *7785*
High school for girls, *2918*
Inheritance tax enacted by a state, *4410*
Internal-combustion engine, *8183*
Lyceum for adult education, *3194*
Malleable iron castings, *1923*
Organized gang of street criminals, *6927*
Overland trip to California, *6063*
President to be buried in a grave, *4247*
Printing instruction at a school, *3193*
Reflecting telescope, *6370*
Rhinoceros to be exhibited, *1365*
Transportation report, *3221*

1827

Actor to appear abroad, *1429*
Anarchist, *7108*
Book commercially bound in cloth, *4447*
Federal dry docks, *8424*
Federal law hostile to lotteries, *1801*
Gourmet restaurant, *1810*
Horticulture society of importance, *1594*
Monument to George Washington to be completed, *7169*
Nautical school, *3195*
Newspaper for African-American readers, *4554*
Nursery school, *2919*
Plastic and reconstructive surgeon, *5340*
Printing press invented in the United States that was successful, *2034*
Spanish newspaper, *4555*
Swimming school, *7908*
Telegraph system, *4841*
Trade union organization established in a city, *7107*

1828

Circus tights, *2239*
Electromagnet, *6535*
Fourdrinier papermaking machine, *2011*
Game manufacturing company, *7724*
Leather belts for transmitting power, *1851*
Magazine for women, *4610*
Manufacturers' fair, *1482*
Native American newspaper, *4556*
Political history book, *7473*
Railroad owned by a state, *8301*
State labor party, *4068*
Strike by women, *7110*
Strike in which a militia was called out, *7109*
Washington news correspondent, *4590*

1829

Bank deposit insurance law enacted by a state, *1720*
Catholic community of African-American nuns, *6264*
City carriage service, *8181*
Coffee mill, *2343*
Collar manufacturer, *2240*
Conjoined twins, *2148*
Cottonseed oil mill, *2322*
Daredevil jumper of note, *1366*
Dental surgery textbook, *5305*
Encyclopedia compiled by American editors, *3186*
File factory, *2646*
Genealogical collective work, *7474*
High school night classes, *2921*
Horse racing magazine, *7792*
Hotel recognized as a modern first-class hotel, *1811*
Library for seamen, *3010*
Locomotive for railroad use, *8331*
Pathology textbook, *5306*
Post office building, *4664*
Revolving gun, *5842*
School for blind students, *2920*
Spoils system of presidential patronage, *4128*
Stone arch railroad bridge, *3235*
Straw paper, *2012*
Typewriter, *1662*
Typewritten letter, *1662*

1830

Adhesive and medicated plaster, *5171*
Antiquarian book business, *4448*
Cakes of soap of uniform weight and individually wrapped, *2210*
Census in which the national population exceeded 10 million, *6152*
Census that included deaf, mute, and blind people, *6153*
Cooperative store for consumers, *2083*
Double-deck railroad coaches, *8347*
Etcher, *1031*
Geological survey for a state government, *6489*
Hospital for treatment of the mentally ill established by a state, *5103*
Interstate railroad, *8303*
Marble statuary group, *1032*
Mormon Church meeting, *6265*
National convention of African-Americans, *6127*
National educational association, *2922*
Observatory established by the federal government, *6372*
Observatory operated by a college, *6371*
Parade held by a mystic society, *1367*
Passenger locomotive, *8332*
Passenger train to run on a regular schedule, *8305*
Penny daily newspaper, *4503*
Platform scale, *1663*
Professional American aeronaut, *7996*
Race between a locomotive and a horse-drawn vehicle, *7793*
Railroad for commercial transportation of passengers and freight, *8302*
Railroad rails of T shape, *8382*
Railroad timetable advertised in a newspaper, *8304*
Split-level buildings, *3264*
Sugar beets, *1597*
Team sport played in America, *7960*
Veterinary hospital, *5403*

1831

Anti-Masonic Party convention, *4055*
Bedspring manufacturing patent, *2545*
Brass wire and tubing, *1924*
Building and loan association, *1721*
Cabinet member who was Catholic, *4176*
Chloroform, *5236*
Coastal shipping service, *2070*
Congress in which 1,000 bills were introduced, *3566*
Congressional chaplain who was Catholic, *3565*
Curling club, *7634*
Cylinder printing press, *2037*
Electromagnetic telegraph, *4842*
Glucose from potato starch, *2344*
Locomotive to burn coal, *8333*
Music book for children, *1232*
Play performed 1,000 times, *1430*
Political activist who was an African-American woman, *7432*
Railroad car with a center aisle, *8348*
Railroad to carry troops, *8306*
Railroad tunnel, *3437*
Reaper machine, *1598*
Sculptor to obtain a federal commission, *1033*
Slave rebellion after the Revolution, *6128*
Stone breaking machine, *3378*
Streetcar company, *8364*
Trade journal, *4611*
Widower of a veteran of the armed services to receive a pension, *5620*

1832

Cholera epidemic, *5093*
College art museum, *3137*

Congressional representative to be censured, *3597*
Democratic Party national convention, *4057*
Guano for use as a soil fertilizer, *1599*
Horticultural magazine, *1600*
Hospital and asylum for African-Americans, *5104*
Lock-stitch sewing machine, *2613*
Machine for manufacturing pins, *2614*
National political convention to adopt the two-thirds rule, *4058*
National political platform, *4056*
Performance of "America the Beautiful," *1233*
Phrenologist, *5021*
Phrenology book, *5307*
Presidential candidate nominated at a national convention, *3801*
Railroad accident, *8307*
Rubber company, *1885*
Streetcar, *8365*
Theater history, *1431*
Toy distribution center, *2178*
Vaccination program by the federal government to protect Native Americans against smallpox, *5154*
Vice president to resign, *4304*

1833

Antislavery book, *6129*
Army cavalry unit, *5417*
Avocado, *1601*
Book for the blind, *7030*
Book jacket, *4449*
Cabinet appointee rejected by the Senate, *4177*
Clipper ship, *8425*
College founded as a Quaker institution, *2739*
College to enroll women and men on equal terms, *2740*
Cutlery factory, *2546*
Fireproof safe, *1664*
First Lady who was the grandmother of a president, *4222*
Free public library established by a city, *3011*
Homeopathic medical society, *5213*
Interstate anticrime pact, *7358*
Locomotive cowcatcher, *8383*
Medical dictionary, *5308*
Pharmaceuticals book written and published in America, *5296*
President to ride on a railroad train, *4292*
School for music teachers, *3196*
State aid to railroads, *8308*
Tenement house, *2525*
Treaty between the federal government and an Asian nation, *3891*

1834

Baseball book, *7481*
Bellows, *1853*
Book trade magazine, *4450*
Boxer to die from blows inflicted in a fight, *7593*
Brass kettles, *2273*
City mayor elected by popular vote, *3521*
Dental amalgam for filling teeth, *5081*
Dental society of a city, *5214*
Diving suit, *6490*
Electric motor using direct current, *6536*
Friction matches, *2547*
Gas meter, *6581*
Geological survey authorized by Congress, *6491*
Homeopathic pharmacy, *5237*
Ice-making machine, *2274*
Iron sailing vessel, *8426*
Labor newspaper, *4504*
Locomotive with six or eight driving wheels, *8334*
Novel about whaling, *1085*
Political cartoon featuring Uncle Sam, *4575*
President to be censured by Congress, *4129*
Presidential protest, *4130*
Rifled gun, *5843*
Sandpaper patent, *1852*
Soda water machine, *2345*
Sportswriter, *4591*
Valentines commercially produced, *2492*
Wire sieves, *2548*

1835

Bible for the blind in embossed form, *6360*
Bowie knife, *5844*
Bridge of cast iron, *3236*
Coke used successfully as a blast furnace fuel, *6582*
Egyptian antiquities collection, *3138*
Flea circus, *1368*
Gardener's manual, *1602*
Homeopathy journal, *5309*
Homeopathy school, *3052*
Laundry, *2211*
Locomotive with a cab, *8335*
Mortised lock, *3265*
Mutual fire insurance company, *1978*
Novel by an American to depict Native Americans in a realistic manner, *1086*
President whose assassination was attempted, *4248*
Sculptor of renown, *1034*
State governor who was Catholic, *4374*
State police, *7359*
Wrench patent, *2647*

1835—*continued*

Zinc, *3379*

1836

Agricultural seed distribution on a national scale, *1603*
Child labor law enacted by a state that included an education requirement, *7111*
City superintendent of schools, *2923*
College for women, *2741*
Cricket game played by a college team, *7630*
Federal treasury surplus to be returned to the states, *4345*
Gag rule in the House of Representatives, *3598*
Hooks and eyes, *2241*
Medical encyclopedia, *5310*
Missionaries to cross the continent, *6064*
Mormon temple, *6266*
Navy officer to become an engineer, *5598*
Numbering system for patents, *3992*
President of the Republic of Texas, *3922*
Railroad sleeping car, *8349*
Revolver pistol, *5845*
Safety fuse, *1854*
Scientific expedition fitted out by the federal government, *6642*
Settlers to cross the continent who were women, *6064*
State legislator who was African-American, *4387*
Steamboat on the Pacific coast, *8427*
Supreme Court justice who was Catholic, *3746*
Tourist guide for train travelers, *1812*
Transcendentalist literary work, *1087*
Whig Party convention, *4059*

1837

African-American physician to graduate from medical school, *5017*
Artificial legs, *5265*
Brass clock works, *2628*
Carpet power loom, *2549*
First Lady who was born an American citizen, *4223*
Fluorspar, *3380*
Gun control law enacted by a state, *6932*
Iron blast furnace to use anthracite coal in smelting, *1925*
Iron piano frame, *1294*
Locomotive steam whistle, *8336*
Magazine for blind readers, *7031*
Music instruction in a public school, *2926*
Physiology society, *5215*
Political cartoon showing the Democratic Party as a donkey, *4576*
Silk power loom, *2128*
State board of education, *2925*
State school for blind students, *2924*
Steel plow with a steel moldboard, *1604*
Threshing machine to employ steam, *1605*
Vice president elected by the Senate, *4305*
Whole-wheat bread, *2346*

1838

African-American magazine, *6130*
Alcohol prohibition law enacted by a state, *7060*
Astronomical observations book, *6776*
Bunting manufacture, *2129*
Embossing press, *2038*
Hebrew spelling book, *3187*
Jewish Sunday school, *6214*
Killing of one congressional representative by another, *3599*
Model laboratory school at a college, *2742*
Phrenology journal, *5311*
Pins manufactured with a solid head, *2615*
Silk dyers, *2130*
Silver mine, *3381*
Steam shovel, *1855*
Steamboat inspection service established by Congress, *8429*
Sugar beet mill, *2347*
Telegraphic system in which dots and dashes represented letters, *4843*
Tool factory, *2648*
Transatlantic steamboat service, *8428*
Watch made by machinery, *2629*
Wooden railroad bridge of a purely truss type, *3237*
Workers' compensation lawsuit involving the rights of an injured servant against his master, *7112*

1839

Astronomy photograph, *6398*
Building with a high steeple, *3266*
Cotton twine factory, *2550*
Cranioscopy book, *5312*
Dental journal, *5313*
Dictionary of American law, *3963*
Envelope manufacturer, *2013*
Express delivery service, *2071*
Fraternity house at a college, *2743*
Iron blast furnace to use anthracite coal successfully, *1926*
Liberty Party convention, *4060*
Military school established by a state, *3103*

National political convention to adopt the unit rule, *4061*
State law allowing married women to own property, *7433*
Statistical society, *6716*
Teacher training school established by a state, *2927*
Teachers' institute, *2928*

1840

Aquatic play, *1432*
Bowling match, *7579*
Camera exposure scale, *4638*
Chiropodist, *5022*
Class photograph, *4619*
Clinic for teaching medical students, *3053*
Commercial photography studio, *4618*
Dental college, *3054*
Electric printing press, *2039*
Electricity journal, *6777*
Embalming book, *5314*
Factory workers' magazine, *7113*
Girder bridge of cast iron, *3238*
Graphite, *3382*
Gutta-percha, *1886*
Lager beer, *2348*
Land mines, *5846*
Library building at a university, *2744*
Line drawing to illustrate a newspaper article, *4577*
National dental society, *5216*
Naval vessel to sail around the Cape of Good Hope, *8529*
Nuts and bolts factory, *2649*
Photograph taken in the United States, *4617*
Presidential candidate to make a campaign speech, *3802*
Radio impulse transmission, *4817*
Seeding machine, *1606*
Tap dancer of renown, *1049*

1841

Advertising agency, *1522*
Attempt to form a newspaper syndicate, *4521*
Baby bottle, *2179*
Collapsible tube, *2650*
Commercial rating agency, *1770*
Dental surgeons to be licensed by a state, *5023*
Detective story, *1088*
Elastic webbing, *2131*
Fire brick to withstand high heat, *3335*
Fire engine with a steam boiler, *7321*
First Lady who attended school, *4224*
General anesthetic, *5049*
Geodetic survey, *6492*
Heavyweight boxing match to last longer than 100 rounds, *7594*
Japanese to enter the United States, *6065*
Life preserver of cork, *7342*
Orthodontia treatise, *5315*
President to die in Washington, *4250*
President whose grandson became president, *4249*
Reclining chair, *2551*
State fair, *4346*
Teaching methodology course at a college, *2745*
Underwater torpedo operated by electric current, *5847*
Venetian blinds to be patented, *2539*
Vice president to succeed to the presidency after the death of a president, *4306*
Wagon train to California, *6066*
Wire rope factory, *1856*

1842

Adhesive postage stamps, *4716*
Boxer to die in the ring, *7593*
Business school, *3197*
Child labor law enacted by a state that regulated hours of employment, *7114*
Cornstarch made commercially from maize, *2349*
Credit protection group, *1483*
Department store, *2084*
Design patent, *3993*
First Lady to die during her husband's term in office, *4225*
Free public art museum in continuous existence, *3139*
Gold discovered in California, *3383*
Hammered iron, *1927*
Illustrated weekly magazine, *4612*
Mutual life insurance company, *1990*
Narcotics tariff enacted by Congress, *7061*
Navy bureau of medicine and surgery, *5196*
Navy officer condemned for mutiny, *5599*
Orchestra of international stature, *1234*
Overland wagon road across the Rocky Mountains, *3412*
Rubber shoe manufacturer, *2242*
State to repudiate a debt, *4347*
Tariff enacted by Congress to prevent the importation of obscene literature and pictures, *4411*
Telegraph cable, *4844*
Wire suspension bridge for general traffic, *3239*

1843

Consul to California, *3892*

1843—*continued*

Egg incubator, *1607*
Floating church, *6267*
Fraternal society for Jews, *7204*
Government on the Pacific Coast, *3451*
Grain elevator operated by steam, *1608*
Harness horse race at night, *7794*
Ice cream freezer, *2350*
Index to books, *4451*
Iron vessel built for the Navy, *8469*
Magazine for and by patients with mental illness, *7032*
Manila paper, *2014*
Minstrel show troupe, *1235*
Photograph of a former president, *4131*
Stained-glass window, *3356*
Telegraph appropriation by Congress, *4845*
Warship with propelling machinery below the waterline, *8470*
Water cures, *5389*

1844

Achromatic lenses, *4639*
Adventist church to accept Saturday as the Sabbath, *6268*
Anesthetic in dentistry, *5050*
Book review editor, *4592*
Branding punishment by a federal court, *6998*
College to feature rowing as a sport, *7877*
Commercial telegraph service, *4847*
Credit report book, *1703*
Cylinder and flatbed combination printing press, *2040*
Express delivery service to the West, *2072*
Game protection society, *7824*
Gas engine, *8184*
Iron steamship built for transatlantic service, *8430*
National psychiatry association, *5217*
News dispatch by telegraph, *4505*
Pharmacy chair at a college, *3045*
President married while in office, *4251*
President who was a "dark horse" candidate, *3803*
Presidential candidate to be assassinated, *3804*
Printing press for polychromatic printing, *2041*
Railroad rails of iron, *8384*
Telegraph station, *4846*
Turbine successfully operated by waterpower, *1857*
Vulcanized rubber, *1887*
Whist rule book, *7725*
Yacht club, *7567*

1845

Anesthetic administered in childbirth, *5051*
Baseball team, *7482*
Building heated by steam, *3267*
Factory for making pocket cutlery, *2546*
Health journal to advocate water cures, *5316*
Iron truss bridge, *3240*
Law book of federal laws then in force, *3964*
Lawyer formally admitted to the bar who was African-American, *3965*
Military school operated by a church, *3104*
Monolithic concrete building, *3268*
National labor congress, *7115*
Naval academy, *3105*
Newspaper with a full page of woodcut engravings, *4578*
Ocean mail contracts, *4665*
Oilcloth factory, *2132*
Opera of importance by an American composer, *1317*
Photograph to gain world fame, *4620*
Presidential veto to be overridden by Congress, *4132*
Pressure-sensitive adhesive, *1888*
Prison matrons for guarding women prisoners, *6999*
Regatta, *7568*
Senator of Jewish descent, *3661*
Silver wire suture, *5172*
Soap powder in packages, *2212*
Spring manufacturer, *1858*
Underwater telegraph cable that was practical, *4848*
Voice synthesizer, *4863*
Wall and floor tiles, *3336*

1846

Applied chemistry professor at a college, *2746*
Artificial leg patent, *5265*
Astronomy magazine, *6778*
Baking soda commercial production, *2351*
Baseball game, *7483*
Bronchitis treatise, *5317*
Cast steel for plows, *1928*
Demonstration of surgery under anesthesia, *5052*
Factory heated by steam, *3269*
Gingham factory, *2133*
Handwriting teaching system widely used in schools, *2929*
Herd book for livestock, *1609*
Humor writer who was a woman, *1089*
Newspaper published on the Pacific Coast, *4506*
Plank road, *3413*
Rotary printing press, *2042*

School to provide separate classrooms for each class, *2930*
Senator elected on an antislavery ticket, *6131*
Supreme Court decision in a state boundary case, *3747*
Tattoo shop, *2460*
Telegrapher who was a woman, *4849*
Unit of American deserters to join an enemy army, *5688*
War correspondent, *4593*
War tax resister, *4412*
War that began before a declaration of war was made by Congress, *5687*
War to receive daily newspaper coverage, *5686*
Warehouse legislation enacted by Congress, *2073*

1847

African-American physician to graduate from an American medical school, *5017*
Bronze statue of full length, *7170*
Chinese students in the U.S., *2755*
Health insurance company, *1980*
National medical society, *5218*
Norwegian newspaper, *4557*
Pathology chair at a college, *3055*
Postage stamps issued by the Post Office Department, *4717*
Reformatory for boys established by a state, *7000*
Silver plating factory, *1929*
Skin grafting, *5341*
Steamship passenger line between American and European ports, *8431*
Synthetic fertilizer, *1610*
Telegraph company, *4850*
Tourist guide with train schedules, *1813*
Vacation fund to send poor children to the country, *2180*
Workday of 10 hours to be mandated by a state, *7116*

1848

Baby carriage, *2181*
Baseball uniforms, *7484*
Bloomers, *2244*
Building constructed wholly of cast iron, *3270*
Chewing gum, *2352*
Child labor law enacted by a state that restricted the age of the worker, *7117*
Chinese immigrants to America, *6067*
Comic weekly, *4613*
Congressional lobbyist who was a woman, *3567*
Dental chair, *5082*
Drinking water conduit to be built underwater, *7404*
Eastern Orthodox cathedral, *6242*
Election day for presidential voting held nationwide, *3805*
Engineering society, *3222*
Father and son who were senators at the same session, *3658*
Free Soil Party convention, *4062*
Gaslight in the White House, *4326*
Macaroni factory, *2353*
Medical school for women, *3056*
Medical society for women, *5219*
National science society, *6717*
Periodical index, *3012*
Pure food and drug law established by Congress, *7238*
Railroad to run west out of Chicago, *8309*
School for children with mental disabilities, *2931*
Shirt factory, *2243*
Spiritualist, *6269*
Steamboat service to California around Cape Horn, *8432*
War fought mostly on foreign soil, *5689*
Woman member of the American Academy of Arts and Sciences, *7198*
Women's rights convention, *7434*

1849

Breech-loading cannon, *5848*
Business economics course at a college, *2747*
Chamber music ensemble, *1236*
Chinese restaurant, *1814*
Department of the Interior, *4178*
Free public libraries authorized by a state, *3013*
Gas mask, *1860*
Ice skating champion, *7838*
Ice skating club, *7839*
Jewish weekly newspaper in English, *4553*
Melodeon patent, *1295*
Percussion rock drill, *1859*
Photograph of a president in office, *4133*
Photography book, *4621*
Physician who was a woman, *5024*
Poultry show, *1611*
President who had received a patent, *4134*
Railroad excursion rates, *8310*
Safety pin, *2552*
Secretary of the interior, *4178*
Senator to serve three states, *3659*
Senator who was returned to the Senate after being defeated for the presidency, *3660*
Social and political newspaper for women, *4507*

1849—*continued*

Tattooed man exhibited as a theatrical attraction, *1369*
Twin covered bridges, *3241*
Watchmaking firm of importance, *2627*
Wire gauge, *2651*

1850

Adding machine to employ depressible keys, *1665*
American history chair at a college, *2748*
Aviation book, *7997*
Billiards book, *7726*
College graduate who was an African-American woman, *2749*
Community leader to exercise the authority of king and high priest, *6068*
Cork manufacturer, *3337*
Derby hat, *2245*
Desk with a roll top, *2553*
Elevator, *3271*
First Lady to graduate from college, *4226*
German daily newspaper, *4551*
Homeopathic hospital, *5105*
Meat biscuit, *2354*
Naturalized citizen who was Japanese, *6065*
Orphan train, *2182*
Paper money issued by the Native Americans, *4022*
Photograph of a star other than the sun, *6399*
Photography magazine, *4622*
Piano wire, *1296*
Private mint authorized by the federal government, *4023*
Private railroad car, *8350*
Public health report commissioned by a state, *7239*
Railroad land grant, *8311*
Signal flares, *5849*
Sparrows, *5942*
State on the Pacific coast to be admitted to the Union, *4348*
Theater ticket scalpers, *1433*
Women's rights national convention, *7434*

1851

Airship bombing plan, *5457*
Artificial eyes, *5266*
Brass and copper seamless tubes, *1930*
Brass spinning, *1931*
Brothers to serve as representatives in Congress simultaneously, *3600*
Cheese factory, *2357*
Chinese laundry, *2213*
Christmas cards, *2493*
College secret society for women, *2751*
College to prohibit discrimination because of race, religion, or color, *2750*
Condensed milk, *2355*
Electric locomotive, *8337*
Escaped slave legally recaptured in New England, *6132*
Felt hats for women, *2246*
Fifty-dollar gold pieces, *4024*
French daily newspaper that was successful, *4552*
Ice cream wholesale dealer, *2356*
Insurance board established by a state government, *1954*
Magazine for and by deaf students, *7033*
Mechanical freezer patent, *2275*
Nail machine, *2652*
Postage stamps depicting the American eagle, *4718*
Scandinavian Methodist Episcopal church, *6270*
Sewing machine equipped with a rocking treadle or double treadle, *2617*
Sewing machine manufacturer, *2616*
State adoption law to consider the interests of the child, *2183*
Telegraph used by a railroad, *4851*
Traveler's aid program, *6069*
Yacht from the United States to win an international yacht race, *7569*
Young Men's Christian Association, *7205*

1852

Beehive with removable frames, *1612*
Body to lie in state in the Capitol rotunda, *3568*
Book to sell more than 1 million copies, *1090*
Chinese theater, *1435*
Chinese theatrical performance, *1434*
College professor who was a woman, *2752*
Compulsory education law enacted by a state, *2932*
Hospital under Jewish auspices, *5106*
Insurance journal, *1955*
Intercollegiate rowing race, *7878*
Matzah made by machine, *2358*
Musician born in America to achieve fame in Europe, *1237*
National civil engineering society, *3223*
National pharmacy society, *5220*
Paper bag machine, *1995*
President to celebrate his silver wedding anniversary at the White House, *4252*
Public bathhouse and washhouse, *7240*
Railroad to run west of the Mississippi River, *8309*
Senator who was Jewish, *3661*
Showboat theater of importance, *1426*

Sprinkler system, *7322*
State temperance society for women, *7062*
Working hours of women to be regulated by a state, *7118*

1853

African-American branch of the YMCA, *7205*
Arctic expedition by an American explorer, *6643*
Art magazine, *1035*
Bank clearinghouse, *1722*
Bronze equestrian statue, *7171*
Circumnavigation of the world by a yacht, *8530*
Coal oil factory, *1889*
College literary society that was coeducational, *2700*
Elevator with safety devices, *3272*
Envelope folding machine, *2015*
Fire department to be paid a salary, *7324*
Fire engine that was practical, *7323*
Horse show, *1370*
Infirmary for women staffed by physicians who were women, *5107*
Mechanics textbook, *6779*
Minister who was a woman, *6271*
Novel by an African-American writer, *1091*
Physical education classes in elementary schools, *2933*
Physiology and hygiene courses at a liberal arts college, *3057*
Plate glass, *3357*
Potato chips, *2359*
Pottery to make sanitary ware, *3358*
Railroad merger, *8312*
Stamped envelopes, *4719*
Terra cotta, *3338*
Trade association, *1484*
Truancy law enacted by a state, *2934*
Union passenger station used by several railroad companies, *8313*
University on the Pacific Coast, *2753*
Vice president sworn in on foreign soil, *4307*
Village improvement society, *7206*
World's fair, *1485*
Zinc commercial production, *3384*

1854

African-American member of a state medical society, *5212*
American to be named a Chevalier of the Legion d'Honneur, *6894*
Asylum for alcoholics, *5109*
Baby show, *2184*
Billiard match, *7727*
Blanket factory, *2554*
Building in which wrought-iron beams were used, *3273*
Children's hospital, *5108*
Chinese labor immigration, *6070*
Chinese newspaper, *4558*
College for African-American students, *2754*
College graduate of Asian ancestry, *2755*
Curved stereotype plate, *2043*
Entomologist hired by a state, *6659*
Entomologist hired by the federal government, *6660*
Folding theater chair, *1436*
Gazetteer of the world, *3188*
Oil company, *6583*
Orphan train from New York, *2182*
Paper collar, *2247*
Paper for printing made from rags and wood-pulp fiber, *2016*
Paper made from wood pulp, *2017*
Parkland purchased by a city, *5988*
Publishing society, *4452*
Republican Party convention, *4063*
Republican Party meeting, *4063*
Rifled breech-loading steel cannon, *5850*
Sewing machine to stitch buttonholes, *2618*
Sociology treatise, *7475*
State governor to be removed from office by a state supreme court, *4375*
Street-cleaning machine, *7405*

1855

African-American to hold elective office, *3767*
Book trade magazine that was successful, *4453*
Calliope, *1297*
Claims court established by the federal government, *3706*
Dental filling made of gold, *5083*
Dentist who was a woman, *5084*
Dissection of a living animal to demonstrate anatomy and physiology, *3058*
Hospital for women, *5110*
Kerosene, *6585*
Lighthouse on the Pacific coast, *7343*
Magazine for professional printers, *2018*
Married woman to keep her maiden name, *2592*
Novel by an African-American woman, *1092*
Oil refinery, *6584*
Phonetic dictionary, *3189*
Poem to win national acclaim, *1093*
Postal directory, *4666*
Quarantine board established by a state, *7241*
Railroad suspension bridge, *3242*
Railroad union, *7119*
Registered mail, *4667*

1855—*continued*

Steel animal traps commercially manufactured, *2653*
Veterinary college, *3059*

1856

Assault by a congressman on a senator, *3662*
Blotting paper, *2019*
Borax, *3385*
Camels imported for military purposes, *5418*
Comparative philology chair at a college, *2756*
Congressman censured for assaulting another, *3601*
Industrial school for girls, *2935*
Kindergarten run informally, *2944*
Know-Nothing (American) Party convention, *4064*
Machine gun, *5852*
Milk purity law enacted by a state, *7242*
Paper folding machine, *2020*
Play in which a horse race was run on stage, *1437*
President who was a bachelor, *4253*
Railroad bridge across the Mississippi River, *3243*
Railroad safety law enacted by a state, *8314*
Republican Party national convention, *4063*
Revolver that was self-cocking, *5851*
Rolled oats, *2360*
Screw machine to make pointed screws, *2654*
Telegraph ticker to print type successfully, *4852*
Tintype camera, *4640*
Underground city sewer system, *7406*

1857

Box spring, *2555*
Brick machine, *3339*
Buddhist temple, *6272*
Chess tournament, *7728*
College for deaf students, *2757*
Dual sewer system for sewage and storm water, *7407*
Elevator with a completely enclosed car, *3274*
Fire alarm system operated by electricity, *7325*
Grape vines planted in California for winemaking, *1613*
Horse bred in the United States to win a major race abroad, *7795*
International chess champion from the United States, *7729*
Literacy qualification for voting, *3768*
Mardi Gras in New Orleans, *2486*
Metal gun cartridge, *5853*
National organization of teachers, *2943*
Oil lamp, *2556*
Pediatrics professor at a college, *3060*
Photograph of a solar eclipse, *6400*
Postage stamp issued with perforations, *4720*
Racing shell, *7879*
School band, *1238*
State agricultural college to open, *2759*
Toilet paper, *2461*
Tuberculosis patients' home, *5124*
Typesetting machine, *2044*
Veterinary college of importance, *3061*

1858

Baseball game in which spectators were charged admission, *7486*
Baseball rules standardizing the game, *7485*
Baseball series, *7487*
Building designed to be used by artists, *3275*
Burglar alarm, *3276*
Cable car, *8366*
Can opener, *2276*
Chemical laboratory at a college, *2758*
Congressional medal awarded to a physician, *3569*
Dinosaur skeleton found in the United States, *6661*
Mason jar, *2557*
Medical college on the Pacific Coast, *3062*
Ornamented soda fountain for restaurants, *1815*
Overland mail service, *4669*
Pencil with an attached eraser, *2677*
Psychiatry textbook, *5318*
Shoe manufacturing machine, *2248*
Steel pens, *2676*
Stone crusher, *3386*
Street letter box, *4668*
Transatlantic telegraph cable, *4853*
Treatise on fossil footprints, *6658*
Washing machine, *2214*

1859

Agricultural college to be chartered by a state, *2759*
Airmail dispatched from a post office in a balloon, *4670*
Church for deaf people, *6258*
Daredevil to cross Niagara Falls on a tightrope, *1371*
Electric light for household illumination, *6537*
Electric range, *2277*
Escalator patent, *3277*
Fishing line factory, *2655*
Gas journal, *6780*
Grand piano with a cast-metal plate, *1298*
Hotel with an elevator, *1816*

Intercollegiate baseball game, *7488*
Intercollegiate regatta, *7880*
International cricket tournament, *7631*
Library newspaper room, *3014*
Mastoid operation, *5342*
Milk inspection law enacted by a state, *7243*
Oil well that was commercially productive, *6586*
Public school for Asian-American children, *2937*
Pullman sleeping car, *8351*
School for blind students to adopt the Braille system, *2936*
Song popular in the Confederate States, *1338*
Temporary insanity defense in a criminal case, *6933*

1860

Aerial photograph, *4623*
Army signal corps, *5419*
Baseball game of record in which a team scored no runs in nine innings, *7502*
Baseball team to tour, *7489*
Boarding school on a Native American reservation, *2938*
Chiropody book, *5319*
Commercial dog food, *2602*
Commercial oil refinery, *6587*
Constitutional Union Party convention, *4065*
Corkscrew patent, *2558*
Cowboy hat, *2249*
Czech newspaper, *4559*
Department store to occupy a city block, *2085*
Doctoral degree awarded by an American university, *2761*
Electrotherapy book, *5320*
Fire escapes for tenements, *7326*
Foreign missionary society organized by women, *6273*
Game preserve, *7825*
Hebrew book other than the Bible, *6361*
Mass-market paperback book, *4454*
News reporter at a political convention who was a woman, *4594*
Physical education and hygiene professorship at a college, *2760*
Pony Express mail, *4671*
Prince of Wales to visit the United States, *3923*
Rabbi to open the House of Representatives with prayer, *3602*
Secession act at the start of the Civil War, *4349*
Silver mill, *1932*
State law of significance to secure property rights for married women, *7435*
State to secede from the Union, *4350*
Tinware manufacturers who were successful, *2270*
Traffic police squad, *7360*

1861

Act inaugurating the Civil War, *5690*
African-American to enlist in the United States armed forces during the Civil War, *5706*
Army balloon corps, *5458*
Army secret service bureau, *5420*
Balloon carrier, *8471*
Battle flag, *3496*
Bibliophile magazine, *4455*
Camp for boys, *2185*
Chromolithograph, *1036*
Civil War attack, *5693*
Civil War bloodshed, *5696*
Civil War call for volunteers, *5695*
Civil War combat action that earned the Medal of Honor, *5502*
Civilian welfare effort for soldiers organized on a large scale, *5702*
Combat action that earned the Medal of Honor, *5501*
Confederate coin, *4025*
Confederate congressional session, *5691*
Confederate cruiser to raid Union commerce, *5699*
Confederate forts to surrender in the Civil War, *5707*
Confederate general killed in the Civil War, *5704*
Confederate government bond, *5692*
Confederate officer killed in the Civil War, *5700*
Confederate paper money, *4026*
Congressional representative to be expelled, *3603*
Constitutional amendment proposal to bear the signature of a president, *3495*
Copyright law on photographs enacted by Congress, *3979*
Creamery for commercial production, *2361*
Divided road, *3414*
Federal law to emancipate slaves, *6133*
Fire in an oil well, *6588*
Fly casting tournament, *7671*
Former president to serve as an official of an enemy government, *4135*
Fund-raising organization to sell stamps, *7207*
Ice yacht club, *7570*
Income tax levied by Congress, *4413*
Land battle in the Civil War, *5701*
Laryngology instruction at a college, *3063*
Major battle of the Civil War, *5705*

1861—*continued*

Mass expulsion from the Senate, *3663*
Military prison on an island, *7001*
Naval battle in the Civil War, *5708*
Naval skirmish in the Civil War, *5694*
Newspaper published by soldiers in the field, *4508*
Newspaper wrappers for mailing newspapers, *4672*
Nursing school to award a diploma, *3065*
Orthopedics chair at a college, *3064*
Paper money issued by the federal government, *4027*
Patent issued by the Confederate States of America, *3994*
Peep show machine, *1372*
Petroleum exported to Europe, *6589*
Photographic attempt to show motion, *1204*
Pin-tumbler cylinder lock, *3278*
Press censorship by military authorities, *4509*
Pretzel bakery, *2362*
Proposal for a Medal of Honor, *5503*
Regiment of free African-Americans organized during the Civil War, *5710*
School for freed slaves, *2940*
Senator to address the Senate in military uniform, *3664*
Teacher training school at which students conducted practice classes, *2939*
Telegram dispatched from an aerial station, *4854*
Transcontinental telegraph line, *4855*
Union naval officer killed in the Civil War, *5703*
Union officer killed in the Civil War, *5698*
Union ship captured in the Civil War, *5709*
Union soldier killed by enemy action in the Civil War, *5697*
Year in which two presidents were elected, *3806*

1862

African-American unit in the Union Army to see combat, *5716*
Army ambulance corps, *5198*
Army field hospital, *5197*
Army field telegraph used in warfare, *5714*
Army general to become an admiral in the Navy, *5440*
Artillery fire to be directed from the air, *5459*
Bill bearing the likeness of a president, *4028*
Chinaware for restaurant use, *1817*
Citizen of the United States to be hanged for treason, *7003*
Confederate ship surrendered to the Union, *5713*
Decalcomania pictures, *2559*
Emancipation proclamation, *6134*
Enclosed baseball park, *7491*
Episcopal cathedral, *6274*
Execution for slave trading carried out by the federal government, *7002*
Folding stepladder, *2560*
Football club, *7685*
Gymnastics instruction at a college for women, *7786*
Homestead law enacted by Congress, *6071*
Hospital ship operated by the Navy, *5199*
Inheritance tax levied by Congress, *4414*
Ironclad naval vessels, *8473*
Ironclad seagoing naval warship, *8474*
Ironclad turreted vessel in the Navy, *8475*
Land grant for an agricultural college, *2762*
Military service by African-Americans to be authorized by Congress, *5421*
Naval battle between ironclad vessels in the Civil War, *5712*
Navy chaplain killed in action, *5711*
Newspaper printed on a train, *4510*
Oil pipeline, *6590*
Paper money fractional currency, *4029*
Passport fee, *6072*
Pediatric clinic, *5064*
Photographs of an American battlefield showing the bodies of the dead, *5715*
Polygamy ban enacted by Congress, *7436*
Postage stamp catalog, *4673*
Railroad post office, *4674*
Rapid-fire machine gun, *5855*
Revenue stamps issued by the federal government, *4415*
Revolving gun turret for ships, *5854*
Scientific publication issued by an agriculture bureau, *1614*
Snowshoe production, *2250*
State governor to be impeached and acquitted, *4376*
Submarine in the U.S. Navy, *8509*
Taps, *1339*
Turreted frigate in the Navy, *8472*
Warship sunk by an underwater torpedo mine, *5717*

1863

Accident insurance company, *1956*
Catholic parish church for African-Americans, *6275*
Cheesemaking society, *2357*
Civil War bloodshed north of the Mason-Dixon Line, *5718*
Compressed pills or tablets, *5238*
Docks owned by a state, *2074*

Draft law enacted by Congress during wartime, 5556
Farmers' institute sponsored by a state, 1615
Free mail delivery in cities, 4675
Gold certificates, 4030
Laryngology clinic, 5065
Medal of Honor awarded to a Marine, 5506
Medal of Honor awarded to a member of the Naval Service, 5505
Medal of Honor awarded to an Army soldier, 5504
Monument to commemorate the Civil War, 7172
National bank, 1723
National science institute, 6718
News reporter tried as a spy, 4595
Newspaper printed on wood-pulp paper, 4511
Notes wholly engraved and printed at the Bureau of Engraving and Printing, 4031
Officer to preside over both of the branches of Congress, 3570
Paper sewing patterns, 2619
Photographs of combat, 4624
Presidential amnesty issued during the Civil War, 4121
Presidential proclamation of a national day of prayer, 2494
Printing press to use a continuous web or roll of paper, 2045
Private school for children with disabilities, 2941
Roller skates, 7872
Thanksgiving Day, 2495
Turkish bath, 7244

1864

African-American daily newspaper, 4554
Bessemer steel converter, 1933
Boiler inspection law enacted by a state, 7327
Cigarette tax, 7063
Circus to feature a car as an attraction, 1373
Coin to use the motto "In God We Trust," 4032
Confederate vessel sunk by an underwater torpedo mine, 5717
File factory to use machines, 2646
Fine arts department in a college, 2763
Fish hatchery, 1616
Hunting license required by a state, 7826
Knights of Pythias meeting, 7208
Mines school at a college, 2765
Money order system, 4676
National hall of fame, 3140
News photographs of distinction, 4625
Oil tank railroad cars, 8352
Ophthalmologist of note, 5025
Periscope, 5856
Physician who was an African-American woman, 5026
Presidential election in which soldiers in the field were allowed to vote, 3807
Professional fraternity at a college, 2764
Railroad rails of steel, 8385
Salmon cannery, 2363
Stamp collection magazine, 4677
State park, 5989
Submarine to sink a warship, 5719
Sugar and glucose from cornstarch, 2364

1865

Advertising magazine, 1523
African-American preacher to deliver a sermon in the House of Representatives, 3604
African-American to earn a Ph.D., 2768
Architecture department at a college, 2766
Army major who was African-American, 5441
Ban by Congress on importation of diseased cattle, 7246
Bank for freed African-American slaves, 1724
Baseball game in which one team scored more than 100 runs, 7492
Bathhouses owned and operated by a city, 7245
Coast Guard serviceman who was African-American, 5543
Coffee percolator, 2278
College to sponsor an endowed lecture series, 2767
Congressional directory, 3571
Entomology journal, 6781
Environmental protection law enacted by a state in connection with advertising, 5906
Execution of a woman by hanging by the federal government, 7004
Figure skater of note, 7840
Judge advocate of the Navy, 5600
Ku Klux Klan meeting, 6135
Lawyer admitted to practice before the Supreme Court who was African-American, 3966
Linen thread factory, 2620
Medal of Honor awarded to a woman, 5508
Medal of Honor winner to receive two awards, 5507
Memoir of life in the White House, 4327
National bank to fail, 1725
National social science society, 6719
Natural gas corporation, 6591
Newspaper published at sea, 4512
Oil pipeline of importance, 6592
Premiums given away with merchandise, 1524
President to be assassinated, 4254

1865—*continued*

President to lie in state in the Capitol rotunda, *4255*
Professor of ophthalmology, *3066*
Pullman sleeping car that was comfortable, *8353*
Robbery of a disabled train, *6934*
Safe deposit vault, *1666*
Secret service established by the federal government, *3842*
Soap in liquid form, *2215*
Streamlined railroad train, *8393*
Sweet crackers, *2365*
Trial of a war criminal by the federal government, *5721*
War in which more than 500,000 American combatants died, *5720*
Woman member of a dental society, *5085*
Zinc sheet mill, *1934*

1866

All-metal roller skate, *7874*
Ambulance service for hospitals, *5044*
Animal humane society, *7210*
Artificial insemination of a woman resulting in conception, *5390*
Bank and train robbery gang, *6935*
Baseball pitcher to throw a curve ball, *7493*
Bicycle with a rotary crank, *7639*
Boiler insurance company, *1957*
Broadway hit musical, *1439*
Civil rights law enacted by Congress, *6136*
Cog railroad, *8315*
College baseball teams for women, *7494*
Commemoration of the birthday of Abraham Lincoln, *2496*
Corrupt election practices law enacted by a state, *3770*
Delegate to a national political convention who was African-American, *4066*
Dentist who was a woman to obtain a D.D.S. degree, *5085*
Dynamite, *1861*
Fur-bearing animals raised commercially, *1617*
General of the U.S. Army, *5442*
Grand Army of the Republic post for veterans of the Civil War, *5622*
Health board with emergency powers established by a city, *7247*
Hotel with safe deposit boxes, *1818*
Indelible pencil, *2678*
Insurance rate standardization, *1958*
Interracial jury, *3707*
Irrigation law enacted by Congress, *1618*
Machine for cutting and straightening wire, *1862*
Metric system usage to be approved by Congress, *1486*
Monument ordered by the federal government from a sculptor who was a woman, *7173*
Mourning postage stamp, *4721*
National voting rights organization to advocate universal voting rights, *3769*
Navy officer to become an admiral, *5601*
News correspondent accredited to the White House, *4596*
Newspaper index separately published, *4513*
Nickel five-cent piece, *4033*
Paleontology chair at a college, *2769*
Queen to visit the United States, *3924*
Refrigerated railroad car to carry fresh fruit, *8354*
Robbery of a train in motion, *6936*
Roller skating rink open to the public, *7873*
Root beer, *2366*
Sewing needles made by machine, *2621*
Sextuplets, *2149*
Soldiers' homes established by Congress, *5621*
State readmitted to the Union after the Civil War, *4351*
Steam car, *8224*
Steam whaler, *8433*
Theater ticket agency, *1438*
Tin can with a key opener, *1996*
Transatlantic yacht race, *7571*
Underwater highway tunnel, *3438*
University for African-American students, *2770*
Young Women's Christian Association, *7209*
Zither factory, *1299*

1867

Animated picture machine, *1192*
Book tour of the United States by an author, *1094*
Cartridge belt patent, *5857*
Collection of spirituals, *1239*
Cow town, *3522*
Dental school to be associated with a medical school, *3067*
Election law granting African-American men the right to vote, *3771*
Elevated railroad, *8316*
Fashion magazine, *2251*
Gallstone operation, *5343*
Greek Orthodox church, *6276*
National organization of farmers, *1619*
Paint ready-mixed, *2656*
Plate-glass insurance, *1959*
Refrigerated railroad car, *8354*

School for deaf students to teach lip-reading, *2909*
Stamp collection society, *4722*
State ban on corporal punishment in schools, *2942*
State governor who had also been governor of a territory, *4377*
State university supported by a direct property tax, *2771*
Stock brokerage concern to use a stock ticker, *1772*
Stock price indicator used on Wall Street, *1771*
Terra cotta factory, *3340*
Territory annexed by the federal government beyond the nation's continental limits, *6074*
Territory annexed by the federal government that was noncontinguous, *6073*
Theological college for Jews, *2773*
Theological school that was multisectarian, *2772*
Trademark for food, *1525*
Transpacific sidewheeler steamer, *8434*
Typewriter that was practical, *1667*
Water supply tunnel for a city, *3439*

1868

Amateur athletic games held indoors, *7937*
Artificial-ice manufacturing plant, *1890*
Athletic club, *7936*
Bicycle school, *7640*
Compressed fresh yeast, *2367*
Dye plant, *1891*
Elks meeting, *7211*
Kindergarten, *2944*
Local baseball team for women, *7494*
Memorial Day, *2497*
National cemetery for Civil War dead, *5722*
National philology society, *6720*
Native American to win territorial concessions from the federal government, *6075*
Nickel plating, *1936*
Office building with an elevator, *3279*
Open-hearth furnace for the manufacture of steel, *1935*
Parade with float tableaux, *1374*
Pediatrics journal, *5321*
President to be impeached, *4136*
Professor of public hygiene, *3049*
Railroad dining car, *8355*
State chamber of commerce, *1487*
Steam-driven motorcycle, *8285*
Tape measure, *2657*
Uniforms for mail carriers, *4678*
Veterinary department at a college, *3068*
Women's professional club, *7212*
Workday of eight hours to be authorized by Congress, *7120*

1869

Air brake, *8386*
Apartment house with a modern layout, *2526*
Architectural patent awarded to a woman, *3226*
Baseball team whose players received a regular salary, *7495*
Bookseller's guide, *4456*
Brokerage office owned by women, *1773*
Celluloid, *1892*
Chain store organization, *2086*
Coal mine disaster, *6594*
Corncob pipe commercial manufacture, *7064*
Dental crown made of gold, *5086*
Diplomat who was African-American, *3893*
Exploration of the Grand Canyon of the Colorado, *6644*
Financial news agency, *4514*
Fraternal group insurance, *1960*
Gymnasium at a YMCA, *7205*
Health board established by a state government, *7248*
Indian Affairs Commissioner who was Native American, *3843*
Intercollegiate football contest, *7686*
Journalism course at a college, *2774*
Jute culture, *1620*
Kindergarten manual, *2945*
Labor bureau established by a state, *7121*
Labor Day, *2498*
Labor union to admit workers other than craft workers, *7123*
Law school at a university to admit women, *2775*
Lawyer who was a woman, *3967*
Lithuanian settlement, *6076*
Movie projector patent, *1205*
National union for women, *7122*
Oil drill offshore rig, *6593*
Patent issued to Thomas Alva Edison, *3995*
Photograph of the sun's corona made during a total solar eclipse, *6400*
Postage stamp depicting the American flag, *4724*
Postage stamps depicting scenes, *4723*
Prehistoric hoax, *1376*
Prepared-food producer, *2368*
Prohibition Party convention, *4067*
Railroad owned by a city, *8317*
Rodeo for roping and tying steers, *1375*
Sawmill to use a band saw, *1863*
School for blind African-American students, *2946*

1869—*continued*

Senate hearing witness who was a woman, *3665*
State dairy association, *1621*
State probation officer for juvenile delinquents, *7005*
State university to grant equal privileges to women, *2776*
Steeplechase, *7796*
Sulfur deposit, *3387*
Supreme Court nominee to die before taking office, *3748*
Toothpick manufacturing machine, *2462*
Transcontinental railroad service, *8318*
Vacuum cleaner that used suction, *2216*
Waffle iron patent, *2279*

1870

African-American cadet admitted to West Point, *3107*
African-American to vote under authority of the 15th Amendment, *3772*
Animated photograph projection before a theater audience, *1193*
Autopsy performed by a woman physician on a male corpse, *2299*
Baking powder manufacturer, *2369*
Boardwalk, *3416*
Brick pavement on a city street, *3415*
Can opener with a cutting wheel, *2276*
Canoe club, *7572*
Check protectors, *1726*
Clearinghouse for stocks and bonds, *1774*
Coin box for streetcars, *8367*
College summer school, *2779*
Congressional representative censured for corruption, *3605*
Congressional representative who was African-American, *3606*
Department of Justice, *4170*
Entomology professor at a college, *2777*
Justice of the peace who was a woman, *3709*
Law school graduate who was a woman, *2780*
Medal of Honor awarded to a Jewish soldier, *5509*
Natural gas for use in manufacturing, *6595*
Newspaper premiums, *1526*
Paper bags with flat bottoms, *1997*
Pension granted to the widow of a president, *4227*
Petroleum jelly, *5239*
Proposal for standard time, *2630*
Railroad signal system with automatic electric block, *8388*
Railroad to install track water tanks, *8387*
Road pavement of sheet asphalt, *3417*
Sandblasting process, *1893*
School for African-American children established by a state, *2947*
Senator who was African-American, *3666*
Sorority at a college, *2778*
Stamp auction, *4725*
State governor to be impeached and convicted, *4378*
State supreme court justice who was African-American, *3708*
Subway, *8376*
Tong organized crime gang, *6937*
Trademark, *3980*
Yiddish newspaper, *4560*

1871

Amateur athletic games held outdoors, *7938*
Art museum to sell reproductions, *3141*
Bandwagon, *1527*
Baseball game between an all-white team and an all-African-American team, *7498*
Baseball league, *7497*
Baseball player to play as a professional, *7496*
Carousel patent, *1001*
Cement, *3341*
Choral concerts featuring spirituals, *1240*
College entrance plan using certified schools, *2784*
Corrugated paper, *2022*
Dermatology chair at a college, *3069*
Elks grand lodge, *7211*
Forest fire of consequence, *5974*
Half holiday on Saturday for factory workers, *7124*
Hebrew newspaper, *4561*
Human cannonball, *1377*
Land grant college for African-American students, *2781*
Lifesaving service established by the federal government, *7344*
Masonic lodge of African-Americans to be recognized, *7196*
Medical chemistry course at a college, *3070*
Narrow-gauge locomotive, *8338*
National rifle society, *7882*
Natural gas plant operated by a city, *6596*
Neurology textbook, *5322*
Oranges of the seedless navel variety, *1622*
Perforated wrapping paper, *2021*
Political economy chair at a college, *2782*
Popcorn snack, *2370*
Relief map, *4484*
Rotary printing press with a continuous-roll feed, *2046*
Speech delivered before the House of Representatives by an African-American representative, *3607*

Surgeon general, *7249*
Surgeon who was a woman, *5027*
Theological school to admit women as students, *2783*
Unitarian woman minister, *6236*
Visible speech method of instruction for deaf students, *2948*

1872

Adding machine to print totals and subtotals, *1668*
African-American midshipman at the Naval Academy, *3118*
African-American to serve as interim state governor, *4383*
Allergy book, *5323*
Arbor Day, *2499*
Ban on sex discrimination in employment enacted by a state, *7437*
Baseball player on a white team who was African-American, *7499*
Bird refuge established by a state, *5943*
Book showing photographs of movements in sequence, *4626*
Burglar alarm system, *3280*
Candy packaged in a factory, *2371*
Cigarette-manufacturing machine, *7065*
Congressional representative to serve a single day, *3608*
Danish newspaper, *4562*
Dental floss dispenser, *2463*
Doughnut cutter, *2280*
Dried milk patent, *2372*
Engineer who was a woman, *3224*
Fish hatchery run by the federal government, *1623*
Labor Reform Party national convention, *4068*
Lawyer who was an African-American woman, *3968*
Liberal Republican convention, *4069*
Lunch wagon, *1819*
Mail fraud law enacted by Congress, *4679*
Mail-order business, *2087*
Mohair, *2134*
National park, *5990*
Natural gas pipeline constructed over a long distance, *6597*
Nurse to receiving formal training, *5028*
Optometry school, *3071*
Patent list, *1488*
Photographs showing action, *4627*
Popular science magazine, *6782*
Presidential candidate nominated by prohibition advocates, *4067*
Presidential candidate who was a woman, *3808*
Presidential candidate who was Catholic, *3810*
Sprinkler system patent, *7328*
Vacuum canning process, *2341*
Vice presidential candidate who was African-American, *3809*

1873

Barbed wire commercial production, *1864*
Brass rod, *1937*
Cable car put into service, *8369*
Collapsible tube machine, *2658*
College president who was a woman, *2786*
Earmuffs, *2252*
Education department at a college, *2785*
Football rules, *7687*
Gas-powered streetcar, *8368*
Hotel that was fireproof, *1820*
Illustrated daily newspaper, *4515*
International football game, *7688*
Linoleum, *2561*
Margarine manufacturer, *2373*
National measurement organization, *1489*
Natural gas for use in ironworking, *6595*
Oratorio by an American, *1241*
Organization to offer free lunches for the poor and sick, *7213*
Patent examiner who was a woman, *3996*
Patent for a gold dental crown, *5086*
Postal card, *4680*
Prison built for women and managed by women, *7006*
Public school kindergarten, *2949*
Railroad coupler, *8389*
Silo, *1624*
Slicing machine, *2281*
State to make Memorial Day a legal holiday, *2497*
Trade dollars, *4034*
Transatlantic crossing attempted by a balloon, *7998*
Water filtration system using sand, *7415*

1874

African-American elected to Phi Beta Kappa, *2791*
Baseball teams to travel abroad, *7500*
Child abuse prevention organization, *7215*
Coeducational medical school in the world, *3056*
Coins manufactured for a foreign government, *4035*
Corset, *2253*
Football goalpost, *7689*
Hospital record system, *5111*
Hutterites, *6277*

1874—*continued*

Ice cream soda, *2374*
International rifle tournament of consequence, *7883*
Label patent, *3997*
Labor union label, *7125*
Lawn tennis, *7917*
Lithuanian newspaper, *4563*
Mechanical engineering laboratory, *2787*
Musical with an American theme and original score, *1440*
National temperance society for women, *7066*
Osteopathic physician, *5029*
Physiology laboratory, *5163*
Political cartoon showing the Republican Party as an elephant, *4579*
Railroad interlocking signal machine, *8390*
Reigning king to visit the United States, *3925*
Screw caliper, *2659*
Sprinkler head, *7329*
Steel arch bridge, *3244*
Store with fixed prices, *2088*
Tin factory, *1938*
Young Men's Hebrew Association, *7214*
Zoo, *3142*

1875

African-American senator to serve a full term, *3666*
Baseball game in which a team had no hits in nine innings, *7502*
Baseball glove, *7501*
Book manuscript that was typewritten, *4457*
Bowling rule standardization, *7580*
Cantilever bridge, *3245*
Cash carrier system, *1669*
Catholic bishop who was African-American, *6279*
Catholic priest from the United States to be made a cardinal, *6278*
Centennial celebration of the Revolution, *2501*
Christmas cards to be printed in color, *2500*
Coaching club, *7961*
College program of study abroad, *2788*
Comic strip in a newspaper, *4580*
Dental drill powered by electricity, *5087*
Dynamo for a direct-current outdoor lighting system, *6538*
Electric tattoo machine, *2464*
Federal law restricting immigration, *6077*
Floating hospital, *5112*
Folding bed, *2562*
Football uniforms worn in a game, *7690*
Former president to become a senator, *4137*
Jim Crow law, *6137*
Kentucky Derby horse race, *7797*
Music professor at a college, *2789*
National banking association, *1727*
National forestry association, *5975*
Nautical school established by a city, *3198*
Oat-crushing machine, *2375*
Pension plan, *7126*
Quintuplets, *2150*
Rabbinical college, *2790*
Railroad parlor car, *8356*
State agricultural experiment station, *1625*
Theosophical society, *7216*
Time lock, *3281*
Tuberculosis sanatorium, *5125*

1876

Actors' home, *1441*
Animal crackers, *2376*
Baseball game that was a shutout, *7503*
Baseball players to hit home runs, *7504*
Bible translation by a woman, *6362*
Bicycle factory, *7641*
Carpet sweeper, *2217*
Centennial exhibition, *1490*
Coach riding, *7962*
Coast Guard officers' training school, *3106*
Cooking school, *3199*
Court tennis, *7918*
Crematory, *2300*
Dermatology treatise, *5324*
Doctoral degree awarded to an African-American by an American university, *2791*
Electric organ, *1300*
Electric turnstile with a rachet, *1671*
Ethical culture society, *7217*
Free kindergarten, *2950*
Greenback Party convention, *4070*
Hair clipper, *2465*
High-speed newspaper printing and folding machine, *2047*
Intercollegiate athletic association, *7939*
Intercollegiate football association, *7692*
Intercollegiate football championship, *7691*
Intercollegiate track meet, *7940*
Library journal, *3015*
Lifesaving medal awarded by the Treasury Department, *7345*
Mimeograph, *2048*
National chemistry organization, *6721*
National library association, *3016*
National political convention to be addressed by a woman, *4071*
Ordained clergyman who was deaf, *6258*
Patent medicine to achieve nationwide popularity, *5240*
Pipe or screw wrench, *2660*
Polo club, *7867*
Polo mallets and balls, *7868*

Public exhibition of postage stamps, *4726*
Research university, *2792*
Sardine cannery, *2377*
State forestry association, *5976*
Stenotype device, *1670*
Symphonic work by an American composer, *1242*
Telephone conversation, *4864*
Telephone conversation over outdoor wires, *4865*
Telephone patent, *4864*
Title guaranty insurance company, *1961*
Torpedo boat, *8476*
Woman elected to the American Medical Association, *5218*
Woman to earn an engineering degree, *3224*

1877

African-American town in continuous existence, *3523*
Amateur open swimming championship meet, *7909*
Bicycle magazine, *7642*
Cabinet member who had served as a Confederate officer, *4179*
Catamaran, *7573*
Chinese language and literature lectureship at a college, *2793*
Cricket magazine, *7632*
District nurse, *5030*
Doctoral degree awarded to a woman, *2794*
Dog show, *1378*
Easter egg roll, *2502*
Federal marshal who was African-American, *7361*
Flag Day, *2503*
Granola, *2397*
Heating system to heat buildings from a central station, *3282*
Interstate telephone call, *4867*
Margarine law, *2378*
Millionaire with a fortune greater than $100 million, *1704*
Monument to an American poet, *7174*
National animal humane society, *7218*
News dispatch by telephone, *4516*
Occupational therapy treatment, *5391*
Organ with color display, *1301*
Socialist Labor Party of North America national convention, *4072*
Strike suppressed by federal troops in peacetime, *7127*
Telephone concert held long-distance, *1243*
Telephone for domestic use, *4866*
Telephone switchboard or exchange, *4868*
Use of the term "First Lady" to refer to the president's wife, *4228*
West Point graduate who was African-American, *3107*

1878

Airship, *7999*
Baseball catcher's mask, *7506*
Baseball catchers' chest protector, *7505*
Bicycle club, *7643*
Coffee in a can, *2379*
College daily newspaper, *4517*
Copper refinery furnace, *1939*
Electric company, *6539*
Electric light in a store, *6540*
Firehouse pole, *7330*
Floating soap, *2466*
Fruit spraying, *1626*
Fuller's earth, *3388*
Hotel for women, *1821*
Milk delivery in glass bottles, *2380*
Modern dancer, *1050*
National society of lawyers, *3969*
Phonograph, *4827*
President to use a telephone, *4138*
Probation system for criminals of all ages, *7007*
Railroad bridge entirely of steel, *3246*
Telephone directory, *4869*
Telephone operator who was a woman, *4870*
Typing school, *3200*
Unassisted triple play in organized baseball, *7507*

1879

African-American nurse to receive formal training, *5028*
Amateur athletic competition, *7941*
Automatic telephone system, *4871*
Cash register, *1672*
Centrifugal cream separator, *2381*
Christian Science church, *6280*
Court case to establish the personhood of Native Americans, *6078*
Electric arc streetlights, *7408*
Electric company organized to produce and sell electricity, *6542*
Electricity generated by Niagara Falls waterpower, *6541*
Factory inspection law enacted by a state, *7128*
Five-cent store, *2089*
Hearing aid, *5267*
Incandescent lamp, *6543*
Indoor ice skating rink, *7841*
Lawyer who was a woman to be admitted to practice before the Supreme Court, *3970*
Locomotive to use oil for fuel, *8339*

1879—*continued*

Milk bottles, *1998*
National archeology organization, *6722*
Photograph taken by incandescent electric light, *4641*
School of prominence for Native American children, *2951*
State ban on the employment of women in a dangerous occupation, *7129*
Sugar substitute, *2382*
Veterinary school established by a state, *3072*

1880

Antibacterial mouthwash, *2467*
Bacteriology textbook, *5325*
Balloon pilot who was a woman, *8000*
Bareknuckle world heavyweight boxing champion, *7595*
City with a population of more than 1 million, *3524*
Clay pigeon target for trapshooting, *7884*
Croquet league, *7963*
Electric streetlight installed in a city, *7410*
Flour rolling mill, *2383*
Greenback Labor Party convention, *4073*
Halftone engraving, *1037*
Horse whose total purses exceeded $100,000, *7798*
Hydroelectric power plant to furnish arc lighting service, *6544*
Incandescent lamp factory, *6545*
Italian newspaper, *4564*
Laryngology journal, *5326*
National bicycle organization, *7644*
National mechanical engineering society, *3225*
Neurasthenia book, *5327*
Obelisk to be brought to the United States, *7175*
Paint mixed to a consistent standard, *2656*
Paint prepared from standard formulas, *2661*
Patent on an electrical hearing aid, *5268*
Pay station telephone service, *4872*
Play presented by a Jewish professional acting troupe, *1442*
Presidential seal, *4139*
Safety razor, *2468*
Salvation Army services, *6281*
Sewage-disposal system separate from the city water system, *7409*
Steam distribution plant, *6598*
Steamboat to employ electric lights successfully, *8435*
Tennis tournament of national scope, *7919*
Tunnel construction using compressed air, *3440*

1881

Architect who was a woman, *3226*
Bonding company, *1962*
Business school at a college, *2795*
Centrifugal cream separator with continuous flow, *2381*
Coast Guard inland station, *5544*
Cold storage plant, *1865*
College baseball player who was African-American, *7508*
Electric light from a power plant in a residence, *6547*
Electric locomotive headlight, *8391*
Film rolls for cameras, *4642*
Fishing magazine, *7672*
Greek drama, *1443*
Halftone printing plate, *2049*
Horse bred in the United States to win the English Derby, *7799*
Incandescent light bulbs in widespread use, *6546*
International commercial telephone service, *4873*
Locomotive to attain a speed of one mile in less than a minute, *8340*
Loganberry, *1627*
Matzah factory, *2358*
National labor organization, *7130*
National tennis championship matches, *7921*
National tennis society, *7920*
Player piano, *1302*
Player piano that was completely automatic, *1303*
Plumbing law enacted by a state, *7411*
President to be treated by a woman medical practitioner, *4266*
President whose mother lived at the White House, *4256*
Presidential candidate to make campaign speeches in a foreign language, *3811*
Psychology laboratory, *5164*
Pure food and drug law enacted by a state, *7251*
Quarantine law for plants enacted by a state, *7250*
Red Cross meeting, *7219*
Rotary jail, *7008*
Statue cast by the federal government, *7176*
Steel-hulled ferryboat, *8436*
Universal constant in physics to be measured by American scientists, *6741*

1882

Accounting society, *1705*
Alcohol abuse programs required in schools by the federal government, *7067*

Bicycle trip of 100 miles sponsored by a club, *7645*
Building shaped like an elephant, *3283*
Christmas tree decorated with electric lights, *2504*
Cooperative store at a college, *2090*
Dynamo that was successful, *6549*
Electric fan, *2563*
Electric power plant operated by a city, *6548*
Electric power station with a central source, *6550*
Federal ban on polygamy that was enforced, *7436*
Flicker animation, *1194*
Forestry book, *5977*
Home economist, *7252*
Honors program offered by a university, *2796*
Hotel to install electric lights, *1822*
Immigration ban enacted by Congress, *6080*
Intercollegiate lacrosse association, *7964*
Knights of Columbus meeting, *7220*
Labor Day parade, *1379*
Lipreading instruction for deaf people, *3201*
Naval attache, *5602*
Newspaper printing plant to install electricity, *2050*
Restrictions by Congress on immigration of Chinese laborers, *6079*
Royal palace, *3926*
Silk sutures and ligatures, *5173*
Steel mill to install an electrical machine, *1940*
Tariff commission established by Congress, *4416*
Theater lighted by electricity, *1445*
Yiddish theater performance, *1444*

1883

Antitrust law enacted by a state, *1491*
Apartment house cooperative, *2527*
Baseball game at night, *7509*
Catalog of government publications, *3844*
Chair of modern pathology at a college, *3055*
Cigar-rolling machine, *7068*
Coronation, *3927*
Correspondence course of a serious nature, *3202*
Crane, *1866*
Cross-country championships, *7943*
Electric elevated railroad, *8319*
Electrical engineering school at a college, *2797*
Fence made of woven wire, *1628*
History of African-Americans, *7476*
Intercollegiate lawn tennis match, *7922*
Labor unions to be legalized by a state, *7131*
Mail chute, *4681*
Major league baseball player who was African-American, *7508*
Missionary training school, *2798*
National animal rights organization, *7221*
Newsboy, *4519*
Newspaper delivery train, *4518*
Opera produced at the Metropolitan Opera House, *1319*
Pharmacist who was a woman to receive a degree from a pharmacy college, *3073*
Plate glass produced on a large scale, *3359*
Recipe for animal crackers, *2376*
Rodeo at which cash prizes were awarded, *1380*
Sports trainer to work professionally, *7942*
Standard time program, *2630*
Steel-cut nails, *2662*
Vaudeville show, *1446*
Wild West Show, *1381*
Wrecking crane, *1867*
Yellow pages telephone directory, *4874*

1884

Albert Medal presented to a person born in America, *6895*
American Derby horse race, *7800*
American poet honored in Westminster Abbey, *1095*
Anti-Monopoly Party convention, *4074*
Baseball championship, *7510*
Bullfight, *7613*
Catholic hillside shrine, *6282*
Chrome tanning process, *2135*
Dean of faculty at a college, *2799*
Drama school, *3204*
Equal Rights Party convention, *4077*
Evaporated milk, *2385*
Fountain pen, *2679*
Glider flight, *8001*
Graduate student who was a woman to receive a university fellowship, *2801*
Keynote speech by an African-American at a major party convention, *4075*
Linotype machine, *2051*
Long-distance telephone call, *4875*
Manual training school entirely financed by public taxes, *3203*
Martini, *2384*
Medical society for African-Americans, *5221*
National political convention of a major party presided over by an African-American, *4076*
Naval Academy graduate to attain the rank of rear admiral, *3108*
Newspaper clipping bureau, *4520*
Newspaper syndicate, *4521*
Parent-teacher assocation, *2952*

1884—*continued*

Photograph of a lightning flash, *6401*
Photograph of a tornado, *5907*
Police bureau of identification, *7362*
Roller coaster, *1002*
Round-the-world bicycle trip, *7646*
Skyscraper, *3284*
State college for women, *2800*
Theater to employ women as ushers, *1447*
Underground burial of electric wires to be required by a state, *7412*
Vending machine that dispensed liquid automatically, *1673*
Vice presidential candidate who was a woman, *3812*
Wall Street stock index, *1775*
Woman presidential candidate who was eligible to hold office, *3808*

1885

Appendectomy, *5344*
Bacteriology lectures for medical students, *3076*
Baseball batting and fielding cage, *7511*
Baseball team of African-American players to play professionally, *7512*
Biology course offered at a college, *2802*
Catalog of first American editions of American authors, *4458*
Clock movement to be electrically wound, *2631*
Cowgirl, *1382*
Dealer in Oriental rugs, *2564*
Economics association, *6723*
Electric streetcars commercially operated, *8370*
Episcopal bishop who was African-American, *6283*
First aid instruction, *7346*
Forest reserve established by a state, *5978*
Gasoline pump, *1868*
Graduate school for women, *2803*
Local anesthetic, *5053*
Local library society, *3017*
Motorboat pleasure craft, *8437*
Movie film, *1206*
Naval war college, *3109*
Nursing society, *5222*
Patent granted to an inventor who was an African-American woman, *3998*
Penalty rule in football, *7693*
Piggyback railroad operation, *8320*
President elected for two nonconsecutive terms, *4140*
Savings group for children, *1728*
Self-service restaurant, *1823*
Special delivery mail service, *4682*
State banking association, *1729*
State gas commission, *6599*
State legislator who was African-American to represent a constituency with a white majority, *4388*
Surfing in Southern California, *7958*
Tuberculosis sanatorium using modern treatment methods, *5126*
Unofficial boxing match under the Marquis of Queensberry rules, *7598*
Yiddish daily newspaper, *4560*

1886

Adding machine successfully marketed, *1674*
African-American Catholic priest assigned to work in the United States, *6284*
Air gun, *5858*
Aluminum pots, *2282*
Avon Lady, *2469*
Bill bearing the likeness of a woman, *4036*
Boat race for fishermen, *7574*
Cola drink, *2386*
College for women to affiliate with a university, *2804*
Construction of the Statue of Liberty on site, *3497*
Coursing club, *7801*
Daredevil to jump off the Brooklyn Bridge and survive, *1383*
Dedication ceremony for the Statue of Liberty, *3498*
Dishwasher, *2218*
Drinking straws, *2565*
Earthquake of consequence to be recorded, *5908*
Economics journal, *6783*
Electric lighthouse, *7347*
Electric power plant using alternating current, *6551*
Electric power plant using alternating current that was commercialy successful, *6551*
Gubernatorial election in which two brothers were the opposing candidates, *4379*
International polo series, *7869*
Labor mediation and arbitration board established by a state, *7132*
Laboratory for the study of parasites in livestock, *5404*
Mineral segregation by oil flotation, *3389*
National accounting society, *1706*
Newspaper page set by linotype, *2052*
Nursing magazine, *5328*
Nursing school for African-American students, *3074*
Organization of newspaper publishers, *4597*
Ostrich farm, *1629*

Phonograph that was practical, *4828*
Playground, *2186*
Settlement house in a poor city neighborhood, *3525*
Social register published, *4459*
Soup company, *2387*
Statue presented to the United States by a foreign country, *7177*
Steel vessels of the Navy, *8477*
Stock exchange at which more than a million shares were traded in one day, *1776*
Ticker-tape parade, *1384*
Tuxedo coat, *2254*
Typewriter ribbon, *1675*
Wedding of a president in the White House, *4257*
Welding by the electric process, *1894*
Yeshivah for Jewish religious study, *2953*

1887

Accident reports by employers, *7134*
Ambassador who was Jewish, *3894*
Antiseptic surgical dressings, *5174*
Bacteriology laboratory, *5165*
Baseball player who was Native American, *7513*
Bauxite, *3390*
Book set by linotype, *4460*
Cancer hospital, *5114*
Credit insurance, *1963*
Ecologist, *7253*
European edition of an American newspaper, *4522*
Fishing rod of telescoping steel tubes, *2663*
Game warden to be paid a salary, *5944*
Hospital designed exclusively for infants, *5113*
Interstate commerce act enacted by Congress, *2075*
Kindergarten for blind children, *2954*
Labor activists to be executed, *7135*
Library school at a college, *2805*
Malted milk, *2388*
Mayor who was a woman, *3526*
Military hospital, *5200*
Monotype machine, *2053*
Mutual liability insurance company, *1964*
National physiology society, *5223*
National tennis championship match for women, *7923*
Navy contract for armor plate, *5582*
Psychology journal, *5329*
Shot tower, *5859*
Sick-leave benefit funds for teachers, *7133*
Silk loom, *2136*
Softball game, *7965*
States to make Labor Day a legal holiday, *2498*
Steel-frame building, *3285*
Train with electric lighting, *8394*

1888

Aluminum in metallic form, *1941*
Armenian newspaper, *4565*
Ball-point pen, *2680*
Bank for African-Americans operated by African-Americans, *1730*
Baseball teams to go on a world tour, *7514*
Camera to use film rolls, *4643*
Catholic seminary under the supervision of the Pope, *2806*
County created by federal law, *6081*
Double-deck ferryboat, *8439*
Electric freight locomotive, *8337*
Electric meter, *6552*
Express delivery service nationwide, *2076*
Geography magazine, *6784*
Health laboratory established by a city, *7254*
Holding companies authorized by a state, *1492*
Hotel transported from one location to another, *1824*
Incubator for premature babies, *5175*
Key time recorder, *1676*
Motorboat with a storage battery, *8438*
Observatory on a mountaintop, *6373*
Phonograph record, *4829*
Presidential nominee who was African-American, *3813*
Psychology professor at a college, *3075*
Race between a horse and a bicycle, *7802*
Revolving door, *3286*
Rodeo to charge admission, *1385*
Seismograph, *6493*
State crematory, *2301*
Sweet potato, *1630*
Union Labor Party convention, *4078*
United Labor Party convention, *4079*
Woman mayor with an all-woman town council, *3526*

1889

Bacteriology courses at a college, *3076*
Bicycle with a back-pedal brake, *7648*
Business high school, *2955*
Centralized refrigeration service, *1895*
Children's department in a library, *3018*
Conference of American republics initiated by the United States, *3890*
County high school, *2956*
Dam disaster of great consequence, *5909*
Department of Agriculture, *4180*

1889—*continued*

Dial time recorder, *1678*
Electric elevator, *3287*
Electric sewing machine, *2622*
Electric tabulating machine, *1677*
Football dummy, *7694*
General medical clinic, *5066*
Golf mixed foursome, *7749*
House majority leader, *3609*
Hydroelectric power plant generating alternating current to operate over a long distance, *6553*
International professional tennis contest, *7924*
Investment trust, *1778*
Jukebox, *4830*
Metal clarinet, *1305*
National holiday, *2505*
Night school for immigrants, *3205*
Pay telephone, *4876*
Photograph of a meteor, *6402*
Pocket lighter, *2566*
Public exhibition of postage stamps by collectors, *4726*
Ready-made clothing for children, *2255*
Ready-mix food, *2389*
Salute to the flag by schoolchildren, *3499*
Saxophone production, *1304*
Secretary of agriculture, *4180*
Sewer district established by a city, *7413*
Six-day bicycle race, *7647*
State law banning trusts and monopolies in business, *1491*
State named for a person born in America, *4353*
States admitted to the Union simultaneously, *4352*
Steam tractor, *1631*
Stock quotation boards, *1777*
Transcontinental daily railroad service, *8321*
World tour by a woman traveling alone, *8531*

1890

Animal husbandry professor at a college, *2807*
Antitrust law enacted by Congress, *1493*
Census compiled by machines, *6154*
Chrome-tanned leather successfully marketed, *2137*
Conservationist of note, *5910*
Crepe paper, *2023*
Dairy school at a college, *2808*
Dam filled with rocks, *3350*
Decalcomania commercial production, *2559*
Egg cream, *2390*
Election law enacted by a state to grant voting rights to women after the adoption of the Constitution, *3773*
Employment service established by a state, *7136*
Execution by electrocution, *7009*
Formal declaration of the closing of the American frontier, *6082*
Golf course with nine holes, *7750*
Hot dog, *2391*
Intercollegiate Army-Navy football game, *7696*
Lawn mower, *2664*
Lipreading school for deaf adults, *3201*
Meat inspection law enacted by Congress, *7255*
Mechanized shooting gallery, *1003*
Milk butterfat tester, *2392*
Movie made in the United States, *1112*
National polo association, *7870*
Naval militia established by a state, *5583*
Photojournalist, *4598*
Pneumatic hammer, *2665*
Power transmission installation using alternating current, *6554*
Prizefighting ban enacted by a state, *7596*
Sewage disposal by chemical precipitation, *7414*
Soccer team entirely made up of Americans, *7898*
State law requiring candidates to file expenditure reports, *3770*
State library society, *3019*
Steel-frame residence, *3288*
Tournament of Roses, *7695*
Web-fed four-color rotary printing press, *2054*
Woman delegate to a national convention of the American Federation of Labor, *7130*

1891

African-American Catholic priest ordained in the United States, *6284*
American woman of European descent to be made a Native American chief, *3928*
Anatomy research institute, *6662*
Boxing match timed by automatic timer, *7597*
Car with an electric storage battery, *8225*
Carborundum, *3391*
Congress to appropriate $1 billion, *3572*
Congressional representative elected by prohibitionists, *3610*
Corkboard patent, *3342*
Correspondence school for workers, *3207*
Deck chair for steamer passengers, *2567*
Diamonds in a meteorite, *3392*
Eye wash commercially manufactured, *5241*
Football book, *7697*

1892

1893

1893—*continued*

College extension courses, *2813*
Commemorative postage stamps, *4727*
First Lady to give birth during her husband's term in office, *4229*
Golf course with 18 holes, *7751*
Grand American Trapshoot tournament using live birds, *7885*
Highway bridge with concrete arches, *3247*
Hindu spiritual leader to visit America, *6285*
Horse race of 1,000 miles, *7803*
Kapok, *2138*
Lynching ban enacted by a state, *6138*
Movie exhibition, *1114*
Movie studio, *1113*
Moving sidewalk, *3419*
Navy medical school, *3078*
Newspaper colored supplement, *4583*
Newspaper with a color page, *4582*
Police officer who was a woman, *7363*
Postage stamps depicting a woman, *4728*
Print patent, *3999*
Railroad safety law enacted by Congress, *8322*
Recitation of the Pledge of Allegiance by adults in a public ceremony, *3501*
Relay race in a college track meet, *7944*
Slide fastener, *2256*
Sunday comics section in a newspaper, *4581*
Surgical repair of a stab wound to the heart, *5345*
Theater operated by a city, *1448*
Trademark character, *1530*
Tuberculosis laboratory established by a city, *7258*
Typewriter to produce a line of writing visible as it was being typed, *1681*
Visiting nurses, *5031*
Water filtration system for bacterial purification of a city water supply, *7415*

1894

Actor to have an exclusive movie contract, *1116*
Amateur golf tournament, *7754*
Antitoxin laboratory established by a public health department, *7261*
Card time recorder, *1682*
Catalog of recordings on disk, *1244*
Chocolate bars, *2395*
Commercial museum, *3144*
Cork for covering steam pipes, *3343*
Designation of Labor Day as a federal holiday, *2498*
Dietary standards issued by the U.S. Department of Agriculture, *7259*
Dog license law enacted by a state, *2603*
Employment office established by a city, *7137*
Full-page magazine advertisement for a food product, *1531*
Golf magazine, *7752*
Greek newspaper, *4566*
Intercollegiate fencing championship competition, *7667*
Labor union discrimination law enacted by a state, *7138*
Leprosy hospital, *5116*
Magic lantern feature show, *1387*
Medical inspection of schoolchildren, *7260*
Monument to a woman financed by women, *7178*
Movie to be copyrighted, *1115*
Music by Native Americans to be recorded, *1245*
National championship stroke-play golf match, *7753*
National golf association, *7755*
National organization of Jewish women, *7204*
Osteopathic physicians who were women, *5032*
Osteopathy journal, *5332*
Pediatrics book written for parents, *2187*
Peep show using film in a vending machine, *1386*
Polio epidemic, *5094*
Postage stamps printed by the Bureau of Engraving and Printing, *4717*
Railroad to use an electric engine, *8323*
Round-the-world bicycle trip by a woman, *7652*
State legislators who were women, *4389*
Steel sailing vessel, *8440*
Tuberculosis research laboratory, *5166*
Vedanta Center, *6285*

1895

Amateur golf championship tournament for women, *7758*
Amateur golf tournament held under the rules of the USGA, *7754*
Automobile club, *8227*
Bathhouses mandated by a state, *7262*
Battleship, *8478*
Cafeteria, *1825*
Canal made of concrete, *3324*
Car magazine, *8226*
Car patent, *8228*
Car race, *7616*
Carbide factory, *1897*
Cat show, *1388*
Cereal sold as a breakfast food, *2397*
Chiropractor, *5033*
College course in the contemporary novel, *2814*

College for women founded as a Catholic institution, 2815
Electric elevated railroad that was permanent, 8319
Glass-blowing machine, 3361
Glider with cambered wings, 8003
Golf book, 7756
Important bowling convention to standardize rules, 7580
Intercollegiate basketball game, 7554
Medicine ball, 7966
Milk pasteurized commercially, 2396
Movie production company, 1119
Movie recorded on film to be shown on a screen, 1117
Movies with color, 1118
National anti-saloon league, 7070
National manufacturing assocation, 1494
Navy submarine contract, 8510
Open golf championship tournament, 7757
Pneumatic tires, 8185
Professional football game, 7700
Rolling lift bridge, 3248
Round-the-world solo sailing journey, 8532
Shoot-the-chutes, 1005
Slot machine, 1802
Statue officially sanctioned by the Pope, 7179
Volleyball, 7967

1896

Absentee voting law enacted by a state, 3775
Actors' union, 7139
Airplane model to make a sustained flight under its own power, 8004
All-fiction pulp magazine, 4614
Audubon society, 5912
Book review newspaper supplement, 4523
Car accident, 8230
Car produced for commercial sale, 8229
Car race on a racetrack, 7617
Certified public accountant, 1707
Chop suey, 2399
College cricket club team to tour England, 7633
Company nurse, 5034
Composer born in America to win an international reputation, 1246
Discus-throwing competition, 7945
Electric alternator, 6555
Electric socket operated by a pull chain, 2569
Electric stove, 2283
Flashlight, 2666
Geologist who was a woman, 6494
Golf player in an official amateur tournament who was African-American, 7759
Golfer to win the United States Women's Amateur Championship, 7760
Health ordinance prohibiting spitting, 7264
Hospice for incurable cancer patients, 5392
Hydroelectric power plant to use a storage battery, 6556
Intercollegiate basketball game with five-man teams, 7554
Intercollegiate bicycle race, 7653
Latvian newspaper, 4567
Life insurance policy rated substandard, 1991
Matchbooks, 2568
Milk sale regulations enacted by a city, 7263
Movie exhibition in a theater to a paying audience, 1121
Movie kiss, 1120
Nonfiction best-seller, 1097
Oil wells successfully drilled in the ocean, 6601
Olympic athlete from the United States to win a gold medal, 7850
Pet cemetery, 2604
Physician who was a Chinese woman, 5035
Pneumatic piano player, 1306
Presidential candidate to ride in a car, 3814
Psychiatric institute, 3079
Recipes using standard measurements, 2398
Rural free mail delivery, 4684
Sawmill driven by electricity, 1870
Silverite national convention, 4082
State senator who was a woman, 4390
Symphonic work by an American woman, 1247
Telephone exchange with a rotating dial, 4871
Tennis champions who were brothers, 7925
Transatlantic trip by rowboat, 8533
Uniforms for working women, 2257
X-ray photograph, 5131

1897

Assistance to blind readers by the Library of Congress, 7034
College to offer training for teachers in Jewish schools, 6214
Comic strip in continuous newspaper publication, 4584
Condensed soup, 2400
Country day school, 2958
Electric taxicabs, 8231
Frontier Day, 2506
Garbage incinerator, 5913
Gelatin dessert, 2401
Hospital for disabled children established by a state, 5117
Ice cream sundae, 2402
Indoor fly casting tournament, 7673
Intercollegiate football game between African-American colleges, 7701
Intercollegiate golf association, 7761

1897—*continued*

Marathon race held annually, *7946*
Milk station operated by a city government, *7265*
Municipal subway, *8377*
National parent-teacher association, *2957*
National Zionist organization, *6286*
Performance of The Stars and Stripes Forever, *1248*
President to appear on film, *4275*
Rock wool insulation factory, *3344*
Settlement house serving an Hispanic population, *3527*
State accounting society, *1708*
Submarine fitted with an internal combustion engine, *8511*
Tuberculosis hospital for the poor established by a city, *5127*
Vending machine to sell food from bulk, *1683*
X-ray of the entire body of a living person made in a single exposure, *5132*
Yeshivah to offer advanced-level learning, *2953*

1898

Ambulance ship operated by the Navy, *5202*
Arabic newspaper, *4568*
Armored car, *8234*
Army officer killed in battle in the Spanish-American War, *5727*
Balloon destroyed by enemy gunfire, *5460*
Cancer laboratory, *5167*
Capture of a ship in the Spanish-American War, *5724*
Car advertisement in a specialty magazine, *1533*
Car driver who was a woman, *8232*
Car exported from the United States, *8233*
Car insurance policy, *1965*
Celluloid photographic film, *4644*
Cornflakes, *2397*
County library, *3020*
Dentist officially employed in the Army, *5201*
Diesel engine built for commercial service, *8186*
Documentary movies of an American war, *5723*
Envelope folding and gumming machine, *2024*
First Lady to earn a college degree in a scientific field, *4230*
Foreign service school in a college, *2817*
Forestry school at a college, *2816*
Interurban streetcar line, *8373*
Island territory annexed by the federal government, *6083*
Land battle in the Spanish-American War, *5728*
Log-rolling national championship tournament, *7968*
Mayor of metropolitan New York City, *3509*
Military campaign medal, *5510*
Military expeditionary force to be sent beyond the Western Hemisphere, *5726*
Monthly cumulative index of books, *4461*
Musical comedy written by African-Americans for African-American performers, *1449*
National optometry society, *5226*
Navy officer killed in action in the Spanish-American War, *5725*
Physiology journal, *5333*
Postcard, *4685*
Roller coaster with a loop-the-loop, *1006*
Social Democracy of America Party national convention, *4083*
State law requiring schoolchildren to salute the American flag, *3502*
Steel dam, *3351*
Submarine that was practical and submersible, *8512*
Truck, *8292*
Truth-in-advertising law enacted by a state, *1532*
Tuberculosis sanatorium established by a state, *5128*
Vending machine law enacted by a city, *1684*

1899

Admiral of the Navy, *5603*
Baseball "Home Run King," *7517*
Bicycle racer to attain the speed of a mile a minute, *7654*
Car accident fatality, *8238*
Car factory, *8235*
Certified public accountant who was a woman, *1709*
Children's museum, *3145*
Clincher tire, *8187*
Driver arrested for speeding, *8236*
Driver license board, *8188*
Golf champion born in America, *7762*
Golf tee, *7763*
Hungarian newspaper, *4569*
Juvenile court, *3710*
Kosher wine, *2403*
Librarian who was African-American, *3021*
Mail truck, *4686*
Medal of Honor awarded to an African-American soldier, *5511*
Message sent by wireless transmission, *4776*
Movie western, *1122*
National physics association, *6724*

Newspaper published at sea to use a radio news service, *4512*
Parade of automobiles, *1389*
Police patrol wagon, *7364*
Portable church, *6287*
Primary election law enacted by a state, *3776*
Public garage, *8237*
Rhodes Scholars, *2819*
Rubber shoe heel, *2258*
Sheet music to sell millions of copies, *1249*
Six-day two-man bicycle race, *7650*
State-sponsored council for the arts, *4356*
Ticker-tape parade for a celebrity, *1390*
Tuberculosis hospital established by Congress, *5129*
Tuberculosis hospital for needy patients, *5130*
University press, *2818*
Vacuum cleaner driven by a motor, *2219*
Voting machines in congressional elections, *3611*
Woman executed in the electric chair, *7009*

1900

Automatic computing pendulum scale, *1685*
Automatic plate-casting and finishing machine for stereotype printing, *2055*
Bonds payable specifically in United States gold coins, *1779*
Books of postage stamps, *4729*
Bowling with duckpins, *7582*
Car advertisement in a national magazine, *1534*
Car show, *8239*
Championship heavyweight boxing title won in the first round, *7599*
Chinese daily newspaper, *4558*
Chiropractic school, *3080*
Grand American Trapshoot tournament with clay targets, *7886*
Hurricane to cause extensive destruction, *5914*
Industrial research laboratory, *1495*
International tennis matches for the Davis Cup challenge trophy, *7926*
Kindergarten for children with disabilities, *2959*
Laborsaving machine approved by a labor union, *7140*
Medal of Honor awarded to an African-American soldier for an action in the Civil War, *5512*
Motorcycle that was practical, *8286*
National business organization for African-Americans, *1496*
National political convention at which a woman made a seconding speech, *4086*
Olympic athlete from the United States to win 10 medals, *7851*
Orthodontists' society, *5227*
Penny restaurant, *1826*
Public school for children with disabilities, *2960*
Revolver shooting tournament, *7887*
Road map for motorists, *4485*
Sightseeing bus, *8218*
Social-Democratic Party of America national convention, *4084*
Union Reform Party convention, *4087*
United Christian Party convention, *4085*
Water-quality standards enacted by a state, *7266*
Wedding by telegraph, *2593*

1901

Academic hall of fame, *3146*
Army dental corps, *5203*
Army nurse corps for women, *5204*
Army war college, *3110*
Bowling tournament sponsored by the American Bowling Congress, *7583*
Building with an all-marble dome, *3290*
Car hill-climbing contest, *7618*
Car to exceed the speed of a mile a minute, *8241*
Catalog cards from the Library of Congress, *3023*
Catholic mass for night workers, *6288*
City government using the commission plan, *3528*
Corporation with a capitalization of $1 billion, *1497*
Daredevil to go over Niagara Falls in a barrel, *1391*
Dean of students at a college, *2820*
Electrical hearing aid, *5268*
Escalator of the modern type, *3289*
License plates for vehicles, *8189*
Long-distance car race, *7619*
Mercury vapor lamp, *6558*
Motorcycle with a built-in gasoline engine, *8287*
Professional open golf championship match, *7764*
Professor at a first-class medical school who was a woman, *3081*
Shaft-driven car, *8240*
Speed limits for motor vehicles, *8190*
State archival agency, *4357*
Steam turbine operated by a public utility to produce electricity, *6557*
Union catalog of books in American libraries, *3022*

1902

Animal crackers packaged in a circus box, *2376*
Arabic daily newspaper, *4568*
Building with a large-scale clear-span dome, *3292*
Cancer research fund, *5118*
Cut glass, *3362*
Envelope with a window, *2025*
Factory with temperature and humidity control, *3291*
Federal penitentiary, *7010*
Fistfight in the Senate, *3667*
Labor dispute resolved through presidential intervention, *7142*
Laboratory for the study of human parasites, *5168*
Motorcycle endurance run, *7846*
Newspaper published daily at sea to carry world news, *4512*
Oil journal, *6785*
Postage stamp depicting an American woman, *4730*
President to ride in a car, *4293*
Restaurant with an automatic arrangement for vending food, *1827*
School nurses in public schools, *5036*
Steel seven-masted schooner, *8441*
Suturing of a heart wound, *5346*
Taxidermy method of stuffing animals, *6663*
Technical college for women, *2821*
Teddy bear, *2188*
Theater to show movies, *1123*
Tournament of Roses intercollegiate football game, *7695*
Trade school for girls, *2961*
Transpacific telegraph cable, *4857*
Workers' compensation insurance law enacted by a state, *7141*
Young Women's Hebrew Association, *7222*

1903

Airplane flight, *8005*
Automobile school, *3208*
Bank president who was a woman, *1732*
Bird reservation established by the federal government, *5946*
Boycott prevention law enacted by a state, *1498*
Department of Commerce and Labor, *4181*
Fashion show, *1392*
Filmpack camera, *4645*
Football stadium, *7702*
Interracial labor union, *7143*
License plate issued by a state, *8192*
Motorcycle association, *7848*
Motorcycle hill-climbing contest, *7847*
Movie star, *1124*
Movie with multiple plot lines, *1125*
Multigraph, *1687*
National political science association, *6725*
Naval radio station, *5584*
Numerical system of insurance rating, *1966*
Nurses to be registered by a state, *5037*
Opera composed by a woman to be performed at the Metropolitan Opera House, *1320*
Printed traffic regulations, *8193*
Professional hockey team, *7828*
Pronghorn antelope, *5945*
Public locker plant, *1686*
Radio distress signal from an American ship, *7348*
Railroad operated by an electric third-rail system, *8324*
Safety razor successfully marketed, *2468*
Secretary of commerce and labor, *4181*
Semitic museum, *3147*
State prison to take fingerprints, *7365*
State to establish statewide primary elections, *3776*
State to require driver licenses, *8191*
Suspension bridge with steel towers, *3249*
Transatlantic radio broadcast in code, *4777*
Transcontinental car trip, *8242*
Transcontinental motorcycle trip, *8288*
Windshield wiper, *8194*
World Series baseball game, *7518*

1904

Banana split, *2404*
Border patrol officer, *6084*
Bulk mail, *4687*
Carnegie Hero Fund Commission awards, *6896*
College varsity sports program, *2822*
Comic books, *1098*
Disease research and treatment organization, *5228*
Fingerprinting in federal penitentiaries, *7367*
Hamburger, *2405*
Hotel with individually controlled air conditioning and heating in every room, *1828*
Hungarian daily newspaper, *4569*
Ice cream cone, *2406*
Installment finance company, *1759*
Intercity trucking service, *2077*
Maternity clothes to be manufactured, *2259*
Monument to commemorate the Spanish-American War, *7180*
Motorboat magazine, *8442*
Motorboat race under organized rules, *7575*
Motorcycle police, *7368*
National arts and letters organization, *7223*

National bibliography organization, *3024*
Olympic Games held in the United States, *7852*
Olympic medalist who was African-American, *7853*
Original cast recording of a stage performance, *1450*
Pharmacists to be regulated by a state, *5038*
Police department to adopt the fingerprinting system, *7366*
Radio distress signal officially established, *7349*
Radium treatment for cancer, *5393*
Rapid-transit subway, *8378*
Real estate board game, *7730*
Rotogravure press, *2056*
School of social work, *2823*
Senator convicted of a crime, *3668*
Socialist Party national convention, *4088*
Tire chains, *8195*
Use of "American" as an adjective, *3503*
Vocational high school for girls, *2962*

1905

Aerial ferry, *3251*
All-electric railroad, *8325*
Bookwagon traveling library, *3025*
Concrete cantilever bridge, *3250*
Factory cooled by air conditioning, *3293*
Fire extinguisher using vaporized chemicals, *7331*
Forest fire lookout tower, *5983*
Gas station, *8196*
Greek daily newspaper, *4566*
Helium in natural gas, *6742*
Independent laboratory for evaluating consumer products, *7297*
Intercollegiate wrestling association, *7969*
International exchange of fingerprints, *7369*
Interstate Commerce Commission Medal of Honor, *6897*
Laxative in candy form, *5242*
Movie spoof, *1127*
Movie theater, *1126*
Municipal ferryboats, *8443*
National sociology society, *6726*
Pizzeria, *1829*
Plywood, *3345*
Radio fax patents, *4467*
Rotary Club meeting, *1499*
Statue of a woman installed in the Capitol's National Statuary Hall, *7181*
Twin-cycle motorcycle, *8289*
World Series baseball game that was a shutout, *7519*

1906

Advertising show to be held annually, *1535*
Air conditioner patent, *1871*
Animated cartoon, *1195*
Balloon cup race won by an American, *7674*
Bank open day and night, *1733*
Bubble gum, *2407*
Cabinet member who was Jewish, *4182*
Consumer protection law enacted by Congress, *1500*
Diamonds in actual rock, *3394*
Double-deck bus, *8219*
Hindu temple, *6289*
Laundry detergent, *2220*
Music synthesizer powered by electricity, *1307*
National college fraternity for African-American men, *2824*
National Geographic Society gold medal, *6899*
National monument designated by the federal government, *7182*
Nobel Prize awarded to an American, *6898*
Nurse appointed to a college professorship, *5039*
President to visit a foreign country while in office, *4312*
Public archive building, *4358*
Radio program broadcast, *4778*
Radio receiver advertised, *4819*
Secret Service agent killed in the line of duty, *3845*
Stadium operated by a city, *3294*

1907

African-American to win a Rhodes Scholarship, *2819*
Airplane unit in the Army, *5461*
Balloon cup race held in the United States, *7674*
Building of pressed structural steel, *3295*
Canned tuna, *2408*
Car with the steering wheel on the left side, *8243*
Carbon microphone used in radio broadcasting, *4820*
Centralized system of medical records, *5119*
Circumnavigation of the globe by a fleet of warships, *8534*
Corrupt election practices law enacted by Congress, *3777*
Dental inlay made of gold, *5088*
Dropping of the ball in Times Square on New Year's Eve, *2507*
Electric washing machine, *2221*
Flemish newspaper, *4570*

1907—*continued*

Fund-raising organization to sell Christmas seals, *7224*
Horse farm operated by the federal government, *1635*
Hygiene department in a public school district, *7267*
Movie star who was a woman, *1128*
Night court, *3711*
Nobel Prize in physics awarded to an American, *6900*
Nonsectarian college under Jewish auspices, *2825*
Postage stamp depicting a Native American, *4731*
Rat extermination throughout an entire city, *7268*
Safety congress, *7269*
Savings bank life insurance, *1992*
Senator who was Native American, *3669*
Singer whose voice was broadcast over radio, *1250*
Squash rackets champion, *7903*
Steam-operated pressing machine, *1872*
Sterilization of humans by a state government as a matter of public policy, *7270*
Thermos bottles made in the United States, *2570*
Transatlantic radio message of the regular westward service, *4779*
Woman member of the National Institute of Arts and Letters, *7223*

1908

Airplane endurance flight exceeding one hour, *8009*
Airship disaster, *8006*
Airship ordered by the federal government, *8008*
Army field range, *5860*
Aviation magazine devoted primarily to airplanes, *8011*
Aviation trophy, *8007*
Baseball league for children, *7520*
Bibles in hotel rooms, *6290*
Brake for four-wheeled cars, *8244*
Car race from New York to Paris, *7620*
Carbon tetrachloride, *1898*
Child hygiene bureau, *7273*
Child welfare congress, *2189*
City manager, *3529*
Confectionary machine, *2409*
Credit union, *1734*
Drinking water supply to be chemically treated with chlorine compounds, *7416*
Ductile tungsten, *3395*
Fatal airplane accident, *8010*
Fireworks law enacted by a city, *7332*
Football uniform numerals, *7703*
Health department of a county organized on a full-time basis, *7272*
Heavyweight boxing champion of the world who was African-American, *7600*
Industrial toxicologist, *7271*
Journalism school at a college, *2826*
Mother's Day, *2508*
Navy admiral who was Jewish, *5604*
Navy mail service, *4688*
Navy nurses' corps, *5205*
Nursing school at a college, *3082*
Olympic athlete from the United States to win the marathon race, *7854*
Outdoor school for children with tuberculosis, *2963*
Paper cup, *2571*
Post office aboard a naval vessel, *4689*
Postage stamps in coils, *4732*
Presidential candidate to appear in movie footage, *3815*
Price regulation law enacted by a state, *1501*
Radio magazine, *6786*
Radio society, *4780*
Savings bank to offer life insurance, *1992*
Shampoo commercially produced, *2471*
Sorority for African-American college women, *2778*
Sousaphone, *1308*
State competency test for drivers, *8197*
State law prohibiting discrimination against soldiers, *5422*
Steel ski jump, *7890*
Turbine-propelled naval ship, *8479*
Workers' compensation insurance law enacted by Congress, *7144*

1909

Airplane purchased by the federal government, *8013*
Airplane race won by an American in Europe, *7675*
Airplane sold commercially, *8012*
Airship race, *7676*
Apartment house to occupy a square city block, *2528*
Apprentice continuation school, *3209*
Army pilot to fly solo in an airplane, *5462*
Baseball with a cork center, *7521*
Bed that could be hidden, *2572*
Bird hunting regulation law enacted by Congress, *7827*
Child delinquency law enacted by a state, *2190*
Christmas savings club at a bank, *1736*

Coin bearing the likeness of a president to enter circulation, *4039*
Corporation tax levied by Congress, *4418*
Credit union law enacted by a state, *1735*
Discount clothing store, *2092*
Discovery of the North Pole, *6646*
Domestic relations court, *3712*
Double-deck bridge, *3252*
Election using the preferential ballot system, *3778*
Fireproof baseball stadium, *7522*
First Lady to attend all her husband's cabinet meetings, *4231*
Formation of a new animal by transplantation, *6664*
Hydroelectric power plant built by the federal government, *6559*
International horseshoe pitching contest, *7970*
Japanese cherry trees, *1636*
Junior high school, *2964*
Memorial postage stamp, *4733*
Milk pasteurization law enacted by a city, *7274*
Monoplane, *8014*
Movie censorship board at the national level, *1129*
Narcotics ban enacted by Congress, *7071*
Naturalized citizen to lie in state in the Capitol rotunda, *3573*
Neurological disease research institute, *5120*
Old age home for pioneers, *6085*
Outboard motor, *8444*
Paint-spraying device, *2667*
Radio SOS call from an American ship, *7350*
State to make Columbus Day a legal holiday, *2491*
Subway car with side doors, *8379*
Thermosetting resin, *1899*
Transcontinental car race, *7621*
Transcontinental car trip by women, *8246*
Transcontinental journey on foot, *7971*
Unassisted triple play in a major league baseball game, *7523*
Union catalog of books in a state library, *3026*
Urban planning instruction at a college, *2827*
Year in which more than 100,000 passenger cars were produced, *8245*

1910

Abstract paintings, *1038*
Air rights lease, *3296*
Airplane bombing experiment, *5463*
Airplane flight from a ship, *8021*
Airplane flight over water, *8019*
Airplane flying school for military officers, *3111*
Airplane round trip, *8017*
Airplane to fly higher than a mile in altitude, *8018*
American woman pilot to make a solo flight, *8028*
Animal disease of American origin, *5406*
Aviation meet, *7677*
Bread factory that was completely automatic, *2412*
Chiropody school of note, *3083*
Chocolate sandwich cookie with creme filling, *2411*
Climatology professor at a college, *2828*
Commerce court established by the federal government, *3713*
Electric-gasoline combination car, *8247*
Father's Day, *2509*
Federal law requiring radios on ships, *8445*
Golf club with a steel shaft, *7765*
License plates with a graphic design, *8198*
Matador of American birth, *7614*
Mayor of a major city who was a Socialist, *3530*
Medical research chair at a college, *3084*
Millionaire who was an African-American woman, *1710*
Movie director who was a woman, *1130*
Movie made in Hollywood, *1131*
Movie star who was an inventor, *1132*
Newsreel, *4524*
Night flight in an airplane, *8016*
Opera by an American composer to be performed at the Metropolitan Opera House, *1321*
Optometry courses at a college, *3085*
Photographic copying machine, *1688*
Pilot from the United States to establish an airplane altitude record, *8015*
Pilot to fire a gun from an airplane, *5464*
President to pitch a ball to open the baseball season, *4141*
Radio broadcast sent from an airplane, *4782*
Radio contest, *4781*
Railroad tank car lined with glass, *8358*
Rayon, *2139*
Russian newspaper, *4571*
School stadium, *2965*
Shipment of merchandise by airplane, *2078*
Speedway with a board track, *7622*
State law prohibiting drunk driving, *8199*
Supreme Court justice to be appointed chief justice, *3749*
Toy pinball game machine, *7864*
Trackless trolley system, *8374*
Transatlantic airship flight, *8020*
Transcontinental solo trip on horseback by a woman, *8182*

1910—*continued*

Vichyssoise, *2410*
Woman police officer hired under civil service rules, *7363*

1911

Advertising association to combat business abuses, *1503*
Advertising campaign based on sex appeal, *1536*
Airmail pilot, *4690*
Airplane flight to the deck of a carrier, *8022*
Airplane flight under a bridge, *8027*
Airplane race between cities, *7678*
Airplane rescue at sea, *8024*
Airplane rescue at sea by another airplane, *8029*
Airplane to land on the White House lawn, *4329*
Baseball players to win the Most Valuable Player award, *7524*
Billionaire, *1711*
Blue-sky laws enacted by a state, *1502*
Boy Scouts of America uniformed troop, *2191*
Coin-operated locker, *1689*
College foreign-language house, *2829*
Congressional representative who was a Socialist, *3612*
Diesel engine in a submarine, *8513*
Electric self-starter used in cars, *8248*
Farm bureau, *1637*
Fatal airplane accident in a solo military airplane, *5466*
Federal cemetery to contain graves of both Union and Confederate soldiers, *2302*
Fingerprint conviction in a crime, *6938*
Gyrocompass installed on an American naval vessel, *8500*
Hail insurance law enacted by a state, *1967*
Hydrogenated vegetable shortening, *2413*
Hydroplane, *8023*
Indianapolis 500 race, *7623*
Jazz composer, *1251*
Klieg light unit for movie production, *1207*
Life insurance group policy, *1993*
Linoleum manufacturing machine, *2573*
Movie censorship board established by a state, *1133*
National squash tennis organization, *7904*
Naval airplane, *5467*
Navy pilot, *5465*
Nontoxic friction matches, *2547*
Photograph taken from an airplane, *4628*
Pilot licensed by the Aero Club of America, *8025*
Pilot licensed by the Aero Club of America who was a woman, *8028*
Radio car for military use, *5423*
Radio license, *4806*
Squash tennis tournament, *7905*
State aviation law, *8026*
State continuation school for adults, *3210*
State welfare program for single mothers, *2192*
State workers' compensation insurance law that was not declared unconstitutional, *7141*
Telegraph message sent around the world by commercial telegraph, *4858*
Traffic lanes designated by painted lines, *8200*
Transcontinental airplane flight made in stages, *8030*
Transcontinental group tour by car, *8249*
Transpacific radio conversation, *4783*

1912

Airplane outfitted with a machine gun, *5468*
Airplane round-trip flight over water, *8032*
Airplane torpedo, *5861*
Baseball strike, *7525*
Bra patent, *2260*
Church without theology, creed, or dogma, *6291*
City government using the manager plan, *3531*
Community chorus, *1252*
Detective who was a woman, *7371*
Director of the Federal Bureau of Investigation, *7370*
Eagle Scout, *2191*
Electric heating pad, *5177*
Electric traffic light, *8201*
Fatal airplane accident involving a woman, *8033*
Federal agency director who was a woman, *3846*
Foreign feature film exhibited, *1136*
Horse race mutuel ticket to pay more than $1,000, *7804*
Marine pilot, *5565*
Minimum wage law enacted by a state, *7145*
Movie censorship law enacted by Congress, *1137*
Movie photographed from an airplane, *1135*
Movie version of a Shakespeare play to be made in the United States, *1134*
Municipal streetcars, *8375*
National safety association, *7276*
National surgery society, *5229*
Navy dental corps, *5206*

Nobel Prize in medicine and physiology awarded to an American, *6901*
Oceanography institution, *6495*
Oil and gas production course at a college, *2830*
Olympic athlete from the United States to win the pentathlon and decathlon, *7855*
Parachute jump from an airplane, *8031*
Parcel post service, *4691*
Progressive Party national convention, *4089*
Quarantine law for plants enacted by Congress, *7275*
Scouting organization for girls, *2193*
Senator expelled for corrupt election practices, *3670*
Stuntman, *1393*
Woman pilot to cross the English Channel in an airplane, *8028*

1913

Aeronautical engineering course at a college, *2831*
African-American fellow of the American College of Surgeons, *5229*
Air combat unit of the Army, *5469*
Airplane loop-the-loop, *8036*
Alien land law, *6086*
Animated cartoon made with cel animation, *1196*
Bird for which a definite crossing of the Atlantic was recorded, *5947*
Bonding law enacted by a state, *1968*
Bowler to make a perfect score of 300, *7584*
Chiropractic regulation law enacted by a state, *5040*
Civic design chair at a college, *2833*
Coast-to-coast paved road, *3420*
College comprehensive senior examination program, *2832*
Crepe, *2140*
Crossword puzzle, *7731*
Demountable tire-carrying rim, *8202*
Dentist in the Navy to serve aboard a naval ship, *5207*
Department of Commerce, *4183*
Department of Labor, *4184*
Electrically propelled naval ship, *8480*
Federal law regulating hunting of migratory birds, *7827*
Gasoline obtained from crude petroleum by the cracking process, *6602*
Gyroscope, *8035*
Ice-loading machinery, *1873*
Immunology society, *5230*
Insulating brick, *3346*
Modern art exhibition, *1039*
Monument to a bird, *7183*
Movie of feature length made in Hollywood, *1138*
Occupational therapy course at a college, *3086*
Oil and gas conservation law enacted by a state, *6603*
Parachute jump from an airplane by a woman, *8034*
Photographs taken under the sea, *4629*
Portable movie projector, *1208*
Professional soccer organization recognized internationally, *7899*
Puffed cereal commercially manufactured, *2414*
Secretary of commerce, *4183*
Secretary of labor, *4184*
Sedan car, *8250*
Senate whip, *3671*
Senator elected by popular vote, *3672*
Serial movie with installments longer than one reel, *1139*
Sex education program for high schools, *2966*
Skyscraper higher than 750 feet, *3297*
Small claims court, *3714*
Strike settlement mediated by the federal Department of Labor, *7146*
Synthetic rubber, *1900*
Tract housing development, *3532*
Veterans of Foreign Wars of the United States meeting, *5623*
Zipper, *2261*

1914

Air-conditioned railroad cars, *8359*
Airplane flying school operated by a woman, *8037*
Alcohol prohibition vote taken in Congress, *7073*
Alkaline dry cell battery, *6560*
American to sail to Europe to fight in World War I, *5729*
Auction duplicate bridge championship, *7732*
Bank to establish a branch in a foreign country, *1737*
Bird banding by federal authorities, *5948*
Community trust charity, *7225*
Deadline for filing individual income tax returns, *4419*
Drug control law enacted by Congress, *7072*
Electric hand drill, *2668*
Electric traffic lights equipped with noise signals, *8204*
Extinction by humans of a native American animal, *5949*
Fashion show for charity, *1392*
Federal reserve banks, *1738*
First Lady whose autobiography was commercially published, *4232*

1914—*continued*

Horseshoe pitching association, *7970*
Hydroplane service, *8038*
Industrial museum, *3149*
International championship figure skating tournament, *7842*
Japanese newspaper in continuous publication, *4572*
Long-distance telephone call over underground cables, *4877*
Movie comedy of feature length, *1140*
Museum of medieval art, *3148*
Music society for the protection of composers and song writers, *1254*
Naval air training school, *3112*
Newspaper circulation audit, *4525*
Newspaper rotogravure sections, *4585*
Nobel Prize in chemistry awarded to an American, *6902*
Nonskid tires, *8203*
Orchestra conductor who was a woman, *1253*
Packaged popcorn sold commercially, *2415*
Passport photographs, *6087*
Police chief who was a woman, *7372*
Presidential proclamation establishing Mother's Day, *2508*
Prison organized into community groups, *7011*
Railroad operated by the federal government, *8326*
Skee-ball alley, *1007*
Vocational guidance chair at a college, *2834*
Woman fellow of the American College of Surgeons, *5229*

1915

American combatant to die in World War I, *5731*
Asphalt-covered racetrack, *7624*
Car finance company, *1760*
Cargo ship from the United States attacked by a German submarine in World War I, *5732*
Chiropody school at a college, *3087*
City orchestra supported by taxes, *1255*
Dental hygienists to be licensed by a state, *5041*
Election using proportional representation, *3779*
Fifty-dollar gold pieces minted by the federal government, *4040*
Filly to win the Kentucky Derby horse race, *7805*
Heat-resistant glass, *3363*
Horseshoe pitching championship tournament, *7970*
Junior chamber of commerce, *1504*
Mobile telephone one-way communication, *4879*
Movie blockbuster, *1141*
Movie shown in the White House, *4330*
Naval vessel equipped to lay mines, *8481*
Orthodontia journal, *5334*
Practical paper beverage carton, *2000*
School of modern dance, *3211*
Ship from the United States lost in World War I, *5730*
Sikh gurdwara, *6292*
Sound-absorbing material made of rigid insulating board, *3347*
State governor who was Jewish, *4380*
Submachine gun, *5862*
Submarine disaster, *8514*
Swimsuit, *2262*
Transatlantic message over radio telephone, *4882*
Transcontinental commercial telephone service, *4880*
Transcontinental demonstration of radio telephone operation, *4881*
Transcontinental telephone demonstration, *4878*
Yeshivah with a secular high school, *2953*

1916

Airplane flight longer than 500 miles, *8039*
Animated cartoon in color, *1197*
Animation for technical purposes, *1198*
Army veterinary corps, *5208*
Bird protection international treaty, *5950*
Birth control clinic, *5067*
Chess champion to play more than 100 games simultaneously, *7733*
Child labor law enacted by Congress, *7147*
Coast Guard aviation unit, *5470*
Concept of food groups, *7277*
Cover of the *Saturday Evening Post* by Norman Rockwell, *1040*
Dental hygiene book, *5335*
Election in which returns were broadcast on radio, *3816*
False eyelashes, *2472*
Golfer to win both the U.S. Open and the U.S. Amateur in the same year, *7766*
Grant-in-aid enacted by Congress to help the states build roads, *3421*
Hybrid seed corn shipment, *1639*
Indian Day, *2510*
Japanese beetle, *1638*
Movie featuring an African-American actor, *1142*
Movie sex shocker, *1143*

National park east of the Mississippi River, *5991*
National park to contain an active volcano, *5992*
National research society, *6727*
Pilot from the United States killed in World War I, *5734*
Pilot from the United States shot down in World War I, *5733*
Presidential flag, *4142*
Professional Golfers Association tournament, *7767*
ROTC unit, *3113*
Self-service grocery store, *2093*
Ship-to-shore conversation over radio telephone, *4883*
Sneakers, *2263*
Supreme Court justice who was Jewish, *3750*
Think tank in the United States, *7226*
Transcontinental motorcycle trip by women, *8290*
Zoning ordinance, *3533*

1917

Air combat unit of the Navy, *5471*
Army division to go into battle in World War I, *5742*
Army gas regiment, *5425*
Army general to fly over enemy lines, *5737*
Army training camp for African-American officers, *5424*
Automatic windshield wiper, *8205*
Bowling tournament for women, *7585*
Congressional representative who was a woman, *3613*
Gyroscopic stabilizer, *8501*
Hockey team from the United States to win the Stanley Cup, *7829*
Home studies for foster and adoptive parents, *2194*
Jazz record, *1256*
Joint stock land bank, *1739*
Liberty loan subscriptions, *1762*
Loan made by the federal Government to a war ally, *1761*
Marine regiment to land in Europe in World War I, *5739*
Maternity clinic, *2151*
Movie for training soldiers, *3114*
Naval vessels to sink an enemy submarine in the Atlantic, *5745*
Navy airship, *8040*
Navy enlisted man killed in World War I action, *5741*
Navy petty officer who was a woman, *5605*
Organization of parents of servicemen and servicewomen, *5740*
Pilot who was African-American, *5472*
Proposal for daylight saving time, *2632*
Pulitzer Prize awarded to a newspaper reporter, *4760*
Pulitzer Prize for a newspaper editorial, *4761*
Pulitzer Prize for fiction, *4762*
Radio telephone communication from an airplane, *4884*
Sale of Girl Scout cookies, *2195*
Shot fired by American infantry in World War I, *5743*
Shot fired by the Navy in World War I, *5736*
Soldiers in the American army killed by German bombers in World War I, *5744*
Soldiers in the American army killed in combat in World War I, *5744*
State legislature to use an electric vote recorder, *4391*
Tax levied by Congress on excess profits of corporations, *4420*
Tomato juice, *2416*
Transatlantic crossing by a submarine under its own power, *8535*
Troops from the United States to sail to Europe in World War I, *5738*
War in which the armed services of the United States were deployed in defense of another nation, *5735*
White bread, *2417*
Wrecking crane operated from a car, *1874*

1918

Ace of Aces from the United States, *5754*
Air combat arm of the Army, *5475*
Air combat unit of the Marine Corps, *5473*
Air squadron of the Army in World War I, *5747*
Airmail regular service, *4692*
Airmail stamps, *4734*
Airplane bombing raid by an American air unit, *5752*
Alcohol prohibition law enacted by Congress, *7075*
American air ace, *5751*
American Bar Association members who were women, *3971*
American division to cross the Rhine River in World War I, *5755*
Armored car in commercial use, *8251*
Army nursing school, *3088*
Army pilot to win a victory over an enemy airplane, *5474*
Army school for chaplains, *3115*
Art museum for children, *3150*
Cargo ship from the United States attacked by a submerged German submarine in World War I, *5732*

Astronomer to measure the size of a fixed star, *6374*
Baseball commissioner, *7528*
Blow dryer for hair, *2473*
Boxing match broadcast on radio, *7601*
Boxing match broadcast on radio from ringside, *7602*
Bras in standard sizes, *2260*
Census to show more people living in cities than in rural areas, *6155*
City radio station, *4807*
City with a population of more than 5 million, *3524*
College radio station, *4809*
Commercial radio station licensed, *4808*
Constitutional amendment proposal guaranteeing women the right to vote, *3780*
Dog racetrack to use an imitation rabbit, *7661*
Farmer Labor Party convention, *4093*
Football game to be broadcast on radio with a play-by-play description, *7705*
Hydroplane international service, *8046*
Indoor curling rink, *7635*
International federation of students, *2967*
Major league baseball player killed in a game, *7526*
News program on radio, *4527*
Olympic gold medalist from the United States who was a woman, *7856*
Orchestra from the United States to make a European tour, *1257*
Postage meter, *4694*
Professional football association, *7704*
Radio compass on a naval airplane, *5477*
Radio telephone commercial service, *4886*
Red scare, *4092*
Sanitary napkin, *2474*
Three-colored traffic signal, *8206*
Ukrainian daily newspaper, *4573*
Unassisted triple play in a World Series baseball game, *7527*
Vacuum cleaner with a disposable bag, *2222*
Wedding broadcast over the radio, *2594*

1921

Airplane bombing experiment to sink a battleship, *5864*
Airship filled with helium gas, *8049*
Bandage with built-in adhesive, *5178*
Beauty pageant to be held nationwide, *1394*
Boxing match to gross $1 million, *7603*
Broad jump to reach more than 25 feet, *7947*
Burial at the Tomb of the Unknown Soldier, *2303*
Certified public accountant who was African-American, *1712*
Cigarette tax enacted by a state, *7076*
Civil rights chair at a college, *2838*
Coin bearing the likeness of a living person to enter circulation, *4041*
Conference of great powers, *3895*
Correspondence school to offer instruction in Braille, *2968*
Father and son to occupy the same Cabinet post, *4185*
Former president to become chief justice of the Supreme Court, *4143*
Geography school at a college, *2837*
Helium plant, *6729*
Immigration quota enacted by Congress, *6088*
International fencing championship competition, *7668*
Judge to impose the death penalty who was a woman, *3716*
Modern art museum, *3152*
Opera broadcast over the radio in its entirety, *1322*
Opera broadcast over the radio with a professional cast, *1322*
Pilot who was an African-American woman, *8048*
Pulitzer Prize for a novel written by a woman, *4766*
Pulitzer Prize for an editorial cartoon, *4767*
Radio broadcast of a baseball game with a play-by-play description, *7529*
Radio church, *6296*
Radio navigation beacons, *8502*
Radio program theme song, *4785*
Religious service broadcast on radio, *6295*
Sales tax enacted by a state, *4422*
Stainless steel flatware, *2574*
Telephone cable deep-sea service, *4887*
Tennis match broadcast on radio, *7927*
Transcontinental airmail flight, *4695*
Transcontinental airplane flight made within 24 hours, *8047*
Weather forecast broadcast on radio, *6496*

1922

Automatic steering gear for ships, *8503*
Catholic nuns in a cloistered community, *6297*
Chain radio broadcast, *4787*
Circumnavigation of the world by a cruise ship, *8536*
Congressional representative who was a mother, *3614*
Daily news program on radio, *4529*
Drama broadcast on radio, *1451*
Election campaign using radio, *3781*
Electric blender, *2285*
Electric power line commercial carrier, *6561*
Golf champion to win both the U.S. Open and the Professional tournaments, *7769*

1922—*continued*

Helicopter flight, *8050*
Hotel administration course at a college, *2839*
Ice cream bar, *2419*
Intercollegiate indoor polo championship, *7871*
International golf match, *7770*
Librarian who was an African-American woman, *3021*
Massacre of strikebreakers by union members, *7148*
Microfilm reading device, *3033*
Modern carillon, *1309*
Movie in Technicolor, *1145*
National arbitration organization, *3972*
National monument to Abraham Lincoln, *7185*
Navy Day, *2512*
Peritonitis preventive, *5347*
Pilot to bail out of a disabled airplane, *8052*
Platypus to be exhibited, *1395*
President to make a radio broadcast, *4277*
President to use a radio, *4276*
Radar observations, *8504*
Radio broadcast of a debate, *4786*
Radio commercial, *1537*
Radio orchestra, *1258*
Senator who was a woman, *3673*
Shopping mall, *2094*
Skywriting advertisement exhibition, *1538*
Soybean processing plant, *1640*
State supreme court justice who was a woman, *3717*
Steel mill to produce continuous sheets, *1943*
Swimmer to cover 100 meters freestyle in less than one minute, *7910*
Taconite production, *3396*
Transatlantic radio fax transmission of a photograph, *4468*
Transcontinental airship flight, *8051*
Treaty among more than two states, *4359*
Water skis, *7990*

1923

Airplane refueling attempt in midair, *8054*
Airport runway illumination, *8055*
Balloon tire production, *8207*
Book completed entirely by one man, *4463*
Business history chair at a college, *2840*
Chinchilla farm, *1641*
Combined newspaper, *4531*
Constitutional amendment proposal mandating equal legal rights for women and men, *7438*
Dance marathon, *7972*
Dance marathon to exceed 200 hours, *7972*
Ethyl gasoline to be marketed, *6604*
Garment with a zipper, *2261*
Milky Way candy bar, *2420*
Mimeographed daily newspaper, *4530*
Movie with sound recorded on the film, *1146*
Movie with sound to feature African-American entertainers, *1142*
Neon advertising sign, *1539*
Parachute-jumping contest, *7680*
Pension laws enacted by a state, *7149*
Portable movie camera, *1209*
Precanceled stamps printed on rotary presses, *4735*
President and First Lady to die during the term for which he had been elected, *4258*
President to visit Alaska and Canada while in office, *4315*
Presidential message to Congress that was broadcast on radio, *4278*
Radio broadcast of an open session of Congress, *3574*
Rigid airship, *8056*
Shopping center in a suburban business area, *2095*
Smokescreen for concealing the movement of troops and ships, *5865*
State law to establish English as an official language, *6089*
Swimmer from the United States to swim the English Channel, *7911*
Transatlantic radio broadcast of a voice, *4777*
Transatlantic radio program received from Great Britain, *4788*
Transcontinental nonstop airplane flight, *8053*

1924

African-American Olympic medalist to win an individual event, *7853*
Bowler to roll two perfect games, *7586*
Caesar salad, *2424*
Cellophane, *2575*
Chromium plating process, *1944*
Citizenship and public affairs school at a college, *2843*
Citizenship statute for Native Americans, *6090*
Coast-to-coast radio hookup, *4789*
Contact lenses, *5269*
Corn-husking championship, *1642*
Crossword puzzle book, *7734*
Diesel-electric locomotive, *8342*
Execution by lethal gas, *7013*
Foreign language course broadcast on radio, *3213*
Frozen food for the mass market, *2421*
Gay rights organization, *7439*

Ice cream cone rolling machine, *2423*
Ink paste, *2026*
Macy's Thanksgiving Day Parade, *1397*
Marriage course at a college, *2841*
Micropaleontology course at a college, *2842*
National Hockey League team from the United States, *7830*
Newsreels showing presidential candidates, *4532*
Political convention to be broadcast on radio, *4094*
Popsicle, *2422*
Portable electric stethoscope, *5179*
Portable radio, *4821*
President buried in Washington, *4259*
President to be born in a hospital, *4260*
President to make a radio broadcast from the White House, *4279*
Radio broadcast from a circus, *1396*
Radio broadcast of a livestock auction, *1643*
Radio network broadcast received on the Pacific Coast, *4791*
Radio network program sponsored by commercial advertising, *1540*
Radio two-way broadcast from an airplane, *4790*
Round-the-world steamboat passenger service, *8448*
Senate majority leader, *3674*
State governor who was a woman, *4381*
Swing band, *1259*
Transcontinental airship flight, *8056*
Transcontinental regular airmail service, *4696*

1925

Airship with an enclosed cabin, *8058*
Arbitration law enacted by Congress, *1505*
Atheist organization, *7227*
Car insurance law enacted by a state, *1970*
Caterpillar Club member who was a woman, *8059*
Citrons, *1644*
City in miniature, *1398*
Congressional representative who was a Jewish woman, *3615*
Cosmic ray to be discovered, *6387*
County airport, *8057*
Diagnostic procedure using radioactive tracers, *5133*
Dry ice manufactured commercially, *1901*
Dry ice used in a restaurant, *1901*
Embossed inlaid linoleum, *2576*
Episcopal bishop deposed for heresy in the United States, *6298*
Explosion of Thermit to break up ice jams, *1875*
Full-length play by an African-American writer, *1452*
Labor union of African-American workers, *7150*
Long-distance radio fax transmission of medical information, *4471*
Machine to make glass light bulbs, *6562*
Miniature television tube, *4986*
Motel, *1830*
Movie of a solar eclipse taken from an airship, *6403*
Musk ox, *5951*
National Spelling Bee event, *2969*
Nationwide highway numbering system, *3422*
Nurse midwife, *2152*
Outdoor museum with nature trails, *3153*
Photoelectric cell, *6563*
Photograph taken from an airplane at night, *4630*
Potato chip manufacturing plant, *2359*
Presidential inauguration to be broadcast on radio, *4280*
Reuben sandwich, *2425*
Sleep laboratory, *5169*
State supreme court in which all the judges were women, *3718*
Telecast of an object in motion, *4923*
Tornado disaster on a large scale, *5915*
Transcontinental radio fax transmission of a photograph, *4469*
Transpacific radio fax transmission, *4470*
Trial of a teacher for violating a state ban on teaching the theory of evolution, *2970*
Woman elected to the National Academy of Sciences, *6718*
Woman's World Fair, *1506*

1926

African-American woman lawyer admitted to practice before the Supreme Court, *3966*
Airplane bombing raid by criminals, *6939*
Airplane flight over the North Pole, *6647*
Book course at a college, *2844*
Book-of-the-Month Club selection, *1099*
Boxing match to attract 100,000 spectators, *7604*
Canned ham, *2426*
Catholic church to become a basilica, *6299*
Coin bearing the likeness of a living president, *4039*
Dance major at a college, *2845*
Electric toaster, *2286*
Federal prison for women, *7014*
Ferryboat built exclusively to transport cars, *8449*
Film-developing machine, *4646*
Gas refrigerator, *2287*

1926—*continued*

Gospel composer, *1260*
Greyhound racing association, *7662*
Hambletonian harness horse race for three-year-olds, *7807*
Mayor of a major city who was a woman, *3534*
Movie showing another planet, *6404*
Movie with sound to be released as a feature, *1147*
National Christmas tree, *2513*
Photographs taken under the sea in natural colors, *4631*
Plastic surgery professor at a college, *3090*
Queen to visit the United States during her reign, *3930*
Radio jingle, *1541*
Radio show with a plot, *4792*
Rocket flight using liquid fuel, *6788*
Science fiction magazine, *4615*
Semiautomatic rifle, *5866*
Senate election in which neither candidate was seated after a recount, *3676*
Senator unseated after a recount, *3675*
Sheet of souvenir postage stamps, *4736*
Sheriff who was a woman, *7374*
Statue to commemorate literary characters, *7186*
Swimmer who was an American woman to swim the English Channel, *7912*
Transatlantic radio fax of a drawing, *4586*
Weather map to be telecast, *4924*

1927

Air conditioner for home use, *2577*
American flag displayed from the right hand of the Statue of Liberty, *3504*
Armored truck holdup, *6940*
Bagel bakery, *2427*
Book on the game of bridge, *7735*
Car to exceed the speed of 200 miles per hour, *8252*
Celebrities to leave handprints at Grauman's Chinese Theatre, *1148*
Congress to enact more than 1,000 laws, *3575*
Corporation to own its own airplane, *8064*
Diplomat to represent the United States in Canada, *3897*
Distinguished Flying Cross, *6903*
Drive-up mailbox, *4697*
Feature film with with recorded music and dialogue, *1149*
Grand Ole Opry broadcast, *4793*
High-speed roller coaster, *1002*
Housing cooperative sponsored by a labor union, *7151*
Image transmitted by television, *4927*
Instant powdered soft drink, *2428*
International airplane passenger station, *8065*
International lifeboat race, *7576*
International radio broadcasting license, *4810*
Iron lung respirator, *5180*
King born in the United States, *3931*
Lightweight brick, *3348*
Monument to the American flag, *7187*
Museum to feature a medieval building, *3154*
Phonograph with an automatic record changer, *4832*
Pilot to die because of a lack of oxygen, *8066*
Propaganda course at a college, *2846*
Scheduled passenger night flight by airplane, *8061*
Snowmobile patent, *7973*
State aviation department, *8062*
Stroboscopic lamp for high-speed photography, *4647*
Telecast of image and sound, *4925*
Traffic rotary, *3423*
Transatlantic commercial telephone service, *4888*
Transatlantic solo airplane flight, *8063*
Underwater highway tunnel with twin tubes, *3442*
Vitamin to be commercially synthesized and manufactured, *5243*
Wind tunnel for testing airplane parts, *8060*
Woman to appear on television, *4926*

1928

Air-conditioned office building, *3298*
Airmail service from ship to shore, *4698*
Airplane diesel engine, *8067*
Animated cartoon with sound, *1199*
Army armored car unit, *5426*
College founded as a Jewish institution, *2847*
Daredevil to go over Niagara Falls in a rubber ball, *1400*
Diesel-electric freight locomotive, *8342*
Electric flashing sign, *1542*
Electric light bulb frosted on the inside, *6564*
Fathometer, *6497*
Fax transmission of movie film, *4472*
Federal judge who was a woman, *3719*
Frog-jumping jubilee, *1399*
Guide dog, *7037*
Hydrogenated peanut butter, *2429*
International dogsled mail, *4699*
Machine-sliced bread, *2430*
Mechanical cotton picker, *1645*
Medical center devoted to teaching, treatment, and research, *3091*
Modeling school, *3214*
Outdoor scenes to be televised, *4931*

Physician to Congress, *3576*
Play to be shown on television, *1454*
Presidential nomination ceremony broadcast on radio, *3817*
Puppet show to be televised, *1453*
Remote television pickup, *4933*
Senator who was Hispanic, *3677*
Squash rackets champion who was a woman, *7906*
Standard broadcast station to transmit a television image, *4932*
Telephone switchboard with Braille markings, *4889*
Television magazine, *6787*
Television programs to be shown regularly, *4930*
Television sets to be installed in homes on an experimental basis, *4928*
Television station, *4929*
Theater built and named for a living actress, *1455*
Transcontinental bus service, *8220*
Transcontinental foot race, *7948*
Tuberculosis vaccine, *5155*
Wedding on television, *2595*

1929

African-American congressional representative from a northern state, *3606*
Airmail letter sheet, *4700*
Airplane bombing raid by a mercenary soldier, *6941*
Airplane flight over the South Pole, *6648*
Airship made completely of metal, *8069*
Allergy journal, *5336*
Ambulance air service, *5045*
Automatic electric stock quotation board, *1780*
Automatic pilot on an airplane, *8071*
Aviation course in a high school, *2971*
Baseball manager to win pennants in both leagues, *7530*
Cabinet member convicted of a crime, *4186*
Car radio, *4822*
Coaxial cable, *4859*
College football player to score 50 points in one game, *7706*
Fireworks law enacted by a state, *7333*
Flight trainer for airplane pilots, *8068*
Fluorescent mineral exhibit, *6498*
History of medicine department at a college, *3092*
Horse to win a $100,000 purse in one race, *7808*
Hospital insurance group plan, *1981*
Hotel at an airport, *1831*
Humanist association, *7228*
Miniature golf course, *7771*
Mobile home, *8293*
Movie by a major company for an African-American audience, *1151*
Movie entertainment shown on an airplane, *1156*
Movie of feature length made outdoors, *1150*
Movie with both sound and color, *1155*
Newsreel theater, *1157*
Night coach, *8221*
Nudist organization, *7974*
Organized crime massacre, *6942*
Oscar for best picture, *1152*
Oscars for best acting, *1153*
Oscars for best movie director, *1154*
Passenger transfer from an airship to an airplane, *8070*
Public demonstration of color television, *4987*
Radio broadcast from the Senate chamber, *3678*
Reindeer, *5952*
School for guide dogs, *7038*
Seatrain, *8451*
Ship-to-shore mobile telephone commercial service, *4890*
State police radio system, *7375*
Submarine emergency air supply container, *8515*
Tax on chain stores enacted by a state, *4423*
Teletypewriter system employed by a police department, *7376*
Traffic cloverleaf, *3424*
Transcontinental air derby for women, *7681*
Tugboat with a diesel-electric engine, *8450*
Tuition insurance for private schools, *1983*
Vice president who was Native American, *4309*
Vice president's widow to receive a pension, *4308*
Yogurt dairy, *2431*

1930

Aerial photograph in natural colors, *4632*
Airline flight attendant who was a woman, *8076*
Airship for private commercial operation, *8077*
Airship to land and take off from an oceangoing steamship, *8079*
Athlete to win the James E. Sullivan Memorial Trophy, *7478*
Bobsled run, *7975*
Bowler who was a woman to obtain a perfect score, *7587*
Catholic saints who were active in North America, *6301*
Cellophane transparent tape, *2578*

1930—*continued*

Check photographing device, *1742*
Clothes dryer, *2223*
Coal mine to be automated, *6605*
Computing device with electronic components, *6422*
Consumer protection medical alert, *5042*
Cow flown in an airplane, *1401*
Deep-sea exploration vessel, *6499*
Demonstration of home reception of television, *4988*
Diesel engine speed record, *8208*
Dutch elm disease breakout, *5985*
Factory without windows, *3299*
Fashion designer to use zippers, *2261*
Floating electric power plant, *6566*
Flying medical clinic, *5068*
Funeral home operated on the cooperative plan, *2304*
Glider flight indoors, *8073*
Glider pilot's license, *8081*
Glider released from an airship, *8072*
Golf champion to hold the four highest golf titles, *7772*
Hydroelectric power plant operated by a county, *6565*
Mosaic pavement, *3425*
Movie of a solar eclipse taken from an airplane, *6405*
Museum to install refrigerated vaults, *3155*
Music magazine published in Braille, *7039*
Nobel Prize in literature awarded to an American, *6904*
Nudist summer camp, *7974*
Passenger ship with a diesel engine, *8452*
Photographic flashbulbs, *4648*
Pinball game machine, *7865*
Planet found beyond Neptune, *6388*
Planetarium open to the public, *6375*
Police bureau of criminal alien investigation, *7378*
Presbyterian elder who was a woman, *6300*
President buried in the National Cemetery, *4261*
Radar detection of airplanes, *8078*
Radio advertising course at a college, *2848*
Rotating milking platform, *1646*
Round-the-world radio broadcast, *4794*
Seaplane glider, *8074*
Speaker to address an organization by television, *4934*
State police officers who were women, *7377*
Streamlined submarine, *8516*
Submarine escape training tank, *8517*
Sulfanilamide production, *5244*
Synthetic rubber for manufacture, *1902*
Tampon to be mass-produced, *2475*
Transcontinental car trip driven entirely in reverse, *8253*
Transcontinental glider tow, *8075*
Transcontinental solo airplane flight by a woman, *8080*
Vehicular tunnel to a foreign country, *3443*
Weather map to be telecast to a transatlantic steamer, *4924*

1931

Absolute monarch to visit the United States, *3932*
Air-conditioned train, *8395*
Airplane race of importance in which both men and women were contestants, *7682*
Anthropology laboratory, *6665*
Automatic swinging doors operated by a photoelectric cell, *3301*
Baha'i house of worship, *6302*
Baseball pitcher who was a woman, *7531*
Basketball game at a large commercial sports arena, *7555*
Crossword game, *7736*
Diesel-powered tractor, *1649*
Electric can opener, *2276*
Electric shaver, *2476*
Fizzing cold remedy, *5245*
Glider license awarded to a woman, *8082*
Heavy water to be identified, *6743*
Infrared photograph, *4633*
Mobster convicted for tax evasion, *6943*
Native American art exhibition, *1041*
Nobel Peace Prize awarded to an American woman, *6905*
Opera broadcast over the radio from the Metropolitan Opera House, *1322*
Parachute jump from an autogiro, *8085*
Plant patent, *1648*
Private hydroponic garden, *1647*
Products made of vinyl, *1903*
Radio variety show with a live studio audience, *4795*
Radio waves from space to be observed, *6389*
Rattlesnake meat in cans, *2432*
Resale price maintenance law enacted by a state, *1507*
Rocket glider flight, *8083*
School of nurse-midwifery, *3093*
Shuffleboard championship tournament, *7976*
Sister city partnership, *3535*
Skyscraper higher than 1,250 feet, *3300*
Teletype commercial service, *4860*
Theater designed and built for the rear projection of movies, *1158*
Transpacific nonstop airplane flight, *8084*

Volcanic eruption to be broadcast on radio, *5916*

1932

Airport manager who was a woman, *8087*
American Olympic champions in four-man bobsled competition, *7975*
American Olympic champions in two-man bobsled competition, *7975*
Antimatter to be observed, *6744*
Artificial lightning demonstration, *6500*
Bridge table to shuffle and deal cards by electricity, *7737*
Camera exposure meter, *4649*
City opera house, *1323*
Cooperative store operated by women, *2097*
Distinguished Flying Cross awarded to a woman, *6903*
Dogsled race on an Olympic demonstration program, *7663*
Electrical timing device for foot races, *7949*
Franchise chain, *1832*
Fruit tree patent, *1650*
Gasoline tax levied by Congress, *4424*
Greek Orthodox college, *2849*
International peace park, *5993*
International ski meet, *7891*
Olympic Games competition to be held in the winter, *7858*
Olympic gold medalist in both the Summer and Winter Olympics, *7857*
Ophthalmology clinic, *5069*
President to invite the president-elect, *4144*
Presidential candidate to give an acceptance speech at a national convention, *3818*
Pulitzer Prize awarded to a musical, *4768*
Radio broadcast from a moving train, *4796*
Railroad mystery excursion, *1402*
Self-computing gasoline pump, *1876*
Self-service supermarket, *2096*
Teletypesetter, *2057*
Transatlantic solo airplane flight by a woman, *8086*
Transcontinental nonstop airplane flight by a woman, *8088*
Unemployment insurance act, *7152*
Woman elected to the Senate, *3673*
Woman to receive a gold medal from the National Geographic Society, *6899*
Wooden money, *4042*
Yellow fever vaccine for human immunization, *5156*

1933

Airplane sleeping berths, *8089*
Airplane with nonconvertible sleeping berths, *8089*
All-star major league baseball game, *7532*
Ballet choreographer of international renown, *1051*
Bank deposit insurance law enacted by Congress, *1743*
Blood serum made of dried human blood, *5054*
Bridge with piers sunk in the open sea, *3253*
Cabinet in which all members were sworn in at the same time and place, *4187*
Cabinet member who was a woman, *4188*
Chocolate chip cookies, *2433*
Constitutional amendment to be repealed, *3505*
Diplomat who was a woman, *3896*
Drama broadcast on radio from a regular stage, *1456*
Drive-in movie theater, *1159*
Electric power contract between a city and the federal government, *6568*
Execution for kidnapping, *7015*
First Lady to undertake a career of public service, *4233*
FM radio, *4823*
Game management chair at a college, *2850*
Glass that was nonreflecting, *3364*
Lung removal, *5348*
Maritime Day, *2514*
Mass-produced picture frames, *2579*
Modern dance troupe that was all-male, *1052*
Museum with interactive exhibits, *3156*
Opera prima donna who was African-American, *1324*
Police radio system, *7379*
Polio vaccine, *5157*
Round-the-world solo airplane flight, *8090*
Savings and loan association established by the federal government, *1744*
Singing telegram, *4861*
Sit-down strike, *7153*
Soap opera on radio, *4797*
Sodium vapor lamps, *6567*
State governor to be granted almost dictatorial power, *4382*
State speaker of the House who was a woman, *4392*
Surgical elevation of the skull to treat epilepsy, *5349*
Swimming pool in the White House, *4332*
Synthetic laundry detergent, *2224*
Transcontinental flight made by African-Americans in their own airplane, *8091*
Walkie-Talkie two-way radio device, *4891*
Wedding by transatlantic telephone, *2596*
Woman director of the U.S. Mint, *4017*

1933—*continued*

World championship professional football game, *7707*

1934

Abrasive for commercial use, *1904*
Aircraft carrier, *8484*
All-star football game, *7708*
Archivist of the United States, *3027*
Athlete depicted on a Wheaties box, *1543*
Blue Cross and Blue Shield plans, *1982*
Cartel of corporations, *1509*
College to dispense with credits, hours, points, and grades, *2852*
Commercial production of hydroponic plants, *1651*
Community to fingerprint its citizens, *7380*
Cyclotron, *6730*
Death penalty authorized by federal law, *7016*
Deposits on bottles, *5917*
Director of a major corporation who was a woman, *1508*
Driving course in a high school, *2972*
Factories operated by the federal government in peacetime, *3847*
Federal credit union, *1746*
Federal gun control regulation, *6944*
Federal justice of the Circuit Court of Appeals who was a woman, *3719*
First Lady to travel in an airplane to a foreign country, *4234*
Fluorescent lamp, *6569*
Fluorescent paint, *2669*
Laundromat, *2225*
Liquor stores run by a state government, *2098*
Locomotive communications headlight, *8392*
Monosodium glutamate commercial production, *2434*
Mosque, *6303*
Movie of the sun, *6406*
Musical comedy broadcast on radio, *1458*
Nationwide highway planning surveys authorized by Congress, *3426*
Negative election campaign run by media specialists, *3782*
Payment by the Federal Deposit Insurance Corporation, *1745*
Pilot who was a woman to fly for a commercial airline, *8093*
Pipeless organ, *1310*
President to conduct religious services as commander-in-chief of the Navy, *4145*
President to go through the Panama Canal while in office, *4146*
President to visit Hawaii while in office, *4317*
President to visit South America while in office, *4316*
Pressure suit, *8092*
Ptarmigan, *5955*
Public Enemy Number 1, *6945*
Radio broadcast heard in both the Arctic and the Antarctic regions, *4798*
Raptor sanctuary, *5953*
Revenue stamp printed by the Post Office Department, *4425*
Rocket to break the sound barrier, *6789*
Ski tow made of rope, *7892*
Snow goose, *5954*
Soapbox derby, *7625*
State legislature with a single chamber in the post-Revolutionary era, *4393*
Streamlined all-steel diesel-motor train, *8397*
Streamlined steam locomotive, *8343*
Symphony on an African-American folk theme, *1261*
Talking book for blind listeners, *7040*
Theater and dramatic criticism course at a college, *2851*
Theatrical presentation sponsored by the federal government, *1457*
Train to run 1,000 miles nonstop, *8396*
Woman to receive the Hubbard medal from the National Geographic Society, *6899*
X-ray photograph of the entire body of a living person taken in a one-second exposure, *5134*
Youth hostel, *2196*

1935

Aerial photograph showing the lateral curvature of the horizon and the beginning of the stratosphere, *4634*
Ambulance service with an incubator, *5046*
Automatic parking meter, *8254*
Baseball game at night by major league teams, *7533*
Beer in cans, *2436*
Bill of $100,000 denomination, *4043*
Bill to depict both sides of the Great Seal of the United States, *4044*
Blood testing laws enacted by a state, *7278*
Book series microfilmed, *3034*
Casein fiber, *1905*
Category 5 hurricane, *5918*
City law requiring reporting of premature births, *2153*
Color film, *4650*
Comic book containing original material, *1098*
Commodity exchange member who was a woman, *1781*
Drama school at a college, *2853*

Drug treatment center for addicts established by Congress, *7077*
Electric guitar, *1311*
Electric typewriter that was commercially successful, *1690*
Fax transmission by a press syndicate direct to newspaper offices, *4533*
Federal family assistance program, *3848*
Football player to win the Heisman Trophy for excellence in college football, *7709*
Heart operation for the relief of angina pectoris, *5351*
Heart pump, *5350*
Identification of human beings from the pattern formed by the blood vessels of the retina, *7381*
Invisible-glass installation, *3365*
Kosher soft drink, *2435*
Lie detector, *6946*
Lightning observatory, *6501*
Lunch box featuring a licensed character, *2580*
Medical college founded as a Jewish institution, *3094*
National conference on crime, *7382*
National identification scheme for American citizens, *3849*
National skeet tournament, *7888*
News correspondent who was African-American, *4599*
Newspaper to store issues on microfilm, *3035*
Organized civil rights protest by people with disabilities, *7041*
Paperback publisher, *4464*
Parachute tower for training jumpers, *8095*
President to read a veto message to Congress, *4147*
Public school classes for children with epilepsy, *2973*
Roller derby, *7875*
Round-the-world telephone conversation, *4892*
Spectrophotometer, *6731*
Streamlined electric locomotive, *8344*
Streamlined ferryboat, *8453*
Transpacific airmail flight, *4701*
Transpacific solo airplane flight by a woman, *8094*
Transport airplane designed for transoceanic service, *8096*
Truck completely streamlined, *8294*
Twelve-step rehabilitation program, *7078*
Virus obtained in crystalline form, *6666*

1936

All-glass windowless structure, *3302*
Bicycle traffic court, *7655*
Bottle with a screw cap, *2001*
Cellulose sponge for household use, *2226*
Comics studio, *1100*
Coxswain of a men's college varsity rowing team who was a woman, *7881*
Electric-eye camera installed at a racetrack, *7809*
Electron tube, *6515*
Execution for the murder of a federal officer, *7016*
Federal administrator who was an African-American woman, *3851*
Federally funded low-income housing project, *3536*
Fuel alcohol plant, *6606*
Giant panda, *5956*
High school to fingerprint its students, *7383*
High-definition telecast, *4990*
Lucite commercially manufactured, *1906*
Magazine of the federal government, *3850*
Medical insurance group policy for college students, *1983*
National Union for Social Justice national convention, *4095*
News magazine featuring photographs, *4535*
Newspaper to microfilm its current issues, *3035*
Olympic athlete from the United States to win four gold medals in one year, *7859*
Pensions paid by the federal government to workers in private industry, *7155*
Pope to visit the United States before his election, *3933*
Radioactive isotope medicine, *5394*
Radioactive substance produced synthetically, *6745*
Round-the-world airplane passenger race, *7683*
Sulfanilamide used in medical treatment, *5244*
Telecast using coaxial cable, *4989*
Textile-wrapped detonating fuse, *1877*
Union Party convention, *4096*
Unscheduled event to be televised as it occurred, *4534*
Work week of 40 hours to be required by Congress, *7154*
X-ray photograph showing the complete arterial circulation in an adult human, *5135*

1937

Animated feature-length cartoon in Technicolor, *1200*
Automatic washing machine, *2227*
Badminton championship tournament, *7977*
Bicycle champion who was a woman, *7656*

1937—*continued*

Birth control clinic run by a state government, *5070*
Blood bank, *5055*
Car-airplane combination, *8255*
Children's church, *6304*
Coast-to-coast radio news broadcast to be recorded, *4537*
Costume museum, *3157*
Electric sign showing an animated cartoon, *1545*
Element created artificially, *6746*
First-day special cancellation of a postage stamp, *4737*
Free port, *2079*
Game preserve appropriation by the federal government, *5958*
Grand jury foreman who was a woman, *3720*
Letter to circumnavigate the world by commercial airmail, *4702*
Lighting designer for the stage, *1459*
Marijuana ban enacted by Congress, *7079*
Mobile television transmitter unit, *4991*
Monument to a comic-strip character, *7188*
Movie associated with a merchandise marketing campaign, *1160*
Movie to earn $1 billion, *1161*
National seashore, *5994*
Newspaper advertisement scented with perfume, *1544*
Newspaper printed on pine-pulp paper in color, *4536*
Okapi, *5957*
Original movie soundtrack recording, *1262*
Photographer to receive the John Simon Guggenheim Memorial Foundation award, *4635*
Photosensitive glass, *3366*
Pituitary hormone, *5246*
President inaugurated on January 20, *4148*
Psychodrama treatment for psychiatric patients, *5395*
Radio astronomer, *6376*
Radio facsimile newspaper, *4538*
Retirement colony, *3537*
Santa Claus school, *2515*
Senate parliamentarian, *3679*
Shopping cart, *1691*
Ski lift, *7893*
Socialist Workers Party organizational meeting, *4097*
State to make Flag Day a legal holiday, *2503*
Submarine cable plow, *4862*
Symphony orchestra devoted exclusively to radio broadcasting, *1263*
Synthetic fiber, *2141*
Trampoline commercially manufactured, *7787*
Vanity license plates, *8209*
X-ray movies of human organs in action, *5136*

1938

Airplane instructor's license, *8097*
Aquarium for large marine animals, *3158*
Archival course at a college, *2854*
Ballet on an American theme by an American choreographer, *1053*
Bank president of a national bank who was a woman, *1747*
Beatification of an American citizen by the Catholic Church, *6309*
Blood tests for marriage license applicants to be required by a state, *7280*
Blood tests for pregnant women to be required by a state, *7279*
Broadway play shown in a television version with its original cast, *1460*
Building built completely inside a factory, *3303*
Cartooning school, *3215*
Cathode-ray tubes, *4936*
Comic book hero with superpowers, *1101*
Copy made by xerography, *2027*
Electric sterilamp, *5181*
Electronic voice mechanism, *4893*
Farm cooperative for artificial insemination of livestock, *1652*
Federal law regulating ages and workload for child labor, *7156*
Fiberglass, *3367*
Jazz concert at Carnegie Hall, *1265*
Minimum wage law enacted by Congress, *7157*
Movie to be shown on a television screen, *1162*
News anchor on radio, *4600*
Nobel Prize in literature awarded to an American woman, *6904*
Passenger ship equipped with radar, *8505*
Pontoon bridge of reinforced concrete, *3254*
Radio broadcast from a tape recording, *4799*
Right-to-die society, *2305*
Skimobile ski lift, *7894*
Soda sold in cans, *2437*
State legislator who was an African-American woman, *4394*
Teflon created in a laboratory, *1907*
Television theater to be licensed, *4935*
Tennis champion to win the Grand Slam, *7928*
Toothbrush with synthetic bristles, *2477*
Transatlantic telegraph cable of a high-speed permalloy, *4862*
White band leader to hire an African-American woman vocalist, *1264*

Woman of American ancestry to become a queen, *3934*

1939

Air-conditioned car, *8257*
Army officer to occupy both the nation's highest military post and the highest nonelective civilian post, *5444*
Batman comic book, *1102*
Battleship equipped with radar, *8485*
Beauty pageant to be shown on television, *1404*
Bicycle race to be shown on television, *7657*
Bluegrass musician of renown, *1266*
Boxing match to be shown on television, *7605*
Broadway play starring an African-American actress, *1461*
Catholic beatification of a Native American, *6305*
Coin-operated mailbox, *4703*
Congressional page who was female, *3616*
Dean of a university graduate school who was a woman, *2855*
Electric starting gate for horse races, *7810*
Electronic digital calculator, *6516*
Fashion show to be shown on television, *1403*
Fiberglass sutures, *5182*
Flea laboratory, *6667*
Food stamps, *3852*
Indoor ski school, *7895*
Intercollegiate football game to be shown on television, *7710*
Judge who was an African-American woman, *3721*
King and queen to be shown on television, *3936*
King of Great Britain to visit the United States, *3935*
Lightning bolt to be scientifically measured, *6503*
Major league baseball game to be shown on television, *7534*
Miniature car, *8256*
Movie premiere festivities to be shown on television, *1163*
Musical comedy to be shown on television, *1462*
National water skiing tournament, *7991*
Nylon, *2142*
Pinball ban enacted by a city, *7866*
President to appear on television, *4281*
President to hold an airplane pilot's license, *4294*
Presidential campaign manager who was a woman, *3819*
Professional football game to be shown on television, *7711*
Public telecast made over telephone wires, *4992*
Radio production course at a college, *2856*
Sports event to be televised live, *4937*
Spray can, *2002*
Submarine from the United States destroyed in World War II, *5756*
Submarine to be refloated, *8518*
Surgical operation televised on a closed circuit for medical students, *5352*
Surrogate birth experiment with an animal, *6668*
Tennis tournament to be shown on television, *7929*
Transatlantic airmail service, *4704*
Transatlantic commercial airplane service, *8098*
Weather forecasting service by telephone, *6502*
Woman pilot to earn an airplane instructor's license, *8097*

1940

Air defense military organization, *5478*
Air raid shelter, *7298*
American base in Antarctica that was permanent, *6649*
Army general who rose from draftee, *5446*
Army general who was African-American, *5445*
Army parachute battalion, *5479*
Basketball game to be shown on television, *7556*
Betatron, *6733*
Boxing referee who was a woman, *7606*
Car with an automatic transmission, *8258*
Census proven to have been inaccurate, *6156*
Circus to be shown on television, *1405*
Comic book versions of literary works, *1103*
Concrete highway median barrier, *3427*
Congress in session a full year, *3577*
Dictionary compiled by a woman, *2264*
Draft law enacted by Congress in preparation for war, *5557*
Electron microscope, *6732*
General purpose military vehicle, *5867*
Helicopter, *8099*
Hockey game to be shown on television, *7831*
Intercollegiate track meet to be shown on television, *7950*
M&M candies, *2438*
Major league no-hitter baseball game on opening day, *7535*
Major museum show of Native American art, *1041*
Nylon stockings, *2265*

1940—*continued*

Oscar awarded to an African-American performer, *1164*
Passover seder to be shown on television, *6307*
Plutonium, *6747*
Pole vaulter to clear the bar at 15 feet, *7951*
Political convention to be televised, *4098*
Postage stamp depicting an African-American, *4738*
President elected for third and fourth terms, *4149*
Professional football championship game broadcast on radio, *7712*
Quetzal bird, *5959*
Radio jingle played nationwide on network radio, *1546*
Registration of aliens by the federal government, *6091*
Religious services to be shown on television, *6306*
Rh factor discovery, *5056*
Social Security monthly payment, *3853*
Song to hit No. 1 in the pop charts, *1340*
Synthetic rubber tires, *8210*
Telecommunication by deaf people that was both visual and oral, *7042*
Television production course at a college, *2857*
Tetraploid (giant) flower, *1653*
Two-handed shovel, *2670*

1941

African-American air unit, *5481*
American losses in the Pacific in World War II, *5761*
Army language school, *3116*
Automatic aircraft cannon, *5868*
Bombing mission by American forces in Asia in World War II, *5767*
Camp for conscientious objectors, *5558*
Capture of a German ship by an American ship in World War II, *5758*
City parking garage, *8260*
Civilian airport owned and operated by the federal government, *8103*
Commercial television licenses, *4938*
Destroyer from the United States torpedoed during convoy duty in World War II, *5760*
Destroyer from the United States torpedoed in World War II, *5760*
Fighter plane from the United States to destroy a Japanese airplane in World War II, *5768*
Film professorship at a college, *2858*
FM radio transmitter to receive a commercial license, *4811*
General of the American armed forces killed in World War II, *5769*
Genetics clinic, *5071*
Health insurance clause in a labor contract, *1984*
Heavy tank, *5869*
Helicopter flight from water, *8102*
Helicopter flight of one-hour duration, *8101*
High-jump standards using electric eye detectors, *7952*
Home health testing kit, *5183*
Liberty ship, *8454*
Magnesium commercially produced from seawater, *3397*
Naval patrol bomber launched like a ship, *5586*
Naval ship constructed as a minelayer, *8481*
Navy admiral killed in action in World War II, *5762*
Navy task force assembled for foreign service, *5585*
Noir film, *1165*
Parachute fatality in the Army, *5480*
Plastic bonded airplane, *8100*
Plastic car, *8259*
Presidential library, *4150*
Purple Heart awarded to a woman, *5517*
Quonset hut, *3304*
Radar used to detect enemy airplanes, *5763*
Railroad to be completely equipped with diesel-electric engines, *8327*
Round-the-world flight by a commercial airplane, *8105*
Ship from the United States sunk by a German submarine in World War II, *5757*
Ship from the United States to sink a Japanese submarine in World War II, *5764*
Ship from the United States to surrender to the Japanese in World War II, *5766*
Submarine from the United States to sink a Japanese ship in World War II, *5771*
Television commercial, *1547*
Test pilot who was a woman, *8104*
Warship convoy across the Atlantic Ocean in World War II, *5759*
Wind turbine, *6633*
World War II ace, *5770*
World War II air hero, *5765*

1942

Air attack against the Japanese homeland in World War II, *5778*
Aircraft carrier from the United States sunk in World War II, *5780*
American expeditionary force to land in Africa in World War II, *5782*

1943

1943—*continued*

Poet to win a Pulitzer Prize four times, *4769*
Police appeal for missing persons to be shown on television, *7384*
President of a Sub-Saharan African country to visit the United States, *3937*
President to fly in an airplane, *4296*
President to visit a foreign country in wartime, *4318*
Presidential pet to star in a movie, *4263*
Soldier's Medal awarded to a woman, *5523*
Submarine from the United States sunk by an enemy submarine, *5793*
Submarine with a pressure hull of high-tensile steel, *8519*
Woman line officer in the Navy with the rank of captain, *5606*

1944

African-American news correspondent accredited to the White House, *4599*
Antibiotic discovered in America, *5247*
Antibiotic manufactured commercially, *5247*
Army generals to wear the five-star insignia, *5448*
Army officer to receive the three highest decorations, *5526*
Capture and boarding of an enemy submarine on the high seas by American forces, *5794*
Chinese person granted citizenship, *6093*
Commercial sunscreen product, *2478*
Execution of an organized crime leader in the electric chair, *7017*
Eye bank, *5057*
Horse stakes race ending in a triple dead heat, *7811*
Jet-propelled fighter plane, *5484*
Mathematical theory of economic decision-making, *6706*
Military band leader who was a woman, *5428*
Movie to premiere on television, *1167*
Musical comedy written for television, *1463*
Navy admirals to wear the five-star insignia, *5607*
Political action committee (PAC), *3820*
Presidential airplane, *4297*
Public service symbol of the federal government, *5919*
Quadruplets delivered by cesarean operation, *2154*
Retail store whose sales in one day exceeded $1 million, *2099*
Rocket airplane for military use, *5485*
Serbian Orthodox cathedral, *6308*
Silver Star awarded to a woman, *5525*
Synthetic quinine, *5248*
Transoceanic newspaper, *4539*
Victory ship launched, *8457*
World War II veterans' society officially recognized by Congress, *5625*

1945

African-American opera singer to sing a white role, *1326*
American civilians killed in the continental United States in World War II, *5795*
American conductor of an American orchestra, *1267*
Atomic bomb explosion, *5871*
Atomic bomb explosion over enemy territory, *5797*
Civilian to die in a nuclear accident, *6617*
Color news photograph transmitted by radio fax for publication, *4587*
Computer bug, *6423*
Department store sales demonstrations using television, *1548*
First Lady appointed to a federal post after the death of her husband, *4235*
Food-O-Mat, *2100*
Frozen meals for air travelers, *2439*
Gas-turbine propeller-driven airplane, *8111*
Household product made entirely of plastic, *2581*
Industrial and labor relations school at a college, *2859*
Instant book, *4465*
Jet-propelled landing on an aircraft carrier, *8112*
Labor antidiscrimination commission established by a state government, *7158*
Legal definition of the presidential seal, *4151*
Marine Corps general in active service to wear four stars, *5567*
Medal of Honor awarded to a conscientious objector, *5528*
Naval bombardment of the Japanese homeland in World War II, *5796*
Naval ship with a mixed company of male and female personnel, *8487*
Presidential citation to an entire armed forces division, *5527*
Professional hockey player to score 50 goals in one season, *7832*
Railroad car with an observation dome, *8360*
School completely irradiated with germicidal lamps, *7281*
Strike to last longer than a year, *7159*
Tape recorders, *4833*
Think tank for research and development, *7229*
Treaty signed by a woman, *3898*
Water supply to be fluoridated, *7417*

1946

Antihistamine drug for allergy symptoms, *5249*
Artificial snow from a natural cloud, *6504*
Atomic bomb dropped from an airplane over water, *5872*
Atomic bomb underwater explosion, *5873*
Baseball play-off series, *7536*
Bone bank, *5058*
CARE packages, *5798*
Casino in Las Vegas, *1803*
Catholic saint who was an American citizen, *6309*
Cellulose sponge for medical and surgical use, *5184*
Coin bearing the likeness of an African-American, *4045*
Coin-operated television receiver, *4993*
College principally for war veterans, *2860*
Commercial program telecast on a network, *4940*
Commercially designed helicopter, *8114*
Drive-in banking service, *1748*
Electric blanket, *2582*
Electronic computer, *6424*
Glider commercial freight service, *8116*
Gospel singer, *1268*
Helicopter hoist rescue, *8113*
Helicopter licensed for commercial use, *8115*
Jet airplane to transport mail, *4705*
Jukebox manufacturer who was successful, *4830*
Long-distance car-to-car telephone conversation, *4896*
Medal of Honor awarded to a chaplain, *5529*
Medal of Honor awarded to a soldier of Japanese ancestry, *5530*
Military think tank, *5799*
Mobile overseas telephone call from a moving vehicle, *4895*
Mobile telephone commercial service, *4894*
Movie trailer to be shown on television, *1549*
News anchor on television, *4601*
Nontwisted sewing thread, *2623*
Nuclear product for peacetime use, *6618*
Poster child for a fundraising campaign, *7230*
President to travel underwater in a captured enemy submarine, *4298*
Radar installation aboard a commercial carrier, *8506*
Radar signal to the moon, *6790*
Religious service to be televised from a church, *6310*
Rocket plane for manned supersonic flight, *5486*
Rocket to attain a 100-mile altitude, *6791*
Soldering gun, *2671*
Television show to be sponsored by a commercial advertiser, *1550*
Television variety talent show series, *4939*
Theme park, *1008*
Transcontinental Pullman sleeping car daily service, *8328*
Transcontinental round-trip airplane flight made within 24 hours, *8117*
Traveling cancer clinic, *5072*

1947

African-American news correspondent admitted to the congressional press gallery, *4599*
Aluminum foil, *2583*
Area code, *4897*
Army officer who was a woman, *5449*
Army specialist corps for women, *5429*
Ballistic missile, *5874*
Book issued on microcards, *3036*
Cancer prevention clinic for children, *5073*
Chemotherapy to successfully achieve remission of cancer, *5396*
Commercial telephone service on railroad trains for passengers, *4899*
Commercial television station west of the Mississippi River, *4941*
Congressional opening session to be televised, *3578*
Deaths from smog, *5920*
Department of Defense, *4190*
Forest fire drenched by artificial rain, *5986*
Freedom ride by civil rights activists, *6139*
Golfer born in America to win the British Women's Amateur Golf Tournament, *7773*
Helicopter freight service, *8132*
Horse to win $1 million in races, *7812*
Independent aviation branch of the U.S. armed forces, *5488*
Instant camera, *4651*
Major league baseball player in the postwar era who was African-American, *7537*
Method of natural childbirth, *2155*
Microwave oven, *2288*
Mobile telephone call between an airplane in flight and a moving car, *4900*
Navy commissioned officer who was African-American, *5608*
Navy jet airplane squadron, *5487*
Nobel Prize shared by an American husband and wife, *6906*
Pilot to break the sound barrier, *8121*
Planned suburban development, *3538*
Presidential address televised from the White House, *4283*
Radar for commercial and private planes, *8118*

1947—*continued*

Round-the-world commercial airplane service, *8119*
Secretary of defense, *4190*
Ship from which a long-range rocket was launched, *8488*
State registry of convicted sex offenders, *7299*
Surgical operation televised on a closed circuit for physicians, *5352*
Television drama program regularly scheduled, *4942*
Tony Awards ceremony, *1464*
Transatlantic flight by a robot airplane, *8120*
Transatlantic mobile telephone call between two cars, *4898*
Tubeless car tires, *8211*
Women to participate in an Antarctic expedition, *6649*
World Series baseball game to be shown on television, *7538*
Writer to win the Pulitzer Prize in both fiction and poetry, *4770*

1948

Airplane with a delta wing, *8122*
Americans to die in a UN peacekeeping mission, *5800*
Anthrax vaccine for human immunization, *5158*
Army nonmedical officer who was a woman, *5449*
Broad-spectrum antibiotic, *5251*
Catholic midnight mass to be televised, *6312*
Cloning of a mammalian cell, *6669*
Commissioned officer in the Marine Corps who was African-American, *5568*
Deodorant soap, *2479*
Doctor in the regular Navy who was a woman, *5210*
Elevator with electronic signal controls, *3306*
Figure skating champion from the United States to compete in the Olympic Games, *7843*
Food in an aerosol can, *2440*
Fungicide used medicinally, *5250*
Gas-turbine-electric locomotive, *8346*
Governor of Puerto Rico to be elected, *3784*
High-speed radio fax transmission, *4473*
House completely heated by solar energy, *2529*
Jockey to win the Triple Crown twice, *7813*
Labor dispute in which the Taft-Hartley Act was invoked, *7160*
Latex paint, *2672*
Long-playing microgroove phonograph records, *4835*
Monument to a Native American, *7191*
Muslim cemetery, *6311*
Navy personnel in the regular Navy who were women, *5587*
Newsreel in color, *4540*
Newsreel telecast presented daily, *4541*
Olympic gold medalist who was an African-American woman, *7860*
Opera to be televised from the Metropolitan Opera House, *1327*
Parcel post domestic air service, *4707*
Parcel post international air service, *4706*
Popcorn, *2441*
Presidential candidate who was renominated after a defeat, *3821*
Public high school to specialize in the performing arts, *2974*
Quantum theory of electromagnetic radiation, *6707*
Radio program simultaneously transmitted, *4800*
Scientific survey of sexual behavior among Americans, *7440*
Senator to win a seat that had been occupied by his father and his mother, *3681*
Super-giant locomotive, *8345*
Symphonic concert to be shown on television, *1269*
Tape recorder built in the United States for commercial use, *4834*
Telephone recording devices, *4901*
Television image using a split screen, *4994*
Transistor, *6517*
United Nations peacekeeping mission in which the United States participated, *5800*
Water pollution law enacted by Congress, *5921*
Western series on television, *4943*
Woman legislator from the Republican Party to serve in both houses of Congress, *3680*

1949

Airmail postal card, *4708*
Airport fog disposal unit, *8124*
Ambassador from the United States who was a woman, *3900*
Ambassador to the United States who was a woman, *3899*
Anesthesiology professor at a college, *3095*
Animated cartoon made for television, *4944*
Automatic streetlight system, *7418*
Ballet technique course at a college, *2861*
Bar code scanner, *1692*
Baseball player who was African-American to win the Most Valuable Player award, *7539*
Belt conveyor more than four miles long, *1878*

Cargo airlines licensed by the Civil Aeronautics Board, *8125*
Congressional standing committee headed by an African-American, *3617*
Cortisone synthesis, *5252*
Court-martial at which the judges included enlisted men, *5551*
Designation of Flag Day as a national holiday, *2503*
Emmy awards for excellence in television, *4946*
Federal directions for sealing birth records of adopted children, *2197*
Federal marshal who was a woman, *7385*
Frozen meals in three-part trays, *2442*
Gas turbine to pump natural gas, *6607*
Gas turbine used by an electrical utility company, *6571*
Heliport commercial base, *8126*
Leaping submarine, *8520*
Long-distance dial telephone service, *4902*
Magazine on microfilm offered to subscribers, *3037*
Marine who was an African-American woman, *5569*
Mosque of importance, *6313*
Museum devoted exclusively to nuclear energy, *3159*
Naval Academy graduate who was African-American, *3118*
Photograph of genes, *5137*
President who had been divorced, *4264*
Radio station owned and operated by African-Americans, *4812*
Railroad dining car powered by electricity, *8361*
Rectangular television tube, *4995*
Refrigeration system for trucks, *8295*
Rocket to reach outer space, *6792*
Round-the-world nonstop flight by an airplane, *8123*
Seat belts in cars, *8261*
Sitcom television show, *4945*
Soap opera on daytime television, *4947*
Synchrotron, *6734*
Tape-recording machine for mass production of tapes, *4836*
Telescope lens 200 inches in diameter, *6377*
Television variety talent show with an African-American cast, *4939*
Transcontinental bicycle trip made in less than three weeks, *7658*
Typesetting machine to dispense with metal type, *2058*
Year in which more than 1 million passenger cars of one make were produced, *8262*

1950

African-American player on an amateur hockey team, *7833*
Babysitters' insurance policy, *1971*
Basketball professional player who was African-American, *7557*
Burglar alarm operated by ultrasonic or radio waves, *3307*
Combat mission in the Korean War, *5802*
Concentrated milk, *2443*
Copy machine, *1693*
Credit card to be nationally accepted, *1763*
Criminal on the FBI's Ten Most Wanted list, *6948*
Disposable diapers, *2198*
Dunkin' Donuts, *1833*
Federal appellate judge who was African-American, *3722*
Halloween collection for UNICEF, *2516*
Helicopter rescue of an American pilot behind enemy lines, *5805*
Hurricanes to receive names, *6505*
Husband and wife to be elected simultaneously to both chambers of a state legislature, *4395*
Illegal television station, *4949*
Local radio network, *4813*
Lunch box featuring a TV character, *2584*
Major studies to show a link between smoking and lung cancer, *7080*
Medal of Honor awarded in the Korean War, *5531*
Medical officer assigned to a naval vessel who was a woman, *5609*
National gay rights organization, *7441*
Nazi collaborator to be deported, *6094*
Nobel Peace Prize awarded to an African-American, *6907*
Nuclear engineering course at a college, *2862*
Nuclear medicine imaging device, *5138*
Officer killed in action in the Korean War, *5804*
Phototransistor, *6518*
Pilot of a jet fighter to win a dogfight in the Korean War, *5807*
Pilot to destroy an enemy airplane in the Korean War, *5801*
Poet who was an African-American woman to win the Pulitzer Prize, *4771*
Postage stamp depicting a Jew, *4739*
Radio paging service, *4903*
Rocket launched from Cape Canaveral, *6793*
Secret Service agent killed while protecting the president from an attempted assassination, *3845*
Soldier killed in action in the Korean War, *5803*

1950—*continued*

Sound trademark, *3982*
Swimmer who was a woman to swim the English Channel in both directions, *7913*
Tank crew to cross the 38th parallel in the Korean War, *5806*
Television remote control, *4996*
Television series in which an African-American performer had a starring role, *4948*
Ten Most Wanted list, *6947*
United Nations delegate who was African-American, *3901*

1951

Ace to fly a jet, *5808*
Adaptive technologies for people with disabilities, *7043*
Air Force Medal of Honor for action in the Korean War, *5533*
Air-to-air rocket, *5876*
All-Star Game of the National Basketball Association, *7558*
Atomic bomb explosion to be shown on television, *5875*
Atomic bomb underground explosion, *5878*
Battery to convert radioactive energy into electrical energy, *6572*
Birth to be shown on closed-circuit television, *2156*
Correction fluid for typewriters, *1694*
Electric power from nuclear energy, *6619*
Electronic computer for commercial use, *6425*
Gambling permit stamp issued by the federal government, *4426*
Jet airplane passenger trip, *8128*
Jewish prayer services to be televised in their entirety, *6315*
Mail delivery car with the steering wheel on the right, *8264*
Major league baseball game to be televised in color, *7534*
Medal of Honor awarded to a Marine in the Korean War, *5532*
Movie showing the inside of a living heart, *5139*
Nuclear reactor used in medical therapy, *5185*
Opera written for television, *1328*
Parking garage that was completely automated, *8263*
Pay television system, *4950*
Peacetime death sentence for espionage, *7018*
Presidential press conference recorded on tape, *4284*
Reform rabbi who was a woman, *6314*
Rock and roll song, *1341*
Rocket to intercept an airplane, *5877*
Sex-change operation performed on an American, *7442*
Telecast from a foreign country, *4954*
Telephone company answering service, *4904*
Television eyewitness allowed to testify in a federal court, *3723*
Television program in color, *4951*
Titanium plant fully self-contained and fully integrated, *1945*
Transcontinental direct-dialed phone call, *4905*
Transcontinental telecast received on the East Coast, *4952*
Transcontinental telecast received on the West Coast, *4953*
Transistors produced commercially for a specific product, *6519*
United Nations postage stamps in U.S. denominations, *4740*
Valeteria, *1695*
Year in which air traffic volume exceeded first-class rail traffic volume, *8127*

1952

Airplane flight to land at the North Pole, *6650*
Antibiotic synthetically manufactured, *5253*
Artificial aortic valve, *5358*
Artificial lens for cataract patients, *5270*
Automatic headlight control, *8212*
Bank to issue a credit card, *1764*
Birth to be televised for the public, *2158*
Boxing referee in a heavyweight championship match who was African-American, *7607*
Bullfighter who was a woman to fight professionally, *7615*
Cloning experiment, *6670*
Coal hydrogenation plant, *1908*
Commonwealth of the United States, *6095*
Copyright registered for a choreographic score, *1055*
Drug treatment center for minors, *7081*
Explorer to set foot on both the North and South Poles, *6651*
Frozen bread, *2445*
Hearing aid using transistors, *5271*
Heart operation in which the deep-freezing technique was employed, *5357*
Holiday Inn, *1834*
Hydrogen bomb, *5879*
Jockey to win the Kentucky Derby five times, *7814*
Microfilm editions of federal publications and documents, *3038*
Microwave oven for home use, *2288*
Mitral valve corrective surgery, *5356*

Mother and son simultaneously elected to Congress, *3618*
Musical composition consisting entirely of silence, *1270*
National Day of Prayer established by Congress, *2517*
Pacemaker, *5353*
Pay television presentation of a sports event, *4955*
Person known to have set foot on the North Pole, *6646*
Presidential election in which a computer was used to predict the outcome, *3823*
Railroad freight cars with compartments, *8362*
Religious radio program broadcast by a husband and wife, *6316*
Sugar-free soft drinks, *2444*
Surgical operation shown on a local television program, *5354*
Surgical operation televised coast-to-coast, *5355*
Test for newborn health, *2157*
Toothpaste with fluoride, *2480*
Transatlantic helicopter flight, *8129*
Umpire in organized baseball who was African-American, *7540*
Vice presidential candidate who was an African-American woman, *3822*
Video recording on high-definition magnetic tape, *4997*
World heavyweight boxing champion to retire undefeated, *7608*
Year in which there were no reported lynchings of African-Americans, *6140*
Yiddish professorship at a college, *2863*

1953

Aluminum-faced building, *3309*
Animated three-dimensional cartoon in Technicolor, *1201*
Artmobile, *3160*
Book censorship board established by a state, *1104*
Building with its roof supported by cables, *3308*
Cabinet conference to be telecast, *4192*
Carpeting of tufted plastic, *2586*
Catholic cardinal whose see was west of the Rockies, *6317*
Coast-to-coast live telecast in color, *4959*
College Bowl competition on radio, *2865*
Conjoined twins separated successfully by surgery, *5359*
Department of Health, Education, and Welfare, *4191*
Discovery of different sleep states, *6671*
Doctor commissioned in the regular Army who was a woman, *5450*
Educational television station, *4958*
Electronic road system, *3428*
Helicopter fully operated by remote control, *8131*
Helicopter passenger service, *8132*
Highway interchange structure with four levels, *3429*
Instant tea, *2446*
Japanese person to receive an immigration visa after World War II, *6096*
Lunch box fully decorated with lithographed art, *2585*
Mountain bike, *7659*
Movie in Cinemascope, *1168*
Movie to be shown simultaneously on pay television and in movie theaters, *1172*
Navy ace in Korea, *5810*
Navy chairman of the Joint Chiefs of Staff, *5610*
Navy-Marine Corps Medal for Heroism awarded to a woman, *5534*
Newspaper advertisement that looked three-dimensional, *1551*
Nobel Peace Prize awarded to a professional soldier, *6908*
Nuclear cannon, *5880*
Nuclear reactor privately operated, *6735*
Oil refinery with a carbon monoxide boiler, *6609*
Oscar awards ceremony to be telecast, *1170*
Passenger to circle the world on commercial airlines in less than 100 hours, *8130*
Phi Beta Kappa chapter at an African-American university, *2706*
Photographic type-composing machine, *2059*
Plastic oil pipeline, *6608*
Plastic wrap, *1909*
Polypeptide hormone synthesized, *5254*
Railroad cars with a superdome observation deck, *8360*
Science fiction course at a college, *2864*
Secretary of health, education, and welfare, *4191*
Sports car with a plastic laminated fiberglass body, *8265*
State law regulating beverage containers, *5922*
Tennis champion who was a woman to win the Grand Slam, *7930*
Three brothers from one family to serve in the Senate, *3682*
Three-dimensional feature movie, *1169*
Three-dimensional feature movie in color, *1171*
Three-dimensional telecast, *4957*

1953—*continued*

Transatlantic solo boat journey by a woman, *8537*
Transcontinental express bus service, *8222*
Transcontinental nonstop two-way airplane service, *8134*
Transcontinental round-trip solo flight between sunrise and sunset, *8133*
Triple jet ace, *5809*
Use of tobacco to produce cancer in laboratory animals, *6672*
Woman pilot to break the sound barrier, *8121*
World figure skating champion from the United States, *7844*
Year in which television industry profits exceeded those of radio, *4956*

1954

African-American athlete to win the James E. Sullivan Memorial Trophy, *7479*
Air Force general who was African-American, *5494*
Army ballistic missile operational unit, *5430*
Army helicopter battalion, *5489*
Birth-control pill, *7443*
Bridge hand in which each player was dealt a perfect hand, *7738*
Cabinet session to be telecast and broadcast, *4193*
Carrier for liquid bulk chemicals, *8458*
Civil defense test held nationwide, *7300*
Civilian pilot wounded in Vietnam, *5811*
Court-martial of an officer for collaborating with his captors, *5552*
Editorial to be broadcast over radio and television, *4542*
Educational television station sponsored by a city, *4960*
Filter cigarette, *7082*
Frozen meals marketed as TV dinners, *2442*
Gas-turbine bus, *8223*
Gas-turbine car, *8267*
Hurricane name to be retired, *6506*
Hydraulic-lift parking garage device, *8266*
Intercollegiate court tennis match, *7931*
Jet airplane used for commercial transport, *8135*
Kidney transplant, *5360*
Major league baseball game in which the majority of the players on one team were African-American, *7541*
Mass immunizations for polio, *5159*
Meteorite known to have struck a person, *6390*
Microbiology laboratory, *5170*
Military heliport, *5490*
Miss America contest to be televised, *1404*
Mobile color television transmitter unit, *4991*
Newspaper vending machine to deliver a single copy, *1696*
Nobel Prize winner to receive awards in two different categories, *6909*
Photoengraving high-speed process, *2060*
Polystyrene, *1910*
Prison commissioner who was a woman, *7019*
Radio network for African-Americans, *4814*
Radio sextant, *8507*
Railroad freight yard that was fully automatic, *8329*
Refugee to arrive under the Refugee Relief Act of 1953, *6097*
Rocket-driven sled on rails, *6794*
Round-the-world flight over the North Pole on a regularly scheduled air route, *8136*
Senator elected by a write-in vote, *3683*
Shot-put toss over 60 feet, *7953*
Single by Elvis Presley, *1342*
Solar energy battery, *6634*
State legislative hearing to be shown on television, *4396*
Supreme Court case in which social-science research was accepted as evidence, *7477*
Television commercial in color to appear on a local show, *1552*
Television receiver that showed two programs simultaneously, *4998*
Terrorist shootings in the Capitol Building, *3579*
Tissue bank, *5059*
Toll collection machine, *3430*
Transistor radio receiver to be mass-produced, *4824*
Truck driving school, *3216*
Tunnel with television monitors, *3444*
Water skier to jump 100 feet, *7992*

1955

Aerocycle, *8139*
African-American minister to a white Methodist congregation, *6232*
Air-conditioned public elementary school, *2976*
Aircraft carrier with an angle deck, *8490*
Bank to operate a window in a subway station, *1749*
Beat Generation literary event, *1105*
Broadway play shown in a television version in color with its original cast, *1460*
Cabinet session held at a place other than the seat of the federal government, *4194*
Checkers champion of renown, *7739*
Corporation with a net income of more than $1 billion in one year, *1510*

1956

1956—*continued*

Motorcycle to exceed 200 miles per hour, *8291*
Network variety show hosted by an African-American, *4964*
Nuclear reactor built for private industrial research, *6622*
Oscar for best picture awarded to a movie that was independently produced, *1173*
Pilot on a scheduled passenger line who was African-American, *8142*
Prefrontal lobotomy, *5362*
Radio receiver with an auxiliary solar-cell power unit, *4825*
Ship outfitted for hurricane research, *6507*
Skyscraper of bronze and glass, *3311*
Space cabin simulator, *6795*
Stock brokerage concern of importance whose president was a woman, *1782*
Synthetic mica, *3398*
Taconite production on a large scale, *3396*
Televised performance by Elvis Presley, *1271*
Transatlantic telephone call carried by the transoceanic telephone cable, *4907*
Transcontinental nonstop helicopter flight, *8141*
Ultrasonic television remote control, *4999*
Video recording on magnetic tape televised coast-to-coast, *4963*
Video tape recorder for sounds and pictures, *5001*

1957

Air Force chairman of the Joint Chiefs of Staff, *5495*
Air-to-ground public telephone service, *4908*
American runner to run a mile in less than four minutes on an outdoor track, *7955*
Balloon flight to rise higher than 100,000 feet, *8144*
Charting of the Northwest Passage, *6653*
Circumnavigation of the North American continent by a ship, *8539*
Circumnavigation of the world by a submarine, *8538*
Civic center with an aluminum geodesic dome, *3312*
College karate club, *7978*
Commercial building with solar heating, *3313*
Electric watch, *2634*
Flying disk for use in throwing games, *7979*
Hospital with circular wards, *5122*
Installment sales law enacted by a state, *1511*
Insurance company to insure the lives of animals exclusively, *1972*
Intermediate-range ballistic missile, *5882*
Laser, *6521*
National curling championship, *7636*
National wheelchair games, *7980*
Nuclear power plant devoted exclusively to peaceful uses, *6624*
Nuclear warhead mounted on a rocket, *5883*
Powdered breakfast drink, *2448*
President to fly in a helicopter, *4299*
Round-the-world nonstop flight by a jet airplane, *8143*
Senate filibuster to last for more than 24 hours, *3684*
Sodium reactor, *6623*
Tennis champion who was African-American, *7932*
Titanium mill, *1947*
Vacuum-cast steel, *1946*
Weight lifter to lift more than 6,000 pounds, *7981*
Welding machine for aluminum pipes, *1879*
Writer to win a Pulitzer Prize four times for drama, *4772*

1958

Air Force academy, *3119*
Airline flight attendant who was an African-American woman, *8076*
Antidepressant, *5255*
Battery-powered pacemaker, *5353*
Bifocal contact lenses, *5272*
Calculation of the surface temperature of Venus, *6391*
Catholic prelate named to the Roman Curia who was American-born, *6319*
Crossing of the North Pole underwater by a submerged submarine, *8540*
Electronic computer with solid-state components, *6426*
Gamma camera for imaging the body, *5140*
Grammy awards for musical recordings, *1272*
Integrated circuit, *6522*
Military computer network, *6427*
Molybdenum centrifugal casting, *1948*
Navy nuclear submarine division, *5589*
Navy task force to fight undersea craft, *5588*
Newspaper advertisement printed on aluminum foil, *1553*
Pension for presidents and their widows, *4152*
Polycarbonate products, *1911*
Presidential Unit Citation award in peacetime, *6910*
Professional hockey player who was African-American, *7833*
Radio broadcast using an orbiting satellite, *4801*
Rocket to intercept a supersonic target missile, *5884*

Satellite placed in orbit by the United States, *6844*
Stock exchange director who was a woman, *1783*
Submarine expressly designed and built to fire guided missiles, *8522*
Telecast from the stratosphere, *5002*
Two-way moving sidewalk, *3431*

1959

Airmail by missile, *4710*
Animals to survive a space flight, *6797*
Astronauts trained by the United States, *6802*
Astronomy photographs in color to be published in a magazine, *6408*
Barbie doll, *2199*
Braille encyclopedia, *3190*
Broadway play written by an African-American woman, *1465*
Canal incorporated into a seaway, *3325*
Color photograph of the earth taken from space, *6410*
Computer-aided manufacturing system, *1880*
Golfer to break 60 for 18 holes in a major tournament, *7774*
Golfer to play 24 hours continuously on a regulation course, *7775*
House with a built-in nuclear bomb shelter, *2531*
Jetway, *8146*
Judge of Asian ancestry, *3724*
Medical slang dictionary, *5337*
Movie premiered simultaneously in major cities throughout the world, *1175*
Movie with scent, *1174*
Neo-Nazi party, *4099*
Nuclear-powered cruiser, *8492*
Nuclear-powered merchant ship, *8461*
Pedestrian shopping mall, *2102*
Photograph from space showing the earth, *6409*
Radar signal bounced off the sun, *6796*
Satellite to transmit photographs of the earth, *6845*
Scooter Pies, *2449*
Senator of Asian ancestry, *3685*
Ship to fire a Polaris missile, *5885*
Ski lifts to be regulated by the state, *7896*
State admitted to the Union that had no border with another state, *4360*
State admitted to the Union that was separated by a substantial body of water, *4361*
Stockholder meetings televised coast-to-coast simultaneously, *1784*
Submarine equipped with ballistic missiles, *8523*
Submarine to surface at the North Pole, *8541*
Tae Kwon Do instructor, *7982*
Telecast received from England, *4965*
Television series broadcast in color in prime time, *4951*
Transcontinental jet airplane passenger service, *8145*
Ultraviolet pictures of the sun, *6407*

1960

American flag to orbit the earth, *3506*
Animated cartoon series on prime-time television, *4966*
Artificial ice skating rink of Olympic size, *7845*
Birth-control pill approved by the FDA, *7443*
Chromosomal abnormality linked to cancer, *6674*
Circumnavigation of the earth by a submerged submarine, *8542*
Civil rights anthem to achieve fame, *1344*
Civil rights sit-in, *6142*
Coast-to-coast solar-powered two-way radio conversation, *4802*
Communications satellite, *6851*
Communications satellite with signal reception and transmission equipment, *6853*
Electronic watch, *2635*
Geodesic dome of substantial size, *3314*
Guided missile launched from a nuclear submarine, *5886*
Interactive computer, *6428*
Multisatellite launching, *6849*
Navigational satellite, *6847*
Nuclear reactor for research and development, *6738*
Nuclear reactor operated commercially, *6625*
Pacemaker to be implanted in a patient's body, *5363*
Parking meter enforcement division of a police department, *7386*
Photograph bounced off a satellite, *4637*
Photograph bounced off the moon, *4636*
Planned nationwide shutdown of air traffic, *8147*
Post office fully mechanized, *4711*
Postage stamp issued jointly by two countries, *4741*
Presidential election debates to be shown on television, *3824*
Professional hockey player to reach a score of more than 1,000 points, *7834*
Public demonstration of a working laser, *6521*
Scientific program to search for extraterrestrial life, *6378*
Senate election race in which both candidates were women, *3686*

1960—*continued*

Space capsule recovered from an orbiting satellite, *6850*
Space capsule recovered in midair from an orbiting satellite, *6852*
Spacecraft placed in solar orbit, *6866*
Spy satellite, *6848*
Submarine to make a submerged passage through the Northwest Passage, *8543*
Submerged submarine to fire a Polaris missile, *5887*
Sulfur mine offshore, *3399*
Television newswoman to cover a national political convention, *4603*
Tranquilizer in the benzodiazepine family, *5256*
Undersea park established by the federal government, *5995*
Weather satellite to provide cloud-cover photographs, *6846*
World heavyweight boxing champion to regain his crown, *7609*

1961

Affirmative action order issued by the federal government, *3855*
Air raid shelter for a community, *7301*
Airline to carry 100 million passengers, *8148*
Airplane passenger service with regular in-flight movies, *1156*
Animal fired into space to orbit the earth, *6798*
Archeoastronomer, *6379*
Astronaut to be launched into space, *6803*
Baseball player to win Most Valuable Player award in both major leagues, *7543*
Basketball team to score more than 10,000 points, *7559*
Building of large size with a retractable roof, *3315*
Cabinet member who was related to the president, *4195*
Championship game of the American Football League, *7713*
Commander of a combat ship who was African-American, *5611*
Cordless electric drill, *2668*
Deaths in an American nuclear reactor, *6626*
Disposable diapers to be mass-marketed, *2198*
District attorney who was African-American, *3725*
Electric toothbrush, *2481*
Federal district court judge who was African-American, *3726*
Football player who was African-American to win the Heisman Memorial Trophy, *7714*
Freedom ride in the 1960s, *6143*
Industrial robot that was practical, *6523*
Jazz composition to appear on the Top 40 charts, *1273*
Minimum wage law established by a city for public contract work, *7163*
Mobile computer center, *6429*
Nuclear-powered aircraft carrier, *8493*
Postage stamp featuring a work of art in true color, *4742*
President who was Catholic, *4265*
Presidential news conference to be televised live, *4286*
Presidential physican who was a woman, *4266*
Private housing development designed as a complete community, *3540*
Quasar to be observed, *6392*
Revolving restaurant, *1836*
Seawater conversion plant, *7419*
Skyjacking of a commercial American airplane, *6951*
Television station owned by a religious organization, *6320*
Troops sent to Vietnam, *5812*
Typewriter without type arms, *1698*
Vending machine to dispense fresh flowers, *1699*

1962

African-American athlete who was a woman to win the James E. Sullivan Memorial Trophy, *7480*
African-American woman elected to a judgeship, *3721*
Air Force Academy graduate who was Native American, *3120*
Aluminum can with a pull-tab pop-top, *2003*
American runner to run a mile in less than four minutes on an indoor track, *7955*
Astronaut to orbit the earth, *6804*
Baseball coach in the major leagues who was African-American, *7545*
Baseball player to steal more than 100 bases in a season, *7544*
Children's hospital for research and treatment of catastrophic childhood diseases, *5123*
Christmas postage stamp regular issue, *4744*
Coast-to-coast telecast by satellite, *5003*
Commercial satellite, *6857*
Computer game, *7741*
Ecology book, *5923*
Exhibition of the *Mona Lisa, 1042*
Geodetic satellite, *6858*
Indoor ski slope, *7897*
International satellite, *6855*
Launching silos for Atlas F missiles, *5889*

Limb reattachment, *5364*
Live telecast to Europe by satellite, *4968*
Navy SEAL units, *5590*
Newspaper reproduced commercially and regularly by radio facsimile, *4543*
Nuclear warhead fired from a Polaris submarine, *5888*
Orbiting solar observatory, *6854*
Pay television dramatic program, *4967*
Pilot of an airplane to qualify as an astronaut by attaining a 50-mile altitude, *8149*
Postage stamp issued on the date of the event it commemorated, *4743*
President with a brother in the Senate, *4267*
Presidential hot line, *4153*
Psychedelic music album, *1274*
Running shoes, *2266*
Satellite from the United States to impact the moon, *6856*
Ship with a floating scientific instrument platform, *6508*
Smog chamber for air pollution research, *5924*
Spacecraft to transmit data from Venus, *6867*
Spider-Man comic book, *1106*
State to have a state sport, *4362*
State to repeal its ban on acts of sodomy, *7445*
Subway train to run automatically without conductors or motormen, *8380*
Swimmer to swim the English Channel underwater, *7914*
Tae Kwon Do school, *7982*
Telephone call conveyed by a privately owned satellite, *4909*
Television news commentator who was African-American, *4602*
Transoceanic telecast by satellite, *5004*
Wal-Mart store, *2103*
World's Fair that was financially successful, *1512*

1963

Air Force Academy graduates who were African-American, *3121*
Air pollution law of importance enacted by Congress, *5925*
Aluminum soda can, *2004*
Amphibious vehicle, *8494*
Armored division transported by airplanes to a foreign country, *5431*
Artificial leather, *2143*
Ascent of Mount Everest by an American, *7983*
Assassination of a president captured on film, *4268*
Ban on sex discrimination in wages enacted by Congress, *7446*
Bank of importance to lease personal property, *1751*
Blockbuster prescription drug, *5256*
Commemorative postage stamp depicting a president's wife, *4746*
Computer graphics software, *6430*
Domed sports stadium, *3316*
Elliptical office building, *3317*
Geosynchronous satellite, *6859*
Golfer to earn over $100,000 in one year, *7776*
Honorary citizenship authorized by Congress, *6098*
Illuminated nine-hole regulation golf course, *7777*
International postal card, *4713*
Liver transplant, *5365*
Lung transplant, *5366*
Murder to be captured live on television, *6952*
Naval War College students who were African-American, *3122*
Nuclear arms-control treaty, *3902*
Nuclear reactor fueled by plutonium, *6627*
Postage stamp with fluorescent tagging, *4745*
President to witness the firing of a Polaris missile, *4154*
State college for the performing arts, *2867*
State lottery, *1804*
Supercomputer, *6431*
Telecast transmitted by satellite to Japan, *4969*
Telephone with push buttons, *4911*
Television newswoman to report from Capitol Hill, *4603*
Television receiver and transmitter operated by laser beam, *5005*
Television show transmitted by laser, *5005*
Trimline telephone, *4910*
Zip codes, *4712*

1964

Atomic-powered lighthouse, *7351*
Automated tanker under the American flag, *8463*
Bridge designed by computer, *3255*
Buffalo wings, *2450*
Campus takeover by student protesters, *2868*
Cargo ship fully automated and flying the American flag, *8462*
Cars with seat belts as standard equipment, *8261*
Catholic mass in English, *6321*
Comprehensive civil rights law enacted by Congress, *6145*
Comprehensive wilderness law, *5926*
Computer-aided design (CAD) software, *6432*
Courtroom verdict to be televised, *3727*
Election in the District of Columbia, *3785*

1964—*continued*

Former president to address the Senate, *4155*
Freeze-dried coffee, *2451*
Large commercial computer network, *6433*
Made-for-TV movie, *4971*
Major government report on tobacco smoking, *7084*
Medal of Honor awarded in the Vietnam war, *5535*
Methadone program, *7083*
Musical to run for more than 3,000 performances, *1466*
Navy divers to submerge for 10 days, *5591*
Navy nuclear task force to circumnavigate the globe without refueling, *5592*
Navy pilot shot down and captured in North Vietnam, *5813*
Nominee who was a woman to receive votes at the national convention of a major party, *4100*
Occupation of federal territory by Native American protesters in the modern era, *6099*
Orbiting geophysical observatory, *6860*
Oscar for best actor awarded to an African-American, *1176*
Performance by a British rock group, *1275*
Photographs of the moon in close-up, *6411*
Picturephone commercial service, *4914*
Postage stamps of four different designs sold as a single sheet, *4747*
Presidential election in which votes were tallied electronically, *3825*
Rocket with an electrostatic (ion) engine, *6799*
Round-the-world solo airplane flight by a woman, *8150*
Russian Orthodox saint canonized in the United States, *6322*
Self-service post office, *4714*
Shelter for abused women, *6953*
Soap opera on prime-time television, *4970*
Spacecraft to transmit close-up photographs of the lunar surface, *6868*
Telecast transmitted by satellite from Japan, *4969*
Town to voluntarily desegregate its schools, *6144*
Toy action figure, *2200*
Transcontinental Picturephone call, *4912*
Transpacific telephone service using the transoceanic cable, *4913*
Transplant of an animal organ into a human being, *5367*
Typewriter that could retype text automatically, *1700*
United Nations ambassador who was a woman, *3903*
Year when citizens of the District of Columbia could vote in a presidential election, *3786*

1965

All-news radio station, *4815*
Ambassador who was an African-American woman, *3904*
Astronaut to converse with an aquanaut, *6807*
Astronaut to orbit the earth on two trips, *6806*
Astronaut to walk in space, *6805*
Astronauts to rendezvous in space with another spacecraft, *6808*
Baseball player to play all nine positions in one game, *7546*
Cabinet meeting attended by a foreign national, *4196*
Cassette audio tape recorder, *4837*
Coins bearing dates other than the year of issue, *4046*
College teach-in against the Vietnam War, *5815*
Congressional page who was African-American, *3622*
Congressional representative who was a woman of Asian descent, *3621*
Demonstration in Washington against the Vietnam War, *5815*
Department of Housing and Urban Development, *4198*
Discotheque, *1838*
Educational computer programming language, *6434*
Federal aid program for primary and secondary schools, *2979*
Flashbulb device with multiple flashbulbs, *4652*
Ground troops sent to Vietnam, *5814*
Health insurance plan enacted by Congress, *3856*
Hotel built over a pier, *1839*
Master skyscraper antenna, *4826*
Minicomputer, *6435*
Narcotics ban enacted by a state, *7085*
National Endowment for the Arts grant, *3858*
Naval ship with a crew of mixed nationalities, *8495*
Perfecta or Exacta horse race, *7815*
Pope to visit the United States, *3938*
Presidential order enforcing affirmative action, *3857*
Satellite with a nuclear reactor to orbit the earth, *6861*
Senate page who was African-American, *3687*
Singles bar, *1837*

Spacecraft to transmit close-up photographs of Mars, *6869*
State department of Indian affairs, *4363*
State law prohibiting discrimination against the disabled in employment, *7044*
State law to end de facto segregation in schools, *6146*
State payments to crime victims, *6954*
State supreme court chief justice who was a woman, *3728*
Surgical operation on a bull to correct a sperm block, *5407*
Swimmer from the United States to make a round-trip crossing of the English Channel, *7915*
Television dramatic series starring an African-American performer, *4972*
Transatlantic undersea radio conversation, *4803*
Women members of the American Stock Exchange, *1783*

1966

Astronaut who was a civilian to orbit the earth, *6809*
Black Panther Party organizational meeting, *4101*
Black Power advocate, *6147*
Cabinet member who was African-American, *4197*
Car with front-wheel drive, *8270*
Catgut substitute, *5186*
Coach of a professional basketball team who was African-American, *7560*
Coast Guard Academy graduate who was African-American, *3123*
Computer modem that was practical, *6436*
Department of Transportation, *4199*
Endangered species list issued by the federal government, *5927*
Federal district court judge who was an African-American woman, *3726*
Hospital to offer sex-change operations, *7442*
Kwanzaa celebration, *2518*
Manned docking of two spacecraft, *6870*
Marathon runner from the United States who was a woman, *7956*
Medal of Honor awarded to a Seabee, *5536*
Motorboat ocean race, *7577*
National Endowment for the Humanities grants, *3859*
Navy captain who was African-American, *5612*
Open-reel video tape recorder for home use, *5006*
Parachute jumper snagged by airplane in midair, *8151*
Photograph of the earth taken from the moon, *6412*
Presidential proclamation establishing Father's Day, *2509*
Rocket-tracking ship, *8496*
Secretary of housing and urban development, *4198*
Senator who was African-American to be elected by popular vote, *3688*
Sergeant major of the Army, *5451*
Space probe to achieve lunar orbit, *6871*
Space treaty signed by the United States, *3905*
X-ray three-dimensional stereo fluoroscopic system, *5141*

1967

Abortion legalized by a state as a medical procedure, *7447*
American Independent Party convention, *4102*
Artificial insemination for women to be permitted by a state, *5397*
Astronauts to die in a spacecraft, *6810*
Attorney general whose father also served as attorney general, *4200*
Be-In, *1406*
Bowling automatic scoring machine, *7588*
British-made television series, *4973*
Championship football game to be televised, *7711*
Computer programming language for children, *6437*
Educational television network operated as a nonprofit corporation, *4974*
Food bank, *7282*
Freezing of a corpse for future resuscitation, *2306*
General killed in Vietnam by enemy fire, *5816*
Gravure-printed postage stamp, *4750*
Heart transplant, *5368*
High school for pregnant teenage girls, *2980*
Horse motel, *1840*
Large-type weekly newspaper, *4544*
Mayor of a major city who was African-American, *3541*
Mayor of Washington who was African-American, *3541*
New York Stock Exchange seat owner who was a woman, *1785*
Postage stamp issued in the United States and canceled by a foreign country, *4748*
Public defender hired by a state, *3973*
Quark to be observed, *6749*
Rock and roll broadcast on FM radio, *1276*
Rock music festival, *1277*
Rock musical, *1467*

1967—*continued*

Secretary of transportation, *4199*
Ship with a combined diesel and gas-turbine engine, *8497*
Super Bowl football game, *7715*
Supreme Court justice who was African-American, *3751*
Twin postage stamps, *4749*
Underground comic book of note, *1107*
Woman to run in the Boston Marathon officially, *7956*
Worldwide live television program, *4975*
Zen Buddhist monastery, *6323*

1968

Ambassador assassinated in office, *3906*
Ambulance equipped for mobile coronary care, *5047*
Armenian Orthodox cathedral, *6324*
Army general who was African-American to lead an infantry brigade in combat, *5452*
Astronaut international rescue agreement, *6811*
Astronauts to orbit the moon, *6812*
Bone marrow transplant, *5369*
Book set into type completely by electronic composition, *4466*
Circus clown training school, *3217*
Clothing designer of international renown, *2267*
Computer mouse, *6438*
Congressional representative who was an African-American woman, *3623*
Emergency 911 phone system, *7302*
Federal employee to win a Nobel Prize, *6911*
Heart transplant to an adult, *5368*
Live telecast from space, *6413*
National political convention to propose African-Americans for the offices of president and vice president, *4103*
Naturalization ceremony in the White House, *6100*
Naval ship to be captured intact, *8498*
Online library database, *3039*
Political convention to be televised in color, *4098*
President who was a Rhodes Scholar, *4269*
Presidential campaigner to be assassinated, *3826*
Presidential candidate who was an African-American woman, *3827*
Professional hockey player to score more than 100 points in one season, *7834*
Rock musical on Broadway, *1467*
Silver Star awarded to a Navy chaplain, *5537*
Smoke alarm, *7335*
Television newsmagazine, *4545*
Use of the term "personal computer," *6439*
Vaccine against a form of cancer, *5160*
West Point instructor who was a woman, *3124*
Woman criminal on the FBI's Ten Most Wanted list, *6948*
Year in which color television sets outsold black and white sets, *4976*

1969

Airplane made primarily of composite materials, *8152*
Army War College graduates who were women, *3125*
Astronauts to land on the moon, *6814*
Astronauts to retrieve a manmade object from the moon, *6816*
Astronauts to transfer from one spacecraft to another while in orbit, *6813*
ATM machine, *1752*
Bowling Triple Crown winner, *7589*
College on a Native American reservation, *2869*
Computer operating system for multiple users, *6441*
Episode of *Sesame Street* to be shown on television, *4977*
Gay rights protest, *7448*
General-purpose computer network, *6442*
Heart transplant using an artificial heart, *5371*
Hijacking of an American airliner by terrorists, *5817*
Hip-replacement operation, *5370*
Hollywood movie directed by an African-American, *1177*
Home computer, *6440*
Horse race parimutuel in which all the jockeys were women, *7817*
Human beings to see the sun eclipsed by the Earth, *6815*
Isolation of a single gene from an organism, *6675*
Jockey who was a woman to win on a regular parimutuel flat track, *7816*
Journey on foot to all seven continents, *7985*
Major solo show of work by an African-American artist, *1043*
Mineral found on the moon before it was found on Earth, *3400*
Mobile telephone call to the moon, *4915*
New York Stock Exchange member who was African-American, *1786*
Oil spill with disastrous consequences, *6612*
Oscar for best picture awarded to an X-rated movie, *1178*

Postage stamp depicting a living American, *4751*
President to attend the launching of a manned space flight, *4156*
Religious ritual on the moon, *6325*
Senator to act in the movies, *3689*
Ship to pass both ways through the Northwest Passage, *8544*
Space-to-ground news conference telecast, *4546*
State to require presidential electors to vote for the candidates of the party for which they were chosen, *3795*
Synthetic fabric that was waterproof and breathable, *2144*
Transatlantic solo trip by rowboat, *8545*
Transpacific solo sailboat crossing by a woman, *8546*
Vacuum telescope, *6380*
Vasectomy outpatient service, *5074*
Vietnam War Moratorium Day demonstration, *5818*
Woman jockey to ride two winners in a day, *7816*

1970

Air Force Reserve officer who was a nun, *5496*
Army general who was a woman, *5453*
Bank to be automated, *1753*
Cabinet member to serve in four different capacities, *4201*
Cars with three-point lap-and-shoulder seat belts, *8261*
Census compiled in part from statistics obtained by mail, *6157*
College to offer a degree in human sexuality studies, *2870*
Congressional representative of Puerto Rican ancestry, *3624*
Disposable diapers with adhesive tabs, *2198*
Earth Day, *2519*
European king buried in the United States, *3939*
Gay pride march, *7449*
Jockey who was a woman to ride in the Kentucky Derby, *7818*
Jumbo jet, *8153*
Lottery in which the top prize was $1 million, *1805*
Microprocessor, *6524*
New York City Marathon, *7957*
No-fault car insurance law enacted by a state, *1973*
No-fault divorce law enacted by a state, *2597*
Nobel Prize in economics awarded to an American, *6912*
Packet radio network, *4804*
Physician with a mobile medical office, *5043*
President of a major university who was African-American, *2871*
President who was a jet pilot, *4270*
Professional football game in which a woman participated, *7716*
Right to Life Party organizational meeting, *4104*
School district to implement court-ordered busing to achieve racial integration, *6148*
Sky marshals, *7387*
State prison commissioner who was a woman, *7019*
Strike of postal employees, *7164*
United Nations Security Council resolution vetoed by the United States, *3907*

1971

Air Force general who was a woman, *5497*
Airport baggage scanning system, *8154*
Astronauts to ride a vehicle on the moon, *6817*
Athlete who was a woman to earn more than $100,000 in one season, *7933*
Books of postage stamps with humidity-resistant adhesive, *4752*
Brokerage firm whose shares were traded by a major stock exchange, *1787*
Christmas postage stamp series with a religious and a secular subject, *4744*
College to offer courses to railroad commuters, *2873*
College whose tuition fees were based on family income, *2872*
Computerized library network, *3040*
Electronic book archive, *3029*
Electronic pocket calculator, *6525*
E-mail, *6443*
Floppy disk, *6444*
Football game to last longer than 80 minutes, *7717*
Laser printer, *6446*
Motorcycle racer who was a woman, *7849*
Off-track betting operation, *1806*
Organization for reuniting birthmothers and adopted children, *2201*
People's Party convention, *4105*
President to visit all 50 states, *4319*
Rape crisis center, *6955*
Satellite launched from the earth to orbit another planet, *6862*
Secret Service agents who were women, *3860*
Skyjacking in which the skyjacker disappeared, *6956*
Soft contact lens, *5273*
Sport played on the moon, *7778*
State bottle deposit law, *5928*
Technical school for Native Americans, *2981*

1971—*continued*

Train to transport passengers and their cars, *8398*
Use of @ in an e-mail address, *6445*
Veterinary hospital established by a city, *5408*
Vote in the House of Representatives to be tallied by machine, *3625*
Woman to serve as patent examiner-in-chief, *3996*

1972

Acupuncture treatment center, *5075*
African-American director of the New York Stock Exchange, *1786*
Air Force ace in Vietnam, *5819*
Attorney general to plead guilty to a criminal offense, *4202*
Bank to provide movies for customers waiting in line, *1754*
Birth rate resulting in negative population growth, *6101*
Chairman of a major political party who was a woman, *4107*
Congressional candidate elected while missing, *3626*
Congressional representative from a Southern state who was an African-American woman, *3623*
Conversation between two computers, *6447*
Digital watch, *2636*
Dow Jones Industrial Average to exceed 1,000 points, *1788*
Electric power using municipal garbage as a boiler fuel, *6573*
Fly-by-wire aircraft, *8155*
Freestanding birth center, *2159*
Geologist to reach the moon, *6509*
Horse race for a purse of more than $1 million, *7819*
Large-scale presidential media event, *4287*
Libertarian Party national convention, *4106*
Metropolitan Opera orchestra conductor who was African-American, *1330*
Minister who was openly gay, *7450*
Navy admiral who was African-American, *5613*
Nobel Prize winner to win twice in the same field, *6913*
Noise-control law enacted by a state, *5929*
Pictorial postal cards, *4715*
President to visit a nation not recognized by the federal government, *4320*
President to visit the Soviet Union, *4320*
Recombinant DNA molecule, *6676*
Sailors assigned to regular Navy shipboard duty who were women, *5593*
Satellite composite map of the United States, *4486*
Snowmobile to exceed a speed of 125 miles per hour, *7984*
Spacecraft to carry an extraterrestrial message, *6872*
State to refuse to host the Olympic Games, *7861*
Stereo telecast, *4978*
Television show with open captions, *7045*
Vice presidential candidate of a major political party to resign before the election, *3828*
Video game, *7742*
Wearable infusion pump, *5187*
Woman ordained as a Reform rabbi, *6314*
World chess champion from the United States, *7743*

1973

Airborne express delivery service, *2081*
Armed occupation by Native American protesters in the modern era, *6102*
Artificial gene, *6677*
Balloon flight powered by solar energy, *8157*
Car equipped with an air bag, *8271*
College to offer athletic scholarships to women, *2874*
Commercial crude-oil carrier, *8464*
Congressional representative to give birth while holding office, *3628*
CT scanner, *5142*
Designated hitter in a major league baseball game, *7547*
Electoral vote for a woman, *3829*
Federal marshals who were women to be hired on a permanent basis, *7385*
First Lady to earn a professional degree, *4236*
Food processor, *2290*
Gene splicing, *6678*
Golfer to earn $100,000 in a contest, *7779*
Haircut in space, *6819*
Hang-gliding national championships, *7684*
Iditarod sled dog race, *7664*
Jockey who was a woman to win a major stakes race, *7820*
Mayor of a major Southern city who was African-American, *3541*
Metric distance markers on a state highway, *3432*
Navy officer who was a woman to hold a major command, *5614*
Nazi death camp guard to be deported, *6103*
Phone call made on a cell phone, *4916*
Photograph of a comet taken from space, *6414*
Physician to practice as an astronaut in space, *6818*

Pilot on a regularly scheduled major airline who was a woman, *8156*
Plastic soda bottle, *2005*
Presidential Citizen Medal, *6914*
Prison guard who was a woman to serve in a maximum security prison for men, *7020*
Role-playing game, *7744*
Secretary of state to serve simultaneously as national security advisor, *4203*
Skyscraper higher than 1,400 feet, *3318*
Space station launched by the United States, *6873*
Vice president chosen under the 25th Amendment, *4310*
Vote in the House of Representatives to be recorded electronically, *3627*
Zoo with twilight conditions, *3161*

1974

African-American manager of a major league baseball team, *7545*
Chairman of the Republican party who was a woman, *4107*
Congressional representative who was a grandmother, *3629*
Democratic Party convention between presidential elections, *4108*
Disco dance suite, *1278*
Free agents in major league baseball, *7548*
Hospice home-care program, *5398*
Magazine about recreational drugs, *7086*
Magazine for home computer users, *6449*
Mayor of a major city with a population over 500,000, *3542*
Merchant Marine Academy cadets who were women, *3126*
Military police officer who was a woman, *5432*
Motorcycle jump across a river canyon, *1408*
Native American superintendent of a Bureau of Indian Affairs agency, *3843*
Openly gay politician elected to public office, *7451*
Personal computer, *6450*
Personal computer operating system, *6448*
Police officer who was a woman to be killed in the line of duty, *7388*
President to receive a presidential pardon, *4159*
President to resign, *4157*
President who came to the office through appointment rather than election, *4158*
Round-the-world journey on foot, *7985*
Self-adhesive postage stamp, *4753*
Senate proceeding to be shown on television, *3691*
Senator who had been an astronaut, *3690*
Speed limit for highway traffic established by Congress, *8213*
State legislator who was openly gay, *7452*
State library to publish a master catalog, *3030*
Tightrope walker to span two skyscrapers, *1407*
Woman elected state governor in her own right, *4381*

1975

Adjustable stadium, *3319*
Astronauts to participate in an international spaceflight, *6820*
Catholic saint who was born in America, *6326*
College commencement exercises in a prison, *2875*
Commercial software for personal computers, *6451*
Computer store, *6454*
Computer virus, *6452*
CT scanner capable of making full-body images, *5142*
Divorce rate of more than 1 million a year, *2598*
Dog hotel, *1841*
Emperor of Japan to visit the United States, *3940*
Laser printer marketed, *6446*
Major city with a freestanding birth center, *2160*
Personal computer users group, *6453*
Postage stamps without a denomination, *4754*
Sex discrimination law enacted by a state that affected high school athletic competitions, *7453*
Spacecraft to land on Mars, *6874*
State services to refugees, *6104*
State supreme court chief justice who was African-American, *3708*
State to recognize unions for farmworkers, *7166*
Strike by physicians against long working hours in hospitals, *7165*
Trial in which lawyers appeared on a Picturephone, *6957*
Video cassette recorder for home use, *5006*
Whooping crane, *5964*

1976

Air Force Academy cadets who were women, *3127*
Ambulance ship for first aid to boaters and pleasure craft, *5048*
Bridge named for a woman, *3256*
Congressional representatives to marry each other, *3630*

1976—*continued*

Designated hitter in a World Series game, *7547*
General of the Armies of the United States with the rank of six stars, *5454*
Home pregnancy test, *5188*
Involuntary sterilization regulation enacted by a state, *7454*
Keynote speech by an African-American woman at a major party convention, *4075*
Metropolitan Opera orchestra conductor who was a woman, *1331*
Naval Academy students who were women, *3128*
Nuclear commercial power plant licensed operator who was a woman, *6628*
PET scanner, *5143*
Photograph taken on Mars, *6415*
Postage stamps of 50 different designs sold as a single sheet, *4755*
Presidential election debate between an incumbent president and a challenger to be televised, *3830*
Radiation attacks against an American embassy, *3908*
Right-to-die law enacted by a state, *2307*
Satellite dish for personal use, *5007*
Soccer player to score 12 points in one game, *7900*
Softball game of 365 innings, *7986*
State dinner televised from the White House, *4333*
State to make marital rape a crime, *6958*
Television network evening news program anchor who was a woman, *4604*
Thread as strong as steel, *2145*
Transatlantic supersonic jet service, *8158*
Underground school, *2982*
Voice reader, *6456*
West Point cadets who were women, *3129*
Woman pilot to earn the rank of captain, *8156*
Word processor for computers, *6455*
Year in which a higher percentage of female than male high school graduates enrolled in college, *2876*
Year in which Nobel Prizes were won by Americans in five of six categories, *6915*

1977

Attorney general to be incarcerated, *4205*
Baby carrier, *2202*
Border-to-border national highway, *3433*
Cabinet member who was an African-American woman, *4204*
Catholic saint who was a male American citizen, *6328*
Coast Guard officers who were women who served aboard ships, *5546*
Computer camp, *6457*
Daughters of the American Revolution member who was African-American, *7231*
Department of Energy, *4206*
Diesel cars to be mass-produced, *8272*
Driver who was a woman to compete in the Indianapolis 500, *7626*
Episcopal priest who was a woman, *6327*
Federally chartered bank owned and managed by women, *1755*
Free atmospheric flight by a space shuttle, *6875*
Gay politician elected to an important local office, *7452*
Golfer to break 60 in a Professional Golfers Association tour, *7780*
Human-powered aircraft, *8159*
Judge who had served time in prison, *3729*
Laser printer for use with a single computer, *6446*
License plate slogan to be challenged, *8214*
Magnetic resonance image of a human body, *5145*
Naval War College president who was a former prisoner of war, *3130*
Orca, *5965*
Parade in which the marching music was supplied by transistor radios, *1409*
President to take the oath of office using a nickname, *4161*
Presidential pardon for a person convicted of treason, *4160*
Radio broadcast in which citizens telephoned the president, *4288*
Radioimmunoassay test, *5144*
Secretary of energy, *4206*
State to experience a natural decrease in population, *4364*
State to require arrests in cases of domestic violence, *6959*
Television show with a regularly appearing gay character, *7461*
Woman boxing referee to judge a heavyweight championship match, *7606*

1978

Astronauts who were women, *6821*
Ballet transmitted by satellite, *1056*
Bilingual report of a congressional committee, *3631*
Casino outside the state of Nevada, *1807*
Child safety seat law enacted by a state, *8273*
Coin bearing the likeness of an American woman, *4047*
Computer bulletin board, *6458*

Designated hitter for all baseball games in a season, *7547*
FBI sting operation against corrupt politicians, *6960*
Football game in which referees were allowed to check television instant replays, *7718*
Graphic novel, *1108*
Iron Man triathlon, *7987*
Marine general who was a woman, *5570*
Medicine produced using recombinant DNA, *5257*
Mormon man ordained to the priesthood who was African-American, *6329*
Newspaper whose contents were transmitted by a communications satellite, *4547*
Postage stamp depicting an African-American woman, *4756*
Sports bra, *2268*
Transatlantic balloon flight, *8160*
University president who was a woman, *2786*

1979

All-politics television network, *4979*
Army general who was an African-American woman, *5455*
Astronaut who was Jewish, *6822*
Astronaut who was of Asian descent, *6823*
Boxer to win five world titles in five weight divisions, *7610*
Casino run by a Native American tribe, *1808*
Coal miner who was a woman to be killed in a mining accident, *6613*
Coast Guard ship commander who was a woman, *5547*
Department of Education, *4208*
Department of Health and Human Services, *4207*
Gay rights march, *7455*
Goalie in a National Hockey League team to score a goal, *7835*
Golfer to shoot below his age, *7781*
Graduated driver licenses for teenagers, *8274*
Hostage crisis in the modern era, *3909*
Light sculpture created with a cityscape, *1044*
Marine general who was African-American, *5571*
Nuclear power plant to sustain a major accident, *6629*
Oceanographer of distinction who was a woman, *6510*
Pen with truly erasable ink, *2681*
Pope to visit the White House, *3941*
Rocket-powered car to break the sound barrier on land, *8275*
Secretary of education, *4208*
Secretary of health and human services, *4207*
Solar-powered long-distance airplane flight, *8161*
Spreadsheet program for computers, *6459*
Train operated exclusively by women, *8399*
Transfusion of artificial blood, *5060*
Year in which more women than men were enrolled in colleges and universities, *2877*

1980

All-news television network, *4548*
American boycott of the Olympic Games, *7862*
Coast Guard Academy graduates who were women, *3131*
Congressional representative expelled for corruption, *3632*
Cuban boatlift, *6105*
Debate among party hopefuls for the presidential nomination to be shown on television, *3831*
Human antibodies produced artificially, *5258*
In-line roller skate that was commercially successful, *7876*
Methodist bishop who was a woman, *6330*
Newspaper to publish an Internet edition, *4549*
Power plant using solar cells, *6636*
President who had been a professional actor, *4271*
Solar-powered airplane to cross the English Channel, *8161*
Sticky notes, *2028*
Subcompact car with front wheel drive, *8276*
Synthetic fuels plant, *6614*
Tank with a turbine engine, *5890*
Television shows with closed captions, *7046*
Transcontinental nonstop balloon flight, *8162*
Transgenic animal, *6679*
Volcano known to claim human life, *5930*
West Point woman graduate who was Jewish, *3097*
Woman Secret Service agent killed in the line of duty, *3845*

1981

AIDS epidemic, *5095*
Astronaut who was Hispanic, *6824*
Baby whose life was saved by surgery while still in the womb, *5373*
Body farm for forensic research, *7389*
Child born in the United States through in vitro fertilization, *2161*
Computer software patent, *6461*
Editor of a major daily newspaper who was a woman, *4605*
Graphical user interface for a commercial computer, *6460*

1981—*continued*

IBM personal computer, *6462*
Isolation of embryonic stem cells in a mammal, *6680*
Mayor of a major city who was of Mexican descent, *3543*
Microwave popcorn, *2452*
Music video on MTV, *1279*
Offshore port for oil supertankers, *6615*
Patent on a living organism, *4000*
Permanent ambassador to the United Nations who was a woman, *3910*
President to be wounded in an unsuccessful assassination attempt while in office, *4272*
Product liability lawsuit to result in a criminal trial, *1513*
Reusable manned spacecraft, *6875*
Supreme Court justice who was a woman, *3752*
Three-dimensional maps of the ocean floor, *6511*
Transdermal patch, *5259*
Transplant of artificial skin, *5372*
Year in which the public debt of the United States exceeded $1 trillion, *3861*

1982

Athlete who was a woman to earn more than $1 million in a year, *7934*
Computer virus in personal computers, *6463*
Emoticon comment sign for computer users, *6464*
Heart transplant using an artificial heart that was intended to be permanent, *5374*
National Navajo Code Talkers Day, *5772*
Poisoning of store merchandise, *6961*
Private space launch, *6876*
Round-the-world helicopter flight, *8163*

1983

Astronaut to fly in space who was African-American, *6826*
Astronaut who was a woman to fly in space, *6825*
Cell phone marketed commercially, *4917*
Cellular telephone system, *4918*
Compact disc players, *4838*
Congressional representatives censured for sexual misconduct, *3633*
Designation of Martin Luther King Day as a national holiday, *2520*
DNA chain polymerization, *6681*
Execution by lethal injection, *7021*
Eyeglasses with polycarbonate lenses, *5274*
Identification of the AIDS virus, *6682*
Openly gay member of Congress, *7456*
Presidential candidate who had been an astronaut, *3832*
Spacecraft to leave the solar system, *6877*
State to have an official hero or heroine, *4365*

1984

Astronaut who was a mother, *6829*
Astronaut who was a woman to walk in space, *6828*
Astronauts to fly free in space, *6827*
Bioterror attack on American soil in modern times, *6962*
Green Party organizational meeting, *4109*
Heart transplant using a baboon heart, *5375*
Methodist bishop who was an African-American woman, *6330*
MTV Video Music Awards, *1281*
Nicotine replacement product approved by the FDA, *7087*
Online college classes, *2878*
Rap album to attract a mass audience, *1280*
Salvage operation in space, *6878*
Satellite repair in orbit, *6863*
State to decriminalize public breastfeeding, *2203*
Thermal inkjet printer, *6465*
Transatlantic solo balloon flight, *8164*
Vice presidential candidate from a major political party who was a woman, *3833*
Woman midshipman at the Naval Academy to graduate first in her class, *3128*
Year in which the average price of a new house topped $100,000, *2532*

1985

African-American woman Army general to rise through the ranks, *5455*
AIDS antidiscrimination law, *5096*
Astronomical phenomenon caused by space debris, *6864*
Cabinet member indicted while in office, *4209*
Desktop publishing software, *6467*
Federal lawsuit against a city for failure to protect a battered woman, *7390*
Fullerenes to be observed, *6750*
Internet domain, *6466*
Senator to fly in space, *6830*
Septuplets, *2162*
Vending machine for art, *1701*
Woman ordained as a Conservative rabbi, *6314*

1986

Bicyclist from the United States to win the Tour de France, *7660*

Fortune 1000 company to be owned and chaired by a woman, *1514*
Genetically altered plants, *1654*
Genetically altered virus approved for use in a vaccine, *6683*
Human chain across the United States, *1410*
Martin Luther King Day, *2520*
MX intercontinental ballistic missile base, *5891*
Poet laureate of the United States, *1109*
Round-the-world nonstop airplane flight without refueling, *8165*
Space shuttle disaster, *6879*

1987

Art museum devoted to work by women, *3162*
Condom commercials on television, *7458*
Drug for treating AIDS, *5260*
Elimination of an entire class of nuclear weapons by treaty, *3911*
Interactive multimedia authoring program, *6468*
National hotline for victims of domestic violence, *6963*
Parental leave law enacted by a state that applied to both mothers and fathers, *7457*
Principal chief of a major Native American tribe who was a woman, *3942*
Superconducting material that operated at relatively high temperatures, *6751*
Swimmer to cross the Bering Strait, *7916*
Trial of a surrogate mother for refusing to give up her baby, *2163*
Undersea hotel, *1842*
Wolf to be reintroduced into the wild, *5966*
Woman legislator from the Democratic Party to serve in both houses of Congress, *3680*
Year in which the federal budget exceeded $1 trillion, *3862*

1988

African-American history trail, *6149*
American to be recognized by Tibetan Buddhists as a reincarnated lama, *6331*
Anti-aging skin cream, *2482*
Ascent of Mount Everest by an American woman, *7983*
Ban on cheap handguns enacted by a state, *6964*
Ban on surrogate motherhood enacted by a state, *2164*
Catholic archbishop who was African-American, *6279*
Compensation of Japanese-Americans interned during World War II, *5820*
Computer hacker to be convicted, *6965*
Cyber cafe, *1843*
E-mail program with a graphic interface, *6469*
Factoring of a 100-digit number, *6708*
High school chapter of Alcoholics Anonymous, *7078*
Major worm attack on the Internet, *6470*
Patent on an animal, *6684*
Slot machine jackpot of more than $1 million, *1802*
Smoking ban on airplane flights, *7088*
SSRI antidepressant, *5261*
Texas Ranger who was African-American, *7359*
Transoceanic fiber-optic telecommunications cable, *4919*
Year when half of the nation's agricultural counties were designated disaster areas, *5931*
Zebra mussels, *5967*

1989

Air bag requirement by the federal government, *8277*
Airship that was certified by the Federal Aviation Administration, *8166*
American mercenaries convicted of planning a terrorist attack within the United States on behalf of a foreign government, *6966*
Chairman of a major political party who was African-American, *4110*
Chairman of the Joint Chiefs of Staff who was African-American, *5456*
Commercial provider of dial-up Internet services, *6471*
Congressional representative who was a Hispanic woman, *3634*
Department of Veterans Affairs, *4210*
Drug control chief appointed by the federal government, *7089*
Global Positioning System (GPS) satellite, *6865*
Human-powered helicopter, *8167*
Human-powered submarine race, *7578*
International cyberespionage case, *6967*
Internet search engine, *6472*
Liver transplant from a live donor, *5376*
Mayor of New York City who was African-American, *3544*
Museum devoted solely to American political memorabilia, *3163*
Power plant generating electricity from peat, *6637*
Secretary of veterans affairs, *4210*
State governor who was African-American, *4383*
Stealth aircraft, *5492*
Surgeon general who was a woman, *7283*

1989—*continued*

World Series disrupted by an earthquake, *7549*

1990

Charles Stark Draper Prize for engineering and technology, *6916*
Chemical arms control treaty, *3912*
Comprehensive civil rights legislation for people with disabilities, *7047*
Death by suicide machine, *2308*
Dolphin-free tuna, *2454*
Electronic anticounterfeiting features in U.S. currency, *4048*
Fat substitute in prepared foods, *2453*
Gene therapy, *5399*
Grammy Award to be retracted, *1282*
Killer bees, *5968*
Machine controlled via the Internet, *6473*
Native American Day, *2521*
Navy officer who was a woman to command a ship at sea, *5615*
Orbiting observatory, *6381*
Physical manipulation of individual atoms, *6752*
Prepaid phone card to require a PIN, *4920*
Pulitzer Prize awarded to a comic book, *4773*
Robot to make pizza, *6526*
Round-the-world solo sailing trip by an African-American, *8547*
Solar-powered car race, *7627*
State to authorize incarceration of convicted sex offenders beyond their prison terms, *7303*
State to inform the public about the residences of released sex offenders, *7304*
Telescope of importance with a compound objective mirror, *6382*
Tomatoes from space, *1655*
Tooth-wear gauge, *5089*

1991

Air Force general who was an African-American woman, *5498*
American to hug the Queen of England, *3943*
Antistalking law enacted by a state, *6968*
Astronaut who was a Hispanic woman, *6831*
Cruise missiles used in war, *5892*
Destruction of an attacking missile by a defensive missile in combat, *5893*
Educational multimedia CD-ROM, *6474*
Grandmother to give birth to her own grandchild, *2165*
Medal of Technology awarded to a woman, *6917*
Ornithopter that succeeded in flying, *8168*
Photograph taken close up of an asteroid in space, *6416*
Pilot to destroy an enemy airplane in the Gulf War, *5822*
Pilot who was a woman to die in a combat zone, *5824*
President whose body was exhumed, *4273*
Pulitzer prize awarded to a science book, *4774*
Scientist to win the Pulitzer Prize twice, *4774*
Serviceman killed in the Gulf War, *5823*
Soccer world champion who was a woman, *7901*
State with electronic toll collection, *3434*
Statewide registration of assault weapons, *6969*
Superconducting motor, *6739*
War that was predicted by pizza orders, *5821*

1992

African-American woman astronaut to fly in space, *6826*
Alternative medicine department in a federal research institution, *5400*
Animated film inducted into the National Film Registry, *1202*
Cablecasts of city meetings with realtime captioning for the hearing-impaired, *7048*
Car fueled by methanol, *8278*
Charter school, *2983*
Criminal conviction of a foreign head of state, *3944*
Food guide pyramid, *7284*
Hospice for animals, *2606*
Husband and wife to fly in space together, *6832*
Library to possess 100 million items, *3031*
Life-sized Barbie doll, *2199*
Liver transplant using a baboon liver, *5377*
Motor vehicles powered by natural gas, *8296*
Nationwide nutritional labeling standards, *7285*
Olympic athlete to win two consecutive heptathlon events, *7863*
Postage stamp whose design was decided by popular vote, *4757*
Professional hockey player who was a woman, *7836*
Senator who was an African-American woman, *3692*
Senators who were Jewish women, *3693*
State to recognize midwifery as a separate profession, *2166*
Transgendered person elected to public office, *7459*
Woman poet laureate, *1109*

1993

1994

1995

1995—*continued*

Municipal Heat-Health Warning forecasting system, *6512*
Natural medicine clinic subsidized by a government, *5076*
Patent on a number, *6711*
Planetary probe to enter the atmosphere of Jupiter, *6881*
Robot to perform surgery, *6528*
School district put under state control by federal court order, *2985*
Spacecraft launched by the United States to dock with a Russian space station, *6880*
Theory of fair division, *6712*
Triplets born several weeks apart, *2167*
TV program broadcast on the Internet, *4980*
West Point cadet who was a woman to graduate at the top of her class, *3132*
Wiki Web site, *6478*

1996

American honored by Yad Vashem, *6919*
Astronaut from the United States who was a woman to live in a space station, *6837*
Auction of radio spectrum for satellite services, *4805*
Basketball leagues for women, *7561*
Boxer who was a woman to earn international recognition, *7612*
Censorship of the Internet, *6481*
Chess computer to beat the world chess champion, *7745*
Commercial DNA bank, *6687*
Company to pay a fine of $100 million for a price-fixing scheme, *1515*
Computer software application on Digital Video Disc, *6480*
Electric car to be mass-produced, *8279*
Green Party national convention, *4109*
HDTV broadcasting license, *4981*
Holiday postage stamp issued jointly by two countries, *4741*
Home screening kit for HIV infection, *5189*
Honorary citizen who was a woman, *6108*
Internet record label, *1283*
Laboratory test to identify patients with Alzheimer's disease, *5146*
Manufactured food product to carry a health claim on its label, *7288*
Medals of Honor awarded to African-American servicemen for service in World War II, *5538*
Minister who was a transsexual, *7460*
Online high school, *2986*
Online library provided by a state, *3032*
Painting by an African-American artist to hang in the White House, *4334*
Pilot of a B-52 bomber who was a woman, *5493*
Player in the Women's National Basketball League, *7562*
Police 311 hotline, *7392*
Political asylum granted to avoid genital mutilation, *6107*
Presidential election in which the winning candidate received a greater percentage of women's votes than men's, *3834*
Scientific evidence for life on Mars, *6800*
Serviceman killed in the peacekeeping mission in Bosnia, *5829*
State economic development agency that was partly privatized, *4366*
Television station to regularly broadcast high-definition television, *4982*
Use of radar to investigate a plane crash, *8170*
Webmail service, *6482*

1997

Ambassador to Vietnam, *3914*
AMBER Alert System, *7393*
Art museum of importance devoted to the work of an individual woman, *3165*
Ban on federal funding for human cloning research, *6689*
Biotechnology treatment for cancer, *5401*
Cigarette maker to agree to a lawsuit settlement, *7091*
Cigarette manufacturer to list ingredients on the label, *7092*
Cloning of a primate from an embryo, *6688*
Coins depicting state symbols, *4049*
Complete DNA sequencing of a free-living organism, *6690*
Comprehensive digital atlas of the human body, *5147*
Dow Jones Industrial Average over 7,000, *1789*
Executive officer of a man-of-war who was a woman, *5617*
Federal prosecution of a hate crime on the Internet, *6974*
First Lady to be depicted on a monument to a president, *4238*
Human embryonic stem cell lines, *6691*
Images of the surface of Mars to be televised live, *6417*
Joint space walk by American and Russian astronauts, *6838*
Juvenile hacker charged under federal law, *6973*
Kosher cyber cafe, *1843*

Mandatory AIDS testing for newborns enacted by a state, *7289*
Movie shown on a television network without interruption by commercials, *4983*
Movie to earn more than $400 million in the United States market, *1183*
Online filing system for registering trademarks, *3983*
President to use the line-item veto, *4163*
Presidential inauguration broadcast live over the Internet, *4289*
Prison to offer training in Vipassana meditation, *7023*
Robot to conduct a roving exploration of the surface of another planet, *6882*
Secretary of state who was a woman, *4212*
Space burial, *2311*
State welfare reform program, *7167*
State with a gross state product of $1 trillion, *4367*
Telephone directory with internet addresses, *4921*
Television network sitcom to feature a lead character who was gay, *7461*
Teraflop computer, *6483*
Tobacco sales to minors to be restricted by federal regulations, *7090*
Transplant of human embryo tissue, *5378*
Vote cast from space in an American election, *3788*
Voting rights in space, *3787*
Women's National Basketball League champions, *7564*
Women's National Basketball League game, *7563*

1998

American Heritage Rivers, *5997*
Billion-dollar settlement in an environmental lawsuit, *5932*
Bounty of $5 million for an enemy of the United States, *5830*
Cancer-preventing drug, *5263*
Capitol Police Officers killed in the line of duty, *3580*
Congresswoman who was a veteran of the armed forces, *3635*
Cultivation of human stem cells in a laboratory, *6692*
Detailed financial statement for the federal government, *3863*
Elected president to be impeached, *4165*
Federal judge to reduce a sentence as a protest against racial profiling, *7024*
Federal online privacy law, *7305*
Federal payment over the Internet, *3865*
Fighter pilot who was a woman to fire a missile in combat, *5831*
Fundraising (semipostal) stamp, *4758*
Genome sequencing of a multicellular organism, *6693*
Government report posted on the Internet before its publication on paper, *3866*
Image of a planet outside Earth's solar system, *6418*
International space station, *6884*
Labor Party national convention, *4111*
Law making identity theft a federal crime, *6975*
Live childbirth broadcast on the Internet, *2168*
Live surgery broadcast on the Internet, *5379*
Magnetic surgery, *5380*
Major network program broadcast in high-definition television, *4984*
Marriage and divorce classes required by a state, *2599*
Midterm election since World War II in which the president's party gained seats in the House of Representatives, *3636*
Movie to earn $1 billion worldwide, *1184*
MP3 player, *4839*
National DNA database, *7394*
Nuclear waste storage site deep underground, *6630*
Octuplets, *2169*
Oral medicine for erectile dysfunction, *5262*
President to give testimony before a grand jury during his term in office, *4164*
Ruling requiring retention of all electronic records of the federal government, *3864*
Solo crossing of the Gulf of Mexico in a paddled boat, *8548*
Spacecraft with ion propulsion system, *6883*
State appeals court decision ordering the extension of insurance benefits to gay partners of government employees, *7462*
State law allowing sealed birth records of adopted children to be opened, *2206*
State to eliminate polling places, *3789*
State to mandate workplace accommodations for breastfeeding mothers, *2205*
Supreme Court decision on inclusion of candidates in televised political debates, *3753*
Teleportation experiment, *6753*
Thought control of a computer, *5275*
Web site constructed to authenticate a film, *1185*

1999

Ambassador who was Muslim, *3915*
Antiglobalization protest of significance, *6980*

1999—*continued*

Arms control treaty rejected by the Senate, *3694*
Bloodless liver transplant from a living donor, *5382*
Chess grandmaster who was African-American, *7746*
Chief White House counsel who was a woman, *4167*
City to derive all its energy needs from renewable sources, *6638*
Coin bearing the likeness of a Native American woman, *4047*
Complete sequencing of a human chromosome, *6695*
Computer virus spread by e-mail, *6484*
Criminal conviction in an airliner crash, *6981*
Customer satisfaction survey by the federal government, *3869*
Cyber university, *2879*
Digital projection of a major motion picture, *1187*
Dow Jones Industrial Average to exceed 10,000 points, *1790*
Family car with its own video entertainment system, *8280*
Feature film to premiere simultaneously in a theater and on the Internet, *1186*
Federal conviction for Internet piracy, *6979*
Former speaker of the House to become a television news commentator, *3637*
Fuel cell car, *8281*
Functioning human organ grown in a laboratory, *5061*
Hand transplant, *5381*
Hybrid car, *8282*
Interactive topographical maps of the United States, *6513*
Internet camera showing the site of a presidential assassination, *4274*
Internet march on Washington, *3868*
Language to have its entire literature digitized, *1110*
Major motion picture produced and exhibited entirely with digital technology, *1188*
Moon burial, *2312*
Murderer convicted on the basis of nationally televised evidence, *6976*
Plant DNA bank, *6694*
President to participate in a live chat over the Internet, *4290*
President to receive a bill from Congress by e-mail, *4166*
Robot to grade essays on a standardized test, *6529*
Robotic chair with balancing capability, *7049*
Sale of an American painting at a price comparable to that of European paintings, *1045*
School voucher plan enacted by a state, *2987*
Sex discrimination case to establish the rights of fathers of newborn babies, *2207*
Smart card, *1765*
Solar system with multiple planets, *6394*
Solo row across an ocean by a woman, *8549*
Space probe mission headed entirely by women, *6885*
State criminal prosecution for the sale of confidential personal information, *6977*
State government to completely privatize its computer services, *4368*
State in which all of the top elected offices were held by women, *4369*
State law decriminalizing hemp cultivation, *1656*
State police department to be monitored for racial profiling, *7395*
Statewide 211 helpline, *7420*
Trial broadcast by the court over the Internet, *6978*
Woman to serve as commander of a space flight, *6834*
Year in which Medicare spending declined, *3867*

2000

Ban on the sale of mercury thermometers, *5933*
Billionaires who were African-American, *1714*
Census to be replicated, *6161*
Census to collect information over the phone, *6158*
Civil lawsuit against American organizations brought by American victims of terrorism, *3730*
Dual kidney and liver transplants from children to a parent, *5383*
Fast-food corporation to require humane animal treatment from its suppliers, *1844*
First Lady elected to the Senate, *3695*
First Lady to run for public office, *4239*
Genome sequencing of a plant, *6696*
Movie on videocassette to be released worldwide in one week, *1189*
Multiracial census category, *6159*
Patent registered in the 21st century, *4001*
Person to be counted in the 2000 census, *6160*
Presidential election in which all candidates operated sites on the Internet, *3835*
Ray gun to shoot down an armed missile, *5894*
Senate candidate elected posthumously, *3696*
State to enact a moratorium on executions, *7025*

State to establish civil unions for gay couples, *7463*
State with $1 trillion in personal income, *4370*
Summit conference of world religions, *6333*
Terrorist attack on the U.S. Navy, *5832*
Trademark registered in the 21st century, *3984*
Year in which people of Hispanic descent became the largest minority group, *6109*

2001

American theater company to perform Shakespeare at Stratford, *1468*
Bioterror attacks by mail, *5833*
Building with a combined heat and power energy system, *3320*
Cloned pet, *2607*
Endangered species to be cloned, *5970*
Execution to be televised, *7026*
Federal execution by lethal injection, *7027*
Governor of Puerto Rico who was a woman, *3790*
HDTV all-digital newsroom, *4981*
Popular vote on a national emblem, *3507*
Presidential inauguration broadcast on live high-definition TV, *4291*
Sea otter, *5969*
Secretary of state who was African-American, *4213*
Self-balancing personal vehicle, *8216*
Self-contained artificial heart, *5384*
Senator to change political control of the Senate by switching parties, *3697*
Space tourist, *6839*
Spacecraft to land on an asteroid, *6886*
Stamp honoring a Muslim holiday, *4759*
State ban on the use of cell phones by drivers, *8215*
State consumer protection agency to combat identity theft, *7307*
State office of homeland security, *7306*
Transatlantic telesurgery, *5385*
Unplanned nationwide shutdown of air traffic, *8171*
Year in which the majority of states were represented by at least one congresswoman, *3638*

2002

American mayor to be knighted, *3945*
Astronaut to fly in space who was Native American, *6840*
Ball game to be declared a national special security event, *7719*
Businessman convicted for importing unsafe toys, *7290*
City with a fleet of personal mobility machines, *3545*
Color-coded federal warning system, *5834*
Company penalized for failing to report a hazardous product, *7291*
Image of Mars at night, *6419*
Islamic terrorist who was born in America, *5835*
Movie to gross $100 million in its opening weekend, *1190*
Municipal downsizing plan, *3546*
Municipal recycling of diapers and incontinence products, *5934*
Museum of children's book illustrations, *3167*
Museum of espionage, *3166*
Oscar for best actress awarded to an African-American, *1176*
Physician convicted of manslaughter for prescribing pain medication, *6982*
Political party leader in Congress who was a woman, *3639*
Powder capable of stopping a lethal hemorrhage, *5190*
Powwow at the National Mall, *1057*
Prepaid disposable cell phone, *4922*
President to visit Cuba, *4322*
Shipment of oil directly from Russia to the United States, *6616*
Solo balloon flight around the world, *8172*
State to allow electric mobility devices on sidewalks, *7050*
State to require child booster seats, *8283*
Transmission of touch signals over a long distance, *6530*
Urban business district with complete video surveillance, *7396*

2003

American civil administrator of a Middle Eastern country, *3916*
Astronaut lost in a U.S. space mission who was not an American, *6841*
Astronauts to make a ground landing in a capsule, *6842*
Bandage capable of stopping a lethal hemorrhage, *5191*
Bionic artificial arm operated by thought control, *5276*
Book to sell 5 million copies in a single day, *1111*
City law restricting police inquiries into immigrant activites protected by the First Amendment, *7397*
City to import prescription drugs, *7292*
City to use desalinated seawater as a source of drinking water, *7421*

2003—*continued*

Congressional representatives who were sisters, *3640*
Conviction by an American jury for crimes against humanity, *6983*
Demonstration of wireless remote vehicle control as an antiterrorism tactic, *7309*
Department of Homeland Security, *4214*
Federal agency overseeing all border control, *3870*
Felony conviction for cruelty against farm animals, *1657*
Ground battle in the Iraq War, *5836*
Heart attack treatment using the patient's own stem cells, *5062*
Ice hotel, *1845*
Image of Earth as seen from Mars, *6420*
Lightweight bulletproof body armor, *5895*
Major league baseball player to hit grand slams from both sides of the plate in one game, *7550*
Manned spacecraft to explode over the U.S. mainland, *6887*
Outbreak of mad cow disease, *7293*
School district to install surveillance cameras in all its classrooms, *2988*
Secretary of homeland security, *4214*
State ban on the sale of violent video games to children, *7308*
State to elect two female governors in a row, *4384*
State to legalize gay marriage, *7464*
Transgenic animal sold as a pet, *2608*
Year in which the heads of both major political parties were graduates of the same college, *4112*
Year in which two different coins showed portraits of the same president, *4050*

2004

American orchestra to play for a Pope at the Vatican, *1284*
City with complete WiFi coverage, *7422*
Civilian pilot to fly a craft into space, *6888*
Comprehensive digital archive of state documents, *4371*
County ban on genetically modified farming, *1658*
Court ruling requiring emergency evacuation plans for people with disabilities, *7051*
Dietary supplement to be banned by the FDA, *7294*
Genome sequencing and analysis of a bird, *6698*
Hybrid sport utility vehicle, *8284*
Hydrogen refueling station, *2104*
Marriage between two people of the same sex, *7464*
Photograph of a planet in another solar system, *6421*
Presidential election observed by international monitors, *3837*
Privately funded spacecraft to fly in space, *6888*
Rediscovery of a bird thought to be extinct, *5971*
Robot Olympics, *6531*
School district to require mention of intelligent design in science classes, *2989*
Senate election in which both candidates were African-American, *3698*
State public health program to provide prescription drugs from Canada and Europe, *7295*
State to approve funding for biomedical research using stem cells derived from human embryos, *6697*
State to offer free cancer treatment for uninsured residents, *5402*
State to require labeling of genetically modified seeds, *1659*
State to require paper receipts for electronic voting machines, *3791*
State to require proof of citizenship for voters, *3792*
State whose businesses were required to offer paid family leave, *2170*
Thought control of mechanical devices, *5277*
Vote cast from space in a presidential election, *3836*
Walk from Canada to Mexico along the West Coast, *7988*
Zoo hospital with a CT scanner, *5409*

2005

American orchestra to make all its recordings downloadable from the Internet, *1285*
American to climb all 14 mountains higher than 8,000 meters, *7989*
Antiterrorism security standards enacted by a state to protect its chemical plants, *7310*
Chef at the White House who was a woman, *4335*
Child removed from life support by court order despite a parent's wishes, *2313*
Chimpanzee fossils, *6702*
Church with a weekly attendance exceeding 30,000, *6334*
City to require "green" construction for low-income housing, *5935*
City with a complete smart-card system, *7423*
City with a free public WiFi system, *7426*

City with a mobile mesh WiFi network for both public and municipal use, *7425*
Coin showing a president in frontal view, *4051*
Comprehensive comparison of the human and chimpanzee genomes, *6701*
Comprehensive database of federal research projects, *3871*
Discovery of a meteorite on another planet, *6395*
Experiment that showed separate brain sites involved in processing nouns and verbs, *6699*
Foreign flag flown at the State Department, *3917*
Fuel cell truck, *8297*
In-flight repair of a space shuttle exterior, *6891*
Law against human smuggling enacted by a state, *6984*
Live concert for astronauts, *1286*
Major city to legalize possession of marijuana, *7093*
Major network news program broadcast in high-definition television, *4550*
Medal of Honor awarded to a soldier in the Iraq war, *5539*
Monument to mothers of fallen soldiers, *7192*
Municipal wireless network paid for by advertisements, *7427*
Muslim prayer service led by a woman acting as Imam, *6336*
Natural disaster to cause the evacuation of an entire city, *5936*
Neanderthal skeleton reconstructed from actual bones, *6700*
Podcast from space, *6843*
President to attend the funeral of a pope, *3946*
Public blood bank for collecting umbilical cord and placental blood for stem cell research, *5063*
Radio station with all-podcast programming, *4816*
Secretary of state who was an African-American woman, *4213*
Silver Star awarded to a woman for actions in combat, *5540*
Solar sail aircraft, *6890*
Solo nonstop nonrefueled powered flight around the world, *8173*
Spacecraft to land on the moon of another planet, *6889*
Sports league to cancel a season over a labor dispute, *7837*
State law banning gifts of free formula to new mothers, *2171*
State legislator expelled for campaign financing violations, *4397*
State to disburse funding for biomedical research using stem cells derived from human embryos, *6703*
State to offer simultaneous access to multiple government databases, *7424*
State to provide financial assistance to college students who are parents, *2880*
TV drama about an actual war in progress, *4985*
UNICEF Halloween collection that raised funds for American children, *2522*
Winner of the Grand Challenge robotic vehicle race, *6532*
Year in which hurricane forecasters ran out of names, *6514*
Year in which Protestants were no longer a majority of the United States population, *6335*

2006

American woman honored by Yad Vashem, *6920*
Animal rights group convicted of terrorism, *6985*
Campaign to promote citywide testing for the AIDS virus, *7296*
Capture of comet particles, *6396*
City to provide free citywide WiFi, *7428*
County to require its public agencies to purchase locally grown organic food, *1660*
Death penalty moratorium imposed by a state legislature, *7028*
Detection of water ice on the surface of a comet, *6397*
Digital-photography highway patrol, *8217*
Domestic violence protection law that included pets, *2609*
FBI raid on the office of a congressional representative, *3641*
Major sports facility named for a woman, *7935*
Medals of Honor issued by a state to honor service members killed in Iraq and Afghanistan, *5541*
Movie sold simultaneously as a downloadable product and a DVD, *1191*
Online high school for gifted students, *2991*
Permanent protective vault for crops and seeds, *1661*
Private space station prototype, *6892*
Proof that a human brain can restore impaired functions by growing new networks of nerve fibers, *6704*
Regeneration of spinal cord connections in animals, *6705*
Rocket built by college students to be launched from Cape Canaveral, *6801*

2006—*continued*

Sportscaster who was a woman to be inducted into the Pro Football Hall of Fame, *7720*
State ban on mercury in children's vaccines, *5162*
State law requiring cats to be neutered, *2610*
State with an online learning requirement, *2990*
Supreme Court with a majority of Catholic justices, *3754*
Wireless microchip receiver-transmitter for making digital information part of a non-digital object, *6533*
Year in which the value of a penny was less than its cost of manufacture, *4052*

2007

State to mandate universal health insurance, *1987*

INDEX BY DAYS

The following is a chronological listing of entries, arranged by month and day. To find an entry in the main body of text, please go to the italicized number.

January 1—*continued*

1898 Mayor of metropolitan New York City, *3509*
1901 Building with an all-marble dome, *3290*
1902 Tournament of Roses intercollegiate football game, *7695*
1909 Milk pasteurization law enacted by a city, *7274*
1910 Chocolate sandwich cookie with creme filling, *2411*
1914 Hydroplane service, *8038*
1924 Ink paste, *2026*
1928 Air-conditioned office building, *3298*
1935 Fax transmission by a press syndicate direct to newspaper offices, *4533*
1936 Newspaper to microfilm its current issues, *3035*
1937 Retirement colony, *3537*
1939 Flea laboratory, *6667*
1948 Newsreel in color, *4540*
1951 Pay television system, *4950*
1953 Railroad cars with a superdome observation deck, *8360*
1954 Mobile color television transmitter unit, *4991*
Refugee to arrive under the Refugee Relief Act of 1953, *6097*
Prison commissioner who was a woman, *7019*
1961 Championship game of the American Football League, *7713*
1962 Navy SEAL units, *5590*
State to repeal its ban on acts of sodomy, *7445*
1977 Episcopal priest who was a woman, *6327*
1991 State with electronic toll collection, *3434*
Antistalking law enacted by a state, *6968*
Statewide registration of assault weapons, *6969*
1995 Commercial domestic air service to ban smoking on all flights, *7088*
2004 State whose businesses were required to offer paid family leave, *2170*
2006 State ban on mercury in children's vaccines, *5162*

January 2

1777 Army chaplain killed in action, *5665*
1795 Cabinet member to serve in two or more cabinet posts, *4173*
1811 Senator to be censured, *3656*
1828 Washington news correspondent, *4590*
1842 Wire suspension bridge for general traffic, *3239*
1854 State governor to be removed from office by a state supreme court, *4375*
1893 Commemorative postage stamps, *4727*
Postage stamps depicting a woman, *4728*
1906 Air conditioner patent, *1871*
1914 Community trust charity, *7225*
1919 Navy destroyer named for a Confederate officer, *8483*
1920 Red scare, *4092*
1921 Religious service broadcast on radio, *6295*
1934 Liquor stores run by a state government, *2098*
1936 Electron tube, *6515*
1970 President of a major university who was African-American, *2871*
2001 Governor of Puerto Rico who was a woman, *3790*

January 3

1831 Building and loan association, *1721*
1872 Patent list, *1488*
1876 Free kindergarten, *2950*
1890 Dairy school at a college, *2808*
1905 Greek daily newspaper, *4566*
1921 Weather forecast broadcast on radio, *6496*
1933 State speaker of the House who was a woman, *4392*
1939 Congressional page who was female, *3616*
1940 Congress in session a full year, *3577*
1943 African-American congressional representative from the Democratic Party, *3606*
1945 School completely irradiated with germicidal lamps, *7281*
1947 Congressional opening session to be televised, *3578*
Cancer prevention clinic for children, *5073*
1953 Three brothers from one family to serve in the Senate, *3682*
1957 Electric watch, *2634*
1959 State admitted to the Union that had no border with another state, *4360*
1961 Deaths in an American nuclear reactor, *6626*

1965 Congressional representative who was a woman of Asian descent, *3621*
1976 Congressional representatives to marry each other, *3630*
1977 Judge who had served time in prison, *3729*
2001 Sea otter, *5969*
2003 Congressional representatives who were sisters, *3640*
Congressional representatives who were sisters, *3640*
State to elect two female governors in a row, *4384*

January 4

1739 Newspaper editor who was a woman, *4589*
1869 School for blind African-American students, *2946*
1885 Appendectomy, *5344*
1896 Actors' union, *7139*
1915 State governor who was Jewish, *4380*
1939 Dean of a university graduate school who was a woman, *2855*
1953 Carpeting of tufted plastic, *2586*
1962 Subway train to run automatically without conductors or motormen, *8380*
1965 Naval ship with a crew of mixed nationalities, *8495*
1996 Manufactured food product to carry a health claim on its label, *7288*
1999 State in which all of the top elected offices were held by women, *4369*
2000 Trademark registered in the 21st century, *3984*
Patent registered in the 21st century, *4001*

January 5

1643 Divorce, *2591*
1885 Piggyback railroad operation, *8320*
1887 Library school at a college, *2805*
1904 Real estate board game, *7730*
1933 Bridge with piers sunk in the open sea, *3253*
1944 Transoceanic newspaper, *4539*
1980 Debate among party hopefuls for the presidential nomination to be shown on television, *3831*
1987 Year in which the federal budget exceeded $1 trillion, *3862*

January 6

1639 Crop surplus destruction ordered by a government, *1563*
1885 State legislator who was African-American to represent a constituency with a white majority, *4388*
1968 Heart transplant to an adult, *5368*
1973 Electoral vote for a woman, *3829*
1987 Woman legislator from the Democratic Party to serve in both houses of Congress, *3680*
2003 Year in which two different coins showed portraits of the same president, *4050*

January 7

1751 Benefit performance of a play, *1419*
1784 Seed business, *1581*
1824 Boxing arena, *7592*
1830 Railroad for commercial transportation of passengers and freight, *8302*
1862 Folding stepladder, *2560*
1869 Bookseller's guide, *4456*
1904 Radio distress signal officially established, *7349*
1906 Hindu temple, *6289*
1908 Health department of a county organized on a full-time basis, *7272*
1913 Gasoline obtained from crude petroleum by the cracking process, *6602*
1927 Transatlantic commercial telephone service, *4888*
1949 Photograph of genes, *5137*
1954 Television receiver that showed two programs simultaneously, *4998*
1955 Metropolitan Opera singer who was African-American, *1329*

January 8

1675 Commercial corporation, *1470*
1833 School for music teachers, *3196*
1838 Telegraphic system in which dots and dashes represented letters, *4843*
1853 Bronze equestrian statue, *7171*
1856 Borax, *3385*
1867 Election law granting African-American men the right to vote, *3771*
1884 Chrome tanning process, *2135*
1889 Electric tabulating machine, *1677*
1901 Bowling tournament sponsored by the American Bowling Congress, *7583*
1918 State to ratify the Prohibition Amendment to the Constitution, *7074*
1925 State supreme court in which all the judges were women, *3718*
1935 Spectrophotometer, *6731*
1962 Exhibition of the *Mona Lisa*, *1042*

January 8—*continued*

1965 State supreme court chief justice who was a woman, *3728*
2001 Endangered species to be cloned, *5970*

January 9

1793 Untethered balloon flight, *7994*
1861 Act inaugurating the Civil War, *5690*
1894 Movie to be copyrighted, *1115*
1935 Blood testing laws enacted by a state, *7278*

January 10

1910 Aviation meet, *7677*
1911 Photograph taken from an airplane, *4628*
1943 President to visit a foreign country in wartime, *4318*
1946 Radar signal to the moon, *6790*
1949 Airmail postal card, *4708*
1951 Jet airplane passenger trip, *8128*
1967 Educational television network operated as a nonprofit corporation, *4974*
1994 Payment by the United States to a foreign nation for destroying nuclear weapons, *3913*
2006 County to require its public agencies to purchase locally grown organic food, *1660*

January 11

1759 Life insurance company, *1988*
1770 Rhubarb, *1579*
1794 Federal law officer killed in the line of duty, *7357*
1875 Nautical school established by a city, *3198*
1913 Sedan car, *8250*
1917 State legislature to use an electric vote recorder, *4391*
1935 Transpacific solo airplane flight by a woman, *8094*
1938 Bank president of a national bank who was a woman, *1747*
1949 Mosque of importance, *6313*
1964 Major government report on tobacco smoking, *7084*

January 12

1773 Public museum, *3133*
1792 Minister plenipotentiary to Great Britain, *3881*
1825 Execution of a white criminal for the murder of a Native American, *6997*
1853 University on the Pacific Coast, *2753*
1876 State forestry association, *5976*
1896 X-ray photograph, *5131*
1910 Pilot from the United States to establish an airplane altitude record, *8015*
1929 Airmail letter sheet, *4700*
Seatrain, *8451*
1932 Woman elected to the Senate, *3673*
1937 Submarine cable plow, *4862*
1944 Victory ship launched, *8457*
1953 Catholic cardinal whose see was west of the Rockies, *6317*
2006 Death penalty moratorium imposed by a state legislature, *7028*

January 13

1794 Changes in the American flag to be authorized by Congress, *3491*
1906 Radio receiver advertised, *4819*
1928 Television sets to be installed in homes on an experimental basis, *4928*
1929 Humanist association, *7228*
1957 Flying disk for use in throwing games, *7979*
1976 Metropolitan Opera orchestra conductor who was a woman, *1331*
Voice reader, *6456*
1984 Nicotine replacement product approved by the FDA, *7087*
1996 Medals of Honor awarded to African-American servicemen for service in World War II, *5538*
2003 Felony conviction for cruelty against farm animals, *1657*

January 14

1639 Constitution to declare that "the foundation of authority is in the free consent of the people", *3455*
1794 Cesarean operation, *5338*
1799 Senator to be expelled, *3654*
1813 State superintendent of schools, *2906*
1938 Right-to-die society, *2305*
2005 Spacecraft to land on the moon of another planet, *6889*

January 15

1825 Tax enacted by a state to support public schools, *2917*
1840 Line drawing to illustrate a newspaper article, *4577*
1852 Hospital under Jewish auspices, *5106*

January 20—*continued*

1952 Bullfighter who was a woman to fight professionally, *7615*
1954 Radio network for African-Americans, *4814*
1961 President who was Catholic, *4265*
1969 Transatlantic solo trip by rowboat, *8545*
1975 College commencement exercises in a prison, *2875*
1977 President to take the oath of office using a nickname, *4161*
1986 Martin Luther King Day, *2520*
1993 Pre-inaugural service at an African-American church, *4162*
1997 Presidential inauguration broadcast live over the Internet, *4289*
1999 Internet march on Washington, *3868*
2000 Person to be counted in the 2000 census, *6160*
2001 Secretary of state who was African-American, *4213*
Presidential inauguration broadcast on live high-definition TV, *4291*

January 21

1677 Medical pamphlet, *5278*
1789 Novel by an American writer to be published in America, *1077*
1853 Envelope folding machine, *2015*
1880 Sewage-disposal system separate from the city water system, *7409*
1918 Air combat unit of the Marine Corps, *5473*
1941 Magnesium commercially produced from seawater, *3397*
1954 Gas-turbine car, *8267*
1961 Cabinet member who was related to the president, *4195*
1970 Jumbo jet, *8153*

January 22

1895 National manufacturing assocation, *1494*
1947 Commercial television station west of the Mississippi River, *4941*
1988 Anti-aging skin cream, *2482*
2006 Digital-photography highway patrol, *8217*

January 23

1780 Town named for George Washington to be incorporated, *3514*
1789 College founded as a Catholic institution, *2719*
1793 Emergency first aid organization, *7339*
1849 Physician who was a woman, *5024*
1907 Senator who was Native American, *3669*
1946 Medal of Honor awarded to a chaplain, *5529*
1964 Transplant of an animal organ into a human being, *5367*
1968 Naval ship to be captured intact, *8498*
1973 Vote in the House of Representatives to be recorded electronically, *3627*
1997 Secretary of state who was a woman, *4212*

January 24

1656 Physician who was Jewish, *5011*
1722 Divinity professor at a college, *2693*
1791 Presidential proclamation, *4118*
1887 Shot tower, *5859*
1899 Rubber shoe heel, *2258*
1922 Ice cream bar, *2419*
1925 Movie of a solar eclipse taken from an airship, *6403*
1935 Beer in cans, *2436*
1949 Federal marshal who was a woman, *7385*
1972 Noise-control law enacted by a state, *5929*
1974 Native American superintendent of a Bureau of Indian Affairs agency, *3843*
1996 Auction of radio spectrum for satellite services, *4805*
2003 Secretary of homeland security, *4214*
Department of Homeland Security, *4214*

January 25

1915 Transcontinental telephone demonstration, *4878*
1929 Vice president's widow to receive a pension, *4308*
1945 Water supply to be fluoridated, *7417*
1949 Emmy awards for excellence in television, *4946*
1951 Presidential press conference recorded on tape, *4284*
1952 Automatic headlight control, *8212*
1959 Transcontinental jet airplane passenger service, *8145*
1961 Presidential physican who was a woman, *4266*
Presidential news conference to be televised live, *4286*

January 31—*continued*

2000 State to enact a moratorium on executions, *7025*
2006 Supreme Court with a majority of Catholic justices, *3754*

February

1653 Colonial provision for the care of orphans and widows, *2172*
1799 Tax rebellion, *4407*
1800 Endowment for social service purposes, *7199*
1824 Supreme Court decision in a commerce case, *3745*
1835 Homeopathy journal, *5309*
1839 State law allowing married women to own property, *7433*
1853 Trade association, *1484*
1895 Cereal sold as a breakfast food, *2397*
1898 Monthly cumulative index of books, *4461*
Physiology journal, *5333*
1910 Air rights lease, *3296*
1915 Car finance company, *1760*
1917 Jazz record, *1256*
1921 Civil rights chair at a college, *2838*
1924 Round-the-world steamboat passenger service, *8448*
1932 Wooden money, *4042*
1933 State governor to be granted almost dictatorial power, *4382*
Polio vaccine, *5157*
1934 Commercial production of hydroponic plants, *1651*
1938 Cartooning school, *3215*
1943 Fire department composed entirely of women, *7334*
1944 Silver Star awarded to a woman, *5525*
1946 Nontwisted sewing thread, *2623*
1950 Nazi collaborator to be deported, *6094*
1954 Photoengraving high-speed process, *2060*
1964 Toy action figure, *2200*
1968 Army general who was African-American to lead an infantry brigade in combat, *5452*
1972 Large-scale presidential media event, *4287*
1978 Computer bulletin board, *6458*
1987 Superconducting material that operated at relatively high temperatures, *6751*
1990 Charles Stark Draper Prize for engineering and technology, *6916*
1994 Genetically engineered product to appear in food, *2455*
1996 American honored by Yad Vashem, *6919*
Boxer who was a woman to earn international recognition, *7612*
1997 Movie to earn more than $400 million in the United States market, *1183*
Telephone directory with internet addresses, *4921*
1999 City to derive all its energy needs from renewable sources, *6638*

February 1

1788 Steamboat patent, *8410*
1790 Supreme Court of the United States, *3732*
1791 Dental dispensary, *5080*
1831 Music book for children, *1232*
1860 Rabbi to open the House of Representatives with prayer, *3602*
1865 Lawyer admitted to practice before the Supreme Court who was African-American, *3966*
1871 Speech delivered before the House of Representatives by an African-American representative, *3607*
1885 Tuberculosis sanatorium using modern treatment methods, *5126*
1893 Movie studio, *1113*
1898 Car insurance policy, *1965*
1907 Horse farm operated by the federal government, *1635*
1911 Fingerprint conviction in a crime, *6938*
1920 Armored car that was completely protected, *8251*
1930 Passenger ship with a diesel engine, *8452*
1936 Medical insurance group policy for college students, *1983*
1937 Free port, *2079*
1949 Court-martial at which the judges included enlisted men, *5551*
Telescope lens 200 inches in diameter, *6377*
1951 Atomic bomb explosion to be shown on television, *5875*
1960 Civil rights sit-in, *6142*
1966 Navy captain who was African-American, *5612*
1968 West Point instructor who was a woman, *3124*
1973 Prison guard who was a woman to serve in a maximum security prison for men, *7020*

1978 Postage stamp depicting an African-American woman, *4756*
1997 Mandatory AIDS testing for newborns enacted by a state, *7289*
2003 Astronaut lost in a U.S. space mission who was not an American, *6841*
Manned spacecraft to explode over the U.S. mainland, *6887*

February 2

1802 Leopard to be exhibited, *1359*
1848 War fought mostly on foreign soil, *5689*
1870 State supreme court justice who was African-American, *3708*
1880 Electric streetlight installed in a city, *7410*
1892 Bottle cap with a cork crown, *1999*
1901 Army dental corps, *5203*
Army nurse corps for women, *5204*
1912 Stuntman, *1393*
1923 Ethyl gasoline to be marketed, *6604*
1935 Lie detector, *6946*
1940 Dictionary compiled by a woman, *2264*
2006 Detection of water ice on the surface of a comet, *6397*

February 3

1690 Paper money, *4003*
1790 Supreme Court clerk, *3733*
1803 Supreme Court decision voiding an act of Congress, *3740*
1836 Whig Party convention, *4059*
1862 Newspaper printed on a train, *4510*
1894 Steel sailing vessel, *8440*
1947 African-American news correspondent admitted to the congressional press gallery, *4599*
1995 Astronaut who was a woman to pilot the space shuttle, *6834*
1996 Serviceman killed in the peacekeeping mission in Bosnia, *5829*
1999 Sex discrimination case to establish the rights of fathers of newborn babies, *2207*
2002 Ball game to be declared a national special security event, *7719*

February 4

1789 President to receive the unanimous vote of the presidential electors, *3794*
1801 Supreme Court chief justice to serve in a presidential cabinet, *3739*
1847 Telegraph company, *4850*
1861 Confederate congressional session, *5691*
1887 Interstate commerce act enacted by Congress, *2075*
1895 Rolling lift bridge, *3248*
1913 Demountable tire-carrying rim, *8202*
1930 Mosaic pavement, *3425*
1932 Olympic Games competition to be held in the winter, *7858*
1936 Radioactive substance produced synthetically, *6745*
1943 Submarine with a pressure hull of high-tensile steel, *8519*
1962 Children's hospital for research and treatment of catastrophic childhood diseases, *5123*

February 5

1644 Branding law, *1565*
1777 Laws of entail and primogeniture to be abolished by a state, *3952*
1778 State to ratify the Articles of Confederation, *3476*
1790 Lawyers admitted to practice before the Supreme Court, *3955*
1825 Magazine for mechanics, *6775*
1826 First Lady to have an occupation, *4221*
1846 Newspaper published on the Pacific Coast, *4506*
1850 Adding machine to employ depressible keys, *1665*
1861 Photographic attempt to show motion, *1204*
Peep show machine, *1372*
1863 News reporter tried as a spy, *4595*
1870 Animated photograph projection before a theater audience, *1193*
1903 Semitic museum, *3147*
1918 Army pilot to win a victory over an enemy airplane, *5474*
1924 President buried in Washington, *4259*
1931 Glider license awarded to a woman, *8082*
1948 Figure skating champion from the United States to compete in the Olympic Games, *7843*

February 6

1778 Alliance between the United States and another country, *3874*
Treaties entered into by the federal government, *3875*
1802 Baked Alaska, *2334*

February 6—*continued*

Macaroni and cheese casserole, *2335*
1815 Railroad charter granted by a state, *8300*
1902 Young Women's Hebrew Association, *7222*
1932 Dogsled race on an Olympic demonstration program, *7663*
1956 Circular school building, *2977*

February 7

1818 Education magazine, *2910*
1821 American to set foot on Antarctica, *6641*
1964 Performance by a British rock group, *1275*
1984 Astronauts to fly free in space, *6827*
1989 American mercenaries convicted of planning a terrorist attack within the United States on behalf of a foreign government, *6966*

February 8

1693 College charter granted by the Crown, *2691*
1837 Vice president elected by the Senate, *4305*
1865 Army major who was African-American, *5441*
1881 Halftone printing plate, *2049*
1889 Steam tractor, *1631*
1898 Envelope folding and gumming machine, *2024*
1915 Movie blockbuster, *1141*
1922 President to use a radio, *4276*
1924 Coast-to-coast radio hookup, *4789*
Execution by lethal gas, *7013*
1944 African-American news correspondent accredited to the White House, *4599*
1996 Censorship of the Internet, *6481*

February 9

1889 Department of Agriculture, *4180*
1893 Theater operated by a city, *1448*
1895 Intercollegiate basketball game, *7554*
1909 Narcotics ban enacted by Congress, *7071*
1918 Army school for chaplains, *3115*
1932 American Olympic champions in two-man bobsled competition, *7975*

February 10

1807 Coast survey, *6059*
1830 Interstate railroad, *8303*
1932 International ski meet, *7891*
1942 Medal of Honor awarded in World War II, *5518*
1962 American runner to run a mile in less than four minutes on an indoor track, *7955*
1976 Radiation attacks against an American embassy, *3908*
1989 Chairman of a major political party who was African-American, *4110*
1996 Chess computer to beat the world chess champion, *7745*
1999 Robot to grade essays on a standardized test, *6529*

February 11

1752 Hospital, *5097*
1801 President elected by the House of Representatives, *4123*
1811 Senate filibuster, *3657*
1836 College for women, *2741*
1837 Physiology society, *5215*
1875 College program of study abroad, *2788*
1878 Bicycle club, *7643*
1889 Six-day bicycle race, *7647*
1945 Gas-turbine propeller-driven airplane, *8111*
1952 Yiddish professorship at a college, *2863*
1958 Airline flight attendant who was an African-American woman, *8076*
1972 Snowmobile to exceed a speed of 125 miles per hour, *7984*
1994 Cosmonaut on an American space mission, *6833*
2004 Rediscovery of a bird thought to be extinct, *5971*
Dietary supplement to be banned by the FDA, *7294*

February 12

1738 Puppet show, *1416*
1793 Fugitive slave law enacted by Congress, *6123*
1795 Gold bullion deposit for coinage, *4020*
1809 President born beyond the boundaries of the original 13 states, *4246*
1838 Killing of one congressional representative by another, *3599*
1865 African-American preacher to deliver a sermon in the House of Representatives, *3604*
1866 Commemoration of the birthday of Abraham Lincoln, *2496*
1873 Trade dollars, *4034*

February 13

February 14

February 15

February 16

February 16—*continued*

1948 Newsreel telecast presented daily, *4541*
1960 Circumnavigation of the earth by a submerged submarine, *8542*
1968 Emergency 911 phone system, *7302*
2005 Sports league to cancel a season over a labor dispute, *7837*

February 17

1761 Milestones between cities, *3512*
1817 Gas streetlights throughout a city, *7403*
1864 Confederate vessel sunk by an underwater torpedo mine, *5717*
Submarine to sink a warship, *5719*
1870 Justice of the peace who was a woman, *3709*
1897 National parent-teacher association, *2957*
1905 Statue of a woman installed in the Capitol's National Statuary Hall, *7181*
1913 Modern art exhibition, *1039*
1925 Congressional representative who was a Jewish woman, *3615*
1927 Diplomat to represent the United States in Canada, *3897*
1934 Driving course in a high school, *2972*
1971 Veterinary hospital established by a city, *5408*
1972 President to visit a nation not recognized by the federal government, *4320*
2003 Heart attack treatment using the patient's own stem cells, *5062*

February 18

1688 Protest against slavery, *6116*
1735 Opera performed in America, *1313*
1804 Land grant university, *2726*
1834 Labor newspaper, *4504*
1856 Play in which a horse race was run on stage, *1437*
Know-Nothing (American) Party convention, *4064*
1908 Postage stamps in coils, *4732*
1930 Cow flown in an airplane, *1401*
Planet found beyond Neptune, *6388*
1953 Three-dimensional feature movie, *1169*
1960 Artificial ice skating rink of Olympic size, *7845*
1978 Iron Man triathlon, *7987*

February 19

1807 Former vice president to be arrested, *4301*
1831 Locomotive to burn coal, *8333*
1836 Navy officer to become an engineer, *5598*
1856 Tintype camera, *4640*
1864 Knights of Pythias meeting, *7208*
1878 Phonograph, *4827*
1953 Book censorship board established by a state, *1104*
2002 Physician convicted of manslaughter for prescribing pain medication, *6982*

February 20

1725 Mass scalping of Native Americans by colonists, *5639*
1768 Fire insurance company to receive a charter, *1976*
1792 Postal service law enacted by Congress, *4660*
1809 Supreme Court decision establishing the power of the federal government, *3742*
1851 Fifty-dollar gold pieces, *4024*
1865 Architecture department at a college, *2766*
1910 Matador of American birth, *7614*
1937 Car-airplane combination, *8255*
1952 Umpire in organized baseball who was African-American, *7540*
1962 Postage stamp issued on the date of the event it commemorated, *4743*
Astronaut to orbit the earth, *6804*
1963 Television receiver and transmitter operated by laser beam, *5005*

February 21

1828 Native American newspaper, *4556*
1846 Telegrapher who was a woman, *4849*
1858 Burglar alarm, *3276*
1862 Execution for slave trading carried out by the federal government, *7002*
1866 Dentist who was a woman to obtain a D.D.S. degree, *5085*
1878 Telephone directory, *4869*
1887 Bacteriology laboratory, *5165*
1921 Transcontinental airplane flight made within 24 hours, *8047*
1932 Camera exposure meter, *4649*
1947 Instant camera, *4651*

February 22

1656 Jewish cemetery, *2294*

1770 Child to be killed in the Revolution, *5643*
1784 Trading ship sent to China, *8525*
1825 Treaty rejected by the Senate, *3888*
1854 Republican Party meeting, *4063*
1872 Presidential candidate nominated by prohibition advocates, *4067*
Labor Reform Party national convention, *4068*
1876 Research university, *2792*
1879 Five-cent store, *2089*
1889 States admitted to the Union simultaneously, *4352*
1898 Arabic newspaper, *4568*
1920 Dog racetrack to use an imitation rabbit, *7661*
1921 Transcontinental airmail flight, *4695*
1923 Chinchilla farm, *1641*
1924 President to make a radio broadcast from the White House, *4279*
1953 Japanese person to receive an immigration visa after World War II, *6096*
1966 Motorboat ocean race, *7577*
1969 Jockey who was a woman to win on a regular parimutuel flat track, *7816*
1990 Fat substitute in prepared foods, *2453*

February 23

1784 American woman to become a countess, *3921*
1821 Pharmacy college, *3050*
1839 Express delivery service, *2071*
1883 Antitrust law enacted by a state, *1491*
National animal rights organization, *7221*
1886 Aluminum pots, *2282*
1892 Student government at a college, *2810*
1905 Rotary Club meeting, *1499*
1910 Radio contest, *4781*
1942 Bombing raid on the continental United States in World War II, *5774*
Naval counterattack by American forces against the Japanese in World War II, *5775*
1954 Mass immunizations for polio, *5159*
1962 African-American athlete who was a woman to win the James E. Sullivan Memorial Trophy, *7480*
1976 Postage stamps of 50 different designs sold as a single sheet, *4755*
1979 Marine general who was African-American, *5571*
1997 Movie shown on a television network without interruption by commercials, *4983*

February 24

1855 Claims court established by the federal government, *3706*
1857 Postage stamp issued with perforations, *4720*
1868 Parade with float tableaux, *1374*
President to be impeached, *4136*
1870 Congressional representative censured for corruption, *3605*
1925 Explosion of Thermit to break up ice jams, *1875*
1949 Rocket to reach outer space, *6792*

February 25

1751 Monkey trained to perform, *1351*
1791 Corporate body chartered by a special act of Congress, *1478*
Bank of the United States, *1716*
1799 Shipbuilding law enacted by Congress, *5580*
Quarantine law enacted by Congress, *7237*
1804 Congressional caucus to meet openly, *3593*
Presidential candidate nominated at a caucus, *3797*
1836 Revolver pistol, *5845*
1859 Temporary insanity defense in a criminal case, *6933*
1863 National bank, *1723*
1901 Corporation with a capitalization of $1 billion, *1497*
1919 Gasoline tax levied by a state, *4421*
1928 Television station, *4929*
1930 Check photographing device, *1742*
1940 Hockey game to be shown on television, *7831*
1952 Copyright registered for a choreographic score, *1055*

February 26

1811 Naval hospital established by Congress, *5194*
1866 Health board with emergency powers established by a city, *7247*
1870 Subway, *8376*
1895 Glass-blowing machine, *3361*
1914 Industrial museum, *3149*
Long-distance telephone call over underground cables, *4877*
1935 Ambulance service with an incubator, *5046*

February 26—*continued*

1938 Passenger ship equipped with radar, *8505*
1940 Air defense military organization, *5478*
1949 Round-the-world nonstop flight by an airplane, *8123*
1953 Photographic type-composing machine, *2059*
1955 Pilot to bail out of an airplane flying at supersonic speed, *8137*
1986 Poet laureate of the United States, *1109*
1993 Bombing of a skyscraper by foreign terrorists, *5826*

February 27

1729 College to have a full faculty, *2694*
1793 Supreme Court nominee who was rejected by the Senate, *3735*
1813 Mail delivery by steamboat, *4662*
Vaccination law enacted by Congress, *5153*
1879 Sugar substitute, *2382*
1883 Cigar-rolling machine, *7068*
1915 American combatant to die in World War I, *5731*
1919 National organization for the hard of hearing, *7035*
1929 Movie by a major company for an African-American audience, *1151*
1947 Surgical operation televised on a closed circuit for physicians, *5352*
1973 Armed occupation by Native American protesters in the modern era, *6102*

February 28

1793 Senate election that was contested, *3652*
1810 Fire insurance joint-stock company, *1977*
1822 Trust company, *1719*
1861 Confederate government bond, *5692*
1866 Ambulance service for hospitals, *5044*
1882 Cooperative store at a college, *2090*
1902 Fistfight in the Senate, *3667*
1940 Basketball game to be shown on television, *7556*
1977 Orca, *5965*
1990 State to authorize incarceration of convicted sex offenders beyond their prison terms, *7303*
State to inform the public about the residences of released sex offenders, *7304*
1997 Tobacco sales to minors to be restricted by federal regulations, *7090*

February 29

1940 Oscar awarded to an African-American performer, *1164*
1980 Tank with a turbine engine, *5890*

March

1540 Baptism in America, *6164*
1624 Cattle to be imported, *1559*
1634 Catholics to settle in the English colonies in America, *6177*
1638 Swedes to arrive in America, *6027*
1639 Printing press, *2029*
Document known to have been printed in America, *3456*
1647 Quarantine law enacted by a colony, *7232*
1753 Arctic expedition to seek the Northwest Passage, *6639*
1776 Identification of human remains using dental evidence, *2296*
Independent government in an American colony, *3450*
1791 Orchestral song to be printed, *1336*
1793 Coins struck by the United States Mint to enter circulation, *4018*
1796 Coast survey book, *5905*
1823 Newspaper for Jewish readers, *4553*
1829 Library for seamen, *3010*
1840 Camera exposure scale, *4638*
1852 Book to sell more than 1 million copies, *1090*
1863 Cheesemaking society, *2357*
Laryngology clinic, *5065*
1865 Zinc sheet mill, *1934*
1874 Lawn tennis, *7917*
1886 Air gun, *5858*
1889 Centralized refrigeration service, *1895*
1893 Grand American Trapshoot tournament using live birds, *7885*
1895 Pneumatic tires, *8185*
1899 Movie western, *1122*
Hungarian newspaper, *4569*
1909 Movie censorship board at the national level, *1129*
1919 Fisheries school at a college, *2835*
1920 Asteroid named for an American president, *6386*

March 1

March 2

March 2—*continued*

1989 International cyberespionage case, *6967*
1997 Cloning of a primate from an embryo, *6688*
1998 Movie to earn $1 billion worldwide, *1184*
2004 County ban on genetically modified farming, *1658*
2006 Animal rights group convicted of terrorism, *6985*

March 3

1791 Internal revenue tax levied by Congress, *4405*
1793 Senator to become a congressional representative, *3651*
1794 Opera of a serious nature, *1316*
1801 State governor of Jewish descent, *4380*
1803 Federal judge to be impeached, *3704*
Grant of federal land to a foreigner, *6057*
1819 Standardization of nomenclature for naval vessels, *5581*
Piracy law enacted by Congress, *6931*
1821 Patent granted to an African-American inventor, *3991*
1842 Child labor law enacted by a state that regulated hours of employment, *7114*
1843 Telegraph appropriation by Congress, *4845*
1845 Law book of federal laws then in force, *3964*
Presidential veto to be overridden by Congress, *4132*
Ocean mail contracts, *4665*
1849 Department of the Interior, *4178*
1863 Gold certificates, *4030*
Notes wholly engraved and printed at the Bureau of Engraving and Printing, *4031*
Draft law enacted by Congress during wartime, *5556*
National science institute, *6718*
1865 Bank for freed African-American slaves, *1724*
1875 Federal law restricting immigration, *6077*
1879 Lawyer who was a woman to be admitted to practice before the Supreme Court, *3970*
1891 Forest planting by the federal government, *5980*
1892 Cattle tuberculosis test, *5405*
1893 Coin bearing the likeness of a foreign monarch, *4038*
1894 Greek newspaper, *4566*
1899 Admiral of the Navy, *5603*
1903 Nurses to be registered by a state, *5037*
State prison to take fingerprints, *7365*
1911 Federal cemetery to contain graves of both Union and Confederate soldiers, *2302*
1913 Air combat unit of the Army, *5469*
1917 Tax levied by Congress on excess profits of corporations, *4420*
1919 International airmail, *4693*
1926 Greyhound racing association, *7662*
1943 Election law lowering the voting age in a state to 18, *3783*
1971 Vote in the House of Representatives to be tallied by machine, *3625*
1973 Iditarod sled dog race, *7664*
2005 Solo nonstop nonrefueled powered flight around the world, *8173*

March 4

1776 Marine engagement in battle, *5656*
1789 Meeting place of Congress, *3553*
Session of Congress, *3554*
Congressional representative appointed to a presidential cabinet, *3581*
Congressional representative who was Catholic, *3582*
Session of the House of Representatives, *3583*
Senate journal, *3643*
Senator who was Catholic, *3644*
Session of the Senate, *3645*
1791 Congressional representative who was Jewish, *3589*
Special session of the Senate, *3650*
State admitted to the Union after the ratification of the Constitution, *4339*
1797 Congressional representative to serve before his 25th birthday, *3591*
President whose son became president, *4242*
1799 Supreme Court chief justice who had been a congressional representative, *3737*
1801 President inaugurated in the city of Washington, *4124*
1809 First Lady to attend her husband's inauguration, *4217*
1813 Vice president who had served in the House of Representatives, *4303*

1825 Former president who was elected to the House of Representatives, *4127*
First Lady who was not born in the United States, *4219*
First Lady who was the mother of a president, *4220*
1829 Spoils system of presidential patronage, *4128*
1831 Congressional chaplain who was Catholic, *3565*
Widower of a veteran of the armed services to receive a pension, *5620*
1838 Jewish Sunday school, *6214*
1840 Commercial photography studio, *4618*
1849 Senator to serve three states, *3659*
Senator who was returned to the Senate after being defeated for the presidency, *3660*
1851 Brothers to serve as representatives in Congress simultaneously, *3600*
1853 Vice president sworn in on foreign soil, *4307*
1861 Battle flag, *3496*
1863 Officer to preside over both of the branches of Congress, *3570*
1873 Illustrated daily newspaper, *4515*
1875 African-American senator to serve a full term, *3666*
Former president to become a senator, *4137*
1880 Halftone engraving, *1037*
1881 President whose mother lived at the White House, *4256*
Quarantine law for plants enacted by a state, *7250*
1891 Congress to appropriate $1 billion, *3572*
Congressional representative elected by prohibitionists, *3610*
International copyright agreement, *3981*
1897 President to appear on film, *4275*
1909 First Lady to attend all her husband's cabinet meetings, *4231*
Bird hunting regulation law enacted by Congress, *7827*
1911 Congressional representative who was a Socialist, *3612*
1913 Department of Commerce, *4183*
Department of Labor, *4184*
Federal law regulating hunting of migratory birds, *7827*
1917 Congressional representative who was a woman, *3613*
1925 Presidential inauguration to be broadcast on radio, *4280*
Transcontinental radio fax transmission of a photograph, *4469*
1927 Congress to enact more than 1,000 laws, *3575*
1928 Transcontinental foot race, *7948*
1929 African-American congressional representative from a northern state, *3606*
Radio broadcast from the Senate chamber, *3678*
Vice president who was Native American, *4309*
1930 Bowler who was a woman to obtain a perfect score, *7587*
1933 Cabinet in which all members were sworn in at the same time and place, *4187*
Cabinet member who was a woman, *4188*
1944 Execution of an organized crime leader in the electric chair, *7017*
1997 Ban on federal funding for human cloning research, *6689*

March 5

1623 Alcohol temperance law enacted by a colony, *7054*
1743 Religious magazine, *6345*
1750 Play by William Shakespeare, *1417*
1770 Engraving to achieve popularity, *1023*
Americans killed by British soldiers in the Revolution, *5644*
1856 Railroad safety law enacted by a state, *8314*
1877 Use of the term "First Lady" to refer to the president's wife, *4228*
1894 Employment office established by a city, *7137*
1913 Secretary of commerce, *4183*
Secretary of labor, *4184*
Dentist in the Navy to serve aboard a naval ship, *5207*
1921 Father and son to occupy the same Cabinet post, *4185*
1923 Pension laws enacted by a state, *7149*
1924 Bowler to roll two perfect games, *7586*
1935 City law requiring reporting of premature births, *2153*
1975 Personal computer users group, *6453*
1977 Radio broadcast in which citizens telephoned the president, *4288*
1999 Cyber university, *2879*

March 6

1775 Mason who was African-American, *7196*
1808 College orchestra, *1227*
1810 Vaccination law enacted by a state, *5152*
1862 Ironclad turreted vessel in the Navy, *8475*
1865 Judge advocate of the Navy, *5600*
1886 Nursing magazine, *5328*
Electric power plant using alternating current, *6551*
1928 Medical center devoted to teaching, treatment, and research, *3091*
1934 First Lady to travel in an airplane to a foreign country, *4234*
1941 Parachute fatality in the Army, *5480*
1961 Affirmative action order issued by the federal government, *3855*
1967 Large-type weekly newspaper, *4544*
1969 Astronauts to transfer from one spacecraft to another while in orbit, *6813*
2000 Ban on the sale of mercury thermometers, *5933*
2006 City to provide free citywide WiFi, *7428*

March 7

1644 Whaling industry established by a city, *1792*
Colonial legislature to establish two chambers, *4386*
1736 Methodist preacher, *6221*
1801 Voting registration law enacted by a state, *3765*
1825 Ambassador to Mexico, *3889*
1854 Sewing machine to stitch buttonholes, *2618*
1865 Coast Guard serviceman who was African-American, *5543*
1876 Telephone patent, *4864*
1893 Print patent, *3999*
1911 Coin-operated locker, *1689*
1955 Broadway play shown in a television version in color with its original cast, *1460*
1958 Submarine expressly designed and built to fire guided missiles, *8522*
1962 Orbiting solar observatory, *6854*
2002 Shipment of oil directly from Russia to the United States, *6616*

March 8

1745 Library building, *3001*
1849 Secretary of the interior, *4178*
1855 Railroad suspension bridge, *3242*
1862 Navy chaplain killed in action, *5711*
1887 Fishing rod of telescoping steel tubes, *2663*
1894 Dog license law enacted by a state, *2603*
1915 Naval vessel equipped to lay mines, *8481*
1946 Helicopter licensed for commercial use, *8115*
1950 Medical officer assigned to a naval vessel who was a woman, *5609*
1959 Neo-Nazi party, *4099*
1965 Ground troops sent to Vietnam, *5814*
1969 Woman jockey to ride two winners in a day, *7816*

March 9

1798 Naval surgeon, *5193*
1799 Government contract authorized by Congress for pistols, *5841*
1842 Gold discovered in California, *3383*
1858 Street letter box, *4668*
1861 Confederate paper money, *4026*
1862 Naval battle between ironclad vessels in the Civil War, *5712*
1889 State law banning trusts and monopolies in business, *1491*
1899 State-sponsored council for the arts, *4356*
1907 Sterilization of humans by a state government as a matter of public policy, *7270*
1926 Mayor of a major city who was a woman, *3534*
1949 Railroad dining car powered by electricity, *8361*
1964 Occupation of federal territory by Native American protesters in the modern era, *6099*
1993 State to guarantee mothers the right to breastfeed in public, *2204*

March 10

1785 Minister plenipotentiary appointed after independence, *3877*
1791 Pile driver, *1847*
1830 Hospital for treatment of the mentally ill established by a state, *5103*
1849 President who had received a patent, *4134*
1862 Bill bearing the likeness of a president, *4028*
1871 Elks grand lodge, *7211*
1876 Telephone conversation, *4864*
1880 Salvation Army services, *6281*

March 15—*continued*

1855 Quarantine board established by a state, *7241*
1867 State university supported by a direct property tax, *2771*
1887 Kindergarten for blind children, *2954*
Game warden to be paid a salary, *5944*
1892 Voting machines, *3774*
1897 Indoor fly casting tournament, *7673*
1909 Transcontinental journey on foot, *7971*
1913 Small claims court, *3714*
1930 Seaplane glider, *8074*
1937 Blood bank, *5055*
Birth control clinic run by a state government, *5070*
1945 Presidential citation to an entire armed forces division, *5527*
1947 Navy commissioned officer who was African-American, *5608*
1948 Parcel post international air service, *4706*
1960 Undersea park established by the federal government, *5995*
1985 Cabinet member indicted while in office, *4209*
Internet domain, *6466*
1988 Catholic archbishop who was African-American, *6279*
1989 Secretary of veterans affairs, *4210*
Department of Veterans Affairs, *4210*
1999 Chess grandmaster who was African-American, *7746*
2005 Child removed from life support by court order despite a parent's wishes, *2313*

March 16

1621 Greeting addressed to the Pilgrims by a Native American, *6018*
1802 Army academy, *3096*
Army engineer corps, *5415*
1810 Supreme Court decision declaring a state law unconstitutional, *3743*
1827 Newspaper for African-American readers, *4554*
1829 High school night classes, *2921*
1877 Occupational therapy treatment, *5391*
1883 Pharmacist who was a woman to receive a degree from a pharmacy college, *3073*
1885 Savings group for children, *1728*
1926 Rocket flight using liquid fuel, *6788*
1929 Tax on chain stores enacted by a state, *4423*
1952 Surgical operation shown on a local television program, *5354*
1966 Astronaut who was a civilian to orbit the earth, *6809*
Manned docking of two spacecraft, *6870*
1980 Television shows with closed captions, *7046*
1995 Astronaut from the United States to live in a space station, *6836*

March 17

1631 Fire prevention law enacted by a colony, *7311*
1762 Saint Patrick's Day parade, *1352*
1854 Parkland purchased by a city, *5988*
1871 Baseball league, *7496*
1881 Locomotive to attain a speed of one mile in less than a minute, *8340*
1884 Glider flight, *8001*
1898 Submarine that was practical and submersible, *8512*
1917 Bowling tournament for women, *7585*
1959 Submarine to surface at the North Pole, *8541*
1970 United Nations Security Council resolution vetoed by the United States, *3907*
1975 Strike by physicians against long working hours in hospitals, *7165*
1995 Chicken pox vaccine, *5161*
1999 Fuel cell car, *8281*

March 18

1543 Flood of record, *5896*
1734 Magician's advertisement, *1519*
1748 Spa at a mineral spring, *5386*
1795 Catholic priest trained in the United States, *6244*
1813 Gas streetlights, *7402*
1877 Federal marshal who was African-American, *7361*
1890 Naval militia established by a state, *5583*
1903 Interracial labor union, *7143*
1910 Opera by an American composer to be performed at the Metropolitan Opera House, *1321*
1911 Hail insurance law enacted by a state, *1967*
1913 Chiropractic regulation law enacted by a state, *5040*
1922 Intercollegiate indoor polo championship, *7871*
1925 Tornado disaster on a large scale, *5915*
1931 Electric shaver, *2476*
1938 Blood tests for pregnant women to be required by a state, *7279*

1945 Professional hockey player to score 50 goals in one season, *7832*
1952 Artificial lens for cataract patients, *5270*
1958 Newspaper advertisement printed on aluminum foil, *1553*
1963 Domed sports stadium, *3316*
1967 Ship with a combined diesel and gas-turbine engine, *8497*
1970 Strike of postal employees, *7164*
1993 Bacterium to be discovered that was visible to the naked eye, *6685*
2005 Muslim prayer service led by a woman acting as Imam, *6336*

March 19

1785 City college, *2716*
1941 African-American air unit, *5481*
1948 Labor dispute in which the Taft-Hartley Act was invoked, *7160*
1949 Museum devoted exclusively to nuclear energy, *3159*
1953 Oscar awards ceremony to be telecast, *1170*
1954 Rocket-driven sled on rails, *6794*
1964 Round-the-world solo airplane flight by a woman, *8150*
1965 Narcotics ban enacted by a state, *7085*
1975 Sex discrimination law enacted by a state that affected high school athletic competitions, *7453*
1979 All-politics television network, *4979*
2003 Ground battle in the Iraq War, *5836*

March 20

1833 Treaty between the federal government and an Asian nation, *3891*
1899 Woman executed in the electric chair, *7009*
1911 Farm bureau, *1637*
National squash tennis organization, *7904*
1914 International championship figure skating tournament, *7842*
1930 Diesel engine speed record, *8208*
1948 Symphonic concert to be shown on television, *1269*
Radio program simultaneously transmitted, *4800*
1954 Newspaper vending machine to deliver a single copy, *1696*
1987 Drug for treating AIDS, *5260*
1997 Cigarette maker to agree to a lawsuit settlement, *7091*

March 21

1791 Navy officer commissioned, *5595*
Federal revenue cutter, *8412*
1866 Soldiers' homes established by Congress, *5621*
1867 Stamp collection society, *4722*
1868 Women's professional club, *7212*
1915 Movie shown in the White House, *4330*
1916 Chess champion to play more than 100 games simultaneously, *7733*
1917 Navy petty officer who was a woman, *5605*
Hockey team from the United States to win the Stanley Cup, *7829*
1924 Foreign language course broadcast on radio, *3213*
1939 Surgical operation televised on a closed circuit for medical students, *5352*
1945 Marine Corps general in active service to wear four stars, *5567*
2004 Robot Olympics, *6531*

March 22

1622 Massacre of settlers by Native Americans, *5634*
1630 Gambling law for residents enacted by a colony, *1798*
1765 Direct tax on Britain's American colonists without their consent, *4402*
1790 Secretary of state, *4171*
1861 Nursing school to award a diploma, *3065*
1872 Ban on sex discrimination in employment enacted by a state, *7437*
1874 Young Men's Hebrew Association, *7214*
1880 Hydroelectric power plant to furnish arc lighting service, *6544*
1882 Federal ban on polygamy that was enforced, *7436*

March 23

1794 Rivet production, *3329*
1858 Cable car, *8366*
1880 Flour rolling mill, *2383*
1919 Orthodox rabbi born in America, *6294*
1925 Trial of a teacher for violating a state ban on teaching the theory of evolution, *2970*

March 24

1629 Hunting law enacted by a colony, *5938*
1792 Artist of American birth to head the Royal Academy of London, *1024*

March 24—*continued*

1828 Railroad owned by a state, *8301*
1887 Ambassador who was Jewish, *3894*
1936 Execution for the murder of a federal officer, *7016*
1940 Religious services to be shown on television, *6306*
1955 Oil drill seagoing rig, *6610*
1958 Navy task force to fight undersea craft, *5588*
1996 Astronaut from the United States who was a woman to live in a space station, *6837*
2002 Oscar for best actress awarded to an African-American, *1176*
2005 State legislator expelled for campaign financing violations, *4397*

March 25

1776 Medal awarded by the Continental Congress, *3551*
1802 Smallpox vaccine clinic, *5150*
1857 Photograph of a solar eclipse, *6400*
1863 Medal of Honor awarded to an Army soldier, *5504*
1867 Water supply tunnel for a city, *3439*
1915 Submarine disaster, *8514*
1937 Newspaper advertisement scented with perfume, *1544*
1960 Guided missile launched from a nuclear submarine, *5886*
1964 Telecast transmitted by satellite from Japan, *4969*
1969 State to require presidential electors to vote for the candidates of the party for which they were chosen, *3795*
1994 Political asylum granted on grounds of sexual orientation, *6106*
1995 Wiki Web site, *6478*

March 26

1790 Naturalization act enacted by Congress, *6049*
1866 Corrupt election practices law enacted by a state, *3770*
1885 Movie film, *1206*
1937 Monument to a comic-strip character, *7188*
1999 Murderer convicted on the basis of nationally televised evidence, *6976*

March 27

1792 Congressional investigation, *3562*
1836 Mormon temple, *6266*
1841 Fire engine with a steam boiler, *7321*
1849 Percussion rock drill, *1859*
1855 Kerosene, *6585*
1860 Corkscrew patent, *2558*
1884 Long-distance telephone call, *4875*
1931 Shuffleboard championship tournament, *7976*
1932 Radio broadcast from a moving train, *4796*
1955 Jewish mobile synagogue, *6318*
1961 Mobile computer center, *6429*
1998 Oral medicine for erectile dysfunction, *5262*

March 28

1827 Federal dry docks, *8424*
1834 President to be censured by Congress, *4129*
1836 Supreme Court justice who was Catholic, *3746*
1848 Child labor law enacted by a state that restricted the age of the worker, *7117*
1865 Environmental protection law enacted by a state in connection with advertising, *5906*
1905 Radio fax patents, *4467*
1922 Microfilm reading device, *3033*
1937 Photographer to receive the John Simon Guggenheim Memorial Foundation award, *4635*
1957 National curling championship, *7636*
1978 Bilingual report of a congressional committee, *3631*
1979 Nuclear power plant to sustain a major accident, *6629*

March 29

1626 Forestry law enacted by a colony, *5972*
1806 Highway built by the federal government, *3411*
1812 Wedding in the White House, *4325*
1839 Military school established by a state, *3103*
1852 Working hours of women to be regulated by a state, *7118*
1914 Newspaper rotogravure sections, *4585*
1927 Car to exceed the speed of 200 miles per hour, *8252*
1928 College founded as a Jewish institution, *2847*
1929 Fireworks law enacted by a state, *7333*
1949 Airport fog disposal unit, *8124*
1999 Dow Jones Industrial Average to exceed 10,000 points, *1790*

March 30

1843 Egg incubator, *1607*

March 31

April

April—*continued*

1969 Computer operating system for multiple users, *6441*
1973 Airborne express delivery service, *2081*
1979 Pen with truly erasable ink, *2681*
1988 Patent on an animal, *6684*
1994 Sailor to become a four-star admiral, *5616*
1999 Solar system with multiple planets, *6394*
2005 City with a complete smart-card system, *7423*

April 1

1621 Colonial treaty with the Native Americans, *6019*
1634 Bridge, *3227*
1769 Type foundry, *2032*
1789 Session of the House of Representatives at which there was a quorum, *3583*
Clerk of the House of Representatives, *3584*
Speaker of the House, *3585*
1826 Internal-combustion engine, *8183*
1843 Magazine for and by patients with mental illness, *7032*
1853 Fire department to be paid a salary, *7324*
1883 Recipe for animal crackers, *2376*
1889 Investment trust, *1778*
1927 Scheduled passenger night flight by airplane, *8061*
1928 Telephone switchboard with Braille markings, *4889*
1930 Speaker to address an organization by television, *4934*
1931 Baseball pitcher who was a woman, *7531*
1934 President to conduct religious services as commander-in-chief of the Navy, *4145*
1949 Television variety talent show with an African-American cast, *4939*
1954 Educational television station sponsored by a city, *4960*
Army helicopter battalion, *5489*
1960 Weather satellite to provide cloud-cover photographs, *6846*
1970 Census compiled in part from statistics obtained by mail, *6157*
1993 Members of a foreign terrorist organization indicted for planning attacks within the United States, *5827*
2005 Fuel cell truck, *8297*

April 2

1789 Congressional committee, *3586*
1792 Coin issued by the U.S. Mint to display the motto E pluribus unum, *4008*
Gold price fixed by Congress, *4012*
Minting of coins by the federal government, *4013*
1794 Arsenal of the federal government, *5677*
1819 Agricultural journal to attain prominence, *1592*
1829 Bank deposit insurance law enacted by a state, *1720*
1877 Easter egg roll, *2502*
1878 Hotel for women, *1821*
1893 Newspaper with a color page, *4582*
1902 Theater to show movies, *1123*
1908 City manager, *3529*
1976 Ambulance ship for first aid to boaters and pleasure craft, *5048*

April 3

1782 Fustians, everlastings, and coating, *2112*
1800 First Lady to receive free mail franking privileges, *4216*
1829 Coffee mill, *2343*
1837 State school for blind students, *2924*
1860 Pony Express mail, *4671*
1863 Medal of Honor awarded to a member of the Naval Service, *5505*
1888 Hotel transported from one location to another, *1824*
1965 Satellite with a nuclear reactor to orbit the earth, *6861*
1973 Zoo with twilight conditions, *3161*
Phone call made on a cell phone, *4916*
2000 Movie on videocassette to be released worldwide in one week, *1189*

April 4

1800 Bankruptcy act, *1479*
1841 President to die in Washington, *4250*
Vice president to succeed to the presidency after the death of a president, *4306*
1859 Song popular in the Confederate States, *1338*
1887 Mayor who was a woman, *3526*
1888 Holding companies authorized by a state, *1492*
1890 State law requiring candidates to file expenditure reports, *3770*
1898 Musical comedy written by African-Americans for African-American performers, *1449*

April 5

April 6

April 7

April 8

April 8—*continued*

2005 President to attend the funeral of a pope, *3946*

April 9

1813 African Methodist church, *6254*
1833 Free public library established by a city, *3011*
1847 Reformatory for boys established by a state, *7000*
1865 War in which more than 500,000 American combatants died, *5720*
1866 Civil rights law enacted by Congress, *6136*
1872 Dried milk patent, *2372*
1905 Aerial ferry, *3251*
1934 Federal justice of the Circuit Court of Appeals who was a woman, *3719*
1963 Honorary citizenship authorized by Congress, *6098*
1992 Criminal conviction of a foreign head of state, *3944*
1998 Ruling requiring retention of all electronic records of the federal government, *3864*
2002 Businessman convicted for importing unsafe toys, *7290*

April 10

1777 Lottery held by the Continental Congress, *1799*
1833 Homeopathic medical society, *5213*
1835 Homeopathy school, *3052*
1846 Gingham factory, *2133*
1849 Safety pin, *2552*
1866 Animal humane society, *7210*
1872 Arbor Day, *2499*
1877 Catamaran, *7573*
1892 Fruit-filled cookies, *2393*
Tuberculosis research and prevention society, *5224*
1904 Motorboat magazine, *8442*
1924 Radio broadcast from a circus, *1396*
1930 Synthetic rubber for manufacture, *1902*
1944 Movie to premiere on television, *1167*
Synthetic quinine, *5248*
1953 Three-dimensional feature movie in color, *1171*
1962 Newspaper reproduced commercially and regularly by radio facsimile, *4543*
1976 Involuntary sterilization regulation enacted by a state, *7454*
1984 Satellite repair in orbit, *6863*

April 11

1640 Colonial election held in defiance of the Royal Courts, *3756*
1816 African Methodist Episcopal bishop, *6255*
1876 Stenotype device, *1670*
1921 Telephone cable deep-sea service, *4887*
Cigarette tax enacted by a state, *7076*
1947 Major league baseball player in the postwar era who was African-American, *7537*
1953 Secretary of health, education, and welfare, *4191*
Department of Health, Education, and Welfare, *4191*
1954 State legislative hearing to be shown on television, *4396*
1965 Federal aid program for primary and secondary schools, *2979*

April 12

1631 Militia, *5635*
1776 Declaration of independence by a colonial government, *3461*
1786 Independent dispensary to furnish free medicine to the needy, *5099*
1799 Comb-cutting machine, *2459*
1811 Settlers to reach the Pacific coast, *6060*
1831 Railroad tunnel, *3437*
1833 Fireproof safe, *1664*
1842 Mutual life insurance company, *1990*
1853 Truancy law enacted by a state, *2934*
1861 Civil War attack, *5693*
Naval skirmish in the Civil War, *5694*
1867 Plate-glass insurance, *1959*
1892 Portable typewriter, *1680*
1900 Wedding by telegraph, *2593*
1926 Senator unseated after a recount, *3675*
1938 Blood tests for marriage license applicants to be required by a state, *7280*
1981 Reusable manned spacecraft, *6875*
1985 Senator to fly in space, *6830*
1990 Dolphin-free tuna, *2454*
2005 State to offer simultaneous access to multiple government databases, *7424*

April 13

1789 House of Representatives election that was contested, *3587*
1796 Elephant to be exhibited, *1357*
1831 Stone breaking machine, *3378*
1869 Air brake, *8386*
1904 Border patrol officer, *6084*
1916 Hybrid seed corn shipment, *1639*

1918 Combat mission of American pilots ordered to battle in World War I, *5748*
1940 Pole vaulter to clear the bar at 15 feet, *7951*
1942 Naval vessel from the United States to sink a German submarine in World War II, *5777*
1943 National monument to Thomas Jefferson, *7189*
1954 Carrier for liquid bulk chemicals, *8458*
1960 Navigational satellite, *6847*
1962 Baseball player to steal more than 100 bases in a season, *7544*
1964 Oscar for best actor awarded to an African-American, *1176*
1965 Senate page who was African-American, *3687*

April 14

1528 Ships built by Europeans in America, *8400*
1775 Abolition organization, *6119*
1792 Congressional apportionment of representatives, *3590*
1813 Hospital for insane patients operated privately, *5100*
1818 Army medical corps, *5195*
1863 Printing press to use a continuous web or roll of paper, *2045*
1865 National bank to fail, *1725*
President to be assassinated, *4254*
Execution of a woman by hanging by the federal government, *7004*
1894 Peep show using film in a vending machine, *1386*
1898 Ambulance ship operated by the Navy, *5202*
1910 President to pitch a ball to open the baseball season, *4141*
1914 Nonskid tires, *8203*
1918 Pilots in American units to participate in air combat in World War I, *5749*
1919 Medal of Honor awarded to a pilot, *5515*
1956 Video tape recorder for sounds and pictures, *5001*

April 15

1788 Worsted mill operated by waterpower, *2116*
1789 Political newspaper of national importance, *4492*
1794 French daily newspaper, *4552*
1817 School for deaf students to be established on a permanent basis, *2909*
Canal of importance, *3323*
1834 Presidential protest, *4130*
1854 Asylum for alcoholics, *5109*
1861 Civil War call for volunteers, *5695*
1884 Newspaper clipping bureau, *4520*
1941 Helicopter flight of one-hour duration, *8101*
1952 Bank to issue a credit card, *1764*
1955 McDonalds restaurant, *1835*
1956 All-color television station to televise live local programs, *4962*
1966 X-ray three-dimensional stereo fluoroscopic system, *5141*
1990 Orbiting observatory, *6381*
1995 TV program broadcast on the Internet, *4980*

April 16

1787 Play by an American writer to be successfully presented by an established company, *1422*
1813 Factory standardization to federal government specification, *3260*
1836 Child labor law enacted by a state that included an education requirement, *7111*
1869 Diplomat who was African-American, *3893*
1900 Books of postage stamps, *4729*
1912 Woman pilot to cross the English Channel in an airplane, *8028*
1926 Book-of-the-Month Club selection, *1099*
1935 Transport airplane designed for transoceanic service, *8096*
1940 Major league no-hitter baseball game on opening day, *7535*
1947 Army specialist corps for women, *5429*
1956 Radio receiver with an auxiliary solar-cell power unit, *4825*
1979 Coast Guard ship commander who was a woman, *5547*

April 17

1629 Commercial fishery, *1791*
1640 Lutheran pastor, *6183*
1704 Newspaper that was successful, *4490*
1776 Capture of an enemy warship by a commissioned American naval officer, *5657*
1844 Cylinder and flatbed combination printing press, *2040*
1860 Fire escapes for tenements, *7326*
1861 Fire in an oil well, *6588*
1895 Canal made of concrete, *3324*
1917 Proposal for daylight saving time, *2632*

April 17—*continued*

1941 Helicopter flight from water, *8102*
1952 National Day of Prayer established by Congress, *2517*
1956 Billiard player to win a match in the first inning, *7740*
1957 Installment sales law enacted by a state, *1511*

April 18

1637 Draft law enacted by a colony, *5553*
1662 Book auction, *4428*
1796 Opera by an American composer, *1317*
1895 Bathhouses mandated by a state, *7262*
1910 Night flight in an airplane, *8016*
1924 Crossword puzzle book, *7734*
1925 Woman's World Fair, *1506*
1930 State police officers who were women, *7377*
1934 Laundromat, *2225*
1942 Air attack against the Japanese homeland in World War II, *5778*
1960 Pacemaker to be implanted in a patient's body, *5363*
1968 Silver Star awarded to a Navy chaplain, *5537*
1975 State supreme court chief justice who was African-American, *3708*

April 19

1739 Astronomer of note, *6364*
1775 Battle in the Revolutionary War, *5649*
1861 Civil War bloodshed, *5696*
1865 President to lie in state in the Capitol rotunda, *4255*
1875 Centennial celebration of the Revolution, *2501*
1897 Marathon race held annually, *7946*
1901 City government using the commission plan, *3528*
1937 Letter to circumnavigate the world by commercial airmail, *4702*
1965 All-news radio station, *4815*
1969 Horse race parimutuel in which all the jockeys were women, *7817*
1995 Bombing by domestic terrorists resulting in large loss of life, *6972*

April 20

1564 Artist to come to America, *1010*
1657 Jew to win full citizenship, *6031*
1721 Editorial apology for false news to appear in a newspaper, *4491*
1767 Comic opera written for the American stage, *1315*
1801 Federal law providing services for people with disabilities, *7029*
1812 Vice president to die in office, *4302*
1837 Carpet power loom, *2549*
1852 State temperance society for women, *7062*
1861 Fund-raising organization to sell stamps, *7207*
1876 National chemistry organization, *6721*
1899 Primary election law enacted by a state, *3776*
1927 Celebrities to leave handprints at Grauman's Chinese Theatre, *1148*
1940 Electron microscope, *6732*
1964 Transcontinental Picturephone call, *4912*
1965 Cabinet meeting attended by a foreign national, *4196*
1977 License plate slogan to be challenged, *8214*
2006 State with an online learning requirement, *2990*

April 21

1712 Calico printery, *2110*
1847 Health insurance company, *1980*
1856 Railroad bridge across the Mississippi River, *3243*
1869 Indian Affairs Commissioner who was Native American, *3843*
1878 Firehouse pole, *7330*
1895 Movie recorded on film to be shown on a screen, *1117*
1899 Juvenile court, *3710*
1923 Precanceled stamps printed on rotary presses, *4735*
1962 World's Fair that was financially successful, *1512*
1980 Cuban boatlift, *6105*
1983 Presidential candidate who had been an astronaut, *3832*
1997 Space burial, *2311*
2003 American civil administrator of a Middle Eastern country, *3916*

April 22

1793 Neutrality proclamation by the federal government, *3884*
1794 Death penalty ban by a state, *6992*
1800 Library of Congress collection, *3003*
1864 Coin to use the motto "In God We Trust", *4032*
1884 Round-the-world bicycle trip, *7646*
1898 Capture of a ship in the Spanish-American War, *5724*
1913 Ice-loading machinery, *1873*

April 23

April 24

April 25

April 26

April 26—*continued*

2000 State to establish civil unions for gay couples, *7463*
2004 State to require labeling of genetically modified seeds, *1659*

April 27

1805 American flag flown over conquered hostile territory, *3492*
1816 Tariff passed by Congress for protection, *4408*
1875 Catholic priest from the United States to be made a cardinal, *6278*
1880 Patent on an electrical hearing aid, *5268*
1899 Tuberculosis hospital established by Congress, *5129*
1927 Woman to appear on television, *4926*
1938 Woman of American ancestry to become a queen, *3934*
1970 Bank to be automated, *1753*
1994 Criminal convicted on the evidence of DNA matching, *6970*
2001 Popular vote on a national emblem, *3507*

April 28

1798 Writer whose livelihood was obtained exclusively by writing, *1080*
1855 Veterinary college, *3059*
1866 Steam whaler, *8433*
1890 Employment service established by a state, *7136*
1909 Child delinquency law enacted by a state, *2190*
Naturalized citizen to lie in state in the Capitol rotunda, *3573*
1919 Parachute known as the "free parachute", *8042*
1930 Movie of a solar eclipse taken from an airplane, *6405*
1932 Yellow fever vaccine for human immunization, *5156*
1937 Electric sign showing an animated cartoon, *1545*
Costume museum, *3157*
1939 Miniature car, *8256*
1968 Armenian Orthodox cathedral, *6324*
2006 Medals of Honor issued by a state to honor service members killed in Iraq and Afghanistan, *5541*

April 29

1607 Episcopal Church act in America, *6171*
1749 Electric cooking experiment, *6534*
1851 College to prohibit discrimination because of race, religion, or color, *2750*
Electric locomotive, *8337*
1854 College for African-American students, *2754*
1864 Professional fraternity at a college, *2764*
1873 Railroad coupler, *8389*
1879 Electric arc streetlights, *7408*
1898 Cancer laboratory, *5167*
1913 Zipper, *2261*
1925 Woman elected to the National Academy of Sciences, *6718*
1931 Absolute monarch to visit the United States, *3932*
1942 Health insurance law enacted by a state, *1986*
1949 Cargo airlines licensed by the Civil Aeronautics Board, *8125*
1953 Three-dimensional telecast, *4957*
1997 Joint space walk by American and Russian astronauts, *6838*
2001 Space tourist, *6839*

April 30

1778 Blockade of enemy ships in the Revolutionary War that was effective, *5670*
1789 President elected under the Constitution, *4113*
Presidential inauguration, *4114*
Cabinet, *4168*
First Lady, *4215*
Army organization under the Constitution, *5414*
1796 Patented pills, *5233*
1798 Department of the Navy, *4174*
Navy yard, *5578*
1802 Land subsidy by Congress for road improvements, *3410*
1803 Territory annexed by the federal government, *6058*
1820 Antislavery magazine, *6126*
1837 State board of education, *2925*
1864 Hunting license required by a state, *7826*
1870 Medal of Honor awarded to a Jewish soldier, *5509*
1879 Factory inspection law enacted by a state, *7128*
1889 National holiday, *2505*
1898 Truth-in-advertising law enacted by a state, *1532*
1939 President to appear on television, *4281*
1963 State lottery, *1804*
1972 Attorney general to plead guilty to a criminal offense, *4202*

May 1—*continued*

1931 Skyscraper higher than 1,250 feet, *3300*
Baha'i house of worship, *6302*
1946 Radar installation aboard a commercial carrier, *8506*
1947 Radar for commercial and private planes, *8118*
1950 Poet who was an African-American woman to win the Pulitzer Prize, *4771*
1961 Skyjacking of a commercial American airplane, *6951*
1963 Ascent of Mount Everest by an American, *7983*

May 2

1843 Government on the Pacific Coast, *3451*
1876 Baseball players to hit home runs, *7504*
1880 Steamboat to employ electric lights successfully, *8435*
1900 United Christian Party convention, *4085*
1917 Liberty loan subscriptions, *1762*
1923 Transcontinental nonstop airplane flight, *8053*
1926 Transatlantic radio fax of a drawing, *4586*
1932 Pulitzer Prize awarded to a musical, *4768*
1940 Boxing referee who was a woman, *7606*
1941 Commercial television licenses, *4938*
1970 Jockey who was a woman to ride in the Kentucky Derby, *7818*
1997 First Lady to be depicted on a monument to a president, *4238*

May 3

1654 Toll bridge, *3228*
1765 Medical college, *3042*
1768 Arbitration tribunal, *1473*
1826 Arcade, *3263*
1845 Lawyer formally admitted to the bar who was African-American, *3965*
1851 Scandinavian Methodist Episcopal church, *6270*
1865 Medal of Honor winner to receive two awards, *5507*
1881 Electric locomotive headlight, *8391*
1902 Workers' compensation insurance law enacted by a state, *7141*
1904 Pharmacists to be regulated by a state, *5038*
1906 Advertising show to be held annually, *1535*
1933 Woman director of the U.S. Mint, *4017*
1943 Poet to win a Pulitzer Prize four times, *4769*
1952 Person known to have set foot on the North Pole, *6646*
Airplane flight to land at the North Pole, *6650*
Explorer to set foot on both the North and South Poles, *6651*
Jockey to win the Kentucky Derby five times, *7814*
1994 Judicial decision allowing physicians to end the lives of terminally ill patients at their request, *2309*
2002 Movie to gross $100 million in its opening weekend, *1190*

May 4

1780 Seal of a military department of the federal government, *3477*
National arts and sciences organization, *7198*
1811 Disciples of Christ church, *6252*
1845 Iron truss bridge, *3240*
1854 Entomologist hired by a state, *6659*
1855 Hospital for women, *5110*
1869 Oil drill offshore rig, *6593*
Railroad owned by a city, *8317*
1884 Photograph of a lightning flash, *6401*
1886 Phonograph that was practical, *4828*
1891 Hospital open to all races as a matter of policy, *5115*
1892 Acetylene gas, *1896*
1928 Federal judge who was a woman, *3719*
1942 Sea battle in World War II fought solely by air power, *5779*
1954 Intercollegiate court tennis match, *7931*
1956 Commemorative postal card, *4709*
1961 Freedom ride in the 1960s, *6143*
1973 Skyscraper higher than 1,400 feet, *3318*
2003 Astronauts to make a ground landing in a capsule, *6842*

May 5

1696 Printer who was a woman, *2008*
1832 Vaccination program by the federal government to protect Native Americans against smallpox, *5154*
1847 National medical society, *5218*
1865 Robbery of a disabled train, *6934*
1894 Intercollegiate fencing championship competition, *7667*
1901 Catholic mass for night workers, *6288*

1908 State law prohibiting discrimination against soldiers, *5422*
1917 Pilot who was African-American, *5472*
1936 Bottle with a screw cap, *2001*
1945 American civilians killed in the continental United States in World War II, *5795*
1961 Astronaut to be launched into space, *6803*
1970 Air Force Reserve officer who was a nun, *5496*
1973 College to offer athletic scholarships to women, *2874*
1995 American banned from the Internet, *6479*
1999 Feature film to premiere simultaneously in a theater and on the Internet, *1186*

May 6

1732 German newspaper, *4551*
1840 Library building at a university, *2744*
1851 Mechanical freezer patent, *2275*
1882 Restrictions by Congress on immigration of Chinese laborers, *6079*
1891 National fencing league, *7666*
1896 Airplane model to make a sustained flight under its own power, *8004*
1916 Ship-to-shore conversation over radio telephone, *4883*
1925 Transpacific radio fax transmission, *4470*
1937 Coast-to-coast radio news broadcast to be recorded, *4537*
1941 Ship from the United States sunk by a German submarine in World War II, *5757*
1957 Writer to win a Pulitzer Prize four times for drama, *4772*
1962 Nuclear warhead fired from a Polaris submarine, *5888*
1964 Election in the District of Columbia, *3785*

May 7

1634 Treason trial by a colony, *6925*
1789 Inaugural ball, *4115*
1907 Postage stamp depicting a Native American, *4731*
1912 Airplane outfitted with a machine gun, *5468*
1947 Television drama program regularly scheduled, *4942*

May 8

1783 Salute fired by Great Britain in honor of an officer of the United States, *3878*
1784 Hailstone shower of record that was fatal, *5904*
1787 Prison reform society, *6990*
1792 Draft of civilians by Congress, *5555*
1816 National bible society, *6256*
1866 Interracial jury, *3707*
1877 Dog show, *1378*
1878 Unassisted triple play in organized baseball, *7507*
1886 Cola drink, *2386*
1895 Cat show, *1388*
1915 Filly to win the Kentucky Derby horse race, *7805*
1931 Resale price maintenance law enacted by a state, *1507*
1939 Electric starting gate for horse races, *7810*
1942 Aircraft carrier from the United States sunk in World War II, *5780*
1952 Coal hydrogenation plant, *1908*
1954 Shot-put toss over 60 feet, *7953*
1961 Seawater conversion plant, *7419*
1964 Former president to address the Senate, *4155*
1980 Transcontinental nonstop balloon flight, *8162*
2003 Image of Earth as seen from Mars, *6420*

May 9

1607 Episcopal Church service in an English colony, *6171*
1754 Newspaper cartoon, *4574*
1783 Purple Heart, *5500*
1796 Senators elected but not seated, *3653*
1825 Theater lighted by gas, *1428*
1860 Constitutional Union Party convention, *4065*
1893 Movie exhibition, *1114*
1933 Diplomat who was a woman, *3896*
1939 Catholic beatification of a Native American, *6305*
1944 Eye bank, *5057*
1946 Television variety talent show series, *4939*
1960 Birth-control pill approved by the FDA, *7443*
1989 Airship that was certified by the Federal Aviation Administration, *8166*
1997 Ambassador to Vietnam, *3914*

May 10

1643 Colonial government federation, *3446*
1775 American capture of a British fort in the Revolutionary War, *5650*
1797 Frigate, *8466*
1800 Cabinet secretaries to be fired, *4175*
1851 Cheese factory, *2357*
1864 Sugar and glucose from cornstarch, *2364*
1869 Transcontinental railroad service, *8318*
1872 Presidential candidate who was a woman, *3808*
Vice presidential candidate who was African-American, *3809*
1876 Centennial exhibition, *1490*
Electric turnstile with a rachet, *1671*
Public exhibition of postage stamps, *4726*
1879 National archeology organization, *6722*
1892 Osteopathy school, *3077*
1894 Monument to a woman financed by women, *7178*
1898 Vending machine law enacted by a city, *1684*
1908 Mother's Day, *2508*
1911 Fatal airplane accident in a solo military airplane, *5466*
1912 Airplane round-trip flight over water, *8032*
1914 Presidential proclamation establishing Mother's Day, *2508*
1927 State aviation department, *8062*
1930 Planetarium open to the public, *6375*
1981 Baby whose life was saved by surgery while still in the womb, *5373*

May 11

1792 Exploration by ship of the mouth of the Columbia River, *6050*
1824 Catholic school for Native Americans, *2916*
1825 National religious tract society, *6263*
1832 National political platform, *4056*
1858 Congressional medal awarded to a physician, *3569*
1892 Locomotive owned by an industrial company, *8341*
1898 Navy officer killed in action in the Spanish-American War, *5725*
1928 Television programs to be shown regularly, *4930*
1946 CARE packages, *5798*
1947 Tubeless car tires, *8211*

May 12

1812 Vice presidential candidate to decline the nomination, *3799*
1860 News reporter at a political convention who was a woman, *4594*
1862 Confederate ship surrendered to the Union, *5713*
1879 Court case to establish the personhood of Native Americans, *6078*
1890 Prizefighting ban enacted by a state, *7596*
1896 Psychiatric institute, *3079*
Health ordinance prohibiting spitting, *7264*
1926 Airplane flight over the North Pole, *6647*
1949 Ambassador to the United States who was a woman, *3899*
1969 Transpacific solo sailboat crossing by a woman, *8546*
1985 Woman ordained as a Conservative rabbi, *6314*
2002 President to visit Cuba, *4322*
2005 American to climb all 14 mountains higher than 8,000 meters, *7989*

May 13

1607 Tobacco cultivation, *1554*
Colonial council, *3445*
Colonial council president, *3445*
Permanent English settlement in America, *6013*
1854 Billiard match, *7727*
1857 State agricultural college to open, *2759*
1908 Navy nurses' corps, *5205*
1916 Indian Day, *2510*
1918 Airmail stamps, *4734*
1942 Long-distance helicopter flight, *8106*
1949 Gas turbine to pump natural gas, *6607*
1964 Town to voluntarily desegregate its schools, *6144*
1998 Nuclear waste storage site deep underground, *6630*

May 14

1634 Property tax levied by a colony, *4398*
1743 Science society of importance, *6713*
1801 War fought by the United States against a foreign power, *5678*
1804 Transcontinental expedition to the Pacific coast, *6640*
1836 Scientific expedition fitted out by the federal government, *6642*
1856 Camels imported for military purposes, *5418*
1874 Football goalpost, *7689*

1884 Anti-Monopoly Party convention, *4074*
1887 Accident reports by employers, *7134*
1888 County created by federal law, *6081*
1897 Performance of The Stars and Stripes Forever, *1248*
1904 Olympic Games held in the United States, *7852*
1921 Judge to impose the death penalty who was a woman, *3716*
1932 Electrical timing device for foot races, *7949*
1942 Army corps for women, *5427*
1963 Television show transmitted by laser, *5005*
1973 Presidential Citizen Medal, *6914*
1996 Home screening kit for HIV infection, *5189*

May 15

1602 Exploration of the New England region by an Englishman, *6011*
1672 Colonial copyright law, *3974*
1685 Judge to be impeached, *3701*
1785 Missionary to the Native Americans who was African-American, *6237*
1797 Special session of Congress, *3563*
1851 College secret society for women, *2751*
1862 Enclosed baseball park, *7491*
1869 Postage stamp depicting the American flag, *4724*
1877 Monument to an American poet, *7174*
1885 Forest reserve established by a state, *5978*
1888 Union Labor Party convention, *4078*
United Labor Party convention, *4079*
1890 Milk butterfat tester, *2392*
1894 Labor union discrimination law enacted by a state, *7138*
1922 National arbitration organization, *3972*
1939 Bicycle race to be shown on television, *7657*
1940 Nylon stockings, *2265*
1941 Camp for conscientious objectors, *5558*
1950 Local radio network, *4813*
1957 Civic center with an aluminum geodesic dome, *3312*

May 16

1691 Colonist hanged for treason, *6989*
1775 State constitution, *3460*
1811 Naval battle in the War of 1812, *5681*
1825 Horse race trotting course, *7791*
1836 Steamboat on the Pacific coast, *8427*
1866 Nickel five-cent piece, *4033*
1876 Greenback Party convention, *4070*
1882 Flicker animation, *1194*
1888 Phonograph record, *4829*
1893 Typewriter to produce a line of writing visible as it was being typed, *1681*
1903 Transcontinental motorcycle trip, *8288*
1914 Horseshoe pitching association, *7970*
1929 Oscar for best picture, *1152*
Oscars for best acting, *1153*
Oscars for best movie director, *1154*
1940 Two-handed shovel, *2670*
1941 Automatic aircraft cannon, *5868*
1959 Golfer to break 60 for 18 holes in a major tournament, *7774*
1973 Balloon flight powered by solar energy, *8157*
2000 First lady to run for public office, *4239*

May 17

1792 Stock exchange, *1767*
1796 Pediatrics monograph, *5290*
Sale of federal land to an individual, *6051*
1853 Railroad merger, *8312*
1875 Kentucky Derby horse race, *7797*
1877 Interstate telephone call, *4867*
Telephone switchboard or exchange, *4868*
1895 Electric elevated railroad that was permanent, *8319*
1913 Oil and gas conservation law enacted by a state, *6603*
1938 Farm cooperative for artificial insemination of livestock, *1652*
1939 Fashion show to be shown on television, *1403*
Coin-operated mailbox, *4703*
Sports event to be televised live, *4937*
1954 Supreme Court case in which social-science research was accepted as evidence, *7477*
1955 Nuclear reactor patent, *6736*
1956 Synthetic mica, *3398*
1973 Navy officer who was a woman to hold a major command, *5614*
2004 Marriage between two people of the same sex, *7464*

May 18

1607 Prefabricated ship built in America, *8402*
1631 Election held in a colony, *3755*
1652 Slavery emancipation law enacted by a colony, *6114*
1713 Book auction catalog, *4432*
1766 United Brethren in Christ meeting, *6225*

May 18—*continued*

1852 Compulsory education law enacted by a state, *2932*
1912 Baseball strike, *7525*
1934 Death penalty authorized by federal law, *7016*
1949 Heliport commercial base, *8126*
1953 Triple jet ace, *5809*
Woman pilot to break the sound barrier, *8121*
1956 Forest horse, *5962*
1967 Artificial insemination for women to be permitted by a state, *5397*
1980 Volcano known to claim human life, *5930*
1994 Genetically altered food, *2456*

May 19

1796 Protection of Native American hunting grounds authorized by Congress, *6052*
1857 Fire alarm system operated by electricity, *7325*
1862 Homestead law enacted by Congress, *6071*
1891 People's Party national convention, *4080*
1898 Postcard, *4685*
1915 Dental hygienists to be licensed by a state, *5041*
1921 Opera broadcast over the radio in its entirety, *1322*
Immigration quota enacted by Congress, *6088*
1928 Frog-jumping jubilee, *1399*
1996 Use of radar to investigate a plane crash, *8170*
1998 Supreme Court decision on inclusion of candidates in televised political debates, *3753*
2003 State ban on the sale of violent video games to children, *7308*

May 20

1639 Property tax established by a colony to support public schools, *2885*
1777 Treaty between states after the Declaration of Independence, *4336*
1785 Land set-aside for schools authorized by the Continental Congress, *2902*
Sale of federal land authorized by Congress, *6045*
Survey of public lands, *6046*
Geographer of the United States, *6488*
1830 Railroad timetable advertised in a newspaper, *8304*
1844 Game protection society, *7824*
1856 Telegraph ticker to print type successfully, *4852*
1865 College to sponsor an endowed lecture series, *2767*
1899 National physics association, *6724*
Driver arrested for speeding, *8236*
1916 Cover of the Saturday Evening Post by Norman Rockwell, *1040*
1918 Warship propelled by electricity, *8482*
1927 Transatlantic solo airplane flight, *8063*
1932 Transatlantic solo airplane flight by a woman, *8086*
1939 Transatlantic airmail service, *4704*
Public telecast made over telephone wires, *4992*
1951 Ace to fly a jet, *5808*
1955 Solar energy battery to be manufactured commercially, *6635*
Offshore radar warning station, *8489*
1956 Hydrogen bomb dropped from an airplane, *5881*
1964 Atomic-powered lighthouse, *7351*

May 21

1788 Coins issued by the United States, *4009*
1819 Bicycles, *7637*
1832 Democratic Party national convention, *4057*
National political convention to adopt the two-thirds rule, *4058*
1853 Circumnavigation of the world by a yacht, *8530*
1861 Newspaper published by soldiers in the field, *4508*
1881 Red Cross meeting, *7219*
National tennis society, *7920*
1888 State crematory, *2301*
1891 Nonprofit land conservation trust, *5911*
Boxing match timed by automatic timer, *7597*
1901 Speed limits for motor vehicles, *8190*
1909 Credit union law enacted by a state, *1735*
1919 Medal of Honor awarded in World War I, *5516*
1927 Corporation to own its own airplane, *8064*
1929 Automatic electric stock quotation board, *1780*
1932 Railroad mystery excursion, *1402*
1934 Community to fingerprint its citizens, *7380*
1936 Lucite commercially manufactured, *1906*

1980 Coast Guard Academy graduates who were women, *3131*
1985 Septuplets, *2162*
1986 Human chain across the United States, *1410*

May 22

1621 Wedding of colonists in New England, *2588*
1649 Corrupt election practices law enacted by a colony, *3759*
1761 Life insurance policy, *1988*
1819 Transatlantic crossing by an American steamboat, *8527*
1841 Reclining chair, *2551*
1856 Assault by a congressman on a senator, *3662*
1861 Union soldier killed by enemy action in the Civil War, *5697*
1900 Automatic computing pendulum scale, *1685*
1930 Airship for private commercial operation, *8077*
1933 Maritime Day, *2514*
1935 President to read a veto message to Congress, *4147*
1947 Ballistic missile, *5874*
1961 Revolving restaurant, *1836*
1972 President to visit the Soviet Union, *4320*
1993 Movie broadcast on the Internet, *1180*

May 23

1785 Bifocal eyeglasses, *5264*
1879 Veterinary school established by a state, *3072*
1891 Railroad chapel car, *8357*
1900 Medal of Honor awarded to an African-American soldier for an action in the Civil War, *5512*
1903 Transcontinental car trip, *8242*
1908 Airship disaster, *8006*
1922 Radio broadcast of a debate, *4786*
1929 Coaxial cable, *4859*
1956 Automaton to operate by long-distance control, *6520*
1962 Limb reattachment, *5364*
1983 State to have an official hero or heroine, *4365*
1984 Woman midshipman at the Naval Academy to graduate first in her class, *3128*
1988 Ban on cheap handguns enacted by a state, *6964*
1994 Reparations awarded to victims of a racially motivated massacre, *6971*
2002 Transmission of touch signals over a long distance, *6530*
2006 FBI raid on the office of a congressional representative, *3641*

May 24

1844 Commercial telegraph service, *4847*
1851 State adoption law to consider the interests of the child, *2183*
1861 Civil War combat action that earned the Medal of Honor, *5502*
Union officer killed in the Civil War, *5698*
1862 Artillery fire to be directed from the air, *5459*
Army field telegraph used in warfare, *5714*
1869 Exploration of the Grand Canyon of the Colorado, *6644*
1874 Steel arch bridge, *3244*
1875 National banking association, *1727*
1893 Anti-saloon organization, *7069*
1899 Public garage, *8237*
1902 Oil journal, *6785*
1913 Strike settlement mediated by the federal Department of Labor, *7146*
1918 Air combat arm of the Army, *5475*
Croix de Guerre awarded to an American, *5513*
1931 Air-conditioned train, *8395*
1935 Baseball game at night by major league teams, *7533*
1945 Food-O-Mat, *2100*
1959 House with a built-in nuclear bomb shelter, *2531*
1960 Spy satellite, *6848*
1976 Transatlantic supersonic jet service, *8158*
2001 Senator to change political control of the Senate by switching parties, *3697*

May 25

1721 Fire insurance agent, *1974*
1790 Copyright law enacted by Congress, *3977*
1793 Catholic priest, *6244*
1829 Typewritten letter, *1662*
1844 News dispatch by telegraph, *4505*
Gas engine, *8184*
1895 Golf book, *7756*
1898 Military expeditionary force to be sent beyond the Western Hemisphere, *5726*
1903 Railroad operated by an electric third-rail system, *8324*
1918 Army nursing school, *3088*

May 25—*continued*

1926 Catholic church to become a basilica, *6299*
1953 Educational television station, *4958*
Nuclear cannon, *5880*
1967 Postage stamp issued in the United States and canceled by a foreign country, *4748*
1972 Fly-by-wire aircraft, *8155*
1973 Physician to practice as an astronaut in space, *6818*
Space station launched by the United States, *6873*

May 26

1647 Ban on Jesuits to be enacted by a colony, *6187*
1836 Gag rule in the House of Representatives, *3598*
1913 College comprehensive senior examination program, *2832*
1934 Train to run 1,000 miles nonstop, *8396*
1941 Film professorship at a college, *2858*
1956 Bank to open a branch in a trailer, *1750*
1981 Computer software patent, *6461*

May 27

1607 Battle between English colonists and Native Americans, *5630*
1647 Execution for witchcraft, *6987*
1652 Colonial act of defiance against the King of England, *3447*
Coins made in colonial America, *4002*
1755 Water pumping plant, *7400*
1825 Brothers to serve simultaneously as governors of their respective states, *4373*
1896 Intercollegiate bicycle race, *7653*
1926 Statue to commemorate literary characters, *7186*
1930 Cellophane transparent tape, *2578*
1936 Coxswain of a men's college varsity rowing team who was a woman, *7881*
1943 President of a Sub-Saharan African country to visit the United States, *3937*
1950 Major studies to show a link between smoking and lung cancer, *7080*

May 28

1734 Fish protection law enacted by a city, *5940*
1754 Bloodshed in the French and Indian War, *5640*
1796 Federal law exempting debtors from prison, *6993*
1870 Stamp auction, *4725*
1879 State ban on the employment of women in a dangerous occupation, *7129*
1881 Pure food and drug law enacted by a state, *7251*
1913 Senate whip, *3671*
1917 Troops from the United States to sail to Europe in World War I, *5738*
1918 Gold Star mothers, *5750*
1922 Radio orchestra, *1258*
1925 Long-distance radio fax transmission of medical information, *4471*
1929 Movie with both sound and color, *1155*
1932 Airport manager who was a woman, *8087*
1953 Animated three-dimensional cartoon in Technicolor, *1201*
1959 Animals to survive a space flight, *6797*
1975 Whooping crane, *5964*
1978 Casino outside the state of Nevada, *1807*
1998 Image of a planet outside Earth's solar system, *6418*

May 29

1827 Nautical school, *3195*
1844 President who was a "dark horse" candidate, *3803*
1909 Domestic relations court, *3712*
1916 Presidential flag, *4142*
1919 Toaster, *2284*
1935 Drug treatment center for addicts established by Congress, *7077*
1948 United Nations peacekeeping mission in which the United States participated, *5800*
1962 Baseball coach in the major leagues who was African-American, *7545*
1977 Driver who was a woman to compete in the Indianapolis 500, *7626*

May 30

1734 Masonic book, *7195*
1806 President who had participated in a duel, *4245*
1821 Fire hose of rubber-lined cotton web, *7320*
1848 Woman member of the American Academy of Arts and Sciences, *7198*
1856 Milk purity law enacted by a state, *7242*
1868 Memorial Day, *2497*

1873 State to make Memorial Day a legal holiday, *2497*
1881 Plumbing law enacted by a state, *7411*
1893 Relay race in a college track meet, *7944*
1896 Car accident, *8230*
1901 Academic hall of fame, *3146*
1903 Motorcycle hill-climbing contest, *7847*
1908 Workers' compensation insurance law enacted by Congress, *7144*
1911 Indianapolis 500 race, *7623*
1922 National monument to Abraham Lincoln, *7185*

May 31

1786 Strike benefit by a union, *7101*
1821 Cathedral, *6261*
1853 Arctic expedition by an American explorer, *6643*
1870 African-American cadet admitted to West Point, *3107*
1880 National bicycle organization, *7644*
1889 Dam disaster of great consequence, *5909*
1918 American air ace, *5751*
1929 Reindeer, *5952*
1938 Movie to be shown on a television screen, *1162*
1941 High-jump standards using electric eye detectors, *7952*
1957 Intermediate-range ballistic missile, *5882*

June

1654 Orphanage, *2173*
1749 Waxworks, *1350*
1779 Oyster propagation, *1580*
1789 Presidential appointment, *4116*
1798 Straw hats, *2233*
1809 Magazine containing a fashion plate, *4608*
1812 Pencil factory, *2674*
1813 Stereotyped book, *4445*
1828 Electromagnet, *6535*
1853 Stamped envelopes, *4719*
1860 Commercial oil refinery, *6587*
1861 Confederate cruiser to raid Union commerce, *5699*
1866 Boiler insurance company, *1957*
1869 Lawyer who was a woman, *3967*
1870 College summer school, *2779*
1871 Half holiday on Saturday for factory workers, *7124*
1876 Intercollegiate athletic association, *7939*
1884 Roller coaster, *1002*
1887 Train with electric lighting, *8394*
1891 Diamonds in a meteorite, *3392*
1892 Electric sign of large dimensions, *1529*
1899 Police patrol wagon, *7364*
1900 Orthodontists' society, *5227*
1903 State to require driver licenses, *8191*
1904 Radium treatment for cancer, *5393*
1907 Building of pressed structural steel, *3295*
1912 City government using the manager plan, *3531*
1913 Insulating brick, *3346*
1926 Electric toaster, *2286*
1928 Television magazine, *6787*
Diesel-electric freight locomotive, *8342*
1930 Nudist summer camp, *7974*
1937 Shopping cart, *1691*
1938 Comic book hero with superpowers, *1101*
1941 Presidential library, *4150*
1943 Hydroelectric power plant to produce a million kilowatts, *6570*
1944 Presidential airplane, *4297*
1950 Burglar alarm operated by ultrasonic or radio waves, *3307*
1953 Electronic road system, *3428*
1954 Truck driving school, *3216*
1957 Charting of the Northwest Passage, *6653*
1966 Black Power advocate, *6147*
1972 Libertarian Party national convention, *4106*
1973 Haircut in space, *6819*
1977 Computer camp, *6457*
1980 All-news television network, *4548*
1984 Rap album to attract a mass audience, *1280*
1992 Car fueled by methanol, *8278*
1993 Mathematical proof of Fermat's last theorem, *6709*
1998 Web site constructed to authenticate a film, *1185*
2004 Thought control of mechanical devices, *5277*

June 1

1638 Earthquake of record, *5898*
1785 Minister to Great Britain, *3881*
1789 Congressional act, *3558*
1802 Book fair, *4440*
1815 Steam-propelled frigate, *8468*
1819 Tightrope performer who was a woman, *1363*
1840 Gutta-percha, *1886*
1847 Steamship passenger line between American and European ports, *8431*
1860 Army signal corps, *5419*

June 1—*continued*

1861 Confederate officer killed in the Civil War, *5700*
1880 Pay station telephone service, *4872*
Bareknuckle world heavyweight boxing champion, *7595*
1881 Horse bred in the United States to win the English Derby, *7799*
1886 Labor mediation and arbitration board established by a state, *7132*
1887 Navy contract for armor plate, *5582*
1888 Seismograph, *6493*
1890 Census compiled by machines, *6154*
1897 Rock wool insulation factory, *3344*
1898 Interurban streetcar line, *8373*
1901 Motorcycle with a built-in gasoline engine, *8287*
1909 Transcontinental car race, *7621*
1911 Life insurance group policy, *1993*
1919 Forest Service aerial patrol, *5984*
1939 Boxing match to be shown on television, *7605*
1949 Magazine on microfilm offered to subscribers, *3037*
1951 Titanium plant fully self-contained and fully integrated, *1945*
1957 American runner to run a mile in less than four minutes on an outdoor track, *7955*
National wheelchair games, *7980*
1960 Parking meter enforcement division of a police department, *7386*
1990 Chemical arms control treaty, *3912*

June 2

1883 Baseball game at night, *7509*
Electric elevated railroad, *8319*
1886 Wedding of a president in the White House, *4257*
1889 Hydroelectric power plant generating alternating current to operate over a long distance, *6553*
1924 Citizenship statute for Native Americans, *6090*
1930 Presbyterian elder who was a woman, *6300*
1933 Swimming pool in the White House, *4332*

June 3

1769 Observatory, *6368*
1800 President to reside in Washington, *4122*
1820 Workers' library, *3008*
1833 Clipper ship, *8425*
1856 Screw machine to make pointed screws, *2654*
1861 Land battle in the Civil War, *5701*
1873 Oratorio by an American, *1241*
1884 Keynote speech by an African-American at a major party convention, *4075*
National political convention of a major party presided over by an African-American, *4076*
1898 Military campaign medal, *5510*
1899 Portable church, *6287*
1916 Supreme Court justice who was Jewish, *3750*
Army veterinary corps, *5208*
1925 Airship with an enclosed cabin, *8058*
1949 Naval Academy graduate who was African-American, *3118*
1953 Cabinet conference to be telecast, *4192*
1965 Astronaut to walk in space, *6805*
1972 Woman ordained as a Reform rabbi, *6314*
1995 West Point cadet who was a woman to graduate at the top of her class, *3132*

June 4

1674 Horse racing ban by a colony, *7789*
1811 Proposal in Congress that states should secede from the Union, *4341*
1816 Double-deck steamboat, *8421*
1820 Mariners' church, *6260*
1825 Natural gas used as an illuminant, *6580*
1845 Opera of importance by an American composer, *1317*
1912 Minimum wage law enacted by a state, *7145*
1917 Pulitzer Prize awarded to a newspaper reporter, *4760*
Pulitzer Prize for a newspaper editorial, *4761*
Pulitzer Prize for fiction, *4762*
1931 Rocket glider flight, *8083*
1934 Factories operated by the federal government in peacetime, *3847*
Aircraft carrier, *8484*
1942 Navy Cross awarded to a Coast Guard officer in World War II, *5519*
1944 Capture and boarding of an enemy submarine on the high seas by American forces, *5794*
1980 West Point woman graduate who was Jewish, *3097*
Woman Secret Service agent killed in the line of duty, *3845*
1990 Death by suicide machine, *2308*
1992 Postage stamp whose design was decided by popular vote, *4757*

1998 Solo crossing of the Gulf of Mexico in a paddled boat, *8548*
2005 Monument to mothers of fallen soldiers, *7192*

June 5

1785 College founded as a Methodist institution, *2717*
1794 Neutrality regulation enacted by Congress that governed the actions of citizens, *3885*
1865 Safe deposit vault, *1666*
1877 Margarine law, *2378*
1918 Pulitzer Prize awarded to a newspaper, *4764*
Pulitzer Prize for drama, *4765*
1938 Electronic voice mechanism, *4893*
1940 Synthetic rubber tires, *8210*
1946 Cellulose sponge for medical and surgical use, *5184*
1952 Boxing referee in a heavyweight championship match who was African-American, *7607*
1963 Air Force Academy graduates who were African-American, *3121*
1975 State to recognize unions for farmworkers, *7166*

June 6

1639 Gunpowder mill, *5837*
1822 Physiologist of note, *5019*
1833 President to ride on a railroad train, *4292*
1840 Presidential candidate to make a campaign speech, *3802*
1877 Doctoral degree awarded to a woman, *2794*
1890 National polo association, *7870*
1891 Polar expedition of which a woman was a member, *6645*
1896 Transatlantic trip by rowboat, *8533*
1904 Disease research and treatment organization, *5228*
1907 Nonsectarian college under Jewish auspices, *2825*
1925 City in miniature, *1398*
1932 Gasoline tax levied by Congress, *4424*
1933 Drive-in movie theater, *1159*
1941 Naval ship constructed as a minelayer, *8481*
1942 Parachute jump using a nylon parachute, *8107*
1962 Air Force Academy graduate who was Native American, *3120*
1968 Presidential campaigner to be assassinated, *3826*
1979 Train operated exclusively by women, *8399*
2000 Ray gun to shoot down an armed missile, *5894*

June 7

1801 Organization of booksellers, *4439*
1860 Mass-market paperback book, *4454*
1862 Citizen of the United States to be hanged for treason, *7003*
1870 Railroad signal system with automatic electric block, *8388*
1882 Tariff commission established by Congress, *4416*
1883 Intercollegiate lawn tennis match, *7922*
1887 Monotype machine, *2053*
1892 Delegates to a national political convention who were women, *4081*
Baseball pinch hitter, *7515*
Bicycle tire made of cord, *7651*
1898 Social Democracy of America Party national convention, *4083*
1938 Broadway play shown in a television version with its original cast, *1460*
1939 King of Great Britain to visit the United States, *3935*
1942 American territory occupied by the Japanese in World War II, *5781*
1954 Microbiology laboratory, *5170*
1955 President to appear on color television, *4281*
1980 Power plant using solar cells, *6636*

June 8

1697 Settler heroine publicly rewarded, *6036*
1786 Ice cream to be made commercially, *2325*
1869 Vacuum cleaner that used suction, *2216*
1872 Mail fraud law enacted by Congress, *4679*
1911 Pilot licensed by the Aero Club of America, *8025*
State aviation law, *8026*
1948 Commissioned officer in the Marine Corps who was African-American, *5568*
1959 Airmail by missile, *4710*
1966 Coast Guard Academy graduate who was African-American, *3123*

June 9

1628 Deportation, *6025*

June 9—*continued*

1772 Naval attack in the Revolutionary War, *5645*
Shot fired by an American combatant to wound a British combatant in the conflict over independence, *5646*
Protestant church west of of the Alleghenies, *6227*
1783 Revolutionary War national veterans' organization, *5619*
1790 Book entered for copyright with the federal government, *3978*
1846 Senator elected on an antislavery ticket, *6131*
1880 Greenback Labor Party convention, *4073*
1902 Restaurant with an automatic arrangement for vending food, *1827*
1909 Transcontinental car trip by women, *8246*
2006 State law requiring cats to be neutered, *2610*

June 10

1682 Tornado of record, *5900*
1760 Medical licensing law enacted by a city, *5015*
1809 Steamboat to make an ocean voyage, *8417*
1851 French daily newspaper that was successful, *4552*
1884 Albert Medal presented to a person born in America, *6895*
1902 Envelope with a window, *2025*
1905 Forest fire lookout tower, *5983*
1910 School stadium, *2965*
1923 Dance marathon to exceed 200 hours, *7972*
1924 Political convention to be broadcast on radio, *4094*
Portable electric stethoscope, *5179*
1932 Artificial lightning demonstration, *6500*
1935 Twelve-step rehabilitation program, *7078*
1936 Telecast using coaxial cable, *4989*
1939 King and queen to be shown on television, *3936*
1944 Horse stakes race ending in a triple dead heat, *7811*
1952 Surgical operation televised coast-to-coast, *5355*
1954 Gas-turbine bus, *8223*
1955 Virus separated into component parts, *6673*
1963 Ban on sex discrimination in wages enacted by Congress, *7446*
1967 Horse motel, *1840*
1977 Golfer to break 60 in a Professional Golfers Association tour, *7780*

June 11

1788 Ship built on the Pacific coast, *8411*
1790 Filibuster in the House of Representatives, *3588*
1813 Surgeon general of the Army, *5436*
1885 State gas commission, *6599*
1889 Business high school, *2955*
1891 Nautical school established by a state, *3206*
1919 Horse to win the Triple Crown, *7806*
1922 Transatlantic radio fax transmission of a photograph, *4468*
1927 Distinguished Flying Cross, *6903*
1928 Guide dog, *7037*
1930 Deep-sea exploration vessel, *6499*
1943 American land victory without infantry in World War II, *5790*
1944 Serbian Orthodox cathedral, *6308*
1963 Lung transplant, *5366*
1970 Army general who was a woman, *5453*
1978 Mormon man ordained to the priesthood who was African-American, *6329*
2001 Execution to be televised, *7026*
Federal execution by lethal injection, *7027*

June 12

1775 National day of prayer, *2487*
Naval battle in the Revolutionary War, *5651*
1796 Unitarian church identified as such in its name, *6236*
1849 Gas mask, *1860*
1880 Obelisk to be brought to the United States, *7175*
1900 Grand American Trapshoot tournament with clay targets, *7886*
1913 Animated cartoon made with cel animation, *1196*
1918 Airplane bombing raid by an American air unit, *5752*
1920 Farmer Labor Party convention, *4093*
1946 Transcontinental round-trip airplane flight made within 24 hours, *8117*
1947 Golfer born in America to win the British Women's Amateur Golf Tournament, *7773*
1950 Nuclear engineering course at a college, *2862*

June 17

1775 Army chief engineer, *5434*
1856 Republican Party national convention, *4063*
1863 Accident insurance company, *1956*
1866 Mourning postage stamp, *4721*
1894 Polio epidemic, *5094*
1912 Horse race mutuel ticket to pay more than $1,000, *7804*
Fatal airplane accident involving a woman, *8033*
1937 Ski lift, *7893*
1942 American expeditionary force to land in Africa in World War II, *5782*
1946 Mobile telephone commercial service, *4894*
1947 Round-the-world commercial airplane service, *8119*
1957 Weight lifter to lift more than 6,000 pounds, *7981*
1991 President whose body was exhumed, *4273*
1994 World Cup soccer tournament held in the United States, *7902*

June 18

1621 Duel, *6923*
1798 Secretary of the Navy, *4174*
1861 Telegram dispatched from an aerial station, *4854*
Civilian welfare effort for soldiers organized on a large scale, *5702*
Fly casting tournament, *7671*
1885 Local library society, *3017*
1895 Carbide factory, *1897*
1908 Savings bank to offer life insurance, *1992*
1910 Commerce court established by the federal government, *3713*
1916 Pilot from the United States shot down in World War I, *5733*
1934 Nationwide highway planning surveys authorized by Congress, *3426*
1936 Bicycle traffic court, *7655*
1959 Telecast received from England, *4965*
1964 Transpacific telephone service using the transoceanic cable, *4913*
1983 Astronaut who was a woman to fly in space, *6825*
1999 Digital projection of a major motion picture, *1187*

June 19

1754 Colonial congress, *3547*
1841 Underwater torpedo operated by electric current, *5847*
1846 Baseball game, *7483*
1849 Melodeon patent, *1295*
1876 Lifesaving medal awarded by the Treasury Department, *7345*
1884 Graduate student who was a woman to receive a university fellowship, *2801*
1905 Movie theater, *1126*
1910 Father's Day, *2509*
1911 Movie censorship board established by a state, *1133*
1913 Immunology society, *5230*
1923 State law to establish English as an official language, *6089*
1931 Automatic swinging doors operated by a photoelectric cell, *3301*
1934 Movie of the sun, *6406*
1939 Pinball ban enacted by a city, *7866*
1956 Federal aid to libraries, *3028*
1977 Catholic saint who was a male American citizen, *6328*
1996 HDTV broadcasting license, *4981*
2006 Permanent protective vault for crops and seeds, *1661*

June 20

1867 Territory annexed by the federal government that was noncontinguous, *6073*
1930 Weather map to be telecast to a transatlantic steamer, *4924*
1945 Naval ship with a mixed company of male and female personnel, *8487*
1960 World heavyweight boxing champion to regain his crown, *7609*
1967 Public defender hired by a state, *3973*

June 21

1607 Episcopal Church parish, *6171*
1622 Alcohol prohibition enforcement officers, *7052*
1768 Physician to receive a Bachelor of Medicine degree, *3044*
1869 Health board established by a state government, *7248*
1875 Catholic bishop who was African-American, *6279*
1913 Parachute jump from an airplane by a woman, *8034*
1922 Taconite production, *3396*
Massacre of strikebreakers by union members, *7148*
1932 Woman to receive a gold medal from the National Geographic Society, *6899*
1943 Soldier's Medal awarded to a woman, *5523*

1948 Long-playing microgroove phonograph records, *4835*
1963 State college for the performing arts, *2867*
1977 Attorney general to be incarcerated, *4205*
1997 Women's National Basketball League game, *7563*
1999 School voucher plan enacted by a state, *2987*
2003 Book to sell 5 million copies in a single day, *1111*
2004 Privately funded spacecraft to fly in space, *6888*
Civilian pilot to fly a craft into space, *6888*
2005 Solar sail aircraft, *6890*

June 22

1775 Paper money issued by the Continental Congress, *4005*
1807 Naval ship to surrender in peacetime, *5680*
1832 Machine for manufacturing pins, *2614*
1843 Grain elevator operated by steam, *1608*
1874 Osteopathic physician, *5029*
1896 Physician who was a Chinese woman, *5035*
1914 Woman fellow of the American College of Surgeons, *5229*
1939 Beauty pageant to be shown on television, *1404*
National water skiing tournament, *7991*
1946 Jet airplane to transport mail, *4705*
1960 Multisatellite launching, *6849*
1977 Coast Guard officers who were women who served aboard ships, *5546*
1993 First Lady who was also a federal official, *4237*

June 23

1775 Book made with American paper, ink, and type, *4437*
1812 Naval battle in the War of 1812 that took place after war was declared, *5681*
1836 Federal treasury surplus to be returned to the states, *4345*
1844 Branding punishment by a federal court, *6998*
1848 Congressional lobbyist who was a woman, *3567*
1869 State probation officer for juvenile delinquents, *7005*
Labor bureau established by a state, *7121*
1871 Natural gas plant operated by a city, *6596*
1887 Hospital designed exclusively for infants, *5113*
1888 Presidential nominee who was African-American, *3813*
1899 Medal of Honor awarded to an African-American soldier, *5511*
1904 Motorboat race under organized rules, *7575*
1916 Pilot from the United States killed in World War I, *5734*
1938 Aquarium for large marine animals, *3158*
Airplane instructor's license, *8097*
1960 Coast-to-coast solar-powered two-way radio conversation, *4802*
1967 High school for pregnant teenage girls, *2980*
1970 Physician with a mobile medical office, *5043*
1989 Human-powered submarine race, *7578*
1998 Congresswoman who was a veteran of the armed forces, *3635*

June 24

1497 European to set foot on the North American continent after the Vikings, *6003*
1579 Christian religious service in English on the Pacific Coast, *6168*
1647 Woman in America to appeal for the right to vote, *3758*
1784 Tethered balloon flight, *7993*
1885 Episcopal bishop who was African-American, *6283*
1898 Army officer killed in battle in the Spanish-American War, *5727*
Land battle in the Spanish-American War, *5728*
1910 Federal law requiring radios on ships, *8445*
1930 Radar detection of airplanes, *8078*
1936 Federal administrator who was an African-American woman, *3851*
1940 Political convention to be televised, *4098*
1948 Presidential candidate who was renominated after a defeat, *3821*
1964 Picturephone commercial service, *4914*
1970 Cabinet member to serve in four different capacities, *4201*
1999 Internet camera showing the site of a presidential assassination, *4274*

June 25

1798 Immigration law enacted by Congress, *6054*
1844 President married while in office, *4251*
1868 Workday of eight hours to be authorized by Congress, *7120*
1873 College president who was a woman, *2786*
1938 Minimum wage law enacted by Congress, *7157*
1953 Passenger to circle the world on commercial airlines in less than 100 hours, *8130*
1967 Worldwide live television program, *4975*
1993 AIDS policy coordinator for the federal government, *7286*
1999 State criminal prosecution for the sale of confidential personal information, *6977*

June 26

1614 Lottery, *1796*
1721 Inoculation against smallpox using material from human smallpox pustules, *5148*
1797 Plow patent, *1587*
1819 Bicycle patent, *7638*
1848 Pure food and drug law established by Congress, *7238*
1870 Boardwalk, *3416*
1894 Round-the-world bicycle trip by a woman, *7652*
1907 Savings bank life insurance, *1992*
1911 Transcontinental group tour by car, *8249*
1919 Bank wholly owned and operated by a state, *1740*
Illustrated tabloid, *4526*
1927 High-speed roller coaster, *1002*
1934 Federal gun control regulation, *6944*
1945 Treaty signed by a woman, *3898*
1947 Transatlantic mobile telephone call between two cars, *4898*
1950 Pilot to destroy an enemy airplane in the Korean War, *5801*
1951 Television program in color, *4951*

June 27

1564 Painting of an American scene by a European painter, *1011*
1652 Traffic law enacted by a colony, *8175*
1775 Paymaster general of the Continental Army, *5435*
1776 Execution by the Army, *5549*
1844 Presidential candidate to be assassinated, *3804*
1861 Union naval officer killed in the Civil War, *5703*
1911 Airplane flight under a bridge, *8027*
1923 Airplane refueling attempt in midair, *8054*
1929 Public demonstration of color television, *4987*
1950 Combat mission in the Korean War, *5802*
1969 Gay rights protest, *7448*
1970 President who was a jet pilot, *4270*
1988 Ban on surrogate motherhood enacted by a state, *2164*
2006 Campaign to promote citywide testing for the AIDS virus, *7296*

June 28

1687 Knighthood conferred on a person born in America, *3918*
1778 Revolutionary War conflict in which American and British troops met on equal terms, *5671*
1794 Warship builder, *5577*
1798 Prize money awarded by the Navy, *5579*
1832 Cholera epidemic, *5093*
1834 Geological survey authorized by Congress, *6491*
1845 Newspaper with a full page of woodcut engravings, *4578*
1877 Cricket magazine, *7632*
1884 American Derby horse race, *7800*
1894 Designation of Labor Day as a federal holiday, *2498*
1925 Caterpillar Club member who was a woman, *8059*
1935 Virus obtained in crystalline form, *6666*
1939 Transatlantic commercial airplane service, *8098*
1940 Registration of aliens by the federal government, *6091*
1956 Nuclear reactor built for private industrial research, *6622*
1962 Tae Kwon Do school, *7982*
1970 Gay pride march, *7449*
1976 Air Force Academy cadets who were women, *3127*
2006 Rocket built by college students to be launched from Cape Canaveral, *6801*

June 29

1810 Foreign missionary society, *6253*
1936 High-definition telecast, *4990*

July—*continued*

1980 Newspaper to publish an Internet edition, *4549*
1987 Principal chief of a major Native American tribe who was a woman, *3942*
1990 Solar-powered car race, *7627*
1991 Astronaut who was a Hispanic woman, *6831*
1992 Liver transplant using a baboon liver, *5377*
1994 High school team to achieve a perfect score in the International Mathematical Olympiad, *2984*
1995 High-resolution maps of the ocean floor, *4487*
Municipal Heat-Health Warning forecasting system, *6512*
1996 State economic development agency that was partly privatized, *4366*
1997 Teraflop computer, *6483*
AMBER Alert System, *7393*
1998 MP3 player, *4839*
2002 Museum of espionage, *3166*
2003 Year in which the heads of both major political parties were graduates of the same college, *4112*
City to import prescription drugs, *7292*

July 1

1731 Social library, *3000*
1776 Congressional vote on a declaration of independence, *3462*
1785 Copper cents minted by a state, *4006*
1795 Supreme Court chief justice whose nomination was not confirmed, *3736*
1827 Spanish newspaper, *4555*
1847 Postage stamps issued by the Post Office Department, *4717*
1851 Insurance board established by a state government, *1954*
1852 Body to lie in state in the Capitol rotunda, *3568*
1855 Registered mail, *4667*
1859 Gas journal, *6780*
Intercollegiate baseball game, *7488*
1862 Inheritance tax levied by Congress, *4414*
Revenue stamps issued by the federal government, *4415*
Passport fee, *6072*
Polygamy ban enacted by Congress, *7436*
1863 Free mail delivery in cities, *4675*
1867 Transpacific sidewheeler steamer, *8434*
1869 Patent issued to Thomas Alva Edison, *3995*
1870 Department of Justice, *4170*
1873 Patent examiner who was a woman, *3996*
1874 Zoo, *3142*
1881 International commercial telephone service, *4873*
1896 Life insurance policy rated substandard, *1991*
1898 Balloon destroyed by enemy gunfire, *5460*
1899 Rhodes Scholars, *2819*
1907 Centralized system of medical records, *5119*
1910 Bread factory that was completely automatic, *2412*
1919 Fire and tornado insurance fund enacted by a state, *1979*
1921 Sales tax enacted by a state, *4422*
1924 Transcontinental regular airmail service, *4696*
1927 Traffic rotary, *3423*
1930 Streamlined submarine, *8516*
1934 X-ray photograph of the entire body of a living person taken in a one-second exposure, *5134*
1937 Senate parliamentarian, *3679*
1941 Television commercial, *1547*
Navy task force assembled for foreign service, *5585*
1945 Labor antidiscrimination commission established by a state government, *7158*
1952 Drug treatment center for minors, *7081*
1961 Air raid shelter for a community, *7301*
1972 Navy admiral who was African-American, *5613*
2002 State to require child booster seats, *8283*
2007 State to mandate universal health insurance, *1987*

July 2

1717 Printed book auction catalog, *4433*
1776 Election law enacted by a colony granting voting rights to women, *3761*
1777 Slavery emancipation law enacted by a state, *6120*
1800 District land office, *6056*
1829 Catholic community of African-American nuns, *6264*
1862 Land grant for an agricultural college, *2762*
1864 National hall of fame, *3140*
1867 Elevated railroad, *8316*

July 5

1776 Printing of the Declaration of Independence, *3465*
1865 Secret service established by the federal government, *3842*
1900 National political convention at which a woman made a seconding speech, *4086*
1916 Transcontinental motorcycle trip by women, *8290*
1944 Rocket airplane for military use, *5485*
1950 Soldier killed in action in the Korean War, *5803*
1952 Vice presidential candidate who was an African-American woman, *3822*
1972 African-American director of the New York Stock Exchange, *1786*

July 6

1776 Newspaper to publish the Declaration of Independence, *3466*
1785 Decimal system of money, *4007*
1798 Deportation of aliens authorized by Congress, *6055*
1858 Shoe manufacturing machine, *2248*
1869 Sawmill to use a band saw, *1863*
1871 Baseball game between an all-white team and an all-African-American team, *7498*
1895 Shoot-the-chutes, *1005*
1899 Driver license board, *8188*
1905 International exchange of fingerprints, *7369*
1933 All-star major league baseball game, *7532*
1955 Seat belt law enacted by a state, *8268*
1961 District attorney who was African-American, *3725*
1970 No-fault divorce law enacted by a state, *2597*
1976 Naval Academy students who were women, *3128*
1997 Robot to conduct a roving exploration of the surface of another planet, *6882*

July 7

1802 Comic magazine, *4607*
1838 Steamboat inspection service established by Congress, *8429*
1849 Free public libraries authorized by a state, *3013*
1920 Radio compass on a naval airplane, *5477*
1935 Identification of human beings from the pattern formed by the blood vessels of the retina, *7381*
1943 Ambassador to Canada, *3897*
1946 Catholic saint who was an American citizen, *6309*
1948 Navy personnel in the regular Navy who were women, *5587*
1960 Public demonstration of a working laser, *6521*
1976 West Point cadets who were women, *3129*
State dinner televised from the White House, *4333*
1980 Solar-powered airplane to cross the English Channel, *8161*
2005 Foreign flag flown at the State Department, *3917*

July 8

1524 Kidnapping, *6921*
1663 Colonial charter of religious freedom for all faiths, *6196*
1693 Police uniforms, *7354*
1776 Public reading of the Declaration of Independence, *3467*
1796 Passport, *6053*
1800 Vaccination against smallpox using cowpox, *5149*
1805 Boxer to win distinction in the ring, *7590*
1809 Vaccination program offered by a city, *5151*
1856 Machine gun, *5852*
1861 Press censorship by military authorities, *4509*
1862 Revolving gun turret for ships, *5854*
1870 Trademark, *3980*
1892 National psychology society, *5225*
1897 Tuberculosis hospital for the poor established by a city, *5127*
1899 Golf champion born in America, *7762*
1916 National park east of the Mississippi River, *5991*
1923 President to visit Alaska and Canada while in office, *4315*
1924 African-American Olympic medalist to win an individual event, *7853*
1950 Officer killed in action in the Korean War, *5804*
1957 Circumnavigation of the world by a submarine, *8538*
1965 Flashbulb device with multiple flashbulbs, *4652*
1967 American Independent Party convention, *4102*

July 9

1776 Publication of the Declaration of Independence in another language, *3468*
1792 Agriculture professor at a college, *2721*
1808 Leather-splitting machine, *2122*
1847 Workday of 10 hours to be mandated by a state, *7116*
1864 Boiler inspection law enacted by a state, *7327*
1872 Doughnut cutter, *2280*
1875 Cantilever bridge, *3245*
1886 Coursing club, *7801*
1893 Surgical repair of a stab wound to the heart, *5345*
1910 Airplane to fly higher than a mile in altitude, *8018*
1914 Auction duplicate bridge championship, *7732*
1922 Swimmer to cover 100 meters freestyle in less than one minute, *7910*
1942 Theater designed for dance performances, *1054*
Capture of an American ship captain by a German submarine in World War II, *5784*
1947 Army officer who was a woman, *5449*
1953 Helicopter passenger service, *8132*
1965 Ambassador who was an African-American woman, *3904*

July 10

1791 Catholic seminary, *2720*
1795 Presidential amnesty issued to rebellious citizens, *4121*
1830 Antiquarian book business, *4448*
1863 Medal of Honor awarded to a Marine, *5506*
1866 Indelible pencil, *2678*
1890 Election law enacted by a state to grant voting rights to women after the adoption of the Constitution, *3773*
1902 Steel seven-masted schooner, *8441*
1908 Presidential candidate to appear in movie footage, *3815*
1933 Police radio system, *7379*
1934 President to visit South America while in office, *4316*
1949 Rectangular television tube, *4995*
1962 Telephone call conveyed by a privately owned satellite, *4909*
Transoceanic telecast by satellite, *5004*
Commercial satellite, *6857*
Swimmer to swim the English Channel underwater, *7914*

July 11

1656 Quakers to arrive in America, *6191*
1798 Army lieutenant general, *5439*
Marine band, *5562*
1832 Congressional representative to be censured, *3597*
1861 Mass expulsion from the Senate, *3663*
1870 School for African-American children established by a state, *2947*
1890 State library society, *3019*
1916 Grant-in-aid enacted by Congress to help the states build roads, *3421*
1919 Prisoners in a federal penitentiary to be employed in industry, *7012*
Golfer to play 180 holes in one day, *7768*
1934 President to go through the Panama Canal while in office, *4146*
1942 Distinguished Service Cross awarded in enemy-occupied territory, *5520*
1966 Sergeant major of the Army, *5451*
1997 Transplant of human embryo tissue, *5378*

July 12

1774 Declaration of independence by citizens of an American colony, *3458*
1798 Marine Corps major, *5560*
1881 Rotary jail, *7008*
1912 Foreign feature film exhibited, *1136*
1928 Outdoor scenes to be televised, *4931*
1957 President to fly in a helicopter, *4299*
1972 Acupuncture treatment center, *5075*
1976 Keynote speech by an African-American woman at a major party convention, *4075*
1984 Vice presidential candidate from a major political party who was a woman, *3833*
2006 Regeneration of spinal cord connections in animals, *6705*

July 13

1763 Germ warfare, *5838*
1787 Slavery ban enacted for a territory of the United States, *6122*
1836 Numbering system for patents, *3992*
1861 Congressional representative to be expelled, *3603*
Confederate general killed in the Civil War, *5704*
1875 Cash carrier system, *1669*
1912 Senator expelled for corrupt election practices, *3670*
1915 City orchestra supported by taxes, *1255*

July 13—*continued*

1936 Pensions paid by the federal government to workers in private industry, *7155*
1938 Television theater to be licensed, *4935*
1964 Nominee who was a woman to receive votes at the national convention of a major party, *4100*

July 14

1798 Tax levied by Congress directly on the states, *4406*
Federal law intended to intimidate the press, *4497*
1820 Lightship, *7341*
1853 World's fair, *1485*
1868 Tape measure, *2657*
1870 Pension granted to the widow of a president, *4227*
1885 Patent granted to an inventor who was an African-American woman, *3998*
1891 Corkboard patent, *3342*
1911 Airplane to land on the White House lawn, *4329*
1943 National monument dedicated to an African-American, *7190*
1945 Naval bombardment of the Japanese homeland in World War II, *5796*
1954 Radio sextant, *8507*
1959 Nuclear-powered cruiser, *8492*
1965 Spacecraft to transmit close-up photographs of Mars, *6869*
1972 Chairman of a major political party who was a woman, *4107*
1983 Openly gay member of Congress, *7456*
2006 Private space station prototype, *6892*

July 15

1792 Bridge on a large scale, *3231*
1856 Congressman censured for assaulting another, *3601*
1913 Senator elected by popular vote, *3672*
1920 Airplane flight between New York and Alaska, *8045*
1922 Platypus to be exhibited, *1395*
1929 Hotel at an airport, *1831*
1933 Round-the-world solo airplane flight, *8090*
1940 Betatron, *6733*
1952 Transatlantic helicopter flight, *8129*
1954 Jet airplane used for commercial transport, *8135*
1975 Astronauts to participate in an international spaceflight, *6820*
1985 Desktop publishing software, *6467*
1994 Movie that cost more than $100 million to make, *1181*
2002 Islamic terrorist who was born in America, *5835*

July 16

1769 Catholic mission in California, *6226*
1779 Revolutionary War bayonet charge, *5672*
1798 Health service established by the federal government, *7236*
1845 Regatta, *7568*
1867 Paint ready-mixed, *2656*
1877 Strike suppressed by federal troops in peacetime, *7127*
1912 Airplane torpedo, *5861*
1920 Radio telephone commercial service, *4886*
1926 Photographs taken under the sea in natural colors, *4631*
1935 Automatic parking meter, *8254*
1936 X-ray photograph showing the complete arterial circulation in an adult human, *5135*
1945 Atomic bomb explosion, *5871*
1946 Mobile overseas telephone call from a moving vehicle, *4895*
1969 Astronauts to land on the moon, *6814*
1971 Air Force general who was a woman, *5497*
1999 President to receive a bill from Congress by e-mail, *4166*

July 17

1734 Catholic infirmary, *5097*
1850 Photograph of a star other than the sun, *6399*
1861 Paper money issued by the federal government, *4027*
1862 Military service by African-Americans to be authorized by Congress, *5421*
1867 Dental school to be associated with a medical school, *3067*
1896 College cricket club team to tour England, *7633*
1933 Transcontinental flight made by African-Americans in their own airplane, *8091*
1953 Navy ace in Korea, *5810*
1954 Major league baseball game in which the majority of the players on one team were African-American, *7541*
1955 Electric power generated from nuclear energy to illuminate a town, *6620*

July 23

1827 Swimming school, *7908*
1829 Typewriter, *1662*
1846 War tax resister, *4412*
1885 State banking association, *1729*
1886 Daredevil to jump off the Brooklyn Bridge and survive, *1383*
1921 Broad jump to reach more than 25 feet, *7947*
1930 Transcontinental car trip driven entirely in reverse, *8253*
1937 Pituitary hormone, *5246*
1945 Railroad car with an observation dome, *8360*
1947 Navy jet airplane squadron, *5487*
1953 Transcontinental round-trip solo flight between sunrise and sunset, *8133*
1962 Live telecast to Europe by satellite, *4968*
1965 Coins bearing dates other than the year of issue, *4046*
1972 Satellite composite map of the United States, *4486*
1996 Television station to regularly broadcast high-definition television, *4982*
1999 Major motion picture produced and exhibited entirely with digital technology, *1188*
Woman to serve as commander of a space flight, *6834*

July 24

1824 Opinion poll, *4502*
1860 Doctoral degree awarded by an American university, *2761*
1866 State readmitted to the Union after the Civil War, *4351*
1934 Ptarmigan, *5955*
1946 Atomic bomb underwater explosion, *5873*
1950 Rocket launched from Cape Canaveral, *6793*
1956 Adaptable railroad freight car, *8363*
1998 Capitol Police Officers killed in the line of duty, *3580*

July 25

1832 Railroad accident, *8307*
1854 Paper collar, *2247*
1863 Monument to commemorate the Civil War, *7172*
1866 General of the U.S. Army, *5442*
Navy officer to become an admiral, *5601*
1871 Carousel patent, *1001*
Perforated wrapping paper, *2021*
1916 Zoning ordinance, *3533*
1918 District attorney who was a woman, *3715*
1923 Mimeographed daily newspaper, *4530*
1934 President to visit Hawaii while in office, *4317*
1939 Musical comedy to be shown on television, *1462*
1952 Commonwealth of the United States, *6095*
1965 Surgical operation on a bull to correct a sperm block, *5407*
1997 Human embryonic stem cell lines, *6691*

July 26

1775 Postmaster general under the Continental Congress, *4657*
1777 Navy recruiting campaign, *5575*
1859 Intercollegiate regatta, *7880*
1865 African-American to earn a Ph.D., *2768*
1866 Irrigation law enacted by Congress, *1618*
1880 Steam distribution plant, *6598*
1908 Olympic athlete from the United States to win the marathon race, *7854*
1947 Department of Defense, *4190*
1958 Telecast from the stratosphere, *5002*
1963 Geosynchronous satellite, *6859*
1990 Comprehensive civil rights legislation for people with disabilities, *7047*

July 27

1775 Surgeon general of the Continental Army, *5436*
1784 French newspaper, *4552*
1789 Department of State, *4171*
1868 Uniforms for mail carriers, *4678*
1874 Musical with an American theme and original score, *1440*
1933 Execution for kidnapping, *7015*
1971 Brokerage firm whose shares were traded by a major stock exchange, *1787*
2005 TV drama about an actual war in progress, *4985*

July 28

1777 Election law enacted by a state to grant universal voting rights to freemen, *3762*
1862 Railroad post office, *4674*
1866 Metric system usage to be approved by Congress, *1486*

Monument ordered by the federal government from a sculptor who was a woman, *7173*
1869 National union for women, *7122*
1875 Baseball game in which a team had no hits in nine innings, *7502*
1882 Accounting society, *1705*
1903 Bank president who was a woman, *1732*
1933 Singing telegram, *4861*

July 29

1773 Schoolhouse west of the Alleghenies, *6227*
1847 Norwegian newspaper, *4557*
1865 Newspaper published at sea, *4512*
1870 Road pavement of sheet asphalt, *3417*
1932 Distinguished Flying Cross awarded to a woman, *6903*
1949 Gas turbine used by an electrical utility company, *6571*
1959 Jetway, *8146*
1978 Football game in which referees were allowed to check television instant replays, *7718*
1980 Human antibodies produced artificially, *5258*
1998 Fundraising (semipostal) stamp, *4758*
2003 Major league baseball player to hit grand slams from both sides of the plate in one game, *7550*

July 30

1619 Colonial legislative assembly, *4385*
1774 Price sheet for commodities, *1521*
1844 Yacht club, *7567*
1850 Meat biscuit, *2354*
1874 Baseball teams to travel abroad, *7500*
1898 Car advertisement in a specialty magazine, *1533*
1909 Airplane purchased by the federal government, *8013*
1946 Rocket to attain a 100-mile altitude, *6791*
1956 Designation of "In God We Trust" as the national motto, *4032*
1965 Health insurance plan enacted by Congress, *3856*

July 31

1790 Patent granted by the federal government, *3987*
1792 Building erected by the federal government, *3839*
1809 Railroad track that was practical, *8381*
1849 Breech-loading cannon, *5848*
1876 Coast Guard officers' training school, *3106*
1912 Movie censorship law enacted by Congress, *1137*
1918 Dish set made in America for the White House, *4331*
1930 Airship to land and take off from an oceangoing steamship, *8079*
1964 Navy nuclear task force to circumnavigate the globe without refueling, *5592*
Photographs of the moon in close-up, *6411*
Spacecraft to transmit close-up photographs of the lunar surface, *6868*
1971 Astronauts to ride a vehicle on the moon, *6817*
1999 Moon burial, *2312*
2004 City with complete WiFi coverage, *7422*

August

1619 African slaves in the English colonies, *6111*
1746 Poetry collection by an African-American writer, *1068*
1777 Mine barrage, *5839*
1787 Songbook of secular songs, *1223*
1788 Cotton mill, *2117*
1791 Supreme Court decision, *3734*
1794 Methodist church for African-Americans in the North, *6238*
1796 Gaslights for display, *1358*
1805 Ice exported, *2337*
1817 Paper made by machine, *2010*
1830 Double-deck railroad coaches, *8347*
1833 Army cavalry unit, *5417*
1861 Camp for boys, *2185*
1870 Clearinghouse for stocks and bonds, *1774*
1894 Actor to have an exclusive movie contract, *1116*
1905 Movie spoof, *1127*
1908 Child hygiene bureau, *7273*
1913 Gyroscope, *8035*
1921 Correspondence school to offer instruction in Braille, *2968*
1932 Cooperative store operated by women, *2097*
1933 Game management chair at a college, *2850*
1934 Pressure suit, *8092*
1941 Plastic car, *8259*
1954 Hurricane name to be retired, *6506*
1962 *Spider-Man* comic book, *1106*
1963 Supercomputer, *6431*

August—*continued*

1973 Nazi death camp guard to be deported, *6103*
1974 Magazine about recreational drugs, *7086*
1979 Astronaut who was Jewish, *6822*
Astronaut who was of Asian descent, *6823*
1981 Astronaut who was Hispanic, *6824*
1987 Swimmer to cross the Bering Strait, *7916*
1992 Food guide pyramid, *7284*
1996 Green Party national convention, *4109*
2003 School district to install surveillance cameras in all its classrooms, *2988*

August 1

1776 Jewish soldier killed in the Revolutionary War, *5658*
1787 Printed copies of the Constitution, *3482*
1790 Census to use racial categories, *6151*
1841 Commercial rating agency, *1770*
1861 Patent issued by the Confederate States of America, *3994*
Former president to serve as an official of an enemy government, *4135*
1872 Natural gas pipeline constructed over a long distance, *6597*
1873 Cable car put into service, *8369*
1874 Label patent, *3997*
1886 Laboratory for the study of parasites in livestock, *5404*
1893 Biscuits of shredded wheat, *2394*
Navy medical school, *3078*
1906 Diamonds in actual rock, *3394*
1907 Airplane unit in the Army, *5461*
1911 Pilot licensed by the Aero Club of America who was a woman, *8028*
1912 Marine pilot, *5565*
1930 Photographic flashbulbs, *4648*
Hydroelectric power plant operated by a county, *6565*
1951 Medal of Honor awarded to a Marine in the Korean War, *5532*
1953 Aluminum-faced building, *3309*
1957 Insurance company to insure the lives of animals exclusively, *1972*
Commercial building with solar heating, *3313*
1960 Submarine to make a submerged passage through the Northwest Passage, *8543*
1963 Postage stamp with fluorescent tagging, *4745*
1972 Vice presidential candidate of a major political party to resign before the election, *3828*
1981 Music video on MTV, *1279*

August 2

1791 Patent granted jointly to a father and son, *3989*
1819 Parachute jump from a balloon, *7995*
1862 Army ambulance corps, *5198*
1923 President and First Lady to die during the term for which he had been elected, *4258*
1937 Marijuana ban enacted by Congress, *7079*
1946 Nuclear product for peacetime use, *6618*
2005 City to require "green" construction for low-income housing, *5935*

August 3

1492 Letter containing a description of America, *3452*
1750 Book on teaching methodology, *2899*
1804 Peace medals struck by the United States Mint, *4021*
1852 Intercollegiate rowing race, *7878*
1861 Balloon carrier, *8471*
1882 Immigration ban enacted by Congress, *6080*
1904 Use of "American" as an adjective, *3503*
1922 Drama broadcast on radio, *1451*
1942 Navy officer commissioned in the U.S. Naval Reserve who was a woman, *5606*
1945 Color news photograph transmitted by radio fax for publication, *4587*
1946 Theme park, *1008*
1949 Designation of Flag Day as a national holiday, *2503*
1958 Crossing of the North Pole underwater by a submerged submarine, *8540*
2005 In-flight repair of a space shuttle exterior, *6891*

August 4

1790 Bonds issued by the federal government, *1766*
Coast guard service, *5542*
Naval protection, *5576*
1894 Railroad to use an electric engine, *8323*
1921 Tennis match broadcast on radio, *7927*
1930 Bobsled run, *7975*
1937 Okapi, *5957*

1942 President to become a godfather to a member of the British royal family, *4262*
1956 Motorcycle to exceed 200 miles per hour, *8291*
1977 Department of Energy, *4206*

August 5

1799 Supreme Court decision in a matter between states, *3738*
1858 Transatlantic telegraph cable, *4853*
1861 Income tax levied by Congress, *4413*
1891 Travelers checks, *1731*
1892 Commemorative coin, *4037*
1909 Corporation tax levied by Congress, *4418*
1911 Airplane race between cities, *7678*
1914 Electric traffic lights equipped with noise signals, *8204*
1921 Pulitzer Prize for an editorial cartoon, *4767*
Radio broadcast of a baseball game with a play-by-play description, *7529*
1923 Swimmer from the United States to swim the English Channel, *7911*
1926 Movie with sound to be released as a feature, *1147*
1963 Nuclear arms-control treaty, *3902*
1964 Navy pilot shot down and captured in North Vietnam, *5813*
1968 Political convention to be televised in color, *4098*
1990 Round-the-world solo sailing trip by an African-American, *8547*
2006 Sportscaster who was a woman to be inducted into the Pro Football Hall of Fame, *7720*

August 6

1727 Catholic convent, *6213*
1776 Shaker religious community, *6230*
1819 Military school, *3101*
1832 Phrenologist, *5021*
1846 Warehouse legislation enacted by Congress, *2073*
1861 Federal law to emancipate slaves, *6133*
1890 Execution by electrocution, *7009*
1912 Progressive Party national convention, *4089*
1914 American to sail to Europe to fight in World War I, *5729*
1926 Swimmer who was an American woman to swim the English Channel, *7912*
1945 Atomic bomb explosion over enemy territory, *5797*
1954 Television commercial in color to appear on a local show, *1552*
1993 Head of one of the armed services who was a woman, *5499*
1996 Scientific evidence for life on Mars, *6800*

August 7

1679 Great Lakes vessel, *8404*
1789 Department of War, *4172*
Lighthouse built after American independence, *7338*
1794 Presidential commission, *4120*
1807 Steamboat to make regular trips, *8416*
1854 Republican Party convention, *4063*
1859 Church for deaf people, *6258*
1869 Photograph of the sun's corona made during a total solar eclipse, *6400*
1888 Revolving door, *3286*
1942 American offensive in the Pacific in World War II, *5785*
1953 Navy-Marine Corps Medal for Heroism awarded to a woman, *5534*
1959 Satellite to transmit photographs of the earth, *6845*
1974 Tightrope walker to span two skyscrapers, *1407*
2005 Podcast from space, *6843*

August 8

1797 Medical journal, *5291*
1865 Streamlined railroad train, *8393*
1866 Queen to visit the United States, *3924*
1876 Mimeograph, *2048*
1900 International tennis matches for the Davis Cup challenge trophy, *7926*
1933 Savings and loan association established by the federal government, *1744*
1942 Enemy saboteurs executed in the United States, *5786*
1950 Swimmer who was a woman to swim the English Channel in both directions, *7913*
1958 Presidential Unit Citation award in peacetime, *6910*

August 9

1607 Thanksgiving worship service, *6172*
1829 Locomotive for railroad use, *8331*
1848 Free Soil Party convention, *4062*
1859 Escalator patent, *3277*
1892 Two-way telegraph, *4856*
1893 Bowling magazine, *7581*
1916 National park to contain an active volcano, *5992*

August 9—*continued*

1939 Tennis tournament to be shown on television, *7929*
1944 Public service symbol of the federal government, *5919*
1971 Airport baggage scanning system, *8154*
1974 President to resign, *4157*
President who came to the office through appointment rather than election, *4158*
1989 Chairman of the Joint Chiefs of Staff who was African-American, *5456*

August 10

1821 State west of the Mississippi River to be admitted to the Union, *4344*
1869 Movie projector patent, *1205*
1885 Electric streetcars commercially operated, *8370*
1886 Welding by the electric process, *1894*
1889 Photograph of a meteor, *6402*
1960 American flag to orbit the earth, *3506*
1976 Soccer player to score 12 points in one game, *7900*
1988 Compensation of Japanese-Americans interned during World War II, *5820*

August 11

1860 Silver mill, *1932*
1861 Senator to address the Senate in military uniform, *3664*
1874 Sprinkler head, *7329*
1896 Electric socket operated by a pull chain, *2569*
1909 Radio SOS call from an American ship, *7350*
1924 Newsreels showing presidential candidates, *4532*
1928 Presidential nomination ceremony broadcast on radio, *3817*
1942 Movie star who was a weapons inventor, *1166*
1951 Major league baseball game to be televised in color, *7534*
1960 Space capsule recovered from an orbiting satellite, *6850*
1972 Sailors assigned to regular Navy shipboard duty who were women, *5593*
1980 Subcompact car with front wheel drive, *8276*
1997 President to use the line-item veto, *4163*

August 12

1585 Letters written in English in America, *3454*
1776 Military intelligence unit, *5659*
1834 Dental amalgam for filling teeth, *5081*
1851 Sewing machine equipped with a rocking treadle or double treadle, *2617*
1898 Island territory annexed by the federal government, *6083*
1918 Airmail regular service, *4692*
Concrete barge, *8447*
1923 Portable movie camera, *1209*
1953 Transatlantic solo boat journey by a woman, *8537*
1955 Minimum hourly wage of one dollar, *7161*
1960 Communications satellite, *6851*
1977 Free atmospheric flight by a space shuttle, *6875*
1981 IBM personal computer, *6462*
2005 Law against human smuggling enacted by a state, *6984*

August 13

1587 Native American to become a Protestant, *6169*
1751 Academy, *2697*
1838 Astronomical observations book, *6776*
1889 Pay telephone, *4876*
1918 Marine reserve member who was a woman, *5566*
Cargo ship from the United States attacked by a submerged German submarine in World War I, *5732*
1928 Airmail service from ship to shore, *4698*
Standard broadcast station to transmit a television image, *4932*
1935 Roller derby, *7875*
1946 Soldering gun, *2671*
1955 Guaranteed 52-week wage in a major industry, *7162*
1970 No-fault car insurance law enacted by a state, *1973*

August 14

1775 Quartermaster of the Continental Army, *5437*
1776 Land grant to deserters from the British Army during the Revolutionary War, *5660*
1820 Eye hospital, *5102*
1834 Ice-making machine, *2274*
1888 Electric meter, *6552*
1911 Airplane rescue at sea by another airplane, *8029*

1917 Gyroscopic stabilizer, *8501*
1924 Radio two-way broadcast from an airplane, *4790*
1934 Revenue stamp printed by the Post Office Department, *4425*
1935 Federal family assistance program, *3848*
National identification scheme for American citizens, *3849*
1936 National Union for Social Justice national convention, *4095*
1959 Photograph from space showing the earth, *6409*
1965 Congressional page who was African-American, *3622*
1966 Photograph of the earth taken from the moon, *6412*
Space probe to achieve lunar orbit, *6871*
1976 Softball game of 365 innings, *7986*
1982 National Navajo Code Talkers Day, *5772*
2005 Chef at the White House who was a woman, *4335*

August 15

1635 Hurricane of record, *5897*
1790 Catholic bishop appointed to serve in the United States, *6240*
1812 West Point graduate killed in action, *3099*
1814 Museum especially constructed as a museum and art gallery, *3136*
1848 Dental chair, *5082*
1908 Navy mail service, *4688*
1911 Hydrogenated vegetable shortening, *2413*
1917 Army gas regiment, *5425*
1930 Submarine escape training tank, *8517*
1936 Federally funded low-income housing project, *3536*
Union Party convention, *4096*
1947 Commercial telephone service on railroad trains for passengers, *4899*
1953 Navy chairman of the Joint Chiefs of Staff, *5610*
1954 Water skier to jump 100 feet, *7992*
1957 Air Force chairman of the Joint Chiefs of Staff, *5495*
1970 Professional football game in which a woman participated, *7716*
1985 AIDS antidiscrimination law, *5096*

August 16

1815 Peace society, *7202*
1829 Conjoined twins, *2148*
1898 Roller coaster with a loop-the-loop, *1006*
1902 Laboratory for the study of human parasites, *5168*
1916 Bird protection international treaty, *5950*
1920 Major league baseball player killed in a game, *7526*
1963 Naval War College students who were African-American, *3122*
1999 Trial broadcast by the court over the Internet, *6978*

August 17

1790 Presidential tribute to freedom of religion, *6241*
1809 Disciples of Christ meeting, *6252*
1835 Wrench patent, *2647*
1859 Airmail dispatched from a post office in a balloon, *4670*
1891 Public bathhouse to offer showers, *7240*
1978 Transatlantic balloon flight, *8160*
1998 President to give testimony before a grand jury during his term in office, *4164*
1999 Ambassador who was Muslim, *3915*

August 18

1587 Child born of English parents in America, *6010*
1734 Physician born in America who was graduated from a foreign medical school, *5013*
1840 Class photograph, *4619*
National dental society, *5216*
1882 Yiddish theater performance, *1444*
1891 Price tags, *2091*
1896 Tennis champions who were brothers, *7925*
1908 Airship ordered by the federal government, *8008*
1913 Veterans of Foreign Wars of the United States meeting, *5623*
1926 Weather map to be telecast, *4924*
1929 Transcontinental air derby for women, *7681*
1931 Plant patent, *1648*
1937 First-day special cancellation of a postage stamp, *4737*
1960 Photograph bounced off a satellite, *4637*
1965 State law to end de facto segregation in schools, *6146*

August 19

1812 Marine who was a woman, *5564*
Naval action of importance in the War of 1812, *5682*
1918 Fighter plane, *5476*
1929 Airship made completely of metal, *8069*
1942 Pilot from the United States to shoot down a German fighter plane in World War II, *5787*
Soldier from the United States to land on French soil in World War II, *5788*
1957 Balloon flight to rise higher than 100,000 feet, *8144*
1960 Space capsule recovered in midair from an orbiting satellite, *6852*
1998 Live surgery broadcast on the Internet, *5379*
1999 Chief White House counsel who was a woman, *4167*

August 20

1833 First Lady who was the grandmother of a president, *4222*
1867 Cartridge belt patent, *5857*
1908 Post office aboard a naval vessel, *4689*
1910 Pilot to fire a gun from an airplane, *5464*
1911 Telegraph message sent around the world by commercial telegraph, *4858*
1912 Quarantine law for plants enacted by Congress, *7275*
1920 Commercial radio station licensed, *4808*
1930 Demonstration of home reception of television, *4988*
1971 Electronic pocket calculator, *6525*
1975 Spacecraft to land on Mars, *6874*
1999 Federal conviction for Internet piracy, *6979*

August 21

1781 Slave to be emancipated by a court, *6121*
1831 Slave rebellion after the Revolution, *6128*
1841 Venetian blinds to be patented, *2539*
1862 Paper money fractional currency, *4029*
1878 National society of lawyers, *3969*
1912 Eagle Scout, *2191*
1914 Newspaper circulation audit, *4525*
1923 Airport runway illumination, *8055*
1928 Puppet show to be televised, *1453*
1959 State admitted to the Union that was separated by a substantial body of water, *4361*
1965 Astronaut to orbit the earth on two trips, *6806*

August 22

1654 Jews to arrive in America, *6030*
1670 Native American preacher of Christianity, *6197*
1771 Dwarf exhibited as a theatrical attraction, *1354*
1822 Printing press for printing wallpaper in color, *2036*
1851 Yacht from the United States to win an international yacht race, *7569*
1865 Soap in liquid form, *2215*
1902 President to ride in a car, *4293*
1909 Airplane race won by an American in Europe, *7675*
1912 Navy dental corps, *5206*
1928 Remote television pickup, *4933*
1939 Spray can, *2002*
1942 Ship transported overland across the Rocky Mountains, *8486*

August 23

1784 State denied admission into the Union, *4338*
1853 Bank clearinghouse, *1722*
1859 Hotel with an elevator, *1816*
1861 African-American to enlist in the United States armed forces during the Civil War, *5706*
1865 Trial of a war criminal by the federal government, *5721*
1892 Printed streetcar transfers, *8372*
1900 National business organization for African-Americans, *1496*
1904 Tire chains, *8195*
1956 Transcontinental nonstop helicopter flight, *8141*
1963 Illuminated nine-hole regulation golf course, *7777*
1977 Human-powered aircraft, *8159*

August 24

1675 Catholic holy orders, *6199*
1676 Court-martial in a colony, *5548*
1853 Village improvement society, *7206*
1869 Waffle iron patent, *2279*
1912 Parcel post service, *4691*
1932 Transcontinental nonstop airplane flight by a woman, *8088*
1950 United Nations delegate who was African-American, *3901*
1951 Air Force Medal of Honor for action in the Korean War, *5533*
1959 Senator of Asian ancestry, *3685*

1964 Catholic mass in English, *6321*
1971 Woman to serve as patent examiner-in-chief, *3996*

August 25

1814 President to face enemy gunfire while in office, *4126*
1828 State labor party, *4068*
1830 Race between a locomotive and a horse-drawn vehicle, *7793*
1831 Bedspring manufacturing patent, *2545*
1840 Seeding machine, *1606*
1886 International polo series, *7869*
1902 Arabic daily newspaper, *4568*
1920 Olympic gold medalist from the United States who was a woman, *7856*
1925 Miniature television tube, *4986*
Labor union of African-American workers, *7150*
1941 Health insurance clause in a labor contract, *1984*
1958 Pension for presidents and their widows, *4152*
1997 Voting rights in space, *3787*

August 26

1776 Pension law enacted by Congress, *7099*
1790 State historical society, *7469*
1857 National organization of teachers, *2943*
1873 Public school kindergarten, *2949*
1884 Linotype machine, *2051*
1920 Constitutional amendment proposal guaranteeing women the right to vote, *3780*
1938 Radio broadcast from a tape recording, *4799*
1939 Major league baseball game to be shown on television, *7534*
1954 Editorial to be broadcast over radio and television, *4542*
1968 National political convention to propose African-Americans for the offices of president and vice president, *4103*

August 27

1650 Expedition of Englishmen to cross the Allegheny Mountains, *6029*
1665 Theatrical performance, *1411*
1667 Cyclone of record, *5899*
1776 Major battle lost by American forces, *5661*
1787 Steamboat to carry a man, *8409*
1856 Industrial school for girls, *2935*
1859 Oil well that was commercially productive, *6586*
1889 Metal clarinet, *1305*
1910 Radio broadcast sent from an airplane, *4782*
1959 Ship to fire a Polaris missile, *5885*
1968 Ambassador assassinated in office, *3906*
2005 Natural disaster to cause the evacuation of an entire city, *5936*

August 28

1798 Vineyard, *1588*
1830 Passenger locomotive, *8332*
1867 Territory annexed by the federal government beyond the nation's continental limits, *6074*
1884 Photograph of a tornado, *5907*
1911 Gyrocompass installed on an American naval vessel, *8500*
1918 American Bar Association members who were women, *3971*
1922 Radio commercial, *1537*
International golf match, *7770*
1929 State police radio system, *7375*
1957 Senate filibuster to last for more than 24 hours, *3684*
1972 Air Force ace in Vietnam, *5819*
1994 Golf champion of African-American and Asian ancestry, *7782*
2000 Summit conference of world religions, *6333*
2006 Major sports facility named for a woman, *7935*

August 29

1758 Reservation for Native Americans established by a state, *6039*
1817 Abolition newspaper, *4501*
1861 Confederate forts to surrender in the Civil War, *5707*
1866 Cog railroad, *8315*
1885 Unofficial boxing match under the Marquis of Queensberry rules, *7598*
1889 International professional tennis contest, *7924*
1892 Baseball player to catch a ball dropped from the Washington Monument, *7516*
1893 Slide fastener, *2256*
1896 Chop suey, *2399*
1916 Coast Guard aviation unit, *5470*
1929 Passenger transfer from an airship to an airplane, *8070*
1958 Air Force academy, *3119*

August 29—*continued*

1962 Television news commentator who was African-American, *4602*
1965 Astronaut to converse with an aquanaut, *6807*
1966 Parachute jumper snagged by airplane in midair, *8151*
1969 Hijacking of an American airliner by terrorists, *5817*
1984 Bioterror attack on American soil in modern times, *6962*
1989 Congressional representative who was a Hispanic woman, *3634*

August 30

1637 Synod held in America, *6180*
1664 Bookbinder, *4429*
1842 Tariff enacted by Congress to prevent the importation of obscene literature and pictures, *4411*
Narcotics tariff enacted by Congress, *7061*
1875 Music professor at a college, *2789*
1884 Theater to employ women as ushers, *1447*
1890 Meat inspection law enacted by Congress, *7255*
1909 Apprentice continuation school, *3209*
1926 Hambletonian harness horse race for three-year-olds, *7807*
1929 Submarine emergency air supply container, *8515*
1931 Airplane race of importance in which both men and women were contestants, *7682*
1962 Presidential hot line, *4153*
1963 International postal card, *4713*
1983 Astronaut to fly in space who was African-American, *6826*
1997 Women's National Basketball League champions, *7564*

August 31

1809 Catholic magazine in English, *6358*
1826 Circumnavigation of the globe by a warship, *8528*
1842 Navy bureau of medicine and surgery, *5196*
1881 National tennis championship matches, *7921*
1886 Earthquake of consequence to be recorded, *5908*
1904 Olympic medalist who was African-American, *7853*
1910 Airplane flight over water, *8019*
1920 News program on radio, *4527*
1934 All-star football game, *7708*
1935 National skeet tournament, *7888*
1955 Microwave television station, *4961*
Solar-powered car, *8269*
1974 Merchant Marine Academy cadets who were women, *3126*
2005 Comprehensive comparison of the human and chimpanzee genomes, *6701*

September

1639 Autopsy officially recorded, *2292*
1782 Die for the Great Seal of the United States, *3478*
Keeper of the Great Seal of the United States, *3479*
1784 Motorboat, *8408*
1786 Illustrations of both sides of the Great Seal of the United States, *3481*
1811 Steamboat to sail down the Mississippi, *8418*
1821 College alumni association, *2733*
1826 Children's magazine of literary merit, *2177*
1829 Horse racing magazine, *7792*
1847 Tourist guide with train schedules, *1813*
1852 College professor who was a woman, *2752*
1854 Orphan train from New York, *2182*
1859 Public school for Asian-American children, *2937*
1867 Theological school that was multisectarian, *2772*
1871 College entrance plan using certified schools, *2784*
1880 Italian newspaper, *4564*
1882 Honors program offered by a university, *2796*
1883 Apartment house cooperative, *2527*
1886 Bill bearing the likeness of a woman, *4036*
1889 County high school, *2956*
1893 Water filtration system for bacterial purification of a city water supply, *7415*
1894 Antitoxin laboratory established by a public health department, *7261*
1895 Movies with color, *1118*
1897 Country day school, *2958*
1898 Diesel engine built for commercial service, *8186*
1903 License plate issued by a state, *8192*
1910 Airplane flying school for military officers, *3111*
1923 Combined newspaper, *4531*
1926 Film-developing machine, *4646*

September 1

September 2

September 3

1639 Lawyer disbarred, *3947*
1777 American flag flown in battle, *3473*
1783 Treaty between the federal government and a nation with which it had been at war, *3879*
1872 Presidential candidate who was Catholic, *3810*
1885 Naval war college, *3109*
1894 National championship stroke-play golf match, *7753*
1895 Professional football game, *7700*
1900 Union Reform Party convention, *4087*
1935 Commodity exchange member who was a woman, *1781*

September 4

1632 Road construction law enacted by a colony, *3402*
1645 Lutheran church, *6185*
1777 American flag on the high seas, *3474*
1804 Members of the U.S. armed forces to die in combat on an overseas mission, *5679*
1813 Religious weekly newspaper, *4499*
1882 Newspaper printing plant to install electricity, *2050*
Dynamo that was successful, *6549*
Electric power station with a central source, *6550*
1883 Newsboy, *4519*
1885 Self-service restaurant, *1823*
1888 Camera to use film rolls, *4643*
1904 Hotel with individually controlled air conditioning and heating in every room, *1828*
1917 Soldiers in the American army killed by German bombers in World War I, *5744*
1919 General of the Armies of the United States, *5443*
1923 Rigid airship, *8056*
1935 Truck completely streamlined, *8294*
1937 Bicycle champion who was a woman, *7656*
1950 Helicopter rescue of an American pilot behind enemy lines, *5805*
1951 Transcontinental telecast received on the East Coast, *4952*
1953 Discovery of different sleep states, *6671*
1956 Congressional representative reelected after serving a prison term, *3619*
1964 Orbiting geophysical observatory, *6860*
1972 Horse race for a purse of more than $1 million, *7819*

September 5

1721 Painter to obtain a public commission, *1017*
1774 Continental Congress session, *3548*
President of the Continental Congress, *3549*
1776 Navy uniforms, *5574*
1836 President of the Republic of Texas, *3922*
1854 Publishing society, *4452*
1867 Cow town, *3522*
1882 Labor Day parade, *1379*
1885 Gasoline pump, *1868*
1923 Smokescreen for concealing the movement of troops and ships, *5865*
1925 Musk ox, *5951*
1943 Airplane human pickup, *8110*
1953 Nuclear reactor privately operated, *6735*
1989 Drug control chief appointed by the federal government, *7089*

September 6

1819 Lathe, *2645*
1866 Delegate to a national political convention who was African-American, *4066*
1869 Coal mine disaster, *6594*
1882 Bicycle trip of 100 miles sponsored by a club, *7645*
1892 Gasoline tractor, *1634*
1920 Boxing match broadcast on radio, *7601*
1947 Ship from which a long-range rocket was launched, *8488*

September 7

1724 Congregation of Brethren, *6210*
1774 Continental Congress assembly to be opened with prayer, *3550*
1776 Submarine built for use in war, *8508*
1792 Mint of the United States, *4014*
1816 Steamboat on the Great Lakes, *8422*
1822 Prison treadmill, *6995*
1880 Clay pigeon target for trapshooting, *7884*
1888 Incubator for premature babies, *5175*
1892 Boxing match under the Marquis of Queensberry rules, *7598*
1896 Car race on a racetrack, *7617*
1899 Parade of automobiles, *1389*
1903 Motorcycle association, *7848*
1909 Junior high school, *2964*
1921 Beauty pageant to be held nationwide, *1394*
1927 Image transmitted by television, *4927*
International lifeboat race, *7576*

1957 Circumnavigation of the North American continent by a ship, *8539*
1993 Surgeon general who was African-American, *7287*
2001 Transatlantic telesurgery, *5385*

September 8

1565 Thanksgiving meal shared by European settlers and Native Americans, *2484*
Permanent European settlement in America, *6008*
Catholic parish, *6167*
1636 College to open in America, *2683*
1760 Knighthood conferred on American soil, *3920*
1866 Sextuplets, *2149*
1868 Athletic club, *7936*
1892 Version of the Pledge of Allegiance, *3500*
1900 Hurricane to cause extensive destruction, *5914*
1949 Marine who was an African-American woman, *5569*
1953 Transcontinental express bus service, *8222*
1965 Baseball player to play all nine positions in one game, *7546*
1974 Motorcycle jump across a river canyon, *1408*
President to receive a presidential pardon, *4159*

September 9

1776 Use of the name United States instead of United Colonies, *3469*
1830 Professional American aeronaut, *7996*
1836 Transcendentalist literary work, *1087*
1841 Heavyweight boxing match to last longer than 100 rounds, *7594*
1843 Ice cream freezer, *2350*
1850 State on the Pacific coast to be admitted to the Union, *4348*
1866 Theater ticket agency, *1438*
1885 Economics association, *6723*
1893 First Lady to give birth during her husband's term in office, *4229*
Child born in the White House who was the offspring of a president, *4328*
1895 Important bowling convention to standardize rules, *7580*
1898 Log-rolling national championship tournament, *7968*
1901 Car hill-climbing contest, *7618*
Long-distance car race, *7619*
1908 Airplane endurance flight exceeding one hour, *8009*
1934 Rocket to break the sound barrier, *6789*
1945 Computer bug, *6423*
1965 Department of Housing and Urban Development, *4198*
1966 Federal district court judge who was an African-American woman, *3726*
1969 Postage stamp depicting a living American, *4751*
1970 School district to implement court-ordered busing to achieve racial integration, *6148*
1982 Private space launch, *6876*

September 10

1785 Treaty entered into by the federal government after independence, *3882*
1794 College that was nondenominational, *2722*
1813 Defeat of a British naval squadron in the War of 1812, *5685*
1842 First Lady to die during her husband's term in office, *4225*
1875 National forestry association, *5975*
1913 Coast-to-coast paved road, *3420*
1960 Planned nationwide shutdown of air traffic, *8147*

September 11

1789 Secretary of the treasury, *4169*
1841 Collapsible tube, *2650*
1850 Theater ticket scalpers, *1433*
Private railroad car, *8350*
1875 Comic strip in a newspaper, *4580*
1883 Mail chute, *4681*
1910 Trackless trolley system, *8374*
1928 Play to be shown on television, *1454*
Transcontinental bus service, *8220*
1946 Long-distance car-to-car telephone conversation, *4896*
1952 Artificial aortic valve, *5358*
1954 Miss America contest to be televised, *1404*
1998 Government report posted on the Internet before its publication on paper, *3866*
2001 Unplanned nationwide shutdown of air traffic, *8171*

September 12

1790 Secretary of war, *4172*
1792 Metal purchased for coinage, *4015*
1808 Bible translated into English in America, *6357*

September 12—*continued*

1866 Broadway hit musical, *1439*
1869 Prohibition Party convention, *4067*
1918 Tank operated by Army troops, *5863*
1935 Medical college founded as a Jewish institution, *3094*
1941 Capture of a German ship by an American ship in World War II, *5758*
1952 Railroad freight cars with compartments, *8362*
1956 Coal pipeline, *6611*
1958 Integrated circuit, *6522*
1975 Adjustable stadium, *3319*
1992 African-American woman astronaut to fly in space, *6826*
Husband and wife to fly in space together, *6832*

September 13

1663 Labor protest in a colony, *7096*
1788 Presidential election, *3793*
1789 Loan to the United States, *1758*
1790 Agricultural dictionary, *1584*
1826 Rhinoceros to be exhibited, *1365*
1842 Boxer to die in the ring, *7593*
1881 Incandescent light bulbs in widespread use, *6546*
1898 Celluloid photographic film, *4644*
1899 Car accident fatality, *8238*
1939 Submarine to be refloated, *8518*
1948 Public high school to specialize in the performing arts, *2974*
1956 Taconite production on a large scale, *3396*
1962 Launching silos for Atlas F missiles, *5889*
1966 Medal of Honor awarded to a Seabee, *5536*
1977 Diesel cars to be mass-produced, *8272*

September 14

1638 College library, *2685*
1716 Lighthouse, *7336*
1778 Minister plenipotentiary, *3877*
1814 Star-Spangled Banner, *3494*
1861 Naval battle in the Civil War, *5708*
1886 Typewriter ribbon, *1675*
1892 Bacteriology diagnostic laboratory in a city health department, *7257*
1908 Journalism school at a college, *2826*
1909 Election using the preferential ballot system, *3778*
1915 Sound-absorbing material made of rigid insulating board, *3347*
1922 Transcontinental airship flight, *8051*
1929 Horse to win a $100,000 purse in one race, *7808*
1940 Draft law enacted by Congress in preparation for war, *5557*
1956 Prefrontal lobotomy, *5362*
1975 Catholic saint who was born in America, *6326*
1984 MTV Video Music Awards, *1281*
1990 Gene therapy, *5399*
2002 Powwow at the National Mall, *1057*
2004 State to offer free cancer treatment for uninsured residents, *5402*

September 15

1817 Iron mill to puddle and roll iron, *1922*
1830 National convention of African-Americans, *6127*
1853 Minister who was a woman, *6271*
1857 Typesetting machine, *2044*
1858 Overland mail service, *4669*
1896 Hospice for incurable cancer patients, *5392*
1902 Suturing of a heart wound, *5346*
1927 Book on the game of bridge, *7735*
1930 Funeral home operated on the cooperative plan, *2304*
1934 Musical comedy broadcast on radio, *1458*
1939 Lightning bolt to be scientifically measured, *6503*
1945 Civilian to die in a nuclear accident, *6617*
1955 Woman cantor in a Reform Jewish temple
1957 Air-to-ground public telephone service, *4908*
1964 Soap opera on prime-time television, *4970*
1965 Television dramatic series starring an African-American performer, *4972*

September 16

1782 Impression made by the Great Seal of the United States, *3480*
1833 Interstate anticrime pact, *7358*
1946 College principally for war veterans, *2860*
1960 Postage stamp issued jointly by two countries, *4741*
1971 Technical school for Native Americans, *2981*
1974 Chairman of the Republican party who was a woman, *4107*

September 17

1607 Slander proceedings, *6922*

1777 Catholic funeral attended by the Continental Congress, *6231*
1778 Treaty entered into by the federal government with Native American tribes, *6041*
1787 Constitution of the United States, *3483*
1792 Episcopal bishop consecrated in America, *6233*
1844 Printing press for polychromatic printing, *2041*
1861 School for freed slaves, *2940*
1872 Sprinkler system patent, *7328*
1895 Battleship, *8478*
1901 Mercury vapor lamp, *6558*
1908 Fatal airplane accident, *8010*
1911 Transcontinental airplane flight made in stages, *8030*
1920 Professional football association, *7704*
1938 Building built completely inside a factory, *3303*
1941 Warship convoy across the Atlantic Ocean in World War II, *5759*
1947 Secretary of defense, *4190*
1953 Conjoined twins separated successfully by surgery, *5359*
1959 Ski lifts to be regulated by the state, *7896*
1961 Building of large size with a retractable roof, *3315*
1996 Honorary citizen who was a woman, *6108*

September 18

1634 Religious leader in the American colonies who was a white woman, *6178*
1769 Harpsichord, *1293*
1891 American woman of European descent to be made a Native American chief, *3928*
1895 Chiropractor, *5033*
1915 Asphalt-covered racetrack, *7624*
1932 Greek Orthodox college, *2849*
1947 Independent aviation branch of the U.S. armed forces, *5488*
1948 Airplane with a delta wing, *8122*
1972 Conversation between two computers, *6447*
1984 Transatlantic solo balloon flight, *8164*
2001 Bioterror attacks by mail, *5833*

September 19

1787 Newspaper to publish the Constitution, *3484*
1862 Photographs of an American battlefield showing the bodies of the dead, *5715*
1876 Carpet sweeper, *2217*
1891 Underwater railroad tunnel to a foreign country, *3441*
1898 Forestry school at a college, *2816*
1928 Animated cartoon with sound, *1199*
Airplane diesel engine, *8067*
1951 Valeteria, *1695*
1982 Emoticon comment sign for computer users, *6464*

September 20

1565 Colonial warfare between European powers in America, *5627*
1777 Warship captured overseas, *5667*
1848 National science society, *6717*
1850 Homeopathic hospital, *5105*
Railroad land grant, *8311*
1853 Elevator with safety devices, *3272*
Union passenger station used by several railroad companies, *8313*
1859 Electric range, *2277*
1860 Prince of Wales to visit the United States, *3923*
1862 Hospital ship operated by the Navy, *5199*
1884 Woman presidential candidate who was eligible to hold office, *3808*
Vice presidential candidate who was a woman, *3812*
Equal Rights Party convention, *4077*
1892 Wire glass, *3360*
1915 Chiropody school at a college, *3087*
1916 National research society, *6727*
1946 Movie trailer to be shown on television, *1549*
1974 Police officer who was a woman to be killed in the line of duty, *7388*

September 21

1782 Bible printed in English, *6347*
1846 Unit of American deserters to join an enemy army, *5688*
1872 African-American midshipman at the Naval Academy, *3118*
1883 Electrical engineering school at a college, *2797*
1942 Navy-Marine Corps Medals for Heroism awarded to Marines, *5521*
1965 Swimmer from the United States to make a round-trip crossing of the English Channel, *7915*

September 22

1656 Jury composed of women, *3700*
1734 Moravian settlement in America, *6219*
1776 American executed as a spy, *5662*
1851 Telegraph used by a railroad, *4851*
1862 Emancipation proclamation, *6134*
1926 Book course at a college, *2844*
1947 Transatlantic flight by a robot airplane, *8120*
1953 Highway interchange structure with four levels, *3429*
1961 Federal district court judge who was African-American, *3726*
1964 Musical to run for more than 3,000 performances, *1466*
1973 Secretary of state to serve simultaneously as national security advisor, *4203*
1995 Movie rated NC-17, *1182*

September 23

1642 Bachelor of Arts degree, *2688*
1679 Labadist community, *6201*
1745 Knighthood conferred on a soldier born in America, *3919*
1779 Naval hero, *5673*
1833 Cabinet appointee rejected by the Senate, *4177*
1845 Baseball team, *7482*
1879 Hearing aid, *5267*
1885 Biology course offered at a college, *2802*
1897 Frontier Day, *2506*
1898 Tuberculosis sanatorium established by a state, *5128*
1911 Airmail pilot, *4690*
1926 Boxing match to attract 100,000 spectators, *7604*
1934 Radio broadcast heard in both the Arctic and the Antarctic regions, *4798*
1951 Transcontinental telecast received on the West Coast, *4953*
1952 Pay television presentation of a sports event, *4955*
World heavyweight boxing champion to retire undefeated, *7608*
1954 Court-martial of an officer for collaborating with his captors, *5552*
1970 New York City Marathon, *7957*
1976 Presidential election debate between an incumbent president and a challenger to be televised, *3830*

September 24

1657 Autopsy with verdict of a coroner's jury, *2295*
1696 Lending library, *2996*
1716 Botanical report on plant hybridization, *6755*
1789 Congressional act declared unconstitutional by the Supreme Court, *3559*
Creation of federal courts, *3702*
Supreme Court chief justice, *3731*
Federal law enforcement agency, *3838*
1799 Territorial legislature, *6042*
1832 Toy distribution center, *2178*
1889 Dial time recorder, *1678*
1906 National monument designated by the federal government, *7182*
1933 Drama broadcast on radio from a regular stage, *1456*
1934 Theater and dramatic criticism course at a college, *2851*
1951 Sex-change operation performed on an American, *7442*
1965 Presidential order enforcing affirmative action, *3857*
1968 Television newsmagazine, *4545*

September 25

1690 Newspaper published in the British colonies, *4489*
Newspaper publisher, *4588*
1789 Constitutional amendments to fail the ratification process, *3489*
1880 Play presented by a Jewish professional acting troupe, *1442*
1924 Micropaleontology course at a college, *2842*
1956 Transatlantic telephone call carried by the transoceanic telephone cable, *4907*
1981 Supreme Court justice who was a woman, *3752*

September 26

1772 Medical licensing law enacted by a colony, *5016*
1789 Attorney of the United States, *3703*
Attorney general of the United States, *4170*
Postmaster general of the United States, *4659*
Federal marshals, *7356*
1831 Play performed 1,000 times, *1430*
Anti-Masonic Party convention, *4055*
1871 Cement, *3341*
1874 International rifle tournament of consequence, *7883*
1903 Boycott prevention law enacted by a state, *1498*

October—*continued*

1884 Baseball championship, *7510*
1888 Geography magazine, *6784*
1889 General medical clinic, *5066*
1893 Aviation magazine, *8002*
1896 All-fiction pulp magazine, *4614*
1902 Newspaper published daily at sea to carry world news, *4512*
1925 Atheist organization, *7227*
1926 Movie showing another planet, *6404*
1930 Coal mine to be automated, *6605*
1931 Diesel-powered tractor, *1649*
1932 Teletypesetter, *2057*
1935 News correspondent who was African-American, *4599*
1939 Electronic digital calculator, *6516*
1946 Baseball play-off series, *7536*
1947 Deaths from smog, *5920*
1949 Cortisone synthesis, *5252*
1951 Air-to-air rocket, *5876*
Transistors produced commercially for a specific product, *6519*
1954 Transistor radio receiver to be mass-produced, *4824*
1955 Air-conditioned public elementary school, *2976*
1968 Ambulance equipped for mobile coronary care, *5047*
1969 Vacuum telescope, *6380*
1977 Daughters of the American Revolution member who was African-American, *7231*
1978 Graphic novel, *1108*
1979 Spreadsheet program for computers, *6459*
1989 Liver transplant from a live donor, *5376*
Surgeon general who was a woman, *7283*
1990 Killer bees, *5968*
Machine controlled via the Internet, *6473*
1998 Thought control of a computer, *5275*
1999 Former speaker of the House to become a television news commentator, *3637*
2000 Dual kidney and liver transplants from children to a parent, *5383*
2001 Building with a combined heat and power energy system, *3320*
2004 School district to require mention of intelligent design in science classes, *2989*
Comprehensive digital archive of state documents, *4371*

October 1

1779 Medal awarded by the Continental Congress to a foreigner, *3552*
1785 City directory, *3517*
1790 Political newspaper to carry partisanship to extremes, *4495*
1810 Cattle fair, *1593*
1823 Gymnasium to offer systematic instruction, *7784*
1834 Locomotive with six or eight driving wheels, *8334*
1848 School for children with mental disabilities, *2931*
1861 Army balloon corps, *5458*
Union ship captured in the Civil War, *5709*
1865 Baseball game in which one team scored more than 100 runs, *7492*
1880 Incandescent lamp factory, *6545*
1883 Missionary training school, *2798*
1884 Drama school, *3204*
1885 Special delivery mail service, *4682*
1892 Sociology professor at a college, *2811*
1896 Rural free mail delivery, *4684*
1903 World Series baseball game, *7518*
1904 Bulk mail, *4687*
1908 Nursing school at a college, *3082*
1913 Monument to a bird, *7183*
1918 Hygiene and public health school at a college, *3089*
1924 President to be born in a hospital, *4260*
1934 Federal credit union, *1746*
College to dispense with credits, hours, points, and grades, *2852*
1940 Army parachute battalion, *5479*
1942 Jet airplane, *8108*
1945 Think tank for research and development, *7229*
1946 Military think tank, *5799*
1947 Helicopter freight service, *8132*
1952 Religious radio program broadcast by a husband and wife, *6316*
1955 Aircraft carrier with an angle deck, *8490*
1961 Television station owned by a religious organization, *6320*
1977 Secretary of energy, *4206*
1979 Pope to visit the White House, *3941*

October 2

1721 Camel exhibited to the public, *1347*
1866 Tin can with a key opener, *1996*
1876 Actors' home, *1441*
1889 Conference of American republics initiated by the United States, *3890*
1936 Fuel alcohol plant, *6606*

1937 X-ray movies of human organs in action, *5136*
1955 African-American minister to a white Methodist congregation, *6232*
1956 Clock to operate by nuclear power, *2633*
1963 Artificial leather, *2143*
1965 Transatlantic undersea radio conversation, *4803*
1979 Coal miner who was a woman to be killed in a mining accident, *6613*
1980 Congressional representative expelled for corruption, *3632*
1996 Police 311 hotline, *7392*

October 3

1632 Tobacco penalty enacted by a colony, *7055*
1805 Pharmacopoeia prepared by a medical association, *5295*
1824 Treaty between the federal government and a South American nation, *3887*
1859 International cricket tournament, *7631*
1875 Rabbinical college, *2790*
1899 Vacuum cleaner driven by a motor, *2219*
1902 Labor dispute resolved through presidential intervention, *7142*
1904 School of social work, *2823*
1922 Senator who was a woman, *3673*
1924 Citizenship and public affairs school at a college, *2843*
1942 Silver Star awarded to a civilian, *5522*
1943 Police appeal for missing persons to be shown on television, *7384*
1949 Radio station owned and operated by African-Americans, *4812*
1952 Video recording on high-definition magnetic tape, *4997*
1967 Underground comic book of note, *1107*
1969 Vasectomy outpatient service, *5074*
1974 African-American manager of a major league baseball team, *7545*

October 4

1881 Player piano that was completely automatic, *1303*
1887 European edition of an American newspaper, *4522*
1895 Open golf championship tournament, *7757*
1909 Airship race, *7676*
1940 Quetzal bird, *5959*
1960 Communications satellite with signal reception and transmission equipment, *6853*
1961 Postage stamp featuring a work of art in true color, *4742*
1965 Pope to visit the United States, *3938*
1968 Use of the term "personal computer", *6439*
2004 State public health program to provide prescription drugs from Canada and Europe, *7295*
2005 American orchestra to make all its recordings downloadable from the Internet, *1285*
Coin showing a president in frontal view, *4051*

October 5

1646 Wolf bounty, *5939*
1843 Harness horse race at night, *7794*
1852 Beehive with removable frames, *1612*
1853 Physiology and hygiene courses at a liberal arts college, *3057*
1854 Baby show, *2184*
1871 Unitarian woman minister, *6236*
1919 Radio broadcast from a submerged submarine, *4784*
Two-way radio conversation between a submerged submarine and another vessel, *4885*
1930 Transcontinental solo airplane flight by a woman, *8080*
1931 Transpacific nonstop airplane flight, *8084*
1933 Airplane with nonconvertible sleeping berths, *8089*
1947 Presidential address televised from the White House, *4283*
1974 Round-the-world journey on foot, *7985*

October 6

1683 Mennonites to arrive in America, *6203*
1780 American imprisoned in the Tower of London as an enemy agent, *5674*
1783 Clock that was self-winding, *2625*
1825 Giant exhibited as a theatrical attraction, *1364*
1837 Locomotive steam whistle, *8336*
1848 Steamboat service to California around Cape Horn, *8432*
1852 National pharmacy society, *5220*
1857 Chess tournament, *7728*
International chess champion from the United States, *7729*
1863 Turkish bath, *7244*
1866 Robbery of a train in motion, *6936*

October 6—*continued*

Steam car, *8224*
1868 Nickel plating, *1936*
1873 Transatlantic crossing attempted by a balloon, *7998*
1876 National library association, *3016*
1911 Transpacific radio conversation, *4783*
1927 Feature film with with recorded music and dialogue, *1149*
1929 Baseball manager to win pennants in both leagues, *7530*
1978 University president who was a woman, *2786*

October 7

1856 Paper folding machine, *2020*
1868 Veterinary department at a college, *3068*
1896 Golfer to win the United States Women's Amateur Championship, *7760*
1919 Electric motorized wheelchair, *7036*
1922 Chain radio broadcast, *4787*
1924 Transcontinental airship flight, *8056*
1930 Glider pilot's license, *8081*
1931 Infrared photograph, *4633*
1950 Tank crew to cross the 38th parallel in the Korean War, *5806*
1955 Beat Generation literary event, *1105*
1964 Made-for-TV movie, *4971*

October 8

1818 Hygiene lectures at a college, *3049*
1871 Forest fire of consequence, *5974*
1873 Prison built for women and managed by women, *7006*
1919 Transcontinental air race, *7679*
1929 Movie entertainment shown on an airplane, *1156*
Automatic pilot on an airplane, *8071*
1936 Pope to visit the United States before his election, *3933*
1945 American conductor of an American orchestra, *1267*
1956 Baseball pitcher to pitch a perfect no-hit, no-run, no-walk World Series game, *7542*
1968 Astronaut international rescue agreement, *6811*
1970 Lottery in which the top prize was $1 million, *1805*
1971 President to visit all 50 states, *4319*
1990 Native American Day, *2521*
2005 Winner of the Grand Challenge robotic vehicle race, *6532*

October 9

1780 Astronomical expedition to record an eclipse of the sun, *6369*
1855 Calliope, *1297*
1865 Oil pipeline of importance, *6592*
1871 Surgeon who was a woman, *5027*
1876 Telephone conversation over outdoor wires, *4865*
1877 National animal humane society, *7218*
1894 Magic lantern feature show, *1387*
1946 Electric blanket, *2582*
1947 Mobile telephone call between an airplane in flight and a moving car, *4900*
1956 Electric portable typewriter, *1697*
1969 Senator to act in the movies, *3689*

October 10

1802 Ashkenazic Jewish congregation, *6247*
1845 Naval academy, *3105*
1863 Catholic parish church for African-Americans, *6275*
1886 Tuxedo coat, *2254*
1896 Book review newspaper supplement, *4523*
1898 National optometry society, *5226*
1916 Professional Golfers Association tournament, *7767*
1918 Church organized by Native Americans, *6293*
1920 Unassisted triple play in a World Series baseball game, *7527*
1933 Synthetic laundry detergent, *2224*
1934 Archivist of the United States, *3027*
1953 College Bowl competition on radio, *2865*
1955 Magazine to contain a phonograph record, *4616*
1967 Bowling automatic scoring machine, *7588*

October 11

1753 Arbitration law, *1472*
1784 Hostage crisis involving a foreign government, *3880*
1811 Steam-propelled ferryboat, *8419*
1881 Film rolls for cameras, *4642*
1886 College for women to affiliate with a university, *2804*
1935 National conference on crime, *7382*
1938 Fiberglass, *3367*
1963 Commemorative postage stamp depicting a president's wife, *4746*
1971 College whose tuition fees were based on family income, *2872*

October 16—*continued*

1916 Birth control clinic, *5067*
1917 Navy enlisted man killed in World War I action, *5741*
1928 Electric light bulb frosted on the inside, *6564*
1939 Indoor ski school, *7895*
1951 Movie showing the inside of a living heart, *5139*
1968 Federal employee to win a Nobel Prize, *6911*
1972 Metropolitan Opera orchestra conductor who was African-American, *1330*
1973 Mayor of a major Southern city who was African-American, *3541*
1975 Trial in which lawyers appeared on a Picturephone, *6957*
1984 Heart transplant using a baboon heart, *5375*

October 17

1777 Major American victory in the Revolutionary War, *5668*
1834 Gas meter, *6581*
1839 Building with a high steeple, *3266*
1907 Transatlantic radio message of the regular westward service, *4779*
1916 Movie sex shocker, *1143*
1941 Destroyer from the United States torpedoed in World War II, *5760*
1949 Long-distance dial telephone service, *4902*
1964 Self-service post office, *4714*
1971 Motorcycle racer who was a woman, *7849*
1979 Secretary of health and human services, *4207*
Department of Health and Human Services, *4207*
Department of Education, *4208*
1989 World Series disrupted by an earthquake, *7549*

October 18

1648 Craft union, *7095*
1842 Telegraph cable, *4844*
1852 Chinese theatrical performance, *1434*
1870 Sandblasting process, *1893*
1873 Football rules, *7687*
1891 Six-day bicycle race for men, *7650*
1904 National bibliography organization, *3024*
Hungarian daily newspaper, *4569*
1926 Queen to visit the United States during her reign, *3930*
Sheet of souvenir postage stamps, *4736*
1929 History of medicine department at a college, *3092*
1971 College to offer courses to railroad commuters, *2873*
1996 Basketball leagues for women, *7561*
2005 Public blood bank for collecting umbilical cord and placental blood for stem cell research, *5063*

October 19

1790 Battle fought by federal troops after the formation of the Union, *5676*
1839 Iron blast furnace to use anthracite coal successfully, *1926*
1915 Practical paper beverage carton, *2000*
1926 Semiautomatic rifle, *5866*
1936 High school to fingerprint its students, *7383*
1941 Wind turbine, *6633*
1950 Illegal television station, *4949*
1953 Plastic oil pipeline, *6608*

October 20

1817 Showboat theater, *1426*
1888 Baseball teams to go on a world tour, *7514*
1922 Pilot to bail out of a disabled airplane, *8052*
1951 Gambling permit stamp issued by the federal government, *4426*
1960 Post office fully mechanized, *4711*
1961 Vending machine to dispense fresh flowers, *1699*

October 21

1639 Medical regulations enacted by a colony, *5010*
1849 Tattooed man exhibited as a theatrical attraction, *1369*
1871 Amateur athletic games held outdoors, *7938*
1879 Incandescent lamp, *6543*
1885 Cowgirl, *1382*
1907 Balloon cup race held in the United States, *7674*
1915 Transatlantic message over radio telephone, *4882*
1917 Army division to go into battle in World War I, *5742*
1921 Radio program theme song, *4785*
1925 Photoelectric cell, *6563*
1929 Ambulance air service, *5045*
1948 High-speed radio fax transmission, *4473*

1963 Trimline telephone, *4910*
1979 Light sculpture created with a cityscape, *1044*
1996 Internet record label, *1283*
1998 Federal online privacy law, *7305*

October 22

1746 College charter granted by a governor, *2696*
1812 Prisoners captured in the War of 1812, *5683*
1883 Opera produced at the Metropolitan Opera House, *1319*
1897 National Zionist organization, *6286*
1938 Copy made by xerography, *2027*
1939 Professional football game to be shown on television, *7711*
1963 Armored division transported by airplanes to a foreign country, *5431*
1973 Commercial crude-oil carrier, *8464*
1996 Minister who was a transsexual, *7460*
1998 Billion-dollar settlement in an environmental lawsuit, *5932*

October 23

1824 Locomotive to pull a train on a track, *8330*
1850 Women's rights national convention, *7434*
1885 Graduate school for women, *2803*
1915 Horseshoe pitching championship tournament, *7970*
1917 Shot fired by American infantry in World War I, *5743*
1924 Radio network broadcast received on the Pacific Coast, *4791*
1947 Nobel Prize shared by an American husband and wife, *6906*
1956 Video recording on magnetic tape televised coast-to-coast, *4963*
1961 Jazz composition to appear on the Top 40 charts, *1273*
1974 Self-adhesive postage stamp, *4753*
1996 Holiday postage stamp issued jointly by two countries, *4741*
Player in the Women's National Basketball League, *7562*
1998 Teleportation experiment, *6753*

October 24

1801 Copper rolling mill, *1920*
1812 National historical society, *7472*
1828 Manufacturers' fair, *1482*
1861 Transcontinental telegraph line, *4855*
1901 Daredevil to go over Niagara Falls in a barrel, *1391*
1931 Mobster convicted for tax evasion, *6943*
1943 Distinguished Service Cross awarded to an animal, *5524*
1945 Department store sales demonstrations using television, *1548*
1951 United Nations postage stamps in U.S. denominations, *4740*
1998 Spacecraft with ion propulsion system, *6883*

October 25

1812 Capture of a British frigate in the War of 1812, *5684*
1848 Railroad to run west out of Chicago, *8309*
1888 Double-deck ferryboat, *8439*
1892 Reply-paid card, *4683*
1905 Municipal ferryboats, *8443*
1929 Cabinet member convicted of a crime, *4186*
1940 Army general who was African-American, *5445*
1945 Legal definition of the presidential seal, *4151*
1954 Cabinet session to be telecast and broadcast, *4193*
1955 Electronic range for domestic use, *2289*
1960 Electronic watch, *2635*
1973 Hang-gliding national championships, *7684*
1994 Banner ads on the Internet, *6477*

October 26

1785 Mule born in the United States, *1583*
1849 Jewish weekly newspaper in English, *4553*
1858 Washing machine, *2214*
1869 Steeplechase, *7796*
1909 Army pilot to fly solo in an airplane, *5462*

October 27

1659 Quakers executed for their religious beliefs, *6193*
1787 Federalist Paper, *3486*
1862 African-American unit in the Union Army to see combat, *5716*
1867 Theological college for Jews, *2773*
1869 State dairy association, *1621*
1904 Rapid-transit subway, *8378*
1922 Navy Day, *2512*
1946 Television show to be sponsored by a commercial advertiser, *1550*
Commercial program telecast on a network, *4940*

October 27—*continued*

1954 Air Force general who was African-American, *5494*
1994 Visit by an American president to a country on the U.S. list of terrorist states, *4321*
Year in which the prison population exceeded 1 million, *7022*
2005 City with a mobile mesh WiFi network for both public and municipal use, *7425*

October 28

1833 College founded as a Quaker institution, *2739*
1886 Ticker-tape parade, *1384*
Dedication ceremony for the Statue of Liberty, *3498*
Statue presented to the United States by a foreign country, *7177*
1901 Catalog cards from the Library of Congress, *3023*
1904 Police department to adopt the fingerprinting system, *7366*
1927 International airplane passenger station, *8065*
1949 Ambassador from the United States who was a woman, *3900*
1958 Stock exchange director who was a woman, *1783*
1964 United Nations ambassador who was a woman, *3903*
1970 Sky marshals, *7387*

October 29

1766 Fox hunting club, *7822*
1796 Ship from the Atlantic coast to anchor in a California port, *8526*
1889 Pocket lighter, *2566*
1904 Intercity trucking service, *2077*
1947 Forest fire drenched by artificial rain, *5986*
1959 Stockholder meetings televised coast-to-coast simultaneously, *1784*
1967 Rock musical, *1467*
1991 Photograph taken close up of an asteroid in space, *6416*
1998 Cancer-preventing drug, *5263*

October 30

1768 Methodist meetinghouse in continuous use, *6223*
1794 Ball bearing commercial installation, *3330*
1888 Ball-point pen, *2680*
1894 Card time recorder, *1682*
1896 Symphonic work by an American woman, *1247*
1903 Printed traffic regulations, *8193*
1918 Ace of Aces from the United States, *5754*
1941 Destroyer from the United States torpedoed during convoy duty in World War II, *5760*
1993 Amateur boxing match for women, *7611*

October 31

1835 Mutual fire insurance company, *1978*
1838 Model laboratory school at a college, *2742*
1950 Halloween collection for UNICEF, *2516*
1952 Hydrogen bomb, *5879*
1956 Airplane flight to land at the South Pole, *6652*
1962 Geodetic satellite, *6858*
2004 Vote cast from space in a presidential election, *3836*
2005 UNICEF Halloween collection that raised funds for American children, *2522*

November

1526 Escape of slaves from a colony in what is now United States territory, *6110*
1618 Comet recorded, *6383*
1811 Magician of note, *1361*
1824 Presidential election in which a loser won, *3800*
1829 Daredevil jumper of note, *1366*
1837 Music instruction in a public school, *2926*
1860 Boarding school on a Native American reservation, *2938*
Foreign missionary society organized by women, *6273*
1863 Thanksgiving Day, *2495*
1873 Hotel that was fireproof, *1820*
1876 Cooking school, *3199*
1881 Presidential candidate to make campaign speeches in a foreign language, *3811*
1886 Soup company, *2387*
1887 Psychology journal, *5329*
1888 Aluminum in metallic form, *1941*
1890 Movie made in the United States, *1112*
Dam filled with rocks, *3350*
1895 Amateur golf championship tournament for women, *7758*
Car magazine, *8226*

1902 Trade school for girls, *2961*
School nurses in public schools, *5036*
1904 Rotogravure press, *2056*
1908 Radio society, *4780*
Steel ski jump, *7890*
Aviation magazine devoted primarily to airplanes, *8011*
1910 Newsreel, *4524*
1919 Editor in chief of a law review who was a woman, *2836*
1929 Allergy journal, *5336*
1930 Floating electric power plant, *6566*
1935 Newspaper to store issues on microfilm, *3035*
1937 Photosensitive glass, *3366*
1940 President elected for third and fourth terms, *4149*
1947 Chemotherapy to successfully achieve remission of cancer, *5396*
1948 Broad-spectrum antibiotic, *5251*
1953 Oil refinery with a carbon monoxide boiler, *6609*
1958 Rocket to intercept a supersonic target missile, *5884*
1963 Elliptical office building, *3317*
1969 Human beings to see the sun eclipsed by the Earth, *6815*
1971 People's Party convention, *4105*
Laser printer, *6446*
1975 Video cassette recorder for home use, *5006*
CT scanner capable of making full-body images, *5142*
1983 Designation of Martin Luther King Day as a national holiday, *2520*
1993 Sheriff who was an African-American woman, *7391*
1995 Isolation of embryonic stem cells in a primate, *6686*
1997 Prison to offer training in Vipassana meditation, *7023*
2001 American theater company to perform Shakespeare at Stratford, *1468*
2002 Museum of children's book illustrations, *3167*
Political party leader in Congress who was a woman, *3639*
Municipal recycling of diapers and incontinence products, *5934*

November 1

1777 American flag saluted by a foreign nation, *3475*
1781 Bank chartered by Congress, *1715*
State medical society, *5212*
1784 Citizenship conferred by special grant, *6044*
1796 Dollar marks, *2033*
1848 Medical school for women, *3056*
1850 Photography magazine, *4622*
1864 Money order system, *4676*
1873 Barbed wire commercial production, *1864*
1879 School of prominence for Native American children, *2951*
1886 Electric lighthouse, *7347*
1894 Catalog of recordings on disk, *1244*
Music by Native Americans to be recorded, *1245*
1895 Automobile club, *8227*
1920 Hydroplane international service, *8046*
1927 Housing cooperative sponsored by a labor union, *7151*
1930 Vehicular tunnel to a foreign country, *3443*
1932 Self-computing gasoline pump, *1876*
1939 Surrogate birth experiment with an animal, *6668*
1940 Air raid shelter, *7298*
1941 Army language school, *3116*
1944 Quadruplets delivered by cesarean operation, *2154*
1950 Secret Service agent killed while protecting the president from an attempted assassination, *3845*
1955 Destruction of an American airliner by a criminal, *6949*
Reconstruction of an airliner during a crash investigation, *8138*
Guided missile cruiser, *8491*
1962 Christmas postage stamp regular issue, *4744*
1964 Russian Orthodox saint canonized in the United States, *6322*
1965 State department of Indian affairs, *4363*
1974 Magazine for home computer users, *6449*
1998 Major network program broadcast in high-definition television, *4984*
2001 State ban on the use of cell phones by drivers, *8215*
2005 Major city to legalize possession of marijuana, *7093*

November 2

1776 American soldier to commit treason, *5663*
1867 Fashion magazine, *2251*
1886 Gubernatorial election in which two brothers were the opposing candidates, *4379*
1904 Fingerprinting in federal penitentiaries, *7367*

November 2—*continued*

1915 Election using proportional representation, *3779*
1917 Soldiers in the American army killed in combat in World War I, *5744*
1926 Senate election in which neither candidate was seated after a recount, *3676*
1929 Newsreel theater, *1157*
1933 Surgical elevation of the skull to treat epilepsy, *5349*
1945 Industrial and labor relations school at a college, *2859*
1948 Woman legislator from the Republican Party to serve in both houses of Congress, *3680*
1954 Senator elected by a write-in vote, *3683*
1957 Titanium mill, *1947*
1967 Gravure-printed postage stamp, *4750*
1988 Major worm attack on the Internet, *6470*
2004 Senate election in which both candidates were African-American, *3698*
State to require paper receipts for electronic voting machines, *3791*
State to require proof of citizenship for voters, *3792*
Presidential election observed by international monitors, *3837*
State to approve funding for biomedical research using stem cells derived from human embryos, *6697*

November 3

1824 State nominating convention, *3766*
1840 Dental college, *3054*
1881 Coast Guard inland station, *5544*
1892 Automatic telephone exchange that was successful, *4871*
1896 State senator who was a woman, *4390*
1900 Car show, *8239*
1906 Secret Service agent killed in the line of duty, *3845*
1911 State continuation school for adults, *3210*
1952 Frozen bread, *2445*
1953 Coast-to-coast live telecast in color, *4959*
1955 Human virus to be crystallized, *6666*
1964 Year when citizens of the District of Columbia could vote in a presidential election, *3786*
Presidential election in which votes were tallied electronically, *3825*
1970 Congressional representative of Puerto Rican ancestry, *3624*
1992 Senator who was an African-American woman, *3692*
Senators who were Jewish women, *3693*
1998 State law allowing sealed birth records of adopted children to be opened, *2206*
Midterm election since World War II in which the president's party gained seats in the House of Representatives, *3636*
State to eliminate polling places, *3789*
2000 Billionaires who were African-American, *1714*
2005 Major network news program broadcast in high-definition television, *4550*

November 4

1661 Evening school for working children, *2891*
1846 Artificial leg patent, *5265*
1862 Rapid-fire machine gun, *5855*
1873 Slicing machine, *2281*
Patent for a gold dental crown, *5086*
1914 Fashion show for charity, *1392*
1924 State governor who was a woman, *4381*
1927 Pilot to die because of a lack of oxygen, *8066*
1939 Air-conditioned car, *8257*
1951 Jewish prayer services to be televised in their entirety, *6315*
1952 Mother and son simultaneously elected to Congress, *3618*
Presidential election in which a computer was used to predict the outcome, *3823*
1958 Molybdenum centrifugal casting, *1948*
1970 European king buried in the United States, *3939*
1979 Hostage crisis in the modern era, *3909*
1980 President who had been a professional actor, *4271*
1997 Vote cast from space in an American election, *3788*
2003 Demonstration of wireless remote vehicle control as an antiterrorism tactic, *7309*

November 5

1639 Post office in a colony, *4653*
1733 Political newspaper, *4492*
1824 Engineering college, *2736*
1852 National civil engineering society, *3223*

1872 Congressional representative to serve a single day, *3608*
1889 Sewer district established by a city, *7413*
1895 Car patent, *8228*
1956 Network variety show hosted by an African-American, *4964*
1968 Congressional representative who was an African-American woman, *3623*
1974 Congressional representative who was a grandmother, *3629*
Senator who had been an astronaut, *3690*
Woman elected state governor in her own right, *4381*
State legislator who was openly gay, *7452*
1992 Transgendered person elected to public office, *7459*
1996 Presidential election in which the winning candidate received a greater percentage of women's votes than men's, *3834*
1998 Bounty of $5 million for an enemy of the United States, *5830*

November 6

1804 Presidential election in which candidates were nominated for the vice presidency, *3798*
1855 Railroad union, *7119*
1868 Native American to win territorial concessions from the federal government, *6075*
1869 Intercollegiate football contest, *7686*
1883 Cross-country championships, *7943*
1894 State legislators who were women, *4389*
1928 Electric flashing sign, *1542*
1934 State legislature with a single chamber in the post-Revolutionary era, *4393*
Locomotive communications headlight, *8392*
1945 Jet-propelled landing on an aircraft carrier, *8112*
1955 Full-length American film to premiere on television, *1167*
1956 Congressional representative of Asian ancestry, *3620*
1962 President with a brother in the Senate, *4267*
1974 Mayor of a major city with a population over 500,000, *3542*

November 7

1848 Election day for presidential voting held nationwide, *3805*
1859 Library newspaper room, *3014*
1874 Political cartoon showing the Republican Party as an elephant, *4579*
1910 Shipment of merchandise by airplane, *2078*
1916 Election in which returns were broadcast on radio, *3816*
1922 Congressional representative who was a mother, *3614*
1942 President to make a radio broadcast in a foreign language, *4282*
1946 Coin-operated television receiver, *4993*
1950 Husband and wife to be elected simultaneously to both chambers of a state legislature, *4395*
1967 Mayor of a major city who was African-American, *3541*
Mayor of Washington who was African-American, *3541*
1972 Congressional candidate elected while missing, *3626*
State to refuse to host the Olympic Games, *7861*
1989 Mayor of New York City who was African-American, *3544*
State governor who was African-American, *4383*
2000 First Lady elected to the Senate, *3695*
Senate candidate elected posthumously, *3696*

November 8

1775 Mail franking privilege, *4658*
1825 National organization of artists, *1030*
1860 Baseball game of record in which a team scored no runs in nine innings, *7490*
1864 Presidential election in which soldiers in the field were allowed to vote, *3807*
1884 Newspaper syndicate, *4521*
1897 Assistance to blind readers by the Library of Congress, *7034*
1926 Ferryboat built exclusively to transport cars, *8449*
1938 State legislator who was an African-American woman, *4394*
1941 Naval patrol bomber launched like a ship, *5586*
1950 Pilot of a jet fighter to win a dogfight in the Korean War, *5807*
1954 Tunnel with television monitors, *3444*
1960 Senate election race in which both candidates were women, *3686*

November 8—*continued*

1962 African-American woman elected to a judgeship, *3721*
1966 Senator who was African-American to be elected by popular vote, *3688*
1973 Golfer to earn $100,000 in a contest, *7779*
1994 State to legalize physician-assisted suicide, *2310*
1999 President to participate in a live chat over the Internet, *4290*
2002 Urban business district with complete video surveillance, *7396*

November 9

1756 Intercity stagecoach service, *8178*
1790 President who had been a senator, *4117*
1820 Mercantile library, *3009*
1835 State police, *7359*
1842 Design patent, *3993*
1964 Postage stamps of four different designs sold as a single sheet, *4747*

November 10

1775 Marines, *5560*
1798 State nullification proceedings to obstruct federal legislation, *4340*
1801 Dueling law enacted by a state, *6929*
1817 Trust, *1481*
1855 Poem to win national acclaim, *1093*
1895 Statue officially sanctioned by the Pope, *7179*
1903 Windshield wiper, *8194*
1914 Bank to establish a branch in a foreign country, *1737*
1919 American Legion convention of veterans of World War I, *5624*
1951 Transcontinental direct-dialed phone call, *4905*
1960 Nuclear reactor operated commercially, *6625*
1969 Episode of "Sesame Street" to be shown on television, *4977*
1971 Christmas postage stamp series with a religious and a secular subject, *4744*

November 11

1647 Colonial law requiring towns to hire teachers and construct schools, *2890*
1817 Sword swallower, *1362*
1865 Medal of Honor awarded to a woman, *5508*
1868 Amateur athletic games held indoors, *7937*
1887 Labor activists to be executed, *7135*
1889 State named for a person born in America, *4353*
1919 Veterans' Day, *2511*
1921 Burial at the Tomb of the Unknown Soldier, *2303*
1925 Cosmic ray to be discovered, *6387*
1926 Dance major at a college, *2845*
1933 Electric power contract between a city and the federal government, *6568*
1934 Streamlined all-steel diesel-motor train, *8397*
1935 Aerial photograph showing the lateral curvature of the horizon and the beginning of the stratosphere, *4634*
1950 National gay rights organization, *7441*
2004 Hydrogen refueling station, *2104*

November 12

1799 Meteor shower on record, *6384*
1861 Petroleum exported to Europe, *6589*
1920 Baseball commissioner, *7528*
1921 Conference of great powers, *3895*
1926 Airplane bombing raid by criminals, *6939*
1927 Underwater highway tunnel with twin tubes, *3442*
1932 President to invite the president-elect, *4144*
1941 Genetics clinic, *5071*
Test pilot who was a woman, *8104*
1946 Drive-in banking service, *1748*
1975 Dog hotel, *1841*
1984 Salvage operation in space, *6878*

November 13

1789 President to tour the country, *4311*
1839 Liberty Party convention, *4060*
1868 National philology society, *6720*
1875 Bowling rule standardization, *7580*
Football uniforms worn in a game, *7690*
1913 African-American fellow of the American College of Surgeons, *5229*
1930 Rotating milking platform, *1646*
1933 Sit-down strike, *7153*
1937 Symphony orchestra devoted exclusively to radio broadcasting, *1263*
1938 Beatification of an American citizen by the Catholic Church, *6309*
1943 Woman line officer in the Navy with the rank of captain, *5606*
1946 Artificial snow from a natural cloud, *6504*
1955 Live telecast from a noncontiguous foreign country, *4954*

1971 Satellite launched from the earth to orbit another planet, *6862*
1998 Labor Party national convention, *4111*
2005 Live concert for astronauts, *1286*

November 14

1784 Episcopal bishop, *6233*
1889 World tour by a woman traveling alone, *8531*
1903 Football stadium, *7702*
1906 President to visit a foreign country while in office, *4312*
1910 Airplane flight from a ship, *8021*
1921 Opera broadcast over the radio with a professional cast, *1322*
1934 Symphony on an African-American folk theme, *1261*
1937 Children's church, *6304*
1967 General killed in Vietnam by enemy fire, *5816*
1969 President to attend the launching of a manned space flight, *4156*
1972 Dow Jones Industrial Average to exceed 1,000 points, *1788*

November 15

1681 Shorthand account of a trial, *3949*
1754 Trombone, *1291*
1777 Articles of Confederation, *3476*
1806 College magazine, *2727*
1807 Evangelical Church conference, *6250*
1849 Poultry show, *1611*
1864 Mines school at a college, *2765*
1882 Naval attache, *5602*
1898 Foreign service school in a college, *2817*
1899 Newspaper published at sea to use a radio news service, *4512*
1931 Parachute jump from an autogiro, *8085*
1948 Gas-turbine-electric locomotive, *8346*
1950 African-American player on an amateur hockey team, *7833*
1954 Round-the-world flight over the North Pole on a regularly scheduled air route, *8136*

November 16

1620 Corn found by English settlers, *1557*
1676 Prison, *6988*
1776 American flag saluted by a foreigner, *3470*
1841 Life preserver of cork, *7342*
1901 Car to exceed the speed of a mile a minute, *8241*
1914 Federal reserve banks, *1738*
1920 Postage meter, *4694*
1943 Submarine from the United States sunk by an enemy submarine, *5793*
1955 Dugong, *5961*
Speedboat to exceed 200 miles per hour, *8460*
1963 President to witness the firing of a Polaris missile, *4154*
1984 Astronaut who was a mother, *6829*

November 17

1774 Military organization formed to oppose the British, *5647*
1800 Session of Congress held in Washington, *3554*
1851 Postage stamps depicting the American eagle, *4718*
1875 Theosophical society, *7216*
1886 Organization of newspaper publishers, *4597*
1889 Transcontinental daily railroad service, *8321*
1917 Naval vessels to sink an enemy submarine in the Atlantic, *5745*
1919 Bank with resources exceeding 1 billion dollars, *1741*
1936 Sulfanilamide used in medical treatment, *5244*
1992 Cablecasts of city meetings with real-time captioning for the hearing-impaired, *7048*

November 18

1805 Women's club, *7200*
1820 Discovery of Antarctica by an American, *6641*
1874 National temperance society for women, *7066*
1883 Standard time program, *2630*
1913 Airplane loop-the-loop, *8036*
1921 International fencing championship competition, *7668*
1943 Cabinet member to address a joint session of Congress, *4189*
1949 Baseball player who was African-American to win the Most Valuable Player award, *7539*
1963 Telephone with push buttons, *4911*
1965 Women members of the American Stock Exchange, *1783*
1967 New York Stock Exchange seat owner who was a woman, *1785*
2003 State to legalize gay marriage, *7464*

November 19

1794 Extradition treaty with a foreign country, *3886*
1806 Senator to serve in contravention to the age limit, *3655*
1867 Book tour of the United States by an author, *1094*
1893 Newspaper colored supplement, *4583*
1916 Airplane flight longer than 500 miles, *8039*
1936 News magazine featuring photographs, *4535*
1954 Toll collection machine, *3430*
1969 Astronauts to retrieve a manmade object from the moon, *6816*

November 20

1620 Child born of English parents in New England, *6017*
1771 Town named for George Washington, *3514*
1776 Naval ship of the line, *8465*
1820 Ship sunk by a whale, *1795*
1866 University for African-American students, *2770*
Bicycle with a rotary crank, *7639*
1888 Key time recorder, *1676*
1914 Passport photographs, *6087*
1925 Photograph taken from an airplane at night, *4630*
1931 Teletype commercial service, *4860*
1978 Newspaper whose contents were transmitted by a communications satellite, *4547*
1979 Transfusion of artificial blood, *5060*
1990 Grammy Award to be retracted, *1282*
1998 International space station, *6884*

November 21

1766 Theater building of brick construction, *1420*
1810 English actor of note to perform in America, *1425*
1824 Reform Jewish congregation, *6262*
1915 Sikh gurdwara, *6292*
1918 Alcohol prohibition law enacted by Congress, *7075*
1922 Circumnavigation of the world by a cruise ship, *8536*
1946 President to travel underwater in a captured enemy submarine, *4298*
1969 General-purpose computer network, *6442*
1973 Federal marshals who were women to be hired on a permanent basis, *7385*
1995 Movie that was entirely computer-animated, *1203*
2001 State consumer protection agency to combat identity theft, *7307*

November 22

1910 Golf club with a steel shaft, *7765*
1927 Snowmobile patent, *7973*
1935 Transpacific airmail flight, *4701*
1955 Cabinet session held at a place other than the seat of the federal government, *4194*
1961 Baseball player to win Most Valuable Player award in both major leagues, *7543*
1963 Assassination of a president captured on film, *4268*
Telecast transmitted by satellite to Japan, *4969*

November 23

1848 Medical society for women, *5219*
1861 Regiment of free African-Americans organized during the Civil War, *5710*
1876 Intercollegiate football association, *7692*
1889 Jukebox, *4830*
1940 Army general who rose from draftee, *5446*
1942 Coast Guard unit for women, *5545*
1968 Naturalization ceremony in the White House, *6100*
1969 Space-to-ground news conference telecast, *4546*
1973 Congressional representative to give birth while holding office, *3628*
1995 Triplets born several weeks apart, *2167*
2002 Astronaut to fly in space who was Native American, *6840*

November 24

1703 Lutheran pastor ordained in American, *6183*
1827 Horticulture society of importance, *1594*
1871 National rifle society, *7882*
1885 Nursing society, *5222*
1896 Absentee voting law enacted by a state, *3775*
1922 Treaty among more than two states, *4359*
1924 Corn-husking championship, *1642*
1963 Murder to be captured live on television, *6952*

December—*continued*

1791 Coin bearing the likeness of a president, *4011*
1795 Macadam road, *3408*
1825 Pharmacy journal, *5304*
1840 Radio impulse transmission, *4817*
Naval vessel to sail around the Cape of Good Hope, *8529*
1841 General anesthetic, *5049*
1844 Book review editor, *4592*
1853 College literary society that was coeducational, *2700*
1856 Kindergarten run informally, *2944*
1861 Bibliophile magazine, *4455*
1879 Photograph taken by incandescent electric light, *4641*
1881 Electric light from a power plant in a residence, *6547*
1882 Christmas tree decorated with electric lights, *2504*
Royal palace, *3926*
1889 Children's department in a library, *3018*
1892 Public speaking department at a college, *2812*
Medical journal published by an African-American, *5331*
College basketball team, *7552*
1905 National sociology society, *6726*
1911 Advertising association to combat business abuses, *1503*
1917 Sale of Girl Scout cookies, *2195*
1930 Sulfanilamide production, *5244*
1931 Electric can opener, *2276*
1934 Pilot who was a woman to fly for a commercial airline, *8093*
1935 Casein fiber, *1905*
1943 African-American member of the National Institute of Arts and Letters, *7223*
1953 Use of tobacco to produce cancer in laboratory animals, *6672*
1969 Airplane made primarily of composite materials, *8152*
1976 PET scanner, *5143*
1999 Customer satisfaction survey by the federal government, *3869*
Space probe mission headed entirely by women, *6885*
Criminal conviction in an airliner crash, *6981*
State police department to be monitored for racial profiling, *7395*
2002 Municipal downsizing plan, *3546*
2003 Transgenic animal sold as a pet, *2608*
2005 Municipal wireless network paid for by advertisements, *7427*

December 1

1751 Manual training courses offered in a school, *2900*
1841 Teaching methodology course at a college, *2745*
1842 Navy officer condemned for mutiny, *5599*
1845 Health journal to advocate water cures, *5316*
1896 Certified public accountant, *1707*
1909 Christmas savings club at a bank, *1736*
1914 Naval air training school, *3112*
1919 American woman to become a member of the British Parliament, *3929*
1921 Airship filled with helium gas, *8049*
1955 Mass boycott by civil rights protesters, *6141*
1956 Stock brokerage concern of importance whose president was a woman, *1782*
1959 Color photograph of the earth taken from space, *6410*
1999 Sale of an American painting at a price comparable to that of European paintings, *1045*
Complete sequencing of a human chromosome, *6695*

December 2

1662 Colonial badges issued to friendly Native Americans, *6032*
1799 Ship constructed by the federal government, *8467*
1816 Savings bank to receive money on deposit, *1718*
1933 Wedding by transatlantic telephone, *2596*
1939 Presidential campaign manager who was a woman, *3819*
1941 Round-the-world flight by a commercial airplane, *8105*
1942 Self-sustaining nuclear chain reaction demonstration, *6748*
1952 Birth to be televised for the public, *2158*
1957 Nuclear power plant devoted exclusively to peaceful uses, *6624*
1982 Heart transplant using an artificial heart that was intended to be permanent, *5374*

December 7—*continued*

1904 Carnegie Hero Fund Commission awards, *6896*
1909 Thermosetting resin, *1899*
1926 Gas refrigerator, *2287*
1928 Senator who was Hispanic, *3677*
1941 Purple Heart awarded to a woman, *5517*
American losses in the Pacific in World War II, *5761*
Navy admiral killed in action in World War II, *5762*
Radar used to detect enemy airplanes, *5763*
Ship from the United States to sink a Japanese submarine in World War II, *5764*
World War II air hero, *5765*
1944 Retail store whose sales in one day exceeded $1 million, *2099*
Army officer to receive the three highest decorations, *5526*
1948 Americans to die in a UN peacekeeping mission, *5800*
1954 Military heliport, *5490*
1983 Execution by lethal injection, *7021*

December 8

1792 Cremation, *2297*
1850 College graduate who was an African-American woman, *2749*
1863 Farmers' institute sponsored by a state, *1615*
Presidential amnesty issued during the Civil War, *4121*
1890 Woman delegate to a national convention of the American Federation of Labor, *7130*
1928 Physician to Congress, *3576*
1929 Ship-to-shore mobile telephone commercial service, *4890*
1940 Professional football championship game broadcast on radio, *7712*
1941 Ship from the United States to surrender to the Japanese in World War II, *5766*
Heavy tank, *5869*
1948 Television image using a split screen, *4994*
1959 Movie with scent, *1174*
1987 Elimination of an entire class of nuclear weapons by treaty, *3911*
1988 Transoceanic fiber-optic telecommunications cable, *4919*

December 9

1621 Sermon to be printed, *6337*
1845 Silver wire suture, *5172*
1861 Proposal for a Medal of Honor, *5503*
1869 Labor union to admit workers other than craft workers, *7123*
1907 Fund-raising organization to sell Christmas seals, *7224*
1909 Monoplane, *8014*
1941 Bombing mission by American forces in Asia in World War II, *5767*
Fighter plane from the United States to destroy a Japanese airplane in World War II, *5768*
1946 Rocket plane for manned supersonic flight, *5486*
1998 State appeals court decision ordering the extension of insurance benefits to gay partners of government employees, *7462*
2004 Genome sequencing and analysis of a bird, *6698*

December 10

1672 Postal route between cities, *4654*
1690 Loan by a colony, *1756*
1810 Boxer of fame who was African-American, *7591*
1815 Naval officers' training school, *3100*
1843 Warship with propelling machinery below the waterline, *8470*
1899 Tuberculosis hospital for needy patients, *5130*
1904 Motorcycle police, *7368*
1924 Gay rights organization, *7439*
1927 *Grand Ole Opry* broadcast, *4793*
1931 Nobel Peace Prize awarded to an American woman, *6905*
1938 Nobel Prize in literature awarded to an American woman, *6904*
1950 Nobel Peace Prize awarded to an African-American, *6907*
1953 Nobel Peace Prize awarded to a professional soldier, *6908*
1954 Nobel Prize winner to receive awards in two different categories, *6909*
1970 Nobel Prize in economics awarded to an American, *6912*
1976 Year in which Nobel Prizes were won by Americans in five of six categories, *6915*
1989 Human-powered helicopter, *8167*

December 11

1719 Aurora borealis display, *6485*
1735 Translation of a classic, *1067*

1775 American woman to be killed in action, *5654*
1844 Anesthetic in dentistry, *5050*
1866 Transatlantic yacht race, *7571*
1872 African-American to serve as interim state governor, *4383*
1882 Theater lighted by electricity, *1445*
1919 Monument to an insect, *7184*
1961 Troops sent to Vietnam, *5812*
1972 Geologist to reach the moon, *6509*
1998 Genome sequencing of a multicellular organism, *6693*

December 12

1789 Catholic Bible in English, *6352*
1796 Nail cutting and heading machine, *2639*
1808 Bible society, *6251*
1862 Warship sunk by an underwater torpedo mine, *5717*
1870 Congressional representative who was African-American, *3606*
1897 Comic strip in continuous newspaper publication, *4584*
1899 Golf tee, *7763*
1906 Cabinet member who was Jewish, *4182*
1910 Supreme Court justice to be appointed chief justice, *3749*
1925 Motel, *1830*
1937 Mobile television transmitter unit, *4991*
1941 General of the American armed forces killed in World War II, *5769*
1944 World War II veterans' society officially recognized by Congress, *5625*

December 13

1621 Furs exported, *5937*
1759 Musical instrument dealer, *1217*
1774 Ground attack in the Revolutionary War, *5648*
1809 Abdominal operation other than a cesarean section, *5339*
1853 Infirmary for women staffed by physicians who were women, *5107*
1893 Tuberculosis laboratory established by a city, *7258*
1918 American division to cross the Rhine River in World War I, *5755*
1920 Astronomer to measure the size of a fixed star, *6374*
1941 World War II ace, *5770*
1978 Coin bearing the likeness of an American woman, *4047*

December 14

1793 Road authorization by a state, *3407*
1807 Meteorite whose landing was recorded, *6385*
1849 Chamber music ensemble, *1236*
1902 Transpacific telegraph cable, *4857*
1934 Streamlined steam locomotive, *8343*
1962 Spacecraft to transmit data from Venus, *6867*
1979 Casino run by a Native American tribe, *1808*
2000 Genome sequencing of a plant, *6696*

December 15

1778 Arbitration law enacted by a state, *1477*
1791 Constitutional amendments to be ratified, *3490*
1792 Life insurance offered by a general insurance company, *1989*
1814 Secession convention during the War of 1812, *4342*
1820 General pharmacopoeia, *5301*
1854 Street-cleaning machine, *7405*
1864 Stamp collection magazine, *4677*
1874 Reigning king to visit the United States, *3925*
Child abuse prevention organization, *7215*
1886 Stock exchange at which more than a million shares were traded in one day, *1776*
1906 National Geographic Society gold medal, *6899*
1944 Army generals to wear the five-star insignia, *5448*
Navy admirals to wear the five-star insignia, *5607*
1965 Astronauts to rendezvous in space with another spacecraft, *6808*
1971 Secret Service agents who were women, *3860*
1999 Hybrid car, *8282*

December 16

1851 Brass spinning, *1931*
1884 Vending machine that dispensed liquid automatically, *1673*
1897 Submarine fitted with an internal combustion engine, *8511*
1899 Children's museum, *3145*
1907 Singer whose voice was broadcast over radio, *1250*
Circumnavigation of the globe by a fleet of warships, *8534*
1908 Credit union, *1734*

December 16—*continued*

1922 State supreme court justice who was a woman, *3717*
1930 Athlete to win the James E. Sullivan Memorial Trophy, *7478*
1941 Submarine from the United States to sink a Japanese ship in World War II, *5771*
1979 Rocket-powered car to break the sound barrier on land, *8275*
1997 Cigarette manufacturer to list ingredients on the label, *7092*
1998 Fighter pilot who was a woman to fire a missile in combat, *5831*
2005 State to disburse funding for biomedical research using stem cells derived from human embryos, *6703*

December 17

1679 Price regulation agreement by colonists, *1471*
1791 One-way street, *3406*
1821 State law abolishing imprisonment for debt, *6994*
1895 National anti-saloon league, *7070*
1903 Airplane flight, *8005*
1924 Diesel-electric locomotive, *8342*
1933 World championship professional football game, *7707*
1937 Radio facsimile newspaper, *4538*
1946 Coin bearing the likeness of an African-American, *4045*
1954 Railroad freight yard that was fully automatic, *8329*
1956 Skyscraper of bronze and glass, *3311*
Pilot on a scheduled passenger line who was African-American, *8142*
1959 Movie premiered simultaneously in major cities throughout the world, *1175*
Scooter Pies, *2449*
1963 Air pollution law of importance enacted by Congress, *5925*
1968 Woman criminal on the FBI's Ten Most Wanted list, *6948*
1998 Magnetic surgery, *5380*

December 18

1777 National day of thanksgiving, *2489*
1796 Sunday newspaper, *4496*
1839 Astronomy photograph, *6398*
1865 Ban by Congress on importation of diseased cattle, *7246*
1924 Radio broadcast of a livestock auction, *1643*
1935 Bill to depict both sides of the Great Seal of the United States, *4044*
1936 Giant panda, *5956*

December 19

1683 Landscape architect, *5901*
1795 Road appropriation of a specific sum by a state, *3409*
1823 Birth registration law enacted by a state, *2147*
1871 Corrugated paper, *2022*
1891 African-American Catholic priest ordained in the United States, *6284*
1903 Suspension bridge with steel towers, *3249*
1910 Rayon, *2139*
1920 Indoor curling rink, *7635*
1939 Movie premiere festivities to be shown on television, *1163*
1945 First Lady appointed to a federal post after the death of her husband, *4235*
1958 Radio broadcast using an orbiting satellite, *4801*
1966 Space treaty signed by the United States, *3905*
1974 Senate proceeding to be shown on television, *3691*
Personal computer, *6450*
1998 Elected president to be impeached, *4165*

December 20

1656 Surgeon appointed by a colony, *5097*
1669 Rebellion by colonists against an English governor, *5638*
1777 Foreign nation to recognize the independence of the United States, *3873*
1780 Conscientious objectors, *5554*
1790 Cotton mill to spin cotton yarn successfully, *2118*
1820 Bachelor tax enacted by a state, *4409*
1860 Secession act at the start of the Civil War, *4349*
State to secede from the Union, *4350*
1869 Supreme Court nominee to die before taking office, *3748*
1870 State governor to be impeached and convicted, *4378*
1893 Lynching ban enacted by a state, *6138*
1928 Theater built and named for a living actress, *1455*
International dogsled mail, *4699*
1938 Cathode-ray tubes, *4936*
1951 Electric power from nuclear energy, *6619*
1961 Nuclear-powered aircraft carrier, *8493*

December 27

1845 Anesthetic administered in childbirth, *5051*

1895 Movie production company, *1119*

1899 Certified public accountant who was a woman, *1709*

1934 Youth hostel, *2196*

1938 Skimobile ski lift, *7894*

1941 Railroad to be completely equipped with diesel-electric engines, *8327*

1951 Mail delivery car with the steering wheel on the right, *8264*

1990 Navy officer who was a woman to command a ship at sea, *5615*

December 28

1832 Vice president to resign, *4304*

1869 Labor Day, *2498*

1912 Municipal streetcars, *8375*

1920 Ambulance ship designed and built by the Navy as a hospital, *5209*

1931 Volcanic eruption to be broadcast on radio, *5916*

1961 Airline to carry 100 million passengers, *8148*

1972 Stereo telecast, *4978*

1981 Child born in the United States through in vitro fertilization, *2161*

1992 Nationwide nutritional labeling standards, *7285*

2004 Court ruling requiring emergency evacuation plans for people with disabilities, *7051*

December 29

1782 Nautical almanac, *8407*

1837 Threshing machine to employ steam, *1605*

1848 Gaslight in the White House, *4326*

1851 Young Men's Christian Association, *7205*

1867 Stock brokerage concern to use a stock ticker, *1772*

1891 Radio patent, *4818*

1908 Brake for four-wheeled cars, *8244*

1913 Serial movie with installments longer than one reel, *1139*

1938 Pontoon bridge of reinforced concrete, *3254*

1952 Hearing aid using transistors, *5271*

1955 Aerocycle, *8139*

1961 Minimum wage law established by a city for public contract work, *7163*

1973 Photograph of a comet taken from space, *6414*

December 30

1731 Concert, *1212*

1828 Strike by women, *7110*

1852 President to celebrate his silver wedding anniversary at the White House, *4252*

1854 Oil company, *6583*

1873 National measurement organization, *1489*

1887 National physiology society, *5223*

1903 National political science association, *6725*

1913 Crepe, *2140*

1943 African-American paratroop unit, *5483*

1954 African-American athlete to win the James E. Sullivan Memorial Trophy, *7479*

1959 Submarine equipped with ballistic missiles, *8523*

1995 Coptic Orthodox Church bishop, *6332*

December 31

1776 Price regulation law enacted by a colony, *1476*

1800 Book with color plates, *4438*

1830 Parade held by a mystic society, *1367*

1841 Dental surgeons to be licensed by a state, *5023*

1907 Dropping of the ball in Times Square on New Year's Eve, *2507*

1923 Transatlantic radio broadcast of a voice, *4777*

1937 Socialist Workers Party organizational meeting, *4097*

1948 Senator to win a seat that had been occupied by his father and his mother, *3681*

1951 Battery to convert radioactive energy into electrical energy, *6572*

1981 Year in which the public debt of the United States exceeded $1 trillion, *3861*

2003 Ice hotel, *1845*

INDEX TO PERSONAL NAMES

The following is a listing of key personal names in the main body of the text, arranged alphabetically by last name. To find an entry in the main body of the text, please go to the italicized number.

A

Arroyo, Domingo: *5825*
Arthur, Chester Alan: *6079*
Arthur, Robert: *5083*
Asbury, Francis: *6232, 6234*
Aserinsky, Eugene: *6671*
Ashburner, Charles Edward: *3529*
Ashcroft, John: *3696*
Ashford, Emmett Littleton: *7540*
Ashley, Hannah Hogeboom: *6121*
Ashley, Maurice: *7746*
Ashmun, Jehudi: *2754*
Ashton, Genevieve: *1805*
Ashton, George: *1805*
Asija, Satya Pal: *6461*
Asing, Norman: *1814*
Aspinwall, Nan Jane: *8182*
Assad, Hafez al-: *4321*
Assing, Norman: *1434*
Astor, John Jacob: *6060*
Astor, Mary: *1147*
Astor, Nancy Witcher Langhorne: *3929*
Astor, Waldorf: *3929*
Atala, Anthony: *5061*
Atanasoff, John Vincent: *6516*
Athenagaros, Archbishop: *2849*
Atherton, Ray: *3897*
Atkins, Charles Grandison: *1623*
Atkinson, William: *6468*
Atkisson, Earl James: *5425*
Attlee, Clement Richard: *4587*
Attucks, Crispus: *5644*
Attwater, Henry Smith: *2735*
Atwater, Robert: *8074*
Atwater, Wilbur Olin: *1625, 7259*
Atwell, W. S.: *7641*
Atwood, Ernestine F.: *6896*
Atwood, Harry Nelson: *4329*
Atwood, Luther: *1889*
Atwood, Margaret: *8246*
Atwood, Wallace Walter: *2837*
Audubon, John James: *5941*
Auste, Louis: *2390*
Austin, Ann: *6191*
Austin, C.: *1295*
Austin, William A.: *8285*
Avebury, Lord: *4779*
Averill, D. R.: *2656*
Avila, John B.: *1630*
Avram, Henriette Davidson: *3039*
Axson, A. Forster: *7241*
Ayers, William: *6035*
Aykroyd, Dan: *1281*
Ayllón, Lucas Vazquez de: *6110*
Aymer, Gilbert Henry: *1118*
Ayres, Thomas N.: *1990*

B

Babbitt, Benjamin Talbert: *1524, 1527, 2212, 2369*
Babcock, Stephen Moulton: *2392*
Baby Fae: *5375*
Bache, Alexander Dallas: *6718*
Bache, Benjamin Franklin: *4481, 4495*
Bache, Franklin: *5296*
Bacon, Augustus Octavius: *3672*
Bacon, Henry: *7185*
Bacon, Thomas: *2900*
Badillo, Herman: *3624*
Badin, Father Stephen Theodore: *6244*
Baekeland, Leo Hendrik: *1899*
Baer, Max: *7605*
Bagley, Sarah G.: *4849*
Bagley, Worth: *5725*
Bagno, Samuel: *3307*
Bailey, Carroll L.: *7976*
Bailey, Ezekiel: *2132*
Bailey, Francis: *3517*
Bailey, John: *3596*
Bailey, Leonard L.: *5375*
Bailey, Theodorus: *7003*
Bainbridge, William: *3100*
Baine, John: *6352*
Baird, Robert Atkinson, III: *4705*
Bakay, Roy: *5275*
Baker, Belle: *4796*
Baker, Edward Dickinson: *3664*
Baker, Ellis Benjamin: *4876*
Baker, Eugene Voy: *7691*
Baker, Howard, Jr.: *3831*
Baker, James: *2321*
Baker, Newton Diehl: *3088*
Baker, Richard: *6323*
Baker, Richard Freligh: *5137*
Baker, Sara Josephine: *7273*
Baker, Sue A.: *3860*
Baker, Vernon: *5538*
Bakken, Earl: *5353*
Balanchine, George: *1051*
Balch, George T.: *3499*
Balcom, Homer Gage: *3300*
Baldacci, James: *2609*
Baldasare, Fred: *7914*
Baldwin, James Fowle: *3222*
Baldwin, John: *6119*
Baldwin, Loammi: *8424*
Baldwin, Luke: *1885*
Baldwin, Simeon Eben: *3969*
Baldwin, Thomas Scott: *7676, 8008*
Balfour, George: *5193*
Ball, Cornelius: *7523*
Ballantyne, William: *8043*

Biardot, Alphonse: *2387*
Biardot, Ernest: *2387*
Biardot, Octave: *2387*
Bibb, William Wyatt: *4041*
Biddle, Clement: *7356*
Biddle, Nicholas: *3470*
Bidwell, George R.: *7649*
Bierstadt, Albert: *1029, 3275*
Bigelow, Erastus Brigham: *2133, 2549*
Bigelow, Robert: *6892*
Biggs, Hermann Michael: *7257, 7258*
Biggs, Wayne: *1840*
Billings, Frank: *5115*
Billings, William: *1220, 1335*
Billington, George: *1718*
Billington, John: *6986*
Billmeyer, Michael: *6353*
Bin Laden, Osama: *5830*
Bingham, A. B.: *5681*
Bingham, Caleb: *3006*
Bingham, William: *3408*
Binney, Horace: *1594, 3008*
Binny, Archibald: *2033, 4443*
Biörck, Erick: *6183*
Birch, William Young: *1590*
Bird, Greenup: *6935*
Bird, Robert Montgomery: *1430*
Bird, William: *6935*
Birdseye, Clarence: *2421*
Birger, Charles: *6939*
Birney, Alice McLellan: *2957*
Birney, James Gillespie: *4060*
Bishop, Bainbridge: *1301*
Bishop, David Wolfe: *7619*
Bishop, Samuel: *4006*
Bissell, Daniel: *5500*
Bissell, Emily Perkins: *7224*
Bissell, George Henry: *6583*
Bissell, Melville Reuben: *2217*
Bitzer, Billy: *1131*
Blaché, Alice Guy: *1130*
Black, Alexander: *1387*
Black, Frank Swett: *2816*
Black, James: *4067*
Black, James Wallace: *4623*
Black, Richard: *6649*
Black, Robert Glennwood: *5589*
Black, S. Duncan: *2668*
Blackford, Isaac: *3706*
Blackton, James Stuart: *1195*
Blackwell, Antoinette Brown: *6271*
Blackwell, Edward: *7665*
Blackwell, Elizabeth: *5024, 5107*
Blackwell, Emily: *5107*
Blackwell, H. M.: *1537*
Blackwell, Henry: *2592*
Blaese, Michael: *5399*
Blagojevich, Rod: *7295*
Blaha, John: *3787*
Blaine, James Gillespie: *3890, 4076*
Blair, David: *1180*
Blair, Izell: *6142*
Blair, John: *3732*
Blair, Joseph Cullen: *2833*
Blair, Montgomery: *4674*
Blair, William Reid: *5957*
Blake, Alexander Vietts: *4441*
Blake, Eli Whitney: *3265, 3386*
Blake, Eubie: *1142*
Blake, James, Jr.: *7467*
Blake, Lemuel: *1885*
Blake, Lyman Reed: *2248*
Blake, Philos: *3265*
Blanchard, Jean Pierre: *7994*
Blanchard, Thomas: *2645*
Blanchfield, Florence Aby: *5449*
Bland, Edward: *6029*
Blassan, Harry: *7868*
Blavatsky, Helena Petrovna: *7216*
Blayton, Jesse Bee: *4812*
Bleibtrey, Ethelda: *7856*
Blessitt, Arthur: *7985*
Blickensderfer, George C.: *1680*
Bliss, Eleanor: *5244*
Bliss, Henry H.: *8238*
Bliss, Raymond Whitcomb: *2530*
Block, Adriaen: *8403*
Blodget, Samuel: *1020*
Blodgett, Katherine Burr: *3364*
Blomberg, Ron: *7547*
Blondel, John F.: *2280*
Blondin, Emile: *1371*
Bloom, Claire V.: *5617*
Bloom, Louis Richard: *5005*
Bloomer, Amelia Jenks: *2244, 4507*
Bloomer, Melville H.: *4862*
Blount, William: *3653, 3654*
Blow, Susan Elizabeth: *2949*
Bluford, Guion: *6826*
Blum, Barbara Davis: *1755*
Blumberg, Baruch Samuel: *5160, 6915*
Blumenthal, Mark: *5106*
Blumgart, Hermann: *5133*
Blunt, Edward March: *5905*
Bly, Nellie: *8531*
Boardman, Alexander: *3416*
Bobbs, John Stough: *5343*
Bochco, Stephen: *4985*
Bock, Jerry: *1466*
Bocock, Thomas Salem: *5691*
Boehm, John Philip: *6211*
Boehm, Martin: *6225*
Boehnisch, George: *6219*
Boeing, William Edward: *4693*

Brand, Bernie: *7972*
Brand, Vance Devoe: *6820*
Brandeis, Louis Dembitz: *1992, 3750*
Brantley, William Theophilus: *2716*
Brattain, Walter Houser: *6517*
Brattle, William: *6759*
Braun, Carol Mosely: *3692*
Braunsteiner Ryan, Hermine: *6103*
Bray, John Randolph: *1196*
Bray, Thomas: *2996, 2997, 2998*
Brayton, George B.: *8368*
Brazzil, Ruth: *3718*
Brearley, William Henry: *4597*
Breck, John: *2471*
Breckinridge, John: *3664, 4340*
Breckinridge, Mary: *2152*
Breedlove, Sarah: *1710*
Breidenbach, Warren: *5381*
Breill, Frank "Pop": *7583*
Breitbart, Charles H.: *7278*
Bremer, L. Paul: *3916*
Brenner, Victor David: *4039*
Brenon, Herbert: *1143*
Brenston, Jackie: *1341*
Brent, Margaret: *3758*
Brewer, Joseph: *2852*
Brewer, Lucy: *5564*
Brewer, Margaret Ann: *5570*
Brewster, Nathaniel: *2688*
Brewster, Sackford: *6029*
Brewster, William: *2993, 6175*
Brezhnev, Leonid I.: *4320*
Brice, Steve: *1845*
Bricklin, Dan: *6459*
Bridgeman, Thomas: *1602*
Bridgers, Frank Hillman: *3313*
Bridges, Robert: *1913*
Bridgwood, Charlotte: *8205*
Brigden, Zechariah: *2689*
Briggs, Emily Edson: *4596*
Briggs, Isaac: *8410*
Briggs, Robert: *6670*
Briggs, Samuel, Jr.: *3989*
Briggs, Samuel, Sr.: *3989*
Bristol, Arthur Leroy: *8484*
Britt, Maurice L.: *5526*
Broadhead, James Overton: *3969*
Broadwick, Georgia: *8034*
Broaker, Frank: *1707*
Brock, Sir Thomas: *1095*
Brodie, Maurice: *5157*
Brodie, Stephen: *1383*
Bronck, Jonas: *6028*
Bronson, Earl D.: *6508*
Bronte, Emily: *4464*
Brooke, Edward William: *3688*
Brooke, Robert: *2601*
Brookhart, Smith Wildman: *3675*
Brookings, Robert Somers: *7226*
Brookins, Walter Richard: *8016, 8018*
Brooks, Charles, Jr.: *7021*
Brooks, Gwendolyn: *4771*
Brooks, Preston: *3601, 3662*
Broome, Joseph: *1519*
Broughton, Nicholson: *5653*
Brousseau, Pierre: *7980*
Brow, John: *6022*
Brower, A.: *8181*
Brown, Adolph: *2652*
Brown, Bailey Thornsberry: *5697*
Brown, Benjamin Gratz: *4069*
Brown, Benjamin Harrison: *2820*
Brown, Charles: *8416*
Brown, Charles Brockden: *1080*
Brown, David: *1669*
Brown, David M.: *6887*
Brown, Ebenezer: *2240, 6259*
Brown, Edgar: *3683*
Brown, Edward Fisher: *5042*
Brown, Edwin Lee: *7218*
Brown, Elisha, Jr.: *2333*
Brown, Felix: *2652*
Brown, Gerald: *3365*
Brown, James: *3964*
Brown, Janice: *8161*
Brown, Jerry: *7166*
Brown, Joe E.: *1155*
Brown, John: *5646*
Brown, Joseph Brantley: *3727*
Brown, Joseph Mansfield: *7878*
Brown, Melvin L.: *5531*
Brown, Moses: *3233, 4020*
Brown, Mrs. Charles R.: *7758*
Brown, O. B.: *1205*
Brown, Rachel: *5250*
Brown, Ronald H.: *4110*
Brown, Russell John: *5807*
Brown, Samuel Robbins: *2755*
Brown, Solyman: *5214, 5315*
Brown, Thomas: *4661*
Brown, Wesley Anthony: *3118*
Brown, William: *5286, 5500*
Brown, William H.: *7008*
Brown, William Henry: *7569*
Brown, William Hill: *1077*
Brown, William Montgomery: *6298*
Brown, William Wells: *1091*
Browne, Ethel: *6664*
Browne, Joseph: *5287*
Browne, William W.: *1730*
Brownell, Francis E.: *5502, 5698*
Brownell, Herbert: *4192*
Brownie, Leon: *1003*
Brubeck, Dave: *1273*

C

Cole, Thomas: *1027, 1029*
Cole, William: *3947*
Coleman, Bessie: *8048*
Coleman, Clyde Jay: *8248*
Coleman, Edward: *6927, 7030*
Coleman, John: *6035*
Coleman, Nancy: *1460*
Coleman, Norman Jay: *4180*
Colfax, Schuyler: *3570*
Colgate, William: *2208*
Collbohm, Frank: *5799*
Collens, Charles: *3148*
Colles, Christopher: *4480*
Colley, Russell: *8092*
Collins, Arnold M.: *1902*
Collins, Eileen Marie: *6834*
Collins, Francis: *6695*
Collins, Isaac: *6995*
Collins, Joseph Lawton: *5878*
Collins, Michael: *3400, 6814*
Collins, Thomas: *3487*
Collins, Warren E.: *5180*
Collins, William: *6069*
Collison, Peter: *6487*
Colman, Benjamin: *1412*
Colombosian, Sarkis: *2431*
Colt, Elizabeth Hart Jarvis: *3139*
Colt, Samuel: *4844, 5845, 5847*
Colton, Walter: *4506*
Columbus, Christopher: *2491, 3452, 3501, 4037, 4727, 4728, 7168*
Colwell, Stephen: *1927*
Comerford, Cristeta: *4335*
Commiskey, Henry Alfred: *5532*
Compson, Betty: *1155*
Compton, Arthur: *6569*
Compton, Karl Taylor: *2059*
Comyn, W. Leslie: *8446*
Coney, William Devoe: *8047*
Confer, Bernard: *6144*
Conn, Charles Gerard: *1304, 1305, 1308*
Connally, Charles M.: *2191*
Connally, John: *3831*
Connolly, Daniel: *4871*
Connolly, James Brendan: *7850*
Connolly, Maureen "Little Mo": *7930*
Connolly, Thomas A.: *4871*
Connor, Robert Digges Wimberley: *3027*
Conrad, Charles, Jr.: *4546, 6806, 6815, 6816, 6818, 6819, 6873*
Conried, Heinrich: *2567*
Converse, Frederick Shepherd: *1321*
Converse, Harriet Maxwell: *3928*
Conwell, Christopher Columbus: *4503*
Conyers, James Henry: *3118*
Cook, Frederick A.: *6646*
Cook, G. S.: *4624*
Cook, James: *1074, 6641, 7958*
Cook, Neil: *1830*
Cook, S. M.: *2956*
Cook, Tom: *6926*
Cooke, George Frederick: *1425*
Cooke, Josiah (Joseph) Parsons: *2758*
Cooke, William D.: *7033*
Cooley, Denton A.: *5371, 5379*
Cooley, James P.: *2462*
Coolidge, Calvin: *1506, 3442, 3719, 4039, 4094, 4278, 4279, 4280, 4469, 4532, 4791, 6903*
Coolidge, Grace: *1506*
Coolidge, William David: *3395*
Cooney, Frank Buckley: *2026*
Cooper, Charles Henry: *7557*
Cooper, D. B.: *6956*
Cooper, Daniel M.: *1682*
Cooper, Elias Samuel: *3062*
Cooper, Gary: *1170*
Cooper, George Marion: *5070*
Cooper, James Fenimore: *1032, 1083*
Cooper, Leon N.: *6913*
Cooper, Leroy Gordon, Jr.: *6802, 6806, 6807*
Cooper, Martin: *4916*
Cooper, Peter: *2750, 3273, 4070, 6558, 7793, 8332*
Cooper, Thomas Apthorpe: *1425*
Copland, Aaron: *1053*
Copland, Patrick: *2682*
Copley, John Singleton: *1019*
Copson, John: *1974*
Corbett, James John: *1116, 7597, 7598*
Corbin, John: *5618*
Corbin, Austin: *1723*
Corbin, Margaret Cochran: *5618*
Cori, Carl Ferdinand: *6906*
Cori, Gerty Theresa: *6906*
Cormack, Allen MacLeod: *5142*
Cormier, Lucia Marie: *3686*
Cornbury, Viscount: *7430*
Cornelia, Miss: *2941*
Cornelissen, Erick: *7233*
Cornelissen, Jan: *7233*
Cornelius, Robert: *4617*
Cornell, Ezra: *4848*
Cornish, James: *5345*
Cornish, John: *2109*
Cornish, Samuel E.: *4554*
Cornwallis, Lord Charles: *1332, 3473, 5433, 5674*
Cornwallis, Thomas: *5636*
Coronado, Francis Vasquez: *6165*
Correll, Charles: *4792*
Corrigan, Mairead: *6915*
Corson, Juliet: *3199*

D

Dacey, Ralph: *5380*
Dacres, James Richard: *5682*
Daggett, Ezra: *2341*
Daghlian, Harry K., Jr.: *6617*
Daguerre, Louis Jacques Mandé: *4617*
Dale, Porter Hinman: *3574*
Dale, Richard: *8467*
Dale, Sir Thomas: *7722*
Dallas, Alexander J.: *3705*
Dalton, John Call: *3058*
Daly, John (Charles): *1404*
Damadian, Raymond: *5145*
Damiani, Philip: *5970*
Damrosch, Walter: *1257, 4793*
Dane, Nathan: *6122*
Daniel, Anthony: *6301*
Danis, Anthony Leo: *5760*
Darby, William: *1411*
Dare, Virginia: *4737, 6010*
Dargue, Herbert Arthur: *5769*
Darley, Felix Octavius Carr: *4613*
Darling, Jay Norwood "Ding": *4425*
Darlington, Harry: *6649*
Darlington, Jennie: *6649*
Darrow, Charles B.: *7730*
Darrow, Clarence: *2970*
Dart, Joseph: *1608*
Dasch, George John: *5786*
Daschle, Tom: *5833*
Davenport, James: *2121*
Davenport, Thomas: *2039, 6536, 6777*
Davenport-Engberg, Mary: *1253*
David, Albert Leroy: *5794*
Davids, Thaddeus: *2675*
Davidson, Ann: *8537*
Davidson, Royal Page: *5423, 8234*
Davies, Arthur Bowen: *1039*
Davies, Charles: *2928*
Davies, Ralph Kenneth: *1509*
Davis, Allan: *2955*
Davis, Benjamin Oliver: *5445*
Davis, Benjamin Oliver, Jr.: *5481, 5494*
Davis, Charles, Jr.: *1885*
Davis, Clifford: *3579*
Davis, David: *4068*
Davis, Dwight Filley: *7926*
Davis, Ernie: *7714*
Davis, G. W.: *7359*
Davis, Harry: *1126*
Davis, Harry Phillips: *4777*
Davis, Isaac: *6928*
Davis, Jefferson: *1338, 1456, 3707, 3806*
Davis, John: *6641, 7114*
Davis, John William: *4532*
Davis, Joseph Edward: *5074*
Davis, Miles Lewis: *2301*
Davis, N. Jan: *6832*
Davis, Phineas: *8333*
Davis, William Augustine: *4674*
Davison, Frederic Ellis: *5452*
Dawes, Billy: *5649*
Dawes, Charles Gates: *4094*
Dawson, Benjamin Frederick: *5321*
Dawson, Geoffrey: *4888*
Dawson, Roy O.: *2096*
Dawson, William Levi: *1261, 3617*
Day, Benjamin: *4519*
Day, Benjamin Henry: *4503, 4612*
Day, Henry: *1888*
Day, Stephen: *1061, 1062, 2029, 2030, 2687, 2888, 3168, 3456, 6338*
Dayton, William Lewis: *4063*
de Bore, Etienne: *1574*
De Bow, James Dunwoody Brownson: *2747*
De Brébeuf, John: *6301*
de Brehant de Galinée, Renée: *6574*
de Cass, François Dollier: *6574*
de Clairac, Louis Andrée de la Mamie: *6762*
De Crow, Sarah: *4656*
de Fleury, François Louis Teisseidre: *3552*
de Florencia, Father Francisco: *6184*
de Foreest, Isaaq: *3403*
de Forest, Jesse: *6020*
De Forest, Lee: *1142, 1146, 1250, 4532, 4780, 4820*
de Franchessin, Jacques Antoine: *5438*
de Gersdorff, George Bruns: *7702*
de Gourges, Dominique: *5628*
de Graeff, Johannes: *3470*
de Graff, Robert: *4464*
De Horne, M.: *5287*
de La Salle, Robert Cavelier, Sieur: *8404*
de la Tour, Sieur Le Blond: *3349*
de Laval, Carl Gustaf Patrik: *2381*
de Lerena, Juan José: *4555*
De Luce, Nathaniel: *1318*
de Mandeville, Bernard Xavier Philippe de Marigny: *1800*
de Mille, Agnes: *1464*
De Mille, Cecil B.: *1138*
de Moksa, Count Agoston Haraszthy: *1613*
de Nancrède, Paul Joseph Guérard: *6350*
de Padilla, Juan: *6165*
de Palm, Joseph Henry Louis: *2300*
De Priest, Oscar Stanton: *3606*
de Rojamón, Felipe: *2291*
de Sequeyra, John: *5011*

E

F

Farmer, Karen Batchelor: *7231*
Farmer, Moses Gerrish: *6537, 7325*
Farmer, Robert: *6029*
Farnham, Ivan Richard: *1876*
Farnsworth, Philo Taylor: *4927*
Farnsworth, Willis S.: *1689*
Farnum, Dustin: *1138*
Farquhar, George: *1415*
Farr, John: *5235*
Farr, William: *5562*
Farragut, David Glasgow: *5601, 7003, 7176*
Farrar, Eugenia H.: *1250*
Fauset, Crystal Bird: *4394*
Fayssoux, Peter: *3133*
Featherstonhaugh, George William: *6491*
Fehrenbach, John: *5127*
Feinstein, Dianne: *3693*
Feld, Irvin: *3217*
Felker, Alfred Charles: *5490*
Feller, Robert William Andrew: *7535*
Fellows, Alvin J.: *2657*
Feltham, Jocelyn: *5650*
Feltman, Charles: *2391*
Felton, Rebecca Latimer: *3673*
Fendall, Josias: *3949*
Fenno, John: *4492*
Fenoaltea, Sergio: *4196*
Fenwick, Millicent Hammond: *3629*
Ferebee, Thomas W.: *5797*
Ferentinos, Paisios: *6276*
Ferguson, Samuel David: *6283*
Fermat, Pierre: *6709*
Fermi, Enrico: *6736, 6748*
Fernald, Walter Elmore: *2931*
Fernandez Larios, Armando: *6983*
Fernow, Bernhard Eduard: *2816*
Ferrar, William: *2589*
Ferraro, Geraldine: *3833*
Ferrer, Jose: *1464*
Ferris, George Washington Gale: *1004*
Ferry, Elisha Peyre: *4353*
Ferry, Jules: *3498*
Fessenden, Reginald Aubrey: *4778*
Fessler, Richard: *5378*
Fetchit, Stephen "Stepin"": *1151*
Feuchtwanger, Lion: *6920*
Few, William: *3645, 5102*
Fey, Charles: *1802*
Feynman, Richard Phillips: *6707*
Fickel, Jacob Earl: *5464*
Field, Ben: *8351*
Field, Cyrus West: *4853*
Field, James Gaven: *4080*
Field, Stephen Johnson: *4855*
Fielden, Samuel: *7135*
Figueroa Cordero, Andrés: *3579*
Filene, Abraham Lincoln: *2092*
Filene, Edward P.: *2092*
Filene, William: *2092*
Fillmore, Abigail Powers: *4221*
Fillmore, Millard: *4064, 4221*
Finch, William Bolton : *8528*
Findley, Paul: *3622*
Finger, Bill: *1102*
Fink, Colin Garfield: *1944*
Finley, James: *3232*
Finn, Father William Joseph: *6306*
Finnegan, Jack: *7599*
Finney, John Miller Turpin: *5229*
Firmstone, William: *6582*
Firzer, Arthur: *1442*
Fischer, Adolph: *7135*
Fischer, Isaac, Jr.: *1852*
Fischer, Louis R.: *1399*
Fischer, Robert James "Bobby": *7743*
Fishbourn, Benjamin: *4116*
Fisher, Alva J.: *2221*
Fisher, Anna L.: *6821, 6829*
Fisher, Carl Graham: *3420, 7623*
Fisher, John Dix: *2920*
Fisher, John Stuchell: *7376*
Fisher, Mary: *6191*
Fiske, Bradley Allen: *3033, 5861*
Fiske, Willard: *2774*
Fiske, William L.: *7975*
Fitch, Asa: *6659*
Fitch, Howard W.: *8481*
Fitch, John: *8409*
Fitch, Samuel Sheldon: *5305*
Fite, Rankin: *7302*
Fitzgerald, Eugenia Tucker: *2751*
Fitzpatrick, John: *5561*
Fitzpatrick, Thomas: *6066*
Fitzsimons, Thomas: *3562, 3582*
Fitzsimons, William Thomas: *5744*
Flagg, Josiah: *5077*
Flagg, Josiah Foster: *5289*
Flaherty, Barney: *4519*
Flanagan, Betsy: *2324*
Fleer, Frank Henry: *2407*
Fleeson, Plunket: *2535*
Fleischmann, Charles: *2367*
Fleming, Harry: *5552*
Fleming, John: *1334*
Fleming, Tommy: *7968*
Fletcher, Francis: *6168*
Fletcher, Joseph Otis: *6646, 6650*
Fletcher, Richard: *6716*
Fletcher, Robert: *3743*
Flick, Lawrence Francis: *5224*
Flinn, Kelly Jean: *5493*
Flipper, Henry Ossian: *3107*
Flora, Ruth: *5587*
Florence, Virginia Proctor Powell: *3021*

G

Gluckman, Richard: *3165*
Glyn, W. E.: *7921*
Goddard, George: *4630*
Goddard, Luther: *2627*
Goddard, Mary Katherine: *4656*
Goddard, Robert Hutchins: *6788*
Godfrey, Thomas: *8499*
Godowsky, Leopold, Jr.: *4650*
Godwin, Mary Wollstonecraft: *3763*
Goenka, S. N.: *7023*
Gof, Frederick Harris: *7225*
Goffigan, Laban: *7338*
Gogarty, Deirdre: *7612*
Golden, John: *1460*
Golden, Millie: *3526*
Goldfaden, Abraham: *1444*
Goldin, Daniel: *6800*
Goldman, Sylvan N.: *1691*
Goldmark, Peter: *4835*
Goldsborough, Louis Malesherbes: *6372*
Goldstein, Bernard: *2870*
Goldstein, Isidore: *7381*
Goldwater, Barry: *3786, 4100*
Goldwyn, Samuel: *1138*
Goler, George Washington: *7265*
Golitzyn, Father Dimitri Augustin: *6244*
Golubok, Leon: *1442*
Gompers, Samuel: *4739*
Gonzales, Ron: *4290*
Good, Robert A.: *5369*
Goodale, Samuel D.: *1372*
Goode, Malvin Russell "Mel": *4602*
Goode, Sarah E.: *3998*
Goodlin, Chalmers: *5486*
Goodman, Benny: *1265*
Goodmanson, Adrienne Lee: *5432*
Goodmon, James F.: *4981*
Goodnow, Frank Johnson: *6725*
Goodrich, Annie Warburton: *3088*
Goodrich, John: *4006*
Goodrich, Joseph: *3268*
Goodwin, George: *2174, 3956*
Goodwin, George W.: *8440*
Goodwin, Hannibal Williston: *4644*
Goodwin, Isabella: *7371*
Goodwin, J. Cheever: *1440*
Goodwin, William Nelson, Jr.: *4649*
Goodyear, Charles: *1887, 2263*
Gorbachev, Mikhail: *3911, 3912*
Gordon, Daisy: *2193*
Gordon, Hugh: *8119*
Gordon, Jacqueline: *7773*
Gordon, Nathaniel: *7002*
Gordon, Richard F., Jr.: *6815*
Gordon, Richard Francis, Jr.: *4546, 6816*
Gordon, Samuel George: *6498*
Gore, Albert: *4212*
Gore, Robert: *2144*
Gore, Wilbert L.: *2144*
Gorges, Sir Ferdinando: *2554, 3508, 6631*
Gorham, Nathaniel: *6048*
Gorman, Margaret: *1394*
Gorrie, John: *2275*
Gorringe, Henry Honeychurch: *7175*
Gorton, Adolphus W.: *8070*
Gosden, Freeman: *4792*
Gosnold, Bartholomew: *6011, 6013, 6171*
Goss, Joe: *7595*
Gossling, Frederick W.: *2364*
Gottschalk, Louis Moreau: *1237*
Gougelman, Pierre: *5266*
Gould, Gordon: *6521*
Gould, James: *3191*
Gould, Stephen Philip: *1905*
Goulding, Ray: *4978*
Gounder, Howard Moyer: *7298*
Gounod, Charles François: *1319*
Goupil, René: *6301*
Gourdin, Edward O.: *7947*
Grace, Robert: *2536*
Grace, William Joseph: *5047*
Graham, Annie Neal Gilliard: *5569*
Graham, Bette Nesmith: *1694*
Graham, Evarts Ambrose: *5348, 7080*
Graham, Jack Gilbert: *6949*
Graham, James R.: *6393*
Graham, John: *1836*
Graham, Lew: *1396*
Graham, Sylvester: *2346, 2397*
Graham, William J.: *1993*
Gram, Hans: *1336*
Gram, Hans Burch: *5020, 5303*
Grandon, F. J.: *1139*
Granger, Francis: *4059*
Grant, George F.: *7763*
Grant, Ray: *4939*
Grant, Ulysses Simpson: *2501, 3570, 3843, 3925, 4683, 5442*
Grant, Ulysses Simpson, III: *4332*
Grant, William West: *5344*
Gras, Norman Scott Brien: *2840*
Grasso, Ella: *4381*
Gratz, Rebecca: *6214*
Grauer, Ben: *1163*
Graupner, Johann Christian Gottlieb: *1214*
Gravelet, Jean François: *1371*
Gravely, Samuel Lee, Jr.: *3122, 5611, 5613*
Graves, James: *6982*
Graves, William J.: *3599*
Gray, Adeline: *8107*
Gray, Clifford B.: *7975*
Gray, Elisha: *1243*
Gray, Hanna Holborn: *2786*

H

Heiser, Richard: *6454*
Heisman, John: *7709*
Helguera, Leon: *4741*
Heller, Dean: *3791*
Hemenway, Harriet Lawrence: *5912*
Hemphill, John: *3663*
Hendee, George M.: *8287*
Henderson, Fletcher: *1259*
Henderson, George: *2813*
Henderson, John Brooks: *4076*
Hendricks, Gerhard: *6116*
Henefelt, Frank: *5363*
Henenberg, Hattie L.: *3718*
Henke, Milburn: *5773*
Henley, David: *5550*
Hennepin, Louis: *6575*
Henriques, J. A.: *3106*
Henry VII, King of England: *6003*
Henry, Charles Lewis: *8373*
Henry, Frederick F.: *5531*
Henry, John: *1422*
Henry, Joseph: *4817, 4842, 6535*
Henry, Sir E. R.: *7362, 7366*
Henry, William: *8406*
Hensley, William Nicholas: *4790*
Henson, Matthew Alexander: *6646*
Herbert, H. L.: *7870*
Herbert, Henry William: *4591*
Herbert, Sister Xavier: *5097*
Hering, Constantine: *3052, 5213*
Herjolffson, Bjarni: *5999*
Herman, Peter: *7602*
Hernández, Joseph Marion: *3595*
Herndon, Hugh, Jr.: *8084*
Herrera, Pete: *7819*
Herreshoff, John Brown : *8476*
Herreshoff, Nathanael Greene: *7573, 8476*
Herrington, John Bennett: *6840*
Herrmann, Augustine: *6026*
Hershey, Milton Snavely: *2395*
Herskovitz, Anatol: *5139*
Herter, Christian Archibald: *6853*
Hertz, Alfred: *1320*
Herz, Wilhelm: *8291*
Hess, Daniel: *2216*
Hessel, John: *4891*
Hesselink, Lambertus: *6476*
Hesselius, Gustavus: *1017*
Hester, Leigh Ann: *5540*
Heuring, Vincent P.: *6475*
Hewitt, Don: *4545*
Hewitt, James: *1316*
Hewitt, John Hill: *1337*
Heyl, Henry Renno: *1193*
Heyward, Dorothy: *1461*
Heyward, DuBose: *1461*
Heyward, Thomas: *3133*
Hiacoomes: *6197*
Hiawatha: *6006*
Hibbard, Frederick Cleveland: *7186*
Hickenlooper, Smith: *3719*
Hickey, Deirdre: *8399*
Hickey, Thomas: *5549*
Hickman, C. N.: *5870*
Hicks, Hassel T.: *8260*
Hicks, James: *5407*
Higgins, Daniel P.: *7189*
Higinbotham, William: *7742*
Higley, John: *4004*
Higley, Samuel: *1916*
Hildebrandt, Martin: *2460*
Hill, Alfred: *5945*
Hill, Frank A.: *5787*
Hill, Ira H.: *4482*
Hill, John: *3172*
Hill, Luther Leonidas: *5346*
Hill, Samuel Eugene: *6290*
Hill, Samuel Lapham: *2950*
Hill, Ureli Corelli: *1234*
Hill, Walter: *5806*
Hillary, Sir Edmund: *7983*
Hillegas, Michael: *1217*
Hiller, Clarence B.: *6938*
Hilles, Samuel: *2739*
Hilliard, David: *4101*
Hillman, Sidney: *3820*
Hillquit, Morris: *4088*
Hilton, William: *5983*
Hinckley, John Warnock, Jr.: *4272*
Hine, Thomas Buck: *5865*
Hines, Edward Norris: *8200*
Hines, Paul: *7507*
Hinkle, Clark: *7706*
Hires, Charles Elmer: *2366*
Hirohito, Emperor: *3940*
Hirschfeld, Harry: *4988*
Hiss, Philip: *2528*
Hitchcock, Edward: *6489, 6658*
Hitchcock, Frank Harris: *4690*
Hitchcock, Lambert: *2543*
Hitchcock, Thomas: *7869*
Hitz, John: *3379*
Hitz, William: *4186*
Hoagland, Herbert Case: *4524*
Hoballah, Mahmoud: *6313*
Hoban, James: *3840*
Hobart, Colonel Aaron: *1292*
Hobbs, Lucy B.: *5085*
Hobby, Oveta Culp: *4191, 4192, 5427*
Hobson, Frank M.: *8515*
Hobson, Joseph: *3441*
Hobson, Julius: *4105*
Hobson, Richmond Pearson: *7073*
Hochmuth, Bruno Arthur: *5816*

I

J

K

Knudsen, William Signius: *5447*
Knussman, Kevin: *2207*
Koch, Louis J.: *1008*
Koenig, Alfred J.: *4470*
Koenig, George Augustus: *3392*
Koester, Heinrich Bernhard: *6206*
Koester, M.: *7585*
Kogel, Marcus David: *3094*
Kohnle, Frederick: *2091*
Kolb, Lawrence: *7077*
Kolb, Robert: *5489*
Koons, Franklin M.: *5788*
Koopman, Elias Bernard: *2566*
Kopsky, Doris: *7656*
Korda, Sir Alexander: *1167*
Korizek, Frank: *4559*
Korn, Arthur: *4468*
Kossuth, Lajos: *2246*
Koster, Henry: *1168*
Kozachenko, Kathy: *7451*
Krafft, Michael: *1367*
Krafft, Michael August: *2336*
Kramer, Stanley: *1175*
Kramer, Walter R.: *7977*
Kreps, Juanita Morris: *1785*
Kreusi, John: *4827*
Krier, Gary E.: *8155*
Krikalev, Sergei K.: *6833*
Kroc, Ray: *1835*
Krone, Julie: *7821*
Kross, Anna Moscowitz: *7019*
Krueger, Otto: *1258*
Kubasov, Valery Nikolayevich: *6820*
Kuchins, Harry: *8073*
Kuehne, Trip: *7782*
Kuhn, Adam: *2702*
Kuhn, Richard J.: *5141*
Kuiken, Todd: *5276*
Kujiraoka, Sozaburo: *6096*
Kulakofsky, Reuben: *2425*
Kunst, David: *7985*
Kunze, Johann Christoff: *6353*
Kunzi, Abraham: *5235*
Kurtz, Thomas: *6434*
Kurzweil, Raymond: *6456*
Kuskof, Ivan Alexandrovich: *6043*
Kwolek, Stephanie L.: *2145*
Kyrides, Lucas Petrou: *1900*

L

La Farge, John: *7223*
La Farge, Oliver: *1041*
La Follette, Philip: *7152*
La Follette, Robert Marion: *4532*
La Mountain, John: *8471*
La Porte, Arthur Earl: *4704*
La Rocca, Nick: *1256*
Labadie, Jean de: *6201*
Laban, Rudolf: *1055*
Ladden, Florence: *2201*
LaDuke, Winona: *4109*
Laessig, Clem H.: *8196*
Lafayette, Marquis de: *6044, 6057*
Lafferty, James V.: *3283*
Lagan, M. D.: *5116*
Lahm, Frank Purdy: *5462, 7674, 8013*
Lake, Simon: *8511*
Lalande, John: *6301*
Lalemant, Gabriel: *6301*
Lallemont, Pierre: *7639*
Lalonde, Donny: *7610*
Lamar, Mirabeau Buonaparte: *3922*
Lamarr, Hedy: *1166*
Lamb, Brian P.: *4979*
Lamb, John: *7137*
Lamb, William Frederick: *3300*
Lamprecht, Chris: *6479*
Lancaster, Burt: *1173*
Land, Edwin Herbert: *4651*
Landes, Bertha Knight: *3534*
Landis, Kenesaw Mountain: *7528*
Landis, Merkel: *1736*
Landreth, Cuthbert: *1600*
Landreth, David: *1581, 1600*
Landsteiner, Karl: *5056*
Lane, Dick: *4941*
Lane, Ephraim: *3376*
Lane, Harriet: *5694*
Lane, James H.: *5716*
Lane, Ralph: *3454*
Lane, Thomas Joseph: *3619*
Lane, William Coolidge: *3024*
Lane, William Henry: *1049*
Langan, Jack: *7592*
Langdon, John: *3645, 3646, 3799, 5572, 8465*
Langdon, Kay Louise: *5587*
Langenheim, Frederick: *4620, 6400*
Langenheim, William: *4620*
Langer, Jerry: *7577*
Langford, Nathaniel Pitt: *5990*
Langley, Samuel Pierpont: *8004*
Langloiserie, Louis: *2695*
Langston, John Mercer: *3767*
Langstroth, Lorenzo Lorraine: *1612*
Lansdowne, Zachary: *8056*
Lansky, Aaron: *1110*
Lansky, Meyer: *1803*
Lanston, Tolbert: *2053*
Lapchick, Joe: *7558*
Lapin, Aaron "Bunny," *2440*
Larkin, Thomas Oliver: *3892*

M

Matisse, Henri: *1039*
Matlack, Charles F.: *5213*
Matthews, Clarence: *7701*
Matthews, John: *2345*
Matthews, Marjorie Swank: *6330*
Matthews, Thomas: *7725*
Matthews, Thomas A.: *6392*
Mature, Victor: *1168*
Mauchly, John W.: *6424*
Maverick, Samuel: *5644*
Maxim, Hiram Percy: *8227*
Maxson, William L.: *2439*
Maxwell, George: *1254*
Maxwell, George Holmes: *2843*
Maxwell, William: *3473*
May, Lewis: *7214*
Mayer, Cornell H.: *6391*
Maynard, Belvin W.: *7679*
Maynard, Lambert: *1818*
Mayor, Bruce: *6957*
Mays, Carl: *7526*
Mays, Melvin Edward: *6966*
Mazor, Stan: *6524*
McAfee, Mildred Helen: *5606*
McAllister, James W.: *6781*
McAllister, John, Sr.: *2082*
McAlpin, Harry: *4599*
McArdle, Joseph: *1441*
McArthur, Bill: *1286*
McAuliffe, Terry: *4112*
McBrearty, Sally: *6702*
McBride, John: *7136*
McBride, Roger L.: *3829*
McCaffery, Dominick F.: *7598*
McCain, Franklin: *6142*
McCambley, Joe: *6477*
McCandless, Bruce: *6827*
McCarthy, George Lewis: *1742*
McCarthy, Joseph Vincent: *7530*
McCarthy, Patrick Henry: *8182*
McCarthy, William: *4690*
McCartney, Paul: *1275, 1286*
McChester, George "Country": *7594*
McClellan, George Brinton: *3807, 5198, 5714, 7621*
McCloskey, John, Cardinal: *6278*
McCloskey, Tanya: *7464*
McClure, Donald: *5755*
McClure, Samuel Sidney: *4521*
McComb, John, Jr.: *7338*
McConnell, Ambrose Moses: *7523*
McConnell, Joseph Christopher: *5809*
McConnell, Matthew: *1767*
McCool, William C.: *6887*
McCormick, Cyrus Hall: *1598*
McCormick, Katherine Dexter: *7443*
McCormick, Patricia: *7615*
McCormick, Robert Rutherford: *4526*
McCoy, George Walter: *5406*
McCoy, Joseph Geating: *3522*
McCoy, Thomas: *7593*
McCullough, W. T.: *8237*
McCurdy, John Alexander Douglas: *8024*
McCusker, Marilyn J.: *6613*
McDaniel, D.: *7796*
McDaniel, Hattie: *1164*
McDaniels, Darryl "DMC" : *1280*
McDermott, John J.: *7946*
McDivitt, James Alton: *6805, 6813*
McDonald, Eugene F., Jr: *4996*
McDonald, J. B.: *8225*
McDonald, Marshall: *3143*
McDonald, Maurice: *1835*
McDonald, Richard: *1835*
McDowell, Ephraim: *5339*
McDowell, Irvin: *5705*
McDowell, John Huber: *2851*
McDowell, Samuel: *7356*
McElroy, James: *8379*
McElroy, Mary: *7015*
McEntire, George W.: *8051*
McFarland, David Ford: *6742*
McFarland, Irene: *8059*
McFatrich, George W.: *3071, 5241*
McFatrich, James: *5241*
McGaffey, Ives W.: *2216*
McGee, Anita Newcomb: *5204*
McGee, John: *6248*
McGee, Walter H.: *7015*
McGee, William: *6248*
McGinnity, Joseph Jerome: *7519*
McGivney, Michael Joseph: *7220*
McGovern, Vincent Howard: *8129*
McGowan, John: *5690*
McGrath, Paul: *1460*
McGraw, John Joseph: *7582*
McGuire, Elwood: *2664*
McHenry, James: *4175*
McHugh, Keith S.: *4902*
McIntyre, James Francis, Cardinal: *6317*
McKean, Thomas: *4113*
McKechnie, William: *7534*
McKenney, William W.: *2566*
McKenzie, John: *2079*
McKenzie, Richard: *6099*
McKhann, J.: *5364*
McKim, Isaac: *8425*
McKinley, William: *3611, 3842, 4275*
McLane, Allan: *7356*
McLaurin, John: *3667*
McLean, Edith Eleanor: *5175*
McLean, James: *1958*
McLean, John: *2734, 5057*
McLoughlin, John: *7724*

N

Nash, Gary: *7931*
Nash, James H.: *5691*
Nash, Simon Augustine: *3712*
Nason, James H.: *2278*
Nason, Joseph: *3267*
Nast, Thomas: *4576, 4579*
Nathan, Theodora: *3829, 4106*
Naugle, Harry Merrill: *3295*
Navratilova, Martina: *7934*
Nawang Gombu: *7983*
Neal, Patricia: *1464*
Neale, Father Leonard: *6246*
Neale, Thomas: *4655*
Neals, Huerta Cortez: *5043*
Needles, William B.: *3071*
Neel, Carr Baker: *7925*
Neel, Samuel R.: *7925*
Neely, Joanne: *7385*
Neff, Mary: *6036*
Neff, Pat Morris: *3718*
Neil, Florence E.: *2195*
Neiligan, Raymond J.: *4905*
Neilson, Martha: *2980*
Nein, Timothy: *5540*
Nelson, Christian K.: *2419*
Nelson, George: *6863*
Nelson, Knute: *3574*
Nelson, Murray: *7413*
Nelson, Ray: *1463*
Nelson, Robert F.: *2306*
Nelson, Rosemary Elaine: *5593*
Nerinck, Charles: *6264*
Nesbitt, John Maxwell: *1989*
Neuberger, Maurine Brown: *4395*
Neuberger, Richard Lewis: *4395*
Neuhauser, Frank L.: *2969*
Neumann, Gustav Adolf: *4551*
Neumann, John Nepomucene: *6328*
New, Harry Stewart: *3781*
Newbold, Charles: *1587*
Newell, William C.: *1376*
Newhouse, Benjamin: *3272*
Newhouse, Sewell: *2653*
Newlands, Francis Griffith: *4082*
Newman, Larry: *8160*
Newman, Samuel: *6340*
Newman, William: *2229*
Newport, Christopher: *3445, 6013, 6171*
Newsom, Gavin: *5935*
Newton, Hubert Anson: *1489*
Newton, Huey: *4101*
Newton, Maurice: *4692*
Ney, Karl Winfield: *5349*
Neyhart, Amos Earl: *2972*
Ng Poon Chew: *4558*
Nicholas, Samuel: *5560, 5561, 5656*
Nichols, Anna R. G.: *3996*
Nichols, J. C.: *2094*
Nichols, Jesse Clyde: *2095*
Nichols, Terry: *6972*
Nichols, William: *1346*
Nicholson, Alfred O. P.: *3663*
Nicholson, Francis: *3448, 6989*
Nicholson, L. A.: *2965*
Nicholson, Samuel Danford: *3574*
Nicholson, Samuel T.: *4087*
Nicholson, William: *2646*
Nickell, Joe: *4980*
Nicola, Lewis: *6762*
Nicoll, Allardyce: *2851*
Nicolls, Richard: *3509, 7788*
Nijmeh, Luie: *5827*
Nijmeh, Saij: *5827*
Nimitz, Chester William: *5607, 5779, 8535*
Nininger, Alexander Ramsey "Sandy", Jr.: *5518*
Nirdlinger, Charles: *4228*
Nirenberg, Marshall Warren: *6911*
Nishino, Kozo: *5774*
Nissen, George P.: *7787*
Nissen, Paul F.: *7787*
Nissly, MaryBelle Johns: *5428*
Nitschmann, David: *6219*
Nixon, John: *3467*
Nixon, Richard Milhous: *3691, 3824, 4156, 4157, 4158, 4159, 4193, 4201, 4202, 4203, 4205, 4287, 4310, 4319, 4320, 4915, 6914, 7164, 7845*
Noah, Mordecai Manuel: *3894*
Nobel, Alfred: *6898*
Nobile, Umberto: *6647*
Noble, Elaine: *7452*
Noble, Silas: *2462*
Noeggerath, Emil Jacob: *5321*
Noel, Garrat: *3176*
Nolan, Beth: *4167*
Nolan, David F.: *4106*
Nolan, Lloyd: *4957*
Norcross, Leonard: *6490*
Noriega, Manuel: *3944*
Norman, John: *3178*
North, Elisha: *5101*
North, Simeon: *3260, 5841*
Norton, Charles Eliot: *6722*
Norton, Oliver Willcox: *1339*
Norton, Thomas: *2652*
Norton, William: *3352*
Norwood, William A.: *1007*
Nova, Lou: *7605*
Novello, Antonia C.: *7283*
Novy, Frederick George: *3076*
Nowel, Peter: *6674*
Noyce, Robert N.: *6522, 6916*
Noyes, Eliot Fette: *1698*

O

P

S

Sewall, Arthur: *4082, 8440*
Sewall, Samuel: *3230*
Sewall, Stephen: *6369*
Sewell, Ike: *1829*
Seymour, Richard: *6172*
Shadrick, Kenneth: *5803*
Shaffer, Donald: *4912*
Shafroth, John Franklin: *5796*
Shaheen, Jeanne: *4290*
Shain, Eva: *7606*
Shakespeare, William: *1417, 1468, 4464, 4967*
Shallenberger, Oliver B.: *6552*
Shallus, Jacob: *3482*
Shank, Robert F.: *4692*
Shantz, Phyllis Frances: *3860*
Shapiro, Ben: *1277*
Sharkey, William L.: *4307*
Sharp, John: *1353*
Sharp, Martha: *6920*
Sharp, Waitstill: *6920*
Shattuck, George Cheyne: *3055*
Shattuck, Lemuel: *7239*
Shavers, Earnie: *7606*
Shaw, Artie: *1264*
Shaw, Louis Agassiz: *5180*
Shaw, Samuel: *3883*
Shaw, William Smith: *3007*
Shawan, Jacob A.: *2964*
Shawn, Ted: *1052, 1054, 3211*
Shays, Daniel: *5675*
Shea, John M.: *7366*
Sheehan, Joseph Eastman: *3090*
Sheeler, Charles: *1039*
Sheen, Monsignor Fulton John: *6306*
Sheffield, Washington Wentworth: *2470*
Sheftall, Mordecai: *7197*
Sheldon, Charles Monroe: *1097*
Sheldon, Edward Austin: *2939*
Sheldon, John P.: *1662*
Shelikhov, Grigori: *6043*
Shelton, Gilbert: *1107*
Shepard, Alan Bartlett, Jr.: *6802, 6803, 7778*
Shepard, Charles H.: *7244*
Sheppard, William: *2215*
Sher, Bartlett: *1468*
Sherburne, Samuel, Jr.: *3703*
Sheridan, Bernard: *2038*
Sheridan, George Augustus: *3608*
Sherman, Frederick Carl: *5780*
Sherman, John: *6083*
Sherman, John Ames: *2024*
Sherman, Roger: *3651*
Sherman, Whitney: *4758*
Sherry, Louis: *2527*
Sherwin, Henry Alden: *2656*
Shew, Joel: *5316, 5389*
Shibe, Benjamin F.: *7521*
Shield, Lansing Peter: *2100*
Shields, James: *3659*
Shields, Marvin Glen: *5536*
Shih Mai-yu: *5035*
Shilders, J.: *6201*
Shima, Masatoshi: *6524*
Shinichiro, Tomonaga: *6707*
Shippee, Amasa: *3493*
Shippee, Lois: *3493*
Shippee, Rhoda: *3493*
Shippen, John M.: *7759*
Shippen, William: *3041, 3042*
Shive, John Northrup: *6518*
Shockley, William: *6517, 6913*
Shoemaker, Eugene M.: *2312, 6886*
Shoemaker, Sherman: *5795*
Shoemaker, Thomas Buckman: *6092*
Sholes, Christopher Latham: *1667*
Short, William: *4116*
Shoukletovich, Doushan Jefta: *6308*
Shrayer, Michael: *6455*
Shreeve, Herbert E.: *4882*
Shreve, Henry Miller: *8421*
Shriver, Robert Sargent: *3828*
Shryrock, George Augustus: *2012*
Shuckburgh, Richard: *1332*
Shugart, Alan: *6444*
Shumway, Norman: *5368*
Shunk, Francis Rawn: *7117*
Shurtleff, Asahel M.: *2463*
Shuster, Joe: *1098, 1101*
Shute, Nevil: *1175*
Siccary, John: *1573*
Sickles, Daniel: *6933*
Siddique, M. Osman: *3915*
Sidi Muhammad ben Abdullah: *3873, 3880*
Siebert, Muriel: *1785*
Siebold, George: *5750*
Siebold, Grace Darling: *5750*
Sieffert, Anton: *6219*
Siegel, Benjamin "Bugsy": *1803*
Siegel, Jerry: *1098, 1101*
Sievert, Frances: *4889*
Sikorsky, Igor Ivan: *8099, 8101, 8102, 8106*
Sikwayi: *4556, 6062*
Silliman, Benjamin: *6772*
Silliman, Benjamin, Jr.: *2746*
Sills, Beverly: *1331*
Silver, Bernard: *1692*
Silver, Jerry: *6705*
Silver, Spencer: *2028*
Simmons, Amelia: *2330*
Simmons, Jean: *1168*
Simmons, John: *2821*
Simmons, Joseph "Run": *1280*

Simms, Ruth Hanna McCormick: *3819*
Simms, William Gilmore: *1086*
Simon, Carleton: *7381*
Simon, Rene: *8029*
Simonds, Frank Herbert: *4761*
Simons, David Goodman: *8144*
Simpson, Albert Benjamin: *2798*
Simpson, Edward: *3108*
Simpson, George B.: *2277*
Simpson, Michael Hodge: *2129*
Sims, James Marion: *5110, 5172, 5390*
Sims, Julia Isabelle: *3720*
Sims, Roger Bernard: *3121*
Simson, Sampson: *5106*
Sinatra, Frank: *1340*
Sinclair, Lee: *3292*
Sinclair, Richard L.: *8263*
Sinclair, Sir Archibald: *5773*
Sinclair, Upton Beall: *3782*
Singer, Isaac Merritt: *2616, 2617*
Singh, Bhola: *6292*
Siprut, Leonard: *4001*
Sirhan, Sirhan Bishara: *3826*
Sissle, Noble: *1142*
Skeen, Anton: *8283*
Skene, John: *7193*
Skinner, John Stuart: *1592, 7792*
Skinner, L. A.: *5870*
Skinner, Michael: *5373*
Skinner, Richard Cort: *5289*
Skinner, Rosa: *5373*
Skinner, Samuel: *7356*
Skrenta, Richard: *6463*
Slack, Leslie: *5885*
Slade, Daniel Denison: *3059*
Slade, Frederick J.: *1935*
Slate, Thomas Benton: *1901*
Slater, Bill: *7538*
Slater, Hannah Wilkinson: *2611, 3990*
Slater, Samuel: *2118, 3990, 7103*
Slaughter, Alanson: *2361*
Slayter, James: *3367*
Slayton, Donald Kent: *6802, 6820*
Slifer, Eli: *5695*
Sloan, John: *1041*
Sloane, Neil J. A.: *6710*
Sloane, Paul: *1151*
Sloat, Jacob: *2550*
Slocum, Joshua: *8532*
Slocum, Samuel: *2615*
Slootsky, Al: *7980*
Slowe, Lucy: *2778*
Small, Abraham: *1590*
Small, Albion Woodbury: *2811*
Small, Elisha: *5599*
Smalley, Daniel S.: *3189*
Smalley, Richard: *6750*
Smalls, Robert: *5713*
Smith, Alex: *7764*
Smith, Alfred Emanuel: *4933*
Smith, Alyssa Leanne: *5376*
Smith, Andrew: *2371*
Smith, Arthur: *8238*
Smith, Bill: *7835*
Smith, C. James: *7621*
Smith, Charles: *7227*
Smith, Charles F.: *5800*
Smith, Charles Shaler: *3245*
Smith, Chester Carl: *5771*
Smith, Cloid: *2415*
Smith, Clyde H.: *3680*
Smith, Dalton F.: *6795*
Smith, Daniel B.: *5220, 5304*
Smith, David Burnell: *4397*
Smith, David L.: *6484*
Smith, E. E. "Doc": *7741*
Smith, Earle: *2441*
Smith, Edward H.: *1451*
Smith, Elihu Hubbard: *1078*
Smith, Elinor: *1543*
Smith, Floyd: *8042*
Smith, Francis Henney: *3103*
Smith, Frederick W.: *2081*
Smith, G. Albert: *1118*
Smith, G. L.: *7811*
Smith, George: *7727*
Smith, George Franklin: *8137*
Smith, Georgette: *6978*
Smith, Hamilton Erastus: *2214*
Smith, Hamilton Lamphere: *4640*
Smith, Hamilton O.: *6690*
Smith, Henry Louis: *5131*
Smith, Howard: *2415*
Smith, Hugh: *2175*
Smith, Isabel: *2196*
Smith, Jack: *6482*
Smith, James: *5150*
Smith, James McCune: *5017*
Smith, James Webster: *3107*
Smith, Jebediah S.: *6063*
Smith, Joan Merriam: *8150*
Smith, John: *1058, 1345, 1424, 1976, 3445, 4731, 7465, 8402*
Smith, John Blair: *2722*
Smith, John T.: *3342*
Smith, Joseph: *3804, 6265, 6266*
Smith, Julia Evelina: *6362*
Smith, Lowell Herbert: *8054*
Smith, M. Susan: *6688*
Smith, Margaret: *1457*
Smith, Margaret Chase: *3680, 3686, 4100*
Smith, Mary Louise: *4107*
Smith, Merle James, Jr.: *3123*
Smith, Michael J.: *6879*

Straus, Nathan: *7256*
Straus, Oscar Solomon: *3894, 4182*
Strauss, Harold A.: *8051*
Strauss, Joseph Baermann: *3253*
Strawbridge, Robert: *6223, 6224*
Strean, Bernard Max: *5592*
Streeter, Alson Jenness: *4078*
Streett, St. Clair: *8045*
Strickland, John: *3494*
Strickland, William: *3221*
Strickler, David: *2404*
Stringham, James: *3047*
Stringham, Silas H.: *5707*
Stritch, Samuel Alphonsus, Cardinal: *6319*
Strite, Charles: *2284*
Strong, Alexander: *8089*
Strong, Caleb: *3645*
Strowger, Almon B.: *4871*
Strube, Gustav: *1255*
Stuart, Gilbert: *4730*
Stuart, James Ewell Brown: *5718*
Stubblefield, Nathan B.: *4775*
Studds, Gerry: *3633, 7456*
Sturgis, Julius: *2362*
Sturtevant, Brereton: *3996*
Stuyvesant, Peter: *2173, 6030, 7313*
Stuyvesant, Rutherford: *2526*
Styles, Edward: *7768*
Suderman, Henry Leonard: *2513*
Suess, Randy: *6458*
Sullivan, Edward Vincent: *1275*
Sullivan, Eugene C.: *3363*
Sullivan, Henry F.: *7911*
Sullivan, Jesse: *5276*
Sullivan, John: *5648*
Sullivan, John Laurence: *4190*
Sullivan, John Lawrence: *7598*
Sullivan, Kathryn D.: *6821, 6828*
Sullivan, Mark: *4902*
Sullivan, Robert Oliver Daniel: *8098*
Sully, Thomas: *7959*
Summerfield, Arthur Ellsworth: *4710*
Summers, Rachael: *3841*
Sumner, Charles: *3601, 3662, 3966*
Sundback, Gideon: *2261*
Surratt, Mary E.: *7004*
Sutherland, Ivan: *6430*
Sutherland, J. B.: *8354*
Sutter, John Augustus: *6043*
Suzuki, Shunryu: *6323*
Swaine, Charles: *6639*
Swallow, Ellen: *7252, 7253, 7266*
Swallow, Silas Comfort: *4085*
Swan, Abraham: *3218*
Swan, William G.: *8083*
Swann, Darius: *6148*
Swann, James: *6148*
Swann, Vera: *6148*
Swanson, Clarke: *2442*
Swanson, Gilbert: *2442*
Swarthout, Cornelius: *2279*
Swarts, Gardner Taber: *7254*
Swayze, John Cameron: *4994*
Sweeney, Michael Francis: *8251*
Sweet, John Edson: *2659*
Swenson, Erin: *7460*
Swift, Joseph Gardner: *3098*
Swinnerton, James: *1098*
Switzer, Joseph: *2669*
Switzer, Katherine: *7956*
Switzer, Robert: *2669*
Swoopes, Sheryl: *7562*
Swope, Herbert Bayard: *4760*
Syer, Robert D'oyly: *1751*
Syle, Henry Winter: *6258*
Symington, William Stuart: *4190*
Syms, Benjamin: *2883*
Szilard, Leo: *6736*
Szold, Henrietta: *3205*

T

Tafel, Adolph J.: *5237*
Taft, Helen Herron: *4231, 4232*
Taft, Mrs. Josiah: *3760*
Taft, William Howard: *1474, 3713, 4141, 4143, 4231, 4232, 4261, 4329*
Taggart, William H.: *5088*
Tainter, Charles Sumner: *4828*
Takeuchi, Ryuji: *4969*
Talbot, Ethelbert: *6298*
Talbot, Paul H.: *5775*
Tallmadge, Benjamin: *7355*
Tally, Thomas Lincoln: *1123*
Taney, Roger Brooke: *3746, 3747, 4176, 4177*
Tanner, Harry Laurence: *8501*
Tanner, Henry Ossawa: *1043, 4334*
Tappan, D.: *6249*
Tappan, Lewis: *1770*
Tarkington, Booth: *4763*
Taub, Sam: *7605*
Taylor, Alan: *6712*
Taylor, Albert Hoyt: *8078, 8504*
Taylor, Alfred Alexander: *4379*
Taylor, Anna Edson: *1391*
Taylor, Carl Rutherford: *2423*
Taylor, Colonel: *7801*
Taylor, Frederick W.: *7921*
Taylor, George Caldwell: *7160*
Taylor, Howard Augustus: *7922*
Taylor, John: *1918*

Tolkien, J. R. R.: *7744*
Tolton, Augustus: *6284*
Tombaugh, Clyde William: *6388*
Tombs, Rudolph, Jr.: *2829*
Tomlinson, Ray: *6443, 6445*
Tommie, Howard: *1808*
Tompson, Benjamin: *1064*
Tong Chick: *1434*
Tools, Robert: *5384*
Topliff, Samuel: *4500*
Torkillus, Reorus: *6183*
Torresola, Griselio: *3845*
Toscanini, Arturo: *1257, 1263, 1269*
Touro, Judah: *3011*
Town, Ithiel: *3261*
Towne, Benjamin: *4494*
Townes, Charles Hard: *6521*
Townsend, Fitzhugh: *7667*
Townsend, Francis Everett: *4096*
Townsend, Kathleen Kennedy: *4290*
Toy, Jim: *7513*
Tracy, Susan Edith: *5391*
Travell, Janet Graeme: *4266*
Travis, Joseph: *6128*
Treadwell, Daniel: *2035*
Tree, Marietta Peabody: *3903*
Trenchard, James: *3481*
Treneer, Maurice: *5245*
Tresse, Thomas: *2006*
Trigunatita: *6289*
Trik, Carl A.: *3247*
Tronson du Coudray, Charles: *6231*
Troost, Gerardt: *3050*
Trotsky, Leon: *4097*
Trout, Robert: *4600*
Trudeau, Edward Livingston: *5126, 5166, 5228*
Trueblood, Thomas Clarkson: *2812*
Truman, Bess Wallace: *3856*
Truman, Harry S.: *2517, 3821, 3845, 3856, 3899, 4045, 4151, 4155, 4235, 4283, 4284, 4298, 4587, 4705, 4952, 5532, 7160, 8521*
Trumbull, Earl: *3238*
Truscott, Lucian: *5524*
Truth, Sojourner: *6882*
Tsibliyev, Vasily: *6838*
Tubman, Harriet: *4756*
Tubman, William Vacanarat Shadrach: *3937*
Tucker, John: *3733*
Tucker, St. George: *3959*
Tucker, Stephen D.: *2046*
Tucker, William: *6021*
Tucker, William Ellis: *3355*
Tudor, Frederick: *2337, 8192*
Tufts, John: *1211*
Tugo, Oscar: *5744*
Tuke, Daniel Hack: *5318*
Tulley, John: *4477*
Tunney, Gene: *7604*
Tunnicliffe, George: *1822*
Tupper, Earl S.: *2581*
Turnbull, Andrew: *6040*
Turner, Bob: *7625*
Turner, Charles W.: *5531*
Turner, Christopher: *8413*
Turner, Cyril: *1538*
Turner, George A.: *2866*
Turner, Henry C.: *7158*
Turner, James Edward: *5109*
Turner, Lana: *4950*
Turner, Nat: *6128*
Turner, Robert: *2006*
Turner, Ted: *4548*
Turner, William: *2411*
Turner, William G.: *2866*
Turpin, Mary: *6215*
Tuscaloosa: *5626*
Tuthill, Richard Stanley: *3710*
Tuttle, Dorothy Edith Lorne: *5545*
T'Vault, William G.: *4506*
Twain, Mark: *1399, 4457, 7223*
Twigg, Atrong: *1344*
Twilight, Alexander Lucius: *2738, 4387*
Twining, Nathan Farragut: *5495*
Tyler, John: *4132, 4135, 4225, 4251, 4306, 4521*
Tyler, Letitia Christian: *4225*
Tyler, Royall: *1422*
Tyng, James Alexander: *7506*
Tytus, John Butler: *1943*

U

Uchytil, Christa: *2165*
Udobi, Iyke Louis: *2169*
Uncles, Charles Randolph: *6284*
Underhill, Isaac: *3372*
Underwood, Charles G.: *2389*
Underwood, John Curtiss: *3707*
Unterberg, Bella: *7222*
Unungoit: *6022*
Upham, John B.: *7749*
Upton, Robert: *1418*
Upton, Roger: *1882*
Urban, Charles: *1118*
Urey, Harold Clayton: *6743*
Usher, Hezekiah: *3948, 4427*
Usher, John: *3974, 7466*

V

W

White, Caroline Earle: *7221*
White, Dan: *7452*
White, David: *2737*
White, Edward Douglass: *3749, 4374*
White, Edward Higgins, II: *6805, 6810*
White, Goodrich Cook: *2706*
White, James: *1122*
White, James Clarke: *3069*
White, John: *1012*
White, Joseph N.: *7727*
White, Josiah: *3234*
White, Peregrine: *6017*
White, Robert Michael: *8149*
White, Samuel S.: *5087*
White, Susanna: *2588*
White, William: *5099, 6251, 6990*
Whitefield, George: *6218*
Whitehead, Gustave: *8005*
Whitehead, Joseph Brown: *1508*
Whitehead, Lettie Pate: *1508*
Whitehead, Mary Beth: *2163*
Whitehouse, James Horton: *3478*
Whiteman, Louis Porter: *1998*
Whiteside, Peter: *8525*
Whiteside, William: *8525*
Whitestone, Heather: *1394*
Whitfield, Malvin Greston: *7479*
Whiting, A. H.: *7617*
Whitlock, David: *5147*
Whitman, Malcolm Douglass: *7926*
Whitman, Marcus: *6064*
Whitman, Narcissa Prentiss: *6064*
Whitmer, Peter: *6265*
Whitney, Amos: *4876*
Whitney, Eli: *1585*
Whitney, F. A.: *2181*
Whitney, Harry Payne: *7805, 7808*
Whitney, William Dwight: *6720*
Whitney, Willis Rodney: *1495*
Whiton, James Morris: *2761*
Whittaker, James W.: *7983*
Whittemore, Benjamin: *3605*
Whittier, Earle Ovando: *1905*
Wichman, John R.: *2594*
Wichterle, Otto: *5273*
Wickes, Lambert: *5664*
Widnall, Sheila E.: *5493, 5499*
Wiebe, Edward: *2945*
Wiener, Alexander S.: *5056*
Wiener, Leo: *1841*
Wigfall, Louis T.: *3663*
Wiggins, Leonard A.: *8081*
Wiggins, Mary E.: *5343*
Wigglesworth, Edward: *2693*
Wignell, Thomas: *1422*
Wilbur, James H.: *2938*
Wilde, Francis E. J.: *1542*
Wilder, L. Douglas: *4383*
Wildey, Thomas: *7203*
Wildman, Ernest Atkins: *5558*
Wiles, Andrew: *6709*
Wiley, David: *1592*
Wiley, Herbert Victor: *8072*
Wilkes, Charles: *6642*
Wilkinson, David: *2649*
Wilkinson, Eugene Parks: *8521*
Wilkinson, Jeremiah: *2638*
Willard, Charles Foster: *7677*
Willard, Emma Hart: *2907*
Willard, Frances Elizabeth: *2786, 7181*
Willard, Jess: *7600*
Willard, Samuel: *4434*
Willerup, Christian B.: *6270*
Willet, Edward: *1351*
Willett, Thomas: *3509*
William, King of England: *4655*
Williams, Anthony A.: *7296*
Williams, Bert: *1142*
Williams, Betty: *6915*
Williams, Charles, Jr.: *4866*
Williams, Daniel Hale: *5115, 5229, 5345*
Williams, Edward Christopher: *3021*
Williams, Elkanah: *3066*
Williams, George Washington: *7476*
Williams, Harvey: *4781*
Williams, Henry J.: *4452*
Williams, Horatio Burt: *5179*
Williams, Isaac: *3885*
Williams, James M.: *5716*
Williams, Jesse: *2357*
Williams, Jesse Lynch: *4765*
Williams, John: *5505*
Williams, John Foster: *8412*
Williams, Jonathan: *3096, 5415*
Williams, Kathlyn: *1139*
Williams, Kendra: *5831*
Williams, Lorraine: *7744*
Williams, Richard F.: *5104*
Williams, Robley Cook: *6673*
Williams, Roger: *3169, 5898, 6178, 6179, 6181, 6196*
Williams, Samuel: *6369*
Williams, Samuel Wells: *2793*
Williams, Terry: *2874*
Williams, Thomas Robinson: *2127*
Williams, Thomas W.: *8433*
Williams, Vanessa: *1394*
Williams, Walter: *2826*
Williamson, James De Long: *7225*
Williamson, John Ernest: *4629*
Williamson, John Finley: *6306*
Willich, Anthony Florian Madinger: *1590*
Willing, Thomas: *1715*
Willis, Nathaniel Parker: *4612*

Woolworth, Frank Winfield: *2089*
Worden, Alfred Merrill: *6817*
Worden, John Lorimer: *5712, 8475*
Workman, Sonny: *7808*
Worthington, John: *7234*
Worthylake, George: *7336*
Wouves, P.R.: *4481*
Wozniak, Steven: *6450, 6453*
Wren, Edward: *5524*
Wren, Solomon: *5563*
Wrenn, Robert D.: *7925*
Wright, Arthur Williams: *2761*
Wright, Carroll Davidson: *1679*
Wright, George: *7494*
Wright, George Green: *5158*
Wright, James: *7215*
Wright, James Hood: *6547*
Wright, John D.: *5109*
Wright, Jonathan Jasper: *3708*
Wright, Orville: *4705, 5461, 8005, 8009, 8010, 8013*
Wright, Silas: *4054*
Wright, Wilbur: *5461, 8005, 8013*
Wright, William Hammond: *6404*
Wu, Maw-Kuen: *6751*
Wunderlich, Frieda: *2855*
Wurlitzer, Rudolph: *4830*
Wyatt, James: *1350*
Wyatt, Sir Francis: *7052, 7054*
Wye, Thomas E.: *3847*
Wyeth, Jamie: *4744*
Wyeth, Nathaniel: *2005*
Wyman, George A.: *8288*
Wyman, Jane: *4264, 4971*
Wyman, Morrill: *5323*
Wyman, Walter: *5129*
Wyman, Walter Scott: *6566*
Wynder, Ernst L.: *6672, 7080*
Wynn, Keenan: *3689*
Wynne, Arthur: *7731*
Wynne, Jim: *7577*
Wythe, George: *2711*

Y

Yalden, James: *1706*
Yale, Linus, Jr.: *3278*
Yalow, Rosalyn Sussman: *5144*
Yannas, Ioannis V.: *5372*
Yate, Esther: *7991*
Yeager, Charles Elwood: *8121*
Yeager, Jeana: *8165*
Yeardley, Sir George: *4385*
Yeaton, Hopley: *5595*
Yeltsin, Boris: *5828*
Yepremian, George: *7717*
Yolton, John Maloney: *8058*
Yost, Charles Woodruff: *3907*
Youk, Thomas: *6976*
Youmans, Edward Livingston: *6782*
Young, Achsah: *6987*
Young, Edna Earle: *5587*
Young, Ella Flagg: *2966*
Young, John Richardson: *5293*
Young, John W.: *6875*
Young, Lee Roy: *7359*
Young, Leo C.: *8078*
Young, Mahonri: *7183*
Young, Perry H.: *8142*
Young, Robert A.: *3729*
Young, Samuel Baldwin Marks: *3110*
Young, William G.: *2350*
Younger, Cole: *6935*
Younger, James: *6935*
Younger, Robert: *6935*
Yount, Harry: *5990*
Yulee, David Levy: *3661*
Yung Wing: *2755*

Z

Zacharie, Issachar: *5319*
Zachos, John Celinergos: *1670*
Zachow, Otto: *8244*
Zaharias, Babe Didrikson: *7773*
Zahniser, Howard: *5926*
Zakariya, Mohamed: *4759*
Zakrzewska, Marie Elizabeth: *5107*
Zane, Ebenezer: *6051*
Zapruder, Abraham: *4268*
Zeisberger, David: *6227*
Zeiss, Carl: *5269*
Zenger, John Peter: *1518, 4478, 4492, 4493, 6758*
Zentzytzki, Stanislaus: *7975*
Zerega, Antoine: *2353*
Zettlein, George: *7501*
Zhou Enlai: *4320*
Zieber, George B.: *2616*
Ziegler, Matilda: *7009*
Ziegler, Walter E.: *5408*
Zinzendorf, Countess Benigna von: *2897*
Ziolkowski, Korczak: *7191*
Zobian-Lindahl, Lisa: *2268*
Zog, King of Albania: *3934*
Zoll, Paul M.: *5353*
Zoller, Frederick: *1759*
Zukor, Adolph: *1136*
Zworykin, Vladimir Kosma: *3428, 4936, 6515, 6732*

GEOGRAPHICAL INDEX

The following is a listing of key locations in the main body of the text, arranged alphabetically by state and city. To find an entry in the main body of the text, please go to the italicized number.

ALASKA—*continued*

Chena Hot Springs

Ice hotel, *1845*

Hot Springs

Rediscovery of a bird thought to be extinct, *5971*

Kodiak Island

Eastern Orthodox church, *6242*
Russian settlement, *6043*

Little Diomede Island

Swimmer to cross the Bering Strait, *7916*

Metlakahtla

President to visit Alaska and Canada while in office, *4315*

Nenana

Railroad operated by the federal government, *8326*

Nome

Airplane flight between New York and Alaska, *8045*

Point Barrow

Crossing of the North Pole underwater by a submerged submarine, *8540*

Red Devil

Iditarod sled dog race, *7664*

Sitka

Eastern Orthodox cathedral, *6242*

Unalakleet

Person to be counted in the 2000 census, *6160*

AMERICAN SAMOA

National park in the Southern Hemisphere, *5996*

ARIZONA

Airplane disaster involving more than 100 persons, *8140*
Exploration of the Grand Canyon of the Colorado, *6644*
Law against human smuggling enacted by a state, *6984*
Movie of feature length made outdoors, *1150*
Muslim traveler in America, *6163*
State in which all of the top elected offices were held by women, *4369*
State supreme court chief justice who was a woman, *3728*
State to elect two female governors in a row, *4384*
State to require proof of citizenship for voters, *3792*
Supreme Court justice who was a woman, *3752*

Apache Pass

Combat action that earned the Medal of Honor, *5501*

Ashfork

Steel dam, *3351*

Flagstaff

Planet found beyond Neptune, *6388*

Marana

Solar-powered long-distance airplane flight, *8161*

Naco

Airplane bombing raid by a mercenary soldier, *6941*

Phoenix

Food bank, *7282*
Medal of Honor awarded to a pilot, *5515*

Prescott

Old age home for pioneers, *6085*
Rodeo to charge admission, *1385*

Scottsdale

Digital-photography highway patrol, *8217*
State legislator expelled for campaign financing violations, *4397*

Tsaile

College on a Native American reservation, *2869*

Tucson

House with solar heating and radiation cooling, *2530*

Yuma

Soldier's Medal awarded to a woman, *5523*

ARKANSAS

Supreme Court decision on inclusion of candidates in televised political debates, *3753*
Surgeon general who was African-American, *7287*

Benton

Fuller's earth, *3388*

Hot Springs

Military hospital, *5200*

Jonesboro

Woman elected to the Senate, *3673*

Lonoke

Army officer to receive the three highest decorations, *5526*

Mountain View

Proof that a human brain can restore impaired functions by growing new networks of nerve fibers, *6704*

Murfreesboro

Diamonds in actual rock, *3394*

Wilmar

Gas turbine to pump natural gas, *6607*

CALIFORNIA

Alien land law, *6086*
Cartel of corporations, *1509*
Congressional representative of Asian ancestry, *3620*
Congressional representatives who were sisters, *3640*
Corrupt election practices law enacted by a state, *3770*
Digital projection of a major motion picture, *1187*
District attorney who was a woman, *3715*
Docks owned by a state, *2074*
Health maintenance organization, *1985*
Kwanzaa celebration, *2518*
Locomotive to use oil for fuel, *8339*
Midterm election since World War II in which the president's party gained seats in the House of Representatives, *3636*
Motor vehicles powered by natural gas, *8296*
National park to contain an active volcano, *5992*
Negative election campaign run by media specialists, *3782*
No-fault divorce law enacted by a state, *2597*
Overland trip to California, *6063*
Political party leader in Congress who was a woman, *3639*
Presidential candidate who was an African-American woman, *3827*
Quarantine law for plants enacted by a state, *7250*
Resale price maintenance law enacted by a state, *1507*
Right-to-die law enacted by a state, *2307*
Secretary of education, *4208*
Senators who were Jewish women, *3693*
State on the Pacific coast to be admitted to the Union, *4348*
State payments to crime victims, *6954*
State registry of convicted sex offenders, *7299*
State to approve funding for biomedical research using stem cells derived from human embryos, *6697*
State to recognize unions for farmworkers, *7166*
State whose businesses were required to offer paid family leave, *2170*
State with $1 trillion in personal income, *4370*
State with a gross state product of $1 trillion, *4367*
Statewide registration of assault weapons, *6969*
Steamboat service to California around Cape Horn, *8432*
Surfing in Southern California, *7958*
Sweet potato, *1630*
Telecast transmitted by satellite to Japan, *4969*
Tournament of Roses intercollegiate football game, *7695*
Transcontinental commercial telephone service, *4880*
War fought mostly on foreign soil, *5689*
Woman to earn an engineering degree, *3224*

Alameda

Hydrogenated peanut butter, *2429*
Swimmer to cover 100 meters freestyle in less than one minute, *7910*
Transcontinental direct-dialed phone call, *4905*

Anaheim

Live concert for astronauts, *1286*
Transcontinental Picturephone call, *4912*

CALIFORNIA—*continued*

Apple Valley

Triple jet ace, *5809*

Arcadia

Transcontinental airship flight, *8051*

Avalon

Airplane round-trip flight over water, *8032*

Bakersfield

Concrete highway median barrier, *3427*
County airport, *8057*

Berkeley

Airship disaster, *8006*
Brown dwarf star to be discovered, *6393*
Campus takeover by student protesters, *2868*
Cyclotron, *6730*
Element created artificially, *6746*
Gamma camera for imaging the body, *5140*
Human virus to be crystallized, *6666*
Medal of Honor awarded in the Korean War, *5531*
Museum to install refrigerated vaults, *3155*
Plutonium, *6747*
Pole vaulter to clear the bar at 15 feet, *7951*
Private hydroponic garden, *1647*
Radioactive isotope medicine, *5394*
Radioactive substance produced synthetically, *6745*
Rape crisis center, *6955*
Synchrotron, *6734*
Underground comic book of note, *1107*
Urban master plan, *3539*
Virus separated into component parts, *6673*

Buena Vista

Grape vines planted in California for wine-making, *1613*

Burbank

Grammy awards for musical recordings, *1272*
Jet-propelled fighter plane, *5484*
Major motion picture produced and exhibited entirely with digital technology, *1188*
Movie that was entirely computer-animated, *1203*

Calaveras County

Frog-jumping jubilee, *1399*

Camp Parks

Coast-to-coast telecast by satellite, *5003*

Camp Selfridge

Airplane flight to the deck of a carrier, *8022*

Capitola

Commercial production of hydroponic plants, *1651*

Cazadero

Russian settlement in the continental United States, *6043*

Century City

Movie on videocassette to be released world-wide in one week, *1189*

Chatsworth

Internet domain, *6466*

Chico

Public locker plant, *1686*

Coronado

Airplane refueling attempt in midair, *8054*

Coronado Beach

Transcontinental nonstop airplane flight, *8053*

Culver City

Movie to gross $100 million in its opening weekend, *1190*
Radar for commercial and private planes, *8118*

Cupertino

Interactive multimedia authoring program, *6468*
Mountain bike, *7659*

Davis

Genetically altered food, *2456*
Mountain bike, *7659*

Downey

Gas-turbine propeller-driven airplane, *8111*

CALIFORNIA—*continued*

Oakland

Bird refuge established by a state, *5943*
Black Panther Party organizational meeting, *4101*
Hotel at an airport, *1831*
Long-distance dial telephone service, *4902*
Popsicle, *2422*
State to require paper receipts for electronic voting machines, *3791*
Tennis champion to win the Grand Slam, *7928*
Transpacific solo airplane flight by a woman, *8094*

Orange

Septuplets, *2162*

Oxnard

Interracial labor union, *7143*

Pacific Palisades

High school chapter of Alcoholics Anonymous, *7078*

Palm Springs

Movie to be shown simultaneously on pay television and in movie theaters, *1172*

Palo Alto

Basketball leagues for women, *7561*
Computer mouse, *6438*
Factoring of a 100-digit number, *6708*
First lady to earn a college degree in a scientific field, *4230*
Graphical user interface for a commercial computer, *6460*
Heart transplant to an adult, *5368*
Laser printer, *6446*
Photographs showing action, *4627*
Presidential nomination ceremony broadcast on radio, *3817*
Recombinant DNA molecule, *6676*
Thermal inkjet printer, *6465*
Wireless microchip receiver-transmitter for making digital information part of a non-digital object, *6533*

Pasadena

Antimatter to be observed, *6744*
College karate club, *7978*
Cosmic ray to be discovered, *6387*
Discovery of a meteorite on another planet, *6395*
Human virus to be crystallized, *6666*
Human-powered aircraft, *8159*
Image of a planet outside Earth's solar system, *6418*
Images of the surface of Mars to be televised live, *6417*
Newsreel in color, *4540*
Nobel Prize winner to receive awards in two different categories, *6909*
Photograph taken on Mars, *6415*
Pilot of a jet fighter to win a dogfight in the Korean War, *5807*
Shelter for abused women, *6953*
Solar sail aircraft, *6890*
Space probe mission headed entirely by women, *6885*
Teleportation experiment, *6753*
Tournament of Roses, *7695*
Transcontinental airplane flight made in stages, *8030*

Petaluma

Coin-operated locker, *1689*

Playa del Rey

Speedway with a board track, *7622*

Primm

Winner of the Grand Challenge robotic vehicle race, *6532*

Redwood City

Concrete seagoing ship, *8446*
Tape recorder built in the United States for commercial use, *4834*
Video tape recorder for sounds and pictures, *5001*

Richmond

Grant-in-aid enacted by Congress to help the states build roads, *3421*

Riverside

Air Force Medal of Honor for action in the Korean War, *5533*
Forest Service aerial patrol, *5984*
Oranges of the seedless navel variety, *1622*
Round-the-world nonstop flight by a jet airplane, *8143*

Sacramento

Demonstration of wireless remote vehicle control as an antiterrorism tactic, *7309*
Pony Express mail, *4671*
Robot to perform surgery, *6528*
State consumer protection agency to combat identity theft, *7307*
Store with fixed prices, *2088*
Union catalog of books in a state library, *3026*

San Anselmo

Islamic terrorist who was born in America, *5835*

San Bernardino

Boxing referee who was a woman, *7606*
Woman pilot to earn an airplane instructor's license, *8097*

San Diego

Airplane loop-the-loop, *8036*
Biotechnology treatment for cancer, *5401*
Caesar salad, *2424*
Catholic mission in California, *6226*
Company penalized for failing to report a hazardous product, *7291*
Double-deck streetcar, *8371*
Exploration of land on the Pacific coast by a European, *6005*
Glider flight, *8001*
Hydroplane, *8023*
Image of Earth as seen from Mars, *6420*
Jet-propelled landing on an aircraft carrier, *8112*
Lighthouse on the Pacific coast, *7343*
Navy officer who was a woman to hold a major command, *5614*
Navy pilot, *5465*
Patent registered in the 21st century, *4001*
Photograph taken from an airplane, *4628*
Ship with a floating scientific instrument platform, *6508*
Swimmer who was a woman to swim the English Channel in both directions, *7913*
Tennis champion who was a woman to win the Grand Slam, *7930*
Transcontinental airplane flight made within 24 hours, *8047*
Transcontinental airship flight, *8056*
Transcontinental glider tow, *8075*
Transcontinental motorcycle trip by women, *8290*
Transcontinental nonstop helicopter flight, *8141*
Transpacific solo sailboat crossing by a woman, *8546*
Walk from Canada to Mexico along the West Coast, *7988*

San Fernando Valley

Helicopter freight service, *8132*

San Francisco

Airline flight attendant who was a woman, *8076*
Army language school, *3116*
Baby whose life was saved by surgery while still in the womb, *5373*
Bank of importance to lease personal property, *1751*
Be-In, *1406*
Beat Generation literary event, *1105*
Bed that could be hidden, *2572*
Biotechnology treatment for cancer, *5401*
Boxing match timed by automatic timer, *7597*
Bridge with piers sunk in the open sea, *3253*
Brown dwarf star to be discovered, *6393*
Buddhist temple, *6272*
Cable car put into service, *8369*
Chinese daily newspaper, *4558*
Chinese immigrants to America, *6067*
Chinese laundry, *2213*
Chinese newspaper, *4558*
Chinese restaurant, *1814*
Chinese theater, *1435*
Chinese theatrical performance, *1434*
Christian religious service in English on the Pacific Coast, *6168*
City opera house, *1323*
City to require "green" construction for low-income housing, *5935*
College to offer a degree in human sexuality studies, *2870*
Condom commercials on television, *7458*
Congressional representative who was a Jewish woman, *3615*
District attorney who was African-American, *3725*
Dugong, *5961*
Dynamite, *1861*
Electric company organized to produce and sell electricity, *6542*
Electric starting gate for horse races, *7810*
Equal Rights Party convention, *4077*
Fifty-dollar gold pieces minted by the federal government, *4040*
Flea laboratory, *6667*
Gay politician elected to an important local office, *7452*
Gene splicing, *6678*

CALIFORNIA—San Francisco—*continued*

Giant panda, *5956*
Hindu temple, *6289*
Image transmitted by television, *4927*
Isolation of embryonic stem cells in a mammal, *6680*
Jetway, *8146*
Jukebox, *4830*
Labor union label, *7125*
Methodist bishop who was an African-American woman, *6330*
Military expeditionary force to be sent beyond the Western Hemisphere, *5726*
Military think tank, *5799*
Minister who was openly gay, *7450*
Modern dancer, *1050*
Movie on videocassette to be released worldwide in one week, *1189*
Municipal streetcars, *8375*
National lesbian organization, *7444*
Navy officer who was a woman to command a ship at sea, *5615*
Newspaper reproduced commercially and regularly by radio facsimile, *4543*
Nominee who was a woman to receive votes at the national convention of a major party, *4100*
Nylon, *2142*
Occupation of federal territory by Native American protesters in the modern era, *6099*
Overland mail service, *4669*
Patent for a gold dental crown, *5086*
President and First Lady to die during the term for which he had been elected, *4258*
Public school for Asian-American children, *2937*
Radio station with all-podcast programming, *4816*
Rat extermination throughout an entire city, *7268*
Robot Olympics, *6531*
Rock and roll broadcast on FM radio, *1276*
Round-the-world bicycle trip, *7646*
Round-the-world flight by a commercial airplane, *8105*
Round-the-world steamboat passenger service, *8448*
Slot machine, *1802*
Solar system with multiple planets, *6394*
Stadium operated by a city, *3294*
Steamboat to employ electric lights successfully, *8435*
Tong organized crime gang, *6937*
Transcontinental air race, *7679*
Transcontinental airmail flight, *4695*
Transcontinental car trip, *8242*
Transcontinental car trip by women, *8246*
Transcontinental daily railroad service, *8321*
Transcontinental express bus service, *8222*
Transcontinental journey on foot, *7971*
Transcontinental nonstop balloon flight, *8162*
Transcontinental regular airmail service, *4696*
Transcontinental solo trip on horseback by a woman, *8182*
Transcontinental telecast received on the East Coast, *4952*
Transcontinental telegraph line, *4855*
Transcontinental telephone demonstration, *4878*
Transpacific airmail flight, *4701*
Transpacific radio conversation, *4783*
Transpacific sidewheeler steamer, *8434*
Transpacific telegraph cable, *4857*
Transport airplane designed for transoceanic service, *8096*
Treaty signed by a woman, *3898*
Underground comic book of note, *1107*
Vice presidential candidate who was a woman, *3812*
Woman presidential candidate who was eligible to hold office, *3808*
World Series disrupted by an earthquake, *7549*
X-ray three-dimensional stereo fluoroscopic system, *5141*

San Gabriel

Flying disk for use in throwing games, *7979*

San Jose

American air ace, *5751*
Machine controlled via the Internet, *6473*
Mayor of a major city with a population over 500,000, *3542*
Navy pilot shot down and captured in North Vietnam, *5813*
Physical manipulation of individual atoms, *6752*

San Leandro

Steam tractor, *1631*

San Luis Obispo

Human-powered helicopter, *8167*
Motel, *1830*

San Mateo

Helicopter rescue of an American pilot behind enemy lines, *5805*

San Pedro

Canned tuna, *2408*
Ship to pass both ways through the Northwest Passage, *8544*

San Rafael

Word processor for computers, *6455*

Santa Ana

Federal prosecution of a hate crime on the Internet, *6974*

Santa Barbara

Avocado, *1601*
Oil spill with disastrous consequences, *6612*
Oil wells successfully drilled in the ocean, *6601*
Transatlantic telesurgery, *5385*

Santa Clara

Medical college on the Pacific Coast, *3062*
Microprocessor, *6524*
Presidential inauguration broadcast live over the Internet, *4289*

Santa Clarita

Municipal recycling of diapers and incontinence products, *5934*

Santa Cruz

Loganberry, *1627*

Santa Monica

Car-airplane combination, *8255*
City to derive all its energy needs from renewable sources, *6638*
Cyber cafe, *1843*
Nuclear warhead mounted on a rocket, *5883*
Pen with truly erasable ink, *2681*
Presidential airplane, *4297*
Space tourist, *6839*
Think tank for research and development, *7229*
Transcontinental air derby for women, *7681*
Transcontinental bicycle trip made in less than three weeks, *7658*

Sausalito

Psychedelic music album, *1274*

Soquel

Patent on a number, *6711*

South Pasadena

Ostrich farm, *1629*

Squaw Valley

Artificial ice skating rink of Olympic size, *7845*

Stanford

Astronaut who was a woman to fly in space, *6825*
Computer modem that was practical, *6436*
Gene splicing, *6678*
Holographic data storage system, *6476*
Human antibodies produced artificially, *5258*
Online high school for gifted students, *2991*
Quark to be observed, *6749*
Radar signal bounced off the sun, *6796*

Stockton

American runner to run a mile in less than four minutes on an outdoor track, *7955*
Sikh gurdwara, *6292*

Sunnyvale

Municipal wireless network paid for by advertisements, *7427*
Video game, *7742*

Sylmar

Hang-gliding national championships, *7684*

Tassajara Springs

Zen Buddhist monastery, *6323*

Tulare County

Animal disease of American origin, *5406*

Vallejo

Streamlined submarine, *8516*

Van Nuys

Boxing referee who was a woman, *7606*
Plastic bonded airplane, *8100*

Vandenberg

American flag to orbit the earth, *3506*

Vandenberg Air Force Base

Satellite with a nuclear reactor to orbit the earth, *6861*
Space capsule recovered from an orbiting satellite, *6850*

CALIFORNIA—*continued*

Venice

Transcontinental group tour by car, *8249*

Washington

Salmon cannery, *2363*

Yosemite

Conservationist of note, *5910*
State park, *5989*

COLORADO

Abortion legalized by a state as a medical procedure, *7447*
Baby carrier, *2202*
Child delinquency law enacted by a state, *2190*
Mineral segregation by oil flotation, *3389*
State legislators who were women, *4389*
States to make Labor Day a legal holiday, *2498*

Aurora

State criminal prosecution for the sale of confidential personal information, *6977*

Boulder

Optical computer, *6475*
Solar system with multiple planets, *6394*

Castlewood

Dam filled with rocks, *3350*

Colorado City

Intercity trucking service, *2077*

Colorado Springs

Air Force academy, *3119*
Air Force Academy cadets who were women, *3127*
Air Force Academy graduate who was Native American, *3120*
Air Force Academy graduates who were African-American, *3121*

Danbury

Hat factory, *2231*

Deer Trail

Rodeo for roping and tying steers, *1375*
Denver
Birth to be televised for the public, *2158*
Centralized refrigeration service, *1895*
Church without theology, creed, or dogma, *6291*
Comprehensive digital atlas of the human body, *5147*
Destruction of an American airliner by a criminal, *6949*
Fatal airplane accident involving a woman, *8033*
Libertarian Party national convention, *4106*
Liver transplant, *5365*
Major city to legalize possession of marijuana, *7093*
Millionaire who was an African-American woman, *1710*
Opera broadcast over the radio in its entirety, *1322*
Pilot on a regularly scheduled major airline who was a woman, *8156*
Pilot who was a woman to fly for a commercial airline, *8093*
Pronghorn antelope, *5945*
Secret Service agent killed in the line of duty, *3845*
Ship transported overland across the Rocky Mountains, *8486*
Snow goose, *5954*
State to refuse to host the Olympic Games, *7861*
Tampon to be mass-produced, *2475*
Train to run 1,000 miles nonstop, *8396*
Tuberculosis hospital for needy patients, *5130*
Veterans of Foreign Wars of the United States meeting, *5623*
Woman pilot to earn the rank of captain, *8156*
Zoo habitat constructed of simulated rock formations without bars, *3151*

Englewood

Cyber university, *2879*

Grand Junction

Election using the preferential ballot system, *3778*

Longmont

Reconstruction of an airliner during a crash investigation, *8138*

Telluride

Power transmission installation using alternating current, *6554*

CONNECTICUT

American executed as a spy, *5662*

Bicycle with a rotary crank, *7639*
Boiler inspection law enacted by a state, *7327*
Branding law, *1565*
Dental hygienists to be licensed by a state, *5041*
Livestock pounds for stray animals, *1567*
Purple Heart, *5500*
Speed limits for motor vehicles, *8190*
State aviation law, *8026*
State law allowing married women to make wills, *7431*
Statewide 211 helpline, *7420*
Steel, *1916*
Vanity license plates, *8209*
Woman elected state governor in her own right, *4381*

Ansonia

Copper refinery furnace, *1939*

Ashford

Military intelligence unit, *5659*

Berlin

Government contract authorized by Congress for pistols, *5841*
Tinware manufacturers, *2270*

Bridgeport

Commercially designed helicopter, *8114*
Electric socket operated by a pull chain, *2569*
Handheld rocket launcher, *5870*
Incandescent light bulbs in widespread use, *6546*
Long-playing microgroove phonograph records, *4835*
Steam car, *8224*
Trading stamp, *1528*

Bristol

Brass clock works, *2628*
Fishing rod of telescoping steel tubes, *2663*
Spring manufacturer, *1858*

Brooklyn

Unitarian woman minister, *6236*

Centerbrook

Comb made of ivory, *2458*

Danielson

Dentist who was a woman, *5084*

Derby

Industrial school, *2911*
Machine for manufacturing pins, *2614*

Easton

Meteorite whose landing was recorded, *6385*

Fairfield

Helicopter hoist rescue, *8113*

Georgetown

Wire sieves, *2548*

Glastonbury

Bible translation by a woman, *6362*

Granby

Copper coins, *4004*
Copper mine, *3370*

Greenwich

Squash rackets champion who was a woman, *7906*

Groton

Diesel engine in a submarine, *8513*
Nuclear-powered submarine, *8521*
Submarine equipped with ballistic missiles, *8523*
Submarine from the United States destroyed in World War II, *5756*

Gurleyville

Silk dyers, *2130*

Hamden

Rubber shoe manufacturer, *2242*

Hartford

Accident insurance company, *1956*
Aircraft liability and property damage insurance, *1969*
Anesthetic in dentistry, *5050*
Baseball catchers' chest protector, *7505*
Belting, *1850*
Bicycle factory, *7641*
Boiler insurance company, *1957*
Book manuscript that was typewritten, *4457*
Book to be afforded copyright protection, *3975*
Brick machine, *3339*
Car insurance policy, *1965*
Children's magazine, *2174*

CONNECTICUT—Hartford—*continued*

Constitution to declare that "the foundation of authority is in the free consent of the people," *3455*
Cookbook by an American author, *2330*
Copyright law enacted by a state, *3976*
Cryptography book, *4442*
Electric alternator, *6555*
Elliptical office building, *3317*
Federal aid to special education, *2913*
Free public art museum in continuous existence, *3139*
Genealogy of an American family, *7467*
Hydroelectric power plant to use a storage battery, *6556*
Intercollegiate lawn tennis match, *7922*
Law book of federal laws, *3956*
Neutrality regulation enacted by Congress that governed the actions of citizens, *3885*
Parachute jump using a nylon parachute, *8107*
Pay telephone, *4876*
Pay telephone installed on a rental basis, *4876*
Pay television dramatic program, *4967*
Pneumatic tires, *8185*
Prayers in sign language, *6258*
President to ride in a car, *4293*
School for deaf students to be established on a permanent basis, *2909*
Secession convention during the War of 1812, *4342*
Silver plating factory, *1929*
State aid to special education, *2912*
State aviation department, *8062*
State government to completely privatize its computer services, *4368*
Steam turbine operated by a public utility to produce electricity, *6557*
Teachers' institute, *2928*
Travel writer, *1074*
Underwater torpedo operated by electric current, *5847*
Watch made by machinery, *2629*
Worsted mill operated by waterpower, *2116*

Hebron

Historical hoaxes, *7468*

Huntington

Tungsten and tellurium, *3376*

Ivoryton

Comb-cutting machine, *2459*

Kensington

Monument to commemorate the Civil War, *7172*

Killingworth

Gem-cutting machine, *3371*
Type foundry, *2032*

Lakeville

Factory for making pocket cutlery, *2546*

Litchfield

Anthology of American literature, *1078*
Clock that was self-winding, *2625*
Law report, *3954*
Law school operated privately, *3191*

Litchfield County

Temperance organization, *7057*

Manchester

Parachute jumper snagged by airplane in midair, *8151*

Mansfield

Silk mill, *2124*
Silk thread, *2612*

Marion

Nuts and bolts factory, *2649*

Meriden

Player piano that was completely automatic, *1303*
Stainless steel flatware, *2574*

Middlebury

Lathe, *2645*

Middletown

Education association, *2903*
Elastic webbing, *2131*
Factory standardization to federal government specification, *3260*
State agricultural experiment station, *1625*
Teaching methodology course at a college, *2745*

Milford

Camp for boys, *2185*

Mystic

Ironclad seagoing naval warship, *8474*

New Canaan

Transatlantic crossing attempted by a balloon, *7998*

New Haven

Acidophilus milk, *2418*
African-American elected to Phi Beta Kappa, *2791*
Applied chemistry professor at a college, *2746*
Arbitration law, *1472*
Baseball batting and fielding cage, *7511*
Blotting paper, *2019*
Blue laws prohibiting activities on Sunday, *6182*
Building in all-Gothic architecture, *3261*
Chinese language and literature lectureship at a college, *2793*
City with a complete smart-card system, *7423*
Class photograph, *4619*
Coins issued by the United States, *4009*
College art museum, *3137*
College course in the contemporary novel, *2814*
College daily newspaper, *4517*
College graduate of Asian ancestry, *2755*
College magazine, *2727*
College to feature rowing as a sport, *7877*
Congressional representative to become a senator, *3651*
Dictionary of the English language compiled by an American, *3184*
Doctoral degree awarded by an American university, *2761*
Doctoral degree awarded to an African-American by an American university, *2791*
Fine arts department in a college, *2763*
First Lady to earn a professional degree, *4236*
Football dummy, *7694*
Football uniforms worn in a game, *7690*
Geography book, *6763*
Hamburger, *2405*
Hospice home-care program, *5398*
Intercollegiate football championship, *7691*
International championship figure skating tournament, *7842*
International football game, *7688*
Knights of Columbus meeting, *7220*
Map of the United States, *4479*
Music magazine, *1222*
National geology society, *6715*
Paleontology chair at a college, *2769*
Pay station telephone service, *4872*
Penalty rule in football, *7693*
Physiology laboratory, *5163*
Pituitary hormone, *5246*
Planetarium built in America, *6365*
Political history book, *7473*
Sprinkler head, *7329*
Stone crusher, *3386*
Tape measure, *2657*
Telephone directory, *4869*
Theater and dramatic criticism course at a college, *2851*
Tornado of record, *5900*
Transgenic animal, *6679*

New London

Capture of a British frigate in the War of 1812, *5684*
Circumnavigation of the earth by a submerged submarine, *8542*
Coast Guard Academy graduate who was African-American, *3123*
Coast Guard Academy graduates who were women, *3131*
Episcopal bishop, *6233*
Eye infirmary, *5101*
Marine engagement in battle, *5656*
Mine barrage, *5839*
Movie of the sun, *6406*
Navy nuclear submarine division, *5589*
Patented pills, *5233*
Steam whaler, *8433*
Submarine emergency air supply container, *8515*
Submarine escape training tank, *8517*
Submarine to surface at the North Pole, *8541*
Toothpaste tube, *2470*

New Milford

Automatic streetlight system, *7418*

North Windham

Fourdrinier papermaking machine, *2011*

Old Mystic

African-American minister to a white Methodist congregation, *6232*

Putnam

Nontwisted sewing thread, *2623*

Riverton

Chair factory, *2543*

Salisbury

Children's library, *3006*

CONNECTICUT—*continued*

Seymour

Screw auger, *2642*

Simsbury

Safety fuse, *1854*
Textile-wrapped detonating fuse, *1877*

South Norwalk

Derby hat, *2245*

Stamford

Ambulance ship for first aid to boaters and pleasure craft, *5048*
Crane, *1866*
Electric shaver, *2476*
Portable typewriter, *1680*
Postage meter, *4694*
Railroad signal system with automatic electric block, *8388*
Shoe measuring stick, *2229*

Stanfield

Cider mill, *2338*

Stonington

Discovery of Antarctica by an American, *6641*

Stratford

Helicopter, *8099*
Helicopter flight from water, *8102*
Helicopter flight of one-hour duration, *8101*
Long-distance helicopter flight, *8106*

Torrington

Brass kettles, *2273*
Brass rod, *1937*
Federal lawsuit against a city for failure to protect a battered woman, *7390*

Trumbull

Fluorspar, *3380*

Wallingford

Coffee mill, *2343*
Powder capable of stopping a lethal hemorrhage, *5190*

Waterbury

Brass, *1921*
Brass spinning, *1931*
Brass wire and tubing, *1924*
Buttons of pewter or block tin, *2232*
Can opener, *2276*
Gilt buttons, *2234*
Hooks and eyes, *2241*
Trade association, *1484*

West Hartford

Museum devoted solely to American political memorabilia, *3163*

West Haven

Automatic swinging doors operated by a photoelectric cell, *3301*
Bagel bakery, *2427*

West Suffield

Cigar factory, *7059*

Westport

Banner ads on the Internet, *6477*

Westville

Mortised lock, *3265*

Wethersfield

Colonial election held in defiance of the Royal Courts, *3756*

Wilton

Internet record label, *1283*

Windham

Legal treatise published in the United States, *3957*

Windsor

Umbrella, *2230*

Windsor Locks

Christmas tree displayed in the United States, *2488*
Helicopter fully operated by remote control, *8131*

Wolcottville

Machine for cutting and straightening wire, *1862*
Sewing needles made by machine, *2621*

DELAWARE

Book intended for circulation in the English colonies, *1063*

Online library provided by a state, *3032*
President elected by the House of Representatives, *4123*
Prize money awarded by the Navy, *5579*
Rebellion by colonists against an English governor, *5638*
State to offer free cancer treatment for uninsured residents, *5402*
State to ratify the federal Constitution, *3487*
Surgeon general of the Army, *5436*

Brandywine

Paper made by machine, *2010*

Cooch's Bridge

American flag flown in battle, *3473*

Fort Christina

Lutheran pastor, *6183*

Georgetown

Parachute jumper snagged by airplane in midair, *8151*

Wilmington

African Methodist church, *6254*
Alfalfa, *1586*
Artificial leather, *2143*
Cancer-preventing drug, *5263*
Concentrated milk, *2443*
Fund-raising organization to sell Christmas seals, *7224*
Iron steamship built for transatlantic service, *8430*
Lucite commercially manufactured, *1906*
Merchant ship commanded by an African-American captain, *8456*
Mobile telephone call between an airplane in flight and a moving car, *4900*
Mobile telephone one-way communication, *4879*
Nylon stockings, *2265*
Plastic soda bottle, *2005*
Sulfanilamide production, *5244*
Swedes to arrive in America, *6027*
Synthetic fabric that was waterproof and breathable, *2144*
Synthetic fiber, *2141*
Synthetic rubber for manufacture, *1902*
Teflon created in a laboratory, *1907*
Thread as strong as steel, *2145*
Toothbrush with synthetic bristles, *2477*
Urban business district with complete video surveillance, *7396*
Woman to serve as patent examiner-in-chief, *3996*
World War II air hero, *5765*

DISTRICT OF COLUMBIA

Washington

Admiral of the Navy, *5603*
Aerial photograph in natural colors, *4632*
Affirmative action order issued by the federal government, *3855*
African-American branch of the YMCA, *7205*
African-American history trail, *6149*
African-American news correspondent accredited to the White House, *4599*
African-American opera singer to sing a white role, *1326*
African-American preacher to deliver a sermon in the House of Representatives, *3604*
African-American to earn a Ph.D., *2768*
Agricultural journal, *1592*
AIDS policy coordinator for the federal government, *7286*
Air attack on Germany by the Army Air Force in World War II, *5789*
Air bag requirement by the federal government, *8277*
Air combat arm of the Army, *5475*
Air Force chairman of the Joint Chiefs of Staff, *5495*
Air Force general who was a woman, *5497*
Air Force general who was African-American, *5494*
Air pollution law of importance enacted by Congress, *5925*
Airmail letter sheet, *4700*
Airmail postal card, *4708*
Airmail stamps, *4734*
Airplane model to make a sustained flight under its own power, *8004*
Airplane to land on the White House lawn, *4329*
Airship filled with helium gas, *8049*
Alcohol abuse programs required in schools by the federal government, *7067*
Alcohol prohibition law enacted by Congress, *7075*
Alcohol prohibition vote taken in Congress, *7073*
Ambassador from the United States who was a woman, *3900*
Ambassador to the United States who was a woman, *3899*
Ambassador who was an African-American woman, *3904*
American boycott of the Olympic Games, *7862*
American to hug the Queen of England, *3943*

Campaign to promote citywide testing for the AIDS virus, *7296*
Capitol Police Officers killed in the line of duty, *3580*
Capture of a ship in the Spanish-American War, *5724*
Casein fiber, *1905*
Catalog cards from the Library of Congress, *3023*
Catalog of government publications, *3844*
Catalog of recordings on disk, *1244*
Catalog of the Library of Congress, *3004*
Censorship of the Internet, *6481*
Census compiled by machines, *6154*
Census compiled in part from statistics obtained by mail, *6157*
Census in which the national population exceeded 10 million, *6152*
Census proven to have been inaccurate, *6156*
Census that included deaf, mute, and blind people, *6153*
Census to be replicated, *6161*
Census to collect information over the phone, *6158*
Census to show more people living in cities than in rural areas, *6155*
Certified public accountant who was African-American, *1712*
Chairman of a major political party who was African-American, *4110*
Chairman of the Republican party who was a woman, *4107*
Chef at the White House who was a woman, *4335*
Chemical arms control treaty, *3912*
Chess champion to play more than 100 games simultaneously, *7733*
Chief White House counsel who was a woman, *4167*
Child born in the White House, *4324*
Child born in the White House who was the offspring of a president, *4328*
Child labor law enacted by Congress, *7147*
Child welfare congress, *2189*
Christmas postage stamp series with a religious and a secular subject, *4744*
Cigarette tax, *7063*
Citizenship statute for Native Americans, *6090*
Civil rights law enacted by Congress, *6136*
Civilian airport owned and operated by the federal government, *8103*
Claims court established by the federal government, *3706*
Coast Guard aviation unit, *5470*
Coast guard service, *5542*
Coast survey, *6059*
Coin bearing the likeness of an African-American, *4045*
Coin showing a president in frontal view, *4051*
College for deaf students, *2757*
College founded as a Catholic institution, *2719*
Color news photograph transmitted by radio fax for publication, *4587*
Color-coded federal warning system, *5834*
Commemoration of the birthday of Abraham Lincoln, *2496*
Commemorative postage stamp depicting a president's wife, *4746*
Commerce court established by the federal government, *3713*
Commercial telegraph service, *4847*
Compensation of Japanese-Americans interned during World War II, *5820*
Comprehensive civil rights law enacted by Congress, *6145*
Comprehensive civil rights legislation for people with disabilities, *7047*
Comprehensive database of federal research projects, *3871*
Comprehensive wilderness law, *5926*
Computer virus, *6452*
Concept of food groups, *7277*
Conference of American republics, *3890*
Conference of American republics initiated by the United States, *3890*
Conference of great powers, *3895*
Congress in session a full year, *3577*
Congress in which 1,000 bills were introduced, *3566*
Congress to appropriate $1 billion, *3572*
Congress to enact more than 1,000 laws, *3575*
Congressional caucus to meet openly, *3593*
Congressional chaplain who was Catholic, *3565*
Congressional directory, *3571*
Congressional lobbyist who was a woman, *3567*
Congressional opening session to be televised, *3578*
Congressional page who was African-American, *3622*
Congressional page who was female, *3616*
Congressional representative censured for assaulting another, *3601*
Congressional representative censured for corruption, *3605*
Congressional representative expelled for corruption, *3632*
Congressional representative of Asian ancestry, *3620*
Congressional representative to be censured, *3597*

Father and son to occupy the same Cabinet post, *4185*
Father and son who were senators at the same session, *3658*
FBI raid on the office of a congressional representative, *3641*
FBI sting operation against corrupt politicians, *6960*
Federal administrator who was an African-American woman, *3851*
Federal agency director who was a woman, *3846*
Federal agency overseeing all border control, *3870*
Federal aid program for primary and secondary schools, *2979*
Federal aid to libraries, *3028*
Federal aid to special education, *2913*
Federal ban on polygamy that was enforced, *7436*
Federal ban on the importation of African slaves, *6125*
Federal directions for sealing birth records of adopted children, *2197*
Federal family assistance program, *3848*
Federal government building built to withstand a nuclear attack, *3854*
Federal gun control regulation, *6944*
Federal law exempting debtors from prison, *6993*
Federal law hostile to lotteries, *1801*
Federal law regulating ages and workload for child labor, *7156*
Federal law regulating hunting of migratory birds, *7827*
Federal law requiring radios on ships, *8445*
Federal law restricting immigration, *6077*
Federal law to emancipate slaves, *6133*
Federal marshal who was African-American, *7361*
Federal marshals who were women, *7385*
Federal online privacy law, *7305*
Federal reserve banks, *1738*
Federal treasury surplus to be returned to the states, *4345*
Federally chartered bank owned and managed by women, *1755*
First Lady appointed to a federal post after the death of her husband, *4235*
First Lady to attend all her husband's cabinet meetings, *4231*
First Lady to attend her husband's inauguration, *4217*
First Lady to be depicted on a monument to a president, *4238*
First Lady to die during her husband's term in office, *4225*
First Lady to earn a college degree in a scientific field, *4230*
First Lady to earn a professional degree, *4236*
First Lady to give birth during her husband's term in office, *4229*
First Lady to graduate from college, *4226*
First Lady to have an occupation, *4221*
First Lady to receive free mail franking privileges, *4216*
First Lady to run for public office, *4239*
First Lady to travel in an airplane to a foreign country, *4234*
First Lady to undertake a career of public service, *4233*
First Lady to write her autobiography, *4218*
First Lady who attended school, *4224*
First Lady who was also a federal official, *4237*
First Lady who was born an American citizen, *4223*
First Lady who was the grandmother of a president, *4222*
First Lady who was the mother of a president, *4220*
First Lady who was not born in the United States, *4219*
First Lady whose autobiography was commercially published, *4232*
Fistfight in the Senate, *3667*
Food guide pyramid, *7284*
Foreign flag flown at the State Department, *3917*
Foreign service school in a college, *2817*
Former First Lady elected to the Senate, *3695*
Former president to address the Senate, *4155*
Former president to become chief justice of the Supreme Court, *4143*
Free mail delivery in cities, *4675*
Freedom ride in the 1960s, *6143*
Fuel cell car, *8281*
Fugitive slave law enacted by Congress, *6123*
Gag rule in the House of Representatives, *3598*
Gaslight in the White House, *4326*
Gasoline tax levied by Congress, *4424*
Gay rights march, *7455*
Gay rights protest on a large scale, *7448*
General of the Armies of the United States, *5443*
General of the Armies of the United States with the rank of six stars, *5454*
General of the U.S. Army, *5442*
Genetically altered plants, *1654*
Genetically altered virus approved for use in a vaccine, *6683*
Geographer of the United States, *6488*
Geography magazine, *6784*

DISTRICT OF COLUMBIA—Washington—*continued*

Geological survey authorized by Congress, *6491*
Gold certificates, *4030*
Gold Star mothers, *5750*
Government of Washington, DC, *3518*
Government report posted on the Internet before its publication on paper, *3866*
Grant of federal land to a foreigner, *6057*
Gravure-printed postage stamp, *4750*
Guide to parliamentary rules of order, *3564*
Health insurance plan enacted by Congress, *3856*
High-speed radio fax transmission, *4473*
Holiday postage stamp issued jointly by two countries, *4741*
Honorary citizenship authorized by Congress, *6098*
Hostage crisis in the modern era, *3909*
Hydraulic-lift parking garage device, *8266*
Hydrogen refueling station, *2104*
Immigration ban enacted by Congress, *6080*
Immigration quota enacted by Congress, *6088*
Income tax levied by Congress, *4413*
Independent aviation branch of the U.S. armed forces, *5488*
Indian Affairs Commissioner who was Native American, *3843*
Inheritance tax levied by Congress, *4414*
International fencing championship competition, *7668*
Internet march on Washington, *3868*
Interstate commerce act enacted by Congress, *2075*
Irrigation law enacted by Congress, *1618*
Japanese cherry trees, *1636*
Jet airplane to transport mail, *4705*
Judge advocate of the Navy, *5600*
Jute culture, *1620*
Killing of one congressional representative by another, *3599*
King of Great Britain to visit the United States, *3935*
Knights of Pythias meeting, *7208*
Laboratory for the study of human parasites, *5168*
Laboratory for the study of parasites in livestock, *5404*
Land grant for an agricultural college, *2762*
Land office established by Congress, *6061*
Law making identity theft a federal crime, *6975*
Lawyer admitted to practice before the Supreme Court who was African-American, *3966*
Lawyer who was a woman to be admitted to practice before the Supreme Court, *3970*
Lawyer who was an African-American woman, *3968*
Legal definition of the presidential seal, *4151*
Liberty loan subscriptions, *1762*
Librarian of Congress, *3005*
Library of Congress collection, *3003*
Library to possess 100 million items, *3031*
Lifesaving service established by the federal government, *7344*
Loan made by the federal Government to a war ally, *1761*
Machine to make glass light bulbs, *6562*
Magazine of the federal government, *3850*
Mail delivery by steamboat, *4662*
Mail fraud law enacted by Congress, *4679*
Major government report on tobacco smoking, *7084*
Major solo show of work by an African-American artist, *1043*
Marijuana ban enacted by Congress, *7079*
Marine reserve member who was a woman, *5566*
Maritime Day, *2514*
Mass expulsion from the Senate, *3663*
Mayor of Washington who was African-American, *3541*
Meat inspection law enacted by Congress, *7255*
Medal of Honor awarded in the Vietnam war, *5535*
Medal of Honor awarded in World War I, *5516*
Medal of Honor awarded to a chaplain, *5529*
Medal of Honor awarded to a Marine in the Korean War, *5532*
Medal of Honor awarded to a Seabee, *5536*
Medal of Honor awarded to an Army soldier, *5504*
Medals of Honor awarded to African-American servicemen for service in World War II, *5538*
Medical society for African-Americans, *5221*
Members of a foreign terrorist organization indicted for planning attacks within the United States, *5827*
Memorial postage stamp, *4733*
Metric system usage to be approved by Congress, *1486*
Microfilm reading device, *3033*
Midterm election since World War II in which the president's party gained seats in the House of Representatives, *3636*
Military campaign medal, *5510*
Military service by African-Americans to be authorized by Congress, *5421*
Minimum hourly wage of one dollar, *7161*

DISTRICT OF COLUMBIA—Washington—*continued*

Secretary of commerce, *4183*
Secretary of commerce and labor, *4181*
Secretary of defense, *4190*
Secretary of education, *4208*
Secretary of energy, *4206*
Secretary of health and human services, *4207*
Secretary of health, education, and welfare, *4191*
Secretary of homeland security, *4214*
Secretary of housing and urban development, *4198*
Secretary of labor, *4184*
Secretary of state to serve simultaneously as national security advisor, *4203*
Secretary of state who was a woman, *4212*
Secretary of state who was African-American, *4213*
Secretary of state who was an African-American woman, *4213*
Secretary of the interior, *4178*
Secretary of transportation, *4199*
Secretary of veterans affairs, *4210*
Senate filibuster, *3657*
Senate hearing witness who was a woman, *3665*
Senate parliamentarian, *3679*
Senate proceeding to be shown on television, *3691*
Senate whip, *3671*
Senator convicted of a crime, *3668*
Senator expelled for corrupt election practices, *3670*
Senator to address the Senate in military uniform, *3664*
Senator to change political control of the Senate by switching parties, *3697*
Session of Congress held in Washington, *3554*
Signal flares, *5849*
Sky marshals, *7387*
Smoking ban on airplane flights, *7088*
Sorority for African-American college women, *2778*
Special delivery mail service, *4682*
Speech delivered before the House of Representatives by an African-American representative, *3607*
Speed limit for highway traffic established by Congress, *8213*
Spoils system of presidential patronage, *4128*
Standard time program, *2630*
Standardization of nomenclature for naval vessels, *5581*
State dinner televised from the White House, *4333*
State police department to be monitored for racial profiling, *7395*
Statue cast by the federal government, *7176*
Statue of a woman installed in the Capitol's National Statuary Hall, *7181*
Stealth aircraft, *5492*
Steamboat inspection service established by Congress, *8429*
Streamlined electric locomotive, *8344*
Strike settlement mediated by the federal Department of Labor, *7146*
Strike suppressed by federal troops in peacetime, *7127*
Supreme Court decision declaring a state law unconstitutional, *3743*
Supreme Court decision establishing the power of the federal government, *3742*
Supreme Court decision in a state boundary case, *3747*
Supreme Court decision on inclusion of candidates in televised political debates, *3753*
Supreme Court decision voiding an act of Congress, *3740*
Supreme Court justice to be appointed chief justice, *3749*
Supreme Court justice to be impeached, *3741*
Supreme Court justice who was a Jewish woman, *3750*
Supreme Court justice who was a woman, *3752*
Supreme Court justice who was Jewish, *3750*
Supreme Court nominee to die before taking office, *3748*
Supreme Court with a majority of Catholic justices, *3754*
Surgeon general, *7249*
Surgeon general who was a woman, *7283*
Surgeon general who was African-American, *7287*
Swimming pool in the White House, *4332*
Tae Kwon Do school, *7982*
Tariff commission established by Congress, *4416*
Tariff enacted by Congress to prevent the importation of obscene literature and pictures, *4411*
Tariff passed by Congress for protection, *4408*
Tax levied by Congress on excess profits of corporations, *4420*
Telecast of an object in motion, *4923*
Telecast of image and sound, *4925*
Telegraph appropriation by Congress, *4845*
Telegraph station, *4846*
Telephone cable deep-sea service, *4887*
Telephone call conveyed by a privately owned satellite, *4909*
Telephone recording devices, *4901*

DISTRICT OF COLUMBIA—Washington—*continued*

Year in which the prison population exceeded 1 million, *7022*
Year in which the public debt of the United States exceeded $1 trillion, *3861*
Year in which two presidents were elected, *3806*
Year when citizens of the District of Columbia could vote in a presidential election, *3786*
Zinc, *3379*
Zip codes, *4712*

FLORIDA

Artist to come to America, *1010*
Autopsy, *2291*
Catholic bishop to exercise episcopal functions, *6170*
Congressional representative who was a Hispanic woman, *3634*
Diplomat who was a woman, *3896*
Land mines, *5846*
Mailbox see-through locker, *4661*
Marriage and divorce classes required by a state, *2599*
Meteor shower on record, *6384*
Muslim traveler in America, *6163*
School voucher plan enacted by a state, *2987*
Secretary of transportation, *4199*
Senator of Jewish descent, *3661*
Solar-powered car race, *7627*
State economic development agency that was partly privatized, *4366*
State to guarantee mothers the right to breastfeed in public, *2204*
Swiss settlement in America, *6034*
Triplets born several weeks apart, *2167*

Anastasia Island

Alligator farm, *1632*

Apalachicola

Mechanical freezer patent, *2275*

Arcadia

American civil administrator of a Middle Eastern country, *3916*
Rattlesnake meat in cans, *2432*

Bonita Springs

Coast Guard officers who were women who served aboard ships, *5546*

Cape Canaveral

African-American woman astronaut to fly in space, *6826*
Animal fired into space to orbit the earth, *6798*
Animals to survive a space flight, *6797*
Astronaut lost in a U.S. space mission who was not an American, *6841*
Astronaut to be launched into space, *6803*
Astronaut to fly in space who was African-American, *6826*
Astronaut to orbit the earth, *6804*
Astronaut to orbit the earth on two trips, *6806*
Astronaut to walk in space, *6805*
Astronaut who was a civilian to orbit the earth, *6809*
Astronaut who was a mother, *6829*
Astronaut who was a woman to pilot the space shuttle, *6834*
Astronauts to die in a spacecraft, *6810*
Astronauts to fly free in space, *6827*
Astronauts to land on the moon, *6814*
Astronauts to orbit the moon, *6812*
Astronauts to participate in an international spaceflight, *6820*
Astronauts to rendezvous in space with another spacecraft, *6808*
Astronauts to retrieve a manmade object from the moon, *6816*
Astronauts to ride a vehicle on the moon, *6817*
Astronauts to transfer from one spacecraft to another while in orbit, *6813*
Color photograph of the earth taken from space, *6410*
Commercial satellite, *6857*
Communications satellite, *6851*
Communications satellite with signal reception and transmission equipment, *6853*
Cosmonaut on an American space mission, *6833*
Geodetic satellite, *6858*
Geologist to reach the moon, *6509*
Geosynchronous satellite, *6859*
Global Positioning System (GPS) satellite, *6865*
Husband and wife to fly in space together, *6832*
Intermediate-range ballistic missile, *5882*
International satellite, *6855*
Live telecast from space, *6413*
Manned docking of two spacecraft, *6870*
Manned spacecraft to explode over the U.S. mainland, *6887*
Multisatellite launching, *6849*
Navigational satellite, *6847*
Orbiting geophysical observatory, *6860*
Orbiting observatory, *6381*

Cocoa Beach

Coral Gables

Daytona Beach

Everglades Holiday Park

Fort Jefferson

Fort Lauderdale

Gainesville

Hialeah

Holiday

Hollywood

Jacksonville

FLORIDA—*continued*

Key Largo

Undersea hotel, *1842*
Undersea park established by the federal government, *5995*

Key West

Airplane rescue at sea, *8024*
Cuban boatlift, *6105*
Hydroplane international service, *8046*
International airplane passenger station, *8065*
President to conduct religious services as commander-in-chief of the Navy, *4145*
President to travel underwater in a captured enemy submarine, *4298*
Telephone cable deep-sea service, *4887*

Melbourne

Rocket built by college students to be launched from Cape Canaveral, *6801*

Miami

Atomic bomb explosion over enemy territory, *5797*
Attorney general who was a woman, *4211*
Bilingual report of a congressional committee, *3631*
Conviction by an American jury for crimes against humanity, *6983*
Criminal conviction of a foreign head of state, *3944*
First Lady to travel in an airplane to a foreign country, *4234*
Greyhound racing association, *7662*
Live telecast from a noncontiguous foreign country, *4954*
Motorboat ocean race, *7577*
President to fly in an airplane, *4296*
President to visit a foreign country in wartime, *4318*
Savings and loan association established by the federal government, *1744*
Skyjacking of a commercial American airplane, *6951*
Transatlantic solo boat journey by a woman, *8537*

Miami Beach

Chairman of a major political party who was a woman, *4107*
Commercial sunscreen product, *2478*
Political convention to be televised in color, *4098*

New Smyrna

Greek settlement, *6040*

North Fort Myers

Journey on foot to all seven continents, *7985*

Orlando

Court-martial at which the judges included enlisted men, *5551*
Live childbirth broadcast on the Internet, *2168*
Major motion picture produced and exhibited entirely with digital technology, *1188*
Prepaid disposable cell phone, *4922*
Professional football game in which a woman participated, *7716*
Trial broadcast by the court over the Internet, *6978*
Twin postage stamps, *4749*

Pace

Physician convicted of manslaughter for prescribing pain medication, *6982*

Palm Beach

World's Fair that was financially successful, *1512*

Pensacola

Air combat unit of the Navy, *5471*
Branding punishment by a federal court, *6998*
Naval air training school, *3112*
Naval battle in the Civil War, *5708*
Navy airship, *8040*

Ponte Vedra

Golf champion of African-American and Asian ancestry, *7782*

Rosewood

Reparations awarded to victims of a racially motivated massacre, *6971*

Sebastian

Bird reservation established by the federal government, *5946*

St. Augustine

African slaves in the English colonies in America, *6111*
Aquarium for large marine animals, *3158*
Billiards, *7721*
Catholic holy orders, *6199*

St. Cloud

St. Marks

St. Petersburg

Tallahassee

Tampa

Tortugas

Venice

West Palm Beach

Winter Park

GEORGIA

Athens

Atlanta

GEORGIA—Atlanta—*continued*

Nursing school for African-American students, *3074*
Official use of the "Coke" trademark, *2447*
Olympic gold medalist who was an African-American woman, *7860*
Pinball ban enacted by a city, *7866*
Prisoners in a federal penitentiary to be employed in industry, *7012*
Radio station owned and operated by African-Americans, *4812*
Thought control of a computer, *5275*

Augusta

Federal law officer killed in the line of duty, *7357*
Steamboat patent, *8410*

Columbus

Parachute fatality in the Army, *5480*
Pilot who was African-American, *5472*

Crisp County

Hydroelectric power plant operated by a county, *6565*

Decatur

Woman criminal on the FBI's Ten Most Wanted list, *6948*

Fort Benning

African-American paratroop unit, *5483*
Army general who rose from draftee, *5446*
Army parachute battalion, *5479*

Grover's Island

Shipbuilding law enacted by Congress, *5580*

Jefferson

Anesthetic administered in childbirth, *5051*
General anesthetic, *5049*

La Fayette

Carpeting of tufted plastic, *2586*

Macon

Baptism in America, *6164*
College secret society for women, *2751*

New Echota

Native American newspaper, *4556*

Plains

President to be born in a hospital, *4260*

Rome

Bauxite, *3390*

Savannah

Agricultural experiment farm, *1572*
Beef export, *2320*
Cattle to be exported, *1575*
Cotton gin, *1585*
Hospital and asylum for African-Americans, *5104*
Interfaith charity organization, *7197*
Iron sailing vessel, *8426*
Methodist preacher, *6221*
Moravian church, *6219*
Patent issued by the Confederate States of America, *3994*
Presidential appointment, *4116*
Protestant Sunday school, *6220*
Scouting organization for girls, *2193*
Silk export, *2111*
Transatlantic crossing by an American steamboat, *8527*

Toccoa

Weight lifter to lift more than 6,000 pounds, *7981*

Washington

Town named for George Washington to be incorporated, *3514*

HAWAII

Congressional representative who was a woman of Asian descent, *3621*
Island territory annexed by the federal government, *6083*
Photograph bounced off the moon, *4636*
President to go through the Panama Canal while in office, *4146*
Queen to visit the United States, *3924*
Senator of Asian ancestry, *3685*
State admitted to the Union that was separated by a substantial body of water, *4361*
Surfing in Hawaii, *7958*
Surfing in Southern California, *7958*

Hilo

President to visit Hawaii while in office, *4317*

Honolulu

Adjustable stadium, *3319*

Coronation, *3927*
Medals of Honor issued by a state to honor service members killed in Iraq and Afghanistan, *5541*
Mobile overseas telephone call from a moving vehicle, *4895*
Packet radio network, *4804*
Public archive building, *4358*
Royal palace, *3926*
Space capsule recovered in midair from an orbiting satellite, *6852*
Submarine disaster, *8514*
Transcontinental demonstration of radio telephone operation, *4881*
Transpacific radio fax transmission, *4470*
Transpacific solo airplane flight by a woman, *8094*
Transpacific telegraph cable, *4857*
Volcanic eruption to be broadcast on radio, *5916*

Kauai

Guided missile launched from a nuclear submarine, *5886*

Kona

Iron Man triathlon, *7987*

Maui

Coast Guard ship commander who was a woman, *5547*

Mauna Kea

Telescope of importance with a compound objective mirror, *6382*

Oahu

Guided missile launched from a nuclear submarine, *5886*
Oceanographer of distinction who was a woman, *6510*
Transpacific telephone service using the transoceanic cable, *4913*
World War II air hero, *5765*

Pearl Harbor

American losses in the Pacific in World War II, *5761*
Circumnavigation of the world by a submarine, *8538*
Navy admiral killed in action in World War II, *5762*
Purple Heart awarded to a woman, *5517*
Radar used to detect enemy airplanes, *5763*
Ship from the United States to sink a Japanese submarine in World War II, *5764*
Submarine from the United States sunk by an enemy submarine, *5793*
Submarine to make a submerged passage through the Northwest Passage, *8543*

IDAHO

Hydroelectric power plant built by the federal government, *6559*
State governor who was Jewish, *4380*
State seal designed by a woman, *4354*

Arco

Electric power generated from nuclear energy to illuminate a town, *6620*

Boise

Air raid shelter for a community, *7301*

Idaho Falls

Deaths in an American nuclear reactor, *6626*
Electric power from nuclear energy, *6619*
Nuclear reactor fueled by plutonium, *6627*

Kellogg

Mimeographed daily newspaper, *4530*

Moscow

County created by federal law, *6081*

Twin Falls

Motorcycle jump across a river canyon, *1408*

Winimac

Product liability lawsuit to result in a criminal trial, *1513*

ILLINOIS

African-American congressional representative from the Democratic Party, *3606*
Air Force Reserve officer who was a nun, *5496*
Ambassador to Canada, *3897*
Ban on sex discrimination in employment enacted by a state, *7437*
Brothers to serve as representatives in Congress simultaneously, *3600*
Congressional representatives censured for sexual misconduct, *3633*
Plumbing law enacted by a state, *7411*
Seat belt law enacted by a state, *8268*
Secretary of veterans affairs, *4210*
Senate election in which both candidates were African-American, *3698*

ILLINOIS—*continued*

Senator expelled for corrupt election practices, *3670*
Senator to act in the movies, *3689*
Senator to serve three states, *3659*
State aid to railroads, *8308*
State ban on the employment of women in a dangerous occupation, *7129*
State law to establish English as an official language, *6089*
State public health program to provide prescription drugs from Canada and Europe, *7295*
State supreme court chief justice who was African-American, *3708*
State to enact a moratorium on executions, *7025*
State to repeal its ban on acts of sodomy, *7445*
State welfare program for single mothers, *2192*
Tax enacted by a state to support public schools, *2917*
Tornado disaster on a large scale, *5915*
Woman elected to the American Medical Association, *5218*

Anna

Refrigerated railroad car to carry fresh fruit, *8354*

Aurora

Motorcycle with a built-in gasoline engine, *8287*

Belleville

Pilot to die because of a lack of oxygen, *8066*

Bloomington

Hybrid seed corn shipment, *1639*

Bridgeview

Civil lawsuit against American organizations brought by American victims of terrorism, *3730*

Brookfield

Forest horse, *5962*

Carthage

Presidential candidate to be assassinated, *3804*

Champaign

Nobel Prize winner to win twice in the same field, *6913*

Chicago

African-American congressional representative from a northern state, *3606*
African-American physician to graduate from an American medical school, *5017*
African-American woman elected to a judgeship, *3721*
African-American woman lawyer admitted to practice before the Supreme Court, *3966*
Air-conditioned car, *8257*
Air-conditioned railroad cars, *8359*
Air-to-ground public telephone service, *4908*
Airplane flight longer than 500 miles, *8039*
Airplane sleeping berths, *8089*
Airport runway illumination, *8055*
All-color television station to televise live local programs, *4962*
All-star football game, *7708*
All-star major league baseball game, *7532*
Ambulance service with an incubator, *5046*
American combatant to die in World War I, *5731*
American Derby horse race, *7800*
American mercenaries convicted of planning a terrorist attack within the United States on behalf of a foreign government, *6966*
Anti-Monopoly Party convention, *4074*
Aquarium with an inland saltwater environment, *3143*
Armored car in commercial use, *8251*
Athlete to win the James E. Sullivan Memorial Trophy, *7478*
Automobile club, *8227*
Badminton championship tournament, *7977*
Ballet on an American theme by an American choreographer, *1053*
Baseball coach in the major leagues who was African-American, *7545*
Baseball game between an all-white team and an all-African-American team, *7498*
Baseball manager to win pennants in both leagues, *7530*
Baseball pitcher to throw a curve ball, *7493*
Baseball players to win the Most Valuable Player award, *7524*
Baseball teams to go on a world tour, *7514*
Baseball with a cork center, *7521*
Bicycle tire made of cord, *7651*
Bifocal contact lenses, *5272*
Bionic artificial arm operated by thought control, *5276*
Birth-control pill approved by the FDA, *7443*

Blood bank, *5055*
Bowling automatic scoring machine, *7588*
Bowling tournament sponsored by the American Bowling Congress, *7583*
Bread factory that was completely automatic, *2412*
Bridge table to shuffle and deal cards by electricity, *7737*
Cafeteria, *1825*
Canal made of concrete, *3324*
Car race, *7616*
Car radio, *4822*
Car with an electric storage battery, *8225*
Caterpillar Club member, *8044*
Catholic prelate named to the Roman Curia who was American-born, *6319*
Cellular telephone system, *4918*
Certified public accountant who was an African-American woman, *1713*
Chinese person granted citizenship, *6093*
City founded by an African-American pioneer, *3516*
City law requiring reporting of premature births, *2153*
Civil lawsuit against American organizations brought by American victims of terrorism, *3730*
Civil rights anthem to achieve fame, *1344*
Clock movement to be electrically wound, *2631*
Coast-to-coast radio hookup, *4789*
Coin bearing the likeness of a foreign monarch, *4038*
College extension courses, *2813*
College varsity sports program, *2822*
Columbus Day, *2491*
Commemorative coin, *4037*
Commemorative postage stamps, *4727*
Communist Labor Party of America convention, *4090*
Communist Party of America convention, *4091*
Computer bulletin board, *6458*
Congressional representative who was a mother, *3614*
Corporation to own its own airplane, *8064*
Cortisone synthesis, *5252*
Criminal on the FBI's Ten Most Wanted list, *6948*
Dental inlay made of gold, *5088*
Deodorant soap, *2479*
Discovery of different sleep states, *6671*
Drive-in banking service, *1748*
Driver license board, *8188*
Electric elevated railroad, *8319*
Electric elevated railroad that was permanent, *8319*
Electric washing machine, *2221*
Envelope with a window, *2025*
Farmer Labor Party convention, *4093*
Fax transmission of movie film, *4472*
Federal district court judge who was African-American, *3726*
Ferris wheel, *1004*
Food processor, *2290*
Gasoline obtained from crude petroleum by the cracking process, *6602*
Gay rights organization, *7439*
Gospel composer, *1260*
Greenback Labor Party convention, *4073*
Hindu spiritual leader to visit America, *6285*
Horse race of 1,000 miles, *7803*
Hospital open to all races as a matter of policy, *5115*
Hotel that was fireproof, *1820*
Industrial toxicologist, *7271*
Jet airplane passenger trip, *8128*
Juvenile court, *3710*
Kapok, *2138*
Keynote speech by an African-American at a major party convention, *4075*
Labor activists to be executed, *7135*
Labor union of African-American workers, *7150*
Law school graduate who was a woman, *2780*
Mail-order business, *2087*
Major league no-hitter baseball game on opening day, *7535*
Mass-produced picture frames, *2579*
Milk pasteurization law enacted by a city, *7274*
Mobster convicted for tax evasion, *6943*
Modeling school, *3214*
Moving sidewalk, *3419*
Museum with interactive exhibits, *3156*
National curling championship, *7636*
National forestry association, *5975*
National organization of Jewish women, *7204*
National political convention of a major party presided over by an African-American, *4076*
National political convention to propose African-Americans for the offices of president and vice president, *4103*
News reporter at a political convention who was a woman, *4594*
Newspaper circulation audit, *4525*
Nobel Peace Prize awarded to an American woman, *6905*
Nobel Prize in physics awarded to an American, *6900*
Nonfiction best seller, *1097*
Novel by a woman of Native American descent, *1096*

ILLINOIS—*continued*

Ottawa

Game preserve, *7825*

Peoria

Armored car, *8234*
Diesel-powered tractor, *1649*
Disposable diapers to be mass-marketed, *2198*

Pullman

Electric freight locomotive, *8337*

Quincy

African-American Catholic priest assigned to work in the United States, *6284*

River Park

Hearing aid, *5267*

Rock Island

Railroad bridge across the Mississippi River, *3243*
United Christian Party convention, *4085*

Schaumburg

Cell phone marketed commercially, *4917*

Shelbyville

Dishwasher, *2218*

Springfield

Congressional page who was African-American, *3622*
Fatal airplane accident involving a woman, *8033*
Medical slang dictionary, *5337*
National surgery society, *5229*
President to lie in state in the Capitol rotunda, *4255*
President who had received a patent, *4134*

Streamwood

Parade in which the marching music was supplied by transistor radios, *1409*

Streator

Soldiers in the American army killed by German bombers in World War I, *5744*

Urbana

Betatron, *6733*
Civic design chair at a college, *2833*

Urbana-Champaign

Electronic book archive, *3029*
E-mail program with a graphic interface, *6469*

Waukegan

Car race, *7616*

Wheaton

Golf course with 18 holes, *7751*
Radio astronomer, *6376*

Williamson County

Airplane bombing raid by criminals, *6939*

Wilmette

Americans to die in a UN peacekeeping mission, *5800*
Baha'i house of worship, *6302*

Winnetka

Correspondence school to offer instruction in Braille, *2968*

INDIANA

Election campaign using radio, *3781*
Gas conservation law enacted by a state, *6600*
Interurban streetcar line, *8373*
Naval bombardment of the Japanese homeland in World War II, *5796*
Organization of parents of servicemen and servicewomen, *5740*
Public Enemy Number 1, *6945*
State governor to be granted almost dictatorial power, *4382*
Sterilization of humans by a state government as a matter of public policy, *7270*
Tax on chain stores enacted by a state, *4423*
Tornado disaster on a large scale, *5915*

Alexandria

Rock wool insulation factory, *3344*

Anderson

Automatic headlight control, *8212*

Bloomington

Bacterium to be discovered that was visible to the naked eye, *6685*
Scientific survey of sexual behavior among Americans, *7440*

State university to grant equal privileges to women, *2776*
TV program broadcast on the Internet, *4980*
Vocational guidance chair at a college, *2834*

Brazil

Army pilot who was African-American to shoot down an Axis airplane in World War II, *5791*

Columbus

Diesel engine speed record, *8208*

Crawfordsville

Rotary jail, *7008*

Elkhart

Fizzing cold remedy, *5245*
Home health testing kit, *5183*
Metal clarinet, *1305*
Saxophone production, *1304*
Sousaphone, *1308*

Evansville

Gas refrigerator, *2287*
Soldiers in the American army killed in combat in World War I, *5744*
Tank crew to cross the 38th parallel in the Korean War, *5806*
Vitamin to be commercially synthesized and manufactured, *5243*

Fort Wayne

Baseball game at night, *7509*
Gasoline pump, *1868*
Sawmill to use a band saw, *1863*
Self-computing gasoline pump, *1876*

French Lick

Tomato juice, *2416*

Gary

Railroad freight yard that was fully automatic, *8329*

Greencastle

Sorority at a college, *2778*

Indianapolis

Driver who was a woman to compete in the Indianapolis 500, *7626*
Execution for the murder of a federal officer, *7016*
Full-page magazine advertisement for a food product, *1531*
Gallstone operation, *5343*
Greenback Party convention, *4070*
Indianapolis 500 race, *7623*
Millionaire who was an African-American woman, *1710*
National skeet tournament, *7888*
Navy commissioned officer who was African-American, *5608*
Prison built for women and managed by women, *7006*
Rapid-fire machine gun, *5855*
Socialist Party national convention, *4088*
SSRI antidepressant, *5261*
Transistor radio receiver to be mass-produced, *4824*
Union passenger station used by several railroad companies, *8313*
White bread, *2417*

La Porte

Automatic telephone exchange that was successful, *4871*

Lafayette

Commissioned officer in the Marine Corps who was African-American, *5568*
Olympic athlete from the United States to win 10 medals, *7851*

Madison County

Execution of a white criminal for the murder of a Native American, *6997*

McCordsville

Gallstone operation, *5343*

New Harmony

Communistic settlement that was not religious, *3520*
Printing instruction at a school, *3193*

Richmond

Lawn mower, *2664*

Santa Claus

Theme park, *1008*

South Bend

Automatic washing machine, *2227*
Cars with seat belts as standard equipment, *8261*
Message sent by wireless transmission, *4776*

INDIANA—South Bend—*continued*

Shot fired by American infantry in World War I, *5743*

Terre Haute

Computer camp, *6457*
Federal execution by lethal injection, *7027*

Vincennes

Department store, *2084*

Wabash

Electric streetlight installed in a city, *7410*

West Baden

Building with a large-scale clear-span dome, *3292*

IOWA

Chairman of the Republican party who was a woman, *4107*
Cigarette tax enacted by a state, *7076*
Senator unseated after a recount, *3675*
Soldier from the United States to land on French soil in World War II, *5788*
State ban on mercury in children's vaccines, *5162*
Woman member of a dental society, *5085*

Alleman

Corn-husking championship, *1642*

Ames

Electronic digital calculator, *6516*
Veterinary school established by a state, *3072*

Cedar Rapids

Mosque, *6303*
Muslim cemetery, *6311*
Photograph bounced off a satellite, *4637*
Radio sextant, *8507*
Trampoline commercially manufactured, *7787*

Davenport

Appendectomy, *5344*
Carousel patent, *1001*
Chiropractic school, *3080*
Chiropractor, *5033*
Portable movie camera, *1209*

Des Moines

Army training camp for African-American officers, *5424*
Car with an electric storage battery, *8225*
Debate among party hopefuls for the presidential nomination to be shown on television, *3831*

Fairfield

Electric power plant operated by a city, *6548*

Fort Des Moines

Military band leader who was a woman, *5428*

Fort Madison

Prison guard who was a woman to serve in a maximum security prison for men, *7020*

Froelich

Gasoline tractor, *1634*

Glidden

Soldiers in the American army killed in combat in World War I, *5744*

Iowa City

Intercollegiate basketball game with five-man teams, *7554*

Kellerton

Horseshoe pitching championship tournament, *7970*

Marion

Concrete cantilever bridge, *3250*

Mount Pleasant

Lawyer who was a woman, *3967*
Photograph of the sun's corona made during a total solar eclipse, *6400*

Onawa

Ice cream bar, *2419*

Oskaloosa

Community to fingerprint its citizens, *7380*

Sioux City

County to require its public agencies to purchase locally grown organic food, *1660*
Joint stock land bank, *1739*
Packaged popcorn sold commercially, *2415*

KANSAS

Blue-sky laws enacted by a state, *1502*
Chiropractic regulation law enacted by a state, *5040*
Movie censorship board established by a state, *1133*
Senate majority leader, *3674*
Senator convicted of a crime, *3668*
State governor to be impeached and acquitted, *4376*
State law banning trusts and monopolies in business, *1491*
Vice president who was Native American, *4309*

Abilene

Cow town, *3522*
Mechanized shooting gallery, *1003*

Argonia

Mayor who was a woman, *3526*

Atchison

Fuel alcohol plant, *6606*
Transatlantic solo airplane flight by a woman, *8086*

Bronson

International horseshoe pitching contest, *7970*

Chapman

County high school, *2956*

Council Grove

Senator who was Native American, *3669*

Dexter

Helium in natural gas, *6742*

Dodge City

Bullfight, *7613*

Fort Riley

Army general who was African-American, *5445*

Girard

Book series of small-size paperbacks, *4462*

Greenleaf

Civilian pilot wounded in Vietnam, *5811*

Haviland

Sheriff who was a woman, *7374*

Kansas City

Chocolate sandwich cookie with creme filling, *2411*
Civilian pilot wounded in Vietnam, *5811*
Horseshoe pitching association, *7970*

Leavenworth

Federal penitentiary, *7010*
Fingerprinting in federal penitentiaries, *7367*

Lyon

Christian martyr on American soil, *6165*

Nicodemus

African-American town in continuous existence, *3523*

Oskaloosa

Woman mayor with an all-woman town council, *3526*

Salina

Launching silos for Atlas F missiles, *5889*
Solo nonstop nonrefueled powered flight around the world, *8173*

Sapling Grove

Wagon train to California, *6066*

Topeka

Congressional representatives to marry each other, *3630*
Coursing club, *7801*
Marine general who was African-American, *5571*
Small claims court, *3714*

Wichita

Ace to fly a jet, *5808*

KENTUCKY

Bourbon whiskey, *2326*
Senator to serve in contravention to the age limit, *3655*
Senator who was returned to the Senate after being defeated for the presidency, *3660*
State law abolishing imprisonment for debt, *6994*
State nullification proceedings to obstruct federal legislation, *4340*

KENTUCKY—*continued*

Tornado disaster on a large scale, *5915*

Ashland

Steel mill to produce continuous sheets, *1943*

Barbourville

Colonial settlement west of the Allegheny Mountains, *6038*

Churchill Downs

Jockey who was a woman to ride in the Kentucky Derby, *7818*

Covington

Horse race mutuel ticket to pay more than $1,000, *7804*

Crab Orchard

Road appropriation of a specific sum by a state, *3409*

Danville

Abdominal operation other than a cesarean section, *5339*

Frankfort

Road authorization by a state, *3407*

Harrodsburg

Cantilever bridge, *3245*

Hodgenville

President born beyond the boundaries of the original 13 states, *4246*

Jefferson County

Health department of a county organized on a full-time basis, *7272*

Lexington

Drug treatment center for addicts established by Congress, *7077*
Vineyard, *1588*

Logan County

Camp meeting, *6248*
President who had participated in a duel, *4245*

Loretto

Catholic convent to admit African-American nuns, *6264*

Louisville

Aluminum foil, *2583*
Baseball game that was a shutout, *7503*
Braille encyclopedia, *3190*
Coast Guard inland station, *5544*
Coin box for streetcars, *8367*
Filly to win the Kentucky Derby horse race, *7805*
Gas mask, *1860*
Hand transplant, *5381*
Jockey to win the Kentucky Derby five times, *7814*
Jockey to win the Triple Crown twice, *7813*
Kentucky Derby horse race, *7797*
National Spelling Bee event, *2969*
President whose body was exhumed, *4273*
Presidential candidate who was Catholic, *3810*
Self-contained artificial heart, *5384*
Solo row across an ocean by a woman, *8549*
Telegraph ticker to print type successfully, *4852*
Terra cotta factory, *3340*

Maysville

Sale of federal land to an individual, *6051*

Murray

Radio broadcast demonstration, *4775*

Rosine

Bluegrass musician of renown, *1266*

Troublesome Creek

Oil well, *6579*

Wendover

Nurse midwife, *2152*

LOUISIANA

African-American to serve as interim state governor, *4383*
Amphibious vehicle, *8494*
Congressional candidate elected while missing, *3626*
FBI raid on the office of a congressional representative, *3641*
Law code adopted by a state, *3962*
Price regulation law enacted by a state, *1501*
Prizefighting ban enacted by a state, *7596*

Quarantine board established by a state, *7241*
Senator to win a seat that had been occupied by his father and his mother, *3681*
State governor who was Catholic, *4374*
Sugar cane, *1574*
Sulfur mine offshore, *3399*
UNICEF Halloween collection that raised funds for American children, *2522*

Calcasieu Parish

Sulfur deposit, *3387*

Carville

Leprosy hospital, *5116*

Ferriday

Exploration of the Mississippi River by a European, *6004*

Gretna

Solo crossing of the Gulf of Mexico in a paddled boat, *8548*

Lake Providence

Congressional representative to serve a single day, *3608*

New Orleans

African-American daily newspaper, *4554*
Artificial-ice manufacturing plant, *1890*
Attempt to establish a free public library, *3011*
Ball game to be declared a national special security event, *7719*
Boxer to die from blows inflicted in a fight, *7593*
Boxing match under the Marquis of Queensberry rules, *7598*
Business economics course at a college, *2747*
Catholic convent, *6213*
Catholic infirmary, *5097*
Catholic nun born in the United States, *6215*
Catholic nun who professed her vows in the United States, *6215*
Catholic nuns, *6212*
Citizen of the United States to be hanged for treason, *7003*
City with a free public WiFi system, *7426*
College for women to affiliate with a university, *2804*
Confederate coin, *4025*
Confederate cruiser to raid Union commerce, *5699*
Conjoined twins separated successfully by surgery, *5359*
Craps, *1800*
Croix de Guerre awarded to an American woman, *5514*
Episcopal bishop deposed for heresy in the United States, *6298*
Freedom ride in the 1960s, *6143*
Gospel singer, *1268*
Greek Orthodox church, *6276*
Heavy water to be identified, *6743*
International chess champion from the United States, *7729*
International exchange of fingerprints, *7369*
Levees, *3349*
Mardi Gras in New Orleans, *2486*
Methodist missionary, *6259*
Mosaic pavement, *3425*
Musician born in America to achieve fame in Europe, *1237*
National political science association, *6725*
Natural disaster to cause the evacuation of an entire city, *5936*
Physician who was African-American, *5017*
Precanceled stamps printed on rotary presses, *4735*
President of a major medical society who was a woman, *5231*
Regiment of free African-Americans organized during the Civil War, *5710*
School for girls, *2896*
Seatrain, *8451*
Senator who was Jewish, *3661*
Ship with a combined diesel and gas-turbine engine, *8497*
Statue officially sanctioned by the Pope, *7179*
Sugar refinery, *2328*
Venetian blinds to be patented, *2539*
War correspondent, *4593*
West Point cadet who was a woman to graduate at the top of her class, *3132*

Port Fourchon

Offshore port for oil supertankers, *6615*

Tangipahoa

Town founded by a woman, *3519*

Watson Brake

Human construction in North America, *5998*

Young's Point

News reporter tried as a spy, *4595*

MAINE

Brothers to serve as representatives in Congress simultaneously, *3600*

MAINE—*continued*

Child born of European parents on American soil, *6001*
European to set foot on the North American continent after the Vikings, *6003*
Revolving library, *3002*
Senate election race in which both candidates were women, *3686*
Ship built by English colonists in America, *8401*
State department of Indian affairs, *4363*
State to require presidential electors to vote for the candidates of the party for which they were chosen, *3795*

Andover

Telephone call conveyed by a privately owned satellite, *4909*
Transoceanic telecast by satellite, *5004*

Augusta

Fur trading post, *6024*
State prison commissioner who was a woman, *7019*

Bangor

Chewing gum, *2352*

Bar Harbor

National park east of the Mississippi River, *5991*
Transatlantic radio fax transmission of a photograph, *4468*

Bath

Navy destroyer named for a Confederate officer, *8483*
Steel sailing vessel, *8440*
Turbine-propelled naval ship, *8479*

Bristol

Knighthood conferred on a person born in America, *3918*
Pirate on the Atlantic seaboard, *6924*

Bucksport

Fish hatchery run by the federal government, *1623*
Floating electric power plant, *6566*

Calais

European settlement in the northeast after the Vikings, *6012*
International commercial telephone service, *4873*

Cape Porpoise

Exploration of the New England region by an Englishman, *6011*

Caribou

Transatlantic solo balloon flight, *8164*

Deblois

Power plant generating electricity from peat, *6637*

Dixfield

Diving suit, *6490*

Eastern Egg Rock

Bird for which a definite crossing of the Atlantic was recorded, *5947*

Eastport

Sardine cannery, *2377*

Farmington

Earmuffs, *2252*

Gardiner

Technical institute, *3192*

Greenville

Forest fire lookout tower, *5983*

Kittery

Knighthood conferred on a soldier born in America, *3919*

Lewiston

International dogsled mail, *4699*

Limerick

Bank president of a national bank who was a woman, *1747*

Machias

Naval battle in the Revolutionary War, *5651*

Minot

International dogsled mail, *4699*

MARYLAND—*continued*

Andrews Field

Transcontinental round-trip airplane flight made within 24 hours, *8117*

Annapolis

African-American midshipman at the Naval Academy, *3118*
Arbitration law enacted by a state, *1477*
Citizenship conferred by special grant, *6044*
Lending library, *2996*
Marine pilot, *5565*
Naval academy, *3105*
Naval Academy graduate to attain the rank of rear admiral, *3108*
Naval Academy graduate who was African-American, *3118*
Naval Academy students who were women, *3128*
Printer who was a woman, *2008*
Woman midshipman at the Naval Academy to graduate first in her class, *3128*

Antietam

Photographs of an American battlefield showing the bodies of the dead, *5715*

Baltimore

African-American Catholic priest ordained in the United States, *6284*
Agricultural journal to attain prominence, *1592*
Airplane used for newspaper reporting, *4528*
American expeditionary force to land in Africa in World War II, *5782*
Anti-Masonic Party convention, *4055*
Automated tanker under the American flag, *8463*
Baseball player to win Most Valuable Player award in both major leagues, *7543*
Bottle cap with a cork crown, *1999*
Bowling with duckpins, *7582*
Cathedral, *6261*
Catholic African-Americans, *6243*
Catholic archdiocese, *6239*
Catholic bishop appointed to serve in the United States, *6240*
Catholic bishop consecrated in the United States, *6246*
Catholic community of African-American nuns, *6264*
Catholic diocese, *6239*
Catholic nuns in a cloistered community, *6297*
Catholic parish church for African-Americans, *6275*
Catholic priest, *6244*
Catholic priest trained in the United States, *6244*
Catholic seminary, *2720*
Chair of modern pathology at a college, *3055*
City orchestra supported by taxes, *1255*
Civil War bloodshed, *5696*
Clipper ship, *8425*
Clock to strike the hours, *2624*
Coast Guard Academy graduate who was African-American, *3123*
College for women founded as a Catholic institution, *2815*
Commercial telegraph service, *4847*
Complete DNA sequencing of a free-living organism, *6690*
Constitutional Union Party convention, *4065*
Country day school, *2958*
Cultivation of human stem cells in a laboratory, *6692*
Democratic Party national convention, *4057*
Dental college, *3054*
Double-deck railroad coaches, *8347*
Egyptian antiquities collection, *3138*
Electric streetcars commercially operated, *8370*
Gas streetlights throughout a city, *7403*
General medical clinic, *5066*
Health board established by a city, *7234*
History of medicine department at a college, *3092*
Horse racing magazine, *7792*
Hospital to offer sex-change operations, *7442*
Human embryonic stem cell lines, *6691*
Hygiene and public health school at a college, *3089*
Ice cream wholesale dealer, *2356*
Intensive care unit, *5121*
Label patent, *3997*
Law magazine, *3960*
Liberty ship, *8454*
Linotype machine, *2051*
Local anesthetic, *5053*
Locomotive with six or eight driving wheels, *8334*
Manual training school entirely financed by public taxes, *3203*
Methodist bishop, *6234*
Methodist churches for African-Americans, *6238*
Methodist minister who was African-American, *6232*
Monument to Christopher Columbus, *7168*
Monument to George Washington, *7169*
Museum especially constructed as a museum and art gallery, *3136*

National political convention to adopt the two-thirds rule, *4058*
National sociology society, *6726*
Naval patrol bomber launched like a ship, *5586*
Night school for immigrants, *3205*
Odd Fellows lodge, *7203*
Ophthalmology book, *5302*
Ophthalmology course at a college, *3051*
Parochial school for Catholic children, *2886*
Passenger locomotive, *8332*
Pharmacy chair at a college, *3045*
Police 311 hotline, *7392*
Postmaster who was a woman, *4656*
President to make a radio broadcast, *4277*
President who was a "dark horse" candidate, *3803*
Presidential candidate nominated at a national convention, *3801*
Professional portrait painter who was African-American, *1026*
Professor at a first-class medical school who was a woman, *3081*
Psychology journal, *5329*
Psychology laboratory, *5164*
Race between a locomotive and a horse-drawn vehicle, *7793*
Railroad car with a center aisle, *8348*
Railroad for commercial transportation of passengers and freight, *8302*
Railroad timetable advertised in a newspaper, *8304*
Railroad to use an electric engine, *8323*
Railroad union, *7119*
Refrigerator, *2271*
Research university, *2792*
Silk sutures and ligatures, *5173*
Smallpox vaccine clinic, *5150*
Star-Spangled Banner, *3494*
Stone arch railroad bridge, *3235*
Submarine fitted with an internal combustion engine, *8511*
Sugar substitute, *2382*
Sulfanilamide used in medical treatment, *5244*
Sunday newspaper, *4496*
Surgical operation televised on a closed circuit for physicians, *5352*
Swedenborgian or New Church temple, *6245*
Tethered balloon flight, *7993*
Tooth-wear gauge, *5089*
Union Reform Party convention, *4087*
University press, *2818*
Woman elected to the National Academy of Sciences, *6718*

Baltimore Harbor

Atomic-powered lighthouse, *7351*

Beltsville

Radio broadcast from a moving train, *4796*

Bethesda

Alternative medicine department in a federal research institution, *5400*
Cloning of a mammalian cell, *6669*
Complete sequencing of a human chromosome, *6695*
Computer software application on Digital Video Disc, *6480*
Cooperative store operated by women, *2097*
Federal employee to win a Nobel Prize, *6911*
Gene therapy, *5399*
Genome sequencing and analysis of a bird, *6698*
Genome sequencing of a multicellular organism, *6693*
Identification of the AIDS virus, *6682*
Laboratory test to identify patients with Alzheimer's disease, *5146*
Tissue bank, *5059*

Bladensburg

Duel between representatives in Congress, *3594*
Killing of one congressional representative by another, *3599*
President to face enemy gunfire while in office, *4126*

Bohemia Manor

Labadist community, *6201*

Boonsboro

Monument to George Washington to be completed, *7169*

Catonsville

Military school operated by a church, *3104*

Cockeysville

West Point woman graduate who was Jewish, *3097*

College Park

Airplane outfitted with a machine gun, *5468*
Army pilot to fly solo in an airplane, *5462*
Helicopter flight, *8050*

MARYLAND—*continued*

Cumberland

Highway built by the federal government, *3411*
Milk bottles, *1998*

Ellicott's Mills

President to ride on a railroad train, *4292*

Fort Meade

Army armored car unit, *5426*

Frederick

Supreme Court justice who was Catholic, *3746*

Frederick County

Direct tax on Britain's American colonists without their consent, *4402*

Gaithersburg

Complete DNA sequencing of a free-living organism, *6690*
Molecular measuring machine, *6740*

Hagerstown

Bookwagon traveling library, *3025*

Hyattsville

Satellite composite map of the United States, *4486*
Single tax adopted by a city for local revenue purposes, *4417*

Laurel

Whooping crane, *5964*

Mount Savage

Fire brick to withstand high heat, *3335*
Railroad rails of iron, *8384*

New Windsor

Methodist meetinghouse, *6223*
Methodist Society in America, *6224*

Oxon Hill

Federal marshals who were women to be hired on a permanent basis, *7385*

Patuxent

Jury composed of women, *3700*

Poolesville

American to be recognized by Tibetan Buddhists as a reincarnated lama, *6331*

Prince Georges County

Painter to obtain a public commission, *1017*

Relay Post Office

Camp for conscientious objectors, *5558*

Silver Spring

Court ruling requiring emergency evacuation plans for people with disabilities, *7051*

Somerset

Semiautomatic rifle, *5866*

St. Johns

Shorthand account of a trial, *3949*

St. Mary's City

Catholic school, *2886*
Lead coffins, *2293*

St. Mary's Village

Catholics to settle in the English colonies in America, *6177*

Sykesville

Railroad to carry troops, *8306*

Talbot County

Manual training courses offered in a school, *2900*

Towson

Cordless electric drill, *2668*
Electric hand drill, *2668*

Warburton Manor

Novel by an American writer to be translated into a foreign language, *1073*

Washington County

Elementary schools to use closed-circuit televisions in teaching, *2978*

Wheaton

Self-service post office, *4714*

MASSACHUSETTS

Accident reports by employers, *7134*
Assault by a congressman on a senator, *3662*
Aurora borealis display, *6485*
Ban on Jesuits to be enacted by a colony, *6187*
Ban on Quakers enacted by a colony, *6192*
Bookbinder, *4429*
Bridge, *3227*
Brothers to serve simultaneously as governors of their respective states, *4373*
Car insurance law enacted by a state, *1970*
Centennial celebration of the Revolution, *2501*
Child labor law enacted by a state that included an education requirement, *7111*
Child labor law enacted by a state that regulated hours of employment, *7114*
Christian worship services organized by African-American slaves, *6205*
Cigarette manufacturer to list ingredients on the label, *7092*
Colonial law banning Christmas, *2485*
Colonial law requiring towns to hire teachers and construct schools, *2890*
Colony to legalize slavery, *6113*
Compulsory education law enacted by a state, *2932*
Compulsory education law in a colony, *2887*
Congressional representative reelected after serving a prison term, *3619*
Congressional representatives censured for sexual misconduct, *3633*
Congressman censured for assaulting another, *3601*
Consul, *3883*
Credit union law enacted by a state, *1735*
Diplomat to represent the United States in Canada, *3897*
Election held in a colony, *3755*
Execution for witchcraft, *6987*
Factory inspection law enacted by a state, *7128*
First Lady to write her autobiography, *4218*
Fork, *2533*
Free trade policy by the federal government, *4403*
Geodetic survey, *6492*
Geological survey for a state government, *6489*
Golf clubs for hitting balls, *7747*
Health board established by a state government, *7248*
History of New England, *7466*
Horse racing ban by a colony, *7789*
Horses, *8174*
Household product made entirely of plastic, *2581*
Independence Day, *2490*
Insurance regulation enacted by a state, *1950*
Iron exportation, *1915*
Iron lung respirator, *5180*
Labor bureau established by a state, *7121*
License plate issued by a state, *8192*
Lifesaving service for distressed mariners, *7337*
Literacy qualification for voting, *3768*
Loan by a colony, *1756*
Locomotive owned by an industrial company, *8341*
Marine insurance law enacted by a state, *1953*
Medal of Honor awarded to an African-American soldier for an action in the Civil War, *5512*
Milk purity law enacted by a state, *7242*
Minimum wage law enacted by a state, *7145*
Missionary society organized in the English colonies, *6222*
Nautical school established by a state, *3206*
No-fault car insurance law enacted by a state, *1973*
Openly gay member of Congress, *7456*
Paper money, *4003*
Paper money issued by the Continental Congress, *4005*
Patent granted by a colony, *3985*
Physician in the New England colonies, *5009*
Poetry collection by an American poet, *1060*
President with a brother in the Senate, *4267*
Quarantine law enacted by a colony, *7232*
Rebellion against the federal government, *5675*
Roll-on-roll-off carrier, *8459*
School for children with mental disabilities, *2931*
Scientific expedition sponsored by a colony, *6366*
Secretary of the Senate, *3647*
Secretary of war, *4172*
Senator to be censured, *3656*
Senator who was African-American to be elected by popular vote, *3688*
Shoes to be manufactured, *2228*
Slavery ban enacted for a territory of the United States, *6122*
State adoption law to consider the interests of the child, *2183*
State board of education, *2925*
State gas commission, *6599*
State law banning gifts of free formula to new mothers, *2171*
State law to end de facto segregation in schools, *6146*
State police officers who were women, *7377*
State probation officer for juvenile delinquents, *7005*

MASSACHUSETTS—*continued*

State seal, *4337*
State to legalize gay marriage, *7464*
State to mandate universal health insurance, *1987*
State to require driver licenses, *8191*
Vaccination law enacted by a state, *5152*
Vice president who had served in the House of Representatives, *4303*
Voting registration law enacted by a state, *3765*
Woodcut, *1013*

Abington

Church bells, *1292*
Shoe manufacturing machine, *2248*
Sprinkler system patent, *7328*

Albany

Colonial congress, *3547*

Amherst

Catalog cards from the Library of Congress, *3023*
Language to have its entire literature digitized, *1110*
Museum of children's book illustrations, *3167*
Physical education and hygiene professorship at a college, *2760*
Treatise on fossil footprints, *6658*

Arlington

Spreadsheet program for computers, *6459*

Auburn

Rocket flight using liquid fuel, *6788*

Becket

Modern dance troupe that was all-male, *1052*
Theater designed for dance performances, *1054*

Belchertown

Semaphore telegraph system, *4840*

Belmont

Nonprofit land conservation trust, *5911*

Beverly

Cotton mill, *2117*

Billerica

Leather-splitting machine, *2122*

Bingham

Watchmaking firm of importance, *2627*

Boston

Actor to receive curtain applause, *1427*
Adding machine to print totals and subtotals, *1668*
Aerial photograph, *4623*
African-American member of a state medical society, *5212*
Agricultural book that was distinctly American, *1576*
All-Star Game of the National Basketball Association, *7558*
Almanac with a continuous existence, *3181*
American gazetteer, *3182*
American history book of importance whose author was a woman, *7470*
Americans killed by British soldiers in the Revolution, *5644*
Anatomy lectures for the public, *3041*
Annulment of a marriage by court decree, *2590*
Antiquarian book business, *4448*
Antislavery book, *6129*
Apples, *1561*
Archeoastronomer, *6379*
Architecture department at a college, *2766*
Arithmetic book by an American-born author, *6757*
Arithmetic book printed in America, *6756*
Art museum for children, *3150*
Artist of importance to be born in America, *1019*
Atheneum, *3007*
Audubon society, *5912*
Automobile school, *3208*
Bacteriology textbook, *5325*
Baseball book, *7481*
Baseball glove, *7501*
Baseball teams to travel abroad, *7500*
Basketball professional player who was African-American, *7557*
Bathhouses owned and operated by a city, *7245*
Battle in the Revolutionary War, *5649*
Bell foundry, *1288*
Bicycle club, *7643*
Bicycle magazine, *7642*
Bicycle trip of 100 miles sponsored by a club, *7645*
Boat race for fishermen, *7574*
Book auction catalog, *4432*

MASSACHUSETTS—Boston—*continued*

Tuberculosis patients' home, *5124*
Tuition insurance for private schools, *1983*
Unitarian church, *6236*
Unitarian prayer book, *6349*
Vaudeville show, *1446*
Vending machine to dispense postage stamps, *1679*
Version of the Pledge of Allegiance, *3500*
Veterinary college, *3059*
Visible speech method of instruction for deaf students, *2948*
Vocal instruction book, *1211*
Vocational high school for girls, *2962*
War song, *1335*
Watchmaking firm of importance, *2627*
Water supply system built for a city, *7399*
Whist rule book, *7725*
Window glass factory, *3353*
Woman to run in the Boston Marathon officially, *7956*
World Series baseball game, *7518*
Worsted mill for making wool yarn, *2109*
Yacht club, *7567*
Young Men's Christian Association, *7205*
Young Women's Christian Association, *7209*

Bradford

Foreign missionary society, *6253*

Braintree

President to be buried in a grave, *4247*

Brant Rock

Radio program broadcast, *4778*

Bridgewater

Textile machine, *2114*

Brookfield

Artificial legs, *5265*

Brookline

American "Robin Hood," *6926*
Commercial provider of dial-up Internet services, *6471*
Indoor curling rink, *7635*
International professional tennis contest, *7924*
International tennis matches for the Davis Cup challenge trophy, *7926*
Safety razor successfully marketed, *2468*

Cambridge

Aeronautical engineering course at a college, *2831*
Almanac, *3168*
American poet honored in Westminster Abbey, *1095*
American to earn a Ph.D., *2730*
Ancient and modern history chair at a college, *2734*
Artificial gene, *6677*
Astronomer of note, *6364*
Bachelor of Arts degree, *2688*
Bacteriology lectures for medical students, *3076*
Bible concordance, *6340*
Bible printed in America, *6339*
Birth-control pill, *7443*
Book privately printed, *4430*
Book published in America, *1061*
Bookseller, *4427*
Broad jump to reach more than 25 feet, *7947*
Broadsides, *4488*
Bronze statue of full length, *7170*
Business history chair at a college, *2840*
Chemical laboratory at a college, *2758*
Climatology professor at a college, *2828*
College entrance requirement other than Greek, Latin, and arithmetic, *2728*
College graduate who was Native American, *2690*
College library, *2685*
College orchestra, *1227*
College president, *2686*
College student to work his way through college, *2689*
College to open in America, *2683*
Comprehensive comparison of the human and chimpanzee genomes, *6701*
Computer bug, *6423*
Computer game, *7741*
Computer graphics software, *6430*
Computer programming language for children, *6437*
Computer-aided manufacturing system, *1880*
Computing device with electronic components, *6422*
Cooperative store at a college, *2090*
Court-martial by the Army, *5550*
Dermatology chair at a college, *3069*
Diagnostic procedure using radioactive tracers, *5133*
Divinity professor at a college, *2693*
Document known to have been printed in America, *3456*
Ecumenical synod, *6186*
E-mail, *6443*
Entomology professor at a college, *2777*

Fire prevention law enacted by a colony, *7311*
Football goalpost, *7689*
Football stadium, *7702*
French instruction at a college, *2695*
Fruit-filled cookies, *2393*
Grand jury, *3699*
Greek drama, *1443*
Gymnastics instruction at a college, *7785*
Haptic computer interface to give a sense of virtual tangibility, *6527*
Head of one of the armed services who was a woman, *5499*
Hebrew instruction at a college, *2684*
Hebrew type, *2030*
Hygiene lectures at a college, *3049*
Hymnbook published in America, *6338*
Instrument for observing radiation in total darkness, *6737*
Interactive computer, *6428*
Internet domain, *6466*
Isolation of a single gene from an organism, *6675*
King born in the United States, *3931*
Law book of colonial laws, *3948*
Law school at a college to be permanently organized, *2711*
Marriage between two people of the same sex, *7464*
Master's degree recipient who was Jewish, *2705*
Medical chemistry course at a college, *3070*
Military computer network, *6427*
Music professor at a college, *2789*
Native American grammar, *3170*
Nobel Prize in chemistry awarded to an American, *6902*
Nobel Prize in economics awarded to an American, *6912*
Patent on an animal, *6684*
Pathology chair at a college, *3055*
Photograph of a meteor, *6402*
Photograph of a star other than the sun, *6399*
Planetarium, *6363*
Play of note written by an American, *1412*
Player piano, *1302*
Political economy chair at a college, *2782*
Primer in a Native American dialect, *3171*
Printing press, *2029*
Protest by college students, *2701*
Pulitzer prize awarded to a science book, *4774*
Racing shell, *7879*
Religious leader in the American colonies who was a white woman, *6178*
ROTC unit, *3113*
Scientist to win the Pulitzer Prize twice, *4774*
Semitic museum, *3147*
Solar system with multiple planets, *6394*
Spelling book, *2888*
Spreadsheet program for computers, *6459*
Stroboscopic lamp for high-speed photography, *4647*
Surrogate birth experiment with an animal, *6668*
Synod held in America, *6180*
Synthetic quinine, *5248*
Telephone conversation over outdoor wires, *4865*
Theology school that was nonsectarian, *2729*
Thesis directory, *2687*
Transmission of touch signals over a long distance, *6530*
Urban planning instruction at a college, *2827*
Use of @ in an e-mail address, *6445*
Vaccination against smallpox using cowpox, *5149*
Voice reader, *6456*
Windmill for grinding grain, *2316*

Cambridgeport

Achromatic lenses, *4639*

Canton

Congressional representative to be refused a seat, *3596*
Copper rolling mill, *1920*

Cape Ann

Schooner built in America, *8405*

Cape Cod

Child born of English parents in New England, *6017*
Naval battle in the War of 1812, *5681*
Transatlantic radio broadcast in code, *4777*

Carver

Divided road, *3414*

Charlestown

College library, *2685*
Identification of human remains using dental evidence, *2296*
Naval officers' training school, *3100*

Chelmsford

School for deaf students to teach lip-reading, *2909*

Cheshire

Cheese factory cooperative, *2333*
Plate glass, *3357*

MASSACHUSETTS—*continued*

Chicopee

Newspaper whose contents were transmitted by a communications satellite, *4547*
Transatlantic helicopter flight, *8129*

Clinton

Gingham factory, *2133*

Colrain

American flag flown over a schoolhouse, *3493*

Concord

Battle in the Revolutionary War, *5649*
Online high school, *2986*
Pencil factory, *2674*
Pile driver, *1847*
Transcendentalist literary work, *1087*
War tax resister, *4412*

Danvers

Self-contained artificial heart, *5384*

Dedham

Canal for creating water power, *3321*

Dennis

Cranberry cultivation, *1596*

Dorchester

Chocolate mill, *2321*
Library appropriation approved by a Town Meeting, *2995*
Property tax established by a colony to support public schools, *2885*
School committee, *2889*
Singing contest, *1226*
Transgendered person elected to public office, *7459*

Dover

House completely heated by solar energy, *2529*

East Walpole

Airship for private commercial operation, *8077*

East Watertown

Synthetic rubber, *1900*

Easthampton

Cloth-covered buttons, *2238*

Fairhaven

Japanese to enter the United States, *6065*

Fitchburg

Factory without windows, *3299*

Florence

Free kindergarten, *2950*

Franklin

Coffee percolator, *2278*
Town named for Benjamin Franklin, *3515*

Gloucester

Frozen food for the mass market, *2421*
Modern carillon, *1309*
Universalist church services, *6229*

Great Barrington

Electric power plant using alternating current, *6551*

Greenfield

Architecture book distinctly American, *3220*
Cutlery factory, *2546*
File factory to use machines, *2646*

Hamilton

Professional open golf championship match, *7764*

Haverhill

Settler heroine publicly rewarded, *6036*

Holyoke

Independent laboratory for evaluating consumer products, *7297*
Volleyball, *7967*

Hopkinton

Shoe peg, *2236*

Hudson

Online high school, *2986*

Jamaica Plain

Ecologist, *7253*
Home economist, *7252*

MASSACHUSETTS—*continued*

Mount Greylock

Artificial snow from a natural cloud, *6504*

Nantucket

Lifeboat, *7340*
Nautical school, *3195*
Novel about whaling, *1085*
Prison, *6988*
Ship sunk by a whale, *1795*
Sperm whale captured at sea, *1793*
Whaling expedition, *1794*
Woman member of the American Academy of Arts and Sciences, *7198*

Natick

Church for Native Americans in New England, *6194*

New Bedford

Coast Guard officers' training school, *3106*

New Plymouth

Income tax levied by a colony, *4399*

Newburyport

Algebra book by an American-born author, *6765*
Coast survey book, *5905*
Cracker bakery, *2329*
Federal revenue cutter, *8412*
Pamphlet produced from a steel plate engraving, *4446*
Wool carding machine, *2120*

Newton Center

World figure skating champion from the United States, *7844*

North Beverly

Reindeer, *5952*

North Woburn

American woman to become a countess, *3921*

Northampton

College basketball game, *7552*
Great Awakening of religious revival, *6218*
Gymnasium to offer systematic instruction, *7784*
Indelible pencil, *2678*
School for deaf students to be established on a permanent basis, *2909*
School for deaf students to teach lip-reading, *2909*
Sugar beet mill, *2347*
Theater operated by a city, *1448*
Whole-wheat bread, *2346*

Northfield

Youth hostel, *2196*

Orleans

Shots fired by German forces to land on American soil in World War I, *5753*

Pecoit

Gunpowder mill, *5837*

Pittsfield

Artificial lightning demonstration, *6500*
Broadcloth, *2119*
Cattle fair, *1593*
Intercollegiate baseball game, *7488*
Lightning observatory, *6501*
Polycarbonate products, *1911*

Plymouth

Cattle to be imported, *1559*
Colonial governor who was born in America, *4372*
Colonial treaty with the Native Americans, *6019*
Congregational church, *6175*
Duel, *6923*
Earthquake of record, *5898*
Execution in America, *6986*
Forestry law enacted by a colony, *5972*
Former president who was elected to the House of Representatives, *4127*
Furs exported, *5937*
Greeting addressed to the Pilgrims by a Native American, *6018*
Hurricane of record, *5897*
Leather tanning, *2105*
Military leader of the English settlers, *5633*
Pension law enacted by a colony, *7094*
Private libraries, *2993*
Property tax levied by a colony, *4398*
Prostitute, *7429*
Thanksgiving Day, *2495*
Wedding of colonists in New England, *2588*

Provincetown

Corn found by English settlers, *1557*

National historical society, *7472*
National psychology society, *5225*
Parkland purchased by a city, *5988*
Piano wire, *1296*
Pocket dictionary, *3180*
Settler heroine publicly rewarded, *6036*
Sewage disposal by chemical precipitation, *7414*
Silk loom, *2136*
Spring winding machine, *1869*
Wearable infusion pump, *5187*
Wire gauge, *2651*
Women's rights national convention, *7434*

MICHIGAN

African-American Olympic medalist to win an individual event, *7853*
Ban on surrogate motherhood enacted by a state, *2164*
Fireworks law enacted by a state, *7333*
Interracial jury, *3707*
License plates with a graphic design, *8198*
Medal of Honor winner to receive two awards, *5507*
Republican Party meeting, *4063*
Solar-powered car race, *7627*
State police radio system, *7375*
State to provide financial assistance to college students who are parents, *2880*
State with an online learning requirement, *2990*
Tournament of Roses intercollegiate football game, *7695*

Adrian

Seeding machine, *1606*

Ann Arbor

Bacteriology courses at a college, *3076*
Book series microfilmed, *3034*
College entrance plan using certified schools, *2784*
College teach-in against the Vietnam War, *5815*
Genetics clinic, *5071*
Honors program offered by a university, *2796*
Medal of Honor awarded to a Marine in World War II, *5518*
Microfilm editions of federal publications and documents, *3038*
Openly gay politician elected to public office, *7451*
Physician who was a Chinese woman, *5035*
Public speaking department at a college, *2812*
State university supported by a direct property tax, *2771*

Battle Creek

Cereal sold as a breakfast food, *2397*
Cornflakes, *2397*
Granola, *2397*

Bay City

Wrecking crane, *1867*

Benton Harbor

Boxing match broadcast on radio, *7601*

Big Beaver Island

Community leader to exercise the authority of king and high priest, *6068*

Dearborn

Plastic car, *8259*

Decatur

Carnegie Hero Fund Commission awards, *6896*

Detroit

Air-conditioned car, *8257*
Airplane diesel engine, *8067*
Boxing match broadcast on radio, *7601*
Car factory, *8235*
Car fueled by methanol, *8278*
Car with an automatic transmission, *8258*
Car with front-wheel drive, *8270*
Car with the steering wheel on the left side, *8243*
Cars with three-point lap-and-shoulder seat belts, *8261*
Catholic magazine in English, *6358*
Cellulose sponge for medical and surgical use, *5184*
Championship heavyweight boxing title won in the first round, *7599*
Commercial radio station licensed, *4808*
Computer-aided design (CAD) software, *6432*
Corporation to own its own airplane, *8064*
Corporation with a net income of more than $1 billion in one year, *1510*
Daughters of the American Revolution member who was African-American, *7231*
Death by suicide machine, *2308*
Designated hitter for all baseball games in a season, *7547*
Diesel cars to be mass-produced, *8272*
Electric car to be mass-produced, *8279*
Electric self-starter used in cars, *8248*
Family car with its own video entertainment system, *8280*

MICHIGAN—Detroit—*continued*

Gas-turbine bus, *8223*
Mitral valve corrective surgery, *5356*
Mobile home, *8293*
News program on radio, *4527*
Organization of newspaper publishers, *4597*
Pneumatic hammer, *2665*
Pneumatic piano player, *1306*
Police officer who was a woman, *7363*
Prince of Wales to visit the United States, *3923*
Professional hockey player to reach a score of more than 1,000 points, *7834*
Professional hockey player to score more than 100 points in one season, *7834*
Public school classes for children with epilepsy, *2973*
Radio orchestra, *1258*
Refrigerated railroad car, *8354*
Sedan car, *8250*
Soda sold in six-packs, *2437*
Telecast from a foreign country, *4954*
Three-colored traffic signal, *8206*
Toy pinball game machine, *7864*
Typewritten letter, *1662*
Vehicular tunnel to a foreign country, *3443*
Wedding broadcast over the radio, *2594*
Wedding by transatlantic telephone, *2596*
Woman delegate to a national convention of the American Federation of Labor, *7130*
Year in which more than 1 million passenger cars of one make were produced, *8262*
Year in which more than 100,000 passenger cars were produced, *8245*
Zebra mussels, *5967*

Dowagiac

Orphan train from New York, *2182*

East Lansing

President of a major university who was African-American, *2871*

Flint

Sports car with a plastic laminated fiberglass body, *8265*

Fort Wayne

Subcompact car with front wheel drive, *8276*

Grand Haven

City with complete WiFi coverage, *7422*

Grand Rapids

Carpet sweeper, *2217*
Game warden to be paid a salary, *5944*
Hydroelectric power plant to furnish arc lighting service, *6544*
Water supply to be fluoridated, *7417*

Grosse Ile

Airship made completely of metal, *8069*

Holland

Antibiotic synthetically manufactured, *5253*

Houghton

Professional hockey team, *7828*

Ishpeming

Ski club association, *7889*

Jackson

College commencement exercises in a prison, *2875*
Trimline telephone, *4910*

Kalamazoo

Dental drill powered by electricity, *5087*
Pedestrian shopping mall, *2102*

Lansing

Car equipped with an air bag, *8271*
Car exported from the United States, *8233*
State agricultural college to open, *2759*

Lenawee County

Fence made of woven wire, *1628*

Mendon

Electric locomotive headlight, *8391*

Midland

Plastic wrap, *1909*

Mount Vernon

Typewriter, *1662*

Olivet

College to dispense with credits, hours, points, and grades, *2852*

Plymouth

Air gun, *5858*

Pontiac

Curling club, *7634*
Movie of the sun, *6406*

Port Huron

Newspaper printed on a train, *4510*
Underwater railroad tunnel to a foreign country, *3441*

Royal Oak

Heart attack treatment using the patient's own stem cells, *5062*

Trenton

Traffic lanes designated by painted lines, *8200*

Tupelo

Electric power contract between a city and the federal government, *6568*

Warren

Smog chamber for air pollution research, *5924*

Waterford Township

Murderer convicted on the basis of nationally televised evidence, *6976*

Wyandotte

Bessemer steel converter, *1933*

MINNESOTA

Aerial ferry, *3251*
Blue Cross and Blue Shield plans, *1982*
Congressional representative elected by prohibitionists, *3610*
Home studies for foster and adoptive parents, *2194*
In-line roller skate that was commercially successful, *7876*
Intercollegiate basketball game, *7554*
Parental leave law enacted by a state that applied to both mothers and fathers, *7457*
Primary election law enacted by a state, *3776*
Senator to serve three states, *3659*
State to mandate workplace accommodations for breastfeeding mothers, *2205*

Austin

Canned ham, *2426*
Sit-down strike, *7153*

Babbitt

Taconite production, *3396*

Chippewa Falls

Supercomputer, *6431*

Crosby

Balloon flight to rise higher than 100,000 feet, *8144*
Telecast from the stratosphere, *5002*

Duluth

Ban on the sale of mercury thermometers, *5933*
Canal incorporated into a seaway, *3325*
Taconite production on a large scale, *3396*

Edina

Enclosed climate-controlled suburban shopping mall, *2101*
Microwave popcorn, *2452*

Faribault

Episcopal cathedral, *6274*

Hutchinson

American expeditionary force to land in Europe in World War II, *5773*

Lake City

Water skis, *7990*

Minneapolis

American Legion convention of veterans of World War I, *5624*
Armored car that was completely protected, *8251*
Athlete depicted on a Wheaties box, *1543*
Battery-powered pacemaker, *5353*
Bone marrow transplant, *5369*
Children's department in a library, *3018*
Delegates to a national political convention who were women, *4081*
Electric toaster, *2286*
Golfer to win both the U.S. Open and the U.S. Amateur in the same year, *7766*
Heart operation in which the deep-freezing technique was employed, *5357*
Home computer, *6440*
Immunology society, *5230*
Ink paste, *2026*
Milky Way candy bar, *2420*
Monthly cumulative index of books, *4461*

MINNESOTA—Minneapolis—*continued*

Navy-Marine Corps Medals for Heroism awarded to Marines, *5521*
Nursing school at a college, *3082*
Radio jingle, *1541*
Stockholder meetings televised coast-to-coast simultaneously, *1784*
Transfusion of artificial blood, *5060*
Vending machine that dispensed liquid automatically, *1673*

New Ulm

Catholic hillside shrine, *6282*

Red Wing

Ambassador from the United States who was a woman, *3900*

Rochester

Centralized system of medical records, *5119*
CT scanner, *5142*
Hip-replacement operation, *5370*
Hospital with circular wards, *5122*

Silver Bay

Taconite production on a large scale, *3396*

St. Paul

Armored car that was completely protected, *8251*
Cellophane transparent tape, *2578*
Charter school, *2983*
Computer software patent, *6461*
Green Party organizational meeting, *4109*
Hospital for disabled children established by a state, *5117*
Radio facsimile newspaper, *4538*
Sound-absorbing material made of rigid insulating board, *3347*
State forestry association, *5976*
Sticky notes, *2028*
Tape-recording machine for mass production of tapes, *4836*
Telecast from the stratosphere, *5002*

Stillwater

Toaster, *2284*

MISSISSIPPI

African-American senator to serve a full term, *3666*
State law allowing married women to own property, *7433*
State to ratify the Prohibition Amendment to the Constitution, *7074*
State to repudiate a debt, *4347*
UNICEF Halloween collection that raised funds for American children, *2522*

Biloxi

School district to install surveillance cameras in all its classrooms, *2988*

Clarksdale

Jet airplane to transport mail, *4705*

Columbus

State college for women, *2800*

Hattiesburg

Medal of Honor awarded to a Marine in the Korean War, *5532*

Jackson

Lung transplant, *5366*
Transplant of an animal organ into a human being, *5367*

Meridian

Reform rabbi who was a woman, *6314*

Natchez

Pilot from the United States to shoot down a German fighter plane in World War II, *5787*
Senator who was African-American, *3666*

Pascagoula

Cargo ship fully automated and flying the American flag, *8462*

Rodney

Land grant college for African-American students, *2781*

Vicksburg

Warship sunk by an underwater torpedo mine, *5717*

MISSOURI

Bachelor tax enacted by a state, *4409*
Congressional representative to be expelled, *3603*
Dental crown made of gold, *5086*
Secretary of agriculture, *4180*
Senator to serve three states, *3659*

State office of homeland security, *7306*
State to require driver licenses, *8191*
State west of the Mississippi River to be admitted to the Union, *4344*
Vice presidential candidate of a major political party to resign before the election, *3828*

Arcadia

Railroad mystery excursion, *1402*

Chillicothe

Machine-sliced bread, *2430*

Columbia

Journalism school at a college, *2826*

De Soto

Newspaper published by soldiers in the field, *4508*

Florissant

Catholic school for Native Americans, *2916*

Glasgow

Railroad bridge entirely of steel, *3246*

Goldman

Senate candidate elected posthumously, *3696*

Hannibal

Railroad post office, *4674*
Statue to commemorate literary characters, *7186*

Independence

Overland wagon road across the Rocky Mountains, *3412*

Jefferson Barracks

Army cavalry unit, *5417*

Kansas City

Baseball player to play all nine positions in one game, *7546*
Democratic Party convention between presidential elections, *4108*
Execution for kidnapping, *7015*
Football game to last longer than 80 minutes, *7717*
Helicopter rescue of an American pilot behind enemy lines, *5805*
National political convention at which a woman made a seconding speech, *4086*
Political convention to be broadcast on radio, *4094*
Shopping center in a suburban business area, *2095*
Shopping mall, *2094*
Soldiers in the American army killed by German bombers in World War I, *5744*
Wedding by telegraph, *2593*
World War II veterans' society officially recognized by Congress, *5625*

Kirksville

Osteopathic physicians who were women, *5032*
Osteopathy journal, *5332*
Osteopathy school, *3077*

Liberty

Bank and train robbery gang, *6935*

Louisiana

Fruit tree patent, *1650*

Macon

Osteopathic physician, *5029*

Marshfield

Horse motel, *1840*

Newton County

National monument dedicated to an African-American, *7190*

Sedalia

Sheet music to sell millions of copies, *1249*

Springfield

City in miniature, *1398*
Federal cemetery to contain graves of both Union and Confederate soldiers, *2302*

St. Joseph

Pony Express mail, *4671*
Ready-mix food, *2389*

St. Louis

Adaptable railroad freight car, *8363*
Adding machine successfully marketed, *1674*
Airmail dispatched from a post office in a balloon, *4670*
Airship race, *7676*
Allergy journal, *5336*
Antibacterial mouthwash, *2467*

MISSOURI—St. Louis—*continued*

Babysitters' insurance policy, *1971*
Balloon cup race held in the United States, *7674*
Baseball game in which a team made no runs in nine innings, *7501*
Baseball play-off series, *7536*
Bowling tournament for women, *7585*
Catholic mass in English, *6321*
Cow flown in an airplane, *1401*
Criminal conviction in an airliner crash, *6981*
Dance marathon to exceed 200 hours, *7972*
Diesel engine built for commercial service, *8186*
Electric power using municipal garbage as a boiler fuel, *6573*
Electron tube, *6515*
Evaporated milk, *2385*
Fiberglass sutures, *5182*
Food in an aerosol can, *2440*
Garbage incinerator, *5913*
Gas station, *8196*
Genetically engineered product to appear in food, *2455*
Geodesic dome of substantial size, *3314*
Glider flight indoors, *8073*
Ice cream cone, *2406*
International exchange of fingerprints, *7369*
Ironclad naval vessels, *8473*
Junior chamber of commerce, *1504*
Law school at a university to admit women, *2775*
Lung removal, *5348*
Magnetic surgery, *5380*
Members of a foreign terrorist organization indicted for planning attacks within the United States, *5827*
Mobile overseas telephone call from a moving vehicle, *4895*
Mobile telephone commercial service, *4894*
National bibliography organization, *3024*
Neanderthal skeleton reconstructed from actual bones, *6700*
Nobel Prize shared by an American husband and wife, *6906*
Olympic Games held in the United States, *7852*
Olympic medalist who was African-American, *7853*
Orthodontia journal, *5334*
Orthodontists' society, *5227*
Parachute jump from an airplane, *8031*
PET scanner, *5143*
Police department to adopt the fingerprinting system, *7366*
Public school kindergarten, *2949*
Railroad mystery excursion, *1402*
Railroad to run west of the Mississippi River, *8309*
School for blind students to adopt the Braille system, *2936*
Senator convicted of a crime, *3668*
Sewing machine to stitch buttonholes, *2618*
Silverite national convention, *4082*
Soccer team entirely made up of Americans, *7898*
Steel arch bridge, *3244*
Transcontinental expedition to the Pacific coast, *6640*
Traveler's aid program, *6069*
Vacuum cleaner driven by a motor, *2219*

Tipton

Overland mail service, *4669*

Washington

Corncob pipe commercial manufacture, *7064*
Zither factory, *1299*

MONTANA

Capitol Police Officers killed in the line of duty, *3580*
Congressional representative who was a woman, *3613*
International peace park, *5993*
Pension laws enacted by a state, *7149*

Fort Laramie

Native American to win territorial concessions from the federal government, *6075*

Poplar

Plastic oil pipeline, *6608*

Superior

Bibles in hotel rooms, *6290*

NEBRASKA

Arbor Day, *2499*
State legislature with a single chamber in the post-Revolutionary era, *4393*
State to make marital rape a crime, *6958*

Beatrice

Homestead law enacted by Congress, *6071*

Chadron

Horse race of 1,000 miles, *7803*

Grand Island

Interstate Commerce Commission Medal of Honor, *6897*

Hastings

Instant powdered soft drink, *2428*

Lincoln

Court case to establish the personhood of Native Americans, *6078*
High school team to achieve a perfect score in the International Mathematical Olympiad, *2984*
Streamlined all-steel diesel-motor train, *8397*

North Platte

Wild West Show, *1381*

Omaha

Frozen meals in three-part trays, *2442*
Frozen meals marketed as TV dinners, *2442*
Log-rolling national championship tournament, *7968*
Reuben sandwich, *2425*
Transcontinental telecast received on the East Coast, *4952*
Vending machine law enacted by a city, *1684*

Swan

Forest planting by the federal government, *5980*

NEVADA

Gambling permit stamp issued by the federal government, *4426*
Narcotics ban enacted by a state, *7085*
State to require paper receipts for electronic voting machines, *3791*

Boulder City

Hydroelectric power plant to produce a million kilowatts, *6570*

Carson City

Execution by lethal gas, *7013*

Frenchman Flat

Atomic bomb explosion to be shown on television, *5875*
Atomic bomb underground explosion, *5878*
Nuclear cannon, *5880*

Henderson

Titanium plant fully self-contained and fully integrated, *1945*

Lake Mead

Speedboat to exceed 200 miles per hour, *8460*

Las Vegas

Casino in Las Vegas, *1803*
Private space station prototype, *6892*

Laughlin

Slot machine jackpot of more than $1 million, *1802*

Reno

Transcontinental regular airmail service, *4696*

Virginia City

Silver mill, *1932*

Yucca Flat

Nuclear warhead mounted on a rocket, *5883*

NEW HAMPSHIRE

Attorney of the United States, *3703*
Certified public accountant who was African-American, *1712*
Federal judge to be impeached, *3704*
Free public libraries authorized by a state, *3013*
Insurance board established by a state government, *1954*
License plate slogan to be challenged, *8214*
Navy officer commissioned, *5595*
Orphan train, *2182*
Paper bags with flat bottoms, *1997*
Senate president pro tempore, *3646*
Senator elected on an antislavery ticket, *6131*
Ski lifts to be regulated by the state, *7896*
State lottery, *1804*
State to allow electric mobility devices on sidewalks, *7050*
Workday of 10 hours to be mandated by a state, *7116*

Centre Harbor

Intercollegiate rowing race, *7878*

Concord

Alarm clock, *2626*
Forest fire drenched by artificial rain, *5986*

NEW HAMPSHIRE—Concord—*continued*

Melodeon patent, *1295*

Dartmouth

Educational computer programming language, *6434*

Derry

Potatoes to be cultivated, *1570*

Dover

Mass scalping of Native Americans by colonists, *5639*
Strike by women, *7110*

Franconia

Ski lift, *7893*

Grafton

Mica, *3375*

Laconia

Water skier to jump 100 feet, *7992*

Lebanon

Intensive care unit, *5121*

Manchester

Credit union, *1734*
Self-balancing personal vehicle, *8216*

Meredith

Artificial leg patent, *5265*

Mount Washington

Botanic expedition, *6656*
Cog railroad, *8315*

Nashua

Tool factory, *2648*

New Castle

Ground attack in the Revolutionary War, *5648*

Newington

Community forest, *5973*

North Conway

Skimobile ski lift, *7894*

North Salem

Use of radar to investigate a plane crash, *8170*

Orford

Internal-combustion engine, *8183*

Peterborough

Free public library established by a city, *3011*
Local baseball team for women, *7494*

Portsmouth

American flag displayed on a man-of-war, *3472*
Leaping submarine, *8520*
Naval ship of the line, *8465*
Navy recruiting campaign, *5575*
Navy yard, *5578*
Submarine to be refloated, *8518*
Submarine to make a submerged passage through the Northwest Passage, *8543*
Submarine with a pressure hull of high-tensile steel, *8519*

Stratham

Senator to become a congressional representative, *3651*

Walpole

Herbal book, *5292*

Washington Center

Adventist church to accept Saturday as the Sabbath, *6268*

Wolfeboro

Summer home, *2524*

NEW JERSEY

Antiterrorism security standards enacted by a state to protect its chemical plants, *7310*
Area code, *4897*
Automatic steering gear for ships, *8503*
Book intended for circulation in the English colonies, *1063*
Coin to use E pluribus unum as a motto, *4008*
Congressional representative who was a grandmother, *3629*
Digital projection of a major motion picture, *1187*
Election law enacted by a colony granting voting rights to women, *3761*
Hammered iron, *1927*

NEW JERSEY—Camden—*continued*

Unscheduled event to be televised as it occurred, *4534*

Camp Kilmer

Aerocycle, *8139*

Carlstadt

Food-O-Mat, *2100*

Clinton

Farm cooperative for artificial insemination of livestock, *1652*

Coytesville

Standard broadcast station to transmit a television image, *4932*

Deptford

Untethered balloon flight, *7994*

Edison

Food for dogs on a special diet, *2605*

Elizabeth

Containerized shipping, *2080*
Flicker animation, *1194*
Miniature television tube, *4986*
Self-service supermarket, *2096*
Serviceman killed in the peacekeeping mission in Somalia, *5825*

Elizabeth Town

Contact between the president and the Congress, *3556*

Elizabethport

Cutlery shears, *2544*
Electric sewing machine, *2622*

Englewood

Figure skating champion from the United States to compete in the Olympic Games, *7843*
Transcontinental direct-dialed phone call, *4905*

Fort Lee

Blockade of enemy ships in the Revolutionary War, *5670*
Movie director who was a woman, *1130*
Underwater telegraph cable that was practical, *4848*

Fort Monmouth

Coast-to-coast solar-powered two-way radio conversation, *4802*
Walkie-Talkie two-way radio device, *4891*

Freehold

Revolutionary War conflict in which American and British troops met on equal terms, *5671*

Greenville

Revolver shooting tournament, *7887*

Hackensack

Transcontinental car trip by women, *8246*

Haddonfield

Dinosaur skeleton found in the United States, *6661*

Hadley Field

Scheduled passenger night flight by airplane, *8061*

High Bridge

Manganese steel, *1942*

Hightstown

Parachute tower for training jumpers, *8095*

Hoboken

Baseball game, *7483*
Harness horse race at night, *7794*
International cricket tournament, *7631*
Locomotive to pull a train on a track, *8330*
Mechanical engineering laboratory, *2787*
Tunnel construction using compressed air, *3440*
Zipper, *2261*

Holmdel

Computer operating system for multiple users, *6441*
Radio waves from space to be observed, *6389*

Jersey City

Armenian newspaper, *4565*
Boxing match to gross $1 million, *7603*
Cornstarch made commercially from maize, *2349*

Kearny

Lakehurst

Mahwah

Maplewood

Margate

Menlo Park

Millville

Morristown

Murray Hill

Navesink

New Brunswick

New Sweden

Newark

North Arlington

Nutley

NEW JERSEY—*continued*

Pahaquarry Mines

Hard-surfaced road, *3404*

Passaic

Life insurance group policy, *1993*

Paterson

Industrial park, *3259*
Linen thread factory, *2620*
Locomotive steam whistle, *8336*
Revolver pistol, *5845*
Strike in which a militia was called out, *7109*

Pennsauken

Traffic rotary, *3423*

Perth Amboy

African-American to vote under authority of the 15th Amendment, *3772*

Pitman

Doctor in the regular Navy who was a woman, *5210*

Plainsboro

Rotating milking platform, *1646*

Princeton

College charter granted by a governor, *2696*
College literary society, *2700*
Discus-throwing competition, *7945*
Electronic road system, *3428*
Intercollegiate lacrosse association, *7964*
Mathematical proof of Fermat's last theorem, *6709*
Mathematical theory of economic decision-making, *6706*
Radio impulse transmission, *4817*
Robot to grade essays on a standardized test, *6529*
Theology school graduate who was African-American, *2731*
Virus obtained in crystalline form, *6666*

Rahway

Antibiotic manufactured commercially, *5247*

Ridgewood

Submarine cable plow, *4862*

Riverton

Japanese beetle, *1638*

Sandy Hook

Transatlantic yacht race, *7571*

Sewell

Illuminated nine-hole regulation golf course, *7777*

Teaneck

Town to voluntarily desegregate its schools, *6144*

Trenton

Actor to have an exclusive movie contract, *1116*
Animal rights group convicted of terrorism, *6985*
Army chaplain killed in action, *5665*
Bioterror attacks by mail, *5833*
Chinaware for restaurant use, *1817*
Croix de Guerre awarded to an American, *5513*
Death penalty moratorium imposed by a state legislature, *7028*
Dish set made in America for the White House, *4331*
Masonic lodge of African-Americans to be recognized, *7196*
National conference on crime, *7382*
Open-hearth furnace for the manufacture of steel, *1935*
Pottery to make sanitary ware, *3358*
Railroad charter granted by a state, *8300*

West Orange

Alkaline dry cell battery, *6560*
Movie kiss, *1120*
Movie made in the United States, *1112*
Movie studio, *1113*
Movie to be copyrighted, *1115*
Movie western, *1122*

Whitehouse Station

Chicken pox vaccine, *5161*

Woodbridge

Fire brick, *3334*
Traffic cloverleaf, *3424*

NEW MEXICO

Native American map of record, *4475*

Senator who was Hispanic, *3677*

Acoma

Settlement in America in continuous habitation, *6002*

Alamogordo

Rocket-driven sled on rails, *6794*

Albuquerque

Atomic bomb explosion, *5871*
Commercial building with solar heating, *3313*
Congresswoman who was a veteran of the armed forces, *3635*
Personal computer, *6450*
Technical school for Native Americans, *2981*
Teraflop computer, *6483*
Transatlantic balloon flight, *8160*

Artesia

Underground school, *2982*

Bat Cave

Popcorn, *2441*

Carlsbad

Nuclear waste storage site deep underground, *6630*

Fort Stanton

Tuberculosis hospital established by Congress, *5129*

Los Alamos

Civilian to die in a nuclear accident, *6617*

Ruidoso

Horse race for a purse of more than $1 million, *7819*

Santa Fe

Anthropology laboratory, *6665*
Art museum of importance devoted to the work of an individual woman, *3165*
Nuclear reactor patent, *6736*
Treaty among more than two states, *4359*

Silver City

Race between a horse and a bicycle, *7802*

Sunspot

Vacuum telescope, *6380*

White Sands

Ballistic missile, *5874*
Ray gun to shoot down an armed missile, *5894*
Rocket to attain a 100-mile altitude, *6791*
Rocket to intercept an airplane, *5877*
Rocket to reach outer space, *6792*
Ultraviolet pictures of the sun, *6407*

NEW YORK

Ambulance air service, *5045*
Audubon society, *5912*
Bank deposit insurance law enacted by a state, *1720*
Bank to establish a branch in a foreign country, *1737*
Bathhouses mandated by a state, *7262*
Blood testing laws enacted by a state, *7278*
Blood tests for marriage license applicants to be required by a state, *7280*
Blood tests for pregnant women to be required by a state, *7279*
Botanist of note who was a woman, *6655*
Canal of importance, *3323*
Chiropody school of note, *3083*
Circus to feature a car as an attraction, *1373*
Coastal shipping service, *2070*
Concrete, *3333*
Congregational Church minister who was African-American, *6235*
Congressional medal awarded to a physician, *3569*
Congressional representative of Puerto Rican ancestry, *3624*
Credit insurance, *1963*
Cross-dresser of note, *7430*
Dental society of a city, *5214*
Dissection of a living animal to demonstrate anatomy and physiology, *3058*
Dog license law enacted by a state, *2603*
Domed sports stadium, *3316*
Education department at a college, *2785*
Environmental protection law enacted by a state in connection with advertising, *5906*
Fire escapes for tenements, *7326*
First Lady to undertake a career of public service, *4233*
Forest reserve established by a state, *5978*
Golf clubs for hitting balls, *7747*
Great Lakes vessel, *8404*
Historical novel, *1083*
Horticulture society, *1594*
Indian Day, *2510*
Installment sales law enacted by a state, *1511*
Labor antidiscrimination commission established by a state government, *7158*

NEW YORK—Buffalo—*continued*

Pacemaker to be implanted in a patient's body, *5363*
Paper made from wood pulp, *2017*
Skin grafting, *5341*
Steamboat on the Great Lakes, *8422*
Vacuum canning process, *2341*

Caldwell's Landing

Heavyweight boxing match to last longer than 100 rounds, *7594*

Canandaigua

Land office, *6048*

Canastota

Tire chains, *8195*

Cardiff

Prehistoric hoax, *1376*

Cato

School completely irradiated with germicidal lamps, *7281*

Central Valley

Nudist summer camp, *7974*

Chappaqua

First lady to run for public office, *4239*

College Point

Sugar-free soft drinks, *2444*

Constitution Island

Blockade of enemy ships in the Revolutionary War that was effective, *5670*

Cooperstown

Prehistoric hoax, *1376*

Corning

Heat-resistant glass, *3363*
Photosensitive glass, *3366*
Telescope lens 200 inches in diameter, *6377*

Creedmoor

International rifle tournament of consequence, *7883*

Cuba

Oil spring, *6574*

East Fishkill

Handwriting teaching system widely used in schools, *2929*

East Rochester

Tract housing development, *3532*

Eastchester Township

Police radio system, *7379*

Easthampton

First Lady who attended school, *4224*

Elizabethport

Meat biscuit, *2354*

Elmira

Automatic aircraft cannon, *5868*

Elmont

Horse stakes race ending in a triple dead heat, *7811*
Horse to win a $100,000 purse in one race, *7808*
Horse to win the Triple Crown, *7806*
Jockey who was a woman to win a Triple Crown race, *7821*

Elmsford

Cocktail, *2324*
Hearing aid using transistors, *5271*

Endicott

Robotic chair with balancing capability, *7049*

Fair Point

Correspondence course of a serious nature, *3202*

Farmingdale

Bicycle racer to attain the speed of a mile a minute, *7654*

Fayette

Mormon Church meeting, *6265*

Fayetteville

Natural cement rock, *3331*

Fishkill

Revolutionary War national veterans' organization, *5619*

Flushing Meadows

Major sports facility named for a woman, *7935*

Fort Salonga

Hospice for animals, *2606*

Fort Ticonderoga

American capture of a British fort in the Revolutionary War, *5650*

Fort Washington

Blockade of enemy ships in the Revolutionary War, *5670*
Military pension awarded to a disabled soldier who was a woman, *5618*

Frankfort

Girder bridge of cast iron, *3238*

Franklin Square

Bank to issue a credit card, *1764*

Fredonia

Natural gas corporation, *6591*
Natural gas used as an illuminant, *6580*

Garden City

Airmail pilot, *4690*
College to offer courses to railroad commuters, *2873*
Fighter plane, *5476*
Helicopter rescue of an American pilot behind enemy lines, *5805*
National water skiing tournament, *7991*
National wheelchair games, *7980*
Transatlantic radio program received from Great Britain, *4788*

Genesee

Daredevil jumper of note, *1366*

Geneva

Abstract paintings, *1038*
College course without Greek or Latin, *2735*

Goshen

Telegraph used by a railroad, *4851*

Greenpoint

Oil drill offshore rig, *6593*

Greenwood Lake

Motorcycle racer who was a woman, *7849*

Hammondsport

Airplane bombing experiment, *5463*
Airplane flying school for military officers, *3111*
Airplane race won by an American in Europe, *7675*
Airplane sold commercially, *8012*
Gyroscope, *8035*
Naval airplane, *5467*
Pilot licensed by the Aero Club of America, *8025*

Hartsdale

Pet cemetery, *2604*

Hastings

Boxer to die in the ring, *7593*

Hempstead Plains

Horse race run on a regular basis, *7788*

Honeoye Falls

Fuel cell truck, *8297*

Hudson

Comic magazine, *4607*

Hyde Park

Presidential library, *4150*

Hydeville

Spiritualist, *6269*

Ilion

Revolver that was self-cocking, *5851*
Typewriter that was practical, *1667*

Irvington

Chief White House counsel who was a woman, *4167*

Ithaca

Discovery of a meteorite on another planet, *6395*
Editor in chief of a law review who was a woman, *2836*

NEW YORK—Ithaca—*continued*

Electrical engineering school at a college, *2797*
Airline flight attendant who was an African-American woman, *8076*
Forestry school at a college, *2816*
Graduate student who was a woman to receive a university fellowship, *2801*
Halftone printing plate, *2049*
Hotel administration course at a college, *2839*
Ice cream sundae, *2402*
Industrial and labor relations school at a college, *2859*
Major worm attack on the Internet, *6470*
National college fraternity for African-American men, *2824*
Ptarmigan, *5955*
Quantum theory of electromagnetic radiation, *6707*
Screw caliper, *2659*
Veterinary department at a college, *3068*

Jerome Park

Steeplechase, *7796*

Johnstown

Ax factory, *2640*
Gloves, *2235*
Leather tanning by the oil tan method, *2123*

Jones Beach

National water skiing tournament, *7991*

Karner

Streamlined steam locomotive, *8343*

Kent

Monument to mothers of fallen soldiers, *7192*

Kinderhook

First Lady who was born an American citizen, *4223*
President born an American citizen, *4241*

Kings Point

Merchant marine academy, *3117*
Merchant Marine Academy cadets who were women, *3126*

Lake Placid

Auction duplicate bridge championship, *7732*
Dogsled race on an Olympic demonstration program, *7663*
International ski meet, *7891*
Olympic Games competition to be held in the winter, *7858*
Olympic gold medalist in both the Summer and Winter Olympics, *7857*

Larchmont

Capture of an American ship captain by a German submarine in World War II, *5784*

Le Roy

Gelatin dessert, *2401*

Levittown

Planned suburban development, *3538*

Lewiston

Inclined railroad, *8298*

Little Falls

Balloon pilot who was a woman, *8000*

Lockport

Heating system to heat buildings from a central station, *3282*

Locust Grove

Bank to open a branch in a trailer, *1750*

Manhattan Beach

Motorcycle association, *7848*

Massapequa

Reform rabbi who was a woman, *6314*

McGraw

Corset, *2253*

Melville

Magnetic resonance image of a human body, *5145*

Merrick

Right to Life Party organizational meeting, *4104*

Mineola

Airmail pilot, *4690*
Monoplane, *8014*
Transcontinental air race, *7679*

NEW YORK—New York—*continued*

City with a population of more than 1 million, *3524*
City with a population of more than 5 million, *3524*
Civilian welfare effort for soldiers organized on a large scale, *5702*
Clinic for teaching medical students, *3053*
Clinical instruction and bedside demonstration, *3048*
Clock to operate by nuclear power, *2633*
Clothing designer of international renown, *2267*
Coach riding, *7962*
Coaching club, *7961*
Coast-to-coast live telecast in color, *4959*
Coast-to-coast paved road, *3420*
Coast-to-coast radio news broadcast to be recorded, *4537*
Coaxial cable, *4859*
Coin-operated mailbox, *4703*
Coin-operated television receiver, *4993*
Collection of spirituals, *1239*
College Bowl competition on radio, *2865*
College foreign-language house, *2829*
College founded as a Jewish institution, *2847*
College graduate who was Jewish, *2705*
College student to receive federal aid as the child of a deceased veteran, *2866*
College to prohibit discrimination because of race, religion, or color, *2750*
College to sponsor an endowed lecture series, *2767*
Colonial provision for the care of orphans and widows, *2172*
Colonist hanged for treason, *6989*
Combined newspaper, *4531*
Comic book hero with superpowers, *1101*
Comic books, *1098*
Comic history of the United States, *7471*
Comic strip in a newspaper, *4580*
Comic strip in continuous newspaper publication, *4584*
Comics studio, *1100*
Commemorative postal card, *4709*
Commercial corporation, *1470*
Commercial crude-oil carrier, *8464*
Commercial photography studio, *4618*
Commercial program telecast on a network, *4940*
Commercial rating agency, *1770*
Commercial telephone service on railroad trains for passengers, *4899*
Commercial television licenses, *4938*
Commodity exchange member who was a woman, *1781*
Composer born in America to win an international reputation, *1246*
Concrete barge, *8447*
Condensed milk, *2355*
Congressional act, *3558*
Congressional act declared unconstitutional by the Supreme Court, *3559*
Congressional chaplain, *3557*
Congressional committee, *3586*
Congressional representative who was an African-American woman, *3623*
Construction of the Statue of Liberty on site, *3497*
Consumer protection medical alert, *5042*
Contact between the president and the Congress, *3556*
Contact lenses, *5269*
Cooking school, *3199*
Cooperative store for consumers, *2083*
Copy made by xerography, *2027*
Copyright registered for a choreographic score, *1055*
Cork for covering steam pipes, *3343*
Cork manufacturer, *3337*
Corkboard patent, *3342*
Corkscrew patent, *2558*
Corporate body chartered by a special act of Congress, *1478*
Corrugated paper, *2022*
Costume museum, *3157*
Courtroom verdict to be televised, *3727*
Cover of the Saturday Evening Post by Norman Rockwell, *1040*
Creation of federal courts, *3702*
Credit card to be nationally accepted, *1763*
Credit protection group, *1483*
Credit report book, *1703*
Crepe, *2140*
Crepe paper, *2023*
Cricket match, *7628*
Cross-country championships, *7943*
Crossword game, *7736*
Crossword puzzle, *7731*
Crossword puzzle book, *7734*
Curfew bell, *7398*
Curved stereotype plate, *2043*
Cylinder and flatbed combination printing press, *2040*
Cylinder printing press, *2037*
Daily news program on radio, *4529*
Dance marathon, *7972*
Danish settlers in America, *6028*
Daredevil to jump off the Brooklyn Bridge and survive, *1383*
Dean of a university graduate school who was a woman, *2855*
Deck chair for steamer passengers, *2567*

NEW YORK—New York—*continued*

Factory with temperature and humidity control, *3291*
Fashion magazine, *2251*
Fashion show, *1392*
Fashion show for charity, *1392*
Fashion show to be shown on television, *1403*
Feature film to premiere simultaneously in a theater and on the Internet, *1186*
Feature film with with recorded music and dialogue, *1149*
Federal district court judge who was an African-American woman, *3726*
Federal judge who was a woman, *3719*
Federal law enforcement agency, *3838*
Federal marshals, *7356*
Federalist Paper, *3486*
Felt hats for women, *2246*
Fiction writer to win the Pulitzer Prize twice, *4763*
Figure skater of note, *7840*
Filibuster in the House of Representatives, *3588*
Film professorship at a college, *2858*
Film-developing machine, *4646*
Financial "corner," *1702*
Financial news agency, *4514*
Fire chief, *7314*
Fire department established by a city, *7313*
Fire department to be paid, *7316*
Fire engine with a steam boiler, *7321*
Fireboats, *7318*
Firehouse pole, *7330*
Fireproof safe, *1664*
First Lady appointed to a federal post after the death of her husband, *4235*
First Lady elected to the Senate, *3695*
First Lady who attended school, *4224*
First Lady whose autobiography was commercially published, *4232*
Fish hatchery, *1616*
Fish protection law enacted by a city, *5940*
Fishing line factory, *2655*
Flashlight, *2666*
Flea circus, *1368*
Floating church, *6267*
Floating hospital, *5112*
FM radio, *4823*
Football book, *7697*
Football game played indoors, *7698*
Football player to win the Heisman Trophy for excellence in college football, *7709*
Football player who was African-American to win the Heisman Memorial Trophy, *7714*
Football rules, *7687*
Foreign feature film exhibited, *1136*
Foreign language course broadcast on radio, *3213*
Formation of a new animal by transplantation, *6664*
Fortune 1000 company to be owned and chaired by a woman, *1514*
Fountain pen, *2679*
Fraternal group insurance, *1960*
Fraternal society for Jews, *7204*
Free port, *2079*
French daily newspaper that was successful, *4552*
Frozen meals for air travelers, *2439*
Full-length American film to premiere on television, *1167*
Full-length play by an African-American writer, *1452*
Game manufacturing company, *7724*
Game protection society, *7824*
Gardener's manual, *1602*
Gas engine, *8184*
Gas journal, *6780*
Gas meter, *6581*
Gas-turbine car, *8267*
Gay pride march, *7449*
Gay rights protest, *7448*
German daily newspaper, *4551*
Giant exhibited as a theatrical attraction, *1364*
Golf book, *7756*
Golf magazine, *7752*
Gourmet restaurant, *1810*
Grand American Trapshoot tournament using live birds, *7885*
Grand American Trapshoot tournament with clay targets, *7886*
Grand piano with a cast-metal plate, *1298*
Graphic novel, *1108*
Greek daily newspaper, *4566*
Greek newspaper, *4566*
Greenhouse, *1578*
Gutta-percha, *1886*
Gymnasium at a YMCA, *7205*
Gyroscopic stabilizer, *8501*
Halftone engraving, *1037*
Health board with emergency powers established by a city, *7247*
Health journal to advocate water cures, *5316*
Health ordinance prohibiting spitting, *7264*
Health service established by the federal government, *7236*
Heart pump, *5350*
Heart transplant, *5368*
Hebrew book other than the Bible, *6361*
Hebrew dictionary, *3185*
Hebrew newspaper, *4561*
Helicopter licensed for commercial use, *8115*

Mines school at a college, *2765*
Minimum wage law established by a city for public contract work, *7163*
Minstrel show troupe, *1235*
Missionary training school, *2798*
Mobile color television transmitter unit, *4991*
Mobile computer center, *6429*
Mobile television transmitter unit, *4991*
Modern art exhibition, *1039*
Monkey trained to perform, *1351*
Monument to an American poet, *7174*
Motorboat magazine, *8442*
Motorboat pleasure craft, *8437*
Motorboat race under organized rules, *7575*
Motorcycle endurance run, *7846*
Motorcycle police, *7368*
Movie by a major company for an African-American audience, *1151*
Movie censorship board at the national level, *1129*
Movie director who was a woman, *1130*
Movie entertainment shown on an airplane, *1156*
Movie exhibition, *1114*
Movie exhibition in a theater to a paying audience, *1121*
Movie in Technicolor, *1145*
Movie photographed from an airplane, *1135*
Movie premiere festivities to be shown on television, *1163*
Movie premiered simultaneously in major cities throughout the world, *1175*
Movie production company, *1119*
Movie recorded on film to be shown on a screen, *1117*
Movie sex shocker, *1143*
Movie showing the inside of a living heart, *5139*
Movie to premiere on television, *1167*
Movie trailer to be shown on television, *1549*
Movie with both sound and color, *1155*
Movie with scent, *1174*
Movie with sound recorded on the film, *1146*
Movie with sound to be released as a feature, *1147*
MTV Video Music Awards, *1281*
Municipal ferryboats, *8443*
Museum of medieval art, *3148*
Music book printed from type, *1219*
Music society for the protection of composers and song writers, *1254*
Music synthesizer powered by electricity, *1307*
Music video on MTV, *1279*
Musical comedy broadcast on radio, *1458*
Musical comedy to be shown on television, *1462*
Musical comedy written by African-Americans for African-American performers, *1449*
Musical comedy written for television, *1463*
Musical instrument capable of making any audible sound, *1312*
Musical to run for more than 3,000 performances, *1466*
Musical with an American theme and original score, *1440*
Musk ox, *5951*
Muslim prayer service led by a woman acting as Imam, *6336*
Mutual life insurance company, *1990*
Nail machine, *2652*
Narcotics ban enacted by Congress, *7071*
National accounting society, *1706*
National arbitration organization, *3972*
National arts and letters organization, *7223*
National bible society, *6256*
National chemistry organization, *6721*
National civil engineering society, *3223*
National dental society, *5216*
National Endowment for the Arts grant, *3858*
National Endowment for the Humanities grants, *3859*
National fencing league, *7666*
National golf association, *7755*
National labor congress, *7115*
National measurement organization, *1489*
National mechanical engineering society, *3225*
National optometry society, *5226*
National organization for the hard of hearing, *7035*
National organization of artists, *1030*
National philology society, *6720*
National physics association, *6724*
National physiology society, *5223*
National polo association, *7870*
National religious tract society, *6263*
National research society, *6727*
National rifle society, *7882*
National squash tennis organization, *7904*
National tennis society, *7920*
National Zionist organization, *6286*
Native American art exhibition, *1041*
Naturalization act enacted by Congress, *6049*
Nautical school established by a city, *3198*
Navy medical school, *3078*
Navy submarine contract, *8510*
Nazi death camp guard to be deported, *6103*
Neon advertising sign, *1539*
Neurasthenia book, *5327*
Neurological disease research institute, *5120*
Neurology textbook, *5322*
New York City Marathon, *7957*

School nurses in public schools, *5036*
School of modern dance, *3211*
School of nurse-midwifery, *3093*
School of social work, *2823*
Science fiction course at a college, *2864*
Science fiction magazine, *4615*
Science journal, *6772*
Seal of a military department of the federal government, *3477*
Seal of a nonmilitary department of the federal government, *3488*
Secret service established in a colony, *7355*
Secretary of state, *4171*
Secretary of the Navy, *4174*
Secretary of the Senate, *3647*
Secretary of the treasury, *4169*
Sedan car, *8250*
Self-adhesive postage stamp, *4753*
Self-service restaurant, *1823*
Senate journal, *3643*
Senate of the United States Congress, *3642*
Senate page who was African-American, *3687*
Senate session at which there was a quorum, *3645*
Serbian Orthodox cathedral, *6308*
Session of Congress, *3554*
Session of the House of Representatives, *3583*
Session of the House of Representatives at which there was a quorum, *3583*
Session of the Senate, *3645*
Settlement house in a poor city neighborhood, *3525*
Sewing machine equipped with a rocking treadle or double treadle, *2617*
Sex-change operation performed on an American, *7442*
Sheet of souvenir postage stamps, *4736*
Ship from the United States sunk by a German submarine in World War II, *5757*
Ship-to-shore mobile telephone commercial service, *4890*
Shoot-the-chutes, *1005*
Sick-leave benefit funds for teachers, *7133*
Sightseeing bus, *8218*
Singer whose voice was broadcast over radio, *1250*
Singing telegram, *4861*
Singles bar, *1837*
Sitcom television show, *4945*
Six-day bicycle race, *7647*
Six-day bicycle race for men, *7650*
Skee-ball alley, *1007*
Skyscraper higher than 1,250 feet, *3300*
Skyscraper higher than 750 feet, *3297*
Skyscraper of bronze and glass, *3311*
Skywriting advertisement exhibition, *1538*
Sneakers, *2263*
Soap in liquid form, *2215*
Soap manufacturer to render fats in his plant, *2208*
Soccer player to score 12 points in one game, *7900*
Social library, *3000*
Social register published, *4459*
Soda water machine, *2345*
Solar energy battery, *6634*
Soldiers in the American army killed by German bombers in World War I, *5744*
Song popular in the Confederate States, *1338*
Sound trademark, *3982*
Soup company, *2387*
Spanish grammar, *3176*
Spanish newspaper, *4555*
Sparrows, *5942*
Spider-Man comic book, *1106*
Sports book, *7823*
Sports event to be televised live, *4937*
Sports league to cancel a season over a labor dispute, *7837*
Sports trainer to work professionally, *7942*
Spray can, *2002*
Squash tennis tournament, *7905*
Stamp auction, *4725*
Stamp collection society, *4722*
Stamped envelopes, *4719*
State accounting society, *1708*
State chamber of commerce, *1487*
State organization of lawyers, *3951*
State to decriminalize public breastfeeding, *2203*
Statue presented to the United States by a foreign country, *7177*
Steam distribution plant, *6598*
Steam-propelled ferryboat, *8419*
Steam-propelled frigate, *8468*
Steamboat service to California around Cape Horn, *8432*
Steamboat to make an ocean voyage, *8417*
Steamship passenger line between American and European ports, *8431*
Steel-frame residence, *3288*
Stenotype device, *1670*
Stereo telecast, *4978*
Stereotype printing that was successful, *2031*
Stereotyped book, *4445*
Stock brokerage concern of importance whose president was a woman, *1782*
Stock brokerage concern to use a stock ticker, *1772*
Stock exchange, *1767*
Stock exchange at which more than a million shares were traded in one day, *1776*
Stock exchange director who was a woman, *1783*

NEW YORK—New York—*continued*

Stock price indicator used on Wall Street, *1771*
Stock quotation boards, *1777*
Stockholder meetings televised coast-to-coast simultaneously, *1784*
Stone pavement, *3403*
Street gangs, *6927*
Street letter box, *4668*
Streetcar, *8365*
Streetcar company, *8364*
Strike by physicians against long working hours in hospitals, *7165*
Strike by workers, *7098*
Strike of postal employees, *7164*
Stuntman, *1393*
Submarine that was practical and submersible, *8512*
Subway, *8376*
Subway car with side doors, *8379*
Subway train to run automatically without conductors or motormen, *8380*
Sugar and glucose from cornstarch, *2364*
Sulfanilamide used in medical treatment, *5244*
Summit conference of world religions, *6333*
Sunday comics section in a newspaper, *4581*
Supreme Court case in which social-science research was accepted as evidence, *7477*
Supreme Court of the United States, *3732*
Surgeon appointed by a colony, *5097*
Surgery manual, *5285*
Surgical elevation of the skull to treat epilepsy, *5349*
Surgical operation televised on a closed circuit for medical students, *5352*
Suspension bridge with steel towers, *3249*
Swimmer who was an American woman to swim the English Channel, *7912*
Swing band, *1259*
Sword swallower, *1362*
Symphony orchestra devoted exclusively to radio broadcasting, *1263*
Talking book for blind listeners, *7040*
Tariff legislation enacted by Congress, *4404*
Tattoo shop, *2460*
Tattooed man exhibited as a theatrical attraction, *1369*
Teddy bear, *2188*
Telecast received from England, *4965*
Telecast transmitted by satellite from Japan, *4969*
Telecast using coaxial cable, *4989*
Telegraph cable, *4844*
Telegraph company, *4850*
Telegraph message sent around the world by commercial telegraph, *4858*
Telegraph system, *4841*
Telephone concert held long-distance, *1243*
Telephone switchboard with Braille markings, *4889*
Television commercial in color to appear on a local show, *1552*
Television drama program regularly scheduled, *4942*
Television eyewitness allowed to testify in a federal court, *3723*
Television image using a split screen, *4994*
Television magazine, *6787*
Television network evening news program anchor who was a woman, *4604*
Television news commentator who was African-American, *4602*
Television newsmagazine, *4545*
Television production course at a college, *2857*
Television receiver that showed two programs simultaneously, *4998*
Television show to be sponsored by a commercial advertiser, *1550*
Television show transmitted by laser, *5005*
Television variety talent show series, *4939*
Tenement house, *2525*
Tennis champion to win the Grand Slam, *7928*
Tennis champion who was a woman to win the Grand Slam, *7930*
Tennis champion who was African-American, *7932*
Tennis tournament of national scope, *7919*
Tennis tournament to be shown on television, *7929*
Terra cotta, *3338*
Test for newborn health, *2157*
Theater built and named for a living actress, *1455*
Theater designed and built for the rear projection of movies, *1158*
Theater history, *1431*
Theater lighted by gas, *1428*
Theater ticket agency, *1438*
Theater ticket scalpers, *1433*
Theater to employ women as ushers, *1447*
Theatrical presentation sponsored by the federal government, *1457*
Theory of fair division, *6712*
Theosophical society, *7216*
Thermos bottles made in the United States, *2570*
Three-dimensional feature movie, *1169*
Three-dimensional feature movie in color, *1171*

NEW YORK—New York—*continued*

Vedanta Center, *6285*
Vending machine for art, *1701*
Vending machine to dispense fresh flowers, *1699*
Veterinary college of importance, *3061*
Veterinary hospital, *5403*
Vice presidential candidate who was African-American, *3809*
Vichyssoise, *2410*
Video recording on magnetic tape televised coast-to-coast, *4963*
Visiting nurses, *5031*
Vulcanized rubber, *1887*
Wall Street stock index, *1775*
Warship propelled by electricity, *8482*
Washington news correspondent, *4590*
Water cures, *5389*
Waxworks, *1350*
Weather forecasting service by telephone, *6502*
Weather map to be telecast to a transatlantic steamer, *4924*
Western series on television, *4943*
White band leader to hire an African-American woman vocalist, *1264*
Woman boxing referee to judge a heavyweight championship match, *7606*
Woman director of the New York Stock Exchange, *1785*
Woman member of the National Institute of Arts and Letters, *7223*
Woman ordained as a Conservative rabbi, *6314*
Woman pilot to cross the English Channel in an airplane, *8028*
Woman to appear on television, *4926*
Women's professional club, *7212*
Workers' compensation agreement, *7097*
Workers' library, *3008*
World heavyweight boxing champion to regain his crown, *7609*
World heavyweight boxing champion to retire undefeated, *7608*
World Series baseball game that was a shutout, *7519*
World Series baseball game to be shown on television, *7538*
World tour by a woman traveling alone, *8531*
World's fair, *1485*
Worldwide live television program, *4975*
Writer to win a Pulitzer Prize four times for drama, *4772*
Writer to win the Pulitzer Prize in both fiction and poetry, *4770*
Writer whose livelihood was obtained exclusively by writing, *1080*
X-ray movies of human organs in action, *5136*
X-ray of the entire body of a living person made in a single exposure, *5132*
Yacht from the United States to win an international yacht race, *7569*
Yeshivah for Jewish religious study, *2953*
Yeshivah to offer advanced-level learning, *2953*
Yeshivah with a secular high school, *2953*
Yiddish daily newspaper, *4560*
Yiddish newspaper, *4560*
Yiddish professorship at a college, *2863*
Yiddish theater performance, *1444*
Young Men's Hebrew Association, *7214*
Young Women's Hebrew Association, *7222*
Zoning ordinance, *3533*

New York City

Rocket to break the sound barrier, *6789*
Television commercial, *1547*

Newburgh

Cakes of soap of uniform weight and individually wrapped, *2210*
Double-deck ferryboat, *8439*
Ice skating champion, *7838*
Prehistoric animal skeleton to be displayed, *6657*
Steel-hulled ferryboat, *8436*

Newhouseville

Fax transmission by a press syndicate direct to newspaper offices, *4533*

Newport

Pin-tumbler cylinder lock, *3278*

Newton Creek

Kerosene, *6585*

Niagara County

Fruit spraying, *1626*

Niagara Falls

Airplane flight under a bridge, *8027*
Daredevil to cross Niagara Falls on a tightrope, *1371*
Daredevil to go over Niagara Falls in a barrel, *1391*
Daredevil to go over Niagara Falls in a rubber ball, *1400*

Electricity generated by Niagara Falls waterpower, *6541*
King of Great Britain to visit the United States, *3935*
Photograph to gain world fame, *4620*
Railroad suspension bridge, *3242*
Two-handed shovel, *2670*
Utilization of Niagara Falls waterpower for industrial purposes, *6632*

North Elba

Bobsled run, *7975*

North Tonawanda

Jukebox manufacturer who was successful, *4830*

Oceanside

Eagle Scout, *2191*

Olean

Natural gas for use in manufacturing, *6595*

Oneida

Steel animal traps commercially manufactured, *2653*

Oneida County

Fur-bearing animals raised commercially, *1617*

Ossining

Execution of an organized crime leader in the electric chair, *7017*
Peacetime death sentence for espionage, *7018*
State prison to take fingerprints, *7365*
Woman executed in the electric chair, *7009*

Oswego

Teacher training school at which students conducted practice classes, *2939*

Pearl River

Broad-spectrum antibiotic, *5251*
Catgut substitute, *5186*

Peekskill

Car hill-climbing contest, *7618*
First aid instruction, *7346*

Pelham Bay

Religious leader in the American colonies who was a white woman, *6178*

Pelham Manor

Stained-glass window, *3356*

Plattsburgh

College principally for war veterans, *2860*
Physiologist of note, *5019*

Pleasantville

Distinguished Service Cross awarded to an animal, *5524*

Port Chester

Frozen bread, *2445*

Port Washington

Seaplane glider, *8074*
Train operated exclusively by women, *8399*
Transatlantic airmail service, *4704*
Transatlantic commercial airplane service, *8098*

Poughkeepsie

Candy packaged in a factory, *2371*
College baseball teams for women, *7494*
Conscientious objectors, *5554*
Ice yacht, *7565*
Ice yacht club, *7570*
Medical insurance group policy for college students, *1983*
Pins manufactured with a solid head, *2615*
Water filtration system using sand, *7415*

Richford

Billionaire, *1711*

Riverdale

Motorcycle hill-climbing contest, *7847*

Rochester

Business school, *3197*
Camera to use film rolls, *4643*
Car patent, *8228*
Card time recorder, *1682*
Check protectors, *1726*
Color film, *4650*
Community chorus, *1252*
Copy machine, *1693*
Filmpack camera, *4645*
Food stamps, *3852*
Infrared photograph, *4633*
Installment finance company, *1759*
Mail chute, *4681*

NEW YORK—Rochester—*continued*

Rockville Center

Rocky Point

Rome

Roosevelt Field

Rye

Sackets Harbor

Saranac Lake

Saratoga

Saratoga Springs

Saugerties

Schenectady

Schuylerville

NEW YORK—*continued*

Wallkill

Creamery for commercial production, *2361*

Wappinger Falls

Surgical operation on a bull to correct a sperm block, *5407*

Warsaw

Liberty Party convention, *4060*

Watertown

Biscuits of shredded wheat, *2394*

Watervliet

Conscientious objectors, *5554*
Shaker religious community, *6230*

West Hempstead

Lottery in which the top prize was $1 million, *1805*

West Milton

Electric power generated from nuclear energy to be sold commercially, *6621*

West Point

African-American cadet admitted to West Point, *3107*
Army academy, *3096*
Blockade of enemy ships in the Revolutionary War that was effective, *5670*
Intercollegiate Army-Navy football game, *7696*
Mechanics textbook, *6779*
Movie for training soldiers, *3114*
President to appear on color television, *4281*
West Point cadet who was a woman to graduate at the top of her class, *3132*
West Point cadets who were women, *3129*
West Point graduate who was African-American, *3107*
West Point graduate who was Jewish, *3097*
West Point graduate who was Native American, *3102*
West Point graduates, *3098*
West Point instructor who was a woman, *3124*
West Point woman graduate who was Jewish, *3097*

Westbury

Amateur golf championship tournament for women, *7758*

Westchester

Telephone directory with internet addresses, *4921*

White Plains

Freeze-dried coffee, *2451*
Powdered breakfast drink, *2448*

Woodhaven

Tinware manufacturers who were successful, *2270*

Yonkers

Amateur golf tournament, *7754*
Golf mixed foursome, *7749*
Thermosetting resin, *1899*

NORTH CAROLINA

American Heritage Rivers, *5997*
Freedom ride by civil rights activists, *6139*
Independent civil government in America, *3449*
National seashore, *5994*
Novel by an African-American woman, *1092*
Nurses to be registered by a state, *5037*
State denied admission into the Union, *4338*
State governor to be impeached and convicted, *4378*
Wolf to be reintroduced into the wild, *5966*
Written constitution adopted by a community of American-born freemen, *3457*

Asheville

Forest management on a professional scale, *5979*
Tuberculosis sanatorium, *5125*

Blakely

Interstate railroad, *8303*

Cabarrus County

Gold nugget, *3374*

Cape Hatteras

Radio SOS call from an American ship, *7350*
Smokescreen for concealing the movement of troops and ships, *5865*
Transatlantic airship flight, *8020*

Chapel Hill

English grammar instruction at a college, *2723*
Marriage course at a college, *2841*

NORTH CAROLINA—*continued*

Union County

President born after the death of his father, *4240*

Washington

Town named for George Washington, *3514*

Winston-Salem

Filter cigarette, *7082*
Functioning human organ grown in a laboratory, *5061*
State college for the performing arts, *2867*

NORTH DAKOTA

Bonding law enacted by a state, *1968*
Fire and tornado insurance fund enacted by a state, *1979*
Hail insurance law enacted by a state, *1967*
State law decriminalizing hemp cultivation, *1656*
States admitted to the Union simultaneously, *4352*

Beulah

Synthetic fuels plant, *6614*

Bismarck

Bank wholly owned and operated by a state, *1740*

Carrington

Woman elected to statewide office, *4355*

Devil's Lake

Clothes dryer, *2223*

Esmond

State speaker of the House who was a woman, *4392*

Fairmont

Tank crew to cross the 38th parallel in the Korean War, *5806*

Fort Yates

Native American superintendent of a Bureau of Indian Affairs agency, *3843*

Jamestown

Telecast from the stratosphere, *5002*

Minot

Pilot of a B-52 bomber who was a woman, *5493*

Portal

Absolute monarch to visit the United States, *3932*

OHIO

African-American to enlist in the United States armed forces during the Civil War, *5706*
Battle fought by federal troops after the formation of the Union, *5676*
Coal pipeline, *6611*
Congressional representative to be censured, *3597*
Court-martial at which the judges included enlisted men, *5551*
Employment service established by a state, *7136*
History of African-Americans, *7476*
Land set-aside for schools authorized by the Continental Congress, *2902*
Land subsidy by Congress for road improvements, *3410*
Medal of Honor awarded to an Army soldier, *5504*
Mother and son simultaneously elected to Congress, *3618*
Movie censorship board established by a state, *1133*
Presidential candidate to make campaign speeches in a foreign language, *3811*
Presidential election in which votes were tallied electronically, *3825*
Robbery of a train in motion, *6936*
Sale of federal land to an individual, *6051*
Secretary of the interior, *4178*
Senator who had been an astronaut, *3690*
State in the North to restrict the civil rights of African-Americans, *6124*
State in which slavery was illegal from the time it was admitted to the Union, *6124*
Telephone company answering service, *4904*
Working hours of women to be regulated by a state, *7118*

Akron

Airship with an enclosed cabin, *8058*
Balloon tire production, *8207*
Clincher tire, *8187*
Glider pilot's license, *8081*
Manufactured food product to carry a health claim on its label, *7288*

Alliance

Ashtabula

Athens

Barberton

Bellefontaine

Brownhelm

Canton

Chillicothe

Cincinnati

Cleveland

OHIO—Cleveland—*continued*

Airplane flight over water, *8019*
Airplane race of importance in which both men and women were contestants, *7682*
American Bar Association members who were women, *3971*
Automatic pilot on an airplane, *8071*
Baseball player who was Native American, *7513*
Car advertisement in a specialty magazine, *1533*
Community trust charity, *7225*
Dutch elm disease breakout, *5985*
Electric arc streetlights, *7408*
Electric traffic lights equipped with noise signals, *8204*
Federal justice of the Circuit Court of Appeals who was a woman, *3719*
Fireworks law enacted by a city, *7332*
Fluorescent paint, *2669*
Fund-raising organization to sell stamps, *7207*
Heart operation for the relief of angina pectoris, *5351*
Heart operation in which the elective cardiac arrest technique was employed, *5361*
Ice cream cone rolling machine, *2423*
Judge to impose the death penalty who was a woman, *3716*
Kindergarten for children with disabilities, *2959*
Mail truck, *4686*
Mayor of a major city who was African-American, *3541*
Multigraph, *1687*
National animal humane society, *7218*
National temperance society for women, *7066*
National Union for Social Justice national convention, *4095*
Paint mixed to a consistent standard, *2656*
Paint prepared from standard formulas, *2661*
Passenger transfer from an airship to an airplane, *8070*
Political convention to be broadcast on radio, *4094*
President to be treated by a woman medical practitioner, *4266*
School district put under state control by federal court order, *2985*
State supreme court justice who was a woman, *3717*
Submachine gun, *5862*
Superconducting motor, *6739*
Transcontinental air derby for women, *7681*
Truck completely streamlined, *8294*
Unassisted triple play in a major league baseball game, *7523*
Unassisted triple play in a World Series baseball game, *7527*
Union Party convention, *4096*
Universal constant in physics to be measured by American scientists, *6741*
Valeteria, *1695*
Zoo hospital with a CT scanner, *5409*

Clyde

Navy officer killed in action in the Spanish-American War, *5725*

Columbus

Ace of Aces from the United States, *5754*
Computerized library network, *3040*
Gorilla, *5963*
Junior high school, *2964*
Labor Reform Party national convention, *4068*
Metric distance markers on a state highway, *3432*
National labor organization, *7130*
Newspaper to publish an Internet edition, *4549*
Ornithopter that succeeded in flying, *8168*
Presidential candidate nominated by prohibition advocates, *4067*
Presidential candidate to make a campaign speech, *3802*
Round-the-world solo airplane flight by a woman, *8150*
Shipment of merchandise by airplane, *2078*
State school for blind students, *2924*

Dayton

Airplane purchased by the federal government, *8013*
Aluminum can with a pull-tab pop-top, *2003*
Cash register, *1672*
Electric motorized wheelchair, *7036*
Ethyl gasoline to be marketed, *6604*
Folding stepladder, *2560*
Parachute known as the "free parachute," *8042*
Pilot to bail out of a disabled airplane, *8052*
Postage stamp with fluorescent tagging, *4745*
Pressure suit, *8092*
Price tags, *2091*
Soapbox derby, *7625*
Soldiers' homes established by Congress, *5621*

Findlay

Woman delegate to a national convention of the American Federation of Labor, *7130*

OHIO—Toledo—*continued*

Funeral home operated on the cooperative plan, *2304*
Glass-blowing machine, *3361*
Major league baseball player who was African-American, *7508*
Officer killed in action in the Korean War, *5804*
Paint-spraying device, *2667*
Practical paper beverage carton, *2000*
Rectangular television tube, *4995*
Sister city partnership, *3535*
Television receivers to project large images, *5000*
Vacuum cleaner with a disposable bag, *2222*

Toronto

Titanium mill, *1947*

Van Wert

County library, *3020*

Vienna

Baby show, *2184*

Wilmington

Airplane human pickup, *8110*
Banana split, *2404*

Worthington

Catholic seminary under the supervision of the Pope, *2806*

Yellow Springs

College literary society that was coeducational, *2700*
College professor who was a woman, *2752*
Physiology and hygiene courses at a liberal arts college, *3057*

Youngstown

Municipal downsizing plan, *3546*

Zanesville

Stone breaking machine, *3378*

OKLAHOMA

Artificial insemination for women to be permitted by a state, *5397*
Court case to establish the personhood of Native Americans, *6078*
Novel by a woman of Native American descent, *1096*
Oil and gas conservation law enacted by a state, *6603*
Paper money issued by the Native Americans, *4022*
State with electronic toll collection, *3434*

Bethany

Astronaut from the United States who was a woman to live in a space station, *6837*

Claremore

Transcontinental foot race, *7948*

Clinton

Medal of Honor awarded in the Korean War, *5531*

Duncan

Permanent ambassador to the United Nations who was a woman, *3910*

El Reno

Church organized by Native Americans, *6293*
Distinguished Service Cross awarded in enemy-occupied territory, *5520*

Guymon

Felony conviction for cruelty against farm animals, *1657*

Kingfisher

Wal-Mart store, *2103*

Mulhall

Cowgirl, *1382*

Muskogee

Sale of Girl Scout cookies, *2195*

Norman

Woman criminal on the FBI's Ten Most Wanted list, *6948*

Oklahoma City

Automatic parking meter, *8254*
Bombing by domestic terrorists resulting in large loss of life, *6972*
Execution to be televised, *7026*
Gas turbine used by an electrical utility company, *6571*
Shopping cart, *1691*
Traveling cancer clinic, *5072*

PENNSYLVANIA—*continued*

Labor dispute resolved through presidential intervention, *7142*
Lawyers admitted to practice before the Supreme Court, *3955*
Liquor stores run by a state government, *2098*
Locomotive to attain a speed of one mile in less than a minute, *8340*
Military pension awarded to a disabled soldier who was a woman, *5618*
Moravian settlement in America, *6219*
Movie censorship board established by a state, *1133*
Natural gas pipeline constructed over a long distance, *6597*
Printed ballot, *3764*
Railroad for freight transportation, *8299*
Rhodes Scholars, *2819*
Secretary of homeland security, *4214*
Secretary of labor, *4184*
Senate election in which neither candidate was seated after a recount, *3676*
Senate election that was contested, *3652*
Sex discrimination law enacted by a state that affected high school athletic competitions, *7453*
Speaker of the House, *3585*
State governor who had also been governor of a territory, *4377*
State to make Flag Day a legal holiday, *2503*
States with populations of more than 1 million, *4343*
Telephone with push buttons, *4911*

Allentown

Cement, *3341*
Homeopathy school, *3052*
Transistors produced commercially for a specific product, *6519*

Altoona

Railroad rails of steel, *8385*

Amesland

Colonial law for the maintenance of an insane patient, *7233*

Ardmore

Shaft-driven car, *8240*

Auburn

Tunnel, *3435*

Avondale

Coal mine disaster, *6594*

Bedford

Truck driving school, *3216*

Bethlehem

Cottonseed oil, *2322*
Horse grooming products sold for human use, *2483*
Moravian bishop, *6219*
Oil drill seagoing rig, *6610*
Orchestra, *1214*
Paper bag machine, *1995*
Postage stamps of four different designs sold as a single sheet, *4747*
Slovak settler in America, *6037*
Tax rebellion, *4407*
Trombone, *1291*
Vacuum-cast steel, *1946*
Water pumping plant, *7400*
Zinc commercial production, *3384*
Zinc sheet mill, *1934*

Braddock

Steel mill to install an electrical machine, *1940*

Bradford

Motorcycle endurance run, *7846*

Brownsville

Bridge of cast iron, *3236*

Brush Run

Disciples of Christ church, *6252*

Bryn Mawr

Biology course offered at a college, *2802*
Dean of faculty at a college, *2799*
Geologist who was a woman, *6494*
Graduate school for women, *2803*
Student government at a college, *2810*

Butler

General purpose military vehicle, *5867*

Carbon County

Anthracite coal, *6577*

Carbondale

Locomotive for railroad use, *8331*

PENNSYLVANIA—Philadelphia—*continued*

Homeopathic pharmacy, *5237*
Horticultural magazine, *1600*
Horticulture society of importance, *1594*
Hospital, *5097*
Hospital for insane patients operated privately, *5100*
Hydrotherapy book, *5279*
Hymnbook compiled by an African-American editor, *6356*
Ice cream soda, *2374*
Ice skating club, *7839*
Illustrations of both sides of the Great Seal of the United States, *3481*
Immigration law enacted by Congress, *6054*
Independent dispensary to furnish free medicine to the needy, *5099*
Influenza epidemic, *5091*
Insurance book, *1949*
Insurance company owned by African-Americans, *1952*
Insurance journal, *1955*
Insurance law treatise, *3953*
Intercity stagecoach service, *8178*
Intercollegiate wrestling association, *7969*
Internal revenue tax levied by Congress, *4405*
Invisible ink, *2673*
Jewish Sunday school, *6214*
Judge to be impeached, *3701*
Keeper of the Great Seal of the United States, *3479*
Know-Nothing (American) Party convention, *4064*
Labor Day, *2498*
Labor union to admit workers other than craft workers, *7123*
Lager beer, *2348*
Law history book, *3950*
Legal treatise analyzing the Constitution, *3959*
Library building, *3001*
Life insurance commercial company, *1988*
Life insurance company, *1988*
Life insurance offered by a general insurance company, *1989*
Life insurance policy, *1988*
Lightning demonstration, *6487*
Lightning rod, *7317*
Lithograph, *1028*
Locomotive with a cab, *8335*
Lottery held by the Continental Congress, *1799*
Lutheran pastor ordained in American, *6183*
Lutheran services in English, *6206*
Macadam road, *3408*
Magazine containing a fashion plate, *4608*
Magazine for and by patients with mental illness, *7032*
Magazine for blind readers, *7031*
Magazine for professional printers, *2018*
Magazine published in America, *4606*
Marine band, *5562*
Marines, *5560*
Masonic book, *7195*
Masonic lodge, *7194*
Masonic magazine, *7201*
Maternity book for women, *2175*
Medal of Technology awarded to a woman, *6917*
Medical book by a Navy medical officer, *5298*
Medical college, *3042*
Medical dictionary, *5308*
Medical education book, *5282*
Medical encyclopedia, *5310*
Medical record of an epidemic, *5092*
Medical research chair at a college, *3084*
Meeting place of Congress that is still in existence, *3560*
Metal purchased for coinage, *4015*
Methodist church for African-Americans in the North, *6238*
Milestones between cities, *3512*
Military dictionary, *5416*
Military drill manual, *5412*
Military field strategy manual, *5410*
Military organization formed to oppose the British, *5647*
Mineral water bottler, *2342*
Minister plenipotentiary, *3877*
Mint of the United States, *4014*
Minting of coins by the federal government, *4013*
Mother's Day, *2508*
Movie to premiere on television, *1167*
Municipal Heat-Health Warning forecasting system, *6512*
Music book by an author born in America, *1218*
Music publishers, *1225*
Musical instrument dealer, *1217*
Mustard, *2323*
Narrow-gauge locomotive, *8338*
National animal rights organization, *7221*
National convention of African-Americans, *6127*
National day of prayer, *2487*
National library association, *3016*
National medical society, *5218*
National organization of teachers, *2943*
National pharmacy society, *5220*
National psychiatry association, *5217*
National science society, *6717*

PENNSYLVANIA—Philadelphia—*continued*

Publishing society, *4452*
Quadruplets delivered by cesarean operation, *2154*
Quarantine law enacted by Congress, *7237*
Quarterly magazine, *4609*
Quartermaster of the Continental Army, *5437*
Quinine, *5235*
Radio contest, *4781*
Railroad owned by a state, *8301*
Railroad track that was practical, *8381*
Reclining chair, *2551*
Regeneration of spinal cord connections in animals, *6705*
Relief map, *4484*
Religious weekly newspaper, *4499*
Republican Party national convention, *4063*
Restaurant with an automatic arrangement for vending food, *1827*
Revolving door, *3286*
Rhubarb, *1579*
Rocking chair, *2538*
Root beer, *2366*
Rosicrucian Order lodge, *6207*
Rotogravure press, *2056*
Sandblasting process, *1893*
Savings bank to receive money on deposit, *1718*
Schwenkfelder to arrive in America, *6216*
Science society of importance, *6713*
Secretary of war, *4172*
Secular song by a composer born in America, *1333*
Seed business, *1581*
Session of Congress held in Philadelphia, *3554*
Sieve, *2540*
Signer of the Declaration of Independence, *3464*
Silver deposit for coinage, *4019*
Slide rule book, *6760*
Sociology treatise, *7475*
Soda water, *2339*
Songbook of secular songs, *1223*
Songbook of secular songs by an American-born composer, *1224*
Special session of Congress, *3563*
Special session of the Senate, *3650*
Split-level buildings, *3264*
Squash rackets champion, *7903*
Standardization of weights and measures for customs, *2067*
State labor party, *4068*
State legislator who was an African-American woman, *4394*
Steam engine for industrial use that was practical, *1849*
Steam shovel, *1855*
Stereotype printing, *2031*
Stomach washing with a tube or syringe, *5388*
Stone arch bridge, *3229*
Story serialized in a newspaper, *1066*
Streamlined all-steel diesel-motor train, *8397*
Street letter box, *4668*
Street-cleaning machine, *7405*
Street-sweeping service, *7401*
Strike benefit by a union, *7101*
Submarine in the U.S. Navy, *8509*
Sulfuric acid, *1881*
Supreme Court decision, *3734*
Surgical operation shown on a local television program, *5354*
Suspension bridge of iron wire, *3234*
Swimmer of note, *7907*
Symphonic concert to be shown on television, *1269*
Symphony on an African-American folk theme, *1261*
Tax levied by Congress directly on the states, *4406*
Territory owned by the federal government, *6042*
Tetraploid (giant) flower, *1653*
Textbook printed in America, *2898*
Textile machinery patent, *2121*
Theater building of brick construction, *1420*
Theological college for Jews, *2773*
Therapeutics book, *5300*
Title guaranty insurance company, *1961*
Tobacco tax enacted by Congress, *7058*
Trade directory, *1475*
Trade union organization established in a city, *7107*
Translation of a classic, *1067*
Transportation report, *3221*
Trotting horse, *8180*
True-crime bestseller, *1081*
Tuberculosis research and prevention society, *5224*
Type specimen book from an American type foundry, *4443*
Unitarian church identified as such in its name, *6236*
University legally designated as such, *2710*
Untethered balloon flight, *7994*
Use of the name United States instead of United Colonies, *3469*
Vaccine against a form of cancer, *5160*
Varnish manufacturer, *1883*
Venetian blinds, *2539*
Voice synthesizer, *4863*
Wall and floor tiles, *3336*

PENNSYLVANIA—*continued*

Rouseville

Fire in an oil well, *6588*

Rush

Vending machine to sell food from bulk, *1683*

Saxonburg

Wire rope factory, *1856*

Scranton

Railroad operated by an electric third-rail system, *8324*

Selinsgrove

Methodist bishop who was a woman, *6330*

Sewickley

Tennis match broadcast on radio, *7927*

Shamokin

Lithuanian newspaper, *4563*

Sharpsburg

Prepared-food producer, *2368*

Shenandoah

Correspondence school for workers, *3207*

Shippingport

Nuclear power plant devoted exclusively to peaceful uses, *6624*

Simpson

Eyeglasses with polycarbonate lenses, *5274*

Skippack

Blackboards for use in schools, *2894*

South Bethlehem

Navy contract for armor plate, *5582*

Springfield

Artist of American birth to head the Royal Academy of London, *1024*

State College

Driving course in a high school, *2972*

Titusville

Oil pipeline of importance, *6592*
Oil well that was commercially productive, *6586*

Uniontown

Battle in the French and Indian War, *5641*
Bloodshed in the French and Indian War, *5640*

Village Forks

Twin covered bridges, *3241*

Villanova

Cattle tuberculosis test, *5405*

Washington

Crematory, *2300*
Disciples of Christ meeting, *6252*

Waynesburg

Baseball league for children, *7520*

Westmoreland County

Suspension bridge, *3232*

Wildwood

Coal mine to be automated, *6605*

York

Locomotive to burn coal, *8333*
Treaties entered into by the federal government, *3875*
Wrecking crane operated from a car, *1874*

PUERTO RICO

Commonwealth of the United States, *6095*
Terrorist shootings in the Capitol Building, *3579*

Fajardo

Surgeon general who was a woman, *7283*

San Juan

Governor of Puerto Rico to be elected, *3784*
Governor of Puerto Rico who was a woman, *3790*
Presidential Citizen Medal, *6914*

RHODE ISLAND

American Heritage Rivers, *5997*

RHODE ISLAND—Providence—*continued*

Religious refuge for people of all faiths, *6179*
Screw machine to make pointed screws, *2654*
Shot fired by an American combatant to wound a British combatant in the conflict over independence, *5646*
Spinning jenny for cotton, *2113*
Straw hats, *2233*
Tap dancer of renown, *1049*
Unassisted triple play in organized baseball, *7507*

Quonset Point

Navy jet airplane squadron, *5487*

Warwick

Corrupt election practices law enacted by a colony, *3759*
Slavery emancipation law enacted by a colony, *6114*

SOUTH CAROLINA

African-American midshipman at the Naval Academy, *3118*
Assault by a congressman on a senator, *3662*
Atlas issued by a state, *4483*
Congressional representative censured for corruption, *3605*
Congressman censured for assaulting another, *3601*
Escape of slaves from a colony in what is now United States territory, *6110*
Fistfight in the Senate, *3667*
House of Representatives election that was contested, *3587*
Indigo crop, *1568*
Marine Corps major, *5560*
Minister plenipotentiary to Great Britain, *3881*
Novel by an American to depict Native Americans in a realistic manner, *1086*
Secession act at the start of the Civil War, *4349*
Senate filibuster to last for more than 24 hours, *3684*
Senator elected by a write-in vote, *3683*
Spanish settlement in the United States, *6110*
State to ratify the Articles of Confederation, *3476*
State to secede from the Union, *4350*
Supreme Court chief justice whose nomination was not confirmed, *3736*
Vice president to resign, *4304*

Barnwell County

Workers' compensation lawsuit involving the rights of an injured servant against his master, *7112*

Beaufort

State supreme court justice who was African-American, *3708*

Charleston

Act inaugurating the Civil War, *5690*
Ambassador to Mexico, *3889*
American imprisoned in the Tower of London as an enemy agent, *5674*
Army major who was African-American, *5441*
Ballet performed in the United States, *1046*
Building of fireproof construction, *3262*
City college, *2716*
Civil rights anthem to achieve fame, *1344*
Civil War attack, *5693*
Confederate ship surrendered to the Union, *5713*
Confederate vessel sunk by an underwater torpedo mine, *5717*
Cotton crop exported, *1577*
Cremation, *2297*
Earthquake of consequence to be recorded, *5908*
Fire insurance company, *1975*
Golf players' club, *7748*
Independent government in an American colony, *3450*
Jewish soldier killed in the Revolutionary War, *5658*
Music society, *1213*
Naval skirmish in the Civil War, *5694*
Navy Cross awarded to a Coast Guard officer in World War II, *5519*
Newspaper editor who was a woman, *4589*
Opera performed in America, *1313*
Passenger train to run on a regular schedule, *8305*
Pastelist, *1016*
Photographs of combat, *4624*
Physician born in America who was graduated from a foreign medical school, *5013*
Price sheet for commodities, *1521*
Public museum, *3133*
Publicly supported lending library, *2998*
Reform Jewish congregation, *6262*
Submarine to sink a warship, *5719*
Weather observations to be systematically recorded, *6486*

Columbia

Library building at a university, *2744*

Dewitt's Corner

Treaty between states after the Declaration of Independence, *4336*

Fort Wagner

Medal of Honor awarded to an African-American soldier for an action in the Civil War, *5512*

Georgetown

Congressional representative who was African-American, *3606*

Greenville

Secular song hit, *1337*

Parris Island

French to arrive in America, *6007*
Marine who was an African-American woman, *5569*

Pineville

African-American minister to a white Methodist congregation, *6232*

Port Royal

Ship built in America to cross the Atlantic Ocean, *8524*

Silver Bluff

Baptist churches for African-Americans, *6228*

Sumter

Act inaugurating the Civil War, *5690*
City government using the manager plan, *3531*

Winnsborough

Hailstone shower of record that was fatal, *5904*

SOUTH DAKOTA

Movie director who was African-American, *1144*
Native American Day, *2521*

Aberdeen

Grandmother to give birth to her own grandchild, *2165*

Custer

Monument to a Native American, *7191*

Howard

Photograph of a tornado, *5907*

Rapid City

Aerial photograph showing the lateral curvature of the horizon and the beginning of the stratosphere, *4634*

Watertown

High school to fingerprint its students, *7383*

White Lake

Aerial photograph showing the lateral curvature of the horizon and the beginning of the stratosphere, *4634*

Wounded Knee

Armed occupation by Native American protesters in the modern era, *6102*

Yankton

Hutterites, *6277*

TENNESSEE

Alcohol prohibition law enacted by a state, *7060*
Cabinet member who had served as a Confederate officer, *4179*
Child safety seat law enacted by a state, *8273*
Congressional representative to serve before his 25th birthday, *3591*
Former president to become a senator, *4137*
Freedom ride by civil rights activists, *6139*
Gubernatorial election in which two brothers were the opposing candidates, *4379*
Jim Crow law, *6137*
Medal of Honor awarded to an Army soldier, *5504*
Senator to be expelled, *3654*
Senators elected but not seated, *3653*
State readmitted to the Union after the Civil War, *4351*

Chattanooga

Baseball pitcher who was a woman, *7531*
Miniature golf course, *7771*

TENNESSEE—*continued*

Clarksville

Jackson

Kingsport

Knoxville

Memphis

Nashville

Oak Ridge

Pulaski

Rogersville

Shiloh

Tuskegee

Vonore

Washington College

TEXAS

Abilene

Arlington

Austin

TEXAS—Houston—*continued*

Long-distance car-to-car telephone conversation, *4896*
Octuplets, *2169*
Oil refinery with a carbon monoxide boiler, *6609*
President who was a jet pilot, *4270*
Private space launch, *6876*
Shipment of oil directly from Russia to the United States, *6616*
Space-to-ground news conference telecast, *4546*
Superconducting material that operated at relatively high temperatures, *6751*
Vote cast from space in a presidential election, *3836*
Vote cast from space in an American election, *3788*
Voting rights in space, *3787*
Women's National Basketball League champions, *7564*

Huntsville

Execution by lethal injection, *7021*

Indianola

Camels imported for military purposes, *5418*

Lampasas

State banking association, *1729*

Lufkin

Microwave television station, *4961*

Marshall

Elimination of an entire class of nuclear weapons by treaty, *3911*

Midland

Airplane made primarily of composite materials, *8152*

Pecos

Rodeo at which cash prizes were awarded, *1380*

Plano

State government to completely privatize its computer services, *4368*

Port Arthur

Cargo ship from the United States attacked by a German submarine in World War I, *5732*

Randolph Air Force Base

Space cabin simulator, *6795*

Raymondville

Freestanding birth center, *2159*

San Angelo

Air-conditioned public elementary school, *2976*

San Antonio

Air-conditioned office building, *3298*
Airplane flying school operated by a woman, *8037*
Fatal airplane accident in a solo military airplane, *5466*
Mayor of a major city who was of Mexican descent, *3543*

Schertz

Liver transplant from a live donor, *5376*

Sweetwater

Pilots of military aircraft who were women, *5482*

Texarkana

Federal credit union, *1746*

Waco

Murder trial to be televised, *6950*

Weatherford

Mechanical cotton picker, *1645*

Ysleta

Matador of American birth, *7614*

UTAH

Bird banding by federal authorities, *5948*
Capture of comet particles, *6396*
Federal ban on polygamy that was enforced, *7436*
Game preserve appropriation by the federal government, *5958*
Polygamy ban enacted by Congress, *7436*
Senator to fly in space, *6830*

Fort Bridger

Natural Bridges National Monument

Promontory

Salt Lake City

Wendover

West Jordan

VERMONT

Bradford

Brandon

Brownington

Burlington

Concord

Dorset

Grandpa's Knob

Ludlow

Middlebury

Montpelier

Norwich

Proctor

Randolph

Rupert

VERMONT—*continued*

Springfield

Sandpaper patent, *1852*

St. Johnsbury

Platform scale, *1663*

Vergennes

State legislator who was African-American, *4387*

Windsor

Election law enacted by a state to grant universal voting rights to freemen, *3762*

Woodstock

Ski tow made of rope, *7892*

VIRGINIA

Alcohol prohibition enforcement officers, *7052*
Alcohol temperance law enacted by a colony, *7054*
Ban on convicts holding public office, *3757*
Book written in America, *1058*
Boxer of fame who was African-American, *7591*
Breech-loading cannon, *5848*
Capture of an enemy warship by a commissioned American naval officer, *5657*
Clerk of the House of Representatives, *3584*
Colonial badges issued to friendly Native Americans, *6032*
Colonial laws making slavery lifelong and hereditary, *6115*
Congressional representative appointed to a presidential cabinet, *3581*
Crop limitation law, *1562*
Crop surplus destruction ordered by a government, *1563*
First Lady to receive mail franking privileges, *4658*
Former president to serve as an official of an enemy government, *4135*
Freedom ride by civil rights activists, *6139*
Fungicide used medicinally, *5250*
Gambling law for ministers enacted by a colony, *1797*
Hemp to be exported, *1571*
History book of the colonial era, *7465*
Horse that was a thoroughbred, *8176*
Hunting law enacted by a colony, *5938*
Inheritance tax levied by a colony, *4401*
Involuntary sterilization regulation enacted by a state, *7454*
Irish to arrive in America, *6035*
Local radio network, *4813*
Lottery, *1796*
Medical regulations enacted by a colony, *5010*
Minister plenipotentiary appointed after independence, *3877*
Motorboat, *8408*
Naval expedition mounted by an English colony, *5631*
Physician in the colony of Virginia, *5008*
Potato, *1558*
Presbyterian church, *6173*
President of the Continental Congress, *3549*
President who had been a senator, *4117*
Rice to be imported, *1566*
Secretary of energy, *4206*
Secretary of state, *4171*
Senator appointed by a governor, *3649*
Silk culture, *2106*
State governor who was African-American, *4383*
State to offer simultaneous access to multiple government databases, *7424*
States with populations of more than 1 million, *4343*
Supreme Court chief justice to serve in a presidential cabinet, *3739*
Supreme Court chief justice who had been a congressional representative, *3737*
Supreme Court decision reversing the ruling of a state supreme court, *3744*
Tomatoes eaten in America, *1573*
Treason trial by a colony, *6925*

Accomack

Salt works, *2315*
Theatrical performance, *1411*

Alexandria

Online filing system for registering trademarks, *3983*
Presidential inauguration broadcast on live high-definition TV, *4291*
Railroad coupler, *8389*
School for African-American children established by a state, *2947*
Toll road, *3405*
Union officer killed in the Civil War, *5698*

Arlington

Building containing 6.5 million square feet of usable space, *3305*
Burial at the Tomb of the Unknown Soldier, *2303*
Capitol Police Officers killed in the line of duty, *3580*

VIRGINIA—*continued*

Williamsburg

College charter granted by the Crown, *2691*
College to confer medals as prizes, *2704*
College to have a full faculty, *2694*
College to use the honor system during examinations, *2707*
College with an elective system of study, *2708*
Cookbook published in America, *2319*
Emperor of Japan to visit the United States, *3940*
English grammar by an American, *3174*
Fencing book, *7665*
Hospital for insane patients established by a colony, *5098*
Italian instruction at a college, *2724*
Jewish physician to head an asylum for the mentally ill, *5011*
Law school at a college, *2711*
Physician who was Jewish, *5011*
Political economy course at a college, *2713*
Scholastic fraternity at a college, *2706*
School for Native Americans to be permanently established, *2895*
School of modern history at a college, *2725*
School of modern languages at a college, *2709*
Statehouse, *3448*
Theater, *1414*
Work of satirical fiction, *1072*

Yorktown

Customhouse, *2063*
Patriotic song to achieve national popularity, *1332*

WASHINGTON

Forest canopy crane to be used in North America, *5987*
Postage stamps depicting a woman, *4728*
State ban on the sale of violent video games to children, *7308*
State named for a person born in America, *4353*
State to authorize incarceration of convicted sex offenders beyond their prison terms, *7303*
State to inform the public about the residences of released sex offenders, *7304*
State to require child booster seats, *8283*
State workers' compensation insurance law that was not declared unconstitutional, *7141*
Trial of a teacher for violating a state ban on teaching the theory of evolution, *2970*
Volcano known to claim human life, *5930*

Bellevue

Educational multimedia CD-ROM, *6474*

Bellingham

Orchestra conductor who was a woman, *1253*

Cape Disappointment

Settlers to reach the Pacific coast, *6060*

Cape Flattery

Walk from Canada to Mexico along the West Coast, *7988*

Cheney

Comprehensive digital archive of state documents, *4371*

Lynnwood

Amateur boxing match for women, *7611*

Mabton

Outbreak of mad cow disease, *7293*

Redmond

Ascent of Mount Everest by an American, *7983*
Webmail service, *6482*

Renton

Jet airplane used for commercial transport, *8135*

Richland

Nuclear reactor for research and development, *6738*

Seattle

American to climb all 14 mountains higher than 8,000 meters, *7989*
Antiglobalization protest of significance, *6980*
City law restricting police inquiries into immigrant activites protected by the First Amendment, *7397*
Commercial aircraft designed by computer, *8169*
Commercial software for personal computers, *6451*
Desktop publishing software, *6467*
Employment office established by a city, *7137*
Fisheries school at a college, *2835*
Hockey team from the United States to win the Stanley Cup, *7829*
International airmail, *4693*

Judicial decision allowing physicians to end the lives of terminally ill patients at their request, *2309*
Jumbo jet, *8153*
Mayor of a major city who was a woman, *3534*
Natural medicine clinic subsidized by a government, *5076*
Pontoon bridge of reinforced concrete, *3254*
Poster child for a fundraising campaign, *7230*
Revolving restaurant, *1836*
Ship from the United States lost in World War I, *5730*
Steam-operated pressing machine, *1872*
Streamlined ferryboat, *8453*
Transcontinental car race, *7621*
World's Fair that was financially successful, *1512*

Shoreline

Prison to offer training in Vipassana meditation, *7023*

Spokane

Eye wash commercially manufactured, *5241*
Father's Day, *2509*

Tacoma

School stadium, *2965*

Tenino

Wooden money, *4042*

Vancouver

Army field range, *5860*
Steamboat on the Pacific coast, *8427*

Walla Walla

College comprehensive senior examination program, *2832*
Dean of students at a college, *2820*
Missionaries to cross the continent, *6064*
Settlers to cross the continent who were women, *6064*

Wenatchee

Transpacific nonstop airplane flight, *8084*

Woodland

Skyjacking in which the skyjacker disappeared, *6956*

Yakima Reservation

Boarding school on a Native American reservation, *2938*

WEST VIRGINIA

Belt conveyor more than four miles long, *1878*
Rural free mail delivery, *4684*
Sales tax enacted by a state, *4422*
State to experience a natural decrease in population, *4364*

Alderson

Federal prison for women, *7014*

Berkeley Springs

Spa at a mineral spring, *5386*

Charles Town

Jockey who was a woman to win on a regular parimutuel flat track, *7816*

Charleston

Brick pavement on a city street, *3415*

Chester

Woman jockey to ride two winners in a day, *7816*

Colliers

Bareknuckle world heavyweight boxing champion, *7595*

Elkins

President to visit all 50 states, *4319*

Grafton

National cemetery for Civil War dead, *5722*
Union soldier killed by enemy action in the Civil War, *5697*

Green Bank

Scientific program to search for extraterrestrial life, *6378*

Hanging Rocks

Civil War call for volunteers, *5695*

Institute

Coal hydrogenation plant, *1908*

Kanawha

Trust, *1481*

WEST VIRGINIA—*continued*

Parsons

Confederate general killed in the Civil War, *5704*

Philippi

Land battle in the Civil War, *5701*

Skin Fork

Soldier killed in action in the Korean War, *5803*

Standard

Tunnel with television monitors, *3444*

Sutton

Tank crew to cross the 38th parallel in the Korean War, *5806*

Welch

City parking garage, *8260*

Wheeling

Double-deck steamboat, *8421*
Natural gas plant operated by a city, *6596*
Sale of federal land to an individual, *6051*
Steel-cut nails, *2662*

White Sulphur Springs

Golfer to break 60 for 18 holes in a major tournament, *7774*

WISCONSIN

Brothers to serve as representatives in Congress simultaneously, *3600*
Congressional representative who was a Socialist, *3612*
State governor to be removed from office by a state supreme court, *4375*
State law prohibiting discrimination against the disabled in employment, *7044*
State services to refugees, *6104*
State to establish statewide primary elections, *3776*
State welfare reform program, *7167*
State workers' compensation insurance law that was not declared unconstitutional, *7141*
Unemployment insurance act, *7152*

Beloit

College whose tuition fees were based on family income, *2872*

Boscobel

Bibles in hotel rooms, *6290*

Cambria

Film rolls for cameras, *4642*

Cambridge

Scandinavian Methodist Episcopal church, *6270*

Chippewa Falls

Steel ski jump, *7890*

Clintonville

Brake for four-wheeled cars, *8244*

Eau Claire

Log-rolling national championship tournament, *7968*

Kenosha

Seat belts in cars, *8261*

Kewaunee

Naval ship to be captured intact, *8498*

La Crosse

Book issued on microcards, *3036*

Lake Geneva

Armored car, *8234*
Radio car for military use, *5423*

Madison

Animal husbandry professor at a college, *2807*
Cultivation of human stem cells in a laboratory, *6692*
Dairy school at a college, *2808*
Dance major at a college, *2845*
Game management chair at a college, *2850*
Isolation of embryonic stem cells in a primate, *6686*
Lightweight brick, *3348*
Milk butterfat tester, *2392*
State legislature to use an electric vote recorder, *4391*
Weather forecast broadcast on radio, *6496*

Milton

Monolithic concrete building, 3268

Milwaukee

American orchestra to make all its recordings downloadable from the Internet, 1285
Lunch box featuring a licensed character, 2580
Major league baseball game in which the majority of the players on one team were African-American, 7541
Mayor of a major city who was a Socialist, 3530
National safety association, 7276
Newspaper advertisement printed on aluminum foil, 1553
Occupational therapy course at a college, 3086
Outboard motor, 8444
Presbyterian elder who was a woman, 6300
Soldiers' homes established by Congress, 5621
Telephone exchange with a rotating dial, 4871

Muskego

Norwegian newspaper, 4557

Neenah

Flour rolling mill, 2383

Peshtigo

Forest fire of consequence, 5974

Portage

Lie detector, 6946

Racine

Bicycle traffic court, 7655
Blow dryer for hair, 2473
Confectionary machine, 2409
Court-martial of an officer for collaborating with his captors, 5552
Czech newspaper, 4559
Electric blender, 2285
Malted milk, 2388
State continuation school for adults, 3210
Strike to last longer than a year, 7159

Sayner

Snowmobile patent, 7973

Watertown

Kindergarten run informally, 2944
Quintuplets, 2150

Waukesha

Newspaper advertisement that looked three-dimensional, 1551
Patent on a living organism, 4000

WYOMING

Election law enacted by a state to grant voting rights to women after the adoption of the Constitution, 3773
National forest, 5981
National park, 5990
State governor who was a woman, 4381

Belle Fourche River

National monument designated by the federal government, 7182

Cheyenne

Frontier Day, 2506
Yellow pages telephone directory, 4874

South Pass

Missionaries to cross the continent, 6064
Settlers to cross the continent who were women, 6064

South Pass City

Justice of the peace who was a woman, 3709

Warren Air Force Base

MX intercontinental ballistic missile base, 5891

WITHDRAWAL